G
1021
.R185
1994

Rand McNally and
Company.

Illustrated atlas of
the world.

$ G
1021
.R185
1994

Rand McNally and
Company.

Illustrated atlas
of the world.

$99.95

DATE	BORROWER'S NAME	

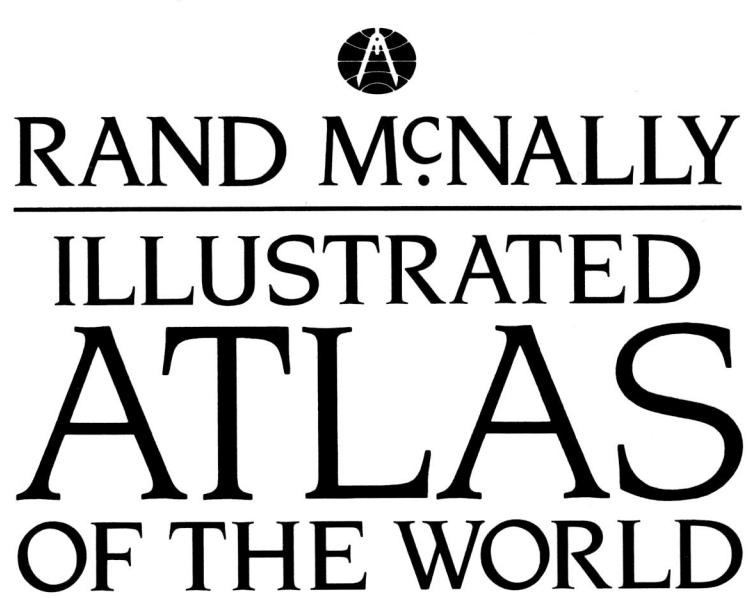

RAND McNALLY

ILLUSTRATED
ATLAS
OF THE WORLD

ILLUSTRATED
ATLAS
OF THE WORLD

 RAND McNALLY & COMPANY

CHICAGO • NEW YORK • SAN FRANCISCO

CONTENTS

ILLUSTRATED ATLAS OF THE WORLD
Copyright © 1992 by Rand McNally & Company
1994 Revised Edition

Pages 1 through 240 and
A·1 through A·144 from
The Great Geographical Atlas
Copyright © 1992 Instituto Geografico De Agostini

Library of Congress Cataloging-in-Publication Data
Rand McNally and Company.
    Illustrated atlas of the world. — 1994 rev. ed.
        p.   cm.
    Shows changes to Czechoslovakia, Yugoslavia, and Eritrea.
    Title on added t.p.: Rand McNally illustrated atlas of the world.
    Includes indexes.
    ISBN 0-528-83492-4
    1. Atlases.   I. Title.   II. Title: Rand McNally illustrated atlas
of the world.   III. Title: Atlas of the world.
G1021.R185   1993   < G&M >
912—dc20   93-504
                                  CIP
                                  MAP

Printed in the United States of America by
Rand McNally & Company

Jacket photo Comstock/Hartman-Dewitt
Title page photo by Ray Atkeson

Our Planet Earth Section

Maps

MAP 1 — WORLD, PHYSICAL 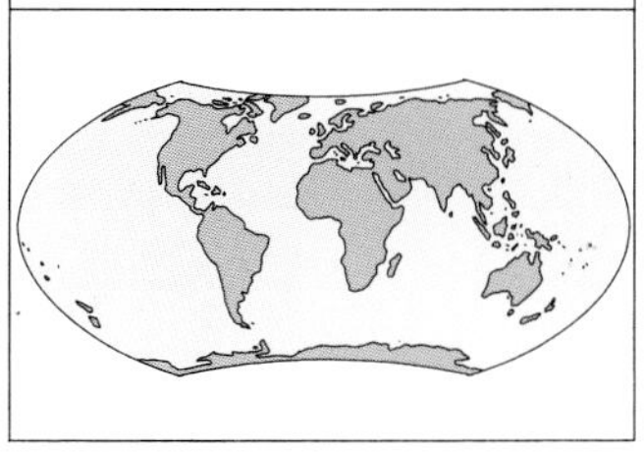
Pages 118–119
Scale 70.000.000

MAP 2 — WORLD, POLITICAL 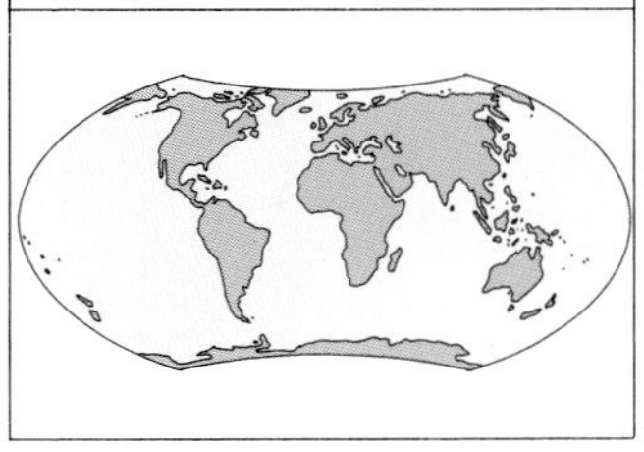
Pages 120–121
Scale 70.000.000

MAP 3 — THE OCEANS 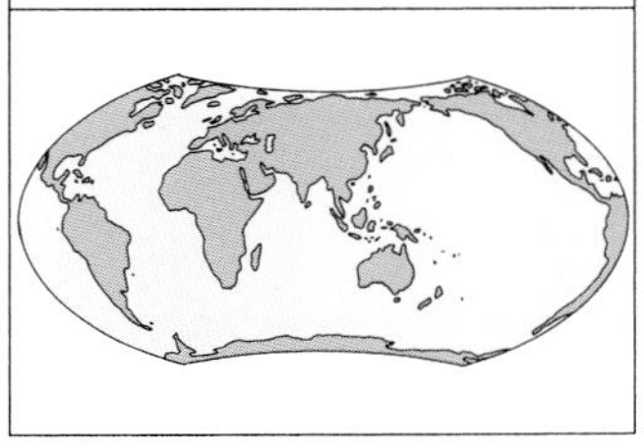
Pages 122–123
Scale 70.000.000

MAP 4 — WORLD TRANSPORTATION AND TIME ZONES 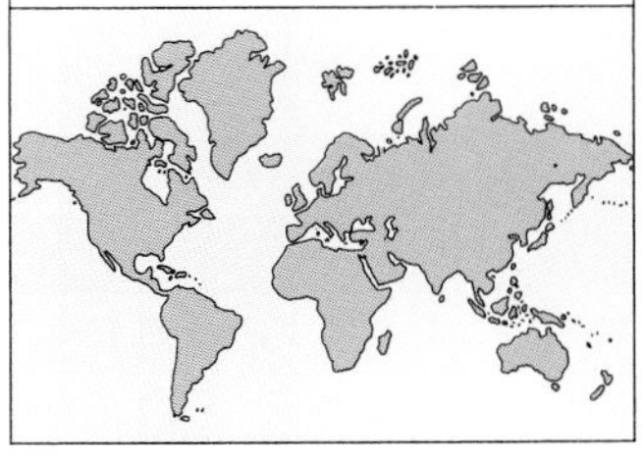
Pages 124–125
Scale 1:90.000.000

MAP 5 — EUROPE, PHYSICAL 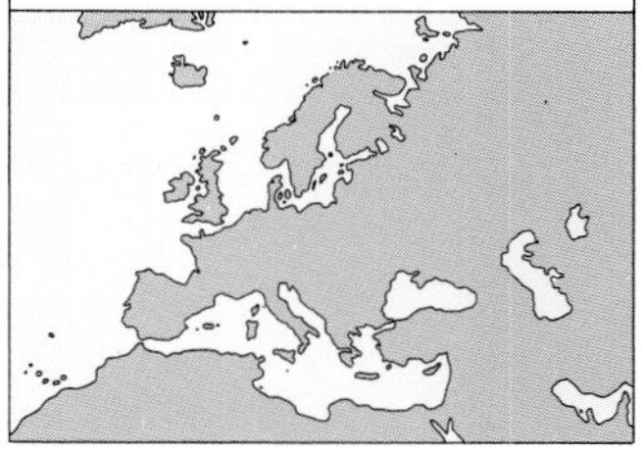
Pages 126–127
Scale 1:15.000.000

MAP 6 — EUROPE, POLITICAL 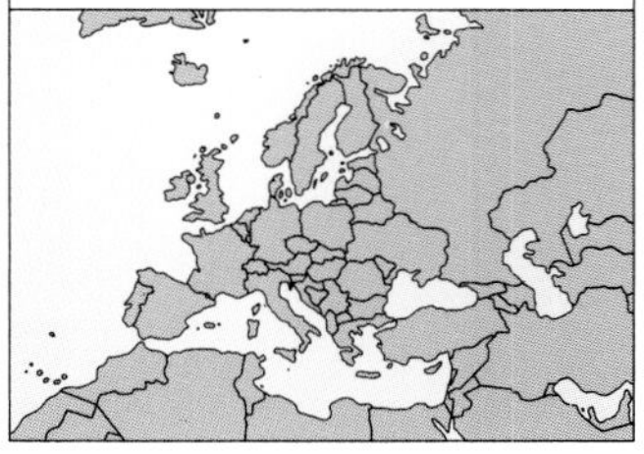
Pages 128–129
Scale 1:15.000.000

MAP 7 — NORTHERN EUROPE
(Belarus)   Latvia
Denmark   Lithuania
Estonia   Norway
Finland   (Russia)
Iceland   Sweden 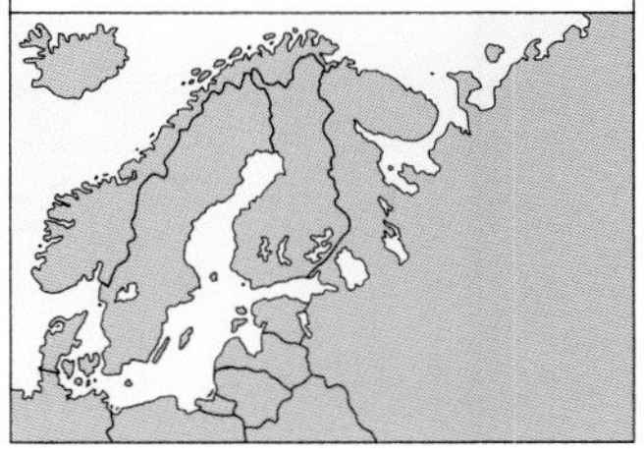
Pages 130–131
Scale 1:6.000.000

MAP 8 — BALTIC REGION
Denmark   Lithuania
Estonia   (Norway)
(Finland)   (Russia)
Latvia   (Sweden) 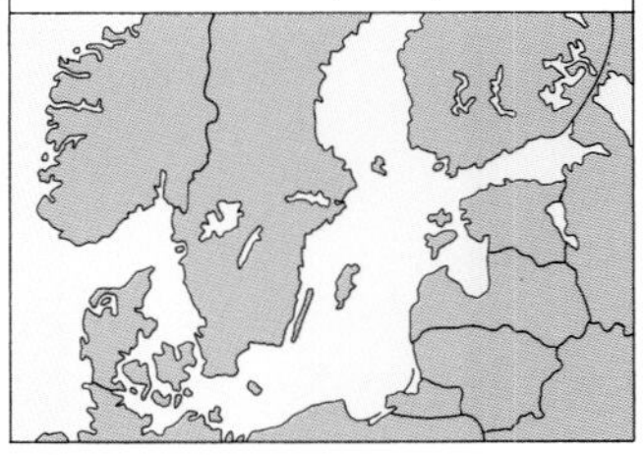
Pages 132–133
Scale 1:3.000.000

MAP 9 — BRITISH ISLES
Ireland
United Kingdom 
Pages 134–135
Scale 1:3.000.000

MAP 10 — CENTRAL EUROPE
Austria   Poland
(Belarus)   (Russia)
(Croatia)   Slovakia
Czech Republic Slovenia
Germany   Switzerland
Hungary   (Ukraine)
Liechtenstein   (Yugoslavia)
Luxembourg
Pages 136–137
Scale 1:3.000.000

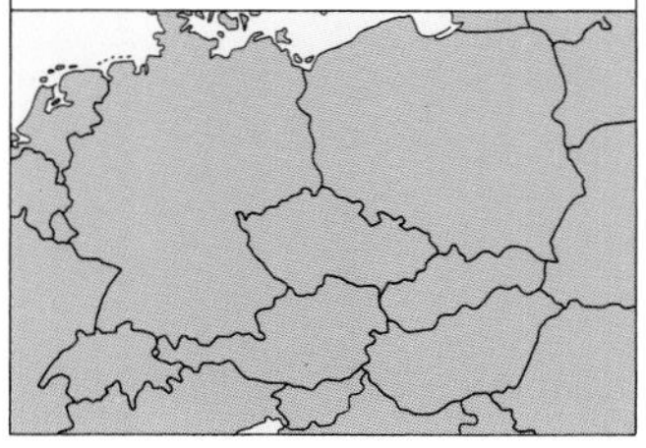

MAP 11 — FRANCE AND BENELUX
Andorra   Monaco
Belgium   Netherlands
France   (Spain)
Luxembourg (United Kingdom) 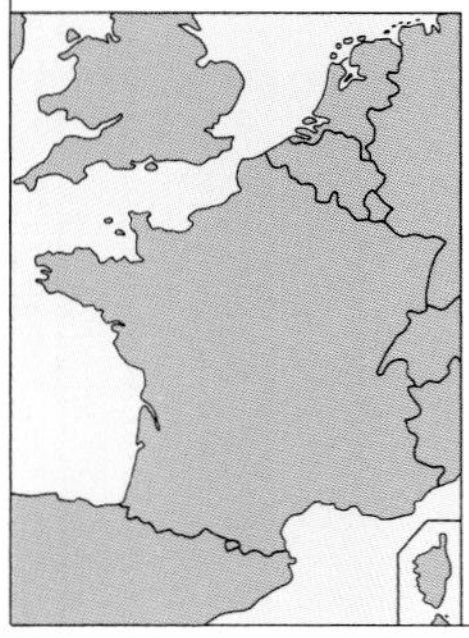
Pages 138–139
Scale 1:3.000.000

MAP 12 — BELGIUM, NETHERLANDS AND LUXEMBOURG
Belgium   Luxembourg
(France)   Netherlands
(Germany)   (United Kingdom) 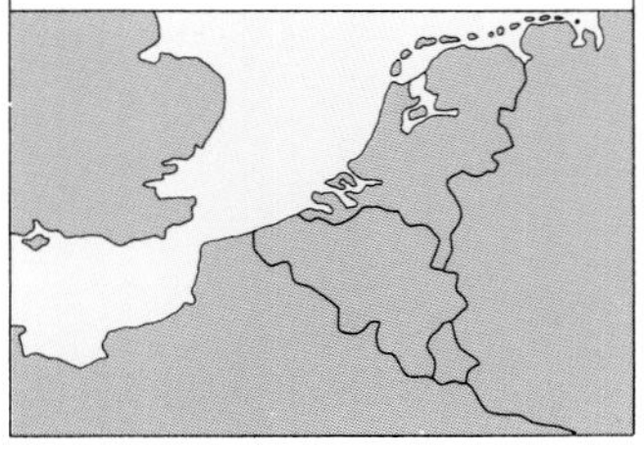
Pages 140–141
Scale 1:1.500.000

MAP 13 — SPAIN AND PORTUGAL
(Algeria)   (Morocco)
Andorra   Portugal
Gibraltar   Spain 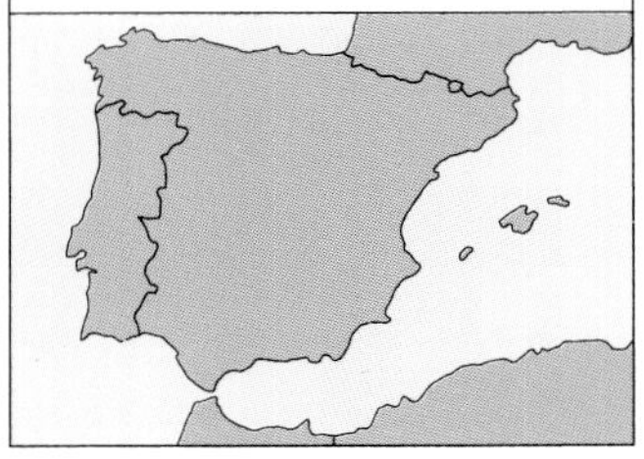
Pages 142–143
Scale 1:3.000.000

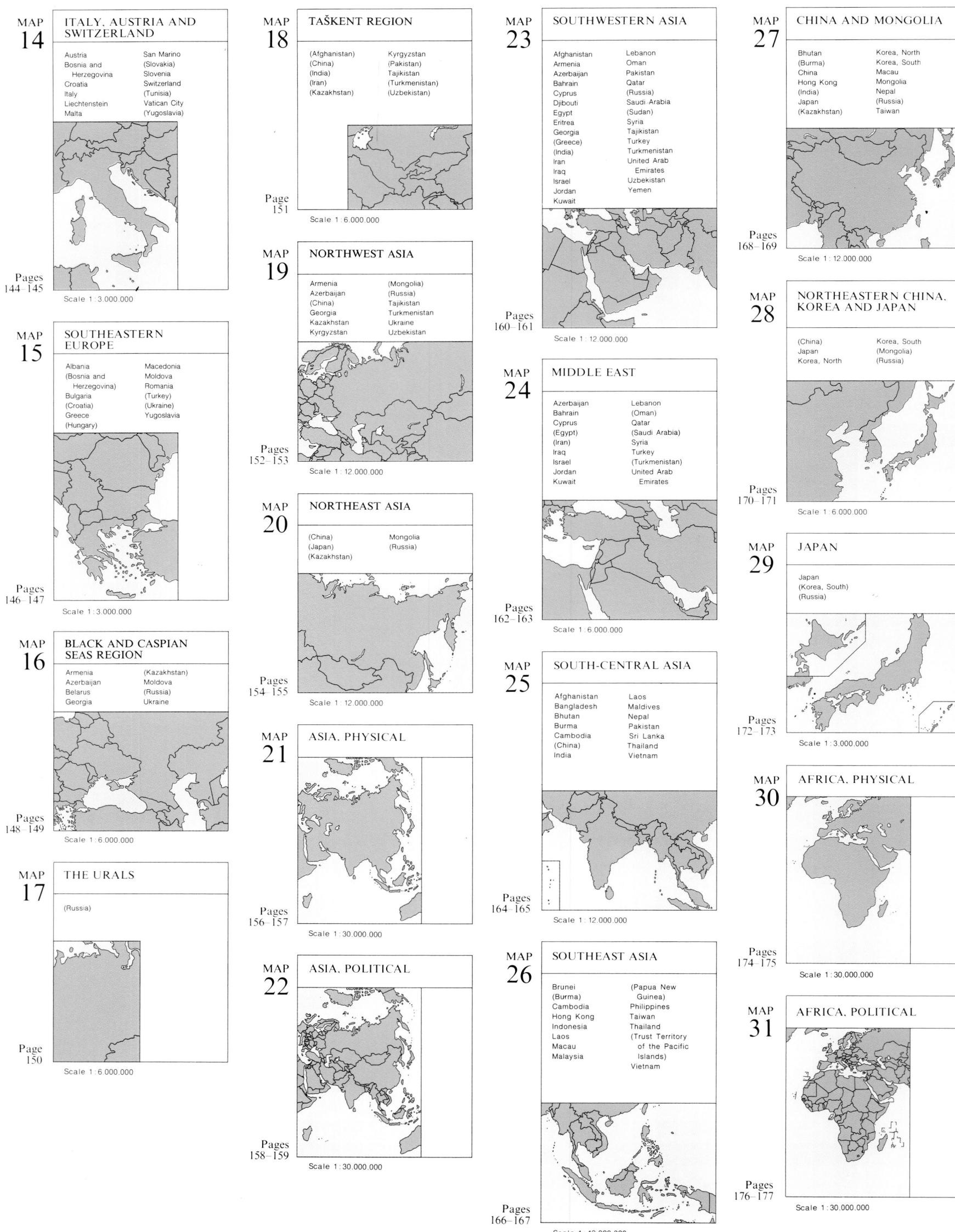

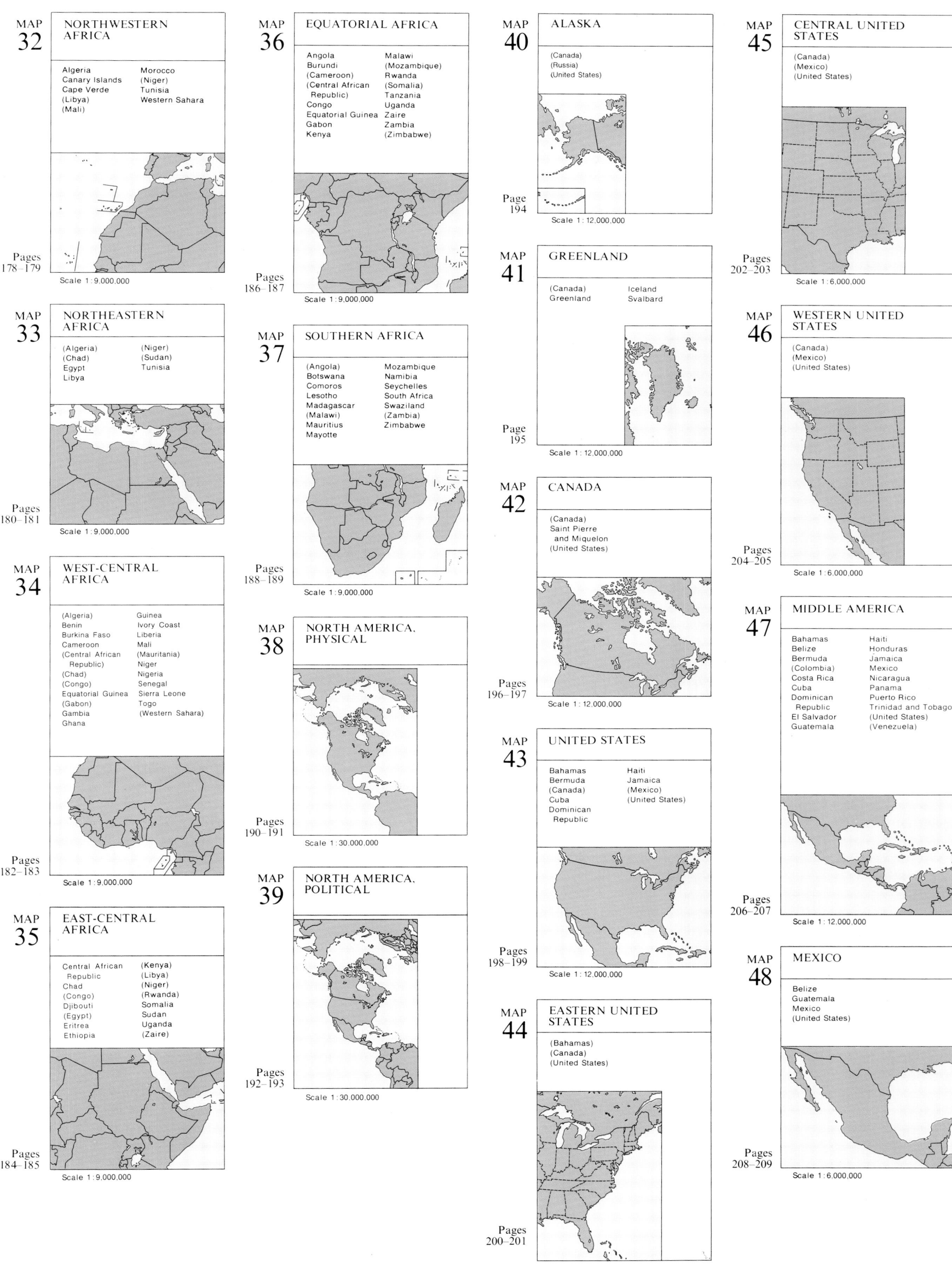

OUR PLANET EARTH SECTION

Part 1

THE EARTH AND THE UNIVERSE

How the universe began · Earth's place in the Solar System
How the Earth became fit for life
Man looks at Earth from outer space

CREATION AND DESTRUCTION

Violent activity pervades our universe and has done so ever since the primordial fireball of creation. Evidence of violence comes from radio telescopes scanning the farthest reaches: entire galaxies may be exploding, torn apart by gravitational forces of unimaginable power. Some very large stars may burst apart in supernovas, spraying interstellar space with cosmic debris. From this violence new stars and new planets are constantly being formed throughout the universe.

The Big Bang theory (left) of the origin of the universe envisages all matter originating from one point in time and space—a point of infinite density. In the intensely hot Big Bang all the material that goes to make up the planets, stars and galaxies that we see now began to expand outward in all directions. This expansion has been likened to someone blowing up a balloon on which spots have been painted. As the air fills and expands the balloon, the spots get farther away from each other. Likewise, clusters of galaxies that formed from the original superdense matter began, and continue, to move away from neighboring clusters. The Big Bang generated enormous temperatures and the remnants of the event still linger throughout space. A leftover, background radiation provides a uniform and measurable temperature of 3°C. It is generally believed that the universe will continue to expand into complete nothingness.

Stars vary enormously in size, temperature and luminosity. The largest, so-called red giants like Antares (1)—the biggest yet known—or Aldebaran (2), are nearing the end of their lives: diminishing nuclear "fuel" causes their thinning envelopes to expand. Rigel (3) is many times brighter than our Sun (4)—a middle-aged star—but both are so-called main-sequence stars. Epsilon Eridani (5) is rather like the Sun. Wolf 359 (6) is a red dwarf.

Our Solar System was formed from a collapsing cloud of gas and dust (A). Collapse made the center hotter and denser (B) until nuclear reactions started. Heat blew matter from the heart of the now flattened, spinning disc (C). Heavier materials condensed closest to the young Sun, now a hot star, eventually forming the inner ring of planets; the lighter ones accumulated farther out, making up the atmosphere and composition of the giant outer planets (D).

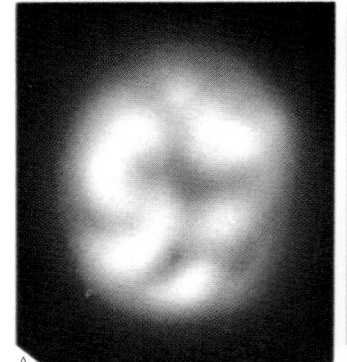

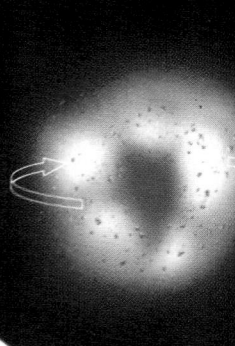

Billions of galaxies exist outside our own Milky Way, each thousands of light-years across and filled with millions of stars. Found in clusters, they are either elliptical or spiral in form. The clusters recede from each other following the space-time geometry, as established by Hubble in 1929, proving that the universe is expanding.

The "exploding" galaxy M82 may be an example of the violence of our universe. Clouds of hydrogen gas, equivalent in mass to 5,000,000 suns, have been ejected from the nucleus at 160 km (100 miles) per second. Black holes may cause the explosions, where gravity sucks in all matter, so that even light cannot escape.

Our own cluster of galaxies (below), the Local Group (A), consists of about 30 members, weakly linked by the force of gravity. Earth lies in the second-largest galaxy, the Milky Way (B)—here shown edge-on and at an angle—which is a spiral galaxy of about 100,000 million stars. Its rotating "arms" are great masses of clouds, dust and stars that sweep around a dense nucleus. In the course of this new stars are regularly created from dust and gas. Our Sun (S)

lies 33,000 light-years from the nucleus and takes 225 million years to complete an orbit. The Andromeda Galaxy (C), known to astronomers as M31, is the largest of our Local Group. It too is a spiral, and lies about two million light-years away. Roughly 130,000 light-years in diameter, it appears as a flattened disc, and indicates how our galaxy would look if viewed from outside. Two smaller elliptical galaxies, M32 and NGC 205, can also be seen.

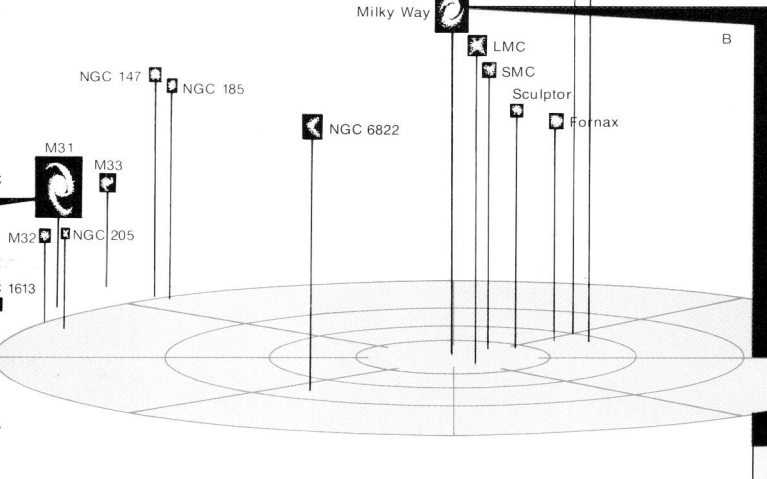

Stars are being born (left) in the Great Nebula of Orion, visible from Earth. The brilliant light comes from a cluster of very hot young stars, the Trapezium, surrounded by a glowing aura of hydrogen gas. Behind the visible nebula there is known to be a dense cloud where radio astronomers have detected emissions from interstellar molecules, and have identified high-density globules. These probably indicate that stars are starting to form.

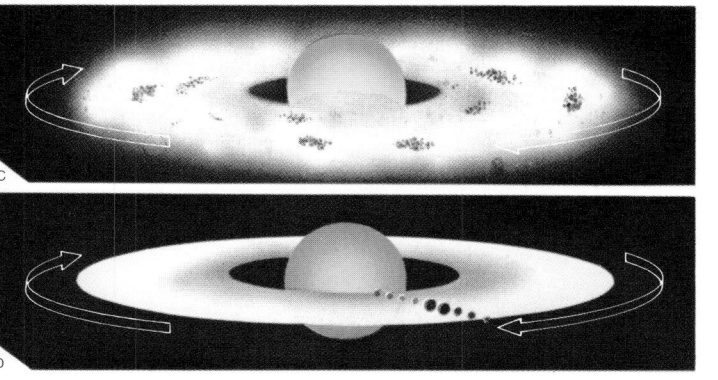

The Making of the Universe

Most astronomers believe that the universe began in a great explosion of matter and energy – the "Big Bang" – about 15,000 million years ago. This event was implied by Einstein's theory of general relativity, as well as by more recent astronomical observations and calculations. But the clinching evidence came in 1965, when two American radio astronomers discovered a faint, uniform, background radiation which permeated all space. This they identified as the remnants of the primordial Big Bang.

The generally accepted explanation for the so-called "cosmic microwave" background, detected by American astronomers Arno Penzias and Robert Wilson, is indeed that it is the echo of the Big Bang itself, the radio noise left over from the fireball of creation. In recognition of their discovery, Penzias and Wilson shared a Nobel Prize in 1978.

The Big Bang has also been identified by astronomers in other ways. All the evidence shows that the universe is expanding, and its constituent parts—clusters of galaxies, each containing thousands of millions of stars like our Sun—are moving away from each other at great speeds. From this and other evidence scientists deduce that long ago the galaxies must have been closer together, in a superdense phase, and that at some time in the remote past all the material in the universe must have started spreading out from a single point. But this "single point" includes not only all three-dimensional matter and space but also the dimension of time, as envisioned in Einstein's revolutionary concept of space-time. Einstein's theory of relativity describes the phenomenon, not in terms of galaxies moving through space in

then reused to form new stars and planets. Thus, from the debris of such explosions new stars can form to repeat the creative cycle, and at each stage more of the heavy elements are produced. Today's heavenly bodies are very much the products of stellar violence in the universe, and indeed the universe itself is now seen to be an area of violent activity. During the past two decades the old idea of the universe as a place of quiet stability has been increasingly superseded by evidence of intense activity on all scales. Astronomers have identified what appear to be vast explosions involving whole galaxies, as well as those of individual stars.

Black holes
The evidence of just why these huge explosions occur is often hard to obtain, because the exploding galaxies may be so far away that light from them takes millions of years to reach telescopes on Earth. But it is becoming increasingly accepted by astronomers that such violent events may be associated with the presence of black holes at the centers of some galaxies.

These black holes are regions in which matter has become so concentrated that the force of gravity makes it impossible for anything—even light itself—to escape. As stars are pulled into super-massive black holes they are torn apart by gravitational forces, and their material forms into a swirling maelstrom from which huge explosions can occur. Collapse into black holes, accompanied by violent outbursts from the maelstrom, may be the ultimate fate of all matter in the universe. For our own Solar System, however, such a fate is far in the future: the Sun in its present form is believed to have enough "fuel" to keep it going for at least another 5,000 million years.

A star is born
The origins of the Earth and the Solar System are intimately connected with the structure of our own galaxy, the Milky Way. There are two main types of galaxies: flattened, disc-shaped spiral galaxies (like the Milky Way), and the more rounded elliptical galaxies, which range in form from near spheres to cigar shapes. The most important feature of a spiral galaxy is that it is rotating, a great mass of stars sweeping around a common center. In our galaxy the Sun, located some way out from the galaxy's center, takes about 225 million years to complete one circuit, called a cosmic year.

New stars are born out of the twisting arms of a spiral galaxy, with each arm marking a region of debris left over from previous stellar explosions. These arms are in fact clouds of dust and gas, including nitrogen and oxygen. As the spiral galaxy rotates over a period of millions of years, the twisting arms are squeezed by a high-density pressure wave as they pass through the cycle of the cosmic year. With two main spiral arms twining around a galaxy such as our own, large, diffuse clouds get squeezed twice during each orbit around the center of the galaxy.

Even if one orbit takes as long as hundreds of millions of years, a score or more squeezes have probably occurred since the Milky Way was first formed thousands of millions of years ago. At a critical point, such repeated squeezing increases the density of a gas cloud so much that it begins to collapse rapidly under the inward pull of its own gravity. A typical cloud of this kind contains enough material to make many stars. As it breaks up it collapses into smaller clouds—which are also collapsing—and these become stars in their own right.

Our own Solar System may have been formed in this way from such a collapsing gas cloud, which went on to evolve into the system of planets that we know today.

the expansion, but as being carried apart by the expansion of space-time itself. Space-time may be imagined as a rubber sheet speckled with paint blobs (galaxies), which move apart as the rubber sheet expands.

Galaxies consist of star systems, dust clouds and gases formed from the hot material exploding outward from the original cosmic fireball. Our own Milky Way system, the band of light that stretches across the night sky, is typical of many galaxies, containing millions of stars slowly rotating around a central nucleus.

Exploding space
The original material of the universe was hydrogen, the simplest of all elements. Nuclear reactions that occurred during the superdense phase of the Big Bang converted about 20 percent of the original hydrogen into helium, the next simplest element. So the first stars were formed from a mixture of about 80 percent hydrogen and 20 percent helium. All other matter in the universe, including the atoms of heavier elements such as carbon and oxygen—which help to make up the human body or the pages of this book—has been processed in further nuclear reactions. The explosion of a star—a relatively rare event called a supernova—scatters material across space, briefly radiating more energy than a trillion suns and ejecting matter into the cosmic reservoir of interstellar space. This is

Earth in the Solar System

The Sun is an ordinary, medium-sized star located some two-thirds of the way from the center of our galaxy, the Milky Way. Yet it comprises more than 99 percent of the Solar System's total mass and provides all the light and heat that make life possible on Earth. This energy comes from nuclear reactions that take place in the Sun's hot, dense interior. The reactions convert hydrogen into helium, with the release of vast amounts of energy – the energy that keeps the Sun shining.

Nuclear reactions in the Sun's core maintain a temperature of some 15,000,000°C and this heat prevents the star from shrinking. The surface temperature is comparatively much lower —a mere 6,000°C. Thermonuclear energy-generating processes cause the Sun to "lose" mass from the center at the rate of four million tonnes of hydrogen every second. This mass is turned into energy (heat), and each gram of matter "burnt" produces the heat equivalent of 100 trillion electric fires. The Sun's total mass is so great, however, that it contains enough matter to continue radiating at its present rate for several thousand million years before it runs out of "fuel."

The Sun's retinue

The Solar System emerged from a collapsing gas cloud. In addition to the Sun there are at least nine planets, their satellites, thousands of minor planets (asteroids), comets and meteors. Most stars occur in pairs, triplets or in even more complicated systems, and the Sun is among a minority of stars in being alone except for its planetary companions. It does seem, however, that a single star with a planetary system offers the greatest potential for the development of life. When there are two or more stars in the same system, any planets are likely to have unstable orbits and to suffer from wide extremes of temperature.

The Solar System's structure is thought to be typical of a star that formed in isolation. As the hot young Sun threw material outward, inner planets (Mercury, Venus, Earth and Mars) were left as small rocky bodies, whereas outer planets (Jupiter, Saturn, Uranus and Neptune) kept their lighter gases and became huge "gas giants." Jupiter has two and a half times the mass of all the other planets put together. Pluto, a small object with a strange orbit, which sometimes carries it within the orbit of Neptune, is usually regarded as a ninth planet, but some astronomers consider it to be an escaped moon of Neptune or a large asteroid.

Planetary relations

Several planets are accompanied by smaller bodies called moons or satellites. Jupiter and Saturn have at least 17 and 22 respectively, whereas Earth has its solitary Moon. Sizes vary enormously, from Ganymede, one of Jupiter's large, so-called Galilean satellites, which has a diameter of 5,000 km (3,100 miles), to Mars' tiny Deimos, which is only 8 km (5 miles) across.

The Earth's Moon is at an average distance of 384,000 km (239,000 miles) and has a diameter of 3,476 km (2,160 miles). Its mass is $\frac{1}{81}$ of the Earth's. Although it is referred to as the Earth's satellite, the Moon is large for a secondary body. Some astronomers have suggested that the Earth/Moon system is a double planet. Certain theories of the origins of the Moon propose that it was formed from the solar nebula in the same way as the Earth was and very close to it. The Moon takes 27.3 days to orbit the Earth—exactly the same time that it takes to rotate once on its axis. As a result, it presents the same face to the Earth all the time.

Our planet's orbit around the Sun is not a perfect circle but an ellipse and so its distance from the Sun varies slightly. More importantly, the Earth is tilted, so that at different times of the year one pole or another "leans" toward the Sun. Without this tilt there would be no seasons. The angle of tilt is not constant: over tens of thousands of years the axis of the Earth "wobbles" like a slowly spinning top, so that the pattern of the seasons varies over the ages. These changes have been linked to recent ice ages, which seem to occur when the northern hemisphere has relatively cool summers.

Patterns of time

The Earth's movements on its axis and around the Sun give us our basic measurements of time—the day and the year—as well as setting the rhythm of the seasons and the ice ages. One rotation of the Earth on its axis—the time from one sunrise to the next—originally defined the day, and the time taken for one complete orbit around the Sun defined the year. Today, however, scientists define both the day and the year in terms of time units "counted" by precision instruments called atomic clocks.

A third basic rhythm is set not by the Sun but by the Moon, which runs through a cycle of phases $29\frac{1}{2}$ days long. This is the basis of the calendar month. But just as the modern calendar cannot cope with months $29\frac{1}{2}$ days long, so too it would have trouble with the precise year, which is, inconveniently, just less than $365\frac{1}{4}$ days long. This is the reason for leap years, by means of which an extra day is added to the month of February every fourth year.

Even this system does not keep the calendar exactly in step with the Sun. Accordingly, the leap year is left out in the years which complete centuries, such as 1900, but retained when they divide exactly by 400. The year 2000 will, therefore, be a leap year. With all these corrections, the average length of the calendar year is within 26 seconds of the year defined by the Earth's movements around the Sun. Thus the calendar will be one day out of step with the heavens in the year 4906.

Cosmic rubble

The other planets are too small and too far away to produce noticeable effects on the Earth, but the smallest members of the Sun's family, the asteroids, can affect us directly. Some of them have orbits that cross the orbit of the Earth around the Sun. From time to time they penetrate the Earth's atmosphere: small fragments burn up high in the atmosphere as meteors, whereas larger pieces may survive to strike the ground as meteorites. These in fact provide an echo of times gone by. All the planets, as the battered face of the Moon shows, suffered collisions from many smaller bodies in the course of their evolution from the collapsing pre-solar gas cloud.

Eclipses occur because the Moon, smaller than the Sun, is closer to Earth and looks just as big. This means that when all three are lined up the Moon can blot out the Sun, causing a solar eclipse. When the Earth passes through the main shadow cone, or umbra, the eclipse is total; in the area of partial shadow, or penumbra, a partial eclipse is seen. A similar effect is produced when Earth passes between the Moon and the Sun, causing a lunar eclipse. At most full moons, eclipses do not occur; the Moon passes either above or below the Earth's shadow, because the Moon's orbit is inclined at an angle of 5° to the orbit of the Earth.

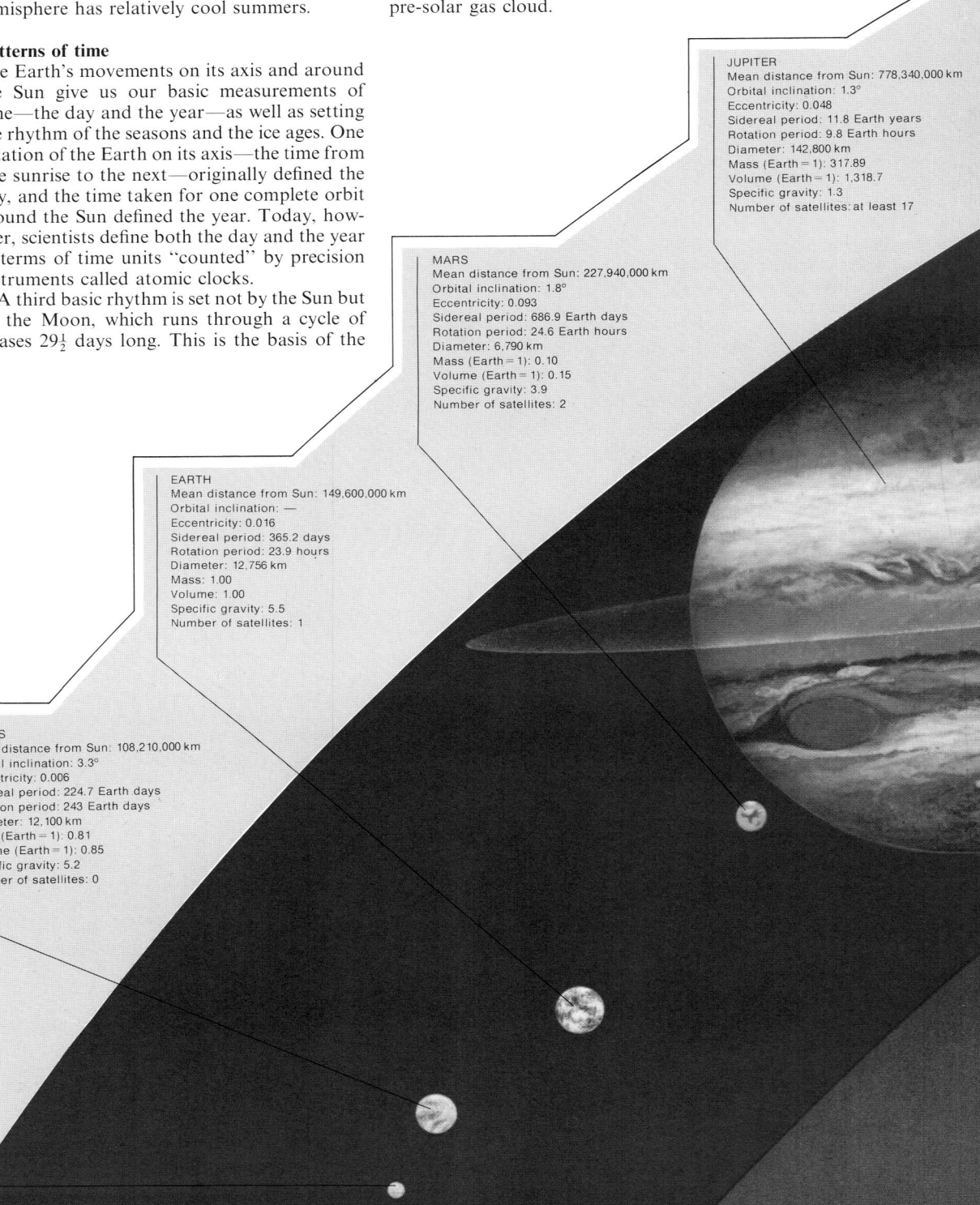

JUPITER
Mean distance from Sun: 778,340,000 km
Orbital inclination: 1.3°
Eccentricity: 0.048
Sidereal period: 11.8 Earth years
Rotation period: 9.8 Earth hours
Diameter: 142,800 km
Mass (Earth = 1): 317.89
Volume (Earth = 1): 1,318.7
Specific gravity: 1.3
Number of satellites: at least 17

MARS
Mean distance from Sun: 227,940,000 km
Orbital inclination: 1.8°
Eccentricity: 0.093
Sidereal period: 686.9 Earth days
Rotation period: 24.6 Earth hours
Diameter: 6,790 km
Mass (Earth = 1): 0.10
Volume (Earth = 1): 0.15
Specific gravity: 3.9
Number of satellites: 2

EARTH
Mean distance from Sun: 149,600,000 km
Orbital inclination: —
Eccentricity: 0.016
Sidereal period: 365.2 days
Rotation period: 23.9 hours
Diameter: 12,756 km
Mass: 1.00
Volume: 1.00
Specific gravity: 5.5
Number of satellites: 1

MEMBERS OF THE SOLAR SYSTEM

The Sun has nine planetary attendants. They are best compared in terms of orbital data (distance from the Sun, inclination of orbit to the Earth's orbit, and eccentricity, which means the departure of a planet's orbit from circularity); planetary periods (the time for a planet to go around the Sun—sidereal periods, and the time it takes for one axial revolution—the rotation period); and physical data (equatorial diameter, mass, volume and density or specific gravity—the weight of a substance compared with the weight of an equal volume of water).

VENUS
Mean distance from Sun: 108,210,000 km
Orbital inclination: 3.3°
Eccentricity: 0.006
Sidereal period: 224.7 Earth days
Rotation period: 243 Earth days
Diameter: 12,100 km
Mass (Earth = 1): 0.81
Volume (Earth = 1): 0.85
Specific gravity: 5.2
Number of satellites: 0

Scale
Diameter of Sun:
1,400,000 km

MERCURY
Mean distance from Sun: 57,910,000 km
Orbital inclination: 7°
Eccentricity: 0.205
Sidereal period: 87.9 Earth days
Rotation period: 58.7 Earth days
Diameter: 4,870 km
Mass (Earth = 1): 0.05
Volume (Earth = 1): 0.05
Specific gravity: 5.5
Number of satellites: 0

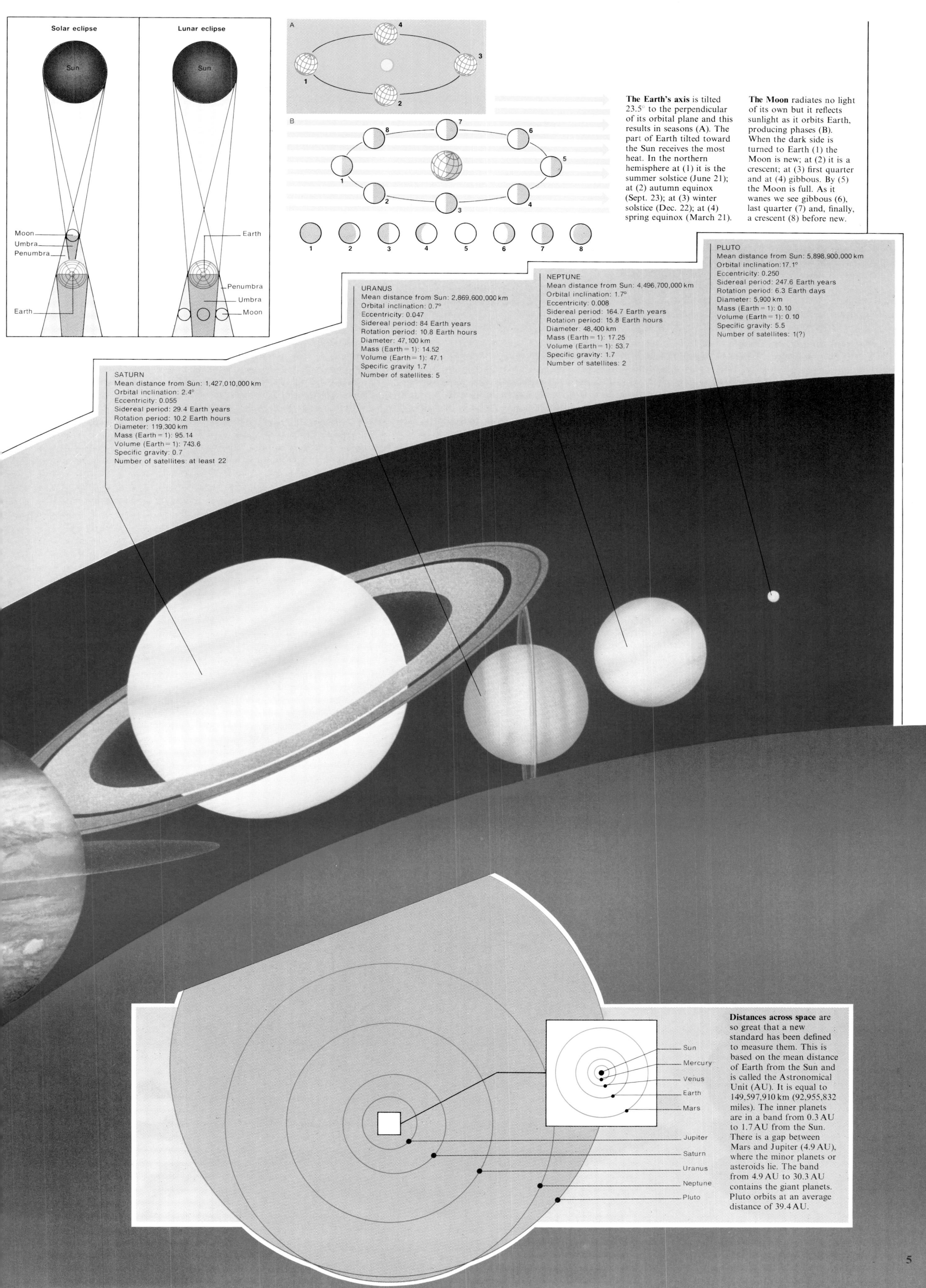

Solar eclipse

Lunar eclipse

Sun

Sun

Moon
Umbra
Penumbra

Earth

Earth

Penumbra
Umbra
Moon

A

4

3

1

2

B

8

7

6

1

5

2

3

4

1 2 3 4 5 6 7 8

The Earth's axis is tilted 23.5° to the perpendicular of its orbital plane and this results in seasons (A). The part of Earth tilted toward the Sun receives the most heat. In the northern hemisphere at (1) it is the summer solstice (June 21); at (2) autumn equinox (Sept. 23); at (3) winter solstice (Dec. 22); at (4) spring equinox (March 21).

The Moon radiates no light of its own but it reflects sunlight as it orbits Earth, producing phases (B). When the dark side is turned to Earth (1) the Moon is new; at (2) it is a crescent; at (3) first quarter and at (4) gibbous. By (5) the Moon is full. As it wanes we see gibbous (6), last quarter (7) and, finally, a crescent (8) before new.

PLUTO
Mean distance from Sun: 5,898,900,000 km
Orbital inclination: 17.1°
Eccentricity: 0.250
Sidereal period: 247.6 Earth years
Rotation period: 6.3 Earth days
Diameter: 5,900 km
Mass (Earth = 1): 0.10
Volume (Earth = 1): 0.10
Specific gravity: 5.5
Number of satellites: 1(?)

NEPTUNE
Mean distance from Sun: 4,496,700,000 km
Orbital inclination: 1.7°
Eccentricity: 0.008
Sidereal period: 164.7 Earth years
Rotation period: 15.8 Earth hours
Diameter: 48,400 km
Mass (Earth = 1): 17.25
Volume (Earth = 1): 53.7
Specific gravity: 1.7
Number of satellites: 2

URANUS
Mean distance from Sun: 2,869,600,000 km
Orbital inclination: 0.7°
Eccentricity: 0.047
Sidereal period: 84 Earth years
Rotation period: 10.8 Earth hours
Diameter: 47,100 km
Mass (Earth = 1): 14.52
Volume (Earth = 1): 47.1
Specific gravity 1.7
Number of satellites: 5

SATURN
Mean distance from Sun: 1,427,010,000 km
Orbital inclination: 2.4°
Eccentricity: 0.055
Sidereal period: 29.4 Earth years
Rotation period: 10.2 Earth hours
Diameter: 119,300 km
Mass (Earth = 1): 95.14
Volume (Earth = 1): 743.6
Specific gravity: 0.7
Number of satellites: at least 22

Sun
Mercury
Venus
Earth
Mars

Jupiter
Saturn
Uranus
Neptune
Pluto

Distances across space are so great that a new standard has been defined to measure them. This is based on the mean distance of Earth from the Sun and is called the Astronomical Unit (AU). It is equal to 149,597,910 km (92,955,832 miles). The inner planets are in a band from 0.3 AU to 1.7 AU from the Sun. There is a gap between Mars and Jupiter (4.9 AU), where the minor planets or asteroids lie. The band from 4.9 AU to 30.3 AU contains the giant planets. Pluto orbits at an average distance of 39.4 AU.

Earth as a Planet

Viewed from space, the Earth appears to be an ordinary member of the group of inner planets orbiting the Sun. But the Earth is unique in the Solar System because it has an atmosphere that contains oxygen. It is the nature of this surrounding blanket of air that has allowed higher life forms to evolve on Earth and provides their life-support system. At the same time the atmosphere acts as a shield to protect living things from the damaging effects of radiation from the Sun.

Any traces of gas that may have clung to the newly formed Earth were soon swept away into space by the heat of the Sun before it attained a stable state powered by nuclear fusion. Farther out in the Solar System, the Sun's heat was never strong enough to blow these gases away into space, so that even today the giant planets retain atmospheres composed of these primordial gases—mostly methane and ammonia.

The evolution of air

Until the Sun "settled down," Earth was a hot, airless ball of rock. The atmosphere and oceans—like the atmospheres of Venus and Mars—were produced by the "outgassing" of material from the hot interior of the planet as the crust cooled. Volcanoes erupted constantly and produced millions of tonnes of ash and lava. They also probably yielded, as they do today, great quantities of gas, chiefly carbon dioxide, and water vapor. A little nitrogen and various sulphur compounds were also released. Other things being equal, we would expect rocky planets, like the young Earth, to have atmospheres rich in carbon dioxide and water vapor. Venus and Mars do indeed have carbon dioxide atmospheres today, but the Earth now has a nitrogen/oxygen atmosphere. This results from the fact that life evolved on Earth, converting the carbon dioxide to oxygen and storing carbon in organic remains such as coal. Some carbon dioxide was also dissolved in the oceans. The Earth's oxygen atmosphere is a clear sign of life; the carbon dioxide atmospheres of Venus and Mars suggest the absence of life. Why did the Earth begin to evolve in a different way from the other inner planets?

When the Sun stabilized, Earth, Venus and Mars started off down the same evolutionary road, and carbon dioxide and water vapor were the chief constituents of the original atmospheres. On Venus the temperature was hot enough for the water to remain in a gaseous form, and both the water vapor and carbon dioxide in the Venusian atmosphere trapped heat by means of the so-called "greenhouse effect." In this process, radiant energy from the Sun passes through the atmospheric gases and warms the ground. The warmed ground re-radiates heat energy, but at infrared wavelengths, with the result that carbon dioxide and water molecules absorb it and stop it escaping from the planet. Instead of acting like a window, the atmosphere acts like a mirror for outgoing energy. As a result, the surface of Venus became hotter still. Today the surface temperature has stabilized at more than 500°C.

Mars, farther out from the Sun than Earth, was never hot enough for the greenhouse effect to dominate. The red planet once had a much thicker atmosphere than it does today, but, being smaller than the Earth, its gravity is too weak to retain a thick atmosphere. As a result, the planet cooled into a frozen desert as atmospheric gases escaped into space. Mars then, in fact, suffered a climatic change. At one time—hundreds of millions of years ago—there must have been running water because traces of old riverbeds still scar the Martian surface. Today, however, Mars has a thin atmosphere of carbon dioxide and surface temperatures below zero.

Earth—the ideal home

On Earth conditions were just right. Water stayed as a liquid and formed the oceans, while some carbon dioxide from outgassing went into the atmosphere, and some dissolved in the oceans. The resulting modest greenhouse effect

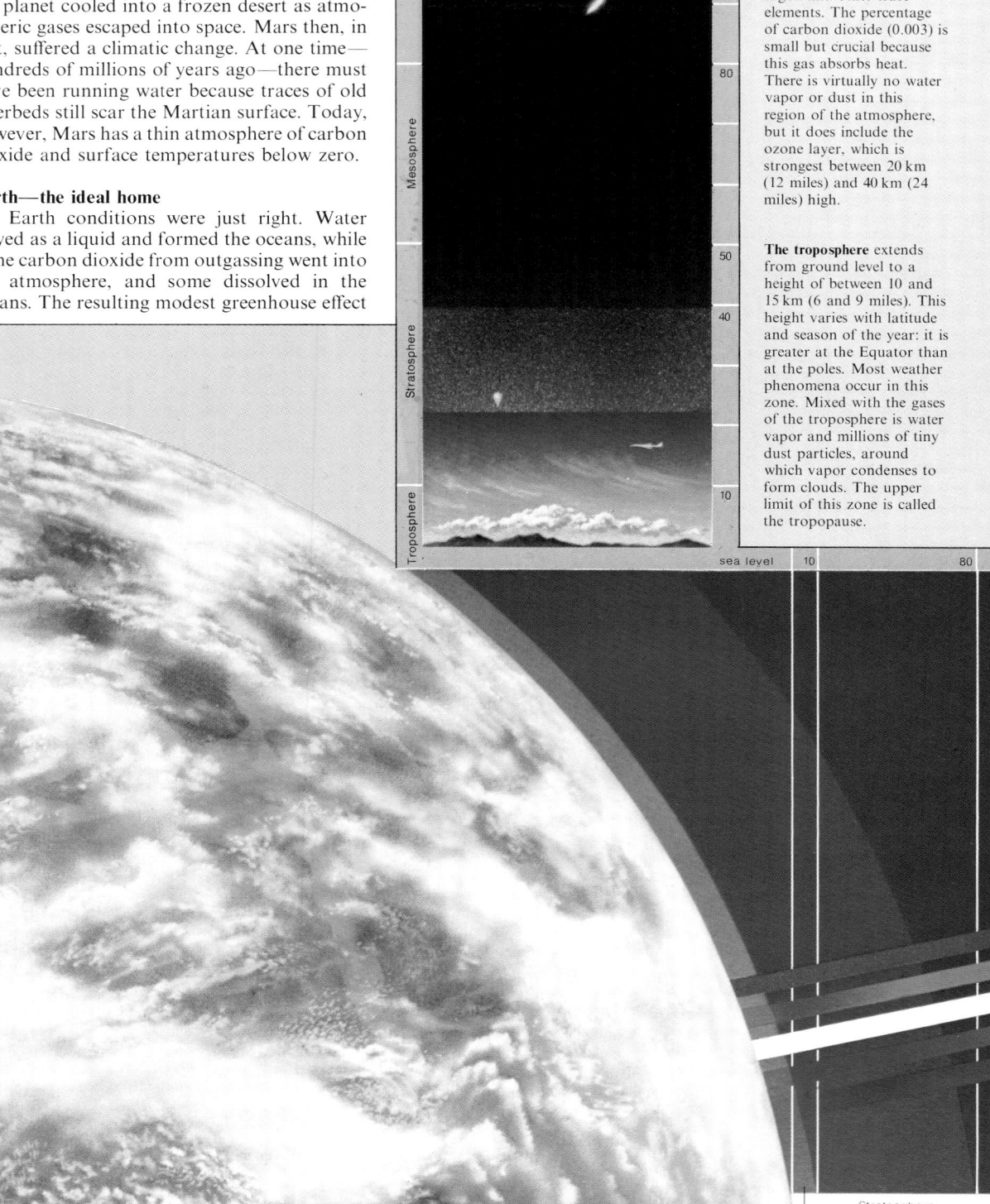

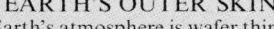

EARTH'S OUTER SKIN

The Earth's atmosphere is wafer thin when compared with the size of the planet. Half of the atmosphere's mass lies in the 5.5 km (3½ miles) nearest the ground and more than 99 percent of it lies within 40 km (24 miles) of the Earth.

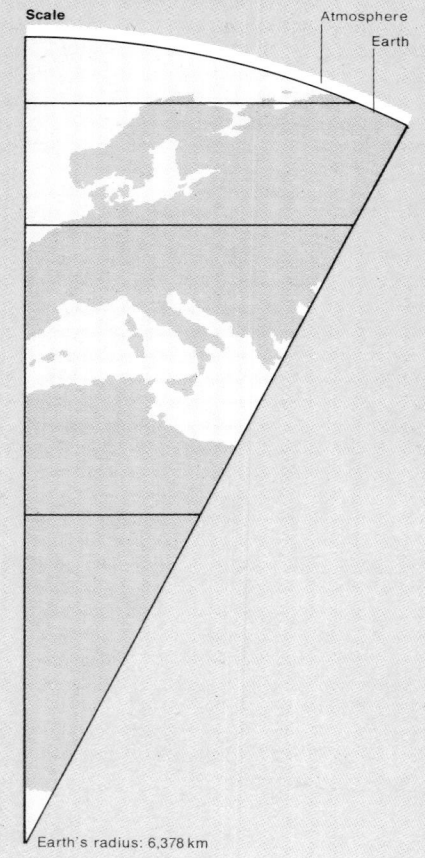

Scale

Atmosphere
Earth

Earth's radius: 6,378 km

Earth reduced by 90% in proportion to this scale

The **thermosphere** extends from 80 km (50 miles) up to 400 km (250 miles). Within this zone temperatures rise steadily with height to as much as 1,650°C (3,000°F), but the air is so thin that temperature is not a meaningful concept. At this height the air is mostly composed of nitrogen molecules to a height of 200 km (125 miles), when oxygen molecules become the dominant constituent.

The **mesosphere** is between 50 and 80 km (30 and 50 miles) above ground level. The stratopause is its lower limit and the mesopause its upper. This zone of the atmosphere is mainly distinguished by its ever decreasing temperatures and, unlike the stratosphere, it does not absorb solar energy.

The **stratosphere** is the level above the troposphere and extends as far as 50 km (30 miles). The chemical composition of the air up to this height is nearly constant and, in terms of volume, it is composed of nitrogen (78%) and oxygen (20%). The rest is mostly argon and other trace elements. The percentage of carbon dioxide (0.003) is small but crucial because this gas absorbs heat. There is virtually no water vapor or dust in this region of the atmosphere, but it does include the ozone layer, which is strongest between 20 km (12 miles) and 40 km (24 miles) high.

The **troposphere** extends from ground level to a height of between 10 and 15 km (6 and 9 miles). This height varies with latitude and season of the year: it is greater at the Equator than at the poles. Most weather phenomena occur in this zone. Mixed with the gases of the troposphere is water vapor and millions of tiny dust particles, around which vapor condenses to form clouds. The upper limit of this zone is called the tropopause.

210 km

160

80

50

40

10

sea level   10   80

Thermosphere

Mesosphere

Stratosphere

Troposphere

Stratosphere
and Mesosphere

Troposphere

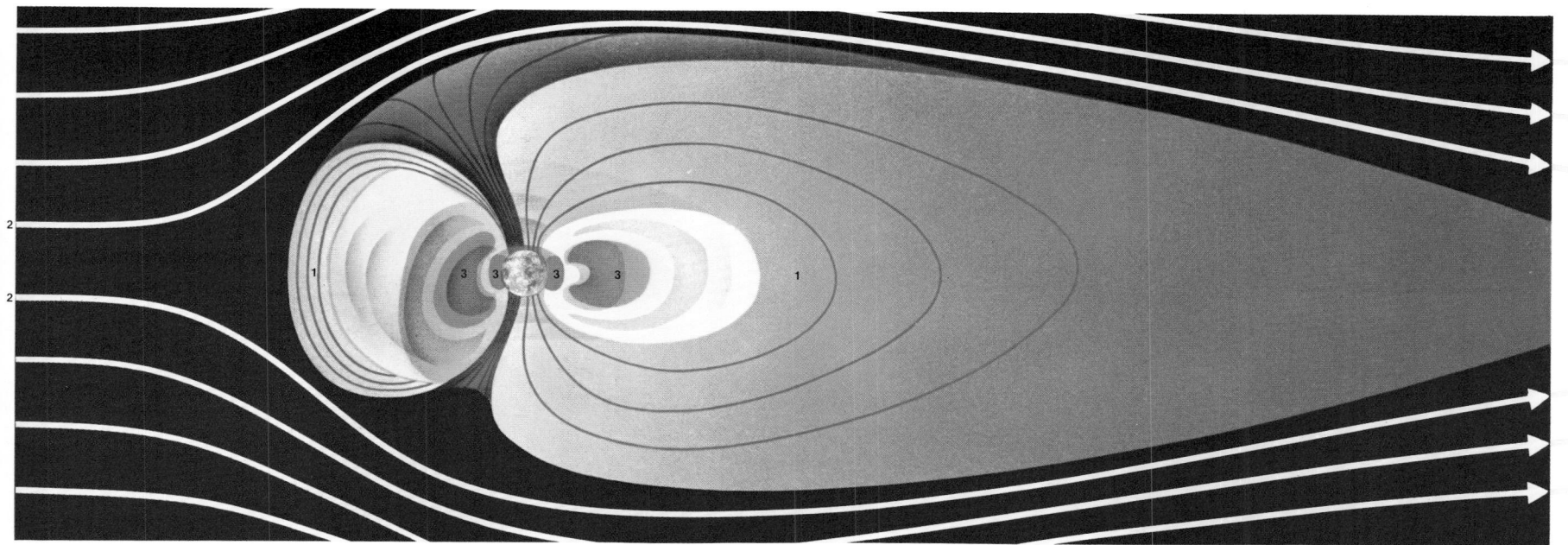

was compensated for by the formation of shiny white clouds of water droplets which reflected some of the Sun's radiation back into space. Our planet stabilized with an average temperature of 15°C. This proved ideal for the emergence of life, which evolved first in the seas and then moved onto land, converting carbon dioxide into oxygen as it did so.

In any view from space, planet Earth is dominated by water—in blue oceans and white clouds—and water is the key to life as we know it. Animal life—oxygen-breathing life—could only evolve after earlier forms of life had converted the atmosphere to an oxygen-rich state. The nature of the air today is a product of life as well as being vital to its existence.

An atmospheric layer cake

Starting at ground level, the first zone of the atmosphere is the troposphere, kept warm near the ground by the greenhouse effect but cooling to a chilly −60°C at an altitude of 15 km (9 miles). Above the troposphere is a warming layer, the stratosphere, in which energy from the Sun is absorbed and temperatures increase to reach 0°C at an altitude of 50 km (30 miles). The energy—in the form of ultraviolet radiation—is absorbed by molecules of ozone, a form of oxygen. Without the ozone layer in the atmosphere, ultraviolet rays would penetrate the

The Earth's magnetic field behaves as if there were a huge bar magnet placed inside the globe, with its magnetic axis tilted at a slight angle to the geographical north–south axis. The speed of rotation of the liquid core differs from that of the mantle, producing an effect like a dynamo (below). The region in which the magnetic field extends beyond the Earth is the magnetosphere (1). Streams of charged particles (2) from the Sun distort its shape into that of a teardrop. Zones of the magnetosphere include the Van Allen Belts (3), which are regions of intense radioactivity where magnetic particles are "trapped."

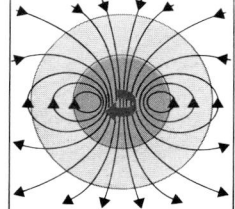

ground and sterilize the land surface: without life, there would be no oxygen from which an ozone layer could form.

Above the stratosphere, another cooling layer, the mesosphere, extends up to 80 km (50 miles), at which point the temperature has fallen to about −100°C. Above this level the gases of the atmosphere are so thin that the standard concept of temperature is no real guide to their behavior, and from the mesosphere outwards the atmosphere is best described in terms of its electrical properties.

In the outer layers of the atmosphere, the Sun's energy is absorbed by individual atoms in such a way that it strips electrons off them, leaving behind positively charged ions, which give the region its name—the ionosphere. A few hundred kilometers above the Earth's surface, gravity is so feeble that electromagnetic forces begin to determine the behavior of the charged particles, which are shepherded along the lines of force in the Earth's magnetic field. Above 500 km (300 miles), the magnetic field is so dominant that yet another region, the magnetosphere, is distinguished. This is the true boundary between Earth and interplanetary space.

The magnetosphere has been likened to the hull of "spaceship Earth." Charged particles (the solar wind) streaming out from the Sun are deflected around Earth by the magnetosphere

like water around a moving ship, while the region of the Earth's magnetic influence in space trails "downstream" away from the Sun like the wake of a ship. The Van Allen Belts, at altitudes of 3,000 and 15,000 km (1,850 and 9,300 miles) are regions of space high above the Equator where particles are trapped by the magnetic field. Particles spilling out of the belts spiral towards the polar regions of Earth, producing the spectacle of the auroras—the northern and southern lights. The Earth and Mercury are the only inner planets with magnetospheres such as this. The cause of the Earth's magnetism is almost certainly the planet's heavy molten core, which is composed of magnetic materials.

The Earth's atmosphere exhibits a great variety of characteristics on a vertical scale. As well as variations of temperature and the electrical properties of the air, there are differences in chemical composition—in the mixture of gases and water vapor—according to altitude. The Earth's gravitational pull means that air density and pressure decrease with altitude. Pressure of about 1,000 millibars at sea level falls to virtually nothing (10^{-42} millibars) by a height of 700 km (435 miles) above the Earth. All these factors, and their interrelationships, help to maintain the Earth's atmosphere as a protective outer covering or radiation shield and an essential life-support system.

The ionosphere is another name for the atmospheric layer beyond 80 km (50 miles). The region is best described in terms of the electrical properties of its constituents rather than by temperature. It is here that ionization occurs. Gamma and X-rays from the Sun are absorbed by atoms and molecules of nitrogen and oxygen and, as a result, each molecule or atom gives up one or more of its electrons, thus becoming a positively charged ion. These ions reflect radio waves and are used to bounce back radio waves transmitted from the surface of the Earth.

The exosphere is the layer above the thermosphere and it extends from 400 km (250 miles) up to about 700 km (435 miles), the point at which, it may be said, space begins. It is almost a complete vacuum because most of its atoms and molecules of oxygen escape the Earth's gravity.

The magnetosphere includes the exosphere, but it extends far beyond the atmosphere—to a distance of between 64,000 and 130,000 km (40,000 and 80,000 miles) above the Earth. It represents the Earth's external magnetic field and its outer limit is called the magnetopause.

The atmosphere protects the Earth from harmful solar radiation and also from bombardment by small particles from space. Most meteors (particles orbiting the Sun) burn up in the atmosphere, but meteorites (debris of minor planets) reach the ground. Of all incoming solar radiation, only visible light, radio waves and infrared rays reach the surface of Earth. X-rays are removed in the ionosphere, and ultraviolet and some infrared radiations are filtered out in the stratosphere. Studies of such radiations have, therefore, to be made from observatories in space.

Man Looks at the Earth

Orbiting satellites keep a detailed watch on the Earth's land surface, oceans and atmosphere, feeding streams of data to meteorologists, geologists, oceanographers, farmers, fishermen and many others. Some information would be unobtainable by any other means. Surveys from orbit are quicker and less expensive than from aircraft, for example, because a satellite can scan a much larger area. And, surprisingly enough, certain features on the ground are easier to see from space.

Landsat (A) circles Earth 14 times every 24 hours at a height of 920 km (570 miles). Every 25 seconds it surveys 34,250 sq km (13,225 sq miles).

1

2

MAPPING AND MEASURING
Man has been looking at Earth from satellites since the beginning of the 1960s, and has firmly established the value of surveys from space to those engaged in a variety of earthly pursuits. Chief of these activities are resource management, ranging from monitoring the spread of deserts and river silting to locating likely mineral deposits; environmental protection, which includes observing delicate ecosystems and natural disasters; and a whole range of mapping and land-use planning.

Satellites give us a greater overview of numerous aspects of life on Earth than any earthbound eye could see.

Of all the information gleaned from satellites, accurate weather forecasts are of particular social and economic value. The first weather satellite was Tiros 1 (Television and Infrared Observation Satellite), launched by the United States in 1960. By the time Tiros 10 ceased operations in 1967, the series had sent back more than half a million photographs, firmly establishing the value of satellite imagery.

Tiros was superseded by the ESSA (Environmental Science Services Administration) and the NOAA (National Oceanic and Atmospheric Administration) satellites. These orbited the Earth from pole to pole, and they covered the entire globe during the course of a day. Other weather satellites, such as the European Meteosat, are placed in geostationary orbit over the Equator, which means they stay in one place and continually monitor a single large region.

Watching the weather
In addition to photographing clouds, weather satellites monitor the extent of snow and ice cover, and they measure the temperature of the oceans and the composition of the atmosphere. Information about the overall heat balance of our planet gives clues to long-term climatic change, and includes the effects on climate of human activities such as the burning of fossil fuels and deforestation.

Infrared sensors allow pictures to be taken at night as well as during the day. The temperature of cloud tops, measured by infrared devices, is a guide to the height of the clouds. In a typical infrared image, high clouds appear white because they are the coldest, lower clouds and land areas appear gray, and oceans and lakes are black. Information on humidity in the atmosphere is provided by sensors tuned to wavelengths between 5.5 and 7 micrometers, at which water vapor strongly absorbs the radiation.

To "see" inside clouds, where infrared and visible light cannot penetrate, satellites use sensors tuned to short-wavelength radio waves (microwaves) around the 1.5 centimeter wavelength. These sensors can reveal whether or not clouds will give rise to heavy rainfall, snow or hail. Microwave sensors are also useful for locating ice floes in polar regions, making use of the different microwave reflections from land ice, sea ice and open water.

Satellites that send out such pictures are in relatively low orbits, at a height of about 1,000 km (620 miles), and they pass over each part of the Earth once every 12 hours. But to build up a global model of the Earth's weather and climate, meteorologists need continual information on wind speed and direction at

various levels in the atmosphere, together with temperature and humidity profiles. This data is provided by geostationary satellites. Cloud photographs taken every half-hour give information on winds, and computers combine this with temperature and humidity soundings to give as complete a model as is possible of the Earth's atmosphere.

Increasing attention is also being paid to the Earth's surface, notably by means of a series of satellites called Landsat (originally ERTS or Earth Resource Technology Satellites), the first of which was launched by the United States in 1972. The third and current Landsat is in a similar pole-to-pole orbit as the weather satellites, but its cameras are more powerful and they make more detailed surveys of the Earth. Landsat rephotographs each part of the Earth's surface every 18 days.

How to map resources
The satellite has two sensor systems: a television camera, which takes pictures of the Earth using visible light; and a device called a multispectral scanner, which scans the Earth at several distinct wavelengths, including visible light and infrared. Data from the various channels of the multispectral scanner can be combined to produce so-called false-color images, in which each wavelength band is assigned a color (not necessarily its real one) to emphasize features of interest.

An important use of Landsat photographs is for making maps, particularly of large countries with remote areas that have never been adequately surveyed from the ground. Several countries, including Brazil, Canada and China, have set up ground stations to receive Landsat data directly. Features previously unknown or incorrectly mapped, including rivers, lakes and glaciers, show up readily on Landsat images. Urban mapping and hence planning are aided by satellite pictures that can distinguish areas of industry, housing and open parkland.

Landsat photographs have also proved invaluable for agricultural land-use planning.

3

They are used for estimates of soil types and for determining land-use patterns. Areas of crop disease or dying vegetation are detectable by their different colors. Yields of certain crops such as wheat can now be accurately predicted from satellite imagery, so that at last it is becoming possible to keep track of the worldwide production of vital food crops. Fresh water, too, is one of our most valuable resources, and knowing its sources and seasonal variation is vital to irrigation projects.

Finally, the geologist and mineral prospector have benefited from remote sensing. Features such as fault lines and different types of sediments and rocks show up clearly on Landsat pictures. This allows geologists to select promising areas in which the prospector can look for mineral deposits.

Another way to study the Earth is by bouncing radar beams off it. Radar sensing indicates the nature of soil or rock on land and movement of water at sea, for example. This was not done by Landsat, but by equipment aboard the United States' Skylab and by a short-lived American satellite called Seasat. The former Soviet Union included Earth surveying in its Salyut program, and resource mapping is also a feature of the spacelab aboard the American space shuttle. All these activities help man to manage the limited resources on our planet and to preserve the environment.

4

5

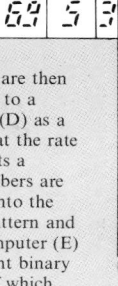

A multispectral scanner (B) has an oscillating mirror (1) that focuses visible and near infrared radiation on to a detector (2). This converts the intensity of the radiation into a voltage. An electronics unit (3) turns the voltage pattern into a series of digitized numbers that can be fed into a computer.

The numbers (C) are then transmitted back to a receiving station (D) as a radio frequency at the rate of 15 million units a second. The numbers are translated back into the digital voltage pattern and converted by computer (E) into the equivalent binary numbers, each of which represents a color.

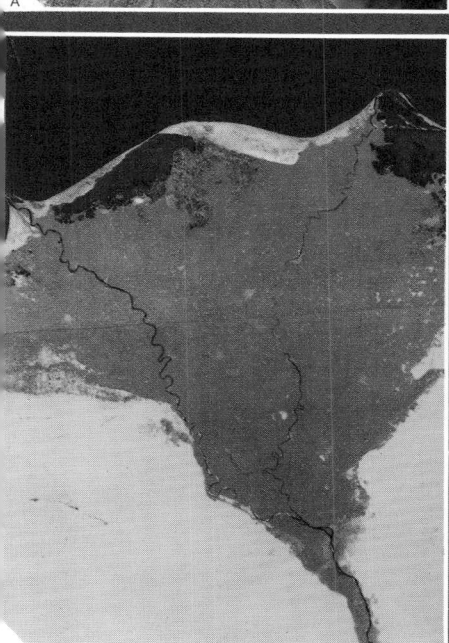

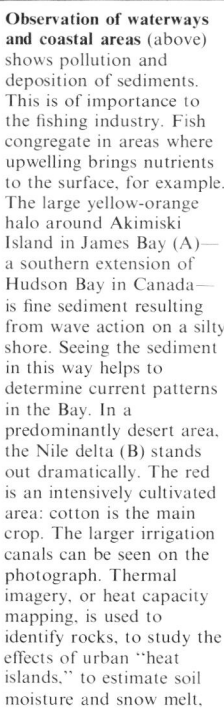

A Landsat image is made up of very many points, each of which is obtained by means of the procedure described above. Each number in the image (F) represents the radiation from a small area of land, or pixel, 0.44 hectares (1.1 acres) in size. A computer then translates the numbers into different colors, or different shades of one color, which are projected on to a TV screen (G) and the image is seen for the first time. Finally, photographs of this false-color image are produced (H). This picture, showing a forest fire in the Upper Peninsula, Michigan, is of use to those engaged in forest management. Other satellite data of use in forestry include types of trees, patterns of growth and the spread of disease.

Observation of waterways and coastal areas (above) shows pollution and deposition of sediments. This is of importance to the fishing industry. Fish congregate in areas where upwelling brings nutrients to the surface, for example. The large yellow-orange halo around Akimiski Island in James Bay (A)—a southern extension of Hudson Bay in Canada—is fine sediment resulting from wave action on a silty shore. Seeing the sediment in this way helps to determine current patterns in the Bay. In a predominantly desert area, the Nile delta (B) stands out dramatically. The red is an intensively cultivated area: cotton is the main crop. The larger irrigation canals can be seen on the photograph. Thermal imagery, or heat capacity mapping, is used to identify rocks, to study the effects of urban "heat islands," to estimate soil moisture and snow melt.

and to map shallow ground water. In this photograph of the northeast coast of North America (C) purple represents the coldest temperatures—in Lakes Erie and Ontario. The coldest parts of the Atlantic Ocean are deep blue, whereas warmer waters near the coast are light blue. Green is the warmer land, but also the Gulf Stream in the lower right part of the image. Brown, yellow and orange represent successively warmer land surface areas. Red is hot regions around cities and coal-mining regions found in eastern Pennsylvania (to the upper left of center in the picture); and, finally, gray and white are the very hottest areas—the urban heat islands of Baltimore, Philadelphia and New York City. Black areas in the upper left are cold clouds. The temperature range of the image is about 30°C (55°F).

The Earth seen from space shows phases just like the Moon, Mercury and Venus do to us. These dramatic photographs were taken from a satellite moving at

- 35,885 km (22,300 miles) above South America at 7.30 am (1), 10.30 am (2), noon (3), 3.30 pm (4) and at 10.30 pm (5), and clearly show the Earth in phase.

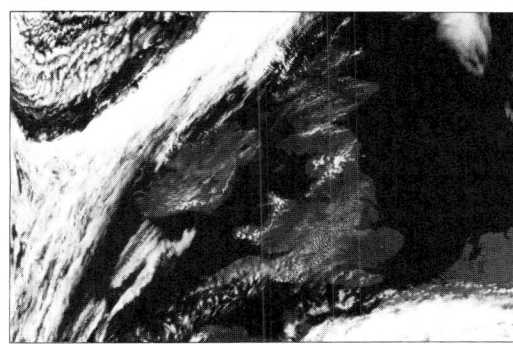
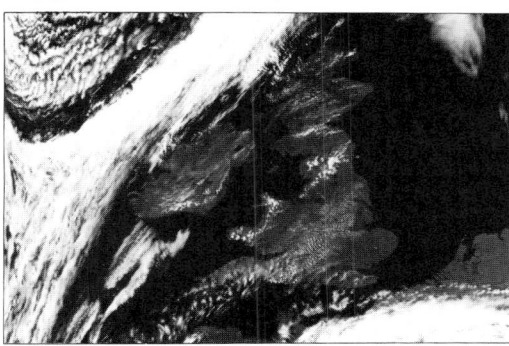

Weather satellite imagery can save lives and property by giving advance warning of bad weather conditions, as well as providing day-to-day forecasts. This Tiros image (left) shows a cold front moving west of Ireland with low-level wave clouds over southern and central England. There are low-pressure systems over northern France and to the northwest of Ireland.

LANDSAT AND THE FARMER

sown	grows	dormant	grows	ripe	harvest

Sep	Oct	Nov	Dec	Jan	Feb	Mar	Apr	May	Jun	Jul	Aug

Agriculturists benefit from "multitemporal analysis" by satellites (left). This is the comparison of data from the same field recorded on two or more dates. It is also able to differentiate crops, which may have an identical appearance, or signature, on one day, but on another occasion exhibit different rates of growth. The pattern of growth is different for small grains than most other crops. A "biowindow" is the period of time in which vegetation is observed. These three biowindows (right) show the emergence and ripening (light blue to red to dark blue) of wheat in May, July and August.

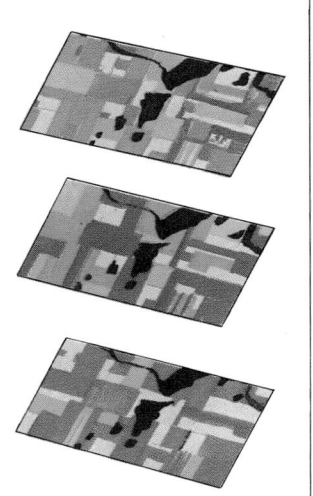

Part 2

MAKING AND SHAPING THE EARTH

The structure and substance of the Earth
Forces that move continents · Forces that fashion Earth's landscapes
How man has changed the face of the Earth

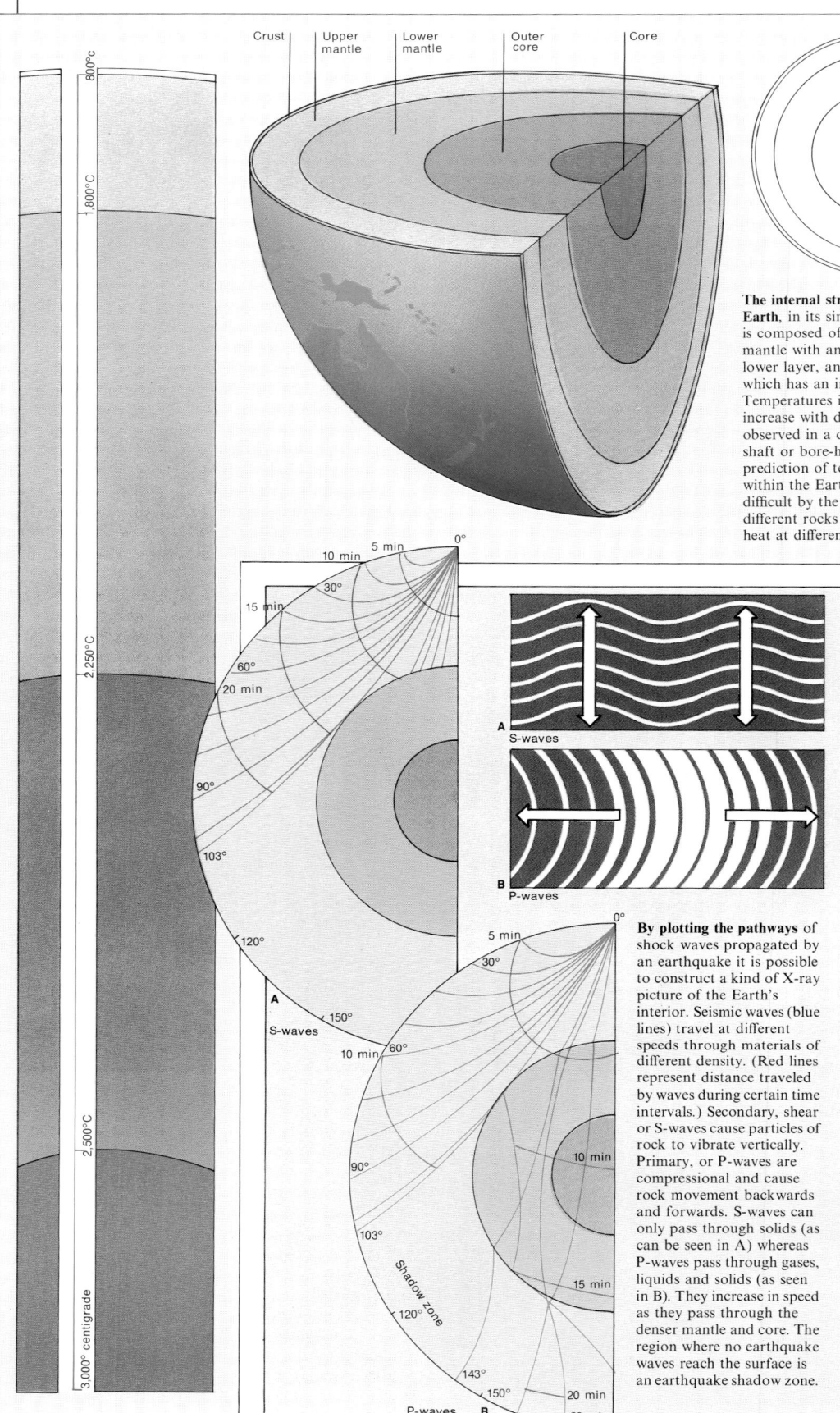

Crust | Upper mantle | Lower mantle | Outer core | Core

0–33 km
(0–19 miles)
33–700 km
(19–435 miles)
700–2,900 km
(435–1,800 miles)
2,900–5,165 km
(1,800–3,205 miles)
5,165–6,385 km
(3,205–3,965 miles)

The internal structure of the Earth, in its simplest form, is composed of a crust, a mantle with an upper and lower layer, and a core, which has an inner region. Temperatures in the Earth increase with depth, as is observed in a deep mine shaft or bore-hole, but the prediction of temperatures within the Earth is made difficult by the fact that different rocks conduct heat at different rates: rock salt, for example, has 10 times the heat conductivity of coal. Also, estimates have to take into account the abundance of heat-generating atoms in a rock. Radioactive atoms are concentrated toward the Earth's surface so the planet has, in effect, a thermal blanket to keep it warm. The temperature at the center of the Earth is believed to be approximately 3,000°C (5,400°F).

A NEW GEOLOGY
A revolution in geological thinking during the first half of this century transformed man's ideas about the structure of the planet Earth. The science of palaeomagnetism, which studies the magnetic properties of rocks and the history of the Earth's magnetic field, and later the new science of marine geology, contributed greatly to the refinement of theories such as continental drift. Man has even looked beyond the Earth for knowledge of this planet's innermost depths.

A
S-waves

B
P-waves

By plotting the pathways of shock waves propagated by an earthquake it is possible to construct a kind of X-ray picture of the Earth's interior. Seismic waves (blue lines) travel at different speeds through materials of different density. (Red lines represent distance traveled by waves during certain time intervals.) Secondary, shear or S-waves cause particles of rock to vibrate vertically. Primary, or P-waves are compressional and cause rock movement backwards and forwards. S-waves can only pass through solids (as can be seen in A) whereas P-waves pass through gases, liquids and solids (as seen in B). They increase in speed as they pass through the denser mantle and core. The region where no earthquake waves reach the surface is an earthquake shadow zone.

A
S-waves

Shadow zone

P-waves   B

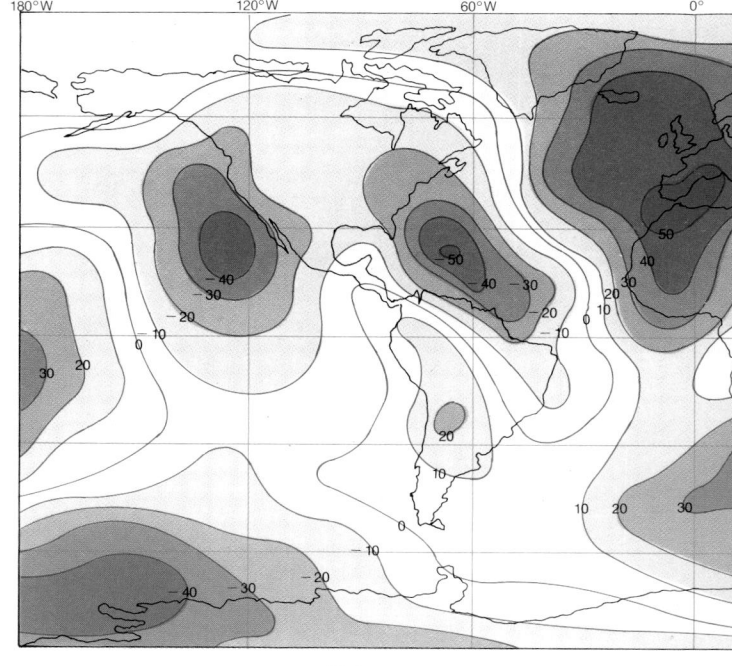

A Silicon
B Aluminum
C Iron
D Calcium
E Magnesium
F Nickel
G Other

The chemical composition of the Earth varies from crust to core. The upper crust of continents (sial) is mainly granite, rich in aluminum and silicon, whereas oceanic crust (sima) is largely basalt, made of magnesium and silicon. The mantle is composed of rocks that are rich in magnesium and iron silicates, whereas the core, it is believed, is made of iron and nickel oxides.

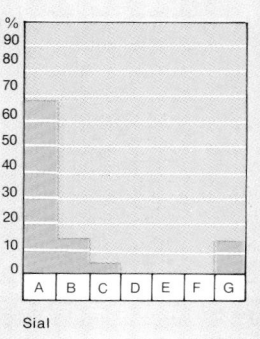

Sial

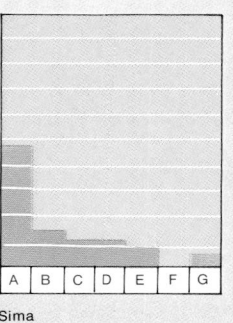

Sima

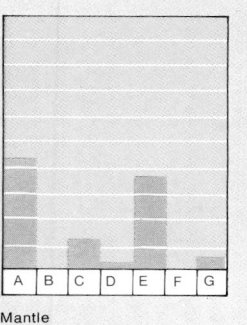

Mantle

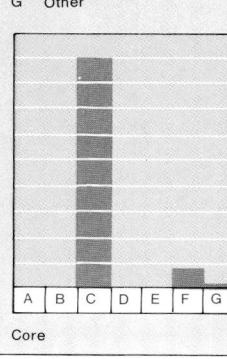

Core

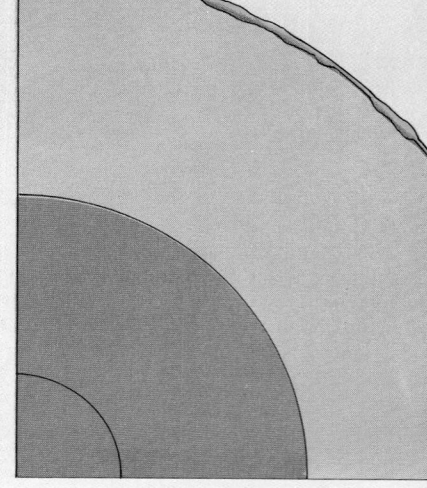

Earth's Structure

The Earth is made up of concentric shells of different kinds of material. Immediately beneath us is the crust; below that is the mantle; and at the center of the globe is the core. Knowledge of the internal structure of Earth is the key to an understanding of the substances of Earth and an appreciation of the forces at work, not only deep in the center of the planet but also affecting the formation of surface features and large-scale landscapes. The workings of all these elements are inextricably linked.

A 17th-century diagram of the Earth shows an internal structure of fire and subterranean rivers.

The Earth is not a sphere but an ellipsoid (below) that is flattened at the poles, where the radius is 6,378 km (3,960 miles), and bulging at the Equator, where the radius is 6,536 km (4,060 miles). This results from the Earth's rapid rotation. But, rather than a perfect ellipsoid, the true shape is a "geoid"—the actual shape of sea level—which is lumpy, with variations away from ellipsoid of up to 80 m (260 ft) (left). This reflects major variations in density in Earth's outer layers.

The Earth as a Geoid

Our knowledge of the Earth is largely restricted to the outer crust. The deepest hole that man has drilled reaches only 10 km (6 miles)—less than 1/600th of the planet's radius—and so our knowledge about the rest of the Earth has had to come via indirect means: by the study of earthquake waves, and a comparison between rocks on Earth and those that make up meteorites—small fragments of asteroids and other minor planetary bodies that originated from similar materials to the Earth.

The Earth's crust

The outermost layer of the Earth is called the crust. The crust beneath the oceans is different from the material that makes up continental crust. Ocean crust is formed at mid-ocean ridges where melted rocks (magma) from the mantle rise up in great quantities and solidify to form a layer a few kilometers thick over the mantle. As this ocean crust spreads out from the ridge it becomes covered with deep-ocean sediments. The ocean crust was initially called "sima," a word made up from the first two letters of the characteristic elements—silicon and magnesium. Sima has a density of 2.9 gm/cc (1 gm/cc is the density of water).

Continental crust was named "sial"—from silicon and aluminum, the most abundant elements. Sial is lighter than sima with a density of 2.7 gm/cc. The continental crust is like a series of giant rafts, 17 to 70 km (9–43 miles) thick. As a result of numerous collisions and breakages, these continental rafts have been bulldozed into their present shape, but they have been forming for at least 4,000 million years. The oldest known rocks, in Greenland, are 3,750 million years old, which is only about 800 million years younger than the Earth itself. The complex history of the continents' evolution over this vast time span makes construction of an ideal cross section difficult, but the rocks of the lower two-thirds of the crust appear to be denser (2.9 gm/cc) than the upper levels.

The Moho, or Mohorovičič discontinuity, discovered in 1909, marks the base of the crust and the beginning of the mantle rocks, where the density increases from 2.9 to 3.3 gm/cc. The Moho is at an average depth of 10 km (6 miles) under the sea and 35 km (20 miles) below land.

The mantle

Our knowledge of the mantle comes from mantle rocks that are sometimes brought to the surface. These are even more enriched in magnesium oxides than the sima, with lesser amounts of iron and calcium oxides. The uppermost mantle to a depth of between 60 and 100 km (40–60 miles), together with the overlying crust, forms the rigid lithosphere, which is divided into plates. Below this is a pasty layer, or asthenosphere, extending to a depth of 700 km (435 miles). The upper mantle is separated from the lower mantle by another discontinuity where the density of the rock increases from 3.3 to 4.3 gm/cc.

Scientists now believe that the mantle is the planetary motor force behind the movements of the continents. By studying in detail the chemistry of the volcanic rocks that have come directly from the mantle, they have gathered much information about this mantle motor. The rocks that come up along oceanic ridges and form new oceanic crust reveal by their chemical composition that they have formed from mantle that has undergone previous melting. By contrast, islands such as Hawaii and Iceland have formed from mantle material that, for the most part, has never been melted before. One explanation for these chemical observations is that, while the top 700 km (435 miles) of the mantle region is moving in accordance with movement of the plates, the mantle beneath it is moving independently and sending occasional rivers of unaltered material through the surface to form islands like volcanic Hawaii.

The core

Structurally, the most important boundary in the Earth lies at a depth of 2,900 km (1,800 miles) below the surface, where the rock density almost doubles from about 5.5 to 9.9 gm/cc. This is known as the Gutenberg discontinuity and was discovered in 1914. Below this level the material must have the properties of a liquid since certain earthquake waves cannot penetrate it. Scientists infer from the composition of meteorites, some of which are composed of iron and nickel, that this deep core material is composed largely of iron, with some nickel and perhaps lighter elements such as silicon. The processes involved in the formation of a planet have been compared to the separation of the metals (the core) from the slag (the mantle and crust) in a blast furnace.

The core has a radius of 3,485 km (2,165 miles) and makes up only one-sixth of the Earth's volume, yet it has one-third of its mass. In the middle of the liquid outer core there is an even denser ball with a radius of 1,220 km (760 miles)—two-thirds the size of the Moon—where, under intense pressure, the metals have solidified. The inner core is believed to be solid iron and nickel and is 20 percent denser (12–13 gm/cc) than the surrounding liquid.

Electric currents in the core are the only possible source of the Earth's magnetic field. This drifts and alters in a way which could arise only from some deeply buried fluid movement. At the top of the core, the pattern of the field moves about 100 m (330 ft) west each day. Every million years or so during the Earth's history, the north–south magnetic poles have switched so that compasses pointed south, not north.

The dynamo that generates magnetism and its strange variations is still not fully understood. Motion in the core may be powered by giant slabs of metal that crystallize out from the liquid and sink to join the inner core. Our knowledge of the Earth's structure has increased greatly over the last 50 years, but many intriguing questions remain to be answered.

● Geomagnetic poles

Oersteds
- 0.20
- 0.25
- 0.30
- 0.35
- 0.40
- 0.45
- 0.50
- 0.55
- 0.60
- 0.65
- 0.70

The Earth's magnetic field is strongest at the poles and weakest in equatorial regions. If the field were simply like a bar magnet inside the globe, lines of intensity would mirror lines of latitude; but the field is inclined at an angle of 11 to the Earth's axis. The geomagnetic poles are similarly inclined and they do not coincide with the geographic poles. In reality, the field is much more complex than that of a bar magnet. In addition, over long periods of time, the magnetic poles and the north–south orientation of the field change slowly. The strength of the Earth's magnetic field is measured in units called oersteds.

Earth's Moving Crust

The top layer of the Earth is known as the lithosphere and is composed of the crust and the uppermost mantle. It is divided into six major rigid plates and several smaller platelets that move relative to each other, driven by movements that lie deep in the Earth's liquid mantle. The plate boundaries correspond to the zones of earthquakes and the sites of active volcanoes. The concept of plate tectonics – that the Earth's crust is mobile despite being rigid – emerged in the 1960s and helped to confirm the early twentieth-century theory of continental drift proposed by Alfred Wegener.

THE DYNAMIC EARTH
As early as the 17th century, the English philosopher Francis Bacon noted that the coasts on either side of the Atlantic were similar and could be fitted together like pieces of a jigsaw puzzle. Three hundred years later Alfred Wegener proposed the theory of continental drift, but no one would believe the Earth's rigid crust could move. Today, geological evidence has provided the basis for the theory of plate tectonics, which demonstrates that the Earth's crust is slowly but continually moving.

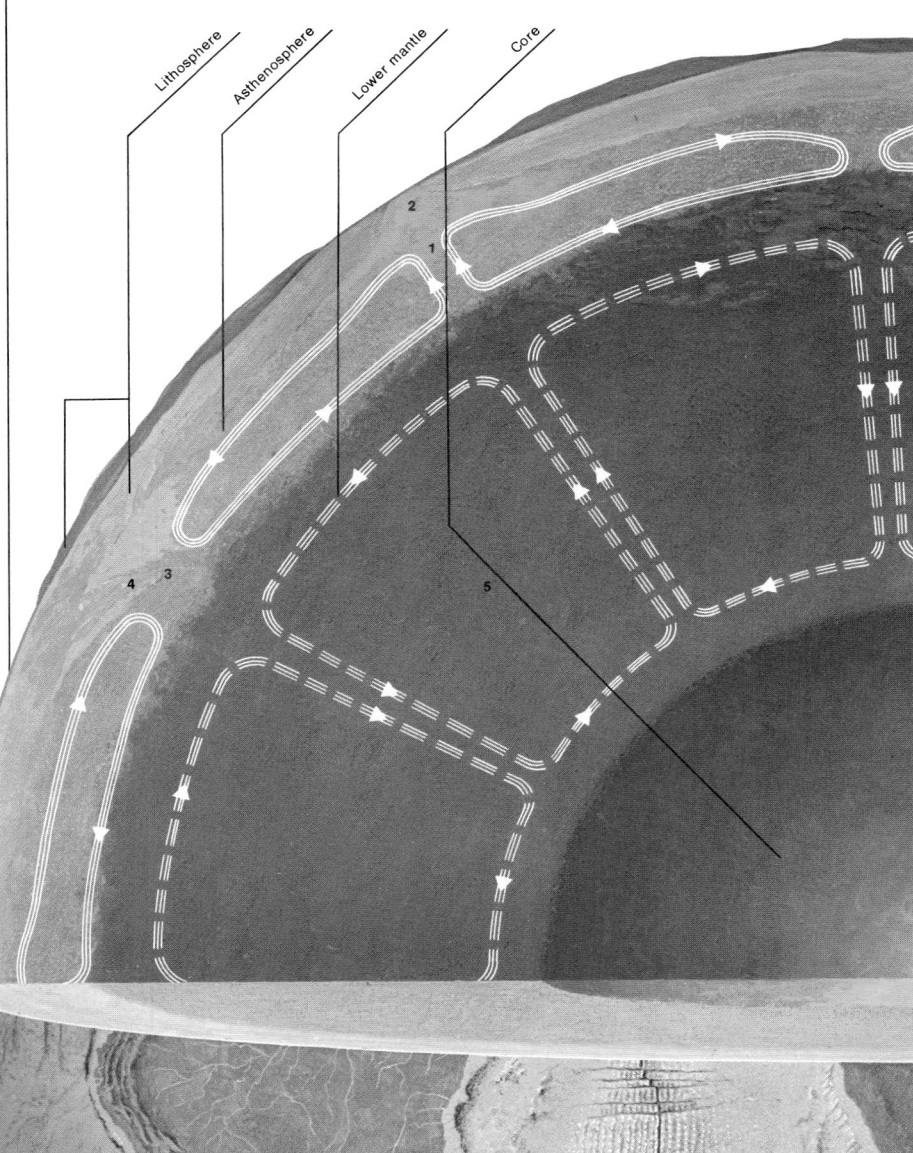

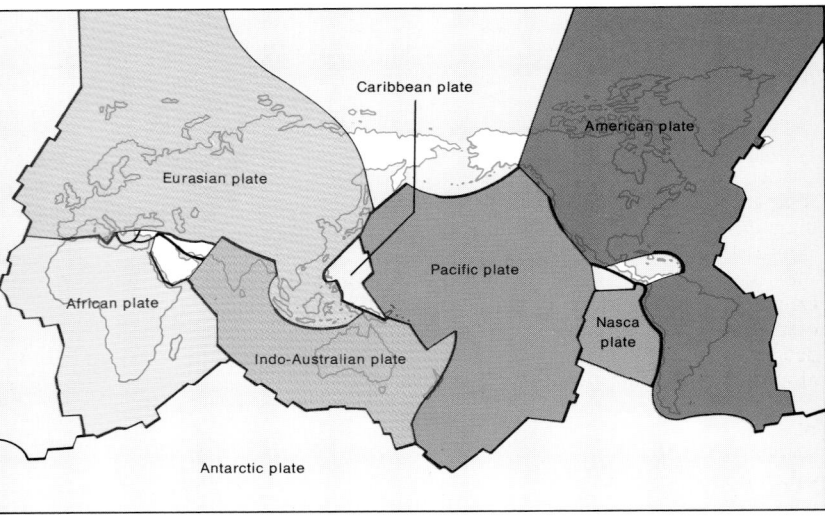

Earth's lithosphere—the rocky shell, or crust—is made up of six major plates and several smaller platelets, each separated from each other by ridges, subduction zones or transcurrent faults. The plates grow bigger by accretion along the mid-ocean ridges, are destroyed at subduction zones beneath the trenches, and slide beside each other along the transcurrent faults. The African and Antarctic plates have no trenches along their borders to destroy any of their crust, so they are growing bigger. This growth is compensated by the subduction zone that is developing to the north of the Tonga Islands and subduction zones in the Pacific. Conversely, the Pacific and Indo-Australian plates are shrinking. Along the plate boundaries magma wells up from the mantle to form volcanoes. Here, too, are the origins of earthquakes as the plates collide or slide slowly past each other.

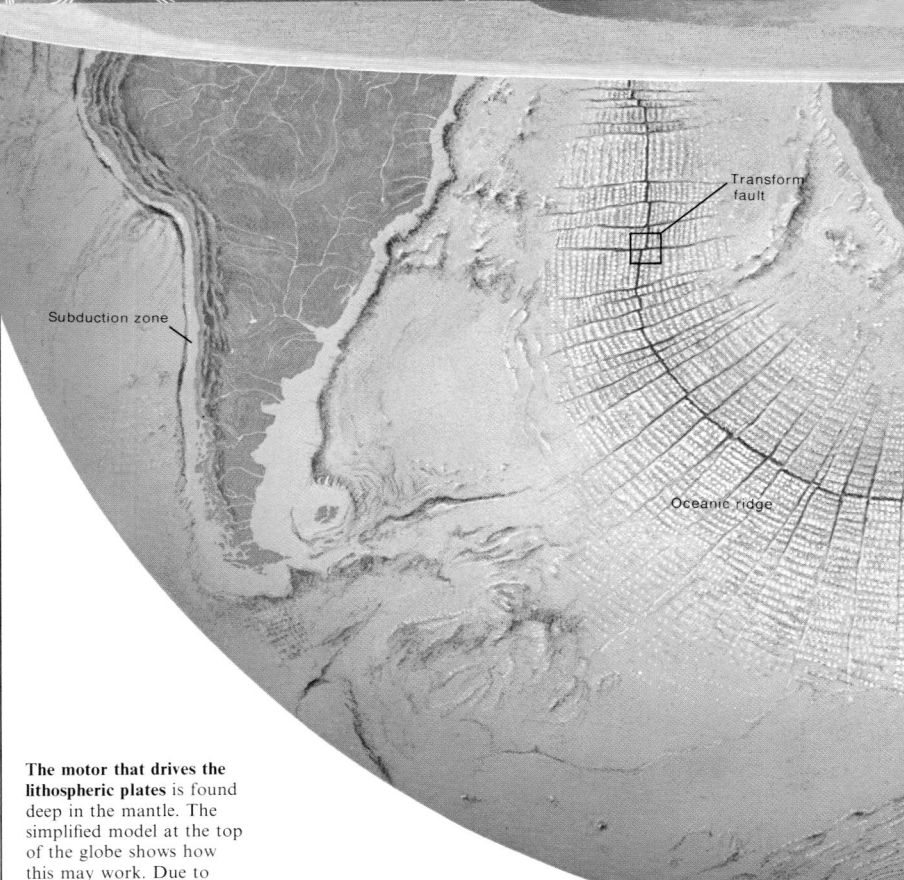

The motor that drives the lithospheric plates is found deep in the mantle. The simplified model at the top of the globe shows how this may work. Due to temperature differences in the mantle, slow convection currents circulate. Where two current cycles move upwards together and separate (1), the plates bulge and move apart along mid-ocean ridges (2). Where there is a downward moving current (3), the plates move together and sometimes one slips under the other to form a subduction zone (4). Another model proposes that the convection currents are found deep in the mantle (5). Only time and more research, however, will reveal the true mechanism of plate movement.

Subduction zones are the sites of destruction of the ocean crust. As one plate passes beneath another down into the mantle, the ocean floor is pulled downward and a deep ocean trench is formed. The movement taking place along the length of the subduction zone causes earthquakes, while melting of the rock at depth produces magma that rises to create the volcanoes that form island arcs.

An oceanic ridge is formed when two plates move away from each other. As they move, molten magma from the mantle forces its way to the surface. This magma cools and is in turn injected with new magma. Thus the oceanic ridge is gradually forming the newest part of Earth's crust.

Transform, or transcurrent, faults are found where two plates slide past each other. They may, for example, link two parts of a ridge (A, B). A study of the magnetic properties of the seabed may suggest a motion shown by the white arrows, but the true movements of the plates are shown by the red arrows. The transform fault is active only between points (2) and (3). Between points (1) and (2) and between (3) and (4) the scar of the fault is healed and the line of the fault is no longer a plate boundary.

The early evidence for continental drift was gathered by Alfred Wegener, a German meteorologist. He noticed that the coastlines on each side of the Atlantic Ocean could be made to fit together, and that much of the geological history of the flanking continents—shown by fossils, structures and past climates—also seemed to match. Wegener compared the two sides of the Atlantic with a sheet of torn newspaper and reasoned that if not just one line of print but 10 lines match then there is a good case for arguing that the two sides were once joined. Yet for 50 years continental drift was generally considered to be a fanciful dream.

Seafloor spreading

In the 1950s the first geological surveys of the oceans began, and a 60,000 km (37,200 mile) long chain of mountains was discovered running down the center of the Atlantic Ocean, all round the Antarctic, up to the Indian Ocean, into the Red Sea and up the Eastern Pacific Ocean into Alaska. Along the axis of this mid-ocean ridge system there was often a narrow, deep rift valley. In places this ridge was offset along sharp fractures in the ocean floor.

The breakthrough in developing the global plate tectonic theory came with the first large-scale survey of the ocean floor. Magnetometers, which were developed during World War II for tracking submarines, showed the ocean floor to be magnetically striped. The ocean floor reveals magnetic characteristics because the ocean crust basalts are full of tiny crystals of the magnetic mineral magnetite. As the basalt cooled, the magnetic field of these crystals aligned itself with the Earth's magnetic field. This would be insignificant if it were not for the fact that the magnetic pole of the Earth has switched from north to south at different times in the past. Half the magnetite compasses of the ocean floor point south rather than north.

In the middle 1960s, two Cambridge geophysicists, Drummond Matthews and Fred Vine, noticed that the pattern of stripes was symmetrical around the mid-ocean ridge. Such an extraordinary and unlikely symmetry could mean only one thing—any two matching stripes must originally have been formed together at the mid-ocean ridge and then moved away from each other as newer crust formed between them to create new stripes. It was soon calculated that the North Atlantic Ocean was growing wider by about 2 cm ($\frac{3}{4}$ in) a year. At last, drifting continents was accepted.

Consumption of the seafloor

Seafloor spreading soon became included in an even more sensational model—plate tectonics. If the oceans are growing wider, then either the whole planet is expanding or the spreading ocean floor is consumed elsewhere. In the late 1950s a global network of seismic stations had been set up to monitor nuclear explosions and earthquakes. For the first time the positions of all earthquakes could be accurately defined.

It was found that the zones of earthquake activity were predominantly narrow, following the mid-ocean ridges and extending along the rim of the Pacific, beneath the island arcs of the

West Pacific and beneath the continental margins in the East Pacific as well as underlying the Alpine-Himalayan Mountain Belt. The seismic zones around the Pacific dipped away from the ocean and continued to depths as great as 700 km (430 miles). They intercepted the surface at the curious arc-shaped deep-ocean trenches. It had been known for 20 years that the pull of gravity over these trenches is strangely reduced, so to survive they must continually be dragged downwards. Here was the site of ocean-floor consumption—now known as a subduction zone. Subduction zones must be efficient at consuming ocean crust because no known ocean crust is older than 200 million years—less than five percent of Earth's lifetime.

The oceanic lithosphere (the Earth's rocky crust) is extraordinarily rigid. Even where the oceanic lithosphere becomes consumed within subduction zones it still maintains its rigidity. As it bends down into the Earth it tends to corrugate, forming very long folds. These corrugations give rise to the pattern of chains of deep-ocean trenches and chains of volcanic islands formed above the subduction zone.

As oceanic lithosphere grows older it cools, contracts and sinks. From the depth of the ocean floor it is possible to make an accurate estimate of the age of the crust beneath. Even the steepness of the subduction zone is a function of the age, and therefore the density, of the lithosphere. The oldest crust provides the strongest downward pull and hence the steepest angle of dip of the subduction zone.

As well as the spreading ridges (constructive margins) and the subduction zones (destructive margins) there is another kind of plate boundary (conservative margins), where the plates slip past one another along a major fault such as the San Andreas Fault of California.

The past positions of the continents

Continental drift is thus the result of the creation and destruction of oceanic lithosphere, but only the continents can record the oceanic plate motions taking place more than 200 million years ago. The discovery of ancient lines of subduction zone volcanoes can testify to the destruction of long-gone oceans. One particularly important technique for finding the positions of the continents is to study the magnetism of certain rocks, particularly lavas, that record the position of the north–south magnetic poles at the time when the rock cooled. If the rock "compass" points, for example, west, then the continent must have rotated by 90°. The vertical dip of the rock compass can reveal the approximate latitude of the rock at its formation (the dip increases from horizontal at the Equator to vertical at the magnetic poles).

As longitude is entirely arbitrary (defined on the position of Greenwich) one can only hope to gain the relative positions of the continents with regard to one another. The best additional information is provided by studies of fossils—if the remains of shallow-water marine organisms are very different latitude they must have been separated by an ocean. The full impact of continental drift on the development of land animals and plants is only beginning to be realized.

THE DRIFTING CONTINENTS

It is now accepted that the continents have changed their positions during the past millions of years, and by studying the magnetism preserved in the rocks the configuration of the continents has been plotted for various geological times. The sequence of continental drifting, illustrated below, begins with one single landmass—the so-called supercontinent Pangaea—and the ancestral Pacific Ocean, called the Panthalassa Ocean. Pangaea first split into a northern landmass called Laurasia and a southern block called Gondwanaland, and subsequently into the continents we see today. The maps illustrate the positions of the continents in the past, where they are now and their predicted positions in 50 million years' time.

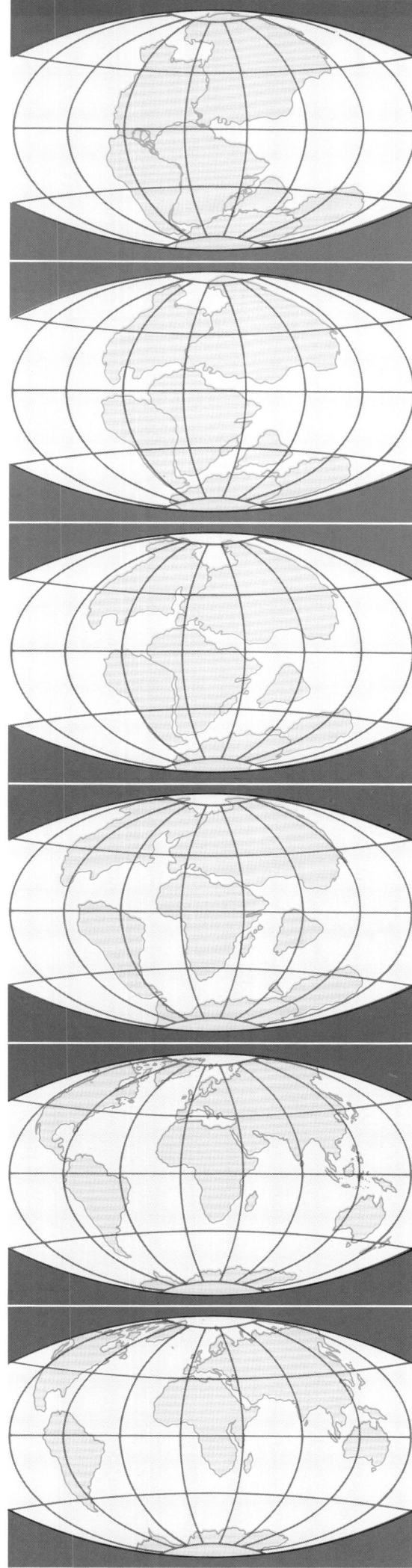

225 million years ago one large landmass, the supercontinent Pangaea, exists and Panthalassa forms the ancestral Pacific Ocean. The Tethys Sea separates Eurasia and Africa and forms an ancestor of the Mediterranean Sea.

180 million years ago Pangaea splits up, the northern block of continents, Laurasia, drifts northwards and the southern block, Gondwanaland, begins to break up. India separates and the South American-African block divides from Australia-Antarctica. New ocean floor is created between the continents.

135 million years ago the Indian plate continues its northward drift and Eurasia rotates to begin to close the eastern end of the Tethys Sea. The North Atlantic and the Indian Ocean have opened up and the South Atlantic is just beginning to form.

65 million years ago Madagascar has split from Africa and the Tethys Sea has closed, with the Mediterranean Sea opening behind it. The South Atlantic Ocean has opened up considerably, but Australia is still joined to the Antarctic and India is about to collide with Asia.

The present day: India has completed its northward migration and collided with Asia, Australia has set itself free from Antarctica, and North America has freed itself from Eurasia to leave Greenland between them. During the past 65 million years (a relatively short geological span of time) nearly half of the present-day ocean floor has been created.

50 million years in the future, Australia may continue its northward drift, part of East Africa will separate from the mainland, and California west of the San Andreas Fault will separate from North America and move northwards. The Pacific Ocean will become smaller, compensating for the increase in size of both the Atlantic and Indian oceans. The Mediterranean Sea will disappear as Africa moves to the north.

Magnetic surveys of the seabed helped build the plate tectonics theory. Research vessels equipped with magnetometers sailed back and forth over a mid-ocean ridge and recorded the varying magnetism of the seabed. The Earth's magnetic pole has switched from north to south at different times in the past, and this mapping revealed a striped magnetic pattern on the seabed. It was noticed that the stripes on either side of the ridge were symmetrical. The explanation was that the matching stripes must have formed together and moved apart as more crust was injected between them—a notion that was subsequently supported by dating of the seafloor.

3   2   1   0   1   3

Time in millions of years

Folds, Faults and Mountain Chains

The continents are great rafts of lighter rock that float in the mantle of the Earth. When drifting continents collide, great mountain chains are thrown up as the continental crust is forced to thicken to absorb the impact of the collision. The highest mountains are formed out of thick piles of sediment that are built up from the debris of erosion constantly washed off the land and deposited on the continental margins. Through the massive deformations of rock faults and folds these remains of old mountains become recycled, thus building new mountains from the remains of old ones.

For the formation of mountain ranges such as the Appalachians or the Himalayas, or the Caledonian mountain chain of Norway, Scotland and Newfoundland, the pattern of development is very much the same. First, a widening ocean with passive margins is located between two continents.

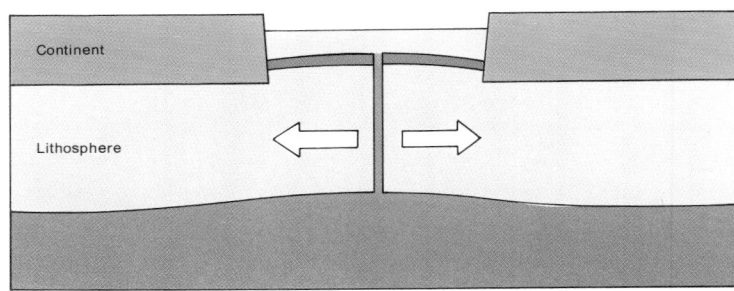

As more ocean floor is created the continents move farther apart, and at the edge of each continent sediment accumulates from the debris of erosion. These piles of thick sediment are known as sedimentary basins.

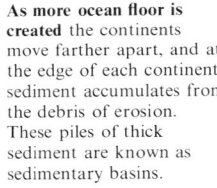
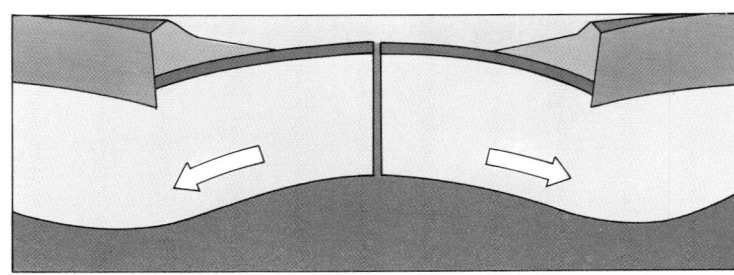

For the formation of the Appalachians, the ancestral Atlantic Ocean began to close, a subduction zone was formed at the ocean–continent boundary, and the oceanic lithosphere began to be absorbed into the mantle. Magma intruded to form granite "plutons" and volcanoes, and much of the sedimentary basin was metamorphosed.

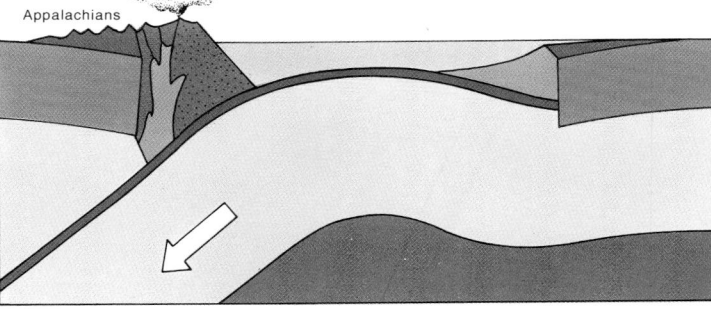

The ocean continued to close until North America and Africa were joined together, further compressing the sediments in the sedimentary basin at the passive ocean margin. The two continents were joined like this between 350 and 225 million years ago.

About 180 million years ago, after the original Appalachians had been worn down in size, the present Atlantic Ocean opened along a new break in the continental crust, offset from the line of the original mountains. As the continents split, so the crust became stretched along great curved faults.

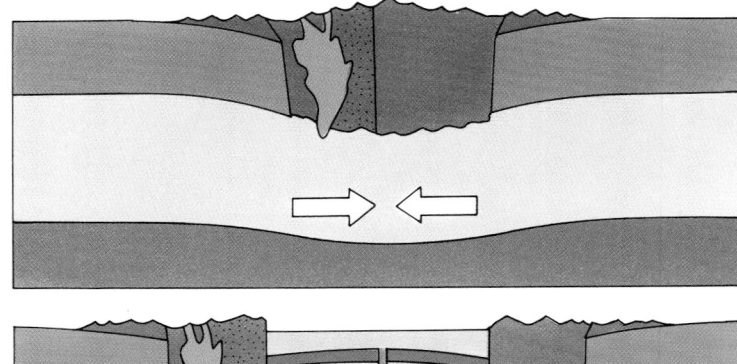
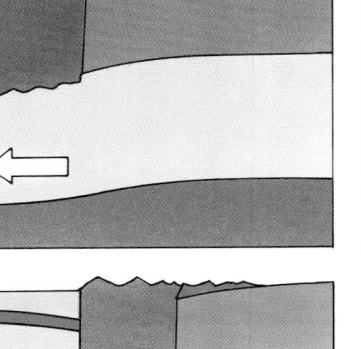

Parts of the ancient Appalachian mountains have been eroded to sea level, leaving the Appalachians, that formed on the edge of the old continent, inland.

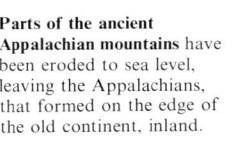
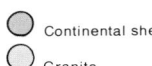

- Continental shelf
- Granite
- Metamorphic rock
- Sediment
- Ocean crust

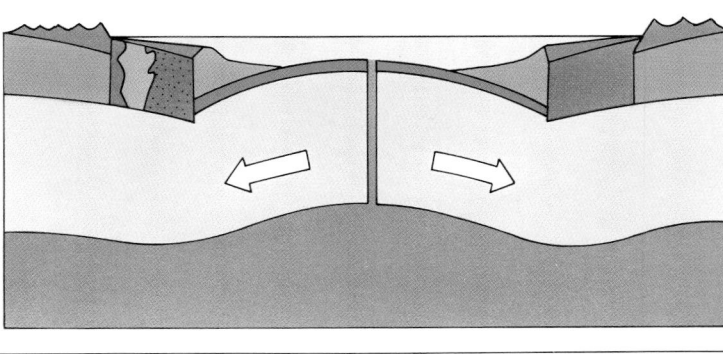

BIRTH AND DEATH OF A MOUNTAIN

Mountains are thrust upward by the pressure exerted by the moving plates of the Earth's crust, and are formed out of the sediments that have been eroded from the continental masses. Young mountains are lofty and much folded, but the agents of erosion and weathering soon begin to reduce their height, and over many millions of years the mountain range is eroded to sea level. This eroded material accumulates in the sea at the edge of the continents and becomes the building material for another phase of mountain building.

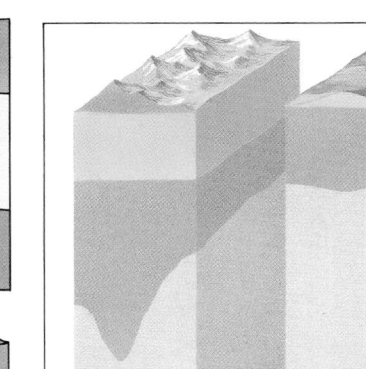

ISOSTASY

The continents float in the Earth's mantle, and because they are only slightly less dense (2.67 g/cc compared to 3.27 g/cc), 85% of their bulk lies below sea level. Thus the higher the mountain the deeper the mountain root. And as the crust can exist only to a maximum depth of about 70 km (43 miles) before it is liquefied in the mantle, mountains can never rise above a maximum of 10 km (6 miles) above sea level.

Folds are generally related to underlying faults. The commonest simple folds are monoclines, formed when a single fault exhibits underlying movement. With continued movement a simple symmetrical anticline (1) may fold unevenly to form an asymmetric anticline (2). More movement bends the strata further into a recumbent fold (3) and eventually the strata break to form an overthrust fold (4). Over a long period an overthrust fold may be pushed many kilometers from its original position to form a nappe (5). Faults are generally of three kinds: faults of tension known as normal faults, when one block drops down (6); faults of horizontal shear (7), known as strike-slip faults; and faults of compression (8), known as thrust faults.

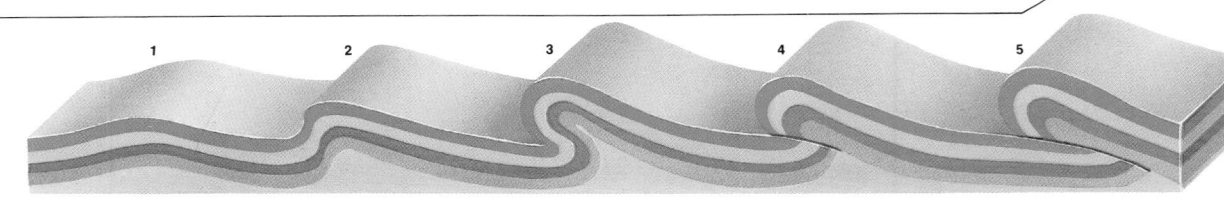

Continents float in the Earth's mantle like icebergs in the sea—more than four-fifths of their bulk lies beneath the surface. The continental crust is 28 km (17 miles) thick at sea level, and where mountains rise above this level there is a corresponding thickening in the crust beneath. The maximum thickness of crust is 70 km (43 miles), so mountains can only ever rise to a maximum height of approximately 10 km (6 miles) above sea level. This relation between upper and underlying crust is known as isostasy, or state of equal pressure.

As mountains become eroded, the process of isostatic rebound allows them to recover about 85 cm (34 in) for every 1 meter (40 in) removed. When, after about 100 million years, a major mountain range has been eroded down to sea level, the rocks exposed at the surface are those that were 15–25 km (9–15 miles) underground when the mountains were at their highest. Such rocks are coarsely crystalline, and make up the fabric of the old, tough continental crust.

Sedimentary basins
As early as the nineteenth century it was noticed that the biggest mountains formed where there had previously been the thickest pile of sediments. According to the principle of isostasy, a thick pile of sediments can form only where the Earth's crust is thin and sinking. The Aegean Sea in the eastern Mediterranean, for example, is at present being pulled apart, and therefore becoming thinner. Over the next few million years, as the Aegean crust sinks, a thick pile of sediments—a sedimentary basin—will accumulate. Most sedimentary basins are at present shallow seas, and form the continental shelves. The depth of water over these shelf seas has been determined by the erosion that accompanied the lowest sea levels of the past 100 million years—about 140 m (460 ft) below the present sea level.

Mountain building
When continents collide, it is the regions of stretched crust that are the first to absorb some of the impact. Such a former sedimentary basin is being turned into the Zagros Mountains of southwestern Iran as Arabia advances northeastward into Asia. The individual blocks of continental crust appear to be sliding back along curved faults, and the sediments that have built up over the thinned crust are now being forced into folds.

Early in the life of such a sedimentary basin sea water may become cut off from the ocean and evaporate to form extensive deposits of salt. Such salt deposits reduce friction and allow the folded pile of sediments overlying the continental blocks to become disconnected and to slide up to 100 km (62 miles) away from the collision zone. In the Zagros Mountains this process has only just begun, but in older mountain ranges, such as the Canadian Rockies or the European Alps, the formation of nappes— disconnected sediment piles forced ahead of the main compression zone—has been widespread.

As mountain ranges often form out of the sedimentary basins along the boundaries between a continent and the ocean, new mountains tend to add on to the fringes of the continents. In North America, for example, the oldest remnants of ranges that make up large tracts of the Canadian shield are found in the center of the continent, while the process of mountain building is continuing in the west.

Other continents show a more complex pattern of mountain ranges through subsequent phases of splitting and amalgamation, and the Himalayas and the Urals have formed where smaller continents have come together to make up the continent of Asia.

The boundary between the continent and the ocean along the western coast of the Atlantic Ocean is not a plate boundary and is therefore termed passive, in contrast to active boundaries such as the eastern coast of the Pacific Ocean, where the ocean plate is moving down into the mantle at a subduction zone beneath the Andean mountain chain. The highest Andean mountains are tall volcanoes of andesite (formed from magmas pouring off the underlying subduction zone). The bulk of the mountain range consists of enormous underground batholiths, in which the magma has solidified before being able to erupt, and compressed and uplifted sedimentary basins formed along the continental margin.

The crustal region immediately beyond the volcanoes that form above subduction zones, however, is very often in tension and in the process of being pulled apart. This appears to be caused by mantle material being dragged down with the oceanic lithosphere. Small ocean basins, such as the Sea of Japan, may open up under such conditions.

Folds and faults
When movement of the Earth's crust has taken place along a planar fracture through sedimentary rocks, it can be easily identified by the breaks in the layers, and such planes of movement are known as faults. Folds form where rock layers bend rather than break. Generally, faults form when rocks are brittle, and folds are found when rocks are plastic.

Sediments close to the surface are often so soft that they behave plastically, as do rocks at depths greater than 15–20 km (9–12 miles), where the continental crust is of sufficiently high temperature and pressure for slow rock flow to take place. Thus most continental faults are found between these levels. All major folds found in soft sediments apparently have a fault of some kind beneath them, and it is the failure of the fault to pass right through to the surface that creates the fold.

Folds are often extremely complicated and some geologists have tended to describe them in extraordinary detail, but in fact they are little more than brush strokes in the overall picture. Pre-existing faults beneath the folds tend to determine the folds' orientation. Once a continental fault has formed, it provides a plane of weakness wherever the continental crust is subject to stress. Many faults around the Mediterranean Sea came into existence during a period of tension, and these are now being reactivated and produce the large earthquakes associated with the continuing collision of Africa with Europe.

At the end of all the complications and intricacies of continental collision, the final phase of mountain building—that involving uplift—remains perhaps the least understood. In the last two million years, for example, while man has been increasingly active on Earth, 2,500,000 sq km (almost 1,000,000 sq miles) of Tibet has risen 4,000 m (2 miles). But the origin of such gigantic and rapid movement lies within the Earth's mantle.

The highest mountains are the product of continental collisions. As the rocks are squeezed, folded and faulted, the original continental crust becomes shortened and thickened. Although the overall extent and height of mountain chains is controlled by mountain building, the whole range can only be viewed from a spacecraft. For the earthbound mountain visitor the familiar shapes of peaks and valleys are those formed by mountain destruction (1). Snow at high altitudes consolidates to form ice that moves slowly downhill in the form of glaciers. To wear away a mountain range at an average of 5 km (3 miles) above sea level requires the removal of more than 20 km (12 miles) of rock, as the thick continental crust that floats in the underlying mantle rises to compensate for the loss of surface mass. Half-eroded mountains (2), such as the Appalachians, pictured above, may linger on for tens of millions of years until, like large regions of the Canadian interior, the mountains are all eroded away and only the hard crystalline surface rocks that were once buried 20 km (12 miles) underground remain (3).

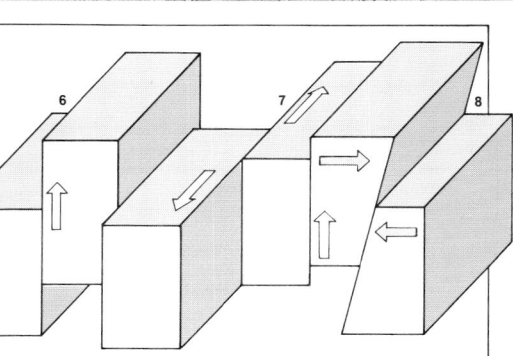

Rock Formation and History

All the rocks on Earth are interrelated through the rock cycle – a never-ending chain of processes that forms and modifies rocks and minerals on the Earth's surface, in its crust and in the mantle. These events are powered both by energy from the Sun and the heat of the Earth itself, and the processes include the forces of nature – from wind and water to the movements of the continents. This geological cycle of creation and destruction is one of the most distinctive features of our planet. Each feature of geological activity, each agent of landscape-making is but a stage of the continuing rock cycle.

CONSTANT CHANGE

The processes of formation and destruction of the three basic rock types—igneous, sedimentary and metamorphic—are linked in an interminable cycle of change. Igneous rocks are thrown up from inside the Earth, are eroded and eventually laid down as sediments. As accumulated sediments sink into the Earth, they are changed by heat and pressure—metamorphosed—before surfacing again in the processes of mountain building.

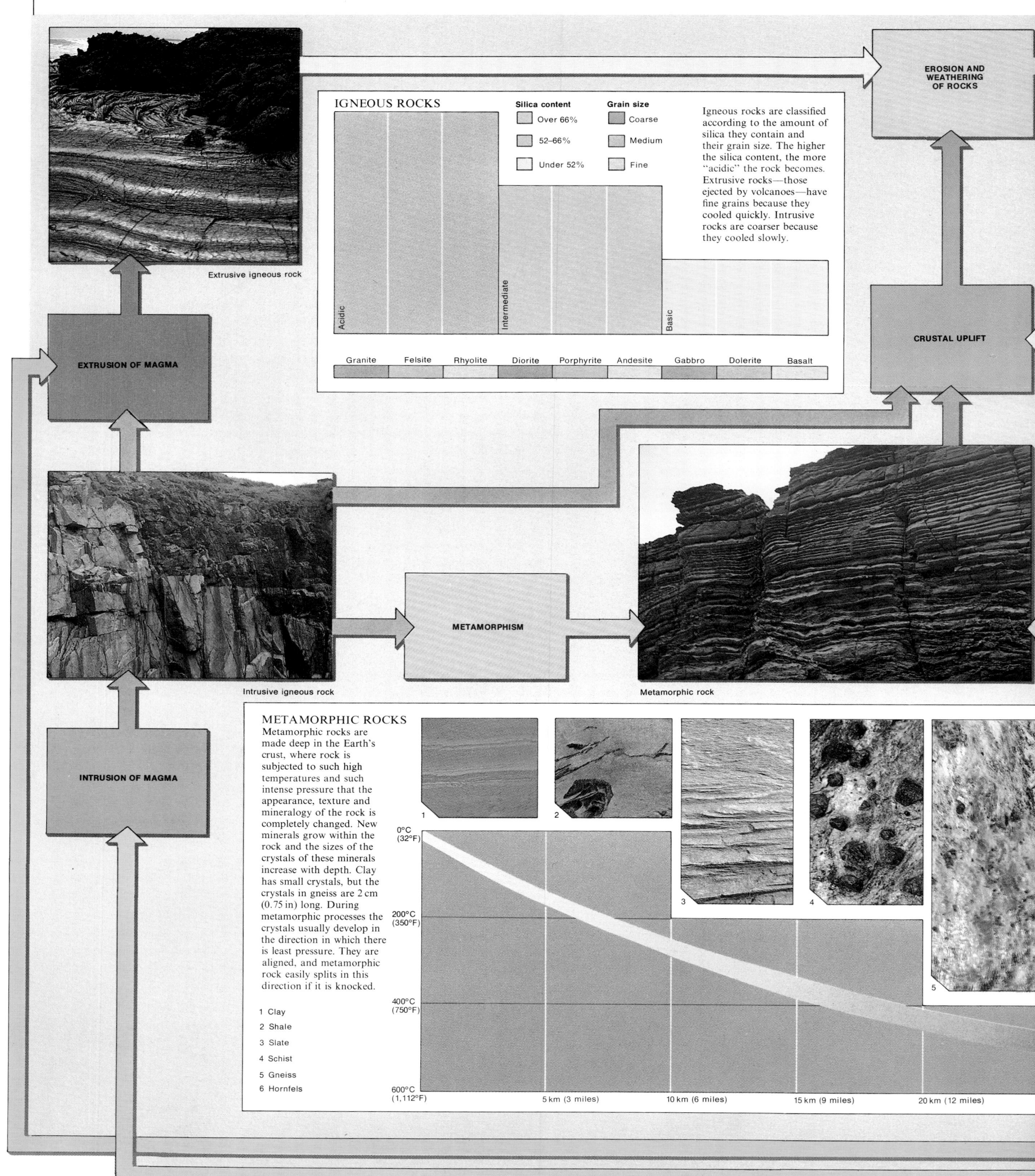

EROSION AND WEATHERING OF ROCKS

IGNEOUS ROCKS

Silica content	
	Over 66%
	52–66%
	Under 52%

Grain size	
	Coarse
	Medium
	Fine

Igneous rocks are classified according to the amount of silica they contain and their grain size. The higher the silica content, the more "acidic" the rock becomes. Extrusive rocks—those ejected by volcanoes—have fine grains because they cooled quickly. Intrusive rocks are coarser because they cooled slowly.

Acidic — Intermediate — Basic

Granite   Felsite   Rhyolite   Diorite   Porphyrite   Andesite   Gabbro   Dolerite   Basalt

Extrusive igneous rock

EXTRUSION OF MAGMA

CRUSTAL UPLIFT

INTRUSION OF MAGMA

Intrusive igneous rock

METAMORPHISM

Metamorphic rock

METAMORPHIC ROCKS
Metamorphic rocks are made deep in the Earth's crust, where rock is subjected to such high temperatures and such intense pressure that the appearance, texture and mineralogy of the rock is completely changed. New minerals grow within the rock and the sizes of the crystals of these minerals increase with depth. Clay has small crystals, but the crystals in gneiss are 2 cm (0.75 in) long. During metamorphic processes the crystals usually develop in the direction in which there is least pressure. They are aligned, and metamorphic rock easily splits in this direction if it is knocked.

1 Clay
2 Shale
3 Slate
4 Schist
5 Gneiss
6 Hornfels

0°C (32°F)
200°C (350°F)
400°C (750°F)
600°C (1,112°F)

5 km (3 miles)   10 km (6 miles)   15 km (9 miles)   20 km (12 miles)

SEDIMENTARY ROCKS

Sediments can be turned into rock by means of three main processes. Cementation is the term used when water percolates between grains of sand. As it does so, any iron oxide, silica or calcium carbonate that were in solution are deposited in thin layers around the grains, thus cementing them into a hard sandstone (1). As more sediment is laid down, the increasing weight of the sediments on top exerts pressure on the underlying layers. Water is squeezed out and a dense rock is formed (2) by the process of compaction. This is the way clay becomes mudstone. Finally, during mountain-building processes forces are exerted on rock minerals that cause them to recrystallize into a solid mass of rock (3) that has no spaces between its mineral constituents.

TRANSPORTATION AND DEPOSITION OF SEDIMENTS

BURIAL AND FORMATION OF ROCK FROM SEDIMENTS (LITHIFICATION)

Sedimentary rock

METAMORPHISM

MELTING

km (15 miles)   30 km (18 miles)

All the rocks on Earth are formed at one stage or another in what is known as the rock cycle. All high ground on the continents suffers erosion; the eroded material is transported and deposited on lower ground; in time, these sediments may be elevated by mountain-building processes and so, in turn, become eroded. If, between their formation and destruction, sediments pass deep into the Earth's crust, they may be transformed by heat or pressure into metamorphic rock; or, at even greater depths, they may melt to form yet another kind of rock—igneous rock.

Materials at the bottom of a thick pile of sediments may be heated enough to melt. If this material then cools and solidifies underground, it is called plutonic rock. Sometimes, however, it escapes to the surface by means of a short cut—a volcano—to become part of the rock cycle. On the other hand, some sediments are lost off the edge of the continents on to the deep ocean floor, and they disappear into the mantle of the Earth by means of the downward movements of the oceanic crust. A measure of the difference between the input and the output of the continental rock cycle is a measure of how fast the continental crust is increasing or decreasing. Scientists believe it is increasing—at a rate of between 0.1 and 1.0 cu km a year.

Types of rock
The range of rock types found on the continents has been classified under three headings: sedimentary, igneous and metamorphic. Sedimentary rocks include all those formed at low temperatures on the Earth's surface; igneous rocks have all solidified from molten rock, or magma; and metamorphic rocks are sedimentary or igneous rocks that have changed their nature under conditions of high temperature and pressure.

There is a certain amount of difficulty in defining the boundaries between the different types. Ash formed from solidified magma falling out of the air after a volcanic eruption is igneous, but what if it should move downhill in a mudslide? If a metamorphic rock is deeply buried it may start to melt and form a "migmatite," which is part liquid and part solid. Is this igneous? And where does the boundary lie between a deeply buried sediment and a metamorphic rock? Coal seams that have been thoroughly metamorphosed from their original peat deposits are found as layers in unaltered sandstones. This classification does, however, provide a useful preliminary guide to understanding the nature of different types of rock.

Rock types are defined by studying their texture, the way they were formed, and their composition. There are interesting textural similarities between evaporites—salt deposits formed as an inland sea dries up—and some plutonic igneous rocks. Both have crystallized directly from a liquid. There are similarities between sandstones and plutonic "cumulates," which form at the base of enormous magma reservoirs where strong magma currents deposit thick layers of crystals. So rock types must be defined in terms of more than just texture.

Rock formation
The simplest sedimentary rocks are those made up of whole fragments of eroded material. "Scree" deposits that accumulate at the base of a cliff or a steep valley side from angular rock fragments that have broken off the rock face above can make a sedimentary "breccia." A rock made from rounded stream pebbles is a "conglomerate." Further erosion reduces the rock into three components: dissolved ions (atoms with an electrical charge) such as those of calcium or magnesium; mineral grains (sand) that cannot be broken down chemically, such as quartz; and a variety of minerals containing sheet-like layers of silicate and alumina (silicon and aluminum oxides)—the minerals that are often the main constituents of clays.

A river carrying these minerals first deposits the sand, and then the clay, while the dissolved ions pass out into the sea, where some are absorbed by living organisms and used to construct protective shells and rigid skeletons. When the creatures die, the shells and bones again become part of the rock cycle, building up great thicknesses of limestone.

Igneous rocks are chemically far more complex than are sedimentary rocks, but are texturally simpler. The slower the magma cools, the larger are the crystals that form within it. If it cools too quickly it may not crystallize at all, forming instead a super-cooled liquid, or glass. A plutonic igneous rock—one cooled deep underground—is coarse grained; a volcanic rock is fine grained. A rock can, however, have both large and small crystals, testifying to a more complex history.

The most striking feature of Earth magmas is their uniformity. With few exceptions, they are all rich in silica. The greater the silica content, the higher their viscosity (resistance to flowing). Those rich in silica tend to solidify underground. The complex chemistry of magmas comes from the melting of the variety of minerals making up the mantle.

The chemistry of metamorphic rocks is like that of their igneous or sedimentary starting materials. As these become more deeply buried and heated, the constituent minerals grow larger. A mudstone metamorphoses to a slate, then to a schist and finally a gneiss. The "slatiness" or "schistosity" of these rocks is provided by micas and other sheet-shaped mineral grains. Such minerals require abundant alumina to form. If this is not present in the starting rock, it will be metamorphosed into more granular material.

A record in the rocks
Rocks contain an unwritten history of the Earth. Sedimentary rocks hold information about climates of the past and fossil relics of organisms that lived when the sediments were laid down. Igneous rocks record periods of crustal activity that relate to the movements of the continents; and metamorphic rocks indicate periods of uplift that exposed previously buried rock. From such information it is possible to construct a geological time scale. Although fossils are a useful means of correlating one pile of sediment with another, good fossils go back only 600 million years. Earlier organisms are believed to have been soft bodied and were not easily fossilized.

The only complete time scale comes from the radioactive "clocks" in many igneous and metamorphic rocks. Certain forms of natural elements, or isotopes, are unstable and emit energy. By measuring the amount of "daughter" atoms that have been formed by the radioactive decay of a larger "parent" atom, it is possible to determine the age of a rock and events in the history of its formation. The dating of rocks from radioactive decay has thus enabled a true time scale for the history of the Earth to be constructed.

Earth's Minerals

Minerals are the basic ingredients of the Earth, from crust to core. They make up not only the ores on which man has based much of his technology, and the gemstones which he values for their beauty or rarity, but also the components of rocks, pebbles and sands. Two million years ago minerals – in the form of stones – provided early man with his first tools. Today, man's use of minerals, such as uranium for nuclear power or silicon for microcomputers, is revolutionizing our lives.

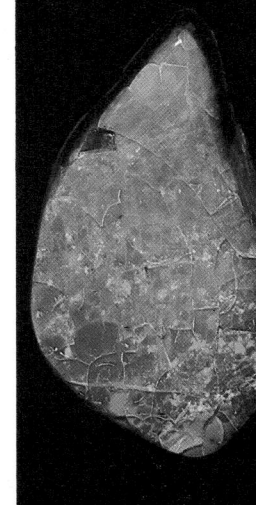

> **SUBSTANCES OF THE EARTH**
> Minerals are made up of chemical elements, arranged according to various crystal structures. Man's chief interest in minerals has been as precious stones and, increasingly, as a resource in the form of useful metal ores. But of the 2,500 minerals so far identified, the majority are rock-forming substances—the material components of the Earth. Relatively infrequent geological processes over vast time spans are responsible for concentrating minerals dispersed through rocks into richer deposits, and it is these economically important ores that have provided man with his supply of workable mineral resources through the ages.

Minerals, and the metals derived from them, have always had an inherent fascination for man, as well as providing the basis for his technology. Gold in particular, which was worked in Egypt as early as 5000 BC, still retains its mysterious attraction. Because of its chemical inactivity it is imperishable, immutable and nontarnishing, and has served as the basis of world trade for almost 2,000 years. Copper has been smelted since the early part of the third millennium BC, to be replaced eventually by harder alloys. Arsenical bronze, for instance, bridged the gap between the Copper and Bronze ages (bronze is an alloy of copper and tin). More complex technology was needed for the working of iron, which began c.1100 BC, whereas brass (an alloy of copper and zinc) did not appear until Roman times.

Although the steel-making process had its roots in antiquity, it was not until the nineteenth century that new techniques changed man's attitude to minerals. Before the modern age of plastics, the capacity to produce steel was the hallmark of industrial development, and together with coal it formed the linchpin of western industrial progress. Today minerals have come to assume their greatest importance as exploitable—but nonrenewable—resources.

Components of the Earth

The terms "mineral," "rock" and "stone" are often used interchangeably, but in fact all rocks are made up of minerals, which are natural and usually inorganic substances with a particular chemical makeup and crystal structure.

Certain stones have properties that satisfy basic human needs for beauty and color. Some possess a flashing sparkle, others have special optical characteristics such as refraction and dispersion ("fire"), or contain inclusions that give rise to phenomena like the "asterism" found in sapphires. About 100 such minerals are classified as gemstones and valued for their beauty, durability or rarity.

Most minerals occur as either pure (ore) deposits or mixed with other minerals in rocks—an economically important difference. Their exploitation has been vastly extended in recent decades through our greater understanding of the mineral-forming processes that take place in the Earth's crust. All mineral ores result from a separation process in which a mineral-rich solution separates into its various components according to the temperature, pressure and composition of the original mixture. Precipitation is the simplest kind of separation, as when calcium salts separate from circulating groundwater to yield stalactites and stalagmites in caves, in the form of calcite crystals.

Mineral formation

Most deposits of metallic ores originate in the intense physicochemical activity that takes place at the boundaries between the Earth's huge crustal plates. Very high concentrations of minerals occur in association with warm solutions coming from springs in the seabed, notably along the spreading zones in the southeastern Pacific Ocean, the Red Sea, the African Rift Valley and the Gulf of Aden. This process also occurs in shallow-water volcanic areas, as near the Mediterranean island of Thira and the submarine volcano of Bahu Wuhu, Indonesia. Cold seawater penetrates the crust and leaches out minerals from the basalts of these "hot spots," returning to the surface of the seabed as hot springs. The minerals then precipitate in the cold, oxygen-rich seawater.

Mineral separation may also occur when part of the deep-seated magma forces its way into the upper layers of the Earth's crust and begins to cool. The great plugs of magma that form the

rock kimberlite, in which diamonds are found, must have come from a depth of at least 100 km (62 miles). If the magma reaches the surface through fissures as extrusive rocks, the pattern of minerals in the surrounding rocks is also changed by a process called contact metamorphism, with various bands or zones of minerals occurring at various distances from the contact boundary.

As rocks become weathered, mineral concentrations that resist weathering may be left. Alternatively, all the weathered materials may be transported by running water, becoming concentrated as they are sorted out according to their different densities. Gold is the best-known example of this alluvial type of mineral deposit—known as a placer deposit. If the minerals are washed into the sea, they may be distributed over deltas or over the seafloor, but when this happens the concentrations of minerals are usually very low.

Mineral energy

Fossil fuels such as coal and petroleum are major mineral sources of energy. But with the twentieth-century discovery of nuclear fission, uranium also became an important energy resource. The richest deposits occur, as with other minerals, as veins deposited in fractures by hot-water movements. These deposits, consisting of a uranium oxide called pitchblende were the first to be mined, for example at Joachimstal (Czech Republic), Great Bear Lake (Canada) and Katanga (Zaire). Weathered products of such rocks, redeposited as sandstones, also contain uranium, as in Wyoming (USA) and in the Niger basin. In many respects uranium is similar to silver: both occur with similar geological abundance, their ores are enriched about 2,000 times during processing, and the metals are recovered by using chemicals to dissolve the metal selectively and then by "stripping" the metal from the solution.

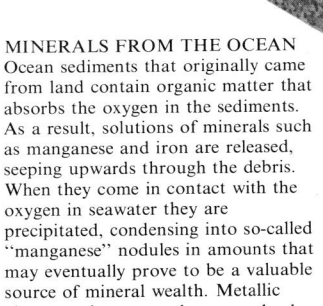

MINERALS FROM THE OCEAN
Ocean sediments that originally came from land contain organic matter that absorbs the oxygen in the sediments. As a result, solutions of minerals such as manganese and iron are released, seeping upwards through the debris. When they come in contact with the oxygen in seawater they are precipitated, condensing into so-called "manganese" nodules in amounts that may eventually prove to be a valuable source of mineral wealth. Metallic elements also accumulate very slowly from the seawater itself.

METAL-RICH BRINES
Scientists have recently discovered deep hollows on the floor of the Red Sea and other similar enclosed basins connected with rift valleys. These prevent normal circulation of water and form undersea pools of hot, high-density brines. The brines contain sulphur and other minerals in very high concentrations, and overlie sediments rich in metals such as zinc, copper, lead, silver and gold. Hot springs in fissures below the pools escape into them, carrying up solutions of the metallic minerals which combine with sulphur to create a concentrated broth rich in metals.

METALS FROM THE INTERIOR
Rift zones on the bed of the Pacific Ocean, where the Earth's crustal plates are slowly separating, provide sensational visual evidence of metallic ores in the actual process of creation. Seawater percolates through the fractured surface to the molten rock below, where it leaches out the soluble metallic components, erupting in superheated hydrothermal springs to form geysers of mineral-rich water. Oxygen in the cold water of the sea-floor causes the minerals to condense out, precipitating in plumes of dark powder. Continental drift, collision and sedimentation over millions of years will eventually incorporate these deposits into the landmasses.

Uranium, chromium and many other minerals are widely distributed through the Earth's crust, but they are valuable as a resource only if the technology exists to extract them economically. In mineral development, the high-grade ores are worked out first, followed by the poorer deposits if demand remains or increases. With uranium, the low-grade deposits contain far more of the total quantity of the mineral, but these are worth exploiting because of uranium's importance and because the technology exists. Chromium, on the other hand, is currently extracted only from high-grade ores. Large deposits of low-grade ores do exist, but technology for exploiting them economically has not yet been developed.

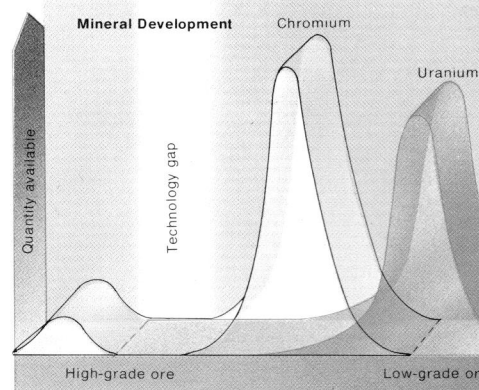

Mineral Development

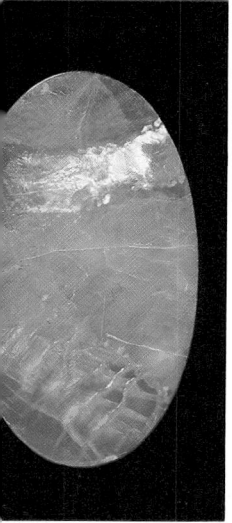

Opal (above), a silica mineral, often contains impurities which give it a range of colors. These flash and change according to the angle of vision, a result of the interference of light along minute internal cracks in the stone.

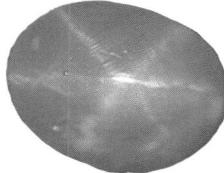

Sapphire gemstone (left), a form of the dull gray mineral corundum (below), owes its color to inclusions of titanium and iron.

MINERALS IN THE SERVICE OF MAN

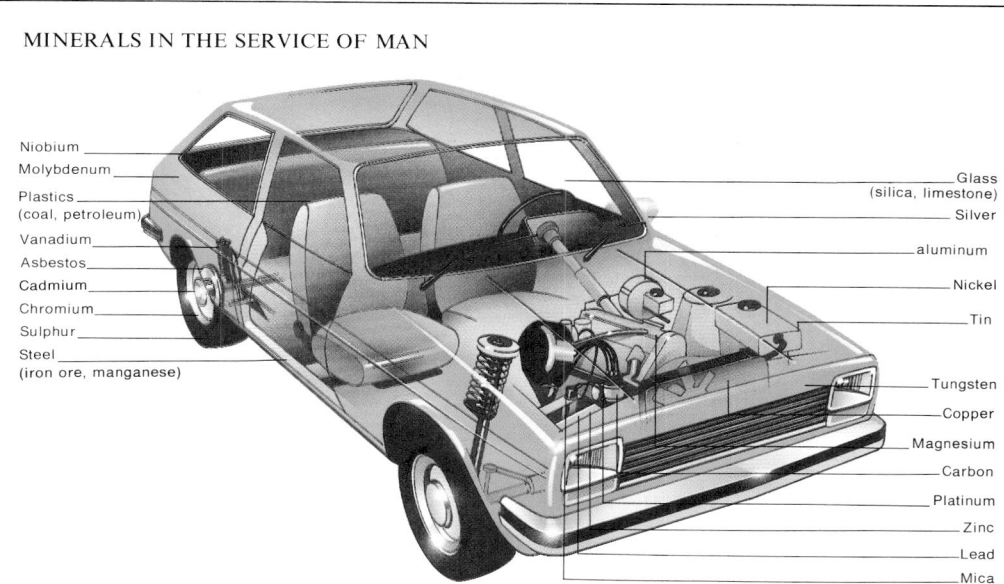

Niobium
Molybdenum
Plastics (coal, petroleum)
Vanadium
Asbestos
Cadmium
Chromium
Sulphur
Steel (iron ore, manganese)

Glass (silica, limestone)
Silver
aluminum
Nickel
Tin
Tungsten
Copper
Magnesium
Carbon
Platinum
Zinc
Lead
Mica

The modern automobile makes use of a whole alphabet of minerals in its composition, from aluminum to zinc. The importance of plastics, made from petroleum and coal, is constantly increasing, but the need for specialist metals is as great as ever. Cadmium, for example, is used in electro-plating; carbon goes into making electrodes and graphite seals; transistors and electric contact points require platinum; sulphur is present in vulcanizing rubber and lubricants; lamp filaments contain tungsten. Of basic metals, iron and steel still account for almost three-quarters of the total quantity of the metals used; lead for 1.19 percent and copper for only 0.94 percent. But the amount of useful metal is often a small fraction of the rock that has to be mined and processed. A copper ore, for instance, only yields about 0.7 percent of metal, so to equip a single car's radiator with copper well over one and a half tonnes of rock will have to be excavated, of which 99.3 percent will simply be discarded.

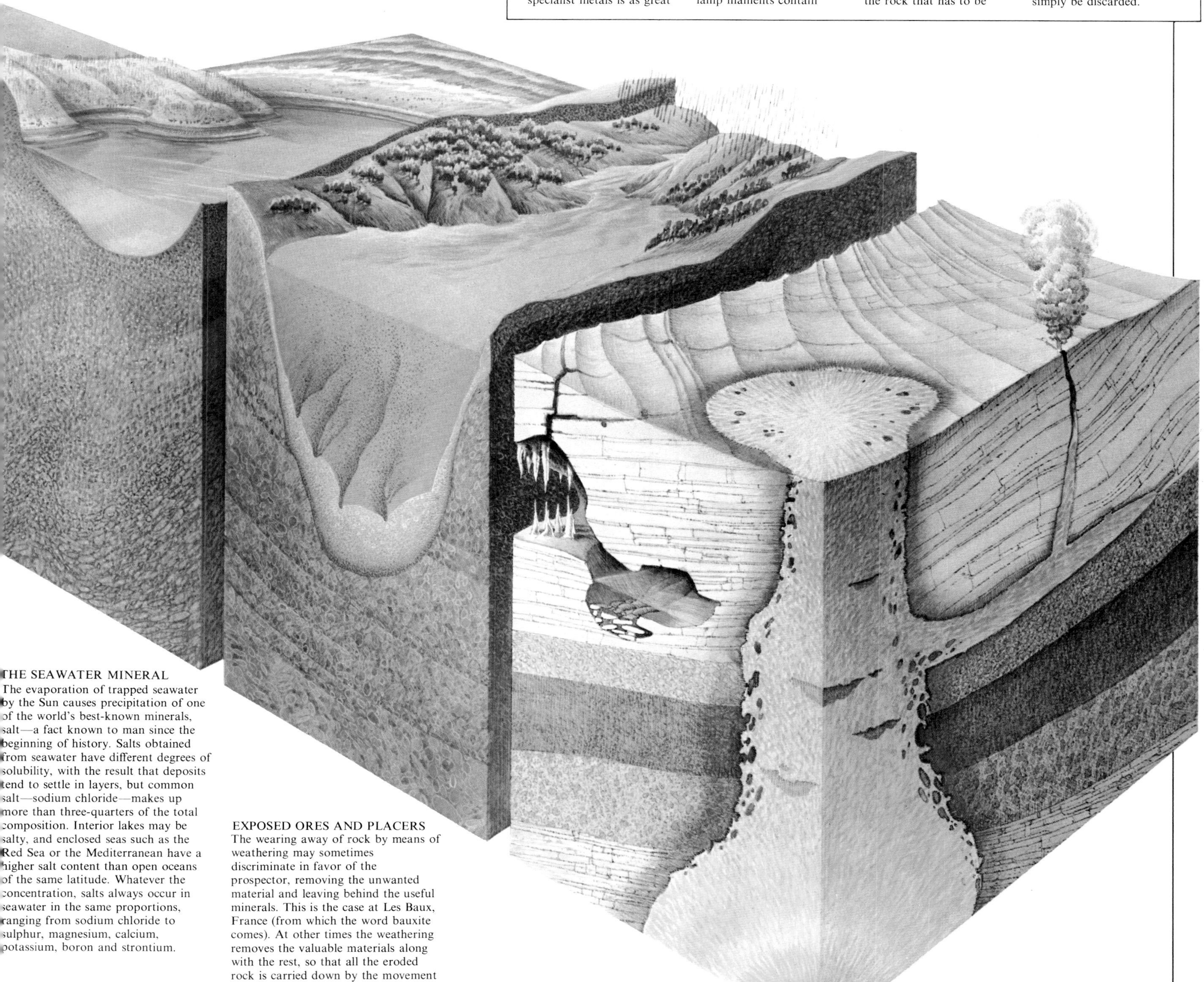

THE SEAWATER MINERAL

The evaporation of trapped seawater by the Sun causes precipitation of one of the world's best-known minerals, salt—a fact known to man since the beginning of history. Salts obtained from seawater have different degrees of solubility, with the result that deposits tend to settle in layers, but common salt—sodium chloride—makes up more than three-quarters of the total composition. Interior lakes may be salty, and enclosed seas such as the Red Sea or the Mediterranean have a higher salt content than open oceans of the same latitude. Whatever the concentration, salts always occur in seawater in the same proportions, ranging from sodium chloride to sulphur, magnesium, calcium, potassium, boron and strontium.

EXPOSED ORES AND PLACERS

The wearing away of rock by means of weathering may sometimes discriminate in favor of the prospector, removing the unwanted material and leaving behind the useful minerals. This is the case at Les Baux, France (from which the word bauxite comes). At other times the weathering removes the valuable materials along with the rest, so that all the eroded rock is carried down by the movement of water until it eventually reaches the sea. So-called "placer" deposits occur where the heavier particles of minerals have become separated, accumulating as deposits of mineral sand and concentrating in riverbeds or estuaries. Gold is the best-known example of this alluvial type of deposit, but tin and other minerals are also found as placers in many parts of the world.

UNDERGROUND PROCESSES

Limestone rock, formed from calcium carbonate, is dissolved by seeping water containing carbon dioxide from the air and the soil. The subsurface water may create vast networks of underground caverns in the limestone, and as the water slowly evaporates it leaves deposits of calcium carbonate, forming stalactites and stalagmites.

VOLCANOES AND MINERALS

Volcanic magma penetrating the Earth's crust may form important mineral deposits. On cooling, the heavy or "basic" minerals are the first to crystallize and sink to the bottom. The minerals may also separate out chemically. The intense heat affects surrounding rocks, causing mineral changes in banded zones.

Earthquakes and Volcanoes

Earthquakes and volcanic eruptions challenge man's faith in the stability of the world, but these violent releases of energy testify to our planet's ever-dynamic activity. Earthquakes are caused when the rigid crust is driven past or over itself by underlying movements that extend deep into the Earth's mantle. Stress builds up until it exceeds the strength of the rocks, when there follows a sudden movement. Volcanoes occur where molten rock, or magma, from the mantle forces its way to the surface through lines of weakness in the crust, often at the lithospheric plate boundaries.

MODIFIED MERCALLI SCALE

I Earthquake not felt, except by a few.

II Felt on upper floors by few at rest. Swinging of suspended objects.

III Quite noticeable indoors, especially on upper floors. Standing cars may sway.

IV Felt indoors. Dishes and windows rattle, standing cars rock. Like a heavy truck hitting a building.

V Felt by nearly all, many wakened. Fragile objects broken, plaster cracked, trees and poles disturbed.

VI Felt by all, many run outdoors. Slight damage, heavy furniture moved, some fallen plaster.

VII People run outdoors. Average homes slightly damaged, substandard ones badly damaged. Noticed by car drivers.

VIII Well-built structures slightly damaged, others badly damaged. Chimneys and monuments collapse. Car drivers disturbed.

IX Well-designed buildings badly damaged, substantial ones greatly damaged, shifted off foundations. Conspicuous ground cracks open up.

X Well-built wood-structures destroyed, masonry structures destroyed. Rails bent, ground cracked, landslides. Rivers overflow.

XI Few masonry structures left standing. Bridges and underground pipes destroyed. Broad cracks in ground. Earth slumps.

XII Damage total. Ground waves seem like sea waves. Line of sight disturbed, objects thrown into the air.

The Earth's crust generally breaks along pre-existing planes of weakness, or faults. Such breakages give rise to an "explosive" release of stress that is familiar to surface dwellers as the vibrations of an earthquake.

Not all earthquakes, however, take place along pre-existing faults, otherwise no new faults would be generated. Many recent large earthquakes have been located immediately north of the Tonga Islands because a giant rent is developing through previously unbroken ocean crust. The crust to the south is being swallowed down into the mantle and that to the north continues at the surface to be subducted farther to the west. Once a fault has formed, however, it remains a plane of weakness even though the two sides tend to become partly resealed, so that when movement does occur there is a considerable release of energy.

Measuring earthquakes

Earthquakes are quantified in two ways. The actual energy release (magnitude) at the source of the earthquake (the focus) is measured on the Richter scale, a log scale where every unit of increase represents approximately 24 times the energy release. A magnitude 7 earthquake is roughly equivalent to the explosion of a one megaton nuclear bomb (one million tonnes of TNT). The strongest earthquake recorded this century was a magnitude 8.5 event in Alaska in 1964. Earthquakes as they are perceived are measured on the Modified Mercalli scale by their impact in terms of the amount of surface destruction. A medium-size earthquake under a town, such as that beneath Tangshan, China, in 1976 which killed more than a quarter of a million people, might record higher on the Mercalli scale than the Alaska event, which affected a large but sparsely populated region.

The magnitude of the earthquake depends on the frictional resistance that has to be overcome before movement can take place. This total frictional resistance, therefore, increases with the area of the fault plane. So the bigger the fault plane that moves, the bigger the earthquake. The largest earthquakes occur on wide fault planes that dip at a very shallow angle and can pass through a great deal of relatively shallow crust that will not deform plastically.

Earthquakes are unlikely to occur where rocks are plastic and can flow to accommodate the buildup of stress. Some faults, such as the San Andreas Fault in the western United States, pass from brittle rocks into a plastic zone at depths of only a few kilometers. Therefore, the next San Francisco earthquake cannot be as great as the 1964 Alaskan one, although this may be of little comfort to the potential victims. Along some sections of the San Andreas Fault the plastic zone comes directly to the surface, and motion occurs without large earthquakes.

Earthquake prediction is still in its infancy, although it is recognized that a number of phenomena may occur before a major earthquake—the ground may swell, the electrical conductivity of groundwater may change, and the water height of wells may rapidly alter.

How volcanoes are formed

Volcanoes, although spectacular, are safer than earthquakes. While an average of 20,000 people are killed each year in earthquakes, only about 400 are killed by volcanoes; and many of the victims die from starvation due to crop failure after heavy ash falls.

Volcanoes are formed when molten rock (magma) escapes through the Earth's crust to the Earth's surface. Most of this magma forms within the upper mantle between 30 and 100 km (20–60 miles) underground. The temperature increases with depth between 20° and 50°C per

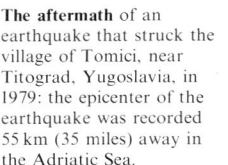

The aftermath of an earthquake that struck the village of Tomici, near Titograd, Yugoslavia, in 1979: the epicenter of the earthquake was recorded 55 km (35 miles) away in the Adriatic Sea.

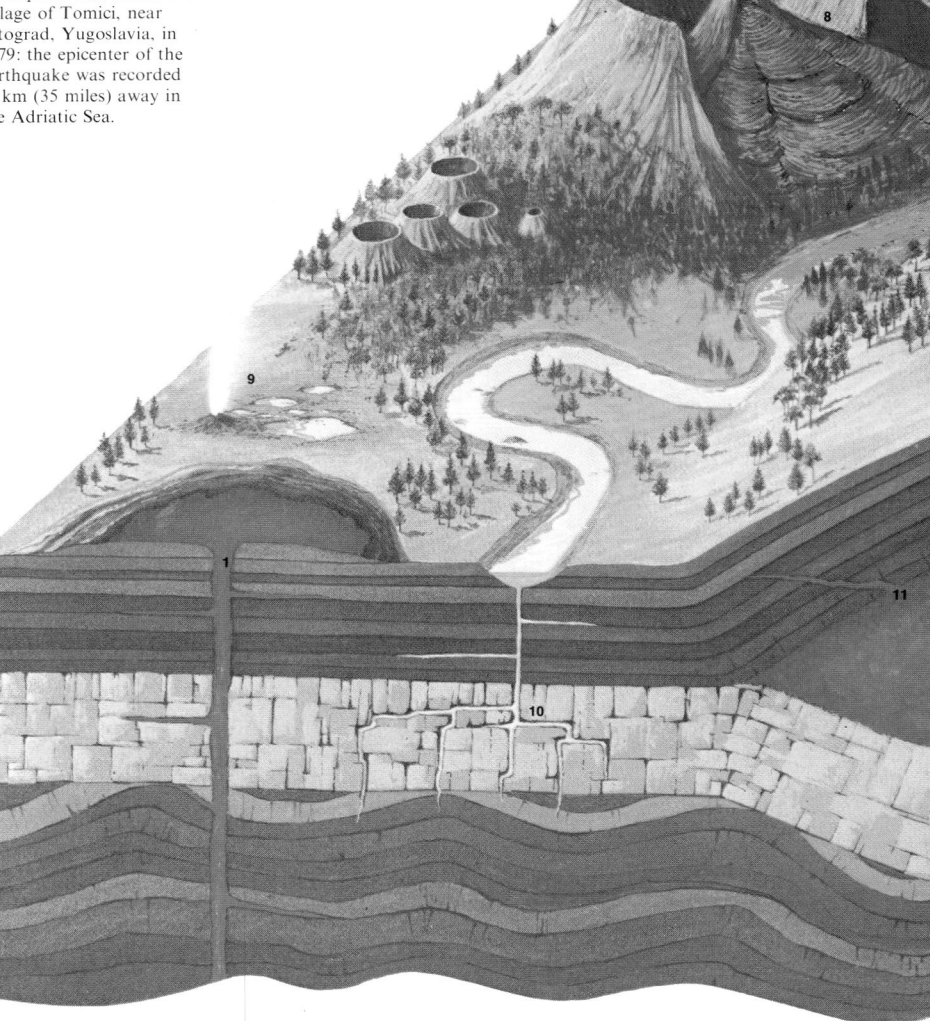

Earthquakes occur when slabs of the Earth's crust move in relation to each other. The focus of the earthquake is the point where movement occurs (1), and the epicenter is the point on the surface directly above it (2). Blue lines represent zones of surface damage as measured on the Modified Mercalli scale.

km (35°–90°F per 3,250 ft) from the crust to the mantle, but even so the rocks are normally not hot enough to melt.

Basaltic magmas, found along mid-ocean spreading ridges and oceanic islands, are formed when hot, deep mantle rises and, on reduction of pressure, begins to melt. Such "basic" magmas generally have low silica and water content, a high temperature and flow easily—often, as in Hawaii, "quietly erupting" to form volcanoes with very gentle gradients known as shield volcanoes. Silica-rich magma forms under continental crust. Ocean crust sucks up water after it has formed at the oceanic spreading ridges and much of this water later becomes taken with the crust down a subduction zone, where it helps to lower the melting point of both mantle and ocean-crust rocks.

By the time these magmas reach the surface they are cooler and have a higher water content than basalts. These "intermediate" or andesite magmas are also more viscous (less willing to

flow) because they contain more silica. The eruptions are more explosive as the water and other gases dissolve out of the magma as it approaches the surface, and the lava remains close to the volcanic vent, building up the archetypal steep-sided conical stratified volcano, such as Mount Fujiyama in Japan. Sometimes the conical form may be destroyed in catastrophic eruptions, as has happened at Mount St Helens in the United States.

The most violent of all eruptions are found where magmas from the mantle have penetrated and melted a great thickness of continental rocks, so as to create highly viscous silica- and water-rich "acid" magmas. As such magmas approach the surface they may turn into a red-hot froth that blasts out from fissures to cover enormous areas in a volcanic material known as ignimbrite. The most extensive eruption known to have occurred in the past 2,000 years was probably on Mount Taupo, on North Island, New Zealand. In AD 150 it discharged some

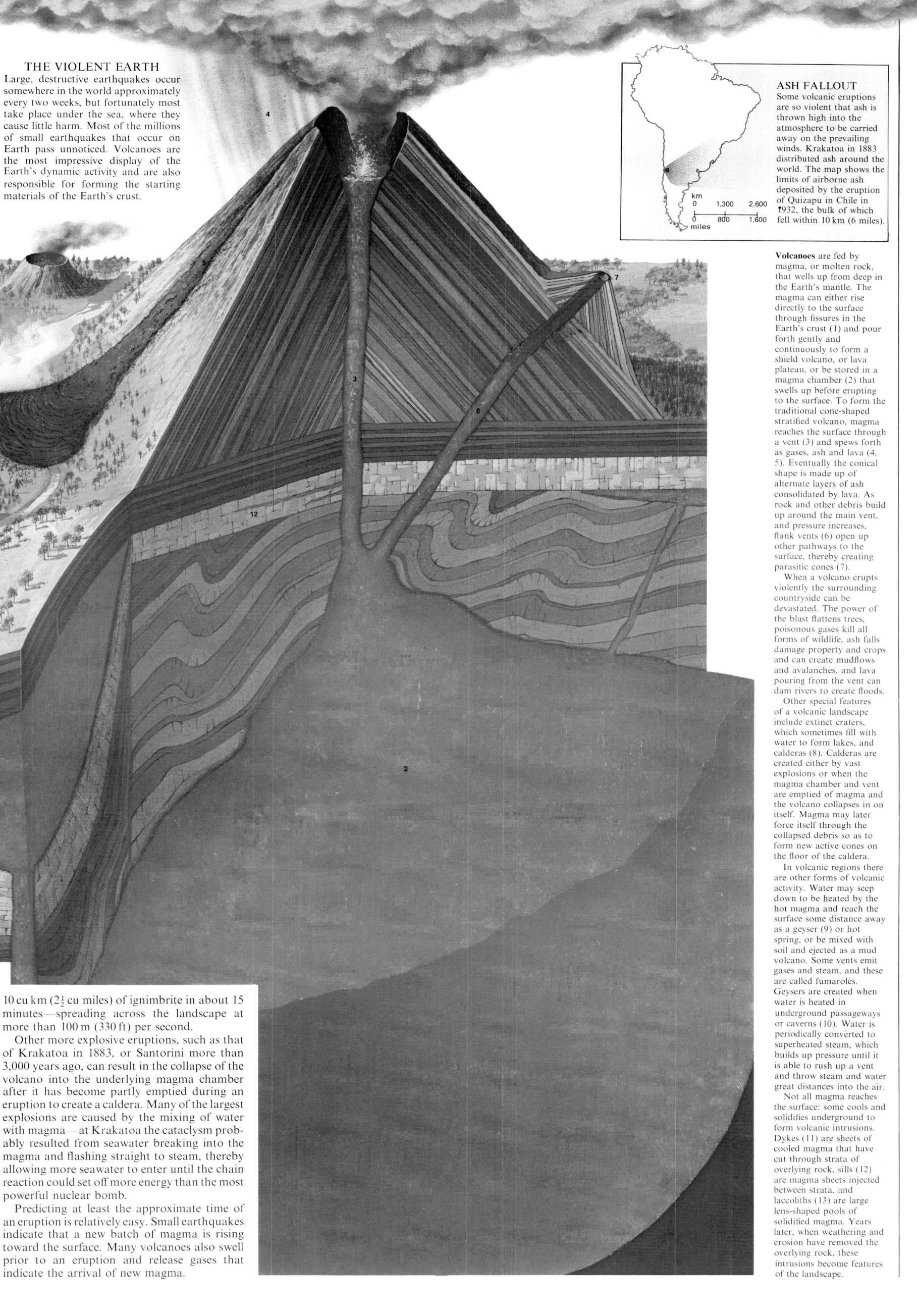

THE VIOLENT EARTH

Large, destructive earthquakes occur somewhere in the world approximately every two weeks, but fortunately most take place under the sea, where they cause little harm. Most of the millions of small earthquakes that occur on Earth pass unnoticed. Volcanoes are the most impressive display of the Earth's dynamic activity and are also responsible for forming the starting materials of the Earth's crust.

Volcanoes are fed by magma, or molten rock, that wells up from deep in the Earth's mantle. The magma can either rise directly to the surface through fissures in the Earth's crust (1) and pour forth gently and continuously to form a shield volcano, or lava plateau, or be stored in a magma chamber (2) that swells up before erupting to the surface. To form the traditional cone-shaped stratified volcano, magma reaches the surface through a vent (3) and spews forth as gases, ash and lava (4, 5). Eventually the conical shape is made up of alternate layers of ash consolidated by lava. As rock and other debris build up around the main vent, and pressure increases, flank vents (6) open up other pathways to the surface, thereby creating parasitic cones (7).

When a volcano erupts violently the surrounding countryside can be devastated. The power of the blast flattens trees, poisonous gases kill all forms of wildlife, ash falls damage property and crops and can create mudflows and avalanches, and lava pouring from the vent can dam rivers to create floods.

Other special features of a volcanic landscape include extinct craters, which sometimes fill with water to form lakes, and calderas (8). Calderas are created either by vast explosions or when the magma chamber and vent are emptied of magma and the volcano collapses in on itself. Magma may later force itself through the collapsed debris so as to form new active cones on the floor of the caldera.

In volcanic regions there are other forms of volcanic activity. Water may seep down to be heated by the hot magma and reach the surface some distance away as a geyser (9) or hot spring, or be mixed with soil and ejected as a mud volcano. Some vents emit gases and steam, and these are called fumaroles. Geysers are created when water is heated in underground passageways or caverns (10). Water is periodically converted to superheated steam, which builds up pressure until it is able to rush up a vent and throw steam and water great distances into the air.

Not all magma reaches the surface: some cools and solidifies underground to form volcanic intrusions. Dykes (11) are sheets of cooled magma that have cut through strata of overlying rock, sills (12) are magma sheets injected between strata, and laccoliths (13) are large lens-shaped pools of solidified magma. Years later, when weathering and erosion have removed the overlying rock, these intrusions become features of the landscape.

10 cu km (2½ cu miles) of ignimbrite in about 15 minutes—spreading across the landscape at more than 100 m (330 ft) per second.

Other more explosive eruptions, such as that of Krakatoa in 1883, or Santorini more than 3,000 years ago, can result in the collapse of the volcano into the underlying magma chamber after it has become partly emptied during an eruption to create a caldera. Many of the largest explosions are caused by the mixing of water with magma—at Krakatoa the cataclysm probably resulted from seawater breaking into the magma and flashing straight to steam, thereby allowing more seawater to enter until the chain reaction could set off more energy than the most powerful nuclear bomb.

Predicting at least the approximate time of an eruption is relatively easy. Small earthquakes indicate that a new batch of magma is rising toward the surface. Many volcanoes also swell prior to an eruption and release gases that indicate the arrival of new magma.

The Oceans

Earth is the water planet. Of all the planets of the solar system only the Earth has abundant liquid water, and 97 percent of this surface water is found in the seas and oceans. The water of the oceans appears to be passive and unchanging, whereas the rain and rivers seem active, but this is far from true. In reality the oceans are a turmoil of giant sluggish rivers – far larger than any of the land rivers – and of circulating surface currents that are driven by the prevailing winds.

No topographic map of the Earth can be drawn unless there is some kind of base line from which to measure depths and heights. This base line has always been taken as the level of the sea, yet the sea is perpetually changing level. One can choose some kind of average to call "sea level," but even today different countries have defined that base line in different ways. The currents found within the sea itself can also give the water surface a slope—the calm Sargasso Sea off the northern coast of South America is, for example, about 1.5 m (5 ft) higher than the water to the west adjacent to the Gulf Stream.

Waves

The changes in the level of the sea, at its surface, provide the most familiar image of motion within the waters. Various changes take place over many different time periods, but the most rapid are those that we call waves.

Waves are produced by the wind moving over the water and catching on the surface. They can move at between 15 and 100 km/hr (10–60 mph) and wave crests may be separated by up to 300 m (1,000 ft) in the open ocean. In general, the greater the wavelength, the faster the wave's speed and the farther the distance traveled by the wave. Waves that have traveled a long way from the winds that created them are known as swell. Without the wind continually pushing them they become symmetrical and smooth. Wind waves produce spilling breakers more like the rapids of a mountain torrent, whereas swell produces giant plunging breakers.

A combination of strong winds and low atmospheric pressure associated with storms can cause yet another kind of wave, known as a storm surge. A storm surge is formed by the water being driven ahead of the wind, and rising as the atmospheric pressure weighing down on the water decreases. Where storms drive water into funnel-shaped coasts, the water can rise more than 10 m (33 ft) above normal sea level, flooding large areas of low-lying land at the head of the bay. Venice, the Netherlands and Bangladesh have been particularly subject to destructive storm surges. Other catastrophic changes in sea level have their origins in the seabed. These are tsunamis (Japanese for "high-water in the harbor") and are generally triggered by underwater earthquakes that suddenly raise or lower large areas of the seafloor.

Tides

As the Earth orbits around the Sun the water in the oceans experiences a changing pull of gravity from both the Moon and the Sun. The Sun is overhead once a day, and because the Moon is itself orbiting the Earth, it is overhead once every 24 hours 50 minutes. The pull of gravity from the Sun is less than half that from the Moon, and so it is the Moon that sets the rhythm of the water movements we call tides. The variation in gravitational pull from the Moon is extremely small, however, and even if the whole of the Earth were covered with deep water a tide of only about 30 cm (12 in) would be produced, rushing around the world keeping

pace with the circling Moon. Yet the tides in shallow coastal regions are often very much higher than this—for example, up to 18 m (60 ft) in the Bay of Fundy, Canada. The seas and bays with the highest tides are located where the whole mass of water is resonating—rebounding backwards and forwards like water in a bath, as the smaller tides in the outlying oceans push it twice each day.

The Bay of Fundy experiences a particularly high tidal range because it happens to have a resonant frequency—a range of movement— very close to the 12½-hour frequency between tides. Large enclosed seas such as the Mediterranean have very small tides because there is no outside push from an ocean to set them resonating. In contrast, where water movement associated with the tides passes through a narrow channel it can produce tidal currents of up to 30 km/hr (19 mph), such as the famous maelstrom of northern Norway.

After these relatively short-lived disturbances the sea returns to its normal, or at least to its average, level again. When the total volume of free water at the Earth's surface alters, or when the shapes of the ocean basins vary, the sea level itself may start to wander.

How does the volume of water vary? It can be buried in rocks—but the steam clouds above volcanoes return such water so it is normally recycled rather than lost. Some vapor can be broken down through radiation in the upper atmosphere and the hydrogen lost to outer space, but this is relatively insignificant. Or it can be frozen and stacked up on land in the form of ice—this is significant as we are still living in an ice age. The lowest ice-age sea levels produced beaches at about 130 m (430 ft) below present sea level, and the low-lying coastal regions of that period have now become flooded to form the continental shelves.

The salt content of the oceans

Average ocean water contains about 35 parts per 1,000 of salts which include 14 elements in concentrations greater than 1 part per million— the most abundant being sodium and chlorine. Where there is considerable surface evaporation, for example in enclosed seas such as the Dead Sea, the salt concentration builds up and the water becomes denser. Where the seasurface is turning to ice the salt also becomes concentrated in the water.

The coldest, saltiest ocean water comes from the Antarctic. As it is also the densest it hugs the ocean bottom as it flows northwards, reaching as far as the latitudes of Spain. A similar current from the Arctic is slightly lighter and therefore rides above it—but traveling southwards, as far as the southern Atlantic. A second slightly lighter body of Antarctic water rides above the Arctic water—again traveling northwards. Where these water movements meet each other they rise up, bringing to the surface oxygenated water that can support a profusion of life in oceans that have been compared to a desert because of their lack of biological activity. Unlikely as it seems, it is the icy, stormy, polar waters that provide the lungs of the oceans.

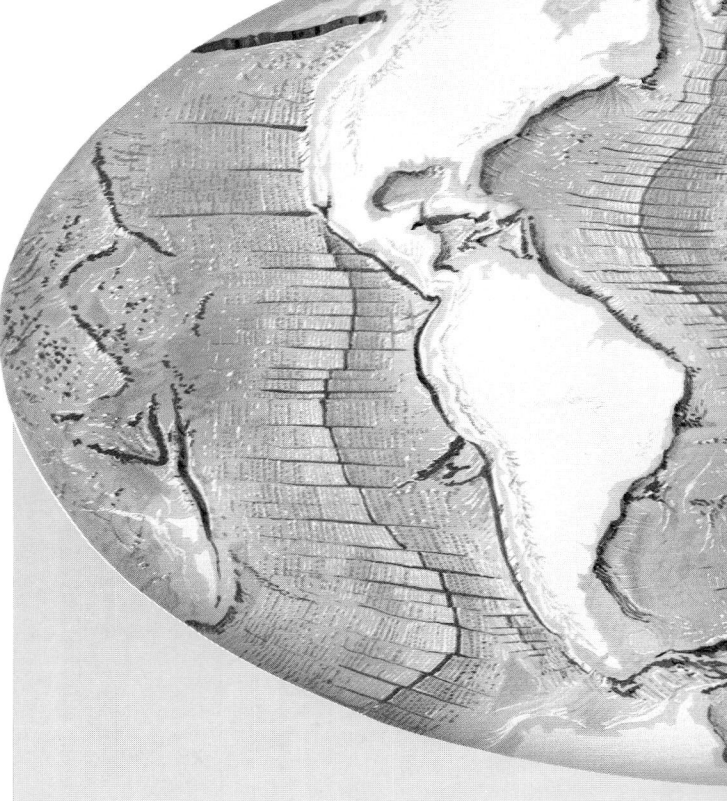

Both the Sun and the Moon exert gravitational pull on the water in the oceans, but the pull of the Sun is less than half that of the Moon. It is the Moon, therefore, that sets the rhythm of the tides. Because the Moon orbits the Earth every 24 hours and 50 minutes, the time of high or low tide advances approximately an hour each day. When the Moon is in its first and last quarters (1, 3) it forms a right angle with the Earth and the Sun and the gravitational fields are opposed, thus causing only a small difference between high and low tide. These are called neap tides. When the Sun, Moon and Earth lie in a straight line (2, 4), at the full and the new Moon, then the high tides become higher and the low tides lower. These are the spring tides. The graph illustrates tidal range over a period of a month.

Depth in meters
0 1 2 3 4 5 6 7 8

Neap tide

Spring tide

Neap tide

Spring tide

Depth in meters

0
1,000
2,000
3,000
4,000
5,000
6,000
7,000
8,000

1 Continent
2 Continental shelf
3 Continental slope
4 Continental rise
5 Submarine canyon
6 Abyssal plain
7 Abyssal hills
8 Mid-ocean ridge
9 Oceanic trench
10 Island arc
11 Continental sea

THE CHANGING OCEANS

Nearly two-thirds of the Earth's surface is covered by the seas and oceans and this great expanse of water is continually in movement. The most familiar movements are waves formed by the wind and the rising and falling tides that respond to the position of the Moon. But even greater movements take place. Currents driven by prevailing winds form whirlpools an ocean in width, and below the surface flow great rivers of colder water. Sea level is also rising as ice melts from the polar caps.

Cl	55.0%
Na	30.6%
SO$_4$	7.7%
Mg	3.7%
Ca	1.5%
K	1.5%

Seawater is about 96% pure water and the rest is made up of dissolved salts. Many elements are present in minute quantities, but only chlorine (Cl), sodium (Na), sulphate (SO$_4$), magnesium (Mg), calcium (Ca) and potassium (K) appear in concentrations of more than 1% of the total dissolved salts.

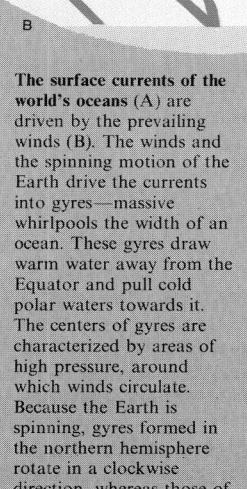

Polar easterlies
Southwesterlies
Northeast trades
Southeast trades
Northwesterlies
Polar easterlies

60° N
30° N
0°
30° S
60°S

B

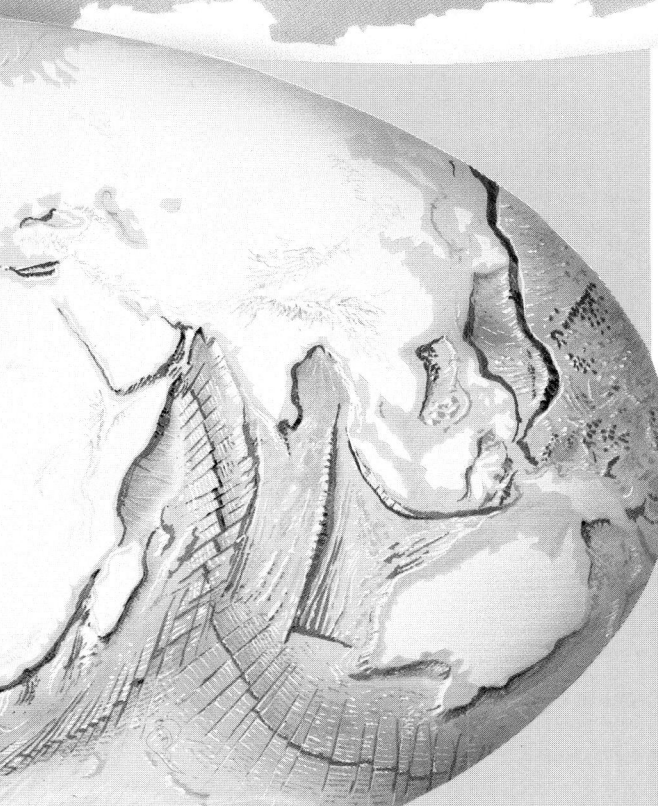

A

The surface currents of the world's oceans (A) are driven by the prevailing winds (B). The winds and the spinning motion of the Earth drive the currents into gyres—massive whirlpools the width of an ocean. These gyres draw warm water away from the Equator and pull cold polar waters towards it. The centers of gyres are characterized by areas of high pressure, around which winds circulate. Because the Earth is spinning, gyres formed in the northern hemisphere rotate in a clockwise direction, whereas those of the southern hemisphere turn anticlockwise. In all, there are five major gyres, made up of the 38 major named currents. The formation of warm (red) and cold (blue) surface currents is not difficult to understand, given the regions from which they flow. However, even in temperate and subtropical regions, the warm waters of the oceans' surfaces have a permanent layer of cold water beneath them. This cold layer has been formed in the polar regions, where, as the ocean waters have been chilled, they have sunk and then spread out into all the other major ocean basins of the world. The warm subtropical and temperate waters float like an oil slick, from 10 m to 550 m (33–1,900 ft) thick, on top of this cold layer. There is very little mixing between the two layers because the warm water is lighter than the cold water.

Much of the Earth's water is locked up as ice and stacked on the land. As the ice melts the sea level rises. Only 20,000 years ago the sea level was a full 100 m (330 ft) lower than it is today, and the continental shelves were dry land. About 10,000 years ago the sea level was rising as fast as 3 cm (1 in) each year. Today the melting ice is causing the sea level to rise about 1 mm (0.04 in) each year: only a small increment, but if all the ice melted, the sea level would rise by about 60 m (197 ft) and would flood many of the world's major cities.

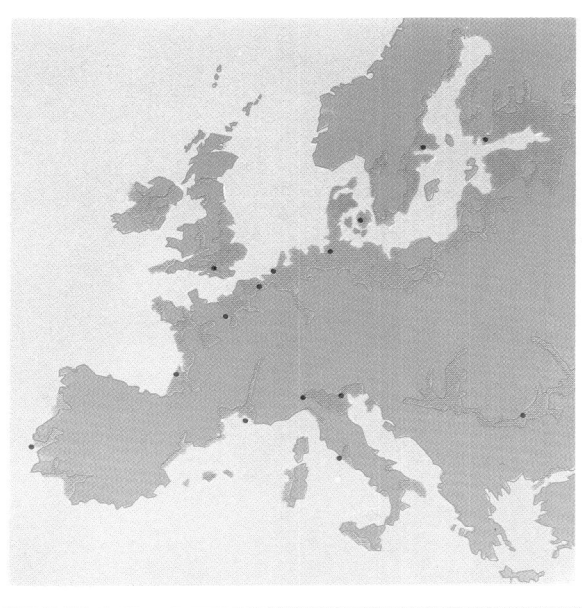

○ < 60 m
○ > 60 m
• Major cities

TSUNAMIS

Tsunamis are generated by massive underwater earthquakes (A) and are common around the Pacific. They can travel at more than 700 km/hr (435 mph) and individual waves may occur at intervals of 15 minutes, or 200 km (125 miles). Low-lying atolls of the Pacific have extremely steep sides underwater, and are generally unharmed, but the gently shelving islands such as Hawaii slow down the tsunami and build it into a giant wave 30 m (100 ft) or more in height. This map plots the hourly position of a tsunami that originated south of Alaska.

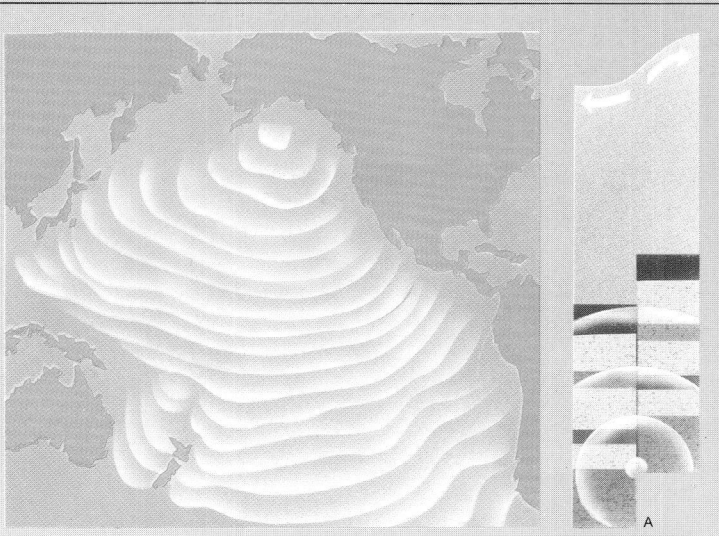

A

The seabed, more uniform than the land surface, also contains a landscape of underwater features that resemble the plains, valleys and mountains of the continents. Off the edge of continents lie the flat, shallow continental shelves, which are bounded by the steeper incline of the continental slope, which meets the true ocean floor at the continental rise.

Here deep submarine canyons may be found. These seem to be in a process of continual erosion from turbidity currents. River water pouring into major estuaries and carrying sediment can also scour out the slope—especially during periods of low sea level. The abyssal plain is rarely interrupted by volcanic hills and

mountains. The largest chains are at the mid-ocean ridge, where two crustal plates are moving apart and new ocean floor is being created. At some ocean margins deep trough-shaped valleys or trenches are the sites of ocean floor consumption at a subduction zone. The volcanic island arcs that form behind it sometimes isolate a continental sea.

Landscape-makers: Water

Of all the natural agents of erosion at work on the Earth's surface, water is probably the most powerful. Many of the finer details of the landscape, from the contouring of hills and valleys to the broad spread of plains, are the work of water. In recent years we have come to understand more fully the subtle factors at work in a river, for example, as it deepens mountain gorges or builds up sedimentary layers in its approach to the sea. The full force of a waterfall, the instability of a meandering stream, the multiple layering of river terraces – all are features of this most versatile landscape-maker.

Ninety-seven percent of the world's water is in the oceans, another two percent is locked up in the ice caps of Greenland and Antarctica, which leaves one percent only on the surface of Earth, under the ground and in the air. The importance of this one percent is, however, inestimable: most life forms could not exist without it, and yet at the same time many are threatened by it, in the form of flood and storm.

The Sun's energy "powers" the evaporation of water from the oceans. Water vapor then circulates in the atmosphere and is precipitated as rain or snow over land, from which it eventually drains back to the oceans. This is the vast, never-ending water cycle. Water in the air that falls as, for example, rain is replaced on average every 12 days. The total water supply remains constant and is believed to be exactly the same as it was 3,000 million years ago.

From raindrops to rivers

Rain falling on to the surface of the land has a great deal of energy: large drops may hit the ground with a terminal velocity of about 35 km/hr (20 mph). If the rain falls on bare soil, it splashes upwards, breaking off and transporting tiny fragments of soil, which come to rest downhill. Vegetation-covered soil breaks the impact and some of the rain may evaporate without ever reaching the ground.

Soil is rather like a sponge. If the holes or pores are very small, rain finds it difficult to penetrate and water runs over the surface of the soil. If the pores are large, rain infiltrates, filling up the pore spaces. Soils that are thin, have low infiltration rates, or already have a lot of water in them, are very susceptible to overland flow. The water may then concentrate into a channel called a gully, and this can have a dramatic effect upon the landscape. The creation of gullies, together with the splash effect, leads to soil erosion. The problem is particularly severe in semiarid regions, where rainfall is sporadic but intense, vegetation is sparse and overgrazing is common. In extreme cases, badlands are formed and by this time recuperation of the land is impossible or is prohibitively expensive.

Where the infiltration rate is high, water percolates through the soil and eventually into the bedrock. There are two well-defined regions, the saturated and the unsaturated. The upper limit of the saturated zone is the water table. Beneath this, water moves at a rate of a few meters a day, but in rocks such as limestone it can move much more quickly along cracks and joints. In most rock types there are some soluble components which are removed as water continually flows through. In limestone regions, the dissolution of calcium salts results in spectacular cave formations.

Groundwater often provides a vital source for domestic consumption. In porous materials, especially chalk, water is stored in large quantities. Such strata are called aquifers and in some areas, notably North Africa, it is believed that water being pumped up now resulted from rainfall when the climate was wetter tens of thousands of years ago.

Water from a number of sources—from overland flow, soil seepage and springs draining aquifers—produces the flow in rivers. Groundwater appears days or even weeks after a heavy rainfall, but overland flow reaches the channel in hours, producing the sudden peak in flow that may cause flooding and occasionally great damage farther downstream. Flood waves usually rise quickly in mountain areas and the wave moves downstream as the river collects more and more water from its tributaries. Eventually, although the volume continues to increase downstream, the flood wave becomes broader and flatter, so it moves more slowly and causes less damage. The most serious floods occur after intense rainfall on already saturated soils where upland rivers issue on to plains.

Rivers at work

The work of a river from its source to its mouth involves three processes, the first of which is erosion. This includes corrasion, or abrasion—the grinding of rocks and stones against the river's banks and bed—which produces both

A RIVER SYSTEM

Rivers form by the accumulation of runoff water, groundwater and from springs and small streams. Few rivers reach the sea without gaining tributaries, thus forming a river system. Highland regions at source are called catchment areas and the total area drained by a river system is the drainage basin.

The course of a river from source to mouth includes distinctive stages and land forms. All rivers flow from high ground to lower ground. Many rise in an upland area where precipitation is heavy. The upper course is where vertical erosion is dominant and the resulting valley is narrow, deep and V-shaped. A gorge is formed if this downcutting is particularly rapid. If the river has a winding course, the valley walls project to produce interlocking spurs. In the middle course erosion is lateral rather than vertical and the valley takes a more open V-shape. The river may start to meander and bluffs are formed as interlocking spurs are eroded. In the lower course the river deposits much material as it meanders across an almost flat flood plain. The bed is sometimes higher than the plain and the river has raised banks, or levées, formed from material deposited when the river is in flood. Ox-bow lakes are common, as is a delta where the slow-flowing river enters the sea.

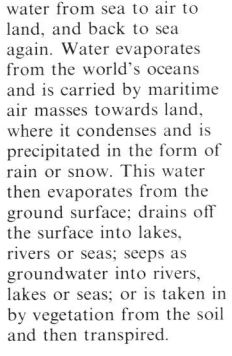

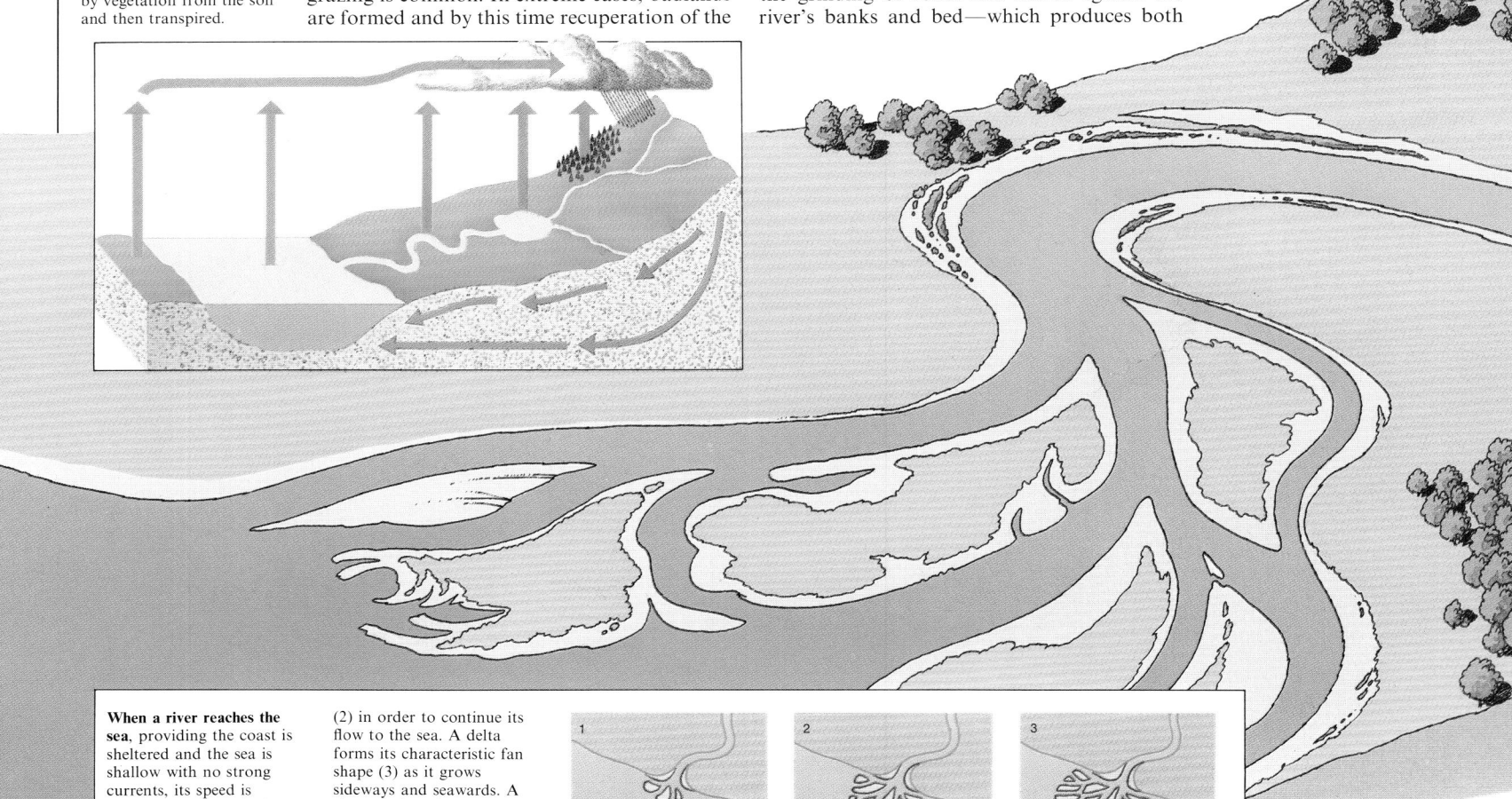

When a river reaches the sea, providing the coast is sheltered and the sea is shallow with no strong currents, its speed is checked and material is deposited (1). The river then forms distributaries (2) in order to continue its flow to the sea. A delta forms its characteristic fan shape (3) as it grows sideways and seawards. A river needs active erosion in its upper course in order to form a delta.

lateral and vertical erosion. Corrosion, or solution, is the chemical dissolution of a rock by water. Hydraulic action is caused by the mechanical loosening of material by the river's flow. Finally, attrition is the wearing away of rock fragments as they are carried along by the river.

The second process is transportation. This is achieved by traction, the rolling of pebbles and stones along the riverbed; saltation, the bouncing of material along the bed; the transportation of finer particles suspended in the water; and the carrying along of dissolved substances such as limestone.

Finally, there is deposition. This happens at all stages along a river's course and usually occurs when the speed of the river's flow is checked. The flow is slowed where there is a break in the slope, where a river enters a lake or the sea, where the valley floor widens, and where a river flows through an arid region.

Transportation routes

Rivers normally flow at between 1 and 3 km/hr (0.9 and 2.7 ft/sec), but a river can pick up and transport material once it attains a speed of only 0.1 km/hr. All the material carried by a river constitutes its "load." The load is greatest at times of flood and most significant in rivers whose basins experience extensive soil erosion.

Deposited material appears first as bars (piles of gravel) on the bends or in the middle of the channel. These bars continually change position, and on a large river like the Mississippi they present a serious hazard to navigation. Sometimes the whole valley floor can be choked with sediment, forming flat expanses of gravel called river terraces. As the river meanders, the terraces are cut back and a new flood plain is formed along the river's course at the latest level. Most sediment is deposited at the mouth of a river. Large accumulations of sediment can create a delta, which has channels that shift as the river seeks out the lines of least resistance to the sea. The shifts of the Hwang-Ho (Yellow River) in China have moved the outlet several hundred kilometers, bringing disaster to the inhabitants of the plains. Deltas are composed of such rich soils, however, that they are among the world's most densely populated regions.

Man's harnessing of flowing water and its resultant land forms is, in fact, extensive. Examples range from the exploitation of fast-flowing streams for the generation of hydroelectricity to the use of rivers for irrigation, industry and domestic purposes, and as transport routes and natural harbors.

Waterfalls develop in the upper and middle courses of rivers and are found where there is a change in gradient. The cause is often a resistant band of rock that forms an obstacle to the river's downcutting action. The force of water erodes material away at the foot, forming a plunge pool. Waterfalls are worn away in time, making a smooth gradient.

Meanders, or large bends, occur in the lower course of a river (1). Bends tend to develop at this stage as a result of the latent instability arising from the river's slight gradient and high volume of flow. The river undercuts the outside bank (undercut slope) and deposits its alluvium on the inside of the bend (slipoff slope) (2). These large meanders eventually become so curved (3) that the river cuts across the narrow neck of land at both ends of the curve, forming what is called an ox-bow lake (4).

When rain falls to Earth, a proportion of it percolates down through joints and cracks in the rock and collects in the form of groundwater. The amount of groundwater depends on the permeability and the porosity of the rock and on the relief of the land. The upper surface of the groundwater is called the water table. Below the water table the rock is totally saturated with water. The height of the water table varies: in dry weather it is lower. A spring is an outlet where groundwater is released on to the surface. This often occurs where layers of impermeable and permeable rock alternate. Spring lines occur where there are several outlets. Springs then drain into rivers.

Landscape-makers: Ice and Snow

A series of glacial periods has punctuated the Earth's history for the last two million years. During the last glacial, the ice covered an area nearly three times larger than that covered by ice sheets and glaciers today. Its remnants are still found in the ice caps of the world: most present-day glacial ice is in Antarctica and Greenland in two great ice sheets which together contain about 97 percent of all the Earth's ice. The rest is in glaciers in Iceland, the Alps and other high mountain chains.

During the Earth's major glacial periods, ice sheets almost as big as that of present-day Antarctica spread over the northern part of North America, reaching as far south as the Ohio River, and over northern Europe as far south as southern England, the Netherlands and southern Poland. Today glacial activity is more restricted, but the mechanisms by which it carves dramatic features of the Earth's landscape remain the same.

Types of glacier
There are six main types of ice mass: cirque glaciers, which occupy basin-shaped depressions in mountain areas; valley glaciers; piedmont glaciers, in which the ice spreads in a lobe over a lowland; floating ice tongues and ice shelves; mountain ice caps; and ice sheets. Climate and relief are responsible for these differences, but glaciers can also be classified according to their internal temperatures.

Cold glaciers are those in which the ice temperature is below freezing point and they are frozen to the rock beneath. This condition, which hinders the movement of glaciers, exists in many parts of Antarctica and Greenland, where air temperatures are low, as well as at high altitudes in some lower-latitude mountain regions. Temperate glaciers, on the other hand, show internal temperatures at or close to the melting point of ice. Unlike cold glaciers, they are not frozen to the rock beneath and can therefore slide over it. Ice melts on the surface of the glacier when the weather is warm, and underneath the glacier as it is warmed by geothermal heat from inside the Earth. Streams collecting meltwater may flow over, through or under the ice and emerge at the ice edge. In other glaciers, cold ice may overlie temperate ice.

Glaciers are formed from snow that, as it accumulates year after year, becomes compacted, turning first into "névé" or "firn" and eventually, after several years or even decades, into glacial ice. This process of accumulation is offset by ablation, through which ice is lost by

melting, evaporation or, in glaciers that end in the sea or in lakes, by calving. If accumulation exceeds ablation, the glacier increases in size; conversely, if ablation is higher, the glacier shrinks and eventually disappears.

Glaciers move because of the force of gravity. The fastest-moving glaciers, for example those of coastal Greenland which descend steeply from areas of great accumulation, move at speeds of more than 20 m (65 ft) a day. A few meters a day is more common, however. Some glaciers move exceptionally quickly in surges, which usually last for a few weeks; rates of more than 100 m (330 ft) a day have been recorded. At the other extreme, some glaciers or parts of glaciers—the central zones of ice sheets and ice caps for example—are virtually motionless. When the ice in a glacier is subject to pressure or tension—as it flows down a valley, for example—it behaves rather like a plastic substance and changes its shape to fit the contours of the valley. Part or all of the movement of a glacier is accomplished by means of this internal deformation. In temperate glaciers, or glaciers whose lower layers are temperate, there is also basal sliding. Movement of a glacier produces cracks or crevasses in areas where stress exceeds the strength of the ice.

The work of glaciers
Glaciers and ice sheets can profoundly modify the landscape by both erosion and deposition. Measured rates of erosion of bedrock may be as much as several millimeters a year. Rock surfaces are scratched, or striated, and worn down by the constant grinding action (abrasion) of rock fragments embedded in the base of the ice. The extreme pressure of thick glacial ice on a basal boulder has been known to rupture solid bedrock beneath it.

The products of bedrock erosion range from fine clays and silts produced by abrasion, to large boulders picked up and transported by the ice. Some rocks have been carried hundreds of kilometers, from southern Scandinavia to

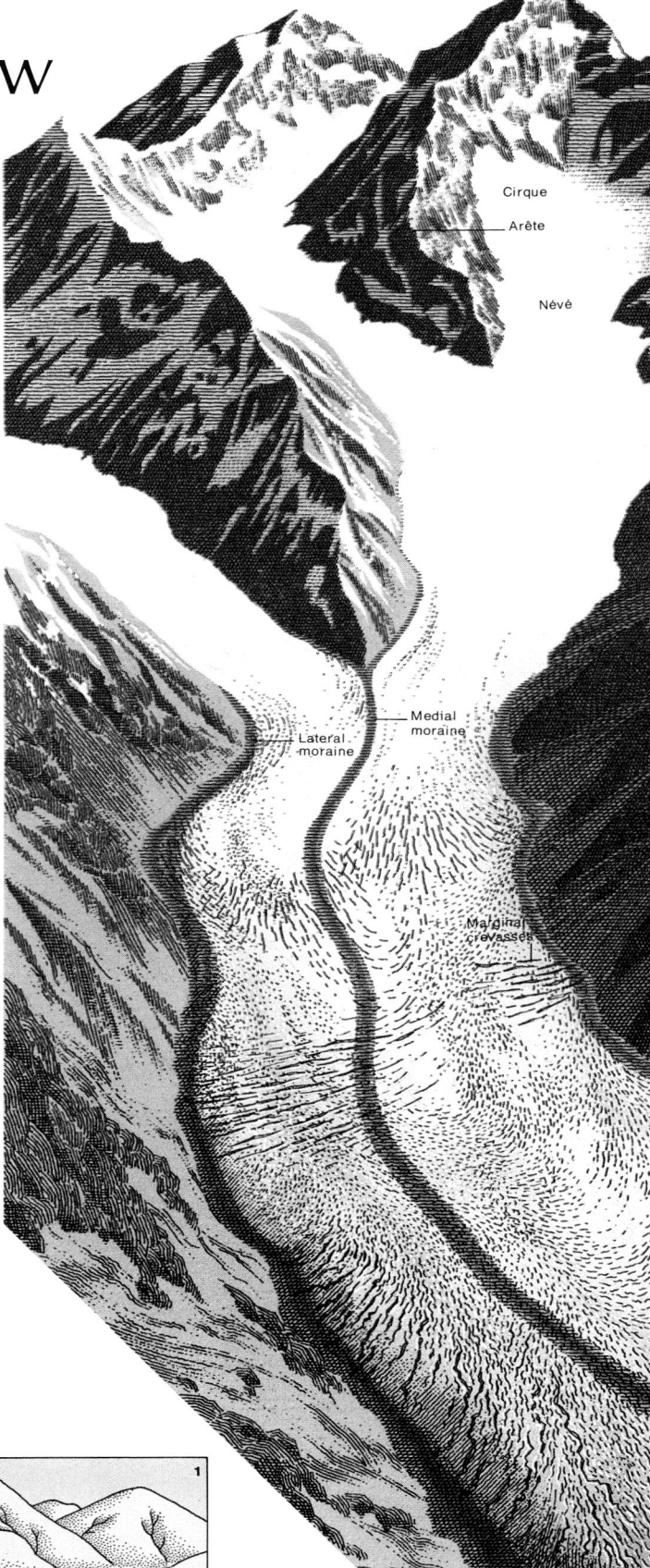

Pyramidal peak

Cirque
Arête
Névé

Medial moraine
Lateral moraine
Marginal crevasses

A U-shaped valley, such as Langdale (below) in the English Lake District, is a clear indication of a glaciated past. The floor is quite flat and the valley sides rise steeply from it.

A crevasse (below left) is created by stress within a glacier. Internally, the ice is rather like plastic but its surface is rigid and brittle. This causes tension and cracking on the surface.

This erratic (below right) is made of Silurian grit, yet it sits on a limestone perch. Ice left Yorkshire 20,000 years ago, since when the limestone surface has been lowered by solution.

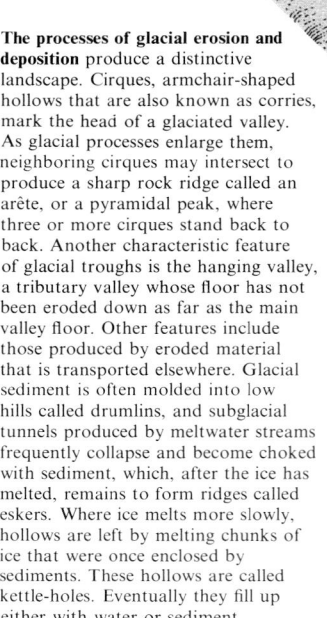

Before the onset of glaciation a mountain region is often sculpted largely by the work of rivers and the processes of weathering. The hills are rounded and the valleys are V-shaped (1). During a period of glacial activity, valleys become filled with snow and eventually

glaciers and, after thousands of years, the region shows a typically glaciated landscape (2). When the ice has finally disappeared there remains a glacial trough (3) with hanging valleys, truncated spurs, waterfalls and all the landforms associated with deposition of material.

The processes of glacial erosion and deposition produce a distinctive landscape. Cirques, armchair-shaped hollows that are also known as corries, mark the head of a glaciated valley. As glacial processes enlarge them, neighboring cirques may intersect to produce a sharp rock ridge called an arête, or a pyramidal peak, where three or more cirques stand back to back. Another characteristic feature of glacial troughs is the hanging valley, a tributary valley whose floor has not been eroded down as far as the main valley floor. Other features include those produced by eroded material that is transported elsewhere. Glacial sediment is often molded into low hills called drumlins, and subglacial tunnels produced by meltwater streams frequently collapse and become choked with sediment, which, after the ice has melted, remains to form ridges called eskers. Where ice melts more slowly, hollows are left by melting chunks of ice that were once enclosed by sediments. These hollows are called kettle-holes. Eventually they fill up either with water or sediment.

THE SNOW LINE

Glaciation is still evident today in regions that are above the snow line—the lowest limit of perpetual snow cover. The height of the snow line varies with latitude: from about 5,200 m (17,000 ft) at the Equator, to 2,700 m (9,000 ft) in the Alps, to 1,200 m (4,000 ft) in Scandinavia and sea level nearer the north and south polar regions.

eastern England, for example, and such far-traveled rocks are termed erratics. The finer sediments, compacted at the base of the glacier by the weight of the overlying ice, form till or boulder clay.

The surface of a glacier is often strewn with rock debris, which either rests on the ice or is within the glacier and revealed as the ice melts. Lateral moraines consist of rock debris that has accumulated along the sides of the glacier as a result of rockfall from, and erosion of, the valley sides. Where two glaciers join, the inner lateral moraines merge to form a medial moraine. In the ablation zone, the surface of the glacier becomes increasingly laden with debris "melting out" so that the ice may become completely buried. At the end of the glacier all rock debris is dumped, forming a terminal moraine.

Meltwater streams pouring out from glaciers or flowing in tunnels beneath them can be powerful agents of erosion and can transport large quantities of sediment. Bedrock surfaces become potholed and carved by channels that are eroded with great speed. As the streams emerge from the edge of the ice, they carry with them and deposit vast quantities of sand and gravel which form flood plains (outwash plains). Alternatively, meltwater streams may deposit sediment between the edge of the glacier and valley side, leaving a "kame terrace" when the ice finally melts. Meltwater streams feeding glacial lakes that are dammed by a glacier or moraine, for example, construct deltas of sand and gravel and lay down finer sediments (varved clays) on the lake floor.

Snow processes

Snow plays a smaller part than glacial ice in landform sculpture. Its most important role is in avalanches, which, in mountain regions, regularly bring down thousands of tonnes of rock debris. The mixture of snow, rock and other debris forms avalanche boulder tongues on the flat ground where the avalanche comes to rest and the snow melts. Gullies (avalanche chutes) on mountain slopes are swept clean of loose debris several times a year and they are gradually enlarged. Snow patches that remain stationary on more gentle slopes or in hollows encourage rock weathering under and around them. Such a process, termed nivation, may lead to deepening and enlargement of hollows and further snow accumulation. This is one way in which new glaciers are formed.

A glaciated valley exhibits a distinctive shape and profile. A cross section shows a U-shape, while longitudinally the valley floor is marked by a series of rocky steps and basins. The zone of accumulation is characterized by a cirque, in which snow collects to produce a firn field. A bergschrund is a type of crevasse that opens up near the top of the firn field where the head of the glacier is pulled away from the cirque walls. A rock step is where the gradient becomes much steeper. The speed of the ice flow is accelerated and consequent tension within the ice creates a number of deep crevasses called an ice fall. The zone of ablation has large accumulations of various kinds of rock debris.

Glacial erosion of rock surfaces is typified by a roche moutonnée, a resistant rock hummock that lies in the path of the ice. The upstream side is smooth as a result of abrasion by rock debris that is frozen into the base of the glacier. This debris scratches and scrapes rock, producing striations. The downstream side is rough as a result of ice plucking. Meltwater removes the small blocks of rock.

A great variety of material arrives at the terminus or snout of a glacier—ranging from large blocks of rock and boulders to very finely ground rock "flour." All the material is dropped in a haphazard way as the ice melts. The mixture of clay and boulders is termed glacial till. If the ice margin remains stationary, till accumulates to form a terminal moraine. If the snout recedes continuously, no ridge forms.

Landscape-makers: The Seas

The coastline is both the birthplace and the graveyard of the land. Over tens of thousands of years, geological uplift of a continent, or a fall in sea level, may create an emerging fringe of new land, whereas a period of submergence drowns the coasts and floods the adjacent river valleys, destroying land but producing some of the most attractive coastal landscapes. More rapid are the changes brought about by the sea itself. Erosion of coastal rocks or beaches can cut back the coastline at a rate of several meters a year, whereas other coastlines are built up at a comparable rate from marine sediments.

Changing coastlines are apparent on a human time scale. In temperate latitudes, beaches tend to be combed down and narrowed by winter waves, only to be restored during the calmer weather of summer. They may be lost one week and replenished the next, demonstrating an invaluable ability to recover from the wounds of all but the most devastating storms. Cliffs are generally much less dynamic, particularly if composed of resistant rock, but any loss that they suffer is permanent because there is no process that is capable of rebuilding them.

Coasts vary greatly around the world. Tropical areas often have wide beaches made up of fine material which in many cases forms broad mangrove swamps that collect sediment and build up the coast. In more exposed tropical zones coral reefs are common, either fringing the shore or (particularly where the sea level is rising) separated from the shore by a lagoon to give a barrier reef. Continued submergence of a small island surrounded by such a reef may produce an atoll. In contrast, Arctic beaches are narrow and coarse, and may be icebound for up to 10 months each year. Recession of soft rock cliffs results more from melting of ice in the ground than from wave erosion.

Waves at work

Across great expanses of open ocean energy is transferred from the wind to the sea surface to produce waves, thus fueling the machine that ultimately creates the coast. Originating as waves with heights of up to 20 or even 30 m (65–100 ft), they lose part of their energy quite rapidly as they travel, and once they have been reduced in height to the lower but more widely spaced ocean swell, they continue to travel across enormous distances.

The coasts of western Europe receive waves produced almost 10,000 km (6,200 miles) away off Cape Horn, and swell reaching California has sometimes crossed more than 11,000 km

Cliffs are attacked by waves at the zone that lies between high tide (HT) and low tide (LT). The rate of erosion depends on the strength and jointing pattern of the rock and the angle at which the strata are presented to the sea. Erosion begins when water and rocks are hurled at the cliff and new fragments are broken off. The pressure of the water also compresses air in joints and cracks to shatter the rock face. As the base of the cliff is attacked, a notch (1) may be cut, and as this is made deeper the cliff above collapses. Eventually a wave-cut platform (2) is created, the top of which is

exposed at low tide. The debris from the cliff is carried along the coast or deposited offshore (3). The shallow seabed now slows down incoming waves: they attack the cliff (4), but their energy is reduced. In calm water, for example at the head of a bay (5), wave energy is diffused and light material such as sand is deposited as beaches.

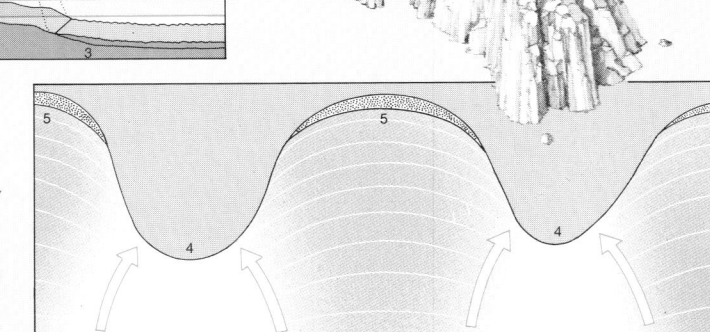

THE SEA COAST

The coastline is continually changing, whether day by day as the tides sift and sort the sand and shingle on the beaches, or over tens of thousands of years as the erosive power of waves carves out headlands and bays. And over millions of years the coastline is subjected to major changes of sea level, whether it is the land uplifting or sinking, or the sea itself rising or receding. Today, interference by man can damage the coast. Dam building and river-channel engineering drastically reduce the amount of sediment reaching the coast; and sea walls built to protect the coast and groynes constructed to retard sand removal both pose a long-term threat to adjacent coasts, which become starved of the sediment that previously supplied their beaches.

When a headland has been created (below), wave erosion continues on both sides and a cave (1) may be formed. After many years of wave action the cave will break through to the other side and an arch (2) may be created.

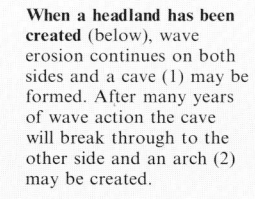

Light material such as mud, sand and shingle is carried by the sea. Waves tend to push the particles obliquely up a beach (right), but the backwash moves the material down again at right-angles to the shore. Thus the materials move in a zigzag fashion along the beach (1). This is known as longshore drift. When the load-carrying capacity of the waves is reduced for any reason, the material is deposited and forms a variety of features. The largest beaches (2) are found in the calmest waters such as in bays or at river mouths, with the finest grains sorted out nearest to the sea and larger pebbles

stranded higher up. Spits (3) and bars (4) are sand ridges deposited across a bay or river mouth. When one end of the ridge is attached to the land it is called a spit. Spits are very often shaped like a hook as waves are refracted around the tip of land. Bars are formed where sand is deposited in shallow water offshore across the entrances to bays and run parallel to the coastline. Dunes, pictured above, are formed when sand on the beach is driven inland by onshore winds. Very often they isolate flooded land behind them to form coastal features such as salt marshes and mud flats.

There are two major kinds of coastline—coastlines of submergence and coastlines of emergence. They are created by either a sinking or an uplift of the land, or by a change in sea level. A coastline with wave-cut cliffs and a river valley (A), for example, that experiences a rise in sea level will produce a new coastline (B) with a drowned estuary, coastal uplands isolated as islands, and a submerged coastal plain. The same coastline subjected to a drop in sea level (C) results in an extended river, abandoned cliffs far inland, and a raised beach that forms a new coastal plain.

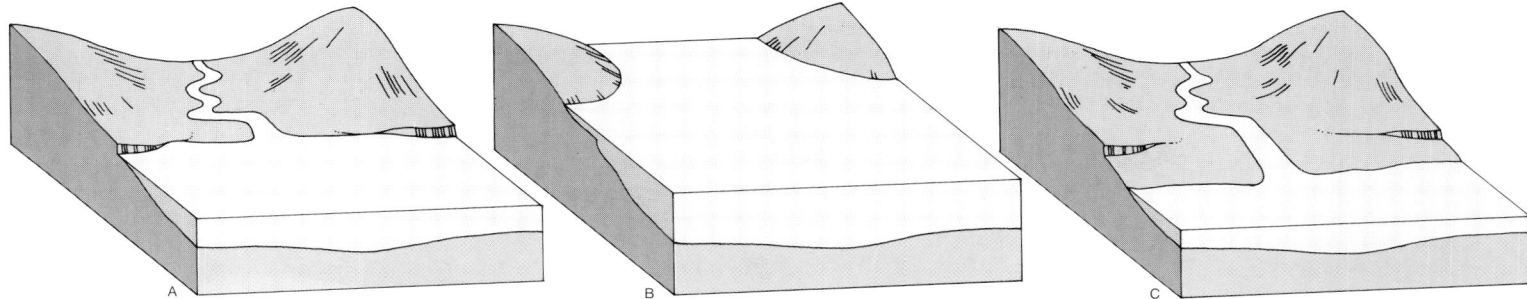

(6,800 miles) of the Pacific from the storm belt south of New Zealand. The waves thus act as a giant conveyor for the energy that is finally used up in a few seconds of intense activity. Few other natural systems gather their energy so widely and then concentrate it so effectively.

A ball floating on the sea surface shows that, although a passing wave form moves forward, the water (and ball) follow a near-circular path and end up almost where they started. Beneath the surface the water follows similar orbits, but the amount of movement becomes progressively less with depth, until it dies out altogether. The greater the wavelength (the distance between crests) the greater is the depth of disturbance.

Long-swell waves approaching a gentle shore start disturbing the seabed far from the coast and these waves slow up, pack closer together and increase in height until they become unstable, thus producing the spilling white surf that carries much sediment to build up wide sandy beaches. Shorter local storm waves disturb the water to less depth, and thus reach much closer inshore before they interact with the seabed. Such waves do not therefore break until they plunge directly down on to the beach, leading to severe erosion, which results in the production of steep pebble beaches.

Waves slow up in shallow water, and so an undulating seabed causes their crests to bend and change their direction of approach. As a result, waves converge toward headlands (where their erosional attack is concentrated), but they diverge as they enter bays, spreading out their energy and encouraging the deposition of the sediment they carry across the seabed close inshore. The high-energy waves at the headlands remove any rock fragments that become detached and transport them to the beaches that form at the bayheads.

Erosional coasts

Much of the local variability of coastal scenery results from differing rates of erosion on different types of rock. Bays are cut back rapidly into soft rocks such as clay, sand or gravel. Headlands are evidence that the sea takes longer to remove higher areas of harder rock such as granite or limestone. Despite the enormous power of storm waves, erosion of resistant rocks is slow and relies on any weakness that the sea can exploit.

Joints, faults and bedding planes are etched out by the water and by rock fragments hurled against them by breaking waves. Air compressed into such crevices by water pressure widens and deepens them into cracks and then into caves. In this way a solid cliff face can be eroded to form the great variety of features.

Resistant rocks can form steep, simple cliffs of great height—more than 600 m (2,000 ft) in some places—and the sea may have to undercut them to produce collapse and retreat. Cliffs of weaker rocks rarely reach 100 m (330 ft) in height and are more rapidly eroded by atmospheric processes, by running water and by landslips. There the role of the sea is largely confined to removing the rock debris from the foot of the cliff. Soft rock cliffs are gently sloping but complex in form.

Coasts of deposition

Although waves bend as they approach the shore, they rarely become completely parallel to the coastline. Wave crests drive sediment obliquely toward the beach, whereas the troughs carry it back directly offshore down the beach slope. In this way, sand and pebbles are transported in a zigzag motion, called longshore drift, away from the areas where they are produced. One such source of material is cliff erosion, but on average about 95 percent of the material moving on to beaches was originally carried to the coast by rivers.

Beaches are built up wherever longshore drift is impeded (for example, by a headland) or where wave and current energy is reduced (as at the head of a bay). An abundant supply of sediment may build a sandbar across the mouth of a bay or in shallow water offshore. Where the coast changes direction, longshore drift may continue in its original direction and build a spit out from the land. Depositional features may become strengthened by vegetation. Plants may take root and bind together newly deposited sediments, but they constitute relatively delicate coasts that are vulnerable to erosion if for any reason they are not continually supplied with fresh deposits of sediment.

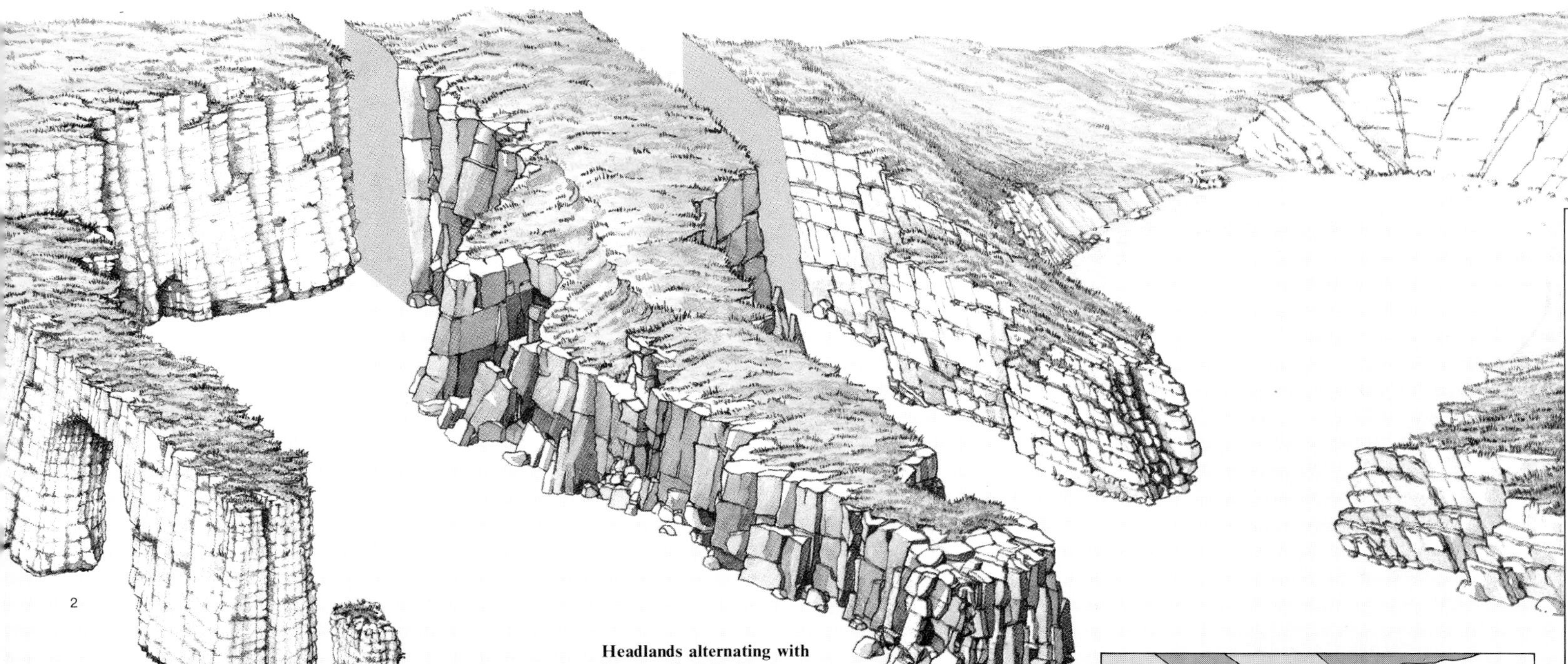

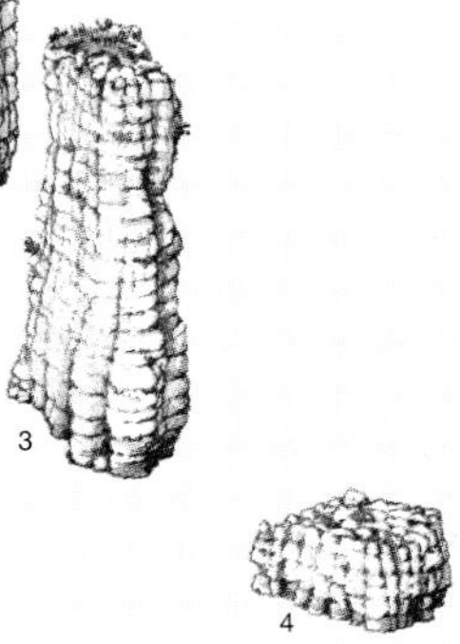

Further wave erosion (above) causes the roof of the arch to collapse, leaving an isolated column of rock called a stack (3). Another cave, and then an arch, may be formed behind the stack, which itself may be eroded to a short stump (4).

Headlands alternating with bays are found where bands of strong (1) and weak (2) rocks meet the coast at an angle and there is a varied resistance to erosion. The bays are first carved out of the softer rock, leaving the waves to attack the headlands of hard rock. If, in contrast, the strata lie parallel to the coast, then the hard rock has few irregular indentations except where the sea has broken through to the soft rock behind and has scoured out a cove (3).

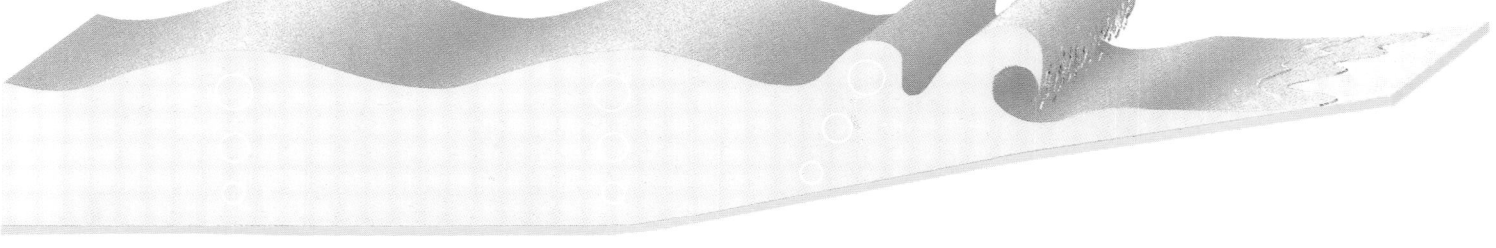

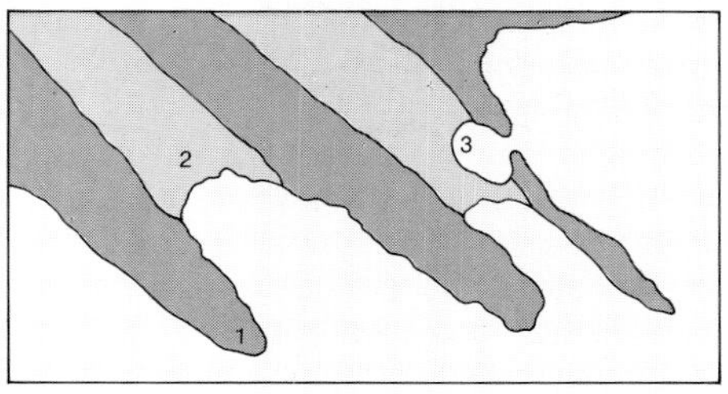

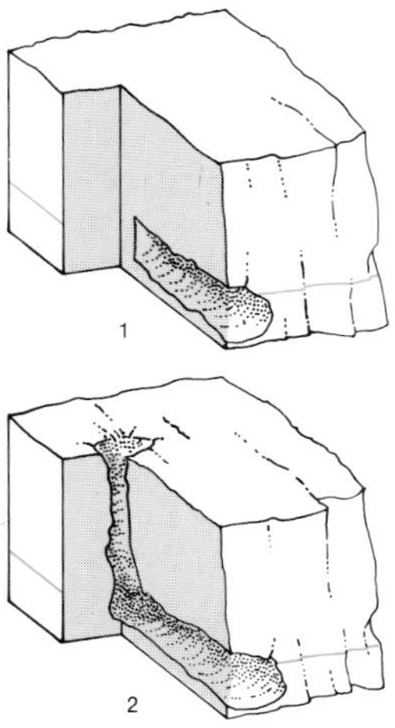

Gloups are formed when waves first erode a cave, then extend it backward as a long shaft running into the cliff (1). If the roof collapses at one point, a blowhole, or gloup (2), is formed. If the whole roof collapses, a deep cleft called a geo is created.

Waves are generated by wind on the surface of the sea. It is the shape of the wave that travels forward—the individual water particles move in near-circular orbits. Disturbance diminishes with depth to about half a wavelength. Waves break when they strike a sloping shore, and the wave height is about the same as the depth of the water.

Landscape-makers: Wind and Weathering

Winds are part of the global circulation of air and they can affect landforms wherever surface material is loose and unprotected by vegetation. The effects of a strong wind are a familiar sight—whether in the dust clouds that rise from a plowed field after a dry spell, or in the sand swept along the beach on a windy day. Weathering is the disintegration and decomposition of rocks through their exposure to the atmosphere. It includes the changes that destroy the original structure of rocks, and few on the Earth's surface have not been weathered at one time or another in the history of our evolving landscape.

Active and fixed dunes in Africa and western Asia

Sand dunes cover only 20 percent of the world's deserts, and tend to be concentrated in a small number of sand seas, or ergs, such as the Erg Bourharet in Algeria (above).

Longitudinal, or seif, dunes (below) are long, narrow ridges that lie parallel to the direction of prevailing winds. Surface heating and wind flow produce vertical spiraling motions of air.

Direction of wind

Most sand seas today are being actively molded by winds. The landscape has long been shaped by wind, and some dune fields produced in dry climates in the distant past may be "fossilized" now by soils and vegetation cover. Desertification often occurs where this vegetation is disturbed by man.

▨ Fixed sand dunes

⸪ Active sand dunes

EROSION AND WEATHERING

Winds result from the differential heating of regions of the globe. They act indirectly as agents of erosion through water or waves, but they also directly affect the surface of the Earth, molding landforms either by erosion or deposition. The nature of weathering processes and the rate at which they operate depend upon climate, the properties of the rock and the conditions of the biosphere. Both wind erosion and the various weathering processes are significant landscape-makers.

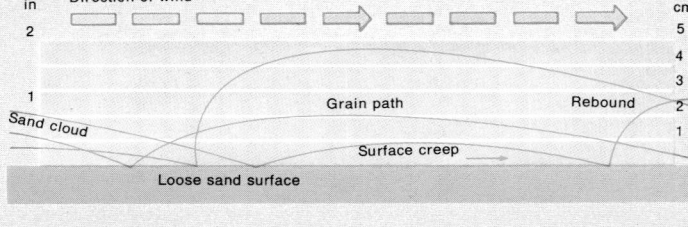

Direction of wind

Sand cloud · Grain path · Rebound · Surface creep · Loose sand surface

Many rocks are formed deep in the Earth, where they are in equilibrium with the forces that created them. If they become exposed at the surface, they are in disequilibrium with atmospheric forces. This brings about the changes —adjustments to atmospheric and organic agents—that we call weathering. Products of weathering are moved by agents of erosion, one of which is the wind. Where the surface is protected, for example by vegetation, the wind has little effect, but where strong winds attack loose surface material that is unprotected, erosion, abrasion and deposition may occur, producing characteristic landforms.

How wind shapes the surface

Strong winds occur in many places, but nowhere are they more effective in forming the surface of the land than in deserts, where their work is largely unhindered by vegetation. There the wind can pick up material and then, charged with sand particles, blast away at the ground, carrying away the debris and depositing it. Many notorious desert winds are associated with sand movement and dust storms—the harmattan of West Africa and the sirocco of the Middle East, for example.

Wind erosion occurs where winds charged with sand attack soils or rock. Dry soils may be broken up and the resulting debris, which includes soil nutrients, is carried away as dust. This poses a serious problem, especially when arid and semiarid lands experience drought. Wind erosion involving the lifting and blowing away of loose material from the ground surface is called deflation.

Erosion by sand and rock fragments carried by winds is called abrasion. In this way winds erode individual surface pebbles into distinctive shapes known as ventifacts. They can also mold larger rock masses into aerodynamic shapes known as yardangs—features that often look rather like upturned rowing boats. Some of these features are so large that they have been identified only since satellite photographs have become available. Finally, winds erode by attrition, which involves the mutual wearing down of particles as they are carried along.

Winds can transport material in three different ways. They can lift loose, sand-sized particles into the air and carry them downwind along trajectories that resemble those of ballistic missiles: the particles rise steeply and descend along gentle flight paths. This produces a bouncing movement known as saltation in a layer extending approximately 1 m (3 ft) above the

Sand particles move in a series of long jumps—a process called saltation. Particles describe a curved path (above), the height and length of which depends upon the mass of the grain, the wind velocity and the number of other particles moving around. Saltation only occurs in a layer extending up to approximately 1 m (3 ft) above the ground surface. Sand grains moving in this way are also responsible for the abraded base of features such as pedestal rocks (right). These landforms are weathered first—for example by the crystallization of salts—and are then eroded by the sand-laden winds.

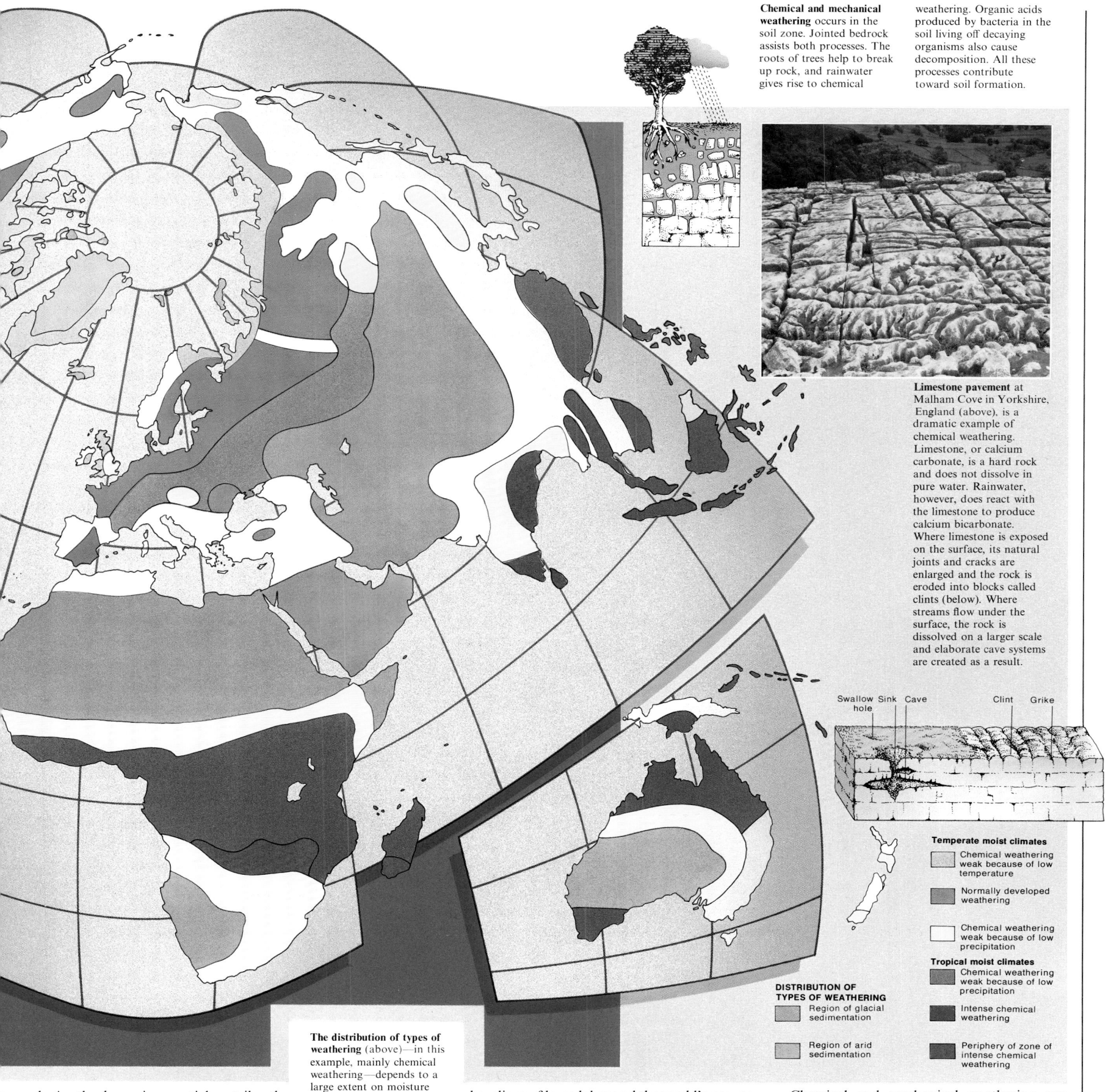

Limestone pavement at Malham Cove in Yorkshire, England (above), is a dramatic example of chemical weathering. Limestone, or calcium carbonate, is a hard rock and does not dissolve in pure water. Rainwater, however, does react with the limestone to produce calcium bicarbonate. Where limestone is exposed on the surface, its natural joints and cracks are enlarged and the rock is eroded into blocks called clints (below). Where streams flow under the surface, the rock is dissolved on a larger scale and elaborate cave systems are created as a result.

Swallow Sink Cave   Clint Grike
hole

Temperate moist climates

Chemical weathering weak because of low temperature

Normally developed weathering

Chemical weathering weak because of low precipitation

Tropical moist climates

Chemical weathering weak because of low precipitation

Intense chemical weathering

Periphery of zone of intense chemical weathering

DISTRIBUTION OF TYPES OF WEATHERING

Region of glacial sedimentation

Region of arid sedimentation

The distribution of types of weathering (above)—in this example, mainly chemical weathering—depends to a large extent on moisture and temperature. When classifying regions with different rates of chemical weathering in terms of climatic zones, many areas of the world can be placed into one of two principal categories: tropical moist climates and temperate moist climates. The white areas on the map are mountain ranges or regions of tectonic activity where there is no appreciable weathering mantle.

ground. As the bouncing particles strike the surface, they push other particles along the ground (creep or drift). Fine particles that are disturbed by saltation rise up into the airflow and are carried away as dust (suspension).

The materials eroded and transported by winds must eventually come to rest in features of deposition, the most extensive of which are sand dunes. Sand seas at first sight appear to be random and complex, rather like a choppy ocean, but their features generally fall into three size groups: small ripples, which have a wavelength of up to 3 m (10 ft) and a height of 20 cm (8 in); dunes, with a wavelength of 20–300 m (65–1,000 ft) and a height of up to 30 m (68 ft); and sand mountains or "draa," which have a wavelength of 1–3 km (0.6–1.5 miles) and rise to a height of up to 200 m (650 ft). Within each size group various forms can be explained in terms of the nature of the sand and the kinds of winds that blow over it. Where winds blow consistently from one direction, long linear dunes form parallel or transverse to the wind direction. Where sand supply is limited, horned "barchan" dunes may form. If winds blow from several directions during a year, then star-shaped dunes and other complex patterns appear. Sand dunes are also common along the shorelines of large lakes and the world's oceans, where onshore winds can pile quite extensive areas of loose drifting sand.

Agents of weathering
Weathering takes two forms: mechanical weathering breaks up rock without altering its mineral constituents, whereas chemical weathering changes in some way the nature of mineral crystals. One agent of mechanical weathering is temperature change. It used to be thought that rocks disintegrated as a result of a huge daily range of temperature (thermal weathering). Despite travelers' tales of rocks splitting in the desert night with cracks like pistol shots, there is little evidence to support this view. In the presence of water, however, alternate heating and cooling of rocks does result in fracture. Frost is also an effective rock breaker. The freezing of water and expansion of ice in the cracks and pores of rocks create disruptive pressures; alternate freezing and thawing eventually causes pieces of rock to break off in angular fragments. Finally, the roots of plants and trees grow into the joints of rock and widen them, thus loosening the structure of the rock. Animals burrowing through the soil can have a similar effect on rocks.

Chemical and mechanical weathering can work hand in hand. In arid regions, for example, the crystallization of salts results in the weathering of rock. As water evaporates from the rock surface, salt crystals grow (from minerals dissolved in the water) in small openings in the rock. In time these crystals bring to bear enough pressure to break off rock fragments from the parent block.

Chemical weathering is most effective in humid tropical climates, however, and it usually involves the decomposition of rocks as a result of their exposure to air and rainwater, which contains dissolved chemicals. Carbon dioxide from the air, for example, becomes dissolved in rainwater, making it into weak carbonic acid. This reacts with minerals such as calcite, which is found in many rocks. Similarly, rocks can be oxidized by oxygen in the air. This happens to rocks that contain iron, for example, if they are exposed on the surface: a reddish iron oxide is produced which causes the rocks to crumble.

Over many thousands, even millions, of years, the processes of mechanical and chemical weathering have affected many of the rocks on the Earth's surface. When rocks are weakened in such a way, they then fall prey to the agents of erosion—water, ice, winds and waves.

Landscape-makers: Man

Man has done much to reshape the face of the planet since his first appearance on Earth more than two million years ago. Early man did little to harm the environment but, with the rise of agriculture, the landscape began to change. An increasing population and the growth of urban settlements gradually created greater demands for agricultural land and living space. But industrialization during the last 200 years has had the biggest impact. Man's search for and exploitation of the Earth's resources has to a large extent transformed the natural landscape and at the same time created totally artificial man-made environments.

Man's major impact on the landscape has been through forest clearance. He made the first attack on natural forests about 8,000 years ago in Neolithic times in northern and western Europe, as revealed by the changing composition of tree pollen deposited in bogs. After Roman times, especially in the Mediterranean region, there was another spate of forest clearance, so that by the Middle Ages little original forest survived in the Old World. As population and emigration increased, it was the turn of trees in the New World and Africa to fall before the axe and plow. Man's present voracious appetite for timber and its products could, if unchecked, clear most of the Earth's great forests by the end of this century.

Forest clearance not only changes the appearance of the landscape but can alter the balance of nature within a region. The hydrological cycle may be affected, and soil erosion may be increased, which in turn chokes rivers with sediment and leads to the silting up of harbors and estuaries. The coastal area of Valencia in Spain, for example, has widened by nearly 4 km (2.5 miles) since Roman times, much of which can be accounted for by forest clearance, and subsequent soil erosion and the deposition of the material by rivers as they near the sea. Reafforestation of an area can reduce soil erosion and the threat of flooding. Landscape management can reduce wind speeds: for example, shelter belts in the Russian steppes have been planted over distances of more than 100 km (62 miles).

Water management
The second great impact of man has been on the waterways of the world. The most spectacular changes are caused by the construction of dams to make vast new lakes. Such projects have frequently had effects far beyond those originally anticipated. The Aswan High Dam on the River Nile was completed in 1970, creating Lake Nasser and making possible the irrigation of an additional 550,000 hectares (1,358,000 acres) in upper Egypt. But some would argue that the dam holds back silt from the rivers and stores it in the lake, a fact that has seriously reduced the rate of silting in the Nile delta. This has resulted in increased salinity and some loss of fertility of the soil, as well as changes to the delta's coastline. The storage of silt in Lake Nasser has caused increased erosion of the riverbed downstream and the undermining of the foundations of bridges and barrages.

Other man-made changes to rivers include straightening and canalization, usually for

Massive power plants (left) symbolize man's modifications to the landscape in modern, industrialized society. Demand for energy and mineral resources has led to the creation of huge holes in the ground like this borax mine (below left) in the Mojave desert in California. The open pit is 100 m (330 ft) deep, 1,460 m (4,800 ft) long and 915 m (3,000 ft) wide. In opening up resource areas in Brazil, the Trans-Amazonian highway has disturbed the forest (below).

Hong Kong's bustling waterfront (below) captures the true essence of urban man. If space is in short supply, he expands his world vertically and maximizes his use of every square meter. Central business districts in the world's major cities reflect this concern with space.

flood protection, but also to prevent the channel from shifting. As long ago as the third millennium BC, during the reign of Emperor Yao, a hydraulic engineer was apparently appointed to control the wandering course of the Hwang-Ho (Yellow River), and the system he devised survived for at least 1,500 years. Even so, over the centuries, the river has changed course radically, and today measures are still being taken to control the fine sediment that the river carries and the flooding caused by its deposition. The Missouri River in the United States is estimated to erode material from an area of about 3,680 hectares (9,000 acres) annually over a length of 1,220 km (758 miles). It is little wonder that engineers attempt to control rivers by means of realignment or try to "train" a river's flow by using concrete stays.

New land from old
The continuing pressure of population on food resources and the need to create new agricultural land illustrate still further the impact of man as a landscape shaper. As part of irrigation projects land is often leveled and new waterways are created in the form of canals. Pakistan has one of the most extensive man-made irrigation systems in the world. It controls almost completely the flow of the Indus, Sutlej and Punjab rivers through some 640 km (400 miles) of linking canals.

A huge demand for rice in many parts of southeastern Asia has led to farmers terracing steep slopes on many mountainous islands. In the Netherlands, about one-third of the entire cultivated area of the country is land that has been reclaimed from the sea. In the future more grandiose schemes are likely. Any large-scale expansion of agricultural land in the former Soviet Union will be mainly dependent on water supply. There have been plans since the 1930s to divert northward-flowing rivers to irrigated areas in the south and west. This idea, which might become a reality by the turn of the century, could have serious implications for the waters of the Arctic Ocean. If the amount of fresh water flowing into the ocean is reduced, salinity will increase, thus affecting the melting of ice floes and, consequently, sea level.

Man has also made his mark along the coastlines, from small-scale measures, such as

the construction of groynes—wooden piles that reduce the amount of sand that is transported along the beach by wave action—to large-scale man-made harbors.

Modern man, the urban dweller of the machine age, has brought great changes to the face of the landscape. The need for materials for the construction of the urban fabric has led to the creation of huge quarries, in which building stone and road-building materials are extracted from the ground. Demand for energy and minerals leads to extensive modification of the landscape, especially where mineral deposits are near the surface and can be extracted by open-cast mining. The largest holes on Earth (excluding ocean basins) are those that result from the extraction of fuel (coal) and minerals.

The side effects of mining can be detrimental to the environment. Land may subside and despoilation of the landscape by slag heaps, for example, is considerable. Escaping coal dust can suffocate vegetation in a mining area, and gases given off during some mining operations can also damage plant and animal life.

Reclamation of spoiled areas is obligatory in many countries. Old open-cast workings are often filled with water to be used for recreational facilities, and slag heaps are treated and planted with vegetation: research has produced certain strains of plants that will grow even in the most acidic soils.

The true impact of man
During the last hundred years or so man has become much more aware of his role as an agent of landscape creation and destruction. The significance of man as the landscape-maker, in comparison with slow, natural changes, is the speed with which he effects transformation, the sheer amount of energy which he can apply to a relatively small area, and the selectiveness and determination with which he applies that energy. Man's increased impact has not been a smooth and continuous process: it has occurred at different rates in different places and at different times. While it can be argued that some landscapes have been constructed which themselves conserve and often beautify the natural environment, man's active role has primarily been destructive: he has transformed the Earth's surface, perhaps irreversibly.

THE DUTCH POLDERS

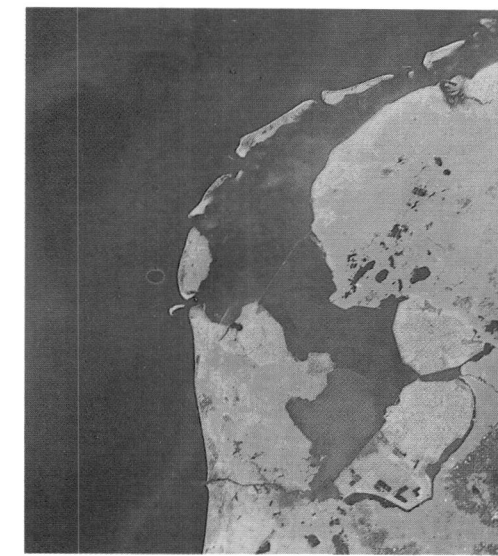

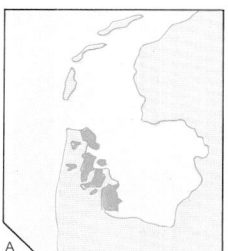
A

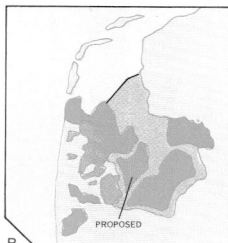
B

PROPOSED

Reclamation of the Dutch polders from the North Sea is an example of man creating land. Many centuries ago a large part of what is now the western Netherlands was beneath the sea. From the 15th to the 17th centuries (A) dykes were constructed to enclose land and protect it against inundation from the sea, and enable it to be farmed. Later, windmills were used to drain away sea water. Further reclamation in the 19th and 20th centuries (B) has brought the total area to

165,000 hectares (408,000 acres). In 1932 a 40 km (25 mile) dam was completed, enclosing the Zuider Zee—which is now a freshwater lake that was renamed the IJsselmeer—and reducing Holland's vulnerable coastline by 320 km (200 miles). To create a polder, a dyke is built and the water pumped out. Reeds are grown to help dry out the soil. After a few years drains are put in to remove water remaining. Newly created polders (light blue) show up well on this satellite image (top).

Man-made environments have become increasingly complex and large scale. Highway construction—this vast interchange (left) is in Chicago—is typical of the extensive use of land for modern transport systems alone. The acreage of land use classified as urban continues to increase. Man's endeavors to make still more land available for his many purposes have extended to cultivating previously inhospitable desert lands (above). More than half the land in Israel is

naturally unproductive because of its aridity. By means of elaborate water carriage and storage schemes and scientifically researched irrigation projects, the desert has been totally transformed from a barren wasteland into intensively cultivated fields. Output from agriculture can also be increased by terracing. In densely populated areas, or mountainous regions, as in Luzon in the Philippines (right), man's skillful landscaping has completely reshaped the topography.

Part 3

THE EMERGENCE OF LIFE

How life on Earth began and developed
How life has evolved and spread over the planet
How man came to inherit the Earth

THE STAGES OF LIFE

Simple organic molecules, the precursors of life, could certainly have evolved in Earth's primitive atmosphere. Energy from the Sun, volcanoes and electric storms had the power to combine the basic chemicals into the amino acids and other molecules that are the constituents of living matter, forming droplets of "pre-life" in pools and on shorelines. Concentrations of droplets collected around some minerals, coagulating in a "soup" of long-chain polymers—proteins and nucleic acids which together form the living cell. Thus far have scientists re-created life's origins, but the combining of proteins and nucleic acids into a living unit remains to be achieved.

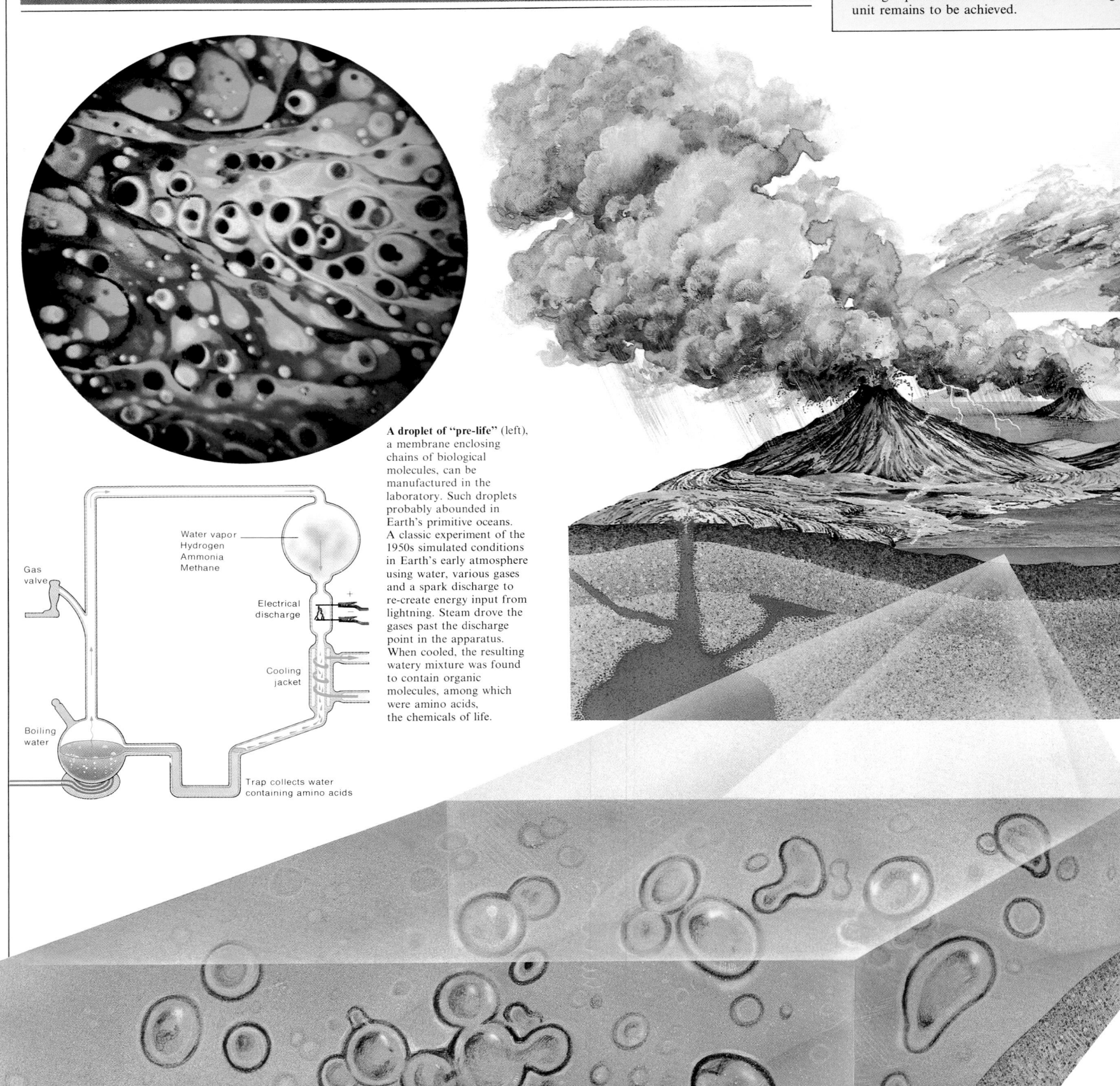

A droplet of "pre-life" (left), a membrane enclosing chains of biological molecules, can be manufactured in the laboratory. Such droplets probably abounded in Earth's primitive oceans. A classic experiment of the 1950s simulated conditions in Earth's early atmosphere using water, various gases and a spark discharge to re-create energy input from lightning. Steam drove the gases past the discharge point in the apparatus. When cooled, the resulting watery mixture was found to contain organic molecules, among which were amino acids, the chemicals of life.

Gas valve

Water vapor
Hydrogen
Ammonia
Methane

Electrical discharge

Cooling jacket

Boiling water

Trap collects water containing amino acids

LIFE BEGINS

A "primordial soup" of organic molecules, each separated from the water by a membrane, formed thick concentrations in Earth's shallow pool From these evolved the long-chain polymers that form proteins and nucle acids in every living cell.

The Source of Life

Life may have come to Earth from outer space – some meteorites contain life-like organic molecules – but the basic constituents of life, the biochemical structures called proteins and nucleic acids, could just as well have formed on Earth itself. By simulating possible primitive conditions on Earth, and applying a likely energy source, American scientists of the 1950s manufactured, from inorganic substances, the amino acids that form the subunits of all living things.

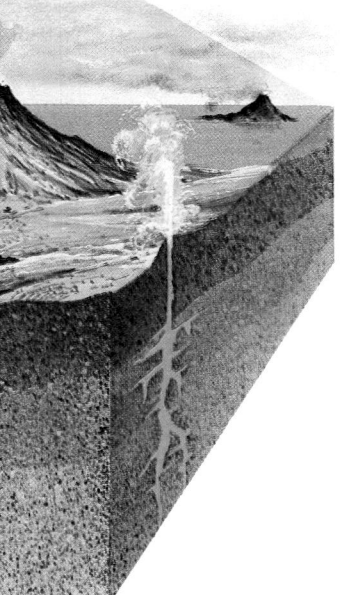

THE RADIANT SUN
A dense atmosphere of water vapor and various gases—but not oxygen—formed round the cooling planet Earth after its creation 4,600 million years ago. Oxygen in the atmosphere would have prevented the evolution of life from nonliving organic matter by blocking the Sun's ultraviolet radiation (which may have provided energy for the forming of organic compounds), and free oxygen would also have destroyed such compounds as they began to accumulate.

THE PRIMITIVE ATMOSPHERE
Volcanic eruptions drove water vapor and gases into the atmosphere of the young Earth; lightning and other discharges of atmospheric electricity accompanied the torrential rain; dissolved minerals collected in the pools. These were some of the preconditions for life on Earth, whereby mixtures of organic compounds in water may have combined to form more complex units essential for life.

Water played a key part in the creation of life on Earth. At first the temperature of the newly formed planet was far too high for water to exist in a liquid state. Instead, it formed a dense atmosphere of steam, which, as the Earth cooled, condensed into droplets of rain that poured down for perhaps thousands of years. This torrential, thundery rain eroded the land and dissolved the minerals, which collected in pools on the surface.

Earth's original atmosphere was also very different from today's. Most importantly, it contained no free oxygen, the gas which makes air-breathing life possible; the primitive atmosphere was composed of carbon monoxide, carbon dioxide, hydrogen and nitrogen. But the absence of oxygen created two conditions that are essential if life is to evolve. First, without oxygen the atmosphere could have no layer of ozone (an oxygen compound), which now acts as a barrier to most of the Sun's high-energy radiation (mainly ultraviolet light). Second, the absence of free oxygen meant that any complex chemicals that might be formed would not immediately break down again. Thus the molecules of life could form.

The chemistry of life

Life may be distinguished from nonlife in three ways: living organisms are able to increase the complexity of their parts through synthetic, self-building reactions; they obtain and use energy by breaking down chemical compounds; and they can make new copies of themselves.

It is the combined properties of the chemicals

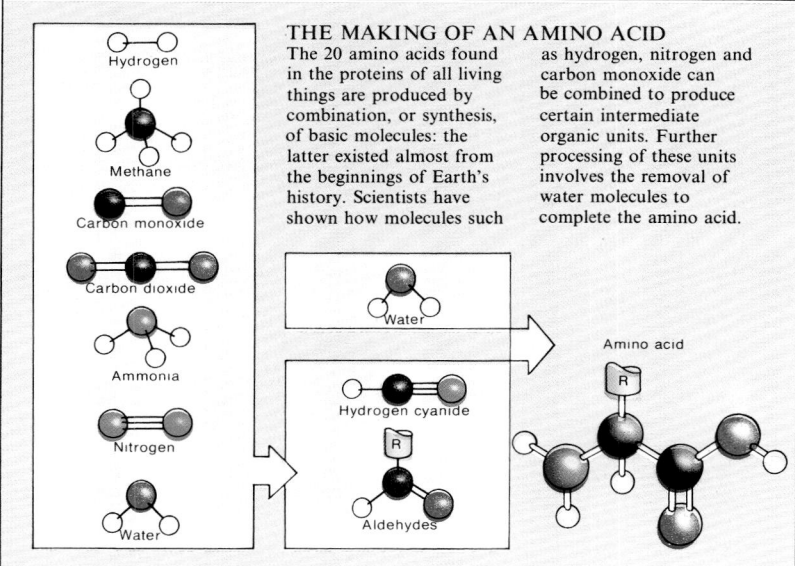

THE MAKING OF AN AMINO ACID
The 20 amino acids found in the proteins of all living things are produced by combination, or synthesis, of basic molecules: the latter existed almost from the beginnings of Earth's history. Scientists have shown how molecules such as hydrogen, nitrogen and carbon monoxide can be combined to produce certain intermediate organic units. Further processing of these units involves the removal of water molecules to complete the amino acid.

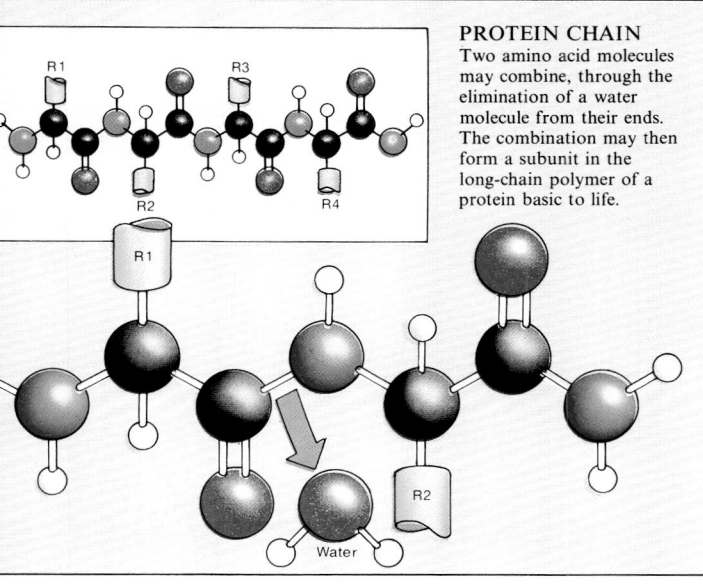

PROTEIN CHAIN
Two amino acid molecules may combine, through the elimination of a water molecule from their ends. The combination may then form a subunit in the long-chain polymer of a protein basic to life.

of life that make them so special, not just the chemicals themselves. Experiments in the last few decades have given us a very good idea of how life could have arisen from the simple, nonliving chemicals which compose it. In the early 1950s, Harold Urey and Stanley Miller simulated the atmosphere of a primitive world by filling a flask with water, ammonia, methane and hydrogen. They supplied it with energy in the form of heat and an electric spark—to simulate lightning—and the experiment was left to run for a week.

Analyzing the mixture formed, they found it contained many chemicals that are associated with living things, particularly nitrogen compounds called amino acids—the really important chemicals of life. Further experiments brought together other gas mixtures, including the one that is now thought to have covered the young Earth, and these gave similar results, as long as there was no free oxygen present. The resulting mixture of organic compounds in water came to be known as the "primordial

soup," and it is from this "soup" that life may have emerged.

Miller and Urey had shown that the basic substances of life can be derived from a primitive atmosphere. But there are still large gaps in our understanding of how these substances became more organized and self-regulating: in other words, how they became alive. More complex molecular structures somehow developed through the linking up of the basic units to form long, chain-like sequences of larger units, called polymers. But how this happened is still not fully understood.

The two most important classes of biological molecules are proteins and nucleic acids, both of which are polymers. Proteins are the building materials of living matter, the chief components of muscles, skin and hair. They also form enzymes—the chemicals that control biochemical reaction in living cells. Nucleic acids—DNA (deoxyribonucleic acid) and RNA (ribonucleic acid)—are so called because they are found in the central nuclei of cells. They are the cell's genetic material, the raw stuff of heredity. They act as the memories and the messengers of life, storing information in units called genes, and releasing that information to the cells when it is needed. Nucleic acids can reproduce themselves and, without this ability, life would not exist or continue.

The basic units that link together to form proteins are amino acids, and all proteins in living organisms are made up of just 20 different amino acids. In chemical terms, a protein molecule is a polymer consisting of a long chain of amino acid units joined together in a particular sequence, and the code to this sequence is held by DNA.

How living chemicals joined

Experiments with simulated primordial conditions have produced many amino acids other than the 20 commonly found in proteins. All amino acids (and other types of chemicals) tend to "stick" onto the surface of clay, but those 20 found in proteins stick particularly well to clays rich in the metal nickel. This suggests that the first proteins may have been formed in pools or on the fringes of seas, where the primordial soup was in contact with nickel-rich clays. There heat from the Sun or a volcano could have combined the amino acids to form a primitive protein.

The four classes of chemicals that form the basic components of nucleic acids have also, like the amino acids, been "cooked up" in a primordial soup, and they too will stick to clay to form long-chain polymers. And, just as nickel-rich clays are best at absorbing the amino acid constituents of protein, so clays rich in zinc absorb the building blocks of nucleic acids. This suggests that such clays could have been the birthplace of genes, which are the "messengers" of inheritance.

However, the coupling of proteins and nucleic acids, which together form the living cell, has yet to be explained, and it is improbable that proteins or nucleic acids alone could have provided the basis for life.

The Russian biochemist I. A. Oparin has shown that, in water, solutions of polymers (such as proteins) have a tendency to form droplets surrounded by an outer membrane very like that which encloses living cells. As these droplets grow by absorbing more polymers, some split in two when they become too large for stability. If such a droplet had protein enzymes to harness energy and make more polymers, and if it had nucleic acids with instructions for making those proteins, and if each new droplet received a complete copy of the nucleic acid instructions, the droplet would be alive—it would be a living cell.

The Structure of Life

All life forms stem from a single cell, and every cell contains in its nucleus instructions for the re-creation of the organism of which it forms a part. These are encoded in chromosomes, which contain the miraculous molecular substance of DNA, sectioned into units of heredity called genes. The genetic code determines in detail the physical characteristics of an individual creature, so that variations in DNA cause variations in the individual. Scientists believe that it is the interaction of the individual variation with the environment that ultimately leads to the evolution of the similar, interbreeding groups of creatures that are known as species.

THE HIDDEN SECRET

Dramatic discoveries in recent decades have revolutionized biology, the primary life science. Scientists can now trace parts of the genetic blueprint that lays down the pattern for every form of life, linking the large-scale unfolding of species that we know as evolution with the ultramicroscopic activity of the molecules within the nucleus of every cell. This may be the secret behind the rich diversity of life on Earth.

Deoxyribonucleic acid (DNA) consists of a "backbone" of alternating sugar and phosphate molecules, and to each sugar is attached one of four nitrogenous bases (adenine, guanine, thymine and cytostine, or A, G, T, C). A single gene might contain 2,000 of these bases, and in the body cell of a human being the 46 chromosomes (thread-like bodies of DNA and protein) run to 3,000 million bases. The sequence of these bases stores the information for making amino acids into proteins, just as the sequence of letters in this sentence stores the information for making a particular verbal structure. But the DNA alphabet has only four letters (A, G, T, C).

The thread of life

DNA is a double molecule, resembling a twisted ladder, its two main strands twining around each other to form the famous double helix. The strands are linked by pairs of bases—A and T, or G and C—whose shape is such that each pair fits together neatly, like pieces of a jigsaw, to form the rungs of the DNA ladder. As a result, the information on the strands can be duplicated by "unzipping" the double helix and making new strands by using the old ones as templates. DNA stores, duplicates and passes on the information that makes life alive.

Cells multiply by splitting in two, and each newly made cell thus gets instructions for its existence by the mechanism of heredity, the gene. But heredity is a word more often applied to the passing on of DNA from an organism to its offspring. In sexual reproduction the offspring gets some of the DNA (usually half) from one parent, and the rest from the other, ending up with a unique mix all of its own.

The laws of heredity

Man has long known that characteristics can be passed on from one generation to the next, for he has been selectively breeding crops and animals for thousands of years. However, it was not until the mid-nineteenth century that an obscure Austrian monk, Gregor Mendel (1822–84), discovered the laws that govern inheritance, and his work was ignored until the beginning of the twentieth century, when more powerful microscopes made possible the direct observation of the cell.

Mendel experimented with pea plants because they had easily recognizable traits, and because, although normally self-fertilizing, they could be cross-fertilized with pollen from a different plant. Mendel made many crosses between different pure-bred plants and found that in the offspring, or hybrids, some characters always prevailed over others: red flowers over white, tall plants over short, and so on. He called the prevailing characters dominant, and the nonprevailing characters recessive. He then let the first-generation hybrids self-fertilize, and found not only that the recessive traits reappeared in the hybrids' offspring, but also that they reappeared in a constant proportion of three dominant to one recessive; the second generation contained three times as many red-flowered peas as white-flowered peas.

To explain his results, Mendel proposed that each plant had two hereditary "factors"— today called alleles—for each character, and that the dominant factor suppressed the recessive factor. If a plant inherited both a dominant and a recessive factor, the dominant one would prevail. Only if both factors were recessive would the recessive character be apparent. Mendel found many other pairs of traits where one form was dominant and the other recessive. He established that permutations arising from the crossing of the two first-generation hybrids allows the dominant gene to be present in three out of four crosses in the second generation; but

in the fourth cross, only the two recessive alleles of the genes are present. So there is always a three-to-one ratio of dominant to recessive.

Theories of evolution

Mendel's work was of course unknown to his contemporaries, Charles Darwin and Alfred Russel Wallace, who even then were providing solutions to the major mystery of biology—the way that species evolve, change and develop over time. Evolution was not a new idea in Darwin's day. In 1809 the French naturalist Jean-Baptiste Lamarck had proposed a theory of the inheritance of acquired characteristics, suggesting that new habits learned by an organism in response to environmental change may become physically incorporated in the animal's descendants. For instance, the fact that the ancestral giraffe had to stretch its neck to reach food might give its offspring long necks to enable them to reach food more easily. Less satisfactory than the "natural selection" theory of Darwin and Wallace (who independently reached the same conclusion), Lamarckism founders on the fact that there is no genetic mechanism enabling acquired characters to pass on in this way.

Darwin's theory of natural selection has three key elements: all individuals vary, and some variations are passed on to the next generation; the gap between the potential and the actual number of offspring reproduced by organisms is very wide and implies that not all will survive. Evolution implies that not all will survive; organisms best adapted to the environment will survive, their offspring will have been selected, and the favorable variation

will spread through the population, perhaps eventually changing it.

Genetic variation, the mainspring of natural selection, is reflected in variations of DNA, the material substance of heredity. Changes in the order of DNA's nitrogenous bases—called mutations—produce changes in the proteins which are usually, but not always, harmful. More important than these is the effect of genes recombining in sexually reproduced offspring.

Sexual reproduction provides the offspring with two sets of DNA, one from each parent. The processes that give rise to a half-set of chromosomes in a sperm or egg shuffle and recombine the genes on each chromosome to provide new combinations. Then, when sperm and egg fuse together at fertilization, the half-sets come together and even more combinations are produced. The world's enormous diversity of life can be explained in terms of a struggle that favors certain genetic combinations.

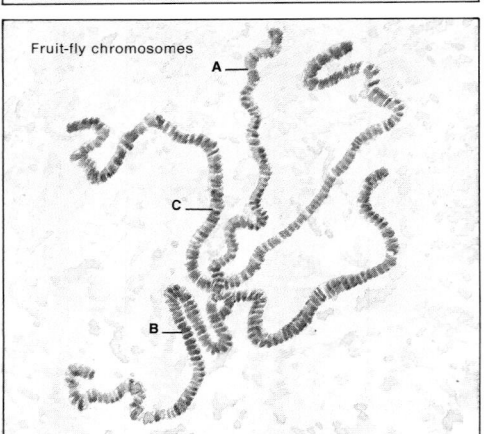

Genes
Chromosomes
Cell
Protein (myoglobin)
Amino acids
Fruit-fly chromosomes

The cell is the basic unit of all life, and every cell contains in its nucleus the thread-like structures, called chromosomes, that control heredity. Each species has its own number of chromosomes, and the number is always the same for that species. Chromosomes are sectioned into genes, units of heredity made of DNA molecules. DNA acts like code, specifying the order and number of amino acids that make up proteins— the organic compounds characteristic of all life.

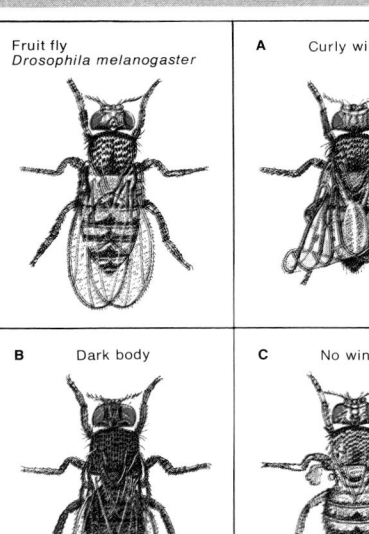

Chromosomes (below left) of the fruit fly, much magnified, show bands of DNA arranged in sections that correspond exactly with specific genes, the chemical units of heredity. The proof of this correspondence came when the American geneticist Hermann Muller introduced the use of ionizing radiation to damage the fruit flies' chromosomes at ultramicroscopic points, causing precise point mutations in offspring of parents whose DNA had been damaged at the places indicated. Random mutations may occur in any organism, and not only as a result of radiation. A gradual accumulation of minor mutations may lead to evolutionary change.

Fruit fly
Drosophila melanogaster
A Curly wings
B Dark body
C No wings

Iiwi
Vestiaria coccinea

Apapane
Himatione
sanguinea

Laysan
finch
Psittiro
cantans

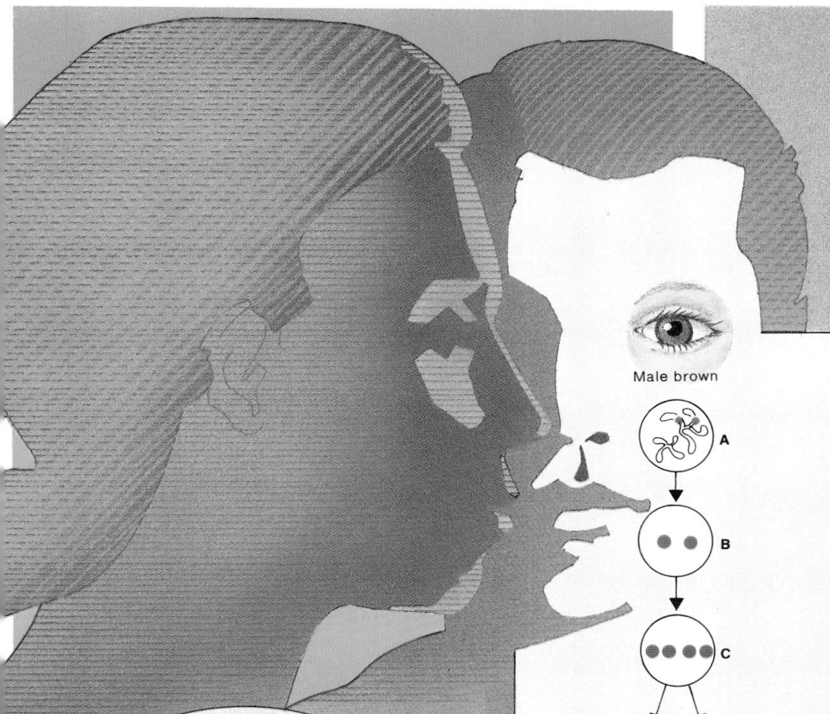

Some human traits, such as eye color, are inherited as single factors (below). In such cases one gene is dominant over the other, recessive, gene, and the gene giving a brown eye color is always dominant over that which gives a blue eye color. The chromosomes carrying eye-color genes (A) pair (B) and duplicate (C, D) before dividing twice (E, F) in the process known as meiosis, or reduction division. This ensures that the offspring gets half the chromosomes from the male and half from the female parent, so each new cell gets both genes when sperm and egg unite. But because brown-eye genes are dominant over blue, all offspring have brown eyes, with the blue-eye gene hidden. But if two brown-eyed parents carry recessive blue-eye genes, half the male sperm cells have blue-eye genes, and the female eggs carry a gene for either blue or brown eyes. So the two recessive genes have a one-in-four chance of being combined to produce a blue-eyed child, no brown-eye genes being present.

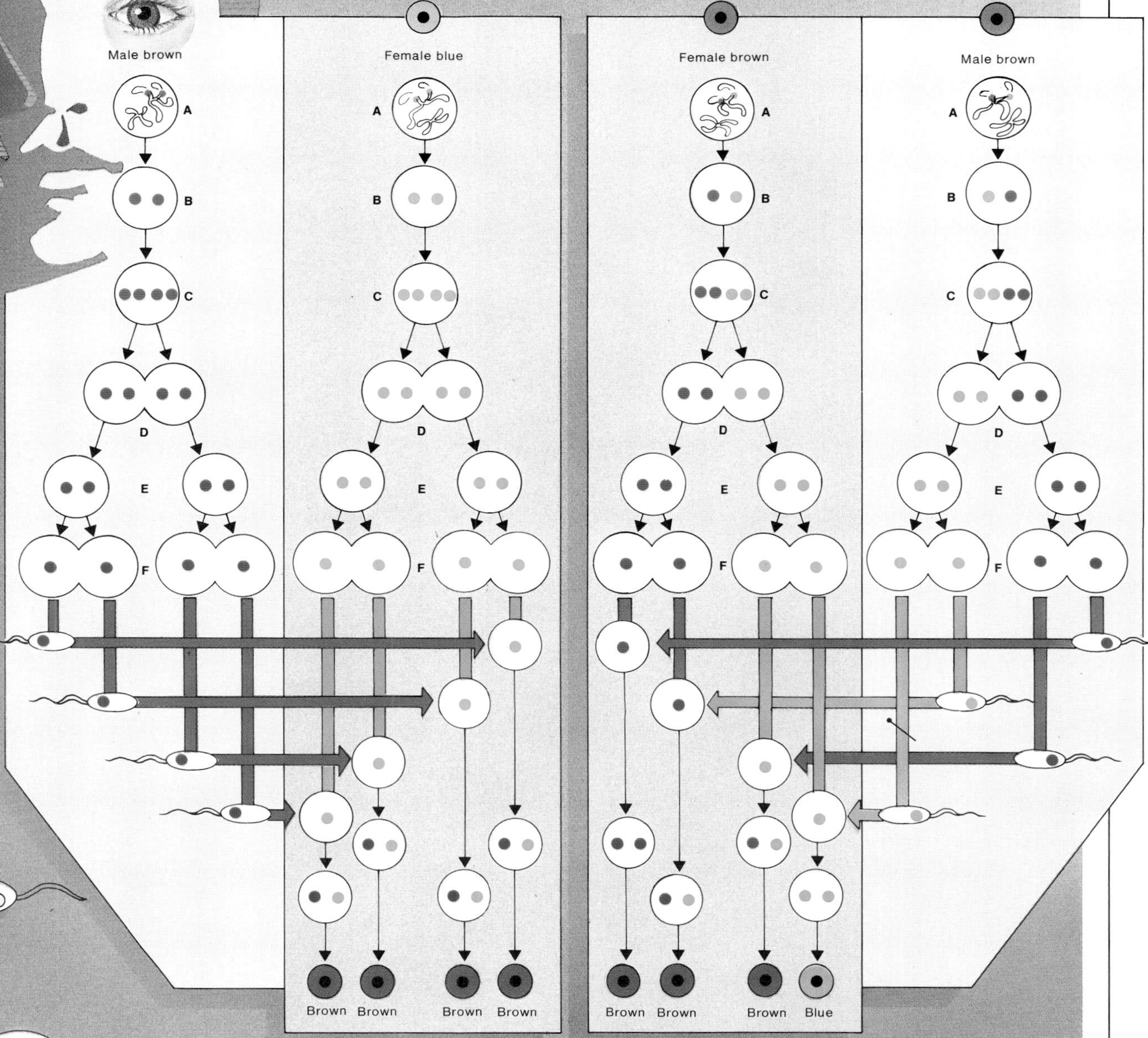

Male brown | Female blue

Female brown | Male brown

A B C D E F

Brown Brown | Brown Brown

Brown Brown | Brown Blue

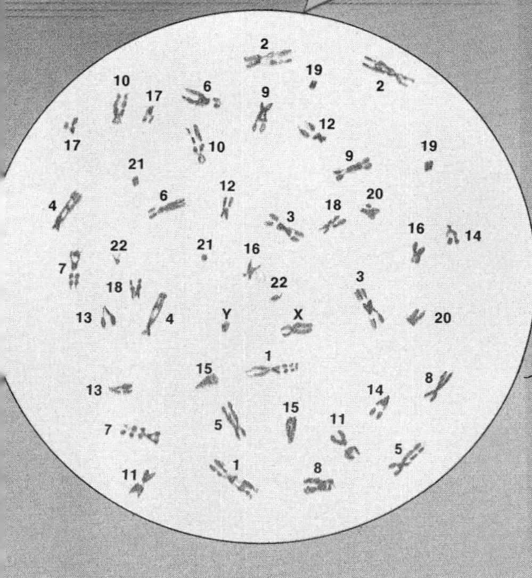

A human body cell (above) contains 46 chromosomes—22 matching pairs and the chromosomes (X, Y) which determine sex. Males have X and Y, females X and X. In sexual reproduction (right) traits carried by the male sperm and the female egg combine in the zygote, the fertilized egg from which new life starts. All growth is the result of repeated cell division, or mitosis, where the nucleus forms paired chromosomes that duplicate themselves; the cell splits, and the chromosomes re-form in the nucleus of the new cells. Sex cells are produced by reduction division, or meiosis, with each cell taking only one from each pair of chromosomes, which exchange corresponding segments in the process called recombination. The genes are thus reshuffled at each generation, so that new combinations of gene traits are available for selection each time meiosis takes place. The result is genetic diversity, with many possibilities for the species to adapt to a changing environment.

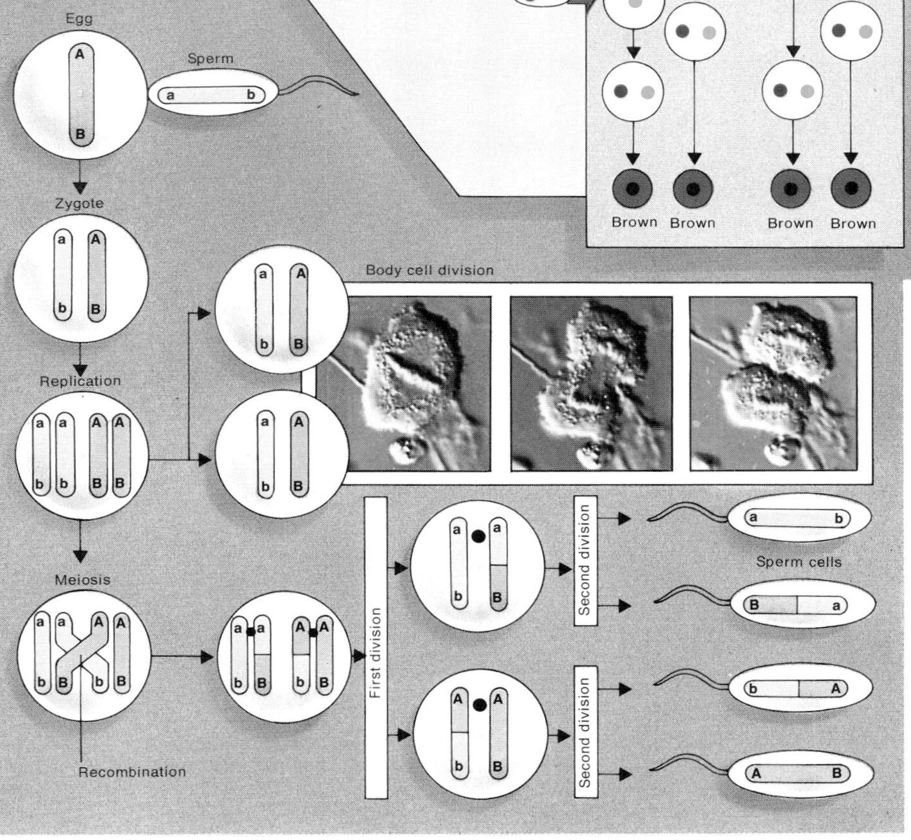

Egg
Sperm
Zygote
Replication
Body cell division
Meiosis
First division
Second division
Sperm cells
Recombination

VARIANT FORMS

Dark forms of many insects, such as the peppered moth *Biston betularia*, have developed widely in industrial areas of the world since the industrial age. The dark variant, resulting from a single genetic mutation, escapes the eye of predators against the black, lichen-free bark of soot-darkened trees (top), whereas the typical pale form is very conspicuous. In rural, unpolluted areas where tree trunks are light and lichen covered (bottom) the well-concealed pale form is much commoner. *Biston*'s rapid evolutionary response is remarkable: in 1849 only one dark example was recorded at Manchester, England, but by 1900 98% of the moths caught in the area were of the dark type. A similar change occurred in other industrial areas, during the period when the most coal was being burned and the population was most rapidly expanding. But with today's clean-air laws the number of pale moths in these areas is once again on the increase.

A diversity of forms (left) has stemmed from a single ancestor of the Hawaiian honeycreeper, which now numbers 14 species. These have adapted in their mid-Pacific isolation to fill niches usually taken by other birds, ranging from the nectar-feeding iiwi to the Laysan finch with its thick beak for cracking seeds, and the short-billed apapane, which includes insects in its diet. But the honeycreepers' success in divergence may have led to overspecialization, with at least eight species now extinct. The Australian marsupial mouse and the Indian spiny mouse (right) look very similar, due to the fact that they fill similar ecological niches, but they belong to groups evolving separately for almost 100 million years.

Indian spiny mouse *Mus platythrix*

Australian marsupial mouse *Sminthopsis murina*

Earliest Life Forms

Earth's original atmosphere lacked oxygen, without which there could be no survival for air-breathing creatures. This vital gas was supplied by life itself, in the form of microscopic organisms that flourished in the atmosphere of the time and emitted oxygen as "waste." In this way a breathable atmosphere built up; increasingly complex life forms were able to develop in the seas; early plants and insects gained a foothold on the shores; and, finally, larger animals could survive on land.

A BREATHABLE ATMOSPHERE

Without oxygen, life as we know it could not exist; yet Earth's original atmosphere contained practically none. The oxygenation of the atmosphere was the work of the planet's first life—primeval bacteria and algae. Of these, some released oxygen as waste while consuming carbon dioxide or nitrogen in photosynthesis. Colonies of algae forming stromatolites ("stony carpets") generated even more oxygen, but this was first taken up by ocean rocks, visible today as "banded iron formations." Once all the ocean rocks were oxidized, an oxygen-rich atmosphere could develop, with an ozone layer to filter out harmful radiation from the Sun.

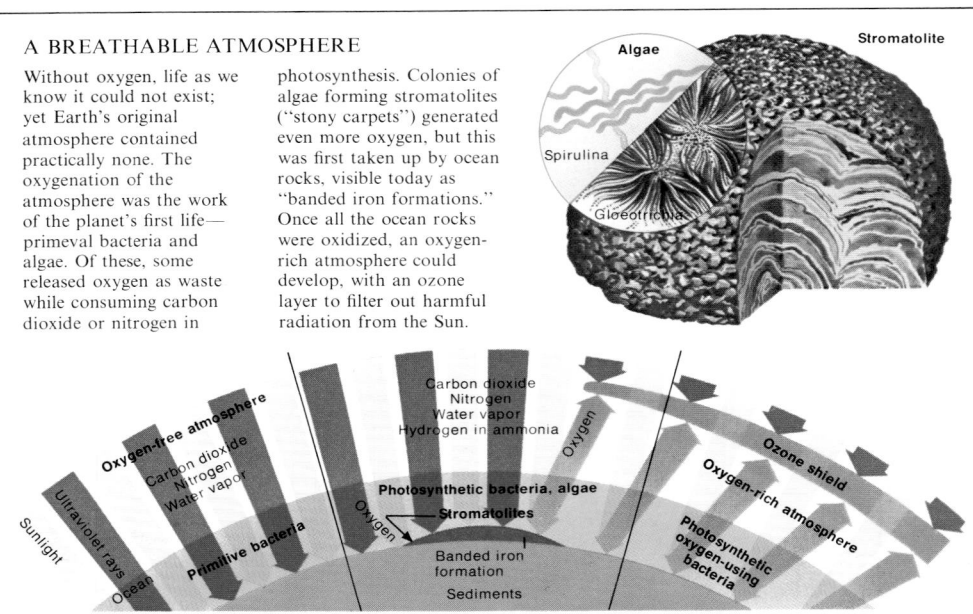

Scientists have identified bacteria-like microfossils in the rocks that were formed more than 3,500 million years ago. Some of these organisms appear to have been capable of photosynthesis—the process of utilizing sunlight, water and carbon dioxide for "food," with release of oxygen as the vitally important by-product. As a result, surplus oxygen very gradually accumulated in the Earth's atmosphere, forming an upper-atmosphere shield of ozone (which kept out damaging ultraviolet radiation from the Sun) and providing an oxygen-rich atmosphere in which breathing life could develop.

At least five types of microfossil have been found in ancient sediments of Western Australia, aged about 3,560 million years, and these provide the earliest evidence of life so far discovered. Other early proof of life comes from the so-called "stromatolites," some of which may date back as far as 3,400 million years. These curious columns, growing in warm, shallow waters, are formed of blue-green algae which have entrapped chalky sediments, bacteria and other microfossils. Their study is made easier by the fact that similar structures have developed at later geological times, and some are even being formed at the present day.

Living below the surface of the water and not initially reliant on oxygen for life, such bacteria and algae were shielded from the Sun's ultraviolet rays as they imperceptibly altered the Earth's atmosphere. For hundreds of millions of years life of this kind persisted, with few obvious developments or changes.

Breathing life
About 1,800 million years ago, the effects of these microscopic photosynthesizers became dramatically apparent in the "rusting" of the ocean sediments, when the red color of the rocks being formed at that time indicates that

there was enough free oxygen on Earth to bring about the process known as oxidation. Once the ocean rocks capable of absorbing oxygen had done so, forming the red "banded iron formations" known to geologists, oxygen could enter the atmosphere in ever greater quantities.

It has been estimated that a breathable atmosphere existed on Earth about 1,700 million years ago, and aerobic (oxygen-using) organisms first became abundant not very long afterwards. These organisms were single celled, and it may have been almost 1,000 million years before multicellular animals evolved. The fossilized remains of animals alive 800 million years ago have been found in many parts of the world, but it is not yet known whether multicellular animals had a long history before these earliest known forms, or whether they had developed and radiated rapidly from a creature capable of feeding as well as photosynthesizing.

One of the earliest collections of animals of this type was discovered in the Ediacara Sandstones of the Flinders Range in Australia, where some 650 million years ago the rocks once formed part of an ancient beach. Here a spectacular collection of soft-bodied animals, similar to today's coelenterates (such as jellyfish) and worms, was washed ashore and preserved in silt from the nearby shallow sea. Comparable, mainly floating forms have been found in other parts of the world in rocks dating from between 650 and 580 million years ago.

The first vertebrates
One of the most important changes in animal life seems to have occurred about 580 million years ago. At that date many creatures evolved hard, protective shells, which also acted as areas of muscle attachment and as support for their bodies—in other words, as external skeletons. Hard shells were more easily preserved as fossils than the soft bodies of earlier animals, so rich collections have been recovered from rocks of the Cambrian Period, beginning 580 million years ago, as well as from later strata.

The first fish-like animals—the earliest true vertebrates—are found in rocks of the Ordovician Period, from about 500 million years ago, and these were in many ways very similar to the lampreys and hagfishes of today. But unlike them, these ancient creatures were heavily armored with external bone. They must have been poor swimmers, living mainly on the seabed and filtering edible particles from the

THE FIRST SHELLED CREATURES
These evolved (right) in the seas when conditions allowed soft-bodied life to form protective casings. In the fossil record of 550 million years ago, soft and shelled forms are found. The trilobites (1, 2, 3)—a now extinct order of woodlouse-like animals—dominated the scene, but other early arthropods (4) included a possible insect ancestor (5), and there may even have been an ancestor to fish (6). Sponges (7), crinoids (8), early moluses (9), bristleworms (10) and lampshells (11) were plentiful, but other creatures (12) are bewilderingly strange.

sediments, which they sucked into their jawless mouths. From them arose true fishes, with backbones, jaws and teeth, and they came to replace the less efficient earlier forms.

During the Devonian Period, about 400 million years ago, the fishes diversified greatly, adapting to fit all kinds of aquatic environments. Some grew to a huge size, such as *Dunkleosteus*, which achieved a length of up to 9 m (29 ft 7 in), although it belonged to a group of fishes that retained heavy armor. Some of these curious creatures probably used their stilt-like pectoral fins to hitch themselves across the beds of the pools in which they lived.

From water to land
The fishes that teemed in the seas and fresh waters of the Devonian world found their way into difficult environments such as swamps and oasis pools, where there was a danger of drying out in the warmer weather. Many of these fishes had rudimentary lungs, and one group developed powerful jointed fins.

Such marginal habitats were not ideal for fishes, but they were nevertheless rich in species, and it is from them that the first land vertebrates developed. When the water dried up they survived, for their strong fins held them up so that they did not flop over helplessly.

They found themselves in a new, dry world, but one which was already inhabited, at least round the water's edges, with plants related to modern liverworts, mosses and club mosses. There were also numerous invertebrate animals such as millipedes, spiders and wingless insects. These plants and animals provided shelter and food, so that the environment was not wholly hostile to larger animals.

The first steps on land probably took the form of strong flexions of the body—desperate swimming movements which swung the fins forward, pegging the animal's position in the drying mud. But in a very short time geologically, animals had evolved in which the rays of the lobe fins had vanished, leaving stubby legs with which the animals—no longer fishes but amphibians—could haul themselves over land. But they still had to return to water to breed and lay eggs.

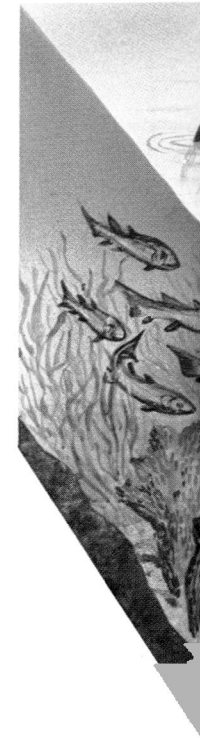

THE FIRST AMPHIBIANS
Amphibians (1) emerged some 345 million years ago (right), inhabiting swampy environments with luxuriant vegetation—club mosses and ferns (2, 3) that made up the early coal forests. Lungfish (4) were well adapted to life in oxygen-poor waters, but the move to land was probably made by related fish with a passage linking nostrils to throat—*Eusthenopteron* (5). Land offered food (6, 7, 8) and suitably damp conditions for a possibly stranded aquatic animal.

Palaeozoic			Mesozoic		Cenozoic
500	400	300	200	100	0

Millions of years ago

A timescale of life on Earth emerges from the record of fossils embedded in rock strata. Major breaks in faunas (animal assemblages) separate eras coinciding roughly with periods of intense mountain-building activity. These eras are broken down into geological periods, which are separated by lesser faunal breaks and which are generally named from the area where rocks of that age were first discovered. The geological eras and periods do not imply particular rock types.

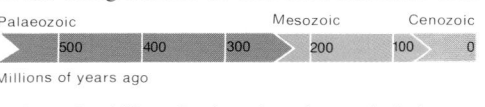

| 600 | Shelled/skeletal animals | ▶ CAMBRIAN | 550 | First fishes | ▶ ORDOVICIAN |

THE AGE OF JELLYFISH

Jellyfish (left) and other soft-bodied animals flourished in the pre-Cambrian seas, more than 600 million years ago. The forms of one group, imprinted on sand, have been preserved as fossils in the Australian Ediacara Sandstones. They include varieties similar to modern jellyfish (1, 2); worm-like crawlers (3); sea pens (4) very like modern types; segmented worms (5); "three-legged" creatures like no known animal (6); and sand casts of burrowing worms (7).

LIFE ON SEA AND LAND

For more than half the Earth's existence, its atmosphere has been hostile to air-breathing life. Then, about 1,600 million years ago, the photosynthesizing action of minute organisms built up enough free oxygen in the atmosphere for more complex oxygen-dependent forms to develop. The first multicellular life led to the soft-bodied animals of the pre-Cambrian time—worms, jellyfish and sea pens. About 580 million years ago many animals developed hard parts, including shells. Over 1,200 new marine species date from this period, and the evolutionary explosion came to fill the Earth's seas with fishes. Some of these had powerful jointed fins and rudimentary lungs, and lived in swamps where primitive plants and insects had already made the move to land. As the pools dwindled the stranded animals could survive by breathing air.

LIVING FOSSILS

Some life forms that emerged 570 million years ago have survived virtually unchanged to the present day. These "living fossils" include *Lingula* (left), today found in warm, brackish coastal waters, poor in oxygen and unsuited to most life, off the Pacific and Indian oceans. *Neopilina* (below), a primitive marine mollusc first found alive in 1952, has features unlike other molluscs but suggesting much closer affinities with the annelids (worms) and arthropods (insects, crabs, etc.).

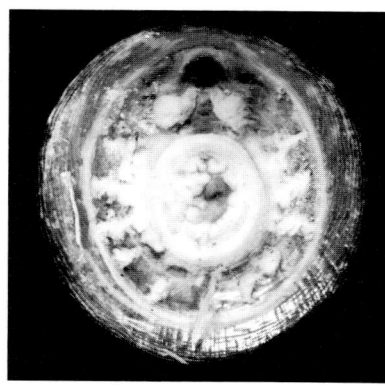

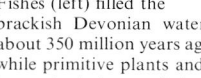

THE AGE OF JELLYFISH
1 Jellyfish (*Ediacaria*)
2 Jellyfish (*Medusina*)
3 Flatworm (*Dickinsonia costata*)
4 Sea pens (*Rangea, Charnia*)
5 Segmented worms (*Spriggina floundersi*)
6 Unknown animal (*Tribrachidium*)
7 Burrowing worm (fossil casts)
8 Sponges and algae (hypothetical)

THE FIRST SHELLED CREATURES
1 Trilobites (*Waptia*)
2 Trilobites (*Marella splendens*)
3 Trilobite (*Olenoides serratus*)
4 Primitive arthropod (*Perspicaris dictynna*)
5 Primitive arthropod (*Aysheaia pedunculata*)
6 Ancestral lancelet fish (*Branchiostoma*)
7 Sponge (*Vauxia*)
8 Crinoids (*Echmatocrinus*)
9 Mollusc (*Wiwaxia*)
10 Bristleworm (*Nereis*)
11 Brachiopod (*Linguiella*)
12 Unknown animal (*Hallucigenia sparsa*)

THE AGE OF FISHES
1 Primitive plant (*Nematophyton*)
2 Psilophite plant (*Asteroxylon*)
3 Psilophite plant (*Rhynia*)
4 Primitive insect (*Rhyniella*)
5 Placoderm fish (*Bothriolepis*)
6 Placoderm fish (*Phyllolepis*)
7 Placoderm fish (*Dunkleosteus*)
8 Early shark (*Cladoselache*)
9 Lungfish (*Dipterus*)
10 Lobe-fin fish (*Osteolepis*)
11 Crustacean (*Montecaris*)

THE FIRST AMPHIBIANS
1 Amphibian (*Ichthyostega*)
2 Club moss (*Cyclostigma*)
3 Fern (*Pseudosporochnus*)
4 Lungfish (*Scaumenacia*)
5 Rhipidistian fish (*Eusthenopteron*)
6 Millipede (*Acantherpestes ornatus*)
7 Early scorpion (*Palaeophonus*)
8 Spider-like creature (*Palaeocharinoides*)
9 Small plant (*Sciadophyton*)

THE AGE OF FISHES

Fishes (left) filled the brackish Devonian waters, about 350 million years ago, while primitive plants and insects had pioneered the land. Giant weeds (1) grew above muddy waters, and vascular plants (2, 3) colonized the shores, sheltering early insects (4). Primitive fishes (5, 6, 7) remained, but ray-finned types (8)—ancestors of modern fish—were dominant. However, it was from the lobe-finned fishes (9, 10) that the first land vertebrates emerged.

The Age of Reptiles

When the Carboniferous Period began, the world was already populated with animals and plants of many kinds. The oceans were full of fishes, invertebrates and aquatic plants. The land, meanwhile, was producing dramatic new species: giant mosses and ferns, spiders and insects and, most important of all, the rapidly evolving amphibians. These creatures were taking the first evolutionary steps on a path that would lead to some of the most remarkable creatures ever to live – the dinosaurs.

The broad, low-lying, swampy plains of the late Carboniferous provided ideal conditions for the world's early plants. They spread and diversified, and some of them grew to enormous size. Giant club mosses, huge horsetails and luxuriant tree ferns took on the proportions of modern-day trees and formed the world's first forests. These new forests were full of animal life: primitive spiders and scorpions hunting their prey, giant dragonflies hovering over the marshy waters and other insects scavenging or hunting on the mossy forest floor or in the branches of the "trees." In the huge coal-forest swamps, the most advanced of all animals, the amphibians, were rapidly evolving. Some of these would ultimately return to life in the water. But others were developing stronger legs and were becoming better able to cope with an existence on dry land.

It was from this second group that the reptiles evolved—the first animals to be equipped with waterproof skins. Unlike their amphibian ancestors, they could stay out of the water indefinitely without losing their body fluids through their skins. They were no longer tied to the water's edge and the pattern of life was revolutionized. The world was soon inhabited by the first wave of land vertebrates—reptiles, which then rapidly diversified.

Included among these first reptiles were creatures known as sailbacks. They had a row of long, bony spines that supported a great fin running down from the back of their heads to the base of their tails. This whole apparatus functioned as a heat-exchange organ: the fin absorbed heat from the atmosphere in the early, cooler parts of the day, when the animal was cold, and blushed off warmth later, when it became overheated. Unlike the cold-blooded reptiles, sailbacked reptiles could, to a certain extent, regulate their body temperatures.

Mammal-like reptiles
It was only about 50 million years later, however, that animals skeletally identical to mammals were found throughout the world. Almost certainly these creatures had a degree of warm-bloodedness. But they were all rather small—the biggest was no larger than a domestic cat—and this may account for their decline. They were destined to be overshadowed for many millions of years by the dinosaurs.

The late Triassic Period, about 200 million years ago, is marked by a sudden decline in the

THE RULING REPTILES
Seymouria and other advanced amphibians evolved to form the first reptiles, such as *Scutosaurus*. From these a multitude of adaptations evolved. Some herbivores, such as *Corythosaurus*, developed 2,000 or more teeth, to help them consume tough, fibrous food plants. Another herbivorous group attained enormous size—*Brachiosaurus* weighed as much as 80 tonnes—and this may have been an adaptation to regulate body temperature (large objects lose and gain heat more slowly than small objects). Another adaptation, but one that developed mainly in the carnivores, was that of offensive weaponry: *Deinonychus* had a huge sickle-shaped claw on each hind foot and the later *Tyrannosaurus* combined a massive body with a jagged mouthful of 60 teeth. Armor plating was a defensive adaptation, produced by herbivores such as *Triceratops*, whereas speed of movement was developed both by some herbivores and by small carnivores such as *Struthiomimus*.

Corythosaurus

Deinonychus

Seymouria

Scutosaurus

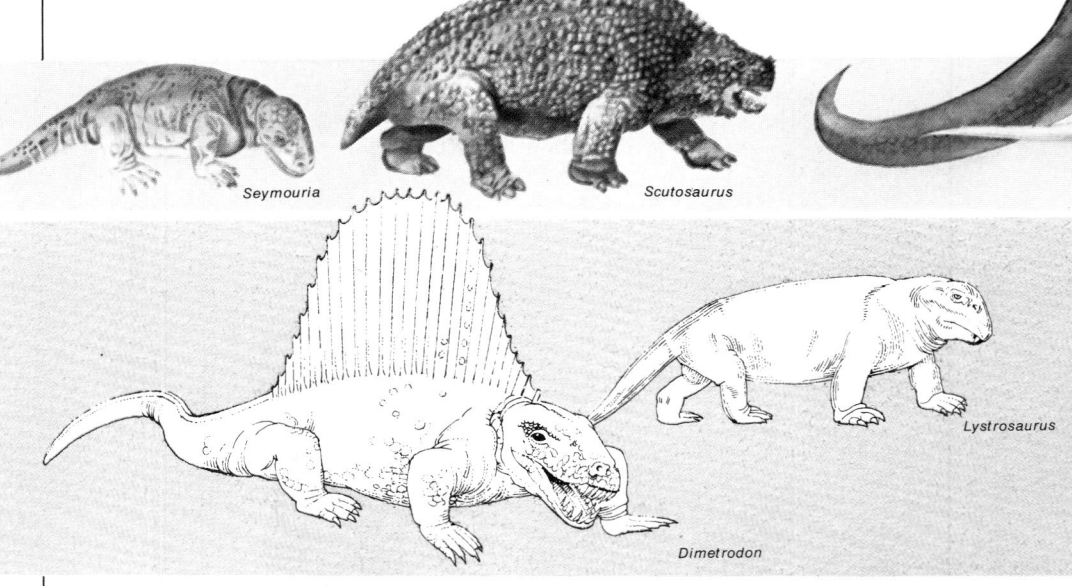

Lystrosaurus

Dimetrodon

THE MAMMAL LINE
Sailbacks such as *Dimetrodon* mark the beginning of mammal history. These reptiles had developed the first method of regulating body temperature—each was equipped with a large fin on its back which acted as a heat-exchange organ, a living solar panel. From these strange creatures, para-mammals such as *Lystrosaurus* evolved, animals with many mammal-like features. Some of the later members of this group, such as *Thrinaxodon*, probably even had fur on their bodies. Then, about 200 million years ago, the first true warm-blooded mammals, such as *Morganucodon*, developed. But by this time the group as a whole was declining in response to reptilian competition. Mammals would have to wait 140 million years before becoming successful again.

Thrinaxodon

Morganucodon

COAL FORMATION
Coal consists of carbon from plant remains and most of it was formed in the swamp-forests from which reptiles emerged. First, peat formed from rotted vegetation. Sea levels rose, ocean covered the peat bogs and marine sediments were laid down. The resulting pressure converted peat to coal. The cycle recurred and the deepest coal seams were compressed and hardened.

Coal-forming forest swamp
Peat layer
Lignite seam
Bituminous seam
Anthracite seam

Palaeozoic   Mesozoic   Cenozoic
500   400   300   200   100   0
Millions of years ago

Three geological eras mark the evolution of life on Earth. It was the Mesozoic era, beginning 230 million years ago, that spanned the age of reptiles. Until then, throughout the Palaeozoic era, life had been slowly evolving from the primitive organisms that appeared 400 million years earlier.

By the Mesozoic, the earliest reptiles had developed. Among their descendants were dinosaurs and early representatives of the mammalian line. Mammals, however, would have to wait another 165 million years, until the Cenozoic, before they achieved dominance.

The plant communities underwent as many developments in the course of the Mesozoic era as did the reptiles. The end of the Palaeozoic saw changes in climate—the Permian Period was much drier than the Carboniferous. Giant horsetails, ferns and club mosses that had formed the world's first forests gave way to other types of plant: early conifers and their relatives

(the gymnosperms) came t[o] the fore. These new specie[s] such as the Cycadales, ha[d] evolved a new, improved method of reproduction— using seeds not spores. By Jurassic times, the climate had changed again and th[e] moist conditions supporte[d] dense forests of ferns and of conifers. The final majo[r] Mesozoic development took place in Cretaceous times, when the flowering plants evolved.

Cycadale

Gingko biloba

CARBONIFEROUS   300   Earliest reptiles ▸ PERMIAN Early conifers   250   First radiation of reptiles ▸ TRIASSIC   First mamma[l]

Once their amphibian ancestors had crawled from the swamps, reptiles rapidly evolved and developed a remarkable range of adaptations: they took to the air, invaded the seas and held dominion over the land. By early Jurassic times, they had firmly established their claim to the title Ruling Reptiles. Another group of early reptile descendants led to the mammals, and although these were long overshadowed by the dinosaurs, they were destined to rise to dominance.

mammal-like reptiles and by the extraordinary evolutionary radiation of the so-called Archosaurs ("ruling reptiles"). These began to fill every available ecological niche. They evolved into carnivores, herbivores and omnivores. They included the Crocodilians, which adapted to a life in the water; the flying pterosaurs, which were the first vertebrates to fly, and, most important of all, the dinosaurs, whose evolutionary reign over the land was to endure for the next 140 million years.

Dinosaurs adapted well to life on the land. They developed "fully erect" limbs (not unlike those of the later higher mammals) rather than the splayed legs found in most other reptiles. The new position of their limbs, which gave them the necessary mobility on dry land, was also accompanied by a general increase in size. But the dinosaurs were not the only land reptiles of the time; many other forms, including tortoises, snakes and lizards, were also carving their niches during the Mesozoic era.

Similarly, the pterosaurs did not remain the only creatures of the sky. By 170 million years ago, birds in the form of claw-winged *Archaeopteryx* had evolved, and these were to prove a serious challenge to the primitive winged reptiles which had poor flying abilities.

Aquatic reptiles

Just as the land and the air were rapidly inhabited by newly evolving forms, so the water produced many new developments. Several of the Mesozoic reptiles began to adapt to aquatic life in ways often parallel to present-day mammals: the long-necked, fish-eating plesiosaurs led a life much like that of seals; the larger

pliosaurs had a streamlined shape similar to that of certain whales; some mollusc-eating placodonts could be likened to the walrus; and the elegant icthyosaurs were in many ways like dolphins. Large invertebrates were also found in the seas. The most dramatic of these were the ammonites—shelled relatives of the octopus—some of which grew to more than 2 m (6 ft) in size. Among fishes a new type emerged, the Teleosts, and these were destined to become the dominant fishes of the modern world.

Wholesale extinction

At the end of the Cretaceous Period, the reptiles were flourishing. Then suddenly, 65 million years ago, a catastrophe occurred. Virtually every species, including all the large animals, were wiped out. Throughout the Mesozoic, a series of dinosaurs and other reptiles had been evolving and slowly becoming extinct, but they were always replaced by other species. This wholesale extinction was unprecedented.

The cause of the catastrophe is unknown, but since the nature of the Earth itself was unchanged, it seems likely that some outside phenomenon was responsible. One theory suggests that a large meteorite collided with the Earth, throwing enough dust into the atmosphere to blot out the sun for several years—long enough to kill almost all the green plants on land and in the sea. If this was the case, only small animals that fed on carrion, decaying vegetation, seeds or nuts could hope to survive. Whatever the cause, the reign of the reptiles was at an end, leaving the small, adaptable mammals and birds to recolonize the virtually empty planet during the Cenozoic era.

Brachiosaurus

Tyrannosaurus rex

Struthiomimus

Triceratops

Rhamphorhynchus

Archaeopteryx

Plesiosaurus

Ichthyornis

Birds are relatives of the reptiles. The first bird, *Archaeopteryx*, evolving in Jurassic times, had many reptilian features—a long, bony tail, toothed mouth and clawed wings. By Cretaceous times, birds such as *Ichthyornis* had a more familiar form.

Plesiosaurs evolved at the same time as the dinosaurs and were as successful in their marine environment as were the dinosaurs on land. They were most common in Jurassic times.

Pterosaurs such as *Rhamphorhynchus* were the first vertebrates to take to the sky. They were not strong fliers and probably glided on air currents much of the time.

Norfolk Island pine *Araucaria heterophylla*

Williamsonia

Common oak *Quercus robur*

Fig tree *Ficus* sp

Plane tree *Platanus* sp

on of reptiles **JURASSIC** First birds | 150 | **CRETACEOUS** First flowering plants | 100 First modern fishes | Extinction of dinosaurs

The Age of Mammals

After the time of the great dying, 65 million years ago, reptiles never regained the importance they had achieved during the Mesozoic era. A new era, the Cenozoic, had begun. On the continental landmasses, mammals and birds, newly released from 160 million years of reptilian domination, began to occupy their niches in the rich, empty habitats. They flourished and diversified, and the cold-blooded reptiles became second-class citizens in a world of warm-blooded animals.

While reptiles still dominated the world, during the late Mesozoic, a new group of mammals had arisen. These were the first creatures on Earth to give birth to fully formed, live young. Until this time, the most advanced of the mammals had been marsupials whose young were still virtually embryos at birth and had to develop in the mother's pouch, or marsupium. The new mammals had evolved a more sophisticated system—the mother retained the fetus safely inside her body until it was fully formed, nourishing it during this time through a special organ, the placenta, developed during pregnancy. These mammals, the placentals, were destined to become the major mammalian group.

Although all the Mesozoic placentals were small, they had already evolved into a number of different forms that existed alongside the dinosaurs. Besides the insectivores, which were the ancestral type, they included early representatives of the Primates (precursors of modern monkeys and apes), the Carnivores, and the now extinct Condylarthrans (primitive hoofed mammals). When suddenly, 65 million years ago, there was no longer competition from the large land reptiles, these early groups rapidly evolved and extravagant forms developed.

But just as the first reptiles had passed through an early evolution, largely to be replaced by a second evolutionary wave, so the first large mammals were, in many cases, superseded by other, more successful lines. In the earliest part of the Cenozoic era, the different groups of placentals, although not closely related, all tended to be heavy limbed and heavy tailed and to walk on the whole length of their feet (as do modern bears) or on thick, stubby toes. These ungainly, thickset mammals soon died out. Some became extinct because their descendants, more efficiently adapted to their environment, overtook and replaced them. Others, such as the powerful taeniodonts and the large rodent-like tillodonts, seem to have been evolutionary blind alleys.

Spectacular developments

It was the Oligocene Period, 36 million years ago, that saw the end of most of these early essays in mammalian gigantism, but, in many parts of the world, they were replaced by others just as spectacular. In South America, the giant sloths and glyptodonts (massive relatives of the armadillos) survived until comparatively recently. The ground sloths, at least, were contemporaries of the first men on the continent.

As each group of early mammals evolved, during the early and middle part of the Cenozoic era, many of their developments closely reflected changes taking place in their environment. The first horse-like creature, for example, was *Hyracotherium*, also called *Eohippus* or "dawn horse." It lived 54 million years ago and was a small, multi-toed creature, well adapted to its densely forested habitat. The teeth of its descendants gradually changed in size and complexity, but it was not until the Miocene Period, nearly 20 million years later, that any radical alterations took place. This was the time when grasses (the Gramineae), until then a rare family of plants, came to the fore. The world's plains suddenly became clothed in a food plant very suitable for the attention of grazing creatures such as the early horses.

Animals of the grasslands

Horses and many other animals moved from the forests to make use of this new and abundant food supply. Once on the plains, different adaptations for survival were required: high-crowned teeth to deal with tough grasses; limbs enabling the animal to run tirelessly without extra, unwanted weight from supporting side toes (which were lost); large eyes capable of seeing for long distances and placed far back on the head for detecting predators approaching from any direction (as a result of which, however, the ability to judge distances ahead had to be sacrificed). Thus, the modern horses are plains-dwelling animals, perfectly adapted to their present way of life.

Mammals reached the climax of diversity during the Pliocene Period, 10 million years ago. But in the following period, the Pleistocene, ice sheets swept down from the polar regions and from the high mountains of the north, bringing massive and sudden changes to the ecology of virtually every region in the world. This dramatic disturbance to the environment brought extinction to an enormous number of species.

The survivors consisted mainly of the smaller species. Unfortunately for many of them, however, they included *Homo sapiens*. Man rose to success at the end of the Pleistocene and has, in the last 10,000 years, taken dominion over virtually every part of the world. During this time, he has proved far more destructive to other animal species than any natural force has ever been. More than 5,000 years ago, the giant sloths may have been a dying species, but there is no doubt that early human hunters hurried on their extinction. Since then, the list of species eliminated by man has grown ever longer. Today the human race is causing the extinction of both animals and plants at a rate comparable to that of 65 million years ago, when some dramatic natural catastrophe swept the dinosaurs from the face of the world. Unless man, the super-efficient species, can curb his numbers and his destructive activities, a new age of dying may soon be upon the world.

By early Cenozoic times, many forms had evolved from the insectivorous mammals of the Mesozoic Period. *Miacis*, *Hyaenodon* and *Oxyaena* were flesh eaters. Plant-eating mammals, such as Taeniodonts, *Arsinoitherium* and *Phenacodus* (one of the first hoofed mammals), had also evolved, while other early forms, such as *Andrewsarchus*, were omnivorous. The early Primates, however, remained insect eaters for millions of years.

Miacis

EARLY STAGES

Andrewsarchus

Hyaenodon

Diatryma

Euryapteryx

CENOZOIC BIRDS
Giant flightless birds came to the fore more than once during the Cenozoic era. *Diatryma*, a massive, flesh-eating bird, ruled the North American grasslands in early Cenozoic times, while mammals were still small, fairly primitive and easily dominated. *Euryapteryx* and its relatives (the moas) evolved in New Zealand, where, because there were no mammals, they filled an empty ecological niche.

The Carnivores diversified into two major types—the cats and their kin (Aeluroidea), and the dogs and their relatives (Arctoidea). During the Oligocene Period, about 36 million years ago, Aeluroidea gave rise not only to early relatives of modern cats, such as sabre-toothed *Hoplophoneus*, but also to two other families, the civets and the hyenas. At the same time, Arctoidea also diversified and produced the dogs, weasels, bears and racoons. It was a complex group, with many forms that were later to become extinct—the massive bear-dogs, such as *Daphoenus*, for example, which lived during the Miocene Period. Cats and dogs evolved to exploit different habitats. The cats adapted to life in forests, and learned to hide and then stalk and ambush their prey. Dogs evolved as plains animals, and used pack-hunting techniques to catch fleet-footed, grassland animals.

Perissodactyls and Artiodactyls were two important groups that evolved from the primitive hoofed mammals; Perissodactyls had an odd number of toes on each foot, Artiodactyls had an even number. These two groups suffered very different fortunes. Artiodactyls are still at the height of their success; the early stock produced the modern pig, camel, deer, giraffe, hippopotamus, antelope, sheep, goat and cow. Perissodactyls, however, are in decline and the only survivors are the horse, rhinoceros and tapir. But they were once important and many, now-extinct, kinds such as *Moropus* and *Brontotherium* existed alongside more familiar types such as *Hyracotherium*. Few remained after the Pliocene Period, however. This was when the Artiodactyls came to the fore. They, too, had had casualties—the pig-like *Archaeotherium* was by then extinct—but many other Artiodactyls, such as the early giraffe, *Palaeotragus*, were evolving. Most important, however, was small *Archaeomeryx*, for it had developed the key to Artiodactyl success—it was a ruminant and this enabled it to make the best possible use of the world's new grasslands.

Three geological eras mark the slow evolution of life on Earth. The Palaeozoic era, 570 million years ago, saw the appearance of the first primitive life forms. By the end of the era, 340 million years later, the reptiles had evolved and the following Mesozoic era was the age of reptilian domination. This reign over the land ended 65 million years ago as the Cenozoic era began. Then mammals came to the fore and the age of mammalian dominance of the world had dawned.

Palaeozoic			Mesozoic	Cenozoic
500	400	300	200	100 0

Millions of years ago

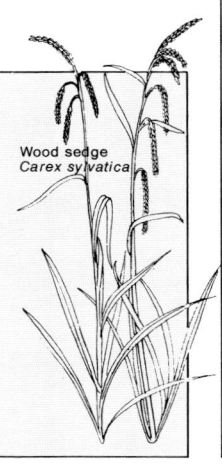

EARLY GRASSES
Grasses first appeared in the densely forested lands of 60 million years ago. Probably similar to the sedges (right) found in wet woodland areas today, they offered an attractive meal to many mammals. But it was not until the Miocene Period, when a change in climate reduced forest cover, that grasses became widespread. Then many forest creatures migrated to grassland areas.

Wood sedge
Carex sylvatica

THE MARSUPIALS
Thylacosmilus and mouse-like *Argyrolagus* were two of the many forms of marsupial mammal that evolved in Cenozoic times in South America. Almost everywhere else, the marsupials, unable to compete with their more efficient placental cousins, met with an early extinction. But in two remote regions—South America (then separate from North America) and Australia—there was no competition from placentals, and there the marsupials flourished.

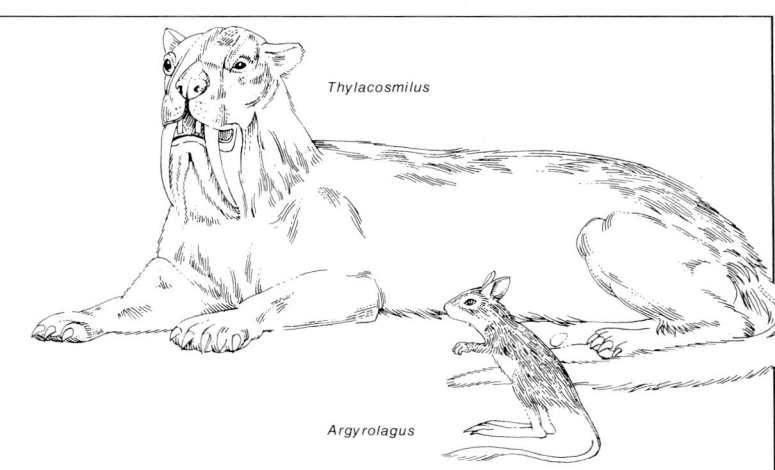

Thylacosmilus

Argyrolagus

TERTIARY	First radiation of mammals and birds		Forest horses				Second radiation of mamm
Palaeocene	60		Eocene	50		40	Oligocene

42

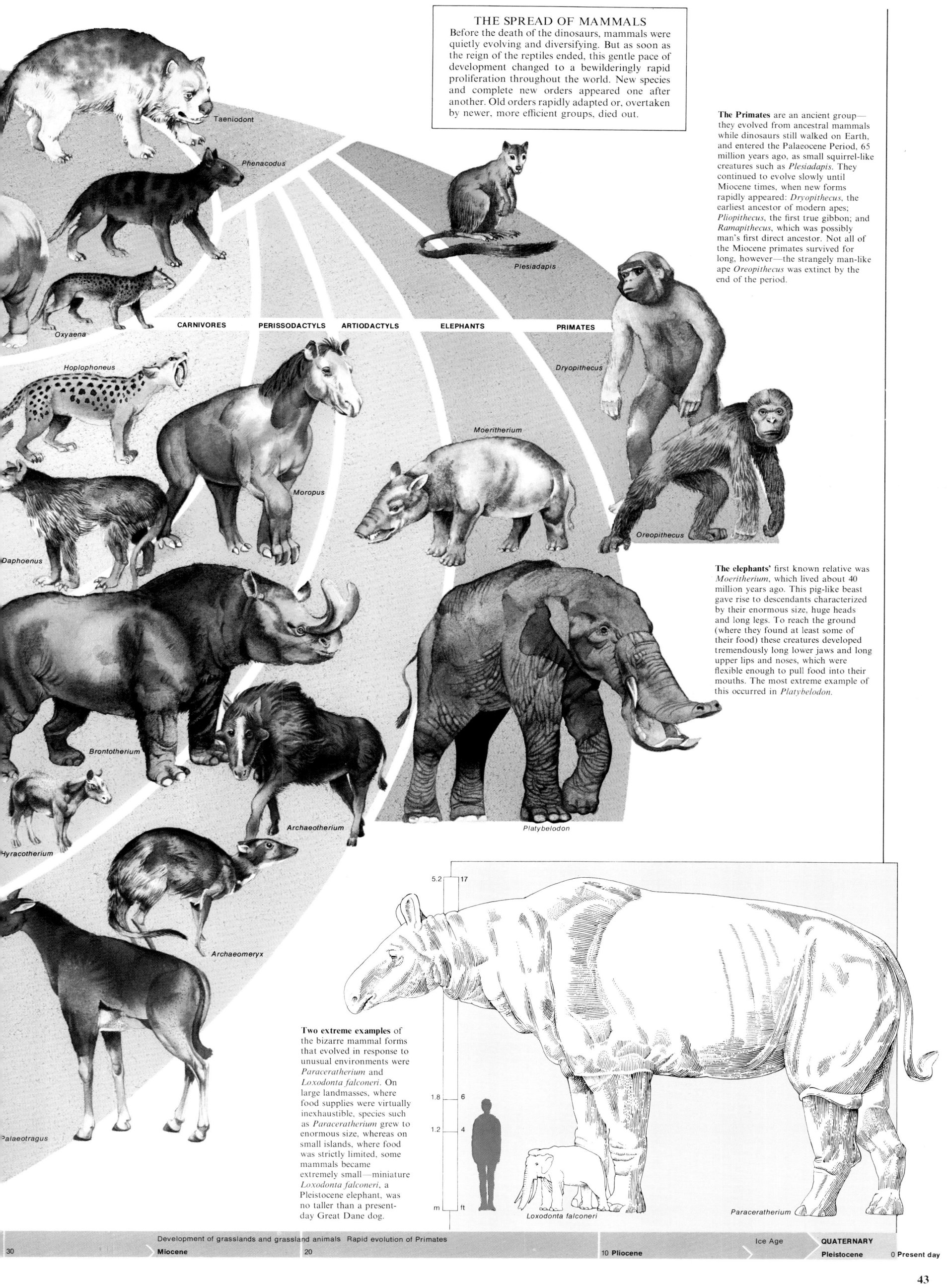

THE SPREAD OF MAMMALS

Before the death of the dinosaurs, mammals were quietly evolving and diversifying. But as soon as the reign of the reptiles ended, this gentle pace of development changed to a bewilderingly rapid proliferation throughout the world. New species and complete new orders appeared one after another. Old orders rapidly adapted or, overtaken by newer, more efficient groups, died out.

The Primates are an ancient group—they evolved from ancestral mammals while dinosaurs still walked on Earth, and entered the Palaeocene Period, 65 million years ago, as small squirrel-like creatures such as *Plesiadapis*. They continued to evolve slowly until Miocene times, when new forms rapidly appeared: *Dryopithecus*, the earliest ancestor of modern apes; *Pliopithecus*, the first true gibbon; and *Ramapithecus*, which was possibly man's first direct ancestor. Not all of the Miocene primates survived for long, however—the strangely man-like ape *Oreopithecus* was extinct by the end of the period.

Taeniodont

Phenacodus

Oxyaena

Plesiadapis

CARNIVORES PERISSODACTYLS ARTIODACTYLS ELEPHANTS PRIMATES

Hoplophoneus

Dryopithecus

Moropus

Moeritherium

Daphoenus

Oreopithecus

The elephants' first known relative was *Moeritherium*, which lived about 40 million years ago. This pig-like beast gave rise to descendants characterized by their enormous size, huge heads and long legs. To reach the ground (where they found at least some of their food) these creatures developed tremendously long lower jaws and long upper lips and noses, which were flexible enough to pull food into their mouths. The most extreme example of this occurred in *Platybelodon*.

Brontotherium

Hyracotherium

Archaeotherium

Platybelodon

Archaeomeryx

Two extreme examples of the bizarre mammal forms that evolved in response to unusual environments were *Paraceratherium* and *Loxodonta falconeri*. On large landmasses, where food supplies were virtually inexhaustible, species such as *Paraceratherium* grew to enormous size, whereas on small islands, where food was strictly limited, some mammals became extremely small—miniature *Loxodonta falconeri*, a Pleistocene elephant, was no taller than a present-day Great Dane dog.

Palaeotragus

Loxodonta falconeri

Paraceratherium

Development of grasslands and grassland animals   Rapid evolution of Primates

| 30 | | 20 | | 10 Pliocene | | Ice Age | **QUATERNARY** |
| **Miocene** | | | | | | | **Pleistocene** | 0 Present day |

Spread of Life

Different parts of the Earth have their own characteristic groups of animals, and this pattern of distribution caused nineteenth-century zoologists to divide the world into zoogeographical regions. Charles Darwin suggested how these assemblages of animals may have come about by the process of evolution. But we now know that movements of the Earth's land surfaces are also responsible for the present-day distribution of many of the world's animal species and groups.

The evolution of a major group of animals, such as the reptiles or the mammals, tends to follow a set pattern in five stages. First the original ancestral group spreads out, with each subgroup adapting to its environment. This process, called adaptive radiation, results in a variety of different kinds of animals, each suited to life in a particular niche or habitat—determined largely by food supply and environmental conditions. The different kinds then move into all of the areas they can reach in which the environment is right, producing the second stage of widespread distribution.

Competition for food or living space, or changes in climate may then cause some forms to decline and disappear from parts of the range, resulting in a third stage of discontinuous distribution. Any further reduction leads to isolated relict populations—the fourth stage—in which the animal exists only in one or two limited areas. The final stage is extinction.

In all distribution patterns, however, there is not only an ecological element but also a historical one, with past events determining where animals are and where they are not. There are thus two basic types of distribution: continuous, where the area is not interrupted by an insurmountable barrier (such as a mountain range), and discontinuous, where the area of distribution is subdivided and there is no way that members of one group can interchange with members of another.

One of these factors—the earliest and most important—is the (continuing) movement of the Earth's tectonic plates. This caused the supercontinent Pangaea to break up, probably in the Triassic Period (225–180 million years ago), and the continental masses to drift apart to their present positions. New oceans developed, separating the Americas from the Euro-African block and splitting both from Antarctica. Madagascar and Australia became islands, India moved north from Africa to join the Asian block, and mountain ranges such as the Alps, Andes, Rockies and Himalayas were thrown up. As a result, animal types that had already evolved on Pangaea or its fragments before they had significantly separated (i.e. all the major invertebrate groups and most of the earlier vertebrates) can be expected to exist on all the present-day continents.

Bridging the continents
Independently of these activities, ice ages occurred from time to time, resulting in the vast accumulations of ice at the poles and a consequent general lowering of the sea level by as much as 100 m (330 ft). This temporarily exposed the previously submerged continental shelves, providing additional land for colonization, and new corridors that linked existing areas, such as the land bridge that appeared between Alaska and Siberia.

Groups that had evolved after the breakup of Pangaea, e.g. the hare, squirrel and dog families, made use of land bridges as the climate allowed, and came to occupy more than one continent. Flying animals—birds and bats—also made intercontinental crossings and established themselves on both sides of oceans, although a surprising number of these have remained very restricted in distribution. But most animals have to stay where they are because of special dietary or environmental requirements, or because they are "trapped" on islands, such as Madagascar and Australia, and cannot get off. These areas have the most distinctive faunas in the world.

Barriers and corridors
The extent to which an expanding group can spread from its original area depends on whether there are barriers, such as mountain ranges, deserts or seas, or corridors that link major areas in which the animals can live. Different animals have different environmental requirements, and so a topographical feature that is a barrier for one may be a corridor for another.

The dispersal of many animals is achieved by "hopping" from lake to lake across a continent, or from island to island across a sea. Some, such as insects, are good at this, whereas others, such as land mammals, are bad. Thus a considerable range of weevils (Curculionidae) are found on islands from New Caledonia to the Marquesas, some 6,500 km (4,000 miles) across the southern Pacific Ocean, whereas the marsupials of the region are concentrated in Australia, Papua New Guinea and a few adjacent islands, with only one genus reaching the Celebes and none crossing Wallace's Line into Borneo.

An example of colonization by "hopping" is seen on the volcanic island of Krakatoa near Java, which exploded in 1883 destroying all life. Within 25 years there were 263 species of animals on the island. Most were insects, but there were three species of land snails, two species of reptiles and 16 of birds. In another 22 years, 46 species of vertebrates had arrived, including two species of rats.

The effect of man
Animal distribution cannot be considered merely as a natural phenomenon, because it has been greatly and increasingly modified by man's impact on the environment. Agricultural practice has made large sections of the land area unsuitable for many of the animals that originally lived there, notably through the clearing of forests and the draining of marshes.

Man has also introduced animals, either deliberately or accidentally, to regions where they were not endemic. The rabbit in Australia and the deer in New Zealand were both deliberately introduced, but rats, cockroaches and many other animals have been accidentally transported throughout the world on ships and aircraft. The enormous growth in human population has driven many animals from their natural homes and into more remote environments, such as mountains. Indeed, in the past century human interference has altered the pattern of animal distribution more drastically than any topographic or climatic change.

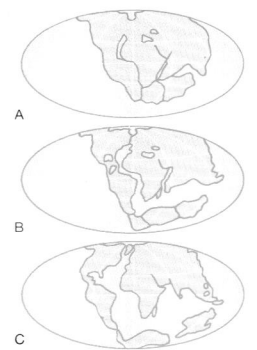

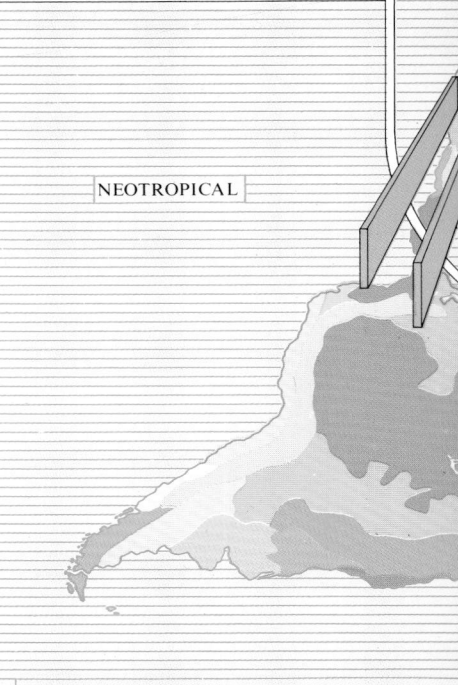

Earth's original single landmass, Pangaea (A), probably began to break up more than 200 million years ago. Species that had already evolved diversified on the Noah's Arks of the drifting supercontinents (B), called Laurasia and Gondwanaland. As the process continued (C), related animals flourished in the separated continents of the southern hemisphere.

PATTERNS OF ANIMALS
Over the ages the shape of the Earth has changed. Whole continents have moved; mountains and deserts have grown; land bridges between continents have opened and closed. These events, together with food supply, climate and other animals, account for the present natural pattern of life in the six zoogeographical regions, each containing a unique mix of animals. But man's activities have drastically affected this natural distribution in all parts of the world.

NEARCTIC

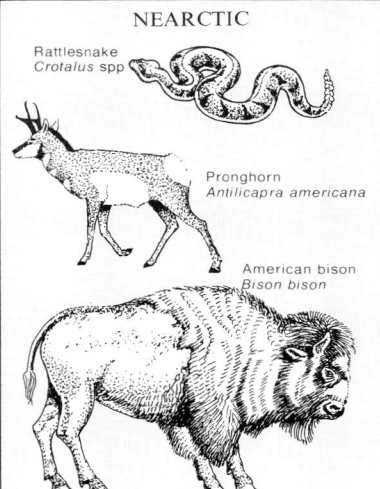

The Nearctic or "New North" region covers all of North America, from the highlands of Mexico in the south to Greenland and the Aleutian Islands in the north. Its climate and vegetation resemble that of the Palearctic region, and many of its mammals crossed over from the Palearctic via the Bering land bridge, which linked Siberia and Alaska when the sea level was lower. Animals unique to the Nearctic group include the pronghorn, an antelope-like mammal that inhabits the grasslands and plains of western and central America, and the bison, another large mammal that inhabits the prairies. Several species of rattlesnake also belong to the Nearctic group, although they are not exclusive to this region.

NEOTROPICAL

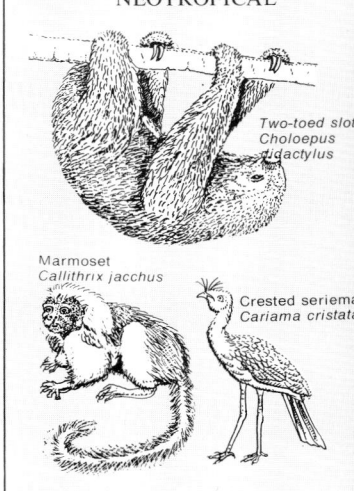

The Neotropical or "New Tropical" region consists of South America, the West Indies and most of Mexico. The climate and vegetation are mostly tropical—only the southern tip is in the temperate zone—and it is linked to the Nearctic by the Central American corridor. The Neotropical region has more distinctive families than any other. These include, among mammals, the sloth, which inhabits the tropical forests and has adapted to an upside-down existence. Among birds, the long-legged crested seriema is also unique to the region. Neotropical monkeys, such as the marmoset, have lateral-facing nostrils, which distinguish them from their downward-nosed relatives found in the Old World.

Land routes around the world have altered with the ages, sometimes allowing invaders to penetrate new lands, or closing to form natural sanctuaries for less efficient animals. The Central American isthmus (A) opened South America to placental mammals from the north. The Sahara desert closed most of Africa (B) to Eurasian species. Asia and Australia (C) share "island hoppers" in the transitional zones, but sea barriers have kept the regions separate.

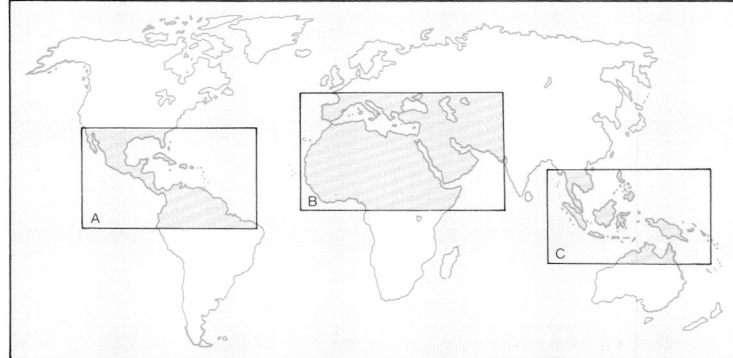

A land bridge between the Americas emerged about three million years ago, breaking the long isolation of the south. The primitive pouched mammals which had developed there were now threatened by more advanced mammals from the north, and many extinctions followed. Northern invaders included peccaries, raccoons and a llama-like camelid. But members of the armadillo and opossum families were successful in making their way to the northern region.

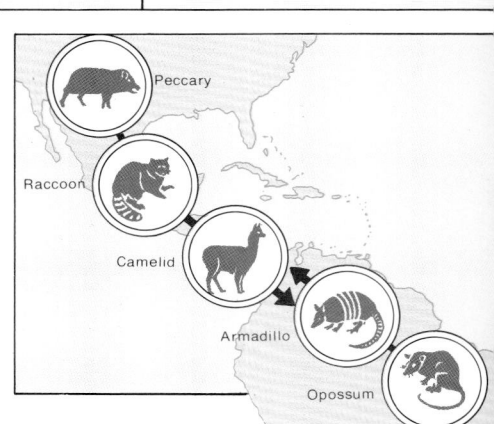

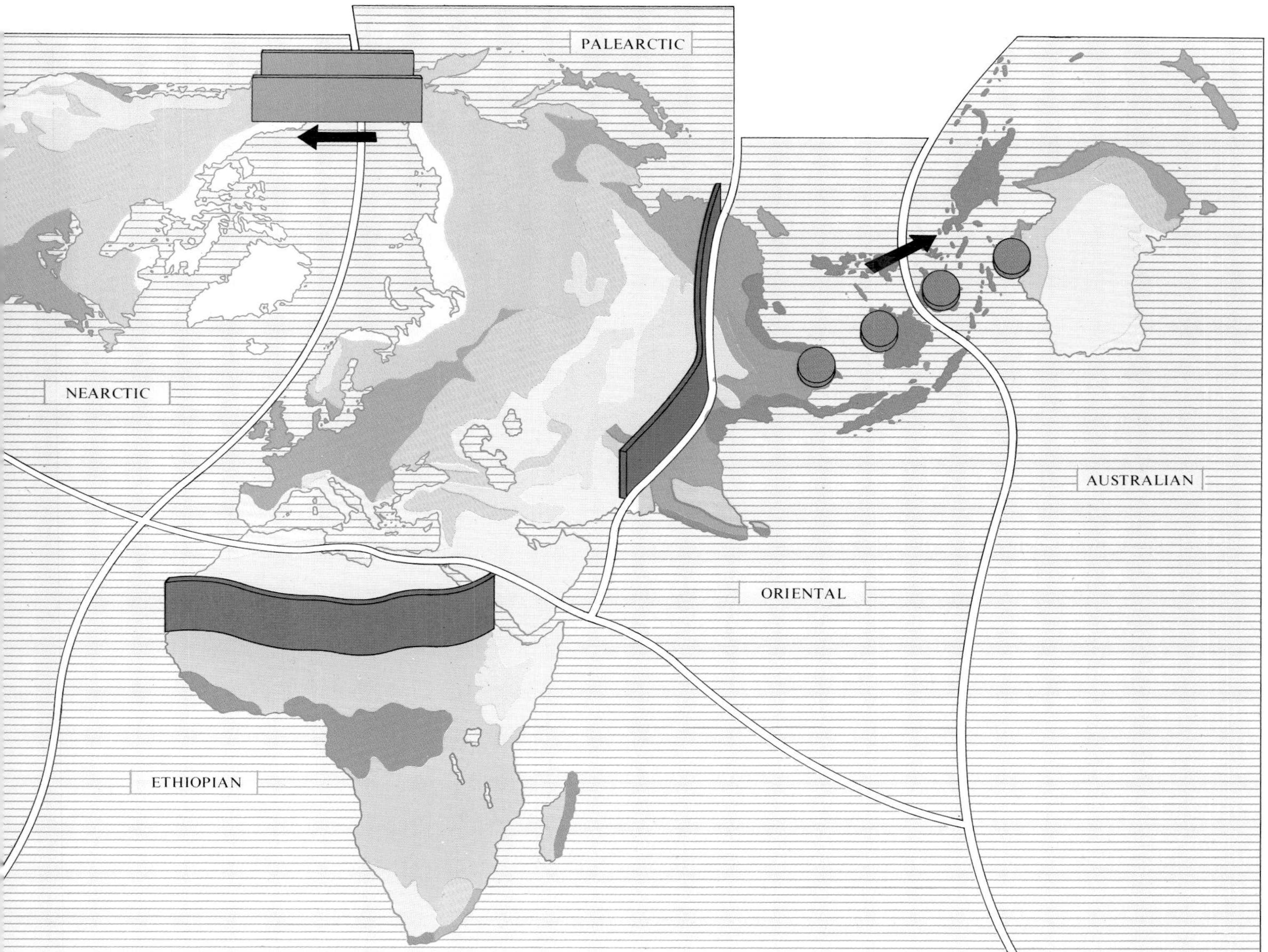

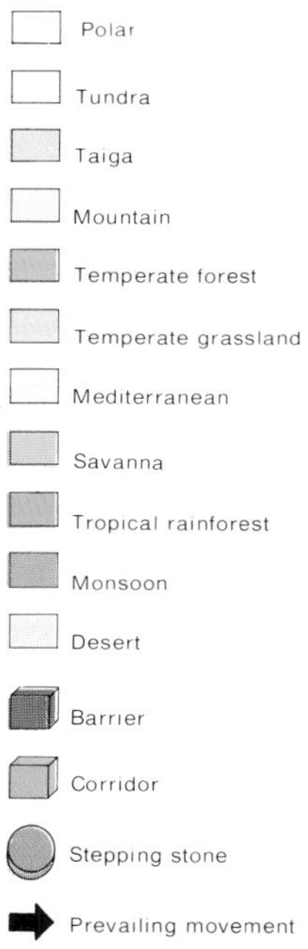

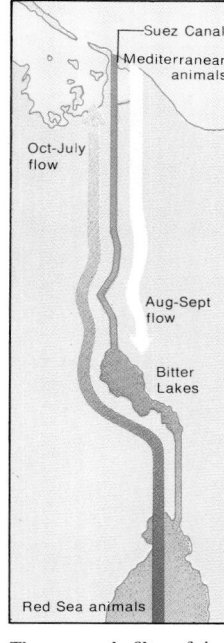

PALEARCTIC

NEARCTIC

ETHIOPIAN

AUSTRALIAN

ORIENTAL

The man-made filter of the Suez Canal, cut in 1869, is an animal corridor between the Mediterranean and Red Sea. But movement is mainly from the latter, for the channel passes through the hot, salty Bitter Lakes, favoring animals adapted to these conditions, and the current flows northwards for 10 months of the year. However, not all the 130 invading species are likely to survive Mediterranean conditions.

Suez Canal
Mediterranean animals
Oct-July flow
Aug-Sept flow
Bitter Lakes
Red Sea animals

PALEARCTIC

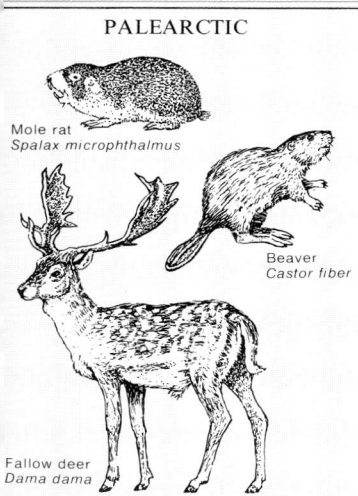

Mole rat
Spalax microphthalmus

Beaver
Castor fiber

Fallow deer
Dama dama

The Palearctic or "Old North" region covers the entire northerly part of the Old World, with seas to the north, east and west. To the south, the Sahara desert and the Himalaya mountains form barriers that separate the Palearctic from the Ethiopian and Oriental regions, although these regions are all part of the same landmass. One of the few species of mammals unique to the Palearctic is the Mediterranean mole rat, a thick-furred rodent. Another Palearctic rodent, the beaver, is shared with the Nearctic region. Fallow deer occur throughout Europe. They have been introduced by man into many other parts of the world, but their origin is almost certainly Mediterranean.

ETHIOPIAN

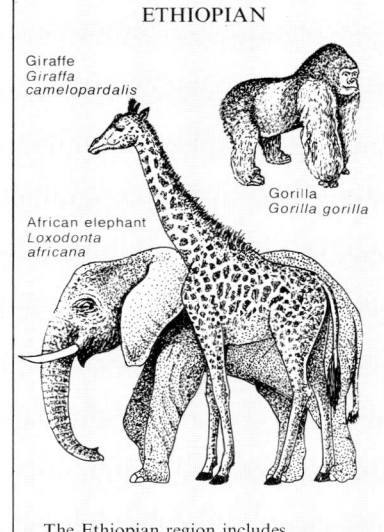

Giraffe
Giraffa camelopardalis

Gorilla
Gorilla gorilla

African elephant
Loxodonta africana

The Ethiopian region includes southern Arabia as well as all Africa south of the Sahara. It resembles in many ways the Neotropical region and is almost as rich in unique families. Its fauna also has much in common with the Oriental region. Unique mammals include the giraffe, at 5.5 m (18 ft) the tallest of living land animals, which inhabits the savanna. The region also supports two of the world's four great apes, the gorilla and the chimpanzee, which are found in the forests of western and central Africa. (The other great apes, the orangutan and the gibbon, are Oriental.) The African elephant is distinguished from its Indian relative by its greater size and by its huge ears and massive tusks.

Polar
Tundra
Taiga
Mountain
Temperate forest
Temperate grassland
Mediterranean
Savanna
Tropical rainforest
Monsoon
Desert
Barrier
Corridor
Stepping stone
Prevailing movement

ORIENTAL

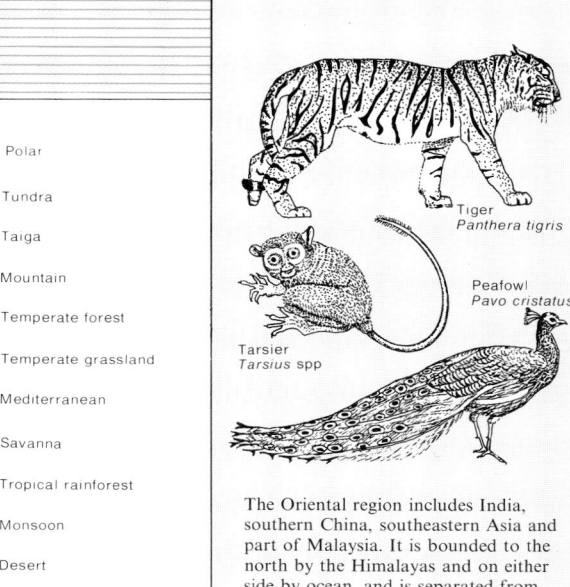

Tiger
Panthera tigris

Tarsier
Tarsius spp

Peafowl
Pavo cristatus

The Oriental region includes India, southern China, southeastern Asia and part of Malaysia. It is bounded to the north by the Himalayas and on either side by ocean, and is separated from the Australian region by a line known as Wallace's Line. It shares a quarter of its mammal families with Africa, but has more primates than any other region. The tarsier, a small relative of the monkey, is unique to southeastern Asia and represents an important early stage of primate evolution. The tiger was once widespread, but its natural habitats are steadily diminishing and the tiger itself is in danger of extinction by man. The peacock is one of the region's many brilliantly colored birds.

AUSTRALIAN

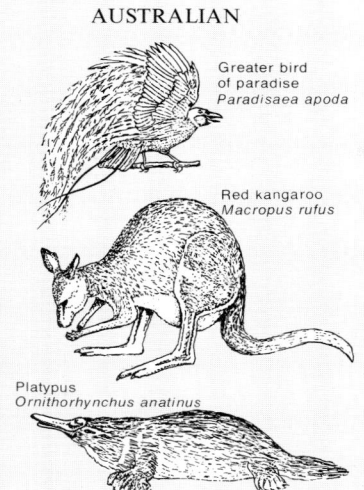

Greater bird of paradise
Paradisaea apoda

Red kangaroo
Macropus rufus

Platypus
Ornithorhynchus anatinus

The Australian region is unique in having no land connection with any other region. Its native fauna has developed in isolation from the rest of the world for at least 50 million years. Most of the mammals are marsupial—animals such as the kangaroo that carry their young in a pouch. Even more of a biological curiosity than the marsupials is the duckbilled platypus, a monotreme or egg-laying mammal. It lives along the banks of streams in Australia and Tasmania, and lays small, leathery eggs like those of snakes and turtles, but it is a true mammal and nurses its young with milk. Some 13 bird families are unique to the region, including the magnificent bird of paradise.

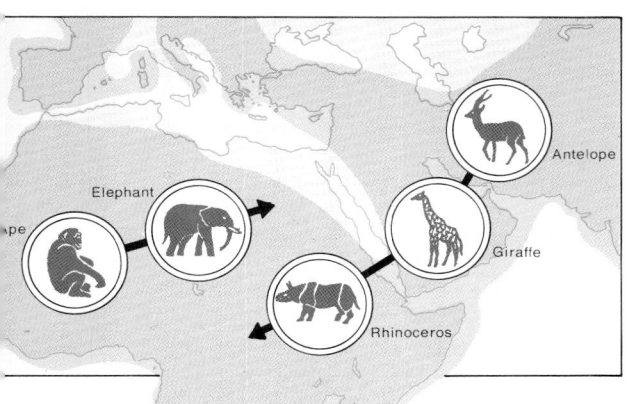

Elephant
Ape
Antelope
Giraffe
Rhinoceros

A desert barrier gradually began to form in northern Africa about nine million years ago, replacing the forest corridor between the Ethiopian and Palearctic regions. During the change, many animals typical of the African plains moved in from the north, including ancestors of today's antelopes, giraffes and rhinoceroses. But African animals also moved up north: early elephants and, much later, apes, which may have been precursors of modern man.

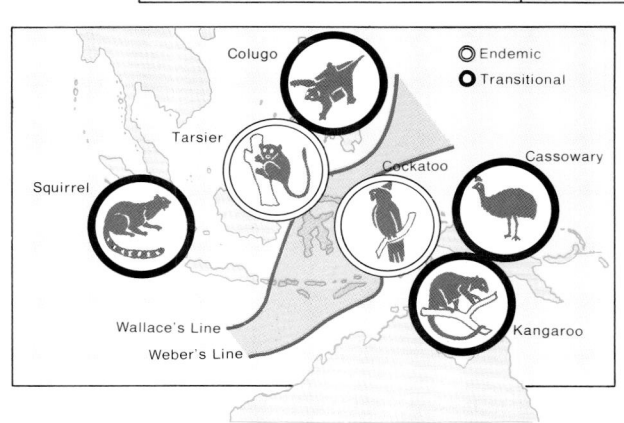

Colugo
Tarsier
Squirrel
Cockatoo
Cassowary
Kangaroo
Wallace's Line
Weber's Line

○ Endemic
● Transitional

The transitional area of "Wallacea" contains animals from both the Oriental and Australian regions, bounded by Wallace's and Weber's Lines, but few have crossed to the other region. Some Oriental mammals, such as tarsiers, are found in Wallacea, but the gliding colugo and varieties of squirrel are not. The Australian cockatoo has reached the transition area, but the flightless cassowary and the tree kangaroo have not.

Spread of Man

Modern Man, *Homo sapiens sapiens*, has proved a highly successful animal since his emergence some 50,000 years ago: today more than 4,000 million members of this subspecies of the *Homo* (Man) group occupy the Earth, living in even the most inhospitable regions. But the fossil record shows that man's lineage goes back millions of years, with different stages of development leading to a greater control of the environment, and with climate itself helping man's ultimate domination of Earth.

Man's lineage may go back at least 14 million years to a small woodland creature known as *Ramapithecus* (Rama's ape). Since the first discoveries of *Ramapithecus* in the Indian subcontinent, its fossils have come to light in many parts of the world, including China, eastern Europe, Turkey and eastern Africa. Fossil remains show that it survived for several million years until, about eight million years ago, there is a tantalizing gap in the fossil record. Then, about four and a half million years later (according to recent discoveries in eastern Africa), we have solid evidence of an upright hominid— a member of man's zoological family. This is "Lucy," a fossil skeleton found in 1973 by Donald Johanson and Tom Gray, and subsequently classified with many other finds as *Australopithecus afarensis*.

This may be man's ancestral "rootstock," but a little later there existed two kinds of "apeman" (*Australopithecus*), and our own direct ancestor Handy Man (*Homo habilis*). Datable volcanic ash found with the fossils provides a time scale and indicates that, about two million years ago, ape-man and "true" man lived side by side in the lush grassland that then covered the eastern African plains.

One and a half million years ago, according to the fossil evidence, there was again only one hominid species. The varieties of australopithecines had died out, and Handy Man (*Homo*

habilis) had apparently evolved into Upright Man (*Homo erectus*). Remains of Upright Man have been found in many regions of the world, from various parts of Africa and Europe to China and Indonesia, although not in the Americas. But there is reason to believe that it was in Africa, well over one million years ago, that he evolved from his ancestor, and began a very gradual expansion out of the continent.

Upright Man had about one million years to spread across the Old World, adapting as he did so to local conditions, just as people of today are adapted in their various ways. He was a nomadic hunter gatherer, socially organized in groups. His skills included the use of fire and cooking, as well as the making of quite large structures out of wood. Recent discoveries suggest that, during the million years of his existence, *Homo erectus* gradually evolved into the next stage of man – *Homo sapiens*.

The next step is revealed most clearly in fossils from more than 100,000 to less than 50,000 years ago. Called Neanderthal Man in Europe, Solo Man in Indonesia, and Rhodesian Man in southern Africa, these types of human being were all descendants of *Homo erectus*.

Variable in brain size, but with prominent eyebrow ridges and receding jaws, they may have been dead ends on the evolutionary road; or some may have led to, or been incorporated in, Modern Man (*Homo sapiens sapiens*).

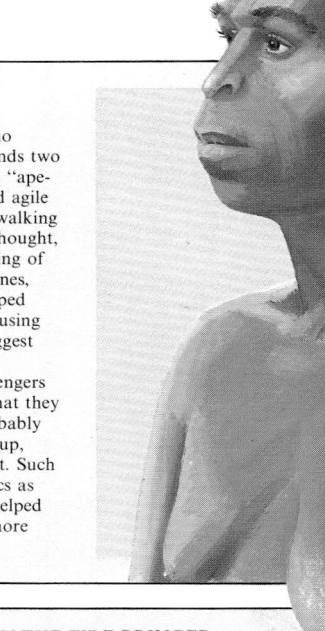

THE AFRICAN CRADLE
Handy Man (*Homo habilis*), who shared the East African grasslands two million years ago with a related "ape-man" species, was a slender and agile creature with a human way of walking and a capacity for conceptual thought, as evidenced in systematic making of tools. Handy Man collected stones, often from far away, and reshaped them into purpose-made tools, using other stones. Fossil remains suggest that these earliest humans were efficient hunters as well as scavengers of larger predators' kills, and that they brought food to campsites, probably sharing it among the whole group, rather than eating it on the spot. Such specifically human characteristics as the sharing of food may have helped our ancestors to survive their more primitive hominid relations.

MAN THE FIRE-BRINGER
Upright Man (*Homo erectus*) emerged about 1.5 million years ago, evolving from his predecessor, Handy Man. For one million years these people developed and adapted, spreading over most of the Old World and following a nomadic hunter-gatherer life-style, assisted by a more sophisticated tool technology. The cooler climates of northern Asia and Europe may have encouraged their most impressive innovation—the use of fire for warmth, cooking and hunting game— and also their ability to construct quite elaborate shelters. It seems likely that they possessed language; and traces of ocher lumps at a campsite perhaps 400,000 years old suggest the possibility of ritual adornment or some kind of body painting.

THE HUMANIZING OF MAN
Modern man's predecessor, although called Wise Man (*Homo sapiens*), was long regarded as more brutish than human. But widespread finds have now changed this image, as can be seen in an old and an updated reconstruction of the same Neanderthal skull (right). Many scientists believe that these people showed a human concern for each other, burying their dead with ceremonial reverence, and looking after disabled members of the group. In their Neanderthal form they inhabited Europe and the Middle East from about 100,000 to 40,000 years ago, and were perhaps adapted to ice-age conditions. *Homo sapiens* counterparts of Neanderthal Man also occur in Africa and southeastern Asia.

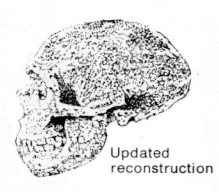
Updated reconstruction

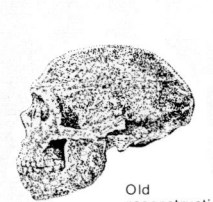
Old reconstruction

The burial of a Neanderthal man took place 60,000 years ago at Shanidar in the Iraq highlands. Fossil traces suggest that the body was laid on a bed of branches, and that flowers were brought to the grave and placed deliberately around the body. The flowers included many varieties still known locally for their medicinal properties. Ritual burials occur at many Neanderthal sites, from the Pyrenees to northern Asia, and indicate a sensitivity that contradicts Neanderthal man's traditional image.

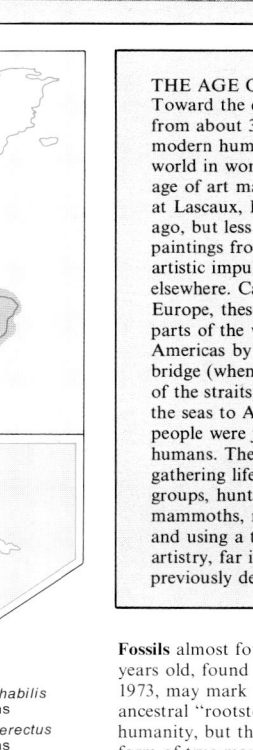

The spread of man (right) from the African heartland of Handy Man (*Homo habilis*) probably began about one million years ago. Remains of Upright Man (*Homo erectus*) have been found all over the Old World, and show a gradual physical and cultural evolution toward a later *Homo sapiens* ancestor, beginning about 350,000 years ago. Between 70,000 and 12,000 years ago, glacial periods locked up the sea water as ice (top), lowering sea levels and opening a land bridge to America that was used by later nomadic peoples. But they had to cross open sea to reach Australia.

Land areas
c. 19,000 years ago
Ice sheets
c. 19,000 years ago
Homo sapiens sapiens remains

Neander Valley
Swanscombe
Steinheim
Terra Amata
Vertesszöllös
La Chapelle
Ambrona
Gibraltar
Petralona
Ternifine
Mount Carmel
Hadar
Omo River
Koobi Fora
Olduvai Gorge
Broken Hill
Central Kazakhstan
Filimoshki
Teshik Tash
Choukoutien
Lantian
Shanidar
Trinil Solo

△ *Homo habilis* remains
▲ *Homo erectus* remains
○ Early *Homo sapiens* remains

THE AGE OF ART
Toward the end of the last Ice Age, from about 35,000 years ago, truly modern humans began to depict their world in wonderfully vivid terms. The age of art may have reached its peak at Lascaux, France, some 15,000 years ago, but less well-preserved cave paintings from Africa show that the artistic impulse was equally present elsewhere. Called Cro-Magnon Man in Europe, these people spread to all parts of the world, crossing to the Americas by way of the Bering land bridge (when ice locked up the water of the straits), and even venturing over the seas to Australia. Physically these people were just like present-day humans. They led a nomadic, hunter-gathering life, living in large, organized groups, hunting such animals as mammoths, reindeer, bison and horses, and using a technology, as well as an artistry, far in advance of anything previously developed.

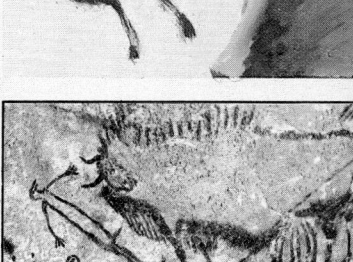

Fossils almost four million years old, found since 1973, may mark the ancestral "rootstock" of humanity, but the earliest form of true man is thought to be *Homo habilis*, who shared his African habitat with "ape-man" relatives some two million years ago. His successor, *Homo erectus*, spread over Asia and Europe, evolving gradually into modern man's predecessors, creatures whose large brow ridges belie their typically human characteristics. These were replaced by Modern Man.

Australopithecus afarensis

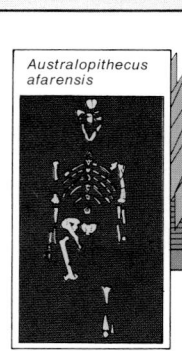

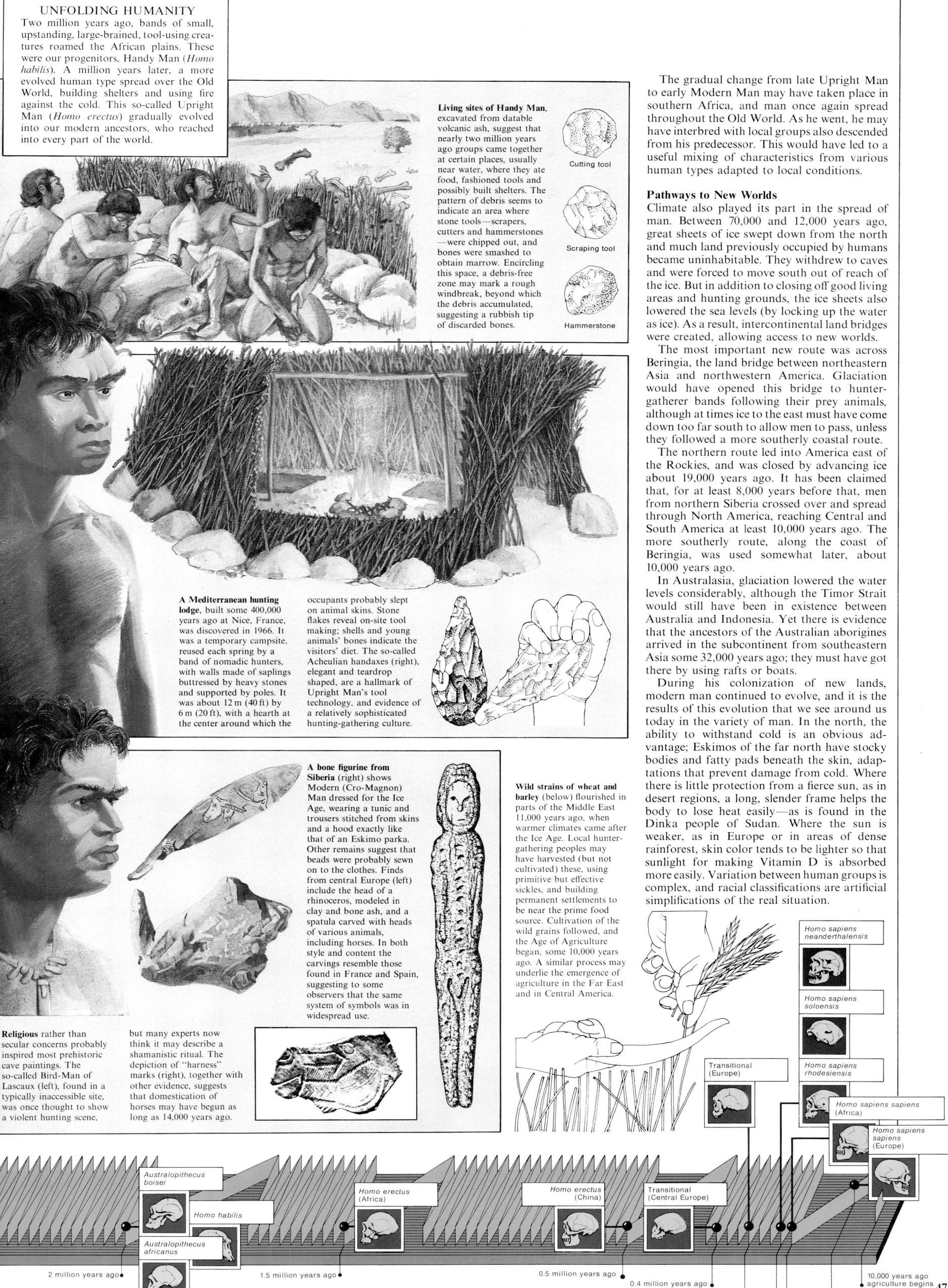

UNFOLDING HUMANITY

Two million years ago, bands of small, upstanding, large-brained, tool-using creatures roamed the African plains. These were our progenitors, Handy Man (*Homo habilis*). A million years later, a more evolved human type spread over the Old World, building shelters and using fire against the cold. This so-called Upright Man (*Homo erectus*) gradually evolved into our modern ancestors, who reached into every part of the world.

Living sites of Handy Man, excavated from datable volcanic ash, suggest that nearly two million years ago groups came together at certain places, usually near water, where they ate food, fashioned tools and possibly built shelters. The pattern of debris seems to indicate an area where stone tools—scrapers, cutters and hammerstones—were chipped out, and bones were smashed to obtain marrow. Encircling this space, a debris-free zone may mark a rough windbreak, beyond which the debris accumulated, suggesting a rubbish tip of discarded bones.

Cutting tool

Scraping tool

Hammerstone

A Mediterranean hunting lodge, built some 400,000 years ago at Nice, France, was discovered in 1966. It was a temporary campsite, reused each spring by a band of nomadic hunters, with walls made of saplings buttressed by heavy stones and supported by poles. It was about 12 m (40 ft) by 6 m (20 ft), with a hearth at the center around which the occupants probably slept on animal skins. Stone flakes reveal on-site tool making; shells and young animals' bones indicate the visitors' diet. The so-called Acheulian handaxes (right), elegant and teardrop shaped, are a hallmark of Upright Man's tool technology, and evidence of a relatively sophisticated hunting-gathering culture.

A bone figurine from Siberia (right) shows Modern (Cro-Magnon) Man dressed for the Ice Age, wearing a tunic and trousers stitched from skins and a hood exactly like that of an Eskimo parka. Other remains suggest that beads were probably sewn on to the clothes. Finds from central Europe (left) include the head of a rhinoceros, modeled in clay and bone ash, and a spatula carved with heads of various animals, including horses. In both style and content the carvings resemble those found in France and Spain, suggesting to some observers that the same system of symbols was in widespread use.

Wild strains of wheat and barley (below) flourished in parts of the Middle East 11,000 years ago, when warmer climates came after the Ice Age. Local hunter-gathering peoples may have harvested (but not cultivated) these, using primitive but effective sickles, and building permanent settlements to be near the prime food source. Cultivation of the wild grains followed, and the Age of Agriculture began, some 10,000 years ago. A similar process may underlie the emergence of agriculture in the Far East and in Central America.

Religious rather than secular concerns probably inspired most prehistoric cave paintings. The so-called Bird-Man of Lascaux (left), found in a typically inaccessible site, was once thought to show a violent hunting scene, but many experts now think it may describe a shamanistic ritual. The depiction of "harness" marks (right), together with other evidence, suggests that domestication of horses may have begun as long as 14,000 years ago.

The gradual change from late Upright Man to early Modern Man may have taken place in southern Africa, and man once again spread throughout the Old World. As he went, he may have interbred with local groups also descended from his predecessor. This would have led to a useful mixing of characteristics from various human types adapted to local conditions.

Pathways to New Worlds

Climate also played its part in the spread of man. Between 70,000 and 12,000 years ago, great sheets of ice swept down from the north and much land previously occupied by humans became uninhabitable. They withdrew to caves and were forced to move south out of reach of the ice. But in addition to closing off good living areas and hunting grounds, the ice sheets also lowered the sea levels (by locking up the water as ice). As a result, intercontinental land bridges were created, allowing access to new worlds.

The most important new route was across Beringia, the land bridge between northeastern Asia and northwestern America. Glaciation would have opened this bridge to hunter-gatherer bands following their prey animals, although at times ice to the east must have come down too far south to allow men to pass, unless they followed a more southerly coastal route.

The northern route led into America east of the Rockies, and was closed by advancing ice about 19,000 years ago. It has been claimed that, for at least 8,000 years before that, men from northern Siberia crossed over and spread through North America, reaching Central and South America at least 10,000 years ago. The more southerly route, along the coast of Beringia, was used somewhat later, about 10,000 years ago.

In Australasia, glaciation lowered the water levels considerably, although the Timor Strait would still have been in existence between Australia and Indonesia. Yet there is evidence that the ancestors of the Australian aborigines arrived in the subcontinent from southeastern Asia some 32,000 years ago; they must have got there by using rafts or boats.

During his colonization of new lands, modern man continued to evolve, and it is the results of this evolution that we see around us today in the variety of man. In the north, the ability to withstand cold is an obvious advantage; Eskimos of the far north have stocky bodies and fatty pads beneath the skin, adaptations that prevent damage from cold. Where there is little protection from a fierce sun, as in desert regions, a long, slender frame helps the body to lose heat easily—as is found in the Dinka people of Sudan. Where the sun is weaker, as in Europe or in areas of dense rainforest, skin color tends to be lighter so that sunlight for making Vitamin D is absorbed more easily. Variation between human groups is complex, and racial classifications are artificial simplifications of the real situation.

Homo sapiens neanderthalensis

Homo sapiens soloensis

Homo sapiens rhodesiensis

Transitional (Europe)

Homo sapiens sapiens (Africa)

Homo sapiens sapiens (Europe)

Australopithecus boisei

Homo habilis

Australopithecus africanus

Homo erectus (Africa)

Homo erectus (China)

Transitional (Central Europe)

2 million years ago

1.5 million years ago

0.5 million years ago

0.4 million years ago

250,000 years ago

100,000 years ago

50,000 years ago

35,000 years ago

10,000 years ago agriculture begins

Part 4

THE DIVERSITY OF LIFE

Earth's habitats from the Poles to the Equator
Plants and animals of the Earth's natural regions
Man the preserver and man the destroyer

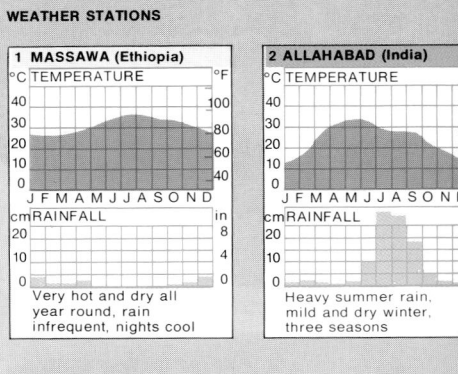

WEATHER STATIONS
1 MASSAWA (Ethiopia)
°C TEMPERATURE °F
40 30 20 10 0
100 80 60 40
J F M A M J J A S O N D
cm RAINFALL in
20 10 0
8 4 0
Very hot and dry all year round, rain infrequent, nights cool
2 ALLAHABAD (India)
°C TEMPERATURE
40 30 20 10 0
J F M A M J J A S O N D
cm RAINFALL
20 10 0
Heavy summer rain, mild and dry winter, three seasons

180° 150° 120° 90° 60° 30° 0° 30° 60° 0° 120° 150°
Arctic Circle
60°
30°
Tropic of Cancer
Equator
Tropic of Capricorn
30°
60°
Antarctic Circle
90° 60° 30° 0° 30° 60° 90° 120° 150°
1
3
4
5
6
7
8
9
10
11
The Natural Regions
Desert
Monsoon
Tropical rainforest
Savanna
Mediterranean
Temperate grassland
Temperate forest
Mountain
Taiga
Tundra
Polar
CLIMATE, RAINFALL AND THE BIOMES
Tundra
Taiga
Temperate grassland
Mediterranean
Temperate forest
Desert
Savanna
Monsoon
Tropical rainforest
–10/26
0°C/32°F
10/37.5
20/68
0 cm/0 in
100/39
200/78
300/117

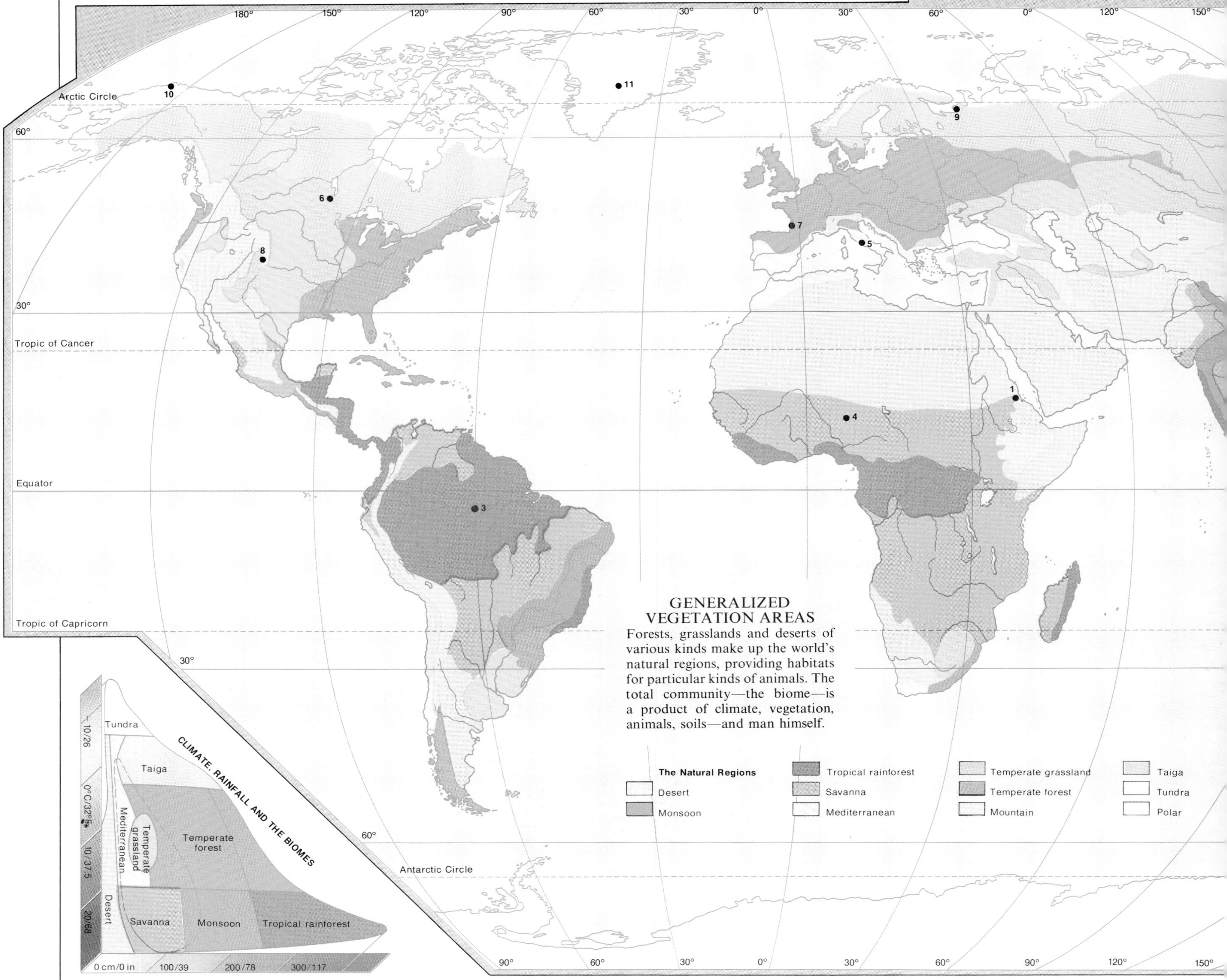

GENERALIZED VEGETATION AREAS
Forests, grasslands and deserts of various kinds make up the world's natural regions, providing habitats for particular kinds of animals. The total community—the biome—is a product of climate, vegetation, animals, soils—and man himself.

Temperature and rainfall (above) govern the world's zones of plant and animal life. Dryness prevents tree growth both in icy tundra and in hot deserts. Wetter conditions cause savannas and grasslands to yield to forest biomes, tropical or temperate (the dotted line indicates zones within which variations occur).

A broad correlation (below) between soil types, climate and vegetation areas shows the interconnections that define the biomes. The soil of the biome is related to climatic conditions and is also modified by plant and animal activity, but soil types are not necessarily confined to any one particular biome.

SOIL AND THE BIOMES
Cold
Cold
Dry
Wet
Tundra soils
High-latitude podsolic soils
Middle-latitude podsolic soils
Middle-latitude chernozemic soils
Desertic soils
Subtropical podsolic soils
Ferruginous soils
Ferralitic soils
Dry
Wet
Hot
Hot

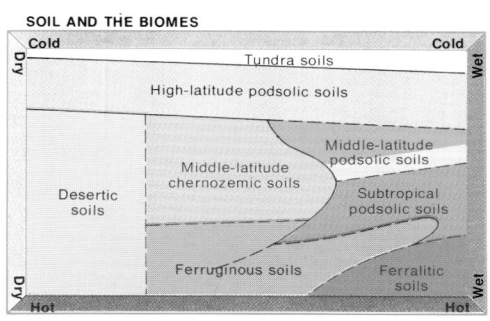

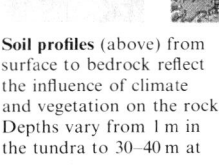

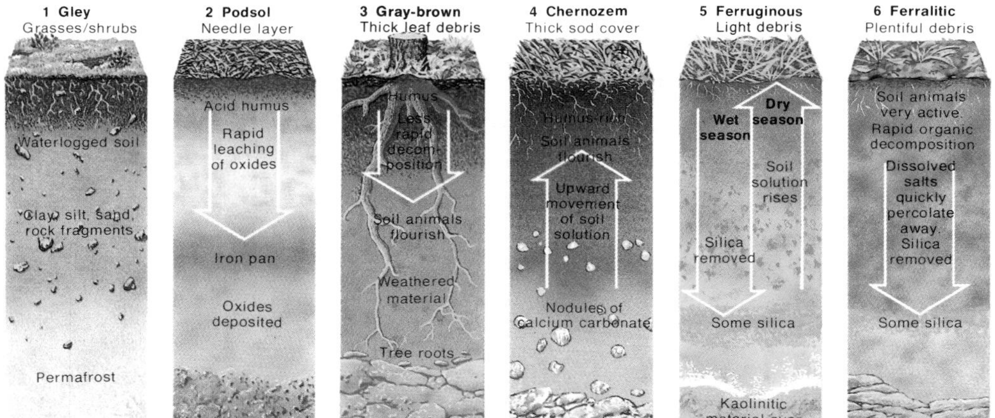

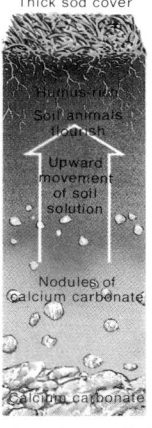

1 Gley
Grasses/shrubs
Waterlogged soil
Clay, silt, sand, rock fragments
Permafrost
2 Podsol
Needle layer
Acid humus
Rapid leaching of oxides
Iron pan
Oxides deposited
Bedrock
3 Gray-brown
Thick leaf debris
Humus
Less rapid decom-position
Soil animals flourish
Weathered material
Tree roots
Bedrock
4 Chernozem
Thick sod cover
Humus-rich
Soil animals flourish
Upward movement of soil solution
Nodules of calcium carbonate
Calcium carbonate
5 Ferruginous
Light debris
Wet season
Dry season
Soil solution rises
Silica removed
Some silica
Kaolinitic material over igneous rocks
6 Ferralitic
Plentiful debris
Soil animals very active. Rapid organic decomposition
Dissolved salts quickly percolate away. Silica removed
Some silica
Bedrock

Soil profiles (above) from surface to bedrock reflect the influence of climate and vegetation on the rock. Depths vary from 1 m in the tundra to 30–40 m at the Equator. Waterlogged gley (1) may form above tundra permafrost. Podsol (2) is typical of taiga forests, where spring snow-melt is heavily leached through a needle layer, sometimes forming an iron "pan." Gray-brown forest soil (3) has rich, organic humus, as has chernozem (4), the typical temperate grassland soil. Ferruginous soils (5) occur in dry-season tropical climates (monsoon, savanna), and ferralitic soils (6) where there is constant rainfall.

ECOSYSTEM DYNAMICS

An ecosystem consists c group of organisms and physical environment. A marshland ecosystem fr North America (right) shows the dynamic interactions between pla and animal communitie and their habitats, whic include climate, soil and water. The energy and food in the system initia derive from the Sun—tl main energy source for living things, notably plants. Plants are food for herbivores, on land and in water; herbivores are food for carnivores; decomposers (bacteria a fungi) nourish plants, breaking down dead bo into compounds.

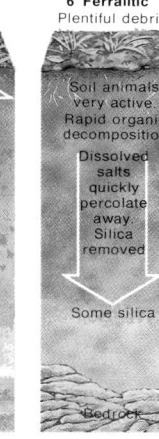

Earth's Natural Regions

Geographers have long looked for ways of classifying conditions such as climate, soil and vegetation to describe the general similarities and differences from area to area throughout the world. By identifying distinctive patterns of climate and vegetation they have provided a convenient global division into natural regions or biomes. And recent developments in ecology – the study of plants and animals in relation to their environments – have given such divisions a greater depth.

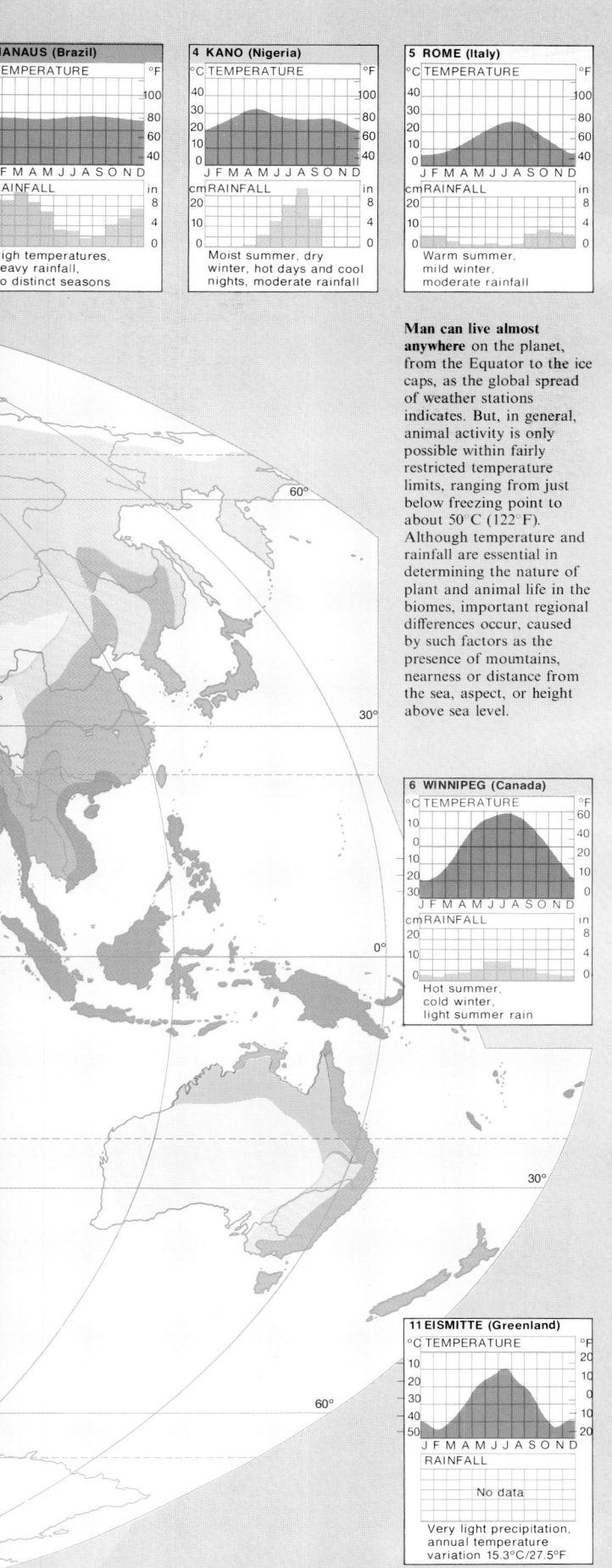

MANAUS (Brazil)
High temperatures, heavy rainfall, no distinct seasons

4 KANO (Nigeria)
Moist summer, dry winter, hot days and cool nights, moderate rainfall

5 ROME (Italy)
Warm summer, mild winter, moderate rainfall

Man can live almost anywhere on the planet, from the Equator to the ice caps, as the global spread of weather stations indicates. But, in general, animal activity is only possible within fairly restricted temperature limits, ranging from just below freezing point to about 50°C (122°F). Although temperature and rainfall are essential in determining the nature of plant and animal life in the biomes, important regional differences occur, caused by such factors as the presence of mountains, nearness or distance from the sea, aspect, or height above sea level.

6 WINNIPEG (Canada)
Hot summer, cold winter, light summer rain

7 BORDEAUX (France)
Warm summer, mild winter, four distinct seasons

8 PIKE'S PEAK (USA)
4,300 m (14,111ft) Temperature decreases with increasing altitude

9 ARKHANGELSK (RUSSIA)
Short summer, long and cold winter, light summer rain

10 BARROW (Alaska)
Brief summer, very long and cold winter, very light rainfall

11 EISMITTE (Greenland)
RAINFALL
No data
Very light precipitation, annual temperature variation 15.3°C/27.5°F

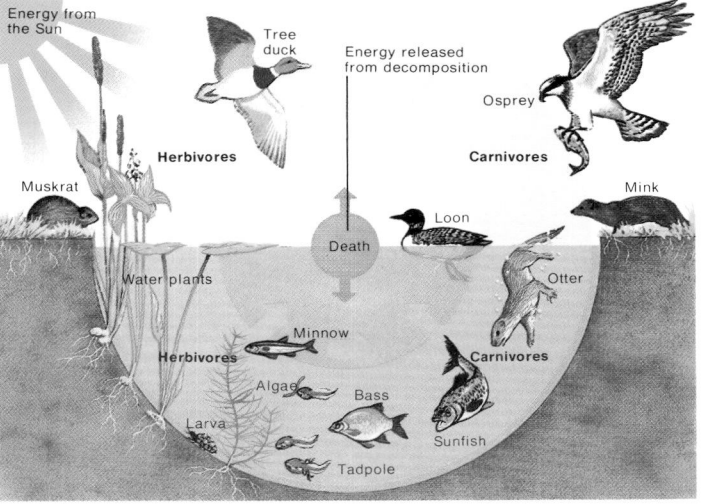

Energy from the Sun — Tree duck — Energy released from decomposition — Osprey — Herbivores — Carnivores — Mink — Muskrat — Loon — Death — Otter — Water plants — Minnow — Herbivores — Carnivores — Algae — Bass — Larva — Sunfish — Tadpole

Divisions according to climate were first suggested by the Greek philosopher Aristotle, and his ideas were still in use until about 100 years ago. Aristotle posited a number of climatic zones—called torrid, temperate and frigid —defined by latitude. But with time it became increasingly apparent that the complex distribution of atmospheric pressure, winds, rainfall and temperature could not be related to such a simple frame. Nineteenth-century scientists divided the world into 35 climatic provinces. Then in 1900 the German meteorologist Wladimir Köppen produced a more sophisticated climatic classification based on temperature and moisture conditions related to the needs of plants. At about the same time other scientists studied the distribution of vegetation types throughout the world. These studies together provided the basis for much of the later work on climatic regions.

An important step forward was made in 1904 by the British geographer A. J. Herbertson. He argued that subdivision of physical environments should take into account the distribution of the various phenomena as they related to each other. He conceived the idea of *natural regions*, each with "a certain unity of configuration (relief), climate and vegetation." His final classification contained four groups or regions: Polar Types, Cool Temperate Types, Warm Temperate Types and Tropical Hot Lands. Herbertson's scheme, controversial at first, was later much used for teaching geography.

Ecology

Meanwhile the study of environmental problems had been advanced by the idea of *ecology*, the relationship of living things between each other and their surroundings. The term was first used in 1868 by Ernst Haeckel, the German biologist, but it was not until the end of the nineteenth century that scientists really began to study life forms in relation to their habitat. In addition to the central ideas of interdependence between the members of plant and animal communities and between the community and the physical environment, there now came the suggestion that communities develop in a sequence that leads to a "climax"—a final step of equilibrium or balance. Their climax stage depends on conditions of climate or soil.

Later the British botanist A. G. Tansley, a leading exponent of ecological thinking, introduced the term *ecosystem* to describe a group of living organisms and its effective environment. Tansley's definition of 1935 referred to the whole system, including "not only the organism complex, but also the whole complex of physical factors forming what we call the environment of the biome." The idea became very influential and has been used in the social sciences as well as in the natural ones. But it is difficult to apply in practice, partly because of the highly complex and often diverse interactions that take place in different parts of the ecosystem.

Ecologists have developed special methods and have given particular attention to the ways in which energy is transferred within the system. The term *biome* refers to the whole complex of organisms, both animals and plants, that live together naturally as a society. By *environment* is meant all the external conditions that affect the life and development of an organism.

Biomes

The biomes shown on the map are broadly drawn generalizations. They should be regarded as idealized regions, within which many local variations may exist—for example, of climate or soil conditions. On a larger scale such features as mountain ranges may cause variations at a regional level. Scientists have tried to work out "hierarchies" that include many levels or orders of scale leading to the major climatic-vegetation realms or biomes. These realms give a broad picture that is useful at the world level of scale, and which forms a starting point for further analysis. Any map of the biomes has to have lines to indicate the boundaries of each region, but these too are generalizations. Although climate and vegetation do sometimes change abruptly from place to place, more often there are transitional zones, and the boundaries on the maps give the broad locations of these.

Herbertson's concept of natural regions attempted also to take account of the influence of man as an important factor in the environment. But he was not totally successful in including man in his analysis, no doubt because of the complexity of the problems involved and because of the immense influence that man has had upon the natural vegetation of the world. The cutting of forests, the drainage and reclamation of land, the introduction, use and spread of cultivated plants, the domestication of animals, the development of sophisticated systems of agriculture and many other actions all create, over large areas of the biomes, landscapes that are more man-made than natural.

Resource systems

An idea that clarifies the study of the interrelations of societies and environments, and the ways in which these change with the passage of time, is that of the *resource system*. This is a model of a population of human beings and their social and economic characteristics, including their technical skills and resources, together with those aspects of the natural environment that affect them and which they influence. The model includes the sequences by which natural materials are obtained, transformed and used. It tries to show how societies are organized according to their natural resources, the effects of that use, and the ways in which natural conditions limit or expand the life and work of the society. But it is easier to apply such a model to societies that have direct relations with natural conditions, through farming, fishing or forestry, than to great urban–industrial complexes.

The sections that follow present a picture of the diversity of habitats from ice caps to equatorial forests, the principal ways man has modified the environment and the problems of maintaining healthy resource systems.

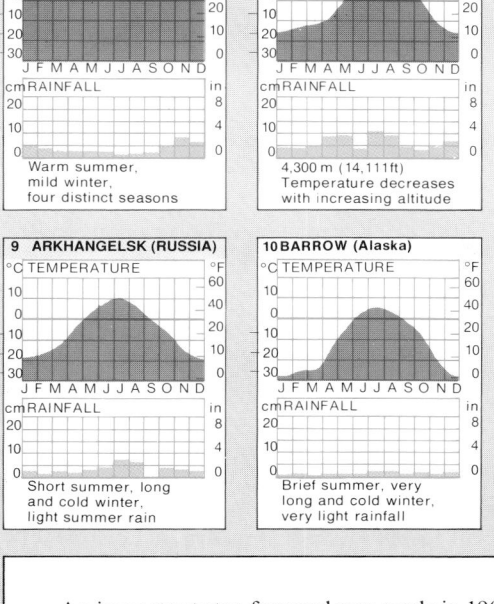

Climate and Weather

The pattern of world climates depends largely on great circulations of air in the atmosphere. These movements of air are driven by energy from the Sun, and they transfer surplus heat from the tropics to the polar regions. Over a long period of time – such as months, seasons or years – they create the climate. Over a short period – day by day, or week by week – they form the weather. Together, climate and weather are among the most significant natural components of the world's diverse environments.

The world's tropical zones receive more heat from the Sun than they re-emit into space, and so their land and sea surfaces become warm. The polar regions, on the other hand, emit more radiation than they receive, and so they become cold. Warm air is less dense than cold air, and this means that atmospheric pressure becomes low at the Equator and high at the poles. As a result, a circulation of air—both vertical and horizontal—is set up. But because of the Earth's rotation and the distribution of land and sea there is not a simple air circulation pattern in each hemisphere; winds are deflected to the right in the northern hemisphere and to the left in the southern hemisphere, a phenomenon known as the Coriolis effect.

A climatic patchwork
When warm air rises it expands and cools and the water vapor it is carrying condenses to form clouds. For this reason heavy, showery rain is frequent in the belt of rising air near the Equator. In the subtropical zones (where the air is sinking), clouds evaporate and the weather is fine. Air moves out of the subtropical high-pressure belts in the lower atmosphere. Some of it flows towards the poles and meets colder air, flowing out of the polar high-pressure region, in a narrow zone called the polar front. This convergence of air is concentrated around low-pressure systems known as depressions.

The pattern of climates does not remain constant throughout the year because of seasonal changes in the amount of radiation from the Sun—the "fuel" of the atmospheric engine. In June, when the northern hemisphere is tilted towards the Sun, the radiation is at a maximum at latitude 23°N and all the climatic belts shift northwards. In December it is summer in the southern hemisphere and all the belts move southwards.

Climate is also affected by the distribution of land and sea across the globe. The temperature of the land changes more quickly than that of

TYPES OF WEATHER
There is a constant flow of air between the world's polar and tropical regions, and this has a prime effect on the weather in other regions. In the high and middle latitudes cold and warm fronts succeed each other, and along coasts sea fogs often form. In temperate and tropical regions thunderstorms are frequent, and the tropics are characterized by the turbulent storms known as hurricanes in the Caribbean area and typhoons in the Pacific.

POLAR WEATHER
Weather in high latitudes is marked by consistently low temperatures—on the ice caps temperatures are nearly always below freezing. At the poles the sun never rises for six months of the year and for the remaining six months it never sets. Even in summer it stays low on the horizon and its rays are so slanted that they bring very little warmth. On the tundra the temperature rises above freezing for a few months in summer, but severe frosts are likely to occur at any time. As well as being bitterly cold, polar weather is predominantly dry. The lower the temperature the less moisture the air can contain. Clouds, when they form, are high, thin sheets of cirrostratus. Composed of ice crystals, they often produce a halo effect around the sun. Snow, when it falls, is usually dry and powdery.

DEPRESSIONS
Low-pressure weather systems, or depressions, form when polar and subtropical air masses converge. Cloud and rain usually occur at the boundary, or front, of the different air masses. Seen in cross section, a fully developed depression shows both warm (A) and cold (B) fronts. As the wave of warm air rises over the cold, its moisture condenses into the "layered" clouds that usually precede a warm front. Behind the warm front, cold air forces under the warm air, producing the wedge-shaped cold front.

FOG
Fogs form as a result of the condensation of water vapor in the air; they may occur when warm, moist air is cooled by its passage over a cold surface. Off the coast of California, for example, air near the surface of the sea is cooled by the cold California current and sea fog is frequent. The air at higher levels is still warm and acts like a lid over the fog, and mountains prevent the fog from dispersing in an easterly direction. Fumes and smoke are trapped by this temperature inversion, creating the notorious Los Angeles smog.

THUNDERSTORMS
These develop when air is unstable to a great height. Particularly violent storms occur when cold, dry air masses meet warm, moist air, causing the latter to rise rapidly. As the warm air surges upwards it cools and its moisture condenses into cumulonimbus, or thunder, clouds. Flat cloud tops mark the level where stable air occurs again. Quickly moving raindrops and hail in the clouds become electrically charged and cause lightning, and the explosion of heated air along the path of the flash creates the sound wave that is heard as thunder.

HURRICANES
These are tropical storms on a vast scale that build up over warm oceans. Their core is an area of low pressure around which large quantities of warm, moist air are carried to the high atmosphere at great speed. The Earth's rotation is responsible for the huge swirling movement: in the northern hemisphere the movement is anticlockwise, in the southern hemisphere it is clockwise. Towering bands of clouds produce torrential rain. The central region, or "eye," of a hurricane, however, has light winds, clear skies and no rainfall.

THE WORLD'S CLIMATIC REGIONS
Climate is the characteristic weather of a region over a long period of time. It is often described in terms of average monthly and yearly temperatures and rainfall. These in turn depend largely on latitude, which determines whether a region is basically hot or cold and whether it has pronounced seasonal changes. Climate is also influenced by prevailing winds, by ocean currents and by geographical features such as the distribution of land and water. Highland climates are influenced by altitude and are always cooler than those of nearby lowland regions. Tropical climates are always warm. Near the Equator rain falls for most of the year, but towards the subtropics the wet and dry seasons are more marked. Temperate climates reflect the conflict between warm and cold air masses. They range from the Mediterranean type with hot, dry summers and mild, moist winters to the cooler, wetter climates of higher latitudes. The subarctic is mainly cold and humid; polar climates are always cold and mainly dry.

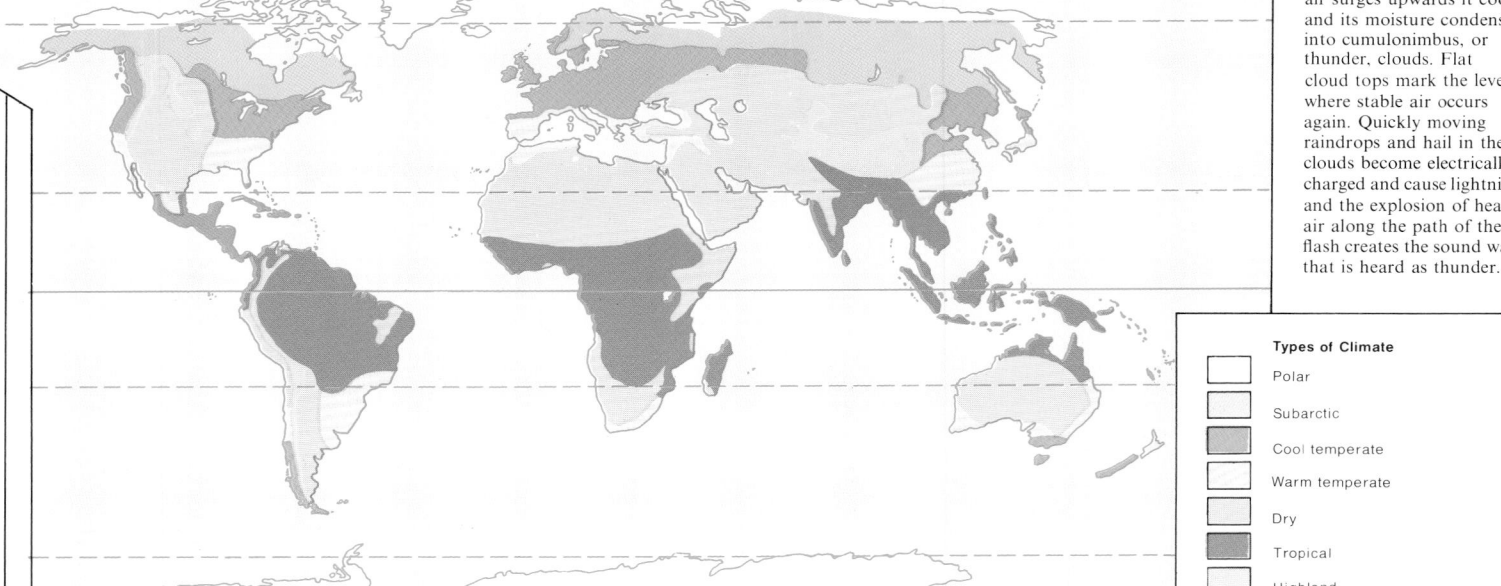

Types of Climate

- Polar
- Subarctic
- Cool temperate
- Warm temperate
- Dry
- Tropical
- Highland

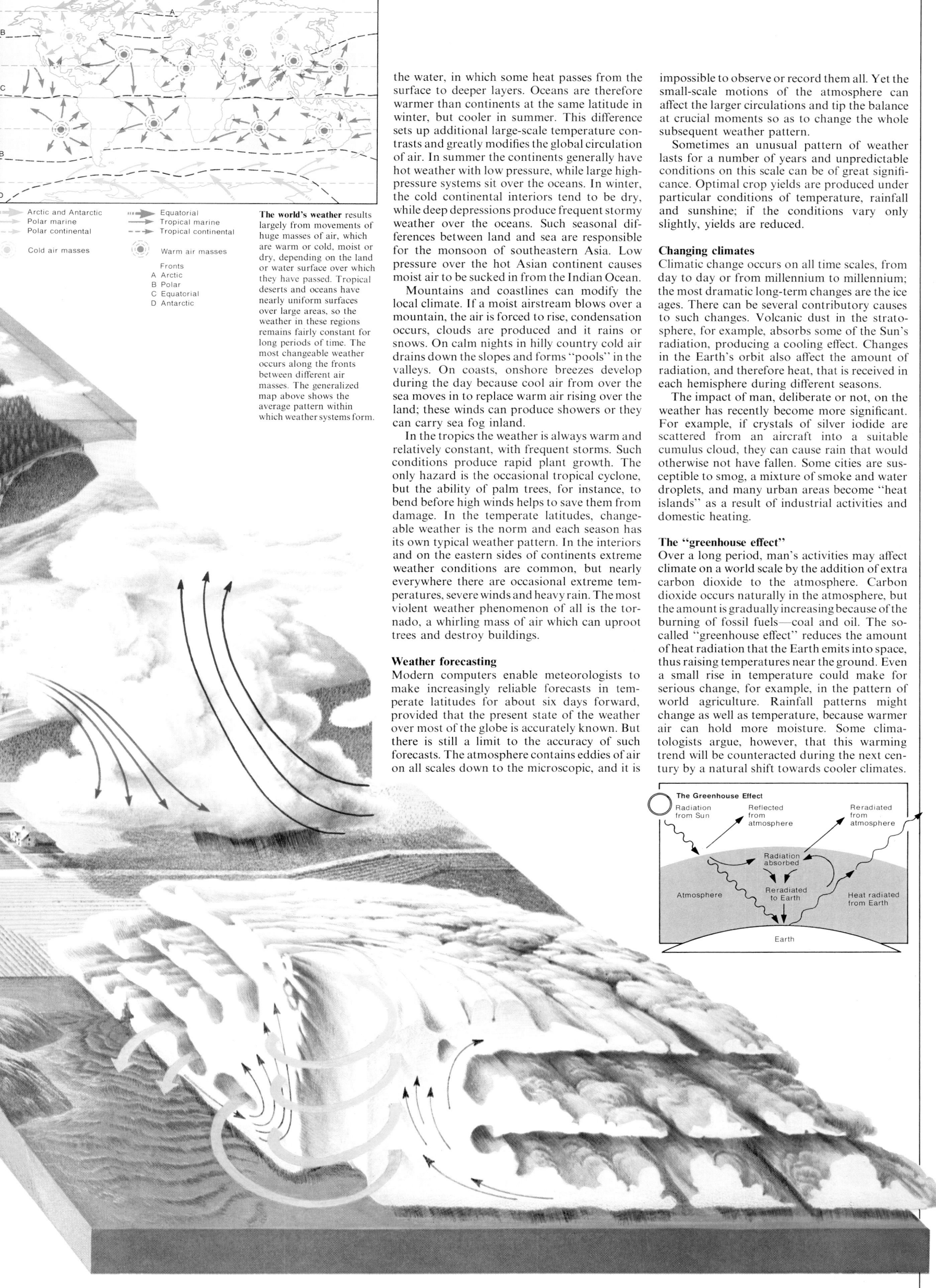

The world's weather results largely from movements of huge masses of air, which are warm or cold, moist or dry, depending on the land or water surface over which they have passed. Tropical deserts and oceans have nearly uniform surfaces over large areas, so the weather in these regions remains fairly constant for long periods of time. The most changeable weather occurs along the fronts between different air masses. The generalized map above shows the average pattern within which weather systems form.

the water, in which some heat passes from the surface to deeper layers. Oceans are therefore warmer than continents at the same latitude in winter, but cooler in summer. This difference sets up additional large-scale temperature contrasts and greatly modifies the global circulation of air. In summer the continents generally have hot weather with low pressure, while large high-pressure systems sit over the oceans. In winter, the cold continental interiors tend to be dry, while deep depressions produce frequent stormy weather over the oceans. Such seasonal differences between land and sea are responsible for the monsoon of southeastern Asia. Low pressure over the hot Asian continent causes moist air to be sucked in from the Indian Ocean.

Mountains and coastlines can modify the local climate. If a moist airstream blows over a mountain, the air is forced to rise, condensation occurs, clouds are produced and it rains or snows. On calm nights in hilly country cold air drains down the slopes and forms "pools" in the valleys. On coasts, onshore breezes develop during the day because cool air from over the sea moves in to replace warm air rising over the land; these winds can produce showers or they can carry sea fog inland.

In the tropics the weather is always warm and relatively constant, with frequent storms. Such conditions produce rapid plant growth. The only hazard is the occasional tropical cyclone, but the ability of palm trees, for instance, to bend before high winds helps to save them from damage. In the temperate latitudes, changeable weather is the norm and each season has its own typical weather pattern. In the interiors and on the eastern sides of continents extreme weather conditions are common, but nearly everywhere there are occasional extreme temperatures, severe winds and heavy rain. The most violent weather phenomenon of all is the tornado, a whirling mass of air which can uproot trees and destroy buildings.

Weather forecasting

Modern computers enable meteorologists to make increasingly reliable forecasts in temperate latitudes for about six days forward, provided that the present state of the weather over most of the globe is accurately known. But there is still a limit to the accuracy of such forecasts. The atmosphere contains eddies of air on all scales down to the microscopic, and it is

impossible to observe or record them all. Yet the small-scale motions of the atmosphere can affect the larger circulations and tip the balance at crucial moments so as to change the whole subsequent weather pattern.

Sometimes an unusual pattern of weather lasts for a number of years and unpredictable conditions on this scale can be of great significance. Optimal crop yields are produced under particular conditions of temperature, rainfall and sunshine; if the conditions vary only slightly, yields are reduced.

Changing climates

Climatic change occurs on all time scales, from day to day or from millennium to millennium; the most dramatic long-term changes are the ice ages. There can be several contributory causes to such changes. Volcanic dust in the stratosphere, for example, absorbs some of the Sun's radiation, producing a cooling effect. Changes in the Earth's orbit also affect the amount of radiation, and therefore heat, that is received in each hemisphere during different seasons.

The impact of man, deliberate or not, on the weather has recently become more significant. For example, if crystals of silver iodide are scattered from an aircraft into a suitable cumulus cloud, they can cause rain that would otherwise not have fallen. Some cities are susceptible to smog, a mixture of smoke and water droplets, and many urban areas become "heat islands" as a result of industrial activities and domestic heating.

The "greenhouse effect"

Over a long period, man's activities may affect climate on a world scale by the addition of extra carbon dioxide to the atmosphere. Carbon dioxide occurs naturally in the atmosphere, but the amount is gradually increasing because of the burning of fossil fuels—coal and oil. The so-called "greenhouse effect" reduces the amount of heat radiation that the Earth emits into space, thus raising temperatures near the ground. Even a small rise in temperature could make for serious change, for example, in the pattern of world agriculture. Rainfall patterns might change as well as temperature, because warmer air can hold more moisture. Some climatologists argue, however, that this warming trend will be counteracted during the next century by a natural shift towards cooler climates.

The Greenhouse Effect

Radiation from Sun
Reflected from atmosphere
Reradiated from atmosphere
Radiation absorbed
Atmosphere
Reradiated to Earth
Heat radiated from Earth
Earth

Resources and Energy

Resources, it has been said, comprise mankind's varying needs from generation to generation and are valued because of the uses societies can make of them. They represent human appraisals and are the products of man's ingenuity and experience. While natural resources remain vitally important in themselves, they must always be regarded as the rewards of human skill in locating, extracting and exploiting them. The development of resources depends on many factors, including the existence of a demand, adequate transport facilities, the availability of capital and the accessibility, quality and quantity of the resource itself.

The world's extraction of its resources highlights the inequality of their distribution. Each resource shown on the map is attributed to the three countries with the largest production percentages of that commodity. So, in 1976, the three leading bauxite producers were Australia (26.69%), Jamaica (14.19%) and Rep. of Guinea (13.9%). Usually, the larger and more wealthy a state the greater its monopoly of resources—although the tiny Pacific island of New Caledonia produces more than 14% of the world's nickel. China is reputed to mine 75% of the world's tungsten and to be increasing its oil supply rapidly. Energy consumption figures are for the year 1976, since when there have been some outstanding changes to patterns of availability, perhaps most noticeably in Britain's new-found oil and gas surplus. Bahrain and Tobago, too small to be shown on this map, also have surpluses of energy production.

A dictionary defines the term "resource" as "a means of aid or support," implying anything that lends support to life or activity. Man has always assessed nature with an eye to his own needs, and it is these varying needs that endow resources with their usefulness. Fossil fuels such as oil have lain long in the Earth, but it was not until about 1900 that the large-scale needs fostered by the rising demands of motor vehicles led to the development of new techniques for locating and extracting this raw material. Today oil has also become precious in the manufacture of a wide variety of industrial products, which themselves are resources that are much used by other industries.

The nature of resources

Resources can be most usefully classified in two groups: "renewable" and "nonrenewable." The latter is composed of materials found at or near the Earth's surface, which are sometimes known as "physical" resources. They include such essential minerals as uranium, iron, copper, nickel, bauxite, gold, silver, lead, mercury and tungsten. Oil, coal and natural gas are the principal nonrenewable fuel and energy resources, but after they have been used for producing heat or power their utility is lost and part of the geological capital of 325 million years of history is gone for ever. Some minerals such as iron and its product, steel, can be recycled and renewed, however. "Renewable" resources are basically biological, being the food and other vegetable matter which life needs to sustain human needs. Provided soil quality is maintained, their productivity may even be increased as better strains of plants and breeds of animals are developed.

Work has long been in progress to improve renewable resources, and has moved forward to manufacturing vegetable-flavored protein (VFP) from soybeans as a meat substitute and to viable experiments to extract protein from leaves. In Brazil, many cars have been converted to run successfully on alcohol extracted from sugar. One renewable resource—the tree—can be closely related to other resources: some conservationists are alarmed at the overuse of firewood as a source of fuel and energy in the semiarid areas of Africa. This may be an important factor in increasing the tendency for the deserts to spread in that continent, and in such a situation there is a new realization of the concept of closely managing resources such as soil, timber and fisheries. This is partly because we have a clearer understanding of the ecology of vegetation and the important interdependence of climate, soil, plants and animal life. Much, however, remains to be done.

The politics of nonrenewable resources

Today we are naturally troubled about the availability of natural resources. Oil is a prime cause for concern. Although many believe that production will grow until the mid-2020s and that new oil reserves will be discovered, oil's scarcity, based on a growing rate of demand and increasingly wasteful use, is now widely accepted. Because, like many resources, it is unevenly distributed, those countries with large and accessible supplies—such as the members of OPEC—have used their political power on a number of occasions to raise oil's price, with adverse effects on the economies of most importers. Ironically, these substantial price rises have had the effect of stimulating exploration and development in many new areas; there are already signs of increased production in China.

Other nonrenewable resources are also distributed unevenly, but have not been mined on any scale comparable with their availability; vast reserves of coal in the former Soviet Union and China have not been worked on any scale resembling their known extent.

New energy sources

As resources such as oil become less available and more expensive, the renewable resources of power such as water, wind, waves and solar energy, all of which are currently under study or development, will receive new injections of capital. Attention will also have to be paid to more widespread nuclear energy production. Energy has been called "the ultimate resource," and it is imperative that we make wise provisions for its future availability.

Future resources

It has been calculated that within four years of the launch of Sputnik I, more than 3,000 products resulting from space research were put into commercial production. These include new alloys, ceramics, plastics, fabrics and chemical compounds. Satellite development have meant that land use can now be measured quickly and potential mineral sources closely identified. A satellite capable of converting solar power to electricity and contributing to the Earth's energy deficit has been widely discussed while the Moon and planets have been mooted as future possible sources of minerals.

Conclusions

Resources are, in the main, the products of man's skill, ingenuity and expertise, and their widespread use, as in the case of timber and iron for shipbuilding, became apparent only as man's needs for them became clear. Our forebears were once concerned about the availability of flint, seaweed, charcoal and natural rubber; countries even went to war over supplies of spices. Today our requirements are slightly different—we no longer depend only on local sites for resources, and improved transport facilities and appropriate technologies have lowered the costs of obtaining materials for manufacture.

Nevertheless, the principles remain the same. A continual search for new resources capable of exploitation and wide application must be maintained, together with a close regard for the value of the renewable resources such as animal and vegetable products required to support man in his search for new resources. Perhaps the most vital consideration is the need for wise policies of conservation relating to the proven reserves of nonrenewable resources still in the ground, and the careful future use of such valuable deposits known or thought to exist.

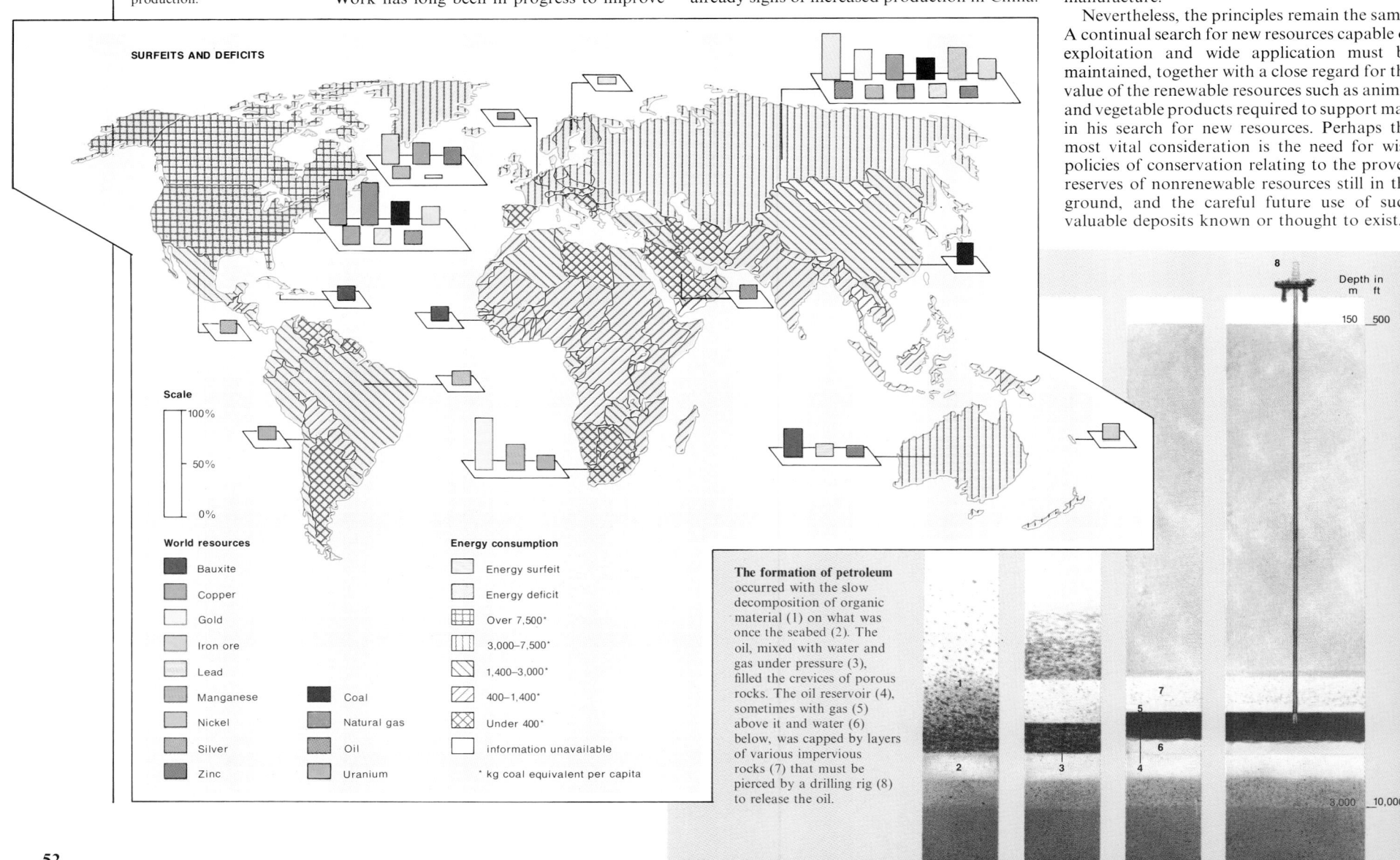

SURFEITS AND DEFICITS

Scale
100%
50%
0%

World resources
- Bauxite
- Copper
- Gold
- Iron ore
- Lead
- Manganese
- Nickel
- Silver
- Zinc
- Coal
- Natural gas
- Oil
- Uranium

Energy consumption
- Energy surfeit
- Energy deficit
- Over 7,500*
- 3,000–7,500*
- 1,400–3,000*
- 400–1,400*
- Under 400*
- information unavailable

*kg coal equivalent per capita

The formation of petroleum occurred with the slow decomposition of organic material (1) on what was once the seabed (2). The oil, mixed with water and gas under pressure (3), filled the crevices of porous rocks. The oil reservoir (4), sometimes with gas (5) above it and water (6) below, was capped by layers of various impervious rocks (7) that must be pierced by a drilling rig (8) to release the oil.

Depth in
m   ft
150 _500
3,000 _10,000

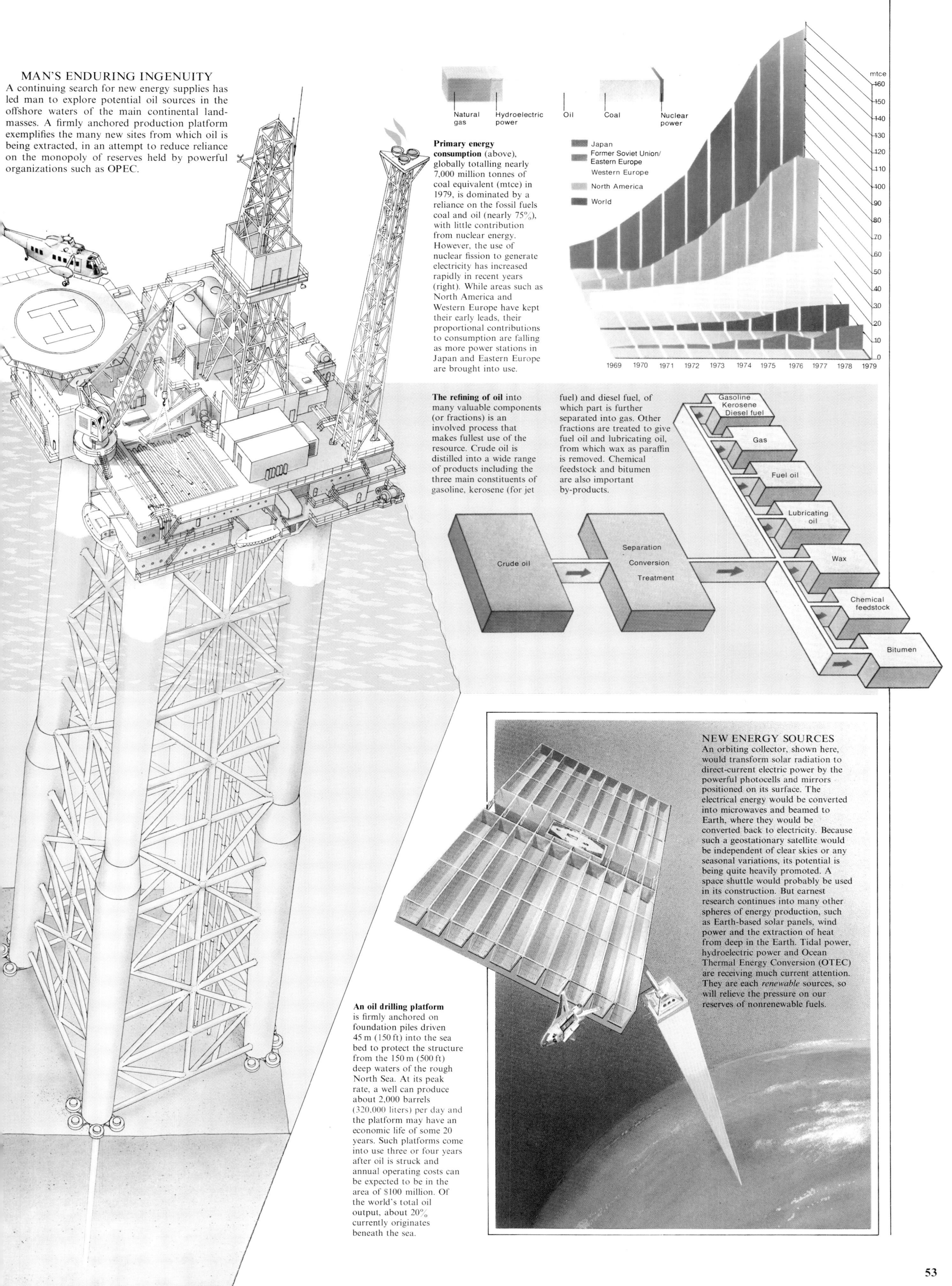

MAN'S ENDURING INGENUITY

A continuing search for new energy supplies has led man to explore potential oil sources in the offshore waters of the main continental land-masses. A firmly anchored production platform exemplifies the many new sites from which oil is being extracted, in an attempt to reduce reliance on the monopoly of reserves held by powerful organizations such as OPEC.

Natural gas   Hydroelectric power   Oil   Coal   Nuclear power

Japan
Former Soviet Union/Eastern Europe
Western Europe
North America
World

Primary energy consumption (above), globally totalling nearly 7,000 million tonnes of coal equivalent (mtce) in 1979, is dominated by a reliance on the fossil fuels coal and oil (nearly 75%), with little contribution from nuclear energy. However, the use of nuclear fission to generate electricity has increased rapidly in recent years (right). While areas such as North America and Western Europe have kept their early leads, their proportional contributions to consumption are falling as more power stations in Japan and Eastern Europe are brought into use.

mtce
160
150
140
130
120
110
100
90
80
70
60
50
40
30
20
10
0

1969 1970 1971 1972 1973 1974 1975 1976 1977 1978 1979

The refining of oil into many valuable components (or fractions) is an involved process that makes fullest use of the resource. Crude oil is distilled into a wide range of products including the three main constituents of gasoline, kerosene (for jet fuel) and diesel fuel, of which part is further separated into gas. Other fractions are treated to give fuel oil and lubricating oil, from which wax as paraffin is removed. Chemical feedstock and bitumen are also important by-products.

Crude oil → Separation Conversion Treatment → Gasoline Kerosene Diesel fuel / Gas / Fuel oil / Lubricating oil / Wax / Chemical feedstock / Bitumen

An oil drilling platform is firmly anchored on foundation piles driven 45 m (150 ft) into the sea bed to protect the structure from the 150 m (500 ft) deep waters of the rough North Sea. At its peak rate, a well can produce about 2,000 barrels (320,000 liters) per day and the platform may have an economic life of some 20 years. Such platforms come into use three or four years after oil is struck and annual operating costs can be expected to be in the area of $100 million. Of the world's total oil output, about 20% currently originates beneath the sea.

NEW ENERGY SOURCES

An orbiting collector, shown here, would transform solar radiation to direct-current electric power by the powerful photocells and mirrors positioned on its surface. The electrical energy would be converted into microwaves and beamed to Earth, where they would be converted back to electricity. Because such a geostationary satellite would be independent of clear skies or any seasonal variations, its potential is being quite heavily promoted. A space shuttle would probably be used in its construction. But earnest research continues into many other spheres of energy production, such as Earth-based solar panels, wind power and the extraction of heat from deep in the Earth. Tidal power, hydroelectric power and Ocean Thermal Energy Conversion (OTEC) are receiving much current attention. They are each *renewable* sources, so will relieve the pressure on our reserves of nonrenewable fuels.

Population Growth

Every minute of every day, more than 250 children are born into the world. The Earth's population now stands at about 4,300 million and is continuing to grow extremely rapidly. The problems associated with such growth are enormous – already, about two-thirds of the world's people are underfed, according to United Nations' recommended standards of nutrition. And an even greater number live in very poor housing conditions, have inadequate access to medical facilities, receive little or no education and, at present, have no hope of improving their lot. As yet, there are no simple or immediate solutions.

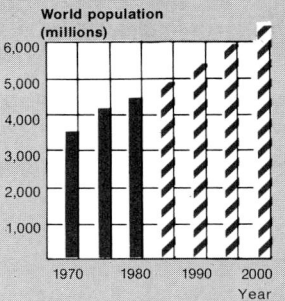

World population (millions)

■ World population
▨ Projected world population

If the world's population continues to grow at its present rate, by the year 2000 there could be more than 6,400 million people on Earth (above). Such growth rates are only a recent phenomenon—for most of mankind's existence on Earth the numbers grew slowly (right). Then in the late 18th century, scientific and industrial developments and the discovery of new food sources (the prairies of the New World) raised living standards. Death rates declined and populations grew rapidly.

Average annual population growth rate 1970–1978

■ 3% and over
▨ 2.5% to less than 3%
▨ 2% to less than 2.5%
▨ 1.0% to less than 2%
▢ Less than 1%
▢ Information unavailable

THE MULTIPLYING PROBLEMS
Populations are increasing most rapidly in the world's poorer nations. Poverty, in fact, seems to be at the heart of many of the complex interrelated problems created by rapid population growth. Poor countries, for example, are the least able to feed increasing numbers of people, while at the same time their lack of educational and medical facilities means that family planning is often inadequate and birth rates remain relatively high.

In 1830, there were only about 1,000 million people on Earth. By 1930, this figure had doubled. And by 1975, it had doubled again. If the present rate of increase continues, it will have doubled again by the year 2020.

This may not happen—it is extremely difficult to predict how world population will behave. What is certain is that it will continue to increase and, moreover, that this increase will not be evenly distributed. Since more than 50 percent of the human race lives in Asia, it is inevitable that the largest population increases will take place there. In fact, by the year 2000, the population of Asia may well have grown from about 2,000 million to more than 3,600 million. Substantial increases, of 400 million or more, will probably also occur in Africa, and Latin America is growing equally quickly.

In more prosperous North America and Europe, however, population growth seems to be stabilizing as women have fewer children and families become smaller—several countries, such as West Germany, now record a zero population growth rate. The poorer countries, the so-called Third World, are therefore gaining, and will probably continue to gain, an increasing share of the world's people. In 1930, about 64 percent of the human race lived in the poor countries of Asia, Africa and Latin America. By 1980, this proportion had increased to more than 75 percent. Population growth in these regions is creating enormous problems. It is estimated that there are now

more than 800 million people living in absolute poverty in the developing world, and these numbers can but increase as populations swell.

An obvious solution is to reduce birth rates, but this cannot be achieved quickly. In much of Africa and Asia, a very high proportion of the population is made up of young people who are, or soon will be, of childbearing age. Population increases are therefore inevitable. This will probably change as family planning becomes more widespread and women have fewer children, but such relief lies in the future and is likely to affect the poorest countries last. The most pressing problem for the growing numbers of impoverished people today is that of hunger.

Food – the fundamental problem
In theory, no food supply problem should exist—already enough food is produced in the world to feed a population of 5,500 million people. In fact, however, two-thirds of this food is consumed by the rich industrialized nations, and supplies are not reaching many of those in need. The developed nations dominate world food markets because developing nations, and people within those nations, are too poor to buy food, and are themselves unable to produce sufficient quantities to feed their growing populations. The answer to undernutrition and malnutrition lies largely in raising the incomes of poor peoples and improving distribution of supplies of food.

At a local level, food produced or imported

by developing countries must reach those in need at a price they can afford. One way of doing this is to encourage the rural poor to produce their own food. Small-scale, intensively farmed plots often prove to be the most efficient form of agriculture in areas where labor is plentiful. At present, many of the rural poor are either without land, or hold plots on extremely unfavorable terms of tenancy. By providing land, appropriate technology (small-scale, inexpensive farming equipment such as windpumps to draw water for irrigation), financial aid and information and education, small farmers could be helped to farm their land as effectively and efficiently as possible.

At a national level, too, developing countries must become more self-sufficient in food. This has already been achieved in some countries. India, although at one time heavily dependent upon imports of one of its staple foodstuffs—rice—has now increased production on such a scale that imports are no longer necessary. Unfortunately, for many developing countries this is not the case. Zaire, for example, was once an exporter of food. Today the country can no longer produce enough to keep pace with the demands of its own expanding population. At a world level, food production must be maintained as well, for unless production is kept high, prices are unstable and at times of bad harvests the poorer nations cannot afford to import essential supplies.

Food alone, however, is not enough to solve

10,000   9000   8000   7000   6000   5000   4000   3000   1000BC   0   AD 1000   2000

FEEDING THE WORLD

How are the growing numbers of people on Earth to be fed when millions are already undernourished? In the short term, the food problem could be solved by improving distribution of supplies that are already available. But the world can also be made to produce more food. Fertilizers and pest control can make land more productive and genetic engineering could produce higher-yielding and more nutritious crops.

The world will have to produce more food than it does today (below) if future populations are to be fed. At present, large areas of the Earth's land surface cannot be farmed—they are either too cold, dry, marshy, mountainous or forested. Cultivatable areas could be extended, given the necessary investment.

THE HEALTH OF NATIONS

Many developing nations are severely short of medical and welfare facilities for their growing populations. Yet these are the very countries with high incidences of disease—mainly because of malnutrition, lack of clean water supplies, and inadequate and overcrowded housing. Furthermore, without health services family planning facilities are not widely available, and expanding populations continue to strain existing resources.

Birth and Death Rates
- High birth rate/ High death rate
- High birth rate/ Moderate or low death rate
- Low birth rate/ Low death rate
- Information unavailable

THE NONPRODUCTIVE LANDS

Areas with no agricultural activity

PATTERNS OF POPULATION GROWTH

FOOD CONSUMPTION

As a country's health facilities improve, its mortality rates decline. Birth rates, however, do not immediately fall (above). Thus, ironically, an improvement in facilities at first exacerbates the problem of rapid growth in population. A country with a declining death rate and a high birth rate gains an increasing percentage of young people who are, or will be, of child-bearing age. Population pyramids (right) plot the percentage balance between age and youth in a nation.

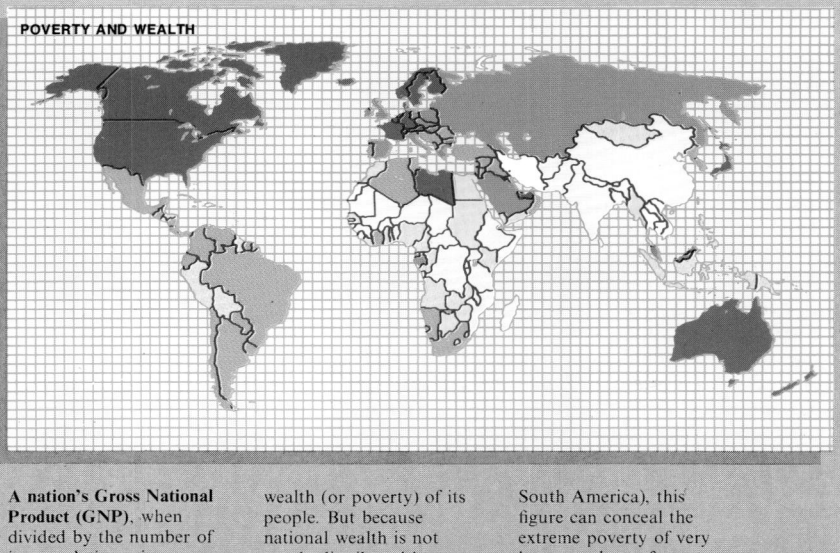

Calories per capita
- Less than 95% of needs
- 95% to 115% of needs
- More than 115% of needs
- Information unavailable

Malnutrition is widespread throughout the developing nations of Africa, Asia and South America. The problem is made worse by the fact that populations in these countries are growing more rapidly than anywhere else in the world.

the problems created by population growth. Broadly based economic development, such as in manufacturing and industry, is essential if developing countries are to have the income and other resources to enable them to cope with their evergrowing numbers of people.

Economic growth

To achieve economic development, certain obstacles must be overcome. First, the Third World needs energy supplies at a price it can afford, for, with the exception of Nigeria and the now-rich Middle East, most developing regions are woefully short of the energy resources needed to fuel growth. Second, for sustained economic development a skilled labor force is required, as are educational facilities to provide the necessary skills from within the nations themselves. Third, investment is required to enable developing nations to exploit the resources they do have—minerals, for example. And this investment must be on terms that are as beneficial to the developing nations as they are to powerful multinational organizations that frequently fund such projects. Finally, and most important, more enlightened social and political outlooks are needed within many countries if their growing populations of impoverished people are to benefit from any economic development and consequent increase in national wealth.

It has been said that wealth is the best method of contraception and, judging by the history of population growth in the rich industrialized nations, this seems to be the case. If it is, economic development of the Third World may well alleviate many of the problems created by population growth.

INCOME

When the income level of a population is raised sufficiently, it seems that birth rates ultimately decline. This has been the pattern that has emerged in the Western world. If this is the case, then economic development of the Third World countries could eventually help to stabilize world population growth, as well as provide nations with the means to cope. It could also help provide for their growing numbers.

POVERTY AND WEALTH

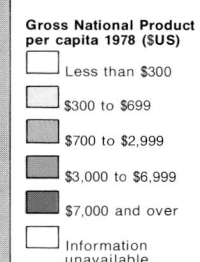

Gross National Product per capita 1978 ($US)
- Less than $300
- $300 to $699
- $700 to $2,999
- $3,000 to $6,999
- $7,000 and over
- Information unavailable

A nation's Gross National Product (GNP), when divided by the number of its population, gives some indication of the relative wealth (or poverty) of its people. But because national wealth is not evenly distributed in many countries (particularly in South America), this figure can conceal the extreme poverty of very large numbers of a nation's people.

EDUCATIONAL RESOURCES

Education is essential if the people of the developing world are to be equipped to improve their lot. Basic education on health and hygiene could dramatically reduce the incidence of disease; education about birth control would help lower birth rates; agricultural advice could help the rural poor to produce more food. Finally, general schooling is required to provide skilled labor.

ILLITERACY

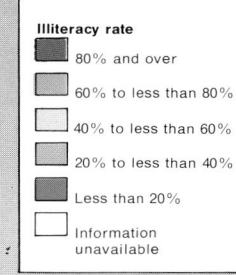

Illiteracy rate
- 80% and over
- 60% to less than 80%
- 40% to less than 60%
- 20% to less than 40%
- Less than 20%
- Information unavailable

Literacy rates are in fact improving in developing countries and national expenditure on schools is growing more quickly than is population. Two major problems are, first, the social traditions that severely restrict the number of girls attending school and, second, the reluctance of many rural poor to send to school children who provide valuable manual labor on the land.

Human Settlement

Man is naturally a gregarious animal. As an agriculturist he first settled in small communities, but it was not long before the emergence of towns and cities. Now nearly half the world's people live in these larger settlements, and by the year 2000, for the first time in history, more people will live in cities than in the countryside. Cities have grown up for various reasons, and are unevenly distributed across the world; but it is in the developing countries that the most rapid rates of urban growth are today taking place.

City life has a long and varied history going back to the early population centers of the Tigris–Euphrates, Indus and Nile valleys. Administrative and political needs led to the development of capital cities. Some, like London and Paris, evolved on conveniently located river crossings; others, such as Canberra, Islamabad and Brasilia, have locations that were deliberately planned.

Types of towns and cities
Market towns were established to exchange produce and, as trade expanded, hierarchies of service centers became established. These ranged from small "central places" that supplied rural areas with simple goods and services from elsewhere, to large cities that provided highly specialized services. Through such centrally placed systems, rural areas became connected with major industrialized areas. Mining towns such as Johannesburg, South Africa, and Broken Hill, Australia, sprang up as man began to exploit the Earth's mineral resources, their locations determined by the presence of rich ore deposits. Fishing ports and settlements dependent on forestry fall into the same group.

Increasing specialization, exemplified by the Black Country, England, and the Ruhr, West Germany, was a feature of European industrial development in the eighteenth and nineteenth centuries, and was based on the availability of capital investment and the presence of sources of fuel and power, especially water and steam power. Such industrialized cities relied on newly developed forms of transport to bring in new materials and to carry away manufactured products. Chicago is a good example of the relationship between the development of rail and water routes and the growth of a city as a market, agricultural processing and manufacturing center. As transport developed, further specialized centers concentrated on locomotive, ship or aircraft construction.

Uneven settlement patterns
Across the world, density and distribution of population are uneven. The land surface of the Earth as a whole has a density of 28 people per sq km (73 per sq mile) although Manhattan, for example, has 26,000 per sq km (63,340 per sq mile) and Australia has only 1.5 per sq km (4 per sq mile). In Brazil, towns and cities are mostly sited in the rich southeast, in contrast to a sparseness of settlement in its interior. Contrasts also occur between Mediterranean North Africa and the deserted Sahara to the south; or Canada of the St. Lawrence and the Canadian Shield to the north. Here the causes are not hard to find: extremes of climate, terrain and vegetation form effective barriers to settlement. Geographers estimate that two-thirds of the world's population lives within 500 km (310 miles) of the sea.

Any true consideration of human settlements must, however, be placed within the context of the economic, political and social systems in which they have evolved. Physical considerations alone cannot fully explain the urban concentrations of Western Europe, Japan or the northeastern USA, or the comparative absence of cities elsewhere. Only 5 percent of Malawi's and 4.7 percent of New Guinea's populations live in towns; in Belgium the percentage is 87, in Australia 86, in the UK 78 and in the USA 73.5. The figure for Norway is only 42 percent. Urbanization is a varied phenomenon and cities grow for many reasons.

The attractions of the city
Cities have always acted as magnets to poor or unemployed rural populations, and migrations from the countryside have assisted high rates of

THE DISTRIBUTION OF POPULATION
THE DISTRIBUTION OF POPULATION
Human settlement is highly uneven because it is related to many social and topographical factors. At first, man was tied to the sites of his crops and the grazing land of his cattle; life in nonrural centers only became a typical feature of population development as specialized services came into demand and towns and cities arose to support these needs. But during the 20th century there has been a vast increase in urban populations, particularly in Third World countries.

Immigration to the United States (below) from Europe was partly responsible for the growth of the vast Washington–Boston urban mass known as "Megalopolis." Since World War II, more immigrants have come from Puerto Rico and Mexico.

Boston
New York City
Philadelphia
Baltimore
Washington DC
Richmond

Immigrants in 000s
Year
1840 1860 1880 1900 1920 1940 1960 1980
(estimated)
0 1,000 2,000 3,000 4,000 5,000 6,000 7,000 8,000 9,000

Oil and gas deposits
Iron ore railroads
Farming
• Towns
⊙ Hydroelectric projects
+++ Iron ore railroads
═══ Current oil and gas pipelines

Ciudad Guayana
Ciudad Bolivar
VENEZUELA
GUYANA

Expanding settlements (above) and new lines of communication are being developed in the poorly populated eastern lowlands of Venezuela in order fully to exploit the resources being discovered there. Huge deposits of iron ore and large supplies of oil and gas have been located, and Ciudad Bolivar and Ciudad Guayana have become steel-making and service centers. To feed the people of these new settlements, agriculture has been greatly expanded.

city growth. Very large cities—Tokyo, New York and Los Angeles—are still found in the northern world, but many cities with far faster growth rates are sited in the Third World, especially in Asia. There the total number of inhabitants living in towns and cities is still much lower than in Europe, but centers such as Shanghai, Karachi, Bandung, New Delhi, Seoul, Jakarta and Manila are among the world's most rapidly expanding urban centers. Perhaps as many as a third of these city dwellers in Asia, Africa and Latin America put up with makeshift housing in shanty towns that present enormous problems of health, sanitation, education and unemployment: city growth in the developing world is a daunting prospect.

People on the move
In the past, one solution to population pressure on the land could be found in the migrations which occurred on a large scale from Asia into Europe, from Europe to the Americas and Australasia, and from China into southeastern Asia. But as claims are being made on almost every habitable area of the Earth, mass migrations have largely declined in importance. Many nations restrict movement to or from

their countries. Australia has strict immigration quotas; Vietnam restricts emigration for largely ideological reasons. Large movements of labor still take place, however, from the poorer regions of the Mediterranean to the industrial cities of France and Germany. Migrant workers from neighboring countries in Africa also play an essential part in the mining economy of South Africa.

New trends in urbanization
In many industrialized countries, a strong process of decentralization is leading to reductions in the populations of cities and corresponding increases in those of the suburbs and beyond. In 1951 the geographer Jean Gottman showed how groups of city regions tend to form chains of functionally linked cities, to which he gave the term "megalopolis." His prime example was Megalopolis, USA, stretching from north of Boston to south of Washington DC. Similar settlements occur in the Tokyo–Yokohama–Osaka area of Japan and the Ruhr megalopolis of northwestern Europe. Ultimately, equally drastic and large-scale patterns are likely to emerge in the already overcrowded human settlements of the Third World.

Migrating refugees, the world total of which increases on average by 2,000–3,000 every day, can affect settlement patterns. The Ugandan children (below) fled to the northern province of Karamoja in the wake of the 1979 war with Tanzania and the resultant famine that occurred in much of Uganda.

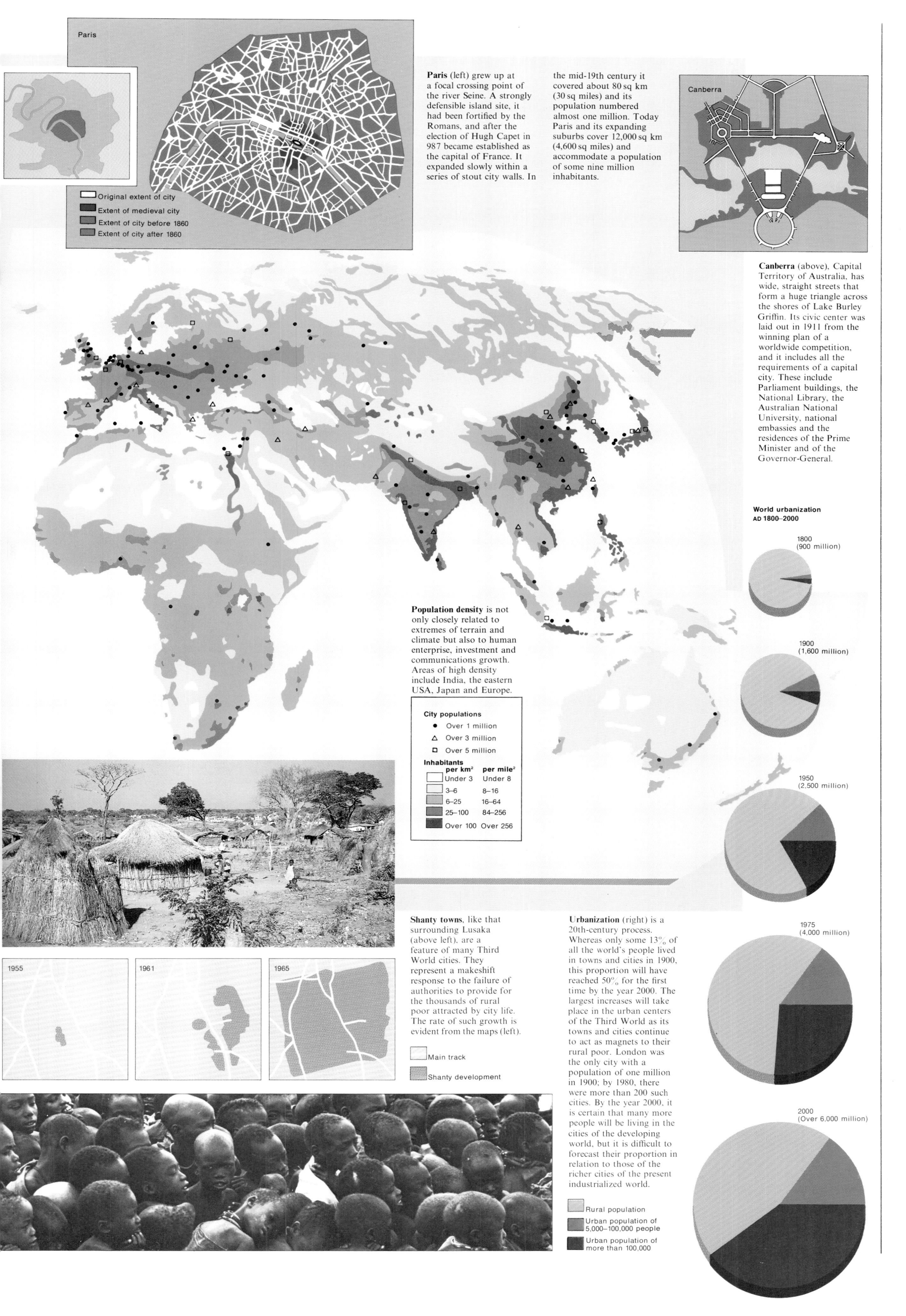

Paris

Paris (left) grew up at a focal crossing point of the river Seine. A strongly defensible island site, it had been fortified by the Romans, and after the election of Hugh Capet in 987 became established as the capital of France. It expanded slowly within a series of stout city walls. In the mid-19th century it covered about 80 sq km (30 sq miles) and its population numbered almost one million. Today Paris and its expanding suburbs cover 12,000 sq km (4,600 sq miles) and accommodate a population of some nine million inhabitants.

☐ Original extent of city
■ Extent of medieval city
■ Extent of city before 1860
■ Extent of city after 1860

Canberra

Canberra (above), Capital Territory of Australia, has wide, straight streets that form a huge triangle across the shores of Lake Burley Griffin. Its civic center was laid out in 1911 from the winning plan of a worldwide competition, and it includes all the requirements of a capital city. These include Parliament buildings, the National Library, the Australian National University, national embassies and the residences of the Prime Minister and of the Governor-General.

Population density is not only closely related to extremes of terrain and climate but also to human enterprise, investment and communications growth. Areas of high density include India, the eastern USA, Japan and Europe.

City populations
● Over 1 million
△ Over 3 million
☐ Over 5 million

Inhabitants

per km²	per mile²
Under 3	Under 8
3–6	8–16
6–25	16–64
25–100	84–256
Over 100	Over 256

World urbanization
AD 1800–2000

1800
(900 million)

1900
(1,600 million)

1950
(2,500 million)

1975
(4,000 million)

2000
(Over 6,000 million)

Shanty towns, like that surrounding Lusaka (above left), are a feature of many Third World cities. They represent a makeshift response to the failure of authorities to provide for the thousands of rural poor attracted by city life. The rate of such growth is evident from the maps (left).

1955   1961   1965

☐ Main track
■ Shanty development

Urbanization (right) is a 20th-century process. Whereas only some 13% of all the world's people lived in towns and cities in 1900, this proportion will have reached 50% for the first time by the year 2000. The largest increases will take place in the urban centers of the Third World as its towns and cities continue to act as magnets to their rural poor. London was the only city with a population of one million in 1900; by 1980, there were more than 200 such cities. By the year 2000, it is certain that many more people will be living in the cities of the developing world, but it is difficult to forecast their proportion in relation to those of the richer cities of the present industrialized world.

☐ Rural population
■ Urban population of 5,000–100,000 people
■ Urban population of more than 100,000

Trade and Transport

It is a commonplace that we live in a "shrinking" world. During the last century the development of communications has been so rapid that man appears almost to have conquered the challenge of distance; but such a concept depends on the kind of area to be covered and the cost of transporting goods in relation to their value, bulk and perishability. People, goods and services become accessible by trade. Transport makes trade possible: trade's demands lead to improvements in transport.

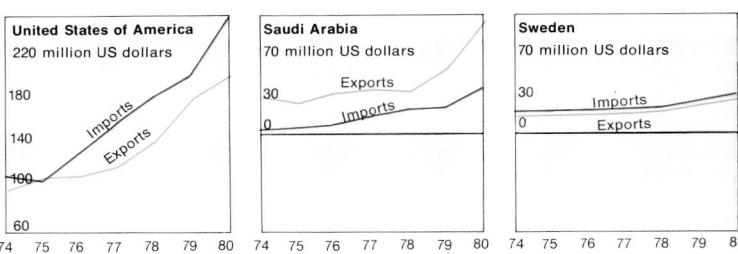

United States of America — 220 million US dollars — Exports / Imports — 74 75 76 77 78 79 80

Saudi Arabia — 70 million US dollars — Exports / Imports — 74 75 76 77 78 79 80

Sweden — 70 million US dollars — Imports / Exports — 74 75 76 77 78 79 8

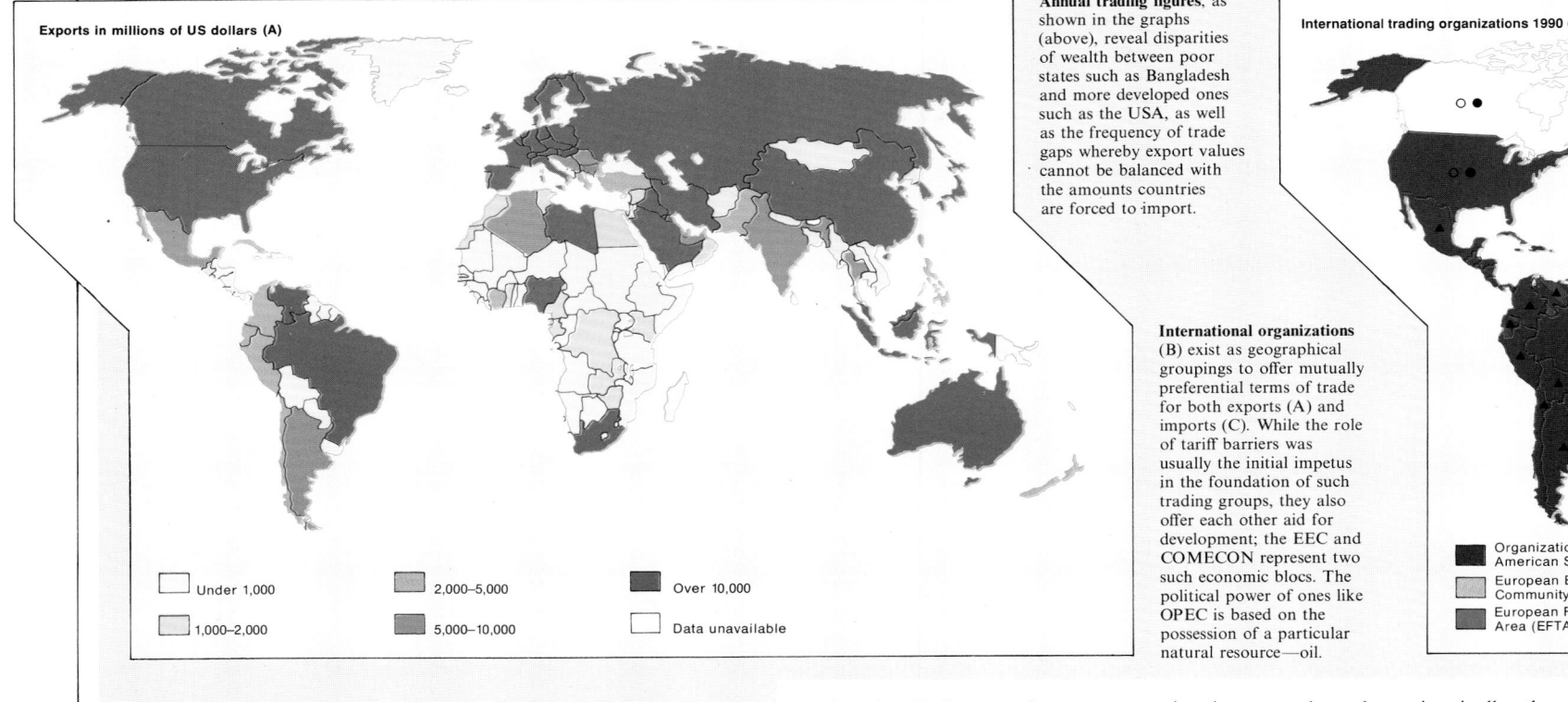

Exports in millions of US dollars (A)

Under 1,000
1,000–2,000
2,000–5,000
5,000–10,000
Over 10,000
Data unavailable

Annual trading figures, as shown in the graphs (above), reveal disparities of wealth between poor states such as Bangladesh and more developed ones such as the USA, as well as the frequency of trade gaps whereby export values cannot be balanced with the amounts countries are forced to import.

International trading organizations 1990 (B)

Organization of American States (OAS)
European Economic Community (EEC)
European Free Trade Area (EFTA)

International organizations (B) exist as geographical groupings to offer mutually preferential terms of trade for both exports (A) and imports (C). While the role of tariff barriers was usually the initial impetus in the foundation of such trading groups, they also offer each other aid for development; the EEC and COMECON represent two such economic blocs. The political power of ones like OPEC is based on the possession of a particular natural resource—oil.

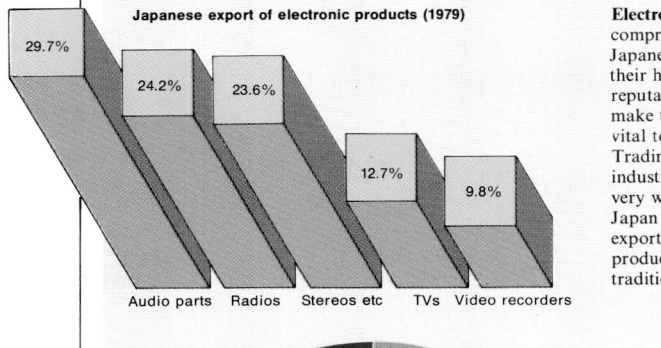

Japanese export of electronic products (1979)

29.7% — Audio parts
24.2% — Radios
23.6% — Stereos etc
12.7% — TVs
9.8% — Video recorders

Electronic products comprise only one-sixth of Japanese exports (left); their high export value and reputation for quality make their sales abroad vital to Japan's economy. Trading links (below) with industrialized countries are very well established; now Japan is mounting new export drives to sell its products to much less traditional markets.

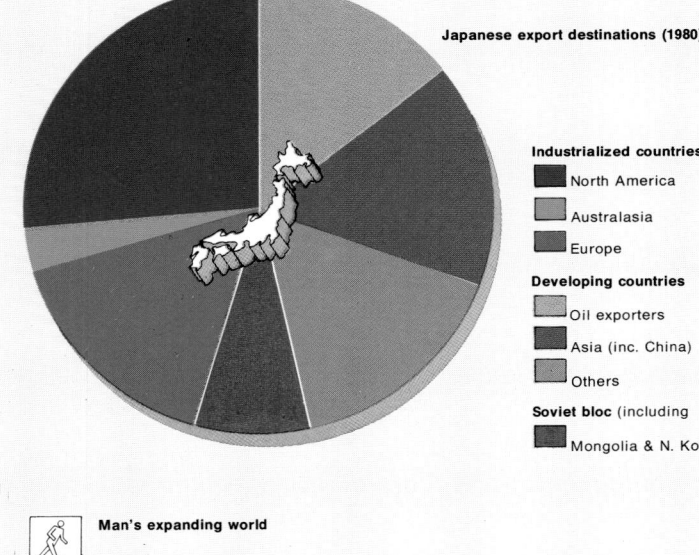

Japanese export destinations (1980)

Industrialized countries
North America
Australasia
Europe

Developing countries
Oil exporters
Asia (inc. China)
Others

Soviet bloc (including Mongolia & N. Korea)

It is only a little more than two centuries since navigators completed the mapping of the world's major landmasses and much less since the mapping of the continental interiors was completed—even today some gaps still remain. Canals like the Suez (1869) and Panama (1915) reduced the extent of long sea voyages—the Suez Canal shortened the distance from northwestern Europe to India by 15,000 km (9,300 miles)—so that in transport terms, the various parts of the world became more accessible, especially as steamships and motor vessels replaced sailing ships, and time distances were reduced still further by the airplane.

Locational advantages

Inland waterways, roads and railroads opened up new areas for mining or specialized agriculture, and created opportunities for the manufacture of goods and for the distribution of the finished products. The contrast, however, between locations such as London, Tokyo or Chicago (which are accessible to all forms of transport) and parts of South America where modern transport hardly penetrates, has become much more marked over the years. New transport developments tend to connect major centers first of all, and thus increase their already high locational status.

Such developments must nevertheless be seen in the light of the demand for communications and trade between different points, the nature of the goods being carried and the actual cost of transport. Transport improvements have allowed different parts of the world to share ideas

and products; ironically, they have also made such places more dissimilar, since each area of the Earth has had the chance to specialize in the services it can provide most efficiently.

Specialization of area

Before the widespread development of canals and railroads, road transport was expensive and towns and villages tended to be more self-sufficient. Railroads played a vital role in reducing transport costs in relation to distance and in providing an opportunity for different areas to specialize. After the emergence of railroad networks in North America, specialized areas of agricultural production quickly developed because they were well adjusted to the climatic conditions needed for growing maize (corn), cotton, fruit and fresh vegetables for the new urban markets. In the southern hemisphere, steamships and the introduction of refrigeration enabled meat, butter and cheese to be kept fresh on their journeys to the north.

This concept of specialization of area is basic to world trading patterns, since regions tend to concentrate on commodities and services that they can exchange for other specialized goods and products from other regional or world markets. Countries and areas do best when they concentrate on products for which they have comparative cost advantages in terms of the presence of natural resources, the availability of the skills to develop them, and a demand for the products. Enterprise in adapting natural conditions for the production of goods at competitive price levels is also important. Settlers in New

Man's expanding world

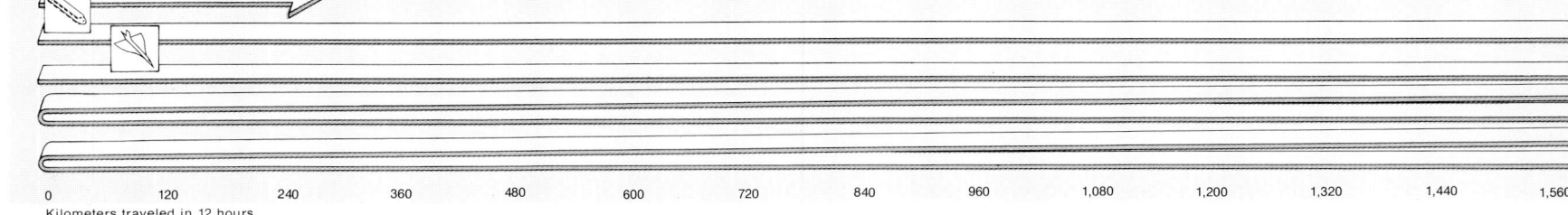

Technological change in transport has resulted in important reductions in the cost of trade. A man trading on foot might travel half the area a

draft horse could cover in a 12-hour day, but it was the acceptance of steam after *The Rocket* (1829) that made trade more reliable and greatly

expanded the potential for international commerce. Modern jet airliners can easily fly thousands of kilometers in half a day, and while they are being

used more and more for freight, most bulk freight is still carried by train or by specialized cargo vessel. The graph below plots changing transport technology.

0   120   240   360   480   600   720   840   960   1,080   1,200   1,320   1,440   1,560
Kilometers traveled in 12 hours

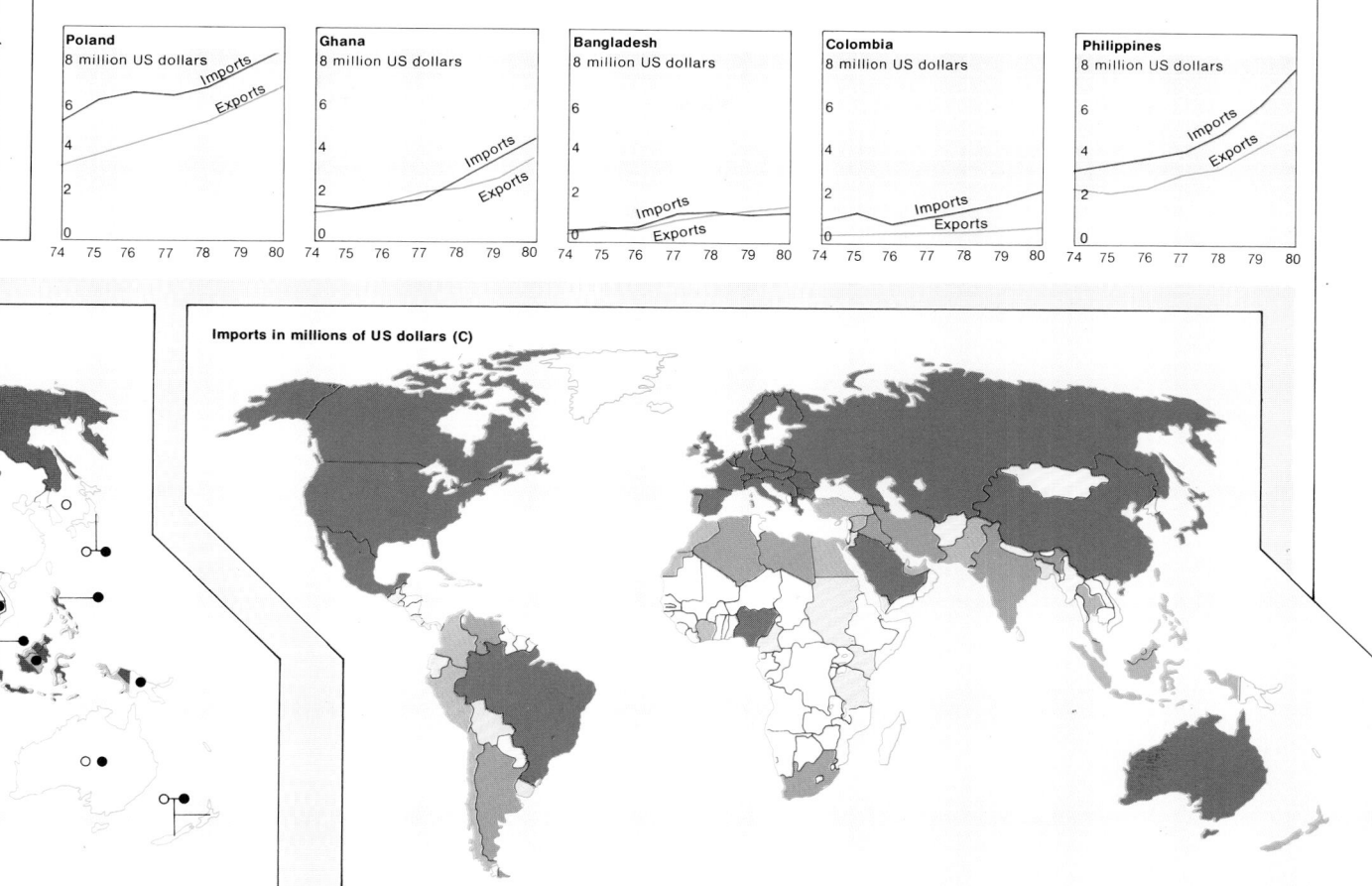

Poland 8 million US dollars — Imports / Exports
Ghana 8 million US dollars — Imports / Exports
Bangladesh 8 million US dollars — Imports / Exports
Colombia 8 million US dollars — Imports / Exports
Philippines 8 million US dollars — Imports / Exports

Imports in millions of US dollars (C)

- Council for Mutual Economic Aid (COMECON)
- Organization of Petroleum Exporting Countries (OPEC)
- Association of South-East Asian Nations (ASEAN)
- Organization for African Unity (OAU)
- ▲ Latin American Free Trade Association (LAFTA)
- ■ Arab League (AL)
- ○ Colombo Plan
- ● Organization for Economic Cooperation and Development (OECD)

- Under 1,000
- 1,000–2,000
- 2,000–5,000
- 5,000–10,000
- Over 10,000
- Data unavailable

Zealand, for example, had little hesitation in clearing the prevailing tussock grass to create a new pastoral environment for their large-scale production of sheep and dairy products.

In the real world, however, there are many impediments to the operation of a free market system, and it is unwise for states like New Zealand to assume that they will always dominate Commonwealth dairy trade.

Impediments to free markets
Countries erect protectionist tariff barriers to assist their home industries and/or to obtain extra revenue. Import or export quotas may be imposed, and trade agreements with other countries give special preference to certain commodities. Problems arise from the exchange of currencies and their fluctuations in value. Tariff barriers may be erected for political, welfare or defense reasons. Sometimes special measures may be adopted to encourage the internal production of certain goods rather than obtaining them more cheaply from abroad, and such methods may be economically important to a new country that has always relied on the export of raw materials for its income but now wishes domestically to manufacture previously imported goods.

Political ties are vital to the groupings of certain countries. For reasons of international politics, countries such as those of the Soviet bloc trade with each other rather than with the outside world; and historical links, as between the UK and the Commonwealth, France and her ex-colonies, and Spain and Portugal with

Latin America, are also influential. The European Economic Community (EEC) is composed of countries that have formed a strong bloc among the developed countries.

Rich man, poor man
The developed countries of "the North" have more than 80 percent of the world's manufacturing income but only a quarter of its population, whereas the poorer peoples of "the South" number 3,000 million and receive only a fifth of world income. Attempts have been made to obtain a better economic balance. The 1948 General Agreement on Tariffs and Trade (GATT) and the United Nations Conference on Trade and Development (UNCTAD) provided mechanisms for multinational trade negotiations, and the World Bank and the International Monetary Fund (IMF) together with the 1960 International Development Association (IDA) have all provided easier loans for less developed states.

The widening gap between rich and poor countries has led to understandable demands for a new international order calling for basic changes in the structure of world production, aid and trade, and the transfer of resources. The 1980 Independent Commission on International Development Issues (The Brandt Commission) advocated just such a transfer to the Third World. But during a major world recession there seems little sign of any international political will strong enough to take action on the scale needed to solve the problems that contrasts in wealth and poverty involve.

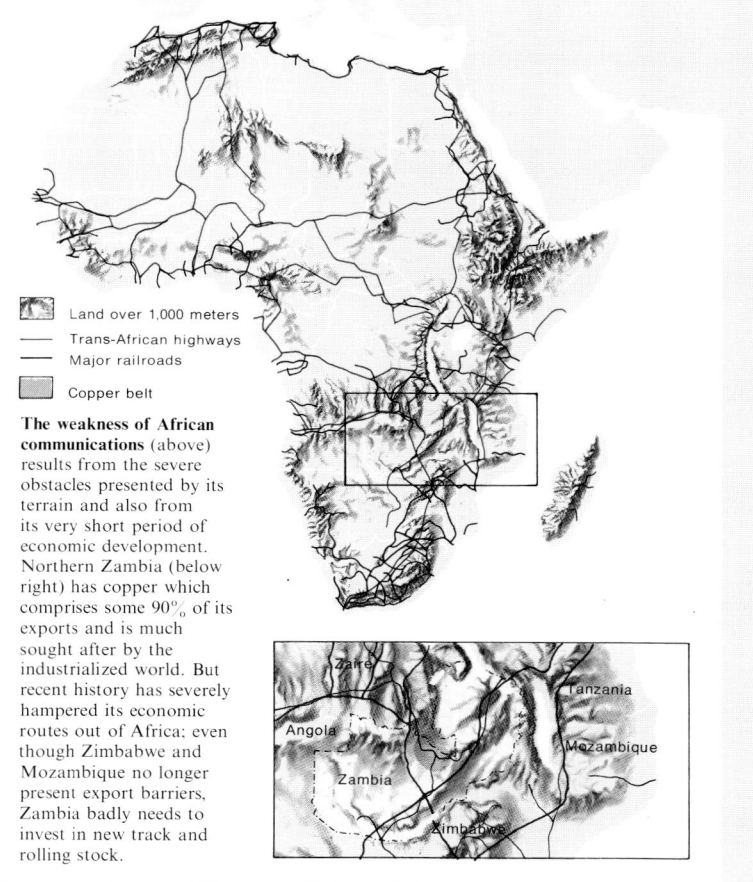

- Land over 1,000 meters
- Trans-African highways
- Major railroads
- Copper belt

The weakness of African communications (above) results from the severe obstacles presented by its terrain and also from its very short period of economic development. Northern Zambia (below right) has copper which comprises some 90% of its exports and is much sought after by the industrialized world. But recent history has severely hampered its economic routes out of Africa; even though Zimbabwe and Mozambique no longer present export barriers, Zambia badly needs to invest in new track and rolling stock.

1,800   1,920   2,040   2,160   2,280   2,400   2,520   2,640   2,760   2,880   3,000   3,120   3,240   3,360

Polar Regions

Sunless in winter, and capped with permanent land ice and shifting sea ice, the world's polar regions present an image of intense and everlasting cold. But permanent ice caps have been the exception rather than the rule in the 4,600 million years of Earth's history. The most recent intensification of the present ice age (which began at least two million years ago) reached its maximum about 20,000 years ago and still continues to fluctuate. Polar conditions preclude all but the toughest life forms on land, but the plankton-rich waters attract many animals, and man is beginning to exploit the polar regions' potential.

There have been about a dozen ice ages since the world began. During the intervening periods there was still a zonal pattern of world temperatures, with hot equatorial regions and cooler poles. But the ice caps, which are both chilling and self-sustaining, were absent altogether—the poles being cold temperate rather than icebound. The shiny ice surfaces of today's poles reflect more than 90 percent of the solar radiation which reaches them from the low-angled summer sun, while in winter the sun never rises at all. Thus the regions are now permanently ice capped.

Antarctica, the great southern polar continent, lies under an ice mantle 14 million sq km (5.4 million sq miles) in area, and sometimes more than 4,000 m (13,000 ft) thick. Many of its neighboring islands also carry permanent ice. In the Arctic, the three islands of Greenland lie under a pall of ice of subcontinental size, more than 1.8 million sq km (700,000 sq miles) in area and up to 3,000 m (9,800 ft) thick.

The ice cover of polar seas varies. The central core of the Arctic Ocean carries a mass of permanent pack ice, slowly circulating within the polar basin, which is added to each winter by a belt of ice forming over the open sea. Currents and winds break this up to form pack ice that also circulates, gradually melting in summer or drifting south. Antarctica too is surrounded by fast ice, which breaks up in spring to form a broad belt of persistent pack ice. Circulating slowly about the continent, the pack ice forms huge gyres spreading far to the north, dotted with tabular bergs that have broken away from the continental ice sheet.

The frozen land

In the present glacial phase, the ice caps reached their farthest spread about 20,000 years ago, and then began the retreat which brought them, some 10,000 to 12,000 years ago, to their current position and size. Since then the climate of the polar regions has been both warmer and colder than it is at the present time.

The fluctuating nature of the polar climates creates very difficult conditions for plants and animals. Very little will grow on the terrestrial ice caps, but water scarcity rather than cold is the most important factor inhibiting plant growth: the small patches of lichens, algae and mosses that occur on rock faces and nunataks (points of rock jutting above the land ice) are usually in the path of a snowmelt runnel. Vegetation patches sometimes contain tiny populations of insects and mites, which may be active for only a few days each year when the sun warms them from a state of dormancy.

However, these tiny scattered plant communities appear all over Antarctica wherever rock surfaces break through the ice cap, and have been seen less than 300 km (190 miles) from the South Pole, and on peaks 2,000 m (6,600 ft) above sea level. Insects and mites occur within 600 km (380 miles) of the Pole itself. In specially favored positions on the Antarctic Peninsula and the offshore islands, carpets of moss and grasses may be seen. Conditions around the northern terrestrial ice cap are similar, with aridity, strong winds and cold discouraging all but the hardiest plants and the smallest, toughest animal colonies.

The frozen seas

The marine ice caps, by contrast, are relatively lively places, especially during summer, when days are long and the sea ice is patchy. Waterlanes between floes are often rich in microscopic algae and the minute zooplanktonic animals that feed on them. These animals in turn attract fish, sea birds and seals in their thousands, as well as whales—including the largest baleen species. Some of the richest patches of sea are close to islands where strong currents stir the water and bring nutrients to the surface, and these attract semipermanent populations of seals and birds. The birds breed on the island cliffs and feed in the sheltered waters among the ice; the seals may breed on the ice itself, producing their pups on a floating nursery where food is close at hand.

Different species of seals are found on inshore and offshore ice environments. In the Arctic, bearded and ringed seals, which produce their young in spring as the inshore ice begins to break up, are often preyed upon by floe-riding polar bears; Eskimos too prize both species for their meat, blubber and skins. Farther out on the offshore pack ice live hooded and harp seals, where their pups are safe from all but the shipborne commercial hunters. In the Antarctic, Weddell seals are the inshore species, whereas crabeater and Ross seals prefer the distant pack ice. Crabeaters, which feed largely on planktonic krill (once thought to be crab larvae), are probably the most numerous of all seal species, with a population estimated at 10 to 15 million.

Sea ice in the north provides a precarious platform on which coastal human populations of the Arctic, such as Eskimos, can extend their winter hunting range. When the land is snowbound and animals are scarce, the sea may still provide food for hunters skilled in fishing, and in stalking seals to their breathing holes.

Nonindigenous inhabitants of the ice caps have greatly increased in recent years, following the discovery and exploitation of oil in the north, as well as other valuable minerals in both the regions. Scientists and technicians today occupy bases and weather stations which in some cases, such as the Amundsen-Scott at the South Pole, are several decades old and have to be maintained by means of aircraft.

The coldness of the poles is caused by the tilt of the Earth's axis, which prevents sunlight from reaching them at all in the winter. Even in summer, little heat is received from the sun because of the low angle at which its rays reach the surface; much even of this is reflected away by the ice.

EARTH'S FROZEN LIMITS

The permanent ice around Earth's poles covers whole oceans, as well as landmasses of immense size. These ice sheets fluctuate, and on land may be thousands of meters thick, sometimes covering all but the highest mountains, and allowing hardly any life. In the circumpolar seas, however, conditions encourage a very rich growth of plankton, and this supports a plentiful and varied range of wildlife. Man, too, is active in the Arctic, where there are indigenous populations. But in the far south the presence of man is confined to scientists and their support groups. The Antarctic Treaty of 1959 has reserved the continent for nonpolitical scientific use.

Arctic spring
Arctic summer
Arctic winter
Arctic autumn

ATLANTIC OCEAN
PACIFIC OCEAN
INDIAN OCEAN
Antarctic convergence

THE FAR SOUTH

A crushing weight of ice (above) permanently covers the continent and seas of Antarctica, forcing much of the land below sea level. The Antarctic convergence (right), the line at which northern and southern water masses meet, marks a sharp change in temperature and marine life. Especially in areas of upwelling, nutrients make these waters rich in plankton. This feeds a multitude of shrimp-like krill that provide food for a huge number of other animals—fish, penguins, flying birds, seals and whales. The Antarctic landmass allows little natural life, but since the 1959 Antarctic Treaty it has proved to be an area of international scientific cooperation.

Whales
Emperor penguin rookeries
Adélie penguins
Antarctic terns and petrels
Ross and crabeater seals
Leopard seals

Scientific research stations

United Kingdom
Former Soviet Union
Japan
Australia
USA
Chile
France
New Zealand
Argentina

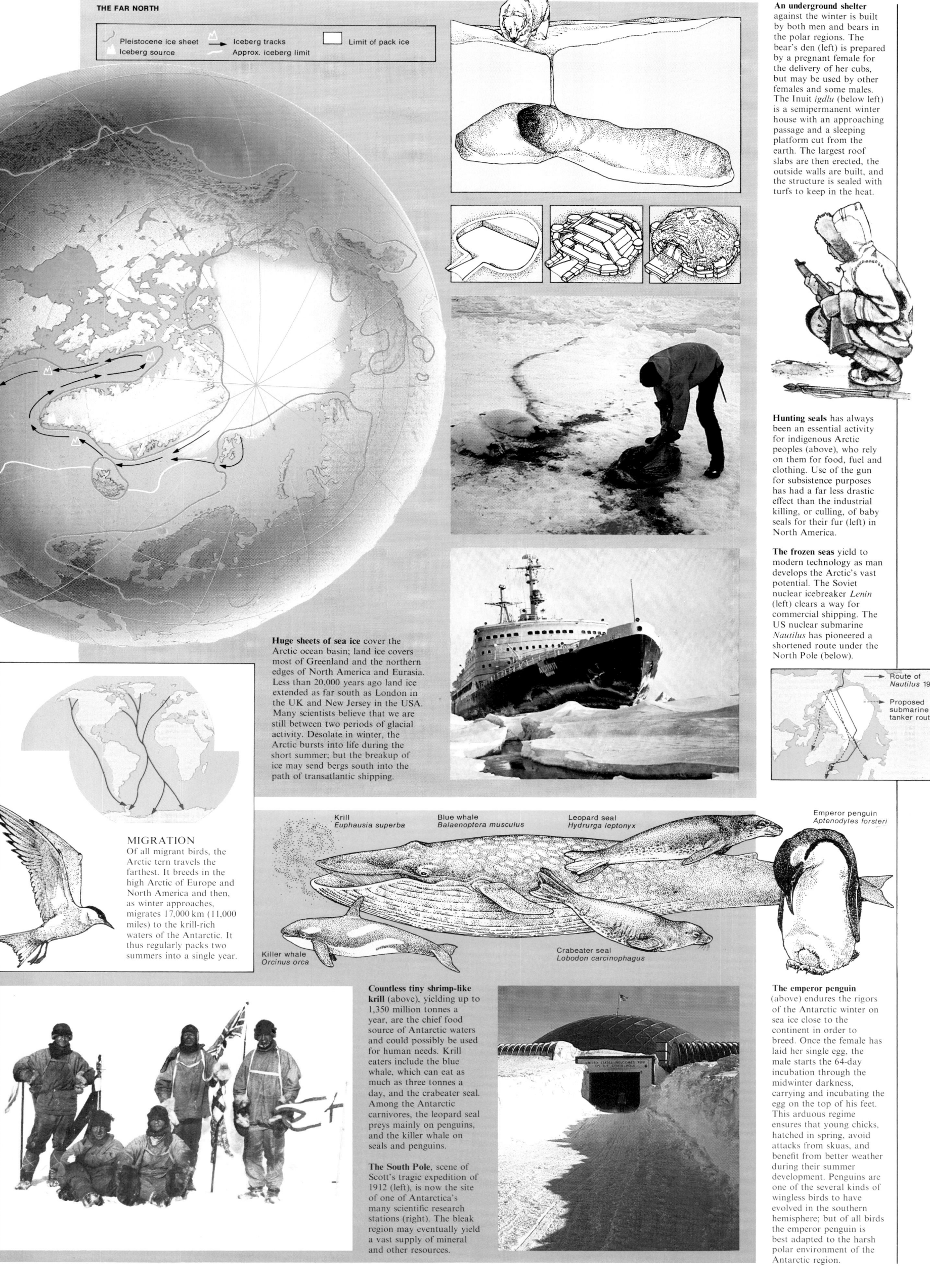

Pleistocene ice sheet → Iceberg tracks ☐ Limit of pack ice

⌂ Iceberg source → Approx. iceberg limit

An underground shelter against the winter is built by both men and bears in the polar regions. The bear's den (left) is prepared by a pregnant female for the delivery of her cubs, but may be used by other females and some males. The Inuit *igdlu* (below left) is a semipermanent winter house with an approaching passage and a sleeping platform cut from the earth. The largest roof slabs are then erected, the outside walls are built, and the structure is sealed with turfs to keep in the heat.

Hunting seals has always been an essential activity for indigenous Arctic peoples (above), who rely on them for food, fuel and clothing. Use of the gun for subsistence purposes has had a far less drastic effect than the industrial killing, or culling, of baby seals for their fur (left) in North America.

The frozen seas yield to modern technology as man develops the Arctic's vast potential. The Soviet nuclear icebreaker *Lenin* (left) clears a way for commercial shipping. The US nuclear submarine *Nautilus* has pioneered a shortened route under the North Pole (below).

Huge sheets of sea ice cover the Arctic ocean basin; land ice covers most of Greenland and the northern edges of North America and Eurasia. Less than 20,000 years ago land ice extended as far south as London in the UK and New Jersey in the USA. Many scientists believe that we are still between two periods of glacial activity. Desolate in winter, the Arctic bursts into life during the short summer; but the breakup of ice may send bergs south into the path of transatlantic shipping.

→ Route of *Nautilus* 1958

⇢ Proposed submarine tanker routes

MIGRATION
Of all migrant birds, the Arctic tern travels the farthest. It breeds in the high Arctic of Europe and North America and then, as winter approaches, migrates 17,000 km (11,000 miles) to the krill-rich waters of the Antarctic. It thus regularly packs two summers into a single year.

Krill
Euphausia superba

Blue whale
Balaenoptera musculus

Leopard seal
Hydrurga leptonyx

Emperor penguin
Aptenodytes forsteri

Killer whale
Orcinus orca

Crabeater seal
Lobodon carcinophagus

Countless tiny shrimp-like krill (above), yielding up to 1,350 million tonnes a year, are the chief food source of Antarctic waters and could possibly be used for human needs. Krill eaters include the blue whale, which can eat as much as three tonnes a day, and the crabeater seal. Among the Antarctic carnivores, the leopard seal preys mainly on penguins, and the killer whale on seals and penguins.

The South Pole, scene of Scott's tragic expedition of 1912 (left), is now the site of one of Antarctica's many scientific research stations (right). The bleak region may eventually yield a vast supply of mineral and other resources.

The emperor penguin (above) endures the rigors of the Antarctic winter on sea ice close to the continent in order to breed. Once the female has laid her single egg, the male starts the 64-day incubation through the midwinter darkness, carrying and incubating the egg on the top of his feet. This arduous regime ensures that young chicks, hatched in spring, avoid attacks from skuas, and benefit from better weather during their summer development. Penguins are one of the several kinds of wingless birds to have evolved in the southern hemisphere; but of all birds the emperor penguin is best adapted to the harsh polar environment of the Antarctic region.

Tundra and Taiga

Tundra is land that has been exposed for only about 8,000 years, since the retreat of the ice caps, and only relatively recently occupied by plants. In consequence, few plants and animals have yet had time to adapt to the virtually soilless and treeless environment. The less rigorous conditions of neighboring taiga forest allow a longer growing season and a somewhat wider range of species. The delicately balanced ecology of both areas is being increasingly threatened, however, by the activities of man.

"Tundra," from a Lapp word meaning "rolling, treeless plain," defines the narrow band of open, low ground that surrounds the Arctic Ocean. It lies north of the line beyond which the temperature of the warmest month usually fails to reach 10°C (50°F). North of this trees do not generally grow well, so the line forms a natural frontier between tundra and the broad band of coniferous forest that circles the northern hemisphere to its south between about 60°N and 48°N. This forest, forming the world's largest and most uninterrupted area of vegetation, is usually referred to by its Russian name of "taiga."

Cheerless landscapes
The tundra presents a desolate and restrictive environment for most of the year: in winter there are several months of semidarkness. While there is considerable variation in the climates of places at the same latitude, temperatures average only −5°C (23°F) and are well below freezing for many months of the year. Frost-free days are restricted to a few weeks in midsummer and even then, although days are warmer, the sun is never high in the sky. Nearly all tundra has been free from ice for only a few thousand years. As a result, it either has no soil at all or has developed only a thin covering of

sandy, muddy or peaty soil, successfully colonized by only a few types of plants.

Trimmed by such grazing animals as hares, musk oxen and reindeer or caribou, and by strong winds carrying abrasive rock dust and ice particles, typical tundra vegetation forms a low, patchy mat a few centimeters deep. Much of it grows on permafrost — ground that thaws superficially in summer but remains perennially frozen beneath the surface. Here drainage is poor, shallow ponds are frequent and the scanty soils tend to be waterlogged and acidic. Nevertheless, a small number of grasses, sedges, mosses and marsh plants may grow well and the summer tundra in flower can be an impressive sight. Knee-high forests of dwarf birch, willow and alder grow in valleys sheltered from the strong and biting wind.

The taiga also is a dark and monotonous habitat. Again, while there is a good deal of variation in climatic conditions, on average the region has somewhat milder summers than the tundra with mean average temperatures of 2–6°C (34–42°F), less wind and a slightly longer growing season. The taiga is mostly older than the tundra, and its soils have had longer to mature. They support a small number of tree species, with coniferous spruce, pine, fir and

larch predominating. Short-season broadleaves such as willows, alders, birches and poplars tend to occur on the better soils of river valleys and the edges of forest lakes.

Animals of the far north
The number of animal species supported throughout the year by tundra and taiga is also comparatively small, with interdependent populations that may fluctuate wildly from season to season. In winter both tundra and taiga are silent, although far from deserted. Mice, voles and lemmings remain active, living in tunnels under the snow, which keeps them well insulated from the wind and subzero temperatures. Above the snow Arctic hares forage; they tend to gather in snow-free areas where food can still be found. Arctic foxes are mainly tundra animals and the musk oxen, too, winter on high, exposed tundra where their dense, shaggy coats protect them from the worst

The circumpolar north that surrounds the permanently frozen ice cap is dominated by tundra—open plain that remains snowfree for only several months in the summer—and taiga, the vast coniferous forest stretching right round the northern hemisphere. The Siberian taiga, for example, is one-third larger than the entire United States.

□ Tundra   □ Taiga

Producers
■ USSR
■ USA

Man's pursuit of resources has accelerated in the past two decades, with the former Soviet Union drastically increasing its outflow of both oil and gas since 1970. North American output has lagged far behind, mainly because the need for exploration and exploitation has only recently become important. In all tundra and taiga areas, gas did not start flowing until the early 1960s. The former Soviet Union's coal output has been rising steadily while that of North America has fluctuated. (In these figures, North America is composed of Alaska and the Yukon and Northwest territories. The former Soviet Union is more loosely defined as "regions of the far north".)

Oil ('000 tonnes)
Coal ('000 tonnes)
Natural gas (1,000,000,000 cu m)

Pollution of Lake Baikal, the world's deepest freshwater lake, is being increasingly threatened by man's indifference to its unique position as a freshwater reservoir. Increasing exploitation of the Siberian taiga for minerals and timber has led to the pollution of the 300 or so rivers discharging effluents into the lake.

Siberian spruce
Picea obovata

Common crossbill
Loxia curvirostra

Adaptation to severe cold by trees of the taiga includes their conical forms that allow snow to be shed easily, and narrow needleleaves that reduce water loss to a minimum. Seeds are protected by closed woody cones; opened by crossbills, they provide a constant supply of food during winter.

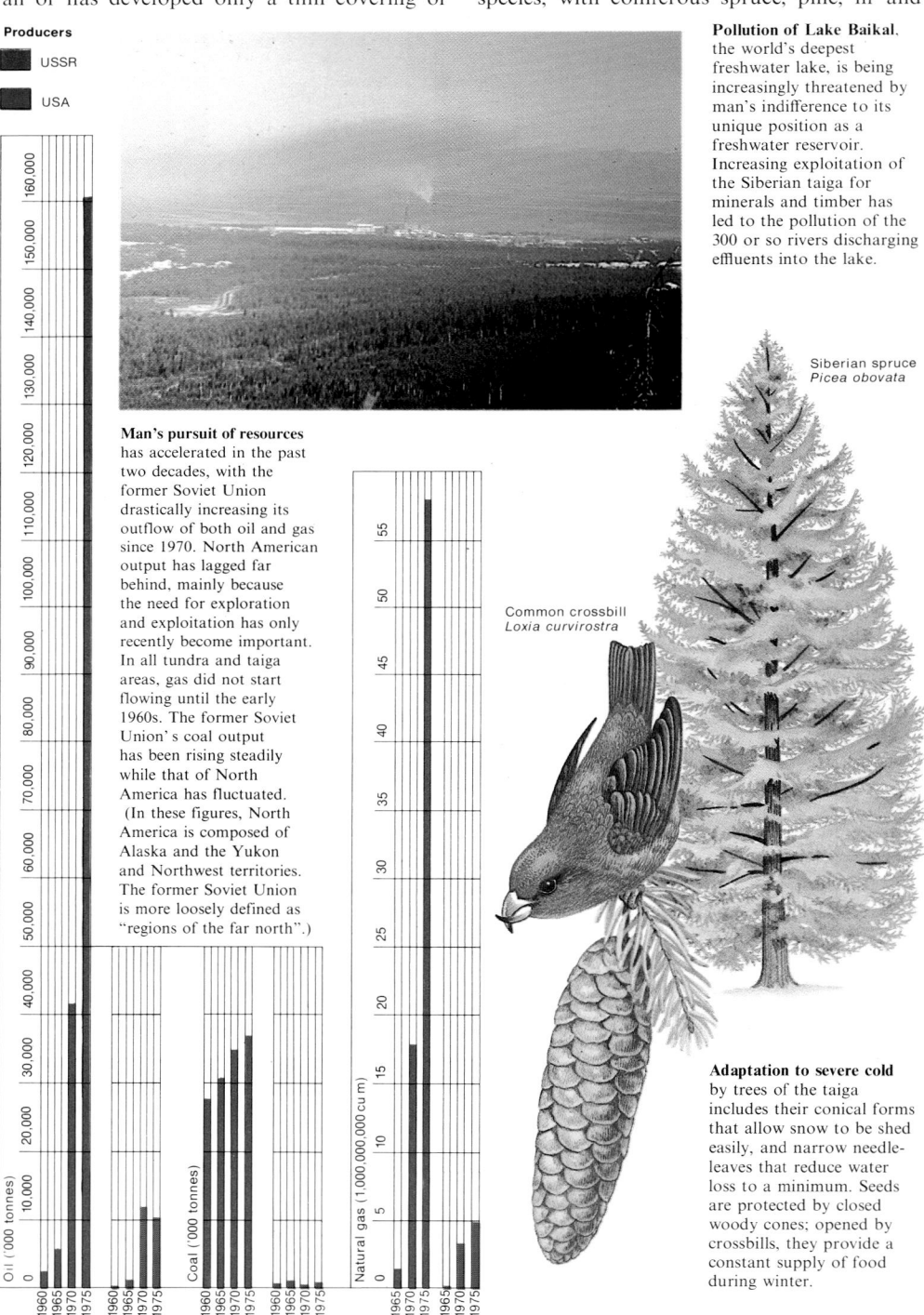

Reindeer or caribou
Rangifer tarandus

Raven
Corvus corax

Arctic fox
Alopex lagopus

Capercaillie
Tetrao urogallus

Snowy owl
Nyctea scandiaca

Brown lemming
Lemmus lemmus

Arctic skua
Stercorarius parasiticus

January
February
March
April
May
June

Movement in these regions takes many directions. The capercaillie spends all winter in the taiga, where it thrives on the abundant conifer needles, buds and shoots. Some move southward into deciduous woods during the summer months. The Arctic skua breeds on the tundra but moves to the warmer oceans in winter, while the tundra movements of the all-scavenging raven and the snowy owl are governed by those of their

prey. The raven picks clean the carcasses left by other predators; the snowy owl feeds on small rodents such as mice and lemmings, as does the Arctic fox. Lemmings remain static and inconspicuous in normal years but some populations expand rapidly every third or fourth year, leading to mass local migration in every direction, possibly caused by an abundance of vegetation that encourages more frequent breeding.

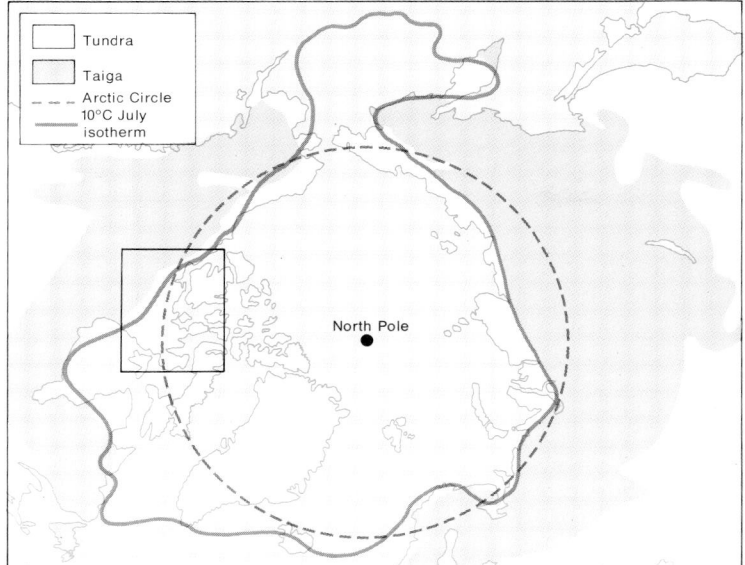

Legend:
- Tundra
- Taiga
- Arctic Circle
- 10°C July isotherm

North Pole

The rough boundary between the tundra and taiga—the tree line—approximates to the 10°C July isotherm, the climatic point north of which trees fail to grow successfully. Seasonal caribou migration in the Canadian barren grounds (boxed) is shown in the main diagram below). Such migration is also undertaken by reindeer in northern Eurasia.

weather. Bears, badgers, beavers and squirrels are common taiga mammals. Elk and reindeer (in North America, moose and caribou) winter in the shelter of the taiga; wolves are mostly woodland animals in winter, following their prey to the open tundra in spring. Red foxes, coyotes, mink and wolverines also move to the tundra in summer.

Snow buntings, ptarmigans and snowy owls live on the tundra throughout the coldest months and are fully adapted to life there. Crossbills and capercaillies are among taiga residents, equipped to live on its abundant conifer buds, seeds and needles. Enormous populations of migrant birds, especially water birds and waders, fly north to both tundra and taiga with the spring thaw. Waxwings, bramblings, siskins and redpolls leave their temperate latitudes to feed on the lush and fast-growing vegetation and the profusion of insects that appear as soon as the snows begin to melt.

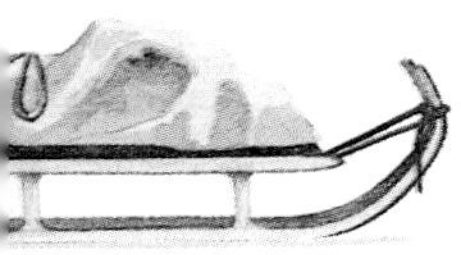

Many Norwegian Lapps (or Samer) derive their income from reindeer, which they domesticated many centuries ago to provide meat, milk and skins. Now they follow them through the seasons along well-worn and familiar routes. Such nomadic life styles are becoming rarer as Samer settle down.

Man in the northlands

These circumpolar regions separate the world's greatest centers of population. They are now crisscrossed with air routes. A total population of about nine million people currently inhabits the tundra and taiga. Numbers have been increased by the immigration of technicians and administrators during the last few decades; oil prospecting and mining, forest exploitation and other activities of these newcomers is altering the seminomadic lives of the million or so aboriginal peoples such as the Khanty (Ostyaks) and Nentsy (Samoyeds) of Russia, the Samer (Lapps) of Scandinavia and Russia, and the Inuit (formerly Eskimos) of North America. New roads, exploitation of minerals and forests, and pipeline construction have disrupted the migration of their reindeer (caribou) and their land has been appropriated for hydroelectric schemes.

In the taiga, Russia is constructing railroads

and towns and extracting huge amounts of timber; they have prospected widely and successfully for gold, nickel, iron, tin, mica, diamonds and tungsten, and have discovered vast reserves of oil and natural gas in western Siberia. Alaskan oil, discovered in 1968, now flows across the state at 54–62°C (130–145°F), and to protect the permafrost from this heat the pipeline has had to be elevated for half its 1,300 km (800 mile) length. The pipe's route to the ice-free port of Valdez has interfered with the migration of caribou; hunting and other pressures have led to a drop in their population from three million to some 200,000 in about 30 years. Only official protection has saved the musk ox from a similar fate. These bleak areas are so vast and inhospitable that living space there will never be threatened. However, if only on a local scale, their ecologies are under increasing pressure from man.

The summer tundra—seen here in Swedish Lapland—provides a wide cover of low plants including "reindeer mosses" and other lichens. Grazing reindeer return minerals to the soil. Shallow ponds form as the frozen ground above the permafrost thaws for a few months in summer. Mountains stay partly snow covered in the warmest weather and are a prominent physical feature of the tundra.

MOVEMENT THROUGH THE SEASONS

Life on tundra and taiga is dominated by the mark of the seasons. In this diagrammatic representation of the north–south migration of the American caribou, each block represents the same area of terrain through the 12 months of the year. From February to April, the caribou move north in a steady file from the forest, emerging to eat the newly exposed lichen and moving to grounds where calving takes place in late May and early June. In the summer months they disperse freely before returning south in smaller groups on a broader front in late July and August. Rutting and mating take place in October/early November before the caribou regain the shelter of the taiga.

Musk ox
Ovibos moschatus

Rock ptarmigan
Lagopus mutus

Arctic hare
Lepus arcticus

Brent goose
Branta bernicla

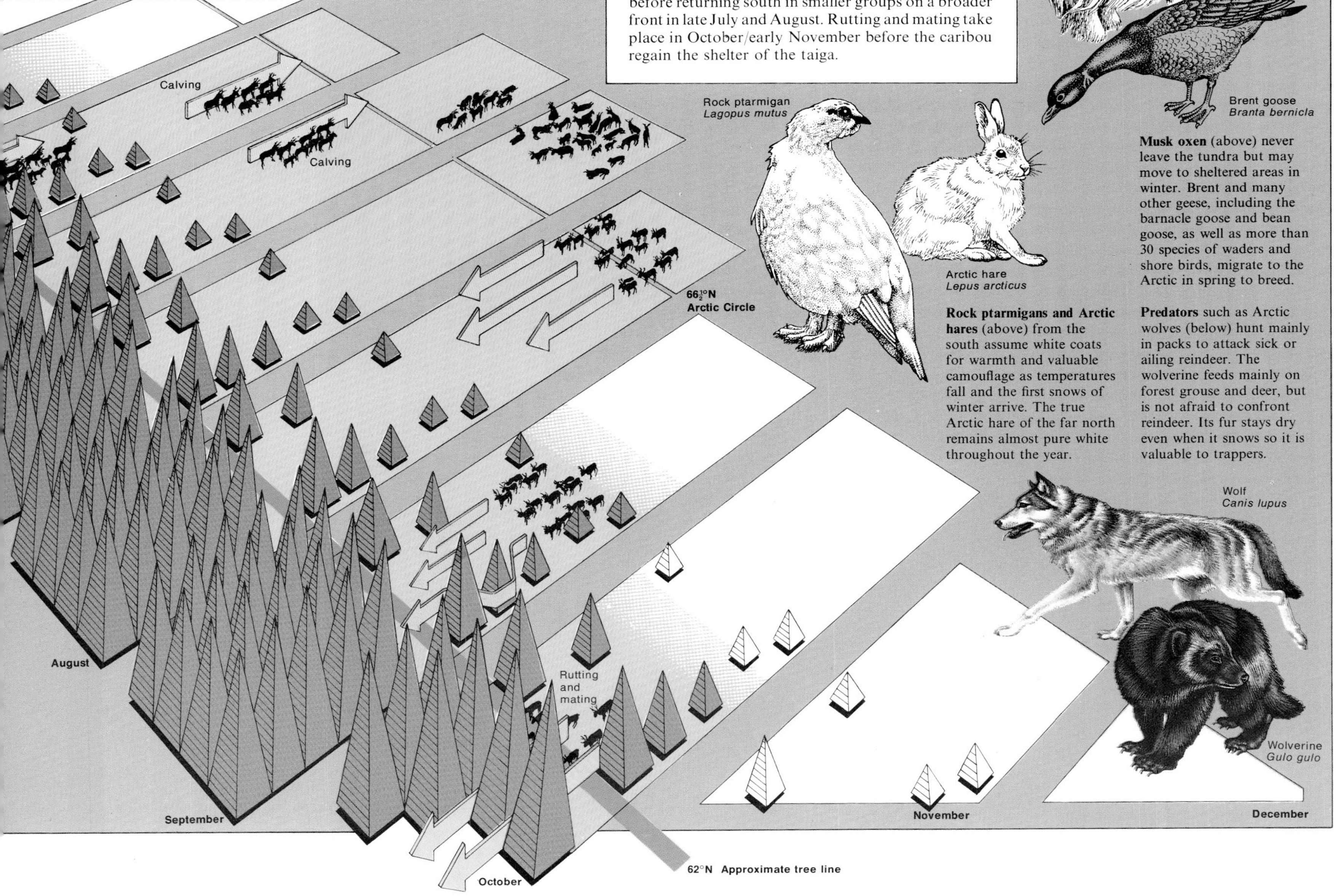

Musk oxen (above) never leave the tundra but may move to sheltered areas in winter. Brent and many other geese, including the barnacle goose and bean goose, as well as more than 30 species of waders and shore birds, migrate to the Arctic in spring to breed.

Rock ptarmigans and Arctic hares (above) from the south assume white coats for warmth and valuable camouflage as temperatures fall and the first snows of winter arrive. The true Arctic hare of the far north remains almost pure white throughout the year.

Predators such as Arctic wolves (below) hunt mainly in packs to attack sick or ailing reindeer. The wolverine feeds mainly on forest grouse and deer, but is not afraid to confront reindeer. Its fur stays dry even when it snows so it is valuable to trappers.

Wolf
Canis lupus

Wolverine
Gulo gulo

Calving

66½°N
Arctic Circle

Rutting and mating

August

September

October

November

December

62°N Approximate tree line

Temperate Forests

At one time, dense, primeval forests blanketed large areas of North America, Europe and eastern Asia. Almost all of the trees that flourished in these temperate regions were deciduous – they shed their leaves in autumn, stood bare branched through winter and produced new foliage every spring. Little of this forest now exists. The few remaining pockets, however, still provide habitats for a large range of shade-loving plants: lichens and fungi, tree-hugging mosses, scrambling creepers and shrubs. And this vegetation in turn provides sanctuary for a surprisingly wide variety of forest creatures.

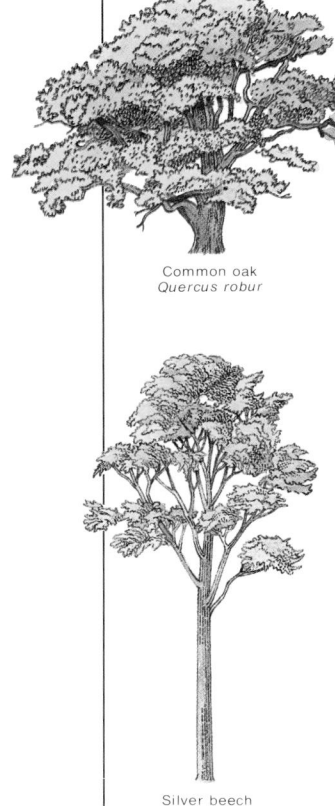

Common oak
Quercus robur

Silver beech
Nothofagus menziesii

Deciduous trees such as the oak (top) make up the temperate forests in cooler temperate regions. In milder, wetter climates, where the seasons are less distinct, evergreens such as southern beech (above) are typical temperate species.

The greater part of the temperate forest zone lies in the northern hemisphere, where winter soil temperatures reduce the ability of plants to absorb water. Hence the trees tend to shed their leaves, which use up moisture through evaporation. In the southern hemisphere, however, the temperate latitudes encourage a type of rainforest in such areas as southern Chile, Tasmania, New Zealand and parts of southeastern Australia. Here the climate is maritime, often with high rainfall and frequent fogs, and evergreen rather than deciduous types of trees grow. Temperate rainforests also occur in the northern hemisphere, in China and in northwestern and northeastern North America.

Deciduous forest consists of a mixture of trees, sometimes with one variety predominant. In central Europe, beech is the leading—and sometimes the only—tree species, whereas oaks mixed with other species made up the forest farther west and east. In North America, beech and maple were once extensive.

The climate in temperate forest zones varies sharply according to seasons—summers tend to be warm, winters moderately cold, and rainfall fairly regular. In fact, the seasonal rhythm is a central feature of temperate forests, and it affects the entire ecosystem—the whole community of plants and animals found there. Soils are generally of the fertile "brown earth" type: the leaf litter of deciduous forests in particular breaks down easily, and is quickly worked into the soil by burrowing animals such as earthworms. In wetter or rockier regions, the soil is more "podsolic"—bleached, sandy and less fertile than the true brown earths.

After the ice
Two million years ago, a series of ice sheets began to extend into the temperate latitudes. In Europe, species moving south before the advancing cold were cut off from the warmer climates by the east–west run of mountains. As a result, many varieties of plants and animals

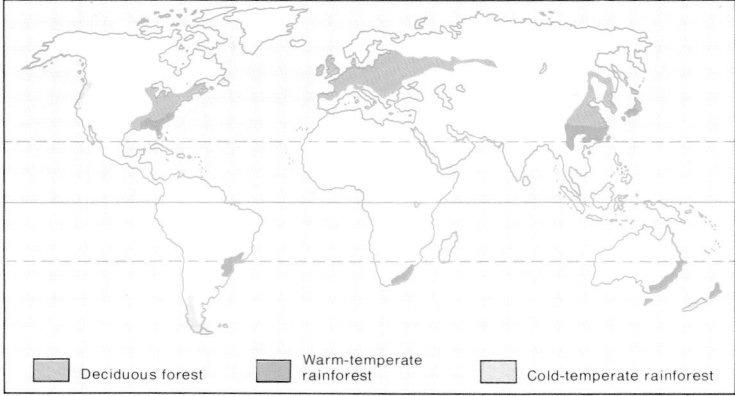

Deciduous forest | Warm-temperate rainforest | Cold-temperate rainforest

Natural distribution: in the northern hemisphere's temperate zone deciduous forests occur in the cooler areas—in eastern USA, northeastern China, Korea, the northern parts of Japan's Honshu island and western Europe. These forests only give way to evergreens in the warmer and wetter parts of the zone. In the southern hemisphere, the climate is generally rather milder throughout the temperate zone and so there are virtually no deciduous forests. Evergreen forests, however, can be found in southeastern South Africa, Chile, New Zealand, Australia and Tasmania.

the eastern USA. But a combination of climatic change and, more recently and importantly, of intense human activity, has meant that the remnants of temperate forest seen today differ greatly from the original forest in both composition and form. Only in remote regions such as the southern Appalachian Mountains do substantial areas of the original forest survive. Elsewhere, regrowth has occurred, but much of this is essentially scrub woodland.

The forest structure
Mature temperate deciduous forest is made up of distinct horizontal layers, particularly where the dominant tree is the oak, which allows enough light for a rich shrub layer to grow beneath it. The largest trees, such as oak, maple or ash, may be 25–50 m (80–160 ft) tall, and beneath them grows a prominent layer of smaller trees such as hazel, hornbeam or yew. Lower down again, a varied ground cover of perennial herbs, ferns, lichens and mosses flourishes in the comparative dampness of the forest floor. Because the trees are bare of leaves in winter, many of the plants growing on the forest floor take advantage of the warmth and light of spring to flower early in the year before the main trees come into full leaf and prevent the sun from reaching them. Various woody climbers, such as ivy and honeysuckle, are also present, growing over the trees and shrubs.

Much of the food supply in temperate forests is locked up in the trees themselves, but the annual fall of leaves in the deciduous forests produces a soil rich in nourishment. This supports a vast quantity of life, ranging in size from earthworms and insects to microscopic bacteria of the soil. The death of individual trees and branches also releases the food supply back to the earth. In shady, damp locations, insects, fungi, bacteria and other decomposing agents break down the leaves and other plant and animal debris more quickly, returning them to the soil as food for new plants.

Creatures of the forest
Temperate forests once contained many varieties of animal life, including several species of large animals. Herbivores such as wild oxen, wood bison, elk and moose ate grass and leaves; scavengers such as wild pigs rooted in the forest floor; predators such as wolves preyed on the other animals. Most of these have now been hunted to extinction by man or are extremely rare. Smaller animals still survive in comparatively large numbers, and include squirrels, chipmunks and raccoons, hedgehogs, wood mice, badgers and foxes.

The bird life of temperate forests is very diverse. Some species are insect eaters, exploring the bark and crevices for insects and grubs. Others, such as the wood pigeon, concentrate on seeds. Yet others, like the tawny owl, are predators. Complex interactions between predators and prey have developed at all levels of the forest, from the high canopy to the rotting ground litter, with each group evolving more efficient techniques of capture or escape in a kind of evolutionary race for survival.

The invertebrate insect life is also extremely varied and numerous, and forms a key component of the ecosystem. Oaks are particularly rich in insect life, and more than 100 species of moths feed on their leaves.

The plant and animal life of the temperate forest is remarkably rich and plentiful. And yet it is only a fraction of what once existed. Ever since man has occupied these regions he has found them so suited to his needs that he has long since cleared most of the original tree cover, replaced it with "civilization" and, in the process, destroyed innumerable species of forest wildlife.

were killed off. Species were reduced still further in islands such as Britain, where the newly formed barriers of the English Channel, Irish Sea and North Sea made recolonization even more difficult after the ice had retreated.

Eastern Asia was one of the few areas in the world that escaped the extreme climatic changes of the ice ages and therefore its temperate forests, unlike those of Europe, still contain an enormous variety of tree species. North America also fared better than Europe, for although glaciers at one time extended deep into the continent, the north–south direction of the mountain ranges allowed relatively easy migration of trees southwards as the climate worsened. Hence most species survived and were able to reoccupy their former territories when the ice retreated. As a result, some 40 species of deciduous trees occur in the North American forests, and contribute to the spectacular display of color during the autumn, notably in

THE SEASONAL CYCLE
It is the cycle of the four seasons that gives the temperate deciduous forest its distinctive character. All animals and plants have adapted their ways of life to cope with the seasonal changes in heat, light, moisture and food. The yearly shedding and regrowth of the forest's leaves is one of the most striking and important of adaptations to the seasonal cycle and one that affects all other life in the forest. In summer the leafy canopy of the trees blocks out the sunlight from the forest floor and creates unsuitable conditions for many other plants to flourish. When the leaves fall they form a layer over the soil and provide winter protection for the plant roots and hibernating animals beneath the ground. Finally, once the dead leaves have been broken down, they give fertility to the soil and provide food for future generations of plants.

SPRING

Between February and April, the low spring sun climbs steadily higher in the sky and, streaming through the still leafless branches of the trees, falls more directly on the forest floor, warming the soil and melting the last frosts. As soon as the days become warmer the sluggish sap in the trees begins to flow more quickly, carrying nutrients to the branches, where leaf buds start to form.

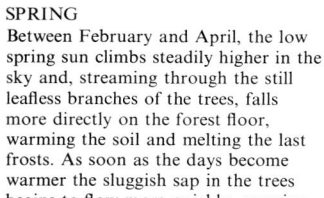

Small plants of the forest floor, such as European bluebells and hepaticas taking advantage of the warm soil and plentiful light, flower in spring.

Bluebell
Endymion non-scriptus

Hepatica
Hepatica nobilis

Forest insects emerge in spring, some, such as the emperor moth, from their winter cocoons, some from hibernation and some newly hatched from eggs.

Small emperor moth
Saturnia pavonia

European blackbird *Turdus merula*

Birds building nests in early spring make use of the forest's winter litter— broken twigs, dead leaves and dried grasses all serve as construction materials.

Woodchuck *Marmota monax*

Western European hedgehog
Erinaceus europaeus

White-tailed deer
Odocoileus virginianus

New plant growth and the increase in insects provide food for such animals as the North American woodchuck and the European hedgehog that wake thin and hungry from months of hibernation. Deer and other non-hibernating animals are also weak and thin— indeed many may have died during the harsh weather. The spring birth of young, however, soon restores their numbers.

SUMMER

By early summer the leaves of the trees are fully grown. They form a dense canopy, blocking out the sun and cooling the soil of the forest floor. Most of the small ground plants have long since finished flowering, but their leaves remain green and they continue actively storing food in their roots ready for their rapid spring growth.

Cranberry *Vaccinium oxycoccus*

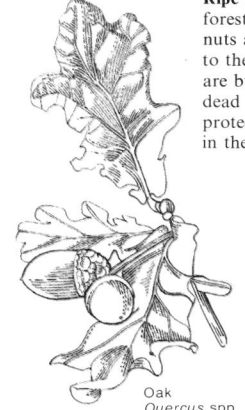
Bramble
Rubus spp

Shrubs and bushes, such as bramble and cranberry, form tangled flowering masses wherever sunlight manages to filter through the forest's gloomy canopy.

Hordes of insects inhabit the forest in summer, living off the vast supply of food plants. The European stag beetle feeds on the sap of chestnut and oak trees.

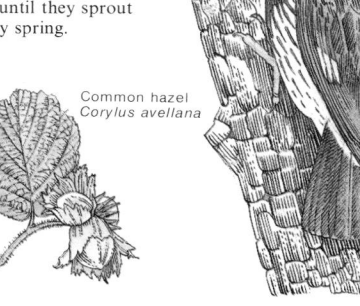
Stag beetle
Lucanus cervus

Willow warbler
Phylloscopus trochilus

The North American pewee and the willow warbler are two of the forest's many summer visitors that feed on the insect population. Some seed-eating birds, finches for example, also take advantage of this summer food supply.

Eastern wood pewee
Contopus virens

Hazel mouse
Muscardinus avellanarius

The hazel mouse protects its young by raising them in a summer nest, which it builds in a tree: almost every creature in the forest is viewed as a source of food by some other animal and the young litters are particularly at risk.

AUTUMN

As the autumn days grow shorter and cooler the forest foliage begins to turn color; the trees are responding to the drop in temperature and are cutting off the food supply to their leaves, which lose their green color and fall to the ground, forming a thick carpet on the forest's floor. Rain, frost, insects, earthworms and fungi then break down the leaves, making them part of the fertile forest soil.

Ripe fruits and seeds of the forest trees—acorns, beech nuts and hazel nuts—drop to the ground, where a few are buried in the layers of dead leaves and remain protected until they sprout in the early spring.

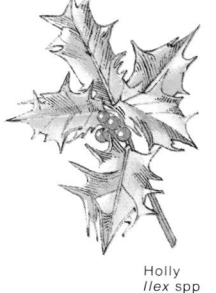
Common hazel
Corylus avellana

Oak
Quercus spp

Preparing for winter, the acorn woodpecker stores seeds in holes that it drills in tree trunks. Chipmunks hide supplies of nuts in their winter nests.

Acorn woodpecker
Melanerpes formicivorus

American black bear
Ursus americanus

Eastern chipmunk
Tamias striatus

The black bear of North America, like other winter hibernators, consumes vast quantities of food during autumn to build up its winter stores of food in the form of body fat.

WINTER

By winter, only evergreen shrubs and a few small hardy plants remain green. Many of the plants of the forest floor lose their green leaves during the first deep frost. The leaves of the trees still lie rotting on the bare ground, but within the soil, beneath the protective layers of leaf litter, plants are growing and spring flowers are developing buds.

Late-fruiting plants, such as holly, mistletoe and dog rose, provide food for winter residents of the temperate forest such as the European hawfinch.

Hawfinch
Coccothraustes coccothraustes

Holly
Ilex spp

Woodcocks are insect-eaters. They can survive winter by prizing insects from the soil with their long beaks, providing that the ground is not too deeply frozen.

European woodcock
Scolopax rusticola

Owls and foxes remain fairly active in winter, regularly leaving their nests or lairs to catch small animals or birds that are also in search of food.

North American screech owl
Otus asio

Red fox
Vulpes vulpes

European badger
Meles meles

European badgers, like racoons, opossums, bears and skunks, are "shallow" hibernators. On mild winter days they wake and go to search for food.

THE EVERGREEN TEMPERATE RAINFORESTS

There are two main kinds of temperate rainforest, the warm temperate, such as can still be found on North Island, New Zealand (left), and the cold temperate, such as that of the Chilean coast. Both of these kinds of forest have one major feature in common: they have enough water for even the most moisture-greedy plants, such as mosses and ferns, to grow throughout the year. The animal life of the forest is also affected by the abundance of rain, so that snails, slugs, frogs and other water-loving creatures flourish. Most temperate rainforest is of the warm-temperate kind, normally found on the edges of subtropical regions, and the vegetation, with palms, lianas, bamboos, as well as ferns and mosses, is similar to, although less rich than, the tropical rainforest's vegetation. The cold-temperate rainforests grow in cooler regions but their coastal position means that the climate is milder and wetter than inland (where deciduous trees dominate). Their vegetation is less lush and less varied than the warm-temperate forests, but mosses and ferns grow in abundance. Broad-leaved evergreens, such as New Zealand's southern beech, are the most common trees of these forests, although on the northwestern coast of North America Douglas firs and other conifers outnumber the broad-leaved evergreen species.

Man and the Temperate Forests

Temperate forests have suffered enormously at the hands of man. For the great civilizations of China, Europe and, later, North America the forests not only yielded cropland for expanding populations but also contributed materials and fuel for early technologies. More recently the demands of industry have reduced the forests still further. But today, scientists believe that this depleted resource could again play an important role in providing energy, food and materials for future generations.

PERMANENT SETTLEMENT
The Bronze Age and, later, the Iron Age laid the foundations of Chinese and Western civilizations. The forest shrank as permanent settlements grew (3) and, with the use of metals and improved technology, agricultural land was extended (4). But the forest was recognized as an important resource and areas were protected. Management techniques were introduced that, especially in medieval Europe, changed dense forest to coppice woods (5).

EARLY INDUSTRIAL TIMES
Sources of cropland and timber had been discovered in the New World, but in the Far East and Europe forests were drastically reduced. Virtually no Chinese forest remained, and in Europe nations began importing timber to serve growing industrial needs (6). To help solve shortages, plantations were established on country estates (7), which were often landscaped into parkland and planted with introduced species of trees (8).

PREHISTORIC FORESTS
Hunter gatherers made clearings in the forest when they cut brushwood for building shelters and for fuel (1): human impact on the temperate forest was small. But 7,000 years ago in Europe, 6,000 years ago in eastern Asia and 1,000 years ago in eastern North America, the first farming communities of the temperate forest (2) began to clear larger pockets of forest to provide land for crops and timber for houses and tools.

The aurochs, or wild ox, was one of the many forest animals that provided food for early hunter gatherers. Once man began to farm the land, he domesticated some of these animals—the wild boar, the aurochs and the wild turkey.

The dwellings of the late Neolithic Chinese were relatively sophisticated, reflecting an increasingly settled way of life that was soon to alter the landscape as forests were felled to provide building materials and land to plant crops.

The fortified villages and the farms of the Eastern Woodland Indians were set in semipermanent clearings cut in the North American forest. Before European settlement, however, human populations were small and deforestation was negligible.

Grain harvesting is depicted in a Chinese tomb image. By the 1st century AD, China contained nearly 60 million people, and agriculture, along with stock raising and metal mining, was drastically depleting the tree cover.

Coppicing and pollarding allowed continual cropping of forests. Branches were cut from trees, the bases of which were left to regrow shoots. This technique reduced the density of tree cover, encouraging a richer growth of ground plants.

Coppicing

Pollarding

Production of charcoal (below), which was a basic raw material for smelting in early industrial times, was responsible for much deforestation of the land.

Human interference with the forests goes back deep into prehistory. There is evidence that fire was used to stampede hunted animals in southern Europe as long as 400,000 years ago. Human populations, while they remained small, had only a slight effect on the vast stretches of primeval forest. Even so, hunting practices and the use of fire to clear land reduced some of the forests of Europe and Asia even before the invention of agriculture. In the New World, too, Eastern Woodland Indians had already affected the North American forests, and early Maori hunters had burned much of the tree cover of New Zealand by the time Europeans arrived.

Nevertheless it was the development of agriculture in Neolithic (New Stone Age) times that had the first really destructive effect on the temperate forests. Clearings were made for crops and the felled trees provided fuel and building material for the new communities. Large forest animals suffered as well, some (such as deer) being hunted for food and others (such as wolves) because they threatened grazing animals. But it was the population increase resulting from the new, settled way of life that caused the extension of man-made cropland deep into former forests.

With man's development of metals, more forests were destroyed: wood and charcoal were used for smelting and the new iron tools made tree clearance easier and more thorough. Firing of forests was also a familiar military ploy, used by such warriors as the Romans.

Medieval woodlands
By medieval times, large tracts of forest had been cleared in Europe and in the Far East, although in the former area there remained extensive royal hunting forest reserves. Local woodlands were carefully managed to serve the needs of the community; the techniques used included pollarding and coppicing.

Pollarding involved the cropping of main branches at a certain height above ground. In coppicing, the "coppice with standards" method was used to harvest the smaller species, such as hazel and hornbeam, whereas the standards (such as oaks) were cut on a longer rotation of 100 years or so. Alternatively, the oak itself could be part of the coppice crop, its stems being cut near ground level so that shoots arose from the stump, to be cut 10 to 20 years later. For local communities, industries and cities, forests provided a variety of materials for building, tanning and fencing, as well as dye-stuffs, charcoal and domestic fuel.

The growth of the iron and shipbuilding industries in the sixteenth century devastated so much woodland and forest that in many regions good timber became scarce and had to be imported from considerable distances. The pressure on woodland continued until the production of coke and cheap coal brought some relaxation, but by the early twentieth century the coppice system had broken down and management of Europe's woodlands had largely been abandoned. In Europe the poor state of the deciduous forests was further worsened by two world wars. Many countries have since set up organizations with the specific task of building reserves of timber. Economic pressures, however, have led to the planting mainly of quick-growing conifers, rather than typical trees of the temperate deciduous forest.

New World forests
The migrants who settled in the New World were the descendants of the people who had largely destroyed the forests of Europe. Confronted by the temperate deciduous forests of eastern North America, they virtually continued where they had left off. Tracts were cleared to create arable and range land and to provide the massive amounts of timber needed for the colonization, industrialization and urbanization of North America. With the opening of the prairie lands for agriculture, however,

Disturbance to the natural vegetation has occurred throughout the temperate forest zone. Exploitation of this biome's greatest resource, its agricultural potential, has been one of the major causes of deforestation. The only forests that have escaped major disturbance are in remote areas, too rocky or too steep for cultivation. Today, intensive farming is still a major economic activity of the temperate forest regions. But farmland is not the only important resource to have disturbed the forests. Mining for key minerals such as copper, iron and coal, all of which made possible the development of Western and Chinese civilization, has also contributed to destruction of the forest cover. For centuries the forests provided man with food, fuel and materials, but, ironically, it has been the removal of the forest that has enabled man to exploit the most important of these regions' resources.

THE CHANGING LANDSCAPE

Mankind has been occupying the temperate forest regions for many thousands of years, at first with little effect on the natural forest ecology. But during the last 2,000 years human activity has destroyed the original tree cover at an accelerating pace. As populations increased and economies developed —at different rates in the three major regions— forests disappeared to be replaced by farms, cities, industries and communications networks. Today, scarcely any of the original forest cover remains.

THE 19TH CENTURY
The Industrial Revolution developed in Europe and the New World, large towns and cities sprang up (9), pushing back the woodlands and forests still farther. This process was aided by the spreading network of railroads (10). Coke, iron and other minerals were replacing timber products as raw materials for growing industries (11), but demands were still made on the forests to provide, for example, railway sleepers and mine pit props.

FORESTS TODAY
The 20th century has seen an increasing trend towards urbanization in areas that were once temperate forest. Housing complexes (12) and new factory sites (13) cover large areas, while roadbuilding (14), industrial agriculture (15) and open-cast mining (16) destroy remaining woodland. Leisure areas (17) and nature reserves protect some woods, but plantations of exotic conifers (18) do not always provide suitable wildlife habitats.

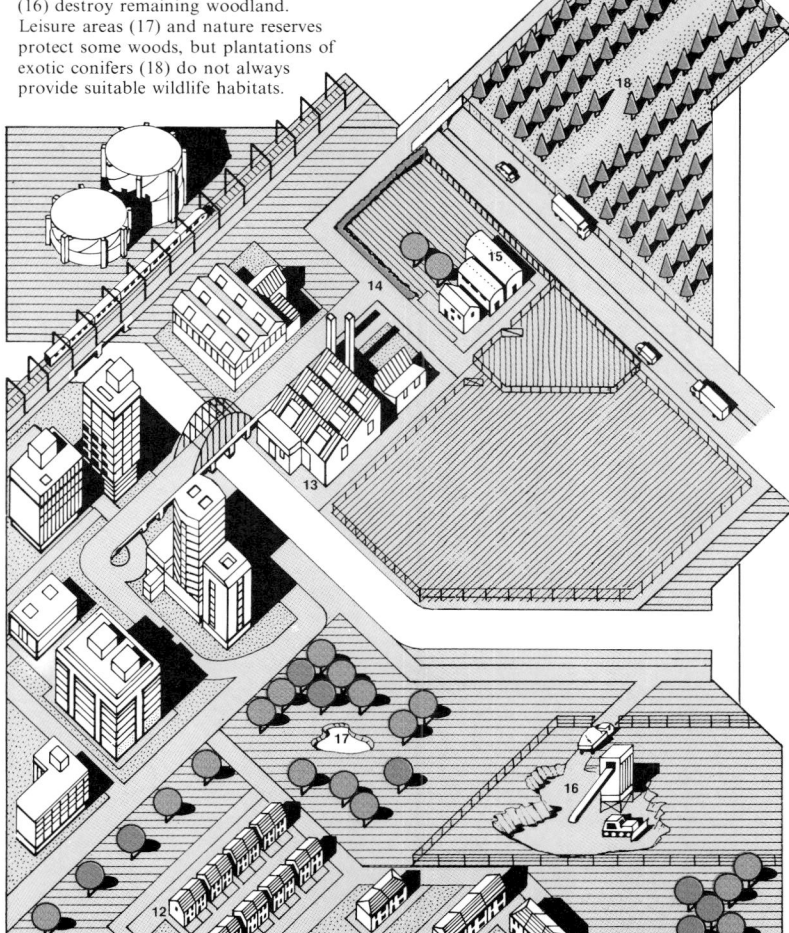

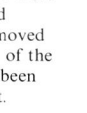
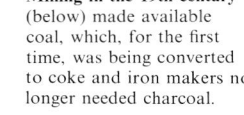
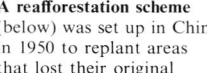
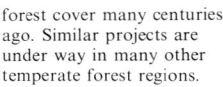

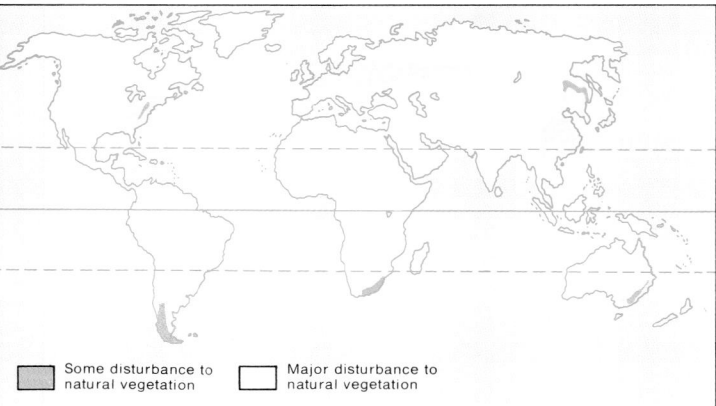

Early pioneers in the USA (below) transformed forestland as they moved west. By 1830 most of the eastern forests had been felled for settlement.

Mining in the 19th century (below) made available coal, which, for the first time, was being converted to coke and iron makers no longer needed charcoal.

Large department stores appeared in 19th-century Chicago, a town that, within 100 years, had been transformed from a remote fort to a city. This rapid growth reflected the huge population increase in many 19th-century towns.

A reafforestation scheme (below) was set up in China in 1950 to replant areas that lost their original forest cover many centuries ago. Similar projects are under way in many other temperate forest regions.

The European wood bison has escaped extinction because one herd of the animals has lived, for centuries, in a royal hunting reserve. Today, wildlife parks throughout temperate regions protect endangered forest species.

Some disturbance to natural vegetation

Major disturbance to natural vegetation

the pressures shifted, some of the east coast deciduous forest grew up again, and it is possible that parts of the eastern USA may have nearly as much forest cover now as when the settlers first arrived. Nevertheless, other areas of forestland have been destroyed in recent decades by strip mining and the creation of a vast road and rail network. In the southern hemisphere, especially in the last 200 years, the temperate rainforests of Australia and New Zealand have been subjected to much the same pattern of events, although on a smaller and somewhat less devastating scale.

Conservation
Today the general need to preserve and extend the woodlands is clearly recognized, but great uncertainty exists about their future. The demand for hardwoods for veneers, quality papermaking and furniture still exceeds supply. Oak is still the preferred material for some types of boat building and, especially in Europe, for joinery work. But one of the major difficulties with forestry as a land use is forecasting future trends within the industry, largely as a result of the long-term nature of the crop—hardwood trees planted today will not yield their timber until well into the next century. Government tax policies can be all important in deciding whether the majority of woodlands are, or will

continue to be, sound economic investments.

Temperate forests and woodlands still exist in sizeable quantities in central Europe and the USA, but many of today's plots, particularly in western Europe, are far too small for efficient conservation of plant and animal life, and are isolated from other woods. As a result, successful breeding and exchange of genetic material is very difficult, especially when modern agriculture is rapidly destroying the linking corridors of hedgerows. The use of woodlands for recreation is also presenting considerable problems. Controlling agencies have been formed to cope with leisure demands, and a start has been made in the multiple use of forests for recreation, conservation and timber felling, but progress still needs to be made in harmonizing these potentially conflicting interests. Meanwhile, natural expanses of woodland and forest are still being lost to agricultural and urban expansion and to plantations of nonnative conifers.

Temperate forests are a biologically efficient form of land use. In terms of biomass—the amount of living material (animal and plant) in any one area—they could still play an important role in the provision of food, materials and even renewable energy. Thus on scientific, economic and aesthetic grounds a strong case can be made for immediate conservation measures.

Mediterranean Regions

Forests of evergreen trees once covered much of the Mediterranean regions. They flourished in spite of the hot, rainless summer months – as the original plant life, they had evolved to survive such harsh conditions. Man, however, has proved to be a greater threat than the climate. He introduced domestic animals and cleared the land to grow crops; the natural vegetation was burned, browsed and plowed into nonexistence. Man's activities left behind tracts of impoverished soil which rapidly became scrubland. Today, scrub is the most typical vegetation in all the Mediterranean climate zones throughout the world.

CONVERGENCE

Isolated from each other by enormous areas of land and ocean, regions with a Mediterranean type of climate rarely have any plant species in common. But, by a process known as "convergent evolution," the plant communities in each of these areas have produced remarkably similar responses to their similar environments. This can be seen in the conifer communities, the broad-leaved evergreen trees, and in the various hardy shrubs and ground plants typical of each of the regions.

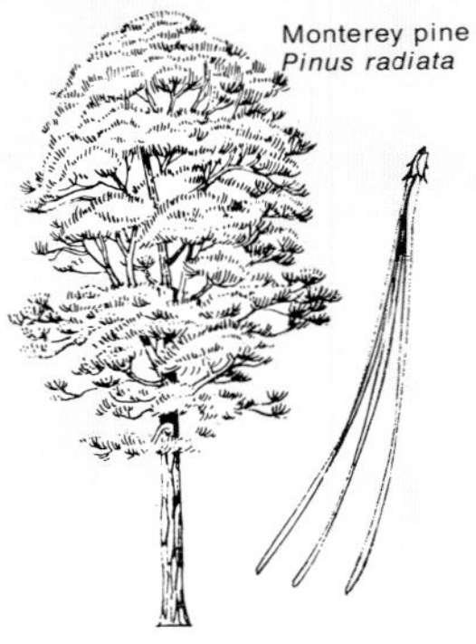

Monterey pine
Pinus radiata

California's Monterey pine and other Mediterranean conifers—South African podocarps and Chile pines, for example—have needle-shaped leaves that prevent rapid loss of water from such trees during drought.

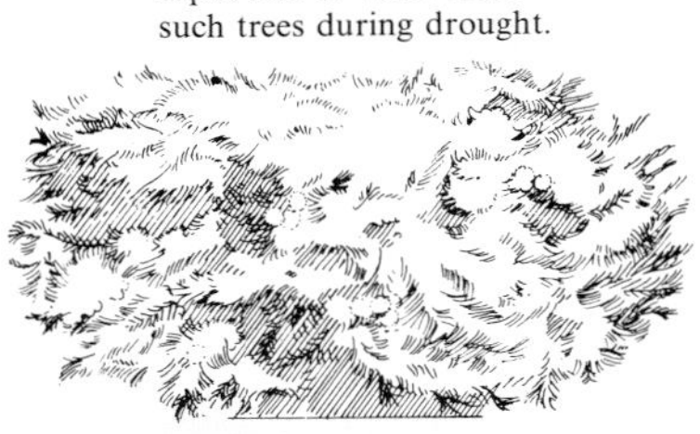

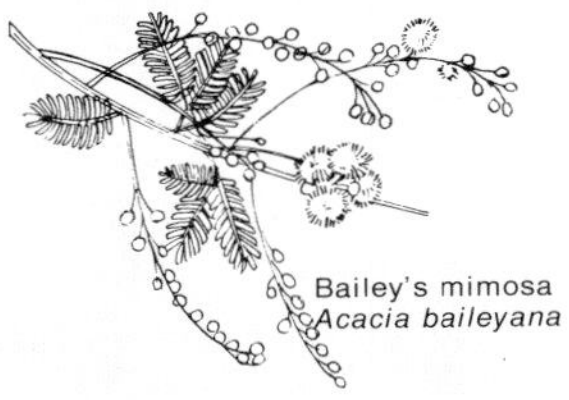

Bailey's mimosa
Acacia baileyana

Nonconiferous evergreens such as Australia's acacias and eucalypts, Chile's *quillajas* and California's evergreen oaks are typical Mediterranean trees. Their leathery leaves limit summer moisture loss.

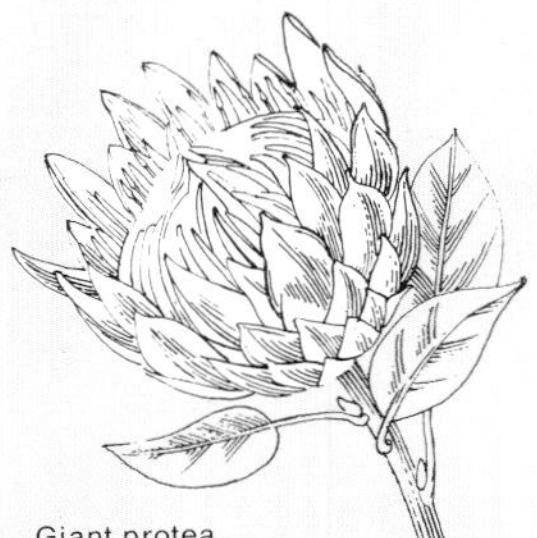

Giant protea
Protea cynaroides

Shrubs and ground plants show various adaptations to drought. South African proteas and Europe's laurel have thick evergreen leaves. Narrow leaves and water-storing roots are other common adaptations.

Long, hot, dry summers and warm, moist winters form the seasonal rhythm of the "Mediterranean" year. This climatic pattern can be found in small areas of nearly every continent in the world, typically on the western side of landmasses and in the mild, temperate latitudes. North America's "Mediterranean" is in California, South America's occurs in Chile and Africa's lies at the southern tip of Cape Province. Australia has two small "Mediterranean" areas, one on the southern coast and one on the western. Europe's Mediterranean region, which has given its name to this climate, covers much of the southern part of the continent and extends into northern Africa.

Wherever Mediterranean conditions prevail, the native plant life has adapted to survive the scanty annual rainfall and the long summer droughts. Some species have developed deep root systems that can tap low summer water tables, and many of the ground plants—such as bulbs and aromatic herbs—grow vigorously only in early summer while rain still moistens the soil. But it is the broad-leaved evergreens with their drought-resistant leaves that are the most typical of the Mediterranean areas.

This natural pattern of vegetation has been drastically altered by man. In southern Europe in particular, almost all the original evergreen forests have long since been destroyed and thickets of fast-growing, tough scrub plants have grown up in their place. This scrub, which once probably covered only small areas, is now so widespread that it is considered the most typically Mediterranean of all kinds of vegetation. It is the *maquis* of France, the *macchia* of Italy and the *mattoral* of Spain. A similar type of vegetation (although containing different species) can also be found in South Africa's fynbos, in California's chapparal, and in Australia's tracts of natural mallee scrub.

Classical land use

Southern Europe, with its long history of human settlement, farming and pastoralism, is the most altered of all the Mediterranean regions. Over the centuries vast tracts of original vegetation have been removed, either by farmers (for crop growing) or by grazing animals. And, particularly on the steep slopes and rocky outcrops, this has resulted in extensive deterioration and erosion of the soil. Agriculture generally has less serious effects upon the vegetation than has animal grazing. Mankind has learned, over many hundreds of years, which are the most suitable crops for the various soils, terrain and climatic conditions of the region. The Mediterranean "triad" of wheat on the lowlands and olives and vines on the hills has been a successful combination since Classical times.

Pastoral plundering of the land, however, has more serious consequences. The virtually omnivorous goat is particularly damaging and can strip a whole forest of its foliage, bark, shrubs, ground plants and grass. After such an assault the vegetation rarely returns to its former condition; normally, a scrubby growth of kermes oak and shrubs springs up to form a typical maquis-type vegetation.

The rise and fall of each great Mediterranean civilization has seen forests destroyed in one area after another. The Greek colonization of southern Italy was provoked by deforestation and soil erosion in Attica. The Romans extended clearance north to the Po valley and into eastern Tunisia. From the seventh century onwards, Muslims made great inroads into the forests of North Africa as well as southern and eastern Spain; and in the north of Spain and southern France, medieval monks cleared forested valleys. During the seventeenth and eighteenth centuries large areas of Provence and Italy were cleared to plant vines and this process continued in the 1800s, when the great wine-producing areas of Languedoc and Algeria were established. During this time the iron industries of Spain and northern Italy, with their growing need for charcoal, were adding to the destruction. Recent reafforestation efforts have been puny compared to past degradation.

Protected species

But throughout this history of forest removal some tree species have been protected. These have been the natural tree crops that have, at times, supported complete peasant economies. The chestnut forests of Corsica, for example, sustained a large rural population until this century; the chestnuts provided flour for bread and fodder for pigs. In Portugal and Sardinia the cork-oak forests are still important today.

It is the olive, however, symbol of peace and of New Testament landscapes, that is the Mediterranean's most characteristic tree crop. Of all the Mediterranean plants, it is the most perfectly adapted to its environment, with its deep roots to search out scarce water and its hard, shiny leaves to conserve what it finds. In fact, the summer drought is essential to olive growers for it encourages the build-up of oil in the fruit. Paradoxically, however, the olive—like the vine, the fig and many other "Mediterranean" crops—did not originate in the Mediterranean but was introduced from Asia Minor.

In spite of massive destruction of the natural landscape, mankind has learned many valuable lessons during his occupation of this region. Ideas that were to become important in laying the foundations of sound land management policy were developed in the Mediterranean area. Hillside terracing, irrigation, crop rotation and manuring were all, from necessity, practiced from early times. The flourishing agricultural industries of the world's other Mediterranean regions—the wine industry of California, the vast soft-fruit plantations of Australia and the citrus industry of South Africa—all owe a considerable debt to the generations of farmers who learned to exploit the red soils of the Mediterranean basin.

The Mediterranean regions occur between the latitudes 30° and 40°, on the western and southwestern sides of the continents. These areas are affected in summer by the high-pressure systems of nearby desert regions, and in winter by wet, low-pressure systems brought in from the oceans and over the land by the prevailing Westerlies. This distinct seasonal shifting of major influences on the climate produces the hot, waterless summers and warm, moist, sometimes stormy winters typical of the Mediterranean climate.

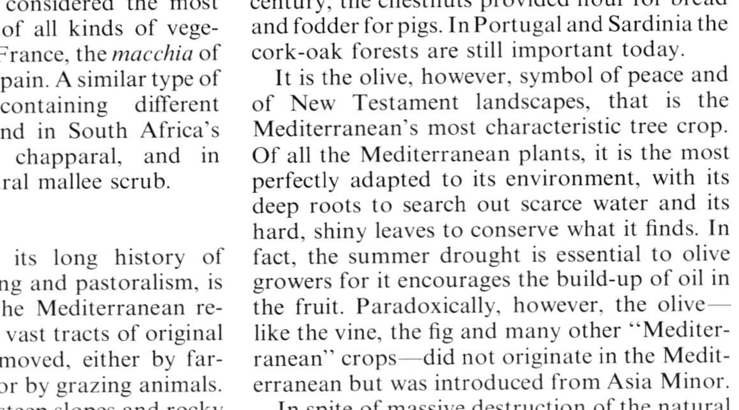

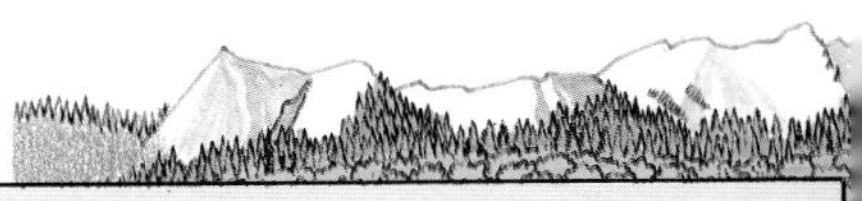

MAN AND THE MEDITERRANEAN

Even by Classical times, the once-forested lands fringing the Mediterranean Sea were suffering from massive deforestation and soil erosion. In the 5th century BC, Plato described the bare, dry hills of Attica, recently stripped of their woodlands. "What now remains," he wrote, "is like the skeleton of a sick man, all the fat and soft earth having been wasted away." By the end of the Classical period, irreparable damage had been done. At the same time, however, mankind was gradually learning through the mistakes he had already made. Suitable patterns of land use, better farming practices and improved land management techniques were slowly being adopted and were enabling man to make better use of the much-altered Mediterranean landscape.

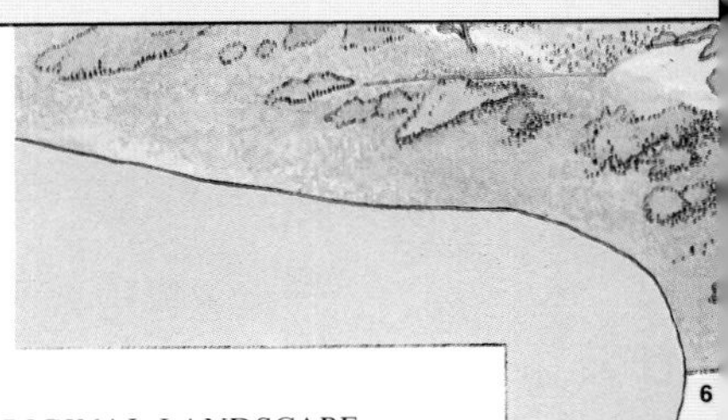

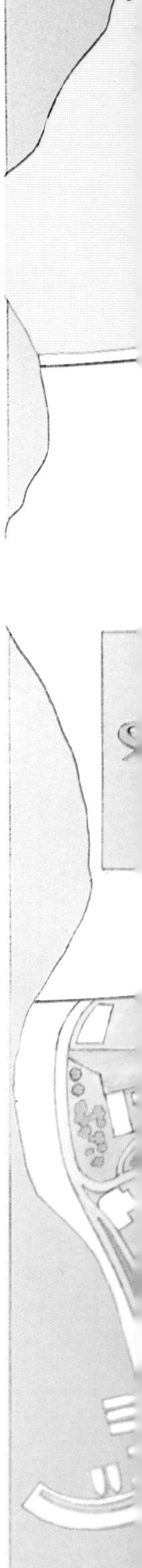

THE ORIGINAL LANDSCAPE
The landscape, unaltered by man, held a rich variety of vegetation. On high mountains, conifers such as black pine and cedar grew. On the lower slopes, these gave way to warmth-tolerant deciduous trees such as Turkey oak. In the foothills and valleys, forests of holm oaks, strawberry trees and other broad-leaved evergreens flourished. Limestone outcrops, common in the area, supported a poorer vegetation. Here, stunted Aleppo pines mixed with herbs such as lavender. Over sandstone, scrubby olives and cork oaks grew and by the sea stood isolated, wind-bent maritime pines.

THE CLASSICAL AGE
Civilizations followed one after another, each taking its toll of the environment. In the mountains, forests were felled, the tall, straight conifers sought after by shipbuilders such as the Phoenicians, and deciduous hardwood timber in demand for charcoal to fuel growing industries. Some replanting did take place, especially as groves of crop trees such as chestnuts. Below in the foothills, agriculture and the grazing of animals had destroyed vast areas of natural forest. Terracing techniques, however, helped to stop soil erosion, and irrigation reached the height of its Classical art with Roman aqueducts and canals. Tree crops, such as olives, were found best suited to the thin hill soils. On the plains, especially where alluvial soils had been deposited, cereals were grown. Meanwhile, towns sprang up and the coastline became densely populated as ships and ports were built and sea trade grew. Exotic food plants, such as pomegranate trees, citron trees and vines, were brought into the region by merchant seamen.

THE MEDITERRANEAN TODAY
The region today bears the scars of many centuries of human activity. The once-forested mountains will never return to their former state, although some regrowth and some replanting (mostly with introduced tree species) has occurred. As in Classical times, hillsides are terraced and planted with vines and fruit trees. But with modern irrigation and fertilizing, land is less readily exhausted and abandoned now. On the plains, native shrubs, such as lavender, are commercially cultivated and grain is widely grown, particularly durum wheat used for making pasta. Cork oaks are planted, especially over dry sandstone areas, but indigenous vegetation has not suffered by this—scrubby woodland is more widespread than ever and can be found throughout the landscape. Perhaps the single most important part of the Mediterranean basin today is the coastline, for this has produced the region's major modern industry—tourism.

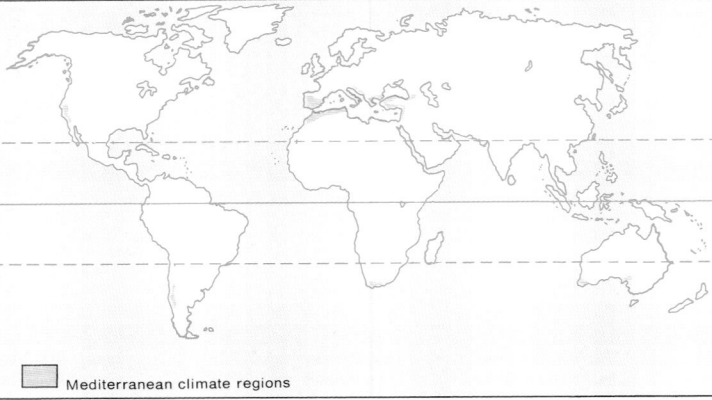

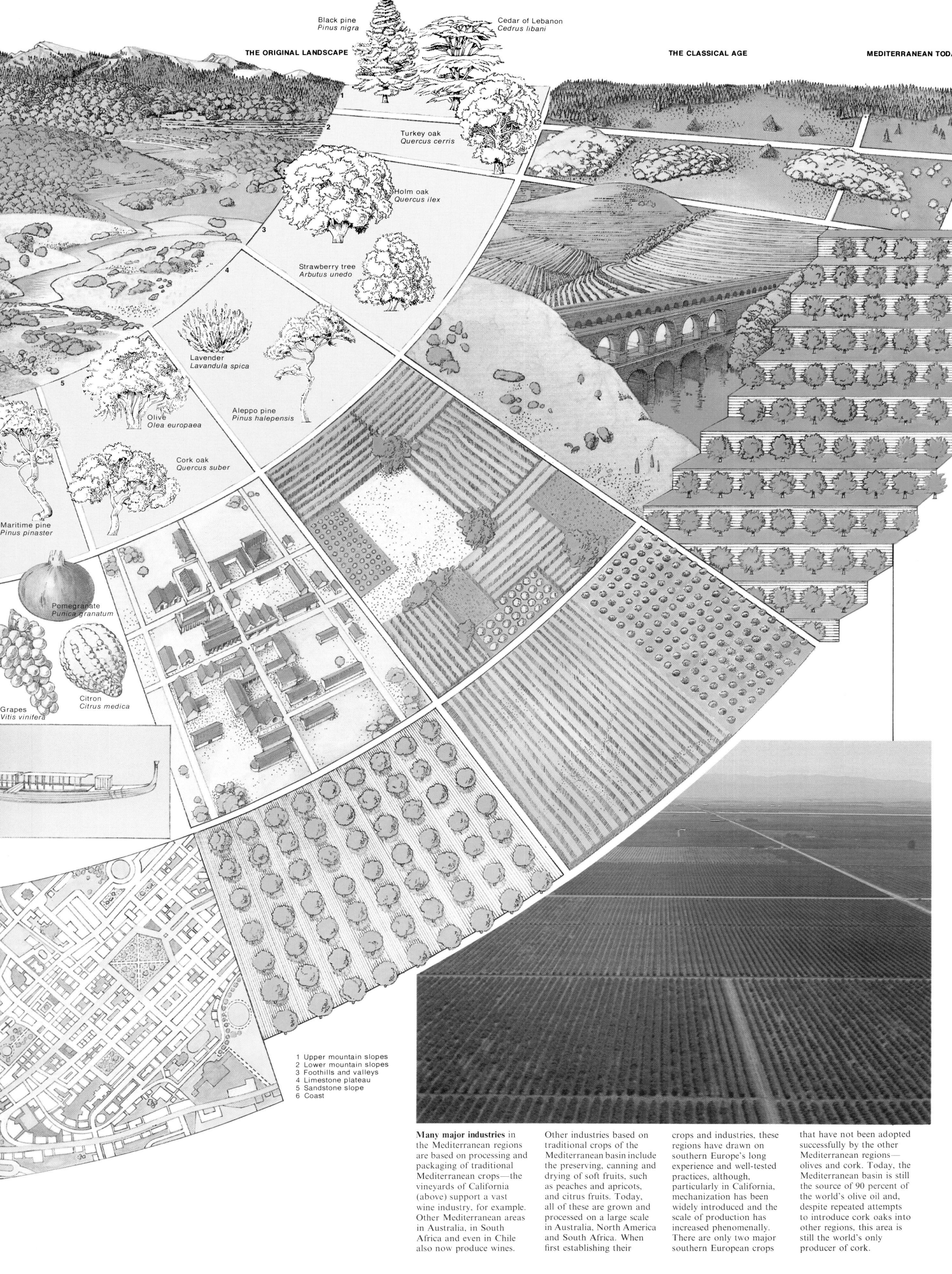

Black pine
Pinus nigra

Cedar of Lebanon
Cedrus libani

Turkey oak
Quercus cerris

Holm oak
Quercus ilex

Strawberry tree
Arbutus unedo

Lavender
Lavandula spica

Aleppo pine
Pinus halepensis

Olive
Olea europaea

Cork oak
Quercus suber

Maritime pine
Pinus pinaster

Pomegranate
Punica granatum

Grapes
Vitis vinifera

Citron
Citrus medica

1 Upper mountain slopes
2 Lower mountain slopes
3 Foothills and valleys
4 Limestone plateau
5 Sandstone slope
6 Coast

Many major industries in the Mediterranean regions are based on processing and packaging of traditional Mediterranean crops—the vineyards of California (above) support a vast wine industry, for example. Other Mediterranean areas in Australia, in South Africa and even in Chile also now produce wines.

Other industries based on traditional crops of the Mediterranean basin include the preserving, canning and drying of soft fruits, such as peaches and apricots, and citrus fruits. Today, all of these are grown and processed on a large scale in Australia, North America and South Africa. When first establishing their

crops and industries, these regions have drawn on southern Europe's long experience and well-tested practices, although, particularly in California, mechanization has been widely introduced and the scale of production has increased phenomenally. There are only two major southern European crops

that have not been adopted successfully by the other Mediterranean regions— olives and cork. Today, the Mediterranean basin is still the source of 90 percent of the world's olive oil and, despite repeated attempts to introduce cork oaks into other regions, this area is still the world's only producer of cork.

Temperate Grasslands

Compared with other flowering plants, grasses are newcomers to the Earth. They appeared only 60 million years ago, but since then they have proved to be an extremely successful family of plants. Today, the grasses dominate large areas of the world's natural vegetation and play a vital part in the intricate balance of plant and animal life in these regions. In spite of the inroads made by man, vast stretches of original grassland still cover the interiors of the North American and Eurasian landmasses.

The prairies of North America and the steppes of Eurasia extend far into the interiors of the northern continents. These are the best known and the most extensive of the world's temperate grasslands. The southern hemisphere, however, has examples in the veld of South Africa and the pampas of South America. Extensive grasslands also occur in southern Australia, although these are sometimes described as semiarid scrub because of the high average temperatures and the prolonged droughts in the region.

Temperate grasslands probably developed wherever the rainfall was too low to support forest and too high to result in semiarid regions, conditions found typically in the interiors of large continents. Continental interiors tend to be somewhat drier than coastal regions, but they are also characterized by extreme changes in temperature from one season to the next. In the North American grasslands, for example, winter temperatures may fall well below freezing whereas summer temperatures of 38°C (100°F) are not unusual. And these sharp fluctuations in seasonal temperature greatly influence how much of the rainfall is made available to plants. In summer particularly, when most of the rain falls, high temperatures, strong winds and lack of protective tree cover cause much of the moisture to evaporate before it can be absorbed into the soil.

Climatic conditions are not the only factor responsible for the distribution and form of the temperate grasslands. There are many pointers that indicate the importance of fire in determining their continuing existence and their extent. Natural fires, caused by lightning and fueled by the dry summer grasses, have always been a feature of these regions, but more recently, man-made fires have been crucial in fixing the boundary between forest and grassland.

Trees and shrubs frequently invade the margins of grasslands, but whenever there is a fire few of them survive. Grasses, however, have certain characteristics that enable them to withstand the potentially destructive impact of fire. The growing point of grasses is at the base of the leaves, close to the ground, and so destruction of the leaves above this point does not interrupt growth—in fact it may stimulate it. These same characteristics also serve to protect grasses from destruction by grazing animals. The large animals of these lands, such as the North American bison and the Eurasian horse, are able to crop the grasses without permanently damaging their food supply.

Grazers and predators

Large migrating herbivores with a strong herd instinct characterize one of the major types of temperate grassland animal. In the North American grasslands the bison (which may have numbered 60 million before being virtually exterminated by settlers) and the antelope-like pronghorn were the major examples of large herbivores. In Eurasia large herds of saiga antelopes, wild horses and asses at one time roamed the steppes, although they too have suffered from human activities, as has South America's largest grassland herd animal, the pampas deer. As these herds of grazing animals have been reduced, so have the carnivorous animals of the grasslands that preyed upon them. At one time, however, these predators played an important part in protecting the grasslands by continually keeping the numbers of grazing herd animals in check.

RUNNING AND LEAPING HERBIVORES

Saiga
Saiga tatarica

American bison
Bison bison

European hare
Lepus europaeus

Guanaco
Lama guanicoe

Springhaas
Pedetes cafer

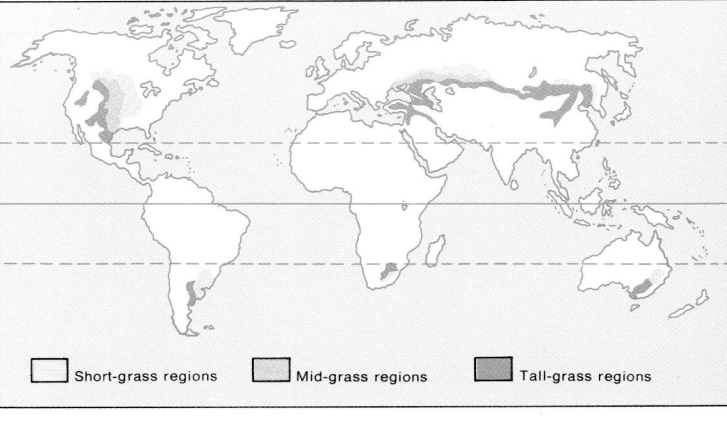

RUNNING CARNIVORES

Maned wolf
Chrysocyon brachyurus

Plains wolf
Canis lupus nubilus

Coyote
Canis latrans

SMALL BURROWING ANIMALS

European souslik
Citellus citellus

Marsupial mole
Notoryctes typhlops

Prairie dog
Cynomys ludovicianus

Viscacha
Lagostomus maximus

SMALL CARNIVORES

Black-footed ferret
Mustela nigripes

Pampas cat
Lynchailurus pajeros

Marbled polecat
Vormela peregusna

Gopher snake
Pituophis melanoleucus

Russian tarragon
Artemisia dracunculoides

Iris
Iris sibirica

Anemone
Anemone patens

The dominant native species of grass varies from area to area. In the undisturbed prairies, for example, tall bluestem and Indian grass grow in the east and in wet central lowlands and mix with switch grass in drier parts. Farther west and on high land in the east, little bluestem and also western wheatgrass grow. June grass grows in the north, and buffalo grass and blue grama grow farthest west.

Many flowering herbs grow in the grasslands and have developed resistance to summer droughts: Russian tarragon has narrow leaves to help prevent moisture evaporation; rhizomes and bulbs, such as Eurasia's iris and anemone, store water in their specialized "root" systems.

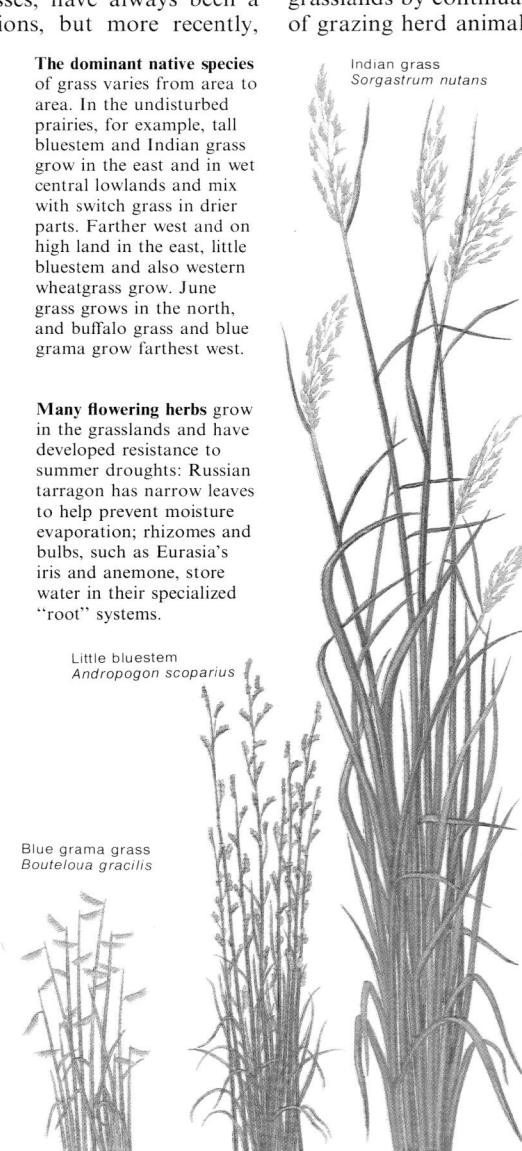

Indian grass
Sorgastrum nutans

Little bluestem
Andropogon scoparius

Blue grama grass
Bouteloua gracilis

The natural distribution of the temperate grasslands is dictated mainly by rainfall: most occur in continental interiors where there is too little rain for forest but enough to prevent desert from forming. Between these limits the large range in rainfall allows three main types of grassland: tall grass in wetter areas, mid-grass, and short grass in drier parts. The largest grasslands exist in North America, Eurasia, South America, in Australia's Murray–Darling river basin and on the South African plateau.

Short-grass regions   Mid-grass regions   Tall-grass regions

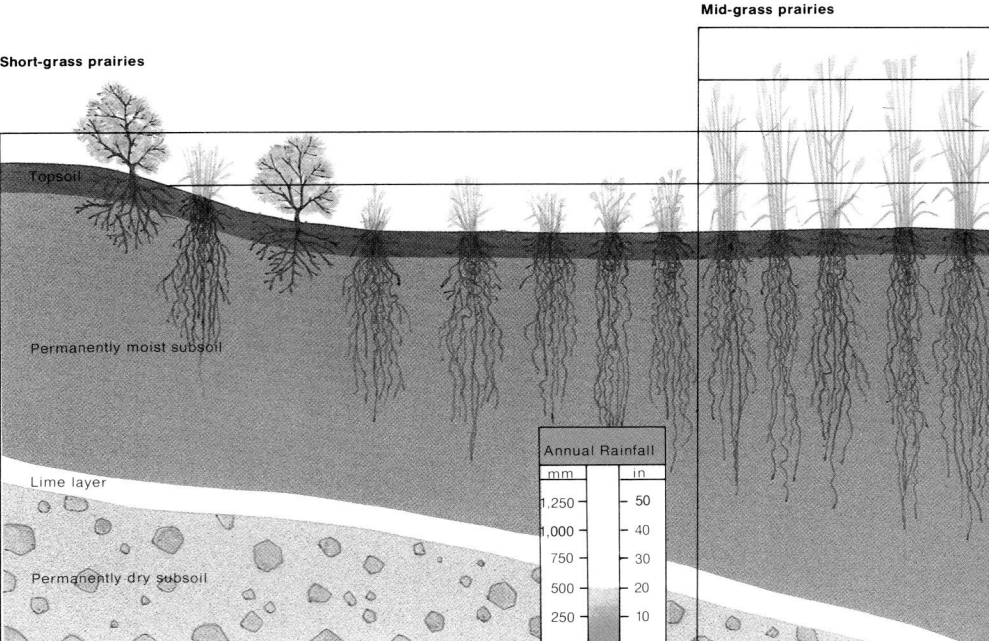

Short-grass prairies

Mid-grass prairies

Topsoil

Permanently moist subsoil

Lime layer

Permanently dry subsoil

Annual Rainfall

mm	in
1,250	50
1,000	40
750	30
500	20
250	10

GRASSLAND ADAPTATION

Animals of these regions have had to adapt to a difficult environment: vast, treeless expanses of grass offer little protection from harsh weather or predators. Different animals have found various answers to the problem and a clearly defined pattern of these adaptations can be traced throughout the grasslands.

Running and leaping herbivores survive because of their ability to move faster than a pursuer. The larger animals such as the Eurasian saiga, North America's bison and pronghorn and the guanaco of South America are runners. The leaping herbivores are usually smaller creatures that escape danger by bounding away to bolt-holes. They include the European hare and the African springhaas.

Running carnivores follow, and prey on, running and leaping herbivores. These animals, such as the coyote and the now extinct plains wolf of North America, and South America's maned wolf, also depend on speed—to enable them to catch their prey.

Small burrowing animals hide from predators by digging under the ground. Some, such as Australia's marsupial mole, spend most of their lives below ground. Others, such as the European souslik, South America's viscacha and North America's prairie dog, live and sleep under the ground but come to the surface to find food.

Small carnivores concentrate on the burrowers as their main source of food. They either, like the pampas cat, rely on surprise attack of their prey, or, like Eurasia's marbled polecat and the grasslands' many kinds of snake, depend on their long, lithe shape to follow creatures into their burrows.

Two distinctive types of grassland bird can be distinguished: the sky birds, which spend long periods of time on the wing, and the ground birds.

Birds of the sky include songbirds such as the skylark which, having no perch from which to proclaim its territory, sings in the sky, and birds of prey such as Eurasia's tawny eagle and North America's red-tailed hawk and prairie falcon, which ride the thermals scanning the ground for their prey.

Ground birds rarely take to the wing, although none has actually lost the ability to fly when necessary. They include birds such as the New World sage grouse and burrowing owl (which lives below ground in abandoned prairie dog burrows), the black grouse of Eurasia and songbirds such as North America's meadowlark.

Insects and other invertebrates have developed many different survival techniques. Some use camouflage: the praying mantis resembles a leaf bud and the tumble bug is the color of the dark grassland soil. Grasshoppers are miniature leaping herbivores and earthworms are small-scale versions of the grassland burrowers.

Skylark
Alauda arvensis

Tawny eagle
Aquila rapax

Red-tailed hawk
Buteo jamaicensis

Prairie falcon
Falco mexicanus

BIRDS OF THE SKY

Burrowing owl
Speotyto cunicularia

Western meadowlark
Sturnella neglecta

Sage grouse
Centrocercus urophasianus

Black grouse
Lyurus tetrix

GROUND BIRDS

Lubber grasshopper
Romalea microptera

Tumble bug
Canthonlaevis drury

Common earthworm
Lumbricus terrestris

Praying mantis
Mantis religiosa

INSECTS AND OTHER INVERTEBRATES

A typical cross section, based on the North American prairies, shows temperate grasslands in relation to rainfall. Annual rainfall determines the depth of the permanently moist subsoil, which in turn dictates the length to which grass roots can grow. Tall grasses have deep root systems and need a considerable depth of moist subsoil. As the rainfall decreases, they gradually give way to shorter grass species. Short grasses require less water and their shallower roots are well suited to drier regions. On dry margins, desert plants start to dominate, and on the wet margins, trees appear.

Another major type of animal found in the temperate grasslands, and one that is better adapted to survive man's activities, is the small, burrowing animal, for example the prairie dog and the gopher of North America, the viscacha of South America and the little ground squirrel known as the souslik in Eurasia.

Unlike the large herd animals, these creatures tend not to migrate. Many of them live together in complex, permanent, underground communities. The colonial "townships" of the prairie dog, for example, may house more than one million individuals, which each year excavate vast quantities of the grassland soil. This has considerable effect upon the structure of the soil. By bringing up earth from lower layers to the surface, these animals are responsible for changing the mineral content of certain areas of topsoil. This then encourages isolated pockets of different plant species to flourish.

A third group of grassland animals, consisting of insects and other invertebrates such as earthworms, has an even more important effect upon the soil. They live in or on the soil and play a vital role in maintaining grassland fertility. These creatures may be herbivores, carnivores or primary (first stage) decomposers (which break down such material as dead grass and animal remains). These three types of activity allow a complete range of organic matter to be processed and incorporated into the earth, where it is further broken down by the second-stage decomposers, the countless millions of soil bacteria. In this way nutrients continuously flow back to the earth and restore its fertility.

Fertile black earths

The topsoil of temperate grassland regions, therefore, contains large amounts of organic material, which is produced every year and is quickly incorporated into the soil. The low and intermittent rainfall and the protective cover of grasses mean that the topsoil undergoes little chemical leaching, a process in which minerals are removed and carried down to lower layers by rainfall percolating through the earth. The soils are thus dark in color, generally fertile and of the "black earth" type ("chernozem" in Russian) which is, at least at first, capable of producing high yields of crops.

The most suitable and most widely grown crops are, predictably, the cultivated grasses, and it is these grasses that provide more food for mankind (either directly as grain or indirectly as animal fodder) than any other source. The temperate grassland biome is therefore an important agricultural resource. Undisturbed natural grasslands, however, are also valuable resources. They need to be preserved both for the information that they can provide about how complex communities of wildlife function efficiently, and because, as a rich source of genetic material, they hold many of the answers to the major agricultural problems that probably lie ahead for the human race.

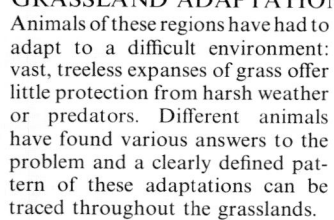

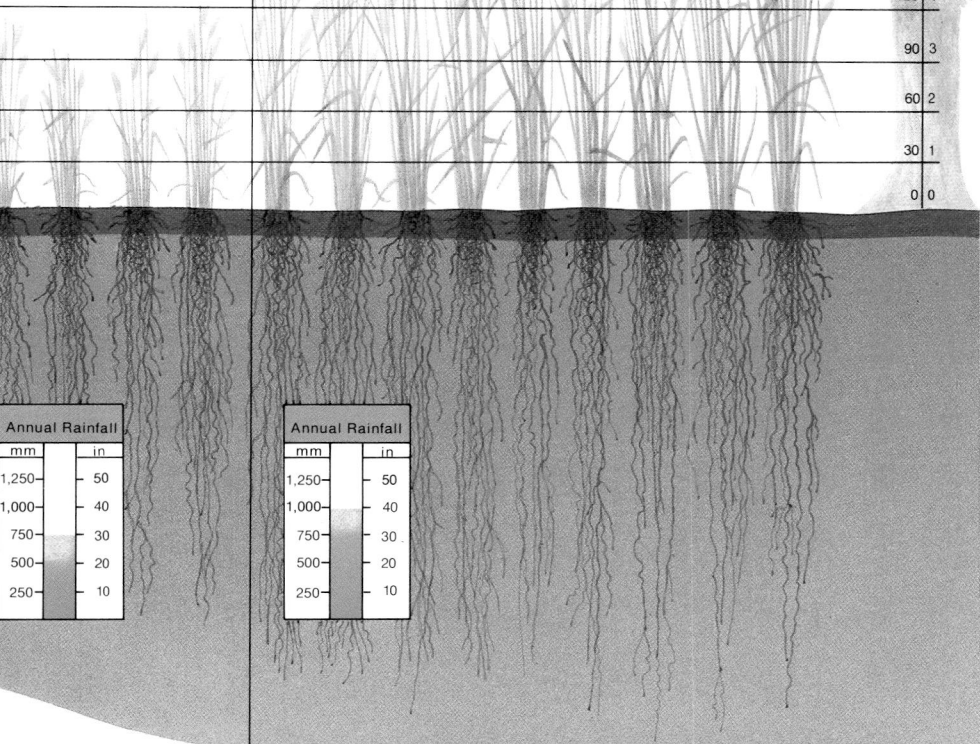

Tall-grass prairies

cm	ft
215	7
180	6
150	5
120	4
90	3
60	2
30	1
0	0

Annual Rainfall

mm		in
1,250		50
1,000		40
750		30
500		20
250		10

Annual Rainfall

mm		in
1,250		50
1,000		40
750		30
500		20
250		10

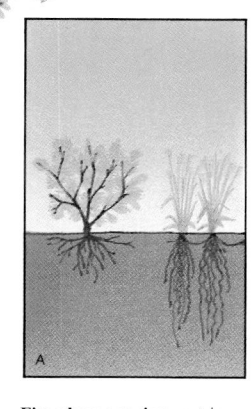
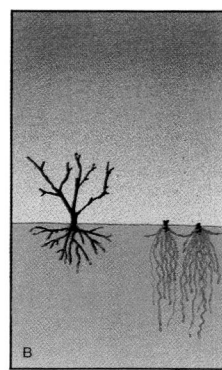
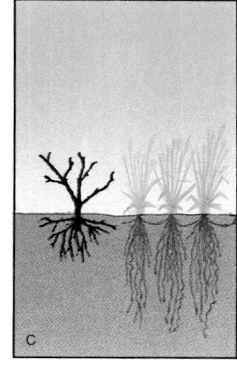

A   B   C

Fire plays a major part in fixing and maintaining the natural boundaries of the temperate grasslands, where tree saplings and shrubs are continually attempting to invade (A). Man-made fires are recent phenomena, natural fires have always occurred. In summer, low-pressure systems build up in continental interiors, causing violent electrical storms. The dry sward of summer grass is easily ignited by lightning and fire is quickly spread by wind. Shrubs and saplings are killed or badly damaged by fire, but grasses, with their growing points close to the soil, remain unharmed (B). They may even benefit from this "pruning" and grow more quickly. Some species grow new buds from their underground shoots. Removal of the main shoot may encourage growth of "tillers" (shoots growing out sideways), which then increase the spread of the grasses as they begin to invade the area left vacant by the dead, or slowly recuperating, shrubs (C).

Man and the Temperate Grasslands

The vast areas of temperate grassland lay virtually empty until the end of the eighteenth century. Over the next 125 years they were occupied by millions of people, most of them migrants from overcrowded Europe. By 1914, the grasslands had become the granaries and the stockyards of the world. Today, they are still the most important food-producing regions on Earth and their riches, properly distributed, are the world's first reserve against the possibility of a hungry future for the human race.

The great nineteenth-century migration to the grasslands proved of immense significance to the human race. It meant that, within a single century, the area of productive land available was suddenly enlarged by thousands of millions of hectares. In all of mankind's history, such a thing had never happened before.

But before the grasslands could be occupied a number of major problems had to be solved. First, in order to reach these regions it was almost always necessary to travel deep into the continental interiors, and there were few navigable rivers and no mechanized forms of transportation for early pioneers. Second, with virtually no indigenous population, newcomers had to learn by their mistakes how best to exploit the new and unfamiliar environment. Third, even if settlers succeeded in using the land, they still had to find markets for their produce.

A number of technological developments, however, that took place in the nineteenth century provided the right combination of circumstances for the opening up of the grasslands. The Industrial Revolution in Europe produced the steamship and the railway locomotive, which created both a means of travel to and from these distant parts and an internal transport system for moving produce to ports and markets. It also produced the kind of machinery needed to plow and farm the great new open spaces; it made it possible for one family to cultivate an area 50 times as large as that which most farmers had known in Europe. Industrialization also threw thousands of Europeans out of work, and therefore provided a large supply of eager migrants. And it crowded further thousands into cities, thus creating vast markets for the settlers' produce.

It was the coming together of these various circumstances that acted as the catalyst and converted, for example, the Russian penetration of the Eurasian steppes in the late eighteenth

THE CRADLE OF AGRICULTURE

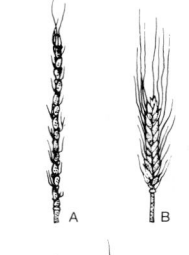
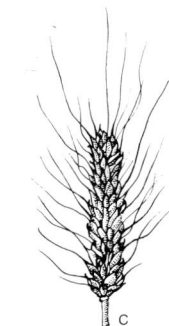

Stands of wild einkorn (A), emmer wheat (B) and wild barleys can be seen today in the grassy foothills that flank the Taurus and the Zagros mountains, and the uplands of northern Israel. It was in this region 10,000 years ago that the world's earliest farmers gathered seeds from these species and sowed the first crops. Wild einkorn is probably the oldest of all wheats and the parent of every modern variety—including the most important and most widely grown kind of grain in the world today, common bread wheat (C).

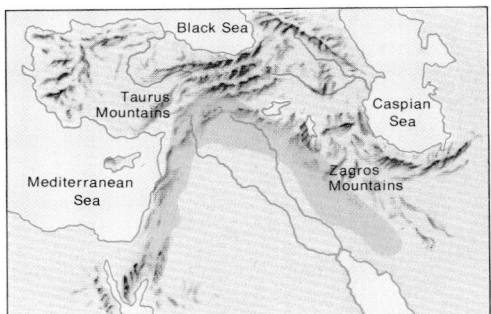

GRASSLAND EXPLOITATION

Today, temperate grasslands provide mankind with a superabundance of food. But the vast potential of these regions was not exploited until the mid-19th century, when mass migration by Europeans, combined with new technology, allowed full-scale development and settlement.

BEFORE EUROPEAN SETTLEMENT
The grasslands were sparsely populated. Most of the indigenous tribespeoples were nomadic hunters and gatherers. They wandered widely over the regions, making temporary camps (1) as they followed the movement of their quarry—the plentiful herds of grazing animals (2). These peoples made little impact on the natural grasslands.

GRASSLAND SETTLERS
Early pioneers relied on animal-drawn transport (3), primitive farm tools (4) and unpredictable free-range livestock grazing (5). During the 19th century, farming became more productive: better equipment cultivated larger areas (6); barbed wire made stock raising efficient (7); railways and the telegraph improved communication (8).

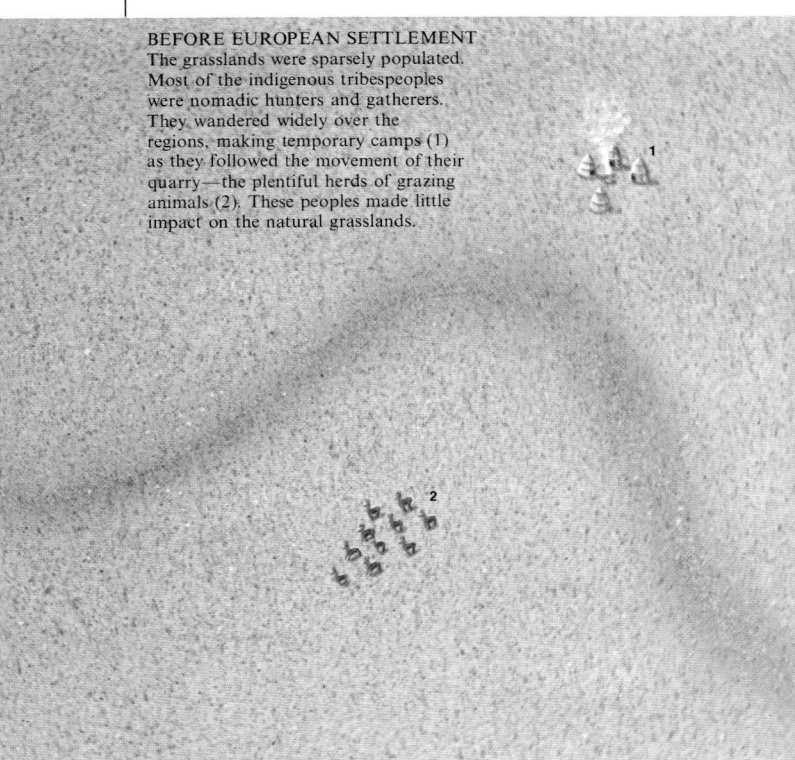
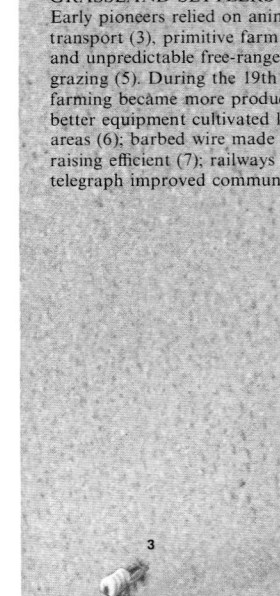
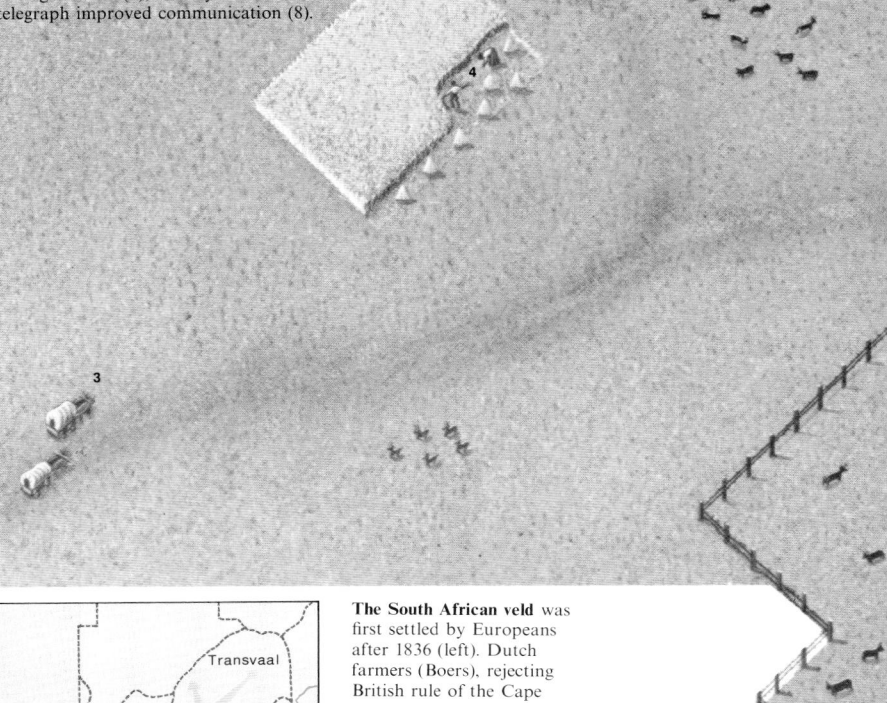

Tehuelche Indians (above) adopted horses for hunting from early Spanish settlers to the pampas. In South Africa and North America, too, the introduced horse became a valued asset for grassland hunters. For people of the Eurasian steppes, for example the Mongols (right), native horses have always been culturally important.

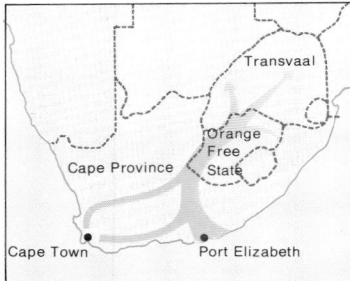

The South African veld was first settled by Europeans after 1836 (left). Dutch farmers (Boers), rejecting British rule of the Cape Colony, trekked north in search of new land. Moving into the Transvaal they discovered rich grassland, recently emptied of its original inhabitants, who had fled to escape the aggressive attentions of neighboring Zulus.

Vaqueros were the original cowboys (left). Tending herds of cattle for the missionaries in 18th-century California, they developed techniques and traditions that served hundreds of later cowboys working the prairie ranges. In other grassland regions, as free-range stock raising became important, similar "cowboy" professions evolved—the Australian stockman and the gaucho of South America.

century into the explosive movement of hundreds of thousands of settlers a few years later. In the USA, too, by the year 1850, settlement had reached and then rapidly crossed the Mississippi. In the Argentine, genuine colonization of the pampas had begun, in South Africa, the Boers had reached the high veld, and in Australia pioneer settlers were moving outwards from the various areas of coastal settlement into the scrub grasslands of the interior.

Farmers or ranchers?

The fundamental question posed for these settlers was whether their newly found land should be used for crops or for livestock. Most grasslands have a dry edge and a wet edge, and it was therefore sensible to use the drier parts for stock raising and the wetter parts for cultivation. But the question was complicated by the fact that most of the newcomers were cultivators, and also that the line dividing dry from wet was vague—worse, it shifted from year to year.

Early attempts to define the dividing line tended to be ignored by the settlers themselves, and they pushed the limit of cultivation into areas where plowing the soil led to its destruction. Several generations of farmers had to learn this bitter lesson, and they learned only slowly: the worst disasters on the American grasslands occurred in the 1930s and created the infamous

Dust Bowl region in the dry grasslands of the Midwest. Similarly, the Soviet Virgin Lands Program for growing cereal crops on the dry steppes was established in 1954 and is still experiencing difficulties.

Special methods are required both for farming and for ranching the grasslands successfully. Farming has to take account of the open, treeless surface, the scanty and variable rainfall and the comparatively shallow topsoil. To minimize the risk of soil erosion, farmers plant windbreaks, plow fields along the contour, and protect the soil with a covering of the previous year's stubble and by planting cover crops in rotation with cereals. Ranchers, too, have learned to live with variable rainfall. They build stock ponds, irrigate areas of fodder crops to be used as a reserve in dry years and avoid overstocking and consequent overgrazing, which destroys the quality of the grass.

Food for the world

Today, the world's principal trading supplies of cereals and meat flow from these lands, over the networks of railway which link the grasslands to mill towns, slaughter yards and ports of shipment such as Adelaide in Australia, Buenos Aires in Argentina and Montreal in Canada. Without these links to large towns, the grasslands would be of little value, for even

today their populations are sparse and the local markets are relatively insignificant.

Throughout most of the world, however, the human population continues to soar and it remains to be seen whether the grasslands can continue to supply these growing numbers with food. Undoubtedly, the output of cereals and meat can be increased, although at considerable cost in fertilizers, new crop strains, more irrigation and more machines. On the other hand, the problem at present is not mainly one of production, nor will it be in the near future. The land can produce more, but there is no point in doing so unless the yields can be made available where they are most needed.

The world's hungry people live in other regions, many of them in countries that are unable to afford imported food supplies, particularly during those years when prices are high. The major importers of temperate grassland produce are the rich industrialized nations, such as those of western Europe. Furthermore, much of the grain imported by these countries is not consumed by humans but used to feed stalled, beef-producing cattle—a highly inefficient way of using these supplies. Consequently, unless producer nations and wealthy importing nations can create a system for produce to reach those in need of it, extra output from the grasslands will be irrelevant.

9

MODERN-DAY FARMING
Livestock feed on carefully selected grasses, which are sown and fertilized by aircraft (9). Fodder crops are grown as reserve animal feed (10), and stock ponds ensure against drought (11). Feedlots (12) fatten stock on grain (13). Cereal farms (14) are highly mechanized, and road and rail serve even the remotest regions (15).

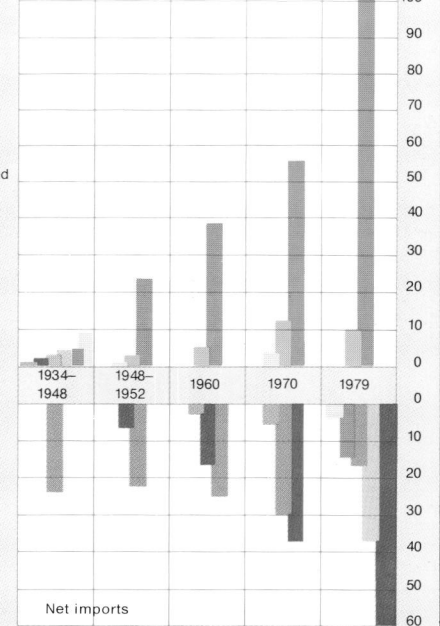

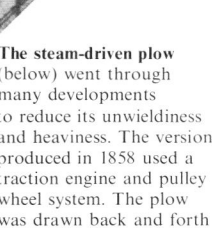

The steam-driven plow (below) went through many developments to reduce its unwieldiness and heaviness. The version produced in 1858 used a traction engine and pulley wheel system. The plow was drawn back and forth between these by a power-driven cable. This design was, however, superseded by the steam tractor, which, although unsuited to small European fields, was ideal for drawing multifurrow plows across the grasslands.

Sand-smothered farms in the heart of the Dust Bowl were rapidly abandoned during the 1930s and 40s (above). This was one costly lesson that man had to learn in the process of developing the grasslands. Traditionally grazing land, the western part of the prairies was first plowed this century. Years of drought arrived, crops died and the desert encroached.

World cereal supplies flow from temperate grasslands (right). North America is the most important producing region, for although almost all nations produce grain, few can grow enough to feed their populations and even fewer have any surplus to export or hold in reserve against poor harvests. But North America, with its prairie cornfields and its small population, exports many millions of tonnes.

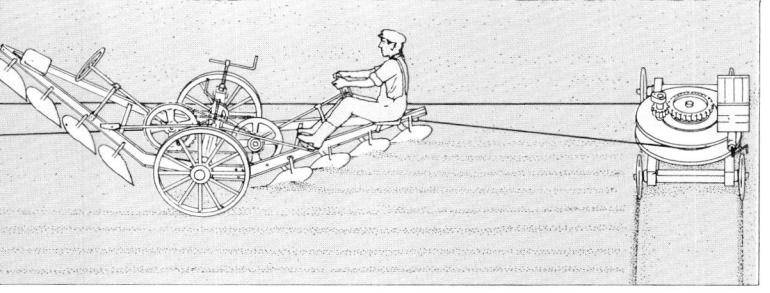

World grain-trading regions

- Africa
- North America
- South America
- Asia
- Western Europe
- Australia and New Zealand
- Former Soviet Union / Eastern Europe

Deserts

Much of the Earth's land surface is so short of water that it is defined as desert. Not all deserts are hot, sandy wastelands; some are cold, some are rocky, but all lack moisture for most of the year. Even so, a surprising variety of plants and animals have adapted to these hostile environments. Plants have developed ingenious ways of surviving long periods of drought, and many desert animals shelter during the intense heat of the day, emerging only at night to feed.

LIFE IN THE DESERT
The overriding need to obtain and conserve water dictates the pattern of desert life. Many plants close their pores during the day and most daytime creatures limit their activity to early morning and late afternoon. At night the temperature drops sharply and dew provides welcome moisture. Some plants bloom at night, and the desert is alive with insects, night-hunting birds, reptiles and small mammals.

DESERTS BY DAY

Many birds are at home in the desert. The lanner falcon of Africa and Asia gets all the moisture it needs from its diet of small birds and rodents. Sandgrouse live in the open deserts of Eurasia and North Africa; mainly seed eaters, they must make long flights each day to find water. Roadrunners, in American deserts, hunt insects, lizards and small rattlesnakes.

Lanner falcon
Falco biarmicus

Pallas's sandgrouse
Syrrhaptes paradoxus

Roadrunner
Geococcyx californianus

Large mammals are nomadic and obtain most of the moisture they need from plants. Camels can go for long periods without food or water because their humped back stores fat which can be drawn on when food is scarce, and water stored in their body tissues prevents dehydration. Addax antelopes survive entirely on plants. They roam remote parts of the Sahara, their broad hooves enabling them to travel easily over soft sand. Gazelles rely on speed. Small and fleet footed, they are able to disperse quickly over great distances to find food and water.

Arabian camel
Camelus dromedarius

Asian camel
Camelus bactrianus

Dorcas gazelle
Gazella dorcas

Addax antelope
Addax nasomaculatus

Insects and reptiles are well adapted to desert life. Desert locusts, when overpopulation threatens their food supply, change from a solitary to a swarming migratory form. Harvester ants store seeds against times of drought; desert tortoises withstand drought by becoming torpid. Lizards are cold blooded and need the sun to warm them, but must shelter from the intense heat of midday. The thorny devil, a small Australian ant-eating lizard, is protected from potential predators by its prickly scales.

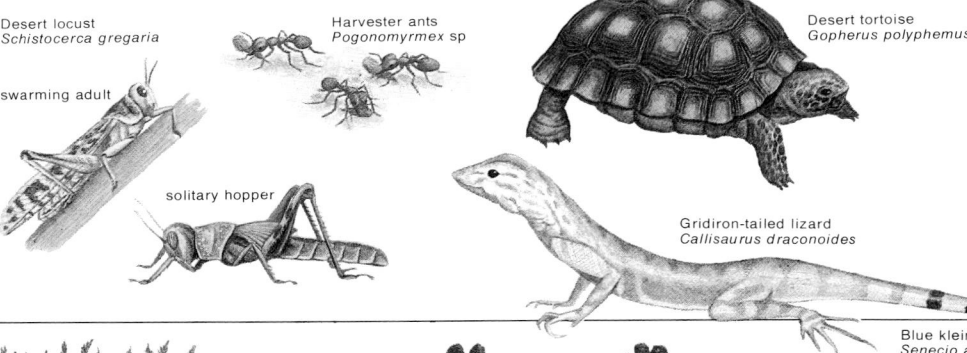

Desert locust
Schistocerca gregaria

swarming adult

solitary hopper

Harvester ants
Pogonomyrmex sp

Desert tortoise
Gopherus polyphemus

Gridiron-tailed lizard
Callisaurus draconoides

Thorny devil
Moloch horridus

Desert plants have evolved various ways of coping successfully with drought. The ocotillo of southwestern America sheds its leaves, reducing its need for water. Euphorbias, and cacti such as the prickly pear, store water in their stems. Blue kleinia, a South African succulent, has a waxy coating that limits water loss. Agaves mature very slowly, building up reserves of food and water in their leaves before they flower. Esparto, a needlegrass, is typical of many desert grasses.

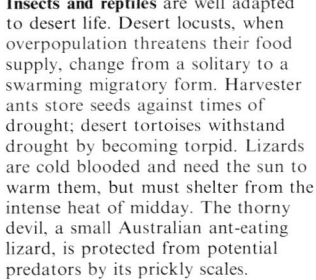

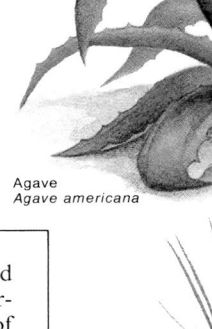

Blue kleinia
Senecio articulatus

Prickly pear
Opuntia ficus-indica

Ocotillo
Fouquieria splendens

Euphorbia
Euphorbia obesa

Agave
Agave americana

Deserts occur where rainfall is low and infrequent and where any moisture quickly evaporates or disappears instantly into the parched ground. In the driest deserts, rainfall rarely exceeds 100 mm (4 in) a year, and is so unreliable that some places may have no rain for 10 years or more. These are deserts in the truest sense of the word: harsh wildernesses that are almost totally without life. Regions with less than 255 mm (10 in) of rain a year are generally classified as arid and those with less than 380 mm (15 in) as semiarid.

Hot deserts have very high daytime temperatures in summer, although they drop sharply at night, and the winters are relatively mild. In the so-called cold deserts the summers are hot but the winters are so cold that temperatures may fall as low as −30°C (−22°F).

Desert climates and landscapes
In the subtropical latitudes, swept by hot, drying winds, high-pressure weather systems prevent rain clouds from forming. In these regions, rain comes only from local storms or follows low-pressure weather systems (often seasonal) when they move in across the desert. Large areas of central Asia have become desert because they are so far from the sea that clouds have shed all their rain before they reach them. Other deserts occur because mountains cut them

off from moisture-bearing winds. The Andes, for example, shelter the drylands of Argentina, and a high sierra stops rain from reaching the Mojave and Great Basin deserts of North America. Rain is also rare on the western sides of continents where cold ocean currents flow from the polar regions towards the Equator.

Desert climates vary not only from place to place but also with time. Over short periods rainfall is much less predictable than it is in temperate regions and droughts are frequent. Some droughts, such as those that occur along the southern fringe of the Sahara, are so severe that it may seem that the climate has changed permanently. But most droughts are short-lived and are followed by years of normal (although sparse) rainfall. Over longer periods of time, however, desert climates do change. Prehistoric cave drawings in the Saharan highlands, for example, show that elephants, rhinoceroses and even hippopotamuses—animals that are at home in wetter climates—lived in these now dry, barren uplands in a more moist period between 7,000 and 4,000 years ago.

Desert landscapes also vary enormously. They are as contrasted as the Colorado canyon country of the United States and the sandy wastes of the Middle East, but most include one or more of several basic features: steep, rocky mountain slopes, broad plains, basin floors

dominated by dry lake beds or sand seas, and canyon-like valleys. In low-lying areas, evaporation sometimes leaves a glistening residue of salt. Where there is soil, it is often sandy or consists of little more than fragmented rock, and because plant life is usually sparse there is little or no humus to enrich the ground.

Where water is life
Plant growth depends on water, and desert plants are usually widely spaced to reduce competition for what little moisture is available. Many plants rely on short, sharp rainstorms; others make use of dew and grow in locations, such as crevices in rocks, where water can accumulate. Some complete their life cycle in a single wet season, producing seeds that lie dormant during the following drought and germinate only when enough moisture is available for them to grow. These are the ephemerals that carpet the desert with a brief but brilliant display of flowers shortly after rain has fallen.

Most desert plants, however, are able to tolerate or resist drought. These are the xerophytes ("dry plants") and phreatophytes ("deep-water plants"). Xerophytic trees and shrubs have a wide-spreading network of shallow roots that take in water from a large area of ground. Many xerophytes also limit the amount of water

Esparto grass
Stipa tenacissima

Adaptations to desert life: kangaroo rats, jerboas and gerbils (A) make prodigious leaps with their long back legs to escape predators, and some desert lizards (B) run at high speed on their hind legs when pursued, using their tail for balance. Spadefoot toads have scoop-like hind feet with which they dig burrows to avoid the intense heat of day. Skinks use flattened toes fringed with scales to "swim" through the sand. Fan-toed geckos have toes that spread into fans at the tips, enabling them to walk easily on sand dunes, and the Namib palmate gecko has webbed feet that support it on loose sand.

The saguaro dominates the desert landscapes of Mexico and southern America. Immensely slow growing, it can take 200 years to reach its full height, and more than four-fifths of its weight may be water stored in its stem to be used in times of drought. To minimize water loss, it opens its pores only at night to absorb carbon dioxide and to help radiate heat accumulated by day.

Five great arid regions are bordered by semi-arid steppe and scrub. Cold deserts—the Gobi in central Asia, the Great Basin in North America and the Patagonian Desert in South America—lie in the higher latitudes. Cold ocean currents also affect climate, causing fogs to form over coastal deserts in southwest Africa, South America and Baja California, Mexico.

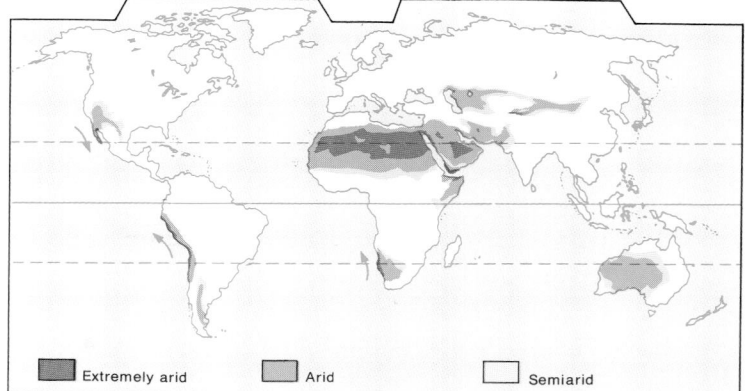

Extremely arid	Arid	Semiarid

Elf owl
Micrathene whitneyi

Great horned owl
Bubo virginianus

White-throated poorwill
Phalaenoptilus nuttallii

Long-nosed bat
Leptonycteris sanborni

Desert hedgehog
Hemiechinus auritus

Kangaroo rat
Dipodomys deserti

Fat sand rat
Psammomys obesus

Fennec fox
Fennecus zerda

Gila monster
Heloderma suspectum

Scorpion
Buthus occitanus

Honey ants
Myrmecocystus melliger

Camel spider
Solifugae

Centipede
Chilopoda

Sidewinder rattlesnake
Crotalus cerastes

Darkling beetle
Tenebrionidae

Night-blooming cereus
Selenicereus spp

Welwitschia
Welwitschia mirabilis

Saguaro cactus
Cereus giganteus

Skink
Scincus scincus

Fan-toed gecko
Ptyodactylus hasselquistii

Palmate gecko
Palmatogecko rangei

Spadefoot toad
Scaphiopus couchi

Owls and nightjars hunt under cover of darkness. Elf owls shelter by day, emerging at dusk to catch insects, and great horned owls often come into the desert at night to hunt. The poorwill, a small desert nightjar, is known to American Indians as "the sleeper." An insect eater, it sometimes survives the rigors of winter, when food is scarce, by hibernating.

Most small animals are active at night. Nectar-eating bats visit plants that blossom at night, pollinating the flowers while they feed. American kangaroo rats obtain water from a dry diet of seeds and conserve moisture by producing very concentrated urine. The sand rat of North Africa feeds on salty succulents and excretes great quantities of extremely salty urine. Hedgehogs are mainly insect eaters; the long ears of desert species help to disperse body heat. The Saharan fennec, the smallest type of desert fox, hunts lizards, rodents and locusts.

Among insects and other invertebrates the hunt for food intensifies at night. Honey ants gather nectar; centipedes and camel spiders hunt insects. The gila monster, a poisonous American lizard, eats centipedes, eggs and sometimes other lizards, and uses its tail to store fat. The sidewinder, a small rattlesnake, is active mainly at night, leaving its distinctive parallel tracks in the sand. Scorpions emerge from their burrows to stalk insects and spiders, and darkling beetles feed on dry, decomposing vegetation.

Some desert plants are nocturnal, in the sense that they bloom only at night or make use of the dew that forms when the temperature falls. The welwitschia, unique to the Namib Desert in southwest Africa, has broad, sprawling leaves on which moisture condenses at night. The night-blooming cereus of the American deserts flowers for a single night in summer. Like other nocturnal plants, its flowers are luminously pale and strongly scented to attract pollinating night insects.

that evaporates from their leaves by having small leaves, or by shedding them in the dry season. Some produce a protective covering of hairs or a coating of wax to prevent loss of moisture and to help to withstand heat.

Succulent plants, such as cacti and euphorbias, store water in their thick stems. Their leaves are usually reduced to spines, and their round or cylindrical shape also helps to reduce water loss. Spines have the added advantage in the desert of discouraging foraging animals.

The drought-resisting phreatophytes—date palms, mesquite and cottonwood trees, for example—have a similar variety of adaptations to dry conditions, but their most typical feature is a long tap root that draws water from great depths. Many plants can also tolerate the presence of salt in the soil. These are the halophytes ("salt plants") such as saltbush and other small shrubs that grow in and around salt pans.

The struggle to survive
Animals, too, need to obtain and conserve water at all costs and to be able to adjust to extremes of temperature. Most are small enough to shelter under stones or in burrows during the intense heat of day; others survive adverse conditions by becoming dormant or by migrating. For most desert creatures it is also an advantage to be inconspicuous, and many are

pale in color so that they are hard to see against their light background of sand or stones.

Many animals, especially those that are active by day, show adaptations that are strikingly similar to those of desert plants. Frogs and toads are activated by rain, emerging from dormancy to feed and mate in temporary pools and then quickly burying themselves until the next rain falls. Mammals have hairy coats that reduce water loss and also help to keep their body temperature at a tolerable level. Most desert insects have a waxy coating that serves much the same purpose.

Some geckos and other lizards store food, in the form of fat, in their tails, and camels store fat in their humped backs to sustain them when food is scarce. Honey ants force-feed nectar to some members of the colony, creating living "honey pots" for the rest of the community to feed from in times of drought. Many creatures are able to survive on the moisture contained in their food, and rarely need to drink. Most desert dwellers also have extremely efficient kidneys that produce very concentrated urine, so that little or no moisture is lost in the process.

Man enjoys no such advantages. Nevertheless, he still seeks to live in deserts, as he has for thousands of years, and the pressures he exerts on the environment may well have irrevocably changed much of the world's desert landscapes.

Man and the Deserts

Water is the key to man's survival in deserts: where water has been available, great civilizations have flourished, and man's dream of making the desert bloom has become a reality. More recently, discoveries of great mineral wealth have spurred the opening up of some of Earth's most inhospitable regions. But while man's ingenuity has made many deserts both habitable and productive, the human tendency to increase the extent of deserts has become a problem of international proportions.

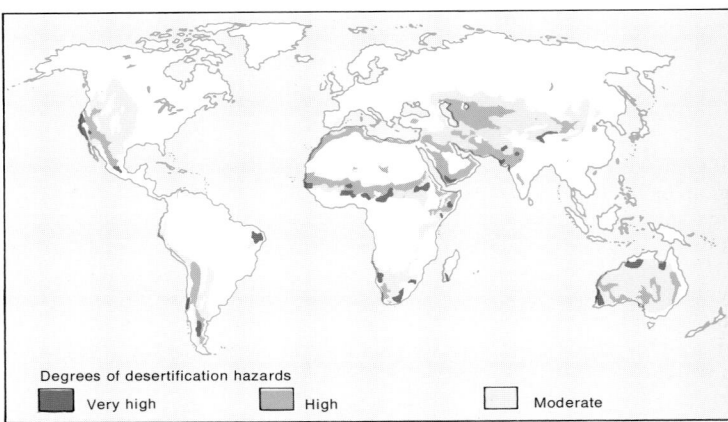

Degrees of desertification hazards

Very high   High   Moderate

Given water, much is possible, and not surprisingly man has tended to settle where water is most readily available: along the courses of rivers (such as the Nile) that rise outside the desert, and around oases fed by springs or by wells that tap groundwater supplies. But desert rainfall is so unreliable that often runoff and spring flow are uncertain in quantity and timing. Much groundwater is either also unreliable or it is fossil water that has accumulated in the geological past and is not being replenished by today's rainfall. Thus in areas such as southern Libya and some of the oasis settlements of the Arabian Gulf, and in America's arid west, groundwater is a nonrenewable resource that is being rapidly depleted.

Making water go farther
Man has also used great ingenuity to secure water supplies and to transport them to where they are needed. Runoff from flash floods that follow rare desert storms may be collected in channels and distributed to crops in nearby fields, and terracing slopes to trap runoff is a traditional way of obtaining the maximum benefit from limited rainfall. Reservoirs, ranging from the small night tanks of the southern Atacama desert in Chile to the massive artificial lakes along the Colorado river in the United States, store seasonally or perennially unreliable runoff. Also, surface runoff may be increased by reducing the permeability of runoff surfaces, a

solution engineered by the Nabataeans in the Negev desert more than 2,000 years ago and being reemployed by the Israelis today.

The transport of water is a fundamental desert activity. Open canals are typical, usually carrying water to irrigated fields—a practice used throughout the fertile crescent of Mesopotamia more than 8,000 years ago and still widespread today. A striking alternative are the ancient qanats, which limit the evaporation of water while it is in transit. Qanats are still found in the Middle East, although today pipelines are increasingly used.

Ultimately the conversion of salt water to fresh water may ensure plentiful supplies for many desert regions. The process is expensive, but large-scale desalination has already become a reality in some affluent communities such as oil-rich Saudi Arabia and Kuwait. Increasing emphasis is also being placed on more efficient use of existing freshwater supplies: in Egypt and Israel, waste water from towns is being purified and recycled for use in agriculture.

Cultivating the desert
The successful control of water has enabled large areas of otherwise arid and semiarid land to be made productive. The Egyptian civilization along the Nile depended, and still depends, on the management of seasonal floodwaters. In North America, the large-scale, long-distance piping of water has made central

Desertification—the advance of desert areas across the Earth—now affects more than 30 million sq km (12 million sq miles) and deserts are continuing to expand at an alarming rate. In recent years, on the southern edge of the Sahara alone, as much as 650,000 sq km (250,900 sq miles) of land that was once productive have been lost, and in places there is little left to show where the Sahara ends and the Sahel–Sudan region begins. Intense and often inappropriate human pressures are major causes frequently aggravated by drought: overcultivating vulnerable land, chopping down trees for fuelwood and grazing too many livestock, especially on the margins of arid lands.

THE SHIFTING SANDS
Recent decades have seen unprecedented changes in the world's deserts. Increasing pressure on the environment, especially from pastoralists and farmers, has caused extensive damage and a rapid expansion of barren land. In many desert regions, nomadism has long been the only way in which man could survive, except in oases. Today, even these traditional ways of life are changing as the exploitation of oil and other mineral resources, and the introduction of new agricultural techniques, are drawing many of the deserts into a spectacular new age of development.

The traditional pastoral response to limited water supplies and forage in desert regions is nomadic livestock herding, still practiced by the Tuareg of the northern Sahara (right) and by tribal groupings in Mongolia (left). The nomadic way of life has, however, become severely restricted in recent years. Long-distance migrations are often incompatible with the requirements of the modern state, and the poor rewards no longer match the incentives to settle in towns and cities.

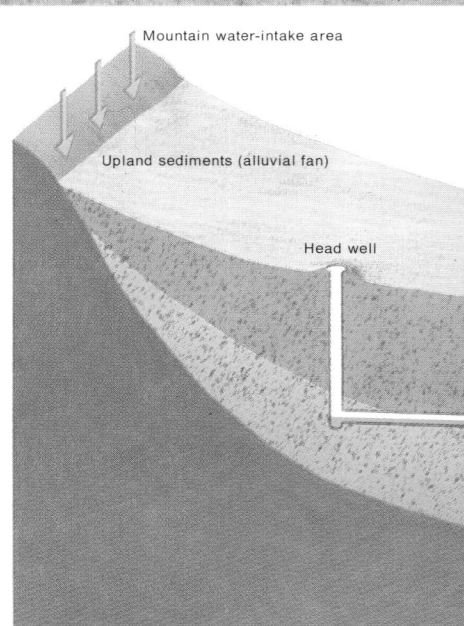

Oases have provided welcome refuges in deserts since ancient times. Secure water supplies from wells or springs make settled life possible in the midst of the most arid landscapes. Many oases are intensively cultivated with three tiers of vegetation: tall date palms shade orchards of citrus fruits, apricots, peaches, pomegranates and figs, and both palms and orchard trees shade the ground crops of vegetables and cereals. Irrigation channels distribute water to the desert soils, which are frequently rich in plant foods although they lack humus. Windbreaks help to protect cultivated land from erosion and from migrating dunes, although many oases are losing the battle with encroaching sands and the oasis people are leaving to find work in the oil fields.

Mountain water-intake area

Upland sediments (alluvial fan)

Head well

California the most productive agricultural region in the world. But while irrigation can bring enormous benefits, it can also create problems. Too much water causes waterlogging of the land, and where water evaporates in the dry desert air, concentrations of dissolved salts build up in the soil.

Farming without irrigation is possible only where rainfall, although meager, is sufficient to sustain crops with a short growing season. Soil moisture is conserved by using dry surface mulches, by fallowing and crop rotation, by planting seeds sparsely and by controlling weeds. Geneticists are also producing new varieties of cereal crops that can survive for weeks without water. Dry farming, however, is precarious. Especially at times of drought it can cause serious problems of soil erosion, chiefly by the action of wind.

Man the desert maker
The extension of dry farming into unsuitable regions, and waterlogging and the accumulation of salts in irrigated areas, are major causes of desertification—the spread of deserts into formerly habitable land. Other major causes are the overgrazing of livestock on land with too little forage and the removal of trees and shrubs for firewood by communities that have no alternative fuel supply. A sequence of drier than normal years does the rest.

Many scientists believe that desertification can be reversed, provided the pressures on the land are reduced sufficiently to allow vegetation to recover. But desertification affects such huge areas, often crossing national frontiers, that broad-scale, international cooperation is needed to coordinate reductions in population and livestock pressures and to improve understanding of drought.

In some countries the battle against desertification has already begun. In China, extensive

planting of drought-tolerant trees has created windbreaks to control sand movement and to protect farmland. In Algeria, a broad belt of trees has been planted to keep the Sahara at bay, and in Iran, advancing dunes have been halted by spraying them with petroleum residue: when the spray dries it forms a mulch that retains moisture and allows vegetation to grow, and much desert land has been reclaimed.

The deserts' riches
The exploitation of resources has also led to an "opening up" of many deserts. The rushes for precious metals in Arizona, Australia and South Africa started man's development of these regions in the nineteenth century. Some minerals, such as the evaporite deposits of Searles Basin in California and the nitrates of the Atacama desert in Chile, are actually products of the arid environment.

A resource that deserts also possess in abundance is solar power, and in many hot, dry regions the heat of the sun is used to evaporate mineral-rich solutions of salts, as well as being harnessed as a source of energy. Sunshine and the dry, clear air are also drawing ever-increasing numbers of tourists to the "sun cities" of the western United States and to Saharan oases, which were, until recently, only remote desert outposts.

No resource, however, has created as much attention or wealth as has oil. Oil has transformed the fortunes of several desert nations and provided an economic boom that has led to rapid industrialization and spectacular urban growth. The benefits of such growth in terms of affluence are substantial. The problems—the weakening of traditional desert societies, the submerging of traditional cities in the concrete labyrinths of modern complexes, and the precariousness of prosperity that is based on finite resources—are also clear.

Mineral wealth provides a powerful incentive for man's development of arid lands, and today the flow of oil rather than water is often a measure of a desert nation's prosperity. In some of the world's most desolate regions, flares signal the presence of modern "oases" where fossil fuels are being extracted—products, like the fossil waters that are sometimes trapped in the same sedimentary rocks, of the desert's geological past. Uranium, another mineral "fuel," also often lies beneath desert sands. Arid environments may also provide a rich harvest of other minerals: potash, phosphates and nitrates, valuable sources of commercial fertilizers; gypsum, manganese and salt; and borax, source of the element boron, used in nuclear reactors.

A "plastic" revolution has helped transform much of Israel's desert hinterland into productive farmland. Plastic cloches, plastic mulches and greenhouses trap moisture and reduce evaporation, and water trickled through thin plastic tubes irrigates the plants' roots with a minimum of wastage. Such innovative agricultural techniques enable Israel to produce most of its own food requirements, and fruit and vegetables grown in the relatively mild desert winters are also exported to Europe, where they command high prices.

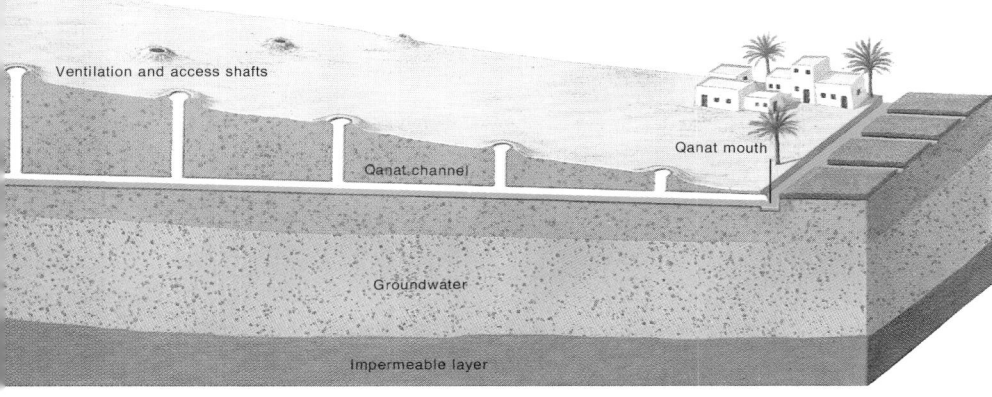

One of the most ingenious ways man has devised of bringing water to desert regions is by the ancient underground system known as the qanat. Invented by the Persians in the first millennium BC, qanats tap groundwater in upland sediments and carry it by gravity to the surface on lower land. The head well is dug first, sometimes to a depth of 100 m (330 ft), until water is reached. A line of shafts is then sunk to provide ventilation and to give access to the channel being tunneled below. Work begins at the mouth end, and a typical channel is 10–20 km (6–12 miles) long when completed, depending on the depth of the head well and the slope of the land. Its slight gradient ensures that water flows freely but gently down to ground level. Surface canals then divert the water to where it is needed. Thousands of such qanats are still in use, their routes marked by mounds of excavated debris.

Ventilation and access shafts

Qanat channel

Qanat mouth

Groundwater

Impermeable layer

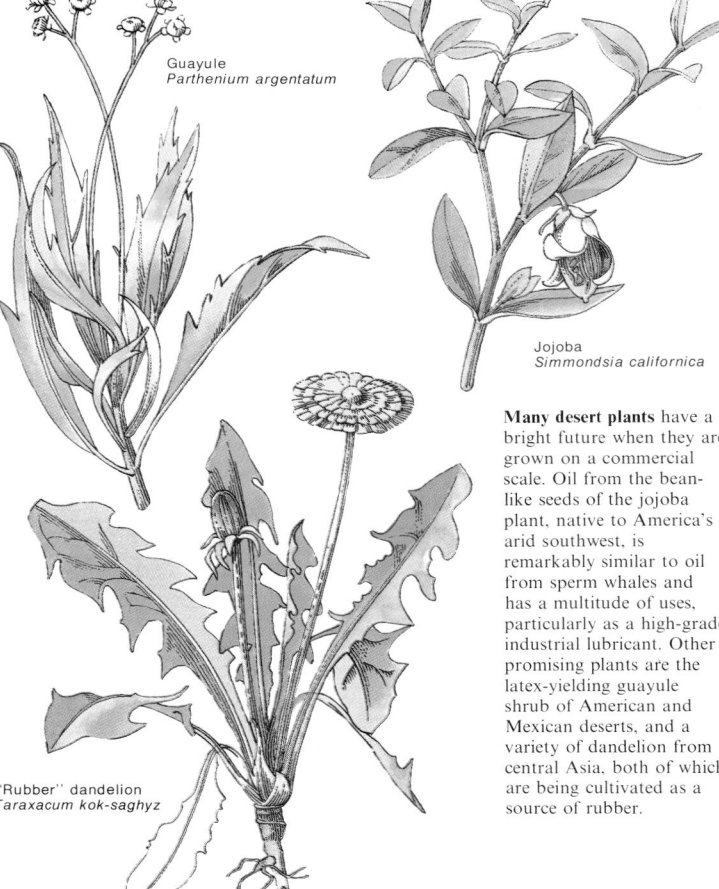

Guayule
Parthenium argentatum

Jojoba
Simmondsia californica

"Rubber" dandelion
Taraxacum kok-saghyz

Many desert plants have a bright future when they are grown on a commercial scale. Oil from the bean-like seeds of the jojoba plant, native to America's arid southwest, is remarkably similar to oil from sperm whales and has a multitude of uses, particularly as a high-grade industrial lubricant. Other promising plants are the latex-yielding guayule shrub of American and Mexican deserts, and a variety of dandelion from central Asia, both of which are being cultivated as a source of rubber.

Savannas

Between the tropical rainforest and desert regions lie large stretches of savanna, which are characterized by seasonal rainfall and long periods of drought. Those nearest to the forests usually take the form of open woodland, whereas those nearest to the deserts consist of widely scattered thorn scrub or tufts of grass. Unlike temperate grasslands, where the summers are hot but the winters are cold, savanna regions are always warm and in the wet season rain falls in heavy tropical downpours.

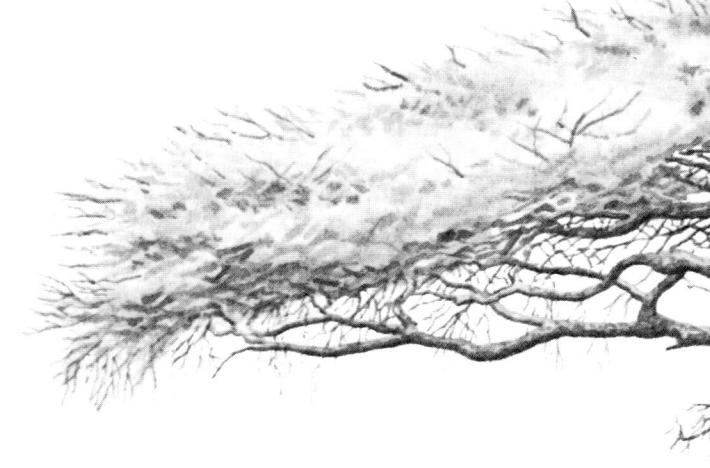

The most extensive areas of savanna are in Africa, north and south of the rainforest, and in South America, where the two main regions are the *llanos* of Venezuela, north of the Amazon rainforest, and the *campos* of Brazil in the south. Smaller areas of savanna also occur in Australia, India and southeastern Asia.

Savannas range from thickly wooded grasslands to almost treeless plains. Some are the result of man's destruction of the forest, and most are maintained in their present state by the high incidence of fire, both natural and man-made. The grasses tend to be taller and coarser than their temperate counterparts and they grow in tufts rather than as a uniform ground cover. In areas of high rainfall some grasses grow up to 4.5 m (15 ft) tall. Trees and bushes are usually widely spaced so that they do not compete with each other for water in the dry season. Humid, or moist, savannas experience 3 to 5 dry months a year, dry savannas 6 to 7 months, and thornbush savannas 8 to 10 months. Rainfall also varies widely, from more than 1,200 mm (47 in) a year in humid savannas to as little as 200 mm (8 in) where the savanna merges into desert.

Types of savannas

Humid woodland savanna presents an abrupt contrast to the rainforest. Trees tend to be scattered and some are so low growing that they are dwarfed by the tall grass that springs up during the summer rains. In the dry season the grass fuels fierce fires, which destroy all except thick-barked, large-leaved deciduous trees. Consequently, the proportion of fire-resistant trees and shrubs is large, and the grass quickly regenerates with the coming of the next rains.

In Africa this type of savanna is known as Guinea savanna north of the rainforest and as miombo savanna south of the rainforest. In South America it is known as *campo cerrado*, from the Portuguese words meaning field (*campo*) and dense. (*Campos sujos* are *campos* in which stretches of open grassland predominate and *campos limpos* are grasslands from which trees are entirely absent.) The *llanos*, or plains, of northern South America are grasslands interspersed with forests and swamps.

North of the Guinea savanna in Africa lies a belt known as Sudan savanna. The annual rainfall is in the range 500 to 1,000 mm (20–40 in) and the dry season lasts from October to April. This is typical dry savanna. Tall grasses between 1 and 1.5 m (3–5 ft) form an almost continuous ground cover and acacias and other thorny trees dot the landscape, together with branching dôm palms and massive water-storing baobab trees. Because of the interrupted tree cover the old name given to many savannas of this type was orchard steppe, and this description gives a good idea of the countryside. Like the humid woodland savannas it is maintained by regular burning of the grass in the dry season, and there is a delicate

balance and interaction between climate, soil, vegetation, animals and fire. On the desert margins the grasses grow in short tufts and the scattered acacias are seldom more than 3 m (10 ft) tall. The scrub and grasses are too widely dispersed for fires to spread, and this type of savanna is modified not by fire but by aridity and blistering heat.

Thorn-scrub and thorn-forest savannas frequently form transitional zones between tropical forests and grasslands. The *caatinga*, or "light forest," of northeastern Brazil is a typical thorn-forest savanna. Long, hot, dry seasons alternate with erratic downpours of rain, and the rate of evaporation is high. Drought-resisting trees and thorny shrubs mix with bromeliads, cacti and palm trees.

Abundance of life

No other environment supports animals so spectacular in size and so immense in numbers as do the African savannas. In spite of the concentration of animal life, however, competition for food is not severe. Each species has its own preferences and feeds from different levels of the vegetation. Giraffes and elephants can easily reach the upper branches of trees, antelopes feed on bushes at different heights from the ground, zebras and impalas eat the grasses and warthogs root for the underground parts of plants. With the onset of the dry season, massed herds assemble for the great migrations that are a major part of savanna life, moving to areas where rain has recently fallen and new grass is plentiful.

Following the grazing animals are the large predators: the lions, leopards and cheetahs. Wild dogs hunt in packs, and the scavengers—jackals, hyenas and vultures—move in to dispose of the remains of the kill.

The savannas of South America and Australia are much poorer in animal species. The only mammal of any size on the South American savanna is the elusive, nocturnal maned wolf, which eats almost anything from small animals to wild fruit. On the Australian savanna the largest inhabitant is the kangaroo, and the prime predator—apart from man—is the dingo, or native dog.

Many of the resident savanna birds are ground-living species such as the ostrich in Africa and its counterparts, the rhea in South America and the emu in Australia. The warm African climate attracts large numbers of visiting birds, which migrate each year across the Sahara to escape from the severe winter of the northern hemisphere.

For many thousands of years man has lived in harmony with the savanna. Within the last century, however, and in recent decades in particular, the savanna has come under increasing pressure. Inevitably, there is competition between the needs of the environment and those of the human population, and the future of the savanna is very much in the balance.

On each side of the Equator are broad tracts of tropical grassland known as savannas. In these regions there are distinct wet and dry seasons and temperatures are high all the year round, seldom falling below 21°C (70°F). Rain falls mainly in the hottest months, whereas the cooler months are generally dry. Thorn-scrub and thorn-forest savannas occur where the rainfall is more erratic; they have relatively little grass cover and trees and bushes can tolerate long periods of drought.

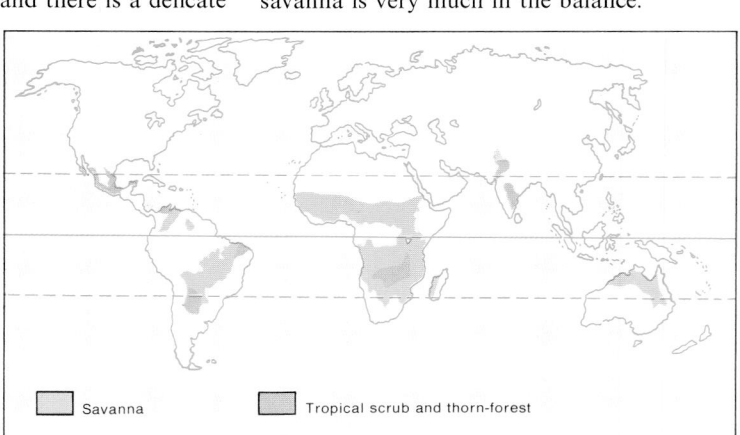

Savanna | Tropical scrub and thorn-forest

THE AFRICAN SAVANNA

More than a third of Africa is savanna, the vast parklike plains and gently rolling foothills providing the setting for a supreme wildlife spectacle. Vegetation is the basis of the immense wealth of animal life. It supports the large herds of grazing animals, and they return nutrients to the grassland in their droppings. The plant eaters, in turn, provide food for the hunters and for the scavengers that play an indispensable role by keeping the savanna free from carrion. Most of the plant-eating animals are agile and swift-footed, which enables them to escape from their enemies, and live in herds, which also provides some protection in the open habitat. Many of the animals, both predators and prey, are camouflaged: stripes or spots, at a distance, help to break up their outline; dappled markings merge with the pattern of sunlight and shade in the undergrowth; and tawny colors make them difficult to see against a background of dry grass.

THE PLANT EATERS
Most plant eaters have adapted to feeding at a particular level of the vegetation. Giraffes browse on acacia tips that other animals cannot reach and elephants use their trunks to tear down succulent branches and leaves, although both feed on low-growing vegetation when it is easily available. Elephants will also uproot trees to gather leaves that are otherwise out of reach. The black rhinoceros plucks low-growing twigs and leaves by grasping them with its upper lip (the white rhinoceros has a broad, square mouth for grazing on grass). Eland often use their horns to collect twigs by twisting and breaking them. Zebra, wildebeest, topi and gazelle all graze on the same grasses, but at different stages of the plants' growth.

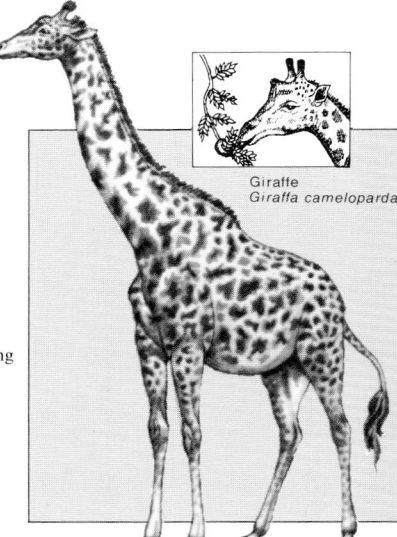

Giraffe
Giraffa camelopardali

HUNTERS OF THE PLAINS
The plant eaters provide rich hunting for the carnivores. Lions kill the largest prey and hunt in family groups; the lioness usually makes the kill but the male is the first to eat. The leopard is a solitary hunter. It lies in ambush or stalks its prey, mainly at night, in brush country where it has ground cover. Cheetahs are the swiftest of all the hunters. They usually hunt in pairs in open grassland, stalking their prey and then charging in a lightning-fast sprint. Hunting dogs travel in well-organized packs. They exhaust their quarry by chasing it to a standstill and attacking as a team. Whereas lions, leopards and cheetahs usually kill by leaping for the neck or throat, packs of hunting dogs characteristically attack from the rear.

Lion
Panthera leo

THE SCAVENGERS
When the hunters have eaten, the scavengers move in. Jackals, small and quick, make darting runs to snatch titbits while packs of hyenas use their powerful bone-crushing jaws to demolish the bulk of the carcass. Hyenas are the most voracious of the carnivores, often driving the primary predator from its kill. Vultures are frequently the first to see a kill as they circle high in the sky, but must await their turn to feed on the skin and scraps because their descent attracts the more aggressive scavengers. Carrion beetles, carrion flies and the larvae of the horn-boring moth dispose of what is left. Most of the large scavengers, particularly the hyenas, also do their own hunting, singling out prey that is small, weak or sickly.

Jackal
Canis aureus

Plants in the savanna are remarkably well adapted to withstand drought, fire and the onslaughts of the animals that eat them. Acacias tolerate both drought and fire, and are armed with sharp thorns—although many animals do feed on them, thorns and all. Red oat grass survives fire because its seeds twist deep into the ground. Bermuda, or sawtooth, grass is a favorite food of many grazers, but it recovers quickly from close cropping because its growing point lies too flat against the ground to be eaten.

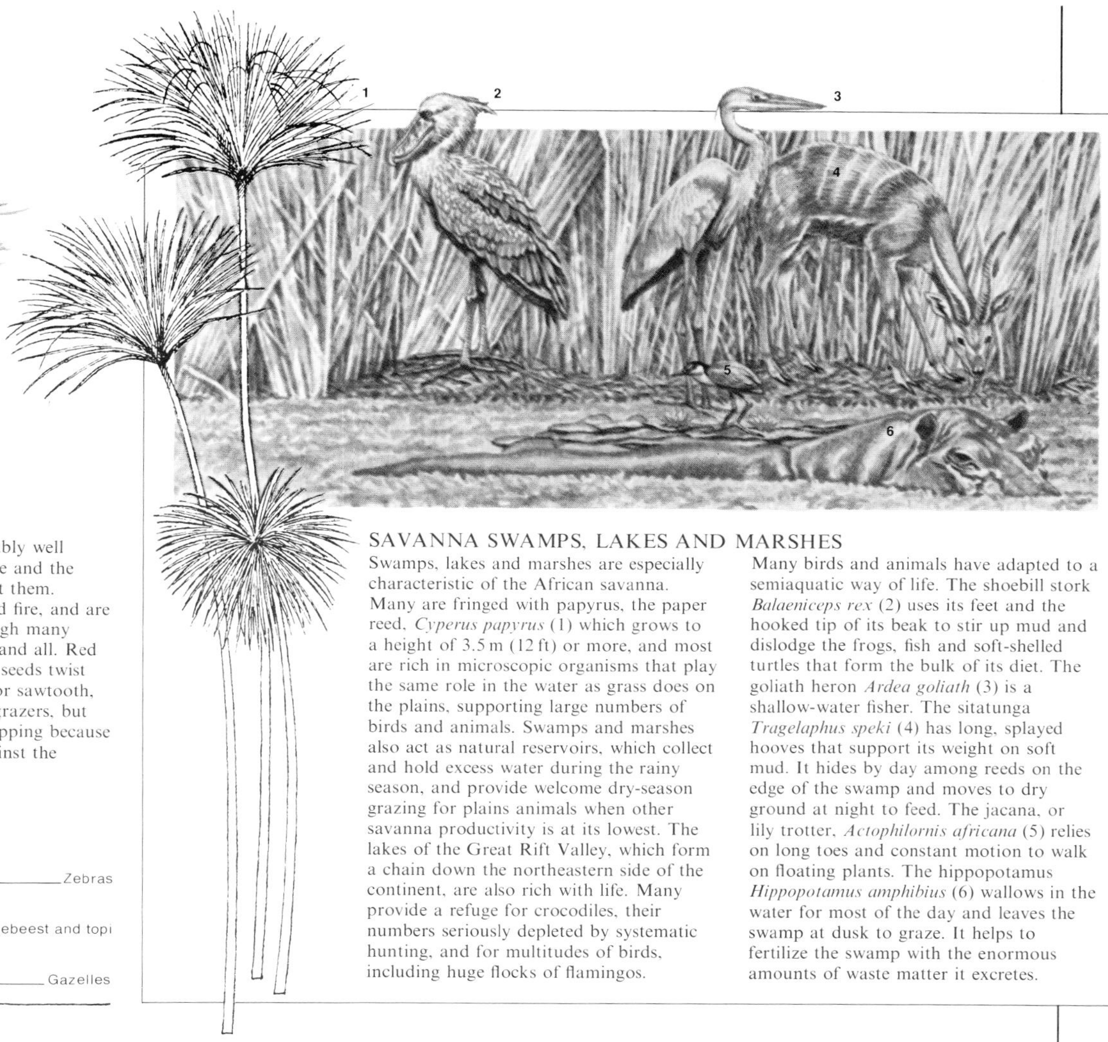

Acacia
Acacia sp

Red oat grass
Themeda triandra

Bermuda grass
Cynodon dactylon

Zebras

Wildebeest and topi

Gazelles

SAVANNA SWAMPS, LAKES AND MARSHES

Swamps, lakes and marshes are especially characteristic of the African savanna. Many are fringed with papyrus, the paper reed, *Cyperus papyrus* (1) which grows to a height of 3.5 m (12 ft) or more, and most are rich in microscopic organisms that play the same role in the water as grass does on the plains, supporting large numbers of birds and animals. Swamps and marshes also act as natural reservoirs, which collect and hold excess water during the rainy season, and provide welcome dry-season grazing for plains animals when other savanna productivity is at its lowest. The lakes of the Great Rift Valley, which form a chain down the northeastern side of the continent, are also rich with life. Many provide a refuge for crocodiles, their numbers seriously depleted by systematic hunting, and for multitudes of birds, including huge flocks of flamingos.

Many birds and animals have adapted to a semiaquatic way of life. The shoebill stork *Balaeniceps rex* (2) uses its feet and the hooked tip of its beak to stir up mud and dislodge the frogs, fish and soft-shelled turtles that form the bulk of its diet. The goliath heron *Ardea goliath* (3) is a shallow-water fisher. The sitatunga *Tragelaphus speki* (4) has long, splayed hooves that support its weight on soft mud. It hides by day among reeds on the edge of the swamp and moves to dry ground at night to feed. The jacana, or lily trotter, *Actophilornis africana* (5) relies on long toes and constant motion to walk on floating plants. The hippopotamus *Hippopotamus amphibius* (6) wallows in the water for most of the day and leaves the swamp at dusk to graze. It helps to fertilize the swamp with the enormous amounts of waste matter it excretes.

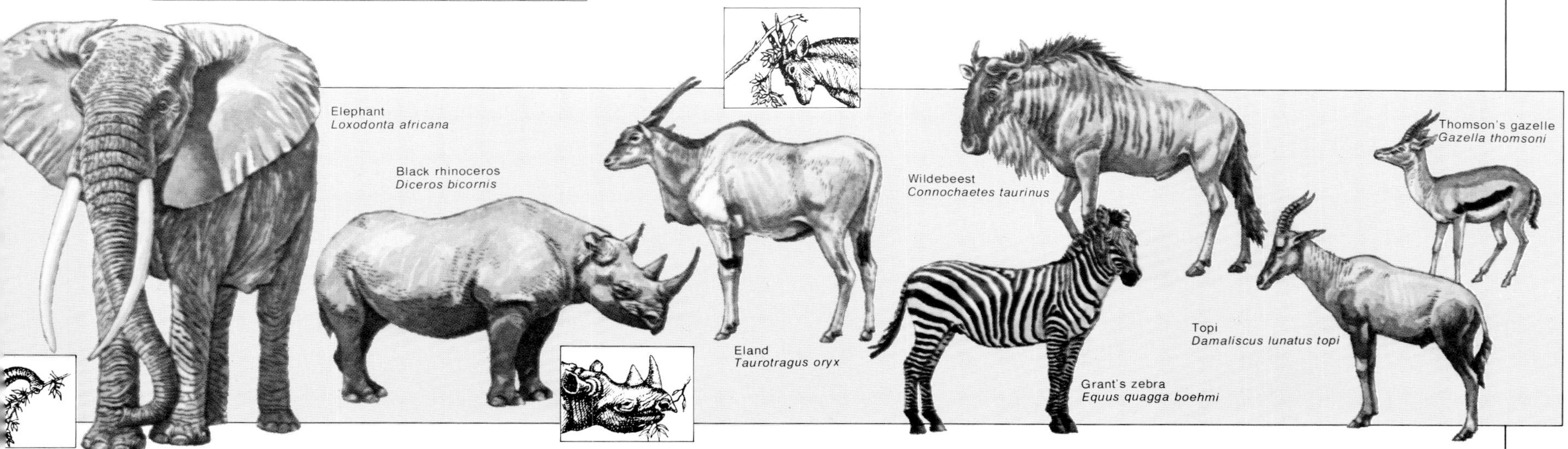

Elephant
Loxodonta africana

Black rhinoceros
Diceros bicornis

Eland
Taurotragus oryx

Wildebeest
Connochaetes taurinus

Grant's zebra
Equus quagga boehmi

Thomson's gazelle
Gazella thomsoni

Topi
Damaliscus lunatus topi

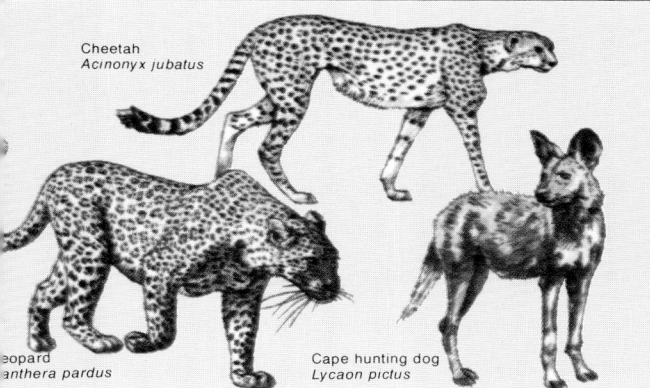

Cheetah
Acinonyx jubatus

Leopard
Panthera pardus

Cape hunting dog
Lycaon pictus

Ostrich
Struthio camelus

Secretary bird
Sagittarius serpentarius

LONG-LEGGED BIRDS
The ostrich, up to 2.4 m (8 ft) tall, can see for great distances across the plains and can outrun most of its enemies. Its territory is often shared with grazing animals, such as wildebeest, which take advantage of the ostrich's keen sight to alert them to danger. The secretary bird (so-called because of its quill-like crest) strides through the grass hunting small mammals, insects and snakes; it kills snakes by battering them with its powerful, long-clawed feet.

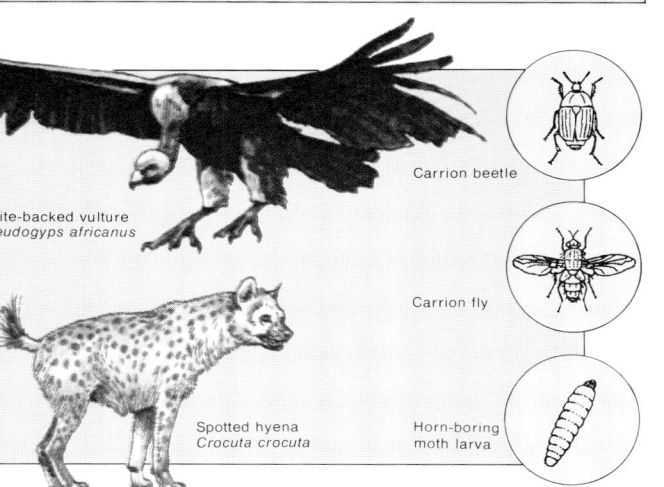

White-backed vulture
Pseudogyps africanus

Spotted hyena
Crocuta crocuta

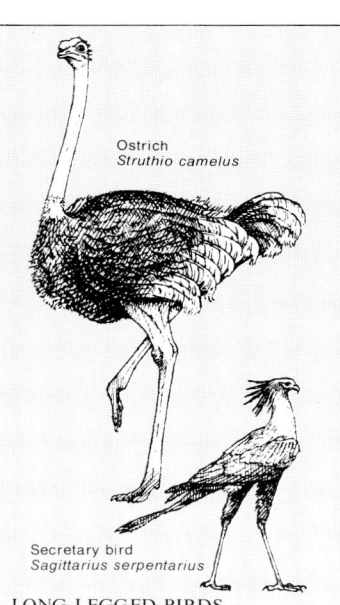

Carrion beetle

Carrion fly

Horn-boring moth larva

Large termite mounds are a distinctive feature of many savanna landscapes. The mounds, or termitaria, are made of soil excavated by the termites and bound with their saliva. Thick walls help to keep the interior at a constant temperature, and some species of termite cultivate fungus "gardens" as a source of food. The royal chamber deep inside the mound is occupied by the colony's queen, grossly distended with eggs, and her consort. Predators include the aardwolf and the aardvark. The aardwolf is related to the hyena but is smaller and has weak jaws; it digs the termites out of their mound and scoops them up with its long sticky tongue. The aardvark, distantly related to the elephant, uses its powerful hoof-like claws to break into termite nests.

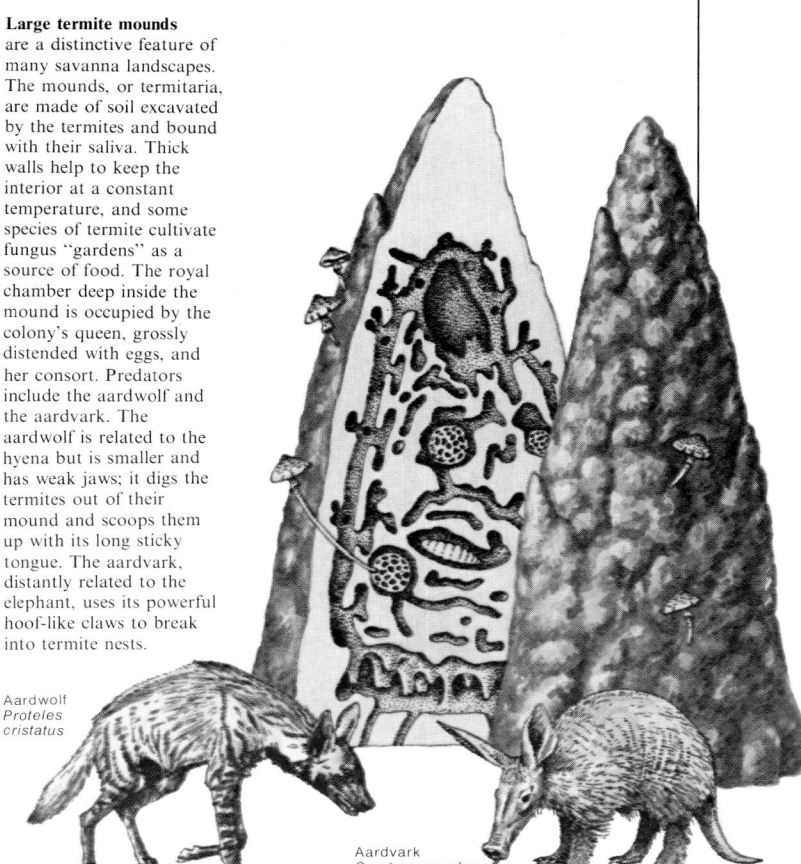

Aardwolf
Proteles cristatus

Aardvark
Orycteropus afer

Man and the Savannas

In their natural state, savannas are among the most strikingly productive of all Earth's regions. Before the coming of man they supported a wealth of animal life that has seldom been surpassed. As yet they are relatively undeveloped, but many of them lie in areas where the pressures of population growth are becoming increasingly acute. Wisely used, they offer great hope for the future, both as cattle lands and for the cultivation of food crops. But without proper management savannas can rapidly turn into wasteland, and man will be the poorer for the loss of such a great natural resource.

Throughout much of the savannas the climate is semiarid and the soils tend to be poor: stripped of their plant cover, they bake hard and crack during the long months of hot sunshine, and during the wet season they often become waterlogged or are washed away by the rains. Man's indiscriminate use of fire, unwise agricultural methods and the unrestricted grazing of domestic animals have already led to much soil loss, and erosion is widespread in tropical Africa, Asia, South America and Australia.

Systematic burning has long been practiced by the people of the savannas. Large areas are burned each year to clear land for agriculture or to remove dead grass and encourage a fresh growth to feed livestock. The resulting ash provides much-needed nutrients for crops, and the grasses rapidly produce new green shoots that provide a rich pasture for domestic herds. But although the short-term effects may be beneficial, repeated burning is harmful to the vegetation, the animals and the soil.

Trees are always more or less damaged by fire. Their trunks become twisted and gnarled, fresh shoots are killed and young trees are prevented from growing. Constant burning can destroy some species altogether, and when they disappear so too does the wildlife that depends on them for food and shelter.

Grasses, on the other hand, may be encouraged by burning, and the lush new growth that springs up when the first rains break the long dry season provides welcome nourishment for domestic herds and game animals alike. But whereas game animals move freely over the range, cropping grasses at various stages of growth, cattle tend to feed on grass only in the neighborhood of wells and other sources of drinking water. They may trample the soil and continue to graze the same area until the grass is completely suppressed.

The hazards of large projects
Cultivation in marginal areas that are unsuited to intensive agriculture also contributes to the impoverishment of the savanna. The Sahel and Sudan savannas on the fringes of the Sahara are particularly vulnerable to large-scale development projects that fail to take account of local climate and soil. Mechanized agriculture in fragile areas bordering the desert may well lead to soil erosion and dustbowl conditions, and large-scale irrigation schemes often result in waterlogging and an accumulation of salts in the soil. Cultivation in the savannas requires understanding and care. Many smaller schemes are safer—and usually more productive—than a few large ones, but not all planners yet realize that agricultural methods that are effective in temperate regions seldom come up to expectations in tropical climates.

Man first inhabited the savannas, as he did many other regions of the world, as a hunter and gatherer. He took from the land only what he needed from day to day, and although he used fire as a hunting tool, his impact was little more than that of any other savanna inhabitant. In East Africa, groups of nomadic Hadza (left) still hunt game and collect roots, fruit and the honey of wild bees, building grass huts as temporary shelters.

Small farms are scattered over much of the savannas. Plots close to houses are farmed continuously; beyond them lie the main fields, where periods of cultivation are usually followed by periods of fallow. Maize, millet and peanuts are the main food crops, and early and late crops are sometimes sown on the same plot to extend the growing season. Most of the work is done by hand, and any surplus to a family's needs is sold.

THE VULNERABLE WILDERNESS
Nowhere has man's impact on the tropical grasslands been felt more keenly than in Africa, although much of what is happening in Africa is happening also in savannas elsewhere. The majority of the people still live on the land, where the determining factor is the length and severity of the annual dry season. In the moister savannas the people are primarily cultivators, while in savannas that are too dry to sustain agriculture the main occupation is raising livestock. Most of the savannas are as yet sparsely settled, but competition is inevitably growing between man and wildlife, particularly in Africa, for the remaining tracts of relatively untouched wilderness.

The development of mineral resources and industries has led to an increasing movement of people—mainly young adults—from rural areas to towns and mining centers, attracted by opportunities for work—often at the expense of agriculture, since the heavy work of farming is left to the women, old people and children. Mining enterprises such as those in the Zambian Copper Belt (above), may recruit large labor forces from the surrounding countryside. Mining also dramatically alters the landscape, especially where the bedrock containing the ore reaches the surface and is quarried in huge terraces. The need for electricity to power mining and other industries leads, in turn, to the development of hydro-electric schemes, many of which entail resettling people whose villages are flooded by the creation of large artificial lakes.

Large areas of savanna have been set aside in East and Central Africa, and to a lesser extent in South America and Australia, as national parks and reserves where the landscape is kept intact and animals can be studied in their natural habitats. In Africa, observation platforms are frequently built close to waterholes where animals congregate to drink, and wardens use light aircraft to patrol the vast areas involved. Camel units are also used to patrol near-desert regions where much of the wildlife flourishes. Animals, such as elephants, whose numbers can grow out of control in the protected environment of the reserves are culled by licensed hunters to prevent the vegetation being destroyed. Culling maintains the health of the community as a whole and is also an economic source of meat in many countries where the people are short of protein foods.

Similarly, the introduction of European breeds of cattle into the savannas has not been an unqualified success. Not only are these breeds more susceptible to tropical pests and diseases than are the local varieties, but they are also adversely affected by the hot climate and their productivity is greatly reduced. In Africa and Brazil, native breeds are replacing more recent importations, and their productivity is being enhanced by selective breeding. In Australia, where most of the cattle are of British stock, tropical zebu, or humped cattle, are being introduced into the herds.

In the future, much more of the savanna may be developed as ranch lands, because the temperate grasslands will become less able to support enough animals to satisfy the world demand for meat. The *llanos* of Venezuela, the *campos* of Brazil and the tropical grasslands of Argentina and Australia already carry large herds of beef cattle. Throughout the savannas, however, ranching is still hampered by lack of water, poor natural pasture and remoteness from markets. In Africa, where herding is mainly nomadic, the sinking of wells by government organizations is changing the traditional ways of life, and cattle raising on a commercial

scale is likely to become increasingly important. In Africa, too, the conservation and controlled cropping of game animals could become one of the most productive—and constructive—forms of land use.

Game as a resource
The value of game animals as a source of food is considerable. Buffaloes, for example, and kangaroos in Australia, can thrive on natural grasses that will not even maintain the weight of domestic stock, and they show greater gains in weight than African and European cattle on most forms of vegetation, while several species of antelopes can survive on a water ration that is wholly inadequate for cattle.

In recent years attention has been directed toward the economics of controlled cropping of wild game, and of ranching animals such as eland, which can be kept as if they were domesticated stock and can convert poor pasture into excellent meat. Game animals are also more resistant than cattle to the tsetse fly, which infests large areas of Africa and transmits the disease trypanosomiasis (known as nagana in cattle and as sleeping sickness in man).

But for the most part game animals are still

considered to be a nuisance by man, and it is perhaps fortunate that by denying much of the savanna to domestic animals—and to man—the tsetse fly has preserved these regions from exploitation at the expense of the game. Many countries have also set aside large tracts of savanna as national parks and game reserves, where the natural environment is preserved and the wildlife can thrive.

Safeguarding the savanna
At a time when the pressure of the expanding human population calls for the development of areas hitherto uninhabited or only sparsely populated, it may seem paradoxical to maintain that the development of national parks and nature reserves is essential to the welfare of mankind. The aim of game conservation, however, is not simply to preserve rare or unusual animals for the enjoyment of posterity, or even for their scientific interest. It is to ensure that the land is put to its most economic and efficient use. The next few decades will show whether the savannas of the world will be developed into major sources of food and revenue for the countries that own them, or whether they will be misused and degraded into desert.

Commercial agriculture is important to the economies of many savanna countries. Cotton and coffee are major cash crops in Africa and Brazil, together with maize, tobacco, sisal and peanuts—crops that need a cycle of wet and dry seasons and year-round warmth. But large-scale cultivation of one crop tends to attract pests and diseases, and dependence on a single crop makes the economy vulnerable to fluctuating world prices.

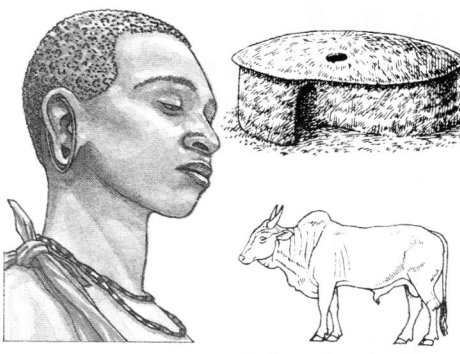

Cattle rearing takes the place of cultivation in areas that are too dry to be cropped successfully. In Africa, people such as the Masai are nomadic herders, moving their cattle long distances in search of pasture. Wealth is counted in terms of the numbers rather than the quality of the cattle they own, but improved management of their herds and better control of animal diseases are now making their cattle much more productive.

SAVANNA FIRES
Fires have been sweeping the savannas for thousands of years. Hunters set fires to flush game from cover, farmers use fire to clear land for crops, and cattle owners burn off parched, unpalatable grasses to make way for a fresh new growth for their stock. At the end of the dry season, when fires are particularly fierce, large areas of savanna lie under a thin haze of smoke.

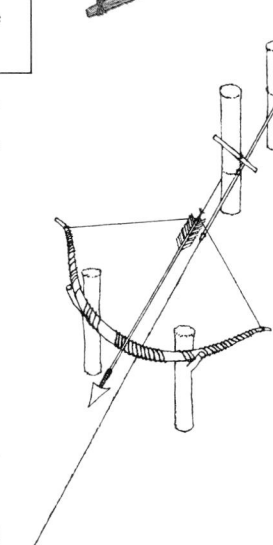

Poaching, together with the takeover of wildlife ranges by farms and livestock, has led many animals to near-extinction in areas where they were once plentiful. Poisoned arrows are capable of killing even the biggest African game: sometimes they are set as traps and are triggered by the animal itself walking into a trip line. More sophisticated poachers use machine-guns and high-powered assault rifles, and airlift their illicit cargos of skins, ivory and rhinoceros horn. Illegal hunting for meat, which is dried and sold, has also become a large, highly organized and very profitable business in many areas.

Game animals also provide the spectacular displays that attract tourists and make tourism an important source of income for many developing nations. Today, most tourists pursue game with cameras instead of guns. The hunting that led to the wholesale slaughter of wildlife in previous years is banned, and so is the traffic in trophies, although even in the sanctuary provided by parks and reserves animals still fall prey to poachers.

Animals are frequently transferred from areas where they are at risk to safer areas such as game parks and reserves. In Kenya, helicopters came to the rescue of a herd of rare antelopes when their range was threatened by a proposed irrigation scheme and moved them to Tsavo National Park. Animals are also moved to introduce new blood to small, isolated herds or to restock areas from which they have been lost.

Tropical Rainforests

Tropical rainforests, extremely rich in both plant and animal life, consist of a series of layered or stratified habitats. These range from the dark and humid forest floor through a layer of shrubs to the emerging tops of the scattered giant trees towering above the dense main canopy of the forest. Each layer of vegetation is a miniature life zone containing a wide selection of animal species. These can be divided into a number of ecological groups according to their various ways of life, and many have evolved special adaptations to enable them to make maximum use of the plentiful food supply surrounding them.

Crested tree swift
Hemiprocne longipennis

Crowned eagle
Stephanoaetus coronatus

Tropical rainforests occur only in the regions close to the Equator; they have a heavy rainfall and a uniformly hot and moist climate. There are slightly more of these forests in the northern half of the world than in the southern half and they occur at altitudes of up to 1,500 m (5,000 ft). Temperatures are normally between 24°C and 30°C (77°–86°F) and rarely fall below 21°C (70°F) or rise above 32°C (90°F). The skies are often cloudy and the rain falls more or less evenly throughout the year. Rainfall is usually more than 2,000 mm (78 in) a year and is never less than 1,500 mm (59 in). A distinctive feature of this tropical, humid climate is that the average daily temperature range is much greater than the range between the hottest and coolest months.

A stratified habitat

There are usually three to five overlapping layers in the mature tropical rainforest. The tallest trees (called "emergents") rise above a closed, dense canopy formed by the crowns of less tall trees, which nevertheless can reach more than 40 m (130 ft) tall. Below this canopy is a third or middle layer of trees—the understory; their crowns do not meet but they still form a dense layer of growth about 5–20 m (16–65 ft) tall. The fourth layer consists of woody shrubs of varying heights between 1–5 m (3–16 ft). The bottom layer comprises decomposers (fungi) that rarely reach 50 cm (20 in) in height.

Although the trees are so tall, few of them have really thick trunks. Nearly all are evergreens, shedding their dark, leathery leaves and growing new ones continuously. Many of the larger species grow buttresses—thin, triangular slabs of hardwood that spread out from the bases of their trunks. These support the trees, so removing the need for a heavy outlay of energy and resources on deep root systems. Hanging lianas (vines), thin and strong as rope, vanish like cables into the mass of foliage. They are especially abundant on riverbanks, where the canopy of trees is thinner; their leaves and flowers appear only among the treetops.

Epiphytes—plants that grow on other plants but do not take their nourishment from them—festoon the trunks and branches of trees, and up to 80 may grow on a single tree. They include many kinds of orchid and bromeliad. Their aerial roots make use of a humus substitute derived from the remains of other plants, often

Tropical rainforests

Tropical rainforests are located in the hot and wet equatorial lands of Latin America, West Africa, Madagascar and Asia. These areas have consistently high temperatures throughout the year and receive high rainfall from the moist and unstable winds blowing in from the oceans.

The hummingbird numbers about 300 species, most of which are confined to the forests of South America. It is renowned for its ability to hover while gathering nectar, a feat achieved by the almost 180° rotations of its wings, which beat rapidly more than 80 times per second.

brought together by ants. The bases of their leaves may be broad and bowl shaped and collect and hold water; they also provide homes for a variety of insects and reptiles.

Rainforest soils are not as fertile as might be supposed by the luxuriance of their vegetation. On the contrary, the silicates and compounds necessary for plant growth are leached away by the rain to leave red or yellow soils of poor quality. This process, known as laterization, is widespread in the humid tropics. Humus is rapidly broken down by bacteria, fungi and termites, while earthworms, which in more temperate regions normally contribute to the mixing of humus with mineral particles, are usually absent.

In rainforests there are often up to 25 different tree species on a single hectare of land (60 species to the acre). Most temperate forests have only a fifth of this number, with nothing like the abundance of plants that grow in the tropics. This incredible variety supports—directly or indirectly—a corresponding variety of animal species which has an abundant food supply because the forest never ceases to be productive. This is why most mammals do not move far; they stay where their food grows.

Life in the canopy

The dense leaves and branches of the canopy provide the most food and so support the greatest number of species. Macaws and toucans (from the American tropics) and parrots and trogons (which live in forests throughout the tropics) eat the fruit growing in the

THE LAYERS OF THE FOREST

Stratification—the existence of distinct layers of forest vegetation—is especially pronounced in the tropics, where there are usually five main storys. These can overlap greatly and may vary in height from area to area. The large differences between the layers present many varied habitats and ecological niches for a very wide range of animals.

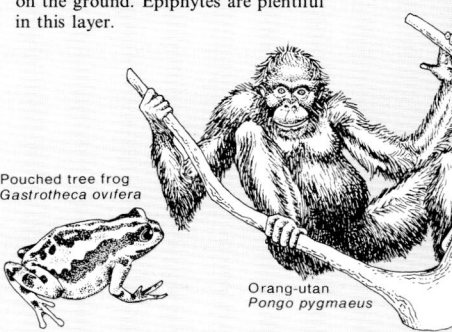

CANOPY LAYER
This dense story exerts a powerful influence on the levels below since its trees, which grow between 20 m (65 ft) and 40 m (130 ft) tall, form such a thick layer of vegetation that they cut off sunlight from the forest below. The canopy is noted for the diversity of its fauna. Many birds and animals are adapted to running along branches to get the flowers, fruits or nuts that form their diets. The pointed tips of canopy leaves encourage rapid drainage.

Sacred langur
Presbytis entellus

Tree shrew
Tupaia glis

MIDDLE LAYER
This understory comprises trees from 5 m (16 ft) to 20 m (65 ft) tall whose long, narrow crowns do not become quite so dense as those of the canopy. There is very often no clear distinction, however, between this level and the canopy. Middle-layer trees are strong enough to bear large animals such as leopards that spend part of their lives on the ground. Epiphytes are plentiful in this layer.

Leopard
Panthera pardus

Pouched tree frog
Gastrotheca ovifera

Orang-utan
Pongo pygmaeus

Moth orchid
Phalaenopsis sanderana

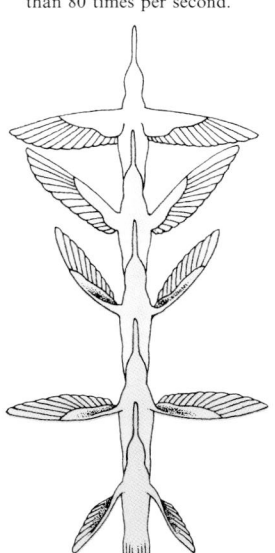

SHRUB LAYER
The vegetation of this level is sparse in comparison with that above it and consists of treelets and woody shrubs that rarely reach 5 m (16 ft). These grow up in any available space between the abundant boles of large trees. Life in this story exists equally well at ground level.

Four-striped squirrel
Funisciurus lemniscatus

Oriental civet
Viverra tangalunga

Tree pangolin
Manis tricuspis

Flowering plants of the forest include epiphytes such as bromeliads and orchids like the species of *Phalaenopsis* illustrated here. Epiphytes grow on other plants such as trees where they can receive sunlight and are nourished by humus in the bark. Many epiphytic orchids have swellings in their roots or at the bases of their leaves where water can be stored. Seventy species of *Phalaenopsis* grow in southeast Asian forests and *P. sanderana*, one of the most beautiful, was first discovered in the Philippines in 1882.

GROUND LAYER
Shade-tolerant herbs, ferns and tree seedlings represent the only flora at ground level; there is no grass there. Light is less than one percent of full daylight so that many mammals are well camouflaged in the gloom, whereas others have compact bodies to facilitate movement through the undergrowth. Ants and termites are well adapted to the high humidity and darkness of the forest floor. Fungi and a host of invertebrates quickly break down the litter of rotting leaves, fruit and fallen branches to provide vital nutrients for the fast-growing trees of the tropical rainforest.

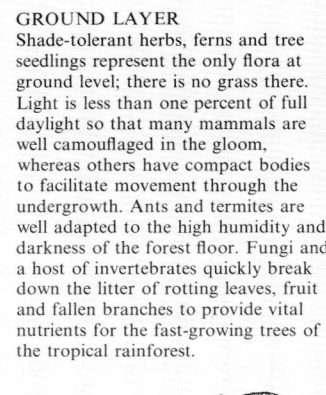

Okapi
Okapia johnstoni

Forest buffalo
Syncerus caffer nanus

Indian tiger
Panthera tigris tigris

Malayan tapir
Tapirus indicus

Congo forest mouse
Deomys ferrugineus

Short-eared elephant shrew
Macroscelides proboscideus

Orange-rumped agouti
Dasyprocta aguti

Mandrill
Mandrillus sphinx

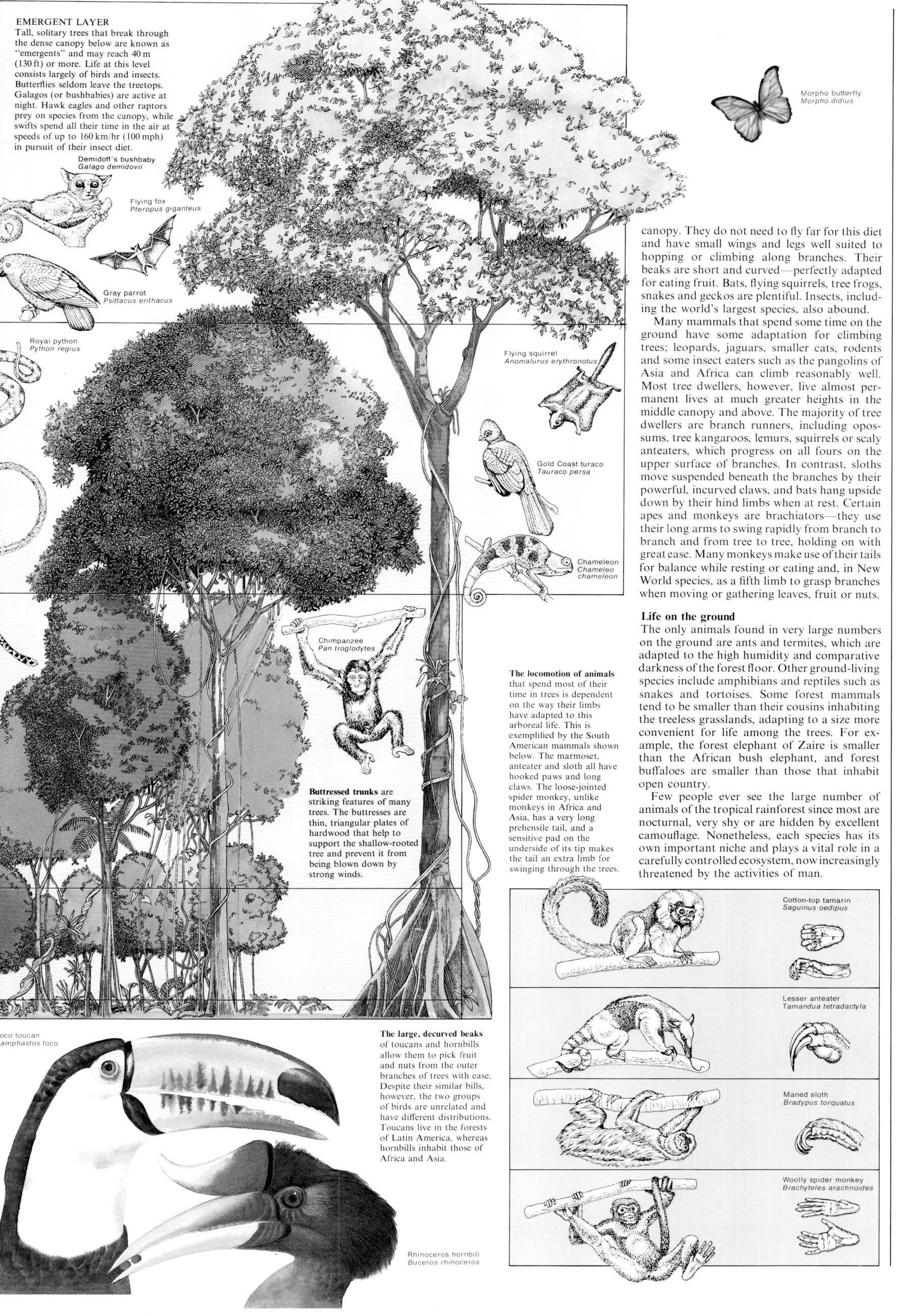

EMERGENT LAYER

Tall, solitary trees that break through the dense canopy below are known as "emergents" and may reach 40 m (130 ft) or more. Life at this level consists largely of birds and insects. Butterflies seldom leave the treetops. Galagos (or bushbabies) are active at night. Hawk eagles and other raptors prey on species from the canopy, while swifts spend all their time in the air at speeds of up to 160 km/hr (100 mph) in pursuit of their insect diet.

Demidoff's bushbaby
Galago demidovii

Flying fox
Pteropus giganteus

Gray parrot
Psittacus erithacus

Morpho butterfly
Morpho didius

Royal python
Python regius

Flying squirrel
Anomalurus erythronotus

Gold Coast turaco
Tauraco persa

Chameleon
Chameleo chameleon

Chimpanzee
Pan troglodytes

Buttressed trunks are striking features of many trees. The buttresses are thin, triangular plates of hardwood that help to support the shallow-rooted tree and prevent it from being blown down by strong winds.

The locomotion of animals that spend most of their time in trees is dependent on the way their limbs have adapted to this arboreal life. This is exemplified by the South American mammals shown below. The marmoset, anteater and sloth all have hooked paws and long claws. The loose-jointed spider monkey, unlike monkeys in Africa and Asia, has a very long prehensile tail, and a sensitive pad on the underside of its tip makes the tail an extra limb for swinging through the trees.

Toco toucan
Ramphastos toco

The large, decurved beaks of toucans and hornbills allow them to pick fruit and nuts from the outer branches of trees with ease. Despite their similar bills, however, the two groups of birds are unrelated and have different distributions. Toucans live in the forests of Latin America, whereas hornbills inhabit those of Africa and Asia.

Rhinoceros hornbill
Buceros rhinoceros

Cotton-top tamarin
Saguinus oedipus

Lesser anteater
Tamandua tetradactyla

Maned sloth
Bradypus torquatus

Woolly spider monkey
Brachyteles arachnoides

canopy. They do not need to fly far for this diet and have small wings and legs well suited to hopping or climbing along branches. Their beaks are short and curved—perfectly adapted for eating fruit. Bats, flying squirrels, tree frogs, snakes and geckos are plentiful. Insects, including the world's largest species, also abound.

Many mammals that spend some time on the ground have some adaptation for climbing trees; leopards, jaguars, smaller cats, rodents and some insect eaters such as the pangolins of Asia and Africa can climb reasonably well. Most tree dwellers, however, live almost permanent lives at much greater heights in the middle canopy and above. The majority of tree dwellers are branch runners, including opossums, tree kangaroos, lemurs, squirrels or scaly anteaters, which progress on all fours on the upper surface of branches. In contrast, sloths move suspended beneath the branches by their powerful, incurved claws, and bats hang upside down by their hind limbs when at rest. Certain apes and monkeys are brachiators—they use their long arms to swing rapidly from branch to branch and from tree to tree, holding on with great ease. Many monkeys make use of their tails for balance while resting or eating and, in New World species, as a fifth limb to grasp branches when moving or gathering leaves, fruit or nuts.

Life on the ground

The only animals found in very large numbers on the ground are ants and termites, which are adapted to the high humidity and comparative darkness of the forest floor. Other ground-living species include amphibians and reptiles such as snakes and tortoises. Some forest mammals tend to be smaller than their cousins inhabiting the treeless grasslands, adapting to a size more convenient for life among the trees. For example, the forest elephant of Zaire is smaller than the African bush elephant, and forest buffaloes are smaller than those that inhabit open country.

Few people ever see the large number of animals of the tropical rainforest since most are nocturnal, very shy or are hidden by excellent camouflage. Nonetheless, each species has its own important niche and plays a vital role in a carefully controlled ecosystem, now increasingly threatened by the activities of man.

Man and the Tropical Rainforests

Every three seconds a portion of original rainforest the size of a football field disappears as man fells the trees and extends his cultivation. Although tropical conditions allow rapid regrowth of secondary forest, the loss of primary forest is destroying thousands of plant and animal species that will never again be seen on Earth. Even by conservative estimates, it is likely that all the world's primary tropical forest will have disappeared within 85 years unless the trend is reversed.

The activities of man have only recently begun to threaten the tropical rainforest. Since pre-historic times, forests have offered shelter to people who, lacking any knowledge of agriculture, have existed as hunters and gatherers. They used only stone and wooden weapons such as bows and arrows to kill their animal prey, and collected berries, fruit and honey from their surroundings. Their influence on the forest environment was minimal and today a few races such as African pygmies and the Punans of Borneo still live in such a simple state of balance with nature. The Punans, for example, have no permanent homes, but use leaves and branches to construct temporary shelters that are used for only a few weeks before being abandoned. The pygmies build similar homes.

Shifting agriculture

Most forest dwellers, however, live in more permanent settlements and grow most of their food in forest clearings they have made. Such people are expert at chopping down trees in order to set fire to them, and this "slash-and-burn" farming results in small areas littered with charred logs and stumps whose ashes enrich the ground. Crops such as wild tapioca (cassava or manioc) are widely grown, but after a year or two the soil loses the little fertility it once had so that a new tract of forest has to be cleared and burned. Such shifting agriculture provides food for more than 200 million inhabitants of the Third World. As a farming system it has been used throughout the world for more than 2,000 years. When there were few farmers per kilometer the land was allowed to lie fallow for at least 10 years so that the soil could recover. Today, however, population pressures are so great that fallow periods have been drastically reduced and a swift repetition of slash-and-burn degrades and removes nutrients from the soil.

Effects on world climate

Tropical forest floors seldom have deep layers of humus so that, once trees are removed, the shallow topsoil is exposed and soon becomes eroded. In turn, this reduces the capacity of the ground to retain moisture, and without this sponge-like effect runoff can become very erratic and lead to floods, such as those that frequently occur in India and Bangladesh. Estuary sedimentation is often greatly increased

Living in harmony with the forest are small groups of hunter gatherers who mainly live on a flesh diet, killing their prey with bows and arrows. Nuts and berries supplement this diet, and leaves gathered from the immediate jungle cover their temporary dome-shaped shelters. These are abandoned as an area becomes exhausted and the tribe moves on. Twenty or so pygmies need about 500 sq km (200 sq miles) to support themselves.

Selective logging by gangs of men seeking out the straightest and most valuable hardwood species has been the most common form of tree extraction, even though 75 percent of the canopy might have to be destroyed to remove just a few important trees. Today heavy axes are being replaced by power saws that have no difficulty in cutting down the large buttresses that were once left behind.

Plantation forestry has made increasing inroads into the forests over the decades. The commercial advantage of products that can be cropped several times during the hardwoods' maturation period is becoming increasingly apparent to farmers in the regions. Many rubber plantations in southeastern Asia consist of small holdings that have tended to encroach upon the forest, and intercropping now takes place between the long-established trees.

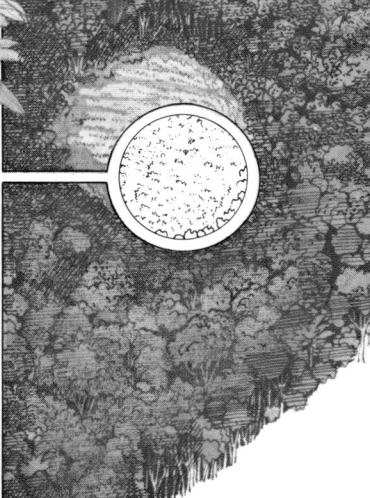

Shifting cultivation converts thousands of square kilometers of primary forest to substandard cultivation every year. Forest is cleared by slash-and-burn, the resulting fertile clearing is cropped with staples such as manioc, and then left to degrade to secondary forest once the ash-strewn ground has lost its poor fertility. Inevitably, the ground becomes permanently degraded. One encouraging antidote to the futility of such shifting agriculture is the recent strategy of agroforestry (as used by countries such as Nigeria and Thailand), which encourages the planting of fast-growing trees at the same time as the farmer's normal crops. Such intercropping offers considerable financial incentives to the small itinerant farmer.

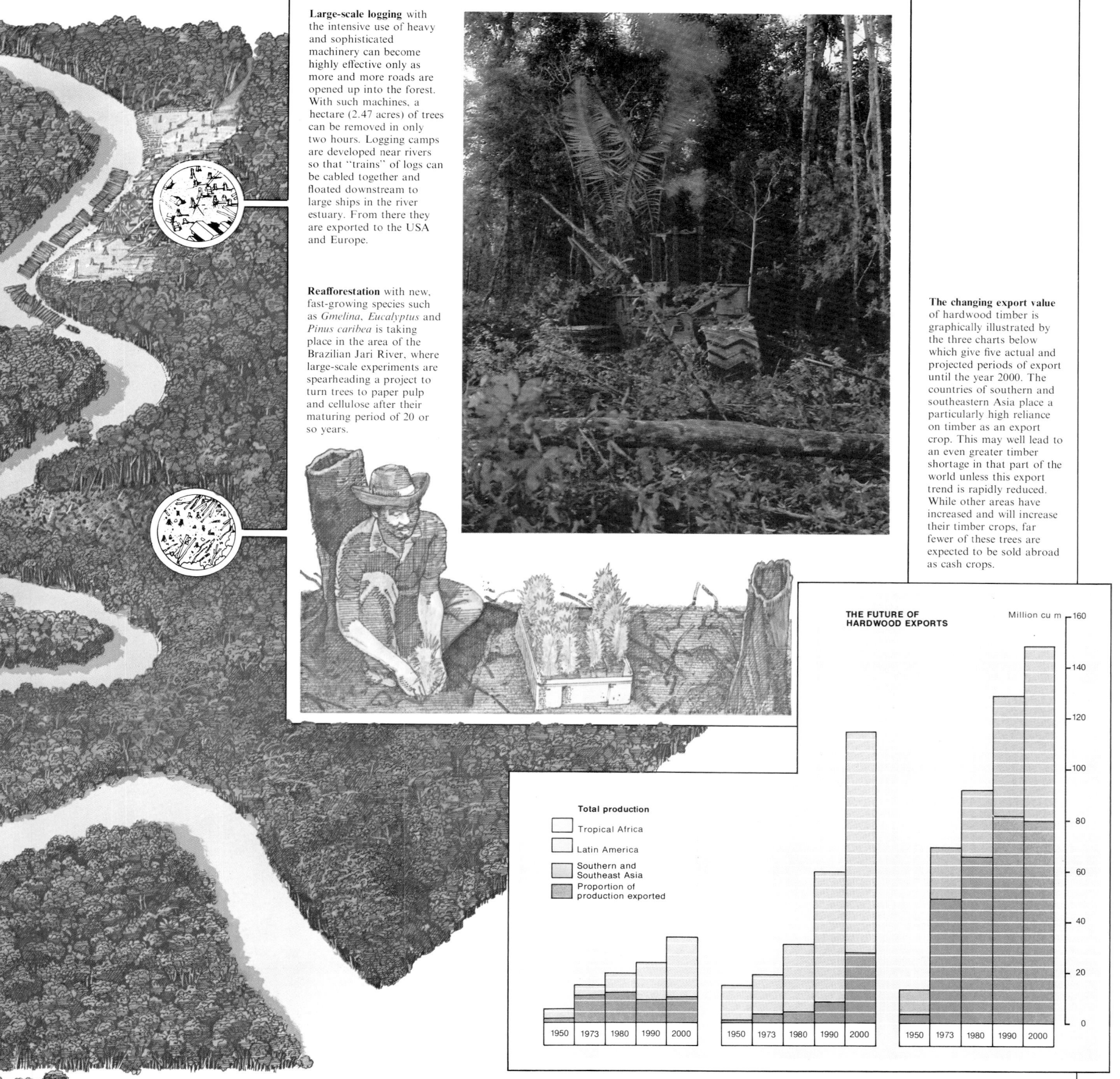

Large-scale logging with the intensive use of heavy and sophisticated machinery can become highly effective only as more and more roads are opened up into the forest. With such machines, a hectare (2.47 acres) of trees can be removed in only two hours. Logging camps are developed near rivers so that "trains" of logs can be cabled together and floated downstream to large ships in the river estuary. From there they are exported to the USA and Europe.

Reafforestation with new, fast-growing species such as *Gmelina*, *Eucalyptus* and *Pinus caribea* is taking place in the area of the Brazilian Jari River, where large-scale experiments are spearheading a project to turn trees to paper pulp and cellulose after their maturing period of 20 or so years.

The changing export value of hardwood timber is graphically illustrated by the three charts below which give five actual and projected periods of export until the year 2000. The countries of southern and southeastern Asia place a particularly high reliance on timber as an export crop. This may well lead to an even greater timber shortage in that part of the world unless this export trend is rapidly reduced. While other areas have increased and will increase their timber crops, far fewer of these trees are expected to be sold abroad as cash crops.

THE FUTURE OF HARDWOOD EXPORTS

Million cu m

Total production
- Tropical Africa
- Latin America
- Southern and Southeast Asia
- Proportion of production exported

1950 1973 1980 1990 2000 | 1950 1973 1980 1990 2000 | 1950 1973 1980 1990 2000

as the forest topsoil is simply washed away by torrential rain. In parts of Asia, deforestation has caused changes in water flow that have interfered with the production of new high-yield rice crops.

Tropical forests contain an enormous store of carbon, and some authorities believe that its release into the air (as carbon dioxide) when the forest is burned down may be as great in volume as that released by the rest of the world's fossil fuels. The higher proportion of carbon dioxide in the atmosphere may lead to an increase in global temperatures, especially at the poles. Trees also release oxygen into the air through photosynthesis, and some scientists have estimated that half of the world's oxygen is derived from this source. Others estimate that half of the rainfall of the Amazon basin is generated by the forest itself, so that any great reduction in tree cover would turn Amazonia into a much drier region.

Threats to Amazonia

Much attention has been paid to the situation of Amazonia, covering as it does some 6.5 million sq km (2½ million sq miles). In an attempt to give better access to timber and mineral reserves, the Brazilian government's building of the TransAmazonian Highway (3,000 km or 1,860 miles long) has opened the way to deforestation, and settlers have been encouraged to make small holdings on the cleared forest beside the road. Between 1966 and 1978, the government calculated that farmers and big business interests had turned 80,000 sq km (31,000 sq miles) of forest into grazing land for 6 million cattle intended for hamburgers. However, like the wholesale extraction of timber, this has proved to be of doubtful economic value. Because costs rise steeply as less accessible areas are tapped, expenses tend to eliminate logging profits.

Threats in Africa

Even greater threats to tropical forest land have come from less cautious and realistic governments, such as that of Ivory Coast. There neither shifting agriculture nor excessive logging for valuable export sales appear to be under any sort of control. Accordingly, between 1966 and 1974, the area of forest declined from 156,000 sq km (60,000 sq miles) to 54,000 sq km (20,000 sq miles), much of the latter being secondary forest that can never be returned to its original status. Like many other developing countries, Ivory Coast has been more keen to cut down and export its profitable timbers than to think about protecting its invaluable forest environment. Inevitably, forest farmers move into cleared areas and often establish plantation cash crops such as coffee, cocoa and rubber, while the establishment of national parks to curtail depletion has often had very little profitable effect. The Malaysian rainforest is also disappearing rapidly, through widescale logging and open-cast mining for bauxite (aluminum ore).

A large proportion of the world's rainforest occurs in tropical countries faced with severe problems of population control. It is therefore inevitable that the pressures on such forests will be great. Human interference does more than merely destroy the primary forest, to be replaced in time by secondary growth; more importantly, the wholesale removal of trees also drastically reduces the vast genetic reservoir contained in the number of plant and animal species the forests harbor. This in itself is a sound ecological argument for preserving forests and for reversing current trends towards monoculture in the tropics. All the warnings about forest depletion appear to be clear, yet there seems little hope that man will heed them until it is too late.

Monsoon Regions

The word monsoon often conjures up the image of torrential rain and steaming tropical jungles. Yet such a view is misleading, for very great contrasts occur in the regions of the tropical world with a monsoon climate. What distinguishes monsoon regions is not so much the amount of rainfall or the permanently high temperatures, but the dramatic contrast between seasons, with an extended dry season as an essential feature. And in fact the word monsoon derives from the Arabic word for season.

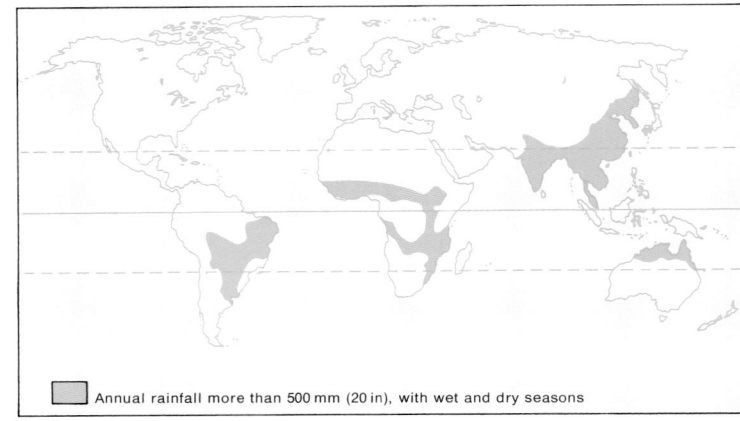

THE SEASON OF RAIN
Life in the monsoon regions balances on the expectation of seasonal heavy rain. In much of India, for instance, 85 percent of the annual rainfall occurs during the limited monsoon periods, and humans as well as plants and animals depend on it wholly. About half the world's people live in these regions, in communities whose rhythm of life necessarily reflects the rains' seasonal nature.

This contrast between wet and dry seasons reflects the reversals of winds over sea and land, which in the northern hemisphere blow from the northeast in the dry winter season, and from the southwest in the wet summer periods.

The monsoon regions occur most widely in southern, southeastern and eastern Asia to the south of latitude 25°N, and in western and central Africa north of the Equator, but there are also smaller regions with a characteristically monsoon climate in eastern Africa, northern Australia and central America. Despite the similar overall climatic pattern, however, the monsoon regions are otherwise very diverse.

Before human settlement the original vegetation of the monsoon regions reflected the dominance of an extended dry season followed by a period of violent rainfall. Typical forest cover was provided by the sal (*Shorea robusta*) deciduous forest, which adjusts to extended periods of moisture deficiency by shedding its leaves. However, within the monsoon region rainfall varies from 200 mm (8 in) a year to more than 20,000 mm (800 in), and the rainy periods may vary between three and nine months.

The range of vegetation found in the monsoon regions reflects this diversity. Where tropical rainforest alters to monsoon forest, as in eastern Java, there is a sharp fall in the total number of plant and animal species, and species adapted to endure seasonal drought begin to be seen. At the other extreme of rainfall the forest thins and shades into semidesert vegetation in India's northwest. But if there is a "type" of monsoon vegetation it is tropical deciduous forest, with sal as the dominant species.

As well as contrasts in climate, the monsoon regions also exhibit pronounced changes in temperature and vegetation as a result of variations in altitude. The Western Ghats of India and the foothills of the Himalayas in Assam both rise to more than 2,500 m (8,200 ft). Temperatures decrease sharply at such altitudes with corresponding changes in vegetation. In southern India on the Nilgiri Hills a wet temperate forest is characteristic, with an intermingling of temperate and tropical species. Magnolias, planes and elms all grow there.

Agriculture in monsoon regions
Despite its extensive area there is no part of the monsoon world that is untouched by man and by man's activities. In southern Asia, agricultural activity can be traced back at least 5,000 years, and there have been agricultural settlements throughout the monsoon regions for at least 1,500 years. Man's activity and the grazing of domesticated animals have interfered with, and progressively modified, the natural vegetation. The range of species indicates that, in the whole of the monsoon biome, there is now virtually no primary forest left. The pace of man's interference has speeded up considerably over the last 100 years. As a result, less than 10 percent of the land in southern Asia is now forested, and other parts of the monsoon

Many parts of the world experience "monsoon" winds, blowing from sea to land in summer, and from land to sea in winter; but typical monsoon vegetation is most clearly seen in the regions of southeastern Asia and the Indian subcontinent. In climatic terms, however, the monsoon circulation of seasonal wind reversals, with wetter summers and dry winters, also affects considerable areas of Africa, South America and northern Australia.

Annual rainfall more than 500 mm (20 in), with wet and dry seasons

regions are similarly losing their forest cover.

Many of today's farming methods incorporate traditional cultivation practices, but there have also been very significant changes in recent decades. Traditional agriculture in the monsoon regions has been developed to take into account the seasonal nature of its rainfall pattern and the total rainfall received. The fundamental role of water throughout the region and the absence of low temperatures have placed great importance on either cultivating crops that can tolerate the seasonal rainfall pattern, or on providing irrigation.

Through most of southern Asia, overwhelmingly the most populous of the monsoon regions, the most important single crop is rice, which covers about one-third of the total cultivated area. Rice needs a great deal of water and for this reason is grown mainly in areas of high irrigation, such as the delta lands of the southern and eastern coasts of India, and in areas where rainfall is more than 1,500 mm (59 in) a year. Its cultivation creates a very distinctive landscape as a result of the fact that rice must spend much of its growing period with a few centimeters of water over the soil.

Rice cultivation gives the monsoon regions their characteristic pattern of paddy fields, but other cereal crops such as wheat, the millets and sorghum are also very important. These can tolerate far drier conditions than can rice and occur in areas such as central India or upland Thailand, where uncertain and less abundant rainfall puts a premium on drought tolerance.

Even with traditional crops, man has often interfered extensively with the environment in order to increase yields and attempt to guarantee successful cropping. Traditional irrigation schemes range from diverting rivers at times of flood, in order to lead water to dry land, to digging wells and building small reservoirs. But recent technological developments have brought a new dimension to agricultural activity in the monsoon regions. Large-scale dam and irrigation canal schemes have become important in Africa as well as in monsoon Asia. The introduction and speed of electric or diesel "pumpsets" have transformed well irrigation in regions with extensive groundwater. The

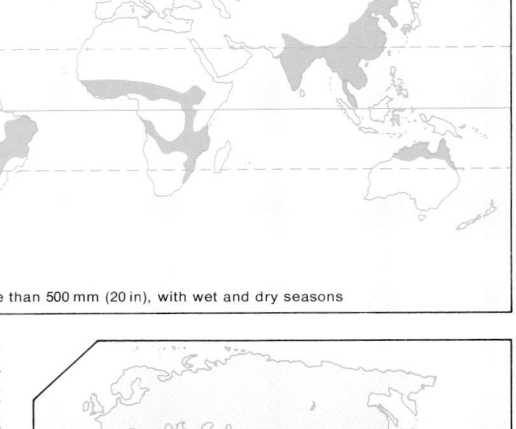

January

July

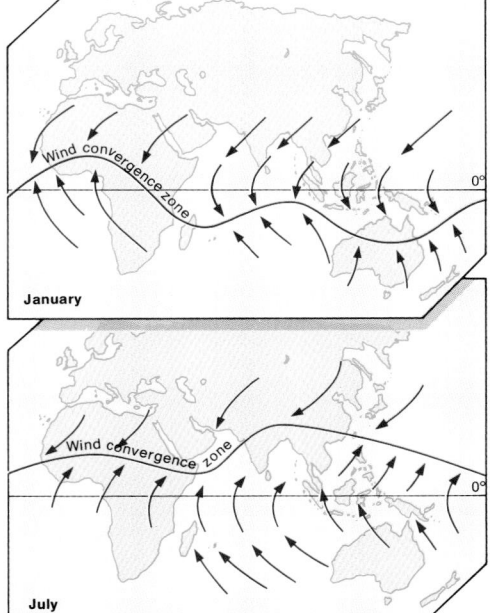

Heat differences in the atmosphere cause the seasonal wind reversals (left) characteristic of monsoon circulation. In January the northern hemisphere is tilted away from the sun, and cold, dry winds blow from the central Asian landmass toward the Equator. Here they change direction (an effect of the Earth's rotation), converge with other winds, and drop their rain. In July the situation is reversed when the heated Asian landmass attracts a flow of cooler air from the equatorial oceans, which moves northward with the sun. The moist air condenses on reaching land, and the monsoon rains descend.

reliable water supply that irrigation can give has brought in its train the opportunity for farmers to adopt a wide range of new farming practices. Chemical fertilizers and new strains of seed have made possible great increases in the productivity of the land in many parts of the monsoon regions, but their use is generally restricted to areas of reliable water supply.

Subsistence cultivation over thousands of years has been by far the most important element in the transformation of the landscape and vegetation of the monsoon world, but the introduction of plantation cultivation during the last centuries has also had a major effect. Tea plantations, for instance, have led to the almost total replacement of natural vegetation in the hills of southern India and Sri Lanka.

Populations in all the countries of the monsoon regions are rapidly increasing, and demands for economic development are constantly growing, placing increasing pressures on the environment, pressures which to date have seemed almost irresistible.

DISAPPEARING ANIMALS
The dwindling wildlife of southeastern Asia includes species that may be regarded locally as pests—a fact that makes their protection difficult outside game reserves. Animals such as the tiger and the wild pig are doubly threatened as human cultivation spreads into the natural habitat: their hunting and foraging grounds are reduced, and their destruction of crops or livestock provides villagers with an obvious incentive for killing them in order to protect their own livelihoods.

Wild pig
Sus scrofa

Tiger
Panthera tigris

SELF-SUFFICIENCY IN CHINA
Local materials are turned into saleable products at a ratan factory in southern China. This factory is not owned by the state but by the village-sized brigade responsible for the manufacturing. The brigade functions as a smaller economic unit within the Ting Chow people's commune of 20 to 30 villages, but is encouraged to act independently, owning what it creates. The commune takes care of such matters as waterways—it contains 82 km (51 miles) of canals.

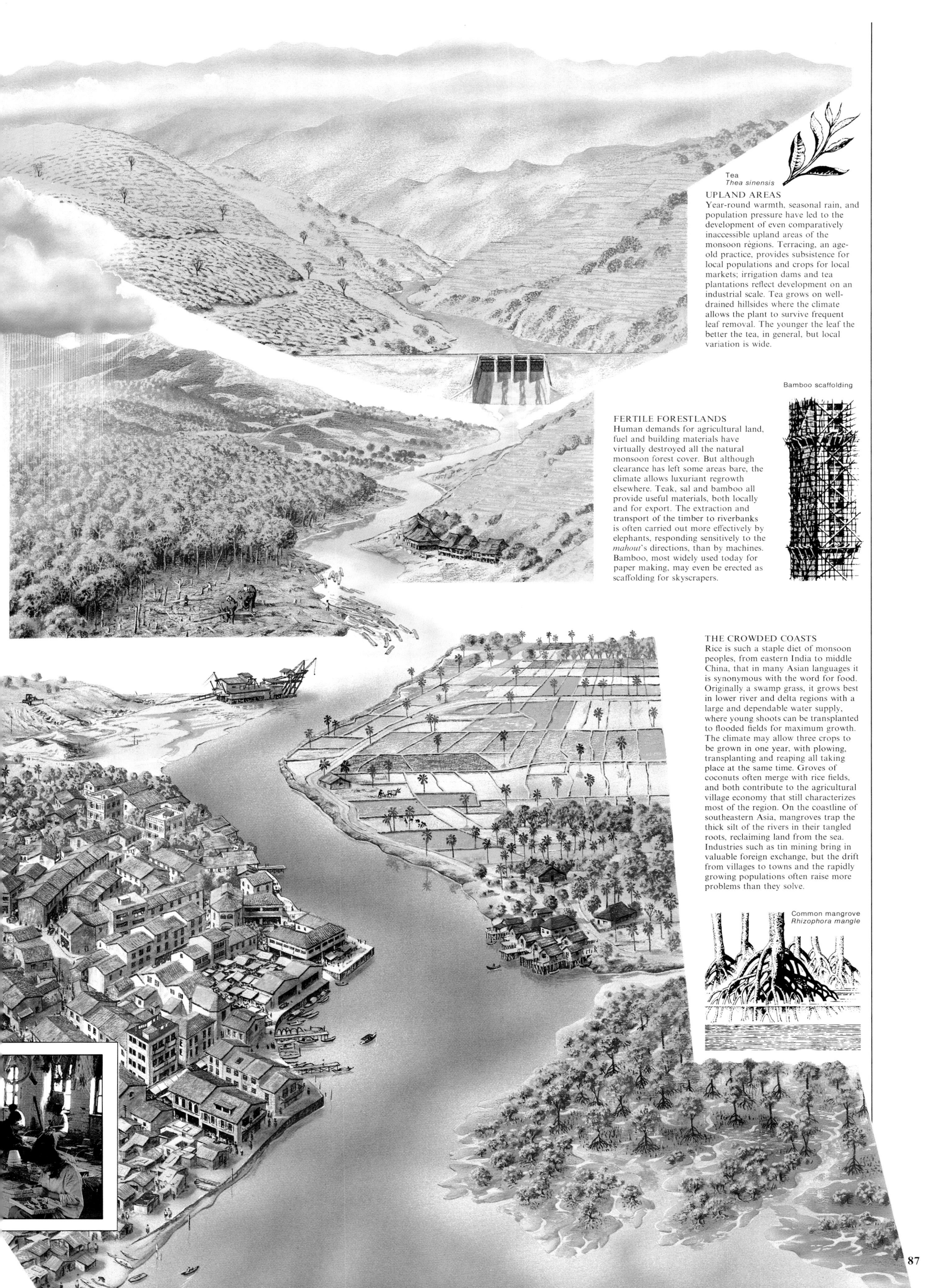

Tea
Thea sinensis

UPLAND AREAS

Year-round warmth, seasonal rain, and population pressure have led to the development of even comparatively inaccessible upland areas of the monsoon régions. Terracing, an age-old practice, provides subsistence for local populations and crops for local markets; irrigation dams and tea plantations reflect development on an industrial scale. Tea grows on well-drained hillsides where the climate allows the plant to survive frequent leaf removal. The younger the leaf the better the tea, in general, but local variation is wide.

Bamboo scaffolding

FERTILE FORESTLANDS

Human demands for agricultural land, fuel and building materials have virtually destroyed all the natural monsoon forest cover. But although clearance has left some areas bare, the climate allows luxuriant regrowth elsewhere. Teak, sal and bamboo all provide useful materials, both locally and for export. The extraction and transport of the timber to riverbanks is often carried out more effectively by elephants, responding sensitively to the *mahout*'s directions, than by machines. Bamboo, most widely used today for paper making, may even be erected as scaffolding for skyscrapers.

THE CROWDED COASTS

Rice is such a staple diet of monsoon peoples, from eastern India to middle China, that in many Asian languages it is synonymous with the word for food. Originally a swamp grass, it grows best in lower river and delta regions with a large and dependable water supply, where young shoots can be transplanted to flooded fields for maximum growth. The climate may allow three crops to be grown in one year, with plowing, transplanting and reaping all taking place at the same time. Groves of coconuts often merge with rice fields, and both contribute to the agricultural village economy that still characterizes most of the region. On the coastline of southeastern Asia, mangroves trap the thick silt of the rivers in their tangled roots, reclaiming land from the sea. Industries such as tin mining bring in valuable foreign exchange, but the drift from villages to towns and the rapidly growing populations often raise more problems than they solve.

Common mangrove
Rhizophora mangle

87

Mountain Regions

A quarter of Earth's land surface lies at heights of 1,000 m (3,300 ft) or more above sea level. But the highland regions are thinly populated by man, who is, generally speaking, a lowland dweller (most major population centers are less than 100 m (330 ft) above sea level). Some formerly lowland animals have fled from man to the harsh refuge of the mountains, joining with specially adapted plants and wildlife, but today man himself is finding the highland regions increasingly useful and desirable.

The world's highest mountain peaks rise to almost 9.6 km (6 miles) above sea level, but these heights are small compared to the total diameter of the Earth. The rough surface of an orange would have mountains higher than the Himalayas if scaled up to world size. But mountain environments, although they vary enormously from system to system, all tend to demand remarkable endurance and adaptability from the plants and animals that inhabit them.

Altitude rather than geological variation determines conditions of life on mountains. The temperature falls by 2°C with every 300 m (3.4°F every 1,000 ft)—hence the snowcapped beauty of the heights—and life forms must be adapted to increasingly harsh conditions as height increases. As a result, zones of different life occur at different levels, from tropical forests (at the base of low-latitude mountains) to arctic-type life in the zone of ice and snow at the summit. The latitude of the mountain affects the heights to which these zones extend: trees occur at 2,300 m (7,500 ft) in the southern Alps, whereas farther north, in central Sweden, trees cannot survive above 1,000 m (3,300 ft).

Life at the top

The specially adapted plant and animal life of the mountains occurs above the tree line, for here the variations in living conditions reach their greatest extremes. A plant that has found a foothold on a bare rock face may have to endure intense heat, even where the average temperature is low, when the summer sun blazing through the clear air warms the slabs to tropical temperatures. But when that part of the mountain falls into shadow, the temperature decreases very rapidly, often assisted by the high winds that blow almost constantly throughout the year in many mountain areas.

Soil necessary for plant life develops with the breakdown of the rock through the agency of water, frost and ice. Lichens, whose acids may aid in this destruction, can survive at very high levels, and as they die may add some humus to the newly forming soil. This may first accumulate in sheltered places where plants requiring high humidity, such as mosses and filmy ferns, are found. Flowering plants follow where a greater depth of soil has formed, although some grow in cracks between rocks.

Flowering plants of the mountains all tend to be small (to avoid harsh, drying winds), deep rooted (to anchor the plant firmly), and abundantly flowering (to benefit from the short growing season). Many unrelated species have independently developed a similar cushion form. This enables them to shed excess rainwater easily and to retain heat better in a tight tangle of stems and leaves, where the temperature may be more than 10°C (18°F) higher than that of the outside air. Insects sheltering there are well placed to perform the vital task of pollination. But pollinating insects are relatively rare at high altitudes, and some mountain plants are wind pollinated. The brilliant color of many others may be to increase their attractiveness for the insects. Nearly all upland plants are very slow-growing perennials, and many are evergreen, with leaves that exploit all available light.

Some large animals, such as the ibex or the Rocky Mountain goat, are adapted to spend their lives among the rocks and slopes. These stocky creatures, with hooves that act rather like suction cups, produce their summer young in the security of the heights, although in winter they descend to the shelter of the upper forests. Among smaller mammals, most of which are rodents, some dig burrows in which they hibernate through the winter. Others have very thick insulating coats, and may stay awake through the coldest weather in burrows under the snow.

Refugees from the lowlands

Some mountain animals, particularly carnivorous mammals and birds, have been driven by human persecution into remote mountain fastnesses. Many birds of prey, which could otherwise survive well in lowland areas, have their last strongholds among the mountains. They survive by feeding on small rodents, many of which are extremely wary. Some upland birds feed on insects or on seeds, but their number is comparatively small. The Alpine chough is one of the most interesting of mountain birds, for it has learned to find food among the scraps provided by climbers and skiers, whom it often follows to very high altitudes.

Insects and other small invertebrates, like their Arctic counterparts, may take several years to mature. Some are wingless, and many tend to fly low in order not to be blown away from their home range. Jumping spiders have been seen at heights of 6,700 m (22,000 ft) on the

slopes of Mount Everest, where they exist on small flies and springtails, but even above this level springtails and glacier "fleas" occur where there are no plants, apparently surviving on wind-blown insects and pollen grains.

Man and the mountains

The remote beauty of the mountains has led many peoples to identify them as the abode of the gods, but man himself prefers to live in the more convenient lowlands. The rarefied atmosphere of the heights makes physical work difficult, although some mountain-dwelling peoples have developed adaptations of the blood system to enable them to carry scarce oxygen more efficiently. The short growing season prevents cultivation of all but the hardiest cereal crops, and most uplanders rely on their livestock—cattle, sheep, llamas or yaks—for their existence. The animals are often driven to high pasture during the summer, descending to the valleys in the winter.

Modern, urbanized man finds the beauty and freshness of mountains increasingly attractive. Climbers have invaded most of the world's mountain regions, and in winter hosts of skiers flock to the resorts. Many important wildlife sanctuaries and national parks, particularly in the United States, are in mountain areas.

Lowland populations often rely on the pure mountain streams for both water and energy. Whole upland valleys are sometimes flooded to store water for distant conurbations. And the forceful flow of the water as it descends from the snow-fed heights is frequently harnessed to produce electricity for entire regions hundreds of kilometers away. The clear mountain air also offers the best conditions for astronomical observation, and most observatories today are built in dry, cloudless mountain areas.

Many peoples have believed that the gods have their abodes in the high places of the world. Tibet (above), one of the highest and most mountainous of all countries, has a large number of religious sites. Modern man also finds the clear, dry air suitable for the study of heavenly bodies: most modern observatories, such as Kitt Peak, USA (right), are built on mountain sites far from cities.

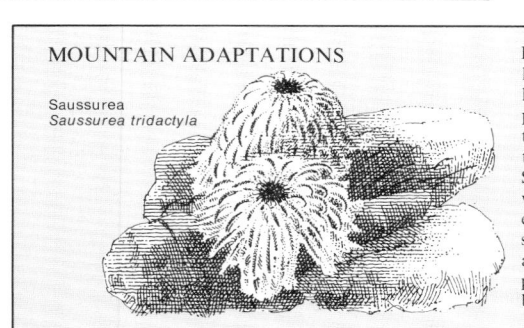

Activity in Earth's crust has produced mountains in every continent (left). Some thrust up sharply, while older mountains have been eroded to rounded shapes. The Scottish Highlands were made by mountain-building forces 400 million years ago (170 million years before the Appalachians and the Urals). The Rockies are 70 million years old and the Alps 15 million years old.

Ancient mountains (Caledonian orogenesis)
Intermediate mountains (Hercynian orogenesis)
Recent mountains (Alpine orogenesis)

MOUNTAIN ADAPTATIONS

Saussurea
Saussurea tridactyla

Ingenious adaptations to harsh mountain conditions have been evolved by many plants, most of which have tiny cells with thick sap that does not freeze easily. Saussurea masks itself with white hair to reduce evaporation from the leaf surface. Alpine soldanellas are active even under snow, pushing up their flowers before the thaw.

Alpine soldanella
Soldanella alpina

7,600 m
25,000 ft

SNOWBOUND PEAKS
Perpetual snow, violent winds and atmospheric dryness impose harsh conditions on life in the high Himalayas. But wind-blown organic debris from the plains does support some life forms—springtails, flies and jumping spiders—where the air is too dry to allow even lichens to survive. Lower down, a cushion plant may take root in a rock-base niche, but there is little other vegetation. Among birds, the Alpine chough is a scavenger that has followed Everest expeditions to heights of 7,900 m (26,000 ft).

Jumping spider
Salticus scenicus

Alpine chough
Pyrrhocorax graculus

Cushion pink
Parrya lanuginosa

4,900 m
16,000 ft

Fly
Diptera sp

Primula
Primula rosea

Blue sheep
Pseudois nayaur

Royle's pika
Ochotona roylei

Himalayan blue poppy
Meconopsis horridula

MOUNTAIN MEADOWS
Between the snow line and the zone of coniferous trees, the Himalayan slopes exhibit a glorious variety of flowering plants during summer. Small and slow growing, these often have bright flowers which attract pollinating insects such as fly-like *Diptera*. The pika and other small, thick-furred rodents are the most common animals, although larger creatures, such as blue (bharal) sheep and yaks, also find summer pasturage at these heights. Snow leopards tend to inhabit the coniferous forests, but they travel up to higher parts to prey on the grazing herds. Few people live within the zone, but some Sherpas take their yak herds as high as 4,600 m (15,000 ft) for summer grazing, and even grow crops of potatoes at this height. Their permanent villages, however, are on the lower alpine slopes.

4,300 m
14,000 ft

Domestic yak
Bos grunniens

Snow leopard
Panthera uncia

3,700 m
12,000 ft

3,000 m
10,000 ft

FORESTED SLOPES
Isolated birches mark the tree line—the transition from meadow to coniferous and rhododendron forest. In the upper parts of the forest, trees are dwarfed by cold and lack of moisture, and are twisted and bent from the wind. These low and tangled masses provide shelter for animals such as the Asian black bear and the red panda. Below the conifers lies a zone of broad-leaved evergreens, and in the foothills these in turn give way to tropical monsoon forests of sal trees (*Shorea robusta*) and thickets of bamboo. The raucous flocks of hill mynahs represent just one of the many kinds of birds found in this zone, which has the widest range of wildlife of all the kinds of mountain vegetation. Unfortunately, many species are in danger of extinction, for here man has settled, cut down forests and terraced hillsides to grow crops.

Rhododendron
Rhododendron sp

2,400 m
8,000 ft

Asiatic black bear
Selenarctos thibetanus

1,800 m
6,000 ft

Red panda
Ailurus fulgens

Hill mynah bird
Gracula religiosa

1,200 m
4,000 ft

- ▢ Permanent snow
- ▢ Alpine meadows
- ▦ Isolated birches
- ▦ Coniferous forest
- ▨ Rhododendron groves
- ▢ Broadleaved evergreen forest
- ▨ Bamboo
- ▢ Tropical monsoon forest

Rocky Mountain goat
Oreamnos americanus

Animals and humans adapt to mountain conditions in many ways. The Rocky Mountain goat (left) has evolved a fleecy undercoat and hooves with concave pads to grip on any surface. Comparison of the blood counts (right) of a lowlander (A) and an Andean (B) shows how the latter has a higher total content and more red cells.

liters pints

The golden eagle *Aquila chrysaetos* (left) epitomizes the grandeur of the heights. Although it lives and nests in remote regions, it could equally well find its food in the lowlands were it not for human competition. An eagle's territory may cover 130 sq km (50 sq miles): it preys on small mammals and even (it is believed) on young deer and lambs. It mates for life and returns each year to the same nest.

Freshwater Environments

Broad, muddy rivers, fast-running streams, miniature ponds and deep, ancient lakes all provide their own distinctive environments for populations of animals and colonies of aquatic plants. And in spite of the fact that these, the world's freshwater systems, contain only a minute proportion of the Earth's total supplies of water, the remarkable variety and richness of the wildlife they support make them among the most valuable and significant of all the world's natural habitats.

Fresh water is never really pure for, like sea water, and indeed like all other natural waters, it contains various dissolved minerals. Fresh water differs from seawater only in the relatively low concentrations of the minerals it contains. But these mineral traces are extremely important; they provide essential nutrients without which freshwater plants could not exist. And without plant life, there would be virtually no animal life either.

Not all parts of every freshwater system are rich in both plants and animals. Large, deep lakes are very similar to oceans—no light can penetrate their gloomy depths, and few plants can live in these conditions. The surface waters, on the other hand, where light is plentiful, teem with microscopic floating plants, mainly single-celled algae such as desmids and diatoms. The edges of lakes provide a different set of conditions again, for here the water is shallow and light can penetrate right through it. Plants can take root in the silt on the bottom, grow up through the water and thrust their leaves out into the light and air. Edges of lakes and, for the same reasons, the waters of small ponds are usually full of such plant life, which in turn supports many freshwater animals.

Running waters

Just as the still waters of lakes and ponds offer a variety of habitats, so the running waters of rivers support many different forms of life, each adapted to the particular conditions of its environment. In the upper reaches, where rivers are scarcely more than upland streams, water is fast flowing and clear of silt. Few plants, except close-clinging mosses, can gain a hold on the bare stony bottom and most of the fish are well muscled and strong bodied to enable them to withstand the constant tug of the current. As a river swells to form a mature lowland water course, however, it becomes slower moving and the water is warmer and richer in nutrients. Plants grow readily in these lower reaches and provide a supply of food for aquatic animals.

Volume of Lakes in cu km (cu miles)	Discharge of Rivers in cu m (cu ft) per second
Huron, North America 3,447 (827)	Ganges, Asia 18,689 (660,000)
Nyasa, Africa 8,373 (2,009)	Brahmaputra, Asia 19,822 (700,000)
Superior, North America 12,153 (2,916)	Yangtze, Asia 21,804 (770,000)
Tanganyika, Africa 19,418 (4,659)	Congo, Africa 39,644 (1,400,000)
Baikal, Asia 23,260 (5,581)	Amazon, South America 212,376 (7,500,000)

The five largest lakes in the world hold more than 53% of all fresh water that flows over the land. The rest of the world's lakes account for another 45%.

The world's largest river, the Amazon, discharges more than one-fifth of all fresh water that flows from the mouths of the world's rivers into the oceans.

With such a wide range of conditions, freshwater environments support an enormous variety of animal life—insects, fishes, amphibians, reptiles, mammals and birds. In some ways insects are the most important of all these creatures: freshwater systems contain more insects and other invertebrates, representing a greater variety of species, than any other kind of animal. Furthermore, these, the smallest representatives of the freshwater animal world, provide one of the most important links in the complex freshwater food chain.

Insects may be the most numerous, but fishes are probably the most familiar of all freshwater creatures, and they certainly show some of the greatest varieties of adaptations to the many different habitats. Their sizes vary from the tiny, 14 mm ($\frac{1}{2}$ in) of the virtually transparent dwarf goby fish found in small streams and lakes in the Philippines to the 4 m (14 ft) of the arapaima found in deep rivers in tropical South America. Their feeding habits vary from those of the ferocious carnivorous piranha of South America to those of the North American paddle fish which, although more than three times the size of the largest piranha, feed solely on microscopic organisms which they filter from the water with their specially adapted throats.

The breeding habits of freshwater fish also vary widely, from the carefully maternal instincts of the African mouthbreeding cichlids—these retain the developing eggs safely in their mouths until the offspring hatch—to the rather more common ejection of eggs into the water, where their fertilization and survival is simply left to chance. Other adaptations include the ability to breathe air (as does the African lungfish), to leap waterfalls (a common practice among migrating salmon) and to emit an electric shock of up to 600 volts (an adaptation of the South American electric eel).

Creatures of the water's edge

Of all the other major groups of animals, amphibians (such as frogs and toads) are probably the most reliant on freshwater systems. Because their skins must not dry out and they have to lay their eggs in water, few amphibians can venture far from the water's edge. And because they cannot tolerate the salt in seawater (it causes them to lose their body fluids through their skins) they are totally dependent upon fresh water for their existence. Reptiles, rather less typical of freshwater environments, range in size from miniature North American terrapins to the giant crocodiles that live along the banks of the Nile. Freshwater mammals, on the other hand, with the considerable exception of the hippopotamus, all tend to be rather small creatures such as otters, beavers, coypus, aquatic moles and water shrews.

Birds are another important group of freshwater creatures. Although few birds are truly aquatic an enormous number of species live in or near freshwater systems and take advantage of the various food supplies: the plants and fish within the waters; the bankside vegetation and small animal life; and the many forms of freshwater insects. Marshes and swamps, for example, provide some of the richest bird habitats in the world.

Also numbered among the species dependent on Earth's freshwater systems is man. And although strictly a nonaquatic, land-living animal, man uses more fresh water than any other creature. His needs seem to be inexhaustible as he harnesses, channels, diverts and often pollutes freshwater systems throughout the world. Unfortunately, the vast requirements of the human race are not always compatible with the rather more humble needs of all other species that depend upon fresh water.

THE UPPER REACHES Here, water flows rapidly. Tumbling over bare rocks and stones, it is chilly, oxygen-rich and free of silt. Bird life attracted to these reaches includes the sure-footed dipper, which walks the stream bed hunting for caddis larvae. Slightly farther downstream, but where the river is still narrow and easily dammed, beavers are found. Few plants can live within the water, but river crowfoot has feathery underwater leaves that remain intact where most other plants would be shredded by the current. Many fish, such as trout, have streamlined bodies to offer the least resistance to the stream's pull, while others survive on the bottom by bracing against the rocks—the bullhead, for example. Insects have various means of anchoring themselves to the stream bed—blackfly larvae have hooks to fix themselves to pebbles.

Dipper
Cinclus cinclus

Beaver
Castor fiber

River crowfoot
Ranunculus fluitans

Brown trout
Salmo trutta

Blackfly larvae
Simulium spp

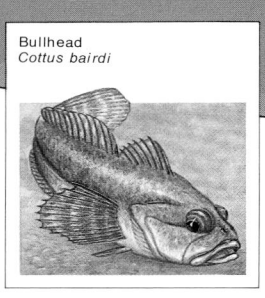

Bullhead
Cottus bairdi

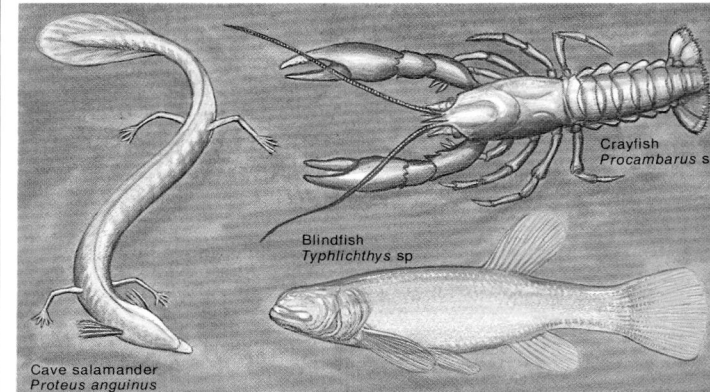

Crayfish
Procambarus sp

Blindfish
Typhlichthys sp

Cave salamander
Proteus anguinus

THE LIFE OF A RIVER

As a river makes its way from its upland source to the sea, it gradually changes its character. And at every stage in its progress, the animals and plants that inhabit the riverbanks and the waters reflect these changes by their adaptations to their environments. Most distinctive and dramatic are those adaptations produced in the wildlife of the upper and lower river reaches.

an spoonbill
lea alba

THE LOWER REACHES
The slowly flowing river and its muddy banks are rich in animals and plants. Many birds live along the water's edge; spoonbills wade in the shallows, filtering food from the water with their beaks. The banks, fringed with reedmaces and other plants, provide habitats for many reptiles, such as the American painted turtle, and mammals, such as the platypus. Plants also grow on the water—they range from large waterlilies to tiny algae that are food for river fishes: Africa's upside-down-feeding catfish, for example. In these waters, mammals as well as fish are to be found—Amazonian manatees live entirely aquatic lives. The plentiful river plants, such as curled pondweed, provide food for water snails and other herbivores, and cover for predators such as pike. Crustacea and insects living in the silt of the river-bed are food for bottom-feeding fish such as the strange-looking North American paddle fish.

Southern painted turtle
Chrysemys picta dorsalis

LAKES: CHANGE AND EVOLUTION
No two lakes are alike: each is virtually a self-contained world for its population of aquatic animals and plants. Furthermore, no individual lake remains the same for long: in every lake, slow, inexorable changes in conditions are gradually but constantly changing the balance of species inhabiting the lake bed, the bankside and the water.

Changing conditions may be caused by one of several processes. Accumulating sediments, one of the most common of these processes, may eliminate a lake altogether. The water becomes shallower as sediments thicken (1) and these sediments are then added to and consolidated by water plants taking root. Ultimately, land plants (2) invade the area.

Lakes develop their own peculiar species when the aquatic wildlife that evolves within them has no means of migrating to other freshwater systems to interbreed. The world's only existing species of freshwater seal, for example, is found in just one lake—isolated Lake Baikal in Asia.

Baikal seal
Phoca sibirica

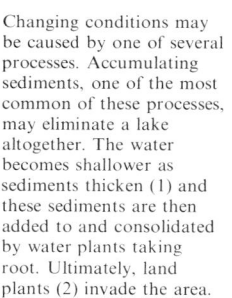

Platypus
Ornithorhynchus anatinus

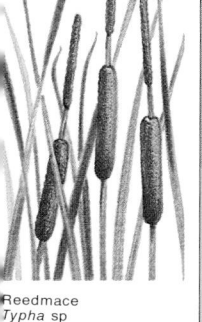

Reedmace
Typha sp

Waterlily
Nymphaea sp

African catfish
Synodontis batensoda

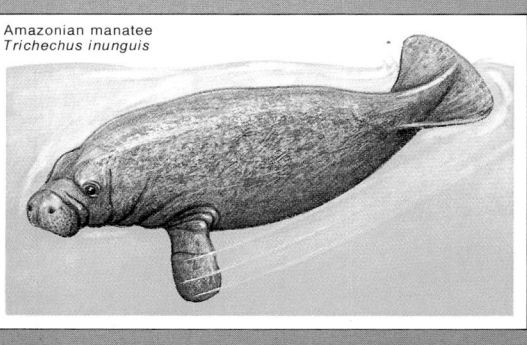

Amazonian manatee
Trichechus inunguis

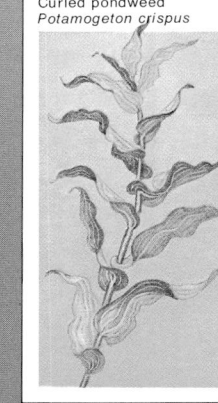

Curled pondweed
Potamogeton crispus

hite ramshorn snail
anorbis albus

Pike
Esox lucius

WETLANDS
Marshes and swamps are the richest of freshwater habitats. Wading birds, such as Asia's painted stork *Ibis leucocephalus* (above), are particularly common. Reptiles include caimans, which lay their eggs in swamps' warm, rotting vegetation. Of the many insects, mosquitoes are probably the most numerous, and of the many fishes, African lungfish are perhaps best adapted to life in wetlands. They survive drought, when marshes dry up, by their ability to breathe air.

ARK WATERS
derground rivers that w through many of the rld's cave systems port surprising numbers creatures that have pted to the permanent kness. Many of these, h as the American cave yfish, have lost the oration of their surface-ng kin. Some, such as ntucky blind fishes, no ger possess eyes. Some amanders are sighted black when born, become blind and orless by adulthood.

Paddle fish
Polydon spathula

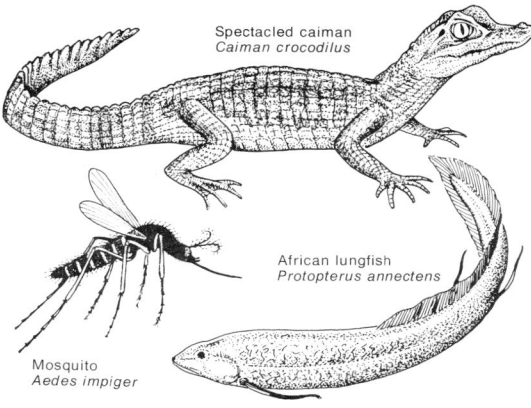

Spectacled caiman
Caiman crocodilus

Mosquito
Aedes impiger

African lungfish
Protopterus annectens

91

Man and the Freshwater Environments

From earliest times, man has been finding new uses for and making new demands upon the world's freshwater resources. Today, the whole of modern society depends upon a vast supply to serve its agricultural, industrial, domestic and other needs. To meet the ever-growing demand for water, man has performed remarkable engineering feats: altering the courses of rivers, creating and destroying lakes, drowning valleys and tapping water sources that lie deep within the Earth.

Water is essential to human life. Simply to remain alive, an active adult living in a temperate climate needs a liquid intake of about two liters ($3\frac{1}{2}$ pints) every day. In warmer climates, the body's fluid requirements are even greater. Consequently, man has always been tied to reliable sources of drinking water—rivers, springs, lakes and ponds—and the availability of these, until very recently, has dictated the routes of all his wanderings and determined the sites of all his settlements.

From the time of the earliest human settlements, however, man has looked upon freshwater systems not simply as a source of drinking water but also as an increasingly useful resource for a multitude of other purposes. Today, water enters into virtually every aspect of modern life, and enormous quantities are used in agriculture, in industry, in the home, in the production of energy, for transport and for recreation.

The farmer's resource

Of all the major activities that rely on fresh water, agriculture is by far the world's largest consumer. In much of Europe and North America, rainfall is usually plentiful and lack of sufficient water for crops is rarely a problem. But in other parts of the world the climate simply does not produce enough rainfall and water shortages are a perennial problem. There, irrigation is not just a sophisticated technique to improve the yields and increase the varieties of crops grown; it is, and always has been, an essential element of agriculture.

Methods of irrigation range from small-scale devices—such as miniature windpumps—used in many developing countries simply to lift water from rivers for bankside crops, to vast dams, reservoirs and canal systems such as the Indus River project in Pakistan, which irrigates 10 million hectares (25 million acres) of land.

Traditional irrigation techniques usually involve using open channels or furrows for conducting water to fields. But one of the major problems with these, particularly in hot climates, is that much of the water evaporates and is lost before it can be used. Several new techniques, such as sprinklers and drip-feed systems, have recently been developed, however, to help make more efficient use of available supplies.

Although the most severe water deficiencies are experienced in the dry subtropical and tropical regions of the world, the temperate regions of North America and Europe, in spite of their relatively wet climates, do suffer shortages. Large towns and cities rarely have enough locally available rainfall or river flow to satisfy both domestic demand and the insatiable needs of industry. In the developed nations, industry consumes more water than any other activity.

Industrial demands

Fresh water is not only an integral part of almost every manufacturing process, it has other important industrial uses. As a source of power, it has been used since the early days of civilization—water wheels were one of man's first industrial inventions. Today, these simple devices are rarely seen in industrial societies, but water power is more important than ever before. Giant dams allow enormous volumes of water to be controlled and the power harnessed to drive turbines and generate electricity.

Freshwater systems have also, for centuries, provided industry with an important means of transporting its goods, and canal systems are still an essential part of industrial infrastructure in many countries of the world: the Europa Canal, when completed, will link three of Europe's major rivers, the Rhine, Main and Danube, and so form a continuous waterway running east–west across the breadth of Europe.

Already, the finished sections of the canal are carrying oil, chemicals, fertilizers, coal, coke and building materials to and from some of Europe's major industrial regions.

Many of Europe's waterways date back to the great canal-building days of the Industrial Revolution. Although a few of these are still used for commerce, many are today considered too narrow to transport economical quantities of goods. Some, however, are now finding a role to play in one of the world's fastest-growing new industries—the leisure market. Today, canals provide a wide range of aquatic activities for holiday makers, tourists and sportsmen.

Recreation and sport

Freshwater systems throughout the world, in fact, are rapidly being recognized and developed as major recreational resources. Lakes and reservoirs are stocked with fish for anglers, silted waterways are dredged to provide sailing and swimming facilities, and old quarries and open-cast workings are landscaped and flooded to provide entirely new freshwater systems purely for leisure pursuits. The projects not only help to rejuvenate previously misused land, they also provide significant incomes to otherwise underdeveloped areas, especially highland regions that are too remote to attract other industries, and are unsuitable for farming.

Unfortunately, however, few of the world's freshwater systems can continue indefinitely to absorb the ever-growing demands that are being made upon them. Overuse of water resources is already a problem and has led to the pollution and destruction of many water systems—in some places overtapping has lowered water tables so drastically that rivers and lakes have been permanently destroyed. Although steps have been taken to protect certain waterways, legislation to guard against misuse and overuse is costly, time consuming and, inevitably, comes up against vested interests. Nevertheless, stringent conservation measures are becoming increasingly necessary if society is to maintain one of its most precious resources.

THE VERSATILE RESOURCE
Every day, more than seven trillion liters (12 trillion pints) of water are removed from the world's freshwater systems. Almost all of this water is then directed to one of four destinations—some is destined for industry, a certain amount is piped to towns and cities for use in public services and in homes, some is fed to agricultural regions, and the rest is stored in reservoirs for future use.

INDUSTRY	19.5%
DOMESTIC	4.4%
AGRICULTURE	73.8%
RESERVOIRS	2.3%

Man obtains fresh water by trapping it as it passes through one of the stages in the hydrological cycle—the never-ending circulation of Earth's waters from the ocean, to the atmosphere, to land. This cycle can be traced from the point at which water evaporates from the sea. The water vapor is blown across the land and falls as rain, hail or snow. Some then evaporates, but the rest completes the cycle by flowing over the land or through the soil or rocks back to the sea. It is at this point in its journey that man obtains his water supplies—from lakes (1), boreholes and wells (2) and dammed rivers (3). These supplies are then either used locally, or are transported by pipe or canal (4) to reservoirs (5) where they are stored ready for distribution.

➡ Movement of water in the hydrological cycle

▬ Water-bearing rock

RESERVOIRS

About 70 trillion liters (15 trillion gallons) of fresh water are held in storage during any one year. Reservoirs ensure a continuous supply of water in spite of the inevitable seasonal fluctuations in demand and in the natural supply from rivers and rainfall. And where reservoirs are formed by damming rivers, there are additional benefits—the vast quantities of water held can be controlled and the power used to generate electricity. The Kariba Dam in Zimbabwe (right) has the potential for producing 8,500 million kilowatt hours of electrical power every year.

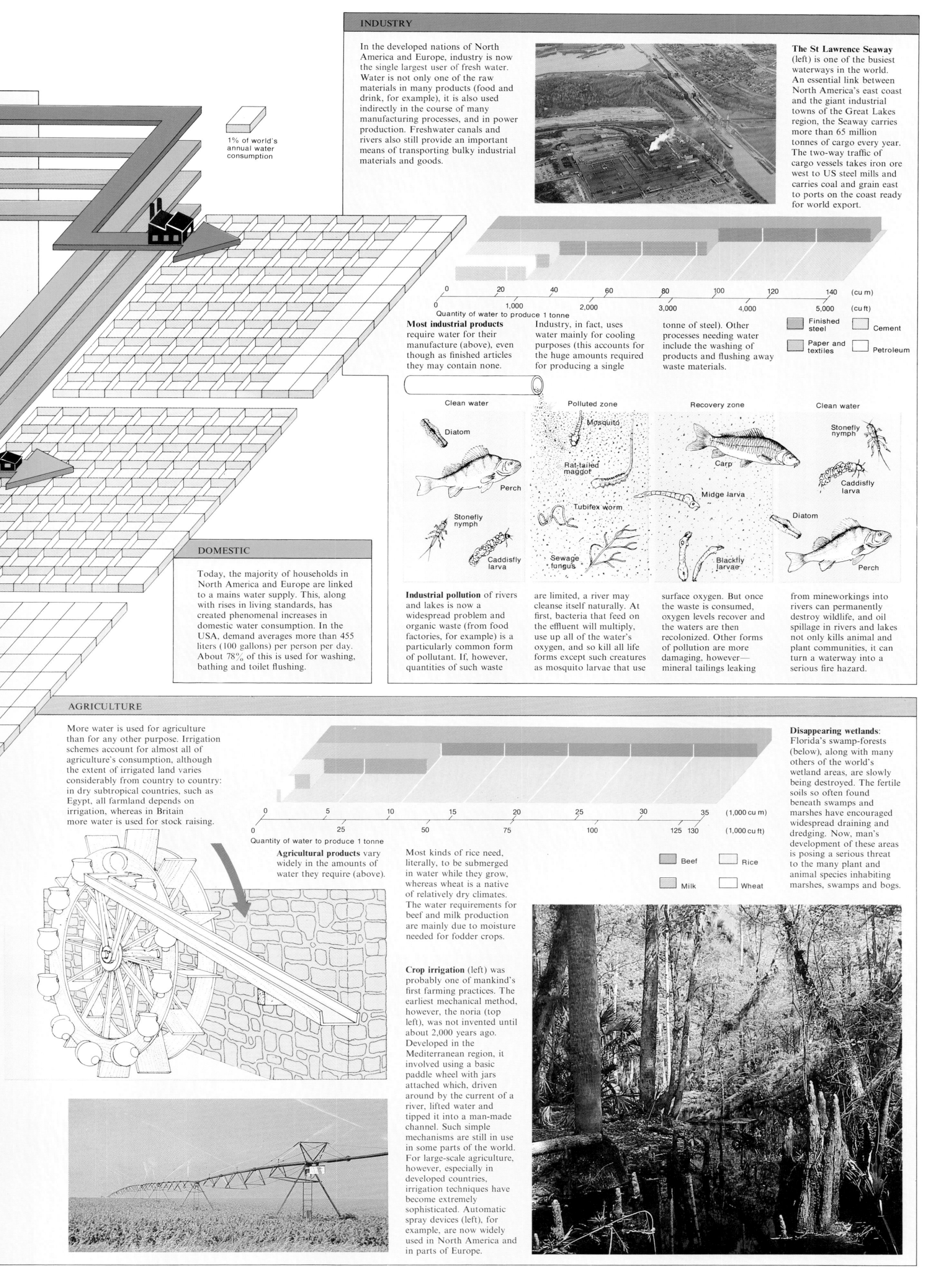

INDUSTRY

In the developed nations of North America and Europe, industry is now the single largest user of fresh water. Water is not only one of the raw materials in many products (food and drink, for example), it is also used indirectly in the course of many manufacturing processes, and in power production. Freshwater canals and rivers also still provide an important means of transporting bulky industrial materials and goods.

1% of world's annual water consumption

The St Lawrence Seaway (left) is one of the busiest waterways in the world. An essential link between North America's east coast and the giant industrial towns of the Great Lakes region, the Seaway carries more than 65 million tonnes of cargo every year. The two-way traffic of cargo vessels takes iron ore west to US steel mills and carries coal and grain east to ports on the coast ready for world export.

| 0 | 20 | 40 | 60 | 80 | 100 | 120 | 140 | (cu m) |
| 0 | 1,000 | 2,000 | 3,000 | 4,000 | 5,000 | (cu ft) |

Quantity of water to produce 1 tonne

Most industrial products require water for their manufacture (above), even though as finished articles they may contain none.

Industry, in fact, uses water mainly for cooling purposes (this accounts for the huge amounts required for producing a single tonne of steel). Other processes needing water include the washing of products and flushing away waste materials.

- Finished steel
- Paper and textiles
- Cement
- Petroleum

Clean water — Diatom, Perch, Stonefly nymph, Caddisfly larva

Polluted zone — Mosquito, Rat-tailed maggot, Tubifex worm, Sewage fungus

Recovery zone — Carp, Midge larva, Blackfly larvae

Clean water — Stonefly nymph, Caddisfly larva, Diatom, Perch

Industrial pollution of rivers and lakes is now a widespread problem and organic waste (from food factories, for example) is a particularly common form of pollutant. If, however, quantities of such waste are limited, a river may cleanse itself naturally. At first, bacteria that feed on the effluent will multiply, use up all of the water's oxygen, and so kill all life forms except such creatures as mosquito larvae that use surface oxygen. But once the waste is consumed, oxygen levels recover and the waters are then recolonized. Other forms of pollution are more damaging, however— mineral tailings leaking from mineworkings into rivers can permanently destroy wildlife, and oil spillage in rivers and lakes not only kills animal and plant communities, it can turn a waterway into a serious fire hazard.

DOMESTIC

Today, the majority of households in North America and Europe are linked to a mains water supply. This, along with rises in living standards, has created phenomenal increases in domestic water consumption. In the USA, demand averages more than 455 liters (100 gallons) per person per day. About 78% of this is used for washing, bathing and toilet flushing.

AGRICULTURE

More water is used for agriculture than for any other purpose. Irrigation schemes account for almost all of agriculture's consumption, although the extent of irrigated land varies considerably from country to country: in dry subtropical countries, such as Egypt, all farmland depends on irrigation, whereas in Britain more water is used for stock raising.

| 0 | 5 | 10 | 15 | 20 | 25 | 30 | 35 | (1,000 cu m) |
| 0 | 25 | 50 | 75 | 100 | 125 | 130 | (1,000 cu ft) |

Quantity of water to produce 1 tonne

Agricultural products vary widely in the amounts of water they require (above).

Most kinds of rice need, literally, to be submerged in water while they grow, whereas wheat is a native of relatively dry climates. The water requirements for beef and milk production are mainly due to moisture needed for fodder crops.

- Beef
- Milk
- Rice
- Wheat

Disappearing wetlands: Florida's swamp-forests (below), along with many others of the world's wetland areas, are slowly being destroyed. The fertile soils so often found beneath swamps and marshes have encouraged widespread draining and dredging. Now, man's development of these areas is posing a serious threat to the many plant and animal species inhabiting marshes, swamps and bogs.

Crop irrigation (left) was probably one of mankind's first farming practices. The earliest mechanical method, however, the noria (top left), was not invented until about 2,000 years ago. Developed in the Mediterranean region, it involved using a basic paddle wheel with jars attached which, driven around by the current of a river, lifted water and tipped it into a man-made channel. Such simple mechanisms are still in use in some parts of the world. For large-scale agriculture, however, especially in developed countries, irrigation techniques have become extremely sophisticated. Automatic spray devices (left), for example, are now widely used in North America and in parts of Europe.

Seawater Environments

The oceans form by far the largest of the world's habitable environments, covering almost three-quarters of the Earth's surface at an average depth of more than 3,500 m (11,500 ft). Little more than a century ago, scientists believed that the deep sea's low temperatures, perpetual darkness and immense pressures made life in these regions completely untenable. But we now know that animals live at all depths in the ocean, even at the bottom of trenches more than 11,000 m (36,000 ft) deep.

THE PATTERN OF MARINE LIFE
The distribution of life in the seas is like a inverted pyramid whose broad base is formed billions of minute single-celled plants—the phytoplankton. Plants need sunlight and nutrient salt so phytoplankton occurs only in the upper, sum layers and where salts are present. Elsewhere, t distribution of marine life thins out rapidly.

Shore life belongs to both land and sea, and thus has to cope with a wide range of conditions. Seaweeds get all their food from the sea and are quite unlike land plants. Many animals take refuge below the surface: tellin shell molluscs sift food particles through special "lips"; lugworms swallow sand, digesting any organic matter; cockles take in food and eject waste through two siphons. Some birds have bills adapted for opening bivalve molluscs.

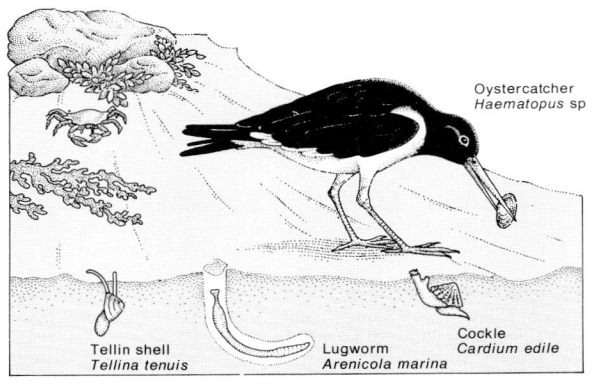

Oystercatcher
Haematopus sp

Tellin shell
Tellina tenuis

Lugworm
Arenicola marina

Cockle
Cardium edile

Marine plant life consists largely of diatoms—minute single-celled specks, each enclosed in a lidded box of silicon. Dinoflagellates, classed as plants but able to swim, dominate warmer waters. Both are food for copepods, the flea-sized grazers whose total weight, in the North Sea alone, is some seven million tonnes.

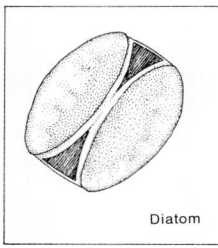

Diatom

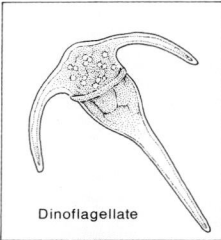

Dinoflagellate

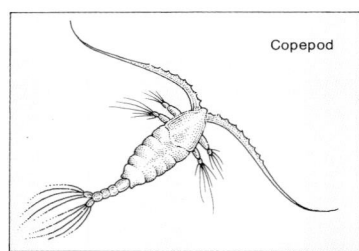

Copepod

A coral atoll, forming in warm shallow water round an extinct volcano, makes up a living aquarium for thousands of tropical marine life forms. Countless billions of tiny polyps, each secreting a hard, calcareous skeleton, form the first layer of the reef, but die as the volcano gradually sinks. Their skeletons provide a base for further layers of corals, which enclose the sinking island to create a shallow, salt water lagoon. Different coral species in the same reef provide homes for a great variety of life.

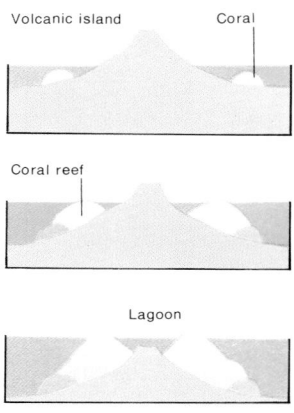

Volcanic island   Coral

Coral reef

Lagoon

Life is by no means evenly distributed throughout the oceans, either vertically or horizontally. The great majority of marine creatures are concentrated in the upper few hundred meters, for the biological organization of life in the seas, as on land, depends on photosynthesis (the process by which plants use the Sun's energy to combine carbon dioxide and water to produce more complex compounds). This near-surface layer is the euphotic ("well-lighted") zone.

Some of the Sun's rays are reflected from the surface of the sea, and those that penetrate are scattered and absorbed as they pass through the water, so that even in the clearest oceanic water there is insufficient light to support photosynthesis at depths greater than about 100 m (330 ft). In turbid inshore regions, where the water is less clear, this near-surface layer may be reduced to a very few meters. So the large seaweeds that anchor themselves to the seabed are restricted to the small areas of the sea where the water is sufficiently shallow to allow them to photosynthesize. Of much greater importance over most of the oceans are the tiny floating plants of the phytoplankton, which live suspended in the sunlit surface layers.

Pastures of the sea
Phytoplankton, like all plant life, requires not only sunlight for survival but also adequate supplies of nutrient salts and chemical trace elements. River waters carry down considerable quantities of dissolved mineral salts and other matter, so that high levels of phytoplankton production may occur locally around major estuaries. But a far more important source of nutrient supply to the euphotic zone is the recycling of salts that have sunk into the deeper layers, locked up in the bodies of plants and animals or in their fecal pellets.

In those areas of the oceans that overlie the continental shelves (about six percent of the total), the depth is nowhere more than about 200 m (650 ft), and the nutrient-rich bottom water is fairly readily brought back to the surface by currents and the stirring effect of storms. This stirring can reach much greater depths in near-polar latitudes, where the "water column" is not layered by temperature but remains more or less uniformly cold from top to bottom. In the Antarctic, cold (and therefore heavy) surface water sinks and is replaced by nutrient-rich water that may surface from depths of 1,000 m (3,300 ft).

In subtropical and tropical regions of the open ocean, where the warm surface layer is only a few tens of meters deep, the temperature falls rapidly with depth. There is little exchange between deep and shallow layers, and the euphotic zone receives an adequate supply of nutrient salts only in certain areas. These occur between westward-flowing and eastward-flowing currents in each of the major oceans. The Earth's rotation causes these currents to diverge so as to create an upwelling of nutrient-rich water along their common boundaries.

Finally, in restricted coastal regions of the tropics and subtropics the local climatic conditions cause an offshore movement of surface water, which is again replaced by upwelling nutrient-rich deep water. The central oceanic regions, including the deep blue subtropical waters, are in effect the deserts of the sea.

Sea grazers and carnivores
The abundance of animals in the oceans closely follows that of the plants. But very few of the larger marine animals can feed directly on the phytoplankton because the individual plants are so small—often only a fraction of a millimeter across. Instead, the phytoplankton supports an amazingly diverse community of planktonic animals, which also spend their lives in mid-water and are swept along by the ocean currents. This community, the zooplankton, includes many different protozoans (single-celled animals), crustaceans, worms and molluscs, and also the juvenile stages of fishes and of many invertebrate animals that live as adults on the seabed. Most members of the zooplankton are very small and many of them graze on the phytoplankton. But some planktonic animals, particularly among the jellyfish and salps, may be a meter or more across and are voracious carnivores feeding on their planktonic neighbors. In turn, the zooplankton provides food for many of the active swimmers such as the fishes and baleen whales, while at the top of the food chain are larger carnivores including

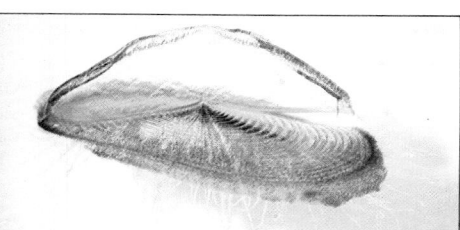

The by-the-wind sailor, *Velella*, is a so-called colonial animal, consisting of a whole collection of animals that function as a single individual. The gas-filled float of its body carries a vertical sail to catch the wind, and below dangle a group of modified polyps specialized for particular roles such as deterrence, reproduction, feeding and digesting.

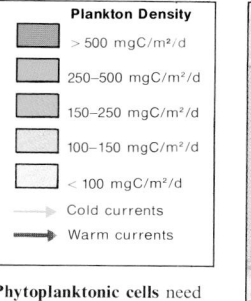

Phytoplanktonic cells need not only sunlight but also nutrient salts, and so they are restricted to areas where these are available: coastal regions, high latitudes (particularly the Antarctic), narrow tongues extending across the tropical regions of the main ocean basins, and a number of subtropical upwelling regions.

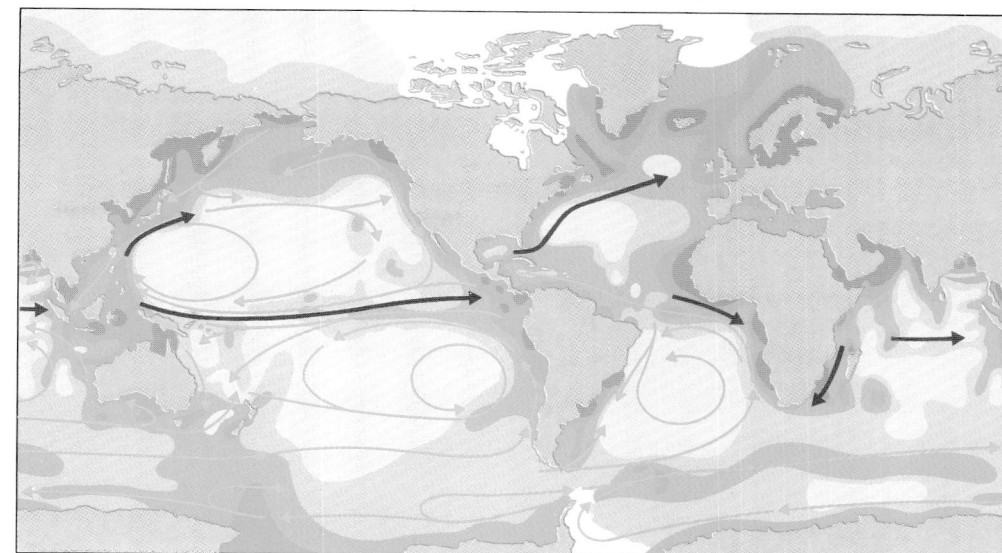

Plankton Density

- > 500 mgC/m²/d
- 250–500 mgC/m²/d
- 150–250 mgC/m²/d
- 100–150 mgC/m²/d
- < 100 mgC/m²/d
- Cold currents
- Warm currents

Zones of life (below) extend from the teeming euphotic ("well-lighted") layer to the sparsely populated bathypelagic ("deep-sea") depths, while benthic ("bottom") life occurs at all seabed levels. Phytoplankton (plant life) (1) dictates the pattern of the rest, flourishing where surface conditions allow nutrient salts to well up from lower depths. Herbivores such as minute zooplankton (2) provide food for a host of surface-layer life, which in turn feeds larger predators. Dead animals and fecal pellets fall to lower levels, where they sustain life, but in far smaller quantity.

1 Phytoplankton
2 Zooplankton
3 Blue whale *Balaenoptera musculus*
4 Herring *Clupea harengus*
5 Gray seal *Halichoerus grypus*
6 Bluefin tuna *Thunnus thynnus*
7 Bottlenosed dolphin *Tursiops truncatus*
8 Mackerel *Scomber scomber*
9 Common squid *Loligo* spp
10 White shark *Carcharadon carcharias*
11 Hatchet fish *Argyropelecus hemigymnus*
12 Giant squid *Architeuthis* spp
13 Sea anemone *Cerianthus orientalis*
14 Tripod fish *Benthosaurus grallator*
15 Scarlet shrimp *Notostomus longirostris*
16 Angler fish *Linophryne bicornis*
17 Brittle star *Ophiothrix fragilis*
18 Sea cucumber class Holothuroidea

Offshore wind

Euphotic zone

500 m (1,650 ft)

Mesopelagic zone

1,000 m (3,300 ft)

Bathypelagic zone

Benthic zone

4,000 m (13,200 ft)

Bizarre life forms new to science live in the sunless depths, where plumes of hot mineral-rich water gush through deep-sea vents in the Earth's crust. These oases of life support huge, gutless tubeworms more than 1.5 m (5 ft) long, which appear to take food particles from the hot vents through blood-red tentacles. Other creatures include blind crabs and large white clams.

sharks, tuna-like fishes and toothed whales.

Beneath the euphotic zone, of course, there can be no herbivores at all, although some animals that spend the daylight hours in the deeper layers move upwards at night to feed in the plankton-rich surface waters. All of the permanent members of the deep-living communities are dependent for food upon material that sinks or is carried downwards from the euphotic zone. Many of them feed on dead animal remains and fecal material as it sinks through the water column or after it reaches the seabed. These detritus eaters in turn support the predatory carnivores that feed upon the detritivores or upon each other.

In shallow areas the food material that reaches the bottom supports complex communities, notably the rich and varied groups of invertebrates and fishes associated with coral reefs. In the deep sea, however, where the euphotic zone is separated from the seabed by several kilometers of water, much of the sinking material is recycled within the water column and relatively little reaches the bottom. Life on the deep-sea floor therefore becomes more and more sparse with increasing depth, but in recent years scientists have discovered that this community includes a surprising number of fishes, some many meters in length. So far man's knowledge of these deep-sea communities is relatively meager, but with our increasing use of the deep oceans we may need to know much more about the life in this environment.

Man and the Seawater Environments

For thousands of years man has used the oceans as a source of food and other materials, and as a repository for wastes. But only in the last 100 years have technological advances and fast-growing human populations had a significant effect, to a point where overfishing and pollution are becoming a cause for concern. Harvesting of krill and seaweeds may ease the pressure on traditional seafoods, but legal restrictions on dumping of wastes or on overfishing are notoriously hard to enforce.

Until about the middle of the nineteenth century the seas had always seemed to be a boundless source of food and of income for fishermen who were brave enough to face the elements with their relatively small sailing ships and primitive gear. But once fishing vessels began to be fitted with steam engines in the 1880s they became relatively independent of the weather, while improvements in the fishing gear itself, such as steam-powered winches in trawling and harpoon guns in whaling, made the whole business of fishing much more efficient.

At first these advances resulted in enormous increases in catches, but in many fisheries this was rapidly followed by a distressing fall in the catch per unit of effort—that is, it was becoming more and more difficult in successive years to catch the same amount of fish as before. In most fisheries the initial response to this situation was to increase the size and number of fishing vessels and to search for new fishing grounds. But as the fishing pressure on the stocks increased, with smaller fish being captured, often before they were able to reproduce, the catch per unit of effort frequently continued to fall.

In many cases attempts were made to counter the effects of overfishing by introducing regulations to control the mesh size of the nets, so allowing the small fish to escape; by establishing closed seasons or quotas of fish which might legitimately be taken from a particular fishing ground in any one year; or even, as in the case of the British herring fishery in the late 1970s, by imposing a complete ban on fishing. Moral questions also sometimes intervene, as in whaling operations, which, many conservationists believe, have driven some species close to extinction despite attempts to rationalize the fisheries.

Fisheries in decline
The North Sea trawl fishery, the first to be affected by the new technology in the nineteenth century, has been declining in terms of catch per unit of effort since the early decades of this century. Dramatic but short-lived improvements after the "closed seasons" of the two world wars proved that fishing pressure had a serious effect on stocks, but by the 1970s many North Sea fishing ports had become almost deserted. This decline put pressure on more distant fishing grounds used by European fishermen, and recent decades have been marked by a series of fishing disputes, with nations fighting for the continued existence of their fisheries despite clear evidence that there are not enough catchable fish to satisfy everyone.

A similar story of declining catches during the present century could be told of many of the old-established fisheries around the world, but at the same time the demand for fish in a protein-hungry world has increased. To satisfy this demand the total annual world catch increased by about seven percent from the end of World War II until the early 1970s, by this time reaching a figure of around 60–70 million tonnes. But this increase was achieved only by exploiting previously unfished stocks or new geographical areas. Such an increase cannot go on indefinitely, for we are rapidly running out of "new" areas and some of the new fisheries have already shown the same symptoms of overfishing as the older ones—and sometimes even more dramatically.

New foods from the sea
The indications are that the present total catch is close to the maximum that can be obtained from relatively conventional fisheries even with careful management, and that, to increase the total, or even to sustain it, we must look to completely new sources such as krill, the shrimp-like food of the whalebone whales.

Estimates of the sustainable annual catch of krill in the Antarctic range from about 50 to 500 million tonnes, that is up to about seven times as much as the current total from all other fisheries put together. Of course, the use of such an enormous quantity of small crustaceans would present considerable problems. Part of it might be converted into a protein-rich paste for human consumption, but much would be used indirectly as a feed for farm animals.

Many larger seaweeds are already cropped in several parts of the world, particularly in Japan, and are used not only for human food but also for animal food and in many industrial processes. About one million tonnes of seaweed are taken each year, but because seaweeds grow naturally only in relatively shallow areas of the oceans this figure could probably not be significantly increased using natural populations. However, seaweeds can be grown artificially on frames floating over deep water. Experiments suggest that, by enriching the surface layers through artificial upwelling of nutrient-rich deep water, each square kilometer of such a floating seaweed farm could produce enough food to feed 1,000–2,000 people, and enough energy and other products to satisfy the needs of a further 1,000. With an estimated 260 million sq km (100 million sq miles) of "arable" surface, the seas might thus support up to 10 times the present world population.

Polluted waters
Of course, the present century has seen an increase not only in what man takes out of the sea but also in the harmful substances that he throws into it. Not only oil but many other substances are dumped into the seas accidentally or intentionally, usually either in the discharged effluent from industrial plant or as a result of agricultural chemicals being leached into rivers and thence into the ocean. In many cases the amounts are very small compared with the amounts present in the oceans as a whole; the problem is that they are usually released, and accumulate, in restricted inshore areas near which we live and from which we obtain most of our sea-caught food.

Since the 1930s there have been both national and international attempts to control pollution by legislation, and since 1958 a series of United Nations conferences has sought agreement on many aspects of international maritime law, including pollution. Despite many prophecies of imminent doom, it does not seem that marine pollution yet poses any general threat to humanity. Nevertheless, with ever-increasing industrialization and the production of more and more toxic materials, including radioactive wastes, it is essential that we monitor the effects of man's activities on the ocean.

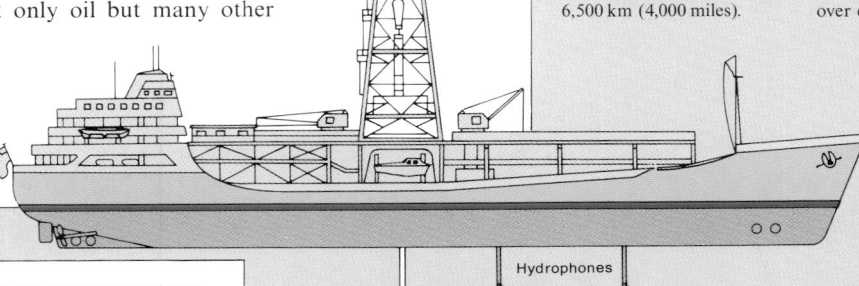

Drilling derrick

Hydrophones

Sonar beacons

Core sample tube

Drilling head

THE MARINE RESOURCES
Modern technology has enabled man to expand his age-old exploitation of the seas to the limit in some areas, and a need for the careful management of our marine resource is imperative. But in some fields, such as energy and the extraction of fresh water, the seas may yield inexhaustible riches.

The ocean is home to the Bajau (above), the "sea gypsies" of southeastern Asia, who inhabit a tract of sea and islands stretching more than 6,500 km (4,000 miles).

Each group has its own clan pattern, blazoned on the sails of their *praus*. The Bajau may live on the open sea in clusters of boats, or in stilt-house villages built over estuaries.

The deep-sea drilling ship *Glomar Challenger* (above) plays an important role in surveying and prospecting the oceans. It can drill in water depths of 7,000 m (23,000 ft) and obtain core samples 1,200 m (4,000 ft) below the ocean bed. The ship is positioned over the drill hole through signals from a sonar beacon to hydrophones in the hull.

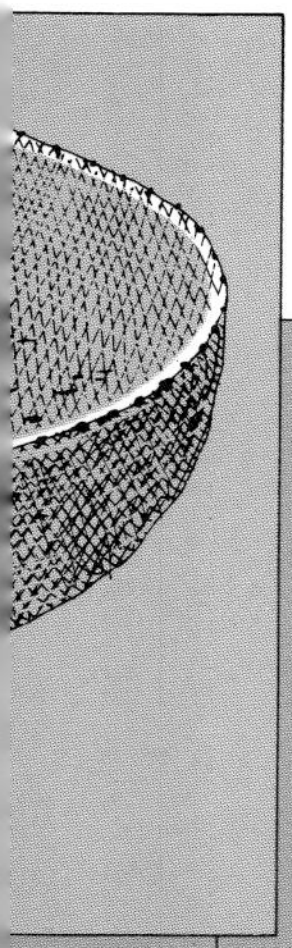

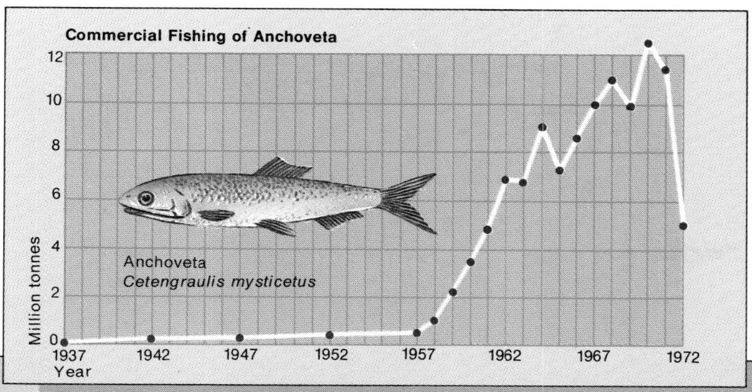

Commercial Fishing of Anchoveta

Anchoveta
Cetengraulis mysticetus

(graph: Million tonnes vs Year, 1937 to 1972)

Purse-seine fishing (left) is used for the capture of surface shoals. Having located the shoal, the boat encircles it, letting out the net until the fish are enclosed. A line is then hauled in to draw together the footrope, thus closing the net's bottom. American tuna-fishing boats use purse seines of huge size.

The Peruvian anchovy fishery's abrupt growth and decline (above) indicates the need for careful management of the food resource, though overfishing is not always the only reason for decline of fish stocks. Processed into animal feed, anchovies supply fish meal for many of the developed nations.

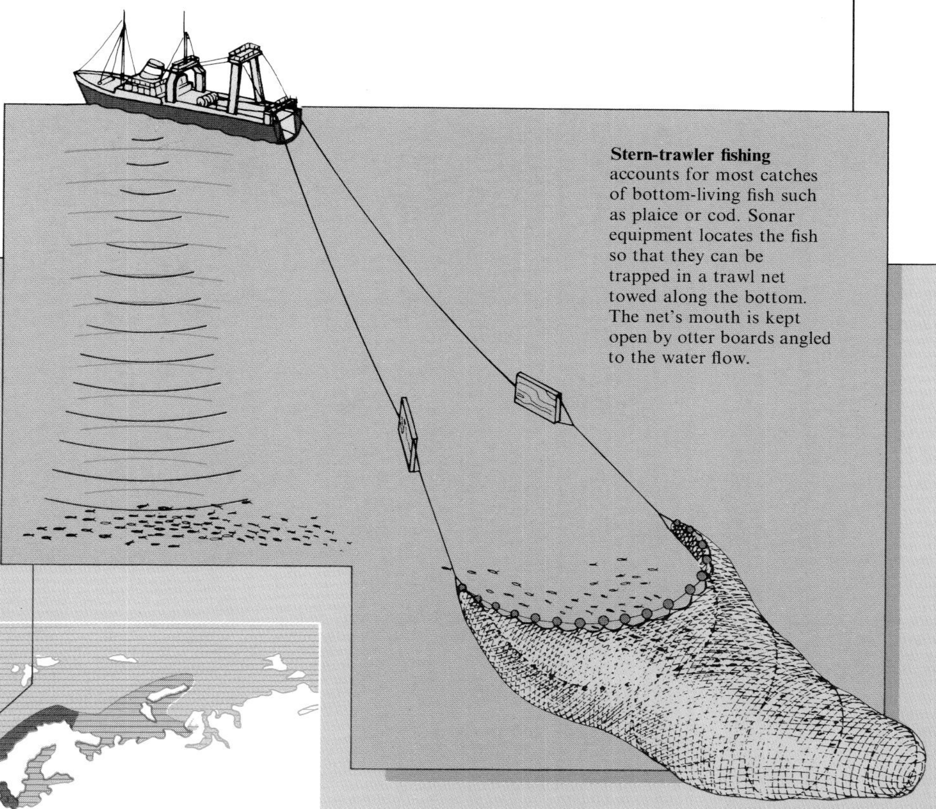

Stern-trawler fishing accounts for most catches of bottom-living fish such as plaice or cod. Sonar equipment locates the fish so that they can be trapped in a trawl net towed along the bottom. The net's mouth is kept open by otter boards angled to the water flow.

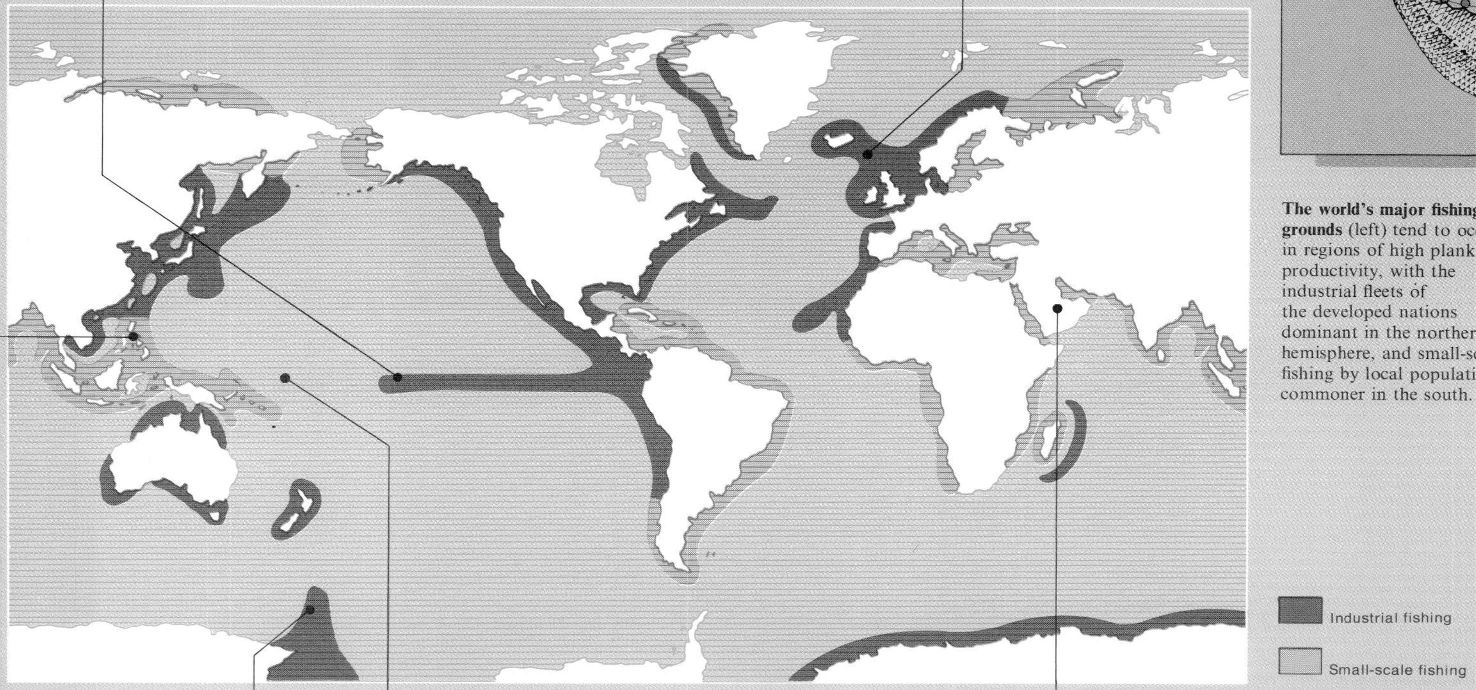

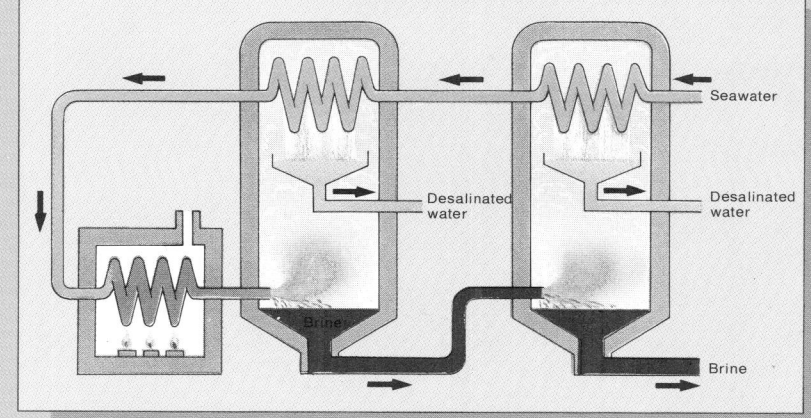

The world's major fishing grounds (left) tend to occur in regions of high plankton productivity, with the industrial fleets of the developed nations dominant in the northern hemisphere, and small-scale fishing by local populations commoner in the south.

Remote fishing grounds can be exploited by industrial fleets, as when whaling vessels operate in the Antarctic waters. But small-scale fishermen from underdeveloped nations in many parts of the world may also venture far from land, often in unpowered boats.

■ Industrial fishing

▨ Small-scale fishing

Minke whales (below) made up 80% of the 1981 permitted commercial take of 13,850 whales, as set by the International Whaling Commission. This figure was less than one-third of the total allowed eight years before, and today large-scale whaling is practiced only by Japan and the former Soviet Union. Protected species include the blue, bowhead, right and humpback whales.

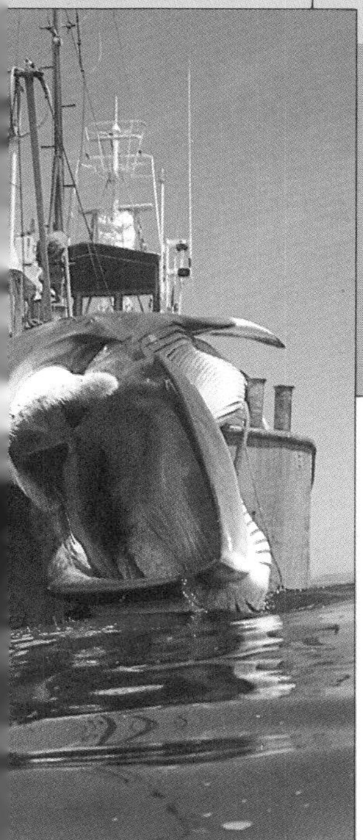

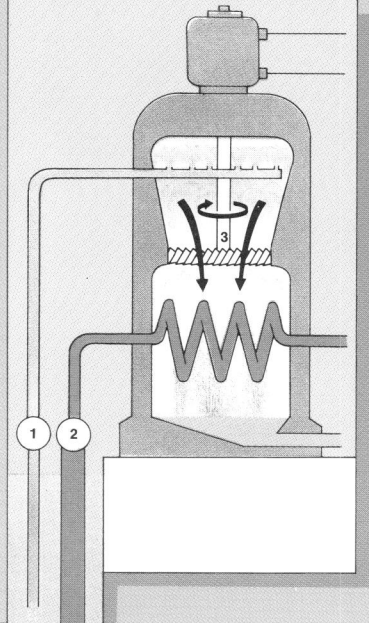

Energy from the oceans (left) can be obtained by Ocean Thermal Energy Conversion (OTEC), which exploits the temperature difference between warm surface water and cold bottom water. The former (1) is evaporated under reduced pressure when a partial vacuum is formed by pumping cold water (2) into the lower chamber. This draws down the vapor, thus turning the turbine (3). The nutrient-rich bottom water may also be a source of food for fish farms. The first commercial OTEC plant, Japanese made, has been constructed for the Pacific island of Nauru, where conditions for operation are ideal.

Seawater

Desalinated water

Desalinated water

Brine

Brine

Fresh water is distilled from the sea (above) at many desalination plants in the Middle East. The cold seawater is heated and then discharged into a vessel at reduced pressure, where the cooling coils of seawater in the upper part condense the water vapor. The briny water that is left passes through several similar stages, at lower pressures, with more water vapor being evaporated and condensed at each stage. Such systems can operate by means of waste steam from electricity generating plants, as at Abu Dhabi.

ENERGY, INDUSTRY AND THE SEAS

The volume of oil carried annually along the world's major tanker routes (below) exceeds 1,400 million tonnes, of which some six million tonnes enter the seas through dumping or accidents. Coastlines of developed nations are worst affected by oil (right) and discharge of industrial wastes.

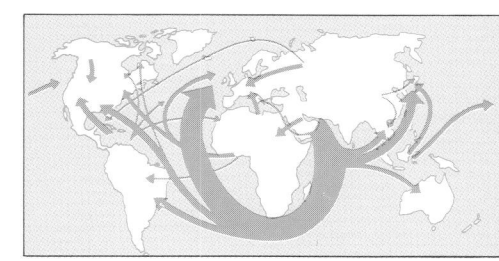

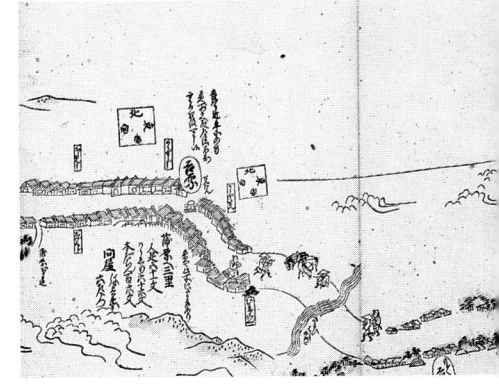

Part 5

UNDERSTANDING MAPS
What maps are and how they are made
New horizons and latest developments in maps and mapmaking
How to read the language of maps

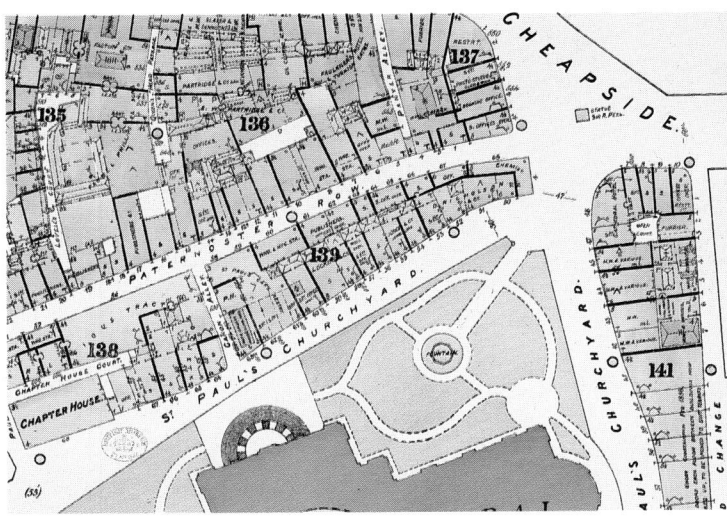

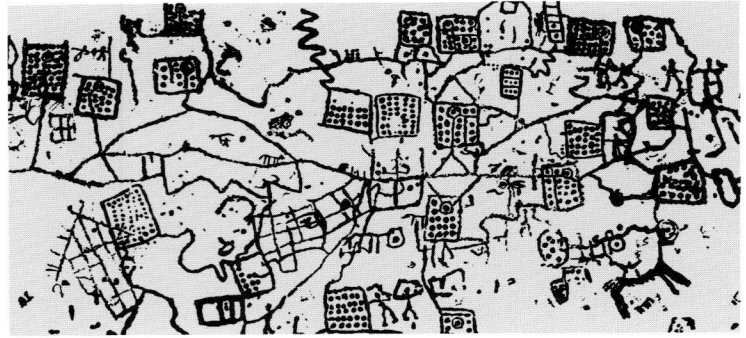

Elegant road maps with pictorial and geographical features have been produced by many different cultures. The woodcut map of the Tōkaidō (detail above), the great Japanese highway, 555 km (345 miles) long, between Edo (Tokyo) and Kyoto, was drawn as a panorama by the famous artist Moronobu in 1690. Its pictorial details do not prevent it being an accurate representation of the road's track. A Mexican map of the Tepetlaoztoc valley (right) drawn in 1583 marks roads with footprints between parallel lines, and hill ranges with wavy lines. Symbols in panels represent place-names.

Maps defining territory and ownership are almost as old as the human territorial instinct itself. The rock-carving maps of the Val Camonica, Italy (above), dating from the second and first millennia BC, show stippled square fields, paths, river lines, houses, and even humans and animals. It is uncertain whether their purpose was legal, but the need to establish ownership is a basic function of many maps, as seen in a detail from Goad's 19th-century insurance map of London (left), where every occupation is recorded.

America first appears as a separate continent (below) in an inset to Martin Waldseemüller's world map of 1507, with the two hemispheres facing each other. Presiding over the Old World is Claudius Ptolemy, the 2nd-century geographer whose remarkably scientific maps, copied and recopied over a thousand years, were revised and emended by Waldseemüller to show some of the results of Portuguese exploration. His New World counterpart is the Italian Amerigo Vespucci, one of the early explorers of the continent, after whom it was named. This is the first map to show the Pacific (not yet named) as an ocean between America and Asia. The west coast of South America, still to be explored by Europeans, seems to be inspired guesswork. The island between the landmasses is Cipango (Japan) known from Marco Polo.

1 2

The earliest surviving Chinese globe (above) was made in 1623 by two Jesuit missionaries, probably for the emperor of China. The long legend in Chinese expresses terms and ideas derived from early Chinese cosmology. It describes the Earth as "floating in the Heavens like the yolk of an egg . . . with all objects having mass tending toward its center"—one of the first known references to gravity.

High-altitude photography (left) allows accurate updating of topographic maps (right), while data gathering by satellites (above) expands the range. Landsat satellites carry electronic remote-sensing equipment that detects the energy emitted by surface materials and translates it into images. Healthy plants may show as bright red, sparse vegetation as pink, barren lands as light gray, and urban areas as green or dark gray. The folded shape of the Appalachians (1) is clearly seen; the Canada–US border (2) is revealed by land-use patterns; silt from the Mississippi (3) builds up the delta. Sudan irrigation (4) shows up as brilliant red.

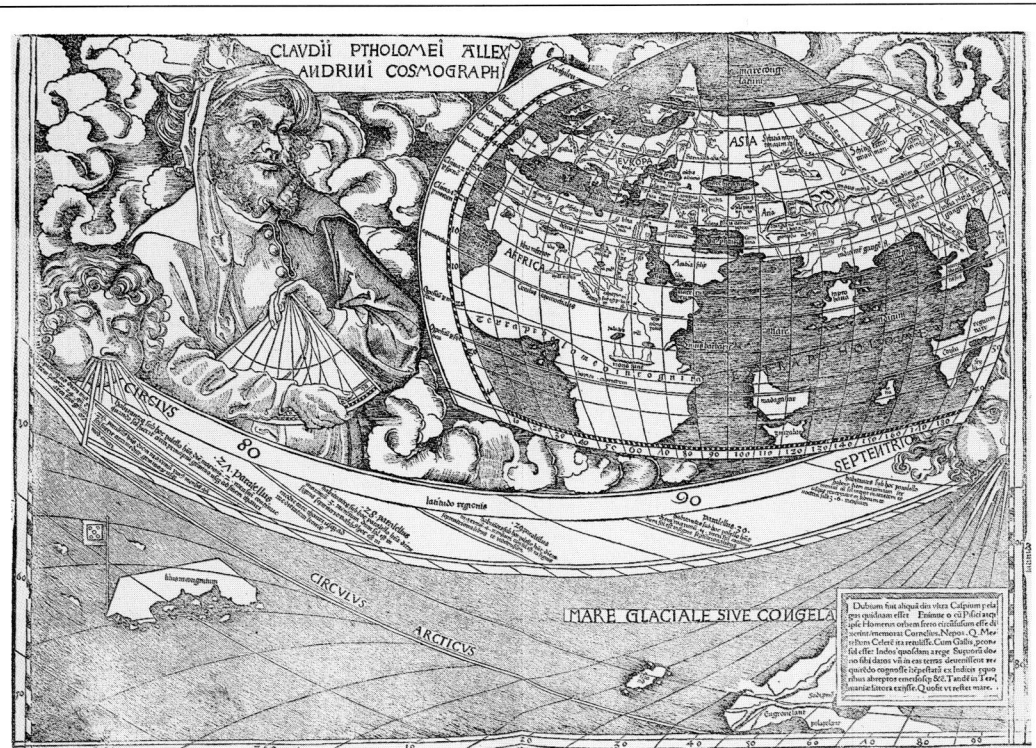

Mapping, Old and New

Mapmaking must have its origins in the earliest ages of human history, since people of preliterate as well as literate cultures possess an innate skill in map drawing. This innate capacity is further indicated by the ease with which almost anyone can sketch in the sand or on paper simple directions for showing the way. But maps may also define territory and express man's idea of the world in graphic representation. Today, modern technology has vastly extended the scope of cartography.

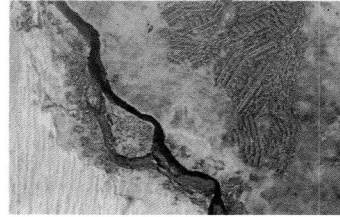

3   4

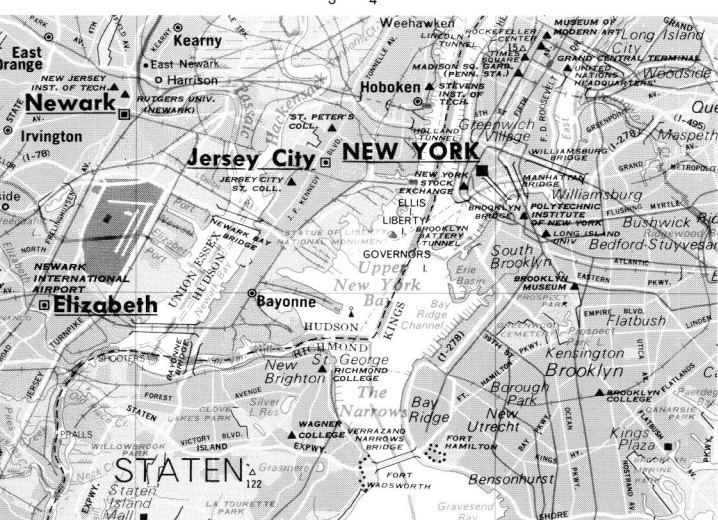

Many non-European cultures developed ingenious route-map techniques: the North American Indians, for example, made sketch maps of routes on birch bark. These were diagrammatic maps in which directions and distances were not accurate but relationships were true, as in New York Subway or London Underground maps. The people of the Marshall Islands in the western Pacific made route maps over the seas, depicting the direction of the main seasonal wave swells in relation to the islands.

Although maps of routes are the simplest type of map in concept, they developed complex forms as cartography progressed. A road map of the whole Roman Empire, drawn about AD 280, survives today in a thirteenth-century copy known as the Peutinger Table. Hernando Cortes, the Spanish conqueror, made his way across Mexico in the 1520s with the help of pre-conquest Mexican maps painted on cloth. These showed roads with double lines or colored bands marked with footprints. Another type of map is the strip map depicting a single road along its entire length. Pictorial maps of the Tōkaidō highway from Edo to Kyoto in Japan, made from a survey of 1651, were popular in the Edo period of Japanese history.

Nautical charts evolved as a special type of direction-finding map to meet the needs of seamen. Those of the late Middle Ages came to be known as "portolan" charts, from the word "portolani," or sailing directions. They showed the sea and adjacent coasts superimposed on a network of radiating compass lines.

Territorial maps

Another basic type of map derives from man's sense of territorial possession. The earliest example of a "cadastral" plan (a map showing land parcels and property boundaries) appears to be that preserved as rock carvings at Bedolina in Val Camonica in northern Italy. However, in the ancient civilizations of Mesopotamia and Egypt, land surveying had become an established profession by 2000 BC. An idea of what Egyptian surveyors' plans of 1000 BC were like can be seen from the "Fields of the Dead" representing the Egyptians' idea of life after death. These show plots of land surrounded by water and intersected by canals. The Romans used cadastral surveys to determine land ownership and assess tax liability.

Another form of map showing territorial demarcations is the map of administrative units. The Chinese in the thirteenth century AD were making official district maps to help in the organization of grain supplies and the collection of taxes. Many of their gazetteers (*fang chih*), written in the form of local geographies and

histories from the eleventh century onward, were illustrated with maps. Political maps showing the boundaries of states were increasingly significant in European cartography from the sixteenth century onward.

A third major class of map is the general or topographical map expressing man's perception of the world, its regions and its place in the universe. A Babylonian world map of the seventh century BC is drawn on a clay tablet and shows the Earth as a circular disc surrounded by the Earthly Ocean. With the ancient Greeks, geography developed on scientific principles. The treatise on mapmaking by Claudius Ptolemy (AD 87–150), later known as the *Geographia*, was the most famous cartographic text of the period. It influenced the Arabic geographers of the Middle Ages, notably Muhammad Ibn Muhammad, Al-Idrisi (1099–1164), and with the revival of Ptolemy in fifteenth-century Europe became one of the major works of the Renaissance. Published, with engraved maps, at Bologna in 1477, the *Geographia* ranks as the first printed atlas in the western world. The invention of techniques of engraving in wood and copper facilitated a wide diffusion of geographical knowledge through the map-publishing trade. The first atlas made up of modern maps to a uniform design was Abraham Ortelius's *Theatrum Orbis Terrarum* published at Antwerp in 1570. From 1492, when Martin Behaim made his "Erdapfel" at Nürnberg, globes also became popular, and globemakers vied with each other to make larger and more elaborate ones to keep pace with the growth of knowledge about the world.

Over the last two hundred years cartography has made rapid and remarkable advances. Observatories built in Paris in 1671 and at Greenwich in 1675 enabled the location of places to be established more exactly with the use of astronomical tables. Improvements in surveying instruments facilitated more accurate and rapid land survey. France was the pioneer in establishing (from 1679 onward) a national survey on a geometrical basis of triangulation. By the end of the eighteenth century national surveys on small and medium scales had been begun by most European countries. In the United States the Geological Survey was set up in 1879 to undertake the topographical and geological mapping of the country.

Mapping today

Since World War II cartographic techniques have undergone a revolution. The use of air survey and photogrammetry has made it possible to map most of the Earth's surface. Electronic distance measurement by laser or light beams in surveying, and digital computers in mapping, are among the most recent advances in methods. Mosaics or air photography are used to produce orthophoto maps which can supplement or substitute for the conventional topographic map. Artificial satellites and manned space craft make it possible to provide a world-wide framework of geodetic networks.

Earth Resource Technology Satellites (ERTS) imagery has made it possible to map mountain ranges in Africa and features on the surface of Antarctica that were hitherto unknown. The imagery is made available by means of remote-sensing instruments, carried by the satellites, that are sensitive to invisible portions of the electromagnetic spectrum—longer and shorter wavelengths than can be sensed by the human eye. Remote-sensing instruments usually work in the infrared bands. They can also pick up the energy emitted by all types of surface material—rocks, soils, vegetation, water and man-made structures—and produce photographs or images from it.

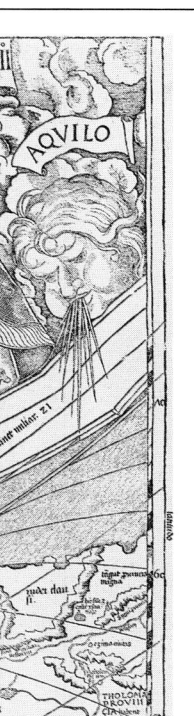
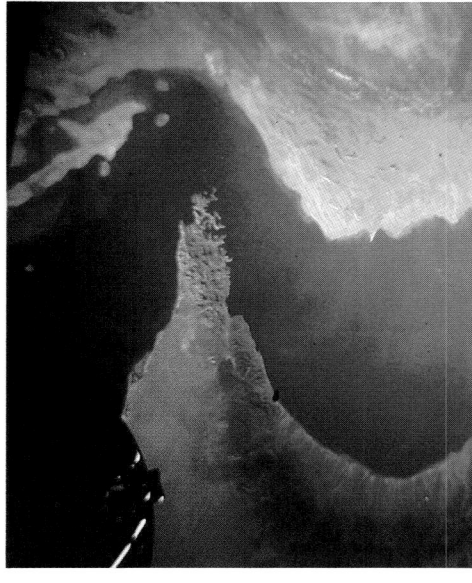
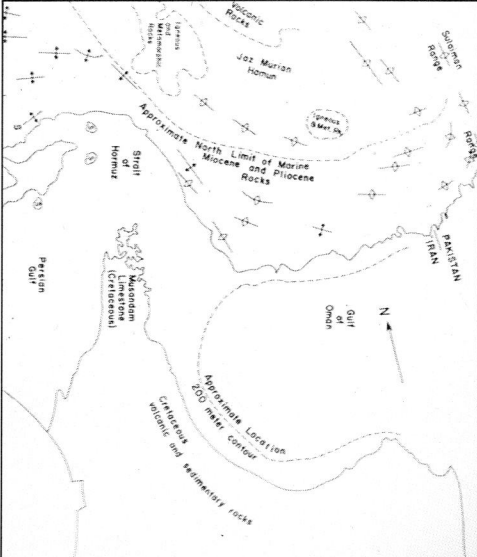

Space technology helps cartographers to map even interior details of the planet: its geology and mineral wealth. A photo (below) taken from Gemini 12 at an altitude of 272 km (168 miles) forms the basis of a geologic sketch map of SW Asia (below right), showing the oil-rich area around the region between the Persian Gulf and the Gulf of Oman. The symbol S on the map indicates salt plugs; diamonds show fold trends; double-headed arrows anticlines.

The Language of Maps

Mapmakers for more than 4,000 years have tried to find the best way to represent the shape and features of the three-dimensional Earth on two-dimensional paper, parchment and cloth. The measurement of distance and direction is a basic requirement for accurate surveys, but until about 1800 theoretical understanding of the method was well in advance of the technical equipment available. Today the use of lasers and light beams sometimes takes the place of direct measurement on the ground.

A reference system must be used to show distance and direction correctly in the construction of maps. The simplest type is the rectangular or square grid. The Chinese mapmaker Pei Xin made a map with a grid in about AD 270, and this system remained in continuous use in China until modern times. The Roman system of centuriation, a form of division of public lands on a square or rectangular basis, was also a "coordinate" system starting from a point of origin at the intersection of two perpendicular axes. Roman surveyors' maps, dating from the first century AD, are the earliest known European maps based on a grid system.

Latitude and longitude

Makers of small-scale regional maps and of world maps in early times also had to take account of the fact that the Earth is a sphere. The Greeks derived from the Babylonians the idea of dividing a circle into 360 degrees. In the second century BC the Greek geographer Eratosthenes (c. 276–194 BC) was the first to calculate the circumference of the globe and was reported to have made a world map based on the concept of the Earth's sphericity. From this the Greeks went on to develop the system of spherical coordinates which remains in use today. The poles at each end of the Earth's axis provide reference points for the Earth in its rotation in relation to the celestial sphere. Parallel circles around the Earth are degrees of latitude and express the idea of distance north or south of the Equator. Lines of longitude running north and south through the poles express east–west distances. One meridian is chosen as the meridian of origin, known as the prime meridian.

Whereas latitude from early times could be observed from the height of the Sun or (in the northern hemisphere) from the position of the Pole Star at night, accurate observations of longitude were not possible until the middle of the eighteenth century, when the chronometer was invented and more accurate astronomical tables were provided. In 1884 most countries agreed, at an international conference in Washington DC, to adopt the prime meridian through the Royal Greenwich Observatory in England and to calculate longitude to 180 degrees east and west of Greenwich.

Projection and distortion

The mathematical system by which the spherical surface of the Earth is transferred to the plane surface of a map is called a map projection. The Greek geographer Ptolemy gave instructions in his geographical treatise of AD 150 for the construction of two projections. When the *Geographia* was revised in Europe in the fifteenth century, and navigators began sailing across the oceans, mapmakers devised new projections more appropriate to the expanding geographical knowledge of the world. The Dutch geographer Gerard Mercator invented the projection named after him, applying it to his world chart of 1569. This cylindrical projection, in which all points are at true compass courses from each other, was of great benefit to navigators and is still one of the most commonly used projections. Another advance was made when Johann Heinrich Lambert of Alsace (1728–1777) invented the azimuthal equal-area projection, in which the sizes of all areas are represented on the projection in correct proportion to one another, and the conformal projection, in which at any point on the map the scale is constant in all directions.

Since all projections involve deformation of the geometry of the globe, the cartographer has to choose the one that best suits the purpose of his map. "Conformal" or "orthomorphic" projections, in which angular relations (or shape) are preserved, are widely used for the construction of topographical maps. "Equivalent" or "equal-area" projections retain relative sizes and are particularly useful for general reference maps displaying economic, historical, political and other geographical phenomena.

Since the mid-fifteenth century, European mapmakers have generally arranged their maps with north at the top of the sheet. Earlier maps, however, were not standardized in this way. The circular world maps of the Middle Ages were orientated with east at the top, because this was where the terrestrial paradise was traditionally sited. Indeed, the word "orientation" originally meant the arrangement of something so as to face east.

Map scale

Scale is another basic property of a map. The scale of a map is the ratio of the distance on the map to the actual distance represented. Whereas the Babylonians, Egyptians, Greeks and Romans drew surveys to scale, in medieval Europe mapmakers used customary methods of estimating. The earliest known local map since Roman times which is drawn to scale (it displays a scale bar) is a plan of Vienna, 1422.

Projection, grid, orientation and scale form the framework of a map. The language of maps in concept and content is much more complex. To represent the surface of the Earth on a map, the cartographer must select and generalize from a vast quantity of material, using symbols and conventional signs as codes.

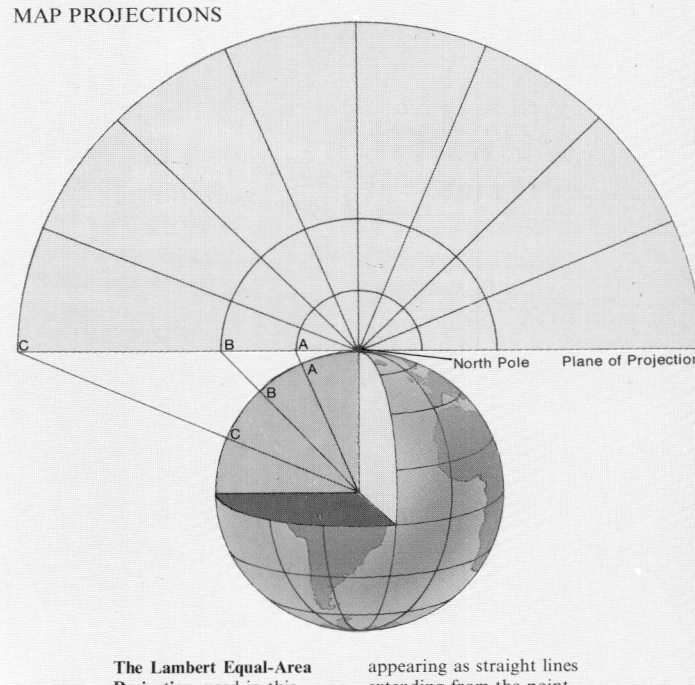

The Lambert Equal-Area Projection, used in this atlas, may be visualized as a flat plane placed at a tangent to the globe, with the lines of longitude appearing as straight lines extending from the point of tangency, the North Pole (above). Deformation increases away from this point (below).

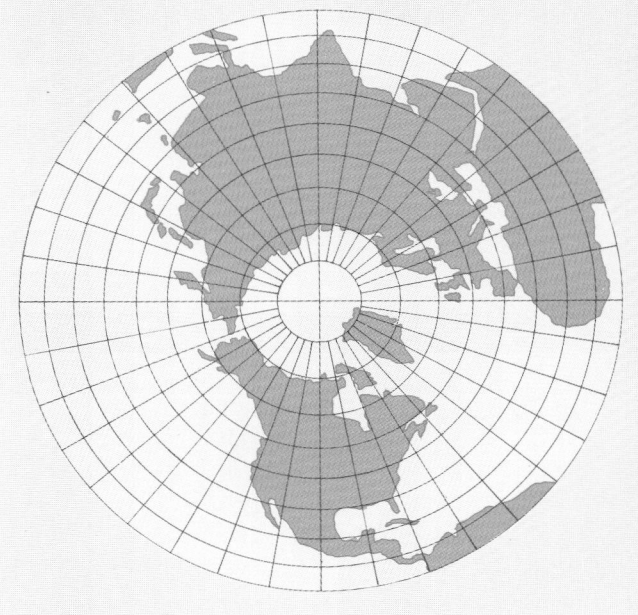

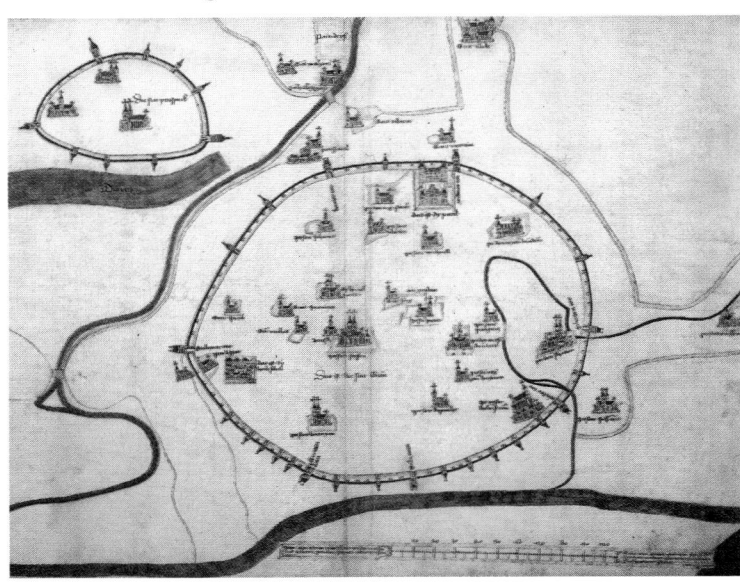

Map scales express the relationship between a distance measured on the map and the true distance on the ground. A plan of Vienna (left), originally made in 1422, is drawn in the bird's-eye-view style typical of early medieval town plans. But the scale bar at its foot shows that it has been explicitly drawn to scale, indicating that the concept of a uniform scale had been grasped in medieval Europe.

Direction and distance are concepts used in the relative location of two or more points (below). These concepts are organized according to a general frame of reference, with direction following the grid system of coordinates. Thus places shown in (A) can be precisely located in terms of longitude and of latitude (B), with the degrees further subdivided into one-sixtieths of minutes.

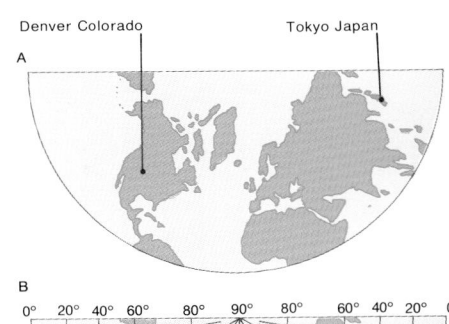

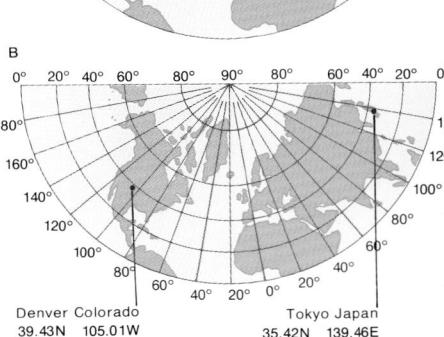

Denver Colorado
39.43N 105.01W

Tokyo Japan
35.42N 139.46E

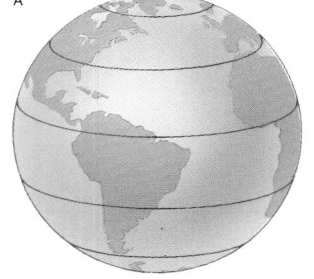

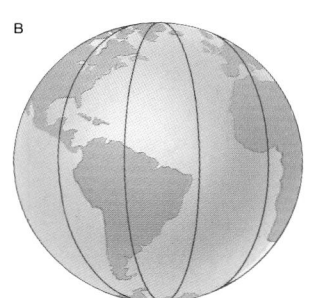

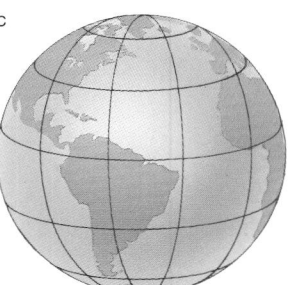

Superimposed on the globe (left), lines of latitude (A) and longitude (B) allow every place to be exactly located in terms of a coordinate system (C). The parallels of latitude measure distance from 0° to 90° north and south of the Equator. The meridians of longitude measure distance from 0° to 180° east and west of a "prime meridian" at Greenwich.

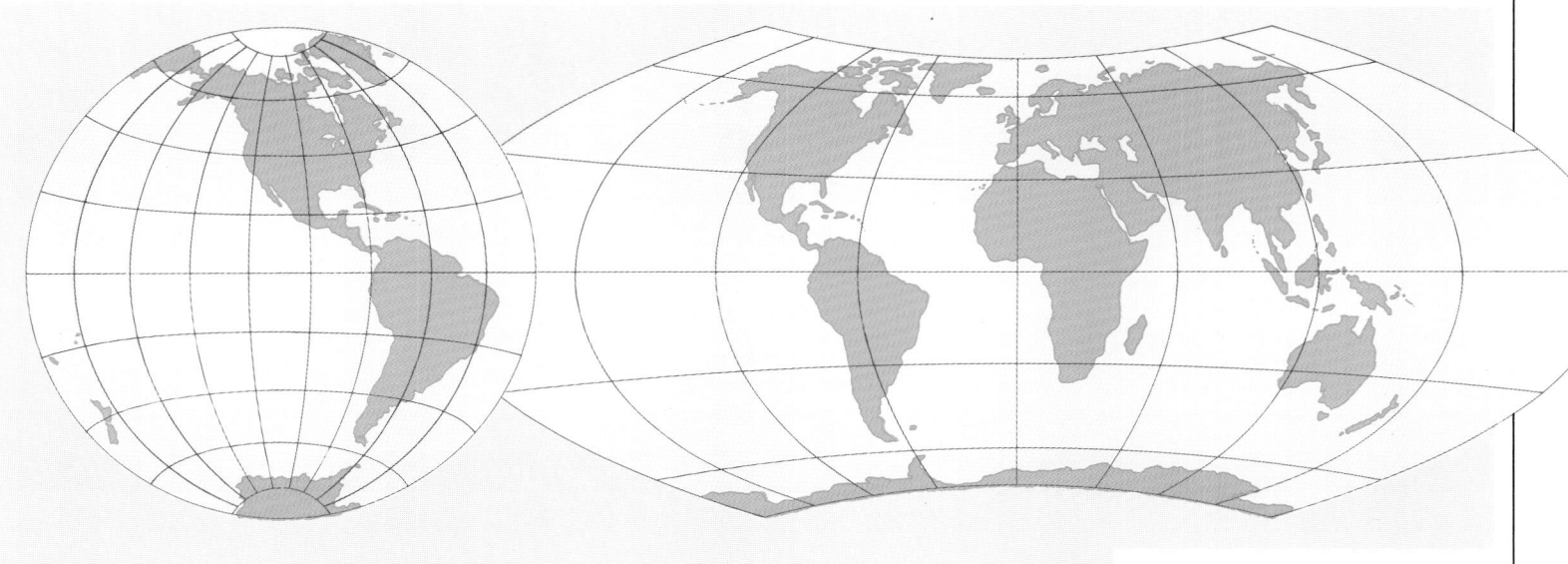

The Hammer Projection (far right), developed from the Lambert Projection of one hemisphere (right), is designed to show the whole world in a single view, and is used in this atlas in a version modified by Wagner and known as the Hammer-Wagner Projection. The Earth appears as an ellipse because the lines of longitude are plotted at twice their horizontal distance from the center line, and numbered at twice their previous values. The central meridian is half the length of the Equator.

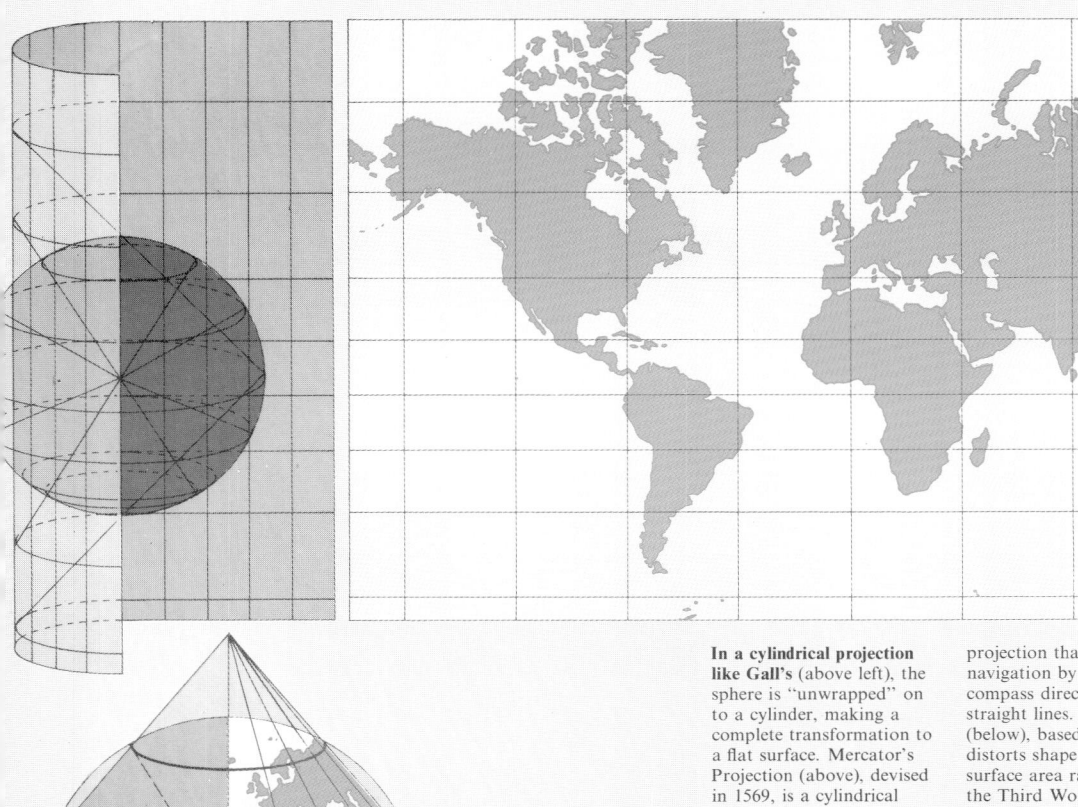

Photogrammetric plotting instruments (above) are now used in the preparation of large-scale accurate topographic maps. These are sophisticated machines that provide very precise measurements, plotting the map data in orthogonal projection.

In a cylindrical projection like Gall's (above left), the sphere is "unwrapped" on to a cylinder, making a complete transformation to a flat surface. Mercator's Projection (above), devised in 1569, is a cylindrical projection that aids navigation by showing all compass directions as straight lines. A projection (below), based on Peters', distorts shape to show land surface area ratios, emphasizing the Third World.

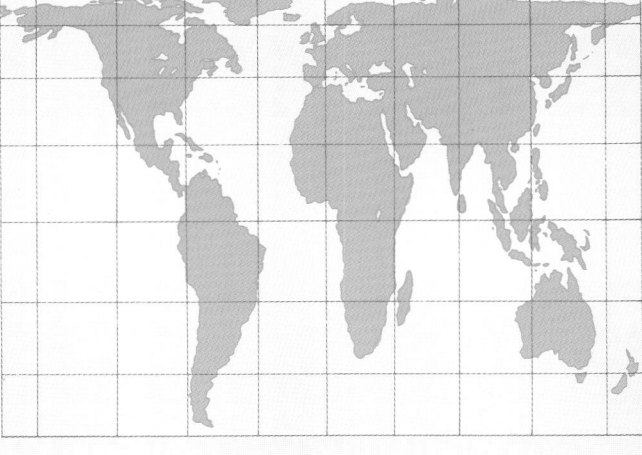

The theodolite (above), a basic surveying instrument dating back to the 16th century, can measure angles and directions horizontally and vertically. A swivel telescope with cross-hairs inside it permits accurate alignment, and it may be used in the field.

Delisle's Conic Projection (right), used in this atlas, intersects the globe at two points (above). Distortion is least at the parallels where the cone "touches" the globe, increasing with distance from them. Thus it is good for mid-latitudes.

EARTH MEASUREMENT THROUGH THE AGES

Surveying—the technique of making accurate measurements of the Earth's surface—is as old as civilization and has been an essential element in mankind's development of his environment. The need to establish land boundaries arose at least 3,500 years ago in the fertile valleys of the Nile, Tigris and Euphrates rivers. Man's urge to explore and to describe the world also led to the development of instruments determining position, distance and direction. The astrolabe, sometimes called the world's oldest scientific instrument, may date to the 3rd century BC. Today's techniques make increasing use of computers.

An Egyptian wall painting (left) from the middle of the second millennium BC shows what appears to be the measurement of a grain field by means of a rope with knots at regular intervals on its length.

The astrolabe (right), used in classical times to observe the positions of celestial bodies, became a navigational instrument in the Middle Ages, when it was developed to permit establishment of latitude.

How to Use Maps

Today maps play a role more important than ever before in increasing our knowledge of the Earth, its regions and peoples. How maps communicate knowledge is now a subject of scientific study. The process comprises the collection and mapping of the data and the reading of the map. In this final stage the map user is all important. Through him the map is transformed into an image in the mind, and the effectiveness of the map depends on the reader being able to understand it.

The cartographer's map has to convey an objective picture of reality. To compile the map the cartographer selects and generalizes information, taking into account the purpose of his map. If he is making a topographical reference map, he has to reduce the three-dimensional landforms of the Earth on to the flat surface of the map. He adds cultural detail such as towns, roads and railroads, and features not apparent to the eye, such as administrative boundaries. On the topographical base map he adds appropriate place-names, using typefaces which reflect their class and significance. All this requires the classification of phenomena, with emphasis to direct the reader's attention.

Themes and symbolization

The cartographer who seeks not merely to represent visible features but to convey geographical ideas about specific phenomena uses the techniques of thematic cartography, where the emphasis is on one or two elements, or themes. Maps today provide one of the most effective means of communicating many kinds of data and ideas relating to the world and its peoples. Their extensive use makes them an important force in education, planning, recreation and in many other human affairs.

The map is designed in code, with symbols to represent features, and a legend, or key, to explain them. There are three types of symbol: point, line and area. Point symbols usually denote places, which may be distinguished into classes by the shape, color and size of the symbol. Line symbols express connections, such as roads or traffic flow, and they may also define and distinguish areas. Area symbols in which variations of color are often combined with patterns of lines or dots are used to depict spatial phenomena, such as types of soil, vegetation and density of population.

How much detail can be shown on a map will depend on its scale, which controls the process of generalization. Scale expresses the relationship of the distance on the map to the distance on the Earth, with the distance on the map always given as the unit ·1. It is denoted in various ways: as a representative fraction such as 1:1,000,000; as a written statement; or by means of a graph or bar. Some map scales have become widely used and are generally familiar to map users. The scale 1:25,000 is ideal for walkers and relief can be shown in detail. That of 1:50,000 is a typical medium scale for national surveys. The publication of an international map of the world on a scale of one to

one million (1:1,000,000) has been in progress since 1909. On this scale 1 mm represents 1 km on the ground. The regional maps of countries in this atlas are drawn on scales of 1:6,000,000, 1:3,000,000 and 1:1,500,000; those of the continents are at 1:30,000,000 and 1:15,000,000. The Map Section index maps show the arrangement.

Terrain depiction

Since the early days of map making in ancient Chinese and classical Greek and Roman civilizations, map makers have been concerned to show the configuration of the land. For many centuries they symbolized mountains and hills by pictorial features often looking like caterpillars or sugar loaves. As topographical mapping developed in Europe from the seventeenth century onward, new techniques were devised to improve the visual impression of the features and to depict them accurately in terms of height and location. The system of hachuring (shading with fine parallel or crossed lines), first used in 1674, gives a good idea of relief but not of height. The use of contours, which became general from the nineteenth century onward, is more exact in representing actual elevation, but for many regions, especially those of irregular relief, the appearance of the land is lost.

The addition of hypsometric tints (tints between contours which show elevation) helps clarify the elevation. Applying shadows to the form of the land through the process called hill shading or relief shading creates a visual impression of the configuration of the land surface. Hypsometric tints combined with hill shading gives both elevation information and surface form of the area being depicted, leading to an almost three-dimensional effect.

Maps are classed (right) as either general (A) or thematic (B,C). The purpose of a general reference map is to provide locational information, showing how the positions of various geographical phenomena relate to each other. Thematic maps concentrate on a particular type of information, or theme, such as the distribution of people (B) or rainfall (C), and are generally based on statistical data.

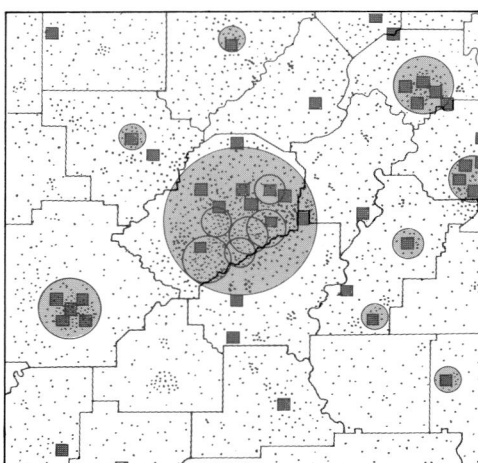
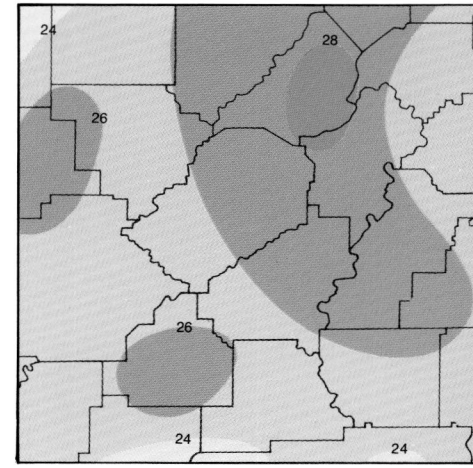

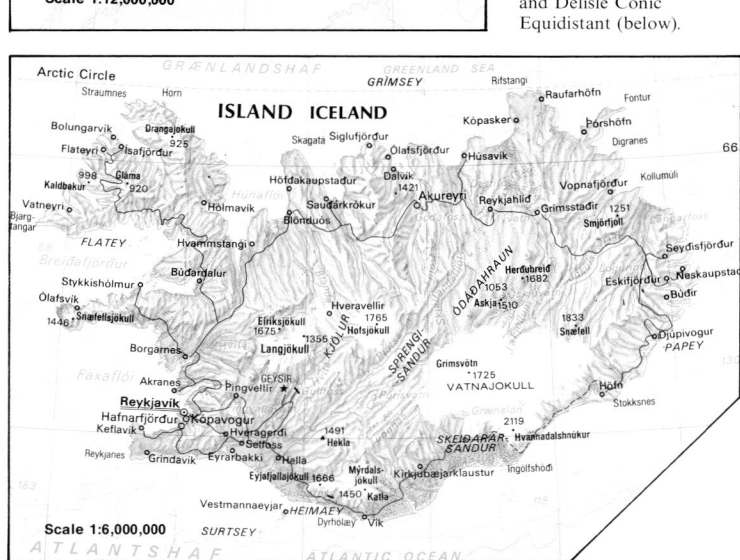

The ratio between a map's dimensions and those of the physical world is defined by the map scale (left and below), with the map distance always given as the unit 1. The larger the reduction, the smaller the scale, so that a scale of 1:6,000,000—1 mm (.04 in) to 6 km (3.74 miles)—is twice that of 1:12,000,000 (.04 in to 7.5 miles). The size of the scale reflects the amount of detail that needs to be shown. The projections are the Lambert Azimuthal Equal-Area (left) and Delisle Conic Equidistant (below).

Scale 1:12,000,000

Scale 1:6,000,000

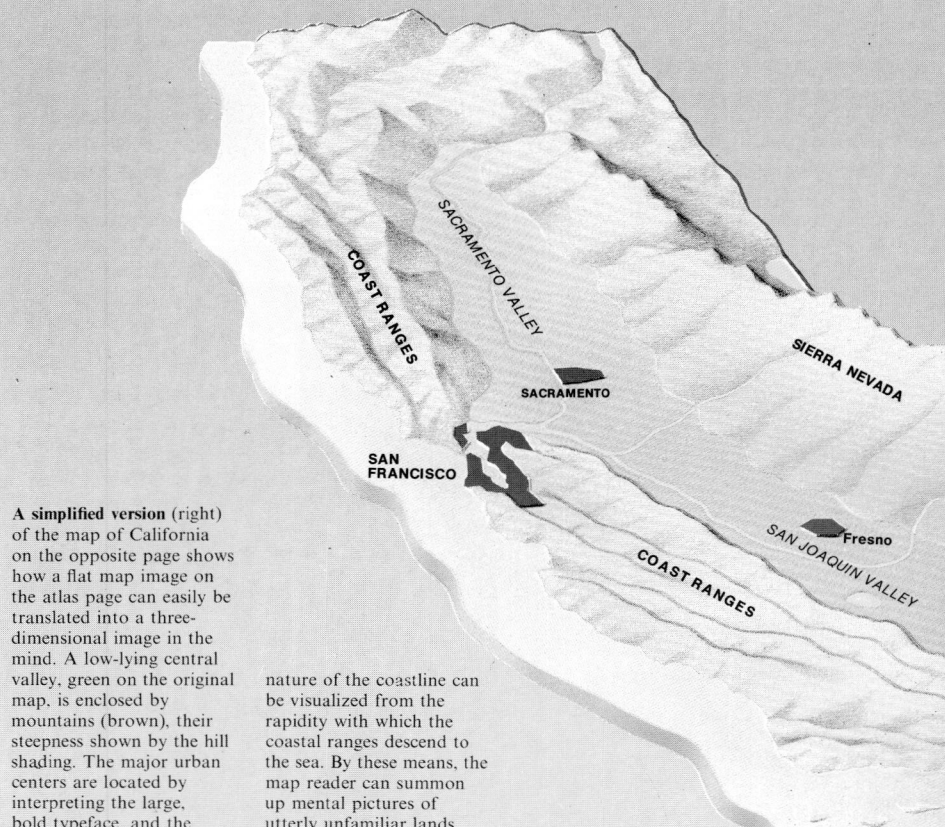

A simplified version (right) of the map of California on the opposite page shows how a flat map image on the atlas page can easily be translated into a three-dimensional image in the mind. A low-lying central valley, green on the original map, is enclosed by mountains (brown), their steepness shown by the hill shading. The major urban centers are located by interpreting the large, bold typeface, and the nature of the coastline can be visualized from the rapidity with which the coastal ranges descend to the sea. By these means, the map reader can summon up mental pictures of utterly unfamiliar lands.

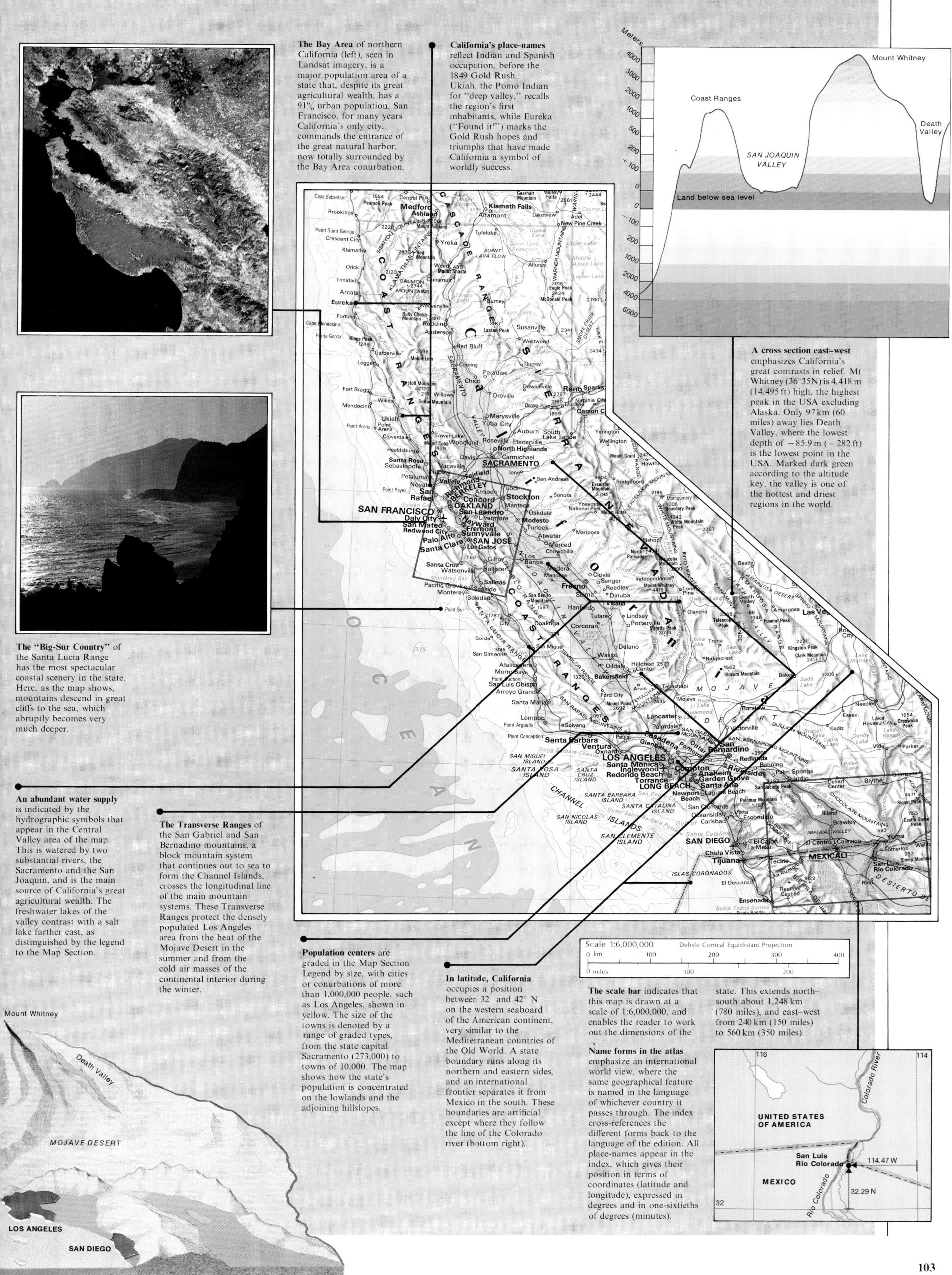

The Bay Area of northern California (left), seen in Landsat imagery, is a major population area of a state that, despite its great agricultural wealth, has a 91% urban population. San Francisco, for many years California's only city, commands the entrance of the great natural harbor, now totally surrounded by the Bay Area conurbation.

California's place-names reflect Indian and Spanish occupation, before the 1849 Gold Rush. Ukiah, the Pomo Indian for "deep valley," recalls the region's first inhabitants, while Eureka ("Found it!") marks the Gold Rush hopes and triumphs that have made California a symbol of worldly success.

A cross section east–west emphasizes California's great contrasts in relief. Mt Whitney (36° 35N) is 4,418 m (14,495 ft) high, the highest peak in the USA excluding Alaska. Only 97 km (60 miles) away lies Death Valley, where the lowest depth of −85.9 m (−282 ft) is the lowest point in the USA. Marked dark green according to the altitude key, the valley is one of the hottest and driest regions in the world.

The **"Big-Sur Country"** of the Santa Lucia Range has the most spectacular coastal scenery in the state. Here, as the map shows, mountains descend in great cliffs to the sea, which abruptly becomes very much deeper.

An abundant water supply is indicated by the hydrographic symbols that appear in the Central Valley area of the map. This is watered by two substantial rivers, the Sacramento and the San Joaquin, and is the main source of California's great agricultural wealth. The freshwater lakes of the valley contrast with a salt lake farther east, as distinguished by the legend to the Map Section.

The Transverse Ranges of the San Gabriel and San Bernadino mountains, a block mountain system that continues out to sea to form the Channel Islands, crosses the longitudinal line of the main mountain systems. These Transverse Ranges protect the densely populated Los Angeles area from the heat of the Mojave Desert in the summer and from the cold air masses of the continental interior during the winter.

Population centers are graded in the Map Section Legend by size, with cities or conurbations of more than 1,000,000 people, such as Los Angeles, shown in yellow. The size of the towns is denoted by a range of graded types, from the state capital Sacramento (273,000) to towns of 10,000. The map shows how the state's population is concentrated on the lowlands and the adjoining hillslopes.

In latitude, California occupies a position between 32° and 42° N on the western seaboard of the American continent, very similar to the Mediterranean countries of the Old World. A state boundary runs along its northern and eastern sides, and an international frontier separates it from Mexico in the south. These boundaries are artificial except where they follow the line of the Colorado river (bottom right).

The scale bar indicates that this map is drawn at a scale of 1:6,000,000, and enables the reader to work out the dimensions of the state. This extends north–south about 1,248 km (780 miles), and east–west from 240 km (150 miles) to 560 km (350 miles).

Name forms in the atlas emphasize an international world view, where the same geographical feature is named in the language of whichever country it passes through. The index cross-references the different forms back to the language of the edition. All place-names appear in the index, which gives their position in terms of coordinates (latitude and longitude), expressed in degrees and in one-sixtieths of degrees (minutes).

Scale 1:6,000,000   Delisle Conical Equidistant Projection
0 km   100   200   300   400
0 miles   100   200

Meters
4000 / 3000 / 2000 / 1000 / 500 / 200 / +100 / 0 / −100 / 200 / 1000 / 2000 / 4000 / 6000

Coast Ranges   Mount Whitney   Death Valley
SAN JOAQUIN VALLEY
Land below sea level

Mount Whitney

Death Valley

MOJAVE DESERT

LOS ANGELES

SAN DIEGO

UNITED STATES OF AMERICA

MEXICO

San Luis Rio Colorado

Colorado River

114.47 W

32.29 N

Rio Colorado

116   114   32

ACKNOWLEDGMENTS

Senior Executive Art Editor
Michael McGuinness

Executive Editor
James Hughes

Coordinating Editor
Dian Taylor

Editors
Lesley Ellis
Judy Garlick
Ken Hewis

Art Editor
Mike Brown

Designers
Sue Rawkins
Lisa Tai

Picture Researcher
Flavia Howard

Researchers
Nicholas Law
Nigel Morrison
Alicia Smith

Editorial Assistant
Barbara Gish

Proofreader
Kathie Gill

Indexers
Hilary and Richard Bird

Production Controller
Barry Baker

Typesetting by Servis Filmsetting
Limited, Manchester, England

Reproduction by Gilchrist
Brothers Limited, Leeds, England

CONTRIBUTORS AND CONSULTANTS

GENERAL CONSULTANT
Professor Michael Wise, CBE, MC, BA, PhD, D.Univ, Professor of
Geography, London School of Economics and Political Science

EDITORIAL CONSULTANT
John Clark

Frances Atkinson, BSc

British Museum (Natural History), Botany Library

Robert W. Bradnock, MA, PhD, Lecturer in Geography with special
reference to South Asia at the School of Oriental and African
Studies, University of London

Michael J. Bradshaw, MA, Principal Lecturer in Geography, College
of St Mark and St John, Plymouth

Dr J. M. Chapman, BSc, ARCS, PhD, MIBiol, Lecturer in Biology,
Queen Elizabeth College, University of London

Dr Jeremy Cherfas, Departmental Demonstrator in Zoology, Oxford
University

Dr M. J. Clark, Senior Lecturer in Geomorphology, Geography
Department, Southampton University

J. L. Cloudsley-Thompson, MA, PhD(Cantab), DSc(Lond),
Hon DSc(Khartoum), Professor of Zoology, Birkbeck College,
University of London

Professor R. U. Cooke, Department of Geography, University
College, London

Professor Clifford Embleton, MA, PhD, Department of Geography,
King's College, University of London

Dr John Gribbin, Physics Consultant to *New Scientist* magazine

Dr John M. Hellawell, BSc, PhD, FIBiol, MIWES, Principal,
Environmental Aspects, Severn Trent Water Authority, Birmingham

Dr Garry E. Hunt, BSc, PhD, DSc, FRAS, FRMetS, FIMA, MBCS,
Head of Atmospheric Physics, Imperial College, London

David K. C. Jones, Lecturer in Geography, London School of
Economics and Political Science

Dr Russell King, Department of Geography, University of Leicester

Dr D. McNally, Assistant Director, University of London
Observatory

Meteorological Office, Berkshire

Dr Robert Muir Wood, PhD

Dr B. O'Connor, Department of Geography, University of London

J. H. Paterson, MA, Professor of Geography in the University of
Leicester

Dr Nigel Pears, Department of Geography, University of Leicester

Joyce Pope, BA

Dr A. L. Rice, Institute of Oceanographic Sciences, Wormley, Surrey

Ian Ridpath, science writer and broadcaster

Royal Geographical Society

Helen Scoging, BSc, Department of Geography, London School of
Economics and Political Science

Bernard Stonehouse, DPhil, MA, BSc, Chairman, Post-Graduate
School of Environmental Science, University of Bradford

Dr Christopher B. Stringer, PhD, Senior Scientific Officer,
Palaeontology Department, British Museum (Natural History)

J. B. Thornes, Professor of Physical Geography and Head of
Department, Bedford College, University of London

UN Information Office and Library

Professor J. E. Webb, DSc, *Emeritus*, Department of Zoology,
Westfield College, University of London

Peter B. Wright, BSc, MPhil

UNDERSTANDING MAPS
Helen Wallis, MA, DPhil, FSA, The Map Librarian, British Library

A great many other individuals, organizations, and institutions have
given invaluable advice and assistance during the preparation of this
Our Planet Earth Section and the publishers wish to extend their
thanks to them all.

ILLUSTRATION CREDITS

Maps in the Our Planet Earth Section by Creative Cartography Limited
unless otherwise specified. Map of the world's climatic regions, page 50,
adapted from *An Introduction to Climate* 4th edition by Trewartha/
Elements of Geography by G. T. Trewartha, A. H. Robinson and
E. H. Hammond © McGraw-Hill Book Co., N.Y., 1967. Used with
permission of McGraw-Hill Book Co. Map diagram page 101 (bottom)
courtesy Doctor Arno Peters.

2-3 *Exploding universe* Product Support (Graphics); *others* Quill.
4-5 Bob Chapman. **6-7** Bob Chapman. **8-9** Mick Saunders;
Landsat diagrams Gary Marsh; *biowindows* Chris Forsey. **10-11**
Mick Saunders. **12-13** Bob Chapman. **14-15** *Diagrams* Chris Forsey;
mountain sequence Donald Myall. **16-17** Colin Salmon. **18-19** Peter
Morter; *graph* Mick Saunders; *car* Peter Owen. **20-21** Bob
Chapman; *diagram* Chris Forsey; *map* Colin Salmon. **22-23** Chris
Forsey (*including maps*). **24-25** Brian Delf. **26-27** Brian Delf.
28-29 Dave Etchell/John Ridyard. **30-31** Creative Cartography Ltd.
32-33 Mick Saunders. **34-35** Chris Forsey; *experiment* Gary Hincks;
others Mick Saunders. **36-37** Chris Forsey; *fruit flies, birds and mice*
Donald Myall. **38-39** Chris Forsey; *time scale* Mick Saunders;
stromatolite and diagram Garry Hincks. **40-41** Donald Myall;
time scale Mick Saunders. **42-43** Donald Myall; *time scale* Mick
Saunders. **44-45** Creative Cartography Ltd. **46-47** Donald Myall;
diagram Kai Choi; *skulls* Jim Robins. **48-49** Creative Cartography
Ltd. **50-51** Peter Morter; *diagram* Marilyn Clark. **52-53** Kai Choi.
54-55 Creative Cartography Ltd. **56-57** Creative Cartography Ltd.
58-59 Creative Cartography Ltd. **60-61** Creative Cartography Ltd;
illustrations Jim Robins. **62-63** *Migration diagram and graph* Kai
Choi; *illustrations* Coral Mula. **64-65** Donald Myall. **66-67**
Landscape diagram Bill le Fever; *illustrations* Russell Barnett. **68-69**
Donald Myall. **70-71** Jim Robins; *plants, bottom left* Andrew
Macdonald. **72-73** Rory Kee; *bottom left* Russell Barnett; *plow*
Kai Choi; *grains and graph* Creative Cartography Ltd. **74-75** Bob
Bampton/The Garden Studio; *animal adaptations* Russell Barnett.
76-77 Donald Myall; *qanat* Bob Chapman. **78-79** David Ashby.
80-81 David Ashby. **82-83** Coral Mula; *trees, orchid, toucan and
hornbill* Donald Myall. **84-85** Jim Robins. **86-87** Creative
Cartography Ltd. **88-89** Brian Delf; *blood counts diagram* Colin
Salmon. **90-91** Bob Chapman; *animal adaptations* Russell Barnett.
92-93 Kai Choi; *hydrological cycle* Bob Chapman. **94-95** Andy
Farmer; *shore and plant life* Russell Barnett; *coral atoll* Colin
Salmon. **96-97** Creative Cartography Ltd. **98-99** *Topographic maps*
Rand McNally; *sketch map* Space Frontiers Ltd. **100-101** *Diagrams*
Creative Cartography Ltd. **102-103** *Maps* Istituto Geografico De
Agostini; Rand McNally; *diagrams* Creative Cartography Ltd.

104

PICTURE CREDITS

Credits read from top to bottom and from left to right on each page. Images that extend over two pages are credited to the left-hand page only.

2 US Naval Observatory; California Institute of Technology and Carnegie Institution of Washington. **3** Both pictures from Royal Observatory, Edinburgh. **8** All pictures from NASA. **9** All pictures from NASA except top and top right, courtesy of Garry Hunt, Laboratory of Planetary Atmospheres, University College, London. **14–15** Maurice and Sally Landre/Colorific! **16–17** All pictures courtesy of Dr Basil Booth, Geoscience Features. **18** Institute of Geological Sciences. **19** Paul Brierley; Institute of Geological Sciences. **20** Camera Press, London. **26** Barnaby's Picture Library; Barnaby's Picture Library; Institute of Geological Sciences. **28** Dr Alan Beaumont. **30** Tom Sheppard/Robert Harding Picture Library; Professor Ronald Cooke. **31** Institute of Geological Sciences. **32** Stuart Windsor; Sefton Photo Library, Manchester; Rio Tinto Zinc; Douglas Botting; Aspect Picture Library. **33** NASA; Mireille Vautier; Explorer/Vision International. **34** Paul Brierley. **37** Paediatric Research Unit, Guy's Hospital Medical School; Dr Laurence Cook, Zoology Department, University of Manchester. **39** Both pictures from British Museum (Natural History). **46** Colophoto Hans Hinz. **47** Dr P. G. Bahn, School of Archaeology and Oriental Studies, University of Liverpool/Musée des Antiquités Nationales, St. Germain-en-Laye. **56** UNICEF (Photo no. 8675 by H. Dalrymple). **57** Dr A. M. O'Connor, Department of Geography, University College, London. **61** International Fund for Animal Welfare; K. Kunov/Novosti Press Agency; Popperfoto; Charles Swithinbank. **62** Alan Robson. **63** Gösta Hakansson/Frank Lane Agency. **65** G. R. Roberts. **67** Anglo-Chinese Educational Trust; Aerofilms. **69** Ted Streshinsky. **72** Engraving from *At Home with the Patagonians.* **73** The Mansell Collection. **76** J. Bitsch/Zefa; Penny Tweedie/Colorific! **77** Alan Hutchison Library; Bill Holden/Zefa. **80** Syndication International; Gerald Cubitt/Bruce Coleman Ltd; Bruce Coleman Ltd. **81** Alan Hutchison Library; R. and M. Borland/Bruce Coleman Ltd; M. P. Kahl/Bruce Coleman Ltd; Jan and Des Bartlett/Bruce Coleman Ltd. **84** J. von Puttkamer/Alan Hutchison Library. **85** Marion Morrison. **86–87** Richard and Sally Greenhill. **88** Alan Hutchison Library; The Association of Universities for Research in Astronomy, Inc. **89** Gunter Ziesler/Bruce Coleman Ltd. **91** Mike Price/Bruce Coleman Ltd. **92** Ian Murphy. **93** Paolo Koch/Vision International; J. Allan Cash; M. Timothy O'Keefe/Bruce Coleman Ltd. **94** Heather Angel. **95** Institute of Oceanographic Sciences. **96** Fritz Prenzel/Bruce Coleman Ltd; Gordon Williamson/Bruce Coleman Ltd. **97** Martin Rogers/Susan Griggs Agency. **98** British Library; British Museum; Centro Camuno di Studi Preistorici; British Library; NASA; NASA; Rand McNally; British Museum; British Museum. **99** British Museum; NASA; NASA; Rand McNally; Space Frontiers Ltd; Paul G. Lowman/NASA Goddard SFC/Space Frontiers Ltd. **100** Historisches Museum, Vienna. **101** Hunting Surveys Ltd; Michael Holford/Science Museum, London; Michael Holford/Science Museum, London. **103** Space Frontiers Ltd; F. Damm/Zefa.

INTERNATIONAL MAP SECTION CREDITS AND ACKNOWLEDGMENTS

Cartographic and Geographic Director
Giuseppe Motta

Geographic Research
G. Baselli
M. Colombo

Toponymy and Translation
C. Carpine
M. Colombo
H. R. Fischer
R. Nuñez de las Cuevas
Rand McNally Cartographic Research Staff
I. Straube

Computerized Data Organization
C. Bardesono
E. Ciano
G. Comoglio
E. Di Costanzo

Index
S. Osnaghi
T. Tomasini

Cartographic Editor
V. Castelli

Cartographic Compilation
G. Albera
L. Cairo
C. Camera
G. Conti
G. Fizzotti
G. Gambaro
M. Mochetti
O. Passarelli
M. Peretti
G. Rassiga
A. Saino
F. Valsecchi

Terrain Illustration
S. Andenna
E. Ferrari

Cartographic Production
F. Tosi
G. Capitini
A. Carnero

Filmsetting
S. Fiorini
P. L. Gatta
E. Geranio
G. Ghezzi
L. Lorena
R. Martelli
E. Morchio
M. Morganti
C. Pezzana
P. Uglietti
D. Varalli

Photographic Processing
G. Fracassina
G. Klaus
L. Mella

Coordination
S. Binda
L. Pasquali
G. Zanetta

The editors wish to thank the many organizations, institutions and individuals who have given their valuable help and advice during the preparation of this International Map Section. Special thanks are extended to the following:

Agenzia Novosti, Rome, Italy
D. Arnold, Acting Chief of Documentation and Terminology Section, United Nations, New York, USA
Australian Bureau of Statistics, Brisbane, Australia
J. Breu, United Nations Group of Experts on Geographical Names, Vienna, Austria
Bureau Hydrographique International, Monaco, Principality of Monaco
Canada Map Office, Ottawa, Canada
Cartactual, Budapest, Hungary
Census and Statistical Department, Tripoli, Libya
Central Bureau of Statistics, Accra, Ghana
Central Bureau of Statistics, Jerusalem, Israel
Central Bureau of Statistics, Ministry of Economic Planning and Development, Nairobi, Kenya
Central Department of Statistics, Riyadh, Saudi Arabia
Central Statistical Board of the USSR, Moscow, USSR
Central Statistical Office, London, UK
Centro de Informaçao e Documentaçao Estadística, Rio de Janeiro, Brazil
Committee for the Reform of Chinese Written Language, Peking, China
Danmark Statistik, Copenhagen, Denmark
Defense Mapping Agency, Distribution Office for Latin America, Miami, USA
Defense Mapping Agency, Washington DC, USA
Department of National Development and Energy, Division of National Mapping, Belconnen ACT, Australia
Department of State Coordinator for Maps and Publications, Washington DC, USA
Department of State Map Division, Sofia, Bulgaria
Department of Statistics, Wellington, New Zealand
Direcçao Nacional de Estadística, Maputo, Mozambique
Dirección de Cartografía Naciónal, Caracas, Venezuela
Dirección de Estadística y Censo de la Repubblica de Panamá, Panama
Dirección General de Estadística, Mexico City, Mexico
Dirección General de Estadística y Censos, San Salvador, El Salvador
Direcţia Centrala de Statistică, Bucharest, Romania
Directorate of National Mapping, Kuala Lumpur, Malaysia
Directorate of Overseas Surveys, London, UK
Elaborazione Dati e Disegno Automatico, Torino, Italy
Federal Office of Statistics, Lagos, Nigeria
Federal Office of Statistics, Prague, Czechoslovakia
Geographical Research Institute, Hungarian Academy of Sciences, Budapest, Hungary
Geological Map Service, New York, USA
G. Gomez de Silva, Chief Conference Services Section, United Nations Environment Programme, New York, USA
Government of the People's Republic of Bangladesh, Statistics Division, Ministry of Planning, Dacca, Bangladesh
High Commissioner for Trinidad and Tobago, London, UK
L. Iarotski, World Health Organization, Geneva, Switzerland
Information Division, Valletta, Malta
Institut für Angewandte Geodäsie, Frankfurt, West Germany
Institut Géographique, Abidjan, Ivory Coast
Institut Géographique du Zaïre, Kinshasa, Zaïre
Institut Géographique National, Brussels, Belgium
Institut Géographique National, Paris, France
Institut Haïtien de Statistique, Port-au-Prince, Haiti
Institut National de Géodésie et Cartographie, Antananarivo, Madagascar
Institut National de la Statistique, Tunis, Tunisia
Institute of Geography, Polish Academy of Sciences, Warsaw, Poland
Instituto Geográfico Militar, Buenos Aires, Argentina
Instituto Nacional de Estadística, La Paz, Bolivia
Instituto Nacional de Estadística, Madrid, Spain
Istituto Centrale di Statistica, Rome, Italy
Istituto Geografico Militare, Florence, Italy
Istituto Idrografico della Marina, Genoa, Italy
Landesverwaltung des Fürstentums, Vaduz, Liechtenstein
Ministère des Affaires Economiques, Brussels, Belgium
Ministère des Ressources Naturelles, des Mines et des Carrières, Kigali, Rwanda
Ministère des Travaux Publics, des Transports et de l'Urbanisme, Ouagadougou, Upper Volta
Ministry of Finance, Department of Statistics and Research, Nicosia, Cyprus

Ministry of Lands, Housing and Urban Development, Surveys and Mapping Division, Dar es Salaam, Tanzania
Ministry of the Interior, Jerusalem, Israel
National Census and Statistics Office, Manila, Philippines
National Central Bureau of Statistics, Stockholm, Sweden
National Geographic Society, Washington DC, USA
National Institute of Polar Research, Tokyo, Japan
National Ocean Survey, Riverdale, Maryland, USA
National Statistical Institute, Lisbon, Portugal
National Statistical Office, Zomba, Malawi
National Statistical Service of Greece, Athens, Greece
J. Novotny, Prague, Czechoslovakia
Office Nationale de la Recherche Scientifique et Technique, Yaoundé, Cameroon
Officina Comercial del Gobierno de Colombia, Rome, Italy
Ordnance Survey of Ireland, Dublin, Ireland
Österreichisches Statistisches Zentralamt, Vienna, Austria
Państwowe Przedsiebiorstwo Wydawnictw Kartograficznych, Warsaw, Poland
Scott Polar Research Institute, University of Cambridge, Cambridge, UK
Secrétariat d'Etat au Plan, Algiers, Algeria
Servicio Geografico Militar, Montevideo, Uruguay
Z. Shiying, Research Institute of Surveying and Mapping, Peking, China
Statistisches Bundesamt, Wiesbaden, West Germany
Statistisk Sentralbyrå, Oslo, Norway
Survey and National Mapping Department, Kuala Lumpur, Malaysia
Ufficio Turismo e Informazioni della Turchia, Rome, Italy
United States Board on Geographic Names, Washington DC, USA
M. C. Wu, Chinese Translation Service, United Nations, New York, USA
Z. Youguang, Committee for the Reform of Chinese Written Language, Peking, China

The editors are also grateful for the assistance provided by the following embassies, consulates and official state representatives:

Angolan Embassy, Rome
Australian Embassy, Rome
Austrian Embassy, Rome
Embassy of Bangladesh, Rome
Brazilian Embassy, Rome
British Embassy, Rome
Burmese Embassy, Rome
Embassy of Cameroon, Rome
Embassy of Cape Verde, Lisbon
Consulate of Chad, Rome
Chilean Embassy, Rome
Embassy of the People's Republic of China in Italy, Rome
Danish Embassy, Rome
Embassy of El Salvador, Rome
Ethiopian Embassy, Rome
Finnish Embassy, Rome
Embassy of the German Democratic Republic, Rome
Greek Embassy, Rome
Honduras Republic Embassy, Rome
Hungarian Embassy, Rome
Consulate General of Iceland, Rome
Embassy of India, Rome
Embassy of the Republic of Indonesia, Rome
Embassy of the Islamic Republic of Iran, Rome

Irish Embassy, Rome
Embassy of Israel, Rome
Japanese Embassy, Rome
Korean Embassy, Rome
Luxembourg Embassy, Rome
Embassy of Malta, Rome
Mexican Embassy, Rome
Moroccan Embassy, Rome
Netherlands Embassy, Rome
Embassy of New Zealand, Rome
Embassy of Niger, Rome
Embassy of Pakistan, Rome
Peruvian Embassy, Rome
Philippine Embassy, Rome
Romanian Embassy, Rome
Somali Embassy, Rome
South African Embassy, Rome
Spanish Embassy, Rome
Consulate General of Switzerland, Milan
Royal Thai Embassy, Rome
Consulate of Upper Volta, Rome
Uruguay Embassy, Rome
Embassy of the Socialist Republic of Vietnam in Italy, Rome
Permanent Mission of Yemen to United Nations Educational, Scientific and Cultural Organization, Paris

INTERNATIONAL MAP SECTION

Hydrographic and Topographic Features
Symboles hydrographiques et morphologiques
Gewässer- und Geländeformen
Idrografia, Morfologia
Hidrografía y morfología

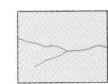

River, Stream
Cours d'eau permanent
Ständig wasserführender Fluß
Corso d'acqua perenne
Corriente de agua de régimen permanente

Lake
Lac d'eau douce
Süßwassersee
Lago d'acqua dolce
Lago de agua dulce

Rocks
Ecueils, Roches
Klippen, Felsriffe
Scogli, Rocce
Escollos, Rocas

Summer Limit of Pack-Ice
Limite du pack en été
Packeisgrenze im Sommer
Limite estivo del pack ghiacciato
Limite estival de banco de hielo

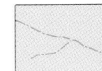

Intermittent Stream
Cours d'eau intermittent
Zeitweilig wasserführender Fluß
Corso d'acqua periodico
Corriente de agua intermitente

Intermittent Lake
Lac d'eau douce temporaire
Zeitweiliger Süßwassersee
Lago d'acqua dolce periodico
Lago de agua dulce intermitente

Reef, Atoll
Barrière, Atoll
Riff, Atoll
Barriera, Atollo
Barrera de arrecifes

Winter Limit of Pack-Ice
Limite du pack en hiver
Packeisgrenze im Winter
Limite invernale del pack ghiacciato
Límite invernal de banco de hielo

Disappearing Stream
Perte de cours d'eau
Versickernder Fluß
Corso d'acqua che si inabissa
Corriente de agua que desaparece

Salt Lake
Lac d'eau salée
Salzsee
Lago d'acqua salata
Lago de agua salada

Mangrove
Mangrove
Mangrove
Mangrovie
Manglar

Limit of Icebergs
Limite des glaces flottantes
Treibeisgrenze
Limite dei ghiacci alla deriva
Limite de hielo a la deriva

Undefined or Fluctuating River Course
Cours d'eau incertain
Fluß mit veränderlichem Lauf
Fiume dal corso incerto
Corriente de agua incerta

Intermittent Salt Lake
Lac d'eau salée temporaire
Zeitweiliger Salzsee
Lago d'acqua salata periodico
Lago de agua salada intermitente

Continental Ice-cap
Glacier continental
Inlandeis. Gletscher
Ghiacciaio continentale
Glaciar continental

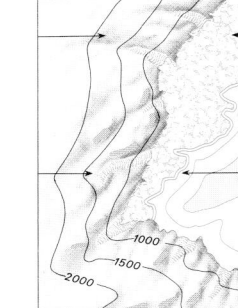

Ice Shelf
Banquise
Schelfeis oder Eisschelf
Banchisa polare (Ice-shelf)
Banquisa

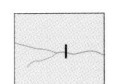

Waterfall, Rapids, Cataract
Chute, Rapide, Cataracte
Wasserfall, Stromschnelle, Katarakt
Cascata, Rapida, Cateratta
Cascada, Rapido, Catarata

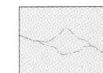

Dry Lake Bed
Lac asséché
Trockener Seeboden
Alveo di lago asciutto
Lecho de lago seco

Glacial Tongue
Langue glaciaire
Gletscherzunge
Lingua di ghiaccio
Lengua de glaciar

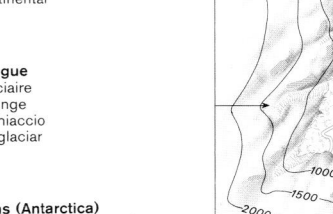

Limit of Ice Shelf
Limite de la banquise
Schelfeisgrenze
Limite della banchisa
Límite de la banquisa

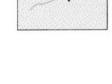

Canal
Canal
Kanal
Canale
Canal

315

Lake Surface Elevation
Cote du lac au-dessus du niveau de la mer
Höhe des Seespiegels
Altitudine del lago
Elevación de lago sobre el nivel del mar

Rocky Areas (Antarctica)
Région de roches (Antarctique)
Eisfreie Gebiete, Gebirge (Antarktika)
Aree rocciose (Antartide)
Area rocosa (Antártida)

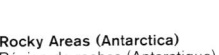

Contour Lines in Continental Ice
Courbes de niveau dans les régions glaciaires
Höhenlinien auf vergletschertem Gebiet
Curve altimetriche nelle aree ghiacciate
Curvas de nivel en aréas heladas

Navigable Canal
Canal navigable
Schiffbarer Kanal
Canale navigabile
Canal navegable

Lake Depth
Profondeur du lac
Seetiefe
Profondità del lago
Profundidad del lago

Defined Shoreline
Trait de côte définie
Küsten- oder Uferlinie
Linea di costa definita
Línea de costa definida

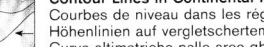

Bathymetric Contour
Courbe bathymétrique
Tiefenlinie
Curva batimetrica
Curva batimétrica

Swamp
Marais
Sumpf
Palude d'acqua dolce
Pantano

Sand Area
Région de sable, Désert
Sandgebiet, Sandwüste
Area sabbiosa, Deserto
Zona arenosa, desierto

Undefined or Fluctuating Shoreline
Trait de côte indéfinie
Unbestimmte oder veränderliche Uferlinie
Linea di costa indefinita
Línea de costa indefinida

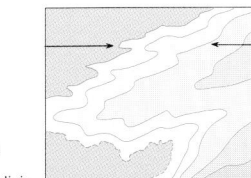

Depth of Water
Valeur de sonde
Tiefenzahl
Quota batimetrica
Cota batimétrica

Salt Marsh
Marais d'eau salée
Salzsumpf
Palude d'acqua salata
Pantano de agua salada

Sandbank, Sandbar
Banc de sable
Sandbank
Bassofondo sabbioso
Banco submarino de arena

Mountain Range
Chaine de montagnes
Bergkette
Catena di monti
Cadena montañosa

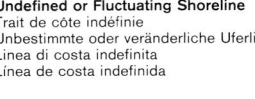

Mountain
Mont
Berg, Bergmassiv
Monte
Monte

Salt Pan
Marais salant
Salzpfanne
Salina
Salina

Port Facilities
Installations portuaires
Hafenanlagen
Impianti portuali
Instalaciones portuarias

Elevation
Cote, Altitude
Höhenzahl
Quota altimetrica
Cota altimétrica

Mountain Pass, Gap
Passage, Col, Port
Paß, Joch, Sattel
Passo, Colle, Valico
Paso, Collado, Puerto de montaña

Key to Elevation and Depth Tints
Hypsométrie, Bathymétrie
Höhenstufen, Tiefenstufen
Altimetria, Batimetria
Altimetría, Batimetría

Scales in Metric and English Measures
Échelle des teintes hypsométriques et bathymétriques
Farbskala der Höhen- und Tiefenstufen
Scala delle tinte Altimetriche e Batimetriche
Escala de tintas hypsométricas y batimétricas

Land Elevation Below Sea Level
Dépression et cote au-dessous du niveau de la mer
Senke mit Tiefenzahl unter dem Meeresspiegel
Depressione e quota sotto il livello del mare
Depresión y elevación bajo el nivel del mar

−155

M 6000 5000 4000 3000 2000 1000 500 +200 0
Ft

0 −200 1000 2000 4000 6000 8000

Map Scale
Échelle
Maßstab
Scala
Escala

1:30,000,000

M 6000 5000 4000 3000 2000 1000 500 +200 0
Ft

0 −100 200 1000 2000 4000 6000 8000

1:15,000,000, 1:12,000,000

M 6000 5000 4000 3000 2000 1000 500 200 +100 0
Ft

0 −100 200 1000 2000 4000 6000 8000

1:9,000,000, 1:6,000,000

M 5000 4000 3000 2000 1500 1000 500 200 +100 0
Ft

0 −100 200 1000 2000 4000 6000 8000

1:3,000,000, 1:1,500,000
1:600,000, 1:300,000

Map Projections
Projections cartographiques
Kartennetzentwürfe
Proiezioni cartografiche
Proyecciones cartográficas

The projections appearing in this atlas have been plotted by computer

Les réseaux des projections ont été obtenus par élaboration automatique à partir de formules mathématiques

Die Kartennetze aller im Atlas vorkommenden Abbildungen wurden mit Hilfe der Datenverarbeitung (EDV) völlig neu errechnet

I disegni delle proiezioni presenti in quest'opera sono stati realizzati interamente ex-novo con l'uso del computer e del plotter a partire dalle formule matematiche

El reticulado de las proyecciones (redes geográficas) incluidas en esta obra han sido obtenidas por proceso automático a partir de las formulas matemáticas

The meanings of the symbols on the Legend pages are in English, French, German, Italian, and Spanish languages to permit the interpretation of the maps by a broad readership.

Boundaries, Capitals
Frontières, Soulignements · Confini, Sottolineature
Grenzen, Unterstreichungen · Límites, Subrayados

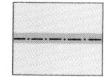

Defined International Boundary
Frontière internationale définie
Staatsgrenze
Confine di Stato definito
Límite de Nación definido

Second-order Political Boundary
Frontière d'État fédéré, Région
Bundesstaats-, Regionsgrenze
Confine di Stato federato, Regione
Límite de Estado federado, Región

International Boundary (Continent Maps)
Frontière internationale (Continents)
Staatsgrenze (Erdteilkarten)
Confine di Stato (Carte dei Continenti)
Límite de Nación (Continentes)

Third-order Political Boundary
Frontière de Province, Comté, Bezirk
Provinz-, Grafschafts-, Bezirksgrenze
Confine di Provincia, Contea, Bezirk
Límite de Provincia, Condado, Bezirk

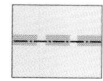

Undefined International Boundary
Frontière internationale indéfinie
Nicht genau festgelegte Staatsgrenze
Confine di Stato indefinito
Límite de Nación indefinido

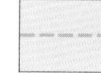

Administrative District Boundary
Frontière de Circonscription
Kreisgrenze
Confine di Circondario
Límite de Circunscripción administrativa

International Ocean Floor Boundary Defined by Treaty or Bilateral Agreement
Frontière d'état en mer définie par traités et conventions bilatéraux
Durch Verträge festgelegte Staatsgrenze im Meeresgebiet
Confine di Stato nel mare definito da trattati e convenzioni bilaterali
Límite de Nación en el Mar definido por los tratados bilaterales

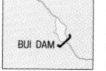

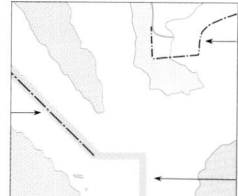

International Ocean Floor Boundary
Frontière d'état en mer
Staatsgrenze im Meeresgebiet
Confine di Stato nel mare
Límite de Nación en el mar

Undefined Ocean Floor Boundary
Frontière indéfinie d'état tracée en meer
Unbstimmte Staatsgrenze im Meeresgebiet
Confine di Stato indefinito nel mare
Límite indefinido de Nación en el mar

ROMA

National Capital
Capitale d'État
Hauptstadt eines unabhängigen Staates
Capitale di Stato
Capital de Nación

Kristiansand

Third-order Capital
Capitale de Province, Comté, Bezirk
Provinz-, Grafschafts-, Bezirkshauptstadt
Capoluogo di Provincia, Contea, Bezirk
Capital de Provincia, Condado, Bezirk

LYON

Dependency or Second-order Capital
Capitale d'État fédéré, Région
Bundesstaats-, Regionshauptstadt
Capitale di Stato federato, Regione
Capital de Estado federado, Región

Anadyr

Administrative District Capital
Capitale de Circonscription
Kreishauptstadt
Capoluogo di Circondario
Capital de Circunscripción administrativa

Other Symbols
Symboles divers · Simboli vari
Sonstige Zeichen · Signos varios

LUTON AIRPORT

International Airport
Aéroport international
Internationaler Flughafen
Aeroporto internazionale
Aeropuerto internacional

SANTAS CREUS

Church, Monastery, Abbey
Monastère, Église, Abbaye
Kloster, Kirche, Abtei
Monastero, Chiesa, Abbazia
Monasterio, Iglesia, Abadía

Lighthouse
Phare
Leuchtturm
Faro
Faro

DAMPIERRE

Castle
Château
Burg, Schloß
Castello
Castillo

BUI DAM

Dam
Barrage
Staudamm, Staumauer
Diga artificiale, Sbarramento
Presa

PAESTUM

Ruin, Archeological Site
Ruine, Centre archéologique
Ruine, Archäologisches Zentrum
Rovina, Zona archeologica
Ruina, Zona arqueológica

L.-GREENWICH
V.-IJmuiden

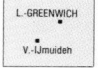

Section of a City
Faubourg
Stadt- oder Ortsteil
Sobborgo urbano
Suburbio

MOLENS VAN KINDERDIJK

Monument, Historic Site, etc.
Monument
Denkmal
Monumento
Monumento

Bidon V

Uninhabited Locality, Hamlet
Ville inhabitée, Ferme, Hameau
Unbewohnte Stadt, Gehöft, Weiler
Città disabitata, Fattoria, Nucleo di case
Ciudad despoblada, Granja, Casar

HADRIAN'S WALL

Wall
Muraille
Wall, Mauer
Vallo, Muraglia
Muralla

Bi'r Nāhid

Periodically Inhabited Oasis
Oasis habitées périodiquement
Zeitweilig bewohnte Oase
Oasi periodicamente abitate
Oasis periodicamente habitados

GIANT'S CAUSEWAY

Point of Interest
Curiosité
Sehenswürdigkeit
Curiosità
Curiosidad

Casey (Australia)

Scientific Station
Base géophysique
Geophysikalische Beobachtungsstation
Base geofisica
Base geofísica

CUEVAS DE ARTÁ

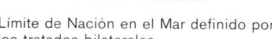

Cave
Grotte, Caverne
Höhle
Grotta, Caverna
Cueva, Gruta

Populated Places
Population · Popolazione
Bevölkerung · Población

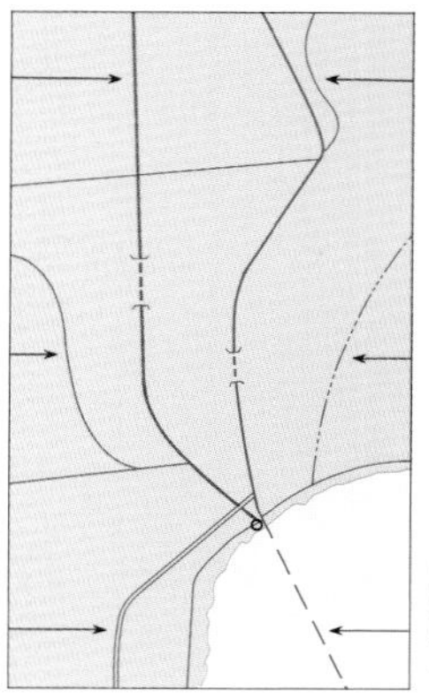

Continent Maps
Cartes des Continents · Carte dei Continenti
Erdteilkarten · Mapas de Continentes

- < 25 000
- 25 000-100 000
- 100 000-250 000
- 250 000-1 000 000
- > 1 000 000

Regional Maps
Cartes à plus grande échelle · Carte di sviluppo
Karten größeren Maßstabs · Mapas a gran escala

- < 10 000
- 10 000-25 000
- 25 000-100 000
- 100 000-250 000
- 250 000-1 000 000
- > 1 000 000

Symbols represent population of inhabited localities
Les symboles représentent le nombre d'habitants des localités
Die Signaturen entsprechen der Einwohnerzahl des Ortes
I simboli sono relativi al valore demografico dei centri abitati
Los símbolos son proporcionales a la población del lugar

Town area symbol represents the shape of the urban area
Le petit plan de la ville reproduit la configuration de l'aire urbaine
Die Plansignatur stellt die Gestalt des Stadtgebietes dar
La piantina della città rappresenta la configurazione dell'area urbana
El pequeño plano de la ciudad representa la forma del area urbana

Transportation
Communications · Comunicazioni
Verkehrsnetz · Comunicaciones

Primary Railway
Chemin de fer principal
Hauptbahn
Ferrovia principale
Ferrocarril principal

Secondary Railway
Chemin de fer secondaire
Sonstige Bahn
Ferrovia secondaria
Ferrocarril secundario

Motorway, Expressway
Autoroute
Autobahn
Autostrada
Autopista

Road
Route de grande communication, Autres Routes
Fernverkehrsstraße, andere Straßen
Strada principale, Altre Strade
Carretera principal, Otras Carreteras

Trail, Caravan Route
Piste, Voie caravanière
Wüstenpiste, Karawanenweg
Pista nel deserto, Carovaniera
Pista en el desierto, Via de Carabanas

Ferry, Shipping Lane
Bac, Ligne maritime
Fähre, Schiffahrtslinie
Traghetto, Linea di navigazione
Transbordador (Ferry), Línea de navegación

Type Styles
Caractères utilisés pour la toponymie · Caratteri usati per la toponomastica
Zur Namenschreibung verwendete Schriftarten · Caracteres utilizados para la toponimia

ITALY
Hessen RIBE

Political Units
Etat, Dépendance, Division administrative
Staat, abhängiges Gebiet, Verwaltungsgliederung
Stato, Dipendenza, Divisione amministrativa
Nación, Dependencia, División administrativa

Ankaratra · Monte Bianco
Tsiafajavona · Ngorongoro Crater
Nevado del Tolima · Kings Peak

Small Mountain Range, Mountain, Peak
Petit massif, Mont, Cime
Bergmassiv, Berg, Gipfel
Piccolo gruppo montuoso, Monte, Vetta
Macizo pequeño, Monte, Cima

LABRADOR SEA
Gulf of Alaska · Hudson Bay
Estrecho de Magallanes

Sea, Gulf, Bay, Strait
Mer, Golfe, Baie, Détroit
Meer, Golf, Bucht, Meeresstraße
Mare, Golfo, Baia, Stretto
Mar, Golfo, Bahía, Estrecho

SAXONY
THRACE · SUSSEX

Historical or Cultural Region
Région historique ou culturelle
Historische oder Kulturlandschaft
Regione storico - culturale
Región histórica y cultural

Cabo de São Vicente · Land's End
Mizen Head · Point Conception
Col de la Perche · Passo della Cisa

Cape, Point, Pass
Cap, Pointe, Passe
Kap, Landspitze, Paß
Capo, Punta, Passo
Cabo, Punta, Paso

West Mariana Basin
Galapagos Fracture Zone
Mid-Atlantic Ridge

Undersea Features
Formes du relief sous-marin
Formen des Meeresbodens
Forme del rilievo sottomarino
Formas del relieve submarino

PATAGONIA
BASSIN DE RENNES
PENÍNSULA DE YUCATÁN

Physical Region (plain, peninsula)
Région physique (plaine, péninsule)
Landschaft (Ebene, Halbinsel)
Regione fisica (pianura, penisola)
Región natural (llanura, península)

MAHÉ · ALDABRA ISLANDS
CORSE · CHANNEL ISLANDS
SULU ARCHIPELAGO

Island, Archipelago
Ile, Archipel
Insel, Archipel
Isola, Arcipelago
Isla, Archipiélago

Tarfaya
Tombouctou
Agadir
Nouakchott
BRAZZAVILLE
CASABLANCA

Size of type indicates relative importance of inhabited localities
La dimension des caractères indique l'importance d'une localité
Die Schriftgröße entspricht der Gesamtbedeutung des Ortes
La grandezza del carattere è proporzionale all'importanza della località
La dimensión de los caracteres de imprenta indica la importancia de la localidad

PYRENEES
CUMBRIAN MOUNTAINS
SIERRA DE GÁDOR · LA SILA

Mountain Range
Chaîne de montagnes
Bergkette, Gebirge
Catena di monti
Cadena montañosa

Thames · Po · Victoria Falls
Lotagipi Swamp · Göta kanal
Lago Maggiore

River, Waterfall, Cataract, Canal, Lake
Fleuve, Chute d'eau, Cataracte, Canal, Lac
Fluß, Wasserfall, Katarakt, Kanal, See
Fiume, Cascata, Cateratta, Canale, Lago
Río, Cascada, Catarata, Canal, Lago

INDEX MAPS

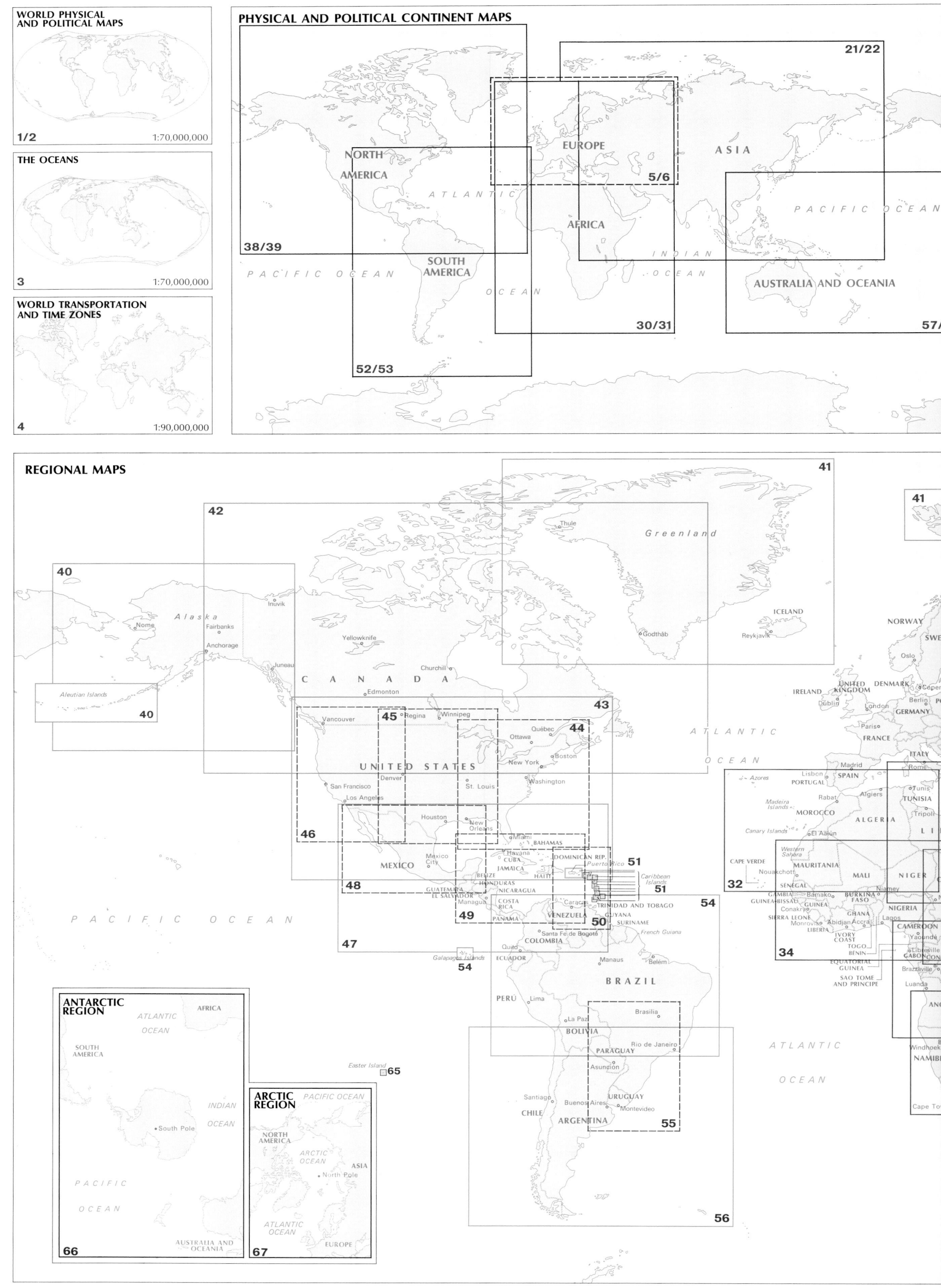

WORLD PHYSICAL AND POLITICAL MAPS

1/2   1:70,000,000

THE OCEANS

3   1:70,000,000

WORLD TRANSPORTATION AND TIME ZONES

4   1:90,000,000

PHYSICAL AND POLITICAL CONTINENT MAPS

21/22

NORTH AMERICA

EUROPE

ASIA

AFRICA

5/6

SOUTH AMERICA

AUSTRALIA AND OCEANIA

38/39

30/31

57/

52/53

REGIONAL MAPS

41

41

42

40

40

Greenland

Alaska

Nome
Inuvik
Fairbanks
Anchorage
Juneau

Yellowknife

ICELAND

NORWAY
SWE

Reykjavik

Godthåb

Thule

Aleutian Islands

CANADA

Churchill
Edmonton

OSLO

Oslo

IRELAND
UNITED KINGDOM
DENMARK
Cöpen

Dublin
London
Berlin
PO
GERMANY

43

Vancouver
Regina
Winnipeg
45
Québec
Ottawa
44

Paris
FRANCE

UNITED STATES
New York
Boston

ATLANTIC

OCEAN

ITALY
Rome

San Francisco
Denver
St. Louis
Washington

Madrid
Lisbon
SPAIN
PORTUGAL
Azores

46

Los Angeles
Houston
New Orleans

Algiers
Tunis
TUNISIA

Rabat
MOROCCO
ALGERIA
LI
Tripoli

Miami
BAHAMAS

Madeira Islands

MEXICO
Mexico City
Havana
CUBA
JAMAICA

Canary Islands
El Aaiún

48

BELIZE
GUATEMALA
HONDURAS

DOMINICAN REP.
HAITI
Puerto Rico
51

Western Sahara

CAPE VERDE

MAURITANIA
MALI
NIGER
N

32

PACIFIC   OCEAN

EL SALVADOR
NICARAGUA
Managua
COSTA RICA
49
PANAMA

Caribbean Islands
51

54

Nouakchott
SENEGAL
Bamako
BURKINA FASO
Niamey
GAMBIA
GUINEA-BISSAU
GUINEA
Conakry
SIERRA LEONE
Monrovia
LIBERIA
IVORY COAST
GHANA
NIGERIA
Accra
Lagos
Abidjan

TRINIDAD AND TOBAGO
GUYANA
SURINAME
French Guiana

Caracas
VENEZUELA
50

47

Santa Fe de Bogotá
COLOMBIA

CAMEROON
Yaoundé
TOGO
BENIN
EQUATORIAL GUINEA
GABON
CONGO

34

Galapagos Islands
54

Quito
ECUADOR

Manaus
Belém

Libreville

B R A Z I L

SAO TOME AND PRINCIPE

Brazzaville

PERÚ
Lima

La Paz
BOLIVIA
Brasília

Luanda

ANG

ANTARCTIC REGION

AFRICA
ATLANTIC OCEAN

PARAGUAY
Rio de Janeiro

ATLANTIC

SOUTH AMERICA

Asunción
URUGUAY

OCEAN

Windhoek

INDIAN OCEAN

Santiago
Buenos Aires
Montevideo

NAMIBI

South Pole

CHILE
ARGENTINA
55

Cape Tow

PACIFIC

OCEAN

Easter Island
65

56

ARCTIC REGION
PACIFIC OCEAN

NORTH AMERICA

ARCTIC OCEAN
ASIA
North Pole

66

ATLANTIC OCEAN

AUSTRALIA AND OCEANIA

67

EUROPE

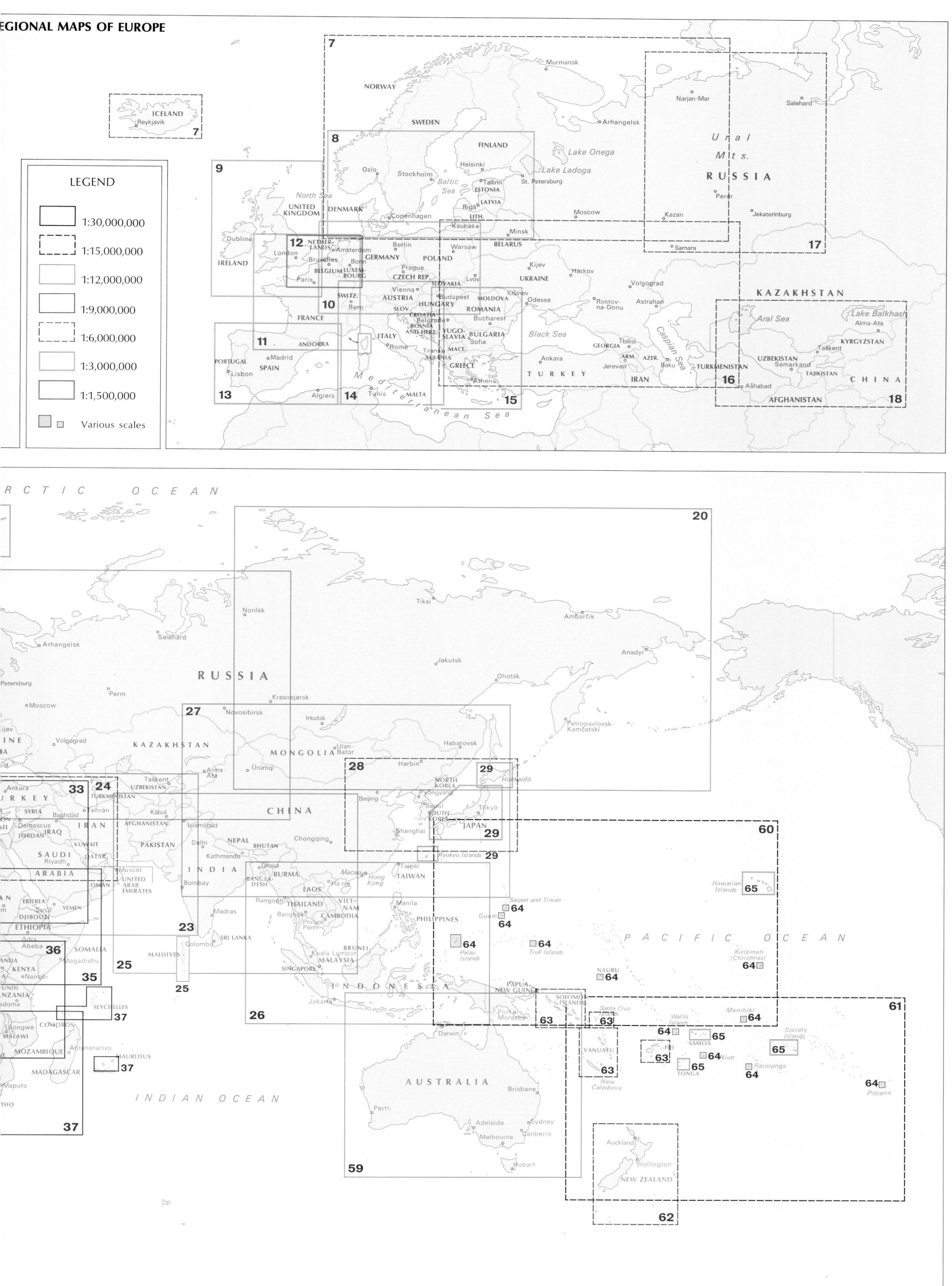

REGIONAL MAPS OF EUROPE

LEGEND

1:30,000,000
1:15,000,000
1:12,000,000
1:9,000,000
1:6,000,000
1:3,000,000
1:1,500,000

Various scales

Map 1 **WORLD, PHYSICAL**

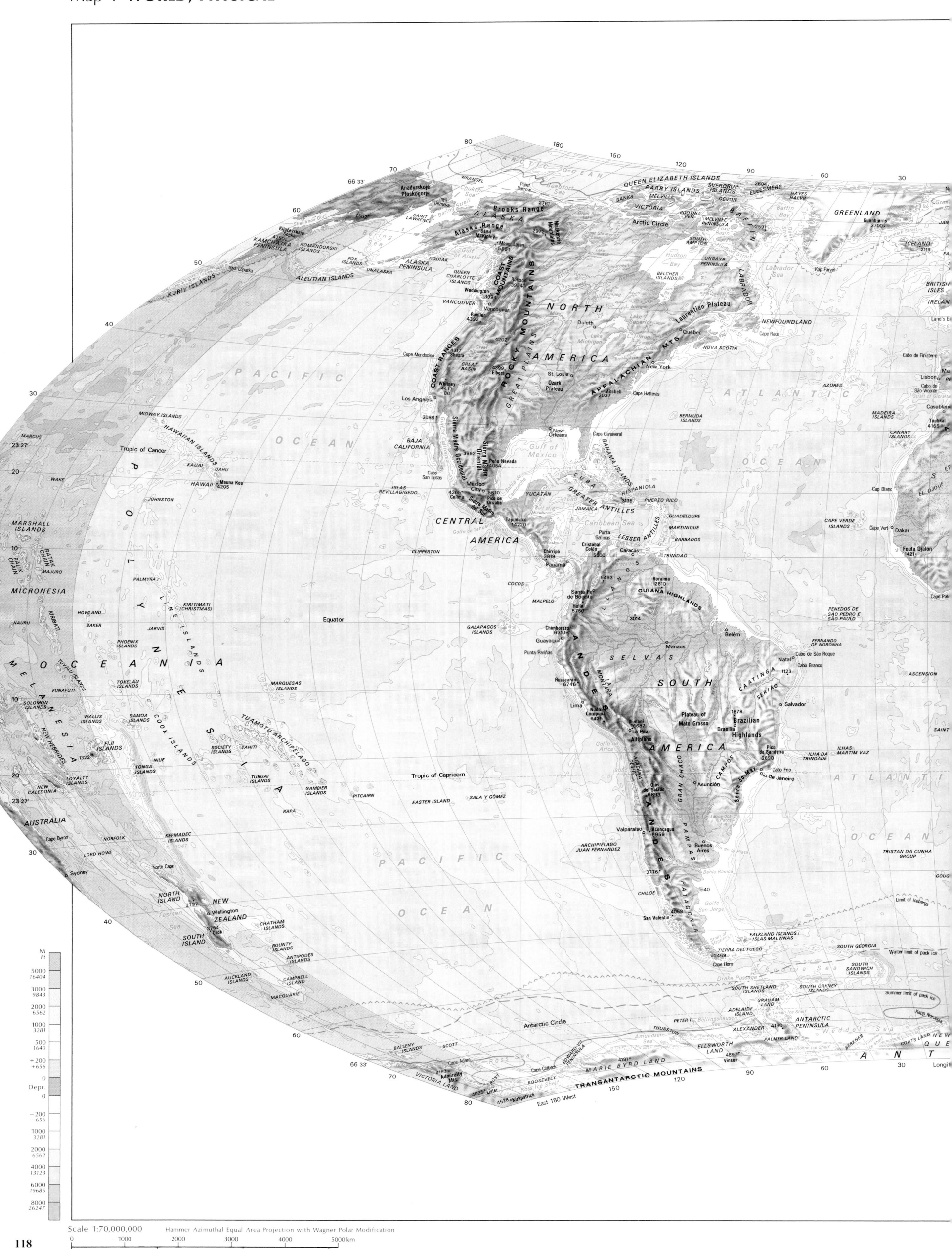

Scale 1:70,000,000
Hammer Azimuthal Equal Area Projection with Wagner Polar Modification

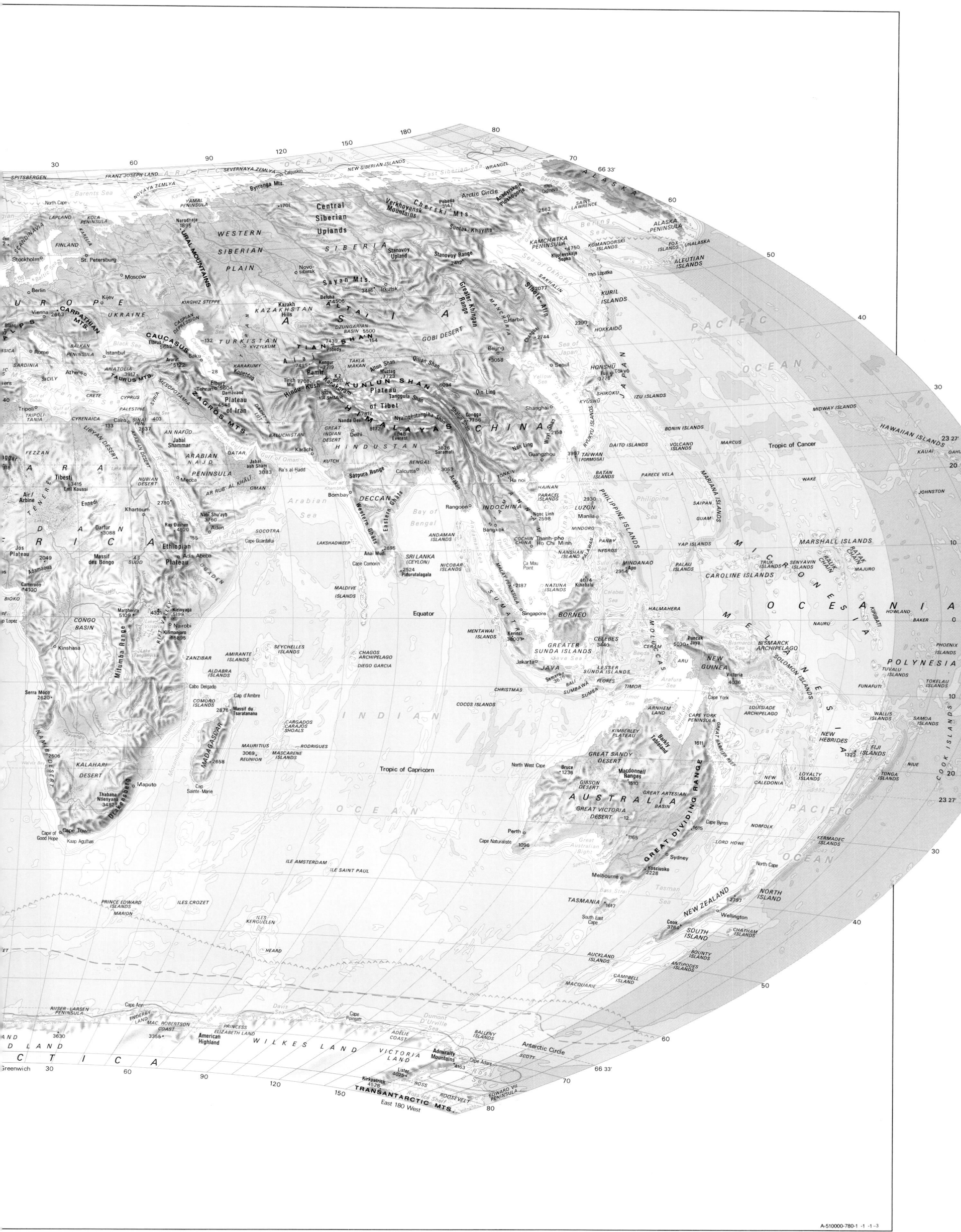

Map 2 **WORLD, POLITICAL**

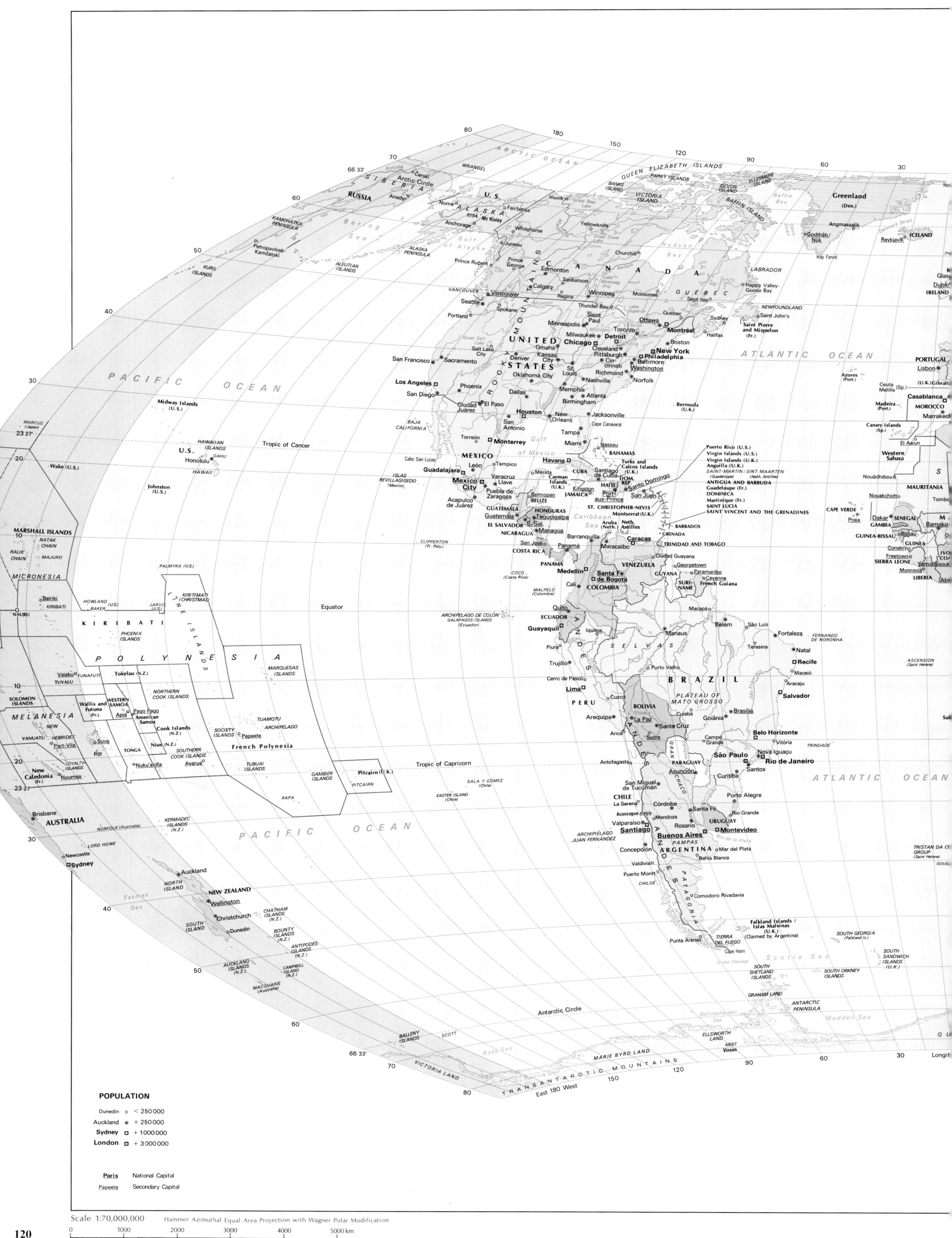

POPULATION

Dunedin	o < 250 000
Auckland	⊕ + 250 000
Sydney	▫ + 1 000 000
London	▣ + 3 000 000

Paris   National Capital

Papeete   Secondary Capital

Scale 1:70,000,000   Hammer Azimuthal Equal Area Projection with Wagner Polar Modification

0	1000	2000	3000	4000	5000 km

0	1000	2000	3000 miles

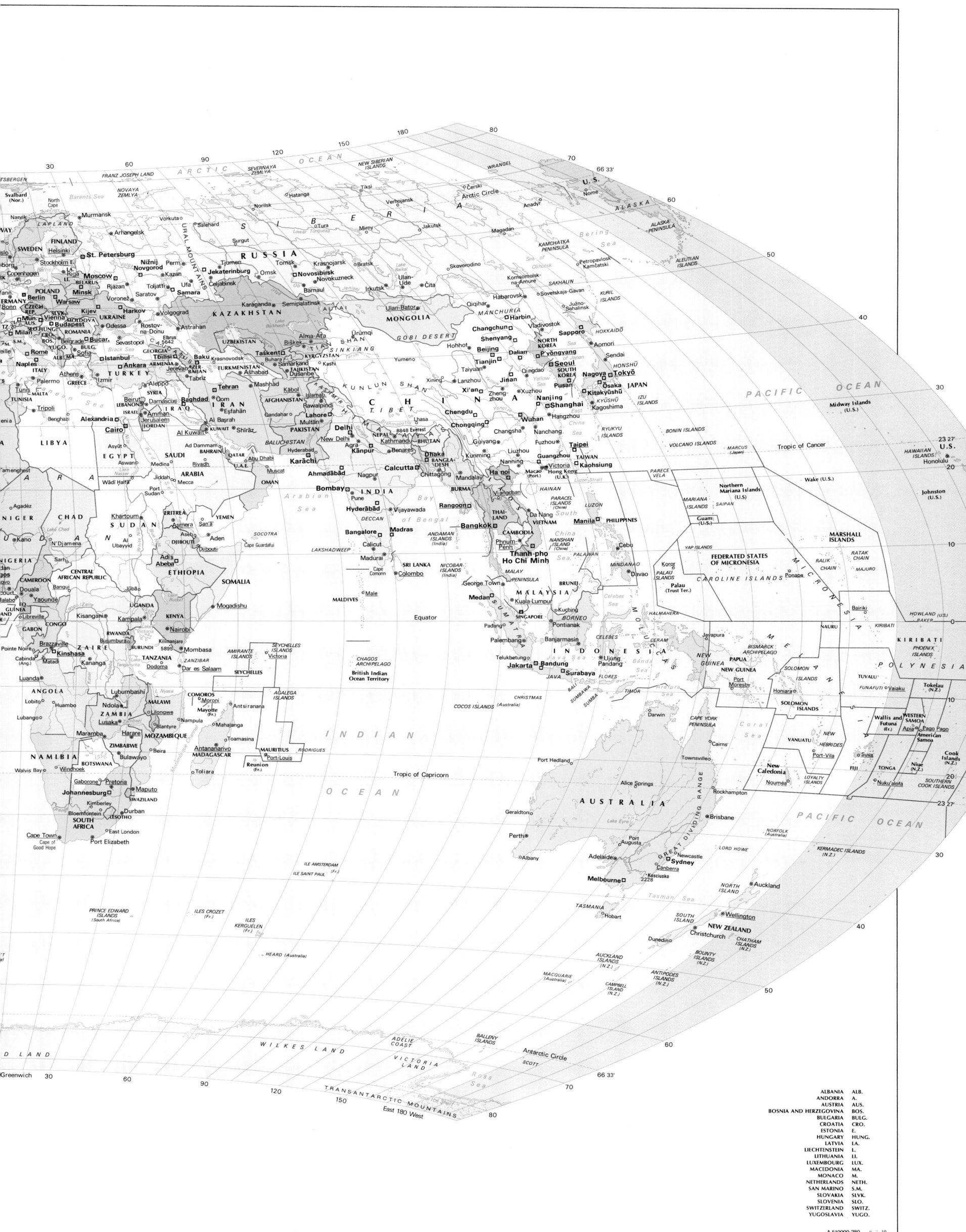

ALBANIA	ALB.
ANDORRA	A.
AUSTRIA	AUS.
BOSNIA AND HERZEGOVINA	BOS.
BULGARIA	BULG.
CROATIA	CRO.
ESTONIA	E.
HUNGARY	HUNG.
LATVIA	LA.
LIECHTENSTEIN	L.
LITHUANIA	LI.
LUXEMBOURG	LUX.
MACEDONIA	MA.
MONACO	M.
NETHERLANDS	NETH.
SAN MARINO	S.M.
SLOVAKIA	SLVK.
SLOVENIA	SLO.
SWITZERLAND	SWITZ.
YUGOSLAVIA	YUGO.

Map 3 **THE OCEANS**

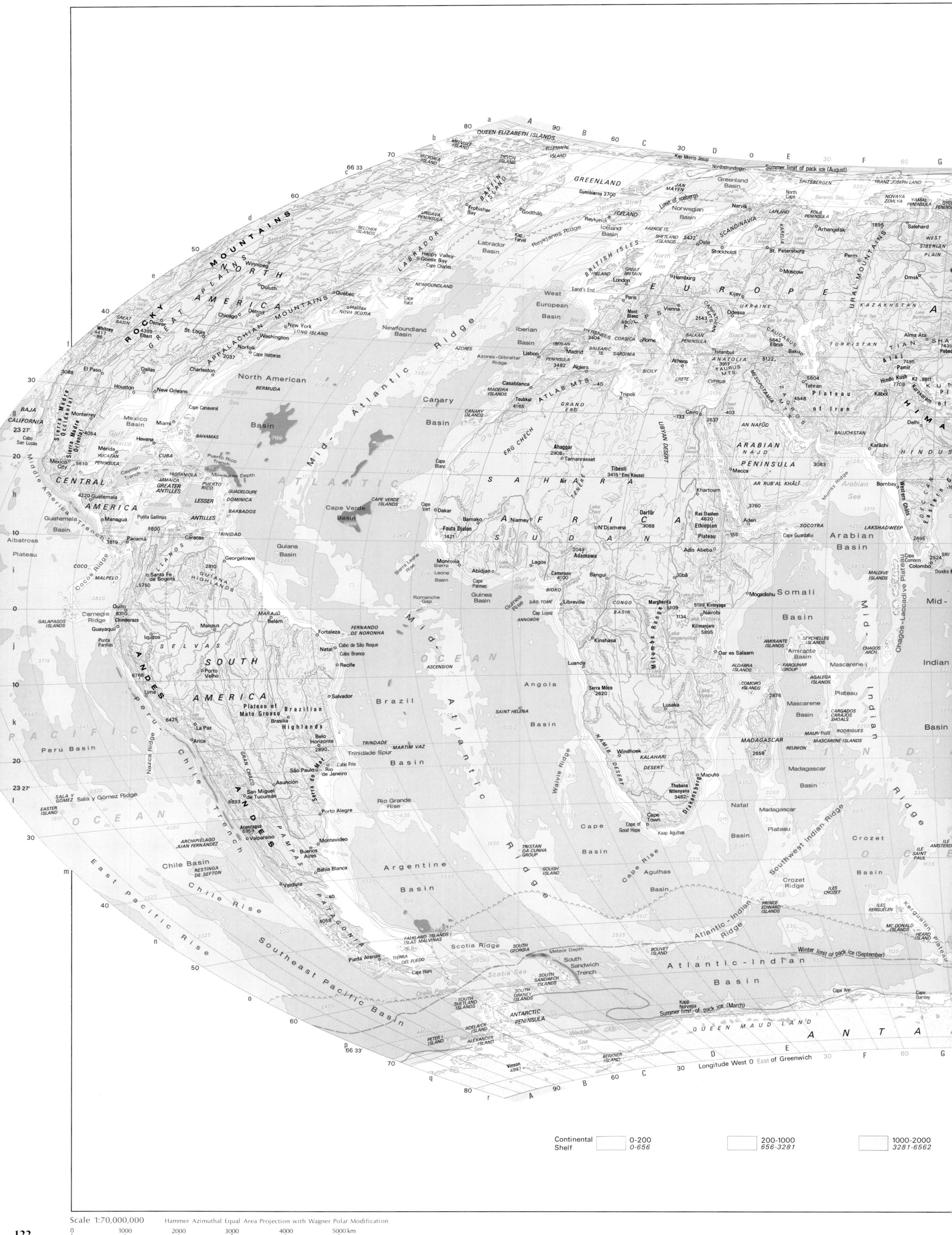

Continental Shelf: 0-200 / 0-656, 200-1000 / 656-3281, 1000-2000 / 3281-6562

Scale 1:70,000,000 Hammer Azimuthal Equal Area Projection with Wagner Polar Modification

0 1000 2000 3000 4000 5000 km

0 1000 2000 3000 miles

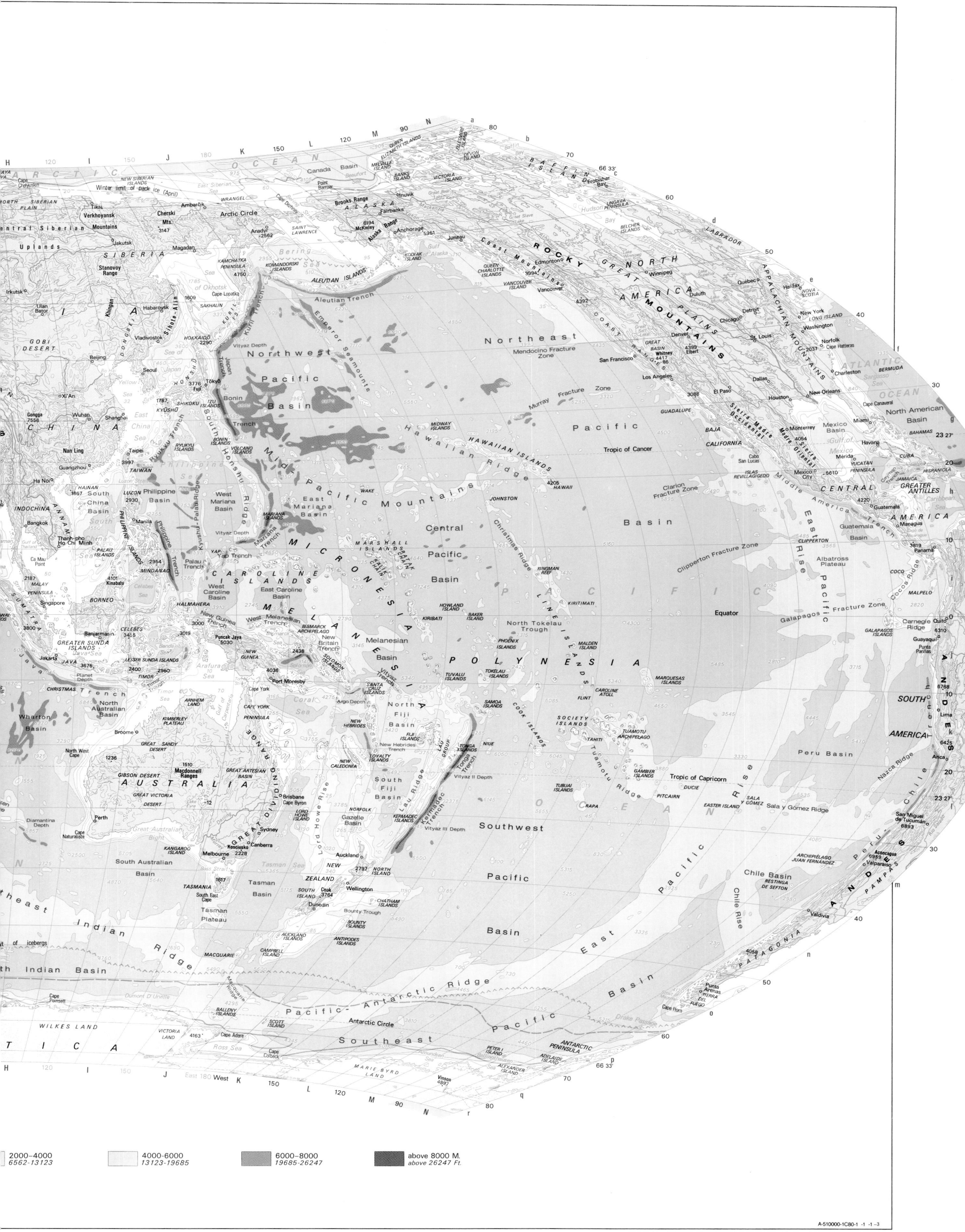

	2000–4000		4000–6000		6000–8000		above 8000 M.
	6562-13123		*13123-19685*		*19685-26247*		*above 26247 Ft.*

Map 4 **WORLD TRANSPORTATION AND TIME ZONES**

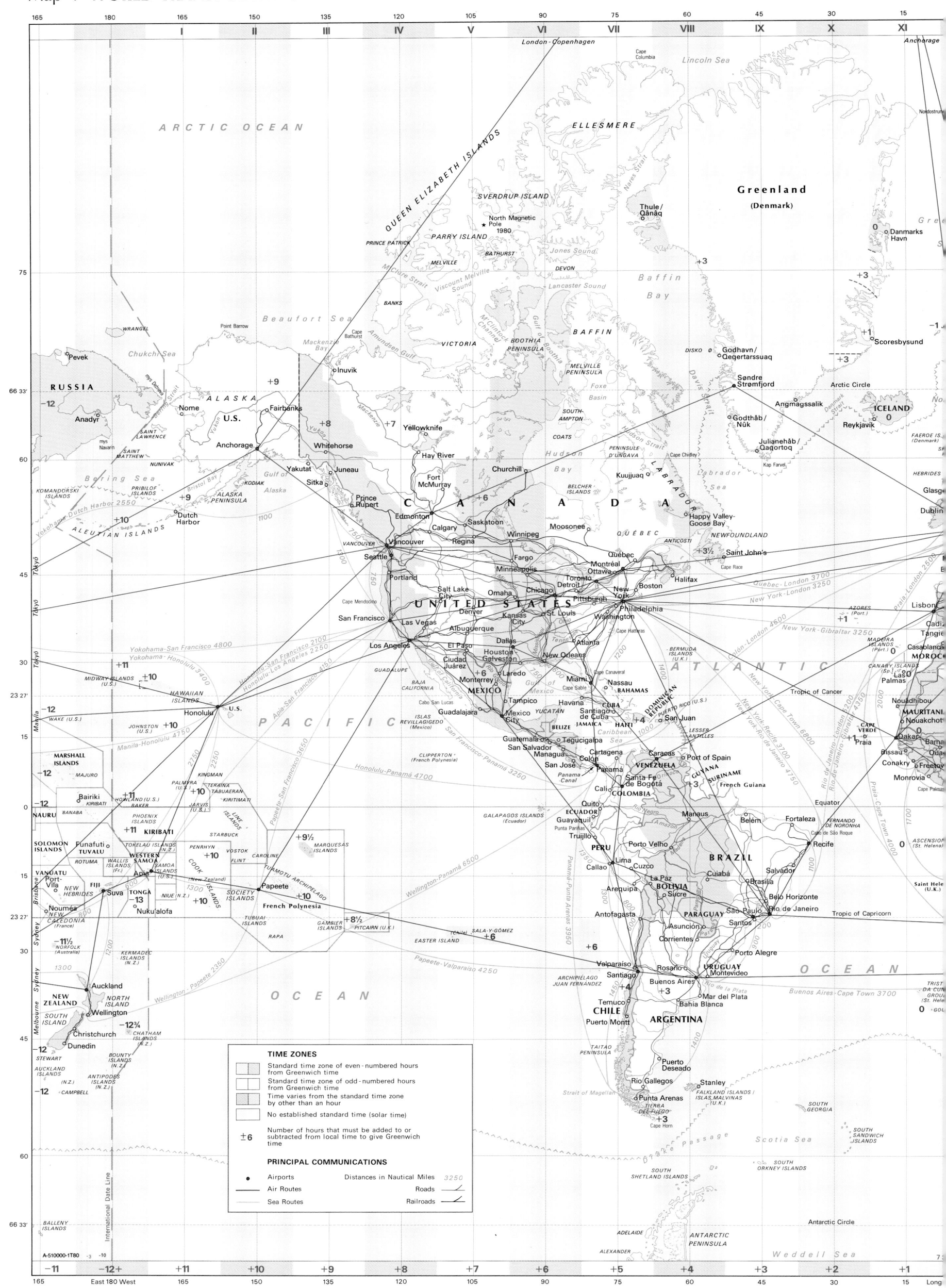

Map 4 WORLD TRANSPORTATION AND TIME ZONES

TIME ZONES

Standard time zone of even-numbered hours from Greenwich time

Standard time zone of odd-numbered hours from Greenwich time

Time varies from the standard time zone by other than an hour

No established standard time (solar time)

±6   Number of hours that must be added to or subtracted from local time to give Greenwich time

PRINCIPAL COMMUNICATIONS

• Airports   Distances in Nautical Miles 3250

— Air Routes   Roads

— Sea Routes   Railroads

A-510000-1T80

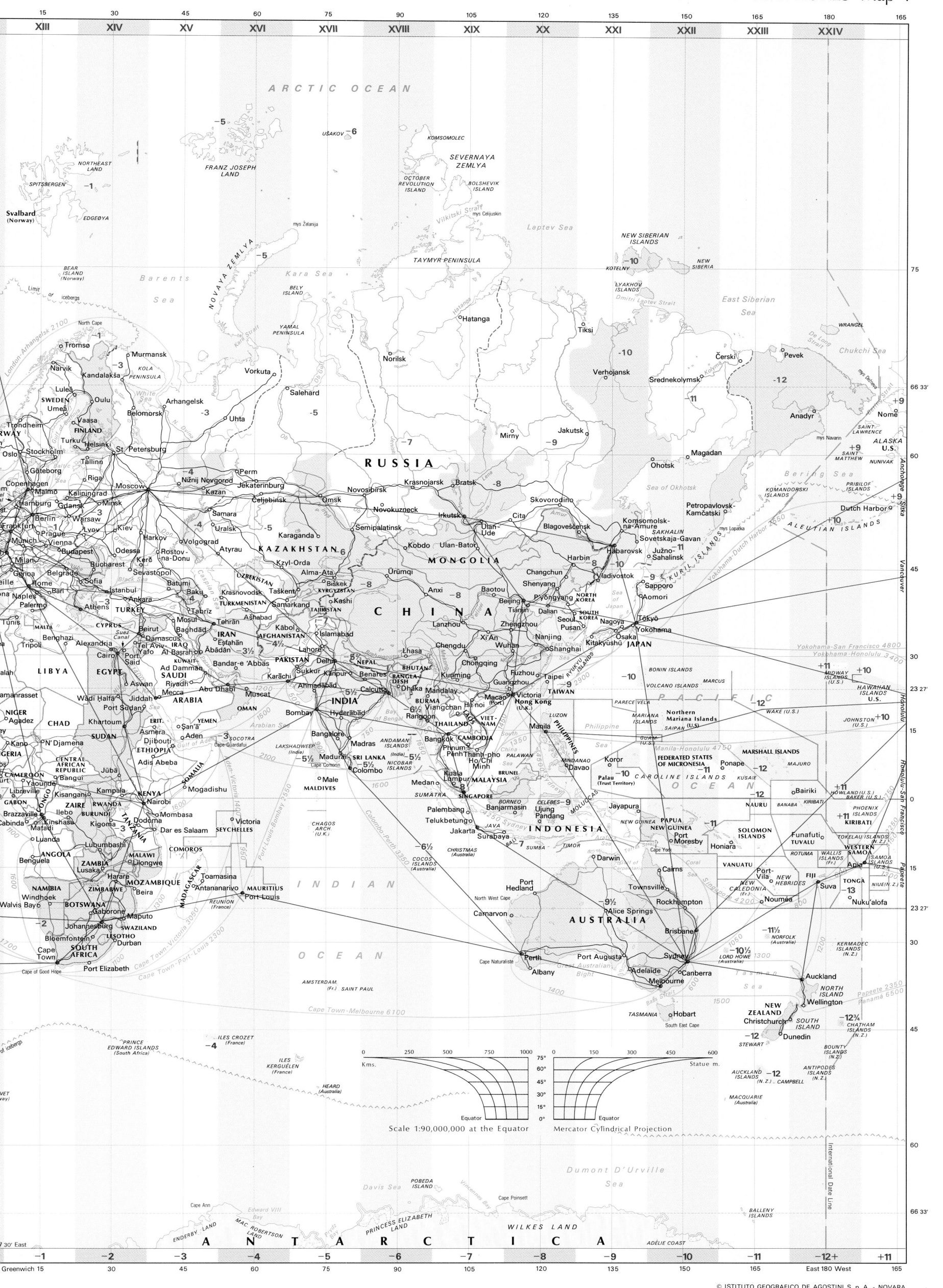

Scale 1:90,000,000 at the Equator   Mercator Cylindrical Projection

Map 5 **EUROPE, PHYSICAL**

Scale 1:15,000,000

Lambert Azimuthal Equal Area Projection

| 0 | 200 | 400 | 600 | 800 | 1000 km |

| 0 | 250 | 500 miles |

Longitude East 0 of Greenwich

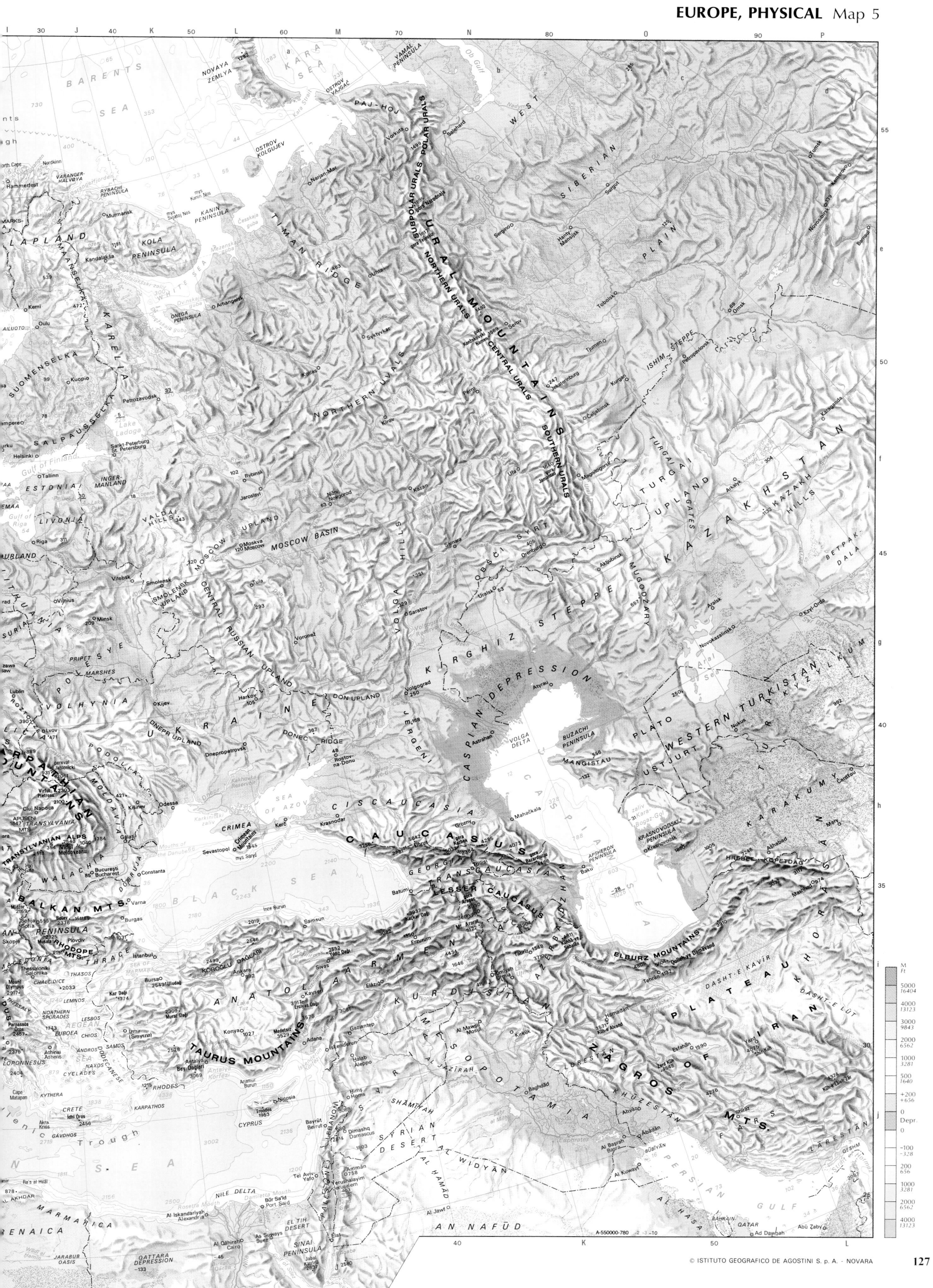

Map 6 **EUROPE, POLITICAL**

A   50   B   40   C   30   D   20   E   10   F   0   G   10   H

King Frederik VI Coast   KING CHRISTIAN IX LAND   Angmagssalik   a

Nanortalik   Frederiksdal   Julianehåb   Qaqortoq   KING FREDERIK VI COAST   b
Narssaq   Ivigtut   d
Narssarssuaq   Godthåb
Kap Farvel   Qaqortoq

G r e e n l a n d
(Den.)

3700

Greenland   Scoresby Sund   Scoresbysund   a

Greenland Sea

55

Denmark Strait

Ísafjörður   Horn   JAN MAYEN   (Norway)

VESTERÅLEN

Akureyri
Reykjavík   **ICELAND**   LOFOTEN   e
VATNAJÖKULL   2119   Seyðisfjörður
Hvannadalshnúkur
Arctic Circle   Bodø

N o r w e g i a n

Mo i Rana

S e a

50   Thorshavn   **Faeroe**   Namsos   NORWAY   Stor

FØROYAR   **Islands**
FÆRØERNE   (Den.)   Kristiansund   Trondheim   Østersund   **SWEDEN**
Ålesund   Molde
SHETLAND   Dombås   Glittertinden   Falun
ISLANDS   2472
ROCKALL   Bergen   Gjøvik   Hamar   f

Thurso   ORKNEY   Haugesund   Oslo   Moss   Västerås
ISLANDS   Stavanger   Drammen   Örebro
HEBRIDES   Skien   Karlstad   Norrk
Inverness   Kristiansand   Lindesnes
Aberdeen   N o r t h   Göteborg   Linköping

45   **Glasgow**   Dundee   S e a   DENMARK   Ålborg   Frederikshavn   Jönköping   f
Edinburgh   Frederikshavn   VÄXJÖ   Kalmar
Londonderry   Herning   Århus   Halmstad   ÖLAND
IRELAND   **Belfast**   Newcastle   Esbjerg   København   Helsingborg   Karlskrona
Galway   upon Tyne   Koldin   Copenhagen   Malmö   BORNHOLM
Sligo   Carlisle   Flensburg   Odense   Trelleborg   (Den.)
Irish   **Middlesbrough**   Kiel   Lübeck   Stralsund   Gdy
Limerick   Sea   Bremerhaven   Rostock   Gdań
Manchester   **Kingston-upon-Hull**   Groningen   Hamburg   (Dan
Waterford   **Liverpool**   **UNITED KINGDOM**   Bremen   Szczecin
Wexford   **Leeds**   Stettin
Cork   Fishguard   **Sheffield**   Hannover   Magdeburg   Berlin   Pozn
Mizen Head   **Leicester**   **Nottingham**   Amsterdam   **GERMANY**   PO
Birmingham   Norwich   NETHERLANDS   Essen   Dortmund   Leipzig   Dresden   Wrocław
Swansea   Oxford   Ipswich   **Amsterdam**   Bremen   Magdeburg   Wałbrzych   Breslau

40   **Cardiff**   **London**   Den Haag   Utrecht   Dortmund   Köln Cologne   Chemnitz   CZE   g
Celtic   Bristol   Rotterdam   Antwerpen   Düsseldorf   Erfurt   Praha   Ostrava
Sea   **Plymouth**   BELGIUM   Brussel   Bonn   Frankfurt   Prague   Katov
Land's End   Southampton   Bruxelles   Wiesbaden   Würzburg   Plzeň   Brno
ISLES OF   Penzance   Brighton   Dover   Liège   Mannheim   Nürnberg   CZECH REP.
SCILLY   CHANNEL   Cherbourg   Le Havre   Amiens   Lille   LUXEMBOURG   Stuttgart   Regensburg   Wien   Brat
ISLANDS   Calais   Mannheim   Augsburg   Linz   Vienna
(U.K.)   Caen   Rouen   Reims   Metz   Strasbourg   München   AUSTRIA   Győr
Pointe de Saint-Mathieu   Saint-Malo   Nancy   Saarbrücken   Freiburg   Munich   Salzburg   Graz
Brest   **Paris**   Troyes   Mulhouse   Zürich   Innsbruck   LIECHTENSTEIN   Klagenfurt   Székesfehérv
Lorient   Rennes   Le Mans   Orléans   Basel   Bern   SWITZERLAND   Bolzano   SLOVENIA   Balaton   Pécs
Nantes   Angers   Tours   Bourges   Dijon   Besançon   Lausanne   Geneva   Verona   Trieste   Ljubljana   Zagreb
Mont Blanc   Milano   Brescia   Venezia   CROATIA
Poitiers   Genève   Lyon   4807   Milan   Verona   Venice   Rijeka
La Rochelle   Limoges   Clermont-   Grenoble   Torino   Parma   BOSNIA
Ferrand   1885   Turin   Genova   Bologna   AND
35   Cabo de Finisterre   **Bordeaux**   Monts Dore   Saint   Genoa   SAN   Zadar   HERZEGO   h
La Coruña   Étienne   Nice   La Spezia   MARINO
Gijón   Bay of Biscay   Toulouse   Avignon   MONACO   Livorno   Firenze   Ancona   Split
Vigo   Oviedo   Santander   San Sebastián   Montpellier   Nîmes   Marseille   Florence   Perugia   ITALY
Braga   León   Bilbao   Bayonne   PYRENEES   Toulon   CORSICA   Pescara   Dúbrovnik
Porto   Burgos   Pamplona   Perpignan   Cabo de Creus   (Fr.)   L'Aquila
Coimbra   Valladolid   Pico de Aneto   ANDORRA   Bastia   VATICAN
PORTUGAL   Salamanca   3404   Andorra   Ajaccio   CITY   Foggia
SPAIN   la Vella   **Roma**   Napoli   **Bari**
Lisboa   **Madrid**   **Barcelona**   Rome   Naples   Tarant   Lecc
Lisbon   Toledo   Zaragoza   Sassari   Olbia   Salerno
Setúbal   Saragossa   Castellón   SARDINIA   Nuoro   Tyrrhenian   Cosenza
i   Evora   Badajoz   de la Plana   BALEARIC   MINORCA   Catanzaro   i
Córdoba   Albacete   **Valencia**   ISLANDS   Cagliari
Huelva   MAJORCA
Faro   **Sevilla**   Murcia   Palma   Sea   Palermo   Messina
Cádiz   Granada   Alicante   IBIZA   Reggio
Málaga   Almería   di Calabria
Algeciras   Cartagena   SICILY   Catania
Tánger   Gibraltar (U.K.)   ISLA DE ALBORAN   Trapani   Siracusa
30   Tanger   Ceuta (Spain)   (Spain)   Al Jazā'ir   Algiers   PANTELLERIA   Capo delle Correnti
Larache   Tétouan   Melilla   Oran   Bizerte   (Italy)
Ksar el Kebir   Mosta-   **Tūnis**   Nabûl
Casablanca   ganem   Blida   Skikda   Annaba   ISOLE PELAGIE
Rabat   Sidi Bel Abbès   Tizi-Ouzou   Sétif   Constantine   Valletta   (Italy)
El Jadida   Taza   Bejaïa   Jijel   Guelma   Tébessa   **MALTA**
Meknès   **Fès**   Oujda   Cheliff   Batna   Sûsah   KERKENNAH
Safi   Relizane   Tiaret   El Qayrawân   Sousse   ISLANDS
Essaouira   Oued Zem   Saïda   Djelfa   Biskra   Sfax   DJERBA
25   **MOROCCO**   Beni   ATLAS   MOUNTAINS   Qafsah   Gulf of Gabès
Marrakech   Mellal   Laghouat   Safāqis   Qâbis
4165   Dar   Air Sefra   **TUNISIA**   Madanīyîn
Jebel   Rachidiya   Touggourt
Toubkal   ALGERIA   Ghardaïa
Agadir   Sidi Ifni   Figuig   Ouargla   Hassi   Tripoli
Guelmine   Béchar   GRAND   Messaoud   Adh Dhahibāt   Al Khums
Zagora   ERG   Hassi   Gharyān   Ra's Misrātah
Tiznit   Abadla   OCCIDENTAL   El Goléa   GRAND   ERG   Messaoud   Mizdah   Misrātah
Sidi Ifni   Tan Tan   Beni Abbès   ORIENTAL   Banī Walīd   Qaryat
Cap   Tindouf   Timimoun   al Qaddāfīyah
Juby   Séguia el Hamra   Tabelbala   GRAND   **TRIPOLITANIA**   Gulf of
Western Sahara   J   As Sidr

GRACIOSA   SÃO JORGE   PICO   Angra do Heroísmo   TERCEIRA   Ponta Delgada   SÃO MIGUEL   SANTA MARIA
Azores   (Portugal)   h

A T L A N T I C

O C E A N

40

MADEIRA   ILHAS DESERTAS   PORTO SANTO   Funchal   ILHAS SELVAGENS
ISLANDS   **Madeira**   (Portugal)   i

LA PALMA   LANZAROTE   FUERTEVENTURA
GOMERA   TENERIFE   Santa Cruz de Tenerife   j
HIERRO   **Canary Islands**   Las Palmas de Gran Canaria
(Spain)   GRAN CANARIA

Dakhla   E

Scale 1:15,000,000   Lambert Azimuthal Equal Area Projection

0   200   400   600   800   1000 km
0   250   500 miles

Longitude East 0 of Greenwich

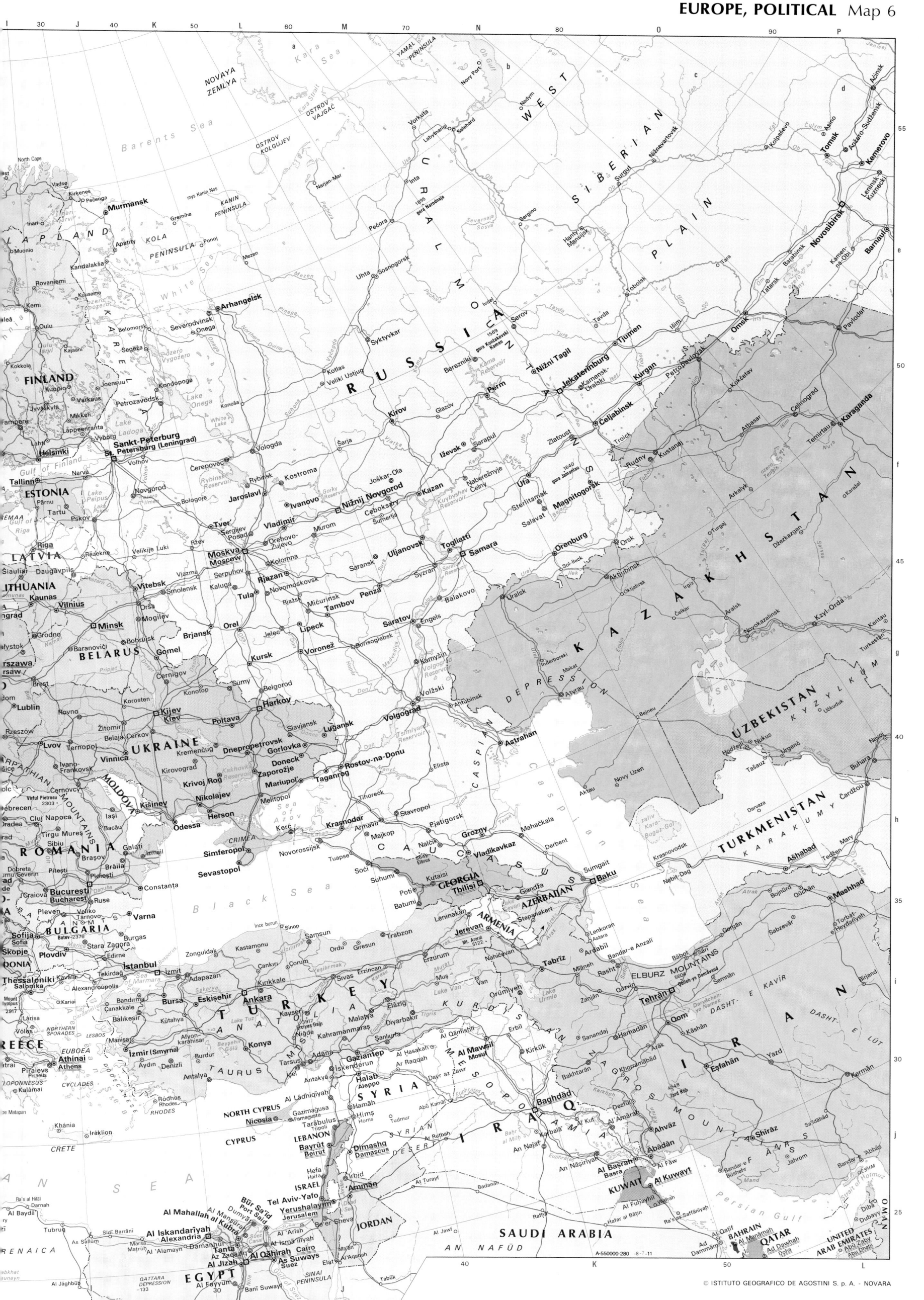

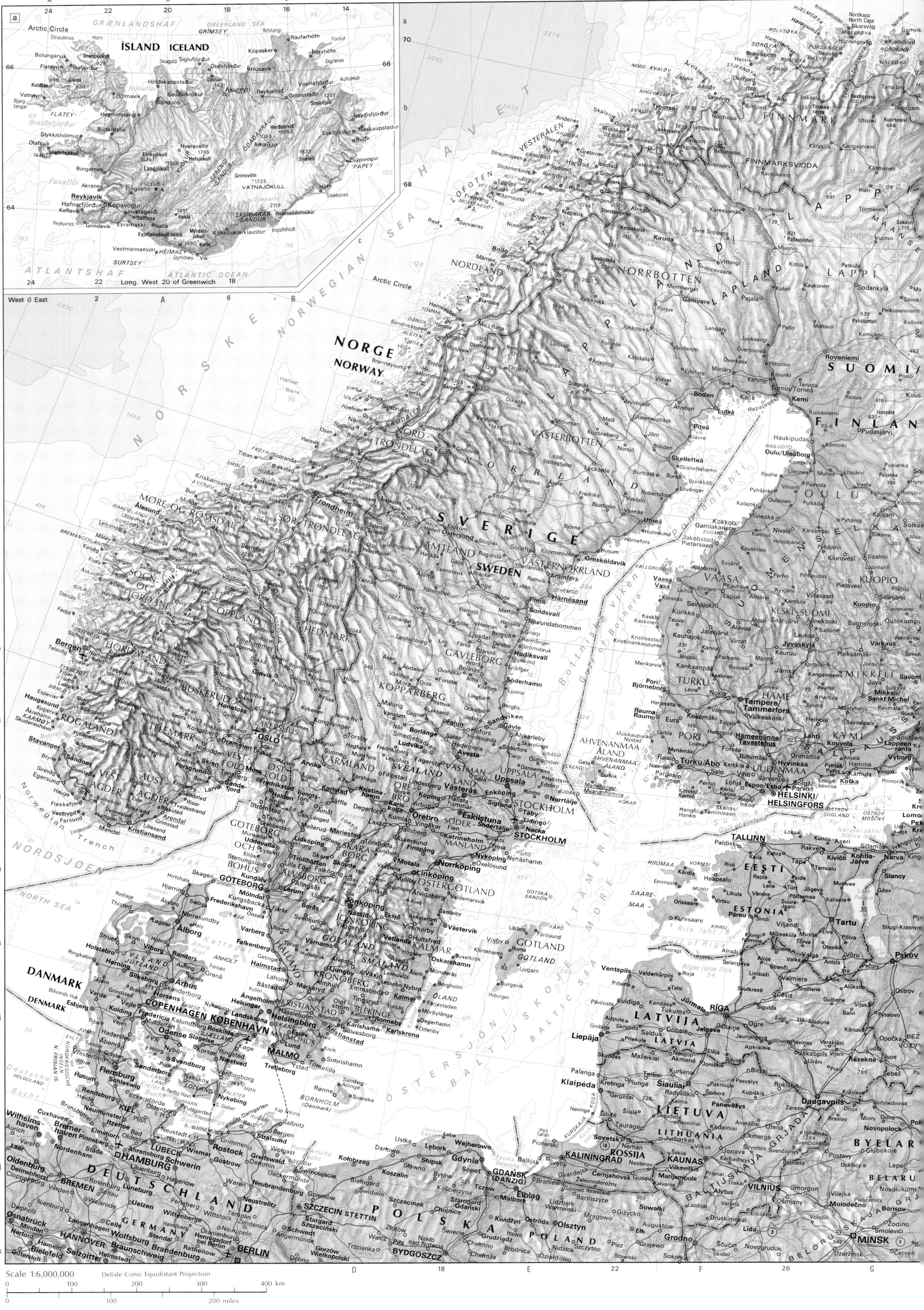

Map 7 **NORTHERN EUROPE**

Iceland Inset

ÍSLAND ICELAND

GRÆNLANDSHAF — GREENLAND SEA

Arctic Circle

Reykjavik
Kópavogur
Hafnarfjörður
Keflavík
Akureyri
Húsavík
VATNAJÖKULL
Vestmannaeyjar HEIMAEY
SURTSEY
ATLANTSHAF — ATLANTIC OCEAN

Long. West 20 of Greenwich

Main Map

NORGE
NORWAY

SVERIGE
SWEDEN

SUOMI
FINLAND

DANMARK
DENMARK

DEUTSCHLAND
GERMANY

POLSKA
POLAND

EESTI
ESTONIA

LATVIJA
LATVIA

LIETUVA
LITHUANIA

ROSSIJA
RUSSIA

BYELARUS
BELARUS

NORSKE-HAVET / NORWEGIAN SEA

NORDSJØEN / NORTH SEA

ØSTERSJÖN / BALTIJSKOJE MORE / BALTIC SEA

Skagerrak
Kattegat

NORRLAND
LAPLAND
LAPPI
NORRBOTTEN
VÄSTERBOTTEN
JÄMTLAND
VÄSTERNORRLAND
GÄVLEBORG
KOPPARBERG
VÄRMLAND
VÄSTMANLAND
UPPLAND
SÖDERMANLAND
ÖSTERGÖTLAND
SMÅLAND
GÖTALAND
SVEALAND
KRONOBERG
BLEKINGE
KRISTIANSTAD
HALLAND
ÄLVSBORG
BOHUS
SKARABORG
ÖREBRO

GOTLAND
ÖLAND
BORNHOLM (Denmark)

OSLO
STOCKHOLM
HELSINKI / HELSINGFORS
TALLINN
RIGA
VILNIUS
KALININGRAD
MINSK
BERLIN
HAMBURG
HANNOVER
BREMEN
COPENHAGEN / KØBENHAVN
GÖTEBORG
MALMÖ
BERGEN
Trondheim
Ålesund
Stavanger
Kristiansand
GDAŃSK (DANZIG)
SZCZECIN STETTIN
BYDGOSZCZ
KAUNAS

Gulf of Riga / Riia laht / Rigas jūras līcis

ÅLAND / AHVENANMAA

TURKU / ÅBO
Tampere / Tammerfors
Vaasa / Vasa
Oulu / Uleåborg
KUOPIO
MIKKELI
HÄME / TAVASTLAND
UUSIMAA
KYMI

FINNMARK
FINNMARKSVIDDA
TROMS
NORDLAND
NORD-TRØNDELAG
SØR-TRØNDELAG
MØRE OG ROMSDAL
SOGN OG FJORDANE
HORDALAND
ROGALAND
VEST-AGDER
AUST-AGDER
TELEMARK
BUSKERUD
OPPLAND
HEDMARK
ØSTFOLD
VESTFOLD

Nordkapp / North Cape

Arctic Circle

Scale 1:6,000,000
Delisle Conic Equidistant Projection

0   100   200   300   400 km
0   100   200 miles

M Ft
2000 / 6562
1000 / 3281
500 / 1640
200 / 656
+100 / +328
0
Depr.
−100 / −328
200 / 656
1000 / 3281
2000 / 6562

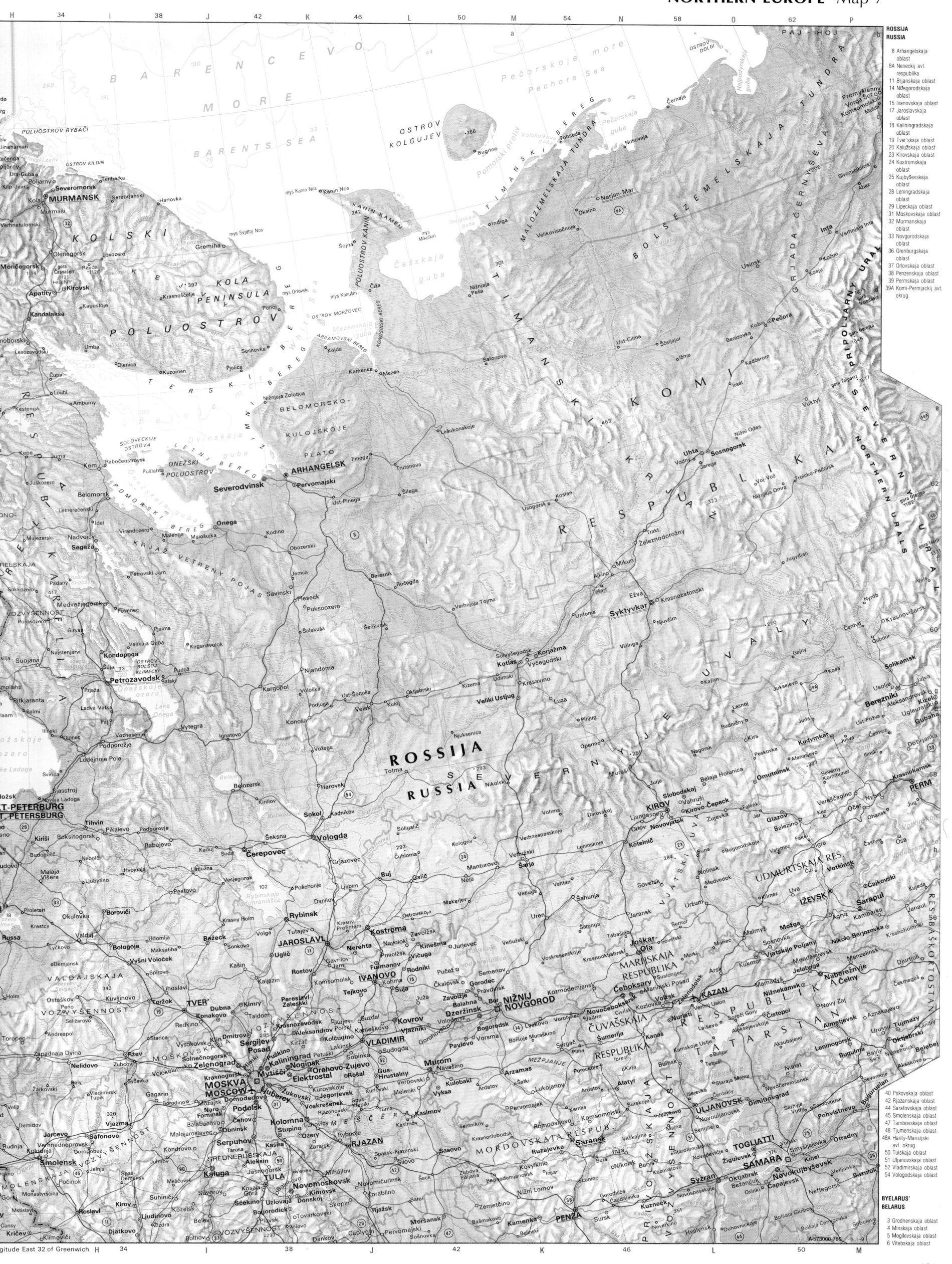

Map 8 **BALTIC REGION**

Scale 1:3,000,000

Delisle Conic Equidistant Projection

0   50   100   150   200 km

0   50   100 miles

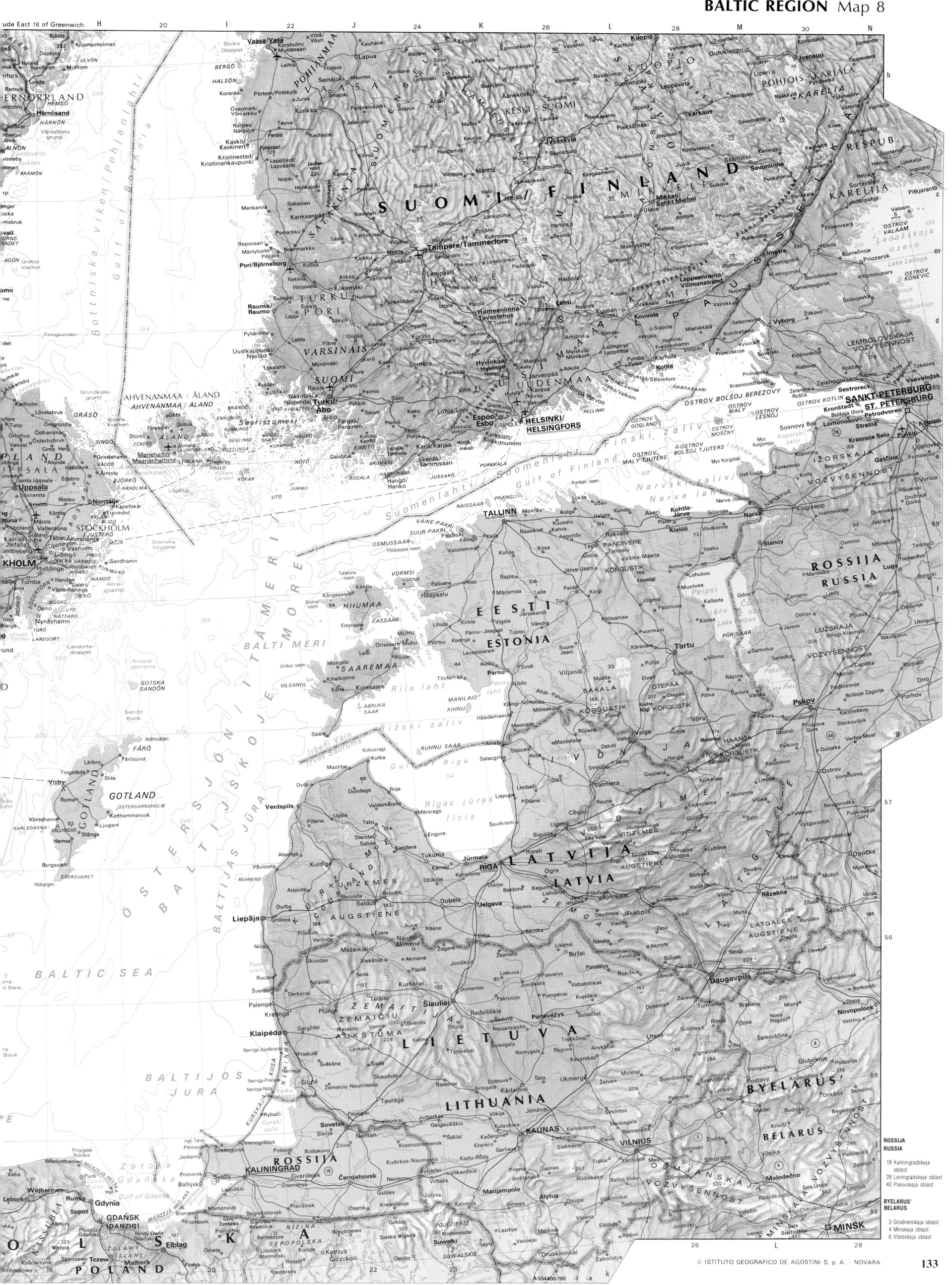

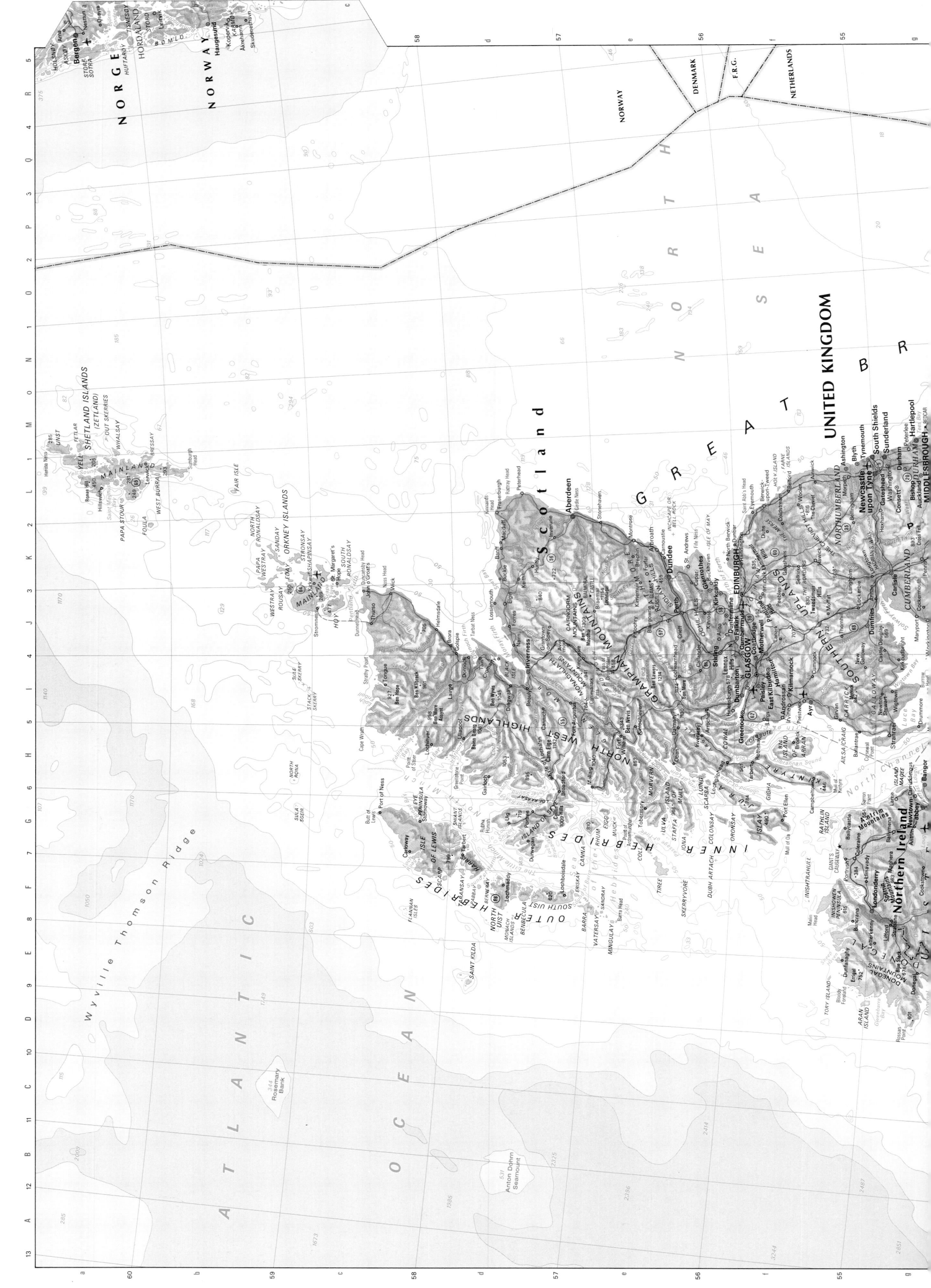

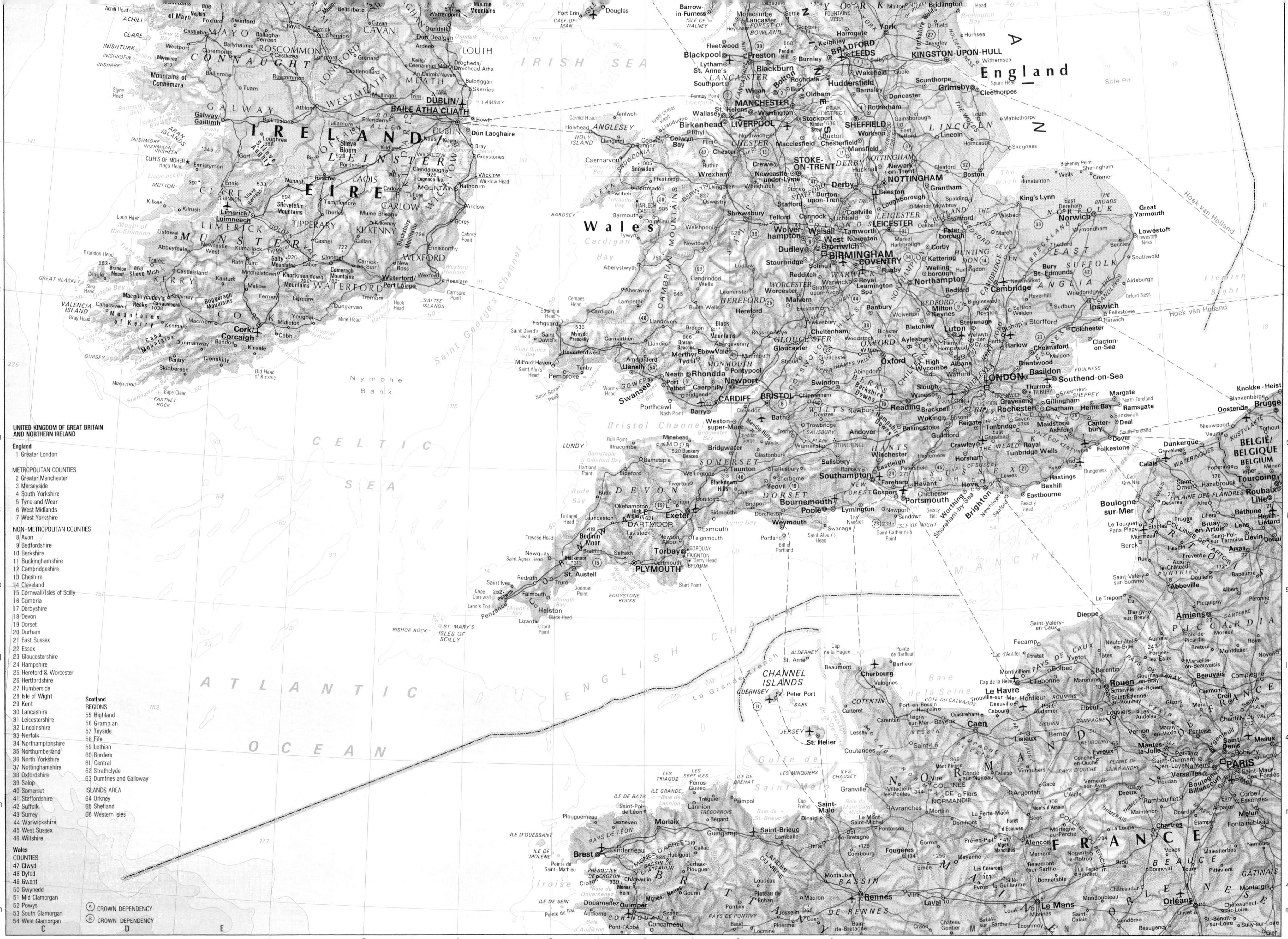
UNITED KINGDOM OF GREAT BRITAIN AND NORTHERN IRELAND
England
1 Greater London
METROPOLITAN COUNTIES
2 Greater Manchester
3 Merseyside
4 South Yorkshire
5 Tyne and Wear
6 West Midlands
7 West Yorkshire
NON-METROPOLITAN COUNTIES
8 Avon
9 Bedfordshire
10 Berkshire
11 Buckinghamshire
12 Cambridgeshire
13 Cheshire
14 Cleveland
15 Cornwall/Isles of Scilly
16 Cumbria
17 Derbyshire
18 Devon
19 Dorset
20 Durham
21 East Sussex
22 Essex
23 Gloucestershire
24 Hampshire
25 Hereford & Worcester
26 Hertfordshire
27 Humberside
28 Isle of Wight
29 Kent
30 Lancashire
31 Leicestershire
32 Lincolnshire
33 Norfolk
34 Northamptonshire
35 Northumberland
36 North Yorkshire
37 Nottinghamshire
38 Oxfordshire
39 Salop
40 Somerset
41 Staffordshire
42 Suffolk
43 Surrey
44 Warwickshire
45 West Sussex
46 Wiltshire
Wales
COUNTIES
47 Clwyd
48 Dyfed
49 Gwent
50 Gwynedd
51 Mid Glamorgan
52 Powys
53 South Glamorgan
54 West Glamorgan
Scotland
REGIONS
55 Highland
56 Grampian
57 Tayside
58 Fife
59 Lothian
60 Borders
61 Central
62 Strathclyde
63 Dumfries and Galloway
ISLANDS AREA
64 Orkney
65 Shetland
66 Western Isles
Ⓐ CROWN DEPENDENCY
Ⓑ CROWN DEPENDENCY
M Ft
1000 3281
500 1640
200 656
+100 +328
0
Depr.
0
−100 −328
200 656
1000 3281
2000 6562
4000 13123
IRELAND / EIRE
England
Wales
FRANCE
IRISH SEA
CELTIC SEA
ATLANTIC OCEAN
ENGLISH CHANNEL
LA MANCHE
CHANNEL ISLANDS
Bristol Channel
Saint George's Channel
LONDON
PARIS
DUBLIN / BAILE ATHA CLIATH
BELGIË / BELGIQUE
Longitude West 0 East of Greenwich

Scale 1:3,000,000 Delisle Conic Equidistant Projection

0 50 100 150 200 km

0 50 100 miles

© ISTITUTO GEOGRAFICO DE AGOSTINI S. p. A. - NOVARA

Map 10 **CENTRAL EUROPE**

Scale 1:3,000,000   Delisle Conic Equidistant Projection

DEUTSCHLAND
GERMANY

LÄNDER
1 Brandenburg
2 Mecklenburg-Vorpommern
3 Sachsen
4 Sachsen-Anhalt
5 Thüringen

Map 11 **FRANCE AND BENELUX**

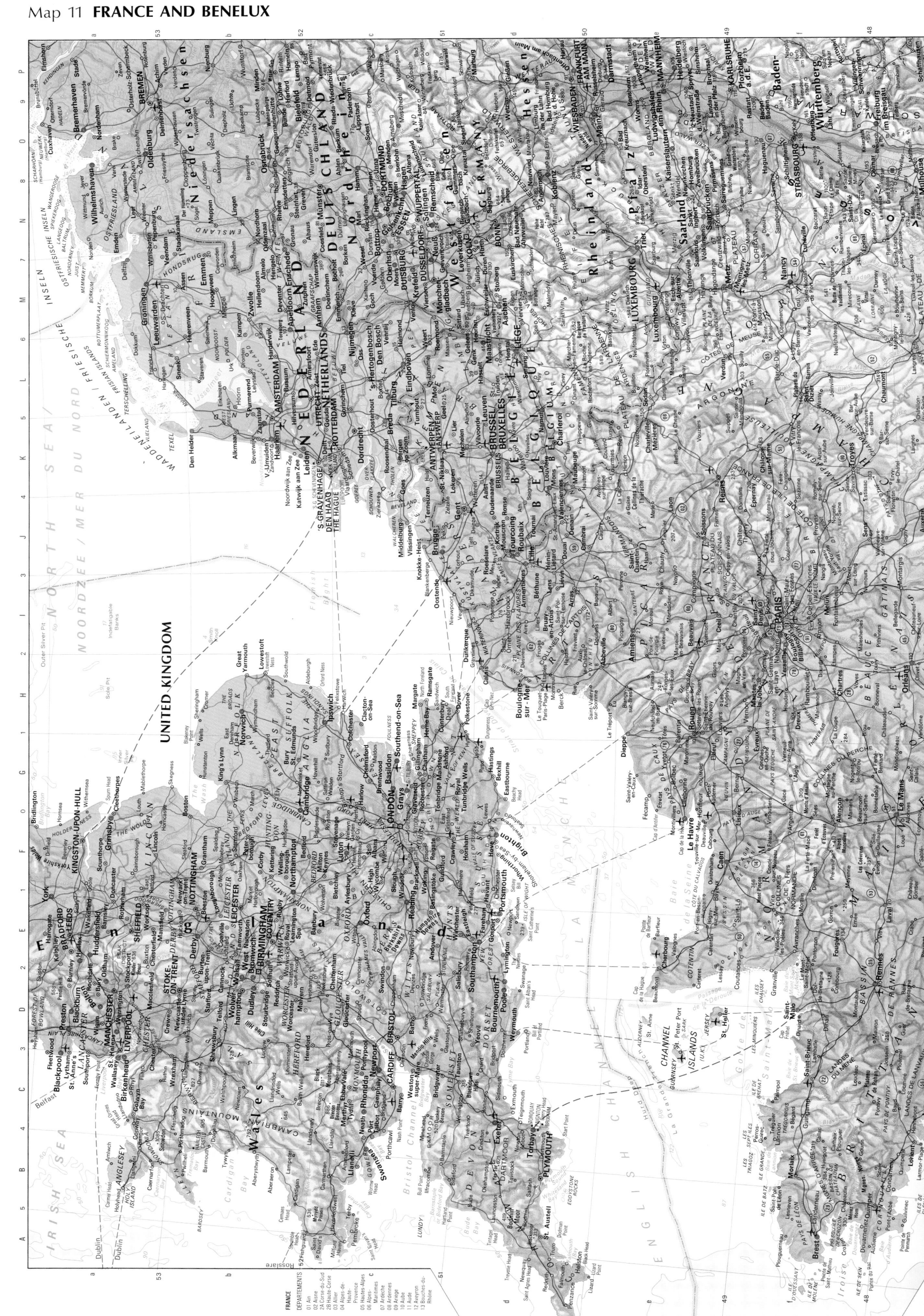

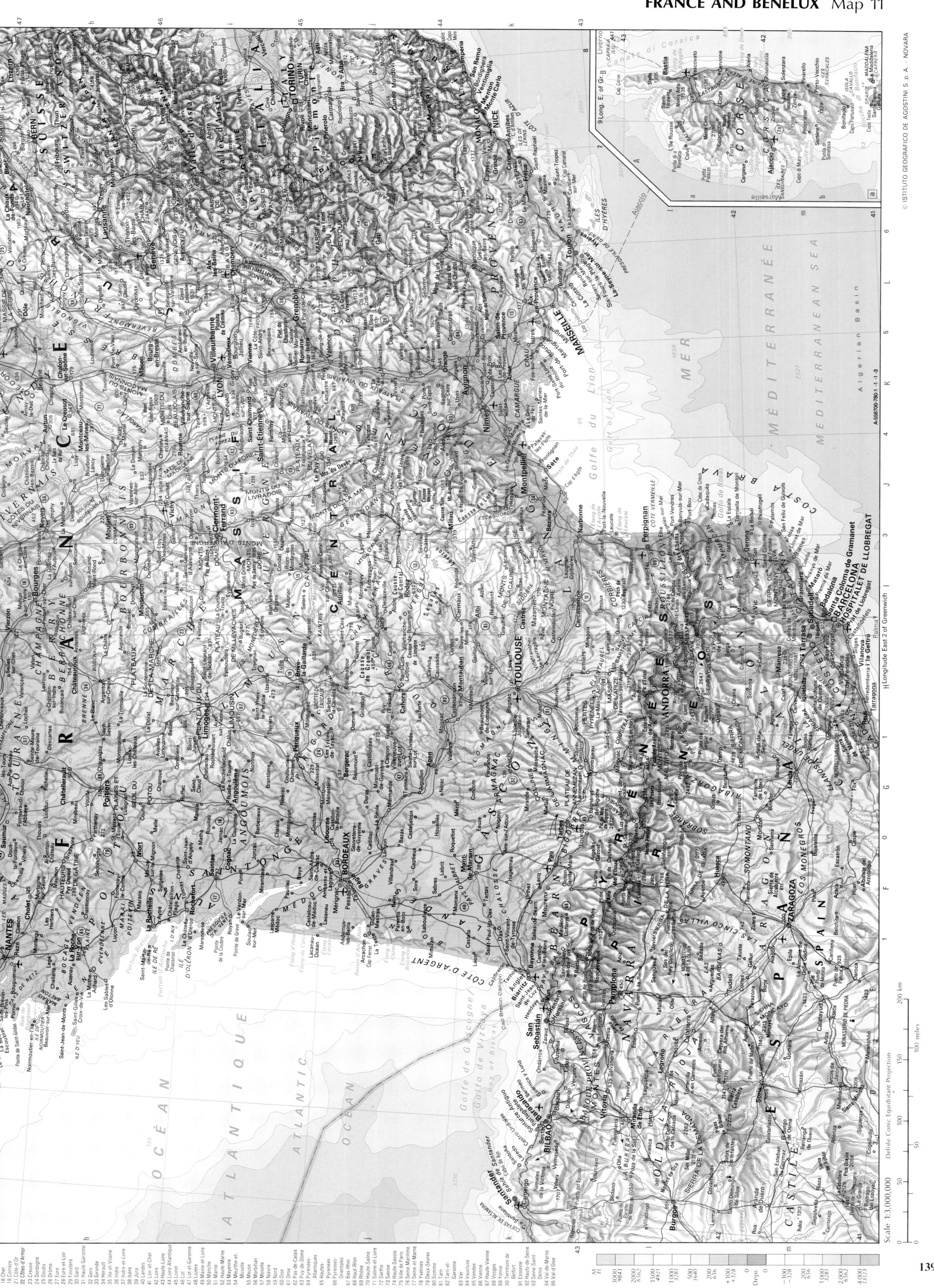

Map 12 BELGIUM, NETHERLANDS AND LUXEMBOURG

UNITED KINGDOM

NORTH SEA / NOORDZEE / MER DU NORD

'S-GRAV

Flemish Bight

ENGLISH CHANNEL / LA MANCHE

Strait of Dover / Pas de Calais

Baie de la Seine / Bay of the Seine

FRANCE

England

LINCOLNSHIRE · NOTTINGHAM · LEICESTERSHIRE · CAMBRIDGESHIRE · NORFOLK · SUFFOLK · EAST ANGLIA · ESSEX · KENT · SURREY · SUSSEX · HAMPSHIRE · BERKSHIRE · HERTFORDSHIRE · BEDFORDSHIRE · BUCKINGHAMSHIRE · OXFORDSHIRE · NORTHAMPTONSHIRE · WARWICKSHIRE · HUNTINGDON

LONDON · Nottingham · Leicester · Derby · Peterborough · Cambridge · Norwich · Ipswich · Colchester · Southampton · Portsmouth · Brighton · Dover · Folkestone · Boulogne-sur-Mer · Calais · Dunkerque · Oostende · Brugge · GENT

ISLE OF WIGHT

PAS-DE-CALAIS · SOMME · PICARDIE · NORMANDIE · SEINE MARITIME · EURE · CALVADOS · MANCHE · ORNE

Le Havre · Rouen · Caen · Amiens · Abbeville · Dieppe · Beauvais · Lille · Roubaix · Tournai · Arras · Cambrai · Saint-Quentin

PARIS · Versailles · Compiègne · Soissons · Laon

FRANCE
DÉPARTEMENTOS
75 Ville de Paris
92 Hauts-de-Seine
93 Seine-Saint-Denis
94 Val-de-Marne

Scale 1:1,500,000
Delisle Conic Equidistant Projection

0   25   50   75   100 km
0   25   50 miles

M Ft
500 1640
200 656
100 328
0
Depr.

Map 12

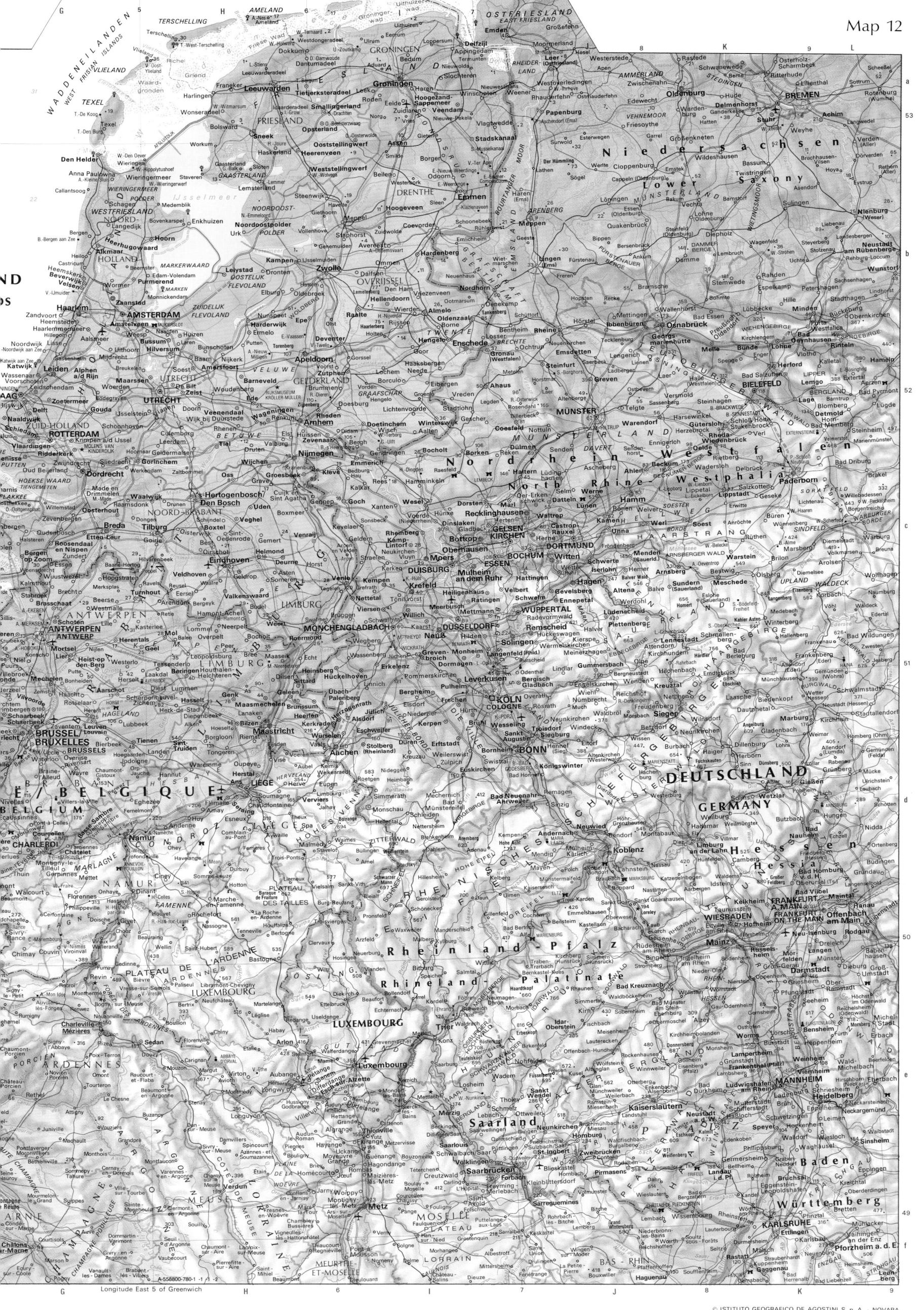

Map 13 **SPAIN AND PORTUGAL**

Longitude West 5 of Greenwich

PORTUGAL

SPAIN

AL MAGHRIB

MOROCCO

OCÉANO ATLÁNTICO

OCEANO ATLÂNTICO

MAR CANTÁBRICO

COSTA VERDE

CORDILLERA CANTÁBRICA

PICOS DE EUROPA

GALICIA

ASTURIAS

LEÓN

OLD CASTILE

NEW CASTILE

SUBMESETA NORTE

SUBMESETA SUR

SIERRA DE GUADARRAMA

SISTEMA CENTRAL

SIERRA DE GREDOS

MONTES DE TOLEDO

EXTREMADURA

SIERRA MORENA

ANDALUCÍA

SISTEMA BÉTICO

SIERRA NEVADA

COSTA DEL SOL

MINHO

TRÁS OS MONTES

DOURO LITORAL

ALTO DOURO

BEIRA ALTA

BEIRA BAIXA

BEIRA LITORAL

ESTREMADURA

RIBATEJO

ALTO ALENTEJO

BAIXO ALENTEJO

ALGARVE

LISBOA / LISBON

PORTO

MADRID

SEVILLA / SEVILLE

CÓRDOBA

GRANADA

MÁLAGA

CÁDIZ

BILBAO

Gibraltar (U.K.)

Ceuta (Sp.)

M
ft
3000 9843
2000 6562
1500 4921
1000 3281
500 1640
200 656
+100 +328
0
−100 −328
200 656
1000 3281
2000 6562
4000 13123

Scale 1:3,000,000 Delisle Conic Equidistant Projection

0   50   100   150   200 km
0   50   100 miles

FRANCE

TOULOUSE

PYRÉNÉES

ANDORRA

ROUSSILLON

Perpignan

NAVARRA

Pamplona

HUESCA

LÉRIDA

CATALUÑA

ZARAGOZA SARAGOSSA

BARCELONA

Santa Coloma de Gramanet

HOSPITALET DE LLOBREGAT

Sabadell

Tarrasa

Manresa

GERONA

Gerona

Costa Brava

Costa Dorada

TARRAGONA

Tarragona

Tortosa

TERUEL

CASTELLON

Castellón de la Plana

Costa del Azahar

ISLAS COLUMBRETES

Sagunto

VALENCIA

Golfo de Valencia

Costa de Valencia

ALBACETE

Albacete

ALICANTE

Alicante

Elche

Costa Blanca

MURCIA

Cartagena

Mar Menor

ISLAS BALEARES

BALEARIC ISLANDS

ISLAS BALEARES

MENORCA / MINORCA

Mahón

MALLORCA / MAJORCA

PALMA

BALEARES

ISLA CABRERA

IBIZA IVIZA

FORMENTERA

ISLA ESPALMADOR

MEDITERRANEAN SEA

Algerian Basin

MARSEILLE

Toulon

Golfe du Lion / Gulf of Lion

PROVENCE

Avignon

Nîmes

Montpellier

Béziers

Narbonne

Carcassonne

AL JAZÃ'IR

ALGIERS / ALGER

ORAN

MOSTAGANEM

TIZI OUZOU

KABYLIE

SÉTIF

ATLAS TELLIEN

ALGERIA / ALGÉRIE / AL JAZÃ'IR

PLAINE DU CHÉLIF

PLAINE DU HODNA

Map 14 **ITALY, AUSTRIA AND SWITZERLAND**

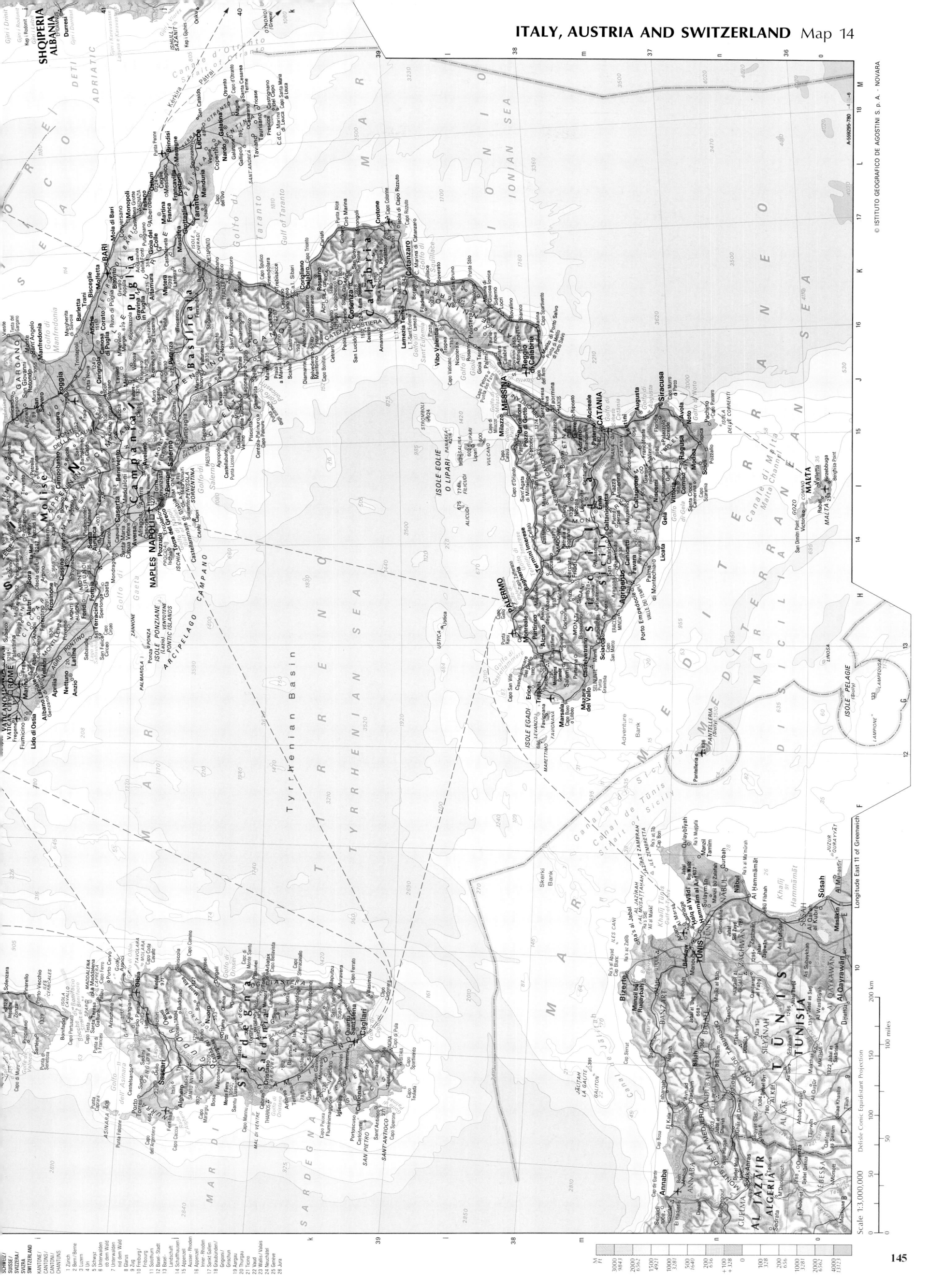

Scale 1:3,000,000

Delisle-Conic Equidistant Projection

Longitude East 11 of Greenwich

Map 15 **SOUTHEASTERN EUROPE**

Map 15

© ISTITUTO GEOGRAFICO DE AGOSTINI S. p. A. - NOVARA

A-559800-780--3   L   29   M   35   N   -6   28   27   26   25   24   23   22   21

MEDITERRANEAN SEA

AKDENIZ

MESOYEIOS THALASSA

Scale 1:3,000,000   Delisle Conic Equidistant Projection   H Longitude East 25 of Greenwich

0   50   100   150   200 km

0   50   100 miles

Map 16 **BLACK AND CASPIAN SEAS REGION**

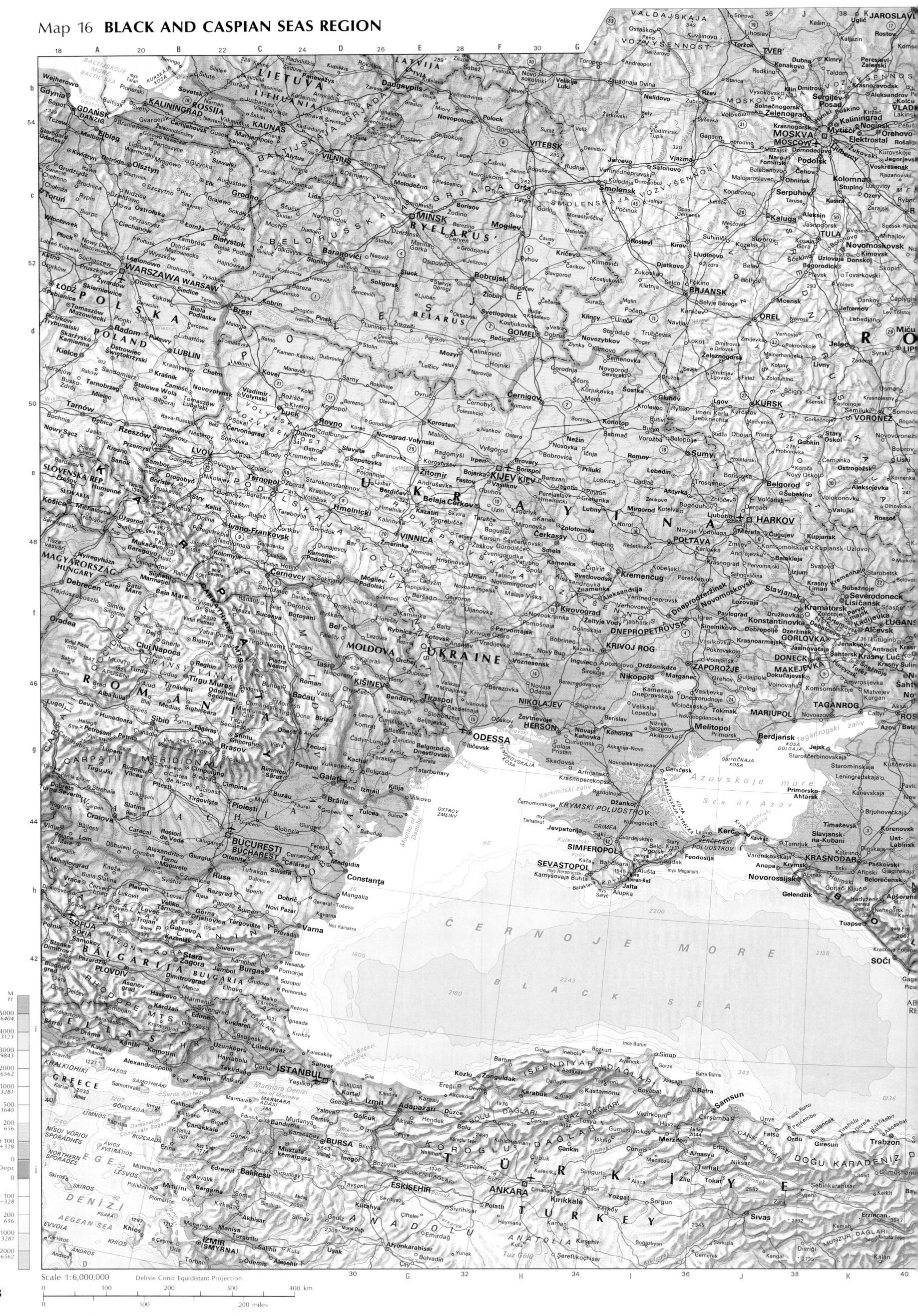

Scale 1:6,000,000   Delisle Conic Equidistant Projection

0   100   200   300   400 km

0   100   200 miles

Map 17 **THE URALS**

ROSSIJA
RUSSIA

8 Arhangelskaja oblast
8A Neneckij avt. respublika
12 Čeljabinskaja oblast
14 Gorkovskaja oblast
23 Kirovskaja oblast
24 Kostromskaja oblast
25 Kujbiševskaja oblast
26 Kurganskaja oblast
35 Omskaja oblast
36 Orenburgskaja oblast
39 Permskaja oblast
39A Komi-Permjackij avt. okrug
44 Saratovskaja oblast
46 Jekaterinburgskaja oblast
48 Tjumenskaja oblast
48A Hanty-Mansijski avt. okrug
48B Jamalo-Neneckij respublika
51 Uljanovskaja oblast
54 Vologodskaja oblast

QAZAQSTAN
KAZAKHSTAN

3 Celinogradskaja oblast
10 Kokčetavskaja oblast
11 Kustanajskaja oblast
15 Severo-Kazahstanskaja oblast
17 Turgajskaja oblast

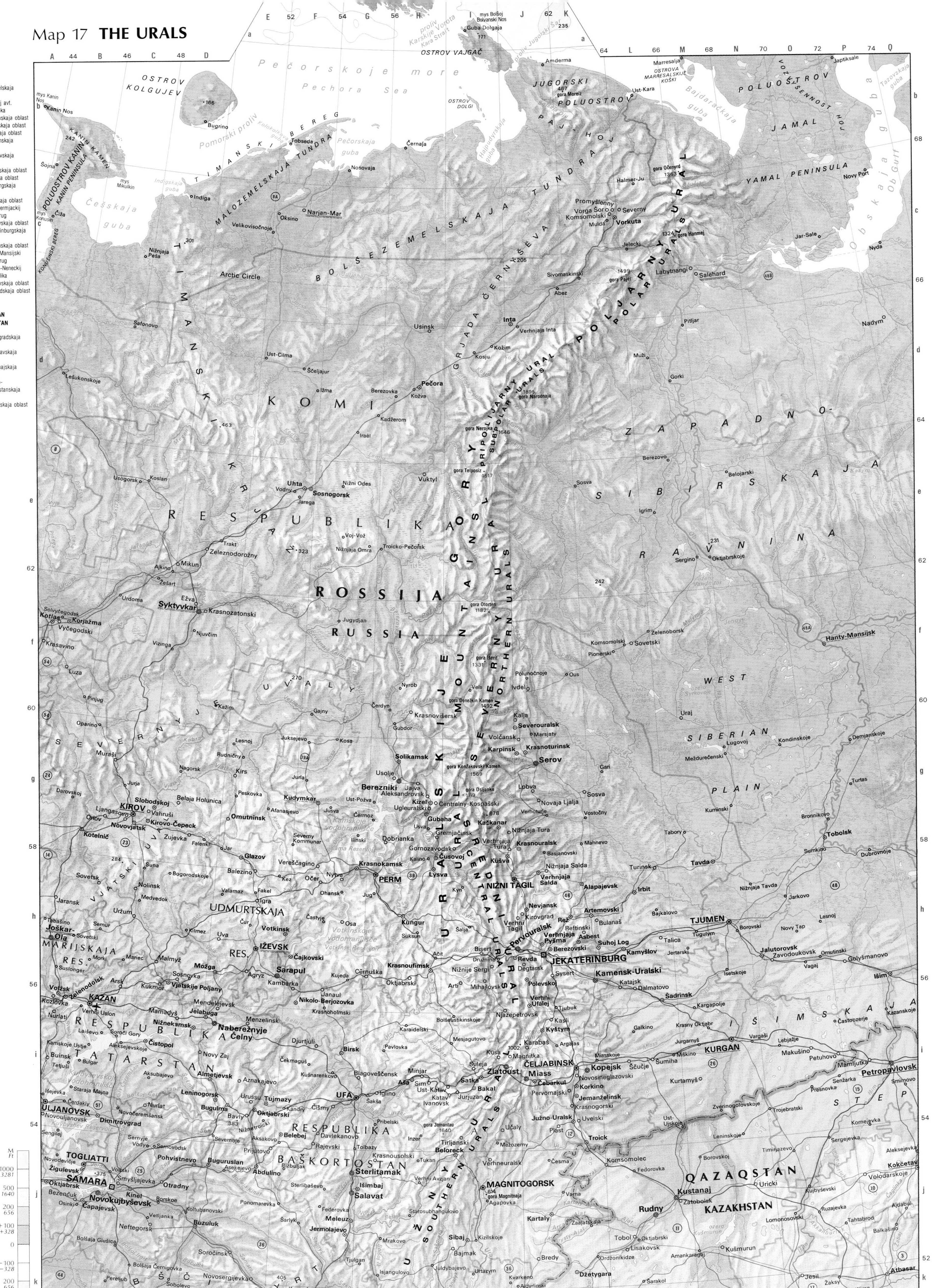

Pečorskoje more
Pechora Sea

OSTROV VAJGAČ

JUGORSKI POLUOSTROV

POLUOSTROV JAMAL
YAMAL PENINSULA

POLJARNY URAL

SUBPOLARNY URAL

RUSSIJA
RUSSIA

KOMI

RESPUBLIKA

SEVERNYJ URAL / NORTHERN URALS

ZAPADNO-SIBIRSKAJA RAVNINA

WEST SIBERIAN PLAIN

SREDNIJ URAL / CENTRAL URALS

JEKATERINBURG

UDMURTSKAJA RES.

RESPUBLIKA TATARSTAN

RESPUBLIKA BAŠKORTOSTAN

JUŽNYJ URAL / SOUTHERN URALS

QAZAQSTAN
KAZAKHSTAN

STEP

Scale 1:6,000,000   Delisle Conic Equidistant Projection

Longitude East 60 of Greenwich

150

© ISTITUTO GEOGRAFICO DE AGOSTINI S. p. A - NOVARA

0   100   200   300   400 km
0   100   200 miles

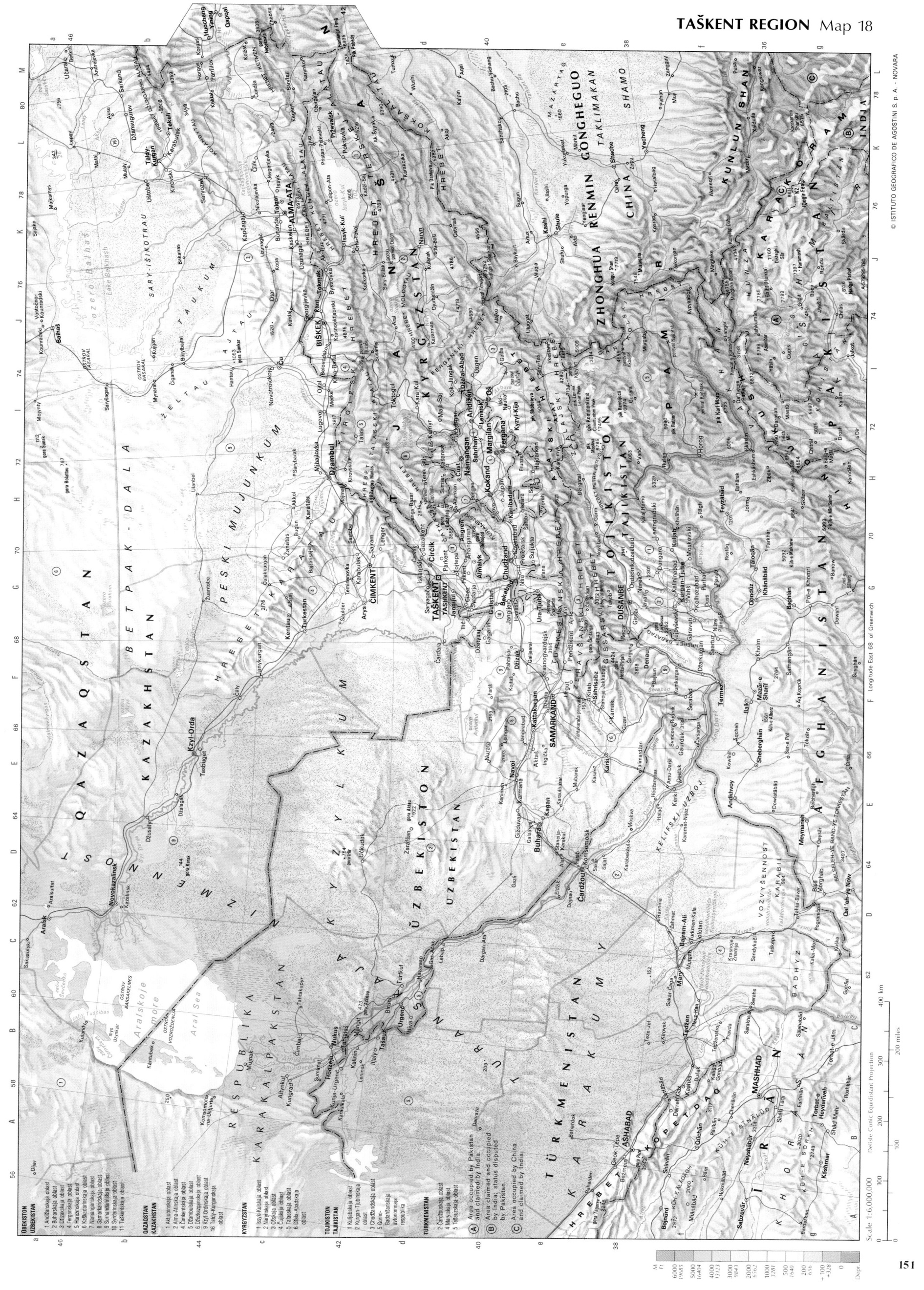

Map 19

152

ROSSIJA
RUSSIA

3 Krasnodarski kraj
3A Adygeja,
    respublika
6 Stavropolski kraj

6A Karačajevo-
   Čerkessakaja
   respublikas
8 Arhangelskaja
   oblast
8A Neneckij avt.res.
9 Astrahanskaja
   oblast
10 Belgorodskaja obl.
11 Brjanskaja obl.
12 Čeljabinskaja obl.
14 Nižegrodskaja
   oblast
15 Ivanovskaja obl.
17 Jaroslavskaja obl.
18 Kaliningradskaja
   oblast
19 Tver'skaja obl.
21 Kalužskaja obl.
23 Kirovskaja obl.
24 Kostromskaja obl.
25 Kujbyševskaja
   oblast
26 Kurganskaja obl.
27 Kurskaja obl.
28 Leningradskaja
   oblast
29 Lipeckaja obl.
30 Pskovskaja obl.
31 Moskovskaja obl.
32 Murmanskaja obl.
33 Novgorodskaja
   oblast
35 Omskaja obl.
36 Orenburgskaja obl.
37 Orlovskaja obl.
38 Penzenskaja obl.
39 Permskaja obl.
39A Komi-Permjackij
    avt. okr.
40 Pskovskaja obl.
41 Rostovskaja obl.
42 Rjazanskaja obl.
44 Saratovskaja obl.
45 Smolenskaja obl.
46 Jekaterinburgskaja
   oblast
47 Tambovskaja obl.
48 Tjumenskaja obl.
48A Hanty-Mansijski
    avt. okr.
50 Tulskaja obl.
51 Uljanovskaja obl.
52 Vladimirskaja obl.
53 Volgogradskaja
   oblast
54 Vologodskaja obl.
55 Voronežskaja obl.

UKRAYINA
UKRAINE

1 Čerkasskaja obl.
2 Černigovskaja obl.
3 Černovickaja obl.
4 Dnepropetrovskaja
   oblast
5 Doneckaja obl.
6 Harkovskaja obl.
7 Hersonskaja obl.
8 Hmelnickaja obl.
9 Ivano-Frankovskaja
   oblast
10 Kijevskaja obl.
11 Kirovogradskaja
   oblast
12 Krym, respublika
13 Lvovskaja obl.
14 Nikolajevskaja obl.
15 Odesskaja obl.
16 Poltavskaja obl.

Scale 1:12,000,000   Delisle Conic Equidistant Projection

0   200   400   600   800 km

0   200   400 miles

Longitude East 55 of Greenwich

Commonwealth of
dependent States (CIS)
s created by republics
he former Soviet Union.

**UKRAYINA
UKRAINE**

17 Rovenskaja obl.
18 Sumskaja obl.
19 Ternopolskaja obl.
20 Vinnickaja obl.
21 Volynskaja obl.
22 Vorošilovgradskaja oblast
23 Zakarpatskaja obl.
24 Zaporožskaja obl.
25 Žitomirskaja obl.

**BYELARUS'
BELARUS**

1 Brestskaja obl.
2 Gomelskaja obl.
3 Grodnenskaja obl.
4 Minskaja obl.
5 Mogilevskaja obl.
6 Vitebskaja obl.

**ÜZBEKISTON
UZBEKISTAN**

1 Andižanskaja obl.
2 Buharskaja obl.
3 Džizakskaja obl.
4 Ferganskaja obl.
5 Horezmskaja obl.
6 Kaškadarinskaja oblast
7 Namanganskaja oblast
8 Samarkandskaja oblast
9 Surhandarinskaja oblast
10 Syrdarinskaja obl.
11 Taškentskaja obl.

**QAZAQSTAN
KAZAKHSTAN**

1 Aktjubinskaja obl.
2 Alma-Atinskaja oblast
3 Celinogradskaja obl.
4 Čimkentskaja obl.
5 Džambulskaja obl.
6 Džezkazganskaja oblast
7 Atyrauskaja obl.
8 Karagandinskaja oblast
9 Kzyl-Ordinskaja oblast
10 Kokčetavskaja obl.
11 Kustanajskaja obl.
12 Mangyšlakskaja obl.
13 Pavlodarskaja obl.
14 Semipalatinskaja oblast
15 Severo-
Kazahstanskaja oblast
16 Taldy-Kurganskaja oblast
17 Turgajskaja obl.
18 Uralskaja obl.
19 Vostočno-
Kazahstanskaja oblast

**SAKARTVELO
GEORGIA**

1 Jugo Osetija

**AZÄRBAYJAN
AZERBAIJAN**

1 Nagorno-
Karabah

KYRGYZSTAN

1 Issyk-Kulskaja oblast
2 Narynskaja obl.
3 Ošskaja obl.
4 Čujskaja oblast
5 Talasskaja obl.
6 Džal-Abadskaja oblast

**TOJIKISTON
TAJIKISTAN**

1 Kuljabskaja obl.
2 Kurgan-Tjubinskaja oblast
3 Chudžandskaja obl.
5 Gorno-
Badahšanskaja avt. respublika

TÜRKMENISTAN

2 Čardžouskaja obl.
3 Balkanskaja oblast
4 Maryjskaja obl.
5 Tašauzskaja obl.

	M	Ft
	6000	19685
	5000	16404
	4000	13123
	3000	9843
	2000	6562
	1000	3281
	500	1640
	+200	+656
	0	0
	Depr.	
	−100	−328
	200	656
	1000	3281
	2000	6562

Map 20

e Commonwealth of
ependent States (CIS)
as created by republics
the former Soviet Union.

**ROSSIJA
RUSSIA**

1 Altajski kraj
1A Gornyj Altaj, respublika
2 Habarovski kraj
2A Evrejskaja avt.
   respublika
4 Krasnojarski kraj
4A Hakasija, respublika
5 Primorski kraj
7 Amurskaja oblast
8A Nenecki avt.
   respublika
13 Čitinskaja oblast
16 Irkutskaja oblast
16A Ust-Ordynski
   Burjatski avt. okrug
21 Kamčatskaja oblast
21A Korjakski avt.
   okrug
22 Kemerovskaja
   oblast
30 Magadanskaja
   oblast
30A Čukotski avt. okrug
34 Novosibirskaja
   oblast
35 Omskaja oblast
43 Sahalinskaja oblast
48 Tjumenskaja oblast
48A Hanty-Mansijski
   avt. okrug
48B Jamalo-Neneckij
   respublika
49 Tomskaja oblast

**QAZAQSTAN
KAZAKHSTAN**

13 Pavlodarskaja
   oblast
14 Semipalatinskaja
   oblast
19 Vostočno-
   Kazahstanskaja
   oblast

Ostrov Kunašir, ostrov Šikotan, ostrov
Iturup and Malaja Kurilskaja Grjada,
occupied since 1945,
are claimed by Japan pending a final
peace treaty.

Longitude East 150 of Greenwich

A-579395-780

© ISTITUTO GEOGRAFICO DE AGOSTINI S.p A. - NOVARA   **155**

Map 21 **ASIA, PHYSICAL**

© ISTITUTO GEOGRAFICO DE AGOSTINI S. p. A. - NOVARA

A-515200-780 -2 --10

Scale 1:30,000,000   Lambert Azimuthal Equal Area Projection   Longitude East 80 of Greenwich

157

Map 22 **ASIA, POLITICAL**

Map 23 **SOUTHWESTERN ASIA**

Scale 1:12,000,000

Delisle Conic Equidistant Projection

0 200 400 600 800 km

0 200 400 miles

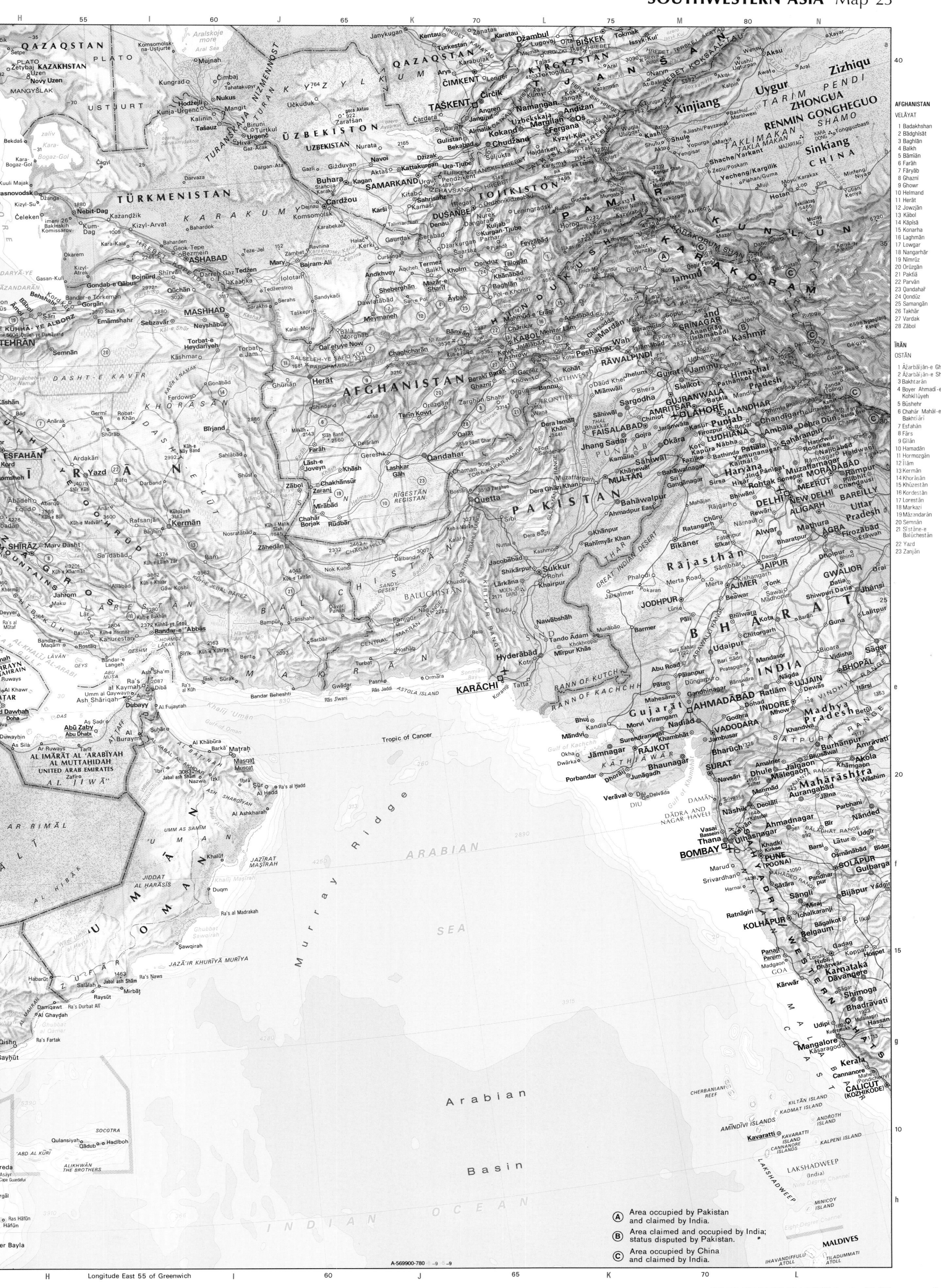

© ISTITUTO GEOGRAFICO DE AGOSTINI S.p.A. - NOVARA

Left margin index:

AL URDUN
JORDAN
MUHĀFAZAT
1 Al Balqā'
2 Al Karak
3 Al Khalīl
4 Al Quds
5 'Ammān
6 Irbid
7 Ma'ān
8 Nābulus

West Bank:
Occupied by
Israel

YISRA'EL
ISRAEL
MEHOZ
1 HaDarom
2 HaMerkaz
3 HaZafon
4 Hefa
5 Tel Aviv
6 Yerushalayim

SŪRĪYAH
SYRIA
MINTAQAT
14 Dimashq
MUHĀFAZAT
1 Al Hasakah
2 Al Lādhiqīyah
3 Al Qunaytirah
4 Ar Raqqah
5 As Suwaydā'
6 Dar'ā
7 Dayr Az Zawr
8 Dimashq
9 Halab
10 Hamāh
11 Hims
12 Idlib
13 Tartūs

Golan Heights:
Occupied by
Israel

KUZEY KIBRIS
NORTH CYPRUS
North Cyprus unilaterally declared
its independence November, 1983.

KÍPROS
CYPRUS

Legend:

▨ Area occupied by Israel

(A) Golan Heights area:
Occupied by Israel since 1967.
Unilaterally annexed by Israel, 1981.

(B) West Bank area:
Unilaterally annexed by Jordan, 1950.
Occupied by Israel since 1967.
Status to be determined.

(C) Gaza Strip:
Occupied by Israel since 1967.
Status to be determined.

Elevation scale:

M	Ft
5000	16404
4000	13123
3000	9843
2000	6562
500	1640
200	656
+100	+328
Depr.	0
−100	−328
1000	3281
2000	6562
4000	13123

162

Scale 1:6,000,000   Delisle Conic Equidistant Projection   Longitude East 40 of Greenwich

0 100 200 300 400 km
0 100 200 miles

A-569495-780-7

Major labels: KARADENIZ / BLACK SEA · TÜRKIYE / TURKEY · ELLAS / GREECE · BÂLGARIJA / BULGARIA · AKDENIZ / AL BAHR AL-MUTAWASSIT / YĀM KHATIKHON / MEDITERRANEAN SEA · SŪRĪYAH / SYRIA · LUBNĀN / LEBANON · YISRA'EL / ISRAEL · AL URDUN / JORDAN · MISR / EGYPT · AL 'ARABĪYAH SAUDI · SYRIAN DESERT / BĀDIYAT ASH SHĀM · SINAI PENINSULA / SĪNĀ' · NILE DELTA · WESTERN DESERT / AS SAHRĀ' AL GHARBĪYAH

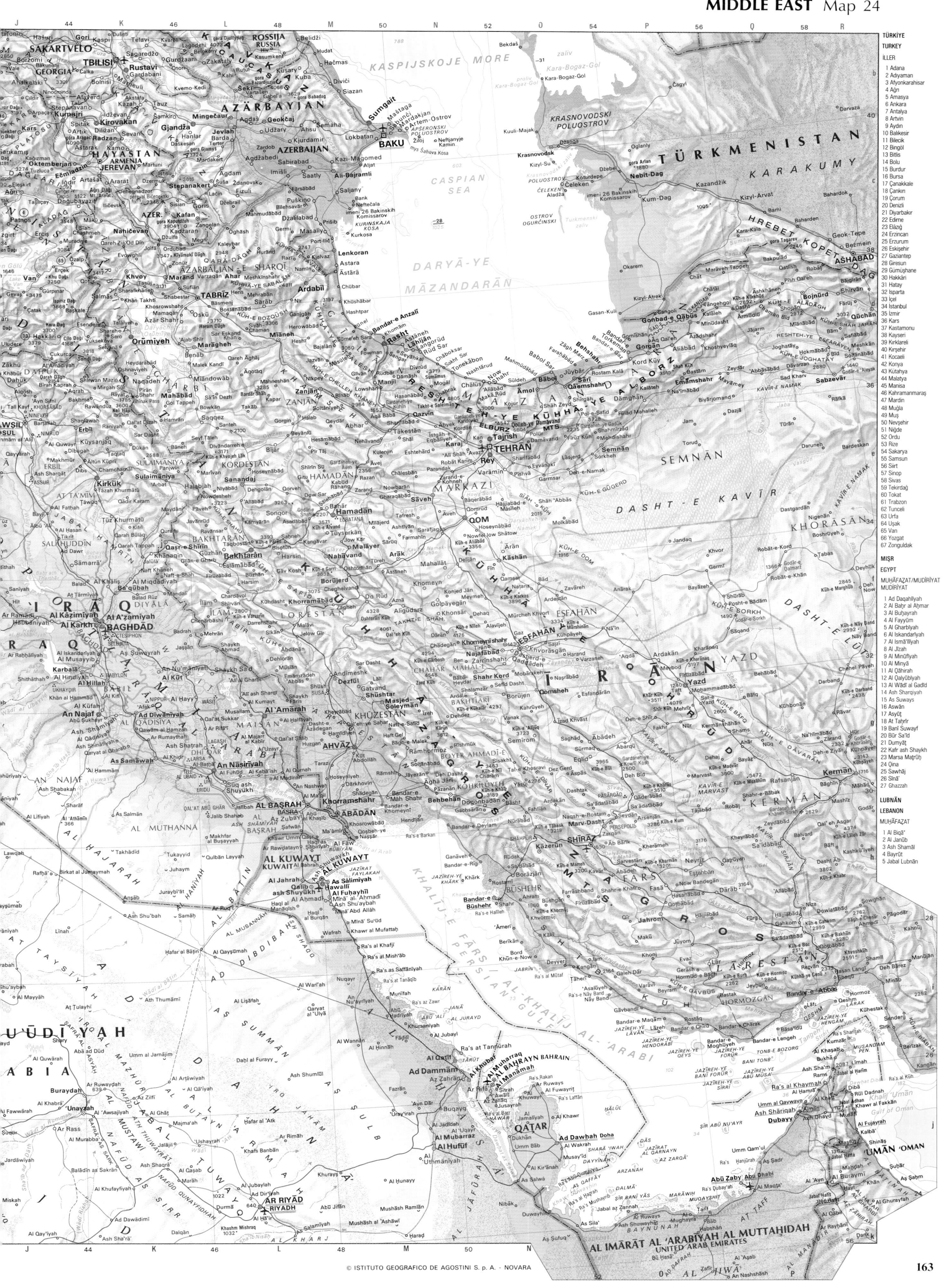

TÜRKİYE
TURKEY
İLLER
1 Adana
2 Adıyaman
3 Afyonkarahisar
4 Ağrı
5 Amasya
6 Ankara
7 Antalya
8 Artvin
9 Aydın
10 Balıkesir
11 Bilecik
12 Bingöl
13 Bitlis
14 Bolu
15 Burdur
16 Bursa
17 Çanakkale
18 Çorum
19 Çorum
20 Denizli
21 Diyarbakır
22 Edirne
23 Elazığ
24 Erzincan
25 Erzurum
26 Eskişehir
27 Gaziantep
28 Giresun
29 Gümüşhane
30 Hakkari
31 Hatay
32 Isparta
33 İçel
34 İstanbul
35 İzmir
36 Kars
37 Kastamonu
38 Kayseri
39 Kırklareli
40 Kırşehir
41 Kocaeli
42 Konya
43 Kütahya
44 Malatya
45 Manisa
46 Kahramanmaraş
47 Mardin
48 Muğla
49 Muş
50 Nevşehir
51 Niğde
52 Ordu
53 Rize
54 Sakarya
55 Samsun
56 Siirt
57 Sinop
58 Sivas
59 Tekirdağ
60 Tokat
61 Trabzon
62 Tunceli
63 Urfa
64 Uşak
65 Van
66 Yozgat
67 Zonguldak

MISIR
EGYPT
MUḤĀFAẒAT/MUDĪRĪYAT
MUDĪRĪYAT
1 Ad Daqahlīyah
2 Al Baḥr al Aḥmar
3 Al Buḥayrah
4 Al Fayyūm
5 Al Gharbīyah
6 Al Iskandarīyah
7 Al Ismāʿīlīyah
8 Al Jīzah
9 Al Minūfīyah
10 Al Minyā
11 Al Qāhirah
12 Al Qalyūbīyah
13 Al Wādī al Gadīd
14 Ash Sharqīyah
15 As Suways
16 Aswān
17 Asyūṭ
18 Aṭ Ṭaḥrīr
19 Banī Suwayf
20 Būr Saʿīd
21 Dumyāṭ
22 Kafr ash Shaykh
23 Marsa Maṭrūḥ
24 Qinā
25 Sawhāj
26 Sīnā
27 Ghazzah

LUBNĀN
LEBANON
MUḤĀFAẒAT
1 Al Biqāʿ
2 Al Janūb
3 Ash Shamāl
4 Bayrūt
5 Jabal Lubnān

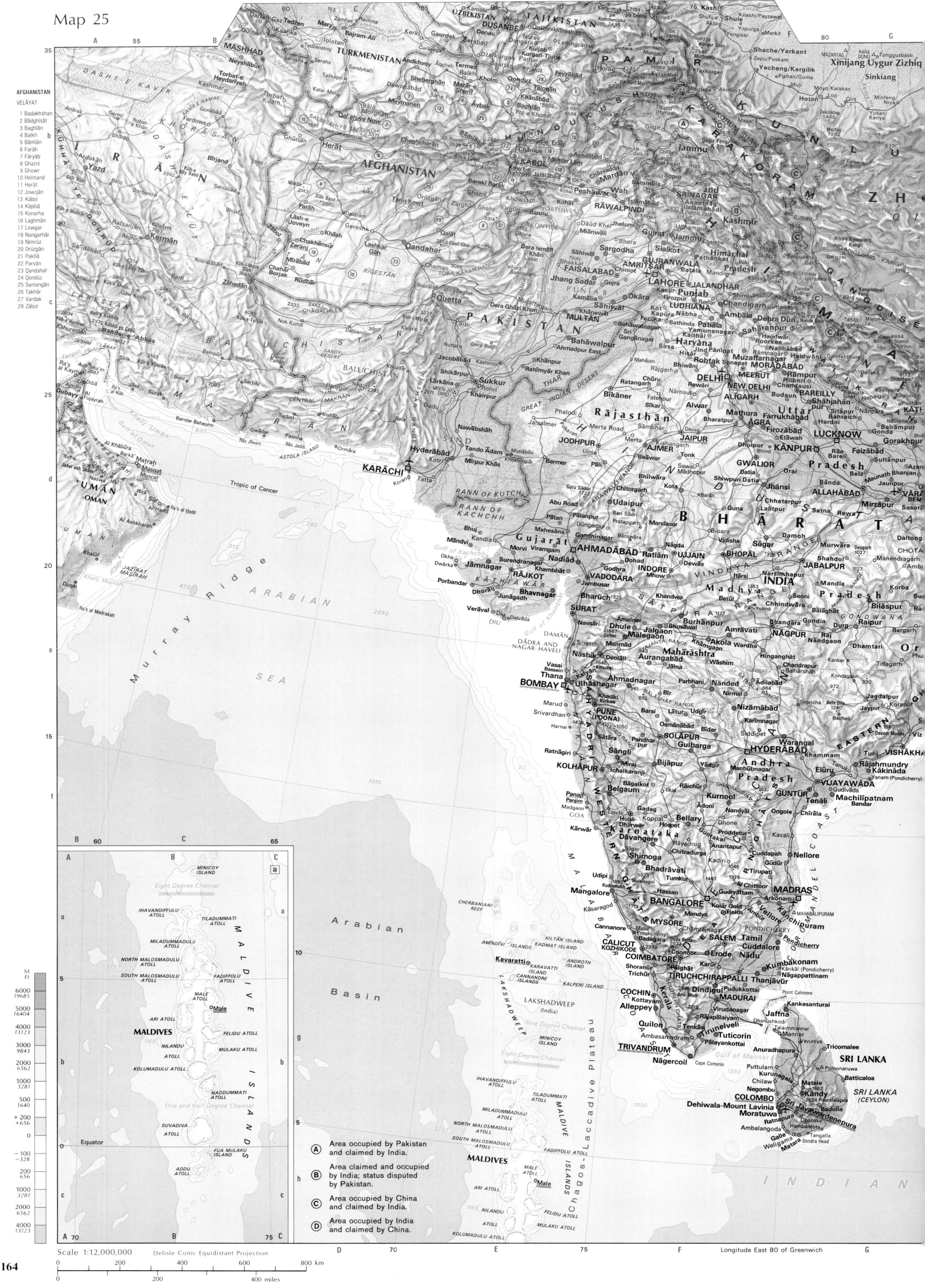

Map 25

AFGHANISTAN
VELĀYAT
1 Badakhshan
2 Bādghīsāt
3 Baghlān
4 Balkh
5 Bāmīān
6 Farāh
7 Fāryāb
8 Ghaznī
9 Ghowr
10 Helmand
11 Herāt
12 Jowzjān
13 Kābol
14 Kāpīsā
15 Konarha
16 Laghmān
17 Lowgar
18 Nangarhār
19 Nīmrūz
20 Orūzgān
21 Paktīā
22 Parvān
23 Qandahār
24 Qondūz
25 Samangān
26 Takhār
27 Vardak
28 Zābol

MALDIVES

Ⓐ Area occupied by Pakistan
and claimed by India.

Ⓑ Area claimed and occupied
by India; status disputed
by Pakistan.

Ⓒ Area occupied by China
and claimed by India.

Ⓓ Area occupied by India
and claimed by China.

M
Ft
6000
19685
5000
16404
4000
13123
3000
9843
2000
6562
500
1640
+ 200
+656
0
− 100
−328
200
656
1000
3281
2000
6562
4000
13123

Scale 1:12,000,000   Delisle Conic Equidistant Projection

0   200   400   600   800 km

0   200   400 miles

Longitude East 80 of Greenwich

Map 26 **SOUTHEAST ASIA**

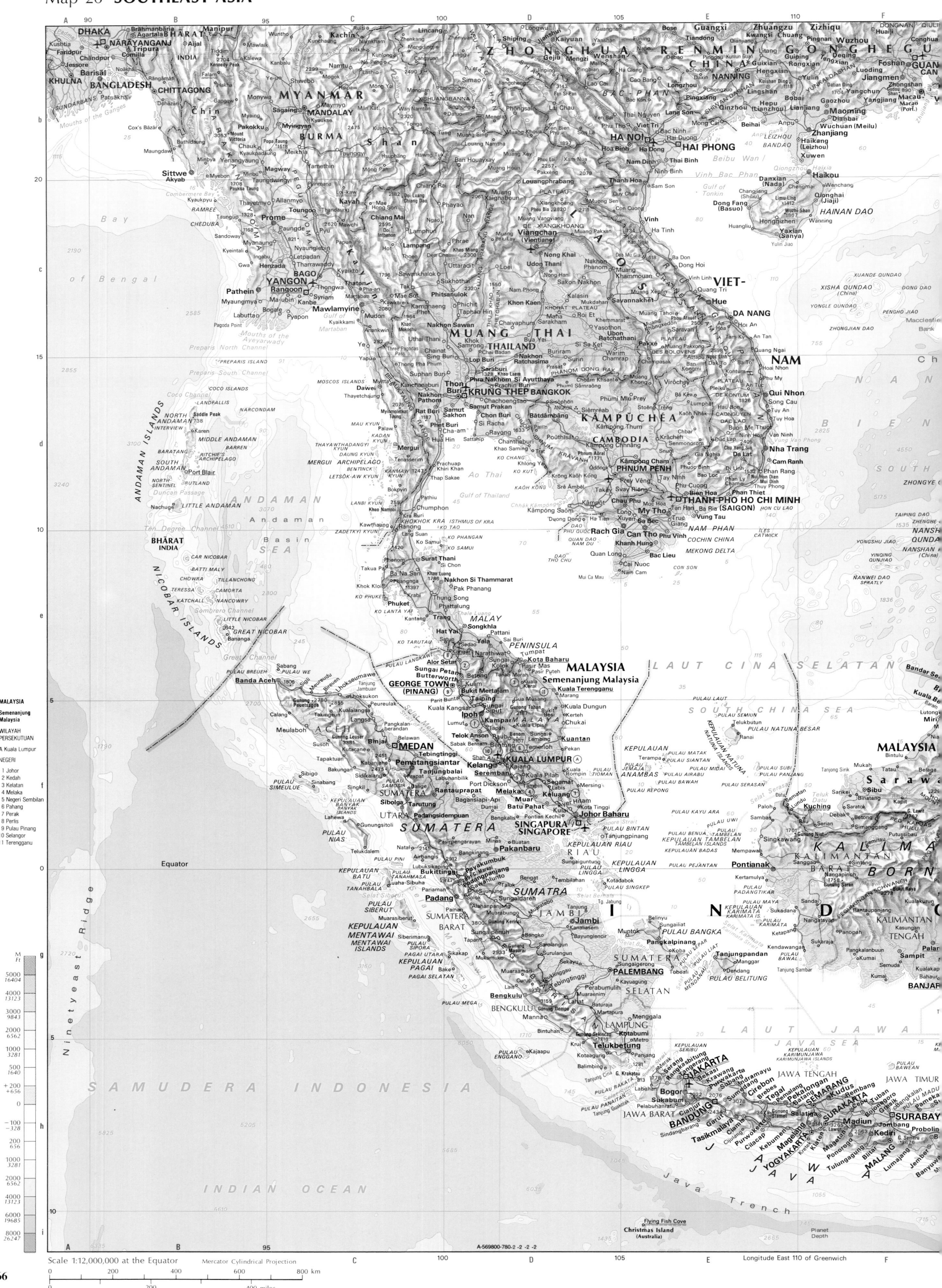

Scale 1:12,000,000 at the Equator

Mercator Cylindrical Projection

Longitude East 110 of Greenwich

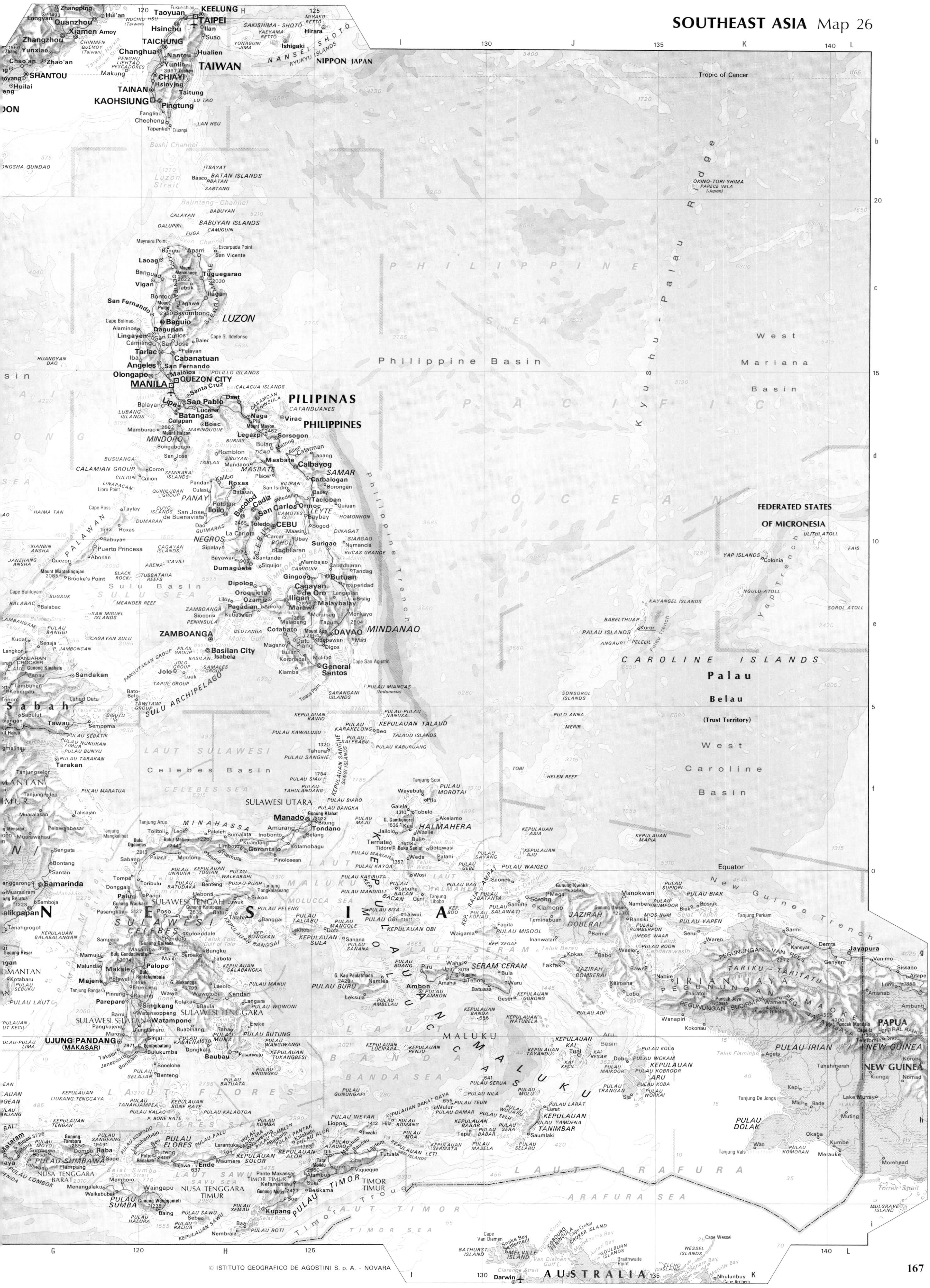

Tropic of Cancer

TAIWAN
KEELUNG
TAIPEI
TAICHUNG
CHIAYI
TAINAN
KAOHSIUNG
Pingtung

NIPPON JAPAN
NANSEI SHOTO
RYUKYU ISLANDS

PHILIPPINE SEA

Philippine Basin

LUZON
Laoag
Vigan
San Fernando
Baguio
Dagupan
Lingayen
Tarlac
Angeles
Olongapo
MANILA
QUEZON CITY
Santa Cruz
San Pablo
Batangas
MINDORO

PILIPINAS
PHILIPPINES

Legazpi
Sorsogon
Naga
Virac
CATANDUANES

MASBATE
Roxas
PANAY
Iloilo
Bacolod
San Carlos
CEBU
NEGROS
Dumaguete
Tacloban
Ormoc
LEYTE
SAMAR
Calbayog
Catbalogan

PACIFIC OCEAN

WEST MARIANA BASIN

FEDERATED STATES
OF MICRONESIA

YAP ISLANDS
Colonia

Surigao
Butuan
Cagayan de Oro
Iligan
Ozamiz
Pagadian
ZAMBOANGA
Basilan City
Isabela
Jolo
SULU ARCHIPELAGO

MINDANAO
Malaybalay
Marawi
Cotabato
DAVAO
Digos
General Santos

CAROLINE ISLANDS
Palau
Belau
(Trust Territory)
PALAU ISLANDS
Koror

West Caroline Basin

Sabah
Sandakan
Lahad Datu
Tawau
Tarakan

LAUT SULAWESI
CELEBES SEA
Celebes Basin

KEPULAUAN TALAUD
TALAUD ISLANDS

PULAU MOROTAI

Manado
Tondano
Gorontalo
SULAWESI UTARA
MINAHASSA

Ternate
Tidore
HALMAHERA

Equator

KEPULAUAN MAPIA

New Guinea Trench

Samarinda
Balikpapan
SULAWESI TENGAH
CELEBES
Palu
Poso

MOLUCCA SEA
LAUT MALUKU

PULAU OBI

LAUT SERAM
CERAM SEA
SERAM
CERAM
Ambon
PULAU BURU

Sorong
JAZIRAH DOBERAI
PULAU MISOOL
PULAU WAIGEO
Manokwari
PULAU BIAK
PULAU YAPEN

IRIAN JAYA
PEGUNUNGAN MAOKE
Jayapura

Makale
Palopo
Majene
Parepare
Singkang
Watampone
SULAWESI TENGGARA
Kendari

UJUNG PANDANG
(MAKASAR)
SULAWESI SELATAN
Baubau
PULAU MUNA
PULAU BUTUNG

LAUT BANDA
BANDA SEA

MALUKU
KEPULAUAN KAI
Tual
KEPULAUAN ARU

PAPUA
NEW GUINEA
PULAU IRIAN

PULAU DOLAK
Merauke

BANDA SEA
KEPULAUAN TANIMBAR
Saumlaki

LAUT FLORES
FLORES SEA
PULAU FLORES
Ende
NUSA TENGGARA TIMUR

PULAU SUMBA
Waingapu

PULAU WETAR
PULAU ALOR
Dili
TIMOR TIMUR
Kupang
PULAU TIMOR

LAUT ARAFURA
ARAFURA SEA

LAUT TIMOR
TIMOR SEA
TIMOR TROUGH

AUSTRALIA
Darwin

Map 27 **CHINA AND MONGOLIA**

Scale 1:12,000,000

Delisle Conic Equidistant Projection

0   200   400   600   800 km

0   200   400 miles

Area occupied by Pakistan
and claimed by India.

Area claimed and occupied by India;
status disputed by Pakistan.

Area occupied by China
and claimed by India.

Area occupied by India
and claimed by China.

Map 28 **NORTHEASTERN CHINA, KOREA AND JAPAN**

MONGOL ARD ULS
MONGOLIA

PUSTYNJA GOBI Nei Mongol Zizhiqu

NEI MONGOL GAOYUAN Inner Mongolia

GOBI DESERT

ZHONGHUA RENMIN GONGHEGUO
CHINA

DA HINGGAN LING / GREATER KHINGAN RANGE

MANCHURIA

YIN SHAN

HEILONGJIANG

HARBIN

CHANGCHUN

JILIN

DONGBEI PINGYUAN

LIAONING

SHENYANG

HOHHOT

DATONG

HEBEI

SHAANXI

SHANXI

TAIYUAN

BEIJING · PEKING

TIANJIN (TIENTSIN)

SHIJIAZHUANG

BAODING

Bo Hai
Gulf of Chihli

LIAODONG BANDAO
LIAOTUNG PENINSULA

DALIAN
Lüshun
Port Arthur

Bohai Haixia

P'YŎNGYANG

SEOUL SŎUL
INCH'ŎN

SHANDONG BANDAO
SHANTUNG PENINSULA

JINAN · TSINAN

SHANDONG

QINGDAO (TSINGTAO)

Yantai

Weifang

HUANG HAI / HWANG-HAE

YELLOW SEA

ZHENGZHOU

KAIFENG

LUOYANG

HENAN

XUZHOU

JIANGSU

HEFEI

ANHUI

HUBEI

WUHAN

NANJING (NANKING)

SHANGHAI

SUZHOU

WUXI

WUHU

HANGZHOU

ZHEJIANG

HUNAN

JIANGXI

NANCHANG

CHANGSHA

DONG HAI / HIGASHI-SHI

EAST CHINA SEA

CHEJU-DO
Cheju

Scale 1:6,000,000   Delisle Conic Equidistant Projection

0   100   200   300   400 km

0   100   200 miles

NIPPON
JAPAN
1 Hokkaidō Ken
2 Aomori Ken
3 Iwate Ken
4 Miyagi Ken
5 Akita Ken
6 Yamagata Ken
7 Fukushima Ken
8 Ibaraki Ken
9 Tochigi Ken
10 Gunma Ken
11 Saitama Ken
12 Chiba To
13 Tōkyō To
14 Kanagawa Ken
15 Niigata Ken
16 Toyama Ken
17 Ishikawa Ken
18 Fukui Ken
19 Yamanashi Ken
20 Nagano Ken
21 Gifu Ken
22 Shizuoka Ken
23 Aichi Ken
24 Mie Ken
25 Shiga Ken
26 Kyōto Fu
27 Ōsaka Fu
28 Hyōgo Ken
29 Nara Ken
30 Wakayama Ken
31 Tottori Ken
32 Shimane Ken
33 Okayama Ken
34 Hiroshima Ken
35 Yamaguchi Ken
36 Tokushima Ken
37 Kagawa Ken
38 Ehime Ken
39 Kōchi Ken
40 Fukuoka Ken
41 Saga Ken
42 Nagasaki Ken
43 Kumamoto Ken
44 Ōita Ken
45 Miyazaki Ken
46 Kagoshima Ken

CHOSŎN M.I.K.
NORTH KOREA
1 Chagang-Do
2 Ch'ŏngjin Si
3 Hamgyŏng-Namdo
4 Hamgyong-Pukto
5 Hwanghae-Namdo
6 Hwanghae-Pukto
7 Kaesŏng Si
8 Kangwŏn-Do
9 P'yŏngan-Namdo
10 P'yŏngan-Pukto
11 P'yŏngyang Si
12 Yanggang-Do

TAEHAN-MIN'GUK
SOUTH KOREA
1 Cheju-Do
2 Chŏlla-Namdo
3 Chŏlla-Pukto
4 Ch'ungch'ŏng-Namdo
5 Ch'ungch'ŏng-Pukto
6 Kangwŏn-Do
7 Kyŏngi-Do
8 Kyŏngsang-Namdo
9 Kyŏngsang-Pukto
10 Pusan Si
11 Sŏul Si

ZHONGHUA RENMIN
GONGHEGUO
CHINA
1 Beijing Shi
2 Shanghai Shi
3 Tianjin Shi

Ⓐ Ostrov Kunašir, ostrov Sikotan,
ostrov Iturup and Malaja Kurilskaja
Grjada, occupied
since 1945, are claimed by Japan
pending a final peace treaty.

A-569600-780-1 -1 -1 -3

Map 29 **JAPAN**

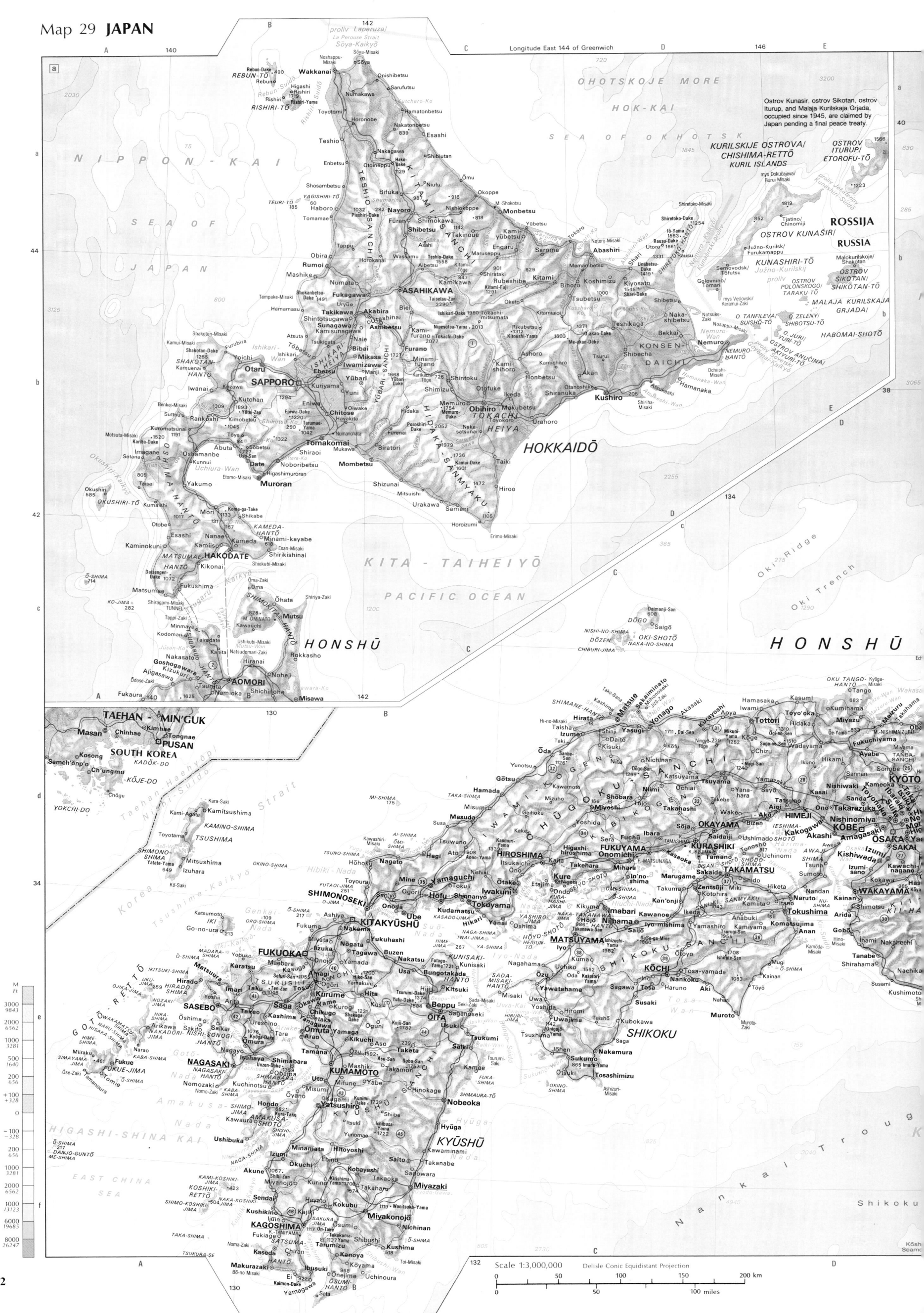

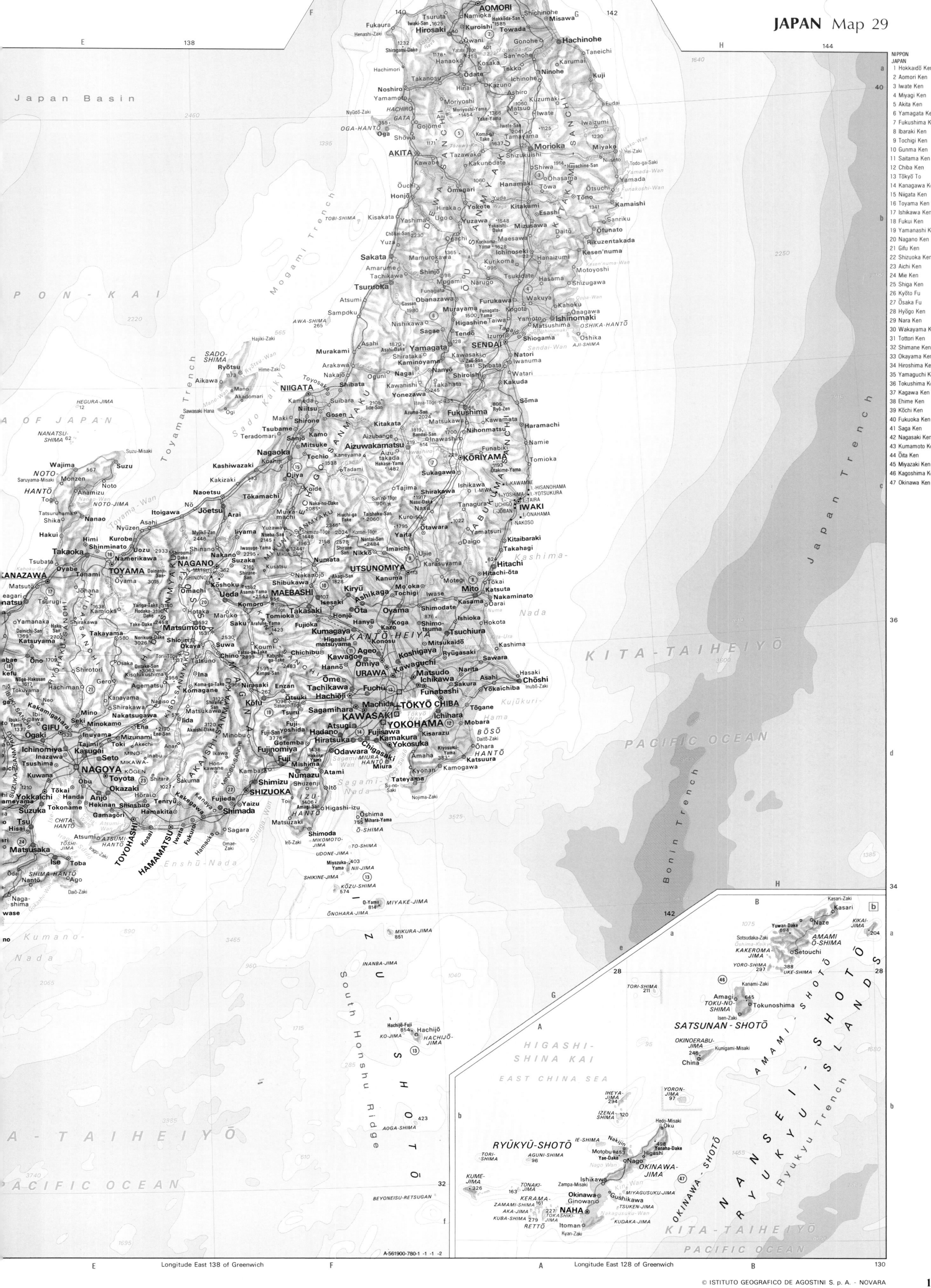

Map 30 **AFRICA, PHYSICAL**

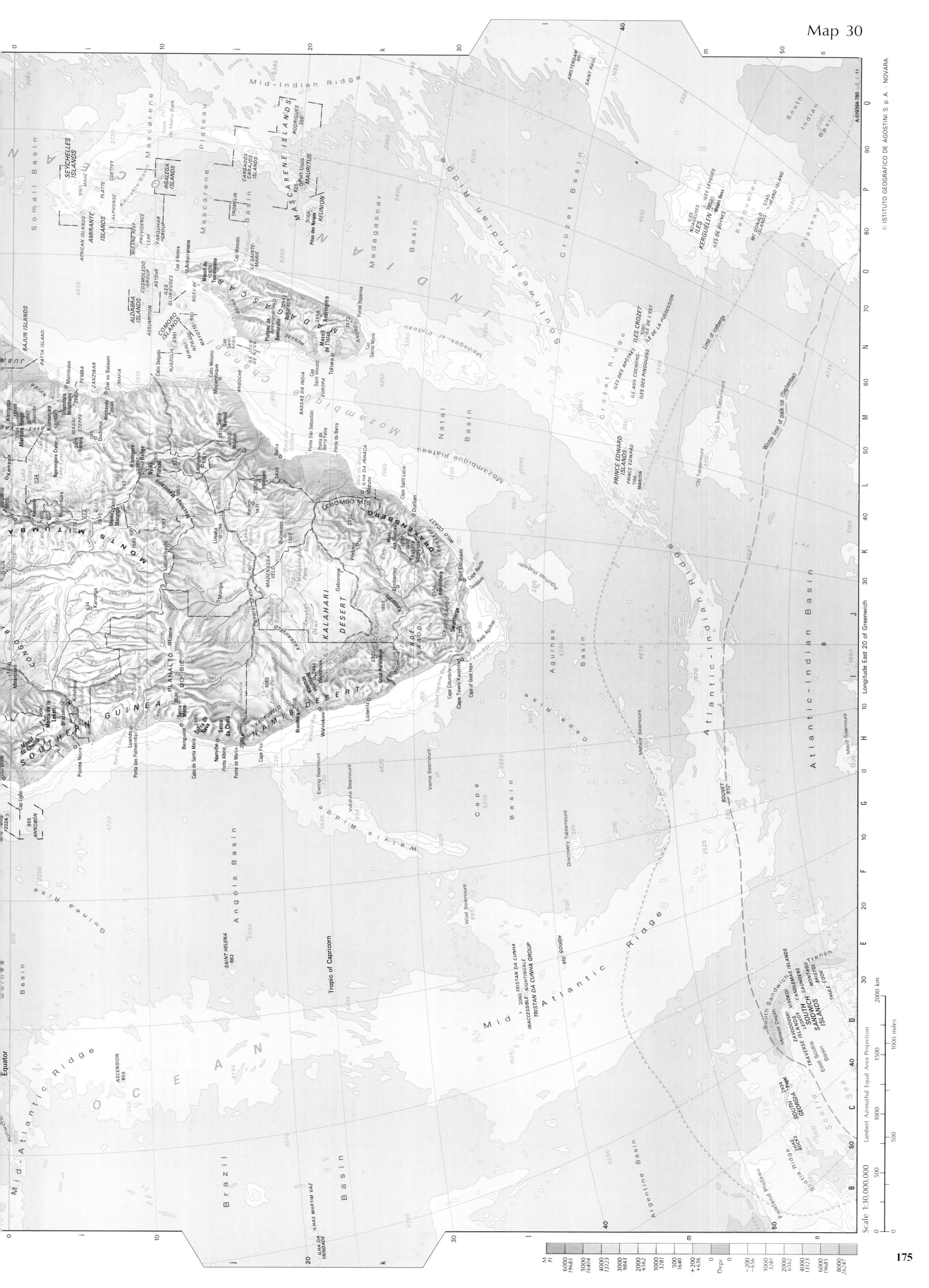

Map 30

A-519394-780 -3.-2 -11

Equator

Mid-Indian Ridge

N

SOMALI Basin

SEYCHELLES ISLANDS

AFRICAN ISLANDS
AMIRANTE ISLANDS
ALDABRA ISLANDS
COSMOLEDO GROUP
ILES GLORIEUSES
COMORO ISLANDS

MASCARENE ISLANDS
RODRIGUES
MAURITIUS
RÉUNION

Mascarene Plateau
Mascarene Basin

AGALEGA ISLANDS
CARGADOS CARAJOS ISLANDS

MADAGASCAR

Madagascar Basin

Madagascar Plateau

Mozambique Plateau

Mozambique Basin

Natal Basin

CROZET Basin

Crozet Ridge
ILES DES APÔTRES
ILE AUX COCHONS
ILES CROZET
ILE DE LA POSSESSION
ILE DE L'EST
ILES DES PINGOUINS

PRINCE EDWARD ISLANDS
PRINCE EDWARD
MARION

South Indian Basin

Southwest Indian Ridge

Limit of icebergs

Winter limit of pack ice (September)

NUAGEUSES
ILES
KERGUÉLEN
ILES LEVÉES
ILES DE BOYNES
MC DONALD ISLANDS
HEARD ISLAND

AMSTERDAM
SAINT PAUL

INDIAN

OCEAN

Atlantic-Indian Basin

Atlantic-Indian Ridge

Longitude East 20 of Greenwich

SOUTHERN GUINEA

CONGO

MONTS MITUMBA

KALAHARI DESERT

NAMIB DESERT

DRAKENSBERG

LEBOMBO MTS

KAROO

GREAT KAROO

Cape Town/Kaapstad
Cape of Good Hope

Aguilhas Basin

Agulhas Plateau

Cape Basin

Walvis Ridge

Angola Basin

Guinea Basin

Mid-Atlantic Ridge

Brazil Basin

ASCENSION

SAINT HELENA

ILHA DA TRINDADE
ILHAS MARTIM VAZ

TRISTAN DA CUNHA
INACCESSIBLE
NIGHTINGALE
TRISTAN DA CUNHA GROUP

GOUGH

Tropic of Capricorn

Mid-Atlantic Ridge

Meteor Seamount

Discovery Tablemount

BOUVET

SOUTH GEORGIA

SOUTH SANDWICH ISLANDS
ZAVODOVSKI
VISOKOI
CANDLEMAS
SAUNDERS
MONTAGU
BRISTOL
THULE/COOK

South Sandwich Trench

Scotia Sea

East Scotia Basin

Scotia Ridge

Falkland Plateau

Argentine Basin

Scale 1:30,000,000   Lambert Azimuthal Equal Area Projection

0   500   1000   1500   2000 km
0   500   1000 miles

M		
Ft		
6000	19685	
5000	16404	
4000	13123	
3000	9843	
2000	6562	
1000	3281	
500	1640	
+200	+656	
0	0	
Depr.		
-200	-656	
500	1640	
1000	3281	
2000	6562	
4000	13123	
6000	19685	
8000	26247	

Map 31 **AFRICA, POLITICAL**

Map 31

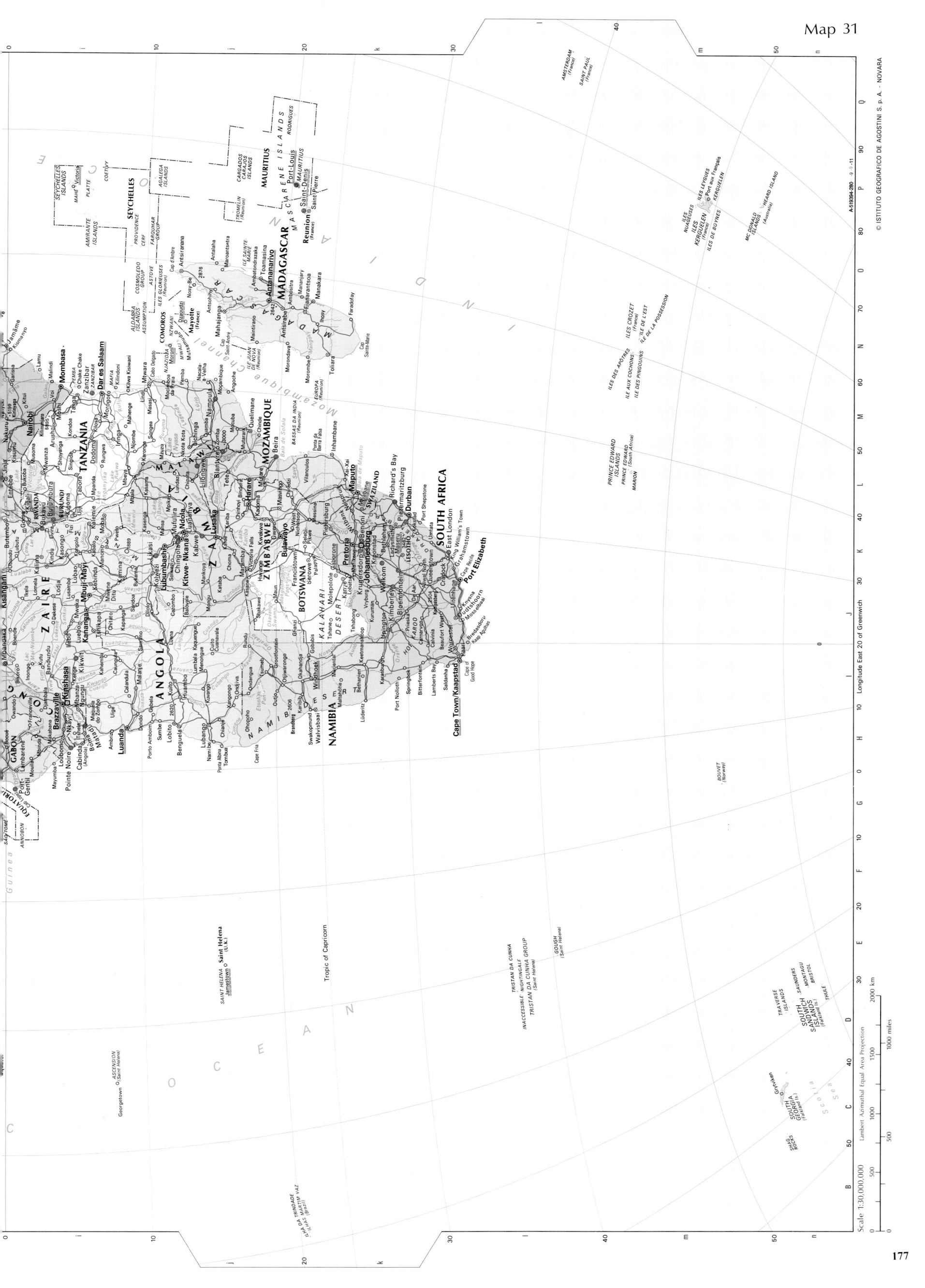

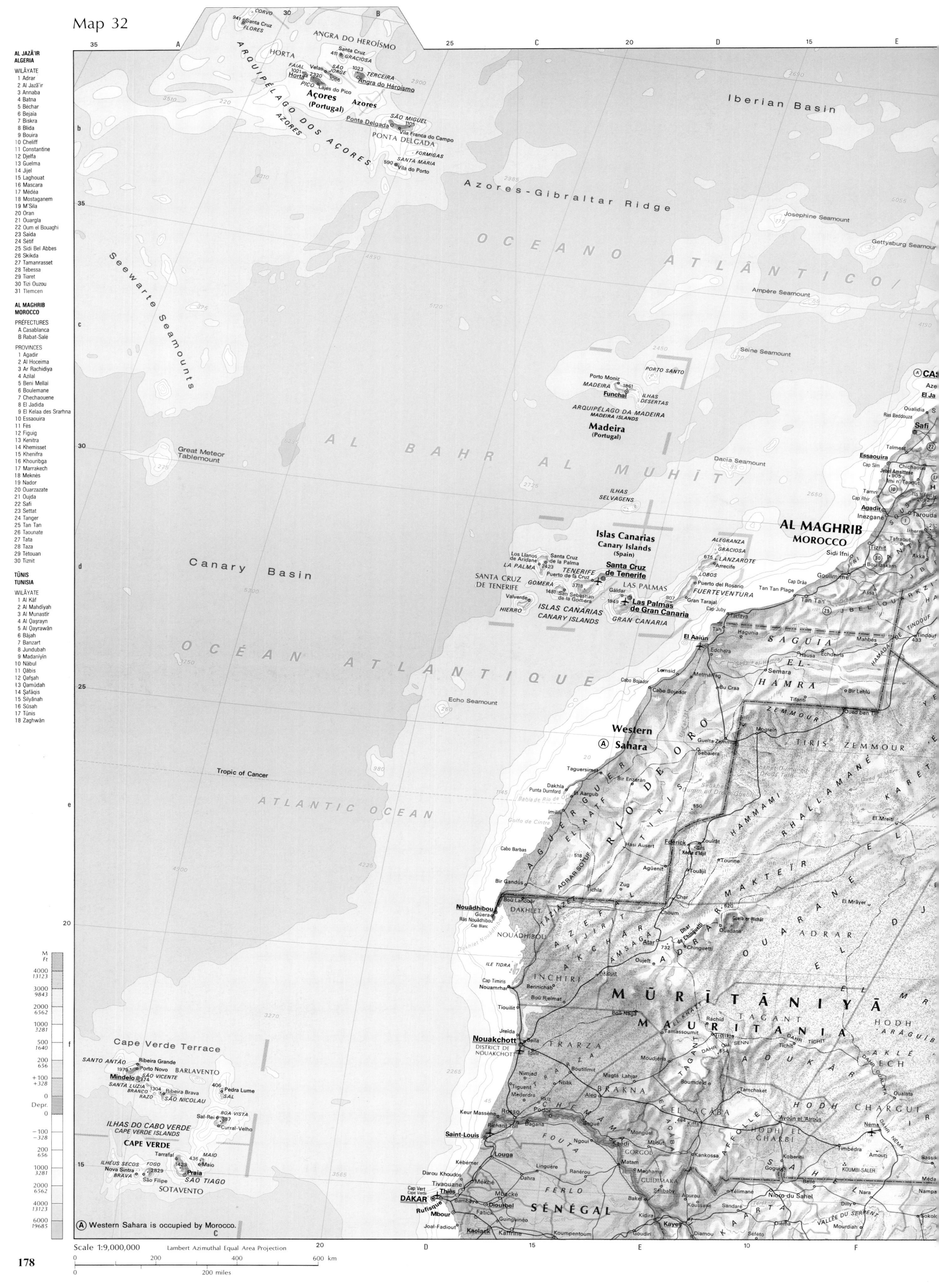

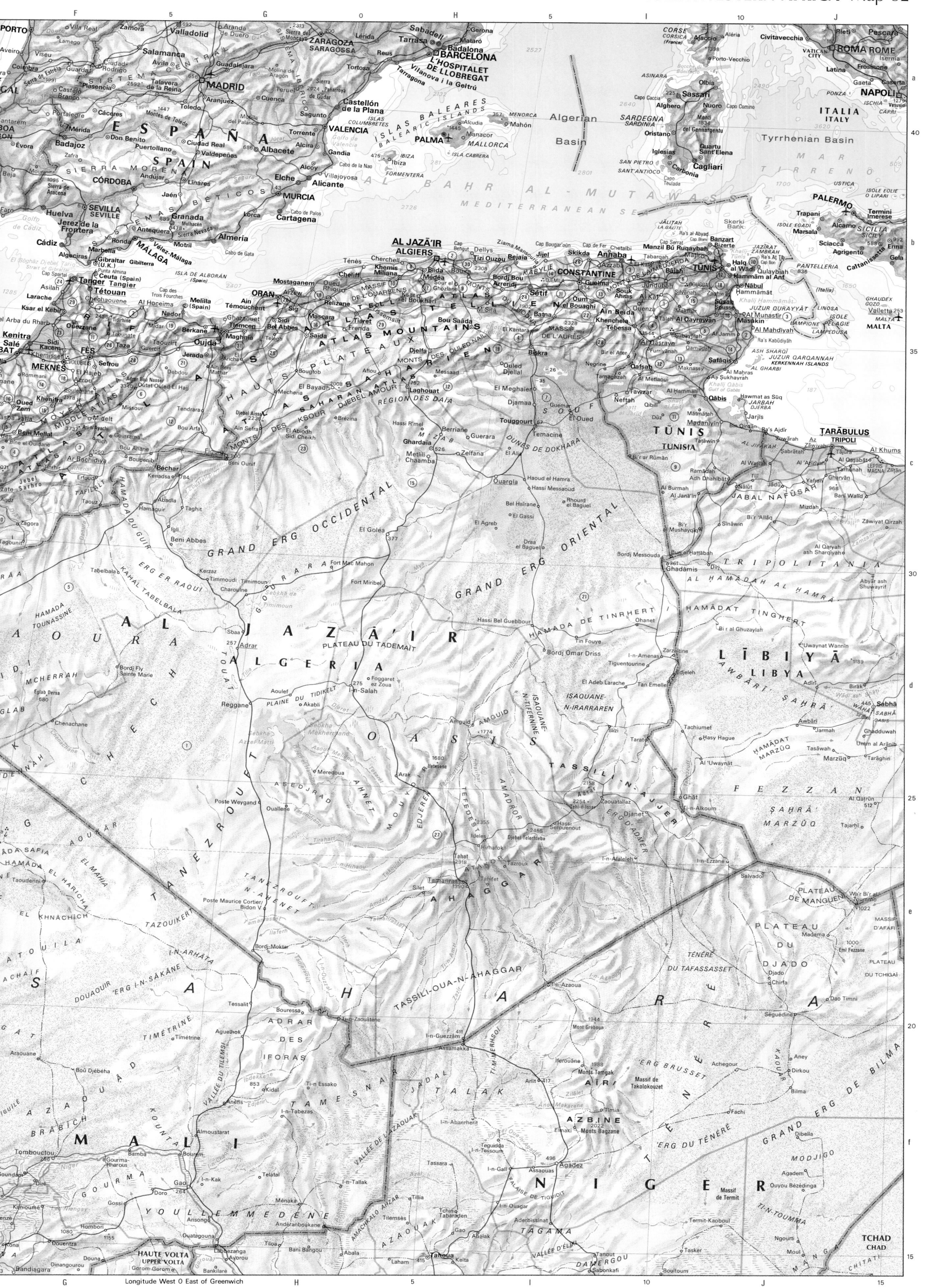

Map 33 **NORTHEASTERN AFRICA**

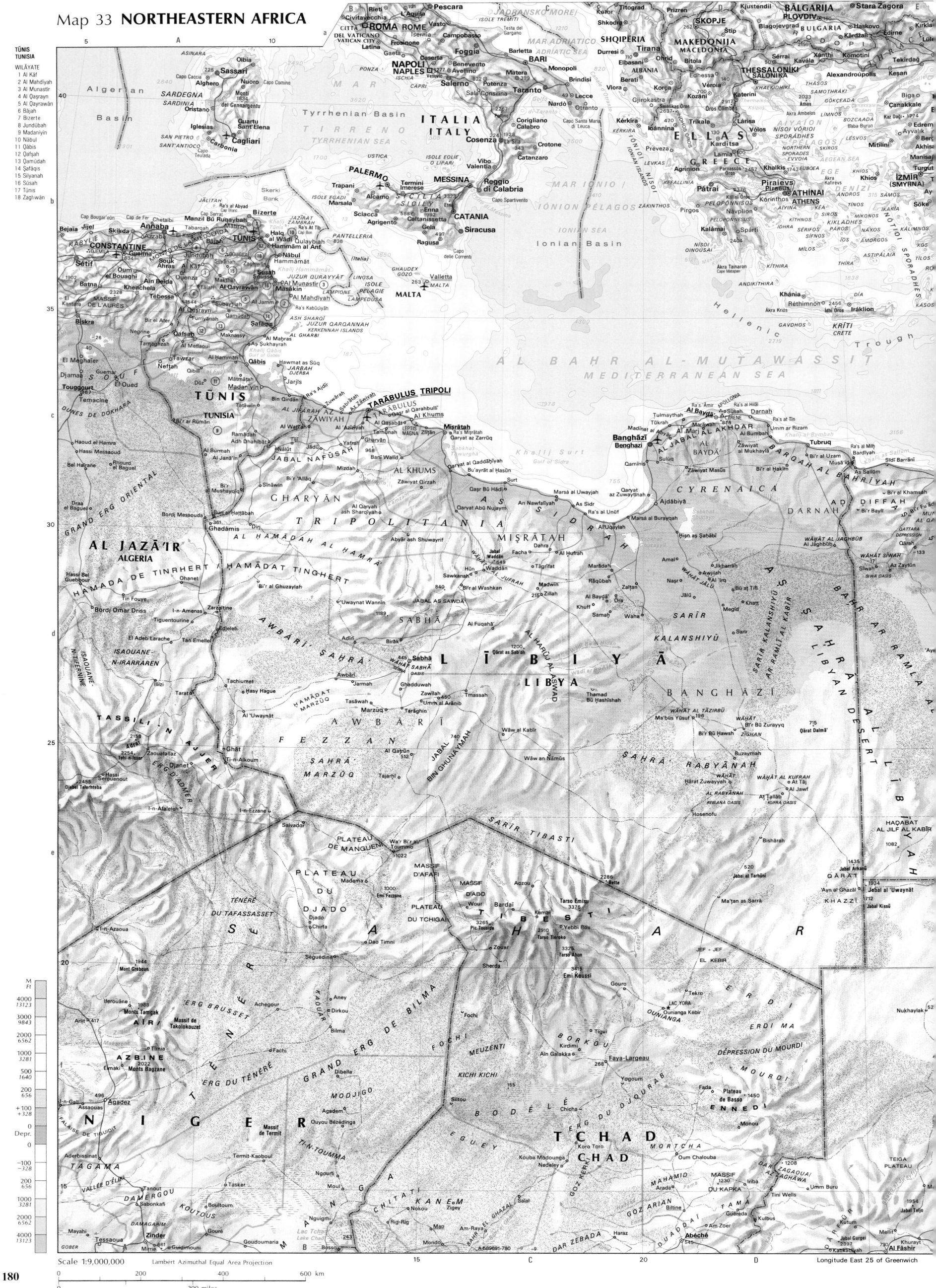

TŪNIS
TUNISIA
WILĀYATE
1 Al Kāf
2 Al Mahdīyah
3 Al Munastīr
4 Al Qaşrayn
5 Al Qayrawān
6 Bājah
7 Bizerte
8 Jundūbah
9 Madaniyin
10 Nābul
11 Qābis
12 Qafşah
13 Qamūdah
14 Şafāqis
15 Silyanah
16 Sūsah
17 Tūnis
18 Zaghiwān

Scale 1:9,000,000
Lambert Azimuthal Equal Area Projection
Longitude East 25 of Greenwich

0   200   400   600 km

0   200 miles

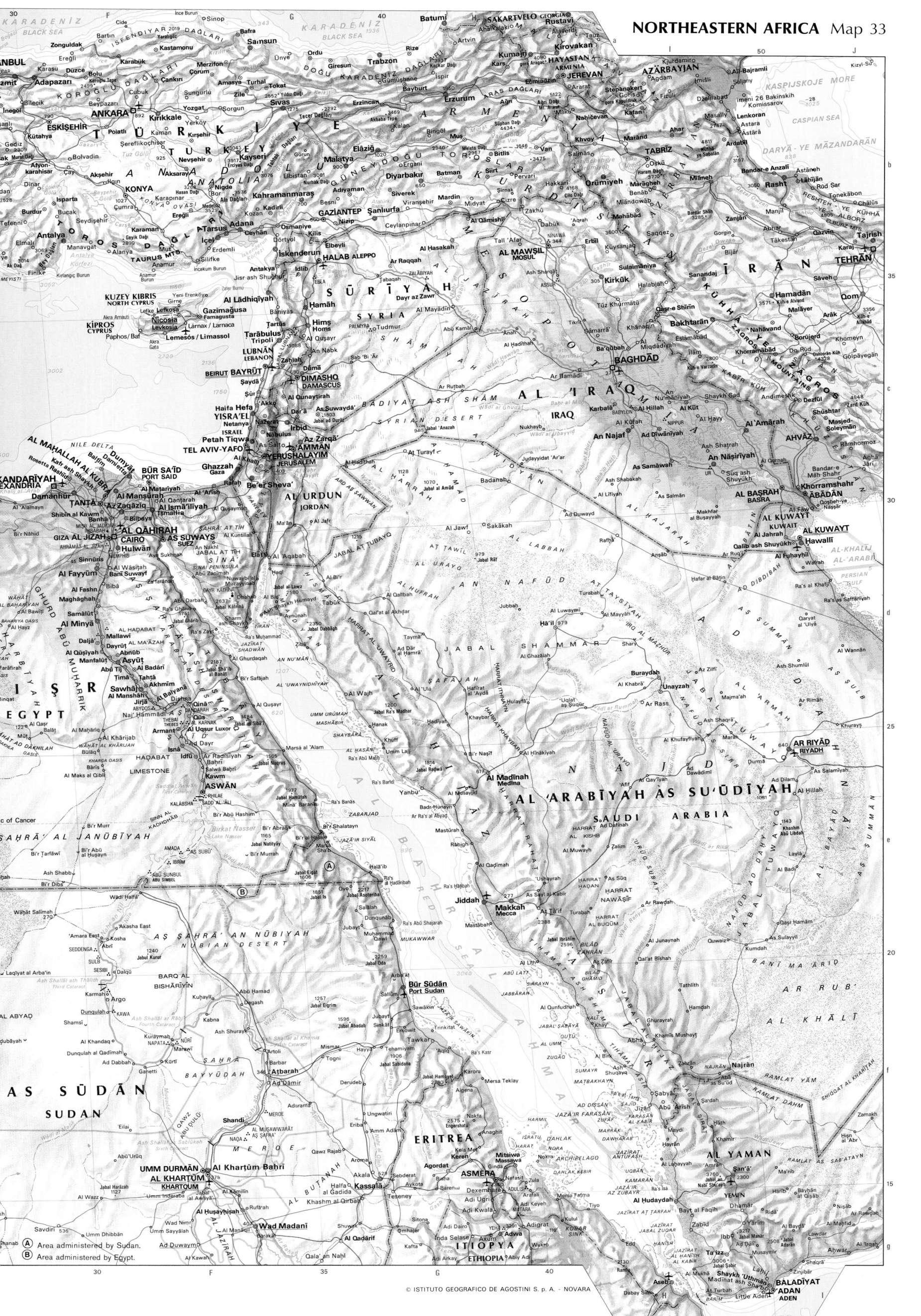

KARADENİZ
Black Sea
KARA DENİZ
Black Sea

İNCE Burun
Sinop
Bafra
Samsun
Ünye
Ordu
Giresun
Trabzon
Rize
Artvin

Batumi
SAKARTVELO GEORGIA@
Rustavi
Ahalkalaki

Kumajri
Kirovakan
HAYASTAN
JEREVAN
ARMENIA
AZÄRBAYJAN

Zonguldak
Ereğli
Karabük
Kastamonu
Çankırı
Çorum
Amasya
Turhal
Tokat

Bartın
Merzifon
Sungurlu

Düzce
Bolu

ANKARA
Kırıkkale
Yerköy
Yozgat
Sorgun

Sivas

Erzincan
Erzurum

Kars
Ağrı
Nahiçevan
Kafan

TÜRKİYE
TURKEY
ANADOLU
ANATOLIA

Kırşehir
Kayseri
Malatya
Elâzığ
Diyarbakır
Batman
Siirt

Van
Bitlis
Hakkâri

Orūmiyeh
Tabrīz

ĪRĀN
TEHRĀN

KONYA
Niğde
Kahramanmaraş
Adıyaman
Mardin
Midyat
Cizre
Zakhū

Al Qāmishlī
Dahūk

ERBİL
Kirkūk

Sanandaj
Hamadān
Qom

Adana
Tarsus
İskenderun
HALAB ALEPPO
Ar Raqqah
AL MAWSIL
MOSUL

ASSUR
Sāmarrā'
Khānaqīn
Eslāmābād

KUZEY KIBRIS
NORTH CYPRUS
KIBRIS
CYPRUS
Nicosia
Levkosía
Lemesós / Limassol

SŪRĪYAH
SYRIA
Ḥamāh
Ḥimṣ Homs

 Dayr az Zawr
PALMYRA
Tudmur
Al Mayādīn
Abū Kamāl
'Ānah

Ba'qūbah
BAGHDĀD

Bakhtarān

Tarābulus
Tripoli
An Nabk
DIMASHQ
DAMASCUS

AL 'IRĀQ

Karbalā'
An Najaf

AHVĀZ

BEIRUT BAYRŪT
LUBNĀN
LEBANON

BADIYAT ASH SHĀM
SYRIAN DESERT
IRAQ

YISRA'EL
ISRAEL
TEL AVIV-YAFO
YERUSHALAYIM
JERUSALEM

As Suwaydā'

AL KUWAYT
KUWAIT
AL KUWAYT

AL MAḤALLAH AL KUBRÁ
KANDARĪYAH
ALEXANDRIA

AL QĀHIRAH
CAIRO
GIZA AL JĪZAH

AL URDUN
JORDAN

AS SUWAYS
SUEZ

SINAI PENINSULA
SĪNĀ'

AN NAFŪD

ḤĀ'IL

JABAL SHAMMAR

AR RIYĀḌ
RIYADH

EGYPT
MIṢR

ŞAḤRĀ' AL JANŪBĪYAH

Lake Nasser
Birkat Nāṣir

NAJD
AL 'ARABĪYAH AS SU'ŪDĪYAH

Al Madīnah
Medina

SAUDI ARABIA

Yanbu'

AL ḤIJĀZ

AṢ ṢAḤRĀ' AN NŪBĪYAH
NUBIAN DESERT

ABŪ SUNBUL
ABU SIMBEL

Jiddah
Makkah
Mecca

AT TĀ'IF

RED SEA

BŪR SŪDĀN
Port Sudan

AR RUB'
AL KHĀLĪ

BARQ AL BISHĀRĪYĪN

AL ABYAḌ

AS SŪDĀN
SUDAN

NAPATA
NŪRĪ

MEROE

UMM DURMĀN
AL KHARTŪM
KHARTOUM

AL YAMAN

ERITREA

ASMERA

AL YAMAN
YEMEN
San'ā'

AL ḤUDAYDAH

ITIOPYA
ETHIOPIA

BALADĪYAT 'ADAN
ADEN

(A) Area administered by Sudan.
(B) Area administered by Egypt.

© ISTITUTO GEOGRAFICO DE AGOSTINI S. p. A. - NOVARA

181

Map 34 **WEST-CENTRAL AFRICA**

LIBERIA

COUNTIES
1 Bong
2 Cape Mount
3 Grand Bassa
4 Grand Gedeh
5 Lofa
6 Maryland
7 Montserrado
8 Nimba
9 Sinoe

CÔTE D'IVOIRE
IVORY COAST

DÉPARTEMENTS
1 Abengourou
2 Abidjan
3 Aboisso
4 Adzopé
5 Agboville
6 Biankouma
7 Bondoukou
8 Bongouanou
9 Bouaflé
10 Bouaké
11 Bouna
12 Boundiali
13 Dabakala
14 Daloa
15 Danané
16 Dimbokro
17 Divo
18 Ferkessédougou
19 Gagnoa
20 Guiglo
21 Issia
22 Katiola
23 Korhogo
24 Lakota
25 Man
26 Mankono
27 Odienné
28 Oumé
29 Sassandra
30 Séguéla
31 Soubré
32 Tengréla
33 Touba
34 Zuenoula

BURKINA FASO

DÉPARTEMENTS
1 Centre
2 Centre-Est
3 Centre-Nord
4 Centre-Ouest
5 Est
6 Hauts-Bassins
7 Komoé
8 Nord
9 Sahel
10 Sud-Ouest
11 Volta Noire

TOGO

RÉGIONS
1 Centre
2 Kara
3 Maritime
4 Plateaux
5 Savanes

BÉNIN

PROVINCES
1 Atakora
2 Atlantique
3 Borgou
4 Mono
5 Ouémé
6 Zou

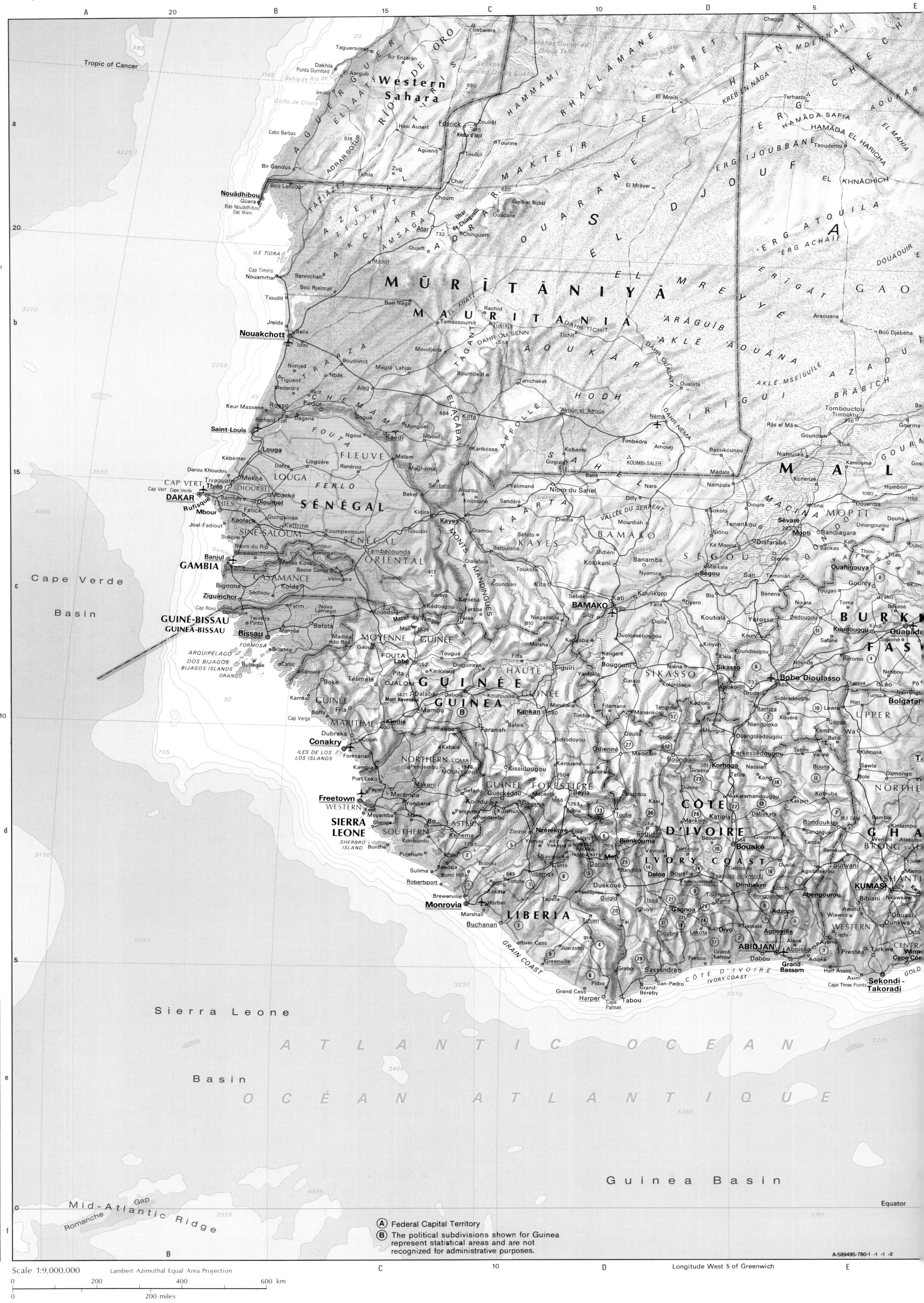

Ⓐ Federal Capital Territory

Ⓑ The political subdivisions shown for Guinea represent statistical areas and are not recognized for administrative purposes.

Scale 1:9,000,000   Lambert Azimuthal Equal Area Projection

Longitude West 5 of Greenwich

A-589495-780-1 -1 -1 -2

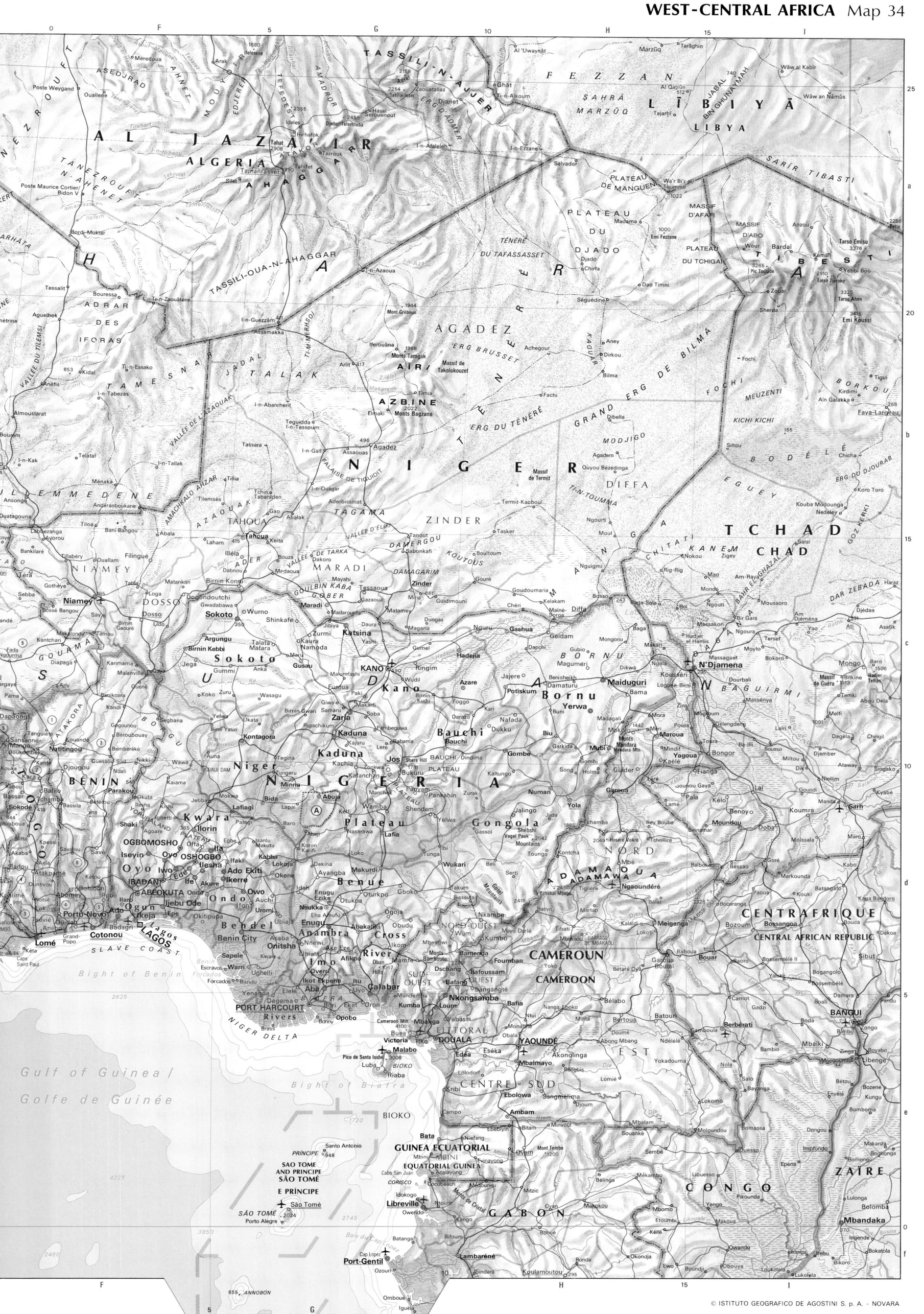

Map 35 **EAST-CENTRAL AFRICA**

Scale 1:9,000,000

Lambert Azimuthal Equal Area Projection

Longitude East 30 of Greenwich

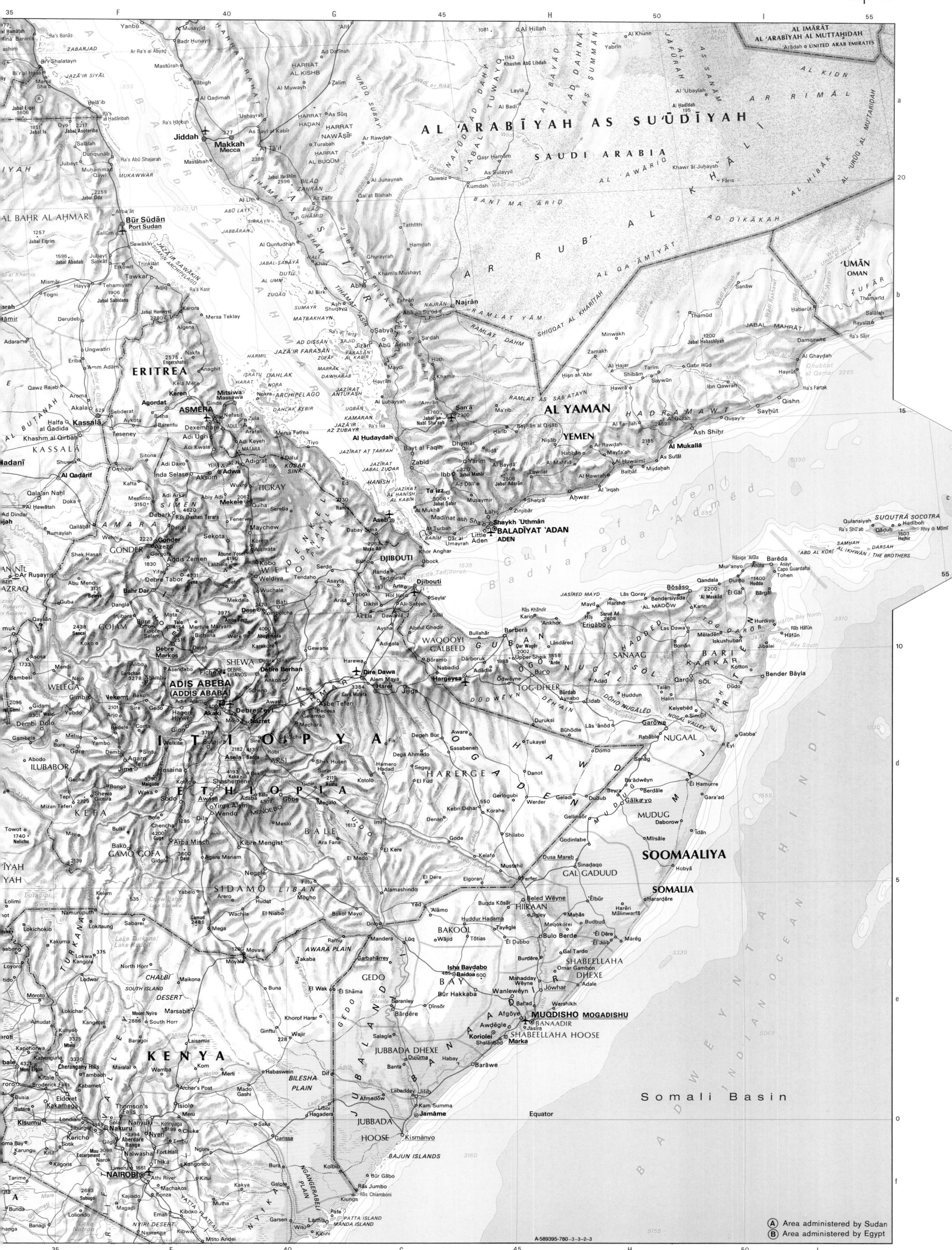

Somali Basin

A Area administered by Sudan
B Area administered by Egypt

Map 36 **EQUATORIAL AFRICA**

Scale 1:9,000,000   Lambert Azimuthal Equal Area Projection

0   200   400   600 km

0   200 miles

A-589500-780-1 -1 -1 -2

© ISTITUTO GEOGRAFICO DE AGOSTINI S. p. A. - NOVARA   **187**

Map 37 **SOUTHERN AFRICA**

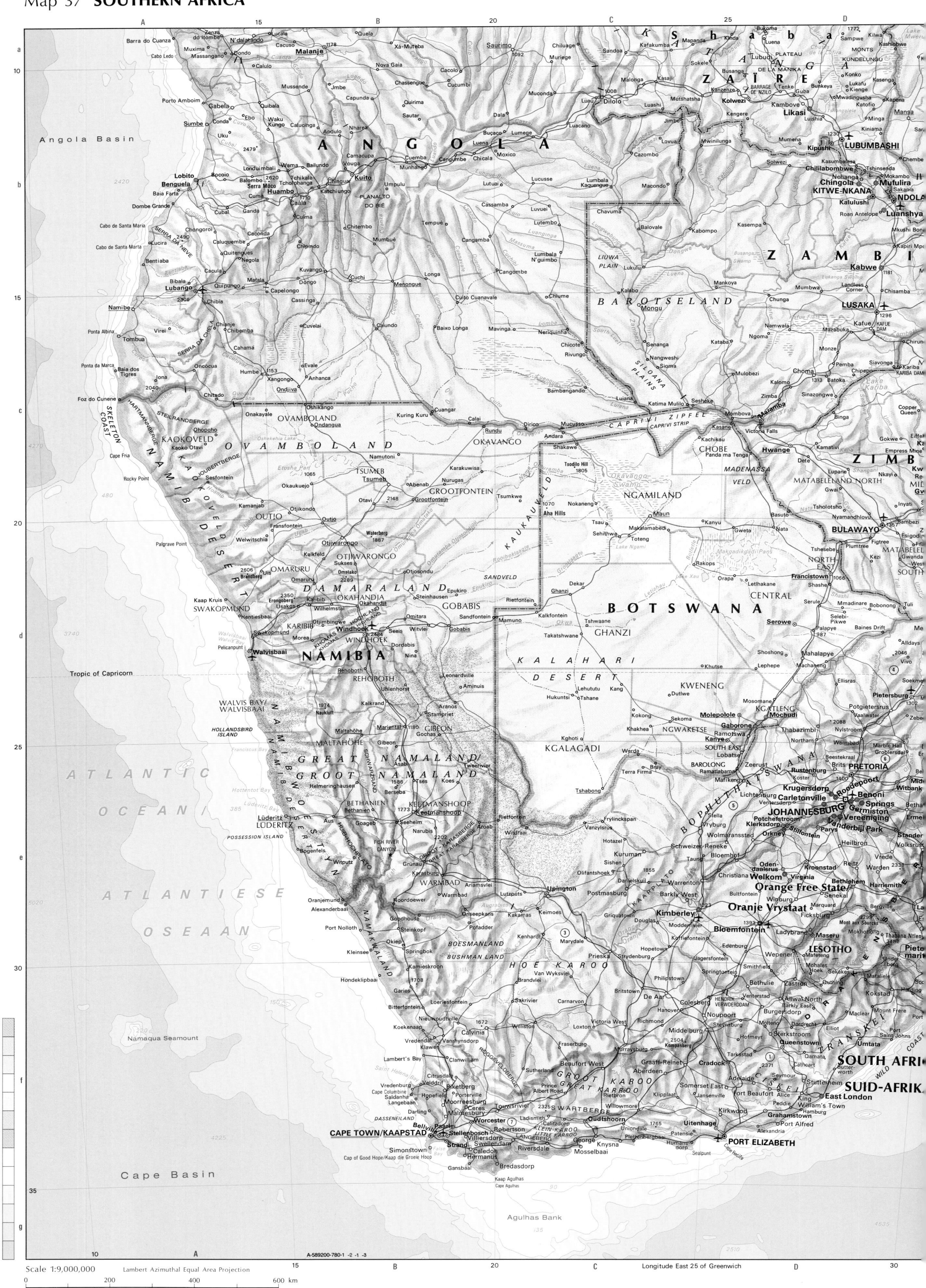

Scale 1:9,000,000   Lambert Azimuthal Equal Area Projection

Longitude East 25 of Greenwich

A-589200-780-1 -2 -1 -3

0   200   400   600 km

0   200 miles

SEYCHELLES

ALDABRA ISLANDS
WEST ISLAND · MIDDLE ISLAND
SOUTH ISLAND · ALDABRA · COSMOLEDO GROUP
ASSUMPTION ISLAND · GROUP · ASTOVE ISLAND

ARCHIPEL DES COMORES / COMORO ISLANDS

COMORES / COMOROS

Mwali · Mutsamudu
Moroni · Mayotte (France)

MADAGASCAR

MADAGASIKARA
MADAGASCAR

Mahajanga

ANTANANARIVO
ANTANANARIVO

Fianarantsoa
FIANARANTSOA

Toamasina
TOAMASINA

Antsiranana
ANTSIRANANA

MOÇAMBIQUE
MOZAMBIQUE

Beira

Quelimane

Nampula

HARARE

Blantyre

Lilongwe

MAPUTO

Richard's Bay

OCEANO ÍNDICO / OCÉAN INDIEN

INDIAN OCEAN / INDIESE OSEAAN

Natal Basin

Mozambique Plateau

Madagascar Plateau

SOUTH AFRICA
SUID-AFRIKA
MAGISTERIAL
DISTRICTS
1 Eastern Cape
2 Eastern Transvaal
3 Northern Cape
4 Northern Transvaal
5 North West
6 Pretoria-
  Witwatersrand-
  Vereeniging
7 Western Cape

SEYCHELLES ISLANDS

BIRD ISLAND · DENIS ISLAND
PRASLIN ISLAND · LA DIGUE ISLAND
SILHOUETTE ISLAND
Victoria
MAHÉ ISLAND

AFRICAN ISLANDS
REMIRE REEF
BENJAMEN · D'ARROS ISLAND
ISLAND · FOUQUET ISLAND
POIVRE ISLANDS · ÎLE DES ROCHES
ETOILE CAY · PLATTE ISLAND
BOUDEUSE CAY · MANIE LOUISE ISLAND
ÎLE DES NOEUF · ISLAND
ALPHONSE ISLAND
BIJOUTIER ISLAND · COETIVY ISLAND
SAINT FRANÇOIS · ISLAND

AMIRANTE ISLANDS

SEYCHELLES

Amirante Basin

INDIAN OCEAN

MAURITIUS

MAURITIUS
Port-Louis
Beau-Bassin · Flacq
Curepipe · Mahébourg
ÎLES MASCAREIGNES/
MASCARENE ISLANDS

Saint-Denis
Saint-Paul
Saint-Pierre · Piton des Neiges
Saint-Benoit
Saint-Joseph
Réunion
(France)

ALDABRA ISLANDS
WEST ISLAND · MIDDLE ISLAND
SOUTH ISLAND · ALDABRA · COSMOLEDO GROUP
ASSUMPTION ISLAND · GROUP · ASTOVE ISLAND

SAINT PIERRE
PROVIDENCE ISLAND
WIZARD REEF
FARQUHAR GROUP · NORTH ISLAND
GOELETTE ISLAND · SOUTH ISLAND

AGALEGA ISLANDS
(Mauritius)

Longitude East 50 of Greenwich

Map 38 **NORTH AMERICA, PHYSICAL**

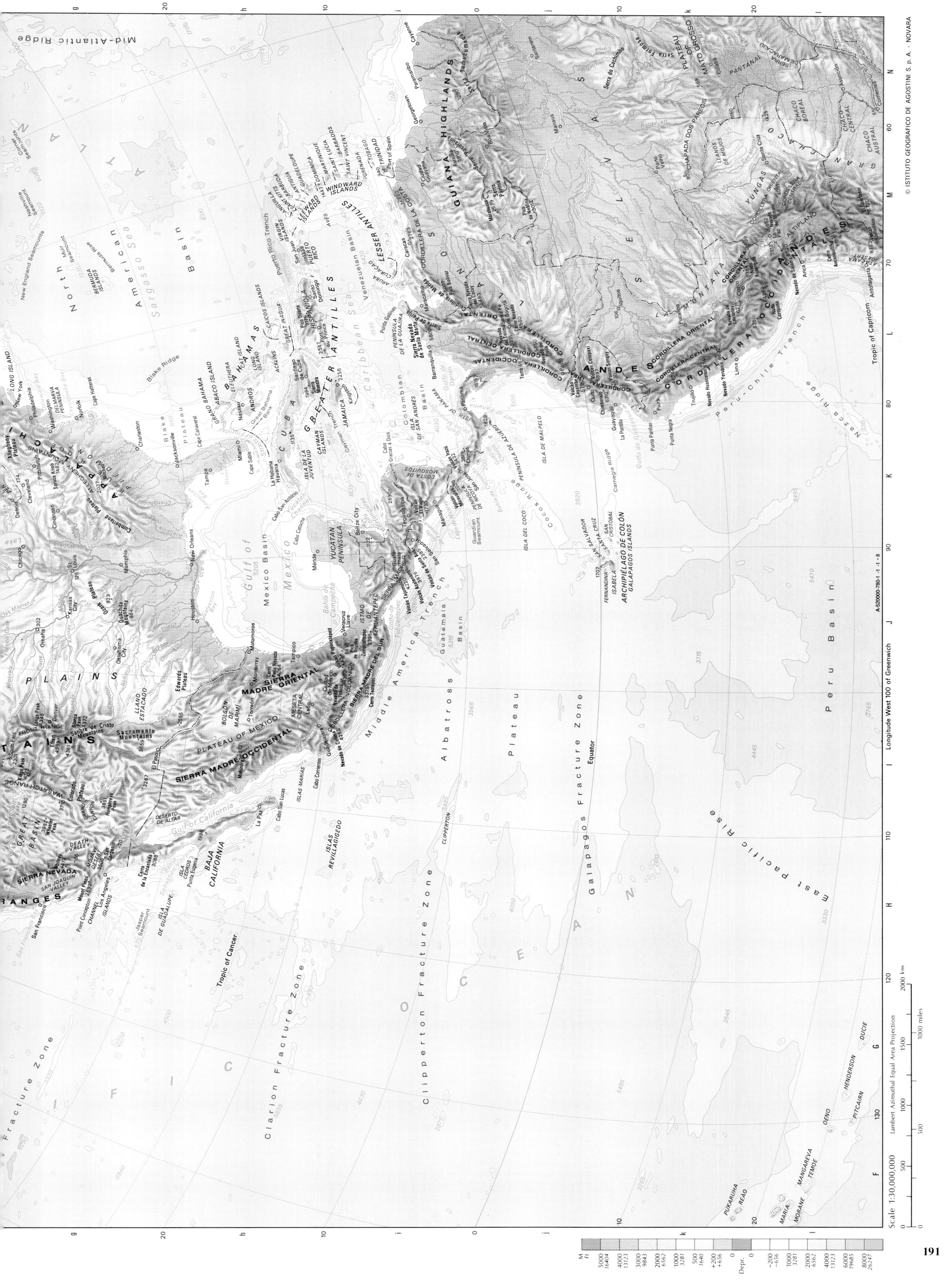

© ISTITUTO GEOGRAFICO DE AGOSTINI S. p. A. - NOVARA

Mid-Atlantic Ridge

North American Basin

Sargasso Sea

Bermuda Rise
New England Seamounts
Muir Seamount
BERMUDA ISLANDS

Blake Ridge

Long Island
New York
Philadelphia
Baltimore
DELMARVA PENINSULA
Norfolk
Cape Hatteras
Washington
ALLEGHENY PLATEAU
Pittsburgh
Cleveland
APPALACHIAN MOUNTAINS
Piedmont
BLUE RIDGE MOUNTAINS
Cumberland
Charleston
Jacksonville
Cape Canaveral
Tampa
Miami
Cape Sable

Cleveland
Chicago
St. Louis
Memphis
Des Moines
Kansas City
Omaha
Oklahoma City
Ozark Plateau
Ouachita Mountains
P L A I N S
New Orleans
Houston

M O U N T A I N S
Denver
Pikes Peak
FRONT RANGE
Sangre de Cristo Mountains
GREAT BASIN
DEATH VALLEY
SIERRA NEVADA
SAN JOAQUIN VALLEY
San Francisco
Point Conception
Los Angeles
CHANNEL ISLANDS
WASATCH RANGE
Colorado Plateau
Mount Whitney
RANGES

Edwards Plateau
LLANO ESTACADO
DESERTO DE ALTAR
BAJA CALIFORNIA
Gulf of California
La Paz
Cabo San Lucas
ISLA CEDROS
ISLA DE GUADALUPE
Punta Eugenia

Matamoros
Monterrey
Tampico
BOLSÓN DE MAPIMÍ
SIERRA MADRE ORIENTAL
MESETA CENTRAL
PLATEAU OF MEXICO
Guadalajara
León
SIERRA MADRE OCCIDENTAL
El Pacífico
Veracruz
Orizaba
Popocatépetl
ISTMO DE TEHUANTEPEC
SIERRA MADRE DEL SUR
Cabo Corrientes
ISLAS MARÍAS
ISLAS REVILLAGIGEDO

GRAND BAHAMA
ABACO ISLAND
ELEUTHERA
LONG ISLAND
B A H A M A S
ANDROS
Nassau
Great Bahama Bank
CAT ISLAND
SAN SALVADOR
ACKLINS
CAICOS ISLANDS
GREAT INAGUA

C U B A
La Habana / Havana
ISLA DE LA JUVENTUD
Cabo San Antonio
YUCATÁN CHANNEL
Cabo Catoche
Mérida
YUCATAN PENINSULA
Bahía de Campeche
Cabo San Lucas
Belize City
Gulfo de Honduras

GREATER ANTILLES
JAMAICA
Kingston
CAYMAN ISLANDS
HISPANIOLA
Santo Domingo
PUERTO RICO
San Juan
Puerto Rico Trench
VIRGIN ISLANDS
ANGUILLA
ANTIGUA
GUADELOUPE
DOMINICA
MARTINIQUE
SAINT LUCIA
SAINT VINCENT
BARBADOS
GRENADA
TOBAGO
TRINIDAD
Port of Spain
LEEWARD ISLANDS
WINDWARD ISLANDS
L E S S E R   A N T I L L E S
AVES

Caribbean Sea
Venezuelan Basin
Colombian Basin
Cayman Trench
ISLA DE SAN ANDRÉS

ARUBA
Maracaibo
Caracas
PENÍNSULA DE LA GUAJIRA
Nevada de Santa Marta
Barranquilla
Cartagena
CORDILLERA DE LA COSTA
Golfo de Darién
Gulf of Panamá
ISTHMUS OF PANAMA
COSTA DE MOSQUITOS
PENÍNSULA DE

V E N E Z U E L A
GUIANA HIGHLANDS
Georgetown
Paramaribo
Cayenne
S E L V A S
Manaus
PLATEAU MATO GROSSO
SERRA DE MATACÃU
SERRA DOS PAREIS
CHAPADA DOS PAREIS
PANTANAL
CHACO BOREAL
CHACO CENTRAL
CHACO AUSTRAL
Corrientes
Asunción
LLANOS DE MOJOS
YUNGAS
A N D E S
L A   M O N T A Ñ A
CORDILLERA OCCIDENTAL
CORDILLERA CENTRAL
CORDILLERA ORIENTAL
ALTIPLANO
Lima
Santa Cruz
Antofagasta
Peru-Chile Trench
Tropic of Capricorn

Middle America Trench
Guatemala Basin
Albatross Plateau
Clipperton Fracture Zone
Galapagos Fracture Zone
Equator
CLIPPERTON
Cocos Ridge
Carnegie Ridge
Galapagos Rise
Guardian Seamount
ISLA DEL COCO
ISLA DE MALPELO
ARCHIPIÉLAGO DE COLÓN
GALAPAGOS ISLANDS
ISABELA
FERNANDINA
SAN CRISTOBAL
SANTA CRUZ
SAN SALVADOR

Peru Basin
East Pacific Rise

P A C I F I C   O C E A N
Clarion Fracture Zone
Fracture Zone
Tropic of Cancer

PUKARUHA
REAO
MARIA
MORANE
TEMOE
MANGAREVA
OENO
HENDERSON
DUCIE
PITCAIRN

A-5000007780-1 -1 -1 -8
Longitude West 100 of Greenwich
Lambert Azimuthal Equal Area Projection
Scale 1:30,000,000

M ft
5000 16404
4000 13123
3000 9843
1000 3281
500 1640
+200 +656
0
Depr. 0
−200 −656
1000 3281
2000 6562
4000 13123
6000 19685
8000 26247

191

Map 39 **NORTH AMERICA, POLITICAL**

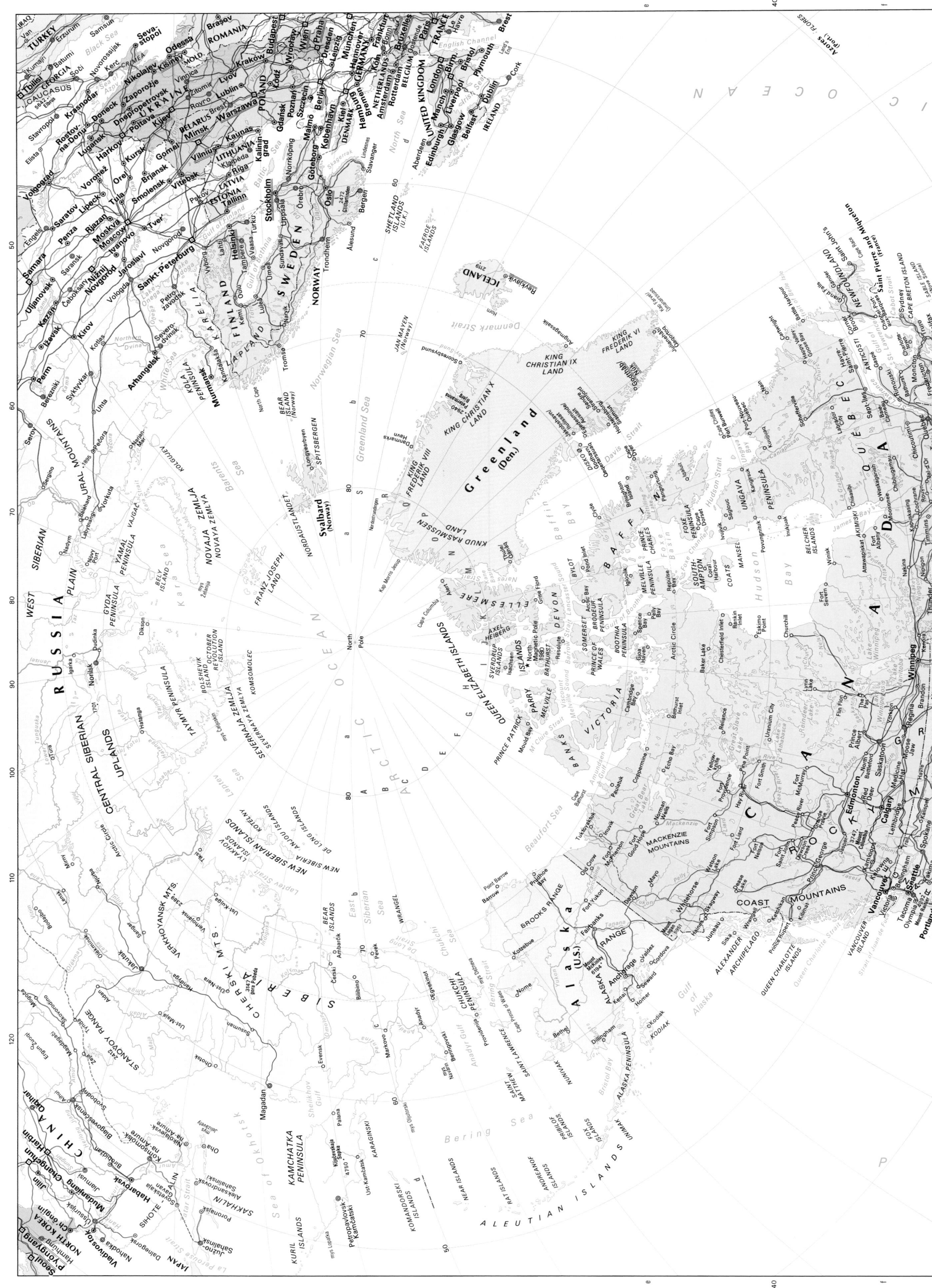

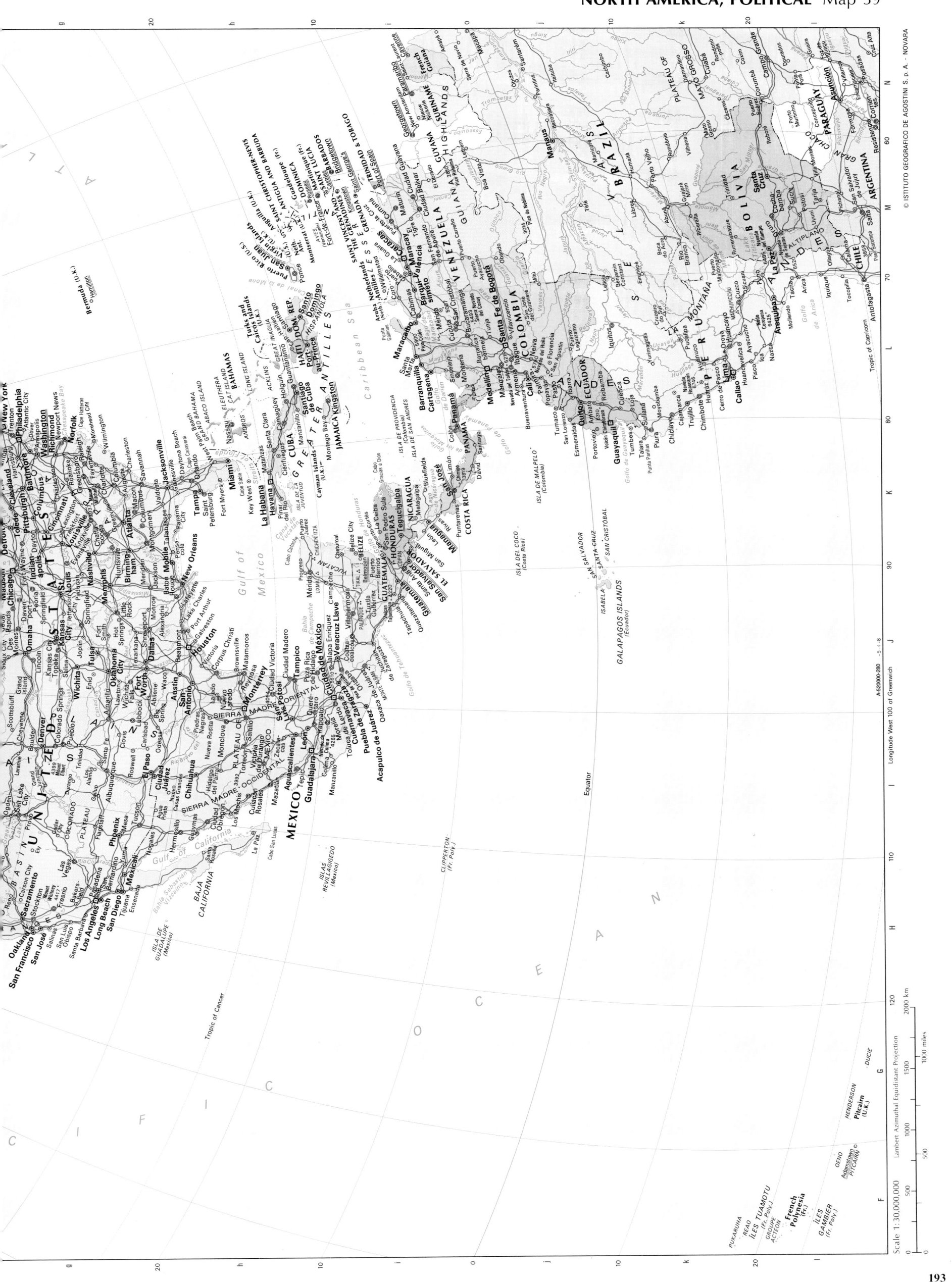

Scale 1:30,000,000

Lambert Azimuthal Equidistant Projection

Map 40 **ALASKA**

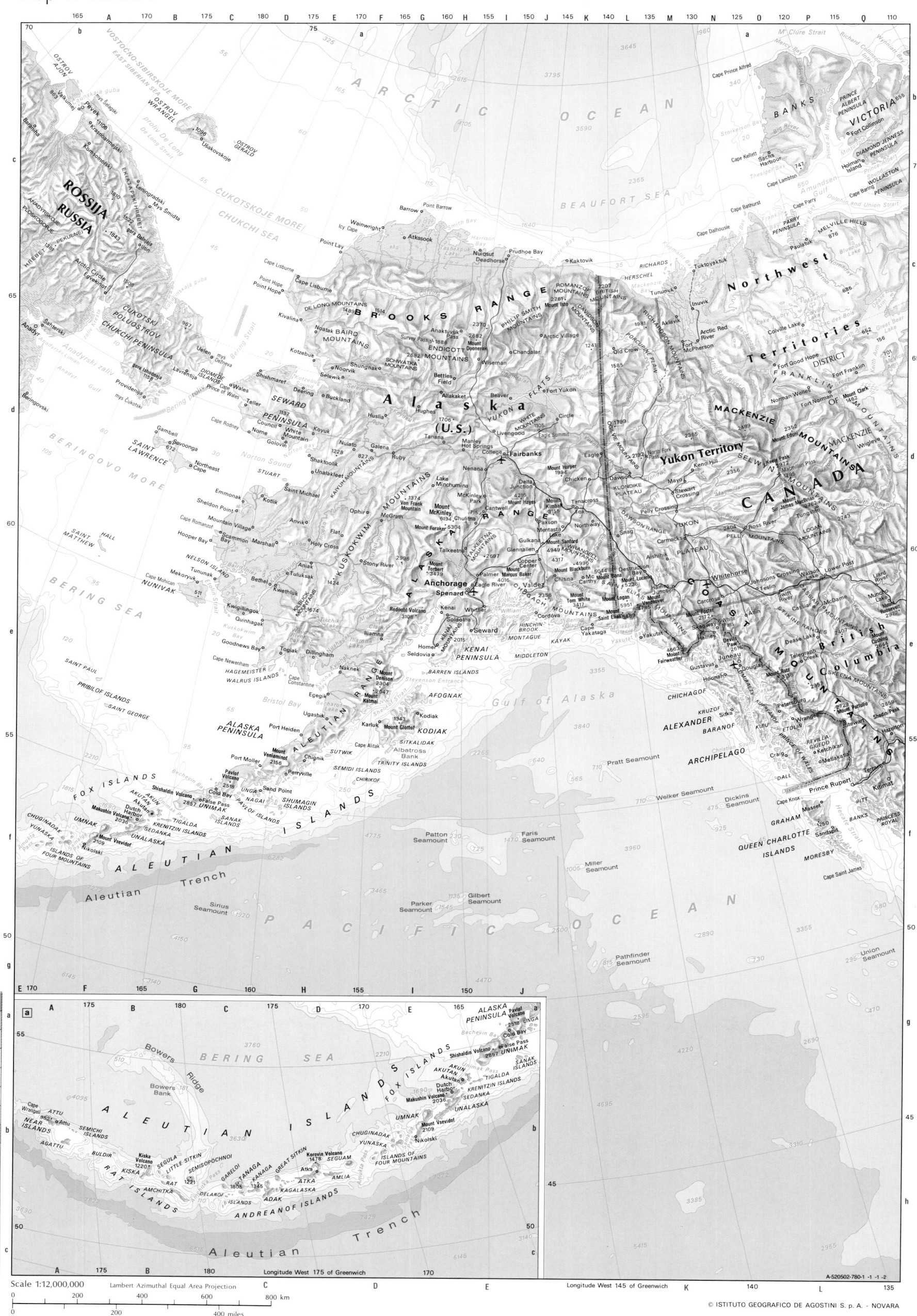

Scale 1:12,000,000   Lambert Azimuthal Equal Area Projection

Longitude West 175 of Greenwich

Longitude West 145 of Greenwich

A-520502-780-1 -1 -1 -2

© ISTITUTO GEOGRAFICO DE AGOSTINI S. p. A. - NOVARA

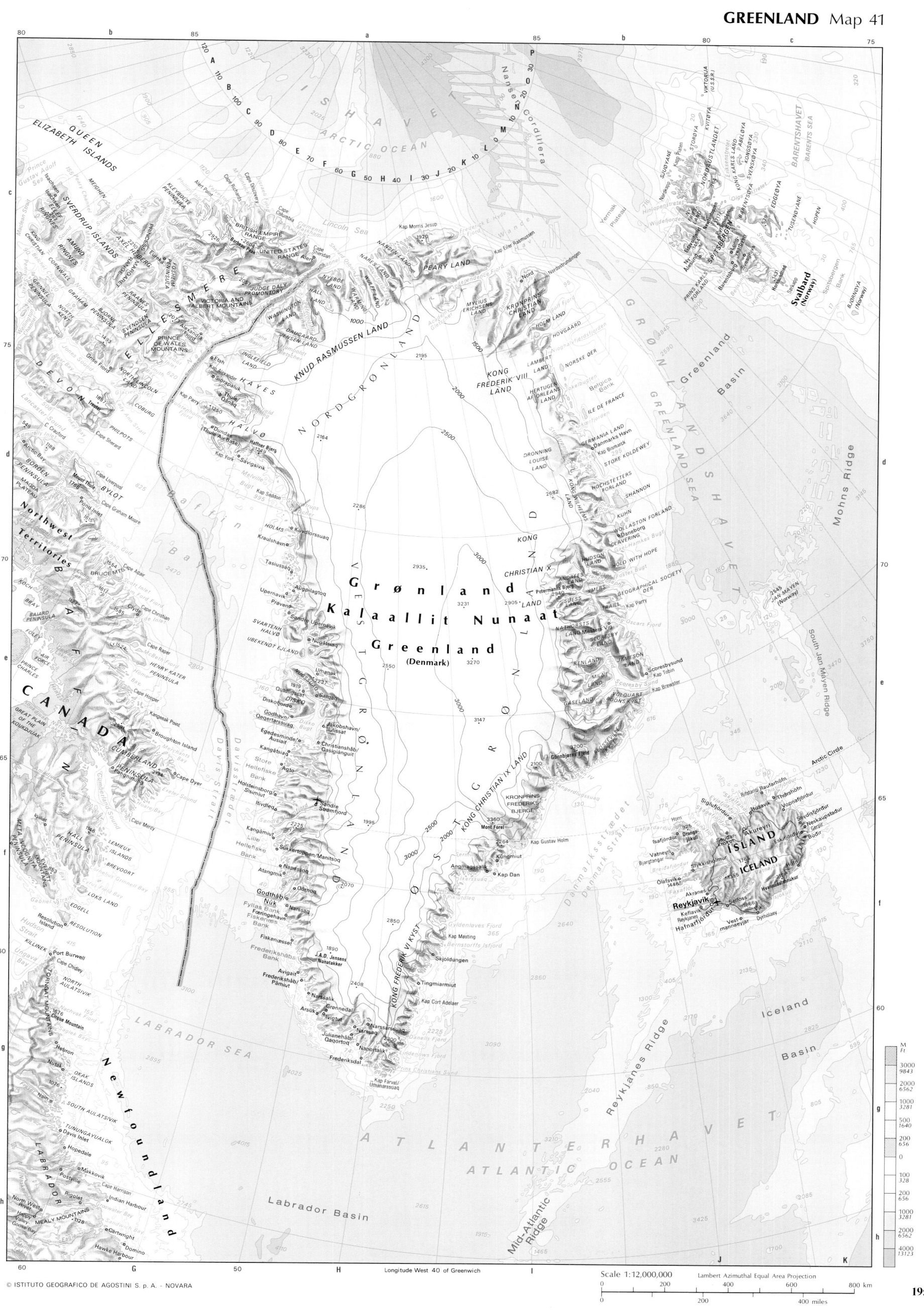

© ISTITUTO GEOGRAFICO DE AGOSTINI S. p. A. - NOVARA

Longitude West 40 of Greenwich

Scale 1:12,000,000 Lambert Azimuthal Equal Area Projection

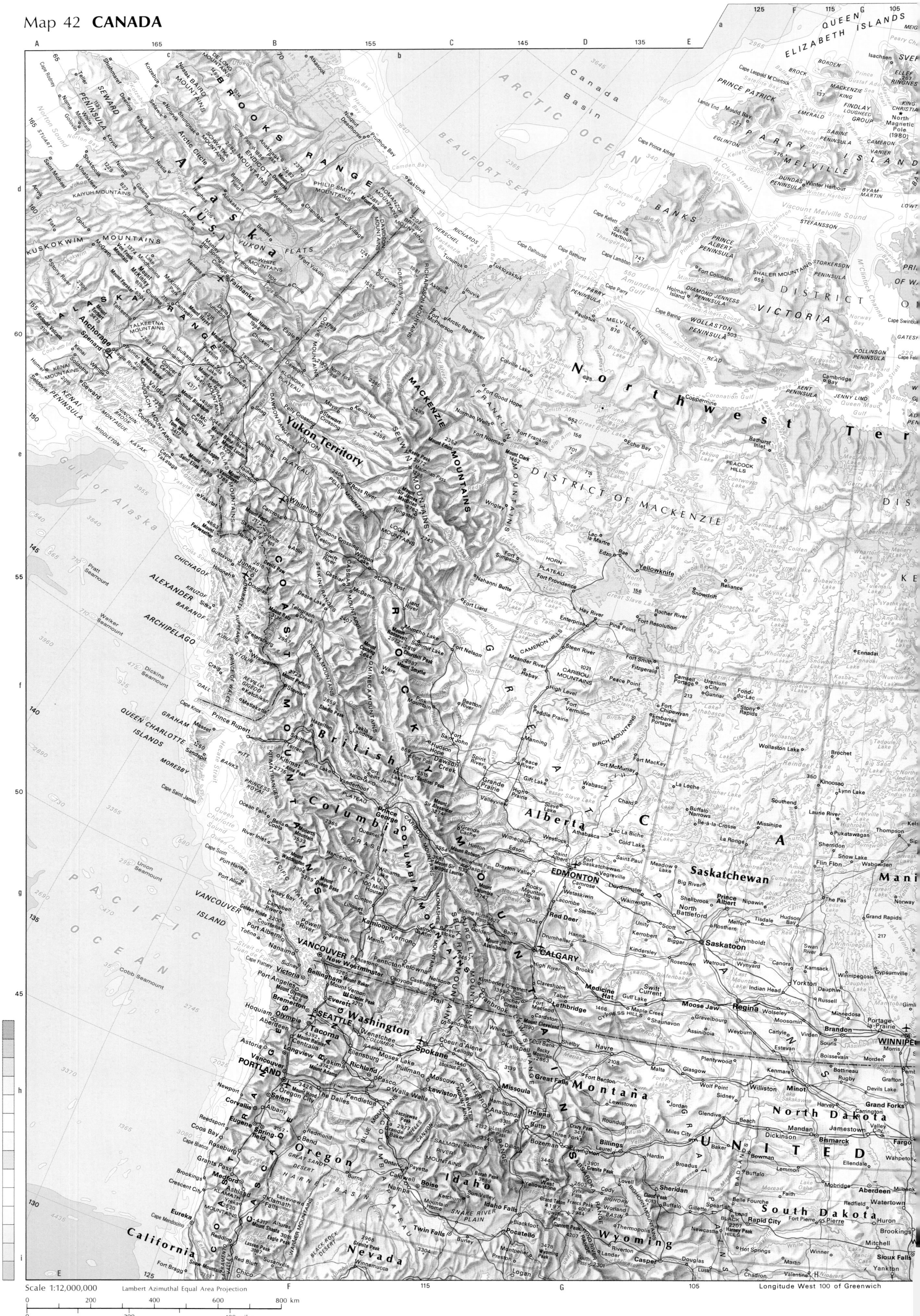

Map 42 **CANADA**

Scale 1:12,000,000   Lambert Azimuthal Equal Area Projection

Longitude West 100 of Greenwich

Map 43 **UNITED STATES**

British Columbia
Alberta
Saskatchewan
Manitoba
Washington
Oregon
Idaho
Montana
Wyoming
North Dakota
South Dakota
Nebraska
Nevada
Utah
Colorado
Kansas
California
Arizona
New Mexico
Oklahoma
Texas
Baja California
Sierra Madre Occidental
Sierra Madre Oriental
MÉXICO

VANCOUVER ISLAND
VANCOUVER
SEATTLE
Tacoma
Olympia
PORTLAND
Salem
Eugene
CALGARY
Saskatoon
Regina
WINNIPEG
Spokane
Missoula
Helena
Butte
Great Falls
Billings
Bismarck
Fargo
Grand Forks
Minot
Aberdeen
Boise
Idaho Falls
Pocatello
Twin Falls
Casper
Cheyenne
Rapid City
Sioux Falls
OMAHA
Lincoln
Reno
Carson City
SACRAMENTO
SAN FRANCISCO
OAKLAND
SAN JOSE
Stockton
Modesto
Fresno
Salt Lake City
Provo
Ogden
DENVER
Colorado Springs
Pueblo
Grand Junction
Wichita
Salina
Dodge City
Garden City
Las Vegas
LOS ANGELES
Long Beach
Pasadena
San Bernardino
Riverside
Santa Barbara
SAN DIEGO
Tijuana
MEXICALI
Yuma
PHOENIX
Mesa
Tucson
Flagstaff
Albuquerque
Santa Fe
Las Vegas
Amarillo
Lubbock
OKLAHOMA CITY
Roswell
EL PASO
CIUDAD JUÁREZ
FORT WORTH
Odessa
Midland
San Angelo
AUSTIN
SAN ANTONIO
Waco
Temple
Corpus Christi
Laredo
Nuevo Laredo
Brownsville
Matamoros
MONTERREY
Saltillo
Torreón
CHIHUAHUA
Hermosillo
Guaymas
Ciudad Obregón
Los Mochis
Culiacán
Mazatlán
La Paz
Durango
Aguascalientes
SAN LUIS POTOSÍ
Ciudad Victoria
TAMPICO
León
GUADALAJARA
Irapuato
Querétaro
Morelia
CIUDAD DE MÉXICO
MEXICO CITY
PUEBLA DE ZARAGOZA
VERACRUZ
Colima
Puerto Vallarta

PACIFIC OCEAN
OCÉANO PACÍFICO
GOLFO DE CALIFORNIA
Tropic of Cancer
Clarion Fracture Zone

ROCKY MOUNTAINS
GREAT BASIN
COLUMBIA PLATEAU
SNAKE RIVER PLAIN
COLORADO PLATEAU
MOJAVE DESERT
DEATH VALLEY
GRAND CANYON
SIERRA NEVADA
GREAT SALT LAKE
LLANO ESTACADO
EDWARDS PLATEAU

M
Ft
5000
16404
4000
13123
3000
9843
2000
6562
1000
3281
500
1640
+ 200
+656
Depr.
0
0
− 100
−328
200
656
1000
3281
2000
6562
4000
13123
6000
19685
8000
26247

Scale 1:12,000,000
Lambert Azimuthal Equidistant Projection
0   200   400   600   800 km
0   200   400 miles
Longitude West 100 of Greenwich

Map 44

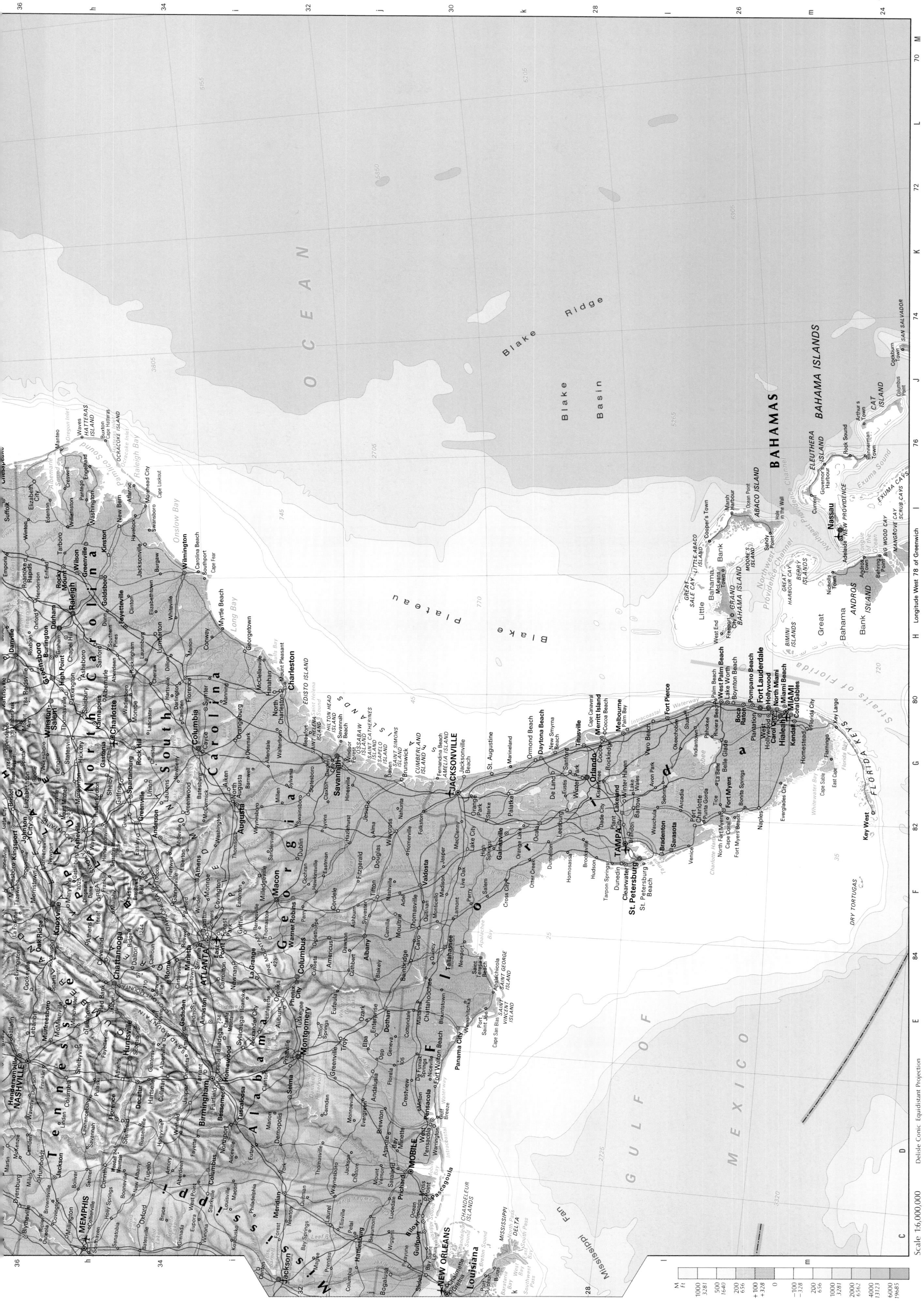

O C E A N

Blake Ridge

Blake Basin

Blake Plateau

BAHAMAS

BAHAMA ISLANDS

ABACO ISLAND

ELEUTHERA

ANDROS

Nassau NEW PROVIDENCE

CAT ISLAND

SAN SALVADOR

Straits of Florida

GULF OF MEXICO

FLORIDA KEYS

DRY TORTUGAS

MISSISSIPPI DELTA

CHANDELEUR ISLANDS

HATTERAS ISLAND

Tennessee

North Carolina

South Carolina

Georgia

Alabama

Mississippi

Louisiana

Florida

APPALACHIAN

MEMPHIS

NASHVILLE

ATLANTA

BIRMINGHAM

MOBILE

NEW ORLEANS

MIAMI

TAMPA

JACKSONVILLE

Charlotte

Raleigh

Columbia

Charleston

Savannah

Montgomery

Knoxville

Chattanooga

Macon

Columbus

Tallahassee

Orlando

St. Petersburg

Fort Lauderdale

Key West

Pensacola

Greensboro

Winston-Salem

Durham

Wilmington

Myrtle Beach

Daytona Beach

West Palm Beach

Longitude West 78 of Greenwich

© ISTITUTO GEOGRAFICO DE AGOSTINI S. p. A. - NOVARA

Scale 1:6,000,000

Delisle Conic Equidistant Projection

400 km

200 miles

Map 45

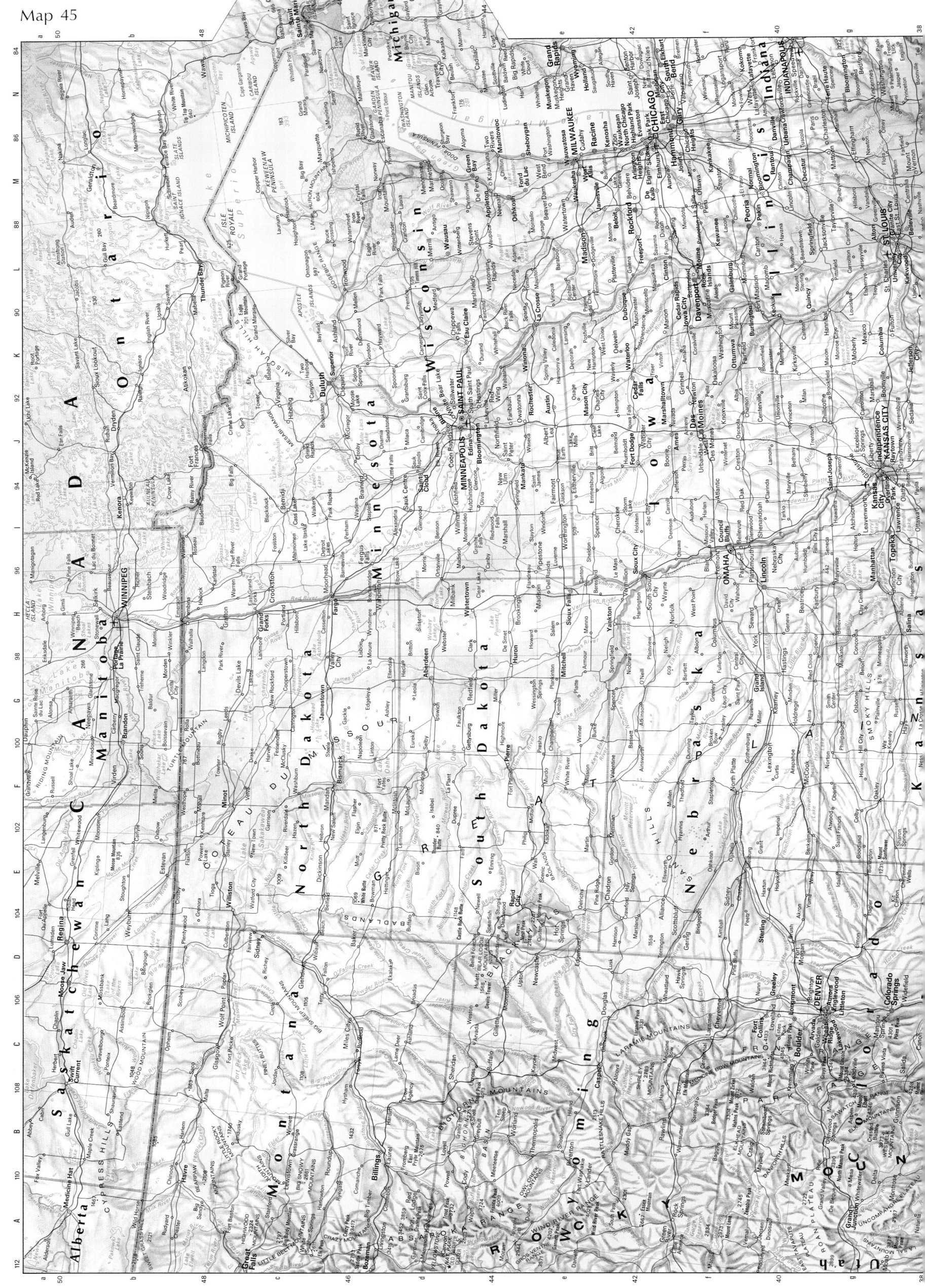

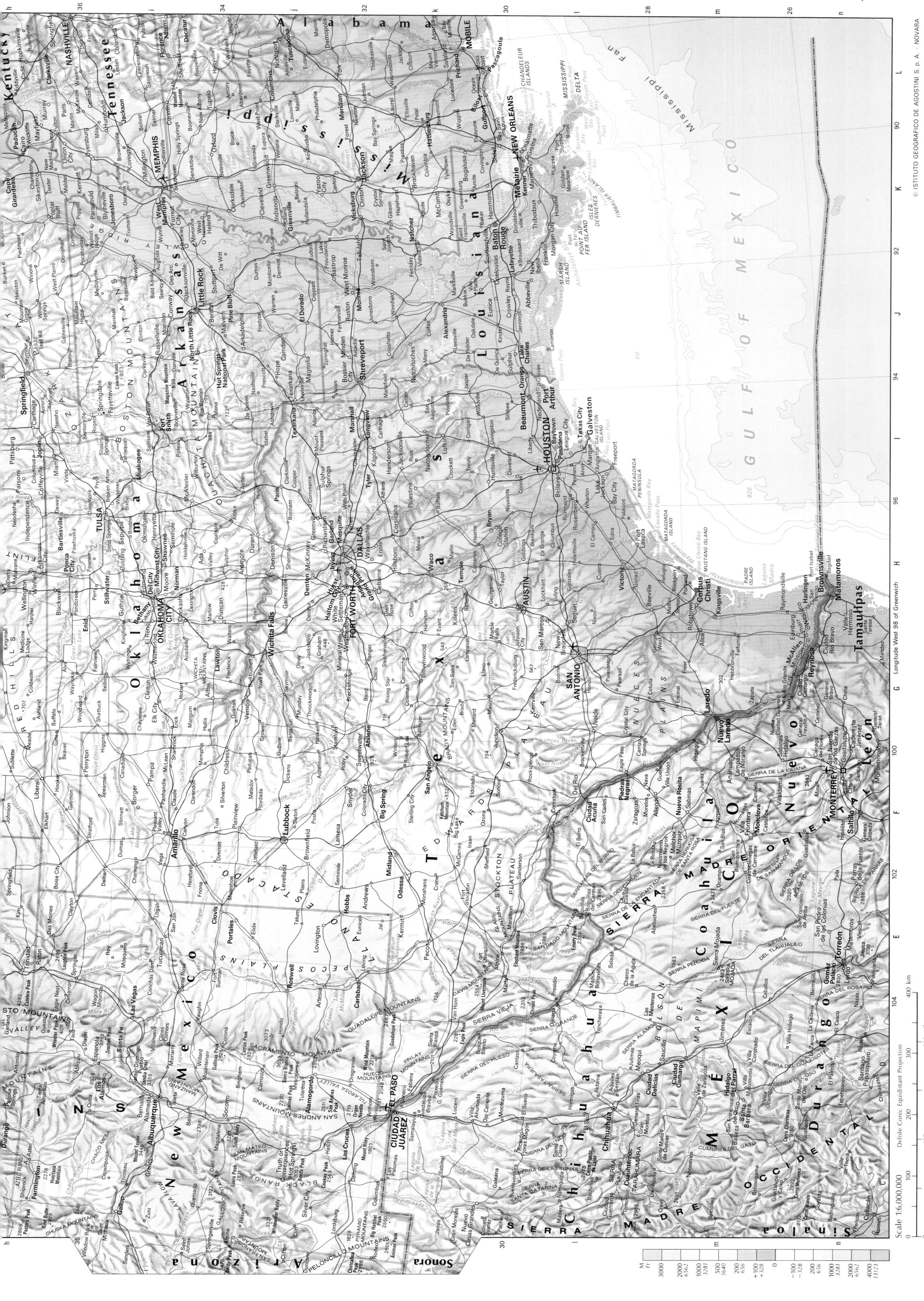

GULF OF MEXICO

Scale 1:6,000,000

Delisle Conic Equidistant Projection

Longitude West 98 of Greenwich

© ISTITUTO GEOGRAFICO DE AGOSTINI S. p. A. - NOVARA

400 km

200 miles

Map 46 **WESTERN UNITED STATES**

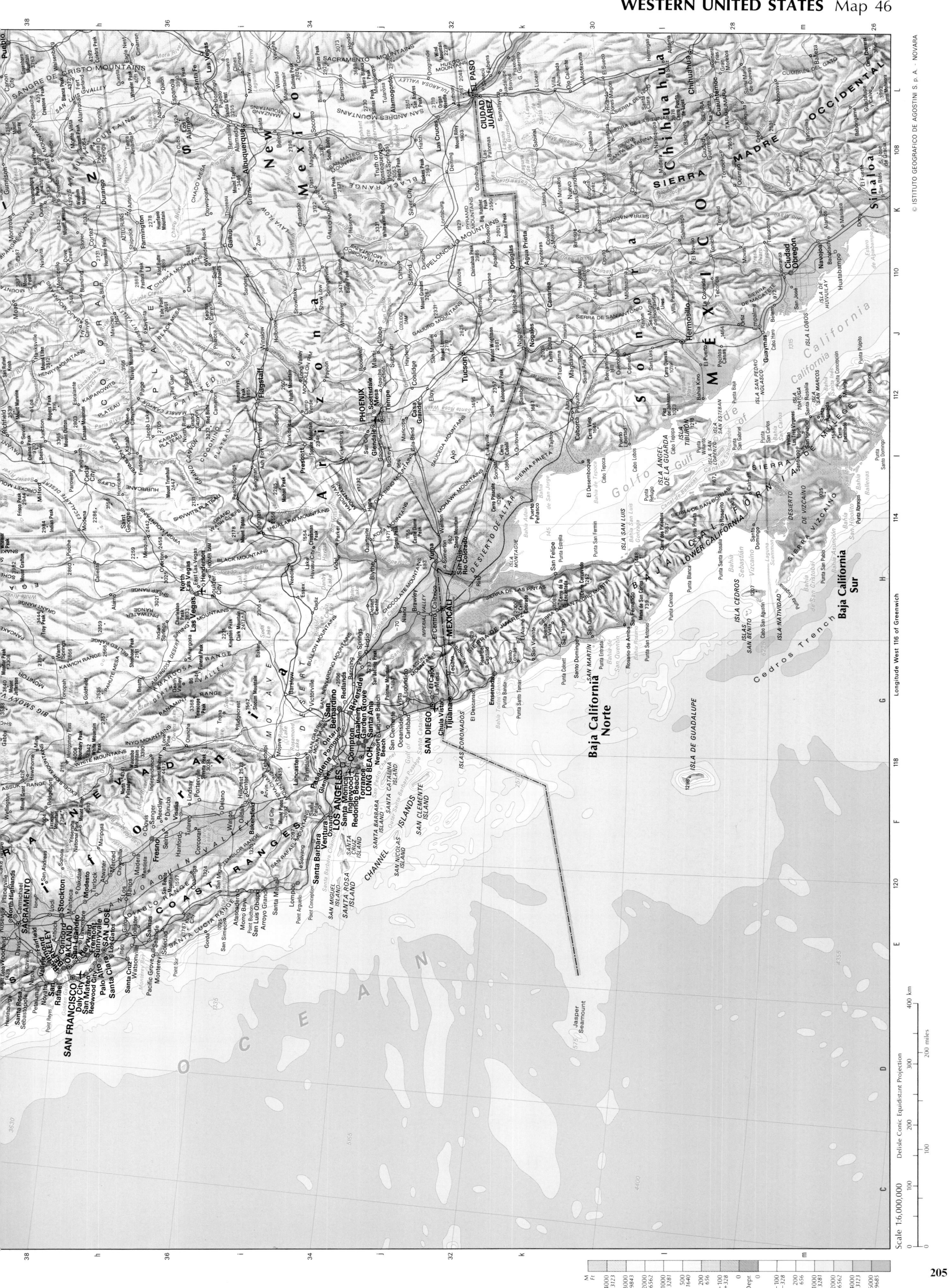

Scale 1:6,000,000

Delisle Conic Equidistant Projection

Longitude West 116 of Greenwich

Map 47 **MIDDLE AMERICA**

MEXICO
ESTADOS

D.F. Distrito Federal
1 Aguascalientes
2 Baja California Norte
3 Baja California Sur
4 Campeche
5 Coahuila
6 Colima
7 Chiapas
8 Chihuahua
9 Durango
10 Guanajuato
11 Guerrero
12 Hidalgo
13 Jalisco
14 Mexico
15 Michoacán
16 Morelos
17 Nayarit
18 Nuevo León
19 Oaxaca
20 Puebla
21 Querétaro
22 Quintana Roo
23 San Luis Potosí
24 Sinaloa
25 Sonora
26 Tabasco
27 Tamaulipas
28 Tlaxcala
29 Veracruz
30 Yucatán
31 Zacatecas

M ft	
5000 16404	
4000 13123	
3000 9843	
2000 6562	
1000 3281	
500 1640	
+200 +656	
Depr.	
−100 −328	
200 656	
1000 3281	
2000 6562	
4000 13123	
6000 19685	
8000 26247	

Scale 1:12,000,000
Lambert Azimuthal Equal Area Projection

0   200   400   600   800 km
0   200   400 miles

A-530000-780-1 -1 -1 -3

Longitude West 90 of Greenwich

San Diego A 116 Brawley 1155·114 966 112 B Maricopa D 110 E 108 F 106 G 104 10

California El Cajon El Centro Castle Dome 593 Superior Casa Grande Coolidge Hayden Duncan Silver City Cookes Peak 2511 Hobbs Artesia Seminole

Tijuana Chula Vista Yuma Gila Bend 862 Eloy San Manuel 2331 Mount Graham Lordsburg Deming 1829 Las Cruces 2719 Carlsbad Loving Eunice Andrews

MEXICALI Tecate Somerton Wellton MOHAWK MOUNTAINS SAUCEDA Tucson 2825 Benson Chiricahua Peak PYRAMID MOUNTAINS Columbus Mount Riley EL PASO Guadalupe Peak 2667 UNITED

San Luis Río Colorado Sheep Mountain Sells 2357 Babóquivari Peak Tombstone Bisbee Douglas CIUDAD JUÁREZ Fabens Kermit Monahans

Ensenada Cerro Pinacate 1206 Sonoita Lukeville Nogales Nogales Agua Prieta Samalayuca Guadalupe Odessa

DESIERTO DE ALTAR Quitovac Sásabe Cananea Fronteras Galeana Pecos River

Santo Tomás El Álamo Tajito Cerro Cíbuta Colonia Morelos Van Horn Fort Davis

Baja California Norte Cerro Colorado Caborca Pitiquito Magdalena Imuris Santa Ana Nuevo Casas Grandes Ojo Caliente Marathon

San Felipe Puerto Peñasco Bahía Adair Benjamin Hill Cumpas Moctezuma Buenaventura Flores Magón El Sueco Sanderson

ISLA TIBURÓN Hermosillo Sabuaripa Madera Namiquipa Chihuahua Cerro Puerto de Lajas Aldama Trincheras La Cuesta

ISLA ÁNGEL DE LA GUARDA Bahía Kino El Novillo SIERRA Cuauhtémoc TARAHUMARA Ciudad Delicias BOLSÓN DE MAPIMÍ Coahuila

ISLA CEDROS Guaymas Ciudad Obregón Chínipas Temores Hidalgo del Parral Jiménez SIERRA MOJADA

Baja California Sur Santa Rosalía Navojoa Álamos ALTIPLANICIE MEXICANA Santa Bárbara Villa Matamoros Torreón Gómez Palacio

Mulegé Huatabampo Masiaca Choix El Fuerte Guadalupe Calvo Durango Zacatecas

La Paz CULIACÁN ROSALES El Dorado Mazatlán Victoria de Durango Aguascalientes

Tropic of Cancer Todos Santos San José del Cabo Cabo San Lucas Tepic Nayarit GUADALAJARA

OCÉANO PACÍFICO ISLAS MARÍAS ISLA ISABELA Puerto Vallarta Jalisco Colima

ISLAS REVILLAGIGEDO (Mexico) ISLA SOCORRO ISLA SAN BENEDICTO ISLA CLARIÓN ISLA ROCA PARTIDA Colima Michoacán

PACIFIC OCEAN

Mathematicians Seamount

Scale 1:6,000,000   Delisle Conic Equidistant Projection
0   100   200   300   400 km
0   100   200 miles

208

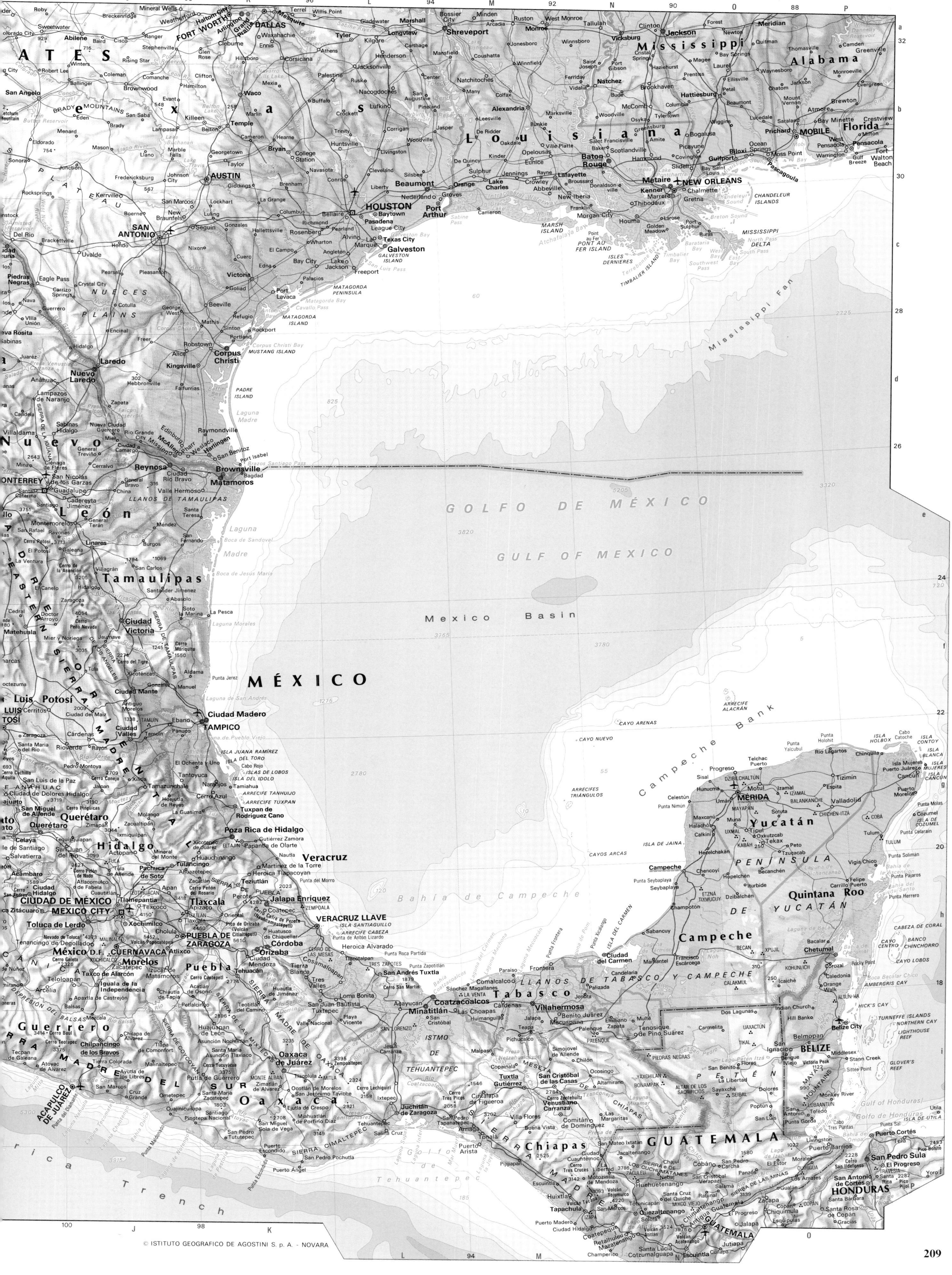

MEXICO

Texas

Mississippi
Alabama
Louisiana
Florida

FORT WORTH
DALLAS
Shreveport
Jackson
Meridian
MOBILE
Pensacola

AUSTIN
SAN ANTONIO
HOUSTON
Galveston
Port Arthur
Lake Charles
Baton Rouge
NEW ORLEANS

Corpus Christi
Laredo
Nuevo Laredo

Brownsville
Matamoros
Reynosa
MONTERREY

Nuevo León
Tamaulipas
Ciudad Victoria

GOLFO DE MÉXICO
GULF OF MEXICO

Mexico Basin

Luis Potosí
SAN LUIS POTOSÍ
Ciudad Madero
TAMPICO

Campeche Bank

Querétaro
Hidalgo
Pachuca de Soto
Poza Rica de Hidalgo
Veracruz

MÉRIDA
Yucatán
PENÍNSULA DE YUCATÁN
Cancún
Quintana Roo

CIUDAD DE MÉXICO
MEXICO CITY
México D.F.
Toluca de Lerdo
CUERNAVACA
Morelos
Tlaxcala
Jalapa Enríquez
PUEBLA DE ZARAGOZA
Puebla
Córdoba
Orizaba
VERACRUZ LLAVE

Guerrero
ACAPULCO DE JUÁREZ
Chilpancingo de los Bravos
Oaxaca de Juárez
Oaxaca

Campeche
Ciudad del Carmen
Chetumal
LLANOS DE TABASCO Y CAMPECHE
Tabasco
Coatzacoalcos
Minatitlán
Villahermosa

ISTMO DE TEHUANTEPEC

San Cristóbal de las Casas
Tuxtla Gutiérrez
Chiapas

BELIZE
Belize City
Belmopan

GUATEMALA
GUATEMALA

HONDURAS
San Pedro Sula

© ISTITUTO GEOGRAFICO DE AGOSTINI S.p.A - NOVARA

209

Map 49 **CENTRAL AMERICA AND WESTERN CARIBBEAN**

UNITED STATES
Florida

GOLFO DE MÉXICO

GULF OF MEXICO

CUBA

LA HABANA
HAVANA

MÉXICO

Yucatán
PENÍNSULA
Quintana Roo
DE YUCATÁN
YUCATÁN
PENÍNSULA
Campeche

Cayman Islands
(U.K.)

Tabasco

Chiapas

GUATEMALA

BELIZE

PETÉN

HONDURAS

LA MOSQUITIA

GUATEMALA

EL SALVADOR

SAN SALVADOR

TEGUCIGALPA

NICARAGUA

SAN ANDRÉS
Y PROVIDENCIA
(Colombia)

OCÉANO PACÍFICO

MANAGUA

SAN JOSÉ

COSTA RICA

PANAMÁ

PACIFIC OCEAN

COSTA RICA

ISTMO DE PANAMÁ
ISTHMUS OF
PANAMA

PANAMÁ

M
Ft
5000
16404
4000
13123
3000
9843
2000
6562
1000
3281
500
1640
200
656
+100
+328
Depr.
0
-100
-328
200
656
1000
3281
2000
6562
4000
13123
6000
19685
8000
26247

Scale 1:6,000,000   Delisle Conic Equidistant Projection

0   100   200   300   400 km

0   100   200 miles

CUBA
PROVINCIAS
1 Camagüey
2 Ciego de Avila
3 Cienfuegos
4 Ciudad de la Habana
5 Granma
6 Guantánamo
7 Holguín
8 La Habana
9 Las Tunas
10 Matanzas
11 Pinar del Río
12 Sancti Spíritus
13 Santiago de Cuba
14 Villaclara

BELIZE
DISTRICTS
1 Belize
2 Cayo
3 Corozal
4 Orange Walk
5 Stann Creek
6 Toledo

GUATEMALA
DEPARTAMENTOS
1 Alta Verapaz
2 Baja Verapaz
3 Chimaltenango
4 Chiquimula
5 El Progreso
6 Escuintla
7 Guatemala
8 Huehuetenango
9 Izabal
10 Jalapa
11 Jutiapa
12 Petén
13 Quezaltenango
14 Quiché
15 Retalhuleu
16 Sacatepéquez
17 San Marcos
18 Santa Rosa
19 Sololá
20 Suchitepéquez
21 Totonicapán
22 Zacapa

HONDURAS
DEPARTAMENTOS
1 Atlántida
2 Choluteca
3 Colón
4 Comayagua
5 Copán
6 Cortés
7 El Paraíso
8 Francisco Morazán
9 Gracias a Dios
10 Intibucá
11 Islas de la Bahía
12 La Paz
13 Lempira
14 Ocotepeque
15 Olancho
16 Santa Bárbara
17 Valle
18 Yoro

NICARAGUA
DEPARTAMENTOS
1 Boaco
2 Carazo
3 Chinandega
4 Chontales
5 Estelí
6 Granada
7 Jinotega
8 León
9 Madriz
10 Managua
11 Masaya
12 Matagalpa
13 Nueva Segovia
14 Río San Juan
15 Rivas
16 Zelaya

COSTA RICA
PROVINCIAS
1 Alajuela
2 Cartago
3 Guanacaste
4 Heredia
5 Limón
6 Puntarenas
7 San José

PANAMÁ
PROVINCIAS
1 Bocas del Toro
2 Chiriquí
3 Coclé
4 Colón
5 Darién
6 Herrera
7 Los Santos
8 Panamá
9 San Blas
10 Veraguas

ATLANTIC OCEAN
BAHAMAS
BAHAMA ISLANDS
Tropic of Cancer
Turks and Caicos Islands (U.K.)
HAÏTI
HISPANIOLA
SANTIAGO DE CUBA
SANTO DOMINGO
PORT-AU-PRINCE
REPÚBLICA DOMINICANA
DOMINICAN REPUBLIC
Puerto Rico (U.S.)
GREATER ANTILLES
MAYORES
CARIBBEAN SEA
CARIBE / MAR DE LAS ANTILLAS
Venezuelan Basin
Colombian Basin
Netherlands Antilles
Nederlandse Antillen
LESSER ANTILLES
ANTILLAS MENORES
COLOMBIA
VENEZUELA
CARACAS
MARACAIBO
CARTAGENA
BARRANQUILLA

© ISTITUTO GEOGRAFICO DE AGOSTINI S.p.A. - NOVARA

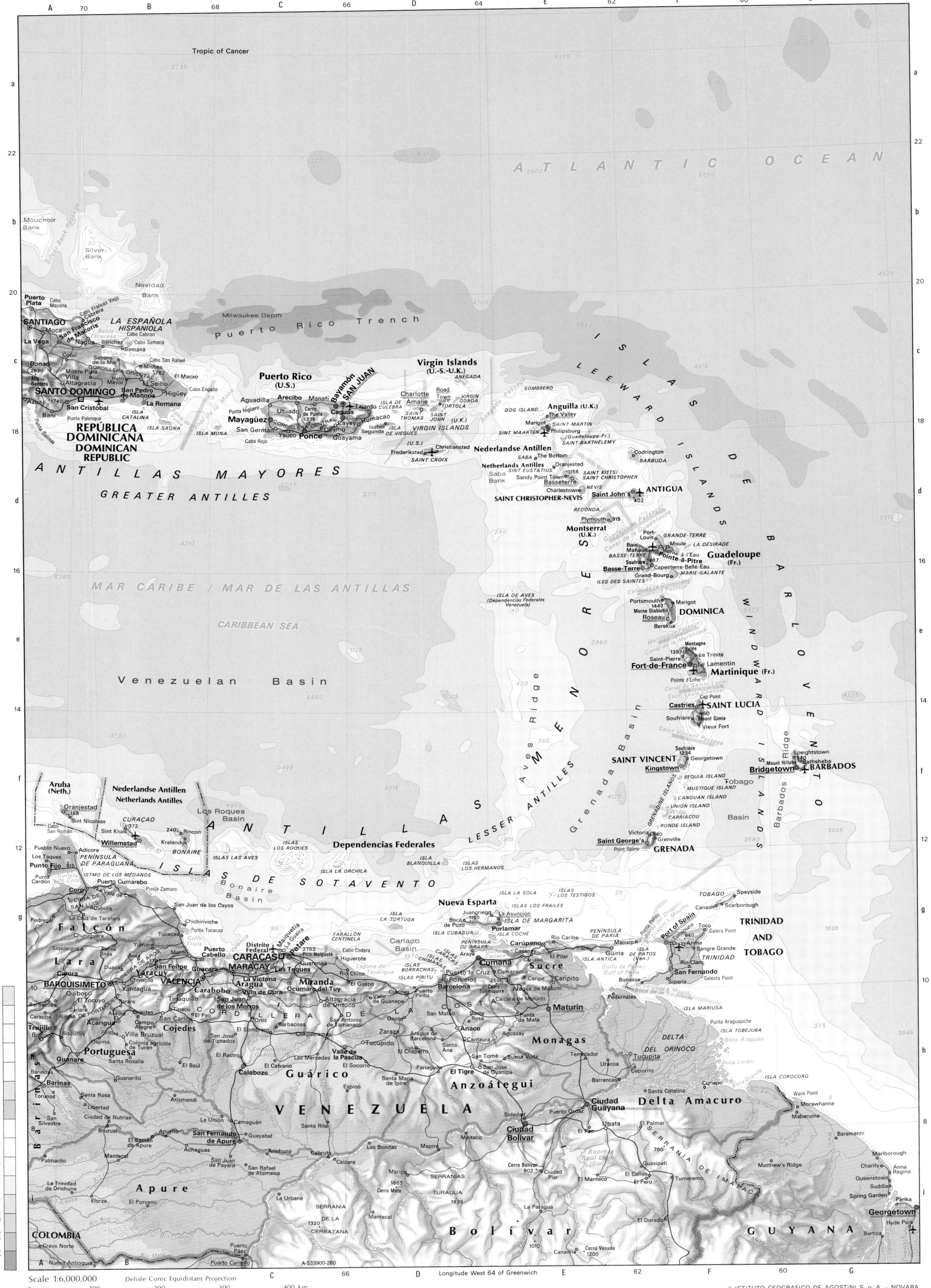

Map 50 EASTERN CARIBBEAN

ATLANTIC OCEAN

Tropic of Cancer

LA ESPAÑOLA
HISPANIOLA

Milwaukee Depth

Puerto Rico Trench

SANTIAGO
La Vega

SANTO DOMINGO
San Cristóbal

REPÚBLICA
DOMINICANA
DOMINICAN
REPUBLIC

Puerto Rico (U.S.)
Mayagüez
Ponce
SAN JUAN

Virgin Islands
(U.S.-U.K.)

Charlotte
Amalie

Road
Town

Anguilla (U.K.)
The Valley

SAINT-MARTIN
Sint Maarten
Philipsburg
SAINT-BARTHÉLEMY

Nederlandse Antillen
Netherlands Antilles

Frederiksted
SAINT CROIX
Christiansted

Barbuda
Codrington

ANTIGUA
Saint John's

SAINT CHRISTOPHER-NEVIS
Basseterre
Charlestown

ANTILLAS MAYORES
GREATER ANTILLES

Montserrat (U.K.)
Plymouth

GRANDE-TERRE
Pointe-à-Pitre
Guadeloupe (Fr.)
Basse-Terre
MARIE-GALANTE

MAR CARIBE / MAR DE LAS ANTILLAS

CARIBBEAN SEA

ISLA DE AVES
(Dependencias Federales Venezuela)

Portsmouth
Roseau
DOMINICA

Saint-Pierre
Fort-de-France
Martinique (Fr.)

Venezuelan Basin

Castries SAINT LUCIA
Soufrière
Vieux Fort

SAINT VINCENT
Kingstown
Georgetown

Bridgetown BARBADOS

Aruba (Neth.)
Oranjestad

Nederlandse Antillen
Netherlands Antilles

CURAÇAO
Willemstad
BONAIRE
Kralendijk

Dependencias Federales

LESSER ANTILLES

Saint George's
GRENADA

PENÍNSULA
DE PARAGUANÁ
Punto Fijo
Coro

Nueva Esparta
Porlamar
ISLA DE MARGARITA

TRINIDAD
AND
TOBAGO

Port of Spain
TRINIDAD
San Fernando

BARQUISIMETO
Falcón
Lara

PUERTO CABELLO
MARACAY
CARACAS
VALENCIA
Aragua
Carabobo
Miranda

Cumaná
Barcelona
Sucre
Maturín
Monagas

VENEZUELA

Guárico
Anzoátegui

Calabozo

San Fernando
de Apure

Apure

Ciudad Guayana
Ciudad Bolívar

Delta Amacuro

DELTA
DEL ORINOCO

Bolívar

COLOMBIA

GUYANA

Georgetown

Scale 1:6,000,000
Delisle Conic Equidistant Projection
0 100 200 300 400 km
0 100 200 miles

Longitude West 64 of Greenwich

© ISTITUTO GEOGRAFICO DE AGOSTINI S. p. A. - NOVARA

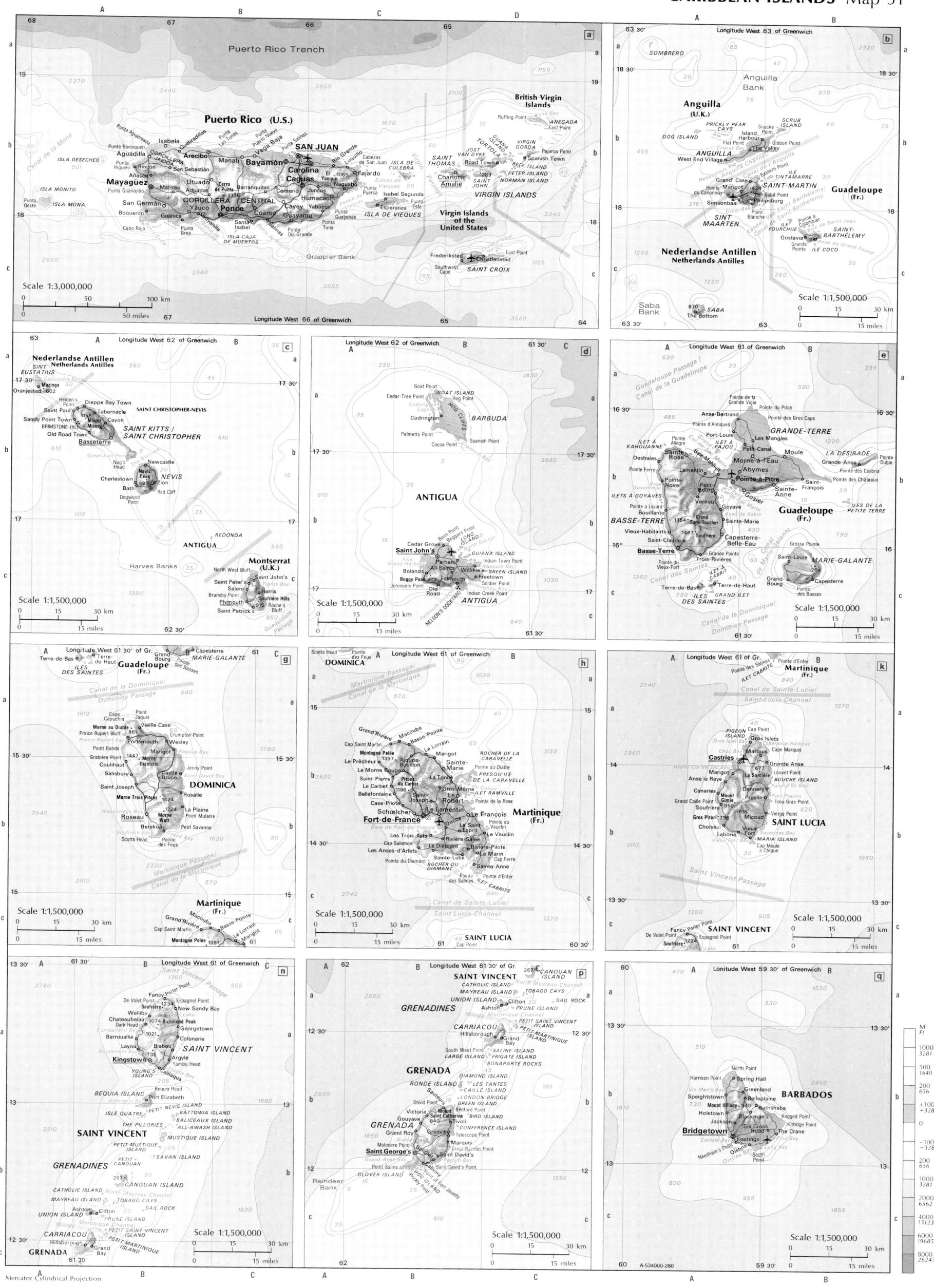

Puerto Rico Trench

Puerto Rico (U.S.)

SAN JUAN
Bayamón
Carolina
Caguas
Ponce
Mayagüez
San Germán
CORDILLERA CENTRAL

ISLA DE MONA
ISLA MONITO
ISLA DESECHEO

British Virgin Islands

SAINT THOMAS
Charlotte Amalie
SAINT JOHN
VIRGIN ISLANDS

Virgin Islands of the United States

ISLA DE VIEQUES

Frederiksted
Christiansted
SAINT CROIX

Scale 1:3,000,000
0 50 100 km
0 50 miles

Longitude West 66 of Greenwich

[a]

[b]
Longitude West 63 of Greenwich

SOMBRERO

Anguilla Bank

Anguilla (U.K.)
West End Village
The Valley

PRICKLY PEAR CAYS
DOG ISLAND
SCRUB ISLAND

SAINT-MARTIN
Marigot
Philipsburg
SINT MAARTEN
Simsonbaai
Gustavia
SAINT-BARTHÉLEMY

Guadeloupe (Fr.)

Nederlandse Antillen
Netherlands Antilles

Saba Bank
SABA
The Bottom

Scale 1:1,500,000
0 15 30 km
0 15 miles

---

[c]
Longitude West 62 of Greenwich

Nederlandse Antillen
Netherlands Antilles
SINT EUSTATIUS
Oranjestad

SAINT CHRISTOPHER-NEVIS
Dieppe Bay Town
Sandy Point Town
BRIMSTONE HILL
Old Road Town
Basseterre
SAINT KITTS / SAINT CHRISTOPHER
Newcastle
Charlestown
NEVIS
Nevis Peak
Bath

REDONDA

ANTIGUA

Montserrat (U.K.)
North West Bluff
Saint Peter's
Salem
Harris
Bransby Point
Plymouth
Soufrière Hills
Saint Patrick's
Roche's Bluff

Harves Banks

Scale 1:1,500,000
0 15 30 km
0 15 miles
62 30'

[d]
Longitude West 62 of Greenwich

Goat Point
Cedar-Tree Point
GOAT ISLAND
Hog Point
HOG CLIFFS
Codrington
BARBUDA
Palmetto Point
Cocoa Point
Spanish Point

ANTIGUA

Cedar Grove
Saint John's
Parham
All Saints
Bolands
Boggy Peak
Freetown
Johnsons Point
Old Road
ANTIGUA

NELSON'S DOCKYARD

Scale 1:1,500,000
0 15 30 km
0 15 miles
61 30'

[e]
Longitude West 61 of Greenwich

Anse-Bertrand
Port-Louis
GRANDE-TERRE
Les Mangles
Petit-Canal
Moule
LA DÉSIRADE
Grande-Anse
Deshaies
Sainte-Rose
Lamentin
Morne-à-l'Eau
Abymes
Pointe-à-Pitre
Pointe-Noire
Petit-Bourg
Sainte-Anne
Saint-François
ILES DE LA PETITE-TERRE
Bouillante
Gosier
Goyave
BASSE-TERRE
Vieux-Habitants
Soufrière
Capesterre-Belle-Eau
Saint-Claude
Basse-Terre
Trois-Rivières
Guadeloupe (Fr.)
Grande Pointe
Vieux-Fort
Terre-de-Bas
Terre-de-Haut
ILES DES SAINTES
Saint-Louis
MARIE-GALANTE
Grand-Bourg
Capesterre

Scale 1:1,500,000
0 15 30 km
0 15 miles
61 30'

---

[g]
Longitude West 61 30' of Gr.

Terre-de-Bas
Terre-de-Haut
Guadeloupe (Fr.)
Grand-Bourg
MARIE-GALANTE
ILES DES SAINTES

Cape Capuchin
Point Jaquot
Morne au Diable
Vieille Case
Prince Rupert Bluff
Portsmouth
Crumpton Point
Point Ronde
Wesley
Grabière Point
Marigot
Coulihaut
Morne Diablotin
Salisbury
Jenny Point
Saint Joseph
Castle Bruce
DOMINICA
Rosalie
Morne Trois Pitons
Roseau
Morne Watt
La Plaine
Berekua
Point Mulatre
Petit Savanne
Scotts Head
Pointe des Fous

Martinique (Fr.)
Grand'Rivière
Macouba
Basse-Pointe
Cap Saint Martin
Le Lorrain
Montagne Pelée
Marigot

Scale 1:1,500,000
0 15 30 km
0 15 miles

[h]
Longitude West 61 of Greenwich

DOMINICA
Scotts Head
Pointe des Fous

Grand'Rivière
Macouba
Basse-Pointe
Cap Saint Martin
Le Lorrain
Montagne Pelée
Marigot
Le Prêcheur
Sainte-Marie
Le Morne Rouge
La Trinité
Saint-Pierre
ROCHER DE LA CARAVELLE
Le Carbet
Gros-Morne
PRESQU'ILE DE LA CARAVELLE
Bellefontaine
Le Robert
Case-Pilote
ILET RAMVILLE
Schœlcher
Le Lamentin
Saint-Joseph
Le François
Fort-de-France
Ducos
Martinique (Fr.)
Les Trois-Îlets
Saint-Esprit
Le Vauclin
Cap Salomon
Rivière-Salée
Les Anses-d'Arlets
Le Diamant
Rivière-Pilote
Sainte-Luce
Le Marin
Pointe du Diamant
Sainte-Anne
ROCHER DU DIAMANT
Pointe d'Enfer
des Salines
ILET CABRITS

Scale 1:1,500,000
0 15 30 km
0 15 miles
61
SAINT LUCIA
Cap Point

[k]
Longitude West 61 of Gr.

Pointe des Sables
Martinique (Fr.)
ILET CABRITS

PIGEON ISLAND
Cap Point
Gros Islets
Grande Anse
Cape Marquis
Castries
Marquis
Marigot
La Sorcière
Anse la Raye
Louvet Point
Canaries
Mount Gimie
Dennery
BOUCHE À L'EAU
Grand Caille Point
Praslin
Trou Gras Point
Soufrière
Vierge Point
Gros Piton
Micoud
Choiseul
SAINT LUCIA
Vieux-Fort
Laborie
MARIA ISLAND
Cap Moule à Chique

Scale 1:1,500,000
0 15 30 km
0 15 miles
13 30'
SAINT VINCENT

---

[n]
Longitude West 61 of Greenwich

Saint Vincent Passage

De Volet Point
Fancy Porter Point
Soufrière
Espagnol Point
New Sandy Bay
Wallibu
Chateaubelair
Richmond Peak
Dark Head
Georgetown
Barrouallie
Colonarie
Layou
Biabou
SAINT VINCENT
Kingstown
Argyle
Calliaqua
Yambou Head
BEQUIA ISLAND
Port Elizabeth
Bequia Head
ISLE QUATRE
PETIT NEVIS ISLAND
BATTOWIA ISLAND
THE PILLORIES
BALICEAUX ISLAND
ALL-AWASH ISLAND
MUSTIQUE ISLAND
SAINT VINCENT
PETIT MUSTIQUE ISLAND
PETIT CANOUAN
SAVAN ISLAND
GRENADINES
CANOUAN ISLAND
CATHOLIC ISLAND
MAYREAU ISLAND
TOBAGO CAYS
UNION ISLAND
Ashton
Clifton
SAIL ROCK
Martinique Channel
CARRIACOU
Hillsborough
PRUNE ISLAND
PETIT SAINT VINCENT
PETIT MARTINIQUE ISLAND
GRENADA
Grand Bay

Scale 1:1,500,000
0 15 30 km
0 15 miles
61 30'

[p]
Longitude West 61 30' of Gr.

CANOUAN ISLAND
SAINT VINCENT
CATHOLIC ISLAND
MAYREAU ISLAND
TOBAGO CAYS
UNION ISLAND
GRENADINES
Ashton
Clifton
PRUNE ISLAND
SAIL ROCK
Martinique Channel
PETIT SAINT VINCENT
CARRIACOU
Hillsborough
PETIT MARTINIQUE ISLAND
Grand Bay
SALINE ISLAND
LARGE ISLAND
FRIGATE ISLAND
BONAPARTE ROCKS
South West Point
DIAMOND ISLAND
GRENADA
RONDE ISLAND
LES TANTES
CAILLE ISLAND
LONDON BRIDGE
GREEN ISLAND
'BIRD ISLAND
Victoria
Mount Saint Catherine
Bedford Point
Tivoli
Gouyave
CONFERENCE ISLAND
Telescope Point
Grand Roy
Grenville
Grenada
Marquis
Molinière Point
Great Bacolet Point
Saint George's
Saint David
Saint David's Point
Grand Anse
Point Saline
Saline
GLOVER ISLAND
Prickly Point
Reindeer Bank

Scale 1:1,500,000
0 15 30 km
0 15 miles
62

[q]
Longitude West 59 30' of Greenwich

North Point
Spring Hall
Harrison Point
Greenland
Speightstown
Belleplaine
BARBADOS
Mount Hillaby
Bathsheba
Holetown
Blackman's
Jackson
Ragged Point
Six Cross Road
Bridgetown
Hastings
The Crane
Oistins
South Point
Long Bay

Scale 1:1,500,000
0 15 30 km
0 15 miles
59 30'

M
Ft
1000 / 3281
500 / 1640
200 / 656
+100 / +328
-100 / -328
200 / 656
1000 / 3281
2000 / 6562
4000 / 13123
6000 / 19685
8000 / 26247

A-534000-280

Mercator Cylindrical Projection

Map 52

SOUTH AMERICA, PHYSICAL

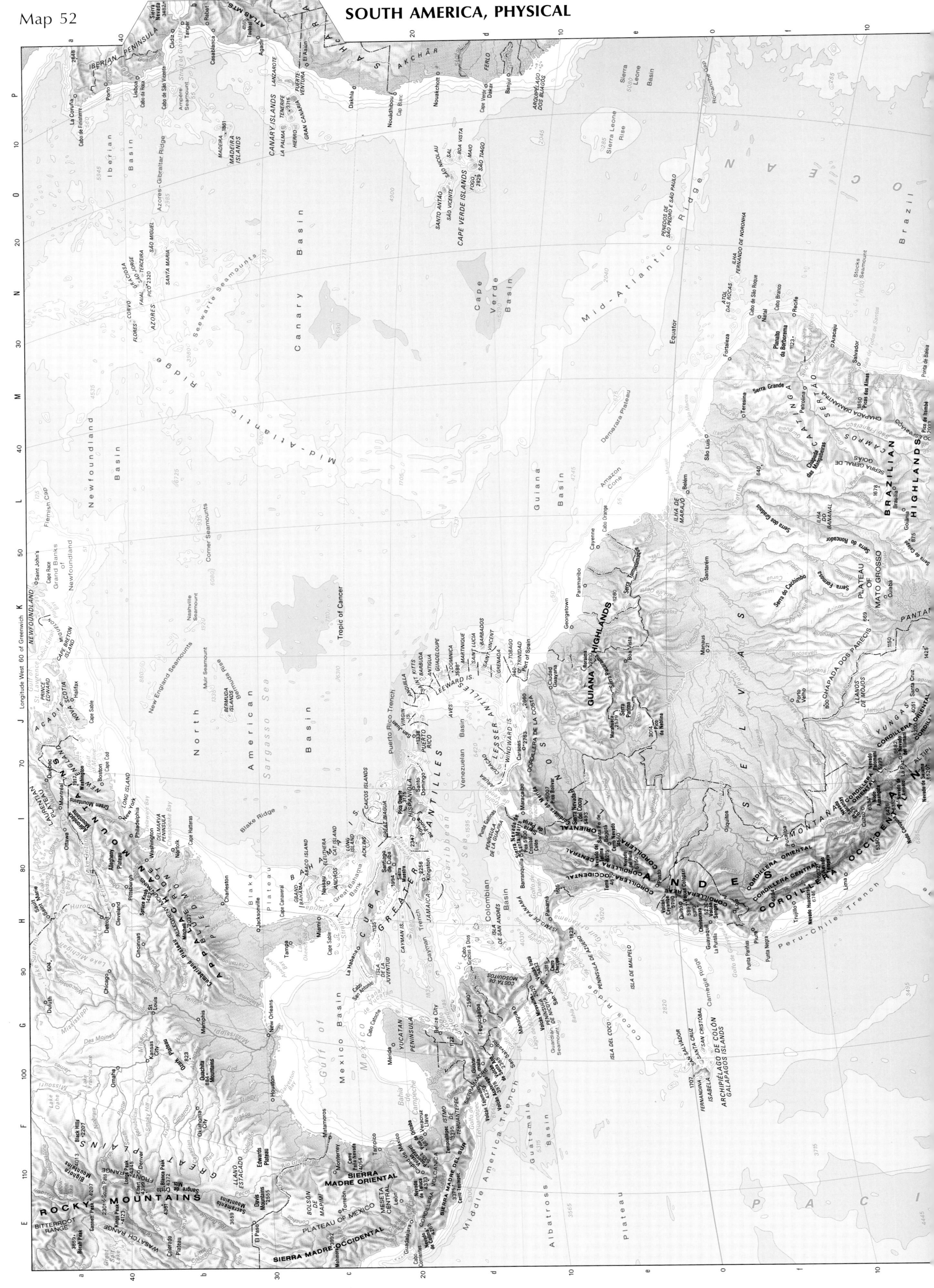

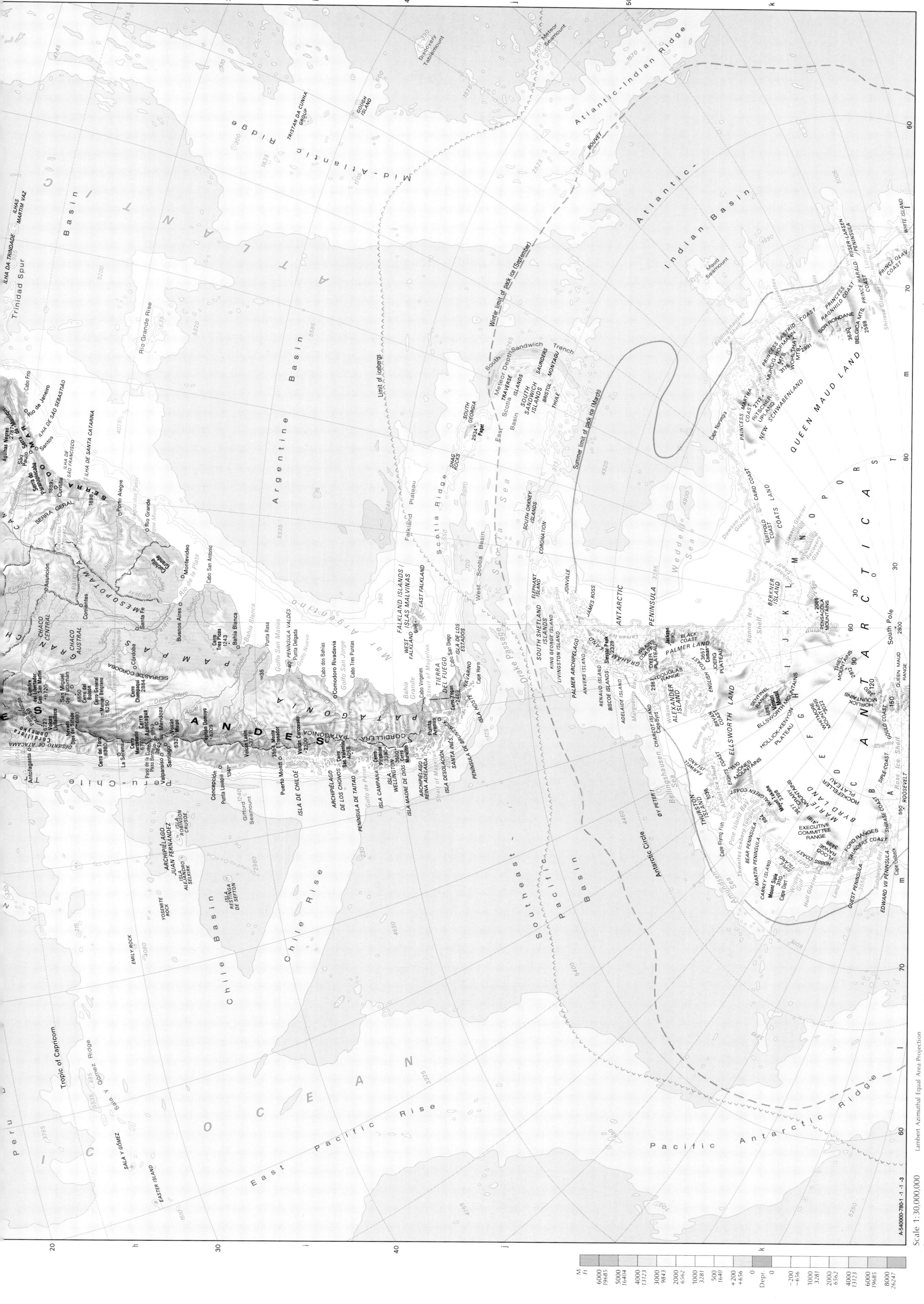

© ISTITUTO GEOGRAFICO DE AGOSTINI S. P. A. - NOVARA

Mid-Atlantic Ridge

Atlantic-Indian Ridge

Atlantic-Indian Basin

TRISTAN DA CUNHA GROUP

GOUGH ISLAND

Trinidad Spur

ILHAS MARTIM VAZ

ILHA DA TRINDADE

Rio Grande Rise

Rio Grande

Porto Alegre

Argentine Basin

Brazil Basin

Winter limit of pack ice (September)

Limit of icebergs

Summer limit of pack ice (March)

BOUVET

Meteor Seamount

Discovery Tablemount

South Sandwich Trench

South Georgia

SOUTH SANDWICH ISLANDS

SAUNDERS

BRISTOL

MONTAGU

THULE

TRAVERSE ISLANDS

SHAG ROCKS

Scotia Sea

East Scotia Basin

West Scotia Basin

Scotia Ridge

Falkland Plateau

FALKLAND ISLANDS (ISLAS MALVINAS)

WEST FALKLAND

EAST FALKLAND

SOUTH ORKNEY ISLANDS

CORONATION

ELEPHANT ISLAND

JOINVILLE

SOUTH SHETLAND ISLANDS

KING GEORGE ISLAND

LIVINGSTON ISLAND

Weddell Sea

QUEEN MAUD LAND

NEW SCHWABENLAND

PRINCESS ASTRID COAST

PRINCESS RAGNHILD COAST

PRINCESS MARTHA COAST

PRINCE HARALD COAST

PRINCE OLAV COAST

RIISER-LARSEN PENINSULA

WHITE ISLAND

Maud Seamount

Cape Norvegia

COATS LAND

LUITPOLD COAST

CAIRD COAST

Filchner Ice Shelf

BERKNER ISLAND

Ronne Ice Shelf

PENSACOLA MOUNTAINS

South Pole

A N T A R C T I C A

ANTARCTIC PENINSULA

GRAHAM LAND

PALMER LAND

PALMER ARCHIPELAGO

ANVERS ISLAND

BISCOE ISLANDS

ADELAIDE ISLAND

ALEXANDER ISLAND

ELLSWORTH LAND

MARIE BYRD LAND

Ronne Ice Shelf

ELLSWORTH MOUNTAINS

SENTINEL RANGE

HORLICK MOUNTAINS

Ross Ice Shelf

EXECUTIVE COMMITTEE RANGE

FORD RANGES

THURSTON ISLAND

Bellingshausen Sea

Antarctic Circle

Drake Passage

Cape Horn

TIERRA DEL FUEGO

ISLA DE LOS ESTADOS

ISLA HOSTE

Strait of Magellan

PENINSULA DE BRUNSWICK

Punta Arenas

ISLA DESOLACION

ISLA SANTA INES

ISLA MADRE DE DIOS

ISLA WELLINGTON

ISLA CAMPANA

ARCHIPIELAGO REINA ADELAIDA

PENINSULA DE TAITAO

ARCHIPIELAGO DE LOS CHONOS

ISLA DE CHILOE

Puerto Montt

Gulf of Penas

CORDILLERA PATAGONICA

P A T A G O N I A

A N D E S

Golfo de Penas

Golfo San Jorge

Comodoro Rivadavia

PENINSULA VALDES

Golfo San Matias

Bahia Blanca

Punta Rasa

P A M P A S

Cerro Tres Picos

Buenos Aires

Rio de la Plata

Montevideo

Cabo San Antonio

Punta del Este

Santa Fe

Cordoba

Cerro Champaqui

SIERRAS DE CORDOBA

Mendoza

Aconcagua

Santiago

Valparaiso

Concepcion

ARCHIPIELAGO JUAN FERNANDEZ

ISLA ALEJANDRO SELKIRK

ISLA ROBINSON CRUSOE

YOSEMITE ROCK

RESTINGA DE SEPTON

EMILY ROCK

SALA Y GOMEZ RIDGE

SALA Y GOMEZ

EASTER ISLAND

Tropic of Capricorn

C h i l e   B a s i n

C h i l e   R i s e

E a s t   P a c i f i c   R i s e

P A C I F I C   O C E A N

Southeast Pacific Basin

Pacific Antarctic Ridge

Ross Sea

ROOSEVELT

Cabo San Diego

SERRA GERAL

MAR DE ESPANHA

Curitiba

ILHA DE SANTA CATARINA

SAO FRANCISCO

Rio de Janeiro

Cabo Frio

São Paulo

Santos

CHACO CENTRAL

CHACO AUSTRAL

Asuncion

Corrientes

M E S O P O T A M I A

Rosario

Desaguadero

Scale 1:30,000,000

Lambert Azimuthal Equal Area Projection

0 500 1000 1500 2000 km

0 500 1000 miles

A-540000-780-1 -1 -1 -3

215

M Ft
6000 19685
5000 16404
4000 13123
3000 9843
2000 6562
1000 3281
500 1640
200 +656
Depr.
0
-200 -656
1000 3281
2000 6562
4000 13123
6000 19685
8000 26247

Map 53

SOUTH AMERICA, POLITICAL

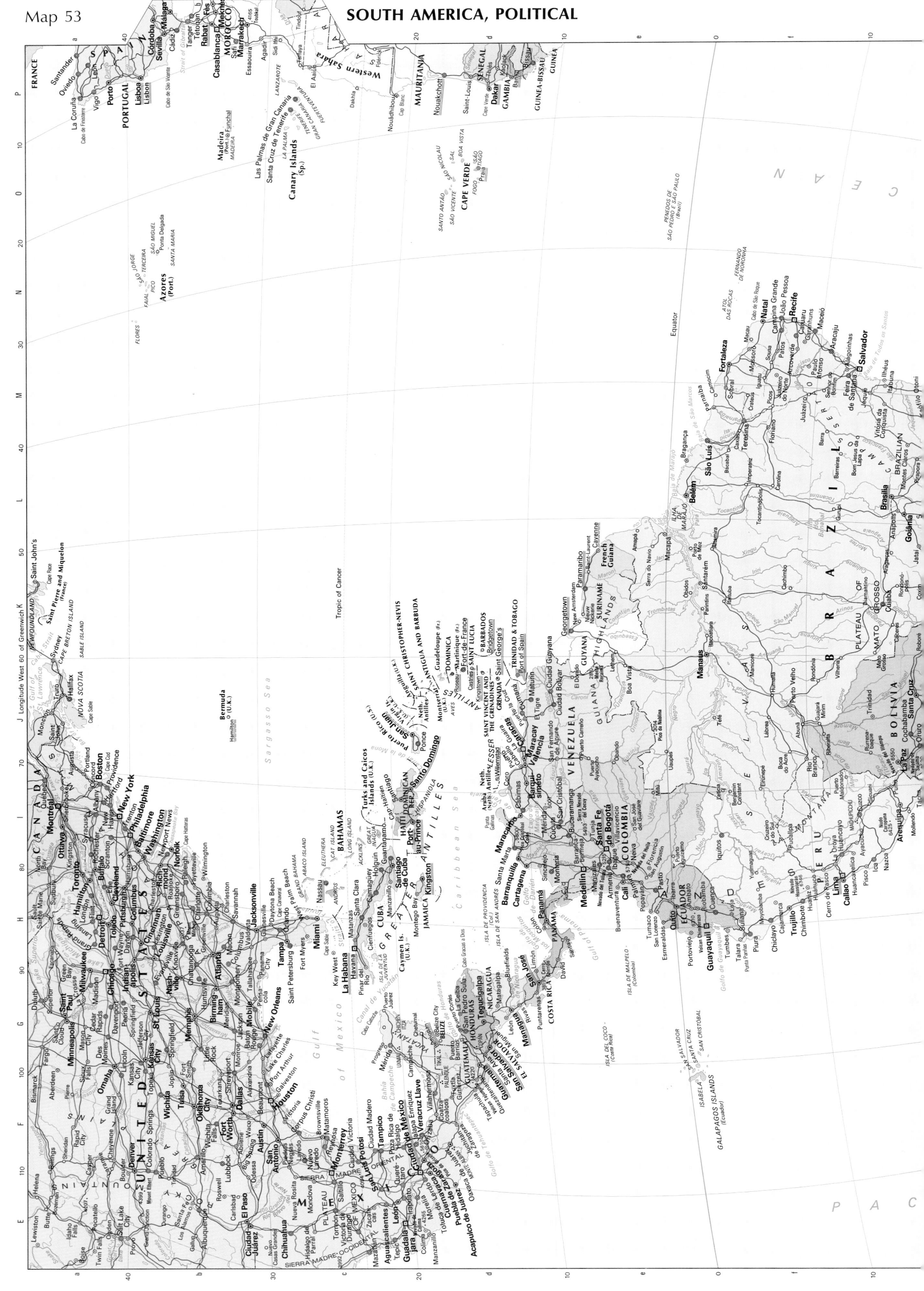

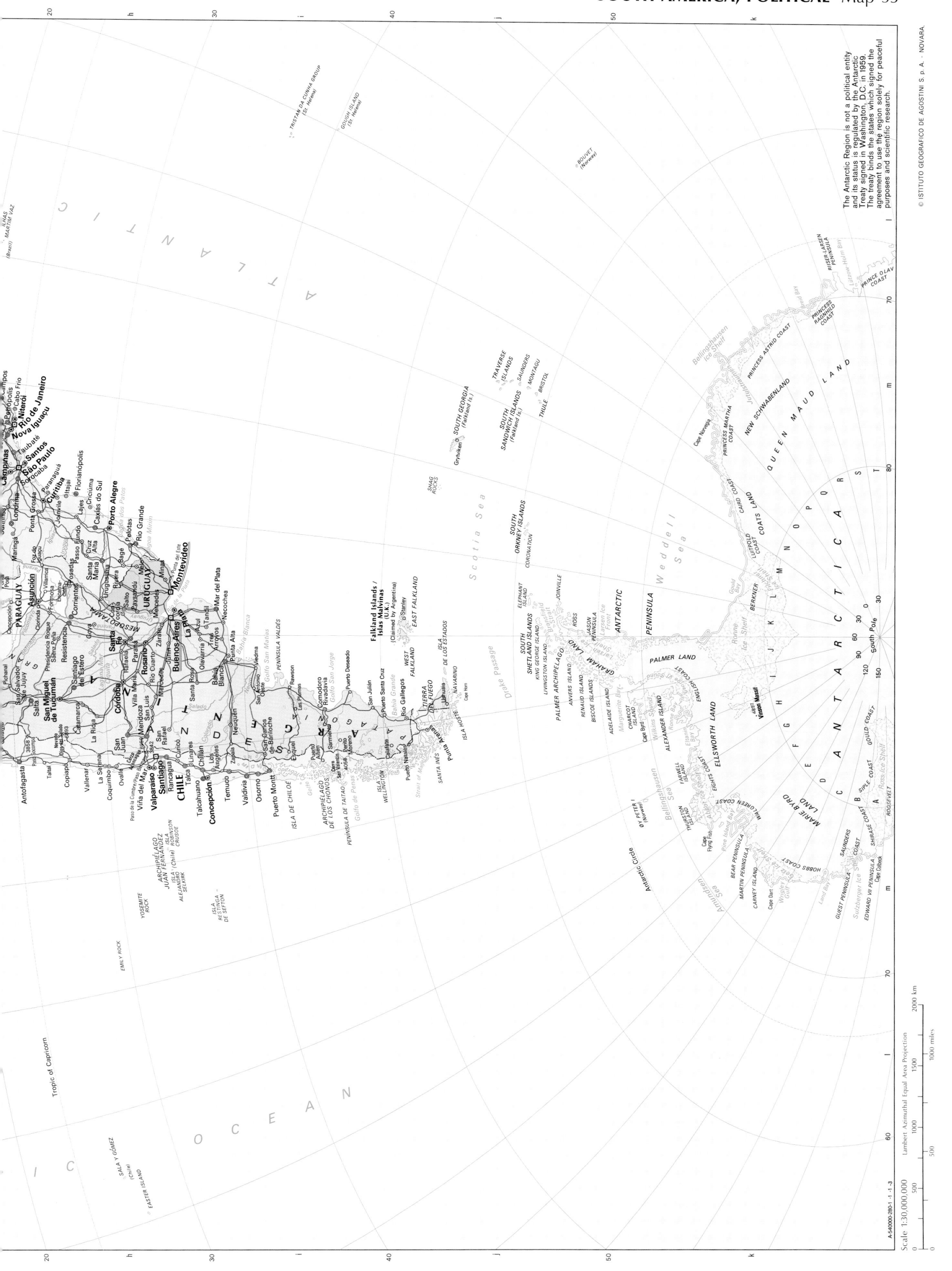

The Antarctic Region is not a political entity and its status is regulated by the Antarctic Treaty signed in Washington, D.C. in 1959. The treaty binds the states which signed the agreement to use the region solely for peaceful purposes and scientific research.

© ISTITUTO GEOGRAFICO DE AGOSTINI S. p. A. - NOVARA.

Scale 1:30,000,000

A-540000-28Q-1.-1.-3

Lambert Azimuthal Equal Area Projection

0   500   1000   1500   2000 km

0   500   1000 miles

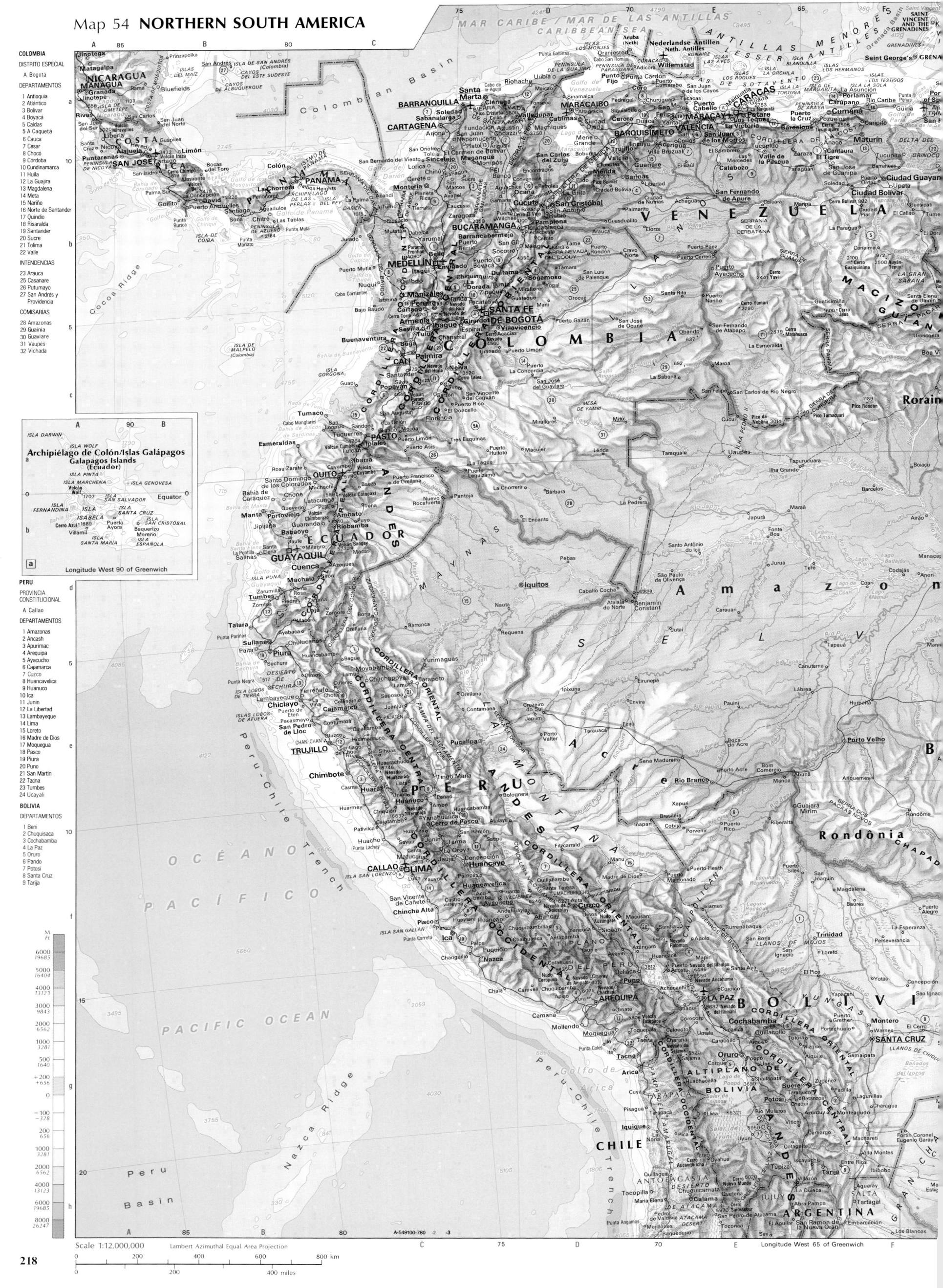

Map 54 NORTHERN SOUTH AMERICA

COLOMBIA

DISTRITO ESPECIAL
A Bogotá

DEPARTAMENTOS
1 Antioquia
2 Atlántico
3 Bolívar
4 Boyacá
5 Caldas
5 A Caquetá
6 Cauca
7 Cesar
8 Chocó
9 Córdoba
10 Cundinamarca
11 Huila
12 La Guajira
13 Magdalena
14 Meta
15 Nariño
16 Norte de Santander
17 Quindío
18 Risaralda
19 Santander
20 Sucre
21 Tolima
22 Valle

INTENDENCIAS
23 Arauca
25 Casanare
26 Putumayo
27 San Andrés y Providencia

COMISARÍAS
28 Amazonas
29 Guainía
30 Guaviare
31 Vaupés
32 Vichada

Archipiélago de Colón/Islas Galápagos
Galapagos Islands
(Ecuador)

ISLA DARWIN
ISLA WOLF
ISLA PINTA
ISLA MARCHENA   ISLA GENOVESA
Volcán Wolf 1707
SAN SALVADOR
ISLA   ISLA
FERNANDINA   SANTA CRUZ   Equator
ISLA   ISLA CRISTÓBAL
ISABELA   Puerto   Baquerizo
Cerro Azul 1689 Ayora   Moreno
Villamil   ISLA
ISLA   ESPAÑOLA
SANTA MARÍA

Longitude West 90 of Greenwich

PERU

PROVINCIA
CONSTITUCIONAL
A Callao

DEPARTAMENTOS
1 Amazonas
2 Ancash
3 Apurímac
4 Arequipa
5 Ayacucho
6 Cajamarca
7 Cuzco
8 Huancavelica
9 Huánuco
10 Ica
11 Junín
12 La Libertad
13 Lambayeque
14 Lima
15 Loreto
16 Madre de Dios
17 Moquegua
18 Pasco
19 Piura
20 Puno
21 San Martín
22 Tacna
23 Tumbes
24 Ucayali

BOLIVIA

DEPARTAMENTOS
1 Beni
2 Chuquisaca
3 Cochabamba
4 La Paz
5 Oruro
6 Pando
7 Potosí
8 Santa Cruz
9 Tarija

M
Ft
6000 / 19685
5000 / 16404
4000 / 13123
3000 / 9843
2000 / 6562
1000 / 3281
500 / 1640
+200 / +656
0
−100 / −328
200 / 656
1000 / 3281
2000 / 6562
4000 / 13123
6000 / 19685
8000 / 26247

Scale 1:12,000,000
Lambert Azimuthal Equal Area Projection
0   200   400   600   800 km
0   200   400 miles

Longitude West 65 of Greenwich

VENEZUELA
DISTRITO FEDERAL
A Caracas
ESTADOS
1 Anzoátegui
2 Apure
3 Aragua
4 Barinas
5 Bolívar
6 Carabobo
7 Cojedes
8 Falcón
9 Guárico
10 Lara
11 Mérida
12 Miranda
13 Monagas
14 Nueva Esparta
15 Portuguesa
16 Sucre
17 Táchira
18 Trujillo
19 Yaracuy
20 Zulia
TERRITORIOS FEDERALES
21 Amazonas
22 Delta Amacuro
23 DEPENDENCIAS FEDERALES
Islas Los Monjes
Isla La Tortuga
Islas Los Frailes
Isla La Sola
Islas Los Testigos
Islas Las Aves
Islas Los Roques
Isla La Orchila
Isla Blanquilla
Islas Los Hermanos
Isla de Patos
Isla de Aves

OCEANO ATLÂNTICO

Guiana Basin

Mid-Atlantic Ridge

ATLANTIC OCEAN

Equator

Georgetown
New Amsterdam
Linden
Paramaribo
SURINAME
GUAYANA
Cayenne
Guyane Française
French Guiana

Amapá
Macapá
Belém
Marajó
ILHA DE MARAJÓ

Pará

Santarém
Óbidos
Parintins
Manaus

Maranhão
São Luís
Parnaíba
FORTALEZA
Ceará
Teresina
Sobral
Piauí
Rio Grande do Norte
NATAL
Paraíba
João Pessoa
RECIFE
Olinda
Pernambuco
Caruaru
Alagoas
Maceió
Sergipe
Aracaju
Bahia
Feira de Santana
SALVADOR

Tocantins
Goiás
BRASÍLIA
Distrito Federal
GOIÂNIA

Mato Grosso
PLANALTO DO MATO GROSSO
Cuiabá

Minas Gerais
BELO HORIZONTE
Uberlândia
Uberaba

Espírito Santo
Vitória

Mato Grosso do Sul
Campo Grande

Paraná
Londrina
Maringá

São Paulo
SÃO PAULO
Campinas
Santos
RIO DE JANEIRO
Niterói
Petrópolis

Tropic of Capricorn

BRAZIL

© ISTITUTO GEOGRAFICO DE AGOSTINI S. p A - NOVARA

219

Map 55 **EAST-CENTRAL SOUTH AMERICA**

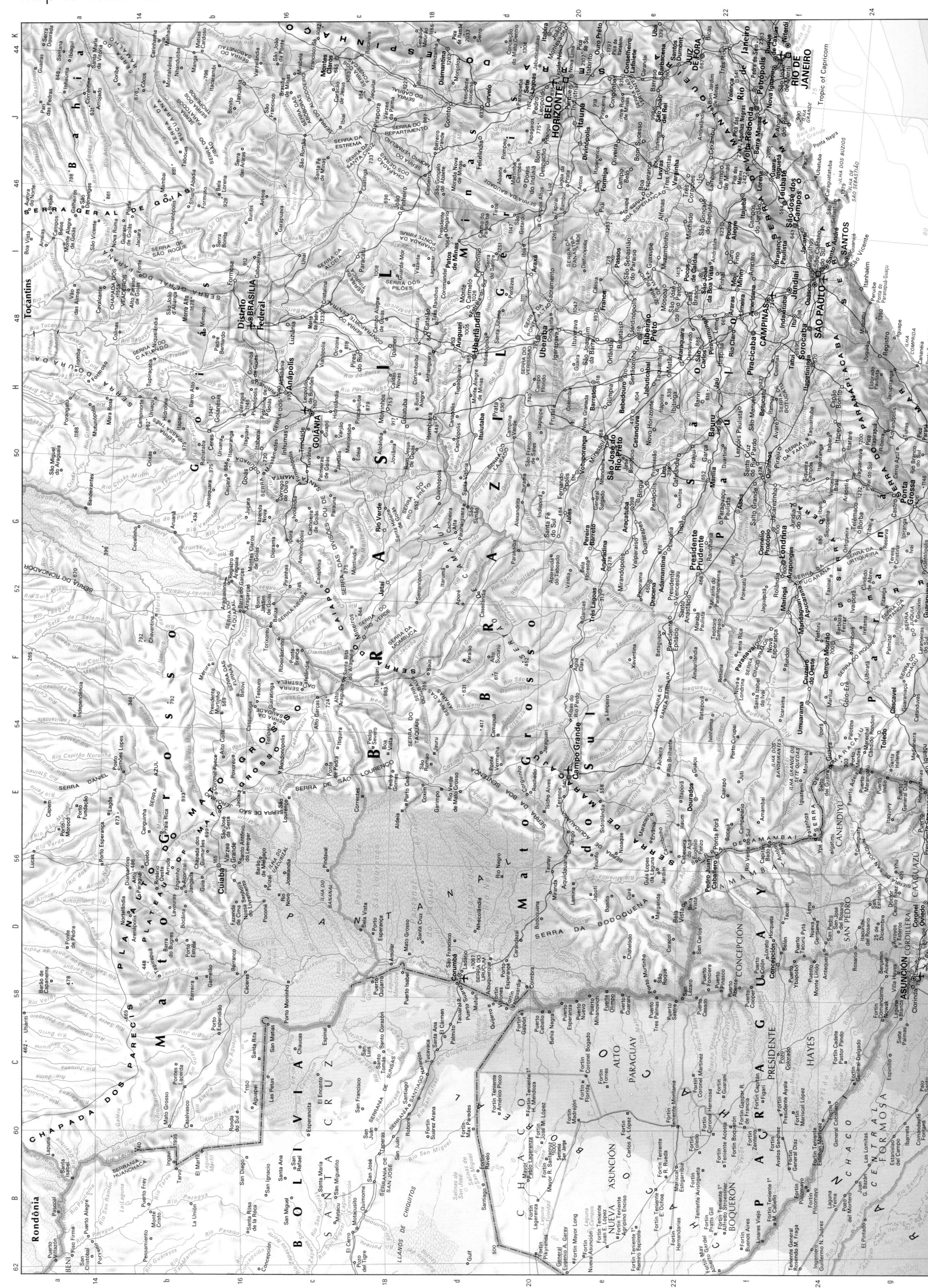

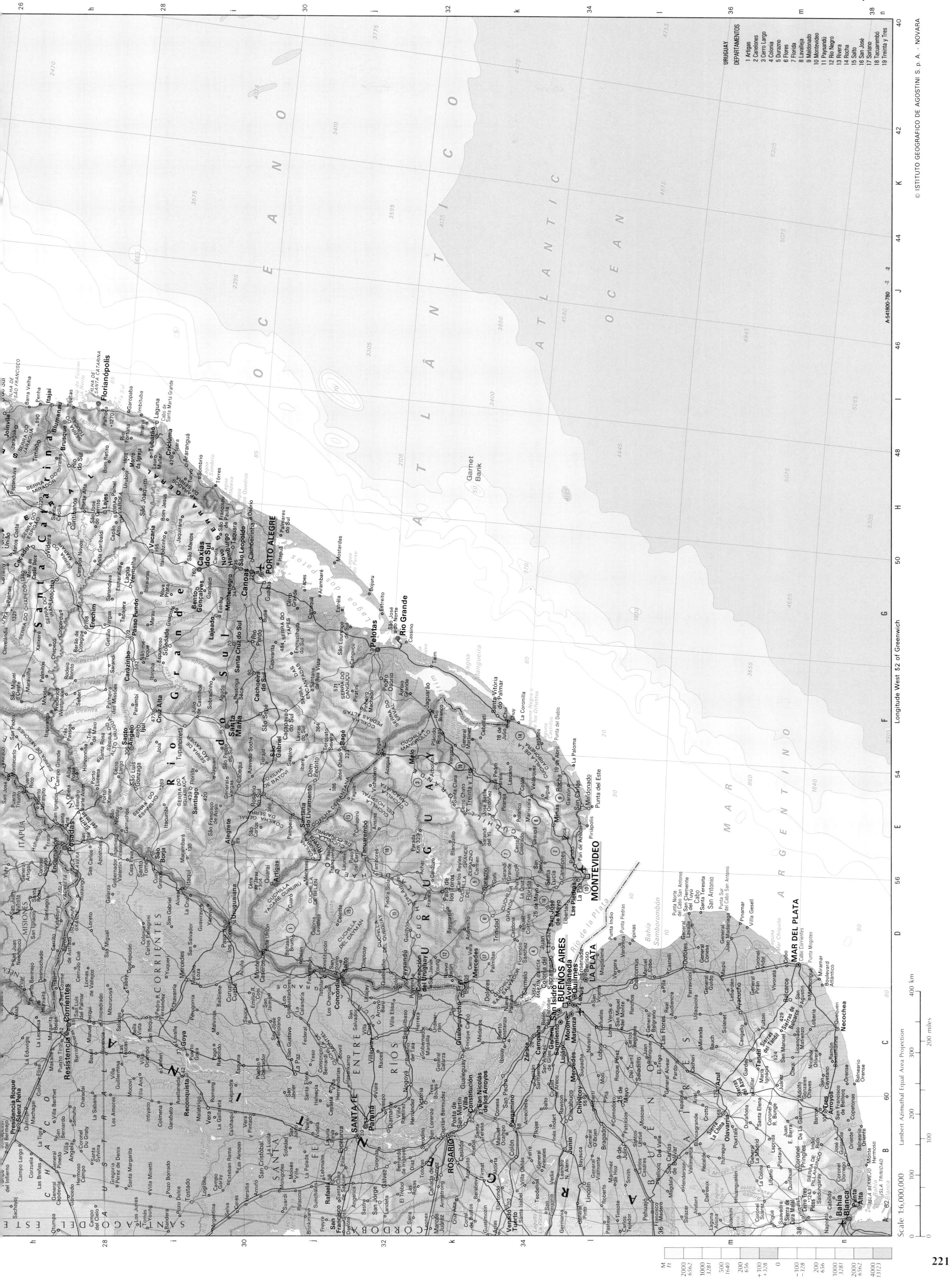

URUGUAY
DEPARTAMENTOS
1 Artigas
2 Canelones
3 Cerro Largo
4 Colonia
5 Durazno
6 Flores
7 Florida
8 Lavalleja
9 Maldonado
10 Montevideo
11 Paysandú
12 Río Negro
13 Rivera
14 Rocha
15 Salto
16 San José
17 Soriano
18 Tacuarembó
19 Treinta y Tres

© ISTITUTO GEOGRAFICO DE AGOSTINI S. p. A. - NOVARA

A T L A N T I C   O C E A N

O C E A N O   A T L A N T I C O

Garnet Bank

Longitude West 52 of Greenwich

PORTO ALEGRE
MONTEVIDEO
BUENOS AIRES
LA PLATA
MAR DEL PLATA
Rosário
Santa Fe
Paraná
Florianópolis
Bahía Blanca
Pelotas
Rio Grande
Resistencia
Corrientes
Reconquista
Presidencia Roque Sáenz Peña

Rio de la Plata
Bahía Samborombón

A R G E N T I N O
M A R

Scale 1:6,000,000
Lambert Azimuthal Equal Area Projection

0   100   200   300   400 km
0   100   200 miles

M ft
2000 6562
1000 3281
500 1640
200 656
+100 +328
0
-100 -328
200 656
1000 3281
2000 6562
4000 13123

221

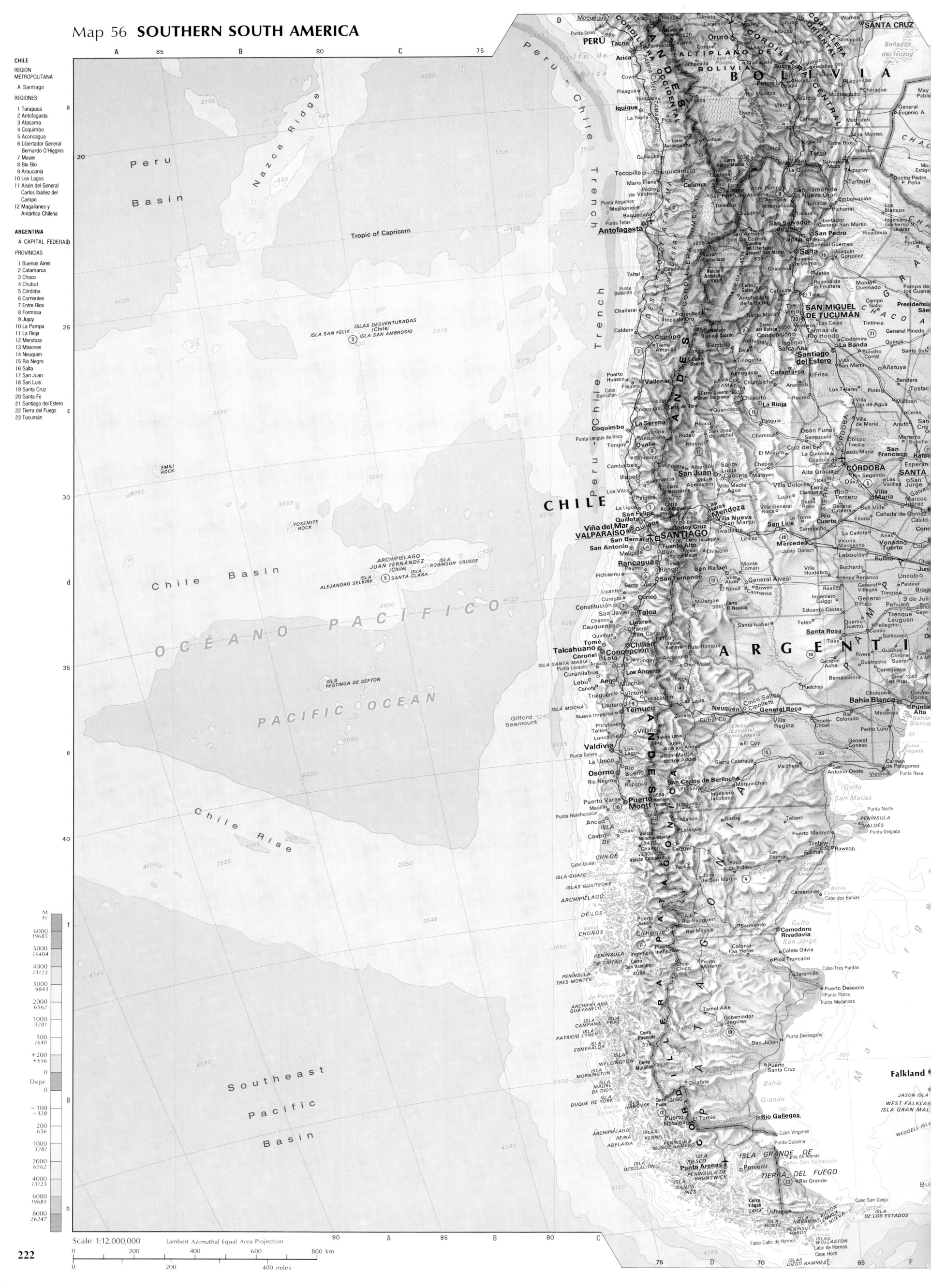

Map 56 **SOUTHERN SOUTH AMERICA**

CHILE
REGIÓN
METROPOLITANA

A Santiago

REGIONES

1 Tarapacá
2 Antofagasta
3 Atacama
4 Coquimbo
5 Aconcagua
6 Libertador General
   Bernardo O'Higgins
7 Maule
8 Bío Bío
9 Araucanía
10 Los Lagos
11 Aisén del General
   Carlos Ibáñez del
   Campo
12 Magallanes y
   Antártica Chilena

ARGENTINA

A CAPITAL FEDERAL

PROVINCIAS

1 Buenos Aires
2 Catamarca
3 Chaco
4 Chubut
5 Córdoba
6 Corrientes
7 Entre Ríos
8 Formosa
9 Jujuy
10 La Pampa
11 La Rioja
12 Mendoza
13 Misiones
14 Neuquén
15 Río Negro
16 Salta
17 San Juan
18 San Luis
19 Santa Cruz
20 Santa Fe
21 Santiago del Estero
22 Tierra del Fuego
23 Tucumán

Scale 1:12,000,000
Lambert Azimuthal Equal Area Projection

OCÉANO ATLÁNTICO

ATLANTIC OCEAN

Argentine Basin

Rio Grande Rise

Falkland Plateau

Scotia Ridge

West Scotia Basin

Map 57 AUSTRALIA AND OCEANIA, PHYSICAL

Scale 1:30,000,000 Lambert Azimuthal Equal Area Projection

A-590000-780

Longitude East 170 of Greenwich

Map 58 **AUSTRALIA AND OCEANIA, POLITICAL**

CHINA

Chengdu, Nanchong, Guangyuan, Hanzhong, Ankang, Nanyang, Xuchang, Kaifeng, Xuzhou, Lianyungang, Nanjing, Nanking, SOUTH KOREA, Taejŏn, Kwangju, Mokp'o, Pusan, Taegu, Okayama, Kōbe, Niigata, Toyama, Nagano, Utsunomiya, Sendai, Iwaki, Tōkyō, Yokohama, JAPAN

Zigong, Chongqing, Wanxian, Yichang, Wuhan, Hefei, Wuhu, Anqing, Wuxi, Shanghai, Hangzhou, Suzhou, Hiro shima, Matsuyama, SHIKOKU, Wakayama, Osaka, Nagoya, Gifu, Shizuoka, IZU ISLANDS (Japan)

Guiyang, Changsha, Xiangtan, Nanchang, Ningbo, Jingdezhen, Shaoxing, Kitakyūshū, KYŪSHŪ, Kumamoto, OSUMI ISLANDS

Kunming, Hengyang, Guilin, Fuzhou, Keelung, Taipei, Taichung, TAIWAN, Kagoshima, TOKARA ISLANDS, AMAMI, RYUKYU ISLANDS (Japan), OKINAWA, Naha, SAKISHIMA ISLANDS, DAITO ISLANDS (Japan)

Nanning, Liuzhou, Wuzhou, Guangzhou, Canton, Shantou, Xiamen (Amoy), Tainan, Kaohsiung, TAIWAN (U.K.)

Hà noi, Haiphong, HAINAN, Haikou, Zhanjiang, New Kowloon, Hong Kong, Victoria (U.K.), Macao (Port.)

THAILAND, VIET-NAM, Da Nang, Qui Nhon, Nha Trang, CAMBODIA, Phnum Penh, Thanh-pho Ho Chi Minh (Saigon), Can Tho

Philippine Sea

Laoag, Aparri, Baguio, Ilagan, Lingayen, Tarlac, Cabanatuan, LUZON, Olongapo, Manila, Quezon City, San Pablo, Batangas, Naga, Legazpi, MINDORO, CALAMIAN GROUP, PANAY, Iloilo, MASBATE, SAMAR, Calbayog, Tacloban, LEYTE, Bacolod, Cebu, NEGROS, BOHOL, PALAWAN, Dipolog, Cagayan de Oro, Butuan, Iligan, MINDANAO, Davao, Zamboanga, Basilan City, SULU ARCHIPELAGO, General Santos

South China Sea

NORTHERN MARIANA ISLANDS (U.S.), FARALLON DE PAJAROS, MAUG, ASUNCION, AGRIHAN, PAGAN, ALAMAGAN, GUGUAN, MARIANA ISLANDS, ANATAHAN, SAIPAN, Administrative Center, TINIAN, ROTA, Agana, Guam (U.S.)

OKINO-TORI (Japan), MINAMI-TORI (Japan), Wake (U.S.), MARSHALL ISLANDS, TAONGI

MICRONESIA

FEDERATED STATES OF MICRONESIA, YAP ISLANDS, ULITHI, FAIS, SOROL, NGULU, GAFERUT, FARAULEP, NAMONUITO, FAYU, HALL ISLANDS, PIKELOT, MINTO, ORGLUK, OLIMARAO, LAMOTREK, PULAP, TRUK ISLANDS, PONAPE, WOLEAI, IFALIK, ELATO, SATAWAL, PULUSUK, LOSAP, SENYAVIN ISLANDS, MOKIL, EAURIPIK, NAMOLUK, MORTLOCK ISLANDS, NGATIK, PINGELAP, SONSOROL, PULO ANNA, MERIR, HELEN, NUKUORO, KAPINGAMARANGI, KOSRAE (KUSAIE), KILI, EBON

Palau, Belau (Trust Territory), PALAU ISLANDS, BABELTHUAP, Koror, ANGAUR, CAROLINE ISLANDS, KAYANGEL

MARSHALL ISLANDS, ENEWETAK, BIKINI, RONGERIK, UTIRIK, AILINGINAE, RONGELAP, LIKIEP, AILUK, WOTHO, KWAJALEIN, UJELANG, UJAE, LAE, ERIKUB, WOTJE, NAMU, AUR, ALINGLAPALAP, MAJURO, ULIGA, NAMORIK, JALUIT, MILI, RALIK CHAIN, RATAK CHAIN

MELANESIA

NAURU, NAOERO, BANABA, BUTARITARI, MARAKEI, ABAIANG, TARAWA, Bairiki, MAIANA, KURIA, ABEMAMA, ARANUKA, NONOUTI, BERU, TABITEUEA, ONOTOA, TAMANA, KIRIBATI

New Guinea / Papua New Guinea

Manokwari, BIAK, Sarmi, NINIGO GROUP, KANIET ISLANDS, SAINT MATTHIAS GROUP, ADMIRALTY ISLANDS, MANUS, NEW HANOVER, TABAR ISLANDS, LIHIR GROUP, Jayapura, Waren, YAPEN, Wewak, BISMARCK ARCHIPELAGO, NEW IRELAND, Rabaul, TANGA ISLANDS, FENI ISLANDS, GREEN ISLANDS, Madang, Dumpu, LONG, UMBOI, NEW BRITAIN, BUKA, NUKUMANU ISLANDS, Nomad, Goroka, Lae, BOUGAINVILLE, Kieta, Panggoe, RONCADOR, ONTONG JAVA, Kikori, Morobe, Tufi, PAPUA NEW GUINEA, Honiara, MALAITA, Auki, CHOISEUL, SANTA ISABEL, SOLOMON ISLANDS, Port Moresby, Samarai, TROBRIAND ISLANDS, D'ENTRECASTEAUX ISLANDS, WOODLARK, NEW GEORGIA, Buala, Kirakira, SAN CRISTOBAL, RENNELL, LOUISIADE ARCHIPELAGO, ROSSEL, TAGULA, GUADALCANAL

INDONESIA

Pontianak, KALIMANTAN, BORNEO, Samarinda, Balikpapan, BRUNEI, MALAYSIA, Kota Kinabalu, Sandakan, Tawau, Sibu, Kuching, Banjarmasin, Sampit, SUMATRA, BANGKA, BELITUNG, Jakarta, Bogor, Bandung, Cirebon, Semarang, Surakarta, Surabaya, MADURA, Yogyakarta, Malang, Tasikmalaya, Kediri, Banyuwangi, BALI, Denpasar, LOMBOK, SUMBAWA, Mataram, FLORES, TIMOR, Kupang, SUMBA, SAWU, ROTI

Manado, MINAHASSA PENINSULA, Gorontalo, Ternate, HALMAHERA, MOROTAI, Sengata, Palu, Poso, CELEBES, Palopo, Parepare, Kendari, Ujung Pandang, Watampone, BUTUNG, Baubau, ASIA, MAPIA, WAIGEO, SALAWATI, Sorong, OBI, MISOOL, SULA ISLANDS, BURU, CERAM, Ambon, MOLUCCAS, Banda Sea, TANIMBAR ISLANDS, DOLAK, ARU ISLANDS, Merauke, Mapi, Agats, Nabire, Puncak Jaya 5030

AUSTRALIA

Darwin, ARNHEM LAND, MELVILLE ISLAND, BATHURST ISLAND, Nhulunbuy, Cape Arnhem, WESSEL ISLANDS, GROOTE EYLANDT, Gulf of Carpentaria, Weipa, CAPE YORK PENINSULA, Cape York, OSPREY, Cooktown, Coen, Musgrave, Mossman, Cairns, Ingham, Townsville, Bowen, Mackay, Rockhampton, Gladstone, Bundaberg, FRASER, Maryborough, Gympie, Brisbane, Gold Coast, Ipswich, Toowoomba

Wyndham, KIMBERLEY, Halls Creek, Katherine, Larrimah, Borroloola, Normanton, Burketown, Georgetown, Croydon, Charters Towers, Hughenden, Winton, Cloncurry, Mount Isa, Dajarra, Longreach, Barcaldine, Blackall, Tambo, Emerald, Roma, Miles, Charleville, Augathella, Cunnamulla, Dirranbandi, Moree, Lismore, Coffs Harbour, Glen Innes, Armidale, Tamworth, Taree

Derby, Broome, Port Hedland, Dampier, Karratha, Onslow, North West Cape, GREAT SANDY DESERT, TANAMI DESERT, Tennant Creek, Barrow Creek, Alice Springs, SIMPSON DESERT, Yaraka, Windorah, Birdsville, GIBSON DESERT, Carnarvon, Shark Bay, Meekatharra, Mount Magnet, Wiluna, Leonora, Kalgoorlie, GREAT VICTORIA DESERT, Coober Pedy, Oodnadatta, Marree, Leigh Creek, Broken Hill, Bourke, Walgett, Nyngan, Dubbo, Nyngan, Wilcannia, Cobar, Ivanhoe

Geraldton, Northam, Moore, Merredin, Southern Cross, NULLARBOR PLAIN, Norseman, Rawlinna, Eucla, Ceduna, Penong, Kyancutta, Port Augusta, Port Pirie, Port Lincoln, GREAT AUSTRALIAN BIGHT, Perth, Bunbury, Northam, Wagin, Katanning, Esperance, Albany, KANGAROO ISLAND, Adelaide, Murray Bridge, Renmark, Mildura, Hay, Wagga Wagga, Goulburn, Canberra, Sydney, Wollongong, Newcastle, Maitland, Orange, Lithgow, Bathurst

Bendigo, Shepparton, Albury, Ballarat, Geelong, Melbourne, Bairnsdale, Morwell, Sale, Horsham, Mount Gambier, Warrnambool, Portland, BASS STRAIT, King Island, FURNEAUX GROUP, Smithton, Devonport, Burnie, Launceston, George Town, TASMANIA, Hobart, South East Cape

VANUATU / NEW CALEDONIA

NEW HEBRIDES, Luganville, SANTO, MALÉKOULA, PENTECÔTE, AMBRYM, EPI, Port-Vila, ÉFATÉ, ERROMANGO, ANIWA, TANNA, FOUTOUNA, ANEITYIUM, RÉCIFS D'ENTRECASTEAUX, ÎLE DES PINS, BELEP, LOYALTY ISLANDS, OUVÉA, LIFOU, MARÉ, Koumac, NEW CALEDONIA, Nouméa, New Caledonia (France), MATTHEW, HUNTER, ÎLE DES PINS, RÉCIFS DE L'ASTROLABE, HUON, ÎLES TORRÉS, VANUA LAVA, ÎLES BANKS, MAÉWO, MIDDLETON, ELIZABETH (Australia), LORD HOWE, BALL'S PYRAMID

SOLOMON ISLANDS / TUVALU

SOLOMON ISLANDS, REEF ISLANDS, SANTA CRUZ ISLANDS, DUFF ISLANDS, NDENI, UTUPUA, VANIKOLO, ANUTA, FATAKA, TIKOPIA, INDISPENSABLE REEFS, NUKUMANU, NANUMEA, NANUMA, NUI, TUVALU

Seas

East China Sea, Philippine Sea, South China Sea, Sulu Sea, Celebes Sea, Molucca Sea, Banda Sea, Ceram Sea, Flores Sea, Java Sea, Timor Sea, Arafura Sea, Gulf of Carpentaria, Coral Sea, Gulf of Papua, Solomon Sea, Tasman Sea, INDIAN OCEAN

LIHOU REEFS AND CAYS, FLINDERS REEFS, SWAIN REEFS, CHESTERFIELD, RÉCIFS BELLONA, CATO

Norfolk (Australia), Kingston, FIJI ISLANDS, YASAWA GROUP, VITI LEVU, ROTUMA, CEVA-I-RA (CONWAY R.)

NEW ZEALAND

Whangarei, North Cape, Auckland, Manukau, Hamilton, NORTH ISLAND, New Plymouth, Nelson, Blenheim, SOUTH ISLAND, Westport, Hokitika, Haast, Mount Cook 3764, Christchurch, Timaru, Wanaka, Manapouri, Dunedin, West Cape, STEWART ISLAND, Invercargill, Southwest Cape

Scale 1:30,000,000 Lambert Azimuthal Equal Area Projection

0 500 1000 1500 2000 km

0 500 1000 miles

H Longitude East 170 of Greenwich

Map 59 AUSTRALIA

INDONESIA

LAUT JAWA
JAWA SEA
PULAU BAWEAN
Kudus
SEMARANG Rembang Cepu Tuban Gresik
Magelang Madiun SURABAYA
SURAKARTA Kediri PULAU MADURA Pamekasan Sumenep
YOGYA-KARTA Tulungagung MALANG Probolinggo Bondowoso
Jember Banjuwangi
JAWA JAVA Lumajang PULAU BALI Singaraja
Denpasar NUSA PENIDA PULAU LOMBOK Mataram
LAUT BALI Tanjung Bumbuk
KEPULAUAN KANGEAN

LAUT FLORES
KEPULAUAN LIUKANG TENGGAYA
KEPULAUAN TENGAH
BONE RATE
PULAU MOYO Gunung Tambora Raba Labuhanbajo PULAU KOMODO Ruteng PULAU FLORES
KEPULAUAN KOMODO Ende
PULAU SUMBAWA Sumbawa Besar
PULAU SUMBA Waingapu LAUT SAWU
Waikabubak KEPULAUAN SAWU
PULAU SUMBA Baing Baa PULAU ROTI

LARANTUKA PULAU LOMBLEN PULAU ALOR Kalabahi
KEPULAUAN SOLOR
Dili Manatuto Atambua Gunung Mutis PULAU TIMOR
Soe Kupang

KEPULAUAN BARAT DAYA
PULAU WETAR PULAU ROMANG KEPULAUAN LETI PULAU SERMATA
Iliwaki

KEPULAUAN TANIMBAR
PULAU YAMDENA
PULAU SELARU
Saumlaki

KEPULAUAN KAI
PULAU TRANGAN

ARAFURA

TIMOR SEA
Timor Trough

HIBERNIA REEF
ASHMORE ISLANDS
CARTIER ISLAND
SERINGAPATAM REEF
SCOTT REEF
BROWSE ISLAND

Cape Van Diemen BATHURST ISLAND MELVILLE ISLAND COBOURG PENINSULA CROKER ISLAND
Snake Bay Cape Croker
Beagle Gulf Port Darwin Darwin
Rum Jungle Batchelor ARNHEM LAND
Adelaide River Mount Evelyn
Katherine Larrim Birdum
Mataranka

North Australian Basin

INDIAN OCEAN

Planet Deep
Java Trench

Corona Bank

D'Artagnan Bank

Holothuria Banks Cape Londonderry Joseph Bonaparte Gulf
BONAPARTE ARCHIPELAGO Kalumburu Mission Wyndham
ADELE ISLAND Kuri Bay Victoria River Downs Top Springs
BUCCANEER ARCHIPELAGO KIMBERLEY Mount Hann Gibb River Turkey Creek Newcastle Waters
Cape Leveque KING LEOPOLD RANGES Mount Ord Mount Well Mount Parker Mount Napier Wave Hill
LACEPEDE ISLANDS DAMPIER LAND KIMBERLEY PLATEAU Mount Amherst
ROWLEY SHOALS Derby Fitzroy Crossing Halls Creek Christmas Creek

Broome
Cape Bossut Roebuck Bay Tanami TANAMI DESERT The Granites
EIGHTY MILE BEACH CANNING BASIN
Larrey Point Pardoo Poissonnier Point
Port Hedland Goldsworthy GREAT SANDY DESERT Barrow Creek
DAMPIER ARCHIPELAGO Marble Bar
MONTE BELLO ISLANDS Dampier Roebourne PATERSON RANGE Nullagine
BARROW ISLAND Whim Creek CHICHESTER RANGE Roy Hill
MUIRON ISLANDS Onslow HAMERSLEY RANGE Brockman Mount Bruce Mount Meharry Mount Leisler
NORTH WEST CAPE Mount Tom Price OPHTHALMIA RANGE Newman MACDONNELL RANGES
Exmouth Paraburdoo ROBERTSON RANGE Mount Zeil
Learmonth Mundiwindi
Point Cloates GIBSON DESERT AUSTRALIA
BARLEE RANGE Docker River George Gill Henbury
Chabujuwardan Bay KENNEDY RANGE Mount Vernon CARNARVON RANGE Mount Essenden RAWLINSON RANGE PETERMANN RANGES Mount Olga
Cape Farquhar Mount Augustus Mount Egerton Mount Aloysius Mount Morris Mount Woodroffe
Minilya WARBURTON RANGE Giles Meteorological Station TOMKINSON RANGES MUSGRAVE RANGES
BERNIER ISLAND Carnarvon Gascoyne Junction ROBINSON RANGE Warburton Mission Simpson Hill Mount Davies
DORRE ISLAND Western Australia BIRKSGATE RANGE Mount Sir Thomas EVERARD RANGES Welbo
Cape Inscription Mount Hale Wiluna Lake Carnegie GREAT VICTORIA DESERT
DIRK HARTOG ISLAND Mount Narryer Mount Murchison Meekatharra Lake Way South
Shark Bay (Denham) NICHOLSON RANGE Cue Lake Austin Sandstone Agnew Maralinga
Bluff Point YELD RANGE Mount Magnet Mount Redcliffe Laverton Oldea
Yalgoo Mount Dalgaranger Leonora Cook
Northampton Wyemandoo Lake Barlee NULLARBOR PLAIN Forrest Nullarbor Colona
Geraldton Mullewa Menzies
HOUTMAN ABROLHOS Morawa Mount Singleton Eucla
Dongara Perenjori Mount Jackson Kalgoorlie Rawlinna Head of Bight
Carnamah Koorda Mukinbudin Zanthus
Watheroo Dalwallinu Coolgardie Fraser Range
Lancelin Moora Bullfinch Kambalda Norseman Balladonia Point Culver
Gingin Goomalling Wyalkatchem Southern Cross Widgiemooltha
P-MINDA Northam Merredin Lake Cowan Lake Lefroy Twilight Cove
PERTH York Cunderdin Bruce Rock Lake Dundas Eyre
FREMANTLE Beverley Corrigin Peak Charles
Rockingham Brookton Pingelly Kondinin Lake King Esperance Great Australian Bight
Mandurah Narrogin Wickepin Ravensthorpe ARCHIPELAGO OF THE RECHERCHE
Harvey Wagin Lake Grace Hopetoun Hood Point
Bunbury Nyabing Gnowangerup Esperance Bay
Cape Naturaliste Kojonup Katanning Cheyne Bay
Busselton Donnybrook Cranbrook STIRLING RANGE King George Sound
Margaret River Bridgetown Mount Barker
Augusta Nannup Manjimup Albany
Cape Leeuwin Pemberton Denmark Bald Head
Point D'Entrecasteaux

INDIAN OCEAN

South Australian Basin

Cuvier Basin

Tropic of Capricorn

Diamantina Deep
Diamantina Trench

Scale 1:12,000,000 Delisle Conic Equidistant Projection
0 200 400 600 800 km
0 200 400 miles

PULAU IRIANII NEW GUINEA

PAPUA NEW GUINEA

PULAU DOLAK

PULAU KOMORAN

NEW IRELAND ISLAND

BISMARCK ARCHIPELAGO

NEW BRITAIN

BOUGAINVILLE ISLAND

SOLOMON SEA

Solomon Basin

New Britian Trench

CHOISEUL ISLAND

SOLOMON ISLANDS

SANTA ISABEL ISLAND

NEW GEORGIA ISLANDS

GUADALCANAL ISLAND

MALAITA ISLAND

Honiara

Port Moresby

Gulf of Papua

Torres Strait

CAPE YORK PENINSULA

Coral Sea

Coral Sea Basin

Coral Sea Islands Territory

Gulf of Carpentaria

GOVE PENINSULA

WESSEL ISLANDS

GROOTE EYLANDT

Cairns

GREAT BARRIER REEF

Townsville

Nouvelle-Calédonie
New Caledonia
(France)

PACIFIC

Mount Isa

Queensland

GREAT ARTESIAN BASIN

GREAT DIVIDING RANGE

Mackay

Rockhampton

Gladstone

Bundaberg

FRASER ISLAND

Maryborough

Tropic of Capricorn

OCEAN

SIMPSON DESERT

STURT DESERT

BRISBANE
Ipswich
Gold Coast

Toowoomba

DARLING DOWNS

tralia

New South Wales

Broken Hill

Armidale

Tamworth

Port Macquarie

LORD HOWE ISLAND
(Australia)

BALL'S PYRAMID
(Australia)

Dubbo

Newcastle

ADELAIDE

SYDNEY
Wollongong

KANGAROO ISLAND

RIVERINA

Wagga Wagga

Albury

Canberra
Australian Capital Territory

Victoria

Bendigo

Ballarat
MELBOURNE
Geelong

GREAT DIVIDING RANGE

TASMAN SEA

BASS STRAIT

KING ISLAND

Tasman Basin

Tasmania

Launceston

Hobart

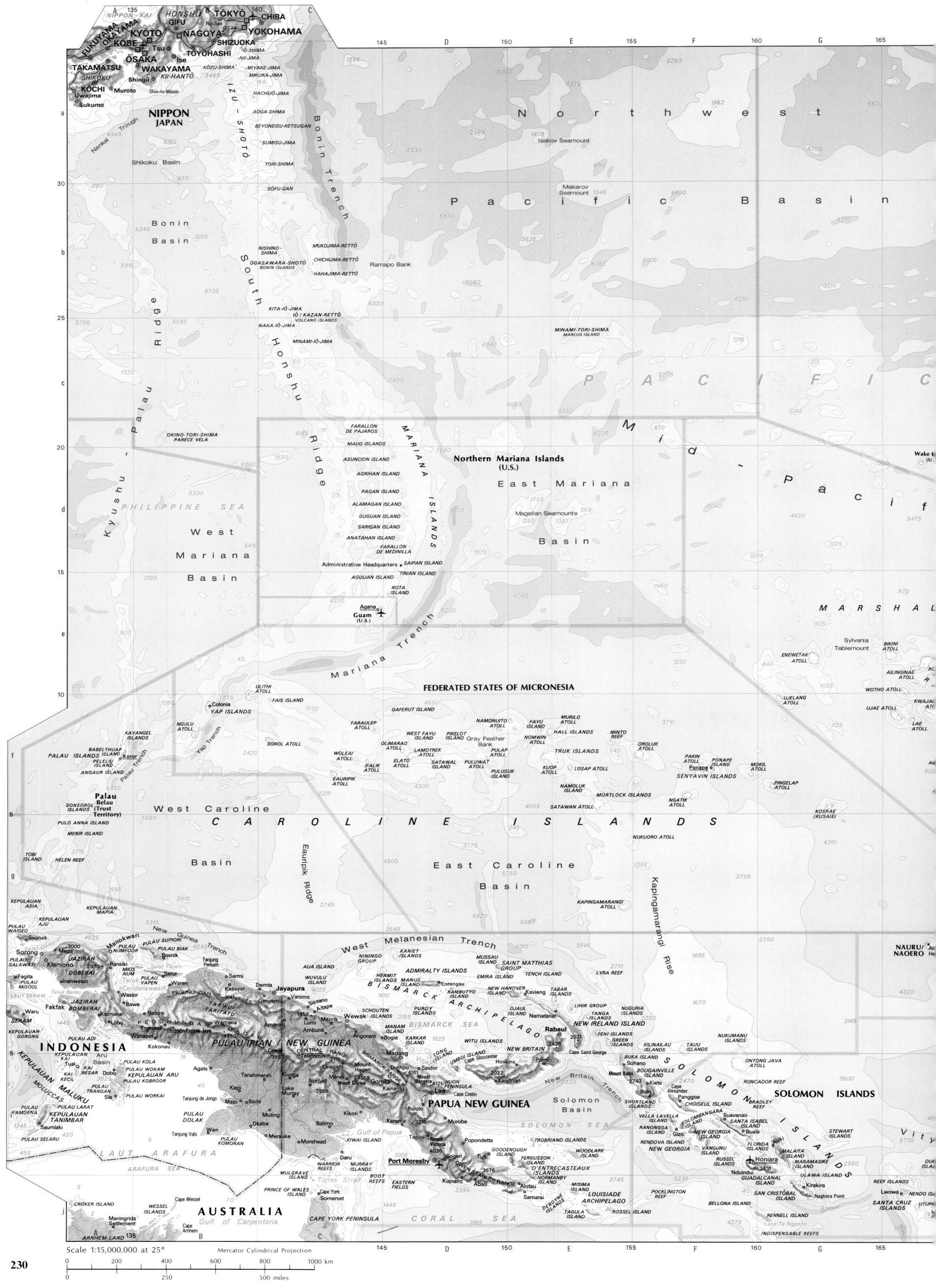

NIPPON
JAPAN

INDONESIA

PAPUA NEW GUINEA

AUSTRALIA

SOLOMON ISLANDS

Northern Mariana Islands
(U.S.)

FEDERATED STATES OF MICRONESIA

CAROLINE ISLANDS

Palau
Belau
(Trust
Territory)

HONSHU TŌKYŌ CHIBA
GIFU NAGOYA YOKOHAMA
KYOTO SHIZUOKA
FUKUYAMA OKAYAMA TOYOHASHI
KŌBE Tsu
ŌSAKA WAKAYAMA
TAKAMATSU
SHIKOKU Shingū
KŌCHI Muroto
Uwajima
Sukumo

Scale 1:15,000,000 at 25°

Mercator Cylindrical Projection

0   200   400   600   800   1000 km

0   250   500 miles

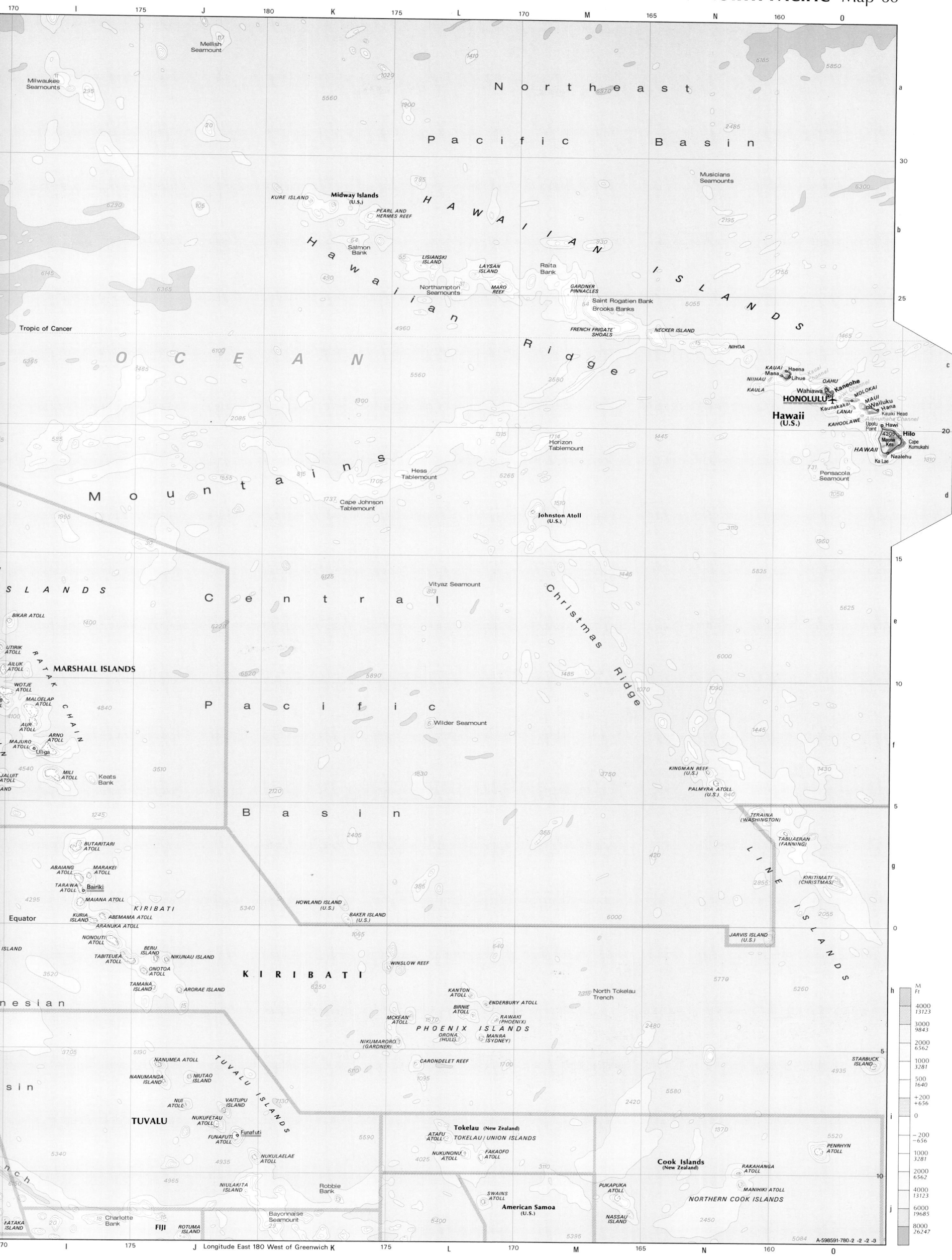

Mellish
Seamount

Milwaukee
Seamounts

Northeast

Pacific Basin

Musicians
Seamounts

KURE ISLAND Midway Islands
(U.S.)

PEARL AND
HERMES REEF

Salmon
Bank

LISIANSKI
ISLAND LAYSAN
ISLAND Raita
Bank

Northampton
Seamounts MARO
REEF GARDNER
PINNACLES

Saint Rogatien Bank
Brooks Banks

FRENCH FRIGATE
SHOALS NECKER ISLAND

NIHOA

HAWAIIAN ISLANDS

HAWAIIAN

Hawaiian Ridge

Tropic of Cancer

O C E A N

KAUAI Haena
Mana Lihue
NIIHAU OAHU
KAULA Wahiawa Kaneohe
HONOLULU MOLOKAI
Kaunakakai MAUI
LANAI Wailuku Hana
Hawaii Kauiki Head
(U.S.) KAHOOLAWE Upolu
Point Hawi
Mauna Hilo
Kea Cape
HAWAII Kumukahi
Ka Lae Naalehu

Horizon
Tablemount

Mountains

Hess
Tablemount

Cape Johnson
Tablemount

Pensacola
Seamount

Johnston Atoll
(U.S.)

ISLANDS

Central

Vityaz Seamount

BIKAR ATOLL

UTIRIK
ATOLL

AILUK
ATOLL MARSHALL ISLANDS

WOTJE
ATOLL

MALOELAP
ATOLL

AUR
ATOLL ARNO
ATOLL

MAJURO
ATOLL
Uliga

JALUIT
ATOLL MILI
ATOLL Keats
Bank

Wilder Seamount

Christmas Ridge

Pacific

KINGMAN REEF
(U.S.)

PALMYRA ATOLL
(U.S.)

Basin

TERAINA
(WASHINGTON)

TABUAERAN
(FANNING)

BUTARITARI
ATOLL

ABAIANG
ATOLL MARAKEI
ATOLL

TARAWA
ATOLL Bairiki

MAIANA ATOLL

KURIA
ISLAND ABEMAMA ATOLL

KIRIBATI

ARANUKA ATOLL

NONOUTI
ATOLL

BERU
ISLAND

TABITEUEA
ATOLL NIKUNAU ISLAND

ONOTOA
ATOLL

TAMANA
ISLAND ARORAE ISLAND

KIRIBATI

HOWLAND ISLAND
(U.S.)

BAKER ISLAND
(U.S.)

KIRITIMATI
(CHRISTMAS)

JARVIS ISLAND
(U.S.)

LINE ISLANDS

Winslow Reef

KANTON
ATOLL

BIRNIE
ATOLL ENDERBURY ATOLL

North Tokelau
Trench

STARBUCK
ISLAND

McKEAN
ATOLL RAWAKI
(PHOENIX)

PHOENIX ISLANDS

NIKUMARORO
(GARDNER) ORONA
(HULL) MANRA
(SYDNEY)

NANUMEA ATOLL

NANUMANGA
ISLAND

NIUTAO
ISLAND

CARONDELET REEF

TUVALU ISLANDS

NUI
ATOLL VAITUPU
ISLAND

TUVALU

NUKUFETAU
ATOLL

FUNAFUTI
ATOLL Funafuti

Tokelau (New Zealand)

TOKELAU / UNION ISLANDS

ATAFU
ATOLL

NUKUNONU
ATOLL FAKAOFO
ATOLL

NUKULAELAE
ATOLL

PENRHYN
ATOLL

NIULAKITA
ISLAND Robbie
Bank

Cook Islands
(New Zealand)

RAKAHANGA
ATOLL

PUKAPUKA
ATOLL

MANIHIKI ATOLL

FATAKA
ISLAND

Charlotte
Bank

FIJI ROTUMA
ISLAND

Bayonnaise
Seamount

SWAINS
ATOLL

American Samoa
(U.S.)

NASSAU
ISLAND

NORTHERN COOK ISLANDS

Longitude East 180 West of Greenwich

Equator

170 175 180 175 170 165 160

M
Ft
4000
13123
3000
9843
2000
6562
1000
3281
500
1640
+200
+656
0
−200
−656
1000
3281
2000
6562
4000
13123
6000
19685
8000
26247

A-598591-780-2 -2 -2 -3

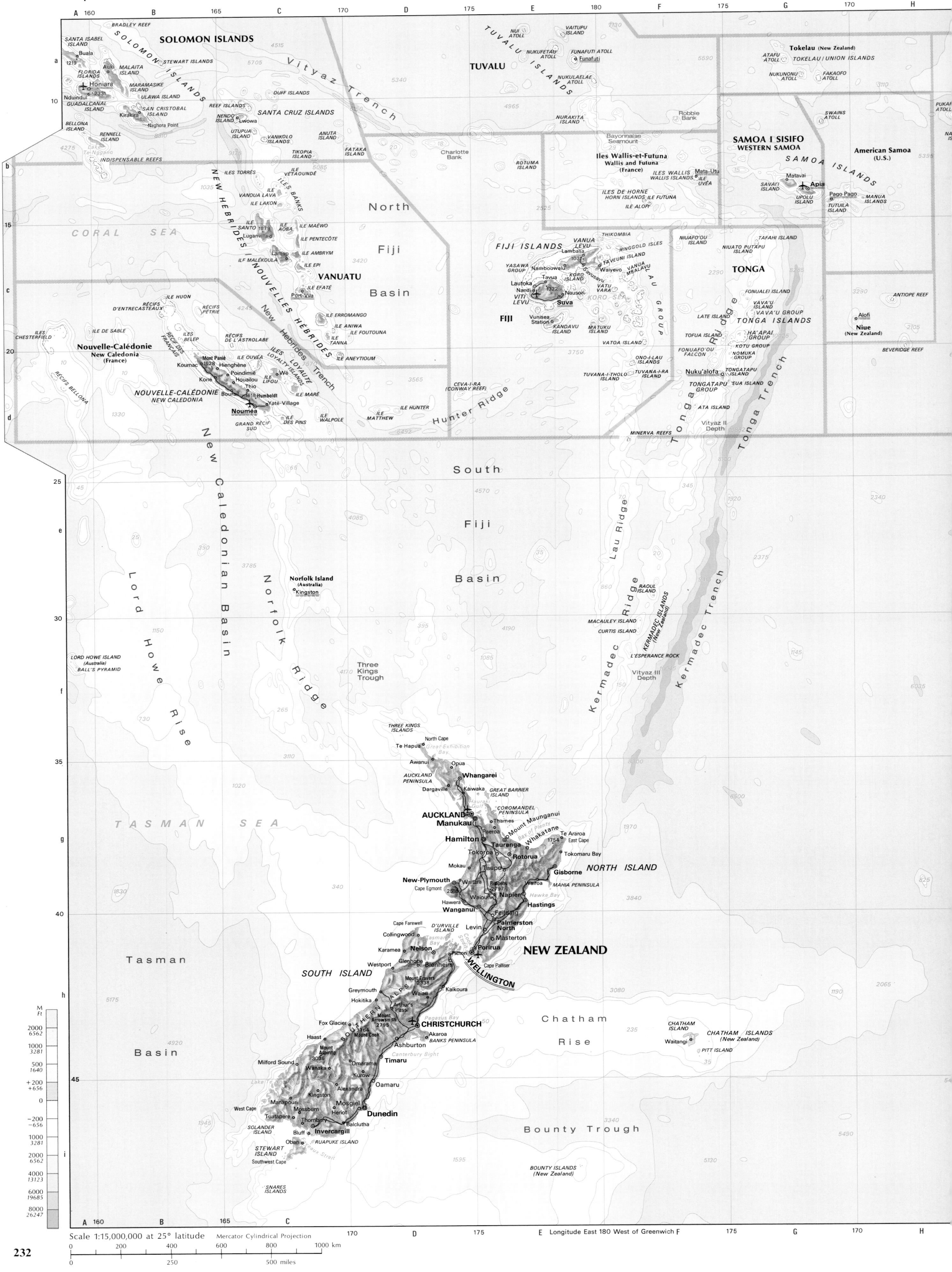

Map 61 **THE SOUTH PACIFIC**

SOLOMON ISLANDS

SANTA ISABEL ISLAND
Buala
1219
FLORIDA ISLANDS
Auki
MALAITA ISLAND
Honiara
2331
Nduindui
GUADALCANAL ISLAND
San Cristobal Island
Kirakira
Naghora Point
BELLONA ISLAND
RENNELL ISLAND
Te Nggano
4275
INDISPENSABLE REEFS
STEWART ISLANDS
MARAMASIKE ISLAND
ULAWA ISLAND
NENDO
Lwowa
REEF ISLANDS
DUFF ISLANDS
SANTA CRUZ ISLANDS
UTUPUA ISLAND
VANIKOLO ISLAND
ANUTA ISLAND
TIKOPIA ISLAND
FATAKA ISLAND

Vityaz Trench

BRADLEY REEF
4515
5705
5085
5340
4965

North

Fiji

Basin

TUVALU ISLANDS
NUI ATOLL
VAITUPU ISLAND
NUKUFETAU ATOLL
FUNAFUTI ATOLL
Funafuti
NUKULAELAE ATOLL
NURAKITA ISLAND
TUVALU

Robbie Bank
5590
3110

TOKELAU (New Zealand)
ATAFU ATOLL
NUKUNONU ATOLL
FAKAOFO ATOLL
TOKELAU / UNION ISLANDS
SWAINS ATOLL
PUKA...

CORAL SEA
4275

ILES TORRÈS
ILES BANKS
ÎLE VÉTAOUNDÉ
VANUA LAVA
ÎLE LAKON
ÎLE SANTO 1879
Luganville
Lamap
ÎLE MALÉKOULA
ÎLE AOBA
ÎLE MAÉWO
ÎLE PENTECÔTE
ÎLE AMBRYM
ÎLE EPI
NEW HEBRIDES
NOUVELLES HÉBRIDES
VANUATU
ÎLE ÉFATÉ
Port-Vila
ÎLE ERROMANGO
ÎLE ANIWA
ÎLE TANNA
ÎLE FOUTOUNA
ÎLE ANEYTIOUM

1035
5085
3420
4245
3565

Charlotte Bank
ROTUMA ISLAND
2525

Bayonnaise Seamount

THIKOMBIA
FIJI ISLANDS
VANUA LEVU
Lambasa
YASAWA GROUP
Namboiowalu
RINGGOLD ISLES
FAVEUNI ISLAND
Waiyevo
VANUA MBALAVU
KORO ISLAND
Laufoka
VITI LEVU
Nandi
1322
Niausori
Suva
FIJI
Vunisea Station
KANDAVU ISLAND
MATUKU ISLAND
KORO SEA
LAU GROUP
VATOA ISLAND
ONO-I-LAU ISLANDS
TUVANA-I-THOLO ISLAND
TUVANA-I-RA ISLAND

ÎLES WALLIS-ET-FUTUNA
Wallis and Futuna (France)
ÎLES WALLIS
WALLIS ISLANDS
ÎLE UVÉA
Mata-Utu
ÎLES DE HORNE
HORN ISLANDS
ÎLE FUTUNA
ÎLE ALOFI

SAMOA I SISIFO
WESTERN SAMOA
SAVAI'I ISLAND
Apia
UPOLU ISLAND
Pago Pago
TUTUILA ISLAND
AMERICAN SAMOA (U.S.)
MANU'A ISLANDS
Matavai
SAMOA ISLANDS
5395

NIUAFO'OU ISLAND
TAFAHI ISLAND
NIUATO PUTAPU ISLAND
TONGA
FONUALEI ISLAND
LATE ISLAND
VAVA'U ISLAND
VAVA'U GROUP
TONGA ISLANDS
TOFUA ISLAND
HA'APAI GROUP
KOTU GROUP
NOMUKA GROUP
FONUAFO'OU FALCON
Nuku'alofa
TONGATAPU GROUP
'EUA ISLAND
ATA ISLAND
TONGATAPU

ANTIOPE REEF
3290
Alofi
NIUE (New Zealand)
2105
BEVERIDGE REEF

NOUVELLE-CALÉDONIE
New Caledonia (France)
RÉCIFS D'ENTRECASTEAUX
ÎLE HUON
RÉCIFS PETRIE
ÎLE DE SABLE
ÎLES BELEP
RÉCIFS DES FRANÇAIS
RÉCIFS DE L'ASTROLABE
Mont Panié
1628
Kournac
Hienghène
Poindimié
Houailou
Kone
Thio
Bourail
Humboldt 1618
NOUVELLE-CALÉDONIE
NEW CALEDONIA
Yaté-Village
Nouméa
ÎLE DES PINS
GRAND RÉCIF SUD
ÎLES LOYAUTÉ
LOYALTY ISLANDS
ÎLE OUVÉA
ÎLE LIFOU
We
ÎLE MARÉ
ÎLE WALPOLE

CEVA-I-RA (CONWAY REEF)
ÎLE HUNTER
ÎLE MATTHEW
Hunter Ridge
MINERVA REEFS
Vityaz II Depth
Tonga Trench

RÉCIFS BELLONA
ÎLES CHESTERFIELD
1330

South

Fiji

Basin

4570
4085
3785

Lord Howe Rise

New Caledonian Basin

Norfolk Ridge

Norfolk Island (Australia)
Kingston

Lau Ridge

Kermadec Ridge

Kermadec Trench

RAOUL ISLAND
MACAULEY ISLAND
CURTIS ISLAND
KERMADEC ISLANDS (New Zealand)
L'ESPERANCE ROCK
Vityaz III Depth

LORD HOWE ISLAND (Australia)
BALL'S PYRAMID

Three Kings Trough

THREE KINGS ISLANDS
North Cape
Te Hapua
Awanui
Great Exhibition Bay
AUCKLAND PENINSULA
Opua
Whangarei
Kaiwaka
Dargaville
GREAT BARRIER ISLAND
AUCKLAND
Manukau
COROMANDEL PENINSULA
Thames
Mount Maunganui
Paeroa
Bay of Plenty
Whakatane
Te Araroa
East Cape
Hamilton
Tauranga
Tokoroa
Rotorua
1754
Tokomaru Bay
Mokau
Taupo
NORTH ISLAND
Gisborne
New-Plymouth
Waitara
2519
MAHIA PENINSULA
Cape Egmont
2797
Wairoa
Hawera
Waiouru
Napier
Hawke Bay
Wanganui
Hastings
Feilding
Cape Farewell
D'URVILLE ISLAND
Levin
Palmerston North
Collingwood
Masterton
Tasman Bay
Karamea
Nelson
Porirua
NEW ZEALAND
Westport
Picton
WELLINGTON
Blenheim
Glenhope
Cape Palliser
Mount Travers
2338
Kaikoura
Greymouth
Hokitika
Arthur's Pass
SOUTH ISLAND
SOUTHERN ALPS
Mount Arrowsmith
2795
Fox Glacier
Mount Cook
3764
Pegasus Bay
CHRISTCHURCH
Haast
Akaroa
BANKS PENINSULA
Mount Aspiring
3036
Ashburton
Milford Sound
Canterbury Bight
Timaru
Wanaka
Omarama
Kurow
Oamaru
West Cape
Manapouri
Alexandra
Kingston
Mosgiel
Tuatapere
Mossburn
Heriot
Dunedin
Balclutha
SOLANDER ISLAND
Thornbury
Obah
Bluff
Invercargill
RUAPUKE ISLAND
STEWART ISLAND
Southwest Cape
SNARES ISLANDS

TASMAN SEA

Tasman

Basin

Chatham Rise

CHATHAM ISLAND
CHATHAM ISLANDS (New Zealand)
Waitangi
PITT ISLAND

Bounty Trough

BOUNTY ISLANDS (New Zealand)

M Ft
2000 6562
1000 3281
500 1640
+200 +656
0 0
−200 −656
1000 3281
2000 6562
4000 13123
6000 19685
8000 26247

Scale 1:15,000,000 at 25° latitude   Mercator Cylindrical Projection
0   200   400   600   800   1000 km
0   250   500 miles

Longitude East 180 West of Greenwich

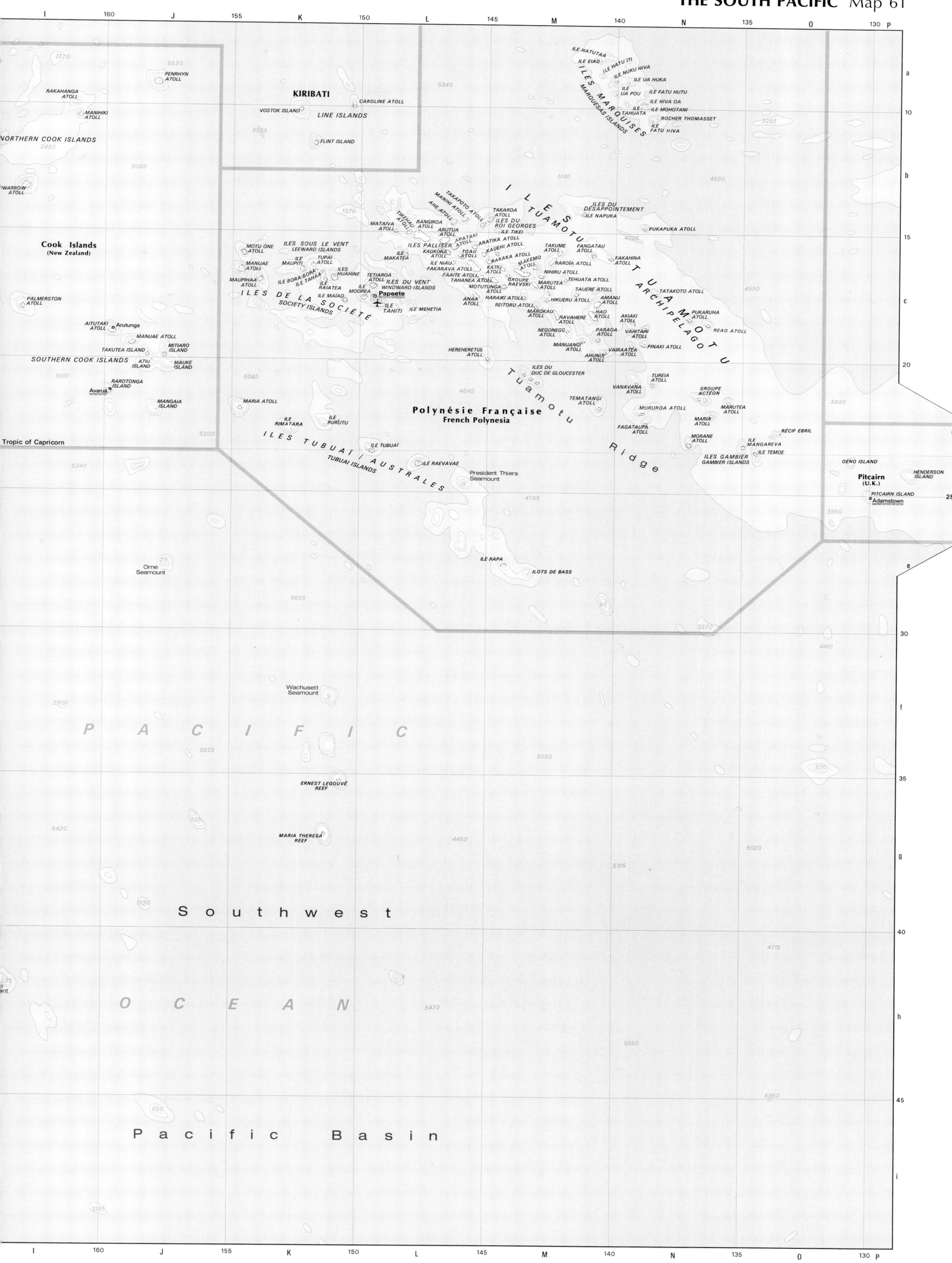

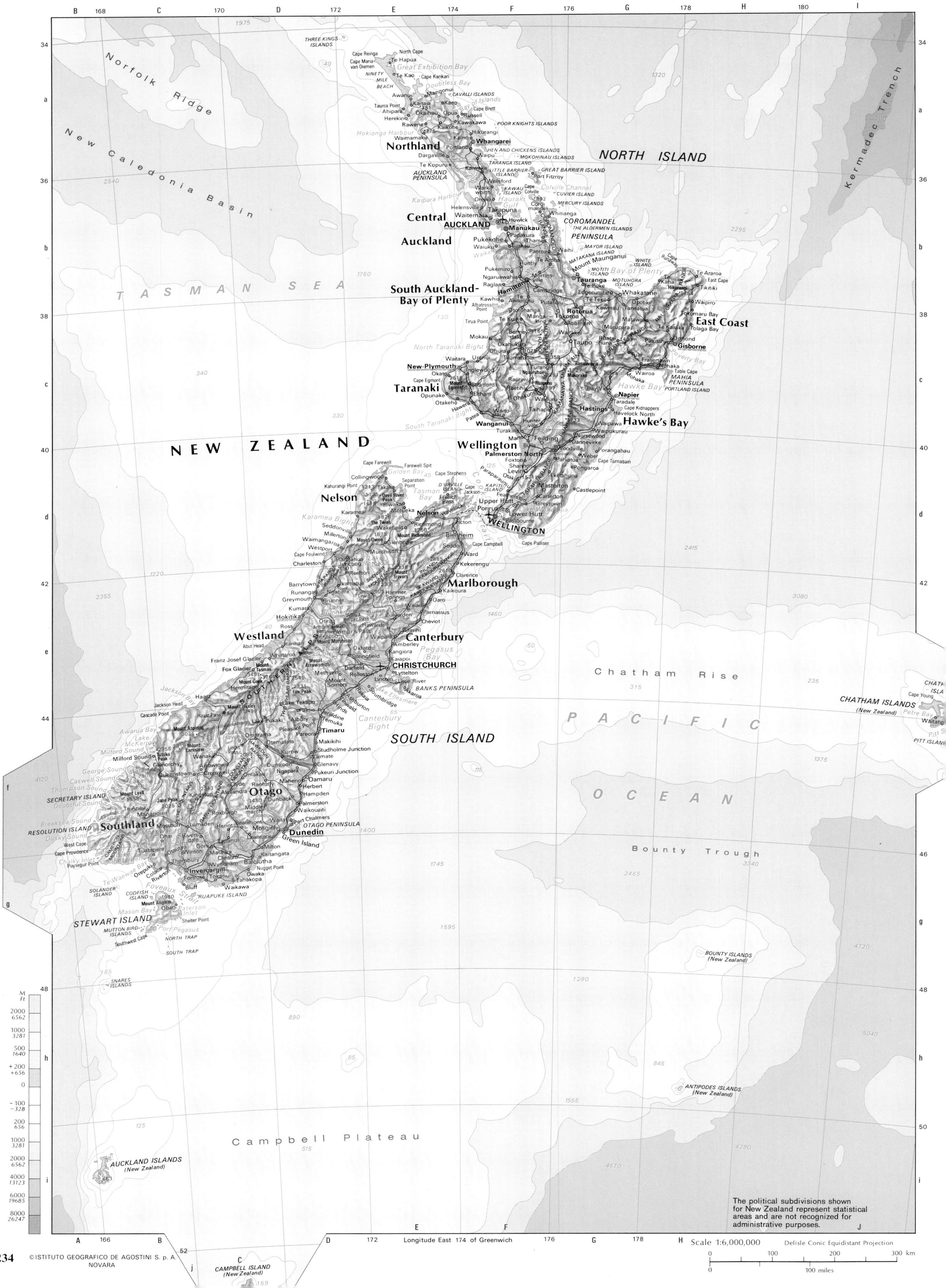

Map 62 **NEW ZEALAND**

NORTH ISLAND

NEW ZEALAND

SOUTH ISLAND

TASMAN SEA

PACIFIC OCEAN

Norfolk Ridge

New Caledonia Basin

Kermadec Trench

Chatham Rise

Bounty Trough

Campbell Plateau

Regions / Statistical Areas

Northland
Central Auckland
Auckland
South Auckland-Bay of Plenty
East Coast
Taranaki
Hawke's Bay
Wellington
Nelson
Marlborough
Westland
Canterbury
Otago
Southland

Cities and towns

AUCKLAND, Manukau, Whangarei, Pukekohe, Waiuku, Hamilton, Tauranga, Whakatane, Rotorua, Taupo, Gisborne, New Plymouth, Wanganui, Napier, Hastings, Palmerston North, WELLINGTON, Upper Hutt, Lower Hutt, Porirua, Masterton, Nelson, Richmond, Blenheim, Picton, Greymouth, Hokitika, Westport, CHRISTCHURCH, Lyttelton, Timaru, Oamaru, Dunedin, Invercargill, Bluff, Queenstown, Alexandra

Features

Cape Reinga, North Cape, Cape Maria van Diemen, Great Exhibition Bay, Doubtless Bay, Three Kings Islands, Ninety Mile Beach, Hokianga Harbour, Kaipara Harbour, Hauraki Gulf, Coromandel Peninsula, Great Barrier Island, Little Barrier Island, Bay of Plenty, White Island, East Cape, Poverty Bay, Mahia Peninsula, Hawke Bay, Cape Kidnappers, Cape Egmont, Mount Egmont, South Taranaki Bight, North Taranaki Bight, Cape Farewell, Farewell Spit, Golden Bay, Tasman Bay, D'Urville Island, Cape Campbell, Cape Palliser, Banks Peninsula, Pegasus Bay, Canterbury Bight, Lake Tekapo, Lake Pukaki, Mount Cook, Mount Aspiring, Milford Sound, Doubtful Sound, Dusky Sound, Foveaux Strait, Stewart Island, Ruapuke Island, Solander Island, Snares Islands, Auckland Islands (New Zealand), Campbell Island (New Zealand), Bounty Islands (New Zealand), Antipodes Islands (New Zealand), Chatham Islands (New Zealand), Pitt Island

Longitude East 174 of Greenwich

Scale 1:6,000,000   Delisle Conic Equidistant Projection

0   100   200   300 km

0   100 miles

The political subdivisions shown for New Zealand represent statistical areas and are not recognized for administrative purposes.

M / Ft
2000 / 6562
1000 / 3281
500 / 1640
+200 / +656
0
-100 / -328
200 / 656
1000 / 3281
2000 / 6562
4000 / 13123
6000 / 19685
8000 / 26247

© ISTITUTO GEOGRAFICO DE AGOSTINI S. p. A. NOVARA

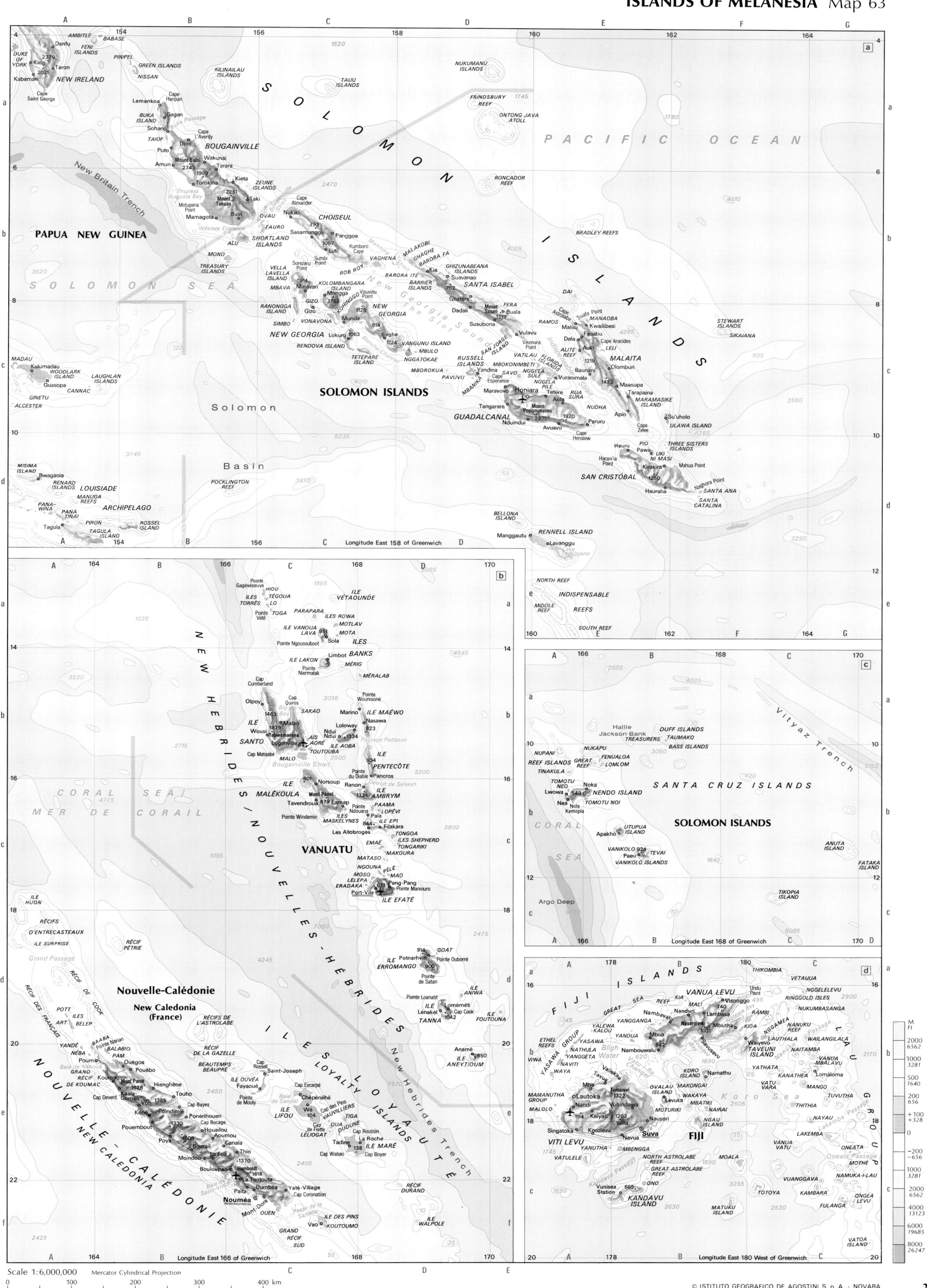

SOLOMON ISLANDS

VANUATU

Nouvelle-Calédonie
New Caledonia
(France)

FIJI

Scale 1:6,000,000   Mercator Cylindrical Projection

0   100   200   300   400 km

0   100   200 miles

Map 64 **ISLANDS OF MICRONESIA-POLYNESIA**

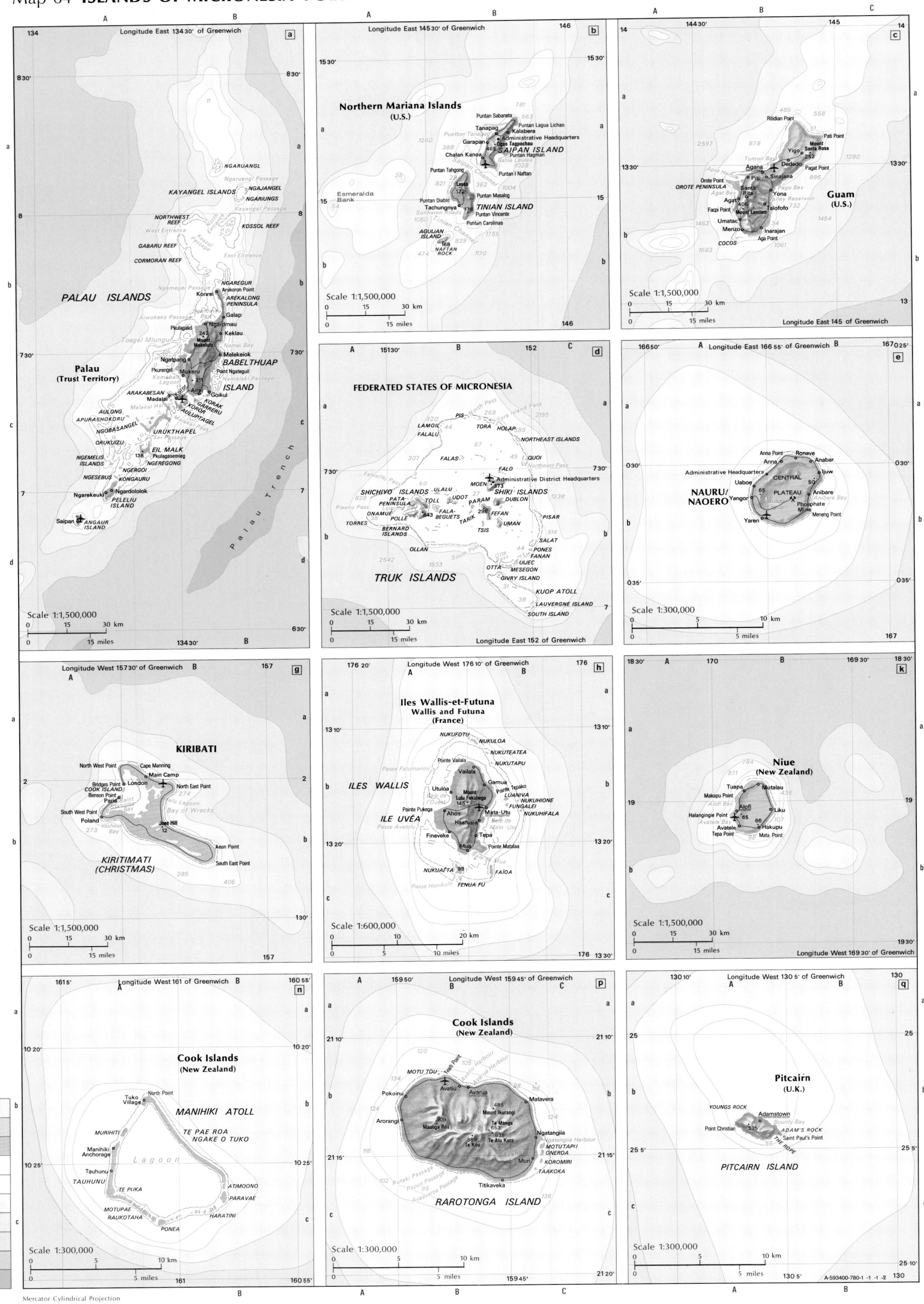

Northern Mariana Islands (U.S.)

Scale 1:1,500,000

Guam (U.S.)

Scale 1:1,500,000

PALAU ISLANDS

Palau (Trust Territory)

Scale 1:1,500,000

FEDERATED STATES OF MICRONESIA

TRUK ISLANDS

Scale 1:1,500,000

NAURU/ NAOERO

Scale 1:300,000

KIRIBATI

KIRITIMATI (CHRISTMAS)

Scale 1:1,500,000

Iles Wallis-et-Futuna Wallis and Futuna (France)

ILES WALLIS

ILE UVÉA

Scale 1:600,000

Niue (New Zealand)

Scale 1:1,500,000

Cook Islands (New Zealand)

MANIHIKI ATOLL

Scale 1:300,000

Cook Islands (New Zealand)

RAROTONGA ISLAND

Scale 1:300,000

Pitcairn (U.K.)

PITCAIRN ISLAND

Scale 1:300,000

Mercator Cylindrical Projection

© ISTITUTO GEOGRAFICO DE AGOSTINI S. p. A. - NOVARA

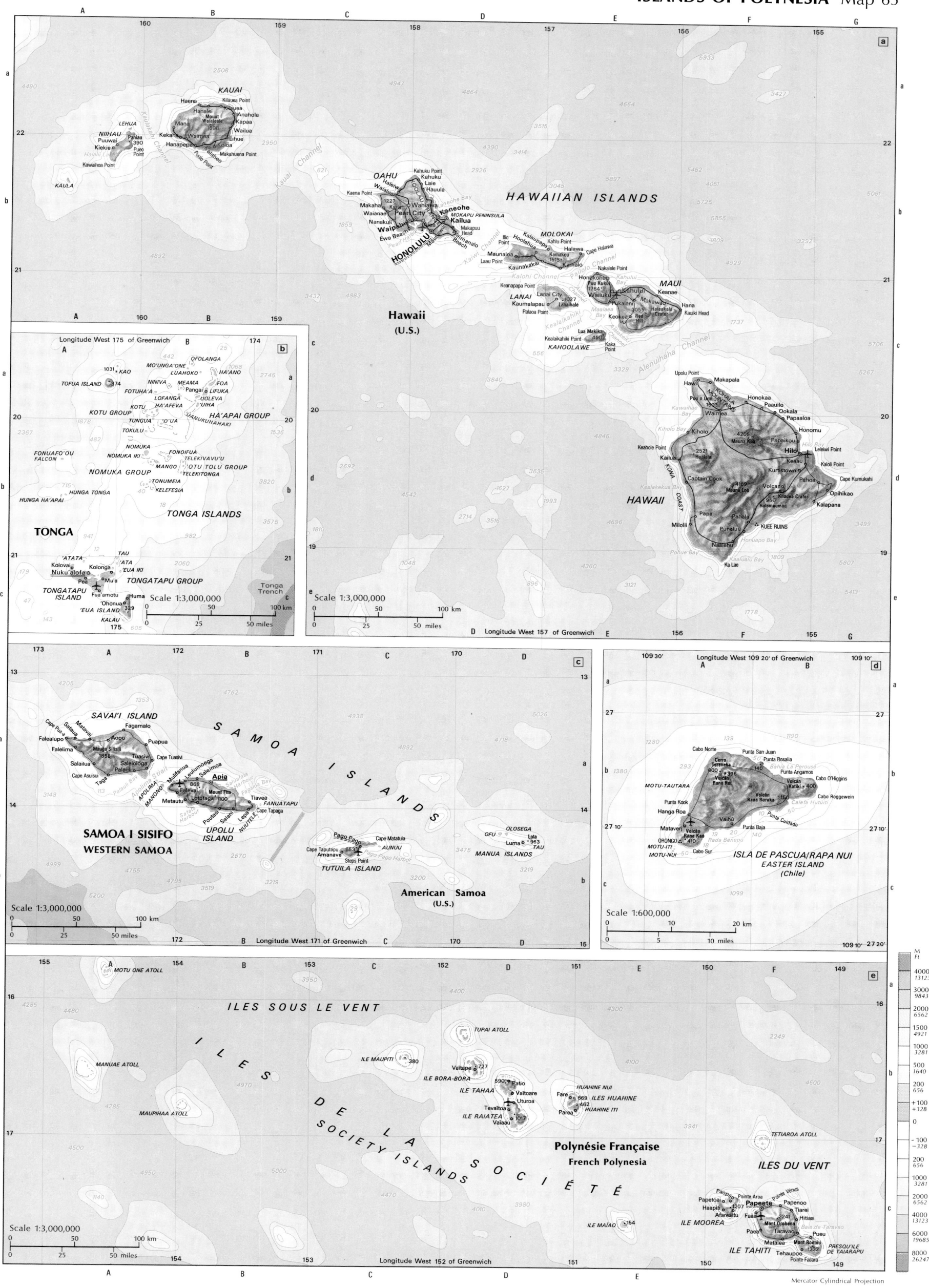

HAWAIIAN ISLANDS

KAUAI

Haena • Kilauea Point
Hanalei • Puuwai
Mana • Mount Waialeale
5666
Kekaha • Waimea • Anahola
• Kapaa
• Wailua
Hanapepe • Koloa • Lihue
Hanamaulu Point
NIIHAU
Puuwai • Pahau
Kiekie • 390
Kawaihoa Point
LEHUA

KAULA

Kawaihoa Point
Pueo Point

OAHU
Kahuku Point
Kahuku
Haleiwa • Laie
Wahiawa • Hauula
Kaena Point • 1227
Makaha • Kaneohe Bay
Makaha • Waianae • Pearl City • **Kaneohe**
Nanakuli • Waipahu • **Kailua**
Waipio • MOKAPU PENINSULA
Ewa Beach • **HONOLULU** • Makapuu Head
• Waimanalo Beach
Pearl Harbor

MOLOKAI
Ilio Point • Kahiku Point
Hoolehua • Kalaupapa • Cape Halawa
Maunaloa • Kamakou • Halawa
1515 • Kamalo
Kaunakakai
Laau Point • Nakalele Point
Kalohi Channel

MAUI
Honolua • Puu Kukui
1764 • Kahului • Keanae
Waihee • Wailuku • Makawao • Hana
Lahaina • Kahului • Haleakala • Kauiki Head
LANAI • Maalaea Bay • Crater
Lanai City • 1027 • Keokea • Red Hill
Kaumalapau • Lanaihale
Palaoa Point
Lua Makika • 4901
KAHOOLAWE
Kaka Point

Kealaikahiki Channel
Alenuihaha Channel

Hawaii (U.S.)

Upolu Point • Makapala
Hawi • KOHALA • Honokaa
Puu o Umi • MOUNTAINS • Paauilo
Waimea • 1625 • Ookala
Kawaihae Bay • Papaaloa
Kiholo Bay • Kiholo • Honomu
4205 • Mount Kea • Papaikou
Keahole Point • 2521 • Hualalai • **Hilo**
Kailua • Kurtistown • Leleiwi Point
Kaloli Point
Captain Cook • 4168 • Volcano • Pahoa
Mount Loa • 1003 • Cape Kumukahi
Papa • Halemaumau • Kilauea Crater • Opihikao
Pahala • 950 • Kalapana
Milolii
KONA COAST
Punaluu • KUEE RUINS
Naalehu
Ka Lae
Honuapo Bay

HAWAII

Scale 1:3,000,000
0 ____ 50 ____ 100 km
0 ____ 25 ____ 50 miles

Longitude West 157 of Greenwich

TONGA

Longitude West 175 of Greenwich

1031 • KAO
MO'UNGA'ONE • OFOLANGA
TOFUA ISLAND • 374 • LUAHOKO • HA'ANO
NINIVA • MEAMA • FOA
FOTUHA'A • Pangai • LIFUKA
LOFANGA • HA'AFEVA • UOLEVA
KOTU GROUP • UIHA
TUNGUA • 'O'UA
TOKULU • VANUKUHAHAKI
NOMUKA
FONUAFO'OU • NOMUKA IKI • FONOIFUA
FALCON • TELEKIVAVU'U
MANGO • OTU TOLU GROUP
NOMUKA GROUP • TONUMEIA • TELEKITONGA
HUNGA HA'APAI • KELEFESIA
HUNGA TONGA

TONGA ISLANDS

'ATATA • TAU
Kolovai • 'ATA • 'EUA IKI
Pea • Kolonga
Nuku'alofa • Mu'a
TONGATAPU • Huma
ISLAND • Fua'amotu
'Ohonua • 329
'EUA ISLAND
KALAU

TONGATAPU GROUP

Tonga Trench

Scale 1:3,000,000
0 ____ 50 ____ 100 km
0 ____ 25 ____ 50 miles

SAMOA ISLANDS

SAVAI'I ISLAND
Cape Puava • Sataua • Matavai • Fagamalo
Falealupo • Aopo • Puapua
Falelima • Mauga Silisili • Tuasivi • Cape Tuasivi
1858
Salailua • Saleaula
Cape Asuisu • Saleimoa • Lealumoega
Tuga • Apolima • Mulifanua • Apia
MANONO • 868 • Faleula
APOLIMA • Metautu • Mount Fito
Lefaga • Lotofaga • 1100 • Tiavea
Poutasi • Salani • Lepa • FANUATAPU
UPOLU • Cape Tapaga
ISLAND • NUUTELE

SAMOA I SISIFO
WESTERN SAMOA

Pago Pago
Cape Matatula
Cape Taputapu • Amanave • 653 • AUNUU
Steps Point
Pago Pago Harbor
TUTUILA ISLAND

OFU • OLOSEGA
Luma • Lata • 1963
• TAU
MANUA ISLANDS

American Samoa (U.S.)

Scale 1:3,000,000
0 ____ 50 ____ 100 km
0 ____ 25 ____ 50 miles

Longitude West 171 of Greenwich

ISLA DE PASCUA/RAPA NUI
EASTER ISLAND (Chile)

Longitude West 109 20' of Greenwich

Cabo Norte • Punta San Juan
• Punta Rosalia
Cerro • Punta Angamos
Terevaka • 500 • Volcán • Cabo O'Higgins
MOTU-TAUTARA • Rana Roi
• Volcán • Cabo Roggewein
Punta Koak • Rana Roraka
Hanga Roa • Vaihu • Punta Baja
Mataveri • Volcán • Punta Cuidado
ORONGO • Rana Kao • Caleta Hutuiti
MOTU-ITI • 410 • Cabo Sur
MOTU-NUI
Rada Benepu

Scale 1:600,000
0 ____ 10 ____ 20 km
0 ____ 5 ____ 10 miles

Polynésie Française
French Polynesia

ILES SOUS LE VENT

MOTU ONE ATOLL

MANUAE ATOLL

MAUPIHAA ATOLL

ILE MAUPITI • 380

TUPAI ATOLL

Vaitape • 727
ILE BORA-BORA
590 • Patio
ILE TAHAA • Vaitoare
Uturoa
Tevaitoa • 669 • Fare
1017 • HUAHINE NUI
ILE RAIATEA • ILES HUAHINE
Vaiaau • Parea • HUAHINE ITI

ILES DE LA SOCIÉTÉ
SOCIETY ISLANDS

TETIAROA ATOLL

ILES DU VENT

ILE MAIAO • 154

Paopao • Pointe Aroa
Papetoai • Pointe Venus
Haapiti • 1207 • **Papeete** • Papenoo
Tiarei
Faaa • 2241 • Hitiaa
Afareaitu
ILE MOOREA • Mont Orohena
Taravao
Mataiea • 1332 • Mont Roonui
Tehaupoo • PRESQU'ILE DE TAIARAPU
Pointe Faaiti
ILE TAHITI

Scale 1:3,000,000
0 ____ 50 ____ 100 km
0 ____ 25 ____ 50 miles

Longitude West 152 of Greenwich

Mercator Cylindrical Projection

M
Ft
4000 / 13123
3000 / 9843
2000 / 6562
1500 / 4921
1000 / 3281
500 / 1640
200 / 656
+100 / +328
0
−100 / −328
200 / 656
1000 / 3281
2000 / 6562
4000 / 13123
6000 / 19685
8000 / 26247

Map 66 **ANTARCTIC REGION**

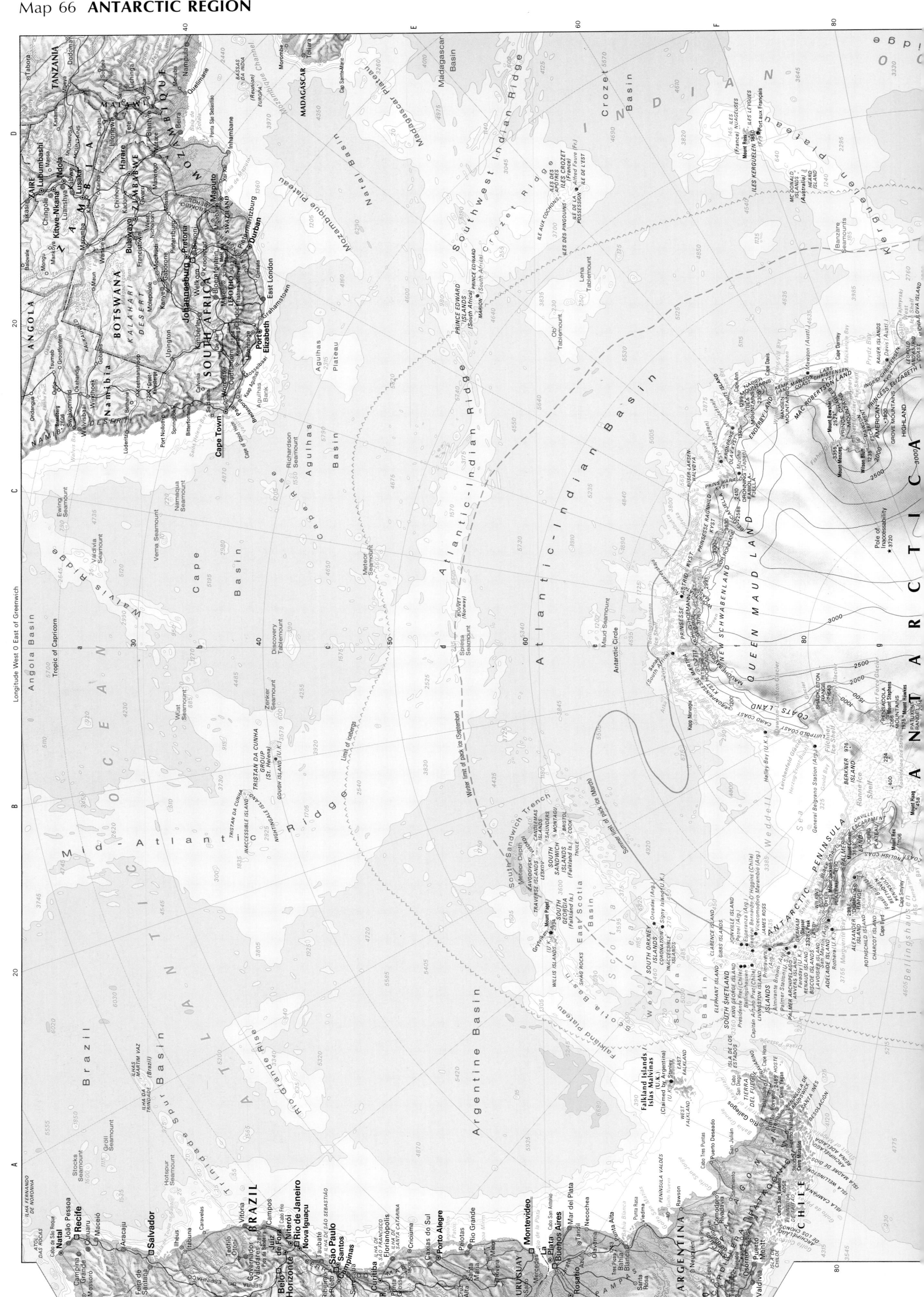

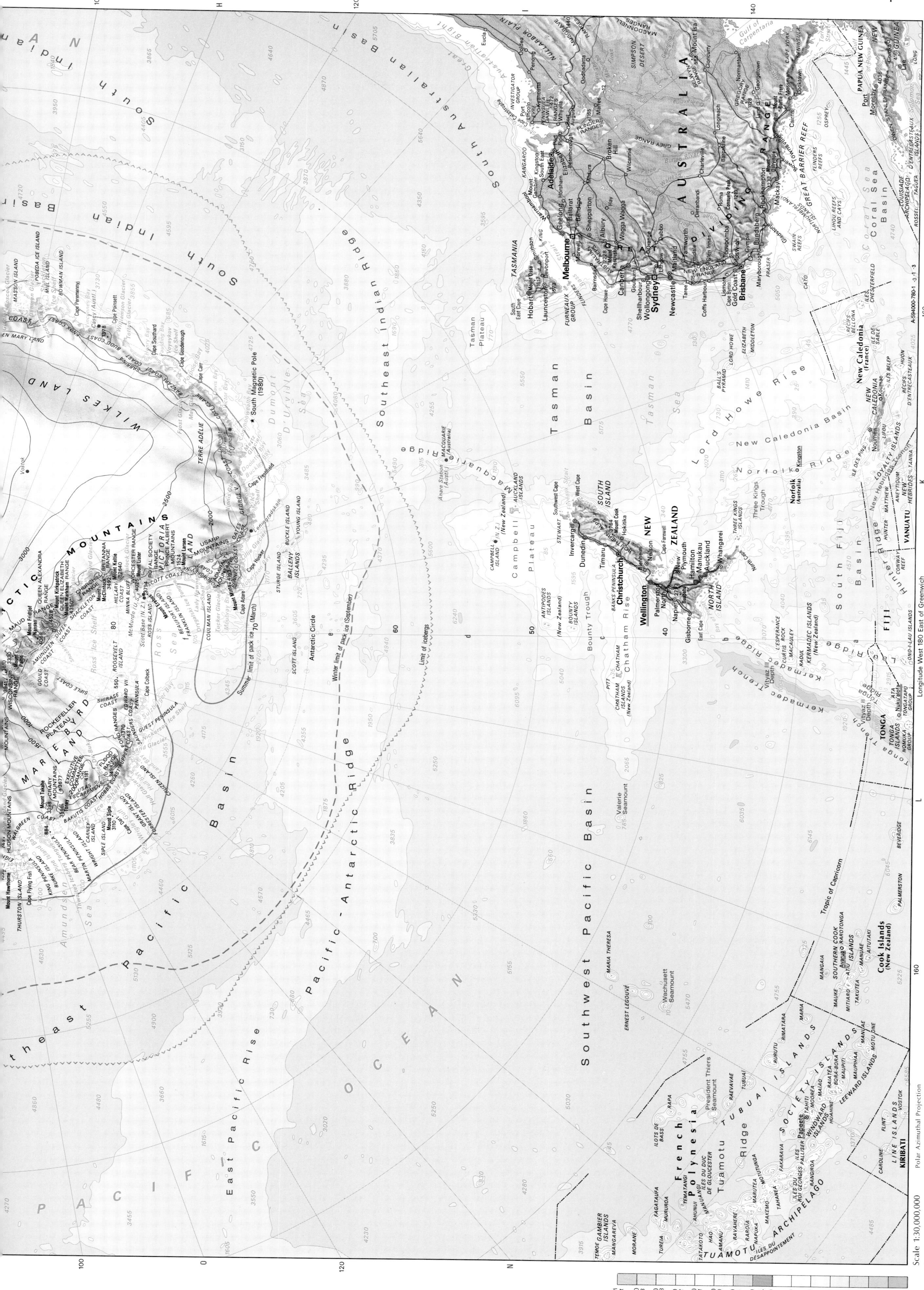

The Antarctic region is not a political entity and its status is regulated by the Antarctic Treaty signed in Washington, D.C. in 1959. The treaty binds the states which signed the agreement to use the region solely for peaceful purposes and scientific research.

Longitude West 180 East of Greenwich

Scale 1:30,000,000

Polar Azimuthal Projection

2000 km
1500
1000
500
0

1000 miles
500
0

AUSTRALIA

TASMANIA

NEW ZEALAND

SOUTH ISLAND

NORTH ISLAND

Melbourne
Sydney
Canberra
Adelaide
Brisbane
Newcastle
Wollongong
Hobart

Wellington
Christchurch
Auckland
Dunedin

New Caledonia (France)

PAPUA NEW GUINEA

Tasman Basin

Tasman Sea

South Australian Basin

Southeast Indian Ridge

South Indian Basin

WILKES LAND

VICTORIA LAND

MARIE BYRD LAND

QUEEN MARY LAND

TRANSANTARCTIC MOUNTAINS

Ross Sea
Ross Ice Shelf

Amundsen Sea

Southwest Pacific Basin

Pacific-Antarctic Ridge

East Pacific Rise

Southeast Pacific Basin

PACIFIC OCEAN

South Magnetic Pole (1980)

Antarctic Circle

Summer limit of pack ice (March)
Winter limit of pack ice (September)
Limit of icebergs

Tropic of Capricorn

French Polynesia

TUAMOTU ARCHIPELAGO

TUBUAI ISLANDS

SOCIETY ISLANDS

SOUTHERN COOK ISLANDS

Cook Islands (New Zealand)

KIRIBATI

LINE ISLANDS

TONGA

FIJI

VANUATU

NEW CALEDONIA

Lord Howe Rise

New Caledonia Basin

Norfolk Ridge

South Fiji Basin

Kermadec Trench

Tonga Trench

Kermadec Ridge

CHATHAM ISLANDS (New Zealand)

Chatham Rise

Bounty Trough

Campbell Plateau

AUCKLAND ISLANDS (Australia)

MACQUARIE (Australia)

Macquarie Ridge

Great Barrier Reef

Coral Sea

GREAT DIVIDING RANGE

Dumont d'Urville Sea

M ft
4000 13123
3000 9843
2000 6562
1000 3281
500 1640
+200 +656
0 0
Depr. 0 0
-200 -656
2000 6562
3000 9843
4000 13123
6000 19685
8000 26247

239

Map 67 **ARCTIC REGION**

PACIFIC OCEAN

Suiko Seamount
Papanin Seamount

Aleutian Trench
ALEUTIAN ISLANDS
ATKA ANDREANOF ISLANDS
RAT ISLANDS
NEAR ISLANDS
FOX ISLANDS
UNIMAK
Bowers Bank
Bowers Ridge
Shishaldin Volcano
PRIBILOF ISLANDS
KOMANDORSKI ISLANDS
Komandorskiye
Ust-Kamčatsk
Petropavlovsk-Kamčatski
KAMCHATKA PENINSULA
Obruchev Rise
Kuril Trench
KURIL ISLANDS
SIMUŠIR URUP ITURUP
PARAMUŠIR ONEKOTAN
JAPAN HONSHŪ
Aomori Hakodate
HOKKAIDŌ Asahikawa
Sapporo Wakkanai
SAKHALIN
Južno-Sahalinsk
Holmsk
Sea of Japan
Vladivostok

ALASKA PENINSULA
Patton Seamount
KODIAK
KENAI PENINSULA
Seward Kenai
Anchorage
Homer
Cordova
Valdez
Fairbanks
NUNIVAK
SAINT MATTHEW
SAINT LAWRENCE
Cape Romanzof
Bethel
Nome
SEWARD PENINSULA
Kotzebue
Point Hope
Barrow
Point Barrow
Prudhoe Bay
KORYAK RANGE
Anadyr
ANADYR RANGE
CHUKCHI PENINSULA
Uelen
Egvekinot
Pevek
Magadan
SREDINNYJ RANGE
Sea of Okhotsk
KOLYMA RANGE
CHERSKI RANGE
VERKHOYANSK RANGE
DZHUGDZHUR RANGE
STANOVOY RANGE
Habarovsk
Komsomolsk-na-Amure
SHANTAR ISLANDS

East Siberian Sea
WRANGEL
BEAR ISLANDS
KOLYMA PLAIN
Jakutsk
Ust-Maja
CENTRAL SIBERIAN PLATEAU
CHINA

De Long Strait
Chukchi Plateau
ARCTIC OCEAN
Canada Basin
DE LONG ISLANDS
NEW SIBERIA
ANJOU ISLANDS
NEW SIBERIAN ISLANDS
LYAKHOV ISLANDS
KOTELNY
Tiksi
Laptev Sea
NORTH SIBERIAN PLAIN

Makarov Basin
Lomonosov Ridge
North Pole
Eurasia Basin
Alpha Cordillera
SEVERNAYA ZEMLJA
BOLSHEVIK ISLAND
OCTOBER REVOLUTION ISLAND
KOMSOMOLEC
TAYMYR PENINSULA
Norilsk
Dudinka
RUSSIA
CENTRAL SIBERIAN UPLANDS
PUTORANA PLATO
Krasnoyarsk

Nansen Basin
Fram Basin
FRANZ JOSEPH LAND
ZEMLJA GEORGA
NOVAJA ZEMLJA
NOVAYA ZEMLYA
Kara Sea
GYDA PENINSULA
YAMAL PENINSULA
WEST SIBERIAN PLAIN
Novosibirsk
Tomsk

VANCOUVER ISLAND
QUEEN CHARLOTTE ISLANDS
ALEXANDER ARCHIPELAGO
Victoria
Vancouver
Seattle
Prince Rupert
Kitimat
Sitka
Juneau
COAST MOUNTAINS
SAINT ELIAS MOUNTAINS
Whitehorse
Skagway
Wrangell
MACKENZIE MOUNTAINS
ROCKY MOUNTAINS
Calgary
Edmonton
Fort Nelson
Fort Liard
Fort Simpson
Hay River
Fort Providence
Yellowknife
Fort Smith
Uranium City
GREAT BEAR LAKE
GREAT SLAVE LAKE
Coppermine
CANADA
Lynn Lake
Churchill
Hudson Bay
Fort Severn
Winisk

BANKS ISLAND
VICTORIA ISLAND
Cambridge Bay
PRINCE OF WALES
KING WILLIAM
BOOTHIA PENINSULA
SOMERSET
Resolute
PRINCE PATRICK
MELVILLE
MACKENZIE KING
ELLEF RINGNES
AXEL HEIBERG
QUEEN ELIZABETH ISLANDS
PARRY ISLANDS
North Magnetic Pole 1980
ELLESMERE
Grise Fiord
Alert
Cape Columbia
Barbeau Peak
PEARY LAND
KNUD RASMUSSEN LAND
Kap Morris Jesup

BAFFIN ISLAND
CUMBERLAND PENINSULA
Frobisher Bay
Broughton Island
Pond Inlet
BYLOT
Clyde
Baffin Bay
PENINSULA D'UNGAVA
UNGAVA PENINSULA
Ivujivik
Fort-George
Inoucdjouac
BELCHER ISLANDS
OTTAWA ISLANDS
COATS
MANSEL
SOUTHAMPTON
Repulse Bay
Chesterfield Inlet
Rankin Inlet
Eskimo Point
Kap York
HAYES HALVØ
Thule / Qânâq

Greenland (Den.)
KING CHRISTIAN IX LAND
KING FREDERIK VI COAST
KING FREDERIK VIII LAND
KING CHRISTIAN X LAND
Godthåb / Nûk
Holsteinsborg / Sisimiut
Jakobshavn / Ilulissat
Egedesminde / Ausiat
Godhavn / Qeqertarssuaq
DISKO
Søndre Strømfjord
Angmagssalik
Scoresbysund
Kap Brewster
Julianehåb / Qaqortoq
Kap Farvel
Ûmânarssuaq
Gunnbjørns Field

Fort-Chimo
Nouveau-Québec
Schefferville
Labrador City
Goose Bay
TORNGAT MOUNTAINS
LABRADOR
Nain
NEWFOUNDLAND
Battle Harbour
Grand Falls
Corner Brook
Saint John's
Cape Race

ATLANTIC OCEAN
Mid-Atlantic Ridge
Reykjanes Ridge
Labrador Basin
Newfoundland Basin
Greenland Basin
Iceland
ICELAND
Reykjavik
Denmark Strait
Norwegian Basin
Faroe Bank
FAEROE IS (Den.)
Iceland Basin
Rockall Rise
ROCKALL
SHETLAND ISLANDS
ORKNEY ISLANDS
HEBRIDES
West European Basin
Porcupine Bank
AZORES (Port.)

JAN MAYEN (Norway)
Svalbard (Norway)
SPITSBERGEN
Barentsburg
NORDAUSTLANDET
EDGEØYA
KVITØYA
BEAR ISLAND (Norway)
Barents Sea
KOLGUJEV
KANIN PENINSULA
Narjan-Mar
TIMAN RIDGE
Vorkuta
URAL MOUNTAINS
Salehard
Hanty-Mansijsk
Tjumen
Jekaterinburg
Perm
Čeljabinsk
Kurgan
Ufa

Murmansk
KOLA PENINSULA
Arhangelsk
NORWAY
SWEDEN
FINLAND
SCANDINAVIA
LAPLAND
KARELIA
Tromsø
Hammerfest
North Cape
VESTERÅLEN
LOFOTEN
Narvik
Bodø
Trondheim
Bergen
Oslo
Stockholm
Helsinki
Turku
Tallinn
Sankt-Peterburg
Moskva
Kirov
Kazan
Samara
Syzran
Saratov
Tambov
Voronež
Rjazán
Tula
Orel
Smolensk
Vitebsk
Minsk
BELARUS
Riga
LATVIA
LITHUANIA
Vilnius
Kaliningrad
Gdansk
ESTONIA
Novgorod
Vologda
Jaroslavl
Tver
Vladimir
Penza

Oulu
Vaasa
Umeå
Örnsköldsvik
Norrköping
Göteborg
Malmö
København
DENMARK
Gotland
BORNHOLM
Baltic Sea
Gulf of Bothnia
Ålesund
Ålborg
Kristiansand
Stavanger
Wick
Aberdeen
Glasgow
Edinburgh
BRITISH ISLES
UNITED KINGDOM
IRELAND
Dublin
Belfast
Liverpool
Manchester
Birmingham
London
Bristol
Plymouth
Cork
Wexford
North Sea
Celtic Sea
NETHERLANDS
Amsterdam
Rotterdam
BELGIUM
Bruxelles
GERMANY
Hamburg
Hannover
Berlin
Leipzig
Frankfurt
Nürnberg
München
Praha
CZECH REP.
POLAND
Warszawa
Poznan
Katowice
Wroclaw
SLOVAKIA
AUSTRIA
Wien
HUNGARY
Budapest
ROMANIA
Bucuresti
Cluj-Napoca
Timisoara
Constanta
MOLDOVA
Kišinev
UKRAINE
Kijev
Lvov
Odessa
Nikolajev
Harkov
Dnepropetrovsk
Sevastopol
CRIMEA
Rostov-na-Donu
Novorossijsk
CAUCASUS
Black Sea
BULGARIA
Sofia
YUGO.
Beograd
CROATIA
Zagreb
SLOV.
BOS.
Sarajevo
Split
ITALY
Venezia
Milano
Torino
Genova
Firenze
FRANCE
Paris
Nantes
Bordeaux
Lyon
Genève
Zürich
Bern
Strasbourg
Luxembourg
Le Havre
Brest
Le Mans
Bay of Biscay
GREECE
Thessaloníki
Izmir
TURKEY
Ankara
Eskişehir
Adana
ANATOLIAN PLATEAU
CYPRUS

Arctic Circle
Summer limit of pack ice (August)
Winter limit of pack ice (April)
Limit of icebergs

Scale 1:30,000,000   Polar Azimuthal Projection
0   500   1000   1500   2000 km
0   500   1000 miles
Longitude West 0 East of Greenwich

Geographical Information and International Map Index

World Nations

This table gives the area, population, population density, form of government, capital and location of every country in the world.

Area figures include inland water.

The populations are estimates made by Rand McNally on the basis of official data, United Nations estimates and other available information.

Besides specifying the form of government for all political areas, the table classifies them into five groups according to their political status. Units labeled

A are independent sovereign nations. Units labeled *B* are independent as regards internal affairs, but for purposes of foreign affairs they are under the protection of another country. Units labeled *C* are colonies, overseas territories, dependencies, etc. of other countries. Units labeled *D* are states, provinces or other major administrative subdivisions of important countries. Units in the table with no letter designations are regions, islands or other areas that do not constitute separate political units by themselves.

Map Plate numbers refer to the International Map section of the atlas.

Country, Division, or Region English (Conventional)	Local Name	Area km²	Area sq mi	Population 1/1/93	Population Density per km²	Population Density per sq mi	Form of Government and Political Status		Capital	Continent and Map Plate	
Afars and Issas, see Djibouti	. . .	. . .	. . .		. . .	. . .	. . . .		. . . .	. . . .	. . .
† AFGHANISTAN	Afghānestān	652,225	251,826	16,290,000	25	65	Islamic republic	A	Kābol	Asia	23
Africa	. . .	30,300,000	11,700,000	668,700,000	22	57	. . . .		. . . .	Africa	30-31
Alabama	Alabama	135,775	52,423	4,128,000	30	79	State (U.S.)	D	Montgomery	N. Amer.	44
Alaska	Alaska	1,700,139	656,424	564,000	0.3	0.9	State (U.S.)	D	Juneau	N. Amer.	40
† ALBANIA	Shqiperia	28,748	11,100	3,305,000	115	298	Republic	A	Tirana	Europe	15
Alberta	Alberta	661,190	255,287	2,839,000	4.3	11	Province (Canada)	D	Edmonton	N. Amer.	42
† ALGERIA	Al Jazā'ir	2,381,741	919,595	26,925,000	11	29	Provisional military government	A	Al Jazā'ir (Algiers)	Africa	32
American Samoa	American Samoa (English) / Amerika Samoa (Samoan)	199	77	52,000	261	675	Unincorporated territory (U.S.)	C	Pago Pago	Oceania	65
Andaman and Nicobar Islands	Andaman and Nicobar Islands	8,293	3,202	302,000	36	94	Territory (India)	D	Port Blair	Asia	25
ANDORRA	Andorra	453	175	56,000	124	320	Coprincipality (Spanish and French protection)	B	Andorra la Vella	Europe	13
† ANGOLA	Angola	1,246,700	481,354	10,735,000	8.6	22	Republic	A	Luanda	Africa	36
ANGUILLA	Anguilla	91	35	7,000	77	200	Dependent territory (U.K. protection)	B	The Valley	N. Amer.	51
Anhui	Anhui	139,000	53,668	58,440,000	420	1,089	Province (China)	D	Hefei	Asia	28
Antarctica	. . .	14,000,000	5,400,000	(1)	. . .	. . .	. . . .		. . . .	Antarctica	66
† ANTIGUA AND BARBUDA	Antigua and Barbuda	442	171	77,000	174	450	Parliamentary state	A	St. John's	N. Amer.	51
Arabian Peninsula	. . .	3,010,000	1,160,000	35,848,000	12	31	. . . .		. . . .	Asia	23
† ARGENTINA	Argentina	2,780,400	1,073,519	32,950,000	12	31	Republic	A	Buenos Aires and Viedma (2)	S. Amer.	56
Arizona	Arizona	295,276	114,006	3,872,000	13	34	State (U.S.)	D	Phoenix	N. Amer.	46
Arkansas	Arkansas	137,742	53,182	2,410,000	17	45	State (U.S.)	D	Little Rock	N. Amer.	45
† ARMENIA	Hayastan	29,800	11,506	3,429,000	115	298	Republic	A	Jerevan	Asia	16
ARUBA	Aruba	193	75	65,000	337	867	Self-governing territory (Netherlands protection)	B	Oranjestad	N. Amer.	49
Ascension	Ascension	88	34	1,200	14	35	Dependency (St. Helena)	C	Georgetown	Africa	30-31
Asia	. . .	44,900,000	17,300,000	3,337,800,000	74	193	. . . .		. . . .	Asia	21-22
† AUSTRALIA	Australia	7,682,300	2,966,155	16,965,000	2.2	5.7	Federal parliamentary state	A	Canberra	Oceania	59
Australian Capital Territory	Australian Capital Territory	2,400	927	282,000	118	304	Territory (Australia)	D	Canberra	Oceania	59
† AUSTRIA	Österreich	83,856	32,377	7,899,000	94	244	Federal republic	A	Wien (Vienna)	Europe	14
† AZERBAIJAN	Azärbayjan	86,600	33,436	7,510,000	87	225	Republic	A	Baku	Asia	16
Azores	Açores	2,247	868	261,000	116	301	Autonomous region	D	Ponta Delgada	Europe	32
Baden-Wurttemberg	Baden-Württemberg	35,751	13,804	9,798,000	274	710	State (Germany)	D	Stuttgart	Europe	10
† BAHAMAS	Bahamas	13,939	5,382	265,000	19	49	Parliamentary state	A	Nassau	N. Amer.	47
† BAHRAIN	Al Baḥrayn	691	267	561,000	812	2,101	Monarchy	A	Al Manāmah (Manama)	Asia	24
Balearic Islands	Islas Baleares	5,014	1,936	743,000	148	384	Province (Spain)	D	Palma	Europe	13
Baltic Republics	. . .	174,000	67,182	8,154,000	47	121	. . . .		. . . .	Europe	8
† BANGLADESH	Bangladesh	143,998	55,598	120,850,000	839	2,174	Republic	A	Dhaka	Asia	25
† BARBADOS	Barbados	430	166	258,000	600	1,554	Parliamentary state	A	Bridgetown	N. Amer.	51
Bavaria	Bayern	70,554	27,241	11,430,000	162	420	State (Germany)	D	München (Munich)	Europe	10
† BELARUS	Byelarus'	207,600	80,155	10,400,000	50	130	Republic	A	Minsk	Europe	16
† BELGIUM	Belgique (French) / België (Flemish)	30,518	11,783	10,030,000	329	851	Constitutional monarchy	A	Bruxelles (Brussels)	Europe	12
† BELIZE	Belize	22,963	8,866	186,000	8.1	21	Parliamentary state	A	Belmopan	N. Amer.	49
Benelux	. . .	74,968	28,945	25,612,000	342	885	Economic union			Europe	12
† BENIN	Bénin	112,600	43,475	5,083,000	45	117	Republic	A	Porto-Novo and Cotonou	Africa	34
Berlin	Berlin	883	341	3,475,000	3,935	10,191	State	D	Berlin	Europe	10
Bermuda	Bermuda	54	21	60,000	1,111	2,857	Dependent territory (U.K.)	C	Hamilton	N. Amer.	47
† BHUTAN	Druk	46,500	17,954	1,680,000	36	94	Monarchy (Indian protection)	B	Thimphu	Asia	25
Bioko	Bioko	2,017	779	75,000	37	96	Province of Equatorial Guinea	D	Malabo	Africa	34
† BOLIVIA	Bolivia	1,098,581	424,165	7,411,000	6.7	17	Republic	A	La Paz and Sucre	S. Amer.	54
Borneo, Indonesian	Kalimantan	539,460	208,287	9,458,000	18	45	Part of Indonesia (4 provinces)		. . . .	Asia	26
† BOSNIA AND HERZEGOVINA	Bosna i Hercegovina	51,129	19,741	4,375,000	86	222	Republic	A	Sarajevo	Europe	14
† BOTSWANA	Botswana	582,000	224,711	1,379,000	2.4	6.1	Republic	A	Gaborone	Africa	37
Brandenburg	Brandenburg	29,060	11,220	2,690,000	93	240	State (Germany)	D	Potsdam	Europe	10
† BRAZIL	Brasil	8,511,996	3,286,500	159,630,000	19	49	Federal republic	A	Brasília	S. Amer.	54-56
Bremen	Bremen	404	156	687,000	1,700	4,404	State (Germany)	D	Bremen	Europe	10
British Columbia	British Columbia (English) / Colombie-Britannique (French)	947,800	365,948	3,665,000	3.9	10	Province (Canada)	D	Victoria	N. Amer.	42
British Indian Ocean Territory	British Indian Ocean Territory	60	23	(1)	. . .	. . .	Dependent territory (U.K.)	C	. . .	Africa	22
† BRUNEI	Brunei	5,765	2,226	273,000	47	123	Monarchy	A	Bandar Seri Begawan	Asia	26
† BULGARIA	Balgarija	110,912	42,823	8,842,000	80	206	Republic	A	Sofija (Sofia)	Europe	15
† BURKINA FASO	Burkina Faso	274,200	105,869	9,808,000	36	93	Provisional military government	A	Ouagadougou	Africa	34
† BURMA	Myanmar	676,577	261,228	43,070,000	64	165	Provisional military government	A	Yangon (Rangoon)	Asia	25
† BURUNDI	Burundi	27,830	10,745	6,118,000	220	569	Republic	A	Bujumbura	Africa	36
California	California	424,002	163,707	31,310,000	74	191	State (U.S.)	D	Sacramento	N. Amer.	46
† CAMBODIA	Kâmpüchéa	181,035	69,898	8,928,000	49	128	Transitional government	A	Phnum Pénh (Phnom Penh)	Asia	26
† CAMEROON	Cameroon (English) / Cameroun (French)	475,442	183,569	12,875,000	27	70	Republic	A	Yaoundé	Africa	34
† CANADA	Canada	9,970,610	3,849,674	30,530,000	3.1	7.9	Federal parliamentary state	A	Ottawa	N. Amer.	42
Canary Islands	Islas Canarias	7,273	2,808	1,613,000	222	574	Part of Spain (2 provinces)		. . . .	Africa	32
† CAPE VERDE	Cabo Verde	4,033	1,557	404,000	100	259	Republic	A	Praia	Africa	32
Cayman Islands	Cayman Islands	259	100	29,000	112	290	Dependent territory (U.K.)	C	Georgetown	N. Amer.	49
Celebes	Sulawesi	189,216	73,057	12,995,000	69	178	Part of Indonesia (4 provinces)		. . . .	Asia	26
† CENTRAL AFRICAN REPUBLIC	Centrafrique	622,984	240,535	3,068,000	4.9	13	Republic	A	Bangui	Africa	35
Central America	. . .	520,000	200,000	30,402,000	58	152	. . . .		. . . .	N. Amer.	49
Ceylon, see Sri Lanka	. . .	. . .	. . .	. . .	. . .	. . .	. . . .		. . . .		. . .
† CHAD	Tchad	1,284,000	495,755	5,297,000	4.1	11	Republic	A	N'Djamena	Africa	35

Country, Division, or Region English (Conventional)	Local Name	Area km²	Area sq mi	Population 1/1/93	Population Density per km²	Population Density per sq mi	Form of Government and Political Status	Capital	Continent	Map Plate
CHANNEL ISLANDS	...	194	*75*	143,000	737	*1,907*	Dependent territory (U.K.)	*B* ...	Europe	9
†CHILE	Chile	756,626	*292,135*	13,635,000	18	*47*	Republic	*A* Santiago	S. Amer.	56
†CHINA (excl. Taiwan)	Zhongguo Renmin Gongheguo	9,556,100	*3,689,631*	1,179,030,000	123	*320*	Socialist republic	*A* Beijing (Peking)	Asia	27
China (Nationalist), see Taiwan	...	...	...	...	...	...	...	...	...	...
Christmas Island	Christmas Island	135	*52*	900	6.7	*17*	External territory (Australia)	*C* Flying Fish Cove	Oceania	26
Cocos (Keeling) Islands	Cocos (Keeling) Islands	14	*5.4*	500	36	*93*	Territory (Australia)	*C* ...	Oceania	22
†COLOMBIA	Colombia	1,141,748	*440,831*	34,640,000	30	*79*	Republic	*A* Santa Fe de Bogotá	S. Amer.	54
Colorado	Colorado	269,620	*104,100*	3,410,000	13	*33*	State (U.S.)	*D* Denver	N. Amer.	45
Commonwealth of Independent States	...	22,031,200	*8,506,294*	281,640,000	13	*33*	Alliance of sovereign states	... Minsk	Eur.-Asia	...
Commonwealth of Nations	...	29,230,000	*11,320,000*	1,498,930,000	51	*132*	...	... London	...	...
†COMOROS (excl. Mayotte)	Al-Qumur (Arabic) / Comores (French)	2,235	*863*	503,000	225	*583*	Federal Islamic republic	*A* Moroni	Africa	37
†CONGO	Congo	342,000	*132,047*	2,413,000	7.1	*18*	Republic	*A* Brazzaville	Africa	36
Connecticut	Connecticut	14,358	*5,544*	3,358,000	234	*606*	State (U.S.)	*D* Hartford	N. Amer.	44
COOK ISLANDS	Cook Islands	236	*91*	18,000	76	*198*	Self-governing territory (New Zealand protection)	*B* Avarua	Oceania	61
Coral Sea Islands Territory	Coral Sea Islands Territory	2.6	*1.0*	(1)	...	...	External territory (Australia)	*C* ...	Oceania	59
Corsica	Corse	8,720	*3,367*	255,000	29	*76*	Part of France	*D* ...	Europe	11
†COSTA RICA	Costa Rica	51,100	*19,730*	3,225,000	63	*163*	Republic	*A* San José	N. Amer.	49
Côte d'Ivoire, see Ivory Coast	...	...	...	...	...	...	...	...	...	...
†CROATIA	Hrvatska	56,538	*21,829*	4,793,000	85	*220*	Republic	... Zagreb	Europe	14
†CUBA	Cuba	110,861	*42,804*	10,900,000	98	*255*	Socialist republic	*A* La Habana (Havana)	N. Amer.	49
Curacao	Curaçao	444	*171*	146,000	329	*854*	Division of Netherlands Antilles (Neth.)	*D* Willemstad	N. Amer.	49
†CYPRUS	Kipros (Greek) / Kıbrıs (Turkish)	5,896	*2,276*	527,000	89	*232*	Republic	*A* Nicosia (Levkosía)	Asia	24
CYPRUS, NORTH	Kuzey Kıbrıs	3,355	*1,295*	193,000	58	*149*	Republic	*A* Nicosia (Lefkoşa)	Asia	24
†CZECH REPUBLIC	Česká Republika	78,864	*30,450*	10,335,000	131	*339*	Republic	*A* Praha (Prague)	Europe	10
Delaware	Delaware	6,447	*2,489*	692,000	107	*278*	State (U.S.)	*D* Dover	N. Amer.	44
†DENMARK	Danmark	43,093	*16,638*	5,169,000	120	*311*	Constitutional monarchy	*A* København (Copenhagen)	Europe	8
Denmark and Possessions	...	2,220,092	*857,182*	5,275,000	2.4	*6.2*	...	...	...	...
District of Columbia	District of Columbia	177	*68*	590,000	3,333	*8,676*	Federal district (U.S.)	*D* Washington	N. Amer.	44
†DJIBOUTI	Djibouti	23,200	*8,958*	396,000	17	*44*	Republic	*A* Djibouti	Africa	35
†DOMINICA	Dominica	790	*305*	88,000	111	*289*	Republic	*A* Roseau	N. Amer.	51
†DOMINICAN REPUBLIC	República Dominicana	48,442	*18,704*	7,591,000	157	*406*	Republic	*A* Santo Domingo	N. Amer.	49
†ECUADOR	Ecuador	283,561	*109,484*	11,055,000	39	*101*	Republic	*A* Quito	S. Amer.	54
†EGYPT	Mişr	1,001,449	*386,662*	57,050,000	57	*148*	Socialist republic	*A* Al Qāhirah (Cairo)	Africa	33
Ellis Islands, see Tuvalu	...	...	...	...	...	...	...	...	...	...
†EL SALVADOR	El Salvador	21,041	*8,124*	5,635,000	268	*694*	Republic	*A* San Salvador	N. Amer.	49
England	England	130,478	*50,378*	48,235,000	370	*957*	Administrative division (U.K.)	*D* London	Europe	9
†EQUATORIAL GUINEA	Guinea Ecuatorial	28,051	*10,831*	394,000	14	*36*	Republic	*A* Malabo	Africa	36
ERITREA	Eritrea	93,679	*36,170*	3,425,000	37	*95*	Republic	*A* Asmera	Africa	35
†ESTONIA	Eesti	45,100	*17,413*	1,613,000	36	*93*	Republic	*A* Tallinn	Europe	8
†ETHIOPIA	Ītiopya	1,157,603	*446,953*	51,715,000	45	*116*	Transitional military government	*A* Ādīs Ābeba (Addis Ababa)	Africa	35
Eurasia	...	54,800,000	*21,100,000*	4,032,700,000	74	*191*	...	...	...	...
Europe	...	9,900,000	*3,800,000*	694,900,000	70	*183*	...	...	Europe	5-6
European Community	...	4,070,000	*1,570,000*	346,800,000	85	*221*	...	... Brussels (Bruxelles)	Europe	5-6
FAEROE ISLANDS	Føroyar	1,399	*540*	49,000	35	*91*	Self-governing territory (Danish protection)	*B* Thorshavn	Europe	6
Falkland Islands (3)	Falkland Islands (English) / Islas Malvinas (Spanish)	12,173	*4,700*	2,100	0.2	*0.4*	Dependent territory (U.K.)	*C* Stanley	S. Amer.	56
†FIJI	Fiji (French) / Viti (Fijian)	18,274	*7,056*	754,000	41	*107*	Republic	*A* Suva	Oceania	63
†FINLAND	Suomi (Finnish) / Finland (Swedish)	338,145	*130,559*	5,074,000	15	*39*	Republic	*A* Helsinki (Helsingfors)	Europe	7
Florida	Florida	170,313	*65,758*	13,630,000	80	*207*	State (U.S.)	*D* Tallahassee	N. Amer.	44
†FRANCE (excl. Overseas Departments)	France	547,026	*211,208*	57,570,000	105	*273*	Republic	*A* Paris	Europe	11
France and Possessions	...	666,866	*257,476*	59,617,000	89	*232*	...	... Paris	...	...
French Guiana	Guyane Française	91,000	*35,135*	131,000	1.4	*3.7*	Overseas department (France)	*C* Cayenne	S. Amer.	54
French Polynesia	Polynésie Française	3,521	*1,359*	208,000	59	*153*	Overseas territory (France)	*C* Papeete	Oceania	61
French West Indies	...	2,880	*1,112*	785,000	273	*706*	...	...	N. Amer.	50
Fujian	Fujian	120,000	*46,332*	31,160,000	260	*673*	Province (China)	*D* Fuzhou	Asia	27
†GABON	Gabon	267,667	*103,347*	1,115,000	4.2	*11*	Republic	*A* Libreville	Africa	36
Galapagos Islands	Archipiélago de Colón (Islas Galápagos)	7,964	*3,075*	8,500	1.1	*2.8*	Province (Ecuador)	*D* Baquerizo Moreno	S. Amer.	54
†GAMBIA	Gambia	10,689	*4,127*	916,000	86	*222*	Republic	*A* Banjul	Africa	34
Gansu	Gansu	450,000	*173,746*	23,280,000	52	*134*	Province (China)	*D* Lanzhou	Asia	27
Georgia	Georgia	153,953	*59,441*	6,795,000	44	*114*	State (U.S.)	*D* Atlanta	N. Amer.	44
GEORGIA	Sakartvelo	69,700	*26,911*	5,593,000	80	*208*	Provisional military government	*A* Tbilisi	Asia	16
†GERMANY	Deutschland	356,955	*137,822*	80,590,000	226	*585*	Federal republic	*A* Berlin and Bonn	Europe	10
†GHANA	Ghana	238,533	*92,098*	16,445,000	69	*179*	Provisional military government	*A* Accra	Africa	34
Gibraltar	Gibraltar	6.0	*2.3*	32,000	5,333	*13,913*	Dependent territory (U.K.)	*C* Gibraltar	Europe	13
Gilbert Islands, see Tuvalu	...	...	...	...	...	...	...	...	...	...
Great Britain, see United Kingdom	...	...	...	...	...	...	...	...	...	...
†GREECE	Ellas	131,957	*50,949*	10,075,000	76	*198*	Republic	*A* Athínai (Athens)	Europe	15
GREENLAND	Kalaallit Nunaat (Inuit) / Grønland (Danish)	2,175,600	*840,004*	57,000	...	*0.1*	Self-governing territory (Danish protection)	*B* Godthåb (Nûk)	N. Amer.	41
†GRENADA	Grenada	344	*133*	97,000	282	*729*	Parliamentary state	*A* St. George's	N. Amer.	51
Guadeloupe (incl. Dependencies)	Guadeloupe	1,780	*687*	413,000	232	*601*	Overseas department (France)	*C* Basse-Terre	N. Amer.	51
Guam	Guam	541	*209*	143,000	264	*684*	Unincorporated territory (U.S.)	*C* Agana	Oceania	64
Guangdong	Guangdong	178,000	*68,726*	65,380,000	367	*951*	Province (China)	*D* Guangzhou (Canton)	Asia	27
†GUATEMALA	Guatemala	108,889	*42,042*	9,705,000	89	*231*	Republic	*A* Guatemala	N. Amer.	49
GUERNSEY (incl. Dependencies)	Guernsey	78	*30*	58,000	744	*1,933*	Crown dependency (U.K. protection)	*B* St. Peter Port	Europe	9
†GUINEA	Guinée	245,857	*94,926*	7,726,000	31	*81*	Provisional military government	*A* Conakry	Africa	34
†GUINEA-BISSAU	Guiné-Bissau	36,125	*13,948*	1,060,000	29	*76*	Republic	*A* Bissau	Africa	34
Guizhou	Guizhou	170,000	*65,637*	33,745,000	199	*514*	Province (China)	*D* Guiyang	Asia	27
†GUYANA	Guyana	214,969	*83,000*	737,000	3.4	*8.9*	Republic	*A* Georgetown	S. Amer.	54
Hainan	Hainan	34,000	*13,127*	6,820,000	201	*520*	Province (China)	*D* Haikou	Asia	27
†HAITI	Haïti	27,750	*10,714*	6,509,000	235	*608*	Provisional military government	*A* Port-au-Prince	N. Amer.	49
Hamburg	Hamburg	755	*292*	1,657,000	2,195	*5,675*	State (Germany)	*D* Hamburg	Europe	10
Hawaii	Hawaii	28,313	*10,932*	1,159,000	41	*106*	State (U.S.)	*D* Honolulu	N. Amer.	60
Hebei	Hebei	190,000	*73,359*	63,500,000	334	*866*	Province (China)	*D* Shijiazhuang	Asia	28
Heilongjiang	Heilongjiang	469,000	*181,082*	36,685,000	78	*203*	Province (China)	*D* Harbin	Asia	27
Henan	Henan	167,000	*64,479*	88,890,000	532	*1,379*	Province (China)	*D* Zhengzhou	Asia	27
Hessia	Hessen	21,114	*8,152*	5,766,000	273	*707*	State (Germany)	*D* Wiesbaden	Europe	10
Hispaniola	La Española	76,192	*29,418*	14,100,000	185	*479*	...	...	N. Amer.	49

Country, Division, or Region English (Conventional)	Local Name	Area km²	Area sq mi	Population 1/1/93	Population Density per km²	Population Density per sq mi	Form of Government and Political Status	Capital	Continent and Map Plate	
Holland, see Netherlands	. . .	. . .	. . .	. . .	. . .	. . .				
† HONDURAS	Honduras	112,088	*43,277*	5,164,000	46	*119*	Republic	A Tegucigalpa	N. Amer.	49
Hong Kong	Hong Kong (English) / Xianggang (Chinese)	1,072	*414*	5,580,000	5,205	*13,478*	Chinese territory under British administration	C Victoria (Hong Kong)	Asia	27
Hubei	Hubei	187,400	*72,356*	56,090,000	299	*775*	Province (China)	D Wuhan	Asia	27
Hunan	Hunan	210,000	*81,081*	63,140,000	301	*779*	Province (China)	D Changsha	Asia	27
† HUNGARY	Magyarország	93,033	*35,920*	10,305,000	111	*287*	Republic	A Budapest	Europe	10
† ICELAND	Ísland	103,000	*39,769*	260,000	2.5	*6.5*	Republic	A Reykjavík	Europe	7
Idaho	Idaho	216,456	*83,574*	1,026,000	4.7	*12*	State (U.S.)	D Boise	N. Amer.	46
Illinois	Illinois	150,007	*57,918*	11,640,000	78	*201*	State (U.S.)	D Springfield	N. Amer.	45
† INDIA (incl. part of Jammu and Kashmir)	India (English) / Bhārat (Hindi)	3,203,975	*1,237,062*	873,850,000	273	*706*	Federal republic	A New Delhi	Asia	25
Indiana	Indiana	94,328	*36,420*	5,667,000	60	*156*	State (U.S.)	D Indianapolis	N. Amer.	44
† INDONESIA	Indonesia	1,948,732	*752,410*	186,180,000	96	*247*	Republic	A Jakarta	Asia	26
Inner Mongolia	Nei Mongol Gaoyuan	1,183,000	*456,759*	22,340,000	19	*49*	Autonomous region (China)	D Hohhot	Asia	27
Iowa	Iowa	145,754	*56,276*	2,821,000	19	*50*	State (U.S.)	D Des Moines	N. Amer.	45
† IRAN	Īrān	1,638,057	*632,457*	60,500,000	37	*96*	Islamic republic	A Tehrān	Asia	23
† IRAQ	Al ʿIrāq	438,317	*169,235*	18,815,000	43	*111*	Republic	A Baghdād	Asia	24
† IRELAND	Ireland (English) / Éire (Gaelic)	70,285	*27,137*	3,525,000	50	*130*	Republic	A Dublin (Baile Átha Cliath)	Europe	9
ISLE OF MAN	Isle of Man	572	*221*	70,000	122	*317*	Crown dependency (U.K. protection)	B Douglas	Europe	9
† ISRAEL (excl. Occupied Areas)	Yisra'el (Hebrew) / Isrāʾīl (Arabic)	20,770	*8,019*	4,593,000	221	*573*	Republic	A Yerushalayim (Jerusalem)	Asia	24
Israeli Occupied Areas [4]	. . .	7,632	*2,947*	2,461,000	322	*835*	None	. . .	Asia	24
† ITALY	Italia	301,277	*116,324*	56,550,000	188	*486*	Republic	A Roma (Rome)	Europe	14
† IVORY COAST	Côte d'Ivoire	322,500	*124,518*	13,765,000	43	*111*	Republic	A Abidjan and Yamoussoukro [2]	Africa	34
† JAMAICA	Jamaica	10,991	*4,244*	2,412,000	219	*568*	Parliamentary state	A Kingston	N. Amer.	49
† JAPAN	Nippon	377,801	*145,870*	124,710,000	330	*855*	Constitutional monarchy	A Tōkyō	Asia	29
Java	Jawa	132,187	*51,038*	107,580,000	814	*2,108*	Part of Indonesia (5 provinces)	. . .	Asia	26
JERSEY	Jersey	116	*45*	85,000	733	*1,889*	Crown dependency (U.K. protection)	B St. Helier	Europe	9
Jiangsu	Jiangsu	102,600	*39,614*	69,730,000	680	*1,760*	Province (China)	D Nanjing (Nanking)	Asia	28
Jiangxi	Jiangxi	166,600	*64,325*	39,270,000	236	*610*	Province (China)	D Nanchang	Asia	27
Jilin	Jilin	187,000	*72,201*	25,630,000	137	*355*	Province (China)	D Changchun	Asia	27
Johnston Atoll	Johnston Atoll	1.3	*0.5*	1,400	1,077	*2,800*	Unincorporated territory (U.S.)	C . . .	Oceania	60
† JORDAN (excl. West Bank)	Al Urdun	91,000	*35,135*	3,632,000	40	*103*	Constitutional monarchy	A ʿAmmān	Asia	24
Kansas	Kansas	213,110	*82,282*	2,539,000	12	*31*	State (U.S.)	D Topeka	N. Amer.	45
Kashmir, Jammu and	Jammu and Kashmir	222,236	*85,806*	11,565,000	52	*135*	Disputed territory (India and Pakistan)	D . . .	Asia	25
† KAZAKHSTAN	Qazaqstan	2,717,300	*1,049,156*	17,190,000	6.3	*16*	Republic	A Alma-Ata	Asia	19
Kentucky	Kentucky	104,665	*40,411*	3,745,000	36	*93*	State (U.S.)	D Frankfort	N. Amer.	44
† KENYA	Kenya	582,646	*224,961*	26,635,000	46	*118*	Republic	A Nairobi	Africa	36
Kerguelen Islands	Iles Kerguélen	6,993	*2,700*	200	. . .	*0.1*	Territory (France)	C . . .	S. Amer.	30-31
KIRIBATI	Kiribati	811	*313*	76,000	94	*243*	Republic	A Bairiki	Oceania	60
† KOREA, NORTH	Chosŏn Minjujuŭi Inmin Konghwaguk	120,538	*46,540*	22,450,000	186	*482*	Socialist republic	A P'yŏngyang	Asia	28
† KOREA, SOUTH	Taehan-min'guk	99,016	*38,230*	43,660,000	441	*1,142*	Republic	A Sŏul (Seoul)	Asia	28
Korea (entire)	. . .	219,554	*84,770*	66,110,000	301	*780*		. . .	Asia	28
† KUWAIT	Al Kuwayt	17,818	*6,880*	2,388,000	134	*347*	Constitutional monarchy	A Al Kuwayt (Kuwait)	Asia	24
Kwangsi	Guangxi Zhuangzu Zizhiqu	236,300	*91,236*	43,975,000	186	*482*	Autonomous region (China)	D Nanning	Asia	27
† KYRGYZSTAN	Kyrgyzstan	198,500	*76,641*	4,613,000	23	*60*	Republic	A Biškek	Asia	18
Labrador	Labrador	292,218	*112,826*	36,000	0.1	*0.3*	Part of Newfoundland province (Canada)	. . .	N. Amer.	42
† LAOS	Lao	236,800	*91,429*	4,507,000	19	*49*	Socialist republic	A Viangchan (Vientiane)	Asia	26
Latin America	. . .	20,500,000	*7,900,000*	461,900,000	23	*58*		. . .	N.A.,S.A.	52-53
† LATVIA	Latvija	63,700	*24,595*	2,737,000	43	*111*	Republic	A Rīga	Europe	8
† LEBANON	Lubnān	10,400	*4,015*	3,467,000	333	*864*	Republic	A Bayrūt (Beirut)	Asia	24
† LESOTHO	Lesotho	30,355	*11,720*	1,873,000	62	*160*	Constitutional monarchy under military rule	A Maseru	Africa	37
Liaoning	Liaoning	145,700	*56,255*	41,035,000	282	*729*	Province (China)	D Shenyang (Mukden)	Asia	28
† LIBERIA	Liberia	99,067	*38,250*	2,869,000	29	*75*	Republic	A Monrovia	Africa	34
† LIBYA	Lībiyā	1,759,540	*679,362*	4,552,000	2.6	*6.7*	Socialist republic	A Ţarābulus (Tripoli)	Africa	33
† LIECHTENSTEIN	Liechtenstein	160	*62*	30,000	188	*484*	Constitutional monarchy	A Vaduz	Europe	14
† LITHUANIA	Lietuva	65,200	*25,174*	3,804,000	58	*151*	Republic	A Vilnius	Europe	8
Louisiana	Louisiana	134,275	*51,843*	4,282,000	32	*83*	State (U.S.)	D Baton Rouge	N. Amer.	45
Lower Saxony	Niedersachsen	47,349	*18,282*	7,420,000	157	*406*	State (Germany)	D Hannover	Europe	10
† LUXEMBOURG	Luxembourg (French) / Lezebuurg (Luxembourgish)	2,586	*998*	392,000	152	*393*	Constitutional monarchy	A Luxembourg	Europe	12
Macao	Macau	17	*6.6*	477,000	28,059	*72,273*	Chinese territory under Portuguese administration	C Macau	Asia	27
MACEDONIA	Makedonija	25,713	*9,928*	2,179,000	85	*219*	Republic	A Skopje	Europe	15
† MADAGASCAR	Madagasikara	587,041	*226,658*	12,800,000	22	*56*	Republic	A Antananarivo	Africa	37
Madeira	Madeira	794	*307*	284,000	358	*925*	Autonomous region (Portugal)	D Funchal	Europe	32
Maine	Maine	91,653	*35,387*	1,257,000	14	*36*	State (U.S.)	D Augusta	N. Amer.	44
† MALAWI	Malaŵi	118,484	*45,747*	9,691,000	82	*212*	Republic	A Lilongwe	Africa	36
Malaya	Semenanjung Malaysia	131,598	*50,810*	15,335,000	117	*302*	Part of Malaysia (11 states)	D . . .	Asia	26
† MALAYSIA	Malaysia	334,758	*129,251*	18,630,000	56	*144*	Federal constitutional monarchy	A Kuala Lumpur	Asia	26
† MALDIVES	Maldives	298	*115*	235,000	789	*2,043*	Republic	A Male	Asia	25
† MALI	Mali	1,248,574	*482,077*	8,754,000	7.0	*18*	Republic	A Bamako	Africa	34
† MALTA	Malta	316	*122*	360,000	1,139	*2,951*	Republic	A Valletta	Europe	14
Manitoba	Manitoba	649,950	*250,947*	1,221,000	1.9	*4.9*	Province (Canada)	D Winnipeg	N. Amer.	42
Maritime Provinces	. . .	134,590	*51,965*	1,983,000	15	*38*		. . .	N. Amer.	42
† MARSHALL ISLANDS	Marshall Islands	181	*70*	51,000	282	*729*	Republic (U.S. protection)	A Uliga	Oceania	60
Martinique	Martinique	1,100	*425*	372,000	338	*875*	Overseas department (France)	C Fort-de-France	N. Amer.	51
Maryland	Maryland	32,135	*12,407*	4,975,000	155	*401*	State (U.S.)	D Annapolis	N. Amer.	44
Massachusetts	Massachusetts	27,337	*10,555*	6,103,000	223	*578*	State (U.S.)	D Boston	N. Amer.	44
† MAURITANIA	Mūrītāniyā (Arabic) / Mauritanie (French)	1,025,520	*395,956*	2,092,000	2.0	*5.3*	Republic	A Nouakchott	Africa	32
† MAURITIUS (incl. Dependencies)	Mauritius	2,040	*788*	1,096,000	537	*1,391*	Republic	A Port-Louis	Africa	37
Mayotte [5]	Mayotte	374	*144*	89,000	238	*618*	Territorial collectivity (France)	C Dzaoudzi and Mamoudzou [2]	Africa	37
Mecklenburg-Vorpommern	Mecklenburg-Vorpommern	23,835	*9,203*	2,000,000	84	*217*	State (Germany)	D Schwerin	Europe	10
† MEXICO	México	1,967,183	*759,534*	86,170,000	44	*113*	Federal republic	A Ciudad de México (Mexico City)	N. Amer.	48
Michigan	Michigan	250,738	*96,810*	9,488,000	38	*98*	State (U.S.)	D Lansing	N. Amer.	44
† MICRONESIA, FEDERATED STATES OF	Federated States of Micronesia	702	*271*	117,000	167	*432*	Republic (U.S. protection)	A Ponape	Oceania	60
Middle America	. . .	2,710,000	*1,050,000*	151,200,000	56	*144*		. . .	N. Amer.	47
Midway Islands	Midway Islands	5.2	*2.0*	500	96	*250*	Unincorporated territory (U.S.)	C . . .	Oceania	60
Minnesota	Minnesota	225,182	*86,943*	4,513,000	20	*52*	State (U.S.)	D St. Paul	N. Amer.	45
Mississippi	Mississippi	125,443	*48,434*	2,616,000	21	*54*	State (U.S.)	D Jackson	N. Amer.	45
Missouri	Missouri	180,546	*69,709*	5,231,000	29	*75*	State (U.S.)	D Jefferson City	N. Amer.	45

Country, Division, or Region: English (Conventional)	Local Name	Area km²	Area sq mi	Population 1/1/93	Population Density per km²	Population Density per sq mi	Form of Government and Political Status	Capital	Continent and Map Plate
† MOLDOVA	Moldova	33,700	*13,012*	4,474,000	133	*344*	Republic	A Kišinev (Kishinev)	Europe 16
MONACO	Monaco	1.9	*0.7*	31,000	16,316	*44,286*	Constitutional monarchy	A Monaco	Europe 11
† MONGOLIA	Mongol Ard Uls	1,566,500	*604,829*	2,336,000	1.5	*3.9*	Republic	A Ulan-Bator (Ulaanbaatar)	Asia 27
Montana	Montana	380,850	*147,046*	821,000	2.2	*5.6*	State (U.S.)	D Helena	N. Amer. 46
Montenegro	Crna Gora	13,812	*5,333*	650,000	47	*122*	Republic (Yugoslavia)	D Titograd	Europe 15
Montserrat	Montserrat	102	*39*	13,000	127	*333*	Dependent territory (U.K.)	C Plymouth	N. Amer. 51
† MOROCCO (excl. Western Sahara)	Al Maghrib	446,550	*172,414*	27,005,000	60	*157*	Constitutional monarchy	A Rabat	Africa 32
† MOZAMBIQUE	Moçambique	799,380	*308,642*	15,795,000	20	*51*	Republic	A Maputo	Africa 37
† NAMIBIA	Namibia	824,272	*318,254*	1,580,000	1.9	*5.0*	Republic	A Windhoek	Africa 37
NAURU	Nauru (English) / Naoero (Nauruan)	21	*8.1*	10,000	476	*1,235*	Republic	A Domaneab	Oceania 64
Navassa Island	Navassa Island	4.9	*1.9*	(1)	...	...	Unincorporated territory (U.S.)	C ...	N. Amer 49
Nebraska	Nebraska	200,358	*77,358*	1,615,000	8.1	*21*	State (U.S.)	D Lincoln	N. Amer. 45
† NEPAL	Nepāl	147,181	*56,827*	20,325,000	138	*358*	Constitutional monarchy	A Kāṭhmāṇḍāũ	Asia 25
† NETHERLANDS	Nederland	41,864	*16,164*	15,190,000	363	*940*	Constitutional monarchy	A Amsterdam and 's-Gravenhage (The Hague)	Europe 12
NETHERLANDS ANTILLES	Nederlandse Antillen	800	*309*	191,000	239	*618*	Self-governing territory (Netherlands protection)	B Willemstad	N. Amer. 50
Nevada	Nevada	286,368	*110,567*	1,308,000	4.6	*12*	State (U.S.)	D Carson City	N. Amer. 46
New Brunswick	New Brunswick (English) / Nouveau-Brunswick (French)	73,440	*28,355*	824,000	11	*29*	Province (Canada)	D Fredericton	N. Amer. 42
New Caledonia	Nouvelle-Calédonie	19,058	*7,358*	177,000	9.3	*24*	Overseas territory (France)	C Nouméa	Oceania 63
New England	New England	186,472	*71,997*	13,488,000	72	*187*	Part of U.S. (6 states)	...	N. Amer. 43
Newfoundland	Newfoundland (English) / Terre-Neuve (French)	405,720	*156,649*	641,000	1.6	*4.1*	Province (Canada)	D St. John's	N. Amer. 42
Newfoundland (island)	Newfoundland (English) / Terre-Neuve (French)	108,860	*42,031*	605,000	5.6	*14*	Part of Newfoundland province (Canada)	...	N. Amer. 42
New Hampshire	New Hampshire	24,219	*9,351*	1,154,000	48	*123*	State (U.S.)	D Concord	N. Amer. 44
New Hebrides, see Vanuatu	...	...	...	...	...	...	...	...	...
New Jersey	New Jersey	22,590	*8,722*	7,898,000	350	*906*	State (U.S.)	D Trenton	N. Amer. 44
New Mexico	New Mexico	314,939	*121,598*	1,590,000	5.0	*13*	State (U.S.)	D Santa Fe	N. Amer. 45
New South Wales	New South Wales	801,600	*309,500*	5,770,000	7.2	*19*	State (Australia)	D Sydney	Oceania 59
New York	New York	141,089	*54,475*	18,350,000	130	*337*	State (U.S.)	D Albany	N. Amer. 44
† NEW ZEALAND	New Zealand	270,534	*104,454*	3,477,000	13	*33*	Parliamentary state	A Wellington	Oceania 62
† NICARAGUA	Nicaragua	129,640	*50,054*	3,932,000	30	*79*	Republic	A Managua	N. Amer. 49
† NIGER	Niger	1,267,000	*489,191*	8,198,000	6.5	*17*	Provisional military government	A Niamey	Africa 34
† NIGERIA	Nigeria	923,768	*356,669*	91,700,000	99	*257*	Provisional military government	A Lagos and Abuja	Africa 34
Ningsia	Ningxia Huizu Zizhiqu	66,400	*25,637*	4,820,000	73	*188*	Autonomous region (China)	D Yinchuan	Asia 27
NIUE	Niue	258	*100*	1,700	6.6	*17*	Self-governing territory (New Zealand protection)	B Alofi	Oceania 64
Norfolk Island	Norfolk Island	36	*14*	2,600	72	*186*	External territory (Australia)	C Kingston	Oceania 61
North America	...	24,700,000	*9,500,000*	438,200,000	18	*46*	...	...	N. Amer. 38-39
North Borneo, see Sabah	...	...	...	...	...	...	...	...	...
North Carolina	North Carolina	139,397	*53,821*	6,846,000	49	*127*	State (U.S.)	D Raleigh	N. Amer. 44
North Dakota	North Dakota	183,123	*70,704*	632,000	3.5	*8.9*	State (U.S.)	D Bismarck	N. Amer. 45
Northern Ireland	Northern Ireland	14,121	*5,452*	1,604,000	114	*294*	Administrative division (U.K.)	D Belfast	Europe 9
NORTHERN MARIANA ISLANDS	Northern Mariana Islands	477	*184*	48,000	101	*261*	Commonwealth (U.S. protection)	B Saipan (island)	Oceania 60
Northern Territory	Northern Territory	1,346,200	*519,771*	176,000	0.1	*0.3*	Territory (Australia)	D Darwin	Oceania 59
North Rhine-Westphalia	Nordrhein-Westfalen	34,068	*13,154*	17,420,000	511	*1,324*	State (Germany)	D Düsseldorf	Europe 10
Northwest Territories	Northwest Territories (English) / Territoires du Nord-Ouest (French)	3,426,320	*1,322,910*	61,000	...	...	Territory (Canada)	D Yellowknife	N. Amer. 42
† NORWAY (incl. Svalbard and Jan Mayen)	Norge	386,975	*149,412*	4,308,000	11	*29*	Constitutional monarchy	A Oslo	Europe 7
Nova Scotia	Nova Scotia (English) / Nouvelle-Écosse (French)	55,490	*21,425*	1,007,000	18	*47*	Province (Canada)	D Halifax	N. Amer. 42
Oceania (incl. Australia)	...	8,500,000	*3,300,000*	26,700,000	3.1	*8.1*	...	...	Oceania 57-58
Ohio	Ohio	116,103	*44,828*	11,025,000	95	*246*	State (U.S.)	D Columbus	N. Amer. 44
Oklahoma	Oklahoma	181,049	*69,903*	3,205,000	18	*46*	State (U.S.)	D Oklahoma City	N. Amer. 45
† OMAN	'Umān	212,457	*82,030*	1,617,000	7.6	*20*	Monarchy	A Masqaṭ (Muscat)	Asia 23
Ontario	Ontario	1,068,580	*412,581*	11,265,000	11	*27*	Province (Canada)	D Toronto	N. Amer. 42
Oregon	Oregon	254,819	*98,386*	2,949,000	12	*30*	State (U.S.)	D Salem	N. Amer. 46
Orkney Islands	Orkney Islands	976	*377*	20,000	20	*53*	Part of Scotland (U.K.)	D Kirkwall	Europe 9
Pacific Islands, Trust Territory of the, see Palau	...	...	...	...	...	...	...	...	...
† PAKISTAN (incl. part of Jammu and Kashmir)	Pākistān	879,902	*339,732*	123,490,000	140	*363*	Federal Islamic republic	A Islāmābād	Asia 25
PALAU	Palau (English) / Belau (Palauan)	508	*196*	16,000	31	*82*	Under U.S. administration	B Koror	Oceania 60
† PANAMA	Panamá	75,517	*29,157*	2,555,000	34	*88*	Republic	A Panamá	N. Amer. 49
† PAPUA NEW GUINEA	Papua New Guinea	462,840	*178,704*	3,737,000	8.1	*21*	Parliamentary state	A Port Moresby	Oceania 60
† PARAGUAY	Paraguay	406,752	*157,048*	5,003,000	12	*32*	Republic	A Asunción	S. Amer. 56
Peking	Beijing	16,800	*6,487*	11,290,000	672	*1,740*	Autonomous city (China)	D Beijing (Peking)	Asia 28
Pennsylvania	Pennsylvania	119,291	*46,058*	12,105,000	101	*263*	State (U.S.)	D Harrisburg	N. Amer. 44
† PERU	Perú	1,285,216	*496,225*	22,995,000	18	*46*	Republic	A Lima	S. Amer. 54
† PHILIPPINES	Pilipinas (Pilipino) / Philippines (English)	300,000	*115,831*	65,500,000	218	*565*	Republic	A Manila	Asia 26
Pitcairn (incl. Dependencies)	Pitcairn	49	*19*	50	1.0	*2.6*	Dependent territory (U.K.)	C Adamstown	Oceania 61
† POLAND	Polska	312,683	*120,728*	38,330,000	123	*317*	Republic	A Warszawa (Warsaw)	Europe 10
† PORTUGAL	Portugal	91,985	*35,516*	10,660,000	116	*300*	Republic	A Lisboa (Lisbon)	Europe 13
Prairie Provinces	Prairie Provinces	1,963,470	*758,100*	5,159,000	2.6	*6.8*	Part of Canada (3 provinces)	...	N. Amer. 42
Prince Edward Island	Prince Edward Island (English) / Île-du Prince-Édouard (French)	5,660	*2,185*	152,000	27	*70*	Province (Canada)	D Charlottetown	N. Amer. 42
PUERTO RICO	Puerto Rico	9,104	*3,515*	3,594,000	395	*1,022*	Commonwealth (U.S. protection)	B San Juan	N. Amer. 51
† QATAR	Qaṭar	11,427	*4,412*	492,000	43	*112*	Monarchy	A Ad Dawḥah (Doha)	Asia 24
Qinghai	Qinghai	720,000	*277,994*	4,585,000	6.4	*16*	Province (China)	D Xining	Asia 27
Quebec	Québec	1,540,680	*594,860*	7,725,000	5.0	*13*	Province (Canada)	D Québec	N. Amer. 42
Queensland	Queensland	1,727,200	*666,876*	3,000,000	1.7	*4.5*	State (Australia)	D Brisbane	Oceania 59
Reunion	Réunion	2,510	*969*	633,000	252	*653*	Overseas department (France)	C Saint-Denis	Africa 37
Rhineland-Palatinate	Rheinland-Pfalz	19,849	*7,664*	3,771,000	190	*492*	State (Germany)	D Mainz	Europe 10
Rhode Island	Rhode Island	4,002	*1,545*	1,026,000	256	*664*	State (U.S.)	D Providence	N. Amer. 44
Rhodesia, see Zimbabwe	...	...	...	...	...	...	...	...	...
Rodrigues	Rodrigues	104	*40*	40,000	385	*1,000*	Part of Mauritius	...	Africa 30-31
† ROMANIA	România	237,500	*91,699*	23,200,000	98	*253*	Republic	A București (Bucharest)	Europe 15
† RUSSIA	Rossija	17,075,400	*6,592,849*	150,500,000	8.8	*23*	Republic	A Moskva (Moscow)	Eur., Asia 19-20
Russia in Europe	...	3,955,818	*1,527,350*	106,980,000	27	*70*	...	...	Europe 19

Country, Division, or Region English (Conventional)	Local Name	Area km²	Area sq mi	Population 1/1/93	Population Density per km²	Population Density per sq mi	Form of Government and Political Status		Capital	Continent and Map Plate	
† RWANDA	Rwanda	26,338	*10,169*	7,573,000	288	*745*	Provisional military government	*A*	Kigali	Africa	36
Saarland	Saar	2,570	*992*	1,085,000	422	*1,094*	State (Germany)	*D*	Saarbrücken	Europe	10
Sabah	Sabah	73,711	*28,460*	1,544,000	21	*54*	State (Malaysia)	*D*	Kota Kinabalu	Asia	26
† ST. CHRISTOPHER-NEVIS	St. Christopher-Nevis	269	*104*	40,000	149	*385*	Parliamentary state	*A*	Basseterre	N. Amer.	51
St. Helena (incl. Dependencies)	St. Helena	314	*121*	7,000	22	*58*	Dependent territory (U.K.)	*C*	Jamestown	Africa	31
† ST. LUCIA	St. Lucia	616	*238*	153,000	248	*643*	Parliamentary state	*A*	Castries	N. Amer.	51
St. Pierre and Miquelon	St.-Pierre et Miquelon	242	*93*	7,000	29	*75*	Territorial collectivity (France)	*C*	Saint-Pierre	N. Amer.	42
† ST. VINCENT AND THE GRENADINES	St. Vincent and the Grenadines	388	*150*	116,000	299	*773*	Parliamentary state	*A*	Kingstown	N. Amer.	51
† SAN MARINO	San Marino	61	*24*	23,000	377	*958*	Republic	*A*	San Marino	Europe	14
† SAO TOME AND PRINCIPE	São Tomé e Príncipe	964	*372*	134,000	139	*360*	Republic	*A*	São Tomé	Africa	34
Sarawak	Sarawak	129,449	*49,981*	1,751,000	14	*35*	State (Malaysia)	*D*	Kuching	Asia	26
Sardinia	Sardegna	24,090	*9,301*	1,681,000	70	*181*	Autonomous region (Italy)	*D*	Cagliari	Europe	14
Saskatchewan	Saskatchewan	652,330	*251,866*	1,099,000	1.7	*4.4*	Province (Canada)	*D*	Regina	N. Amer.	42
† SAUDI ARABIA	Al 'Arabīyah as Su'ūdīyah	2,149,690	*830,000*	15,985,000	7.4	*19*	Monarchy	*A*	Ar Riyāḍ (Riyadh)	Asia	23
Saxony	Sachsen	18,338	*7,080*	4,993,000	272	*705*	State (Germany)	*D*	Dresden	Europe	10
Saxony-Anhalt	Sachsen-Anhalt	20,444	*7,893*	3,021,000	148	*383*	State (Germany)	*D*	Magdeburg	Europe	10
Scandinavia	. . .	1,320,000	*510,000*	23,479,000	18	*46*	. . .		. . .	Europe	7
Schleswig-Holstein	Schleswig-Holstein	15,730	*6,073*	2,643,000	168	*435*	State (Germany)	*D*	Kiel	Europe	10
Scotland	Scotland	78,789	*30,421*	5,145,000	65	*169*	Administrative division (U.K.)	*D*	Edinburgh	Europe	9
† SENEGAL	Sénégal	196,712	*75,951*	7,849,000	40	*103*	Republic	*A*	Dakar	Africa	34
Serbia	Srbija	88,361	*34,116*	10,020,000	113	*294*	Republic (Yugoslavia)	*D*	Belgrade (Beograd)	Europe	15
† SEYCHELLES	Seychelles	453	*175*	70,000	155	*400*	Republic	*A*	Victoria	Africa	37
Shaanxi	Shaanxi	205,000	*79,151*	34,215,000	167	*432*	Province (China)	*D*	Xi'an (Sian)	Asia	27
Shandong	Shandong	153,000	*59,074*	87,840,000	574	*1,487*	Province (China)	*D*	Jinan	Asia	27
Shanghai	Shanghai	6,200	*2,394*	13,875,000	2,238	*5,796*	Autonomous city (China)	*D*	Shanghai	Asia	28
Shanxi	Shanxi	156,000	*60,232*	29,865,000	191	*496*	Province (China)	*D*	Taiyuan	Asia	27
Shetland Islands	Shetland Islands	1,433	*553*	22,000	15	*40*	Part of Scotland (U.K.)	*D*	Lerwick	Europe	9
Sichuan	Sichuan	570,000	*220,078*	111,470,000	196	*507*	Province (China)	*D*	Chengdu	Asia	27
Sicily	Sicilia	25,709	*9,926*	5,270,000	205	*531*	Autonomous region (Italy)	*D*	Palermo	Europe	14
† SIERRA LEONE	Sierra Leone	72,325	*27,925*	4,424,000	61	*158*	Transitional military government	*A*	Freetown	Africa	34
† SINGAPORE	Singapore (English) / Singapura (Malay)	636	*246*	2,812,000	4,421	*11,431*	Republic	*A*	Singapore	Asia	26
Sinkiang	Xingiang Uygur Zizhiqu	1,600,000	*617,764*	15,755,000	9.8	*26*	Autonomous region (China)	*D*	Ürümqi	Asia	27
† SLOVAKIA	Slovenská Republika	49,035	*18,933*	5,287,000	108	*279*	Republic	*A*	Bratislava	Europe	10
† SLOVENIA	Slovenija	20,251	*7,819*	1,965,000	97	*251*	Republic	*A*	Ljubljana	Europe	14
† SOLOMON ISLANDS	Solomon Islands	28,370	*10,954*	366,000	13	*33*	Parliamentary state	*A*	Honiara	Oceania	63
† SOMALIA	Soomaaliya	637,657	*246,201*	6,000,000	9.4	*24*	None	*A*	Muqdisho (Mogadishu)	Africa	35
† SOUTH AFRICA	South Africa (English) / Suid-Afrika (Afrikaans)	1,220,018	*471,090*	42,407,000	35	*90*	Republic	*A*	Pretoria, Cape Town, and Bloemfontein	Africa	37
South America	. . .	17,800,000	*6,900,000*	310,700,000	17	*45*	. . .		. . .	S. Amer.	52-53
South Australia	South Australia	984,000	*379,925*	1,410,000	1.4	*3.7*	State (Australia)	*D*	Adelaide	Oceania	59
South Carolina	South Carolina	82,898	*32,007*	3,616,000	44	*113*	State (U.S.)	*D*	Columbia	N. Amer.	44
South Dakota	South Dakota	199,745	*77,121*	718,000	3.6	*9.3*	State (U.S.)	*D*	Pierre	N. Amer.	45
South Georgia (incl. Dependencies)	South Georgia	3,755	*1,450*	(1)	. . .	. . .	Dependent territory (U.K.)	*C*	. . .	S. Amer.	56
South West Africa, see Namibia	. . .	. . .	. . .	. . .	. . .	. . .	. . .		. . .	. . .	. . .
† SPAIN	España	504,750	*194,885*	39,155,000	78	*201*	Constitutional monarchy	*A*	Madrid	Europe	13
Spanish North Africa (6)	Plazas de Soberanía en el Norte de África	32	*12*	144,000	4,500	*12,000*	Five possessions (Spain)	*C*	. . .	Africa	13
Spanish Sahara, see Western Sahara	. . .	. . .	. . .	. . .	. . .	. . .	. . .		. . .	. . .	. . .
† SRI LANKA	Sri Lanka	64,652	*24,962*	17,740,000	274	*711*	Socialist republic	*A*	Colombo and Sri Jayawardenapura	Asia	25
† SUDAN	As Sūdān	2,505,813	*967,500*	28,760,000	11	*30*	Provisional military government	*A*	Al Kharṭūm (Khartoum)	Africa	35
Sumatra	Sumatera	473,606	*182,860*	36,455,000	77	*199*	Part of Indonesia (7 provinces)		. . .	Asia	26
† SURINAME	Suriname	163,820	*63,251*	413,000	2.5	*6.5*	Republic	*A*	Paramaribo	S. Amer.	54
† SWAZILAND	Swaziland	17,364	*6,704*	925,000	53	*138*	Monarchy	*A*	Mbabane and Lobamba	Africa	37
† SWEDEN	Sverige	449,964	*173,732*	8,619,000	19	*50*	Constitutional monarchy	*A*	Stockholm	Europe	7
SWITZERLAND	Schweiz (German) / Suisse (French) / Svizzera (Italian)	41,293	*15,943*	6,848,000	166	*430*	Federal republic	*A*	Bern (Berne)	Europe	14
† SYRIA	Sūrīyah	185,180	*71,498*	14,070,000	76	*197*	Socialist republic	*A*	Dimashq (Damascus)	Asia	24
TAIWAN	Taiwan	36,002	*13,900*	20,985,000	583	*1,510*	Republic	*A*	Taipei	Asia	27
† TAJIKISTAN	Tojikiston	143,100	*55,251*	5,765,000	40	*104*	Republic	*A*	Dušanbe (Dushanbe)	Asia	18
† TANZANIA	Tanzania	945,087	*364,900*	28,265,000	30	*77*	Republic	*A*	Dar es Salaam and Dodoma (2)	Africa	36
Tasmania	Tasmania	67,800	*26,178*	456,000	6.7	*17*	State (Australia)	*D*	Hobart	Oceania	59
Tennessee	Tennessee	109,158	*42,146*	5,026,000	46	*119*	State (U.S.)	*D*	Nashville	N. Amer.	44
Texas	Texas	695,676	*268,601*	17,610,000	25	*66*	State (U.S.)	*D*	Austin	N. Amer.	45
† THAILAND	Muang Thai	513,115	*198,115*	58,030,000	113	*293*	Constitutional monarchy	*A*	Krung Thep (Bangkok)	Asia	26
Thuringia	Thüringen	16,251	*6,275*	2,734,000	168	*436*	State (Germany)	*D*	Erfurt	Europe	10
Tibet	Xizang Zizhiqu	1,220,000	*471,045*	2,235,000	1.8	*4.7*	Autonomous region (China)	*D*	Lhasa	Asia	27
Tientsin	Tianjin	11,300	*4,363*	9,170,000	812	*2,102*	Autonomous city (China)	*D*	Tianjin (Tientsin)	Asia	28
† TOGO	Togo	56,785	*21,925*	4,030,000	71	*184*	Provisional military government	*A*	Lomé	Africa	34
Tokelau	Tokelau	12	*4.6*	1,800	150	*391*	Island territory (New Zealand)	*C*	. . .	Oceania	61
TONGA	Tonga	747	*288*	103,000	138	*358*	Constitutional monarchy	*A*	Nuku'alofa	Oceania	61
† TRINIDAD AND TOBAGO	Trinidad and Tobago	5,128	*1,980*	1,307,000	255	*660*	Republic	*A*	Port of Spain	N. Amer.	50
Tristan da Cunha	Tristan da Cunha	104	*40*	300	2.9	*7.5*	Dependency (St. Helena)	*C*	Edinburgh	Africa	30-31
† TUNISIA	Tunisie (French) / Tūnis (Arabic)	163,610	*63,170*	8,495,000	52	*134*	Republic	*A*	Tūnis	Africa	32
† TURKEY	Türkiye	779,452	*300,948*	58,620,000	75	*195*	Republic	*A*	Ankara	Eur.,Asia	24
Turkey in Europe	. . .	23,764	*9,175*	8,805,000	371	*960*	. . .		. . .	Europe	24
† TURKMENISTAN	Türkmenistan	488,100	*188,456*	3,884,000	8.0	*21*	Republic	*A*	Ašhabad	Asia	19
Turks and Caicos Islands	Turks and Caicos Islands	500	*193*	13,000	26	*67*	Dependent territory (U.K.)	*C*	Grand Turk	N. Amer.	49
TUVALU	Tuvalu	26	*10*	10,000	385	*1,000*	Parliamentary state	*A*	Funafuti	Oceania	60
† UGANDA	Uganda	241,139	*93,104*	17,410,000	72	*187*	Republic	*A*	Kampala	Africa	36
† UKRAINE	Ukrayina	603,700	*233,090*	51,990,000	86	*223*	Republic	*A*	Kijev (Kiev)	Europe	16
† UNITED ARAB EMIRATES	Al Imārāt al 'Arabīyah al Muttaḥidah	83,600	*32,278*	2,590,000	31	*80*	Federation of monarchs	*A*	Abū Ẓaby (Abu Dhabi)	Asia	23
† UNITED KINGDOM	United Kingdom	244,154	*94,269*	57,890,000	237	*614*	Constitutional monarchy	*A*	London	Europe	9
United Kingdom and Possessions	. . .	259,753	*100,291*	63,860,000	246	*637*	. . .		. . .	. . .	. . .
† UNITED STATES	United States	9,809,431	*3,787,425*	256,420,000	26	*68*	Federal republic	*A*	Washington	N. Amer.	43
United States and Possessions	. . .	9,820,617	*3,791,744*	260,380,000	27	*69*	. . .		. . .	. . .	. . .
Upper Volta, see Burkina Faso	. . .	. . .	. . .	. . .	. . .	. . .	. . .		. . .	. . .	. . .
† URUGUAY	Uruguay	177,414	*68,500*	3,151,000	18	*46*	Republic	*A*	Montevideo	S. Amer.	55
Utah	Utah	219,902	*84,904*	1,795,000	8.2	*21*	State (U.S.)	*D*	Salt Lake City	N. Amer.	46
† UZBEKISTAN	Ŭzbekiston	447,400	*172,742*	21,885,000	49	*127*	Republic	*A*	Taškent (Tashkent)	Asia	19
† VANUATU	Vanuatu	12,190	*4,707*	157,000	13	*33*	Republic	*A*	Port-Vila	Oceania	63

Country, Division, or Region English (Conventional)	Local Name	Area km²	Area sq mi	Population 1/1/93	Population Density per km²	Population Density per sq mi	Form of Government and Political Status	Capital	Continent and Map Plate	
VATICAN CITY	Città del Vaticano	0.4	0.2	800	2,000	4,000	Monarchical-sacerdotal state	A Vatican City	Europe	14
† VENEZUELA	Venezuela	912,050	352,145	19,085,000	21	54	Federal republic	A Caracas	S. Amer.	54
Vermont	Vermont	24,903	9,615	590,000	24	61	State (U.S.)	D Montpelier	N. Amer.	44
Victoria	Victoria	227,600	87,877	4,273,000	19	49	State (Australia)	D Melbourne	Oceania	59
† VIETNAM	Viet Nam	330,036	127,428	69,650,000	211	547	Socialist republic	A Ha Noi	Asia	26
Virginia	Virginia	110,771	42,769	6,411,000	58	150	State (U.S.)	D Richmond	N. Amer.	44
Virgin Islands of the United States	Virgin Islands	344	133	104,000	302	782	Unincorporated territory (U.S.)	C Charlotte Amalie	N. Amer.	51
Virgin Islands, British	British Virgin Islands	153	59	13,000	85	220	Dependent territory (U.K.)	C Road Town	N. Amer.	51
Wake Island	Wake Island	7.8	3.0	200	26	67	Unincorporated territory (U.S.)	C . . .	Oceania	60
Wales	Wales	20,766	8,018	2,906,000	140	362	Administrative division (U.K.)	D Cardiff	Europe	9
Wallis and Futuna	Îles Wallis et Futuna	255	98	17,000	67	173	Overseas territory (France)	C Mata-Utu	Oceania	61
Washington	Washington	184,674	71,303	5,052,000	27	71	State (U.S.)	D Olympia	N. Amer.	46
Western Australia	Western Australia	2,525,500	975,101	1,598,000	0.6	1.6	State (Australia)	D Perth	Oceania	59
Western Sahara	. . .	266,000	102,703	200,000	0.8	1.9	Occupied by Morocco	C El Aaiŭn	Africa	32
† WESTERN SAMOA	Western Samoa (English) / Samoa i Sisifo (Samoan)	2,831	1,093	197,000	70	180	Constitutional monarchy	A Apia	Oceania	65
West Indies	West Indies (English) / Indias Occidentales (Spanish)	235,000	91,000	34,627,000	147	381	. . . .	. . . .	N. Amer.	47
West Virginia	West Virginia	62,759	24,231	1,795,000	29	74	State (U.S.)	D Charleston	N. Amer.	44
Wisconsin	Wisconsin	169,653	65,503	5,000,000	29	76	State (U.S.)	D Madison	N. Amer.	45
Wyoming	Wyoming	253,349	97,818	462,000	1.8	4.7	State (U.S.)	D Cheyenne	N. Amer.	46
† YEMEN	Al Yaman	527,968	203,850	12,215,000	23	60	Republic	A Şan'ā'	Asia	23
YUGOSLAVIA	Jugoslavija	102,173	39,449	10,670,000	104	270	Republic	A Beograd (Belgrade)	Europe 14-15	
Yukon Territory	Yukon Territory	483,450	186,661	31,000	0.1	0.2	Territory (Canada)	D Whitehorse	N. Amer.	42
Yunnan	Yunnan	394,000	152,124	38,450,000	98	253	Province (China).	D Kunming	Asia	27
† ZAIRE	Zaire	2,345,095	905,446	39,750,000	17	44	Republic	A Kinshasa	Africa	36
† ZAMBIA	Zambia	752,614	290,586	8,475,000	11	29	Republic	A Lusaka	Africa	36
Zanzibar	Zanzibar	2,461	950	434,000	176	457	Part of Tanzania	. . . Zanzibar	Africa	36
Zhejiang	Zhejiang	101,800	39,305	43,150,000	424	1,098	Province (China).	D Hangzhou	Asia	27
† ZIMBABWE	Zimbabwe	390,759	150,873	10,000,000	26	66	Republic	A Harare	Africa	37
WORLD	. . .	150,100,000	57,900,000	5,477,000,000	36	95	. . . .	. . . . .	. . . .	1-2

† Member of the United Nations (1992).
. . . None, or not applicable.
(1) No permanent population.
(2) Future capital.
(3) Claimed by Argentina.
(4) Includes West Bank, Golan Heights, and Gaza Strip.
(5) Claimed by Comoros.
(6) Comprises Ceuta, Melilla, and several small islands.

World Geographical Tables

The Earth: Land and Water

	Total Area		Area of Land			Area of Oceans and Seas		
	km²	sq mi	km²	sq mi	%	km²	sq mi	%
Earth	510,100,000	197,100,000	150,100,000	57,900,000	29.4	360,200,000	139,100,000	70.6
N. Hemisphere	255,050,000	98,500,000	106,571,000	41,109,000	41.6	148,762,600	57,448,300	58.4
S. Hemisphere	255,050,000	98,500,000	43,529,000	16,791,000	17.0	211,437,400	81,651,700	83.0

The Continents

Continent	Area km² sq mi	Population Estimate (1/1/93)	Population per km² sq mi	Mean Elevation m ft	Highest Elevation m/ft	Lowest Elevation m/ft (below sea level)	Highest Recorded Temperature °C/°F	Lowest Recorded Temperature °C/°F
Europe	9,900,000 3,800,000	694,700,000	70 183	300 980	gora Elbrus, Russia 5,642/18,510	Caspian Sea, Asia-Europe −28/−92	Sevilla, Spain 50°/122°	Ust-Ščugor, Russia −55°/−67°
Asia	44,900,000 17,300,000	3,337,800,000	74 193	910 3,000	Everest, China-Nepal 8,848/29,028	Dead Sea, Israel-Jordan −403/−1,322	Tirat Zevi, Israel 54°/129°	Ojmjakon and Verkhoyansk, Russia −68°/−90°
Africa	30,300,000 11,700,000	668,700,000	22 57	580 1,900	Kilimanjaro, Tanzania 5,895/19,340	Lac Assal, Djibouti −157/−515	Al 'Azīzīyah, Libya 58°/136°	Ifrane, Morocco −24°/−11°
North America	24,700,000 9,500,000	438,200,000	18 46	610 2,000	Mt. McKinley, U.S. 6,194/20,320	Death Valley, U.S. −86/−282	Death Valley, U.S. 57°/134°	Northice, Greenland −66°/−87°
South America	17,800,000 6,900,000	310,700,000	17 45	550 1,800	Cerro Aconcagua, Argentina 6,960/22,835	Salinas Chicas −42/−138	Rivadavia, Argentina 49°/120°	Sarmiento, Argentina −33°/−27°
Oceania, incl. Australia	8,500,000 3,300,000	26,700,000	3 8	....	Mt. Wilhelm, Papua New Guinea 4,509/14,793	Lake Eyre, Australia −12/−39	Cloncurry, Australia 53°/128°	Charlotte Pass, Australia −22°/−8°
Australia	7,682,300 2,966,155	16,965,000	2 6	300 1,000	Mt. Kosciusko, Australia 2,228/7,310	Lake Eyre, Austraila −12/−39	Cloncurry, Australia 53°/128°	Charlotte Pass, Australia −22°/−8°
Antarctica	14,000,000 5,400,000	....	... ...	1,830 6,000	Vinson Massif 4,897/116,06	sea level	Vanda Station 15°/59°	Vostok −89°/−129°
World	150,100,000 57,900,000	5,477,000,000	36 95	....	Everest, China-Nepal 8,848/29,028	Dead Sea, Israel-Jordan −403/−1,322	Al 'Azīzīyah, Libya 58°/136°	Vostok −89°/−129°

Principal Mountains

Mountain	Country	Height m	ft
Europe			
Elbrus, gora	△Russia	5,642	18,510
Dyhtau, gora	Russia	5,204	17,073
Blanc, Mont	△France-△Italy	4,807	15,771
Rosa, Monte	Italy-△Switzerland	4,634	15,203
Matterhorn	Italy-Switzerland	4,478	14,692
Grossglockner	△Austria	3,797	12,457
Teide, Pico de	△Spain (Canary Is.)	3,718	12,198
Aneto, Pico de	Spain	3,404	11,168
Etna	Italy	3,323	10,902
Zugspitze	Austria-△Germany	2,963	9,721
Ólimbos, Óros	△Greece	2,917	9,570
Corno Grande	Italy	2,912	9,554
Gerlachovský štít	△Slovakia	2,663	8,737
Glittertind	△Norway	2,472	8,110
Kebnekaise	△Sweden	2,111	6,926
Narodnaja, gora	Russia	1,895	6,217
Nevis, Ben	△United Kingdom	1,343	4,406
Asia			
Everest	△China-△Nepal	8,848	29,028
K2 (Qogir Feng)	China-△Pakistan	8,611	28,250
Kanchenjunga	△India-Nepal	8,598	28,208
Makalu	China-Nepal	8,481	27,825
Dhaulagiri	Nepal	8,172	26,810
Annapurna	Nepal	8,078	26,504
Muztag	China	7,723	25,338
Tirich Mīr	Pakistan	7,690	25,230
Kommunizma, pik (Communism Peak)	△Tajikistan	7,495	24,590
Pobedy, pik	China-Russia	7,439	24,406
Damāvand, Qolleh-ye	△Iran	5,604	18,386
Ağrı Dağı, Büyük (Mt. Ararat)	△Turkey	5,122	16,804
Jaya, Puncak	△Indonesia	5,030	16,503
Ključevskaja Sopka, vulkan	Russia	4,750	15,584
Kinabalu, Gunong	△Malaysia	4,101	13,455
Yushan	△Taiwan	3,997	13,114
Fuji-San	△Japan	3,776	12,388
Nabī Shu'ayb, Jabal an	△Yemen	3,760	12,336
Apo, Mt.	△Philippines	2,954	9,692
Shaykh, Jabal ash- (Mt. Hermon)	Lebanon-△Syria	2,814	9,232
Mayon, Mt.	Philippines	2,462	8,077
Chili-san	△South Korea	1,915	6,283
Meron, Hare	△Israel	1,208	3,963

Mountain	Country	Height m	ft
Africa			
Kilimanjaro	△Tanzania	5,895	19,340
Kirinyaga (Mt. Kenya)	△Kenya	5,199	17,058
Margherita	△Uganda-△Zaire	5,109	16,762
Ras Dashan Terara	△Ethiopia	4,620	15,158
Toubkal, Jebel	△Morocco	4,165	13,665
Cameroon, Mt.	△Cameroon	4,100	13,451
North America			
McKinley, Mt.	△United States	6,194	20,320
Logan, Mt.	△Canada	5,951	19,524
Orizaba, Pico de	△Mexico	5,610	18,406
Popocatépetl, Volcán	Mexico	5,452	17,887
Whitney, Mt.	United States	4,417	14,491
Elbert, Mt.	United States	4,399	14,433
Rainier, Mt.	United States	4,392	14,410
Shasta, Mt.	United States	4,317	14,162
Pikes Pk.	United States	4,301	14,110
Tajumulco, Volcán	△Guatemala	4,220	13,845
Mauna Kea	United States	4,205	13,796
Grand Teton	United States	4,197	13,770
Waddington, Mt.	Canada	3,994	13,104
Robson, Mt.	Canada	3,954	12,972
Chirripó, Cerro	△Costa Rica	3,819	12,530
Gunnbjørns Fjeld	△Greenland	3,700	12,139
Duarte, Pico	△Dominican Rep.	3,175	10,417
Mitchell, Mt.	United States	2,037	6,684
Marcy, Mt.	United States	1,629	5,344
South America			
Aconcagua, Cerro	△Argentina	6,960	22,835
Ojos del Salado, Nevado	Argentina-△Chile	6,863	22,516
Huascarán, Nevado	△Peru	6,746	22,133
Illimani, Nevado del	△Bolivia	6,682	21,923
Chimborazo, Volcán	△Ecuador	6,310	20,702
Cristóbal Colón, Pico	△Colombia	5,800	19,029
Neblina, Pico da	△Brazil-Venezuela	3,014	9,888
Oceania			
Wilhelm, Mt.	△Papua New Guinea	4,509	14,793
Cook, Mt.	△New Zealand	3,764	12,349
Kosciusko, Mt.	△Australia	2,228	7,310
Antarctica			
Vinson Massif	△Antarctica	4,897	16,066
Kirkpatrick, Mt.	Antarctica	4,528	14,856

△ Highest mountain in country.

Oceans, Seas, and Gulfs

Name	Area km²	Area sq mi	Greatest Depth m	Greatest Depth ft
Pacific Ocean	165,200,000	63,800,000	11,020	36,155
Atlantic Ocean	82,400,000	31,800,000	9,220	30,249
Indian Ocean	74,900,000	28,900,000	7,450	24,442
Arctic Ocean	14,000,000	5,400,000	5,450	17,881
Arabian Sea	3,864,000	1,492,000	5,800	19,029
South China Sea	3,447,000	1,331,000	5,560	18,241
Caribbean Sea	2,753,000	1,063,000	7,680	25,197
Mediterranean Sea	2,505,000	967,000	5,020	16,470
Bering Sea	2,269,000	876,000	4,096	13,438
Bengal, Bay of	2,173,000	839,000	5,258	17,251
Okhotsk, Sea of	1,603,000	619,000	3,372	11,063
Norwegian Sea	1,546,000	597,000	4,020	13,189
Mexico, Gulf of	1,544,000	596,000	4,380	14,370
East China Sea	1,248,000	482,000	4,424	14,514
Hudson Bay	1,230,000	475,000	259	850

Waterfalls

Waterfall	Country	River	Height m	Height ft
Angel	Venezuela	Churún	972	3,189
Tugela	South Africa	Tugela	948	3,110
Yosemite	United States	Yosemite Creek	739	2,425
Sutherland	New Zealand	Arthur	579	1,900
Gavarnie	France	Gave de Pau	421	1,381
Lofoi	Zaire	Lofoi	384	1,260
Krimml	Austria	Krimml	381	1,250
Takakkaw	Canada	Yoho	380	1,248
Staubbach	Switzerland	Staubbach	305	1,001
Mardalsfoss	Norway	. . .	297	974
Gersoppa	India	Sharavati	253	830
Kaieteur	Guyana	Potaro	247	810

Principal Rivers

River	Continent	Length km	Length mi
Nile	Africa	6,671	4,145
Amazon-Ucayali	South America	6,400	4,000
Yangtze (Chang Jiang)	Asia	6,300	3,900
Yellow (Huang He)	Asia	5,464	3,395
Ob-Irtyš	Asia	5,410	3,362
Río de la Plata-Paraná	South America	4,876	3,030
Congo (Zaire)	Africa	4,700	2,900
Paraná	South America	4,500	2,800
Amur (Heilong Jiang)	Asia	4,416	2,744
Lena	Asia	4,400	2,700
Mekong	Asia	4,200	2,600
Niger	Africa	4,200	2,600
Jenisej	Asia	4,092	2,543
Mississippi	North America	3,779	2,348
Missouri	North America	3,726	2,315
Volga	Europe	3,531	2,194
São Francisco	South America	3,199	1,988
Rio Grande	North America	3,034	1,885
Indus	Asia	2,900	1,800
Danube	Europe	2,858	1,776
Yukon	North America	2,849	1,770
Brahmaputra	Asia	2,849	1,770
Salween (Thanlwin)	Asia	2,816	1,750
Zambezi	Africa	2,700	1,700
Tocantins	South America	2,639	1,640
Orinoco	South America	2,600	1,600
Paraguay	South America	2,591	1,610
Amudarja	Asia	2,540	1,578
Murray	Australia	2,520	1,566
Ganges	Asia	2,511	1,560
Euphrates	Asia	2,430	1,510
Ural	Asia	2,428	1,509
Arkansas	North America	2,348	1,459
Colorado	North America (U.S.-Mex.)	2,334	1,450
Syrdarja	Asia	2,205	1,370
Tarim	Asia	2,137	1,328
Orange	Africa	2,100	1,300
Negro	South America	2,100	1,300
Irrawaddy (Ayeyarwady)	Asia	2,100	1,300
Red	North America	2,044	1,270
Columbia	North America	2,000	1,200
Xingu	South America	1,979	1,230
Ucayali	South America	1,963	1,220
Saskatchewan-Bow	North America	1,939	1,205
Peace	North America	1,923	1,195
Tigris	Asia	1,899	1,180
Sungari	Asia	1,835	1,140
Pechora	Europe	1,809	1,124
Limpopo	Africa	1,800	1,100
Snake	North America	1,670	1,038

Principal Islands

Island	Area km²	Area sq mi	Name	Highest Point m	Highest Point ft
Grønland (Greenland)	2,175,600	840,000	Gunnbjørns Fjeld	3,700	12,139
New Guinea	800,000	309,000	Puncak Jaya	5,030	16,503
Borneo	744,100	287,300	Gunong Kinabalu	4,101	13,455
Madagascar	587,000	227,000	Maromokotro	2,876	9,436
Baffin Island	507,451	195,928	Unnamed	2,591	8,501
Sumatera (Sumatra)	473,606	182,860	Gunung Kerinci	3,800	12,467
Honshū	230,966	89,176	Fuji-San	3,776	12,388
Great Britain	229,978	88,795	Ben Nevis	1,343	4,406
Victoria Island	217,291	83,897	Mt. Bumpus	655	2,149
Ellesmere Island	196,236	75,767	Barbeau Peak	2,604	8,543
Sulawesi (Celebes)	189,216	73,057	Bulu Rantekombola	3,455	11,335
South Island	149,883	57,870	Mt. Cook	3,764	12,349
Jawa (Java)	132,187	51,038	Gunung Semeru	3,676	12,060
North Island	114,669	44,274	Mt. Ruapehu	2,797	9,177
Cuba	110,800	42,800	Pico Turquino	1,994	6,542
Newfoundland	108,860	42,031	Unnamed	814	2,670
Luzon	104,688	40,420	Mt. Pulog	2,930	9,613
Ísland (Iceland)	103,000	39,800	Hvannadalshnúkur	2,119	6,952
Mindanao	94,630	36,537	Mt. Apo	2,954	9,692
Ireland	84,400	32,600	Carrauntoohil	1,038	3,406
Hokkaidō	83,515	32,245	Taisetsu-Zan	2,290	7,513
Novaja Zemlja (Novaya Zemlya)	82,600	31,900	Unnamed	1,547	5,075
Sahalin, ostrov (Sakhalin)	76,400	29,500	gora Lopatina	1,609	5,279
Hispaniola	76,000	29,300	Pico Duarte	3,175	10,417
Banks Island	70,028	27,038	Unnamed	747	2,451
Tasmania	67,800	26,200	Mt. Ossa	1,617	5,305
Sri Lanka	64,600	24,900	Pidurutalagala	2,524	8,281
Devon Island	55,247	21,331	Unnamed	1,887	6,191
Tierra del Fuego, Isla Grande de	48,200	18,600	Cerro Yogan	2,469	8,100

Major Lakes

Lake	Location	Area km²	Area sq mi	Depth m	Depth ft
Caspian Sea	Asia-Europe	370,990	143,240	1,025	3,363
Superior, L.	Canada-U.S.	82,100	31,700	406	1,332
Victoria, L.	Africa	69,463	26,820	85	279
Aral'skoje more (Aral Sea)	Asia	64,100	24,700	68	223
Huron, L.	Canada-U.S.	60,000	23,000	229	750
Michigan, L.	U.S.	57,800	22,300	282	924
Tanganyika. L.	Africa	31,986	12,350	1,463	4,800
Bajkal, ozero (L. Baikal)	Russia	31,500	12,200	1,620	5,315
Great Bear Lake	Canada	31,326	12,095	413	1,356
Nyasa, L.	Africa	28,878	11,150	695	2,280
Great Slave Lake	Canada	28,568	11,030	614	2,015
Erie, L.	Canada-U.S.	25,667	9,910	62	204
Winnipeg, L.	Canada	24,387	9,416	28	92
Ontario, L.	Canada-U.S.	19,529	7,540	243	798
Balhaš, ozero (L. Balkhash)	Kazakhstan	18,300	7,100	26	85
Chad, L.	Africa	16,300	6,300	7	24
Onežskoje ozero (L. Onega)	Russia	9,720	3,753	127	417
Eyre, L.	Australia	9,500	3,700	1	4
Titicaca, Lago	Bolivia-Peru	8,300	3,200	302	990
Nicaragua, Lago de	Nicaragua	8,158	3,150	70	230
Mai-Ndombe, Lac	Zaire	8,000	3,100	11	36
Athabasca, L.	Canada	7,935	3,064	124	407
Reindeer Lake	Canada	6,650	2,568	219	720
Tônlé Sab, Bœng	Cambodia	6,500	2,500	12	39
Rudolf, L.	Ethiopia-Kenya	6,405	2,473	219	720
Torrens, L.	Australia	5,900	2,300	☼	☼
Albert, L.	Uganda-Zaire	5,594	2,160	51	168
Vänern	Sweden	5,584	2,156	99	325

☼ Intermittently dry lake

Drainage Basins

Name	Continent	Area km²	Area sq mi
Amazon	South America	6,151,000	2,375,000
Congo (Zaïre)	Africa	3,823,000	1,476,000
Mississippi-Missouri	North America	3,230,000	1,247,000
Río de la Plata-Paraná	South America	3,100,000	1,197,000
Ob'-Irtyš	Asia	2,989,000	1,154,000
Nile	Africa	2,802,000	1,082,000
Lena	Asia	2,489,000	961,000
Amur-Argun	Asia	2,051,000	792,000
Niger	Africa	1,891,000	730,000
Yangtze (Chang Jiang)	Asia	1,826,000	705,000
Mackenzie	North America	1,572,000	607,000
Volga	Europe	1,360,000	525,000
Zambezi	Africa	1,331,000	514,000
St. Lawrence	North America	1,303,000	503,000

World Geographical Tables

Historical Population of the World

AREA	1650	1750	1800	1850	1900	1914	1920	1939	1950	1993
Europe	*100,000,000*	*140,000,000*	*190,000,000*	265,000,000	400,000,000	470,000,000	453,000,000	526,000,000	530,000,000	694,700,000
Asia	*335,000,000*	*476,000,000*	*593,000,000*	754,000,000	932,000,000	1,006,000,000	1,000,000,000	1,247,000,000	1,418,000,000	3,337,800,000
Africa	*100,000,000*	*95,000,000*	*90,000,000*	95,000,000	118,000,000	130,000,000	140,000,000	170,000,000	199,000,000	668,700,000
North America	*5,000,000*	*5,000,000*	*13,000,000*	39,000,000	106,000,000	141,000,000	147,000,000	186,000,000	219,000,000	438,200,000
South America	*8,000,000*	*7,000,000*	*12,000,000*	20,000,000	38,000,000	55,000,000	61,000,000	90,000,000	111,000,000	310,700,000
Oceania, incl. Australia	*2,000,000*	*2,000,000*	*2,000,000*	*2,000,000*	6,000,000	8,000,000	9,000,000	11,000,000	13,000,000	26,700,000
Australia					4,000,000	5,000,000	6,000,000	7,000,000	8,000,000	16,965,000
World	*550,000,000*	*725,000,000*	*900,000,000*	*1,175,000,000*	1,600,000,000	1,810,000,000	1,810,000,000	2,230,000,000	2,490,000,000	5,477,000,000

Figures in italics represent very rough estimates.

Largest Countries: Population

Country	Population 1/1/93
1. China	1,179,030,000
2. India	873,850,000
3. United States	256,420,000
4. Indonesia	186,180,000
5. Brazil	159,630,000
6. Russia	150,500,000
7. Japan	124,710,000
8. Pakistan	123,490,000
9. Bangladesh	120,850,000
10. Nigeria	91,700,000
11. Mexico	86,170,000
12. Germany	80,590,000
13. Vietnam	69,650,000
14. Philippines	65,500,000
15. Iran	60,500,000
16. Turkey	58,620,000
17. Thailand	58,030,000
18. United Kingdom	57,890,000
19. France	57,570,000
20. Egypt	57,050,000
21. Italy	56,550,000
22. Ukraine	51,990,000
23. Ethiopia	51,715,000
24. South Korea	43,660,000
25. Burma	43,070,000
26. South Africa	42,407,000
27. Zaire	39,750,000
28. Spain	39,155,000
29. Poland	38,330,000
30. Colombia	34,640,000
31. Argentina	32,950,000
32. Canada	30,530,000
33. Sudan	28,760,000
34. Tanzania	28,265,000
35. Morocco	27,005,000
36. Algeria	26,925,000
37. Kenya	26,635,000
38. Romania	23,200,000
39. Peru	22,995,000
40. North Korea	22,450,000
41. Uzbekistan	21,885,000
42. Taiwan	20,985,000
43. Nepal	20,325,000
44. Venezuela	19,085,000
45. Iraq	18,815,000

Largest Countries: Area

Country	km²	sq mi
1. Russia	17,075,400	6,592,849
2. Canada	9,970,610	3,849,674
3. United States	9,809,431	3,787,425
4. China	9,556,100	3,689,631
5. Brazil	8,511,996	3,286,500
6. Australia	7,682,300	2,966,155
7. India	3,203,975	1,237,062
8. Argentina	2,780,400	1,073,519
9. Kazakhstan	2,717,300	1,049,156
10. Sudan	2,505,813	967,500
11. Algeria	2,381,741	919,595
12. Zaire	2,345,095	905,446
13. Greenland	2,175,600	840,004
14. Saudi Arabia	2,149,690	830,000
15. Mexico	1,967,183	759,534
16. Indonesia	1,948,732	752,410
17. Libya	1,759,540	679,362
18. Iran	1,638,057	632,457
19. Mongolia	1,566,500	604,829
20. Peru	1,285,216	496,225
21. Chad	1,284,000	495,755
22. Niger	1,267,000	489,191
23. Mali	1,248,574	482,077
24. Angola	1,246,700	481,354
25. South Africa	1,220,118	471,090
26. Ethiopia	1,157,603	446,953
27. Colombia	1,141,748	440,831
28. Bolivia	1,098,581	424,165
29. Mauritania	1,025,520	395,956
30. Egypt	1,001,449	386,662
31. Tanzania	945,087	364,900
32. Nigeria	923,768	356,669
33. Venezuela	912,050	352,145
34. Pakistan	879,902	339,732
35. Namibia	824,272	318,254
36. Mozambique	799,380	308,642
37. Turkey	779,452	300,948
38. Chile	756,626	292,135
39. Zambia	752,614	290,586
40. Burma	676,577	261,228
41. Afghanistan	652,225	251,826
42. Somalia	637,657	246,201
43. Central African Republic	622,984	240,535
44. Ukraine	603,700	233,090
45. Madagascar	587,041	226,658

Smallest Countries: Population

Country	Population 1/1/93
1. Vatican City	800
2. Niue	1,700
3. Anguilla	7,000
4. Nauru	10,000
Tuvalu	10,000
5. Palau	16,000
6. Cook Islands	18,000
7. San Marino	23,000
8. Liechtenstein	30,000
9. Monaco	31,000
10. St. Christopher-Nevis	40,000
11. Northern Mariana Islands	48,000
12. Faeroe Islands	49,000
13. Marshall Islands	51,000
14. Andorra	56,000
15. Greenland	57,000
16. Guernsey	58,000
17. Aruba	65,000
18. Isle of Man	70,000
Seychelles	70,000
19. Kiribati	76,000
20. Antigua and Barbuda	77,000
21. Jersey	85,000
22. Dominica	88,000
23. Grenada	97,000
24. Tonga	103,000
25. St. Vincent and the Grenadines	116,000
26. Micronesia, Federated States of	117,000
27. Sao Tome and Principe	134,000
28. St. Lucia	153,000
29. Vanuatu	157,000
30. Belize	186,000
31. Netherlands Antilles	191,000
32. Cyprus, North	193,000
33. Western Samoa	197,000
34. Maldives	235,000
35. Barbados	258,000
36. Iceland	260,000
37. Bahamas	265,000
38. Brunei	273,000
39. Malta	360,000
40. Solomon Islands	366,000
41. Luxembourg	392,000
42. Equatorial Guinea	394,000
43. Djibouti	396,000

Smallest Countries: Area

Country	km²	sq mi
1. Vatican City	0.4	0.2
2. Monaco	1.9	0.7
3. Nauru	21	8.1
4. Tuvalu	26	10
5. San Marino	61	24
6. Guernsey	78	30
7. Anguilla	91	35
8. Jersey	116	45
9. Liechtenstein	160	62
10. Marshall Islands	181	70
11. Aruba	193	75
12. Cook Islands	236	91
13. Niue	258	100
14. St. Christopher-Nevis	269	104
15. Maldives	298	115
16. Malta	316	122
17. Grenada	344	133
18. St. Vincent and the Grenadines	388	150
19. Barbados	430	166
20. Antigua and Barbuda	442	171
21. Andorra	453	175
Seychelles	453	175
22. Northern Mariana Islands	477	184
23. Palau	508	196
24. Isle of Man	572	221
25. St. Lucia	616	238
26. Singapore	636	246
27. Bahrain	691	267
28. Micronesia, Federated States of	702	271
29. Tonga	747	288
30. Dominica	790	305
31. Netherlands Antilles	800	309
32. Kiribati	811	313
33. Sao Tome and Principe	964	372
34. Faeroe Islands	1,399	540
35. Mauritius	2,040	788
36. Comoros	2,235	863
37. Luxembourg	2,586	998
38. Western Samoa	2,831	1,093
39. Cyprus, North	3,355	1,295
40. Cape Verde	4,033	1,557
41. Trinidad and Tobago	5,128	1,980
42. Brunei	5,765	2,226
43. Cyprus	5,896	2,276

Highest Population Densities

Country	km²	sq mi		Country	km²	sq mi
1. Monaco	16,316	44,286		16. Tuvalu	385	1,000
2. Singapore	4,421	11,431		17. San Marino	377	958
3. Vatican City	2,000	4,000		18. Netherlands	363	940
4. Malta	1,139	2,951		19. Aruba	337	867
5. Bangladesh	839	2,174		20. Lebanon	333	864
6. Bahrain	812	2,101		21. Japan	330	855
7. Maldives	789	2,043		22. Belgium	329	851
8. Guernsey	744	1,933		23. St. Vincent and the Grenadines	299	773
9. Jersey	733	1,889		24. Rwanda	288	745
10. Barbados	600	1,554		25. Grenada	282	729
11. Taiwan	583	1,510		Marshall Islands	282	729
12. Mauritius	537	1,391		26. Sri Lanka	274	711
13. Nauru	476	1,235		27. India	273	706
14. Korea, South	441	1,142		28. El Salvador	268	694
15. Puerto Rico	395	1,022		29. Trinidad and Tobago	255	660

Lowest Population Densities

Country	km²	sq mi		Country	km²	sq mi
1. Greenland		0.1		16. Niue	6.6	17
2. Mongolia	1.5	3.9		17. Bolivia	6.7	17
3. Namibia	1.9	5.0		18. Mali	7.0	18
4. Mauritania	2.0	5.3		19. Congo	7.1	18
5. Australia	2.2	5.7		20. Saudi Arabia	7.4	19
6. Botswana	2.4	6.1		21. Oman	7.6	20
7. Iceland	2.5	6.5		22. Turkmenistan	8.0	21
Suriname	2.5	6.5		23. Belize	8.1	21
8. Libya	2.6	6.7		Papua New Guinea	8.1	21
9. Canada	3.1	7.9		24. Angola	8.6	22
10. Guyana	3.4	8.9		25. Russia	8.8	23
11. Chad	4.1	11		26. Somalia	9.4	24
12. Gabon	4.2	11		27. Algeria	11	29
13. Central African Republic	4.9	13		28. Norway	11	29
14. Kazakhstan	6.3	16		29. Zambia	11	29
15. Niger	6.5	17				

... Less than 0.1

Major Metropolitan Areas of the World

This table lists the major metropolitan areas of the world according to their estimated population on January 1, 1993. For convenience in reference, the areas are grouped by major region with the total for each region given. The number of areas by population classification is given in parentheses with each size group.

For ease of comparison, each metropolitan area has been defined by Rand McNally according to consistent rules. A metropolitan area includes a central city, neighboring communities linked to it by continuous built-up areas, and more distant communities if the bulk of their population is supported by commuters to the central city. Some metropolitan areas have more than one central city; in such cases each central city is listed.

SIZE	ANGLO AMERICA	LATIN AMERICA	WESTERN EUROPE	EASTERN EUROPE / RUSSIA	WEST ASIA	EAST ASIA	AFRICA / OCEANIA
Over 15,000,000 (6)	New York	Ciudad de México (Mexico City) São Paulo				Ōsaka-Kōbe-Kyōto Sŏul (Seoul) Tōkyō-Yokohama	
10,000,000- 15,000,000 (13)	Los Angeles	Buenos Aires Rio de Janeiro	London Paris	Moskva (Moscow)	Bombay Calcutta Delhi-New Delhi	Jakarta Manila Shanghai	Al-Qāhirah (Cairo)
5,000,000- 10,000,000 (21)	Chicago Philadelphia-Trenton- Wilmington San Francisco- Oakland-San Jose	Lima Santa Fe de Bogotá Santiago	Essen-Dortmund- Duisburg (Ruhr Area)	Sankt-Peterburg (St. Petersburg)	Dhaka (Dacca) İstanbul Karāchi Madras Tehrān	Beijing (Peking) Krung Thep (Bangkok) Nagoya Tianjin (Tientsin) T'aipei Victoria (Hong Kong)	Johannesburg Lagos
3,000,000- 5,000,000 (37)	Boston Dallas-Fort Worth Detroit-Windsor Houston Miami-Fort Lauderdale Montréal San Diego-Tijuana Toronto Washington	Belo Horizonte Caracas Guadalajara Porto Alegre	Barcelona Berlin Madrid Milano (Milan) Roma (Rome)	Athínai (Athens) Kijev (Kiev)	Ahmadābād Baghdād Bangalore Hyderābād Lahore	Guangzhou (Canton) Pusan Shenyang (Mukden) Singapore Thanh Pho Ho Chi Minh (Saigon) Wuhan Yangon (Rangoon)	Al-Iskandarīyah (Alexandria) Casablanca Kinshasa Melbourne Sydney
2,000,000- 3,000,000 (64)	Atlanta Baltimore Cleveland Minneapolis-St. Paul Phoenix Pittsburgh St. Louis Seattle-Tacoma	Fortaleza La Habana (Havana) Medellín Monterrey Recife Salvador San Juan Santo Domingo	Amsterdam Birmingham Bruxelles (Brussels) Frankfurt am Main Hamburg Leeds-Bradford Lisboa (Lisbon) Liverpool Manchester München (Munich) Napoli (Naples) Stuttgart Wien (Vienna)	București (Bucharest) Budapest Char'kov (Kharkov) Doneck-Makejevka Katowice-Bytom- Gliwice Nižnij Novgorod (Gorkiy) Warszawa (Warsaw)	Ankara Baku Colombo Dimashq (Damascus) İzmir Kānpur Pune (Poona) Taškent	Bandung Changchun Chengdu (Chengtu) Chongqing (Chungking) Dalian (Dairen) Fukuoka Harbin Kuala Lumpur Nanjing (Nanking) P'yongyang Sapporo-Otaru Surabaya Taegu Xi'an (Sian)	Abidjan Adis Abeba Al-Khartūm-Umm Durmān (Khartoum- Omdurman) Cape Town Durban El Djazaïr (Algiers)
1,500,000- 2,000,000 (48)	Cincinnati Denver El Paso-Ciudad Juárez Portland Vancouver	Brasília Cali Curitiba Guatemala Guayaquil Montevideo San José	Glasgow København (Copenhagen) Köln (Cologne) Mannheim Stockholm	Beograd (Belgrade) Dnepropetrovsk Jekaterinburg (Sverdlovsk) Minsk Novosibirsk	'Amman Ar-Riyad (Riyadh) Bayrūt (Beirut) Chittagong Faisalabad Halab (Aleppo) Jaipur Jiddah Kābol (Kabul) Lucknow Mashhad Nāgpur Rāwalpindi- Islāmābād Surat Tbilisi Tel Aviv-Yafo	Hiroshima-Kure Jinan (Tsinan) Kaohsiung Kitakyūshū- Shimonoseki Medan Qingdao (Tsingtao) Taiyuan	Accra Dakar Rabat-Salé
1,000,000- 1,500,000 (119)	Buffalo-Niagara Falls- St. Catharines Columbus Hartford-New Britain Indianapolis Kansas City Milwaukee New Orleans Norfolk-Newport News Sacramento St. Petersburg- Clearwater San Antonio	Asuncíon Barranquilla Belém Campinas Córdoba Goiânia La Paz Manaus Maracaibo Puebla Quito Rosario San Salvador Santos Valencia Vitória	Antwerpen (Antwerp) Dublin (Baile Átha Cliath) Düsseldorf Hannover Helsinki Lille-Roubaix Lyon Marseille Newcastle-Sunderland Nürnberg Porto Rotterdam Sevilla Torino (Turin) Valencia	Čel'abinsk (Chelyabinsk) Łódź Kazan' Kraków Krasnojarsk Odessa Omsk Perm Praha (Prague) Rīga Rostov-na-Donu Samara (Kuybyshev) Saratov Sofija (Sofia) Ufa Volgograd Voronež	Adana Agra Allahābād Al-Kuwayt (Kuwait) Alma-Ata Asansol Bhopāl Cochin Coimbatore Esfahān Indore Jerevan Ludhiāna Madurai Patna Shīrāz Tabrīz Vadodara Vārānasi (Benares) Vishākhapatnam	Anshan Baotou Changsha Fushun Guiyang Hangzhou Ha Noi Jilin (Kirin) Kunming Kwangju Lanzhou Nanchang Palembang Qiqihar (Tsitsihar) Semarang Sendai Shijiazhuang Shizuoka-Shimizu Taejŏn Tangshan Ujung Pandang Ürümqi Zhengzhou Zibo	Adelaide Antananarivo Brisbane Dar es Salaam Douala Harare Ibadan Kampala Luanda Lusaka Maputo Nairobi Perth Pretoria Tarābulus (Tripoli) Tunis
Total by region (308)	38	42	41	33	57	64	33

Populations of Major Cities

The largest and most important of the world's major cities are listed in the following table. Also included are some smaller cities because of their regional significance.

Local official name forms have been used throughout the table. When a commonly used "conventional" name form exists, it has been featured within parentheses, following the official name. Each city name is followed by the English name of its country. Names in the United States, the United Kingdom, and Canada are further distinguished by the name of the state, region, or province in which they are located.

Many cities have population figures within parentheses following the country name. These are metropolitan populations, comprising the central city and its suburbs. When a city is within the metropolitan area of another city the name of the metropolitan central city is specified in parentheses preceded by a *. The symbol † identifies a political district population which includes some rural population. For these cities the estimated city population has been based upon the district figure.

The population of each city has been dated for ease of comparison. The date is followed by a letter designating: Census (C) or Official Estimate (E).

City and Country	Population	Date
Aachen, Germany (535,000) . . .	233,255	89E
Ābādān, Iran	296,081	76C
Abidjan, Ivory Coast	1,950,000	83E
Abū Ẓaby (Abu Dhabi), United Arab Emirates	242,975	80C
Acapulco [de Juárez], Mexico	301,902	80C
Accra, Ghana (1,250,000)	949,113	87C
Adana, Turkey	931,555	90C
Ad Dawḥah (Doha), Qatar (310,000)	217,294	86E
Addis Ababa, see Ādīs Ābeba		
Adelaide, Australia (1,036,747)	12,340	89E
Aden, see Baladiyad 'Adan		
Ādīs Ābeba (Addis Ababa), Ethiopia (1,760,000)	1,686,300	88E
Agana, Guam (44,000)	896	80C
Āgra, India (955,684)	899,195	91C
Aguascalientes, Mexico	293,152	80C
Ahmadābād, India (3,297,655)	2,872,865	91C
Ahvāz, Iran	579,826	86C
Akita, Japan	302,359	90C
Akron, Oh., U.S. (*Cleveland)	223,019	90C
Albany, N.Y., U.S. (874,304) . . .	101,082	90C
Al Baṣrah, Iraq	616,700	85E
Albuquerque, N.M., U.S. (480,557)	384,736	90C
Aleppo, see Halab		
Alexandria, see Al Iskandarīyah		
Algiers, see Al Jazā'ir		
Al Iskandarīyah (Alexandria), Egypt (3,350,000)	2,917,327	86C
Al Jazā'ir (Algiers), Algeria (2,547,983)	1,507,241	87E
Al Jīzah (Giza), Egypt (*Al Qāhirah)	1,870,508	86C
Al Khartūm (Khartoum), Sudan (1,450,000)	476,218	83C
Al Kuwayt (Kuwait), Kuwait (1,375,000)	44,335	85C
Allahābād, India (858,213)	806,447	91C
Alma-Ata, Kazakhstan (1,190,000)	1,128,000	89C
Al Madīnah (Medina), Saudi Arabia	290,000	80E
Al Maḥallah al Kubrā, Egypt	358,844	86C
Al Manāmah (Manama), Bahrain (224,643)	115,054	81C
Al Manṣūrah, Egypt (375,000)	316,870	86C
Al Mawṣil (Mosul), Iraq	570,926	85E
Al Qāhirah (Cairo), Egypt (9,300,000)	6,052,836	86C
Amagasaki, Japan (*Ōsaka) . . .	498,998	90C
'Ammān, Jordan (1,450,000) . . .	936,300	89E
Amritsar, India	709,456	91C
Amsterdam, Netherlands (1,860,000)	696,500	89E
Anchorage, Ak., U.S.	226,338	90C
Andorra la Vella, Andorra	20,437	91E
Ankara, Turkey (2,650,000) . . .	2,553,209	90C
Annaba (Bône), Algeria	305,526	87C
Anshan, China	1,330,000	88E
Antananarivo, Madagascar . . .	663,000	85E
Antwerpen (Antwerp), Belgium (1,100,000)	479,748	87E
Apia, Western Samoa	33,170	81C
Arequipa, Peru (446,942)	108,023	81C
Arhangelsk, Russia	416,000	89C
Arnhem, Netherlands (296,362)	129,000	89E
Ar Riyāḍ (Riyadh), Saudi Arabia	1,250,000	80E
Asansol, India (763,845)	261,836	91C
Ashabad, Turkmenistan	398,000	89C
As Suways (Suez), Egypt	326,820	86C
Astrahan, Russia	509,000	89C

City and Country	Population	Date
Asunción, Paraguay (700,000)	477,100	85E
Athínai (Athens), Greece (3,027,331)	885,737	81C
Atlanta, Ga., U.S. (2,833,511)	394,017	90C
Auckland, New Zealand (850,000)	149,046	86C
Augsburg, Germany (405,000)	247,731	89E
Austin, Tx., U.S. (781,572)	465,622	90C
Baghdād, Iraq	3,841,268	87C
Bakhtaran, Iran	560,514	86C
Baku, Azerbaijan (2,020,000)	1,150,000	89C
Baladiyat 'Adan (Aden), Yemen (318,000)	176,100	84E
Balikpapan, Indonesia (†279,852)	208,040	80C
Baltimore, Md., U.S. (2,382,172)	736,014	90C
Bamako, Mali	646,163	87C
Bandar Seri Begawan, Brunei (64,000)	22,777	81C
Bandung, Indonesia (1,800,000)	1,633,000	85E
Bangalore, India (4,086,548) . . .	2,650,659	91C
Banghāzī (Benghazi), Libya . . .	466,250	88E
Bangkok, see Krung Thep		
Bangui, Cen. Afr. Rep.	473,817	84E
Banjul, Gambia (95,000)	44,188	83C
Barcelona, Spain (4,040,000)	1,714,355	88E
Barnaul, Russia (665,000)	602,000	89C
Barquisimeto, Venezuela	497,635	81C
Barranquilla, Colombia (1,140,000)	899,781	85C
Basel, Switzerland (575,000) . . .	169,587	90E
Basse-Terre, Guadeloupe (26,000)	13,656	82C
Basseterre, St. Chris.-Nevis . . .	14,725	80C
Baton Rouge, La., U.S. (528,264)	219,531	90C
Bayrūt (Beirut), Lebanon (1,675,000)	509,000	82E
Beijing (Peking), China (7,320,000)	6,710,000	88E
Beirut, see Bayrūt		
Belém, Brazil (1,200,000)	1,116,578	85E
Belfast, N. Ire., U.K. (685,000)	303,800	87E
Belgrade, see Beograd		
Belize City, Belize	47,000	85E
Belmopan, Belize	4,500	85E
Belo Horizonte, Brazil (2,950,000)	2,114,429	85E
Benares, see Vārānasi		
Bengbu, China (†612,600)	403,900	86E
Benxi, China	860,000	88E
Beograd (Belgrade), Yugoslavia (1,400,000)	1,130,000	87E
Bergamo, Italy (345,000)	118,959	87E
Berlin, Germany (3,825,000) . . .	3,352,848	89E
Bern (Berne), Switzerland (298,363)	134,393	90E
Bhopāl, India	1,063,662	91C
Bielefeld, Germany (515,000)	311,946	89E
Bilbao, Spain (985,000)	384,733	88E
Billings, Mt., U.S. (113,419) . . .	81,151	90C
Birmingham, Eng., U.K. (2,675,000)	1,013,995	81C
Birmingham, Al., U.S. (907,810)	265,968	90C
Biškek Kirghizia	616,000	89C
Bissau, Guinea-Bissau	125,000	88E
Blackpool, Eng., U.K. (280,000)	146,297	81C
Bloemfontein, South Africa (235,000)	104,381	85C
Bogor, Indonesia (560,000) . . .	246,946	80C
Boise, Id., U.S. (205,775)	125,738	90C
Bologna, Italy (525,000)	432,406	87E
Bombay, India (12,571,720) . . .	9,909,547	91C
Bonn, Germany (570,000)	282,190	89E
Bordeaux, France (640,012) . . .	208,159	82C

City and Country	Population	Date
Boston, Ma., U.S. (4,171,643)	574,283	90C
Brasília, Brazil	1,567,709	85E
Bratislava, Slovakia	442,999	90E
Braunschweig, Germany (330,000)	253,794	89E
Brazzaville, Congo	585,812	84C
Bremen, Germany (800,000) . . .	5,325,058	89E
Brest, France (201,145)	156,060	82C
Bridgetown, Barbados (115,000)	7,466	80C
Brighton, Eng., U.K. (420,000)	134,581	81C
Brisbane, Australia (1,273,511)	744,828	89E
Bristol, Eng., U.K. (630,000) . . .	413,861	81C
Bruxelles / Brussel (Brussels), Belgium (2,385,000)	136,920	87E
Bucaramanga, Colombia (550,000)	352,326	85C
Bucureşti (Bucharest), Romania (2,275,000)	1,989,823	86E
Budapest, Hungary (2,565,000)	2,016,132	90E
Buenos Aires, Argentina (10,750,000)	2,922,829	80C
Buffalo, N.Y., U.S. (1,189,288)	328,123	90C
Bujumbura, Burundi	273,000	86E
Bulawayo, Zimbabwe	429,000	83E
Burlington, Vt., U.S. (131,439)	39,127	90C
Bursa, Turkey	838,323	90C
Būr Saʿīd (Port Said), Egypt . . .	399,793	86C
Cádiz, Spain (240,000)	156,591	88E
Cagliari, Italy (305,000)	220,574	87E
Cairo, see Al Qāhirah		
Calcutta, India (11,605,833) . . .	4,388,262	91C
Calgary, Alta., Can. (671,326)	636,104	86C
Cali, Colombia (1,400,000)	1,350,565	85C
Calicut (Kozhikode), India (800,913)	419,531	91C
Callao, Peru (*Lima)	264,133	81C
Campinas, Brazil (1,125,000)	841,016	85E
Canberra, Australia (271,362)	247,194	86C
Cannes, France (295,525)	72,259	82C
Canton, see Guangzhou		
Cape Town, South Africa (1,790,000)	776,617	85C
Caracas, Venezuela (3,600,000)	1,816,901	81C
Cardiff, Wales, U.K. (625,000)	262,313	81C
Cartagena, Colombia	531,426	85C
Casablanca, Morocco (2,475,000)	2,139,204	82C
Castries, St. Lucia	53,933	87E
Catania, Italy (550,000)	372,486	87E
Cayenne, French Guiana	38,091	82C
Cebu, Philippines (720,000) . . .	610,000	90C
Čeljabinsk (Chelyabinsk), Russia (1,325,000)	1,143,000	89C
Chandīgarh, India (574,646) . . .	502,992	91C
Changchun, China (†2,000,000)	1,822,000	88E
Changshu, China (†998,000)	281,300	86E
Changzhou, China	522,700	86E
Chao'an, China (†1,214,500)	265,400	86E
Charleston, W.V., U.S. (250,454)	57,287	90C
Charlotte, N.C., U.S. (1,162,093)	395,934	90C
Chattanooga, Tn., U.S. (433,210)	152,466	90C
Chengdu, China (†2,960,000)	1,884,000	88E
Chiba, Japan (*Tōkyō)	829,467	90C
Chicago, Il., U.S. (8,065,633)	2,783,726	90C
Chiclayo, Peru (279,527)	213,095	81C
Chihuahua, Mexico	385,603	80C
Chittagong, Bangladesh (1,391,877)	980,000	81C
Ch'ŏngjin, N. Korea	490,000	81E
Chongqing (Chungking), China (†2,890,000)	2,502,000	88E
Chŏnju, S. Korea	426,473	85C

City and Country	Population	Date
Christchurch, New Zealand (320,000)	168,200	86C
Chungking, see Chongqing		
Cincinnati, Oh., U.S. (1,744,124)	364,040	90C
Ciudad de México, Mexico (14,100,000)	8,831,079	80C
Ciudad Juárez, Mexico (*El Paso)	544,496	80C
Clermont-Ferrand, France (256,189)	147,361	82C
Cleveland, Oh., U.S. (2,759,823)	505,616	90C
Cochin, India (1,139,543)	564,038	91C
Coimbatore, India (1,135,549)	853,402	91C
Cologne, see Köln		
Colombo, Sri Lanka (2,050,000)	683,000	86E
Columbia, S.C., U.S. (453,331)	98,052	90C
Columbus, Oh., U.S. (1,377,419)	632,910	90C
Conakry, Guinea	800,000	86E
Concepción, Chile (675,000)	267,891	82C
Constanța, Romania	327,676	86C
Constantine, Algeria	440,842	87C
Córdoba, Argentina (1,070,000)	993,055	80C
Córdoba, Spain	302,301	88E
Cotonou, Benin	478,000	84E
Coventry, Eng., U.K. (645,000)	318,718	81C
Cúcuta, Colombia (445,000)	379,478	85C
Cuernavaca, Mexico	192,770	80C
Curitiba, Brazil (1,700,000)	1,279,205	85E
Cusco, Peru (184,550)	89,563	81C
Dakar, Senegal	1,447,642	88C
Dalian (Lüda), China	2,280,000	88E
Dallas, Tx., U.S. (3,885,415)	1,006,877	90C
Dandong, China	579,800	86E
Danzig, see Gdańsk		
Daqing, China (†880,000)	640,000	88E
Dar es Salaam, Tanzania	1,300,000	84E
Darmstadt, Germany (305,000)	136,067	89E
Datong, China (†1,040,000)	810,000	88E
Davao, Philippines (*850,000)	569,300	90C
Dayton, Oh., U.S. (951,270)	182,044	90C
Delhi, India (8,375,188)	7,174,755	91C
Denver, Co., U.S. (1,848,319)	467,610	90C
Des Moines, Ia., U.S. (392,928)	193,187	90C
Detroit, Mi., U.S. (4,665,236)	1,027,974	90C
Dhaka, Bangladesh (3,430,312)	2,365,695	81C
Dhānbād, India (817,549)	151,334	91C
Dimashq (Damascus), Syria (1,950,000)	1,326,000	88E
Djibouti, Djibouti	120,000	76E
Dnepropetrovsk, Ukraine (1,600,000)	1,179,000	89C
Doneck, Ukraine (2,200,000)	1,110,000	89C
Dongguan, China (†1,208,500)	254,900	86E
Dortmund, Germany (*Essen)	587,328	89E
Douala, Cameroon	1,029,731	86E
Dresden, Germany (670,000)	518,057	89E
Dublin (Baile Átha Cliath), Ireland (1,140,000)	502,749	86C
Duisburg, Germany (*Essen)	527,447	89E
Durban, South Africa (1,550,000)	634,301	85C
Dušanbe, Tajikistan	595,000	89C
Düsseldorf, Germany (1,190,000)	569,641	89E
Ecatepec de Morelos, Mexico (*Ciudad de México)	741,821	80C
Edinburgh, Scot., U.K. (630,000)	433,200	89E
Edmonton, Alta., Can. (785,465)	573,982	86C
El Paso, Tx., U.S. (1,211,300)	515,342	90C
Enschede, Netherlands (288,000)	145,200	89E
Erbīl, Iraq	333,903	85E
Eṣfahān (Isfahan), Iran (1,175,000)	986,753	86C
Essen, Germany (4,950,000)	620,594	89E
Faisalabad, Pakistan	1,104,209	81C
Fargo, N.D., U.S (153,296)	74,111	90C
Fès, Morocco (535,000)	488,823	82C
Firenze (Florence), Italy (640,000)	425,835	87E
Florianópolis, Brazil (365,000)	178,400	85E
Fortaleza, Brazil (1,825,000)	1,582,414	85E
Fort-de-France, Martinique (116,017)	99,844	82C
Fort Worth, Tx., U.S. (*Dallas)	447,619	90C
Frankfurt am Main, Germany (1,855,000)	625,258	89E
Freetown, Sierra Leone (525,000)	469,776	85C
Fukuoka, Japan (1,750,000)	1,237,107	90C
Funabashi, Japan (*Tōkyō)	533,273	90C
Funafuti, Tuvalu	2,191	79C
Fushun, China	1,290,000	88E
Fuxian, China (†960,700)	246,200	86E
Fuxin, China	700,000	88E
Fuzhou, China (†1,240,000)	910,000	88E
Gaborone, Botswana	107,677	87E
Gdańsk (Danzig), Poland (909,000)	461,500	89E
General Sarmiento, Argentina (*Buenos Aires)	502,926	80C
Genève (Geneva), Switzerland (470,000)	165,404	90E
Genova (Genoa), Italy (805,000)	727,427	87E
Gent (Ghent), Belgium (465,000)	233,856	87E
Georgetown, Cayman Islands	13,700	88E
Georgetown, Guyana (188,000)	78,500	83E
George Town (Pinang), Malaysia (495,000)	248,241	80C
Gifu, Japan	410,318	90C
Giza, see Al Jīzah		
Glasgow, Scot., U.K. (1,800,000)	695,630	89E
Godthåb (Nûk), Greenland	12,217	90E
Goiânia, Brazil (990,000)	923,333	85E
Gorki, see Nižnij Novgorod		
Göteborg, Sweden (710,894)	431,840	90E
Granada, Spain	263,334	88E
Graz, Austria (325,000)	243,166	81C
Grenoble, France (392,021)	156,637	82C
Guadalajara, Mexico (2,325,000)	1,626,152	80C
Guadalupe, Mexico (*Monterrey)	370,524	80C
Guangzhou (Canton), China (†3,420,000)	3,100,000	88E
Guarulhos, Brazil (*São Paulo)	571,700	86E
Guatemala, Guatemala (1,400,000)	1,057,210	89E
Guayaquil, Ecuador (1,580,000)	1,572,615	87C
Guilin, China (†457,500)	342,200	86E
Guiyang, China (†1,430,000)	1,030,000	88E
Gujranwala, Pakistan (658,753)	600,993	81C
Gwalior, India (720,068)	692,982	91C
Haicheng, China (†984,800)	210,700	86E
Haikou, China (†289,600)	209,200	86E
Hai Phong, Vietnam (†1,447,523)	351,919	89C
Halab (Aleppo), Syria (1,261,000)	1,261,000	88E
Halifax, N.S., Can. (295,990)	113,577	86C
Hamamatsu, Japan	534,624	90C
Hamburg, Germany (2,225,000)	1,603,070	89E
Hamilton, Bermuda (15,000)	1,676	85E
Hamilton, Ont., Can. (557,029)	306,728	86C
Handan, China (†1,030,000)	870,000	88E
Hannover, Germany (1,000,000)	498,495	89E
Ha Noi (Hanoi), Vietnam (1,275,000)	905,939	89C
Hāora (Howrah), India (*Calcutta)	946,732	91C
Harare, Zimbabwe (890,000)	681,000	83E
Harbin, China	2,710,000	88E
Harkov, Ukraine (1,940,000)	1,611,000	89C
Hartford, Ct., U.S. (1,085,837)	139,739	90C
Havana, see La Habana		
Ḥefa (Haifa), Israel (435,000)	222,600	89E
Hefei, China (†930,000)	740,000	88E
Hegang, China	588,300	86E
Helsinki, Finland (1,040,000)	490,034	88E
Hibli, India	647,640	91C
Ḥims (Homs), Syria	447,000	88E
Hiroshima, Japan (1,575,000)	1,085,677	90C
Hohhot, China (†830,000)	670,000	88E
Hong Kong, see Victoria		
Honiara, Solomon Is.	30,413	86C
Honolulu, Ha., U.S. (836,231)	365,272	90C
Houston, Tx., U.S. (3,711,043)	1,630,553	90C
Huainan, China (†1,110,000)	700,000	88E
Hyderābād, India (4,280,261)	2,991,884	91C
Ibadan, Nigeria	1,144,000	87E
Ilorin, Nigeria	380,000	87E
Inch'ŏn, S. Korea (*Seoul)	1,628,000	89E
Indianapolis, In., U.S. (1,249,822)	731,327	90C
Indore, India (1,104,065)	1,086,673	91C
Irkutsk, Russia	626,000	89C
Isfahan, see Eṣfahān		
Islāmābād, Pakistan (*Rāwalpindi)	204,364	81C
İstanbul, Turkey (7,550,000)	6,748,435	90C
Iževsk, Russia	635,000	89C
İzmir, Turkey (1,900,000)	1,762,849	90C
Jabalpur, India (887,188)	739,961	91C
Jackson, Ms., U.S. (395,396)	196,637	90C
Jacksonville, Fl., U.S. (906,727)	635,230	90C
Jaipur, India (1,514,425)	1,454,678	91C
Jakarta, Indonesia (10,000,000)	9,200,000	89E
Jamshedpur, India (834,535)	461,212	91C
Jaroslavl, Russia	633,000	89C
Jekaterinburg, Russia (1,620,000)	1,367,000	89C
Jerevan, Armenia (1,315,000)	1,199,000	89C
Jiaozuo, China (†509,900)	335,400	86E
Jiddah, Saudi Arabia	1,300,000	80E
Jinan, China (†2,140,000)	1,546,000	88E
Jinzhou, China (†810,000)	710,000	88E
Jixi, China (†820,000)	700,000	88E
João Pessoa, Brazil (550,000)	348,500	85E
Jodhpur, India	648,621	91C
Johannesburg, South Africa (3,650,000)	632,369	85C
Kābol, Afghanistan	1,424,400	88E
Kagoshima, Japan	536,685	90C
Kaifeng, China (†629,100)	458,800	86E
Kaliningrad, Russia	401,000	89C
Kampala, Uganda	1,008,707	90E
Kano, Nigeria	538,300	87E
Kānpur, India (2,111,284)	1,958,282	91C
Kansas City, Mo., U.S. (1,566,280)	435,146	90C
Kaohsiung, Taiwan (1,845,000)	1,342,797	88E
Karāchi, Pakistan (5,300,000)	4,901,627	81C
Karaganda, Kazakhstan	614,000	89C
Karl-Marx-Stadt, Germany (450,000)	311,765	89E
Kāthmāndau, Nepal (320,000)	235,160	81C
Katowice, Poland (2,778,000)	365,800	88C
Kawasaki, Japan (*Tōkyō)	1,173,606	60C
Kayseri, Turkey	416,276	90C
Kazan, Russia (1,140,000)	1,094,000	89C
Keelung (Chilung), Taiwan	348,541	88E
Kemerovo, Russia	520,000	89C
Khartoum, see Al Kharṭum		
Khulna, Bangladesh	648,359	81C
Kiel, Germany (335,000)	240,675	89E
Kigali, Rwanda	181,600	83E
Kijev (Kiev), Ukraine (2,900,000)	2,587,000	89C
Kingston, Jamaica (770,000)	646,400	87E
Kingston-upon-Hull, Eng., U.K. (350,000)	322,144	81C
Kingstown, St. Vin. and the Gren. (28,936)	19,028	87E
Kinshasa, Zaire	3,000,000	86E
Kisangani (Stanleyville), Zaire	282,650	84C
Kišinev, Moldavia	665,000	89C
Kitakyūshū, Japan (1,525,000)	1,026,467	90C
Kitchener, Ont., Can. (311,195)	150,604	86C
Kitwe-Nkana, Zambia (283,962)	207,500	80C
Knoxville, Tn., U.S. (604,816)	165,121	90C
Kōbe, Japan (*Ōsaka)	1,477,423	90C
København (Copenhagen), Denmark (1,685,000)	466,723	90E
Köln (Cologne), Germany (1,760,000)	937,482	89E
Kowloon, Hong Kong (*Victoria)	774,781	88C
Kraków, Poland (828,000)	743,700	89E
Krasnodar, Russia	620,000	89C
Krasnojarsk, Russia	912,000	89C
Krivoj Rog, Ukraine	713,000	89C
Krung Thep (Bangkok), Thailand (7,025,000)	5,845,152	89E
Kuala Lumpur, Malaysia (1,475,000)	919,610	80C
Kujbyšev, see Samara		
Kumamoto, Japan	579,305	90C
Kumasi, Ghana (600,000)	385,192	87C
Kunming, China (†1,550,000)	1,310,000	88E
Kuwait, see Al Kuwayt		
Kwangju, S. Korea (975,000)	1,165,000	89E
Kyōto, Japan (*Ōsaka)	1,461,140	90C
Lagos, Nigeria (3,800,000)	1,213,000	87E
La Habana (Havana), Cuba (2,125,000)	2,036,800	87E
Lahore, Pakistan (3,025,000)	2,707,215	81C
Lansing, Mi., U.S. (432,674)	127,321	90C
Lanzhou, China (†1,420,000)	1,297,000	88E
La Paz, Bolivia	1,057,200	88E
La Plata, Argentina (*Buenos Aires)	477,175	80C
Las Palmas de Gran Canaria, Spain (†366,347)	319,000	88E
Las Vegas, Nv., U.S. (741,459)	258,295	90C
Lausanne, Switzerland (263,442)	122,600	90E
Leeds, Eng., U.K. (1,540,000)	445,242	81C
Le Havre, France (254,595)	199,388	82C

...politan area populations are shown in parentheses.

... is located within the metropolitan area of another city; for example, Kyōto, Japan is located in the Ōsaka metropolitan area.

...ulation of entire municipality or district, including rural area.

C Census
E Official estimate

...litan area populations are shown in parentheses.
...s located within the metropolitan area of another city; for example, Kyōto, Japan is located in the Ōsaka metropolitan area.
...tion of entire municipality or district, including rural area.

C Census
E Official estimate

A • 15

Transliteration Systems

Toponymy: Criteria Used for the Writing of Names on the Maps

The language of geography is a language which defines geographic features in universally recognized terms. In creating this language, toponymy experts and cartographers have confronted complex problems in finding terms which are universally acceptable. So that the reader can fully understand the maps in this atlas, here is a brief explanation of how the toponyms (place-names for geographic features) have been written, particularly those relating to regions or countries where the Roman alphabet is not used. Among these are the Slavic-speaking nations such as Russia, Yugoslavia and Bulgaria; and China and Japan, which use ideographic characters. Of the European countries, Greece has its own alphabet, which is totally different from the Roman alphabet. Many of the Islamic countries use Arabic, with variations derived from local dialects.

There are two basic systems for Romanizing writing. The first is by phonetic transcription, using combinations of different alphabetical signs for each language when the phonetic sound in other languages should be maintained. For example, the Italian sound "sc" (which must be followed by an "e" or "i" to remain soft) in French is "ch," in English is "sh," and in German is "sch."

The second system is transliteration, in which the words, letters or characters of one language are represented or spelled in the letters or characters of another language.

Chinese, Japanese and Arabic Languages

Various Asian and African countries use non-Roman forms in their writing. For example, the Chinese and Japanese languages use ideographic characters instead of an alphabet, and these ideographic characters are transformed into the Roman alphabet through phonetic transcription. Until recently, one of the methods used for transforming Chinese was the Wade-Giles system, named for its English authors. Used in this atlas is the Pinyin system, which was approved by the Chinese government in 1958 and has been incorporated into the official maps of the People's Republic of China. The Pinyin system also has been adopted by the United States Board on Geographic Names and is used in official United Nations documents. The Pinyin names, however, often are accompanied by the Wade-Giles form, as the latter was widely known.

In Japan, ideographic characters are used, although the Roman alphabet is used in many Japanese scientific works. Japan uses two principal systems for standardizing names. They are the Kunreisiki, used by the government in official publications, and the Hepburn method. Adopted for this atlas is the Hepburn method, the system used in international English-language publications and by the United States Board on Geographic Names.

Romanization of the Arabic alphabet, which is used in many Islamic countries, is by transliteration. Since English and French are still used as international languages in many Arab countries, the name forms proposed by the major English and French sources have been taken into consideration. Generally, the systems proposed by the United States Board on Geographic Names and the Permanent Committee on Geographical Names have been used for most Asian countries and Arab-speaking countries.

Greek, Russian and Other Slavic Languages

Practically all written languages in Europe use the Roman alphabet. The differences in phonetics and grammar are shown by the use of diacritical marks and by groupings of consonants, vocals and syllables which give meaning to the various tones in the language. According to a centuries-old tradition, each written language maintains its formal characters, using the translated form rather than the phonetic transcription when a geographical term must be given in another language. This system, therefore, makes it more a translation than a transliteration.

In the Aegean area, Greek and the Greek alphabet are particularly significant because of historical links to the beginning of European civilization. The 1962 United States Board on Geographic Names and the Permanent Committee on Geographical Names systems, based on modern Greek pronunciation, have been used in transcribing toponyms from official sources for these maps. (The table that follows has an example indicating essential norms for Romanizing the modern Greek alphabet.)

A different situation arises in countries using the Cyrillic alphabet. Six principal Slavic languages using this alphabet are Russian, Byelorussian, Ukrainian, Bulgarian, Serbian, and Macedonian. The Cyrillic alphabet also is used by some non-Slavic people of the former Soviet Union. The nomenclature of these regions has been transliterated in accordance with the system proposed by the International Organization for Standardization, taking into consideration sounds and letters and uses of the diacritical marks normal in Slavic languages. The International Organization for Standardization method is accepted and used in bibliographical works and international documents. (The table which follows gives the relationship between the letters of the Cyrillic and Roman alphabets for the above six languages.)

Special Cases: Conventional Forms and Multilinguals

Cartographic nomenclature generally derives from the official nomenclature of the sovereign and nonsovereign countries, although a number of cases need explanation.

In numerous situations, English conventional forms are used along with the local or conventional name in referring to a geographical entity used outside the official English language area. For example, Vienna, Prague, Copenhagen and Moscow are English forms for Wien, Praha, København and Moskva, respectively. There are cases, however, where the conventional or historical form commonly used in English cartography has been applied with the same meaning. Thus, Peking and Nanking are the English conventional forms for Beijing and Nanjing, while Tsinan, Tientsin and Mukden are the former conventional spellings or names for Jinan, Tianjin and Shenyang, respectively. Other examples are Saigon, the former name for Ho Chi Minh, Vietnam; and Bangkok, the name for Krung Thep, which is used in Thailand.

The lack of reliable data for countries, especially ex-colonies without a firm national cartographic tradition, has made it necessary to utilize mapping skills of former colonial nations such as France, the United Kingdom and Belgium. A lack of data has led to the adoption of French and British forms in many areas, as these two languages are widely used for official purposes.

Another special case is that of the multilingual areas. Many countries and areas officially recognize two or more written and spoken languages; therefore, all of the principal written forms appear on the maps. This is true, for example, of Belgium where the official languages are French and Dutch (e.g. Bruxelles/Brussel) and of Italian regions such as Valle d'Aosta and Alto Adige, where French, German and Italian are used (e.g. Aosta/Aoste) (Bolzano/Bozen).

In preparing this atlas, each of these special cases has been taken into full consideration within the limits of the scale, space and readability of the maps.

Transliteration of the Cyrillic Alphabet
(International System—ISO)

Cyrillic Letter	Roman Letter		Cyrillic Letter	Roman Letter	
А а	a		О о	o	
Б б	b		П п	p	
В в	v		Р р	r	
Г г	g		С с	s	
Д д	d		Т т	t	
Е е	e	initially, after a vowel or after the mute sign "Ъ", becomes "je"	У у	u	
			Ф ф	f	
			Х х	h	
Ё ё	ë		Ц ц	c	
Ж ж	ž		Ч ч	č	
З з	z		Ш ш	š	
И и	i		Щ щ	šč	
Й й	j	not written if preceded by "И" or "Ы"	Ъ ъ	—	not written
			Ы ы	y	
К к	k		Ь ь	—	not written
Л л	l		Э э	e	
М м	m		Ю ю	ju	
Н н	n		Я я	ja	

Transcription of Modern Greek
(U. S. B. G. N. / P. C. G. N.)

Greek Letter (or combination)	Roman Letter (or combination)		Greek Letter (or combination)	Roman Letter (or combination)	
Α α	a		μπ	b	beginning a word
αι	ai			mb	within a word
αυ	av		Ν ν	n	
Β β	v		ντ	d	beginning a word
Γ γ	g			nd	within a word
γγ	ng		Ξ ξ	x	
γκ	g	beginning a word	Ο ο	o	
	ng	within a word	οι	oi	
			ου	ou	
Δ δ	d		Π π	p	
Ε ε	e		Ρ ρ	r	
ει	i		Σ σ	s	
ευ	ev		ς	s	ending a word
Ζ ζ	z		Τ τ	t	
Η η	i		τζ	tz	
ηυ	iv		Υ υ	i	
Θ θ	th		υι	i	
Ι ι	i		Φ φ	f	
Κ κ	k		Χ χ	kh	
Λ λ	l		Ψ ψ	ps	
Μ μ	m		Ω ω	o	

The "Geographical Glossary" lists the principal geographical terms used on the maps. All of these terms, including abbreviations, prefixes and suffixes, appear in the cartographic table as they appear on the maps. Terms are listed in accordance with the English alphabet, without consideration of diacritical marks on letters or of particular groups of letters.

Prefixes and suffixes relating to principal names or forming part of geographical toponyms are followed or preceded by a dash and the language to which they refer: e.g. Chi-/Dan. (Chi, a Danish prefix, means large); -bor/Slvn. (-bor, a Slovakian suffix, means city). Suffixes can also appear as words in themselves. In this case, the suffix and primary word are coupled together: e.g. Berg, -berg (Berg, which means mountain, can be used alone or as part of another word, such as Hapsberg).

Certain terms are followed or preceded by their abbreviation used on the maps. Both instances are listed: e.g. Fjord, Fj. and Fj., Fjord.

All geographical terms are identified by the language or languages to which each belongs. The language or languages in italics follows the term: e.g. Abbey/*Eng.*; -bad/*Nor., Dut., Swed., Germ.* Each term is translated into a corresponding English term or terms.

Below is a table identifying the abbreviations of various language names used on the maps. Note that certain abbreviations represent a group of languages, instead of one language: e.g. Ural. is the abbreviation for Uralic, a group word for Udmurt, Komi, and Nenets.

Alt. = Altaic (Turkmen, Tatar, Bashkir, Kazakh, Karalpak, Nogai, Kirghiz, Uzbek, Uigur, Altaic, Yakut, Khakass)

Ban. = Bantu (KiSwahili, ChiLuba, Lingala, KiKongo)

Cauc. = Caucasian (Chechen, Ingush, Kalmuck, Georgian)
Iran. = Iranian (Baluchi, Tagus)
Mel. = Melanesian (Fijian, New Caledonian, Micronesian, Nauruan)
Mong. = Mongolian (Buryat, Khalka Mongol)
Poly. = Polynesian (Maori, Samoan, Tongan, Tahitian, Hawaiian)
Sah. = Saharan (Kanuri, Tubu)
Som. = Somalian (Somali, Galla)
Sud. = Sudanese (Peul, Ehoué, Mossi, Yoruba, Ibo)
Ural. = Uralic (Udmurt, Komi, Nenets).

Because of their technical application to geography, some geographical terms may not fully correspond with the meaning given for them in some dictionaries.

Abbreviations of Language Names

Abbreviations in English	English	Abbreviations in English	English	Abbreviations in English	English	Abbreviations in English	English	Abbreviations in English	English	Abbreviations in English	English
Afr.	Afrikaans	Bulg.	Bulgarian	Fr.	French	Khm.	Khmer	Pers.	Persian	Som.	Somalian
A.I.	American Indian	Burm.	Burmese	Gae.	Gaelic	Kor.	Korean	Pol.	Polish	Sp.	Spanish
Alb.	Albanian	Cat.	Catalan	Georg.	Georgian	K.S.	Khoi-San	Poly.	Polynesian	Sud.	Sudanese
Alt.	Altaic	Cauc.	Caucasian	Germ.	German	Laot.	Laotian	Port.	Portuguese	Swa.	Swahili
Amh.	Amharic	Chin.	Chinese	Gr.	Greek	Lapp.	Lappish	Prov.	Provençal	Swed.	Swedish
Ar.	Arabic	Cz.	Czech	Hebr.	Hebrew	Latv.	Latvian	Rmsh.	Romansh	Tam.	Tamil
Arm.	Armenian	Dan.	Danish	Hin.	Hindi	Lith.	Lithuanian	Rom.	Romanian	Thai	Thai
Az.	Azerbaidzhani	Dut.	Dutch	Hung.	Hungarian	Mal.	Malay	Rus.	Russian	Tib.	Tibetan
Ban.	Bantu	Eng.	English	Icel.	Icelandic	Malag.	Malagasy	Sah.	Saharan	Tur.	Turkish
Bas.	Basque	Esk.	Eskimo	Indon.	Indonesian	Mel.	Melanesian	S.C.	Serbo-Croatian	Ural.	Uralic
Beng.	Bengali	Est.	Estonian	Ir.	Irish	Mong.	Mongolian			Urdu	Urdu
Ber.	Berber	Far.	Faroese	Iran.	Iranian	Nep.	Nepalese	Sin.	Sinhalese	Viet.	Vietnamese
Br.	Breton	Finn.	Finnish	It.	Italian	Nor.	Norwegian	Slvk.	Slovak	Wall.	Walloon
		Fle.	Flemish	Jap.	Japanese	Pash.	Pashto	Slvn.	Slovene	Wel.	Welsh

Glossary of Geographical Terms

Local Form	English	Local Form	English	Local Form	English	Local Form	English
A		Aït / *Ar.; Ber.*	sons	Ard- / *Gae.*	high	Badwêynta / *Som.*	ocean
		Aivi, -aivi / *Lapp.*	mountain	Areg / *Ar.*	dune	Badyarada / *Som.*	gulf
A- / *Ban.*	people	Ak / *Tur.*	white	Areia / *Port.*	beach	Baeg / *Kor.*	white
A' / *Icel.*	river	'Aklé / *Ar.*	dunes	Arena / *Sp.*	beach	Bæk / *Dan.*	brook
Å / *Dan.; Nor.; Swed.*	stream	Akmeņs / *Latv.*	stone	Argent / *Fr.*	silver	Bælt / *Dan.*	strait
a-, an / *Germ.*	on	Ákra / *Gr.*	point	Arhipelag / *Rus.*	archipelago	Bagni / *It.*	thermal springs
Aa / *Germ.*	stream	Akti / *Gr.*	coast	Arkhaíos / *Gr.*	old, antique	Baharu / *Mal.*	new
Aache / *Germ.*	stream	Ala / *Malag.*	forest	Arm / *Eng.; Germ.*	branch	Bahia / *Port.*	bay
Aaiún / *Ar.*	springs	Ala / *Finn.*	low, lower	Arquipélago / *Port.*	archipelago	Bahía / *Sp.*	bay
Aan / *Dut.; Fle.*	on	Alan / *Tur.*	field	Arr., Arroyo / *Sp.*	stream	Bahir / *Ar.*	river, lake, sea
Āb / *Pers.*	stream	Alb / *Rom.*	white	Arrecife / *Sp.*	reef	Bahnhof / *Germ.*	railway station
Ābād / *Pers.*	city, town	Albo / *Sp.*	white	Arroio / *Port.*	stream	Baḥr / *Ar.*	wadi
Abad, -abad / *Pers.*	city, town	Albufera / *Sp.*	lagoon	Art / *Tur.*	pass, watershed	Baḥr / *Ar.*	river, lake, sea
Ābār / *Ar.*	spring	Alcalá / *Sp.*	castle	Aru / *Sin.; Tam.*	river	Baḥrat / *Ar.*	lake
Abbadia / *It.*	abbey	Alcázar / *Sp.*	castle	Ås / *Dan.; Nor.; Swed.*	hills	Bahri / *Ar.*	north, northern
Abbaye / *Fr.*	abbey	Aldea / *Sp.*	village	Asfar / *Ar.*	yellow	Baḥrī / *Ar.*	north
Abbazia / *It.*	abbey	Alföld / *Hung.*	lowland	Asif / *Ber.*	river	Bahriyah / *Ar.*	northern
Abbi / *Amh.*	great	Ali / *Amh.*	mountain	Asky / *Alt.*	lower	Bai / *Chin.*	white
Abd / *Ar.*	servant	Alia / *Poly.*	stream	Áspros / *Gr.*	white	Băi / *Rom.*	thermal springs
Abeba / *Amh.*	flower	Alin / *Mong.*	range	Assa / *Ber.*	wadi	Baia / *Port.*	bay
Aber / *Br.; Wel.*	estuary	Alm / *Germ.*	mountain	Atalaya / *Sp.*	frontier	Baie / *Fr.*	bay
Abhang / *Germ.*	slope		pasture	Áth / *Gae.*	ford	Baigne / *Fr.*	seaside resort
Abū / *Ar.*	father, master	Alor / *Mal.*	river	Átha / *Gae.*	ford	Baile / *Gae.*	city, town
Abyad / *Ar.*	white	Alp / *Germ.*	mountain	Atol / *Port.*	atoll	Bain / *Fr.*	thermal springs
Abyaḍ / *Ar.*	white		pasture	Au / *Germ.*	meadow	Bains / *Fr.*	thermal springs
Abyār / *Ar.*	well	Alpe / *Germ.; Fr.; It.*	mountain	Aue / *Germ.*	irrigated field	Baixo / *Port.*	low, lower
Abyss / *Eng.*	ocean depth, deep		pasture	Aust / *Nor.*	east	Bajan / *Mong.*	rich
Ach / *Germ.*	stream	Alps / *Eng.*	mountains	Austur / *Icel.*	east	Bajo / *Sp.*	low
Achaïf / *Ar.*	dunes	Alsó / *Hung.*	low, lower	Ava / *Poly.*	canal	Bajrak / *Alb.*	tribe
Ache / *Germ.*	stream	Alt / *Germ.*	old	Aven / *Fr.*	doline, sink	Bakhtīyārī / *Pers.*	western
Achter / *Afr.; Dut.; Fle.*	back	Altin / *Tur.*	lower	Awa / *Poly.*	bay	Bakki / *Icel.*	hill
Acqua / *It.*	water	Altiplano / *Sp.*	plateau	Ayios / *Gr.*	saint	Bālā / *Pers.*	high
Açu / *A.I.*	great	Alto / *Sp.; It.; Port.*	high	'Ayn / *Ar.*	spring, well	Bald / *Eng.*	peak
Açude / *Port.*	reservoir, dam	Altopiano / *It.*	plateau	'Ayoûn / *Ar.*	springs, wells	Balka / *Rus.*	gorge
Ada / *Tur.*	island	Älv / *Swed.*	river	'Ayoūn / *Ar.*	spring	Balkan / *Bulg.; Tur.*	mountain range
Adalar / *Tur.*	archipelago	Am / *Kor.*	mountain, peak	Aza / *Ber.*	wadi	Ballin / *Gae.*	mouth
Adasr / *Tur.*	island	Amane / *Ber.*	water	Azraq / *Ar.*	light blue	Ballon / *Fr.*	dome
Addis / *Amh.*	new	Amba / *Amh.*	mountain	Azul / *Port.; Sp.*	light blue	Bally / *Gae.*	city, town
Adi / *Amh.*	village	Ambato / *Malag.*	rock	Azur / *Fr.*	light blue	Balta / *Rom.*	marsh
Adrar / *Ber.*	mount, mountains	An / *Gae.*	of			Báltos / *Gr.*	marsh
		An, a. / *Germ.*	on			Ban / *Laot.*	village
Aéroport / *Fr.*	airport	Ana / *Poly.*	grotto	**B**		Bana / *Jap.*	promontory
Aeroporto / *It.; Port.*	airport	Anatolikós / *Gr.*	eastern			Baña / *Slvk.*	mine
Aeropuerto / *Sp.*	airport	Äng / *Swed.*	meadow	B., Bay / *Eng.*	bay	Bañados / *Sp.*	marsh
Af / *Som.*	mouth, gorge	Angra / *Port.*	bay, anchorage	b., bei / *Germ.*	by	Banc / *Fr.*	bank
Afsluitdijk / *Dut.*	dam	Ani- / *Malag.*	center	B., Bucht / *Germ.*	bay	Banco / *It.; Sp.*	bank
Agadir / *Ber.*	castle	Áno / *Gr.*	upper	Ba / *Sud.*	river	Band / *Pers.*	dam, mountain range
Aǧiz / *Tur.*	mouth	Ánou / *Ber.*	well	Ba- / *Ban.*	people	Bandao / *Chin.*	peninsula
Agro / *Sp.; It.*	plain	Anse / *Fr.*	inlet	Ba / *Mel.*	hill, mountain	Bandar / *Ar.; Mal.; Pers.*	port, market
Agua / *Sp.*	water	Ant- / *Malag.*	center	Baai / *Afr.*	bay	Bang / *Indon.; Mal.*	stream
Aguja / *Sp.*	needle	Ao / *Chin.; Khm.; Thai*	gulf	Bab / *Ar.*	gate	Bangou / *Sah.*	well
Agulha / *Port.*	needle, promontory	'Āouâna / *Ar.*	well	Bac / *Viet.*	north	Banhado / *Port.*	marsh
Ahal / *Georg.*	new	Apă / *Rom.*	water	Bach / *Germ.*	brook, torrent	Bani / *Ar.*	sons
Aḥmar / *Ar.*	red	'Aqabat / *Ar.*	pass	Bacino / *It.*	reservoir	Banja / *Bulg.; S.C.; Slvn.*	thermal springs
Ahrāmāt / *Ar.*	pyramids	Aqueduc / *Fr.*	aqueduct	Back / *Eng.*	ridge	Banjaran / *Mal.*	mountain range
Ahzar / *Ber.*	wadi	Ar / *Mong.*	north	Back / *Swed.*	brook	Banka / *Rus.*	sandbank
Aigialós / *Gr.*	coast	Ar / *Sin.; Tam.*	river	Bäck / *Swed.*	brook	Banke / *Dan.*	bank
Aigue / *Prov.*	water	'Arâguîb / *Ar.*	hills	Backe / *Swed.*	hill	Baño / *Sp.*	thermal springs
Aiguille / *Fr.*	needle	Arba / *Amh.*	mount	Bad, -bad / *Dan.; Germ.; Nor.; Swed.*	thermal springs	Bansky / *Cz.*	upper
Ain / *Ar.*	spring	Arbore / *It.*	tree	Baden, -baden / *Germ.*	thermal springs	Bánya / *Hung.*	mine
		Archipiélago / *Sp.*	archipelago	Bādiyat / *Ar.*	desert	Bar / *Gae.*	peak
		Arcipelago / *It.*	archipelago			Bar / *Eng.*	sandbar
		Arḍ / *Ar.*	region				

Geographical Glossary

Local Form	English
Bar / Hin.	great
Bāra / Hin.	great
Bara / S.C.	pond
Barā / Urdu	great
Baraji / Tur.	dam
Barat / Indon.; Mal.	west, western
Barkas / Lith.	castle, city, town
Barlovento / Sp.	windward
Barq / Ar.	hill
Barra / Port.; Sp.	bar, bank
Barrage / Fr.	dam
Barragem / Port.	reservoir
Barranca / Sp.	gorge
Barranco / Port.; Sp.	gorge
Barre / Fr.	bar
Barun / Mong.	western
Bas / Fr.	low
-bas / Rus.	reservoir
Bassa / Port.	flat
Bassejn / Rus.	reservoir
Bassin / Fr.	basin
Bassure / Fr.	flat
Bassurelle / Fr.	flat
Bašta / S.C.	garden
Bataille / Fr.	battle
Batalha / Port.	battle
Batang / Indon.; Mal.	river
Batha / Sah.	stream
Batin / Ar.	depression
Bātlāq / Pers.	marsh
Batu / Mal.	rock
Bayan / Mong.	rich
Bayır / Tur.	mountain, slope
Bayou / Fr.	branch, stream
Bayt / Ar.	house
Bazar / Pers.	market
Be / Malag.	great
Beau / Fr.	beautiful
Becken / Germ.	basin
Bed / Eng.	river bed
Beek / Dut.	creek
Be'er / Hebr.	spring
Bei / Chin.	north
Bei, b. / Germ.	by
Beida / Ar.	white
Beinn / Gae.	mount
Bel / Ar.	son
Bel / Bulg.	white
Bel / Tur.	pass
Beled / Ar.	village
Belen / Tur.	mount
Belet / Ar.	village
Beli / S.C.; Slvn.	white
Beli / Tur.	pass
Bellah / Sah.	well
Belogorje / Rus.	mountains
Belt / Dan.; Germ.	strait
Bely / Rus.	white
Bělý / Cz.	white
Ben / Ar.	son
Ben / Gae.	mount
Bender / Pers.	port, market
Bendi / Tur.	dam
Beni / Ar.	son
Beo / S.C.	white
Bereg / Rus.	bank
Berg, -berg / Afr.; Dut.; Fle.; Germ.; Nor.; Swed.	mount
Berge / Afr.	mountain
Bergen / Dut.; Fle.	dunes
Bergland / Germ.	upland
Bermejo / Sp.	red
Besar / Mal.	great
Betsu / Jap.	river
Betta / Tam.	mountain
Bhani / Hin.	community
Bharu / Mal.	new
Bheag / Gae.	little
Biābān / Pers.	desert
Biały / Pol.	white
Bianco / It.	white
Bien / Viet.	lake
Bight / Eng.	bay
Bijeli / S.C.	white
Bill / Eng.	promontory
Bilo / S.C.	range
Bilý / Cz.	white
Binnen / Dut.; Fle.; Germ.	inner
Biqā' / Ar.	valley
Bir / Ar.	well
Bi'r / Ar.	well
Birkat / Ar.	pond
Bistrica / Bulg.; S.C.; Slvn.	stream
Bjarg / Icel.	rock
Bjerg / Dan.	mount
Bjeshkët / Alb.	mountain pasture
Blaauw / Afr.	blue
Blanc / Fr.	white
Blanco / Sp.	white
Blau / Germ.	blue
Bleu / Fr.	blue
Bluff / Eng.	cliff
Bo- / Ban.	people
Bo / Chin.	white
Bo / Swed.	habitation
Boca / Sp.	gap, mouth
Bôca / Port.	gap, mouth
Bocage / Fr.	forest
Bocca / It.	gap, pass
Bocchetta / It.	gap, pass
Bodden / Germ.	bay, lagoon
Boden / Germ.	soil
Bœng / Khm.	lake, marsh
Bog / Eng.	marsh
Bogaz / Alt.; Az.; Tur.	strait
Bogāzi / Tur.	strait
Bogdo / Mong.	high
Bogen / Nor.	bay
Bois / Fr.	forest
Boka / S.C.	channel
Boloto / Rus.	marsh
Bolšoj / Rus.	great
Bolsón / Sp.	basin
Bom / Port.	good
Bong / Kor.	peak
Bongo / Malag.	upland
Bor / Cz.; Rus.	coniferous forest
Bór / Pol.	forest
-bor / Slvn.	city, town
Bóras / Gr.	north
Börde / Germ.	fertile plain
Bordj / Ar.	fort
Bóreios / Gr.	northern
Borg, -borg / Dan.; Nor.; Swed.	castle
Borgo / It.	village
Born / Germ.	spring
Bory / Pol.	forest
Bosch / Dut.; Fle.	forest
Bosco / It.	wood
Bosque / Sp.	forest
Bosse / Fr.	hill
Both / Nor.	bay
Bou / Ar.	father, master
Bouche / Fr.	mouth
Boula / Sud.	well
Bourg / Fr.	city, town
Bourne, - bourne / Eng.	frontier
Boven / Afr.	upper
Boz / Tur.	grey
Bozorg / Pers.	great
Brána / Cz.	gate
Braňa / Sp.	mountain pasture
Branche / Fr.	branch
Branco / Port.	white
Bratul / Rom.	branch
Bravo / Sp.	wild
Brazo / Sp.	branch
Brdo / Cz.; S.C.	hill
Bre / Nor.	glacier
Bredning / Dan.	bay
Breg / Alb.; Bulg.; S.C.	hill, coast
Brjag / Bulg.	bank
Bro / Dan.; Nor.; Swed.	bridge
Brod / Bulg.; Cz.; Rus.; S.C.; Slvk.; Slvn.	ford
Bród / Pol.	ford
Bron / Afr.	spring
Bronn / Germ.	spring
Bru / Nor.	bridge
Bruch / Germ.	peat-bog
Bruchzone / Germ.	fracture zone
Bruck, -bruck / Germ.	bridge
Brücke / Germ.	bridge
Brug / Dut.; Fle.	bridge
Brugge / Dut.; Fle.	bridge
Bruk / Nor.	factory
Brunn / Swed.	spring
-brunn / Swed.	spring
Brunnen / Germ.	spring
Brygg / Swed.	bridge
Brzeg / Pol.	coast
Bü / Ar.	father, master
Bucht, B. / Germ.	bay
Bugt / Dan.	bay
Buhayrat / Ar.	lake, lagoon
Bühel / Germ.	hill
Bühl / Germ.	hill
Buhta / Rus.	bay
Bukit / Mal.	mountain, peak
Bukt / Nor.; Swed.	bay
Buku / Indon.	hill, mountain
Bulag / Mong.; Tur.	spring
Bulak / Mong.; Tur.	spring
Būlāq / Tur.	spring
Bult / Afr.	hill
Bulu / Indon.	mountain
Bur / Som.	mount
Bür / Ar.	port
Burg, - burg / Afr.; Ar.; Dut.; Eng.; Germ.	castle
Burgh / Eng.	city, town
Burgo / Sp.	village
Burha / Hin.	old
Bûri / Thai	city, town
Burj / Ar.	village
Burn / Eng.	stream
Burnu / Tur.	promontory
Burqat / Ar.	mount, marsh
Burun / Tur.	cape
Busen / Germ.	bay
Busu / Ban.	land
Bütat / Ar.	lake, pond
Butte / Eng.; Fr.	flat-topped hill
Büyük / Tur.	great
By / Eng.	near
By, -by / Dan.; Nor.; Swed.	city, town
Bystrica / Cz.; Slvk.	stream
Bystrzyca / Pol.	stream

C

Local Form	English
C., Cap / Cat.; Fr.; Rom.	cape
C., Cape / Eng.	cape
C., Colle / It.	pass
Caatinga / A.I.	forest
Cabeça / Port.	peak
Cabeço / Port.	peak
Cabeza / Sp.	peak
Cabezo / Sp.	peak, mountain
Cabo / Port.; Sp.	cape
Cachoeira / Port.	waterfall, rapids
Cachopo / Port.	reef
Cadena / Sp.	range
Caer / Wel.	castle
Cagan / Cauc.; Mong.	white
Cairn / Gae.	hill
Čāj / Az.; Tur.	river
Cajdam / Mong.	salt marsh
Caka / Chin.	lake
Cala / Sp.; It.	inlet
Calar / Sp.	plateau
Caldas / Sp.; Port.	thermal springs
Caleta / Sp.	inlet
Camp / Cat.; Fr.; Eng.	field
Campagna / It.	plain
Campagne / Fr.	plain
Campo / Sp.; It.; Port.	field
Cañada / Sp.	gorge, ravine
Canale / It.	canal, channel
Caño / Sp.	branch
Cañón / Sp.	gorge
Canyon / Sp.	gorge
Cao / Viet.	mountain
Cap, C. / Cat.; Fr.; Rom.	cape
Car / Gae.	castle
Càrn / Gae.	peak
Carrera / Sp.	road
Carrick / Gae.	rock
Casale / It.	hamlet
Cascada / Sp.	waterfall
Cascata / It.	waterfall
Castel / It.	castle
Castell / Cat.	castle
Castello / It.	castle
Castelo / Port.	castle
Castillo / Sp.	castle
Castro / Sp.; It.	village
Catarata / Sp.	cataract
Catena / It.	mountain range
Catinga / Port.	degraded forest
Cauce / Sp.	river bed
Causse / Fr.	highland
Cava / It.	stone quarry
Çay / Tur.	river
Cay / Eng.	islet, island
Caye / Fr.	island
Cayo / Sp.	islet, island
Ceann / Gae.	promontory
Centralny / Rus.	middle
Čeren / Alb.	black
Černi / Bulg.	black
Černý / Cz.	black
Čërny / Rus.	black
Cerrillo / Sp.	hill
Cerrito / Sp.	hill
Cerro / Sp.; Port.	hill, mountain
Cêrro / Port.	hill, mountain
Červen / Bulg.	red
Červony / Rus.	red
Cetate / Rom.	city, town
Chaco / Sp.	scrubland
Chāh / Pers.	well
Chaîf / Ar.	dunes
Chaîne / Fr.	mountain range
Champ / Fr.	field
Chang / Chin.	highland
Chapada / Port.	highland
Chapadão / Port.	highland
Château / Fr.	castle
Châtel / Fr.	castle
Chăy / Tur.	river
Chedo / Kor.	archipelago
Chenal / Fr.	canal
Cheng / Chin.	city, town, wall
Cheon / Kor.	city, river
Chergui / Ar.	eastern
Cherry, -cherry / Hin.; Tam.	city, town
Chew / Amh.	salt mine, salt
Chhâk / Khm.	bay
Chhotla / Hin.	little
Chi- / Ban.	great
Chi / Chin.	marsh, lake
Chi / Kor.	lake, pond
Chi- / Swa.	land
Chiang / Thai	city, town
Chico / Sp.	little
Chine / Eng.	ridge
Ch'on / Kor.	station
Ch'ŏn / Kor.	river
Chŏsuji / Kor.	reservoir
Chott / Ar.	salt marsh
Chu / Chin.; Viet.	mountain, hill
Chuŏr phnum / Khm.	mountain range
Chute / Fr.	waterfall
Chutes / Fr.	waterfalls
Cidade / Port.	city, town
Ciems / Latv.	village
Čierny / Slvk.	black
Cime / Fr.	peak
Cîmp / Rom.	field
Cîmpie / Rom.	plain
Cinco / Sp.; Port.	five
Citeli / Georg.	red
Città / It.	city, town
Ciudad / Sp.	city, town
Ckali / Georg.	water
Ckaro / Georg.	spring
Co / Chin.	lake
Col / Cat.; Fr.	pass
Colina / Port.; Sp.	hill
Coll / Cat.	hill
Collado / Sp.	pass
Colle, C. / It.	pass
Collina / It.	hill
Colline / Fr.	hill
Colonia / Sp.; It.	colony
Coma / Sp.	hill country
Comb / Eng.	basin
Comba / Sp.	basin
Combe / Fr.	basin
Comté / Fr.	county, shire
Con / Viet.	island
Conca / It.	depression
Condado / Sp.	county, shire
Cone / Eng.	volcanic cone
Cône / Fr.	volcanic cone
Contraforte / Port.	front range
Cordal / Sp.	crest
Cordilheira / Port.	mountain range
Cordillera / Sp.	mountain range
Coring / Chin.	lake
Corixa / A.I.	stream
Corno / It.	peak
Cornone / It.	peak
Corrente / It.; Port.	stream
Corriente / Sp.	stream
Costa / Sp.; It.; Port.	coast
Côte / Fr.	coast
Coteau / Fr.	height, slope
Coxilha / Port.	ridge
Craig / Gae.	rock
Cratère / Fr.	crater
Cresta / Sp.; It.	crest
Crêt / Fr.	crest
Crête / Fr.	crest
Crkva / S.C.	church
Crni / S.C.; Slvn.	black
Crven / S.C.	red
Csatorna / Hung.	canal
Cuchilla / Sp.	ridge
Cuenca / Sp.	basin
Cuesta / Sp.	escarpment
Cueva / Sp.	cave
Čuka / Bulg.; S.C.	peak
Çukur / Tur.	well
Cu Lao / Viet.	island
Cumbre / Sp.	peak
Cun / Chin.	village
Cura / A.I.	stone
Curr / Alb.	rock
Cy., City / Eng.	city, town
Czarny / Pol.	black

D

Local Form	English
Da / Chin.	great
Da / Viet.	mountain, peak
Daal / Dut.; Fle.	valley
Daba / Mong.	pass
Daba / Som.	hill
Daban / Chin.; Mong.	pass
Dae / Kor.	great
Dağ / Tur.	mountain
Dağ., Dağı / Tur.	mountain
Dāgh / Pers.; Tur.	mountain
Dağı, Dağ. / Tur.	mountain
Dağları / Tur.	mountain range
Dahar / Ar.	hill
Dahr / Ar.	plateau, escarpment
Dai / Chin.; Jap.	great
Daiet / Ar.	marsh
Dak / Viet.	stream
Dake / Jap.	mountain
Dakhla / Ar.	depression
Dakhlet / Ar.	depression, bay
Dal, -dal / Afr.; Dan.; Dut.; Fle.; Nor.; Swed.	valley
Dala / Alt.	steppe, plain
Dalaj / Mong.	lake, sea
Dalan / Mong.	wall
Dallol / Sud.	valley, torrent
Dalur / Icel.	valley
Damm / Germ.	dam
Dan / Kor.	point

Local Form	English
Danau / *Indon.*	lake
Danda / *Nep.*	mountains
Dao / *Chin.*	island, peninsula
Dao / *Viet.*	island
Dar / *Ar.*	house, region
Dar / *Swa.*	port
Dara / *Tur.*	torrent, valley
Darb / *Ar.*	track
Darja / *Alt.*	river, sea
Darya, Daryā / *Pers.*	river, sea
Daryācheh / *Pers.*	lake, sea
Daš / *Alt.; Az.*	rock
Dasht / *Pers.*	desert, plain
Dawḩat / *Ar.*	bay
Dayr / *Ar.*	convent
De / *Sp.; Fr.*	of
Deal / *Rom.*	hill
Dearg / *Gae.*	red
Debre / *Amh.*	hill, monastery
Dega / *Som.*	stone
Deh / *Pers.*	village
Dēh / *Som.*	stream
Deich / *Germ.*	dike
Dél / *Hung.*	south
Delft / *Dut.; Fle.*	deep
Delger / *Mong.*	wide, market
-den / *Eng.*	city, town
Deniz / *Tur.*	sea
Denizi / *Tur.*	sea
Dent / *Fr.*	peak
Deo / *Laot.; Viet.*	pass
Dépression / *Fr.*	depression
Depressione / *It.*	depression
Der / *Som.*	high
Dera / *Hin.; Urdu*	temple
Derbent / *Tur.*	gorge, pass
Dere / *Tur.*	river, valley
Désert / *Fr.*	desert
Desfiladero / *Sp.*	pass
Desh / *Hin.*	land, country
Desierto / *Sp.*	desert
Det / *Alb.*	sea
Détroit / *Fr.*	strait
Deux / *Fr.*	two
Dezh / *Pers.*	castle
Dhar / *Ar.*	heights, hills
Dhār / *Hin.; Urdu*	mountain
Dhitikós / *Gr.*	western
Dien / *Khm.; Viet.*	rice-field
Diep / *Dut.; Fle.*	deep, strait
Dijk, -dijk / *Dut.; Fle.*	dam
Ding / *Chin.*	mountain, peak
Dique / *Sp.*	dam
Di Sopra / *It.*	upper
Di Sotto / *It.*	lower
Distrito / *Sp.; Port.*	district
Diu / *Hin.*	island
Diz / *Pers.*	castle
Djebel / *Ar.*	mountain
Dji / *Ban.*	water
Djup / *Swed.*	deep
Do / *Kor.*	Island
Do / *S.C.*	valley
Dō / *Jap.*	island, administrative division
Dōho / *Som.*	valley
Doi / *Thai*	mountain, peak
Dol / *Bulg.; Cz.; Rus.; S.C.*	valley
Doł / *Pol.*	valley
Dolen / *Bulg.*	low
Dolgi / *Rus.*	long
Dolina / *Bulg.; Cz.; Pol.; Rus.; S.C.; Slvn.*	valley
Dolni / *Bulg.*	low
Dolni / *Pol.*	lower
Dolny / *Pol.*	lower
Domb / *Hung.*	hill
Dôme / *Fr.*	dome
Dong / *Chin.; Viet.*	east
Dong / *Kor.*	city, town
Dong / *Thai*	mountain
Dong / *Viet.*	marsh, plain
Donji / *S.C.*	low, lower
Dorf, -dorf / *Germ.*	village
Doroga / *Rus.*	road
Dorp, -dorp / *Afr.; Dut.; Fle.*	village
Dos / *Rom.*	ridge
Dos / *Sp.*	two
Douarn / *Br.*	land
Dougou / *Sud.*	settlement
Doukou / *Sud.*	settlement
Down / *Eng.*	hill
Drâa / *Ar.*	dunes, hills
Dracht / *Germ.*	sandbank
Draw / *Eng.*	ravine, valley
Drif / *Afr.*	ford
Drift / *Afr.*	ford
Droichead / *Gae.*	bridge
Droûs / *Ar.*	crest
Dry / *Pash.*	river
Dubh / *Gae.*	black
Dugi / *S.C.*	long
Dugu / *Sud.*	settlement
Dun / *Gae.*	castle
Duna / *Sp.; It.*	dune
Düne / *Germ.*	dune
Dungar / *Hin.*	mountain
Düngar / *Hin.*	mountain
Duong / *Viet.*	stream
Durchbruch / *Germ.*	gorge
Ḍurg / *Hin.*	castle
-durga / *Hin.*	castle
Duży / *Pol.*	great
Dvor / *Cz.*	court
Dvorec / *Rus.*	castle
Dvůr / *Cz.*	castle
Dwór / *Pol.*	court
Džebel / *Bulg.*	mountain
Dzong / *Tib.*	fort, monastery

E

Local Form	English
Ea / *Thai*	river
Eau / *Fr.*	water
Ebe / *Ban.*	forest
Ebene / *Germ.*	plain
Eck / *Germ.*	point
Eclusa / *Sp.*	lock
Écluse / *Fr.*	lock
Écueil / *Fr.*	cliff
Edeien / *Ber.*	sand desert
Edjérir / *Ber.*	wadi
Egg / *Germ.; Nor.*	crest, point
Eglab / *Ar.*	hills
Ehi / *Sah.*	mountain
Eid / *Nor.*	isthmus
Eiland / *Afr.*	island
Eisen / *Germ.*	iron
Eisenerz / *Germ.*	iron ore
El / *Amh.*	well
Elv, -elv / *Nor.*	river
Embalse / *Sp.*	reservoir
Embouchure / *Fr.*	mouth
Emi / *Sah.*	mountain
En / *Fr.*	in
Ende / *Germ.*	end
Enneri / *Sah.*	stream
Ennis / *Gae.*	island
Enseada / *Port.*	Bay, inlet
Ensenada / *Sp.*	bay, inlet
Ér / *Hung.*	stream
Erdö / *Hung.*	forest
Erg / *Ar.*	sand desert
Erz / *Germ.*	ore
Espigão / *Port.*	plateau
Ēstān / *Pers.*	land
Este / *Sp.*	east
Estero / *Sp.*	estuary, marsh
Estrecho / *Sp.*	strait
Estreito / *Port.*	strait
Estuaire / *Fr.*	estuary
Estuário / *Port.*	estuary
Estuario / *Sp.; It.*	estuary
Észak / *Hung.*	north
Étang / *Fr.*	pond
Ewaso / *Ban.*	river
Ey / *Icel.*	island
Eyja / *Icel.*	island
Eyjar / *Icel.*	islands
Eylandt / *Dut.*	island
Ežeras / *Lith.*	lake
Ezers / *Latv.*	lake

F

Local Form	English
Fa / *Mel.*	stream
Falaise / *Fr.*	cliff
Fall, -fall / *Germ.; Eng.; Swed.*	waterfall
Falls / *Eng.*	waterfall
Falu / *Hung.*	village
-falva / *Hung.*	village
Fan / *Sah.*	village
Faraglione / *It.*	cliff
Farallón / *Sp.*	cliff
Faro / *Sp.; It.*	lighthouse
Farvand / *Dan.*	strait
Fehér / *Hung.*	white
Fehn / *Germ.*	peat fen, peat-bog
Fekete / *Hung.*	black
Feld / *Dan.; Germ.*	field
Fell / *Eng.*	upland moor
Fell / *Icel.*	mountain
Fels / *Germ.*	rock
Fen / *Eng.*	marsh, peat-bog
Feng / *Chin.*	mountain, peak
Feste / *Germ.*	fort
Festung / *Germ.*	fort
Fier / *Rom.*	iron
Firn / *Germ.*	snow-field
Firth / *Eng.*	estuary, fjord
Fiume / *It.*	river
Fjäll / *Swed.*	mountain
Fjärd / *Swed.*	fjord
Fjell / *Nor.*	mountain
Fjöll / *Icel.*	mountain
Fjord, Fj. / *Dan.; Nor.; Swed.*	fjord
Fjörður / *Icel.*	fjord, bay
Fleuve / *Fr.*	river
Fließ / *Germ.*	torrent
Fljót / *Icel.*	river
Flói / *Icel.*	bay, gulf
Floresta / *Sp.; Port.*	forest
Flow / *Eng.*	strait
Flughafen / *Germ.*	airport
Fluß / *Germ.*	river
Fo / *Mel.*	stream
Foa / *Mel.*	stream
Foa / *Poly.*	cove
Foce / *It.*	mouth
Föld / *Hung.*	plain
Fonn / *Nor.*	glacier
Fontaine / *Fr.*	fountain
Fonte / *It.; Port.*	spring
Fontein / *Afr.; Dut.*	spring
Foort / *Afr.; Dut.*	ford
Forca / *It.*	pass
Forcella / *It.*	defile
Ford / *Rus.*	fjord
Förde / *Germ.*	fjord, gulf
Foreland / *Eng.*	promontory
Foresta / *It.*	forest
Forêt / *Fr.*	forest
Fors / *Swed.*	rapids, waterfall
Forst / *Germ.; Dut.*	forest
Forte / *It.; Port.*	fort
Fortin / *Sp.*	fort
Fosa / *Sp.*	trench
Foss / *Icel.; Nor.*	rapids, waterfall
Fossé / *Fr.*	trench
Foum / *Ar.*	pass
Fourche / *Fr.*	pass
Foz / *Sp.; Port.*	mouth
Frei / *Germ.*	free
Fronteira / *Port.*	frontier
Frontera / *Sp.*	frontier
Frontón / *Sp.*	promontory
Fuente / *Sp.*	spring
Fuerte / *Sp.*	fort
Fuji / *Jap.*	mountain
Fūlat / *Ar.*	marsh
Furt / *Germ.*	ford
Fushë / *Alb.*	plain

G

Local Form	English
G., Gora / *Bulg.; Rus.; S.C.*	mountain, hill
G., Gunung / *Indon.*	mountain
Ga / *Jap.*	bay
Ga / *Mel.*	mountain, peak
Gabel / *Germ.*	pass
Gaissa / *Lapp.*	mountain
Gala / *Sin.; Tam.*	mountain
Gam / *Hin.; Urdu*	village
Gamle / *Nor.; Swed.*	old
Gana / *Sud.*	little
Gang / *Germ.*	passage
Gang / *Chin.*	port, bay
Gang / *Kor.*	stream, bay
Gang / *Tib.*	glacier
Ganga / *Hin.*	river
Ganj / *Hin.; Urdu*	market
-gaon / *Hin.*	city, town
Gaoyuan / *Chin.*	plateau
Gap / *Kor.*	point
Gar / *Hin.*	house
Gara / *Bulg.*	station
Gara / *Ar.*	hills, range
Gară / *Rom.*	station
Garaet / *Ar.*	marsh, intermittent lake
Garam / *Beng.; Hin.; Urdu*	village
-gard / *Pol.*	city, town
Gård, -gård / *Dan.; Nor.; Swed.*	farmhouse
Gardaneh / *Pers.*	pass
Gare / *Fr.*	railway station
Garet / *Ar.*	hill
Garh, -garh / *Hin.; Urdu*	castle
Garhi / *Hin.; Nep.; Urdu*	fort
Garten / *Germ.*	garden
Gat / *Dan.; Fle.; Dut.*	strait
Gata / *Jap.*	bay, lake
Gau, -gau / *Germ.*	district
Gäu, -gäu / *Germ.*	district
Gavan / *Rus.*	port
Gave / *Bas.*	torrent
Gawa / *Jap.*	river
Geb., Gebirge / *Germ.*	mountain range
Gebergte / *Afr.; Dut.*	mountain range
Gebirge, Geb. / *Germ.*	mountain range
Geç., Geçit / *Tur.*	pass
Geçidi / *Tur.*	pass
Geçit, Geç. / *Tur.*	pass
Geysir / *Icel.*	geyser
Ghar / *Hin.; Urdu*	house
Ghar / *Pash.*	mountain, mountain range
Gharbīyah / *Ar.*	western
Ghat / *Hin.; Nep.; Urdu*	pass
Ghubbat / *Ar.*	bay
Ghurd / *Ar.*	dune
Gi / *Kor.*	peninsula
Giang / *Viet.*	stream
Giri / *Hin.; Urdu*	mountain, hill
Girlo / *Rus.*	branch
Gjebel / *Ar.*	mountain
Gji / *Alb.*	bay
Glace / *Fr.*	ice
Glaciar / *Sp.*	glacier
Glacier / *Eng.; Fr.*	glacier
Glen / *Gae.*	valley
Gletscher / *Germ.*	glacier
Gobi / *Mong.*	desert
Godār / *Pers.*	ford
Gok / *Kor.*	river
Gök / *Tur.*	blue
Gol / *Cauc.; Mong.*	river
Göl / *Tur.*	lake
Gola / *It.*	gorge
Gold / *Germ.; Eng.*	gold
Golet / *S.C.*	mountain
Golf / *Germ.*	gulf
Golfe / *Fr.*	gulf
Golfete / *Sp.*	inlet
Golfo / *Sp.; It.; Port.*	gulf
Goljam / *Bulg.*	great
Gölü / *Tur.*	lake
Gong / *Tib.*	high
Gonggar / *Tib.*	mountain
Gongo / *Ban.*	mountain
Góra / *Pol.*	mountain
Gora, G. / *Bulg.; Rus.; S.C.*	mountain, hill
Gorica / *S.C.; Slvn.*	hill
Gorje / *S.C.*	mountain range
Gorlo / *Rus.*	gorge
Gorm / *Gae.*	blue
Gorni / *Bulg.; S.C.; Slvn.*	upper
Gornji / *S.C.; Slvn.*	upper
Górny / *Pol.*	high
Gorod / *Rus.*	city, town
Gorodok / *Rus.*	village
Gorski / *Bulg.*	upper
Gory / *Rus.*	mountains
-gou / *Chin.*	river
Goulbi / *Sud.*	river, lake
Goulbin / *Sud.*	wadi
Goulet / *Fr.*	gap
Gour / *Ar.*	hills, range
Gourou / *Sud.*	wadi
Goz / *Sah.*	dune
Graafschap / *Dut.*	county, shire
Graben / *Germ.*	ditch, canal
Gracht / *Dut.*	canal
Grad, -grad / *Bulg.; Rus.; S.C.; Slvn.*	city, town, castle
Gradac / *S.C.*	castle
Gradec / *Bulg.*	village
Gradec / *Slvn.*	castle
Græn / *Icel.*	green
Gran / *Sp.; It.*	great
Grande / *Sp.; It.; Port.*	great
Grao / *Cat.; Sp.*	gap
Grat / *Germ.*	crest
Grève / *Fr.*	beach
Grind / *Germ.*	peak
Grjada / *Rus.*	range
Gród, -gród / *Pol.*	castle, city, town
Grön / *Icel.*	green
Grond / *Afr.*	soil
Gronden / *Dut.; Fle.*	flat
Groot / *Afr.; Dut.; Fle.*	great
Groß / *Germ.*	great
Grotta / *It.*	grotto
Grotte / *Fr.; Germ.*	grotto
Grube / *Germ.*	mine
Grün / *Germ.*	green
Grunn / *Nor.*	ground
Gruppe / *Germ.*	mountain system
Gruppo / *It.*	mountain system
Gua / *Mal.*	cave
Guaçu / *A.I.*	great
Guan / *Chin.*	pass
Guazú / *A.I.*	great
Guba / *Rus.*	bay
Guchi / *Jap.*	strait
Guelb / *Ar.*	hill, mountain
Guelta / *Ar.*	well
Guic / *Br.*	village
Güney / *Tur.*	south, southern
Gunong / *Mal.*	mountain
Guntō / *Jap.*	archipelago
Gunung, G. / *Indon.*	mountain
Guo / *Chin.*	state, land
Gur / *Rom.*	mountain
Guri / *Jap.*	cliff
Gurud / *Ar.*	hills, dunes
Gyár / *Hung.*	factory

H

Local Form	English
Haag / *Dut.; Fle.*	hedge
-håb / *Dan.*	port
Haḑabat / *Ar.*	highland
Hadd / *Ar.*	point
Hadjer / *Ar.*	hill, mountain
Hae / *Kor.*	bay, sea
Haehyeop / *Kor.*	strait

Geographical Glossary

Local Form	English
Haf / Icel.	sea
Ḥafar / Ar.	well
Hafen / Germ.	port
Haff / Germ.	lagoon
Hafir / Ar.	spring, ditch
Hafnar / Icel.	port
Ḥāfūn / Som.	bay
Hage / Dan.	point
Hage / Dut.; Fle.	hedge
Hågna / Swed.	peak
Hai / Chin.	sea, lake, bay
Hain / Germ.	forest
Haixia / Chin.	strait
Ḥajar / Ar.	hill, mountain
Hajar / Ar.	hill country
Halbinsel / Germ.	peninsula
Halma / Hung.	hill
Halom / Hung.	hill
Halq / Ar.	gap
Hals / Nor.	peninsula
Halvø / Dan.	peninsula
Halvøy / Nor.	peninsula
Hama / Jap.	beach
Hamāda / Ar.	rocky desert
Ḥamādah / Ar.	plateau
Ḥamādat / Ar.	plateau
Hammam / Ar.	thermal springs
Ḥammām / Ar.	well
Hamn / Nor.; Swed.	port
Hamrā' / Ar.	red
Hāmūn / Jap.	salt lake
Hana / Jap.	cape
Hana / Poly.	bay
Hane / Tur.	house
Hang / Kor.	port
Hank / Ar.	escarpment, plateau
Hantō / Jap.	peninsula
Har / Hebr.	mountain
Hara / Mong.	black
Harar / Swa.	well
Ḥarrah / Ar.	lava field
Ḥarrat / Ar.	lava field
Hasi / Ar.	well
Ḥasi / Ar.	well
Hassi / Ar.	well
Ḥasy / Ar.	well
Haug / Nor.	hill
Haupt- / Germ.	principal
Haure / Lapp.	lake
Haus / Germ.	house
Hausen / Germ.	village
Haut / Fr.	high
Hauteur / Fr.	hill
Hauts Plateaux / Fr.	highlands
Hauz / Pers.	reservoir
Hav / Dan.; Nor.; Swed.	sea, gulf
Haven / Eng.; Fle.; Dut.	port
Havn / Dan.; Nor.	port
Havre / Fr.	port
Hawr / Ar.	lake, marsh
Ház / Hung.	house
-háza / Hung.	house
Hazm / Ar.	height, mountain range
He / Chin.	river
Head / Eng.	headland
Hed / Dan.; Swed.	heath
Hegy / Hung.	mountain
Hegység / Hung.	mountain
Hei / Nor.	heath
Heide / Germ.	heath
Heijde / Dut.; Fle.	heath
Heilig / Germ.	saint
Heim, -heim / Germ.; Nor.	house
Heiya / Jap.	plain
-hely / Hung.	locality
Hem / Swed.	home
Hen / Br.	old
Higashi / Jap.	east, eastern
Hima / Hin.	ice
Himal / Nep.	peak
Hisar / Tur.	castle
Ho / Chin.	reservoir, river
Ho / Kor.	river, reservoir
Hō / Jap.	mountain
Hoch / Germ.	high, upper
Hochland / Germ.	highland
Hochplato / Afr.	highland
Hodna / Ar.	highland
Hoek / Dut.; Fle.	cape
Hof / Dut.; Germ.	court
Höfn / Icel.	port
Høg / Nor.	peak
Hög / Swed.	mountain
Hogna / Nor.	peak
Höhe / Germ.	peak
Høj / Dan.	hill
Hoj / Ural.	mountain range
Hok / Jap.	north
Hoku / Jap.	north, northern
Holm / Dan.; Nor.; Swed.	island
Holz / Germ.	forest
Hon / Viet.	island, point
Hong / Chin.; Viet.	red
Hono / Poly.	bay, anchorage
Hoog / Afr.; Dut.; Fle.	high
Hook / Eng.	point
Hoorn / Afr.; Dut.; Fle.	cape, point

Local Form	English
Hora / Cz.; Slvk.	point
Horn / Eng.; Germ.; Icel.; Nor.; Swed.	point
Horni / Cz.	high
Horný / Slvk.	upper
Horst / Germ.	mountain
Horvot / Hebr.	ruins
Hory / Cz.; Slvk.	mountain range
Hout / Dut.; Fle.	forest
Hovd, -hovd / Dan.; Nor.	cape
Ḥowz / Pers.	basin
Hrad / Cz.; Slvk.	castle, city, town
Hradiště / Cz.	citadel
Hřeben / Cz.	crest
Hrebet / Rus.	mountain range
Hu / Rmsh.	lake
Huang / Chin.	yellow
Hude / Germ.	pasture
Huerta / Sp.	market garden
Hügel / Germ.	hill
Hügelland / Germ.	hill country
Huis, -huis / Afr.; Dut.; Fle.	house
Huisie / Afr.	house
Huizen, -huizen / Dut.	houses
Huk / Afr.; Dan.; Swed.	cape
Hum / S.C.	hill
Hurst / Eng.	grove
Hus / Dut.; Nor.; Swed.	house
Huta / Pol.; Slvk.	hut
Hütte / Germ.	hut
Hver / Icel.	crater
Hvit / Icel.	white
Hvost / Rus.	spit

I

Local Form	English
I., Island / Eng.	island
Ierós / Gr.	holy
Igarapé / A.I.	river
Ighazer / Ber.	torrent
Ighil / Ber.	hill
Iguidi / Ber.	dunes
Ih / Mong.	great
Ike / Jap.	pond
Ile / Fr.	island
Ilha / Port.	island
Iller / Tur.	administrative division
Ilot / Fr.	islet
Imi / Ar.	spring
I-n / Ber.	well
Inch / Gae.	island
Inder / Dan.; Nor.	inner
Indre / Nor.	inner
Inferiore / It.	lower
Inish / Gae.	island
Insel / Germ.	island
Insulă / Rom.	island
Inver / Gae.	mouth
Irhazér / Ber.	wadi
Irmak / Tur.	river
'Irq / Ar.	dunes
Is / Nor.	glacier
Ís / Icel.	ice
Isblink / Dan.	glacier
Ishi / Jap.	rock
Iske / Alt.	old
Isla / Sp.	island
Iso / Finn.	great
Iso / Jap.	cliff
Isola / It.	island
Isthmós / Gr.	isthmus
Istmo / Sp.; It.	isthmus
Ita / A.I.	stone
Itä / Finn.	east
Itivdleq / Esk.	isthmus
Iwa / Jap.	rock, cliff
Iztočni / Bulg.	eastern
Izvor / Bulg.; Rom.; S.C.; Slvn.	spring

J

Local Form	English
J., Jazīrat / Ar.	island
J., Jiang / Chin.	river
Jabal / Ar.	mountain
Jaha / Ural.	river
Jam / Ural.	lake, river
Jama / Rus.	cave
Jan / Alt.	great
Janga / Tur.	north
Jangi / Alt.; Iran.	new
Janūbīyah / Ar.	southern
Jar / Rus.	bank
Järv / Est.	lake
Järve / Finn.	lake
Järvi / Finn.	lake
Jasiréd / Som.	island
Jaun / Latv.	new
Jaur / Lapp.	lake
Jaure / Lapp.	lake
Javr / Lapp.	lake
Javrre / Lapp.	lake

Local Form	English
Jazā'ir / Ar.	islands
Jazīrat, J. / Ar.	island
Jazovir / Bulg.	reservoir
Jbel / Ar.	mountain
Jebel / Ar.	mountain
Jedid / Ar.	new
Jedo / Kor.	archipelago
Jezero / S.C.; Slvn.	lake
Jezioro / Pol.	lake
Jhil / Hin.; Urdu	lake
Jian / Chin.	mountain
Jiang, J. / Chin.	river
Jiao / Chin.	cape, cliff
Jibāl / Ar.	mountain
Jih / Cz.	south
Jima / Jap.	island
Jin / Kor.	cove
Jing / Chin.	spring
Jisr / Ar.	bridge
Joch / Germ.	pass
Jōgi / Est.	river
Jøkel / Nor.	glacier
Joki / Finn.	river
Jokka / Lapp.	river
Jökull / Icel.	glacier
Jord, -jord / Nor.	earth
Ju / Ural.	river
Judeţ / Rom.	district
Jugan / Ural.	river
Jura / Lith.	sea
Jūra / Latv.	sea
Jūras Līcis / Latv.	bay
Jūrmala / Latv.	beach
Jurt / Cauc.	village
Južni / Bulg.; S.C.; Slvn.	southern
Južny / Rus.	southern
Juzur / Ar.	islands

K

Local Form	English
Ka / Poly.	lake
Kaap / Afr.	cape
Kabīr / Ar.	great
Kae / Kor.	inlet
Kāf / Ar.	peak, mountain
Kafr / Ar.	village
Kaga / Ban.	hills, mountain range
Kahal / Ar.	plateau, escarpment
Kai / Jap.	sea
Kaikyō / Jap.	strait
Kaise / Lapp.	mountain
Kal / Pers.	stream
Kala / Az.; Kor.	fort
Kala / Finn.	river
Kala / Hin.	black
Kala / Tur.	castle
Kalaa / Ar.	castle
Kalaki / Georg.	city, town
Kale / Tur.	castle
Kali / Hin.	black
Kali / Indon.; Mal.	bay, river
Kallio / Finn.	rock
Kaln / Latv.	mountain
Kalós / Gr.	beautiful, good
Kamen / Bulg.; Rus.; S.C.; Slvn.	mountain, peak
Kámen / Cz.	rock
Kameň / Slvk.	rock
Kami / Jap.	upper
Kamień / Pol.	rock
Kamm / Germ.	crest
Kamp / Germ.	field
Kâmpóng / Khm.	village
Kámpos / Gr.	field
Kampung / Indon.; Mal.	village
Kan., Kanal / Alb.; Dan.; Germ.; Nor.; Rus.; S.C.; Slvn.; Swed.; Tur.	canal, channel
Kanaal / Dut.; Fle.	canal
Kanał / Pol.	canal
Kanal, Kan. / Alb.; Dan.; Germ.; Nor.; Rus.; S.C.; Slvn.; Swed.; Tur.	canal, channel
Kand, -kand / Pers.; Tur.	city, town
Kang / Chin.; Kor.	bay, river
Kangas / Fle.	heath
Kange / Esk.	east
Kangri / Tib.	snow-capped mountain
Kantara / Ar.	bridge
Kaōh / Khm.	island
Kap / Dan.; Germ.	cape
Kapija / S.C.	gate, gorge
Kapp / Nor.	cape
Kar / Tib.	white
Kar / Ural.	city, town
Kara / Tur.	black
Karang / Indon.; Mal.	sandbank, cliff
Kari / Finn.	cliff
Kariba / Ban.	gorge
Kariet / Ar.	village
Karki / Finn.	peninsula
Kastel / Germ.	castle
Kástron / Gr.	fort, city, town
Káto / Gr.	lower

Local Form	English
Kaupstadur / Icel.	city, town
Kaupunki / Finn.	city, town
Kavīr / Pers.	salt desert
Kawa / Jap.	river
Kawm / Ar.	hill
Kebir / Ar.	great
Kedi / Georg.	mountain range
Kédia / Ar.	mountain, plateau
Kedim / Ar.	old
Kef / Ar.	mountain
Kefála / Gr.	mountain, peak
Kefar / Hebr.	village
Kei / Jap.	river
Kelet / Hung.	east
Ken / Gae.	cape
Kent / Alt.; Iran.; Tur.	city, town
Kenya / Swa.	fog
Kep / Alb.	cape
Kep., Kepulauan / Mal.	archipelago
Kepulauan, Kep. / Mal.	archipelago
Kereszt / Hung.	cross
Kerk / Dut.; Fle.	church
Keski / Finn.	middle
Kette / Germ.	mountain range
Keur / Sud.	village
Key / Eng.	coral island
Kha / Tib.	valley
Khal / Hin.	canal
Khalīj / Ar.	gulf
Khand / Hin.	district
Khao / Thai	hill, mountain
Kharābeh / Pers.	ruins
Khashm / Ar.	promontory
Khatt / Ar.	wadi
Khawr / Ar.	mouth, bay
Khazzān / Ar.	dam
Khemis / Ar.	fifth
Khersónisos / Gr.	peninsula
Khirbat / Ar.	ruins
Khlong / Thai	stream, mouth
Khokhok / Thai	isthmus
Khor / Ar.	mouth, bay
Khóra / Gr.	land
Khorion / Gr.	village
Khowr / Pers.	bay
Khrısós / Gr.	gold
Ki- / Ban.	little
Kibali / Sud.	river
Kil / Gae.	church
Kilde / Dan.	spring
Kilima / Swa.	mountain
Kill / Gae.	strait
Kilwa / Ban.	lake
Kin / Gae.	cape
Kinn / Nor.	cape, point
Kirche / Germ.	church
Kirk / Eng.	church
Kis / Hung.	little
Kisiwa / Swa.	island
Kita / Jap.	north, northern
Kızıl / Tur.	red
Klein / Afr.; Dut.; Germ.	little
Kliff / Germ.	cliff
Klint / Dan.	reef
Klip / Afr.; Dut.	rock, cliff
Klit / Dan.	dune
Kloof / Afr.; Dut.	gorge
Kloster / Dan.; Germ.; Nor.; Swed.	convent
Knob / Eng.	mountain
Knock / Gae.	mountain, hill
Ko / Jap.	bay, lake, little
Ko / Sud.	stream
Ko / Thai	island, point
Købing / Dan.	town
Kogel / Germ.	dome
Kōgen / Jap.	plateau
Koh / Hin.; Pers.	mountain, mountain range
Kol / Alt.	river, valley
Kol / Alt.; Tur.	lake
Koll / Nor.	peak
Kólpos / Gr.	gulf
Kong / Dan.; Nor.; Swed.	king
Kong / Indon.; Mal.	mountain
Kong / Viet.	mountain, hill
Konge / Ban.	river
König / Germ.	king
Koog / Germ.	polder
Kop / Nor.	hill
Kopec / Cz.; Slvk.	hill
Kopf / Germ.	peak
Köping / Swed.	town
Köprü / Tur.	bridge
Körfezi / Tur.	gulf
Korfi / Gr.	rock
Koro / Mel.	mountain, island
Koro / Sud.	old
Koru / Tur.	forest
Kosa / Rus.	spit
Koška / Rus.	cliff
Koski / Finn.	rapids
Kosui / Jap.	lake
Kot / Urdu	castle
Kota / Mal.	city, town
Kotal / Pash.; Pers.	pass
Kotar / S.C.	cultivated area
Kotlina / Pol.	basin

Local Form	English
Kotlovina / Rus.	basin, plain
Kou / Chin.	mouth, pass
Kourou / Sud.	well
Kowr / Pers.	river
Kowtal / Pers.	pass
Koy / Tur.	bay
Köy / Tur.	village
Kraal / Afr.	village
Kraina / Pol.	land
Kraj / Rus.; S.C.	land
Kraj / Rus.	administrative division
Krajina / S.C.	land
Krak / Ar.	hill, castle
Krans / Afr.	mountain
Kras / S.C.; Slvn.	karst landscape
Krasny / Rus.	red
Kreb / Ar.	hills, mountain range
Kriaž / Ar.	mountain range
Krš / S.C.	karst area, limestone area
Krung / Thai	city, town
Ksar / Ar.	castle
Ksour / Ar.	fortified village
Ku- / Ban.	river branch
Kuala / Mal.	river, mouth
Kubra / Ar.	bridge
Küçük / Tur.	little
Kuduk / Tur.	spring
Küh / Pers.	mountain
Kühhā / Pers.	mountain range
Kul / Alt.; Iran.; Tur.	lake
Kulam, -kulam / Hin.; Tam.	pond
Kulle / Swed.	hill
Kulm / Germ.	peak
Kultuk / Rus.	bay
Kum / Tur.	dunes, sand desert
Kuppe / Germ.	dome, seamount
Kurayb / Ar.	hill
Kurgan / Alt.	hill
Kurgan / Tur.	fort
Kuro / Jap.	black
Kurort / Bulg.; Germ.; Rus.	spa
Kust / Dut.; Fle.	coast
Kust- / Swed.	coast
Küste / Germ.	coast
Kút / Hung.	spring
Kuyu / Tur.	spring
Kvemo / Georg.	low, lower
Kwa / Ban.	village
Kylä / Finn.	village
Kyle / Gae.	strait, channel
Kyō / Jap.	strait
Kyrka / Swed.	church
Kyst / Dan.; Nor.	coast
Kyun / Burm.	island
Kyūryō / Jap.	hills, mountains
Kyzyl / Tur.	red
Kzyl / Tur.	red

L

Local Form	English
L., Lake, Lago / Eng.; It.; Port.; Sp.	lake
La / Tib.	pass
Laagte / Afr.	stream, valley
Labuan / Indon.; Mal.	bay, port
Lac / Fr.	lake
Lach / Som.	stream, wadi
Lacul / Rom.	lake
Lae / Poly.	cape, point
Laem / Thai	bay, port
Låg / Nor.; Swed.	low, lower
Lag / Swed.	stream, wadi
Läge / Swed.	beach
Lagh / Som.	stream, wadi
Lago, L. / It.; Port.; Sp.	lake
Lagoa / Port.	lagoon
Laguna / Alb.; It.; Rus.; Sp.	lagoon, lake
Lagune / Fr.	lagoon
Laht / Est.	bay
Lahti / Finn.	bay, gulf
Laks / Finn.	bay
Lalla / Ar.	saint
Lampi / Finn.	pond
Lande / Fr.	heath
Lang / Afr.; Dut.; Germ.	long
Lang / Viet.	village
Lao / Chin.	old
Lapa / Poly.	mountain range, peak
Largo / Port.; Sp.	basin
Las / Pol.	forest
Las, Läs / Som.	well
Laut / Mal.	sea
Law / Gae.	hill, mountain
Lázně / Cz.	thermal springs
Lednik / Rus.	glacier
Leite / Germ.	coast
Lekh / Nep.	mountain range

Local Form	English
Les / Bulg.; Cz.; Rus.; Slvk.	forest
Leso / Rus.	forested
Levante / It.; Sp.	eastern
Levkós / Gr.	white
Levy / Rus.	left
Lha / Tib.	temple
Lhari / Hin.; Nep.	mountain
Lho / Tib.	south
Lido / It.	sandbar
Liedao / Chin.	archipelago
Liehtao / Chin.	archipelago
Liels / Latv.	great
Lilla / Swed.	little
Lille / Dan.; Nor.	little
Liman / Alb.; Rus.; Tur.	lagoon, bay
Liman / Tur.	bay, port
Limin / Gr.	port
Limni / Gr.	lake
Ling / Chin.	mountain range, peak
Linna / Finn.	castle
Liqen / Alb.	lake
Lithos / Gr.	stone
Litoral / Port.; Sp.	littoral
Litorale / It.	littoral
Llan / Wel.	church
Llano / Sp.	plain
Llanura / Sp.	plain
Lo- / Ban.	river
Loch / Gae.	lake, inlet
Loch / Germ.	grotto
Loka / Slvn.	forest
Loma / Sp.	hill
Long / Indon.	stream
Loo / Dut.; Fle.	clearing
Lough / Gae.	lake
Loutrá / Gr.	thermal springs
Ložbina / Rus.	depression
Lu- / Ban.	river
Lua / Ban.	river
Lua / Mel.	island, reef
Lua / Poly.	crater
Luang / Thai	yellow
Luch / Germ.	peat-bog
Lücke / Germ.	pass
Lug / Rus.	meadow
Luka / S.C.; Slvn.	port
Lule / Lapp.	east, eastern
Lum / Alb.	river
Lund / Dan.; Swed.	forest
Lung / Rom.	long
Lung / Tib.	valley
Luoto / Finn.	shoal
Lurg / Pers.	salt flat
Lut / Pers.	desert

M

Local Form	English
M., Monte / It.; Port.; Sp.	mountain
Ma / Ar.	water
Ma- / Ban.	people
Maa / Est.; Finn.	island, land
Ma'arrat / Ar.	height
Machi / Jap.	district
Macizo / Sp.	massif
Madhya / Hin.	central
Madīnah / Ar.	city, town
Madīq / Ar.	strait
Mado / Swa.	well
Madu / Tam.	pond
Mae / Thai	stream
Mae nam / Thai	stream, mouth
Magh / Gae.	plain
Mägi / Est.	mountain
Măgura / Rom.	height
Mahā / Hin.	great
Mahal / Hin.; Urdu	palace
Mai / Amh.; Ban.	stream
Majdan / S.C.	quarry
Mäki / Finn.	mountain, hill
Makrós / Gr.	long
Mala / Hin.; Tam.	mountain
Malai / Hin.; Tam.	mountain
Malal / A.I.	fence
Malhão / Port.	dome
Mali / Alb.	mountain
Mali / S.C.; Slvn.	little
Malki / Bulg.	little
Malla / Tam.	mountain
Maly / Rus.	little
Malý / Cz.; Slvk.	little
Mały / Pol.	little
Man / Kor.	bay
Manastir / Bulg.; S.C.	monastery
Manche / Fr.	channel
Mar / It.; Port.; Sp.	sea
Mar / Tib.	red
Mar / Ural.	city, town
Marais / Fr.	marsh
Marché / Fr.	market
Mare / Fr.	pond
Mare / It.; Rom.	sea
Mare / Rom.	great
Marea / Rom.	sea
Marécage / Fr.	marsh
Marios / Lith.	reservoir

Local Form	English
Marisma / Sp.	marsh
Mark / Dan.; Nor.; Swed.	land
Markt / Germ.	market
Marsa / Ar.	anchorage, bay
Marsch / Germ.	marsh
Maru / Jap.	mountain
Mas / Prov.	farmhouse
Maşabb / Ar.	mouth
Mashra' / Ar.	landing, pier
Masivul / Rom.	massif
Massiv / Germ.; Rus.	massif
Mata / Poly.	point
Mata / Port.; Sp.	forest
Mata / Som.	waterfall
Mato / Port.; Sp.	forest
Matsu / Jap.	point
Mauna / Poly.	mountain
Mávros / Gr.	black
Mayo / Sud.	river
Maza / Lith.	little
Mazar / Pers.; Tur.	sanctuary
Mazs / Latv.	little
Me / Khm.	river
Me / Mel.	hill, mountain
Me / Thai	great
Medina / Ar.	city, town
Medjez / Ar.	ford
Meer / Dut.; Fle.	lake
Meer / Germ.	lake, sea
Megálos / Gr.	great
Mégas / Gr.	great
Megye / Hung.	district
Mélas / Gr.	black
Melkosopočnik / Rus.	hill country
Mellan / Swed.	central
Men / Chin.	gate, channel
Ménez / Br.	mountain
Menzel / Ar.	bivouac
Meos / Indon.	island
Mer / Fr.	sea
Mercato / It.	market
Merdja / Ar.	lagoon, marsh
Meri / Est.; Finn.	sea
Meridional / Rom.; Sp.	southern
Merin / A.I.	little
Merja / Ar.	lagoon, marsh
Mers / Ar.	port
Mersa / Ar.	port
Mesa / Sp.	mesa, tableland
Meseta / Sp.	plateau
Mésos / Gr.	central
Mesto / Bulg.; S.C.; Slvk.; Slvn.	city, town
Město / Cz.	city, town
Mestre / Port.	principal
Meydan / Tur.	square
Mezad / Hebr.	castle
Mező / Hung.	field
Mgne., Montagne / Fr.	mountain
Mgnes., Montagnes / Fr.	mountains
Miao / Chin.	temple
Miasto / Pol.	city, town
Mic / Rom.	little
Middel / Afr.; Dut.; Fle.	middle
Midi / Fr.	noon, south
Między / Pol.	central
Miedzyrzecze / Pol.	interfluve
Mierzeja / Pol.	sand spit
Mifraz / Hebr.	bay, gulf
Miftah / Ar.	gorge
Mikrós / Gr.	little
Mina / Port.; Sp.	mine
Mīnā' / Ar.	port
Minami / Jap.	south, southern
Minamoto / Jap.	spring
Minato / Jap.	port
Mine / Jap.	peak
Mirim / A.I.	little
Misaki / Jap.	cape
Mittel- / Germ.	middle
Mo / Chin.	sand desert
Mo / Nor.; Swed.	heath
Moana / Poly.	lake
Mogila / Bulg.; Rus.	hill
Moku / Poly.	island
Mølle / Dan.	mill
Monasterio / Sp.	monastery
Mond / Afr.; Dut.; Fle.	mouth
Mong / Burm.; Thai; Viet.	city, town
Moni / Gr.	monastery
Mont / Cat.; Fr.	mountain
Montagna / It.	mountain
Montagne, Mgne. / Fr.	mountain
Montagnes, Mgnes. / Fr.	mountains
Montaña / Sp.	mountain
Monte, M. / It.; Port.; Sp.	mountain
Monts, Mts. / Fr.	mountains
Moos / Germ.	moor
Mòr / Gae.	great
More / Bulg.; Rus.; S.C.	sea
More / Gae.	great
Mori / Jap.	mountain, forest
Morne / Fr.	mountain
Moron / Mong.	river
Morro / Port.; Germ.	hill, peak
Morrón / Sp.	mountain
Morze / Pol.	sea

Local Form	English
Most / Bulg.; Cz.; Pol.; Rus.; S.C.; Slvn.	bridge
Moto / Jap.	spring
Motte / Fr.	hill
Motu / Mel.; Poly.	island, rock
Moutier / Fr.	monastery
Movilă / Rom.	hill
Moyen / Fr.	central
Mta / Georg.	mountain
Mts., Monts, Mountains / Eng.; Fr.	mountains
Muang / Laot.; Thai	city, town, land
Muara / Indon.; Mal.	mouth
Muela / Sp.	mountain
Mühle / Germ.	mill
Mui / Mel.	point
Mui / Viet.	point, cape
Muiden / Dut.; Fle.	mouth
Muir / Gae.	sea
Mukh / Hin.	mouth
Mull / Gae.	promontory
Münde / Germ.	mouth
Mündung / Germ.	mouth
Municipiul / Rom.	commune
Munkhafaḍ / Ar.	depression
Münster / Germ.	monastery
Munte / Rom.	mountain
Muntelé / Rom.	mountain
Munţii / Rom.	mountain range
Muren / Mong.	river
Mushāsh / Ar.	spring
Muz / Tur.	ice
Muztagh / Tur.	snow-capped mountain
Mwambo / Ban.	rock, cliff
Myit / Burm.	stream
Mynydd / Wel.	mountain
Myo / Burm.	city, town
Mýri / Icel.	marsh
Mys / Rus.	cape

N

Local Form	English
Na / Cz.; Pol.; Rus.; S.C.; Slvn.	on
Nab / Ar.	spring
Nad / Cz.; Pol.; Rus.	on
Nada / Jap.	bay, sea
Nadi, -nadi / Hin.; Urdu	river
Næs / Dan.	point
Nafūd / Ar.	dunes
Nag / Tib.	black
Nagar, -nagar / Hin.; Tib.	city, town
Nagaram / Hin.; Tam.	city, town
Nagorje / Rus.	plateau, mountains
Nagy / Hung.	great
Nahr / Ar.	river
Naikai / Jap.	sea
Naka / Jap.	central
Nakhon / Thai	city, town
Nam / Burm.; Laot.; Thai	river
Nam / Kor.	south
Namakzar / Pers.	salt desert
Nan / Chin.	south
Narrows / Eng.	strait
Narssaq / Esk.	plain, valley
Näs / Swed.	cape
Nationalpark / Swed.; Germ.	national park
Nau / Lith.	new
Nauja / Lith.	new
Navolok / Rus.	cape, promontory
Ne / Jap.	cliff
Neder / Fle.; Dut.	low
Neem / Est.	cape
Negro / Port.; Sp.	black
Negru / Rom.	black
Nehir / Tur.	river
Nei / Chin.	inner
Nene, -nene / Ban.	great
Néos / Gr.	new
Nero / It.	black
Nes / Icel.; Nor.	cape
Ness / Gae.	promontory
Neu / Germ.	new
Neuf / Fr.	new
Nevado / Sp.	snow-capped mountain
Nez / Fr.	cape
Ngok / Viet.	mountain, peak
Ngolo / Ber.	great
Ni / Kor.	village
Niecka / Pol.	basin
Niemi / Finn.	peninsula
Nieuw / Fle.; Dut.	new
Nij / Dut.	new
Nīl / Hin.	blue
Nishi / Jap.	west
Niski / Pol.	lower
Nisko / S.C.	low
Nisoi / Gr.	islands
Nisos / Gr.	island
Nizina / Pol.	lowland
Nižina / Cz.	depression
Nizký / Cz.	low, lower

Geographical Glossary

Local Form	English
Nizmennost / *Rus.*	lowland, depression
Nižni / *Rus.*	low, lower
Nižný / *Slvk.*	low, lower
No / *Mel.*	stream
Nock / *Gae.*	ridge
Noir / *Fr.*	black
Non / *Thai*	hill
Nong / *Thai*	lake, marsh
Noord / *Afr.; Fle.; Dut.*	north
Noordoost / *Afr.; Fle.; Dut.*	northeast
Nor / *Arm.*	new
Nord / *Fr.; It.; Germ.*	north
Nördlich / *Germ.*	northern
Nørdre / *Dan.; Nor.*	northern
Norra / *Swed.*	northern
Nørre / *Dan.*	northern
Norte / *Sp.*	north
Nos / *Bulg.; Rus.; S.C.; Slvn.*	cape
Nosy / *Malag.*	island
Nótios / *Gr.*	southern
Nou / *Rom.*	new
Novi / *Bulg.; S.C.; Slvn.*	new
Novo / *Port.*	new
Novy / *Rus.*	new
Nový / *Cz.; Slvk.*	new
Now / *Pers.*	new
Nowy / *Pol.*	new
Nudo / *Sp.*	mountain
Nuevo / *Sp.*	new
Nui / *Viet.*	mountain
Numa / *Jap.*	marsh, lake
Nummi / *Finn.*	heath
Nunatak / *Esk.*	peak
Nuovo / *It.*	new
Nur / *Chin.*	lake
Nusa / *Mal.*	island
Nut, -nut / *Nor.*	peak
Nuwara / *Sin.; Tam.*	city, town
Nuwe / *Afr.*	new
Nyanza / *Ban.*	water, river, lake
Nyasa / *Ban.*	lake
Nyeong / *Kor.*	pass
Nyika / *Ban.*	upland
Nyŏng / *Kor.*	mount, pass
Nyugat / *Hung.*	west

O

Local Form	English
Ō / *Jap.*	great
Ó / *Hung.*	old
Ö / *Swed.*	island
Ø, -ø / *Dan.; Nor.*	island
Öar / *Swed.*	islands
Ober / *Germ.*	upper
Oblast / *Rus.*	province
Obo / *Mong.*	mountain, hill
Occidental / *Fr.; Rom.; Sp.*	western
Océan / *Fr.*	ocean
Océano / *Sp.*	ocean
Oceano / *It.; Port.*	ocean
Ocnă / *Rom.*	salt mine
Odde / *Dan.; Nor.*	promontory
Oeste / *Port.; Sp.*	west
Oever / *Fle.; Dut.*	bank
Oewer / *Afr.*	bank
Oie / *Germ.*	islet
Ojos / *Sp.*	spring
Oka / *Jap.*	coast
Oke / *Sud.*	height
Okean / *Rus.*	ocean
Oki / *Jap.*	bay
Okrug / *Rus.*	district
Ola / *Alt.*	city, town
Omuramba / *K.S.*	stream
Onder / *Afr.*	under
Oni / *Malag.*	river
Oos / *Afr.*	east
Oost / *Fle.; Dut.*	east
Oostelijk / *Dut.*	eastern
Opatija / *Slvn.*	abbey
Or / *Fr.*	gold
Oraş / *Rom.*	city, town
Óri / *Gr.*	mountains
Oriental / *Fr.; Port.; Rom.; Sp.*	eastern
Orientale / *It.*	eastern
Orilla / *Sp.*	bank
Órmos / *Gr.*	bay
Óros / *Gr.*	mountain
Ország / *Hung.*	land
Ort / *Germ.*	cape
Orta / *Tur.*	central
Orto / *Alt.*	central
Oseaan / *Afr.*	ocean
Ōshima / *Jap.*	large island
Ost / *Dan.; Germ.*	east
Öst / *Swed.*	east
Ostān, -ostān / *Pers.*	province
Øster / *Dan.; Nor.*	east, eastern
Öster / *Swed.*	east, eastern
Östlich / *Germ.*	eastern
Ostrog / *Rus.*	castle
Ostrov / *Rus.*	island
Ostrovul / *Rom.*	island
Ostrów / *Pol.*	island
Ostrvo / *S.C.*	island
Otok / *S.C.; Slvn.*	island
Otrog / *Rus.*	front range (mountains)
Oua / *Mel.*	stream
Ouar / *Ar.*	rocky desert
Oud / *Fle.; Dut.*	old
Oued / *Ar.*	wadi
Ouest / *Fr.*	west
Ouled / *Ar.*	son
Oum / *Ar.*	mother
Ouro / *Port.*	gold
Outu / *Poly.*	cape
Ova / *Ban.*	people
Ova / *Tur.*	plain
Ovasi / *Tur.*	plain
Øver / *Nor.*	over
Över / *Swed.*	over
Övre / *Swed.*	over
Øy / *Dan.; Nor.*	island
oz., Ozero / *Rus.*	lake
Ozek / *Alt.*	hollow
Ozera / *Rus.*	lakes
Ozero, oz. / *Rus.*	lake

P

Local Form	English
P., Pulau / *Mal.; Indon.*	island
Pää / *Finn.*	principal
Pad / *Rus.*	valley
Padang / *Indon.*	plain
Padiş / *Rom.*	upland
Padół / *Pol.*	valley
Pădure / *Rom.*	forest
Pahorek / *Cz.*	hill
Pahorkatina / *Cz.*	plateau, hills
Pais / *Port.; Sp.*	land, country
Pak / *Thai*	mouth
Pala / *It.*	peak
Palaiós / *Gr.*	old
Palanka / *S.C.*	village
Pali / *Poly.*	cliff
-palli / *Hin.*	village
Pampa / *Sp.*	plain, prairie
Panda / *Swa.*	junction
Panev / *Cz.*	basin
Pantanal / *Sp.*	swamp
Pantano / *Sp.*	swamp, lake
Pao / *Mel.*	hill
Pará / *A.I.*	river
Paramera / *Sp.*	desert highland
Páramo / *Sp.*	moor
Paraná / *A.I.*	river
Parbat / *Hin.; Urdu*	mountain
Parc / *Fr.*	park
Parco / *It.*	park
Parco Nazionale / *It.*	national park
Pardo / *Port.*	grey
Parque / *Sp.*	park
Parque Nacional / *Sp.; Port.*	national park
Pas / *Fr.; Rom.*	pass, strait
Pasaje / *Sp.*	passage
Pasir / *Mal.*	sand, beach
Paso / *Sp.*	pass
Passágem / *Port.*	passage
Passe / *Fr.*	pass
Passo / *It.; Port.*	pass
Pasul / *Rom.*	pass
Patak / *Hung.*	stream
Patam, -patam / *Hin.*	city, town
Patnā / *Hin.*	city, town
Patnam, -patnam / *Hin.*	city, town
Pattinam, -pattinam / *Hin.*	city, town
Pays / *Fr.*	land, country
Pazar / *Tur.*	market
Pea / *Est.*	cape
Pech / *Cat.*	hill
Pedhiás / *Gr.*	plain
Pedra / *Port.*	rock, mountain
Peg., Pegunungan / *Mal.; Indon.*	mountain range
Pegunungan, Peg. / *Mal.; Indon.*	mountain range
Pélagos / *Gr.*	sea
Pele / *Poly.*	peak, hill
Pen / *Br.*	principal
Pen / *Br.; Gae.*	cape, mountain
Peña / *Sp.*	peak
Pendi / *Chin.*	basin
Pendiente / *Sp.*	slope
Penha / *Port.*	peak
Peninsula / *Port.; Sp.*	peninsula
Péninsule / *Fr.*	peninsula
Penisola / *It.*	peninsula
Peñon / *Sp.*	rock, island
Pente / *Fr.*	slope
Perekop / *Rus.*	channel
Pereval / *Rus.*	pass
Perevoz / *Rus.*	ford
Pertuis / *Fr.*	strait
Peščara / *S.C.*	sandy soil
Peski / *Rus.*	sand desert
Petit / *Fr.*	little
Pétra / *Gr.*	rock
Phanom / *Thai; Khm.*	mountain range, mountain
Phau / *Laot.*	mountain
Phnum / *Khm.*	hill, mountain
Phu / *Viet.*	mountain, hill
Phum / *Thai*	forest
Phumĭ / *Khm.*	village
Pi / *Chin.*	cape
Piana, Pianura / *It.*	plain
Piano / *It.*	plain
Piatră / *Rom.*	stone
Pic / *Cat.; Fr.*	peak
Picacho / *Sp.*	peak
Piccolo / *It.*	little
Pico / *Port.; Sp.*	peak
Piedra / *Sp.*	rock, cliff
Pietra / *It.*	stone
Pieve / *It.*	parish
Pik / *Rus.*	peak
Pils / *Latv.*	city, town
Pinar / *Sp.*	pine forest
Pingyuan / *Chin.*	plain
Pioda / *It.*	crest
Pirgos / *Gr.*	tower, peak
Pish / *Pers.*	anterior, before
Pitkä / *Finn.*	great
Piton / *Fr.*	mountain, peak
Piz / *Rmsh.*	peak
Pizzo / *It.*	peak
Pjasăci / *Bulg.*	beach
Plaat / *Fle.; Dut.*	sandbank
Plage / *Fr.*	beach
Plaine / *Fr.*	plain
Plan / *Fr.*	plain
Planalto / *Port.*	plateau
Planina / *Bulg.*	mountain
Plano / *Sp.*	plain
Plas / *Dut.; Fle.*	lake, marsh
Plato / *Bulg.; Rus.*	plateau
Platosu / *Tur.*	plateau
Platte / *Germ.*	plain, plateau
Plav / *S.C.*	blue
Plavnja / *Rus.*	marsh
Playa / *Sp.*	beach
Ploskogorje / *Rus.*	plateau
Plou / *Br.*	church
Po / *Kor.*	port
Po / *Chin.*	lake, white
P'o / *Kor.*	bay, lake
Poa / *Mel.*	hill
Poarta / *Rom.*	pass
Poartă / *Rom.*	gate
Pobla / *Cat.*	village
Pobrzeże / *Pol.*	littoral, coast
Poço / *Port.*	well
Poço / *Port.*	point
Pod / *Cz.; Pol.; Rus.; S.C.; Slvn.*	bridge
Podkamenny / *Rus.*	stony
Poggio / *It.*	hill
Pohja / *Finn.*	north, northern
Pohjois- / *Finn.*	north
Pojezierze / *Pol.*	lake region
Pol / *Pers.*	bridge
Pol, -pol / *Rus.*	city, town
Pola / *Port.; Sp.*	village
Polder / *Fle.; Dut.*	reclaimed land
Pole / *Pol.*	field
Pólis / *Gr.*	city, town
Poljana / *Bulg.; Rus.; S.C.; Slvn.*	field, terrace
Poljarny / *Rus.*	polar
Polje / *S.C.; Slvn.*	valley, field, basin
Poluostrov / *Rus.*	peninsula
Pomorije / *Bulg.*	littoral
Pomorze / *Pol.*	littoral
Ponente / *It.*	western
Pont / *Cat.; Fr.*	bridge
Ponta / *Port.*	point
Ponte / *It.; Port.*	bridge
Póntos / *Gr.*	sea
Poort / *Afr.; Fle.; Dut.*	pass
Pore, -pore / *Hin.; Urdu*	city, town
Porog / *Rus.*	rapids
Porte / *Fr.*	gate
Portile / *Rom.*	gorge
Portillo / *Sp.*	pass
Portiţa / *Rom.*	small gate
Porto / *It.*	port
Pôrto / *Port.*	port
Posht / *Pers.*	back, posterior
Potjo / *Indon.*	peak
Potok / *Bulg.; Cz.; Pol.; Rus.; S.C.; Slvn.*	stream
Póvoa / *Port.*	village
Pozo / *Sp.*	well
Pozzo / *It.*	well
Pradesh / *Hin.*	region, state
Prado / *Sp.*	meadow
Praia / *Port.*	beach
Prato / *It.*	meadow
Pré / *Fr.*	meadow
Prealpi / *It.*	prealps
Presa / *Sp.*	reservoir
Presqu'île / *Fr.*	peninsula
Prêto / *Port.*	black
Priehradní nádrž / *Cz.*	reservoir
Pripoljarny / *Rus.*	subpolar
Pristan / *Rus.*	port
Prohod / *Bulg.*	pass
Proliv / *Rus.*	strait
Promontoire / *Fr.*	promontory
Průchod / *Cz.*	pass
Przedgorze / *Pol.*	front range (mountains)
Przełęcz / *Pol.*	pass
Przemysł / *Pol.*	industry
Przylądek / *Pol.*	cape
Pua / *Mel.*	hill
Puebla / *Sp.*	village
Puente / *Sp.*	bridge
Puerto / *Sp.*	port, pass
Puig / *Cat.*	peak
Puits / *Fr.*	well
Pul / *Pash.*	bridge
Pulau, P. / *Mal.; Indon.*	island
Pulau Pulau / *Mal.*	islands
Pulo / *Mal.; Indon.*	island
Puna / *A.I.*	upland
Puncak / *Indon.*	mountain
Punjung / *Mal.; Indon.*	mountain
Punt / *Afr.*	point
Punta / *It.; Sp.*	point
Pur, -pur / *Hin.; Urdu*	city, town
-pura / *Hin.; Urdu*	city, town
Pura / *Indon.*	city, town, temple
Puri, -puri / *Hin.; Urdu*	city, town
Pus / *Alb.*	spring
Pušča / *Rus.*	forest
Pustynja / *Rus.*	desert
Puszcza / *Pol.*	heath
Puszta / *Hung.*	lowland
Put / *Afr.*	well
Put / *Rus.; S.C.*	road
Putra, -putra / *Hin.*	son
Puu / *Poly.*	mountain, volcano
Puy / *Fr.*	peak
Pwell / *Wel.*	pond
Pyeong / *Kor.*	plain
Pyhä / *Finn.*	saint

Q

Local Form	English
Qagan / *Mong.*	white
Qala / *Pash.*	fortified town
Qal'at / *Ar.*	castle
Qalb / *Ar.*	hill
Qalīb / *Ar.*	spring
Qalīq / *Ar.*	spring
Qanāt / *Ar.*	canal
Qantara / *Ar.*	bridge
Qaqortoq / *Esk.*	white
Qar / *Som.*	mountain
Qara / *Pers.*	black
Qarah / *Tur.*	black
Qārat / *Ar.*	height, mountain
Qāret / *Ar.*	village, hill
Qaryah / *Ar.*	village
Qaryat / *Ar.*	village
Qaşr / *Ar.*	castle
Qawz / *Ar.*	dunes
Qeqertarssuaq / *Esk.*	peninsula
Qezel / *Tur.*	red
Qi / *Chin.*	river
Qing / *Chin.*	blue, green
Qiryat / *Hebr.*	city, town
Qolleh / *Pers.*	mountain, peak
Qu / *Chin.*	river, canal
Quan dao / *Viet.*	islands
Quebracho / *Sp.*	stream
Quebrada / *Sp.*	gorge, stream
Quedas / *Port.*	waterfalls
Qulbān / *Ar.*	well
Qundao / *Chin.*	archipelago
Qūr / *Ar.*	height, hill
Qytet / *Alb.*	city, town
Qyteti / *Alb.*	city, town

R

Local Form	English
R., Rio, River / *Eng.; Sp.*	river
Rada / *It.; Sp.*	anchorage
Rade / *Fr.*	anchorage
Rags / *Latv.*	cape
Rahad / *Ar.*	lake, pond
Rajon / *Rus.*	district
Rak / *Fle.; Dut.*	strait
Rakai / *Poly.*	reef
Ramla / *Ar.*	sand
Rancho / *Port.; Sp.*	farm, ranch
Rand / *Afr.; Germ.*	escarpment
Range / *Eng.*	mountain range
Rann / *Urdu*	marsh
Rano / *Malag.*	water
Ranta / *Finn.*	bank, beach
Rapide / *Fr.*	rapids
Ras / *Amh.*	peak
Rās / *Ar.*	point, cape

Local Form	English
Ras, Ràs / Ar.	promontory, peak
Răsiga / Som.	promontory
Rass / Ar.	promontory, peak
Rassa / Lapp.	mountain
Ráth / Gae.	castle
Raunina / Bulg.; Rus.	plain
Raz / Fr.	strait
Razliv / Rus.	flood plain
Récif / Fr.	reef
Recife / Port.	reef
Reede / Germ.; Dut.; Slvn.	anchorage
Reek / Afr.; Gae.	mountain range
Reg / Pash.	dunes
Région / Fr.	region
Rei / Port.	king
Reka / Bulg.; Rus.; S.C.; Slvn.	river
Řeka / Cz.	river
Réma / Gr.	torrent
Renne / Dan.; Nor.	deep
Reprêsa / Port.	dam, reservoir
Represa / Sp.	dam, reservoir
República / Port.; Sp.	republic
République / Fr.	republic
Rés., Réservoir / Fr.	reservoir
Res., Reservoir / Eng.	reservoir
Réservoir, Rés. / Fr.	reservoir
Reshteh / Pers.	mountain range
Respublika / Rus.	republic
Restinga / Port.	cliff, sandbank
Retsugan / Jap.	reef
Rettō / Jap.	archipelago
Rev / Dan.; Nor.; Swed.	reef
Rey / Sp.	king
Ri / Tib.	mountain
Ria / Sp.	estuary
Riacho / Port.	stream
Rialto / It.	plateau
Rialto / It.	rise
Riba / Port.	bank
Ribeira / Port.	river
Ribeirão / Port.	stream
Ribeiro / Port.	stream
Ribera / Sp.	coast
Ribnik / Slvn.	pond
Rid / Bulg.	mountain range
Rif / Icel.	cliff
Riff / Germ.	reef
Rīg / Pash.	dunes
Rijeka / S.C.	river
Rimäl / Ar.	sand desert
Rincón / Sp.	peninsula between two rivers
Ring / Tib.	long
Rinne / Germ.	trench
Rio / Port.	river
Rio, R. / Sp.	river
Riu / Rom.	river
Riva / It.	bank
Rive / Fr.	bank
Rivera / Sp.	brook, stream
Rivier, -rivier / Afr.; Dut.; Fle.	river
Riviera / It.	coast
Rivière / Fr.	river
Roads / Eng.	anchorage
Roc / Fr.	rock
Roca / Port.; Sp.	rock
Rocca / It.	castle
Roche / Fr.	rock
Rocher / Fr.	rock
Rock / Eng.	rock
Rod / Pash.	river
Rode / Germ.	tilled soil
Rodnik / Rus.	spring
Rog / Rus.; S.C.; Slvn.	peak
Roi / Fr.	king
Rojo / Sp.	red
Roque / Sp.	rock
Rot / Germ.	red
Roto / Poly.	lake
Rouge / Fr.	red
Równina / Pol.	plain
Rt / S.C.; Slvn.	cape
Ru / Tib.	mountain
Ruck / Germ.	ridge
Rücken / Germ.	ridge
Rud / Pers.	river
Ruda / Cz.; Slvk.	mine
Ruda / Pol.	ore
Rüdbär / Pers.	river
Rudha / Gae.	point
Rudnik / Rus.; S.C.; Slvn.	mine
Rug / Fle.; Dut.	ridge
Ruggen / Afr.	ridge
Ruina / Sp.	ruins
Ruíne / Fr.; Dut.; Germ.	ruins
Rujm / Ar.	hill
Run / Eng.	stream

S

Local Form	English
S., See / Germ.	lake, sea
Saar / Est.	island

Local Form	English
Saari / Finn.	island
Sabbia / It.	sand
Sabkhat / Ar.	salt flat, salt marsh
Sable / Fr.; Eng.	beach
Sacca / It.	anchorage
Saco / Port.	bay
Sad / Cz.; Slvk.	park
Sad / Pers.	wall
Sadd / Ar.; Pers.	cataract, dam
Safid / Pash.; Urdu; Hin.	white
Şafrā' / Ar.	desert
Sāgar / Hin.	reservoir
Saguia / Ar.	irrigation canal
Sahara / Ar.	desert
Sahel / Ar.	plain, coast
Sahr / Iran.	city, town
Şaḥrā' / Ar.	desert
Said / Ar.	sweet
Saj / Alt.	stream, valley
Saki / Jap.	point
Sala / Latv.; Lith.	island
Saladillo / Sp.	salt desert
Salar / Sp.	salt lake
Sale / Ural.	village
Salina / It.; Sp.	salt flat, salt marsh
Saline / Dut.; Fr.; Germ.	salt flat, salt marsh
Salmi / Finn.	strait
Salseleh-ye Kūh / Pers.	mountain range
Salto / Port.; Sp.	waterfall, rapids
Salz / Germ.	salt
Samudera / Indon.	ocean
Samudra / Hin.	lake
Samut / Thai	sea
San / Jap.; Kor.	mountain
San / It.; Sp.	saint
Sanchi / Jap.	mountain range
Sand / Dan.; Eng.; Nor.; Swed.; Germ.	beach
Šand / Mong.	spring
Sandur / Icel.	sand
Sank / Pers.	rock
Sankt, St. / Germ.; Swed.	saint
Sanmaeg / Kor.	mountain range
Sanmyaku / Jap.	mountain range
Sansanné / Sud.	campsite
Santo / It.; Port.; Sp.	saint
Santuario / It.	sanctuary
São / Port.	saint
Sar / Pers.	cape; peak
Šar / Rus.; Tur.	strait
Saraf / Ar.	well
Sari / Finn.	island
Sari / Tur.	yellow
Sarīr / Ar.	rocky desert
Sary / Tur.	yellow
Sasso / It.	stone
Sat / Rom.	village
Sattel / Germ.	pass
Saurum / Latv.	strait
Schleuse / Germ.	lock
Schloß / Germ.	castle
Schlucht / Germ.	gorge
Schnee / Germ.	snow
Schwarz / Germ.	black
Scoglio / It.	cliff
Se / Jap.	bank, shoal
Sebkha / Ar.	salt flat
Sebkhet / Ar.	salt flat
Sed / Ar.	dam
Seda / Ural.	mountain
See, S. / Germ.	lake, sea
Sefra / Ar.	yellow
Segara / Indon.	lagoon
Şehir / Tur.	city, town
Seki / Jap.	dam
Selat / Mal.; Indon.	strait
Selatan / Indon.	southern
Selkä / Finn.	ridge, lake
Sella / It.	pass
Selo / Bulg.; Rus.; S.C.; Slvn.	village
Selsela Kohe / Pers.	mountain range
Selva / It.; Sp.	forest
Semenanjung / Mal.	peninsula
Sen / Jap.	mountain
Seong / Kor.	castle
Sep / Alt.	canal
Serīr / Ar.	rocky desert
Serra / Cat.; Port.	mountain range
Serra / It.	mountain
Serrania / Sp.	mountain range
Sertão / Port.	steppe
Seto / Jap.	strait
Sett., Settentrionale / It.	northern
Settentrionale, Sett. / It.	northern
Seuil / Fr.	sill
Sev / Arm.	black
Sever / Rus.	north
Severny / Rus.	northern
Sfint / Rom.	saint
Sfintu / Rom.	saint
Sgeir / Gae.	cliff
Sha'b / Ar.	cliff
Shahr / Pers.; Hin.	city, town
Sha'īb / Ar.	stream
Shallāl / Ar.	cataract

Local Form	English
Shām / Ar.	north; northern
Shamo / Chin.	sand desert
Shan / Chin.	mountain, mountain range
Shan / Gae.	old
Shand / Mong.	spring
Shankou / Chin.	pass
Shaqq / Ar.	wadi
Sharm / Ar.	bay
Sharqī / Ar.	east, eastern
Sharqīyah / Ar.	eastern
Shatt / Ar.	river, salt lake
Shatt / Tur.	stream
Shën / Alb.	saint
Sheng / Chin.	province
Shi / Chin.	city, town
Shibīn / Ar.	village
Shih / Chin.	rock
Shima / Jap.	island
Shimo / Jap.	lower
Shin / Jap.	new
Shō / Jap.	island
Shotō / Jap.	archipelago
Shū / Jap.	administrative division
Shui / Chin.	river
Shuiku / Chin.	reservoir
Shur / Pers.	salt
Sidhiros / Gr.	iron
Sidi / Ar.	master
Sieben / Germ.	seven
Sierra / Sp.	mountain range
Sikt / Ural.	village
Sillon / Fr.	furrow
Šine / Mong.	new
Sink / Eng.	depression
Sinn / Ar.	point
Sint / Dut.; Fle.	saint
Sirt / Tur.	mountain range
Sirtlar / Tur.	mountain range
Sistema / It.; Sp.	mountain system
Sīyäh / Pers.	black
Sjø / Nor.	lake
Sjö / Swed.	lake, sea
Skag / Icel.	peninsula
Skala / Bulg.; Rus.	rock
Skála / Slvk.	rock
Skar / Nor.	pass
Skär / Swed.	cliff
Skeir / Gae.	cliff
Skerry / Gae.	cliff
Skog / Nor.; Swed.	forest
Skóg / Icel.	forest
Skov / Dan.; Nor.	forest
Slatina / S.C.; Slvn.	mineral water
Slätt / Swed.	plain
Slieve / Gae.	mountain
Slot / Dut.; Fle.	castle
Slott / Nor.; Swed.	castle
Slough / Eng.	creek, pond, marsh
Sluis / Dut.; Fle.	sluice
Små / Swed.	little
Sne / Nor.	snow
Sneeuw / Afr.; Dut.	snow
Snežny / Rus.	snowy
Snø / Nor.	snow
So / Kor.	little
Sø / Dan.; Nor.	lake; sea
So / Ural.	passage
Söder / Swed.	south
Södra / Swed.	southern
Solončak / Rus.	salt flat
Sommet / Fr.	peak
Son / Viet.	mountain
Sønder / Dan.; Nor.	southern
Søndre / Dan.	southern
Sone / Jap.	bank
Song / Viet.	river
Sopka / Rus.	volcano
Sopočnik / Rus.	mountain system
Soprana / It.	upper
Šor, Sor / Alt.	salt marsh
Sos / Ar.	upon
Sotavento / Sp.	leeward
Sotoviento / Sp.	leeward
Sottana / It.	lower
Souk / Ar.	market
Souq / Ar.	market
Sour / Ar.	rampart
Source / Eng.; Fr.	spring
Souto / Port.	forest
Spitze / Germ.	peak
Spruit / Afr.	current
Sreden / Rus.	central
Sredni / Rus.	central
Średni / Pol.	central
Srednji / S.C.; Slvn.	central
St., Saint, Sankt / Eng.; Fr.; Germ.; Swed.	saint
Stadhur / Icel.	city, town
Stadt, -stadt / Germ.	city, town
Stag / Eng.	city, town
Stagno / It.	pond
-stan / Hin.; Pers.; Urdu	land
Star / Bulg.	old
Stari / S.C.; Slvn.	old

Local Form	English
Stary / Pol.; Rus.	old
Starý / Cz.; Slvk.	old
Stat / Afr.; Dan.; Fle.; Nor.; Dut.; Swed.	city, town
Stathmós / Gr.	railway station
Stausee / Germ.	reservoir
Stavrós / Gr.	cross
Sted / Dan.; Nor.	place
Stedt / Germ.	place
Stein, -stein / Nor.; Germ.	stone
Sten / Nor.; Swed.	stone
Stena / S.C.; Slvn.	rock
Stěna / Cz.	mountain range
Stenón / Gr.	strait, pass
Step / Rus.	steppe
-sthān / Hin.; Pers.; Urdu	land
Stift / Germ.	foundation
Štít / Cz.; Slvk.	peak
Stock / Germ.	massif
Stok / Pol.	slope
Stor / Dan.; Nor.; Swed.	great
Store / Dan.	great
Stræde / Dan.	strait
Strana / Rus.	land
Strand / Germ.; Nor.; Swed.; Afr.; Dan.	beach
Straße / Germ.	street, road
Strath / Gae.	valley
Straum / Nor.; Swed.	stream
Střední / Cz.	central
Středný / Slvk.	central
Strelka / Rus.	spit
Stret / Nor.	strait
Stretto / It.	strait
Strom / Germ.	stream
Strøm / Nor.	stream
Ström / Swed.	stream
Stroom / Dut.	stream
Su / Jap.	sandbank
Su / Tur.	river
Suando / Finn.	pond
Suid / Afr.	south
Suidō / Jap.	strait
Sul / Port.	south
Sund / Dan.; Nor.; Swed.; Germ.	strait
Sungai / Mal.	river
Sunn / Nor.	south
Sūq / Ar.	market
Sur / Fr.	on
Sur / Sp.	south
Surkh / Pers.	red
Suu / Finn.	mouth, river mouth
Suur / Cat.	great
Svart / Nor.; Swed.	black
Sveti / S.C.; Slvn.	saint
Swa / Ban.	great
Swart / Afr.	black
Świety / Pol.	saint
Syrt / Alt.	ridge
Szállás / Hung.	village
Szczyt / Pol.	peak
Szeg / Hung.	bend
Székes / Hung.	residence
Szent / Hung.	saint
Sziget / Hung.	river island

T

Local Form	English
Tadi / Ban.	rock, cliff
Tae / Kor.	great
Tafua / Poly.	mountain
Tag / Alt.; Tur.	mountain
Tahta / Ar.	lower
Tahti / Ar.	lower
Tai / Chin.; Jap.	great
Taipale / Finn.	isthmus
Tajga / Rus.	forest
Take / Jap.	mountain
Tal / Germ.	valley
Tala / Mong.	plain, steppe
Tala / Ber.	spring
Tall / Ar.	hill
Talsperre / Germ.	dam
Tam / Viet.	stream
Tamgout / Ber.	peak
Tan / Chin.; Kor.	sandbank
Tana / Malag.	city, town
Tanana / Malag.	city, town
Tandjung / Mal.	cape, point
Tanezrouft / Ber.	desert
Tang / Tib.	upland
Tangeh / Pers.	strait
Tanjong / Mal.	cape, point
Tanjung, Tg. / Indon.	cape, point
Tanout / Ber.	well
Tao / Chin.	island
Taourirt / Ber.	peak
Targ / Pol.	market
Tãrg / Bulg.	market
Tarn / Eng.	glacial lake
Tarso / Sah.	crater
Taš / Alt.	stone

Geographical Glossary

Local Form	English
Tassili / *Ber.*	upland
Tau / *Tur.*	mountain
Taung / *Burm.*	mountain
Ṭawîl / *Ar.*	hill
Tégi / *Sah.*	hill
Teguidda / *Ber.*	well
Tehi / *Ber.*	pass, mountain
Teich / *Germ.*	pond
Tell / *Tur.*	hill
Telok / *Mal.*	bay, port
Teluk / *Mal.*	bay, port
Tempio / *It.*	temple
Ténéré / *Ber.*	rocky desert
Tengah / *Indon.; Mal.*	central
Tepe / *Tur.*	hill
Tepesi / *Tur.*	hill
Termas / *Sp.*	thermal springs
Terme / *It.*	thermal springs
Terra / *It.; Dut.*	land, earth
Terrazzo / *It.*	guyot, tablemount
Terre / *Fr.*	land, earth
Teso / *Cat.*	hill
Téssa / *Ber.*	wadi, depression
Testa / *It.*	point
Tête / *Fr.*	peak
Tetri / *Georg.*	white
Teu / *Poly.*	reef
Teze / *Alt.*	new
Tg., Tanjung / *Indon.*	cape, point
Thaba / *Ban.*	mountain
Thabana / *Ban.*	mountain
Thal / *Germ.*	valley
Thálassa / *Gr.*	sea
Thale / *Thai*	lagoon
Thamad / *Ar.*	well
Theós / *Gr.*	god
Thermes / *Fr.*	thermal springs
Thog / *Tib.*	high, upper
Tian / *Chin.*	field
Tiefe / *Germ.*	deep
Tierra / *Sp.*	land, earth
Timur / *Indon.; Mal.*	eastern
Tind / *Nor.*	mountain
Tinto / *Sp.*	black
Tirg / *Rom.*	market
Tis / *Amh.*	new
Tizgui / *Ber.*	forest
Tizi / *Ber.*	pass
Tjåkko / *Lapp.*	mountain
Tjärn / *Swed.*	tarn, glacial lake
Tji / *Mal.*	stream
To / *Kor.*	island
To / *Mel.*	stream
Tō / *Jap.*	island
Tó / *Hung.*	lake
To / *Ural.*	lake
Tobe / *Tur.*	hill
Tofua / *Poly.*	mountain
Tog / *Som.*	valley
Tōge / *Jap.*	pass
Tokoj / *Alt.*	forest
Tônle / *Khm.*	stream, lake
Tope / *Dut.*	peak
Toplice / *S.C.; Slvn.*	thermal springs
Topp / *Nor.*	peak
Tor / *Gae.*	rock
Tor / *Germ.*	gate
Torbat / *Pers.*	tomb
Törl / *Germ.*	pass
Torp / *Swed.*	hut
Torre / *Cat.; It.; Sp.; Port.*	tower
Torrente / *It.; Sp.*	torrent, stream
Tossa / *Cat.*	mountain, peak
Tota / *Sin.*	port
Tour / *Fr.*	tower
Traforo / *It.*	tunnel
Träsk / *Swed.*	lake
Trg / *S.C.*	market
Trog / *Germ.*	trough, trench
Trois / *Fr.*	three
Trung / *Viet.*	central
Tse / *Tib.*	peak, point
Tsi / *Chin.*	pond
Tskali / *Georg.*	river
Tsu / *Jap.*	bay
Tulūl / *Ar.*	hills
Tünel / *Pers.*	tunnel
Tunturi / *Lapp.*	mountain, tundra
Tur'ah / *Ar.*	irrigation canal
Turm / *Germ.*	tower
Turn / *Rom.*	tower
Turó / *Cat.*	dome
Tuz / *Tur.*	salt
Týn / *Cz.*	fortress

U

Local Form	English
U., Unter-, Upon / *Eng.; Germ.*	under, lower
Uaimh / *Gae.*	cave
Uchi / *Jap.*	bay
Udde / *Swed.*	cape
Údolní nádrž / *Cz.*	reservoir

Local Form	English
Uebi / *Som.*	river
Új- / *Hung.*	new
Ujście / *Pol.*	mouth
Ujung / *Indon.*	point, cape
Ul / *Chin.; Mong.*	mountain, mountain range
Ula / *Mong.*	mountain range
Ulan / *Mong.*	red
Uls / *Mong.*	state
Umi / *Jap.*	bay
Umm / *Ar.*	mother, spring
Umne / *Mong.*	south
Under / *Mong.*	mountain, peak
Ungur / *Alt.*	cave
Unter-, U. / *Germ.*	under, lower
Upar / *Hin.*	river
'Uqlat / *Ar.*	well
Ūr / *Tam.*	city, town
Ura / *Jap.*	bay, coast
Ura / *Alt.*	depression
Urd / *Mong.*	south
Uru / *Tam.*	city, town
Ušće / *S.C.*	mouth
Uske / *Alt.*	upper
Ust / *Rus.*	mouth
Ústí / *Cz.*	mouth
Ustup / *Rus.*	terrace
Utan / *Indon.; Mal.*	forest
Utara / *Indon.*	north, northern
Uusi / *Finn.*	new
Uval / *Rus.*	height
Úval / *Cz.*	mountain
'Uwaynāt / *Ar.*	well
Uzboj / *Alt.*	river bed
Uzun / *Tur.*	long
Užūrekis / *Lith.*	gulf

V

Local Form	English
Va / *Alb.*	ford
Va / *Ural.*	water, river
Vaara / *Finn.*	mountain
Väärti / *Finn.*	bay
Vad / *Rom.*	ford
Vær / *Nor.*	port
Våg / *Nor.*	bay
Vähä / *Finn.*	little
Väike / *Est.*	little
Väin / *Est.*	strait
Val / *Fr.; It.*	valley
Val / *Rom.; Rus.*	wall
Valico / *It.*	pass
Vall / *Cat.*	valley
Vall / *Swed.*	pasture
Valle / *It.; Sp.*	valley
Vallée / *Fr.*	valley
Vallei / *Afr.*	valley
Vallo / *It.*	wall
Valta / *Finn.*	cape
Váltos / *Gr.*	marsh
Valul / *Rom.*	wall
Vann / *Dan.; Nor.*	water, lake
Vanua / *Mel.*	land
Vár / *Hung.*	fort
Vara / *Finn.*	mountain
Varoš / *S.C.*	city, town
Város / *Hung.*	city, town
Varre / *Lapp.*	mountain
Vary / *Cz.*	spring
Vas / *S.C.; Slvn.*	village
Vásár / *Hung.*	market
Väst / *Swed.*	west
Väster / *Swed.*	western
Vatn / *Icel.; Nor.*	lake
Vatten / *Swed.*	water, lake
Vatu / *Mel.; Poly.*	island, reef
Vdhr., Vodohranilišče / *Rus.*	reservoir
Vechiu / *Rom.*	old
Vecs / *Latv.*	old
Veen / *Dut.; Fle.*	moor
Vega / *Sp.*	irrigated crops
Veld / *Afr.; Dut.; Fle.*	field
Veli / *S.C.; Slvn.*	great
Velik / *Bulg.*	great
Veliki / *Rus.; S.C.; Slvn.*	great
Veliký / *Cz.*	great
Vel'ky / *Slvk.*	great
Vella / *Cat.*	old
Ver / *Ural.*	forest
Verde / *It.; Sp.*	green
Verh / *Rus.*	peak
Verhni / *Rus.*	upper
Verk / *Swed.*	factory
Vermelho / *Port.*	red
Vert / *Fr.*	green
Ves / *Cz.*	village
Vesi / *Finn.*	water, lake
Vest / *Dan.; Nor.*	west
Vester / *Dan.; Nor.*	western
Vestur / *Icel.*	west
Vetta / *It.*	summit
Viaduc / *Fr.*	viaduct

Local Form	English
Vidda / *Nor.*	upland
Vidde / *Nor.*	upland
Viejo / *Sp.*	old
Vier / *Germ.*	four
Viertel / *Germ.*	quarter
Vieux / *Fr.*	old
Vig / *Dan.*	bay
Vik / *Icel.; Nor.; Swed.*	gulf, bay
Vila / *Port.*	city, town
Villa / *Sp.*	city, town
Ville, -ville / *Eng.; Fr.*	city, town
Vinh / *Viet.*	bay
Virful / *Rom.*	peak, mountain
Virta / *Finn.*	river
Višni / *Rus.*	high
Visok / *S.C.*	high
Viz / *Hung.*	water
Viztárolò / *Hung.*	reservoir
Vlakte / *Dut.; Fle.*	plain
Vlei / *Afr.*	pond
Vliet / *Dut.; Fle.*	river
Vloer / *Afr.*	depression
Voda / *Bulg.; Cz.; Rus.; S.C.; Slvn.*	water
Vodny put / *Rus.*	stream, canal
Vodohranilišče, vdhr. / *Rus.*	reservoir
Vodopad / *Rus.*	waterfall
Volcan / *Fr.*	volcano
Volcán / *Sp.*	volcano
Voll / *Nor.*	meadow
Vórios / *Gr.*	northern
Vorota / *Rus.*	gate
Vorrás / *Gr.*	north
Vostočny / *Rus.*	eastern
Vostok / *Rus.*	east
Vötn / *Icel.*	lake, water
Vož / *Ural.*	mouth
Vozvyšennost / *Rus.*	upland
Vpadina / *Rus.*	depression
Vrah / *Bulg.*	peak
Vrata / *Bulg.; S.C.; Slvn.*	pass
Vrch / *Cz.; Slvk.*	mountain
Vrch / *S.C.; Slvn.*	peak
Vrchni- / *Cz.*	upper
Vrchovina / *Cz.*	upland
Vulcan / *Rom.; Rus.*	volcano
Vulcano / *It.*	volcano
Vulkan / *Germ.; Rus.*	volcano
Vuopio / *Lapp.*	bend
Vuori / *Finn.*	rock
Východný / *Cz.*	eastern
Vyšný / *Slvk.*	upper
Vysoki / *Rus.*	high
Vysoky / *Cz.; Slvk.*	high
Vyšší / *Cz.*	high

W

Local Form	English
W., Wādī / *Ar.*	wadi
Wa / *Ban.*	people
Wabe / *Amh.*	stream
Wad / *Ar.*	wadi
Wad / *Dut.*	tidal flat
Wādī, W. / *Ar.*	wadi
Wāḥāt / *Ar.*	oasis
Wai / *Mel.; Poly.*	stream
Wal / *Afr.*	wall
Wala / *Hin.*	mountain range
Wald / *Germ.*	forest
Wan / *Burm.*	village
Wan / *Chin.; Jap.*	bay
Wand / *Germ.*	bluff
War / *Som.*	pond
Wär / *Ar.*	desert
-waram / *Hin.; Tam.*	village
Wasser / *Germ.*	water
Wat / *Pol.*	wall
Wat / *Thai*	church
Waterval / *Afr.; Dut.*	waterfall
Watt / *Germ.*	tidal flat
Wāw / *Ar.*	oasis
Weald / *Eng.*	wooded country
Webi / *Som.*	stream
Weg / *Germ.*	way, road
Wei / *Chin.*	cape, point
Weide / *Germ.*	pasture
Weiler / *Germ.*	village
Weiß / *Germ.*	white
Weon / *Kor.*	field
Wer / *Som.*	pond
Werder / *Germ.*	river island
Werk / *Germ.*	factory
Wes / *Afr.*	west
Westlich / *Germ.*	western
Westr- / *Sca.*	western
Wēyn / *Som.*	great
Wēyne / *Som.*	great
Wick / *Eng.*	village
Wiek / *Germ.*	bay
Wielki / *Pol.*	great
Wieś / *Pol.*	village
Wijk / *Dut.; Fle.*	quarter, district
-willer / *Germ.*	village

Local Form	English
Woda / *Pol.*	water
Woestyn / *Afr.*	desert
Wold / *Dut.; Fle.; Eng.*	forest
Wörth / *Germ.*	river island
Woud / *Dut.; Fle.*	forest
Wschodni / *Pol.*	eastern
Wysoczyzna / *Pol.*	upland
Wysoki / *Pol.*	upper
Wyspa / *Pol.*	island
Wyżyna / *Pol.*	highland
Wzgórze / *Pol.*	hill

X

Local Form	English
Xi / *Chin.*	west
Xia / *Chin.*	gorge, strait
Xian / *Chin.*	county, shire
Xiang / *Chin.*	village
Xiao / *Chin.*	little
Xin / *Chin.*	new
Xu / *Chin.*	island

Y

Local Form	English
Yam / *Hebr.*	lake, sea
Yama / *Jap.*	mountain
Yan / *Chin.*	mountain
Yang / *Chin.*	strait, ocean
Yani / *Tur.*	new
Yar / *Tur.*	gorge
Yarimada / *Tur.*	peninsula
Yazı / *Tur.*	plain
Yegge / *Sah.*	well
Yeni / *Tur.*	new
Yeon / *Kor.*	sea
Yeong / *Kor.*	mountain
Yeşil / *Tur.*	green
Ylä / *Finn.*	upper
Yli- / *Finn.*	upper
Yō / *Jap.*	ocean
Yobe / *Sud.*	great
Yŏm / *Kor.*	island
Yoma / *Burm.*	mountain range
Yŏn / *Kor.*	lake, pond
Yŏng / *Kor.*	mountain, peak
Ytter / *Nor.; Swed.*	outer
Yttre / *Swed.*	outer
Yu / *Chin.*	old
Yu / *Chin.*	island
Yu / *Jap.*	thermal spring
Yüan / *Chin.*	spring, river
Yunhe / *Chin.*	canal

Z

Local Form	English
Zāb / *Ar.*	river
Zachodni / *Pol.*	western
Zaki / *Jap.*	cape
Zalew / *Pol.*	gulf
Zaliv / *Bulg.; Rus.; S.C.; Slvn.*	gulf
Zaljev / *Slvn.*	bay
Zámek / *Cz.*	castle
Zan / *Jap.*	mountain
Zand / *Dut.; Fle.*	sand
Zandt / *Dut.; Fle.*	sand
Zangbo / *Chin.*	river
Zapad / *Rus.*	west
Zapaden / *Bulg.*	western
Zapadni / *S.C.; Slvn.*	western
Západní / *Cz.*	western
Zapadny / *Rus.*	western
Zapovednik / *Rus.*	reserve
Zatoka / *Pol.*	gulf
Zavod / *Rus.*	roadstead
Zāwiyat / *Ar.*	monastery
Zdrój / *Pol.*	thermal springs
Ze / *Jap.*	islet
Zee / *Dut.; Fle.*	sea
Zelëny / *Rus.*	green
Žem / *Lith.*	land, country
Zemé / *Cz.; Slvk.*	land, country
Zemlja / *Rus.*	land
Zen / *Jap.*	mountain
Zhan / *Chin.*	mountain
Zhen / *Chin.*	market
Zhong / *Chin.*	central
Zhou / *Chin.*	quarter, district
Zhuang / *Chin.*	village
Ziemia / *Pol.*	land
Zigos / *Gr.*	pass
Zipfel / *Germ.*	tip, point
Ziwa / *Swa.*	marsh
Zizhiqu / *Chin.*	autonomous region
Zlato / *Bulg.*	gold
Zuid / *Dut.; Fle.*	south
Zuidelijk / *Dut.*	southern
Żuława / *Pol.*	marsh
Zun / *Mong.*	east
Zwart / *Dut.*	black
Zwei / *Germ.*	two

International Map Index

All of the toponyms (place-names) which appear on the maps are listed in the International Map Index. Each entry includes the following: Place-name and, where applicable, other forms by which it is written or known; a symbol, where applicable, indicating what kind of feature it is; the number of the map on which it appears; and the map-reference letters and geographical coordinates indicating its location on the map.

Toponyms

Each toponym, or place-name, is written in full, with accents and diacritical marks. Since many countries have more than one official language, many of these forms are included on the maps. For example, many Belgian place-names are listed as follows: Bruxelles/Brussel; Antwerpen/Anvers, and vice versa, Brussel/Bruxelles; Anvers/Antwerpen. In Italy, certain regions have a special status—they are largely autonomous and officially bilingual. As a result, Index listings appear as follows: Aosta/Aoste; Alto Adige/Sud Tirol, and vice versa. One name, however, may be the only name on the map.

In China, the written forms of commonly used regional languages have been taken into account. These forms are enclosed in parenthesis following the official name: e.g. Xiangshan (Dancheng). However, when the regional is listed first, it is linked to the official name with an→: e.g. Dancheng→Xiangshan. The same style is used for former or historical name forms: e.g. Rhodesia→Zimbabwe and Zimbabwe (Rhodesia).

Place-names for major features (countries, major cities, and large physical features), where applicable, include the English conventional form identified by (EN) and linked in the local name or names with an = sign: e.g. Italia=Italy (EN), and vice versa, Italy (EN)=Italia. Former English names are linked in the Index to the conventional form by an→.

Symbols

The last component with the place-name is a symbol, where applicable, specifying the broad category of the feature named. A table preceding the Index lists all of the symbols used and their meanings; this information also appears as a footnote on each page of the Index. Place-names without symbols are cities and towns.

Alphabetization

Place-names are listed in English alphabetical order—26 letters, from A to Z—because of its international usage. Names including two or more words are listed alphabetically according to the first letter of the word: e.g. De Ruyter is listed under D; Le Havre is listed under L. Names with the prefix Mc are listed as if spelled Mac. The generic portion of a name (lake, sierra, mountain, etc.) is placed after the name: e.g. Lake Erie is listed as Erie, Lake; Sierra Morena is listed as Morena, Sierra. In Spanish, "ch" and "ll" groups and the letter "ñ" are included respectively under C, L, and N, without any distinction.

The same place-name sometimes is listed in the Index several times. It may because of the various translations of a name, or it may be that several places have the same name.

Various translations of a name appear as follows:

Danube (EN) = Dunav   Danube (EN) = Donau
Danube (EN) = Dunărea   Danube (EN) = Dunaj

Several places with the same name appear as follows; however, only in these cases is the location—abbreviated and enclosed in brackets—included. A table of these abbreviations precedes the Index.

Abbeville [U.S.]   Aberdeen [Scot.-U.K.]
Abbeville [Fr.]   Aberdeen [N.C.-U.S.]
Aberdeen [S. Afr.]

Map Number

Each map in the atlas is identified by a number. Where multiple maps are on one page, each map is additionally identified by a boxed letter in the upper-right-hand corner of the map. In the Index listing following the place-name and its variations in language and spelling, where applicable, is the number of the map on which it appears. If the map is one of several on a page, the Index listing includes the map number and letter.

Although a place-name may appear on one or more maps, it is indexed to only one map. Most places are indexed to the regional maps. However, if a place-name appears on either the physical or political continental maps, it is indexed to one of the two types of map. For example, a river or mountain would be indexed to a physical continental map; a city or state would be indexed to a political continental map.

Map-Reference Letters and Geographical Coordinates

The next elements in the Index listing are the map-reference letters and the geographical coordinates, respectively, locating the place on the map.

Map-reference letters consist of a capital and a lowercase letter. Capital letters are across the top and bottom of the maps; lowercase letters are down the sides. The map-reference letters assigned to each place-name refer to the location of the name within the area formed by grid lines connecting the geographical coordinates on either sides of the letters.

Geographical coordinates are the latitude (N for North, S for South) and longitude (E for East, W for West) expressed in degrees and minutes and based on the prime meridian, Greenwich.

Map-reference letters and coordinates for extensive geographical features, such as mountain ranges and countries, are given for the approximate central point of the area. Those for waterways, such as canals and rivers, are given for the mouth of the river, the point where it enters another river or where the feature reaches the map margin. On this page are sample maps showing points to which features are indexed according to map-reference letters and coordinates.

On most maps there is not enough space to place all of the names of administrative subdivisions. In these cases the location of the place is shown on the map by a circled letter or number and the place-name and circled letter or number are listed in the map margin. The map-reference numbers and coordinates for these places refer to the location of the circled letter or number on the map.

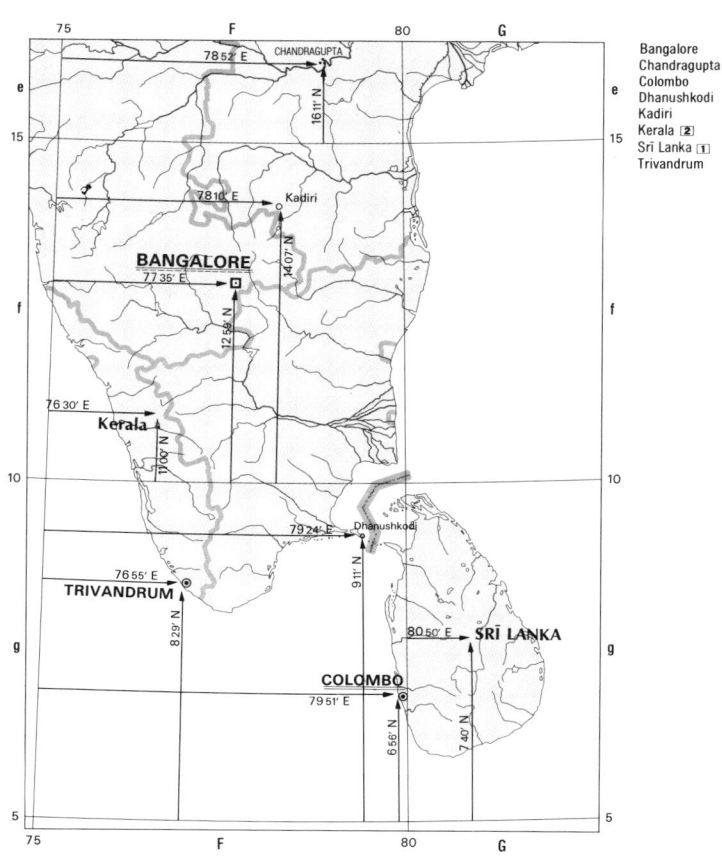

Bangalore	25 Ff	12°59'N	77°35'E
Chandragupta ▣	35 Fe	16°11'N	78°52'E
Colombo	25 Fg	6°56'N	79°51'E
Dhanushkodi	25 Fg	9°11'N	79°24'E
Kadiri	25 Ff	14°07'N	78°10'E
Kerala ②	25 Ff	11°00'N	76°30'E
Sri Lanka ①	25 Gg	7°40'N	80°50'E
Trivandrum	25 Fg	8°29'N	76°55'E

Alaska ▣	38 Dc	65°00'N	153°00'W
Alaska, Gulf of- ◖	38 Ed	58°00'N	146°00'W
Alexander Archipelago ▣	38 Fd	56°30'N	134°00'W
Barrow, Point- ▶	38 Db	71°23'N	156°30'W
Bering Strait ▤	38 Cc	65°30'N	169°00'W
Coast Mountains ▲	38 Gd	55°00'N	129°00'W
Kodiak ✦	38 Dd	57°30'N	153°30'W
Yukon ⬎	38 Cc	62°33'N	163°59'W

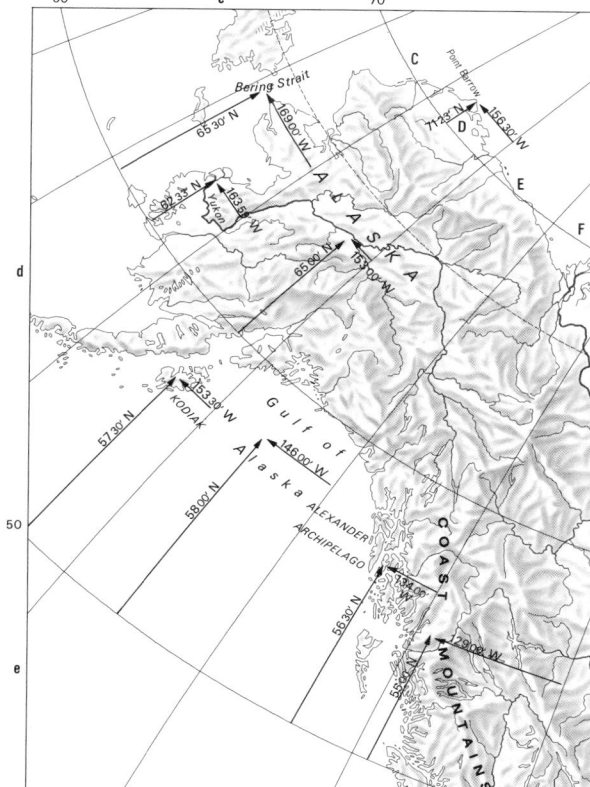

List of Abbreviations

Afg. Afghanistan
Afr. Africa
Agl. Anguilla
Ak.-U.S. Alaska, U.S.
Al.-U.S. Alabama, U.S.
Alb. Albania
Alg. Algeria
Alta.-Can. Alberta, Canada
Am. Sam. American Samoa
And. Andorra
Ang. Angola
Ant. Antarctica
Ar.-U.S. Arkansas, U.S.
Arg. Argentina
Asia Asia
Atg. Antigua and Barbuda
Aus. Austria
Austl. Australia
Az.-U.S. Arizona, U.S.
Azr. Azores
Bah. Bahamas
Bar. Barbados
B.A.T. British Antarctic Territory
B.C.-Can. British Columbia, Canada
Bel. Belgium
Ben. Benin
Ber. Bermuda
Bhr. Bahrain
Bhu. Bhutan
Blz. Belize
Bnd. Burundi
Bngl. Bangladesh
Bol. Bolivia
Bots. Botswana
Braz. Brazil
Bru. Brunei
Bul. Bulgaria
Bur. Burma
Burkina Burkina Faso
B.V.I. British Virgin Islands
Ca.-U.S. California, U.S.
Cam. Cameroon
C. Amer. Central America
Can. Canada
Can. Is. Canary Islands
C.A.R. Central African Republic
Cay. Is Cayman Islands
Chad Chad
Chan. Is. Channel Islands
Chile Chile
China China
Co.-U.S. Colorado, U.S.
Cocos Is. Cocos Islands
Col. Colombia
Con. Congo
Cook Cook Islands
Cor. Sea Is. Coral Sea Islands
C.R. Costa Rica
Ct.-U.S. Connecticut, U.S.
Cuba Cuba
C.V. Cape Verde
Cyp. Cyprus
Czech. Czech Republic

D.C.-U.S. District of Columbia, U.S.
De.-U.S. Delaware, U.S.
Den. Denmark
Dji. Djibouti
Dom. Dominica
Dom. Rep. Dominican Republic
Ec. Ecuador
Eg. Egypt
El Sal. El Salvador
Eng.-U.K. England, U.K.
Eq. Gui. Equatorial Guinea
Est. Estonia
Eth. Ethiopia
Eur. Europe
Falk. Is. Falkland Islands
Far. Is. Faeroe Islands
Fiji Fiji
Fin. Finland
Fl.-U.S. Florida, U.S.
Fr. France
Fr. Gui. French Guiana
Fr. Poly. French Polynesia
F.S.M. Federated States of Micronesia
Ga.-U.S. Georgia, U.S.
Gabon Gabon
Gam. Gambia
Geor. Georgia
Ger. Germany
Ghana Ghana
Gib. Gibraltar
Grc. Greece
Gren. Grenada
Grld. Greenland
Guad. Guadeloupe
Guam Guam
Guat. Guatemala
Gui. Guinea
Gui. Bis. Guinea Bissau
Guy. Guyana
Haiti Haiti
Hi.-U.S. Hawaii, U.S.
H.K. Hong Kong
Hond. Honduras
Hun. Hungary
Ia.-U.S. Iowa, U.S.
I.C. Ivory Coast
Ice. Iceland
Id.-U.S. Idaho, U.S.
Il.-U.S. Illinois, U.S.
In.-U.S. Indiana, U.S.
India India
Indon. Indonesia
I. of M. Isle of Man
Iran Iran
Iraq Iraq
Ire. Ireland
Isr. Israel
It. Italy
Jam. Jamaica
Jap. Japan
Jor. Jordan
Kam. Cambodia
Kenya Kenya
Ker. Is. Kermadec Islands

Kir. Kiribati
Ks.-U.S. Kansas, U.S.
Kuw. Kuwait
Ky.-U.S. Kentucky, U.S.
La.-U.S. Louisiana, U.S.
Laos Laos
Lat. Latvia
Lbr. Liberia
Leb. Lebanon
Les. Lesotho
Lib. Libya
Liech. Liechtenstein
Lith. Lithuania
Lux. Luxembourg
Ma.-U.S. Massachusetts, U.S.
Mac. Macao
Mad. Madagascar
Mala. Malaysia
Mald. Maldives
Mali Mali
Malta Malta
Man.-Can. Manitoba, Canada
Mar. Is. Marshall Islands
Mart. Martinique
Maur. Mauritius
May. Mayotte
Mco. Monaco
Md.-U.S. Maryland, U.S.
Me.-U.S. Maine, U.S.
Mex. Mexico
Mi.-U.S. Michigan, U.S.
Mid. Is. Midway Islands
Mn.-U.S. Minnesota, U.S.
Mo.-U.S. Missouri, U.S.
Mong. Mongolia
Mont. Montserrat
Mor. Morocco
Moz. Mozambique
Ms.-U.S. Mississippi, U.S.
Mt.-U.S. Montana, U.S.
Mtna. Mauritania
Mwi. Malawi
Nam. Namibia
N. Amer. North America
Nauru Nauru
N.B.-Can. New Brunswick, Canada
Nb.-U.S. Nebraska, U.S.
N.C.-U.S. North Carolina, U.S.
N. Cal. New Caledonia
N.D.-U.S. North Dakota, U.S.
Nep. Nepal
Neth. Netherlands
Neth. Ant. Netherlands Antilles
Newf.-Can. Newfoundland, Canada
N.H.-U.S. New Hampshire, U.S.
Nic. Nicaragua
Nig. Nigeria
Niger Niger

N. Ire.-U.K. Northern Ireland, U.K.
N.J.-U.S. New Jersey, U.S.
N. Kor. North Korea
N.M.-U.S. New Mexico, U.S.
N. M. Is. Northern Mariana Islands
Nor. Norway
Nor. I. Norfolk Island
N.S.-Canada Nova Scotia, Canada
Nv.-U.S. Nevada, U.S.
N.W.T.-Can. Northwest Territories, Canada
N.Y.-U.S. New York, U.S.
N.Z. New Zealand
Ocn. Oceania
Oh.-U.S. Ohio, U.S.
Ok.-U.S. Oklahoma, U.S.
Oman Oman
Ont.-Ont. Ontario, Canada
Or.-U.S. Oregon, U.S.
Pa.-U.S. Pennsylvania, U.S.
Pak. Pakistan
Pal. Palau
Pan. Panama
Pap. N. Gui. Papua New Guinea
Par. Paraguay
Pas. Pascua
P.E.I.-Can. Prince Edward Island, Canada
Peru Peru
Phil. Philippines
Pit. Pitcairn
Pol. Poland
Port. Portugal
P.R. Puerto Rico
Qatar Qatar
Que.-Can. Quebec, Canada
Reu. Reunion
R.I.-U.S. Rhode Island, U.S.
Rom. Romania
Rwn. Rwanda
S. Afr. South Africa
S. Amer. South America
Sao T.P. Sao Tome and Principe
Sask.-Can. Saskatchewan, Canada
Sau. Ar. Saudi Arabia
S.C.-U.S. South Carolina, U.S.
Scot.-U.K. Scotland, U.K.
S.D.-U.S. South Dakota, U.S.
Sen. Senegal
Sey. Seychelles
Sing. Singapore
S. Kor. South Korea
S.L. Sierra Leone
S. Lan. Sri Lanka
S.M. San Marino
S.N.A. Spanish North Africa
Sol. Is. Solomon Islands
Som. Somalia
Sp. Spain

St. C.N. Saint Christopher-Nevis
St. Hel. Saint Helena
St. Luc. Saint Lucia
St. P.M. Saint Pierre and Miquelon
St. Vin. Saint Vincent and the Grenadines
Sud. Sudan
Sur. Suriname
Sval. Svalbard
Swe. Sweden
Switz. Switzerland
Syr. Syria
Tai. Taiwan
Tan. Tanzania
T.C. Is. Turks and Caicos Islands
Thai. Thailand
Tn.-U.S. Tennessee, U.S.
Togo Togo
Ton. Tonga
Trin. Trinidad and Tobago
T.T.P.I. Trust Territory of the Pacific Islands
Tun. Tunisia
Tur. Turkey
Tuv. Tuvalu
Tx.-U.S. Texas, U.S.
U.A.E. United Arab Emirates
Ug. Uganda
U.K. United Kingdom
Ukr. Ukraine
Ur. Uruguay
U.S. United States
Ut.-U.S. Utah, U.S.
Va.-U.S. Virginia, U.S.
Van. Vanuatu
V.C. Vatican City
Ven. Venezuela
Viet. Vietnam
V.I.U.S. Virgin Islands of the U.S.
Vt.-U.S. Vermont, U.S.
Wa.-U.S. Washington, U.S.
Wake Wake Island
Wales-U.K. Wales, U.K.
W.F. Wallis and Futuna
Wi.-U.S. Wisconsin, U.S.
W. Sah. Western Sahara
W. Sam. Western Samoa
W.V.-U.S. West Virginia, U.S.
Wy.-U.S. Wyoming, U.S.
Yem. Yemen
Yugo. Yugoslavia
Yuk.-Can. Yukon, Canada
Zaire Zaire
Zam. Zambia
Zimb. Zimbabwe

List of Symbols

Plains and Associated Features
Plain, Basin, Lowland
Delta
Salt Flat

Valleys and Depressions
Valley, Gorge, Ravine, Canyon
Cave, Crater, Quarry
Karst Features
Depression
Polder, Reclaimed Marsh

Vegetational Features
Desert, Dunes
Forest, Woods
Heath, Steppe, Tundra, Moor
Oasis

Political/Administrative Units
[1] Independent Nation
[2] State, Canton, Region
[3] Province, Department, County, Territory, District
[4] Municipality
[5] Colony, Dependency, Administered Territory

Geographical Regions
Continent
Physical Region
Historical or Cultural Region

Mountain Features
Mount, Mountain, Peak
Volcano
Hill
Mountains, Mountain Range
Hills, Escarpment
Plateau, Highland, Upland
Pass, Gap

Coastal Features
Cape, Point
Coast, Beach
Cliff
Peninsula, Promontory
Isthmus
Sandbank, Tombolo, Sandbar

Islands Rocks, Reefs
Island
Atoll
Rock, Reef
Islands, Archipelago
Rocks, Reefs
Coral Reef

Hydrographic Features
Well, Spring
Geyser, Fumarole
River, Stream, Brook
Waterfall, Rapids, Cataract
River Mouth, Estuary
Lake
Salt Lake
Intermittent Lake, Dry Lake Bed
Reservoir, Artificial Lake
Swamp, Marsh, Pond
Irrigation Canal, Navigable Canal, Ditch, Aqueduct

Ice Features
Glacier, Snowfield
Ice Shelf, Pack Ice

Marine Features
Ocean
Sea
Gulf, Bay
Strait, Fjord, Sea Channel
Lagoon, Anchorage

Submarine Features
Bank, Shoal
Seamount
Rise, Plateau, Tablemount
Seamount Chain, Ridge
Platform, Shelf
Basin, Depression
Escarpment, Slope, Sea Scarp
Fracture
Trench, Abyss, Valley, Canyon

Other Features
National Park, Nature Reserve
Scenic Area, Point of Interest
Recreation Site, Sports Arena
Cave, Cavern
Historic Site, Memorial, Mausoleum, Museum
Ruins
Wall, Walls, Tower, Castle, Fortress
Church, Abbey, Cathedral, Sanctuary
Temple, Synagogue, Mosque
Research or Scientific Station
Airport, Heliport
Port, Dock
Lighthouse
Mine
Tunnel
Dam, Bridge

A

Name	Pg	Grid	Lat	Long
Å	7	Cc	67.53N	12.59 E
Aa [Eur.] ◁	12	Ic	51.50N	6.25 E
Aa [Fr.] ◁	11	Ic	51.01N	2.06 E
Aa [Fr.]	12	Dd	50.44N	2.18 E
Aa [Ger.] ◁	12	Kb	52.07N	8.41 E
Aa [Ger.]	12	Jb	52.15N	7.18 E
Aachen	10	Cf	50.46N	6.06 E
Aalen	10	Gh	48.50N	10.06 E
A'âli an Nîl ③	35	Ed	9.15N	33.00 E
Aalsmeer	12	Gb	52.15N	4.45 E
Aalst/Alost	11	Kd	50.56N	4.02 E
Aalten	12	Ic	51.55N	6.35 E
Aalter	12	Fc	51.05N	3.27 E
Äänekoski	7	Fe	62.36N	25.44 E
Aa of Weerijs ◁	12	Gc	51.35N	4.46 E
Aar ◁	12	Kd	50.23N	8.00 E
Aarau	14	Cc	47.25N	8.02 E
Aarbergen	12	Kd	50.13N	8.03 E
Aare ◁	14	Cc	47.37N	8.13 E
Aargau ②	14	Cc	47.30N	8.10 E
Aarlen/Arlon	11	Le	49.41N	5.49 E
Aarschot	11	Kd	50.59N	4.50 E
Aat/Ath	11	Jd	50.38N	3.47 E
Aazanèn	13	Ii	35.06N	3.02W
Åb ◁	24	Md	36.00N	48.05 E
Aba [Nig.]	31	Hh	5.07N	7.22 E
Aba [Zaire]	31	Hk	3.52N	30.14 E
Aba/Ngawa	27	He	32.55N	101.45 E
Abâ ad Dûd	24	Ki	27.02N	44.04 E
Abâ as Su'ûd	23	Ff	17.28N	44.06 E
Abacaxis, Rio- ◁	54	Gd	3.54 S	58.50W
Abaco Island ●	38	Lg	26.25N	77.10W
Abadab, Jabal- ▲	49	Kd	18.03N	73.47W
	35	Fb	18.53N	35.59 E
Åbâdân	22	Gf	30.10N	48.50 E
Åbâdeh [Iran]	23	Hc	31.10N	52.37 E
Åbâdeh [Iran]	24	Oh	29.08N	52.52 E
Abadiânia	55	Hc	16.06 S	48.48W
Abadla	31	Ge	31.01N	2.43W
Abaeté	55	Jd	19.09 S	45.27W
Abaeté, Rio- ◁	55	Jd	18.02 S	45.12W
Abaetetuba	54	Id	1.42 S	48.54W
Abagnar Qi (Xilin Hot)	22	Ne	43.58N	116.08 E
Abag Qi (Xin Hot)	27	Jc	44.01N	114.59 E
Abai	55	Eh	26.01 S	55.57W
Abaiang Atoll ◉	57	Id	1.51N	172.58 E
Abaj	19	Hf	49.38N	72.50 E
Abaji	34	Gd	8.28N	6.57 E
Abajo Mountains ▲	46	Kh	37.50N	109.25W
Abakaliki	34	Gd	6.20N	8.03 E
Abakan ◁	20	Ef	53.43N	91.30 E
Abakan	22	Ld	53.43N	91.26 E
Abakwasimbo	36	Eb	0.36N	28.43 E
Abala [Con.]	36	Cc	1.21 S	15.30 E
Abala [Niger]	34	Fc	14.56N	3.26 E
Abalak	34	Gb	15.27N	6.17 E
Aban	20	Ee	56.40N	96.10 E
Abancay	54	Df	13.35 S	72.55W
Abancourt	12	De	49.42N	1.46 E
Abanga ◁	36	Bb	0.13N	10.28 E
Abano Terme	14	Fe	45.21N	11.47 E
Åbâr al Jidd	24	Hf	32.50N	39.50 E
Abarqû	23	Hc	31.08N	53.17 E
Abarqu, Kavîr-e- ◎	24	Og	31.00N	53.50 E
Abashiri	27	Pc	44.01N	144.17 E
Abashiri-Gawa ◁	29a Db	43.56N	144.09 E
Abashiri-Ko ◎	29a Da	44.00N	144.10 E
Abashiri-Wan ◁	29a Da	44.00N	144.35 E
Abasolo	48	Je	24.04N	98.22W
Abatski	19	Hd	56.18N	70.28 E
Abau	60	Dj	10.11 S	148.42 E
Abava ◁	7	Eh	57.06N	21.54 E
Abay = Blue Nile (EN) ◁	35	Kg	15.38N	32.31 E
Abaya, Lake- ◎	30	Kh	6.20N	37.55 E
Abaza	20	Ef	52.39N	90.06 E
Abbadia San Salvatore	14	Fg	42.53N	11.41 E
Abbah Qușûr	14	Co	35.57N	8.50 E
Åb Bârik	24	Oh	29.45N	52.37 E
'Abbâsâbâd	24	Qd	36.20N	56.25 E
Abbekås	8	Fc	55.24N	13.36 E
Abberton Reservoir ◎	12	Cc	51.50N	0.55 E
Abbeville [Fr.]	11	Hd	50.06N	1.50 E
Abbeville [La.-U.S.]	45	Jl	29.58N	92.08W
Abbeville [S.C.-U.S.]	44	Fh	34.10N	82.23W
Abbey	46	Ka	50.43N	108.45W
Abbeyfeale/Mainistir na Féile	9	Di	52.24N	9.18W
Abbiategrasso	14	Ce	45.24N	8.54 E
Abbot, Mount- ▲	59	Jd	20.03 S	147.45 E
Abbot Ice Shelf ◙	66	Pf	72.45 S	90.00W
'Abd Al 'Azîz, Jabal- ▲	24	Id	36.25N	40.20 E
'Abd al Kurî ●	21	Hh	12.12N	52.13 E
Åbdânân	24	Lf	32.57N	47.26 E
Abdul Ghadir	35	Gc	10.42N	42.59 E
Abdulino	19	Fe	53.42N	53.38 E
Abe, Lake- ◎	35	Gc	11.10N	41.45 E
Abéché	31	Jg	13.49N	20.49 E
Abeek ◁	12	Hc	51.15N	6.00 E
Abe-Gawa ◁	29	Fd	34.55N	138.22 E
Abeløya ●	41	Pc	79.00N	30.15 E
Abelvær	7	Cd	64.44N	11.11 E
Abemama Atoll ◉	57	Id	0.21N	173.51 E
Abenab	37	Bc	19.12 S	18.06 E
Abengourou	34	Ed	6.35N	3.25W
Abengourou	31	Gh	6.44N	3.29W
Åbenrå	8	Bi	55.02N	9.26 E
Åbenrå Fjord ◁	8	Ci	55.05N	9.35 E
Åb-e-Pany ◁	23	If	37.06N	68.20 E
Aberayron	9	Ij	52.15N	4.15W
Aberdare Range ▲	30	Ki	0.25 S	36.38 E
Aberdeen [Id.-U.S.]	46	Ie	42.57N	112.50W
Aberdeen [Md.-U.S.]	44	If	39.30N	76.14W
Aberdeen [Ms.-U.S.]	45	Lj	33.49N	88.33W
Aberdeen [N.C.-U.S.]	44	Hh	35.08N	79.26W
Aberdeen [S.Afr.]	37	Cf	32.29 S	24.03 E
Aberdeen [Scot.-U.K.]	6	Fd	57.10N	2.04W
Aberdeen [S.D.-U.S.]	39	Je	45.28N	98.29W
Aberdeen [Wa.-U.S.]	43	Cb	46.59N	123.50W
Aberdeen Lake ◎	42	Hd	64.28N	99.00W
Abergavenny	9	Kj	51.50N	3.00W
Aberystwyth	9	Ii	52.25N	4.05W
Abetone	14	Ef	44.08N	10.40 E
Abez	19	Gb	66.32N	61.46 E
Abhâ	22	Gh	18.13N	42.30 E
Abhainn an Chláir/Clare ◁	9	Dh	53.20N	9.03W
Abhainn an Lagáin/ Lagan ◁	9	Hg	54.37N	5.53W
Abhainn na Bandan/ Bandon ◁	9	Ej	51.40N	8.30W
Abhainn na Deirge/Derg ◁	9	Fg	54.40N	7.25W
Abhar	24	Md	36.02N	49.45 E
Abhar	23	Gb	36.09N	49.13 E
Abhazskaja republika	19	Eg	43.00N	41.10 E
Abibe, Serrania de- ▲	54	Cb	8.00N	76.30W
Abidjan	31	Gh	5.19N	4.02W
Abidjan ③	34	Ed	5.30N	4.30W
Abilene [Ks.-U.S.]	45	Hg	38.55N	97.13W
Abilene [Tx.-U.S.]	39	Jf	32.27N	99.44W
Abingdon	9	Lj	51.41N	1.17W
Abinsk	16	Kg	44.52N	38.10 E
Abiquiu	45	Ch	36.12N	106.19W
Abiquiu Reservoir ◎	45	Dh	36.18N	106.32W
Abisko	7	Eb	68.20N	18.51 E
Abitibi, Lake- ◎	42	Jf	51.04N	80.55W
Abiy Adi	38	Le	48.42N	79.45W
Abiyata, Lake- ◎	35	Fc	13.37N	39.01 E
Abja-Paluoja	35	Fd	7.38N	38.36 E
Åbnûb	8	Kf	58.02N	25.14 E
Åbo/Turku	33	Fd	27.16N	31.09 E
Abo, Massif d'- ▲	6	Ic	60.27N	22.17 E
Abóboras, Serra das- ▲	35	Ba	21.41N	16.08 E
Abodo	55	Jc	16.12 S	44.35W
Aboisso ③	35	Ed	7.50N	34.25 E
Aboisso	34	Ed	5.28N	3.02W
Abomey	34	Ed	5.28N	3.12W
Abong Mbang	31	Hh	7.11N	1.59 E
Abony	34	He	3.59N	13.11 E
Aborigen, Pik- ▲	10	Pi	47.11N	20.00 E
Aborlar	20	Jd	62.05N	149.10 E
Aborrebierg ▲	26	Ge	9.26N	118.33 E
Abou Deia	8	Ej	54.59N	12.32 E
Abou Goulem	35	Bc	11.27N	19.17 E
Abovjan	35	Cc	13.37N	21.38 E
Abråd, Wâdî- ◁	16	Ni	40.14N	44.37 E
Abraham's Bay	23	Gf	15.51N	46.05 E
Abramovski Bereg ●	49	Kb	22.21N	72.55W
Abrántes	7	Kc	66.25N	43.05 E
Abra Pampa	13	De	39.28N	8.12W
Abrego	56	Gb	22.43 S	65.42W
Abreojos, Punta- ▶	49	Ki	8.04N	73.14W
'Abrî	47	Bc	26.42N	113.35W
Abrolhos, Arquipélago dos- ◻	35	Ea	20.48N	30.20 E
Abrud	54	Kg	18.00 S	38.40W
Abruka, Ostrov-/Abruka Saar ●	15	Gc	46.16N	23.04 E
Abruka Saar/Abruka, Ostrov- ●	8	Jf	58.08N	22.25 E
Abruzzi ②	8	Jf	58.08N	22.25 E
Absaroka Range ▲	14	Hh	42.20N	13.45 E
Abtenau	43	Fc	44.45N	109.50W
Abû, Hâd, Wâdî- ◁	14	Hc	47.33N	13.21 E
Abû ad Duhûr	24	Ei	27.46N	33.30 E
Abû 'Alî ●	24	Ge	35.44N	37.02 E
Abû al Khașîb	24	Mi	27.20N	49.33 E
Abû an Na'am	24	Lg	30.27N	47.59 E
Abû 'Arîsh	24	Hj	25.14N	38.49 E
Abû Ballaș ▲	23	Ff	16.58N	42.50 E
Abû Daghmah	33	Ee	24.26N	27.39 E
Abû Darbah	24	Hd	36.25N	38.15 E
Abû Dhabi (EN) = Abû Ẓaby	33	Hf	28.29N	33.20 E
Abû Ḥadrîyah	22	Hg	24.28N	54.22 E
Abû Ḥamad	24	Mi	27.20N	48.58 E
Abû Ḥammâd	31	Kg	19.32N	33.19 E
Abû Ḥarbah, Jabal- ▲	24	Dg	30.32N	31.40 E
Abû Ḥashâ'ifah, Khalîj- ◁	24	Ei	27.17N	33.13 E
Abuja	33	Bi	31.16N	27.25 E
Abû Jâbirah	31	Hh	9.10N	7.11 E
Abû Jifân	35	Dc	11.04N	26.51 E
Abû Kabîr	24	Lj	24.31N	47.43 E
Abû Kamâl	33	Dg	30.44N	31.40 E
Abukuma-Gawa ◁	24	Fc	34.27N	40.55 E
Abukuma-Sanchi ▲	29	Gb	38.06N	140.52 E
Abû Latt ●	29	Gc	37.20N	140.45 E
Abû Libdah, Khashm- ▲	33	Hf	19.58N	40.08 E
Abû Maṭâriq	35	Dc	10.58N	26.17 E
Abu Mendi	35	Fc	11.47N	35.42 E
Abumonbazi	36	Db	3.42N	22.10 E
Abû Muḥarrik, Ghurd- ◎	33	Ed	27.00N	30.00 E
Abû Mûsâ, Jazîreh-ye- ●	23	Id	25.52N	55.03 E
Abunã	53	Jf	9.42 S	65.23W
Abunã, Rio- ◁	54	Ef	9.41 S	65.23W
Abune Yosef ▲	35	Fc	12.09N	39.12 E
Abû Qîr	33	Dd	31.19N	30.04 E
Abû Qîr, Khalîj- ◁	33	Dd	31.20N	30.15 E
Abû Qumayyis, Ra's- ▶	24	Nj	24.34N	51.30 E
Abu Road	25	Ed	24.29N	72.47 E
Abû Sawmah, Ra's- ▶	33	Ee	26.51N	33.59 E
Abû Shanab	35	Dc	13.57N	27.47 E
Abu Simbel (EN) = Abû Sumbul ◻	33	Ee	22.22N	31.38 E
Abû Şukhayr	24	Kg	31.52N	44.27 E
Abû Sumbul = Abu Simbel (EN) ◻	33	Ee	22.22N	31.38 E
Abut Head ▶	62	Dc	43.06 S	170.15 E
Abû Tîj	33	Fd	27.02N	31.19 E
Abû Ṭurṭûr, Jabal- ▲	24	Cj	25.20N	30.00 E
Abû'Urûq	35	Fd	15.54N	30.27 E
Abuyemeda ▲	35	Fc	10.38N	39.43 E
Abû Zabad	35	Dc	12.21N	29.15 E
Abû Ẓaby = Abu Dhabi (EN)	22	Hg	24.28N	54.22 E
Abû Zanîmah	33	Fd	29.03N	33.06 E
Abwong	35	Ed	9.07N	32.12 E
Åby	8	Gf	58.40N	16.11 E
Abyaḍ	35	Dc	13.46N	26.28 E
Abyaḍ, Al Baḥr al-= White Nile (EN) ◁	30	Kg	15.38N	32.31 E
Abyaḍ, Al Baḥr al-= White Nile (EN) ③	35	Ec	12.40N	32.30 E
Abyaḍ, Ar Ra's al- ▶	23	Ee	23.32N	38.32 E
Abyaḍ, Jabal- ▲	35	Db	18.55N	28.40 E
Abyaḍ, Ra's al-= Blanc, Cape- (EN) ▶	30	He	37.20N	9.50 E
Abyâr Alî	24	Hj	24.25N	39.33 E
Abyâr ash Shuwayrif	33	Bd	29.59N	14.16 E
Åbybro	7	Bh	57.09N	9.45 E
Abydos ◻	33	Fd	26.11N	31.55 E
Abyei	35	Dd	9.36N	28.26 E
Abymes	24	Nd	36.02N	50.31 E
Acacias	51e Ab	16.16N	61.31W
Academy Gletscher ◙	54	Dc	3.59N	73.47W
Acadie ◻	41	Ib	81.45N	33.35W
Acaill/Achill ●	38	Me	46.00N	65.00W
Acajutla	9	Dh	54.00N	10.00W
Acalayong	49	Cg	13.36N	89.50W
Acámbaro	34	Ge	1.05N	9.40 E
Acandí	47	Dd	20.02N	100.44W
Acaponeta	54	Cb	8.31N	77.17W
Acaponeta, Rio- ◁	47	Cc	22.30N	105.22W
Acapulco de Juárez	48	Gf	22.20N	105.37W
Acará	39	Jh	16.51N	99.55W
Acaraú	54	Id	1.57 S	48.11W
Acaray, Rio- ◁	54	Gc	1.50N	57.40W
Acari, Serra- ▲	54	Jd	2.53 S	40.07W
Acari, Rio- [Braz.] ◁	55	Eg	25.29 S	54.42W
Acari, Rio- [Braz.] ◁	54	Gc	5.18 S	59.42W
Acarigua	55	Jb	16.00 S	45.03W
Acatenango, Volcán- ▲	54	Eb	9.33N	69.12W
Acatlán de Osorio	38	Jh	14.30N	91.40W
Acayucan	48	Ih	18.12N	98.03W
Accéglio	47	Fe	17.57N	94.55W
Ac̆c̆itau, Gora- ▲	14	Af	44.28N	7.00 E
Accomac	18	Cc	42.07N	60.31 E
Accra	44	Jg	37.43N	75.40W
Acebal	31	Gh	5.33N	0.13W
Acebuches	55	Bk	33.45 S	60.50W
Aceguá [Braz.]	48	Hc	28.15N	102.43W
Aceguá [Ur.]	55	Ej	31.52 S	54.09W
Aceh ②	55	Ej	31.52 S	54.12W
Acerenza	26	Cf	4.10N	96.50 E
Acerra	14	Jj	40.48N	15.56 E
Achacachi	14	Jj	40.57N	14.22 E
Achaguas	54	Eg	16.03 S	68.43W
Achaif, 'Erg- ▲	54	Eb	7.46N	68.14W
Achao	34	Ea	20.49N	4.34W
Achegour	56	Ff	42.28 S	73.30W
Acheng	34	Hb	19.03N	11.53 E
Acheux-en-Amiénois	27	Mb	45.32N	126.56 E
Achiet-le-Grand	12	Ed	50.04N	2.32 E
Achill/Acaill ●	12	Ed	50.08N	2.47 E
Achilleion	9	Dh	54.00N	10.00W
Achim ◁	15	Cj	39.34N	19.55 E
Achim	10	Fc	53.02N	9.01 E
Achterwasser ◻	35	Bb	15.53N	19.31 E
Açı Gölü ◎	10	Jb	54.00N	13.57 E
Ačinsk	24	Cd	37.50N	29.54 E
Acıpayam	22	Ld	56.17N	90.30 E
Acireale	24	Cd	37.25N	29.22 E
Aciş	14	Jm	37.37N	15.10 E
Ačisaj	15	Fb	47.32N	22.47 E
Ačit	18	Gc	43.33N	68.53 E
Açit-Nur ◎	17	Hh	56.48N	57.54 E
Acklins ●	27	Fb	49.30N	90.30 E
Acklins, The Bight of- ◁	38	Lg	22.25N	74.00W
Acle	49	Jb	22.30N	74.15W
Acobamba	9	Ni	52.38N	1.33 E
Acolin ◁	54	Df	12.48 S	74.34W
Aconcagua ②	11	Jh	46.49N	3.23 E
Aconcagua, Cerro- ▲	56	Ff	32.15 S	70.50W
Açor, Serra de- ▲	52	Jf	32.39 S	70.00W
Açôres = Azores (EN) ③	13	Ed	40.13N	7.48W
Açores, Arquipélago dos-= Azores (EN) ◻	31	Ee	38.30N	28.00W
Acorizal	55	Dc	15.12 S	56.22W
Acoyapa	49	Ii	11.58N	85.10W
Acquapendente	14	Fh	42.44N	11.52 E
Acquasanta Terme	14	Gh	42.46N	13.24 E
Acquasparta	14	Gh	42.41N	12.33 E
Acquaviva delle Fonti	14	Kj	40.54N	16.50 E
Acqui Terme	14	Cf	44.41N	8.28 E
Acraman, Lake- ◎	59	Hf	32.05 S	135.25 E
Acre ②	54	Ee	9.00 S	70.00W
Acre, Rio- ◁	52	Jf	8.45 S	67.22W
Acri	14	Kk	39.29N	16.23 E
Actéon, Groupe- ◻	57	Ng	21.20 S	136.30W
Actopan	48	Jg	20.16N	98.56W
Açu	54	Ke	5.34 S	36.54W
Acuña	56	Di	29.55 S	57.58W
Ada [Ghana]	34	Fd	5.47N	0.38 E
Ada [Ok.-U.S.]	43	Ih	34.46N	96.41W
Ada [Yugo.]	15	Dd	45.48N	20.08 E
'Adâd	35	Fd	7.03N	39.31 E
'Adâdle	35	Gd	9.45N	44.41 E
Adair, Bahía- ◁	48	Cb	31.30N	113.50W
Adair, Cape- ▶	42	Kc	71.31N	71.24W
Adal ▲	16	Kc	41.32N	4.52W
'Adale	35	He	2.46N	46.20 E
Ådalen ◁	8	Ga	63.20N	17.30 E
Adalselv ◁	8	Dd	60.04N	10.11 E
Adam, Mount- ▲	56	Hl	51.34 S	60.04W
Adamantina	55	Ge	21.42 S	51.04W
Adamaoua = Adamawa (EN) ▲	30	Ih	7.00N	15.00 E
Adamawa (EN) = Adamaoua ▲	30	Ih	7.00N	15.00 E
Adamello ▲	14	Ed	46.09N	10.30 E
Adams	45	Le	43.58N	89.49W
Adams, Mount- ▲	43	Cb	46.12N	121.28W
Adams Lake ◎	46	Fa	51.13N	119.33W
Adams River ◁	42	Ff	50.54N	119.33W
Adam's Rock ●	64d Ab	25.04 S	130.05W
Adamstown	58	Ng	25.04 S	130.05W
Adamuz	13	Hf	38.02N	4.31W
Adana	22	Ff	37.01N	35.18 E
Adapazarı	24	Db	40.46N	30.24 E
Adarama	35	Eb	17.05N	34.54 E
Adárán, Jabal- ▲	33	Ig	13.46N	45.08 E
Adare, Cape- ▶	66	Kf	71.17 S	170.14 E
Adavale	59	Ie	25.55 S	144.36 E
Adda [It.] ◁	5	Gf	45.08N	9.53 E
Adda [Sud.] ◁	35	Cd	9.51N	24.50 E
Ad Dab'ah	33	Ec	31.02N	28.26 E
Ad Dabbah	35	Eb	18.03N	30.57 E
Ad Dafinah	33	He	23.18N	41.58 E
Aḍ Ḍafrah ◎	24	Ok	23.25N	53.25 E
Ad Dahnâ' ◎	24	Nh	24.30N	48.10 E
Addala-Šuhgelmeer, Gora- ▲	16	Oh	42.20N	46.15 E
Aḍ Ḍâli'	33	Hg	13.42N	44.44 E
Ad Damazin	35	Ec	11.49N	34.23 E
Aḍ Ḍâmir	35	Eb	17.35N	33.58 E
Ad Dammâm	22	Hg	26.26N	50.07 E
Ad Dâr al Ḥamrâ'	23	Ed	27.19N	37.44 E
Ad Dawâdimî	23	Fe	24.28N	44.18 E
Ad Dawḥah = Doha (EN)	22	Hg	25.17N	51.32 E
Ad Dawr	24	Je	34.27N	43.47 E
Ad Dayr	23	Ee	22.50N	32.35 E
Ad Dibdibah ◎	24	Lh	28.00N	46.30 E
Aḍ Ḍiffah ◎	33	Ec	30.30N	25.30 E
Ad Dikâkah ◎	35	Ih	19.25N	51.30 E
Ad Dilam	23	Ge	23.59N	47.10 E
Ad Dindar ◁	35	Ec	13.20N	34.05 E
Ad Dir'îyah	24	Lj	24.48N	46.32 E
Ad Dissân ●	33	Hf	16.56N	41.41 E
Addis Zemen	35	Fc	12.05N	37.44 E
Ad Dîwânîya	23	Fc	31.59N	44.56 E
Addu Atoll ◉	21	Jj	0.25 S	73.10 E
Ad Du'ayn	35	Dc	11.26N	26.09 E
Ad Duwayd	24	Jg	30.13N	42.18 E
Ad Duwaym	35	Ec	14.00N	32.19 E
Adel [Ga.-U.S.]	44	Fj	31.18N	83.25W
Adel [Or.-U.S.]	46	Fe	42.11N	119.54W
Adelaide [Austl.]	58	Eh	34.56 S	138.36 E
Adelaide [Bah.]	44	Jm	25.00N	77.31W
Adelaide [S.Afr.]	37	Df	32.42 S	26.20 E
Adelaide Island ●	66	Qe	67.15 S	68.30W
Adelaide Peninsula ▶	42	Hc	68.05N	97.50W
Adelaide River	58	Ef	13.15 S	131.06 E
Adelay	35	Cd	7.07N	22.49 E
Adelboden	14	Bd	46.30N	7.33 E
Adèle Island ●	59	Cc	15.30 S	123.10 E
Adélie, Terre- ◻	66	Ie	67.00 S	139.00 E
Ademuz	30	Ad	40.04N	1.17W
Aden (EN) = Baladiyat 'Adan	22	Gh	12.46N	45.01 E
Aden, Gulf of- ◁	30	Lg	12.00N	48.00 E
Aden, Gulf of- (EN) = 'Adméd, Badyarada- ◻	30	Lg	12.00N	48.00 E
Adenau	12	Id	50.23N	6.56 E
Ader ◎	30	Hg	14.10N	5.05 E
Aderbissinat	34	Gb	15.37N	7.52 E
Adhan, Jabal- ▲	24	Oj	25.27N	56.13 E
Adh Dhahîbât	32	Jc	32.01N	10.42 E
Adh Dhayd	24	Pj	25.17N	55.53 E
Adhelfi ●	15	Gj	39.08N	23.59 E
'Adhrîyât, Jibâl- al- ◎	24	Jm	36.25N	26.37 E
Adi, Pulau- ●	49	Jg	30.25N	36.48 E
Adiaké	34	Ed	5.16N	3.17W
Adi Arkay	35	Fc	13.31N	38.00 E
Adicora	54	Ea	11.57N	69.48W
Adi Dairo	35	Fc	14.21N	38.12 E
Adigala	35	Gc	10.24N	42.18 E
Adige/Etsch ◁	5	Gf	45.10N	12.20 E
Adi Keyeh	35	Fc	14.16N	39.28 E
Adi Kwala	35	Fc	14.37N	38.51 E
Adilâbâd	25	Fe	19.40N	78.32 E
Adîrî	31	If	27.30N	13.16 E
Adirondack Mountains ▲	38	Le	44.00N	74.00W
Adis Abeba	31	Kh	9.01N	38.46 E
Adis Alem	35	Fd	9.03N	38.24 E
Adi Ugri	35	Fc	14.53N	38.49 E
Adıyaman	22	Fe	37.46N	38.17 E
Adjud	15	Hc	46.06N	27.10 E
Adjuntas	51a Bb	18.09N	66.43W
'Adméd, Badyarada- = Aden, Gulf of- (EN) ◻	30	Lg	12.00N	48.00 E
Admer, Erg d'- ◎	32	Ie	24.10 S	138.30W
Admiralty Bay ◁	40	Me	57.50N	134.30W
Admiralty Gulf ◁	51b Ba	10.00N	61.16W
Admiralty Inlet ◁	59	Fb	14.20 S	125.50 E
Admiralty Islands ◻	42	Jc	72.30N	86.00W
Admiralty Mountains ▲	58	Ff	2.10 S	147.00 E
Admont	66	Kf	71.45 S	168.30 E
Ado	14	Ic	47.34N	14.27 E
Ado Ekiti	34	Gd	6.37N	2.56 E
Adolfo Gonzales Chaves	34	Gd	7.38N	5.12 E
Adolfo López Mateos, Presa- ◎	55	Bh	38.02 S	60.06W
Adonara, Pulau- ●	26	Hh	8.20 S	123.10 E
Adra	48	Gc	25.05N	107.20W
Adrano	15	Mi	40.52N	29.07 E
Adrar	14	Im	37.40N	14.50 E
Adrar ▲	31	Ff	20.30N	13.30W
Adrar	31	Gf	27.54N	0.17W
Adrar ▲	30	Hf	25.12N	8.10 E
Adrar [Alg.] ③	32	Gd	27.00N	1.00W
Adrar [Mtna.] ③	32	Ee	21.00N	11.00W
Adré	35	Cc	13.28N	22.12 E
Adria	14	Ge	45.03N	12.03 E
Adrian	44	Ee	41.54N	84.02W
Adrianópolis	55	Hg	24.41 S	48.50W
Adriatic, Deti- = Adriatic Sea (EN) ◁	5	Hg	43.00N	16.00 E
Adriatico, Mar-= Adriatic Sea (EN) ◁	5	Hg	43.00N	16.00 E
Adriatic Sea (EN) = Adriatic, Deti- ◁	5	Hg	43.00N	16.00 E
Adriatico, Mar- ◁	5	Hg	43.00N	16.00 E
Adriatic Sea (EN) = Jadransko More ◁	5	Hg	43.00N	16.00 E
Aduard	12	Ia	53.15N	6.25 E
Adula ▲	14	Dd	46.30N	9.05 E
Adulis ◻	35	Fb	15.15N	39.37 E
Adur ◁	12	Bd	50.49N	0.16W
Adusa	36	Eb	1.23N	28.01 E
Adventure Bank (EN) ◻	14	Gm	37.20N	12.10 E
Adwa	31	Kg	14.10N	38.55 E
Adyča ◁	21	Pc	68.13N	135.03 E
Adygalah	20	Jd	62.57N	146.25 E
Adygeja, respublika	19	Eg	44.30N	40.05 E
Adžarskaja respublika	19	Ej	41.40N	42.10 E
Adzopé ③	34	Ed	6.15N	3.45W
Adzopé	34	Ed	6.06N	3.52W
Adzva ◁	17	Ic	66.36N	59.28 E
Aegean Sea (EN) = Aiyaion Pélagos ◁	5	Ih	39.00N	25.00 E
Aegean Sea (EN) = Ege Denizi ◁	5	Ih	39.00N	25.00 E
Aegina (EN) = Aíyina ●	15	Gl	37.40N	23.30 E
Aegviidu	8	Ke	59.17N	25.37 E
Aeon Point ▶	64g Bb	1.46N	157.11W
Aerfort na Sionainne/ Shannon ✈	9	Ei	52.43N	8.57W
Ære ●	8	Dj	54.55N	10.20 E
Æreskøbing	8	Dj	54.53N	10.25 E
Aerzen	12	Lb	52.02N	9.16 E
Afafi, Massif d'- ▲	34	Ha	22.15N	15.00 E
'Afak	24	Kf	32.04N	45.15 E
Afanasjevo	7	Mg	58.54N	53.16 E
Afareaitu	65e Fc	17.33 S	149.47W
Afars and Issas → Djibouti ①	31	Lg	11.30N	43.00 E
Aff ◁	11	Dg	47.43N	2.07W
Affollé ▲	30	Fg	16.55N	10.25W
Affrica, Scoglio d'- ●	14	Eh	42.20N	10.05 E
Afghanistan ①	22	If	33.00N	65.00 E
Afgooye	35	He	2.09N	45.07 E
'Afîf	23	Fe	23.55N	42.56 E
Afikpo	34	Gd	5.53N	7.55 E
Afipski	16	Kg	44.52N	38.50 E
Aflou	32	Hc	34.07N	2.06 E
Afmadow	35	Ge	0.29N	42.06 E
Afognak ●	40	Ie	58.15N	152.30W
Afonso Cláudio	54	Jh	20.05 S	41.08W
Afon Teifi ◁	9	Ij	52.06N	4.43W
Afon Tywi ◁	9	Jj	51.40N	4.15W
Afragola	14	Ij	40.55N	14.18 E
Afrêrâ, Lake- ◎	35	Gc	13.20N	41.03 E
Africa ◻	30	Ih	10.00N	22.00 E
African Islands ◻	30	Mi	4.53 S	43.24 E
Afșin	24	Gc	38.36N	36.55 E
Afsluitdijk ✶	11	La	53.00N	5.15 E
Afton	46	Je	42.44N	110.56W
Afuá	54	Hd	0.10 S	50.23W
'Afula	24	Ff	32.36N	35.17 E
Afyonkarahisar	22	Ff	38.45N	30.40 E
Agadem	31	Ig	16.50N	13.17 E
Agadez	31	Ig	16.58N	7.59 E
Agadez ②	34	Gb	19.45N	10.15 E
Agadir ③	32	Ge	30.25N	9.37W
Agadir	31	Fe	30.00N	9.00W
Agadyr	22	Je	48.17N	72.53 E
Agalega Islands ◻	30	Mj	10.24 S	56.30 E
Agalta, Sierra de- ▲	47	Se	85.00N	85.53W
Agana	58	Fc	13.28N	144.45 E
Agano-Gawa ◁	29	Gd	37.57N	139.07 E
Aga Point ▶	64c Bb	13.14N	144.43 E
Agapovka	17	Lj	53.18N	59.10 E
Agaro	35	Fd	7.53N	36.36 E
Agartala	22	La	23.49N	91.16 E
Agassiz Pool ◎	45	Mb	48.95N	95.58W
Agat	64c Bb	13.23N	144.39 E
Agat Bay ◁	64c Bb	13.23N	144.38 E
Agats	58	Ee	5.33 S	138.08 E
Agattu ●	40a Ab	52.25N	173.35 E
Agawa Bay	44	Eb	47.22N	84.33W
Agawa Bay ◁	44	Eb	47.20N	84.42W
Agboville ③	34	Ed	5.56N	4.13W
Agboville	34	Ed	6.00N	4.15W
Agdam	16	Oi	39.58N	46.57 E
Agdaš	16	Oi	40.38N	47.29 E
Agde	11	Jk	43.19N	3.28 E
Agde, Cap d'- ▶	11	Jk	43.16N	3.30 E
Agdz ◻	8	Cf	58.25N	8.15 E
Agedabia ◻	16	Nc	30.27N	47.28 E
Agematsu	29	Eb	35.45N	137.41 E
Agen	11	Gj	44.12N	0.38 E
Ageo	29	Fc	35.58N	139.35 E
Agepsta, Gora- ▲	16	Lh	43.32N	40.32 E
Agere Mariam	35	Fd	5.38N	38.15 E
Agerso ●	8	Di	55.10N	11.10 E
Agger ◁	12	Jd	50.48N	7.11 E
Aghireșu	15	Gc	46.53N	23.15 E
Agiabampo, Estero de- ◁	48	Dc	26.15N	109.15W
Ağın	24	Gc	38.57N	38.43 E

Index Symbols

①	Independent Nation	◻	Historical or Cultural Region	✕	Pass, Gap	◻	Depression	◻	Coast, Beach	◻	Rock, Reef	◁	Waterfall Rapids	◻	Canal	◻	Lagoon	◻	Escarpment, Sea Scarp	◻	Historic Site	◻	Port
②	State, Region	▲	Mount, Mountain	◻	Plain, Lowland	◻	Polder	◻	Cliff	◻	Islands, Archipelago	◻	River Mouth, Estuary	◻	Glacier	◻	Bank	◻	Fracture	◻	Ruins	◻	Lighthouse
③	District, County	▲	Volcano	◻	Delta	◻	Desert, Dunes	◻	Peninsula	◻	Rocks, Reefs	◎	Lake	◻	Ice Shelf, Pack Ice	◻	Seamount	◻	Trench, Abyss	◻	Wall, Walls	◻	Mine
④	Municipality	◻	Hill	◻	Salt Flat	◻	Forest, Woods	◻	Isthmus	◻	Coral Reef	◻	Salt Lake	◻	Ocean	◻	Tablemount	◻	National Park, Reserve	◻	Church, Abbey	◻	Tunnel
⑤	Colony, Dependency	▲	Mountains, Mountain Range	◻	Valley, Canyon	◻	Heath, Steppe	◻	Sandbank	◻	Well, Spring	◻	Intermittent Lake	◻	Sea	◻	Ridge	◻	Point of Interest	◻	Temple	◻	Dam, Bridge
◻	Continent	◻	Hills, Escarpment	◻	Crater, Cave	◻	Oasis	◻	Island	◻	Geyser	◻	Reservoir	◻	Gulf, Bay	◻	Shelf	◻	Recreation Site	◻	Scientific Station		
◻	Physical Region	◻	Plateau, Upland	◻	Karst Features	◻	Cape, Point	◉	Atoll	◁	River, Stream	◻	Swamp, Pond	◻	Strait, Fjord	◻	Basin	◻	Cave, Cavern	◻	Airport		

Aginskoje 20 Gf 51.03N 114.33 E
Agnew 59 Ee 28.01S 120.30 E
Agnibilékrou 34 Ed 7.08N 3.12W
Agnita 15 Hd 45.58N 24.37 E
Agno 14 Fe 45.32N 11.21 E
Agnone 14 Ii 41.48N 14.22 E
Ago 29 Ed 34.19N 136.50 E
Agoare 34 Fd 8.30N 3.25 E
Agogna 14 Ce 45.04N 8.54 E
Agön 8 Gc 61.35N 17.25 E
Agordat 31 Kg 15.32N 37.53 E
Agordo 14 Gd 46.17N 12.02 E
Agout 11 Hk 43.47N 1.41 E
Āgra 22 Jg 27.11N 78.01 E
Agrahanski Poluostrov 16 Oh 43.45N 47.35 E
Agramunt 13 Nc 41.47N 1.06 E
Agreda 13 Kc 41.51N 1.56W
Ağrı 23 Fb 39.44N 43.03 E
Ağrı Dağı = Mount Ararat (EN) 21 Gf 39.40N 44.24 E
Agričaj 16 Oi 41.17N 46.43 E
Agrigento 6 Hh 37.19N 13.34 E
Agrihan Island 57 Fc 18.46N 145.40 E
Agrij 15 Gb 47.15N 23.16 E
Agrinion 15 Ek 38.38N 21.25 E
Agropoli 14 Ij 40.21N 14.59 E
Agro Pontino 14 Gi 41.25N 12.55 E
Agryz 7 Mh 56.31N 53.01 E
Agto 41 Ge 67.37N 53.49W
Agua Brava, Laguna- 48 Gf 22.10N 105.32W
Agua Caliente, Cerro- 47 Cc 26.27N 106.12W
Aguachica 54 Db 8.18N 73.38W
Agua Clara 55 Fe 20.27S 52.52W
Aguada de Pasajeros 49 Gb 22.23N 80.51W
Aguadez, Irhazer Oua-n- 34 Gb 17.28N 6.26 E
Aguadilla 49 Nd 18.26N 67.09W
Aguadulce 49 Gi 8.15N 80.33W
Agua Fria River 46 Ij 33.23N 112.21W
Agua Limpa, Rio- 55 Gb 14.58S 51.20W
Aguán, Rio- 49 Ef 15.57N 85.44W
Aguanaval, Rio- 48 Hf 25.28N 102.53W
Aguapei 55 Cc 16.12S 59.43W
Aguapei, Rio- 56 Jb 21.03S 51.47W
Aguapei, Rio- 55 Cb 15.53S 58.25W
Agua Prieta 39 If 31.18N 109.34W
Aguaray 56 Hb 22.16S 63.44W
Aguaray Guazú, Rio- [Par.] 55 Dg 24.05S 56.40W
Aguaray Guazú, Rio- [Par.] 55 Dg 24.47S 57.19W
Aguasay 50 Eh 9.25N 63.44W
Aguascalientes 39 Ig 21.53N 102.18W
Aguascalientes [2] 47 Dd 22.00N 102.30W
Aguasvivas 13 Lc 41.20N 0.25W
Água Verde, Rio- 55 Da 13.42S 56.43W
Agua Vermelha, Représa- 56 Ja 19.53S 50.17W
Agudo [Braz.] 55 Fi 29.38S 53.15W
Agudo [Sp.] 13 Hf 38.59N 4.52W
Agueda 13 Fc 41.02N 6.56W
Águeda 13 Dd 40.34N 8.27W
Aguelhok 34 Fb 19.28N 0.51 E
Agüenit 32 Ee 22.11N 13.08W
Aguerguer 30 Ff 23.09N 16.01W
Aguijan Island 57 Fc 14.51N 145.34 E
Aguilar de Campóo 13 Hb 42.48N 4.16W
Aguilar de la Frontera 13 Hg 37.31N 4.39W
Aguilas 13 Kg 37.24N 1.35W
Aguililla 48 Hh 18.44N 102.44W
Aguirre, Rio- 50 Fh 8.28N 61.02W
Aguja, Cabo de la- 54 Da 11.21N 73.59W
Agujereada, Punta- 51a Ab 18.31N 67.08W
Agul 20 Ee 55.40N 95.45 E
Agulhas, Cape-(EN) = Agulhas, Kaap- 30 Jl 34.50S 20.00 E
Agulhas, Kaap- = Agulhas, Cape-(EN) 30 Jl 34.50S 20.00 E
Agulhas Negras, Pico das- 52 Lh 22.23S 44.38W
Agulhas Plateau (EN) 30 Jm 40.00S 26.00 E
Agung, Gunung- 26 Gh 8.21S 115.30 E
Aguni-Shima 27 Mf 26.35N 127.15 E
Agupey, Rio- 55 Di 29.07S 56.36W
Agustin Codazzi 54 Da 10.02N 73.15W
Ağva 24 Cb 41.05N 29.50 E
Ahaggar 30 Hf 23.10N 5.50 E
Ahaggar, Tassili-oua-n- 30 Hf 20.30N 5.00 E
Aha Hills 37 Cc 19.45S 21.10 E
Ahalcihe 19 Eg 41.38N 42.59 E
Ahalkalaki 19 Eg 41.25N 43.29 E
Ahangaran 18 Gd 40.57N 69.37 E
Ahar 23 Gb 38.28N 47.04 E
Ahat 15 Mk 38.39N 29.47 E
Ahaus 10 Cd 52.04N 7.00 E
Ahe Atoll 57 Mf 14.30S 146.18W
Ahenet, Tanezrouft-n- 32 He 22.00N 1.00 E
Ahini 20 Ff 53.18N 105.01 E
Ahipara 62 Ea 35.10S 173.09 E
Ahja Jõgi 8 Lf 58.19N 27.15 E
Ahlat 24 Jc 38.45N 42.29 E
Ahlen 10 De 51.45N 7.55 E
Ahmadābād 22 Jg 23.02N 72.37 E
Aḥmadī 24 Qi 27.56N 56.42 E
Ahmadnagar 25 Ee 19.05N 74.44 E
Ahmadpur East 25 Ec 29.09N 71.16 E
Ahmar 30 Lh 9.23N 41.13 E
Aḥmar, Al Baḥr al- = Red Sea (EN) 30 Kf 25.00N 38.00 E
Ahmeta 16 Nh 42.02N 45.11 E
Ahmetli 15 Kk 38.31N 27.57 E
Ahnet 32 He 24.35N 3.15 E
Ahoa 64h Ab 13.17S 176.12W
Ahome 48 Ee 25.55N 109.11W
Ahon, Tarso- 35 Bb 18.35N 18.18 E
Ahr 10 Df 50.33N 7.17 E
Ahram 24 Nh 28.52N 51.16 E
Ahrāmāt al Jīzah 33 Fd 29.55N 31.05 E
Ahrensburg 10 Gc 53.41N 10.15 E
Ahrgebirge 12 Id 50.31N 6.54 E
Ahse 12 Jc 51.42N 7.51 E
Ahsu 16 Pi 40.35N 48.26 E
Ähtäri 7 Ee 62.02N 21.20 E
Ähtärinjärvi 8 Kb 62.40N 24.05 E
Ähtävänjoki 7 Fe 63.38N 22.48 E
Ahtopol 15 Kg 42.06N 27.57 E
Ahtuba 5 Kf 46.42N 48.00 E
Ahtubinsk 6 Kf 48.14N 46.14 E
Ahtyrka 19 De 50.19N 34.55 E
Ahuacapán 49 Cg 13.55N 89.51W
Ahuazotepec 48 Jg 20.03N 98.09W
Ahunui Atoll 57 Mf 19.35S 140.28W
Åhus 7 Di 55.55N 14.17 E
Ahvāz 22 Gf 31.19N 48.42 E
Ahvenanmaa/Åland [2] 7 Ef 60.15N 20.00 E
Ahvenanmaa/Åland = Aland Islands (EN) 5 Hc 60.15N 20.00 E
Ahvenanmeri 8 Hd 60.00N 19.30 E
Aḥwar 23 Gg 13.31N 46.42 E
Aibag Gol 28 Ad 41.42N 110.24 E
Aibetsu 29a Cb 43.55N 142.33 E
Aichach 10 Hh 48.28N 11.08 E
Aichi Ken [2] 28 Ng 35.00N 137.07 E
Aiea 65a Db 21.23N 157.56W
Aigle 14 Ad 46.20N 6.59 E
Aigoual, Mont- 11 Jj 44.07N 3.35 E
Aiguá 55 El 34.12S 54.45W
Aigues 11 Kj 44.07N 4.43 E
Aigues-Mortes 11 Kk 43.34N 4.11 E
Aiguilles 11 Mj 44.47N 6.52 E
Aiguillon 11 Gj 44.18N 0.21 E
Aigurande 11 Hh 46.26N 1.50 E
Ai He 28 Hd 40.13N 124.30 E
Aihui (Heihe) 22 Od 50.13N 127.26 E
Aikawa 29 Fb 38.02N 138.14 E
Aiken 43 Ke 33.34N 81.44W
Ailao Shan 27 Hg 23.15N 102.20 E
Ailette 12 Fe 49.35N 3.10 E
Ailinginae Atoll 57 Hc 11.08N 166.24 E
Aillte an Mhothair/Moher, Cliffs of- 9 Di 52.58N 9.27W
Ailly-le-Haut-Clocher 12 Dd 50.05N 1.59 E
Ailly-sur-Noye 12 Ee 49.45N 2.22 E
Ailsa Craig 9 Hf 55.16N 5.07W
Ailuk Atoll 57 Hc 10.20N 169.56 E
Aim 20 Ie 58.48N 134.12 E
Aimogasta 56 Gc 28.33S 66.49W
Aimorés 54 Jg 19.30S 41.04W
Ain 11 Lh 46.10N 5.20 E
Ain 11 Li 45.48N 5.10 E
Ainazi/Ajnazi 7 Fh 57.52N 24.25 E
Ain Beida 32 Ib 35.48N 7.24 E
Ain Ben Mathar 32 Gc 34.01N 2.01W
Ain Bessem 13 Ph 36.18N 3.40 E
Ain Boucif 13 Pi 35.53N 3.09 E
Ain Defla 13 Nh 36.16N 1.58 E
Ain el Berd 13 Li 35.21N 0.31W
Ain el Hammam 13 Qh 36.34N 4.19 E
Ain el Turck 13 Li 35.44N 0.46W
Ain Galakka 35 Bb 18.05N 18.31 E
Ainos Óros 15 Dk 38.07N 20.40 E
Ain Oulmene 13 Ri 35.55N 5.18 E
Ain Oussera 13 Oi 35.27N 2.54 E
Ain Sefra 31 Ge 32.45N 0.35W
Ainsworth 45 Ge 42.33N 99.52W
Ain Taghrout 13 Rh 36.08N 5.05 E
Ain Tedeles 13 Mh 36.00N 0.18 E
Ain Témouchent 32 Gb 35.18N 1.08W
Ain Tolba 13 Ki 35.15N 1.15W
Aioi 29 Dd 34.49N 134.28 E
Aiquile 54 Eg 18.10S 65.10W
Air/Azbine 30 Hg 18.00N 8.30 E
Airabu, Pulau- 26 Ef 2.46N 106.14 E
Airai 64a Bc 7.21N 134.34 E
Airaines 12 De 49.58N 1.57 E
Airão 54 Fd 1.56S 61.22W
Airbangis 26 Cf 0.12N 99.23 E
Airdrie 46 Ha 51.18N 114.02W
Aire 11 Id 50.38N 2.24 E
Aire [Eng.-U.K.] 9 Mh 53.44N 0.54W
Aire [Fr.] 11 Ke 49.19N 4.49 E
Aire, Canal d'- 11 Id 50.38N 2.25 E
Aire, Isla del- 13 Qe 39.47N 4.16 E
Aire-sur-l'Adour 11 Fk 43.42N 0.16W
Air Force 42 Kc 67.55N 74.05W
Airolo 14 Cd 46.33N 8.35 E
Ais 63b Cb 15.26S 167.15 E
Aisch 10 Hg 49.46N 11.01 E
Aisén del General Carlos Ibáñez del Campo [2] 56 Fg 46.00S 73.00W
Aishihik 42 Dd 61.34N 137.30W
Ai-Shima 29 Bd 34.30N 131.18 E
Aisne [3] 11 Je 49.30N 3.30 E
Aisne 11 Ie 49.26N 2.50 E
Aisne à la Marne, Canal de l'- 11 Je 49.24N 3.55 E
Aïssa, Djebel- 32 Gc 32.51N 0.30W
Aitana, Pico- 13 Lf 38.39N 0.16W
Aitape 60 Ch 3.08S 142.21 E
Aitolikón 15 Ek 38.26N 21.21 E
Aitutaki Atoll 57 Lf 18.52S 159.45W
Ait Youssef ou Ali 13 Ii 35.09N 3.55W
Aiud 15 Gc 46.18N 23.43 E
Aiviekste 7 Fh 56.36N 25.44 E
Aiviekste/Ajviekste 7 Fh 56.36N 25.44 E
Aiwokako Passage 64a Bb 7.39N 134.33 E
Aix, Ile d'- 11 Eh 46.01N 1.10W
Aix-en-Provence 11 Lk 43.32N 5.26 E
Aixe-sur-Vienne 11 Hi 45.48N 1.08 E
Aix-les-Bains 11 Li 45.42N 5.55 E
Aiyaion Pélagos = Aegean Sea (EN) 5 Ih 39.00N 25.00 E
Aiyina 15 Gl 37.45N 23.26 E
Aiyina = Aegina (EN) 15 Gl 37.40N 23.30 E
Aiyinion 15 Fi 40.30N 22.33 E
Aiyion 15 Fk 38.15N 22.05 E
Aizawl 25 Id 23.44N 92.43 E
Aizenay 11 Eh 46.44N 1.37W
Aizpute/Ajzpute 7 Eh 56.45N 21.39 E
Aizubange 29 Fc 37.34N 139.49 E
Aizutakada 29 Fc 37.29N 139.48 E
Aizuwakamatsu 28 Of 37.30N 139.56 E
Ajā', Jabal- 24 Ii 27.30N 41.30 E
'Ajab Shīr 24 Kd 37.28N 45.54 E
Ajaccio 6 Gg 41.55N 8.44 E
Ajaccio, Golfe d'- 11a Ab 41.50N 8.41 E
Ajaguz 22 Ke 47.58N 80.27 E
Ajakli 20 Eb 70.13N 95.55 E
Ajan 20 Fe 59.38N 106.45 E
Ajan 20 Ie 56.27N 138.10 E
Ajanka 20 Ld 63.40N 167.30 E
Ajanta Range 25 Fd 20.30N 76.00 E
Ajat 17 Kj 52.54N 62.50 E
Ajax Peak 46 Id 45.20N 113.40W
Ajdābiyā 31 Je 30.46N 20.14 E
Ajdabul 19 Ge 52.42N 69.01 E
Ajdar 16 Ke 48.42N 39.13 E
Ajdar, Solončak- 18 Fd 40.50N 66.50 E
Ajdovščina 14 He 45.53N 13.53 E
Ajdyrlinski 17 Ij 52.03N 59.50 E
Ajhal 20 Gc 66.00N 111.32 E
Ajigasawa 28 Pd 40.47N 140.12 E
Aji-Shima 29 Gb 38.15N 141.30 E
Ajjer, Tassili-n- 30 Hf 25.30N 9.00 E
Ajka 10 Ni 47.06N 17.34 E
Ajke, Ozero- 16 Vd 50.55N 61.35 E
Ajkino 17 De 62.15N 49.56 E
'Ajlūn 24 Ff 32.20N 35.45 E
'Ajmah, Jabal al- 24 Fh 29.12N 34.02 E
'Ajmān 23 Id 25.25N 55.27 E
Ajmer 22 Jg 26.27N 74.38 E
Ajnaži/Ainaži 7 Fh 57.52N 24.25 E
Ajni 18 Ge 39.23N 68.36 E
Ajo 43 Ee 32.22N 112.52W
Ajo, Cabo de- 13 Ia 43.31N 3.35W
Ajon, Ostrov- 21 Sc 69.50N 168.40 E
Ajoupa-Bouillon 51h Ab 14.50N 61.08W
Ajsary 19 He 53.05N 71.00 E
Ajtos 15 Kg 42.42N 27.15 E
Aju, Kepulauan- 26 Jf 0.28N 131.03 E
'Ajūz, Jabal al- 24 Dj 25.49N 30.43 E
Ajviekste 7 Fh 56.36N 25.44 E
Ajviekste 7 Fh 56.36N 25.44 E
Ajzkraukle (Stučka) 7 Fh 56.36N 25.17 E
Ajzpute/Aizpute 7 Eh 56.45N 21.39 E
Akaba 34 Fd 7.57N 1.03 E
Akabira 28 Qc 43.30N 142.04 E
Akabli 32 Hd 26.42N 1.22 E
Akademika Obručeva, Hrebet- 20 Ef 51.30N 96.45 E
Akadomari 29 Fc 37.54N 138.24 E
Aka-Gawa 29 Fb 38.54N 139.50 E
Akagi-San 29 Fc 36.33N 139.11 E
Akaishi-Dake 29 Fd 35.27N 138.09 E
Akaishi-Sanmyaku 29 Fd 35.25N 138.10 E
Akajaure 7 Dc 67.42N 17.30 E
Aka-Jima 29b Ab 26.14N 127.17 E
Akaki 35 Fd 8.51N 38.48 E
Akala 35 Fb 15.38N 36.12 E
Akan 29a Db 43.08N 144.07 E
Akan-Gawa 29a Db 43.00N 144.16 E
Akar 24 Dc 38.38N 31.06 E
Akarnaniká Óri 15 Dk 38.45N 21.00 E
Akaroa 61 Dh 43.48S 172.59 E
Akasaki 29 Cd 35.31N 133.38 E
'Akasha East 35 Ea 21.05N 30.43 E
Akashi 28 Mg 34.38N 134.59 E
Akbaba Tepe 24 Hc 39.32N 39.33 E
Akbajtal, Pereval- 19 Hh 38.31N 73.41 E
Akbou 13 Qh 36.28N 4.32 E
Akbulak 19 Fe 51.03N 55.37 E
Akbura 18 Id 40.34N 72.45 E
Akçaabat 24 Hb 40.59N 39.34 E
Akçadağ 24 Gc 38.21N 37.59 E
Akçakale 24 Hd 36.41N 38.56 E
Akçakara Dağı 24 Ic 38.40N 40.52 E
Akçakoca 24 Db 41.05N 31.09 E
Akçaova [Tur.] 15 Mh 41.03N 29.57 E
Akçaova [Tur.] 15 Ll 37.30N 28.02 E
Akčatau 19 Hf 47.59N 74.02 E
Akçay 15 Ll 37.50N 28.15 E
Akçay 15 Mm 36.36N 29.45 E
Akchār 30 Ff 20.20N 14.28W
Ak Dağ [Tur.] 24 Ib 40.35N 41.46 E
Ak Dağ [Tur.] 23 Cb 36.32N 29.34 E
Akdağ [Tur.] 24 Gd 37.53N 37.56 E
Akdağ [Tur.] 24 Fb 40.57N 35.55 E
Akdağ [Tur.] 24 Cc 39.15N 28.49 E
Akdağ [Tur.] 15 Ll 37.42N 28.56 E
Akdağ [Tur.] 15 Mk 38.18N 29.58 E
Akdağ [Tur.] 15 Jk 38.33N 26.30 E
Ak Dağlar 24 Gc 39.30N 36.00 E
Ak Dağları 24 Ic 38.40N 40.12 E
Akdağmadeni 24 Fc 39.40N 35.54 E
Akdeniz = Mediterranean Sea (EN) 5 Hh 35.00N 20.00 E
Ak-Dovurak 20 Ef 51.10N 90.40 E
Akechi 29 Ed 35.18N 137.22 E
Ake Eze 34 Gd 5.55N 7.40 E
Akera 16 Oj 39.09N 46.48 E
Åkersberga 8 He 59.29N 18.18 E
Akershus [2] 7 Cf 60.00N 11.10 E
Aketi 31 Jh 2.44N 23.46 E
Akharnai 15 Gk 38.05N 23.44 E
Akhdar, al Jabal al- 21 Hg 23.30N 57.00 E
Akhḍar, Al Jabal al- 30 Je 32.30N 21.30 E
Akhḍar, Wādī al- 24 Gh 28.35N 36.35 E
Akhelóös 15 Ej 38.18N 21.10 E
Akhisar 23 Cb 38.55N 27.51 E
Akhmīm 33 Fd 26.34N 31.44 E
Akhtarin 24 Gd 36.31N 37.20 E
Aki 29 Ce 33.30N 133.53 E
Akiaki Atoll 61 Nc 18.30S 139.12W
Akiéni 36 Bc 1.11S 13.53 E
Akimiski 38 Kd 53.00N 81.20W
Akimovka 16 If 46.42N 35.09 E
Aki-Nada 29 Cd 34.05N 132.40 E
Åkirkeby 8 Fi 55.04N 14.56 E
Akita 22 Qf 39.43N 140.07 E
Akita Ken [2] 28 Pe 39.45N 140.20 E
Akjoujt 31 Fg 19.44N 14.22W
Akka 32 Fd 29.25N 8.15W
Akkanburluk 17 Mj 52.46N 66.35 E
'Akko 23 Ec 32.55N 35.05 E
Akkol 18 Hc 43.25N 70.47 E
Akköy 24 Bd 37.29N 27.15 E
Akkystau 19 Ff 47.17N 51.03 E
Aklavik 42 Dc 68.14N 135.02W
Aklé Mséiguilé 34 Eb 16.20N 4.45W
Akmenė/Akmene 8 Jh 56.14N 22.43 E
Akmenrags/Akmenrags 8 Ih 56.54N 20.55 E
Akmenrags/Akmenrags 8 Ih 56.54N 20.55 E
Akmeqit 27 Cd 37.05N 76.55 E
Akniste 8 Kh 56.10N 25.54 E
Akō 29 Dd 34.45N 134.23 E
Akobo 30 Kh 7.48N 33.03 E
Akobo 31 Kh 7.47N 33.01 E
Akola 22 Jg 20.44N 77.00 E
Akonolinga 34 He 3.46N 12.15 E
Akosombo Dam 34 Fd 6.16N 0.03 E
Akpatok 42 Kd 60.24N 68.05W
Akqi 27 Cc 40.50N 78.01 E
Ákra Ámbelos 15 Gj 39.56N 23.56 E
Ákra Kambanós 15 Hl 37.59N 24.45 E
Akranes 7a Ab 64.19N 22.06W
Ákra Spathí 15 Gl 37.27N 23.31 E
Åkrehamn 7 Ag 59.16N 5.11 E
Akritas, Ákra- = Akritas, Cape- (EN) 15 Em 36.43N 21.53 E
Akritas Cape- (EN) = Akritas, Ákra- 15 Em 36.43N 21.53 E
Akron [Co.-U.S.] 45 Ef 40.10N 103.13W
Akron [Oh.-U.S.] 43 Kc 41.04N 81.31W
Akrotiri 24 Ee 34.36N 32.57 E
Akša 20 Gf 50.17N 113.17 E
Aksaj 16 Oh 43.32N 46.55 E
Aksaj 19 Fe 51.13N 53.01 E
Aksaj 16 Kf 47.15N 39.52 E
Aksakal 15 Li 40.09N 28.07 E
Aksakovo 17 Gi 54.02N 54.09 E
Aksaray 23 Db 38.23N 34.03 E
Aksay 27 Fd 39.28N 94.15 E
Akşehir 23 Db 38.21N 31.25 E
Akşehir Gölü 24 Dc 38.30N 31.28 E
Akseki 24 Dd 37.02N 31.48 E
Aksenovo-Zilovskoje 20 Gf 53.00N 117.35 E
'Aks-e Rostam 24 Ph 28.23N 54.52 E
Aksoran, Gora 19 Hf 48.25N 75.30 E
Akstafa 16 Ni 41.13N 45.27 E
Akstafa 16 Ni 41.06N 45.28 E
Aksu [China] 22 Ke 41.09N 80.15 E
Aksu 19 He 52.28N 71.59 E
Aksu 18 Lb 45.34N 79.30 E
Aksu 19 Hf 46.20N 78.15 E
Aksu [Tur.] 15 Ll 37.56N 28.56 E
Aksu [Tur.] 24 Dd 36.51N 30.54 E
Aksuat 19 If 47.48N 82.50 E
Aksubajevo 7 Mi 54.52N 50.50 E
Aksu He 21 Ke 40.28N 80.52 E
Aksum 35 Fc 14.07N 38.44 E
Ak-Šyjrak 18 Ld 41.49N 78.44 E
Aktag 27 Dd 36.45N 84.40 E
Aktaš 20 Df 50.18N 87.44 E
Aktaš 19 Gh 39.55N 65.53 E
Aktau 19 He 50.16N 73.07 E
Aktau (Ševčenko) 22 He 43.35N 51.05 E
Aktau, Gora- 19 Gg 41.45N 64.30 E
Aktjubinsk 6 Le 50.17N 57.10 E
Aktjubinskaja Oblast [3] 19 Ff 48.00N 58.00 E
Ak-Tjuz 18 Kc 42.50N 76.07 E
Akto 27 Cd 39.05N 76.02 E
Aktogaj 19 Hf 47.01N 79.40 E
Akula 36 Db 2.22N 20.11 E
Akun 40a Eb 54.12N 165.35W
Akune 28 Kh 32.01N 130.11 E
Akure 34 Gd 7.15N 5.12 E
Akureyri 6 Eb 65.40N 18.06W
Akuseki-Jima 28 Jj 29.28N 129.33 E
Akutan 40a Eb 54.10N 165.55W
Akutan 40a Eb 54.08N 165.46W
Akyab Sittwe 22 Lg 20.09N 92.54 E
Akyazı 24 Db 40.41N 30.37 E
Akžajkyn, Ozero- 18 Fb 44.55N 67.45 E
Akžal 19 If 49.13N 81.30 E
Ål 8 Cd 60.38N 8.34 E
Alà, Monti di- 14 Dj 40.35N 9.16 E
Alabama 38 Kf 31.08N 87.57W
Alabama [2] 43 Je 32.50N 87.30W
Al'Abbāsīyah 35 Ec 12.10N 31.18 E
Alaca 24 Fb 40.10N 34.51 E
Alaçam Dağlari 15 Lj 39.20N 28.32 E
Alaçan 24 Fd 41.37N 35.37 E
Alaçati 15 Jk 38.16N 26.23 E
Aladağ 24 Jc 43.35N 39.20 E
Ala Dağ [Tur.] 24 Jb 40.11N 42.49 E
Ala Dağ [Tur.] 24 Ed 37.58N 32.04 E
Alādāgh, Kūh-e- 24 Qd 37.13N 57.30 E
Ala Dağları 24 Fd 37.55N 35.13 E
Aladža 16 Rj 39.21N 53.12 E
Aladža Manastir 15 Lf 43.17N 28.01 E
Alagir 16 Nh 43.01N 44.12 E
Alagna Valsesia 14 Be 45.51N 7.56 E
Alagnon 11 Ji 45.27N 3.19 E
Alagoas [2] 54 Ke 9.30S 36.30W
Alagoinhas 53 Mg 12.07S 38.26W
Alagón 13 Kc 41.46N 1.07W
Alagón 13 Fe 39.44N 6.53W
Ala Gou 27 Ec 42.42N 89.12 E
Alahanpanjang 26 Dg 1.05S 100.47 E
Alahärmä 7 Fe 63.14N 22.51 E
Al Aḥmadī 24 Mh 29.05N 48.04 E
Alaid, Vulkan 20 Kf 50.50N 155.33 E
Alajärvi 7 Fe 63.00N 23.49 E
Alajku 19 Hg 40.18N 74.29 E
Alajski Hrebet 21 Jf 39.45N 72.30 E
Alajuela [3] 49 Eh 10.30N 84.30W
Alajuela 47 Hf 10.01N 84.13W
Alajuela, Lago- 49 Hi 9.05N 79.24W
Alakol, Ozero- 21 Ke 46.05N 81.50 E
Alakurtti 7 Hc 66.59N 30.20 E
Alalakeiki Channel 65a Ec 20.35N 156.30W
Al 'Alamayn 31 Je 30.49N 28.57 E
Alalau, Rio- 54 Fd 0.30S 61.10W
Al Amādīyah 24 Jd 37.06N 43.29 E
Alamagan Island 57 Fc 17.36N 145.50 E
Al 'Amārah 23 Gc 31.50N 47.09 E
'Alam ar Rūm, Ra's- 24 Bg 31.22N 27.21 E
Alāmarvdasht 24 Oi 27.52N 52.34 E
Alamashindo 35 Ge 4.51N 42.04 E
Alamata 35 Fc 12.25N 39.37 E
Alameda 45 Ci 35.11N 106.37W
Alaminos 26 Gc 16.10N 119.59 E
Al 'Āmirīyah 24 Cg 31.01N 29.48 E
Alamito Creek 45 Dl 29.31N 104.17W
Alamitos, Sierra de los- 48 Hd 26.20N 102.15W
'Alāmo 35 Ge 4.23N 43.09 E
Alamo 46 Hh 37.22N 115.10W
Alamogordo 43 Fe 32.54N 105.57W
Alamos 47 Cc 27.01N 108.56W
Alamos, Sierra- 48 Gc 28.25N 105.00W
Alamosa 43 Fd 37.28N 105.52W
Al Anbār [3] 24 If 34.00N 42.00 E
Åland/Ahvenanmaa [2] 7 Ef 60.15N 20.00 E
Åland/Ahvenanmaa = Aland Islands (EN) 5 Hc 60.15N 20.00 E
Aland Islands (EN) = Ahvenanmaa/Åland 5 Hc 60.15N 20.00 E
Aland Islands (EN) = Åland/Ahvenanmaa 5 Hc 60.15N 20.00 E
Ålandsbro 8 Gb 62.40N 17.50 E
Ålandshav 8 Hd 60.00N 19.30 E
Alange 13 Ff 38.47N 6.15W
Alanje 49 Fi 8.24N 82.33W
Alanya 23 Db 36.33N 32.01 E
Alaotra, Lac- 37 Hc 17.30S 48.30 E
Alapaha River 44 Fj 30.26N 83.06W
Alapajevsk 19 Gd 57.52N 61.42 E
Alapli 24 Db 41.08N 31.25 E
Al 'Aqabah = Aqaba (EN) 23 Dd 29.31N 35.00 E
Al 'Aqabah aş Şaghīrah 24 Ej 24.14N 32.53 E
Al 'Arabīyah As-Su'ūdīyah = Saudi Arabia (EN) [1] 22 Gg 25.00N 45.00 E
Alarcón, Embalse de- 13 Je 39.45N 2.20W
Al 'Arīsh 33 Fc 31.08N 33.48 E
Al 'Armah 24 Lj 25.30N 46.30 E
Al Arṭāwīyah 24 Ki 26.30N 45.20 E
Alas, Selat- 26 Gh 8.40S 116.40 E
Al 'Aşab 24 Pk 23.20N 54.10 E
Alaşehir 24 Cc 38.21N 28.32 E
Al Ashkharah 23 Ie 21.47N 59.30 E
Al 'Āshūrīyah 24 Jg 31.02N 43.05 E
Alaska [2] 40 Ic 65.00N 153.00W
Alaska 38 Dc 65.00N 153.00W
Alaska, Gulf of- 38 Ed 58.00N 146.00W
Alaska Peninsula 38 Dd 57.00N 158.00W
Alaska Range 38 Ec 62.30N 150.00W
Alassio 14 Cf 44.00N 8.10 E
Alastaro 8 Jd 60.57N 22.51 E
Alat 18 De 39.26N 63.48 E
Alataw Shan 27 Cb 45.00N 80.00 E
Alataw Shankou = Dzungarian Gate (EN) 21 Ke 45.25N 82.25 E
Al 'Athāmīn 24 Jg 30.35N 43.40 E
Alatri 14 Hi 41.43N 13.21 E
Al 'Aṭrun 31 Jg 18.11N 26.36 E
Alatyr 7 Li 54.52N 46.36 E
Alatyr 19 Ee 54.50N 46.36 E
Álava [3] 13 Jb 42.50N 2.45W
Alava, Cape- 46 Cb 48.10N 124.43W
Alaverdi 19 Eg 41.08N 44.37 E
Alavijeh 24 Nf 33.03N 51.05 E
Alavo/Alavus 7 Fe 62.35N 23.37 E
Alavus/Alavo 7 Fe 62.35N 23.37 E
Al 'Awāliq 23 Gg 14.15N 46.30 E
Al 'Awāriq 35 Ha 20.25N 48.40 E
Al 'Awsajīyah 24 Ki 26.04N 44.08 E
'Ālayh 24 Ff 33.48N 35.36 E
Al 'Ayn [Sau.Ar.] 24 Hj 25.04N 38.06 E
Al 'Ayn [U.A.E.] 24 Pj 24.13N 55.45 E
Alayor 13 Qe 39.56N 4.08 E
Al 'Ayyāț 24 Dh 29.37N 31.15 E
Al A'ẓamīyah 24 Kf 33.23N 44.22 E
Alazani 16 Oi 41.03N 46.40 E
Alazeja 20 Kb 70.55N 153.40 E
Al'Azīzīyah 33 Bc 32.32N 13.01 E
Alazores, Puerto de los- 13 Hg 37.05N 4.15W
Alb [Ger.] 12 Ke 49.04N 8.20 E
Alb [Ger.] 10 Ei 47.35N 8.08 E
Alba 15 Gc 46.08N 23.30 E
Alba 14 Cf 44.42N 8.02 E
Alba Adriatica 14 Hh 42.50N 13.56 E
Al Bāb 24 Gd 36.22N 37.31 E
Albac 15 Fc 46.27N 22.58 E
Albacete 6 Fh 38.59N 1.51W
Albacete [3] 13 Kf 38.50N 2.00W
Al Badārī 33 Fd 26.59N 31.25 E
Alba de Tormes 13 Gd 40.49N 5.31W
Al Badi 33 Ie 22.02N 46.34 E
Al Bādī 24 Ie 35.56N 41.32 E
Ålbæk 8 Dg 57.36N 10.25 E
Ålbæk Bugt 8 Dg 57.35N 10.30 E
Al Bahrah 24 Lh 29.40N 47.52 E
Al Baḥr al Aḥmar [3] 35 Fb 19.50N 35.30 E
Al Baḥrayn 21 Hg 26.00N 50.30 E

Index Symbols

[1] Independent Nation
[2] State, Region
[3] District, County
[4] Municipality
[5] Colony, Dependency
Continent
Physical Region
Historical or Cultural Region
Mount, Mountain
Volcano
Hill
Mountains, Mountain Range
Hills, Escarpment
Plateau, Upland
Pass, Gap
Plain, Lowland
Delta
Salt Flat
Valley, Canyon
Crater, Cave
Karst Features
Depression
Polder
Desert, Dunes
Forest, Woods
Heath, Steppe
Oasis
Cape, Point
Coast, Beach
Cliff
Peninsula
Isthmus
Sandbank
Island
Atoll
Rock, Reef
Islands, Archipelago
Rocks, Reefs
Coral Reef
Well, Spring
Geyser
River, Stream
Waterfall Rapids
River Mouth, Estuary
Lake
Salt Lake
Intermittent Lake
Reservoir
Swamp, Pond
Canal
Glacier
Ice Shelf, Pack Ice
Ocean
Sea
Gulf, Bay
Strait, Fjord
Lagoon
Bank
Seamount
Tablemount
Ridge
Shelf
Basin
Escarpment, Sea Scarp
Fracture
Trench, Abyss
National Park, Reserve
Point of Interest
Recreation Site
Cave, Cavern
Historic Site
Ruins
Wall, Walls
Church, Abbey
Temple
Scientific Station
Airport
Port
Lighthouse
Mine
Tunnel
Dam, Bridge

Index Symbols

[1] Independent Nation · [2] State, Region · [3] District, County · [4] Municipality · [5] Colony, Dependency · [6] Continent · [7] Physical Region · Historical or Cultural Region · Mount, Mountain · Volcano · Hill · Mountains, Mountain Range · Hills, Escarpment · Plateau, Upland · Pass, Gap · Plain, Lowland · Delta · Salt Flat · Valley, Canyon · Crater, Cave · Karst Features · Depression · Polder · Desert, Dunes · Forest, Woods · Heath, Steppe · Oasis · Cape, Point · Coast, Beach · Cliff · Peninsula · Isthmus · Sandbank · Island · Atoll · Rock, Reef · Islands, Archipelago · Rocks, Reefs · Coral Reef · Well, Spring · Geyser · River, Stream · Waterfall Rapids · River Mouth, Estuary · Lake · Salt Lake · Intermittent Lake · Réservoir · Swamp, Pond · Canal · Glacier · Ice Shelf, Pack Ice · Ocean · Sea · Ridge · Strait, Fjord · Lagoon · Bank · Seamount · Tablemount · Shelf · Basin · Escarpment, Sea Scarp · Fracture · Trench, Abyss · National Park, Reserve · Point of Interest · Recreation Site · Cave, Cavern · Historic Site · Ruins · Wall, Walls · Mine · Church, Abbey · Temple · Scientific Station · Airport · Port · Lighthouse · Tunnel · Dam, Bridge

Al Maḩallah al Kubrá	33	Fc	30.58N	31.10 E
Al Maḩāriq	33	Fd	25.37N	30.39 E
Al Mahdīyah	32	Jb	35.30N	11.04 E
Al Mahdīyah [3]	32	Jb	35.35N	11.00 E
Al Maḩfīd	33	Ig	14.03N	46.55 E
Al Mahrah	23	Hf	16.56N	52.15 E
Al Maḩras	32	Jc	34.32N	10.30 E
Al Majarr al Kabīr	24	Lg	31.34N	47.10 E
Almajului, Munţii-	15	Fe	44.43N	22.12 E
Al Maks al Qiblī	13	Fe	24.35N	30.38 E
Almalyk	19	Gg	40.49N	69.38 E
Al Manādir	24	Pk	23.10N	55.10 E
Al Manāmah = Manama (EN)	22	Hg	26.13N	50.35 E
Al Manāqil	35	Ec	14.15N	32.59 E
Almanor, Lake-	46	Ef	40.15N	121.08W
Almansa	13	Kf	38.52N	1.05W
Almansa, Puerto de-	13	Lf	38.49N	0.58W
Al Manshāh	33	Fd	26.28N	31.48 E
Almansor	13	Df	38.56N	8.54W
Al Manşūrah	33	Fc	31.03N	31.23 E
Al Manzilah	24	Dg	31.09N	31.56 E
Almanzor, Pico de-	13	Gd	40.15N	5.18W
Almanzora	13	Jg	37.21N	2.08W
Al Ma'qil	24	Lg	30.33N	47.48 E
Al Maqnah	24	Fh	28.24N	34.45 E
Al Maqţa'	24	Pj	24.25N	54.29 E
Almar	13	Gd	40.54N	5.29W
Al Marāghah	24	Di	26.42N	31.36 E
Al Marsá	14	En	36.53N	10.20 E
Al Mary	31	Je	32.30N	20.54 E
Almaş	15	Gb	47.14N	23.19 E
Almas, Picos de-	52	Lg	13.33S	41.56W
Almas, Rio das-	54	If	14.35S	49.02W
'Al Maskād	35	Hc	11.18N	49.41 E
Al Maţarīyah	33	Fc	31.11N	32.02 E
Al Mawşil = Mosul (EN)	22	Gf	36.20N	43.08 E
Al Mayādīn	24	Ie	35.01N	40.27 E
Al Mayyāh	24	Ji	27.51N	42.47 E
Almazán	13	Jc	41.29N	2.32W
Al Mazār	24	Eg	31.23N	33.23 E
Almazny	20	Gd	62.19N	114.04 E
Almazora	13	Le	39.57N	0.03W
Al Mazra'ah	24	Fg	31.16N	35.31 E
Alme, Brilon-	12	Kc	51.27N	8.37 E
Almeida	13	Fc	41.16N	6.04W
Almeirim [Braz.]	54	Hd	1.32S	52.34W
Almeirim [Port.]	13	De	39.12N	8.38W
Al Mellem	35	Dd	9.49N	28.45 E
Almelo	11	Mb	52.21N	6.39 E
Almenara, Sierra de la-	13	Kg	37.35N	1.31W
Almendra, Embalse de-	13	Fc	41.13N	6.10W
Almendralejo	13	Ff	38.41N	6.24W
Almería [3]	13	Jg	37.10N	2.20W
Almeria	6	Fh	36.50N	2.27W
Almería, Golfo de-	13	Jh	36.46N	2.30W
Almetjevsk	19	Fe	54.54N	52.20 E
Al Metlaoui	32	Ic	34.20N	8.24 E
Älmhult	7	Dh	56.33N	14.08 E
Almijara, Sierra de-	13	Ih	36.55N	3.55W
Almina, Punta-	13	Gi	35.54N	5.17W
Al Minyā [Eg.]	24	Dh	29.45N	31.18 E
Al Minyā [Eg.]	31	Kf	28.06N	30.45 E
Al Miqdādīyah	24	Kf	33.59N	44.56 E
Almirante	49	Fi	9.18N	82.24W
Almirante Brown	66	Qe	64.53S	62.53W
Almirós	15	Fj	39.11N	22.46 E
Almiroú, Órmos-	15	Hn	35.23N	24.20 E
Almodôvar	13	Dg	37.31N	8.04W
Almodóvar del Campo	13	Hf	38.43N	4.10W
Almodóvar del Río	13	Gg	37.48N	5.01W
Almonte	13	Fg	37.15N	6.31W
Almonte	13	Fe	39.42N	6.28W
Almora	25	Fc	29.37N	79.40 E
Almoustarat	34	Fb	17.22N	0.07 E
Älmsta	8	He	59.58N	18.48 E
Al Mubarraz	23	Gd	25.25N	49.35 E
Al Mudawwarah	24	Fh	29.19N	35.59 E
Al Mudharī, Rujm-	24	Hf	32.45N	39.08 E
Al Mughayrā' [Sau.Ar.]	24	Gh	29.17N	37.41 E
Al Mughayrā' [U.A.E.]	24	Oj	24.05N	53.32 E
Al Muglad	31	Jg	11.02N	27.44 E
Al Muḩarraq	24	Ni	26.16N	50.37 E
Al Mukallā	22	Gh	14.32N	49.08 E
Al Mukhā	23	Fg	13.19N	43.15 E
Al Munastīr [3]	32	Jb	35.40N	10.50 E
Al Munastīr	32	Jb	35.47N	10.50 E
Almuñécar	13	Ih	36.43N	3.41W
Al Murabba'	24	Kj	25.43N	44.18 E
Almus	24	Gb	40.23N	36.55 E
Al Musannāh	24	Lh	29.02N	47.12 E
Al Muşawwarāt aş Şafrā'	35	Eb	16.25N	33.22 E
Al Musayjīd	24	Hj	24.05N	39.06 E
Al Musayyib	24	Kf	32.47N	44.18 E
Al Mustawī	24	Kj	25.55N	44.40 E
Al Muthanna	24	Kg	30.50N	45.20 E
Al Muwayh	33	He	22.45N	41.35 E
Al Muwaylih	24	Fi	27.41N	35.28 E
Alnön	8	Gb	62.25N	17.25 E
Alnwick	9	Lf	55.25N	1.42W
Ālō	8	Jd	60.20N	22.15 E
Aloândia	55	Hc	17.43S	49.29W
Alofi	58	Kf	19.03S	169.56W
Alofi, Ile-	57	Jf	14.19S	178.02W
Alofi Bay	64k	Bb	19.01S	169.56W
Aloja	7	Fh	57.44N	24.59 E
Along	25	Ic	28.10N	94.46 E
Alönnisos	15	Gj	39.13N	23.55 E
Alonsa	45	Ga	50.47N	99.00W
Alonso, Rio-	55	Gg	24.05S	51.35W
Alor, Kepulauan-	26	Hh	8.15S	124.30 E
Alor, Pulau-	21	Oj	8.15S	124.45 E
Alora	13	Hh	36.48N	4.42W
Alor Setar	22	Mi	6.07N	100.22 E
Alost/Aalst	11	Kd	50.56N	4.02 E
Alotau	60	Ej	10.31S	150.43 E
Aloysius, Mount-	59	Fe	26.00S	128.34 E
Alpen = Alps (EN)	5	Gf	46.25N	10.00 E
Alpena	43	Kb	45.04N	83.26W
Alpera	13	Kf	38.58N	1.13W
Alpes = Alps (EN)	5	Gf	46.25N	10.00 E
Alpes Bernoises/Berner Alpen = Bernese Alps (EN)	14	Bd	46.25N	7.30 E
Alpes Cottiennes	14	Af	44.45N	7.00 E
Alpes de Haute-Provence [3]	11	Lj	44.10N	6.00 E
Alpes Grées/Alpi Graie	14	Be	45.30N	7.10 E
Alpes Mancelles	11	Ff	48.25N	0.10W
Alpes Maritimes	14	Bf	44.15N	7.10 E
Alpes-Maritimes [3]	11	Nk	44.00N	7.10 E
Alpes Pennines/Alpi Pennine	14	Bd	46.05N	7.50 E
Alpes Valaisannes/Walliser Alpen	14	Bd	46.10N	7.30 E
Alpha Cordillera (EN)	67	Re	85.30N	125.00W
Alphen aan der Rijn	12	Gb	52.08N	4.42 E
Alphonse Island	30	Mi	7.00S	52.45 E
Alpi = Alps (EN)	5	Gf	46.25N	10.00 E
Alpi Apuane	14	Ef	44.05N	10.20 E
Alpi Aurine	10	Hi	47.00N	11.55 E
Alpi Carniche	14	Gd	46.40N	13.00 E
Alpi Cozie	14	Af	44.45N	7.00 E
Alpi Graie/Alpes Grées	14	Be	45.30N	7.10 E
Alpi Lepontine	14	Cd	46.25N	8.40 E
Alpi Liguri	14	Cf	44.10N	8.05 E
Alpi Marittime	14	Bf	44.15N	7.10 E
Alpine [Az.-U.S.]	46	Kj	33.51N	109.09W
Alpine [Tx.-U.S.]	43	Ge	30.22N	103.40W
Alpine [Wy.-U.S.]	46	Je	43.15N	110.59W
Alpi Orobie	14	Dd	46.00N	10.00 E
Alpi Pennine/Alpes Pennines	14	Bd	46.05N	7.50 E
Alpi Retiche = Rhaetian Alps (EN)	14	Dd	46.30N	10.00 E
Alpi Ticinesi	14	Cd	46.20N	8.45 E
Alpi Venoste	10	Gj	46.45N	10.55 E
Alprech, Cap d'-	12	Dd	50.42N	1.34 E
Alps (EN) = Alpen	5	Gf	46.25N	10.00 E
Alps (EN) = Alpes	5	Gf	46.25N	10.00 E
Alps (EN) = Alpi	5	Gf	46.25N	10.00 E
Al qa 'Āmiyāt	35	Hb	18.50N	48.30 E
Al Qābil	24	Pk	23.56N	55.49 E
Al Qaḑārif	31	Kg	14.02N	35.24 E
Al Qaḑimah	23	Ee	22.21N	39.09 E
Al Qādisīya [3]	24	Kg	31.50N	45.00 E
Al Qādisīya	24	Kg	31.42N	44.28 E
Al Qadmūs	24	Ge	35.05N	36.10 E
Al Qaffāy	24	Nj	24.35N	51.44 E
Al Qāhirah = Cairo (EN)	31	Ke	30.03N	31.15 E
Al Qāhirah-Imbabah	33	Fc	30.05N	31.13 E
Al Qāhirah-Mişr al Jadīdah	33	Fc	30.06N	31.20 E
Al Qā'iyah	24	Ki	26.27N	45.35 E
Al Qal'ah al Kubrá	14	Eo	35.52N	10.32 E
Al Qalībah	23	Ed	28.24N	37.42 E
Al Qāmishlī	23	Fb	37.02N	41.14 E
Al Qanţarah	33	Fc	30.52N	32.19 E
Al Qaryah ash Sharqīyah	33	Bc	30.24N	13.36 E
Al Qaryatayn	24	Ge	34.14N	37.14 E
Al Qaşab	24	Kj	25.18N	45.30 E
Al Qaşabāt	33	Bc	32.35N	14.03 E
Al Qa'şah	24	Ch	28.25N	28.56 E
Al Qash	35	Fb	16.48N	35.51 E
Al Qaşr	33	Ed	25.42N	28.53 E
Al Qaşrayn	32	Ib	35.11N	8.48 E
Al Qaşrayn [3]	32	Ib	35.15N	9.00 E
Al Qaţīf	24	Mi	26.33N	50.00 E
Al Qaţrānī	24	Gg	31.15N	36.03 E
Al Qaţrūn	33	Be	24.56N	14.38 E
Al Qay'īyah	23	Fe	24.18N	43.30 E
Al Qayrawān	32	Jb	35.41N	10.07 E
Al Qayrawān [3]	32	Ib	35.30N	10.00 E
Al Qayşūmah [Sau.Ar.]	24	Jh	29.11N	42.58 E
Al Qayşūmah [Sau.Ar.]	23	Gd	28.16N	46.03 E
Alqōsh	24	Jd	36.44N	43.06 E
Al Qubayyāt	24	Ge	34.34N	36.17 E
Al Qunayţirah	23	Ec	33.07N	35.49 E
Al Qunfudhah	23	Ff	19.08N	41.05 E
Al Qurayyah	24	Gh	28.45N	36.12 E
Al Qurnah	24	Lg	31.00N	47.26 E
Al Quşaymah	33	Fc	30.40N	34.22 E
Al Quşayr [Eg.]	31	Kf	26.06N	34.17 E
Al Quşayr [Syr.]	24	Ge	34.31N	36.35 E
Al Qūşīyah	33	Fd	27.26N	30.49 E
Al Quşūr	14	Co	35.54N	8.53 E
Al Quţayfah	24	Gf	33.44N	36.36 E
Al Quwārah	24	Ji	26.47N	43.28 E
Al Quwayr	24	Jd	36.03N	43.30 E
Al Quzah	35	Hb	15.06N	49.08 E
Als	8	Ci	55.00N	9.55 E
Alsace	11	Nf	48.30N	7.30 E
Alsace, Ballon d'-	11	Mg	47.50N	6.51 E
Alsasua	13	Jb	42.54N	2.10W
Alsdorf	12	Id	50.53N	6.10 E
Alsea River	46	Cd	44.26N	124.05W
Alsenz	12	Je	49.49N	7.51 E
Alsfeld	10	Ff	50.45N	9.16 E
Alsina, Laguna-	55	Am	36.52S	62.07W
Alsten	7	Cd	65.57N	12.36 E
Alsterån	8	Gh	56.55N	16.26 E
Alsunga	8	Ig	57.02N	21.28 E
Alta	7	Fb	69.58N	23.14 E
Altaelva	7	Fb	69.58N	23.23 E
Altafjorden	7	Fa	70.12N	23.06 E
Altagracia	54	Da	10.07N	71.14W
Alta Gracia	56	Hd	31.40S	64.26W
Altagracia de Orituco	50	Ch	9.52N	66.23W
Altai (EN) = Altay Shan	21	Le	46.30N	93.00 E
Altaj	22	Le	46.20N	96.17 E
Altaj	21	Kd	51.30N	90.00 E
Altajski	20	Df	51.58N	85.30 E
Altajskij Kraj [3]	20	Df	52.00N	82.30 E
Altamaha River	43	Ke	31.19N	81.17W
Altamira	53	Kf	3.12S	52.12W
Altamira, Cuevas de-	13	Ha	43.23N	4.05W
Altamira, Sierra de-	13	Ge	39.35N	5.10W
Altamirano	48	Mi	16.53N	92.09W
Altamont	46	Ee	42.12N	121.44W
Altamura	14	Kj	40.49N	16.33 E
Altamura, Isla de-	48	Ee	25.00N	108.10W
Altan Bulag	27	Jc	44.19N	113.28 E
Altan-Emel → Xin Barag Youqi	27	Kb	48.41N	116.47 E
Altan Xiret → Ejin Horo Qi	27	Id	39.31N	109.45 E
Altar	48	Db	30.43N	111.44W
Altar, Desierto de-	38	Hf	31.50N	114.15W
Altar, Rio-	48	Db	30.39N	111.55W
Altar de los Sacrificios	49	Be	16.28N	90.32W
Altata	47	Cd	24.38N	107.55W
Alta Verapaz [3]	49	Bf	15.40N	90.00W
Altavista	44	Hg	37.07N	79.18W
Altay	22	Ke	47.52N	88.07 E
Altay Shan = Altai (EN)	21	Le	46.30N	93.00 E
Altdorf	14	Cd	46.53N	8.40 E
Altea	13	Lf	38.36N	0.03W
Altena	10	De	51.18N	7.40 E
Altenberge	12	Jb	52.03N	7.28 E
Altenburg	10	If	50.59N	12.27 E
Altenglan	12	Je	49.33N	7.28 E
Altenkirchen (Westerwald)	12	Jd	50.42N	7.39 E
Alter do Chão	13	Ee	39.12N	7.40W
Altevatnet	7	Eb	68.32N	19.30 E
Altındağ	24	Ec	39.56N	32.52 E
Altinoluk	15	Jj	39.34N	26.44 E
Altinova	15	Jj	39.13N	26.47 E
Altıntaş	24	Dc	39.04N	30.07 E
Altinyayla	15	Mm	36.59N	29.33 E
Altkirch	11	Ng	47.37N	7.15 E
Altmark	10	Hd	52.40N	11.20 E
Altmühl	10	Hh	48.55N	11.52 E
Alto, Morro-	55	Ib	13.46S	46.50W
Alto, Pico-	54	Kd	4.20S	39.00W
Alto Alentejo	13	Ef	38.50N	7.40W
Alto Araguaia	54	Hg	17.19S	53.12W
Alto Coité	55	Eb	15.47S	54.20W
Alto Garças	55	Fc	16.56S	53.32W
Alto Longá	54	Je	5.15S	42.12W
Alto Molócuè	37	Fc	15.38S	37.42 E
Altomonte	14	Kk	39.42N	16.08 E
Alton [Eng.-U.K.]	12	Bc	51.08N	0.59W
Alton [Il.-U.S.]	43	Id	38.54N	90.10W
Altona, Hamburg-	10	Fc	53.33N	9.57 E
Altoona	43	Lc	40.32N	78.23W
Alto Paraguai	54	Gf	14.30S	56.31W
Alto Paraguay [3]	55	Ce	21.00S	59.00W
Alto Paraíso de Goiás	55	Ib	14.12S	47.38W
Alto Paraná [3]	55	Eg	25.00S	54.50W
Alto Parnaíba	54	Ie	9.06S	45.57W
Alto Purús, Rio-	54	De	9.34S	70.36W
Alto Rio Senguerr	56	Fg	45.02S	70.50W
Altos	54	Jd	5.03S	42.28W
Alto Sucuriú	55	Fd	19.19S	52.47W
Altötting	10	Ih	48.14N	12.41 E
Alto Uruguai, Serra do-	55	Fh	27.35S	53.40W
Altun Ha	49	Ce	17.50N	88.20W
Āltūn Kūpri	24	Ke	35.45N	44.09 E
Altun Shan	21	Kf	38.00N	88.00 E
Alturas	43	Cc	41.29N	120.32W
Alturitas	49	Ki	9.45N	72.25W
Altus	43	He	34.38N	99.20W
Altynkan	18	Hd	41.03N	70.43 E
Altynkul	18	Bc	43.07N	58.55 E
Alu	63a	Bb	7.05S	155.47 E
Al 'Ubaylah	35	Ia	21.59N	50.57 E
Al Ubayyiḑ	31	Kg	13.11N	30.13 E
Alucra	24	Hb	40.20N	38.46 E
Al 'Udaysāt	24	Ej	25.35N	32.29 E
Al Uḑayyah	35	Dc	12.03N	28.17 E
Alūksne/Aluksne	7	Gh	57.26N	27.01 E
Aluksne/Alūksne	7	Gh	57.26N	27.01 E
Aluksne Ozero	8	Lg	57.22N	27.10 E
Aluksne Ozero/Alūksnes Ezers	8	Lg	57.22N	27.10 E
Alūksnes Ezers/Aluksne Ozero	8	Lg	57.22N	27.10 E
'Alūla	35	Ic	11.58N	50.48 E
Al 'Ulá	23	Ed	26.37N	37.52 E
Al Umm	33	Hf	18.18N	40.45 E
Alunda	8	Hd	60.04N	18.05 E
Alupka	19	Dg	44.24N	34.03 E
Al'Uqaylah	33	Cc	30.16N	19.12 E
Al 'Uqaylāt	24	Ii	26.43N	41.43 E
Al 'Uqayr	24	Nj	25.39N	50.13 E
Al Uqşur = Luxor (EN)	33	Fd	25.41N	32.39 E
Al Urayq	24	Hh	29.00N	39.10 E
Al Urdun = Jordan (EN) [1]	22	Ff	31.00N	36.00 E
Al 'Urūq al Mu'Tariḑah	35	Ia	21.00N	54.00 E
Alūs	24	Ie	34.02N	42.26 E
Alušta	19	Dg	44.42N	34.20 E
Al 'Uthmānīyah	24	Mj	25.15N	49.22 E
Al'Uwaynāt	33	Bd	25.48N	10.33 E
Al 'Uwaynidhīyah	24	Gi	26.38N	36.05 E
Al 'Uwayqīlah	24	Jg	30.21N	42.14 E
Al 'Uyūn	24	Hj	24.33N	39.35 E
Al Uzayin	24	Ke	34.02N	44.20 E
Al 'Uzayr	24	Lg	31.19N	47.25 E
Alva	43	Hd	36.48N	98.40W
Alva	13	Dd	40.18N	8.15W
Alvand, Kūh-e-	24	Me	34.41N	48.28 E
Älvängen	8	Eg	57.56N	12.09 E
Alvaro Obregón, Presa	48	Ed	28.00N	109.45W
Alvdal	7	Ce	62.07N	10.39 E
Älvdalen	8	Ed	60.30N	13.00 E
Älvdalen	7	Df	61.14N	14.02 E
Alvear	55	Di	29.06S	56.33W
Alvelos, Serra de-	13	De	39.55N	8.01W
Alvesta	7	Dh	56.54N	14.33 E
Alvik	8	Gb	62.25N	17.24 E
Ålvik	7	Bf	60.26N	6.26 E
Alvin	45	Il	29.25N	95.15W
Älvkarleby	7	Df	60.34N	17.27 E
Alvord Valley	46	Fe	42.45N	118.25W
Alvoy	8	Ad	60.35N	4.50 E
Älvros	8	Fb	62.03N	14.39 E
Älvsborg [2]	7	Cg	58.00N	12.30 E
Älvsbyn	7	Ed	65.40N	21.00 E
Al Wāḩidī	23	Gg	14.20N	47.50 E
Al Wajh	22	Fg	26.14N	36.28 E
Al Wakrah	24	Nj	25.10N	51.36 E
Al Wannān	24	Mi	26.55N	48.24 E
Alwar	25	Fc	27.34N	76.36 E
Al Warī'ah	24	Li	27.50N	47.29 E
Al Wāsiţah	33	Fd	29.20N	31.12 E
Al Waslātīyah	14	Do	35.51N	9.35 E
Al Watī'ah	33	Bc	32.28N	11.46 E
Al Wazz	35	Eb	15.01N	30.10 E
Al Widyān	21	Gf	31.10N	40.45 E
Alxa Youqi (Ehen Hudag)	27	Hd	39.12N	101.40 E
Alxa Zuoqi (Bayan Hot)	27	Id	38.50N	105.32 E
Al Yaman = Yemen (EN)	22	Gh	15.00N	44.00 E
Al Yaman ad Dīmuqrāţīyah → Yemen (EN)	22	Gh	15.00N	44.00 E
Alyangula	59	Hb	13.50S	136.25 E
Alygdžer	20	Ef	53.38N	98.16 E
Alymka	17	Ng	59.01N	68.40 E
Alytus/Alitus	19	Ce	54.25N	24.08 E
Alz	10	Ih	48.10N	12.48 E
Alzamaj	20	Ee	55.33N	98.39 E
Alzey	10	Eg	49.45N	8.07 E
Alzira/Alcira	13	Le	39.09N	0.26W
Amachkalo Ahzar	34	Fb	15.30N	3.20 E
Amacuro, Rio-	54	Fb	8.32N	60.28W
Amada	33	Fe	22.45N	32.10 E
Amadeus, Lake-	57	Eg	24.50S	130.45 E
Amadi [Sud.]	35	Ed	5.31N	30.20 E
Amadi [Zaire]	36	Eb	3.35N	26.47 E
Amadjuak Lake	42	Kd	64.55N	71.00W
Amadora	13	Cf	38.45N	9.14W
Amadror	32	Ie	24.50N	6.25 E
Amadror	32	Id	26.00N	5.21W
Amagasaki	29	Dd	34.42N	135.25 E
Amager	8	Ei	55.35N	12.35 E
Amagi [Jap.]	29	Be	33.26N	130.39 E
Amagi [Jap.]	29b	Bb	27.47N	128.52 E
Amagi-San	29	Fd	34.51N	139.00 E
Amaha	29	Fd	35.13N	139.51 E
Amahai	26	Ig	3.20S	128.55 E
Amain, Monts d'-	11	Gf	48.39N	0.20 E
Amajac, Rio-	48	Jg	21.15N	98.46W
Amakusa-Nada	28	Jh	32.25N	129.40 E
Amakusa-Shotō	28	Kh	32.22N	130.12 E
Amal	33	Dd	29.25N	21.10 E
Åmål	7	Cg	59.03N	12.42 E
Amalfi	14	Ij	40.38N	14.36 E
Amaliás	15	El	37.48N	21.21 E
Amalner	25	Fd	21.03N	75.04 E
Amambai	54	Gh	23.05S	55.13W
Amambai, Rio-	55	Ff	23.22S	53.56W
Amambai, Serra de-	55	Ef	23.10S	55.30W
Amambay [3]	55	Df	23.00S	56.00W
Amami Islands (EN) = Amami-Shotō	21	Og	28.16N	129.21 E
Amami-Ō-Shima	27	Mf	28.15N	129.20 E
Amami-Shotō = Amami Islands (EN)	21	Og	28.16N	129.21 E
Amån	8	Fc	61.12N	14.45 E
Amanā, Lago-	54	Fd	2.35S	64.40W
Amana, Rio-	50	Eh	9.45N	62.39W
Amanave	65c	Cb	14.19S	170.49W
Amangeldy	19	Ge	50.10N	65.13 E
Amankaragaj	17	Lj	52.27N	64.08 E
Amantea	14	Kk	39.07N	16.08 E
Amanu Atoll	57	Mf	17.48S	140.46W
Amanzimtoti	37	Ef	30.05S	30.53 E
Amapá	53	Ke	2.03N	50.48W
Amapá	54	Hc	1.30N	52.00W
Amapala	49	Dg	13.17N	87.40W
Amara	15	Ke	44.37N	27.19 E
Amara	30	Kg	11.30N	37.45 E
Amaradia	15	Ge	44.22N	23.43 E
'Amara East	35	Ea	20.48N	30.23 E
Amarante [Braz.]	54	Je	6.14S	42.50W
Amarante [Port.]	13	Dc	41.16N	8.05W
Amaranth	45	Ga	50.36N	98.43W
Amargosa	46	Gh	36.18N	116.25W
Amargosa Desert	46	Gh	36.40N	116.30W
Amargosa Range	46	Gh	36.30N	116.45W
Amargosa River	46	Gh	36.13N	116.48W
Amarillo	39	If	35.13N	101.49W
Amário	15	Hn	35.14N	24.39 E
Amarume	29	Fb	38.50N	139.54 E
Amasra	24	Eb	41.45N	32.34 E
Amasya	23	Ea	40.39N	35.51 E
Amathus	24	Ee	34.42N	33.08 E
Amatique, Bahia de-	49	Cf	15.55N	88.45W
Amatlán de Cañas	48	Gg	20.52N	104.27W
Amatrice	14	Hh	42.38N	13.17 E
Amaurilandia	55	Ff	22.10S	52.38W
Amay	12	Hd	50.33N	5.19 E
Amazar	20	Hf	53.54N	120.57 E
Amazon (EN) = Amazonas, Rio- (Solimões)	52	Lf	0.10S	49.00W
Amazon, Mouths of the- (EN)	52	Le	0.10S	49.00W
Amazonas [Braz.] [2]	54	Fd	5.00S	63.00W
Amazonas [Col.] [2]	54	Dd	1.00S	72.00W
Amazonas [Peru] [2]	54	Ce	5.00S	77.00W
Amazonas [Ven.] [2]	54	Ec	3.30N	66.00W
Amazonas, Rio- = Amazon (EN)	52	Lf	0.10S	49.00W
Amazonas, Rio- (Solimões) = Amazon (EN)	52	Lf	0.10S	49.00W
Amazon Cone (EN)	52	Ke	4.30N	52.00W
Amba Ferit	35	Fc	10.55N	38.55 E
Ambāla	25	Fb	30.21N	76.50 E
Ambalangoda	25	Gg	6.14N	80.03 E
Ambalavao	37	Hd	21.50S	46.57 E
Ambam	34	He	2.23N	11.17 E
Ambanja	37	Hb	13.39S	48.27 E
Ambarčik	22	Sc	69.39N	162.20 E
Ambarès-et-Lagrave	11	Fj	44.55N	0.29W
Ambargasta, Salinas de-	56	Hc	29.20S	64.30W
Ambarny	19	Db	65.54N	33.41 E
Ambasamudram	25	Fg	8.42N	77.28 E
Ambato	53	If	1.15S	78.37W
Ambato-Boéni	37	Hc	16.28S	46.40 E
Ambatofinandrahana	37	Hd	20.33S	46.47 E
Ambatolampy	37	Hc	19.23S	47.25 E
Ambatondrazaka	31	Lj	17.48S	48.26 E
Ambatosoratra	37	Hc	17.36S	48.32 E
Ambelau, Pulau-	26	Ig	3.51S	127.12 E
Amberg	10	Hg	49.27N	11.52 E
Ambergris Cay	49	Dd	18.03N	87.56W
Ambergris Cays	49	Lc	21.18N	71.37W
Ambérieu-en-Bugey	11	Li	45.57N	5.21 E
Amberley [Eng.-U.K.]	12	Bd	50.55N	0.32W
Amberley [N.Z.]	62	Ee	43.09S	172.45 E
Ambert	11	Ji	45.33N	3.45 E
Ambikāpur	25	Gd	23.07N	83.12 E
Ambila	37	Hd	21.58S	47.59 E
Ambilobe	37	Hb	13.11S	49.03 E
Ambitle	63a	Aa	4.05S	153.40 E
Ambjörby	8	Ed	60.30N	13.10 E
Ambla	8	Ke	59.10N	25.44 E
Amblève	11	Ld	50.28N	5.36 E
Amblève/Amel	12	Id	50.21N	6.10 E
Ambo	54	Cf	10.07S	76.10W
Amboasary Sud	37	He	25.01S	46.23 E
Ambodifototra	37	Hc	16.58S	49.52 E
Ambohimahasoa	37	Hd	21.08S	47.12 E
Ambohimanarina	37	He	18.52S	47.29 E
Ambohitralanana	37	Ic	15.15S	50.28 E
Amboise	11	Gg	47.25N	0.59 E
Ambon	58	De	3.43S	128.12 E
Ambon, Pulau-	26	Ig	3.40S	128.10 E
Ambongo	37	Gc	16.50S	45.00 E
Amboseli, Lake-	36	Gc	2.37S	37.08 E
Ambositra	31	Lk	20.30S	47.14 E
Ambovombe	37	He	25.09S	46.06 E
Ambre, Cap d'- = Ambre, Cape d'-(EN)	30	Lj	11.57S	49.17 E
Ambre, Cape d'-(EN) = Ambre, Cap d'-	30	Lj	11.57S	49.17 E
Ambre, Montagne d-'	37	Hb	12.30S	49.10 E
Ambriz	31	Ii	7.50S	13.08 E
Ambrolauri	16	Mh	42.31N	43.05 E
Ambrym, Ile-	57	Hf	16.15S	168.07 E
Ambunti	60	Ch	4.14S	142.50 E
Āmbūr	25	Ff	12.47N	78.42 E
Amchitka	40a	Bb	51.30N	179.00 E
Amchitka Pass	40a	Cb	51.30N	179.30W
Am Dafok	35	Cc	10.28N	23.17 E
Am Dam	35	Cc	12.46N	20.29 E
Amded	32	He	22.10N	3.15 E
Amderma	19	Gb	69.45N	61.39 E
Am Djéména	35	Bc	13.06N	17.19 E
Amdo	27	Fe	32.29N	91.47 E
Ameca	47	Dd	20.33N	104.02W
Ameca, Rio-	48	Gg	20.41N	105.18W
Amel/Amblève	12	Id	50.21N	6.09 E
Ameland	12	Ha	53.26N	5.48 E
Ameland	11	La	53.25N	5.45 E
Ameland- Nes	12	Ha	53.26N	5.48 E
Amelia Island	44	Gj	30.37N	81.27W
Amélie-les-Bains-Palaloa	11	Il	42.28N	2.40 E
Amendola	14	Hh	42.59N	13.21 E
Amendolara	14	Kk	39.57N	16.35 E
'Āmerī	24	Nh	28.30N	51.05 E
Americana	55	If	22.45S	47.20W
American Falls	46	Ie	42.47N	112.51W
American Falls Reservoir	46	Ie	43.00N	113.00W
American Fork	46	Jf	40.23N	111.48W
American Highland	66	Ff	72.30S	78.00 E
American Samoa [5]	58	Kf	14.50S	170.00W
Americus	43	Ke	32.04N	84.14W
Amersfoort	11	Lb	52.09N	5.24 E
Amery Ice Shelf	66	Fe	69.30S	72.00 E
Ames	43	Ic	42.02N	93.37W
Amfilokhía	15	Ek	38.52N	21.10 E
Ámfissa	15	Fk	38.32N	22.23 E
Amfreville-la-Campagne	12	Ce	49.13N	0.57 E
Amga	20	Id	60.52N	131.50 E
Amga	21	Pc	62.40N	134.59 E
Amgalang → Xin Barag Zuoqi	27	Kb	48.13N	118.14 E
Am Géréda	35	Cc	12.52N	21.10 E
Amgu	28	Nb	45.51N	137.41 E
Amguema	20	Nc	68.03N	177.55W
Amguid	32	Id	26.30N	5.36 E
Amguid	31	Hf	26.26N	5.22 E
Amgun	21	Pd	52.56N	139.40 E
Amherst	42	Lg	45.49N	64.14W
Amherst, Mount-	59	Fc	18.11S	126.59 E
Amherst Island	44	Ic	44.12N	76.42W
Amiata, Monte-	14	Fh	42.53N	11.37 E
Amiens	6	Gf	49.54N	2.18 E
Āmij, Wādī-	24	If	33.48N	41.46 E
Amik Gölü	24	Gd	36.22N	36.17 E
Amik Ölü	24	Gd	36.15N	36.12 E
Amili	25	Jc	28.26N	95.52 E
Amindivi Islands	25	Ef	11.23N	72.23 E
Aminuis	37	Bd	23.43S	19.21 E
'Āmir, Ra's-	30	Je	32.57N	21.43 E
Amirante Islands	30	Mi	6.00S	53.10 E
Amirante Trench (EN)	37	Bb	6.00S	52.30 E
Amisk Lake	42	Hf	54.35N	102.15W
Amistad, Presa de la-	45	Fl	28.34N	101.15W
Amistad Reservoir	43	Gf	28.34N	101.15W
Amite	45	Kk	30.44N	90.30W
Amlekhganj	25	Gc	27.17N	84.59 E
Amlia	40a	Db	52.06N	173.30W
Amlwch	9	Ih	53.25N	4.20W

Index Symbols

[1] Independent Nation	Historical or Cultural Region	Pass, Gap	Depression	Coast, Beach	Rock, Reef	Waterfall Rapids	Canal	Lagoon	Escarpment, Sea Scarp	Historic Site	Port
[2] State, Region	Mount, Mountain	Plain, Lowland	Polder	Cliff	Islands, Archipelago	River Mouth, Estuary	Glacier	Bank	Fracture	Ruins	Lighthouse
[3] District, County	Volcano	Delta	Desert, Dunes	Peninsula	Rocks, Reefs	Lake	Ice Shelf, Pack Ice	Seamount	Trench, Abyss	Wall, Walls	Mine
[4] Municipality	Hill	Salt Flat	Forest, Woods	Isthmus	Coral Reef	Salt Lake	Ocean	Tablemount	National Park, Reserve	Church, Abbey	Tunnel
[5] Colony, Dependency	Mountains, Mountain Range	Valley, Canyon	Heath, Steppe	Sandbank	Well, Spring	Intermittent Lake	Sea	Ridge	Point of Interest	Temple	Dam, Bridge
Continent	Hills, Escarpment	Crater, Cave	Oasis	Island	Geyser	Reservoir	Gulf, Bay	Shelf	Recreation Site	Scientific Station	
Physical Region	Plateau, Upland	Karst Features	Cape, Point	Atoll	River, Stream	Swamp, Pond	Strait, Fjord	Basin	Cave, Cavern	Airport	

'Amm Adām	35	Fb	16.22N	36.09 E
'Ammān	22	Ff	31.57N	35.56 E
Ammanford	9	Jj	51.48N	3.59W
Ammarnäs	7	Dd	65.58N	16.12 E
Åmmeberg	8	Ff	58.52N	15.00 E
Ammer	10	Hi	47.57N	11.08 E
Ammerån	8	Ga	63.09N	16.13 E
Ammerland	10	Dc	53.15N	8.00 E
Ammersee	10	Hi	48.00N	11.08 E
Ammi-Moussa	13	Ni	35.52N	1.07 E
Ammokhostos → Famagusta (EN)	23	Dc	35.07N	33.57 E
Amnja	17	Me	63.45N	67.07 E
Amnok-kang	27	Ld	39.55N	124.20 E
Āmol	23	Hb	36.23N	52.20 E
Amolar	55	Dd	18.01S	57.30W
Amorgós	15	Im	36.50N	25.53 E
Amorgós	15	Im	36.50N	25.59 E
Amorinópolis	55	Gc	16.36S	51.08W
Amory	45	Lj	33.59N	88.29W
Amos	42	Jg	48.34N	78.07W
Amot [Nor.]	8	Be	59.35N	8.00 E
Amot [Nor.]	7	Bg	59.54N	9.54 E
Amotfors	8	Ee	59.46N	12.22 E
Amoucha	13	Rh	36.23N	5.25 E
Amouliani	15	Gi	40.20N	23.55 E
Amour, Djebel-	32	Hc	33.45N	1.45 E
Amourj	32	Ff	16.10N	7.35W
Ampanihy	37	Gd	24.40S	44.45 E
Amparafaravola	37	Hc	17.36S	48.12 E
Amparo	55	If	22.42S	46.47W
Amper	10	Hh	48.10N	11.50 E
Ampère Seamount (EN)	5	Eh	35.05N	12.13W
Amphitrite Point	46	Cb	48.56N	125.35W
Amposta	13	Md	40.43N	0.35 E
Ampthill	12	Bb	52.02N	0.29W
Ampurdán/L'Empordà	13	Ob	42.12N	2.45 E
Ampurias	13	Pb	42.10N	3.05 E
Amqui	44	Na	48.28N	67.26W
'Amrān	23	Ff	15.41N	43.55 E
Amrāvati	22	Jg	20.56N	77.45 E
Am-Raya	35	Bc	14.05N	16.30 E
Amritsar	22	Jf	31.35N	74.53 E
Amrum	8	Cj	54.40N	8.20 E
Amsaga	32	Ee	20.07N	14.10W
Amsittene, Jebel-	32	Fc	31.11N	9.40W
Amstel	12	Gb	52.22N	4.56 E
Amstelveen	12	Gb	52.18N	4.53 E
Amsterdam	30	Ol	37.57S	77.40 E
Amsterdam [Neth.]	6	Ge	52.22N	4.54 E
Amsterdam [N.Y.-U.S.]	44	Jd	42.56N	74.12W
Amsterdam-Rijnkanaal	12	Hc	51.57N	5.25 E
Amstetten	14	Ib	48.07N	14.52 E
Am Timan	31	Jg	11.02N	20.17 E
Amūd, Jabal al-	23	Ec	30.59N	39.20 E
Āmūdā	24	Id	37.05N	40.54 E
Amu-Darja	18	Ef	37.57N	65.15 E
Amudarja = Amu Darya (EN)	21	He	43.40N	59.01 E
Āmū Daryā = Amu Darya (EN)	21	He	43.40N	59.01 E
Amu Darya (EN) = Amudarja	21	He	43.40N	59.01 E
Amu Darya (EN) = Āmū Daryā	21	He	43.40N	59.01 E
Amudat	36	Fb	1.58N	34.56 E
Amukta Pass	40a	Db	52.25N	172.00W
Amun	63a	Ba	5.57S	154.45 E
Amund Ringnes	42	Ha	78.15N	97.00W
Amundsen Bay	66	Ee	66.55S	50.00 E
Amundsen Coast	66	Mg	85.30S	159.00W
Amundsen Glacier	66	Mg	85.35S	159.00W
Amundsen Gulf	38	Gb	71.00N	124.00W
Amundsen-Scott Station	66	Bg	90.00S	0.00
Amundsen Sea (EN)	66	Of	72.30S	112.00W
Amungen	8	Fc	61.10N	15.40 E
Amuntai	22	Nj	2.26S	115.15 E
Amur	21	Qd	52.56N	141.10 E
'Amūr, Wādī	35	Eb	18.56N	33.34 E
Amurang	26	Hf	1.11N	124.35 E
Amursk	20	If	50.16N	136.55 E
Amurskaja Oblast [3]	20	Hf	54.00N	128.00 E
Amurzet	20	Ig	47.41N	131.07 E
Amvrakia, Gulf of- (EN) = Amvrakikós Kólpos	15	Dk	39.00N	21.00 E
Amvrakikós Kólpos = Amvrakia, Gulf of- (EN)	15	Dk	39.00N	21.00 E
Amvrosijevka	16	Kf	47.44N	38.31 E
Am Zoer	35	Cc	14.13N	21.23 E
Anaa Atoll	61	Lc	17.25S	145.30W
Anabar	64e	Ba	0.29S	166.57 E
Anabar	21	Nb	73.08N	113.36 E
Anabarskoje Ploskogorje	21	Mc	70.00N	108.00 E
An Abhainn Dubh/Blackwater	9	Gh	53.39N	6.43W
An Abhainn Mhór/Blackwater [Ire.]	9	Fj	51.51N	7.50W
An Abhainn Mhór/Blackwater [N.Ire.-U.K.]	9	Gg	54.30N	6.35W
Anabuki	29	Dd	34.02N	134.11 E
Ancasti	56	Gc	28.49S	65.30W
Anaco	54	Fb	9.27N	64.28W
Anaconda	43	Eb	46.08N	112.57W
Anacortes	46	Db	48.30N	122.37W
Anadarko	45	Gi	35.04N	98.15W
Anadolu = Anatolia (EN)	21	Ff	39.00N	35.00 E
Anadyr	21	Tc	64.55N	176.05 E
Anadyr	22	Tc	64.45N	177.29 E
Anadyr Gulf (EN) = Anadyrski Zaliv	21	Uc	64.00N	179.00W
Anadyr Range (EN) = Anadyrskoje Ploskogorje	21	Tc	67.00N	174.00 E
Anadyrski Liman	20	Md	64.30N	178.00 E
Anadyrski Zaliv = Anadyr Gulf (EN)	21	Uc	64.00N	179.00W
Anadyrskoje Ploskogorje = Anadyr Range (EN)	21	Tc	67.00N	174.00 E
Anáfi	15	Im	36.22N	25.47 E
Anaghit	35	Fb	16.20N	38.39 E
Anagni	14	Hi	41.44N	13.09 E
'Ānah	23	Fc	34.28N	41.56 E
Anaheim	46	Gj	33.51N	117.57W
Anahola	65a	Ba	22.09N	159.19W
Anáhuac	48	Id	27.14N	100.09W
Anahuac, Meseta de-	47	Dd	21.30N	101.00W
An Aird/Ards Peninsula	9	Hg	54.30N	5.30W
Anaj Mudi	21	Jh	10.10N	77.04 E
Anaktuvuk Pass	40	Ic	68.10N	151.50W
Analalava	37	Hb	14.38S	47.45 E
Analavelona	37	Gd	22.37S	44.10 E
Ana Maria, Golfo de-	49	Hc	21.25N	78.40W
Anambas, Kepulauan- = Anambas Islands (EN)	21	Mi	3.00N	106.00 E
Anambas Islands (EN) = Anambas, Kepulauan-	21	Mi	3.00N	106.00 E
Anambra [2]	34	Gd	6.30N	7.30 E
Anamé	63b	De	20.08S	169.49 E
Anamizu	28	Nf	37.14N	136.54 E
Anamur	23	Db	36.06N	32.50 E
Anamur Burun	23	Db	36.03N	32.48 E
Anan [Jap.]	29	Dd	33.54N	134.39 E
Anan [Jap.]	29	Ed	35.19N	137.48 E
Anane, Djebel-	13	Mi	35.12N	0.47 E
Anánes	15	Hm	36.31N	24.08 E
Ananjev	16	Ff	47.43N	29.59 E
Anankwin	25	Je	15.41N	97.59 E
Anantapur	25	Ff	14.41N	77.36 E
Anantnāg (Islāmābād)	25	Fb	33.44N	75.09 E
Anapa	19	Dg	44.53N	37.19 E
Anapo	14	Jm	37.03N	15.16 E
Anápolis	53	Lg	16.20S	48.58W
Anapu, Rio-	54	Hd	2.15S	51.30W
Anār	23	Ic	30.53N	55.18 E
Anārak	23	Hc	33.20N	53.42 E
Anare Station	66	Jd	54.30S	158.55 E
Anaro, Rio-	49	Lj	7.48N	70.12W
Añasco	51a	Ab	18.17N	67.10W
Anatahan Island	57	Fc	16.22N	145.40 E
Anatolia (EN) = Anadolu	21	Ff	39.00N	35.00 E
Anatolikí Rodhópi	15	Ih	41.44N	25.31 E
Añatuya	56	Hc	28.28S	62.50W
Anauá, Rio-	54	Fc	0.58N	61.21W
Anazarba	24	Fd	37.15N	35.45 E
An Baile Meánach/Ballymena	9	Gg	54.52N	6.17W
An Bhanna/Bann	9	Gf	55.10N	6.46W
An Bhearú/Barrow	9	Gi	52.10N	7.00W
An Bhinn Bhui/Benwee Head	9	Dg	54.21N	9.48W
An Bhograch/Boggeragh Mountains	9	Ei	52.05N	9.00W
An Bhóinn/Boyne	9	Gh	53.43N	6.15W
An Bhrosnach/Brosna	9	Fh	53.13N	7.58W
An Blascaod Mór/Great Blasket	9	Ci	52.05N	10.32W
Anbyŏn	28	Ie	39.02N	127.32 E
An Cabhán/Cavan [2]	9	Fh	53.55N	7.30W
An Cabhán/Cavan	9	Fg	54.00N	7.21W
An Caisleán Nua/Newcastle	9	Hg	54.12N	5.54W
An Caisleán Nua/Newcastle West	9	Di	52.27N	9.03W
An Caisleán Riabhach/Castlerea	9	Eh	53.46N	8.29W
An Caoláire Rua/Killary Harbour	9	Dh	53.38N	9.55W
Ancares, Sierra de-	13	Fb	42.46N	6.54W
Ancash [2]	54	Ce	9.30S	77.45W
Ancenis	11	Eg	47.22N	1.10W
An Chathair/Caher	9	Fi	52.22N	7.55W
An Cheacha/Caha Mountains	9	Dj	51.45N	9.45W
Anchorage	39	Ec	61.13N	149.53W
An Chorr Chríochach/Cookstown	9	Gg	54.39N	6.45W
Anci (Langfang)	27	Kd	39.29N	116.40 E
An Clár/Clare [2]	9	Ei	52.50N	9.00W
An Cóbh/Cóbh	9	Ej	51.51N	8.17W
Ancohuma, Nevado-	54	Eg	15.51S	68.36W
Ancona	6	Hg	43.38N	13.30 E
Ancón de Sardinas, Bahía de-	54	Cc	1.30N	79.50W
Ancre	11	Ie	49.54N	2.28 E
Ancuabe	37	Fb	12.58S	39.51 E
Ancud	56	Ff	41.52S	73.50W
Ancud, Golfo de-	56	Ff	42.05S	73.00W
Anda	27	Mb	46.24N	125.20 E
Anda (Sartu)	28	Ha	46.35N	125.00 E
Andacollo [Arg.]	56	Fe	37.11S	70.41W
Andacollo [Chile]	56	Fd	30.14S	71.06W
Andahuaylas	54	Df	13.39S	73.23W
An Daingean/Dingle	9	Ci	52.08N	10.15W
Andalgalá	56	Gc	27.36S	66.19W
Åndalsnes	7	Be	62.34N	7.42 E
Andalucia = Andalusia (EN)	13	Hg	37.30N	4.30W
Andalucia = Andalusia (EN)	5	Fh	37.30N	4.30W
Andalusia	43	Je	31.19N	86.29W
Andalusia (EN) = Andalucia	13	Hg	37.30N	4.30W
Andalusia (EN) = Andalucia	5	Fh	37.30N	4.30W
Andaman and Nicobar [3]	25	If	12.30N	92.45 E
Andaman Basin (EN)	21	Lh	10.00N	94.00 E
Andaman Islands	21	Lh	12.30N	92.43 E
Andaman Sea (EN)	21	Lh	10.00N	95.00 E
Andamooka	59	Hf	30.27S	137.12 E
'Andān, Wādī-	23	Ie	21.05N	58.23 E
Andant	55	Am	36.34S	62.07W
Andapa	37	Hb	14.38S	49.33 E
Andara	37	Cc	18.03S	21.27 E
Andelle	12	De	49.19N	1.14 E
Andenes	7	Db	69.19N	16.08 E
Andenne	12	Hd	50.29N	5.06 E
Andenne-Namêche	12	Hd	50.28N	5.00 E
Andéranboukane	34	Fb	15.26N	3.02 E
Anderlecht	12	Gd	50.50N	4.18 E
Anderlues	12	Gd	50.24N	4.16 E
Andermatt	14	Cd	46.38N	8.37 E
Andernach	10	Df	50.26N	7.24 E
Andernos-les-Bains	11	Ej	44.44N	1.06W
Anderson	42	Ec	69.42N	129.01W
Anderson [Ca.-U.S.]	46	Df	40.27N	122.18W
Anderson [In.-U.S.]	43	Jc	40.10N	85.41W
Anderson [S.C.-U.S.]	43	Ke	34.30N	82.39W
Anderstorp	8	Eg	57.17N	13.38 E
Andes (EN) = Andes, Cordillera de los-	52	Jh	20.00S	67.00W
Andes, Cordillera de los- = Andes (EN)	52	Jh	20.00S	67.00W
Andevoranto	37	Hc	18.48S	49.02 E
Andfjorden	7	Db	69.10N	16.20 E
Andhra Pradesh [3]	25	Fe	16.00N	79.00 E
Andia, Sierra de-	13	Kb	42.45N	2.00W
Andikhásia Óri	15	Ej	39.47N	21.55 E
Andikira	15	Fk	38.23N	22.38 E
Andikithira = Andikithira (EN)	15	Gn	35.52N	23.18 E
Andikithira (EN) = Andikithira	15	Gn	35.52N	23.18 E
Andikíthiron, Stenón-	15	Gn	35.45N	23.25 E
Andilamena	37	Hc	17.01S	48.32 E
Andilanatoby	37	Hc	17.56S	48.14 E
Andímeshk	24	Mf	32.27N	48.21 E
Andímilos	15	Hm	36.47N	24.14 E
Andíparos	15	Il	37.00N	25.03 E
Andípaxoi	15	Dj	39.08N	20.14 E
Andípsara	15	Ik	38.33N	25.24 E
Andir He	27	Dd	38.00N	83.36 E
Andırın	24	Gd	37.34N	36.20 E
Andirlangar	27	Dd	37.36N	83.50 E
Andirrion	15	Ek	38.20N	21.46 E
Andítilos	15	Km	36.22N	27.28 E
Andižan	22	Je	40.45N	72.22 E
Andižanskaja Oblast [3]	19	Hg	40.45N	72.20 E
Andkhvoy	23	Kb	36.56N	65.08 E
Andŏng	27	Md	36.36N	128.44 E
Andorra (Valls d'Andorra) [1]	6	Gg	42.30N	1.30 E
Andorra la Vella	6	Gg	42.31N	1.31 E
Andover	9	Lj	51.13N	1.28W
Andøya	7	Db	69.08N	15.54 E
Andradas	55	If	22.05S	46.35W
Andradina	56	Jb	20.54S	51.23W
Andraitx	13	Oe	39.35N	2.25 E
Andreanof Islands	38	Bd	52.00N	176.00W
Andreapol	7	Hh	56.39N	32.16 E
Andrées Land	41	Jd	73.20N	26.30W
Andrejevka	19	If	45.47N	80.35 E
Andrejevka	16	Je	49.32N	36.40 E
Andrejevo-Ivanovka	15	Nb	47.31N	30.21 E
Andrejevsk	20	Ge	58.10N	114.15 E
Andrelândia	55	Je	21.44S	44.18W
Andresito	55	Dk	33.08S	57.09W
Andrespol	10	Pe	51.43N	19.40 E
Andrews	45	Ej	32.19N	102.33W
Andria	14	Ki	41.13N	16.17 E
Andriamena	37	Hc	17.28S	47.29 E
Andriba	37	Hc	17.36S	46.53 E
Andrijevica	15	Cg	42.44N	19.48 E
Andringitra	30	Lk	22.10S	46.55 E
Andritsaina	15	El	37.29N	21.54 E
Androka	37	Gd	24.59S	44.04 E
Andropov → Rybinsk	6	Jd	58.03N	38.52 E
Ándros	5	Ih	37.50N	24.50 E
Andros	38	Lg	24.25N	78.00W
Ándros	15	Hl	37.50N	24.56 E
Androscoggin River	44	Md	43.55N	69.55W
Androssan	9	If	55.40N	4.55W
Andros Town	47	Id	24.43N	77.47W
Androth Island	25	Ef	10.50N	73.41 E
Androy	30	Lk	25.00S	45.40 E
Andruševka	16	Fe	49.59N	29.01 E
Andrychów	10	Pg	49.52N	19.21 E
Andselv	7	Eb	69.04N	18.30 E
Andudu	36	Eb	2.29N	28.41 E
Andújar	13	Hf	38.03N	4.04W
Andulo	36	Ce	11.28S	16.43 E
Andu Tan	26	Fe	7.35N	114.15 E
Anduze	11	Jj	44.03N	3.59 E
An Ea agail/Errigal	9	Ef	55.02N	8.07W
Aneby	8	Fg	57.50N	14.48 E
Anéfis	34	Fb	18.03N	0.36 E
Anegada	47	Le	18.45N	64.20W
Anegada, Bahia-	56	Hf	40.15S	62.15W
Anegada Passage	47	Le	18.30N	63.40W
Anécho	34	Fd	6.14N	1.36 E
An Éirne/Erne	9	Eg	54.30N	8.15W
An Eithne/Inny	9	Fh	53.35N	7.50W
An Eoghanach/Annalee	9	Fg	54.02N	7.25W
Anet	12	Df	48.51N	1.26 E
Aneto, Pico de-	5	Gg	42.38N	0.40 E
Aney	34	Hb	19.24N	12.56 E
Aneytioum, Ile-	57	Hg	20.12S	169.49 E
An Feabhal	9	Ff	55.04N	7.15W
An Fhéil/Feale	9	Di	52.28N	9.40W
An Fheoir/Nore	9	Gi	52.25N	6.58W
Angamos, Punta- [Chile]	56	Fb	23.01S	70.32W
Angamos, Punta- [Pas.]	65d	Bb	27.04S	109.17W
Angara	21	Ld	58.06N	93.00 E
Angarsk	22	Md	52.34N	103.54 E
Angarski, Pereval-	16	Ig	44.47N	34.25 E
Angarskij Krjaž	20	Fe	57.30N	103.00 E
Angathonisi	15	Jl	37.28N	27.00 E
Angaur Island	57	Ed	6.54N	134.09 E
Ånge	7	De	62.31N	15.37 E
Ånge	8	Fa	63.27N	14.03 E
An Gearran/Garron Point	9	Hf	55.05N	5.58W
Ángel, Cerro-	48	Hf	22.49N	102.34W
Ángel, Salto- = Angel Falls (EN)	52	Je	5.57N	62.30W
Angelburg	12	Kd	50.47N	8.25 E
Ángel de la Guarda, Isla-	47	Bc	29.20N	113.25W
Angeles	26	Hc	15.09N	120.35 E
Ángeles, Sierra de los-	48	Jf	23.10N	99.20W
Angel Falls (EN) = Ángel, Salto-	52	Je	5.57N	62.30W
Angel Falls (EN) = Churún Merú	52	Je	5.57N	62.30W
Ängelholm	7	Ch	56.15N	12.51 E
Angélica	55	Bj	31.33S	61.33W
Angeln	10	Fb	54.40N	9.45 E
Ängelsberg	8	Ge	59.58N	16.02 E
Anger	35	Fd	9.40N	36.06 E
Angereb	35	Fc	13.44N	36.28 E
Ångermanälven	5	Hc	62.48N	17.56 E
Angermünde	10	Jc	53.02N	14.00 E
Angers	6	Ff	47.28N	0.33W
Angkor	25	Kf	13.26N	103.52 E
Angikuni Lake	42	Hd	62.10N	99.55W
Angistrion	15	Gl	37.40N	23.20 E
Anglem, Mount-	62	Bg	46.44S	167.54 E
Anglés	13	Oc	41.57N	2.39 E
Anglesey	5	Fe	53.18N	4.20W
Anglet	11	Ek	43.29N	1.32W
Angleton	45	Il	29.10N	95.26W
Anglin	11	Gh	46.42N	0.52 E
Anglona	14	Cj	40.45N	8.45 E
Angmagssalik	67	Mc	65.45N	37.30W
Ango	36	Eb	4.02N	25.52 E
Angoche	31	Kj	16.12S	39.54 E
Angoche, Ilha-	30	Kj	16.20S	39.51 E
Angol	56	Fe	37.48S	72.43W
Angola [1]	31	Ij	12.30S	18.30 E
Angola	44	Ee	41.38N	85.00W
Angola Basin (EN)	3	Ek	15.00S	3.00 E
Angoram	60	Ch	4.04S	144.04 E
Angostura	48	Ee	25.22N	108.11W
Angostura, Presa de la-	48	Mi	16.30N	92.30W
Angostura, Salto-	54	Dc	2.43N	70.57W
Angostura Reservoir	43	Gc	43.18N	103.27W
Angoulême	11	Gi	45.39N	0.09 E
Angoumois	11	Fi	45.30N	0.10W
Angra do Heroismo [3]	32	Bb	38.42N	27.15W
Angra do Heroismo	31	Ee	38.39N	27.13W
Angra dos Reis	55	Jf	23.00S	44.18W
Angren	19	Hg	41.03N	70.10 E
Angu	36	Db	3.33N	24.28 E
Anguang	28	Gb	45.36N	123.48 E
Anguilla [5]	39	Mh	18.15N	63.05W
Anguilla	38	Mh	18.15N	63.05W
Anguilla, Canal de l'- = Anguilla Channel (EN)	51b	Ab	18.09N	63.04W
Anguilla Bank (EN)	51b	Ab	18.30N	63.03W
Anguilla Cays	49	Hb	23.31N	78.33W
Anguilla Channel (EN) = Anguilla, Canal de l'-	51b	Ab	18.09N	63.04W
Anguli Nur	28	Cd	41.23N	114.30 E
Anguo	28	Ce	38.25N	115.20 E
Anhanca	36	Cf	16.47S	15.33 E
Anhanguera	55	Hd	18.21S	48.17W
An Hoa	25	Le	15.46N	108.03 E
Anholt	7	Ch	56.40N	11.35 E
Anhua (Dongping)	27	Jf	28.27N	111.15 E
Anhui Sheng (An-hui Sheng) = Anhwei (EN) [2]	27	Ke	32.00N	117.00 E
An-hui Sheng → Anhui Sheng = Anhwei (EN) [2]	27	Ke	32.00N	117.00 E
Anhwei (EN) = Anhui Sheng (An-hui Sheng) [2]	27	Ke	32.00N	117.00 E
Anhwei (EN) = An-hui Sheng → Anhui Sheng [2]	27	Ke	32.00N	117.00 E
Ani	29	Gb	39.59N	140.25 E
Aniak	40	Hd	61.34N	159.30W
An Iarmhi/Westmeath [2]	9	Fh	53.30N	7.30W
Anibare	64e	Bb	0.32S	166.57 E
Anibare Bay	64e	Bb	0.32S	166.57 E
Aniche	12	Fd	50.20N	3.15 E
Ánidros	15	Im	36.37N	25.41 E
Anié	34	Fd	7.45N	1.12 E
Anie, Pic d'-	11	Fl	42.57N	0.43W
Aniene	14	Gi	41.56N	12.30 E
Anijangying → Luanping	28	Dd	40.55N	117.19 E
Anikščiaj/Anykščiai	7	Fi	55.31N	25.08 E
Animas Peak	45	Bk	31.35N	108.47W
Anina	15	Ed	45.05N	21.51 E
Anita Garibaldi	55	Gh	27.37S	51.05W
Anittepe	15	Kh	41.21N	27.42 E
Aniva	20	Jg	46.41N	142.35 E
Aniva, Zaliv-	20	Jg	46.20N	142.40 E
Anivorano Nord	37	Hb	12.43S	49.12 E
Aniwa, Ile-	57	Hf	19.16S	169.35 E
Anizy-le-Château	12	Fe	49.30N	3.27 E
Anjala	7	Gf	60.41N	26.50 E
Anji	28	Ei	30.39N	119.41 E
Anjiang → Qianyang	27	Jf	27.19N	110.13 E
Anjō	29	Ed	34.57N	137.05 E
Anjou	11	Fg	47.20N	0.30W
Anjou, Ostrova- = Anjou Islands (EN)	21	Qb	75.30N	143.00 E
Anjouan → Nzwani	30	Lj	12.15S	44.25 E
Anjou Islands (EN) = Anjou, Ostrova-	21	Qb	75.30N	143.00 E
Anjozorobe	37	Hc	18.24S	47.52 E
Anju	27	Md	39.37N	125.40 E
Anjuj	20	Ig	49.20N	136.20 E
Anjujski Hrebet	20	Lc	67.20N	166.00 E
Anjou, Val d'-	11	Fg	47.25N	0.15W
Anka	34	Gc	12.07N	5.55 E
Ankang (Xing'an)	22	Mf	32.37N	109.03 E
Ankara	22	Ff	39.56N	32.52 E
Ankaratra	30	Lj	19.25S	47.12 E
Ankarsrum	7	Dh	57.42N	16.19 E
Ankavandra	37	Hc	18.45S	45.18 E
Ankazoabo	37	Gd	22.16S	44.30 E
Ankazobe	37	Hc	18.17S	47.05 E
Ankeny	45	Jf	41.44N	93.36W
Ankhor	35	Hc	10.47N	46.18 E
Anklam	10	Jc	53.52N	13.42 E
Ankober	35	Fd	9.40N	39.44 E
Ankoro	36	Ed	6.45S	26.57 E
Ankum	12	Jb	52.33N	7.53 E
An Laoi/Lee	9	Ej	51.55N	8.30W
Anlong	27	If	25.02N	105.30 E
An Longfort/Longford [2]	9	Fh	53.40N	7.40W
An Longfort/Longford	9	Fh	53.44N	7.47W
An Lorgain/Lurgan	9	Gg	54.28N	6.20W
Anlu	27	Je	31.12N	113.46 E
An Mhí/Meath [2]	9	Gh	53.35N	6.40W
An Mhuaidh/Moy	9	Dg	54.12N	9.08W
An Mhuir Cheilteach = Celtic Sea (EN)	5	Fe	51.00N	7.00W
An Muileann gCearr/Mullingar	9	Fh	53.32N	7.20W
An Muirthead/Mullet Peninsula	9	Cg	54.15N	10.04W
Ånn	7	Ce	63.15N	12.35 E
Ånn	8	Ea	63.19N	12.33 E
Ann, Cape- [Ant.]	66	Ee	66.10S	51.22 E
Ann, Cape- [Ma.-U.S.]	44	Ld	42.39N	70.38W
Anna [Il.-U.S.]	45	Lh	37.28N	89.15W
Anna [Nauru]	64e	Ba	0.29S	166.56 E
Anna	19	Ee	51.29N	40.26 E
Annaba	31	He	36.54N	7.46 E
Annaba [3]	32	Ib	36.35N	8.00 E
An Nabaţīyah at Taḩtā	24	Gf	33.23N	35.29 E
Annaberg-Buchholz	10	If	50.34N	13.00 E
An Nabī Şāliḩ	24	Eh	28.38N	33.59 E
An Nabk	23	Ec	34.01N	36.44 E
An Nabk Abū Qaşr	24	Hg	30.21N	38.34 E
An Nafīdah	14	En	36.08N	10.23 E
An Nafūd	21	Gg	28.30N	41.00 E
An Najaf	22	Gf	31.59N	44.20 E
An Najaf [3]	24	Kg	31.20N	44.07 E
An Nakhl	33	Fd	29.55N	33.45 E
Annalee/An Eoghanach	9	Fg	54.02N	7.25W
Annam (EN) = Trung Phan	21	Me	15.00N	108.00 E
Annamitique, Chaîne-	25	Le	17.00N	106.00 E
Annan	9	Jg	54.59N	3.16W
Annan	9	Jg	55.00N	3.16W
Anna Paulowna	12	Gb	52.52N	4.52 E
Anna Paulowna-Kleine Sluis	12	Gb	52.52N	4.52 E
Anna Point	64e	Ba	0.29S	166.56 E
Annapolis	39	Lf	38.59N	76.30W
Annapolis Royal	44	Oc	44.45N	65.31W
Annapurna	21	Kg	28.34N	83.50 E
Ann Arbor	43	Kc	42.18N	83.45W
Anna Regina	50	Gi	7.16N	58.30W
An Nás/Naas	9	Gh	53.13N	6.39W
An Nashshāsh	24	Pk	23.05N	54.02 E
An Nashwah	24	Lg	30.49N	47.36 E
An Nāşirīyah	23	Gc	31.02N	46.16 E
An Nasser	21	Fg	24.36N	32.58 E
An Nawfalīyah	33	Cc	30.47N	17.50 E
Annecy	11	Mi	45.54N	6.07 E
Annecy, Lac d'-	11	Mi	45.51N	6.11 E
Annemasse	11	Mh	46.12N	6.15 E
Annevoie-Rouillon	12	Gd	50.21N	4.50 E
An Nīl [3]	35	Ea	20.10N	33.00 E
An Nīl al Azraq [3]	35	Ed	12.20N	34.15 E
Anning	27	Hg	24.58N	102.29 E
Anniston	43	Je	33.40N	85.50W
Annobón	30	Hi	1.32S	5.38 E
Annonay	11	Ki	45.14N	4.40 E
Annotto Bay	49	Id	18.16N	76.46W
An Nu'ayrīyah	24	Mi	27.28N	48.27 E
An Nuhūd	31	Jg	12.42N	28.26 E
An Nu' Mān	24	Fi	27.06N	35.46 E
An Nu'mānīyah	24	Kf	32.32N	45.25 E
Annweiler am Trifels	12	Je	49.12N	7.58 E
Anoia/Noya	13	Nc	41.28N	1.56 E
Anoka	45	Jd	45.11N	93.23W
An Ómaigh/Omagh	9	Fg	54.36N	7.18W
Anori	54	Fd	3.47S	61.38W
Anosyennes, Chaînes-	37	Hd	24.20S	47.00 E
Ánou Makarene	34	Gb	18.07N	7.35 E
Áno Viánnos	15	In	35.03N	25.25 E
Anóyia	15	Hn	35.15N	24.54 E
Anping [China]	28	Ce	38.13N	115.32 E
Anping [China]	28	Gd	41.10N	123.25 E
An Pointe/Warrenpoint	9	Gg	54.06N	6.15W
Anpu	27	Ig	21.30N	110.00 E
Anpu Gang	27	Ig	21.25N	109.40 E
Anqing	22	Nf	30.32N	116.59 E
Anqiu	28	Ef	36.25N	119.12 E
An Ráth/Ráth Luirc	9	Ei	52.21N	8.41W
An Ribhéar/Kenmare River	9	Dj	51.50N	9.50W
Anröchte	12	Kc	51.34N	8.20 E
Ans	12	Hd	50.39N	5.32 E
Anşāb	23	Fd	29.11N	44.43 E
Ansauvillers	12	Ee	49.34N	2.24 E
Ansbach	10	Gg	49.18N	10.35 E
An Sciobairin/Skibbereen	9	Dj	51.33N	9.15W
An Seancheann/Kinsale, Old Head of-	9	Ej	51.36N	8.32W
Anse-à-Veau	49	Kd	18.30N	73.19W
Anse-Bertrand	51e	Ab	16.29N	61.31W
Anse-d'Hainault	49	Jd	18.30N	74.27W
Anse la Raye	51k	Ab	13.57N	61.03W
Anshan	22	Oe	41.08N	122.59 E
Anshun	22	Mg	26.15N	105.58 E
Ansina	56	Id	31.54S	55.28W
Ansley	45	Gf	41.18N	99.23W
Anson Bay	59	Gb	13.20S	130.05 E
Ansongo	34	Fb	15.40N	0.31 E
An Srath Bán/Strabane	9	Fg	54.49N	7.27W
Anta	54	Df	13.29S	72.09W

Index Symbols

[1] Independent Nation
[2] State, Region
[3] District, County
[4] Municipality
[5] Colony, Dependency
Continent
Physical Region

Historical or Cultural Region
Mount, Mountain
Volcano
Hill
Mountains, Mountain Range
Hills, Escarpment
Plateau, Upland

Pass, Gap
Plain, Lowland
Delta
Salt Flat
Valley, Canyon
Crater, Cave
Karst Features

Depression
Polder
Desert, Dunes
Forest, Woods
Heath, Steppe
Oasis
Cape, Point

Coast, Beach
Cliff
Peninsula
Isthmus
Sandbank
Island
Atoll

Rock, Reef
Islands, Archipelago
Rocks, Reefs
Coral Reef
Well, Spring
Geyser
River, Stream

Waterfall Rapids
River Mouth, Estuary
Lake
Salt Lake
Intermittent Lake
Reservoir
Swamp, Pond

Canal
Glacier
Ice Shelf, Pack Ice
Ocean
Sea
Gulf, Bay
Strait, Fjord

Lagoon
Bank
Seamount
Tablemount
Ridge
Shelf
Basin

Escarpment, Sea Scarp
Fracture
Trench, Abyss
National Park, Reserve
Point of Interest
Recreation Site
Cave, Cavern

Historic Site
Ruins
Wall, Walls
Church, Abbey
Temple
Scientific Station
Airport

Port
Lighthouse
Mine
Tunnel
Dam, Bridge

Antabamba	54	Df	14.19S	72.55W
Antakya=Antioch (EN)	23	Eb	36.14N	36.07 E
Antalaha	31	Mj	14.55S	50.15 E
Antalya	22	Ff	36.53N	30.42 E
Antalya, Gulf of- (EN)= Antalya Körfezi	23	Db	36.30N	31.00 E
Antalya Körfezi=Antalya, Gulf of- (EN)	23	Db	36.30N	31.00 E
An Tan	25	Le	15.26N	108.39 E
Antananarivo	31	Lj	18.55S	47.30 E
Antananarivo [3]	37	Hc	19.00S	46.40 E
Antanimora	37	Hd	24.48S	45.39 E
An tAonach/Nenagh	9	Ei	52.52N	8.12W
Antarctica (EN)	66	Bg	90.00S	0.00
Antarctic Peninsula (EN)	66	Qe	69.30S	65.00W
Antas, Cachoeira das-	55	Ha	13.06S	48.09W
Antas, Rio das-	55	Gi	29.04S	51.21W
An Teampall Mór/ Templemore	9	Fi	52.48N	7.50W
Antela, Laguna de-	13	Eb	42.07N	7.41W
Antelao	14	Gd	46.27N	12.16 E
Antelope Creek	46	Me	43.29N	105.23W
Anten	8	Ef	58.03N	12.30 E
Antequera [Par.]	55	Dg	24.08S	57.07W
Antequera [Sp.]	13	Hg	37.01N	4.33W
Anthony	45	Cj	32.00N	106.34W
Anti-Atlas	30	Ge	30.00N	8.30W
Antibes	11	Nk	43.35N	7.07 E
Antibes, Cap d'-	11	Nk	43.32N	7.07 E
Antica, Isla-	50	Eg	10.24N	62.43W
Anticosti, Ile d'-	38	Me	49.30N	63.00W
Antigo	45	Ld	45.09N	89.09W
Antigonish	42	Lg	45.37N	61.58W
Antigua	38	Mh	17.03N	61.48W
Antigua and Barbuda	39	Mh	17.03N	61.48W
Antigua Guatemala	47	Ff	14.34N	90.44W
Antiguo Cauce del Rio Bermejo	56	Hc	25.39S	60.11W
Antiguo Morelos	48	Jf	22.30N	99.05W
Antilla	49	Jc	20.50N	75.45W
Antillas, Mar de las-/Caribe, Mar-=Caribbean Sea (EN)	38	Lh	15.00N	73.00W
Antillas Mayores=Greater Antilles (EN)	38	Lh	20.00N	74.00W
Antillas Menores=Lesser Antilles (EN)	38	Mh	15.00N	61.00W
Antilles, Mer des-/Caraibe, Mer-=Caribbean Sea (EN)	38	Lh	15.00N	73.00W
An tInbhear Mór/Arklow	9	Gi	52.48N	6.09W
Antioch	46	Eg	38.00N	121.49W
Antioch (EN)=Antakya	23	Eb	36.14N	36.07 E
Antioche, Pertuis d'-	11	Eh	46.05N	1.20W
Antiope Reef	57	Kf	18.18S	168.40W
Antioquia [2]	54	Cb	7.00N	75.30W
Antipajeta	20	Cc	69.09N	77.00 E
Antipodes Islands	57	Ii	49.40S	178.50 E
Antiques, Pointe d'-	51e	Ab	16.26N	61.33W
An t-Iúr/Newry	9	Gg	54.11N	6.20W
Antler River	45	Fb	49.08N	101.00W
Antlers	45	Ii	34.14N	95.37W
Antofagasta [2]	56	Gb	23.30S	69.00W
Antofagasta	53	Ih	23.39S	70.24W
Antofagasta de la Sierra	56	Gc	26.04S	67.25W
Antofalla, Salar de-	56	Gc	25.44S	67.45W
Antofalla, Volcán-	56	Gc	25.34S	67.55W
Antoing	12	Fd	50.34N	3.27 E
Antón	49	Gi	8.24N	80.16W
Anton Dohrn Seamount (EN)	9	Cd	57.30N	11.00W
Antongil, Baie d'-	30	Lj	15.45S	49.50 E
Antonina	56	Kc	25.27S	48.43W
Antônio João	55	Ef	23.15S	55.31W
Antonito	45	Dh	37.05N	106.00W
Antón Lizardo, Punta de-	48	Lh	19.03N	95.58W
Antony	12	Ef	48.45N	2.18 E
Antopol	10	Ud	52.12N	24.53 E
Antracit	16	Ke	48.06N	39.06 E
Antreff	12	Ld	50.52N	9.15 E
Antrim/Aontroim	9	Gg	54.43N	6.13W
Antrim Mountains	9	Gf	55.00N	6.10W
Antrodoco	14	Hh	42.25N	13.05 E
Antsakabary	37	Hc	15.03S	48.56 E
Antsalova	37	Gc	18.42S	44.33 E
Antseranana [3]	37	Hb	13.40S	49.15 E
An tSionainn/Shannon	5	Fe	52.36N	9.41W
Antsirabe	31	Lj	19.51S	47.01 E
Antsiranana	31	Lj	12.17S	49.17 E
An tSiúir/Suir	9	Gi	52.15N	7.00W
Antsla	7	Gh	57.52N	26.33 E
An tSláine/Slaney	9	Gi	52.21N	6.30W
Antsohihy	31	Lj	14.52S	47.58 E
An tSuca/Suck	9	Eh	53.16N	8.03W
Anttola	8	Lc	61.35N	27.39 E
Antu (Songjiang)	28	Jc	42.33N	128.20 E
An Tuc	25	Lf	13.57N	108.39 E
Antufash, Jazīrat-	33	Hf	15.42N	42.25 E
An Tulach/Tullow	9	Gi	52.48N	6.44W
An Tulach Mhór/Tullamore	9	Fh	53.16N	7.30W
Antwerp (EN)=Antwerpen/ Anvers	6	Ge	50.38N	5.34 E
Antwerp (EN)=Anvers/ Antwerpen	6	Ge	50.38N	5.34 E
Antwerpen [3]	12	Gc	51.10N	4.30 E
Antwerpen/Anvers= Antwerp (EN)	6	Ge	50.38N	5.34 E
Antwerpen-Ekeren	11	Kc	51.17N	4.25 E
Antwerpen-Hoboken	12	Gc	51.10N	4.21 E
Antwerpen-Merksem	12	Gc	51.15N	4.27 E
Antykan	20	If	54.55N	135.13 E
An Uaimh/Navan	9	Gh	53.39N	6.41W
Anuradhapura	25	Gg	8.21N	80.23 E
Anuta Island	57	Hf	11.38S	169.50 E
Anvers/Antwerpen= Antwerp (EN)	6	Ge	50.38N	5.34 E
Anvers Island	66	Qe	64.33S	63.35W
Anvik	40	Gd	62.40N	160.12W
Anxi	22	Le	40.30N	96.00 E
Anxiang	27	Jf	29.26N	112.11 E
Anxin	28	Ce	38.55N	115.56 E
Anxious Bay	59	Gf	33.25S	134.35 E
Anyang (Zhangde)	22	Nf	36.01N	114.25 E
A'nyêmaqen Shan	21	Lf	34.30N	100.00 E
Anyi	28	Cj	28.50N	115.31 E
Anykščiai/Anikščjaj	7	Fi	55.31N	25.08 E
Anyva, Mys-	20	Jg	46.00N	143.25 E
Anza	14	Ce	46.00N	8.17 E
Anze	28	Bf	36.09N	112.14 E
Anzegem	12	Fd	50.50N	3.28 E
Anžero-Sudžensk	22	Kd	56.07N	86.00 E
Anzi	36	Dc	0.52S	23.24 E
Anzio	14	Gi	41.27N	12.37 E
Anzoátegui [2]	54	Fb	9.00N	64.30W
Anzob, Pereval-	18	Ge	39.07N	68.53 E
Aoba, Ile-	61	Cc	15.25S	167.50 E
Ao Ban Don	25	Jg	9.20N	99.25 E
Aoga-Shima	27	Oe	32.30N	139.50 E
Aohan Qi (Xinhui)	28	Ec	42.18N	119.53 E
Aoiz	13	Kb	42.47N	1.22W
Aoji	28	Kc	42.31N	130.24 E
Aola	63a	Ec	9.32S	160.29 E
Aomen/Macau=Macao (EN) [5]	22	Ng	22.10N	113.33 E
Aomen/Macau=Macao (EN)	27	Jg	22.12N	113.33 E
Aomori	22	Qe	40.49N	140.45 E
Aomori Ken [2]	28	Pd	40.40N	140.40 E
Aono-Yama	29	Bd	34.27N	131.48 E
Aontroim/Antrim	9	Gg	54.43N	6.13W
Aopo	65c	Aa	13.29S	172.30W
Aôral, Phnum-	25	Kf	12.02N	104.10 E
Aoré	63b	Cb	15.35S	167.10 E
Aosta / Aoste	14	Be	45.44N	7.20 E
Aosta, Val d'-	14	Be	45.45N	7.20 E
Aoste / Aosta	14	Be	45.44N	7.20 E
Aouk, Bahr-	30	Ih	8.51N	18.53 E
Aoukalé	35	Cd	9.10N	20.30 E
Aoukâr [Afr.]	32	Ge	24.00N	2.30W
Aoukâr [Mtna.]	30	Gg	17.30N	9.30W
Aoulef	32	Hd	26.58N	1.05 E
Aoumou	63b	Be	21.24S	165.49 E
Aourou	34	Cc	14.28N	11.34W
Aoya	29	Cd	35.32N	133.59 E
Aozou	31	If	21.49N	17.25 E
Apa, Rio-	56	Ib	22.06S	58.00W
Apača	20	Kf	52.50N	157.10 E
Apache	46	Kk	31.44N	109.07W
Apache Junction	46	Jj	33.26N	111.32W
Apahida	15	Gc	46.49N	23.45 E
Apakho	63b	Bb	11.25S	166.32 E
Apalachee Bay	38	Kg	29.30N	84.00W
Apalachicola	44	Ek	29.44N	84.59W
Apalachicola River	44	Ek	29.44N	84.59W
Apan	48	Jh	19.43N	98.25W
Apaporis, Rio-	52	Jf	1.23S	69.25W
Aparecida do Taboado	54	Hg	20.05S	51.05W
Aparri	22	Oh	18.22N	121.39 E
Apataki Atoll	57	Mf	15.26S	146.20W
Apatin	15	Bd	45.40N	18.59 E
Apatity	6	Jb	67.34N	33.18 E
Apatzingán de la Constitucion	47	De	19.05N	102.21W
Apaxtla de Castrejón	48	Jh	18.09N	99.52W
Ape	7	Gh	57.32N	26.42 E
Apeldoorn	11	Lb	52.13N	5.58 E
Apeldoorn-Nieuw Milligen	12	Hb	52.14N	5.45 E
Apen	12	Ja	53.13N	7.48 E
Apennines (EN) = Appennini	5	Hg	43.00N	13.00 E
Apere, Rio-	54	Ef	13.44S	65.18W
Aphrodisias	24	Cd	37.45N	28.40 E
Api	21	Kf	30.00N	80.57 E
Api	36	Eb	3.40N	25.26 E
Apia	58	Jf	13.50S	171.44W
Apiacás, Serra dos-	54	Gf	10.15S	57.15W
Apio	63a	Ec	9.39S	161.23 E
Apipé Grande, Isla-	55	Di	27.30S	56.54W
Apizaco	48	Jh	19.25N	98.09W
Aplao	54	Dc	16.05S	72.31W
Apo, Mount-	21	Oi	6.59N	125.16 E
Apodi	54	Ke	5.39S	37.48W
Apolda	10	He	51.01N	11.30 E
Apolima	65c	Aa	13.49S	172.07W
Apolima Strait	65c	Aa	13.50S	172.10W
Apollo Bay	59	Ig	38.45S	143.40 E
Apollonia [Alb.]	15	Ci	40.43N	19.27 E
Apollonia [Lib.]	33	Dc	32.54N	21.58 E
Apolo	54	Ef	14.43S	68.31W
Apón, Rio-	49	Kh	10.06N	72.23W
Apopka, Lake-	44	Gk	28.37N	81.38W
Aporé	55	Fd	18.58S	52.01W
Aporé, Rio-	54	Hg	19.27S	50.57W
Apostle Islands	43	Ib	46.50N	90.30W
Apostoles	56	Ic	27.55S	55.46W
Apostolovo	16	Hf	47.39N	33.43 E
Apoteri	54	Gc	4.02N	58.34W
Apôtres, Iles des-	30	Mm	45.40S	50.20 E
Appalachia	44	Fg	36.54N	82.48W
Appalachian Mountains	38	Lc	41.00N	77.00W
Äppelbo	8	Ed	60.30N	14.00 E
Appennini = Apennines (EN)	5	Hg	43.00N	13.00 E
Appennino Abruzzese	14	Hh	42.00N	13.55 E
Appennino Calabro	14	Kl	39.00N	16.30 E
Appennino Campano	14	Ii	40.50N	14.45 E
Appennino Ligure	14	Cf	44.30N	9.00 E
Appennino Lucano	14	Jj	40.30N	16.00 E
Appennino Tosco-Emiliano	14	Fg	44.00N	11.30 E
Appennino Umbro-Marchigiano	14	Gg	43.20N	12.55 E
Appenzell	14	Dc	47.20N	9.25 E
Appenzell Ausser-Rhoden [2]	14	Dc	47.20N	9.20 E
Appenzell Inner-Rhoden [2]	14	Dc	47.15N	9.25 E
Appingedam	12	Ia	53.19N	6.52 E
Appleby	9	Kg	54.36N	2.29W
Appleton	43	Jc	44.16N	88.25W
Appomattox	44	Hg	37.21N	78.51W
Apra Harbor	64c	Bb	13.27N	144.38 E
Apricena	14	Ji	41.47N	15.27 E
Aprilia	14	Gi	41.36N	12.39 E
Apšeronsk	19	Dg	44.27N	39.44 E
Apšeronski Poluostrov= Apsheron Peninsula (EN)	5	Lg	41.00N	50.50 E
Apsheron Peninsula (EN)= Apšeronski Poluostrov	5	Lg	41.00N	50.50 E
Apt	11	Lk	43.53N	5.24 E
Apucarana	56	Jb	23.33S	51.29W
Apucarana, Serra da-	55	Gf	23.50S	51.20W
Apuka	20	Ld	60.23N	169.45 E
Apuka	20	Ld	60.25N	169.35 E
Apulia (EN) = Puglia [2]	14	Ki	41.15N	16.15 E
Apurashokoru	64a	Ac	7.17N	134.18 E
Apure [2]	54	Eb	7.10N	68.50W
Apure, Rio-	52	Je	7.37N	66.25W
Apurimac [2]	54	Df	14.00S	73.00W
Apurimac, Rio-	52	Ig	12.17S	73.56W
Apurito	50	Bi	7.56N	68.27W
Apuseni, Munţii-=Apuseni Mountains (EN)	5	If	46.30N	22.30 E
Apuseni Mountains (EN)= Apuseni, Munţii-	5	If	46.30N	22.30 E
Āq	24	Kc	38.59N	45.27 E
Āqā	24	Me	35.00N	47.00 E
Aqaba (EN)=Al 'Aqabah	23	Dd	29.31N	35.00 E
Aqaba, Gulf of- (EN)= 'Aqabah, Khalīj al-	30	Kf	29.00N	34.40 E
Āqā Bāba	24	Md	36.20N	49.46 E
'Aqabah, Khalīj al-=Aqaba, Gulf of- (EN)	30	Kf	29.00N	34.40 E
Āqcheh	23	Kb	36.56N	66.11 E
'Aqdā	24	Of	32.26N	53.37 E
'Aqīq	35	Fb	18.14N	38.12 E
Aqitag	27	Fc	41.49N	90.38 E
Āqotāq	24	Ld	37.10N	47.05 E
Āq Qal'eh	24	Pd	37.01N	54.30 E
Aqqikkol Hu	27	Ed	37.00N	88.20 E
'Aqrah	24	Jd	36.45N	43.54 E
Aqrin, Jabal-	24	Hg	31.32N	38.18 E
Āq Sū	24	Ke	34.35N	44.31 E
Aquidabã, Rio-	55	De	20.58S	57.50W
Aquidabán, Rio-	55	Df	23.11S	57.32W
Aquidauana	54	Gh	20.28S	55.48W
Aquidauana, Rio-	54	Gg	19.44S	56.50W
Aquidauana, Serra de-	55	Ee	20.50S	55.30W
Aquiles Serdán	48	Gc	28.36N	105.53W
Aquin	49	Kd	18.16N	73.24W
Aquitaine, Bassin d'-= Aquitane Basin (EN)	5	Fg	44.00N	0.10W
Aquitane Basin (EN)= Aquitaine, Bassin d'-	5	Fg	44.00N	0.10W
Ara	13	Mb	42.25N	0.09 E
'Arab, Baḩr al-	30	Jh	9.02N	29.28 E
'Arab, Khalīj al-	33	Ec	30.55N	29.05 E
'Arab, Shaţţ al-	21	Gf	30.28N	47.59 E
'Arabah, Wādī-	24	Eh	29.07N	32.39 E
'Arabah, Wādī al-	24	Fg	30.58N	32.24 E
Arabatskaja Strelka, Kosa-	16	Ig	45.40N	35.05 E
'Arabestān	24	Mg	30.30N	50.00 E
Arabian Basin (EN)	3	Gh	11.30N	65.00 E
Arabian Desert (EN)= Sharqiyah, Aş Şaḩrā' ash-	30	Kf	28.00N	32.00 E
Arabian Peninsula (EN)	21	Gg	25.00N	45.00 E
Arabian Sea (EN)	21	Ih	15.00N	65.00 E
Araç	24	Eb	41.15N	33.21 E
Aracá, Rio-	54	Fd	0.25S	62.55W
Aracaju	53	Mg	10.55S	37.04W
Aracataca	49	Jh	10.35N	74.13W
Aracati	54	Kd	4.34S	37.46W
Araçatuba	53	Kh	21.12S	50.25W
Aracena	13	Fg	37.53N	6.33W
Aracena, Sierra de-	13	Fg	37.56N	6.50W
Aracides, Cape-	63a	Ec	8.39S	161.01 E
Aracruz	54	Jg	19.49S	40.16W
Araçuai	54	Jg	16.52S	42.04W
Arad	6	If	46.11N	21.19 E
'Arad	24	Fg	31.15N	35.13 E
Arad [2]	15	Ec	46.11N	21.25 E
Arada	35	Cb	15.01N	20.40 E
'Arādah	35	Ia	22.59N	53.26 E
Arafali	35	Fb	15.04N	39.45 E
Ara Fana	35	Gd	6.01N	41.11 E
Arafune-Yama	29	Fc	36.12N	138.38 E
Arafura, Laut-=Arafura Sea (EN)	57	Ee	9.00S	133.00 E
Arafura, Sea (EN)=Arafura, Laut-	57	Ee	9.00S	133.00 E
Aragac, Gora-	5	Kg	40.31N	44.10 E
Aragarças	53	Kg	15.55S	52.15W
Aragón	13	Kb	42.13N	1.44W
Aragón	5	Fg	41.00N	1.00W
Aragón	13	Lc	41.00N	1.00W
Aragona	14	Hm	37.24N	13.37 E
Aragua [2]	54	Eb	10.00N	67.10W
Araguacema	54	Ie	8.50S	49.34W
Aragua de Barcelona	50	Dh	9.28N	64.49W
Aragua de Maturin	50	Eh	9.58N	63.29W
Araguaia, Rio-	52	Lf	5.21S	48.41W
Araguaiana	55	Gb	16.49S	53.05W
Araguaina	54	Ie	7.12S	48.12W
Araguao, Boca-	54	Fb	9.17N	60.48W
Araguao, Caño-	50	Fh	9.15N	60.50W
Araguapiche, Punta-	50	Fh	9.29N	60.56W
Araguari	54	Ig	18.38S	48.11W
Araguari, Rio- [Braz.]	52	Le	1.15N	49.55W
Araguari, Rio- [Braz.]	55	Hd	18.21S	48.40W
Araguatins	54	Ie	5.38S	48.07W
'Arāguīb	32	Ff	18.50N	7.45W
Aragvi	16	Ni	41.50N	44.43 E
Arai	28	Of	37.09N	138.06 E
Árainn/ Inishmore	9	Dh	53.07N	9.45W
Árainn Mhór/Aran Island	9	Ef	55.00N	8.30W
Araioses	54	Jd	2.53S	41.55W
Arāk	22	Gf	34.05N	49.41 E
Arak	32	Hd	25.18N	3.45 E
Arakabesan	64a	Ac	7.21N	134.27 E
Arakan [2]	25	Ie	19.00N	94.15 E
Arakan Yoma	21	Lh	19.00N	94.40 E
Arakawa	29	Fb	38.09N	139.25 E
Ara-Kawa [Jap.]	29	Fb	38.09N	139.23 E
Ara-Kawa [Jap.]	29	Fc	37.11N	138.15 E
Árakhthos	15	Ej	39.01N	21.03 E
Araks	21	Gf	39.56N	48.20 E
Aral [China]	27	Dc	40.38N	81.24 E
Aral	19	Hg	41.48N	74.25 E
Aral Sea (EN)=Aralskoje More	21	He	45.00N	60.00 E
Aralsk	22	Ie	46.48N	61.40 E
Aralskoje More=Aral Sea (EN)	21	He	45.00N	60.00 E
Aralsor, Ozero-	16	Pe	49.05N	48.15 E
Aralsulfat	19	Gf	46.50N	61.59 E
Aramac	59	Jd	22.59S	145.14 E
Arambaré	55	Gj	30.55S	51.29W
Ārān	24	Ne	34.03N	51.30 E
Aranda de Duero	13	Ic	41.41N	3.41W
Arandelovac	15	De	44.18N	20.35 E
Arandilla	13	Ic	41.40N	3.41W
Aran Island/Árainn Mhór	9	Dh	53.07N	9.43W
Aran Islands	9	Ef	55.00N	8.30W
Aranjunez	13	Id	40.02N	3.36W
Aranos	37	Bd	24.09S	19.09 E
Arañuelo, Campo-	13	Ge	39.55N	5.30W
Aranuka Atoll	57	Id	0.11N	173.36 E
Arao	29	Be	32.59N	130.27 E
Araouane	31	Gg	18.53N	3.35W
Arapahoe	45	Gf	40.18N	99.54W
Arapey Grande, Rio-	55	Dj	30.55S	57.49W
Arapiraca	54	Ke	9.45S	36.39W
Arápis, Ákra-	15	Gi	40.27N	24.00 E
Arapkir	24	Hc	39.03N	38.30 E
Arapoim, Rio-	55	Kb	15.45S	43.39W
Arapongas	56	Jb	23.23S	51.27W
Arapoti	55	Hg	24.08S	49.50W
'Ar'ar	24	Ig	30.59N	41.02 E
'Ar'ar, Wādī	24	Jg	31.23N	42.26 E
Araranguá	56	Kc	28.56S	49.29W
Araraquara	53	Lh	21.47S	48.10W
Araras	55	If	22.22S	47.23W
Araras, Açude-	54	Jd	4.20S	40.30W
Araras, Serra das-	55	Fd	18.45S	53.00W
Ararat	19	Eh	39.50N	44.43 E
Ararat [Austl.]	59	Ig	37.17S	142.56 E
Ararat, Mount- (EN)=Büyük Ağri Daği	21	Gf	39.40N	44.24 E
Arari	54	Jd	3.28S	44.47W
Arari, Lago-	54	Id	0.37S	49.07W
Aras	21	Gf	39.56N	48.20 E
Aras Dağlari	24	Jc	40.00N	43.00 E
Aratika Atoll	57	Mf	15.32S	145.32W
Aratürük/Yiwu	27	Fc	43.15N	94.35 E
Arauca [2]	54	Db	6.30N	71.00W
Arauca	54	Db	7.03N	70.47W
Arauca, Rio-	52	Je	7.24N	66.35W
Araucania [2]	56	Fe	37.50S	73.15W
Arauco	56	Fe	37.15S	73.19W
Araure	50	Bh	9.38N	69.15W
Aravaca, Madrid-	13	Id	40.27N	3.47W
Aravis	11	Mi	45.53N	6.28 E
Arawali Range	21	Jg	25.00N	73.30 E
Araxá	54	Ig	19.35S	46.55W
Áraxos, Ákra-	15	Ek	38.10N	21.23 E
Araya	50	Dg	10.34N	64.15W
Araya, Peninsula de-	54	Fa	10.35N	64.00W
Arba	13	Kc	41.52N	1.18W
Arba'āt	35	Fb	19.50N	37.03 E
Arba'īn, Darb al-	24	Di	26.40N	30.50 E
Arbaj-Here	27	Hb	46.15N	102.48 E
Arba Minch	31	Kh	5.59N	37.38 E
'Arbat	24	Ke	35.25N	45.35 E
Arbatax	14	Dk	39.56N	9.42 E
Arboga	7	Dg	59.24N	15.50 E
Arbogaån	8	Ge	59.26N	16.04 E
Arbois	11	Lh	46.54N	5.46 E
Arboletes	49	Ii	8.52N	76.25W
Arbolito	55	Ek	32.39S	54.15W
Arbon	14	Dc	47.30N	9.26 E
Arbore	15	Ib	47.44N	25.56 E
Arborea	14	Ck	39.46N	8.35 E
Arborea	14	Ck	39.50N	8.50 E
Arborg	45	Ha	50.55N	97.15W
Arbrå	7	Dc	61.29N	16.23 E
Arbroath	9	Ke	56.34N	2.35W
Arbus	14	Ck	39.32N	8.36 E
Arc [Fr.]	11	Mi	45.34N	6.12 E
Arc [Fr.]	11	Lk	43.31N	5.07 E
Arcachon	11	Ej	44.39N	1.10W
Arcachon, Bassin d'-	11	Ej	44.42N	1.09W
Arcadia [Fl.-U.S.]	44	Gl	27.14N	81.52W
Arcadia [La.-U.S.]	45	Jj	32.33N	92.55W
Arcagly-Ajat	17	Jj	53.00N	61.50 E
Arcas, Cayos-	47	Fd	20.12N	91.58W
Arcata	46	Cf	40.52N	124.05W
Arcelia	48	Ih	18.17N	100.16W
Arcen, Arcen en Velden-	12	Ic	51.28N	6.11 E
Arcevia	14	Gg	43.30N	12.56 E
Archangel (EN)= Archangelsk	6	Kc	64.34N	40.32 E
Archaringa Creek	59	He	28.15S	135.15 E
Archer River	59	Ib	13.28S	141.41 E
Archer's Post	36	Gb	0.39N	37.41 E
Archidona	13	Hg	37.05N	4.23W
Arcidosso	14	Fh	42.52N	11.33 E
Arcipelago Campano	5	Hg	40.30N	13.20 E
Arcipelago Toscano= Tuscan Archipelago (EN)	5	Hg	42.45N	10.20 E
Arcis-sur-Aube	11	Kf	48.32N	4.08 E
Arciz	16	Fg	45.59N	29.27 E
Arco [Id.-U.S.]	46	Ie	43.38N	113.18W
Arco [It.]	14	Ee	45.55N	10.53 E
Arconce	11	Jh	46.27N	4.00 E
Arcos	55	Je	20.17S	45.32W
Arcos de Jalón	13	Jc	41.13N	2.16W
Arcos de la Frontera	13	Gh	36.45N	5.48W
Arcos de Valdevez	13	Dc	41.51N	8.25W
Arcoverde	53	Mf	8.25S	37.04W
Arctic Bay	39	Kb	73.02N	85.11W
Arctic Ocean	67	Be	85.00N	170.00 E
Arctic Ocean (EN)= Ishavet	67	Be	85.00N	170.00 E
Arctic Ocean (EN)=Severny Ledovity Okean	67	Be	85.00N	170.00 E
Arctic Red River	42	Ec	67.27N	133.45W
Arctic Red River	42	Ec	67.22N	133.30W
Arctic Village	40	Jc	68.08N	145.19W
Arda [Eur.]	15	Jh	41.39N	26.29 E
Arda [It.]	14	Ee	45.02N	10.02 E
Ardabil [Iran]	22	Gf	38.15N	48.18 E
Ardabil [Iraq]	24	Ie	34.24N	40.59 E
Ardahan	24	Jb	41.07N	42.41 E
Ardakāh	23	Hc	32.19N	53.59 E
Ardakān	24	Og	30.16N	52.01 E
Ardal	24	Ng	31.59N	50.39 E
Ardales	13	Hh	36.52N	4.51W
Ardalsfjorden	8	Bc	61.15N	7.30 E
Årdalstangen	7	Bf	61.14N	7.43 E
Ardanuç	24	Jb	41.08N	42.03 E
Ardatov	7	Ki	55.17N	43.12 E
Ardatov	7	Li	54.53N	46.13 E
'Arde	35	Hd	9.58N	46.04 E
Ardèche	11	Kj	44.16N	4.39 E
Ardèche [3]	11	Kj	44.40N	4.20 E
Ardee/Béal Atha Fhirdhia	9	Gh	53.52N	6.33W
Ardencaple Fjord	41	Jd	75.20N	20.10W
Ardenne, Plateau de l'-/ Ardennen, Plateau van der- =Ardennes (EN)	5	Ge	50.10N	5.45 E
Ardennen, Plateau van der-/ Ardenne, Plateau de l'-= Ardennes (EN)	5	Ge	50.10N	5.45 E
Ardennes [3]	11	Ke	49.40N	4.40 E
Ardennes (EN)=Ardenne, Plateau de l'-/Ardennen, Plateau van der-	5	Ge	50.10N	5.45 E
Ardennes (EN)=Ardennen, Plateau van der-/Ardenne, Plateau de l'-	5	Ge	50.10N	5.45 E
Ardennes, Canal des-	11	Ke	49.26N	4.02 E
Ardennes, Forêt des-	12	Ge	49.48N	4.50 E
Ardentes	11	Hh	46.45N	1.50 E
Ardeşen	24	Ib	41.12N	41.00 E
Ardestān	24	Of	33.22N	52.23 E
Ardhas	15	Jh	41.39N	26.29 E
Ardila	13	Ef	38.12N	7.28W
Ard Mhacha/Armagh	9	Gg	54.21N	6.39W
Ardmore	43	He	34.10N	97.08W
Ardnamurchan, Point of-	9	Ge	56.45N	6.30W
Ardon	16	Nh	43.07N	44.13 E
Ardooie	12	Fd	50.59N	3.12 E
Ardre	12	Fe	49.18N	3.40 E
Ardres	12	Dd	50.51N	1.59 E
Ards Peninsula/An Aird	9	Hg	54.30N	5.30W
Ar Dub'al Khālī	21	Hg	21.00N	51.00 E
Ardud	15	Fb	47.38N	22.53 E
Arebi	36	Eb	2.50N	29.38 E
Arecibo	47	Ke	18.28N	66.43W
Areen en Valden	12	Ic	51.28N	6.11 E
Areen en Velden-Arcen	12	Ic	51.28N	6.11 E
Arégala/Ariogala	8	Ji	55.13N	23.30 E
Areia, Ribeirão da-	55	Jc	16.07S	45.52W
Areia Branca	54	Kd	4.57S	37.08W
Arekalong Peninsula	64a	Bb	7.40N	134.38 E
Aremberg	12	Id	50.25N	6.49 E
Arena	26	He	9.14N	120.46 E
Arena, Point-	43	Cd	38.57N	123.44W
Arena, Punta-	47	Cd	23.30N	109.30W
Arena de la Ventana, Punta-	47	Cd	24.04N	109.52W
Arenápolis	54	Gf	14.26S	56.49W
Arenas, Cayo-	47	Fd	22.08N	91.24W
Arenas, Punta de-	56	Gh	53.09S	68.13W
Arenas de San Pedro	13	Gd	40.12N	5.05W
Arenberg	12	Jb	52.42N	7.20 E
Arendal	7	Bg	58.27N	8.48 E
Arendonk	12	Hc	51.19N	5.05 E
Arénys de Mar/Arenys de Mar	13	Oc	41.35N	2.33 E
Arenys de Mar/Arénys de Mar	13	Oc	41.35N	2.33 E
Areópolis	15	Fm	36.40N	22.23 E
Areq, Sebkha bou-	13	Ji	35.10N	2.45W
Arequipa	53	Ig	16.24S	71.33W
Arequipa [2]	54	Dg	16.00S	72.30W
Arequito	55	Bk	33.09S	61.28W
Arero	35	Fe	4.44N	38.50 E
Ares, Muela de-	13	Ld	40.28N	0.07W
Åreskutan	8	Ea	63.26N	13.06 E
Åreskutan	7	Ce	63.24N	13.06 E
Arévalo	13	Hc	41.04N	4.43W
Arezzo	14	Fg	43.25N	11.53 E
Arga	13	Kb	42.18N	1.47W
Argajaš	17	Ji	55.31N	60.55 E
Argamasilla de Alba	13	Ie	39.07N	3.06W
Argan	27	Ec	40.09N	88.22 E
Arganda	13	Id	40.18N	3.26W
Arga-Sala	20	Gc	68.37N	112.05 E
Argelès-Gazost	11	Fk	43.01N	0.06W
Argelès-sur-Mer	11	Jl	42.33N	3.01 E
Argens	11	Mk	43.24N	6.44 E

Index Symbols

[1] Independent Nation
[2] State, Region
[3] District, County
[4] Municipality
[5] Colony, Dependency
Continent
Physical Region
Historical or Cultural Region
Mount, Mountain
Volcano
Hill
Mountains, Mountain Range
Hills, Escarpment
Plateau, Upland
Pass, Gap
Plain, Lowland
Delta
Salt Flat
Valley, Canyon
Crater, Cave
Karst Features
Depression
Polder
Desert, Dunes
Forest, Woods
Heath, Steppe
Oasis
Cape, Point
Coast, Beach
Cliff
Peninsula
Isthmus
Sandbank
Island
Atoll
Rock, Reef
Islands, Archipelago
Rocks, Reefs
Coral Reef
Well, Spring
Geyser
River, Stream
Waterfall Rapids
River Mouth, Estuary
Lake
Salt Lake
Intermittent Lake
Reservoir
Swamp, Pond
Canal
Glacier
Ice Shelf, Pack Ice
Ocean
Sea
Gulf, Bay
Strait, Fjord
Lagoon
Bank
Seamount
Tablemount
Ridge
Shelf
Basin
Escarpment, Sea Scarp
Fracture
Trench, Abyss
National Park, Reserve
Point of Interest
Recreation Site
Cave, Cavern
Historic Site
Ruins
Wall, Walls
Church, Abbey
Temple
Scientific Station
Airport
Port
Lighthouse
Mine
Tunnel
Dam, Bridge

Argent, Côte d'- 11 Ej 44.00N 1.30W
Argenta 14 Ff 44.37N 11.50 E
Argentan 11 Ff 48.45N 0.01W
Argentario, Monte- 14 Fh 42.24N 11.09 E
Argentat 11 Hi 45.06N 1.56 E
Argentera 14 Bf 44.10N 7.18 E
Argenteuil 11 If 48.57N 2.15 E
Argentiera, Capo dell'- 14 Cj 40.44N 8.08 E
Argentina 55 Ai 29.33S 62.17W
Argentina [1] 53 Ji 34.00S 64.00W
Argentine Basin (EN) 3 Cn 45.00S 45.00W
Argentino, Lago- 52 Ik 50.13S 72.25W
Argentino, Mar- 52 Kj 46.00S 59.40W
Argenton 11 Fg 47.05N 0.13W
Argenton-Château 11 Fh 46.59N 0.27W
Argenton-sur-Creuse 11 Hh 46.35N 1.31 E
Arges 15 Jd 44.04N 26.37 E
Arges [2] 15 Hd 45.00N 24.50 E
Arghandāb 23 Jc 31.27N 64.23 E
Argo 35 Eb 19.31N 30.25 E
Argo Depth (EN) 3 Jk 12.10S 165.40W
Argolikós Kólpos = Argolis, Gulf of- (EN) 15 Fl 37.20N 22.55 E
Argolis, Gulf of- (EN) = Argolikós Kólpos 15 Fl 37.20N 22.55 E
Argonne 12 He 49.30N 5.00 E
Argonne 11 Ke 49.30N 5.00 E
Árgos 15 Fl 37.38N 22.44 E
Árgos Orestikón 15 Ei 40.30N 21.16 E
Argostólion 15 Dk 38.11N 20.29 E
Arguedas 13 Kb 42.10N 1.36W
Argueil-Fry 12 De 49.37N 1.31 E
Arguello, Point- 46 Ei 34.35N 120.39W
Arguenon 11 Df 48.35N 2.13W
Argun 16 Nh 43.16N 45.52 E
Argun 21 Od 53.20N 121.28 E
Argungu 34 Fc 12.45N 4.31 E
Argyle 51n Ba 13.10N 61.10W
Argyle, Lake- 57 Df 16.15S 128.40 E
Argyll 9 Ie 56.20N 5.00W
Arhangelsk = Archangel (EN) 6 Kc 64.34N 40.32 E
Arhangelskaja Oblast [3] 19 Ec 63.30N 43.00 E
Arhara 20 Ig 49.30N 130.09 E
Arhavi 24 Ib 41.22N 41.16 E
Arholma 8 He 59.50N 19.05 E
Ar Horqin Qi (Tianshan) 27 Lc 43.55N 120.05 E
Århus [2] 8 Dh 56.10N 10.15 E
Århus 6 Hd 56.09N 10.13 E
Århus Bugt 8 Dh 56.10N 10.20 E
Arhust 27 Ib 47.42N 107.50 E
Ariadnoje 20 Ig 45.08N 134.25 E
Ariake-Kai 28 Kh 32.55N 130.27 E
Ariamsvlei 37 Be 28.08S 19.50 E
Ariano Irpino 14 Ji 41.09N 15.05 E
Ariari, Rio- 54 Dc 2.35N 72.47W
Arias 56 Hd 33.38S 62.25W
Ari Atoll 25a Bb 3.30N 72.45 E
Aribinda 34 Ec 14.14N 0.52W
Arica 53 Ig 18.29S 70.20W
Arica, Golfo de- 52 Ig 18.30S 70.30W
Arichuna 50 Ci 7.42N 67.08W
Arid, Cape- 59 Ef 34.00S 123.09 E
Arida 28 Mg 34.05N 135.07 E
Arida-Gawa 29 Dd 34.05N 135.06 E
Aridhaia 15 Fi 40.59N 22.04 E
Ariège 11 Hk 43.31N 1.25 E
Ariège [3] 11 Hk 43.00N 1.30 E
Ariel 55 Cm 36.32S 59.54W
Arieş 15 Gc 46.26N 23.59 E
Ariguani 54 Db 9.50N 74.01W
Ariguani, Rio- 49 Ki 9.35N 73.46W
Arīḩā [Jor.] 24 Fg 31.52N 35.27 E
Arīḩā [Syr.] 24 Ge 35.48N 36.36 E
Arikaree River 45 Ff 40.01N 101.56W
Arikawa 29 Ae 32.59N 129.07 E
Arilje 15 Df 43.45N 20.06 E
Arima 54 Fa 10.38N 61.17W
Arinos 55 Ib 15.55S 46.04W
Arinos, Rio- 52 Kg 10.25S 58.20W
Arinos Novo, Rio- 55 Db 14.14S 56.01W
Ariogala/Arėgala 8 Ji 55.13N 23.30 E
Aripuanã 54 Fe 9.10S 60.38W
Aripuanã, Rio- 52 Jf 5.07S 60.24W
Ariquemes 54 Fe 9.56S 63.04W
Arisa 35 Gc 11.11N 41.38 E
'Arish, Wādī al- 24 Eg 31.09N 33.49 E
Arismendi 49 Mi 8.29N 68.22W
Arita 29 Ae 33.11N 129.52 E
Aritzo 14 Dk 39.57N 9.12 E
Arixang/Wenquan 27 Dc 44.59N 81.04 E
Ariza 13 Jc 41.19N 2.03W
Arizaro, Salar de- 56 Gb 24.42S 67.45W
Arize, Massif de l'- 11 Hl 42.50N 1.30 E
Arizona [2] 43 Ee 34.00N 112.00W
Arizpe 48 Db 30.20N 110.10W
Årjäng 7 Cg 59.23N 12.08 E
Arjeplog 7 Dc 66.03N 17.54 E
Arjo 35 Fd 8.45N 36.30 E
Arjona 54 Ca 10.15N 75.21W
Arkadak 19 Ee 51.58N 43.28 E
Arkadelphia 43 Ie 34.07N 93.04W
Arkalyk 22 Id 50.13N 66.50 E
Arkansas 38 Jf 33.48N 91.04W
Arkansas [2] 43 Id 34.50N 93.40W
Arkansas City 43 Hd 37.04N 97.02W
Arkanū, Jabal- 33 De 22.15N 24.45 E
Arkatag 21 Kf 36.45N 89.10 E
Arkhángelos 15 Lm 36.12N 28.08 E
Árki 15 Jl 37.22N 26.45 E
Arklow/An tInbhear Mór 9 Gi 52.48N 6.09W
Arkona, Kap- 10 Jb 54.41N 13.26 E
Arkonam 25 Ff 13.06N 79.40 E
Arkösund 8 Gf 58.30N 16.56 E
Arkoúdhion 15 Dk 38.33N 20.43 E
Arktičeskoga Instituta, Ostrova- = Arkticheski Institut Islands (EN) 20 Da 75.20N 81.50 E
Arkticheski Institut Islands (EN) = Arktičeskoga Instituta, Ostrova- 20 Da 75.20N 81.50 E
Arlan, Gora- 16 Sj 39.43N 54.40 E
Arlanza 13 Hb 42.06N 4.09W
Arlanzón 13 Hb 42.03N 4.17W
Arlberg 14 Ec 47.08N 10.12 E
Arles 11 Kk 43.40N 4.38 E
Arlington [Or.-U.S.] 46 Ed 45.46N 120.13W
Arlington [Tx.-U.S.] 45 Hj 32.44N 97.07W
Arlington [Va.-U.S.] 43 Ld 38.52N 77.05W
Arlington Heights 45 Me 42.05N 87.59W
Arlit 31 Hg 19.00N 7.38 E
Arlon/Aarlen 11 Le 49.41N 5.49 E
Arlöv 8 Ei 55.39N 13.05 E
Arly 34 Fc 11.35N 1.28 E
Armagh/Ard Mhacha 9 Gg 54.21N 6.39W
Armagnac 11 Gk 43.45N 0.10 E
Armagnac, Collines de l'- 11 Gk 43.30N 0.30 E
Armah, Wādī- 23 Hf 18.12N 51.02 E
Arman 20 Ke 59.43N 150.12 E
Armançon 11 Jg 47.57N 3.30 E
Armandale, Perth- 59 Df 32.09S 116.00 E
Armant 33 Fd 25.37N 32.32 E
Armáthia 15 Jn 35.26N 26.52 E
Armavir 6 Kf 45.00N 41.08 E
Armenia 53 Ie 4.31N 75.41W
Armenia (EN) = Ermenistan 23 Fb 39.10N 43.00 E
Armenia (EN) = Ermenistan 21 Gf 39.10N 43.00 E
Armenia (EN) = Hayastan 19 Eg 40.00N 45.00 E
Armentières 11 Id 50.41N 2.53 E
Armeria 48 Gh 18.56N 103.58W
Armi, Capo dell'- 14 Jm 37.57N 15.41 E
Armidale 58 Gh 30.31S 151.39 E
Armisvesi 8 Lb 62.30N 26.35 E
Armjansk 16 Hf 46.05N 33.41 E
Armjanskaja Sovetskaja Socialističeskaja Respublika → Hayastan 19 Eg 40.00N 45.00 E
Armjanskaja SSR/Haikakan Sovetaken Socialistakan Respublika → Hayastan 19 Eg 40.00N 45.00 E
Armjanskaja SSR → Hayastan 19 Eg 40.00N 45.00 E
Armoricain, Massif- = Armorican Massif (EN) 5 Ff 48.00N 3.00W
Armorican Massif (EN) = Armoricain, Massif- 5 Ff 48.00N 3.00W
Armour 45 Ge 43.19N 98.21W
Arm River 46 Ma 50.46N 105.00W
Armstrong [Arg.] 55 Bk 32.47S 61.36W
Armstrong [B.C.-Can.] 46 Fa 50.27N 119.12W
Armstrong [Ont.-Can.] 42 If 50.18N 89.02W
Ārmūdlū 24 Qd 37.15N 56.05 E
Armutçuk Dağ 15 Ki 40.05N 27.23 E
Armutlu 15 Li 40.31N 28.50 E
Armutova 15 Jj 39.23N 26.50 E
Arnaia 15 Gi 40.29N 23.36 E
Arnaud 42 Kd 60.00N 69.55W
Arnautis, Akrotērion- 24 Ee 35.06N 32.17 E
Arnay-le-Duc 11 Kg 47.08N 4.29 E
Arnedo 13 Jb 42.13N 2.06W
Årnes 7 Cf 60.09N 11.28 E
Arnhem 11 Lc 51.59N 5.55 E
Arnhem, Cape- 57 Ef 12.21S 136.21 E
Arnhem Bay 59 Hb 12.20S 136.10 E
Arnhem Land 57 Ef 13.10S 134.30 E
Arno 14 Eg 43.41N 10.17 E
Arno Atoll 57 Id 7.05N 171.41 E
Arnold 12 Aa 53.00N 1.08W
Arnon 11 Ig 47.13N 2.01 E
Arnøy 7 Ea 70.08N 20.36 E
Arnprior 44 Ic 45.26N 76.21W
Arnsberg 10 Ee 51.23N 8.05 E
Arnsberger Wald 12 Kc 51.26N 8.10 E
Arnsberg-Oeventrop 12 Kc 51.24N 8.08 E
Arnsburg 12 Kd 50.29N 8.48 E
Arnstadt 10 Gf 50.50N 10.57 E
Aro, Rio- 50 Di 8.01N 64.11W
Aroa 50 Bg 10.26N 68.54W
Aroa, Pointe- 65e Fc 17.28S 149.46W
Aroa, Rio- 50 Bg 10.41N 68.18W
Aroa, Sierra de- 50 Bg 10.15N 68.55W
Aroab 37 Be 26.47S 19.40 E
Aroánia Óri 15 Fl 37.57N 22.13 E
Aroche 13 Fg 37.57N 6.57W
Aroche, Pico de- 13 Ff 38.01N 6.56W
Aroeira 55 Ee 21.41S 54.25W
Arolsen 12 Lc 51.22N 9.01 E
Aroma 35 Fb 15.49N 36.08 E
Aron 11 Jh 46.50N 3.27 E
Arona 14 Ce 45.46N 8.34 E
Aroostook River 44 Nb 46.48N 67.45W
Arorae Island 57 Ie 2.38S 176.49 E
Arorangi 64p Bb 21.13S 159.49W
Aros, Rio- 48 Ec 29.30N 109.15W
Arosa 14 Dd 46.47N 9.40 E
Arosa, Ría de- 13 Db 42.28N 8.57W
Aros Papigochic, Rio- 48 Ec 29.09N 108.35W
Årøsund 8 Ci 55.15N 9.43 E
Arouca 13 Dd 40.56N 8.15W
Arpaçay 24 Jb 40.45N 43.25 E
Arpajon 11 If 48.35N 2.15 E
Arpino 14 Hi 41.39N 13.36 E
Arquata Scrivia 14 Cf 44.41N 8.53 E
Arque 54 Eg 17.48S 66.23W
Arques-la-Bataille 12 De 49.53N 1.08 E
Ar Rachidiya 32 Gc 31.55N 4.40W
Ar Rachidiya [3] 32 Gc 31.00N 4.00W
Ar Radīsīyah Baḩrī 33 Fe 24.57N 32.53 E
Arrah 25 Gc 25.34N 84.40 E
Ar Rahad 35 Ec 12.43N 30.39 E
Ar Rahad 30 Kg 14.28N 33.31 E
Arraias 54 If 12.56S 46.57W
Arraias, Rio- [Braz.] 54 Hf 11.10S 53.35W
Arraias, Rio- [Braz.] 55 Ia 12.28S 47.18W
Arraiolos 13 Ef 38.43N 7.59W
Ar Ramādī 23 Fc 33.25N 43.17 E
Ar Ramlah 24 Fh 29.32N 35.57 E
Ar Ramlī al Kabīr 33 Dd 26.30N 22.10 E
Arran, Island of- 9 Hf 55.35N 5.15W
Ar Rank 35 Ec 11.45N 32.48 E
Ar Raqqah 23 Eb 35.56N 39.01 E
Arras 11 Id 50.17N 2.47 E
Ar Rāshidah 24 Cj 25.35N 28.56 E
Ar Rass 24 Jj 25.52N 43.28 E
Ar Rastān 24 Ge 34.55N 36.44 E
Arrats 11 Gj 44.06N 0.52 E
Ar Rawḑah [Sau.Ar.] 33 He 21.16N 42.50 E
Ar Rawḑatayn 24 Lh 29.53N 47.44 E
Ar Rayhānī 24 Pk 23.37N 55.58 E
Arrecife 32 Ed 28.57N 13.32W
Arrecife Alacrán 47 Gd 22.24N 89.42W
Arrecifes 56 Hd 34.03S 60.07W
Arrecifes, Rio- 55 Ck 33.46S 59.31W
Arrée, Montagnes d'- 11 Cf 48.26N 3.55W
Arresø 8 Ei 55.55N 12.05 E
Arriaga 48 Mi 16.14N 93.54W
Ar Rifā'ī 24 Lg 31.43N 46.07 E
Ar Rihāb 24 Kg 30.52N 45.30 E
Ar Rimāḩ 24 Lj 25.34N 47.09 E
Ar Rimāl 21 Hg 22.00N 52.50 E
Ar Riyāḑ = Riyadh (EN) 22 Gg 24.38N 46.43 E
Arrochar 9 Ie 56.12N 4.45W
Arroio Grande 55 Fk 32.14S 53.05W
Arrojado 55 Ja 13.29S 44.37W
Arrojado, Rio- 55 Ja 13.24S 44.20W
Arromanches-les-Bains 12 Be 49.20N 0.37W
Arros 11 Gk 43.40N 0.02 E
Arroscia 14 Cg 44.03N 8.11 E
Arroux 11 Jh 46.29N 3.58 E
Arrow, Lough-/Loch Arabhach 9 Eg 54.05N 8.20W
Arrowsmith, Mount- 61 Dh 43.21S 170.59 E
Arrowtown 62 Cf 44.56S 168.50 E
Arroyo Barú 55 Cj 31.52S 58.26W
Arroyo de la Luz 13 Fe 39.29N 6.35W
Arroyo Grande 46 Ei 35.07N 120.34W
Arroyos y Esteros 55 Dg 25.04S 57.06W
Arruda 55 Db 15.02S 56.07W
Arrufó 56 Hd 30.15S 61.45W
Ar Rumaythah 24 Kg 31.32N 45.12 E
Ar Ruq'ī 24 Lh 29.01N 46.33 E
Ar Ruṣāfah 24 He 35.02N 36.17 E
Ar Ruṣayriş 31 Kg 11.51N 34.23 E
Ar Ruṭbah 23 Fc 33.02N 40.17 E
Ar Ruwaydah 24 Ki 26.23N 44.14 E
Ar Ruways [Qatar] 23 Hd 26.08N 51.13 E
Ar Ruways [U.A.E.] 23 He 24.08N 52.45 E
Ar Ruzayqāt 24 Ej 25.35N 32.28 E
Års 8 Ch 56.48N 9.32 E
Arsenjān 24 Oh 29.56N 53.18 E
Arsenjev 20 Ih 44.12N 133.20 E
Arsi [3] 35 Fd 7.10N 40.00 E
Arsk 7 Lh 56.07N 49.52 E
Årskogen 8 Gb 62.05N 17.20 E
Arslanköy 24 Fd 37.01N 34.17 E
Ars-sur-Moselle 12 Ie 49.05N 6.04 E
Arsuk 41 Hf 61.11N 48.30W
Årsunda 8 Gd 60.32N 16.44 E
Art 63b Ad 19.43S 163.39 E
Artá 13 Pe 39.42N 3.21 E
Arta 35 Gc 11.31N 42.50 E
Árta 15 Dj 39.09N 20.59 E
Artá, Cuevas de- 13 Pe 39.40N 3.24 E
Artašat 16 Nj 39.59N 44.33 E
Arteaga 48 Hh 18.28N 102.25W
Artem 20 Ih 43.23N 132.10 E
Artemisa 47 Hd 22.49N 82.46W
Artemón 15 Hm 36.57N 24.43 E
Artem-Ostrov 19 Fg 40.28N 50.18 E
Artemovsk 20 Ef 54.23N 93.30 E
Artemovsk 16 Ke 48.33N 38.03 E
Artemovski 17 Jh 57.25N 61.58 E
Artesa de Segre 13 Nc 41.54N 1.03 E
Artesia 43 Ge 32.51N 104.24W
Arthur 45 Ff 41.35N 101.31W
Arthur Creek 59 Hd 23.00S 136.58 E
Arthur River 59 Ih 41.00S 144.55 E
Arthur's Pass 61 Dh 42.57S 171.34 E
Arthur's Pass 62 De 42.54S 171.34 E
Arthur's Town 49 Ja 24.38N 75.32W
Arti 17 Ih 56.26N 58.32 E
Artibonite, Rivière de l'- 49 Kd 19.15N 72.47W
Artigas 56 Id 30.42S 56.28W
Artigas [2] 55 Dj 30.35S 57.00W
Artijarvi/Artsjö 8 Ld 60.45N 26.05 E
Artik 16 Mi 40.36N 43.58 E
Artillery Lake 42 Gd 63.08N 107.45W
Artois 11 Id 50.30N 2.30 E
Artois, Collines de l'- 11 Id 50.30N 2.15 E
Artoli 35 Eb 18.19N 33.54 E
Artsjö/Artjarvi 8 Ld 60.45N 26.05 E
Artux 27 Cd 39.40N 76.10 E
Artvin 23 Fa 41.11N 41.49 E
Artyk 20 Jd 64.12N 145.15 E
Aru 36 Fb 2.52N 30.51 E
Aru, Kepulauan- = Aru Islands (EN) 57 Ee 6.00S 134.30 E
Arua 31 Kh 3.01N 30.55 E
Aruanã 55 Gb 14.54S 51.05W
Aruba 54 Ea 12.30N 70.00W
Aruba 39 Lh 12.30N 71.00W
Aru Islands (EN) = Aru, Kepulauan 57 Ee 6.00S 134.30 E
Arukoron Point 64a Bb 7.43N 134.38 E
Arun 9 Mk 50.48N 0.33W
Arunāchal Pradesh [3] 25 Ic 27.50N 94.50 E
Arundel 12 Bd 50.51N 0.33W
Arun He 27 Lb 47.36N 124.06 E
Arun Qi 27 Lb 48.09N 123.29 E
Arus, Tanjung- 26 Hf 1.24N 125.06 E
Arusha [3] 36 Gc 3.30S 36.00 E
Arusha 31 Ki 3.22S 36.41 E
Arutua Atoll 61 Lc 15.18S 146.44W
Arutunga 61 Jc 18.52S 159.46W
Aruwimi 30 Jh 1.13N 23.36 E
Arvada [Co.-U.S.] 45 Dg 39.50N 105.05W
Arvada [Wy.-U.S.] 46 Ld 44.40N 106.03W
Arve 11 Mh 46.12N 6.08 E
Arvert, Presqu'île d'- 11 Ei 45.45N 1.05W
Arvida 42 Kg 48.26N 71.11W
Arvidsjaur 7 Ed 65.35N 19.10 E
Arvika 7 Cg 59.39N 12.36 E
Årviksand 7 Ea 70.12N 20.32 E
Arvin 46 Fi 35.12N 118.50W
Aryānah 14 En 36.52N 10.11 E
Arys 18 Gc 42.48N 68.15 E
Arys 19 Gg 42.26N 68.48 E
Arys, Ozero- 18 Fb 45.50N 66.20 E
Arz 11 Dg 47.39N 2.06W
Arzachena 14 Di 41.05N 9.23 E
Arzamas 19 Ed 55.23N 43.50 E
Arzanah 24 Oj 24.47N 52.34 E
Aržano 14 Kg 43.35N 16.59 E
Arzew 32 Gb 35.51N 0.19W
Arzew, Golfe d'- 13 Li 35.50N 0.10W
Arzew, Salines d'- 13 Li 35.42N 0.18W
Arzfeld 12 Id 50.05N 6.16 E
Arzgir 19 Ef 45.22N 44.13 E
Arzúa 13 Db 42.56N 8.09W
As 12 Hc 51.01N 5.35 E
Ås 8 De 59.40N 10.48 E
Aš 10 If 50.13N 12.12 E
Aša 19 Fd 55.02N 57.18 E
Aså 8 Dg 57.09N 10.25 E
Asab 37 Be 25.29S 17.59 E
Asaba 34 Gd 6.11N 6.45 E
Asad, Buḩayrat al- 24 He 35.57N 38.10 E
Asadābād [Afg.] 23 Lc 34.52N 71.09 E
Asadābād [Iran] 24 Me 34.47N 48.07 E
Asafik 35 Bc 13.10N 19.26 E
Asahi [Jap.] 29 Fb 38.15N 139.30 E
Asahi [Jap.] 29a Ca 44.08N 142.35 E
Asahi [Jap.] 29 Gd 35.43N 140.35 E
Asahi [Jap.] 29 Ec 36.57N 137.34 E
Asahi-Dake 29 Fb 38.16N 139.55 E
Asahi-Gawa 29 Cd 34.36N 133.58 E
Asahikawa 22 Qe 43.46N 142.22 E
Asaka-Drainage 29 Gc 37.30N 140.15 E
Asale, Lake- 35 Gc 14.00N 40.20 E
'Asalūyeh 24 Oi 27.28N 52.37 E
Asama-Yama 28 Of 36.27N 138.30 E
Asan-Man 28 If 36.56N 126.51 E
Asansol 22 Kg 23.41N 86.59 E
Asarna 7 De 62.39N 14.21 E
Asarum 8 Fh 56.12N 14.50 E
'Asāyr = Guardafui, Cape- (EN) 30 Mg 11.49N 51.15 E
Asayta 35 Gc 11.33N 41.27 E
Asbest 17 Jh 57.01N 61.31 E
Asbestos 44 Lc 45.46N 71.57W
Asbe Teferi 35 Gd 9.05N 40.51 E
Asbury Park 44 Je 40.14N 74.01W
Ascension 30 Fi 7.57S 14.22W
Ascensión, Bahía de la- 47 Ge 19.40N 87.30W
Ascensión, Bahía de la- 48 Ph 19.40N 87.30W
Ascensión, Laguna de la- 48 Fb 31.05N 107.55W
Aschaffenburg 10 Fg 49.59N 9.09 E
Ascheberg 12 Jc 51.47N 7.37 E
Aschendorf (Ems), Papenburg- 12 Ja 53.04N 7.22 E
Aschersleben 10 He 51.45N 11.28 E
Aščikol, Ozero- 18 Fb 45.05N 67.20 E
Aščiozek 16 Pe 49.12N 48.06 E
Ascoli Piceno 14 Hh 42.51N 13.34 E
Ascoli Satriano 14 Ji 41.12N 15.34 E
Ascot 12 Bc 51.24N 0.40W
Aseb 31 Lg 13.00N 42.44 E
Åseda 7 Dh 57.10N 15.20 E
Asedjrad 30 Hf 24.42N 1.40 E
Asekejevo 16 Rc 53.36N 52.51 E
Asela 31 Kh 7.58N 39.08 E
As Ela 35 Gc 11.06N 42.06 E
Asele 7 Dd 64.10N 17.20 E
Åsen [Nor.] 7 Ce 63.36N 11.03 E
Åsen [Swe.] 7 Cf 61.17N 13.50 E
Asendabo 35 Fd 9.47N 37.36 E
Asendorf 12 Kb 52.46N 9.00 E
Asenovgrad 15 Hg 42.01N 24.52 E
Åsensbruk 8 Ef 58.48N 12.25 E
Åseral 8 Bf 58.37N 7.25 E
Aseri/Azeri 7 Gg 59.29N 26.51 E
Asfeld 12 Ge 49.28N 4.07 E
Asfūn al Maṭā'inah 24 Ej 25.23N 32.32 E
Åsgårdstrand 8 De 59.21N 10.28 E
Ashabad 22 Hf 37.57N 58.23 E
Ashanti [3] 34 Ed 6.45N 1.30W
Ashburn 44 Fj 31.43N 83.39W
Ashburton 61 Dh 43.54S 171.45 E
Ashburton River 57 Cg 21.40S 114.56 E
Ashdod 24 Fg 31.49N 34.39 E
Ashdown 45 Ij 33.41N 94.08W
Asheboro 44 Hh 35.42N 79.49W
Asheroft 46 Ea 50.43N 121.17W
Asheville 43 Kd 35.34N 82.33W
Ashford 9 Nj 51.09N 0.53 E
Ashford Airport 12 Cc 51.10N 0.59 E
Ash Fork 46 Ii 35.13N 112.29W
Ashibetsu 28 Qc 43.31N 142.11 E
Ashikaga 29 Fc 36.21N 139.27 E
Ashington 9 Lf 55.11N 1.34W
Ashiro 29 Ga 40.06N 141.01 E
Ashiya 29 Be 33.53N 130.40 E
Ashizuri-Misaki 28 Lh 32.44N 133.01 E
Ashkal, Qar'at al- 14 Dm 37.10N 9.40 E
Āshkhāneh 24 Qd 37.28N 57.00 E
Ashland [Ks.-U.S.] 45 Gh 37.11N 99.46W
Ashland [Ky.-U.S.] 43 Kd 38.28N 82.38W
Ashland [Mt.-U.S.] 46 Ld 45.35N 106.16W
Ashland [Oh.-U.S.] 44 Fe 40.52N 82.19W
Ashland [Or.-U.S.] 43 Cc 42.12N 122.42W
Ashland [Wi.-U.S.] 43 Ib 46.35N 90.53W
Ashland, Mount- 46 De 42.05N 122.43W
Ashley 45 Gc 46.02N 99.22W
Ashmore Islands 57 Df 12.15S 123.05 E
Ashmūn 24 Dg 30.18N 30.58 E
Ashoro 29a Cb 43.14N 143.31 E
Ashqelon 24 Fg 31.40N 34.35 E
Ash Shabakah 24 Jg 30.49N 43.39 E
Ash Shabb 33 Ee 22.19N 29.46 E
Ash Shā'ib 24 Gh 28.59N 37.07 E
Ash Sha'm 23 Id 26.02N 56.05 E
Ash Shamālīyah [3] 35 Db 18.40N 30.00 E
Ash 'Shāmīyah 24 Kg 31.57N 44.36 E
Ash Shāmīyah 24 Lg 30.15N 46.55 E
Ash Shaqq 24 Lh 28.20N 47.30 E
Ash Shaqrā' 23 Gd 25.15N 45.15 E
Ash Sha'rā' 24 Kj 24.16N 44.11 E
Ash Sharīqah 23 Id 25.22N 55.23 E
Ash Sharqāţ 23 Fb 35.27N 43.16 E
Ash Sharqī 24 Jc 34.45N 11.15 E
Ash Sharqī 24 Ge 34.00N 36.30 E
Ash Sharqīyah 23 Ie 22.15N 58.30 E
Ash Shatrah 24 Lg 31.25N 46.10 E
Ash Shawbak 24 Fg 30.32N 35.34 E
Ash Shaykh Ḩumayd 24 Fh 28.07N 34.34 E
Ash Shifā 24 Fh 28.30N 35.30 E
Ash Shiḩr 23 Gg 14.44N 49.35 E
Ash Shināfiyah 24 Kg 31.35N 44.39 E
Ash Shu'aybah [Kuw.] 24 Mh 29.03N 48.08 E
Ash Shu'aybah [Sau.Ar.] 24 Ji 27.53N 42.43 E
Ash Shu'bah 24 Kh 28.54N 44.44 E
Ash Shumlūl 24 Li 26.31N 47.20 E
Ash Shuqayq 23 Ff 17.44N 42.01 E
Ash Shurayk 35 Eb 18.48N 33.34 E
Ash Shuwayhāt 24 Oj 24.05N 52.28 E
Ash Shuwaykh 24 Lh 29.21N 47.55 E
Ashtabula 43 Kc 41.53N 80.47W
Ashtabula, Lake- 45 Hc 47.11N 97.58W
Ashtīyān 24 Me 34.30N 49.55 E
Ashton [Id.-U.S.] 46 Jd 44.04N 111.27W
Ashton [St.Vin.] 51n Bb 12.36N 61.27W
Ashuanipi 42 Kf 52.55N 66.00W
Ashuanipi Lake 42 Kf 52.45N 66.10W
Asia 21 Ke 40.00N 85.00 E
Asia, Kepulauan- 26 Jf 1.03N 131.18 E
Asiago 14 Fe 45.52N 11.30 E
Asiago, Altopiano di- 14 Fe 45.54N 11.30 E
Asilah 32 Fb 35.28N 6.02W
Asinara 5 Gg 41.04N 8.15 E
Asinara, Golfo dell'- 14 Cj 41.00N 8.35 E
Asino 20 De 56.58N 86.09 E
'Asīr 23 Ff 19.00N 42.00 E
Aškadar 17 Hi 53.37N 56.01 E
Aškale 24 Ic 39.55N 40.42 E
Askanija-Nova 16 Hf 46.27N 33.52 E
Asker 8 De 59.50N 10.26 E
Askersund 7 Dg 58.53N 14.54 E
Askī Al Mawṣil 24 Jd 36.34N 42.42 E
Askim [Nor.] 8 De 59.35N 11.10 E
Askim [Swe.] 8 Dg 57.38N 11.56 E
Áskion Óros 15 Ei 40.22N 21.34 E
Askiz 20 Ef 53.08N 90.32 E
Askja 5 Eb 65.03N 16.48W
Askola 8 Kd 60.32N 25.36 E
Äsköping 8 Ge 59.09N 16.04 E
Askøy 8 Ad 60.30N 5.05 E
Askøy 8 Ad 60.24N 5.11 E
Askrova 8 Ac 61.30N 4.55 E
Askvoll 7 Af 61.21N 5.04 E
Asl 24 Eh 29.30N 32.43 E
Aslanapa 15 Mj 39.13N 29.52 E
Asmara (EN) = Asmera 31 Kg 15.19N 38.57 E
Asmera = Asmara (EN) 31 Kg 15.19N 38.57 E
Åsnen 8 Fh 56.40N 14.40 E
Asni 32 Fc 31.15N 7.59W
Asnières-sur-Seine 12 Ef 48.55N 2.17 E
Aso 14 Hg 43.06N 13.51 E
Aso 29 Be 32.58N 131.02 E
Asola 14 Ee 45.13N 10.24 E
Asosa 31 Kg 10.02N 34.32 E
Aso-San 29 Be 32.53N 131.06 E
Asoteriba, Jabal- 35 Fa 21.51N 36.30 E
Asouf Mellene 32 Hd 25.40N 2.08 E
Asō-Wan 29 Ad 34.20N 129.15 E
Äspäs 24 Og 30.40N 52.24 E
Aspe 13 Lf 38.21N 0.46W
Aspen 43 Fd 39.11N 106.49W
Aspermont 45 Fj 33.08N 100.14W
Aspiring, Mount- 61 Ch 44.23S 168.44 E
Aspromonte 14 Jl 38.10N 16.00 E
Assa 32 Fd 28.37N 9.25W
Aş Şadr 23 He 24.40N 54.41 E
Aş Şaff 24 Dh 29.34N 31.17 E
Aş Şāfī 24 Fg 31.02N 35.28 E
As Safīrah 24 Gd 36.04N 37.22 E
Aş Şahm 24 Qj 24.10N 56.53 E
Assahoun 34 Fd 6.27N 0.55 E
Aş Şa'īd 30 Kf 26.00N 32.00 E
Assal, Lac- 35 Gc 11.40N 42.22 E
As Salamīyah [Sau.Ar.] 23 Ge 24.12N 47.23 E
As Salamīyah [Syr.] 24 Ge 35.01N 37.03 E
Aş Şāliḩīyah 24 Ie 34.44N 40.45 E
As Sallūm 31 Je 31.34N 25.09 E
As Salmān 24 Kg 30.26N 44.30 E
As Salt 24 Ff 32.03N 35.44 E
As Salwā 23 He 24.45N 50.49 E

Index Symbols

[1] Independent Nation
[2] State, Region
[3] District, County
[4] Municipality
[5] Colony, Dependency
Continent
Physical Region
Historical or Cultural Region
Mount, Mountain
Volcano
Hill
Mountains, Mountain Range
Hills, Escarpment
Plateau, Upland
Pass, Gap
Plain, Lowland
Delta
Salt Flat
Valley, Canyon
Crater, Cave
Karst Features
Depression
Polder
Desert, Dunes
Forest, Woods
Heath, Steppe
Oasis
Cape, Point
Coast, Beach
Cliff
Peninsula
Isthmus
Sandbank
Island
Atoll
Rock, Reef
Islands, Archipelago
Rocks, Reefs
Coral Reef
Well, Spring
Geyser
River, Stream
Waterfall Rapids
River Mouth, Estuary
Lake
Salt Lake
Intermittent Lake
Reservoir
Swamp, Pond
Canal
Glacier
Ice Shelf, Pack Ice
Ocean
Sea
Gulf, Bay
Strait, Fjord
Lagoon
Bank
Seamount
Tablemount
Ridge
Shelf
Basin
Escarpment, Sea Scarp
Fracture
Trench, Abyss
National Park, Reserve
Point of Interest
Recreation Site
Cave, Cavern
Historic Site
Ruins
Wall, Walls
Church, Abbey
Temple
Scientific Station
Airport
Port
Lighthouse
Mine
Tunnel
Dam, Bridge

Index Symbols

[1] Independent Nation	Historical or Cultural Region	Pass, Gap	Depression
[2] State, Province	Mount, Mountain	Plain, Lowland	Polder
[3] District, County	Volcano	Delta	Desert, Dunes
[4] Municipality	Hill	Salt Flat	Forest, Woods
[5] Colony, Dependency	Mountains, Mountain Range	Valley, Canyon	Heath, Steppe
■ Continent	Hills, Escarpment	Crater, Cave	Oasis
Physical Region	Plateau, Upland	Karst Features	Cape, Point

Coast, Beach	Rock, Reef	Waterfall Rapids	Canal
Cliff	Islands, Archipelago	River Mouth, Estuary	Bank
Peninsula	Rocks, Reefs	Lake	Glacier
Isthmus	Coral Reef	Salt Lake	Ice Shelf, Pack Ice
Sandbank	Well, Spring	Intermittent Lake	Ocean
Island	Geyser	Reservoir	Sea
Atoll	River, Stream	Swamp, Pond	Shelf
			Strait, Fjord

Lagoon	Escarpment, Sea Scarp	Historic Site	Port
Bank	Fracture	Ruins	Lighthouse
Seamount	Trench, Abyss	Wall, Walls	Mine
Tablemount	National Park, Reserve	Church, Abbey	Tunnel
Ridge	Point of Interest	Temple	Dam, Bridge
Basin	Recreation Site	Scientific Station	
	Cave, Cavern	Airport	

Ayeyarwady 25 Ie 17.00N 95.00 E
Ayeyarwady = Irrawaddy (EN) 21 Lg 15.50N 95.06 E
Ayiá 15 Fj 39.43N 22.46 E
Ayia Marina 15 Jl 37.09N 26.52 E
Ayiásos 15 Jj 39.06N 26.22 E
Áyion Óros = Athos, Mount- (EN) 15 Hi 40.15N 24.15 E
Áyios Evstrátios 15 Hj 39.31N 25.00 E
Áyios Ioánnis, Ákra- 15 In 35.20N 25.46 E
Áyios Kirikos 15 Jl 37.35N 26.14 E
Áyios Minás 15 Jl 37.36N 26.34 E
Áyios Nikólaos 15 In 35.11N 25.43 E
Áyios Yeóryios 15 Gl 37.28N 23.56 E
Aykota 35 Fb 15.10N 37.03 E
Aylesbury 9 Mj 51.50N 0.50W
Ayllón, Sierra de- 13 Ic 41.15N 3.25W
Aylmer Lake 42 Gd 64.05N 108.30W
Aylsham 12 Db 52.47N 1.15 E
Ayna 13 Jf 38.33N 2.05W
'Aynabo 35 Hd 8.57N 46.30 E
'Ayn ad Darāhim 14 Cn 36.47N 8.42 E
'Ayn al Baydā 24 Ge 34.32N 37.55 E
'Ayn al Ghazāl [Eg.] 24 Dj 25.46N 30.38 E
'Ayn al Ghazāl [Lib.] 31 Jf 21.50N 24.55 E
'Ayn al Shigi 24 Ci 27.01N 28.02 E
'Ayn al Wādī 24 Ci 27.23N 28.13 E
'Ayn Bū Sālim 14 Cn 36.37N 8.59 E
'Ayn Dāllah 33 Ed 27.19N 27.20 E
'Ayn Dār 24 Mj 25.58N 49.14 E
'Ayn Dīwār 24 Jd 37.17N 42.11 E
'Ayn Ilwān 24 Dj 25.44N 30.25 E
'Ayn Khalīfah 24 Bi 26.46N 27.47 E
'Ayn Sifnī 24 Jd 36.42N 43.21 E
'Ayn Sukhnah 33 Fd 29.30N 32.10 E
'Aynūnah 23 Ed 28.05N 35.08 E
Ayod 35 Ed 8.08N 31.24 E
Ayora 13 Ke 39.04N 1.03W
Ayorou 34 Fc 14.44N 0.55 E
'Ayoûn el 'Atroûs 31 Gg 16.38N 9.36W
Ayr 9 If 55.29N 4.28W
Ayr [Austl.] 59 Jc 19.35 S 147.24 E
Ayr [Scot.-U.K.] 9 If 55.28N 4.38W
Ayre, Point of- 9 Ig 54.26N 4.22W
Ayrolle, Étang de l'- 11 Jk 43.16N 3.30 E
Aysha 35 Gc 10.45N 42.35 E
Aytré 11 Eh 46.08N 1.06W
Ayutla 48 Gg 20.07N 104.22W
Ayutla de los Libres 48 Ji 16.54N 99.13W
Ayvacık 24 Gb 41.00N 36.45 E
Ayvacik 15 Jj 39.36N 26.24 E
Ayvalık 23 Cb 39.18N 26.41 E
Aywaille 12 Hd 50.28N 5.40 E
Āzādshahr 24 Pd 37.05N 55.08 E
Azahar, Costa del- 13 Me 39.58N 0.01 E
Azaila 13 Lc 41.17N 0.29W
Azambuja 13 De 39.04N 8.52W
Azamgarh 25 Gc 26.04N 83.11 E
Azángaro 54 Df 14.55 S 70.13W
Azannes-et-Soumazannes 12 He 49.18N 5.28 E
Azaouâd = Azaouad (EN) 30 Gg 19.00N 3.00W
Azaouad (EN) = Azaouâd 30 Gg 19.00N 3.00W
Azaouak 34 Fb 15.30N 3.18 E
Azaouak 30 Hg 15.20N 4.55 E
Azaouak, Vallée de l'- 30 Hg 17.30N 3.40 E
Azar 34 Fb 16.02N 4.04 E
Āžarbāijān-e Gharbī 23 Fb 37.00N 45.00 E
Āžarbāijān-e Sharqī 23 Gb 37.00N 47.00 E
Azarbaijčan SSR → Azärbayjan 19 Eg 40.30N 47.30 E
Azärbayjan = Azerbaijan (EN) 19 Eg 40.30N 47.30 E
Azare 34 Hc 11.41N 10.12 E
Āzār Shahr 24 Kd 37.45N 45.59 E
Azay-le-Rideau 11 Gg 47.16N 0.28 E
A 'zāz 24 Gd 36.35N 37.03 E
Azazga 13 Qh 36.44N 4.22 E
Azbine/Aïr 30 Hg 18.00N 8.30 E
Azdaak, Gora- 16 Ni 40.13N 44.59 E
Azdavay 24 Eb 41.39N 33.18 E
Azefal 30 Ff 21.00N 14.45W
Azeffoun 13 Qh 36.53N 4.25 E
Azemmour 32 Fc 33.17N 8.21W
Azerbaijan (En) = Azärbayjan 19 Eg 40.30N 47.30 E
Azerbajdžanskaja Sovetskaja Socialističeskaja Respublika → Azärbayjan 19 Eg 40.30N 47.30 E
Azerbajdžanskaja SSR/ Azarbaijčan Sovet Socialistik Respublicasy → Azärbayjan 19 Eg 40.30N 47.30 E
Azerbajdžanskaja SSR → Azärbayjan 19 Eg 40.30N 47.30 E
Azeri/Aseri 7 Gg 59.29N 26.51 E
Azevedo Sodré 55 Ej 30.04S 54.36W
Azezo 35 Fc 12.33N 37.25 E
Azilal 32 Fc 32.09N 6.05W
Azilal 32 Fc 31.58N 6.35W
Aznā 24 Mf 33.56N 49.24 E
Aznakajevo 7 Mi 54.56N 53.04 E
Azogues 54 Cd 2.44 S 78.48W
Azores (EN) = Açores 31 Ee 38.30N 28.00W
Azores (EN) = Açores, Arquipélago dos- 30 Ee 38.30N 28.00W
Azores-Gibraltar Ridge (EN) 3 Df 37.00N 16.00W
Azoum, Bahr- 30 Jg 10.53N 20.15 E
Azov 19 Df 47.05N 39.25 E
Azov, Sea of- (EN) = Azovskoje More 5 Jf 46.00N 36.00 E
Azovskoje More = Azov, Sea of- (EN) 5 Jf 46.00N 36.00 E
Azpeitia 13 Ja 43.11N 2.16W
Azrak, Bahr- 35 Bc 10.50N 19.50 E
Azraq, Al Baḩr al- = Blue Nile (EN) 30 Kg 15.38N 32.31 E
Azraq ash Shīshān 24 Gg 31.50N 36.49 E
Azrou 32 Fc 33.26N 5.13W
Aztec 45 Ch 36.49N 107.59W
Aztec Ruins 46 Kh 36.51N 108.10W
Azua 49 Ld 18.27N 70.44W
Azuaga 13 Gf 38.16N 5.41W
Azuar 13 Ie 39.08N 3.36W
Azuero, Península de- = Azuero Peninsula (EN) 38 Ki 7.40N 80.30W
Azuero Peninsula (EN) = Azuero, Península de- 38 Ki 7.40N 80.30W
Azul 53 Ki 36.45 S 59.50W
Azul, Arroyo del- 55 Cm 36.15 S 59.07W
Azul, Cerro- 54a Ab 0.54 S 91.21W
Azul, Cordillera- 54 Ce 8.30 S 76.00W
Azul, Rio- 48 Oi 17.54N 88.52W
Azul, Serra- 55 Eb 14.50 S 54.50W
Azul, Sierras del- 55 Cm 37.02 S 59.55W
Azūm 35 Cc 10.53N 20.15 E
Azuma-San 29 Gc 37.44N 140.08 E
Azur, Côte d'- 11 Mk 43.30N 7.00 E
Azurduy 54 Fg 19.59 S 64.29W
Azzaba 32 Ib 36.44N 7.06 E
Az Zāb al Kabīr 23 Fb 36.00N 43.21 E
Az Zāb aş Şaghīr 23 Fb 35.12N 43.25 E
Az Zabdānī 24 Gf 33.43N 36.05 E
Az Zabū 24 Ch 28.22N 28.56 E
Aẓ Ẓafīr 23 Ff 19.57N 41.30 E
Az Zaghāwa 35 Cb 15.15N 23.14 E
Aẓ Ẓāhirah 24 Qk 23.30N 56.15 E
Az Zallāq 24 Ni 26.03N 50.29 E
Az Zaqāzīq 33 Fc 30.35N 31.31 E
Az Zarqā' 24 Oj 24.53N 53.04 E
Az Zarqā' 24 Gf 32.05N 36.06 E
Az Zāwiyah 33 Bc 32.40N 12.10 E
Az Zāwiyah 33 Bc 32.45N 12.44 E
Az Zaytūn 33 Ed 29.09N 25.47 E
Azzel Matti, Sebkha- 30 Hf 26.00N 0.55 E
Az Zilfī 24 Ki 26.18N 44.48 E
Az Zubayr 24 Lg 30.23N 47.43 E

B

Baa 26 Hi 10.43 S 123.03 E
Baaba 63b Ae 20.03 S 163.58 E
Ba'ādwēyn 35 Hd 7.12N 47.24 E
Bá an Daingin/Dingle Bay 9 Ci 52.05N 10.15W
Baar 10 Ei 48.00N 8.30 E
Baarle-Hertog 12 Gc 51.27N 4.56 E
Baarn 12 Hb 52.14N 5.17 E
Baas, Bassure de- 12 Dd 50.30N 1.15 E
Bāb 24 Ok 23.55N 53.45 E
Baba 35 Bd 6.25N 17.07 E
Baba 15 Ei 40.55N 21.10 E
Baba Burun [Tur.] 24 Db 41.18N 31.26 E
Baba Burun [Tur.] 24 Bc 39.29N 26.04 E
Babadağ 15 Ll 37.48N 28.52 E
Baba Dağ 15 Mm 36.32N 29.10 E
Babadag 15 Le 44.54N 28.43 E
Babadag, Gora- 16 Pi 41.01N 48.29 E
Babaeski 24 Bb 41.26N 27.06 E
Bābā-Ḩeydar 24 Nf 32.20N 50.28 E
Babajevo 19 Dd 59.24N 35.55 E
Babajtag, Gora- 18 Hd 41.13N 70.16 E
Babajurt 16 Oh 43.35N 46.47 E
Bāb al Māndab = Bab el Mandeb (EN) 30 Lg 12.35N 43.25 E
Babanūsah 35 Dc 11.20N 27.48 E
Babao → Qilian 27 Hd 38.14N 100.15 E
Babaoyo 54 Cd 1.50 S 79.30W
Babar, Kepulauan- 26 Ih 7.50 S 129.45 E
Babar, Pulau- 57 De 7.55 S 129.45 E
Babase 63a Aa 4.01 S 153.42 E
Babatag, Hrebet- 18 Ge 38.00N 68.10 E
Babati 36 Gc 4.13 S 35.45 E
Babbitt 45 Kc 47.43N 91.57W
B'abdā 24 Ff 33.50N 35.32 E
Bab el Mandeb (EN) = Bāb al Māndab 30 Lg 12.35N 43.25 E
Babelthuap Island 57 Ed 7.30N 134.36 E
Babenhausen [Ger.] 10 Gh 48.09N 10.15 E
Babenhausen [Ger.] 12 Ke 49.58N 8.57 E
Babeni 15 He 44.59N 24.15 E
Baberton 44 Ge 41.02N 81.38W
Bá Bheanntrai/Bantry Bay 9 Dj 51.38N 9.48W
Babian Jiang = Black River (EN) 21 Mg 20.17N 106.34 E
Babil 24 Kf 32.40N 44.50 E
Babine Lake 42 Ef 54.45N 126.00W
Babino Polje 14 Lh 42.43N 17.33 E
Babit Point 51b Ab 18.03N 63.02W
Babo 26 Jg 2.33 S 133.25 E
Bābol 23 Hb 36.34N 52.42 E
Babol Sar 24 Od 36.43N 52.39 E
Baboquivari Peak 46 Jk 31.46N 111.35W
Babor, Djebel- 13 Rh 36.32N 5.28 E
Baborigame 48 Fd 26.27N 107.16W
Baboua 35 Ad 5.48N 14.49 E
Babozero, Ozero- 7 Ic 66.30N 37.25 E
Babu → Hexian 27 Jg 24.28N 111.34 E
Babuna 15 Eh 41.30N 21.40 E
Babuyan 26 Hc 19.32N 121.57 E
Babuyan 26 Gd 10.01N 118.58 E
Babuyan Channel 26 Hc 18.44N 121.40 E
Babuyan Islands 21 Oh 19.15N 121.40 E
Babylon 23 Fc 32.32N 44.25 E
Bač 15 Cd 45.23N 19.14 E
Bacabachi 48 Ed 26.55N 109.24W
Bacabal 53 Lf 4.14 S 44.47W
Ba-Cagan 27 Gb 45.40N 99.30 E
Bacajá, Rio- 54 Hd 3.25 S 51.50W
Bacalar 48 Oh 18.43N 88.27W
Bacalar, Laguna de- 48 Oh 18.43N 88.22W
Bacalar Chico, Boca- 49 Dd 18.12N 87.53W
Bacan, Kepulauan- 26 Ig 0.35 S 127.30 E
Bacan, Pulau- 26 Ig 0.35 S 127.30 E
Bacău 15 Jc 46.36N 27.00 E
Bacău 6 If 46.34N 26.54 E
Baccarat 11 Mf 48.27N 6.45 E
Bacchiglione 14 Ge 45.11N 12.14 E
Baceşti 15 Kc 46.51N 27.14 E
Bachaquero 49 Li 9.56N 71.08W
Bacharach 12 Jd 50.04N 7.46 E
Bacheli 25 Ge 18.40N 81.15 E
Bachiniva 48 Fc 28.45N 107.15W
Bachu/Maralwexi 27 Cd 39.46N 78.15 E
Back 38 Jd 67.15N 95.15W
Bačka 15 Cd 45.50N 19.30 E
Bac Kan 25 Ld 22.08N 105.49 E
Bačka Palanka 15 Cd 45.15N 19.22 E
Bačka Topola 15 Cd 45.49N 19.39 E
Bäckefors 8 Ef 58.48N 12.10 E
Bäckhammar 8 Fe 59.10N 14.11 E
Backnang 10 Fh 48.57N 9.26 E
Bačkovski Manastir 15 Hh 41.56N 24.51 E
Bac Lieu 25 Lg 9.17N 105.43 E
Bac Ninh 25 Ld 21.11N 106.03 E
Bacolet 51p Bb 12.02N 61.41W
Bacolod 22 Oh 10.40N 122.57 E
Bac-Phan = Tonkin (EN) 21 Mg 22.00N 105.00 E
Bacqueville, Lac- 42 Ke 58.00N 74.00W
Bacqueville-en Caux 12 Ce 49.47N 1.00 E
Bácsalmás 10 Pj 46.08N 19.20 E
Bács-Kiskun 10 Pj 46.30N 19.25 E
Bacton 12 Db 52.51N 1.28 E
Bād 23 Hc 33.41N 52.01 E
Badagara 25 Ff 11.36N 75.35 E
Badagri 34 Fd 6.25N 2.53 E
Badain Jaran Shamo 21 Me 40.20N 101.40 E
Badajós, Lago- 54 Fd 3.15 S 62.45W
Badajoz 6 Fh 38.53N 6.58W
Badajoz 13 Ff 38.40N 6.10W
Badakhshan 23 Lb 36.45N 72.00 E
Badalona 13 Oc 41.27N 2.15 E
Badanah 23 Fc 30.59N 41.02 E
Badaohao 28 Fd 41.50N 121.59 E
Badas, Kepulauan- 26 Ef 0.35N 107.06 E
Bad Aussee 14 Hc 47.36N 13.47 E
Bad Axe 44 Fd 43.48N 83.00W
Bad Bergzabern 10 Dg 49.06N 8.00 E
Bad Berleburg 12 Kc 51.04N 8.24 E
Bad Bertrich 12 Jd 50.03N 7.02 E
Bad Bramstedt 10 Fc 53.55N 9.53 E
Bad Brückenau 10 Ff 50.18N 9.45 E
Badda 35 Fd 7.55N 39.23 E
Baddo 25 Cc 27.59N 64.21 E
Bad Doberan 10 Hb 54.06N 11.54 E
Bad Driburg 12 Lc 51.44N 9.01 E
Bad Düben 10 Ie 51.36N 12.35 E
Bad Dürkheim 12 Ke 49.28N 8.12 E
Bade 26 Kh 7.10 S 139.35 E
Bademli 15 Lk 38.04N 28.04 E
Baden [Aus.] 14 Kb 48.01N 16.14 E
Baden [Switz.] 14 Cc 47.28N 8.18 E
Baden-Baden 10 Eh 48.45N 8.15 E
Badenoch 9 Je 56.50N 4.00W
Baden-Württemberg 10 Eh 48.30N 9.00 E
Bad Essen 12 Kb 52.19N 8.20 E
Bad Freienwalde 10 Kd 52.47N 14.02 E
Badgastein 14 Hc 47.07N 13.08 E
Bādghīsat 23 Jc 35.00N 63.45 E
Bad Gleichenberg 14 Jd 46.52N 15.54 E
Bad Godesberg, Bonn- 10 Df 50.41N 7.09 E
Bad Hall 14 Ib 48.02N 14.12 E
Bad Harzburg 10 Ge 51.53N 10.34 E
Bad Herrenalb 12 Kf 48.48N 8.25 E
Bad Hersfeld 10 Ff 50.52N 9.42 E
Bad Homburg 10 Ef 50.13N 8.37 E
Bad Honnef 12 Jd 50.38N 7.12 E
Bá Dhún na nGall/Donegal Bay 5 Fe 54.30N 8.30W
Badhyz 18 Cg 35.50N 62.00 E
Badiraguato 48 Fe 25.22N 107.31W
Bad Ischl 14 Hc 47.43N 13.37 E
Bad Kissingen 10 Gf 50.12N 10.05 E
Bad Kreuznach 10 Dg 49.50N 7.52 E
Badlands [S.D.-U.S.] 45 Ee 43.30N 102.20W
Badlands [U.S.] 43 Gb 46.45N 103.30W
Bad Langensalza 10 Ge 51.06N 10.39 E
Bad Lautenberg am Harz 10 Ge 51.38N 10.28 E
Bad Liebenwerda 10 Je 51.31N 13.24 E
Bad Liebenzel 12 Kf 48.46N 8.44 E
Bad Mergentheim 10 Fg 49.29N 9.46 E
Bad Mondorf/Mondorf-les-Bains 12 Ie 49.30N 6.17 E
Bad Münster am Stein Ebernburg 12 Je 49.49N 7.51 E
Bad Münstereifel 12 Id 50.34N 6.45 E
Bad Muskau 10 Ke 51.33N 14.43 E
Bad Nauheim 12 Kd 50.22N 8.45 E
Bad Neuenahr-Ahweiler 10 Df 50.33N 7.08 E
Bad Neustadt an der Saale 10 Gf 50.20N 10.13 E
Bad Oeynhausen 12 Kb 52.12N 8.48 E
Bad Oldesloe 10 Gc 53.49N 10.23 E
Ba Don 25 Le 17.45N 106.27 E
Badou [China] 28 Df 36.27N 117.56 E
Badou [Togo] 34 Fd 7.35N 0.36 E
Bad Pyrmont 10 Fe 51.59N 9.15 E
Bad Ragaz 14 Dc 47.00N 9.30 E
Badrah 24 Kf 33.06N 45.58 E
Bad Reichenhall 10 Ii 47.44N 12.53 E
Badr Ḩunayn 23 Ee 23.44N 38.46 E
Bad River 45 Fd 44.22N 100.22W
Bad Salzuflen 12 Kb 52.05N 8.46 E
Bad Salzungen 10 Gf 50.49N 10.14 E
Bad Schwartau 10 Gc 53.55N 10.42 E
Bad Segeberg 10 Gc 53.56N 10.19 E
Bad Tölz 10 Hi 47.46N 11.34 E
Badulla 25 Gg 6.59N 81.03 E
Bad Wildungen 10 Fe 51.07N 9.07 E
Bad Wimpfen 10 Fg 49.14N 9.08 E
Baena 13 Hg 37.37N 4.19W
Baeza [Ec.] 54 Cd 0.28 S 77.53W
Baeza [Sp.] 13 Ig 37.59N 3.28W
Baf/Paphos 24 Ee 34.50N 32.35 E
Bafang 34 Hd 5.09N 10.11 E
Bafatá 31 Fg 12.10N 14.40W
Bafélé 34 Cc 10.09N 10.08W
Baffin 38 Mc 68.00N 70.00W
Baffin Bay 38 Mb 73.00N 65.00W
Bafia 34 He 4.45N 11.14 E
Bafilo 34 Fd 9.21N 1.16 E
Bafing [Afr.] 30 Fg 13.49N 10.50W
Bafing [I.C.] 34 Dd 7.52N 7.07W
Bafoulabé 34 Cc 13.48N 10.50W
Bafoussam 31 Ih 5.28N 10.25 E
Bāfq 23 Ic 31.35N 55.24 E
Bāfq, Kūh-e- 24 Pg 31.20N 55.10 E
Bafra 23 Ea 41.34N 35.56 E
Bāft 24 Qh 29.14N 56.38 E
Bafwaboli 36 Eb 0.39N 26.10 E
Bafwasende 36 Eb 1.05N 27.16 E
Baga 34 Hc 13.06N 13.50 E
Bagaces 49 Eh 10.31N 85.15W
Bagagem, Rio- 55 Ha 13.58 S 48.21W
Bagajevski 16 Lf 47.19N 40.25 E
Bāgalkot 25 Fe 16.11N 75.42 E
Bagamoyo 36 Gd 6.26 S 38.54 E
Bagansiapi-Api 26 Df 2.09N 100.49 E
Bağarasi 15 Kl 37.42N 27.33 E
Baga Sola 35 Ac 13.32N 14.19 E
Bagata 36 Cc 3.44 S 17.57 E
Bagdad 48 Ke 25.57N 97.09W
Bagdarin 20 Gf 54.30N 113.36 E
Bagdati (Majakovski) 16 Mh 42.02N 42.47 E
Bağdere 24 Ic 38.10N 40.45 E
Bagé 53 Ki 31.20 S 54.06W
Bages et de Sigean, Étang de- 11 Jk 43.05N 3.01 E
Baggs 46 Lf 41.02N 107.39W
Bâgh Baile na Sgealg/ Ballinskelligs Bay 9 Cj 51.50N 10.15W
Baghdād 24 Kf 33.18N 44.36 E
Baghdād 22 Gf 33.21N 44.23 E
Baghdādī, Ra's- 24 Fj 24.40N 35.06 E
Bāgh-e Chenār 24 Qh 28.11N 56.54 E
Bāgh-e-Malek 24 Mg 31.32N 49.55 E
Bagheria 14 Hl 38.05N 13.30 E
Bāghīn 23 Ic 30.12N 56.48 E
Baghlān 23 Kb 35.45N 69.00 E
Baghlān 23 Kb 36.13N 68.46 E
Bāglung 25 Gc 28.16N 83.36 E
Bagn 8 Cd 60.49N 9.34 E
Bagnara Calabra 14 Jl 38.17N 15.48 E
Bagnères-de-Bigorre 11 Gk 43.04N 0.09 E
Bagnères-de-Luchon 11 Gl 42.47N 0.36 E
Bagni di Lucca 14 Ef 44.01N 10.35 E
Bagno di Romagna 14 Fg 43.50N 11.57 E
Bagnolo Mella 14 Ee 45.26N 10.10 E
Bagnols-sur-Cèze 11 Kj 44.10N 4.37 E
Bago 22 Lh 17.30N 96.30 E
Bagoé 30 Gg 12.36N 6.34W
Bagolino 14 Ee 45.49N 10.28 E
Bagrationovsk 8 Ij 54.23N 20.40 E
Bagrax/Bohu 27 Ec 41.58N 86.29 E
Bagrax Hu/Bosten 21 Ke 42.00N 87.00 E
Bagua 54 Ce 5.40 S 78.31W
Baguio 22 Oh 16.25N 120.36 E
Baguirmi 30 Ig 11.40N 16.20 E
Bagzane, Monts- 30 Hg 17.43N 8.45 E
Bahama Islands 38 Lg 24.15N 76.00W
Bahamas 39 Lg 24.15N 76.00W
Bahamas, Canal Viejo de- = Old Bahama Channel (EN) 49 Ib 22.30N 78.05W
Bahār 24 Me 34.54N 48.26 E
Baharampur 25 Hd 24.06N 88.15 E
Baharden 19 Fh 38.28N 57.28 E
Bahardok 19 Fh 38.51N 58.24 E
Baharīyah, Wāḩāt al- 33 Ed 28.10N 29.00 E
Bahariya Oasis (EN) = Baḩarīyah, Wāḩāt al- 33 Ed 28.15N 28.57 E
Bahaur 26 Fg 3.20N 114.00 E
Bahāwalnagar 25 Ec 29.59N 73.16 E
Bahāwalpur 22 Jg 29.24N 71.41 E
Bahčisaraj 16 Hg 44.45N 33.51 E
Bahę 24 Gd 37.14N 36.34 E
Bahi 36 Gd 5.39 S 35.19 E
Bahia 54 Jf 12.00 S 42.00W
Bahía, Islas de la- 47 Ge 16.20N 86.30W
Bahia Blanca 53 Ji 38.44 S 62.16W
Bahia de Caráquez 54 Bd 0.37 S 80.25W
Bahia Kino 47 Bc 28.50N 111.55W
Bahia Negra 56 Ib 20.15 S 58.12W
Bahias, Cabo dos- 52 Jj 44.55 S 65.32W
Bahīj 24 Cg 30.56N 29.35 E
Bahinga 36 Ed 5.57 S 27.06 E
Bahi Swamp 36 Gd 6.05 S 35.10 E
Bahlui 15 Kb 47.08N 27.44 E
Bahmač 19 De 51.11N 32.50 E
Bahoruco, Sierra de- 49 Ld 18.10N 71.25W
Bahraich 25 Gc 27.35N 81.36 E
Bahrain (EN) = Al Baḩrayn 22 Hg 26.00N 50.29 E
Baḩr al Ghazāl 35 Dd 8.15N 26.50 E
Bahr ar Ramla al Kabīr 33 Ed 27.00N 26.00 E
Baḩrayn, Khalij al- 24 Nj 25.45N 50.40 E
Bahr Dar 31 Kg 11.36N 37.22 E
Bahta 20 Dd 62.20N 89.15 E
Bahusi 15 Jc 46.43N 26.42 E
Baia 15 Le 44.43N 28.40 E
Baia de Aramă 15 Fe 45.00N 22.50 E
Baia de Fier 15 Gd 45.10N 23.46 E
Baia dos Tigres 36 Bf 16.35 S 11.43 E
Baia Farta 36 Be 12.37 S 13.26 E
Baia Mare 15 Gb 47.40N 23.35 E
Baião 54 Id 2.41 S 49.41W
Baia Sprie 15 Gb 47.40N 23.42 E
Baibiene 55 Ci 29.36 S 58.10W
Baïbokoum 35 Bd 7.45N 15.41 E
Baicheng 22 Oe 45.34N 122.49 E
Baicheng/Bay 27 Dc 41.46N 81.52 E
Băicoi 15 Id 45.02N 25.51 E
Băiculeşti 15 Hd 45.04N 24.42 E
Baidoa (EN) = Isha Baydabo 31 Lh 3.04N 43.48 E
Baïdou 35 Cd 5.52N 20.41 E
Baie-Comeau 39 Me 49.13N 68.10W
Baie-Mahault 50 Fd 16.16N 61.35W
Baie-Saint-Paul 42 Kg 47.27N 70.30W
Baie-Trinité 44 Na 49.24N 67.19W
Baie Verte 42 Lg 49.55N 56.11W
Baiguan → Shangyu 28 Fi 30.01N 120.53 E
Baihe 27 Je 32.46N 110.06 E
Bai He [China] 28 Bh 32.10N 112.20 E
Bai He [China] 28 Dd 40.43N 116.33 E
Baikal, Lake- (EN) = Bajkal, Ozero- 21 Md 53.00N 107.40 E
Baikal Range (EN) = Bajkalski Hrebet 21 Md 55.00N 108.40 E
Baile an Chaistil/ Ballycastle 118 Gf 55.12N 6.15W
Baile an Róba/Ballinrobe 118 Dh 53.37N 9.13W
Baile Átha Cliath/Dublin 9 Gh 53.20N 6.15W
Baile Átha Cliath/Dublin 6 Fe 53.20N 6.15W
Baile Átha Luain/Athlone 9 Fh 53.25N 7.56W
Baile Átha Troim/Trim 9 Gh 53.34N 6.47W
Băile Borşa 15 Hb 47.41N 24.43 E
Baile Brigin/Balbriggan 9 Gh 53.37N 6.11W
Băile Govora 15 Hd 45.05N 24.11 E
Baile Locha Riach/Loughrea 9 Eh 53.12N 8.34W
Baile Mhistéala/ Mitchelstown 9 Ei 52.16N 8.16W
Bailén 13 If 38.06N 3.46W
Baile na Mainistreach/ Newtownabbey 9 Hg 54.42N 5.54W
Baile Nua na hArda/ Newtownards 9 Hg 54.36N 5.41W
Băile Olăneşti 15 Hd 45.12N 24.14 E
Băileşti 15 Ge 44.01N 23.21 E
Bailleul 12 Ce 49.12N 0.26 E
Bailleul 12 Ed 50.44N 2.44 E
Ba Illi 35 Bc 10.31N 16.29 E
Bailong Jiang 27 Ie 32.42N 105.15 E
Bailundo 36 Ce 12.10 S 15.56 E
Baima 27 He 33.05N 100.29 E
Bain 12 Ba 53.04N 0.12W
Bainbridge 43 Ke 30.54N 84.34W
Bain-de-Bretagne 11 Eg 47.50N 1.41W
Baines Drift 37 Dd 22.30 S 28.43 E
Baing 26 Hi 10.14 S 120.34 E
Baingoin 27 Ee 31.36N 89.48 E
Baiquan 27 Mb 47.38N 126.04 E
Bā'ir 24 Gg 30.46N 36.41 E
Bā'ir, Wādī- 24 Gg 31.12N 37.31 E
Baird 45 Gj 32.24N 99.24W
Baird Inlet 40 Gd 60.45N 164.00W
Baird Mountains 40 Gc 67.35N 161.30W
Baird Peninsula 42 Jc 69.00N 75.15W
Bairiki 58 Id 1.20N 173.01 E
Bairin Youqi (Daban) 27 Kc 43.30N 118.37 E
Bairin Zuoqi (Lindong) 27 Kc 43.59N 119.22 E
Bairnsdale 58 Fh 37.50 S 147.38 E
Bais 26 He 9.35N 123.07 E
Bai Shan 27 Fc 40.53N 93.48 E
Baisogala/Bajsogala 8 Ji 55.35N 23.44 E
Baitou Shan 21 Oe 42.00N 128.00 E
Baitoushan Tian Chi 28 Jc 42.00N 128.03 E
Baixiang 28 Cf 37.29N 114.44 E
Baixo Alentejo 13 Dg 37.55N 8.10W
Baixo Guandu 54 Jg 19.31 S 41.01W
Baixo Longa 36 Cf 15.42 S 18.38 E
Baiyanghe 27 Ec 43.12N 88.28 E
Baiyü 27 Ge 31.13N 98.51 E
Baja 10 Oj 46.11N 18.58 E
Baja, Punta- [Mex.] 48 Dc 28.25N 111.45W
Baja, Punta- [Pas.] 65d Ab 27.10 S 109.22W
Baja California = Lower California (EN) 38 Hg 28.00N 112.00W
Baja California Sur 47 Bd 25.50N 111.50W
Bājah 32 Ib 36.30N 9.30 E
Bājah 32 Ib 36.44N 9.11 E
Bajalān 24 Md 37.18N 48.47 E
Bajan 27 Jb 49.15N 111.58 E
Bajanaul 19 He 50.47N 75.42 E
Bajandaj 20 Ff 53.04N 105.30 E
Bajan-Delger 27 Jb 45.55N 112.15 E
Bajangol 20 Ff 50.40N 103.25 E
Bajan-Hongor 22 Me 46.20N 100.40 E
Bajan-Ula [Mong.] 27 Jb 49.07N 112.45 E
Bajan-Ula [Mong.] 27 Gb 47.05N 95.15 E
Bajan-Under 27 Gc 44.45N 98.45 E
Baja Verapaz 49 Bf 15.05N 90.20W
Bajawa 26 Hh 8.47 S 120.59 E
Bajčunas 16 Rf 47.17N 53.03 E
Bajdarackaja Guba 20 Bc 69.00N 67.30 E
Bajdarata 17 Nb 68.12N 68.18 E
Bajdrag Gol 27 Hb 45.10N 100.45 E
Bājgīrān 24 Rd 37.36N 58.24 E
Baj-Haak 20 Ef 51.07N 94.34 E
Bajiazi 28 Jc 42.41N 129.13 E
Bajina Bašta 15 Cf 43.58N 19.34 E
Bajkal 20 Ff 51.53N 104.47 E
Bajkal, Ozero- = Baikal, Lake- (EN) 21 Md 53.00N 107.40 E
Bajkalovo 17 Kh 57.24N 63.40 E
Bajkalsk 20 Ff 51.30N 104.05 E
Bajkalski Hrebet = Baikal Range (EN) 21 Md 55.00N 108.40 E
Bajkit 20 Ed 61.41N 96.25 E
Bajkonur 19 Gf 47.50N 66.07 E
Bajmak 19 Fe 52.36N 58.19 E
Bajmba, Mount- 59 Ke 29.20 S 152.05 E
Bajmok 15 Cd 45.58N 19.26 E
Bajo Baudó 54 Cc 4.58N 77.22W

Index Symbols

Independent Nation
State, Region
District, County
Municipality
Colony, Dependency
Continent
Physical Region
Historical or Cultural Region
Mount, Mountain
Volcano
Hill
Mountains, Mountain Range
Hills, Escarpment
Plateau, Upland
Pass, Gap
Plain, Lowland
Delta
Salt Flat
Valley, Canyon
Crater, Cave
Karst Features
Depression
Polder
Desert, Dunes
Forest, Woods
Heath, Steppe
Oasis
Cape, Point
Coast, Beach
Cliff
Peninsula
Isthmus
Sandbank
Island
Atoll
Rock, Reef
Islands, Archipelago
Rocks, Reefs
Coral Reef
Well, Spring
Geyser
River, Stream
Waterfall Rapids
River Mouth, Estuary
Lake
Salt Lake
Intermittent Lake
Reservoir
Swamp, Pond
Canal
Glacier
Ice Shelf, Pack Ice
Ocean
Sea
Gulf, Bay
Strait, Fjord
Lagoon
Bank
Seamount
Tablemount
Ridge
Shelf
Basin
Escarpment, Sea Scarp
Fracture
Trench, Abyss
National Park, Reserve
Point of Interest
Recreation Site
Cave, Cavern
Historic Site
Ruins
Wall, Walls
Church, Abbey
Temple
Scientific Station
Airport
Port
Lighthouse
Mine
Tunnel
Dam, Bridge

Bajo Boquete 49 Fi 8.46N 82.26W
Bajram-Ali 19 Gh 37.39N 62.12 E
Bajram Curri 15 Dg 42.21N 20.04 E
Bajsogala/Baisogala 8 Ji 55.35N 23.44 E
Bajsun 18 Fe 38.14N 67.12 E
Bajun Islands 30 Li 0.50S 42.15 E
Bajžansaj 18 Gc 43.13N 69.56 E
Baka 35 Ee 4.33N 30.05 E
Bakacak 15 Ki 40.12N 27.05 E
Bakadžicite 15 Jg 42.25N 26.43 E
Bakal 19 Fe 54.56N 58.48 E
Bakala 35 Cd 6.11N 20.22 E
Bakanas 19 Hg 44.48N 76.15 E
Bakar 14 Ie 45.18N 14.32 E
Bakčar 20 De 57.01N 82.10 E
Bake 26 Dg 3.03S 100.16 E
Bakel 34 Cc 14.54N 12.27W
Baker [Ca.-U.S.] 46 Gi 35.15N 116.02W
Baker [La.-U.S.] 45 Kk 30.35N 91.10W
Baker [Mt.-U.S.] 43 Gb 46.22N 104.17W
Baker [Or.-U.S.] 43 Dc 44.47N 117.50W
Baker, Mount- 43 Cb 48.47N 121.49W
Baker Island 57 Jd 0.15N 176.27W
Baker Lake 39 Jc 64.10N 95.30W
Baker Lake 38 Jc 64.10N 95.30W
Bakersfield 39 Hf 35.23N 119.01W
Bâ Kêv 25 Lf 13.42N 107.12 E
Bakhma 24 Kd 36.38N 44.17 E
Bakhtarān (Kermānshāh) 22 Gf 34.19N 47.04 E
Bakhtarān [3] 23 Gc 34.15N 47.20 E
Bakhtegān, Daryāchech-ye 24 Ph 29.20N 54.05 E
Bakhūn, Kūh-e- 23 Id 27.56N 56.18 E
Bakir 24 Bc 38.55N 27.00 E
Bakırköy, İstanbul 15 Li 40.59N 28.52 E
Baklan 15 Ml 37.58N 29.36 E
Bako 35 Fd 7.19N 35.08 E
Bako [Eth.] 35 Fd 9.05N 37.07 E
Bako [Eth.] 35 Fd 5.50N 36.37 E
Bakony = Bakony Mountains (EN) 5 Hf 47.15N 17.50 E
Bakony Mountains (EN) = Bakony 5 Hf 47.15N 17.50 E
Bakool [3] 35 Ge 4.10N 43.50 E
Bakouma 35 Cd 5.42N 22.47 E
Bakoye 34 Cc 13.49N 10.50W
Bakpulād 24 Qc 38.10N 57.00 E
Baksan 16 Mh 43.40N 43.28 E
Baksan 16 Nh 43.42N 44.03 E
Baku 6 Kg 40.23N 49.51 E
Bakum 12 Kb 52.44N 8.11 E
Bakungan 26 Cf 2.56N 97.30 E
Bakuriani 16 Mi 41.43N 43.31 E
Bakutis Coast 66 Of 74.45S 120.00W
Balâ 24 Ec 39.34N 33.08 E
Bala, Cerros de- 54 Ef 14.30S 67.40W
Balabac 26 Ge 7.59N 117.04 E
Balabac 26 Ge 7.57N 117.01 E
Balabac, Selat- = Balabac Strait (EN) 21 Ni 7.40N 117.00 E
Balabac Strait (EN) = Balabac, Selat- 21 Ni 7.40N 117.00 E
Ba'labakk 24 Ge 34.00N 36.12 E
Balabalangan, Kepulauan- 26 Gg 2.20S 117.25 E
Balaban DaGı 24 Hb 40.28N 39.15 E
Balabanovo 16 Jb 55.11N 36.40 E
Balabio 63b Be 20.07S 164.11 E
Balaci 15 He 44.21N 24.55 E
Bal'ad 35 He 2.22N 45.24 E
Balad 24 Ke 34.01N 44.01 E
Balādīn as Sakrān 24 Kj 25.12N 44.37 E
Baladiyat 'Adan = Aden (EN) 22 Gh 12.46N 45.01 E
Balad Rūz 24 Kf 33.42N 45.05 E
Balagannoje 20 Je 59.43N 149.15 E
Balagansk 20 Ff 53.58N 103.02 E
Bālāghāt 25 Gd 21.48N 80.11 E
Bālāghāt Range 25 Fe 18.45N 76.30 E
Balagne 11a Aa 42.35N 8.50 E
Balaguer 13 Mc 41.47N 0.49 E
Balahna 7 Kh 56.31N 43.37 E
Balahta 20 Ee 55.24N 91.37 E
Balaka 36 Fe 14.59S 34.57 E
Balaklava 16 Hg 44.31N 33.34 E
Balakleja 19 Df 49.27N 36.52 E
Balakovo 6 Ke 52.02N 47.45 E
Balama 37 Fb 13.16S 38.36 E
Balambangam, Pulau- 26 Ge 7.17N 116.55 E
Bālā Morghāb 23 Jb 35.35N 63.20 E
Balan Daği 15 Lm 36.52N 28.20 E
Balankanche 48 Og 20.45N 88.30W
Balasan 26 Hd 11.28N 123.05 E
Balasore → Bāleshwar 25 Hd 21.30N 86.56 E
Balašov 19 Ee 51.33N 43.10 E
Balassagyarmat 10 Ph 48.05N 19.18 E
Balāţ 33 Ed 25.33N 29.16 E
Balaton 5 Hf 46.50N 17.45 E
Balatonfüred 10 Nj 46.57N 17.53 E
Balatonkeresztúr 10 Nj 46.42N 17.23 E
Balaurin 26 Hh 8.15S 123.43 E
Bălăuşeri 15 Hc 46.24N 24.41 E
Balayan 26 Hd 13.57N 120.44 E
Balazote 13 Jf 38.53N 2.08W
Balbi, Mount- 60 Ei 5.55S 154.59 E
Balboa Heights 47 Ig 8.57N 79.33W
Balbriggan/Baile Brigin 9 Gh 53.37N 6.11W
Balby 8 Ei 55.40N 13.20 E
Balcarce 56 Ie 37.50S 58.15W
Balcarce, Sierras de- 55 Cm 37.50S 58.40W
Bălceşti 15 Ge 44.37N 23.57 E
Balčik 15 Lf 43.25N 28.10 E
Balclutha 61 Ci 46.14S 169.44 E
Bald Eagle Mountain 44 Ie 41.00N 77.45W
Bald Head 59 Dg 35.07S 118.01 E
Bald Knob 44 Hg 37.56N 79.51W
Bald Knob 45 Ki 35.19N 91.34W
Baldo, Monte- 14 Ee 45.40N 10.50 E
Baldock 12 Bc 51.59N 0.11W
Baldone 8 Kh 56.41N 24.22 E
Baldur 45 Gb 49.23N 99.15W
Baldwin 44 Ed 43.54N 85.51W
Baldy Peak 43 Fe 33.55N 109.35W
Bale [3] 35 Gd 6.00N 41.00 E
Bâle/Basel 6 Gf 47.30N 7.30 E
Baleares [3] 13 Oe 39.30N 3.00 E
Balearic Islands (EN) = Bâleares, Islas-/Balears, Illes- 5 Gh 39.30N 3.00 E
Balearic Islands (EN) = Balears, Illes-/Baleares, Islas- 5 Gh 39.30N 3.00 E
Balears, Illes-/Baleares, Islas- = Balearic Islands (EN) 5 Gh 39.30N 3.00 E
Balease, Gunung- 26 Hg 2.24S 120.33 E
Baleia, Ponta de- 52 Mg 17.40S 36.07W
Baleine, Rivière à la- 42 Ke 58.15N 67.38W
Balej 20 Gf 51.35N 116.38 E
Balen 12 Hc 51.10N 5.09 E
Baler 26 Hc 15.46N 121.34 E
Bāleshwar 25 Hd 21.30N 86.56 E
Balezino 19 Fd 57.59N 53.02 E
Balfate 49 Df 15.48N 86.25W
Bălgarija = Bulgaria (EN) [1] 6 Ig 43.00N 25.00 E
Balgazyn 20 Ef 50.58N 95.12 E
Balguntay 27 Ec 42.45N 86.18 E
Balḩāf 23 Fg 13.58N 48.11 E
Balhaš 22 Je 46.49N 74.59 E
Balhaš, Ozero- = Balkhash, Lake- (EN) 21 Je 46.00N 74.00 E
Balho 35 Gc 12.00N 42.10 E
Balholm 7 Bf 61.12N 6.33 E
Bali [3] 26 Gh 8.30S 115.00 E
Bali, Laut- = Bali Sea (EN) 21 Nj 7.45S 115.30 E
Bali, Pulau- 21 Nj 8.20S 115.00 E
Bali, Selat- = Bali Strait (EN) 26 Fh 8.18S 114.25 E
Baliceaux Island 51n Bb 12.57N 61.08W
Baliem 26 Kg 4.25S 138.59 E
Balige 26 Cf 2.20N 99.04 E
Balikesir 23 Cb 39.39N 27.53 E
Balık Gölü 24 Jc 39.45N 43.36 E
Balīkh, Nahr- 24 He 35.53N 39.10 E
Balikpapan 22 Nj 1.17S 116.50 E
Balimbing 26 Dh 5.55S 104.34 E
Balimo 60 Ci 8.03S 142.56 E
Balingen 10 Eh 48.17N 8.51 E
Balinqiao 28 Ec 43.16N 118.38 E
Balintang Channel 26 Hc 19.49N 121.40 E
Bali Sea (EN) = Bali, Laut- 21 Nj 7.45S 115.30 E
Bali Strait (EN) = Bali, Selat- 26 Fh 8.18S 114.25 E
Balitung, Palau- 21 Mj 2.50S 107.55 E
Baliza 55 Fc 16.15S 52.25W
Balk, Gaasterland- 12 Hb 52.54N 5.36 E
Balkan Mountains (EN) = Stara Planina 5 Ig 43.15N 25.00 E
Balkan Peninsula (EN) 5 Ig 41.30N 23.00 E
Balkanskaja oblast 19 Fh 39.50N 55.00 E
Balkašino 19 Ge 52.32N 68.46 E
Balkh 23 Kb 36.46N 66.54 E
Balkh [3] 23 Kb 36.30N 67.00 E
Balkhash, Lake- (EN) = Balhaš, Ozero- 21 Je 46.00N 74.00 E
Balladonia 59 Ef 32.27S 123.51 E
Ballagen 7 Db 68.20N 16.50 E
Ballaghaderreen/Bealach an Doirin 9 Eh 53.55N 8.35W
Ballantrae 9 If 55.06N 5.00W
Ballantyne Strait 42 Ga 77.30N 115.00W
Ballarat 58 Fh 37.34S 143.52 E
Ballard, Lake- 59 Ee 29.25S 120.55 E
Ballé 34 Db 15.20N 8.36W
Ballenas, Bahia- 48 Cd 26.45N 113.25W
Ballenas, Canal de- 48 Cc 29.10N 113.25W
Ballenero, Canal- 56 Fh 54.50S 71.00W
Ballenita, Punta- 56 Fc 25.46S 70.44W
Balleny Islands 66 Ke 66.35S 162.50 E
Balleroy 12 Be 49.11N 0.50W
Balleza 48 Fd 26.57N 106.21W
Balli 15 Ki 40.50N 27.03 E
Ballia 25 Gc 25.45N 84.10 E
Ballina 59 Ke 28.52S 153.33 E
Ballina/Béal an Átha 9 Dg 54.07N 9.09W
Ballinasloe/Béal Átha na Sluaighe 9 Eh 53.20N 8.13W
Ballinger 45 Gk 31.44N 99.57W
Ballinrobe/Baile an Róba 9 Dh 53.37N 9.13W
Ballinskelligs Bay/Bágh Baile na Sgealg 9 Cj 51.50N 10.15W
Ballshi 15 Ci 40.36N 19.44 E
Ball's Pyramid 57 Gh 31.45S 159.15 E
Ballycastle/Baile an Chaistil 9 Gf 55.12N 6.15W
Ballyhaunis/Béal Átha hAmhnais 9 Eh 53.46N 8.46W
Ballymena/An Baile Meànach 9 Gg 54.52N 6.17W
Ballyshannon/Béal Átha Seanaidh 9 Eg 54.30N 8.11W
Balmazújváros 10 Ri 47.37N 21.21 E
Balmoral Castle 9 Jd 57.02N 3.15W
Balneario Orense 55 Cn 38.49S 59.46W
Balneario Oriente 55 Bn 38.55S 60.32W
Balombo 36 Be 12.21S 14.43 E
Balonne River 57 Fg 28.47S 147.56 E
Balota, Vîrful- 15 Gd 45.18N 23.53 E
Balovale 31 Jj 13.33S 23.07 E
Balrāmpur 25 Gc 27.26N 82.11 E
Balranald 59 If 34.38S 143.33 E
Balş 15 He 44.21N 24.06 E
Balsas [Braz.] 54 Ie 7.31S 46.02W
Balsas [Mex.] 48 Jh 18.00N 99.47W
Balsas, Depresión del- 48 Ih 18.00N 100.10W
Balsas, Rio- [Mex.] 38 Ih 17.55N 102.10W
Balsas, Rio- [Pan.] 49 Ii 8.15N 77.59W
Balsas, Rio das- [Braz.] 54 Ie 9.58S 47.52W
Balsas, Rio das- [Braz.] 54 Je 7.14S 44.33W
Bålsta 8 Ge 59.35N 17.30 E
Balsthal 14 Bc 47.19N 7.42 E
Balta 16 Ff 47.57N 29.38 E
Baltanás 13 Hc 41.56N 4.15W
Baltasar Brum 56 Id 30.44S 57.19W
Baltaţi 15 Kb 47.13N 27.09 E
Baltic Sea (EN) = Baltijas Jūra 5 Hd 57.00N 19.00 E
Baltic Sea (EN) = Baltijos Jura 5 Hd 57.00N 19.00 E
Baltic Sea (EN) = Balti Meri 5 Hd 57.00N 19.00 E
Baltic Sea- (EN) = Baltiskoje More 5 Hd 57.00N 19.00 E
Baltic Sea (EN) = Bałtyckie, Morze- 5 Hd 57.00N 19.00 E
Baltic Sea (EN) = Itämeri 5 Hd 57.00N 19.00 E
Baltic Sea (EN) = Östersjön 5 Hd 57.00N 19.00 E
Baltic Sea (EN) = Østersøen 5 Hd 57.00N 19.00 E
Baltic Sea (EN) = Ostsee 5 Hd 57.00N 19.00 E
Baltijas Jūra = Baltic Sea (EN) 5 Hd 57.00N 19.00 E
Baltijos Jura = Baltic Sea (EN) 5 Hd 57.00N 19.00 E
Baltijsk 19 Be 54.40N 19.58 E
Baltijskaja Grjada 7 Fi 55.00N 25.00 E
Balţīm 33 Fc 31.33N 31.05 E
Balti Meri = Baltic Sea (EN) 5 Hd 57.00N 19.00 E
Baltimore 39 Lf 39.17N 76.37W
Baltiskoje More = Baltic Sea (EN) 5 Hd 57.00N 19.00 E
Baltit (Hunza) 25 Ea 36.20N 74.40 E
Baltoj Voke 8 Kj 54.24N 25.16 E
Baltrum 10 Dc 53.44N 7.23 E
Bałtyckie, Morze- = Baltic Sea (EN) 5 Hd 57.00N 19.00 E
Baluarte, Río- 48 Ff 22.49N 106.02W
Baluchistān = Baluchistan (EN) 21 Ig 28.00N 63.00 E
Baluchistān = Baluchistan (EN) [3] 25 Cc 28.00N 63.00 E
Baluchistan (EN) = Baluchistān [3] 25 Cc 28.00N 63.00 E
Baluchistan (EN) = Baluchistān 21 Ig 28.00N 63.00 E
Balupe 8 Lh 56.54N 27.02 E
Balurghat 25 Hc 25.13N 88.46 E
Balvard 24 Qh 29.25N 56.06 E
Balve 12 Jc 51.20N 7.52 E
Balver Wald 12 Jc 51.21N 7.51 E
Balvi/Balvy 7 Gh 57.08N 27.20 E
Balvy/Balvi 7 Gh 57.08N 27.20 E
Balya 24 Bc 39.45N 27.35 E
Balygyčan 20 Kd 64.00N 154.10 E
Balykši 16 Qf 47.02N 51.55 E
Bām 24 Qd 36.58N 57.59 E
Bam 23 Id 29.06N 58.21 E
Bama 34 Hc 11.31N 13.41 E
Bamaji Lake 45 Ka 51.09N 91.25W
Bamako 31 Gg 12.38N 8.00W
Bamako [3] 34 Dc 13.00N 8.00W
Bamba 34 Eb 17.02N 1.24W
Bambama 36 Bc 2.32S 13.33 E
Bambana, Río- 49 Fg 13.27N 83.50W
Bambangando 36 Df 16.59S 20.57 E
Bambari 31 Jh 5.45N 20.40 E
Bamberg 10 Gg 49.42N 10.52 E
Bambesa 36 Eb 3.28N 25.43 E
Bambesi 35 Ed 9.45N 34.44 E
Bambey J4 Bc 14.42N 16.28W
Bambezi 37 Dc 19.57S 28.55 E
Bambili 36 Eb 3.39N 26.07 E
Bambio 35 Be 3.54N 16.59 E
Bamboi 34 Ed 8.10N 2.02W
Bambouti 35 Dd 5.24N 27.12 E
Bambouto, Monts- 30 Ih 5.44N 10.04 E
Bambui 55 Je 20.01S 45.58W
Bam Co 27 Fe 31.15N 90.32 E
Bamenda 34 Hd 5.56N 10.10 E
Bāmīān [3] 23 Kc 34.45N 67.15 E
Bāmīān 23 Kc 34.50N 67.50 E
Bamiancheng 28 Gc 43.15N 124.00 E
Bamiantong → Muling 28 Kb 44.55N 130.32 E
Bamingui 35 Cd 7.34N 20.11 E
Bamingui 30 Ih 8.33N 19.05 E
Bamingui-Bangoran [3] 35 Cd 7.50N 20.15 E
Bampūr 23 Jd 27.12N 60.27 E
Bampūr 23 Id 27.18N 59.06 E
Banaadir 30 Lh 1.00N 44.00 E
Banaadir [3] 35 He 2.00N 45.15 E
Banaba Island 57 He 0.52S 169.35 E
Banabuiú, Açude- 54 Ke 5.20S 39.00W
Banagi 36 Fc 2.16S 34.51 E
Banalia 36 Eb 1.33N 25.20 E
Banamba 34 Dc 13.32N 7.27W
Bananal, Ilha do- [Braz.] 52 Kg 11.30S 50.15W
Bananal, Ilha do- [Braz.] 55 Dc 17.05S 56.25W
Bananga 25 Ig 6.57N 93.54 E
Banarli 15 Kh 41.04N 27.20 E
Banās 25 Fc 25.54N 76.45 E
Banās, Ra's- 30 Kf 23.54N 35.48 E
Banat 5 If 45.30N 21.00 E
Banat 15 Dd 45.30N 21.00 E
Banaz 24 Cc 38.46N 29.46 E
Banaz 24 Cc 38.12N 29.14 E
Banbar 27 Fe 30.48N 94.52 E
Banbridge/Droichead na Banna 9 Gg 54.21N 6.16W
Banbury 9 Li 52.04N 1.20W
Banco, Punta- 49 Fi 8.23N 83.09W
Bancroft 44 Ic 45.03N 77.51W
Bānda 25 Gc 25.29N 80.20 E
Banda, Kepulauan- = Banda Islands (EN) 26 Ig 4.35S 129.55 E
Banda, Laut- = Banda Sea (EN) 57 De 5.00S 128.00 E
Banda, Punta- 48 Ab 31.45N 116.45W
Banda Aceh 22 Li 5.34N 95.20 E
Bandai-San 29 Gc 37.38N 140.04 E
Banda Islands (EN) = Banda, Kepulauan- 26 Ig 4.35S 129.55 E
Bandak 8 Ce 59.25N 8.15 E
Bandama 30 Gh 5.10N 4.58W
Bandama Blanc 34 Dd 6.54N 5.31W
Bandar Behestī 23 Jd 25.18N 60.37 E
Bandar-e 'Abbās 22 Hg 27.11N 56.17 E
Bandar-e Anzalī 23 Gb 37.28N 49.27 E
Bandar-e Būshehr 22 Hq 28.59N 50.50 E
Bandar-e Chīrū 24 Oi 26.43N 53.43 E
Bandar-e Deylam 23 Hg 30.05N 50.07 E
Bandar-e-Gaz 24 Od 36.47N 53.59 E
Bandar-e-Khomeynī 24 Mg 30.25N 49.08 E
Bandar-e Lengeh 23 Hd 26.33N 54.53 E
Bandar-e Māh Shahr 23 Gc 30.33N 49.12 E
Bandar-e Maqām 23 Hd 26.56N 53.29 E
Bandar-e Moghūyeh 24 Pi 26.35N 54.31 E
Bandar-e-Rīg 24 Nh 29.29N 50.38 E
Bandar-e-Torkeman 23 Gf 30.45N 51.33 E
Bandar Seri Begawan 22 Ni 4.53N 114.56 E
Banda Sea (EN) = Banda, Laut- 57 De 5.00S 128.00 E
Bande 13 Eb 42.02N 7.58W
Bandeira, Pico da- 52 Lh 20.26S 41.47W
Bandeirantes 55 Ga 13.41S 50.48W
Bandeirantes, Ilha dos- 55 Ff 23.22S 53.50W
Bandera 56 Hc 28.54S 62.16W
Bandera, Alto- 49 Ld 18.49N 70.37W
Banderas, Bahia de- 47 Cd 20.40N 105.25W
Bandiagara 34 Ec 14.20N 3.37W
Bandiat 11 Gi 45.46N 0.20 E
Bandırma 23 Ca 40.20N 27.58 E
Bandirma Körfezi 15 Ki 40.25N 28.00 E
Bandol 11 Lk 43.08N 5.45 E
Bandon 46 Ce 43.07N 124.25W
Bandon/Abhainn na Bandan 9 Ej 51.40N 8.30W
Bandon/Droichead na Bandan 9 Ej 51.45N 8.45W
Ban Don, Ao- 25 Jg 9.20N 99.25 E
Bandundu [2] 36 Cc 5.00S 17.00 E
Bandundu 31 Ii 3.18S 17.20 E
Bandung 22 Mj 6.54S 107.36 E
Bāneh 24 Ke 35.59N 45.53 E
Banes 47 Id 20.58N 75.43W
Banff [Alta.-Can.] 42 Ff 51.10N 115.34W
Banff [Scot.-U.K.] 9 Kd 57.40N 2.31W
Banfora 34 Ec 10.38N 4.46W
Banga 36 Dd 5.57S 20.28 E
Bangalore 22 Jh 12.59N 77.35 E
Bangangté 34 Hd 5.09N 10.31 E
Bangar 26 Gf 4.43N 115.04 E
Bangassou 31 Jh 4.44N 22.49 E
Bangeta, Mount- 60 Di 6.16S 147.04 E
Banggai 26 Hg 1.34S 123.30 E
Banggai, Kepulauan- = Banggai Archipelago (EN) 26 Hg 1.30S 123.15 E
Banggai, Selat- 26 Hg 1.55S 124.00 E
Banggai Archipelago (EN) = Banggai, Kepulauan- 26 Hg 1.30S 123.15 E
Banggi, Pulau- 26 Ge 7.17N 117.12 E
Banghāzī = Benghazi (EN) 31 Je 32.07N 20.04 E
Banghāzī = Benghazi (EN) [3] 33 Dd 27.00N 20.30 E
Bangka, Pulau- [Indon.] 26 If 1.48N 125.09 E
Bangka, Pulau- [Indon.] 21 Mj 2.15S 106.00 E
Bangka, Selat- = Bangka Strait (EN) 26 Eg 2.20S 105.45 E
Bangkalan 26 Fh 7.02S 112.44 E
Bangka Strait (EN) = Bangka, Selat- 26 Eg 2.20S 105.45 E
Bangkinang 26 Df 0.21N 101.02 E
Bangko 26 Dg 2.05S 102.17 E
Bangkok (EN) = Krung Thep 22 Mh 13.45N 100.31 E
Bangladesh [1] 22 Kg 24.00N 90.00 E
Bangli 26 Gh 8.27S 115.21 E
Bangolo 34 Dd 7.01N 7.09W
Bangong Co 27 Ce 33.45N 79.15 E
Bangor [Me.-U.S.] 43 Nc 44.49N 68.47W
Bangor [Wales-U.K.] 9 Ih 53.13N 4.08W
Bangor/Beannchar 9 Hg 54.40N 5.40W
Bangoran 35 'Bd 8.42N 19.06 E
Bangsund 7 Cd 64.24N 11.24 E
Bangu 36 Dd 9.05S 23.44 E
Bangued 26 Hc 17.36N 120.37 E
Bangui [C.A.R.] 31 Ih 4.22N 18.35 E
Bangui [Phil.] 26 Hc 18.32N 120.46 E
Bangweulu, Lake- 30 Jj 11.05S 29.45 E
Bangweulu Swamps 36 Fe 11.30S 30.15 E
Banhā 33 Fc 30.28N 31.11 E
Ban Houayxay 25 Kd 20.18N 100.26 E
Bani 30 Gg 14.30N 4.12W
Baní 47 Je 18.17N 70.20W
Bani, Jbel- 30 Gf 28.30N 9.00W
Bani Bangou 34 Fb 15.03N 2.42 E
Banie 10 Kc 53.08N 14.38 E
Banifing 34 Dc 12.43N 6.25W
Banī Forūr, Jazīreh-ye- 24 Pi 26.07N 54.28 E
Banihal Pass 25 Fb 33.15N 75.09 E
Banija 14 Ke 45.10N 16.10 E
Banikoara 34 Fc 11.18N 2.26 E
Banī ma 'Āriḑ 33 Ie 20.42N 47.42 E
Banī Mazār 33 Fd 28.30N 30.48 E
Banī Muḩammadīyāt 24 Di 27.17N 31.05 E
Banī Suwayf 33 Fd 29.05N 31.05 E
Banī Tonb 24 Pi 26.12N 54.56 E
Banī Walīd 33 Bc 31.46N 13.59 E
Bāniyās 23 Ec 33.15N 35.41 E
Banja 15 Hg 42.33N 24.50 E
Banja Koviljača 15 Ce 44.30N 19.11 E
Banja Luka 14 Lf 44.46N 17.10 E
Banjarmarsin 22 Nj 3.20S 114.35 E
Banjul 31 Fg 13.27N 16.35W
Bank 16 Pj 39.27N 49.14 E
Bankas 34 Ec 14.05N 3.31W
Bankeryd 8 Fg 57.51N 14.07 E
Banket 37 Ec 17.23S 30.24 E
Bankhead Lake 44 Di 33.30N 87.15W
Bankilaré 34 Fc 14.35N 0.44 E
Bankja 15 Gg 42.42N 23.08 E
Ban Kongmi 25 Lf 14.31N 106.55 E
Banks [Can.] 38 Gb 73.15N 121.30W
Banks [Can.] 42 Ef 53.25N 130.10W
Banks, Iles- = Banks Islands (EN) 57 Hf 13.50S 167.35 E
Banks Island 59 Ib 10.10S 142.15 E
Banks Islands (EN) = Banks, Iles- 57 Hf 13.50S 167.35 E
Banks Lake 46 Fc 47.45N 119.15W
Banks Peninsula 57 Ii 43.40S 172.40 E
Banks Strait 59 Jh 40.40S 148.10 E
Bann/An Bhanna 9 Gf 55.10N 6.46W
Ban Na San 25 Jg 8.53N 99.17 E
Bannerman Town 44 Im 24.09N 76.09W
Banning 46 Gj 33.56N 116.52W
Bannock Range 46 Ie 42.30N 112.20W
Bannu 25 Eb 32.59N 70.36 E
Bañolas/Banyoles 13 Ob 42.07N 2.46 E
Bánovce nad Bebravou 10 Oh 48.44N 18.15 E
Banqiao 27 Hf 25.28N 104.02 E
Banská Bystrica 10 Ph 48.44N 19.09 E
Banská Štiavnica 10 Oh 48.27N 18.55 E
Bansko 15 Gh 41.50N 23.29 E
Bānswāra 25 Ed 23.33N 74.27 E
Banta 35 Ge 1.13N 42.30 E
Bantenan, Tanjung- 26 Fh 8.47S 114.33 E
Bantry/Beanntrai 9 Dj 51.41N 9.27W
Bantry Bay/Bá Bheanntrai 9 Dj 51.38N 9.48W
Bañuela 13 Hf 38.24N 4.11W
Banyak, Kepulauan- = Banyak Islands (EN) 26 Cf 2.10N 97.15 E
Banyak Islands (EN) = Banyak, Kepulauan- 26 Cf 2.10N 97.15 E
Banyo 34 Hd 6.45N 11.49 E
Banyoles/Bañolas 13 Ob 42.07N 2.46 E
Banyuls-sur-Mer 11 Jl 42.29N 3.08 E
Banyuwangi 22 Nj 8.12S 114.21 E
Banzare Coast 66 Ie 67.00S 126.00 E
Banzare Seamounts (EN) 66 Df 58.50S 77.44 E
Banzart [3] 32 Ib 37.00N 9.30 E
Banzart = Bizerte (EN) 31 He 37.17N 9.52 E
Banzart, Buḩayrat- 14 Dm 37.11N 9.52 E
Bao'an 27 Jg 22.35N 114.10 E
Bao'an → Zhidan 27 Id 36.48N 108.46 E
Baochang → Taibus Qi 27 Kc 41.55N 115.22 E
Baode 27 Jd 38.59N 111.07 E
Baodi 28 De 39.43N 117.18 E
Baoding 22 Nf 38.47N 115.30 E
Baofeng [China] 27 Je 33.48N 113.14 E
Baofeng [China] 28 Bh 33.52N 113.04 E
Baoji 22 Mf 34.26N 107.12 E
Baokang 27 Je 31.49N 111.13 E
Baokang → Horqin Zuoyi Zhongqi 27 Lc 44.06N 123.19 E
Bao Loc 25 Lf 11.32N 107.48 E
Baoqing 27 Nb 46.20N 132.11 E
Baoro 35 Bd 5.40N 15.58 E
Baoshan 22 Lg 25.09N 99.12 E
Baotou 22 Me 40.38N 110.00 E
Baoulé [Afr.] 30 Gg 12.35N 6.34W
Baoulé [Mali] 30 Gg 13.33N 9.54W
Baoying 28 Eh 33.15N 119.18 E
Bapaume 11 Id 50.06N 2.51 E
Baqên (Dartang) 27 Fe 31.58N 94.00 E
Bāqerābād 24 Ne 34.56N 50.50 E
Ba'qūbah 23 Fc 33.45N 44.38 E
Baquedano 56 Gb 23.20S 69.51W
Bar 12 Ge 49.42N 4.50 E
Bar 16 Ee 49.02N 27.40 E
Bar [Yugo.] 15 Cg 42.05N 19.06 E
Barabai 26 Gg 2.35S 115.23 E
Barabevú 55 Bk 33.20S 61.52W
Barabinsk 22 Jd 55.21N 78.21 E
Barabinskaja Step 20 Ce 55.00N 79.00 E
Baraboo 45 Le 43.28N 89.45W
Baracaldo 13 Ja 43.18N 2.59W
Baracoa 47 Jd 20.21N 74.30W
Bărăganului, Cîmpia- 15 Ke 44.55N 27.15 E
Baragoi 36 Gb 1.47N 36.47 E
Bārah 35 Ec 13.42N 30.22 E
Barahona 47 Je 18.12N 71.06W
Barak 24 Gd 36.51N 37.59 E
Baraka 35 Fb 18.13N 37.35 E
Barakah 35 Fb 18.13N 37.35 E
Barakāt 35 Ec 14.20N 33.36 E
Barakī Barak 23 Kc 33.58N 68.58 E
Baram 26 Ff 4.36N 113.59 E
Baram 26 Ff 4.36N 113.58 E
Baramanni 50 Gi 7.50N 59.13W
Barama River 50 Gi 7.40N 59.15W
Barāmūla 25 Eb 34.12N 74.21 E
Bāran 25 Fc 25.06N 76.31 E
Baran 7 Hi 54.29N 30.19 E
Baraniha 20 Lc 68.31N 168.25 E
Baranja 14 Me 46.00N 18.30 E
Baranoa 49 Jh 10.49N 75.03W
Baranof 40 Le 57.00N 135.00W

Index Symbols

[1] Independent Nation
[2] State, Region
[3] District, County
[4] Municipality
[5] Colony, Dependency
Continent
Physical Region
Historical or Cultural Region
Mount, Mountain
Volcano
Hill
Mountains, Mountain Range
Hills, Escarpment
Plateau, Upland
Pass, Gap
Plain, Lowland
Delta
Salt Flat
Valley, Canyon
Crater, Cave
Karst Features
Depression
Polder
Desert, Dunes
Forest, Woods
Heath, Steppe
Oasis
Cape, Point
Coast, Beach
Cliff
Peninsula
Isthmus
Sandbank
Island
Atoll
Rock, Reef
Islands, Archipelago
Rocks, Reefs
Coral Reef
Well, Spring
Geyser
River, Stream
Waterfall Rapids
River Mouth, Estuary
Lake
Salt Lake
Intermittent Lake
Reservoir
Swamp, Pond
Canal
Glacier
Ice Shelf, Pack Ice
Ocean
Sea
Gulf, Bay
Strait, Fjord
Lagoon
Bank
Seamount
Tablemount
Ridge
Shelf
Basin
Escarpment, Sea Scarp
Fracture
Trench, Abyss
National Park, Reserve
Point of Interest
Recreation Site
Cave, Cavern
Historic Site
Ruins
Wall, Walls
Church, Abbey
Temple
Scientific Station
Airport
Port
Lighthouse
Mine
Tunnel
Dam, Bridge

Index Symbols

- [1] Independent Nation
- [2] State, Region
- [3] District, County
- Municipality
- Colony, Dependency
- Continent
- Physical Region
- Historical or Cultural Region
- Mount, Mountain
- Volcano
- Hill
- Mountains, Mountain Range
- Hills, Escarpment
- Plateau, Upland
- Pass, Gap
- Plain, Lowland
- Delta
- Salt Flat
- Valley, Canyon
- Crater, Cave
- Karst Features
- Depression
- Polder
- Desert, Dunes
- Forest, Woods
- Heath, Steppe
- Oasis
- Cape, Point
- Coast, Beach
- Cliff
- Peninsula
- Isthmus
- Sandbank
- Island
- Rock, Reef
- Islands, Archipelago
- Rocks, Reefs
- Coral Reef
- Well, Spring
- Geyser
- River, Stream
- Waterfall Rapids
- River Mouth, Estuary
- Lake
- Salt Lake
- Intermittent Lake
- Sea
- Swamp, Pond
- Canal
- Glacier
- Ice Shelf, Pack Ice
- Ocean
- Tableland
- Ridge
- Shelf
- Basin
- Lagoon
- Bank
- Seamount
- Trench, Abyss
- National Park, Reserve
- Point of Interest
- Recreation Site
- Cave, Cavern
- Escarpment, Sea Scarp
- Fracture
- Wall, Walls
- Church, Abbey
- Temple
- Scientific Station
- Airport
- Historic Site
- Ruins
- Mine
- Tunnel
- Dam, Bridge
- Port
- Lighthouse

Béal Átha na Muice/Swinford 9 Eh 53.57N 8.57W
Béal Átha na Sluaighe/Ballinasloe 9 Eh 53.20N 8.13W
Béal Átha Seanaidh/Ballyshannon 9 Eg 54.30N 8.11W
Beale, Cape- 46 Cb 48.44N 125.20W
Béal Easa/Foxford 9 Dh 53.59N 9.07W
Béal Feirste/Belfast 6 Fe 54.35N 5.55W
Beal Range 59 Ie 25.30S 141.30E
Béal Tairbirt/Belturbet 9 Fg 54.06N 7.26W
Beanna Boirche/Mourne Mountains 9 Gg 54.10N 6.04W
Beannchar/Bangor 9 Hg 54.40N 5.40W
Beanntrai/Bantry 9 Dj 51.41N 9.27W
Bear Bay 42 Ia 75.45N 86.30W
Beardmore 45 Mb 49.36N 87.57W
Beardstown 45 Kg 39.59N 90.26W
Bear Island (EN)=Björnöya 5 Ha 74.30N 19.00E
Bear Islands (EN)=Medveži, Ostrova- 21 Sb 70.52N 161.26E
Bear Lake 43 Ec 42.00N 111.20W
Bear Lodge Mountains 45 Dd 44.35N 104.15W
Béarn 11 Fk 43.20N 0.45W
Bearpaw Mountains 46 Kb 48.15N 109.30W
Bear Peninsula 66 Of 74.36S 110.50W
Bear River 46 If 41.30N 112.08W
Bearskin Lake 42 If 53.57N 90.59W
Beās 25 Eb 31.10N 74.59E
Beas de Segura 13 Jf 38.15N 2.53W
Beata, Cabo- 47 Je 17.36N 71.25W
Beata, Isla- 49 Le 17.35N 71.31W
Beata Ridge (EN) 47 Je 16.00N 72.30W
Beatrice 43 Hc 40.16N 96.44W
Beatrice, Cape- 59 Hb 14.15S 137.00E
Beatton 42 Fe 56.06N 120.22W
Beatton River 42 Fe 56.10N 120.25W
Beatty 43 Dd 36.54N 116.46W
Beattyville 44 Ia 48.52N 77.10W
Beatys Butte 46 Fe 42.23N 119.20W
Beau-Bassin 37a Bb 20.13S 57.27E
Beaucaire 11 Kk 43.48N 4.38E
Beaucamps-le-Vieux 12 De 49.50N 1.47E
Beaucanton 44 Ha 49.05N 79.15W
Beauce 11 Hf 48.22N 1.50E
Beaudesert 59 Ke 27.59S 153.00E
Beaufort [Mala.] 26 Ge 5.20N 115.45E
Beaufort [S.C.-U.S.] 44 Gi 32.26N 80.40W
Beaufort/Befort 12 Ie 49.50N 6.18E
Beaufort, Massif de- 11 Mi 45.50N 6.40E
Beaufort Island 66 Kf 76.57S 166.56E
Beaufort Sea 67 Eb 73.00N 140.00W
Beaufort West 31 Jl 32.20S 22.33E
Beaugency 11 Hg 47.47N 1.38E
Beaujolais, Monts du- 11 Kh 46.00N 4.22E
Beauly 9 Id 57.29N 4.29W
Beaumesnil 12 Ce 49.01N 0.43E
Beaumetz-lès-Loges 12 Ed 50.14N 2.39E
Beaumont [Bel.] 12 Gd 50.14N 4.14E
Beaumont [Fr.] 11 Gj 44.46N 0.46E
Beaumont [Fr.] 11 Ee 49.40N 1.51W
Beaumont [Fr.] 12 Hf 48.51N 5.47E
Beaumont [Ms.-U.S.] 45 Lk 31.11N 88.55W
Beaumont [N.Z.] 62 Cf 45.49S 169.32E
Beaumont [Tx.-U.S.] 39 Jf 30.05N 94.06W
Beaumont-de-Lomagne 11 Gk 43.53N 0.59E
Beaumont-en-Argonne 12 He 49.32N 5.03E
Beaumont-le-Roger 12 Ce 49.05N 0.47E
Beaumont-sur-Oise 12 Ee 49.08N 2.17E
Beaumont-sur-Sarthe 11 Gf 48.13N 0.08E
Beaune 11 Kg 47.02N 4.50E
Beaupré 44 Lb 47.03N 70.53W
Beauraing 12 Gd 50.07N 4.48E
Beaurepaire 11 Li 45.20N 5.03E
Beausejour 42 Hf 50.04N 96.33W
Beautemps Beaupré 63b Ce 20.25S 166.08E
Beauvais 11 Ie 49.26N 2.05E
Beauval 12 Ed 50.06N 2.20E
Beauvoir-sur-Mer 11 Dh 46.55N 2.03W
Beaver [Ak.-U.S.] 40 Jc 66.22N 147.24W
Beaver [Ok.-U.S.] 45 Fh 36.48N 100.30W
Beaver [Ut.-U.S.] 43 Ed 38.17N 112.38W
Beaver Creek [Co.-U.S.] 45 Ef 40.20N 103.33W
Beaver Creek [U.S.] 45 Ec 47.20N 103.39W
Beaver Creek [U.S.] 45 Gf 40.04N 99.20W
Beaver Creek [U.S.] 45 Ee 43.25N 103.59W
Beaver Dam 45 Le 43.28N 88.50W
Beaver Falls 44 Ge 40.45N 80.21W
Beaverhead Mountains 46 Id 45.00N 113.20W
Beaver Island 44 Ec 45.40N 85.31W
Beaver Lake 45 Jh 36.20N 93.55W
Beaver River [U.S.] 45 Gh 36.10N 98.45W
Beaver River [Ut.-U.S.] 46 Ig 39.10N 112.57W
Beaverton 46 Dd 45.29N 122.48W
Beāwar 25 Ec 26.06N 74.19E
Bebedouro 56 Kb 20.56S 48.28W
Becan 48 Oh 18.37N 89.35W
Becanchén 48 Oh 19.50N 89.22W
Beccles 9 Oi 52.28N 1.34E
Bečej 15 Dd 45.37N 20.03E
Beceni 15 Jd 45.23N 26.47E
Becerreá 13 Eb 42.51N 7.10W
Becerro, Cayos- 49 Ff 15.57N 83.17W
Béchar 31 Ge 31.37N 2.13W
Béchar 32 Gd 30.00N 2.00W
Becharof Lake 40 He 58.00N 156.30W
Bechet 15 Gf 43.46N 23.57E
Bechevin Bay 40 Ge 55.00N 163.27W
Bechyně 10 Kg 49.18N 14.28E
Beckingen 12 Ie 49.24N 6.42E
Beckley 43 Kd 37.46N 81.12W
Beckum 10 Ee 51.45N 8.02E
Beckumer Berge 12 Kc 51.43N 8.10E
Beclean 15 Hb 47.11N 24.11E
Bédarieux 11 Jk 43.37N 3.09E
Bedburg-Hau 12 Ic 51.46N 6.11E
Bedele 35 Fd 8.27N 36.22E
Bedesa 35 Gd 8.53N 40.46E
Bedford 9 Mi 52.10N 0.50W
Bedford [Eng.-U.K.] 9 Mi 52.08N 0.29W
Bedford [In.-U.S.] 44 Df 38.52N 86.29W
Bedford [Pa.-U.S.] 44 He 40.00N 78.31W
Bedford [Va.-U.S.] 44 Hg 37.20N 79.31W
Bedford Level 9 Ni 52.30N 0.05E
Bedford Point 51p Bb 12.13N 61.36W
Bedfordshire 9 Mi 52.05N 0.20W
Bednja 14 Kd 46.18N 16.45E
Bednodemjanovsk 16 Mc 53.55N 43.12E
Bedourie 59 Hd 24.21S 139.28E
Bedum 12 Ia 53.18N 6.39E
Beech Grove 44 Df 39.43N 86.03W
Beecroft Head 59 Kg 35.01S 150.50E
Beef Island 51a Db 18.27N 64.31W
Beelitz 10 Id 52.14N 12.58E
Beemster 12 Gb 52.34N 4.56E
Beerfelden 12 Ke 49.34N 8.59E
Beernem 12 Fc 51.09N 3.20E
Beerse 12 Gc 51.19N 4.52E
Beersel 12 Gd 50.46N 4.18E
Beersheba (EN)=Be'er Shevà 23 Dc 31.14N 34.47E
Be'er Shevà=Beersheba (EN) 23 Dc 31.14N 34.47E
Beerze 12 Hc 51.36N 5.19E
Beeskow 10 Kd 52.10N 14.14E
Beestekraal 37 De 25.23S 27.38E
Beeston 9 Li 52.56N 1.12W
Beethoven Peninsula 66 Qf 71.40S 73.45W
Beetsterzwaag, Opsterland- 12 Ia 53.03N 6.04E
Beeville 43 Hf 28.24N 97.45W
Befale 36 Db 0.28N 20.58E
Befandriana Nord 37 Hc 15.15S 48.32E
Befandriana Sud 37 Gd 22.06S 43.54E
Befori 36 Db 0.06N 22.17E
Befort/Beaufort 12 Ie 49.50N 6.18E
Bega 15 Dd 45.13N 20.19E
Bega 58 Fh 36.40S 149.50E
Bégard 11 Cf 48.38N 3.18W
Begejski kanal 15 Dd 45.27N 20.27E
Beggars Point 51d Bb 17.10N 61.48W
Bègle 11 Fj 44.48N 0.32W
Begna 7 Bf 60.35N 10.00E
Begoml 8 Mj 54.46N 28.14E
Begunicy 8 Me 59.31N 29.30E
Behābād 24 Pg 31.52N 55.57E
Behbehān 23 Hc 30.35N 50.14E
Behring Point 49 Ia 24.27N 77.43W
Behshahr 23 Hb 36.43N 53.34E
Bei'an 27 Oe 48.16N 126.29E
Beibu Wan=Tonkin, Gulf of- (EN) 21 Mh 20.00N 108.00E
Beida He 27 Gc 40.18N 99.01E
Beihai 22 Mg 21.31N 109.07E
Bei Hulsan Hu 27 Gd 36.55N 95.55E
Bei Jiang 27 Jg 23.02N 112.58E
Beijing=Peking (EN) 22 Nf 39.55N 116.23E
Beijing Shi (Pei-ching Shih) 27 Kc 40.15N 116.30E
Beïla 32 Df 18.10N 15.53W
Beilen 12 Ib 52.52N 6.32E
Beiliutang He 28 Eg 34.12N 119.33E
Beilrstroom 12 Ib 52.41N 6.12E
Beilsteim 12 Jd 50.07N 7.15E
Beilu He 27 Fe 34.34N 94.00E
Beinamar 35 Bd 8.40N 15.23E
Beine-Nauroy 12 Ge 49.15N 4.13E
Beipiao 27 Lc 41.49N 120.45E
Beira 31 Kj 19.50S 34.52E
Beira Alta 13 Ed 40.40N 7.35W
Beira Baixa 13 Ee 39.55N 7.30W
Beira Litoral 13 Dd 40.15N 8.25W
Beiru He 28 Bh 33.40N 113.35E
Beirut (EN)=Bayrūt 22 Ff 33.53N 35.30E
Bei Shan 21 Le 41.30N 96.00E
Beitstad 7 Cd 64.05N 11.22E
Beiuş 15 Fc 46.40N 22.21E
Beiwei Tan 27 Kg 21.10N 116.10E
Beizhen [China] 27 Kd 37.24N 117.59E
Beizhen [China] 27 Fd 41.36N 121.47E
Beja 13 Ef 38.01N 7.52W
Beja 13 Eg 37.58N 7.50W
Bejaia 32 Ib 36.40N 5.10E
Bejaïa 31 He 36.45N 5.05E
Bejaïa, Golfe de- 13 Rh 36.45N 5.20E
Béjar 13 Gd 40.23N 5.46W
Beji 25 Dc 29.47N 67.58E
Bejneu 19 Ff 45.15N 55.05E
Bejsug 16 Kf 46.02N 38.35E
Bejsugski Liman 16 Kf 46.05N 38.25E
Bekabad 19 Gg 40.13N 69.14E
Bekasi 26 Eh 6.14S 106.59E
Bekdaš 19 Fg 41.31N 52.40E
Békés 10 Rj 46.46N 21.08E
Békés 10 Qj 46.45N 21.00E
Békéscsaba 10 Rj 46.41N 21.06E
Bekilli 15 Mk 38.14N 29.26E
Bekily 37 Hd 24.12S 45.18E
Bekkai 29a Db 43.25N 145.07E
Bekoji 35 Fd 7.32N 39.15E
Bekopaka 37 Gc 19.08S 44.45E
Bekovo 16 Mc 52.29N 43.45E
Bela [India] 25 Gc 25.56N 81.59E
Bela [Pak.] 25 Dc 26.14N 66.19E
Bélabo 34 He 4.52N 13.10E
Bela Crkva 15 Ee 44.54N 21.26E
Bela Dila 25 Ge 18.40N 80.55E
Bela Floresta 55 Ge 20.36S 51.16W
Belaga 26 Ff 2.42N 113.47E
Belaja 20 Mc 65.30N 173.15E
Belaja 5 Ld 56.00N 54.32E
Belaja 16 Kg 45.03N 39.25E
Belaja Cerkov 6 Jf 49.49N 30.07E
Belaja Gora 20 Jc 68.30N 146.15E
Belaja Holunica 19 Fd 58.53N 50.50E
Belaja Kalitva 19 Ef 48.09N 40.49E
Bela Krajina 14 Je 45.35N 15.15E
Bela Lorena 55 Ib 15.13S 46.01W
Belang 26 Hf 0.57N 124.47E
Bela Palanka 15 Ff 43.13N 22.19E
Belarbi 13 Pi 35.09N 0.27W
Belarus (EN) = Byelarus' 19 Ce 53.50N 28.00E
Belasica 15 Fh 41.21N 22.50E
Belau → Palau (EN) 58 Ed 7.30N 134.30E
Bela Vista [Braz.] 54 Gh 22.06S 56.31W
Bela Vista [Braz.] 55 Dc 17.37S 57.01W
Bela Vista [Moz.] 37 Ee 26.20S 32.40E
Belawan 26 Cf 3.47N 98.41E
Běła Woda/Weißwasser 10 Ke 51.31N 14.38E
Belayan 26 Gg 0.14S 116.36E
Belbo 14 Cf 44.54N 8.31E
Bel'c' 19 Cf 47.46N 27.55E
Bełchatow 10 Pe 51.22N 19.21E
Belcher Channel 42 Ia 77.20N 4.30W
Belcher Islands 38 Ld 56.20N 79.30W
Belchite 13 Lc 41.18N 0.45W
Bełczyna 10 Ne 51.25N 17.50E
Belebej 19 Fe 54.10N 54.07E
Belecke, Warstein- 12 Kc 51.29N 8.20E
Beled 10 Ni 47.28N 17.06E
Beled Wēyne 31 Lh 4.47N 45.12E
Bélel 34 Hd 7.03N 14.26E
Belém [Moz.] 37 Fb 14.08S 35.58E
Belém [Braz.] 53 Lf 1.27S 48.29W
Belem [Mex.] 48 Dd 27.45N 110.28W
Belém de São Francisco 54 Ke 8.46S 38.58W
Belen 43 Fe 34.40N 106.46W
Belén [Arg.] 56 Gc 27.39S 67.02W
Belén [Nic.] 49 Eh 11.30N 85.53W
Belén [Par.] 55 Df 23.30S 57.06W
Belén [Ur.] 55 Dj 30.47S 57.47W
Belén, Cuchilla de- 55 Dj 30.55S 56.30W
Belén de Escobar 55 Cl 34.21S 58.47W
Belene 15 If 43.39N 25.07E
Bélep, Iles- 57 Hf 19.45S 163.40E
Beles 35 Fc 10.55N 35.10E
Belev 16 Jc 53.50N 36.10E
Beleye 35 Fc 11.24N 36.10E
Belfast [Me.-U.S.] 44 Mc 44.27N 69.01W
Belfast [S.Afr.] 37 Ee 25.43S 30.03E
Belfast/Béal Feirste 6 Fe 54.35N 5.55W
Belfast Lough/Loch Lao 9 Hg 54.40N 5.50W
Belfield 45 Ec 46.53N 103.12W
Belford 9 Lf 55.36N 1.49W
Belfort 11 Mg 47.45N 7.00E
Belgaum 22 Jh 15.52N 74.30E
Belgica Bank (EN) 67 Ld 78.28N 15.00W
Belgicafjella 66 Df 72.35S 31.10E
België/Belgique=Belgium (EN) 6 Ge 50.30N 4.30E
Belgique/België=Belgium (EN) 6 Ge 50.30N 4.30E
Belgium (EN)=België/Belgique 6 Ge 50.30N 4.30E
Belgium (EN)=Belgique/België 6 Ge 50.30N 4.30E
Belgorod 6 Je 50.36N 36.35E
Belgorod-Dnestrovski 19 Df 46.12N 30.17E
Belgorodskaja Oblast 19 De 50.45N 37.30E
Belgrade (EN) = Beograd 6 Ig 44.50N 20.30E
Bel Haïrane 32 Ic 31.17N 6.20E
Beli 34 Hd 7.52N 10.58E
Belice 14 Gm 37.35N 12.52E
Beli Drim 15 Dg 42.05N 20.20E
Belidži 16 Pi 41.53N 48.20E
Beli Lom 15 If 43.41N 26.00E
Beli Manastir 14 Me 45.46N 18.37E
Belimbegovo 15 Eh 42.00N 21.35E
Belin 11 Fj 44.30N 0.47W
Belinga 36 Bb 1.04N 13.12E
Belinski 16 Mc 52.58N 43.29E
Belinyu 26 Eg 1.38S 105.46E
Beliş 15 Gc 46.39N 23.02E
Beli Timok 15 Ff 43.55N 22.18E
Belize 39 Kh 17.15N 88.45W
Belize (British Honduras) 39 Kh 17.15N 88.45W
Belize City 39 Kh 17.30N 88.12W
Belize River 49 Ce 17.32N 88.14W
Beljajevka 16 Gf 46.29N 30.14E
Beljanica 15 Ee 44.07N 21.43E
Belka 8 Mg 57.40N 29.47E
Belkovski, Ostrov- 20 Ia 75.30N 136.00E
Bellac 11 Hh 46.07N 1.03E
Bella Coola 42 Ef 52.22N 126.46W
Bellagio 14 De 45.59N 9.15E
Bellaire [Oh.-U.S.] 44 Ge 40.02N 80.46W
Bellaire [Tx.-U.S.] 45 Il 29.43N 95.28W
Bellaria-Igea Marina 14 Gf 44.09N 12.28E
Bellary 22 Jh 15.09N 76.56E
Bella Unión 55 Dj 30.15S 57.35W
Bella Vista [Arg.] 56 Ic 28.30S 59.03W
Bella Vista [Par.] 55 Df 22.08S 56.31W
Bellavista, Capo- 14 Dk 39.56N 9.43E
Bell Bay 42 Jb 71.10N 84.55W
Belle-Anse 49 Kd 18.13N 72.04W
Belledonne 11 Mi 45.18N 6.08E
Bellefontaine [Mart.] 51h Ab 14.40N 61.10W
Bellefontaine [Oh.-U.S.] 44 Fe 40.22N 83.45W
Belle Fourche 43 Gc 44.40N 103.51W
Belle Fourche River 45 Ed 44.26N 102.19W
Bellegarde 11 If 47.59N 2.26E
Bellegarde-sur-Valserine 11 Lh 46.06N 5.49E
Belle Glade 44 Gl 26.41N 80.40W
Belle Ile 5 Ff 47.19N 3.11W
Belle Isle 42 Lf 51.55N 55.20W
Belle Isle, Strait of- 38 Nd 51.35N 56.30W
Bellencombre 12 De 49.42N 1.14E
Belleplaine 51q Ab 13.15N 59.34W
Belleville [Fr.] 11 Kh 46.06N 4.45E
Belleville [Il.-U.S.] 45 Lg 38.31N 90.00W
Belleville [Ks.-U.S.] 45 Hg 39.49N 97.38W
Belleville [Ont.-Can.] 42 Jh 44.10N 77.23W
Bellevue [Nb.-U.S.] 45 If 41.09N 95.54W
Bellevue [Wa.-U.S.] 46 Dc 47.37N 122.12W
Belley 11 Li 45.46N 5.41E
Bellheim 12 Ke 49.12N 8.17E
Bellin → Kangirsuk 39 Lc 60.00N 70.01W
Bellingham [Eng.-U.K.] 9 Kf 55.09N 2.16W
Bellingham [Wa.-U.S.] 39 Ge 48.46N 122.29W
Bellingsfors 8 Ef 58.59N 12.15E
Bellingshausen 66 Re 62.12S 58.56W
Bellingshausen Ice Shelf 66 Ce 71.00S 89.00W
Bellingshausen Sea (EN) 66 Pf 71.00S 85.00W
Bellinzona 14 Dd 46.11N 9.02E
Bello 54 Cb 6.19N 75.34W
Bellocq 55 Bl 35.55S 61.32W
Bellona, Récifs- 57 Gg 21.00S 159.00E
Bellona Island 60 Fj 11.17S 159.47E
Bellot Strait 42 Ib 72.00N 94.30W
Bellow Falls 44 Kd 43.08N 72.28W
Bell Peninsula 42 Jd 63.45N 81.30W
Bell River 42 Jg 49.49N 77.39W
Bell Rock → Inchcape 9 Ke 56.26N 2.24W
Bellsund 41 Nc 77.39N 14.15E
Belluno 14 Gd 46.09N 12.13E
Bell Ville 56 Hd 32.37S 62.42W
Bellville 37 Bf 33.53S 18.36E
Belmond 45 Je 42.51N 93.37W
Belmont 44 Hd 42.14N 78.02W
Belmonte [Braz.] 54 Kg 15.51S 38.54W
Belmonte [Port.] 13 Ed 40.21N 7.21W
Belmonte [Sp.] 13 Je 39.34N 2.42W
Belmopan 39 Kh 17.15N 88.46W
Beloeil 12 Fd 50.35N 3.43E
Belogorsk 22 Od 50.57N 128.25E
Belogorsk 16 Ig 45.01N 34.33E
Belogradčik 15 Ff 43.38N 22.41E
Belogradčiški 15 Ff 43.38N 22.28E
Belo Horizonte 53 Lg 19.55S 43.56W
Beloit [Ks.-U.S.] 45 Gg 39.28N 98.06W
Beloit [Wi.-U.S.] 43 Jc 42.31N 89.02W
Belojarovo 20 Hf 51.35N 128.55E
Belojarski 19 Gc 63.40N 66.45E
Beloje More=White Sea (EN) 5 Kb 66.00N 44.00E
Beloje Ozero=White Lake (EN) 5 Jc 60.11N 37.35E
Belokany 16 Oi 41.43N 46.28E
Belomorsk 6 Jc 64.29N 34.43E
Belomorsko-Baltijski Kanal=White Sea-Baltic Canal (EN) 5 Jc 63.30N 34.48E
Belomorsko-Kulojskoje Plato 7 Jd 65.20N 41.50E
Beloozersk 16 Dc 52.28N 25.13E
Belopolje 16 Id 51.09N 34.18E
Belorečensk 16 Kg 44.43N 39.52E
Beloreck 19 Fe 53.58N 58.24E
Belorusskaja Grjada 16 Ec 53.50N 27.00E
Belorusskaja Sovetskaja Socialističeskaja Respublika → Belarus 19 Ce 53.50N 28.00E
Belorusskaja SSR/Belaruskaja Sovetskaja Socialistyčnaja Respublika → Belarus 19 Ce 53.50N 28.00E
Belorusskaja SSR → Belarus 19 Ce 53.50N 28.00E
Belo-sur-Mer 37 Gd 20.44S 44.00E
Belo-sur-Tsiribihina 37 Gc 19.39S 44.32E
Belot, Lac- 42 Ec 66.50N 126.20W
Belovo 20 Df 54.25N 86.18E
Belovodsk 16 Ke 49.10N 39.33E
Belovodskoe 18 Jc 42.47N 74.13E
Belozersk 19 Dd 60.03N 37.48E
Belper 12 Aa 53.02N 1.28W
Belted Range 46 Gh 37.25N 116.10W
Belton [Mo.-U.S.] 45 Ig 38.49N 94.32W
Belton [Tx.-U.S.] 45 Hk 31.04N 97.28W
Belton Lake 45 Hk 31.08N 97.32W
Belturbet/Béal Tairbirt 9 Fg 54.06N 7.26W
Beluha 21 Ke 49.48N 86.35E
Belvedere Marittimo 14 Jk 39.37N 15.52E
Belvidere 45 Le 42.15N 88.50W
Bely 7 Hi 55.50N 32.58E
Bely, Ostrov-=Bely Island (EN) 21 Jb 73.10N 70.45E
Belyando River 59 Jd 21.38S 146.50E
Bely Čeremoš 15 Ia 48.06N 25.04E
Bely Island (EN)=Bely, Ostrov- 21 Jb 73.10N 70.45E
Bely Jar 20 De 58.26N 85.03E
Belyje Berega 16 Ic 53.12N 34.42E
Belz 16 Dd 50.23N 24.03E
Bełżec 10 Tf 50.24N 23.26E
Belzoni 45 Kj 33.11N 90.29W
Bełżyce 10 Se 51.11N 22.18E
Bemaraha, Plateau de- 30 Lj 19.00S 45.15E
Bembe 36 Bd 7.02S 14.18E
Bembéréké 34 Fc 10.13N 2.40E
Bembézar 13 Gg 37.45N 5.13W
Bembridge 12 Ad 50.41N 1.05W
Bemidji 43 Ib 47.29N 94.53W
Ben 24 Nf 32.32N 50.45E
Benāb 23 Gb 37.18N 46.05E
Benabarre/Benavarn 13 Mb 42.07N 0.29E
Bena Dibele 36 Dc 4.07S 22.50E
Benaize 11 Hh 46.34N 1.04E
Benalla 59 Jg 36.33S 145.59E
Benares → Vārānasi 22 Kg 25.20N 83.00E
Benasc/Benasque 13 Mb 42.36N 0.32E
Benasque/Benasc 13 Mb 42.36N 0.32E
Benavarn/Benabarre 13 Mb 42.07N 0.29E
Benavente 13 Gc 42.00N 5.41W
Benbecula 9 Fd 57.27N 7.20W
Bencheng → Luannan 28 Ee 39.30N 118.42E
Ben-Chicao, Col de- 13 Oh 36.12N 2.51E
Bend 43 Cc 44.03N 121.19W
Bendaja 34 Cd 7.10N 11.15W
Bendel 34 Gd 6.00N 5.50E
Bendela 36 Cc 3.18S 17.36E
Bender Bäyla 31 Mh 9.30N 50.30E
Bendersiyada 35 Hc 11.14N 48.57E
Bendery 19 Cf 46.48N 29.22E
Bendigo 58 Fh 36.45S 144.17E
Bendorf 12 Jd 50.26N 7.34E
Bēne/Bene 8 Jh 56.28N 23.01E
Bene/Bēne 8 Jh 56.28N 23.01E
Bénéna 34 Ec 13.06N 4.22W
Benepú, Rada- 65d Ac 27.10S 109.25W
Benešov 10 Kg 49.47N 14.40E
Benevento 14 Ii 41.08N 14.45E
Bengal 21 Kg 24.00N 90.00E
Bengal, Bay of- (EN) 21 Kh 15.00N 90.00E
Bengamisa 36 Eb 0.57N 25.10E
Bengbis 34 He 3.27N 12.27E
Bengbu 22 Nf 32.47N 117.23E
Benghazi (EN)=Banghāzī 31 Je 32.07N 20.04E
Benghazi (EN)=Banghāzī 33 Dd 27.00N 20.30E
Benghisa Point 14 Io 35.50N 14.35E
Bengkalis 26 Df 1.28N 102.08E
Bengkulu 26 Dg 3.48S 102.16E
Bengkulu 22 Mj 3.48S 102.16E
Bengo, Baía do- 30 Ii 8.43S 13.21E
Bengo He 28 Eg 35.04N 118.22E
Bengough 46 Mb 49.24N 105.08W
Bengtsfors 7 Cg 59.02N 12.13E
Benguela 31 Ij 12.35S 13.26E
Benguela 36 Be 12.00S 15.00E
Benguerir 32 Fc 32.14N 7.57W
Benguérua, Ilha- 37 Fd 21.53S 35.26E
Bengue Viejo 49 Ce 17.05N 89.08W
Bengut, Cap- 32 Hb 36.55N 3.54E
Beni 31 Jh 0.30N 29.28E
Beni 54 Ef 14.00S 65.30W
Beni, Rio- 52 Jg 10.23S 65.24W
Beni Abbes 32 Gc 30.08N 2.10W
Beni Baufrah 13 Hi 35.05N 4.18W
Benicarló 13 Md 40.25N 0.26E
Benicasim 13 Md 40.03N 0.04E
Beni Chougran, Monts des- 13 Mi 35.30N 0.15E
Benidorm 13 Lf 38.32N 0.08W
Beni Enzar 13 Ji 35.14N 2.57W
Beni Haoua 13 Nh 36.32N 1.34E
Beni Mellal 31 Ge 32.20N 6.21W
Beni Mellal 32 Fc 32.30N 6.30W
Benin 34 Gd 5.45N 5.04E
Bénin=Benin (EN) 31 Hh 9.30N 2.15E
Bénin (Dahomey) 31 Hh 9.30N 2.15E
Benin (EN)=Bénin 31 Hh 9.30N 2.15E
Benin, Bight of- 30 Hh 5.30N 4.00E
Benin City 31 Hh 6.20N 5.38E
Beni Ounif 32 Gc 32.03N 1.15W
Benisa 13 Mf 38.43N 0.03E
Beni Saf 13 Ki 35.19N 1.23W
Benisheikh 34 Hc 11.48N 12.29E
Benito Juárez 48 Mi 17.50N 92.32W
Benito Juárez, Presa- 48 Li 16.27N 95.30W
Benjamen Island 37b Bb 5.27S 53.21E
Benjamin 45 Gj 33.35N 99.48W
Benjamin Aceval 55 Dg 24.58S 57.34W
Benjamin Constant 53 If 4.22S 70.02W
Benjamin Hill 48 Db 30.10N 111.10W
Benkei-Misaki 29a Bb 42.50N 140.11E
Benkelman 45 Ff 40.03N 101.32W
Benkovac 14 Jf 44.02N 15.37E
Ben Mehidi 14 Bn 36.46N 7.54E
Bennett, Lake- 59 Gd 23.50S 131.00E
Bennett, Ostrov- 20 Ja 76.45N 149.00E
Benneydale 62 Fc 38.31S 175.21E
Bennichab 32 Df 19.26N 15.21W
Bennington 44 Kd 42.53N 73.12W
Benom 26 Df 3.50N 102.06E
Benoni 31 Jk 26.19S 28.27E
Bénoué=Benue (EN) 30 Hh 7.48N 6.46E
Benoy 35 Bd 8.59N 16.19E
Benrath 12 Ic 51.10N 6.52E
Bensekrane 13 Ki 35.04N 1.13W
Bensheim 12 Ke 49.41N 8.37E
Ben Slimane 32 Fc 33.37N 7.07W
Benson [Az.-U.S.] 46 Jk 31.58N 110.18W
Benson [Mn.-U.S.] 45 Id 45.19N 95.36W
Benson Point 64g Ab 1.56N 157.30W
Bent 23 Id 26.17N 59.31E
Benteng [Indon.] 26 Hg 0.24S 121.59E
Benteng [Indon.] 26 Hh 6.08N 120.27E
Bentheim 10 Dd 52.19N 7.10E
Bentiaba 36 Be 14.29S 12.50E
Bentinck 25 Jf 11.45N 98.03E
Bentinck Island 59 Hc 17.05S 139.30E
Bentiu 35 Dd 9.14N 29.50E
Bento Gonçalves 56 Jc 29.10S 51.31W
Bento Gomes, Rio- 55 Dc 16.40S 57.12W
Benton [Ar.-U.S.] 45 Ji 34.34N 92.35W
Benton [Il.-U.S.] 45 Lg 38.01N 88.55W
Bentong 26 Df 3.32N 101.55E
Benton Harbor 44 Dd 42.07N 86.27W
Bentonville 45 Ih 36.22N 94.13W
Benua, Pulau- 26 Ef 0.56N 107.27E
Benue 34 Gd 7.15N 8.20E
Benue 30 Hh 7.48N 6.46E
Benue (EN)=Bénoué 30 Hh 7.48N 6.46E
Benwee Head/An Bhinn Bhui 9 Dg 54.21N 9.48W
Benxi 22 Oe 41.16N 123.48E
Beo 26 If 4.15N 126.48E
Beograd = Belgrade (EN) 6 Ig 44.50N 20.30E
Beograd-Krnjača 15 De 44.52N 20.28E
Beograd-Zemun 15 De 44.53N 20.25E
Béoumi 34 Dd 7.40N 5.34W

Index Symbols

1 Independent Nation
2 State, Region
3 District, County
4 Municipality
5 Colony, Dependency
Continent
Physical Region
Historical or Cultural Region
Mount, Mountain
Volcano
Hill
Mountains, Mountain Range
Hills, Escarpment
Plateau, Upland
Pass, Gap
Plain, Lowland
Delta
Salt Flat
Valley, Canyon
Crater, Cave
Karst Features
Depression
Polder
Desert, Dunes
Forest, Woods
Heath, Steppe
Oasis
Cape, Point
Coast, Beach
Cliff
Peninsula
Isthmus
Sandbank
Island
Atoll
Rock, Reef
Islands, Archipelago
Rocks, Reefs
Coral Reef
Well, Spring
Geyser
River, Stream
Waterfall Rapids
River Mouth, Estuary
Lake
Salt Lake
Intermittent Lake
Reservoir
Swamp, Pond
Canal
Glacier
Ice Shelf, Pack Ice
Ocean
Sea
Gulf, Bay
Strait, Fjord
Lagoon
Bank
Seamount
Tablemount
Ridge
Shelf
Basin
Escarpment, Sea Scarp
Fracture
Trench, Abyss
National Park, Reserve
Point of Interest
Recreation Site
Cave, Cavern
Historic Site
Ruins
Wall, Walls
Church, Abbey
Temple
Scientific Station
Airport
Port
Lighthouse
Mine
Tunnel
Dam, Bridge

Beppu 27 Ne 33.17N 131.30 E
Beppu-Wan 29 Be 33.20N 131.35 E
Bequia Head 51n Ba 13.03N 61.12W
Bequia Island 50 Ff 13.01N 61.13W
Beraketa 37 Hd 24.11S 45.42 E
Berati 15 Ci 40.42N 19.57 E
Beratus, Gunung- 26 Gg 1.02S 116.20 E
Berau, Teluk- = McCluer Gulf (EN) 26 Jg 2.30S 132.30 E
Berberá 31 Lg 10.25N 45.02 E
Berbérati 31 Ih 4.16N 15.47 E
Berberia, Cabo- 13 Nf 38.38N 1.23 E
Berbice River 54 Gb 6.17N 57.32W
Berca 15 Jd 45.17N 26.41 E
Berchères-sur-Vesgre 12 Df 48.51N 1.33 E
Berchtesgaden 10 Ii 47.38N 13.00 E
Berck [Fr.] 12 Dd 50.24N 1.36 E
Berck [Fr.] 11 Hd 50.24N 1.34 E
Berck- Berck Plage 12 Dd 50.24N 1.34 E
Berck-Plage, Berck- 12 Dd 50.24N 1.34 E
Berda 16 Jf 46.47N 36.52 E
Berdāle 35 Hd 7.04N 47.51 E
Berdičev 19 Cf 49.53N 28.36 E
Berdigestjah 20 Hd 62.03N 126.50 E
Berdjansk 19 Df 46.43N 36.48 E
Berdsk 20 Df 54.47N 83.05 E
Beregomet 15 Ia 48.10N 25.24 E
Beregovo 19 Cf 48.13N 22.41 E
Bereku 36 Gc 4.27S 35.44 E
Berekua 50 Fe 15.14N 61.19W
Berekum 34 Ed 7.27N 2.35W
Berens 42 Hf 52.21N 97.01W
Berens River 42 Hf 52.22N 97.02W
Beresford 45 He 43.05N 96.47W
Berestečko 10 Vf 50.16N 25.14 E
Bereşti 15 Kc 46.06N 27.53 E
Berettyó 15 Ec 46.59N 21.07 E
Berettyóújfalu 10 Ri 47.13N 21.33 E
Bereza 19 Ce 52.33N 24.58 E
Berezan 16 Gd 50.19N 31.31 E
Berežany 16 De 49.29N 25.00 E
Berezina 16 Dc 53.48N 25.59 E
Berezina 5 Je 52.33N 30.14 E
Berezino 16 Fc 53.51N 29.00 E
Berezino 8 Mj 54.55N 28.16 E
Berezino 15 Mc 46.16N 29.11 E
Bereznegovatoje 16 Hf 47.20N 32.49 E
Bereznik 19 Ec 62.53N 42.42 E
Berezniki 6 Ld 59.24N 56.46 E
Berezno 16 Ed 51.01N 26.45 E
Berezovka 10 Vc 53.40N 25.37 E
Berezovka 17 Hd 64.59N 56.29 E
Berezovka 19 Df 47.12N 30.56 E
Berezovka Višerka 17 Hf 60.55N 56.50 E
Berezovo 19 Gc 63.58N 65.00 E
Berezovski 17 Jh 56.55N 60.50 E
Berezovski 20 De 55.39N 86.16 E
Berezovy 20 If 51.41N 135.52 E
Berga [Sp.] 13 Nb 42.06N 1.51 E
Berga [Swe.] 8 Gg 57.13N 16.02 E
Bergama 23 Cb 39.07N 27.10 E
Bergamo 14 De 45.41N 9.43 E
Bergantiños 13 Da 43.20N 8.45W
Bergby 7 Df 60.56N 17.02 E
Bergen [Ger.] 10 Jb 54.25N 13.26 E
Bergen [Neth.] 12 Gb 52.40N 4.42 E
Bergen [Nor.] 6 Gc 60.23N 5.20 E
Bergen/Mons 11 Jd 50.27N 3.56 E
Bergen aan Zee, Bergen- 12 Gb 52.40N 4.38 E
Bergen-Bergen aan Zee 12 Gb 52.40N 4.38 E
Bergen op Zoom 11 Kc 51.30N 4.17 E
Bergerac 11 Gj 44.51N 0.29 E
Bergeyk 12 Hc 51.19N 5.22 E
Bergh 12 Ic 51.53N 6.16 E
Bergheim 10 Cf 50.58N 6.39 E
Bergh-s'Heerenberg 12 Ic 51.53N 6.16 E
Bergisches Land 10 De 51.07N 7.10 E
Bergisch Gladbach 10 Df 50.59N 7.08 E
Bergkvara 8 Gh 56.23N 16.05 E
Bergneustadt 12 Jc 51.02N 7.39 E
Bergö 8 Ib 62.55N 21.10 E
Bergsjö 7 Df 61.59N 17.04 E
Bergslagen 8 Fd 60.05N 14.30 E
Bergstraße 12 Ke 49.40N 8.40 E
Bergues 12 Ed 50.58N 2.26 E
Bergum, Tietjerksteradeel- 12 Ha 53.12N 6.00 E
Bergviken 8 Gc 61.10N 16.45 E
Bergville 37 De 28.52S 29.18 E
Berh 27 Jb 47.45N 111.07 E
Berhala, Selat- 26 Dg 0.48S 104.25 E
Berici, Monti- 14 Fe 45.26N 11.31 E
Berīkān 24 Nh 28.17N 51.14 E
Berikulski 20 De 55.32N 88.08 E
Beringa, Ostrov- = Bering Island (EN) 20 Lf 55.00N 166.10 E
Beringen 12 Hc 51.03N 5.13 E
Bering Glacier 40 Kd 60.15N 143.30W
Bering Island (EN) = Beringa, Ostrov- 20 Lf 55.00N 166.10 E
Beringovo More = Bering Sea (EN) 38 Bd 60.00N 175.00W
Beringovski 22 Tc 63.07N 179.19 E
Bering Proliv = Bering Strait (EN) 38 Cc 65.30N 169.00W
Bering Sea 38 Bd 60.00N 175.00W
Bering Sea (EN) = Beringovo More 38 Bd 60.00N 175.00W
Bering Strait 38 Cc 65.30N 169.00W
Bering Strait (EN) = Bering Proliv 38 Cc 65.30N 169.00W
Berislav 16 Hf 46.51N 33.29 E
Berisso 55 Dl 34.52S 57.53W
Berit Dağı 24 Gc 38.01N 36.52 E
Berīzak 24 Qi 26.06N 57.15 E
Berja 13 Jh 36.51N 2.57W
Berkåk 7 Be 62.50N 10.00 E
Berkane 32 Gc 34.56N 2.20W
Berkel 10 Cd 52.09N 6.12 E
Berkeley 43 Cd 37.57N 122.18W
Berkhamsted 12 Bc 51.45N 0.33W
Berkner Island 66 Rf 79.30S 49.30W
Berkovica 15 Gf 43.14N 23.07 E
Berks 9 Lj 51.15N 1.20W
Berkshire [3] 9 Lj 51.30N 1.10W
Berkshire Downs 9 Lj 51.35N 1.25W
Berkshire Hills 44 Kd 42.20N 73.10W
Berlaimont 12 Fd 50.12N 3.49 E
Berlanga de Duero 13 Jc 41.28N 2.51W
Berlengas, Ilhas- 13 Ce 39.25N 9.30W
Berlevåg 7 Ga 70.51N 29.06 E
Berlin [N.H.-U.S.] 43 Mc 44.29N 71.10W
Berlin [Ger.] 6 He 52.31N 13.24 E
Berlin (Ost) = Berlin 6 He 52.31N 13.24 E
Berlin (West) = Berlin 6 He 52.31N 12.24 E
Berlin-Pankow 10 Jd 52.34N 13.24 E
Bermeja, Sierra- 13 Gh 36.30N 5.15W
Bermejillo 47 Dc 25.53N 103.37W
Bermejito, Rio- 55 Bg 25.39S 60.11W
Bermejo, Isla- 55 An 39.01S 62.01W
Bermejo, Paso-/Cumbre, Paso de la- 52 Ii 32.50S 70.05W
Bermejo, Rio- [Arg.] 52 Ji 31.52S 67.22W
Bermejo, Rio- [S.Amer.] 52 Kh 26.52S 58.23W
Bermen, lac- 42 Kf 53.35N 68.55W
Bermeo 13 Ja 43.26N 2.43W
Bermillo de Sayago 13 Fc 41.22N 6.06W
Bermuda [5] 39 Mf 32.20N 64.45W
Bermuda Islands 39 Mf 32.20N 64.45W
Bermuda Rise (EN) 38 Mf 32.30N 65.00W
Bern [2] 14 Bd 46.55N 7.40 E
Bern/Berne 6 Gf 46.55N 7.30 E
Bernalda 14 Kj 40.24N 16.41 E
Bernalillo 45 Ci 35.18N 106.33W
Bernard Islands 64d Bb 7.18N 151.32 E
Bernardo de Irigoyen 55 Bk 32.10S 61.09W
Bernardo do Irigoyen 56 Jc 26.15S 53.39W
Bernasconi 56 He 37.54S 63.43W
Bernau bei Berlin 10 Jd 52.40N 13.35 E
Bernaville 12 Ed 50.08N 2.10 E
Bernay 11 Ge 49.06N 0.36 E
Bernburg 10 He 51.48N 11.44 E
Berndorf 14 Kc 47.57N 16.06 E
Berne [Ger.] 12 Ka 53.11N 8.29 E
Berne [In.-U.S.] 44 Ee 40.39N 84.57W
Berne/Bern 6 Gf 46.55N 7.30 E
Berner Alpen/Alpes Bernoises = Bernese Alps (EN) 14 Bd 46.25N 7.30 E
Berneray 9 Fd 57.43N 7.15W
Bernese Alps (EN) = Alpes Bernoises/Berner Alpen 14 Bd 46.25N 7.30 E
Bernese Alps (EN) = Berner Alpen/Alpes Bernoises 14 Bd 46.25N 7.30 E
Bernesga 13 Gb 42.28N 5.31W
Bernesq 12 Be 49.16N 0.56W
Bernier Bay 42 Ib 71.08N 88.00W
Bernier Island 59 Cd 24.50S 113.10 E
Bernina 14 Ed 46.25N 10.01 E
Bernina 5 Gf 46.22N 9.50 E
Berninapaß 14 Ed 46.25N 10.01 E
Bernissart 12 Fd 50.28N 3.38 E
Bernkastel-Kues 10 Dg 49.55N 7.04 E
Bernstorffs Isfjord 41 Hf 63.10N 40.45W
Berón de Astrada 55 Dh 27.33S 57.32W
Beroroha 37 Hd 21.39S 45.10 E
Béroubouay 34 Fc 10.32N 2.44 E
Beroun 10 Kg 49.58N 14.04 E
Berounka 10 Kg 50.00N 14.24 E
Berovo 15 Fh 41.43N 22.51 E
Berre, Étang de- 11 Lk 43.27N 5.08 E
Berriane 32 Hc 32.50N 3.46 E
Berrouaghia 13 Oh 36.08N 2.55 E
Berry 11 Hh 47.00N 2.00 E
Berry-au-Bac 12 Fe 49.24N 3.54 E
Berryessa, Lake- 46 Dg 38.37N 122.16W
Berry Head 9 Jk 50.24N 3.29W
Berry Islands 47 Ic 25.34N 77.45W
Berry River 46 Ja 50.50N 111.36W
Beršad 19 Cf 48.23N 29.33 E
Berseba 37 Be 26.01S 17.41 E
Bersenbrück 12 Jb 52.33N 7.56 E
Berthierville 44 Kb 46.05N 73.11W
Bertincourt 12 Ed 50.05N 2.59 E
Bertogne 12 Hd 50.05N 5.40 E
Bertolinia 54 Je 7.38S 43.57W
Bertoua 31 Ih 4.35N 13.41 E
Bertraghboy Bay 9 Dh 53.23N 9.50W
Bertrix 12 He 49.51N 5.15 E
Beru Island 57 Ie 1.20S 176.00 E
Berwick-upon-Tweed 9 Lf 55.46N 2.00W
Berwyn 9 Ji 52.53N 3.24W
Besalampy 37 Gc 16.44S 44.24 E
Besançon 6 Gf 47.15N 6.02 E
Besar, Gunung- 26 Gg 1.25S 115.39 E
Besbre 11 Jh 46.33N 3.44 E
Besed 16 Gc 52.38N 31.11 E
Besikama 26 Hh 9.36S 124.57 E
Beskid Mountains (EN) 5 Hf 49.40N 20.00 E
Beskid Niski 10 Rg 49.20N 21.30 E
Beskid Średni 10 Pg 49.45N 19.20 E
Beskid Wysoki 10 Pg 49.32N 20.00 E
Beskidy Wschodnie 10 Sg 49.20N 22.30 E
Beskidy Zachodnie 10 Pg 49.30N 19.30 E
Beskol 18 Ma 46.06N 81.01 E
Beslan 19 Eg 43.10N 44.35 E
Besna Kobila 15 Fg 42.32N 22.14 E
Besni 24 Gd 37.41N 37.52 E
Besparmak Dağ 15 Kl 37.30N 27.35 E
Bessao 35 Bd 7.53N 15.59 E
Bessarabia (EN) = Bessarabija 15 Lb 47.00N 28.30 E
Bessarabija = Bessarabia (EN) 15 Lb 47.00N 28.30 E
Bessarabka 16 Ff 46.20N 28.59 E
Bességes 11 Kj 44.17N 4.06 E
Bessemer 43 Je 33.25N 86.57W
Bessin 11 Fe 49.10N 1.00W
Bessines-sur-Gartempe 11 Hh 46.06N 1.22 E
Besšoki, Gora- 16 Rh 43.57N 52.30 E
Best 12 Hc 51.30N 5.24 E
Bestjah 20 Hc 66.00N 123.35 E
Bestjah 20 Hd 61.17N 128.50 E
Bestobe 19 He 52.30N 73.05 E
Bestwig 12 Kc 51.22N 8.24 E
Betafo 37 Hc 19.49S 46.50 E
Betanzos [Bol.] 54 Eg 19.34S 65.27W
Betanzos [Sp.] 13 Da 43.17N 8.12W
Betanzos, Ria de- 13 Da 43.23N 8.15W
Bétaré Oya 34 Hd 5.36N 14.05 E
Bétérou 34 Fd 9.12N 2.16 E
Beteta 13 Jd 40.34N 2.04W
Bethal 37 De 26.27S 29.28 E
Bethanien [3] 37 Be 26.30S 17.00 E
Bethanien 31 Ik 26.32S 17.11 E
Bethany [Mo.-U.S.] 45 If 40.16N 94.02W
Bethany [Ok.-U.S.] 45 Hi 35.31N 97.38W
Bethel 39 Cc 60.48N 161.46W
Béthenville 12 Ge 49.18N 4.22 E
Bethlehem [Pa.-U.S.] 44 Je 40.36N 75.22W
Bethlehem [S.Afr.] 31 Jk 28.15S 28.15 E
Bethlehem (EN) = Bayt Laḥm 24 Fg 31.43N 35.12 E
Bethulie 37 Df 30.32S 25.59 E
Béthune 11 Id 50.32N 2.38 E
Béthune 11 He 49.53N 1.09 E
Betioky 37 Gd 23.42S 44.22 E
Betong 25 Kg 5.45N 101.05 E
Betor 35 Fc 11.37N 39.00 E
Bétou 36 Cb 3.03N 18.31 E
Betpak-Dala 21 Ie 46.00N 70.00 E
Betroka 37 Hd 23.15S 46.05 E
Bet She'an 24 Ff 32.30N 35.30 E
Betsiamites, Rivière- 42 Kg 48.56N 68.38W
Betsiboka 30 Lj 16.03S 46.36 E
Bette 30 If 22.00N 19.12 E
Bettembourg/Bettemburg 12 Ie 49.31N 6.06 E
Bettemburg/Bettembourg 12 Ie 49.31N 6.06 E
Bettendorf 45 Kf 41.32N 90.30W
Bettles Field 40 Ic 66.53N 151.51W
Bettna 8 Gf 58.55N 16.38 E
Bettola 14 Df 44.47N 9.36 E
Betūl 25 Fd 21.55N 77.54 E
Betuwe 11 Lc 51.55N 5.30 E
Betwa 25 Hc 25.55N 80.12 E
Betz 12 Ee 49.09N 2.57 E
Betzdorf 10 Df 50.47N 7.53 E
Beulah 44 Dc 44.38N 86.06W
Beult 12 Cc 51.13N 0.26 E
Beuvron 11 Hg 47.29N 1.15 E
Beuzeville 12 Ce 49.20N 0.21 E
Beveland 11 Jc 51.30N 3.40 E
Beveren 12 Gc 51.13N 4.15 E
Beveridge Reef 57 Kg 20.00S 168.00W
Beverley [Austl.] 59 Df 32.06S 116.56 E
Beverley [Eng.-U.K.] 9 Mh 53.51N 0.26W
Beverwijk 11 Kb 52.28N 4.40 E
Bewsher, Mount- 66 Ff 70.54S 65.28 E
Bexhill 9 Nk 50.50N 0.29 E
Bexley, London- 12 Cc 51.26N 0.09 E
Beyağaç 15 Ll 37.13N 28.57 E
Beyānlū 24 Ld 36.02N 47.53 E
Bey Dağı 24 Hc 38.15N 38.22 E
Bey Dağları 23 Db 36.40N 30.15 E
Beykoz 24 Cb 41.08N 29.05 E
Beyla 34 Dd 8.41N 8.38W
Beyoğlu, İstanbul 15 Lh 41.02N 28.59 E
Beyoneisu-Retsugan 27 Oe 31.55N 139.55 E
Beypazari 24 Db 40.10N 31.55 E
Beyra 35 Hd 6.57N 47.19 E
Beyram 24 Oi 27.26N 53.31 E
Beyşehir 24 Dd 37.41N 31.43 E
Beyşehir Gölü 23 Db 37.40N 31.30 E
Bezaha 37 Gd 23.29S 44.30 E
Bežanickaja Vozvyšennost 7 Gh 56.45N 29.30 E
Bežanicy 7 Gh 56.58N 29.57 E
Bezdan 15 Bd 45.51N 18.56 E
Bezděz 10 Kf 50.32N 14.43 E
Bezdež 10 Vd 52.18N 25.20 E
Bežeck 19 Dd 57.50N 36.41 E
Bezenčuk 7 Lj 53.01N 49.24 E
Bezerra, Rio- 55 Ia 13.16S 47.31W
Bezerros 54 Ke 8.14S 35.45W
Beziers 11 Jk 43.21N 3.15 E
Bezmein 19 Fh 38.05N 58.12 E
Bežta 19 Eg 42.08N 46.08 E
Bhadrak 25 Hd 21.04N 86.30 E
Bhadrāvati 25 Ff 13.52N 75.43 E
Bhāgalpur 22 Kg 25.15N 87.00 E
Bhairawa 25 Gc 27.31N 83.24 E
Bhaironghati 25 Fb 31.01N 78.53 E
Bhakkar 25 Eb 31.38N 71.04 E
Bhamo 25 Jd 24.16N 97.14 E
Bhandāra 25 Fd 21.10N 79.39 E
Bhanjan 25 Gc 25.47N 83.36 E
Bhārat Juktarashtra = India (EN) [1] 22 Jh 20.00N 77.00 E
Bharatpur 25 Fc 27.13N 77.29 E
Bharūch 25 Ed 21.46N 72.54 E
Bhatinda → Bathinda 25 Eb 30.12N 74.57 E
Bhātpāra 25 Hd 22.52N 88.24 E
Bhavnagar 22 Jg 21.46N 72.09 E
Bhera 25 Eb 32.29N 72.55 E
Bheri 25 Gc 28.44N 81.16 E
Bhīlwāra 25 Ec 25.21N 74.38 E
Bhīma 21 Jh 16.25N 77.17 E
Bhind 25 Fc 26.34N 78.48 E
Bhiwāni 25 Fc 28.47N 76.08 E
Bhopāl 22 Jg 23.16N 77.24 E
Bhubaneshwar 22 Kg 20.14N 85.50 E
Bhuj 25 Dd 23.16N 69.40 E
Bhusāwal 25 Fd 21.03N 75.46 E
Bhutan (Druk-Yul) [1] 22 Lg 27.30N 90.30 E
Bia 34 Ed 5.21N 3.11W
Bia, Phou- 21 Mh 18.36N 103.01 E
Biá, Rio- 54 Ed 3.28S 67.23W
Bīābān, Kūh-e- 24 Qi 26.30N 57.25 E
Biabou 51n Ba 13.12N 61.09W
Biafra 30 Hh 5.00N 7.30 E
Biafra, Bight of- 30 Hh 3.20N 9.20 E
Biak 26 Kg 1.10S 136.06 E
Biak, Pulau- 57 Ee 1.00S 136.00 E
Biała Piska 10 Sc 53.37N 22.04 E
Biała Podlaska [2] 10 Td 52.00N 23.05 E
Biała Podlaska 10 Td 52.02N 23.06 E
Białobrzegi 10 Qe 51.40N 20.57 E
Białogard 10 Lb 54.01N 16.00 E
Białostocka, Wysoczyzna- 10 Tc 53.23N 23.10 E
Białowieża 10 Td 52.41N 23.50 E
Białystok 6 Ie 53.09N 23.09 E
Białystok [2] 10 Tc 53.10N 23.10 E
Biancavilla 14 Im 37.38N 14.52 E
Bianco 14 Kl 38.05N 16.09 E
Bianco, Monte- 5 Gf 45.50N 6.52 E
Biankouma 34 Dd 7.44N 7.37W
Biankouma [3] 34 Dd 7.43N 7.40W
Bianzhuang → Cangshan 28 Eg 34.51N 118.03 E
Biaro, Pulau- 26 If 2.05N 125.20 E
Biarritz 11 Ek 43.29N 1.34W
Biasca 14 Cd 46.22N 8.57 E
Bibā 33 Fd 28.55N 30.59 E
Bibai 27 Pc 43.19N 141.52 E
Bibala 36 Be 14.50S 13.30 E
Biban, Chaine des- 13 Qh 36.12N 4.25 E
Bibbiena 14 Fg 43.42N 11.49 E
Biberach an der Riß 10 Fh 48.06N 9.48 E
Bibiani 34 Ed 6.28N 2.20W
Bic 44 Ma 48.22N 68.42W
Bicaj 15 Dh 41.59N 20.25 E
Bicas 55 Ke 21.43S 43.04W
Bicaz 15 Jc 46.55N 26.04 E
Bicaz, Pasul- 15 Ic 46.49N 25.52 E
Bičenekski, Pereval- 16 Nj 39.33N 45.48 E
Bicester 9 Lj 51.54N 1.09W
Bichena 35 Fc 10.21N 38.14 E
Bickerton Island 59 Hb 13.45S 136.10 E
Bicske 10 Oi 47.29N 18.38 E
Bičura 20 Ff 50.36N 107.35 E
Bīd 24 Qd 36.33N 57.35 E
Bida 31 Hh 9.05N 6.01 E
Bidar 25 Fe 17.54N 77.33 E
Bidasoa 13 Ka 43.22N 1.47W
Biddeford 43 Mc 43.30N 70.26W
Bideford 9 Ij 51.01N 4.13W
Bideford Bay → Barnstaple Bay 9 Ij 51.05N 4.20W
Bidon V/Poste Maurice Cortier 32 He 22.18N 1.05 E
Bié [3] 36 Ce 13.00S 17.30 E
Bié, Planalto do- 30 Ij 13.00S 17.02 E
Biebrza 10 Sc 53.13N 22.28 E
Biecz 10 Rg 49.44N 21.14 E
Biedenkopf 10 Ef 50.55N 8.32 E
Biei 29a Cb 43.35N 142.28 E
Biel/Bienne 14 Bc 47.10N 7.15 E
Bielefeld 10 Ed 52.02N 8.32 E
Bielefeld-Brackwede 12 Kc 51.59N 8.31 E
Bielefeld-Sennestadt 12 Kc 51.57N 8.35 E
Biella 14 Ce 45.34N 8.03 E
Bielsk 10 Pd 52.40N 19.49 E
Bielska, Wysoczyzna- 10 Sd 52.35N 23.00 E
Bielsko [2] 10 Og 49.50N 19.00 E
Bielsko-Biała 10 Pg 49.49N 19.02 E
Bielsk Podlaski 10 Td 52.47N 23.12 E
Bien Dong = South China Sea (EN) 21 Ni 10.00N 113.00 E
Bien Hoa 25 Lf 10.57N 106.49 E
Bienne 11 Lh 46.20N 5.38 E
Bienne/Biel 14 Bc 47.10N 7.15 E
Bienvenida 13 Jd 40.30N 2.30W
Bienville, Lac- 42 Ke 55.20N 72.40W
Bierbeek 12 Gd 50.50N 4.46 E
Bieszczady 10 Sg 49.10N 22.35 E
Bièvre 12 He 49.56N 5.01 E
Biferno 14 Ji 41.59N 15.02 E
Bifoum 36 Bc 0.20S 10.23 E
Bifuka 28 Qb 44.29N 142.21 E
Biga 24 Bb 40.13N 27.14 E
Bigadiç 24 Cc 39.23N 28.08 E
Big Bald Mountain 44 Nb 47.37N 66.38W
Big Baldy Mountain 46 Jc 46.58N 110.37W
Big Bay [Mi.-U.S.] 44 Db 46.49N 87.44W
Big Bay [Van.] 63b Cb 15.05S 166.54 E
Big Beaver House 42 If 52.58N 89.57W
Big Belt Mountains 46 Jc 46.40N 111.25W
Big Black River 45 Kj 32.00N 91.05W
Big Blue River 43 Hd 39.11N 96.32W
Big Creek Peak 46 Id 44.28N 113.32W
Big Dry Creek 46 Lc 47.30N 106.19W
Big Falls 45 Jb 48.11N 93.46W
Biggar 42 Gf 52.04N 108.00W
Biggenden 59 Ke 25.30S 152.00 E
Biggleswade 9 Mi 52.05N 0.17W
Big Hatchet Peak 45 Bk 31.37N 108.20W
Big Hole River 46 Id 45.34N 112.20W
Bighorn Basin 43 Fc 44.15N 108.10W
Bighorn Lake 46 Kd 45.08N 108.10W
Bighorn Mountains 38 Ie 44.00N 107.30W
Bighorn River 43 Fb 46.09N 107.28W
Bight, Head of- 59 Gf 31.30S 131.10 E
Big Island 42 Kd 62.43N 70.40W
Big Lake 44 Nc 45.10N 67.40W
Big Lake 45 Fk 31.12N 101.28W
Big Lost River 46 Ie 43.50N 112.44W
Big Muddy Creek 46 Mb 48.08N 104.36W
Big Muddy Lake 46 Mb 49.08N 104.54W
Bignona 34 Bc 12.49N 16.14W
Bigorre 11 Gk 43.06N 0.05 E
Big Porcupine Creek 46 Lc 46.17N 106.47W
Big Quill Lake 42 Hf 51.51N 104.18W
Big Rapids 44 Ed 43.42N 85.29W
Big River 42 Gf 53.50N 107.01W
Big River 42 Fb 72.50N 125.00W
Big Sand Lake 42 He 57.45N 99.45W
Big Sandy 46 Jb 48.11N 110.07W
Big Sandy Creek 45 Eg 38.06N 102.29W
Big Sandy River [Az.-U.S.] 46 Ii 34.19N 113.31W
Big Sandy River [Wy.-U.S.] 46 Kf 41.50N 109.48W
Big Sheep Mountains 46 Mc 47.03N 105.43W
Big Sioux River 43 Hc 42.30N 96.25W
Big Smoky Valley 43 Dd 38.30N 117.15W
Big Snowy Mountains 46 Kc 46.50N 109.30W
Big Spring 39 If 32.15N 101.28W
Big Spruce Knob 44 Gf 38.16N 80.12W
Big Stone Lake 45 Hd 45.25N 96.40W
Big Timber 46 Kd 45.50N 109.57W
Big Trout Lake 42 If 53.45N 90.00W
Biguglia, Étang de- 11a Ba 42.36N 9.29 E
Big Wood Cay 49 Ia 24.21N 77.44W
Big Wood River 46 He 42.52N 114.55W
Bihać 14 Jf 44.49N 15.52 E
Bihār [3] 25 Hd 25.00N 86.00 E
Bihār 25 Hc 25.11N 85.31 E
Biharamulo 36 Fc 2.38S 31.20 E
Bihor [2] 15 Ec 47.00N 22.00 E
Bihoro 27 Pc 43.49N 144.07 E
Bihorului, Munţii- 15 Fc 46.40N 22.45 E
Bija 21 Kd 52.25N 85.05 E
Bijagós, Arquipélago dos- = Bijagos Islands (EN) 30 Fg 11.15N 16.05W
Bijagós Islands (EN) = Bijagós, Arquipélago dos- 30 Fg 11.15N 16.05W
Bijapur 25 Fe 16.50N 75.42 E
Bijār 23 Gb 35.52N 47.36 E
Bijeljina 14 Nf 44.45N 19.13 E
Bijelo Polje 15 Cf 43.02N 19.45 E
Bijiang (Zhiziluo) 27 Gf 26.39N 99.00 E
Bijie 27 If 27.15N 105.16 E
Bijlikol, Ozero- 18 Hc 43.05N 70.40 E
Bijou Creek 45 Ef 40.17N 103.52W
Bijoutier Island 37b Bb 7.04S 52.45 E
Bijsk 22 Kd 52.34N 85.15 E
Bikāner 22 Jg 28.01N 73.18 E
Bikar Atoll 57 Ic 12.15N 170.06 E
Bikeqi 28 Ad 40.45N 111.17 E
Bikin 20 Ig 46.43N 134.02 E
Bikin 20 Ig 46.51N 134.02 E
Bikini Atoll 57 Hc 11.35N 165.23 E
Bikoro 31 Ii 0.45S 18.07 E
Bilād Ghāmid 33 Hf 19.58N 41.38 E
Bilād Zahrān 33 He 20.15N 41.15 E
Bilāspur 22 Kg 22.03N 82.10 E
Bilate 35 Fd 6.34N 38.04 E
Bilauktaung Range 21 Lh 13.00N 99.00 E
Bilbao 6 Fg 43.15N 2.58W
Bilbays 33 Fc 30.25N 31.34 E
Bileća 14 Mh 42.53N 18.26 E
Bilecik 23 Ca 40.09N 29.59 E
Bilehsavār 24 Mc 39.28N 48.20 E
Bílé Karpaty = White Carpathians (EN) 10 Nh 48.55N 17.50 E
Bilesha Plain 36 Hb 0.35N 40.45 E
Biłgoraj 10 Sf 50.34N 22.43 E
Bili 36 Db 4.50N 22.29 E
Bili 36 Eb 4.09N 25.10 E
Bilibino 22 Sc 68.03N 166.20 E
Biliran 26 Hd 11.35N 124.28 E
Bilishti 15 Di 40.37N 20.59 E
Biliu He 28 Ge 39.30N 122.36 E
Bill Baileys Bank (EN) 9 Ca 60.40N 10.20W
Billerbeck 12 Jc 51.58N 7.18 E
Billericay 12 Cc 51.37N 0.35 E
Billingen 8 Ef 58.24N 13.45 E
Billings 39 Jf 37.04N 93.33W
Billings, Represa- 55 If 23.45S 46.40W
Billingshurst 12 Bc 51.01N 0.27W
Bill Williams River 46 Hi 34.17N 114.03W
Billy Chinook, Lake- 46 Ed 44.33N 121.20W
Bilma 31 Ig 18.41N 12.56 E
Biloela 59 Kd 24.24S 150.30 E
Bilo Gora 14 Le 45.50N 17.10 E
Biloku 54 Gc 1.46N 58.33W
Biloxi 43 Je 30.24N 88.53W
Bilqās Qism Awwal 24 Dg 31.13N 31.21 E
Bilteni 15 Ge 44.52N 23.17 E
Biltine 35 Cc 14.32N 20.55 E
Biltine [3] 35 Cc 15.00N 21.00 E
Bilzen 12 Hd 50.51N 5.31 E
Bima 36 Eb 3.23N 25.09 E
Bimbān 24 Ej 24.26N 32.53 E
Bimberi Peak 59 Jg 35.40S 148.47 E
Bimbila 34 Fd 8.51N 0.04 E
Bimbo 35 Be 4.18N 18.33 E
Bimini Islands 47 Ic 25.44N 79.15W
Bināb 24 Md 36.35N 48.41 E
Binačka Morava 15 Eg 42.27N 21.47 E
Binaiya, Gunung- 26 Ig 3.11S 129.26 E
Binatang 26 Ff 2.10N 111.38 E
Binboğa Dağı 24 Gc 38.21N 36.32 E
Binche 12 Gd 50.24N 4.10 E
Binder 27 Jb 48.35N 110.36 E
Bindura 31 Kj 17.17S 31.20 E
Bine el Ouidane 32 Fc 32.08N 6.28W
Binéfar 13 Mc 41.51N 0.18 E
Binem 35 Bb 18.43N 19.40 E
Binga [Zaire] 36 Db 2.23N 20.30 E
Binga [Zimb.] 37 Dc 17.37S 27.20 E

Index Symbols

[1] Independent Nation
[2] State, Region
[3] District, County
[4] Municipality
[5] Colony, Dependency
Continent
Physical Region
Historical or Cultural Region
Mount, Mountain
Volcano
Hill
Mountains, Mountain Range
Hills, Escarpment
Plateau, Upland
Pass, Gap
Plain, Lowland
Delta
Salt Flat
Valley, Canyon
Crater, Cave
Karst Features
Depression
Polder
Desert, Dunes
Forest, Woods
Heath, Steppe
Oasis
Cape, Point
Coast, Beach
Cliff
Peninsula
Isthmus
Sandbank
Island
Atoll
Rock, Reef
Islands, Archipelago
Rocks, Reefs
Coral Reef
Well, Spring
Geyser
River, Stream
Waterfall Rapids
River Mouth, Estuary
Lake
Salt Lake
Intermittent Lake
Reservoir
Swamp, Pond
Canal
Glacier
Ice Shelf, Pack Ice
Ocean
Sea
Gulf, Bay
Strait, Fjord
Lagoon
Bank
Seamount
Tablemount
Ridge
Shelf
Basin
Escarpment, Sea Scarp
Fracture
Trench, Abyss
National Park, Reserve
Point of Interest
Recreation Site
Cave, Cavern
Historic Site
Ruins
Wall, Walls
Church, Abbey
Temple
Scientific Station
Airport
Port
Lighthouse
Mine
Tunnel
Dam, Bridge

Index Symbols

[1] Independent Nation	Historical or Cultural Region	Pass, Gap	Depression	Coast, Beach
[2] State, Region	Mount, Mountain	Plain, Lowland	Polder	Cliff
[3] District, County	Volcano	Delta	Desert, Dunes	Peninsula
[4] Municipality	Hill	Salt Flat	Forest, Woods	Isthmus
[5] Colony, Dependency	Mountains, Mountain Range	Valley, Canyon	Heath, Steppe	Sandbank
■ Continent	Hills, Escarpment	Crater, Cave	Oasis	Island
⬯ Physical Region	Plateau, Upland	Karst Features	Cape, Point	Atoll

Rock, Reef	Waterfall Rapids	Canal	Lagoon
Islands, Archipelago	River Mouth, Estuary	Bank	Escarpment, Sea Scarp
Rocks, Reefs	Lake	Seamount	Fracture
Coral Reef	Salt Lake	Tablemount	Trench, Abyss
Well, Spring	Intermittent Lake	Ridge	National Park, Reserve
Geyser	Reservoir	Shelf	Point of Interest
River, Stream	Swamp, Pond	Basin	Recreation Site
			Cave, Cavern

Historic Site	Port
Ruins	Lighthouse
Wall, Walls	Mine
Church, Abbey	Tunnel
Temple	Dam, Bridge
Scientific Station	
Airport	

Index Symbols

[1]	Independent Nation		Historical or Cultural Region		Pass, Gap		Depression		Coast, Beach		Rock, Reef		Waterfall Rapids		Canal		Lagoon		Escarpment, Sea Scarp		Historic Site		Port
[2]	State, Region		Mount, Mountain		Plain, Lowland		Polder		Cliff		Islands, Archipelago		River Mouth, Estuary		Glacier		Bank		Fracture		Ruins		Lighthouse
[3]	District, County		Volcano		Delta		Desert, Dunes		Peninsula		Rocks, Reefs		Lake		Ice Shelf, Pack Ice		Seamount		Trench, Abyss		Wall, Walls		Mine
[4]	Municipality		Hill		Salt Flat		Forest, Woods		Isthmus		Coral Reef		Salt Lake		Ocean		Tablemount		National Park, Reserve		Church, Abbey		Tunnel
[5]	Colony, Dependency		Mountains, Mountain Range		Valley, Canyon		Heath, Steppe		Sandbank		Well, Spring		Intermittent Lake		Sea		Ridge		Point of Interest		Temple		Dam, Bridge
	Continent		Hills, Escarpment		Crater, Cave		Oasis		Island		Geyser		Reservoir		Gulf, Bay		Shelf		Recreation Site		Scientific Station		
	Physical Region		Plateau, Upland		Karst Features		Cape, Point		Atoll		River, Stream		Swamp, Pond		Strait, Fjord		Basin		Cave, Cavern		Airport		

Bougtob 32 Hc 34.02N 0.05 E
Bouguenais 11 Eg 47.11N 1.37W
Bougzoul 13 Oi 35.42N 2.51 E
Bou Hadjar 14 Cn 36.30N 8.06 E
Bouhalla, Jbel- 13 Gi 35.06N 5.07W
Bou Hamed 13 Hi 35.19N 4.58W
Bouillante 51e Ab 16.08N 61.46W
Bouillon 11 Le 49.48N 5.04 E
Bouira 32 Hb 36.23N 3.54 E
Bouira [3] 32 Hb 36.15N 4.10 E
Bou Ismaïl 13 Oh 36.38N 2.41 E
Bou Izakarn 32 Fd 29.10N 9.44W
Bou Kadir 13 Nh 36.04N 1.07 E
Boukombé 34 Fc 10.11N 1.06 E
Boû Lanouâr 32 De 21.16N 16.30W
Boulay-Moselle 12 Ie 49.11N 6.30 E
Boulder [Co.-U.S.] 39 Ie 40.01N 105.17W
Boulder [Mt.-U.S.] 46 Ic 46.14N 112.07W
Boulder City 46 Hi 35.59N 114.50W
Boulemane 32 Gc 33.22N 4.45W
Boulemane [3] 32 Gc 33.02N 4.04W
Boulevard Atlántico 55 Dn 38.19S 57.59W
Boulia 59 Hd 22.54S 139.54 E
Bouligny 11 Le 49.17N 5.45 E
Boulogne 11 Eg 47.05N 1.40W
Boulogne-Billancourt 11 If 48.50N 2.15 E
Boulogne-sur-Mer 11 Hd 50.43N 1.37 E
Boulonnais 11 Hd 50.42N 1.40 E
Bouloupari 63b Ce 21.52S 166.03 E
Boulsa 34 Ec 12.39N 0.34W
Boultoum 34 Hc 14.40N 10.18 E
Bou Maad, Djebel- 13 Oh 36.26N 2.08 E
Boumba 34 Ie 2.02N 15.12 E
Boumdeid 32 Ef 17.26N 11.21W
Boum Kabir 35 Bc 10.11N 19.24 E
Boumort 13 Nb 42.14N 1.08 E
Bouna 31 Gh 9.16N 3.00W
Bouna [3] 34 Ed 9.15N 3.20W
Boû Nâga 32 Ef 19.00N 13.13W
Bou Nasser, Adrar- 32 Gc 33.35N 3.53W
Boundary Peak 46 Fh 37.51N 118.21W
Boundiali [3] 34 Dd 9.23N 6.32W
Boundiali 34 Dd 9.31N 6.29W
Boundji 36 Cc 1.03S 15.22 E
Boungou 35 Cd 6.45N 22.06 E
Bountiful 43 Ec 40.53N 111.53W
Bounty Bay 64q Ab 25.03S 130.05W
Bounty Islands 57 Ii 47.45S 179.05 E
Bounty Trough (EN) 3 Jn 46.00S 178.00 E
Bourail 61 Cd 21.34S 165.30 E
Bourbon-Lancy 11 Jh 46.37N 3.47 E
Bourbonnais 11 Ih 46.30N 3.00 E
Bourbonne-les-Bains 11 Lg 47.57N 5.45 E
Bourbourg 12 Ed 50.57N 2.12 E
Bourbre 11 Li 45.47N 5.11 E
Bourem 34 Eb 16.58N 0.21W
Bouressa 34 Fa 20.01N 2.18 E
Bourg-Achard 12 Ce 49.21N 0.49 E
Bourganeuf 11 Hi 45.57N 1.45 E
Bourgar'oûn, Cap- 32 Ib 37.06N 6.28 E
Bourg-de-Péage 11 Li 45.02N 5.03 E
Bourg-en-Bresse 11 Lh 46.12N 5.13 E
Bourges 6 Gf 47.05N 2.24 E
Bourget, Lac du- 11 Li 45.44N 5.52 E
Bourgneuf, Baie de- 11 Dg 47.05N 2.13W
Bourgogne 12 Ge 49.21N 4.04 E
Bourgogne = Burgundy (EN) 5 Gf 47.00N 4.30 E
Bourgogne = Burgundy (EN) 11 Kg 47.00N 4.30 E
Bourgogne, Canal de- 11 Jg 47.58N 3.30 E
Bourgogne, Porte de- 11 Mg 47.38N 6.52 E
Bourgoin-Jallieu 11 Li 45.35N 5.17 E
Bourgtheroulde-Infreville 12 Ce 49.18N 0.53 E
Bourguébus 12 Be 49.07N 0.18W
Boû Rjeimat 32 Df 19.04N 15.08W
Bourke 58 Fh 30.05S 145.56 E
Bourne 12 Bb 52.46N 0.23W
Bournemouth 9 Lk 50.43N 1.54W
Bourtanger Moor 12 Jb 52.50N 7.06 E
Bourth 12 Cf 48.46N 0.49 E
Bou Saâda 32 Hb 35.12N 4.11 E
Bou Sellam 13 Qh 36.26N 4.34 E
Boussac 11 Ih 46.21N 2.13 E
Boussé 34 Ec 12.39N 1.53W
Boussens 11 Gk 43.11N 0.58 E
Bousso 35 Bc 10.29N 16.43 E
Bouthaleb, Djebel- 13 Ri 35.48N 5.12 E
Boutilimit 32 Ef 17.33N 14.42W
Bou-Tlélis 13 Li 35.34N 0.54W
Boutonne 11 Fi 45.55N 0.49W
Bouvet 66 Cd 54.26S 3.24 E
Bouxwiller 12 Jf 48.49N 7.29 E
Bouza 34 Gc 14.25N 6.02 E
Bouzanne 11 Hh 46.38N 1.28 E
Bouzghaïa 13 Nh 36.20N 1.15 E
Bouzonville 12 Ie 49.18N 6.32 E
Bovalino 14 Kl 38.09N 16.11 E
Bovec 14 Hd 46.20N 13.33 E
Bovenkarspel 12 Hb 52.42N 5.17 E
Boves 12 Ee 49.51N 2.23 E
Bovino 14 Ji 41.15N 15.20 E
Bovril 55 Cj 31.21S 59.26W
Bowa → Muli 27 Hf 27.55N 101.13 E
Bowen [Arg.] 56 Ge 35.02S 67.31W
Bowen [Austl.] 58 Fg 20.01S 148.15 E
Bowers Bank (EN) 40a Bb 54.00N 180.00
Bowers Ridge (EN) 40a Bb 54.30N 180.00
Bowie 45 Hj 33.34N 97.51W
Bowkān 24 Ld 36.31N 46.12 E
Bowland, Forest of- 9 Kh 54.00N 2.35W
Bowling Green [Ky.-U.S.] 43 Jd 37.00N 86.27W
Bowling Green [Oh.-U.S.] 44 Fe 41.22N 83.40W
Bowman 43 Gb 46.11N 103.24W
Bowman Bay 42 Kc 65.33N 73.40W
Bowman Island 66 He 65.17S 103.08 E
Bowman, Mount- 46 Ea 51.10N 121.55W
Bowo/Bomi 27 Ge 30.02N 95.39 E
Bowokan, Kepulauan- 26 Hg 2.05S 123.35 E
Bowral 59 Kf 34.28S 150.25 E
Bow River 42 Gg 49.56N 111.42W
Box Elder Creek 46 Kc 46.57N 108.04W
Boxelder Creek 46 Nd 45.59N 103.57W
Boxholm 7 Dg 58.12N 15.03 E
Boxian 27 Ke 33.46N 115.44 E
Boxing 27 Kd 37.07N 118.04 E
Boxmeer 12 Hc 51.39N 5.57 E
Boxtel 11 Lc 51.35N 5.20 E
Boyabat 24 Fb 41.28N 34.47 E
Boyabo 36 Cb 3.43N 18.46 E
Boyacá [2] 54 Db 5.30N 72.50W
Boyang 27 Kf 29.00N 116.41 E
Boyer, Cap- 63b De 21.37S 168.07 E
Boyer Ahmadī-e Kohkīlūyeh [3] 23 Hc 31.00N 50.30 E
Boyle/Mainistir na Búille 9 Eh 53.58N 8.18W
Boyne/An Bhóinn 9 Gh 53.43N 6.15W
Boyne City 44 Ec 45.13N 85.01W
Boynes, Iles de- 30 Nm 49.58S 69.59 E
Boynton Beach 44 Gl 26.32N 80.03W
Boysen Reservoir 46 Ke 43.19N 108.11W
Boz, Kūh-e- 24 Pi 27.46N 55.54 E
Bozburun 15 Li 40.32N 28.46 E
Bozburun 15 Lm 36.41N 28.04 E
Bozburun Daği 24 Dd 37.18N 31.03 E
Bozcaada 24 Bc 39.50N 26.04 E
Bozcaada 24 Bc 39.49N 26.03 E
Bozdağ 15 Lk 38.20N 28.06 E
Boz Daği [Tur.] 24 Cd 37.18N 29.12 E
Boz Daği [Tur.] 24 Cc 38.19N 28.08 E
Boz Dağlari 15 Kj 38.20N 27.45 E
Bozdoğan 15 Ll 37.40N 28.19 E
Bozeman 39 He 45.41N 111.02W
Bozen / Bolzano 6 Hf 46.31N 11.22 E
Bozene 36 Cb 2.56N 19.12 E
Bozhen 28 De 38.04N 116.34 E
Bozkol, Zaliv- 18 Cb 45.20N 61.45 E
Bozkurt 24 Fb 41.57N 34.01 E
Bozok Platosu 24 Fc 39.05N 35.05 E
Bozouls 11 Ij 44.28N 2.43 E
Bozoum 31 Ih 6.19N 16.23 E
Bozova 24 Hd 37.22N 38.31 E
Bozovici 15 Ee 44.56N 22.00 E
Bozqūsh, Kūh-e- 24 Ld 37.45N 47.40 E
Bra 14 Bf 44.42N 7.51 E
Braås 8 Fg 57.04N 15.03 E
Braathen, Cape- 66 Pf 71.48S 96.05W
Brabant 11 Lc 51.10N 5.05 E
Brabant [3] 12 Gd 50.45N 4.30 E
Brabant-les-Villers 12 Gf 48.51N 4.59 E
Brâbich 34 Eb 17.30N 3.00W
Brač 14 Kg 43.19N 16.40 E
Bracadale, Loch- 9 Gd 57.20N 6.35W
Bracciano 14 Gh 42.06N 12.10 E
Bracciano, Lago di- 14 Gh 42.05N 12.15 E
Bräcke 7 De 62.43N 15.27 E
Brackettville 45 Fl 29.19N 100.24W
Bracki Kanal 14 Kg 43.24N 16.40 E
Brackley 12 Ab 52.02N 1.09W
Bracknell 9 Mj 51.26N 0.46W
Brackwede, Bielefeld- 12 Kc 51.59N 8.31 E
Brad 15 Fc 46.08N 22.47 E
Bradano 14 Kj 40.23N 16.51 E
Bradenton 43 Kf 27.29N 82.34W
Bradford [Eng.-U.K.] 9 Lh 53.48N 1.45W
Bradford [Pa.-U.S.] 44 He 41.57N 78.39W
Bradley Reef 60 Gi 6.52S 160.48 E
Brady 43 He 31.08N 99.20W
Brady Mountains 45 Gk 31.20N 99.40W
Brædstrup 8 Ci 55.58N 9.37 E
Braemar 9 Jd 57.01N 3.24W
Braga [2] 13 Dc 41.35N 8.25W
Braga 6 Fg 41.33N 8.26W
Bragadiru 15 If 43.46N 25.31 E
Bragado 56 He 35.08S 60.30W
Bragança [2] 13 Fc 41.30N 6.45W
Bragança [Braz.] 53 Lf 1.03S 46.46W
Bragança [Port.] 13 Fc 41.49N 6.45W
Bragança Paulista 55 If 22.57S 46.34W
Brahestad/Raahe 7 Fd 64.41N 24.29 E
Brāhmanbāria 25 Id 23.59N 91.07 E
Brahmapur 22 Kh 19.19N 84.47 E
Brahmaputra 21 Lg 24.02N 90.59 E
Brăila [2] 15 Kd 45.13N 27.43 E
Brăila 6 If 45.16N 27.59 E
Brăilei, Balta- 15 Ke 45.00N 28.00 E
Braine 12 Fe 49.20N 3.32 E
Braine-l'Alleud/Eigenbrakel 12 Gd 50.41N 4.22 E
Brainerd 43 Ib 46.21N 94.12W
Braintree 12 Cc 51.53N 0.34 E
Braithwaite Point 59 Gb 11.58S 134.00 E
Brake (Unterweser) 10 Ec 53.20N 8.29 E
Brakel [Bel.] 12 Fd 50.47N 3.45 E
Brakel [Ger.] 12 Lc 51.43N 9.11 E
Brakna [3] 32 Ef 17.30N 13.30W
Brålanda 8 Ef 58.34N 12.22 E
Bralorne 46 Da 50.47N 122.49W
Bramming 8 Ci 55.28N 8.42 E
Brämön 8 Gb 62.10N 17.40 E
Brampton 44 Hd 43.41N 79.46W
Bramsche 10 Dd 52.24N 7.59 E
Bran, Pasul- 15 Id 45.26N 25.17 E
Branco 32 Cf 16.39N 24.41W
Branco, Cabo- 52 Mf 7.09S 34.47W
Branco, Rio- [Braz.] 52 Jf 1.24S 61.51W
Branco, Rio- [Braz.] 55 De 21.00S 57.48W
Branco ou Cabixi, Rio- 55 Ba 13.55S 60.10W
Brandberg 30 Ik 21.08S 14.35 E
Brandbu 7 Cf 60.26N 10.28 E
Brande 7 Bi 55.57N 9.07 E
Brandenburg 10 Id 52.25N 12.33 E
Brandenburg 10 Jd 52.10N 13.30 E
Brändö 8 Id 60.25N 21.05 E
Brandon [Eng.-U.K.] 12 Cb 52.27N 0.37 E
Brandon [Fl.-U.S.] 44 Fl 27.56N 82.17W
Brandon [Man.-Can.] 39 Je 49.50N 99.57W
Brandon [Vt.-U.S.] 44 Kd 43.47N 73.05W
Brandon Head/Na Machairí 9 Ci 52.16N 10.15W
Brandon Mount/Cnoc Bréanainn 9 Ci 52.14N 10.15W
Brandval 8 Ed 60.19N 12.02 E
Brandvlei 37 Cf 30.25S 20.30 E
Brandýs nad Labem-Stará Boleslav 10 Kf 50.11N 14.40 E
Brăneşti 15 Je 44.27N 26.20 E
Braniewo 10 Pb 54.24N 19.50 E
Bransby Point 51c Bc 16.43N 62.14W
Bransfield Strait 66 Re 63.00S 59.00W
Brańsk 10 Sd 52.45N 22.51 E
Branson 45 Jh 36.39N 93.13W
Brantevik 8 Fi 55.31N 14.21 E
Brantford 42 Jh 43.08N 80.16W
Brantôme 11 Gi 45.22N 0.39 E
Bras d'Or Lake 42 Lg 45.50N 60.50W
Brasil = Brazil (EN) [1] 53 Kf 9.00S 53.00W
Brasil, Planalto do- = Brazilian Highlands (EN) 52 Lg 17.00S 45.00W
Brasiléia 54 Ef 11.00S 68.44W
Brasília 53 Lg 15.47S 47.55W
Brasília de Minas 55 Jc 16.12S 44.26W
Brasla 8 Kg 57.08N 24.50 E
Braslav 7 Gi 55.37N 27.05 E
Braşov 15 Id 45.40N 25.10 E
Braşov [2] 15 Id 45.38N 25.35 E
Brass 34 Ge 4.19N 6.14 E
Brassac 11 Ik 43.38N 2.30 E
Brasschaat 12 Gc 51.17N 4.27 E
Brasstown Bald 44 Fh 34.52N 83.48W
Brastavăţu 15 Hf 43.55N 24.24 E
Brataj 15 Ci 40.16N 19.40 E
Bråte 8 De 59.43N 11.27 E
Bratea 15 Fc 46.56N 22.37 E
Bratislava 6 Hf 48.09N 17.07 E
Bratsk 22 Md 56.05N 101.48 E
Bratskoje Vodohranilišče = Bratsk Reservoir (EN) 20 Fe 56.30N 102.00 E
Bratsk Reservoir (EN) = Bratskoje Vodohranilišče 20 Fe 56.30N 102.00 E
Brattleboro 43 Mc 42.51N 72.36W
Brattvåg 8 Bb 62.36N 6.27 E
Braubach 12 Jd 50.17N 7.40 E
Braunau am Inn 14 Hb 48.16N 13.02 E
Braunschweig 10 Gd 52.16N 10.32 E
Brava 30 Eg 14.52N 24.43W
Brava, Costa- 13 Pc 41.45N 3.04 E
Bråviken 8 Gf 58.40N 16.30 E
Bravo del Norte, Rio- = Grande, Rio- (EN) 38 Jg 25.57N 97.09W
Brawley 43 De 32.59N 115.34W
Bray 42 Jc 69.20N 77.00W
Bray 37 Ce 25.26S 23.38 E
Bray/Bré 9 Gh 53.12N 6.06W
Bray, Pays de- 11 He 49.46N 1.26 E
Bray-Dunes 12 Ec 51.05N 2.31 E
Braye 11 Gg 47.45N 0.42 E
Bray Head 9 Cj 51.53N 10.25W
Bray-sur-Somme 12 Ee 49.56N 2.43 E
Brazi 15 Je 44.52N 26.01 E
Brazil 44 Df 39.32N 87.08W
Brazil (EN) = Brasil [1] 53 Kf 9.00S 53.00W
Brazil Basin (EN) 3 Dk 15.00S 25.00W
Brazilian Highlands (EN) = Brasil, Planalto do- 52 Lg 17.00S 45.00W
Brazos 38 Jg 28.53N 95.23W
Brazos Santiago Pass 45 Hm 26.05N 97.16W
Brazzaville 31 Ii 4.16S 15.17 E
Brčko 14 Mf 44.52N 18.49 E
Brda 10 Oc 53.07N 18.08 E
Brdy 10 Jg 49.35N 13.50 E
Bré/Bray 9 Gh 53.12N 6.06W
Brea, Punta- 51a Bc 17.54N 66.55W
Breaden, Lake- 59 Fe 25.45S 125.40 E
Breaksea Sound 62 Bf 45.35S 166.40 E
Breaza [Rom.] 15 Id 45.11N 25.40 E
Breaza [Rom.] 15 Ib 47.37N 25.20 E
Breaza, Virful- 15 Hb 47.22N 24.02 E
Brebes 26 Eh 6.53S 109.03 E
Brêche 12 Ee 49.16N 2.30 E
Brechin 9 Ke 56.44N 2.40W
Brecht 12 Gc 51.21N 4.38 E
Brechte 12 Jb 52.15N 7.10 E
Breckenridge [Mn.-U.S.] 45 Hc 46.16N 96.35W
Breckenridge [Tx.-U.S.] 45 Gj 32.45N 98.54W
Breckland 9 Ni 52.30N 0.35 E
Břeclav 10 Mh 48.46N 16.54 E
Brecon 9 Jj 51.57N 3.24W
Brecon Beacons 9 Jj 51.53N 3.31W
Breda 11 Kc 51.35N 4.46 E
Bredaryd 8 Eg 57.10N 13.44 E
Bredasdorp 31 Jl 34.32S 20.02 E
Brede 12 Cd 50.55N 0.43 E
Bredene 12 Ec 51.14N 2.58 E
Bredstedt 10 Eb 54.37N 8.59 E
Bredy 19 Ge 52.26N 60.21 E
Bree 12 Hc 51.08N 5.36 E
Breg 10 Ei 47.57N 8.31 E
Bregalnica 15 Eh 41.36N 21.56 E
Bregenz 14 Dc 47.30N 9.46 E
Bréhat, Ile de- 11 Df 48.51N 3.00W
Breiðafjörður 5 Db 65.15N 23.15W
Breimsvatnet 8 Bc 61.40N 6.25 E
Breisach am Rhein 10 Dh 48.02N 7.35 E
Breisund 8 Ab 62.30N 6.00 E
Breit Bridge 37 Dd 22.12S 29.59 E
Breivikbotn 7 Fa 70.37N 22.29 E
Brejão 55 Ia 12.50S 44.51W
Brekken 7 Ce 62.39N 11.53 E
Brekstad 7 Be 63.41N 9.41 E
Bremangerlandet 7 Af 61.50N 5.00 E
Brembana, Val- 14 De 45.55N 9.40 E
Brembo 14 De 45.35N 9.32 E
Bremen [2] 10 Ec 53.05N 8.50 E
Bremen [Ger.] 6 Ge 53.05N 8.48 E
Bremen [In.-U.S.] 44 De 41.27N 86.09W
Bremerhaven 6 Ge 53.33N 8.35 E
Bremerton 43 Cb 47.34N 122.38W
Bremervörde 10 Fc 53.29N 9.08 E
Brendel 46 Kg 38.57N 109.50W
Brenham 45 Hk 30.10N 96.24W
Brenne 11 Hh 46.44N 1.14 E
Brennero, Passo del- = Brenner Pass (EN) 5 Hf 47.00N 11.30 E
Brennerpaß = Brenner Pass (EN) 5 Hf 47.00N 11.30 E
Brenner Pass (EN) = Brennero, Passo del- 5 Hf 47.00N 11.30 E
Brenner Pass (EN) = Brennerpaß 5 Hf 47.00N 11.30 E
Brenta 14 Ge 45.11N 12.18 E
Brentwood 9 Nj 51.38N 0.18 E
Brescia 6 Hf 45.33N 10.15 E
Breskens 12 Fc 51.24N 3.33 E
Breslau (EN) = Wrocław 6 He 51.06N 17.00 E
Bresle 11 Hd 50.04N 1.22 E
Bressanone / Brixen 14 Fd 46.43N 11.39 E
Bressay 9 La 60.08N 1.05W
Bresse 11 Lh 46.30N 5.15 E
Bressuire 11 Fh 46.51N 0.29W
Brest 6 Ie 52.06N 23.42 E
Brest [Fr.] 6 Ff 48.24N 4.29W
Brestova 14 Ie 45.08N 14.14 E
Brestskaja Oblast [3] 19 Ce 52.20N 25.30 E
Bretagne = Brittany (EN) 11 Df 48.00N 3.00W
Bretagne = Brittany (EN) 5 Ff 48.00N 3.00W
Breţcu 15 Jc 46.03N 26.18 E
Breteuil [Fr.] 12 Cf 48.50N 0.55 E
Breteuil [Fr.] 11 Ie 49.38N 2.18 E
Breton, Marais- 11 Eh 46.56N 2.00W
Breton, Pertuis- 11 Eh 46.16N 1.22W
Breton Sound 45 Ll 29.30N 89.30W
Brett 12 Cc 51.58N 0.57 E
Brett, Cape- 62 Fa 35.10S 174.20 E
Bretten 12 Ke 49.03N 8.42 E
Bretteville-sur-Laize 12 Be 49.03N 0.20W
Breueh, Pulau- 26 Be 5.41N 95.05 E
Breuil Cervinia 14 Be 45.56N 7.38 E
Breukelen 12 Db 52.10N 5.01 E
Breuna 12 Lc 51.25N 9.11 E
Breves 54 Hd 1.40S 50.29W
Brevik 7 Bg 59.04N 9.42 E
Brevoort 42 Ld 63.30N 64.20W
Brewarrina 59 Je 29.57S 146.52 E
Brewerville 34 Cd 6.25N 10.47W
Brewster 46 Fb 48.06N 119.47W
Brewster, Kap- 67 Md 70.10N 21.30W
Brewton 43 Je 31.07N 87.04W
Brežice 14 Je 45.54N 15.35 E
Brézina 32 Hc 33.05N 1.16 E
Březnice 10 Jg 49.33N 13.57 E
Breznik 15 Fg 42.44N 22.54 E
Brezno 10 Ph 48.49N 19.39 E
Brezoi 15 Hd 45.21N 24.15 E
Brezolles 12 Df 48.41N 1.04 E
Brezovo 15 Ig 42.21N 25.05 E
Bria 31 Jh 6.32N 21.59 E
Briance 11 Hi 45.47N 1.12 E
Briançon 11 Mj 44.54N 6.39 E
Brianza 14 De 45.45N 9.15 E
Briare, Canal de- 11 If 48.02N 2.43 E
Bribie Island 59 Ke 27.00S 153.05 E
Bričany 15 Ka 48.18N 27.04 E
Bride 9 Fi 52.05N 7.50W
Bridgend 9 Jj 51.31N 3.35W
Bridgeport [Ca.-U.S.] 46 Fg 38.10N 119.13W
Bridgeport [Ct.-U.S.] 43 Mc 41.11N 73.11W
Bridgeport [Nb.-U.S.] 45 Ef 41.40N 103.06W
Bridge River 46 Ea 50.45N 121.55W
Bridger Peak 46 Lf 41.12N 107.02W
Bridges Point 64g Bb 1.58N 157.28W
Bridgeton 44 Jf 39.26N 75.14W
Bridgetown [Austl.] 59 Df 33.57S 116.08 E
Bridgetown [Bar.] 39 Nh 13.06N 59.37W
Bridgewater 42 Lh 44.23N 64.31W
Bridgwater 9 Kj 51.08N 3.00W
Bridgwater Bay 9 Jj 51.16N 3.12W
Bridlington 9 Mg 54.05N 0.12W
Bridlington Bay 9 Mg 54.04N 0.08W
Bridport 9 Kk 50.44N 2.46W
Brie 11 Jf 48.40N 3.30 E
Brielle 12 Gc 51.54N 4.10 E
Brienzer-See 14 Bd 46.45N 7.55 E
Briey 11 Le 49.15N 5.56 E
Brig 14 Bd 46.20N 8.00 E
Brigach 10 Ei 47.58N 8.30 E
Brigham City 43 Ec 41.31N 112.01W
Brighstone 12 Ad 50.38N 1.23W
Bright 59 Jg 36.44S 146.58 E
Brightlingsea 12 Dc 51.48N 1.02 E
Brighton [Co.-U.S.] 45 Dg 39.59N 104.49W
Brighton [Eng.-U.K.] 6 Fe 50.50N 0.10W
Brignoles 11 Mk 43.24N 6.04 E
Brihuega 13 Jd 40.45N 2.52W
Brijuni 14 Hf 44.55N 13.46 E
Brikama 34 Bc 13.16N 16.39W
Brilhante, Rio- 54 Hh 21.58S 54.18W
Brilon 12 Kc 51.24N 8.35 E
Brilon-Alme 12 Kc 51.27N 8.37 E
Brimstone Hill 51c Ab 17.21N 62.49W
Brindisi 6 Hg 40.38N 17.56 E
Brinkley 45 Ki 34.53N 91.12W
Brinkmann 55 Aj 30.52S 62.02W
Brionne 12 Ce 49.12N 0.43 E
Brioude 11 Ji 45.18N 3.24 E
Brisbane 58 Gg 27.28S 153.02 E
Brisighella 14 Ff 44.13N 11.46 E
Bristol 66 Ad 59.02S 26.31W
Bristol [Eng.-U.K.] 6 Fe 51.27N 2.35W
Bristol [Tn.-U.S.] 44 Fg 36.36N 82.11W
Bristol Bay 38 Dd 58.00N 159.00W
Bristol Channel 5 Fe 51.20N 4.00W
Bristol Lake 46 Hi 34.28N 115.41W
Bristow 45 Hi 35.50N 96.23W
Britannia Range 66 Jf 80.00S 158.00 E
British Columbia [3] 42 Fe 55.00N 125.00W
British Honduras → Belize 49 Ce 17.35N 88.35W
British Indian Ocean Territory [5] 22 Jj 7.00S 72.00 E
British Isles 5 Fd 54.00N 4.00W
British Mountains 40 Kc 69.20N 140.20W
British Solomon Islands → Solomon Islands [1] 58 Ge 8.00S 159.00 E
British Virgin Islands [5] 39 Mh 18.20N 64.50W
Brits 37 De 25.40S 27.46 E
Britstown 37 Cf 30.37S 23.30 E
Britt 45 Je 43.06N 93.48W
Brittany (EN) = Bretagne 11 Df 48.00N 3.00W
Brittany (EN) = Bretagne 5 Ff 48.00N 3.00W
Britton 45 Hd 45.48N 97.45W
Brive-la-Gaillarde 11 Hi 45.09N 1.32 E
Briviesca 13 Ib 42.33N 3.19W
Brixen / Bressanone 14 Fd 46.43N 11.39 E
Brixham 9 Jk 50.24N 3.30W
Brjansk 6 Je 53.15N 34.22 E
Brjanskaja Oblast [3] 19 De 52.50N 33.20 E
Brjuhoveckaja 16 Kg 45.46N 39.01 E
Brjukoviči 10 Jg 49.52N 24.00 E
Brno 6 Hf 49.12N 16.37 E
Broa, Ensenada de la- 49 Fb 22.35N 82.00W
Broad Bay 9 Gc 58.15N 6.15W
Broadford 9 Hd 57.14N 5.54W
Broad Sound 59 Jd 22.10S 149.45 E
Broadstairs 12 Dc 51.22N 1.27 E
Broadus 43 Fb 45.27N 105.25W
Brocēni/Broceny 8 Jh 56.41N 22.30 E
Broceny/Brocēni 8 Jh 56.41N 22.30 E
Brochet 42 He 57.53N 101.40W
Brochu, Lac- 44 Ja 48.26N 74.15W
Brock 42 Ga 77.55N 114.30W
Brocken 10 Ge 51.48N 10.36 E
Brockman, Mount- 59 Dd 22.28S 117.18 E
Brockton 44 Ld 42.05N 71.01W
Brockville 42 Jh 44.35N 75.41W
Brod 15 Eh 41.31N 21.14 E
Brodarevo 15 Cf 43.14N 19.43 E
Broderick Falls 36 Fb 0.37N 34.46 E
Brodeur Peninsula 38 Kb 73.00N 88.00W
Brodick 9 Hf 55.35N 5.09W
Brodnica 10 Pc 53.16N 19.23 E
Brody 10 Dd 50.04N 25.12 E
Broglie 12 Ce 49.01N 0.32 E
Brok 10 Rd 52.43N 21.52 E
Brok 10 Rd 52.38N 21.55 E
Broken Arrow 45 Ih 36.03N 95.48W
Broken Bow 45 Gf 41.24N 99.38W
Broken Bow Lake 45 Ii 34.10N 94.40W
Broken Hill 58 Fh 31.57S 141.27 E
Broken Ridge (EN) 3 Hm 31.30S 95.00 E
Brokind 8 Ff 58.13N 15.40 E
Brokopondo 54 Hb 5.04N 55.00W
Bromarv 8 Je 59.55N 23.00 E
Bromley, London- 12 Cc 51.25N 0.01 E
Bromölla 7 Dh 56.04N 14.28 E
Brønderslev 8 Cg 57.16N 9.58 E
Brong-Ahafo [3] 34 Ed 7.45N 1.30W
Bronnikovo 17 Ng 58.29N 68.27 E
Brønnøysund 7 Cd 65.28N 12.13 E
Bronte 14 Im 37.47N 14.50 E
Brooke's Point 26 Ge 8.47N 117.50 E
Brookfield 45 Jg 39.47N 93.04W
Brookhaven 45 Kk 31.35N 90.26W
Brookings [Or.-U.S.] 43 Cc 42.03N 124.17W
Brookings [S.D.-U.S.] 43 Hc 44.19N 96.48W
Brooks 42 Gf 50.35N 111.53W
Brooks Banks (EN) 60 Mc 24.05N 166.50W
Brooks Range 38 Dc 68.00N 154.00W
Brookston 45 Jc 46.50N 92.32W
Brooksville 44 Fk 28.33N 82.23W
Brookton 59 Df 32.22S 117.01 E
Brookville [In.-U.S.] 44 Ef 39.25N 85.01W
Brookville [Pa.-U.S.] 44 He 41.10N 79.06W
Broom 9 Hd 57.45N 5.05W
Broom, Loch- 9 Hd 57.55N 5.15W
Broome 58 Df 17.58S 122.14 E
Brora 9 Jc 58.00N 3.50W
Brora 9 Jc 58.01N 3.51W
Brosna/An Bhrosnach 9 Fh 53.13N 7.58W
Broşteni 15 Ib 47.14N 25.42 E
Brou 11 Hf 48.13N 1.11 E
Brough 9 Kg 54.32N 2.19W
Broughton Island 39 Mc 67.35N 63.50W
Broussard 45 Kk 30.09N 91.58W
Brovary 16 Gd 50.32N 30.48 E
Brovst 8 Cg 57.06N 9.32 E
Brown Bank (EN) = Bruine Bank 12 Fb 52.35N 3.20 E
Brownfield 43 Ge 33.11N 102.16W
Browning 46 Ib 48.34N 113.01W
Browns Bank (EN) 42 Kh 42.40N 66.05W
Brownsville [Tn.-U.S.] 44 Ch 35.36N 89.15W
Brownsville [Tx.-U.S.] 39 Jg 25.54N 97.30W
Brownwood 43 He 31.43N 98.59W
Browse Island 59 Eb 14.05S 123.35 E
Broye 14 Bd 46.55N 7.02 E
Bruay-en-Artois 11 Id 50.29N 2.33 E
Bruay-sur-l'Escaut 12 Fd 50.23N 3.32 E
Bruce 45 Lj 33.59N 89.21W
Bruce, Mount- 57 Cg 22.36S 118.08 E
Bruce Crossing 44 Cb 46.32N 89.10W
Bruce Peninsula 42 Jh 44.59N 81.20W
Bruce Rock 59 Df 31.53S 118.09 E
Bruche 11 Nf 48.34N 7.43 E

Index Symbols

[1] Independent Nation
[2] State, Region
[3] District, County
[4] Municipality
[5] Colony, Dependency
Continent
Physical Region
Historical or Cultural Region
Mount, Mountain
Volcano
Hill
Mountains, Mountain Range
Hills, Escarpment
Plateau, Upland
Pass, Gap
Plain, Lowland
Delta
Salt Flat
Valley, Canyon
Crater, Cave
Karst Features
Depression
Polder
Desert, Dunes
Forest, Woods
Heath, Steppe
Oasis
Cape, Point
Coast, Beach
Cliff
Peninsula
Isthmus
Sandbank
Island
Atoll
Rock, Reef
Islands, Archipelago
Rocks, Reefs
Coral Reef
Well, Spring
Geyser
River, Stream
Waterfall Rapids
River Mouth, Estuary
Lake
Salt Lake
Intermittent Lake
Reservoir
Swamp, Pond
Canal
Glacier
Ice Shelf, Pack Ice
Ocean
Sea
Gulf, Bay
Strait, Fjord
Lagoon
Bank
Seamount
Tablemount
Ridge
Shelf
Basin
Escarpment, Sea Scarp
Fracture
Trench, Abyss
National Park, Reserve
Point of Interest
Recreation Site
Cave, Cavern
Historic Site
Ruins
Wall, Walls
Church, Abbey
Temple
Scientific Station
Airport
Port
Lighthouse
Mine
Tunnel
Dam, Bridge

Bruchhausen Vilsen	12	Lb	52.50N	9.01 E
Bruchmühlbach Miesau	12	Je	49.23N	7.28 E
Bruchsal	10	Eg	49.08N	8.36 E
Bruck an der Leitha	14	Kb	48.01N	16.46 E
Bruck an der Mur	14	Jc	47.25N	15.17 E
Brue	9	Kj	51.13N	3.00W
Bruges/Brugge	11	Jc	51.13N	3.14 E
Brugg	14	Cc	47.29N	8.12 E
Brugge/Bruges	11	Jc	51.13N	3.14 E
Brugge-Assebroek	12	Fc	51.12N	3.16 E
Brüggen	12	Ic	51.15N	6.11 E
Brugge-Sint-Andries	12	Fc	51.12N	3.10 E
Brühl [Ger.]	12	Ke	49.24N	8.32 E
Brühl [Ger.]	12	Id	50.50N	6.54 E
Bruine Bank = Brown Bank (EN)	12	Fb	52.35N	3.20 E
Bruin Point	43	Ed	39.39N	110.22W
Brule River	44	Cc	45.57N	88.12W
Brumado	54	Jf	14.13S	41.40W
Brummen	12	Ib	52.06N	6.10 E
Brummo	8	Ef	58.50N	13.40 E
Brumunddal	7	Cf	60.53N	10.56 E
Bruna	14	Eh	42.45N	10.53 E
Brune	12	Fe	49.45N	3.47 E
Bruneau	46	He	42.53N	115.48W
Bruneau River	46	He	42.57N	115.58W
Bruneck / Brunico	14	Fd	46.48N	11.56 E
Brunehamel	12	Ge	49.46N	4.11 E
Brunei [5]	22	Ni	4.30N	114.40 E
Brunei, Teluk-	21	Ni	5.05N	115.18 E
Brunette Downs	59	Hc	18.38S	135.57 E
Brunflo	8	Fa	63.05N	14.49 E
Brunico / Bruneck	14	Fd	46.48N	11.56 E
Brunna	8	Ge	59.52N	17.25 E
Brunner	62	De	42.26S	171.19 E
Brunner, Lake-	62	De	42.35S	171.25 E
Brunnsberg	8	Ec	61.17N	13.55 E
Brunsbüttel	10	Fc	53.54N	9.07 E
Brunssum	12	Hd	50.57N	5.57 E
Brunswick [Ga.-U.S.]	43	Ke	31.10N	81.29W
Brunswick [Me.-U.S.]	43	Nc	43.55N	69.58W
Brunswick, Peninsula de-	52	Ik	53.30S	71.25W
Brunswick Lake	44	Fa	49.00N	83.23W
Bruntál	10	Ng	49.59N	17.28 E
Bruny Island	59	Jh	43.30S	147.05 E
Brus	15	Ef	43.23N	21.02 E
Brus, Laguna de-	49	Ef	15.50N	84.35W
Brush	43	Gc	40.15N	103.37W
Brus Laguna	49	Ef	15.47N	84.35W
Brusque	56	Kc	27.06S	48.56W
Brussel/Bruxelles = Brussels (EN)	6	Ge	50.50N	4.20 E
Brussels (EN) = Brussel/Bruxelles	6	Ge	50.50N	4.20 E
Brussels (EN) = Bruxelles/Brussel	6	Ge	50.50N	4.20 E
Brusset, 'Erg-	34	Hb	18.55N	10.30 E
Brusturi	15	Fb	47.09N	22.15 E
Brusy	10	Nc	53.53N	17.45 E
Bruxelles/Brussel = Brussels (EN)	6	Ge	50.50N	4.20 E
Bruzual	50	Bh	8.03N	69.19W
Bryan [Oh.-U.S.]	44	Ee	41.30N	84.34W
Bryan [Tx.-U.S.]	43	He	30.40N	96.22W
Bryan Coast	66	Pf	73.35S	84.00W
Bryne	7	Ag	58.44N	5.39 E
Brza Palanka	15	Fe	44.28N	22.27 E
Brzava kanal	15	Dd	45.16N	20.49 E
Brzeg	10	Nf	50.52N	17.27 E
Brzeg Dolny	10	Me	51.15N	16.40 E
Brzeziny	10	Pe	51.48N	19.46 E
Brzozów	10	Sg	49.42N	22.02 E
Bsharri	24	Ge	34.15N	36.01 E
Bû	12	Df	48.48N	1.30 E
Bua	8	Eg	57.14N	12.07 E
Buada Lagoon	64e	Ab	0.32S	166.54 E
Buala	58	Ge	8.10S	159.35 E
Bū al Ḥidān, Wādī-	33	Cd	27.25N	19.22 E
Buapinang	26	Hg	4.46S	121.34 E
Buatan	26	Df	0.44N	101.51 E
Bū aṭ Ṭifl	33	Dd	28.54N	22.30 E
Bua Yai	25	Ke	15.34N	102.24 E
Bu'ayrāt al Ḥasūn	33	Cc	31.24N	15.44 E
Bubanza	36	Ec	3.06S	29.23 E
Bubaque	34	Bc	11.17N	15.50W
Būbīyan	24	Mh	29.45N	48.15 E
Bubu	36	Gd	6.03S	35.19 E
Bubye	37	Ed	22.20S	31.07 E
Buca	15	Kk	38.22N	27.11 E
Bučač	16	De	49.04N	25.23 E
Bucačača	20	Gf	52.59N	116.55 E
Bucak	24	Dd	37.28N	30.36 E
Bucaramanga	53	Ie	7.08N	73.09W
Bucas Grande	26	Ie	9.40N	125.58 E
Buccament Bay	51n	Ba	13.12N	61.17W
Buccaneer Archipelago	59	Ec	16.17S	123.20 E
Bucecea	15	Jb	47.46N	26.26 E
Buchanan	31	Fh	5.53N	10.03W
Buchanan, Lake- [Austl.]	59	Jd	21.30S	145.50 E
Buchanan, Lake- [Tx.-U.S.]	45	Gk	30.48N	98.25W
Buchanan Bay	42	Ka	78.55N	75.00W
Buchan Gulf	42	Kb	71.48N	74.06W
Buchardo	56	Hd	34.43S	63.31W
Bucharest (EN) = Bucureşti	6	Ig	44.26N	26.06 E
Buchen	10	Fg	49.31N	9.20 E
Buchholz in der Nordheide	10	Fc	53.20N	9.52 E
Buchon, Point-	46	Ei	35.15N	120.54W
Buchs	14	Dc	47.10N	9.30 E
Buchy	12	De	49.35N	1.22 E
Bückeburg	12	Lb	52.16N	9.03 E
Buckeye	46	Ij	33.22N	112.35W
Buckhaven	9	Je	56.11N	3.03W
Buckie	9	Kd	57.40N	2.58W
Buckingham [Eng.-U.K.]	12	Bb	52.00N	0.59W
Buckingham [Que.-Can.]	44	Jc	45.35N	75.25W
Buckingham Bay	59	Hb	12.10S	135.46 E
Buckinghamshire [3]	9	Mj	51.50N	0.55W
Buckland	40	Gc	66.16N	161.20W
Buckle Island	66	Ke	66.47S	163.14 E
Buckley Bay	66	Je	68.16S	148.12 E
Bucks	9	Mj	51.50N	0.55W
Bucksport	44	Mc	44.34N	68.48W
Buco Zau	36	Bc	4.50S	12.33 E
Bu Craa	32	Ed	26.17N	12.46W
Bucureşti [2]	15	Je	44.30N	26.05 E
Bucureşti = Bucharest (EN)	6	Ig	44.26N	26.06 E
Bucy-lès-Pierrepont	12	Fe	49.39N	3.54 E
Bucyrus	44	Fe	40.47N	82.57W
Bud	7	Be	62.55N	6.55 E
Budacu, Vîrful-	15	Ib	47.07N	25.41 E
Buda-Koševelo	16	Gc	52.43N	30.39 E
Budapest [2]	10	Pi	47.30N	19.05 E
Budapest	6	Hf	47.30N	19.05 E
Búdardalur	7a	Bb	65.07N	21.46W
Budaun	25	Fc	28.03N	79.07 E
Budbud	35	He	4.13N	46.31 E
Budd Coast	66	He	66.30S	113.00 E
Buddusò	14	Di	40.35N	9.15 E
Bude [Eng.-U.K.]	9	Ik	50.50N	4.33W
Bude [Ms.-U.S.]	45	Kk	31.28N	90.51W
Bude Bay	9	Ik	50.50N	4.37W
Budel	12	Hc	51.16N	5.30 E
Budennovsk	19	Eg	44.45N	44.08 E
Budeşti	15	Je	44.14N	26.27 E
Budia	13	Jd	40.38N	2.45W
Büdingen	10	Ff	50.18N	9.07 E
Búðir	7a	Cb	64.56N	14.01W
Budjala	36	Cb	2.39N	19.42 E
Budkowiczanka	10	Nf	50.52N	17.33 E
Budogošč	7	Hg	59.19N	32.29 E
Budrio	14	Ff	44.32N	11.32 E
Budslav	8	Lj	54.49N	27.32 E
Budva	15	Bg	42.17N	18.51 E
Budyšin/Bautzen	10	Ke	51.11N	14.26 E
Budžjak	15	Lc	46.15N	28.45 E
Buea	34	Ge	4.09N	9.14 E
Buech	11	Lj	44.12N	5.57 E
Buenaventura [Col.]	53	Ie	3.53N	77.04W
Buenaventura [Mex.]	47	Cc	29.51N	107.29W
Buenaventura, Bahía de-	54	Cc	3.45N	77.15W
Buenavista	48	Ef	23.39N	109.42W
Buena Vista [Co.-U.S.]	45	Cg	38.50N	106.08W
Buena Vista [Mex.]	48	Mi	16.05N	93.00W
Buena Vista [Mex.]	48	Bb	31.10N	115.40W
Buena Vista [Ven.]	50	Eh	9.02N	63.49W
Buenavista, Bahía de-	49	Hb	22.30N	79.08W
Buendia, Embalse de-	13	Jd	40.25N	2.43W
Buenópolis	55	Jc	17.54S	44.11W
Buenos Aires [2]	56	Ie	36.00S	60.00W
Buenos Aires [Arg.]	53	Ki	34.36S	58.27W
Buenos Aires [C.R.]	49	Fi	10.04N	84.26W
Buenos Aires, Lago-	52	Ij	46.30S	72.00W
Buffalo	42	Fe	60.52N	115.03W
Buffalo [N.Y.-U.S.]	39	Le	42.54N	78.53W
Buffalo [Ok.-U.S.]	45	Gh	36.50N	99.38W
Buffalo [S.D.-U.S.]	43	Gb	45.35N	103.33W
Buffalo [Tx.-U.S.]	45	Hk	31.28N	96.04W
Buffalo [Wy.-U.S.]	43	Fc	44.21N	106.42W
Buffalo Bill Reservoir	46	Kd	44.29N	109.13W
Buffalo Lake	42	Fd	60.12N	115.25W
Buffalo Narrows	42	Ge	55.51N	108.30W
Buffalo Pound Lake	46	Ma	50.38N	105.20W
Buffels	37	Be	29.41S	17.04 E
Bū Fishah	14	En	36.18N	10.28 E
Buford	44	Fh	34.07N	84.00W
Buftea	15	Ie	44.34N	25.57 E
Bug	5	Ie	52.31N	21.05 E
Buga	54	Cc	3.55N	76.18W
Bugarach, Pech de-	11	Il	42.52N	2.23 E
Bugeat	11	Hi	45.36N	1.56 E
Bugene	36	Fc	1.35S	31.08 E
Bugey	11	Li	45.48N	5.30 E
Bugojno	23	Ff	44.03N	17.27 E
Bugøynes	7	Gb	69.58N	29.39 E
Bugrino	17	Db	68.48N	49.09 E
Bugsuk	26	Ge	8.15N	117.18 E
Bugt	27	Lb	48.47N	121.55 E
Bugulma	19	Fe	54.33N	52.48 E
Bugun	18	Hc	43.22N	70.10 E
Bugun	18	Gc	42.56N	68.36 E
Bügür/Luntai	27	Dc	41.46N	84.10 E
Buguruslan	19	Fe	53.39N	52.30 E
Buhara	22	If	39.49N	64.25 E
Buharskaja Oblast [3]	19	Gg	41.20N	64.20 E
Bū Ḥaṣā'	24	Ok	23.20N	53.20 E
Buhera	37	Ec	19.18S	31.29 E
Buh He	27	Gd	36.58N	99.48 E
Buhl	46	He	42.36N	114.46W
Bühl	10	Eh	48.42N	8.09 E
Bühödle	35	Hd	8.15N	46.20 E
Buhtarminskoje Vodohranilišče	19	If	49.10N	84.00 E
Bui Dam	34	Ed	8.22N	2.10W
Builth Wells	9	Ji	52.09N	3.24W
Buin [Chile]	56	Fd	33.44S	70.44W
Buin [Pap.N.Gui.]	60	Fi	6.50S	155.44 E
Buinsk	19	Ee	54.59N	48.17 E
Buir Nur	27	Kb	47.48N	117.42 E
Buitrago del Lozoya	13	Id	41.00N	3.38W
Buj	17	Gh	56.15N	54.12 E
Buj	19	Ed	58.29N	41.31 E
Bujalance	13	Hg	37.54N	4.22W
Bujanovac	15	Eg	42.28N	21.47 E
Bujaraloz	13	Lc	41.30N	0.09W
Buje	14	He	45.24N	13.40 E
Bujnaksk	19	Eg	42.49N	47.07 E
Bujukly	20	Jg	49.33N	142.55 E
Bujumbura	31	Ji	3.23S	29.22 E
Bujunda	20	Kd	62.00N	153.30 E
Buk	10	Md	52.22N	16.31 E
Bük	10	Mi	47.23N	16.45 E
Buk	10	Hb	54.10N	11.42 E
Buka Island	57	Ge	5.15S	154.35 E
Bukakata	36	Fc	0.18S	32.02 E
Bukama	31	Ji	9.12S	25.51 E
Buka Passage	63a	Ba	5.25S	154.41 E
Bukavu	31	Ji	2.30S	28.52 E
Bukene	36	Fc	4.14S	32.53 E
Bukhā	24	Qi	26.10N	56.09 E
Bukit Besi	26	Df	4.46N	103.12 E
Bukit Mertajam	26	De	5.22N	100.28 E
Bukittinggi	22	Mj	0.19S	100.22 E
Bükk	10	Qh	48.05N	20.30 E
Bukoba	31	Ki	1.20S	31.49 E
Bukovina	15	Ia	48.00N	25.30 E
Bukowiec	10	Ld	52.23N	15.20 E
Bukuru	34	Gd	9.48N	8.52 E
Būl, Kūh-e-	23	Hc	30.48N	52.45 E
Bulajevo	19	He	54.53N	70.26 E
Bulan	26	Hd	12.40N	123.52 E
Bulanaš	17	Kh	57.16N	62.02 E
Bulancak	24	Hb	40.57N	38.14 E
Bulanık	24	Jc	39.05N	42.15 E
Būlāq	33	Fd	25.12N	30.32 E
Bulawayo	31	Jk	20.09S	28.34 E
Buldan	24	Cc	38.03N	28.51 E
Bulgan [Mong.]	27	Hc	44.05N	103.32 E
Bulgan [Mong.]	27	Hb	48.45N	103.34 E
Bulgan [Mong.]	27	Fb	46.05N	91.34 E
Bulgar (Kujbyšev)	7	Li	55.01N	49.06 E
Bulgaria (EN) = Bălgarija [1]	6	Ig	43.00N	25.00 E
Buli	26	If	0.53N	128.18 E
Buli, Teluk-	26	If	0.45N	128.30 E
Buliluyan, Cape-	26	Ge	8.20N	117.11 E
Bulki	35	Fd	6.01N	36.36 E
Bullahār	35	Gc	10.23N	44.27 E
Bullange/Büllingen	12	Id	50.25N	6.16 E
Bullaque	13	Hf	38.59N	4.17W
Bulla Regia	14	Cn	36.33N	8.45 E
Bullas	13	Kf	38.03N	1.40W
Bulle	14	Bd	46.37N	7.04 E
Buller	62	Dd	41.44S	171.35 E
Bullfinch	59	Df	30.59S	119.06 E
Büllingen/Bullange	12	Id	50.25N	6.16 E
Bullion Mountains	46	Hi	34.25N	116.00W
Bulloo River	57	Fg	28.43S	142.30 E
Bull Point [Eng.-U.K.]	9	Ij	51.12N	4.10W
Bull Point [Falk.Is.]	56	Ih	52.19S	59.18W
Bulls	62	Fd	40.10S	175.23 E
Bulls Bay	44	Hi	32.59N	79.33W
Bull Shoals Lake	45	Jh	36.30N	92.50W
Bully Choop Mountain	46	Df	40.35N	122.45W
Bully-les-Mines	12	Ed	50.26N	2.43 E
Bulo Berde	35	He	3.52N	45.40 E
Bulolo	60	Di	7.12S	146.39 E
Bulqiza	15	Dh	41.30N	20.21 E
Bulter	45	Ig	38.16N	94.20W
Bultfontein	37	De	28.20S	26.05 E
Bulukumba	26	Hh	5.33S	120.11 E
Bulungu [Zaire]	36	Cc	4.33S	18.36 E
Bulungu [Zaire]	36	Dd	6.04S	21.54 E
Bumba	31	Jh	2.11N	22.28 E
Bumbah, Khalīj al-	33	Dc	32.25N	23.06 E
Buna	15	Ch	41.52N	19.22 E
Buna	36	Gb	2.47N	39.31 E
Bunbury	58	Ch	33.19S	115.38 E
Buncrana/Bun Cranncha	9	Ff	55.08N	7.27W
Bun Cranncha/Buncrana	9	Ff	55.08N	7.27W
Bunda	36	Fc	2.03S	33.52 E
Bundaberg	58	Gg	24.52S	152.21 E
Bünde	10	Ed	52.12N	8.35 E
Bundesrepublik Deutschland = Germany	6	Ge	51.00N	10.00 E
Bun Dobhráin/Bundoran	9	Eg	54.28N	8.17W
Bundoran/Bun Dobhráin	9	Eg	54.28N	8.17W
Bungay	12	Db	52.27N	1.27 E
Bungku	26	Hg	2.33S	121.58 E
Bungo	36	Cd	7.26S	15.24 E
Bungo Strait (EN) = Bungo-Suidō	28	Lh	32.40N	132.18 E
Bungo-Suidō = Bungo Strait (EN)	28	Lh	32.40N	132.18 E
Bungotakada	29	Be	33.33N	131.27 E
Bungsberg	10	Gb	54.12N	10.43 E
Buni	34	Hc	11.12N	12.02 E
Bunja	31	Kh	1.34N	30.15 E
Bunji	25	Ea	35.40N	74.36 E
Bunker	45	Kh	37.27N	91.13W
Bunker Group	59	Kd	23.50S	152.20 E
Bunkeya	36	Ee	10.24S	26.58 E
Bunkie	45	Jk	30.57N	92.11W
Bunnerfjällen	8	Ea	63.10N	12.34 E
Buñol	13	Le	39.25N	0.47W
Bunschoten	12	Hb	52.14N	5.24 E
Buntingford	12	Bc	51.57N	0.01W
Buntok	26	Fg	1.42S	114.48 E
Bünyan	24	Fc	38.51N	35.52 E
Bunyu, Pulau-	26	Gf	3.30N	117.50 E
Buon Me Thuot	25	Lf	12.40N	108.03 E
Buor-Haja, Guba-	20	Ib	71.00N	131.00 E
Buotama	20	Hd	61.17N	128.55 E
Buqayaq	23	Gd	25.56N	49.40 E
Buqda Kōsār	35	Ge	4.31N	44.49 E
Bur	20	Hb	71.40N	123.40 E
Bura	36	Gc	1.06S	39.57 E
Buram	31	Jg	10.49N	25.10 E
Buran	19	If	48.04N	85.15 E
Burang	27	De	30.18N	81.08 E
Burāq	24	Gf	33.10N	36.29 E
Buras	45	Ll	29.21N	89.32W
Buraydah	22	Gg	26.20N	43.59 E
Burbach	12	Kd	50.43N	8.03 E
Būrdab	35	Hd	9.05N	46.30 E
Burdekin River	59	Jc	19.39S	147.30 E
Burdēre	35	He	3.30N	45.37 E
Burdur	23	Db	37.43N	30.17 E
Burdur Gölü	24	Dd	37.44N	30.12 E
Burdwood Bank (EN)	56	Ih	54.15S	59.00W
Bure	12	Db	52.38N	1.45 E
Bure [Eth.]	35	Fd	8.20N	35.08 E
Bure [Eth.]	35	Fc	10.43N	37.03 E
Bureå	7	Ed	64.37N	21.12 E
Bureinski Hrebet = Bureya Range (EN)	21	Pd	50.40N	134.00 E
Bureja	20	Hg	49.43N	129.51 E
Bureja	21	Oe	49.25N	129.35 E
Büren	10	Ee	51.33N	8.34 E
Buren-Cogt	27	Jb	46.45N	111.30 E
Bureya Range (EN) = Bureinski Hrebet	21	Pd	50.40N	134.00 E
Burfjord	7	Fb	69.56N	22.03 E
Būr Gābo	35	Gf	1.10S	41.50 E
Burgas	6	Ig	42.30N	27.28 E
Burgas [2]	15	Kg	42.30N	27.20 E
Burgas, Gulf of- (EN) = Burgaski Zaliv	15	Kg	42.30N	27.33 E
Burgaski Zaliv = Burgas, Gulf of- (EN)	15	Kg	42.30N	27.33 E
Burg auf Fehmarn	10	Hb	54.26N	11.12 E
Burg auf Fehmarn-Puttgarden	10	Hb	54.30N	11.13 E
Burgaw	44	Ih	34.33N	77.56W
Burgaz Daği	15	Mk	38.25N	29.46 E
Burg bei Magdeburg	10	Hd	52.16N	11.51 E
Burgdorf [Ger.]	10	Gd	52.27N	10.01 E
Burgdorf [Switz.]	14	Bc	47.04N	7.37 E
Burgenland [2]	14	Kc	47.30N	16.25 E
Burgersdorp	37	Df	31.00S	26.20 E
Burgess Hill	12	Bd	50.58N	0.08W
Burgfjället	7	Dd	64.56N	15.03 E
Burghausen	10	Ih	48.10N	12.50 E
Burghūth, Sabkhat al-	24	Ie	34.58N	41.06 E
Burglengenfeld	10	Ig	49.12N	12.02 E
Burgos [3]	13	Ib	42.20N	3.40W
Burgos [Mex.]	48	Je	24.57N	98.57W
Burgos [Sp.]	6	Fg	42.21N	3.42W
Burg-Reuland	12	Id	50.12N	6.09 E
Burgsvik	7	Eh	57.03N	18.16 E
Burgundy (EN) = Bourgogne	5	Gf	47.00N	4.30 E
Burgundy (EN) = Bourgogne	11	Kg	47.00N	4.30 E
Burgwald	12	Kd	50.57N	8.48 E
Būr Hakkaba	35	Ge	2.43N	44.10 E
Burhaniye	24	Bc	39.30N	26.58 E
Burhānpur	22	Jg	21.18N	76.14 E
Burias	26	Hd	12.57N	123.08 E
Buribaj	17	Ij	51.57N	58.11 E
Burica, Punta-	47	Hg	8.03N	82.53W
Burien	46	Dc	47.27N	122.21W
Burin Peninsula	42	Lg	47.00N	55.40W
Buriram	25	Kf	14.59N	103.08 E
Buriti, Rio-	55	Ca	12.50S	58.28W
Buriti Alegre	55	Hd	18.09S	49.03W
Buriti Bravo	54	Je	5.50S	43.50W
Buriti dos Lopes	54	Jd	3.10S	41.52W
Buritis	55	Ib	15.37S	46.26W
Burj al Ḥaṭṭābah	32	Ic	30.20N	9.30 E
Burjasot	13	Le	39.31N	0.25W
Burjatija, respublika	20	Ff	53.00N	110.00 E
Burj Şāfitā	24	Ge	34.49N	36.07 E
Burkandja	20	Jd	63.27N	147.27 E
Burkburnett	45	Gi	34.06N	98.34W
Burke	45	Ge	43.11N	99.18W
Burke, Mount-	46	Ha	50.18N	114.30W
Burke Island	66	Of	73.08S	105.06W
Burke River	59	Hd	23.12S	139.33 E
Burketown	58	Ef	17.44S	139.22 E
Burkina Faso [1]	31	Gg	13.00N	2.00W
Burley	43	Ec	42.32N	113.48W
Burli	16	Rd	51.28N	52.44 E
Burlingame	45	Ig	38.45N	95.50W
Burlington [Co.-U.S.]	43	Gd	39.18N	102.16W
Burlington [Ia.-U.S.]	43	Ic	40.49N	91.07W
Burlington [Ks.-U.S.]	45	Ig	38.12N	95.45W
Burlington [N.C.-U.S.]	44	Hg	36.06N	79.26W
Burlington [Ont.-Can.]	44	Hd	43.19N	79.43W
Burlington [Vt.-U.S.]	43	Mc	44.28N	73.14W
Burlington [Wi.-U.S.]	45	Le	42.41N	88.17W
Burma [1]	22	Lg	22.00N	98.00 E
Burma [1] (Myanmar-Nainggan-Daw)	22	Lg	22.00N	98.00 E
Burnazului, Cîmpia-	15	Ie	44.10N	25.50 E
Burnett River	59	Kd	24.46S	152.25 E
Burney	46	Ef	40.53N	121.40W
Burnham Market	12	Cb	52.57N	0.44 E
Burnham-on-Crouch	12	Cc	51.37N	0.50 E
Burnie	59	Jh	41.04S	145.54 E
Burnley	9	Kh	53.48N	2.14W
Burns	43	Dc	43.35N	119.03W
Burnside	42	Gc	66.51N	108.04W
Burnside, Lake-	59	Ee	25.20S	123.10 E
Burns Lake	42	Ef	54.14N	125.46W
Burnsville	44	Fh	35.55N	82.18W
Burnt Lava Flow	46	Ef	41.35N	121.35W
Burnt River	44	Hc	44.35N	78.46W
Burntwood	42	He	56.08N	96.33W
Bur'o	31	Lh	9.30N	45.34 E
Burqin	27	Eb	47.43N	86.53 E
Burqin He	27	Eb	47.42N	86.50 E
Burqūm, Ḥarrat al-	33	He	20.54N	42.00 E
Burra	59	Hf	33.40S	138.56 E
Burragorang Lake	59	Kf	34.00S	150.25 E
Burreli	15	Ch	41.37N	20.00 E
Burrendong Reservoir	59	Jf	32.40S	149.10 E
Burriana	13	Le	39.53N	0.05W
Burro, Serranias del	48	Ic	28.50N	101.35W
Burrow Head	9	Ig	54.41N	4.24W
Bursa	22	Ee	40.11N	29.04 E
Būr Sa'īd = Port Said (EN)	31	Ke	31.16N	32.18 E
Burscheid	12	Jc	51.06N	7.07 E
Bürstadt	12	Ke	49.38N	8.27 E
Burštyn	16	De	49.16N	24.37 E
Būr Sūdān = Port Sudan (EN)	31	Kg	19.37N	37.14 E
Burt Lake	44	Ec	45.27N	84.40W
Burtnieku, Ozero-	8	Kg	57.35N	25.10 E
Burtnieku, Ozero-/Burtnieku Ezers	8	Kg	57.35N	25.10 E
Burtnieku Ezers	8	Kg	57.35N	25.10 E
Burtnieku Ezers/Burtnieku, Ozero-	8	Kg	57.35N	25.10 E
Burton	44	Fd	43.02N	83.36W
Burton Latimer	12	Bb	52.21N	0.40W
Burton-upon-Trent	9	Li	52.49N	1.36W
Burträsk	7	Ed	64.31N	20.39 E
Buru, Pulau-	57	De	3.24S	126.40 E
Burullus, Buḥayrat al-	24	Dg	31.30N	30.50 E
Burultokay/Fuhai	27	Eb	47.06N	87.23 E
Burum Gana	34	Hc	13.00N	11.57 E
Burūn, Ra's-	24	Eg	31.14N	33.04 E
Burundaj	19	Hg	43.20N	76.49 E
Burundi [1]	31	Ki	3.15S	30.00 E
Bururi	36	Ec	3.57S	29.37 E
Burutu	34	Gd	5.21N	5.31 E
Bury	9	Kh	53.36N	2.17W
Burylbajtal	18	Ib	44.56N	73.59 E
Buryn	16	Hd	51.13N	33.48 E
Bury Saint Edmunds	9	Ni	52.15N	0.43 E
Burzil Pass	25	Ff	34.54N	75.06 E
Busalla	14	Cf	44.34N	8.57 E
Busanga [Zaire]	36	Ee	10.12S	25.23 E
Busanga [Zaire]	36	Dc	0.51S	22.04 E
Busanga Swamp	36	Ee	14.10S	25.50 E
Buşayrah	24	Ie	35.09N	40.26 E
Būsh	24	Dh	29.09N	31.08 E
Būshehr [3]	23	Hd	28.00N	52.00 E
Būshgān	24	Nh	28.48N	51.42 E
Bushimaie	29	Ji	6.02S	23.45 E
Bushmanland (EN) = Boesmanland	37	Be	29.30S	19.00 E
Busia	36	Fb	0.28N	34.06 E
Busigny	12	Fd	50.02N	3.28 E
Businga	36	Db	3.20N	20.53 E
Busira	30	Ii	0.15S	18.59 E
Busk	16	Dd	50.01N	24.37 E
Buskerud [2]	7	Bf	60.30N	9.10 E
Busko-Zdrój	10	Qf	50.28N	20.44 E
Busoga [3]	36	Fb	0.45N	33.30 E
Buşrá ash Shām	24	Gf	32.31N	36.29 E
Busselton	59	Df	33.39S	115.20 E
Bussum	11	Lb	52.16N	5.10 E
Bustamante, Bahía-	56	Gg	45.07S	66.27W
Buşteni	15	Id	45.24N	25.32 E
Busto Arsizio	14	Ce	45.37N	8.51 E
Buštyna	10	Th	48.03N	23.28 E
Busuanga	26	Hd	12.05N	120.05 E
Busu-Djanoa	36	Db	1.43N	21.23 E
Büsum	10	Eb	54.08N	8.51 E
Buta	31	Jh	2.48N	24.44 E
Butajira	35	Fd	8.08N	38.27 E
Buta Ranquil	56	Ge	37.03S	69.50W
Butare	36	Ec	2.36S	29.44 E
Butaritari Atoll	57	Id	3.03N	172.49 E
Bute, Island of-	9	Hf	55.50N	5.05W
Bute Inlet	46	Ca	50.37N	124.53W
Butembo	31	Jh	0.09N	29.17 E
Butera	14	Im	37.11N	14.11 E
Butere	36	Fb	0.13N	34.30 E
Butha Qi (Zalantum)	27	Lb	48.02N	122.42 E
Buthidaung	25	Id	20.52N	92.32 E
Butiá	56	Jd	30.07S	51.58W
Butiaba	36	Fb	1.49N	31.19 E
Butler	44	He	40.51N	79.55W
Butser Hill	12	Bd	50.57N	0.59W
Butte	39	He	46.00N	112.32W
Butterworth [Mala.]	26	Df	5.25N	100.24 E
Butterworth [S.Afr.]	37	Df	32.23S	28.04 E
Button Bay	42	Ie	58.45N	94.25W
Butuan	22	Oi	8.57N	125.33 E
Butung, Palau-	21	Oj	5.00S	122.55 E
Buturlinovka	16	Ld	50.48N	40.45 E
Butzbach	12	Kd	50.26N	8.41 E
Bützow	10	Hc	53.50N	11.59 E
Buxtehude	10	Fc	53.27N	9.42 E
Buxton [Eng.-U.K.]	9	Lh	53.15N	1.55W
Buxton [N.C.-U.S.]	44	Jh	35.16N	75.32W
Buyo	34	Dd	6.16N	7.03W
Büyük Ağri Daği = Ararat, Mount- (EN)	21	Gf	39.40N	44.24 E
Büyükanafarta	15	Ji	40.17N	26.22 E
Büyükçekmece	15	Lh	41.01N	28.34 E
Büyükkariştiran	15	Kh	41.18N	27.32 E
Büyük Kemikli Burun	15	Ji	40.18N	26.14 E
Büyük Mahya	15	Kh	41.47N	27.36 E
Büyük Menderes	23	Cb	37.57N	28.58 E
Büyükorhan	15	Lj	39.45N	28.55 E
Buyun Shan	27	Lc	40.06N	122.42 E
Buzači, Poluostrov-	19	Ff	45.00N	52.00 E
Buzan	16	Pf	46.18N	49.06 E
Buzançais	11	Hh	46.53N	1.25 E
Buzancy	12	Ge	49.25N	4.57 E
Buzău [2]	15	Jd	45.09N	26.50 E
Buzău	15	Jd	45.09N	26.50 E
Buzău	15	Kd	45.26N	27.44 E
Buzaymah	33	De	24.55N	22.02 E
Buzen	29	Be	33.37N	131.08 E
Buzet	14	He	45.24N	13.59 E
Būzhān	24	Le	34.09N	47.05 E
Búzi	37	Ec	19.51S	34.30 E
Búzi	37	Ec	19.52S	34.46 E
Buziaş	15	Ed	45.39N	21.36 E
Búzios, Ilha dos-	55	Jf	23.48S	45.08W
Bužora, Gora-	10	Th	48.24N	23.15 E
Buzuluk	19	Fe	52.46N	52.17 E
Buzuluk	16	Md	50.13N	42.12 E
Buzuluk	16	Rc	52.47N	52.16 E
Buzzards Bay	44	Le	41.33N	70.47W

Index Symbols

- [1] Independent Nation
- [2] State, Region
- [3] District, County
- [4] Municipality
- [5] Colony, Dependency
- Continent
- Physical Region
- Historical or Cultural Region
- Mount, Mountain
- Volcano
- Hill
- Mountains, Mountain Range
- Hills, Escarpment
- Plateau, Upland
- Pass, Gap
- Plain, Lowland
- Delta
- Salt Flat
- Valley, Canyon
- Crater, Cave
- Karst Features
- Depression
- Polder
- Desert, Dunes
- Forest, Woods
- Heath, Steppe
- Oasis
- Cape, Point
- Coast, Beach
- Cliff
- Peninsula
- Isthmus
- Sandbank
- Island
- Atoll
- Rock, Reef
- Islands, Archipelago
- Rocks, Reefs
- Coral Reef
- Well, Spring
- Geyser
- River, Stream
- Waterfall Rapids
- River Mouth, Estuary
- Lake
- Salt Lake
- Intermittent Lake
- Reservoir
- Swamp, Pond
- Canal
- Glacier
- Ice Shelf, Pack Ice
- Ocean
- Sea
- Gulf, Bay
- Strait, Fjord
- Lagoon
- Bank
- Seamount
- Tablemount
- Ridge
- Shelf
- Basin
- Escarpment, Sea Scarp
- Fracture
- Trench, Abyss
- National Park, Reserve
- Point of Interest
- Recreation Site
- Cave, Cavern
- Historic Site
- Ruins
- Wall, Walls
- Church, Abbey
- Temple
- Scientific Station
- Airport
- Port
- Lighthouse
- Mine
- Tunnel
- Dam, Bridge

Bwagaoia 63a Ad 10.42S 152.50 E
Byälven 8 Ee 59.06N 12.54 E
Byam Martin 42 Ha 75.15N 104.15W
Byam Martin Channel 42 Ha 76.00N 105.00W
Bychawa 10 Se 51.01N 22.32 E
Byczyna 10 Oe 51.07N 18.11 E
Bydgoszcz [2] 10 Nc 53.10N 18.00 E
Bydgoszcz 6 He 53.08N 18.00 E
Byelarus' =
Belarus (EN) 19 Ce 53.50N 28.00 E
Bygdin 8 Cc 61.20N 8.35 E
Bygland [Nor.] 7 Bg 58.51N 7.51 E
Bygland [Nor.] 8 Bf 58.41N 7.48 E
Byglandsfjorden 8 Bf 58.50N 7.50 E
Byhov 19 De 53.31N 30.15 E
Byk 15 Mc 46.55N 29.25 E
Bykovec 15 Lb 47.12N 28.18 E
Bykovo 16 Ne 49.47N 45.25 E
Bykovski 20 Hb 71.56N 129.05 E
Bylot 38 Lb 73.13N 78.34W
Byrd, Cape- 66 Qe 69.38S 76.07W
Byrdbreen 66 Df 71.35S 26.00 E
Byrd Glacier 66 Jg 80.15S 160.20 E
Byron, Cape- 57 Gg 28.39S 153.38 E
Byron Bay 42 Gc 68.55N 108.25W
Byron Bay 59 Ke 28.39S 153.37 E
Byrranga Gory=Byrranga
Mountains (EN) 21 Mb 75.00N 104.00 E
Byrranga Mountains (EN)=
Byrranga Gory 21 Mb 75.00N 104.00 E
Bystraja 20 Kf 52.40N 156.10 E
Bystreyca 10 Se 51.40N 22.33 E
Bystřice 10 Lf 50.11N 15.30 E
Bystrovka 18 Jc 42.45N 75.43 E
Bystrzyca [Pol.] 10 Se 51.16N 22.45 E
Bystrzyca [Pol.] 10 Me 51.13N 16.54 E
Bystrzyca Kłodzka 10 Mf 50.19N 16.39 E
Bytantaj 20 Ic 68.40N 134.50 E
Bytča 10 Og 49.14N 18.35 E
Byten 10 Vd 52.49N 25.33 E
Bytom 10 Of 50.22N 18.54 E
Bytów 10 Nb 54.11N 17.30 E
Byumba 36 Fc 1.35S 30.04 E
Byxelkrok 7 Dh 57.20N 17.00 E
Bzura 10 Qd 52.23N 20.09 E
Bzyb 16 Lh 43.12N 40.15 E

C

Cà, Sông- 25 Le 18.40N 105.40 E
Caacupé 56 Ic 25.23S 57.09W
Čaadajevka 16 Nc 53.09N 45.56 E
Caaguazú 56 Ic 25.26S 56.02W
Caaguazú [3] 55 Eg 25.00S 55.45W
Caála 36 Ce 12.55S 15.35 E
Caapucú 55 Dh 26.13S 57.12W
Caarapó 55 Ef 22.38S 54.48W
Caatinga 54 Ig 17.10S 45.53W
Caatinga 52 Lf 9.00S 42.00W
Caatinga, Rio- 55 Jc 17.10S 45.52W
Caazapá [3] 55 Dh 26.10S 56.00W
Caazapá 56 Ic 26.09S 56.24W
Cabaçal, Rio- 55 Db 16.00S 57.42W
Cabadbaran 26 Ie 9.10N 125.38 E
Cabaiguán 49 Hb 22.05N 79.30W
Caballeria, Cabo de- 13 Qd 40.05N 4.05 E
Caballo Cocha 54 Dd 3.54S 70.32W
Caballo Reservoir 45 Cj 32.58N 107.18W
Cabañas 13 Jg 37.40N 3.00W
Cabanatuan 22 Oh 15.29N 120.58 E
Cabano 44 Mb 47.41N 68.54W
Čabar 14 Ie 45.36N 14.39 E
Cabeceira do Apa 55 Ef 22.01S 55.46W
Cabeceiras 55 Ib 15.48S 46.59W
Cabeceiras de Basto 13 Ec 41.31N 7.59W
Cabeza, Arrecife- 48 Lh 19.04N 95.50W
Cabeza de Buey 13 Gf 38.43N 5.13W
Cabildo 55 Bn 38.29S 61.54W
Cabimas 53 Id 10.23N 71.28W
Cabinda 31 Ii 5.35S 12.13 E
Cabinda [3] 36 Bd 5.00S 12.30 E
Cabinet Mountains 46 Hb 48.08N 115.46W
Cabo Bojador 32 Ed 26.08N 14.30W
Cabo Frio 53 Lh 22.53S 42.01W
Cabo Gracias a Dios 49 Ff 14.59N 83.10W
Cabonga, Réservoir- 42 Jg 47.20N 76.35W
Caboolture 59 Ke 27.05S 152.50 E
Cabora Bassa, Dique de- 37 Ec 15.34S 32.42 E
Cabora Bassa, Lago-=
Cabora Bassa, Lake-(EN)
30 Kj 15.40S 31.40 E
Cabora Bassa, Lake-(EN)=
Cabora Bassa, Lago- 30 Kj 15.40S 31.40 E
Caborca 47 Bb 30.37N 112.06W
Cabot Strait 38 Ne 47.20N 59.30W
Cabourg 11 Fe 49.17N 0.08W
Cabo Verde=Cape Verde
(EN) [1] 31 Eg 16.00N 24.00W
Cabo Verde, Ilhas do-=Cape
Verde Islands (EN) 30 Eg 16.00N 24.10W
Cabra 13 Hg 37.28N 4.27W
Cabral, Serra do- 55 Jc 17.45S 44.22W
Cabras 14 Ck 39.56N 8.32 E
Cabras, Stagno di- 14 Ck 39.55N 8.30 E
Cabreira 13 Dc 41.39N 8.04W
Cabrejas, Puerto de- 13 Jd 40.08N 2.25W
Cabrera 49 Md 19.38N 69.54W
Cabrera, Isla- 13 Oe 39.09N 2.56 E
Cabrera, Sierra de la- 13 Fb 42.10N 6.25W
Cabri 46 Ka 50.37N 108.28W
Cabriel 13 Ke 39.14N 1.03W
Cabrit, Ilet 'a- 51e Ac 15.53N 61.36W
Cabrits, Ilet- 51h Bc 14.23N 60.52W
Cabrón, Cabo- 49 Md 19.22N 69.12W
Cabruta 50 Ci 7.38N 66.15W
Čabulja 14 Lg 43.30N 17.35 E
Cabure 49 Mh 11.08N 69.38W
Cacacas, Islas- 50 Dg 10.22N 64.26W
Caçador 56 Jc 26.47S 51.00W
Čačak 15 Df 43.54N 20.21 E
Caçapava dó Sul 56 Jd 30.30S 53.30W
Caccamo 14 Hm 37.56N 13.40 E
Caccia, Capo- 14 Cj 40.34N 8.09 E
Cacequi 55 Ei 29.53S 54.49W
Cáceres [3] 13 Ge 39.40N 6.00W
Cáceres [Braz.] 53 Kg 16.04S 57.41W
Cáceres [Sp.] 13 Fe 39.29N 6.22W
Cáceres, Laguna- 55 Dd 18.56S 57.48W
Cachari 56 Ie 36.24S 59.32W
Cache Peak 46 Ie 42.11N 113.40W
Cacheu 34 Bc 12.10N 16.21W
Cachimbo 53 Kf 9.08S 55.10W
Cachimbo, Serra do- 52 Kf 8.30S 55.50W
Cachimo 36 Dd 8.20S 21.21 E
Cáchira 49 Kj 7.46N 73.03W
Cáchira, Rio- 49 Kj 7.52N 73.40W
Cachoeira 54 Kf 12.36S 38.58W
Cachoeira Alta 55 Gd 18.48S 50.58W
Cachoeira de Goiás 55 Gc 16.44S 50.38W
Cachoeira do Arari 54 Id 1.01S 48.58W
Cachoeira do Sul 56 Jc 29.58S 52.54W
Cachoeira Dourada, Represa
de- 54 Ig 18.30S 49.00W
Cachoeirinha 55 Gi 29.57S 51.05W
Cachoeiro de Itapemirim 54 Jh 20.51S 41.06W
Cacinbinho 55 Ee 21.50S 55.43W
Căciulaţi 15 Je 44.38N 26.10 E
Cacolo 36 Ce 10.08S 19.18 E
Caconda 36 Ce 13.45S 15.05 E
Cacuaco 36 Bd 8.47S 13.21 E
Cacuchi 36 Ce 14.23S 16.59 E
Cacula 36 Be 14.29S 14.10 E
Caculé 54 Jf 14.30S 42.13W
Caculuvar 36 Bf 16.46S 14.56 E
Cacuso 36 Cd 9.26S 15.45 E
Čadan 20 Ef 51.17N 91.40 E
Cadaqués 13 Pb 42.17N 3.17 E
Čadca 10 Og 49.26N 18.48 E
Caddo Lake 45 Ij 32.42N 94.01W
Cadena Costero Catalana/
Serralada Litoral Catalana
=Catalan Coastal Range
(EN) 5 Gg 41.35N 1.40 E
Cadereyta Jiménez 48 Ie 25.36N 100.00W
Cadí, Serra del-/Cadí, Sierra
del- 13 Nb 42.17N 1.42 E
Cadibarrawirracanna, Lake-
59 He 28.50S 135.25 E
Cadibona, Colle di- 14 Cf 44.20N 8.22 E
Cadillac [Fr.] 11 Fj 44.38N 0.19W
Cadillac [Mi.-U.S.] 43 Jc 44.15N 85.24W
Cadí, Sierra del/Cadí, Serra
del- 13 Nb 42.17N 1.42 E
Cadiz 26 Hd 10.57N 123.18 E
Cádiz [3] 13 Gh 36.30N 5.45W
Cádiz 6 Fh 36.32N 6.18W
Cadiz [Ca.-U.S.] 46 Hi 34.30N 115.30W
Cadiz [Ky.-U.S.] 44 Dg 36.52N 87.50W
Cádiz, Bahía de- 13 Fh 36.32N 6.16W
Cádiz, Golfo de- 5 Fh 36.50N 7.10W
Cadiz Lake 46 Hi 34.18N 115.24W
Cadore 14 Gd 46.30N 12.20 E
Cadwell 43 Dc 43.40N 116.41W
Čadyr-Lunga 16 Ff 46.04N 28.52 E
Caen 6 Ff 49.11N 0.21W
Caen, Campagne de- 11 Fe 49.05N 0.20W
Caernarvon 9 Ih 53.08N 4.16W
Caernarvon Bay 9 Ih 53.05N 4.30W
Caerphilly 9 Jj 51.35N 3.14W
Caetité 54 Jf 14.04S 42.29W
Cafayate 56 Gc 26.05S 65.58W
Cafelândia [Braz.] 55 Fc 16.40S 53.25W
Cafelândia [Braz.] 55 Ie 21.49S 49.35W
Cafundó, Serra do- 55 Hb 14.40S 48.23W
Čagan 19 He 50.30N 79.10 E
Cagan-Aman 16 Ff 47.32N 46.43 E
Cagan-Nur [Mong.] 27 Eb 49.40N 89.55 E
Cagan-Nur [Mong.] 27 Ia 50.25N 105.15 E
Cagan-Ula 27 Gb 49.35N 98.25 E
Cagatá, Arroyo- 55 Df 23.26S 56.36W
Cagayan 26 Hc 18.22N 121.37 E
Cagayan de Oro 22 Oi 8.29N 124.39 E
Cagayan Islands 26 He 9.40N 121.16 E
Cagayan Sulu 26 Ge 7.01N 118.30 E
Čagda 20 Ie 58.42N 130.37 E
Cageri 16 Mh 42.39N 42.42 E
Çağış 15 Lj 39.30N 28.01 E
Cagli 14 Gg 43.33N 12.39 E
Cagliari 6 Gh 39.13N 9.07 E
Cagliari, Golfo di- 14 Dk 39.10N 9.10 E
Cagliari, Stagno di- 14 Dk 39.15N 9.05 E
Čaglinka 17 Nj 53.59N 69.47 E
Cagnes-sur-Mer 11 Nk 43.40N 7.09 E
Čagoda 7 Ig 59.12N 35.13 E
Čagodošča 7 Ig 58.58N 36.37 E
Caguas 47 Ke 18.14N 66.02W
Čagyl 19 Fg 40.43N 55.25 E
Cahama 36 Bf 16.16S 14.17 E
Caha Mountains/An
Cheacha 9 Dj 51.45N 9.45W
Caher/An Chathair 9 Fi 52.22N 7.55W
Cahersiveen/Cathair
Saidhbhin 9 Cj 51.57N 10.13W
Cahore Point/Rinn
Chathóir 9 Gi 52.34N 6.11W
Cahors 11 Hj 44.26N 1.26 E
Cai, Rio- 55 Gi 29.56S 51.16W
Caia 37 Fc 17.49S 35.20 E
Caia 13 Ef 38.50N 7.05W
Caiabis, Serra dos- 54 Gf 11.40S 56.30W
Caiapó, Rio- 55 Gb 15.49S 51.53W
Caiapó, Serra do- 52 Kg 17.00S 52.00W
Caiapônia 55 Gc 16.57S 51.49W
Caibarién 47 Id 22.31N 79.28W
Caiçara 55 Gb 15.34S 50.12W
Caicara 54 Eb 7.37N 66.10W
Caicara de Maturin 50 Eh 9.49N 63.36W
Caicó 54 Ke 6.27S 37.06W
Caicos Bank (EN) 47 Jd 21.35N 71.55W
Caicos Islands 38 Lg 21.45N 71.35W
Caicos Passage 47 Jd 22.00N 72.30W
Caille Island 51p Bb 12.17N 61.35W
Caimanera 49 Jd 19.59N 75.09W
Caine, Rio- 54 Eg 18.23S 65.21W
Cai Nuoc 25 Lg 8.56N 105.01 E
Caird Coast 66 Af 76.00S 24.30W
Cairngorms Mountains 9 Jd 57.06N 3.30W
Cairns 58 Ff 16.55S 145.46 E
Cairo [Ga.-U.S.] 44 Ej 30.53N 84.12W
Cairo [Il.-U.S.] 43 Jd 37.00N 89.11W
Cairo (EN)=Al Qāhirah 31 Ke 30.03N 31.15 E
Cairo Montenotte 14 Cf 44.24N 8.16 E
Caiseal/Cashel 9 Fi 52.31N 7.53W
Caisleán an Bharraigh/
Castlebar 9 Dh 53.52N 9.17W
Caister-on-Sea 12 Db 52.40N 1.45 E
Caiundo 36 Cf 15.42S 17.27 E
Caiúva, Lagoa- 55 Fk 32.24S 52.30W
Caiyuanzhen → Shengsi 28 Gi 30.42N 122.29 E
Caizi Hu 28 Di 30.48N 117.05 E
Čaja 20 De 58.17N 82.45 E
Cajabamba 54 Ce 7.58S 77.59W
Caja de Muertos, Isla- 51a Bc 17.53N 66.31W
Cajamarca 53 If 7.10S 78.31W
Cajamarca [2] 54 Ce 6.15S 78.50W
Cajapió 54 Jd 2.58S 44.48W
Cajarc 11 Hj 44.29N 1.51 E
Cajatambo 54 Cf 10.29S 77.02W
Čajkovski 19 Fd 56.47N 54.09 E
Çakırgöl Dağ 24 Hb 40.34N 39.42 E
Çakmak 24 Fd 37.37N 34.19 E
Çakmak Dağı 24 Jc 39.46N 42.12 E
Čakor 15 Dg 42.40N 20.02 E
Čakovec 14 Kd 46.23N 16.26 E
Čakrani 15 Ci 40.36N 19.37 E
Çal 24 Cc 38.05N 29.24 E
Cal, Rio de la- 55 Cc 17.27S 58.15W
Calabar 31 Hh 4.57N 8.19 E
Calabozo 54 Eb 8.56N 67.26W
Calabozo, Ensenada de- 49 Lh 11.30N 71.45W
Calabria [2] 14 Kl 39.00N 16.30 E
Calaburras, Punta de- 13 Hh 36.30N 4.38W
Calacoto 54 Eg 17.18S 68.39W
Calacuccia 11a Ba 42.20N 9.01 E
Calaf 13 Nc 41.44N 1.31 E
Calafat 15 Ff 43.59N 22.56 E
Calafate 53 Ik 50.20S 72.16W
Cala Figuera, Cabo de- 13 Oe 39.27N 2.31 E
Calagua Islands 26 Hd 14.27N 122.55 E
Calahorra 13 Kb 42.18N 1.58W
Calai 36 Cf 17.50S 19.20 E
Calais [Fr.] 6 Ge 50.57N 1.50 E
Calais [Me.-U.S.] 44 Nc 45.11N 67.17W
Calais, Pas de-=Dover,
Strait of- (EN) 5 Ge 51.00N 1.30 E
Calakmul 48 Oh 18.05N 89.55W
Calalaste, Sierra de- 56 Gc 25.30S 67.30W
Calama 53 Jh 22.28S 68.56W
Calamar 49 Jh 10.14N 74.56W
Calamian Group 21 Nh 12.00N 120.00 E
Calamocha 13 Kd 40.55N 1.18W
Călan 15 Fd 45.44N 22.59 E
Calanda 13 Ld 40.56N 0.14W
Calang 26 Cf 4.30N 95.40 E
Calangiánus 14 Dj 40.56N 9.11 E
Calapan 26 Hd 13.25N 121.10 E
Calar Alto 13 Jg 37.15N 2.25W
Călăraşi 15 Ke 44.12N 27.20 E
Cala Ratjada 13 Pe 39.42N 3.25 E
Calar del Mundo 13 Jf 38.31N 2.28W
Calatafimi 14 Gm 37.55N 12.52 E
Calatañazor 13 Jc 41.42N 2.49W
Calatayud 13 Kc 41.21N 1.38W
Calatrava 13 If 38.35N 3.48W
Calatrava, Campo de- 13 Hf 38.50N 4.15W
Calavà, Capo- 14 Il 38.10N 14.55 E
Calavon 11 Kk 43.51N 5.00 E
Calayan 26 Hc 19.20N 121.27 E
Calbayog 22 Oh 12.04N 124.36 E
Calchaqui 56 Hc 29.54S 60.18W
Calçoene 54 Hc 2.30N 50.57W
Calcutta 22 Kg 22.32N 88.22 E
Caldaro / Kaltern 14 Fd 46.25N 11.14 E
Caldas [2] 54 Cb 5.15N 75.30W
Caldas da Rainha 13 Ce 39.24N 9.08W
Caldas Novas 55 Hc 17.45S 48.38W
Caldeirão, Serra de- 13 Dg 37.19N 8.04W
Calder 9 Lh 53.44N 1.21W
Caldera 56 Fc 27.04S 70.50W
Calderina, Sierra de la- 13 Ie 39.19N 3.48W
Caldes de Mombúy 13 Oc 41.38N 2.10 E
Caldwell 44 Gf 39.44N 81.32W
Caledon 37 Bf 34.12S 19.23 E
Caledon 30 Jl 30.32S 26.05 E
Caledonia [Blz.] 49 Cd 18.14N 88.29W
Caledonia [Mn.-U.S.] 45 Ke 43.38N 91.29W
Caledonian Canal 9 Id 57.20N 4.30W
Calella 13 Oc 41.37N 2.40 E
Caleta Olivia 56 Gg 46.26S 67.32W
Calexico 46 Hj 32.40N 115.30W
Çalgal Dağı 24 Hc 39.06N 38.05 E
Calgary 39 Hd 51.03N 114.05W
Calhoun 44 Eh 34.30N 84.57W
Cali 53 Ie 3.27N 76.31W
Calicut (Kozhikode) 22 Jh 11.19N 75.46 E
Caliente 43 Ed 37.37N 114.31W
California [2] 43 Dd 37.30N 119.30W
California, Golfo de-=
California, Gulf of- (EN) 38 Hg 28.00N 112.00W
California, Gulf of- (EN)=
California, Golfo de- 38 Hg 28.00N 112.00W
Căliman, Munţii- 15 Ib 47.07N 25.03 E
Călimăneşti 15 Hd 45.14N 24.20 E
Calimere, Point- 25 Ff 10.18N 79.52 E
Calingasta 56 Gd 31.19S 69.25W
Calispell Peak 46 Gb 48.26N 117.30W
Calitri 14 Jj 40.54N 15.26 E
Calitzdorp 37 Cf 33.33S 21.42 E
Caliviny 51p Bb 12.01N 61.43W
Calixtlahuaca 48 Jh 19.15N 99.45W
Calka 16 Ni 41.35N 44.05 E
Calkini 48 Ng 20.22N 90.03W
Callabonna, Lake- 59 Ie 29.45S 140.05 E
Callac 11 Cf 48.24N 3.26W
Callaghan, Mount- 46 Gg 39.42N 116.57W
Callainn/Callan 9 Fi 52.33N 7.23W
Callan/Callainn 9 Fi 52.33N 7.23W
Callander [Ont.-Can.] 44 Hb 46.13N 79.23W
Callander [Scot.-U.K.] 9 Ie 56.15N 4.13W
Callantsoog 12 Gb 52.50N 4.41 E
Callao 53 Ig 12.02S 77.05W
Callao [2] 54 Cf 2.04S 77.09W
Calliaqua 51n Ba 13.08N 61.12W
Callosa de Ensarriá 13 Lf 38.39N 0.07W
Callosa de Segura 13 Lf 38.08N 0.52W
Calmalli 48 Cc 28.14N 113.33W
Călmăţui [Rom.] 15 If 43.46N 25.10 E
Călmăţui [Rom.] 15 Ke 44.50N 27.50 E
Calonne 12 Ce 49.17N 0.12 E
Calore 14 Ii 41.11N 14.28 E
Čalovo → Veľký Meder 10 Ni 47.52N 17.47 E
Calpe 13 Mf 38.39N 0.03 E
Caltabellotta 14 Hm 37.34N 13.13 E
Caltagirone 14 Im 37.14N 14.31 E
Caltanissetta 14 Im 37.29N 14.04 E
Caltilibük 15 Lj 39.57N 28.36 E
Čaltyr 16 Kf 47.17N 39.29 E
Caluago 36 Cd 8.15S 19.38 E
Calucinga 36 Ce 11.19S 16.13 E
Călugareni 15 Ie 44.11N 25.59 E
Calulo 36 Bd 9.59S 14.54 E
Caluquembe 36 Be 13.46S 14.41 E
Calvados [3] 11 Fe 49.10N 0.30W
Calvados, Côte du- 11 Fe 49.22N 0.30W
Calvert Island 46 Ba 51.35N 128.00W
Calvert River 59 Hc 16.17S 137.44 E
Calvi 11a Aa 42.34N 8.45 E
Calvillo 48 Hg 21.51N 102.43W
Calvinia 31 Il 31.25S 19.45 E
Calvitero 13 Gd 40.20N 5.43W
Cam 9 Ni 52.21N 0.15 E
Camabatela 36 Cd 8.13S 15.23 E
Camacã 54 Kg 15.24S 39.30W
Camacupa 36 Ce 12.01S 17.22 E
Camaguán 50 Ch 8.06N 67.36W
Camagüey [3] 49 Ic 21.30N 78.10W
Camagüey 39 Lg 21.23N 77.55W
Camagüey, Archipiélago de-
47 Id 22.18N 78.00W
Camaiore 14 Eg 43.56N 10.18 E
Camajuani 49 Hb 22.28N 79.44W
Camamu 54 Kf 13.57S 39.07W
Camaná 54 Dg 16.37S 72.42W
Camapuã 55 Ed 19.30S 54.05W
Camapuã, Sertão de- 52 Kg 19.00S 51.30W
Camaquã 56 Jd 30.51S 51.49W
Camaquã, Rio- 55 Gj 31.17S 51.47W
Camarat, Cap- 11 Mk 43.12N 6.41 E
Camargo [Bol.] 54 Eh 20.39S 65.13W
Camargo [Sp.] 13 Ia 43.24N 3.54W
Camargos, Represa- 55 Je 21.20S 44.30W
Camargue 11 Kk 43.31N 4.34 E
Camariñas 13 Ca 43.07N 9.10W
Camarón, Cabo- 47 He 16.00N 85.04W
Camarones 56 Gf 44.48S 65.42W
Camarones, Bahía- 56 Gf 44.45S 65.34W
Camas [Sp.] 13 Fg 37.24N 6.02W
Camas [Wa.-U.S.] 46 Dd 45.35N 122.24W
Camatagua, Embalse de- 50 Ch 9.48N 66.55W
Ca Mau, Mui-=Ca Mau
Point (EN) 21 Mi 8.38N 104.44 E
Ca Mau Point (EN)=Ca
Mau, Mui- 21 Mi 8.38N 104.44 E
Cambados 13 Db 42.30N 8.48W
Camberg 12 Kd 50.18N 8.16 E
Camberley 12 Bc 51.21N 0.44W
Cambo 36 Cd 7.40S 17.17 E
Cambodia (EN) =
Kampuchea 22 Mh 13.00N 105.00 E
Cambo-les-Bains 11 Ek 43.22N 1.24W
Cambrai 11 Jd 50.10N 3.14 E
Cambremer 12 Ce 49.09N 0.03 E
Cambrésis 12 Fd 50.15N 3.05 E
Cambrian Mountains 5 Fe 52.35N 3.35W
Cambridge 9 Ni 52.25N 0.10 E
Cambridge [Eng.-U.K.] 9 Ni 52.12N 0.07 E
Cambridge [Id.-U.S.] 46 Gd 44.34N 116.41W
Cambridge [Ma.-U.S.] 44 Ld 42.22N 71.06W
Cambridge [Md.-U.S.] 44 If 38.34N 76.04W
Cambridge [Mn.-U.S.] 45 Jd 45.31N 93.14W
Cambridge [N.Z.] 62 Fb 37.53S 175.28 E
Cambridge [Oh.-U.S.] 44 Ge 40.02N 81.36W
Cambridge Airport 12 Cb 52.10N 0.08 E
Cambridge Bay 39 Ic 69.03N 105.05W
Cambridge Gulf 59 Fb 14.55S 128.15 E
Cambridgeshire [3] 9 Mi 52.25N 0.05W
Cambutal, Cerro- 49 Gj 7.16N 80.36W
Camden [Al.-U.S.] 44 Dj 32.00N 87.17W
Camden [Ar.-U.S.] 43 Ie 33.35N 92.50W
Camden [N.J.-U.S.] 44 Jf 39.57N 75.07W
Camden [S.C.-U.S.] 44 Gh 34.16N 80.36W
Camden [Tn.-U.S.] 44 Cg 36.04N 88.06W
Camden Bay 40 Kb 70.00N 145.00W
Camdenton 45 Jg 38.00N 92.45W
Camel 9 Ik 50.33N 4.55W
Çameli 24 Cd 37.05N 29.20 E
Camerino 14 Hg 43.08N 13.04 E
Cameron 42 Ha 76.15N 104.00W
Cameron [Az.-U.S.] 46 Ji 35.51N 111.25W
Cameron [La.-U.S.] 45 Jl 29.48N 93.19W
Cameron [Mo.-U.S.] 45 Ig 39.44N 94.14W
Cameron [Tx.-U.S.] 45 Hk 30.51N 96.59W
Cameron [Wi.-U.S.] 45 Kd 45.25N 91.44W
Cameron Hills 42 Fe 60.00N 118.00W
Cameron Mountains 62 Bf 46.00S 166.55 E
Cameroon (EN)=
Cameroun [1] 31 Ih 6.00N 12.00 E
Cameroon, Mount- (EN)=
Cameroun 30 Hh 4.12N 9.11 E
Camerota 14 Jj 40.02N 15.22 E
Cameroun=Cameroon (EN)
[1] 31 Ih 6.00N 12.00 E
Cameroun=Cameroon,
Mount-(EN) 30 Hh 4.12N 9.11 E
Cametá 54 Id 2.15S 49.30W
Camiguin [Phil.] 26 Hc 18.56N 121.55 E
Camiling 26 Hc 15.42N 120.24 E
Camilla 44 Ej 31.14N 84.12W
Caminha 13 Dc 41.52N 8.50W
Camissombo 36 Dd 8.10S 20.39 E
Camoapa 49 Eg 12.23N 85.31W
Camocim 53 Lf 2.54S 40.50W
Camonica, Val- 14 Ed 46.00N 10.20 E
Camooweal 59 Hc 19.55S 138.07 E
Camopi 54 Hc 3.13N 52.28W
Camorta 25 Ig 8.08N 93.30 E
Campagne-lès-Hesdin 12 Dd 50.24N 1.52 E
Campana 55 Cl 34.10S 58.57W
Campana, Isla- 52 Ij 48.20S 75.15W
Campanario 13 Gf 38.52N 5.37W
Campanário 55 Ef 22.48S 55.03W
Campania [2] 14 Ii 41.00N 14.30 E
Campanquiz, Cerros- 54 Cd 4.30S 77.40W
Campbell, Cape- 62 Fd 41.44S 174.16 E
Campbell Island 62 Ci 52.30S 169.10 E
Campbell Plateau (EN) 57 Ij 51.00S 170.00 E
Campbell River 42 Ef 50.01N 125.15W
Campbellsville 44 Eg 37.21N 85.20W
Campbellton 42 Kg 48.00N 66.40W
Campbelltown, Sydney- 59 Kf 34.04S 150.49 E
Campbeltown 9 Hf 55.26N 5.36W
Campeche 39 Jh 19.51N 90.32W
Campeche [2] 47 Fe 19.00N 90.30W
Campeche, Bahía de-=
Campeche, Gulf of- (EN)
38 Jg 20.00N 94.00W
Campeche, Gulf of- (EN)=
Campeche, Bahía de- 38 Jg 20.00N 94.00W
Campeche Bank (EN) 47 Fd 22.00N 90.00W
Campechuela 49 Ic 20.14N 77.17W
Camperdown 59 Ig 38.14S 143.09 E
Campidano 14 Ck 39.30N 8.45 E
Campiglia Marittima 14 Eg 43.03N 10.37 E
Campillos 13 Hg 37.03N 4.51W
Campina Grande 53 Mf 7.13S 35.53W
Campinas 53 Lh 22.54S 47.05W
Campina Verde 55 Hd 19.31S 49.28W
Campine/Kempen 11 Lc 51.10N 5.20 E
Campinorte 55 Hb 14.20S 49.08W
Campione d'Italia 14 Ce 45.59N 8.59 E
Campo 34 Ge 2.22N 9.49 E
Campo Alegre 50 Bh 9.15N 68.25W
Campo Alegre de Goiás 55 Ic 17.36S 47.46W
Campobasso 14 Ii 41.34N 14.39 E
Campo Belo 55 Je 20.53S 45.16W
Campo de Criptana 13 Ie 39.24N 3.07W
Campo de la Cruz 49 Jh 10.23N 74.52W
Campo del Cielo 55 Bh 27.53S 61.49W
Campo Florido 55 Hd 19.46S 48.34W
Campo Formoso 54 Jf 10.31S 40.20W
Campo Gallo 56 Hc 26.35S 62.51W
Campo Garay 55 Bi 29.41S 61.37W
Campo Grande [Arg.] 55 Eh 27.13S 54.58W
Campo Grande [Braz.] 53 Kh 20.27S 54.37W
Campo Largo [Arg.] 55 Bh 26.48S 60.50W
Campo Largo [Braz.] 55 Hg 25.26S 49.32W
Campo Maior [Braz.] 54 Jd 4.49S 42.10W
Campo Maior [Port.] 13 Ee 39.01N 7.04W
Campomarino 14 Ji 41.57N 15.02 E
Campo Mourão 56 Jb 24.03S 52.22W
Campos 53 Lh 21.45S 41.18W
Campos [Braz.] 52 Lg 15.00S 44.30W
Campos [Braz.] 52 Kh 21.00S 51.00W
Campos, Laguna- 55 Be 20.50S 61.31W
Campos, Tierra de- 13 Hb 42.10N 4.50W
Campos Altos 55 Id 19.41S 46.10W
Campos Belos 55 Ia 13.03S 46.53W
Campos do Jordão 55 Jf 22.44S 45.35W
Campos Novos 55 Gh 27.24S 51.12W
Campos Sales 54 Je 7.04S 40.23W
Campo Tures / Sand in
Taufers 14 Fd 46.55N 11.57 E
Camp Verde 43 Ee 34.34N 111.51W
Cam Ranh 25 Lf 11.54N 109.13 E
Camrose 42 Gf 53.01N 112.50W
Camseil 42 Fc 65.40N 118.07W
Camsell Portage 42 Ge 59.38N 109.42W
Çan 24 Bb 40.02N 27.03 E
Canaan [Ct.-U.S.] 44 Kd 42.02N 73.20W
Canaan [Trin.] 50 Fg 11.09N 60.49W
Canaan Mountain 46 Jh 37.45N 111.51W
Cana Brava, Ribeirão- 55 Ic 16.35S 46.34W
Cana Brava, Rio- [Braz.] 55 Ib 14.40S 47.07W
Cana Brava, Rio- [Braz.] 55 Ha 12.12S 48.40W
Cana Brava, Rio- [Braz.] 55 Ha 13.11S 48.11W
Canada [1] 39 Jc 60.00N 95.00W
Cañada 13 Fb 42.50N 6.05W
Canada Basin (EN) 67 Ad 80.00N 145.00W
Cañada de Gomez 56 Hd 32.49S 61.24W
Canadian 45 Fi 35.55N 100.23W
Canadian River 38 Jf 35.27N 95.03W
Canaguá, Rio- 49 Mj 7.57N 69.36W
Canaima 54 Db 9.49N 70.56W

Index Symbols

[1] Independent Nation
[2] State, Region
[3] District, County
[4] Municipality
[5] Colony, Dependency
Continent
Physical Region
Historical or Cultural Region
Mount, Mountain
Volcano
Hill
Mountains, Mountain Range
Hills, Escarpment
Plateau, Upland
Pass, Gap
Plain, Lowland
Delta
Salt Flat
Valley, Canyon
Crater, Cave
Karst Features
Depression
Polder
Desert, Dunes
Forest, Woods
Heath, Steppe
Oasis
Cape, Point
Coast, Beach
Cliff
Peninsula
Isthmus
Sandbank
Island
Atoll
Rock, Reef
Islands, Archipelago
Rocks, Reefs
Coral Reef
Well, Spring
Geyser
River, Stream
Waterfall Rapids
River Mouth, Estuary
Lake
Salt Lake
Intermittent Lake
Reservoir
Swamp, Pond
Canal
Glacier
Ice Shelf, Pack Ice
Ocean
Sea
Gulf, Bay
Strait, Fjord
Lagoon
Bank
Seamount
Tablemount
Ridge
Shelf
Basin
Escarpment, Sea Scarp
Fracture
Trench, Abyss
National Park, Reserve
Point of Interest
Recreation Site
Cave, Cavern
Historic Site
Ruins
Wall, Walls
Church, Abbey
Temple
Scientific Station
Airport
Port
Lighthouse
Mine
Tunnel
Dam, Bridge

Canakkale Boğazi = Dardanelles (EN)	5	Ig	40.15N	26.25 E
Canala	63b	Be	21.32S	165.57 E
Canandaigua	44	Id	42.53N	77.19W
Cananea	47	Bb	30.57N	110.18W
Cananéia	55	Ig	25.01S	47.57W
Canapolis	55	Hd	18.44S	49.13W
Canarias, Islas- = Canary Islands (EN) [5]	31	Ff	28.00N	15.30W
Canarias, Islas- = Canary Islands (EN)	30	Ff	28.00N	15.30W
Canaries	51k	Ab	13.55N	61.04W
Canaronero, Laguna-	48	Ff	23.00N	106.15W
Canarreos, Archipiélago de los-	47	Hd	21.50N	82.30W
Canary Basin (EN)	3	Dg	30.00N	25.00W
Canary Islands (EN) = Canarias, Islas-	30	Ff	28.00N	15.30W
Canary Islands (EN) = Canarias, Islas- [5]	31	Ff	28.00N	15.30W
Cañas [C.R.]	49	Eh	10.25N	85.07W
Cañas [Pan.]	49	Gj	7.27N	80.16W
Canastra, Serra da-	55	Ie	20.00S	46.20W
Canatlán	48	Ge	24.31N	104.47W
Cañaveral	13	Fe	39.47N	6.23W
Canaveral, Cape-	38	Kg	28.30N	80.35W
Canavese	14	Be	45.20N	7.40 E
Canavieiras	54	Kg	15.39S	38.57W
Canazei	14	Fd	46.28N	11.46 E
Canberra	58	Fh	35.17S	149.08 E
Canby [Mn.-U.S.]	45	Hd	44.43N	96.16W
Canby [Or.-U.S.]	46	Dd	45.16N	122.42W
Cance	11	Ki	45.12N	4.48 E
Canche	11	Hd	50.31N	1.39 E
Cancon	11	Gj	44.32N	0.37 E
Cancún	47	Gd	21.05N	86.46W
Cancún, Isla-	48	Pg	21.05N	86.46W
Çandarli	15	Jk	38.56N	26.56 E
Çandarli Körfezi	15	Jk	38.52N	26.55 E
Candé	11	Eg	47.34N	1.02W
Candela	48	Id	26.50N	100.40W
Candelaria	48	Nh	18.18N	91.21W
Candelaria, Cerro-	48	Hf	23.25N	103.43W
Candelaria, Río- [Bol.]	55	Cc	17.17S	58.39W
Candelaria, Río- [Mex.]	48	Nh	18.38N	91.15W
Candelaro	14	Ji	41.34N	15.53 E
Cândido de Abreu	55	Gg	24.35S	51.20W
Cândido Mendes	54	Id	1.27S	45.43W
Candlemas Islands	66	Ad	57.03S	26.40W
Candói	55	Fg	25.43S	52.11W
Čandyr	16	Jj	38.13N	55.44 E
Canela	56	Jc	29.22S	50.50W
Canelli	14	Cf	44.43N	8.17 E
Canelones [2]	55	El	34.35S	56.00W
Canelones	55	Dl	34.32S	56.17W
Canendiyu [3]	55	Eg	24.20S	55.00W
Cañete [Chile]	56	Fe	37.48S	73.24W
Cañete [Sp.]	13	Kd	40.03N	1.39W
Cangallo	55	Cm	37.13S	58.42W
Cangamba	36	Ce	13.44S	19.53 E
Cangas	13	Db	42.16N	8.47W
Cangas de Narcea	13	Fa	43.11N	6.33W
Cangas de Onís	13	Ga	43.21N	5.07W
Cangola	36	Cd	7.58S	15.53 E
Cangombe	36	Ce	14.24S	19.59 E
Cangshan (Bianzhuang)	28	Eg	34.51N	118.03 E
Canguçu	55	Fj	31.24S	52.41W
Canguçu, Serra do-	55	Fj	31.20S	52.40W
Canguinha	55	Eb	14.42S	55.40W
Cangumbe	36	Ce	12.00S	19.09 E
Cangyuan	27	Gg	23.10N	99.15 E
Cangzhou	27	Kd	38.14N	116.58 E
Cani, Iles-	14	Em	37.21N	10.07 E
Caniapiscau	38	Md	57.40N	69.30W
Caniapiscau, Lac-	42	Kf	54.00N	70.10W
Canicatti	14	Hm	37.21N	13.51 E
Canigou, Pic du-	11	Il	42.31N	2.27 E
Canik Dağları	24	Gb	40.50N	37.10 E
Canim Lake	46	Ea	51.52N	120.45W
Canindé	54	Kd	4.22S	39.19W
Canindé, Rio-	54	Je	6.15S	42.52W
Cañitas de Felipe Pescador	48	Hf	23.36N	102.43W
Çankaya	24	Ec	39.56N	32.52 E
Çankırı	23	Da	40.36N	33.37 E
Canna	9	Gd	57.03N	6.33W
Cannac	63a	Ac	9.15S	153.29 E
Çannakale	23	Ca	40.09N	26.24 E
Cannanore	25	Ff	11.51N	75.22 E
Cannanore Islands	25	Ef	10.05N	72.10 E
Cannes	11	Nk	43.33N	7.01 E
Cannich	9	Id	57.20N	4.45W
Canning Basin	59	Ed	20.10S	123.00 E
Cannobio	14	Cd	46.04N	8.42 E
Cannock	9	Ki	52.42N	2.01W
Cannonball River	45	Fc	46.26N	100.38W
Cann River	59	Jg	37.34S	149.10 E
Caño, Isla del-	49	Fi	8.44N	83.53W
Canoas	56	Jc	29.56S	51.11W
Canoas, Punta-	48	Bc	29.25N	115.10W
Canoas, Rio-	56	Jc	27.36S	51.25W
Canoeiros	54	Ig	18.02S	45.31W
Canoinhas	55	Gh	26.10S	50.24W
Canoinhas, Rio-	55	Gh	26.07S	50.22W
Cañoles	13	Le	39.02N	0.29W
Canon City	43	Fd	38.27N	105.14W
Canon Fiord	42	Ja	80.15N	83.00W
Canonnier, Pointe du-	51b	Ab	18.04N	63.10W
Canora	42	Hf	51.37N	102.26W
Canosa di Puglia	14	Ki	41.13N	16.04 E
Canouan Island	50	Ff	12.43N	61.20W
Canourgue	11	Jj	44.25N	3.13 E
Canso, Strait of -	42	Lg	45.35N	61.23W
Canta	54	Cf	11.25S	76.38W
Cantabrian Mountains (EN) = Cantábrica, Cordillera-	5	Fg	43.00N	5.00W
Cantábrica, Cordillera- = Cantabrian Mountains (EN)	5	Fg	43.00N	5.00W
Cantal	5	Gf	45.10N	2.50 E
Cantal [3]	11	Ii	45.05N	2.40 E
Cantalejo	13	Ic	41.15N	3.55W
Cantanhede	13	Dd	40.21N	8.36W
Cantaura	54	Fb	9.19N	64.21W
Cantavieja	13	Ld	40.32N	0.24W
Cantavir	15	Cd	45.55N	19.46 E
Canterbury [2]	62	De	43.30S	171.50 E
Canterbury	9	Oj	51.17N	1.05 E
Canterbury Bight	57	Ii	44.10S	172.00 E
Can Tho	22	Mi	10.02N	105.47 E
Cantiles, Cayo-	49	Fc	21.36N	82.02W
Canto do Buriti	54	Je	8.07S	42.58W
Canton [Il.-U.S.]	45	Kf	40.33N	90.02W
Canton [Mo.-U.S.]	45	Kf	40.08N	91.32W
Canton [Ms.-U.S.]	45	Kj	32.37N	90.02W
Canton [N.Y.-U.S.]	44	Jc	44.37N	75.11W
Canton [Oh.-U.S.]	43	Kc	40.48N	81.23W
Canton [S.D.-U.S.]	45	He	43.18N	96.35W
Canton (EN) = Guangzhou	22	Ng	23.07N	113.18 E
Cantù	14	De	45.44N	9.08 E
Cantwell	40	Jd	63.23N	148.57W
Cañuelas	55	Cl	35.03S	58.44W
Canumã, Rio-	52	Kf	3.55S	59.10W
Canutama	54	Fe	6.32S	64.20W
Canvey	12	Cc	51.31N	0.36 E
Čany	20	Ce	55.19N	76.56 E
Čany, Ozero-	21	Jd	54.50N	77.30 E
Cany-Barville	12	Ce	49.47N	0.38 E
Canyon [Mn.-U.S.]	45	Jc	47.02N	92.29W
Canyon [Tx.-U.S.]	43	Ge	34.59N	101.55W
Canyon [Wy.-U.S.]	46	Jd	44.44N	110.30W
Canyon Lake	45	Gl	29.52N	98.16W
Canzar	36	Dd	7.36S	21.33 E
Cao Bang	25	Ld	22.40N	106.15 E
Caojiahe → Qichun	28	Ci	30.15N	115.26 E
Caojian	27	Gf	25.38N	99.07 E
Caombo	36	Cd	8.42S	16.33 E
Caorle	14	Ge	45.36N	12.53 E
Caoxian	28	Cg	34.49N	115.33 E
Caozhou → Heze	27	Kd	35.14N	115.28 E
Capaccio	14	Jj	40.25N	15.05 E
Čapajev	19	Fe	50.14N	51.08 E
Čapajevsk	19	Ee	53.01N	49.36 E
Capanaparo, Río-	54	Eb	7.01N	67.07W
Capanema [Braz.]	54	Id	1.12S	47.11W
Capanema [Braz.]	55	Fg	25.40S	53.48W
Capanema, Serra do-	55	Fh	26.05S	53.16W
Capão Alto	55	Gh	27.56S	50.30W
Capão Bonito	55	Hf	24.01S	48.20W
Capão Doce, Morro do-	55	Gh	26.43S	51.25W
Caparo, Río-	49	Lj	7.46N	70.23W
Capatárida	49	Lh	11.11N	70.37W
Capbreton	11	Ek	43.38N	1.26W
Cap Breton Canyon (EN)	11	Ek	43.40N	1.50W
Čapčama, Pereval-	18	Hd	41.34N	70.50 E
Cap-Chat	44	Na	49.06N	66.42W
Capcir	11	Il	42.45N	2.10 E
Cap-de-la-Madeleine	42	Kg	46.22N	72.32W
Capdenac-Gare	11	Ij	44.34N	2.05 E
Cape Barren Island	59	Jh	40.25S	148.10 E
Cape Basin (EN)	3	Em	37.00S	7.00 E
Cape Breton Island	38	Me	46.00N	60.30W
Cape Charles	44	Jg	37.17N	76.00W
Cape Coast	31	Gh	5.06N	1.15W
Cape Cod Bay	44	Le	41.52N	70.22W
Cape Coral	44	Gl	26.33N	81.58W
Cape Dorset	39	Lc	64.14N	76.32W
Cape Dyer	39	Mc	66.30N	61.18W
Cape Fear River	44	Ii	33.53N	78.00W
Cape Girardeau	43	Jd	37.19N	89.32W
Cape Johnson Tablemount (EN)	57	Jc	17.08N	177.15W
Capel	12	Bc	51.08N	0.19W
Cape Lisburne	40	Fc	68.52N	166.05W
Capelka	8	Mf	58.02N	29.07 E
Capelongo	36	Ce	14.54S	15.05 E
Capem	55	Ea	13.14S	55.14W
Cape May	44	Jf	38.56N	74.54W
Cape Mount [3]	34	Cd	7.05N	10.50W
Cape Rise (EN)	3	En	42.00S	15.00 E
Cape Smith	42	Jd	60.44N	78.29W
Capesterre	51e	Bc	15.54N	61.13W
Capesterre-Belle-Eau	50	Fd	16.03N	61.34W
Cape Town / Kaapstad	31	Il	33.55S	18.22 E
Cape Verde (EN) = Cabo Verde [1]	31	Eg	16.00N	24.00W
Cape Verde (EN) = Cap Vert [3]	34	Bc	14.45N	17.20W
Cape Verde Basin (EN)	3	Ch	15.00N	30.00W
Cape Verde Islands (EN) = Cabo Verde, Ilhas do-	30	Eg	16.00N	24.10W
Cape Yakataga	40	Kd	60.04N	142.26W
Cape York Peninsula	57	Ff	14.00S	142.30 E
Cap-Haïtien	39	Lh	19.45N	72.15W
Capiibary, Arroyo-	55	Dg	24.06S	56.26W
Capiibary, Río-	55	Eg	25.30S	55.33W
Capim, Rio-	52	Lf	1.40S	47.47W
Capinópolis	55	Hd	18.41S	49.35W
Capira	49	Hi	8.45N	79.53W
Capital Federal [2]	56	Id	34.36S	58.27W
Capitán Arturo Prat	66	Re	62.29S	59.39W
Capitán Bado	56	Ib	23.16S	55.32W
Capitán Bermúdez	55	Bk	32.49S	60.43W
Capitán Sarmiento	55	Cl	34.10S	59.48W
Capitão Noronha, Rio-	55	Ea	13.19S	54.36W
Capivara, Represa da-	55	Gf	22.40S	50.57W
Capivari, Rio-	55	Dd	19.16S	57.10W
Capivarita	55	Fj	30.18S	52.19W
Cap Lopez, Baie du-	36	Ac	0.40S	9.00 E
Čaplygin	16	Kc	53.17N	39.59 E
Cappeln (Oldenburg)	12	Kb	52.49N	8.07 E
Cap Point	50	Fe	14.07N	60.57W
Capraia	14	Dg	43.05N	9.50 E
Caprara, Punta-	14	Ci	41.07N	8.19 E
Capreol	44	Gb	46.43N	80.56W
Caprera	14	Di	41.10N	9.30 E
Capri	14	Ij	40.35N	14.15 E
Capri	14	Ij	40.33N	14.14 E
Capricorn, Cape-	59	Kd	23.30S	151.15 E
Capricorn Channel	59	Kd	22.15S	151.30 E
Capricorn Group	57	Gg	23.30S	152.00 E
Caprivi Strip (EN) = Caprivi Zipfel	30	Jj	18.00S	23.00 E
Caprivi Zipfel = Caprivi Strip (EN)	30	Jj	18.00S	23.00 E
Captain Cook	65a	Fd	19.30N	155.55W
Captains Flat	59	Jg	35.35S	149.27 E
Captieux	11	Fj	44.17N	0.15W
Capua	14	Ii	41.06N	14.12 E
Capuchin, Cape-	51g	Ba	15.38N	61.28W
Capunda	36	Ce	10.41S	17.23 E
Cap Vert = Cape Verde (EN) [3]	34	Bc	14.45N	17.20W
Caquetá [2]	54	Dc	1.00N	74.00W
Čara	21	Oc	60.17N	120.40 E
Čara	20	Ge	56.58N	118.17 E
Čara	20	Ge	58.54N	118.12 E
Carabobo [2]	54	Ea	10.10N	68.05W
Caracal	15	He	44.07N	24.21 E
Caracaraí	54	Fc	1.50N	61.08W
Caracas	53	Jd	10.30N	66.56W
Carache	49	Li	9.38N	70.14W
Caracol	55	De	21.59S	57.02W
Caracol, Rio-	55	Df	22.13S	57.03W
Caracollo	54	Eg	17.39S	67.10W
Cara Droma Rúisc/Carrick-on-Shannon	9	Eh	53.57N	8.05W
Caraguatá, Cuchilla-	55	Ek	32.05S	54.54W
Caraguatatuba	55	Jf	23.37S	45.25W
Caraïbe, Mer-/Antilles, Mer des- = Caribbean Sea (EN)	38	Lh	15.00N	73.00W
Carajas, Serra dos-	54	He	6.00S	51.20W
Caramoan Peninsula	26	Hd	13.48N	123.40 E
Caramulo, Serra do-	13	Dd	40.34N	8.11W
Caraná, Rio-	55	Ca	13.20S	59.17W
Carandaí	55	Ke	20.57S	43.48W
Carandazal	55	Dd	19.50S	57.09W
Caransebeş	15	Fd	45.25N	22.13 E
Carapá, Río-	55	Eg	24.30S	54.20W
Carapelle	14	Ji	41.30N	15.55 E
Caraş	15	Ee	44.49N	21.20 E
Caraş Severin [2]	15	Ed	45.20N	22.00 E
Caratasca, Cayo-	49	Fe	16.02N	83.20W
Caratasca, Laguna de-	47	He	15.20N	83.50W
Caratinga	54	Jg	19.47S	42.08W
Carauari	54	Ed	4.52S	66.54W
Caraúbas	54	Ke	5.47S	37.34W
Caravaca	13	Kf	38.06N	1.51W
Caravelas	53	Mg	17.45S	39.15W
Caraveli	54	Dg	15.46S	73.22W
Caravelle, Presqu'île de la-	51h	Bb	14.45N	60.55W
Caravelle, Rocher de la-	51h	Bb	14.48N	60.53W
Caràzinho	56	Jc	28.18S	52.48W
Carazo [3]	49	Dh	11.45N	86.15W
Carballino	13	Db	42.26N	8.04W
Carballo	13	Da	43.13N	8.41W
Carberry	45	Gb	49.52N	99.20W
Carbet, Pitons du-	51h	Ab	14.42N	61.07W
Carbon, Cap- [Alg.]	13	Rh	36.47N	5.06 E
Carbon, Cap- [Alg.]	13	Li	35.54N	0.20W
Carbonara, Capo-	14	Dk	39.06N	9.31 E
Carbondale [Il.-U.S.]	43	Jd	37.44N	89.13W
Carbondale [Pa.-U.S.]	44	Je	41.35N	75.31W
Carbonera, Cuchilla de la-	55	El	34.10S	54.00W
Carboneras	13	Kh	36.59N	1.54W
Carboneras, Cerro-	48	Ih	18.10N	101.10W
Carbones	13	Gg	37.36N	5.39W
Carbonia	14	Ck	39.10N	8.31 E
Carcans, Étang de-	11	Ei	45.06N	1.07W
Carcar	26	Hd	10.06N	123.38 E
Carcarañá, Río-	55	Bk	32.27S	60.48W
Carcassonne	11	Ik	43.13N	2.21 E
Carcross	42	Ed	60.10N	134.42W
Çardak [Tur.]	15	Ji	40.22N	26.43 E
Çardak [Tur.]	24	Cd	37.48N	29.40 E
Čardara	19	Gg	41.15N	68.01 E
Čardarinskoje Vodohranilišče	18	Gd	41.05N	68.15 E
Cárdenas [Cuba]	47	Hd	23.02N	81.12W
Cárdenas [Mex.]	47	Ed	22.00N	99.40W
Cárdenas [Mex.]	48	Mi	17.59N	93.22W
Cárdenas, Bahia de-	49	Gb	23.05N	81.10W
Cardener/Cardoner	13	Nc	41.41N	1.51 E
Cardiel, Lago-	56	Fg	48.55S	71.15W
Cardiff	6	Fe	51.30N	3.13W
Cardigan	9	Ii	52.06N	4.40W
Cardigan Bay	5	Fe	52.30N	4.20W
Cardona [Sp.]	13	Nc	41.55N	1.41 E
Cardona [Ur.]	55	Dk	33.54S	57.22W
Cardoner/Cardener	13	Nc	41.41N	1.51 E
Cardozo	55	Dk	32.38S	56.21W
Cardston	42	Gg	49.12N	113.18W
Čardžou	22	If	39.06N	63.34 E
Čardžouskaja Oblast [3]	19	Gh	39.00N	63.00 E
Carei	15	Fb	47.41N	22.28 E
Careiro	54	Gd	3.12S	59.45W
Carentan	11	Ee	49.18N	1.14W
Carey	46	Ie	43.20N	113.58W
Carey, Lake-	57	Dg	29.05S	122.15 E
Cargados Carajos Islands	30	Mj	16.35S	59.40 E
Cargese	11a	Aa	42.08N	8.35 E
Carhaix-Plouguer	11	Cf	48.17N	3.35W
Cari	14	Hi	41.23N	13.50 E
Caria	15	Ll	37.30N	29.00 E
Cariacica	54	Jh	20.16S	40.25W
Cariaco	50	Eg	10.29N	63.33W
Cariaco, Golfo de-	50	Eg	10.30N	64.00W
Cariaco Basin (EN)	50	Dg	10.37N	65.10W
Cariati	14	Kk	39.30N	16.57 E
Caribana, Punta-	49	Ii	8.37N	76.52W
Caribbean Sea	38	Lh	15.00N	73.00W
Caribbean Sea (EN) = Antillas, Mar de las-/Caribe, Mar-	38	Lh	15.00N	73.00W
Caribbean Sea (EN) = Antilles, Mer des-/Caraïbe, Mer-	38	Lh	15.00N	73.00W
Caribbean Sea (EN) = Caribe, Mar-/Antillas, Mar de las-	38	Lh	15.00N	73.00W
Caribe, Mar-/Antillas, Mar de las- = Caribbean Sea (EN)	38	Lh	15.00N	73.00W
Cariboo Mountains	42	Ff	53.00N	121.00W
Caribou	42	Ie	59.20N	94.45W
Caribou	44	Mb	46.52N	68.01W
Caribou Island	44	Eb	47.27N	85.52W
Caribou Lake	45	La	50.25N	89.00W
Caribou Mountains	38	Hd	59.12N	115.40W
Caribou Range	46	Je	43.05N	111.15W
Caričin Grad	15	Eg	42.57N	21.45 E
Carignan	11	Le	49.38N	5.10 E
Carignano	14	Bf	44.55N	7.40 E
Cariñena	13	Kc	41.20N	1.13W
Carinhanha	54	Jf	14.08S	43.47W
Carinhanha, Rio-	55	Kb	14.20S	43.47W
Carini	14	Hl	38.08N	13.11 E
Carinola	14	Hi	41.11N	13.58 E
Carinthia (EN) = Kärnten [2]	14	Hd	46.45N	14.00 E
Carinthia (EN) = Kärnten	14	Hd	46.45N	14.00 E
Caripe	50	Eg	10.21N	63.29W
Caripito	54	Fa	10.08N	63.06W
Caris, Río-	50	Eh	8.09N	63.46W
Carlet	13	Le	39.14N	0.31W
Carleton Place	44	Ic	45.07N	76.08W
Carletonville	37	De	26.23S	27.22 E
Carlin	46	Gf	40.43N	116.07W
Carling	12	Ie	49.10N	6.43 E
Carlingford Lough/Loch Cairlinn	9	Gg	54.05N	6.14W
Carlinville	45	Lg	39.17N	89.53W
Carlisle [Eng.-U.K.]	6	Fe	54.54N	2.55W
Carlisle [Pa.-U.S.]	44	Ie	40.12N	77.12W
Carlisle Bay	51q	Ab	13.05N	59.37W
Carloforte	14	Ck	39.08N	8.18 E
Carlos Beguerie	55	Cl	35.29S	59.06W
Carlos Casares	56	He	35.38S	61.21W
Carlos Chagas	54	Jg	17.43S	40.45W
Carlos Reyles	55	Dk	33.03S	56.29W
Carlos Tejedor	55	Al	35.23S	62.25W
Carlow/Ceatharlach	9	Gi	52.50N	6.55W
Carlow/Ceatharlach [2]	9	Gi	52.50N	7.00W
Carloway	9	Gc	58.17N	6.47W
Carlsbad [Ca.-U.S.]	46	Gj	33.10N	117.21W
Carlsbad [N.M.-U.S.]	39	If	32.25N	104.14W
Carlyle	42	Hg	49.38N	102.16W
Carlyle Lake	45	Lg	38.40N	89.18W
Carmacks	42	Dd	62.05N	136.18W
Carmagnola	14	Bf	44.51N	7.43 E
Carmarthen	9	Ij	51.52N	4.19W
Carmarthen Bay	9	Ij	51.40N	4.30W
Carmaux	11	Ij	44.03N	2.09 E
Carmel Head	9	Ih	53.24N	4.34W
Carmelita	49	Be	17.21N	90.10W
Carmelo	56	Id	34.00S	58.17W
Carmen	55	Dk	33.15S	56.01W
Carmen, Isla-	47	Bc	25.57N	111.12W
Carmen, Isla del-	48	Nh	18.42N	91.40W
Carmen, Laguna del-	48	Mh	18.15N	93.50W
Carmen, Río del-	48	Fb	30.42N	106.29W
Carmen, Sierra del-	48	Hc	29.00N	102.30W
Carmen de Patagones	56	Hf	40.48S	62.59W
Carmensa	56	Ge	35.08S	67.38W
Carmi	45	Lg	38.07N	88.10W
Carmichael	46	Eg	38.38N	121.19W
Carmo de Minas	55	Jf	22.07S	45.08W
Carmo do Paranaíba	55	Id	18.59S	46.21W
Carmona	13	Gg	37.28N	5.38W
Carnac	11	Cg	47.35N	3.05W
Carnamah	59	De	29.42S	115.53 E
Carnarvon [Austl.]	58	Cg	24.53S	113.40 E
Carnarvon [S.Afr.]	31	Jl	30.56S	22.08 E
Carnarvon Range	59	Ee	25.10S	121.00 E
Carnatic (EN)	21	Jh	10.30N	79.00 E
Carnegie, Lake-	57	Dg	26.10S	122.30 E
Carnegie Ridge (EN)	3	Nj	1.00S	85.00W
Carn Eige	9	Hd	57.30N	5.05W
Carney Island	66	Nf	73.57S	121.00W
Carnia	14	Gd	46.25N	13.00 E
Car Nicobar	25	Ig	9.10N	92.47 E
Carnot	35	Be	4.48N	16.03 E
Carnoustie	9	Ke	56.30N	2.44W
Carnsore Point/Ceann an Chairn	9	Gi	52.10N	6.22W
Carn Ui Néid/Mizen Head	5	Fe	51.27N	9.49W
Caro	44	Fd	43.29N	83.24W
Carol City	44	Gm	25.56N	80.16W
Carolina [Braz.]	53	Lf	7.20S	47.28W
Carolina [P.R.]	51a	Cb	18.24N	65.57W
Carolina [S.Afr.]	37	Ee	26.05S	30.06 E
Carolina Beach	44	Ih	34.02N	77.54W
Carolinas, Puntan-	64b	Bb	14.54N	145.38 E
Caroline Atoll	57	Le	9.58S	150.13W
Caroline Islands	57	Fd	8.00N	147.00 E
Carondelet Reef	57	Je	5.34S	173.51W
Caroni, Río-	52	Je	8.21N	62.43W
Caronie → Nebrodi	14	Im	37.55N	14.35 E
Carora	54	Da	10.11N	70.05W
Carpathian Mountains (EN)	5	If	48.00N	24.00 E
Carpathian Mountains (EN) = Carpaţii Occidentali	15	Fc	46.30N	22.10 E
Carpathian Mountains (EN) = Carpaţii Orientali	15	Ib	47.30N	25.30 E
Carpaţii Meridionali = Transylvanian Alps (EN)	5	If	45.30N	22.10 E
Carpaţii Occidentali = Carpathian Mountains (EN)	15	Fc	46.30N	22.10 E
Carpaţii Orientali = Carpathian Mountains (EN)	15	Ib	47.30N	25.30 E
Carpen	15	Ge	44.20N	23.15 E
Carpentaria, Gulf of-	57	Ef	14.00S	139.00 E
Carpentras	11	Lj	44.03N	5.03 E
Carpi	14	Ef	44.47N	10.53 E
Carpina	54	Ke	7.51S	35.15W
Carr, Cape-	66	Ie	66.07S	130.51 E
Carraig Fhearghais/Carrickfergus	9	Hg	54.43N	5.44W
Carraig na Siúire/Carrick-on-Suir				
Carrara	14	Ef	44.05N	10.06 E
Carrauntoohil	5	Fe	52.00N	9.45W
Carreiro, Rio-	55	Gi	29.07S	51.43W
Carreño	13	Ga	43.35N	5.46W
Carreta, Punta-	54	Cf	14.13S	76.18W
Carretero, Puerto-	13	Ig	37.28N	3.40W
Carriacou	50	Ff	12.30N	61.27W
Carrick	9	If	55.15N	4.40W
Carrickfergus/Carraig Fhearghais	9	Hg	54.43N	5.44W
Carrick-on-Shannon/cara Droma Rúisc	9	Eh	53.57N	8.05W
Carrick-on-Suir/Carraig na Siúire	9	Fi	52.21N	7.25W
Carrington	43	Hb	47.27N	99.08W
Carrión	13	Hc	41.53N	4.32W
Carrión de los Condes	13	Hb	42.20N	4.36W
Carrizal	49	Kh	11.58N	72.12W
Carrizo Peak	45	Dj	33.20N	105.38W
Carrizos	48	Gc	29.58N	105.16W
Carrizo Springs	45	Gl	28.31N	99.52W
Carrizo Wash	46	Ki	34.36N	109.26W
Carrizozo	45	Dj	33.38N	105.53W
Carroll	45	Ie	42.04N	94.52W
Carroll Inlet	66	Qf	73.18S	78.30W
Carrollton [Ga.-U.S.]	44	Ei	33.35N	85.05W
Carrollton [Il.-U.S.]	45	Kg	39.18N	90.24W
Carrollton [Ky.-U.S.]	44	Ef	38.41N	85.11W
Carrollton [Mo.-U.S.]	45	Jg	39.22N	93.30W
Carron, Loch-	9	Hd	57.30N	5.40W
Carrot	42	Hf	53.50N	101.18W
Carrowmore Lough	9	Dg	54.12N	9.47W
Çarşamba	24	Gb	41.12N	36.44 E
Çarşamba	24	Ed	37.53N	32.37 E
Čaršanga	19	Gh	37.31N	66.03 E
Čarsk	19	If	49.35N	81.05 E
Carson	46	Ed	45.44N	121.49W
Carson City	39	Hf	39.10N	119.46W
Carson Lake	46	Fg	39.19N	118.43W
Carson Sink	46	Fg	39.45N	118.30W
Cartagena [Col.]	53	Id	10.25N	75.32W
Cartagena [Sp.]	6	Fh	37.36N	0.59W
Cartago [3]	49	Fi	9.50N	83.45W
Cartago [Col.]	54	Cc	4.46N	75.56W
Cartago [C.R.]	47	Hg	9.52N	83.55W
Cartaxo	13	De	39.09N	8.47W
Carter, Mount-	59	Ib	13.05S	143.15 E
Carteret	11	Ee	49.23N	1.47W
Cartersville	44	Eh	34.10N	85.05W
Carterton	62	Fd	41.01S	175.31 E
Carthage [Mo.-U.S.]	45	Ih	37.11N	94.19W
Carthage [Tx.-U.S.]	45	Ij	32.09N	94.20W
Cartier	44	Gb	46.42N	81.32W
Cartier Island	57	Df	12.30S	123.30 E
Caruaru	53	Mf	8.17S	35.58W
Carúpano	54	Fa	10.40N	63.14W
Carutapera	54	Id	1.13S	46.01W
Čarvak	18	Gd	41.38N	69.56 E
Carvin	12	Ed	50.29N	2.58 E
Carvoeiro, Cabo-	13	Ce	39.21N	9.24W
Čaryn	18	Lc	43.50N	79.12 E
Čaryš	20	Df	52.22N	83.45 E
Casablanca [2]	32	Fc	33.37N	7.35W
Casablanca	31	Ge	33.36N	7.37W
Casa Branca	55	Ie	21.46S	47.05W
Casa Grande	43	Ee	32.53N	111.45W
Casalbordino	14	Ih	42.09N	14.35 E
Casale Monferrato	14	Ce	45.08N	8.27 E
Casalmaggiore	14	Ef	44.59N	10.26 E
Casalvasco	55	Cb	15.19S	59.59W
Casal Velino	14	Jj	40.11N	15.06 E
Casamance	34	Bc	12.33N	16.46W
Casamance [3]	34	Bc	12.50N	15.00W
Casanare [2]	54	Db	5.20N	72.00W
Casanare, Río-	54	Eb	6.02N	69.51W
Casanay	50	Eg	10.30N	63.25W
Casa Nova	54	Je	9.25S	41.08W
Casarano	14	Mj	40.00N	18.10 E
Casas Grandes, Río-	48	Eb	30.22N	107.31W
Casas-Ibáñez	13	Ke	39.17N	1.28W
Casca, Rio da-	55	Eb	14.52S	55.52W
Cascade	46	Hd	44.31N	115.59W
Cascade Point	62	Cf	44.01S	168.22 E
Cascade Range	38	Ge	45.00N	121.30W
Cascais	13	Cf	38.42N	9.25W
Cascavel	56	Jb	24.57S	53.28W
Cascia	14	Hh	42.43N	13.01 E
Casciana Terme	14	Eg	43.32N	10.38 E
Cascina	14	Eg	43.41N	10.33 E
Casentino	14	Fg	43.40N	11.50 E

Index Symbols

- [1] Independent Nation
- [2] State, Region
- [3] District, County
- [4] Municipality
- [5] Colony, Dependency
- Continent
- Physical Region
- Historical or Cultural Region
- Mount, Mountain
- Volcano
- Hill
- Mountains, Mountain Range
- Hills, Escarpment
- Plateau, Upland
- Pass, Gap
- Plain, Lowland
- Delta
- Salt Flat
- Valley, Canyon
- Crater, Cave
- Karst Features
- Depression
- Polder
- Desert, Dunes
- Forest, Woods
- Heath, Steppe
- Oasis
- Cape, Point
- Coast, Beach
- Cliff
- Peninsula
- Isthmus
- Sandbank
- Island
- Atoll
- Rock, Reef
- Islands, Archipelago
- Rocks, Reefs
- Coral Reef
- Well, Spring
- Geyser
- River, Stream
- Waterfall Rapids
- River Mouth, Estuary
- Lake
- Salt Lake
- Intermittent Lake
- Reservoir
- Swamp, Pond
- Canal
- Glacier
- Ice Shelf, Pack Ice
- Ocean
- Sea
- Gulf, Bay
- Strait, Fjord
- Lagoon
- Bank
- Seamount
- Tablemount
- Ridge
- Shelf
- Basin
- Escarpment, Sea Scarp
- Fracture
- Trench, Abyss
- National Park, Reserve
- Point of Interest
- Recreation Site
- Cave, Cavern
- Historic Site
- Ruins
- Wall, Walls
- Church, Abbey
- Temple
- Scientific Station
- Airport
- Port
- Lighthouse
- Mine
- Tunnel
- Dam, Bridge

Case-Pilote 51h Ab 14.38N 61.08W
Caserta 14 Ii 41.04N 14.20 E
Casey 66 He 66.17S 110.32 E
Casey Bay 66 Ee 67.00S 48.00 E
Cashel/Caiseal 9 Fi 52.31N 7.53W
Casigua 49 Ki 8.46N 72.30W
Casilda 56 Hd 33.03S 61.10W
Casimcea 15 Le 44.24N 28.33 E
Casino 59 Ke 28.52S 153.03 E
Casiquiare, Brazo- 54 Ec 2.01N 67.07W
Čáslav 10 Lg 49.55N 15.25 E
Casma 54 Ce 9.28S 78.19W
Časnačorr, Gora- 7 Hc 67.45N 33.29 E
Čašniki 7 Gi 54.52N 29.08 E
Casoli 14 Ih 42.07N 14.18 E
Casoria 14 Ij 40.54N 14.17 E
Caspe 13 Lc 41.14N 0.02W
Casper 39 Ie 42.51N 106.19W
Caspian Depression (EN) = Prikaspijskaja Nizmennost 5 Lf 48.00N 52.00 E
Caspian Sea (EN) = Kaspijskoje More 5 Lg 42.00N 50.30 E
Caspian Sea (EN) = Māzandarān, Daryā-ye- 5 Lg 42.00N 50.30 E
Cassai 30 Ii 3.02S 16.57 E
Cassamba 36 De 13.04S 20.25 E
Cassange, Rio- 55 Dc 17.06S 57.23W
Cassano allo Ionio 14 Kk 39.47N 16.19 E
Cass City 44 Fd 43.36N 83.10W
Cassel 12 Ed 50.47N 2.29 E
Casselton 45 Hc 46.54N 97.13W
Cássia 55 Ie 20.36S 46.56W
Cassiar 42 Ee 59.16N 129.40W
Cassiar Mountains 38 Gd 59.00N 129.00W
Cassilândia 54 Hg 19.09S 51.45W
Cassino [Braz.] 55 Fk 32.11S 52.10W
Cassino [It.] 14 Hi 41.30N 13.49 E
Cassis 11 Lk 43.13N 5.32 E
Cass Lake 45 Ic 47.23N 94.36W
Cass River 44 Fd 43.23N 83.59W
Cassununga 55 Fc 16.03S 53.38W
Castagneto Carducci 14 Eg 43.10N 10.36 E
Castagniccia 11a Ba 42.25N 9.30 E
Castañar, Sierra del- 13 He 39.35N 4.10W
Castanhal 54 Id 1.18S 47.55W
Castaños 48 Id 26.47N 101.25W
Castelbuono 14 Im 37.56N 14.05 E
Castel di Sangro 14 Ii 41.47N 14.06 E
Castelfidardo 14 Hg 43.28N 13.33 E
Castelfranco Veneto 14 Fe 45.40N 11.55 E
Casteljaloux 11 Gj 44.19N 0.06 E
Castellabate 14 Ij 40.17N 14.57 E
Castellammare, Golfo di- 14 Gl 38.10N 12.55 E
Castellammare del Golfo 14 Gl 38.01N 12.53 E
Castellammare di Stabia 14 Ij 40.42N 14.29 E
Castellana Grotte 14 Lj 40.53N 17.10 E
Castellane 11 Mk 43.51N 6.31 E
Castellaneta 14 Kj 40.38N 16.56 E
Castelldefels 13 Nc 41.17N 1.58 E
Castelli [Arg.] 56 Hc 25.57S 60.37W
Castelli [Arg.] 55 Dm 36.06S 57.47W
Castelló de la Plana/Castellón de la Plana 6 Fh 39.59N 0.02W
Castellón [3] 13 Ld 40.10N 0.10W
Castellón de la Plana/Castelló de la Plana 6 Fh 39.59N 0.02W
Castellón de la Plana-El Grao 13 Me 39.58N 0.01 E
Castellote 13 Ld 40.48N 0.19W
Castelnaudary 11 Hk 43.19N 1.57 E
Castelnau-de-Médoc 11 Fi 45.02N 0.48W
Castelnovo ne' Monti 14 Ef 44.26N 10.24 E
Castelo Branco [2] 13 Ee 40.00N 7.30W
Castelo Branco 13 Ee 39.49N 7.30W
Castelo de Vide 13 Ee 39.25N 7.27W
Castelo do Piauí 54 Je 5.20S 41.33W
Castel San Giovanni 14 De 45.04N 9.26 E
Castelsardo 14 Cj 40.55N 8.43 E
Castelsarrasin 11 Hj 44.02N 1.06 E
Casteltermini 14 Hm 37.32N 13.39 E
Castelvetrano 14 Gm 37.41N 12.47 E
Castets 11 Ek 43.53N 1.09W
Castiglione del Lago 14 Gg 43.07N 12.03 E
Castiglione della Pescaia 14 Eh 42.46N 10.53 E
Castiglion Fiorentino 14 Fg 43.20N 11.55 E
Castilla la Nueva = New Castile (EN) 13 Id 40.00N 3.45W
Castilla la Vieja = Old Castile (EN) 13 Ic 41.30N 4.00W
Castillejo 13 Gc 41.14N 5.30W
Castillon-la-Bataille 11 Fj 44.51N 0.02W
Castillonnès 11 Gj 44.39N 0.36 E
Castillos 56 Jd 34.12S 53.50W
Castillos, Laguna de- 55 Fl 34.20S 53.54W
Castlebar/Caisleán an Bharraigh 9 Dh 53.52N 9.17W
Castle Bruce 51g Bb 15.26N 61.16W
Castle Dome Peak 46 Hj 33.05N 114.08W
Castle Douglas 9 Jg 54.57N 3.56W
Castlegar 42 Fg 49.19N 117.40W
Castleisland/Oiléan Ciarrai 9 Di 52.14N 9.27W
Castlemaine 59 Ig 37.04S 144.13 E
Castle Peak 46 Hd 44.03N 114.32W
Castlepoint 62 Gd 40.55S 176.13 E
Castlepollard 9 Fh 53.41N 7.17W
Castlerea/An Caisleán Riabhach 9 Eh 53.46N 8.29W
Castlereagh Bay 59 Hb 12.10S 135.10 E
Castle Rock Butte 45 Ed 45.00N 103.27W
Castle Rock Lake 45 Le 43.56N 89.58W
Častoozerje 17 Mi 55.34N 67.53 E
Castor 46 Ja 52.13N 111.53W
Castres 11 Ik 43.36N 2.15 E
Castricum 12 Gb 52.33N 4.42 E
Castries 39 Mh 14.01N 61.00W
Castrignano del Capo 14 Mk 39.50N 18.20 E
Castro [Braz.] 56 Jb 24.47S 50.03W
Castro [Chile] 56 Ff 42.29S 73.46W
Castro Alves 54 Kf 12.45S 39.26W
Castrocaro Terme e Terra del Sole 14 Ff 44.10N 11.57 E
Castro Daire 13 Ed 40.54N 7.56W
Castro del Río 13 Hg 37.41N 4.28W
Castrojeriz 13 Hb 42.17N 4.08W
Castropol 13 Ea 43.32N 7.02W
Castrop-Rauxel 12 Jc 51.33N 7.19 E
Castro Urdiales 13 Ia 43.23N 3.13W
Castro Verde 13 Dg 37.42N 8.05W
Castrovillari 14 Kk 39.49N 16.12 E
Castrovirreyna 54 Cf 13.16S 75.19W
Castuera 13 Gf 38.43N 5.33W
Častyje 17 Gh 57.19N 54.59 E
Casupá 55 El 34.09S 55.38W
Caswell Sound 62 Bf 45.00S 167.10 E
Čat 24 Ic 39.40N 41.02 E
Čata 10 Oi 47.58N 18.40 E
Catacamas 49 Ef 14.54N 85.56W
Catahoula Lake 45 Jk 31.30N 92.06W
Çatak 24 Jc 38.01N 43.07 E
Çatak 24 Jd 37.53N 42.39 E
Catalan Coastal Range (EN) = Cadena Costero Catalana /Serralada Litoral Catalana 5 Gg 41.35N 1.40 E
Catalan Coastal Range (EN) = Serralada Litoral Catalana/Cadena Costero Catalana 5 Gg 41.35N 1.40 E
Catalão 54 Ig 18.10S 47.57W
Çatal Balkan 15 Jg 42.46N 27.00 E
Çatalca 15 Lh 41.09N 28.27 E
Çatal Dağ 15 Lj 39.51N 28.20 E
Catalina 56 Gc 25.13S 69.43W
Catalina, Isla- 49 Md 18.21N 69.00W
Catalina, Punta- 56 Gh 52.32S 68.47W
Catalonia (EN) = Cataluña/Catalunya 5 Gg 42.00N 2.00 E
Catalonia (EN) = Cataluña/Catalunya 13 Nc 42.00N 2.00 E
Catalonia (EN) = Catalunya/Cataluña 5 Gg 42.00N 2.00 E
Catalonia (EN) = Catalunya/Cataluña 13 Nc 42.00N 2.00 E
Cataluña/Catalunya = Catalonia (EN) 5 Gg 42.00N 2.00 E
Cataluña/Catalunya = Catalonia (EN) 13 Nc 42.00N 2.00 E
Catalunya/Cataluña = Catalonia (EN) 13 Nc 42.00N 2.00 E
Catalunya/Cataluña = Catalonia (EN) 5 Gg 42.00N 2.00 E
Çatalzeytin 24 Fb 41.57N 34.13 E
Catamarca 53 Jh 28.30S 65.45W
Catamarca [2] 56 Gc 27.00S 67.00W
Catanduanes 21 Oh 13.45N 124.15 E
Catanduva 56 Kb 21.08S 48.58W
Catanduvas 55 Fg 25.12S 53.08W
Catania 6 Hh 37.30N 15.06 E
Catania, Golfo di- 14 Jm 37.25N 15.10 E
Catania, Piana di- 14 Im 37.25N 14.50 E
Catanzaro 6 Hh 38.54N 16.35 E
Catarman 26 Hd 12.30N 124.38 E
Catastrophe, Cape- 57 Eh 35.00S 136.00 E
Catatumbo, Río- 49 Li 9.21N 71.45W
Catbalogan 26 Hd 11.46N 124.53 E
Catemaco, Lago- 48 Lh 18.25N 95.05W
Catete 36 Bd 9.07S 13.41 E
Cathair na Mart/Westport 9 Dh 53.48N 9.32W
Cathair Saidhbhin/Cahersiveen 9 Cj 51.57N 10.13W
Cathcart 37 Df 32.18S 27.09 E
Catherine, Mount- 46 Ig 39.05N 112.04W
Catholic Island 51n Bb 12.40N 61.24W
Catio 34 Bc 11.17N 15.15W
Cat Island 38 Lg 24.30N 75.30W
Čatkal 18 Hd 41.36N 70.05 E
Čatkalski Hrebet 19 Hg 41.30N 70.50 E
Cat Lake 42 If 51.40N 91.52W
Catoche, Cabo- 38 Kg 21.36N 87.07W
Cato Island 57 Gg 23.15S 155.35 E
Catolé do Rocha 54 Ke 6.21S 37.45W
Catoute 13 Fb 42.45N 6.20W
Catria 14 Gg 43.28N 12.42 E
Catriló 56 He 36.26S 63.24W
Catrimani, Rio- 54 Fc 0.28N 61.44W
Catskill Mountains 44 Jd 42.10N 74.30W
Cattenom 12 Ie 49.25N 6.15 E
Cattolica 14 Gg 43.58N 12.44 E
Catu 54 Kf 12.21S 38.23W
Catuane 37 Ee 26.48S 32.14 E
Catumbela 36 Be 12.27S 13.29 E
Catur 37 Fb 13.45S 35.37 E
Catwick, Iles- 25 Lg 10.00N 109.00 E
Catwright 39 Nd 53.50N 56.45W
Catyrkël, Ozero- 18 Jd 40.35N 75.20 E
Catyrtaš 18 Kd 40.52N 76.23 E
Cauca [2] 54 Cc 2.30N 77.00W
Cauca, Río- 52 Ie 8.54N 74.28W
Caucasia 54 Cb 7.59N 75.13W
Caucasus (EN) = Kavkaz, Bolšoj- 5 Kg 42.30N 45.00 E
Caucete 56 Gd 31.38S 68.16W
Caudebec-en-Caux 12 Ce 49.32N 0.44 E
Caudete 13 Lf 38.42N 0.59W
Caudry 11 Jd 50.08N 3.25 E
Caulonia 14 Kl 38.23N 16.24 E
Caumont-l'Eventé 12 Be 49.05N 0.48W
Caungula 31 Ii 8.26S 18.37 E
Čaunskaja Guba 20 Lc 69.30N 170.00 E
Caupolican 54 Ef 13.30S 68.30W
Cauquenes 56 Fe 35.58S 72.21W
Caura, Río- 52 Je 7.38N 64.53W
Causapscal 44 Na 48.22N 67.14W
Caussade 11 Hj 44.10N 1.32 E
Čausy 16 Gc 53.50N 30.59 E
Cauterets 11 Fl 42.53N 0.07W
Cauto, Río- 49 Ic 20.33N 77.15W
Cauvery 21 Jh 11.09N 78.52 E
Caux, Pays de- 11 Ge 49.40N 0.40 E
Cávado 13 Dc 41.32N 8.48W
Cavaillon 11 Lk 43.50N 5.02 E
Cavalcante 55 Ia 13.48S 47.30W
Cavalese 14 Fd 46.17N 11.27 E
Cavalli Islands 62 Ea 35.00S 173.55 E
Cavallo, Isola- 11a Bb 41.22N 9.16 E
Cavallo Pass 45 Hl 28.25N 96.26W
Cavally 30 Gh 4.22N 7.32W
Cavan/An Cabhán 9 Fg 54.00N 7.21W
Cavan/An Cabhán [2] 9 Fh 53.55N 7.30W
Cavarzere 14 Ge 45.08N 12.05 E
Çavdarhisar 15 Mj 39.12N 29.37 E
Çavdir 15 Ml 37.09N 29.42 E
Caviana, Ilha- 54 Hc 0.10N 50.05W
Cavili 26 He 9.17N 120.50 E
Cavour, Canale- 14 Be 45.11N 7.54 E
Cavtat 14 Mh 42.35N 18.13 E
Caxambu 55 Je 21.59S 44.56W
Caxias 53 Lf 4.50S 43.21W
Caxias do Sul 53 Kh 29.10S 51.11W
Caxito 36 Bd 8.34S 13.40 E
Çay 24 Dc 38.35N 31.02 E
Cayambe 54 Cc 0.05N 78.08W
Cayambe, Volcán- 52 Ie 0.02N 77.59W
Cayastá 55 Bj 31.12S 60.10W
Cayce 44 Gi 33.59N 81.04W
Çaycuma 24 Eb 41.25N 32.05 E
Çayeli 24 Ib 41.05N 40.44 E
Cayenne 53 Ke 4.56N 52.20W
Cayeux-Sur-Mer 12 Dd 50.11N 1.29 E
Cayey 49 Nd 18.07N 66.10W
Çayırlı 24 Ic 39.48N 40.01 E
Çaykara 24 Ib 40.45N 40.19 E
Caylus 11 Hj 44.14N 1.47 E
Cayman Brac 47 Ie 19.43N 79.49W
Cayman Islands [5] 39 Kh 19.30N 80.30W
Cayman Islands 38 Kh 19.30N 80.30W
Cayman Ridge (EN) 47 He 19.30N 80.30W
Cayman Trench (EN) 3 Bh 19.00N 80.00W
Cayo 49 Ce 17.10N 88.50W
Cayon 51c Ab 17.21N 62.43W
Cayones, Cayos- 49 Fe 16.05N 83.12W
Cay Sal Bank 47 Hd 23.45N 80.00W
Cayuga Lake 44 Id 42.45N 76.45W
Cazalla de la Sierra 13 Gg 37.56N 5.45W
Caza Pava 55 Di 28.17S 56.07W
Cazaux, Étang de- 11 Ej 44.29N 1.10W
Cazombo 31 Jj 11.54S 22.53 E
Cazorla 13 Jg 37.55N 3.00W
Cazorla, Sierra de- 13 Jf 37.55N 2.55W
Cea 13 Gb 42.00N 5.36W
Ceahlău 15 Ib 47.03N 25.58 E
Ceanannas Mór/Kells 9 Gh 53.44N 6.53W
Ceanna Cailligh/Hags Head 9 Di 52.57N 9.28W
Ceann Acla/Achill Head 9 Ch 53.59N 10.13W
Ceann an Chairn/Carnsore Point 9 Gi 52.10N 6.22W
Ceann Chill Mhantáin/Wicklow Head 9 Hi 52.58N 6.00W
Ceann Gólaim/Slyne Head 9 Ch 53.24N 10.13W
Ceann Iorrais/Erris Head 5 Fe 54.19N 10.00W
Ceann Léime/Loop Head 9 Di 52.34N 9.56W
Ceann Ros Eoghain/Rossan Point 9 Eg 54.42N 8.48W
Ceann Sléibhe/Slea Head 9 Ci 52.06N 10.27W
Ceann Toirc/Kanturk 9 Ei 52.10N 8.55W
Ceará [2] 54 Kd 5.00S 39.30W
Ceará-Mirim 54 Ke 5.38S 35.26W
Ceatharlach/Carlow [2] 9 Gi 52.50N 7.00W
Ceatharlach/Carlow 9 Gi 52.50N 6.55W
Cébaco, Isla- 49 Gj 7.32N 81.09W
Ceballos 48 Gd 26.32N 104.09W
Čebarkul 17 Ji 54.58N 60.25 E
Čeboksary 6 Kd 56.09N 47.15 E
Cebollati 55 Fk 33.16S 53.47W
Cebollati, Río- 55 Fk 33.09S 53.38W
Cebollera, Sierra- 13 Jc 42.00N 2.40W
Ceboruco, Volcán- 48 Gg 21.09N 104.30W
Cebreros 13 Hd 40.27N 4.28W
Cebrikovo 15 Nb 47.09N 30.02 E
Cebu 21 Oh 10.20N 123.45 E
Cebu 26 Hd 10.18N 123.54 E
Cece 10 Oj 46.46N 18.39 E
Čečen, Ostrov- 16 Og 44.00N 47.45 E
Čečeno respublika 19 Eg 43.15N 45.30 E
Cecen-Ula 27 Gb 49.20N 95.55 E
Cecerleg 22 Me 47.30N 101.27 E
Čečersk 16 Gc 52.56N 30.58 E
Čechy = Bohemia (EN) 5 Hf 50.00N 14.30 E
Čechy = Bohemia (EN) 10 Kf 50.00N 14.30 E
Cecina 14 Eg 43.18N 10.29 E
Cecina 14 Eg 43.10N 10.31 E
Čečuisk 20 Fe 58.07N 108.32 E
Cedar City 39 Hf 37.41N 113.04W
Cedar Creek 45 Fc 46.07N 101.18W
Cedar Creek Reservoir 45 Hj 32.20N 96.10W
Cedar Falls 43 Ic 42.32N 92.27W
Cedar Grove 51d Bb 17.10N 61.49W
Cedar Lake 42 Hf 53.25N 100.00W
Cedar Rapids 39 Je 41.59N 91.40W
Cedar River [Nb.-U.S.] 45 Hf 41.22N 97.57W
Cedar River [U.S.] 43 Ic 41.17N 91.20W
Cedartown 44 Eh 34.01N 85.15W
Cedar-Tree Point 51d Ba 17.42N 61.53W
Cedeira 13 Da 43.39N 8.03W
Cedral 48 If 23.48N 100.44W
Cedrino 14 Dj 40.23N 9.44 E
Cedro 54 Ke 6.36S 39.03W
Cedrón 13 Ie 39.48N 3.33W
Cedros, Isla- [Mex.] 47 Ac 28.12N 115.15W
Cedros, Isla [Mex.] = Cedros Island (EN) 38 Hg 28.10N 115.15W
Cedros Island (EN) = Cedros, Isla [Mex.] 38 Hg 28.10N 115.15W
Cedros Trench (EN) 47 Ac 27.45N 115.45W
Ceduna 59 Gf 32.07S 133.40 E
Cedynia 10 Kd 52.50N 14.14 E
Cefalù 14 Il 38.02N 14.01 E
Cega 13 Hc 41.33N 4.46W
Čegdomyn 22 Pd 51.07N 133.05 E
Čegem 16 Mh 43.36N 43.48 E
Cegléd 10 Pi 47.10N 19.48 E
Ceglie Messapico 14 Lj 40.39N 17.31 E
Cehegin 13 Kf 38.06N 1.48W
Cehotina 15 Bf 43.31N 18.45 E
Čehov 7 Ii 55.11N 37.29 E
Čehov 20 Jg 47.24N 142.05 E
Ceica 15 Fc 46.51N 22.11 E
Çekerek 24 Fb 40.34N 35.46 E
Çekerek 24 Fb 40.04N 35.31 E
Čekmaguš 17 Gi 55.10N 54.40 E
Celano 14 Hh 42.05N 13.33 E
Celaya 47 Dd 20.31N 100.37W
Čelbas 16 Kf 46.06N 38.59 E
Cèlè 11 Hj 44.28N 1.38 E
Celebes/Sulawesi 21 Oj 2.00S 121.10 E
Celebes Basin (EN) 26 Hf 4.00N 122.00 E
Celebes Sea (EN) = Sulawesi, Laut- 21 Oj 3.00N 122.00 E
Čeleken 19 Fh 39.27N 53.10 E
Čeleken, Poluostrov- 16 Rj 39.25N 53.35 E
Celendín 54 Ce 6.52S 78.09W
Celerain, Punta- 48 Pg 20.16N 86.59W
Celeste 55 Dj 31.18S 57.04W
Celestún 48 Ng 20.52N 90.24W
Celinograd 22 Jd 51.10N 71.30 E
Celinogradskaja Oblast [3] 19 Gh 51.00N 70.00 E
Čeljabinsk 22 Id 55.10N 61.24 E
Čeljabinskaja Oblast [3] 19 Ge 54.00N 61.00 E
Celje 14 Jd 46.14N 15.16 E
Celjuskin, Mys- 21 Mb 77.45N 104.20 E
Čelkar 19 Ff 47.50N 59.29 E
Celldömölk 10 Ni 47.15N 17.09 E
Celle 10 Gd 52.37N 10.05 E
Celles 12 Fd 50.43N 3.27 E
Celles, Houyet- 12 Hd 50.19N 5.01 E
Cellina 14 Ge 46.02N 12.47 E
Celone 14 Ji 41.36N 15.41 E
Celorico da Beira 13 Ed 40.38N 7.23W
Celtic Sea 5 Fe 51.00N 7.00W
Celtic Sea (EN) = An Mhuir Cheilteach 5 Fe 51.00N 7.00W
Cemaes Head 9 Ii 52.07N 4.44W
Čemal 20 Df 51.25N 86.05 E
Čemdalsk 20 Fe 59.45N 103.18 E
Cemernica 14 Lf 44.30N 17.15 E
Cemerno 15 Df 43.36N 20.26 E
Çemişkezek 24 Hc 39.04N 38.55 E
Cenajo, Embalse de- 13 Kf 38.20N 1.55W
Cenderawasih, Teluk- 26 Kg 2.25S 135.10 E
Cengel 27' Eb 48.56N 89.10 E
Çengel Geçidi 24 Kc 39.45N 44.02 E
Ceno 14 Ef 44.41N 10.05 E
Centenary 37 Ec 16.44S 31.07 E
Centennial 46 Lf 41.51N 106.07W
Centennial Lake 44 Ic 45.15N 77.00W
Centennial Mountains 46 Jd 44.35N 111.55W
Center 45 Ik 31.48N 94.11W
Center Hill Lake 44 Eg 36.00N 85.45W
Centerville 45 Jf 40.43N 92.52W
Centinela, Farallón- 50 Cg 10.49N 66.05W
Centinela, Picacho del- 47 Dc 29.07N 102.27W
Cento 14 Ff 44.43N 11.17 E
Centrafrique = Central African Republic (EN) [1] 31 Jh 7.00N 21.00 E
Central [Bots.] [3] 37 Dd 21.30S 26.00 E
Central [Ghana] [3] 34 Ed 5.30N 1.00W
Central [Kenya] [3] 36 Gc 0.45S 37.00 E
Central [Mwi.] [3] 36 Fe 13.30S 34.00 E
Central [Par.] [3] 55 Dg 25.30S 57.30W
Central [Scot.-U.K.] [3] 9 Ie 56.15N 4.10W
Central [Ug.] [3] 36 Fb 0.10N 32.05 E
Central [Zam.] [3] 36 Ee 15.00S 29.00 E
Central, Chaco- 52 Kh 25.00S 59.45W
Central, Cordillera- [Dom.Rep.] 47 Je 18.45N 70.30W
Central, Cordillera- [P.R.] 49 Nd 18.10N 66.35W
Central, Massif- 5 Gf 45.00N 3.10 E
Central, Meseta- 38 Ig 23.00N 103.00W
Central African Republic (EN) = Centrafrique [1] 31 Jh 7.00N 21.00 E
Central Auckland [2] 62 Fb 36.45S 174.40 E
Central Brāhui Range 25 Dc 29.20N 66.55 E
Central City 45 Hf 41.07N 98.00W
Centralia [Il.-U.S.] 45 Lg 38.31N 89.08W
Centralia [Wa.-U.S.] 43 Cb 46.43N 122.58W
Central Lowland 38 Ke 40.20N 90.00W
Central Makrān Range 21 Ig 26.40N 64.30 E
Centralno Tungusskoje Plato 20 Fd 61.15N 102.00 E
Centralny-Kospašski 17 Hg 59.03N 57.50 E
Central Pacific Basin (EN) 3 Ki 5.00N 175.00W
Central Plateau 64e Bb 0.32S 166.56 E
Central Point 46 De 42.23N 122.57W
Central Range 57 Fe 5.00S 142.30 E
Central Russian Uplands (EN) = Srednerusskaja Vozvyšennost 5 Je 52.00N 38.00 E
Central Siberian Uplands (EN) = Srednesibirskoje Ploskogorje 21 Mc 65.00N 105.00 E
Central Urals (EN) = Srednij Ural 5 Ld 58.00N 59.00 E
Centre [Togo] [3] 34 Fd 9.15N 1.00 E
Centre [U.V.] [3] 34 Ec 12.00N 1.00W
Centre, Canal du- 11 Jh 46.28N 3.59 E
Centre-Est [3] 34 Ec 11.30N 0.20W
Centre-Nord [3] 34 Ec 13.20N 0.55W
Centre-Ouest [3] 34 Ec 12.00N 2.20W
Centre-Sud [3] 34 He 3.30N 11.50 E
Centro, Cayo- 48 Ph 18.35N 87.20W
Centuripe 14 Im 37.37N 14.44 E
Čepca 19 Fd 58.35N 50.05 E
Čepelare 15 Hh 41.44N 24.41 E
Cephalonia (EN) = Kefallinía 5 Ih 38.15N 20.35 E
Čepin 14 Me 45.32N 18.34 E
Ceplenița 15 Jb 47.23N 26.58 E
Cepu 26 Fh 7.09S 111.35 E
Cer 15 Ce 44.37N 19.28 E
Ceram Sea (EN) = Seram, Laut- 57 De 2.30S 128.00 E
Cerbatana, Serranía de la- 54 Eb 6.50N 66.15W
Cerbicales, Iles- 11a Bb 41.33N 9.22 E
Cercal 13 Dg 37.47N 8.42W
Čerchov 10 Rg 49.10N 21.05 E
Čerdakly 7 Li 54.23N 48.51 E
Čerdyn 17 Hf 60.25N 56.29 E
Cère 11 Hj 44.55N 1.49 E
Čereha 7 Gh 57.47N 28.22 E
Čeremhovo 22 Md 53.09N 103.05 E
Čerepanovo 20 Df 54.13N 83.32 E
Čerepovec 6 Jd 59.08N 37.54 E
Ceres [Arg.] 56 Hc 29.53S 61.57W
Ceres [Braz.] 54 Ig 15.17S 49.35W
Ceres [S.Afr.] 37 Bf 33.21S 19.18 E
Céret 11 Il 42.29N 2.45 E
Cereté 54 Cb 8.53N 75.47W
Cerf Island 30 Mi 9.31S 51.01 E
Cerfontaine 12 Gd 50.10N 4.25 E
Cergy 12 Ee 49.02N 2.04 E
Cerignola 14 Ji 41.16N 15.54 E
Čerikov 16 Gc 53.35N 31.25 E
Cérilly 11 Ih 46.37N 2.50 E
Čerkasskaja Oblast [3] 19 Df 49.15N 31.15 E
Čerkassy 19 Df 49.26N 32.04 E
Çerkeş 24 Eb 40.50N 32.54 E
Čerkessk 19 Eg 44.14N 42.04 E
Čerkesskaja respublika 19 Eg 43.45N 41.45 E
Çerkezköy 15 Kh 41.17N 28.00 E
Čerlak 19 He 54.09N 74.58 E
Čerlakski 19 He 53.47N 74.31 E
Čermasan 17 Gi 55.10N 55.20 E
Čermei 15 Ec 46.33N 21.51 E
Čermenika 15 Dh 41.03N 20.20 E
Čermoz 17 Hg 58.47N 56.10 E
Cerna [Rom.] 15 Ge 44.37N 23.57 E
Cerna [Rom.] 15 Fd 44.42N 22.25 E
Cerna [Rom.] 15 Fe 45.53N 22.58 E
Černaja 17 Hb 68.35N 56.31 E
Černaja 17 Hb 68.35N 56.30 E
Černaja 15 Mb 47.39N 29.11 E
Černa Skala, Prohod- 15 Fg 42.02N 22.47 E
Černatica 15 Hh 41.53N 24.33 E
Černavčicy 10 Td 52.11N 23.47 E
Cernavoda 15 Le 44.22N 28.01 E
Cernay 11 Ng 47.49N 7.10 E
Cernay-en-Dormois 12 Ge 49.13N 4.46 E
Černevo 8 Mf 58.35N 28.23 E
Černigov 6 Je 51.30N 31.18 E
Černigovskaja Oblast [3] 19 De 51.20N 32.00 E
Černi Lom 15 If 43.33N 25.57 E
Černi vrăh 15 Gg 42.35N 23.15 E
Černjahovsk 19 Ce 54.38N 21.48 E
Černjanka 16 Jd 50.55N 37.49 E
Černobyl 19 De 51.17N 30.13 E
Černogorsk 20 Ef 53.45N 91.18 E
Černoje More = Black Sea (EN) 5 Jg 43.00N 35.00 E
Černo More = Black Sea (EN) 5 Jg 43.00N 35.00 E
Černomorskoje 16 Hg 45.31N 32.42 E
Černovcy 6 If 48.18N 25.56 E
Černovickaja Oblast [3] 19 Cf 48.20N 26.10 E
Černuška 19 Fd 56.31N 56.03 E
Černy Jar 16 Oe 48.03N 46.05 E
Černyje Zemli 16 Nf 45.55N 46.00 E
Černyševa, Grjada- 17 Ic 66.20N 59.45 E
Černyševa, Zaliv- 18 Bb 45.50N 59.10 E
Černyševsk 20 Gf 52.35N 117.02 E
Černyševski 20 Gd 62.58N 112.15 E
Černyškovski 16 Me 48.27N 42.14 E
Cérou 11 Hj 44.08N 1.52 E
Cerralvo 48 Jd 26.06N 99.37W
Cerralvo, Isla- 47 Cd 24.15N 109.55W
Cerredo, Torre de- 13 Ha 43.13N 4.50W
Cerriku 15 Ch 41.02N 19.57 E
Cerrito [Col.] 54 Db 6.51N 72.42W
Cerrito [Par.] 55 Dh 27.19S 57.40W
Cerritos 48 Dd 22.26N 100.17W
Cerro Azul 48 Kg 21.12N 97.44W
Cerro Azul 56 Kb 24.50S 49.15W
Cerro Chato 55 Ek 33.06S 55.08W
Cerro Colorado 55 Ek 33.52S 55.33W
Cerro de las Mesas 48 Kh 18.47N 96.05W
Cerro de Pasco 53 Ig 10.41S 76.16W
Cêrro Grande 55 Gj 30.36S 51.45W
Cerro Largo 56 Jc 28.09S 54.45W
Cerro Largo [2] 55 Ek 32.30S 54.20W
Cerron, Cerro- 49 Lh 10.19N 70.39W
Cerro San Valentín 52 Ij 46.36S 73.20W
Cerros Colorados, Embalse- 56 Ge 38.35S 68.40W
Cerro Vera 55 Dk 33.11S 57.28W
Cerrudo Cué 55 Dh 27.34S 57.57W
Čerski 22 Sc 68.45N 161.45 E
Čerskogo, hrebet- 20 Gf 52.00N 114.00 E
Čerskogo, hrebet- = Cherski Mountains 21 Qc 65.00N 145.00 E

Index Symbols

[1] Independent Nation
[2] State, Region
[3] District, County
[4] Municipality
[5] Colony, Dependency
Continent
Physical Region
Historical or Cultural Region
Mount, Mountain
Volcano
Hill
Mountains, Mountain Range
Hills, Escarpment
Plateau, Upland
Pass, Gap
Plain, Lowland
Delta
Salt Flat
Valley, Canyon
Crater, Cave
Karst Features
Depression
Polder
Desert, Dunes
Forest, Woods
Heath, Steppe
Oasis
Cape, Point
Coast, Beach
Cliff
Peninsula
Isthmus
Sandbank
Island
Atoll
Rock, Reef
Islands, Archipelago
Rocks, Reefs
Coral Reef
Well, Spring
Geyser
River, Stream
Waterfall Rapids
River Mouth, Estuary
Lake
Salt Lake
Intermittent Lake
Reservoir
Swamp, Pond
Canal
Glacier
Ice Shelf, Pack Ice
Ocean
Sea
Gulf, Bay
Strait, Fjord
Lagoon
Bank
Seamount
Tablemount
Ridge
Shelf
Basin
Escarpment, Sea Scarp
Fracture
Trench, Abyss
National Park, Reserve
Point of Interest
Recreation Site
Cave, Cavern
Historic Site
Ruins
Wall, Walls
Church, Abbey
Temple
Scientific Station
Airport
Port
Lighthouse
Mine
Tunnel
Dam, Bridge

Certaldo 14 Fg 43.33N 11.02 E
Čertkovo 16 Le 49.20N 40.12 E
Cervaro 14 Ji 41.30N 15.52 E
Cervati 14 Jj 40.17N 15.29 E
Červeh 15 Jf 43.37N 26.02 E
Červen 16 Fc 53.43N 28.29 E
Červen brjag 15 Hf 43.16N 24.06 E
Cervera 13 Nc 41.40N 1.17 E
Cervera del Río Alhama 13 Kb 42.01N 1.57W
Cervera de Pisuerga 13 Hb 42.52N 4.30W
Cerveteri 14 Gh 42.00N 12.06 E
Cervia 14 Gf 44.15N 12.22 E
Cervin/Cervino 14 Be 45.58N 7.39 E
Cervino/Cervin 14 Be 45.58N 7.39 E
Cervione 11a Ba 42.20N 9.29 E
Červonoarmejsk 10 Vf 50.03N 25.18 E
Červonoarmejskoje 15 Ld 45.50N 28.38 E
Červonograd 19 Ce 50.24N 24.12 E
Cesano 14 Hg 43.45N 13.10 E
Cesar [2] 54 Db 9.50N 73.30W
César, Río- 49 Ki 9.00N 73.58W
Cesena 14 Gf 44.08N 12.15 E
Cesenatico 14 Gf 44.12N 12.24 E
Cēsis/Cesis 19 Cd 57.18N 25.18 E
Cesis/Cēsis 19 Cd 57.18N 25.18 E
Česká Lípa 10 Kf 50.42N 14.32 E
Česká Republika = Czech Republic (EN) 6 Hf 50.00N 13.00 E
Česká Třebová 10 Mg 49.54N 16.27 E
Ceské Budějovice 10 Kh 48.58N 14.29 E
České středohoří 10 Jf 50.35N 14.00 E
Ceské země [2] 10 Kg 49.45N 15.00 E
Českomoravská Vrchovina = Moravian Upland (EN) 5 Hf 49.20N 15.30 E
Český Krumlov 10 Kh 48.49N 14.19 E
Český Les = Bohemian Forest (EN) 10 Ig 49.50N 12.30 E
Cesma 14 Kf 45.35N 16.29 E
Česma 17 Jj 53.50N 60.40 E
Çeşme 24 Bc 38.18N 26.19 E
Çeşme Yarimadasi 15 Jk 38.30N 26.30 E
Češskaja Guba = Chesha Bay (EN) 5 Kb 67.20N 46.30 E
Cessnock 59 Kf 32.50S 151.21 E
Cestos 30 Gh 5.27N 9.35W
Cesvaine/Cesvajne 8 Lh 56.55N 26.20 E
Cesvajne/Cesvaine 8 Lh 56.55N 26.20 E
Cetate 15 Ge 44.06N 23.03 E
Cetiná 14 Kg 43.27N 16.42 E
Cetinje 15 Bg 42.24N 18.55 E
Çetinkaya 24 Gc 39.15N 37.38 E
Cetraro 14 Jk 39.31N 15.56 E
Cetynia 10 Sd 52.33N 22.26 E
Ceuta [5] 31 Ge 35.53N 5.19W
Ceva-i-Ra (Conway Reef) 57 Ig 21.45S 174.35 E
Cevedale/Zufallspitze 14 Ed 46.27N 10.37 E
Cévennes 5 Gg 44.40N 4.00 E
Ceyhan 23 Eb 36.45N 35.42 E
Ceyhan 23 Eb 37.04N 35.47 E
Ceylanpınar 24 Id 36.51N 40.02 E
Ceylon → Srī Lanka [1] 22 Ki 7.40N 80.50 E
Cézallier 11 Ii 45.20N 3.00 E
Cèze 11 Kj 44.06N 4.42 E
Chaalis, Abbaye de- 12 Ee 49.10N 2.40 E
Cha-am 25 Jf 12.48N 99.58 E
Chabanais 11 Gi 45.52N 0.43 E
Chabjuwardoo Bay 59 Cd 22.55S 113.50 E
Chablais 11 Mh 46.20N 6.30 E
Chāboksar 24 Nd 36.58N 50.34 E
Chabówka 10 Pg 49.34N 19.58 E
Chacabuco 56 Hd 34.38S 60.29W
Chachan, Nevado- 54 Dg 16.12S 71.33W
Chachapoyas 54 Ce 6.13S 77.51W
Chachoengsao 25 Kf 13.41N 101.03 E
Chaco [2] 56 Hc 26.00S 60.30W
Chaco [3] 55 Bd 20.00S 60.30W
Chaco, Gran- 52 Jh 23.00S 60.00W
Chaco Mesa 45 Ci 35.50N 107.35W
Chaco River 45 Bh 36.46N 108.39W
Chad (EN) = Tchad [1] 31 Ig 15.00N 19.00 E
Chad, Lake- (EN) = Tchad, Lac- 30 Ig 13.20N 14.00 E
Chādegān 24 Nf 32.46N 50.38 E
Chadileuvú, Río- 56 Ee 38.49S 64.57W
Chadiza 36 Fe 14.04S 32.26 E
Chadron 43 Gc 42.50N 103.02W
Chaeryŏng 28 He 38.24N 125.37 E
Chafarinas, Islas- 13 Ji 35.11N 2.26W
Chāgai Hills 21 Ig 29.30N 64.15 E
Chagang-Do [2] 28 Ie 40.50N 126.30 E
Chaghcharān 22 If 34.31N 65.15 E
Chagny 11 Kh 46.55N 4.45 E
Chagos Archipelago 21 Jj 6.00S 72.00 E
Chagos-Laccadive Plateau (EN) 3 Gi 3.00N 73.00 E
Chagu, Serra do- 55 Fg 25.10S 52.40W
Chaguaramas 50 Ch 9.20N 66.16W
Chahār Borjak 23 Jc 30.17N 62.03 E
Chahār Mahāl-e Bakhtīārī [3] 23 Hc 32.00N 50.00 E
Chahbounia 13 Oi 35.33N 2.36 E
Ch'aho 28 Jd 40.12N 128.38 E
Chai Badan 25 Ke 15.05N 101.04 E
Chaibāsa 25 Hd 22.34N 85.49 E
Chaigoubu → Huai'an 28 Cd 40.40N 114.25 E
Chai He 28 Gc 42.20N 123.51 E
Chaillu, Massif du- 30 Ii 2.32S 11.10 E
Chainat 25 Ke 15.10N 100.10 E
Chaitén 56 Ff 42.55S 72.43W
Chaiyaphum 25 Ke 16.09N 102.02 E
Chajul 49 Bf 15.30N 91.02W
Chakari 37 Dc 18.09S 29.52 E
Chak Chak 35 Dd 8.40N 26.54 E
Chake Chake 31 Ki 5.15S 39.46 E
Chakhānsūr 23 Jc 31.10N 62.04 E
Chala 54 Dg 15.52S 74.16W
Chalais 11 Gi 45.17N 0.02 E
Chalaltenango 49 Cf 14.03N 88.56W
Chalan Kanoa 64b Ba 15.08N 145.43 E
Chālūs 22 Gf 37.16N 49.36 E
Chalbi Desert 30 Kh 3.00N 37.20 E
Chalchuapa 49 Cg 13.59N 89.41W
Chalcidice (EN) = Khalkidhikí 5 Ig 40.25N 23.25 E
Chālesbān 24 Ne 35.18N 50.03 E
Chaleur Bay 42 Kg 47.50N 65.30W
Chalhuanca 54 Df 14.17S 73.15W
Chaling 27 Jf 26.47N 113.32 E
Chalky Inlet 62 Bg 46.05S 166.30 E
Challans 11 Eh 46.51N 1.53W
Challapata 54 Eg 18.54S 66.47W
Challis 46 Hd 44.30N 114.14W
Chalmette 45 Ll 29.56N 89.58W
Châlons-sur-Marne 11 Kf 48.57N 4.22 E
Châlon-sur-Saône 11 Kh 46.47N 4.51 E
Chaltubo 16 Mh 42.19N 42.34 E
Chālūs 23 Hb 36.38N 51.26 E
Châlus 11 Gi 45.39N 0.59 E
Cham 10 Ig 49.13N 12.40 E
Chama 36 Fe 11.12S 33.10 E
Chama, Río- 45 Ch 36.03N 106.05W
Chama, Río- 49 Li 9.03N 71.37W
Chaman 25 Db 30.55N 66.27 E
Chaman Bīd 24 Qd 37.25N 56.38 E
Chamba [India] 25 Fb 32.34N 76.08 E
Chamba [Tan.] 36 Ge 11.35S 36.58 E
Chambal 21 Jg 26.29N 79.15 E
Chambaran, Plateau de- 11 Li 45.10N 5.20 E
Chambas 49 Hb 22.12N 78.55W
Chamberlain 45 Ge 43.49N 99.20W
Chamberlain Lake 44 Mb 46.17N 69.20W
Chamberlain River 59 Fc 15.35S 127.51 E
Chambersburg 44 If 39.57N 77.40W
Chambéry 11 Li 45.34N 5.56 E
Chambeshi 30 Jj 11.53S 29.48 E
Chambley-Bussières 12 He 49.03N 5.54 E
Chambly 12 Ee 49.10N 2.15 E
Chambois 12 Cf 48.48N 0.07 E
Chambon, Lac de- 11 Ih 45.35N 2.55 E
Chambord 11 Hg 47.37N 1.31 E
Chamchamal 24 Ke 35.32N 44.50 E
Chame, Punta- 49 Hi 8.39N 79.42W
Chamela 48 Gh 19.32N 105.05W
Chamela, Bahia- 48 Gh 19.30N 105.10W
Chamelecón, Río- 49 Df 15.51N 87.49W
Chamical 56 Gd 30.21S 66.19W
Chamiss Bay 46 Ba 50.07N 127.22W
Chamoli 25 Fb 30.24N 79.21 E
Chamonix-Mont-Blanc 11 Mi 45.55N 6.52 E
Chamouchouane, Rivière- 44 Ka 48.40N 72.20W
Champagne 5 Gf 49.00N 4.30 E
Champagne 11 Kf 49.00N 4.30 E
Champagne Berrichonne 11 Hh 47.00N 2.00 E
Champagne Humide 11 Kf 48.20N 4.30 E
Champagne Pouilleuse 11 Kf 48.40N 4.20 E
Champagnole 11 Lh 46.45N 5.55 E
Champaign 43 Jc 40.07N 88.14W
Champaquí, Cerro- 52 Ji 31.59S 64.56W
Champasak 25 Lf 14.53N 105.52 E
Champaubert 12 Ff 48.53N 3.47 E
Champdoré, Lac- 42 Ke 55.55N 65.45W
Champeigne 11 Gg 47.15N 0.50 E
Champerico 49 Bf 14.18N 91.55W
Champlain, Lake- 43 Mc 44.45N 73.15W
Champlitte-et-le-Prélot 11 Lg 47.37N 5.31 E
Champotón 47 Fe 19.21N 90.43W
Champsaur 11 Mj 44.45N 6.10 E
Chāmrājnagar 25 Ff 11.55N 76.57 E
Chañaral 56 Fc 26.21S 70.37W
Chança 13 Eg 37.33N 7.31W
Chan Chan 54 Ce 8.07S 79.02W
Chanco 56 Fe 35.44S 72.32W
Chandalar 40 Jc 66.36N 145.48W
Chandalar 40 Jc 67.30N 148.30W
Chandausi 25 Fc 28.27N 78.46 E
Chandeleur Islands 43 Jf 29.48N 88.51W
Chandeleur Sound 45 Ll 29.55N 89.10W
Chandīgarh 22 Jf 30.44N 76.55 E
Chandler 42 Lg 48.21N 64.41W
Chandless, Rio 54 Ee 9.08S 69.51W
Chāndpur 25 Id 23.13N 90.39 E
Chandragupta 25 Fe 16.11N 78.52 E
Chandrapur 22 Jh 19.57N 79.18 E
Chang, Ko- 25 Kf 12.00N 102.23 E
Changajn Nuruu → Hangaj, Hrebet- = Khangai Mountains (EN) 21 Le 47.30N 100.00 E
Chang'an → Rong'an 27 If 25.16N 109.23 E
Changane 30 Kk 24.43S 33.32 E
Changbai 28 Jd 41.25N 128.11 E
Changbai Shan 21 Oe 42.00N 128.00 E
Changchun 22 Oe 43.51N 125.20 E
Changdao(Sihou) 28 Ff 37.56N 120.42 E
Changde 22 Ng 29.04N 111.42 E
Ch'angdo 28 Ie 38.30N 127.45 E
Changfeng (Shuijiahu) 28 Dh 32.29N 117.10 E
Changge 28 Bg 34.12N 113.45 E
Changhang 28 If 36.01N 126.42 E
Chang He 28 Ei 31.21N 118.21 E
Changhowŏn 28 If 37.07N 127.38 E
Changhua 27 Lg 24.05N 120.32 E
Changhŭng 28 Ig 34.40N 126.54 E
Changji 27 Ec 44.01N 87.16 E
Chang Jiang 28 Dj 28.59N 116.42 E
Changjiang (Shiliu) 27 Ih 19.20N 109.03 E
Chang Jiang (Yangtze Kiang) 21 Of 31.48N 121.10 E
Changjiang Kou 27 Le 31.24N 121.59 E
Changjin-gang 28 Id 40.30N 127.12 E
Changjin-ho 28 Id 40.30N 127.12 E
Changjin-ŭp 27 Mc 40.23N 127.15 E
Changli 28 Ee 39.43N 119.10 E
Changling 27 Lc 44.15N 123.58 E
Changlung 25 Fb 34.56N 77.29 E
Changping 28 Dd 40.14N 116.13 E
Changsha 22 Ng 28.12N 113.02 E
Changshan 28 Ej 28.55N 118.31 E
Changshan Qundao 28 Ge 39.10N 122.34 E
Changshu 28 Fi 31.38N 120.44 E
Changsŏng 28 Ig 35.19N 126.48 E
Changting 28 Jb 44.27N 128.50 E
Changtu 28 Hc 42.47N 124.08 E
Changuillo 54 Cf 14.40S 75.12W
Changuinola 49 Fi 9.26N 82.31W
Changwu 27 Id 35.17N 107.52 E
Changxing 28 Ei 31.01N 119.55 E
Changxing Dao 28 Fe 39.35N 121.42 E
Changyi 28 Ef 36.52N 119.25 E
Changyŏn 27 Md 38.15N 125.05 E
Changyuan 28 Cg 35.12N 114.40 E
Changzhi 27 Jd 36.07N 113.10 E
Changzhou 28 Ei 31.46N 119.56 E
Channel Islands [5] 9 Kl 49.20N 2.20W
Channel Islands [Chan.Is.] 5 Ff 49.20N 2.20W
Channel Islands [U.S.] 38 Hf 34.00N 120.00W
Channel Port-aux-Basques 39 Ne 47.35N 59.11W
Channel Rock 49 Ib 23.00N 77.55W
Channing 45 Ei 35.41N 102.20W
Chantada 13 Eb 42.37N 7.46W
Chantengo, Laguna- 48 Ji 16.35N 99.10W
Chanthaburi 25 Kf 12.35N 102.06 E
Chantilly 11 Ie 49.12N 2.28 E
Chantonnay 11 Eh 46.41N 1.03W
Chantrey Inlet 38 Jc 67.48N 96.20W
Chanute 45 Ih 37.41N 95.27W
Chanza 13 Eg 37.33N 7.31W
Chao'an (Chaozhou) 27 Kg 23.41N 116.37 E
Chaobai Xinhe 28 De 39.07N 117.41 E
Chao He 28 Dd 40.36N 117.08 E
Chao Hu 28 Di 31.31N 117.33 E
Chao Phraya 21 Mh 13.32N 100.36 E
Chaor He 27 Lb 46.49N 123.45 E
Chaoxian 27 Ke 31.37N 117.49 E
Chaoyang [China] 22 Oe 41.35N 120.26 E
Chaoyang [China] 27 Kg 23.17N 116.37 E
Chaoyang → Huinan 28 Ic 42.41N 126.03 E
Chaoyang → Jiayin 27 Nb 48.52N 130.21 E
Chaoyangchuan 28 Jc 42.53N 129.23 E
Chaoyangcun 27 La 50.01N 124.22 E
Chaozhong 27 La 50.53N 121.23 E
Chaozhou → Chao'an 27 Kg 23.41N 116.37 E
Chapada dos Guimarães 54 Gg 15.26S 55.45W
Chapadinha 54 Jd 3.44S 43.21W
Chapais 44 Ja 49.47N 74.56W
Chapala 48 Hg 20.18N 103.12W
Chapala, Lago de- 38 Ig 20.15N 103.00W
Chaparral 54 Cc 3.43N 75.28W
Chapecó 56 Jc 27.06S 52.36W
Chapecó, Rio- 55 Fh 27.06S 53.01W
Chapecó, Serra do- 55 Gh 26.44S 51.54W
Chapel Hill 44 Hh 35.55N 79.04W
Chapicuy 55 Dj 31.40S 57.55W
Chapleau 42 Jg 47.50N 83.24W
Chaplin 46 La 50.28N 106.40W
Chaplin Lake 46 La 50.18N 106.35W
Chapman, Cape - 42 Ic 69.15N 89.27W
Chappell 45 Ef 41.06N 102.28W
Chāpra 25 Gc 25.46N 84.45 E
Chapultepec 48 Hf 23.27N 103.04W
Chaqui 54 Eg 19.36S 65.32W
Char 32 Ee 21.31N 12.51W
Charadai 55 Ch 27.38S 59.54W
Charagua 54 Fg 19.48S 63.13W
Charām 24 Ng 30.45N 50.44 E
Charaña 54 Eg 17.36S 69.28W
Charcas 48 If 23.08N 101.07W
Charco de la Aguja 48 Gc 28.25N 104.01W
Charcot Island 66 Qe 69.45S 75.15W
Chard [Alta.-Can.] 42 Ge 55.48N 111.10W
Chard [Eng.-U.K.] 9 Kk 50.53N 2.58W
Chardāvol 24 Lf 33.45N 46.38 E
Chardonnières 49 Jd 18.16N 74.10W
Charente [3] 11 Gi 45.40N 0.05 E
Charente 11 Ei 45.57N 1.05W
Charente-Maritime [3] 11 Fi 45.30N 0.45W
Charentonne 12 Ce 49.07N 0.44 E
Chari 30 Ig 12.58N 14.31 E
Chari-Baguirmi [3] 35 Bc 12.00N 17.00 E
Chārīkār 23 Kb 35.01N 69.11 E
Charing 12 Cc 51.12N 0.48 E
Chariton 45 Jf 41.00N 93.19W
Chariton River 45 Jg 39.19N 92.57W
Charity 54 Gb 7.24N 58.36W
Charleroi 11 Kd 50.25N 4.26 E
Charleroi-Jumet 11 Kd 50.27N 4.26 E
Charleroi-Marcinelle 12 Gd 50.25N 4.28 E
Charles 42 Kd 62.38N 74.15W
Charles, Cape- [Can.] 38 Nd 52.13N 55.40W
Charles, Cape- [Va.-U.S.] 43 Ld 37.08N 75.58W
Charles, Peak- 59 Ef 32.52S 121.11 E
Charlesbourg 44 Lb 46.52N 71.16W
Charles City 43 Ic 43.04N 92.40W
Charles de Gaulle, Aéroport- = Charles de Gaulle Airport (EN) 12 Ee 49.02N 2.35 E
Charles de Gaulle Airport (EN) = Charles de Gaulle, Aéroport- 12 Ee 49.02N 2.35 E
Charleston [Il.-U.S.] 45 Lg 39.30N 88.10W
Charleston [Mo.-U.S.] 45 Lh 36.55N 89.21W
Charleston [Ms.-U.S.] 45 Ki 34.01N 90.04W
Charleston [N.Z.] 62 Dd 41.54S 171.27 E
Charleston [S.C.-U.S.] 39 Lf 32.48N 79.57W
Charleston [W.V.-U.S.] 39 Kf 38.21N 81.38W
Charleston Peak 43 Dd 36.16N 115.42W
Charles Town 44 If 39.18N 77.52W
Charlestown 50 Ed 17.12N 62.35W
Charleval 12 De 49.22N 1.23 E
Charleville 58 Fg 26.24S 146.15 E
Charleville-Mézières 11 Ke 49.46N 4.43 E
Charleville Mézières-Mohon 12 Ge 49.46N 4.43 E
Charlevoix 44 Ec 45.19N 85.16W
Charlieu 11 Kh 46.09N 4.11 E
Charlotte [Mi.-U.S.] 44 Ed 42.36N 84.50W
Charlotte [N.C.-U.S.] 39 Kf 35.14N 80.50W
Charlotte Amalie 47 Le 18.21N 64.56W
Charlotte Bank (EN) 57 If 11.47S 173.13 E
Charlotte Harbor 44 Fl 26.45N 82.12W
Charlottenberg 8 Ee 59.53N 12.17 E
Charlottesville 43 Ld 38.02N 78.29W
Charlottetown 39 Me 46.14N 63.08W
Charlton 59 Ig 36.16S 143.21 E
Charlton 42 Jf 52.00N 79.26W
Charly 12 Ff 48.58N 3.17 E
Charmes 11 Mf 48.22N 6.17 E
Charnley River 59 Ec 16.20S 124.53 E
Charny-sur-Meuse 12 He 49.12N 5.22 E
Charollais 11 Kh 46.26N 4.16 E
Charouïne 32 Gd 29.01N 0.16W
Charroux 11 Gh 46.09N 0.24 E
Chārsadda 25 Eb 34.09N 71.44 E
Charters Towers 58 Fg 20.05S 146.16 E
Chartres 11 Hf 48.27N 1.30 E
Charzykowskie, Jezioro- 10 Nc 53.47N 17.30 E
Chascomus 56 Ie 35.34S 58.01W
Chase 46 Fa 50.49N 119.41W
Chasŏng 28 Id 41.25N 126.35 E
Chassengue 36 Ce 10.26S 18.32 E
Chassezac 11 Kj 44.26N 4.19 E
Chassiron, Pointe de- 11 Eh 46.03N 1.24W
Chat 24 Pd 37.59N 55.16 E
Châtaigneraie 11 Ij 44.45N 2.20 E
Chātāl 24 Pd 37.40N 55.45 E
Château-Arnoux 11 Lj 44.06N 6.00 E
Chateaubelair 51n Ba 13.17N 61.15W
Châteaubriant 11 Eg 47.43N 1.23W
Château-Chinon 11 Jg 47.04N 3.56 E
Château-du-Loir 11 Gg 47.42N 0.25 E
Châteaudun 11 Hf 48.05N 1.20 E
Château-Gontier 11 Fg 47.50N 0.42W
Châteaulin 11 Bf 48.12N 4.05W
Châteaulin, Bassin de- 11 Cf 48.18N 3.50W
Châteaumeillant 11 Ih 46.34N 2.12 E
Châteauneuf-de-Randon 11 Jj 44.39N 3.04 E
Châteauneuf-sur-Cher 11 Ih 46.51N 2.19 E
Châteauneuf-sur-Loire 11 Ig 47.52N 2.14 E
Château-Porcien 12 Ge 49.32N 4.15 E
Châteaurenard 11 Kk 43.53N 4.51 E
Château-Renault 11 Gg 47.35N 0.54 E
Châteauroux 11 Hh 46.49N 1.42 E
Château-Salins 11 Mf 48.49N 6.30 E
Château-Thierry 11 Je 49.03N 3.24 E
Châteaux, Pointe des- 51e Bb 16.15N 61.11W
Châtelaillon-Plage 11 Eh 46.04N 1.05W
Châtelet 12 Gd 50.24N 4.31 E
Châtelguyon 11 Ji 45.55N 3.04 E
Châtellerault 11 Gh 46.48N 0.32 E
Chatelodo 55 De 21.19S 57.28W
Chatham [Eng.-U.K.] 9 Nj 51.23N 0.32 E
Chatham [N.B.-Can.] 42 Kg 47.02N 65.26W
Chatham [Ont.-Can.] 42 Jh 42.24N 82.11W
Chatham [Va.-U.S.] 44 Hg 36.49N 79.26W
Chatham Island 57 Ji 44.00S 176.30W
Chatham Islands 57 Ji 44.00S 176.30W
Chatham Rise (EN) 57 Ii 43.30S 180.00
Chatham Strait 40 Me 57.30N 134.45W
Châtillon-en-Bazois 11 Jg 47.03N 3.40 E
Châtillon-sur-Indre 11 Hh 46.59N 1.10 E
Châtillon-sur-Marne 12 Fe 49.06N 3.45 E
Châtillon-sur-Seine 11 Kg 47.51N 4.33 E
Chatom 44 Cj 31.28N 88.16W
Chatsworth 37 Ec 19.38S 30.50 E
Chattahoochee 44 Ej 30.42N 84.51W
Chattahoochee 38 Kf 30.52N 84.57W
Chattanooga 39 Kf 35.03N 85.19W
Chatteris 12 Cb 52.27N 0.03 E
Chaucas 55 Cc 16.46S 58.44W
Chaudfontaine 12 Hd 50.35N 5.38 E
Chaudière, Rivière- 44 Lb 46.43N 71.17W
Chauk 25 Id 20.53N 94.49 E
Chaulnes 12 Ee 49.49N 2.48 E
Chaumont 11 Lf 48.07N 5.08 E
Chaumont-en-Vexin 12 De 49.16N 1.53 E
Chaumont-Gistoux 12 Gd 50.41N 4.44 E
Chaumont-Porcien 12 Ge 49.39N 4.15 E
Chaumont-sur-Aire 12 Hf 48.56N 5.15 E
Chaumont-sur-Loire 11 Hg 47.29N 1.11 E
Chauny 11 Je 49.37N 3.13 E
Chau Phu 25 Lf 10.42N 105.07 E
Chausey, Iles- 11 Ef 48.53N 1.50W
Chauvigny 11 Gh 46.34N 0.39 E
Chavantina 54 Hf 14.40S 52.21W
Chavarría 55 Ci 28.57S 58.35W
Chaves [Braz.] 54 Id 0.10S 49.55W
Chaves [Port.] 13 Ec 41.44N 7.28W
Chavigny, Lac - 42 Je 58.00N 75.05W
Chavuma 36 De 13.05S 22.42 E
Chazelles-sur-Lyon 11 Ki 45.38N 4.23 E
Chbar 25 Lf 12.46N 107.10 E
Cheaha Mountain 44 Ei 33.30N 85.47W
Cheat River 44 Hf 39.45N 79.55W
Cheb 10 If 50.04N 12.23 E
Cheboygan 43 Kb 45.39N 84.29W
Chech, 'Erg- 30 Gf 25.00N 3.00W
Chechaouene [3] 32 Fb 35.00N 5.00W
Chechaouene 32 Fb 35.10N 5.16W
Checheng 27 Lg 22.05N 120.42 E
Che-Chiang Sheng → Zhejiang Sheng [2] 27 Kf 29.00N 120.00 E
Chech'ŏn 28 Jf 37.08N 128.12 E
Chęciny 10 Qf 50.48N 20.28 E
Cheddar Gorge 9 Kj 51.13N 2.47W
Cheduba 25 Ie 18.48N 93.38 E
Chée 12 Gf 48.45N 4.39 E
Cheektowaga 44 Hd 42.57N 78.38W
Chefu 37 Ed 22.27S 32.45 E
Chegga 31 Gf 25.22N 5.49W
Cheghelvandī 24 Mf 33.42N 48.25 E
Chehel Pāyeh 24 Qg 31.54N 57.14 E
Cheju 27 Me 33.31N 126.32 E
Cheju-Do 21 Of 33.25N 126.30 E
Cheju-Do [2] 28 Ih 33.25N 126.30 E
Cheju-Haehyŏp 28 Ih 33.40N 126.28 E
Chela, Serra da- 30 Ij 16.00S 13.10 E
Chelan 46 Ec 47.51N 120.01W
Chelan, Lake- 46 Eb 48.05N 120.30W
Chelforó, Arroyo- 55 Cm 36.55S 58.12W
Cheliff [3] 32 Hb 36.10N 1.45 E
Cheliff 30 He 36.02N 0.08 E
Cheliff 32 Hb 36.10N 1.20 E
Cheliff, Plaine du- 13 Mi 35.57N 0.45 E
Chellalat el Adhaouara 13 Pi 35.56N 3.25 E
Chelleh Khāneh, Kūh-e- 24 Md 36.52N 48.36 E
Chełm [2] 10 Te 51.10N 23.30 E
Chełm 10 Te 51.10N 23.28 E
Chelmer 12 Cc 51.44N 0.42 E
Chełmińskie, Pojezierze- 10 Oc 53.20N 19.00 E
Chełmno 10 Oc 53.22N 18.26 E
Chelmsford 9 Nj 51.44N 0.28 E
Chełmża 10 Oc 53.12N 18.37 E
Cheltenham 9 Kj 51.54N 2.04W
Chelva 13 Le 39.45N 0.59W
Chemainus 46 Db 48.55N 123.43W
Chemâma 32 Ef 16.50N 14.00 E
Chemba 37 Ec 17.09S 34.53 E
Chembe 36 Ee 11.58S 28.45 E
Chemillé 11 Fg 47.13N 0.43W
Chemnitz = Karl-Marx-Stadt 6 He 50.50N 12.55 E
Chemult 46 Ee 43.13N 121.47W
Chenachane 32 Gd 26.00N 4.15W
Chenārbāshi 24 Lf 33.20N 46.20 E
Chen Barag Qi (Bayan Hure) 27 Kb 49.21N 119.25 E
Chencha 35 Fd 6.17N 37.40 E
Chencoyi 48 Nh 19.48N 90.14W
Cheney 46 Gc 47.29N 117.34W
Cheney Reservoir 45 Hh 37.45N 97.50W
Cheng'an 28 Cf 36.27N 114.41 E
Chengde 27 Kc 41.00N 117.57 E
Chengdu 22 Mf 30.45N 104.04 E
Chengkou 27 Ie 31.54N 108.37 E
Chengmai 27 Ih 19.50N 109.59 E
Chengshan Jiao 27 Ld 37.24N 122.42 E
Chengxi Hu 28 Dh 32.22N 116.12 E
Chengzitan 27 Ld 39.31N 122.28 E
Cheňisckali 16 Mh 42.06N 42.16 E
Chenjiagang 28 Eg 34.22N 119.48 E
Chenonceaux 11 Hg 47.20N 1.04 E
Chenxi 27 Jf 28.02N 110.15 E
Chenxian 27 Jf 25.49N 113.05 E
Chenying → Wannian 28 Dj 28.42N 117.04 E
Chépénéhé 63b Ce 20.47S 167.09 E
Chepes 56 Gd 31.21S 66.36W
Chepo 49 Hi 9.10N 79.06W
Cher [3] 11 Ig 47.00N 2.30 E
Cher 5 Gf 47.21N 0.29 E
Cheradi, Isole- 14 Lj 40.25N 17.10 E
Cherangany Hills 36 Gb 1.15N 35.27 E
Cheraw 44 Hh 34.42N 79.53W
Cherbaniani Reef 25 Ef 12.18N 71.53 E
Cherbourg 6 Ff 49.39N 1.39W
Cherchell 32 Hb 36.36N 2.12 E
Chère 11 Eg 47.42N 1.50W
Chergui, Chott Ech- 30 He 34.21N 0.30 E
Chéri 34 Hc 13.26N 11.21 E
Cherlen → Kerulen 21 Ne 48.48N 117.00 E
Cherokee 45 Ie 42.45N 95.33W
Cherokees, Lake O' the- 45 Ih 36.39N 94.49W
Cherksi Mountains (EN) = Čerskogo, hrebet- 21 Qc 65.00N 145.00 E
Chesterfield Inlet 39 Jc 63.21N 90.42W
Chertsey 12 Bc 51.23N 0.30W
Cherwell 9 Lj 51.44N 1.15W
Chesapeake 44 Ig 36.45N 76.15W
Chesapeake Bay 38 Lf 38.40N 76.25W
Chesapeake Bay Bridge-Tunnel 44 Ig 37.00N 76.02W
Chesha Bay (EN) = Češskaja Guba 5 Kb 67.20N 46.30 E
Chesham 12 Bc 51.42N 0.36W
Cheshire [3] 9 Kh 53.15N 2.30W
Cheshire Plain 9 Kh 53.20N 2.40W
Cheshunt 12 Bc 51.42N 0.02W
Chester 9 Kh 53.10N 2.55W
Chester [Eng.-U.K.] 9 Kh 53.12N 2.54W
Chester [Il.-U.S.] 45 Lh 37.55N 89.49W
Chester [Mt.-U.S.] 46 Jb 48.31N 110.58W
Chester [Pa.-U.S.] 44 Jf 39.50N 75.23W
Chester [S.C.-U.S.] 44 Gh 34.40N 81.12W
Chesterfield 9 Lh 53.15N 1.25W
Chesterfield, Ile- 37 Gc 16.20S 43.58 E
Chesterfield, Récifs et Iles- = Chesterfield Reefs and Islands (EN) 57 Gf 20.00S 159.00 E
Chesterfield Inlet 38 Jc 63.25N 90.45W
Chesterfield Reefs and Islands (EN) = Chesterfield, Récifs et Iles- 57 Gf 20.00S 159.00 E
Chesterton Range 59 Je 25.30S 147.30 E
Chestnut Ridge 44 He 40.10N 79.25W
Chesuncook Lake 44 Mb 46.00N 69.20W
Chetaibi 32 Ib 37.04N 7.23 E
Chetumal 39 Kh 18.35N 88.07W
Chetumal, Bahía de 47 Ge 18.20N 88.05W
Cheviot 62 Ee 42.49S 173.16 E
Chew Bahir = Stefanie, Lake- (EN) 30 Kh 4.38N 36.50 E
Chewelah 46 Gb 48.17N 117.43W
Cheyenne [Ok.-U.S.] 45 Gi 35.37N 99.40W

Index Symbols

[1] Independent Nation
[2] State, Region
[3] District, County
[4] Municipality
[5] Colony, Dependency
Continent
Physical Region
Historical or Cultural Region
Mount, Mountain
Volcano
Hill
Mountains, Mountain Range
Hills, Escarpment
Plateau, Upland
Pass, Gap
Plain, Lowland
Delta
Salt Flat
Valley, Canyon
Crater, Cave
Karst Features
Depression
Polder
Desert, Dunes
Forest, Woods
Heath, Steppe
Oasis
Cape, Point
Coast, Beach
Cliff
Peninsula
Isthmus
Sandbank
Island
Atoll
Rock, Reef
Islands, Archipelago
Rocks, Reefs
Coral Reef
Well, Spring
Geyser
River, Stream
Waterfall Rapids
River Mouth, Estuary
Lake
Salt Lake
Intermittent Lake
Reservoir
Swamp, Pond
Canal
Glacier
Ice Shelf, Pack Ice
Ocean
Sea
Gulf, Bay
Strait, Fjord
Lagoon
Bank
Seamount
Tablemount
Ridge
Shelf
Basin
Escarpment, Sea Scarp
Fracture
Trench, Abyss
National Park, Reserve
Point of Interest
Recreation Site
Cave, Cavern
Historic Site
Ruins
Wall, Walls
Church, Abbey
Temple
Scientific Station
Airport
Port
Lighthouse
Mine
Tunnel
Dam, Bridge

Cheyenne [Wy.-U.S.] 39 Ie 41.08N 104.49W
Cheyenne River 43 Gc 44.40N 101.15W
Cheyenne Wells 45 Eg 38.51N 102.11W
Cheyne Bay 59 Df 34.35S 118.50 E
Chhatarpur 25 Fd 24.54N 79.36 E
Chhindwāra 25 Fd 22.04N 78.56 E
Chi 25 Ke 15.11N 104.43 E
Chiamboni, Rās- 35 Gf 1.38S 41.36 E
Chiana, Val di- 14 Fg 43.15N 11.50 E
Chianciano Terme 14 Fg 43.02N 11.49 E
Chiang-hsi Sheng→Jangxi Sheng=Kiangsi (EN) [2] 27 Kf 28.00N 116.00 E
Chiang Mai 22 Lh 18.46N 98.58 E
Chiang Rai 22 Lh 19.54N 99.50 E
Chiang-su Sheng→Jiangsu Sheng=Kiangsu (EN) [2] 27 Ke 33.00N 120.00 E
Chiani 14 Gh 42.44N 12.07 E
Chianje 31 Ij 15.45S 13.54 E
Chianti 14 Fg 43.30N 11.25 E
Chiapa, Rio- 48 Mj 16.30N 93.10W
Chiapas [2] 47 Fe 16.30N 92.30W
Chiapas, Meseta de- 47 Fe 16.30N 92.00W
Chiaramonte Gulfi 14 Im 37.02N 14.42 E
Chiaravalle 14 Hg 43.36N 13.19 E
Chiaromonte 14 Kj 40.07N 16.13 E
Chiautla de Tapia 48 Jh 18.17N 98.36W
Chiavari 14 Df 44.19N 9.19 E
Chiavenna 14 Dd 46.19N 9.24 E
Chiayi 27 Lg 23.29N 120.27 E
Chiba 27 Pd 35.36N 140.07 E
Chiba Ken [2] 28 Pg 35.40N 140.20 E
Chibemba 36 Bf 15.45S 14.06 E
Chibia 36 Bf 15.11S 13.41 E
Chibougamau 39 Le 49.53N 74.21W
Chibougamau, Lac- 44 Ja 49.50N 74.15W
Chibougamau, Rivière- 44 Ja 49.50N 74.25W
Chiburi-Jima 28 Lf 36.00N 133.02 E
Chibuto 37 Ed 24.42S 33.33 E
Chicago 39 Ke 41.53N 87.38W
Chicago Heights 45 Mf 41.30N 87.38W
Chicala 36 Ce 11.59S 19.30 E
Chicapa 30 Ji 6.25S 20.48 E
Chic-Chocs, Monts- 44 Na 48.55N 66.45W
Chicha 35 Bb 16.52N 18.33 E
Chichagof 40 Le 57.30N 135.30W
Chichancanab, Laguna de- 48 Oh 19.54N 88.46W
Chichaoua 32 Fc 31.32N 8.46W
Chichas, Cordillera de- 54 Eh 20.30S 66.30W
Chicheng 27 Kc 40.55N 115.47 E
Chichén Itzá 39 Kg 20.40N 88.35W
Chichester 9 Mk 50.50N 0.48W
Chichester Range 59 Dd 22.20S 119.20 E
Chichibu 28 Og 35.59N 139.05 E
Chichigalpa 49 Dg 12.34N 87.02W
Chichijima-Rettō 60 Cb 27.06N 142.12 E
Chichilla de Monte-Aragón 13 Kf 38.55N 1.43W
Chichiriviche 49 Mh 10.56N 68.16W
Chickasawhay River 45 Lk 31.00N 88.45W
Chickasha 43 Hd 35.02N 97.58W
Chicken 40 Kd 64.04N 141.56W
Chiclana de la Frontera 13 Fh 36.25N 6.08W
Chiclayo 53 If 6.46S 79.50W
Chico 43 Cd 39.44N 121.50W
Chico, Rio- [Arg.] 52 Jj 43.48S 66.25W
Chico, Rio- [Arg.] 52 Jj 49.56S 68.32W
Chicoana 56 Gc 25.06S 65.33W
Chicomo 37 Ed 24.31S 34.17 E
Chiconono 37 Fb 12.57S 35.45 E
Chicopee 44 Kd 42.10N 72.36W
Chicote 36 Df 16.01S 21.48 E
Chicoutimi 39 Le 48.26N 71.04W
Chicoutimi Nord 44 La 48.29N 71.02W
Chicualacuala 37 Ed 22.05S 31.42 E
Chidenguele 37 Ed 24.55S 34.10 E
Chidley, Cape- 38 Mc 60.25N 64.30W
Chiemsee 10 Ii 47.54N 12.29 E
Chiengi 36 Ed 8.39S 29.10 E
Chienti 14 Hg 43.18N 13.45 E
Chieri 14 Be 45.01N 7.49 E
Chiers 12 He 49.39N 5.00 E
Chiese 14 Ee 45.08N 10.25 E
Chieti 14 Ih 42.21N 14.10 E
Chiévres 12 Fd 50.35N 3.48 E
Chifeng/Ulanhad 27 Kc 42.16N 118.57 E
Chifumage 36 De 12.10S 22.30 E
Chifwefwe 36 Fe 13.35S 29.35 E
Chigasaki 29 Fd 35.19N 139.24 E
Chignik 40 He 56.18N 158.23W
Chigombe 37 Ed 23.26S 33.19 E
Chigorodó 49 Ij 7.41N 76.41W
Chigubo 37 Ed 22.50S 33.31 E
Chigu Co 27 Ff 28.40N 91.50 E
Chi He 28 Dh 32.51N 117.59 E
Chihli, Gulf of- (EN)=Bo Hai 21 Nf 38.30N 120.00 E
Chihuahua [2] 47 Cc 28.30N 106.00W
Chihuahua 39 Ig 28.38N 106.05W
Chii-san 28 Ig 35.20N 127.44 E
Chikaskia River 45 Hh 36.37N 97.15W
Chikugo 29 Be 33.13N 130.30 E
Chikugo-Gawa 29 Be 33.10N 130.21 E
Chikuma-Gawa 29 Fc 37.00N 138.35 E
Chikwana 36 Ff 16.03S 34.48 E
Chilapa de Alvarez 48 Ji 17.36N 99.10W
Chilās 25 Ea 35.26N 74.05 E
Chilaw 25 Fg 7.34N 79.47 E
Chilcotin 42 Ff 51.46N 122.22W
Childers 59 Ke 25.14S 152.17 E
Childress 43 Ge 34.25N 100.13W
Chile [1] 53 Ii 30.00S 71.00W
Chile Basin (EN) 3 Mm 33.00S 90.00W
Chile Chico 56 Fg 46.33S 71.44W
Chilecito [Arg.] 56 Gd 33.53S 69.03W
Chilecito [Arg.] 56 Gc 29.10S 67.30W
Chile Rise (EN) 3 Mm 40.00S 90.00W
Chili 35 Cb 16.44N 20.53 E
Chilia, Braţul- 15 Md 45.13N 29.43 E
Chililabombwe 36 Ee 12.22S 27.50 E
Chi-lin Sheng→Jilin Sheng=Kirin (EN) [2] 27 Mc 43.00N 126.00 E
Chilko Lake 46 Ca 51.20N 124.05W
Chilko River 46 Da 52.00N 123.40W
Chillán 53 Ii 36.36S 72.07W
Chillar 56 Ie 37.18S 59.59W
Chillicothe [Il.-U.S.] 45 Lf 40.55N 89.29W
Chillicothe [Mo.-U.S.] 45 Jg 39.48N 93.33W
Chillicothe [Oh.-U.S.] 43 Kd 38.20N 82.59W
Chilliwack 46 Eb 49.10N 121.57W
Chiloé, Isla de- 52 Ij 42.30S 73.55W
Chilón 48 Mi 17.14N 92.25W
Chiloquin 46 Ee 42.35N 121.52W
Chilpancingo de los Bravos 47 Ee 17.33N 99.30W
Chiltern Hills 9 Mj 51.42N 0.48W
Chilton 45 Ld 44.02N 88.10W
Chiluage 36 Dd 9.31S 21.46 E
Chilumba 36 Fe 10.27S 34.16 E
Chilwa, Lake- 36 Fc 15.12S 35.50 E
Chimala 36 Fd 8.51S 34.01 E
Chimaltenango 49 Bf 14.39N 90.49W
Chimaltenango [3] 49 Bf 14.40N 90.55W
Chimán 49 Hi 8.42N 78.37W
Chimanas, Islas- 50 Dg 10.17N 64.38W
Chimay 12 Gd 50.03N 4.19 E
Chimborazo, Volcán- 52 If 1.28S 78.48W
Chimbote 53 If 9.05S 78.36W
Chimichagua 49 Ki 9.16N 73.49W
Chimoio 37 Ec 19.00S 33.23 E
Chimorra 13 Hf 38.18N 4.53W
Chin [2] 25 Id 22.00N 93.30 E
China [Jap.] 29b Bb 27.20N 128.36 E
China [Mex.] 48 Je 25.42N 99.14W
China (EN)=Zhonghua Renmin Gongheguo [1] 22 Mf 35.00N 105.00 E
Chinacates 48 Ge 25.00N 105.13W
China Lake 46 Gi 35.46N 117.39W
Chinandega 47 Gf 12.37N 87.09W
Chinandega [3] 49 Dg 12.45N 87.05W
Chinati Peak 45 Dl 29.57N 104.29W
Chincha Alta 54 Cf 13.27S 76.08W
Chinchaga 42 Fe 58.52N 118.19W
Chinchilla 59 Ke 26.45S 150.38 E
Chinchón 13 Id 40.08N 3.25W
Chinchorro, Banco- 47 Ge 18.35N 87.20W
Chincoteague 44 Jg 37.55N 75.23W
Chinde 31 Kj 18.34S 36.27 E
Chin-Do 28 Ig 34.25N 126.15 E
Chindu 27 Ge 33.30N 96.31 E
Chindwinn 21 Lg 21.26N 95.15 E
Ch'ing-hai Sheng→Qinghai Sheng=Tsinghai (EN) [2] 27 Gd 36.00N 96.00 E
Chingil 35 Bc 10.33N 18.57 E
Chingola 31 Jj 12.32S 27.52 E
Chinguar 36 Ce 12.33S 16.22 E
Chinguetti 32 Ee 20.27N 12.21W
Chinguetti, Dahr de- 32 Ee 20.43N 12.20W
Chinhae 28 Jg 35.08N 128.40 E
Chiniot 25 Eb 31.43N 72.59 E
Chinipas 48 Ed 27.23N 108.32W
Chinju 27 Md 35.11N 128.05 E
Chinko 30 Jh 4.50N 23.53 E
Chinle 46 Kh 36.09N 109.33W
Chinle Creek 46 Kh 37.12N 109.43W
Chinmen 27 Kg 24.25N 118.25 E
Chino 29 Fd 36.00N 138.09 E
Chinon 11 Gg 47.10N 0.15 E
Chinook 46 Kb 48.35N 109.14W
Chinquila 48 Pg 21.30N 87.25W
Chinsali 36 Fe 10.33S 32.04 E
Chinteche 36 Fe 11.50S 34.10 E
Chinú 54 Cb 9.06N 75.24W
Chinvali 19 Eg 42.13N 43.57 E
Chiny 12 He 49.44N 5.20 E
Chinyŏng 28 Jg 35.18N 128.44 E
Chioco 37 Ec 16.25S 32.50 E
Chioggia 14 Ge 45.13N 12.17 E
Chios (EN)=Khios 5 Ih 38.22N 26.00 E
Chipata 31 Kj 13.39S 32.40 E
Chipepo 36 Ef 16.49S 27.50 E
Chipindo 36 Ce 13.48S 15.48 E
Chiping 28 Df 36.35N 116.16 E
Chipinge 37 Ed 20.12S 32.38 E
Chipman 44 Ob 46.11N 65.53W
Chippenham 9 Kj 51.28N 2.07W
Chippewa, Lake- 45 Kd 45.56N 91.13W
Chippewa Falls 43 Ic 44.56N 91.24W
Chippewa River [Wi.-U.S.] 45 Id 44.56N 95.44W
Chippewa River [U.S.] 45 Jd 44.25N 92.10W
Chipping Ongar 12 Cc 51.42N 0.15 E
Chiputneticook Lakes 44 Mc 45.45N 68.45W
Chiquián 54 Cf 10.09S 77.11W
Chiquimula [3] 49 Cf 14.40N 89.25W
Chiquimula 49 Cf 14.48N 89.33W
Chiquimulilla 49 Bf 14.05N 90.23W
Chiquinquirá 54 Db 5.37N 73.50W
Chiquitos, Llanos de- 54 Fg 18.00S 61.30W
Chirāla 25 Ge 15.49N 80.21 E
Chiran 29 Bf 31.22N 130.27 E
Chiredzi 31 Kk 21.03S 31.45 E
Chirfa 34 Ha 20.57N 12.21 E
Chirgua, Rio- 50 Bh 8.30N 68.01W
Chiricahua Peak 43 Fe 31.52N 109.20W
Chiriguaná 49 Ki 9.22N 73.37W
Chirikof 40 He 55.50N 155.35W
Chiriquí [3] 49 Fi 8.30N 82.00W
Chiriquí, Golfo de- 38 Ki 8.00N 82.20W
Chiriquí, Laguna de- 47 Hg 9.03N 82.00W
Chiriquí Grande 49 Fi 8.57N 82.07W
Chirnogi 15 Je 44.07N 26.84 E
Chiromo 36 Gf 16.33S 35.08 E
Chirripó, Cerro- 38 Ki 9.29N 83.29W
Chirripó, Río- [C.R.] 49 Fh 10.03N 83.16W
Chirripó, Río- [C.R.] 49 Fh 10.41N 83.41W
Chirundu 37 Dc 15.59S 28.54 E
Chisamba 36 Ee 14.59S 28.23 E
Chisāpāni Garhi 25 Hc 27.34N 85.08 E
Chisenga 36 Fd 9.56S 33.26 E
Chisasibi 39 Ld 53.50N 79.00W
Chishui 27 If 28.30N 105.44 E
Chişineu Criş 15 Ec 46.32N 21.31 E
Chisone 14 Bf 44.49N 7.25 E
Chitado 36 Bf 17.18S 13.54 E
Chita-Hantō 29 Ed 34.50N 136.50 E
Chitati 35 Ac 14.40N 14.30 E
Chitato 31 Jl 7.22S 20.49 E
Chita-Wan 29 Ed 34.50N 136.55 E
Chitembo 36 Ce 13.31S 16.45 E
Chitina 40 Kd 61.31N 144.27W
Chitipa 36 Fd 9.43S 33.16 E
Chitorgarh 25 Ed 24.53N 74.38 E
Chitose 28 Pc 42.49N 141.39 E
Chitradurga 25 Ff 14.14N 76.24 E
Chitrāl 25 Ea 35.51N 71.47 E
Chitré 47 Hg 7.58N 80.26W
Chittagong 22 Lg 22.20N 91.50 E
Chittoor 25 Ff 13.12N 79.07 E
Chiumbe 30 Ji 6.59S 21.12 E
Chiume 36 Df 15.08S 21.12 E
Chiusi 14 Fg 43.01N 11.57 E
Chiusi, Lago di- 14 Fg 43.05N 12.00 E
Chiva 13 Le 39.28N 0.43W
Chivacoa 50 Bg 10.10N 68.54W
Chivapuri, Rio- 50 Ci 6.25N 66.23W
Chivasso 14 Be 45.11N 7.53 E
Chivay 54 Dg 15.38S 71.36W
Chivilcoy 56 Hd 34.53S 60.01W
Chixoy o Negro, Rio- 49 Be 16.28N 90.33W
Chizou→Guichi 27 Ke 30.38N 117.30 E
Chizu 29 Dd 35.15N 134.14 E
Chôâm Khsant 25 Kf 14.13N 104.56 E
Choapa, Rio- 56 Fd 31.38S 71.34W
Chobe 30 Jj 17.47S 25.10 E
Choc Bay 51k Ba 14.03N 60.59W
Choch'iwŏn 28 If 36.36N 127.18 E
Chocó [2] 54 Cb 6.00N 77.00W
Chocolate Mountains 46 Hj 33.25N 114.10W
Chodecz 10 Pd 52.24N 19.01 E
Chodov 10 If 50.15N 12.45 E
Chodzież 10 Md 52.59N 16.56 E
Choele-Choel 56 Ge 39.16S 65.41W
Choique 56 He 38.28S 62.43W
Choiseul 51k Ab 13.47N 61.03W
Choiseul Island 57 Ge 7.00S 157.00 E
Choix 48 Ed 26.43N 108.17W
Chojna 10 Kd 52.58N 14.28 E
Chojnice 10 Nc 53.42N 17.34 E
Chojnów 10 Le 51.17N 15.56 E
Chŏkai-San 21 Qf 39.10N 140.02 E
Choke 30 Kg 10.45N 37.35 E
Chókué 37 Ed 24.27S 32.55 E
Cho La 27 Ge 31.52N 98.51 E
Cholet 11 Fg 47.04N 0.53W
Chŏlla-Namdo [2] 28 Ig 34.45N 127.00 E
Chŏlla-Pukto [2] 28 Ig 35.45N 127.15 E
Cholo 36 Gf 16.04S 35.08 E
Cholula 48 Jh 19.04N 98.18W
Choluteca 47 Gf 13.18N 87.12W
Choluteca [3] 49 Dg 13.20N 87.10W
Choluteca, Rio- 49 Dg 13.07N 87.19W
Choma 31 Jj 16.49S 26.59 E
Chomo/Yadong 27 Ef 27.38N 89.03 E
Chomo Lhari 27 Ef 27.50N 89.16 E
Chomutov 10 Jf 50.28N 13.25 E
Ch'ŏnan 27 Md 36.48N 127.09 E
Chon Buri 25 Kf 13.22N 100.59 E
Chone 54 Bd 0.42S 80.07W
Ch'ŏngch'ŏn-gang 28 He 39.35N 125.28 E
Ch'ŏngjin 22 Oe 41.46N 129.49 E
Ch'ŏngjin Si [2] 28 Jd 41.45N 129.45 E
Chŏngju 27 Md 39.51N 125.15 E
Ch'ŏngju 27 Md 36.38N 127.30 E
Chongli (Xiwanzi) 28 Cd 40.57N 115.12 E
Chongming 28 Fi 31.38N 121.24 E
Chongming Dao 28 Fi 31.36N 121.33 E
Chongoroi 36 Be 13.34S 13.55 E
Chongqing (Yuzhou)=Chungking (EN) 22 Mg 29.34N 106.27 E
Chongqing→Yuzhou=Chungking (EN) 22 Mg 29.34N 106.27 E
Ch'ŏngsan-Do 28 Ig 34.11N 126.54 E
Chŏngŭp 28 Ig 35.34N 126.51 E
Chongyang 28 Cj 29.32N 114.02 E
Chongzuo 27 Ig 12.29N 107.22 E
Chŏnju 27 Md 35.49N 127.09 E
Choni (Culukidze) 16 Mh 42.18N 42.25 E
Chonos, Archipiélago de los- 52 Ij 45.00S 74.00W
Chontaleña, Cordillera- 49 Eh 11.50N 85.00W
Chontales [3] 49 Eg 12.05N 85.10W
Chopim, Rio- 55 Fg 25.35S 53.05W
Chopinzinho 55 Fg 25.51S 52.30W
Chorito, Sierra del- 13 He 39.25N 4.25W
Choroszcz 10 Sc 53.09N 22.59 E
Chorreras, Cerro- 48 Fd 26.02N 106.21W
Ch'ŏrwŏn 27 Md 38.15N 127.13 E
Chorzele 10 Qc 53.16N 20.55 E
Chorzów 10 Of 50.19N 18.57 E
Ch'osan 28 Hd 40.45N 125.50 E
Chośebuz/Cottbus 10 Ke 51.46N 14.20 E
Chōshi 28 Pg 35.44N 140.50 E
Chos Malal 56 Fe 37.23S 70.16W
Chosŏn M.I.K.=North Korea (EN) [1] 22 Oe 40.00N 127.30 E
Chosŏn Minjuju-Inmin-Konghwaguk=Chosŏn M.I.K. [1] 22 Oe 40.00N 127.30 E
Choszczno 10 Lc 53.10N 15.26 E
Chota 54 Ce 6.33S 78.39W
Chotanagpur Plateau 21 Kg 22.00N 86.00 E
Choteau 46 Ic 47.49N 112.11W
Chotla, Cerro de- 48 Ii 17.55N 101.31W
Choukchot, Djebel- 13 Qh 36.01N 4.11 E
Choum 32 Ee 21.18N 12.59W
Chovd→Kobdo 27 Fb 48.06N 92.11 E
Chövsgöl nuur→Hubsugul Nur 21 Md 51.00N 100.30 E
Chowchilla 46 Eh 37.07N 120.16W
Chowra 25 Ig 8.27N 93.02 E
Chréa 13 Oh 36.25N 2.53 E
Chřiby 10 Ng 49.10N 17.20 E
Christchurch 58 Ii 43.32S 172.37 E
Christian, Cape- 42 Kb 70.32N 68.18W
Christian, Point- 64q Ab 25.04S 130.07W
Christiana 37 De 27.52S 25.08 E
Christian IV Gletscher 41 Ie 68.40N 30.20W
Christiansburg 44 Gg 37.07N 80.26W
Christiansfeld 8 Ci 55.21N 9.29 E
Christianshåb/Qasigiánguit 41 Ge 68.45N 51.30W
Christiansø 8 Fi 55.20N 15.10 E
Christian Sound 40 Me 55.56N 134.40W
Christiansted 50 Dd 17.45N 64.40W
Christiansted Harbor 51a Dc 17.46N 64.42W
Christie Bay 42 Gd 62.45N 110.15W
Christmas→Kiritimati Atoll 57 Ld 1.52N 157.20W
Christmas Creek 59 Fc 18.29S 125.23 E
Christmas Creek 59 Fc 18.53S 125.55 E
Christmas Island [5] 22 Mk 10.30S 105.40 E
Christmas Ridge (EN) 3 Ki 10.00N 165.00W
Chrudim 10 Lg 49.57N 15.47 E
Chrzanów 10 Pf 50.09N 19.24 E
Chrząstowa 10 Mc 53.35N 16.58 E
Chuansha 28 Fi 31.11N 121.42 E
Chúbar 24 Mc 38.11N 48.51 E
Chubut [2] 56 Gf 44.00S 69.00W
Chubut, Rio- 52 Jj 43.20S 65.03W
Chugach Mountains 40 Jd 61.00N 145.00W
Chudžand (Leninabad) 22 Ie 40.17N 69.37 E
Chudžandskaja oblast 19 Gh 40.00N 69.10 E
Chu He 28 Eh 32.15N 119.03 E
Chuhuichupa 48 Ec 29.38N 108.22W
Chui 55 Fk 33.41S 53.27W
Chuka 36 Gc 0.20S 37.39 E
Chukai 26 Df 4.15N 103.25 E
Chukchi Peninsula (EN)=Čukotski Poluostrov 21 Uc 66.00N 175.00W
Chukchi Plateau (EN) 67 Bd 78.00N 165.00W
Chukchi Sea 67 Bd 69.00N 171.00W
Chukchi Sea (EN)=Čukotskoje More 67 Bd 69.00N 171.00W
Chula Vista 46 Gj 32.39N 117.05W
Chulitna 40 Jd 62.55N 149.39W
Chullo 13 Jg 37.10N 2.57W
Chulucanas 54 Be 5.06S 80.10W
Chumbicha 56 Gc 28.52S 66.14W
Chumphon 25 Jf 10.32N 99.13 E
Chumunjin 28 Jf 37.53N 128.49 E
Ch'unch'ŏn 27 Md 37.52N 127.44 E
Chunga 36 Ef 15.03S 26.00 E
Ch'ungch'ŏng-Namdo [2] 28 If 36.30N 127.00 E
Ch'ungch'ŏng-Pukto [2] 28 Jf 36.45N 128.00 E
Ch'ungju 27 Md 36.58N 127.56 E
Chungking (EN)=Chongqing (Yuzhou) 22 Mg 29.34N 106.27 E
Chungking (EN)=Yuzhou→Chongqing 22 Mg 29.34N 106.27 E
Ch'ungmu 28 Jg 34.51N 128.26 E
Chunya 36 Fd 8.32S 33.25 E
Chuquibamba 54 Dg 15.50S 72.39W
Chuquibambilla 54 Df 14.07S 72.43W
Chuquicamata 56 Gb 22.19S 68.56W
Chuquisaca [2] 54 Fg 20.00S 64.20W
Chur/Cuera 14 Dd 46.50N 9.35 E
Churchill 39 Jd 58.46N 94.10W
Churchill [Can.] 38 Md 53.30N 60.10W
Churchill [Can.] 38 Jd 58.47N 94.12W
Churchill, Cape- 42 Ie 58.46N 93.12W
Churchill Falls 42 Lf 53.30N 64.10W
Churchill Lake 42 Ge 56.05N 108.15W
Churchill Peak 42 Ee 58.20N 125.02W
Churchill Range 66 Jg 81.30S 158.30 E
Chūru 25 Ec 28.18N 74.57 E
Churuguara 54 Ea 10.49N 69.32W
Churún Merú=Angel Falls (EN) 52 Je 5.57N 62.30W
Chuska Mountains 46 Kh 36.15N 108.50W
Chute-des Passes 42 Kg 49.50N 71.00W
Chuxian 27 Ke 32.16N 118.15 E
Chuxiong 27 Hf 25.02N 101.32 E
Chuy 55 Fk 33.41S 53.27W
Chyncěšť (Kotovsk) 16 Ff 46.49N 28.33 E
Ciamis 26 Eh 7.20S 108.21 E
Cianjur 26 Eh 6.49S 107.08 E
Ciarrai/Kerry [2] 9 Di 52.10N 9.30W
Čiatura 16 Mh 42.17N 43.15 E
Cibuta, Cerro- 48 Db 31.02N 110.58W
Ćićarija 14 He 45.28N 13.54 E
Ćićevac 15 Ef 43.43N 21.27 E
Cicicleja 15 Nb 47.23N 30.50 E
Cicolano 14 Hh 42.15N 13.10 E
Cidacos 13 Kb 42.19N 1.55W
Cide 24 Eb 41.54N 33.00 E
Cidlina 10 Lf 50.09N 15.12 E
Ciechanów 10 Qd 52.53N 20.38 E
Ciechanów [2] 10 Qd 52.55N 20.40 E
Ciechanowiec 10 Sd 52.42N 22.31 E
Ciechanowska, Wysoczyzna- 10 Qc 53.10N 20.30 E
Ciego de Ávila 47 Id 21.51N 78.46W
Ciego de Ávila [3] 49 Hb 22.00N 78.40W
Ciénaga 54 Da 11.00N 74.14W
Ciénaga de Flores 48 Ie 25.57N 100.11W
Ciénaga de Oro 49 Ji 8.53N 75.38W
Cieneguita 48 Fd 27.57N 106.59W
Cienfuegos [3] 49 Gb 22.15N 80.30W
Cienfuegos 39 Kg 22.09N 80.27W
Cies, Islas de- 13 Db 42.13N 8.54W
Cieszanów 10 Tf 50.16N 23.08 E
Cieza 13 Kf 38.14N 1.25W
Çifteler 24 Dc 39.22N 31.03 E
Cifuentes 13 Jd 40.47N 2.37W
Čiganak 19 Hf 45.05N 73.58 E
Čigirin 16 He 49.03N 32.42 E
Cigüela 13 Ie 39.08N 3.44W
Cihanbeyli 24 Ec 38.40N 32.56 E
Cihanbeyli Platosu 24 Ec 38.40N 32.45 E
Čihareši 16 Mh 42.47N 43.02 E
Cihuatlán 48 Gh 19.14N 104.35W
Čiily 19 Gg 44.13N 66.46 E
Cijara, Embalse de- 13 He 39.18N 4.52W
Cijulang 26 Eh 7.44S 108.27 E
Čik 15 Dd 45.42N 20.04 E
Čikoj 20 Ff 51.02N 106.39 E
Čikurački, Vulkan- 20 Kf 50.15N 155.29 E
Cilacap 26 Eh 7.44S 109.00 E
Çıldır 24 Jb 41.08N 43.07 E
Çıldır Gölü 24 Jb 41.04N 43.15 E
Cilento 14 Jj 40.20N 15.20 E
Čilik 18 Lc 43.42N 78.14 E
Čilik 19 Hg 43.35N 78.12 E
Cill Airne/Killarney 9 Di 52.03N 9.30W
Cill Chainnigh/Kilkenny 9 Fi 52.39N 7.15W
Cill Chainnigh/Kilkenny [2] 9 Fi 52.40N 7.20W
Cill Chaoi/Kilkee 9 Di 52.41N 9.38W
Cill Dara/Kildare [2] 9 Gh 53.15N 6.45W
Cill Dara/Kildare 9 Gh 53.10N 6.55W
Cill Mhantáin/Wicklow 9 Gi 52.59N 6.03W
Cill Mhantáin/Wicklow [2] 9 Gi 53.00N 6.30W
Cill Mocheallóg/Kilmallock 9 Ei 52.25N 8.35W
Cill Rois/Kilrush 9 Di 52.39N 9.29W
Cilma 17 Fd 65.25N 52.05 E
Cilo Daği 24 Kd 37.30N 44.00 E
Cimaltepec, Sierra- 47 Ee 16.00N 96.40W
Cimarron 38 Jf 36.10N 96.17W
Cimarron 45 Dh 36.31N 104.55W
Čimbaj 19 Fg 42.59N 59.47 E
Cimini, Monti- 14 Gh 42.24N 12.12 E
Čimišlija 16 Ff 46.32N 28.46 E
Čimkent 22 Ie 42.18N 69.36 E
Čimkentskaja Oblast [3] 19 Gg 43.00N 68.40 E
Cimljansk 19 Ef 47.37N 42.04 E
Cimljanskoje Vodohranilišče=Tsimlyansk Reservoir (EN) 5 Kf 48.00N 43.00 E
Cimone 5 Hg 44.12N 10.40 E
Cîmpeni 15 Gc 46.22N 23.03 E
Cîmpia Turzii 15 Gc 46.33N 23.53 E
Cîmpina 15 Id 45.08N 25.44 E
Cîmpulung 15 Id 45.16N 25.03 E
Cîmpulung Moldovenesc 15 Ib 47.32N 25.34 E
Čimtarga, Gora- 18 Ge 39.14N 68.12 E
Cina, Tanjung- 26 Dh 5.55S 104.35 E
Çinar 24 Id 37.39N 40.06 E
Cinarcik 15 Mi 40.39N 29.06 E
Cinaruco, Rio- 50 Ci 6.41N 67.07W
Cina Selatan, Laut-=South China Sea (EN) 21 Ni 10.00N 113.00 E
Činaz 18 Gd 40.56N 68.45 E
Cinca 13 Mc 41.26N 0.21 E
Cincar 14 Lg 43.54N 17.04 E
Cincinnati 39 Kf 39.06N 84.31W
Cinco Irmãos, Serra dos- 55 Ff 22.55S 52.50W
Cinco Saltos 56 Ge 38.49S 68.04W
Cindrelu, Vîrful- 15 Gd 45.35N 23.48 E
Çine 24 Cd 37.36N 28.04 E
Çine 15 Kl 37.46N 27.49 E
Ciney 11 Ld 50.18N 5.06 E
Cîngirlau 19 Fe 51.07N 54.05 E
Cingoli 14 Hg 43.22N 13.13 E
Cintalapa de Figueroa 48 Mi 16.44N 93.43W
Cinto, Monte- 5 Gg 42.23N 8.56 E
Cintra, Golfo de- 32 De 23.00N 16.15W
Cinzas, Rio das- 55 Gf 22.56S 50.32W
Ciociaria 14 Hi 41.45N 13.15 E
Cionn Mhálanna/Malin Head 9 Fd 55.23N 7.24W
Cionn tSáile/Kinsale 9 Ej 51.42N 8.32W
Ciorani 15 Je 44.49N 26.25 E
Čiovo 14 Kg 43.30N 16.18 E
Cipa 20 Ge 55.20N 115.55 E
Cipikan 20 Gf 54.58N 113.21 E
Cipó 54 Kf 11.06S 38.31W
Cipolletti 56 Ge 38.56S 67.59W
Čiprovci 15 Ff 43.23N 22.53 E
Čir 16 Me 48.35N 42.55 E
Circeo, Capo- 14 Hi 41.14N 13.03 E
Čirčik 19 Gg 41.28N 69.35 E
Circle [Ak.-U.S.] 40 Kc 65.50N 144.04W
Circle [Mt.-U.S.] 46 Mc 47.25N 105.35W
Circleville 44 Ff 39.36N 82.57W
Cirebon 22 Mj 6.44S 108.34 E
Cirencester 9 Lj 51.44N 1.59W
Ciriè 14 Be 45.14N 7.36 E
Čirinda 20 Fc 67.30N 100.35 E
Čirip, Vulkan- 20 Jg 45.20N 147.58 E
Čirka-Kem 7 Hd 64.45N 32.10 E
Cirò 14 Lk 39.23N 17.04 E
Cirò Marina 14 Lk 39.22N 17.08 E
Ciron 11 Fj 44.36N 0.18W
Čirpan 15 Ig 42.12N 25.20 E
Cirque Mountain 42 Le 58.55N 63.33W
Cisa, Passo della- 14 Df 44.28N 9.55 E
Ciscaucasia (EN) 5 Kf 45.00N 43.00 E
Cisco 45 Gj 32.23N 98.59W
Ciskei [1] 37 Df 31.30S 26.40 E
Čišmy 19 Fe 54.35N 55.25 E
Cisnădie 15 Hd 45.43N 24.09 E
Cisne, Islas del- 47 He 17.22N 83.51W
Cistern Point 49 Ib 24.40N 77.45W
Cistierna 13 Gb 42.48N 5.07W
Čistoozernoje 20 Cf 54.43N 76.43 E
Čistopol 19 Fd 55.23N 50.39 E
Čita 22 Nd 52.03N 113.30 E
Çitak 15 Mk 38.08N 29.39 E

Index Symbols

[1] Independent Nation
[2] State, Region
[3] District, County
[4] Municipality
[5] Colony, Dependency
Continent
Physical Region
Historical or Cultural Region
Mount, Mountain
Volcano
Hill
Mountains, Mountain Range
Hills, Escarpment
Plateau, Upland
Pass, Gap
Plain, Lowland
Delta
Salt Flat
Valley, Canyon
Crater, Cave
Karst Features
Depression
Polder
Desert, Dunes
Forest, Woods
Heath, Steppe
Oasis
Cape, Point
Coast, Beach
Cliff
Peninsula
Isthmus
Sandbank
Island
Atoll
Rock, Reef
Islands, Archipelago
Rocks, Reefs
Coral Reef
Well, Spring
Geyser
River, Stream
Waterfall Rapids
River Mouth, Estuary
Lake
Salt Lake
Intermittent Lake
Reservoir
Swamp, Pond
Canal
Glacier
Ice Shelf, Pack Ice
Ocean
Sea
Gulf, Bay
Strait, Fjord
Lagoon
Bank
Seamount
Tablemount
Ridge
Shelf
Basin
Escarpment, Sea Scarp
Fracture
Trench, Abyss
National Park, Reserve
Point of Interest
Recreation Site
Cave, Cavern
Historic Site
Ruins
Wall, Walls
Church, Abbey
Temple
Scientific Station
Airport
Port
Lighthouse
Mine
Tunnel
Dam, Bridge

Čona 21 Mc 62.00N 110.00 E
Cona 27 Ff 28.01N 91.57 E
Co Nag 27 Fe 32.00N 91.25 E
Conakry 31 Fh 9.31N 13.43W
Conara Junction 59 Jh 41.50S 147.26 E
Concarneau 11 Cg 47.52N 3.55W
Conceição da Barra 54 Kg 18.35S 39.45W
Conceição do Araguaia 54 Ie 8.15S 49.17W
Conceição do Mato Dentro 55 Kd 19.01S 43.25W
Concepción [3] 55 Df 23.00S 57.00W
Concepción [Arg.] 56 Gc 27.20S 65.35W
Concepción [Arg.] 55 Di 28.23S 57.53W
Concepción [Bol.] 54 Fg 16.15S 62.04W
Concepción [Chile] 53 Ii 36.50S 73.03W
Concepción [Par.] 53 Kh 23.25S 57.17W
Concepción [Peru] 54 Cf 11.55S 75.17W
Concepción [Ven.] 49 Lh 10.25N 71.41W
Concepción, Bahía- 48 Dd 26.40N 111.48W
Concepción, Laguna- 54 Fg 17.30S 61.25W
Concepción, Punta- 48 Dd 26.50N 111.50W
Concepción, Río- 55 Ab 15.46S 62.10W
Concepción del Bermejo 55 Bh 26.36S 60.57W
Concepción del Oro 47 Dd 24.38N 101.25W
Concepción del Uruguay 56 Id 32.29S 58.14W
Conception, Point- 38 Gf 34.27N 120.27W
Conception Bay 42 Mg 48.00N 52.50W
Conception Island 49 Jb 23.52N 75.03W
Concha 49 Li 9.02N 71.45W
Conchas 55 Hf 23.01S 48.00W
Conchas Dam 45 Di 35.22N 104.11W
Conchas Lake 45 Di 35.25N 104.14W
Conches-en-Ouche 11 Gf 48.58N 0.56 E
Concho River 45 Gk 31.32N 99.43W
Conchos, Río- 38 Ig 29.35N 104.25W
Concoran 46 Fh 36.06N 119.33W
Concord [Ca.-U.S.] 46 Eh 37.59N 122.00W
Concord [N.H.-U.S.] 39 Le 43.12N 71.32W
Concordia [Arg.] 53 Ki 31.24S 58.02W
Concordia [Braz.] 55 Fh 27.14S 52.01W
Concordia [Ks.-U.S.] 45 Hg 39.34N 97.39W
Concordia [Mex.] 48 Ff 23.17N 106.04W
Concordia Baai 51c Aa 17.31N 62.58W
Con Cuong 25 Ke 19.02N 104.54 E
Conda 36 Be 11.06S 14.20 E
Condamine River 59 Je 27.00S 149.50 E
Condat 11 Ii 45.22N 2.46 E
Conde 54 Kf 11.49S 37.37W
Condé-en-Brie 12 Fe 49.01N 3.33 E
Condega 49 Dg 13.21N 86.24W
Condé-sur-l'Escaut 12 Fd 50.27N 3.35 E
Condé-sur-Marne 12 Ge 49.03N 4.11 E
Condé-sur-Noireau 11 Ff 48.51N 0.33W
Condobolin 59 Jf 33.05S 147.09 E
Condom 11 Gk 43.58N 0.22 E
Condon 46 Ed 45.14N 120.11W
Condor, Cordillera del- 54 Cd 4.20S 78.30W
Condroz/Condruzisch Plateau 11 Kd 50.25N 5.00 E
Condruzisch Plateau/ Condroz 11 Kd 50.25N 5.00 E
Conecuh River 44 Dj 30.58N 87.14W
Conegliano 14 Ge 45.53N 12.18 E
Conejera, Isla- [Sp.] 13 Nf 38.59N 1.12 E
Conejera, Isla- [Sp.] 13 Oe 39.11N 2.57 E
Conejo 48 De 24.05N 111.00W
Conejo, Cerro- 48 Jg 21.24N 99.06W
Conero 14 Hg 43.33N 13.36 E
Conesa 55 Bk 33.36S 60.21W
Conference Island 51p Bb 12.09N 61.35W
Conflans-en-Jarnisy 12 He 49.10N 5.51 E
Conflans-Sainte-Honorine 12 Ef 48.59N 2.06 E
Confolens 11 Gh 46.01N 0.40 E
Confuso, Río- 55 Dg 25.09S 57.34W
Conghua 27 Jg 23.31N 113.30 E
Congo [1] 31 Ii 1.00S 15.00 E
Congo 30 Ii 6.04S 12.24 E
Congo, Dem. Rep. of the- → Zaïre [1] 31 Ji 1.00S 25.00 E
Congo Basin (EN) 30 Ih 0.00 17.00 E
Congonhas 55 Ke 20.30S 43.52W
Conil de la Frontera 13 Fh 36.16N 6.05W
Coniston 44 Gb 46.29N 80.51W
Conn, Lough-/Loch Con 9 Dg 54.04N 9.20W
Connacht/Connaught 9 Eh 53.30N 9.00W
Connaught/Connacht 9 Eh 53.30N 9.00W
Conneaut 44 Ge 41.58N 80.34W
Connecticut [2] 43 Mc 41.45N 72.45W
Connecticut River 43 Mc 41.17N 72.21W
Connell 46 Fc 46.40N 118.52W
Connellsville 44 He 40.02N 79.38W
Connemara, Mountains of- 9 Dh 53.30N 9.45W
Connersville 44 Ef 39.39N 85.08W
Conn Lake 42 Kb 70.30N 73.30W
Connors Range 59 Jd 21.40S 149.10 E
Conon 9 Id 57.35N 4.30W
Conquista 55 Id 19.56S 47.33W
Conrad 46 Jb 48.10N 111.57W
Conroe 45 Ik 30.19N 95.27W
Conroe Lake 45 Ik 30.25N 95.37W
Conscripto Bernardi 55 Cj 31.03S 59.05W
Conselheiro Lafaiete 54 Jh 20.40S 43.48W
Conselice 14 Ff 44.31N 11.49 E
Consett 9 Lg 54.51N 1.49W
Consolación del Sur 49 Fb 22.30N 83.31W
Con Son 25 Lg 8.43N 106.36 E
Constance, Lake- (EN)= Bodensee 5 Gf 47.35N 9.25 E
Constanța [2] 15 Le 44.30N 28.30 E
Constanța 6 Ig 44.11N 28.39 E
Constantina 13 Gg 37.52N 5.37W
Constantine [3] 32 Ib 36.20N 6.35 E
Constantine 31 He 36.22N 6.37 E
Constantine, Cape- 40 He 58.25N 158.50W
Constitución [Chile] 56 Fe 35.20S 72.25W
Constitución [Ur.] 55 Dj 31.05S 57.50W
Consuegra 13 Ie 39.28N 3.36W
Consuelo Peak 57 Fg 24.58S 148.10 E
Contamana 54 De 7.15S 74.54W
Contas, Rio de- 52 Mg 14.17S 39.01W
Contoy, Isla- 48 Pg 21.30N 86.48W
Contraforte Central, Serra do- 55 Ic 17.15S 47.50W
Contramaestre 49 Ic 20.18N 76.15W
Contraviesa, Sierra- 13 Ih 36.50N 3.10W
Contreras, Embalse de- 13 Ke 39.32N 1.30W
Contreras, Islas- 49 Gj 7.50N 81.47W
Contreras, Puerto de- 13 Ke 39.32N 1.30W
Contres 11 Hg 47.25N 1.26 E
Contumazá 54 Ce 7.22S 78.49W
Contursi 14 Jj 40.39N 15.14 E
Contwig 12 Je 49.15N 7.26 E
Contwoyto Lake 42 Gc 65.40N 110.40W
Conty 12 Ee 49.44N 2.09 E
Convención 54 Db 8.28N 73.20W
Conversano 14 Lj 40.58N 17.07 E
Conway 9 Jh 53.17N 3.50W
Conway [Ar.-U.S.] 43 Id 35.05N 92.26W
Conway [N.H.-U.S.] 44 Ld 43.58N 71.07W
Conway [S.C.-U.S.] 44 Hi 33.51N 79.04W
Conway [Wales-U.K.] 9 Jh 53.17N 3.50W
Conway, Mount- 59 Gd 23.45S 133.25 E
Conway Reef → Ceva-i-Ra 57 Ig 21.45S 174.35 E
Conyers 44 Fi 33.40N 84.00W
Conza, Sella di- 14 Jj 40.50N 15.18 E
Coober Pedy 58 Eg 29.01S 134.43 E
Cooch Behār → Koch Bihār 25 Hc 26.19N 89.26 E
Cook 66 Ad 59.27S 27.10W
Cook 59 Gf 30.37S 130.25 E
Cook, Bahía- 56 Fi 55.10S 70.10W
Cook, Cap- 63b Dd 19.32S 169.30 E
Cook, Cape- 46 Ba 50.08N 127.55W
Cook, Mount- 57 Hi 43.36S 170.09 E
Cook, Récif de- 63b Ad 19.25S 163.50 E
Cooke, Mount- 59 Df 32.25S 116.18 E
Cookes Peak 45 Cj 32.32N 107.44W
Cookeville 44 Eg 36.10N 85.31W
Cook Ice Shelf 66 Je 68.40S 152.30 E
Cook Inlet 38 Dc 60.30N 152.00W
Cook Island 64g Bb 1.57N 157.28W
Cook Islands [5] 58 Lf 20.00S 158.00W
Cookstown/An Chorr Chríochach 9 Gg 54.39N 6.45W
Cook Strait 57 Ii 41.20S 174.25 E
Cooktown 58 Ff 15.28S 145.15 E
Coolgardie 59 Ef 30.57S 121.10 E
Coolidge [Az.-U.S.] 43 Ee 32.59N 111.31W
Coolidge [Ks.-U.S.] 45 Fg 38.03N 101.59W
Coolidge Dam 46 Jj 33.12N 110.32W
Cooma 59 Jg 36.14S 149.08 E
Coonabarabran 59 Jf 31.16S 149.17 E
Coonamble 59 Jf 30.57S 148.23 E
Coonoor 25 Ff 11.21N 76.49 E
Coon Rapids 45 Jd 45.09N 93.18W
Cooper 45 Ij 33.23N 95.35W
Cooper, Mount- 46 Ga 50.13N 117.12W
Cooper Creek 57 Eg 28.29S 137.46 E
Cooper's Town 44 Il 26.51N 77.31W
Cooperstown [N.D.-U.S.] 45 Gc 47.27N 98.07W
Cooperstown [N.Y.-U.S.] 44 Jd 42.43N 74.56W
Coosa River 44 Di 32.30N 86.16W
Coos Bay 43 Cc 43.22N 124.13W
Coos Bay 46 Ce 43.23N 124.16W
Cootamundra 59 Jf 34.39S 148.02 E
Čop 16 Ce 48.26N 22.14 E
Copaipó, Río- 56 Fc 27.19S 70.56W
Copainalá 48 Mi 17.05N 93.12W
Copán [3] 49 Cf 14.50N 89.00W
Copan 39 Kh 14.50N 89.09W
Copán 49 Cf 14.50N 89.12W
Copenhagen (EN)= København 6 Hi 55.40N 12.35 E
Copertino 14 Mj 40.16N 18.03 E
Copetonas 55 Bn 38.43N 60.27W
Copiapó 53 Ih 27.22S 70.20W
Çöpköy 15 Jh 41.13N 26.49 E
Coporito 50 Fh 8.56N 62.00W
Coporolo 36 Be 12.56S 13.00 E
Copparo 14 Ff 44.54N 11.49 E
Copper 40 Kd 60.30N 144.50W
Copperbelt [3] 36 Ee 13.00S 28.00 E
Copper Center 40 Jd 61.58N 145.19W
Copper Cliff 42 Jg 46.28N 81.04W
Copper Harbor 44 Db 47.27N 87.53W
Coppermine 39 Hc 67.50N 115.05W
Coppermine 38 Hc 67.49N 115.04W
Coppermine Point 44 Eb 46.59N 84.47W
Copper Queen 37 Dc 17.31S 29.20 E
Coqên (Maindong) 27 Ee 31.15N 85.13 E
Coquet 9 Lf 55.22N 1.37W
Coquetá, Rio- 52 Jf 3.08S 64.46W
Coquille 46 Ce 43.11N 124.11W
Coquimbo [2] 56 Fd 31.00S 71.00W
Coquimbo 53 Ih 29.58S 71.21W
Corabia 15 Hf 43.47N 24.30 E
Coração de Jesus 55 Jc 16.42S 44.22W
Coradi o Cheradi, Isole- 14 Lj 40.27N 17.09 E
Corail 49 Kd 18.34N 73.53W
Corail, Mer de-=Coral Sea (EN) 57 Gf 20.00S 158.00 E
Coral, Cabeza de- 48 Ph 18.47N 87.19W
Coral Gables 43 Kf 25.45N 80.16W
Coral Harbour 39 Kc 64.08N 83.10W
Coral Sea 57 Gf 20.00S 158.00 E
Coral Sea (EN)=Corail, Mer de- 57 Gf 20.00S 158.00 E
Coral Sea Basin (EN) 57 Gf 14.00S 152.00 E
Coral Sea Islands Territory 59 Lc 18.00S 158.00 E
Coralville 45 Kf 41.40N 91.35W
Coralville Lake 45 Kf 41.47N 91.48W
Corantijn River 54 Gc 5.55N 57.05W
Corato 14 Ki 41.09N 16.25 E
Corbara, Lago di- 14 Gh 42.45N 12.15 E
Corbeil-Essones 11 If 48.36N 2.29 E
Corbie 12 Ee 49.55N 2.30 E
Corbières 11 Il 42.55N 2.38 E
Corbigny 11 Jg 47.15N 3.40 E
Corby 9 Mi 52.29N 0.40W
Corcaigh/Cork [2] 9 Ej 52.00N 8.30W
Corcaigh/Cork 6 Fe 51.54N 8.28W
Corcoran 46 Gi 35.45N 117.23W
Corcovado, Cerro- 48 Bb 30.40N 114.55W
Corcovado, Golfo 56 Ff 43.30S 73.30W
Corcovado, Golfo- 52 Ij 43.30S 73.30W
Corcovado, Volcán- 52 Ij 43.12S 72.48W
Corcubión 13 Cb 42.57N 9.11W
Corcubión, Ría de- 13 Cb 42.54N 9.09W
Cordele 43 Ke 31.58N 83.47W
Cordes 11 Hj 44.04N 1.57 E
Cordevole 14 Gd 46.05N 12.04 E
Cordilheiras, Serra das- 54 Ie 7.30S 48.30W
Cordillera [3] 55 Dg 25.15S 57.00W
Cordillera Central [Phil.] 26 Hc 17.20N 120.57 E
Cordillera Central [S.Amer.] 52 If 8.00S 77.00W
Cordillera Occidental 52 Ig 14.00S 74.00W
Cordillera Oriental 52 If 7.00S 76.00W
Córdoba [3] 13 Hf 38.00N 4.50W
Córdoba [Arg.] [2] 56 Hd 32.00S 64.00W
Córdoba [Arg.] 53 Ji 31.25S 64.10W
Córdoba [Col.] [2] 54 Cb 8.20N 75.40W
Córdoba [Mex.] 47 Ee 18.53N 96.56W
Córdoba [Sp.] 6 Fh 37.53N 4.46W
Córdoba, Sierras de- 52 Ji 31.15S 64.00W
Cordova 39 Ec 60.33N 145.46W
Corfu (EN)=Kérkira 5 Hh 39.40N 19.45 E
Corfu, Strait of- (EN) = Kerkíras, Stenón- 15 Dj 39.35N 20.05 E
Corguinho 55 Ed 19.53S 54.52W
Coria 13 Fe 39.59N 6.32W
Coria del Rio 13 Fg 37.16N 6.03W
Coribe 55 Ja 13.50S 44.28W
Coricudgy, Mount- 59 Kf 32.50S 150.22 E
Corigliano Calabro 14 Kk 39.36N 16.31 E
Coringa Islets 59 Jc 17.00S 150.00 E
Corinne 46 Ma 50.06N 104.32W
Corinth 43 Je 34.56N 88.31W
Corinth (EN) = Kórinthos 15 Fl 37.55N 22.53 E
Corinth, Gulf of- (EN)= Korinthiakós Kólpos 5 Ih 38.12N 22.30 E
Corinth Canal (EN) = Korinthou, Dhiórix- 15 Fl 37.57N 22.58 E
Corinto [Braz.] 54 Jg 18.21S 44.27W
Corinto [Nic.] 49 Dg 12.29N 87.10W
Corisco 34 Ge 0.55N 9.19 E
Cork/Corcaigh 6 Fe 51.54N 8.28W
Cork/Corcaigh [2] 9 Ej 52.00N 8.30W
Cork Harbour 9 Ej 51.45N 8.15W
Corleone 14 Hm 37.49N 13.18 E
Çorlu 23 Ca 41.09N 27.48 E
Çorlu 15 Kh 41.12N 27.28 E
Cormeilles 12 Ce 49.15N 0.23 E
Cormoran Reef 64a Bb 7.50N 134.32 E
Cornelio 48 Dc 29.55N 111.08W
Cornélio Procopio 56 Jb 23.08S 50.39W
Cornelius Grinnel Bay 42 Ld 63.20N 64.50W
Corner Brook 39 Ne 48.57N 57.57W
Corner Seamounts (EN) 38 Nf 35.30N 51.30W
Cornia 14 Eh 42.57N 10.33 E
Corning [Ar.-U.S.] 45 Kh 36.24N 90.35W
Corning [Ca.-U.S.] 46 Dg 39.56N 122.11W
Corning [N.Y.-U.S.] 44 Id 42.10N 77.04W
Corno Grande 14 Hh 42.28N 13.34 E
Cornouaille 11 Cg 48.00N 4.00W
Cornwall [3] 9 Ik 50.30N 4.30W
Cornwall 42 Kg 45.02N 74.44W
Cornwall 42 Ia 73.30N 95.00W
Cornwall 9 Hk 50.20N 5.05W
Cornwall 5 Fe 50.30N 4.40W
Cornwall, Cape- 9 Hk 50.08N 5.43W
Cornwallis 42 Ia 75.15N 95.00W
Coro 53 Jd 11.25N 69.41W
Coro, Golfete de- 49 Mh 11.34N 69.53W
Corocoro 54 Eg 17.12S 68.28W
Corocoro, Isla- 50 Fh 8.31N 60.05W
Corod 15 Kd 45.54N 27.37 E
Čoroh 23 Fa 41.36N 41.35 E
Coroico 54 Eg 16.10S 67.44W
Coromandel [Braz.] 55 Id 18.28S 47.13W
Coromandel [N.Z.] 62 Fb 36.46S 175.30 E
Coromandel Coast 21 Kh 14.00N 80.10 E
Coromandel Peninsula 61 Eg 36.50S 175.35 E
Coromandel Range 62 Fb 37.00S 175.40 E
Coron 26 Hd 12.00N 120.12 E
Corona 45 Di 34.15N 105.36W
Corona Bank (EN) 59 Db 12.20S 118.30 E
Coronado, Bahía de- 38 Ki 9.00N 83.50W
Coronados, Isla- 48 Aa 32.25N 117.15W
Coronados, Isla- 48 Dd 26.07N 111.17W
Coronation 66 Re 60.37S 45.35W
Coronation 46 Ja 52.05N 111.27W
Coronation, Cap- 63b Cf 22.15S 167.02 E
Coronation Gulf 38 Ic 68.25N 110.00W
Coronda 55 Bj 31.58S 60.55W
Coronda, Laguna- 55 Bk 32.06S 60.52W
Coronel 56 Fe 37.01S 73.08W
Coronel Bogado 56 Ic 27.11S 56.18W
Coronel Dorrego 56 He 38.42S 61.17W
Coronel du Graty 55 Bh 27.40S 60.56W
Coronel Fabriciano 54 Jg 19.31S 42.38W
Coronel Oviedo 56 Ic 25.25S 56.27W
Coronel Ponce 55 Eb 15.34S 55.01W
Coronel Pringles 56 He 37.58S 61.22W
Coronel Rodolfo Bunge 55 Bm 37.34S 60.08W
Coronel Suárez 56 He 37.28S 61.55W
Coronel Vidal 55 Dm 37.27S 57.43W
Coronel Vivida 55 Fg 25.58S 52.34W
Corpuna, Nudo- 52 Ig 15.30S 72.41W
Çorovoda 15 Di 40.30N 20.13 E
Corozal [Blz.] 49 Cd 18.24N 88.24W
Corozal [Blz.] 49 Cd 18.15N 88.17W
Corozal [Col.] 49 Ji 9.18N 75.17W
Corpus Christi 39 Jg 27.48N 97.24W
Corpus Christi, Lake- 45 Hl 28.10N 97.53W
Corpus Christi Bay 45 Hm 27.48N 97.20W
Corque 54 Eg 18.21S 67.42W
Corral de Bustos 55 Ak 33.17S 62.12W
Corrèggio 14 Ef 44.46N 10.47 E
Córrego do Ouro 55 Gc 16.18S 50.32W
Corrente 54 If 10.27S 45.10W
Corrente, Rio- [Braz.] 54 Hg 19.19S 50.50W
Corrente, Rio- [Braz.] 55 Ka 13.08S 43.28W
Corrente, Rio- [Braz.] 55 Ib 14.14S 46.58W
Correntes 55 Ec 17.37S 54.59W
Correntes, Rio- 55 Ec 17.38S 55.08W
Correnti, Capo delle- 5 Hh 36.40N 15.05 E
Correntina 54 Jf 13.20S 44.39W
Corrèze 11 Hi 45.10N 1.28 E
Corrèze [3] 11 Hi 45.15N 1.50 E
Corrib, Lough-/Loch Coirib 9 Dh 53.05N 9.10W
Corrientes [2] 56 Ic 29.00S 58.00W
Corrientes 53 Kh 27.30S 58.50W
Corrientes, Cabo- [Arg.] 55 Dn 38.01S 57.32W
Corrientes, Cabo- [Col.] 54 Cb 5.30N 77.34W
Corrientes, Cabo- [Cuba] 49 Ec 21.45N 84.31W
Corrientes, Cabo- [Mex.] 38 Ig 20.25N 105.42W
Corrientes, Ensenada de- 49 Ec 21.45N 84.31W
Corrientes, Río- [Arg.] 55 Cj 30.21S 59.33W
Corrientes, Río- [Peru] 54 Dd 3.43S 74.40W
Corrieyairack Pass 9 Id 57.05N 4.40W
Corrigan 45 Ik 31.00N 94.50W
Corrigin 59 Df 32.21S 117.52 E
Corry 44 He 41.56N 79.39W
Corryong 59 Jg 36.12S 147.54 E
Corse=Corsica (EN) 5 Gg 42.00N 9.00 E
Corse, Cap- 5 Gg 43.00N 9.23 E
Corse-du-Sud [3] 11a Ab 41.50N 9.00 E
Corsewall Point 9 Hf 55.02N 5.05W
Corsica (EN)=Corse 5 Gg 42.00N 9.00 E
Corsica, Canale di- 14 Dh 42.45N 9.45 E
Corsicana 43 He 32.06N 96.28W
Cort Adelaer, Kap- 41 Hf 61.45N 42.00W
Corte 11a Ba 42.18N 9.09 E
Cortegana 13 Fg 37.55N 6.49W
Cortés [3] 49 Cf 15.30N 88.00W
Cortes 13 Kc 41.55N 1.25W
Cortez 43 Fd 37.21N 108.35W
Cortina d'Ampezzo 14 Gd 46.32N 12.08 E
Čortkov 16 De 48.59N 25.50 E
Cortland 44 Id 42.36N 76.10W
Cortona 14 Fg 43.16N 11.59 E
Corubal 34 Bc 11.57N 15.06W
Coruche 13 Df 38.57N 8.31W
Çoruh 23 Fa 41.36N 41.35 E
Çorum 24 Fb 40.29N 35.36 E
Çorum 23 Da 40.33N 34.58 E
Corumbá 53 Kg 19.01S 57.39W
Corumbá, Rio- 54 Ig 18.19S 48.55W
Corumbá de Goiás 55 Hb 15.55S 48.48W
Corumbáiba 55 Hd 18.09S 48.34W
Corumo, Rio- 50 Fi 6.49N 60.52W
Corvallis 43 Cc 44.34N 123.16W
Corvo 30 De 39.42N 31.06W
Corzuela 55 Bh 26.57S 60.58W
Cosalá 48 Fe 24.23N 106.41W
Cosamaloapan 48 Lh 18.22N 95.48W
Cosenza 6 Hh 39.18N 16.15 E
Coshocton 44 Ge 40.16N 81.53W
Cosigüina, Punta- 49 Dg 12.54N 87.41W
Cosmoledo Group 30 Li 9.43S 47.35 E
Cosne-sur-Loire 11 Ig 47.24N 2.55 E
Cosquín 56 Hd 31.15S 64.29W
Cossato 14 Ce 45.34N 8.10 E
Costa, Cordillera de la- 52 Je 9.50N 66.00W
Costa Rica [1] 39 Ki 10.00N 84.00W
Costa Verde 13 Ga 43.40N 5.40W
Costești 15 He 44.40N 24.53 E
Costiera, Catena- 14 Kk 39.25N 16.10 E
Coswig 10 Je 51.08N 13.35 E
Cotabato 26 He 7.13N 124.15 E
Cotagaita 54 Eh 20.50S 65.41W
Cotahuasi 54 Dg 15.12S 72.56W
Côte d'Ivoire=Ivory Coast (EN) [1] 31 Gh 8.00N 5.00W
Côte d'Or 11 Kg 47.10N 4.50 E
Côte-d'Or [3] 11 Kg 47.30N 4.50 E
Cotentin 5 Ff 49.30N 1.30W
Côtes-d'Armor 11 Df 48.25N 2.40W
Cotiella 13 Mb 42.31N 0.19 E
Cotmeana 15 He 44.24N 24.45 E
Cotmeana 15 He 44.58N 24.37 E
Cotonou 31 Hh 6.21N 2.26 E
Cotopaxi, Volcán- 52 If 0.40S 78.26W
Cotswold Hills 9 Kj 51.45N 2.10W
Cottage Grove 46 De 43.48N 123.03W
Cottbus/Chośebuz 10 Ke 51.46N 14.20 E
Cottenham 12 Cb 52.17N 0.08 E
Cottondale 44 Ej 30.48N 85.23W
Cottonwood Wash 46 Ji 35.05N 110.22W
Cotui 49 Ld 19.03N 70.09W
Cotulla 45 Gl 28.26N 99.14W
Coubre, Pointe de la- 11 Ei 45.42N 1.14W
Couburg 10 Gf 50.15N 10.58 E
Coucy-le-Château-Auffrique 12 Fe 49.31N 3.19 E
Coudekerque-Branche 12 Ec 51.02N 2.24 E
Coudersport 44 He 41.46N 78.01W
Couedic, Cape du- 59 Hg 36.10S 136.40 E
Couesnon 11 Ef 48.37N 1.31W
Couhé 11 Gh 46.18N 0.11 E
Couilly-Pont-aux-Dames 12 Ef 48.53N 2.52 E
Coulee Dam 46 Fb 48.00N 118.59W
Coulihaut 51g Bb 15.30N 61.29W
Coulman Island 66 Kf 73.28S 169.45 E
Coulogne 12 Dd 50.55N 1.53 E
Coulommiers 11 Jf 48.49N 3.05 E
Coulonge, Rivière- 44 Ic 45.51N 76.45W
Coulounieix-Chamiers 11 Gi 45.10N 0.42 E
Council 46 Gd 44.44N 116.26W
Council Bluffs 43 Hc 41.16N 95.52W
Courcelles 12 Gd 50.28N 4.22 E
Courcelles-Chaussy 12 Ie 49.07N 6.24 E
Courland (EN) =Kurzeme 5 Id 57.00N 20.30 E
Courmayeur 14 Ae 45.47N 6.58 E
Cours 11 Kh 46.06N 4.19 E
Courseulles-sur-Mer 12 Be 49.20N 0.27W
Courtenay 42 Fg 49.41N 125.00W
Courtisols 12 Gf 48.59N 4.31 E
Courtrai/Kortrijk 11 Jd 50.50N 3.16 E
Coushatta 45 Jj 32.00N 93.21W
Cousin 11 Kh 46.58N 4.15 E
Coutances 11 Ee 49.03N 1.26W
Couto de Magalhães, Rio- 55 Fa 13.37S 53.09W
Coutras 11 Fi 45.02N 0.08W
Couture, Lac- 42 Jd 60.05N 75.20W
Couvin 12 Gd 50.03N 4.20 E
Couvin-Mariembourg 12 Gd 50.06N 4.31 E
Covarrubias 13 Ib 42.04N 3.31W
Covasna [2] 15 Id 46.00N 26.00 E
Covasna 15 Jd 45.51N 26.11 E
Coveñas 49 Ji 9.25N 75.42W
Coventry 9 Li 52.25N 1.30W
Covilhã 13 Ed 40.17N 7.30W
Covington [Ga.-U.S.] 44 Fi 33.37N 83.51W
Covington [Ky.-U.S.] 43 Kd 39.05N 84.30W
Covington [La.-U.S.] 45 Kk 30.29N 90.06W
Covington [Tn.-U.S.] 44 Ch 35.34N 89.39W
Covington [Va.-U.S.] 44 Hg 37.48N 79.59W
Cowal 9 He 56.05N 5.10W
Cowan, Lake- 59 Ef 31.50S 121.50 E
Cowan Knob 45 Ji 35.52N 93.29W
Cowell 59 Hf 33.41S 136.55 E
Cowes 12 Ad 50.46N 1.18W
Cowichan Lake 46 Cb 48.54N 124.20W
Cowra 59 Jf 33.50S 148.41 E
Coxim 53 Kg 18.30S 54.45W
Coxim, Rio- 55 Ed 18.34S 54.46W
Cox's Bāzār 25 Id 21.26N 91.59 E
Coyah 34 Cd 9.43N 13.23W
Coyame 48 Gc 29.28N 105.06W
Coyanosa Draw 45 Ek 31.18N 103.06W
Coycoyan, Sierra de- 48 Ji 17.30N 98.20W
Coyle—Coig, Río- 56 Gh 50.58S 69.11W
Coyote, Río- 48 Cb 30.48N 112.35W
Coyotitán 48 Ff 23.47N 106.35W
Coyuca, Laguna de- 48 Ii 16.57N 100.05W
Cozia, Pasul- 15 Hd 45.15N 24.15 E
Cozumel 48 Pg 20.31N 86.55W
Cozumel, Isla de- 47 Gd 20.25N 86.55W
Cradock 31 Jl 32.08S 25.36 E
Craig [Ak.-U.S.] 40 Me 55.29N 133.09W
Craig [Co.-U.S.] 45 Cf 40.31N 107.33W
Craigmont 46 Gc 46.15N 116.28W
Craigs Range 59 Ke 26.40S 151.30 E
Crailsheim 10 Gg 49.09N 10.05 E
Craiova 6 Ig 44.19N 23.48 E
Cranbrook [Austl.] 59 Df 34.18S 117.32 E
Cranbrook [B.C.-Can.] 42 Fg 49.31N 115.46W
Cranbrook [Eng.-U.K.] 12 Cc 51.05N 0.32 E
Crandon 45 Ld 45.34N 88.54W
Crane [Or.-U.S.] 46 Fe 43.25N 118.35W
Crane [Tx.-U.S.] 45 Ek 31.24N 102.21W
Crane Lake 45 Jb 48.16N 92.28W
Crane Lake 46 Ka 50.06N 109.06W
Cranleigh 12 Bc 51.08N 0.29W
Craon 11 Fg 47.51N 0.57W
Craonne 12 Fe 49.26N 3.47 E
Crapaud, Puy- 11 Fh 46.40N 0.40W
Crary Mountains 66 Of 76.48S 117.40W
Crasna 15 Fa 48.09N 22.20 E
Crasna [Rom.] 15 Kc 46.31N 27.51 E
Crasna [Rom.] 15 Fb 47.10N 22.54 E
Crater Lake [Or.-U.S.] 46 Dd 42.56N 122.06W
Crater Lake [St.Vin.] 51n Ba 13.19N 61.11W
Crateús 53 Lf 5.10S 40.40W
Crati 14 Kk 39.43N 16.31 E
Crato [Braz.] 54 Ke 7.14S 39.23W
Crato [Port.] 13 Ee 39.17N 7.39W
Crau 11 Kk 43.36N 4.50 E
Crauford, Cape- 42 Jb 73.44N 84.51W
Cravo Norte 54 Db 6.17N 70.12W
Crawford 45 Ee 42.41N 103.25W
Crawfordsville 44 De 40.02N 86.54W
Crawley 9 Mj 51.07N 0.12W
Crazy Mountains 46 Jc 46.08N 110.20W
Crazy Peak 43 Eb 46.01N 110.16W
Creciente, Isla- 48 De 24.23N 111.37W
Crécy-en-Ponthieu 12 Dd 50.15N 1.53 E
Crécy-la-Chapelle 12 Ef 48.51N 2.55 E
Crécy-sur-Serre 12 Fe 49.42N 3.37 E
Crediton 9 Jk 50.47N 3.39W
Cree [Sask.-Can.] 42 Ge 58.50N 105.40W
Cree [Scot.-U.K.] 9 Ig 54.52N 4.20W
Creede 45 Ch 37.51N 106.56W
Creel 47 Cc 27.45N 107.38W
Cree Lake 42 Ge 57.30N 106.30W
Creglingen 10 Gg 49.28N 10.02 E
Creil 11 Ie 49.16N 2.29 E
Crema 14 De 45.22N 9.41 E
Cremenea, Brațul- 15 Ke 44.57N 27.54 E
Crémieu, Plateau de- 11 Li 45.40N 5.30 E
Cremona 14 Ee 45.07N 10.02 E
Crepaja 15 Dd 45.01N 20.39 E
Crepori, Rio- 54 Ge 5.42S 57.08W
Crépy-en-Valois 11 Ie 49.14N 2.54 E
Cres 14 If 44.40N 14.25 E
Cres 14 If 44.58N 14.24 E
Crescent 46 Ee 43.29N 121.41W
Crescent City 43 Cc 41.45N 124.12W
Crescent Lake 44 Gk 29.28N 81.30W
Crespo 55 Bk 32.02S 60.19W

Index Symbols

[1] Independent Nation
[2] State, Region
[3] District, County
[4] Municipality
[5] Colony, Dependency
Continent
Physical Region
Historical or Cultural Region
Mount, Mountain
Volcano
Hill
Mountains, Mountain Range
Hills, Escarpment
Plateau, Upland
Pass, Gap
Plain, Lowland
Delta
Salt Flat
Valley, Canyon
Crater, Cave
Karst Features
Depression
Polder
Desert, Dunes
Forest, Woods
Heath, Steppe
Oasis
Cape, Point
Coast, Beach
Cliff
Peninsula
Isthmus
Sandbank
Island
Atoll
Rock, Reef
Islands, Archipelago
Rocks, Reefs
Coral Reef
Well, Spring
Geyser
River, Stream
Waterfall Rapids
River Mouth, Estuary
Lake
Salt Lake
Intermittent Lake
Reservoir
Swamp, Pond
Canal
Glacier
Ice Shelf, Pack Ice
Ocean
Sea
Gulf, Bay
Strait, Fjord
Lagoon
Bank
Seamount
Tablemount
Ridge
Shelf
Basin
Escarpment, Sea Scarp
Fracture
Trench, Abyss
National Park, Reserve
Point of Interest
Recreation Site
Cave, Cavern
Historic Site
Ruins
Wall, Walls
Church, Abbey
Temple
Scientific Station
Airport
Port
Lighthouse
Mine
Tunnel
Dam, Bridge

Crest 11 Lj 44.44N 5.02 E
Crested Butte 45 Cg 38.52N 106.59W
Creston [B.C.-Can.] 46 Gb 49.06N 116.31W
Creston [Ia.-U.S.] 43 Ic 41.04N 94.22W
Crestone Peak 45 Dh 37.58N 105.36W
Crestview 43 Je 30.46N 86.34W
Creswell 44 Ih 35.52N 76.23W
Creswell Bay 42 Ib 72.40N 93.30W
Creswell Creek 59 Hc 18.10S 135.11 E
Crete 45 Hf 40.38N 96.58W
Crete (EN) = Kriti 5 Ih 35.15N 24.45 E
Crete (EN) = Kriti [2] 15 Hn 35.35N 25.00 E
Crete, Sea of- (EN) = Kritikón Pélagos 15 Hn 36.00N 25.00 E
Créteil 11 If 48.47N 2.28 E
Cretin, Cape- 60 Di 6.40S 147.52 E
Creus, Cabo de-/Creus, Cap de- 5 Gg 42.19N 3.19 E
Creus, Cap de-/Creus, Cabo de- 5 Gg 42.19N 3.19 E
Creuse [3] 11 Hh 46.05N 2.00 E
Creuse 11 Gg 47.00N 0.34 E
Creutzwald 11 Me 49.12N 6.41 E
Crevecoeur-en-Auge 12 Ce 49.07N 0.01 E
Crévecoeur-le-Grand 12 Ee 49.36N 2.05 E
Crevillente 13 Lf 38.15N 0.48W
Crewe 9 Kh 53.05N 2.27W
Crézancy 12 Fe 49.03N 3.30 E
Criciúma 53 Lh 28.40S 49.23W
Cricket Mountains 46 Ig 38.50N 113.00W
Crieff 9 Je 56.23N 3.52W
Criel-sur-Mer 12 Dd 50.01N 1.19 E
Criel sur Mer-Mesnil Val 12 Dd 50.03N 1.20 E
Crikvenica 14 Ie 45.11N 14.42 E
Crillon 12 De 49.31N 1.56 E
Crimea (EN)=Krymski Poluostrov 5 Jf 45.00N 34.00 E
Crimean Mountains (EN)= Krymskije Gory 5 Jg 44.45N 34.30 E
Crimmitschau 10 If 50.49N 12.23 E
Criquetot-l'Esneval 12 Ce 49.39N 0.16 E
Crissolo 14 Bf 44.42N 7.09 E
Cristal, Monts de- 36 Bb 0.30N 10.30 E
Cristal, Sierra del- 49 Jc 20.33N 75.31W
Cristalândia 54 If 10.36S 49.11W
Cristalina 54 Ig 16.45S 47.36W
Cristalino, Rio- 54 Hf 12.40S 50.40W
Cristallo 14 Gd 46.34N 12.12 E
Cristóbal Colón, Pico 52 Id 10.50N 73.45W
Cristuru Secuiesc 15 Ic 46.35N 25.47 E
Crişu Alb 15 Ec 46.42N 21.16 E
Crişu Negru 15 Ec 46.42N 21.16 E
Crişu Repede 15 Dc 46.55N 20.59 E
Crixás 55 Hb 14.27S 49.58W
Crixás-Açu, Rio- 54 Hf 13.19S 50.36W
Crixás Mirim, Rio- 55 Ga 13.28S 50.36W
Crkvena Planina 15 Fg 42.48N 22.22 E
Crna Gora 15 Eg 42.16N 21.35 E
Crna Gora 15 Ce 44.05N 19.50 E
Crna Gora = Montenegro (EN) [2] 15 Cg 42.30N 19.18 E
Crna Gora=Montenegro (EN) 15 Cg 42.30N 19.18 E
Crna Reka 15 Ef 43.50N 21.55 E
Crna reka 15 Eh 41.33N 21.59 E
Crni Drim 15 Dg 42.05N 20.23 E
Crni Timok 15 Ff 43.55N 22.18 E
Črni Vrh 14 Jd 46.29N 15.14 E
Crni vrh 14 Kf 44.36N 16.30 E
Črnomelj 14 Je 45.34N 15.12 E
Croatia (EN) = Hrvatska 14 Jf 45.00N 15.30 E
Croatia (EN) = Hrvatska 5 Hf 45.00N 15.30 E
Croatia (EN) = Hrvatska 14 Je 45.00N 15.30 E
Crocker, Banjaran- 26 Ge 5.40N 116.20 E
Crockett 45 Ik 31.19N 95.28W
Crocq 11 Ii 45.52N 2.22 E
Crocus Bay 51b Ab 18.13N 63.05W
Croisette, Cap- 11 Lk 43.13N 5.20 E
Croisic, Pointe du- 11 Dg 47.17N 2.33W
Croisilles 12 Ed 50.12N 2.53 E
Croissy-sur-Celle 12 Ee 49.42N 2.11 E
Croix, Lac la- 45 Jb 48.21N 92.05W
Croix-Haute, Col de la- 11 Lj 44.43N 5.40 E
Croker, Cape- 59 Gb 10.58S 132.35 E
Croker Bay 42 Jb 74.38N 83.15W
Croker Island 59 Gb 11.10S 132.30 E
Cromarty 9 Id 57.40N 4.02W
Cromer 9 Oi 52.56N 1.18 E
Cromwell 62 Cf 45.03S 169.14 E
Crooked Island 47 Jd 22.45N 74.13W
Crooked Island Passage 47 Jd 22.55N 74.35W
Crooked River 46 Ed 44.34N 121.16W
Crookston 43 Hb 47.47N 96.37W
Crosby [Mn.-U.S.] 45 Jc 46.28N 93.57W
Crosby [N.D.-U.S.] 45 Eb 48.55N 103.18W
Cross 34 Ge 4.55N 8.15 E
Cross City 44 Fk 29.32N 83.07W
Crossett 45 Kj 33.08N 91.58W
Cross Fell 9 Kg 54.42N 2.29W
Cross Lake 42 Hf 54.47N 97.22W
Crossman Peak 46 Hi 34.32N 114.07W
Cross River [2] 34 Gd 5.40N 8.10 E
Cross Sound 40 Le 58.10N 136.30W
Crotone 14 Lk 39.05N 17.08 E
Crotto 55 Bm 36.35S 60.10W
Crouch 12 Cc 51.37N 0.53 E
Crow Agency 46 Ld 45.36N 107.27W
Crowborough 12 Cc 51.03N 0.09 E
Crow Creek 45 Df 40.23N 104.29W
Crowell 45 Gj 33.59N 99.43W
Crow Lake 45 Jb 49.12N 93.57W
Crowley 45 Jk 30.13N 92.22W
Crowley, Lake- 46 Fh 37.37N 118.44W
Crowley Ridge 45 Ki 35.45N 90.45W
Crownpoint 45 Bi 35.42N 108.07W
Crown Prince Frederik 42 Ic 70.05N 86.40W
Crowsnest Pass 42 Gg 49.00N 114.30W
Crows Nest Peak 45 Ed 44.03N 103.58W
Croydon 59 Ic 18.12S 142.14 E
Croydon, London- 9 Mj 51.23N 0.07W
Crozet, Iles- 30 Mm 46.30S 51.00 E
Crozet Basin (EN) 3 Gm 39.00S 60.00 E
Crozet Ridge (EN) 3 Fn 45.00S 45.00 E
Crozon 11 Bf 48.15N 4.29W
Crozon, Presqu'île de- 11 Bf 48.15N 4.25W
Crucero, Cerro- 48 Gg 21.41N 104.25W
Cruces 49 Gb 22.21N 80.16W
Crump Lake 46 Fe 42.17N 119.50W
Crumpton Point 51g Ba 15.35N 61.19W
Cruz, Cabo- 47 Ie 19.51N 77.44W
Cruz Alta [Arg.] 55 Bk 33.01S 61.49W
Cruz Alta [Braz.] 53 Kh 28.39S 53.36W
Cruz del Eje 56 Hd 30.44S 64.48W
Cruzeiro do Oeste 56 Jb 23.46S 53.04W
Cruzeiro do Sul 53 If 7.38S 72.36W
Cruzen Island 66 Mf 74.47S 140.42W
Cruz Grande 48 Ji 16.44N 99.08W
Crvanj 14 Mg 43.25N 18.11 E
Crvenka 15 Cd 45.39N 19.28 E
Crystal Brook 59 Hf 33.21S 138.13 E
Crystal City [Man.-Can.] 45 Gb 49.08N 98.57W
Crystal City [Tx.-U.S.] 45 Gl 28.41N 99.50W
Crystal Falls 44 Cb 46.06N 88.20W
Crystal Springs 45 Kk 31.59N 90.21W
Csákvár 10 Oi 47.24N 18.27 E
Cserhat 10 Pi 47.55N 19.30 E
Csongrád [2] 10 Qj 46.25N 20.15 E
Csongrad 10 Qj 46.42N 20.09 E
Csorna 10 Ni 47.37N 17.15 E
Csurgó 10 Nj 46.16N 17.06 E
Ctesiphon 24 Kf 33.05N 44.35 E
Ču 21 Ie 45.00N 67.44 E
Ču 22 Je 43.33N 73.45 E
Cuajinicuilapa 48 Ji 16.28N 98.25W
Cuale 36 Cd 7.40S 17.01 E
Cuamba 31 Kj 14.49S 36.33 E
Cuan an Fhóid Duibh/Blacksod Bay 9 Dg 54.08N 10.00W
Cuanavale 36 Cf 15.07S 19.14 E
Cuan Bhaile Átha Cliath/Dublin Bay 9 Gh 53.20N 6.06W
Cuan Chill Ala/Killala Bay 9 Dg 54.15N 9.10W
Cuan Dhun Dealgan/Dundalk Bay 9 Gh 53.57N 6.17W
Cuan Dhún Droma/Dundrum Bay 9 Hg 54.13N 5.45W
Cuando 30 Jj 18.27S 23.32 E
Cuando-Cubango [3] 36 Df 16.00S 20.30 E
Cuan Eochaille/Youghal Harbour 9 Fj 51.52N 7.50W
Cuangar 36 Cf 17.36S 18.37 E
Cuango 30 Ii 3.14S 17.22 E
Cuango [Ang.] 36 Cd 9.07S 18.05 E
Cuango [Ang.] 36 Cd 6.17S 16.41 E
Cuan Loch Garman/Wexford Harbour 9 Gi 52.20N 6.25W
Cuan Mó/Clew Bay 9 Dh 53.50N 9.50W
Cuan na Gaillimhe/Galway Bay 5 Fe 53.10N 9.15W
Cuan na gCaorach/Sheep Haven 9 Ff 55.10N 7.52W
Cuan Phort Láirge/Waterford Harbour 9 Gi 52.10N 6.57W
Cuan Shligigh/Sligo Bay 9 Eg 54.20N 8.40W
Cuanza 30 Ii 9.19S 13.08 E
Cuanza Norte [3] 36 Bd 8.50S 14.30 E
Cuanza Sul [3] 36 Be 10.50S 14.50 E
Cuareim, Arroyo- 55 Dj 30.12S 57.36W
Cuaró 55 Dj 30.37S 56.54W
Cuaró Grande, Arroyo- 55 Dj 30.18S 57.12W
Cuarto, Rio- 56 Hd 33.25S 63.02W
Cuatir 36 Cf 17.01S 18.09 E
Cuatro Ciénegas de Carranza 48 Hd 26.59N 102.05W
Cuauhtémoc 47 Cc 28.25N 106.52W
Cuautitlán 48 Jh 19.40N 99.11W
Cuay Grande 55 Di 28.40S 56.17W
Cuba 38 Lg 21.30N 80.00W
Cuba 39 Lg 21.30N 80.00W
Cuba [Mo.-U.S.] 45 Kg 38.04N 91.24W
Cuba [N.M.-U.S.] 45 Ch 36.01N 107.04W
Cuba [Port.] 13 Ef 38.10N 7.53W
Cubabi, Cerro- 48 Cb 31.42N 112.46W
Cubagua, Isla- 50 Dg 10.49N 64.11W
Cubal 36 Be 13.03S 14.15 E
Cubal [Ang.] 36 Be 11.29S 13.48 E
Cubal [Ang.] 36 Bf 15.22S 12.39 E
Cubango 30 Jj 18.53N 22.24 E
Çubuk 24 Eb 40.59N 32.05 E
Čubukulah, Gora- 20 Kc 66.23N 153.59 E
Cucalón, Sierra de- 13 Kd 40.59N 1.10W
Cuchi 36 Ce 14.40S 16.52 E
Cuchi 30 Ij 15.28S 17.21 E
Cuchibi 36 De 15.00S 20.45 E
Cuchilla Aquila, Cerro- 48 Ig 21.27N 101.03W
Cuchivero, Rio- 50 Di 7.40N 65.57W
Cuchumatanes, Sierra de los- 49 Bf 15.35N 91.25W
Cuckfield 12 Bc 51.01N 0.08W
Cuckmere 12 Cd 50.45N 0.09 E
Cucui 54 Ec 1.12N 66.50W
Cucumbi 36 Ce 10.17S 19.03 E
Cucurpe 48 Db 30.20N 110.43W
Cúcuta 53 Ie 7.54N 72.31W
Cudahy 45 Me 42.57N 87.52W
Cudalbi 15 Kd 45.47N 27.42 E
Cuddalore 22 Jh 11.45N 79.45 E
Cuddapah 25 Ff 14.28N 78.49 E
Čudovo 19 Dd 59.08N 31.41 E
Čudskoje Ozero=Peipus, Lake- (EN) 5 Id 58.45N 27.30 E
Cue 59 De 27.25S 117.54 E
Cuebe 36 Cf 15.48S 17.30 E
Cuelei 36 Cf 15.33S 17.21 E
Cuéllar 13 Hc 41.29N 4.19W
Cuemba 36 Ce 12.09S 18.07 E
Cuenca [3] 13 Ke 40.00N 2.00W
Cuenca [Ec.] 53 If 2.53S 78.59W
Cuenca [Sp.] 13 Jd 40.04N 2.08W
Cuenca, Serrania de- 5 Fg 40.10N 1.55W
Cuencamé de Ceniceros 48 He 24.53N 103.42W
Cuera/Chur 14 Dd 46.50N 9.35 E
Cuerda del Pozo, Embalse de la- 13 Jc 41.51N 2.44W
Cuernavaca 39 Jh 18.55N 99.15W
Cuero 45 Hl 29.06N 97.18W
Cuevas del Almanzora 13 Kg 37.18N 1.53W
Cugir 15 Gd 45.50N 23.22 E
Cugo 36 Cd 7.22S 17.06 E
Čugujev 16 Je 49.50N 36.41 E
Čugujevka 28 Mb 44.08N 133.53 E
Čuhloma 12 Ed 58.47N 42.41 E
Cuiabá 53 Kg 15.35S 56.05W
Cuiabá, Rio- 52 Kg 17.05S 56.36W
Cuiabá Mirim, Rio- 55 Ec 16.20S 55.55W
Cuidado, Punta- 65d Bb 27.08S 109.19W
Cuijk, Cuijk en Sint Agatha- 12 Hc 51.44N 5.52 E
Cuijk en Sint Agatha-Cuijk 12 Hc 51.44N 5.52 E
Cuilapa 49 Bf 14.17N 90.18W
Cuillin Hills 9 Gd 57.14N 6.15W
Cuilo 30 Ii 3.22S 17.22 E
Cúil Raithin/Coleraine 9 Gf 55.08N 6.40W
Cuiluan 27 Mb 47.39N 128.34 E
Cuima 36 Ce 13.14S 15.38 E
Cuito 30 Jj 18.01S 20.48 E
Cuito Cuanavale 31 Ij 15.13S 19.08 E
Cuitzeo, Lago de- 48 Ih 19.55N 101.05W
Cuiuni, Rio- 54 Fd 0.45S 63.07W
Cujmir 15 Fe 44.13N 22.56 E
Čujskaja oblast 19 Hg 42.30N 73.50 E
Čukotski avtonomnyj okrug [3] 20 Mc 66.00N 172.30 E
Čukotski Poluostrov= Chukchi Peninsula (EN) 21 Uc 66.00N 175.00W
Čukotskoje More=Chukchi Sea (EN) 67 Bd 69.00N 171.00W
Çukurca 24 Jd 37.15N 43.37 E
Çukurdağı 15 Ll 37.58N 28.44 E
Čulakkurgan 19 Gg 43.48N 69.12 E
Culan 11 Ih 46.33N 2.21 E
Cu Lao, Hon- 25 Lf 10.30N 109.13 E
Culasi 26 Hd 11.26N 122.03 E
Culbertson 46 Mb 48.09N 104.31W
Culebra, Isla de- 49 Od 18.19N 65.17W
Culebra, Sierra de la- 13 Fc 41.55N 6.20W
Culebra Peak 45 Dh 37.06N 105.10W
Culemborg 12 Hc 51.57N 5.14 E
Culiacán, Rio de- 48 Fe 24.31N 107.41W
Culiacán Rosales 39 Ig 24.48N 107.24W
Culion 26 Gd 11.50N 119.55 E
Culion 26 Hd 11.53N 120.01 E
Culiseu, Rio- 54 Hf 12.14S 53.17W
Cullera 13 Le 39.10N 0.15W
Cullman 43 Je 34.11N 86.51W
Čulman 22 Od 56.52N 124.52 E
Culpeper 44 Hf 38.28N 78.01W
Culuene, Rio- 52 Kg 12.56S 52.51W
Culver, Point- 59 Ef 32.54S 124.43 E
Culverden 62 Ee 42.46S 172.51 E
Čulym 20 De 55.06N 80.58 E
Čulym 21 Kd 57.40N 83.50 E
Čulyšman 20 Df 51.20N 87.45 E
Cuma 36 Ce 12.52S 15.04 E
Cumaná 53 Jd 10.28N 64.10W
Cumanacoa 50 Eg 10.15N 63.55W
Cumaovası 15 Kk 38.15N 27.09 E
Cumbal, Volcán- 54 Cc 0.57N 77.52W
Cumberland 9 Kg 54.40N 2.50W
Cumberland 38 Kf 37.09N 88.25W
Cumberland [B.C.-Can.] 46 Cb 49.37N 125.01W
Cumberland [Md.-U.S.] 43 Ld 39.39N 78.46W
Cumberland [Va.-U.S.] 44 Hg 37.31N 78.16W
Cumberland, Cap- 63b Cb 14.39S 166.37 E
Cumberland, Lake- 44 Eg 36.57N 84.55W
Cumberland Bay 51n Ba 13.16N 61.17W
Cumberland Island 44 Gj 30.51N 81.27W
Cumberland Islands 59 Jd 20.40S 149.10 E
Cumberland Lake 42 Hf 54.00N 102.20W
Cumberland Peninsula 38 Mc 66.50N 64.00W
Cumberland Plateau 38 Kf 36.00N 85.00W
Cumberland Sound 38 Mc 65.10N 65.30W
Cumbernauld 9 Jf 55.58N 3.59W
Cumbre, Paso de la-/Bermejo, Paso- 52 Ii 32.50S 70.05W
Cumbria [3] 9 Kg 54.35N 2.45W
Cumbrian Mountains 9 Jg 54.30N 3.05W
Čumerna 15 Ig 42.47N 25.58 E
Čumikan 20 If 54.42N 135.19 E
Cummins 59 Hf 34.16S 135.44 E
Cumnock 9 If 55.27N 4.16W
Cumpas 48 Eb 30.02N 109.48W
Çumra 24 Ed 37.34N 32.48 E
Čumyš 20 Df 53.30N 83.10 E
Čuna 21 Ld 57.42N 95.35 E
Cunagua 49 Hb 22.05N 78.20W
Cuñapirú 55 Ej 31.32S 55.35W
Cuñapirú, Arroyo- 55 Ej 31.12S 55.31W
Cuñapirú, Cuchilla de- 55 Ej 31.12S 55.36W
Cunaviche, Rio- 50 Ci 7.19N 67.11W
Cunderdin 59 Df 31.39S 117.15 E
Cundinamarca [2] 54 Db 5.00N 74.00W
Čundža 19 Hg 43.32N 79.28 E
Cunene [3] 36 Cf 16.30S 15.00 E
Cunene=Kunene (EN) 30 Ij 17.20S 11.50 E
Cuneo 14 Bf 44.23N 7.32 E
Čunja 21 Lc 61.30N 96.20 E
Cunnamulla 58 Fg 28.04S 145.41 E
Čunski 20 Ee 56.03N 99.48 E
Čunski 20 Ee 57.23N 97.40 E
Cuorgné 14 Be 45.23N 7.39 E
Čupa 19 Db 66.17N 33.01 E
Cupar 9 Je 56.19N 3.01W
Cupica, Golfo de- 54 Cb 6.35N 77.30W
Ćuprija 15 Ef 43.56N 21.22 E
Cupula, Pico- 48 De 24.47N 110.50W
Čur 7 Mh 57.11N 53.01 E
Curaçá 54 Ke 8.59S 39.54W
Curacao 52 Jd 12.11N 69.00W
Curacautin 56 Fe 38.26S 71.53W
Curâ Malal, Sierra de- 55 Am 37.44S 62.16W
Curanilahue 56 Fe 37.28S 73.21W
Čurapča 20 Id 61.56N 132.18 E
Curaray, Rio- 54 Dd 2.20S 74.05W
Curcúbata, Vîrful- 15 Fc 46.25N 22.35 E
Curdimurka 58 Eg 29.30S 137.10 E
Curé 55 De 21.25S 56.25W
Cure 11 Jg 47.40N 3.41 E
Curepipe 37a Bb 20.19S 57.31 E
Curepto 56 Fe 35.05S 72.01W
Curiapo 54 Fb 8.33N 61.00W
Curicó 53 Ii 34.59S 71.14W
Curicuriari, Rio- 54 Ed 0.14S 66.48W
Curitabanos 56 Jc 27.18S 50.36W
Curitiba 53 Lh 25.25S 49.15W
Curoca 36 Bf 15.43S 11.55 E
Currais Novos 54 Ke 6.15S 36.31W
Curralinho 54 Id 1.48S 49.47W
Curral-Velho 32 Cf 15.59N 22.48W
Current River 45 Kh 36.15N 90.57W
Currie 59 Ig 39.56S 143.52 E
Curtea de Argeş 15 Hd 45.08N 24.41 E
Curtici 15 Ec 46.21N 21.18 E
Curtis 45 Ff 40.38N 100.31W
Curtis Channel 59 Kd 23.55S 152.05 E
Curtis Island 57 Jh 30.35S 178.36W
Curtis Island [Austl.] 59 Kd 23.40S 151.10 E
Curuá, Rio- 55 Ga 13.26S 51.24W
Curuá, Rio- [Braz.] 54 Gd 1.55S 55.07W
Curuá, Rio- [Braz.] 52 Kf 5.23S 54.22W
Curuçá 54 Id 0.43S 47.50W
Curuçá, Rio- 54 Dd 4.27S 71.23W
Curuguaty 56 Ib 24.31S 55.42W
Curuguaty, Arroyo- 55 Dg 24.06S 56.02W
Curup 26 Dg 3.28S 102.32 E
Curupira, Sierra de- 54 Fc 1.25N 64.30W
Cururupu 54 Jd 1.50S 44.52W
Curuzú Cuatiá 56 Ic 29.47S 58.03W
Curvelo 54 Jg 18.45S 44.25W
Cusco → Cuzco 53 Ig 13.31S 71.59W
Cushing 45 Hi 35.59N 96.46W
Cushing, Mount- 42 Ee 57.36N 126.51W
Čusovaja 5 Ld 58.13N 56.30 E
Čusovoj 19 Fd 58.17N 57.50 E
Cusset 11 Jh 46.08N 3.28 E
Cusseta 44 Ei 32.18N 84.47W
Čust 18 Hd 41.00N 71.15 E
Custer 45 Ee 43.46N 103.36W
Cutato 36 Cc 10.33S 16.48 E
Cut Bank 43 Eb 48.38N 112.20W
Cutervo 54 Ce 6.22S 78.51W
Cuthbert 44 Ej 31.46N 84.48W
Cutral Có 56 Ge 38.56S 69.14W
Cutro 14 Kk 39.02N 16.59 E
Cuttack 22 Kg 20.30N 85.50 E
Čuvašskaja respublika 19 Ed 55.30N 47.10 E
Cuvelai 36 Cf 15.40S 15.47 E
Cuvette [3] 36 Cc 0.10S 15.30 E
Cuvier Basin (EN) 59 Cd 22.00S 111.00 E
Cuvier Island 62 Fb 36.25S 175.45 E
Cuvo ou Queve 30 Ij 10.50S 13.47 E
Cuxhaven 10 Ec 53.53N 8.42 E
Cuya 56 Fa 19.07S 70.08W
Cuyahoga Falls 44 Ge 41.08N 81.55W
Cuyo Islands 26 Hd 11.04N 120.57 E
Cuyubini, Rio- 50 Fh 8.20N 60.20W
Cuyuni, Rio 52 Ke 6.23N 58.41W
Cuyutlán, Laguna 48 Gh 19.00N 104.10W
Cuzco (Cusco) 53 Ig 13.31S 71.59W
Cuzco [2] 54 Df 12.30S 72.30W
Cuzna 13 Hf 38.04N 4.41W
Cvikov 10 Kf 50.48N 14.40 E
Čvrsnica 14 Lg 43.35N 17.35 E
Cyangugu 36 Ec 2.29S 28.54 E
Cybinka 10 Kd 52.12N 14.48 E
Cyclades (EN) = Kikládhes [2] 5 Ih 37.00N 25.10 E
Čyjyrčyk, Pereval- 18 Id 40.15N 73.20 E
Cypress Hills 38 Ie 49.40N 109.30W
Cypress Lake 46 Kb 49.28N 109.29W
Cyprus (EN)=Kıbrıs/Kypros [1] 22 Ff 35.00N 33.00 E
Cyprus (EN)=Kıbrıs/Kypros 21 Ff 35.00N 33.00 E
Cyprus (EN)=Kypros/Kıbrıs [1] 22 Ff 35.00N 33.00 E
Cyprus (EN)=Kypros/Kıbrıs 21 Ff 35.00N 33.00 E
Cyrenaica (EN)=Barqah 33 Dc 31.00N 22.30 E
Cyrenaica (EN)=Barqah 30 Je 31.00N 23.00 E
Cyrene 33 Dc 32.48N 21.59 E
Cyrus Field Bay 42 Ld 62.50N 65.00W
Cysoing 12 Fd 50.34N 3.13 E
Cythera (EN)=Kíthira 15 Fm 36.09N 23.00 E
Czaplinek 10 Mc 53.34N 16.14 E
Czarna [Pol.] 10 Pe 51.12N 19.53 E
Czarna [Pol.] 10 Rf 50.30N 21.15 E
Czarna Białostocka 10 Tc 53.18N 23.19 E
Czarna Dąbrówka 10 Nb 54.20N 17.32 E
Czarna Hańcza 10 Tc 53.50N 23.47 E
Czarnków 10 Md 52.55N 16.34 E
Czchów 10 Qg 49.50N 20.39 E
Czechowice-Dziedzice 10 Og 49.54N 19.00 E
Czech Republic (EN) = Česká Republika 6 Hf 50.00N 13.00 E
Czeremcha 10 Td 52.32N 23.15 E
Czersk 10 Nc 53.48N 18.00 E
Częstochowa 6 He 50.49N 19.06 E
Częstochowa [2] 10 Pf 50.50N 19.05 E
Człopa 10 Mc 53.06N 16.08 E
Człuchów 10 Nc 53.41N 17.21 E

D

Da, Sông-=Black River (EN) 21 Mg 20.17N 106.34 E
Da'an (Dalai) 27 Lb 45.35N 124.16 E
Dabaga 36 Gd 8.07S 35.55 E
Dabakala 34 Ed 8.22N 4.26W
Dabakala [3] 34 Ed 8.27N 4.28W
Daban→Bairin Youqi 27 Kc 43.30N 118.37 E
Dabas 10 Pi 47.11N 19.19 E
Daba Shan 21 Mf 32.15N 109.00 E
Dabat 35 Fc 12.58N 37.45 E
Dabay Sima 35 Gc 12.43N 42.17 E
Dabba/Daocheng 27 Hf 29.01N 100.26 E
Dabbāgh, Jabal- 23 Ed 27.52N 35.45 E
Dabeiba 54 Cb 7.02N 76.16W
Dąbie 10 Od 52.06N 18.49 E
Dabie, Jezioro- 10 Kc 53.29N 14.40 E
Dabie Shan 21 Nf 31.15N 115.00 E
Dabl, Wādī- [Sau.Ar.] 24 Gh 28.35N 39.04 E
Dabl, Wādī- [Sau.Ar.] 24 Gh 29.05N 36.14 E
Dabnou 34 Gc 14.09N 5.22 E
Dabola 34 Cc 10.45N 11.07W
Daborow 35 Hd 6.11N 48.22 E
Dabou 34 Ed 5.19N 4.23W
Dabqig→Uxin Qi 27 Id 38.27N 109.08 E
Dabraš 15 Gh 41.40N 23.50 E
Dąbrowa Białostocka 10 Tc 53.40N 23.20 E
Dąbrowa Górnicza 10 Pf 50.20N 19.11 E
Dąbrowa Tarnowska 10 Qf 50.11N 21.00 E
Dabsan Hu 27 Fd 36.58N 95.00 E
Dăbuleni 15 Hf 43.48N 24.05 E
Dabus 35 Fc 10.38N 35.10 E
Dacata 35 Gd 7.16N 42.15 E
Dacca → Dhaka 22 Lg 23.43N 90.25 E
Dachangzhen 28 Eh 32.13N 118.44 E
Dachau 10 Hh 48.16N 11.26 E
Dachen Dao 28 Fj 28.29N 121.53 E
Dachstein 14 Hc 47.30N 13.36 E
Dacia Seamount (EN) 5 Ei 31.10N 13.42W
Dačice 10 Lg 49.05N 15.26 E
Dac Lac, Caonguyen- 25 Lf 12.50N 108.05 E
Đacovica 15 Dg 42.23N 20.26 E
Dadali 63a Dc 8.07S 159.06 E
Dadanawa 54 Gc 2.50N 59.30W
Daday 24 Eb 41.28N 33.28 E
Dade City 44 Fk 28.22N 82.12W
Dadou 11 Hk 43.44N 1.49 E
Dādra and Nagar Haveli [3] 25 Ed 20.20N 72.50 E
Dadu 25 Dc 26.44N 67.47 E
Dadu He 21 Mg 29.32N 103.44 E
Dadukou 28 Di 30.30N 117.03 E
Dăeni 15 Le 44.50N 28.07 E
Daet 26 Hd 14.05N 122.55 E
Dafang 27 If 27.06N 105.32 E
Dafeng (Dazhongji) 28 Fh 33.11N 120.27 E
Dagana 34 Bb 16.31N 15.30W
Dagana 35 Bc 13.05N 16.00 E
Daga Post 35 Ed 9.13N 33.58 E
Dağardi 15 Lj 39.26N 29.00 E
Dagash 35 Eb 19.22N 33.24 E
Dagda 8 Lh 56.04N 27.36 E
Dagéla 35 Bc 10.40N 18.26 E
Dagestanskaja respublika 19 Eg 43.00N 47.00 E
Dagestanskije Ogni 19 Eg 42.06N 48.12 E
Dagu 28 De 38.58N 117.40 E
Daguan 27 Hf 27.48N 103.54 E
Dagu He 28 Ff 37.34N 121.17 E
Daguokui Shan 28 Jb 45.19N 129.50 E
Dagupan 26 Hc 16.03N 120.20 E
Dagxoi → Yidun 27 Ge 30.25N 99.28 E
Dagzê 27 Ff 29.41N 91.24 E
Dagzê Co 27 Ee 31.54N 87.29 E
Daheiding Shan 27 Mb 47.58N 129.10 E
Dahei He 28 Ad 40.34N 111.05 E
Da Hinggan Ling=Greater Khingan Range (EN) 21 Oe 49.00N 122.00 E
Dahlak Archipelago 30 Lg 15.40N 40.30 E
Dahlak Kebir 35 Gb 15.38N 40.11 E
Daḥl al Furayy 24 Li 26.45N 47.03 E
Dahlem 12 Id 50.23N 6.33 E
Dahlonega Plateau 44 Fh 34.30N 83.45W
Dahm, Ramlat- 33 If 16.25N 45.45 E
Dahme 10 Je 51.52N 13.26 E
Dahmouni 13 Ni 35.25N 1.29 E
Dahn 12 Je 49.09N 7.47 E
Dahomey → Bénin [1] 31 Hh 9.30N 2.15 E
Dahongliutan 27 Cd 36.00N 79.12 E
Dahra 13 Mh 36.18N 0.55 E
Dahra [Lib.] 33 Cd 29.40N 17.40 E
Dahra [Sen.] 34 Bb 15.21N 15.29W
Dahra, Massif de- 13 Oh 36.30N 2.05 E
Dahūk [3] 24 Jd 36.57N 43.00 E
Dahūk 24 Jd 36.52N 43.00 E
Dahushan 28 Gd 41.37N 122.09 E
Daḥy, Nafūd ad- 33 Ie 22.00N 45.25 E
Dai 63a Eb 7.53S 160.37 E
Daia 15 If 44.00N 25.59 E
Daia, Région des- 32 Hc 33.30N 3.25 E
Daicheng 28 De 38.42N 116.37 E
Daigo 28 Pf 36.46N 140.21 E
Dai Hai 28 Bd 40.31N 112.43 E
Dailekh 25 Gc 28.50N 81.44 E
Daimanji-San 29 Cc 36.15N 133.19 E
Daimiel 13 Ie 39.04N 3.37W

Index Symbols

[1] Independent Nation
[2] State, Region
[3] District, County
[4] Municipality
[5] Colony, Dependency
Continent
Physical Region
Historical or Cultural Region
Mount, Mountain
Volcano
Hill
Mountains, Mountain Range
Hills, Escarpment
Plateau, Upland
Pass, Gap
Plain, Lowland
Delta
Salt Flat
Valley, Canyon
Crater, Cave
Karst Features
Depression
Polder
Desert, Dunes
Forest, Woods
Heath, Steppe
Oasis
Cape, Point
Coast, Beach
Cliff
Peninsula
Isthmus
Sandbank
Island
Atoll
Rock, Reef
Islands, Archipelago
Rocks, Reefs
Coral Reef
Well, Spring
Geyser
River, Stream
Waterfall Rapids
River Mouth, Estuary
Lake
Salt Lake
Intermittent Lake
Reservoir
Swamp, Pond
Canal
Glacier
Ice Shelf, Pack Ice
Ocean
Sea
Gulf, Bay
Strait, Fjord
Lagoon
Bank
Seamount
Tablemount
Ridge
Shelf
Basin
Escarpment, Sea Scarp
Fracture
Trench, Abyss
National Park, Reserve
Point of Interest
Recreation Site
Cave, Cavern
Historic Site
Ruins
Wall, Walls
Church, Abbey
Temple
Scientific Station
Airport
Port
Lighthouse
Mine
Tunnel
Dam, Bridge

Name	Pg	Grid	Lat	Long
Dainanji-San [▲]	29	Ec	36.36N	137.42 E
Dainichi-San [▲]	29	Ec	36.09N	136.30 E
Dainkog	27	Ge	32.31N	97.59 E
Daiō-Zaki [►]	28	Ng	34.22N	136.53 E
Dairan (EN) = Dalian (Luda)	22	Of	38.55N	121.39 E
Dairan (EN) = Lüda→Dalian	22	Of	38.55N	121.39 E
Dairbhre/Valentia [✦]	9	Cj	51.55N	10.20W
Daireaux	55	Bm	36.36 S	61.45W
Dai-Sen [▲]	29	Cd	35.24N	133.34 E
Daisengen-Dake	29a	Bc	41.35N	140.09 E
Daishan (Gaotingzhen)	28	Gi	30.15N	122.13 E
Daitō [Jap.]	29	Gb	35.19N	132.58 E
Daitō [Jap.]	29	Gb	39.02N	141.22 E
Daito Islands (EN) = Daitō Shotō [▪]	21	Pg	25.00N	131.15 E
Daitō Shotō = Daito Islands (EN) [▪]	21	Pg	25.00N	131.15 E
Daitō-Zaki [►]	29	Gd	35.18N	140.24 E
Daixian	28	Be	39.03N	112.57 E
Daiyue→Shanyin	28	Be	39.30N	112.48 E
Dajabón	49	Ld	19.33N	71.42W
Dajarra	58	Eg	21.42 S	139.31 E
Dajtit, Mali i- [▲]	15	Ch	41.22N	19.55 E
Daka [⊾]	34	Ed	8.19N	0.13W
Dakar	31	Fg	14.40N	17.26W
Dākhilah, Wāḥāt al- = Dakhla Oasis (EN) [▫]	30	Jf	25.30N	29.10 E
Dakhla Oasis (EN) = Dākhilah, Wāḥāt al- [▫]	30	Jf	25.30N	29.10 E
Dakhlet Nouâdhibou [3]	32	De	20.30N	16.00W
Dakla	31	Ff	23.42N	15.56W
Dakoro	34	Gc	14.30N	6.25 E
Đakovo	14	Me	45.19N	18.25 E
Daksti	8	Kg	57.38N	25.32 E
Dak To	25	Lf	14.42N	107.51 E
Dal [⊾]	8	Dd	60.15N	11.12 E
Dal, Jökulsá á- [⊾]	7a	Cb	65.40N	14.20W
Đala	15	Dc	46.09N	20.07 E
Dala [Ang.]	36	De	11.03 S	20.17 E
Dala [Sol.Is.]	63a	c	8.36 S	160.41 E
Dalaba	34	Cc	10.42N	12.15W
Dalai → Da'an	27	Lb	45.35N	124.16 E
Dalai Nur [⊾]	27	Kc	43.18N	116.15 E
Dala-Järna	8	Fd	60.33N	14.21 E
Dālaki [⊾]	24	Nh	29.19N	51.06 E
Dalälven [⊾]	5	Hc	60.38N	17.27 E
Dalaman	24	Cd	36.40N	28.45 E
Dalaman [⊾]	15	Lm	36.44N	28.49 E
Dalâmi	35	Ec	11.52N	30.28 E
Dalán	24	Kj	24.15N	45.47 E
Dalan-Dzadgad	22	Me	43.47N	104.29 E
Dalane [⊾]	8	Bf	58.35N	6.20 E
Dalarna [▪]	8	Fd	61.00N	14.05 E
Dalarö	8	He	59.08N	18.24 E
Da Lat	22	Mh	11.56N	108.25 E
Dâlbandin	25	Cc	28.53N	64.25 E
Dalbosjön [⊾]	8	Ef	58.45N	12.50 E
Dalboslätten [⊾]	8	Ef	58.35N	12.25 E
Dalby	59	Ke	27.11 S	151.16 E
Dale [Nor.]	7	Af	60.35N	5.49 E
Dale [Nor.]	7	Af	61.22N	5.25 E
Dale Hollow Lake [⊾]	44	Eg	36.36N	85.19W
Dalen	7	Bg	59.27N	8.00 E
Dalfsen	12	Ib	52.30N	6.14 E
Dalgaranger, Mount- [▲]	59	De	27.51 S	117.06 E
Dälgopol	15	Kf	43.03N	27.21 E
Dalhart	43	Gd	36.04N	102.31 W
Dalhousie	42	Kg	48.04N	66.23W
Dalhousie, Cape- [►]	42	Eb	70.15N	129.41W
Dali [China]	22	Mg	25.43N	100.07 E
Dali [China]	27	Ie	34.55N	110.00 E
Dalian (Lüda) = Dairan (EN)	22	Of	38.55N	121.39 E
Dalias	13	Jh	36.49N	2.52W
Daling He [⊾]	28	Fd	40.56N	121.44 E
Dalizi	27	Mc	41.45N	126.50 E
Dalj	14	Me	45.29N	18.59 E
Daljä'	33	Fd	27.39N	30.42 E
Dalkowskie, Wzgórza- [⊾]	10	Le	51.35N	15.50 E
Dall [Ak.-U.S.] [◆]	40	Mf	54.50N	132.55W
Dall [Can.] [◆]	2	Ef	55.00N	133.00W
Dallas [Or.-U.S.]	46	Dd	44.55N	123.19W
Dallas [Tx.-U.S.]	39	Jf	32.47N	96.48W
Dalmā [◆]	24	Oj	24.30N	52.20 E
Dalmā', Qārat- [▲]	33	Dd	25.32N	23.57 E
Dalmacija	14	Kg	43.00N	17.00 E
Dalmacija = Dalmatia (EN) [▪]	5	Hg	43.00N	17.00 E
Dalmaj, Hawr- [⊾]	24	Kf	32.20N	45.28 E
Dalmally	9	Ie	56.24N	4.58W
Dalmatia (EN) = Dalmacija [▪]	5	Hg	43.00N	17.00 E
Dalmatovo	17	Kh	56.16N	63.00 E
Dalnegorsk	22	Pe	44.31N	135.31 E
Dalnerečensk	22	Pe	45.55N	133.45 E
Dalni	20	Kf	53.15N	157.30 E
Dalni	20	Ih	44.57N	135.03 E
Dalnjaja, Gora- [▲]	20	Mc	68.08N	179.53 E
Daloa	34	Dd	6.53N	6.23W
Daloa	31	Gh	6.53N	6.27W
Dalou Shan [⊾]	21	Mg	28.00N	106.40 E
Dalqū	35	Ea	20.07N	30.35 E
Dalrymple, Mount- [▲]	57	Fg	21.02 S	148.38 E
Dalsbruk	8	Jd	60.02N	22.31 E
Dalsbruk/Taalintendas	8	Jd	60.02N	22.31 E
Dalsfjorden [⊾]	8	Ac	61.20N	5.05 E
Dalsjöfors	8	Eg	57.43N	13.05 E
Dalsland [▪]	8	Df	58.55N	12.55 E
Dalslands kanal [⊾]	8	Ef	58.50N	12.25 E
Dals Långed	7	Cg	58.55N	12.18 E
Dalton	44	Eh	34.47N	84.58W
Daltonganj	25	Gd	24.02N	84.04 E
Dalul [⊾]	35	Gc	14.22N	40.21 E
Daluo	27	Hg	21.38N	100.15 E
Dalupiri [◆]	26	Hc	19.05N	121.12 E
Dalvík	7a	Bb	65.58N	18.32W
Dalwallinu	59	Df	30.17 S	116.40 E
Dalyan	15	Lm	36.50N	28.39 E
Daly Bay [◄]	42	Id	64.00N	89.40W
Daly City	46	Dh	37.42N	122.29W
Daly River [⊾]	57	Ef	13.20 S	130.19 E
Daly Waters	59	Gc	16.15 S	133.22 E
Damã, Wādi- [⊾]	24	Fi	27.09N	35.47 E
Damagarim [⊾]	34	Gc	13.42N	9.00 E
Damän [3]	25	Ed	20.10N	73.00 E
Damanhûr	33	Fc	31.02N	30.28 E
Damar, Pulau- [◆]	26	Ih	7.09 S	128.40 E
Damara	35	Be	4.58N	18.42 E
Damaraland [▪]	37	Bd	21.00 S	17.30 E
Damas Cays [◆]	49	Hb	23.58N	79.55W
Damascus (EN) = Dimashq	22	Ff	33.30N	36.15 E
Dāmāsh	24	Md	36.46N	49.46 E
Damaturu	34	Hc	11.45N	11.58 E
Damävand	34	He	35.56N	52.08 E
Damävand, Qolleh-ye- [▲]	21	Hf	35.56N	52.08 E
Damba	36	Cd	6.50 S	15.07 E
Dambaslar	15	Kh	41.13N	27.14 E
Dame Marie, Cap- [►]	47	Je	18.36N	74.26W
Damergou [⊾]	30	Hg	15.00N	9.00 E
Dämghän	24	Pd	36.09N	54.22 E
Damianópolis	55	Ib	14.33 S	46.10W
Damiao	34	He	30.52N	104.38 E
Damietta (EN) = Dumyät	31	Ke	31.25N	31.48 E
Daming	28	Cf	36.17N	115.09 E
Daming Shan [▲]	27	Jg	23.23N	108.30 E
Damir Qâbû	24	Id	36.54N	41.47 E
Dammartin en Goële	12	Ee	49.03N	2.41 E
Dammastock [▲]	14	Cd	46.38N	8.25 E
Damme [Bel.]	12	Fc	51.15N	3.17 E
Damme [Ger.]	12	Kb	52.31N	8.12 E
Dammer Berge [⊾]	12	Kb	52.35N	8.17 E
Damoh	25	Fd	23.50N	79.27 E
Damongo	34	Ed	9.05N	1.49W
Damous	13	Nh	36.33N	1.42 E
Dampier	58	Cg	20.39 S	116.45 E
Dampier, Selat- = Dampier Strait (EN) [⊾]	26	Jg	0.40 S	130.40 E
Dampier Archipelago [◆]	59	Dd	20.35 S	116.35 E
Dampier Land [◆]	59	Ec	17.30 S	122.55 E
Dampierre [⊾]	12	Df	48.42N	1.59 E
Dampier Strait [◄]	59	Ja	5.36 S	148.12 E
Dampier Strait (EN) = Dampier, Selat- [⊾]	26	Jg	0.40 S	130.40 E
Damqawt	23	Hf	16.34N	52.50 E
Damqog Kanbab/Maquan He [⊾]	27	Df	29.36N	84.09 E
Dam Qu [⊾]	27	He	33.56N	92.41 E
Damville	12	Df	48.52N	1.04 E
Damvillers	12	He	49.20N	5.24 E
Damwoude, Dantumadeel-	12	Ha	53.18N	5.59 E
Damxoi → Comai	27	Ff	28.26N	91.32 E
Damxung	27	Fe	30.34N	91.16 E
Danakil = Danakil Plain (EN) [⊾]	30	Lg	12.25N	40.30 E
Danakil Plain (EN) = Danakil [⊾]	30	Lg	12.25N	40.30 E
Danané [3]	34	Dd	7.25N	8.09W
Đananê	34	Dd	7.16N	8.09W
Da Nang	22	Mh	16.04N	108.13 E
Danba/Rongzhag	27	He	30.48N	101.54 E
Danbury	44	Kc	41.23N	73.27W
Danby Lake [⊾⊾]	46	Hi	34.14N	115.07W
Dancheng	28	Ch	33.36N	115.14 E
Dancheng → Xiangshan	28	Jh	29.29N	121.52 E
Dandarah [▪]	33	Fd	26.10N	32.39 E
Dandeldhura	25	Gc	29.18N	80.35 E
Dandenong, Melbourne-	59	Jg	37.59 S	145.12 E
Dandong	22	Oe	40.10N	124.15 E
Dandu	41	Jd	74.25N	20.10W
Danells Fjord [⊾]	41	Hf	60.45N	42.45W
Daneti	15	Hf	43.59N	24.03 E
Danfeng (Longjuzhai)	27	Je	33.44N	110.22 E
Danforth Hills [⊾]	45	Cf	40.15N	108.00W
Dangara	19	Je	38.09N	69.22 E
Dangchengwan → Subei	27	Fd	39.36N	94.58 E
Dang He [⊾]	27	Fc	40.30N	94.42 E
Dangjin Shankou [⊾]	21	Lf	39.15N	94.30 E
Dangla	35	Fc	11.16N	36.50 E
Dangla Shan → Tanggula Shan [⊾]	21	Lf	33.00N	92.00 E
Dangoura, Mount- [▲]	35	Dd	6.12N	26.27 E
Dangrek Range (EN) = Dong Rak, Phanom- [⊾]	21	Mh	14.25N	104.30 E
Dangshan	27	Ke	34.22N	116.21 E
Dangtu	28	Ii	31.33N	118.30 E
Dangu	12	De	49.15N	1.42 E
Dangyang	28	Ai	30.49N	111.47 E
Dan He [⊾]	28	Bg	35.05N	112.59 E
Daniel	46	Ke	42.52N	110.04W
Daniel, Serra- [▲]	55	Ea	13.40 S	54.55W
Danielskuil	37	De	28.11 S	23.33 E
Danilov	19	Ed	58.12N	40.13 E
Danilovgrad	15	Gg	42.33N	19.07 E
Danilovka	16	Nd	50.21N	44.06 E
Danjiang → Junxian	27	Jd	36.31N	110.45 E
Danjiangkou Shuiku [⊾]	27	Jd	32.31N	111.32 E
Danjo-Guntō [◆]	27	Me	32.00N	128.20 E
Dank	24	Qk	23.33N	56.16 E
Dankov	16	Kc	53.16N	39.07 E
Danli	49	Df	14.00N	86.35W
Danmark = Denmark (EN) [1]	5	Gf	56.00N	10.00 E
Danmark Fjord [⊾]	67	Me	81.10N	23.20W
Danmarks Havn	67	Ld	76.50N	18.30W
Dannemora	8	Hd	60.12N	17.48 E
Dannenberg	11	Mc	53.06N	11.06 E
Dannevirke	62	Gd	40.12 S	176.06 E
Danot	35	Hd	7.33N	45.17 E
Dan Sai	25	Kf	17.16N	101.09 E
Dantewara	25	Ge	18.54N	81.21 E
Dantumadeel [⊾]	12	Ha	53.18N	5.59 E
Dantumadeel-Damwoude	12	Ha	53.18N	5.59 E
Danube (EN) = Donau [⊾]	5	If	45.20N	29.40 E
Danube (EN) = Duna [⊾]	5	If	45.20N	29.40 E
Danube (EN) = Dunaj [⊾]	5	If	45.20N	29.40 E
Danube (EN) = Dunărea [⊾]	5	If	45.20N	29.40 E
Danube (EN) = Dunav [⊾]	5	If	45.20N	29.40 E
Danube, Mouths of the- (EN) = Dunării, Delta- [⊾]	5	If	45.30N	29.45 E
Danville [Ar.-U.S.]	45	Ji	35.03N	93.24W
Danville [Il.-U.S.]	43	Jc	40.08N	87.37W
Danville [In.-U.S.]	44	Df	39.46N	86.32W
Danville [Ky.-U.S.]	43	Kd	37.39N	84.46W
Danville [Va.-U.S.]	43	Ld	36.34N	79.25W
Danxian (Nada)	21	Ih	19.38N	109.32 E
Danyang	28	Bi	32.00N	119.33 E
Danzig (EN) = Gdańsk	6	Ie	54.23N	18.40 E
Dao [⊾]	26	Hd	10.31N	121.57 E
Dào [⊾]	13	Cd	40.20N	8.11W
Daocheng/Dabba	27	He	29.01N	100.26 E
Daokou → Huaxian	28	Cg	35.33N	114.30 E
Daosa	25	Fc	26.53N	76.20 E
Dao Shui [⊾]	28	Ci	30.42N	114.40 E
Dao Timni	34	Ha	20.38N	13.39 E
Daoura [⊾]	32	Gd	29.03N	4.33W
Daoxian	27	Jf	25.37N	111.36 E
Dapaong	34	Fc	10.52N	0.12 E
Dapchi	34	Hc	12.29N	11.29 E
Daqing Shan [⊾]	28	Ad	41.00N	111.00 E
Daqin Tal → Naiman Qi	27	Lc	42.49N	120.38 E
Daquing Shan [▲]	28	Ed	40.30N	119.38 E
Dar'ā	23	Gc	32.37N	36.06 E
Dārāb	24	Ph	28.45N	54.34 E
Darabani	15	Ja	48.11N	26.35 E
Daraçya Yarimadasi [⊾]	15	Lm	36.40N	28.10 E
Daräfisah	35	Ec	13.23N	31.59 E
Dārān	24	Nf	32.59N	50.24 E
Darasun	20	Gf	51.39N	113.59 E
Đaravica [▲]	15	Gg	42.32N	20.08 E
Darāw	24	Ej	24.25N	32.56 E
Darazo	34	Hc	11.00N	10.25 E
Darband, Kūh-e- [▲]	24	Qg	31.34N	57.08 E
Darbandi Khān, Sad ad- [⊡]	24	Ke	35.07N	45.50 E
Darbat Alī, Ra's- [►]	23	Hf	16.43N	53.33 E
Darbénai/Darbenas	8	Ih	56.02N	21.08 E
Dar Ben Karriche el Bahri	13	Sh	35.51N	5.21W
Darbhanga	25	Hc	26.10N	85.54 E
Dārboruk	35	Gd	9.44N	44.31 E
Darby	46	Ki	46.01N	114.11W
Darchan → Darhan	22	Me	49.33N	106.21 E
Darda	14	Me	45.38N	18.42 E
Dardanelle Lake [⊾]	45	Ji	35.25N	93.20W
Dardanelles (EN) = Çanakkale Boğazi [⊾]	5	Jg	40.15N	26.25 E
Dardo/Kangding	27	He	30.01N	101.58 E
Dar el Kouti [▪]	30	Jh	8.50N	21.50 E
Đarende	24	Gc	38.34N	37.30 E
Dar es Salaam [3]	36	Ge	6.50 S	39.02 E
Dar es Salaam	31	Ki	6.48S	39.17 E
Darfo Boario Terme	14	Ee	43.29 S	172.07 E
Dārfūr [▪]	30	Jg	12.40 N	24.20 E
Dārfūr al Janūbīyah [3]	35	Dc	11.30N	25.10 E
Dārfūr ash Shamālīyah [3]	35	Db	16.00N	25.30 E
Dargan-Ata	19	Ig	40.29N	62.12 E
Dargaville	61	Dg	35.56 S	173.52 E
Darhan (Darchan)	22	Me	49.33N	106.21 E
Darhan Muminggan Lianheqi	27	Jc	41.45N	110.24 E
Darica [Tur.]	15	Kj	40.00N	27.50 E
Darica [Tur.]	15	Mi	40.45N	29.23 E
Darién	47	Ig	8.30N	77.30W
Darien	44	Gj	31.22N	81.26W
Darién [3]	49	Ii	8.10N	77.45W
Darién, Golfo de- [◄]	52	Ie	8.25N	76.53W
Darién, Serranía del- [⊾]	47	Jg	8.30N	77.30W
Dariense, Cordillera- [⊾]	49	Eg	12.55N	85.30W
Darja [⊾]	18	Ee	38.13N	65.46 E
Darjeeling → Dārjiling	25	Hc	27.02N	88.16 E
Dārjiling	25	Hc	27.02N	88.16 E
Dar-Kebdani	13	Jh	35.07N	3.21W
Dark Head [►]	51n	Ba	13.17N	61.17W
Dārkhovin	24	Mg	30.45N	48.25 E
Darlag	27	Ge	33.49N	99.08 E
Darling Downs [⊾]	59	Ke	27.30 S	150.30 E
Darling Range [⊾]	57	Ch	32.00 S	116.30 E
Darling River [⊾]	57	Fh	34.07 S	141.55 E
Darlington [Eng.-U.K.]	9	La	54.31N	1.34W
Darlington [S.C.-U.S.]	44	Hh	34.18N	79.53W
Darłowo	10	Mb	54.26N	16.23 E
Darmouth	13	Jk	50.21N	3.35W
Darmstadt	10	Jk	49.52N	8.39 E
Darnah	31	Je	32.46N	22.39 E
Darnah [3]	33	Dc	31.00N	23.40 E
Darnétal	12	De	49.27N	1.09 E
Darney	11	Mf	48.05N	6.03 E
Darnley, Cape- [►]	66	Fc	67.43 S	69.30 E
Darnley Bay [◄]	42	Fc	69.45N	123.45W
Daroca	13	Kc	41.07N	1.25W
Darou Khoudos	34	Bb	15.06N	16.50W
Darovskoj	7	Jg	58.47N	47.59 E
Darrah, Mount- [▲]	46	Hb	49.00N	114.35W
Darregueira	56	Hf	37.42 S	63.10W
Darrehshahr	24	Lf	33.10N	47.18 E
D'Arros Island [◆]	37b	Bb	5.24 S	53.18 E
Dar Rounga [▪]	35	Cc	12.11N	21.21 E
Dar Sila [▪]	35	Cc	12.00N	21.00 E
Darß [⊾]	10	Ka	54.26N	12.31 E
Darßer Ort [►]	10	Ka	54.29N	12.31 E
Dart [⊾]	9	Jk	50.20N	3.33W
Dart, Cape- [►]	66	Nf	73.06 S	126.20W
D'Artagnan Bank (EN) [⊾]	59	Eb	13.00 S	121.00 E
Dartang → Bagên	27	Ff	31.50N	92.00 E
Dartford	12	Cc	51.27N	0.13 E
Dartmoor [⊾]	9	Jk	50.35N	3.58W
Dartmouth	42	Lh	44.40N	63.34W
Dartuch, Cabo- [►]	13	Pe	39.55N	3.48 E
Daru	60	Ci	9.04 S	143.12 E
Daruneh	24	Qe	35.10N	57.18 E
Daruvar	14	Le	45.35N	17.14 E
Darvaza	19	Fg	40.15N	58.24 E
Darvel, Teluk- [◄]	26	Gf	4.50N	118.30 E
Darwin	58	Ef	12.28 S	130.50 E
Darwin, Bahia- [◄]	56	Fg	45.27 S	74.40W
Darwin, Isla- [◆]	54a	Aa	1.39N	92.00W
Darwin, Port- [◄]	59	Gb	12.23 S	130.40 E
Dar Zagaoua [⊾]	35	Cb	15.15N	23.14 E
Dar Zebada [3]	35	Bc	13.45N	18.50 E
Dās [◆]	24	Oj	25.09N	52.53 E
Dašava	10	Uj	49.13N	24.05 E
Daš-Balbar	27	Jb	49.31N	114.21 E
Dasha He [⊾]	28	Ce	38.27N	114.39 E
Dashengtang Shan [⊾]	28	Dc	42.07N	117.12 E
Dashennongjia [⊾]	27	Je	31.47N	114.12 E
Dashennongjia [▲]	28	Ai	31.26N	110.18 E
Dashiqiao → Yingkou	28	Gd	40.39N	122.31 E
Dashitou	28	Jc	43.18N	128.29 E
Dasht	24	Qf	31.17N	56.04 E
Dasht Äb	24	Qh	28.59N	56.32 E
Dashtak	24	Qg	30.23N	52.30 E
Dasht-e Äzädegan	16	Oi	40.30N	46.03 E
Daškesan	37	Bf	33.26 S	18.05 E
Dasseneiland [◆]	37	Bf	33.26 S	18.05 E
Dastgardän	24	Qe	34.19N	56.51 E
Dastjerd-e Qaddädeh	24	Nf	32.44N	51.32 E
Datça	24	Be	36.45N	27.40 E
Date	29	Bc	42.27N	140.51 E
Datia	25	Fc	25.40N	78.28 E
Datian Ding [▲]	27	Jg	22.17N	111.13 E
Datil	45	Ci	34.09N	107.47W
Datong [China]	27	Hd	36.56N	101.40 E
Datong [China]	22	Nf	40.09N	113.17 E
Datteln	12	Jc	51.40N	7.23 E
Datteln-Hamm Kanal [⊾]	12	Jc	51.39N	7.21 E
Datu	21	Mi	2.05N	109.39 E
Datu, Teluk- [◄]	21	Ni	2.00N	111.00 E
Datu Plang	26	Hf	6.58N	124.40 E
Däüd Khel	25	Eb	32.53N	71.34 E
Daudzeva	8	Kh	56.28N	25.18 E
Daugaard-Jensen Land [◆]	41	Fb	80.10N	63.30W
Daugai/Daugai	8	Kj	54.20N	24.28 E
Daugava = Dvina (EN) [⊾]	19	Cd	57.04N	24.03 E
Daugavpils	6	Id	55.53N	26.32 E
Daule	54	Cd	1.50 S	79.57W
Daun	10	Cf	50.12N	6.50 E
Daung Kyun [◆]	25	Jf	12.14N	98.05 E
Daunia, Monti della- [⊾]	14	Ji	41.25N	15.05 E
Dauphin	42	Hf	51.09N	100.03W
Dauphiné [▪]	11	Lj	44.50N	6.00 E
Dauphin Lake [⊾]	42	Hf	51.15N	99.45W
Daura	34	Gc	13.02N	8.18 E
Dautphetal	12	Kd	50.52N	8.33 E
Dävangere	25	Ff	14.28N	75.55 E
Davao	22	Oi	7.04N	125.36 E
Davao Gulf [◄]	21	Oi	6.40N	125.55 E
Davenport [Ia.-U.S.]	24	Qg	30.40N	56.15 E
Davenport [Wa.-U.S.]	46	Gc	47.39N	118.09W
Davenport Range [⊾]	59	Gc	20.45 S	134.50 E
Daventry	12	Ab	52.15N	1.10W
Davert [⊾]	12	Jc	51.51N	7.36 E
David	47	Ik	8.25N	82.27W
David City	45	Hf	41.15N	97.08W
David-Gorodok	16	Gc	52.03N	27.13 E
David Point [►]	51p	Bb	12.14N	61.39W
Davidson	42	He	51.18N	105.59W
Davidson Mountains [⊾]	40	Kc	68.45N	142.10W
Davies, Mount- [▲]	59	Fe	26.14 S	129.16 E
Davis	46	Eg	38.33N	121.44W
Davis [◈]	66	Fc	68.35 S	77.58 E
Davis, Cape- [►]	66	Ee	66.24 S	56.50 E
Davis, Mount- [▲]	44	Hf	39.47N	79.10W
Davis Bay [◄]	66	Ie	66.08 S	134.05 E
Davis Inlet	42	Le	56.00N	61.30W
Davis Mountains [⊾]	45	Ek	30.35N	104.00W
Davis Sea (EN) [⊹]	66	Ge	66.00 S	92.00 E
Davisstraedet = Davis Strait (EN) [⊾]	38	Nc	68.00N	58.00W
Davis Strait (EN) = Davisstraedet [⊾]	38	Nc	68.00N	58.00W
Davlekanovo	19	Fe	54.13N	55.03 E
Davo [⊾]	34	Dd	5.06N	6.08W
Davos/Tavau	14	Dd	46.47N	9.50 E
Davutlar	15	Kl	37.43N	27.17 E
Dawa	33	Dc	31.00N	23.40 E
Dawanlè	35	Gc	11.06N	42.38 E
Dawäsir, Wādī ad-	24	Jm	20.24N	46.29 E
Dawei	22	Lh	14.05N	98.12 E
Dawen He [⊾]	28	Eg	35.37N	116.23 E
Dawharab [▲]	35	Hf	16.17N	41.57 E
Dawson [Ga.-U.S.]	44	Ei	31.47N	84.26W
Dawson [Yuk.-Can.]	38	Fc	64.04N	139.25W
Dawson, Mount- [▲]	46	Ea	51.09N	117.25W
Dawson Creek	38	Gd	55.45N	120.07W
Dawson Range [⊾]	40	Dd	65.15N	137.45W
Dawson River [⊾]	57	Gg	23.38 S	149.46 E
Dawu	27	He	30.59N	101.07 E
Dawu → Maqên	27	Gd	34.29N	100.01 E
Dawu	28	Ci	31.33N	114.07 E
Dawukou → Shizuishan	27	Id	39.04N	106.24 E
Dax	11	Ek	43.43N	1.03W
Da Xi [⊾]	28	Lf	28.10N	120.14 E
Daxian	27	Ie	31.15N	107.28 E
Daxing	28	Df	39.44N	116.21 E
Daxinggou	28	Jc	43.23N	129.39 E
Daxue Shan [▲]	21	Mf	30.30N	101.30 E
Dayan → Lijiang	22	Mg	26.56N	100.15 E
Dayang He [⊾]	28	Ge	39.52N	123.40 E
Dayao	27	Hf	25.49N	101.18 E
Daye	28	Ci	30.05N	114.58 E
Dayishan → Guanyun	28	Eg	34.18N	119.14 E
Daymán, Cuchilla del- [⊾]	55	Dj	31.38S	57.10W
Daymán, Rio- [⊾]	55	Dj	31.40 S	58.02W
Dayong	27	Je	29.09N	110.30 E
Dayr, Jabal ad- [▲]	35	Ec	12.27N	30.45 E
Dayr az Zawr	22	Gf	35.20N	40.09 E
Dayr Ḥāfir	24	Gd	36.09N	37.42 E
Dayr Kätrīnä = Saint Catherine Monastery of- (EN) [▲]	33	Fd	28.31N	33.57 E
Dayr Mawās	24	Di	27.38N	30.51 E
Dayrūț	33	Fd	27.33N	30.49 E
Dayton [Oh.-U.S.]	39	Kf	39.45N	84.15W
Dayton [Wa.-U.S.]	46	Gc	46.19N	117.59W
Daytona Beach	39	Kg	29.12N	80.59W
Dayu	27	Jf	25.29N	114.22 E
Da Yunhe → Grand Canal (EN) [⊾]	21	Nf	39.54N	116.44 E
Dayville	46	Fd	44.28N	119.32W
Dayyinah [◆]	24	Oj	24.57N	52.24 E
Dazhongji → Dafeng	28	Fh	33.11N	120.27 E
Dazhu	27	Ie	30.42N	107.12 E
Dazjä	24	Pe	35.50N	55.46 E
Dazkiri	24	Cd	37.54N	29.42 E
De Aar	31	Jl	30.39S	24.00 E
Dead	9	Ei	52.40N	8.30W
Deadhorse	40	Jb	70.11N	148.27W
Deadmans Cay	49	Jb	23.14N	75.14W
Dead Sea (EN) = Mayyit, Al Baḥr al- [⊾]	21	Ff	31.30N	35.30 E
Deadwood	45	Ed	44.23N	103.44W
Deal	12	Dc	51.13N	1.24 E
Dealu Mare [▲]	15	Jb	47.27N	26.40 E
De'an	28	Cj	29.19N	115.45 E
Deán Funes	56	Hd	30.26 S	64.21W
Dearborn	44	Fd	42.18N	83.10W
Dearg, Beinn- [▲]	9	Id	57.48N	4.57W
Dease [⊾]	46	Gc	46.52N	116.31W
Dease Arm [◄]	42	Fc	66.50N	120.00W
Dease Lake	39	Fd	58.35N	130.02W
Dease Strait [⊾]	42	Gc	69.00N	107.00W
Death Valley	38	Hf	36.30N	117.00W
Death Valley	46	Gh	36.20N	116.50W
Deauville	11	Ge	49.22N	0.04 E
Debak	26	Ff	1.34N	111.25 E
Debal	15	Ke	48.20N	38.29 E
Debao	27	Ig	23.17N	106.21 E
Debar	15	Dh	41.32N	20.32 E
Debark	35	Fc	13.08N	37.53 E
Debdou	32	Gc	33.59N	3.03W
Debed [⊾]	16	Nf	41.22N	44.58 E
Deben [⊾]	12	Db	52.01N	1.22 E
De Beque	45	Bg	39.20N	108.13W
Đebica	10	Rf	50.04N	21.24 E
De Bilt	12	Hb	52.06N	5.11 E
Deblin	20	Kd	62.18N	150.47 E
Dębno	10	Kc	52.45N	14.40 E
Débo, Lac- [⊾]	34	Eb	15.18N	4.09W
Deborah East, Lake- [⊾]	59	Df	30.45 S	119.10 E
Deborah West, Lake- [⊾]	59	Df	30.45 S	119.05 E
Deboyne Islands [◆]	57	Gf	10.43 S	152.22 E
Debrc	15	Ca	44.37N	19.54 E
Debre Berhan	35	Fd	9.41N	39.33 E
Debrecen [2]	6	If	47.32N	21.38 E
Debrecen	10	Ri	47.31N	21.41 E
Debre Libanos [▲]	35	Fd	9.43N	38.52 E
Debre Markós	35	Kg	10.10N	37.36 E
Debre Sina	35	Fd	9.51N	39.46 E
Debre Tabor	35	Fc	11.51N	38.00 E
Debre Zeyt	31	Kh	8.47N	39.00 E
De-Buka, Glacier- [⊾]	66	Nf	76.00 S	131.00W
Decatur [Al.-U.S.]	43	Je	34.36N	86.59W
Decatur [Ga.-U.S.]	44	Ei	33.46N	84.18W
Decatur [Il.-U.S.]	43	Jd	39.51N	89.32W
Decatur [In.-U.S.]	44	Ee	40.50N	84.56W
Decatur [Tx.-U.S.]	45	Ij	33.14N	97.35W
Decazeville	11	Ij	44.33N	2.15 E
Deccan [⊾]	21	Jh	14.00N	77.00 E
Decelles, Reservoir- [⊾]	44	Hb	47.40N	78.08W
Deception Bay [◄]	59	Ia	7.07 S	144.05 E
Dechang	27	Hf	27.22N	102.12 E
Děčín	10	Kf	50.47N	14.13 E
Decize	11	Jh	46.50N	3.28 E
Decorah	45	Ke	43.18N	91.48W
Deda	15	Hc	46.56N	24.54 E
Dedemsvaart, Avereest-	12	Ib	52.37N	6.27 E
Dedopolis-Ckaro	16	Oi	40.26N	46.06 E
Dédougou	34	Ec	12.28N	3.28W
Dedovići	7	Gh	53.59N	29.58 E
Dedza	36	Fe	14.22 S	34.20 E
Dee [Eng.-U.K.] [⊾]	9	Kd	53.19N	3.11W
Dee [Scot.-U.K.] [⊾]	9	Kd	57.08N	2.04W
Dee [Scot.-U.K.] [⊾]	9	Ig	54.50N	4.03W
Deep Creek Range [⊾]	46	If	40.00N	113.57W
Deering	40	Fc	66.05N	162.43W
Deer Isle [◆]	44	Mc	44.13N	68.41W
Deer Lake [Newf.-Can.]	42	Ig	49.10N	57.25W
Deer Lake [Ont.-Can.]	42	If	52.40N	94.30W
Deer Park	46	Gc	47.57N	117.28W
Defiance	44	Ee	41.17N	84.21W
De Funiak Springs	44	Dj	30.43N	86.07W
Dega Ahmedo	35	Gd	7.50N	42.53 E
Degeberg	8	Gh	56.21N	14.26 E
Degeh Bur	35	Gd	8.13N	43.34 E
Degema	34	Ge	4.45N	6.46 E
Degerfors	7	Dg	59.14N	14.26 E
Degerhamn	7	Dh	56.21N	16.24 E
Deggendorf	10	Jh	48.50N	12.58 E

Index Symbols

[1] Independent Nation	[◻] Historical or Cultural Region	[◻] Pass, Gap	[◻] Depression
[2] State, Region	[◻] Mount, Mountain	[◻] Plain, Lowland	[◻] Polder
[3] District, County	[◻] Volcano	[▽] Delta	[◻] Desert, Dunes
[4] Municipality	[◻] Hill	[◻] Salt Flat	[◻] Forest, Woods
[5] Colony, Dependency	[◻] Mountains, Mountain Range	[▽] Valley, Canyon	[◻] Heath, Steppe
[◻] Continent	[◻] Hills, Escarpment	[◻] Crater, Cave	[◻] Oasis
[◻] Physical Region	[◻] Plateau, Upland	[◻] Karst Features	[►] Cape, Point

[◻] Coast, Beach	[◻] Rock, Reef	[◻] Waterfall Rapids	[◻] Canal
[◻] Cliff	[◻] Islands, Archipelago	[◻] River Mouth, Estuary	[◻] Glacier
[◻] Peninsula	[◻] Rocks, Reefs	[◻] Lake	[◻] Ice Shelf, Pack Ice
[◻] Isthmus	[◻] Coral Reef	[◻] Salt Lake	[◻] Ocean
[◻] Sandbank	[◻] Well, Spring	[◻] Intermittent Lake	[◻] Sea
[◻] Island	[◻] Geyser	[◻] Reservoir	[◻] Gulf, Bay
[◻] Atoll	[◻] River, Stream	[◻] Swamp, Pond	[◻] Strait, Fjord

[◻] Lagoon	[◻] Escarpment, Sea Scarp	[◻] Historic Site	[◻] Port
[◻] Bank	[◻] Fracture	[◻] Ruins	[◻] Lighthouse
[◻] Seamount	[◻] Trench, Abyss	[◻] Wall, Walls	[◻] Mine
[◻] Tablemount	[◻] National Park, Reserve	[◻] Church, Abbey	[◻] Tunnel
[◻] Ridge	[◻] Point of Interest	[◻] Temple	[◻] Dam, Bridge
[◻] Shelf	[◻] Recreation Site	[◻] Scientific Station	
[◻] Basin	[◻] Cave, Cavern	[◻] Airport	

Değirmendere	15	Kk	38.06N	27.09 E
De Gray Lake	45	Ji	34.15N	93.15W
De Grey River	59	Dd	20.12S	119.11 E
Degtarsk	17	Jh	56.42N	60.06 E
De Haan	12	Fc	51.16N	3.02 E
Dehaj	24	Pg	30.42N	54.53 E
Dehaq	24	Nf	32.55N	50.57 E
Deh Bārez	24	Qi	27.26N	57.12 E
Deh Bīd	24	Og	30.38N	53.13 E
Deh Dasht	24	Ng	30.47N	50.34 E
Dehdez	24	Ng	31.43N	50.17 E
Deh-e-Namak	24	Oe	35.25N	52.50 E
Deh-e Shīr	24	Og	31.29N	53.45 E
Deh-e Ziyār	24	Qg	30.40N	57.00 E
Dehgolān	24	Le	35.17N	47.25 E
Dehiwala-Mount Lavinia	25	Fg	6.50N	79.52 E
Dehlorān	24	Lf	32.41N	47.16 E
Deh Now	24	Qf	33.01N	57.41 E
Dehra Dūn	25	Fb	30.19N	78.02 E
Dehui	27	Mc	44.33N	125.38 E
Deinze	11	Jd	50.59N	3.32 E
Dej	15	Gb	47.09N	23.52 E
Deje	8	Ee	59.36N	13.28 E
Dejen	35	Fc	10.05N	38.11 E
Dejës, Mali i-	15	Dh	41.42N	20.10 E
Dejnau	19	Gh	39.18N	63.11 E
De Jongs, Tanjung-	26	Kh	6.56S	138.32 E
De Kalb	45	Lf	41.56N	88.45W
Dekar	37	Cd	21.30S	21.58 E
Dekese	31	Ji	3.27S	21.24 E
Dekina	34	Gd	7.42N	7.01 E
Dékoa	35	Bd	6.19N	19.04 E
De Koog, Texel-	12	Ga	53.07N	4.46 E
De La Garma	55	Bm	37.58S	60.25W
De Land	44	Gk	29.02N	81.18W
Delano	43	Dd	35.41N	119.15W
Delano Peak	43	Ed	38.22N	112.23W
Delārām	23	Jc	32.11N	63.25 E
Delarof Islands	40a	Cb	51.30N	178.45W
Delaware	44	Fe	40.18N	83.06W
Delaware	45	Ek	32.00N	104.00W
Delaware [2]	43	Ld	39.10N	75.30W
Delaware Bay	38	Lc	39.05N	75.15W
Delaware River	43	Ld	39.20N	75.25W
Delbrück	12	Kc	51.46N	8.34 E
Del Carril	55	Cl	35.31S	59.30W
Delčevo	15	Fh	41.58N	22.47 E
Del City	45	Hi	35.27N	97.27W
Delegate	59	Jg	37.03S	148.58 E
Delémont/Delsberg	14	Bc	47.22N	7.21 E
Delet/Teili	8	Id	60.15N	20.35 E
Delfinópolis	55	Ie	20.20S	46.51W
Delft	11	Kb	52.00N	4.21 E
Delfzijl	11	Ma	53.19N	6.56 E
Delgada, Punta-	52	Jj	42.46S	63.38W
Delgado, Cabo-=Delgado, Cape-(EN)	30	Lj	10.40S	40.38 E
Delgado, Cabo-=Delgado, Cape-(EN) [3]	37	Fb	12.30S	39.00 E
Delgado, Cape-(EN)= Delgado, Cabo-	30	Lj	10.40S	40.38 E
Delgado, Cape-(EN)= Delgado, Cabo- [3]	37	Fb	12.30S	39.00 E
Delger Muren	27	Hb	49.17N	100.40 E
Delhi [Co.-U.S.]	45	Eh	37.42N	103.58W
Delhi [India]	25	Jg	28.40N	77.13 E
Delhi [N.Y.-U.S.]	44	Jd	42.17N	74.57W
Deliblatska Peščara	15	Dd	45.00N	21.00 E
Delice	24	Fc	39.58N	34.02 E
Deliceırmak	24	Fb	40.28N	34.10 E
Delicias [Cuba]	49	Ic	21.11N	76.34W
Delicias [Mex.]	47	Cc	28.13N	105.28W
Delījān	24	Nf	33.59N	50.40 E
Delingha	27	Gd	37.26N	97.25 E
Dēliņkalns/Delinkalns, Gora-	8	Lg	57.30N	27.02 E
Delinkalns, Gora-/ Dēliņkalns	8	Lg	57.30N	27.02 E
Delitzsch	10	Ie	51.32N	12.21 E
Deljatin	15	Ha	48.29N	24.45 E
Delle	11	Mg	47.30N	7.00 E
Dell Rapids	45	He	43.50N	96.43W
Dellys	32	Hb	36.55N	3.55 E
Delmarva Peninsula	38	Lf	38.50N	75.30W
Delme	12	Ka	53.05N	8.40 E
Delme	12	If	48.53N	6.24 E
Delmenhorst	10	Ec	53.03N	8.37 E
Delnice	14	Ie	45.24N	14.48 E
Delo	35	Fd	5.49N	37.57 E
De Long Strait (EN)= Longa, Proliv-	21	Tb	70.20N	178.00 E
De-Longa, Ostrova-=De Long Islands (EN)	21	Rb	76.30N	153.00 E
De Long Islands (EN)=De-Longa, Ostrova-	21	Rb	76.30N	153.00 E
De Long Mountains	40	Gc	68.20N	162.00W
Deloraine	59	Jh	41.31S	146.39 E
Delorme, Lac-	42	Kf	54.35N	69.55W
Delphi (EN) = Dhelfoi	15	Fk	38.29N	22.30 E
Del Rio	43	Gf	29.22N	100.54W
Delsberg/Delémont	14	Bc	47.22N	7.21 E
Delsbo	7	Dc	61.48N	16.35 E
Delta [Co.-U.S.]	43	Fd	38.44N	108.04W
Delta [Ut.-U.S.]	43	Ed	39.21N	112.35W
Delta Amacuro [2]	54	Fb	8.30N	61.30W
Delta Junction	40	Jd	64.02N	145.41W
Delvāda	25	Ed	20.46N	71.02 E
Del Valle	55	Bl	35.54S	60.43W
Delvina	15	Dj	39.57N	20.06 E
Dëma	17	Gi	54.42N	55.58 E
Demanda, Sierra de la-	13	Ib	42.15N	3.05W
Demba	36	Dd	5.30S	22.16 E
Dembi	35	Fd	8.05N	36.28 E
Dembia	35	Cd	5.07N	24.25 E
Dembi Dolo	35	Ed	8.32N	34.49 E
De Medinilla, Farallon-	57	Fc	16.01N	146.04 E

Demer	11	Kd	50.58N	4.45 E
Demerara Plateau (EN)	52	Le	4.30N	44.00W
Demerara River	50	Gi	6.48N	58.10W
Demidov	16	Gb	55.15N	31.29 E
Demidovka	10	Vf	50.20N	25.27 E
Deming	43	Fe	32.16N	107.45W
Demini, Rio-	54	Fd	0.46S	62.56W
Demirci	24	Cc	39.03N	28.40 E
Demir Kapija	15	Fh	41.25N	22.15 E
Demirköy	15	Kh	41.49N	27.15 E
Demirtaş	15	Mi	40.16N	29.06 E
Demjanka	19	Gd	59.34N	69.20 E
Demjansk	7	Hh	57.38N	32.29 E
Demjanskoje	19	Gd	59.36N	69.18 E
Demmin	10	Jc	53.54N	13.02 E
Demopolis	44	Di	32.31N	87.50W
Dempo, Gunung-	21	Mj	4.02S	103.09 E
Demta	26	Lg	2.20S	140.08 E
Denain	11	Jd	50.20N	3.23 E
Denan	35	Gd	6.30N	43.30 E
Denau	19	Gh	38.18N	67.55 E
Den Bosch/'s-Hertogenbosch	11	Lc	51.41N	5.19 E
Den Burg, Texel-	12	Ga	53.03N	4.47 E
Den Chai	25	Ke	17.59N	100.04 E
Dendang	26	Eg	3.05S	107.54 E
Dender/Dendre	11	Kc	51.02N	4.06 E
Dendermonde/Termonde	12	Gc	51.02N	4.07 E
Dendre/Dender	11	Kc	51.02N	4.06 E
Dendtler Island	66	Pf	72.58S	89.57W
Denekamp	12	Jb	52.23N	7.00 E
Denežkin Kamen, Gora-	19	Fc	60.25N	59.31 E
Dengarh	25	Hd	23.50N	81.42 E
Dêngkagoin→Têwo	27	He	34.03N	103.21 E
Dengkou (Bayan Gol)	22	Me	40.25N	106.59 E
Dêngqên	27	Ge	31.29N	95.32 E
Dengzhou→Penglai	27	Ld	37.44N	120.45 E
Den Haag/'s-Gravenhage= The Hague (EN)	6	Ge	52.06N	4.18 E
Den Ham	12	Ib	52.28N	6.32 E
Denham→Shak Bay	59	Ce	25.55S	113.32 E
Denham, Mount-	49	Id	18.13N	77.32W
Denham Range	59	Jd	21.55S	147.45 E
Denham Sound	59	Ce	25.40S	113.15 E
Den Helder	11	Kb	52.54N	4.45 E
Denia	13	Mf	38.51N	0.07 E
Deniliquin	59	Ig	35.32S	144.58 E
Denio	46	Ff	41.59N	118.39W
Denis Island	37b	Ca	3.48S	55.40 E
Denison [Ia.-U.S.]	43	Hc	42.01N	95.20W
Denison [Tx.-U.S.]	43	He	33.45N	96.33W
Denison, Mount-	40	Ie	58.25N	154.27W
Denizli	23	Cb	37.46N	29.06 E
Denklingen, Reichshoft-	12	Jd	50.55N	7.39 E
Denman Glacier	66	Ge	66.45S	99.25 E
Denmark [Austl.]	59	Df	34.57S	117.21 E
Denmark [S.C.-U.S.]	44	Gi	33.19N	81.09W
Denmark (EN)=Danmark [1]	6	Gd	56.00N	10.00 E
Denmark Strait (EN)= Danmarksstraedet	38	Qc	67.00N	25.00W
Dennery	51k	Bb	13.55N	60.54W
Den Oever, Wieringen-	12	Hb	52.56N	5.02 E
Denpasar	22	Nj	8.39S	115.13 E
Denton	43	He	33.13N	97.08W
D'Entrecasteaux, Point-	59	Df	34.50S	116.00 E
D'Entrecasteaux Islands	57	Ge	9.35S	150.40 E
Denver	39	If	39.43N	105.01W
Deoghar	25	Hd	24.29N	86.42 E
Deolāli	25	Ee	19.54N	73.50 E
De Pajaros, Farallon-	57	Fb	20.32N	144.54 E
De Panne/La Panne	12	Ec	51.06N	2.35 E
De Pere	45	Ld	44.27N	88.04W
Deputatski	20	Ic	69.13N	139.55 E
Dêqên	27	Gf	28.32N	98.50 E
Deqing	27	Jg	23.14N	111.42 E
De Queen	45	Ii	34.02N	94.21W
De Quincy	45	Jk	30.27N	93.26W
Dequing	28	Fi	30.34N	120.05 E
Dera, Lach-	35	Ge	0.15N	42.17 E
Dera, Lagh-	30	Lh	0.15N	42.17 E
Dera Bugti	25	Dc	29.02N	69.09 E
Dera Ghāzi Khan	22	Jf	30.03N	70.38 E
Dera Ismāil Khan	25	Eb	31.50N	70.54 E
Derbent	6	Kg	42.00N	48.18 E
Derbent [Tur.]	15	Lk	38.11N	28.33 E
Derby	9	Lh	53.05N	1.40W
Derby [Austl.]	58	Df	17.18S	123.38 E
Derby [Eng.-U.K.]	9	Li	52.55N	1.30W
Derby [Ks.-U.S.]	45	Hh	37.33N	97.16W
Derbyshire [3]	9	Lh	53.10N	1.35W
Đerdap	15	Fe	44.41N	22.10 E
Derecske	10	Ri	47.21N	21.34 E
Dereköy	15	Kh	41.56N	27.21 E
Dereli	24	Hb	40.45N	38.27 E
Derg/Abhainn na Deirge	9	Fg	54.40N	7.25W
Đerg, Lough-/Loch Deirgeirt	9	Ei	53.00N	8.20W
Dergači	16	Pd	51.13N	48.46 E
Dergači	16	Jd	50.09N	36.09 E
Der Grabow	10	Ib	54.23N	12.50 E
De Ridder	45	Jk	30.51N	93.17W
Derik	24	Id	37.22N	40.17 E
Derkul	16	Qd	51.17N	51.15 E
Dermott	45	Kj	33.32N	91.26W
Dernieres, Isles-	45	Kl	29.02N	90.47W
Derong	27	Gf	28.44N	99.18 E
De Rose Hill	59	Ge	26.25S	133.15 E
Déroute, Passage de la-	11	Ee	49.12N	1.51W
Dersa, Eglab-	32	Gd	26.45N	4.26W
Dersca	15	Jb	47.59N	26.12 E
Dersingham	12	Cb	52.51N	0.30 E
Derudeb	35	Fb	17.32N	36.06 E
Derventa	14	Lf	44.59N	17.55 E
Derwent [Eng.-U.K.]	9	Mg	54.10N	0.40W
Derwent [Eng.-U.K.]	12	Ab	52.53N	1.17W
Derwent River	59	Jh	43.03S	147.22 E
Deržavinsk	19	Ge	51.03N	66.19 E

Desaguadero, Río-	52	Ji	34.13S	66.47W
Désappointement, Iles du-	57	Mf	14.10S	141.20W
Des Arc	45	Ki	34.58N	91.30W
Desborough	12	Bb	52.26N	0.49W
Descalvado	55	Ie	21.54S	47.37W
Descartes	11	Gh	46.58N	0.45 E
Deschambault Lake	42	Hf	54.50N	103.30W
Deschutes River	43	Cb	45.38N	120.54W
Descoberto, Rio-	55	Hc	16.20S	48.19W
Dese	31	Kg	11.07N	39.38 E
Deseado, Río-	52	Jj	47.45S	65.54W
Desecheo, Isla-	51a	Ab	18.25N	67.28W
Desengaño, Punta-	56	Gg	49.15S	67.37W
Desengano del Garda	14	Ee	45.28N	10.32 E
Desert Center	46	Hj	33.42N	115.26W
Desert Peak	46	If	40.28N	112.38W
Deshaies [Guad.]	51e	Ab	16.18N	61.48W
Deshaies [Guad.]	51e	Ab	16.18N	61.47W
Desiderio, Rio-	55	Ja	12.20S	44.50W
Desmaraisville	44	Ia	49.31N	76.10W
De Smet	45	Hd	44.23N	97.33W
Desmochado	55	Ch	27.07S	58.06W
Des Moines	38	Je	40.22N	91.26W
Des Moines [Ia.-U.S.]	39	Je	41.35N	93.37W
Des Moines [N.M.-U.S.]	45	Eh	36.46N	103.50W
Desmoronado, Cerro-	47	Dd	20.21N	105.01W
Desna	5	Je	50.33N	30.32 E
Desnăţui	15	Ge	43.53N	23.35 E
Desolación, Isla-	52	Ik	53.00S	74.10W
De Soto	45	Kg	38.08N	90.33W
Despeñaperros, Desfiladero de-	13	If	38.24N	3.30W
Des Roches, Ile-	37b	Bb	5.41S	53.41 E
Dessau	10	Ie	51.50N	12.15 E
Destruction Bay	42	Dd	61.20N	139.00W
Desvres	11	Hd	50.40N	1.50 E
Deta	15	Ed	45.24N	21.14 E
Dete	37	Dc	18.37S	26.51 E
Detmold	10	Ee	51.56N	8.53 E
Detour, Point-	44	Dc	45.36N	86.37W
Detroit [Mi.-U.S.]	39	Ke	42.20N	83.03W
Detroit [Or.-U.S.]	46	Dd	44.42N	122.10W
Detroit Lakes	45	Ic	46.49N	95.51W
Dettifoss	7a	Cb	65.49N	16.24W
Detva	10	Ph	48.34N	19.25 E
Deûle	12	Ed	50.44N	2.56 E
Deurdeur	13	Oh	36.14N	2.16 E
Deurne	12	Hc	51.28N	5.48 E
Deutsche Bucht	10	Db	54.30N	7.30 E
Deutsche Demokratische Republik = Germany	6	Ge	51.00N	10.00 E
Deutschlandsberg	14	Jd	46.49N	15.13 E
Deux-Bassins, Col des-	13	Ph	36.27N	3.18 E
Deux Sèvres [3]	11	Fh	46.30N	0.15W
Deva	15	Fd	45.53N	22.54 E
Dévaványa	10	Qi	47.02N	20.58 E
Deveci Dağları	24	Gb	40.05N	36.00 E
Devecser	10	Ni	47.06N	17.26 E
Develi	24	Fc	38.22N	35.06 E
Deventer	11	Mb	52.15N	6.10 E
Deverd, Cap-	63b	Be	20.46S	164.22 E
Deveron	9	Kd	57.40N	2.30W
Devès, Monts du-	11	Jj	44.57N	3.46 E
Devetak	14	Mg	43.58N	19.00 E
Devil River Peak	62	Ed	40.58S	172.39 E
Devil's Hole	9	Ne	56.38N	0.40 E
Devil's Island (EN)=Diable, Ile du-	54	Hb	5.17N	52.35W
Devils Lake	43	Hb	48.07N	98.59W
Devils Lake	45	Gb	48.01N	98.52W
Devils Paw	40	Me	58.44N	133.50W
Devils River	45	Fl	29.39N	100.58W
Devils Tower	46	Md	44.31N	104.57W
Devin	15	Hh	41.45N	24.24 E
Devizes	9	Lj	51.22N	1.59W
Devnja	15	Kf	43.13N	27.33 E
Devodi Munda	25	Ge	17.37N	82.57 E
De Volet Point	51n	Ba	13.22N	61.13W
Devolli	15	Ci	40.49N	19.51 E
Devolli	15	Di	40.30N	20.50 E
Dévoluy	11	Lj	44.39N	5.53 E
Devon [3]	9	Jk	50.50N	3.50W
Devon	9	Jk	50.50N	4.00W
Devon	38	Kb	75.00N	87.00W
Devon	12	Ba	53.04N	0.49W
Devonport	57	Fi	41.11S	146.21 E
Devoto	55	Aj	31.24S	62.19W
Devrek	24	Db	41.13N	31.57 E
Devrez	24	Fb	41.06N	34.25 E
Dewa	30	Lh	4.11N	42.06 E
Dewar Lakes	42	Kc	68.00N	73.00W
Dewās	25	Fd	22.58N	76.04 E
Dewa-Sanchi	29	Gb	39.30N	140.15 E
Dewey	45	Ih	36.48N	95.56W
De Witt	45	Ki	34.18N	91.20W
Dexemhare	35	Fb	15.04N	39.03 E
Dexing	28	Dj	28.55N	117.33 E
Dexter	45	Lh	36.48N	89.57W
Deyang	27	He	31.07N	104.25 E
Dey-Dey, Lake-	59	Ge	29.15S	131.05 E
Deyhūk	24	Qf	33.17N	57.30 E
Deyyer	23	Hd	27.50N	51.55 E
Dez	24	Mg	31.39N	48.52 E
Dezfūl	22	Gf	32.23N	48.24 E
Dez Gerd	24	Ng	30.45N	51.57 E
Dezhou	27	Kd	37.28N	116.18 E
Dháfni	15	Fl	37.46N	22.02 E
Dhahab	33	Fd	28.29N	34.32 E
Dhaka	22	Lg	23.43N	90.25 E
Dhamār	23	Fg	14.37N	44.23 E
Dhamtari	25	Gd	20.41N	81.34 E
Dhānbād	25	Hd	23.48N	86.27 E

Dhanushkodi	25	Fg	9.11N	79.24 E
Dhaulagiri	21	Kg	28.44N	83.25 E
Dhekeleia	24	Ee	35.03N	33.40 E
Dhelfoi = Delphi (EN)	15	Fk	38.29N	22.30 E
Dhelvinákion	15	Dj	39.56N	20.28 E
Dhenkanal	25	Hd	20.40N	85.36 E
Dheskáti	15	Ej	39.55N	21.49 E
Dhespotikó	15	Hm	36.58N	25.00 E
Dhiapóndioi Nísoi	15	Cj	39.50N	19.25 E
Dhībān	24	Fg	31.30N	35.47 E
Dhidhimótikhon	15	Jh	41.21N	26.30 E
Dhikti Óros	15	In	35.15N	25.30 E
Dhílos	15	Il	37.24N	25.16 E
Dhílos	15	Il	37.24N	25.16 E
Dhimitsána	15	Fl	37.36N	22.03 E
Dhionisiádhes, Nísoi-	15	Jn	35.21N	26.10 E
Dhiórix Potidhaia	15	Gi	40.10N	23.20 E
Dhī-Qar [3]	24	Lg	31.10N	46.10 E
Dhī-Qar	24	Kf	32.14N	44.22 E
Dhírfis Óros	15	Gk	38.38N	23.50 E
Dhísoron Óros	15	Fh	41.11N	22.57 E
Dhivounia	15	Jn	35.50N	26.28 E
Dhodhekánisos = Dodecanese (EN)	15	Jm	36.20N	27.00 E
Dhodhóni = Dodona (EN)	15	Dj	39.33N	20.46 E
Dholpur	25	Fc	26.42N	77.54 E
Dhomokós	15	Fj	39.08N	22.18 E
Dhone	25	Fe	15.25N	77.53 E
Dhonoúsa	15	Il	37.10N	25.50 E
Dhorāij	25	Ed	21.44N	70.27 E
Dhoxáton	15	Hh	41.06N	24.14 E
Dhragónisos	15	Il	37.27N	25.29 E
Dhuburi	25	Hc	26.02N	89.58 E
Dhule	22	Jg	20.54N	74.47 E
Dhuliān	25	Hd	24.41N	87.58 E
Dia	15	In	35.27N	25.13 E
Diable, Ile du-=Devil's Island (EN)	54	Hb	5.17N	52.35W
Diable, Morne au-	51g	Ba	15.37N	61.27W
Diable, Pointe du- [Mart.]	51h	Bb	14.47N	60.54W
Diable, Pointe du- [Van.]	63b	Dc	16.01S	168.12 E
Diablo, Punta del-	55	Fl	34.22S	53.46W
Diablo, Puntan-	64b	Ba	15.00N	145.34 E
Diablo Range	46	Eh	36.45N	121.20W
Diafarabé	34	Ec	14.10N	5.00W
Dialafara	34	Cc	13.27N	11.23W
Diamant, Pointe du-	51h	Ac	14.27N	61.04W
Diamant, Rocher du-	51h	Ac	14.27N	61.03W
Diamante [Arg.]	56	Hd	32.04S	60.39W
Diamante [It.]	14	Jk	39.41N	15.49 E
Diamante, Punta del-	48	Ji	16.47N	99.52W
Diamantina	54	Jg	18.15S	43.36W
Diamantina, Chapada-	52	Lg	11.30S	41.10W
Diamantina, Rio-	55	Fc	16.42S	52.45W
Diamantina Depth (EN)	3	Hm	33.30S	102.00 E
Diamantina Lakes	59	Id	23.46S	141.09 E
Diamantina River	57	Eg	26.45S	139.10 E
Diamantina Trench (EN)	3	Hm	36.00S	104.00 E
Diamantino	53	Kg	14.25S	56.27W
Diamantino, Rio-	55	Fc	16.08S	52.28W
Diamond Harbour	25	Hd	22.12N	88.12 E
Diamond Island	51p	Bb	12.20N	61.35W
Diamond Jenness Peninsula	42	Fb	71.00N	117.00W
Diamond Peak [Nv.-U.S.]	46	Hg	39.40N	115.48W
Diamond Peak [Or.-U.S.]	46	De	43.33N	122.09W
Diamond Peak [U.S.]	46	Id	44.09N	113.05W
Diamond Peak [U.S.]	46	Gc	46.07N	117.32W
Diamou	34	Cc	14.05N	11.16W
Diana, Baie-	42	Kd	61.00N	70.00W
Dianbai	27	Jg	21.33N	110.58 E
Dianbu → Feidong	28	Di	31.53N	117.29 E
Diancang Shan	27	Hf	25.42N	100.02 E
Dian Chi	27	Hg	24.50N	102.45 E
Diane, Étang de-	11a	Ba	42.07N	9.32 E
Dianjiang	27	Ie	30.19N	107.25 E
Diano Marina	14	Cg	43.54N	8.05 E
Dianópolis	54	If	11.38S	46.50W
Dianra	34	Dd	8.45N	6.18W
Diapaga	34	Fc	12.04N	1.47 E
Diaz	55	Bk	32.22S	61.05W
Dibā, Dawḩat-	24	Qk	25.38N	56.18 E
Dībagah	24	Je	35.52N	43.49 E
Dibang	25	Jc	27.50N	95.32 E
Dibaya	36	Dd	6.30S	22.57 E
Dibaya-Lubue	36	Cc	4.09S	19.52 E
Dibella	34	Hb	17.31N	12.59 E
Dibrugarh	22	Lg	27.29N	94.54 E
Dibs	24	Ke	35.40N	44.04 E
Dibsī Afnān	24	Ee	35.55N	38.16 E
Dickens	45	Fj	33.37N	100.50W
Dickinson	43	Gb	46.53N	102.47W
Dickins Seamount (EN)	40	Lf	54.30N	137.00W
Dickson	44	Dg	36.05N	87.23W
Dicle	24	Ic	38.22N	40.04 E
Dicle=Tigris (EN)	21	Gf	31.00N	47.25 E
Didam	12	Ic	51.56N	6.09 E
Didao	28	Kb	45.22N	130.48 E
Didcot	12	Ac	51.36N	1.15W
Didesa	35	Fd	9.30N	35.32 E
Didiéni	34	Dc	13.23N	8.05W
Didyma	15	Kl	37.21N	27.13 E
Die	11	Lj	44.45N	5.22 E
Dieburg	10	Eg	49.54N	8.51 E
Diecinueve de Abril	55	El	34.22S	54.04W
Dieciocho de Julio	55	Fk	33.41S	53.33W
Diefenbaker Lake	42	Gf	51.00N	107.00W
Diège	11	Ii	45.36N	2.16 E
Diego Garcia	21	Jj	6.20S	72.20 E
Diego Ramírez, Islas	56	Gi	56.30S	68.44W
Diekirch	11	Me	49.53N	6.10 E
Die Lewitz	10	Hc	53.30N	11.30 E
Diéma	34	Dc	14.33N	9.11W
Diemel	10	Fe	51.39N	9.27 E
Diemelsee	12	Kc	51.19N	8.43 E
Diemelstadt	12	Lc	51.27N	9.01 E

Dien Bien Phu	25	Kd	21.23N	103.01 E
Diepenbeek	12	Hd	50.54N	5.24 E
Diepholz	10	Ed	52.36N	8.22 E
Dieppe	11	He	49.56N	1.05 E
Dieppe Bay Town	51c	Ab	17.25N	62.48W
Dierdorf	12	Jd	50.33N	7.40 E
Dieren, Rheden-	12	Ib	52.03N	6.08 E
Di'er Songhua Jiang	27	Lc	45.26N	124.39 E
Diest	12	Hd	50.59N	5.03 E
Dieulefit	11	Lj	44.31N	5.04 E
Dieulouard	12	If	48.51N	6.04 E
Dieuze	11	Mf	48.49N	6.43 E
Dieveniškes	8	Kj	54.10N	25.44 E
Die Ville	12	Id	50.40N	6.55 E
Diez	12	Kd	50.22N	8.01 E
Dif	36	Hb	0.59N	40.57 E
Diffa [2]	34	Hb	16.00N	13.30 E
Diffa	34	Hc	13.19N	12.37 E
Differdange/Differdingen	11	Le	49.32N	5.52 E
Differdingen/Differdange	11	Le	49.32N	5.52 E
Digby	42	Kh	44.40N	65.50W
Dighton	45	Fg	38.29N	100.28W
Digne	11	Mj	44.06N	6.14 E
Digoin	11	Jh	46.29N	3.59 E
Digora	16	Nh	43.07N	44.06 E
Digos	26	Ie	6.45N	125.20 E
Digranes	7a	Ca	66.02N	14.45W
Digul	26	Kh	7.07S	138.42 E
Dihāng	25	Jc	27.48N	95.30 E
Dijar	16	Tf	46.33N	56.05 E
Dijlah=Tigris (EN)	21	Gf	31.00N	47.25 E
Dijle	11	Kd	50.53N	4.42 E
Dijon	6	Gf	47.19N	5.01 E
Dik	35	Bd	9.58N	17.31 E
Dikanäs	7	Dd	65.14N	16.00 E
Dikhil	35	Gc	11.06N	42.22 E
Dikili	24	Bc	39.04N	26.53 E
Dikli	8	Kg	57.30N	25.00 E
Diksmuide/Dixmude	11	Ic	51.02N	2.52 E
Dikson	22	Kb	73.30N	80.35 E
Dikwa	34	Hc	12.02N	13.55 E
Dila	35	Fd	6.23N	38.19 E
Dilbeek	12	Gd	50.51N	4.16 E
Dili	22	Oj	8.33S	125.34 E
Di Linh	25	Lf	11.35N	108.04 E
Diližan	16	Ni	40.46N	44.55 E
Dilj	14	Me	45.16N	18.01 E
Dill	12	Kd	50.33N	8.29 E
Dillenburg	10	Ef	50.44N	8.17 E
Dillia	30	Ig	14.09N	12.50 E
Dilling	31	Jg	12.03N	29.39 E
Dillingen (Saar)	12	Ie	49.21N	6.44 E
Dillingham	39	Dd	59.02N	158.29W
Dillon [Mt.-U.S.]	43	Eb	45.13N	112.38W
Dillon [S.C.-U.S.]	44	Hh	34.25N	79.22W
Dilly	34	Dc	14.57N	7.43W
Dilolo	31	Jj	10.42S	22.20 E
Dilsen	12	Hc	51.02N	5.44 E
Dimashq=Damascus (EN)	22	Ff	33.30N	36.15 E
Dimbelenge	36	Dd	5.30S	23.53 E
Dimbokro [3]	34	Ed	6.50N	4.45W
Dimbokro	34	Ed	6.39N	4.42W
Dimboola	59	Ig	36.27S	142.02 E
Dîmboviţa	15	Je	44.14N	26.27 E
Dîmboviţa [2]	15	Ie	44.55N	25.30 E
Dîmbovnic	15	Ie	44.20N	25.40 E
Dimitrovgrad [Bul.]	15	Ig	42.03N	25.36 E
Dimitrovgrad	19	Ee	54.14N	49.42 E
Dimitrovgrad [Yugo.]	15	Fg	43.01N	22.47 E
Dimmitt	45	Ei	34.33N	102.19W
Dimona	24	Fg	31.04N	35.02 E
Dimovo	15	Ff	43.44N	22.44 E
Dinagat	26	Id	10.12N	125.35 E
Dinājpur	25	Hc	25.38N	88.38 E
Dinan	11	Df	48.27N	2.02W
Dinangourou	34	Ec	14.27N	2.14W
Dinant	11	Kd	50.16N	4.55 E
Dinar	24	Dc	38.04N	30.10 E
Dīnar, Kūh-e-	24	Ng	30.50N	51.35 E
Dinara	14	Kf	44.04N	16.23 E
Dinara=Dinaric Alps (EN)	5	Hg	43.50N	16.35 E
Dinard	11	Df	48.38N	2.04W
Dinaric Alps (EN)= Dinara	5	Hg	43.50N	16.35 E
Dindar, Nahr ad-	35	Ec	14.06N	33.40 E
Dinder	35	Ec	14.06N	33.40 E
Dindigul	25	Ff	10.21N	77.57 E
Dindima	34	Hc	10.14N	10.09 E
Dinga	36	Cd	5.19S	16.34 E
Dingbian	27	Id	37.35N	107.37 E
Dingden, Hamminkeln-	12	Ic	51.46N	6.37 E
Dinggyê	27	Ef	28.25N	87.45 E
Dinghai	27	Le	30.05N	122.07 E
Dingle	8	Df	58.32N	11.34 E
Dingle/An Daingean	9	Ci	52.08N	10.15W
Dingle Bay/Bá an Daingin	9	Ci	52.05N	10.15W
Dingolfing	10	Ih	48.38N	12.30 E
Dingshuzhen	28	Ei	31.16N	119.50 E
Dingtao	28	Cg	35.04N	115.35 E
Dinguiraye	34	Cc	11.18N	10.43W
Dingwall	9	Id	57.35N	4.26W
Dingxi	27	Hd	35.33N	104.32 E
Dingxian	27	Jd	39.29N	115.00 E
Dingxiang	28	Be	38.32N	112.59 E
Dingxing	27	Kd	39.11N	115.48 E
Dingyuan	28	Dh	32.32N	117.41 E
Dingzi Gang	28	Ff	36.33N	120.59 E
Dinh, Mui-	21	Mh	11.22N	109.01 E
Dinkel	12	Ib	52.30N	6.58 E
Dinosaur	45	Bf	40.15N	109.01W
Dinskaja	16	Kg	45.09N	39.12 E
Dinslaken	12	Ic	51.34N	6.44 E
Dīnsōr	35	Ge	2.23N	42.58 E
Dintel	12	Gc	51.39N	4.24 E
Dinuba	46	Fh	36.36N	119.27W

Index Symbols

[1] Independent Nation
[2] State, Region
[3] District, County
[4] Municipality
[5] Colony, Dependency
Continent
Physical Region
Historical or Cultural Region
Mount, Mountain
Volcano
Hill
Mountains, Mountain Range
Hills, Escarpment
Plateau, Upland
Pass, Gap
Plain, Lowland
Delta
Salt Flat
Valley, Canyon
Crater, Cave
Karst Features
Depression
Polder
Desert, Dunes
Forest, Woods
Heath, Steppe
Oasis
Cape, Point
Coast, Beach
Cliff
Peninsula
Isthmus
Sandbank
Island
Atoll
Rock, Reef
Islands, Archipelago
Rocks, Reefs
Coral Reef
Well, Spring
Geyser
River, Stream
Waterfall Rapids
River Mouth, Estuary
Lake
Salt Lake
Intermittent Lake
Reservoir
Swamp, Pond
Canal
Glacier
Ice Shelf, Pack Ice
Ocean
Sea
Gulf, Bay
Strait, Fjord
Lagoon
Bank
Seamount
Tablemount
Ridge
Shelf
Basin
Escarpment, Sea Scarp
Fracture
Trench, Abyss
National Park, Reserve
Point of Interest
Recreation Site
Cave, Cavern
Historic Site
Ruins
Wall, Walls
Church, Abbey
Temple
Scientific Station
Airport
Port
Lighthouse
Mine
Tunnel
Dam, Bridge

Index Symbols

[1] Independent Nation
[2] State, Region
[3] District, County
[4] Municipality
[5] Colony, Dependency
Continent
Physical Region
Historical or Cultural Region
Mount, Mountain
Volcano
Hill
Mountains, Mountain Range
Hills, Escarpment
Plateau, Upland
Pass, Gap
Plain, Lowland
Delta
Salt Flat
Valley, Canyon
Crater, Cave
Karst Features
Depression
Polder
Desert, Dunes
Forest, Woods
Heath, Steppe
Oasis
Cape, Point
Coast, Beach
Cliff
Peninsula
Isthmus
Sandbank
Island
Atoll
Rock, Reef
Islands, Archipelago
Rocks, Reefs
Coral Reef
Well, Spring
Geyser
River, Stream
Waterfall Rapids
River Mouth, Estuary
Lake
Salt Lake
Intermittent Lake
Reservoir
Swamp, Pond
Canal
Glacier
Ice Shelf, Pack Ice
Ocean
Sea
Gulf, Bay
Strait, Fjord
Lagoon
Bank
Seamount
Tablemount
Ridge
Shelf
Basin
Escarpment, Sea Scarp
Fracture
Trench, Abyss
National Park, Reserve
Point of Interest
Recreation Site
Cave, Cavern
Historic Site
Ruins
Wall, Walls
Church, Abbey
Temple
Scientific Station
Airport
Port
Lighthouse
Mine
Tunnel
Dam, Bridge

Index Symbols

[1] Independent Nation	Historical or Cultural Region	Pass, Gap
[2] State, Region	Mount, Mountain	Plain, Lowland
[3] District, County	Volcano	Delta
[4] Municipality	Hill	Salt Flat
[5] Colony, Dependency	Mountains, Mountain Range	Valley, Canyon
[6] Continent	Hills, Escarpment	Crater, Cave
[7] Physical Region	Plateau, Upland	Karst Features

Depression	Coast, Beach	Rock, Reef
Polder	Cliff	Islands, Archipelago
Desert, Dunes	Peninsula	Rocks, Reefs
Forest, Woods	Isthmus	Coral Reef
Heath, Steppe	Sandbank	Well, Spring
Oasis	Island	Geyser
Cape, Point	Atoll	River, Stream

Waterfall Rapids	Canal	Lagoon
River Mouth, Estuary	Glacier	Bank
Lake	Ice Shelf, Pack Ice	Seamount
Salt Lake	Ocean	Tablemount
Intermittent Lake	Sea	Ridge
Reservoir	Gulf, Bay	Shelf
Swamp, Pond	Strait, Fjord	Basin

Escarpment, Sea Scarp	Historic Site	Port
Fracture	Ruins	Lighthouse
Trench, Abyss	Wall, Walls	Mine
National Park, Reserve	Church, Abbey	Tunnel
Point of Interest	Temple	Dam, Bridge
Recreation Site	Scientific Station	
Cave, Cavern	Airport	

Index Symbols

[1]	Independent Nation
[2]	State, Region
[3]	District, County
[4]	Municipality
[5]	Colony, Dependency
	Continent
	Physical Region
	Historical or Cultural Region
	Mount, Mountain
	Volcano
	Hill
	Mountains, Mountain Range
	Hills, Escarpment
	Plateau, Upland
	Pass, Gap
	Plain, Lowland
	Delta
	Salt Flat
	Valley, Canyon
	Crater, Cave
	Karst Features
	Depression
	Polder
	Desert, Dunes
	Forest, Woods
	Heath, Steppe
	Oasis
	Cape, Point
	Coast, Beach
	Cliff
	Peninsula
	Isthmus
	Sandbank
	Island
	Islands, Archipelago
	Rocks, Reefs
	Coral Reef
	Well, Spring
	Geyser
	Atoll
	Rock, Reef
	Waterfall Rapids
	River Mouth, Estuary
	Lake
	Salt Lake
	Intermittent Lake
	Sea
	Gulf, Bay
	Strait, Fjord
	Canal
	Glacier
	Ice Shelf, Pack Ice
	Ocean
	Ridge
	Shelf
	Basin
	Lagoon
	Bank
	Seamount
	Tablemount
	National Park, Reserve
	Point of Interest
	Recreation Site
	Cave, Cavern
	Escarpment, Sea Scarp
	Trench, Abyss
	Fracture
	River, Stream
	Swamp, Pond
	Reservoir
	Historic Site
	Ruins
	Wall, Walls
	Church, Abbey
	Temple
	Scientific Station
	Airport
	Port
	Lighthouse
	Mine
	Tunnel
	Dam, Bridge

Index Symbols

[1] Independent Nation	Historical or Cultural Region
[2] State, Region	Mount, Mountain
[3] District, County	Volcano
[4] Municipality	Hill
[5] Colony, Dependency	Mountains, Mountain Range
Continent	Hills, Escarpment
Physical Region	Plateau, Upland

Pass, Gap	Depression
Plain, Lowland	Polder
Delta	Desert, Dunes
Salt Flat	Forest, Woods
Valley, Canyon	Heath, Steppe
Crater, Cave	Oasis
Karst Features	Cape, Point

Coast, Beach	Rock, Reef
Cliff	Islands, Archipelago
Peninsula	Rocks, Reefs
Isthmus	Coral Reef
Sandbank	Well, Spring
Island	Geyser
Atoll	River, Stream

Waterfall Rapids	Canal
River Mouth, Estuary	Glacier
Lake	Ice Shelf, Pack Ice
Salt Lake	Ocean
Intermittent Lake	Sea
Reservoir	Gulf, Bay
Swamp, Pond	Strait, Fjord

Lagoon	Escarpment, Sea Scarp
Bank	Fracture
Seamount	Trench, Abyss
Tablemount	National Park, Reserve
Ridge	Point of Interest
Shelf	Recreation Site
Basin	Cave, Cavern

Historic Site	Port
Ruins	Lighthouse
Wall, Walls	Mine
Church, Abbey	Tunnel
Temple	Dam, Bridge
Scientific Station	
Airport	

Name	Page	Grid	Lat	Long
Eshowe	37	Ee	28.50S	31.29 E
Eshetehård	24	Ne	35.44N	50.23 E
Esigodini	37	Dd	20.18S	28.56 E
Esino ⌐	14	Hg	43.39N	13.22 E
Esk ⌐	9	Jg	54.58N	3.04W
Eskifjördur	7a	Cb	65.04N	14.01W
Eskimo Point	39	Jc	61.07N	94.03W
Eskişehir	22	Ff	39.46N	30.32 E
Esla ⌐	13	Fc	41.29N	6.03W
Eslâmâbâd	23	Gc	34.11N	46.35 E
Eşler Dağı ▲	15	Ml	37.24N	29.43 E
Eslohe (Sauerland)	12	Kc	51.15N	8.10 E
Eslöv	7	Ci	55.50N	13.20 E
Esme	24	Cc	38.24N	28.59 E
Esmeralda [Braz.]	55	Gi	28.03S	51.12W
Esmeralda [Cuba]	49	Hc	21.51N	78.07W
Esmeralda, Isla- ▪	56	Eg	48.57S	75.25W
Esmeralda Bank (EN) ▪	65b	Ab	14.57N	145.15 E
Esmeraldas	53	Ie	0.59N	79.42W
Esnagami Lake ▪	45	Ma	50.21N	86.48W
Esneux	12	Hd	50.32N	5.34 E
Espada, Punta- ▪	49	Lg	12.05N	71.07W
Espagnol Point ▪	51n	Ba	13.22N	61.09W
Espalion	11	Ij	44.31N	2.46 E
Espalmador, Isla- ▪	13	Nf	38.47N	1.26 E
España=Spain (EN) ▪	6	Fg	40.00N	4.00W
Espanola [N.M.-U.S.]	45	Ch	36.06N	106.02W
Espanola [Ont.-Can.]	44	Gb	46.15N	81.46W
Española, Isla- ▪	54a	Bb	1.25S	89.42W
Espardell, Isla- ▪	13	Nf	38.47N	1.27 E
Esparta	49	Ei	9.59N	84.40W
Espeland	8	Ad	60.23N	5.28 E
Espelkamp	10	Ed	52.25N	8.37 E
Esperance	58	Dh	33.51S	121.53 E
Esperance, Cape- ▪	63a	Dc	9.15S	159.43 E
Esperance Bay ▪	59	Ef	33.50S	121.55 E
Esperance Harbour ▪	51k	Ba	14.04N	60.55W
Esperancita	55	Bc	16.55S	60.06W
Esperantina	54	Jd	3.54S	42.14W
Esperanza ⊠	66	Re	63.26S	57.00W
Esperanza [Arg.]	56	Hd	31.27S	60.56W
Esperanza [Mex.]	48	Ed	27.35N	109.56W
Esperanza [P.R.]	51a	Cb	18.06N	65.29W
Esperanza, Sierra la- ▪	49	Ef	15.40N	85.45W
Espevær	7	Ag	59.36N	5.10 E
Espichel, Cabo- ▪	13	Cf	38.25N	9.13W
Espiel	13	Gf	38.12N	5.01W
Espigão Serra do- ▲	55	Gh	26.55S	50.25W
Espinal [Bol.]	55	Cc	17.13S	58.43W
Espinal [Col.]	54	Dc	4.10N	74.54W
Espinazo del Diablo, Sierra- ▲	48	Ff	24.00N	106.00W
Espinhaço, Serra do- ▲	52	Lg	17.30S	43.30W
Espinho	13	Dc	41.01N	8.38W
Espinilho, Serra do- ▲	55	Ei	28.30S	55.06W
Espinillo	55	Ca	24.58S	58.34W
Espino	50	Dh	8.34N	66.01W
Espinosa	54	Jf	14.56S	42.50W
Espinouse ▲	11	Ik	43.32N	2.46 E
Espírito Santo ▪	54	Jg	20.00S	40.30W
Espíritu Santo, Bahía del- ▪	48	Ph	19.20N	87.35W
Espíritu Santo, Isla- ▪	48	De	24.30N	110.22W
Espita	48	Og	21.01N	88.19W
Esplanada	54	Kf	11.47S	37.57W
Espoo/Esbo	7	Ff	60.13N	24.40 E
Espoo-Tapiola	8	Kd	60.11N	24.49 E
Esposende	13	Dc	41.32N	8.47W
Espumoso	55	Fi	28.44S	52.51W
Espuña, Sierra de- ▲	13	Kg	37.52N	1.34W
Espungabera	37	Ed	20.28S	32.46 E
Esquel	53	Ij	42.55S	71.20W
Esquina	56	Id	30.01S	59.32W
Esquinapa de Hidalgo	47	Cd	22.51N	105.48W
Esquipular	49	Cf	14.34N	89.21W
Essandsjøen ▪	8	Da	63.05N	12.00 E
Essaouira	31	Ge	31.31N	9.46W
Essaouira ▪	32	Fc	31.04N	9.03W
Essen [Bel.]	12	Gc	51.28N	4.28 E
Essen [Ger.]	6	Ge	51.27N	7.01 E
Essen (Oldenburg)	12	Jb	52.42N	7.55 E
Essendon, Mount- ▲	59	Ed	24.55S	120.28 E
Essequibo River ⌐	52	Ke	6.50N	58.30W
Essex	46	Hi	34.42N	115.12W
Essex ▪	9	Nj	51.50N	0.30 E
Essex ▪	9	Mj	51.50N	0.35W
Essex Mountain ▲	46	Ke	42.02N	109.13W
Esslingen am Neckar	10	Fh	48.45N	9.18 E
Esso	20	Ke	55.55N	158.40 E
Essonne	11	If	48.37N	2.29 E
Essonne ▪	11	If	48.36N	2.20 E
Est [Cam.] ▪	34	He	4.00N	14.00 E
Est	34	Fc	12.00N	1.00 E
Est, Canal de l'- ⌐	11	Lf	48.45N	5.35 E
Est, Cap- ▪	37	Ic	15.16S	50.29 E
Est, Ile de l'- ▪	30	Mm	46.15S	52.05 E
Est, Pointe de l'- ▪	42	Lg	49.08N	61.41W
Estaca de Bares, Punta de la- ▪	5	Fg	43.46N	7.42W
Estados, Isla de los-=Staten Island (EN) ▪	52	Jk	54.47S	64.15W
Estados Unidos Mexicanos ▪	39	Ig	23.00N	102.00W
Esţahbân	24	Ph	29.08N	54.04 E
Estaimpuis	12	Fd	50.42N	3.15 E
Estância	54	Kf	11.16S	37.26W
Estancias, Sierra de las- ▲	13	Jg	37.35N	2.20W
Estanislao del Campo	55	Bg	25.03S	60.06W
Estarreja	13	Dd	40.45N	8.34W
Estats, Pica d'- ▲	11	Hn	42.40N	1.24 E
Estats, Pica d'-/Estats, Pico d'- ▲	11	Hn	42.40N	1.24 E
Estats, Pico d'- ▲	11	Hn	42.40N	1.24 E
Estats, Pico d'-/Estats, Pica d'- ▲	11	Hn	42.40N	1.24 E
Estcourt	37	De	29.01S	29.52 E
Este	14	Fe	45.14N	11.39 E
Este, Punta- ▪	51a	Cb	18.08N	65.16W
Este, Punta del- ▪	56	Jd	34.59S	54.57W
Esteban Rams	55	Bi	29.47S	61.29W
Esteli	47	Gi	13.05N	86.23W
Esteli ▪	49	Dg	13.10N	86.20W
Estella	13	Jb	42.40N	2.02W
Estepa	13	Hg	37.18N	4.54W
Estepona	13	Gh	36.26N	5.08W
Estérel ▲	11	Mk	43.30N	6.50 E
Esternay	12	Ff	48.44N	3.34 E
Esterri d'Aneu/Esterri de Aneu	13	Nb	42.38N	1.08 E
Esterri d'Aneu/Esterri d'Aneu	13	Nb	42.38N	1.08 E
Esterwegen	12	Jb	52.59N	7.37 E
Estes Park	45	Df	40.23N	105.31W
Este Sudeste, Cayos del- ▪	47	Hf	12.26N	81.27W
Estevan	39	Jg	49.07N	103.05W
Estherville	45	Ie	43.24N	94.50W
Estissac	11	Jf	48.16N	3.49 E
Eston	46	Ka	51.10N	108.46W
Estonia (EN) ▪	5	Id	59.00N	26.00 E
Estonia (EN) = Eesti	19	Cd	59.00N	26.00 E
Estonskaja Sovetskaja Socialistiĉeskaja Respublika → Eesti	19	Cd	59.00N	26.00 E
Estonskaja SSR/Eesti Nôukogude Socialistlik Vabarijk → Eesti	19	Cd	59.00N	26.00 E
Estoril	13	Cf	38.42N	9.24W
Estrées-Saint-Denis	12	Ee	49.26N	2.39 E
Estreito	55	Gj	31.50S	51.44W
Estreito, Reprêsa do- ▪	55	Ie	20.15S	47.09W
Estrêla [Braz.]	55	Gi	29.29S	51.58W
Estrêla [Braz.]	55	Gj	31.15S	21.45W
Estrela, Arroyo- ⌐	55	Df	22.05S	56.25W
Estrela, Serra da- ▲	55	Fc	16.27S	53.24W
Estrêla, Serra da- ▲	5	Fg	40.20N	7.38W
Estrêla do Sul	55	Id	18.21S	47.49W
Estrella	13	If	38.28N	3.35W
Estrella, Punta- ▪	48	Bb	30.55N	114.40W
Estrema, Serra da- ▲	55	Jc	16.50S	45.07W
Estremadura ▪	13	Ce	39.15N	9.10W
Estremoz	13	Ef	38.51N	7.35W
Estrondo, Serra do- ▲	54	Ie	9.00S	48.45W
Estry	12	Hf	48.54N	0.44W
Estuaire ▪	36	Ab	0.10N	10.00 E
Esztergom	10	Oi	47.48N	18.45 E
Etah	41	Ec	78.19N	72.38W
Étain	11	Le	49.13N	5.38 E
Etajima	29	Cd	34.15N	132.29 E
Etalle	12	He	49.41N	5.36 E
Étampes	11	If	48.26N	2.09 E
Étaples	11	Hd	50.31N	1.39 E
Etāwah	25	Fc	26.46N	79.02 E
Ethe, Virton-	12	He	49.35N	5.35 E
Ethel Reefs ▪	63d	Ab	16.56S	177.13 E
Ethiopia (EN)=Itiopiya ▪	31	Kh	9.00N	39.00 E
Ethiopian Plateau (EN) ▲	30	Kg	10.00N	38.10 E
Etive, Loch- ⌐	9	He	56.35N	5.15W
Etna	8	Dd	60.50N	10.03 E
Etna ▲	5	Hh	37.50N	14.55 E
Etne	8	Ae	59.40N	5.56 E
Etoile Cay ▪	37b	Bb	5.53S	53.01 E
Etolin Island ▪	40	Me	56.08N	132.20W
Etolin Strait ⌐	40	Fd	60.20N	165.15W
Etomo-Misaki ▪	29a	Bb	42.20N	140.55 E
Etorofu Tō/Iturup, Ostrov- ▪	21	Qe	44.54N	147.30 E
Etosha Pan ⌐	30	Ij	18.50S	16.20 E
Etoumbi	36	Bb	0.01N	14.57 E
Etrépagny	12	De	49.18N	1.37 E
Étretat	11	Ge	49.42N	0.12 E
Etropole	15	Gd	42.50N	24.00 E
Etruria	56	Md	32.56S	63.15W
Etsch/Adige ⌐	5	Hf	45.10N	12.20 E
Ettelbrück/Ettelbruck	12	Ie	49.51N	6.07 E
Ettelbruck/Ettelbrück	12	Ie	49.51N	6.07 E
Etten-Leur	12	Gc	51.35N	4.39 E
Ettersberg ▲	10	He	51.03N	11.15 E
Ettlingen	12	Kf	48.57N	8.24 E
Etzatlán	48	Nh	19.35N	90.13W
Eu	11	Hd	50.03N	1.25 E
'Eua Iki ▪	65b	Bc	21.07S	174.59W
Eua Island ▪	61	Gd	21.22S	174.56W
Euboea (EN)=Évvoia ▪	5	Ih	38.30N	24.00 E
Eucla	58	Dh	31.43S	128.52 E
Euclid	44	Gc	41.34N	81.33W
Euclides da Cunha	54	Kf	10.31S	39.01W
Eucumbene, Lake- ⌐	59	Jg	36.05S	148.45 E
Eudora	45	Kj	30.07N	91.16W
Eufaula	44	Ej	31.54N	85.09W
Eufaula Lake ⌐	45	Ii	35.17N	95.31W
Euganei, Colli- ▲	14	Fe	45.19N	11.40 E
Eugene	39	Gf	44.02N	123.05W
Eugenia, Punta- ▪	38	Hg	27.50N	115.03W
Eugênio Penzo	55	Ef	22.13S	55.53W
Eugmo ▪	7	Fe	63.49N	22.45 E
Eume ⌐	13	Da	43.25N	8.08W
Eunice [La.-U.S.]	45	Jk	30.30N	92.26W
Eunice [N.M.-U.S.]	45	Ej	32.26N	103.09W
Eupen	11	Md	50.38N	6.02 E
Euphrates (EN)=Al Furāt ⌐	21	Gf	31.00N	47.25 E
Euphrates (EN)=Firat ⌐	23	Fb	37.00N	38.00 E
Eupora	45	Lj	33.32N	89.16W
Eura	7	Ff	61.08N	22.08 E
Eurajoki	8	Ic	61.12N	21.44 E
Eurasia Basin (EN) ▪	62	Ge	87.00N	80.00 E
Eure ▪	11	He	49.18N	1.12 E
Eure ⌐	11	He	49.18N	1.12 E
Eure-et-Loir ▪	11	Hf	48.30N	1.30 E
Eureka [Ca.-U.S.]	39	Gf	40.47N	124.09W
Eureka [Ks.-U.S.]	45	Hh	37.49N	96.17W
Eureka [Mt.-U.S.]	46	Hb	48.53N	115.03W
Eureka [Nv.-U.S.]	43	Dd	39.31N	115.58W
Eureka [N.W.T.-Can.]	42	Ia	80.00N	85.59W
Eureka [S.D.-U.S.]	45	Gd	45.46N	99.38W
Eureka [Ut.-U.S.]	46	Ig	39.57N	112.07W
Eureka Sound ⌐	42	Ia	79.00N	87.00W
Europa ▪	30	Lk	22.20S	40.22 E
Europa, Picos de- ▲	5	Fg	43.12N	4.48W
Europe ■	1	e	50.00N	20.00 E
Europoort	11	Jc	51.58N	4.00 E
Euskirchen	10	Cf	50.40N	6.47 E
Eustis	44	Gk	28.51N	81.41W
Eutaw	44	Di	32.50N	87.53W
Eutin	10	Gb	54.08N	10.37 E
Euzkadi/Vascongadas= Basque Provinces (EN) ▪	13	Ja	43.00N	2.30W
Evale	36	Cf	16.33S	15.44 E
Evans, Lac- ⌐	42	Jf	50.50N	77.00W
Evans, Mount- ▲	46	Ic	46.05N	113.07W
Evans Strait ⌐	42	Jd	63.20N	82.00W
Evanston [Il.-U.S.]	45	Me	42.03N	87.42W
Evanston [Wy.-U.S.]	43	Ec	41.16N	110.58 E
Evansville	39	Kf	37.58N	87.35W
Evart	45	Gk	31.29N	98.09W
Evaux-les-Bains	44	Ed	43.54N	85.14W
Evaz	11	Ah	46.10N	2.29 E
Evciler [Tur.]	24	Oi	27.46N	53.59 E
Evciler [Tur.]	15	Jj	39.46N	26.46 E
Evelyn, Mount- ▲	15	Mk	38.03N	29.54 E
Evensk	59	Gb	13.36S	132.53 E
Everard, Lake- ⌐	22	Rc	61.57N	159.14 E
Everard Ranges ▲	59	Hf	31.25S	135.05 E
Everest, Mount- (EN)= Qomolangma Feng ▲	59	Ge	27.05S	132.30 E
Everest, Mount- (EN)= Saragmatha ▲	21	Kg	27.59N	86.56 E
Everett	21	Kg	27.59N	86.56 E
Everett Mountains ▲	43	Cb	47.59N	122.13W
Evergem	42	Kd	62.45N	67.10W
Evergem-Sleidinge	12	Fc	51.07N	3.42 E
Everglades City	12	Fc	51.08N	3.41 E
Evergreen	44	Dj	31.26N	86.57W
Evertsberg	8	Ec	61.08N	13.57 E
Evesham	9	Li	52.05N	1.56W
Evesham, Vale of- ⌐	9	Li	52.05N	1.50W
Evian-les-Bains	11	Mh	46.36N	6.35 E
Evijärvi	7	Fe	63.22N	23.29 E
Evinayong	34	He	1.27N	10.34 E
Evinos ⌐	15	Ek	38.19N	21.32 E
Evje	7	Bg	58.36N	7.51 E
Évora	5	Fh	38.34N	7.54W
Évora ▪	13	Ef	38.35N	7.50W
Evoron	20	If	51.23N	136.23 E
Evowghlī	24	Kc	38.43N	45.13 E
Evre ⌐	11	Eg	47.22N	1.02W
Evrecy	12	Be	49.06N	0.30W
Evrejskaja avtonomnaja respublika	20	Ig	48.30N	132.00 E
Evreux	11	He	49.01N	1.09 E
Evron	11	Ff	48.01N	0.24W
Evrótas ⌐	15	Fm	36.48N	22.41 E
Evry	11	If	48.38N	2.27 E
Évvoia=Euboea (EN) ▪	5	Ih	38.30N	24.00 E
Évvoia, Gulf of- (EN)= Vórios Evvoïkós Kólpos ⌐	15	Gk	38.45N	23.10 E
Evzonoi	15	Fh	41.06N	22.33 E
Ewa Beach	65a	Cb	21.19N	158.00W
Ewing Seamount (EN) ▪	30	Hk	23.20S	8.45 E
Ewo	36	Bc	0.55S	14.49 E
Excelsior Mountain ▲	46	Fg	38.02N	119.18W
Excelsior Mountains ▲	46	Fg	38.10N	118.30W
Excelsior Springs	45	Jg	39.20N	94.13W
Exe ⌐	9	Jk	50.37N	3.25W
Executive Committee Range ▲	66	Nf	76.50S	126.00W
Exeter [Eng.-U.K.]	6	Fe	50.43N	3.31W
Exeter [N.H.-U.S.]	44	Le	42.59N	70.56W
Exeter Sound ⌐	42	Lc	66.10N	62.00W
Exmoor ▪	9	Jj	51.10N	3.45W
Exmouth [Austl.]	59	Cc	21.55S	114.07 E
Exmouth [Eng.-U.K.]	9	Jk	50.37N	3.25W
Exmouth Gulf ⌐	57	Cg	22.00S	114.20 E
Exmouth Plateau (EN) ▪	57	Cc	16.00S	114.00 E
Expedition Range ▲	59	Jd	24.30S	149.05 E
Explorer Tablemount (EN) ▪	47	He	16.55N	83.15W
Externsteine ▪	12	Kc	51.52N	8.55 E
Extertal	12	Lb	52.04N	9.07 E
Extertal-Bösingfeld	12	Lb	52.04N	9.07 E
Extremadura ▪	13	Ge	39.00N	6.00W
Exuma Cays ▪	47	Id	24.00N	76.20W
Exuma Cays ▪	49	Ia	24.20N	76.40W
Exuma Sound ⌐	47	Id	24.15N	76.00W
Eyasi, Lake- ⌐	30	Ki	3.40S	35.05 E
Eydehavn	8	Dh	58.31N	8.53 E
Eye	12	Db	52.19N	1.09 E
Eyemouth	9	Kf	55.52N	2.06W
Eye Peninsula ▪	9	Gc	58.13N	6.05W
Eygurande	11	Ii	45.40N	2.28 E
Eyjafjallajökull ▲	7a	Bc	63.38N	19.36W
Éyl	31	Lh	8.00N	49.51 E
Eymoutiers	11	Hi	45.44N	1.44 E
Eynesil	24	Hb	41.03N	39.08 E
Eyrarbakki	7a	Bc	63.52N	21.09W
Eyre	59	Ff	32.15S	126.18 E
Eyre, Lake- ⌐	57	Eg	28.43S	137.11 E
Eyre Creek ⌐	59	Ge	24.30S	139.00 E
Eyre Mountains ▲	62	Cf	45.20S	168.20 E
Eyre North, Lake- ⌐	59	He	28.30S	137.10 E
Eyre Peninsula ▪	57	Eh	34.00S	135.45 E
Eyre South, Lake- ⌐	59	He	29.30S	137.20 E
Eyrieux ⌐	11	Ki	44.58N	4.49 E
Eystrup	12	Lc	52.47N	9.13 E
Eythvana	11	Dc	51.11N	1.17 E
Eyvänaki	24	Oe	35.24N	51.56 E
Ezequiel Ramos Mexia, Embalse- ⌐	56	Ge	39.30S	69.00W
Ezere	8	Jh	56.27N	22.17 E
Ezerelis	8	Jj	54.50N	23.38 E
Ezine	24	Bc	39.47N	26.20 E
Eznas/Jieznas	8	Kj	54.34N	24.17 E
Ežva	17	Ef	61.47N	50.40 E

F

Name	Page	Grid	Lat	Long
Faaa	65e	Fc	17.33S	149.36W
Faaite Atoll ▪	61	Lc	16.45S	145.14W
Fabens	45	Ck	31.30N	106.10W
Fåberg	8	Dc	61.10N	10.24 E
Faber Lake ⌐	42	Fd	63.55N	117.15W
Fåborg	7	Ci	55.06N	10.15 E
Fabriano	14	Gg	43.20N	12.54 E
Fäcäeni	15	Ke	44.34N	27.54 E
Facatativá	54	Dc	4.49N	74.22W
Facha	33	Cd	29.30N	17.20 E
Fachi	31	Ig	18.06N	11.34 E
Facpi Point ▪	64c	Bb	13.20N	144.38 E
Fada	31	Jg	17.14N	21.33 E
Fada N'Gourma	31	Hg	12.04N	0.21 E
Faddeja, Zaliv- ⌐	20	Fa	76.30N	107.30 E
Faddejevski, Ostrov- ▪	20	Ja	75.30N	144.00 E
Fadfifolu Atoll ▪	25a	Ba	5.25S	73.30 E
Fägäli	24	Mi	26.58N	49.15 E
Faeara, Pointe- ▪	65e	Fc	17.52S	149.11W
Færce Bank (EN) ▪	9	Ea	60.55N	8.40W
Faeroe-Iceland Ridge (EN) ▪	5	Fc	64.00N	10.00W
Faeroe Islands (EN)= Føroyar/Færøerne ▪	5	Fc	62.00N	7.00W
Faeroe Islands (EN)= Færøerne/Føroyar ▪	6	Fc	62.00N	7.00W
Faeroe Islands (EN) = Føroyar/Færøerne ▪	5	Fc	62.00N	7.00W
Færøerne/Føroyar=Faeroe Islands (EN) ▪	5	Fc	62.00N	7.00W
Færøerne/Føroyar=Faeroe Islands (EN) ▪	6	Fc	62.00N	7.00W
Fafa ▪	35	Bd	7.18N	18.16 E
Fafe	13	Dc	41.27N	8.10W
Fafen ⌐	30	Lh	5.47N	44.11 E
Faga ⌐	34	Dc	13.45N	0.58 E
Fagaloa Bay ⌐	65c	Ba	13.54S	171.28W
Fagamalo	65c	Aa	13.25S	172.21W
Fagåraş	15	Hd	45.51N	24.58 E
Fagårasului, Muntii- ▲	15	Hd	45.35N	25.00 E
Fagataufa Atoll ▪	57	Ng	22.14S	138.45W
Fagatogo	65c	Ba	14.16S	170.41W
Fageira ▪	8	Fh	56.15N	15.57 E
Fagelmara	8	Fh	56.15N	15.40 E
Fagerhult	8	Bf	60.59N	9.15 E
Fagersta	7	Df	60.00N	15.47 E
Fåget	15	Fd	45.51N	22.11 E
Fagita	26	Jg	1.48S	130.25 E
Fagnano, Lago- ⌐	56	Gä	54.38S	68.00W
Fagne ▪	11	Kd	50.10N	4.25 E
Faguibine, Lac- ⌐	30	Gg	16.45N	3.54W
Fahlian	24	Ng	30.12N	51.28 E
Fahner Höhe ▲	10	He	51.10N	10.45 E
Faial	30	Ge	38.34N	28.42W
Faial ▪	32	Bc	38.34N	28.42W
Fa'id	24	Je	30.19N	32.19 E
Faioa ▪	64b	Bc	13.23S	176.08W
Fairbairn Reservoir ⌐	59	Jd	23.40S	148.00 E
Fairbanks	39	Ec	64.51N	147.43W
Fairborn	44	Ef	39.48N	84.03W
Fairbury	43	Gc	40.08N	97.11W
Fairchild	45	Kd	44.36N	90.58W
Fairfield [Al.-U.S.]	44	Di	33.29N	86.55W
Fairfield [Ca.-U.S.]	46	Eg	38.15N	122.01W
Fairfield [Ia.-U.S.]	45	Kf	41.00N	91.57W
Fairfield [Id.-U.S.]	46	Hd	43.21N	114.48W
Fairfield [Il.-U.S.]	45	Lg	38.23N	88.22W
Fair Isle ▪	9	Lb	59.30N	1.40W
Fairlie	62	Cf	44.06S	170.50 E
Fairmont [Mn.-U.S.]	43	Ic	43.39N	94.28W
Fairmont [W.V.-U.S.]	44	Gf	39.28N	80.08W
Fair Ness ▪	42	Kd	63.24N	72.05W
Fairview [Mt.-U.S.]	46	Mc	47.51N	104.03W
Fairview [Ok.-U.S.]	45	Gh	36.16N	98.29W
Fairview Peak ▲	46	Fg	38.22N	122.39W
Fairweather, Mount- ▲	38	Fd	58.54N	137.32W
Fais Island ▪	57	Hd	9.46N	140.31 E
Faistós ▪	15	Hn	35.03N	24.48 E
Faith	43	Gb	45.02N	102.02W
Faizābād	25	Gc	26.47N	82.08 E
Fajardo	49	Id	18.20N	65.39W
Fajou, Ilet 'a- ▪	51e	Ab	16.17N	61.33W
Fakahina Atoll ▪	57	Mf	15.59S	140.08W
Fakaofo Atoll ▪	57	Je	9.22S	171.14W
Fakarava Atoll ▪	57	Mf	16.05S	145.37W
Fakaura ▪	57	Fa	40.38N	139.55 E
Fakel	17	Gf	57.36N	53.05 E
Fakenham	12	Cb	52.50N	0.50 E
Fakfak	26	Jg	2.55S	132.18 E
Fakfak ▪	26	Jg	3.00S	132.30 E
Fakse Bugt ⌐	8	Ei	55.10N	12.15 E
Fakse Ladeplads	8	Ei	55.15N	12.08 E
Faku	27	Je	42.30N	123.24 E
Fala-Beguets ▪	64d	Bb	7.21N	151.40 E
Falaise	11	Ff	48.54N	0.12W
Falaise de Tiguidit ▲	34	Gb	16.22N	7.45 E
Falakrón Óros ▲	5	Ih	41.20N	24.00 E
Falam	25	Id	22.55N	93.41 E
Falas ▪	64d	Ba	7.32N	151.42 E
Fälciu	15	Lc	46.18N	28.08 E
Falcón ▪	54	Ea	11.00N	69.50W
Falcon, Cap- ▪	13	Li	35.46N	0.48W
Falcon, Presa- ⌐	45	Gm	26.37N	99.11W
Falconara Marittima	14	Hg	43.37N	13.24 E
Falcone, Punta- ▪	14	Cj	40.58N	8.12 E
Falcon Reservoir ⌐	43	Hf	26.37N	99.11W
Faléa ▪	34	Cc	12.16N	11.15W
Faleallep Pass ⌐	64d	Bb	7.26N	151.34 E
Falealupo	65c	Aa	13.30S	172.48W
Falelima	65c	Aa	13.32S	172.41W
Falémé ⌐	30	Fg	14.46N	12.14W
Falenki	7	Mg	58.23N	51.36 E
Falerum	8	Gf	58.09N	16.13 E
Falešty	16	Ef	47.35N	27.44 E
Falevai	65c	Ba	13.55S	171.59W
Falfurrias	43	Hf	27.14N	98.09W
Falkenberg	7	Ch	56.54N	12.28 E
Falkensee	10	Jd	52.34N	13.05 E
Falkirk	9	Jf	56.00N	3.48W
Falkland Islands/Malvinas, Islas- ▪	53	Kk	51.45S	59.00W
Falkland Islands/Malvinas, Islas- ▪	52	Kk	51.00S	59.00W
Falkland Plateau (EN) ▪	52	Lk	51.00S	50.00W
Falkland Sound ⌐	56	Ih	51.45S	59.25W
Falkonéra ▪	15	Gm	36.50N	23.53 E
Falköping	7	Cg	58.10N	13.31 E
Fallingbostel	10	Fd	52.52N	9.42 E
Fallon [Mt.-U.S.]	46	Mc	46.48N	105.00W
Fallon [Nv.-U.S.]	46	Fg	39.28N	118.47W
Fall River	43	Mc	41.43N	71.08W
Falls City	43	Hc	40.03N	95.36W
Falmouth [Atg.]	51d	Bb	17.01N	61.46W
Falmouth [Eng.-U.K.]	9	Hk	50.08N	5.04W
Falmouth [Jam.]	49	Id	18.30N	77.39W
Falmouth [Ky.-U.S.]	44	Ef	38.40N	84.20W
Falmouth Bay ⌐	9	Hk	50.10N	5.05W
Falmouth Harbour ⌐	51d	Bb	17.01N	61.46W
Falo ▪	64d	Bb	7.29N	151.53 E
False Bay ⌐	30	Il	34.15S	18.35 E
False Pass	40	Gf	54.52N	163.24W
Falset	49	Gf	42.48N	0.49 E
Falso, Cabo- [Dom.Rep.] ▪	49	Le	17.47N	71.41W
Falso, Cabo- [Hond.] ▪	49	Ff	15.12N	83.20W
Falso, Cabo- [Mex.] ▪	47	Cc	22.52N	109.58W
Falso Cabo de Hornos ▪	56	Gi	55.43S	68.05W
Falster ▪	7	Ci	54.50N	12.00 E
Falsterbo	8	Ci	55.25N	12.50 E
Fälticeni	15	Jb	47.27N	26.18 E
Falun	6	Hc	60.36N	15.38 E
Fama ⌐	35	Cb	15.20N	20.34 E
Famagusta (EN)= Gazimağusa	23	Dc	35.07N	33.57 E
Famatina, Nevados de- ▲	56	Gc	29.00S	67.51W
Famenne ▪	11	Ld	50.15N	5.15 E
Fana	34	Dc	12.45N	6.57W
Fanan ▪	64d	Bb	7.11N	151.59 E
Fanchang	27	Ke	31.00N	118.11 E
Fancheng	27	Je	33.09N	113.05 E
Fandriana	37	Hd	20.13S	47.20 E
Fangak	35	Ed	9.04N	30.53 E
Fangatau Atoll ▪	57	Mf	15.50S	140.52W
Fangcheng	27	Je	33.09N	113.05 E
Fangliao	25	Mg	22.16N	120.25 E
Fangshan	28	Ce	39.43N	115.58 E
Fangxian	27	Je	32.03N	110.41 E
Fangzheng	27	Mb	45.50N	128.49 E
Fangzi	28	Hc	36.36N	119.08 E
Fanjiatun	28	Hc	43.42N	125.05 E
Fanjing Shan ▲	27	If	27.57N	108.50 E
Fannārden ▪	8	Bc	61.31N	7.55 E
Fanning → Tabuaeran Atoll ▪	57	Ld	3.52N	159.20W
Fano	14	Hg	43.50N	13.01 E
Fanø ▪	8	Cc	55.25N	8.25 E
Fanø Bugt ⌐	8	Cc	55.25N	8.10 E
Fanshi	28	Ce	39.11N	113.16 E
Fan Si Pan ▲	21	Mg	22.15N	103.50 E
Fan Si Pan ▲	25	Kd	22.18N	103.46 E
Fanuatapu ▪	65c	Ba	13.55S	171.20W
Fanxian	28	Gc	35.53N	115.29 E
Faqūs	24	Jf	30.44N	31.48 E
Farab	18	Hd	39.12N	63.38 E
Faraba	34	Cc	12.52N	11.23W
Faraday ⊠	66	Qa	65.15S	64.15W
Faradje	36	Eb	3.44N	29.43 E
Faradofay	37	Hd	25.01S	46.59 E
Farafangana	37	Hd	22.48S	47.50 E
Farafra Oasis (EN) ▪	30	Jf	27.15N	28.10 E
Farafra Oasis (EN) ▪	30	Jf	27.15N	28.10 E
Farāfirah, Wāḩāt al- ▪	31	Jf	29.15N	28.10 E
Farah	21	Jg	32.22N	62.07 E
Farah ▪	23	Jc	33.00N	62.30 E
Farah ⌐	23	Jc	31.29N	61.24 E
Fara'h, Wādī al- ⌐	24	Od	36.47N	53.06 E
Farahābād	24	Od	36.47N	53.06 E
Faranah	34	Cc	10.00N	10.44W
Farasan ▪	30	Lg	16.42N	42.02 E
Farasan, Jazā'ir- ▪	21	Gh	16.48N	41.54 E
Farasān al Kabīr ▪	33	Hf	16.42N	41.48 E
Faraulep Atoll ▪	57	Hd	8.36N	144.33 E
Farcău, Vîrful- ▲	15	Hb	47.55N	24.22 E
Farciennes	12	Gd	50.26N	4.33 E
Fardes ⌐	13	Jg	37.20N	3.16W
Fare	65e	Db	16.42S	151.01W
Farewell, Cape- ▪	57	Ii	40.30S	172.43 E
Farewell Spit ▪	62	Ed	40.30S	172.50 E
Färgelanda	8	Df	58.34N	11.59 E
Fargo	39	Jf	46.52N	96.48W
Faribault	43	Ic	44.18N	93.16W
Faribault, Lac- ⌐	42	Ke	58.00N	72.00W

Index Symbols

- [1] Independent Nation
- [2] State, Region
- [3] District, County
- [4] Municipality
- ■ Colony, Dependency
- ■ Continent
- ▪ Physical Region
- ■ Historical or Cultural Region
- ▲ Mount, Mountain
- ▲ Volcano
- ▲ Hill
- ▲ Mountains, Mountain Range
- ▲ Hills, Escarpment
- ▲ Plateau, Upland
- ⊃ Pass, Gap
- ⊃ Plain, Lowland
- ⊃ Delta
- ⊃ Salt Flat
- ⊃ Valley, Canyon
- ⊃ Crater, Cave
- ⊃ Karst Features
- □ Depression
- □ Polder
- □ Desert, Dunes
- □ Forest, Woods
- □ Heath, Steppe
- □ Oasis
- □ Cape, Point
- ⌐ Coast, Beach
- ⌐ Cliff
- ⌐ Peninsula
- ⌐ Isthmus
- ⌐ Coral Reef
- ⌐ Sandbank
- ⌐ Island
- ⌐ Rock, Reef
- ⌐ Islands, Archipelago
- ⌐ Rocks, Reefs
- ⌐ Coral Reef
- ⌐ Well, Spring
- ⌐ Geyser
- ⌐ River, Stream
- ⌐ Waterfall Rapids
- ⌐ River Mouth, Estuary
- ⌐ Lake
- ⌐ Salt Lake
- ⌐ Intermittent Lake
- ⌐ Reservoir
- ⌐ Swamp, Pond
- ⌐ Canal
- ⌐ Glacier
- ⌐ Ice Shelf, Pack Ice
- ⌐ Ocean
- ⌐ Sea
- ⌐ Gulf, Bay
- ⌐ Strait, Fjord
- ⌐ Lagoon
- ⌐ Bank
- ⌐ Seamount
- ⌐ Tablemount
- ⌐ Ridge
- ⌐ Shelf
- ⌐ Basin
- ⌐ Escarpment, Sea Scarp
- ⌐ Fracture
- ⌐ Trench, Abyss
- ⌐ National Park, Reserve
- ⌐ Point of Interest
- ⌐ Recreation Site
- ⌐ Cave, Cavern
- ⌐ Historic Site
- ⌐ Ruins
- ⌐ Wall, Walls
- ⌐ Church, Abbey
- ⌐ Temple
- ⊠ Scientific Station
- ⌐ Airport
- ⌐ Port
- ⌐ Lighthouse
- ⌐ Mine
- ⌐ Tunnel
- ⌐ Dam, Bridge

Index Symbols

- [1] Independent Nation
- [2] State, Region
- [3] District, County
- Municipality
- Colony, Dependency
- Continent
- Physical Region
- Historical or Cultural Region
- Mount, Mountain
- Volcano
- Hill
- Mountains, Mountain Range
- Hills, Escarpment
- Plateau, Upland
- Pass, Gap
- Plain, Lowland
- Delta
- Salt Flat
- Valley, Canyon
- Crater, Cave
- Karst Features
- Depression
- Polder
- Desert, Dunes
- Forest, Woods
- Heath, Steppe
- Oasis
- Cape, Point
- Coast, Beach
- Cliff
- Peninsula
- Isthmus
- Sandbank
- Island
- Atoll
- Rock, Reef
- Islands, Archipelago
- Rocks, Reefs
- Coral Reef
- Well, Spring
- Geyser
- River, Stream
- Waterfall Rapids
- River Mouth, Estuary
- Lake
- Salt Lake
- Intermittent Lake
- Reservoir
- Swamp, Pond
- Canal
- Glacier
- Ice Shelf, Pack Ice
- Ocean
- Sea
- Gulf, Bay
- Strait, Fjord
- Lagoon
- Bank
- Seamount
- Tablemount
- Ridge
- Shelf
- Basin
- Escarpment, Sea Scarp
- Fracture
- Trench, Abyss
- National Park, Reserve
- Point of Interest
- Recreation Area
- Cave, Cavern
- Historic Site
- Ruins
- Wall, Walls
- Church, Abbey
- Temple
- Scientific Station
- Airport
- Port
- Lighthouse
- Mine
- Tunnel
- Dam, Bridge

Florida City 44 Gm 25.27N 80.29W
Florida Islands 60 Gi 9.00S 160.10 E
Florida Keys 43 Kg 24.45N 81.00W
Floridia 14 Jm 37.05N 15.09 E
Florido, Río- 48 Gd 27.43N 105.10W
Flórina 15 Ei 40.47N 21.24 E
Flörsheim 12 Kd 50.01N 8.26 E
Flotte, Cap de- 63b Ce 21.11S 167.24 E
Floydada 45 Fj 33.59N 101.20W
Fluessen 11 Lb 52.57N 5.30 E
Flumen 13 Lc 41.43N 0.09W
Flumendosa 14 Dk 39.26N 9.37 E
Fluminimaggiore 14 Ck 39.26N 8.30 E
Flumini Mannu 14 Ck 39.16N 9.00 E
Flums 14 Dc 47.05N 9.20 E
Fluvià 13 Pb 42.12N 3.07 E
Flying Fish, Cape- 66 Of 72.06S 102.29W
Fly River 57 Fe 8.00S 142.21 E
Fnideq 13 Gi 35.50N 5.22W
Fnjóská 7a Bb 65.54N 18.07W
Foa 65b Ba 19.45S 174.18W
Foam Lake 46 Na 51.39N 103.33W
Foça 15 Jk 38.39N 26.46 E
Foča 14 Mg 43.31N 18.47 E
Fochi 15 Bb 18.25N 15.40 E
Fochi 35 Bb 18.56N 15.57 E
Focşani 15 Kd 45.42N 27.11 E
Fodda 13 Nh 36.14N 1.33 E
Fodé 35 Cd 5.29N 23.18 E
Færingehavn 41 Gf 63.45N 51.28W
Foga, Dallol- 34 Fc 12.05N 3.32 E
Foggaret ez Zoua 32 Hd 27.22N 2.50 E
Foggia 6 Hg 41.27N 15.34 E
Foggo 34 Gc 11.23N 9.57 E
Foglia 14 Gg 43.55N 12.54 E
Föglö 8 Ie 60.00N 20.25 E
Fogo [Can.] 42 Mg 49.40N 54.10W
Fogo [C.V.] 30 Eg 14.55N 24.25W
Fohnsdorf 14 Ic 47.12N 14.41 E
Föhr 10 Eb 54.45N 8.30 E
Föhren 12 Ie 49.51N 6.46 E
Foix 11 Hl 42.58N 1.36 E
Fojnica 23 Fg 43.58N 17.54 E
Fokino 16 Ic 53.27N 34.26 E
Folda 7 Dc 67.36N 14.50 E
Folégandros 15 Hm 36.38N 24.54 E
Foley 42 Kc 68.30N 75.00W
Foleyet 42 Jg 48.16N 82.30W
Folgefonni 7 Bf 60.00N 6.20 E
Foligno 14 Gh 42.57N 12.42 E
Folkestone 9 Oj 51.05N 1.11 E
Folkingham 12 Bb 52.52N 0.24W
Folkston 44 Fj 30.50N 82.01W
Folldals verk 7 Bb 62.08N 10.00 E
Follebu 7 Cf 61.14N 10.17 E
Föllinge 7 De 63.40N 14.37 E
Follo 8 De 59.55N 10.55 E
Follonica 14 Eh 42.55N 10.45 E
Follonica, Golfo di- 14 Eh 42.55N 10.40 E
Folschviller 12 Ie 49.04N 6.41 E
Fomboni 37 Gb 12.16S 43.45 E
Fomento 49 Hb 22.06N 79.43W
Fond d'Or Bay 51k Bb 13.56N 60.54W
Fond-du-Lac 42 Ge 59.19N 107.10W
Fond-du-Lac 42 Ge 59.17N 106.00W
Fond du Lac 43 Jc 43.47N 88.27W
Fondi 14 Hi 41.21N 13.25 E
Fongen 8 Da 63.11N 11.38 E
Fongoro 35 Cc 11.30N 22.25 E
Fonni 14 Dj 40.07N 9.15 E
Fonoifua 65b Bb 20.17S 174.38W
Fonsagrada 13 Ea 43.08N 7.04W
Fonseca 54 Da 10.53N 72.50W
Fonseca, Golfo de- 38 Kh 13.08N 87.40W
Fonsecas, Serra dos- 55 Jc 17.02S 44.13W
Fontaine-Bellenger 12 De 49.11N 1.16 E
Fontainebleau 11 If 48.24N 2.42 E
Fontaine-Henry, Château de- 12 Be 49.17N 0.27W
Fontaine-le-Dun 12 Ce 49.49N 0.51 E
Fontaine-l'Evêque 12 Gd 50.25N 4.19 E
Fontas 42 Fe 58.17N 121.46W
Fonte Boa 54 Ed 2.32S 66.01W
Fontenay-le-Comte 11 Fh 46.28N 0.49W
Fontenay Trésigny 12 Ef 48.42N 2.52 E
Fontenelle Reservoir 46 Je 42.05N 110.06W
Fontevraud-l'Abbaye 11 Gg 47.11N 0.03 E
Fontur 5 Eb 66.23N 14.32W
Fonuafo'ou Falcon 61 Fd 20.19S 175.25W
Fonualei Island 57 Jf 18.01S 174.19W
Fonyód 10 Nj 46.44N 17.33 E
Foraker, Mount- 40 Id 62.56N 151.26W
Forbach 11 Me 49.11N 6.54 E
Forbes 59 Jf 33.23S 148.01 E
Forbes, Mount- 46 Ga 51.52N 116.56W
Forcados 34 Gd 5.23N 5.19 E
Forcados 34 Gd 5.21N 5.25 E
Forcalquier 11 Lk 43.58N 5.47 E
Forchheim 10 Hg 49.43N 11.04 E
Ford City 46 Fi 35.09N 119.27W
Førde 7 Af 61.27N 5.52 E
Førdefjorden 8 Ac 61.30N 5.40 E
Ford Ranges 66 Mf 77.00S 145.00W
Fordyce 45 Jj 33.49N 92.25W
Forécariah 34 Cd 9.26N 13.06W
Forel, Mont- 67 Mc 67.05N 36.55W
Forelshogna 8 Db 62.41N 10.47 E
Forest 45 Lj 32.22N 89.28W
Forest Park 44 Ei 33.37N 84.22W
Forestville 44 Ma 48.45N 69.06W
Forez, Monts du- 11 Ji 45.35N 3.48 E
Forez, Plaine du- 11 Ki 45.50N 4.10 E
Forfar 9 Ke 56.38N 2.54W
Forges-les-Eaux 11 He 49.37N 1.33 E
Forggensee 10 Gi 47.36N 10.44 E
Forks 46 Cc 47.57N 124.23W
Forlì 14 Gf 44.13N 12.03 E
Forlì, Bocca di- 14 Ii 41.45N 14.10 E
Formby Point 9 Jh 53.33N 3.06W
Formentera 5 Gh 38.42N 1.28 E
Formentor, Cabo de-/Formentor, Cap de- 13 Pe 39.58N 3.12 E
Formentor, Cap de-/Formentor, Cabo de- 13 Pe 39.58N 3.12 E
Formerie 12 De 49.39N 1.44 E
Formia 14 Hi 41.15N 13.37 E
Formiga 54 Ih 20.27S 45.25W
Formigas 32 Cb 37.16N 24.47W
Formosa [2] 56 Ib 25.00S 60.00W
Formosa [Arg.] 53 Kh 26.10S 58.11W
Formosa [Braz.] 54 Ig 15.32S 47.20W
Formosa [Gui. Bis.] 34 Bc 11.45N 16.05W
Formosa [Tai.]→Taiwan 21 Og 23.30N 121.00 E
Formosa, Serra- 52 Kg 12.00S 55.00W
Formosa Bay 36 Hc 2.45S 40.20 E
Formosa Strait (EN)= Taiwan Haixia 21 Ng 24.00N 119.00 E
Formoso [Braz.] 55 Ib 14.57S 46.14W
Formoso [Braz.] 55 Ha 13.37S 48.54W
Formoso, Rio- [Braz.] 55 Ja 13.26S 44.14W
Formoso, Rio- [Braz.] 55 If 10.34S 49.59W
Formoso, Rio- [Braz.] 55 Fd 18.25S 52.28W
Fornæs 7 Ch 56.27N 10.58 E
Fornosovo 8 Ne 59.31N 30.45 E
Fornovo di Taro 14 Ef 44.42N 10.06 E
Föroyar/Færøerne=Faeroe Islands (EN) [5] 6 Fc 62.00N 7.00W
Föroyar/Færøerne=Faeroe Islands (EN) 5 Fc 62.00N 7.00W
Forres 9 Jd 57.37N 3.38W
Forrest 59 Ff 30.51S 128.06 E
Forrest City 45 Ki 35.01N 90.47W
Forrester Island 66 Nf 74.06S 132.00W
Forsayth 59 Ic 18.35S 143.36 E
Forsbacka 8 Gd 60.37N 16.53 E
Forserum 8 Fg 57.42N 14.28 E
Forshaga 7 Cg 59.32N 13.28 E
Forsnäs 7 Ec 66.14N 18.39 E
Forssa 7 Ff 60.49N 23.38 E
Forst/Baršć 10 Ke 51.44N 14.38 E
Forsyth 46 Lc 46.16N 106.41W
Fort Albany 39 Kd 52.15N 81.37W
Fortaleza 53 Mf 3.43S 38.30W
Fortaleza, Ribeirão- 55 Fd 19.50S 53.25W
Fort Augustus 9 Id 57.09N 4.41W
Fort Beaufort 37 Df 32.46S 26.40 E
Fort Benton 43 Eb 47.49N 110.40W
Fort Bragg 43 Cd 39.26N 123.48W
Fort Bridger 46 Jf 41.19N 110.23W
Fort-Carnot 37 Hd 21.53S 48.26 E
Fort Chipewyan 42 Ge 58.42N 111.08W
Fort Cobb Reservoir 45 Gi 35.12N 98.29W
Fort Collins 43 Fc 40.35N 105.05W
Fort Collinson 42 Fb 71.37N 117.57W
Fort Coulogne 44 Ic 45.51N 76.44W
Fort Davis 45 Ek 30.35N 103.54W
Fort-de-France 39 Mh 14.36N 61.05W
Fort-de-France, Baie de- 51h Ab 14.34N 61.04W
Fort Dodge 43 Ic 42.30N 94.10W
Forte 55 Ib 14.16S 47.17W
Forte dei Marmi 14 Eg 43.57N 10.10 E
Fortescue River 57 Cg 21.00S 116.06 E
Fort Frances 39 Je 48.36N 93.24W
Fort Franklin 42 Fc 65.12N 123.26W
Fort Garland 45 Dh 37.26N 105.26W
Fort Gibson Lake 45 Ih 36.00N 95.18W
Fort Good-Hope 39 Gc 66.15N 128.38W
Forth 9 Je 56.04N 3.42W
Forth, Firth of- 5 Fd 56.05N 2.55W
Fort Hall 36 Gc 0.43S 37.09 E
Fort Hope 42 If 51.32N 88.00W
Fortin Avalos Sanchez 55 Bf 23.28S 60.07W
Fortín Boquerón 55 Cf 22.47S 59.57W
Fortín Buenos Aires 55 Bf 22.57S 61.51W
Fortín Cadete Pastor Pando 55 Cg 24.20S 58.54W
Fortín Capitán Figari 55 Cf 23.12S 59.32W
Fortín Carlos A. Lopez 55 Ce 21.19S 59.44W
Fortín Comandante Nowak 55 Cg 24.51S 58.15W
Fortín Coronel Bogado 55 Ce 20.46S 59.09W
Fortín Coronel Eugenio Garay 56 Hb 20.31S 62.08W
Fortín Coronel Hermosa 55 Bf 22.33S 60.01W
Fortín Coronel Martínez 55 Cf 22.15S 59.09W
Fortín Florida 55 Ce 20.45S 59.17W
Fortín Galpón 55 Cd 19.51S 58.16W
Fortín Gaspar Rodriguez de Francia 55 Cf 23.01S 59.57W
Fortín General Caballero 55 Cg 24.08S 59.30W
Fortín General Delgado 55 Cg 24.28S 59.15W
Fortín General Diaz 56 Hb 23.31S 60.34W
Fortín Guaraní 55 Cf 22.44S 59.30W
Fortín Hernandarias 55 Bf 21.58S 61.30W
Fortín José M. López 55 Be 20.07S 60.15W
Fortín Lagerenza 55 Be 20.06S 61.03W
Fortín Madrejón 55 Ce 20.38S 59.52W
Fortín Mariscal López 55 Cf 23.09S 59.44W
Fortín Max Paredes 55 Cd 19.16S 59.58W
Fortín May Alberto Gardel 55 Af 22.46S 62.12W
Fortín Mayor Long 55 Ae 20.33S 62.01W
Fortín Mayor R. Santacruz 55 Be 20.15S 60.37W
Fortín Nueva Asunción 55 Be 20.42S 61.55W
Fortín Pikyrenda 55 Be 20.05S 61.48W
Fortín Pilcomayo [Par.] 55 Bf 23.44S 60.51W
Fortín Pilcomayo [Arg.] 55 Bf 23.52S 60.53W
Fortín Pratts Gill 55 Bf 22.41S 61.33W
Fortín Presidente Ayala 55 Cf 23.30S 59.46W
Fortín Ravelo 55 Bd 19.18S 60.35W
Fortín Suarez Arana 55 Bd 18.40S 60.09W
Fortín Teniente 1° Alfredo Stroessner 55 Bf 22.45S 61.32W
Fortín Teniente 1° H. Mendoza 55 Cd 19.54S 59.47W
Fortín Teniente 1° M. Cabello 55 Bf 23.28S 61.19W
Fortín Teniente 1° Ramiro Espinola 55 Be 21.28S 61.18W
Fortín Teniente Acosta 55 Bf 22.41S 60.32W
Fortín Teniente Agripino Enciso 55 Be 21.12S 61.34W
Fortín Teniente Américo Picco 55 Cd 19.35S 59.43W
Fortín Teniente Aristigueta 55 Bf 22.21S 60.38W
Fortín Teniente E. Ochoa 55 Be 21.42S 61.02W
Fortín Teniente Esteban Martinez 55 Cg 24.02S 59.51W
Fortín Teniente Juan E. López 55 Be 21.05S 61.48W
Fortín Teniente Montania 55 Cf 22.04S 59.57W
Fortín Teniente R. Rueda 55 Be 21.49S 60.49W
Fortín Toledo 55 Bf 22.20S 60.21W
Fortín Torres 55 Ce 21.01S 59.30W
Fortín Vanguardia 55 Cd 19.39S 58.10W
Fortín Vitiones 55 Cd 19.30S 58.06W
Fortín Zenteno 55 Cf 23.10S 59.59W
Fort Jeuedy, Point of- 51p Bb 12.00N 61.42W
Fort Kent 44 Mb 47.15N 68.36W
Fort Knox 44 Eg 37.53N 85.55W
Fort Lamy→N'djamena 31 Ig 12.07N 15.03 E
Fort Lauderdale 43 Kf 26.07N 80.08W
Fort Liard 39 Gc 60.15N 123.28W
Fort-Liberté 49 Ld 19.38N 71.57W
Fort MacKay 42 Ge 57.08N 111.42W
Fort Macleod 42 Gg 49.43N 113.25W
Fort Mac Mahon 32 Hd 29.46N 1.37 E
Fort Madison 45 Kf 40.38N 91.21W
Fort-Mahon-Plage 12 Dd 50.21N 1.34 E
Fort McMurray 39 Hd 56.44N 111.23W
Fort McPherson 39 Fc 67.27N 134.53W
Fort Miribel 32 Hd 29.26N 3.00 E
Fort Morgan 45 Ef 40.15N 103.48W
Fort Myers 39 Kg 26.37N 81.54W
Fort Myers Beach 44 Gl 26.27N 81.57W
Fort Nelson 39 Gd 58.49N 122.39W
Fort Nelson 42 Fe 59.33N 124.01W
Fort Norman 42 Ed 64.56N 125.22W
Fortore 14 Ji 41.55N 15.17 E
Fort Payne 44 Eh 34.27N 85.43W
Fort Peck 46 Lb 48.01N 106.27W
Fort Peck Lake 43 Fb 47.45N 106.50W
Fort Pierce 43 Kf 27.27N 80.20W
Fort Pierre 43 Gc 44.21N 100.22W
Fort Portal 36 Fb 0.39N 30.17 E
Fort Providence 39 Hc 61.21N 117.39W
Fort Qu'Appelle 46 Na 50.56N 103.09W
Fort Resolution 42 Gd 61.10N 113.40W
Fortrose 62 Cg 46.34S 168.48 E
Fort Saint James 42 Ff 54.26N 124.15W
Fort Saint John 39 Gd 56.15N 120.51W
Fort Sandeman 25 Db 31.20N 69.27 E
Fort Saskatchewan 42 Gf 53.43N 113.13W
Fort Scott 45 Ih 37.50N 94.42W
Fort-Ševčenko 19 Fg 44.30N 50.14 E
Fort Severn 39 Kd 56.00N 87.38W
Fort Simpson 39 Gc 61.52N 121.23W
Fort Smith [Ar.-U.S.] 39 Jf 35.23N 94.25W
Fort Smith [N.W.T.-Can.] 39 Hd 60.00N 111.53W
Fort Stockton 43 Ge 30.53N 102.53W
Fort Sumner 45 Di 34.28N 104.15W
Fortuna 46 Cf 40.36N 124.09W
Fortuna, Rio de la- 55 Cc 16.36S 58.46W
Fortune Bay 42 Lg 47.15N 55.40W
Fort Vermilion 42 Fe 58.24N 116.00W
Fort Walton Beach 43 Je 30.25N 86.36W
Fort Washakie 46 Ke 43.00N 108.53W
Fort Wayne 39 Ke 41.04N 85.09W
Fort William 9 He 56.49N 5.07W
Fort Worth 39 Jf 32.45N 97.20W
Fort Yates 45 Fc 46.05N 100.38W
Fort Yukon 39 Ec 66.34N 145.17W
Forūr, Jazīreh-ye- 24 Pi 26.17N 54.32 E
Foshan 22 Ng 22.59N 113.05 E
Fosheim Peninsula 42 Ja 80.00N 84.30W
Fosnavåg 8 Ab 62.21N 5.39 E
Fosnøy 8 Ad 60.45N 4.55 E
Fossacesia 14 Ih 42.15N 14.29 E
Fossano 14 Bf 44.33N 7.43 E
Fossato, Colle di- 14 Gg 43.20N 12.49 E
Fossberg 8 Cc 61.50N 8.34 E
Fossil 46 Ed 44.59N 120.13W
Fossil Bluff 66 Qf 71.20S 68.17W
Fossombrone 14 Gg 43.41N 12.48 E
Fosston 45 Ic 47.35N 95.45W
Fos-sur-Mer 11 Kk 43.26N 4.57 E
Foster 59 Jg 38.39S 146.12 E
Foster, Mount- 40 Le 59.48N 135.29W
Foster Bugt 41 Jd 73.40N 21.40W
Fostoria 44 Fe 41.10N 83.25W
Fotuha'a 65b Ba 19.49S 174.44W
Foucarmont 12 De 49.51N 1.34 E
Fougamou 36 Bc 1.13S 10.36 E
Fougères 11 Ef 48.21N 1.12W
Foul, Khalīj- 33 Ge 23.30N 35.40 E
Foula 9 Ka 60.10N 2.05W
Foul Bay 51q Bb 13.06N 59.27W
Fouligny 12 Ie 49.06N 6.30 E
Foulness 9 Nj 51.36N 0.55 E
Foulness Point 12 Cc 51.37N 0.57 E
Foulwind, Cape- 62 Dd 41.45S 171.28 E
Foumban 34 Hd 5.43N 10.55 E
Foumbouni 37 Gb 11.50S 43.30 E
Foum Zguid 32 Fc 30.05N 6.52W
Foundation Ice Stream 66 Qg 83.15S 60.00W
Fountains Abbey 9 Lg 54.07N 1.34W
Fouquet Island 37b Bb 5.25S 53.20 E
Fourchambault 11 Jg 47.01N 3.05 E
Fourchue, Île- 51b Bc 17.57N 62.55W
Fourmiers 11 Kd 50.00N 4.03 E
Four Mountains, Islands of the- 40a Db 52.50N 170.00W
Foúrnoi 15 Jl 37.34N 26.30 E
Fouron/Voeren 12 Hd 50.45N 5.48 E
Fours 11 Jh 46.49N 3.43 E
Fourth Cataract (EN)= Rabi', Ash Shallāl ar- 30 Kg 18.47N 32.03 E
Fous, Pointe des- 51g Bb 15.12N 61.20W
Fouta 34 Cb 16.18N 14.48W
Fouta Djalon 30 Fg 11.30N 12.30W
Foutouna, Ile- 57 If 19.32S 170.13 E
Foux, Cap-à- 49 Kd 19.45N 73.27W
Fouzon 11 Hg 47.16N 1.27 E
Foveaux Strait 57 Hi 46.40S 168.10 E
Fowler [Co.-U.S.] 45 Eg 38.08N 104.00W
Fowler [In.-U.S.] 44 De 40.37N 87.19W
Fowlers Bay 59 Gf 32.00S 132.25 E
Fowman 24 Md 37.13N 49.19 E
Foxe Basin 38 Lc 68.25N 77.00W
Foxe Channel 38 Lc 64.30N 80.00W
Foxen 8 De 59.25N 11.55 E
Foxe Peninsula 38 Lc 65.00N 76.00W
Foxford/Béal Easa 9 Dh 53.59N 9.07W
Fox Glacier 61 Ch 43.28S 170.00 E
Fox Islands 38 Cd 54.00N 168.00W
Fox Peak 62 De 43.50S 170.47 E
Fox River 45 Lf 41.21N 88.50W
Foxton 62 Fd 40.28S 175.17 E
Fox Valley 46 Ka 50.29N 109.28W
Foyle 9 Ff 55.04N 7.15W
Foyle, Lough-/Loch Feabhail 9 Ff 55.05N 7.10W
Foz do Cunene 36 Bf 17.15S 11.48 E
Foz do Iguaçu 53 Kh 25.33S 54.35W
Fraga 13 Mc 41.31N 0.21 E
Fragoso, Cayo 49 Hb 22.44N 79.30W
Fraire, Walcourt- 12 Gd 50.16N 4.30 E
Fram 55 Eh 27.06S 55.58W
Fram Basin (EN) 67 He 88.00N 80.00 E
Framlingham 12 Db 52.13N 1.20 E
Franca 56 Kb 20.32S 47.24W
Franca-Josifa, Zemlja-= Franz Joseph Land (EN) 21 Ha 81.00N 55.00 E
Francavilla al Mare 14 Ih 42.25N 14.17 E
Francavilla Fontana 14 Lj 40.32N 17.35 E
France [1] 6 Gf 46.00N 2.00 E
Frances 42 Ed 60.16N 129.11W
Francés, Punta- 49 Fc 21.38N 83.12W
Francesi, Punta di li- 14 Di 41.08N 9.02 E
Francés Viejo, Cabo- 49 Md 19.39N 69.55W
Franceville 31 Ii 1.38S 13.35 E
Franche-Comté 11 Lh 47.00N 6.00 E
Franches Montagnes/ Freiberge 14 Ac 47.15N 7.00 E
Francia 55 Dk 32.34S 36.38W
Francia, Sierra de- 13 Fd 40.35N 6.05W
Francis Case, Lake- 38 Je 43.15N 99.00W
Francisco Beltrão 56 Jc 26.05S 53.04W
Francisco Escárcega 48 Nh 18.37N 90.43W
Francisco I. Madero 48 Ge 24.32N 104.22W
Francisco Madero 55 Al 35.52S 62.03W
Francisco Morazán [3] 49 Df 14.15N 87.15W
Francisco Sá 54 Jg 16.28S 43.30W
Franciscus Bay 37 Ae 25.00S 14.50 E
Francistown 31 Jk 21.09S 27.31 E
Francofonte 14 Im 37.14N 14.53 E
Franconian Jura (EN)= Fränkische Alb 5 Hf 49.00N 11.30 E
Francs Peak 43 Fc 43.58N 109.20W
Franeker 11 La 53.11N 5.32 E
Frankenau 12 Kc 51.06N 8.56 E
Frankenberg (Eder) 10 Ee 51.04N 8.40 E
Frankenhöhe 10 Gg 49.15N 10.15 E
Frankenthal (Pfalz) 12 Ke 49.32N 8.21 E
Frankenwald 10 Hf 50.18N 11.36 E
Frankfort [In.-U.S.] 44 De 40.17N 86.31W
Frankfort [Ky.-U.S.] 39 Kf 38.12N 84.52W
Frankfort [Mi.-U.S.] 44 Dc 44.38N 86.14W
Frankfort on the Main (EN) =Frankfurt am Main 6 Ge 50.07N 8.41 E
Frankfurt 10 Kd 52.21N 14.33 E
Frankfurt am Main= Frankfort on the Main (EN) 6 Ge 50.07N 8.41 E
Fränkische Alb=Franconian Jura(EN) 5 Hf 49.00N 11.30 E
Fränkische Saale 10 Ff 50.03N 9.42 E
Fränkische Schweiz 10 Hg 49.45N 11.20 E
Franklin [In.-U.S.] 44 Df 39.29N 86.03W
Franklin [Ky.-U.S.] 44 Dg 36.43N 86.35W
Franklin [La.-U.S.] 45 Kl 29.48N 91.30W
Franklin [N.C.-U.S.] 44 Fh 35.11N 83.23W
Franklin [N.H.-U.S.] 44 Ld 43.27N 71.39W
Franklin [Pa.-U.S.] 44 He 41.24N 79.49W
Franklin [Tn.-U.S.] 44 Dh 35.55N 86.52W
Franklin, District of- [3] 42 Hb 72.00N 96.00W
Franklin Bay 38 Gc 68.45N 125.35W
Franklin Delano Roosevelt Lake 43 Db 48.20N 118.10W
Franklin Island 66 Kf 76.05S 168.11 E
Franklin Lake [Nv.-U.S.] 46 Hf 40.24N 115.12W
Franklin Lake [N.W.T.-Can.] 42 Hc 66.55N 96.05W
Franklin Mountains 38 Gc 63.15N 123.30W
Franklin Strait 42 Hb 71.30N 96.30W
Fransfontein 37 Bd 20.12S 15.01 E
Fränsta 8 Gb 62.30N 16.09 E
Franz Josef Glacier 62 De 43.23S 170.11 E
Franz Joseph Land (EN)= Franca-Josifa, Zemlja- 21 Ha 81.00N 55.00 E
Frascati 14 Gi 41.48N 12.41 E
Fraser [Can.] 38 Ge 49.09N 123.12W
Fraser [Newf.-Can.] 42 Le 56.39N 63.08W
Fraserburg 37 Cf 31.55S 21.30 E
Fraserburgh 9 Ld 57.42N 2.00W
Fraserdale 42 Jg 49.51N 81.38W
Fraser Island 57 Gg 25.15S 153.10 E
Fraser Plateau 38 Gd 51.30N 122.00W
Fraser Range 59 Ef 32.03S 122.48 E
Frasertown 62 Gc 38.58S 177.24 E
Frasnes-les-Anvaing 12 Fd 50.40N 3.36 E
Frauenfeld 14 Cc 47.35N 8.54 E
Fray Bentos 56 Id 33.08S 58.18W
Frechen 12 Id 50.55N 6.49 E
Frechilla 13 Hb 42.08N 4.50W
Fredericia 7 Bi 55.35N 9.46 E
Frederick [Md.-U.S.] 44 If 39.25N 77.25W
Frederick [Ok.-U.S.] 45 Gi 34.23N 99.01W
Frederick E. Hyde Fjord 41 Jb 82.40N 25.45W
Frederick Reef 57 Gg 21.00S 154.25 E
Fredericksburg [Tx.-U.S.] 45 Gk 30.17N 98.52W
Fredericksburg [Va.-U.S.] 44 If 38.18N 77.30W
Fredericktown 45 Kh 37.33N 90.18W
Frederico Westphalen 55 Fh 27.22S 53.24W
Fredericton 39 Me 45.58N 66.39W
Frederiksborg [2] 8 Ei 55.55N 12.15 E
Frederiksdal 41 Hf 60.15N 45.30W
Frederikshåb/Pâmiut 41 Hf 62.00N 49.45W
Frederikshåbs Bank (EN) 41 Hf 62.16N 49.45W
Frederikshavn 6 Hd 57.26N 10.32 E
Frederikssund 8 Ei 55.50N 12.04 E
Frederiksted 50 Dd 17.42N 64.48W
Frederiksværk 8 Ei 55.58N 12.02 E
Fredonia 46 Ih 36.57N 112.32W
Fredrika 7 Ed 64.05N 18.24 E
Fredriksberg 7 Df 60.08N 14.23 E
Fredrikshamn/Hamina 7 Gf 60.34N 27.12 E
Fredrikstad 7 Cg 59.13N 10.57 E
Fredvang 7 Cb 68.05N 13.10 E
Freeling Heights 59 Hf 30.10S 139.25 E
Freels, Cape- 42 Mg 49.13N 53.29W
Freeport [Bah.] 47 Ic 26.30N 78.45W
Freeport [Il.-U.S.] 43 Jc 42.17N 89.36W
Freeport [N.Y.-U.S.] 44 Ke 40.40N 73.35W
Freeport [Tx.-U.S.] 43 Hf 28.55N 95.22W
Freer 45 Gm 27.53N 98.37W
Freetown [Atg.] 51d Bb 17.03N 61.42W
Freetown [S.L.] 31 Fh 8.30N 13.15W
Fregenal de la Sierra 13 Ff 38.10N 6.39W
Fregene 14 Gi 41.51N 12.12 E
Frei 8 Ba 63.01N 7.48 E
Freiberg 10 Jf 50.55N 13.22 E
Freiberge/Franches Montagnes 14 Ac 47.15N 7.00 E
Freiberger Mulde 10 Ie 51.10N 12.48 E
Freiburg/Fribourg 14 Bd 46.50N 7.10 E
Freiburg im Breisgau 6 Gf 48.00N 7.51 E
Freilassing 10 Ii 47.51N 12.59 E
Freirina 56 Fc 28.30S 71.06W
Freisen 12 Je 49.33N 7.15 E
Freising 10 Hh 48.24N 11.44 E
Freistadt 14 Ib 48.30N 14.30 E
Freital 10 Je 51.01N 13.39 E
Fréjus 11 Mk 43.26N 6.44 E
Fréjus, Col du- 11 Mi 45.07N 6.40 E
Fremantle, Perth- 59 Df 32.03S 115.45 E
Fremont [Ca.-U.S.] 43 Cd 37.34N 122.01W
Fremont [Nb.-U.S.] 43 Hc 41.26N 96.30W
Fremont [Oh.-U.S.] 44 Fe 41.21N 83.08W
Fremont River 46 Jg 38.24N 110.42W
French Frigate Shoals 57 Kb 23.45N 166.10W
French Guiana (EN) = Guyane Française [5] 53 Ke 4.00N 53.00W
French Lick 44 Df 38.33N 86.37W
Frenchman Creek 45 Ff 40.13N 100.50W
Frenchman River 43 Fb 48.24N 107.05W
French Pass 62 Ed 40.55S 173.50 E
French Plain (EN) 5 Gf 47.00N 1.00 E
French Polynesia (EN)= Polynésie Française [5] 58 Mf 16.00S 145.00W
French River 44 Gc 45.56N 80.54W
Frenda 32 Hb 35.04N 1.02 E
Frénel, Cap- 11 Df 48.42N 2.19W
Frentani, Monti dei- 14 Ii 41.55N 14.30 E
Freren 12 Jb 52.29N 7.33 E
Fresco 34 Dd 5.05N 5.34W
Fresco, Rio- 54 He 6.39S 52.00W
Freshfield, Cape- 66 Je 68.22S 151.05 E
Fresnes-en-Woëvre 12 He 49.06N 5.37 E
Fresnillo de Gonzales Echeverria 47 Dd 23.10N 102.53W
Fresno 39 Hf 36.45N 119.45W
Fresno, Portillo del- 13 Ib 42.35N 3.40W
Fresno River 46 Eh 37.05N 120.33W
Fresquel 11 Ik 43.14N 2.24 E
Fresvikbreen 8 Bc 61.02N 6.45 E
Freu, Cabo- 13 Pe 39.45N 3.27 E
Freudenberg 12 Jd 50.54N 7.52 E
Freudenstadt 10 Eh 48.26N 8.25 E
Frévent 11 Id 50.16N 2.17 E
Freycinet Estuary 59 Ce 26.25S 113.45 E
Freycinet Peninsula 59 Jh 42.15S 148.20 E
Freyming-Merlebach 12 Ie 49.09N 6.47 E
Freyre 55 Aj 31.10S 62.02W
Freyung 10 Jh 48.48N 13.33 E
Fri 15 Jn 35.25N 26.56 E
Fria 34 Cc 10.27N 13.32W
Fria, Cape- 30 Ij 18.27S 12.01 E
Frias 56 Gc 28.39S 65.09W
Fribourg [2] 14 Bd 46.40N 7.10 E
Fribourg/Freiburg 14 Bd 46.50N 7.10 E
Fridtjof Nansen, Mount- 66 Lg 85.21S 167.33W
Friedberg [Aus.] 14 Kc 47.26N 16.03 E
Friedberg 10 Ef 50.21N 8.46 E
Friedrichshafen 10 Fi 47.39N 9.29 E
Friedrichsthal 12 Je 49.19N 7.06 E
Friesach 14 Id 46.57N 14.24 E
Friese Gat 12 Ia 53.30N 6.05 E
Friese Wad 12 Ha 53.25N 5.50 E
Friese Wad 12 Ha 53.24N 5.45 E
Friesland [3] 12 Ha 53.03N 5.45 E
Friesland 11 La 53.05N 6.00 E
Friesland 5 Ge 53.05N 6.00 E

Index Symbols

[1] Independent Nation
[2] State, Region
[3] District, County
[4] Municipality
[5] Colony, Dependency
Continent
Physical Region

Historical or Cultural Region
Mount, Mountain
Volcano
Hill
Mountains, Mountain Range
Hills, Escarpment
Plateau, Upland

Pass, Gap
Plain, Lowland
Delta
Salt Flat
Valley, Canyon
Crater, Cave
Karst Features

Depression
Polder
Desert, Dunes
Forest, Woods
Heath, Steppe
Oasis
Cape, Point

Coast, Beach
Cliff
Peninsula
Isthmus
Sandbank
Island
Atoll

Rock, Reef
Islands, Archipelago
Rocks, Reefs
Coral Reef
Well, Spring
Geyser
River, Stream

Waterfall Rapids
River Mouth, Estuary
Lake
Salt Lake
Intermittent Lake
Reservoir
Swamp, Pond

Canal
Glacier
Ice Shelf, Pack Ice
Ocean
Sea
Gulf, Bay
Strait, Fjord

Lagoon
Bank
Seamount
Tablemount
Ridge
Shelf
Basin

Escarpment, Sea Scarp
Fracture
Trench, Abyss
National Park, Reserve
Point of Interest
Recreation Site
Cave, Cavern

Historic Site
Ruins
Wall, Walls
Church, Abbey
Temple
Scientific Station
Airport

Port
Lighthouse
Mine
Tunnel
Dam, Bridge

Friesoythe 10 Dc 53.01N 7.51 E
Frigate Island 51p Cb 12.25N 61.29W
Friggesund 8 Gc 61.54N 16.32 E
Frignano 14 Ef 44.20N 10.50 E
Frindsbury Reef 63a Da 5.00S 159.07 E
Frinnaryd 8 Fg 57.56N 14.49 E
Frinton-on-Sea 12 Dc 51.50N 1.15 E
Frio, Cabo- 52 Lh 22.53S 42.00W
Frio, Rio- 49 Eh 11.08N 84.46W
Frio Draw 45 Ei 34.50N 102.08W
Friona 45 Ei 34.38N 102.43W
Frio River 45 Gl 28.30N 98.10W
Frisco Peak 46 Ig 38.31N 113.14W
Frisian Islands (EN) 5 Ge 54.00N 7.00 E
Fristad 8 Eg 57.50N 13.01 E
Fritsla 8 Eg 57.33N 12.47 E
Fritzlar 10 Fe 51.08N 9.17 E
Friuli 14 Ge 46.00N 13.00 E
Friuli-Venezia Giulia [2] 14 Gd 46.00N 13.00 E
Frobisher Bay 38 Mc 62.30N 66.00W
Frobisher Lake 42 Ge 56.20N 108.20W
Froidchapelle 12 Gd 50.09N 4.20 E
Froissy 12 Ee 49.34N 2.13 E
Frolovo 19 Ef 49.45N 43.39 E
Fromberg 46 Kd 45.23N 108.54W
Frombork 10 Pb 54.22N 19.41 E
Frome 9 Kj 51.14N 2.20W
Frome, Lake- 57 Eh 30.50S 139.50 E
Frondenberg 12 Jc 51.28N 7.46 E
Fronteira 13 Ee 39.03N 7.39W
Fronteiras 54 Je 7.05S 40.37W
Frontera 48 Mh 18.32N 92.38W
Frontera, Punta- 48 Mh 19.36N 92.42W
Fronteras 48 Eb 30.56N 109.31W
Frontignan 11 Jk 43.27N 3.45 E
Frontino, Paramo- 54 Cb 6.28N 76.04W
Front Range 38 If 39.45N 105.45W
Front Royal 44 Hf 38.56N 78.13W
Frosinone 14 Hi 41.38N 13.19 E
Frösö 8 Fa 63.11N 14.32 E
Frostburg 44 Hf 39.39N 78.56W
Frost Glacier 66 Ie 67.05S 129.00 E
Frövi 8 Fe 59.28N 15.22 E
Frøya 7 Be 63.43N 8.42 E
Frøysjøen 8 Ac 61.50N 5.05 E
Frozen Strait 42 Jc 65.50N 84.30W
Fruges 11 Id 50.31N 2.08 E
Frunze → Biškek 22 Je 42.54N 74.36 E
Frunze 18 Hd 40.06N 71.45 E
Frunzovka 15 Mb 47.20N 29.37 E
Fruška Gora 15 Cd 45.10N 19.35 E
Frutal 54 Ih 20.02S 48.55W
Frutigen 14 Bd 46.35N 7.40 E
Fry Canyon 46 Jh 37.38N 110.08W
Frýdek Mistek 10 Og 49.41N 18.22 E
Frylinckspan 37 Ce 26.46S 22.28 E
Ftéri 15 Ej 39.09N 21.33 E
Fua'amotu 65b Ac 21.15S 175.08W
Fua Mulaku Island 25a Bc 0.15S 73.30 E
Fu'an 27 Kf 27.10N 119.44 E
Fu-chien Sheng → Fujian Sheng=Fukien (EN) [2] 27 Kf 26.00N 118.00 E
Fuchskauten 10 Ef 50.40N 8.05 E
Fuchū [Jap.] 29 Cd 34.34N 133.14 E
Fuchū [Jap.] 29 Fd 35.41N 139.28 E
Fuchun-Jiang 28 Fi 30.15N 120.15 E
Fuchunjiang-Shuiku 28 Ej 29.29N 119.31 E
Fucino, Conca del- 14 Hj 42.01N 13.31 E
Fudai 29 Ga 40.01N 141.52 E
Fuding 27 Lf 27.19N 120.08 E
Fuengirola 13 Hh 36.32N 4.37W
Fuente Alto 56 Fd 33.37S 70.35W
Fuente del Maestre 13 Ff 38.32N 6.27W
Fuente-Obejuna 13 Gf 38.16N 5.25W
Fuentesaúco 13 Gc 41.14N 5.30W
Fuentes de Andalucia 13 Gg 37.28N 5.21W
Fuentes de Cantos 13 Ff 38.15N 6.18W
Fuerte 47 Cc 25.54N 109.22W
Fuerte, Isla- 49 Ii 9.23N 76.11W
Fuerte, Sierra del- 48 Hd 27.30N 102.45W
Fuerte Olimpo 56 Ib 21.02S 57.54W
Fuerteventura 30 Ff 28.20N 14.00W
Fuga 26 Hc 18.52N 121.22 E
Fugong 27 Gf 27.03N 98.57 E
Fugou 28 Cg 34.04N 114.23 E
Fugu 27 Jd 39.02N 111.03 E
Fuguo → Zhanhua 28 Ef 37.42N 118.08 E
Fuhai/Burultokay 27 Eb 47.06N 87.23 E
Fuhayrī, Wādī- 23 Hf 16.04N 52.11 E
Fu He 28 Dj 28.36N 116.04 E
Fuji 28 Og 35.09N 138.38 E
Fujian Sheng (Fu-chien Sheng)=Fukien (EN) [2] 27 Kf 26.00N 118.00 E
Fujieda 29 Fd 34.51N 138.15 E
Fuji-Gawa 29 Fd 35.07N 138.38 E
Fujin 27 Nb 47.15N 132.01 E
Fujinomiya 29 Fd 35.12N 138.38 E
Fujioka 29 Fc 36.15N 139.03 E
Fuji-San 21 Pf 35.26N 138.43 E
Fujisawa 29 Fd 35.21N 139.27 E
Fuji-yoshida 29 Fd 35.29N 138.47 E
Fukagawa 27 Pc 43.43N 142.03 E
Fūkah 24 Bg 31.04N 27.55 E
Fukang 27 Ec 44.10N 87.59 E
Fuka-Shima 29 Be 32.43N 131.56 E
Fukiage 29 Bf 31.30N 130.20 E
Fukien (EN)=Fu-chien Sheng → Fujian Sheng [2] 27 Kf 26.00N 118.00 E
Fukien (EN)=Fujian Sheng (Fu-chien Sheng) [2] 27 Kf 26.00N 118.00 E
Fukuchiyama 28 Mg 35.18N 135.07 E
Fukue 28 Jh 32.41N 128.50 E
Fukueichiao 27 Lf 25.19N 121.34 E
Fukue-Jima 28 Jh 32.41N 128.48 E
Fukui 27 Od 36.04N 136.13 E
Fukui Ken [2] 28 Ng 36.00N 136.20 E
Fukuma 29 Be 33.47N 130.28 E
Fukuoka 22 Pf 33.35N 130.24 E
Fukuoka Ken [2] 28 Kh 33.28N 130.45 E
Fukuroi 29 Ed 34.45N 137.54 E
Fukushima [Jap.] 27 Pd 37.45N 140.28 E
Fukushima [Jap.] 27 Pc 41.29N 140.15 E
Fukushima Ken [2] 28 Pf 37.25N 140.10 E
Fukuyama 27 Ne 34.29N 133.22 E
Fūlādī, Kūh-e- 23 Kc 34.38N 67.32 E
Fūlād Mahalleh 24 Od 36.02N 53.44 E
Fulanga 63d Cc 19.08S 178.34W
Fulda 5 Ge 51.25N 9.39 E
Fulda 10 Ff 50.33N 9.40 E
Fuliji 28 Dh 33.47N 116.59 E
Fulin → Hanyuan 27 Hf 29.25N 102.12 E
Fuling 27 If 29.40N 107.21 E
Fullerton 45 Hf 41.22N 97.58W
Fulton [Arg.] 55 Cm 37.25S 58.48W
Fulton [Il.-U.S.] 45 Kf 41.52N 90.11W
Fulton [Ky.-U.S.] 44 Cg 36.30N 88.53W
Fulton [Mo.-U.S.] 45 Kg 38.52N 91.57W
Fulton [N.Y.-U.S.] 44 Id 43.20N 76.26W
Fulufjället 8 Ec 61.33N 12.43 E
Fumaiolo 14 Gg 43.47N 12.04 E
Fumay 11 Kd 50.00N 4.42 E
Fumel 11 Gj 44.30N 0.58 E
Funabasi 28 Og 35.42N 139.59 E
Funabiki 29 Gc 37.26N 140.35 E
Funafuti 58 Ie 8.01S 178.00 E
Funafuti Atoll 57 Ie 8.31S 179.08 E
Funagata 29 Gb 38.42N 140.18 E
Funagata-Yama 29 Gb 38.27N 140.37 E
Funakoshi-Wan 29 Hb 39.25N 142.00 E
Funan 28 Ch 32.38N 115.35 E
Funäsdalen 7 Ce 62.32N 12.33 E
Funchal 31 Fe 32.38N 16.54W
Fundación 54 Da 10.29N 74.12W
Fundão 13 Ed 40.08N 7.30W
Fundy, Bay of- 38 Me 45.00N 66.00W
Funeral Peak 46 Gh 36.08N 116.37W
Fungalei 64h Bb 13.17S 176.07W
Funhalouro 37 Ed 23.05S 34.24 E
Funing [China] 27 Ig 23.39N 105.33 E
Funing [China] 28 Eh 33.48N 119.47 E
Funing [China] 28 Ee 39.56N 119.15 E
Funiu Shan 27 Je 33.40N 112.10 E
Funtua 34 Gc 11.32N 7.19 E
Fuping 28 Ce 38.49N 114.15 E
Fuqing 27 Kf 25.47N 119.24 E
Furancungo 37 Eb 14.54S 33.37 E
Furano 28 Qc 43.21N 142.23 E
Füren 29a Ca 44.17N 142.25 E
Furenai 29a Cb 42.43N 142.15 E
Füren-Ko 29a Db 43.20N 145.20 E
Fürg 24 Ph 28.18N 55.13 E
Fur Jiang 28 Hc 42.37N 125.33 E
Furmanov 7 Jh 57.16N 41.07 E
Furnas, Represa de- 54 Ih 21.20S 45.50W
Furnas, Serra das- 55 Fb 15.45S 53.20W
Furneaux Group 57 Fi 40.10S 148.05 E
Furnes/Veurne 11 Ic 51.04N 2.40 E
Furqlus 24 Ge 34.36N 37.05 E
Furriyānah 32 Ic 34.57N 8.34 E
Fürstenau 12 Jb 52.31N 7.43 E
Fürstenauer Berge 12 Jb 52.35N 7.45 E
Fürstenfeld 14 Kc 47.03N 16.05 E
Fürstenfeldbruck 10 Hh 48.11N 11.15 E
Fürstenlager 12 Ke 49.42N 8.38 E
Fürstenwalde 10 Kd 52.22N 14.04 E
Fürth [Ger.] 10 Gg 49.28N 11.00 E
Fürth [Ger.] 12 Ke 49.39N 8.47 E
Furth im Wald 10 Ig 49.18N 12.51 E
Furubira 29a Bb 43.16N 140.39 E
Furudal 7 Df 61.10N 15.08 E
Furukawa 27 Pd 38.34N 140.58 E
Furusund 8 He 59.40N 18.55 E
Fury and Hecla Strait 42 Jc 69.55N 84.00W
Fushan [China] 27 Ff 37.30N 121.15 E
Fushan [China] 28 Ag 35.58N 111.51 E
Fushë-Arëzi 15 Dg 42.04N 20.02 E
Fushë-Lura 15 Dh 41.48N 20.13 E
Fu Shui 28 Cj 29.52N 115.26 E
Fushun 22 Oe 41.46N 123.56 E
Fusong 27 Mc 42.20N 127.17 E
Füsselberg 12 Je 49.32N 7.14 E
Füssen 10 Gi 47.34N 10.42 E
Futa, Passo della- 14 Ff 44.05N 11.17 E
Futago-Yama 29 Be 33.35N 131.38 E
Futaoi-Jima 29 Bd 34.06N 130.47 E
Futog 15 Cd 45.15N 19.42 E
Futuna, Ile- 57 Jf 14.17S 178.09W
Fuwah 24 Dg 31.12N 30.33 E
Fuxian (Wafangdian) 27 Ld 39.38N 121.59 E
Fuxian Hu 27 Hg 24.30N 102.55 E
Fuxin 22 Oe 41.59N 121.38 E
Fuxin Monggolzu Zizhixian 28 Fc 42.06N 121.46 E
Fuyang 27 Ke 32.47N 115.46 E
Fuyang He 28 Dd 38.14N 116.05 E
Fuyang Zhan 28 Ch 32.56N 115.53 E
Fuyu [China] 27 Lb 45.10N 124.52 E
Fuyu [China] 27 Lb 47.48N 124.26 E
Fuyuan [China] 27 Lc 42.44N 124.57 E
Fuyuan [China] 27 Nb 48.21N 134.18 E
Fuyuan [China] 27 Hf 25.43N 104.20 E
Fuyun/Koktokay 22 Ke 47.13N 89.39 E
Füzesabony 10 Qi 47.45N 20.25 E
Fuzhou [China] 22 Ng 26.10N 119.20 E
Fuzhou [China] 27 Kf 27.58N 116.20 E
Fuzhou He 28 Fe 39.36N 121.35 E
Fyllas Bank (EN) 41 Gf 64.00N 53.00W
Fyn 5 Hd 55.20N 10.30 E
Fyn [2] 8 Di 55.20N 10.30 E
Fyne, Loch- 9 He 56.10N 5.20W
Fyresdal 7 Bg 59.11N 8.06 E
Fyresvatn 8 Ce 59.05N 8.10 E
Fzāra, Gara'et- 14 Bn 36.47N 7.30 E

G

Gaasbeek 12 Gd 50.48N 4.10 E
Gaasterland 12 Hb 52.54N 5.36 E
Gaasterland 12 Hb 52.53N 5.35 E
Gaasterland-Balk 12 Hb 52.54N 5.36 E
Gabaru Reef 64a Bb 7.53N 134.31 E
Gabas 11 Fk 43.46N 0.42W
Gabba' 35 Id 8.02N 50.08 E
Gabbs 46 Gg 38.52N 117.55W
Gabela 31 Ij 10.52S 14.23 E
Gabel'a (Kutkašen) 16 Oi 40.58N 47.52 E
Gabès, Gulf of-(EN)=Qābis, Khalīj- 30 Ie 34.00N 10.25 E
Gabon 36 Ab 0.25N 9.20 E
Gabon [1] 31 Ii 1.00S 11.45 E
Gaborone 31 Jk 24.40S 25.55 E
Gabras 35 Dc 10.16N 26.14 E
Gabriel Strait 42 Kd 61.50N 65.40W
Gabriel y Galán, Embalse de- 13 Fd 40.15N 6.15W
Gabrovo 15 Ig 42.52N 25.19 E
Gabrovo [2] 15 Ig 42.52N 25.19 E
Gacé 11 Gf 48.48N 0.18 E
Gachsārān 24 Ng 30.12N 50.47 E
Gackle 45 Gc 46.38N 99.09W
Gacko 14 Mg 43.10N 18.32 E
Gadag 25 Fe 15.25N 75.37 E
Gäddede 7 Dd 64.30N 14.09 E
Gadé 27 Ge 34.13N 99.29 E
Gadjač 16 Id 50.22N 34.01 E
Gádor, Sierra de- 13 Jh 36.55N 2.45W
Gadsden 43 Je 34.02N 86.02W
Gadūk, Gardaneh-ye- 24 Oe 35.55N 52.55 E
Gadzi 35 Be 4.47N 16.42 E
Gael Hamkes Bugt 41 Jd 74.00N 22.00W
Găeşti 15 Ie 44.43N 25.19 E
Gaeta 14 Hi 41.12N 13.35 E
Gaeta, Golfo di- 14 Hi 41.05N 13.30 E
Gaferut Island 57 Fd 9.14N 145.23 E
Gaffney 44 Gh 35.05N 81.39W
Gagan 63a Ba 5.14S 154.37 E
Gagarin 19 Dd 55.35N 35.01 E
Gagarin 18 Gd 40.40N 68.05 E
Gagévésouva, Pointe- 63b Ca 13.04S 166.32 E
Gaggenau 12 Kf 48.48N 8.20 E
Gagnef 7 Df 60.35N 15.04 E
Gagnoa 31 Gh 6.08N 5.56W
Gagnoa [3] 34 Dd 6.03N 6.00W
Gagnon 42 Kf 51.55N 68.10W
Gagra 19 Eg 43.17N 40.15 E
Gahkom 24 Ph 28.12N 55.50 E
Gahkom, Kūh-e- 24 Ph 28.10N 55.57 E
Gaiba, Laguna- 55 Dc 17.45S 57.43W
Gail 14 Hd 46.36N 13.53 E
Gaillac 11 Hk 43.54N 1.55 E
Gaillefontaine 12 De 49.39N 1.37 E
Gaillimh/Galway 6 Fe 53.16N 9.03W
Gaillimh/Galway [2] 9 Eh 53.20N 9.00W
Gaillon 12 De 49.10N 1.20 E
Gailtaler Alpen 14 Gd 46.40N 13.00 E
Gaiman 56 Gf 43.17S 65.29W
Găineşti 15 Ib 47.25N 25.55 E
Gainesville [Fl.-U.S.] 39 Kg 29.40N 82.20W
Gainesville [Ga.-U.S.] 43 Ke 34.18N 83.50W
Gainesville [Mo.-U.S.] 45 Jh 36.36N 92.26W
Gainesville [Tx.-U.S.] 43 He 33.37N 97.08W
Gainsborough 9 Mh 53.24N 0.46W
Gairdner, Lake- 57 Eh 31.35S 136.00 E
Gairloch 9 Hd 57.43N 5.40W
Gaizina Kalns/Gajzinkalns 8 Kh 56.50N 25.59 E
Gaj 19 Fe 51.31N 58.30 E
Gajny 19 Fc 60.20N 54.15 E
Gajsin 19 Cf 48.50N 29.27 E
Gajvoron 16 Fe 48.22N 29.52 E
Galaasija 18 Ee 39.52N 64.27 E
Gălăbovo 15 Ig 42.08N 25.51 E
Gala Golü 15 Ji 40.45N 26.12 E
Galaico, Macizo- 13 Eb 42.30N 7.20W
Galán, Cerro- 56 Gc 25.55S 66.52W
Galana 30 Li 3.09S 40.08 E
Galanta 10 Nh 48.12N 17.44 E
Galap 64a Bb 7.38N 134.39 E
Galápagos, Islas-/Colón, Archipiélago de-=Galapagos Islands (EN) 52 Gf 0.30S 90.30W
Galapagos Fracture Zone (EN) 3 Mi 0.00 100.00W
Galápagos Islands (EN)=Colon, Archipiélago de-/Galápagos, Islas- 52 Gf 0.30S 90.30W
Galapagos Islands (EN)=Galápagos, Islas-/Colón, Archipiélago de- 52 Gf 0.30S 90.30W
Galarza 55 Di 28.06S 56.41W
Galashiels 9 Kf 55.37N 2.49W
Galaţi [2] 15 Kd 45.33N 27.56 E
Galaţi 6 If 45.27N 28.03 E
Galatina 14 Mj 40.10N 18.10 E
Galatone 14 Mj 40.09N 18.04 E
Galatzó 13 Oe 39.38N 2.29 E
Galdar 32 Dd 28.09N 15.39W
Galdhøpiggen 7 Bf 61.37N 8.17 E
Galeana [Mex.] 48 Fb 30.07N 107.38W
Galeana [Mex.] 48 Ie 24.50N 100.04W
Galeh Dār 24 Oi 27.38N 52.42 E
Galela 58 Dd 1.50N 127.50 E
Galena [Ak.-U.S.] 40 Hd 64.44N 156.57W
Galena [Il.-U.S.] 45 Ke 42.25N 90.26W
Galeota Point 50 Fg 10.08N 60.59W
Galera, Punta- 56 Fe 39.59S 73.43W
Galera, Rio- 55 Bb 14.25S 60.07W
Galera Point 50 Fg 10.49N 60.55W
Galesburg 43 Ic 40.57N 90.22W
Galga 10 Pi 47.33N 19.43 E
Gal Gaduud [3] 35 Hd 5.00N 47.00 E
Galheirão, Rio- 55 Ja 12.23S 45.05W
Galheiros 55 Ia 13.18S 46.25W
Gali 16 Lh 42.36N 41.42 E
Galič 19 Ed 58.23N 42.21 E
Galič 16 De 49.06N 24.43 E
Galicea Mare 15 Ge 44.06N 23.18 E
Galicia 5 Fg 43.00N 8.00W
Galicia 13 Eb 43.00N 8.00W
Galicia (EN)=Galicija 5 If 49.50N 21.00 E
Galicia (EN)=Galicija [Eur.] 10 Qg 49.50N 21.00 E
Galicia (EN)=Galicja 10 Qg 49.50N 21.00 E
Galicia (EN)=Galicja 5 If 49.50N 21.00 E
Galicija [Eur.]=Galicia (EN) 10 Qg 49.50N 21.00 E
Galicija 10 Jg 49.00N 24.00 E
Galicija=Galicia (EN) 5 If 49.50N 21.00 E
Galicja=Galicia (EN) 5 If 49.50N 21.00 E
Galicja=Galicia (EN) 10 Qg 49.50N 21.00 E
Galilee, Lake- 59 Jd 22.20S 145.55 E
Galimy 20 Kd 62.19N 156.00 E
Galina Point 49 Id 18.24N 76.53W
Galion 44 Fe 40.44N 82.46W
Galion, Baie du- 51h Bb 14.44N 60.57W
Galiton 14 Cm 37.30N 8.52 E
Galiuro Mountains 46 Jj 32.40N 110.20W
Gâlka'yo 31 Lh 6.49N 47.23 E
Galkino 17 Ki 55.40N 62.55 E
Gallarate 14 Ce 45.40N 8.47 E
Gallatin 44 Dg 36.24N 86.27W
Gallatin Range 46 Jd 45.15N 111.05W
Gallatin River 46 Jd 45.56N 111.29W
Galle 22 Ki 6.02N 80.13 E
Gállego 13 Lc 41.39N 0.51W
Gallegos, Rio- 52 Jk 51.36S 68.59W
Gallinas, Punta- 52 Id 12.25N 71.40W
Gallinas Peak 45 Di 34.15N 105.45W
Gallipoli 14 Lj 40.03N 17.58 E
Gallipoli Peninsula (EN)=Gelibolu Yarimadası 15 Ji 40.20N 26.30 E
Gallipolis 44 Ff 38.49N 82.14W
Gällivare 6 Ib 67.08N 20.42 E
Galljaaral 18 Fd 40.02N 67.35 E
Gallo 13 Jd 40.48N 2.09W
Gällö 7 De 62.55N 15.14 E
Gallo, Capo- 14 Hl 38.15N 13.19 E
Gallo Mountains 45 Bi 34.00N 108.15W
Galloway 9 If 55.00N 4.25W
Galloway, Mull of- 9 Ig 54.38N 4.50W
Gallup 39 If 35.32N 108.44W
Gallur 13 Kc 41.52N 1.19W
Gallura 14 Dj 41.00N 9.15 E
Galmaarden/Gammerages 12 Fd 50.45N 3.58 E
Galole 36 Hc 1.30S 40.02 E
Galt 44 Gd 43.22N 80.19W
Gal Tardo 35 He 3.37N 45.58 E
Galtasen 8 Eg 57.48N 13.30 E
Galty Mountains/Na Gaibhlte 9 Ei 52.23N 8.11W
Galut 27 Hb 46.43N 100.08 E
Galveston 39 Jg 29.18N 94.48W
Galveston Bay 38 Jg 29.36N 94.57W
Galveston Island 45 Il 29.13N 94.55W
Gálvez 56 Hd 32.02S 61.13W
Galway/Gaillimh [2] 9 Eh 53.20N 9.00W
Galway/Gaillimh 6 Fe 53.16N 9.03W
Galway Bay/Cuan na Gaillimhe 5 Fe 53.10N 9.15W
Gamaches 12 De 49.59N 1.33 E
Gamagōri 29 Ed 34.49N 137.13 E
Gamarra 54 Db 8.19N 73.44W
Gamba [China] 27 Ef 28.17N 88.31 E
Gamba [Gabon] 36 Ac 2.37S 10.00 E
Gambaga 34 Ec 10.32N 0.26W
Gambela 31 Kh 8.15N 34.36 E
Gambell 40 Ed 63.46N 171.46W
Gambia 30 Fg 13.28N 16.34W
Gambia [1] 31 Fg 13.25N 16.00W
Gambie 34 Bc 13.28N 16.34W
Gambier, Iles-=Gambier Islands (EN) 57 Ng 23.09S 134.58W
Gambier Islands (EN)=Gambier, Iles- 57 Ng 23.09S 134.58W
Gambo 35 Ce 4.39N 22.16 E
Gamboma 36 Cc 1.53S 15.51 E
Gamboula 35 Be 4.08N 15.09 E
Gamda → Zamtang 27 He 32.23N 101.05 E
Gamelão 55 Db 15.29S 57.50W
Gamkonora, Gunung- 26 If 1.21N 127.31 E
Gamlakarleby/Kokkola 6 Ic 63.50N 23.07 E
Gamla Uppsala 8 Ge 59.54N 17.38 E
Gamleby 7 Dh 57.54N 16.24 E
Gamo Gofa [3] 35 Fd 5.45N 37.20 E
Gamua 64h Bb 13.15S 176.08W
Gamud 35 Fe 4.05N 38.06 E
Gamvik 7 Ga 71.03N 28.14 E
Ganāne, Webi-=Juba (EN) 30 Lh 0.15S 42.38 E
Gananoque 44 Ic 44.20N 76.10W
Ganāveh 24 Nh 29.32N 50.31 E
Gancedo 55 Bh 27.30S 61.42W
Gancevići 16 Ec 52.45N 26.29 E
Gand/Gent=Ghent (EN) 11 Jc 51.03N 3.43 E
Ganda 36 Be 12.59S 14.40 E
Gandadiwata, Bulu- 26 Gg 2.42S 119.27 E
Gandajika 36 Dd 6.45S 23.57 E
Gandak 25 Hc 25.39N 85.13 E
Gander 39 Ne 48.57N 54.34W
Ganderkesee 12 Ka 53.04N 8.33 E
Gandesa 13 Mc 41.03N 0.26 E
Gandhinagar 22 Jg 23.21N 72.40 E
Gāndhi Sāgar 25 Fd 24.30N 75.30 E
Gandia 13 Lf 38.58N 0.11W
Gandia-Grao de Gandia 13 Lf 38.59N 0.09W
Gandisê Shan 21 Kf 31.00N 83.00 E
Gandu 54 Kf 13.45S 39.30W
Ganetti 35 Eb 17.58N 31.13 E
Ganga=Ganges (EN) 21 Lg 23.20N 90.30 E
Gangaw 25 Id 22.10N 94.08 E
Gangca (Shaliuhe) 27 Hd 37.30N 100.14 E
Ganges 11 Jk 43.56N 3.42 E
Ganges (EN)=Ganga 21 Lg 23.20N 90.30 E
Ganges, Mouths of the- (EN) 21 Lg 23.20N 90.30 E
Gangi 14 Im 37.48N 14.12 E
Gango 36 Cd 9.48S 15.40 E
Gangtok 22 Kg 27.20N 88.37 E
Gangu 27 Ie 34.45N 105.12 E
Gangziyao 28 Cf 36.17N 114.06 E
Gan He 27 Mb 49.12N 125.14 E
Ganhe 27 La 50.43N 123.00 E
Gani 26 Ig 0.47S 128.13 E
Ganjgah 24 Md 37.42N 48.16 E
Gan Jiang 21 Ng 29.12N 116.00 E
Ganjig → Horqin Zuoyi Houqi 27 Lc 42.57N 122.14 E
Gannan 27 Lb 47.53N 123.26 E
Gannat 11 Jh 46.06N 3.12 E
Gannett Peak 38 Ie 43.10N 109.40W
Gansbaai 37 Bf 34.35S 19.22 E
Gansu Sheng (Kan-su Sheng)=Kansu (EN) [2] 27 Hd 38.00N 102.00 E
Ganta 34 Dd 7.14N 8.59W
Gantang → Taiping 28 Ei 30.18N 118.07 E
Ganyu (Qingkou) 28 Eg 34.50N 119.07 E
Ganzhou 22 Ng 25.49N 114.56 E
Gao [3] 34 Eb 18.15N 1.00W
Gao [Mali] 31 Hg 16.15N 0.01 E
Gao [Niger] 34 Gb 15.25N 5.45 E
Gao'an 27 Kf 28.27N 115.24 E
Gaobeidian → Xincheng 28 Ce 39.20N 115.50 E
Gaocheng 28 Ce 38.02N 114.50 E
Gaolan (Shidongsi) 27 Hd 36.23N 103.55 E
Gaoliangjian → Hongze 27 Ke 33.10N 119.58 E
Gaoligong Shan 27 Gf 25.45N 98.45 E
Gaolou Ling 27 Ig 24.47N 106.48 E
Gaomi 28 Ef 36.23N 119.45 E
Gaoping 27 Jd 35.46N 112.55 E
Gaoqing (Tianzhen) 28 Df 37.10N 117.50 E
Gaotai 27 Gd 39.20N 99.58 E
Gaotingzhen → Daishan 28 Gi 30.15N 122.13 E
Gaoua 34 Ec 10.20N 3.11W
Gaoual 34 Cc 11.45N 13.12W
Gaoyang 28 Ce 38.42N 115.47 E
Gaoyi 28 Cf 37.37N 114.37 E
Gaoyou 28 Eh 32.46N 119.27 E
Gaoyou Hu 27 Ke 32.50N 119.15 E
Gaozhou 27 Jg 21.56N 110.47 E
Gap 11 Mj 44.34N 6.05 E
Gar 27 Ce 32.12N 79.57 E
Gara, Lough-/Loch Ui Ghadra 9 Eh 53.55N 8.30W
Gara'ad 35 Hd 6.54N 49.20 E
Garabato 55 Bi 28.56S 60.09W
Garachiné 49 Hi 8.04N 78.22W
Garachiné, Punta- 49 Hi 8.06N 78.25W
Gara Dragoman 15 Fg 42.55N 22.56 E
Ga'raet el Oubeira 14 Cn 36.50N 8.23 E
Gara Kostenec 15 Gg 42.18N 23.52 E
Garalo 34 Dc 11.00N 7.26W
Gara Muleta 35 Gd 9.05N 41.43 E
Garanhuns 53 Mf 8.54S 36.29W
Garapan 64b Ba 15.12N 145.43 E
Garapuava 55 Ic 16.06S 46.33W
Garavuti 18 Gf 37.36N 68.29 E
Garba 35 Cd 9.12N 20.30 E
Garbahārrey 35 Ge 3.20N 42.17 E
Garberville 46 Df 40.06N 123.48W
Gārbosh, Kūh-e- 24 Nf 32.36N 50.04 E
Garça 55 Hf 22.14S 49.37W
Garças, Rio das- 55 Fb 15.54S 52.16W
Garcias 55 Fe 20.34S 52.13W
Gard [3] 11 Jj 44.00N 4.00 E
Gard 11 Kk 43.51N 4.37 E
Garda 14 Ee 45.34N 10.42 E
Garda, Lago di-=Garda, Lake- (EN) 5 Hf 45.35N 10.35 E
Garda, Lake- (EN)=Garda, Lago di- 5 Hf 45.35N 10.35 E
Gardabani 16 Ni 41.29N 45.05 E
Garde, Cap de- 14 Bn 36.58N 7.47 E
Gardelegen 10 Hd 52.32N 11.22 E
Garden City [Ga.-U.S.] 44 Gi 32.06N 81.09W
Garden City [Ks.-U.S.] 43 Gd 37.58N 100.53W
Garden Grove 46 Gj 33.46N 117.57W
Garden Peninsula 44 Dc 45.40N 86.35W
Gardermoen 8 Dd 60.13N 11.06 E
Gardey 55 Cm 37.17S 59.21W
Gardēz 23 Kc 33.37N 69.07 E
Gardiner 46 Jd 45.02N 110.42W
Gardiner Range 59 Fc 19.15S 128.50 E
Gardner → Nikumaroro Atoll 57 Je 4.40S 174.32W
Gardner Pinnacles 57 Kb 25.00N 167.55W
Gardno, Jezioro- 10 Nb 54.43N 17.05 E
Gardone Riviera 14 Ee 45.37N 10.34 E
Gardždai/Gargždaj 7 Ei 55.43N 21.24 E
Gareloi 40a Cb 51.47N 178.48W
Garessio 14 Cf 44.12N 8.02 E
Garfagnana 14 Ef 44.05N 10.30 E
Gargaliánoi 15 El 37.04N 21.38 E
Gargano 5 Hg 41.50N 16.00 E
Gargano, Testa del- 14 Ki 41.35N 16.12 E
Gargantua, Cape- 44 Eb 47.36N 85.02W
Gargždaj/Gargždai 7 Ei 55.43N 21.24 E
Gari 19 Gd 59.28N 62.25 E
Garibaldi 55 Gi 29.15S 51.32W
Garibaldi, Mount- 46 Db 49.51N 123.01W
Garies 37 Bf 30.30S 18.00 E
Garigliano 14 Hi 41.13N 13.45 E
Garimpo 55 Ed 18.41S 54.50W
Garissa 31 Ki 0.28S 39.38 E

Index Symbols

[1] Independent Nation
[2] State, Region
[3] District, County
[4] Municipality
[5] Colony, Dependency
Continent
Physical Region
Historical or Cultural Region
Mount, Mountain
Volcano
Hill
Mountains, Mountain Range
Hills, Escarpment
Plateau, Upland
Pass, Gap
Plain, Lowland
Delta
Salt Flat
Valley, Canyon
Crater, Cave
Karst Features
Depression
Polder
Desert, Dunes
Forest, Woods
Heath, Steppe
Oasis
Cape, Point
Coast, Beach
Cliff
Peninsula
Isthmus
Sandbank
Island
Atoll
Rock, Reef
Islands, Archipelago
Rocks, Reefs
Coral Reef
Well, Spring
Geyser
River, Stream
Waterfall Rapids
River Mouth, Estuary
Lake
Salt Lake
Intermittent Lake
Reservoir
Swamp, Pond
Canal
Glacier
Ice Shelf, Pack Ice
Ocean
Sea
Gulf, Bay
Strait, Fjord
Lagoon
Bank
Seamount
Tablemount
Ridge
Shelf
Basin
Escarpment, Sea Scarp
Fracture
Trench, Abyss
National Park, Reserve
Point of Interest
Recreation Site
Cave, Cavern
Historic Site
Ruins
Wall, Walls
Church, Abbey
Temple
Scientific Station
Airport
Port
Lighthouse
Mine
Tunnel
Dam, Bridge

Garkida 34 Hc 10.25N 12.34 E
Garland 45 Hj 32.54N 96.39W
Garlasco 14 Ce 45.12N 8.55 E
Garliava/Garljava 8 Jj 54.46N 23.55 E
Garljava/Garliava 8 Jj 54.46N 23.55 E
Garm 18 He 39.02N 70.18 E
Garmisch-Partenkirchen 10 Hi 47.30N 11.06 E
Garmsar 24 Oe 35.20N 52.13 E
Garnet Bank (EN) 55 Hk 33.05S 49.25W
Garnet Range 46 Ic 46.45N 113.15W
Garnett 45 Ig 38.17N 95.14W
Garonne 5 Ff 45.02N 0.36W
Garonne, Canal latéral à la- 11 Fj 44.34N 0.09W
Garopába 55 Hi 28.04S 48.40W
Garoua 31 Ih 9.18N 13.24 E
Garoua Boulaï 35 Ad 5.53N 14.33 E
Garoubi 34 Fc 13.07N 2.18 E
Garōwe 31 Lh 8.25N 48.33 E
Garpenberg 8 Gd 60.19N 16.12 E
Garphyttan 8 Fe 59.19N 14.56 E
Garrel 12 Kb 52.57N 8.01 E
Garreru 64a Bc 7.20N 134.33 E
Garri, Kūh-e- 24 Mf 33.59N 48.25 E
Garrigues 11 Kj 44.10N 4.30 E
Garrison 45 Fc 47.40N 101.25W
Garron Point/An Gearran 9 Hf 55.05N 5.58W
Garrovillas 13 Fe 39.43N 6.33W
Garruchos 55 Ei 28.11S 55.39W
Garry 9 Je 56.45N 3.45W
Garry Bay 42 Ic 69.00N 85.10W
Garry Lake 38 Jc 66.00N 100.00W
Garsen 36 Hc 2.16S 40.07 E
Gartar/Qianning 27 He 30.27N 101.29 E
Gartempe 11 Gh 46.47N 0.50 E
Gartog → Markam 27 Gf 29.32N 98.33 E
Garut 26 Eh 7.13S 107.54 E
Garuva 55 Hh 26.01S 48.51W
Garvie Mountains 62 Cf 45.30S 168.50 E
Garwa 25 Gd 24.11N 83.49 E
Garwolin 10 Re 51.54N 21.37 E
Gary 43 Jc 41.36N 87.20W
Garyarsa 27 De 31.40N 80.26 E
Garzê 27 Ge 31.42N 99.58 E
Garzón [Col.] 54 Cc 2.13N 75.38W
Garzón [Ur.] 56 Jd 34.36S 54.33W
Gasan-Kuli 19 Fh 37.29N 53.59 E
Gascogne = Gascony (EN) 11 Gk 43.30N 0.10 E
Gasconade River 45 Kg 38.40N 91.33W
Gascony (EN) = Gascogne 11 Gk 43.30N 0.10 E
Gascoyne Junction 59 De 25.03S 115.12 E
Gascoyne River 57 Cg 24.52S 113.37 E
Gasefjord 41 Je 70.00N 27.30W
Gaseland 41 Jd 70.20N 29.00W
Gash 30 Kg 16.48N 35.51 E
Gas Hu 27 Fd 38.08N 90.45 E
Gashua 31 Ig 12.52N 11.03 E
Gaspar Strait (EN)=Kelasa, Selat- 26 Eg 2.40S 107.15 E
Gaspé 39 Me 48.50N 64.29W
Gaspé, Cap de- 42 Lg 48.45N 64.10W
Gaspé, Péninsule de-= Gaspe Peninsula (EN) 38 Me 48.30N 65.00W
Gaspe Peninsula (EN)= Gaspé, Péninsule de- 38 Me 48.30N 65.00W
Gassan 29 Gb 38.34N 140.01 E
Gassol 34 Hd 8.32N 10.28 E
Gaston, Lake- 44 Ig 36.35N 78.00W
Gastonia 43 Kd 35.16N 81.11W
Gastoúni 15 El 37.51N 21.15 E
Gastre 56 Gf 42.17S 69.14W
Gästrikland 8 Gd 60.30N 16.30 E
Gata, Akrōtērion- 24 Ee 34.34N 33.02 E
Gata, Cabo de- 5 Fh 36.43N 2.12W
Gata, Sierra de- 13 Fd 40.15N 6.45W
Gātaia 15 Ed 45.26N 21.26 E
Gatčina 19 Dd 59.34N 30.09 E
Gate 45 Fh 36.51N 100.01W
Gate City 44 Fg 36.38N 82.37W
Gateshead 9 Lg 54.58N 1.37W
Gateshead 42 Hb 70.35N 100.15W
Gathemo 12 Bf 48.46N 0.58W
Gâtinais 11 If 48.00N 2.20 E
Gâtine, Hauteurs de- 11 Fh 46.38N 0.38W
Gatineau, Rivière- 42 Jg 45.27N 75.42W
Gatlinburg 44 Fh 35.43N 83.31W
Gato, Cumbres del- 48 Fd 27.00N 106.35W
Gattinara 14 Ce 45.37N 8.22 E
Gatún 49 Hi 9.16N 79.55W
Gatún, Lago-=Gatun Lake (EN) 47 Ig 9.12N 79.55W
Gatun Lake (EN)=Gatún, Lago- 47 Ig 9.12N 79.55W
Gatvand 24 Mf 32.15N 48.50 E
Gatwick Airport 12 Bc 51.08N 0.12W
Gaucín 13 Gh 36.31N 5.19W
Gauhati → Guwāhāti 22 Lg 26.11N 91.44 E
Gauiena/Gaujiena 8 Lg 57.25N 26.28 E
Gauja 7 Fh 57.10N 24.16 E
Gaujiena/Gauiena 8 Lg 57.25N 26.28 E
Gaula [Nor.] 8 Da 63.21N 10.14 E
Gaula [Nor.] 8 Ac 61.22N 5.41 E
Gauldalen 8 Db 63.00N 11.00 E
Gauley River 44 Gf 38.10N 81.12W
Gau-Odernheim 12 Ke 49.46N 8.12 E
Gaurdak 19 Gh 37.49N 66.01 E
Gausdal 8 Cc 61.20N 9.55 E
Gausta 7 Bg 59.50N 8.39 E
Gāvbandī 24 Oi 27.12N 53.04 E
Gāvbūs, Kūh-e- 24 Oi 27.10N 54.00 E
Gavdhopoúla 15 Go 34.56N 24.00 E
Gávdhos 5 Ii 34.50N 24.05 E
Gāveh 24 Le 35.00N 46.58 E
Gavere 12 Fd 50.56N 3.40 E
Gavkhūnī, Bāṭlāq-e- 24 Of 32.06N 52.52 E
Gāv Kosh 24 Le 34.00N 48.00 E
Gävle 6 Hc 60.40N 17.10 E
Gävleborg [2] 7 Df 61.30N 16.15 E
Gävlebukten 8 Gd 60.40N 17.20 E
Gavorrano 14 Eh 42.55N 10.54 E
Gavri 8 Lh 56.49N 27.58 E
Gavrilov-Jam 7 Jh 57.19N 39.51 E
Gāw Koshi 23 Id 28.38N 57.12 E
Gawler 59 Hf 34.37S 138.44 E
Gawler Ranges 57 Eh 32.30S 136.00 E
Gaxun Nur 21 Me 42.25N 101.00 E
Gaya [India] 22 Kg 24.47N 85.00 E
Gaya [Niger] 34 Fc 11.53N 3.27 E
Gaya He 28 Jc 42.58N 129.52 E
Gaylord 44 Ec 45.02N 84.40W
Gayndah 59 Ke 25.37S 151.36 E
Gaz 24 Nf 32.48N 51.37 E
Gaza [3] 37 Ed 23.30S 33.00 E
Gaz-Ačak 19 Gg 41.11N 61.27 E
Gazalkent 18 Gd 41.33N 69.46 E
Gazaoua 34 Gc 13.32N 7.55 E
Gazelle, Récif de la- 63b Be 20.11S 165.27 E
Gaziantep 22 Ff 37.05N 37.22 E
Gaziemir 15 Kk 38.19N 27.10 E
Gazimağusa = Famagusta (EN) 23 Dc 35.07N 33.57 E
Gazipaşa 24 Ed 36.17N 32.20 E
Gazli 19 Gg 40.09N 63.23 E
Gbarnga 31 Gh 7.00N 9.29W
Gboko 34 Gd 7.21N 8.58 E
Gbon 34 Dd 9.50N 6.27W
Gdańsk [2] 10 Ob 54.25N 18.40 E
Gdańsk=Danzig (EN) 6 He 54.23N 18.40 E
Gdansk, Gulf of- (EN)= Gdanska, Zatoka- 5 He 54.40N 19.15 E
Gdov 7 Gg 58.47N 27.54 E
Gdynia 6 He 54.32N 18.33 E
Gearhart Mountain 46 Ee 42.30N 120.53W
Gêba 34 Bc 11.58N 15.00W
Gebe, Pulau- 26 Ig 0.05S 129.20 E
Gebze 24 Cb 40.48N 29.25 E
Gecha 35 Fd 7.29N 35.25 E
Geçitkale 25 Ee 35.15N 33.45 E
Gedi 36 Hc 3.18S 40.01 E
Gedinne 12 Ge 49.59N 4.56 E
Gediz 24 Cc 39.02N 29.25 E
Gedo 35 Ge 2.20N 41.20 E
Gedo [3] 35 Ge 3.00N 42.00 E
Gedo 35 Fd 9.00N 37.29 E
Gedser, Sydfalster- 7 Ci 54.35N 11.57 E
Gedser Odde 8 Dj 54.34N 11.59 E
Geel 11 Kc 51.10N 5.00 E
Geelong 58 Fh 38.08S 144.21 E
Geelvink Channel 59 Ce 28.30S 114.10 E
Geer 12 Hd 50.51N 5.42 E
Geeste 12 Jb 52.36N 7.16 E
Geesthacht 10 Gc 53.26N 10.22 E
Gê'gyai 27 De 32.29N 80.52 E
Ge Hu 28 Ei 31.36N 119.51 E
Geidam 34 Hc 12.53N 11.56 E
Geigar 35 Ec 11.59N 32.46 E
Geihoku 29 Cd 34.44N 132.17 E
Geikie 42 He 57.48N 103.46W
Geilo 7 Bf 60.31N 8.12 E
Geiranger 8 Bb 62.06N 7.12 E
Geisenheim 12 Je 49.59N 7.58 E
Geislingen an der Steige 10 Fh 48.37N 9.51 E
Geita 36 Fc 2.52S 32.10 E
Geithus 7 Bg 59.57N 9.59 E
Geiyo-Shotō 29 Cd 34.15N 132.45 E
Gejiu 22 Mg 23.22N 103.14 E
Gel [Sud.] 30 Jh 7.46N 29.36 E
Gel [Sud.] 35 Ed 6.08N 31.17 E
Gela 14 Im 37.04N 14.15 E
Gela, Golfo di- 14 Im 37.05N 14.10 E
Geladi 35 Hd 6.57N 46.25 E
Geldenaken/Jodoigne 12 Gd 50.43N 4.52 E
Gelderland [3] 12 Hb 52.10N 5.50 E
Geldermalsen 12 Hc 51.53N 5.19 E
Geldern 10 Ce 51.31N 6.20 E
Geldrop 12 Hc 51.25N 5.33 E
Geleen 11 Ld 50.58N 5.52 E
Gelembé 15 Kj 39.10N 27.50 E
Gelemso 35 Gd 8.48N 40.32 E
Gelendžik 19 Dg 44.33N 38.06 E
Gelengdeng 35 Bc 10.56N 15.32 E
Gelgaudiškis 8 Ji 55.02N 22.58 E
Gelibolu 24 Bb 40.24N 26.40 E
Gelibolu Yarimadası = Gallipoli Peninsula (EN) 15 Ji 40.20N 26.30 E
Gélise 11 Gj 44.11N 0.17 E
Gellinsör 35 Hd 6.24N 46.46 E
Gelnhausen 10 Ff 50.12N 9.11 E
Gelsenkirchen 10 De 51.31N 7.06 E
Gemena 31 Ih 3.15N 19.46 E
Gemerek 24 Gc 39.11N 36.05 E
Gemert 12 Hc 51.33N 5.41 E
Gemi, Jabal- 35 Ed 9.01N 34.09 E
Gemlik 24 Cb 40.26N 29.09 E
Gemlik Körfezi 24 Cb 40.25N 28.55 E
Gemona del Friuli 14 Hd 46.16N 13.09 E
Gemünden (Felda) 12 Ld 50.42N 9.03 E
Gemünden (Wohra) 12 Kd 50.58N 8.58 E
Gemünden am Main 10 Ff 50.03N 9.42 E
Genale 30 Lh 0.15S 42.38 E
Genç 24 Ic 38.46N 40.35 E
Gendringen 12 Ic 51.52N 6.23 E
Gendringen-Ulft 12 Ic 51.54N 6.24 E
Genemuiden 12 Ib 52.37N 6.02 E
General Acha 56 He 37.23S 64.36W
General Alvear [Arg.] 56 Gd 34.58S 67.42W
General Alvear [Arg.] 56 He 36.03S 60.01W
General Arenales 55 Bl 34.18S 61.18W
General Artigas 55 Dh 26.53S 56.17W
General Belgrano 56 Ie 35.46S 58.30W
General Belgrano Station 66 Af 77.50S 38.00W
General Bernardo O'Higgins 66 Re 63.19S 57.54W
General Bravo 48 Je 25.48N 99.10W
General Cabrera 56 Hd 32.48S 63.52W
General Capdevila 55 Bh 27.26S 61.28W
General Carneiro 55 Gh 26.28S 51.25W
General Carrera, Lago- 52 Ij 46.30S 72.00W
General Cepeda 48 Ie 25.23N 101.27W
General Conesa [Arg.] 55 Dm 36.30S 57.20W
General Conesa [Arg.] 56 Hf 40.06S 64.26W
General Enrique Martinez 55 Fk 33.12S 53.50W
General Galarza 55 Ck 32.43S 59.24W
General Güemes 56 Hb 24.40S 65.00W
General Guide 56 Ie 36.40S 57.46W
General José de San Martin 55 Ch 26.33S 59.21W
General Juan Madariaga 56 Ie 37.00S 57.09W
General La Madrid 56 He 37.16S 61.17W
General Lavalle 56 Ie 36.24S 56.58W
General Manuel Belgrano, Cerro- 52 Jh 29.01S 67.49W
General O'Brien 55 Bl 34.54S 60.45W
General Pico 56 He 35.40S 63.44W
General Pinedo 56 Hc 27.19S 61.17W
General Pinto 55 Bl 34.46S 61.53W
General Pirán 55 Dm 37.16S 57.45W
General Roca 56 Ge 39.02S 67.35W
General Salgado 56 Ge 20.39S 50.22W
General Santos 22 Oi 6.05N 125.10 E
General Sarmiento 55 Cl 34.33S 58.43W
General Terán 48 Je 25.16N 99.41W
General-Toševo 15 Lf 43.42N 28.02 E
General Treviño 48 Jd 26.14N 99.29W
General Trias 48 Fc 28.21N 106.22W
General Vargas 55 Ei 29.42S 54.40W
General Viamonte 55 Bl 35.01S 61.01W
General Villegas 56 He 35.02S 63.01W
Genesee River 44 Id 43.16N 77.36W
Geneseo 44 Id 42.46N 77.49W
Geneva [Al.-U.S.] 44 Ej 31.02N 85.52W
Geneva [Nb.-U.S.] 45 Hf 40.32N 97.36W
Geneva [N.Y.-U.S.] 44 Id 42.53N 76.59W
Geneva (EN) = Genève 6 Gf 46.10N 6.10 E
Geneva, Lake- (EN) = Léman, Lac- 5 Gf 46.25N 6.30 E
Genève 14 Ad 46.10N 6.15 E
Genève = Geneva (EN) 6 Gf 46.10N 6.10 E
Genevois 11 Mh 46.00N 6.10 E
Genhe → Ergun Zuoqi 22 Od 50.47N 121.32 E
Geni 35 Ed 8.31N 33.10 E
Geničesk 19 Df 46.12N 34.48 E
Genil 13 Gg 37.42N 5.19W
Genk 11 Ld 50.58N 5.30 E
Genkai-Nada 29 Ae 33.45N 130.00 E
Gennargentu 5 Gg 40.00N 9.20 E
Gennep 12 Hc 51.42N 5.59 E
Genoa (EN) = Genova 6 Gg 44.25N 8.57 E
Genoa, Gulf of- (EN) = Genova, Golfo di- 5 Gg 44.10N 8.55 E
Genova = Genoa (EN) 6 Gg 44.25N 8.57 E
Genova, Golfo di- = Genoa, Gulf of- (EN) 5 Gg 44.10N 8.55 E
Genova-Nervi 14 Df 44.23N 9.02 E
Genova-Voltri 14 Cf 44.26N 8.45 E
Genovesa, Isla- 54a Ba 0.20N 89.58W
Gent/Gand=Ghent (EN) 11 Jc 51.03N 3.43 E
Gentbrugge, Gent- 12 Fc 51.03N 3.45 E
Gent-Gentbrugge 12 Fc 51.03N 3.45 E
Genthin 10 Id 52.24N 12.10 E
Gent-Sint-Amandsberg 12 Fc 51.04N 3.45 E
Genū, Kūhhā-ye- 23 Id 27.25N 56.09 E
Genyem 26 Lg 2.46S 140.12 E
Genzano di Lucania 14 Kj 40.51N 16.02 E
Genzano di Roma 14 Fi 41.42N 11.41 E
Geographe Bay 57 Ch 33.35S 115.15 E
Geographe Channel 59 Cd 24.40S 113.20 E
Geographical Society Øer 41 Jd 72.40N 22.20W
Geokčaj 16 Oi 40.40N 47.42 E
Geok-Tepe 19 Fh 38.10N 57.58 E
Geomagnetic Pole (1975) (EN) 66 Hf 78.40S 109.33 E
Georga, Zemlja- 21 Ga 80.30N 49.00 E
George 38 Md 58.30N 66.00W
George 37 Cf 33.58S 22.24 E
George, Lake- [Austl.] 59 Jg 35.05S 149.25 E
George, Lake- [Fl.-U.S.] 44 Gk 29.17N 81.36W
George, Lake- [Ug.] 36 Fc 0.00 30.12 E
George, Lake- [U.S.] 44 Kd 43.35N 73.35W
George Gill Range 59 Gd 24.15S 131.35 E
Georges Bank (EN) 43 Nc 41.15N 67.30W
George Sound 62 Bf 44.50S 167.20 E
George Town [Austl.] 58 Fi 41.06S 146.50 E
George Town [Cay.Is.] 47 He 19.18N 81.23W
George Town [Indon.] 22 Mi 5.25N 100.20 E
George Town [Tx.-U.S.] 45 Hk 30.38N 97.41W
Georgetown [Austl.] 58 Ff 18.18S 143.33 E
Georgetown [Bah.] 49 Jb 23.30N 75.46W
Georgetown [De.-U.S.] 44 Jf 38.42N 75.23W
Georgetown [Gam.] 31 Fg 13.32N 14.46W
Georgetown [Guy.] 53 Ke 6.48N 58.10W
Georgetown [Ky.-U.S.] 44 Ef 38.13N 84.33W
Georgetown [Oh.-U.S.] 44 Ff 38.52N 83.54W
Georgetown [S.C.-U.S.] 43 Le 33.23N 79.18W
Georgetown [St.Hel.] 31 Fj 7.56S 14.25W
Georgetown [St.Vin.] 50 Ff 13.16N 61.08W
George V Coast 66 Je 68.30S 147.30 E
George VI Sound 66 Qf 71.00S 68.00W
George West 45 Gl 28.20N 98.07W
Georgia [2] 43 Ke 32.50N 83.15W
Georgia (EN) 5 Kg 42.00N 44.00 E
Georgia (EN) = Sakartvelo 19 Eg 42.00N 44.00 E
Georgia, Strait of 42 Fg 49.00N 123.20W
Georgia del Sur/South Georgia 66 Ad 54.15S 36.45W
Georgian Bay 38 Ke 45.15N 80.50W
Georgijevka 19 Hg 43.02N 74.43 E
Georgijevka 19 If 49.19N 81.35 E
Georgijevsk 16 Mg 44.09N 43.28 E
Georgina River 57 Eg 23.30S 139.47 E
Georgsmarienhütte 10 Ed 52.16N 8.02 E
Gera 10 Ge 51.08N 10.56 E
Gera 10 If 50.52N 12.05 E
Geraardsbergen/Grammont 12 Fd 50.46N 3.52 E
Gerais, Chapadão dos- 55 Jc 17.40S 45.35W
Geral, Serra- [Braz.] 55 Gi 29.10S 50.15W
Geral, Serra- [Braz.] 52 Kh 26.30S 50.30W
Geral, Serra- [Braz.] 55 Gf 23.54S 50.46W
Geral da Serra, Coxilha- 55 Ej 30.20S 55.15W
Geral de Goiás, Serra- 52 Lg 13.00S 46.15W
Geraldine 62 Df 44.05S 171.15 E
Geral do Paraná, Serra- 55 Ib 14.45S 47.30W
Geraldton [Austl.] 58 Cg 28.46S 114.36 E
Geraldton [Ont.-Can.] 42 Ig 49.44N 86.57W
Gérardmer 11 Mf 48.04N 6.53 E
Gerāsh 24 Pi 27.40N 54.06 E
Gerbiči, Gora- 20 Fc 66.39N 105.02 E
Gerca 15 Ja 48.10N 26.17 E
Gercüş 24 Id 37.34N 41.23 E
Gerecse 10 Oi 47.41N 18.29 E
Gerede 24 Eb 40.52N 32.39 E
Gerede 24 Eb 40.48N 32.12 E
Gerês, Serra do- 13 Ec 41.48N 8.00W
Gereshk 23 Jc 31.48N 64.34 E
Gérgal 13 Jg 37.07N 2.33W
Gering 45 Ef 41.50N 103.40W
Gerlachovský štít 10 Qg 49.12N 20.09 E
Gerlogubi 35 Hd 6.56N 45.03 E
Gerlos 14 Gc 47.14N 12.02 E
Gerlovo 15 Kf 43.03N 27.35 E
German Democratic Republic = Germany 6 Ge 51.00N 10.00 E
Germania 55 Al 34.34S 62.03W
Germania Land 41 Kc 76.50N 20.00W
Germany, Federal Republic of = Germany 6 Ge 51.00N 10.00 E
Germencik 15 Kl 37.51N 27.37 E
Germersheim 12 Ke 49.13N 8.22 E
Germī 23 Hc 33.32N 54.58 E
Germi 24 Mc 39.01N 48.03 E
Germiston 37 De 26.15S 28.05 E
Gernsbach 12 Kf 48.46N 8.19 E
Gernsheim 12 Ke 49.45N 8.29 E
Gero 28 Ng 35.48N 137.14 E
Gerolstein 12 Id 50.13N 6.40 E
Gerona [3] 13 Ob 42.10N 2.40 E
Gerona/Girona 13 Oc 41.59N 2.49 E
Gerpinnes 12 Gd 50.20N 4.31 E
Gers 11 Gj 44.09N 0.39 E
Gers [3] 11 Gk 43.40N 0.30 E
Gersprenz 12 Le 49.59N 9.04 E
Gêrzê 27 De 32.20N 84.04 E
Gerze 24 Fb 41.48N 35.12 E
Gescher 12 Jc 51.57N 7.00 E
Geseke 12 Kc 51.39N 8.31 E
Geser 26 Jg 3.53S 130.54 E
Gesunda 8 Fd 60.54N 14.32 E
Gesunden 8 Fa 63.10N 15.55 E
Geta 7 Ef 60.23N 19.50 E
Getafe 13 Id 40.18N 3.43W
Gete 12 Ld 50.55N 5.08 E
Getinge 7 Ch 56.49N 12.44 E
Gettysburg 45 Gd 45.01N 99.57W
Gettysburg Seamount (EN) 32 Eb 36.32N 11.37W
Getúlio Vargas 55 Fh 27.50S 52.16W
Getz Ice Shelf 66 Nf 74.15S 125.00W
Geul 12 Hd 50.40N 5.43 E
Gévaudan 11 Jj 44.27N 3.30 E
Gevelsberg 12 Jc 51.19N 7.20 E
Gevgelija 15 Fh 41.08N 22.31 E
Gévora 13 Ff 38.53N 6.57W
Gevsjön 8 Ea 63.25N 12.40 E
Gewane 35 Gc 10.10N 40.39 E
Gex 11 Mh 46.20N 6.04 E
Gexianzhuang → Qinghe 28 Cf 37.03N 115.39 E
Geyersberg 10 Fg 49.50N 9.30 E
Geyik Dağı 24 Ed 36.54N 32.10 E
Geyikli 15 Jj 39.48N 26.12 E
Geyser, Banc du- 37 Hb 12.25S 46.25 E
Geysir 5 Dc 64.19N 20.18W
Geyve 24 Db 40.30N 30.18 E
Ghabāri, Darb al- 24 Cj 25.10N 29.50 E
Ghadāmis 31 He 30.08N 9.30 E
Ghadduwah 33 Bd 26.26N 14.18 E
Ghaghara 21 Kg 24.52N 84.55 E
Ghaghe 63a Db 7.23S 158.12 E
Ghallah, Wādī al- 30 Jg 10.25N 27.32 E
Ghamrah, Wādī al- 24 Hj 25.47N 38.45 E
Ghana [1] 31 Gh 8.00N 2.00W
Ghanzi 31 Jk 21.42S 21.38 E
Ghanzi [3] 37 Cd 22.00S 23.00 E
Ghār ad Dimā' 14 Cn 36.27N 8.26 E
Gharaqābād 24 Me 35.06N 49.50 E
Gharbī, Al Hajar al- 24 Qj 24.10N 56.15 E
Gharbīyah, Aṣ Ṣaḥrā' al-= Western Desert (EN) 30 Jf 27.30N 28.00 E
Ghardaia 31 He 32.29N 3.40 E
Ghārib, Jabal- 33 Fd 28.07N 32.54 E
Gharrāf, Shaṭṭ al- 24 Kf 32.30N 45.48 E
Gharsah, Shaṭṭ al- 32 Ic 34.06N 7.50 E
Gharyān 33 Bc 32.10N 13.01 E
Gharyān [3] 33 Bc 30.35N 12.00 E
Ghāt 31 If 24.58N 10.11 E
Ghatere 63a Db 7.58S 159.01 E
Ghaṭṭī 24 Gg 31.16N 37.31 E
Ghazāl, Baḥr al- 35 Ed 9.31N 30.25 E
Ghazal, Bahr el- 30 Ig 13.01N 15.28 E
Ghazal, Bahr el- 35 Bc 14.00N 16.30 E
Ghazaouet 32 Gb 35.06N 1.51W
Ghazipur 25 Gc 25.35N 83.34 E
Ghaznī 22 If 33.33N 68.26 E
Ghaznī [3] 23 Kc 33.00N 68.00 E
Ghent (EN) = Gand/Gent 11 Jc 51.03N 3.43 E
Gheorghe Gheorghiu-Dej → Onești 15 Jc 46.12N 26.46 E
Gheorghieni 15 Ic 46.43N 25.37 E
Gheorghiu-Dej → Liski 19 De 51.00N 39.31 E
Gherla 15 Gb 47.02N 23.55 E
Ghidigeni 15 Kc 46.03N 27.30 E
Ghidole (EN)=Gidole 35 Fd 5.37N 37.29 E
Ghilarza 14 Cj 40.07N 8.50 E
Ghimeș, Pasul- 15 Jc 46.33N 26.07 E
Ghisonaccia 11a Ba 42.00N 9.24 E
Ghizunabeana Islands 63a Db 7.33S 158.45 E
Ghowr [3] 23 Jc 34.00N 65.00 E
Ghriss 13 Mi 35.15N 0.10 E
Ghubbat al Qamar 21 Hh 16.00N 52.30 E
Ghudāf, Wādī al- 24 Jf 32.56N 43.30 E
Ghurāb, Jabal al- 24 Hf 34.00N 38.42 E
Ghurayrah 33 Hf 18.37N 42.41 E
Ghūriān 23 Jc 34.21N 61.30 E
Ghurrah, Jabal al- 14 Cn 36.36N 8.23 E
Ghuzayyil, Sabkhat- 33 Dd 29.50N 19.45 E
Giaginskaja 16 Lg 44.47N 40.05 E
Giala, Jabal- 24 Ef 27.20N 32.57 E
Gialo Oasis (EN)=Jālū, Wāḥāt- 30 Jf 29.00N 21.20 E
Gialoúsa 24 Fe 35.35N 34.15 E
Gia Nghia 25 Lf 11.59N 107.42 E
Giannutri 14 Fh 42.15N 11.05 E
Giant's Causeway/Clochán an Aifir 9 Gf 55.15N 6.35W
Giarre 14 Jm 37.43N 15.11 E
Gibara 49 Ic 21.07N 76.08W
Gibbon Point 51b Bb 18.14N 63.00W
Gibb River 59 Fc 16.25S 126.25 E
Gibbs Islands 66 Re 61.30S 55.31W
Gibellina 14 Gm 37.47N 12.58 E
Gibeon [3] 37 Bd 25.00S 18.30 E
Gibeon 37 Be 25.09S 17.43 E
Gibostad 7 Db 69.21N 18.00 E
Gibraleón 13 Fg 37.23N 6.58W
Gibraltar 6 Fh 36.11N 5.22W
Gibraltar [5] 6 Fh 36.11N 5.22W
Gibraltar, Estrecho de-= Gibraltar, Strait of- (EN) 5 Fh 35.57N 5.36W
Gibraltar, Strait of- (EN)= Djebel Ṭāriq, El Bōghāz- 5 Fh 35.57N 5.36W
Gibraltar, Strait of- (EN)= Gibraltar, Estrecho de- 5 Fh 35.57N 5.36W
Gibson Desert 57 Dg 24.30S 126.00 E
Gidami 35 Ed 8.58N 34.40 E
Giddings 45 Hk 30.11N 96.56W
Gidigić 15 Lb 47.04N 28.38 E
Gidole=Ghidole (EN) 35 Fd 5.37N 37.29 E
Gien 11 Ig 47.42N 2.38 E
Giens, Presqu'île de- 11 Mk 43.02N 6.08 E
Gier 11 Ki 45.35N 4.46 E
Gießen 10 Ef 50.35N 8.39 E
Gieten 12 Ia 53.01N 6.48 E
Giethoorn 12 Ib 52.43N 6.07 E
Gifford 42 Jb 70.21N 83.05W
Gifford Seamount (EN) 52 Hi 39.00S 82.00W
Gifhorn 10 Gd 52.29N 10.33 E
Gift Lake 42 Fe 55.49N 115.57W
Gifu 22 Pf 35.25N 136.45 E
Gifu Ken [2] 28 Ng 35.50N 137.00 E
Gigant 16 Lf 46.29N 41.20 E
Giganta, Cerro- 47 Bc 26.07N 111.36W
Giganta, Sierra de la- 47 Bc 26.18N 111.39W
Gigante 54 Cc 2.24N 75.34W
Gigen 15 Hf 43.42N 24.29 E
Gigha 9 Hf 55.41N 5.44W
Giglio 14 Eh 42.20N 10.55 E
Gijón 6 Fg 43.32N 5.40W
Gikongoro 36 Ec 2.30S 29.35 E
Gila Bend 46 Ij 32.57N 112.43W
Gila Bend Mountains 46 Ij 33.10N 113.10W
Gilān [3] 23 Gb 37.00N 49.50 E
Gilān-e-Gharb 24 Ke 34.08N 45.55 E
Gila River 43 Ee 32.43N 114.33W
Gilbert, Mount- 46 Ca 50.51N 124.20W
Gilbert River 59 Ic 16.35S 141.15 E
Gilbert Seamount (EN) 40 If 52.50N 150.10W
Gilbués 54 Ie 9.50S 45.21W
Gilé 37 Fc 16.09S 38.19 E
Giles Meteorological Station 59 Fe 25.02S 128.18 E
Gilford Island 46 Ba 50.45N 126.25W
Gilgandra 59 Jf 31.42S 148.39 E
Gilgău 15 Gb 47.17N 23.43 E
Gilgil 36 Gc 0.30S 36.19 E
Gilgit 25 Ea 35.44N 74.38 E
Gilgit 22 Jf 35.55N 74.18 E
Giljuj 20 Hf 54.17N 127.05 E
Gillam 42 Ie 56.21N 94.43W
Gilleleje 8 Eh 56.07N 12.19 E
Gillen, Lake- 59 Ee 26.10S 124.40 E
Gillenfeld 12 Id 50.07N 6.54 E
Gillette 43 Fc 44.18N 105.30W
Gillian, Lake - 42 Jc 69.30N 75.30W
Gillingham 9 Nj 51.24N 0.33 E
Gilo 35 Ed 8.10N 33.15 E
Gilort 15 Ge 44.36N 23.27 E
Gilroy 46 Eh 37.00N 121.34W
Giluwe, Mount- 60 Ci 6.04S 143.53 E
Gilvān 24 Md 36.47N 49.08 E
Gimån 8 Gb 62.28N 16.20 E
Gimbi 35 Fd 9.10N 35.51 E
Gimie, Mount- 50 Ff 13.52N 61.01W
Gimli 42 Hf 50.39N 97.00W
Gimo 8 Hd 60.11N 18.11 E
Gimolskoje, Ozero- 7 He 63.00N 32.15 E
Gimone 11 Hk 44.00N 1.06 E
Ginda 35 Fb 15.27N 39.06 E
Ginetu 63a Ac 9.30S 152.43 E

Index Symbols

- [1] Independent Nation
- [2] State, Region
- [3] District, County
- [4] Municipality
- [5] Colony, Dependency
- Continent
- Physical Region
- Historical or Cultural Region
- Mount, Mountain
- Volcano
- Hill
- Mountains, Mountain Range
- Hills, Escarpment
- Plateau, Upland
- Pass, Gap
- Plain, Lowland
- Delta
- Salt Flat
- Valley, Canyon
- Crater, Cave
- Karst Features
- Depression
- Polder
- Desert, Dunes
- Forest, Woods
- Heath, Steppe
- Oasis
- Cape, Point
- Coast, Beach
- Cliff
- Peninsula
- Isthmus
- Sandbank
- Island
- Atoll
- Rock, Reef
- Islands, Archipelago
- Rocks, Reefs
- Coral Reef
- Well, Spring
- Geyser
- River, Stream
- Waterfall Rapids
- River Mouth, Estuary
- Lake
- Salt Lake
- Intermittent Lake
- Reservoir
- Swamp, Pond
- Canal
- Glacier
- Ice Shelf, Pack Ice
- Ocean
- Sea
- Gulf, Bay
- Strait, Fjord
- Lagoon
- Bank
- Seamount
- Tablemount
- Ridge
- Shelf
- Basin
- Escarpment, Sea Scarp
- Fracture
- Trench, Abyss
- National Park, Reserve
- Point of Interest
- Recreation Site
- Cave, Cavern
- Historic Site
- Ruins
- Wall, Walls
- Church, Abbey
- Temple
- Scientific Station
- Airport
- Port
- Lighthouse
- Mine
- Tunnel
- Dam, Bridge

Index Symbols

[1] Independent Nation	[⊟] Historical or Cultural Region	[⊏] Pass, Gap	[◻] Depression	[◻] Coast, Beach	[◻] Rock, Reef	[◻] Waterfall Rapids
[2] State, Region	[▲] Mount, Mountain	[◁] Plain, Lowland	[◻] Polder	[◻] Cliff	[◻] Islands, Archipelago	[◻] River Mouth, Estuary
[3] District, County	[▲] Volcano	[◁] Delta	[◻] Desert, Dunes	[◻] Peninsula	[◻] Rocks, Reefs	[◻] Lake
[4] Municipality	[●] Hill	[◻] Salt Flat	[◻] Forest, Woods	[◻] Isthmus	[◻] Coral Reef	[◻] Salt Lake
[5] Colony, Dependency	[▲] Mountains, Mountain Range	[⊏] Valley, Canyon	[◻] Heath, Steppe	[◻] Sandbank	[◻] Well, Spring	[◻] Intermittent Lake
[◆] Continent	[▲] Hills, Escarpment	[⊡] Crater, Cave	[◻] Oasis	[◻] Island	[◻] Geyser	[◻] Reservoir
[◇] Physical Region	[▲] Plateau, Upland	[⊠] Karst Features	[◻] Cape, Point	[◻] Atoll	[◻] River, Stream	[◻] Swamp, Pond

[◻] Canal	[◻] Lagoon	[◻] Escarpment, Sea Scarp	[◻] Historic Site	[◻] Port		
[◻] Bank	[◻] Glacier	[◻] Fracture	[◻] Ruins	[◻] Lighthouse		
[◻] Seamount	[◻] Ice Shelf, Pack Ice	[◻] Trench, Abyss	[◻] Wall, Walls	[◻] Mine		
[◻] Tablemount	[◻] Ocean	[◻] National Park, Reserve	[◻] Church, Abbey	[◻] Tunnel		
[◻] Ridge	[◻] Sea	[◻] Point of Interest	[◻] Temple	[◻] Dam, Bridge		
[◻] Shelf	[◻] Gulf, Bay	[◻] Recreation Site	[◻] Scientific Station			
[◻] Basin	[◻] Strait, Fjord	[◻] Cave, Cavern	[◻] Airport			

Goulburn Islands 59 Gb 11.50 S 133.30 E
Gould Bay 66 Rf 78.10 S 44.00 W
Gould Coast 66 Mg 84.30 S 150.00 W
Goulia 34 Dc 10.01 N 7.11 W
Goulimine 32 Ed 28.59 N 10.04 W
Gouménissa 15 Fi 40.57 N 22.27 E
Gouna 34 Hd 8.32 N 13.34 E
Gounda 35 Cd 9.09 N 21.15 E
Goundam 34 Eb 16.24 N 3.38 W
Goundi 35 Bd 9.22 N 17.22 E
Goundoumaria 34 Hc 13.42 N 11.10 E
Gounou Gaya 35 Bd 9.38 N 15.31 E
Gourara 32 Hd 29.30 N 0.40 E
Gouraya 13 Nh 36.34 N 1.55 E
Gourcy 34 Ec 13.13 N 2.21 W
Gourdon 11 Hj 44.44 N 1.23 E
Gouré 31 Ig 13.58 N 10.18 E
Gourin 11 Cf 48.08 N 3.36 W
Gourma [Mali] 30 Gg 15.45 N 2.00 W
Gourma 30 Hg 12.20 N 1.30 E
Gourma-Rharous 34 Eb 16.52 N 1.55 W
Gournay-en-Bray 11 He 49.29 N 1.44 E
Gourniá 15 In 35.06 N 25.48 E
Gouro 35 Bb 19.40 N 19.28 E
Gourrama 32 Gc 32.20 N 4.05 W
Goussainville 12 Ee 49.01 N 2.28 E
Gouyave 51p Bb 12.10 N 61.44 W
Gouzeaucourt 12 Fd 50.03 N 3.07 E
Gouzon 11 Ih 46.11 N 2.14 E
Govena, Mys- 20 Le 59.47 N 166.02 E
Gove Peninsula 59 Hb 13.02 S 136.50 E
Goverla, Gora- 19 Cf 48.10 N 24.32 E
Governador Valadares 53 Lg 18.51 S 41.56 W
Governor's Harbour 47 Ic 25.10 N 76.14 W
Gowanda 44 Hd 42.28 N 78.57 W
Gower 9 Ij 51.36 N 4.10 W
Gowganda 44 Gb 47.38 N 80.46 W
Goya 53 Kh 29.10 S 59.20 W
Goyave 51e Ab 16.08 N 61.34 W
Goyaves, Ilets 'a- 51e Ab 16.10 N 61.48 W
Goyder River 59 Hb 12.38 S 135.05 E
Göynücek 24 Fb 40.24 N 35.32 E
Göynük 15 Ni 40.20 N 30.05 E
Göynük 24 Db 40.24 N 30.47 E
Gozaisho-Yama 29 Ed 35.01 N 136.24 E
Goz Arian 35 Bc 14.35 N 20.00 E
Goz Beïda 35 Cc 12.13 N 21.25 E
Gozha Co 27 De 34.59 N 81.06 E
Goz Kerki 35 Bb 15.30 N 18.50 E
Gözlü Baba Dağı 15 Lk 38.15 N 28.28 E
Gozo 5 Hh 36.05 N 14.15 E
Graaff-Reinet 37 Cf 32.14 S 24.32 E
Graafschap 11 Mb 52.05 N 6.30 E
Graben Neudorf 12 Ke 49.10 N 8.28 E
Grabia 10 Oe 51.26 N 18.56 E
Grabière Point 51g Bb 15.30 N 61.29 W
Grabowa 10 Mb 54.26 N 16.20 E
Gračac 14 Jf 44.18 N 15.51 E
Gračanica 14 Mf 44.42 N 18.18 E
Gračanica, Manastir- 15 Eg 42.36 N 21.12 E
Gracias 49 Cf 14.35 N 88.35 W
Gracias a Dios 49 Ef 15.20 N 84.20 W
Gracias a Dios, Cabo 38 Kh 15.00 N 83.08 W
Graciosa [Azr.] 30 Ee 39.04 N 28.00 W
Graciosa [Can.Is.] 32 Ed 29.15 N 13.30 W
Gradačac 14 Mf 44.53 N 18.26 E
Gradaús, Serra dos- 52 Kf 8.00 S 50.45 W
Grado [It.] 14 He 45.40 N 13.23 E
Grado [Sp.] 13 Fa 43.23 N 6.04 W
Grænalon 7a Cb 64.10 N 17.24 W
Grænlandshaf = Greenland Sea (EN) 67 Ld 77.00 N 1.00 W
Grafenau 10 Jh 48.51 N 13.24 E
Grafham Water 12 Bb 52.19 N 0.10 W
Grafing bei München 10 Hh 48.03 N 11.58 E
Grafschaft Bentheim 12 Jb 52.30 N 7.05 E
Grafton [Austl.] 59 Ke 29.41 S 152.56 E
Grafton [N.D.-U.S.] 43 Hb 48.25 N 97.25 W
Grafton [W.V.-U.S.] 44 Hf 39.21 N 80.00 W
Grafton, Mount- 46 Hg 38.40 N 114.45 W
Graham 42 Ef 53.40 N 132.30 W
Graham [N.C.-U.S.] 44 Hg 36.05 N 79.25 W
Graham [Tx.-U.S.] 45 Gj 33.06 N 98.35 W
Graham, Mount- 46 Ke 32.42 N 109.52 W
Graham Land (EN) 66 Qe 66.00 S 63.30 W
Graham Moore, Cape - 42 Jb 72.51 N 76.05 W
Grahamstown 31 Jl 33.19 S 26.31 E
Grain Coast 30 Gh 5.00 N 9.00 W
Graisivaudan 11 Li 45.15 N 5.50 E
Grajaú 54 Ie 5.49 S 46.08 W
Grajaú, Rio- 54 Jd 3.41 S 44.48 W
Grajewo 10 Sc 53.39 N 22.27 E
Gram 8 Ci 55.17 N 9.04 E
Gramalote 49 Kj 7.54 N 72.48 W
Gramat 11 Hj 44.47 N 1.43 E
Gramat, Causse de- 11 Hj 44.40 N 1.50 E
Graminha, Represa da- 55 Ie 21.33 S 46.38 W
Grammerages/Galmaarden 12 Fd 50.45 N 3.58 E
Grammichele 14 Im 37.13 N 14.38 E
Grammont/Geraardsbergen 12 Fd 50.46 N 3.52 E
Grámmos Óros 15 Di 40.20 N 20.45 E
Grampian 9 Kd 57.25 N 2.35 W
Grampian Mountains 5 Fd 56.45 N 4.00 W
Gramshi 15 Di 40.52 N 20.11 E
Gran 8 Dd 60.22 N 10.34 E
Granada [Col.] 54 Dc 3.33 N 73.44 W
Granada [Nic.] 49 Eh 11.50 N 86.00 W
Granada [Nic.] 47 Gf 11.56 N 85.57 W
Granada [Sp.] 13 Ig 37.15 N 3.15 W
Granada [Sp.] 6 Fh 37.13 N 3.41 W
Granada, Vega de- 13 Ig 37.15 N 4.00 W
Gránard/Granard 9 Fh 53.47 N 7.30 W
Granard/Gránard 9 Fh 53.47 N 7.30 W
Granby 42 Kg 45.24 N 72.43 W
Gran Canaria 30 Ff 28.00 N 15.36 W
Gran Chaco 52 Jh 23.00 S 60.00 W
Grand Anse Bay 51p Bb 12.02 N 61.45 W
Grand Bahama 38 Lg 26.40 N 78.20 W
Grand Ballon 11 Ng 47.55 N 7.08 E
Grand Bank 42 Lg 47.06 N 55.47 W
Grand Banks (EN) 38 Oe 45.00 N 50.00 W
Grand Bassa 34 Dd 6.10 N 9.40 W
Grand-Bassam 31 Gh 5.12 N 3.44 W
Grand Bay 51g Bb 15.14 N 61.19 W
Grand Bay 51p Cb 12.29 N 61.23 W
Grand-Béréby 34 De 4.38 N 6.55 W
Grand-Bourg 50 Fe 15.53 N 61.19 W
Grand Cache 42 Ff 53.14 N 119.00 W
Grand Caille Point 51k Ab 13.52 N 61.05 W
Grandcamp-Maisy 12 Ae 49.23 N 1.02 W
Grand Canal 9 Gh 53.21 N 6.14 W
Grand Canal (EN) = Da Yunhe 21 Nf 39.54 N 116.44 E
Grand Canyon 43 Ed 36.03 N 112.09 W
Grand Canyon 38 Hc 36.10 N 112.45 W
Grand' Case 51b Ab 18.06 N 63.03 W
Grand Cayman 47 He 19.20 N 81.15 W
Grand Cess 34 De 4.24 N 8.13 W
Grand Chartreuse 11 Li 45.22 N 5.50 E
Grand Colombier 11 Li 45.54 N 5.46 E
Grand Coulee 46 Fc 47.56 N 119.00 W
Grand-Couronne 12 De 49.21 N 1.01 E
Grandcourt 12 De 49.55 N 1.30 E
Grand Cul de Sac Bay 51k Ab 13.59 N 61.02 W
Grand Cul-de-Sac Marin 51e Ab 16.20 N 61.35 W
Grande, Arroyo- 55 Dm 37.32 S 57.34 W
Grande, Bahia- 52 Jk 50.45 S 68.45 W
Grande, Boca- 54 Fb 8.45 N 60.35 W
Grande, Cachoeira- 55 Gb 15.37 S 51.48 W
Grande, Cerro- 48 If 23.40 N 100.40 W
Grande, Ciénaga- 49 Ji 9.13 N 75.46 W
Grande, Corixa- 55 Cc 17.10 S 58.20 W
Grande, Cuchilla- [Arg.] 55 Cj 31.45 S 58.35 W
Grande, Cuchilla- [Ur.] 52 Ki 33.15 S 55.07 W
Grande, Ile- 11 Cf 48.48 N 3.35 W
Grande, Ilha 54 Jh 23.10 S 44.10 W
Grande, Rio- [Ven.] 54 Fb 8.39 N 60.59 W
Grande, Rio- [Braz.] 52 Lg 11.05 S 43.09 W
Grande, Rio- [N.Amer.] 38 Jg 25.57 N 97.09 W
Grande, Rio- (EN) = Bravo del Norte, Río- 38 Jg 25.57 N 97.09 W
Grande, Rio- o Guapay, Río- 52 Jg 15.51 S 64.39 W
Grande, Serra- 52 Lf 6.00 S 40.52 W
Grande, Sierra- 48 Gc 29.40 N 104.55 W
Grande-Anse 51e Bb 16.18 N 61.04 W
Grande Anse 51k Ba 14.01 N 60.54 W
Grande Briere 11 Dg 47.22 N 2.15 W
Grande Casse 11 Mi 45.24 N 6.50 E
Grande Cayemite 49 Kd 18.37 N 73.45 W
Grande Comore → Njazidja 30 Lj 11.35 S 43.20 E
Grande de Santa Marta, Ciénaga- 49 Jh 10.50 N 74.25 W
Grande de Santiago, Río- 38 Ig 21.36 N 105.26 W
Grande do Gurupa, Ilha- 54 Hd 1.00 S 51.30 W
Grande Inferior, Cuchilla- 55 Dk 33.50 S 56.10 W
Grande Kabylie 13 Ph 36.45 N 4.00 E
Grande ou Sete Quedas, Ilha- 55 Ef 23.45 S 54.03 W
Grande Pointe [Guad.] 51b Bc 17.50 N 62.50 W
Grande Pointe [Guad.] 51e Ac 15.59 N 61.38 W
Grande Prairie 39 Hd 55.10 N 118.48 W
Grand Erg de Bilma 30 Ig 18.30 N 13.50 E
Grand Erg Occidental 30 He 30.20 N 0.01 E
Grand Erg Oriental 30 He 30.00 N 7.00 E
Grande Rio- 52 Kh 20.06 S 51.04 W
Grande Rivière à Goyaves 51e Ab 16.18 N 61.37 W
Grande Rivière de la Baleine 38 Ld 55.15 N 77.45 W
Grande Rivière du Nord 49 Kd 19.35 N 72.11 W
Grande Ronde River 46 Gc 46.05 N 116.59 W
Grandes, Salinas- 52 Ji 30.05 S 65.05 W
Grande Sebkha d'Oran 13 Li 35.32 N 0.48 W
Grandes Rousse 11 Mi 45.06 N 6.07 E
Grande-Synthe 12 Ec 51.01 N 2.17 E
Grand Etang 51p Bb 12.06 N 61.42 W
Grande-Terre 50 Fd 16.20 N 61.25 W
Grande Vigie, Pointe de la- 51e Ba 16.31 N 61.28 W
Grand Falls [N.B.-Can.] 42 Kg 47.03 N 67.44 W
Grand Falls [Newf.-Can.] 39 Ne 48.56 N 55.40 W
Grand Forks [B.C.-Can.] 46 Fb 49.02 N 118.27 W
Grand Forks [N.D.-U.S.] 39 Je 47.55 N 97.03 W
Grand Found, Anse du- 51b Bc 17.53 N 62.49 W
Grand Gedeh 34 Dd 5.45 N 8.05 W
Grand Haven 44 Dd 43.04 N 86.10 W
Grand Ilet 51e Ac 15.50 N 61.36 W
Grand Island 39 Je 40.55 N 98.21 W
Grand Junction 39 If 39.05 N 108.33 W
Grand-Lahou 34 Dd 5.08 N 5.01 W
Grand Lake [La.-U.S.] 45 Kl 29.55 N 91.35 W
Grand Lake [La.-U.S.] 45 Jl 29.55 N 92.47 W
Grand Lake [N.B.-Can.] 44 Nc 45.42 N 66.05 W
Grand Lake [Newf.-Can.] 42 Lg 49.00 N 57.20 W
Grand Lake [Oh.-U.S.] 44 Ee 40.30 N 84.32 W
Grand Lake Victoria 44 Ib 47.35 N 77.33 W
Grand Lieu, Lac de- 11 Eg 47.05 N 1.40 W
Grand Manan Channel 44 Nc 44.45 N 66.52 W
Grand Manan Island 42 Kh 44.40 N 66.50 W
Grand Marais [Mi.-U.S.] 44 Eb 46.40 N 85.59 W
Grand Marais [Mn.-U.S.] 45 Kc 47.45 N 90.20 W
Grand-Mère 44 Kb 46.37 N 72.41 W
Grand Morin 11 If 48.54 N 2.50 E
Grândola 13 Df 38.10 N 8.34 W
Grândola, Serra de- 13 Df 38.06 N 8.38 W
Grand Passage 63b Ad 18.45 S 163.10 E
Grand-Popo 34 Fd 6.17 N 1.50 E
Grand Portage 45 Lc 47.58 N 89.41 W
Grand Prairie 43 He 32.45 N 96.59 W
Grandpré 12 Ge 49.20 N 4.52 E
Grand Rapids [Man.-Can.] 42 Hf 53.10 N 99.17 W
Grand Rapids [Mi.-U.S.] 39 Ke 42.58 N 85.40 W
Grand Rapids [Mn.-U.S.] 43 Ib 47.14 N 93.31 W
Grand Récif Sud 61 Cd 22.38 S 167.00 E
Grand River [Mi.-U.S.] 44 Dd 43.04 N 86.15 W
Grand River [Mo.-U.S.] 45 Jg 39.23 N 93.06 W
Grand River [Ont.-Can.] 44 Hd 42.51 N 79.34 W
Grand River [S.D.-U.S.] 45 Fd 45.40 N 100.32 W
Grand'Rivière 51h Ab 14.52 N 61.11 W
Grand Roy 51p Bb 12.08 N 61.45 W
Grand-Sans-Toucher 51e Ab 16.06 N 61.41 W
Grand Teton 43 Ec 43.44 N 110.48 W
Grand Traverse Bay 43 Jb 45.02 N 85.30 W
Grand Turk 49 Lc 21.30 N 71.10 W
Grand Turk 47 Jd 21.28 N 71.09 W
Grand Union Canal 12 Bc 51.30 N 0.02 W
Grand Valley 45 Bg 39.27 N 108.03 W
Grandview [Man.-Can.] 45 Fa 51.10 N 100.45 W
Grandview [Mo.-U.S.] 45 Ig 38.53 N 94.32 W
Grandvilliers 12 De 49.40 N 1.56 E
Grand Wash Cliffs 46 Ii 35.45 N 113.45 W
Grand Wintersberg 11 Ne 48.59 N 7.37 E
Granger 46 Ec 46.21 N 120.11 W
Grängesberg 8 Fd 60.05 N 14.59 E
Grangeville 46 Gd 45.56 N 116.07 W
Gran Guardia 56 Ic 25.52 S 58.53 W
Granite City 45 Kg 38.42 N 90.09 W
Granite Falls 45 Id 44.49 N 95.33 W
Granite Pass 46 Ld 44.38 N 107.30 W
Granite Peak [Nv.-U.S.] 43 Dc 41.40 N 117.35 W
Granite Peak [U.S.] 43 Fb 45.10 N 109.48 W
Granite Range 46 Ff 41.00 N 119.35 W
Granitola, Punta- 14 Gm 37.34 N 12.41 E
Grankulla/Kauniainen 8 Kd 60.13 N 24.45 E
Granma 49 Ic 20.30 N 77.00 W
Gran Malvina, Isla-/West Falkland 52 Kk 51.40 S 60.00 W
Gran Morelos [Mex.] 48 Eb 30.40 N 108.35 W
Gran Morelos [Mex.] 48 Fc 28.15 N 106.30 W
Gränna 8 Ff 58.01 N 14.28 E
Granollers/Granollérs 13 Oc 41.37 N 2.18 E
Granollérs/Granollers 13 Oc 41.37 N 2.18 E
Gran Paradis/Gran Paradiso 14 Be 45.32 N 7.16 E
Gran Paradiso/Gran Paradis 14 Be 45.32 N 7.16 E
Gran Pilastro/Hochfeiler 14 Fd 46.58 N 11.44 E
Gran San Bernardo 14 Be 45.50 N 7.10 E
Gran Sasso d'Italia 5 Hg 42.25 N 13.40 E
Grant 45 Ff 40.50 N 101.56 W
Grant, Mount- 46 Fg 38.34 N 118.48 W
Gran Tarajal 32 Ed 28.12 N 14.01 W
Grantham 9 Mi 52.54 N 0.38 W
Grant Island 66 Nf 74.24 S 131.20 W
Grantown-on-Spey 9 Jd 57.20 N 3.38 W
Grant Range 46 Hg 38.25 N 115.30 W
Grants 43 Fd 35.09 N 107.52 W
Grantsburg 45 Jd 45.47 N 92.41 W
Grants Pass 43 Cc 42.26 N 123.19 W
Granville 11 Ef 48.50 N 1.36 W
Granville Lake 42 He 56.00 N 100.20 W
Granvin 8 Bd 60.33 N 6.43 E
Grao de Gandía, Gandía- 13 Lf 38.59 N 0.09 W
Grao de Sagunto, Sagunto- 13 Le 39.40 N 0.16 W
Grappa, Monte- 14 Fe 45.52 N 11.48 E
Grappler Bank (EN) 51a Cc 17.48 S 65.55 W
Graskop 37 Ed 24.58 S 30.49 E
Gräsmark 8 Ee 59.57 N 12.55 E
Gräsö 7 Ef 60.25 N 18.25 E
Grasse 11 Mk 43.40 N 6.55 E
Grasset, Lac- 44 Ha 49.58 N 78.10 W
Grassrange 46 Kc 47.01 N 108.48 W
Gråsten 7 Bi 54.55 N 9.36 E
Grästorp 8 Ef 58.20 N 12.40 E
Graubünden 14 Dd 46.35 N 9.35 E
Graulhet 11 Hk 43.46 N 2.00 E
Graus 13 Mb 42.11 N 0.20 E
Grave 12 Hc 51.45 N 5.45 E
Grave, Pointe de- 11 Ei 45.34 N 1.04 W
Gravedona 14 Dd 46.09 N 9.18 E
Gravelbourg 42 Gg 49.53 N 106.34 W
Gravelines 11 Id 50.59 N 2.07 E
Gravenhurst 44 Hc 44.55 N 79.22 W
Gravenor Bay 51d Ba 17.33 N 61.45 W
Graves 11 Fj 44.35 N 0.30 W
Gravesend 9 Nj 51.27 N 0.24 E
Gravesend-Tilbury 9 Nj 51.28 N 0.23 E
Gravina in Puglia 14 Kj 40.49 N 16.25 E
Gravone 11a Ab 41.55 N 8.47 E
Gray 11 Lg 47.27 N 5.35 E
Gray Feather Bank (EN) 60 Df 8.00 N 148.40 E
Grayling 44 Ec 44.40 N 84.43 W
Grays Harbor 46 Cc 46.56 N 124.05 W
Grayson 44 Ff 38.20 N 82.57 W
Grays Peak 45 Fd 39.37 N 105.45 W
Graz 6 Hf 47.04 N 15.27 E
Grazalema 13 Gh 36.46 N 5.22 W
Grdelica 15 Fg 42.54 N 22.04 E
Greåker 8 De 59.16 N 11.02 E
Great 51p Bb 12.10 N 61.38 W
Great Artesian Basin 57 Fg 25.00 S 143.00 E
Great Astrolabe Reef 63d Bc 18.52 S 178.31 E
Great Australian Bight 57 Eh 35.00 S 130.00 E
Great Bacolet Point 51p Bb 12.05 N 61.37 W
Great Bahama Bank (EN) 38 Lg 23.15 N 78.00 W
Great Bardfield 12 Cc 51.56 N 0.29 E
Great Barrier Island 57 Ih 36.10 S 175.25 E
Great Barrier Reef 57 Ff 19.10 S 149.00 E
Great Basin 38 Hf 40.00 N 117.00 W
Great Bay 47 Jf 39.30 N 74.23 W
Great Bear 42 Ed 64.54 N 125.35 W
Great Bear Lake 38 Hc 66.00 N 120.00 W
Great Belt (EN) = Store Bælt 5 Hd 55.30 N 11.00 E
Great Bend 43 Hd 38.22 N 98.46 W
Great Blasket/An Blascaod Mór 9 Ci 52.05 N 10.32 W
Great Britain 5 Fd 54.00 N 3.00 W
Great Central Lake 46 Cb 49.27 N 125.12 W
Great Channel 21 Li 6.00 N 94.00 E
Great Chesterford 12 Cb 52.04 N 0.12 E
Great Dismal Swamp 44 Ig 36.30 N 76.30 W
Great Dividing Range 57 Fg 25.00 S 147.00 E
Great Dunmow 12 Cc 51.53 N 0.22 E
Greater Accra 34 Fd 5.45 N 0.10 E
Greater Antilles (EN) = Antillas Mayores 38 Lh 20.00 N 74.00 W
Greater Khingan Range (EN) = Da Hinggan Ling 21 Oe 49.00 N 122.00 E
Greater London 9 Mj 51.35 N 0.05 W
Greater Manchester 9 Kh 53.35 N 2.10 W
Greater Sunda Islands (EN) 21 Nj 3.52 S 111.20 E
Great Exhibition Bay 61 Df 34.40 S 173.00 E
Great Exuma Island 47 Id 23.32 N 75.50 W
Great Falls 39 He 47.30 N 111.17 W
Great Harbour Cay 44 Im 25.45 N 77.52 W
Great Inagua 38 Lg 21.02 N 73.20 W
Great Indian Desert/Thar 21 Ig 27.00 N 70.00 E
Great Karasberge (EN) = Groot-Karasberge 30 Ik 27.20 S 18.45 E
Great Karroo (EN) = Groot Karoo 30 Jl 33.00 S 22.00 E
Great Lake 59 Jh 41.52 S 146.45 E
Great Namaland/Groot Namaland 37 Be 26.00 S 17.00 E
Great Nicobar 21 Li 7.00 N 93.50 E
Great North East Channel 59 Ia 9.30 S 143.25 E
Great Ormes Head 9 Jh 53.21 N 3.52 W
Great Ouse 9 Ni 52.44 N 0.23 E
Great Plain of the Koukdjuak 42 Kc 66.25 N 72.50 W
Great Plains 38 Je 42.00 N 100.00 W
Great Reef 63c Bb 10.14 S 166.02 E
Great Ruaha 30 Ki 7.56 S 37.52 E
Great Sacandaga Lake 44 Jd 43.08 N 74.10 W
Great Sale Cay 44 Hl 27.00 N 78.12 W
Great Salt Lake 38 He 41.10 N 112.30 W
Great Salt Lake Desert 43 Ec 40.40 N 113.30 W
Great Salt Plains Lake 45 Gh 36.44 N 98.12 W
Great Salt Pond 51c Ab 17.15 N 62.38 W
Great Sandy Desert [Austl.] 57 Dg 21.30 S 125.00 E
Great Sandy Desert [U.S.] 43 Cc 43.35 N 120.15 W
Great Sea Reef 63d Bb 16.15 S 178.33 E
Great Shelford 12 Cb 52.07 N 0.08 E
Great Sitkin 40a Cb 52.03 N 176.07 W
Great Slave Lake 38 Hd 61.30 N 114.00 W
Great Smoky Mountains 44 Fh 35.35 N 83.30 W
Great Stour 9 Oj 51.19 N 1.15 E
Great Valley [U.S.] 44 Ie 40.15 N 76.50 W
Great Valley [U.S.] 43 Kd 36.30 N 82.00 W
Great Victoria Desert 57 Dg 28.30 S 127.45 E
Great Yarmouth 9 Oi 52.37 N 1.44 E
Grebbestad 7 Cg 58.42 N 11.15 E
Grebenka 16 Hd 50.07 N 32.25 E
Gréboun, Mont- 34 Gb 20.00 N 8.35 E
Greci 15 Ld 45.11 N 28.14 E
Gredos, Sierra de- 13 Gd 40.20 N 5.05 W
Greece (EN) = Elläs 6 Ih 39.00 N 22.00 E
Greeley [Co.-U.S.] 43 Gc 40.25 N 104.42 W
Greeley [Nb.-U.S.] 45 Gf 41.33 N 98.32 W
Greely Fiord 42 Ja 80.40 N 85.00 W
Greem-Bell 21 Ia 81.10 N 64.00 E
Green 46 De 43.07 N 123.28 W
Green Bay 43 Jb 45.00 N 87.30 W
Green Bay 39 Ke 44.30 N 88.01 W
Greencastle 44 Df 39.38 N 86.52 W
Green Cay 49 Ia 24.02 N 77.11 W
Greeneville 44 Fg 36.10 N 82.50 W
Greenfield [In.-U.S.] 44 Ef 39.47 N 85.46 W
Greenfield [Ma.-U.S.] 44 Kd 42.36 N 72.36 W
Greenhorn Mountain 45 Dh 37.57 N 105.00 W
Green Island 62 Df 45.54 S 170.26 E
Green Island [Atg.] 51d Bb 17.03 N 61.40 W
Green Island [Gren.] 51p Bb 12.14 N 61.35 W
Green Islands 57 Ge 4.30 S 154.10 E
Greenland 51q Ab 13.15 N 59.34 W
Greenland (EN) = Grønland/Kalaallit Nunaat 38 Pb 70.00 N 40.00 W
Greenland (EN) = Grønland/Kalaallit Nunaat 39 Pb 70.00 N 40.00 W
Greenland (EN) = Kalaallit Nunaat/Grønland 38 Pb 70.00 N 40.00 W
Greenland (EN) = Kalaallit Nunaat/Grønland 39 Pb 70.00 N 40.00 W
Greenland Basin (EN) 3 Gb 77.00 N 0.00
Greenland Sea (EN) = Grænlandshaf 67 Ld 77.00 N 1.00 W
Greenland Sea (EN) = Grønlandshavet 67 Ld 77.00 N 1.00 W
Green Lookout Mountain 46 Dd 45.52 N 122.08 W
Green Mountains 38 Le 43.45 N 72.45 W
Greenock 9 If 55.57 N 4.45 W
Greenough River 59 Ce 28.51 S 114.38 E
Green Peter Lake 46 Dd 44.28 N 122.30 W
Green River [U.S.] 44 Dg 37.55 N 87.30 W
Green River [U.S.] 38 If 38.11 N 109.53 W
Green River [Ut.-U.S.] 43 Ed 38.59 N 110.10 W
Green River [Wy.-U.S.] 43 Fc 41.32 N 109.28 W
Green River Lake 44 Eg 37.15 N 85.15 W
Greensboro 39 Lf 36.04 N 79.47 W
Greensburg [In.-U.S.] 44 Ef 39.20 N 85.29 W
Greensburg [Ks.-U.S.] 45 Gh 37.36 N 99.18 W
Greensburg [La.-U.S.] 45 Kk 30.51 N 90.42 W
Greenstone Point 9 Hd 57.55 N 5.40 W
Greenvale 59 Jc 18.55 S 145.05 E
Greenville [Al.-U.S.] 44 Dj 31.50 N 86.38 W
Greenville [Il.-U.S.] 45 Lg 38.53 N 89.25 W
Greenville [Lbr.] 31 Gh 4.59 N 9.02 W
Greenville [Me.-U.S.] 44 Mc 45.28 N 69.35 W
Greenville [Ms.-U.S.] 43 Ie 33.25 N 91.05 W
Greenville [N.C.-U.S.] 43 Ld 35.37 N 77.23 W
Greenville [Oh.-U.S.] 44 Ee 40.06 N 84.37 W
Greenville [Pa.-U.S.] 44 Ge 41.24 N 80.24 W
Greenville [S.C.-U.S.] 39 Kf 34.51 N 82.23 W
Greenville [Tx.-U.S.] 43 He 33.08 N 96.07 W
Greenwich 44 Fe 41.02 N 82.32 W
Greenwich, London- 9 Mj 51.28 N 0.00
Greenwood [Ms.-U.S.] 43 Ie 33.31 N 90.11 W
Greenwood [S.C.-U.S.] 44 Fh 34.12 N 82.10 W
Greenwood, Lake- 44 Gh 34.15 N 82.00 W
Greer 44 Fh 34.55 N 82.14 W
Greers Ferry Lake 45 Ji 35.30 N 92.10 W
Greeson, Lake- 45 Ji 34.10 N 93.45 W
Grefrath 12 Ic 51.18 N 6.19 E
Gregoria Pérez de Denis 55 Bi 28.14 S 61.32 W
Gregorio, Rio- 54 De 6.50 S 70.46 W
Gregório, Rio- 55 Ha 13.42 S 49.58 W
Gregory, Lake- 59 He 28.55 S 139.00 E
Gregory Lake 59 Fd 20.10 S 127.20 E
Gregory Range 57 Ff 19.00 S 143.00 E
Gregory River 59 Hc 17.53 S 139.17 E
Greifenburg 14 Hd 46.45 N 13.11 E
Greifswald 10 Jb 54.06 N 13.23 E
Greifswalder Bodden 10 Jb 54.15 N 13.35 E
Greifswalder Oie 10 Jb 54.14 N 13.55 E
Grein 14 Ib 48.13 N 14.51 E
Greiz 10 If 50.39 N 12.12 E
Grēko, Akrōtērion- 24 Fe 34.56 N 34.05 E
Gremiha 6 Jb 68.03 N 39.29 E
Gremjačinsk 17 Hg 58.34 N 57.51 E
Grenå 7 Ch 56.25 N 10.53 E
Grenada 39 Mh 12.07 N 61.40 W
Grenada 38 Mh 12.07 N 61.40 W
Grenada 45 Lj 33.47 N 89.55 W
Grenada Basin (EN) 47 Lf 13.30 N 62.00 W
Grenada Lake 45 Lj 33.50 N 89.40 W
Grenadines 47 Lf 12.40 N 61.15 W
Grenchen 14 Bc 47.11 N 7.25 E
Grenen 5 Hd 57.44 N 10.40 E
Grenfell 45 Ea 50.25 N 102.56 W
Grenoble 6 Gf 45.10 N 5.43 E
Grenora 45 Eb 48.37 N 103.56 W
Grense-Jakobselv 7 Hb 69.47 N 30.50 E
Grenville 50 Ff 12.07 N 61.37 W
Grenville, Cape- 59 Ib 12.00 S 143.15 E
Gréoux-les-Bains 11 Lk 43.45 N 5.53 E
Gresham 46 Dd 45.30 N 122.26 W
Gresik 26 Fh 7.09 S 112.38 E
Gressoney-la-Trinité 14 Be 45.50 N 7.49 E
Gretas Klackar 8 Gc 61.34 N 17.50 E
Gretna 45 Kl 29.55 N 90.03 W
Grevelingen 12 Fc 51.45 N 4.00 E
Greven 10 Dd 52.06 N 7.37 E
Grevená 15 Ei 40.05 N 21.25 E
Grevenbroich 10 Ce 51.05 N 6.35 E
Grevenbrück, Lennestadt- 12 Kc 51.08 N 8.01 E
Grevenmacher 12 Ie 49.41 N 6.27 E
Grevesmühlen 10 Hc 53.52 N 11.11 E
Grey 62 De 42.26 S 171.11 E
Greybull 46 Kd 44.30 N 108.03 W
Greybull River 46 Kd 44.28 N 108.03 W
Grey Islands 42 Lf 50.50 N 55.35 W
Greymouth 61 Dh 42.27 S 171.12 E
Grey Range 57 Fg 27.00 S 143.35 E
Greystones/Ná Clocha Liatha 9 Gh 53.09 N 6.04 W
Greytow 37 Ee 29.07 S 30.30 E
Greytown 62 Fd 41.05 S 175.28 E
Gribanovski 16 Ld 51.29 N 41.58 E
Gribb Bank (EN) 66 Ge 63.00 S 90.30 E
Gribës, Mali i- 15 Ci 40.34 N 19.34 E
Gribingui 35 Bd 7.00 N 19.30 E
Gribingui 35 Bd 8.33 N 19.05 E
Griend 12 Ha 53.15 N 5.20 E
Griesheim 12 Ke 49.52 N 8.33 E
Grieskirchen 14 Hb 48.14 N 13.50 E
Griffin 43 Ke 33.15 N 84.16 W
Griffith 59 Jf 34.17 S 146.03 E
Grigoriopol 15 Mb 47.09 N 29.13 E
Grijalva 38 Jh 18.36 N 92.39 W
Grim, Cape- 59 Ih 40.41 S 144.41 E
Grimari 35 Cd 5.44 N 20.03 E
Grimbergen 12 Gd 50.56 N 4.23 E
Grimma 10 Ie 51.14 N 12.43 E
Grimmen 10 Jb 54.06 N 13.03 E
Grimsby 9 Mh 53.35 N 0.05 W
Grimsey 7a Ca 66.33 N 18.00 W
Grimsstadir 7a Cb 65.39 N 16.07 W
Grimstad 7 Bg 58.20 N 8.36 E
Grimsvotn 7a Cb 64.24 N 17.22 W
Grindavik 7a Ac 63.50 N 22.30 W
Grindelwald 14 Cd 46.38 N 8.03 E
Grindsted 7 Bi 55.45 N 8.56 E
Grinnell 45 Jf 41.45 N 92.43 W
Grinnel Peninsula 42 Ia 76.40 N 95.00 W
Grintavec 14 Id 46.22 N 14.32 E
Griquatown 37 Ce 28.49 S 23.15 E
Grise Fiord 39 Kb 76.10 N 83.15 W
Gris-Nez, Cap- 11 Hd 50.52 N 1.35 E
Grisslehamn 8 Hd 60.06 N 18.50 E
Grjazi 19 De 52.29 N 39.57 E
Grjazovec 19 Ed 58.53 N 40.15 E
Grmeč 14 Kf 44.43 N 16.15 E
Grobiņa/Grobinja 7 Eh 56.33 N 21.11 E
Grobinja/Grobiņa 7 Eh 56.33 N 21.11 E
Groblersdal 37 De 25.15 S 29.25 E
Grocka 15 De 44.41 N 20.43 E
Grodk/Spremberg 10 Ke 51.33 N 14.22 E
Grodków 10 Nf 50.43 N 17.22 E
Grodnenskaja Oblast 19 Ce 53.45 N 25.10 E
Grodno 6 Ie 53.42 N 23.50 E
Grodzisk Mazowiecki 10 Qd 52.07 N 20.37 E
Grodzjanka 16 Fc 53.34 N 28.48 E
Groeie Hoop, Kaap die-/Good Hope, Cape of- 30 Il 34.21 S 18.28 E

Index Symbols

- [1] Independent Nation
- [2] State, Region
- [3] District, County
- [4] Municipality
- [5] Colony, Dependency
- Continent
- Physical Region
- Historical or Cultural Region
- Mount, Mountain
- Volcano
- Hill
- Mountains, Mountain Range
- Hills, Escarpment
- Plateau, Upland
- Pass, Gap
- Plain, Lowland
- Delta
- Salt Flat
- Valley, Canyon
- Crater, Cave
- Karst Features
- Depression
- Polder
- Desert, Dunes
- Forest, Woods
- Heath, Steppe
- Oasis
- Cape, Point
- Coast, Beach
- Cliff
- Peninsula
- Isthmus
- Sandbank
- Island
- Atoll
- Rock, Reef
- Islands, Archipelago
- Rocks, Reefs
- Coral Reef
- Well, Spring
- Geyser
- River, Stream
- Waterfall Rapids
- River Mouth, Estuary
- Lake
- Salt Lake
- Intermittent Lake
- Reservoir
- Swamp, Pond
- Canal
- Glacier
- Ice Shelf, Pack Ice
- Ocean
- Sea
- Gulf, Bay
- Strait, Fjord
- Lagoon
- Bank
- Seamount
- Tablemount
- Ridge
- Shelf
- Basin
- Escarpment, Sea Scarp
- Fracture
- Trench, Abyss
- National Park, Reserve
- Point of Interest
- Recreation Site
- Cave, Cavern
- Historic Site
- Ruins
- Wall, Walls
- Church, Abbey
- Temple
- Scientific Station
- Airport
- Port
- Lighthouse
- Mine
- Tunnel
- Dam, Bridge

Groenlo	12	Ib	52.04N	6.39 E
Groesbeek	12	Hc	51.47N	5.56 E
Grofa, Gora-	15	Ha	48.34N	24.03 E
Groix	11	Cg	47.38N	3.28W
Groix, Ile de-	11	Cg	47.38N	3.28W
Grójec	10	Qe	51.52N	20.52 E
Gröll Seamount (EN)	54	Lf	14.00S	32.00W
Gromnik	10	Nf	50.42N	17.07 E
Gronau (Westfalen)	10	Dd	52.12N	7.02 E
Grong	7	Cd	64.30N	12.27 E
Groningen [3]	12	Ia	53.13N	6.33 E
Groningen [Neth.]	6	Ge	53.13N	6.33 E
Groningen [Sur.]	54	Gb	5.48N	55.28W
Groninger-wad	12	Ia	53.25N	6.25 E
Groningerwad	12	Ia	53.25N	6.30 E
Grønland/Kalaallit Nunaat= Greenland (EN)	38	Pb	70.00N	40.00W
Grønland/Kalaallit Nunaat= Greenland (EN) [5]	67	Nd	70.00N	40.00W
Grønlandshavet=Greenland Sea (EN)	67	Ld	77.00N	1.00W
Grønnedal	41	Hf	61.20N	47.45W
Grönskara	8	Fg	57.05N	15.44 E
Groot	30	Jl	33.45S	24.58 E
Groot Baai	51b	Ab	18.01N	63.04W
Groote Eylandt	57	Ef	14.00S	136.40 E
Grootfontein	31	Ij	19.32S	18.05 E
Grootfontein [3]	37	Bc	19.00S	19.00 E
Groot-Karasberge=Great Karasberge (EN)	30	Ik	27.20S	18.45 E
Groot Karoo=Great Karroo (EN)	30	Jl	33.00S	22.00 E
Grootlaagte	37	Cd	20.55S	21.27 E
Groot Namaland/Great Namaland	37	Be	26.00S	17.00 E
Grootvloer	37	Ce	30.00S	20.40 E
Gropeni	15	Kd	45.05N	27.54 E
Gros Caps, Pointe des-	51e	Bb	16.28N	61.25W
Gros Islet Bay	51k	Ba	14.05N	60.58W
Gros Islets	51k	Ba	14.05N	60.58W
Gros-Morne	51h	Ab	14.43N	61.01W
Gros-Morne	42	Lg	49.00N	57.22W
Grosne	11	Kh	46.42N	4.56 E
Gros Piton	51k	Ab	13.49N	61.04W
Große Aa	12	Jb	52.25N	7.23 E
Große Aue	12	Kb	52.30N	8.38 E
Großefehn	12	Ja	53.24N	7.33 E
Große Laaber	10	Ih	48.50N	12.30 E
Großenhain	10	Je	51.17N	13.33 E
Großenkneten	12	Kb	52.57N	8.16 E
Grosse Pointe	51e	Bb	16.01N	61.17W
Großer Arber	10	Jg	49.07N	13.07 E
Großer Gleichberg	10	Gf	50.23N	10.35 E
Großer Inselsberg	10	Gf	50.52N	10.28 E
Grosseto	14	Fh	42.46N	11.08 E
Grosseto, Formiche di-	14	Eh	42.40N	10.55 E
Groß-Gerau	10	Eg	49.55N	8.29 E
Großglockner	5	Hf	47.04N	12.42 E
Großräschen	10	Je	51.35N	14.00 E
Groß-Umstadt	12	Ke	49.52N	8.56 E
Großvenediger	14	Gc	47.06N	12.21 E
Grostenquin	12	If	48.59N	6.44 E
Gros Ventre Range	46	Je	43.30N	110.15W
Groswater Bay	38	Nd	54.20N	57.30W
Grøtavær	7	Db	68.58N	16.16 E
Grote Nete	12	Gc	51.07N	4.34 E
Grotli	7	Be	62.01N	7.40 E
Grottaglie	14	Lj	40.32N	17.26 E
Grottammare	14	Hh	42.59N	13.52 E
Groumania	34	Ed	7.55N	4.00W
Groundhog River	44	Ga	49.43N	81.58W
Grouse Creek Mountains	46	If	41.55N	113.50W
Grove Mountains	66	Ff	72.53S	74.53 E
Groves	45	Jl	29.57N	93.55W
Grovfjord	7	Db	68.41N	17.09 E
Grow, Idaarderadeel-	12	Ha	53.06N	5.50 E
Grozny	6	Kg	43.20N	45.42 E
Grubišno Polje	14	Le	45.42N	17.10 E
Grudovo	15	Kg	42.21N	27.10 E
Grudziądz	10	Oc	53.29N	18.45 E
Grumento Nova	14	Jj	40.17N	15.53 E
Grumo Appula	14	Ki	41.01N	16.42 E
Grums	8	Ee	59.21N	13.06 E
Grünau	37	Be	27.47S	18.23 E
Grünberg	12	Kd	50.36N	8.57 E
Gründau	12	Ld	50.14N	9.05 E
Grundy	44	Fg	37.17N	82.06W
Grunidera	48	Ie	24.15N	101.58W
Grünstadt	12	Ke	49.34N	8.10 E
Grunwald	10	Qc	53.30N	20.05 E
Gruppo di Brenta	14	Ed	46.10N	10.55 E
Gruyère	14	Bd	46.40N	7.10 E
Gruža	15	Df	43.54N	20.47 E
Gruzinskaja Sovetskaja Socialističeskaja Respublika → Sakartvelo	19	Eg	42.00N	44.00 E
Gruzinskaja SSR/ Sakartvelos Sabčata Socialisturi Respublica →	19	Eg	42.00N	44.00 E
Sakartvelo	19	Eg	42.00N	44.00 E
Gruzinskaja SSR → Georgia (EN)	19	Eg	42.00N	44.00 E
Grybów	10	Qg	49.38N	20.56 E
Grycksbo	8	Fd	60.41N	15.28 E
Gryfice	10	Lc	53.56N	15.12 E
Gryfino	10	Kc	53.15N	14.30 E
Grythyttan	8	Fe	59.42N	14.32 E
Grytviken	66	Ad	54.17S	36.31W
Gstaad	14	Bd	46.28N	7.17 E
Guacanayabo, Golfo de-	47	Id	20.28N	77.30W
Guacara	50	Cg	10.14N	67.53W
Guaçu	55	Ef	22.11S	54.31W
Guadaioz	13	Hg	37.50N	4.51W
Guadaira	13	Fg	37.20N	6.01W
Guadalajara [3]	13	Jd	40.50N	2.30W
Guadalajara [Mex.]	39	Ig	20.40N	103.20W
Guadalajara [Sp.]	13	Id	40.38N	3.10W
Guadalbullón	13	Ig	37.59N	3.47W
Guadalcanal	13	Gf	38.06N	5.49W
Guadalcanal Island	57	He	9.32S	160.12 E
Guadalén	13	If	38.05N	3.32W
Guadalentín o Sangonera	13	Kg	37.59N	1.04W
Guadalete	13	Fh	36.35N	6.13W
Guadalfeo	13	Ih	36.43N	3.35W
Guadalimar	13	Ig	37.59N	3.44W
Guadalmena	13	Jf	38.20N	2.55W
Guadalmez	13	Gf	38.46N	5.04W
Guadalope	13	Lc	41.15N	0.03W
Guadalquivir	5	Fh	36.47N	6.22W
Guadalupe [Mex.]	47	Dc	25.41N	100.15W
Guadalupe [Mex.]	48	Hf	22.45N	102.31W
Guadalupe [Mex.]	48	Id	26.12N	101.23W
Guadalupe [Sp.]	13	Ge	39.27N	5.19W
Guadalupe, Isla de-	38	Hg	29.00N	118.16W
Guadalupe, Sierra de-	13	Ge	39.25N	5.25W
Guadalupe Bravos	48	Fb	31.23N	106.07W
Guadalupe Mountains	45	Dj	32.20N	105.00W
Guadalupe Peak	43	Ge	31.50N	104.52W
Guadalupe River	45	Hl	28.30N	96.53W
Guadalupe Victoria, Presa-	48	Gf	23.50N	104.55W
Guadalupe y Calvo	48	Fd	26.06N	106.58W
Guadarrama	13	He	39.53N	4.10W
Guadarrama, Puerto de-	13	Hd	40.43N	4.10W
Guadarrama, Sierra de-	13	Id	40.55N	4.00W
Guadazaón	13	Ke	39.42N	1.36W
Guadeloupe	38	Mh	16.15N	61.35W
Guadeloupe [5]	39	Mh	16.15N	61.35W
Guadeloupe, Canal de la-= Guadeloupe Passage (EN)	47	Le	16.40N	61.50W
Guadeloupe Passage	50	Fd	16.40N	61.50W
Guadeloupe Passage (EN)= Guadeloupe, Canal de la-	47	Le	16.40N	61.50W
Guadiana	5	Fh	37.14N	7.22W
Guadiana, Canal del-	13	Ie	39.20N	3.20W
Guadiana, Ojos del-	13	Ie	39.08N	3.31W
Guadiana Menor	13	Ig	37.56N	3.15W
Guadiaro	13	Gh	36.17N	5.17W
Guadiela	13	Jd	40.22N	2.49W
Guadix	13	Ig	37.18N	3.08W
Guafo, Boca del-	56	Ff	43.40S	74.15W
Guafo, Isla-	56	Ff	43.36S	74.43W
Guaiba	56	Jd	30.06S	51.19W
Guaíba, Rio-	55	Gj	30.15S	51.12W
Guaimaca	49	Df	14.52N	86.51W
Guaimorato, Laguna de-	49	Ef	15.58N	85.55W
Guainía [2]	54	Ec	2.30N	69.00W
Guainía, Rio-	52	Je	2.01N	67.07W
Guaiquinima, Cerro-	54	Fb	5.49N	63.40W
Guaira [3]	55	Dg	25.45S	56.30W
Guaíra [Braz.]	56	Jb	24.04S	54.15W
Guaíra [Braz.]	55	He	20.19S	48.18W
Guaira Falls (EN) = Sete Quedas, Saltos das-	56	Jb	24.02S	54.16W
Guairas	55	Ja	12.39S	44.16W
Guaire/Gorey	9	Gi	52.40N	6.18W
Guaitecas, Islas-	56	Ff	43.57S	73.50W
Guajaba, Cayo-	49	Ic	21.50N	77.30W
Guajará Mirim	53	Jg	10.48S	65.22W
Guajira, Península de la-	52	Id	12.00N	71.30W
Guajolotes, Sierra del-	48	Ge	26.00N	105.15W
Guakolak, Tanjung-	26	Eh	6.50S	105.14 E
Gualaco	49	Df	15.06N	86.07W
Gualán	49	Cf	15.08N	89.22W
Gualdo Tadino	14	Gg	43.14N	12.47 E
Gualeguay	55	Ck	33.09S	59.20W
Gualeguay, Rio-	55	Ck	33.19S	59.39W
Gualeguaychu	56	Id	33.01S	58.31W
Gualeguaychú, Rio-	55	Ck	33.05S	58.25W
Gualicho, Salina del-	56	Gf	40.24S	65.15W
Guam [5]	58	Fc	13.28N	144.47 E
Guam	57	Fc	13.28N	144.47 E
Guamini	56	He	37.02S	62.25W
Guampi, Sierra de-	54	Eb	6.00N	65.35W
Guamuchil	47	Cc	25.22N	108.22W
Gua Musang	26	Df	4.53N	101.58 E
Gu'an	28	De	39.24N	116.10 E
Guanabacoa	49	Fb	23.07N	82.18W
Guanabara, Baia de-	55	Kf	22.50S	43.10W
Guanacaste [3]	49	Eh	10.30N	85.15W
Guanacaste, Cordillera de-	49	Eh	10.45N	85.05W
Guanacevi	48	Ge	25.56N	105.57W
Guanahacabibes, Golfo de-	49	Eb	22.08N	84.35W
Guanahacabibes, Peninsula de-	49	Ec	21.57N	84.35W
Guana Island	51a	Db	18.29N	64.34W
Guanaja	49	Ee	16.27N	85.54W
Guanaja, Isla de-	49	Ee	16.30N	85.55W
Guanajay	49	Fb	22.55N	82.42W
Guanajibo	51a	Ab	18.10N	67.09W
Guanajibo, Punta-	51a	Ab	18.12N	67.10W
Guanajuato	47	Dd	21.01N	101.15W
Guanajuato [2]	47	Dd	21.00N	101.00W
Guanambi	54	Jf	14.13S	42.47W
Guanare	54	Eb	9.03N	69.45W
Guanare, Rio-	50	Ch	8.13N	67.46W
Guanare Viejo, Rio-	49	Mi	8.19N	68.10W
Guanarito	50	Bh	8.42N	69.12W
Guandacol	56	Gc	29.31S	68.32W
Guandi Shan	27	Jd	38.09N	111.27 E
Guane	47	Hd	22.12N	84.05W
Guangde	27	Ke	30.51N	119.26 E
Guangdong Sheng (Kuang-tung Sheng)= Kwangtung (EN) [2]	27	Jg	23.00N	113.00 E
Guangfeng	28	Ej	28.27N	118.12 E
Guanghua	27	Je	32.18N	111.45 E
Guangji (Wuxue)	27	Kf	29.58N	115.32 E
Guangling	28	Ce	39.46N	114.16 E
Guangmao Shan	27	Hf	26.48N	100.56 E
Guangming Ding	28	Ei	30.09N	118.11 E
Guangnan	27	Ig	24.02N	105.04 E
Guangrao	28	Ef	37.03N	118.25 E
Guangshan	28	Ci	32.02N	114.53 E
Guangshui	28	Ci	31.37N	114.01 E
Guangxi Zhuangzu Zizhiqu (Kuang-hsi-chuang-tsu Tzu-chih-ch'ü)=Kwangsi Chuang (EN) [2]	27	Ig	24.00N	109.00 E
Guangyuan	22	Mf	32.27N	105.55 E
Guangzhou=Canton (EN)	22	Ng	23.07N	113.18 E
Guan He	28	Ch	32.18N	115.44 E
Guánica	51a	Bc	17.59N	66.56W
Guanipa, Rio-	50	Eh	9.56N	62.26W
Guannan (Xin'anzhen)	28	Eg	34.04N	119.21 E
Guantánamo [3]	49	Jc	20.10N	75.00W
Guantanamo	39	Lg	20.08N	75.12W
Guantánamo, Bahia de-	49	Jd	20.00N	75.10W
Guantánamo Bay	47	Id	20.00N	75.10W
Guantanamo Bay Naval Station	49	Jd	20.00N	75.08W
Guantao (Nanguantao)	28	Cf	36.33N	115.18 E
Guanting Shuiku	28	Cd	40.13N	115.36 E
Guanxian	22	Mf	31.00N	103.38 E
Guanyun (Dayishan)	28	Eg	34.18N	119.14 E
Guapé	55	Je	20.47S	45.55W
Guapi	54	Cc	2.35N	77.55W
Guápiles	49	Fh	10.13N	83.46W
Guapó	55	Hc	16.51S	49.33W
Guaporé	55	Gi	29.10S	51.54W
Guaporé	56	Jc	28.51S	51.54W
Guaporé, Rio-	52	Jg	11.55S	65.04W
Guaqui	54	Eg	16.35S	68.51W
Guará	55	Gg	25.23S	51.17W
Guara, Sierra de-	13	Lb	42.17N	0.10W
Guarabira	54	Ke	6.51S	35.29W
Guaranda	54	Cd	1.35S	78.59W
Guaraniaçu	56	Jc	25.06S	52.52W
Guarani de Goiás	55	Ia	13.57S	46.28W
Guarapiche, Rio-	50	Eh	9.57N	62.52W
Guarapuava	56	Jc	25.23S	51.27W
Guaraqueçaba	55	Hg	25.17S	48.21W
Guararapes	55	Ge	21.15S	50.38W
Guaratinguetá	55	Jf	22.49S	45.13W
Guaratuba	55	Hg	25.54S	48.34W
Guarayos, Rio-	55	Bb	14.38S	62.11W
Guarda	13	Ed	40.32N	7.16W
Guarda [2]	13	Ed	40.40N	7.10W
Guardafui, Cape-(EN)= 'Asäyr	30	Mg	11.49N	51.15 E
Guardal	13	Jg	37.36N	2.45W
Guarda-Mor	55	Ic	17.47S	47.06W
Guardiagrele	14	Ih	42.11N	14.13 E
Guardian Seamount (EN)	38	Ki	9.32N	87.40W
Guardo	13	Hb	42.47N	4.50W
Guardunha, Serra da-	13	Ed	40.05N	7.31W
Guarei, Rio-	55	Ff	22.40S	53.34W
Guareña	13	Gc	41.29N	5.23W
Guarenas	50	Cg	10.28N	66.37W
Guaribas, Rio-	55	Jc	16.22S	45.03W
Guaribe, Rio-	50	Dh	9.53N	65.11W
Guárico [2]	54	Eb	8.40N	66.35W
Guárico, Embalse del-	50	Ch	9.00N	67.20W
Guarico, Rio-	54	Eb	7.55N	67.23W
Guariquito, Rio-	50	Ci	7.40N	66.18W
Guarita, Rio-	55	Fh	27.11S	53.44W
Guaritico, Caño-	50	Bi	7.52N	68.53W
Guaritire, Rio-	55	Ba	13.43S	60.38W
Guarujá	55	If	24.00S	46.16W
Guarulhos	56	Kb	23.28S	46.32W
Guasave	47	Cc	25.34N	108.27W
Guasdualito	54	Db	7.15N	70.44W
Guasipati	54	Fb	7.28N	61.54W
Guasopa	63a	Ac	9.14S	152.55 E
Guastalla	14	Ef	44.55N	10.39 E
Guatemala	39	Jh	14.38N	90.31W
Guatemala [3]	49	Bf	14.40N	90.30W
Guatemala [1]	39	Jh	14.38N	90.31W
Guatemala Basin (EN)	3	Mh	11.00N	95.00W
Guateque [Col.]	54	Db	5.05N	73.30W
Guateque [Col.]	54	Db	5.00N	73.28W
Guatimozin	55	Ak	33.27S	62.27W
Guatisimiña	54	Fc	4.33N	63.57W
Guatraché	56	He	37.40S	63.32W
Guaviare	54	Dc	2.00N	72.00W
Guaviravi	55	Di	29.22S	56.50W
Guaxupé	55	Ie	21.18S	46.42W
Guayabal [Cuba]	49	Ic	20.42N	77.36W
Guayabal [Ven.]	50	Ci	8.00N	67.24W
Guayabero, Rio-	52	Je	4.03N	67.44W
Guayalejo, Rio-	48	Kf	22.13N	97.52W
Guayama	49	Ne	17.59N	66.07W
Guayana, Macizo de la-= Guiana Highlands (EN)	52	Ke	5.00N	60.00W
Guayana Basin (EN)	3	Ci	10.00N	52.00W
Guayaneco, Archipiélago-	56	Eg	47.45S	75.10W
Guayanés, Punta-	51a	Cb	18.04N	65.48W
Guayanilla	51a	Bb	18.02N	66.47W
Guayanilla, Bahía de-	51a	Bc	17.58N	66.45W
Guayape, Rio-	49	Df	14.26N	86.02W
Guayaquil	53	If	2.10S	79.50W
Guayaquil, Golfo de-	52	Hf	3.00S	80.30W
Guaycurú, Rio-	55	Ch	27.19S	58.45W
Guaymas	39	Hg	27.56N	110.54W
Guayquiraró, Rio-	55	Cj	30.10S	58.34W
Guba [Eth.]	35	Fc	11.15N	35.20 E
Guba [Zaire]	36	Ee	10.38S	26.25 E
Guba Dolgaja	19	Fa	70.19N	58.45 E
Gubaha	19	Fd	58.52N	57.36 E
Guban	30	Lg	10.15N	44.26 E
Gubbio	14	Gg	43.21N	12.55 E
Gubdor	17	Hf	60.15N	56.35 E
Guben	10	Ke	51.57N	14.43 E
Gubin	10	Ke	51.56N	14.45 E
Gubio	34	Hc	12.30N	12.47 E
Gubkin	19	De	51.17N	37.33 E
Gúdar, Sierra de-	13	Ld	40.27N	0.42W
Gudara	19	Hh	38.23N	72.42 E
Gudauta	16	Lh	43.07N	40.37 E
Gudbrandsdalen	7	Bf	61.30N	10.00 E
Gudenå	8	Dh	56.29N	10.13 E
Gudermes	19	Eg	43.22N	46.08 E
Gudivāda	25	Ge	16.27N	80.59 E
Gudiyāttam	25	Ff	12.57N	78.52 E
Gudou Shan	27	Jg	22.12N	112.57 E
Güdül	24	Eb	40.13N	32.15 E
Güdür	25	Ff	14.08N	79.51 E
Gudvangen	8	Bd	60.52N	6.50 E
Guebwiller	11	Ng	47.55N	7.12 E
Guékédou	34	Cd	8.33N	10.09W
Guelma [3]	32	Ib	36.15N	7.30 E
Guelma	32	Ib	36.28N	7.26 E
Guelph	42	Jh	43.33N	80.15W
Guelta Zemmur	32	Ed	25.08N	12.22W
Guemar	32	Ic	33.29N	6.48 E
Guémené-Penfao	11	Eg	47.38N	1.50W
Guénange	12	Ie	49.18N	6.11 E
Guéné	34	Fc	11.44N	3.13 E
Guer	11	Dg	47.54N	2.07W
Guéra [3]	35	Bc	11.30N	18.30 E
Güera	32	De	20.52N	17.03W
Guéra, Massif de-	30	Ig	11.55N	18.12 E
Guérande	11	Dg	47.20N	2.26W
Guerara	32	Hc	32.48N	4.30 E
Guercif	32	Gc	34.14N	3.22W
Guerdjoumane, Djebel-	13	Oh	36.25N	2.51 E
Güere, Rio-	50	Dh	9.50N	65.08W
Guéréda	35	Cc	14.31N	22.05 E
Guéret	11	Hh	46.10N	1.52 E
Guérin-Kouka	34	Fd	9.41N	0.37 E
Guernica y Luno	13	Ja	43.19N	2.41W
Guernsey	9	Kl	49.27N	2.35W
Guerrero [2]	47	De	17.40N	100.00W
Guerrero	48	Ic	28.20N	100.26W
Guessou-Sud	34	Fc	10.03N	2.38 E
Guest Peninsula	66	Mf	76.18S	148.00W
Guge	35	Fd	6.12N	37.30 E
Gügerd, Küh-e-	24	Oe	34.50N	53.00 E
Guglionesi	14	Ii	41.55N	14.55 E
Guguan Island	57	Fc	17.19N	145.51 E
Guia	55	Db	15.22S	56.14W
Guia Lopes da Laguna	55	De	21.26S	56.07W
Guiana Highlands (EN) = Guayana, Macizo de la-	52	Ke	5.00N	60.00W
Guiana Island	51d	Bb	17.06N	61.44W
Guichi (Chizhou)	27	Ke	30.38N	117.30 E
Guichón	55	Dk	32.21S	57.12W
Guide	27	Hd	36.00N	101.30 E
Guider	34	Hd	9.56N	13.57 E
Guidimaka [3]	32	Ef	15.30N	12.00W
Guidimouni	34	Gc	13.42N	9.30 E
Guiding	27	If	26.33N	107.16 E
Guidong	27	Jf	26.11N	113.58 E
Guiers	11	Li	45.37N	5.37 E
Guiglo	34	Dd	6.33N	7.29W
Guiglo [3]	34	Dd	6.30N	7.40W
Guijá	37	Ed	24.29S	33.00 E
Güija, Lago de-	49	Cf	14.13N	89.34W
Gui Jiang	21	Ng	23.28N	111.18 E
Guijk en Sint Agatha	12	Hc	51.44N	5.52 E
Guijuelo	13	Gd	40.33N	5.40W
Guil	11	Mj	44.40N	6.36 E
Guildford	9	Mj	51.14N	0.35W
Guiler Gol	28	Ga	46.03N	122.06 E
Guilin	22	Ng	25.21N	110.15 E
Guillaume Delisle, Lac-	42	Je	56.25N	76.00W
Guillestre	11	Mj	44.40N	6.39 E
Guilvinec	11	Bg	47.47N	4.17W
Guimarães [Braz.]	54	Jd	2.08S	44.36W
Guimarães [Port.]	13	Dc	41.27N	8.18W
Guimaras	26	Hd	10.35N	122.37 E
Guinchos Cay	49	Hb	22.45N	78.06W
Guinea (EN)=Guinée [1]	31	Fg	11.00N	10.00W
Guinea, Gulf of-	30	Hh	2.00N	2.30 E
Guinea, Gulf of- (EN)= Guinée, Golfe de-	30	Hh	2.00N	2.30 E
Guinea Basin (EN)	3	Di	0.00	5.00W
Guinea-Bissau (EN)=Guiné-Bissau [1]	31	Fg	12.00N	15.00W
Guinea Ecuatorial= Equatorial Guinea (EN) [1]	31	Hh	2.00N	9.00 E
Guinea Rise (EN)	3	Dj	4.00S	0.00
Guiné-Bissau=Guinea-Bissau (EN) [1]	31	Fg	12.00N	15.00W
Guinée=Guinea (EN) [1]	31	Fg	11.00N	10.00W
Guinée, Golfe de-=Guinea, Gulf of- (EN)	30	Hh	2.00N	2.30 E
Guinée Forestière [3]	34	Dd	8.40N	9.50W
Guinée Maritime [3]	34	Cc	10.00N	14.00W
Guînes	12	Dd	50.52N	1.52 E
Güines	47	Hd	22.50N	82.02W
Guingamp	11	Cf	48.33N	3.09W
Guinguinéo	34	Bc	14.16N	15.57W
Guiones, Punta-	49	Eh	9.54N	85.41W
Guiping	27	Ig	23.23N	110.00 E
Guipúzcoa [3]	13	Ja	43.10N	2.10W
Guir, Hamada du-	30	Ge	31.00N	3.20W
Güira de Melena	49	Fb	22.48N	82.30W
Guiratinga	54	Hg	16.21S	53.45W
Güiria	54	Fa	10.34N	62.18W
Guiscard	12	Fe	49.39N	3.03 E
Guise	11	Je	49.54N	3.38 E
Guitiriz	13	Ea	43.11N	7.54W
Guiuan	26	Id	11.02N	125.43 E
Guixi	27	Kf	28.18N	117.15 E
Guixian	27	Ig	23.10N	109.35 E
Guiyang	22	Mg	26.38N	106.43 E
Guizhou Sheng (Kuei-chou Sheng)=Kweichow (EN) [2]	27	If	27.00N	107.00 E
Gujan-Mestras	11	Ej	44.38N	1.04W
Gujarāt [3]	25	Ed	22.51N	71.30 E
Gujarāt	21	Jg	22.51N	71.30 E
Gujrānwāla	22	Jf	32.09N	74.11 E
Gujrāt	25	Eb	32.34N	74.05 E
Gukovo	16	Ke	48.04N	39.58 E
Gulang	27	Hd	37.30N	102.54 E
Gulbarga	22	Jh	17.20N	76.50 E
Gulbene	19	Cd	57.12N	26.49 E
Gulča	19	Hg	40.19N	73.33 E
Gulf	55	Ad	19.08S	62.01W
Gulf Breeze	44	Dj	30.22N	87.07W
Gulf Coastal Plain	38	Jf	31.00N	92.00W
Gulfport	43	Je	30.22N	89.06W
Gulian	27	La	52.58N	122.09 E
Gulin	27	If	28.02N	105.47 E
Gulistan	19	Gg	40.30N	68.45 E
Guliya Shan	27	Lb	49.48N	122.25 E
Gulja	20	Hf	54.43N	121.03 E
Gulja/Yining	27	Dc	43.54N	81.21 E
Guljajpole	16	Jf	47.37N	36.18 E
Gulkana	40	Jd	62.16N	145.23W
Gulkeviči	16	Lg	45.19N	40.44 E
Gull Bay	45	Lb	49.47N	89.02W
Gulleråsen	8	Fc	61.04N	15.11 E
Gullfoss	7a	Bb	64.20N	20.08W
Gullkronafjärd	8	Jd	60.05N	22.15 E
Gull Lake	42	Gf	50.08N	108.27W
Gullringen	8	Fg	57.48N	15.42 E
Gull River	45	Lb	49.50N	89.04W
Gullspång	8	Ff	58.59N	14.06 E
Güllü	15	Mk	38.16N	29.07 E
Güllük	24	Bd	37.14N	27.36 E
Gülpinar	15	Jj	39.32N	26.07 E
Gülşehir	24	Fc	38.45N	34.38 E
Gulstav	8	Dj	54.43N	10.41 E
Gulu	31	Kh	2.47N	32.18 E
Guma /Pishan	27	Cd	37.38N	78.19 E
Gumbiri, Jabal-	35	Ee	4.18N	30.57 E
Gumel	34	Gc	12.38N	9.23 E
Gummersbach	10	De	51.02N	7.33 E
Gummi	34	Gc	12.09N	5.07 E
Gümüşçey	15	Ki	40.17N	27.17 E
Gümüşhacıköy	24	Fb	40.53N	35.14 E
Gümüşhane	23	Ea	40.27N	39.29 E
Gümüşsu	15	Nk	38.14N	30.01 E
Guna	35	Fc	11.44N	38.15 E
Guna	25	Fd	24.19N	77.19 E
Gundagai	59	Jg	35.04S	148.07 E
Gundji	36	Db	2.05N	21.27 E
Gündoğdu	15	Ki	40.15N	27.07 E
Gündoğmuş	24	Ed	36.48N	32.01 E
Güney	15	Mk	38.09N	29.05 E
Güneydoğu Toroslar	21	Gf	38.30N	41.00 E
Gungu	36	Cd	5.44S	19.19 E
Gunma Ken [2]	28	Of	36.20N	139.05 E
Gunnar	42	Ge	59.23N	108.53W
Gunnbjørns Fjeld	67	Mc	68.55N	29.20W
Gunnedah	59	Kf	30.59S	150.15 E
Gunnison	43	Fd	38.33N	106.56W
Gunt	18	Hf	37.30N	71.03 E
Guntakal	25	Fe	15.10N	77.23 E
Guntersville	44	Dh	34.21N	86.18W
Guntersville Lake	44	Dh	34.45N	86.03W
Guntür	22	Kh	16.18N	80.27 E
Gunungapi, Pulau-	26	Ih	6.38S	126.40 E
Gunungsitoli	26	Cf	1.17N	97.37 E
Günz	10	Gh	48.27N	10.16 E
Günzburg	10	Gh	48.27N	10.16 E
Gunzenhausen	10	Gg	49.06N	10.45 E
Guo He	28	Dh	32.58N	117.13 E
Guojiadian	28	Hc	43.20N	124.37 E
Guoyang	28	Dh	33.31N	116.12 E
Guozhen	28	Bj	29.24N	113.09 E
Gurahonţ	15	Fc	46.16N	22.21 E
Gura Humorului	15	Ib	47.33N	25.54 E
Gurban Obo	27	Jc	43.06N	112.28 E
Gurbantünggüt Shamo	27	Eb	45.30N	87.30 E
Gurdžaani	16	Ni	41.43N	45.48 E
Güre	15	Mk	38.39N	29.10 E
Gurgei, Jabal-	35	Cc	13.50N	24.19 E
Gurghiului, Munţii-	15	Ic	46.41N	25.12 E
Gurgueia, Rio-	52	Lf	6.50S	43.24W
Guri — Raúl Leoni, Represa-	54	Fb	7.30N	63.00W
Gurjev — Atyrau	6	Lf	47.07N	51.56 E
Gurjevsk	20	Df	54.20N	86.00 E
Gurk	14	Id	46.36N	14.31 E
Gurk	14	Id	46.52N	14.18 E
Gurktaler Alpen	14	Hd	46.55N	14.00 E
Guro	37	Ec	17.26S	33.20 E
Gürpınar	24	Jc	38.18N	43.25 E
Gurskoje	20	If	50.20N	138.05 E
Gurskøy	7	Ae	62.15N	5.40 E
Gürsu	15	Mi	40.13N	29.12 E
Guruè	37	Fc	15.28S	36.59 E
Gurumeti	36	Fc	2.05S	33.57 E
Gürün	24	Gc	38.43N	37.17 E
Gurupá	54	Hd	1.25S	51.39W
Gurupi	53	Lg	11.43S	49.04W
Gurupi, Rio-	52	Lf	1.13S	46.06W
Gurupi, Serra do-	54	Id	5.00S	47.30W
Guru Sikhar	25	Ed	24.39N	72.46 E
Gus	7	Ji	55.00N	41.12 E
Gusau	31	Hg	12.10N	6.40 E
Gusev	19	Ce	54.37N	22.12 E
Gushan	28	Ge	39.54N	123.36 E
Gushi	27	Ke	32.02N	115.39 E
Gushikawa	29b	Ab	26.21N	127.52 E
Gushk	24	Ph	28.13N	55.52 E
Gus-Hrustalny	7	Ji	55.38N	40.40 E
Gusinaja, Guba-	20	Kb	72.00N	150.00 E
Gusinaja Zemlja, Poluostrov-	19	Fa	71.50N	52.00 E
Gusinje	15	Cg	42.34N	19.50 E
Gusinoozersk	20	Ff	51.17N	106.30 E
Guspini	14	Ck	39.32N	8.37 E
Güssing	14	Kc	47.04N	16.20 E
Gustav Holm, Kap-	41	Ie	66.45N	34.00W
Gustavia	51b	Bc	17.54N	62.52W

Index Symbols

[1] Independent Nation
[2] State, Region
[3] District, County
[4] Municipality
[5] Colony, Dependency
Continent
Physical Region
Historical or Cultural Region
Mount, Mountain
Volcano
Hill
Mountains, Mountain Range
Hills, Escarpment
Plateau, Upland
Pass, Gap
Plain, Lowland
Delta
Salt Flat
Valley, Canyon
Crater, Cave
Karst Features
Depression
Polder
Desert, Dunes
Forest, Woods
Heath, Steppe
Oasis
Cape, Point
Coast, Beach
Cliff
Peninsula
Isthmus
Sandbank
Island
Atoll
Rock, Reef
Islands, Archipelago
Rocks, Reefs
Coral Reef
Well, Spring
Geyser
River, Stream
Waterfall Rapids
River Mouth, Estuary
Lake
Salt Lake
Intermittent Lake
Reservoir
Swamp, Pond
Canal
Glacier
Ice Shelf, Pack Ice
Ocean
Sea
Gulf, Bay
Strait, Fjord
Lagoon
Bank
Seamount
Tablemount
Ridge
Shelf
Basin
Escarpment, Sea Scarp
Fracture
Trench, Abyss
National Park, Reserve
Point of Interest
Recreation Site
Cave, Cavern
Historic Site
Ruins
Wall, Walls
Church, Abbey
Temple
Scientific Station
Airport
Port
Lighthouse
Mine
Tunnel
Dam, Bridge

Gustavs/Kustavi 8 Id 60.30N 21.25 E
Gustavs/Kustavi 8 Id 60.33N 21.21 E
Gustavsfors 8 Ee 59.12N 12.06 E
Gustavus 40 Le 58.25N 135.44W
Güstrow 10 Ic 53.48N 12.10 E
Gusum 8 Gf 58.16N 16.29 E
Gütersloh 10 Ee 51.54N 8.23 E
Guthrie [Ok.-U.S.] 45 Hi 35.53N 97.25W
Guthrie [Tx.-U.S.] 45 Fj 33.37N 100.19W
Gutian 27 Kf 26.40N 118.42 E
Gutiérrez Zamora 48 Kg 20.27N 97.05W
Gutii, Vîrful- 15 Gb 47.42N 23.52 E
Guting → Yutai 28 Dg 35.00N 116.40 E
Gutu 37 Ec 19.39S 31.10 E
Guwāhāti 22 Lg 26.11N 91.44 E
Guyana 53 Ke 5.00N 59.00W
Guyane Française = French Guiana (EN) [5] 53 Ke 4.00N 53.00W
Guyang 27 Jc 41.02N 110.04 E
Guyenne 11 Gj 44.35N 1.00 E
Guymon 43 Gd 36.41N 101.29W
Guyonneau, Anse- 51e Ab 16.14N 61.47W
Guyuan 27 Id 36.01N 106.17 E
Guyuan (Pingdingbu) 28 Cd 41.40N 115.41 E
Guzar 18 Fe 38.37N 66.18 E
Güzelyurt 24 Ee 35.12N 32.59 E
Güzhān 24 Le 34.20N 46.57 E
Guzhen 28 Dh 33.20N 117.19 E
Guzhou → Rongjiang 27 If 25.58N 108.30 E
Guzmán, Laguna de- 48 Fb 31.20N 107.30W
Gvardejsk 7 Ei 54.40N 21.03 E
Gvardejskoje 16 Hg 45.06N 33.59 E
Gvary 8 Ce 59.23N 9.09 E
Gwa 25 Ie 17.36N 94.35 E
Gwadabawa 34 Gc 13.22N 5.14 E
Gwādar 22 Ig 25.07N 62.19 E
Gwai 30 Jj 17.59S 26.52 E
Gwai 37 Dc 19.17S 27.39 E
Gwalior 22 Jg 26.13N 78.10 E
Gwanda 37 Dd 20.56S 29.00 E
Gwane 36 Eb 4.43N 25.50 E
Gwda 10 Mc 53.04N 16.44 E
Gweebarra Bay/Béal an Bheara 9 Eg 54.52N 8.20W
Gwent 9 Kj 51.45N 2.55W
Gweru 31 Jj 19.27S 29.49 E
Gweta 37 Dd 20.13S 25.14 E
Gwydir River 59 Je 29.27S 149.48 E
Gwynedd [3] 9 Ji 52.50N 3.50W
Gyaca 27 Ff 29.09N 92.38 E
Gya'gya → Saga 27 Ef 29.22N 85.15 E
Gyai Qu 27 Fe 31.30N 94.40 E
Gyaisi/Jiulong 27 Hf 28.58N 101.33 E
Gya La 27 Gf 29.05N 98.41 E
Gyala Shankou 27 Gf 29.05N 98.41 E
Gyangzê 27 Ef 29.00N 89.38 E
Gyaring Co 27 Ee 31.10N 88.15 E
Gyaring Hu 27 Ge 34.55N 98.00 E
Gyda 20 Cb 70.52N 78.30 E
Gydanskaja Guba 20 Cb 71.20N 76.30 E
Gydanski Poluostrov = Gyda Peninsula (EN) 21 Jb 70.50N 79.00 E
Gyda Peninsula (EN) = Gydanski Poluostrov 21 Jb 70.50N 79.00 E
Gyigang → Zayü 27 Gf 28.43N 97.25 E
Gyirong (Zongga) 27 Ef 28.57N 85.12 E
Gyldenløves Fjord 41 Hf 64.10N 40.30W
Gyldenløves Høj 8 Di 55.33N 11.52 E
Gympie 58 Gg 26.11S 152.40 E
Gyoma 10 Qj 46.56N 20.50 E
Gyöngyös 10 Pi 47.47N 19.56 E
Györ 6 Hf 47.41N 17.38 E
Györ [2] 10 Ni 47.40N 17.39 E
Győr-Moson-Sopron 10 Ni 47.40N 17.15 E
Gypsumville 42 Hf 51.45N 98.35W
Gysinge 8 Gd 60.17N 16.53 E
Gyttorp 8 Fe 59.31N 14.58 E
Gyula 10 Rj 46.39N 21.17 E

H

Haacht 12 Gd 50.59N 4.38 E
Häädemeeste/Hjademeste 8 Uf 58.00N 24.28 E
Ha'afeva 65b Ba 19.57S 174.43W
Haafusia 64h Bb 13.18S 176.09W
Haag, Mount- 66 Qf 77.40S 79.00W
Haaksbergen 12 Ib 52.09N 6.45 E
Haamstede, Westerschouwen- 12 Fc 51.42N 3.45 E
Haanja Kõrgustik 8 Lg 57.30N 27.30 E
Ha'ano 65b Ba 19.40S 174.17W
Ha'apai Group 57 Jf 19.47S 174.27W
Haapajärvi 7 Fe 63.45N 25.20 E
Haapamäki 8 Kb 62.15N 24.28 E
Haapasaari 8 Ld 60.15N 27.10 E
Haapaselkä [Fin.] 8 Mc 61.35N 28.15 E
Haapaselkä [Fin.] 8 Mb 62.10N 28.10 E
Haapiti 65e Fc 17.34S 149.52W
Haapsalu 19 Cd 58.57N 23.32 E
Ha'arava 24 Fg 30.58N 32.24 E
Haardt 10 Dg 49.15N 8.00 E
Haardtkopf 12 Je 49.51N 7.04 E
Haaren, Wünnenberg- 12 Kc 51.34N 8.44 E
Haarlem 11 Kb 52.23N 4.38 E
Haarlemmermeer 12 Gb 52.20N 4.41 E
Haarlerberg 12 Ib 52.20N 6.25 E
Haarstrang 12 Kc 51.30N 8.20 E
Haast 58 Hi 43.52S 169.01 E
Haast Pass 62 Cf 44.06S 169.21 E
Habahe/Kaba 27 Eb 47.53N 86.12 E
Habarovsk 22 Pe 48.27N 135.06 E
Habarovski Kraj [3] 20 If 53.00N 137.00 E
Ḩabarūt 23 Hf 17.22N 52.42 E
Ḩabashīyah, Jabal- 35 Ib 16.45N 50.05 E
Habaswein 36 Gb 1.01N 39.29 E
Habay [Alta.-Can.] 42 Fe 58.52N 118.45W
Habay [Bel.] 12 He 49.45N 5.38 E
Habay [Som.] 35 Ge 1.08N 43.46 E
Ḩabbān 35 Hc 14.21N 47.05 E
Ḩabbānīyah, Hawr al- 24 Jf 33.17N 43.29 E
Habibas, Iles- 13 Ki 35.44N 1.08W
Habichtswald 10 Fe 51.20N 9.25 E
Habo 8 Fg 57.55N 14.04 E
Haboro 27 Pc 44.22N 141.42 E
Ḩabshān 24 Ok 23.50N 53.37 E
Hache 10 Ec 53.05N 8.50 E
Hachenburg 12 Jd 50.39N 7.50 E
Hachijō 29 Fe 35.15N 139.45 E
Hachijō-Fuji 29 Fe 33.08N 139.46 E
Hachijō-Jima 27 Oe 33.05N 139.50 E
Hachiman 29 Ed 35.46N 136.57 E
Hachimori 29 Fa 40.22N 140.00 E
Hachinohe 22 Qe 40.30N 141.29 E
Hachiōji 29 Fd 35.39N 139.18 E
Hachiro-Gata 29 Fa 40.00N 140.00 E
Hacibey De 24 Kd 36.58N 44.18 E
Hackar Daği 24 Ib 40.50N 41.10 E
Hackås 7 De 62.55N 14.31 E
Håckren 8 Ea 63.10N 13.35 E
Hačmas 19 Eg 41.25N 48.52 E
Hadagang 28 Kb 45.24N 131.12 E
Hadamar 12 Kd 50.27N 8.03 E
Ḩaḑan, Ḩarrat- 33 He 21.30N 41.23 E
Hadano 29 Fd 35.22N 139.14 E
Ḩaḑāribah, Ra's al- 35 Fa 22.04N 36.54 E
Hadd, Ra's al- 21 Hg 22.32N 59.59 E
Haddad 30 Ig 14.40N 18.46 E
Ḩadded 35 Hc 10.10N 48.28 E
Haddington 9 Kf 55.58N 2.47W
Haddummati Atoll 25a Bb 1.45N 73.30 E
Hadejia 34 Hc 12.27N 10.03 E
Hadejia 34 Hc 12.50N 10.51 E
Hadeland 8 Dd 60.25N 10.35 E
Hadeln 10 Ec 53.45N 8.45 E
Hadera 24 Ff 32.26N 34.55 E
Haderslev 7 Bi 55.15N 9.30 E
Hadībah 23 Hg 12.39N 54.02 E
Hadım 24 Ed 36.59N 32.28 E
Hadimköy 24 Cb 41.09N 28.37 E
Hadīyah 23 Ed 25.34N 38.41 E
Hadjer el Hamis 35 Ac 12.51N 14.50 E
Hadjout 13 Oh 36.31N 2.25 E
Hadleigh 12 Cb 52.03N 0.56 E
Hadley Bay 42 Gb 72.30N 108.30W
Ha Dong 25 Ld 20.58N 105.46 E
Ḩaḑramawt 21 Gh 15.00N 50.00 E
Hadrian's Wall 9 Kg 54.59N 2.26W
Hadsten 8 Dh 56.20N 10.03 E
Hadsund 8 Dh 56.43N 10.07 E
Hadytajaha 17 Nc 66.57N 69.12 E
Hadyžensk 16 Kg 44.25N 39.31 E
Hadzibeiski Liman 15 Nc 46.40N 30.30 E
Haedo, Cuchilla de- 55 Dj 31.40S 56.18W
Haeju 28 He 38.02N 125.42 E
Haena 60 Oc 22.13N 159.34W
Ḩafar al 'Atk 24 Lj 25.56N 46.47 E
Ḩafar al Bāṭin 23 Gd 28.27N 46.00 E
Haffner Bjerg 41 Fc 76.30N 63.00W
Ḩaffūz 14 Do 35.38N 9.40 E
Hafik 24 Gc 39.52N 37.24 E
Ḩafirat al 'Aydā 23 Ed 26.26N 39.12 E
Ḩafit 24 Pk 23.59N 55.49 E
Ḩafit, Jabal- 24 Pj 24.03N 55.46 E
Hafnarfjördur 7a Bb 64.04N 21.57W
Haft Gel 24 Mg 31.27N 49.27 E
Hāfūn 35 Ic 10.10N 51.05 E
Hāfūn, Rās- = Hafun, Ras- (EN) 30 Mg 10.27N 51.24 E
Hafun, Ras-(EN) = Hāfūn, Rās- 30 Mg 10.27N 51.24 E
Hāfūn Bay North 35 Ic 10.37N 51.15 E
Hāfūn Bay South 35 Ic 10.15N 51.05 E
Hagadera 36 Hb 0.02N 40.17 E
Hagby 8 Gh 56.33N 16.10 E
Hageland 12 Gd 50.55N 4.45 E
Hagemeister 40 Ge 58.40N 161.00W
Hagen 10 De 51.21N 7.28 E
Hagenow 10 Hc 53.26N 11.12 E
Hagere Hiywet 35 Fd 8.58N 37.53 E
Hagerman 46 He 42.49N 114.54W
Hagerstown 43 Ld 39.39N 77.43W
Hagetmau 11 Fk 43.40N 0.35W
Hagfors 7 Cf 60.02N 13.42 E
Häggenås 8 Fa 63.24N 14.55 E
Hagi 28 Kg 34.24N 131.25 E
Ha Giang 25 Kd 22.50N 104.59 E
Hágios Theódóros 24 Fe 35.20N 34.01 E
Hagman, Puntan- 64b Ba 15.09N 145.48 E
Hagondange 11 Me 49.15N 6.10 E
Hags Head/Ceanna Cailliqhe 9 Di 52.57N 9.28W
Hague, Cap de la- 5 Ff 49.43N 1.57W
Haguenau 11 Nf 48.49N 7.47 E
Hagunia 32 Ed 27.26N 12.24W
Hahajima-Rettō 60 Cb 26.37N 142.10 E
Hahns Peak 45 Cf 40.56N 107.01W
Hahót 10 Mj 46.38N 16.56 E
Hai'an 28 Fh 32.33N 120.26 E
Haicheng 27 Lc 40.51N 122.43 E
Haidenaab 10 Ig 49.35N 12.08 E
Hai Duong 25 Ld 20.56N 106.19 E
Haifa (EN) = Hefa 22 Ff 32.50N 35.00 E
Haifeng 27 Kg 22.58N 115.21 E
Haiger 12 Kd 50.45N 8.13 E
Hai He 28 De 38.57N 117.43 E
Haikakan Sovetakan Socialistakan Respublika/ Armjanskaja SSR → Hayastan 19 Eg 40.00N 45.00 E
Haikang (Leizhou) 27 Jg 20.56N 110.06 E
Haikou 22 Ng 20.05N 110.20 E
Hā'il 22 Gg 27.33N 41.42 E
Hailar 22 Ne 49.14N 119.42 E
Hailar He 21 Ne 49.30N 117.50 E
Hailin 27 Mc 44.35N 129.22 E
Hailong (Meihekou) 27 Mc 42.32N 125.37 E
Hailsham 12 Cd 50.52N 0.16 E
Hailun 27 Mb 47.29N 126.55 E
Hailuoto/Karlö 5 Ib 65.02N 24.42 E
Haima Tan 27 Kd 10.52N 116.53 E
Haimen [China] 28 Fi 31.53N 121.10 E
Haimen [China] 28 Fj 28.40N 121.27 E
Haina 12 Kc 51.03N 8.56 E
Hainan Dao 21 Mh 19.00N 109.00 E
Hainaut 11 Jd 50.20N 3.50 E
Hainaut [3] 12 Fd 50.30N 4.00 E
Hainburg an der Donau 14 Kb 48.09N 16.56 E
Haines 39 Fd 59.14N 135.27W
Haines Junction 42 Dd 60.45N 137.30W
Hainich 10 Ge 51.05N 10.27 E
Hainleite 10 Ge 51.20N 10.48 E
Hai Phong 22 Mg 20.52N 106.41 E
Haiti = Haïti (EN) [1] 39 Lh 19.00N 72.25W
Haiti (EN) = Haïti [1] 39 Lh 19.00N 72.25W
Haixing (Suji) 28 De 38.10N 117.29 E
Haixin Shan 27 Hd 37.00N 100.03 E
Haiyan (Sanjiaocheng) 27 Hd 36.58N 100.50 E
Haiyan (Wuyuanzhen) 28 Fi 30.31N 120.56 E
Haiyang (Dongcun) 28 Ff 36.46N 121.09 E
Haiyang Dao 28 Ge 39.03N 123.12 E
Haiyou → Sanmen 27 Lf 29.08N 121.22 E
Haiyuan 27 Id 36.35N 105.40 E
Haizhou 28 Eg 34.34N 119.08 E
Haizhou Wan 27 Nf 35.00N 119.30 E
Ḩajar Banga 35 Cc 11.30N 23.00 E
Hajdarken 19 Hh 39.55N 71.24 E
Hajdú-Bihar [2] 10 Ri 47.25N 21.30 E
Hajdúböszörmény 10 Ri 47.40N 21.31 E
Hajdúhadház 10 Ri 47.41N 21.40 E
Hajdúnánás 10 Ri 47.51N 21.26 E
Hajdúság 10 Ri 47.35N 21.30 E
Hajdúszoboszló 10 Ri 47.27N 21.24 E
Hajihi-Zaki 29 Fb 38.19N 138.31 E
Ḩājjiābād [Iran] 24 Ph 28.19N 55.55 E
Ḩājjiābād [Iran] 24 Ph 28.22N 54.27 E
Ḩājjiābād-e Māsileh 24 Ne 34.49N 51.13 E
Hajnówka 10 Td 52.45N 23.36 E
Hajós 10 Pj 46.24N 19.07 E
Hajpudyrskaja Guba 17 Ib 68.40N 59.30 E
Hakase-Yama 29 Fc 37.22N 139.43 E
Hakasija, respublika 20 Df 53.30N 90.00 E
Hakata-Wan 29 Be 33.40N 130.20 E
Hakefjord 8 Dg 57.41N 11.44 E
Hakha 25 Id 22.39N 93.37 E
Hakkâri 23 Fb 37.34N 43.45 E
Hakken-Zan 29 Dd 34.10N 135.54 E
Hakköda San 29 Ga 40.40N 140.53 E
Hako-Dake 29a Ca 44.40N 142.25 E
Hakodate 22 Qe 41.45N 140.43 E
Hakone-Yama 29 Fd 35.13N 139.00 E
Hakui 28 Nf 36.53N 136.47 E
Hakupu 64k Bb 19.06S 169.50W
Haku-San 29 Ec 36.09N 136.45 E
Hal/Halle 11 Kd 50.44N 4.14 E
Halab 24 Md 36.17N 48.03 E
Ḩalab = Aleppo (EN) 22 Ff 36.12N 37.10 E
Ḩalabjah 24 Ke 35.10N 45.59 E
Halač 19 Gh 39.04N 64.53 E
Halachó 48 Ng 20.29N 90.05W
Halahei 28 Ga 46.11N 122.46 E
Ḩalā'ib 31 Kf 22.13N 36.38 E
Halalii Lake 65a Ab 21.52N 160.11W
Halanginie Point 64k Bb 19.03S 169.58W
Hålaveden 8 Ff 58.05N 14.45 E
Halawa 65a Eb 21.10N 156.44W
Halawa, Cape- 65a Eb 21.10N 156.43W
Ḩalbā 24 Ge 34.33N 36.05 E
Halberstadt 10 He 51.54N 11.03 E
Halcon, Mount- 26 Hd 13.16N 121.00 E
Haldean-Sogotyn-Daba 27 Gb 49.05N 97.55 E
Halden 7 Cg 59.09N 11.23 E
Haldensleben 10 Hd 52.18N 11.25 E
Haldia 25 Hd 22.08N 88.05 E
Haldwani 25 Fc 29.13N 79.31 E
Hale, Mount- 59 De 26.00S 117.10 E
Haleakala Crater 65a Ec 20.43N 156.12W
Haleiwa 65a Cb 21.36N 158.06W
Halemaumau 65a Fd 19.24N 155.17W
Hale River 59 Hd 24.56S 135.53 E
Halesworth 12 Db 52.21N 1.30 E
Haleyville 44 Dh 34.14N 87.37W
Ḩalfā al Gadīda 31 Kg 15.19N 35.34 E
Half Assini 34 Ed 5.03N 2.53W
Halfeti 24 Gd 37.15N 37.52 E
Halfway 42 Fe 56.13N 121.26W
Halh-Gol 27 Kb 48.01N 118.10 E
Haliburton 44 Hc 45.03N 78.33W
Halifax 39 Me 44.39N 63.36W
Halifax, Mount- 59 Jc 19.05S 146.20 E
Halifax Bay 59 Jc 18.50S 146.30 E
Ḩālil 23 Id 27.28N 58.44 E
Ḩalīleh, Ra's-e- 24 Nh 28.46N 50.56 E
Halilovo 16 Ud 51.27N 58.10 E
Ḩalin 35 Hd 9.08N 48.47 E
Haliut → Urad Zhonghou Lianheqi 27 Ic 41.34N 108.32 E
Haljala 8 Le 59.22N 26.09 E
Haljasavej 20 Cd 63.20N 78.30 E
Hall 20 Ed 60.40N 173.05W
Halladale 9 Jc 58.30N 3.50W
Hallam Peak 46 Fa 52.11N 118.46W
Halland 8 Eh 57.00N 12.45 E
Halland [2] 7 Ch 56.45N 13.00 E
Hallandsås 8 Eh 56.23N 13.00 E
Halla-san 28 Ih 33.22N 126.32 E
Ḩallat 'Ammār 24 Gh 29.08N 36.02 E
Hall Beach 42 Jc 68.10N 81.56W
Halle 10 He 51.30N 12.00 E
Halle/Hal 11 Kd 50.44N 4.14 E
Halle (Westfalen) 12 Kb 52.05N 8.22 E
Halleberg 8 Ef 58.23N 12.25 E
Hallefors 8 Fe 59.47N 14.30 E
Hälleforsnäs 8 Ge 59.10N 16.30 E
Hallein 14 Hc 47.41N 13.06 E
Hällekis 8 Ef 58.38N 13.25 E
Hallen 7 De 63.11N 14.05 E
Hallenberg 12 Kc 51.07N 8.38 E
Hallencourt 12 De 49.59N 1.53 E
Halle-Neustadt 10 He 51.31N 11.53 E
Hallertau 10 Hh 48.35N 11.50 E
Hällestad 8 Ff 58.44N 15.34 E
Hallettsville 45 Hl 29.27N 96.57W
Halley Bay 66 Af 75.31S 26.38W
Halli 8 Kc 61.52N 24.50 E
Hallie-Jackson Bank (EN) 63c Ba 9.45S 166.10 E
Halligen 10 Eb 54.35N 8.35 E
Hallingdal 7 Bf 60.40N 9.15 E
Hallingdalselva 8 Cd 60.23N 9.35 E
Hallingskarvet 5 Gc 60.37N 7.45 E
Hall Islands 57 Gd 8.37N 152.00 E
Halliste Jõgi 8 Kf 58.23N 24.25 E
Hall Lake 42 Jc 68.40N 82.20W
Hall Land 41 Fb 81.12N 61.10W
Hallock 45 Hb 48.47N 96.57W
Hall Peninsula 38 Mc 63.30N 66.00W
Hallsberg 7 Dg 59.04N 15.07 E
Halls Creek 58 Df 18.13S 127.40 E
Hallstahammar 7 Dg 59.37N 16.13 E
Hallstatt 14 Hb 47.33N 13.39 E
Hallstavik 7 Ef 60.03N 18.36 E
Halluin 12 Fd 50.47N 3.08 E
Halmahera 57 Dd 1.00N 128.00 E
Halmahera, Laut- = Halmahera Sea (EN) 57 De 1.00S 129.00 E
Halmahera Sea (EN) = Halmahera, Laut- 57 De 1.00S 129.00 E
Halmer-Ju 19 Gb 67.58N 64.40 E
Halmeu 15 Gb 47.58N 23.01 E
Halmstad 6 Hd 56.39N 12.50 E
Haloze 14 Jd 46.20N 15.50 E
Ḩalq al Wādī 32 Jb 36.49N 10.18 E
Hals 7 Cg 57.00N 10.19 E
Hälsingland 8 Gc 61.30N 17.00 E
Halsön 8 Ib 62.50N 21.10 E
Halstead 12 Cc 51.57N 0.38 E
Halsteren 12 Gc 51.32N 4.16 E
Haltang He 27 Fd 39.00N 94.40 E
Halten Bank (EN) 7 Bd 64.45N 8.45 E
Haltern 12 Jc 51.44N 7.11 E
Haltiatunturi 7 Eb 69.18N 21.16 E
Haltom City 45 Hj 32.48N 97.16W
Halturin → Orlov 19 Ed 58.35N 48.55 E
Hälül 24 Oj 25.40N 52.25 E
Halver 12 Jc 51.12N 7.29 E
Ham 11 Je 49.45N 3.04 E
Ham, Roches de- 12 Ae 49.02N 1.02W
Hamada 29 Cd 34.53N 132.03 E
Hamadān 22 Gf 34.48N 48.30 E
Hamadān [3] 23 Gb 35.00N 48.40 E
Hamadia 13 Ni 35.28N 1.52 E
Hamaguir 32 Gc 30.54N 3.02W
Hamāh 23 Eb 35.08N 36.45 E
Hamakita 29 Ed 34.49N 137.45 E
Hamamasu 29a Bb 43.36N 141.21 E
Hamamatsu 27 Oe 34.42N 137.44 E
Hamanaka 29a Db 43.05N 145.05 E
Hamanaka-Wan 29a Db 43.07N 145.10 E
Hamana-Ko 29 Ed 34.45N 137.34 E
Hamanen, Oued el- 32 Hd 25.52N 1.26 E
Hamaoka 29 Fd 34.39N 138.07 E
Hamar 6 Hc 60.48N 11.06 E
Hamar-Daran, Hrebet- 20 Ff 51.10N 105.00 E
Hamasaka 29 Dd 35.38N 134.27 E
Ḩamāṭah, Jabal- 33 Ge 24.12N 35.00 E
Hamatonbetsu 28 Qb 45.07N 142.23 E
Hambantota 25 Gg 6.10N 81.07 E
Hambre, Cayos del- 49 Fb 22.15N 82.47W
Hamburg [2] 10 Fc 53.35N 10.00 E
Hamburg [Ger.] 6 Ge 53.33N 10.00 E
Hamburg [S.Afr.] 37 Df 33.18S 27.28 E
Hamburg-Altona 10 Fc 53.33N 9.57 E
Hamburg-Harburg 10 Fc 53.28N 10.00 E
Hamburgsund 8 Df 58.33N 11.16 E
Ḩamḑah 33 Hf 19.02N 43.36 E
Ḩamḑh, Wādī al- 21 Fg 25.58N 36.42 E
Häme 7 Ff 61.30N 24.30 E
Häme 8 Kc 61.30N 25.30 E
Hämeenkangas 8 Jc 61.45N 22.40 E
Hämeenlinna/Tavastehus 7 Ff 61.00N 24.27 E
Hämeenselkä 8 Kb 62.30N 25.00 E
Hamelin Pool 59 Ce 26.15S 114.05 E
Hameln 10 Fd 52.06N 9.21 E
Hamero Hadad 35 Gd 7.28N 42.13 E
Hamersley Range 59 Dd 21.55S 116.45 E
Hamgyŏng-Namdo [2] 28 Id 40.00N 127.30 E
Hamgyŏng-Pukto [2] 28 Jd 41.45N 129.50 E
Hamgyŏng-Sanmaek 28 Jd 41.00N 128.45 E
Hamhŭng 22 Of 39.54N 127.32 E
Hami/Kumul 22 Le 42.48N 93.27 E
Ḩamīdīyeh 24 Mg 31.29N 48.26 E
Hamilton [Austl.] 59 Ig 37.45S 142.02 E
Hamilton [Ber.] 39 Mf 32.17N 64.46W
Hamilton [Mt.-U.S.] 43 Eb 46.15N 114.09W
Hamilton [N.Z.] 58 Ih 37.47S 175.17 E
Hamilton [Oh.-U.S.] 43 Kd 39.23N 84.33W
Hamilton [Ont.-Can.] 39 Le 43.15N 79.51W
Hamilton [Scot.-U.K.] 9 If 55.47N 4.03W
Hamilton [Tx.-U.S.] 45 Gk 31.42N 98.07W
Hamilton, Lake- 45 Ji 34.30N 93.05W
Hamilton, Mount- 46 Hg 39.14N 115.32W
Hamilton River 59 Hd 23.30S 139.47 E
Ḩamīn, Wādī al- 33 Dc 30.28N 22.00 E
Hamina/Fredrikshamn 7 Gf 60.34N 27.12 E
Hamm 10 De 51.41N 7.48 E
Ḩammām al 'Alīl 24 Jd 36.10N 43.16 E
Ḩammām al Anf 32 Jb 36.44N 10.20 E
Ḩammāmāt 32 Jb 36.24N 10.37 E
Ḩammāmāt, Khalīj- 32 Jb 36.05N 10.40 E
Hammam Bou Hadjar 13 Li 35.23N 0.58W
Hammami 30 Ff 23.03N 11.30W
Hammam Righa 13 Oh 36.23N 2.24 E
Ḩammār, Hawr al- 23 Gc 30.50N 47.10 E
Hammarstrand 8 Ga 63.06N 16.21 E
Hamme 12 Gc 51.06N 4.08 E
Hammelburg 10 Ff 50.07N 9.54 E
Hammerdal 7 De 63.36N 15.21 E
Hammeren 8 Fi 55.18N 14.47 E
Hammerfest 6 Ia 70.40N 23.45 E
Hamminkeln 12 Ic 51.44N 6.35 E
Hamminkeln-Dingden 12 Ic 51.46N 6.37 E
Hammond [In.-U.S.] 44 De 41.36N 87.30W
Hammond [La.-U.S.] 43 Ie 30.30N 90.28W
Hammonton 44 Jf 39.38N 74.48W
Hamont, Hamont-Achel- 12 Hc 51.15N 5.33 E
Hamont-Achel 12 Hc 51.15N 5.33 E
Hamont-Achel-Hamont 12 Hc 51.15N 5.33 E
Hamoyet, Jabal- 30 Kg 17.33N 38.02 E
Hampden 62 Df 45.20S 170.49 E
Hampshire 9 Lk 51.00N 1.10W
Hampshire Downs 9 Lj 51.15N 1.15W
Hampton [Ia.-U.S.] 45 Je 42.45N 93.12W
Hampton [Va.-U.S.] 44 Ig 37.02N 76.23W
Hampton Butte 46 Ee 43.46N 120.17W
Hamp'yong 28 Ig 35.04N 126.31 E
Hamrā' 35 Dc 10.54N 29.54 E
Hamra [R.S.F.S.R.] 20 Gd 60.17N 114.10 E
Hamra [Swe.] 8 Fc 61.39N 15.00 E
Ḩamrā', Al Ḩamādah al- 30 If 29.30N 12.00 E
Hamra, Saguia el- 30 Ff 27.24N 13.43W
Hamrān 24 Kd 36.22N 45.44 E
Ḩamrat ash Shaykh 35 Dc 14.35N 27.58 E
Ḩamrīn, Jabal- 24 Ke 34.30N 44.30 E
Hāmūn-e Hirmand, Daryācheh-ye- 23 Jc 31.30N 61.20 E
Han 34 Ec 10.41N 2.27W
Hana 60 Oc 20.45N 155.59W
Hanahan 44 Hi 32.55N 80.00W
Hanaizumi 29 Gb 38.51N 141.12 E
Ḩanak 23 Ed 25.33N 36.56 E
Hanalei 65a Ba 22.13N 159.30W
Hanamaki 28 Pe 39.23N 141.07 E
Hanang 30 Ki 4.26S 35.24 E
Hanaoka 29 Ga 40.21N 140.34 E
Hanapepe 65a Bb 21.55N 159.35W
Hanau 10 Ef 50.08N 8.55 E
Han-Bogdo 27 Ic 43.12N 107.10 E
Hanceville 42 Ff 51.55N 123.02W
Hancheng 27 Jd 35.30N 110.25 E
Hanchuan 28 Bi 30.39N 113.46 E
Hancock 44 Cb 47.07N 88.35W
Handa 29 Ed 34.53N 136.56 E
Handan 22 Nf 36.35N 114.28 E
Handen 8 He 59.10N 18.08 E
Handeni 36 Gd 5.26S 38.01 E
Handlová 10 Oh 48.44N 18.46 E
Handöl 8 Ea 63.16N 12.26 E
Handyga 22 Pc 62.40N 135.36 E
Hanegev = Negev Desert (EN) 24 Fg 30.30N 34.55 E
Hanford 46 Fh 36.20N 119.39W
Hangaj, Hrebet- (Changajn Nuruu) = Khangai Mountains (EN) 21 Le 47.30N 100.00 E
Han-gang 27 Md 37.45N 126.11 E
Hanga Roa 65d Ab 27.09S 109.26W
Hang'bu He 28 Di 31.33N 117.05 E
Hanggin Houqi (Xamba) 27 Ic 40.59N 107.07 E
Hanggin Qi (Xin Zhen) 27 Id 39.54N 108.55 E
Hangö/Hanko 7 Fg 59.50N 22.57 E
Hangöudde/Hankoniemi 8 Je 59.50N 23.10 E
Hangu 28 De 39.16N 117.50 E
Hangzhou 22 Of 30.18N 120.11 E
Hangzhou Wan 28 Fi 30.25N 121.00 E
Ḩanīsh 33 Hg 13.45N 42.45 E
Ḩanīsh al Kabīr, Jazīrat al- 33 Hg 13.43N 42.45 E
Hanja, Vozvyšennost- 8 Lg 57.30N 27.30 E
Ḩanjūrah, Ra's- 24 Pj 24.44N 54.39 E
Hanka, Ozero- = Khanka Lake (EN) 21 Pe 45.00N 132.24 E
Hankasalmi 8 Lb 62.23N 26.26 E
Hankensbüttel 10 Gd 52.44N 10.36 E
Hanko/Hangö 7 Fg 59.50N 22.57 E
Hankoniemi/Hangöudde 8 Je 59.50N 23.10 E
Hankou, Wuhan- 28 Ci 30.35N 114.16 E
Hanksville 46 Jg 38.25N 110.10W
Hanlar 16 Oi 40.34N 46.20 E
Hanmej, Gora- 17 Lc 67.08N 66.00 E
Hanmer Springs 62 Ee 42.31S 172.50 E
Hann, Mount- 59 Fc 15.50S 125.50 E
Hanna [Alta.-Can.] 42 Gf 51.38N 111.54W
Hanna [Wy.-U.S.] 46 Lf 41.52N 106.34W
Hannah Bay 42 Jf 51.15N 79.50W
Hannibal 43 Id 39.42N 91.22W
Hanningfield Reservoir 12 Cc 51.37N 0.28 E
Hannō 29 Fd 35.53N 139.17 E
Hannover 6 Ge 52.22N 9.43 E
Hann River 59 Fc 17.10S 126.10 E
Hannut/Hannuit 12 Hd 50.40N 5.05 E
Hannuit/Hannut 12 Hd 50.40N 5.05 E
Hano 8 Fi 56.00N 14.50 E
Hanöbukten 8 Fi 55.45N 14.30 E
Ha Noi 22 Mg 21.02N 105.51 E
Hanover [N.H.-U.S.] 44 Kd 43.42N 72.17W
Hanover [Ont.-Can.] 44 Gc 44.09N 81.02W
Hanover [Pa.-U.S.] 44 If 39.47N 76.59W
Hanover [S.Afr.] 37 Cf 31.04S 24.29 E
Hanover, Isla- 56 Fh 51.00S 74.40W
Hanpan, Cape- 59 Ka 5.01S 154.37 E
Han Pijesak 14 Mf 44.05N 18.57 E

Index Symbols

[1] Independent Nation
[2] State, Region
[3] District, County
[4] Municipality
[5] Colony, Dependency
Continent
Physical Region
Historical or Cultural Region
Mount, Mountain
Volcano
Hill
Mountains, Mountain Range
Hills, Escarpment
Plateau, Upland
Pass, Gap
Plain, Lowland
Delta
Salt Flat
Valley, Canyon
Crater, Cave
Karst Features
Depression
Polder
Desert, Dunes
Forest, Woods
Heath, Steppe
Oasis
Cape, Point
Coast, Beach
Cliff
Peninsula
Isthmus
Sandbank
Island
Atoll
Rock, Reef
Islands, Archipelago
Rocks, Reefs
Coral Reef
Well, Spring
Geyser
River, Stream
Waterfall Rapids
River Mouth, Estuary
Lake
Salt Lake
Intermittent Lake
Reservoir
Swamp, Pond
Canal
Glacier
Ice Shelf, Pack Ice
Ocean
Sea
Gulf, Bay
Strait, Fjord
Lagoon
Bank
Seamount
Tablemount
Ridge
Shelf
Basin
Escarpment, Sea Scarp
Fracture
Trench, Abyss
National Park, Reserve
Point of Interest
Recreation Site
Cave, Cavern
Historic Site
Ruins
Wall, Walls
Church, Abbey
Temple
Scientific Station
Airport
Port
Lighthouse
Mine
Tunnel
Dam, Bridge

Hansen Mountains 66 Ee 68.16S 58.47E
Hanshan 28 Ei 31.43N 118.07E
Hanshou 28 Aj 28.55N 111.58E
Han Shui 21 Nf 30.34N 114.17E
Hanstholm 8 Cg 57.07N 8.38E
Han Sum 28 Eb 44.33N 119.58E
Han-sur-Lesse, Rochefort- 12 Hd 50.08N 5.11E
Han-sur-Nied 12 If 48.59N 6.26E
Hantajskoje, Ozero- 20 Ec 68.25N 91.00E
Hantau 19 Hg 44.13N 73.48E
Hantengri Feng 27 Dc 42.03N 80.11E
Hants 9 Lj 51.10N 1.10W
Hanty-Mansijsk 22 Ic 61.00N 69.06E
Hanty-Mansijski avtonomnyj okrug 19 Hc 62.00N 72.30E
Hantzsch 42 Kc 67.32N 72.26W
Hanušovice 10 Mf 50.05N 16.55E
Hanwang 27 He 31.25N 104.13E
Hanyang 28 Ci 30.34N 114.01E
Hanyang, Wuhan- 28 Ci 30.33N 114.16E
Hanyū 29 Fc 36.11N 139.32E
Hanyuan (Fulin) 27 Hf 29.25N 102.12E
Hanzhong [China] 22 Mf 32.59N 107.11E
Hanzhong [China] 27 Ie 33.07N 107.00E
Hanzhuang 28 Dg 34.38N 117.23E
Hao Atoll 57 Mf 18.15S 140.54W
Hāora 22 Kg 22.35N 88.20E
Haoud el Hamra 32 Ic 31.58N 5.59E
Haoxue 28 Bi 30.02N 112.25E
Haparanda 7 Fd 65.50N 24.10E
Hapčeranga 20 Gg 49.42N 112.20E
Happy Valley-Goose Bay 39 Md 53.19N 60.24W
Hapsu 28 Jd 41.13N 128.51E
Ḩaql 24 Fh 29.18N 34.57E
Ḩaql al Barqan 24 Lh 28.55N 47.57E
Ḩaql al Manāqish 24 Lh 29.02N 47.32E
Ḩaql as Şābirīyah 24 Lh 29.48N 47.50E
Hara, Zaliv-/Hara Laht 8 Ke 59.35N 25.30E
Hara-Ajrag 27 Ib 45.50N 109.20E
Harabali 19 Ef 47.25N 47.16E
Ḩaraḑ 23 Ge 24.14N 49.11E
Haraiki Atoll 57 Mf 17.28S 143.27W
Hara Laht/Hara, Zaliv- 8 Ke 59.35N 25.30E
Haramachi 28 Pf 37.38N 140.58E
Haram Dāgh 23 Gb 37.35N 46.43E
Harami, Pereval- 16 Oh 42.48N 46.12E
Harand 24 Of 32.34N 52.26E
Harani'ia Point 63a Ed 10.21S 161.16E
Hara Nur 27 Fb 48.05N 93.12E
Hararḑēre 35 He 4.32N 47.53E
Harare 31 Kj 17.50S 31.10E
Harat 35 Fb 16.05N 39.28E
Hara-Tas, Krjaž- 20 Fb 72.00N 107.00E
Haratini 64n Bc 10.28S 160.58W
Ḩarat Zuwayyah 31 Jf 24.14N 21.59E
Hara-Us-Nur 27 Fb 48.00N 92.10E
Haraz 35 Bc 13.57N 19.26E
Harāz 24 Od 36.40N 52.43E
Harāzah, Jabal- 35 Eb 15.03N 30.27E
Haraze 35 Cd 9.55N 20.48E
Harbel 34 Cd 6.16N 10.21W
Harbin 22 Oe 45.45N 126.37E
Harbor Beach 44 Fd 43.51N 82.39W
Harbour Breton 42 Lg 47.29N 55.50W
Harbour Grace 42 Mg 47.41N 53.15W
Harburg, Hamburg- 10 Fc 53.28N 10.00E
Harcourt 44 Ob 46.30N 65.15W
Harcuvar Mountains 46 Ii 34.00N 113.30W
Harcyzsk 16 Kf 47.59N 38.11E
Hardanger 8 Bd 60.20N 6.30E
Hardangerfjorden 5 Gc 60.10N 6.00E
Hardangerjøkulen 8 Bd 60.35N 7.25E
Hardangervidda 7 Bf 60.20N 7.30E
Hardelot Plage, Neufchâtel Hardelot- 12 Dd 50.38N 1.35E
Hardenberg 12 Ib 52.34N 6.37E
Harderwijk 11 Lb 52.21N 5.36E
Hardin 43 Fb 45.44N 107.37W
Harding 37 Df 30.34S 29.58E
Hardinsburg 44 Dg 37.47N 86.28W
Härdler 12 Kc 51.06N 8.14E
Hardoi 25 Gc 27.25N 80.07E
Hardy, Peninsula- 56 Gi 55.25S 68.30W
Hareid 8 Bb 62.22N 6.02E
Hareidlandet 7 Ae 62.20N 5.55E
Hare Indian 42 Ec 66.18N 128.38W
Harelbeke 12 Fd 50.51N 3.18E
Haren 12 Ja 53.11N 6.38E
Haren (Ems) 12 Jb 52.47N 7.14E
Harer 31 Lh 9.18N 42.08E
Harerge [3] 35 Gd 9.00N 41.30E
Harēri Mālinwarfā 35 He 4.34N 47.21E
Harewa 35 Gd 9.54N 41.58E
Harfleur 12 Ce 49.30N 0.12E
Harg 8 Hd 60.11N 18.24E
Hargeysa 31 Lh 9.30N 44.03E
Harghiţa [2] 15 Ic 46.25N 25.45E
Harghita, Munţii- 15 Ic 46.31N 25.33E
Harghita, Vîrful- 15 Ic 46.27N 25.35E
Hargla 8 Lg 57.31N 26.25E
Harhorin 27 Hb 47.13N 102.50E
Har Hu 38.15N 97.40E
Ḩarīb 23 Gg 14.56N 45.30E
Haridwār 25 Fc 29.58N 78.10E
Harihari 62 De 43.09S 170.34E
Hari Kurk 8 Je 59.00N 22.50E
Harim 24 Gd 36.12N 36.31E
Harīm, Jabal al- 24 Qj 25.58N 56.14E
Harima-Nada 29 Dd 34.30N 134.35E
Haringey, London- 12 Bc 51.36N 0.06W
Harirūd 21 If 37.24N 60.38E
Härjångsfjället 8 Ea 63.01N 12.35E
Harjavalta 7 Ff 61.19N 22.08E
Härjedalen 8 Eb 62.20N 13.05E
Härjehågna 8 Ec 61.44N 12.08E
Hårkan 8 Fa 63.20N 14.55E
Harkov 6 Je 50.00N 36.15E
Harkovskaja Oblast [3] 19 Df 49.40N 36.30E
Harlan [Ia.-U.S.] 45 If 41.39N 95.19W
Harlan [Ky.-U.S.] 44 Fg 36.51N 83.19W
Harlan County Lake 45 Gf 40.04N 99.16W
Harlech Castle 9 Ii 52.52N 4.07W
Harlem 46 Kb 48.32N 108.47W
Harleston 12 Db 52.24N 1.18E
Harlingen [Neth.] 11 La 53.10N 5.24E
Harlingen [Tx.-U.S.] 43 Hf 26.11N 97.42W
Harlovka 7 Ib 68.47N 37.20E
Harlovka 7 Ib 68.47N 37.15E
Harlow 9 Nj 51.47N 0.08E
Harlowton 46 Kc 46.26N 109.50W
Harlu 7 Hf 61.51N 30.54E
Hărman 15 Id 45.43N 25.41E
Harmancık 24 Cc 39.41N 29.10E
Harmånger 7 Df 61.56N 17.13E
Harmanli 15 Ih 41.56N 25.54E
Harmil 35 Gb 16.30N 40.12E
Harmony 45 Ke 43.33N 91.59W
Harnai 25 Ee 17.48N 73.06E
Harney Basin 38 Ge 43.15N 120.40W
Harney Lake 43 Dc 43.14N 119.07W
Harney Peak 43 Gc 44.00N 103.30W
Härnön 8 Gb 62.35N 18.00E
Härnösand 6 Hc 62.38N 17.56E
Haro 13 Jb 42.35N 2.51W
Harovsk 19 Ed 59.59N 40.11E
Harøya 8 Bb 62.45N 6.25E
Harøyfjorden 8 Bb 62.45N 6.35E
Harpenden 12 Bc 51.48N 0.21W
Harper [Ks.-U.S.] 45 Gh 37.17N 98.01W
Harper [Lbr.] 31 Gh 4.22N 7.43W
Harper, Mount- 40 Kd 64.14N 143.50W
Harper Pass 62 De 42.44S 171.53E
Harplinge 8 Eh 56.45N 12.43E
Harqin Qi (Jinshan) 28 Ed 41.57N 118.40E
Harqin Zuoyi Monggolzu Zizhixian 28 Ed 41.05N 119.40E
Ḩarrah 23 Hg 14.57N 50.19E
Ḩarrat al 'Uwayrid 23 Ed 27.00N 37.30E
Harricana 42 Jf 51.10N 79.47W
Harricana, Rivière- 44 Ha 51.10N 79.45W
Harrington-Harbour 42 Lf 50.26N 59.30W
Harris 9 Gd 57.53N 6.55W
Harris 51c Bc 16.28N 62.10W
Harris, Lake- 44 Gk 28.46N 81.49W
Harris, Sound of- 9 Fd 57.45N 7.08W
Harrisburg 39 Le 40.16N 76.52W
Harrismith 37 De 28.18S 29.03E
Harrison [Ar.-U.S.] 45 Jh 36.14N 93.07W
Harrison [Mi.-U.S.] 44 Ec 44.01N 84.48W
Harrison [Nb.-U.S.] 45 Ee 42.41N 103.53W
Harrison, Cape- 42 Lf 54.56N 57.55W
Harrison Bay 40 Ib 70.30N 151.30W
Harrisonburg 44 Hf 38.27N 78.54W
Harrison Lake 46 Eb 49.31N 121.59W
Harrison Point 51q Ab 13.18N 59.38W
Harrisonville 45 Ig 38.39N 94.21W
Harrisville [Mi.-U.S.] 44 Fc 44.39N 83.17W
Harrisville [W.V.-U.S.] 44 Gf 39.13N 81.04W
Harrodsburg 44 Eg 37.46N 84.51W
Harrogate 9 Lh 54.00N 1.33W
Harrow, London- 12 Bc 51.36N 0.20W
Harry S. Truman Reservoir 45 Jg 38.00N 93.45W
Har Sai Shan 27 Gd 35.26N 97.41E
Harsewinkel 12 Kc 51.58N 8.14E
Harshō 35 Hc 11.17N 47.30E
Harsim 24 Lf 33.48N 46.50E
Harsin 24 Le 34.16N 47.35E
Harstad 7 Db 68.47N 16.30E
Harsvik 7 Cd 64.03N 10.02E
Hart 44 Dd 43.42N 86.22W
Hart 42 Dc 65.51N 136.22W
Hartao 28 Gc 42.30N 122.08E
Hartbees 30 Jk 28.45S 20.33E
Hartberg 14 Jc 47.17N 15.58E
Hårteigen 8 Bd 60.12N 7.04E
Hartford [Ct.-U.S.] 39 Le 41.46N 72.41W
Hartford [Ky.-U.S.] 44 Dg 37.27N 86.55W
Hartford City 44 Ee 40.29N 85.23W
Hartington 45 He 42.37N 97.16W
Hartland 44 Nb 46.18N 67.32W
Hartland Point 9 Ij 51.02N 4.31W
Hartlepool 9 Lg 54.42N 1.11W
Hartmannberge 37 Ac 17.30S 12.23E
Hartola 7 Gf 61.35N 26.01E
Harts 28.24S 24.18E
Hartselle 44 Dh 34.27N 86.56W
Harts Range 59 Gd 23.05S 134.55E
Hartsville 44 Gh 34.23N 80.04W
Hartwell 44 Fh 34.21N 82.56W
Hartwell Lake 44 Fh 34.30N 82.55W
Harun, Bukit- 26 Gf 4.06N 115.46E
Haruno 29 Ce 33.30N 133.30E
Harves Bank (EN) 51c Ac 16.52N 62.35W
Harvey [Austl.] 59 Df 33.05S 115.54E
Harvey [N.D.-U.S.] 43 Hb 47.47N 99.56W
Harvey Bay 59 Kd 25.00S 153.00E
Harwich 9 Oj 51.57N 1.17E
Haryana [3] 25 Fc 29.30N 76.30E
Harz 5 He 51.45N 10.30E
Hasaki 29 Gd 35.44N 140.48E
Hasama 29 Gb 38.42N 141.13E
Hasan 20 Ih 42.26N 130.39E
Ḩasanābād [Iran] 24 Ph 28.47N 54.19E
Ḩasanābād [Iran] 24 Nd 36.28N 50.17E
Hasan Dağı 23 Db 38.08N 34.12E
Ḩasan Langī 24 Qi 27.22N 56.52E
Hasavjurt 16 Oh 43.16N 46.35E
Hāsbayyā 24 Ff 33.43N 33.52E
Hasdo 25 Hd 21.44N 82.44E
Hase 10 Dd 52.41N 7.18E
Hasekijata 15 Kg 42.08N 27.30E
Hasenkamp 55 Cj 31.31S 59.51W
Hashimoto 29 Dd 34.19N 135.37E
Hashtpar 24 Md 37.48N 48.55E
Hasi Hausert 32 Ee 22.35N 14.18W
Haskell 43 He 33.10N 99.44W
Haskerland 12 Hb 52.58N 5.47E
Haskerland-Joure 12 Hb 52.58N 5.47E
Haskovo 15 Ih 41.56N 25.33E
Haskovo [2] 15 Ih 41.50N 25.55E
Hasle 8 Fi 55.11N 14.43E
Haslemere 9 Mj 51.06N 0.43W
Haslev 8 Di 55.20N 11.58E
Hășmașu Mare, Vîrful- 15 Ic 46.30N 25.50E
Haspengouws Plateau/Hesbaye 11 Ld 50.30N 5.10E
Haspres 12 Fd 50.15N 3.25E
Hassa 24 Gd 36.50N 36.29E
Hassan 25 Ff 13.00N 76.05E
Hassberge 10 Gf 50.12N 10.29E
Hassela 7 De 62.07N 16.42E
Hassel Sound 42 Ha 78.30N 99.00W
Hasselt 11 Ld 50.56N 5.20E
Hassi Bel Guebbour 32 Id 28.30N 6.41E
Hassi el Ghella 13 Ki 35.27N 1.03W
Hassi-Mamèche 13 Mi 35.51N 0.04E
Hassi Messaoud 31 He 31.43N 6.03E
Hassi R'mel 32 Hc 32.55N 3.16E
Hassi Serouenout 32 Ie 24.00N 7.50E
Hässleholm 7 Ch 56.09N 13.46E
Hasslö 8 Fh 56.05N 15.25E
Haßloch 12 Ke 49.23N 8.16E
Hastière 12 Gd 50.13N 4.50E
Hastière-Hastière par-delà 12 Gd 50.13N 4.50E
Hastière-par-delà, Hastière- 12 Gd 50.13N 4.50E
Hastings [Bar.] 51q Ab 13.04N 59.35W
Hastings [Eng.-U.K.] 9 Nk 50.51N 0.36E
Hastings [Mi.-U.S.] 44 Ed 42.39N 85.17W
Hastings [Mn.-U.S.] 45 Jd 44.44N 92.51W
Hastings [Nb.-U.S.] 43 Hc 40.35N 98.23W
Hastings [N.Z.] 61 Eg 39.38S 176.50E
Hästveda 8 Eh 56.16N 13.56E
Hašuri 16 Mi 41.59N 43.33E
Hasvik 7 Fa 70.29N 22.09E
Ḩasy al Qaţţār 33 Ec 30.14N 27.11E
Ḩasy Hague 33 Bd 26.17N 10.31E
Hat'ae-Do 28 Hg 34.23N 125.17E
Hatanga 22 Mb 71.58N 102.30E
Hatanga 21 Mb 72.55N 106.00E
Hatch 45 Cj 32.40N 107.09W
Hatches Creek 59 Hd 20.56S 135.12E
Haţeg 15 Fd 45.37N 22.57E
Hatgal 27 Ha 50.26N 100.09E
Ḩaţībah, Ra's- 23 Ee 21.59N 38.55E
Ha Tien 25 Kf 10.23N 104.29E
Ha Tinh 25 Le 18.20N 105.54E
Hato Mayor 49 Md 18.46N 69.15W
Ḩattā, Jabal- 24 Qj 24.45N 56.04E
Hattem 12 Ib 52.28N 6.06E
Hatten 12 Ka 53.03N 8.23E
Hatteras, Cape- 38 Lf 35.13N 75.32W
Hatteras Inlet 44 Jh 35.00N 75.40W
Hatteras Island 43 Ld 35.25N 75.30W
Hattfjelldal 7 Cd 65.36N 14.00E
Hattiesburg 43 Je 31.19N 89.16W
Hattingen 12 Jc 51.24N 7.10E
Hatu Iti, Ile- 61 Ma 8.42S 140.43W
Hatutaa, Ile- 57 Me 7.30S 140.38W
Hatvan 10 Pi 47.40N 19.41E
Hat Yai 25 Kg 7.01N 100.27E
Hatyrka 20 Md 62.03N 175.05E
Hau Bon 25 Lf 13.24N 108.27E
Haubourdin 12 Ed 50.36N 2.59E
Hauge 7 Bg 58.21N 6.17E
Haugesund 6 Gd 59.25N 5.18E
Hauho 8 Kc 61.10N 24.33E
Hauhungaroa Range 62 Fc 38.40S 175.35E
Haukeligrend 7 Bg 59.51N 7.11E
Haukipudas 7 Fd 65.15N 25.28E
Haukivesi 5 Ic 62.05N 28.30E
Haukivuori 8 Lb 62.01N 27.13E
Hauraha 63a Ed 10.49S 161.57E
Hauraki Gulf 61 Eg 36.35S 175.00E
Hauroko, Lake- 62 Bf 45.55S 167.20E
Hausa 32 Ed 27.06N 11.01W
Hausruck 14 Hb 48.07N 13.35E
Haut, Isle au- 44 Mc 44.03N 68.38W
Haut Atlas=High Atlas (EN) 30 Ge 32.00N 6.00W
Haute-Champagne 12 Ge 49.18N 4.15E
Haute-Corse [3] 11a Aa 42.30N 9.00E
Haute-Garonne [3] 11 Hk 43.25N 1.30E
Haute-Guinée [3] 34 Dc 11.30N 10.00W
Haute-Kotto [3] 35 Cd 7.00N 23.00E
Haute-Loire [3] 11 Ji 45.05N 4.00E
Haute-Marne [3] 11 Lf 48.05N 5.10E
Hauterive 44 Ma 49.11N 68.16W
Hautes-Alpes [3] 11 Mj 44.40N 6.30E
Haute-Sangha [3] 35 Be 4.30N 16.00E
Haute-Saône [3] 11 Mg 47.40N 6.10E
Haute-Saône, Plateau de- 11 Lg 47.50N 6.00E
Haute-Savoie [3] 11 Mi 46.00N 6.20E
Hautes Fagnes/Hoge Venen 10 Bf 50.30N 6.00E
Hautes-Pyrénées [3] 11 Gk 43.00N 0.10E
Haute Vienne [3] 11 Hi 45.50N 1.10E
Haute Volta→Burkina Faso 31 Gg 13.00N 2.00W
Haut-Mbomou [3] 35 Dd 6.00N 26.00E
Hautmont 11 Jd 50.15N 3.56E
Haut-Ogooué [3] 36 Bc 2.00S 14.00E
Haut Rhin [3] 11 Ng 48.00N 7.20E
Hauts-Bassins [3] 34 Ec 12.30N 4.30W
Hauts-de-Seine [3] 11 If 48.50N 2.11E
Hauts-Plateaux 30 He 34.00N 0.01E
Haut-Zaïre [2] 36 Eb 2.30N 25.30E
Hauula 65a 21.36N 157.54W
Hauz-Han 18 Cf 37.16N 61.15E
Hauz-Hanskoje Vodohr. 18 Cf 37.10N 61.20E
Havana 45 Kf 40.18N 90.04W
Havana (EN)=La Habana 39 Kg 23.08N 82.22W
Havant 9 Mk 50.51N 0.59W
Havast 18 Gd 40.16N 68.51E
Havasu, Lake- 46 Hi 34.30N 114.20W
Havel 10 Hd 52.53N 11.58E
Havelange 12 Hd 50.23N 5.14E
Havelange-Méan 12 Hd 50.22N 5.20E
Havelberg 10 Id 52.49N 12.05E
Havelland 10 Id 52.25N 12.45E
Havelländisches Luch 10 Id 52.40N 12.40E
Havelock [N.C.-U.S.] 44 Ih 34.53N 76.54W
Havelock [N.Z.] 62 Ed 41.17S 173.46E
Havelock North 62 Gc 39.40S 176.53E
Havelte 12 Ib 52.46N 6.16E
Haverfordwest 9 Ij 51.49N 4.58W
Haverhill [Eng.-U.K.] 9 Ni 52.05N 0.26E
Haverhill [Ma.-U.S.] 44 Ld 42.47N 71.05W
Havering, London- 12 Cc 51.36N 0.11E
Havířov 10 Og 49.48N 18.27E
Havlíčkův Brod 10 Lg 49.36N 15.34E
Havøysund 7 Fa 71.03N 24.40E
Havran 24 Bc 39.33N 27.06E
Havre 39 Ie 48.33N 109.41W
Havre-Saint-Pierre 39 Md 50.15N 63.36W
Havsa 15 Jh 41.33N 26.49E
Havza 24 Fb 41.05N 35.45E
Hawaii [2] 58 Kb 24.00N 167.00W
Hawaiian Islands 57 Kb 24.00N 167.00W
Hawaiian Ridge (EN) 3 Kg 24.00N 165.00W
Hawaii Island 57 Lc 19.30N 155.30W
Ḩawallī 23 Gd 29.19N 48.02E
Ḩawār 24 Nj 25.40N 50.45E
Hawarden 62 Ee 42.56S 172.39E
Ḩawashīyah, Wādī- 24 Eh 28.31N 32.58E
Hawaymi, Sha'īb al- 24 Kg 30.58N 44.15E
Hawd 30 Lh 7.40N 47.43E
Ḩawḑ Al Waqf 24 Ei 26.03N 32.22E
Hawea, Lake- 62 Cf 44.30S 169.20E
Hawera 61 Dg 39.35S 174.17E
Hawi 58 Lb 20.14N 155.50W
Hawick 9 Kf 55.25N 2.47W
Ḩawīzah, Hawr al- 24 Lg 31.35N 47.38E
Hawkdun Range 62 Cf 44.50S 170.00E
Hawke Bay 61 Eg 39.25S 177.20E
Hawke Harbour 42 Lf 53.01N 55.50W
Hawker 59 Hf 31.53S 138.25E
Hawkes, Mount- 66 Rg 83.55S 56.05W
Hawke's Bay [2] 62 Gc 39.30S 176.40E
Hawkesbury 44 Jc 45.36N 74.37W
Hawkhurst 12 Cc 51.02N 0.30E
Hawkinsville 44 Fi 32.17N 83.28W
Hawksbill 44 Hf 38.33N 78.23W
Hawk Springs 46 Mf 41.48N 104.09W
Ḩawmat as Sūq 32 Jc 33.53N 10.51E
Hawng Tuk 25 Jd 20.28N 99.56E
Ḩawrā' 35 Hb 15.43N 48.18E
Ḩawrān, Wādī al- 23 Fc 33.58N 42.34E
Ḩawsh 'Īsá 24 Dg 30.55N 30.17E
Hawthorne 43 Dd 38.32N 118.38W
Hawthorne, Mount- 66 Pf 72.10S 98.39W
Haxtun 45 Ef 40.39N 102.38W
Hay 58 Fh 34.30S 144.51E
Hay 38 Hc 60.51N 115.44W
Hayachine-San 29 Gb 39.34N 141.29E
Hayakita 29a Bb 42.45N 141.48E
Hayange 11 Me 49.20N 6.03E
Hayastan = Armenia (EN) 19 Eg 40.00N 45.00E
Hayato 29 Bf 31.45N 130.43E
Haybān 35 Ec 11.13N 30.31E
Haybān, Jabal- 35 Ec 11.15N 30.31E
Hayden 46 Jj 33.00N 110.47W
Hayes [Man.-Can.] 42 Ie 57.00N 92.15W
Hayes [N.W.T.-Can.] 42 Hc 67.20N 95.02W
Hayes, Mount- 40 Jd 63.37N 146.43W
Hayes Halvø=Hayes Peninsula (EN) 67 Od 77.40N 64.30W
Hayes Peninsula (EN)=Hayes Halvø 67 Od 77.40N 64.30W
Ḩayl 24 Qj 24.33N 56.06E
Hayl, Wādī al- 24 He 34.47N 39.18E
Hayling Island 12 Bd 50.48N 0.58W
Haymana 24 Ec 39.27N 32.30E
Haymana Platosu 24 Ec 39.25N 32.45E
Haynin 23 Gf 15.50N 48.18E
Hayrabolu 24 Bb 41.12N 27.06E
Ḩayrān 33 Hf 16.02N 42.49E
Hay River 59 Hd 25.00S 138.00E
Hay River 39 Hc 60.51N 115.40W
Hayrüt 35 Ib 15.59N 52.09E
Hays 43 Hd 38.53N 99.20W
Hay Springs 45 Ee 42.41N 102.41W
Haystack Peak 46 Ig 39.50N 113.55W
Hayward [Ca.-U.S.] 46 Dh 37.40N 122.05W
Hayward [Wi.-U.S.] 45 Kc 46.01N 91.29W
Haywards Heath 12 Bc 51.00N 0.06W
Hazar, Wādī- 35 Hb 17.50N 49.07E
Hazarasp 18 Cd 41.19N 61.08E
Hazard 44 Fg 37.15N 83 12W
Hazar Gölü 24 Hc 38.30N 39.25E
Hazāribāgh 25 Hd 23.59N 85.21E
Hazebrouck 11 Id 50.43N 2.32E
Hazelton 42 Ee 55.15N 127.40W
Hazen 45 Fc 47.18N 101.38W
Hazen Strait 42 Ga 77.15N 110.00W
Ḩazeva 24 Fg 30.48N 35.15E
Hazlehurst [Ga.-U.S.] 44 Fj 31.52N 82.36W
Hazlehurst [Ms.-U.S.] 45 Kk 31.52N 90.24W
Hazleton 44 Je 40.58N 76.00W
Hazlett, Lake- 59 Fd 21.30S 128.50E
Hazrah, Ra's al- 24 Nj 24.22N 51.36E
Hazro 24 Ic 38.15N 40.47E
Heacham 12 Cb 52.55N 0.29E
Headley 12 Bc 51.07N 0.49W
Healdsburg 46 Dg 38.37N 122.52W
Heanor 12 Aa 53.00N 1.18W
Heard Island 30 On 53.00S 73.35E
Hearne 45 Hk 30.53N 96.36W
Hearst 42 Jg 49.41N 83.40W
Heart River 45 Fc 46.47N 100.51W
Heathrow Airport London 12 Bc 51.28N 0.30W
Hebbronville 45 Gm 27.18N 98.41W
Hebei Sheng (Ho-pei Sheng) =Hopeh (EN) [2] 27 Kd 39.00N 116.00E
Heber City 46 Jf 40.30N 111.25W
Hebi 27 Jd 35.53N 114.09E
Hebian 27 Jd 38.35N 113.06E
Hebiji 28 Cf 36.00N 114.08E
Hebrides 5 Fd 57.00N 6.30W
Hebrides, Sea of the- 9 Ge 57.00N 7.00W
Hebron [N.D.-U.S.] 45 Ec 46.54N 102.03W
Hebron [Newf.-Can.] 42 Le 58.15N 62.35W
Heby 8 Ge 59.56N 16.53E
Hecate Strait 42 Ef 53.20N 131.00W
Hecelchakán 48 Ng 20.10N 90.08W
Hechi (Jnchengjiang) 27 Ig 24.44N 108.02E
Hechingen 10 Eh 48.21N 8.59E
Hechuan 27 Ie 30.07N 106.15E
Hecla 45 Gd 45.43N 98.09W
Hecla and Griper Bay 42 Ga 76.00N 111.30W
Hecla Island 45 Ha 51.08N 96.45W
Heddalsvatnet 8 Ce 59.30N 9.15E
Hede 7 Ce 62.25N 13.30E
Hede→Sheyang 28 Fh 33.47N 120.15E
Hedemarken 8 Dd 60.50N 11.20E
Hedemora 7 Df 60.17N 15.59E
Hedensted 8 Ci 55.46N 9.42E
Hedesunda 7 Df 60.25N 17.00E
Hedesunda fjärdarna 8 Gd 60.20N 17.00E
Hedmark [2] 7 Cf 61.30N 11.45E
Hedo-Misaki 29b Bb 26.52N 128.16E
Heemskerk 12 Gb 52.30N 4.42E
Heemstede 12 Gb 52.21N 4.37E
Heerenveen 11 Lb 52.57N 5.55E
Heerhugowaard 12 Gb 52.40N 4.50E
Heerlen 11 Ld 50.54N 5.59E
Hefa=Haifa (EN) 22 Ff 32.50N 35.00E
Hefei 22 Nf 31.47N 117.15E
Hefeng 27 Jf 29.49N 110.01E
Hegang 22 Pe 47.20N 130.12E
Hegau 10 Ei 47.50N 8.45E
Hegura Jima 27 Od 37.50N 136.55E
Heide 10 Fb 54.12N 9.06E
Heidelberg 10 Eg 49.25N 8.42E
Heidenheim an der Brenz 10 Gh 48.41N 10.09E
Heidenreichstein 14 Jb 48.52N 15.07E
Hei-Gawa 29 Gb 39.38N 141.58E
Heigun-Tō 29 Ce 33.47N 132.15E
Hei He 27 Hd 38.15N 100.15E
Heihe→Aihui 22 Od 50.13N 127.26E
Heilbron 37 De 27.21S 27.58E
Heilbronn 10 Fg 49.08N 9.13E
Heiligenblut 14 Gd 47.02N 12.50E
Heiligenhafen 10 Gb 54.22N 10.59E
Heiligenhaus 12 Ic 51.19N 6.58E
Heiligenstadt 10 Ge 51.23N 10.08E
Heilinzi 28 Ib 44.33N 126.41E
Heilong Jiang 21 Qd 52.56N 141.10E
Heilongjiang Sheng (Hei-lung-chiang Sheng)= Heilungkiang (EN) [2] 27 Mb 48.00N 128.00E
Heiloo 12 Gb 52.36N 4.43E
Hei-lung-chiang Sheng→Heilongjiang Sheng=Heilungkiang (EN) [2] 27 Mb 48.00N 128.00E
Heilungkiang (EN)= Heilongjiang Sheng (Hei-lung-chiang Sheng) [2] 27 Mb 48.00N 128.00E
Heilungkiang (EN)=Hei-lung-chiang Sheng→Heilongjiang Sheng [2] 27 Mb 48.00N 128.00E
Heimæy 7a c 63.26N 20.17W
Heimbach 12 Id 50.38N 6.29E
Heimdal 7 Ce 63.21N 10.22E
Heimsheim 12 Kf 48.48N 8.51E
Heinävesi 7 Ge 62.26N 28.36E
Heinola 7 Gf 61.13N 26.02E
Heinsberg 12 Ic 51.04N 6.05E
Heishan 28 Gd 41.42N 122.07E
Heishan Xia 27 Hd 37.18N 104.39E
Heishui [China] 28 Ec 42.06N 119.22E
Heishui [China] 27 He 32.03N 103.05E
Heist, Knokke- 12 Fc 51.21N 3.15E
Heist-op-den-Berg 12 Gc 51.05N 4.43E
Hei-Zaki 29 Hb 39.39N 142.00E
Hejgijaha 17 Pd 65.27N 72.50E
Hejian 28 De 38.27N 116.05E
Hejing 27 Ec 42.18N 86.18E
Hejjaha 17 Kb 68.18N 62.32E
Hekimhan 24 Gc 38.49N 37.56E
Hekinan 29 Ed 34.52N 136.58E
Hekla 5 Ec 64.00N 19.40W
Hekou 28 Ci 31.20N 114.25E
Hekou → Yanshan 28 Dj 28.18N 117.41E
Hel 10 Ob 54.37N 18.48E
Helagsfjället 7 Ce 62.55N 12.27E
Helan 27 Id 38.35N 106.16E
Helan Shan 27 Id 39.00N 106.00E
Helden's Point 51c Ab 17.24N 62.50W
Helena [Ar.-U.S.] 43 Ie 34.32N 90.35W
Helena [Guy.] 54 Gb 6.41N 57.55W
Helena [Mt.-U.S.] 39 He 46.36N 112.01W
Helen Glacier 66 Ge 66.40S 93.55E
Helen Reef 57 Ed 2.35N 131.47E
Helensburgh 9 Ie 56.01N 4.44W
Helensville 62 Fb 36.40S 174.27E
Helgaå 8 Fi 55.53N 14.08E
Helgasjön 8 Fh 56.55N 14.45E
Helgeland 7 Cd 66.15N 13.05E
Helgoland 10 Db 54.12N 7.53E

Index Symbols

[1] Independent Nation
[2] State, Region
[3] District, County
[4] Municipality
[5] Colony, Dependency
Continent
Physical Region
Historical or Cultural Region
Mount, Mountain
Volcano
Hill
Mountains, Mountain Range
Hills, Escarpment
Plateau, Upland
Pass, Gap
Plain, Lowland
Delta
Salt Flat
Valley, Canyon
Crater, Cave
Karst Features
Depression
Polder
Desert, Dunes
Forest, Woods
Heath, Steppe
Oasis
Cape, Point
Coast, Beach
Cliff
Peninsula
Isthmus
Sandbank
Island
Atoll
Rock, Reef
Islands, Archipelago
Rocks, Reefs
Coral Reef
Well, Spring
Geyser
River, Stream
Waterfall Rapids
River Mouth, Estuary
Lake
Salt Lake
Intermittent Lake
Reservoir
Swamp, Pond
Canal
Glacier
Ice Shelf, Pack Ice
Ocean
Sea
Gulf, Bay
Strait, Fjord
Lagoon
Bank
Seamount
Tablemount
Ridge
Shelf
Basin
Escarpment, Sea Scarp
Fracture
Trench, Abyss
National Park, Reserve
Point of Interest
Recreation Site
Cave, Cavern
Historic Site
Ruins
Wall, Walls
Church, Abbey
Temple
Scientific Station
Airport
Port
Lighthouse
Mine
Tunnel
Dam, Bridge

Helgoländer Bucht 10 Eb 54.10N 8.04 E
Helikón Óros 15 Fk 38.20N 22.50 E
Helixi 28 Ei 30.39N 119.01 E
Heljulja 8 Nc 61.37N 30.38 E
Hella 7a Bc 63.50N 20.24W
Hellberge 10 Hd 52.34N 11.17 E
Hèlleh 24 Nh 29.10N 50.40 E
Hellendoorn 11 Mb 52.24N 6.26 E
Hellendoorn-Nijverdal 12 Ib 52.22N 6.27 E
Hellenic Trough (EN) 5 Ii 35.00N 24.00 E
Hellental 12 Id 50.29N 6.26 E
Hellesylt 7 Be 62.05N 6.54 E
Hellin 13 Kf 38.31N 1.41W
Hells Canyon 43 Db 45.20N 116.45W
Hellweg 12 Kc 51.40N 8.00 E
Helmand 21 If 31.12N 61.34 E
Helmand [3] 23 Jc 31.00N 64.00 E
Helme 10 He 51.20N 11.20 E
Helmeringhausen 37 Be 25.54S 16.57 E
Helmond 11 Lc 51.29N 5.40 E
Helmsdale 9 Jc 58.10N 3.40W
Helmsdale 9 Jc 58.07N 3.40W
Helmstedt 10 Gd 52.14N 11.00 E
Helong 27 Mc 42.32N 129.00 E
Helpe Majeure 12 Fd 50.11N 3.47 E
Helpringham 12 Bb 52.56N 0.18W
Helpter Berge 10 Jc 53.30N 13.36 E
Helsingborg 6 Hd 56.03N 12.42 E
Helsinge 8 Eh 56.01N 12.12 E
Helsingfors/Helsinki 6 Ic 60.10N 24.58 E
Helsingør 7 Ch 56.02N 12.37 E
Helsinki/Helsingfors 6 Ic 60.10N 24.58 E
Helska, Mierzeja- 10 Ob 54.45N 18.39 E
Helston 9 Hk 50.05N 5.16W
Helvecia 55 Bj 31.06S 60.05W
Helwān (EN)=Ḩulwān 33 Fd 29.51N 31.20 E
Ḩemār 24 Qg 31.42N 57.31 E
Hemčik 20 Ef 51.40N 92.10 E
Hemel Hempstead 9 Mj 51.46N 0.28W
Hemer 12 Jc 51.23N 7.46 E
Hemnesberget 7 Cc 66.14N 13.38 E
Hemsby 12 Db 52.41N 1.42 E
Hemse 8 Hg 57.14N 18.22 E
Hemsedal 8 Cd 60.50N 8.40 E
Hemsö 7 Ee 62.45N 18.05 E
Hen 8 Dd 60.13N 10.14 E
Henan 27 He 34.33N 101.55 E
Hen and Chickens Islands 62 Fa 35.55S 174.45 E
Henan Sheng (Ho-nan Sheng)=Honan (EN) [2] 27 Je 34.00N 114.00 E
Henares 13 Id 40.24N 3.30W
Henashi-Zaki 29 Fa 40.37N 139.51 E
Henbury 59 Gd 24.35S 133.15 E
Hendaye 11 Ek 43.22N 1.47W
Hendek 24 Db 40.48N 30.45 E
Henderson [Arg.] 55 Bm 36.18S 61.43W
Henderson [Ky.-U.S.] 44 Dg 37.50N 87.35W
Henderson [N.C.-U.S.] 44 Hg 36.20N 78.25W
Henderson [Nv.-U.S.] 43 Dd 36.02N 115.01W
Henderson [Tx.-U.S.] 45 Ij 32.09N 94.48W
Henderson Island 57 Og 24.22S 128.19W
Henderson Seamount (EN) 43 Df 25.34N 119.33W
Hendersonville [N.C.-U.S.] 44 Fh 35.19N 82.28W
Hendersonville [Tn.-U.S.] 44 Dg 36.18N 86.37W
Hendījān 24 Mg 30.14N 49.43 E
Hendorābī, Jazīreh-ye- 24 Oi 26.40N 53.37 E
Hendrik Verwderddam 30 Km 46.36S 37.55 E
Hengām, Jazīreh-ye- 24 Pi 26.39N 55.53 E
Hengduan Shan 21 Lg 27.30N 99.00 E
Hengelo [Neth.] 11 Mb 52.15N 6.45 E
Hengelo [Neth.] 12 Ib 52.03N 6.20 E
Heng Shan [China] 27 Jd 39.42N 113.45 E
Hengshan [China] 27 Jf 27.16N 112.51 E
Heng Shan [China] 27 Jf 27.18N 112.41 E
Hengshan [China] 27 Id 37.51N 109.20 E
Hengshan [China] 28 Kb 45.24N 131.01 E
Hengshui 27 Kd 37.39N 115.46 E
Hengxian 27 Ig 22.46N 109.15 E
Hengyang 22 Ng 26.56N 112.35 E
Henik Lakes 42 Hd 61.05N 97.20W
Hénin-Liétard 11 Id 50.25N 2.56 E
Henley-on-Thames 12 Bc 51.32N 0.54W
Hennan 8 Fb 62.05N 15.45 E
Hennan 7 De 62.02N 15.54 E
Hennebont 11 Cg 47.48N 3.17W
Hennef (Sieg) 12 Jd 50.47N 7.17 E
Hennigsdorf bei Berlin 10 Jd 52.38N 13.12 E
Henrietta Maria, Cape - 42 Je 55.09N 82.19W
Henrietty, Ostrov- 20 Ka 77.00N 157.00 E
Henry, Mount- 46 Hb 48.53N 115.31W
Henry Bay 66 Ie 66.40S 120.40 E
Henryetta 45 Ii 35.27N 95.59W
Henry Kater Peninsula 42 Kk 69.15N 67.30W
Henry Mountains 46 Jh 37.55N 110.50W
Henrys Fork River 46 Je 43.45N 111.56W
Henslow, Cape- 63a Ec 9.56S 160.38 E
Hentej 21 Me 48.50N 109.00 E
Hentiesbaai 37 Ad 22.08S 14.18 E
Henzada 22 Lh 17.38N 95.28 E
Heping→Yanhe 27 If 28.31N 108.28 E
Heppenheim (Bergstraße) 12 Ke 49.38N 8.39 E
Heppner 46 Fd 45.21N 119.33W
Hepu (Lianzhou) 27 Ig 21.40N 109.12 E
Hequ 27 Jd 39.22N 111.15 E
Herakol Dağı 24 Id 37.45N 42.35 E
Heralds Cays 59 Jc 16.55S 149.10 E
Herāt 23 Jc 34.20N 62.00 E
Herāt 22 If 34.20N 62.12 E
Hérault [3] 11 Jk 43.40N 3.30 E
Hérault 11 Jk 43.17N 3.26 E
Herbert [N.Z.] 62 Df 45.13S 170.46 E
Herbert [Sask.-Can.] 46 La 50.26N 107.12W
Herberton 59 Jc 17.23S 145.23 E
Herbert River 59 Jc 18.32S 146.17 E
Herborn 10 Ef 50.41N 8.19 E
Herby 10 Of 50.45N 18.40 E
Hercegnovi 15 Bg 42.27N 18.32 E
Hercegovina 14 Lg 43.00N 17.50 E
Herdubreid 7a Cb 65.11N 16.21W
Heredia [3] 49 Fh 10.30N 84.00W
Heredia 47 Hf 10.00N 84.07W
Hereford 9 Ki 52.15N 2.50W
Hereford [Eng.-U.K.] 9 Ki 52.04N 2.43W
Hereford [Tx.-U.S.] 43 Ge 34.49N 102.24W
Hereford and Worcester [3] 9 Ki 52.10N 2.35W
Hereheretue Atoll 57 Mf 19.54S 144.58W
Hereke 15 Mi 40.48N 29.39 E
Herekino 62 Ea 35.16S 173.13 E
Herent 12 Gd 50.54N 4.40 E
Herentals 12 Gc 51.11N 4.50 E
Herfølge 8 Ei 55.25N 12.10 E
Herford 10 Ed 52.08N 8.41 E
Héricourt 11 Mg 47.35N 6.45 E
Herington 45 Hg 38.40N 96.57W
Heriot 61 Ci 45.51S 169.16 E
Heris 24 Lc 38.14N 47.07 E
Herisau 14 Dc 47.24N 9.16 E
Herk 12 Hd 50.58N 5.07 E
Herk-de-Stad 12 Hd 50.56N 5.10 E
Herkimer 44 Jd 43.02N 74.59W
Herlen He 27 Kb 48.48N 117.00 E
Hermagor 14 Hd 46.37N 13.22 E
Hermanas 48 Id 27.14N 101.14W
Herma Ness 9 Ma 60.50N 0.54W
Hermano Peak 45 Bh 37.17N 108.48W
Hermansverk 8 Bc 61.11N 6.51 E
Hermanus 37 Bf 34.25S 19.16 E
Hermeskeil 12 Ie 49.39N 6.57 E
Hermiston 46 Fd 45.51N 119.17W
Hermitage 62 De 43.44S 170.05 E
Hermit Islands 57 Fe 1.32S 145.05 E
Hermosa de Santa Rosa, Sierra- 48 Id 28.00N 101.45W
Hermosillo 39 Hg 29.04N 110.58W
Hermoso Campo 55 Bh 27.36S 61.21W
Hérnad 10 Qh 48.00N 20.58 E
Hernandarias 56 Jc 25.22S 54.45W
Hernández [Arg.] 55 Bk 32.21S 60.02W
Hernández [Mex.] 48 Hf 23.02N 102.02W
Hernani 13 Ka 43.16N 1.58W
Herne 10 De 51.33N 7.13 E
Herne Bay 9 Oj 51.23N 1.08 E
Herning 6 Gd 56.08N 8.59 E
Heroica Alvarado 48 Lh 18.46N 95.46W
Heroica Tlapacoyan 48 Kh 19.58N 97.13W
Heroica Zitácuaro 48 Ih 19.24N 100.22W
Herouville-Saint-Clair 12 Be 49.12N 0.19W
Herowābād 24 Md 37.37N 48.32 E
Herradura 55 Ch 26.29S 58.18W
Herre 8 Ce 59.06N 9.34 E
Herrera 55 Ck 32.26S 58.38W
Herrera [3] 49 Gj 7.54N 80.38W
Herrera del Duque 13 Ge 39.10N 5.03W
Herrera de Pisuerga 13 Hb 42.36N 4.20W
Herrero, Punta- 48 Ph 19.10N 87.30W
Herrljunga 8 Ef 58.05N 13.02 E
Hers 11 Hk 43.47N 1.20 E
Herschel 42 Dc 69.35N 139.05W
Herselt 12 Gc 51.03N 4.53 E
Herserange 12 He 49.31N 5.47 E
Hershey 44 Ie 40.17N 76.39W
Hersilia 55 Bj 30.00S 61.51W
Herson 6 Jf 46.38N 32.35 E
Hersonesski, Mys- 16 Hg 44.33N 33.25 E
Hersonskaja Oblast [3] 19 Df 46.40N 33.30 E
Herstal 11 Ld 50.40N 5.38 E
Herten 12 Jc 51.36N 7.08 E
Hertford 9 Mj 51.50N 0.05W
Hertford 9 Mj 51.48N 0.05W
Hertfordshire [3] 9 Mj 51.45N 0.20W
Hertugen Af Orleans Land 41 Jc 78.15N 21.12W
Hervás 13 Gd 40.16N 5.51W
Herve 12 Hd 50.38N 5.48 E
Herve, Plateau van-/Herveland 12 Hd 50.40N 5.50 E
Herveland/Herve, Plateau van- 12 Hd 50.40N 5.50 E
Hervey Bay 59 Ke 25.15S 152.50 E
Herzberg 10 Je 51.41N 13.14 E
Herzberg am Harz 10 Ge 51.39N 10.20 E
Herzebrock 12 Kc 51.53N 8.15 E
Herzegovina (EN) 5 Hg 43.00N 17.50 E
Herzele 12 Fd 50.53N 3.53 E
Herzliyya 24 Ff 32.10N 34.51 E
Herzogenrath 12 Id 50.52N 6.06 E
Herzog-Ernst-Bucht (Vahsel Bay) 66 Af 77.48S 34.39W
Hesāmābād 24 Me 35.52N 48.25 E
Hesbaye/Haspengouws Plateau 11 Ld 50.35N 5.10 E
Hesdin 11 Id 50.22N 2.02 E
Hesel 12 Ja 53.18N 7.36 E
Heshī 24 Md 37.30N 48.15 E
Heshun 27 Jd 37.18N 113.32 E
Hesse (EN)=Hessen [2] 10 Ff 50.30N 9.15 E
Hesselberg 10 Gg 49.05N 10.35 E
Hesselø 8 Dh 56.10N 11.45 E
Hessen 12 Ke 49.47N 8.08 E
Hessen=Hesse (EN) [2] 10 Ff 50.30N 9.15 E
Hess Tablemount (EN) 57 Jc 17.50N 174.15W
Heta 21 Mb 71.54N 102.00 E
Heta 20 Eb 71.35N 99.45 E
Hettange-Grande 12 Ie 49.24N 6.09 E
Hettinger 45 Ec 46.00N 102.39W
Heuberg 10 Eh 48.06N 8.55 E
Heuchin 12 Ed 50.28N 2.16 E
Heuru 63a Ed 10.12S 161.25 E
Hève, Cap de la- 11 Fe 49.31N 0.04W
Heves 10 Qi 47.36N 20.17 E
Heves [2] 10 Qi 47.50N 20.15 E
Hexham 9 Kg 54.58N 2.06W
Hexi 27 Hf 27.44N 102.09 E
Hexian 28 Ei 31.43N 118.22 E
Hexian (Babu) 27 Jg 24.28N 111.34 E
Hexigten Qi (Jingfeng) 27 Kc 43.15N 117.31 E
Heydarābād 24 Kd 37.06N 45.27 E
Heysham 9 Kg 54.02N 2.54W
Heyuan 27 Jg 23.41N 114.43 E
Heywood 59 Ig 38.08S 141.38 E
Heze (Caozhou) 27 Kd 35.14N 115.28 E
Hezuo 27 Hd 35.02N 102.57 E
Hialeah 44 Gm 25.49N 80.17W
Hiawatha 45 Ig 39.51N 95.32W
Hibara-Ko 29 Gc 37.42N 140.03 E
Hibbing 43 Ib 47.25N 92.56W
Hibernia Reef 59 Eb 12.00S 123.25 E
Hibiki-Nada 29 Bd 34.15N 130.40 E
Hibiny 7 Hc 67.40N 33.35 E
Hiburi-Jima 29 Ce 33.10N 132.18 E
Hickman 44 Cg 36.34N 89.11W
Hickory 44 Gh 35.44N 81.21W
Hick's Cay 49 Ce 17.39N 88.08W
Hida-Gawa 29 Ed 35.25N 137.03 E
Hidaka [Jap.] 28 Qc 42.53N 142.28 E
Hidaka [Jap.] 29 Dd 35.28N 134.47 E
Hidaka-Gawa 29 De 33.53N 135.08 E
Hidaka Sanmyaku 28 Qc 42.25N 142.50 E
Hidalgo [2] 47 Ed 20.30N 99.00W
Hidalgo [Mex.] 47 Ed 24.15N 99.26W
Hidalgo [Mex.] 48 Jd 27.47N 99.52W
Hidalgo del Parral 39 Ig 26.56N 105.40W
Hida-Sanchi 29 Ec 36.20N 137.00 E
Hida-Sanmyaku 28 Nf 36.10N 137.30 E
Hiddensee 10 Jb 54.33N 13.07 E
Hidra 8 Bf 58.15N 6.35 E
Hidrolândia 55 Hc 16.58S 49.16W
Hidrolina 55 Hb 14.37S 49.25W
Hieflau 14 Ic 47.36N 14.44 E
Hiei-Zan 29 Dd 35.05N 135.50 E
Hienghène 61 Cd 20.35S 164.56 E
Hierro 30 Ff 27.45N 18.00W
Higashi 29b b 26.38N 128.08 E
Higashihiroshima 29 Cd 34.25N 132.43 E
Higashi-izu 29 Fd 34.48N 139.02 E
Higashi-matsuyama 29 Fc 36.02N 139.22 E
Higashimuroran 29a Bb 42.21N 141.02 E
Higashine 28 Pe 38.26N 140.24 E
Higashiōsaka 29 Dd 34.40N 135.42 E
Higashi Rishiri 29a Ba 45.16N 141.15 E
Higashi-Shina-Kai=East China Sea (EN) 21 Og 29.00N 125.00 E
Higgins 45 Fh 36.07N 100.02W
Higgins Ferrers 12 Bb 52.18N 0.35W
High Atlas (EN)=Haut Atlas 30 Ge 32.00N 6.00W
Highland [3] 9 Id 57.30N 5.00W
Highland Park 45 Me 42.11N 87.48W
High Level 42 Fe 58.30N 117.05W
Highmore 45 Gd 44.31N 99.27W
High Plains 38 If 38.30N 103.00W
High Point 43 Ld 35.58N 79.59W
High Prairie 42 Fe 55.27N 116.30W
High River 42 Gf 50.35N 113.52W
Highrock Lake 42 He 55.49N 100.23W
High Springs 44 Fk 29.50N 82.36W
High Tatra (EN)=Vysoké Tatry 10 Pg 49.10N 20.00 E
High Willhays 9 Jk 50.41N 3.59W
Highwood Mountains 46 Jc 47.25N 110.30W
High Wycombe 9 Mj 51.38N 0.46W
Higuera de Zaragoza 48 Ee 25.59N 109.16W
Higüero, Punta- 49 Nd 18.22N 67.16W
Higuerote 50 Cg 10.29N 66.06W
Higüey 49 Md 18.37N 68.43W
Hiidenvesi 8 Kd 60.20N 24.10 E
Hii-Gawa 29 Cd 35.26N 132.52 E
Hiiraan [3] 35 He 4.00N 45.30 E
Hiitola 7 Gf 61.16N 29.42 E
Hiiumaa/Hiiuma 5 Id 58.50N 22.40 E
Hijar 13 Lc 41.10N 0.27W
Ḩijāz 23 Ee 24.30N 38.30 E
Ḩijāz, Jabal al- 33 Hf 19.45N 41.55 E
Hiji 29 Be 33.22N 131.32 E
Hiji-Gawa 29 Ce 33.36N 132.29 E
Hikami 29 Dd 35.11N 135.02 E
Hikari 28 Kh 33.58N 131.56 E
Hiketa 29 Dd 34.13N 134.24 E
Hikiā 8 Kd 60.45N 24.55 E
Hiki-Gawa 29 De 33.35N 135.26 E
Ḩikmah, Ra's al- 24 Bg 31.17N 27.44 E
Hikone 28 Ng 35.15N 136.15 E
Hiko-San 29 Be 33.29N 130.56 E
Hikueru Atoll 61 Mc 17.36S 142.37W
Hikurangi 62 Hb 37.55S 178.04 E
Hikurangi 62 Fa 35.36S 174.17 E
Hila 26 Ih 7.35S 127.24 E
Hilāl, Ra's al- 33 Dc 32.55N 22.11 E
Hiland 46 Le 43.08N 107.18W
Hilchenbach 12 Kc 51.00N 8.06 E
Hildburghausen 10 Gf 50.25N 10.45 E
Hilden 12 Ic 51.10N 6.56 E
Hildesheim 10 Fd 52.09N 9.58 E
Hillaby, Mount- 50 Gf 13.12N 59.35W
Hillared 8 Eg 57.38N 13.09 E
Hillary Coast 66 Kf 79.00S 161.00 E
Hill Bank 49 Ce 17.35N 88.42W
Hill City 45 Gg 39.22N 99.51W
Hillcrest Center 46 Fi 35.23N 118.57W
Hille 12 Kb 52.20N 8.45 E
Hillegom 12 Gb 52.18N 4.35 E
Hillekrog 8 Dj 54.36N 11.30 E
Hillerød 8 Ei 55.56N 12.19 E
Hillerstorp 8 Eg 57.19N 13.52 E
Hillesheim 12 Id 50.19N 6.41 E
Hillingdon, London- 12 Bc 51.31N 0.27W
Hillsboro [Il.-U.S.] 45 Lg 39.09N 89.29W
Hillsboro [N.D.-U.S.] 45 Hc 47.26N 97.03W
Hillsboro [Oh.-U.S.] 44 Ff 39.12N 83.37W
Hillsboro [Or.-U.S.] 46 Dd 45.31N 122.59W
Hillsboro [Tx.-U.S.] 45 Hj 32.01N 97.08W
Hillsborough 51p Cb 12.29N 61.26W
Hillsdale 44 Ee 41.55N 84.38W
Hillsville 44 Gg 36.46N 80.44W
Hillswich 9 La 60.28N 1.30W
Hilo 65a Fd 19.44N 155.05W
Hilo Bay 65a Fd 19.44N 155.05W
Hilok 21 Md 51.19N 106.59 E
Hilok 20 Gf 51.22N 110.30 E
Hilton Head Island 44 Gi 32.12N 80.45W
Hiltrup, Münster- 12 Jc 51.54N 7.38 E
Hilvan 24 Hd 37.30N 38.58 E
Hilvarenbeek 12 Hc 51.29N 5.08 E
Hilversum 11 Lb 52.14N 5.10 E
Himāchal Pradesh [3] 25 Fb 31.00N 78.00 E
Himalaya=Himalayas (EN) 21 Kg 29.00N 83.00 E
Himalayas (EN)=Himalaya 21 Kg 29.00N 83.00 E
Himara 15 Ci 40.07N 19.44 E
Himeji 27 Ne 34.49N 134.42 E
Hime-Jima 29 Be 33.43N 131.40 E
Hime-Kawa 29 Ec 37.02N 137.50 E
Hime-Shima 29 Ae 32.49N 128.41 E
Hime-Zaki 29 Fb 38.05N 138.34 E
Himi 28 Nf 36.51N 136.59 E
Himki 7 Ii 55.56N 37.28 E
Himmelbjerget 8 Ch 56.06N 9.42 E
Himmerfjärden 8 Gg 59.00N 17.43 E
Himmerland 8 Ch 56.50N 9.45 E
Himo 36 Gc 3.23S 37.33 E
Ḩimş=Homs (E) 22 Ff 34.44N 36.43 E
Ḩims, Bahrat- 24 Ge 34.39N 36.34 E
Hinai 29 Ga 40.13N 140.35 E
Hinca Renancó 56 Hd 34.50S 64.23W
Hinche 49 Kd 19.09N 72.01W
Hinchinbrook 40 Jd 60.22N 146.30W
Hinchinbrook Island 59 Jc 18.25S 146.15 E
Hinckley 12 Ab 52.32N 1.22W
Hindås 8 Eg 57.42N 12.27 E
Hindhead 12 Bc 51.06N 0.44W
Hindi, Badwēynta-=Indian Ocean (EN) 3 Gl 21.00S 82.00 E
Hindmarsh, Lake- 59 Ig 36.05S 141.55 E
Hinds 62 Df 44.00S 171.34 E
Hindsholm 8 Di 55.33N 10.40 E
Hindukush 21 Jf 35.00N 71.00 E
Hindustan 21 Jg 25.00N 79.00 E
Hinesville 44 Gj 31.51N 81.36W
Hinganghāt 25 Fd 20.34N 78.50 E
Hinis 24 Ic 39.22N 41.44 E
Hinis 24 Jc 39.18N 42.12 E
Hinlopenstretet 41 Oc 79.15N 21.00 E
Hinnøya 5 Hb 68.30N 16.00 E
Hino-Gawa 29 Cd 35.27N 133.22 E
Hinojosa del Duque 13 Gf 38.30N 5.09W
Hinokage 29 Be 32.39N 131.24 E
Hi-no-Misaki 29 Cd 35.26N 132.38 E
Hino-Misaki 29 De 33.53N 135.04 E
Hinterrhein 14 Dd 46.49N 9.25 E
Hinton 42 Ff 53.25N 117.34W
Hi-Numa 29 Gc 36.16N 140.30 E
Hınzır Burun 24 Fb 36.22N 35.45 E
Hiou 63b Ca 13.08S 166.33 E
Hipólito 48 Ie 25.41N 101.26W
Hippolytushoef, Wieringen- 12 Gb 52.54N 4.59 E
Hippone 14 Bn 36.52N 7.44 E
Hirado 28 Jh 33.22N 129.33 E
Hirado-Shima 28 Jh 33.19N 129.32 E
Hiraka 29 Gb 39.16N 140.29 E
Hirakata 29 Dd 34.48N 135.38 E
Hirākud 25 Gd 21.15N 84.15 E
Hiraman 36 Gc 1.07S 39.55 E
Hiranai 29a Bc 40.54N 140.57 E
Hirara 27 Mg 24.48N 125.17 E
Hira-Shima 29 Ae 33.01N 129.15 E
Hirata 29 Cd 35.26N 132.49 E
Hiratsuka 29 Fd 35.19N 139.19 E
Hirfanlı barajı Gölü 24 Ec 39.10N 33.32 E
Hirgis 27 Fb 49.32N 93.48 E
Hirgis-Nur 21 Le 49.12N 93.24 E
Hirhafok 32 Ie 23.29N 5.45 E
Hîrlău 15 Jb 47.26N 26.54 E
Hiromi 29 Ce 33.15N 132.38 E
Hiroo 27 Pc 42.17N 143.19 E
Hirosaki 27 Pc 40.35N 140.28 E
Hiroshima 22 Pf 34.24N 132.27 E
Hiroshima Ken [2] 28 Lg 34.35N 132.50 E
Hiroshima-Wan 29 Cd 34.10N 132.20 E
Hirschhorn (Neckar) 12 Ke 49.27N 8.54 E
Hirson 11 Ke 49.55N 4.05 E
Hirşova 15 Ke 44.41N 27.56 E
Hirtibaciu 15 Hd 45.44N 24.14 E
Hirtshals 7 Bh 57.35N 9.58 E
Hirvensalmi 8 Lc 61.38N 26.48 E
Ḩīs 35 Hc 10.50N 46.54 E
Hisai 29 Ed 34.40N 136.28 E
Hisaka-Shima 29 Ae 32.48N 128.52 E
Hisar 15 Jg 42.35N 27.00 E
Hisar 25 Fc 29.10N 75.43 E
Hisarcik 15 Mj 39.15N 29.15 E
Hisarja 15 Hg 42.30N 24.42 E
Ḩismā 24 Fh 28.30N 35.50 E
Ḩişn al 'Abr 33 If 16.08N 47.14 E
Ḩişn aş Şahābī 33 Dc 30.01N 20.48 E
Hispaniola (EN)=La Española 38 Lh 19.00N 71.00W
Histon 12 Cb 52.15N 0.06 E
Histria 15 Le 44.30N 28.45 E
Hīt 24 Jf 33.38N 42.49 E
Hita 28 Kh 33.19N 130.56 E
Hitachi 28 Pf 36.36N 140.39 E
Hitachi-ōta 29 Gc 36.32N 140.31 E
Hitchin 12 Bc 51.57N 0.16W
Hitiaa 65e Fc 17.36S 149.18W
Hitotsuse-Gawa 29 Be 32.03N 131.31 E
Hitoyoshi 28 Kh 32.15N 130.45 E
Hitra 5 Gc 63.30N 8.45 E
Hiuchi-ga-Take 29 Fc 36.57N 139.17 E
Hiuchi-Nada 29 Cd 34.05N 133.15 E
Hiumaa/Hiiumaa 5 Id 58.50N 22.40 E
Hiv 16 Oi 41.46N 47.57 E
Hiva 19 Gg 41.25N 60.23 E
Hiva Oa, Ile- 57 Ne 9.45S 139.00W
Hiw 24 Ei 26.01N 32.16 E
Hjademeste/Häädemeeste 8 Uf 58.00N 24.28 E
Hjallerup 8 Dg 57.10N 10.09 E
Hjälmare kanal 8 Fe 59.25N 15.55 E
Hjälmaren 5 Hd 59.15N 15.45 E
Hjelm 8 Dh 56.10N 10.50 E
Hjelmelandsvågen 7 Bg 59.15N 6.10 E
Hjelmsøya 7 Fa 71.05N 24.43 E
Hjerkinn 8 Cb 62.13N 9.32 E
Hjo 7 Dg 58.18N 14.17 E
Hjørring 7 Bh 57.28N 9.59 E
Hlatikulu 37 Ee 26.58S 31.19 E
Hlavní město Praha [3] 10 Kf 50.05N 14.25 E
Hlavní město SSR Bratislava [3] 10 Nh 48.10N 17.10 E
Hlinsko 10 Lg 49.46N 15.54 E
Hlohovec 10 Nh 48.25N 17.48 E
Hluhluwe 37 Ee 28.02S 32.17 E
Hmelnickaja Oblast [3] 19 Cf 49.30N 27.00 E
Hmelnicki 19 Cf 49.24N 26.57 E
Hmelnik 16 Ee 49.33N 27.59 E
Hnilec 10 Rh 48.53N 21.01 E
Ho 34 Fd 6.36N 0.28 E
Hoa Binh 25 Ld 20.50N 105.20 E
Hoai Nhon 25 Lf 14.26N 109.01 E
Hoanib 37 Ac 19.23S 13.06 E
Hoare Bay 42 Lc 65.30N 63.10W
Hoback Peak 46 Je 43.10N 110.33W
Hobart [Austl.] 58 Fi 42.53S 147.19 E
Hobart [Ok.-U.S.] 45 Gi 35.01N 99.06W
Hobbs 43 Ge 32.42N 103.08W
Hobbs Coast 66 Nf 74.50S 131.00W
Hobda 16 Sd 50.55N 54.38 E
Hoboken, Antwerpen- 12 Gc 51.10N 4.21 E
Hoboksar 27 Eb 46.47N 85.43 E
Hobq Shamo 27 Ic 40.30N 108.00 E
Hobro 7 Bh 56.38N 9.48 E
Hoburgen 7 Eh 56.55N 18.07 E
Hobyā 31 Lh 5.20N 48.38 E
Hocalar 15 Mk 38.37N 29.57 E
Hochalmspitze 14 Hc 47.01N 13.19 E
Hochfeiler/Gran Pilastro 14 Fd 46.58N 11.44 E
Hochgolling 14 Hc 47.16N 13.45 E
Hochschwab 14 Jc 47.36N 15.05 E
Höchstadt an der Aisch 10 Gg 49.42N 10.44 E
Hochstetters Forland 41 Kc 75.45N 20.00W
Höchst im Odenwald 12 Ke 49.48N 9.00 E
Hochtor 14 Gc 47.05N 12.48 E
Hockenheim 12 Ke 49.19N 8.33 E
Hodaka-Dake 29 Ec 36.17N 137.39 E
Hodda 35 Ic 11.30N 50.45 E
Hoddesdon 12 Cc 51.45N 0.00
Hodgenville 44 Eg 37.34N 85.44W
Hodh 30 Gg 16.10N 8.40W
Hodh ech Chargui [3] 32 Ff 17.00N 7.15W
Hodh el Gharbi [3] 32 Ff 16.30N 10.00W
Hódmezővásárhely 10 Qj 46.25N 20.20 E
Hodna, Chott el- 32 Hb 35.25N 4.45 E
Hodna, Monts du- 32 Hb 35.50N 4.50 E
Hodna, Plaine du- 13 Qi 35.35N 4.35 E
Hodonín 10 Nh 48.52N 17.08 E
Hodorov 16 De 49.25N 24.18 E
Hodžambas 18 Ee 38.06N 65.01 E
Hodža-Pirjah, Gora- 18 Fe 38.47N 67.35 E
Hodžejli 19 Fg 42.23N 59.20 E
Hœdic, Ile de- 11 Dg 47.20N 2.52W
Hoegaarden 12 Gd 50.47N 4.53 E
Hoei/Huy 11 Ld 50.31N 5.14 E
Hoë Karoo 30 Jl 30.00S 21.30 E
Hoek van Holland 11 Kc 51.59N 4.09 E
Hoeselt 12 Hd 50.51N 5.29 E
Hof 10 Hf 50.19N 11.55 E
Höfðakaupstadur 7a Bb 65.50N 20.19W
Hofgeismar 10 Fe 51.29N 9.24 E
Hofheim 12 Kd 50.05N 8.27 E
Hofmeyr 37 Df 31.39S 25.50 E
Höfn 7a Cb 64.15N 15.13W
Hofsjökull 5 Ec 64.49N 18.48W
Hōfu 28 Kg 34.03N 131.34 E
Höganäs 8 Eh 56.12N 12.33 E
Hogarth, Mount- 59 Hd 21.48S 136.58 E
Hogback Mountain 46 Id 44.54N 112.07W
Hog Cliffs 51d Ba 17.38N 61.44W
Hoge Venen/Hautes Fagnes 10 Bf 50.30N 6.00 E
Högfors/Karkkila 7 Ff 60.32N 24.11 E
Hog Island 51p Bb 12.00N 61.44W
Hogne, Somme-Leuze- 12 Hd 50.15N 5.17 E
Hog Point 51d Ba 17.43N 61.48W
Högsby 7 Dh 57.10N 16.02 E
Høgste Breakulen 8 Bc 61.41N 7.02 E
Høgstegia 8 Db 62.23N 10.08 E
Hogsty Reef 49 Kc 21.41N 73.49W
Hōhang-nyōng 28 Jd 41.48N 128.20 E
Hohe Acht 10 Cf 50.23N 7.00 E
Hohe Eifel 12 Id 50.16N 6.50 E
Hohenau 55 Eh 27.05S 55.45W
Hohenems 14 Dc 47.22N 9.41 E
Hohenloher Ebene 10 Fg 49.20N 9.40 E
Hohes Venn 10 Bf 50.30N 6.00 E
Hohe Tauern 14 Gc 47.10N 12.30 E
Hohhot 22 Ne 40.51N 111.38 E
Höhoku 29 Bd 34.17N 130.57 E
Höhr-Grenzhausen 12 Jd 50.26N 7.40 E
Höhtiäinen 8 Mb 62.50N 29.40 E
Hoh Xil Hu 27 Fd 35.35N 91.06 E
Hoh Xil Shan 21 Lf 35.20N 91.00 E
Hoi An 25 Le 15.52N 108.19 E

Index Symbols

[1] Independent Nation
[2] State, Region
[3] District, County
[4] Municipality
[5] Colony, Dependency
Continent
Physical Region
Historical or Cultural Region
Mount, Mountain
Volcano
Hill
Mountains, Mountain Range
Hills, Escarpment
Plateau, Upland
Pass, Gap
Plain, Lowland
Delta
Salt Flat
Valley, Canyon
Crater, Cave
Karst Features
Depression
Polder
Desert, Dunes
Forest, Woods
Heath, Steppe
Oasis
Cape, Point
Coast, Beach
Cliff
Peninsula
Isthmus
Sandbank
Island
Atoll
Rock, Reef
Islands, Archipelago
Rocks, Reefs
Coral Reef
Well, Spring
Geyser
River, Stream
Waterfall Rapids
River Mouth, Estuary
Lake
Salt Lake
Intermittent Lake
Reservoir
Swamp, Pond
Canal
Glacier
Ice Shelf, Pack Ice
Ocean
Sea
Gulf, Bay
Strait, Fjord
Lagoon
Bank
Seamount
Tablemount
Ridge
Shelf
Basin
Escarpment, Sea Scarp
Fracture
Trench, Abyss
National Park, Reserve
Point of Interest
Recreation Site
Cave, Cavern
Historic Site
Ruins
Wall, Walls
Church, Abbey
Temple
Scientific Station
Airport
Port
Lighthouse
Mine
Tunnel
Dam, Bridge

Index Symbols

[1] Independent Nation	Historical or Cultural Region	Pass, Gap	Depression
[2] State, Region	Mount, Mountain	Plain, Lowland	Polder
[3] District, County	Volcano	Delta	Desert, Dunes
[4] Municipality	Hill	Salt Flat	Forest, Woods
[5] Colony, Dependency	Mountains, Mountain Range	Valley, Canyon	Heath, Steppe
● Continent	Hills, Escarpment	Crater, Cave	Oasis
◆ Physical Region	Plateau, Upland	Karst Features	Cape, Point

Coast, Beach	Rock, Reef	Waterfall Rapids	Canal
Cliff	Islands, Archipelago	River Mouth, Estuary	Glacier
Peninsula	Rocks, Reefs	Lake	Ice Shelf, Pack Ice
Isthmus	Coral Reef	Salt Lake	Ocean
Sandbank	Well, Spring	Intermittent Lake	Sea
Island	Geyser	Reservoir	Gulf, Bay
Atoll	River, Stream	Swamp, Pond	Strait, Fjord

Lagoon	Escarpment, Sea Scarp	Historic Site	Port
Bank	Fracture	Ruins	Lighthouse
Seamount	Trench, Abyss	Wall, Walls	Mine
Tablemount	National Park, Reserve	Church, Abbey	Tunnel
Ridge	Point of Interest	Temple	Dam, Bridge
Shelf	Recreation Site	Scientific Station	
Basin	Cave, Cavern	Airport	

Hude (Oldenburg) 12 Ka 53.07N 8.28 E
Huder 27 Lb 49.59N 121.30 E
Hudiksvall 6 Hc 61.44N 17.07 E
Hudson 38 Le 40.42N 74.02W
Hudson [Fl.-U.S.] 44 Fk 28.22N 82.42W
Hudson [N.Y.-U.S.] 44 Kd 42.15N 73.47W
Hudson, Lake- 45 Ih 36.20N 95.05W
Hudson Bay 42 Hf 52.52N 102.23W
Hudson Bay 38 Kd 60.00N 86.00W
Hudson Canyon (EN) 44 Kf 39.27N 72.12W
Hudson Hope 42 Fe 56.02N 121.55W
Hudson Land 41 Jd 73.45N 22.30W
Hudson Mountains 66 Pf 74.32S 99.20W
Hudson Strait 38 Lc 62.30N 72.00W
Hudžirt 27 Hb 47.05N 102.45 E
Hue 22 Mh 16.28N 107.36 E
Huebra 13 Fc 41.02N 6.48W
Huechucuicui, Punta- 56 Ff 41.47S 74.02W
Hueco Montains 45 Dj 32.05N 105.55W
Huedin 15 Gc 46.52N 23.03 E
Huehuetenango [3] 49 Bf 15.40N 91.35W
Huehuetenango 47 Fe 15.20N 91.28W
Huejutla de Reyes 48 Jg 21.08N 98.25W
Huelgoat 11 Cf 48.22N 3.45W
Huelma 13 Ig 37.39N 3.27W
Huelva [3] 13 Fg 37.40N 7.00W
Huelva 6 Fh 37.16N 6.57W
Huelva, Ribera de- 13 Gg 37.27N 6.00W
Huércal Overa 13 Kg 37.23N 1.57W
Huerfano Mountain 45 Bh 36.30N 108.10W
Huertas, Cabo de- 13 Lf 38.21N 0.24W
Huerva 13 Lc 41.39N 0.52W
Huesca 13 Lb 42.08N 0.25W
Huesca [3] 13 Lb 42.10N 0.10W
Huéscar 13 Jg 37.49N 2.32W
Hueso, Sierra del- 48 Gb 30.15N 105.20W
Huesos, Arroyo de los- 55 Cm 36.30S 59.09W
Huetamo de Núñez 48 Ih 18.35N 100.53W
Huete 13 Jd 40.08N 2.41W
Ḩufrat an Naḩās 35 Cd 9.45N 24.19 E
Huftarøy 8 Ad 60.05N 5.15 E
Hugh Butler Lake 45 Ff 40.22N 100.42W
Hughenden 58 Fg 20.51S 144.12 E
Hughes 40 Ic 66.03N 154.16W
Hughes Range 46 Hb 49.55N 115.28W
Hugo 45 Ii 34.01N 95.31W
Huguan 28 Bf 36.05N 113.12 E
Huhur He 28 Fc 43.55N 120.47 E
Hui'an 27 Kf 25.07N 118.47 E
Huiarau Range 62 Gc 38.35S 177.10 E
Huib-Hochplato 37 Be 27.10S 16.50 E
Huichang 27 Kf 25.33N 115.45 E
Huicheng → Shexian 28 Ej 29.53N 118.27 E
Huicholes, Sierra de los- 48 Gf 22.00N 104.00W
Huich'ŏn 27 Mc 40.10N 126.17 E
Huifa He 28 Ic 43.06N 126.53 E
Hui He [China] 27 Kb 48.51N 119.12 E
Hui He [China] 28 Be 39.21N 112.37 E
Huiji He 28 Ch 33.53N 115.37 E
Huila [2] 54 Cc 2.30N 75.45W
Huila [3] 36 Ce 15.00S 15.00 E
Huila, Nevado del- 52 Ie 3.00N 76.00W
Huilai 27 Kg 23.05N 116.18 E
Huili 27 Hf 26.37N 102.19 E
Huimanguillo 48 Mi 17.51N 93.23W
Huimin 27 Kd 37.29N 117.30 E
Huinan (Chaoyang) 28 Ic 42.41N 126.03 E
Huisne 11 Gg 47.59N 0.11 E
Huissen 12 Hc 51.56N 5.55 E
Huiten Nur 27 Fd 35.30N 91.55 E
Huittinen 8 Jc 61.11N 22.42 E
Huivuilay, Isla de- 48 Dd 27.03N 110.01W
Huixian [China] 28 Bg 35.27N 113.47 E
Huixian [China] 27 Ie 33.46N 106.06 E
Huixtla 47 Fe 15.09N 92.28W
Huize 27 Hf 26.28N 103.18 E
Huizen 12 Hb 52.18N 5.16 E
Huizhou 27 Jg 23.02N 114.28 E
Hukou 28 Dj 29.44N 116.14 E
Hu Kou 28 Cf 36.09N 110.20 E
Hŭksan-Chedo 27 Me 34.30N 125.20 E
Hukuntsi 37 Cd 23.59S 21.44 E
Hulan 27 Mb 46.03N 126.36 E
Hulan He 27 Mb 45.54N 126.42 E
Ḩulayfā' 23 Fd 26.00N 40.47 E
Hulett 46 Md 44.41N 104.36W
Hulga 17 Jd 64.15N 60.58 E
Hulin 27 Nb 45.52N 132.58 E
Hulin He 28 Hb 45.19N 124.06 E
Hull 42 Jg 45.26N 75.43W
Hull → Kingston-upon-Hull 6 Fe 53.45N 0.20W
Hull → Orona Atoll 57 Je 4.29S 172.10W
Hull Bay 66 Nf 74.55S 137.40W
Hull Glacier 66 Nf 75.05S 137.15W
Hull Mountain 46 Dg 39.31N 122.59W
Hüls, Krefeld- 12 Ic 51.22N 6.31 E
Hultsfred 7 Dh 57.29N 15.50 E
Huludao 27 Lc 40.44N 120.59 E
Hulun Nur 21 Ne 49.00N 117.30 E
Ḩulwān = Helwān (EN) 33 Fd 29.51N 31.20 E
Hulwāt, Qūr al- 24 Hh 28.49N 38.50 E
Huma [China] 27 Ma 51.44N 126.36 E
Huma [Ton.] 65b Bc 21.19S 174.56W
Humacao 49 Od 18.09N 65.50W
Huma He 27 Ma 51.42N 126.42 E
Humaitá [Braz.] 53 Jf 7.31S 63.02W
Humaitá [Par.] 56 Ic 27.03S 58.33W
Humansdorp 37 Cf 34.02S 24.46 E
Humbe 36 Bf 16.42S 14.54 E
Humber 9 Fe 53.40N 0.10W
Humberside [3] 9 Mh 53.55N 0.30W
Humbolat River 18 He 40.02N 118.31W
Humboldt 61 Cd 21.53S 166.25 E
Humboldt [Ia.-U.S.] 45 Ie 42.43N 94.13W
Humboldt [Nb.-U.S.] 45 If 40.10N 95.57W
Humboldt [Sask.-Can.] 42 Gf 52.12N 105.07W
Humboldt [Tn.-U.S.] 44 Ch 35.49N 88.55W
Humboldt Gletscher 41 Fc 79.40N 63.45W
Humboldt Range 46 Ff 40.15N 118.10W
Hume, Lake- 59 Jg 36.05S 147.05 E
Humenné 10 Rh 48.56N 21.55 E
Hummelfjell 8 Db 62.27N 11.17 E
Hümmling, Der- 10 Dd 52.52N 7.31 E
Humphreys Peak 38 Hf 35.20N 111.40W
Humppila 7 Ff 60.56N 23.22 E
Humuya, Rio- 49 Df 15.13N 87.57W
Hün 31 If 29.07N 15.56 E
Húnaflói 5 Db 65.50N 20.50W
Hunan Sheng (Hu-nan Sheng) [3] 27 Jf 28.00N 112.00 E
Hu-nan Sheng → Hunan Sheng [3] 27 Jf 28.00N 112.00 E
Hunchun 28 Kc 42.52N 130.21 E
Hundested 8 Di 55.58N 11.52 E
Hunedoara [2] 15 Fd 45.45N 22.52 E
Hünfeld 10 Ff 50.40N 9.46 E
Hünfelden 12 Kd 50.19N 8.11 E
Hunga Ha'apai 65b Ab 20.33S 175.24W
Hungary (EN) = Magyarország [1] 6 Hf 47.00N 20.00 E
Hunga Tonga 65b Ab 20.32S 175.23W
Hungen 12 Kd 50.28N 8.54 E
Hüngnam 27 Md 39.50N 127.38 E
Hungry Horse Reservoir 46 Ib 48.15N 113.50W
Hun He [China] 28 Be 39.47N 113.15 E
Hun He [China] 28 Gd 40.41N 122.12 E
Hunhedoara 15 Fd 45.45N 22.54 E
Hunish, Rubha- 9 Gd 57.43N 6.20W
Hun Jiang 28 Hd 40.52N 125.42 E
Hunjiang 27 Mc 41.55N 126.27 E
Hunneberg 8 Ef 58.20N 12.27 E
Hunnebostrand 8 Df 58.27N 11.18 E
Hunsrück 10 Cg 49.50N 6.40 E
Hunstanton 9 Ni 52.57N 0.30 E
Hunte 10 Ed 52.30N 8.19 E
Hunter, Ile- 57 Ig 22.24S 172.03 E
Hunter Island 59 Ih 40.30S 144.45 E
Hunter Ridge (EN) 57 Ig 21.30S 174.30 E
Hunter River 59 Kf 32.30S 151.42 E
Hunterville 62 Fc 39.56S 175.34 E
Huntingdon 9 Mi 52.30N 0.10W
Huntingdon [Eng.-U.K.] 9 Mi 52.20N 0.12W
Huntingdon [Pa.-U.S.] 44 He 40.31N 78.02W
Huntingdon [Que.-Can.] 44 Jc 45.05N 74.08W
Huntington [In.-U.S.] 44 Ee 40.53N 85.30W
Huntington [W.V.-U.S.] 43 Kd 38.24N 82.26W
Huntly [N.Z.] 62 Fb 37.33S 175.10 E
Huntly [Scot.-U.K.] 9 Kd 57.27N 2.47W
Huntsville [Al.-U.S.] 39 Kf 34.44N 86.35W
Huntsville [Ont.-Can.] 42 Jg 45.20N 79.13W
Huntsville [Tx.-U.S.] 43 He 30.43N 95.33W
Hunucmá 48 Og 21.01N 89.52W
Hünxe 12 Ic 51.39N 6.47 E
Hunyani 37 Ec 15.37S 30.39 E
Hunyuan 27 Jd 39.38N 113.44 E
Hunza → Baltit 25 Ea 36.20N 74.40 E
Hunze 11 Ma 53.13N 6.40 E
Huocheng (Shuiding) 27 Dc 44.03N 80.49 E
Huojia 28 Bg 35.16N 113.39 E
Huolongmen 27 Mb 49.49N 125.49 E
Huolu 28 Ce 38.05N 114.18 E
Huon, Ile- 57 Hf 18.01S 162.57 E
Huon Gulf 59 Ja 7.10S 147.25 E
Huon Peninsula 60 Di 6.25S 147.30 E
Huonville 59 Jh 43.01S 147.02 E
Huoqin 28 Dh 32.21N 116.17 E
Huoshan 27 Ke 31.19N 116.20 E
Huo Shan [China] 27 Jd 37.00N 111.52 E
Huo Shan [China] 27 Ke 31.06N 116.12 E
Huoxian 27 Jd 36.39N 111.47 E
Hupeh (EN) = Hubei Sheng (Hu-pei Sheng) [2] 27 Je 31.00N 112.00 E
Hu-pei Sheng → Hubei Sheng = Hopeh (EN) [2] 27 Je 31.00N 112.00 E
Hür 24 Qg 30.50N 57.07 E
Hurama → Hongyuan 27 He 32.45N 102.38 E
Huränd 24 Lc 38.40N 47.20 E
Hurd, Cape- 44 Gc 45.13N 81.44W
Hurdalssjøen 8 Dd 60.20N 11.05 E
Hurd Deep = La Grande Trench (EN) 9 Kl 49.40N 3.00W
Hurdiyo 35 Ic 10.32N 51.08 E
Hurepoix 11 If 48.40N 2.10 E
Hure Qi 28 Fc 42.44N 121.44 E
Hurkett 45 Lb 48.50N 88.29W
Hurmuli 20 If 51.01N 136.56 E
Huroizumi 29a Cb 42.01N 143.07 E
Huron 43 Hc 44.22N 98.13W
Huron, Lake- 38 Ke 44.30N 82.15W
Huron Mountains 44 Db 46.45N 87.45W
Hurricane 46 Ih 37.11N 113.17W
Hurricane Cliffs 46 Ih 37.00N 113.05W
Hurrungane 8 Bc 61.27N 7.51 E
Hursley 12 Ac 51.01N 1.24W
Hurst 45 Hj 32.49N 97.09W
Hurstpierpoint 12 Bd 50.55N 0.10W
Hürth 10 Cf 50.52N 6.52 E
Hurum 8 De 59.35N 10.35 E
Hurunui 62 Ee 42.54S 173.18 E
Hurup 8 Ch 56.45N 8.25 E
Huş 15 Lc 46.41N 28.04 E
Húsavik 7a Ca 66.03N 17.21W
Hushan → Cixi 28 Fi 30.10N 121.14 E
Huskvarna 8 Fg 57.48N 14.16 E
Huslia 40 Hc 65.42N 156.25W
Husnes 8 Ae 59.52N 5.46 E
Husnesfjorden 8 Ae 59.50N 5.35 E
Hussigny-Godbrange 12 He 49.29N 5.52 E
Hust 16 Ce 48.10N 23.27 E
Hustadvika 8 Ba 63.00N 7.05 E
Husum [Ger.] 10 Fb 54.28N 9.03 E
Husum [Swe.] 7 Ee 63.20N 19.10 E
Hutag 27 Hb 49.23N 102.43 E
Hutchinson [Ks.-U.S.] 43 Hd 38.05N 97.56W
Hutchinson [Mn.-U.S.] 45 Id 44.54N 94.22W
Hutch Mountain 46 Ji 34.47N 111.22W
Hüth 33 Hf 16.14N 43.58 E
Hutou 27 Nb 46.00N 133.36 E
Hutte Sauvage, Lac de la- 42 Ke 55.57N 65.45W
Hutton, Mount- 59 Je 25.51S 148.20 E
Hutubi 27 Ec 44.07N 86.57 E
Hutuiti, Caleta- 65d Bb 27.07S 109.17W
Hutuo He 28 De 38.14N 116.05 E
Huvhojtun, Gora- 20 Le 57.44N 160.45 E
Huxley, Mount- 62 Cf 44.04S 169.41 E
Huy 10 Gd 51.55N 10.55 E
Huy/Hoei 11 Ld 50.31N 5.14 E
Huzhou → Wuxing 27 Le 30.47N 120.07 E
Hvaler 8 De 59.05N 11.00 E
Hvalynsk 19 Ee 52.30N 48.07 E
Hvammstangi 7a Bb 65.24N 20.57W
Hvannadalshnúkur 5 Ec 64.01N 16.41W
Hvar 14 Kg 43.07N 16.45 E
Hvar 14 Kg 43.11N 16.27 E
Hvarski kanal 14 Kg 43.15N 16.37 E
Hvatovka 16 Oc 52.21N 46.36 E
Hveragerdi 7a Bb 64.00N 21.12W
Hveravellir 7a Bb 64.54N 19.35W
Hvide Sande 8 Ci 55.59N 8.08 E
Hvitá [Ice.] 7a Bb 64.35N 21.46W
Hvitá [Ice.] 7a Bb 64.00N 20.58W
Hvittingfoss 8 De 59.29N 10.01 E
Hvojnaja 7 Ig 58.56N 34.31 E
Hwach'on-ni 28 Ie 38.58N 126.02 E
Hwang-Hae = Yellow Sea (EN) 21 Of 36.00N 124.00 E
Hwanghae-Namdo [2] 28 He 38.15N 125.30 E
Hwanghae-Pukto [2] 28 Ie 38.30N 126.25 E
Hwangju 28 He 38.40N 125.45 E
Hyannis [Ma.-U.S.] 44 Le 41.39N 70.17W
Hyannis [Nb.-U.S.] 45 Ff 42.00N 101.44W
Hybo 8 Gc 61.48N 16.12 E
Hyde Park 50 Gi 6.30N 58.16W
Hyderābād [India] 22 Jh 17.23N 78.28 E
Hyderābād [Pak.] 22 Ig 25.22N 68.22 E
Hyères 11 Mk 43.07N 6.07 E
Hyères, Iles d'- 11 Ml 43.00N 6.20 E
Hyesan 27 Mc 41.24N 128.10 E
Hyltebruk 7 Ch 57.00N 13.14 E
Hyndman Peak 46 He 43.50N 114.10W
Hyōgo Ken [2] 28 Mg 34.50N 134.48 E
Hyrov 10 Sg 49.32N 22.48 E
Hyrulä 8 Kd 60.24N 25.02 E
Hyrum 46 Jf 41.38N 111.51W
Hyrynsalmi 7 Gd 64.40N 28.32 E
Hysham 46 Lc 46.18N 107.14W
Hythe [Eng.-U.K.] 12 Ad 50.52N 1.24W
Hythe [Eng.-U.K.] 9 Oj 51.05N 1.05 E
Hyūga 28 Kh 32.25N 131.38 E
Hyūga-Nada 29 Be 32.25N 131.45 E
Hyvinge/Hyvinkää 7 Ff 60.38N 24.52 E
Hyvinkää/Hyvinge 7 Ff 60.38N 24.52 E

I

Iaco, Rio- 54 Ee 9.03S 68.35W
Iacobeni 15 Ib 47.26N 25.19 E
Iakora 37 Hd 23.08S 46.38 E
Ialomiţa [2] 15 Ke 44.30N 27.30 E
Ialomiţa 15 Kd 44.42N 27.51 E
Ialomiţei, Balta- 15 Ke 44.30N 28.00 E
Iapó, Rio- 55 Gg 24.30S 50.24W
Iaşi 6 If 47.10N 27.36 E
Iaşi [2] 15 Kb 47.07N 27.39 E
Iba 26 Gc 15.20N 119.58 E
Ibadan 31 Hh 7.23N 3.54 E
Ibague 53 Ie 4.27N 75.14W
Ibaiti 56 Jb 23.50S 50.10W
Iballja 15 Cg 42.11N 20.00 E
Ibans, Laguna de- 49 Ef 15.53N 84.52W
Ibar 15 Df 43.44N 20.45 E
Ibara 29 Cd 34.36N 133.28 E
Ibaraki 29 Dd 34.49N 135.34 E
Ibaraki Ken [2] 28 Pf 36.25N 140.30 E
Ibaré 55 Ej 30.49S 54.16W
Ibarra 53 Ie 0.21N 78.07W
Ibarreta 56 Ic 25.13S 59.51W
Ibb 22 Gh 13.58N 44.12 E
Ibba 35 De 4.48N 29.06 E
Ibba 35 Dd 7.09N 28.41 E
Ibbenbüren 10 Dd 52.16N 7.44 E
Ibdekkene 34 Fb 18.28N 0.38 E
Ibembo 36 Db 2.38N 23.37 E
Ibenga 36 Cb 2.20N 18.08 E
Iberá, Esteros del- 55 Di 28.05S 57.05W
Iberá, Laguna- 55 Di 28.30S 57.09W
Iberian Basin (EN) 3 De 40.00N 16.00W
Iberian Mountains (EN) = Sistema Ibérico 5 Fg 41.30N 2.30W
Iberian Peninsula (EN) = Peninsula Ibérica 5 Fg 40.00N 4.00W
Iberville, Lac d'- 42 Ke 56.00N 73.10W
Ibestad 7 Db 68.48N 17.08 E
Ibi [Nig.] 34 Gd 8.11N 9.45 E
Ibi [Sp.] 13 Lf 38.38N 0.34W
Ibiá 54 Ig 19.29S 46.32W
Ibiagui 55 Ja 13.03S 44.12W
Ibiai 55 Jc 16.51S 44.55W
Ibibobo 54 Fh 21.35S 62.58W
Ibicaraí 54 Kf 14.51S 39.36W
Ibicuí, Rio- 52 Kh 29.25S 56.47W
Ibicuí da Armada, Rio- 55 Ej 30.16S 54.54W
Ibicuy 55 Ck 33.44S 59.10W
Ibicuy, Rio- 55 Ck 33.48S 59.10W
Ibigawa 29 Ed 35.29N 136.34 E
Ibipetuba 54 Jf 11.00S 44.32W
Ibiraiaras 55 Gi 28.22S 51.39W
Ibirama 55 Hh 27.04S 49.31W
Ibirapuitã, Rio- 55 Ei 29.22S 55.57W
Ibirocai, Arroio- 55 Di 29.26S 56.43W
Ibiruba 55 Fi 28.38S 53.06W
Ibitinga 55 He 21.45S 48.49W
Ibitinga, Reprêsa- 55 He 21.41S 49.05W
Ibity 37 Hd 20.10S 46.58 E
Ibiza 13 Nf 38.54N 1.26 E
Ibiza/Eivissa = Iviza (EN) 5 Gh 39.00N 1.25 E
Iblei, Monti- 14 Im 37.10N 14.55 E
Ibn Hānī', Ra's- 24 Fe 35.35N 35.43 E
Ibn Qawrah 35 Ib 15.43N 50.32 E
Ibo 37 Gb 12.22S 40.36 E
Ibo-Gawa 29 Dd 34.46N 134.35 E
Iboundji, Mont- 36 Bc 1.08S 11.48 E
Ibrā' 23 Ie 22.38N 58.40 E
Ibrah 35 Dc 10.36N 25.20 E
Ibrāhīm, Jabal- 21 Gg 20.27N 41.09 E
Ibresi 7 Li 55.18N 47.05 E
'Ibrī 23 Ie 23.16N 56.32 E
Ibrim 33 Fe 22.39N 32.05 E
Ibshawāy 24 Dh 29.22N 30.41 E
Ibuki-Sanchi 29 Ed 35.35N 136.25 E
Ibuki-Yama 29 Ed 35.25N 136.24 E
Ibusuki 28 Ki 31.16N 130.39 E
Ića 20 Ke 55.28N 155.58 E
Ica [2] 54 Cf 14.20S 75.30W
Ica 53 Ig 14.04S 75.42W
Iça, Rio- 52 Jf 3.07S 67.58W
Icaiché 48 Oh 18.05N 89.10W
Icamaquã, Rio- 55 Ei 28.34S 56.00W
Icana, Rio- 54 Ec 0.26N 67.19W
Icara 55 Hi 28.42S 49.18W
Icaraíma 55 Ff 23.23S 53.41W
İçel 23 Db 36.48N 34.38 E
Iceland (EN) = Island 5 Eb 65.00N 18.00W
Iceland Basin (EN) 3 Dc 60.00N 20.00W
Ichalkaranji 25 Ee 16.42N 74.28 E
Ichibusa-Yama 29 Be 32.19N 131.06 E
Ichihara 28 Pg 35.31N 140.05 E
Ichi-Kawa 29 Dd 34.46N 134.43 E
Ichikawa 29 Fd 35.44N 139.55 E
Ichinohe 28 Pd 40.13N 141.17 E
Ichinomiya 28 Ng 35.18N 136.48 E
Ichinoseki 28 Pe 38.55N 141.08 E
Ich'ŏn [N.Kor.] 28 Ie 38.29N 126.53 E
Ich'ŏn [S.Kor.] 28 If 37.17N 127.27 E
Ichtegem 12 Fc 51.06N 3.00 E
Icigemsk Hrebet 20 Ld 63.30N 164.00 E
Icinskaja Sopka, Vulkan- 21 Rd 55.39N 157.40 E
Ićnja 19 De 50.52N 32.25 E
Icó 54 Ke 6.24S 38.51W
Icy Cape 40 Gb 70.20N 161.52W
Idaarderadeel 12 Ha 53.06N 5.50 E
Idaarderadeel-Grow 12 Ha 53.06N 5.50 E
Idabel 45 Ij 33.54N 94.50W
Idah 34 Gd 7.06N 6.44 E
Idaho [2] 43 Ec 45.00N 115.00W
Idaho Falls 39 He 43.30N 112.02W
Idalia 45 Eg 39.43N 102.14W
Idān 35 Hd 6.03N 49.01 E
Idanha-a-Nova 13 Ee 39.55N 7.14W
Idar-Oberstein 10 Dg 49.42N 7.18 E
Idarwald 12 Je 49.50N 7.13 E
Idel 7 Id 64.08N 34.12 E
Ideles 32 Ie 23.49N 5.55 E
Ider 27 Hb 49.16N 100.41 E
Idfū 33 Fe 24.58N 32.52 E
Idhi Óros 5 Ih 35.15N 24.45 E
Idhra 15 Gl 37.20N 23.30 E
Idhra 15 Gl 37.21N 23.28 E
Idhras, Kólpos- 15 Gl 37.22N 23.22 E
Idice 14 Ff 44.35N 11.49 E
İdil 24 Id 37.21N 41.54 E
Idini 32 Df 17.58N 15.40W
Idiofa 36 Cc 4.59S 19.36 E
Idjil, Kédia d'- 32 Ee 22.38N 12.33W
Idkerberget 8 Fd 60.23N 15.14 E
Idle 9 Mh 53.27N 0.48W
Idlib 23 Eb 35.55N 36.38 E
Idokogo 36 Ab 0.35N 9.19 E
Idolo, Isla del- 48 Kg 21.25N 97.27W
Idre 8 Ec 61.52N 12.43 E
Idrica 8 Mh 56.18N 28.55 E
Idrija 14 Id 46.00N 14.02 E
Idro, Lago d'- 14 Ee 45.47N 10.30 E
Idstein 10 Ef 50.14N 8.16 E
Idževan 16 Ni 40.52N 45.04 E
Iecava 8 Jh 56.40N 24.08 E
Iecava 8 Kh 56.33N 24.11 E
Iepê 55 Gf 22.40S 51.05W
Ieper/Ypres 11 Id 50.51N 2.53 E
Ierápetra 15 In 35.01N 25.45 E
Ierisós 15 Gi 40.24N 23.53 E
Ierisoú, Kólpos- 15 Gi 40.26N 23.55 E
Iernut 15 Hc 46.27N 24.15 E
Ie-Shima 29b Ab 26.43N 127.47 E
Ieshima-Shotō 29 Dd 34.40N 134.30 E
Iesolo 14 Ge 45.32N 12.38 E
Iezerul, Virful- 15 Hd 45.28N 24.57 E
Ifakara 36 Gd 8.08S 36.41 E
Ifaki 36 Gd 7.48N 5.14 E
'Ifāl, Wādī al- 24 Fh 28.07N 35.02 E
Ifalik Atoll 57 Fd 7.15N 144.27 E
Ifanadiana 37 Hd 21.17S 47.38 E
Ife 34 Fd 7.28N 4.34 E
Iferouâne 31 Hg 19.04N 8.24 E
Ifetesene 32 Hd 25.30N 4.33 E
Ifni 32 Ed 29.15N 10.08W
Ifon 34 Gd 6.58N 5.55 E
Iforas, Adrar des- 30 Hg 19.00N 2.00 E
Iga 29 Ed 34.49N 136.12 E
Igal 10 Nj 46.32N 17.57 E
Iganga 36 Fb 0.37N 33.29 E
Igara Paraná, Rio- 54 Dd 2.09N 71.47W
Igarapava 55 Ie 20.03S 47.47W
Igarapé-Açu 54 Id 1.07S 47.37W
Igarapé-Miri 54 Id 1.59S 48.58W
Igarka 22 Kc 67.28N 86.35 E
Igatimí 56 Ib 24.05S 55.30W
Igawa 36 Fd 8.46S 34.23 E
Igbetti 34 Fd 8.45N 4.08 E
Iğdır 24 Kc 39.56N 44.02 E
Iggesund 7 Df 61.38N 17.04 E
Iglesias 14 Ck 39.19N 8.32 E
Iglesiente 14 Ck 39.20N 8.40 E
Igli 32 Gc 30.27N 2.18W
Iglim al Janūbīyah = Southern Region (EN) [2] 35 Dd 6.00N 30.00 E
Iglino 17 Hi 54.50N 56.28 E
Igloolik 39 Kc 69.24N 81.49W
Ignace 42 Ig 49.26N 91.41W
Ignalina 7 Gi 55.22N 26.13 E
Ignatovo 7 If 60.49N 37.48 E
Iğneada 24 Bb 41.50N 27.58 E
Iğneada Burun 15 Lh 41.54N 28.03 E
Igombe 36 Fc 4.25S 31.58 E
Igoumenitsa 15 Dj 39.30N 20.16 E
Igra 19 Fd 57.33N 53.10 E
Igreja, Morro de- 55 Hi 28.08S 49.30W
Igren 16 Ie 48.29N 35.13 E
Igrim 19 Gc 63.12N 64.29 E
Iguaçu, Rio- 52 Kh 25.36S 54.36W
Igualada 13 Nc 41.35N 1.38 E
Iguala de la Independencia 47 Ee 18.21N 99.32W
Iguana, Sierra de la- 48 Id 26.30N 100.15W
Iguape 55 Ig 24.43S 47.33W
Iguariaça, Serra do- 55 Ei 29.03S 55.15W
Iguassu Falls (EN) = Iguazú, Cataratas del- 52 Kh 25.41S 54.26W
Iguatemi 54 If 14.35S 49.02W
Iguatemi, Rio- 55 Ef 23.55S 54.10W
Iguatu 53 Mf 6.22S 39.18W
Iguazú, Cataratas del- = Iguassu Falls (EN) 52 Kh 25.41S 54.26W
Iguéla 36 Ac 1.55S 9.19 E
Iguidi, 'Erg- 30 Gf 27.00N 6.00W
Ihavandiffulu Atoll 25a Ba 7.00N 72.55 E
Iheya-Jima 29b Ab 27.03N 127.57 E
Ih-Hajrhan 27 Ib 46.56N 105.56 E
Ihiala 34 Gd 5.51N 6.51 E
Ihirene 32 He 20.28N 4.37 E
Ihnāsiyat al Madīnah 24 Dh 29.05N 30.56 E
Ih-Obo-Ula 27 Gc 44.55N 95.20 E
Ihosy 31 Lk 22.25S 46.07 E
Ihotry, Lac- 37 Gd 21.56S 43.41 E
Ihrhove, Westoverledingen- 12 Ja 53.10N 7.27 E
Ihsaniye 24 Dc 36.55N 34.46 E
Ihtiman 15 Gg 42.26N 23.49 E
Ih-Ula 27 Hb 49.27N 101.27 E
Ii 7 Fd 65.19N 25.27 E
Iida 28 Ng 35.31N 137.50 E
Iide-San 29 Fc 37.52N 139.41 E
Iijoki 7 Fd 65.20N 25.17 E
Iisaku/Isaku 8 Le 59.14N 27.41 E
Iisalmi 7 Ge 63.34N 27.11 E
Iisvesi 8 Lb 62.45N 26.50 E
Iittala 8 Kc 61.04N 24.10 E
Iivaara 7 Gd 65.47N 29.40 E
Iiyama 29 Fc 36.52N 138.20 E
Iizuka 29 Be 33.38N 130.41 E
Ija 20 Fe 55.02N 101.00 E
Ijebu Ode 34 Fd 6.49N 3.56 E
IJmuiden, Velsen- 12 Gb 52.28N 4.35 E
Ijoubbâne, 'Erg- 34 Da 22.30N 6.00W
IJssel 11 Lb 52.30N 6.00 E
IJsselmeer 11 Lb 52.45N 5.25 E
IJsselmuiden 12 Hb 52.34N 5.56 E
IJsselstein 12 Hb 52.01N 5.02 E
Ijui 56 Jc 28.23S 53.55W
Ijuí, Rio- 55 Eh 27.58S 55.20W
Ijūin 29 Bf 31.37N 130.24 E
Ijuizinho, Rio- 55 Ei 28.20S 54.28W
Ijuw 64e Bb 0.31S 166.57 E
Ijzendijke 12 Fc 51.20N 3.37 E
IJzer 11 Ic 51.09N 2.43 E
Ik 5 Ld 55.55N 52.36 E
Ikaalinen 7 Ff 61.46N 23.03 E
Ikalamavony 37 Hd 21.10S 46.32 E
Ikamatua 62 De 42.17S 171.42 E
Ikaria 15 Jl 37.35N 26.10 E
Ikarion Pélagos 15 Jl 37.30N 26.35 E
Ikast 8 Ch 56.08N 9.10 E
Ikatski Hrebet 20 Gf 54.00N 111.15 E
Ikawa 29 Fd 35.13N 138.14 E
Ikeda [Jap.] 29 Cd 34.01N 133.48 E
Ikeda [Jap.] 27 Pc 42.55N 143.27 E
Ikeda-Ko 27 Bf 31.14N 130.34 E
Ikej 20 Ff 54.12N 100.04 E
Ikeja 34 Fd 6.36N 3.21 E
Ikela 31 Ji 1.11S 23.16 E
Ikelemba 36 Cb 0.07N 18.17 E
Ikerre 34 Gd 7.30N 5.14 E
Ikerssuaq 41 Ie 65.10N 39.45W
Iki 29 Ae 33.45N 129.45 E
Iki-Kaikyō 28 Jh 33.45N 129.50 E
Ikitsuki-Shima 29 Ae 33.25N 129.25 E
İkizdere 24 Ib 40.47N 40.33 E
Ikom 34 Gd 5.58N 8.42 E
Ikongo 36 Gd 9.04S 36.51 E
Ikopa 37 Hc 16.50S 46.50 E
Ikot Ekpene 34 Gd 5.10N 7.43 E
Ikuno 29 Dd 35.10N 134.48 E
Ikurangi, Mount- 64p Bb 21.12S 159.45W
Ila 34 Fd 7.40N 4.40 E
Ilaferh 32 He 21.50N 1.20 E
Ilagan 22 Oh 17.10N 121.54 E
Ilām 25 Hc 26.54N 87.56 E
Ilām 23 Gc 33.38N 46.26 E
Ilām 23 Gc 33.00N 47.00 E
Ilan 27 Lg 24.45N 121.44 E
Ilanski 20 Ee 56.10N 96.03 E
Ilaro 34 Fd 6.53N 3.01 E
Iława 10 Pc 53.37N 19.33 E

Index Symbols

[1] Independent Nation
[2] State, Region
[3] District, County
[4] Municipality
[5] Colony, Dependency
Continent
Physical Region
Historical or Cultural Region
Mount, Mountain
Volcano
Hill
Mountains, Mountain Range
Hills, Escarpment
Plateau, Upland
Pass, Gap
Plain, Lowland
Delta
Salt Flat
Valley, Canyon
Crater, Cave
Karst Features
Depression
Polder
Desert, Dunes
Forest, Woods
Heath, Steppe
Oasis
Cape, Point
Coast, Beach
Cliff
Peninsula
Isthmus
Sandbank
Island
Atoll
Rock, Reef
Islands, Archipelago
Rocks, Reefs
Coral Reef
Well, Spring
Geyser
River, Stream
Waterfall Rapids
River Mouth, Estuary
Lake
Salt Lake
Intermittent Lake
Reservoir
Swamp, Pond
Canal
Glacier
Ice Shelf, Pack Ice
Ocean
Sea
Gulf, Bay
Strait, Fjord
Lagoon
Bank
Seamount
Tablemount
Ridge
Shelf
Basin
Escarpment, Sea Scarp
Fracture
Trench, Abyss
National Park, Reserve
Point of Interest
Recreation Site
Cave, Cavern
Historic Site
Ruins
Wall, Walls
Church, Abbey
Temple
Scientific Station
Airport
Port
Lighthouse
Mine
Tunnel
Dam, Bridge

Name	Ref	Lat	Long
Ilbengja	20 Hd	62.55N	124.10 E
Ile-à-la-Crosse	42 Ge	55.27N	107.53W
Ilebo	31 Ji	4.44S	20.33 E
Ile de France [■]	11 Ie	49.00N	2.20 E
Ile de France [◆]	41 Kc	77.45N	27.45W
Ile de France, Côte de l'- [▲]	11 Jf	48.55N	3.50 E
Ilek	19 Fe	51.32N	53.27 E
Ilek [≈]	5 Le	51.30N	53.20 E
Ileksa [≈]	7 Ie	62.30N	36.57 E
Ilerh [≈]	32 He	21.40N	2.22 E
Ileša [≈]	7 Le	62.37N	46.35 E
Ilesha [Nig.]	34 Fd	8.55N	3.25 E
Ilesha [Nig.]	34 Fd	7.37N	4.44 E
Ilet [≈]	7 Li	55.57N	48.14 E
Ilfov [2]	15 Je	44.30N	26.20 E
Ilfracombe	9 Ij	51.13N	4.08W
Ilgaz	24 Eb	40.56N	33.38 E
Ilgaz Dağları [▲]	24 Eb	41.00N	33.35 E
Ilgın	24 Dc	38.17N	31.55 E
Ilha Grande	54 Ed	0.27 S	65.02W
Ilha Grande, Baia da- [◖]	55 Jf	23.09S	44.30W
Ilhas Desertas [◻]	32 Dc	32.30N	16.30W
Ilhavo	13 Dd	40.36N	8.40W
Ilhéus	53 Mg	14.49S	39.02W
Ili [≈]	21 Je	45.24N	74.08 E
Ilia	15 Fd	45.56N	22.39 E
Iliamna	40 Ie	59.45N	154.54W
Iliamna Lake [≈]	40 He	59.30N	155.00W
Ilič	24 Hc	39.28N	38.34 E
Ilić	18 Gd	40.55N	68.29 E
Ilica	15 Kj	39.52N	27.46 E
Iličevsk	16 Nj	39.33N	44.59 E
Iličevsk	19 Df	46.18N	30.37 E
Ilidža	14 Mg	43.50N	18.19 E
Iligan	22 Oi	8.14N	124.14 E
Iligan Bay [◖]	26 He	8.25N	124.05 E
Ilim [≈]	20 Fe	56.50N	103.25 E
Ilimskoje Vodohranilišče [▭]	20 Fe	57.20N	102.30 E
Ilinski	7 Hf	61.02N	32.42 E
Ilinski	20 Jg	47.59N	142.21 E
Ilinski	17 Gg	58.35N	55.41 E
Ilion	44 Jd	43.01N	75.04W
Ilio Point [▶]	65a Db	21.13N	157.16W
Ilir	20 Fe	55.13N	100.45 E
Ilirska Bistrica	14 Ie	45.34N	14.16 E
Iljaly	18 Bd	41.53N	59.40 E
Ilkal	25 Fe	15.58N	76.08 E
Ilkeston	12 Ab	52.58N	1.18W
Ill [≈]	11 Nf	48.40N	7.53 E
Illampu, Nevado del- [▲]	54 Eg	15.50S	68.34W
Illana Bay [◖]	26 He	7.25N	123.45 E
Illapel	56 Fd	31.38S	71.10W
Illbillee, Mount- [▲]	59 Ge	27.02S	132.30 E
Ille [≈]	11 Ef	48.08N	1.40W
Ille-et-Vilaine [3]	11 Ef	48.10N	1.30W
Illéla	34 Gc	14.28N	5.15 E
Iller [≈]	10 Fh	48.23N	9.58 E
Illescas	13 Id	40.07N	3.50W
Ille-sur-Têt	11 Il	42.40N	2.37 E
Illi, Ba- [≈]	35 Bc	10.44N	16.21 E
Illimani, Nevado de- [▲]	52 Jg	16.39S	67.48W
Illingen	12 Je	49.22N	7.03 E
Illinois	38 Jf	38.58N	90.27W
Illinois [2]	43 Jd	40.00N	89.00W
Illinois Peak [▲]	46 Hc	47.02N	115.04W
Illizi	31 Hf	26.29N	8.28 E
Ilm [≈]	10 He	51.07N	11.40 E
Ilmajoki	8 Jd	62.44N	22.34 E
Ilmen, Ozero- [▭]	5 Jd	58.20N	31.20 E
Ilmenau	10 Gf	50.41N	10.54 E
Ilmenau [≈]	10 Gc	53.23N	10.10 E
Il Montello [▲]	14 Ge	45.49N	12.07 E
Ilo	54 Dg	17.38S	71.20W
Iloilo	22 Oh	10.42N	122.34 E
Ilok	14 Ne	45.13N	19.23 E
Ilomantsi	7 He	62.40N	30.55 E
Ilorin	31 Hh	8.30N	4.33 E
Iloron, Cerro³ [▲]	48 Gg	20.57N	104.22W
Ilova [≈]	14 Ke	45.25N	16.45 E
Ilovik [◆]	14 If	44.27N	14.33 E
Ilovlja	16 Ne	49.18N	44.01 E
Ilovlja [≈]	16 Me	49.14N	43.54 E
Ilpyrski	20 Le	59.52N	164.12 E
Ilski	16 Kg	44.51N	38.32 E
Iltin	20 Nc	67.52N	178.48W
Ilubabor [3]	35 Gd	7.50N	35.00 E
Ilükste/Ilukste	8 Li	55.58N	26.26 E
Ilukste/Ilūkste	8 Li	55.58N	26.26 E
Ilulissat/Jakobshavn	67 Nc	69.20N	50.50W
Ilwaki	26 Ih	7.56 S	126.26 E
Ilyč [≈]	17 He	62.32N	56.40 E
Ilz [≈]	10 Jh	48.35N	-13.30 E
Ilžanka [≈]	10 Re	51.14N	21.47 E
Imabari	28 Lg	34.03N	133.00 E
Imagane	28 Pc	42.26N	140.01 E
Imaichi	28 Of	36.43N	139.41 E
Imán, Sierra del- [▲]	55 Eh	27.42S	55.28W
Imanburluk [≈]	17 Mj	53.40N	67.15 E
Imandra, Ozero- [▭]	5 Jb	67.30N	33.00 E
Imano-Yama [▲]	29 Ce	32.51N	132.49 E
Imari	28 Jh	33.16N	129.53 E
Imarui	55 Hi	28.21S	48.49W
Imataca, Serrania de- [▲]	50 Fi	7.45N	61.00W
Imatra	7 Gf	61.10N	28.46 E
Imazu	29 Gd	35.24N	136.01 E
Imbabah, Al Qāhirah-	33 Fc	30.05N	31.13 E
Imba-Numa [▭]	29 Gd	35.45N	140.14 E
Imbert	49 Ld	19.45N	70.50W
Imbituba	56 Kc	28.14S	48.40W
Imeni 26 Bakinskih Komissarov	19 Eh	39.19N	49.12 E
Imeni 26 Bakinskih Komissarov	19 Fh	39.21N	54.12 E
Imeni Gastello	20 Jd	61.35N	147.59 E
Imeni Karla Liebknechta	16 Jd	51.38N	35.29 E
Imeni Mariny Raskovoj	20 Jd	62.05N	146.30 E
Imeni Poliny Osipenko	20 If	52.23N	136.25 E

Name	Ref	Lat	Long
Imi	31 Lh	6.28N	42.11 E
Imilili	32 De	22.50N	15.54W
Imi n'Tanout	32 Fc	31.03N	8.08W
Imišli	19 Eh	39.53N	48.03 E
Imjin-gang [≈]	28 If	37.47N	126.40 E
Imlay	46 Ff	40.42N	118.07W
Immenstadt im Allgäu	10 Gi	47.34N	10.13 E
Imo [2]	34 Gd	5.30N	7.20 E
Imola	14 Ff	44.21N	11.42 E
Imotski	14 Lg	43.27N	17.13 E
Imperatriz	53 Lf	5.32 S	47.29W
Imperia	14 Cg	43.53N	8.03 E
Imperial	45 Ff	40.31N	101.39W
Imperial de Aragón, Canal- [≈]	13 Kb	42.02N	1.33W
Imperial Valley [✓]	46 Nj	32.50N	115.30W
Impfondo	31 Ih	1.37N	18.04 E
Imphál	22 Lg	24.49N	93.57 E
Imphy	11 Jk	46.56N	3.15 E
Imrali Adasi [◆]	15 Li	40.32N	28.32 E
Imst	14 Ec	47.14N	10.44 E
Imtan	24 Gf	32.24N	36.49 E
Imuris	48 Db	30.47N	110.52W
Im-Zouren	13 Ii	35.04N	3.50W
Ina	28 Ng	35.50N	137.57 E
Ina [≈]	10 Kc	53.32N	14.38 E
I-n-Abanrherit	34 Gb	17.58N	6.05 E
Inabu	29 Ed	35.13N	137.30 E
Inaccessible Islands [◆]	66 Re	60.34S	46.44W
Inacessible Island [◆]	30 Fi	37.17S	12.45W
Inagawa	29 Fc	37.23N	139.18 E
I-n-Afaleleh	32 Ie	23.34N	9.12 E
I-n Naftah, Puntan- [▶]	64b Ba	15.05N	145.45 E
Ina-Gawa [≈]	29 Fc	37.23N	139.18 E
I-n-Amenas	31 Hf	28.03N	9.33 E
Inami	29 De	33.48N	135.12 E
Inanba-Jima [◆]	29 Fe	33.39N	139.18 E
Inangahua Junction	62 Dd	41.52S	171.56 E
Inanwatan	26 Jg	2.08 S	132.10 E
Iñapari	54 Ef	10.57S	69.35W
Inarajan	64c Bb	13.16N	144.45 E
I-n-Arhâta [≈]	34 Ea	21.09N	0.18W
Inari	6 Ib	68.54N	27.01 E
Inari, Lake- (EN) = Inarijärvi [▭]	5 Ib	69.00N	28.00 E
Inarijärvi = Inari, Lake- (EN) [▭]	5 Ib	69.00N	28.00 E
Inawashiro	29 Gc	37.34N	140.05 E
Inawashiro-Ko [▭]	28 Pf	37.30N	140.03 E
I-n Azaoua [≈]	34 Ga	20.47N	7.31 E
I-n-Azaoua	32 Ga	20.54N	7.28 E
Inazawa	29 Ed	35.15N	136.47 E
Inca	13 Oe	39.43N	2.54 E
Inca de Oro	56 Gc	26.45S	69.54W
Incaguasi	56 Fc	29.13S	71.03W
İnce Burun [▶]	15 Ki	40.28N	27.16 E
İnce Burun [▶]	24 Ed	36.13N	33.58 E
İncekum Burun [▶]	15 Ml	37.42N	29.35 E
Inceler	34 Fb	16.23N	0.10 E
Inchcape (Bell Rock) [≈]	9 Ke	56.26N	2.24W
Inchʼon	32 Df	20.00N	15.00W
Inchiri [3]	22 Df	37.28N	126.38 E
Incirliova	15 Kl	37.50N	27.43 E
Incudine [▲]	11a Bb	41.51N	9.12 E
Indaiá, Rio- [≈]	55 Jd	18.27S	45.22W
Indaia Grande, Ribeirão- [≈]	59 Ie	19.31S	52.29W
Indaiatuba	55 Jf	23.05S	47.14W
Indal	8 Gb	62.34N	17.06 E
Indalsälven [≈]	7 Ed	62.31N	17.27 E
Inda Selase	35 Fc	14.06N	38.17 E
Indawgyi	25 Jc	25.08N	96.20 E
Indefatigable Banks [≈]	9 Ph	53.35N	2.20 E
Independence [Ca.-U.S.]	46 Fh	36.48N	118.12W
Independence [Ia.-U.S.]	45 Ke	42.28N	91.54W
Independence [Ks.-U.S.]	43 Hd	37.13N	95.42W
Independence [Mo.-U.S.]	45 Jg	39.05N	94.04W
Independence [Va.-U.S.]	44 Gg	36.38N	81.11W
Independence Fjord	67 Me	82.00N	30.25W
Independence Mountains [▲]	46 Gf	41.15N	116.05W
Independência [Braz.]	54 Je	5.23 S	40.19W
Independência [Braz.]	51 Fa	13.34 S	53.57W
Independenta	15 Kd	45.29N	27.45 E
Inder → Jalaid Qi	27 Lb	46.41N	122.52 E
Inder, Ozero- [▭]	16 Qe	48.25N	51.55 E
Inderborski	6 Lf	48.32N	51.47 E
India (EN) [1]	21 Jh	20.00N	77.00 E
India (EN) = Bhārat			
India Muerta, Arroyo de la- [≈]	55 Fk	33.40S	54.04W
Indiana [2]	43 Jc	40.00N	86.15W
Indiana	44 He	40.39N	79.11W
Indianapolis	39 Kf	39.46N	86.09W
Indian Church	49 Ce	17.45N	88.40W
Indian Creek Point [▶]	51d Bb	17.00N	61.43W
Indian Harbour	42 Lf	54.27N	57.13W
Indian Head	42 Hf	50.32N	103.40W
Indian Ocean [≈]	3 Gl	21.00 S	82.00 E
Indian Ocean (EN) = Hindi, Badwëynta- [≈]	3 Gl	21.00 S	82.00 E
Indian Ocean = Indico, Oceano- [≈]	3 Gl	21.00 S	82.00 E
Indian Ocean = Indien, Océan- [≈]	3 Gl	21.00 S	82.00 E
Indian Ocean = Indiese Oseaan- [≈]	3 Gl	21.00 S	82.00 E
Indian Ocean (EN) = Indonesia, Samudera- [≈]	3 Gl	21.00 S	82.00 E
Indianola	45 Kj	33.40 S	90.39W
Indianópolis	55 Jd	19.02S	47.55W
Indian Peak [▲]	46 Ig	38.16N	113.53W
Indian Rock [▲]	51 Bd	17.20N	62.50W
Indian Springs	43 Dd	36.34N	115.40W
Indian Town Point [▶]	51d Bb	17.06N	61.40W
Indiapora	55 Gd	19.57 S	50.17W

Name	Ref	Lat	Long
Indias Occidentales = West Indies (EN) [◻]	47 Je	19.00N	70.00W
Indico, Oceano- = Indian Ocean (EN) [≈]	3 Gl	21.00 S	82.00 E
Indiese, Oseaan- = Indian Ocean (EN) [≈]	3 Gl	21.00 S	82.00 E
Indiga	19 Eb	67.41N	49.00 E
Indigirka [≈]	21 Qb	70.48N	148.54 E
Indigskaja Guba [◖]	17 Dc	67.45N	48.20 E
Indija	15 Dd	45.03N	20.05 E
Indio	43 De	33.43N	116.13W
Indio, Rio- [≈]	49 Fh	10.57N	83.44W
Indio Rico	55 Bn	38.19S	60.53W
Indispensable Reefs [≈]	57 Hf	12.40S	160.25 E
Indispensable Strait [≈]	63a Ec	9.00S	160.30 E
Indochina (EN) [◻]	21 Mh	16.00N	107.00 E
Indonesia [1]	22 Nj	5.00S	120.00 E
Indonesia, Samudera- = Indian Ocean (EN) [≈]	3 Gl	21.00 S	82.00 E
Indore	22 Jg	22.43N	75.50 E
Indra	8 Li	55.53N	27.40 E
Indragiri [≈]	26 Dg	0.22 S	103.26 E
Indramayu	26 Eh	6.20 S	108.19 E
Indrāvati [≈]	25 Ge	18.44N	80.16 E
Indre [≈]	11 Gg	47.14N	0.11 E
Indre [3]	11 Hh	46.50N	1.40 E
Indre Arna	8 Ad	60.26N	5.30 E
Indre-et-Loire [3]	11 Gg	47.15N	0.45 E
Indus [≈]	21 Ig	24.20N	67.47 E
İnebolu	23 Da	41.58N	33.46 E
İnece	15 Kh	41.41N	27.04 E
İnecik	15 Ki	40.56N	27.16 E
İnegöl	23 Ca	40.05N	29.31 E
Inés Indart	55 Bl	34.24S	60.33W
Ineu	15 Hb	47.32N	24.53 E
Ineu, Vîrful- [▲]	15 Hb	47.32N	24.53 E
I-n-Ezzane	32 Je	23.29N	11.15 E
Inferior, Laguna- [▭]	48 Li	16.15N	94.45W
Infiernillo, Presa del- [▭]	47 De	18.35N	101.45W
Infiesto	13 Ga	43.21N	5.22W
Infreschi, Punta degli- [▶]	14 Jk	39.59N	15.25 E
Ingá	54 Ke	7.17S	35.36W
Inga	36 Bd	5.39S	13.39 E
Ingá/Inkoo	7 Ff	60.03N	24.01 E
Ingabu	25 Je	17.49N	95.16 E
Ingai, Rio- [≈]	55 Ja	21.10S	44.52W
Ingal	34 Gb	16.47N	6.56 E
Ingarö [◆]	8 He	59.15N	18.30 E
Ingavi	55 Bb	15.02S	60.29W
Ingelheim am Rhein	12 Ke	49.59N	8.02 E
Ingelmunster	12 Fd	50.55N	3.15 E
Ingelstad	8 Fh	56.45N	14.55 E
Ingende	36 Cc	0.15S	18.57 E
Ingeniero Guillermo N. Juarez	56 Hb	23.54 S	61.51W
Ingeniero Jacobacci	56 Gf	41.18S	69.33W
Ingeniero Luiggi	56 He	35.25S	64.29W
Ingenio Santa Ana	56 Gc	27.28S	65.41W
Ingermanland (EN) [◻]	5 Id	59.00N	30.00 E
Ingham	58 Ff	18.39S	146.10 E
Ingička	18 Ee	39.47N	65.58 E
Inglefield Bredning [≈]	41 Fc	77.40N	65.00W
Inglefield Land [◻]	41 Fc	78.44N	68.20W
Inglewood [Austl.]	59 Ke	28.25S	151.05 E
Inglewood [Ca.-U.S.]	46 Fj	33.58N	118.21W
Inglewood [N.Z.]	62 Fc	39.09S	174.12 E
Ingolf Fjord [≈]	41 Kb	80.35N	17.35W
Ingólfshöði [▶]	7 a Cc	63.48N	16.39W
Ingolstadt	10 Hh	48.46N	11.26 E
Ingrāj Bāzār	25 Hc	25.00N	88.09 E
I-n-Guezzâm	19 Nj	19.32N	5.42 E
Ingul [≈]	16 Gf	47.02N	31.59 E
Ingulec	16 Hf	46.41N	32.48 E
Ingulec [≈]	19 Df	47.43N	33.10 E
Inguri [≈]	16 Lh	42.24N	41.32 E
Ingusskaja respublika [3]	19 Eg	43.15N	45.30 E
Inhaca, Ilha da- [◆]	30 Kk	26.02S	32.58 E
Inhambane	37 Ed	23.00S	34.30 E
Inhambane [3]	37 Fd	23.50S	35.20 E
Inhambane, Baia de- [◖]	37 Fc	18.25S	35.01 E
Inhandui-Guaçu, Rio- [≈]	55 Fe	21.37S	52.59W
Inhanduizinho, Rio- [≈]	55 Fe	21.34 S	53.36W
Inhassoro	37 Fd	24.28S	35.01 E
Inhaúma	37 Fd	21.32 S	35.12 E
I-n-Hihaou [≈]	34 Ja	13.01 S	44.39W
Inhobi, Rio- [≈]	32 He	23.00N	2.00 E
Inhumas	55 Gd	16.22S	49.30W
Inió [◆]	8 Id	60.25N	21.25 E
Inirida, Rio- [≈]	52 Ja	3.55N	67.52W
Inis/Ennis	9 Ei	52.50N	8.59W
Inis Airc/Inishark [◆]	9 Ch	53.37N	10.16W
Inis Bó Finne/Inishbofin [◆]	9 Ch	53.38N	10.12W
Inis Ceithleann/Enniskillen	9 Fg	54.21N	7.38W
Inis Córthaidh/Enniscorthy	9 Gi	52.30N	6.34W
Inis Diomáin/Ennistymon	9 Di	52.57N	9.13W
Inis Eoghain/Inishowen Peninsula [▲]	9 Ff	55.15N	7.20W
Inishark/Inis Airc [◆]	9 Ch	53.37N	10.16W
Inishbofin/Inis Bó Finne [◆]	9 Ch	53.38N	10.12W
Inisheer/Inis Oírr [◆]	9 Dh	53.03N	9.31W
Inishkea [◆]	9 Dg	54.08N	10.11W
Inishmaan/Inis Meáin [◆]	9 Dh	53.05N	9.35W
Inishmore/Árainn [◆]	9 Dh	53.07N	9.45W
Inishmurray/Inis Muirígh [◆]	9 Eg	54.26N	8.40W
Inishowen Peninsula/Inis Eoghain [▲]	9 Ff	55.15N	7.20W
Inishtrahull [◆]	9 Ff	55.27N	7.14W
Inishturk/Inis Toirc [◆]	9 Ch	53.38N	9.59W
Inis Meáin/Inishmaan [◆]	9 Dh	53.05N	9.35W
Inis Muirígh/Inishmurray [◆]	9 Eg	54.26N	8.40W
Inis Oírr/Inisheer [◆]	9 Dh	53.03N	9.31W
Inis Toirc/Inishturk [◆]	9 Ch	53.43N	10.05W
Inja	20 Je	59.22N	144.50 E

Name	Ref	Lat	Long
Inja	20 Je	59.30N	144.48 E
Inja	20 Df	50.27N	86.42 E
Injeüp	28 Je	38.04N	128.10 E
Injibara	35 Fc	10.55N	36.58 E
Injune	59 Je	25.51 S	148.34 E
I-n-Kak	34 Fb	16.20N	0.17 E
Inkisi [≈]	36 Bc	4.46 S	14.52 E
Inkoo/Ingå	7 Ff	60.03N	24.01 E
Inland Kaikoura Range [▲]	62 Ee	42.00S	173.35 E
Inland Sea (EN) = Setonaikai [≈]	21 Pf	34.10N	133.00 E
Inn [≈]	5 Hf	48.35N	13.28 E
Innamincka	59 Ie	27.45S	140.44 E
Inner Hebrides [◆]	9 Ge	57.00N	6.45W
Inner Mongolia (EN) = Nei Monggol Zizhiqu (Nei-meng-ku Tzu-chih-ch'ü) [2]	27 Jc	44.00N	112.00 E
Inner Silver Pit [≈]	9 Nh	53.30N	0.40 E
Inner Sound [≈]	9 Hd	57.30N	5.55W
Innerste [≈]	10 Fd	52.15N	9.50 E
Innisfail [Alta.-Can.]	46 Ia	52.02N	113.57W
Innisfail [Austl.]	59 Jc	17.32S	146.02 E
Innokentjevka	20 Ig	49.42N	136.55 E
Innokentjevski	20 Jg	48.38N	140.12 E
Innoko [≈]	40 Hd	62.14N	159.45W
Innsbruck	6 Hf	47.16N	11.24 E
Innviertel [▲]	14 Ad	48.15N	13.15 E
Innvikfjorden [≈]	8 Bc	61.50N	6.35 E
Inny/An Eithne [≈]	9 Fh	53.35N	7.50W
Ino	29 Ce	33.33N	133.26 E
Inobonto	26 Hf	0.52N	123.57 E
Inongo	31 Ii	1.57 S	18.16 E
Inoni	36 Cc	3.04S	15.39 E
Inönü	15 Nj	39.48N	30.09 E
I-n-Ouagar	34 Gb	16.12N	6.54 E
I-n-Ouzzal [≈]	32 He	21.34N	1.59 E
I-n-Salah	31 Hf	27.13N	2.28 E
Insar	7 Kj	54.42N	45.18 E
Insar [≈]	7 Kj	53.52N	44.23 E
Inscription, Cape- [▶]	57 Cg	25.30S	112.59 E
Insjön	8 Fd	60.41N	15.05 E
Insko	10 Lc	53.27N	15.33 E
Instruč [≈]	8 Ij	54.39N	21.48 E
Insурãţei	15 Ke	44.55N	27.36 E
Inta	6 Mb	66.05N	60.08 E
I-n-Tabezas	34 Fb	17.54N	1.50 E
I-n-Tallak	34 Fb	16.19N	3.15 E
Intepe	15 Ji	40.00N	26.20 E
Interlaken	14 Bd	46.41N	7.52 E
International Falls	43 Ib	48.36N	93.25W
Interview [◆]	25 If	12.55N	92.43 E
Inthanon, Doi- [▲]	25 Je	18.35N	98.30 E
Intibucá [3]	49 Cf	14.20N	88.15W
Intiyaco	56 Hc	28.39S	60.05W
Intorsura Buzaului	15 Jd	45.41N	26.02 E
Intracoastal Waterway [≈]	45 Im	28.45N	95.40W
Inubō-Zaki [▶]	29 Gd	35.42N	140.52 E
Inukjuak	39 Ld	58.30N	78.15W
Inutil, Bahía- [◖]	56 Gh	53.30N	70.10W
Inuvik	38 Ec	68.25N	133.30W
Inuyama	29 Ed	35.23N	136.56 E
Inva [≈]	17 Gg	58.59N	55.40 E
Inveraray	9 He	56.13S	5.05W
Invercargill	59 Ke	29.47S	151.07 E
Inverell	46 Kb	80.35N	17.35W
Inverness	6 Fd	57.27N	4.15W
Inverurie	9 Kd	57.17N	2.23W
Investigator Group [◻]	57 Sh	33.45S	134.30 E
Investigator Strait [≈]	59 Hg	35.25S	137.10 E
Inyangani [▲]	30 Kj	18.18S	32.51 E
Inyangani	37 Ec	18.13S	32.46 E
Inyati	37 Dc	19.40S	28.51 E
Inyazura	37 Ec	18.43S	32.10 E
Inyo Mountains [▲]	46 Gh	36.50N	117.45W
Inza	19 Ee	53.53N	46.28 E
Inzá	54 Cc	2.33N	76.04W
Inžavino	16 Mc	52.19N	42.31 E
Inzer	17 Hi	54.14N	57.34 E
Inzer [≈]	17 Hi	54.14N	57.34 E
Inzer	54 Cc	3.45S	17.57 E
Ió/Kazan-Rettō = Volcano Islands (EN) [◻]	21 Qg	25.00N	141.00 E
Ioánnina	6 Ih	39.40N	20.50 E
Ioanninon, Limni- [▭]	15 Dj	39.40N	20.53 E
Iokanga [≈]	7 Jb	68.03N	39.40 E
Iola	45 Ih	37.55N	95.24W
Iolotan	19 Gh	37.18N	62.21 E
Iona [◆]	9 Ge	56.19N	6.25W
Iona	36 Bf	16.52S	12.34 E
Ionava/Jonava	15 Ke	44.07N	27.48 E
Ion Corvin	15 Ke	44.07N	27.48 E
Ionia	44 Ed	42.59N	85.04W
Ionian Basin (EN) [≈]	5 Hh	36.00N	20.00 E
Ionian Islands (EN) = Iónioi Nísoi [◻]	5 Ih	38.30N	20.30 E
Ionian Sea (EN) = Ionio, Mar- [≈]	5 Hh	39.00N	19.00 E
Ionian Sea (EN) = Iónion Pélagos [≈]	5 Hh	39.00N	19.00 E
Ionio, Mar- = Ionian Sea (EN) [≈]	5 Hh	39.00N	19.00 E
Iónioi Nísoi = Ionian Islands (EN) [◻]	15 Dk	38.40N	20.10 E
Iónion Pélagos = Ionian Sea (EN) [≈]	5 Hh	39.00N	19.00 E
Iori [≈]	16 Ki	41.03N	46.17 E
Ios	15 Im	36.44N	25.18 E
Íos [◆]	15 Im	36.42N	25.20 E
Ió-Shima [◆]	28 Ki	31.51N	130.13 E

Name	Ref	Lat	Long
Iowa [2]	43 Ic	42.15N	93.15W
Iowa City	43 Ic	41.40N	91.32W
Iowa Falls	45 Je	42.31N	93.15W
Iowa Park	45 Gj	33.57N	98.40W
Iowa River [≈]	45 Kf	41.10N	91.02W
Ió-Yama [▲]	29a Da	44.10N	145.10 E
Ipa [≈]	16 Fc	52.07N	29.12 E
Ipameri	54 Ig	17.43S	48.09W
Ipatovo	19 Ef	45.43N	42.53 E
Ipaumirim	54 Ke	6.47S	38.43W
Ipel' [≈]	10 Oi	47.49N	18.52 E
Ipiales	54 Cc	0.50N	77.37W
Ipiaú	54 Kf	14.08S	39.44W
Ipiranga	55 Gg	25.01S	50.35W
Ipiros [2]	15 Dj	39.30N	20.40 E
Ipiros = Epirus (EN) [▲]	15 Dj	39.30N	20.40 E
Ipiros = Epirus (EN) [2]	5 Ih	39.30N	20.40 E
Ipixuna, Rio- [≈]	54 Fe	5.50 S	63.00W
Ipixuna	54 De	7.34 S	72.36W
Ipoh	22 Mi	4.35N	101.05 E
Ipoly [≈]	10 Oi	47.49N	18.52 E
Iporá	55 Ff	23.59 S	53.37W
Iporá	54 Hg	16.28 S	51.07W
Ippy	35 Cd	6.15N	21.12 E
Ipsala	24 Bb	40.55N	26.23 E
Ipsizonos Óros [▲]	15 Gi	40.28N	23.34 E
Ipswich [Austl.]	58 Gg	27.36S	152.46 E
Ipswich [Eng.-U.K.]	6 Ge	52.04N	1.10 E
Ipswich [S.D.-U.S.]	45 Gd	45.27N	99.02W
Ipu	54 Jd	4.20 S	40.42W
Iqaluit	39 Mc	63.44N	68.28W
Iquique	53 Ih	20.13 S	70.10W
Iquitos	53 If	3.50 S	73.15W
Iraan	45 Fk	30.54N	101.54W
Ira Banda	35 Cd	5.57N	22.06 E
Irabu-Jima [◆]	27 Mg	24.50N	125.10 E
Iracoubo	54 Hb	5.29N	53.13W
Iraël	17 Gd	64.27N	55.08 E
Iráklia [◆]	15 Im	36.50N	25.26 E
Iráklia [◆]	15 Gi	40.28N	23.34 E
Iráklion	6 Ih	35.20N	25.08 E
Irán = Iran (EN) [1]	22 Hf	32.00N	53.00 E
Iran (EN) = Irán [1]	22 Hf	32.00N	53.00 E
Iran, Pegunungan = Iran Mountains (EN) [▲]	21 Ni	2.05N	114.55 E
Iran, Plateau of- (EN) [▲]	21 Hf	32.00N	56.00 E
Irani, Serra do- [≈]	55 Fh	27.00S	52.12W
Iran Mountains (EN) = Iran, Pegunungan- [▲]	21 Ni	2.05N	114.55 E
Iránshahr	21 Ig	27.13N	60.41 E
Irapa	50 Fg	10.34N	62.35W
Irapuá, Arroio- [≈]	55 Fj	30.15 S	53.10W
Iraputo	39 Ig	20.41N	101.28W
Iraq (EN) = Al 'Irāq [1]	22 Gf	33.00N	44.00 E
'Irāq al 'Arabi [◻]	24 Kg	31.50N	45.50 E
Irati	13 Kb	42.35N	1.16W
Irati	56 Jc	25.27S	50.39W
Irazú, Volcán- [▲]	38 Ki	9.59N	83.51W
Irbeni Väin [≈]	5 Ig	57.48N	22.05 E
Irbid	23 Ec	32.33N	35.51 E
Irbiktepe	15 Ji	41.00N	26.30 E
Irbit [≈]	17 Kh	57.42N	63.07 E
Irbit	19 Gd	57.41N	63.03 E
Irebu	36 Cc	0.37S	17.45 E
Irecê	54 Jf	11.18S	41.52W
Iregua [≈]	13 Jb	42.27N	2.24W
Ireland/Éire [1]	5 Fe	53.00N	8.00W
Ireland/Éire [1]	6 Fe	53.00N	8.00W
Ireland Trough (EN) [≈]	5 Ed	55.00N	12.40W
Iren [≈]	17 Hi	57.27N	56.59 E
Ireng River [≈]	54 Gc	3.33N	59.51W
Irês Corações	54 Ih	21.42S	45.16W
Irgiz	54 Jf	24.27S	52.02W
Irgiz [≈]	19 Gf	48.13N	62.68 E
Irgiz	19 Gf	48.36N	61.16 E
Irharrhar [Alg.] [≈]	30 Hf	28.00N	6.15 E
Irharrhar [Alg.] [≈]	32 Ie	21.01N	6.01 E
Irherm	32 Fc	30.04N	8.26W
Iri	28 Jg	35.56N	126.57 E
Iriba	31 Jg	15.07N	22.15 E
Irigui [▲]	30 Eg	16.43N	5.30W
Iriklinski	16 Ud	51.39N	58.38 E
Iriklinskoje Vodohranilišče [▭]	16 Ud	51.45N	58.45 E
Iringa	36 Gd	8.00S	35.30 E
Iringa [3]	31 Ki	7.46S	35.42 E
Irinjalakuda	55 Fe	58.20N	104.30 E
Irinomote Jima [◆]	23 Jm	24.20N	123.50 E
Iriona	49 Ef	15.57N	85.11W
Iriri, Rio- [≈]	52 Kf	3.52 S	52.37W
Irish Sea [≈]	5 Fe	53.30N	5.20W
Irish Sea (EN) = Muir Eireann [≈]	5 Fe	53.30N	5.20W
Irituia	54 Id	1.46S	47.26W
Irkeštam	18 Ie	39.38N	73.55 E
Irkutsk	53 Md	52.16N	104.20 E
Irkutskaja Oblast [3]	20 Fe	56.00N	104.00 E
Irlir, Gora- [▲]	18 Dc	42.40N	63.03 E
Irminio [≈]	14 In	36.46N	14.36 E
Irnijärvi [▭]	8 Jb	65.38N	29.05 E
Iro, Lac- [▭]	35 Bc	10.06N	19.25 E
Iroise [≈]	11 Bf	48.15N	4.55W
Iron Gate (EN) = Portile de Fier [≈]	5 Ig	44.41N	22.31 E
Iron Knob	59 Hf	32.44S	137.08 E
Iron Mountain	43 Jb	45.49N	88.04W
Iron Mountains [≈]	44 Fg	36.50N	7.50W
Iron River [Mi.-U.S.]	43 Jb	46.05N	88.39W
Iron River [Wi.-U.S.]	45 Kc	46.34N	91.24W
Ironside Mountain [▲]	46 Kf	44.19N	118.08W
Ironton [Mo.-U.S.]	45 Kh	37.36N	90.38W
Ironton [Oh.-U.S.]	44 Ef	38.32N	82.41W
Ironwood	43 Ib	46.27N	90.10W
Iroquois Falls	42 Jg	48.46N	80.41W
Irō-Zaki [▶]	28 Og	34.35N	138.55 E

Index Symbols

[1] Independent Nation	[▲] Historical or Cultural Region	[▷] Pass, Gap	[▭] Depression	[≈] Coast, Beach	[≈] Rock, Reef	[≈] Waterfall Rapids	[≈] Canal
[2] State, Region	[▲] Mount, Mountain	[▲] Plain, Lowland	[▭] Polder	[▭] Cliff	[◆] Islands, Archipelago	[≈] River Mouth, Estuary	[▭] Glacier
[3] District, County	[▲] Volcano	[▼] Delta	[▭] Desert, Dunes	[▶] Peninsula	[≈] Rocks, Reefs	[▭] Lake	[▭] Ice Shelf, Pack Ice
[4] Municipality	[▲] Hill	[▭] Salt Flat	[▭] Forest, Woods	[▭] Isthmus	[≈] Coral Reef	[▭] Salt Lake	[▭] Ocean
[5] Colony, Dependency	[▲] Mountains, Mountain Range	[▽] Valley, Canyon	[▭] Heath, Steppe	[▭] Sandbank	[≈] Well, Spring	[▭] Intermittent Lake	[▭] Sea
[◻] Continent	[▲] Hills, Escarpment	[▲] Crater, Cave	[▭] Oasis	[◆] Island	[≈] Geyser	[▭] Reservoir	[▭] Gulf, Bay
[▲] Physical Region	[▲] Plateau, Upland	[▲] Karst Features	[▶] Cape, Point	[○] Atoll	[≈] River, Stream	[▭] Swamp, Pond	[≈] Strait, Fjord

[▭] Lagoon	[▭] Escarpment, Sea Scarp	[▲] Historic Site	[▭] Port
[▭] Bank	[▭] Fracture	[▲] Ruins	[▭] Lighthouse
[▭] Seamount	[▭] Trench, Abyss	[▲] Wall, Walls	[▲] Mine
[▭] Tablemount	[▲] National Park, Reserve	[▲] Church, Abbey	[▭] Tunnel
[▭] Ridge	[▲] Point of Interest	[▲] Temple	[▭] Dam, Bridge
[▭] Shelf	[▲] Recreation Site	[▲] Scientific Station	
[▭] Basin	[▲] Cave, Cavern	[▲] Airport	

A • 71

Irpen 19 De 50.31N 30.16 E
Irpinia 14 Ij 40.55N 15.00 E
Irrawaddy → Ayeyarwady 25 Ie 17.00N 95.00 E
Irrawaddy (EN) = Ayeyarwady 21 Lg 15.50N 95.06 E
Irrel 12 Ie 49.51N 6.28 E
Irsâva 10 Th 48.15N 23.05 E
Irsina 14 Kj 40.45N 16.14 E
Irtek 16 Rd 51.29N 52.42 E
Irthlingborough 12 Bb 52.19N 0.36W
Irtyš 21 Ic 61.04N 68.52 E
Irtyšsk 19 He 53.21N 75.27 E
Irumu 36 Eb 1.27N 29.52 E
Irún 13 Ka 43.21N 1.47W
Irurzun 13 Kb 42.55N 1.50W
Irves Šaurums 8 Ig 57.48N 22.05 E
Irvine 9 If 55.37N 4.40W
Irving 45 Hj 32.49N 96.56W
Is, Jabal- 35 Fa 21.49N 35.39 E
Isa, Ra's- 33 Hf 15.11N 42.39 E
Isabel 45 Fd 45.24N 101.26W
Isabel, Bahia- 54a Ab 0.38S 91.25W
Isabela 51a Ab 18.31N 67.07W
Isabela → Basilan City 26 He 6.42N 121.58 E
Isabela, Cabo- 49 Ld 19.56N 71.01W
Isabela, Isla- [Ec.] 52 Gf 0.30S 91.06W
Isabela, Isla- [Mex.] 48 Gg 21.51N 105.55W
Isabella, Cordillera- 47 Gf 13.30N 85.30W
Isabel Segunda 49 Od 18.09N 65.27W
Isabey 15 Ml 38.00N 29.24 E
Isaccea 15 Ld 45.16N 28.28 E
Isachsen 39 Ib 78.50N 103.30W
Isafjörður 6 Db 66.03N 23.09W
Isahaya 28 Jh 32.50N 130.03 E
Isakov, Seamount (EN) 57 Ga 31.35N 151.07 E
Isana, Rio- 54 Ec 0.26N 67.19W
Isandja 36 Dc 2.59S 22.00 E
Isanga 36 Dc 1.26S 22.18 E
Isangi 36 Db 0.46N 24.15 E
Isanlu Makutu 34 Gd 8.16N 5.48 E
Isaouane-n-Irrarraren 32 Id 27.15N 8.00 E
Isaouane-n-Tifernine 32 Id 27.00N 7.30 E
Isar 10 Ih 48.49N 12.58 E
Isarco/Eisack 14 Fd 46.27N 11.18 E
Isarco, Valle-/Eisacktal 14 Fd 46.45N 11.35 E
Isbergues 12 Ed 50.37N 2.27 E
Iscayachi 54 Eh 21.31S 65.03W
Ischgl 14 Ec 47.01N 10.17 E
Ischia 14 Hj 40.45N 13.55 E
Ischia 14 Hj 40.44N 13.57 E
Ise 27 Oe 34.29N 136.42 E
Isefjord 8 Di 55.50N 11.50 E
Išejevka 7 Li 54.28N 48.17 E
Isen 10 Ih 48.20N 12.45 E
Isenach 12 Ke 49.38N 8.28 E
Isen-Zaki 29b Bb 27.39N 128.55 E
Iseo, Lago d'- 14 Ee 45.45N 10.05 E
Iseran, Col de l'- 11 Ni 45.25N 7.02 E
Isère 11 Kj 44.59N 4.51 E
Isère [3] 11 Li 45.10N 5.50 E
Išerit, Gora- 17 If 61.08N 59.10 E
Iserlohn 10 De 51.22N 7.42 E
Isernia 14 Ii 41.36N 14.14 E
Isesaki 29 Fc 36.19N 139.12 E
Iset 21 Id 56.36N 66.24 E
Isetskoje 17 Lh 56.29N 65.21 E
Ise-Wan 28 Ng 34.40N 136.42 E
Iseyin 34 Fd 7.58N 3.36 E
Isfahan (EN) = Eşfahān 22 Hf 32.40N 51.38 E
Isfana 18 Ge 39.51N 69.32 E
Isfara 18 Hd 40.07N 70.38 E
Isfendiyar Dağları 23 Da 41.45N 34.10 E
Isfjorden 41 Nc 78.15N 15.00 E
Isha Baydabo = Baidoa (EN) 31 Lh 3.04N 43.48 E
Ishasha River 36 Ec 0.50S 29.40 E
Ishavet = Arctic Ocean (EN) 67 Be 85.00N 170.00 E
Isherton 54 Gc 2.19N 59.22W
Ishigaki 27 Lg 24.20N 124.09 E
Ishikari 29a Bb 43.13N 141.18 E
Ishikari-Dake 29a Cb 43.33N 143.00 E
Ishikari-Gawa 29a Bb 43.15N 141.20 E
Ishikari-Heiya 29a Bb 43.00N 141.40 E
Ishikari-Wan 27 Pc 43.25N 141.00 E
Ishikawa [Jap.] 27 Mf 26.27N 127.50 E
Ishikawa [Jap.] 29 Gc 37.09N 140.27 E
Ishikawa Ken [2] 28 Nf 36.35N 136.40 E
Ishim Steppe (EN) = Išimskaja Step 21 Id 55.00N 67.30 E
Ishinomaki 27 Pd 38.25N 141.18 E
Ishinomaki-Wan 28 Ge 38.20N 141.15 E
Ishioka 28 Pf 36.11N 140.16 E
Ishitate-San 28 De 33.44N 134.03 E
Ishizuchi-Yama 29 Ce 33.45N 133.05 E
Ishodnaja, Gora- 20 Nd 64.50N 173.26W
Ishpeming 44 Db 46.30N 87.40W
Isidro Alves 55 Ee 20.09S 55.12W
Isigny-sur-Mer 11 Ee 49.19N 1.06W
Isii 29 Dd 34.04N 134.26 E
Işıklar Dağı 24 Bb 40.50N 27.05 E
Işıkli 15 Mk 38.19N 29.51 E
Isikli Göl 15 Mk 38.14N 29.55 E
Isili 14 Dk 39.44N 9.06 E
Isilkul 19 He 54.55N 71.16 E
Išim 22 Id 56.09N 69.27 E
Išim 21 Jd 57.45N 71.12 E
Išimbaj 19 Fe 53.28N 56.02 E
Išimskaja Step = Ishim Steppe (EN) 21 Id 55.00N 67.30 E
Isinga 20 Gf 52.55N 112.00 E
Isiolo 36 Gb 0.21N 37.35 E
Isiro 31 Jh 2.48N 27.41 E
Isisford 59 Id 24.16S 144.26 E
Isjangulovo 17 Hj 52.12N 56.36 E
Iskandar 18 Gd 41.35N 69.43 E
Iskăr, Jazovir- 15 Gg 42.25N 23.35 E
Iškašim 19 Hh 36.44N 71.39 E
İskenderun = Alexandretta (EN) 22 Ff 36.37N 36.07 E
İskenderun Körfezi = Alexandretta, Gulf of- (EN) 23 Eb 36.30N 35.40 E
İskilip 24 Fb 40.45N 34.29 E
Iski-Naukat 18 Id 40.14N 72.41 E
Iskininski 16 Rf 47.13N 52.36 E
Iskitim 20 Df 54.38N 83.18 E
Iskushuban 35 Ic 10.13N 50.14 E
Iskut 42 Ee 56.45N 131.48W
Isla-Cristina 13 Eg 37.12N 7.19W
İslâhiye 24 Gd 37.26N 36.41 E
Islāmābād 22 Jf 33.42N 73.10 E
Islāmābād → Anantnāg 25 Fb 33.44N 75.09 E
Isla Mujeres 48 Pg 21.12N 86.43W
Island = Iceland (EN) [1] 6 Eb 65.00N 18.00W
Island = Iceland (EN) 5 Eb 65.00N 18.00W
Island Harbour 51b Ab 18.16N 63.02W
Island Lagoon 59 Hf 31.30S 136.40 E
Island Lake 42 If 53.45N 94.30W
Island Lake 42 If 53.58N 94.46W
Island Pond 44 Lc 44.50N 71.53W
Islands, Bay of - [Can.] 42 Lg 49.10N 58.15W
Islands, Bay of- [N.Z.] 62 Fa 35.10S 174.10 E
Islao, Massif de l'- 30 Lk 22.30S 45.20 E
Islas de la Bahía [3] 49 De 16.20N 86.30W
Islay 5 Fd 55.46N 6.10W
Islaz 15 Hf 43.44N 24.45 E
Isle 11 Fj 44.55N 0.15W
Isle of Man [5] 9 Ig 54.15N 4.30W
Isle of Wight [3] 9 Lk 50.40N 1.15W
Isleta 45 Ci 34.55N 106.42W
Isle-Verte 44 Ma 48.01N 69.22W
Ismael Cortinas 55 Dk 33.56S 57.08W
Ismailia (EN) = Al Ismā'īlīyah 33 Fc 30.35N 32.16 E
Ismailly 16 Pi 40.47N 48.13 E
Ismantorps Borg 8 Gh 56.45N 16.40 E
Isnā 31 Kf 25.18N 32.33 E
Isny im Allgäu 10 Gi 47.42N 10.02 E
Isojärvi 8 Ic 61.45N 21.45 E
Isojoki 7 Ee 62.07N 21.58 E
Isojoki/Storå 7 Ee 62.07N 21.58 E
Isoka 36 Fe 10.08S 32.38 E
Isola del Liri 14 Hi 41.41N 13.34 E
Isola di Capo Rizzuto 14 Ll 38.58N 17.05 E
Isonzo 14 He 45.43N 13.33 E
Isonzo (EN) = Soča 14 He 45.43N 13.33 E
Isosyöte 7 Gd 65.37N 27.35 E
Isparta 23 Db 37.46N 30.33 E
Isperih 15 Jf 43.43N 26.50 E
Ispica 14 In 36.47N 14.55 E
İspir 24 Ib 40.29N 41.00 E
İspiriz Dağı 24 Jc 38.03N 43.55 E
Israel (EN) = Yisra'el [1] 22 Ff 31.30N 35.00 E
Isratu 35 Fb 16.20N 39.55 E
Issa 8 Mh 56.55N 28.50 E
Issano 54 Gb 5.49N 59.25W
Issaran, Ra's- 24 Eh 28.50N 32.56 E
Issel 10 Cd 52.00N 6.10 E
Isser 13 Ph 36.51N 3.40 E
Issia [3] 34 Dd 6.30N 6.35W
Issia 34 Dd 6.29N 6.35W
Issoire 11 Ji 45.33N 3.15 E
Issoudun 11 Hh 46.57N 2.00 E
Issyk 18 Kc 43.20N 77.28 E
Issyk-Kul' (Rybačje) 19 Hg 42.28N 76.11 E
Issyk-Kul, Ozero- 21 Je 42.25N 77.15 E
Issyk-Kulskaja Oblast [3] 19 Hg 42.10N 78.00 E
Ist 14 If 44.17N 14.47 E
İstanbul 22 Ee 41.01N 28.58 E
İstanbul-Bakırköy 15 Li 40.59N 28.52 E
İstanbul-Beyoğlu 15 Lh 41.02N 28.59 E
İstanbul Boğazi = Bosporus (EN) 5 Ig 41.00N 29.00 E
İstanbul-Kadıköy 15 Mi 40.59N 29.01 E
Isteren 8 Db 62.00N 11.50 E
Istgāh-e Eqbālīyeh 24 Ne 35.50N 50.45 E
Isthilart 55 Dj 31.11S 57.58W
Istiaia 15 Gk 38.57N 23.09 E
Istisu 16 Nj 39.57N 46.00 E
Istmina 54 Cb 5.09N 76.42W
Isto, Mount- 38 Ec 69.12N 143.48W
Istok 15 Dg 42.47N 20.29 E
Istokpoga, Lake- 44 Gl 27.22N 81.17W
Istra = Istria (EN) 5 Hf 45.00N 14.00 E
Istres 11 Kk 43.31N 4.59 E
Istria 15 Le 44.34N 28.43 E
Istria (EN) = Istra 5 Hf 45.00N 14.00 E
Isulan 26 He 7.02N 124.29 E
Itabaiana 54 Kf 10.41S 37.26W
Itabaianinha 54 Kf 11.16S 37.47W
Itaberá 55 Hf 23.51S 49.09W
Itaberaba 54 Jf 12.32S 40.18W
Itaberai 55 Ic 16.02S 49.48W
Itabira 54 Jg 19.37S 43.13W
Itabirito 55 Ke 20.15S 43.48W
Itabuna 53 Mg 14.48S 39.16W
Itacaiuna, Rio- 54 Ie 5.21S 49.08W
Itacarambi 55 Jb 15.01S 44.03W
Itacoatiara 53 Kf 3.08S 58.25W
Itacolomi, Pico do- 55 Ke 20.26S 43.29W
Itacuai, Rio- 54 Dd 4.20S 70.12W
Itacumbi 55 Ei 28.44S 55.08W
Itacurubí del Rosario 55 Dg 24.29S 56.41W
Itaguari, Rio- 55 Jb 14.11S 44.40W
Itaguaru 55 Hb 15.44S 49.37W
Itagüí 54 Cb 6.12N 75.40W
Itaimbézinho 55 Gi 28.38S 50.34W
Itaituba 53 Kf 4.17S 55.59W
Itajaí 53 Lh 26.53S 48.39W
Itajaí Açu, Rio- 55 Hh 26.54S 48.33W
Itajubá 54 Ih 22.26S 45.27W
Itajuípe 54 Kf 14.41S 39.22W
Itaka 20 Gf 53.54N 118.42 E
Italia = Italy (EN) [1] 6 Hg 42.50N 12.50 E
Itálica 13 Fg 37.25N 6.05W
Italy (EN) = Italia [1] 6 Hg 42.50N 12.50 E
Itambacuri 54 Jg 18.01S 41.42W
Itambé, Pico de- 52 Lg 18.23S 43.21W
Itämeri = Baltic, Sea (EN) 5 Hd 57.00N 19.00 E
Itampolo 37 Gd 24.41S 43.57 E
Itanagar 25 Ic 26.57N 93.15 E
Itanará, Rio- 55 Eg 24.00S 55.53W
Itanhaém 56 Kb 24.11S 46.47W
Itano 29 Dd 34.09N 134.28 E
Itapaci 55 Hb 14.57S 49.34W
Itapagé 54 Kd 3.41S 39.34W
Itapajipe 55 Hd 19.54S 49.22W
Itaparaná, Rio- 54 Fe 5.47S 63.03W
Itapebi 54 Kg 15.56S 39.32W
Itapecerica 55 Je 20.28S 45.07W
Itapecuru-Mirim 54 Jd 3.24S 44.20W
Itapemirim 54 Jh 21.01S 40.50W
Itaperina, Pointe- 30 Lk 24.59S 47.06 E
Itaperuna 54 Jh 21.12S 41.54W
Itapetinga 54 Jg 15.15S 40.15W
Itapetininga 56 Kb 23.36S 48.03W
Itapetininga, Rio- 55 Hf 23.35S 48.27W
Itapeva 55 Hf 23.58S 48.52W
Itapeva, Lagoa- 55 Hi 29.30S 49.55W
Itapicuru, Rio- [Braz.] 54 Kf 11.47S 37.32W
Itapicuru, Rio- [Braz.] 52 Lf 2.52S 44.12W
Itapipoca 54 Kd 3.31S 39.33W
Itapiranga [Braz.] 54 Gd 2.45S 58.01W
Itapiranga [Braz.] 55 Fh 27.08S 53.43W
Itapirapuã, Pico- 55 Hg 24.17S 49.12W
Itápolis 55 He 21.35S 48.46W
Itaporã 55 Ef 22.01S 54.54W
Itaporanga [Braz.] 55 Hf 23.42S 49.29W
Itaporanga [Braz.] 54 Ke 7.18S 38.10W
Itapúa [3] 55 Eh 26.50S 55.50W
Itapuã 55 Gj 30.16S 51.01W
Itapuranga 54 Ig 15.35S 49.59W
Itaqui 56 Ic 29.08S 56.33W
Itaquyry 55 Eg 24.56S 55.13W
Itararé 55 Hg 24.07S 49.20W
Itararé, Rio- 55 Hf 23.10S 49.42W
Itārsi 25 Fd 22.37N 77.45 E
Itarumã 55 Gd 18.42S 51.25W
Itati 55 Ch 27.16S 58.15W
Itatinga 55 Hf 23.07S 48.36W
Itatski 20 De 56.07N 89.20 E
Itaum 55 Ef 22.00S 55.20W
Itaúna 54 Jh 20.04S 44.34W
Itaya-Tōge 29 Gc 37.50N 140.13 E
Itbāy 30 Kf 22.00N 35.30 E
Itbayat 26 Hb 20.46N 121.50 E
Itchen 12 Ad 50.57N 1.22W
Ite 54 Dg 17.50S 70.58W
Itéa 15 Fk 38.26N 22.25 E
Ithaca 43 Lc 42.26N 76.30W
Ithaca (EN) = Itháki 15 Dk 38.24N 20.40 E
Itháki 15 Dk 38.22N 20.43 E
Itháki = Ithaca (EN) 15 Dk 38.24N 20.40 E
Ith Hils 10 Fd 52.05N 9.35 E
Ithnayn, Harrat- 24 Ii 26.40N 40.10 E
Itigi 36 Fd 5.42S 34.29 E
Itimbiri 30 Jh 2.02N 22.44 E
Itiopya = Ethiopia (EN) [1] 31 Kh 9.00N 39.00 E
Itiquira 54 Hg 17.05S 54.56W
Itiquira, Rio- 52 Kg 17.18S 56.44W
Itirapina 55 If 22.15S 47.49W
Itiúba 54 Kf 10.43S 39.51W
Itivdleq 41 Ge 66.38N 53.51W
Itō 28 Og 34.58N 139.05 E
Itoigawa 28 Nf 37.02N 137.51 E
Itoko 36 Dc 1.00S 21.45 E
Itoman 29b Ab 26.07N 127.40 E
Iton 11 Hf 49.09N 1.12 E
Itremo, Massif de l'- 37 Hd 20.45S 46.30 E
Itsā 24 Dh 29.15N 30.48 E
Itsukaichi 29 Cd 34.22N 132.22 E
Itsuki 29 Be 32.24N 130.50 E
Ittiri 14 Cj 40.36N 8.34 E
Itu [Braz.] 55 If 23.16S 47.19W
Itu [Nig.] 34 Gd 5.12N 7.59 E
Itu, Rio- 55 Ei 29.25S 55.51W
Ituí, Rio- 54 Dd 4.38S 70.19W
Ituiutaba 54 Ig 18.58S 49.28W
Itula 36 Ec 3.29S 27.52 E
Itumbiara 54 Ig 18.25S 49.13W
Itumkale 16 Nh 42.43N 45.35 E
Ituna 46 Na 51.10N 103.30W
Itungi Port 36 Fd 9.35S 33.56 E
Itupiranga 54 Ie 5.09S 49.20W
Iturama 55 Gd 19.44S 50.11W
Iturbide 48 Oh 19.40N 89.37W
Ituri 30 Jh 1.40N 27.01 E
Iturregui 55 Bm 36.50S 61.08W
Iturup, Ostrov- 21 Qe 44.54N 147.30 E
Iturup, Ostrov-/Etorofu Tō 21 Qe 44.54N 147.30 E
Itutinga 55 Je 21.18S 44.40W
Ituverava 56 Kb 20.20S 47.47W
Ituxi, Rio- 52 Jf 7.18S 64.51W
Ituzaingó 55 Dh 27.36S 56.41W
Itz 10 Gg 49.58N 10.52 E
Itzehoe 10 Fc 53.55N 9.31 E
Ivacevići 16 Dc 52.43N 25.21 E
Ivai 55 Gg 25.01S 50.52W
Ivaí, Rio- [Braz.] 55 Fi 29.08S 53.16W
Ivaí, Rio- [Braz.] 52 Kh 23.18S 53.42W
Ivaiporã 55 Gg 24.15S 51.45W
Ivajlovgrad 15 Jh 41.32N 26.08 E
Ivakoany, Massif de l'- 37 Hd 23.50S 46.25 E
Ivalojoki 7 Gc 68.43N 27.36 E
Ivančice 10 Mg 49.06N 16.22 E
Ivangorod 7 Gg 59.23N 28.20 E
Ivangrad 15 Cg 42.51N 19.52 E
Ivanhoe 58 Fh 32.54S 144.18 E
Ivanić-Grad 14 Ke 45.42N 16.24 E
Ivaniči 10 Uf 50.38N 24.24 E
Ivanjica 15 Df 43.35N 20.14 E
Ivanjska 14 Lf 44.55N 17.04 E
Ivankov 16 Fd 50.57N 29.58 E
Ivano-Frankovo 10 Tg 49.52N 23.46 E
Ivano-Frankovsk 6 If 48.55N 24.43 E
Ivano-Frankovskaja Oblast [3] 19 Cf 48.40N 24.40 E
Ivanovka 20 Hf 50.18N 127.59 E
Ivanovka 16 Gf 46.57N 30.28 E
Ivanovo 16 Dc 52.10N 25.32 E
Ivanovo 6 Kd 57.00N 40.59 E
Ivanovskaja Oblast [3] 19 Ed 57.00N 41.50 E
Ivanovskoje 8 Me 59.12N 28.59 E
Ivanšćica 14 Kd 46.11N 16.10 E
Ivdel 19 Gc 60.42N 60.28 E
Ivenec 8 Lk 53.55N 26.49 E
Ivigtut 41 Hf 61.15N 48.00W
Ivindo 30 Ii 0.09S 12.09 E
Ivinheima 55 Ff 22.10S 53.37W
Ivinheima, Rio- 54 Hh 23.14S 53.42W
Ivinski razliv 7 If 61.10N 35.00 E
Iviza (EN) = Eivissa/Ibiza 5 Gh 39.00N 1.25 E
Iviza (EN) = Ibiza/Eivissa 5 Gh 39.00N 1.25 E
Ivje 10 Vc 53.55N 25.51 E
Ivohibe 37 Hd 22.29S 46.52 E
Ivoire, Côte d'- = Ivory Coast (EN) 30 Gh 5.00N 5.00W
Ivolândia 55 Gc 16.34S 50.51W
Ivory Coast (EN) = Côte d'Ivoire [1] 31 Gh 8.00N 5.00W
Ivory Coast (EN) = Ivoire, Côte d'- 30 Gh 5.00N 5.00W
Ivösjön 8 Fh 56.05N 14.25 E
Ivrea 14 Be 45.28N 7.52 E
Ivrindi 15 Kj 39.34N 27.29 E
Ivry-la-Bataille 12 Df 48.53N 1.28 E
Ivry-sur-Seine 12 Ef 48.49N 2.23 E
Ivujivik 39 Lc 62.25N 77.54W
Iwai-Shima 29 Be 33.47N 131.58 E
Iwaizumi 28 Pe 39.50N 141.48 E
Iwaki 22 Qf 36.55N 140.48 E
Iwaki-Gawa 29 Ga 41.01N 140.22 E
Iwaki-Hisanohama 29 Gc 37.09N 140.59 E
Iwaki-Jōban 29 Gc 37.02N 140.50 E
Iwaki-Kawamae 29 Gc 37.12N 140.45 E
Iwaki-Miwa 29 Gc 37.09N 140.42 E
Iwaki-Nakoso 29 Gc 36.56N 140.48 E
Iwaki-Onahama 29 Gc 36.57N 140.53 E
Iwaki-San 29 Ga 40.40N 140.20 E
Iwaki-Taira 29 Gc 37.05N 140.55 E
Iwaki-Uchigō 29 Gc 37.04N 140.50 E
Iwaki-Yoshima 29 Gc 37.05N 140.50 E
Iwaki-Yotsukura 29 Gc 37.07N 140.58 E
Iwakuni 27 Ne 34.09N 132.11 E
Iwami 29 Dd 35.35N 134.20 E
Iwami-Kōgen 29 Cd 35.00N 132.30 E
Iwamizawa 27 Pc 43.12N 141.46 E
Iwanai 28 Pc 42.58N 140.30 E
Iwanuma 29 Gb 38.07N 140.52 E
Iwase 29 Gc 36.21N 140.06 E
Iwasuge-Yama 29 Fc 36.44N 138.32 E
Iwata 29 Ed 34.42N 137.48 E
Iwate 28 Pe 39.30N 141.30 E
Iwate Ken [2] 28 Pe 39.30N 141.15 E
Iwate San 28 Pe 39.49N 141.26 E
Iwo 34 Fd 7.38N 4.11 E
Iwŏn 27 Mc 40.19N 128.37 E
Iwuy 12 Fd 50.14N 3.19 E
Ixiamas 54 Ef 13.45S 68.09W
Ixmiquilpan 48 Jg 20.29N 99.14W
Ixopo 37 Ef 30.08S 30.00 E
Ixtapa, Punta- 48 Ii 17.39N 101.40W
Ixtepec 47 Ee 16.34N 95.06W
Ixtlahuacán del Río 48 Hg 20.52N 103.15W
Ixtlán del Río 47 Dd 21.02N 104.22W
Iyah 35 Hd 9.00N 49.38 E
Iyo 28 Lh 33.46N 132.42 E
Iyo-mishima 29 Ce 33.58N 133.33 E
Iyo-Nada 29 Ce 33.40N 132.15 E
Iž 7 Mh 56.00N 52.41 E
Iž 14 Jf 44.03N 15.06 E
Izabal [3] 49 Cf 15.30N 89.00W
Izabal, Lago de- 47 Ge 15.30N 89.10W
Izad Khvāst 24 Og 31.31N 52.07 E
Izamal 47 Gd 20.56N 89.01W
Izamal 48 Og 20.56N 89.01W
Izapa 47 Ff 14.55N 92.10W
'Izbat al Jājah 24 Dj 24.48N 30.35 E
'Izbat Dush 24 Dj 24.34N 30.42 E
Izberbaš 19 Eg 42.33N 47.52 E
Izbiceni 15 Hf 43.50N 24.39 E
Izborsk 8 Mg 57.39N 28.01 E
Izegem 12 Fd 50.55N 3.12 E
Izeh 24 Mg 31.50N 49.50 E
Izena-Shima 29b Ab 26.56N 127.56 E
Iževsk 6 Ld 56.51N 53.14 E
Izjaslav 16 Ed 50.09N 26.51 E
Izjum 19 Df 49.12N 37.17 E
Izki 23 Ie 22.57N 57.49 E
Izma 5 Lb 65.19N 52.54 E
Izma 17 Fd 65.02N 53.55 E
Izmail 6 If 45.21N 28.50 E
İzmir = Smyrna (EN) 22 Ef 38.25N 27.09 E
İzmir, Gulf of- (EN) = İzmir Körfezi 24 Bc 38.30N 26.50 E
İzmir-Bornova 24 Bc 38.27N 27.14 E
İzmir Körfezi = İzmir, Gulf of- (EN) 24 Bc 38.30N 26.50 E
İzmit 22 Ee 40.46N 29.55 E
İzmit Körfezi 24 Cb 40.45N 29.35 E
İzmor 24 Ab 40.11N 25.55 E
Iznajar, Embalse de- 13 Hg 37.15N 4.30W
Iznalloz 13 Ig 37.23N 3.31W
İznik 24 Cb 40.26N 29.43 E
İznik Gölü 23 Ca 40.26N 29.30 E
Izobilny 16 Lg 45.19N 41.42 E
Izola 14 He 45.32N 13.40 E
Izōrskaja Vozvyšennost 8 Me 59.35N 29.30 E
Izozog, Bañados del- 54 Fg 18.50S 62.10W
Izra' 24 Gf 32.51N 36.15 E
Izsák 10 Pj 46.48N 19.22 E
Iztočni Rodopi 15 Ih 41.44N 25.31 E
Izúcar de Matamoros 48 Jh 18.36N 98.28W
Izu-Hantō 28 Og 34.55N 138.55 E
Izuhara 28 Jg 34.12N 129.17 E
Izu Islands (EN) = Izu-shotō 21 Pf 32.00N 140.00 E
Izumi [Jap.] 28 Kh 32.05N 130.22 E
Izumi [Jap.] 29 Dd 34.29N 135.26 E
Izumi [Jap.] 29 Gb 38.19N 140.51 E
Izumi-sano 29 Dd 34.24N 135.18 E
Izumo 28 Lg 35.22N 132.46 E
Izu-Shotō = Izu Islands (EN) 21 Pf 32.00N 140.00 E
Izvesti CIK, Ostrova- = Izvestiya Tsik Islands (EN) 20 Da 75.55N 82.30 E
Izvestiya Tsik Islands (EN) = Izvesti CIK, Ostrova- 20 Da 75.55N 82.30 E

J

Jaala 8 Lc 61.03N 26.29 E
Jaama/Jama 8 Lf 58.59N 27.45 E
Jääsjärvi 8 Lc 61.35N 26.05 E
Jaba 24 Qe 35.55N 56.35 E
Jabal, Baḩr al- = Mountain Nile (EN) 30 Kh 9.30N 30.30 E
Jabal Abū Rujmayn 24 Ge 34.50N 37.56 E
Jabal al Awliyā' 35 Eb 15.14N 32.30 E
Jabal az Zannah 24 Oj 24.11N 52.38 E
Jabalón 13 Hf 38.53N 4.05W
Jabalpur 22 Jg 23.10N 79.57 E
Jabal Şabāyā 33 Hf 18.35N 41.03 E
Jabālyah 24 Fg 31.32N 34.29 E
Jabal Zuqar, Jazīrat- 33 Hg 14.00N 42.45 E
Jabbārah 33 Hf 19.27N 40.03 E
Jabbeke 12 Fc 51.11N 3.05 E
Jabjabah, Wādī- 35 Ea 22.37N 33.17 E
Jablah 24 Fe 35.21N 35.55 E
Jablanac 14 If 44.43N 14.53 E
Jablanica 15 Dh 41.15N 20.30 E
Jablanica [Bul.] 15 Hf 43.01N 24.06 E
Jablanica 14 Lg 43.39N 17.45 E
Jabločny 20 Jg 47.09N 142.03 E
Jablonec nad Nisou 10 Lf 50.44N 15.10 E
Jablonicki, Pereval- 5 If 48.18N 24.28 E
Jablonovo 20 Gf 51.51N 112.50 E
Jablonovy Hrebet = Yablonovy Range (EN) 21 Nd 53.30N 115.00 E
Jablunkovský průsmyk 10 Og 49.31N 18.45 E
Jaboatão 54 Ke 8.07S 35.01W
Jaboti 55 De 20.48S 56.23W
Jabrin 24 Ni 27.51N 51.26 E
Jabuka 14 Jg 43.05N 15.28 E
Jabung, Tanjung- 26 Dg 1.01S 104.22 E
Jabuticabal 56 Kb 21.16S 48.19W
Jabuticatubas 55 Kd 19.30S 43.45W
Jaca 13 Lb 42.34N 0.33W
Jacaltenango 49 Bf 15.40N 91.44W
Jacaré, Rio- 55 Je 21.03S 45.16W
Jacarei 55 Jf 23.19S 45.58W
Jacarezinho 56 Kb 23.09S 49.59W
Jáchal, Rio- 52 Ji 30.44S 68.08W
Jaciara [Braz.] 55 Ib 14.12S 46.41W
Jaciara [Braz.] 55 Eb 15.59S 54.57W
Jackman 44 Lc 45.38N 70.16W
Jack Mountain 46 Eb 48.47N 120.57W
Jackpot 46 Hf 41.59N 114.09W
Jacksboro 45 Gj 33.13N 98.10W
Jacks Mountain 44 Ie 40.45N 77.30W
Jackson [Al.-U.S.] 44 Dj 31.31N 87.53W
Jackson [Bar.] 51q Ab 13.10N 59.43W
Jackson [Ky.-U.S.] 44 Fg 37.33N 83.23W
Jackson [Mi.-U.S.] 43 Kc 42.15N 84.24W
Jackson [Mn.-U.S.] 45 Ie 43.37N 94.59W
Jackson [Mo.-U.S.] 45 Lh 37.23N 89.40W
Jackson [Ms.-U.S.] 39 Jf 32.18N 90.12W
Jackson [Oh.-U.S.] 44 Ff 39.03N 82.40W
Jackson [Tn.-U.S.] 43 Jd 35.37N 88.49W
Jackson [Wy.-U.S.] 46 Je 43.29N 110.38W
Jackson, Cape- 62 Fd 40.59S 174.19 E
Jackson, Mount- [Ant.] 66 Qf 71.23S 63.22W
Jackson, Mount- [Austl.] 59 Df 30.15S 119.16 E
Jackson Bay 62 Ce 43.55S 168.40 E
Jackson Head 62 Ce 43.58S 168.37 E
Jackson Lake 46 Je 43.55N 110.40W
Jacksonville [Ar.-U.S.] 45 Ji 34.52N 92.07W
Jacksonville [Fl.-U.S.] 39 Kf 30.20N 81.40W
Jacksonville [Il.-U.S.] 45 Kg 39.44N 90.14W
Jacksonville [N.C.-U.S.] 43 Le 34.45N 77.26W
Jacksonville [Tx.-U.S.] 43 He 31.58N 95.17W
Jacksonville Beach 43 Ke 30.18N 81.24W
Jacmel 47 Je 18.14N 72.32W
Jacobābād 25 Dc 28.17N 68.26 E
Jacobina 54 Jf 11.11S 40.31W
Jacob Lake 46 Ih 36.45N 112.13W
Jacobs 45 La 50.15N 89.46W
Jacona de Plancarte 48 Hh 19.57N 102.16W
Jacques-Cartier, Détroit de - 42 Lg 50.00N 63.30W
Jacques Cartier, Mont - 42 Kg 48.58N 65.57W
Jacuba, Rio- 55 Fd 18.25S 52.28W
Jacuí, Rio- 52 Ki 30.02S 51.15W
Jacuí-Mirim, Rio- 55 Fi 28.51S 53.07W
Jacundá 54 Id 4.33S 49.28W
Jacundá, Rio- 54 Hd 1.57S 50.26W
Jacupiranga 56 Kb 24.42S 48.00W
Jada 34 Hd 8.46N 12.09 E
Jadal 34 Fb 18.37N 5.00 E

Index Symbols

[1] Independent Nation
[2] State, Region
[3] District, County
[4] Municipality
[5] Colony, Dependency
Continent
Physical Region
Historical or Cultural Region
Mount, Mountain
Volcano
Hill
Mountains, Mountain Range
Hills, Escarpment
Plateau, Upland
Pass, Gap
Plain, Lowland
Delta
Salt Flat
Valley, Canyon
Crater, Cave
Karst Features
Depression
Polder
Desert, Dunes
Forest, Woods
Heath, Steppe
Oasis
Cape, Point
Coast, Beach
Cliff
Peninsula
Isthmus
Sandbank
Island
Atoll
Rock, Reef
Islands, Archipelago
Rocks, Reefs
Coral Reef
Well, Spring
Geyser
River, Stream
Waterfall Rapids
River Mouth, Estuary
Lake
Salt Lake
Intermittent Lake
Reservoir
Swamp, Pond
Canal
Glacier
Ice Shelf, Pack Ice
Ocean
Sea
Gulf, Bay
Strait, Fjord
Lagoon
Bank
Seamount
Tablemount
Ridge
Shelf
Basin
Escarpment, Sea Scarp
Fracture
Trench, Abyss
National Park, Reserve
Point of Interest
Recreation Site
Cave, Cavern
Historic Site
Ruins
Wall, Walls
Church, Abbey
Temple
Scientific Station
Airport
Port
Lighthouse
Mine
Tunnel
Dam, Bridge

Jadar [Yugo.] 15 Ce 44.38N 19.16 E
Jaddi, Rās- 25 Cc 25.14N 63.31 E
Jade 10 Ec 53.25N 8.05 E
Jadebusen 10 Ec 53.30N 8.10 E
Jadīd Ra's al Fīl 35 Dc 12.40N 25.43 E
Jadito Wash 46 Ji 35.22N 110.50W
J.A.D. Jensens Nunatakker 41 Hf 62.45N 48.20W
Jädraås 8 Gd 60.51N 16.28 E
Jadransko More = Adriatic Sea (EN) 5 Hg 43.00N 16.00 E
Jadrin 7 Li 55.57N 46.11 E
Jādū 33 Bc 31.57N 12.01 E
Ja'ël 35 Ic 10.56N 51.09 E
Jaén [3] 13 If 38.00N 3.30W
Jaén 13 Ig 37.46N 3.47W
Jæren 8 Af 58.45N 5.45 E
Jærens rev 8 Af 58.45N 5.29 E
Jaffa, Cape- 59 Hg 36.58S 139.40 E
Jaffna 22 Ji 9.40N 80.00 E
Jafr, Qā' al- 24 Gg 30.17N 36.20 E
Jägala Jõgi 8 Ke 59.28N 25.04 E
Jagdalpur 22 Kh 19.04N 82.02 E
Jagdaqi 27 La 50.26N 124.02 E
Jaghbūb, Wāḥāt al- = Jarabub Oasis (EN) 30 Jf 29.41N 24.43 E
Jagotin 16 Gd 50.17N 31.47 E
Jagst 10 Fg 49.14N 9.11 E
Jaguapitã 55 Gf 23.07S 51.33W
Jaguaquara 54 Kf 13.32S 39.58W
Jaguarão 56 Jd 32.34S 53.23W
Jaguarão, Rio- 55 Fk 32.39S 53.12W
Jaguarari 54 Jf 10.16S 40.12W
Jaguari 55 Ei 29.30S 54.41W
Jaguari, Rio- [Braz.] 55 Ei 29.42S 55.07W
Jaguari, Rio- [Braz.] 55 If 22.41S 47.17W
Jaguariaíva 56 Kb 24.15S 49.42W
Jaguaribe 54 Ke 5.53S 38.37W
Jaguaribe, Rio 52 Mf 4.25S 37.45W
Jaguaruana 54 Kd 4.50S 37.47W
Jagüey Grande 49 Gb 22.32N 81.08W
Jahadyjaha 17 Pc 67.03N 72.01 E
Jahām, 'Irq- 24 Li 26.12N 47.00 E
Jahorina 14 Mg 43.42N 18.35 E
Jahrom 23 Hd 28.31N 53.33 E
Jaice 23 Ff 44.21N 17.17 E
Jaicoa, Cordillera- 51a Ab 18.25N 67.05W
Jaicós 54 Je 7.21S 41.08W
Jailolo 26 If 1.05N 127.30 E
Jailolo, Selat- 26 If 0.05N 129.05 E
Jaina, Isla de- 48 Ng 20.14N 90.40W
Jainca 27 Hd 35.57N 102.00 E
Jaipur 22 Jg 26.55N 75.49 E
Jaisalmer 25 Ec 26.55N 70.54 E
Jaja 20 De 56.12N 86.26 E
Jājarm 24 Qd 36.58N 56.27 E
Jajdúdorog 10 Ri 47.49N 21.30 E
Jajere 34 Hc 11.59N 11.26 E
Jajpan 18 Hd 40.23N 70.50 E
Jajsan 16 Td 50.51N 56.14 E
Jajva 19 Fd 59.20N 57.16 E
Jajva 17 Hg 59.16N 56.42 E
Jakarta 22 Mj 6.10S 106.46 E
Jakobshavn/Ilulissat 67 Nc 69.20N 50.50W
Jakobstad/Pietarsaari 7 Fe 63.40N 22.42 E
Jakoruda 15 Gg 42.02N 23.40 E
Jakupica 15 Eh 41.43N 21.26 E
Jakutsk 22 Oc 62.13N 129.49 E
Jakutskaja ASSR → Saha (Jakutija), respublika 20 Hc 67.00N 130.00 E
Jal 45 Ej 32.07N 103.12W
Jalaid Qi (Inder) 27 Lb 46.41N 122.52 E
Jalājil 24 Kj 25.41N 45.28 E
Jalālābād 23 Lc 34.26N 70.28 E
Jalālah al Baḥrīyah, Jabal al- 24 Eh 29.20N 32.20 E
Jalālah al Qiblīyah, Jabal al- 24 Eh 28.42N 32.22 E
Jalán, Río- 49 Df 15.43N 87.34W
Jalandhar 22 Jf 31.19N 75.34 E
Jalapa [3] 49 Cf 14.35N 89.55W
Jalapa [Guat.] 47 Gf 14.38N 89.59W
Jalapa [Mex.] 48 Mi 17.43N 92.49W
Jalapa [Nic.] 47 Gf 13.55N 86.08W
Jalapa Enriquez 39 Jh 19.32N 96.55W
Jalasjarvi 7 Fe 62.30N 22.45 E
Jales 55 Ge 20.16S 50.33W
Jālgaon 25 Fd 21.01N 75.34 E
Jalhay 12 Hd 50.34N 5.58 E
Jalībah 24 Lg 30.35N 46.32 E
Jalib Shahab 24 Lg 30.23N 46.09 E
Jalingo 34 Hd 8.53N 11.22 E
Jalisco [2] 47 Dd 20.20N 103.40W
Jāliṭah = La Galite (EN) 30 He 37.32N 8.56 E
Jāliṭah, Canal de- 14 Cm 37.20N 9.00 E
Jallas 13 Cb 42.54N 9.08W
Jālna 25 Fe 19.50N 75.53 E
Jalón 13 Kc 41.47N 1.04W
Jalostotitlán 48 Hg 21.12N 102.28W
Jalpa 48 Hg 21.38N 102.58W
Jalpaiguri 25 Hc 26.31N 88.44 E
Jalpan 48 Jg 21.14N 99.29W
Jalpug, Ozero- 16 Fg 45.25N 28.40 E
Jalta 19 Dg 44.30N 34.10 E
Jaltepec, Rio- 48 Li 17.26N 94.59W
Jālū 33 Dd 28.30N 21.05 E
Jālū, Wāḥāt- = Gialo Oasis (EN) 30 Jf 29.00N 21.20 E
Jaluit Atoll 57 Hd 6.00N 169.35 E
Jalūlā' 24 Ke 34.16N 45.10 E
Jalutorovsk 19 Gd 56.40N 66.18 E
Jam [Iran] 24 Pe 35.45N 55.02 E
Jam [Iran] 24 Oi 27.50N 52.22 E
Jama/Jaama 8 Lf 58.59N 27.45 E
Jamaari 30 Ig 12.06N 10.14 E
Jamaica 49 Jc 20.12N 75.09W
Jamaica 38 Lh 18.15N 77.30W
Jamaica [1] 39 Lh 18.15N 77.30W
Jamaica Channel 47 Ie 18.00N 75.30W
Jamaica Channel (EN) = Jamaïque, Canal de- 49 Jd 18.00N 75.30W
Jamaïque, Canal de- = Jamaica Channel (EN) 49 Jd 18.00N 75.30W
Jamal, Poluostrov- = Yamal Peninsula (EN) 21 Ib 70.00N 70.00 E
Jamalo-Neneckij respublika 20 Cc 67.00N 75.00 E
Jamālpur 25 Hd 24.55N 89.56 E
Jamāme 31 Lh 0.04N 42.46 E
Jamantau, Gora- 5 Le 54.15N 58.06 E
Jamanxim, Rio- 52 Kf 4.43S 56.18W
Jamari, Rio- 54 Fe 8.27S 63.30W
Jamarovka 20 Gf 50.38N 110.16 E
Jambi 22 Oj 1.38S 123.42 E
Jambi [3] 26 Dg 1.36S 103.37 E
Jambol [2] 15 Jg 42.15N 26.35 E
Jambol 15 Jg 42.29N 26.30 E
Jambongan, Pulau- 26 Ge 6.41N 117.25 E
Jambuair, Tanjung- 26 Ce 5.16N 97.30 E
Jambusar 25 Ed 22.03N 72.48 E
James Bay 38 Kd 51.00N 80.30W
Jameson Land 41 Jd 70.45N 23.45W
James River [U.S.] 38 Je 42.52N 97.18W
James River [U.S.] 44 Ig 36.56N 76.27W
James Ross 66 Re 64.15S 57.45W
James Ross Strait 42 Hc 69.50N 96.30W
Jamestown [Austl.] 59 Hf 33.12S 138.36 E
Jamestown [N.D.-U.S.] 43 Hb 46.54N 98.42W
Jamestown [N.Y.-U.S.] 43 Lc 42.05N 79.15W
Jamestown [St.Hel.] 31 Gj 15.56S 5.43W
Jamestown Reservoir 45 Gc 47.15N 98.40W
Jamm 8 Mf 58.24N 28.15 E
Jammer Bugt 7 Bh 57.20N 9.30 E
Jammu 22 Jf 32.44N 74.52 E
Jammu and Kashmir [3] 25 Fb 34.00N 76.00 E
Jāmnagar 22 Jg 22.28N 70.04 E
Jamno, Jezioro- 10 Mb 54.15N 16.10 E
Jampol 16 Fe 48.16N 28.17 E
Jämsä 7 Ff 61.52N 25.12 E
Jamsah 24 Ei 27.38N 33.35 E
Jämsänkoski 8 Kc 61.55N 25.11 E
Jamshedpur 22 Kg 22.48N 86.11 E
Jamsk 20 Ke 59.37N 154.10 E
Jämtland [2] 7 De 63.00N 14.00 E
Jämtland 8 Fa 63.25N 14.05 E
Janā 24 Mi 27.22N 49.54 E
Jana 21 Pb 71.31N 136.32 E
Janakpur 25 Hc 26.42N 85.55 E
Janaucu, Ilha- 54 Hc 0.30N 50.10W
Janaul 17 Gh 56.16N 54.59 E
Janda, Laguna de la- 13 Gh 36.15N 5.51W
Jandaia 55 Gc 17.06S 50.07W
Jandaq 24 Pe 34.02N 54.26 E
Jandiatuba, Rio- 54 Ed 3.28S 68.42W
Jandowae 59 Ke 26.47S 151.06 E
Jandula 13 Hf 38.03N 4.06W
Jane Peak 62 Cf 45.20S 168.19 E
Janesville 43 Jc 42.41N 89.01W
Jangada 55 Db 15.14S 56.29W
Jangada, Rio- 55 Db 15.12S 56.24W
Jangao Shan 27 Gf 25.31N 98.08 E
Jange 27 Ie 31.59N 105.28 E
Jangijer 18 Gd 40.18N 68.50 E
Jangijul 18 Gd 41.07N 69.03 E
Jangirabad 18 Gd 40.03N 65.59 E
Jango 55 Ee 20.27S 55.29W
Jangxi Sheng (Chiang-hsi Sheng) = Kiangsi (EN) [2] 27 Kf 28.00N 116.00 E
Jangy-Bazar 18 Hd 41.40N 70.52 E
Janikowo 10 Od 52.45N 18.07 E
Janīn 24 Ff 32.28N 35.18 E
Janisjarvi, Ozero- 7 He 62.00N 31.00 E
Janja 14 Nf 44.40N 19.19 E
Jan Mayen 5 Fa 71.00N 8.30W
Jan Mayen Ridge (EN) 5 Fb 69.00N 8.00W
Jano-Indigirskaja Nizmennost 20 Ib 71.00N 139.30 E
Janos 47 Cb 30.56N 108.08W
Jánoshalma 10 Pj 46.18N 19.20 E
Jánosháza 10 Ni 47.07N 17.10 E
Janów Lubelski 10 Sf 50.43N 22.24 E
Janów Podlaski 10 Td 52.11N 23.11 E
Jansenville 37 Cf 32.56S 24.40 E
Jansha Jang 21 Mg 28.46N 104.38 E
Janski Zaliv 21 Pb 72.00N 136.00 E
Jantarny 8 Hj 54.53N 19.55 E
Jantra 15 If 43.38N 25.34 E
Januária 54 Jg 15.29S 44.22W
Janūbīyah, Aş Şaḥrā' al- = Southern Desert (EN) 30 Jf 24.00N 30.00 E
Janykurgan 19 Gg 43.55N 67.14 E
Janzhang Ansha 27 Ke 9.30N 116.59 E
Japan (EN) 21 Pf 35.00N 135.00 E
Japan (EN) = Nippon [1] 22 Pf 38.00N 137.00 E
Japan, Sea of- (EN) = Japonskoje More 21 Pf 40.00N 134.00 E
Japan, Sea of- (EN) = Nippon Kai 21 Pf 40.00N 134.00 E
Japan, Sea of- (EN) = Tong-Hae 21 Pf 40.00N 134.00 E
Japan Basin (EN) 27 Nc 40.00N 135.00 E
Japan Trench (EN) 3 If 37.00N 143.00 E
Japiim 54 De 7.37S 72.54W
Japonskoje More = Japan, Sea of- (EN) 21 Pf 40.00N 134.00 E
Jäppilä 8 Lb 62.23N 27.26 E
Japtiksale 17 Pb 69.25N 72.29 E
Japurá 54 Ed 1.24S 69.25W
Japurá, Rio- 52 Jf 3.08S 64.46W
Jaqué 49 Hj 7.31N 78.10W
Jaquet, Point- 51g Ba 15.38N 61.26W
Jaquirana 55 Gi 28.54S 50.23W
Jar 7 Mg 58.17N 52.06 E
Jarabub Oasis (EN) = Jaghbūb, Wāḥāt al- 30 Jf 29.41N 24.43 E
Jarābulus 24 Hd 36.49N 38.01 E
Jaraguá [Braz.] 55 Hb 15.45S 49.20W
Jaraguá [Braz.] 55 Hh 26.29S 49.04W
Jaraguá, Serra do- 55 Hh 26.40S 49.15W
Jaraguari 55 Ee 20.09S 54.25W
Jaraiz de la Vera 13 Gd 40.04N 5.45W
Jarama 13 Id 40.02N 3.39W
Jaramillo 56 Gg 47.11S 67.09W
Jarandilla 13 Gd 40.08N 5.39W
Jaransk 19 Ed 57.18N 47.55 E
Jaränwäla 25 Eb 31.20N 73.26 E
Jarash 24 Ff 32.17N 35.54 E
Jarau, Cêrro do- 55 Dj 30.18S 56.32W
Jarbah 30 Ie 33.48N 10.54 E
Järbo 7 Df 60.43N 16.36 E
Jarcevo 16 Hb 55.05N 32.45 E
Jarcevo 20 Ed 60.15N 90.10 E
Jardāwīyah 24 Jj 25.24N 42.42 E
Jardim 54 Gh 21.28S 56.09W
Jardine River 59 Ib 11.10S 142.30 E
Jardines de la Reina, Archipiélago de los- 47 Id 20.50N 78.55W
Jardinópolis 55 Ie 21.02S 47.46W
Jarega 17 Fe 63.27N 53.29 E
Jaremča 16 De 48.31N 24.33 E
Jarenga 7 Le 62.08N 49.03 E
Jarez de Garcias Salinas 47 Dd 22.39N 103.00W
Järfälla 8 Ge 59.24N 17.50 E
Jargava 15 Lc 46.27N 28.27 E
Jari, Rio- 52 Kf 1.09S 51.54W
Jarīd, Shaṭṭ al- 30 He 33.42N 8.26 E
Jarīr, Wādī- 24 Jj 25.38N 42.30 E
Jarjis 32 Jc 33.30N 11.07 E
Jarkovo 17 Mh 57.26N 67.05 E
Jarmah 33 Bd 26.32N 13.04 E
Järna 8 Ge 59.06N 17.34 E
Jarnac 11 Fi 45.41N 0.10W
Järnlunden 8 Ff 58.10N 15.40 E
Jarny 11 Le 49.09N 5.53 E
Jarocin 10 Ne 51.59N 17.31 E
Jaroměř 10 Lf 50.21N 15.55 E
Jaroměřice nad Rokytnou 10 Lg 49.06N 15.54 E
Jaroslavl 6 Jd 57.37N 39.52 E
Jaroslavskaja Oblast [3] 19 Dd 57.45N 39.15 E
Jaroslavski 28 Lb 44.10N 132.13 E
Jarosław 10 Sf 50.02N 22.42 E
Järpen 8 Ea 63.21N 13.29 E
Jarrāḥī 24 Mg 30.44N 48.46 E
Jarroto, Ozero- 17 Oc 67.55N 71.40 E
Jar-Sale 20 Cc 66.50N 70.50 E
Jartai 27 Id 39.45N 105.46 E
Jartai Yanchi 27 Id 39.45N 105.40 E
Jarudej 17 Od 65.50N 71.50 E
Jarud Qi (Lubei) 27 Lc 44.30N 120.55 E
Järva-Jaani/Jarva-Jani 8 Ke 59.00N 25.49 E
Jarva-Jani/Järva-Jaani 8 Ke 59.00N 25.49 E
Järvakandi/Jarvakandi 8 Kf 58.45N 24.44 E
Jarvakandi/Järvakandi 8 Kf 58.45N 24.44 E
Järvenpää 7 Ff 60.28N 25.06 E
Jarvis Island 57 Ke 0.23S 160.01W
Järvsö 7 Df 61.43N 16.10 E
Jašćera 8 Ne 59.05N 30.00 E
Jaselda 16 Ec 52.07N 26.29 E
Jasień 10 Le 51.46N 15.01 E
Jasikan 34 Fd 7.24N 0.28 E
Jasinja 10 Uh 48.14N 24.31 E
Jasinovataja 16 Je 48.05N 37.57 E
Jasiołka 10 Rg 49.47N 21.30 E
Jasira 35 He 1.57N 45.16 E
Jasired Mayd 35 Hc 11.12N 47.13 E
Jašk 23 Id 25.38N 57.46 E
Jaškul 16 Nf 46.17N 45.10 E
Jaškul 16 Nf 46.11N 45.17 E
Jasło 10 Rg 49.45N 21.29 E
Jasmund 10 Jb 54.32N 13.35 E
Jasnogorsk 16 Jb 54.29N 37.42 E
Jasny 16 Fe 51.01N 59.59 E
Jasny 20 Hf 53.18N 128.03 E
Jason Islands 56 Hh 51.00S 61.00W
Jasper [Alta.-Can.] 39 Hd 52.53N 118.05W
Jasper [Al.-U.S.] 43 Je 33.50N 87.17W
Jasper [Fl.-U.S.] 44 Fj 30.31N 82.57W
Jasper [In.-U.S.] 44 Df 38.24N 86.56W
Jasper [Tn.-U.S.] 44 Eh 35.04N 85.38W
Jasper [Tx.-U.S.] 45 Jk 30.55N 93.59W
Jasper Seamount (EN) 38 Gf 30.32N 122.42W
Jaşşān 24 Kf 32.58N 45.53 E
Jastrebarsko 14 Je 45.40N 15.39 E
Jastrowie 10 Mc 53.26N 16.49 E
Jastrzebie Zdrój 10 Og 49.58N 18.34 E
Jászapáti 10 Qi 47.31N 20.09 E
Jászárokszállás 10 Pi 47.38N 19.59 E
Jászberény 10 Pi 47.30N 19.55 E
Jász-Nagykun-Szolnok 10 Qi 47.15N 20.30 E
Jászság 10 Pi 47.25N 20.00 E
Jatai 53 Kg 17.53S 51.43W
Jatapu, Rio- 54 Gd 2.30S 58.17W
Játiva/Xàtiva 13 Lf 38.59N 0.31W
Jatobá, Rio- 55 Ea 12.23S 54.07W
Jaú 56 Kb 22.18S 48.33W
Jaú, Rio- 54 Fd 1.55S 61.25W
Jaua, Cerro- 54 Fc 4.48N 64.26W
Jauaperi, Rio- 52 Jf 1.26S 61.35W
Jauja 54 Cf 11.48S 75.30W
Jaumave 48 Jf 23.25N 99.23W
Jaunanna 8 Lg 57.13N 27.10 E
Jaunelgava/Jaunjelgava 7 Fh 56.37N 25.06 E
Jaunfeld 14 Id 46.35N 14.45 E
Jaungulbene 8 Lh 57.00N 26.42 E
Jaunjelgava/Jaunelgava 7 Fh 56.37N 25.06 E
Jaunpiebalga 8 Lg 57.05N 26.03 E
Jaunpur 25 Gc 25.44N 82.41 E
Jauru 55 Ed 18.35S 54.17W
Jauru, Rio- [Braz.] 54 Hg 18.40S 54.36W
Jauru, Rio- [Braz.] 55 Dc 16.22S 57.46W
Java (EN) = Jawa 21 Mj 7.20S 110.00 E
Javalambre 13 Ld 40.06N 1.00W
Javalambre, Sierra de- 13 Ld 40.05N 1.00W
Javan 18 Ge 38.19N 69.01 E
Javānrūd 24 Le 34.48N 46.30 E
Javari, Rio- 52 If 4.21S 70.02W
Java Sea (EN) = Jawa, Laut- 21 Mj 5.00S 110.00 E
Java Trench (EN) 3 Hk 10.30S 110.00 E
Jávea 13 Mf 38.47N 0.10 E
Javier 13 Kb 42.36N 1.13W
Javor 14 Mf 44.07N 18.59 E
Javorie 10 Ph 48.27N 19.18 E
Javornik 10 Jh 48.10N 13.35 E
Javorníky 10 Og 49.20N 18.20 E
Javorov 16 Cd 50.00N 23.27 E
Javorová skála 10 Kg 49.31N 14.30 E
Jävre 7 Ed 65.09N 21.29 E
Jawa = Java (EN) 21 Mj 7.20S 110.00 E
Jawa, Laut- = Java Sea (EN) 21 Mj 5.00S 110.00 E
Jawa Barat [3] 26 Eh 7.00S 107.00 E
Jawa Tengah [3] 26 Eh 7.30S 110.00 E
Jawa Timur [3] 26 Fh 8.00S 113.00 E
Jawf, Wādī- 33 If 15.50N 45.30 E
Jawor 10 Me 51.03N 16.11 E
Jaworzno 10 Pf 50.13N 19.15 E
Jaya, Puncak- 57 Ee 4.10S 137.00 E
Jayapura 58 Fe 2.32S 140.42 E
Jayawijaya, Pegunungan- 26 Kg 4.30S 139.30 E
Jāyezān 24 Mg 30.50N 49.52 E
Jaypur 25 He 18.51N 82.35 E
Jazāyer va Banāder-e Khalīj-e Fārs va Daryā-ye Omān → Hormozgān 23 Id 27.30N 56.00 E
Jaz Mūrīān, Hāmūn-e- 23 Id 27.20N 58.55 E
Jazva 17 Hf 60.23N 56.50 E
Jazvān 24 Md 36.58N 48.40 E
Jazykovo 7 Li 54.20N 47.22 E
Jazzīn 24 Ff 33.32N 35.34 E
Jdiouia 13 Mi 35.56N 0.50 E
Jeannetty, Ostrov- 20 Ka 76.45N 158.25 E
Jean-Rabel 49 Kd 19.52N 73.11W
Jebala 13 Gi 35.25N 5.30W
Jebal Bārez, Kūh-e- 23 Id 28.30N 58.20 E
Jebba 34 Fd 9.08N 4.50 E
Jebel 15 Ed 45.33N 21.14 E
Jebha 13 Hi 35.13N 4.40W
Jedincy 16 Ee 48.06N 27.19 E
Jedisa 16 Nh 42.32N 44.14 E
Jędrzejów 10 Qf 50.39N 20.18 E
Jeetze 10 Hc 53.09N 11.04 E
Jefferson 45 Ie 42.01N 94.23W
Jefferson, Mount- [Nv.-U.S.] 43 Dd 38.46N 116.55W
Jefferson, Mount- [Or.-U.S.] 46 Ed 44.40N 121.47W
Jefferson City 39 Jf 38.34N 92.10W
Jefferson River 46 Jd 45.56N 111.30W
Jeffersonville 44 Ef 38.17N 85.44W
Jef-Jef el Kebir 35 Ca 20.30N 21.25 E
Jefremov 16 Jc 53.11N 38.07 E
Jega 34 Fc 12.13N 4.23 E
Jegersfontein 37 De 29.44S 25.29 E
Jegorjevsk 7 Ji 55.25N 39.07 E
Jegorlyk 16 Lf 46.32N 41.52 E
Jegorlykskaja 16 Lf 46.34N 40.44 E
Jehegnadzor 16 Nj 39.47N 45.18 E
Jeja 16 Kf 46.39N 38.36 E
Jejsk 19 Df 46.42N 38.16 E
Jēkabpils 19 Cd 56.30N 25.59 E
Jekaterinburg (Sverdlovsk) 22 Id 56.51N 60.36 E
Jekaterinburgskaja oblast 19 Gd 59.00N 62.00 E
Jekaterinovka 16 Nc 52.04N 44.30 E
Jelabuga 19 Fd 55.48N 52.05 E
Jelai 26 Fg 2.59S 110.45 E
Jelan 16 Md 50.57N 43.43 E
Jelancy 20 Ff 52.44N 106.27 E
Jelanec 16 Gf 47.42N 31.50 E
Jelcz 10 Ne 51.01N 17.18 E
Jelec 6 Je 52.37N 38.30 E
Jeleckj 17 Lc 67.03N 64.15 E
Jelenia Góra 10 Lf 50.55N 15.46 E
Jelenia Góra [2] 10 Lf 50.55N 15.45 E
Jelgava 19 Cd 56.39N 23.41 E
Jelica 15 Df 43.47N 20.20 E
Jelin vrh 15 Cf 43.02N 19.27 E
Jelizavety, Mys- 5 Qd 54.30N 142.40 E
Jelizovo 16 Fc 53.24N 29.00 E
Jelizovo 20 Kf 53.06N 158.20 E
Jelling 8 Ci 55.45N 9.26 E
Jelnja 16 Hb 54.35N 33.12 E
Jeloguj 20 Dd 63.10N 87.45 E
Jelow Gīr 24 Lf 32.58N 47.48 E
Jeløy 8 De 58.30N 10.40 E
Jelsk 16 Fd 51.49N 29.13 E
Jelva 17 Ee 63.05N 50.50 E
Jemaja, Pulau- 26 Ef 2.55N 105.45 E
Jemanželinsk 19 Ge 54.45N 61.20 E
Jember 26 Fh 8.10S 113.42 E
Jemca 7 Je 63.32N 41.56 E
Jemca 7 Je 63.04N 40.18 E
Jemeppe-sur-Sambre 12 Gd 50.28N 4.40 E
Jeminay 27 Eb 47.28N 85.48 E
Jemnice 10 Lg 49.01N 15.35 E
Jena 10 Hf 50.56N 11.35 E
Jenakijevo 16 Ke 48.12N 38.18 E
Jenašimski Polkan, Gora- 20 Ee 59.50N 92.45 E
Jendyr 17 Mf 61.38N 67.20 E
Jeneponto 26 Gh 5.41S 119.42 E
Jenisej = Yenisey (EN) 21 Kb 71.50N 82.40 E
Jenisejsk 20 Ee 58.27N 92.10 E
Jenisejski Krjaž = Yenisey Ridge (EN) 21 Ld 59.00N 92.30 E
Jenisejski Zaliv = Yenisey Bay (EN) 20 Db 72.00N 81.00 E
Jennersdorf 14 Kd 46.56N 16.08 E
Jennings 45 Jk 30.13N 92.39W
Jenny Lind 42 Hc 68.50N 101.30W
Jenny Point 51g Bb 15.28N 61.15W
Jensen 46 Kf 40.22N 109.17W
Jens Munk 42 Jc 69.40N 79.40W
Jequié 53 Lg 13.51S 40.05W
Jequitaí 55 Jc 17.15S 44.28W
Jequitaí, Rio 55 Jc 17.04S 44.50W
Jequitinhonha, Rio- 52 Mg 15.51S 38.53W
Jerada 32 Gc 34.19N 2.09W
Jeralijev 19 Fg 43.12N 51.43 E
Jerbogačēn 20 Fd 61.15N 107.57 E
Jérémie 47 Je 18.39N 74.08W
Jeremoabo 54 Kf 10.04S 38.21W
Jerer 35 Gd 7.40N 43.48 E
Jerevan 6 Kg 40.11N 44.30 E
Jerez, Punta- 48 Kf 22.54N 97.46W
Jerez de la Frontera 13 Fh 36.41N 6.08W
Jerez de los Caballeros 13 Ff 38.19N 6.46W
Jergeni 5 Kf 47.00N 44.00 E
Jericho 59 Jd 23.36S 146.08 E
Jermak 19 He 52.02N 76.55 E
Jermakovskoje 20 Ef 53.16N 92.24 E
Jermentau 19 He 51.38N 73.10 E
Jermolajevo (Kumertau) 19 Fe 52.46N 55.47 E
Jeroaquara 55 Gb 15.23S 50.25W
Jerofej Pavlovič 20 Hf 53.58N 121.57 E
Jerome 46 He 42.43N 114.31W
Jersa 17 Fc 66.19N 52.32 E
Jersey 9 Kl 49.15N 2.10W
Jersey City 43 Mc 40.44N 74.04W
Jerseyville 45 Kg 39.07N 90.20W
Jeršov 19 Ee 51.20N 48.17 E
Jertarski 17 Lh 56.47N 64.25 E
Jerte 13 Fe 39.58N 6.17W
Jerusalem (EN) = Yerushalayim 22 Ff 31.46N 35.14 E
Jeruslan 16 Od 50.20N 46.25 E
Jervis Bay 59 Kg 35.05S 150.44 E
Jerzu 14 Dk 39.47N 9.31 E
Jesberg 12 Lc 51.00N 9.09 E
Jesenice 14 Jf 44.14N 15.34 E
Jesenice 14 Id 46.27N 14.04 E
Jesenik 10 Nf 50.14N 17.12 E
Jesi 14 Hg 43.31N 13.14 E
Jesil 19 Ge 51.58N 66.24 E
Jeskianhor, Kanal- 18 Fe 39.15N 66.00 E
Jessej 20 Fc 68.29N 102.10 E
Jessentuki 16 Mg 44.03N 42.51 E
Jessheim 7 Cf 60.09N 11.11 E
Jessore 25 Hd 23.10N 89.13 E
Ještěd 10 Kf 50.42N 14.59 E
Jestro, Wabe- 30 Lh 4.11N 42.09 E
Jesup 43 Ke 31.36N 81.53W
Jesús Carranza 48 Li 17.26N 95.02W
Jesús Maria 56 Hd 30.59S 64.06W
Jesús Maria, Boca de- 48 Ke 24.29N 97.40W
Jesús Maria, Rio- 48 Gg 21.55N 104.30W
Jetmore 45 Gg 38.03N 99.54W
Jever 10 Dc 53.35N 7.54 E
Jevgenjevka 18 Kc 43.27N 77.40 E
Jevišovka 10 Mh 48.52N 16.36 E
Jevlah 19 Eg 40.35N 47.10 E
Jevnaker 7 Cf 60.15N 10.28 E
Jevpatorija 19 Df 45.12N 33.18 E
Jeyḥūn 24 Pi 27.16N 55.12 E
Jeypore → Jaypur 25 He 18.51N 82.35 E
Jezercës 5 Hg 42.26N 19.49 E
Jezero 14 Lf 44.21N 17.10 E
Jeziorak, Jezioro- 10 Pc 53.50N 19.35 E
Jeziorany 10 Qc 53.58N 20.46 E
Jeziorka 10 Rd 52.10N 21.06 E
Jhang Sadar 25 Eb 31.16N 72.19 E
Jhānsi 22 Jg 25.26N 78.35 E
Jhelum 25 Eb 32.56N 73.44 E
Jhelum 21 Jf 31.12N 72.08 E
Jiaji → Qionghai 27 Jh 19.25N 110.28 E
Jialing Jiang 21 Mg 29.34N 106.35 E
Jiamusi 22 Pe 46.49N 130.21 E
Ji'an [China] 27 Mc 41.08N 126.10 E
Ji'an [China] 22 Ng 27.12N 114.59 E
Jianchang 28 Ed 40.49N 119.46 E
Jianchuan 27 Gf 26.32N 99.53 E
Jiande (Baisha) 27 Kf 29.31N 119.17 E
Jiang'an 27 If 28.40N 105.07 E
Jiangao Shan 27 Gf 25.31N 98.08 E
Jiangbiancun 27 Kf 27.13N 115.57 E
Jiangcheng 27 Hg 22.37N 101.48 E
Jiangdu (Xiannümiao) 28 Eh 32.30N 119.33 E
Jianghua (Shuikou) 27 Jg 24.58N 111.56 E
Jiangjin 27 If 29.15N 106.18 E
Jiangle 27 Kf 26.48N 117.29 E
Jiangling (Jingzhou) 27 Je 30.21N 112.10 E
Jiangmen 27 Jg 22.35N 113.02 E
Jiangpu 28 Eh 32.03N 118.37 E
Jiangshan 28 Ej 28.45N 118.37 E
Jiangsu Sheng (Chiang-su Sheng) = Kiangsu (EN) [2] 27 Ke 33.00N 120.00 E
Jiangyou (Zhongba) 27 He 31.48N 104.39 E
Jianhu 28 Eh 33.28N 119.47 E
Jianli 27 Jf 29.50N 112.55 E
Jian'ou 27 Kf 27.08N 118.20 E
Jianping (Yebaishou) 27 Kc 41.55N 119.37 E
Jianshi 27 Ie 30.32N 109.43 E
Jianshui 27 Hg 23.39N 102.46 E
Jianyang 27 Kf 27.23N 118.03 E
Jiaocheng 27 Jd 37.32N 112.09 E
Jiaoding Shan 27 Lc 41.11N 120.01 E
Jiaohe [China] 27 Mc 43.43N 127.20 E
Jiaohe [China] 28 De 38.01N 116.17 E
Jiaolai He [China] 28 Ef 37.07N 119.35 E
Jiaolai He [China] 28 Fc 43.02N 120.48 E
Jiaoliu He 28 Gb 45.21N 122.48 E
Jiaonan (Wanggezhuang) 28 Eg 35.53N 119.58 E

Index Symbols

[1] Independent Nation
[2] State, Region
[3] District, County
[4] Municipality
[5] Colony, Dependency
Continent
Physical Region
Historical or Cultural Region
Mount, Mountain
Volcano
Hill
Mountains, Mountain Range
Hills, Escarpment
Plateau, Upland
Pass, Gap
Plain, Lowland
Delta
Salt Flat
Valley, Canyon
Crater, Cave
Karst Features
Depression
Polder
Desert, Dunes
Forest, Woods
Heath, Steppe
Oasis
Cape, Point
Coast, Beach
Cliff
Peninsula
Isthmus
Sandbank
Island
Atoll
Rock, Reef
Islands, Archipelago
Rocks, Reefs
Coral Reef
Well, Spring
Geyser
River, Stream
Waterfall Rapids
River Mouth, Estuary
Lake
Salt Lake
Intermittent Lake
Reservoir
Swamp, Pond
Canal
Glacier
Ice Shelf, Pack Ice
Ocean
Sea
Gulf, Bay
Strait, Fjord
Lagoon
Bank
Seamount
Tablemount
Ridge
Shelf
Basin
Escarpment, Sea Scarp
Fracture
Trench, Abyss
National Park, Reserve
Point of Interest
Recreation Site
Cave, Cavern
Historic Site
Ruins
Wall, Walls
Church, Abbey
Temple
Scientific Station
Airport
Port
Lighthouse
Mine
Tunnel
Dam, Bridge

International Map Index

Index Symbols

[1] Independent Nation	Historical or Cultural Region	Pass, Gap
[2] State, Region	Mount, Mountain	Plain, Lowland
[3] District, County	Volcano	Delta
[4] Municipality	Hill	Salt Flat
[5] Colony, Dependency	Mountains, Mountain Range	Valley, Canyon
[■] Continent	Hills, Escarpment	Crater, Cave
[C] Physical Region	Plateau, Upland	Karst Features

Depression	Coast, Beach	Rock, Reef
Polder	Cliff	Islands, Archipelago
Desert, Dunes	Peninsula	Rocks, Reefs
Forest, Woods	Isthmus	Coral Reef
Heath, Steppe	Sandbank	Well, Spring
Oasis	Island	Geyser
Cape, Point	Atoll	River, Stream

Waterfall Rapids	Canal	Lagoon
River Mouth, Estuary	Glacier	Bank, Seamount
Lake	Ice Shelf, Pack Ice	Fracture
Salt Lake	Ocean	Trench, Abyss
Intermittent Lake	Sea	Tableland
Reservoir	Gulf, Bay	Ridge
Swamp, Pond	Strait, Fjord	Shelf
		Basin

Escarpment, Sea Scarp	Historic Site	Port
National Park, Reserve	Ruins	Lighthouse
Point of Interest	Wall, Walls	Mine
Recreation Site	Church, Abbey	Tunnel
Cave, Cavern	Temple	Dam, Bridge
	Scientific Station	
	Airport	

Kabunga	36	Ec	1.42S	28.08 E
Kaburuang, Pulau-	26	If	3.48N	126.48 E
Kabwe	31	Jj	14.27S	28.27 E
Kača	16	Hg	44.44N	33.32 E
Kačanik	15	Eg	42.14N	21.15 E
Kačanovo	8	Lg	57.24N	27.53 E
Kaçergine	8	Jj	54.53N	23.49 E
Kachchh, Gulf of	21	Ig	22.36N	69.30 E
Kachchh, Rann of	25	Dd	23.51N	70.30 E
Kachia	34	Gd	9.52N	7.57 E
Kachikau	37	Cc	18.09S	24.29 E
Kachin [2]	25	Jc	26.00N	97.30 E
Kachul (Kagul)	19	Cf	45.53N	28.14 E
Kačiry	19	He	53.04N	76.07 E
Kačkanar	19	Fd	58.42N	59.35 E
Kačug	20	Ff	54.00N	105.52 E
Kaczawa	10	Me	51.18N	16.27 E
Kadada	16	Oc	53.09N	46.01 E
Kadaň	10	Jf	50.23N	13.16 E
Kadan Kyun	25	Jf	12.30N	98.22 E
Kadei	30	Ih	3.31N	16.03 E
Kadijevka	19	Df	48.32N	38.40 E
Kadiköy	24	Bb	40.51N	26.50 E
Kadıköy, İstanbul	15	Mi	40.59N	29.01 E
Kadina	59	Hf	33.58S	137.43 E
Kadınhanı	24	Ec	38.15N	32.14 E
Kadiolo	34	Dc	10.34N	5.45W
Kadiri	25	Ff	14.07N	78.10 E
Kadirli	23	Eb	37.23N	36.05 E
Kadja	35	Cc	12.02N	22.28 E
Kadmat Island	25	Ef	11.14N	72.47 E
Kadnikov	7	Jg	59.30N	40.24 E
Kadoka	45	Fe	43.50N	101.31W
Kaduj	7	Ig	59.14N	37.09 E
Kaduna [2]	34	Gc	11.00N	7.30 E
Kaduna	30	Hh	8.45N	5.48 E
Kaduna	31	Hg	10.31N	7.26 E
Kāduqlī	31	Jg	11.01N	29.43 E
Kadykčan	20	Jd	63.05N	146.58 E
Kadžaran	16	Oj	39.11N	46.10 E
Kadžerom	17	Gd	64.41N	55.54 E
Kadži-Saj	18	Kc	42.08N	77.10 E
Kaech'ŏn	28	He	39.42N	125.53 E
Kaédi	31	Fg	16.08N	13.31W
Kaélé	34	Hc	10.07N	14.27 E
Kaena Point	65a	Cb	21.35N	158.17W
Kaeo	62	Ea	35.06S	173.47 E
Kaesŏng	22	Of	37.58N	126.33 E
Kaesŏng Si [2]	28	Ie	38.05N	126.30 E
Kāf	24	Gg	31.24N	37.29 E
Kafakumba	36	Dd	9.41S	23.44 E
Kafan	19	Eh	39.12N	46.28 E
Kafanchan	34	Gd	9.35N	8.18 E
Kaffrine	34	Bc	14.06N	15.33W
Kafia Kingi	35	Cd	9.16N	24.25 E
Kafiréos, Dhiékplous-	15	Hl	38.00N	24.40 E
Kafirévs, Ákra-	15	Hk	38.10N	24.35 E
Kafr ad Dawwār	24	Dg	31.08N	30.07 E
Kafr ash Shaykh	33	Fc	31.07N	30.56 E
Kafta	35	Fc	13.54N	37.11 E
Kafu	36	Fb	1.39N	32.05 E
Kafue	30	Ef	15.56S	28.55 E
Kafue	31	Jj	15.47S	28.11 E
Kafue Dam	36	Ef	15.45S	28.28 E
Kafue Flats	36	Ef	15.40S	26.25 E
Kafufu	36	Fd	7.12S	31.31 E
Kaga	28	Nf	36.18N	136.18 E
Kaga Bandoro	35	Bd	7.02N	19.13 E
Kagalaska	40a	Cb	51.47N	176.23W
Kagalnik	16	Kf	47.04N	39.18 E
Kagami	29	Be	32.34N	130.40 E
Kagan	19	Gh	39.43N	64.32 E
Kagarlyk	16	Ge	49.53N	30.56 E
Kagawa Ken [2]	28	Mg	34.15N	134.15 E
Kagera	30	Ki	0.57S	31.47 E
Kağızman	24	Jb	40.09N	43.07 E
Kagoshima	22	Pf	31.36N	130.33 E
Kagoshima Bay (EN) = Kagoshima-Wan	28	Ki	31.27N	130.40 E
Kagoshima Ken [2]	28	Ki	31.45N	130.40 E
Kagoshima-Taniyama	29	Bf	31.31N	130.31 E
Kagoshima-Wan = Kagoshima Bay (EN)	28	Ki	31.27N	130.40 E
Kagul → Kachul	19	Cf	45.53N	28.14 E
Kahal Tabelbala	32	Gd	28.45N	2.15W
Kahama	36	Fc	3.50S	32.36 E
Kahemba	31	Ii	7.17S	19.00 E
Kahi	16	Oi	41.23N	46.59 E
Kahiu Point	65a	Eb	21.13N	156.58W
Kahler Asten	10	Ee	51.11N	8.29 E
Kahnūj	24	Qi	27.58N	57.47 E
Kahoku	29	Gb	38.30N	141.20 E
Kahoku-Gata	29	Ec	36.40N	136.40 E
Kahoolawe Island	57	Lb	20.33N	156.35W
Kahouanne, Ilet à-	51e	Ab	16.22N	61.47W
Kahovka	19	Df	46.47N	33.32 E
Kahovskoje Vodohranilišče = Kakhovka Reservoir (EN)	5	Jf	47.25N	34.10 E
Kahramanmaraş	23	Eb	37.36N	36.55 E
Kahrūyeh	24	Ng	31.43N	51.48 E
Kâhta	24	Hd	37.46N	38.36 E
Kahuku	65a	Db	21.41N	157.57W
Kahuku Point	65a	Db	21.43N	157.59W
Kahului	65a	Ec	20.53N	156.27W
Kahului Bay	65a	Ec	20.55N	156.30W
Kahurangi Point	62	Ed	40.46S	172.13 E
Kai, Kepulauan-	57	Ee	5.35S	132.45 E
Kaiama	34	Fd	9.36N	3.57 E
Kaiapoi	62	Ee	43.23S	172.39 E
Kaibab Plateau	46	Ih	36.30N	112.15W
Kai Besar	26	Jh	5.35S	133.00 E
Kaidu He/Karaxabar He	27	Ec	41.55N	86.38 E
Kaieteur Falls	54	Gc	5.10N	59.28W
Kaifeng	22	Nf	34.45N	114.25 E
Kaihua	28	Ej	29.10N	118.24 E
Kai Kecil	26	Jh	5.45S	132.40 E
Kaikohe	62	Ea	35.24S	173.48 E
Kaikoura	61	Dh	42.25S	173.41 E
Kaili	27	If	26.35N	107.59 E
Kailu	27	Lc	43.37N	121.19 E
Kailua [Hi.-U.S.]	65a	Fd	19.39N	155.59W
Kailua [Hi.-U.S.]	65a	Db	21.23N	157.44W
Kaimana	26	Jg	3.39S	133.45 E
Kaimanawa Mountains	62	Fc	39.15S	176.00 E
Kaimon-Dake	29	Bf	31.10N	130.32 E
Kain, Tournai-	12	Fd	50.38N	3.22 E
Kainach	14	Jd	46.54N	15.31 E
Kainan [Jap.]	29	Dd	34.09N	135.12 E
Kainan [Jap.]	29	De	33.36N	134.22 E
Kainantu	60	Di	6.15S	145.53 E
Kainji Dam	34	Fd	9.55N	4.40 E
Kainji Reservoir	34	Fc	10.30N	4.35 E
Kaipara Harbour	62	Fb	36.25S	174.15 E
Kaiparowits Plateau	46	Jh	37.20N	111.15W
Kaiser Franz Josephs Fjord	41	Jd	73.30N	24.00W
Kaisersesch	12	Jd	50.14N	7.09 E
Kaiserslautern	10	Dg	49.27N	7.45 E
Kaiserstuhl	10	Dh	48.06N	7.40 E
Kaishantun	27	Mc	42.43N	129.37 E
Kaišiadorys/Kajšjadoris	7	Fi	54.53N	24.31 E
Kaita	29	Cd	34.20N	132.32 E
Kaitaia	62	Ea	35.07S	173.14 E
Kaitangata	62	Cg	46.17S	169.51 E
Kaithal	25	Fc	29.48N	76.23 E
Kaitong → Tongyu	27	Lc	44.47N	123.05 E
Kaituma River	50	Gh	8.11N	59.41W
Kaiwaka	61	Dg	36.10S	174.26 E
Kaiwi Channel	60	Oc	21.13N	157.30W
Kaixian	27	Ie	31.10N	108.25 E
Kaiyuan [China]	27	Lc	42.33N	124.04 E
Kaiyuan [China]	27	Hg	23.47N	103.15 E
Kaiyuh Mountains	40	Hd	64.00N	158.00W
Kaja	30	Jg	12.02N	22.28 E
Kajaani	6	Ic	64.14N	27.41 E
Kajaapu	26	Dh	5.26S	102.24 E
Kajabbi	58	Fg	20.02S	140.02 E
Kajak	20	Fb	71.30N	103.15 E
Kajang	26	Df	2.59N	101.47 E
Kajdak, Sor-	16	Rg	44.40N	53.30 E
Kajerkan	20	Dc	69.25N	87.30 E
Kajiado	36	Gc	1.51S	36.47 E
Kajiki	29	Bf	31.44N	130.40 E
Kajmakčalan	15	Ei	40.58N	21.48 E
Kajnar	15	Lb	47.50N	28.06 E
Kajo Kaji	35	Ee	3.53N	31.40 E
Kajrakkumskoje Vodohranilišče	18	Hd	40.20N	70.05 E
Kajrakty	19	Hf	48.31N	73.14 E
Kajšjadoris/Kaišiadorys	7	Fi	54.53N	24.31 E
Kajuru	34	Gc	10.19N	7.41 E
Kaka	35	Fd	7.28N	39.06 E
Kākā	35	Ec	10.36N	32.11 E
Kakagi Lake	45	Jb	49.13N	93.52W
Kakamas	37	Ce	28.45S	20.33 E
Kakamega	36	Fb	0.17N	34.45 E
Kakamigahara	29	Ed	35.25N	136.50 E
Kakanj	14	Mf	44.08N	18.05 E
Kaka Point	65a	Ec	20.32N	156.33W
Kakata	34	Cd	6.32N	10.21W
Kake	29	Cd	34.36N	132.19 E
Kakegawa	29	Ed	34.46N	138.00 E
Kakenge	36	Dc	4.51S	21.55 E
Kakeroma-Jima	29b	Ba	28.08N	129.15 E
Kakhovka Reservoir (EN) = Kahovskoje Vodohranilišče	5	Jf	47.25N	34.10 E
Kākī	24	Nh	28.19N	51.34 E
Kākināda	22	Kh	16.56N	82.13 E
Kakisa Lake	42	Fd	60.55N	117.40W
Kakizaki	29	Fc	37.16N	138.22 E
Kaklkan	24	Cd	36.15N	29.24 E
Kakogawa	29	Dd	34.46N	134.51 E
Kakpin	34	Ed	8.39N	3.48W
Kaktovik	40	Kb	70.08N	143.37W
Kakuda	29	Gc	37.58N	140.47 E
Kakuma	36	Fb	3.43N	34.52 E
Kakunodate	28	Pe	39.40N	140.32 E
Kakva	17	Jg	59.37N	60.50 E
Kakya	36	Gc	1.36S	39.02 E
Kalaa	13	Mi	35.35N	0.20 E
Kalaa Khasba	14	Co	35.38N	8.36 E
Kalaallit Nunaat/Grønland = Greenland (EN) [5]	39	Pb	70.00N	40.00W
Kalaallit Nunaat/Grønland = Greenland (EN)	38	Pb	70.00N	40.00W
Kalabahi	26	Hh	8.13S	124.31 E
Kalabáka	15	Ej	39.42N	21.38 E
Kalabera	64b	Ba	15.14N	145.48 E
Kalabo	36	De	14.58S	22.41 E
Kalâbsha	33	Fe	23.33N	32.50 E
Kalač	19	Ee	50.23N	41.01 E
Kalačinsk	19	Hd	55.03N	74.34 E
Kalač-na-Donu	19	Ef	48.43N	43.32 E
Kaladan	25	Id	20.09N	92.57 E
Ka Lae	60	Od	18.55N	155.41W
Kalahari Desert	30	Jk	23.00S	22.00 E
Kalaheo	65a	Bb	21.56N	159.32W
Kalai-Mor	19	Gh	35.37N	62.31 E
Kalaj Humo	18	He	38.25N	70.47 E
Kalajoki	7	Fd	64.15N	23.57 E
Kalakan	20	Ge	55.10N	116.45 E
Kalaldi	34	Hd	6.30N	14.04 E
Kalāleh	24	Pd	37.25N	55.40 E
Kalámai	6	Ih	37.02N	22.07 E
Kalamákion	15	Gl	37.55N	23.43 E
Kalamazoo	43	Jc	42.17N	85.32W
Kalambo Falls	36	Fd	8.36S	31.14 E
Kalamitski Zaliv	16	Hg	45.00N	33.25 E
Kálamos	15	Dk	38.37N	20.55 E
Kalamunda, Perth-	59	Df	31.57S	116.03 E
Kalan	23	Eb	39.07N	39.32 E
Kalanshiyū, Sarīr-	30	Jf	27.00N	21.30 E
Kalao, Pulau-	26	Hh	7.18S	120.58 E
Kalaotoa, Pulau-	26	Hh	7.22S	121.47 E
Kalapana	65a	Gd	19.21N	154.59W
Kalaraš	16	Ff	47.16N	28.16 E
Kälarne	8	Gb	62.59N	16.05 E
Kalarski Hrebet	20	Ge	56.30N	118.50 E
Kalasin [Indon.]	26	Ff	0.12N	114.16 E
Kalasin [Thai.]	25	Ke	16.29N	103.31 E
Kalāt	25	Dc	29.02N	66.35 E
Kalāteh	24	Pd	36.29N	54.10 E
Kalau	65b	Bc	21.28S	174.57W
Kalaupapa	65a	Eb	21.12N	156.59W
Kalaus	16	Ng	45.43N	44.07 E
Kalavárdha	15	Km	36.20N	27.57 E
Kálavrita	15	Fk	38.02N	22.07 E
Kalbā'	24	Qj	25.03N	56.21 E
Kalbīyah, Sabkhat al-	14	Eo	35.51N	10.17 E
Kaldbakur	7a	Ab	65.49N	23.39W
Kaldygajty	16	Re	49.20N	52.38 E
Kale [Tur.]	24	Cd	37.26N	28.51 E
Kale [Tur.]	24	Cd	36.14N	29.59 E
Kalecik	24	Eb	40.06N	33.25 E
Kalehe	36	Ec	2.06S	28.55 E
Kalemie	31	Ji	5.56S	29.12 E
Kāl-e Shur	23	Jb	35.05N	60.59 E
Kalevala	19	Db	65.12N	31.10 E
Kalewa	25	Id	23.12N	94.18 E
Kaleybar	24	Lc	38.47N	47.02 E
Kalgoorlie	58	Dh	30.45S	121.28 E
Kaliakoúdha	15	Ek	38.48N	21.46 E
Kaliakra, Nos-	15	Lf	43.18N	28.30 E
Kalibo	26	Hd	11.43N	122.22 E
Kali Limni	15	Kn	35.35N	27.08 E
Kalima	31	Ji	2.34S	26.37 E
Kalimantan/Borneo	21	Ni	1.00N	114.00 E
Kalimantan Barat [3]	26	Ff	0.01N	110.30 E
Kalimantan Selatan [3]	26	Gg	2.30S	115.30 E
Kalimantan Tengah [3]	26	Fg	2.00S	113.30 E
Kalimantan Timur [3]	26	Gf	1.30N	116.30 E
Kálimnos	15	Jm	36.57N	26.59 E
Kalinin → Tver'	6	Jd	56.52N	35.55 E
Kalinin	19	Fg	42.07N	59.40 E
Kalininabad	18	Gf	37.53N	68.57 E
Kaliningrad	6	Ie	54.43N	20.30 E
Kaliningrad	7	Ii	55.55N	37.57 E
Kaliningradskaja oblast	19	Ce	54.45N	21.20 E
Kalinino → Tašir	16	Ni	41.08N	44.14 E
Kalinino	16	Kg	45.05N	38.59 E
Kalininsk	15	Ka	48.07N	27.16 E
Kalininsk	16	Nd	51.30N	44.30 E
Kalinkoviči	19	Ce	52.07N	29.23 E
Kalino	17	Hg	58.15N	57.35 E
Kalinovik	14	Mg	43.31N	18.26 E
Kalinovka	16	Fe	49.29N	28.32 E
Kaliro	36	Fb	0.54N	33.30 E
Kalispell	39	He	48.12N	114.19W
Kalisz	10	Of	51.45N	18.05 E
Kalisz [2]	10	Oe	51.46N	18.06 E
Kalisz Pomorski	10	Lc	53.19N	15.54 E
Kalitva	16	Le	48.10N	40.46 E
Kaliua	36	Fd	5.04S	31.48 E
Kalix	7	Fd	65.51N	23.08 E
Kalixälven	7	Fc	65.47N	23.13 E
Kalja	17	Jf	60.20N	60.01 E
Kaljazin	19	Dd	57.15N	37.55 E
Kalkandere	24	Ib	40.55N	40.28 E
Kalkar	12	Ic	51.44N	6.18 E
Kalkaska	44	Ec	44.44N	85.11W
Kalkfeld	37	Bd	20.53S	16.11 E
Kalkfontein	37	Cd	22.07S	20.54 E
Kalkim	15	Kj	39.48N	27.13 E
Kalkrand	37	Bd	24.03S	17.33 E
Kall	7	Ce	63.28N	13.15 E
Kållands Halvö	8	Ef	58.35N	13.05 E
Kållandsö	8	Ef	58.40N	13.10 E
Kallaste	7	Gg	58.41N	27.08 E
Kallavesi	5	Ic	62.50N	27.45 E
Kalletal	12	Kb	52.08N	8.57 E
Kallhäll	8	Ge	59.27N	17.48 E
Kallidhromon Óros	15	Fk	38.44N	22.34 E
Kallinge	7	Dh	56.14N	15.17 E
Kallonis, Kolpos-	15	Jj	39.07N	26.08 E
Kallsjön	7	Ce	63.35N	13.00 E
Kalmar	6	Hd	56.40N	16.22 E
Kalmar [2]	7	Dh	57.20N	16.00 E
Kalmarsund	7	Dh	56.40N	16.25 E
Kalmit	12	Ke	49.19N	8.05 E
Kalmius	16	Jf	47.03N	37.34 E
Kalmthout	12	Gc	51.23N	4.28 E
Kalmykija, respublika	19	Ef	46.30N	45.30 E
Kalmykovo	16	Qe	49.05N	51.47 E
Kalnciems	8	Jh	56.48N	23.34 E
Kalnik	14	Kd	46.10N	16.30 E
Kalocsa	10	Oj	46.32N	19.00 E
Kalofer	15	Hg	42.37N	24.59 E
Kalohi Channel	65a	Ec	21.00N	156.56W
Kaloko	36	Ed	6.47S	25.47 E
Kalole	36	Ec	3.42S	27.22 E
Kaloli Point	65a	Gd	19.37N	154.57W
Kalomo	36	Ef	17.02S	26.30 E
Kalpa	25	Fb	31.37N	78.10 E
Kalpákion	15	Dj	39.53N	20.35 E
Kalpeni Island	25	Ef	10.05N	73.38 E
Kalpin	27	Cc	40.31N	79.03 E
Kalsūbai	21	Jh	19.36N	73.43 E
Kaltern/Caldaro	14	Fd	46.25N	11.14 E
Kaltungo	34	Hd	9.49N	11.19 E
Kaluga	6	Je	54.31N	36.16 E
Kalulushi	36	Ee	12.50S	28.05 E
Kalumburu Mission	59	Fb	14.18S	126.39 E
Kalundborg	7	Ci	55.41N	11.06 E
Kaluš	19	Cf	49.03N	24.23 E
Kałuszyn	10	Rd	52.13N	21.49 E
Kalužskaja Oblast [3]	19	De	54.20N	35.30 E
Kalvåg	8	Ac	61.46N	4.53 E
Kalvarija	7	Fi	54.27N	23.14 E
Kalya	36	Fd	6.28S	30.03 E
Kalyān	25	Ee	19.15N	73.09 E
Kám	10	Mi	47.06N	16.53 E
Kama	36	Ec	3.32S	27.07 E
Kama	17	Nf	60.27N	69.00 E
Kama	5	Ld	55.45N	52.00 E
Kamae	29	Be	32.48N	131.56 E
Kamaï	35	Ba	21.12N	17.30 E
Kamaing	25	Jc	25.31N	96.44 E
Kamaishi	28	Pe	39.16N	141.53 E
Kamakou	65a	Eb	21.07N	156.52W
Kamakura	29	Fd	35.19N	139.32 E
Kamālia	25	Eb	30.44N	72.39 E
Kamalo	65a	Eb	21.03N	156.53W
Kaman	24	Ec	39.25N	33.45 E
Kamand, Āb-e-	24	Mf	33.28N	49.04 E
Kamanjab	37	Ac	19.35S	14.51 E
Kamanyola	36	Ec	2.46S	29.00 E
Kamaran	23	Ff	15.12N	42.35 E
Kamarang	54	Fb	5.53N	60.35W
Kama Reservoir (EN) = Kamskoje Vodohranilišče	5	Ld	58.50N	56.15 E
Kamaši	19	Gh	38.48N	66.29 E
Kamativi	37	Dc	18.19S	27.03 E
Kambalda	59	Ef	31.10S	121.37 E
Kambalnaja Sopka, Vulkan-	20	Kf	51.17N	156.57 E
Kambara	29	Fd	35.07N	138.36 E
Kambara	63d	Cc	18.57S	178.57W
Kambarka	7	Nh	56.18N	54.14 E
Kambia	34	Cd	9.07N	12.55W
Kambja	8	Lf	58.11N	26.43 E
Kambove	36	Ee	10.52S	26.35 E
Kamčatka	20	Le	56.10N	162.30 E
Kamčatka, Poluostrov- = Kamchatka Peninsula (EN)	21	Rd	56.00N	160.00 E
Kamčatskaja Oblast [3]	20	Kf	54.50N	159.00 E
Kamčatski Zaliv	20	Le	55.30N	163.00 E
Kamchatka Peninsula (EN) = Kamčatka, Poluostrov-	21	Rd	56.00N	160.00 E
Kamčija	15	Kf	43.02N	27.53 E
Kamčijska Plato	15	Kg	42.56N	27.32 E
Kameda [Jap.]	29	Fc	37.52N	139.06 E
Kameda [Jap.]	29a	Bc	41.49N	140.46 E
Kameda-Hantō	29a	Bc	41.45N	141.00 E
Kámeiros	15	Km	36.18N	27.56 E
Kamelik	16	Pc	52.06N	49.30 E
Kamen	12	Jc	51.36N	7.40 E
Kaménai	15	Im	36.25N	25.25 E
Kamende	36	Dd	6.28S	24.33 E
Kamenec	10	Td	52.23N	23.49 E
Kamenec-Podolski	19	Cf	48.39N	26.33 E
Kamenijak, Rt-	14	Hf	44.46N	13.56 E
Kamenka	16	Qd	51.07N	50.20 E
Kamenka	16	Fe	48.03N	28.45 E
Kamenka	16	Kd	50.43N	39.25 E
Kamenka	19	Ee	53.13N	44.03 E
Kamenka	7	Kd	65.54N	44.04 E
Kamenka	2C	Nb	44.28N	136.01 E
Kamenka	19	Df	49.03N	32.06 E
Kamenka-Bugskaja	10	Uf	50.01N	24.25 E
Kamenka-Dneprovskaja	16	If	47.29N	34.29 E
Kamen-Kaširski	16	Dd	51.36N	24.59 E
Kamen-na-Obi	20	Df	53.47N	81.20 E
Kamennogorsk	7	Gf	60.59N	29.12 E
Kamennoje, Ozero-	7	Hd	64.30N	30.15 E
Kamennomostski	16	Lg	44.17N	40.12 E
Kamen-Rybolov	28	Kb	44.45N	132.04 E
Kamenskoje	20	Ld	62.30N	166.12 E
Kamensk-Šahtinski	16	Le	48.18N	40.16 E
Kamensk-Uralski	22	Id	56.28N	61.54 E
Kamenz	10	Ke	51.16N	14.06 E
Kameoka	29	Dd	35.00N	135.35 E
Kameškovo	7	Jh	56.22N	41.01 E
Kamet	25	Fd	30.55N	79.35 E
Kameyama	29	Ed	34.51N	136.27 E
Kami-Agata	29	Ad	34.38N	129.25 E
Kamiah	46	Gc	46.14N	116.02W
Kamicharo	29a	Cb	43.11N	143.52 E
Kamienna	10	Re	51.06N	21.47 E
Kamienna Góra	10	Mf	50.47N	16.01 E
Kamień Pomorski	10	Kc	53.58N	14.46 E
Kamieńsk	10	Pe	51.12N	19.30 E
Kamieskroon	37	Bf	30.09S	17.56 E
Kami-furano	29a	Cb	43.29N	142.27 E
Kamiiso	28	Pd	41.49N	140.39 E
Kamiita	29	Dd	34.08N	134.24 E
Kamiji	36	Dd	6.39S	23.17 E
Kamikawa	29a	Cb	43.50N	142.47 E
Kami-Koshiki-Jima	29	Af	31.50N	129.55 E
Kamina	31	Ji	8.44S	24.59 E
Kaminak Lake	42	Id	62.13N	95.00W
Kaminokuni	29a	Bc	41.48N	140.05 E
Kamino-Shima	29	Ad	34.30N	129.25 E
Kaminoyama	28	Pe	38.09N	140.17 E
Kaminuriak Lake	42	Hd	63.00N	95.45W
Kamioka	28	Nf	36.16N	137.18 E
Kami-shihoro	29a	Cb	43.13N	143.16 E
Kamisunagawa	29a	Bb	43.28N	141.58 E
Kamitsushima	29	Ad	34.39N	129.28 E
Kamituga	36	Ec	3.04S	28.11 E
Kamiyama	29	De	33.58N	134.21 E
Kami-yūbetsu	29a	Ca	44.11N	143.34 E
Kamjenc/Kamenz	10	Ke	51.16N	14.06 E
Kamloops	39	Gd	50.40N	120.20W
Kamloops Plateau	46	Ea	50.10N	120.35W
Kamnik	14	Id	46.14N	14.37 E
Kamo	16	Ni	40.22N	45.05 E
Kamo [Jap.]	29	Fc	37.39N	139.03 E
Kamo [N.Z.]	62	Fa	35.41S	174.17 E
Kamōda-Misaki	29	De	33.50N	134.45 E
Kamogawa	29	Gd	35.06N	140.05 E
Kamp	14	Jb	48.23N	15.48 E
Kampala	31	Kh	0.19N	32.35 E
Kampar	26	Df	4.18N	101.09 E
Kampar	26	Mi	0.32N	103.08 E
Kampen	11	Lb	52.33N	5.54 E
Kampene	36	Ec	3.36S	26.40 E
Kamphaeng Phet	25	Je	16.26N	99.33 E
Kamp-Lintfort	12	Ic	51.30N	6.32 E
Kamp'o	28	Jg	35.48N	129.30 E
Kâmpóng Cham	22	Mh	12.00N	105.27 E
Kâmpóng Chhnăng	25	Kf	12.15N	104.40 E
Kâmpóng Saôm	22	Mh	10.38N	103.30 E
Kâmpóng Saôm, Chhâk-	25	Kf	10.50N	103.32 E
Kâmpóng Thum	25	Kf	12.42N	104.54 E
Kâmpôt	25	Kf	10.37N	104.11 E
Kampti	34	Ec	10.08N	3.27W
Kampuchea → Cambodia	22	Mh	13.00N	105.00 E
Kamrau, Teluk-	26	Jg	3.32S	133.37 E
Kamsack	42	Hf	51.34N	101.54W
Kamsar	34	Cc	10.40N	14.36W
Kamskoje Ustje	7	Li	55.14N	49.16 E
Kamskoje Vodohranilišče = Kama Reservoir (EN)	5	Ld	58.50N	56.15 E
Kam Summa	35	Ge	0.21N	42.44 E
Kamuenai	29a	Bb	43.08N	140.26 E
Kamui-Dake	29a	Cb	42.25N	142.52 E
Kamui-Misaki	27	Pc	43.20N	140.20 E
Kámuk, Cerro-	49	Fi	9.17N	83.04W
Kamvoúnia Óri	15	Ei	40.00N	21.52 E
Kāmyārān	24	Le	34.47N	46.56 E
Kamyšin	6	Ke	50.06N	45.24 E
Kamyšlov	19	Gd	56.52N	62.43 E
Kamyšovaja Buhta	16	Hg	44.31N	33.33 E
Kamysty-Ajat	17	Jj	53.01N	61.35 E
Kamyzjak	19	Ef	46.06N	48.05 E
Kan	24	Ne	35.45N	51.16 E
Kan	20	Ee	56.31N	93.47 E
Kana	37	Dc	18.32S	27.24 E
Kanaaupscow	42	Jf	54.01N	76.32W
Kanaaupscow	42	Jf	53.40N	77.08W
Kanab	43	Ed	37.03N	112.32W
Kanab Creek	46	Ih	36.24N	112.38W
Kanaga	40a	Cb	51.45N	177.10W
Kanagawa Ken [2]	28	Og	35.30N	139.10 E
Kanaliasem	26	Dg	1.44S	103.35 E
Kanami-Zaki	29b	Bb	27.53N	128.58 E
Kananga	31	Ji	5.54S	22.25 E
Kanariktok	42	Le	55.03N	60.10W
Kanaš	7	Li	55.31N	47.31 E
Kanathea	63d	Cb	17.16S	179.09W
Kanaya	29	Fd	34.48N	138.07 E
Kanayama	29	Ed	35.39N	137.09 E
Kanazawa	22	Pf	36.34N	136.39 E
Kanbalu	25	Jd	23.12N	95.31 E
Kanbe	25	Je	16.42N	96.01 E
Kanchanaburi	25	Jf	14.02N	99.33 E
Känchenjunga	21	Kg	27.42N	88.08 E
Kānchipuram	25	Ff	12.50N	79.43 E
Kandalakša	6	Jb	67.09N	32.21 E
Kandalaksha, Gulf of- (EN) = Kandalakšski Zaliv	5	Jb	66.35N	32.45 E
Kandalakšski Zaliv = Kandalaksha, Gulf of- (EN)	5	Jb	66.35N	32.45 E
Kandangan	26	Gg	2.47S	115.16 E
Kándanos	15	Gn	35.20N	23.44 E
Kandava	7	Fh	57.03N	22.46 E
Kandavu Island	57	If	19.00S	178.13 E
Kandavu Passage	63d	Ac	18.45S	178.00 E
Kandel	12	Ke	49.05N	8.12 E
Kandel	10	Eh	48.04N	8.01 E
Kandheloúsa	15	Jm	36.30N	26.58 E
Kandi	31	Hg	11.08N	2.56 E
Kandıra	24	Db	41.04N	30.09 E
Kandla	25	Ed	23.02N	70.14 E
Kando-Gawa	29	Cd	35.22N	132.40 E
Kandovān, Gardaneh-ye-	24	Nd	36.09N	51.18 E
Kandrian	60	Di	6.13S	149.33 E
Kandry	17	Gi	54.34N	54.10 E
Kandy	22	Ki	7.18N	80.38 E
Kane	44	He	41.40N	78.48W
Kane Bassin	67	Od	79.35N	67.00W
Kaneh	24	Pi	27.04N	54.18 E
Kanem [3]	35	Bc	15.00N	16.00 E
Kanem	30	Ig	14.45N	15.30 E
Kaneohe	60	Oc	21.25N	157.48W
Kaneohe Bay	65a	Db	21.28N	157.48W
Kánestron, Ákra-	15	Gj	39.56N	23.45 E
Kanev	16	Ge	49.42N	31.29 E
Kanevskaja	19	Df	46.06N	38.58 E
Kaneyama	29	Fc	37.27N	139.30 E
Kang	37	Cd	23.44S	22.50 E
Kangaba	34	Dc	11.56N	8.25W
Kangal	24	Gc	39.15N	37.24 E
Kangalassy	20	Hd	62.17N	129.58 E
Kangâmiut	41	Ge	65.39N	53.55W
Kangān [Iran]	24	Oi	27.50N	52.03 E
Kangān [Iran]	24	Qj	25.48N	57.28 E
Kangar	26	De	6.26N	100.12 E
Kangaré	34	Dc	11.37N	8.08W
Kangaroo Island	57	Eh	35.50S	137.05 E
Kangasala	8	Kc	61.28N	24.05 E
Kangasniemi	7	Gf	61.59N	26.38 E
Kangâtsiaq	41	Ge	68.20N	53.18W
Kangāvar	24	Le	34.30N	47.58 E
Kangbao	28	Cd	41.51N	114.37 E
Kangding/Dardo	27	He	30.01N	101.58 E
Kangean, Kepulauan- = Kangean Islands (EN)	26	Gh	6.55S	115.30 E
Kangean, Pulau-	26	Gh	6.54S	115.20 E
Kangean Islands (EN) = Kangean, Kepulauan-	26	Gh	6.55S	115.30 E
Kangeeak Point	42	Lc	68.10N	65.44W
Kangen	30	Kh	6.47N	33.09 E
Kangerdlugssuaq	41	Ie	68.20N	31.40W
Kangetet	36	Gb	1.58N	36.06 E

Index Symbols

[1] Independent Nation
[2] State, Region
[3] District, County
[4] Municipality
[5] Colony, Dependency
Continent
Physical Region

Historical or Cultural Region
Mount, Mountain
Volcano
Hill
Mountains, Mountain Range
Hills, Escarpment
Plateau, Upland

Pass, Gap
Plain, Lowland
Delta
Salt Flat
Valley, Canyon
Crater, Cave
Karst Features

Depression
Polder
Desert, Dunes
Forest, Woods
Heath, Steppe
Oasis
Cape, Point

Coast, Beach
Cliff
Peninsula
Isthmus
Sandbank
Island
Atoll

Rock, Reef
Islands, Archipelago
Rocks, Reefs
Coral Reef
Well, Spring
Geyser
River, Stream

Waterfall Rapids
River Mouth, Estuary
Lake
Salt Lake
Intermittent Lake
Reservoir
Swamp, Pond

Canal
Glacier
Ice Shelf, Pack Ice
Ocean
Sea
Gulf, Bay
Strait, Fjord

Lagoon
Bank
Seamount
Tablemount
Ridge
Shelf
Basin

Escarpment, Sea Scarp
Fracture
Trench, Abyss
National Park, Reserve
Point of Interest
Recreation Site
Cave, Cavern

Historic Site
Ruins
Wall, Walls
Church, Abbey
Temple
Scientific Station
Airport

Port
Lighthouse
Mine
Tunnel
Dam, Bridge

Kanggup'o	28	Id	41.07N	127.31 E
Kanggye	27	Mc	40.58N	126.36 E
Kangi	35	Dd	8.10N	27.39 E
Kangjin	28	Ig	34.38N	126.46 E
Kangiqsualujjuaq	39	Md	58.35N	65.59W
Kangiqsujuaq	42	Kd	61.36N	71.57W
Kangirsuk	39	Lc	60.00N	70.01W
Kangmar	27	Ef	28.32N	89.43 E
Kangnŭng	27	Md	37.44N	128.54 E
Kango	36	Bb	0.09N	10.08 E
Kangondu	36	Gc	1.06S	37.42 E
Kangping	28	Gc	42.45N	123.20 E
Kangrinboqê Feng	27	De	31.04N	81.30 E
Kangto	25	Ic	27.52N	92.30 E
Kangwŏn-Do [N.Kor.] [2]	28	Ie	38.45N	127.35 E
Kangwŏn-Do [S.Kor.] [2]	28	Jf	37.45N	128.15 E
Kani	34	Dd	8.29N	6.36W
Kaniama	36	Dd	7.31S	24.11 E
Kanibadam	18	Hd	40.17N	70.25 E
Kaniet Islands	57	Fe	0.53S	145.30 E
Kanija	15	Lc	46.16N	28.13 E
Kanimeh	18	Ed	40.18N	65.09 E
Kanina	15	Ci	40.26N	19.31 E
Kanin Kamen	17	Bb	68.15N	45.15 E
Kanin Nos	19	Eb	68.39N	43.14 E
Kanin Nos, Mys-	5	Kb	68.39N	43.16 E
Kanin Peninsula (EN) = Kanin Poluostrov	5	Kb	68.00N	45.00 E
Kanin Poluostrov = Kanin Peninsula (EN)	5	Kb	68.00N	45.00 E
Kanioumé	34	Eb	15.46N	3.09W
Kanita	29a	Bc	41.02N	140.38 E
Kanjiža	15	Dc	46.04N	20.03 E
Kankaanpää	7	Ff	61.48N	22.25 E
Kankakee	43	Jc	41.07N	87.52W
Kankakee River	45	Lf	41.23N	88.16W
Kankalabé	34	Cc	11.00N	12.00W
Kankan	31	Gg	10.23N	9.18W
Kanker	25	Gd	20.17N	81.29 E
Kankesanturai	25	Gg	9.49N	80.02 E
Kankossa	32	Ef	15.55N	11.31W
Kankunski	20	He	57.39N	126.25 E
Kanla	10	Hf	50.48N	11.35 E
Kanmav Kyun	25	Jf	11.40N	98.28 E
Kanmon-Kaikyō	29	Bd	33.56N	130.57 E
Kanmuri-Yama	29	Cd	34.28N	132.05 E
Kannapolis	43	Kd	35.30N	80.37W
Kannone-Jima	28	Jj	28.51N	128.58 E
Kannonkoski	8	Kb	62.58N	25.15 E
Kannus	7	Fe	63.54N	23.54 E
Kano [2]	34	Gc	12.00N	9.00 E
Kano	31	Hg	12.00N	8.31 E
Kanona	36	Fe	13.04S	30.38 E
Kan'onji	29	Cd	34.07N	133.39 E
Kanoya	28	Ki	31.23N	130.51 E
Kanozero, Ozero-	7	Ic	67.00N	34.05 E
Kānpur	22	Kg	26.28N	80.21 E
Kansas	38	Jf	39.07N	94.36W
Kansas [2]	43	Hd	38.45N	98.15W
Kansas City [Ks.-U.S.]	39	Jf	39.07N	94.39W
Kansas City [Mo.-U.S.]	39	Jf	39.05N	94.35W
Kanshi	27	Kg	24.57N	116.52 E
Kansk	22	Ld	56.13N	95.41 E
Kansŏng	28	Je	38.22N	128.28 E
Kansu (EN) = Gansu Sheng (Kan-su Sheng) [2]	27	Hd	38.00N	102.00 E
Kansu (EN) = Kan-su Sheng → Gansu Sheng [2]	27	Hd	38.00N	102.00 E
Kan-su Sheng → Gansu Sheng = Kansu (EN) [2]	27	Hd	38.00N	102.00 E
Kansyat	26	Kg	2.15S	138.51 E
Kant	18	Jc	42.52N	74.50 E
Kantang	25	Jg	7.23N	99.32 E
Kantchari	34	Fc	12.29N	1.31 E
Kanté	34	Fd	9.57N	1.03 E
Kantemirovka	19	Df	49.45N	39.53 E
Kantō-Heiya	29	Fc	36.00N	139.30 E
Kanton Atoll	57	Je	2.50S	171.41W
Kantō-Sanchi	29	Fc	36.00N	138.45 E
Kantubek	18	Bb	45.06N	59.16 E
Kanturk/Ceann Toirc	9	Ei	52.10N	8.55W
Kanuma	29	Fc	36.34N	139.45 E
Kanye	31	Jk	24.58S	25.21 E
Kanyu	37	Cd	20.04S	24.36 E
Kanzenze	36	Ee	10.31S	25.12 E
Kao	65b	Aa	19.40S	175.01W
Kaohsiung	22	Og	22.38N	120.17 E
Kaôk Nhêk	25	Lf	13.05N	107.04 E
Kaoko Otavi	37	Ac	18.15S	13.37 E
Kaokoveld [3]	37	Ac	18.00S	13.00 E
Kaokoveld	30	Ij	19.30S	13.30 E
Kaolack	31	Fg	14.09N	16.04W
Kao Neua, Col de-	25	Le	18.23N	105.10 E
Kaouadja	35	Cd	8.00N	23.14 E
Kaouar	34	Hb	19.05N	12.52 E
Kapaa	65a	Ba	22.05N	159.19W
Kapanga	31	Ji	8.21S	22.35 E
Kapar	24	Ld	36.32N	47.30 E
Kapčagaj	19	Hg	43.52N	77.03 E
Kapčagajskoje Vodohranilišče	19	Hg	43.45N	78.00 E
Kapchorwa	36	Fb	1.24N	34.27 E
Kap Dan	41	Ie	65.32N	37.30W
Kapelle	12	Fc	51.39N	3.57 E
Kapellskär	8	He	59.43N	19.04 E
Kapena	36	Ee	10.47S	28.20 E
Kapenguria	36	Gb	1.14N	35.07 E
Kapfenberg	14	Jc	47.26N	15.18 E
Kapıdağı Yarımadası	15	Ki	40.28N	27.50 E
Kapiri Mposhi	36	Ee	13.58S	28.41 E
Kāpīsā [3]	23	Kc	34.45N	69.30 E
Kapit	26	Ff	2.01N	112.56 E
Kapiti Island	62	Fd	40.50S	174.55 E
Kapka, Massif du-	35	Cb	15.07N	21.45 E
Kapoeta	31	Kh	4.47N	33.35 E
Kapona	36	Ed	7.11S	29.09 E
Kapos	10	Oj	46.44N	18.29 E
Kaposvár	10	Nj	46.22N	17.48 E
Kapp	8	Dd	60.42N	10.52 E
Kappeln	10	Fb	54.40N	9.56 E
Kapša	7	Hg	59.52N	33.45 E
Kapsan	28	Jd	41.05N	128.18 E
Kapuas [Indon.]	26	Mj	0.25S	109.40 E
Kapuas [Indon.]	26	Fg	3.01S	114.20 E
Kapuas Hulu, Pegunungan- = Kapuas Mountains (EN)	26	Ff	1.25N	113.15 E
Kapuas Mountains (EN) = Kapuas Hulu, Pegunungan	26	Ff	1.25N	113.15 E
Kapugargin	15	Lm	36.40N	28.50 E
Kapušany	10	Rg	49.03N	21.21 E
Kapuskasing	39	Ke	49.25N	82.26W
Kapustin Jar	16	Ne	48.35N	45.45 E
Kapustoje	7	Ic	67.17N	34.12 E
Kaputdžuh, Gora-	16	Oj	39.12N	46.01 E
Kapuvár	10	Ni	47.36N	17.02 E
Kara	17	Lb	69.10N	64.45 E
Kara	34	Fd	9.33N	1.12 E
Kara [3]	34	Fd	9.35N	1.05 E
Kara Ada [Tur.]	15	Km	36.58N	27.28 E
Kara Ada [Tur.]	15	Jk	38.25N	26.20 E
Kara-Balta	19	Hg	42.49N	73.57 E
Karabas	19	Hf	49.30N	73.00 E
Karabaš	17	Ji	55.29N	60.13 E
Karabekaul	19	Gh	38.28N	64.10 E
Karabiga	15	Ki	40.24N	27.18 E
Karabil, Vozvyšennost-	18	Df	36.20N	63.30 E
Kara-Bogaz-Gol	19	Fg	41.01N	52.59 E
Kara-Bogaz-Gol, proliv-	16	Ri	41.04N	52.59 E
Kara-Bogaz-Gol, Zaliv-	5	Lg	41.00N	53.15 E
Karabuk	23	Da	41.12N	32.37 E
Karabulak	18	Lb	44.54N	78.29 E
Karabulak	19	Gg	42.31N	69.47 E
Kara Burun	15	Km	36.32N	27.58 E
Karaburun [Tur.]	24	Cb	41.21N	28.40 E
Karaburun [Tur.]	24	Bc	38.37N	26.31 E
Karabutak	19	Gf	49.57N	60.08 E
Karacabey	24	Cb	40.13N	28.21 E
Karaca Dağ	24	Hd	37.40N	39.50 E
Karačajevo-Čerkessakaja respublika	19	Eg	43.45N	41.45 E
Karačajevsk	16	Lh	43.44N	41.58 E
Karacaköy	24	Cb	41.22N	28.22 E
Karacaoğlan	15	Kh	41.32N	27.04 E
Karacasu	24	Cd	37.43N	28.37 E
Karačev	19	De	53.04N	34.59 E
Karāchi	22	Ig	24.52N	67.03 E
Kara Dağ [Tur.]	24	Jd	37.40N	43.42 E
Kara Dağ [Tur.]	24	Ed	37.23N	33.10 E
Karadah	16	Oh	42.29N	46.54 E
Karadeniz = Black Sea (EN)	5	Jg	43.00N	35.00 E
Kara Dong	27	Dd	38.26N	81.50 E
Karagajly	19	Hf	49.20N	75.48 E
Karaganda	22	Je	49.50N	73.10 E
Karagandinskaja Oblast [3]	19	Hf	50.00N	74.00 E
Karaginski, Ostrov-	21	Sd	58.48N	164.05 E
Karaginski Zaliv	21	Sd	58.50N	164.00 E
Kara Gölü	15	Mm	36.42N	29.50 E
Karagoš, Gora-	20	Df	51.44N	89.24 E
Karahalli	15	Mk	38.20N	29.32 E
Karaidelski	17	Hi	55.49N	57.05 E
Kara-Irtyš	21	Ke	47.52N	84.16 E
Karaisali	24	Fd	37.16N	35.03 E
Karaj	24	Ne	35.48N	50.59 E
Karaj	24	Ne	35.07N	51.35 E
Karak, Gora-	19	Gg	40.13N	63.05 E
Kara-Kala	19	Fh	38.28N	56.18 E
Karakalpakstan respublika	19	Fg	43.30N	59.00 E
Karakax/Moyu	27	Cd	37.17N	79.42 E
Karakax He	27	Dd	38.06N	80.24 E
Karakaya Barajı	24	Hc	38.25N	38.45 E
Karakeçi	24	Hd	37.26N	39.26 E
Karakelong, Pulau-	26	If	4.15N	126.48 E
Karakoçan	24	Ic	38.02N	40.07 E
Karakoin, Ozero-	18	Ga	46.10N	68.40 E
Karakojsu	16	Oh	42.30N	47.05 E
Karakolka	18	Kd	41.29N	77.24 E
Karakoram	21	Jf	34.00N	78.00 E
Karakoram Pass	21	Jf	35.30N	77.50 E
Karakore	35	Gc	10.25N	40.01 E
Karakoro	34	Cc	14.43N	12.03 E
Karakorum Shan	27	Cd	36.00N	76.00 E
Karakorum Shankou	27	Cd	35.30N	77.50 E
Karaköy	24	Ic	39.04N	41.42 E
Kara-Kul	18	Id	41.34N	72.47 E
Karakul, Ozero-	19	Hh	39.05N	73.25 E
Karakumski kanal imeni V.I. Lenina	19	Gh	37.42N	64.20 E
Karakumy	21	Hf	39.00N	60.00 E
Karakuwisa	37	Bc	18.56S	19.40 E
Karam	20	Fe	55.09N	107.37 E
Karama	26	Gg	2.18S	119.06 E
Karaman	23	Db	37.11N	33.14 E
Karamanli	15	Ml	37.22N	29.49 E
Karamay	22	Ke	45.30N	84.55 E
Karamea	61	Dh	41.15S	172.06 E
Karamea Bight	62	Dd	41.25S	171.50 E
Karamet-Nijaz	19	Gh	37.43N	64.31 E
Karamiran He	27	Dd	37.50N	84.35 E
Karamiran Shankou	27	Ed	36.15N	87.05 E
Karamiševo	8	Mg	57.44N	28.50 E
Karamoja [3]	36	Fb	2.45N	34.15 E
Karamürsel	15	Mi	40.42N	29.36 E
Kara-myk	19	Hh	39.30N	71.51 E
Karamyš	16	Nd	51.18N	45.00 E
Karān	24	Mi	27.43N	49.49 E
Karaova	15	Kl	37.05N	27.40 E
Karapınar	24	Ed	37.43N	33.33 E
Kara-Saki	29	Ad	34.40N	129.29 E
Kara-Sal	16	Mf	47.18N	43.36 E
Karasay	27	Dd	36.48N	83.48 E
Karasburg	31	Ik	28.00S	18.43 E
Kara Sea (EN) = Karskoje More	67	Hd	76.00N	80.00 E
Karašica	14	Me	45.36N	18.36 E
Karasjok	7	Fb	69.27N	25.30 E
Kara Strait (EN) = Karskije Vorota, Proliv-	21	Hb	70.30N	58.00 E
Karasu	24	Db	41.04N	30.47 E
Karasu [Tur.]	21	Ff	38.52N	38.48 E
Karasu [Tur.]	24	Ic	38.49N	41.28 E
Karasu [Tur.]	24	Jc	38.32N	43.10 E
Karasu Dağları	24	Ic	39.30N	40.45 E
Karasuk	20	Cf	53.44N	78.08 E
Karasuk	20	Cf	53.35N	77.30 E
Karasuyama	29	Gc	36.39N	140.08 E
Karatá, Laguna-	49	Fg	13.56N	83.30W
Karatal	19	Hf	46.26N	77.10 E
Karataş [Tur.]	24	Fd	36.36N	35.21 E
Karataş [Tur.]	15	Lk	38.34N	28.17 E
Karataş Burun	24	Fb	36.35N	35.22 E
Karatau	19	Hg	43.10N	70.29 E
Karatau, Hrebet-	21	Ie	43.40N	69.00 E
Karatj	7	Ec	66.43N	18.33 E
Karatobe	16	Re	49.42N	53.33 E
Karaton	19	Ff	46.25N	53.34 E
Karatsu	28	Jh	33.26N	130.00 E
Karatsu-Wan	29	Be	33.30N	130.00 E
Kara-Turgaj	18	Ie	48.01N	62.45 E
Karaul	19	Hf	49.00N	79.20 E
Karaul	20	Db	70.10N	83.08 E
Karaulbazar	18	Ee	39.29N	64.47 E
Karaulkala	18	Bc	42.18N	58.41 E
Karava	15	Ej	39.19N	21.36 E
Karavanke	14	Id	46.25N	14.25 E
Karavastase, Gjiri i-	15	Ci	40.55N	19.30 E
Karavastase, Laguna e-	15	Ci	40.55N	19.30 E
Karavi	15	Gm	36.45N	23.35 E
Karavonisia	15	Jn	35.59N	26.26 E
Karawa	36	Db	3.20N	20.18 E
Karaxabar He/Kaidu He	27	Ec	41.55N	86.38 E
Karažal	19	Hf	47.59N	70.53 E
Karbalā'	22	Gf	32.36N	44.02 E
Karbalā [3]	24	Jf	32.30N	43.45 E
Kårbole	7	Df	61.59N	15.19 E
Karcag	10	Qi	47.19N	20.56 E
Kardeljevo (Ploče)	14	Lg	43.04N	17.26 E
Kardhámaina	15	Km	36.47N	27.09 E
Kardhámila	15	Jk	38.31N	26.06 E
Kardhiotissa	15	Im	36.38N	25.01 E
Kardhitsa	15	Ej	39.22N	21.55 E
Kärdla/Kjardla	7	Fg	59.01N	22.42 E
Kårdžali	15	Ih	41.39N	25.22 E
Kårdžali [2]	15	Ih	41.30N	25.30 E
Kareha, Jbel-	13	Gi	35.15N	5.30W
Karelia (EN)	5	Jc	64.00N	32.00 E
Karelija, respublika	19	Dc	63.30N	33.30 E
Karema	36	Fd	6.49S	30.26 E
Karen — Kayin	25	Je	17.30N	97.45 E
Karen	25	If	12.51N	92.53 E
Karesuando	7	Fb	68.27N	22.29 E
Karêt	30	Gf	24.00N	7.30W
Karevere/Kjarevere	8	Lf	58.23N	26.30 E
Kargala	16	Sd	51.59N	55.10 E
Kargapazarı Dağı	24	Ib	40.07N	41.35 E
Kargapolje	17	Li	55.57N	64.27 E
Kargasok	20	De	59.07N	81.01 E
Kargat	20	De	55.10N	80.17 E
Kargı	24	Fb	41.08N	34.30 E
Kargil	25	Fb	34.34N	76.06 E
Kargilik/Yecheng	22	Jf	37.54N	77.26 E
Kargopol	19	Dc	61.32N	38.58 E
Karhula	7	Gf	60.31N	26.57 E
Kari	34	Hc	11.14N	10.34 E
Kariai	6	Ig	40.15N	24.15 E
Kariba	31	Jj	16.30S	28.45 E
Kariba, Lake-	30	Jj	17.00S	28.00 E
Kariba-Dake	29a	Ab	42.37N	139.56 E
Kariba Dam	37	Dc	16.30S	28.50 E
Karibib	31	Ik	21.58S	15.51 E
Karibib [3]	37	Bd	22.00S	16.00 E
Kariet-Arkmane	13	Ji	35.06N	2.45W
Karigasniemi	7	Fb	69.24N	25.50 E
Karijärvi	8	Jc	61.35N	22.30 E
Karikachi Tōge	29a	Cb	43.10N	142.40 E
Karikāl	25	Ff	10.55N	79.50 E
Karikari, Cape-	62	Ea	34.47S	173.24 E
Karima (EN) = Kuraymah	31	Kg	18.33N	31.51 E
Karimama	34	Fc	12.04N	3.11 E
Karimata, Kepulauan- = Karimata Islands (EN)	26	Eg	1.25S	109.05 E
Karimata, Pulau-	26	Eg	1.36S	108.55 E
Karimata, Selat- = Karimata Strait (EN)	21	Mj	2.05S	108.40 E
Karimata Islands (EN) = Karimata, Kepulauan-	26	Eg	1.25S	109.05 E
Karimata Strait (EN) = Karimata, Selat-	21	Mj	2.05S	108.40 E
Karimganj	25	Id	24.42N	92.33 E
Karīmnagar	25	Fe	18.26N	79.09 E
Karimunjawa, Kepulauan- = Karimunjawa Islands (EN)	26	Fh	5.50S	110.25 E
Karimunjawa Islands (EN) = Karimunjawa, Kepulauan-	26	Fh	5.50S	110.25 E
Karin [Som.]	35	Hc	10.59N	49.13 E
Karin [Som.]	35	Hc	10.51N	45.45 E
Karis/Karjaa	7	Ff	60.05N	23.40 E
Karisimbi	30	Ji	1.30S	29.27 E
Káristos	15	Hk	38.01N	24.25 E
Karkār	35	Hd	9.57N	49.20 E
Karkaralinsk	19	Hf	49.23N	75.31 E
Karkar Island	57	Fe	4.40S	146.00 E
Karkas, Kūh-e	24	Nf	33.27N	51.48 E
Karkheh	23	Gc	31.31N	47.55 E
Karkinitski zaliv	5	Jf	45.55N	33.00 E
Karkkila/Högfors	7	Ff	60.32N	24.11 E
Karkku	8	Jc	61.25N	23.01 E
Kärkölä	8	Kd	60.55N	25.15 E
Kärla/Kjarla	8	Jf	58.16N	22.05 E
Karlholm	8	Gd	60.31N	17.37 E
Karlik Shan	21	Le	43.00N	94.30 E
Karlino	10	Lb	54.03N	15.51 E
Karliova	24	Ic	39.18N	41.01 E
Karl Marx, Pik-	19	Hh	37.08N	72.29 E
Karl-Marx-Stadt — Chemnitz	6	He	50.50N	12.55 E
Karlö/Hailuoto	5	Ib	65.02N	24.42 E
Karlobag	14	Jf	44.32N	15.05 E
Karlovac	14	Je	45.29N	15.33 E
Karlovka	16	Ie	49.28N	35.08 E
Karlovo	15	Hg	42.38N	24.48 E
Karlovy Vary	10	If	50.14N	12.52 E
Karlsbad	12	Kf	48.55N	8.35 E
Karlsborg	7	Df	58.32N	14.31 E
Karlshamn	7	Dh	56.10N	14.51 E
Karlskoga	7	Dg	59.20N	14.31 E
Karlskrona	6	Hd	56.10N	15.35 E
Karlsöarna	8	Gg	57.15N	18.00 E
Karlsruhe	10	Eg	49.01N	8.24 E
Karlstad [Mn.-U.S.]	45	Hb	48.35N	96.31W
Karlstad [Swe.]	6	Hd	59.22N	13.30 E
Karluk	40	Ie	57.34N	154.28W
Karmah = Kerma (EN)	35	Eb	19.38N	30.25 E
Karmana	18	Ed	40.09N	65.15 E
Karmøy	7	Ag	59.15N	5.15 E
Karnāli	25	Gc	28.45N	81.16 E
Karnataka (Mysore) [3]	25	Ff	13.30N	76.00 E
Karnobat	15	Jg	42.39N	26.59 E
Kärnten = Carinthia (EN) [2]	14	Hd	46.45N	14.00 E
Kärnten = Carinthia (EN)	14	Hd	46.45N	14.00 E
Karoi	37	Dc	16.50S	29.40 E
Karonga	31	Ki	9.56S	33.56 E
Karora	35	Fb	17.39N	38.22 E
Káros	15	Im	36.53N	25.39 E
Kárpathos	15	Kn	35.30N	27.14 E
Kárpathos = Karpathos (EN)	5	Ih	35.40N	27.10 E
Karpathos (EN) = Kárpathos	5	Ih	35.40N	27.10 E
Karpathou, Stenón-	15	Kn	35.50N	27.30 E
Karpenision	15	Ek	38.55N	21.47 E
Karpinsk	17	Jg	59.45N	60.01 E
Karpuzlu	15	Kl	37.33N	27.50 E
Kars	23	Fa	40.37N	43.05 E
Karsakpaj	19	Gf	47.48N	66.45 E
Kärsämäki	7	Fe	64.00N	25.46 E
Karsava/Kårsava	7	Gh	56.47N	27.42 E
Kårsava/Karsava	7	Gh	56.47N	27.42 E
Karši	22	If	38.53N	65.48 E
Karşiyaka	15	Ki	40.26N	28.00 E
Karsiyaka	15	Kk	38.27N	27.07 E
Karskije Vorota, Proliv- = Kara Strait (EN)	21	Hb	70.30N	58.00 E
Karskoje More = Kara Sea (EN)	67	Hd	76.00N	80.00 E
Kars Platosu	24	Jb	40.40N	43.07 E
Karst (EN) = Kras	5	Hf	45.48N	14.00 E
Kårsta	8	He	59.39N	18.14 E
Karstula	7	Fe	62.52N	24.47 E
Kartal	24	Cb	40.53N	29.10 E
Kartaly	19	Ge	53.03N	60.40 E
Kartaly-Ajat	17	Jj	53.01N	61.50 E
Karttula	8	Lb	62.53N	26.58 E
Kartuzy	10	Ob	54.20N	18.12 E
Karumai	29	Ga	40.20N	141.28 E
Karumba	59	Ic	17.29S	140.50 E
Karūn	21	Gf	30.25N	48.12 E
Karungi	7	Fc	66.03N	23.57 E
Karungu	36	Fc	0.51S	34.09 E
Karunki	7	Fc	66.02N	24.01 E
Karūr	25	Ff	10.57N	78.05 E
Karvia	7	Fe	62.08N	22.34 E
Karviná	10	Og	49.51N	18.32 E
Kārwār	25	Ef	14.48N	74.08 E
Karwendel Gebirge	14	Fc	47.28N	11.20 E
Karymskoje	20	Gf	51.37N	114.21 E
Kas	35	Cc	12.34N	24.17 E
Kaş	24	Cd	36.12N	29.38 E
Kasaba [Tur.]	15	Mm	36.18N	29.44 E
Kasaba [Zam.]	36	Ee	10.44S	29.43 E
Kasado-Shima	29	Be	33.57N	131.50 E
Kasah	16	Mi	40.03N	43.52 E
Kasai	29d	Dd	34.56N	134.49 E
Kasai	30	Ii	3.02S	16.57 E
Kasai Occidental [2]	36	Dc	5.00S	21.30 E
Kasai Oriental [2]	36	Dc	3.00S	23.00 E
Kasaji	36	De	10.22S	23.27 E
Kasaku	36	Ec	1.55S	25.50 E
Kasama [Jap.]	29	Gc	36.22N	140.16 E
Kasama [Zam.]	31	Kj	10.13S	31.12 E
Kasan	18	Ee	39.01N	65.35 E
Kasane	31	Jj	17.48S	25.09 E
Kasanga	36	Fd	8.28S	31.09 E
Kasangulu	36	Bc	4.36S	15.10 E
Kasansaj	18	Hd	41.10N	71.32 E
Kasaoka	29	Cd	34.30N	133.29 E
Käsaragod	25	Ef	12.30N	75.00 E
Kasari	29b	Ba	28.27N	129.41 E
Kašary	16	Le	49.02N	41.03 E
Kasatori-Yama	29	Ce	33.33N	132.55 E
Kasba Lake	42	Hd	60.20N	102.10W
Kasba Tatla	32	Fc	32.36N	6.16W
Kaseda	28	Ki	31.25N	130.19 E
Kasempa	36	Ee	13.27S	25.50 E
Kasenga	31	Jj	10.22S	28.37 E
Kasenye	36	Fb	1.24N	30.26 E
Kasese [Ug.]	36	Fb	0.10N	30.05 E
Kasese [Zaire]	36	Ec	1.38S	27.07 E
Kashaf	23	Jb	35.58N	61.07 E
Kāshān	22	Hf	33.59N	51.29 E
Kashi	22	Jf	39.29N	75.58 E
Kashihara	29	Dd	34.31N	135.47 E
Kashima [Jap.]	29	Cd	35.31N	132.59 E
Kashima [Jap.]	29	Gd	35.58N	140.38 E
Kashima [Jap.]	29	Be	33.07N	130.07 E
Kashima-Nada	29	Gc	36.30N	140.45 E
Kashiobwe	36	Ed	9.39S	28.37 E
Kashiwazaki	28	Of	37.25N	138.30 E
Kashkū'iyeh	24	Qh	28.58N	56.37 E
Kāshmar	23	Ib	35.12N	58.27 E
Kashmir	21	Jf	34.00N	76.00 E
Kashmor	25	Dc	28.26N	69.35 E
Kasimov	19	Ee	54.59N	41.28 E
Kašin	19	Dd	57.23N	37.37 E
Kasindi	36	Eb	0.02N	29.43 E
Kašira	7	Ji	54.52N	38.11 E
Kasiruta, Pulau-	26	Ig	0.25S	127.12 E
Kasisty	20	Fb	73.40N	109.45 E
Kaškadarinskaja Oblast [3]	19	Gh	38.50N	66.10 E
Kaškadarja	18	Ee	39.35N	64.38 E
Kaskaskia River	45	Lh	37.59N	89.56W
Kaskelen	19	Hg	43.09N	76.37 E
Kaskö/Kaskinen	7	Ee	62.23N	21.13 E
Kasli	17	Ji	55.53N	60.48 E
Kaslo	46	Gb	49.55N	116.55W
Kasongo	31	Ji	4.27S	26.40 E
Kasongo-Lunda	36	Cd	6.28S	16.49 E
Kásos	15	Jn	35.25N	26.55 E
Kásou, Stenon-	15	Jn	35.25N	26.35 E
Kaspi	16	Ni	41.58N	44.25 E
Kaspičan	15	Kf	43.18N	27.11 E
Kaspijsk	19	Eg	42.57N	47.35 E
Kaspijski	19	Ef	45.25N	47.22 E
Kaspijskoje More = Caspian Sea (EN)	5	Lg	42.00N	50.30 E
Kasplja	16	Gb	55.24N	30.43 E
Kasr, Ra's-	35	Fb	18.04N	38.33 E
Kassaar/Kassar	8	Jf	58.47N	22.40 E
Kassalā	31	Kg	15.28N	36.24 E
Kassalā [3]	35	Fc	14.40N	35.30 E
Kassándra	15	Gi	40.00N	23.30 E
Kassandra, Gulf of- (EN) = Kassándras, Kólpos-	15	Gi	40.05N	23.30 E
Kassándras, Ákra-	15	Gj	39.57N	23.21 E
Kassándras, Kólpos- = Kassandra, Gulf of- (EN)	15	Gi	40.05N	23.30 E
Kassel	10	Fe	51.19N	9.30 E
Kassiópi	15	Cj	39.47N	19.55 E
Kastamonu	23	Da	41.22N	33.47 E
Kastanéai	15	Jh	41.39N	26.28 E
Kastellaun	12	Jd	50.04N	7.27 E
Kastéllion [Grc.]	15	In	35.12N	25.20 E
Kastéllion [Grc.]	15	Gn	35.30N	23.39 E
Kastéllos, Ákra-	15	Kn	35.23N	27.09 E
Kasterlee	12	Gc	51.15N	4.57 E
Kastlösa	8	Gh	56.28N	16.25 E
Kastoria	15	Ei	40.31N	21.16 E
Kastorias, Limni-	15	Ei	40.31N	21.18 E
Kastornoje	16	Kd	51.51N	38.07 E
Kastós	15	Dk	38.35N	20.55 E
Kasuga	29	Be	33.32N	130.27 E
Kasugai	29	Ed	35.14N	136.58 E
Kasulu	36	Fc	4.34S	30.06 E
Kasumbalesa	36	Ee	12.13S	27.48 E
Kasumi	29	Dd	35.38N	134.38 E
Kasumi-ga-Ura	28	Pf	36.00N	140.25 E
Kasumkent	16	Pi	41.42N	48.10 E
Kasungan	26	Fg	1.58S	113.24 E
Kasungu	36	Fe	13.02S	33.29 E
Kasupe	36	Gf	15.10S	35.18 E
Kasūr	25	Eb	31.07N	74.27 E
Kaszuby	10	Ob	54.10N	18.15 E
Kataba	31	Jj	16.05S	25.10 E
Katahdin, Mount-	43	Nb	45.55N	68.55W
Katajsk	17	Kh	56.18N	62.35 E
Katako-Kombe	36	Dc	3.24S	24.25 E
Katanga	36	Ed	10.00S	25.30 E
Katanga	20	Fd	60.10N	102.10 E
Katangli	20	Jf	51.43N	143.16 E
Katanning	59	Df	33.42S	117.33 E
Katav-Ivanovsk	17	Ii	54.47N	58.15 E
Katchall	25	Ig	7.57N	93.22 E
Katchi	32	Ef	17.00N	13.55W
Katende, Chutes de-	36	Dd	6.30S	22.10 E
Katerini	15	Fi	40.16N	22.30 E
Katesh	36	Gc	4.31S	35.23 E
Katete	36	Fe	14.06S	32.05 E
Katha	25	Jd	24.11N	96.21 E
Katherine	58	Ef	14.28S	132.16 E
Katherine River	59	Gb	14.39S	131.42 E
Kāthiāwār	21	Jg	21.58N	70.30 E
Kāthmāndāu = Kathmandu (EN)	22	Kg	27.43N	85.19 E
Kathmandu → Kāthmāndāu	22	Kg	27.43N	85.19 E
Kathua	36	Gc	1.17S	39.03 E
Kati	34	Dc	12.43N	8.05W
Katihār	25	Hc	25.32N	87.35 E
Katiki, Volcán-	65d	Bb	27.06S	109.16W
Katima Mulilo	36	Df	17.28S	24.14 E
Katiola	34	Dd	8.08N	5.06W
Katiola [3]	34	Dd	8.13N	5.02W
Katiu Atoll	61	Mc	16.26S	144.22W
Katla	7a	Bc	63.36N	18.58W
Katlabuh, Ozero-	15	Ld	45.25N	29.00 E
Katlanovo	15	Eh	41.54N	21.41 E
Katmai, Mount-	40	Ie	58.17N	154.56W
Káto Akhaia	15	Ek	38.09N	21.33 E
Katofio	36	Ee	11.02S	28.01 E
Katompi	36	Ed	6.11S	26.20 E
Katonga	36	Fb	0.10N	30.40 E
Katon-Karagaj	19	If	49.11N	85.37 E
Káto Ólimbos	15	Fj	39.55N	22.28 E
Katoomba	59	Kf	33.42S	150.18 E
Katopasa, Gunung-	26	Hg	1.14S	121.25 E

Index Symbols

[1] Independent Nation
[2] State, Region
[3] District, County
[4] Municipality
[5] Colony, Dependency
Continent
Physical Region
Historical or Cultural Region
Mount, Mountain
Volcano
Hill
Mountains, Mountain Range
Hills, Escarpment
Plateau, Upland
Pass, Gap
Plain, Lowland
Delta
Salt Flat
Valley, Canyon
Crater, Cave
Karst Features
Depression
Polder
Desert, Dunes
Forest, Woods
Heath, Steppe
Oasis
Cape, Point
Coast, Beach
Cliff
Peninsula
Isthmus
Sandbank
Island
Atoll
Rock, Reef
Islands, Archipelago
Rocks, Reefs
Coral Reef
Well, Spring
Geyser
River, Stream
Waterfall Rapids
River Mouth, Estuary
Lake
Salt Lake
Intermittent Lake
Reservoir
Swamp, Pond
Canal
Glacier
Ice Shelf, Pack Ice
Ocean
Sea
Gulf, Bay
Strait, Fjord
Lagoon
Bank
Seamount
Tablemount
Ridge
Shelf
Basin
Escarpment, Sea Scarp
Fracture
Trench, Abyss
National Park, Reserve
Point of Interest
Recreation Site
Cave, Cavern
Historic Site
Ruins
Wall, Walls
Church, Abbey
Temple
Scientific Station
Airport
Port
Lighthouse
Mine
Tunnel
Dam, Bridge

Index Symbols

[1]	Independent Nation
[2]	State, Region
[3]	District, County
[4]	Municipality
[5]	Colony, Dependency
◆	Continent
◇	Physical Region
≡	Historical or Cultural Region
▲	Mount, Mountain
▲	Volcano
▲	Hill
▲	Mountains, Mountain Range
⬯	Hills, Escarpment
≡	Plateau, Upland
⬯	Pass, Gap
⬯	Plain, Lowland
⬯	Delta
⬯	Salt Flat
⬯	Valley, Canyon
⬯	Crater, Cave
✸	Karst Features
▭	Depression
⬯	Polder
⬯	Desert, Dunes
⬯	Forest, Woods
⬯	Heath, Steppe
⬯	Oasis
⬯	Cape, Point
⬯	Coast, beach
⬯	Cliff
⬯	Peninsula
⬯	Isthmus
⬯	Sandbank
⬯	Island
⬯	Atoll
⬯	Rock, Reef
⬯	Islands, Archipelago
⬯	Rocks, Reefs
⬯	Coral Reef
⬯	Well, Spring
⬯	Geyser
⬯	River, Stream
⬯	Waterfall Rapids
⬯	River Mouth, Estuary
⬯	Lake
⬯	Salt Lake
⬯	Intermittent Lake
⬯	Reservoir
⬯	Swamp, Pond
⬯	Canal
⬯	Glacier
⬯	Ice Shelf, Pack Ice
⬯	Ocean
⬯	Sea
⬯	Gulf, Bay
⬯	Strait, Fjord
⬯	Lagoon
⬯	Bank
⬯	Seamount
⬯	Tablemount
⬯	Ridge
⬯	Shelf
⬯	Basin
⬯	Escarpment, Sea Scarp
⬯	Fracture
⬯	Trench, Abyss
⬯	National Park, Reserve
⬯	Point of Interest
⬯	Recreation Site
⬯	Cave, Cavern
⬯	Historic Site
⬯	Ruins
⬯	Wall, Walls
⬯	Church, Abbey
⬯	Temple
⬯	Scientific Station
⬯	Airport
⬯	Port
⬯	Lighthouse
⬯	Mine
⬯	Tunnel
⬯	Dam, Bridge

Index Symbols

- [1] Independent Nation
- [2] State, Region
- [3] District, County
- [4] Municipality
- [5] Colony, Dependency
- Continent
- Physical Region
- Historical or Cultural Region
- Mount, Mountain
- Volcano
- Hill
- Mountains, Mountain Range
- Hills, Escarpment
- Plateau, Upland
- Pass, Gap
- Plain, Lowland
- Delta
- Salt Flat
- Valley, Canyon
- Crater, Cave
- Karst Features
- Depression
- Polder
- Desert, Dunes
- Forest, Woods
- Heath, Steppe
- Oasis
- Cape, Point
- Coast, Beach
- Cliff
- Peninsula
- Isthmus
- Sandbank
- Island
- Islands, Archipelago
- Rocks, Reefs
- Coral Reef
- Well, Spring
- Geyser
- River, Stream
- Rock, Reef
- Waterfall, Rapids
- River Mouth, Estuary
- Lake
- Salt Lake
- Intermittent Lake
- Reservoir
- Swamp, Pond
- Canal
- Glacier
- Ice Shelf, Pack Ice
- Ocean
- Sea
- Gulf, Bay
- Strait, Fjord
- Lagoon
- Bank
- Seamount
- Tablemount
- Ridge
- Shelf
- Basin
- Escarpment, Sea Scarp
- Fracture
- Trench, Abyss
- National Park, Reserve
- Point of Interest
- Recreation Site
- Cave, Cavern
- Historic Site
- Ruins
- Wall, Walls
- Church, Abbey
- Temple
- Scientific Station
- Airport
- Port
- Lighthouse
- Mine
- Tunnel
- Dam, Bridge

Name	Page	Grid	Lat.	Long.
Kisújszállás	10	Qi	47.13N	20.46 E
Kisuki	29	Cd	35.17N	132.54 E
Kisumu	31	Ki	0.06S	34.45 E
Kisvárda	10	Sh	48.13N	22.05 E
Kita	31	Gg	13.03N	9.30W
Kitab	19	Gh	39.08N	66.54 E
Kita-Daitō-Jima	27	Nf	25.55N	131.20 E
Kitaibaraki	28	Pf	36.48N	140.45 E
Kita-Iō-Jima	60	Cb	25.26N	141.17 E
Kitaj, Ozero-	15	Md	45.35N	29.15 E
Kitakami	27	Pd	39.30N	141.10 E
Kitakami-Gawa	29	Gb	38.25N	141.19 E
Kitakami-Sanchi	29	Gb	39.30N	141.30 E
Kitakata	28	Of	37.39N	139.52 E
Kitakyushū	22	Pf	33.53N	130.50 E
Kitale	31	Kh	1.01N	35.00 E
Kitamaiaioi	29a	Cb	43.33N	143.57 E
Kitami	27	Pc	43.48N	143.54 E
Kitami-Fuji	29a	Cb	43.42N	143.14 E
Kitami-Sanchi	28	Qb	44.30N	142.30 E
Kitami Tōge	29a	Cb	43.55N	142.55 E
Kitan-Kaikyō	29	Dd	34.15N	135.00 E
Kita-Taiheiyō=Pacific Ocean (EN)	60	Ch	22.00N	167.00 E
Kita-Ura	29	Gc	36.00N	140.34 E
Kit Carson	45	Eg	38.46N	102.48W
Kitchener	42	Jh	43.27N	80.29W
Kitee	7	He	62.06N	30.09 E
Kitessa	35	Dd	5.22N	25.22 E
Kitgum	36	Fb	3.19N	32.53 E
Kithira=Cythera (EN)	15	Fm	36.09N	23.00 E
Kithira=Kythera (EN)	5	Ih	36.15N	23.00 E
Kithira Channel (EN)= Kithiron Dhiékplous	15	Fm	36.00N	23.00 E
Kithiron, Dhiékplous-= Kithira Channel (EN)	15	Fm	36.00N	23.00 E
Kithnos	15	Hl	37.25N	24.26 E
Kithnos	15	Hl	37.25N	24.25 E
Kithnou, Stenón-	15	Hl	37.25N	24.30 E
Kitimat	39	Gd	54.05N	128.38W
Kitimat Ranges	42	Ef	53.58N	128.39W
Kitoushi-Yama	29a	Cb	43.27N	143.25 E
Kitriani	15	Hm	36.54N	24.44 E
Kitridge Point	51q	Bb	13.09N	59.25W
Kitros	15	Fi	40.22N	22.35 E
Kitsuki	29	Be	33.25N	131.37 E
Kittanning	44	He	40.49N	79.31W
Kittery	44	Ld	43.05N	70.45W
Kittilä	7	Fc	67.40N	24.54 E
Kitui	31	Ki	1.22S	38.01 E
Kitunda	36	Fd	6.48S	33.13 E
Kitutu	36	Ec	3.17S	28.05 E
Kitwe-Nkana	31	Jj	12.49S	28.13 E
Kitzbühel	14	Gc	47.27N	12.23 E
Kitzbüheler Alpen	14	Gc	47.20N	12.20 E
Kitzingen	10	Gg	49.44N	10.10 E
Kiunga [Kenya]	36	Hc	1.45S	41.29 E
Kiunga [Pap.N.Gui.]	60	Ci	6.07S	141.18 E
Kiuruvesi	7	Ge	63.39N	26.37 E
Kivalina	40	Gc	67.59N	164.33W
Kivercy	16	Dd	50.50N	25.31 E
Kivijärvi [Fin.]	8	Ld	60.55N	27.40 E
Kivijärvi [Fin.]	7	Fe	63.10N	25.09 E
Kivik	7	Di	55.41N	14.15 E
Kiviöli/Kiviyli	7	Gg	59.23N	26.59 E
Kiviyli/Kiviöli	7	Gg	59.23N	26.59 E
Kivu [2]	36	Ec	2.30S	27.30 E
Kivu, Lac-=Kivu, Lake- (EN)	30	Ii	2.00S	29.10 E
Kivu, Lake- (EN)=Kivu, Lac-	30	Ii	2.00S	29.10 E
Kiwai Island	60	Ci	8.30S	143.25 E
Kiyāmakī Dāgh	24	Kc	38.47N	45.51 E
Kiyiköy	24	Cb	41.25N	28.01 E
Kiyosato	29a	Db	43.51N	144.35 E
Kizel	19	Fd	59.03N	57.40 E
Kizema	7	Kf	61.09N	44.46 E
Kizilcabölük	15	Ml	37.37N	29.01 E
Kızılca Dağı	24	Cd	36.55N	29.52 E
Kızılcahaman	24	Eb	40.28N	32.39 E
Kızıl Dağ	24	Ed	36.25N	32.42 E
Kizilhisar	15	Ml	37.33N	29.18 E
Kizilirmak	21	Fe	41.45N	35.59 E
Kızılırmak	24	Eb	40.22N	33.59 E
Kiziljurt	16	Oh	43.13N	46.55 E
Kizilskoje	17	Ij	52.44N	58.54 E
Kızıltepe	24	Id	37.12N	40.36 E
Kizimen, Vulkan-	20	Le	55.03N	160.27 E
Kižinga	20	Ff	51.51N	109.55 E
Kizir	20	Ef	54.10N	93.30 E
Kizljar	19	Eg	43.50N	46.42 E
Kizljarski Zaliv	16	Og	44.35N	46.55 E
Kizukuri	29a	Bc	40.48N	140.22 E
Kizyl-Arvat	19	Fh	39.01N	56.20 E
Kizyl-Atrek	19	Fh	37.38N	54.47 E
Kizyl-Su	19	Fh	39.46N	53.01 E
Kjahta	20	Ff	50.26N	106.25 E
Kjalvaz	16	Pj	38.38N	48.20 E
Kjardla/Kärdla	7	Fg	59.01N	22.42 E
Kjarevere/Kärevere	8	Lf	58.23N	26.30 E
Kjarla/Kärla	8	Jf	58.16N	22.05 E
Kjellerup	8	Ch	56.17N	9.26 E
Kjøllefjord	7	Ga	70.56N	27.27 E
Kjölur	7a	Bb	64.50N	19.25W
Kjøpsvik	7	Db	68.06N	16.21 E
Kjubjume	20	Jd	63.28N	140.30 E
Kjurdamir	19	Eg	40.20N	48.07 E
Kjusjur	20	Hb	70.35N	127.45 E
Kjustendil	15	Fg	42.17N	22.41 E
Kjustendil [2]	15	Fg	42.17N	22.41 E
Kjyosumi-Yama	29	Gd	35.10N	140.09 E
Klabat, Gunung-	26	If	1.28N	125.02 E
Kladanj	23	Gf	44.14N	18.42 E
Kladno	10	Kf	50.09N	14.07 E
Kladovo	15	Fe	44.37N	22.37 E
Klagenfurt	6	Hf	46.38N	14.18 E
Klaipėda/Klajpeda	6	Id	55.43N	21.07 E
Klajpeda/Klaipėda	6	Id	55.43N	21.07 E
Klamath	46	Cf	41.32N	124.02W
Klamath Falls	39	Ge	42.13N	121.46W
Klamath Mountains	43	Cc	41.40N	123.20W
Klamath River	46	Cf	41.33N	124.04W
Klamono	26	Jg	1.08S	131.30 E
Klarälven	5	Hd	59.23N	13.32 E
Klaten	26	Fh	7.42S	110.35 E
Klatovy	10	Jg	49.24N	13.19 E
Klavreström	8	Fg	57.08N	15.08 E
Klawer	37	Bf	31.44S	18.36 E
Klazienaveen, Emmen-	12	Jb	52.44N	7.01 E
Kleck	16	Ec	53.03N	26.40 E
Kłecko	10	Nd	52.38N	17.26 E
Kleinblittersdorf	12	Je	49.09N	7.02 E
Kleine Nete	12	Gc	51.08N	4.34 E
Kleine Sluis, Anna Paulowna-	12	Gb	52.52N	4.52 E
Klein-Karoo=Little Karroo (EN)	37	Cf	33.42S	21.20 E
Kleinsee	37	Be	29.40S	17.05 E
Klekovača	14	Kf	44.26N	16.31 E
Kléla	34	Dc	11.40N	5.40W
Kleppe	8	Af	58.46N	5.40 E
Klerksdorp	37	De	26.58S	26.39 E
Kletnja	19	De	53.27N	33.17 E
Kletski	16	Me	49.19N	43.04 E
Kleve	10	Ce	51.47N	6.09 E
Klibreck, Ben-	9	Ic	58.19N	4.30W
Klička	20	Gf	50.24N	118.01 E
Klimoviči	19	De	53.37N	32.01 E
Klimovo	16	Hc	52.23N	32.16 E
Klin	19	Dd	56.20N	36.42 E
Klina	15	Dg	42.37N	20.35 E
Klincy	19	De	52.46N	32.17 E
Klingbach	12	Ke	49.11N	8.24 E
Klingenthal	10	If	50.22N	12.28 E
Klinovec	10	If	50.24N	12.58 E
Klintehamn	7	Eh	57.24N	18.12 E
Klippan	8	Eh	56.08N	13.06 E
Klipplaat	37	Cf	33.02S	24.21 E
Kliškovcy	15	Ja	48.23N	26.13 E
Klisura	15	Hg	42.42N	24.27 E
Klitmøller	8	Cg	57.02N	8.31 E
Kljazma	5	Kd	56.10N	42.58 E
Ključevskaja Sopka, Vulkan-	21	Sd	56.04N	160.38 E
Kljuci	20	Le	56.14N	160.58 E
Kłobuck	10	Of	50.55N	18.57 E
Kłodawa	10	Od	52.16N	18.55 E
Kłodzka, Kotlina-	10	Mf	50.30N	16.35 E
Kłodzko	10	Mf	50.28N	16.40 E
Kløfta	8	Dd	60.04N	11.09 E
Kloga/Klooga	8	Ke	59.24N	24.10 E
Kłomnice	10	Pf	50.56N	19.21 E
Klondike Plateau	42	Dd	63.10N	139.55W
Klondike River	42	Dd	64.03N	139.26W
Klooga/Kloga	8	Ke	59.24N	24.10 E
Kloosteezande, Hontenisse-	12	Gc	51.23N	4.00 E
Klosi	15	Dh	41.29N	20.06 E
Klosterneuburg	14	Kb	48.18N	16.19 E
Klosters/Claustra	14	Dd	46.52N	9.52 E
Kloten	14	Cc	47.27N	8.35 E
Klotz, Lac-	42	Kd	60.40N	73.00W
Kluane Lake	42	Dd	61.15N	138.40W
Kluczbork	10	Of	50.59N	18.13 E
Knaben	8	Bf	58.39N	7.04 E
Knäred	8	Eh	56.32N	13.19 E
Kneža	15	Hf	43.30N	24.05 E
Knife River	45	Fc	47.20N	101.23W
Knin	14	Kf	44.02N	16.12 E
Knislinge	8	Fh	56.11N	14.05 E
Knittelfeld	14	Ic	47.13N	14.49 E
Knivsta	8	Ge	59.43N	17.48 E
Knjaževac	15	Ff	43.34N	22.15 E
Knobly Mountain	44	Hf	39.15N	79.05W
Knockmealdown Mountains/ Cnoc Mhaoldonn	9	Fi	52.15N	8.00W
Knokke-Heist [Bel.]	12	Fc	51.21N	3.15 E
Knokke-Heist [Bel.]	11	Jc	51.21N	3.17 E
Knokke-Westkapelle	12	Fc	51.19N	3.18 E
Knolls grund	8	Gg	57.30N	17.30 E
Knøsen	8	Dg	57.12N	10.18 E
Knosós = Cnossus (EN)	15	In	35.18N	25.10 E
Knox, Cape-	42	Ef	54.11N	133.05W
Knox Coast	66	He	66.30S	105.00 E
Knoxville [Ia.-U.S.]	45	Jf	41.19N	93.06W
Knoxville [Tn.-U.S.]	39	Kf	35.58N	83.56W
Knud Rasmussen Land	67	Nd	80.00N	55.00W
Knüllgebirge	10	Ff	50.50N	9.30 E
Knutsholstind	8	Cc	61.26N	8.34 E
Knysna	31	Jl	34.02S	23.02 E
Ko, Kut	25	Kf	11.40N	102.35 E
Koartac	42	Kd	60.50N	69.30W
Koba	26	Eg	2.29S	106.24 E
Koba, Pulau-	26	Jh	6.25S	134.28 E
Kobar Sink	35	Gc	14.00N	40.30 E
Kobayashi	28	Ki	31.59N	130.59 E
Kobdo	22	Le	48.01N	91.38 E
Kobdo (Chovd)	27	Fb	48.06N	92.11 E
Kōbe	22	Pf	34.41N	135.10 E
Kobeljaki	16	Ie	49.08N	34.12 E
København [2]	8	Ei	55.40N	12.10 E
København=Copenhagen (EN)	6	Hi	55.40N	12.35 E
Kobenni	32	Ff	15.55N	9.05W
Kobern-Gondorf	12	Jd	50.19N	7.28 E
Kobjaj	20	Hd	63.30N	126.26 E
Koblenz	10	Df	50.21N	7.36 E
Kobo	35	Fc	12.09N	39.39 E
Koboldo	20	If	52.58N	132.42 E
Kobra	7	Mg	59.19N	50.54 E
Kobrin	19	Ce	52.13N	24.23 E
Kobrinskoje	8	Ne	59.22N	30.14 E
Kobroor, Pulau-	26	Jh	6.12S	134.32 E
Kobuk	38	Cc	66.45N	161.00W
Kobuleti	16	Li	41.47N	41.45 E
Koca	24	Eb	41.41N	32.15 E
Kocabaş	24	Bb	40.22N	27.19 E
Koca Çay	15	Lj	38.43N	28.30 E
Koca Çay [Tur.]	24	Bb	40.08N	27.57 E
Koca Çay [Tur.]	24	Cd	36.17N	29.16 E
Koca Çay/Orhaneli	15	Lj	39.56N	28.32 E
Kočani	15	Fh	41.55N	22.25 E
Kocasu	15	Mj	39.42N	29.31 E
Kočečum	20	Fd	64.17N	100.10 E
Kočetovka	16	Lc	53.01N	40.31 E
Kočevje	14	Ie	45.39N	14.51 E
Kočevski rog	14	Ie	45.41N	15.00 E
Koch	42	Jc	69.35N	78.20W
Kŏch'ang	28	Ig	35.41N	127.55 E
Ko Chang	25	Kf	12.00N	102.23 E
Koch Bihār	25	Hc	26.19N	89.26 E
Kochi	27	Ne	33.33N	133.33 E
Kōchi Ken [2]	28	Lh	33.20N	133.30 E
Kochisar Ovası	24	Ec	38.50N	33.30 E
Kock	10	Se	51.39N	22.27 E
Kočkorka	18	Jc	42.11N	75.45 E
Kočmar	15	Kf	43.41N	27.28 E
Kočubej	19	Eg	44.23N	46.31 E
Kočubejevskoje	16	Lg	44.41N	41.50 E
Kodiak	39	Dd	57.48N	152.23W
Kodiak	38	Dd	57.30N	153.30W
Kodino	7	Je	63.44N	39.40 E
Kodok	35	Ed	9.53N	32.07 E
Kodomari	29a	Bc	41.08N	140.18 E
Kodori	16	Lh	42.49N	41.10 E
Kodry	15	Lb	47.15N	28.15 E
Kodyma	16	Ge	48.01N	30.48 E
Kodža Balkan	15	Jg	42.50N	27.00 E
Koekenaap	37	Bf	31.29S	18.19 E
Koes	37	Be	25.59S	19.08 E
Kofa Mountains	46	Ij	33.20N	114.00W
Kofarli	15	Kl	37.45N	27.42 E
Kofaz	24	Bb	41.58N	27.12 E
Koffiefontein	37	Ce	29.30S	25.00 E
Kofiau, Pulau-	26	Ig	1.11S	129.50 E
Köflach	14	Jc	47.04N	15.05 E
Koforidua	31	Gh	6.05N	0.15W
Kōfu [Jap.]	29	Cd	35.18N	133.29 E
Kōfu [Jap.]	27	Od	35.39N	138.35 E
Koga	29	Fc	36.12N	139.42 E
Kogaluc	42	Je	59.38N	77.30W
Kōge	29	Dd	35.24N	134.15 E
Køge	7	Ci	55.27N	12.11 E
Køge Bugt	8	Ei	55.30N	12.20 E
Kogel	17	He	62.38N	57.07 E
Kogilnik	15	Md	45.51N	29.38 E
Kogilnik (Kunduk)	15	Md	45.51N	29.38 E
Kogon	34	Cc	11.09N	14.42W
Kogota	29	Gb	38.32N	141.01 E
Kohala Mountains	65a	Fc	20.05N	155.43W
Kohāt	25	Eb	33.35N	71.26 E
Kohila	8	Ke	59.11N	24.40 E
Kohima	25	Ic	25.40N	94.07 E
Koh-i Mārān	25	Dc	29.05N	66.50 E
Kohinggo	63a	Cc	8.13S	157.10 E
Kohma	7	Jh	56.57N	41.07 E
Kohtla-Jarve/Kohtla-Järve	19	Cd	59.25N	27.14 E
Kohu Dağı	15	Mm	36.30N	29.50 E
Kohunlich	48	Oh	18.30N	88.55W
Koide	29	Fc	37.14N	138.57 E
Koigi/Kojgi	8	Kf	58.49N	25.40 E
Koin	17	Ee	63.10N	51.15 E
Koindu	34	Cd	8.28N	10.20W
Koitere	7	He	62.58N	30.45 E
Kojā	23	Jd	25.34N	61.13 E
Kojandytau	18	Lb	44.20N	78.45 E
Kojda	7	Kc	66.23N	42.31 E
Koje-Do	28	Jg	34.52N	128.37 E
Kojetín	10	Ng	49.21N	17.20 E
Kojgi/Koigi	8	Kf	58.49N	25.40 E
Ko-Jima [Jap.]	29	Fe	33.07N	139.40 E
Ko-Jima [Jap.]	28	Od	41.22N	139.47 E
Kojō	27	Md	38.57N	127.52 E
Kojonup	59	Df	33.50S	117.09 E
Kojtaš	18	Fd	40.14N	67.22 E
Kojtezek, Pereval-	18	If	37.29N	72.45 E
Kojur	24	Nd	36.23N	51.43 E
Kojva	17	Ig	58.15N	58.14 E
Kokab	35	Cc	10.03N	22.04 E
Kokai-Gawa	29	Gd	35.52N	140.08 E
Kokand	22	Je	40.33N	70.57 E
Kökar	7	Eg	59.55N	20.55 E
Kökarsfjärden	8	Ie	59.55N	20.45 E
Kokas	26	Jg	2.42S	132.26 E
Kokava nad Rimavicou	10	Ph	48.34N	19.50 E
Kokawa	29	Dd	34.17N	135.26 E
Kokčetav	22	Id	53.17N	69.25 E
Kokčetavskaja Oblast [3]	19	Ge	53.30N	70.00 E
Kokemäenjoki	8	Ic	61.33N	21.42 E
Kokemäki/Kumo	7	Ff	61.15N	22.21 E
Kok-Jangak	19	Hg	40.59N	73.15 E
Kokkina	24	Ee	35.10N	32.36 E
Kokkola/Gamlakarleby	6	Ic	63.50N	23.07 E
Koko [Eth.]	35	Fc	10.20N	36.04 E
Koko [Nig.]	34	Fc	11.26N	4.30 E
Kokomo	43	Jc	40.29N	86.08W
Kokonau	26	Kg	4.43S	136.26 E
Kokong	37	Cd	24.27S	23.03 E
Koko Nor (EN)=Qinghai Hu	21	Mf	37.00N	100.20 E
Kokpekty	19	If	48.45N	82.24 E
Kokšaal-Tau, Hrebet-	19	Hg	41.00N	78.00 E
Kokšenga	7	Kf	61.27N	42.38 E
Koksijde	12	Ec	51.06N	2.39 E
Koksoak	42	Ke	58.31N	68.11W
Kokstad	31	Jl	30.32S	29.29 E
Koktal	18	Lb	44.05N	79.44 E
Koktokay/Fuyun	22	Ke	47.13N	89.39 E
Kokubu	28	Ki	31.44N	130.46 E
Kola	19	Db	68.53N	33.01 E
Kola, Pulau-	26	Jh	5.30S	134.35 E
Kolahun	34	Cd	8.17N	10.05W
Kolaka	26	Hg	4.03S	121.36 E
Kolamadulu Atoll	25a	Bb	2.25N	73.10 E
Kola Peninsula (EN)=Kolski Poluostrov	5	Jb	67.30N	37.00 E
Kolār Gold Fields	25	Ff	12.55N	78.17 E
Kolari	7	Fc	67.20N	23.48 E
Kolárovo	10	Ni	47.55N	18.00 E
Kolašin	15	Cg	42.49N	19.32 E
Kolbäck	8	Ge	59.34N	16.15 E
Kolbäcksån	8	Ge	59.32N	16.16 E
Kolbio	36	Hc	1.09S	41.12 E
Kolbuszowa	10	Rf	50.15N	21.47 E
Kolby	8	Di	55.48N	10.33 E
Kolčugino	7	Jh	56.16N	39.23 E
Kolda	34	Cc	12.53N	14.57W
Kolding	6	Gd	55.31N	9.29 E
Kole [Zaire]	36	Dc	3.31S	22.27 E
Kole [Zaire]	36	Eb	2.07N	25.26 E
Koléa	13	Oh	36.38N	2.46 E
Kolendo	20	Jf	53.43N	142.57 E
Kolente	34	Cd	8.55N	13.08W
Kolesnoje	15	Mc	46.04N	29.45 E
Kolga	8	Ke	59.28N	25.29 E
Kolga, Zaliv-/Kolga Laht	8	Ke	59.30N	25.15 E
Kolga Laht/Kolga, Zaliv-	8	Ke	59.30N	25.15 E
Kolgompja, Mys-	8	Me	59.44N	28.35 E
Kolgujev, Ostrov-	5	Kb	69.05N	49.15 E
Kolhāpur	22	Jh	16.42N	74.13 E
Kolhozabad	18	Gf	37.35N	68.39 E
Kolhozbentskoje, Vodohranilišče-	18	Df	37.10N	62.30 E
Koli	7	Ge	63.06N	29.53 E
Kolimbiné	34	Cc	14.45N	11.00 E
Kolín	10	Lf	50.02N	15.13 E
Kolito	35	Fd	7.25N	38.07 E
Koljučinskaja Guba	20	Nc	66.50N	174.30W
Kolka	8	Jg	57.44N	22.27 E
Kolkasrags	7	Fh	57.46N	22.37 E
Kolki	16	Dd	51.07N	25.42 E
Kollinai	15	Fl	37.17N	22.22 E
Kollumúli	7a	Cb	65.47N	14.21W
Kolmården	8	Gf	58.41N	16.35 E
Köln=Cologne (EN)	6	Ge	50.56N	6.57 E
Köln-Lövenich	12	Id	50.57N	6.50 E
Kolno	10	Rc	53.25N	21.56 E
Köln-Porz	10	Df	50.53N	7.03 E
Koło	10	Od	52.12N	18.38 E
Koloa	65a	Bb	21.54N	159.28W
Kołobrzeg	10	Lb	54.12N	15.33 E
Kolodnja	16	Hb	54.49N	32.11 E
Kologriv	7	Kg	58.51N	44.17 E
Kolokani	34	Dc	13.34N	8.03W
Koloko	34	Dc	11.05N	5.19W
Kolokolkova Guba	17	Fb	68.30N	52.30 E
Kololo	35	Gd	7.27N	41.59 E
Kolombangara Island	60	Fi	8.00S	157.05 E
Kolomna	6	Jd	55.05N	38.49 E
Kolomyja	19	Cf	48.32N	25.01 E
Kolondiéba	34	Dc	11.06N	6.53W
Kolonga	65b	Ac	21.08S	175.04W
Kolonodale	26	Hg	2.00S	121.19 E
Kolosovka	19	Hd	56.28N	73.36 E
Kolossa	34	Dc	13.52N	7.35W
Kolovai	65b	Ac	21.06S	175.20W
Kolozero, Ozero-	7	Hb	68.15N	33.15 E
Kolp	7	Ig	59.20N	36.50 E
Kolpaševo	22	Kd	58.20N	82.50 E
Kolpino	7	Hg	59.45N	30.33 E
Kolpny	16	Jc	52.16N	37.00 E
Kolski Poluostrov=Kola Peninsula (EN)	5	Jb	67.30N	37.00 E
Koltubanovski	16	Rc	52.57N	52.02 E
Kolubara	15	De	44.40N	20.15 E
Koluszki	10	Pe	51.44N	19.49 E
Koluton	19	Ge	51.42N	69.25 E
Kolva	19	Fb	65.55N	57.20 E
Kolva	17	Hf	60.22N	56.33 E
Kolvickoje, Ozero-	7	Hc	67.05N	33.30 E
Kolvrå	8	Ch	56.18N	9.08 E
Kolwezi	31	Jj	10.43S	25.28 E
Kolyma	21	Sc	69.30N	161.00 E
Kolyma Plain (EN) = Kolymskaja Nizmennost	21	Rc	68.30N	154.00 E
Kolyma Range (EN)= Kolymskoje Nagorje	21	Rc	62.30N	155.00 E
Kolymskaja Nizmennost= Kolyma Plain (EN)	21	Rc	68.30N	154.00 E
Kolymskoje Nagorje= Kolyma Range (EN)	21	Rc	62.30N	155.00 E
Kolyšlej	16	Nc	52.40N	44.31 E
Kolžat	19	Ig	43.29N	80.37 E
Kom	15	Gf	43.10N	23.03 E
Kom	36	Gb	1.05N	38.02 E
Komádi	10	Rj	47.00N	21.30 E
Komadugu Gana	34	Hc	13.05N	12.24 E
Komadugu Yobe	30	Ig	13.42N	13.24 E
Komagane	29	Ed	35.43N	137.54 E
Koma-ga-Take [Jap.]	29	Fd	35.45N	138.13 E
Koma-ga-Take [Jap.]	29	Gb	39.47N	140.50 E
Koma-ga-Take [Jap.]	29a	Bb	42.04N	140.40 E
Komandorski Islands (EN) =Komandorskije Ostrova	21	Sd	55.00N	167.00 E
Komandorskije Ostrova= Komandorski Islands (EN)	21	Sd	55.00N	167.00 E
Komandorskiye Basin (EN)	20	Le	57.00N	168.00 E
Komarin	16	Gd	51.27N	30.32 E
Komarno	10	Tg	49.34N	23.43 E
Komárno	10	Oi	47.46N	18.09 E
Komárom	10	Oi	47.44N	18.07 E
Komárom-Esztegom	10	Oi	47.40N	18.15 E
Komatipoort	37	Ee	25.25S	31.55 E
Komatsu	27	Od	36.24N	136.37 E
Komatsujima	29	Dd	34.01N	134.35 E
Komba, Pulau-	26	Hh	7.47S	123.35 E
Kombissiri	34	Ec	12.04N	1.20W
Kombolcha	35	Fc	11.05N	39.45 E
Komebail Lagoon	64a	Ac	7.24N	134.27 E
Komen/Comines	12	Ed	50.46N	2.59 E
Komi respublika	19	Fc	64.00N	55.00 E
Komi-Permijackij avtonomnyj okrug	19	Fd	60.00N	54.30 E
Komló	10	Oj	46.12N	18.16 E
Kommunarsk (Alčevsk)	16	Ke	48.27N	38.52 E
Kommunary	8	Nd	60.55N	30.10 E
Kommunizma, Pik-= Communism Peak (EN)	21	Jf	38.57N	72.08 E
Komodo, Pulau-	26	Gh	8.36S	119.30 E
Komoé	30	Gh	5.12N	3.44W
Komoé [3]	34	Ec	10.25N	4.20W
Komono	36	Bc	3.15S	13.14 E
Komoran, Pulau-	26	Kh	8.18S	138.45 E
Komoro	29	Fc	36.19N	138.24 E
Komotini	15	Ih	41.07N	25.24 E
Komovi	15	Cg	42.41N	19.39 E
Kompasberg	30	Jl	31.46S	24.32 E
Komrat	16	Ff	46.17N	28.38 E
Komsa	20	Dd	61.40N	89.25 E
Komsomolec	17	Kj	53.45N	62.02 E
Komsomolec, Ostrov-	21	La	80.30N	95.00 E
Komsomolec, Zaliv-	16	Rg	45.30N	52.45 E
Komsomolsk	7	Jh	57.02N	40.22 E
Komsomolsk	20	De	57.25N	86.02 E
Komsomolsk	19	Gh	39.02N	63.36 E
Komsomolski	19	Ff	47.20N	53.44 E
Komsomolski	16	Og	45.22N	46.01 E
Komsomolski	7	Ki	54.27N	45.45 E
Komsomolski	19	Gb	67.35N	63.47 E
Komsomolski	17	Kf	61.20N	63.15 E
Komsomolski	20	Mc	69.12N	172.55 E
Komsomolsk-na-Amure	22	Pd	50.36N	137.02 E
Komsomolsk-na-Ustjurte	19	Fg	44.07N	58.17 E
Komsomolskoje [Ukraine]	16	Je	49.36N	36.33 E
Komsomolskoje [Ukraine]	16	Kf	47.37N	38.05 E
Komsomolskoj Pravdy, Ostrova-	20	Fa	77.15N	107.30 E
Kŏmun-Do	28	Ig	34.02N	127.19 E
Kömür Burun	15	Jk	38.39N	26.25 E
Komusan	27	Mc	42.07N	129.42 E
Kona	34	Ec	14.57N	3.53W
Kona Coast	65a	Fd	19.35N	155.56W
Konakovo	19	Dd	56.42N	36.46 E
Konar	23	Lc	34.25N	70.32 E
Konārak	25	Hh	19.54N	86.07 E
Konarha [3]	23	Lb	35.15N	71.00 E
Konda	19	Gc	60.40N	69.46 E
Kondagaon	25	Ge	19.36N	81.40 E
Kondinin	59	Df	32.30S	118.16 E
Kondinskoje	17	Mg	59.40N	67.25 E
Kondoa	31	Ki	4.54S	35.47 E
Kondopoga	6	Jc	62.13N	34.17 E
Kondratjevo	8	Md	60.36N	28.02 E
Kondrovo	19	De	54.49N	35.55 E
Kondurča	7	Mj	53.31N	50.24 E
Koné	61	Bd	21.04S	164.52 E
Konečnaja	19	He	50.45N	78.27 E
Konevic, Ostrov-	8	Nd	60.50N	30.45 E
Kong	34	Ed	9.09N	4.37W
Kông	25	Lf	13.32N	105.58 E
Kŏng, Kaôh-	25	Kf	11.20N	103.00 E
Konga/Koonga	8	Jf	58.34N	24.00 E
Kongauru	64a	Ac	7.04N	134.17 E
Kong Christian IX Land = King Christian IX Land (EN)	67	Mc	68.00N	36.30W
Kong Christian X Land = King Christian X Land (EN)	67	Md	72.20N	32.30W
Kongeå	8	Ci	55.23N	8.39 E
Kong Frederik VIII Land = King Frederik VIII Land (EN)	67	Md	78.30N	28.00W
Kong Frederik VI Kyst = King Frederik VI Coast (EN)	67	Nc	63.00N	43.30W
Konginkangas	8	Kb	62.46N	25.48 E
Kongju	28	If	36.27N	127.08 E
Kong Karls Land	41	Oc	78.50N	28.00 E
Kong Kong	35	Ed	7.26N	33.14 E
Kongolo	31	Ji	5.23S	27.00 E
Kongor	35	Ed	7.10N	31.21 E
Kong Oscars Fjord	67	Md	72.20N	23.00W
Kongoussi	34	Ec	13.19N	1.32W
Kongsberg	7	Bg	59.39N	9.39 E
Kongsøya	41	Oc	78.55N	28.40 E
Kongsvinger	7	Cf	60.12N	12.00 E
Kongur Shan	21	Jf	38.40N	75.21 E
Kongwa	36	Gd	6.12S	36.25 E
Kong Wilhelms Land	41	Jc	75.48N	23.15W
Koniecpol	10	Pf	50.48N	19.41 E
Königslutter am Elm	10	Gd	52.15N	10.49 E
Königswinter	12	Jd	50.41N	7.11 E
Königs Wusterhausen	10	Jd	52.17N	13.37 E
Konin	10	Od	52.13N	18.16 E
Konin [2]	10	Od	52.15N	18.15 E
Konispoli	15	Dj	39.39N	20.10 E
Kónitsa	15	Di	40.03N	20.45 E
Konj	14	Kg	43.43N	16.55 E
Konjed Jān	24	Nf	33.30N	50.27 E
Konjic	14	Lg	43.39N	17.58 E
Konjuh	14	Mf	44.18N	18.33 E
Konkan	25	Ee	18.05N	73.25 E
Konkiep	37	Be	28.00S	17.23 E
Konko	36	Ed	10.12S	27.27 E
Konkouré	34	Cd	9.58N	13.42W
Konnevesi	8	Lb	62.40N	26.35 E
Konnevesi	8	Lb	62.37N	26.19 E
Konnivesi	8	Lc	61.10N	26.10 E
Konoša	6	Kc	60.58N	40.15 E

Index Symbols

[1] Independent Nation
[2] State, Region
[3] District, County
[4] Municipality
[5] Colony, Dependency
Continent
Physical Region
Historical or Cultural Region
Mount, Mountain
Volcano
Hill
Mountains, Mountain Range
Hills, Escarpment
Plateau, Upland
Pass, Gap
Plain, Lowland
Delta
Salt Flat
Valley, Canyon
Crater, Cave
Karst Features
Depression
Polder
Desert, Dunes
Forest, Woods
Heath, Steppe
Oasis
Cape, Point
Coast, Beach
Cliff
Peninsula
Isthmus
Sandbank
Island
Atoll
Rock, Reef
Islands, Archipelago
Rocks, Reefs
Coral Reef
Well, Spring
Geyser
River, Stream
Waterfall Rapids
River Mouth, Estuary
Lake
Salt Lake
Intermittent Lake
Reservoir
Swamp, Pond
Canal
Glacier
Ice Shelf, Pack Ice
Ocean
Sea
Gulf, Bay
Strait, Fjord
Lagoon
Bank
Seamount
Tablemount
Ridge
Shelf
Basin
Escarpment, Sea Scarp
Fracture
Trench, Abyss
National Park, Reserve
Point of Interest
Recreation Site
Cave, Cavern
Historic Site
Ruins
Wall, Walls
Church, Abbey
Temple
Scientific Station
Airport
Port
Lighthouse
Mine
Tunnel
Dam, Bridge

International Map Index

Index Symbols

[1] Independent Nation	▣ Historical or Cultural Region
[2] State, Region	▲ Mount, Mountain
[3] District, County	▲ Volcano
[4] Municipality	⌂ Hill
[5] Colony, Dependency	⛰ Mountains, Mountain Range
▬ Continent	⌒ Hills, Escarpment
◨ Physical Region	▭ Plateau, Upland

◱ Pass, Gap	▱ Depression
▭ Plain, Lowland	▭ Polder
▽ Delta	▦ Desert, Dunes
▭ Salt Flat	▩ Forest, Woods
⋁ Valley, Canyon	⋈ Heath, Steppe
⋂ Crater, Cave	▨ Oasis
⌗ Karst Features	◁ Cape, Point

▭ Coast, Beach	⊞ Rock, Reef
⊏ Cliff	⊟ Islands, Archipelago
⊢ Peninsula	⊡ Rocks, Reefs
⊣ Isthmus	⊠ Coral Reef
▥ Sandbank	⊙ Atoll
⊡ Island	

⋓ Waterfall Rapids	⊟ Canal
⋗ River Mouth, Estuary	⊟ Glacier
⊝ Lake	⊟ Ice Shelf, Pack Ice
⊟ Salt Lake	⊟ Ocean
⊟ Intermittent Lake	⊟ Sea
⊟ Reservoir	⊟ Gulf, Bay
⊟ Swamp, Pond	⊟ Strait, Fjord
⊟ Well, Spring	
⊙ Geyser	
≈ River, Stream	

▭ Lagoon	⊞ Escarpment, Sea Scarp
⊟ Bank	⊟ Fracture
⊟ Seamount	⊟ Trench, Abyss
⊟ Tablemount	⊟ National Park, Reserve
⊟ Ridge	⊟ Point of Interest
⊟ Shelf	⊟ Recreation Site
⊟ Basin	⊟ Cave, Cavern

⊟ Historic Site	⊟ Port
⊟ Ruins	⊟ Lighthouse
⊟ Wall, Walls	⊠ Mine
⊟ Church, Abbey	⊟ Tunnel
⊟ Temple	⊟ Dam, Bridge
⊟ Scientific Station	
⊟ Airport	

Krokom 7 De 63.20N 14.28 E
Krolevec 16 Hd 51.32N 33.30 E
Kroměříž 10 Ng 49.18N 17.22 E
Krompachy 10 Qh 48.56N 20.52 E
Kronach 10 Hf 50.14N 11.19 E
Kröng Kaôh Köng 25 Kf 11.37N 102.59 E
Kronoberg [2] 7 Dh 56.40N 14.40 E
Kronockaja Sopka, Vulkan- 20 Lf 54.47N 160.35 E
Kronocki, Mys- 20 Lf 54.43N 162.07 E
Kronocki Zaliv 20 Lf 54.00N 161.00 E
Kronoki 20 Lf 54.33N 161.14 E
Kronprins Christian Land 41 Jb 80.45N 22.00W
Kronprinsesse Mærtha Kyst 66 Bf 72.00S 7.30W
Kronprins Frederiks Bjerge 41 Ie 67.20N 34.00W
Kronprins Olav Kyst 66 Ee 68.30S 42.30 E
Kronštadt 19 Cc 60.01N 29.44 E
Kroonstad 31 Jk 27.46S 27.12 E
Kropotkin 19 Ef 45.26N 40.34 E
Kropotkin 20 Ge 58.36N 115.27 E
Kroppefjäll 8 Ef 58.40N 12.13 E
Krośniewice 10 Pd 52.16N 19.10 E
Krosno 10 Rg 49.42N 21.46 E
Krosno [2] 10 Rg 49.40N 21.45 E
Krosno Odrzańskie 10 Ld 52.04N 15.05 E
Krossfjorden 8 Ad 60.10N 5.05 E
Krotoszyn 10 Ne 51.42N 17.26 E
Kroviga, Gora- 20 Ed 60.40N 91.30 E
Krško 14 Je 45.58N 15.28 E
Krstača 15 Dg 42.58N 20.08 E
Krugersdorp 31 Jk 26.05S 27.35 E
Krui 26 Dh 5.11S 103.56 E
Kruibeke 12 Gc 50.10N 4.19 E
Kruiningen 12 Gc 51.27N 4.02 E
Kruja 15 Ch 41.30N 19.48 E
Krulevščina 8 Li 55.03N 27.52 E
Krumbach 10 Gh 48.15N 10.22 E
Krumovgrad 15 Ih 41.28N 25.39 E
Krung Thep=Bangkok (EN) 22 Mh 13.45N 100.31 E
Krupanj 15 Ce 44.22N 19.22 E
Krupinica 10 Oh 48.05N 18.54 E
Krupinská vrchovina 10 Ph 48.20N 19.15 E
Kruså 8 Cj 54.50N 9.25 E
Krušedol 15 Cd 45.07N 19.57 E
Kruševac 15 Ef 43.35N 21.20 E
Kruševo 15 Eh 41.22N 21.15 E
Krušné Hory=Ore Mountains (EN) 5 He 50.30N 13.15 E
Krustpils 8 Lh 56.29N 26.00 E
Kruzof 40 Le 57.10N 135.40W
Krym 16 Jg 45.23N 36.36 E
Krym, respublika 19 Dg 45.15N 34.20 E
Krymsk 19 Dg 44.54N 37.57 E
Krymskije Gory=Crimean Mountains (EN) 5 Jg 44.45N 34.30 E
Krymski Poluostrov=Crimea (EN) 5 Jf 45.00N 34.00 E
Krynica 10 Qg 49.25N 20.56 E
Krzemieniucha 10 Sb 54.12N 22.54 E
Krzepice 10 Of 50.58N 18.44 E
Krzna 10 Td 52.08N 23.31 E
Krzywiń 10 Me 51.58N 16.49 E
Krzyż 10 Md 52.53N 16.01 E
Ksar el Boukhari 32 Hb 35.53N 2.45 E
Ksar el Kebir 32 Fc 35.00N 5.59W
Ksar es Srhir 13 Gi 35.51N 5.34W
Ksenjevka 20 Gf 53.34N 118.44 E
Kšenski 16 Jd 51.52N 37.44 E
Ksour, Monts des- 32 Gc 32.45N 0.10W
Kū', Wādī al- 35 Dc 12.12N 25.43 E
Kuai He 28 Dh 33.09N 117.32 E
Kuala Belait 26 Ff 4.35N 114.11 E
Kuala Dungun 26 Df 4.47N 103.26 E
Kuala Kangsar 26 Df 4.46N 100.56 E
Kualakapuas 26 Fg 3.01S 114.21 E
Kuala Kerai 26 De 5.32N 102.12 E
Kualakurun 26 Fg 1.07S 113.53 E
Kualalangsa 26 Cf 4.32N 98.01 E
Kuala Lipis 26 Df 4.11N 102.03 E
Kuala Lumpur 22 Mi 3.10N 101.42 E
Kuala Pilah 26 Df 2.44N 102.15 E
Kuala Rompin 26 Df 2.49N 103.29 E
Kuala Terengganu 22 Mi 5.20N 103.08 E
Kuancheng 28 Ed 40.37N 118.31 E
Kuandang 26 Hf 0.52N 122.55 E
Kuandian 27 Lc 40.45N 124.48 E
Kuang-hsi-chuang-tsu Tzu-chih-ch'ü→Guangxi Zhuangzu Zizhiqu=Kwangsi Chuang (EN) [2] 27 Ig 24.00N 109.00 E
Kuang-tun Sheng→Guangdong Sheng=Kwangtung (EN) [2] 27 Jg 23.00N 113.00 E
Kuantan 26 Df 3.48N 103.20 E
Kuba 19 Eg 41.20N 48.35 E
Kuban 5 Jf 45.20N 37.30 E
Kuba-Shima 29b b 26.10N 127.15 E
Kubaysah 24 Jf 33.35N 42.37 E
Kubbum 35 Cc 11.47N 23.47 E
Kubena 7 Jg 59.37N 39.48 E
Kubenskoje, Ozero- 7 Jg 59.40N 39.30 E
Kubnja 7 Li 55.32N 48.28 E
Kubokawa 28 Lh 33.12N 133.08 E
Kubolta 15 Lb 47.48N 28.03 E
Kubrat 15 Jf 43.48N 26.30 E
Kubumesaai 26 Gf 1.31N 115.06 E
Kučaj 15 Ef 43.53N 21.44 E
Kučevo 15 Ee 44.29N 21.41 E
Kutching 22 Ni 1.33N 110.20 E
Kuchinotsu 29 Be 32.36N 130.12 E
Kuçova (Qyteti Stalin) 15 Ci 40.48N 19.54 E
Kuçukçekmece 15 Li 40.59N 28.46 E
Küçükerenköy 24 Ee 35.22N 33.45 E
Küçükkuyu 15 Jj 39.32N 26.36 E
Küçuk Menderes 15 Kl 37.57N 27.16 E
Kučurgan 15 Mc 46.35N 29.55 E
Kudaka-Jima 29b Ab 26.10N 127.54 E
Kudamatsu 29 Bd 34.01N 131.53 E
Kudat 26 Ge 6.53N 116.50 E
Kudeb 8 Mg 57.30N 28.16 E
Kudirkos-Naumestis 8 Jj 54.43N 22.49 E
Kudowa-Zdrój 10 Mf 50.27N 16.20 E
Kudremukh 25 Ff 13.08N 75.16 E
Kudus 26 Fh 6.48S 110.50 E
Kudymkar 19 Fd 59.01N 54.37 E
Kuee Ruins 65a Fd 19.12N 155.23W
Kuei-chou Sheng→Guizhou Sheng=Kweichow (EN) [2] 27 If 27.00N 107.00 E
Kufi 24 Cc 38.10N 29.43 E
Kufrah, Wāḩāt al-=Kufra Oasis (EN) 30 Jf 24.10N 23.15 E
Kufra Oasis (EN)=Kufrah, Wāḩāt al- 30 Jf 24.10N 23.15 E
Kufstein 14 Gc 47.35N 12.10 E
Kuganavolok 7 Ie 62.16N 36.55 E
Kugmallit Bay 42 Ek 69.30N 133.20W
Kugojeja 16 Kf 46.33N 39.38 E
Kūh, Ra's al- 23 Id 25.48N 57.19 E
Kuḩaylī 35 Eb 19.29N 32.49 E
Kūhbonān 24 Qg 31.23N 56.19 E
Kūhdasht 24 Lf 33.32N 47.36 E
Kūh-e Būrh 24 Pi 27.22N 54.40 E
Kūh-e Gāvbūs 24 Oi 27.10N 54.00 E
Kūh-e Karkas 24 Nf 33.27N 51.48 E
Kūh-e Kārūn 24 Ng 31.27N 50.18 E
Kūhestak 24 Qi 26.47N 57.02 E
Kūhīn, Gardaneh-ye- 24 Md 36.23N 49.37 E
Kühlungsborn 10 Hb 54.09N 11.43 E
Kuhmo 7 Gd 64.08N 29.31 E
Kuhmoinen 8 Kc 61.34N 25.11 E
Kuhn 41 Kd 74.45N 19.45W
Kūhpāyeh 23 Ic 30.35N 57.15 E
Kūhpāyeh [Iran] 24 Of 32.43N 52.26 E
Kūhpāyeh [Iran] 24 Qg 30.43N 57.30 E
Kūhrān, Kūh-e- 23 Id 26.46N 58.12 E
Kuhtuj 20 Je 59.23N 143.10 E
Kuhva 8 Mg 57.17N 28.17 E
Kuiseb 37 Ad 23.00S 14.33 E
Kuishan Ding 27 Jg 22.32N 109.52 E
Kuito 31 Ij 12.23S 16.56 E
Kuiu 40 Me 57.45N 134.10W
Kuivaniemi 7 Fd 65.35N 25.11 E
Kujang 27 Md 39.52N 126.01 E
Kujawy 10 Od 52.45N 18.30 E
Kujawy 10 Od 52.45N 18.35 E
Kujbyšev → Samara 6 Le 53.12N 50.09 E
Kujbyšev → Bulgar 7 Li 55.01N 49.06 E
Kujbyšev 20 Ce 55.27N 78.29 E
Kujbyševskaja Oblast [3] 19 Fe 53.20N 50.30 E
Kujbyševski 19 Ge 53.15N 66.51 E
Kujbyševski 18 Gf 37.53N 68.44 E
Kujbyševskoje Vodohranilišče=Kuybyshev Reservoir (EN) 5 Ke 53.50N 49.00 E
Kujeda 17 Gh 56.26N 55.35 E
Kujgan 19 Hf 45.22N 74.10 E
Kuji 28 Pd 40.11N 141.46 E
Kuji-Gawa 29 Gc 36.30N 140.37 E
Kujtun 20 Ff 54.21N 101.35 E
Kujūkuri-Hama 29 Gd 35.40N 140.30 E
Kujū-San 28 Kh 33.09N 131.15 E
Kūkalār, Kūh-e- 24 Ng 31.50N 50.53 E
Kukalaya, Rio- 49 Fg 13.39N 83.37W
Kukësi 15 Dg 42.05N 20.24 E
Kukkia 8 Kc 61.20N 24.40 E
Kukmor 7 Mh 56.13N 50.52 E
Kükürt Dağı 24 Ib 41.07N 41.27 E
Kula [Bul.] 15 Ff 43.53N 22.31 E
Kula [Tur.] 24 Cc 38.30N 28.40 E
Kula [Yugo.] 15 Cd 45.37N 19.32 E
Kulai 26 Df 1.40N 103.36 E
Kulanak 18 Jd 41.18N 75.34 E
Kulandy 19 Ff 46.08N 59.31 E
Kular 20 Ib 70.32N 134.26 E
Kular, Hrebet- 20 Ic 69.00N 133.30 E
Kulata 15 Gh 41.23N 23.22 E
Kulautuva 8 Jj 54.55N 23.43 E
Kulbus 35 Cc 14.24N 22.31 E
Kuldiga/Kuldīga 19 Cd 56.59N 21.59 E
Kuldīga/Kuldiga 19 Cd 56.59N 21.59 E
Kuldur 20 Ig 49.10N 131.40 E
Kulebaki 7 Ki 55.26N 42.32 E
Kulenjin 24 Me 35.40N 49.30 E
Kulen Vakuf 14 Kf 44.33N 16.06 E
Kulgera 58 Eg 25.50S 133.18 E
Kulikov 10 Ug 49.55N 24.06 E
Kulim 26 De 5.22N 100.34 E
Kuljab 19 Gh 37.55N 69.47 E
Kuljabskaja Oblast [3] 19 Gh 38.00N 69.40 E
Kullaa 8 Jc 61.28N 22.10 E
Kullen 7 Ch 56.18N 12.26 E
Kulmasa 34 Ed 9.35N 2.27W
Kulmbach 10 Hf 50.06N 11.27 E
Kuloj 7 Kf 61.03N 42.30 E
Kuloj 19 Eb 66.00N 43.30 E
Kuloj 7 Kf 61.01N 42.12 E
Kulp 24 Ic 38.30N 41.02 E
Kulsary 19 Ff 46.57N 54.02 E
Kultuk 20 Ff 51.44N 103.42 E
Kulu 20 Jd 62.15N 147.45 E
Kulu [India] 25 Fb 31.58N 77.06 E
Kulu [Tur.] 24 Ec 39.06N 33.05 E
Kulumadau 63a Ac 9.03S 152.43 E
Kulunda 20 Cf 52.35N 78.57 E
Kulundinskaja Step 20 Cf 52.45N 79.00 E
Kulundinskoje, Ozero- 20 Cf 53.00N 79.30 E
Kum 24 Bc 38.38N 27.32 E
Kum, Kūh-e- 24 Oh 29.55N 53.45 E
Kuma 29 Ce 33.39N 132.54 E
Kuma 17 Mg 59.33N 66.40 E
Kuma 7 Hc 66.15N 31.02 E
Kuma 5 Kg 44.56N 47.00 E
Kumagaya 28 Of 36.08N 139.23 E
Kumai [Indon.] 26 Fg 2.44S 111.43 E
Kumai [Indon.] 26 Fg 3.23S 112.33 E
Kumaishi 29a Ab 42.08N 139.59 E
Kumajri (Leninakan) 6 Kg 40.47N 43.50 E
Kumak 16 Vd 51.33N 60.08 E
Kumamoto 22 Pf 32.48N 130.43 E
Kumamoto Ken [2] 28 Kh 32.30N 130.50 E
Kumano 28 Nh 33.54N 136.05 E
Kumano-Gawa 29 De 33.45N 135.59 E
Kumano-Nada 29 Ee 34.00N 136.30 E
Kumanovo 15 Eg 42.08N 21.43 E
Kumara [N.Z.] 62 De 42.38S 171.11 E
Kumara 20 Hf 51.35N 126.45 E
Kumasi 31 Gh 6.41N 1.37W
Kumba 34 Ge 4.38N 9.25 E
Kumbakonam 25 Ff 10.58N 79.23 E
Kumbe 26 Lh 8.21S 140.13 E
Kumbo 34 Hd 6.12N 10.40 E
Kumboro Cape 63a Cb 7.18S 157.32 E
Kümch'ŏn 28 Ie 38.10N 126.30 E
Kum-Dag 19 Fh 39.13N 54.40 E
Kumdah 33 Ie 20.23N 45.05 E
Kumertau → Jermolajevo 19 Fe 52.46N 55.47 E
Kumhwa 28 Ie 38.17N 127.28 E
Kumihama 29 Dd 35.36N 134.54 E
Kuminski 19 Gd 58.40N 65.55 E
Kumköy (Kilyos) 15 Mh 41.15N 29.02 E
Kumkuduk 27 Fc 40.15N 91.55 E
Kumkurgan 18 Ff 37.50N 67.35 E
Kumla 7 Dg 59.08N 15.08 E
Kumlinge 8 Id 60.15N 20.45 E
Kumluca 24 Dd 36.22N 30.18 E
Kummerower See 10 Ic 53.49N 12.52 E
Kumo/Kokemäki 7 Ff 61.15N 22.21 E
Kumo-Manyčski Kanal 16 Ng 45.27N 44.38 E
Kumon Taung 21 Lg 26.30N 96.50 E
Kumora 20 Ge 55.56N 111.13 E
Kumru 24 Gb 40.53N 37.17 E
Kumu 36 Eb 3.04N 25.09 E
Kumuh 16 Oh 42.11N 47.07 E
Kumukahi, Cape- 60 Od 19.31N 154.49W
Kumul/Hami 22 Le 42.48N 93.27 E
Kümüx 27 Ec 42.15N 88.10 E
Kumzār 24 Qj 26.20N 56.25 E
Kunashiri-Tō/Kunašir, Ostrov- 21 Qe 44.05N 145.51 E
Kunašir, Ostrov-/Kunashiri-Tō 21 Qe 44.05N 145.51 E
Kunaširski Proliv=Nemuro Strait (EN) 20 Jh 43.50N 145.30 E
Kunchaung 25 Jd 23.50N 96.35 E
Kunda 7 Gg 59.30N 26.30 E
Kunda Jõgi 8 Le 59.25N 26.27 E
Kundelungu, Monts- 36 Ed 9.30S 28.00 E
Kundiawa 59 Ia 6.00S 145.00 E
Kunduchi 36 Gd 6.40S 39.13 E
Kunduk 15 Md 45.51N 29.38 E
Kunduk→Kogilnik 15 Md 45.51N 29.38 E
Kunduk→Sasyk, Ozero- 16 Fg 45.45N 29.40 E
Kunene 30 Ij 17.20S 11.50 E
Kunene (EN)=Cunene 30 Ij 17.20S 11.50 E
Künes/Xinyuan 27 Dc 43.24N 83.18 E
Künes He 27 Dc 43.32N 82.29 E
Kungälv 7 Ch 57.52N 11.58 E
Kungej-Alatau, Hrebet- 19 Hg 42.50N 77.15 E
Küngmiut 41 Ie 65.50N 36.45W
Kungrad 19 Fg 43.06N 58.54 E
Kungsbacka 7 Ch 57.29N 12.04 E
Kungsbackafjorden 8 Eg 57.25N 12.04 E
Kungshamn 8 Df 58.21N 11.15 E
Kungsör 8 Ge 59.25N 16.05 E
Kungu 36 Cb 2.47N 19.12 E
Kungur 19 Fd 57.25N 56.57 E
Kunhegyes 10 Qi 47.22N 20.38 E
Kunhing 25 Jd 21.18N 98.26 E
Kunigami 29b Bb 26.45N 128.11 E
Kunigami-Misaki 29b Bb 27.26N 128.43 E
Kunimi-Dake 29 Be 32.33N 131.01 E
Kunisaki 29 Be 33.33N 131.45 E
Kunisaki-Hantō 29 Be 33.30N 131.40 E
Kunja 7 Hh 57.09N 31.10 E
Kunja-Urgenč 19 Fg 42.20N 59.12 E
Kunlong 25 Jd 23.25N 98.39 E
Kunlun Guan 27 Ig 23.06N 108.40 E
Kunlun Shan 21 Kf 36.00N 84.00 E
Kunlun Shankou 27 Gd 35.40N 94.03 E
Kunming 22 Mg 25.08N 102.43 E
Kunnui 29a Bb 42.26N 140.19 E
Kunovat 17 Ld 64.59N 65.35 E
Kunsan 27 Md 35.59N 126.43 E
Kunshan 28 Fi 31.22N 120.57 E
Kuntaur 34 Cc 13.40N 14.53W
Kununurra 59 Fc 15.47S 128.44 E
Kunyao 36 Gb 1.47N 35.03 E
Kunyu Shan 28 Ff 37.15N 121.46 E
Künzelsau 10 Fg 49.17N 9.41 E
Kuohijärvi 8 Kc 61.15N 24.55 E
Kuolimo 8 Lc 61.15N 27.35 E
Kuop Atoll 64d Bb 7.03N 151.56 E
Kuopio [2] 7 Ge 63.20N 27.35 E
Kuopio 6 Ic 62.54N 27.41 E
Kuorboaivi 7 Gb 69.41N 27.45 E
Kuortane 8 Jb 62.48N 23.30 E
Kupa 14 Je 45.28N 16.24 E
Kupang 22 Ok 10.10S 123.35 E
Kupiano 60 Dj 10.10S 148.02 E
Kupičev 10 Uf 50.58N 24.52 E
Kupino 20 Cf 54.22N 77.18 E
Kupiškis 7 Fi 55.49N 25.01 E
Kupjansk 19 Df 49.42N 37.37 E
Kupjansk-Uzlovoj 16 Je 49.39N 37.45 E
Küplü [Tur.] 15 Jh 41.07N 26.21 E
Küplü [Tur.] 15 Mi 40.06N 30.00 E
Kuppenheim 12 Kf 48.50N 8.15 E
Kupreanof 40 Me 56.50N 133.30W
Kuqa 22 Ke 41.43N 82.57 E
Kura 16 Mh 44.05N 44.45 E
Kura 5 Kh 39.20N 49.25 E
Kuragaty 18 Ic 43.55N 73.34 E
Kuragino 20 Ef 53.53N 92.40 E
Kurahashi-Jima 29 Cd 34.08N 132.31 E
Kuraminski Hrebet 18 Hd 40.50N 70.30 E
Kurashiki 28 Lg 34.35N 133.46 E
Kurashiki-Kojima 29 Cd 34.28N 133.48 E
Kurashiki-Tamashima 29 Cd 34.33N 133.40 E
Kura-Take 29 Be 32.27N 130.20 E
Kuraymah=Karima (EN) 31 Kg 18.33N 31.51 E
Kurayoshi 28 Lg 35.28N 133.49 E
Kurbneshi 15 Dh 41.47N 20.05 E
Kurčatov 16 Id 51.41N 35.42 E
Kurdaj 18 Jc 43.18N 74.59 E
Kurdistan 21 Gf 37.00N 44.00 E
Kurdistan 23 Fb 37.00N 44.00 E
Kurdufān 30 Jg 13.00N 30.00 E
Kurdufān al Janūbīyah [3] 35 Dc 11.00N 29.30 E
Kurdufān ash Shamālīyah [3] 35 Dc 14.50N 29.40 E
Kure 28 Lg 34.14N 132.34 E
Küre 24 Eb 41.48N 33.43 E
Kure Island 57 Jb 28.25N 178.25W
Kurejka 21 Kc 66.25N 87.12 E
Kuresaare (Kingissepp) 19 Cd 58.17N 22.29 E
Kurgaldžinski 19 He 50.30N 70.03 E
Kurgan 22 Id 55.26N 65.18 E
Kurganinsk 16 Lg 44.57N 40.35 E
Kurganskaja Oblast [3] 19 Gd 55.00N 65.00 E
Kurgan-Tjube 19 Gh 37.51N 68.46 E
Kurgan-Tjubinskaja Oblast [3] 19 Gh 37.30N 68.30 E
Kuria Island 57 Id 0.14N 173.25 E
Kuria Muria Islands (EN)=Khurīyā Murīyā, Jazā'ir 21 Hh 17.30N 56.00 E
Kuri Bay 59 Ec 15.35S 124.50 E
Kurikka 7 Fe 62.37N 22.25 E
Kurikoma 29 Gb 38.50N 140.59 E
Kurikoma-Yama 29 Gb 38.57N 140.47 E
Kuril Basin (EN) 20 Jg 47.00N 150.00 E
Kuril Islands (EN)=Kurilskije Ostrova 21 Re 46.10N 152.00 E
Kurilo 15 Gg 42.49N 23.21 E
Kurilsk 20 Jg 45.16N 147.58 E
Kurilskije Ostrova=Kuril Islands (EN) 21 Re 46.10N 152.00 E
Kuril Trench (EN) 3 Je 47.00N 155.00 E
Kuring Kuru 37 Bc 17.38S 18.33 E
Kurino 29 Bf 31.57N 130.43 E
Kurinskaja Kosa 16 Pj 39.05N 49.10 E
Kurinwás, Río- 49 Fg 12.49N 83.41W
Kuriyama 29a Bb 43.03N 141.45 E
Kūrkhūd, Kūh-e- 24 Qd 37.15N 56.30 E
Kurkosa 16 Pj 38.59N 49.08 E
Kurkūmā, Ra's- 24 Gj 25.51N 36.39 E
Kurkur 24 Ek 23.54N 32.19 E
Kurlovski 7 Ji 55.29N 40.39 E
Kurmuk 35 Ec 10.33N 34.17 E
Kurnool 22 Jh 15.50N 78.03 E
Kurobe 28 Nf 36.51N 137.26 E
Kurobe-Gawa 29 Ec 36.55N 137.26 E
Kurogi 29 Be 33.14N 130.40 E
Kuroishi 28 Pd 40.38N 140.36 E
Kuroiso 28 Pf 36.58N 140.03 E
Kuromatsunai 28 Pc 42.43N 140.20 E
Kurono-Seto 29 Be 32.05N 130.10 E
Kurort Družba 15 Kf 43.12N 28.00 E
Kurort Slănčev brjag 15 Kg 42.40N 27.42 E
Kurort Zlatni pjasăci 15 Lf 43.16N 28.02 E
Kuro-Shima 28 Ji 31.52N 129.58 E
Kurovskoje 7 Ji 55.35N 38.59 E
Kurow 61 Dh 44.44S 170.28 E
Kurów 10 Se 51.25N 22.10 E
Kurpiowska, Puszcza- 10 Rc 53.20N 21.30 E
Kuršėnai/Kuršenaj 19 Cd 56.03N 22.58 E
Kuršenaj/Kuršėnai 19 Cd 56.03N 22.58 E
Kuršiu užūrekis 8 Ii 55.05N 21.00 E
Kursk 6 Je 51.42N 36.12 E
Kurskaja Kosa 7 Ei 55.18N 21.00 E
Kurskaja Oblast [3] 19 De 51.45N 36.15 E
Kurski zaliv 7 Ei 55.05N 21.00 E
Kuršumlija 15 Ef 43.09N 21.16 E
Kurtalan 24 Id 37.57N 41.42 E
Kurtamyš 19 Ge 54.55N 64.27 E
Kürti 31 Kg 18.07N 31.33 E
Kurtistown 65 Fd 19.36N 155.04W
Kurty 18 Kb 44.19N 76.42 E
Kuru 8 Jc 61.52N 23.44 E
Kuru 35 Dd 9.08N 26.57 E
Kuruşile 24 Eb 41.51N 32.43 E
Kuruktag 27 Ec 41.30N 89.00 E
Kuruman 30 Jk 26.56S 20.39 E
Kuruman 31 Jk 27.28S 23.28 E
Kurume 28 Kh 33.19N 130.31 E
Kurunegala 25 Gg 7.29N 80.22 E
Kurur, Jabal- 35 Ea 20.31N 31.32 E
Kurzeme=Courland (EN) 8 Ih 56.50N 22.00 E
Kurzemes Augstiene/Kurzemskaja Vozvyšennost 8 Jh 56.45N 22.15 E
Kurzemskaja Vozvyšennost/Kurzemes Augstiene 8 Jh 56.45N 22.15 E
Kusa 17 Ii 55.20N 59.29 E
Kuşada Körfezi 15 Kl 37.50N 27.08 E
Kuşadasi 24 Bd 37.51N 27.15 E
Kusagaki-Guntō 27 Me 31.00N 129.00 E
Kusaie→Kosrae 57 Hd 5.19N 162.59 E
Kusalu/Kuusalu 8 Ke 59.23N 25.25 E
Kusary 16 Pi 41.24N 48.29 E
Kusatsu [Jap.] 29 Fc 36.37N 138.35 E
Kusatsu [Jap.] 29 Dd 35.03N 135.59 E
Kuščevskaja 16 Kf 46.33N 39.37 E
Kuščinski 16 Oi 40.33N 46.06 E
Kusel 12 Je 49.33N 7.24 E
Kuş Gölü 24 Bb 40.10N 27.59 E
Kushida-Gawa 29 Ed 34.36N 136.34 E
Kushikino 28 Ki 31.44N 130.16 E
Kushima 28 Ki 31.29N 131.14 E
Kushimoto 28 Mh 33.28N 135.47 E
Kushiro 22 Qe 42.58N 144.23 E
Kushiro-Gawa 29a Db 42.59N 144.23 E
Kushtia 25 Hd 23.55N 89.07 E
Kuška 18 Dg 35.16N 62.18 E
Kuskokwim 38 Cc 60.17N 162.27W
Kuskokwim Bay 38 Cd 59.45N 162.25W
Kuskokwim Mountains 38 Dc 62.30N 156.00W
Kušmurun 19 Ge 52.27N 64.40 E
Kušmurun, Ozero- 19 Ge 52.40N 64.45 E
Kušnarenkovo 17 Gi 55.06N 55.22 E
Kušnica 16 Ce 48.29N 23.20 E
Kusŏng 27 Md 39.59N 125.16 E
Kussharo Ko 28 Rc 43.35N 144.15 E
Kustanaj 22 Id 53.10N 63.35 E
Kustanajskaja Oblast [3] 19 Ge 53.00N 64.00 E
Kustavi 8 Id 60.30N 21.25 E
Kustavi/Gustavs 8 Id 60.30N 21.25 E
Küstenkanal 10 Dd 52.57N 7.18 E
Kūstī 31 Kg 13.10N 32.40 E
Kustvlakte=Coast Plain (EN) 11 Ic 51.00N 2.30 E
Kusu 28 Be 33.16N 131.09 E
Kušva 19 Fd 58.18N 59.45 E
Kut, Ko- 25 Kf 11.40N 102.35 E
Kūt 'Abdollāh 24 Mg 31.13N 48.39 E
Kutacane 26 Cf 3.30N 97.48 E
Kutahya 23 Cb 39.25N 29.59 E
Kutaisi 6 Kg 42.15N 42.40 E
Kutch, Gulf of-→Kachchh, Gulf of 21 Ig 22.36N 69.30 E
Kutch, Rann of- 25 Ed 24.05N 70.10 E
Kutchan 28 Pc 42.54N 140.45 E
Kutcharo-Ko 29a Ca 45.10N 142.20 E
Kutina 14 Ke 45.29N 16.47 E
Kutkai 25 Jd 23.27N 97.56 E
Kutkašen → Gabel'a 16 Oi 40.58N 47.52 E
Kutná Hora 10 Lg 49.57N 15.16 E
Kutno 10 Pd 52.15N 19.23 E
Kutse, Gora-/Kuutse Mägi 8 Lg 57.58N 26.24 E
Kuttara-Ko 29a Bb 42.30N 141.10 E
Kutu 31 Ii 2.44S 18.09 E
Kutum 35 Cc 14.12N 24.40 E
Küty 10 Nh 48.40N 17.01 E
Kuty 15 Ia 48.13N 25.15 E
Kuujjuaq 39 Md 58.10N 68.30W
Kuujjuarapik 42 Je 55.20N 76.50W
Kuuli-Majak 19 Fg 40.16N 52.45 E
Kuurne 12 Fd 50.51N 3.17 E
Kuusalu/Kusalu 8 Ke 59.23N 25.25 E
Kuusamo 6 Ib 66.00N 29.11 E
Kuusankoski 8 Ld 60.54N 26.38 E
Kuutse Mägi/Kutse, Gora- 8 Lg 57.58N 26.24 E
Kuvandyk 16 Td 51.29N 57.28 E
Kuvdlorssuaq 41 Gd 74.38N 56.40W
Kuvšinovo 7 Ih 57.03N 34.13 E
Kuwait (EN)=Al Kuwayt [1] 22 Gg 29.30N 47.45 E
Kuwait (EN)=Al Kuwayt 22 Gg 29.20N 47.59 E
Kuwana 29 Ed 35.04N 136.39 E
Kuybyshev Reservoir (EN)=Kujbyševskoje Vodohranilišče 5 Ke 53.50N 49.00 E
Küysanjaq 24 Kd 36.05N 44.38 E
Kuytun 27 Dc 44.25N 84.58 E
Kuyucak 15 Ll 37.55N 28.28 E
Kuzey Kibris = North Cyprus 23 Db 35.15N 33.40 E
Kuzneck 19 Ee 53.07N 46.36 E
Kuznecki Alatau 21 Kd 54.45N 88.00 E
Kuznečnoje 8 Mc 61.04N 29.58 E
Kuźnia Raciborska 10 Of 50.11N 18.15 E
Kuzomen 19 Db 66.18N 36.49 E
Kuzovatovo 7 Lj 53.33N 47.41 E
Kuzumaki 29 Ga 40.02N 141.26 E
Kuzuryū-Gawa 29 Ec 36.13N 136.08 E
Kvænangen 7 Ea 70.05N 21.13 E
Kvaløy 7 Eb 69.40N 18.30 E
Kvaløya 7 Fa 70.37N 23.52 E
Kvalsund 7 Fa 70.30N 24.00 E
Kvam 8 Cc 61.40N 9.42 E
Kvareli 16 Ni 41.57N 45.47 E
Kvarkeno 17 Ij 52.05N 59.40 E
Kvarnbergsvattnet 7 Dd 64.36N 14.03 E
Kvarner 14 If 44.45N 14.15 E
Kvarnerić 14 If 44.45N 14.35 E
Kvichak Bay 40 He 58.48N 157.30W
Kvemo-Kedi 16 Oi 41.22N 46.31 E
Kvenna 8 Bd 60.01N 7.56 E
Kvichak 40 He 59.10N 156.40W
Kvikkjokk 7 Dc 66.57N 17.47 E
Kvina 8 Bf 58.17N 6.56 E
Kvinesdal 7 Bg 58.19N 6.57 E
Kvissleby 8 Gb 62.17N 17.21 E
Kviteggia 8 Bb 62.05N 6.45 E
Kviteseid 8 Ce 59.24N 8.30 E
Kvitøya 67 Je 80.08N 32.35 E
Kwa 30 Ii 3.10S 16.11 E
Kwahu Plateau 34 Ed 6.30N 0.30W
Kwailibesi 63a Ec 8.25S 160.40 E
Kwajalein Atoll 57 Hd 9.05N 167.20 E
Kwakoegron 54 Gb 5.15N 55.20W
Kwale [Kenya] 36 Gc 4.11S 39.27 E
Kwale [Nig.] 34 Gd 5.45N 6.25 E
Kwamouth 36 Cc 3.10S 16.12 E
Kwa Mtoro 36 Gd 5.14S 35.26 E
Kwando 36 Df 18.27S 23.32 E
Kwangdae-ri 27 Mc 40.34N 127.33 E
Kwangju 22 Of 35.09N 126.55 E
Kwango 30 Ii 3.14S 17.22 E

Index Symbols

[1] Independent Nation
[2] State, Region
[3] District, County
[4] Municipality
[5] Colony, Dependency
Continent
Physical Region
Historical or Cultural Region
Mount, Mountain
Volcano
Hill
Mountains, Mountain Range
Hills, Escarpment
Plateau, Upland
Pass, Gap
Plain, Lowland
Delta
Salt Flat
Valley, Canyon
Crater, Cave
Karst Features
Depression
Polder
Desert, Dunes
Forest, Woods
Heath, Steppe
Oasis
Cape, Point
Coast, Beach
Cliff
Peninsula
Isthmus
Sandbank
Island
Atoll
Rock, Reef
Islands, Archipelago
Rocks, Reefs
Coral Reef
Well, Spring
Geyser
River, Stream
Waterfall Rapids
River Mouth, Estuary
Lake
Salt Lake
Intermittent Lake
Reservoir
Swamp, Pond
Canal
Glacier
Ice Shelf, Pack Ice
Ocean
Sea
Gulf, Bay
Strait, Fjord
Lagoon
Bank
Seamount
Tablemount
Ridge
Shelf
Basin
Escarpment, Sea Scarp
Fracture
Trench, Abyss
National Park, Reserve
Point of Interest
Recreation Site
Cave, Cavern
Historic Site
Ruins
Wall, Walls
Church, Abbey
Temple
Scientific Station
Airport
Port
Lighthouse
Mine
Tunnel
Dam, Bridge

Kwangsi Chuang (EN) = Guangxi Zhuangzu Zizhiqu (Kwang-hsi-chuang-tsu Tzu-chih-ch'ü) [2] 27 Ig 24.00N 109.00 E
Kwangsi Chuang (EN) = Kuang-hsi-chuang-tsu Tzu-chih-ch'ü → Guangxi Zhuangzu Zizhiqu [2] 27 Ig 24.00N 109.00 E
Kwangtung (EN) = Guangdong Sheng (Kuang-tung Sheng) [2] 27 Jg 23.00N 113.00 E
Kwangtung (EN) = Kuang-tun Sheng → Guangdong Sheng [2] 27 Jg 23.00N 113.00 E
Kwanmo-bong 28 Jd 41.42N 129.13 E
Kwara [2] 34 Fd 8.30N 5.00 E
Kweichow (EN) = Guizhou Sheng (Kuei-chou Sheng) [2] 27 If 27.00N 107.00 E
Kweichow (EN) = Kuei-chou Sheng → Guizhou Sheng 27 If 27.00N 107.00 E
Kwekwe 31 Jj 18.55S 29.49 E
Kweneng [3] 37 Cd 24.00S 24.00 E
Kwenge 30 Ii 4.50S 18.44 E
Kwethluk 40 Gd 60.49N 161.27W
Kwidzyn 10 Oc 53.45N 18.56 E
Kwigillingok 40 Ge 59.51N 163.08W
Kwilu 30 Ii 3.22S 17.22 E
Kwisa 10 Le 51.35N 15.25 E
Kwoka, Gunung- 26 Jg 0.31S 132.27 E
Kyabé 31 Ih 9.27N 18.57 E
Kyabram 59 Jg 36.19S 145.03 E
Kyaikkami 25 Je 16.04N 97.34 E
Kyaikto 25 Je 17.18N 97.01 E
Kyaka 36 Fc 1.16S 31.25 E
Kyancutta 58 Eh 33.08S 135.34 E
Kyan-Zaki 29b Ab 26.05N 127.40 E
Kyaukpyu 25 Id 20.51N 92.58 E
Kyaukse 25 Jd 21.36N 96.08 E
Kybartai/Kibartaj 8 Jj 54.38N 22.44 E
Kyeintali 25 Ie 18.00N 94.29 E
Kyelang 25 Fb 32.35N 77.02 E
Kyfhauser 10 He 51.25N 11.10 E
Kyjov 10 Ng 49.01N 17.08 E
Kyle, Lake- 37 Ed 20.12S 31.00 E
Kyle of Lochalsh 9 Hd 57.17N 5.43W
Kyll 10 Cg 49.48N 6.42 E
Kyllburg 12 Id 50.02N 6.35 E
Kymi [2] 7 Gf 61.00N 28.00 E
Kymijoki 8 Ld 60.30N 26.52 E
Kyn 17 Ih 57.52N 58.32 E
Kynnefjäll 8 Df 58.42N 11.41 E
Kynsivesi 8 Lb 62.25N 26.10 E
Kyoga, Lake- 30 Kh 1.30N 33.00 E
Kyōga-Dake 29 Be 33.00N 130.05 E
Kyōga-Misaki 28 Mg 35.45N 135.11 E
Kyonan 29 Fd 35.07N 139.49 E
Kyŏnggi-Do [2] 28 If 37.30N 127.15 E
Kyŏnggi-man 28 Hf 37.25N 126.00 E
Kyŏngju 27 Md 35.50N 129.13 E
Kyŏngsang-Namdo [2] 28 Jg 35.15N 128.30 E
Kyŏngsang-Pukto [2] 28 Jf 36.20N 128.40 E
Kyŏngsŏng 28 Jd 41.40N 129.40 E
Kyōto 22 Pf 35.00N 135.45 E
Kyōto Fu 28 Mg 35.25N 135.15 E
Kypros → Kípros = Cyprus (EN) 23 Db 35.01N 33.00 E
Kyra 20 Gg 49.36N 111.58 E
Kyren 20 Ef 51.41N 102.10 E
Kyrenia 24 Ee 35.20N 33.19 E
Kyrgesaara/Kõrgesaare 8 Je 59.00N 22.25 E
Kyrgyz Sovetik Socialistik Respublikasy/Kirgizskaja SSR → Kyrgyzstan 19 Hg 41.30N 75.00 E
Kyrgyzstan 19 Hg 41.30N 75.00 E
Kyritz 10 Id 52.57N 12.24 E
Kyrkheden 8 Ed 60.10N 13.29 E
Kyrksæterora 7 Be 63.17N 9.06 E
Kyrkslått/Kirkkonummi 8 Kd 60.07N 24.26 E
Kyrö 8 Jd 60.42N 22.45 E
Kyrönjoki 8 Ia 63.14N 21.45 E
Kyrösjärvi 8 Jc 61.45N 23.10 E
Kyröskoski 8 Jc 61.40N 23.11 E
Kyštym 19 Gd 55.42N 60.34 E
Kysucké Nové Mesto 10 Og 49.18N 18.48 E
Kythera (EN) = Kíthira 5 Ih 36.15N 23.00 E
Kythraia 24 Ee 35.15N 33.29 E
Kyuquot Sound 46 Bb 49.55N 127.25W
Kyūshū 21 Pf 32.50N 131.00 E
Kyushu-Palau Ridge (EN) 3 Ih 20.00N 136.00 E
Kyūshū-Sanchi 29 Be 32.40N 131.10 E
Kyyjärvi 7 Fe 63.02N 24.34 E
Kyyvesi 8 Lc 61.55N 27.05 E
Kyzikos 24 Bb 40.28N 27.47 E
Kyzyl 22 Ld 51.42N 94.27 E
Kyzylart, Pereval- 19 Hh 39.22N 73.20 E
Kyzyl-Kija 19 Hg 40.14N 72.12 E
Kyzylkum 21 Ie 42.00N 64.00 E
Kyzylrabot 19 Hh 37.28N 74.45 E
Kyzylsu 19 Gf 37.22N 69.22 E
Kyzylsu 18 He 39.17N 71.25 E
Kyzylžar 19 Gf 48.17N 69.49 E
Kzyl-Orda 22 Ie 44.48N 65.28 E
Kzyl-Ordinskaja Oblast [3] 19 Gf 45.00N 65.00 E
Kzyltu 19 He 53.41N 72.15 E

L

Laa an der Thaya 14 Kb 48.43N 16.23 E
Laakdal 12 Gc 51.05N 4.59 E
La Alberca 13 Fd 40.29N 6.06W
La Alcarria 13 Jd 40.31N 2.45W
La Almunia de Doña Godina 13 Kc 41.29N 1.22W
La Ametlla de Mar 13 Md 40.54N 0.48 E
La Ardilla, Cerro- 48 Hf 22.15N 102.40W
La Armuña 13 Gc 41.05N 5.35W
Laasphe 12 Kd 50.56N 8.24 E
La Asunción 54 Fa 11.02N 63.53W
Laau Point 65a Db 21.06N 157.16W
Laayoune 13 Ni 35.42N 2.00 E
Lab 15 Eg 42.45N 21.01 E
Laba 16 Kg 45.10N 39.40 E
La Babia 48 Hc 28.34N 102.04W
Laba Dağı 15 Kl 37.22N 27.33 E
Labaddey 35 Ge 0.32N 42.45 E
Labadie Bank 9 Ek 50.30N 8.15W
La Banda 56 Hc 27.44S 64.15W
La Bañeza 13 Gb 42.18N 5.54W
La Barca 48 Hg 20.17N 102.34W
Labardén 55 Cm 36.57S 58.06W
La Barge 46 Je 42.16N 110.12W
La Barra, Punta- 49 Lh 11.30N 70.10W
La-Barre-en-Ouche 12 Cf 48.57N 0.40 E
La Baule-Escoublac 11 Dg 47.17N 2.24W
Labbezanga 34 Fc 14.59N 0.43 E
Labé 31 Fg 11.19N 12.17W
Labe = Elbe (EN) 5 Ge 53.50N 9.00 E
La Belle 44 Gl 26.46N 81.26W
Labelle 44 Jb 46.17N 74.45W
La Berzosa 13 Fd 40.35N 6.40W
Labin 14 Ie 45.05N 14.08 E
Labinsk 19 Eg 44.35N 40.44 E
Labis 26 Df 2.23N 103.02 E
La Bisbal/La Bisbal d'Empordà 13 Pc 41.57N 3.03 E
La Bisbal d'Empordà/La Bisbal 13 Pc 41.57N 3.03 E
La Blanca, Laguna- 55 Bj 30.14S 60.38W
Laboe 10 Gb 54.24N 10.13 E
Laborec 10 Rh 48.31N 21.54 E
Laborie 51k Bb 13.45N 61.00W
Labota 26 Hg 2.52S 122.10 E
Labouheyre 11 Fj 44.13N 0.55W
Laboulaye 56 Hd 34.07S 63.24W
Labra, Peña- 13 Ha 43.03N 4.26W
Labrador 38 Md 55.00N 70.00W
Labrador, Coast of- 38 Me 56.00N 60.35W
Labrador Basin (EN) 3 Dd 53.00N 48.00W
Labrador City 39 Md 52.57N 66.54W
Labrador Sea 38 Nd 57.00N 53.00W
Labrang → Xiahe 27 Hd 35.18N 102.30 E
Lábrea 53 Jf 7.16S 64.46W
Labrieville 44 Ma 49.19N 69.34W
Labrit 11 Fj 44.06N 0.33W
Labuan, Pulau- 26 Ge 5.19N 115.13 E
Labudalin → Ergun Youqi 27 La 50.16N 120.09 E
Labuha 26 Ig 0.37S 127.29 E
Labuhan 26 Eh 6.22S 105.50 E
Labuhanbajo 26 Gh 8.29S 119.54 E
Labuhanbilik 26 Df 2.31N 100.10 E
Labuk, Teluk- 26 Ge 6.10N 117.50 E
La Bureba 13 Ib 42.36N 3.24W
Labutta 25 Ie 16.09N 94.46 E
Labytnangi 22 Ic 66.39N 66.21 E
Lac [3] 35 Ac 13.30N 14.20 E
Lača, Ozero- 7 Jf 61.20N 38.50 E
La Cadena 48 Ge 25.53N 104.12W
La Calamine/Kelmis 12 Hd 50.43N 6.00 E
La Calandria 55 Cj 30.48S 58.39W
Lac Allard 42 Lf 50.30N 63.30W
La Campiña 13 Hg 37.45N 4.45W
Lacanau 11 Ej 44.59N 1.05W
Lacanau, Étang de- 11 Ej 44.58N 1.07W
Lacanau-Océan 11 Ei 45.00N 1.12W
Lacantún, Río- 48 Ni 16.36N 90.39W
La-Capelle 11 Je 49.58N 3.55 E
Lacarak 15 Ce 45.00N 19.34 E
La Carlota [Arg.] 56 Hd 33.26S 63.18W
La Carlota [Phil.] 26 Hd 10.25N 122.55 E
La Carlota [Sp.] 13 Hg 37.40N 4.56W
La Carolina 13 If 38.15N 3.37W
Lacaune 11 Ik 43.43N 2.42 E
Lacaune, Monts de- 11 Ik 43.40N 2.36 E
Laccadive Islands → Lakshadweep 21 Jh 11.00N 72.00 E
La Ceiba [Hond.] 39 Kh 15.47N 86.50W
La Ceiba [Ven.] 49 Li 9.28N 71.04W
Lacepede Bay 59 Hg 36.45S 139.45 E
Lacepede Islands 59 Ec 16.50S 122.10 E
La Cerdaña/La Cerdanya 13 Nb 42.24N 1.40 E
La Cerdanya/La Cerdaña 13 Nb 42.24N 1.40 E
Lacey 46 Dc 47.07N 122.49W
Lac Giao → Buon Me Thuot 25 Lf 12.40N 108.03 E
La Chaise-Dieu 11 Ji 45.19N 3.42 E
La Charité-sur-Loire 11 Jg 47.11N 3.01 E
La Châtre 11 Hh 46.35N 1.59 E
La Chaux-de-Fonds 14 Ac 47.06N 6.50 E
Lachay, Punta- 54 Cf 11.18S 77.39W
La China, Sierra- 55 Bm 36.47S 60.34W
Lachine 44 Kc 45.26N 73.40W
Lachlan River 57 Fh 34.21S 143.57 E
La Chorrera [Col.] 54 Dd 0.45S 73.00W
La Chorrera [Pan.] 47 Ig 8.53N 79.47W
Laçi 15 Ch 41.38N 19.43 E
Lačin 16 Oj 39.39N 46.33 E
La Ciotat 11 Lk 43.10N 5.36 E
Łąck 10 Pd 52.28N 19.40 E
Lackawanna 44 Hd 42.49N 78.49W
Lac La Biche 42 Gf 54.46N 111.58W
Lac la Martre 42 Fd 63.21N 117.00W
Lac Mégantic 44 Lc 45.35N 70.53W
La Colina 55 Bm 37.20S 61.32W
La Coloma 49 Fb 22.15N 83.34W
La Colorada 48 Dc 28.41N 110.25W
Lacombe 42 Gf 52.28N 113.44W
Lacon 45 Lf 41.02N 89.24W
La Concepción [Pan.] 49 Fi 8.31N 82.37W
La Concepción [Ven.] 49 Lh 10.48N 71.46W
La Concha 48 Gg 21.46N 105.29W
Laconi 14 Dk 39.51N 9.03 E
Laconia 43 Mc 43.32N 71.29W
Laconia, Gulf of- (EN) = Lakonikós Kólpos 15 Fm 36.35N 22.40 E
La Coronilla 55 Fk 33.44S 53.31W
La Coruña 6 Fg 43.22N 8.23W
La Coruña [3] 13 Da 43.10N 8.25W
La Côte-Saint-André 11 Li 45.23N 5.15 E
La Couronne 11 Gi 45.37N 0.06 E
La Courtine-le-Trucq 11 Ii 45.42N 2.16 E
Lacq 11 Fk 43.25N 0.38W
Lacroix-sur-Meuse 12 Hf 48.58N 5.31 E
La Crosse [Ks.-U.S.] 45 Gg 38.32N 99.18W
La Crosse [Wi.-U.S.] 39 Je 43.49N 91.15W
La Cruz [Arg.] 56 Ic 29.10S 56.38W
La Cruz [C.R.] 49 Eh 11.04N 85.39W
La Cruz [Mex.] 47 Cd 23.55N 106.54W
La Cruz [Ur.] 56 Id 33.56S 56.15W
La Cruz de Río Grande 49 Eg 13.06N 84.10W
La Cruz de Taratara 49 Mh 11.03N 69.44W
La Cuesta 48 Hc 28.45N 102.25W
La Cumbre 56 Hd 30.58S 64.30W
Lac Yora 35 Cb 19.08N 20.35 E
Ladário 55 Dd 19.01S 57.35W
Ladbergen 12 Jb 52.08N 7.45 E
Lądek-Zdrój 10 Mf 50.21N 16.50 E
Ladenburg 12 Ke 49.28N 8.37 E
La Désirade 50 Fd 16.19N 61.03W
La Digue Island 37b Ca 4.21S 55.50 E
Lâdik 24 Fb 40.36N 36.45 E
Ladismith 37 Cf 33.30S 21.16 E
Ladispoli 14 Gi 41.56N 12.05 E
Lado, Jabal- 35 Ed 5.06N 31.35 E
Ladoga, Lake- (EN) = Ladožkoje Ozero 5 Jc 61.00N 31.00 E
Ladong 27 Ig 24.49N 109.34 E
La Dorada 54 Db 5.22N 74.42W
Ladožkoje Ozero = Ladoga, Lake (EN) 5 Jc 61.00N 31.00 E
Ladrones, Islas- 49 Fj 7.52N 82.26W
Ladušin 8 Ij 54.35N 20.10 E
Ladva-Vetka 7 If 61.20N 34.29 E
Lady Ann Strait 42 Ja 75.45N 80.00W
Ladybrand 37 De 29.19S 27.25 E
Lady Evelyn Lake 44 Gb 47.20N 80.10W
Lady Newnes Ice Shelf 66 Kf 73.40S 167.30 E
Ladysmith [B.C.-Can.] 46 Db 48.58N 123.49W
Ladysmith [S.Afr.] 31 Jk 28.34S 29.45 E
Ladysmith [Wi.-U.S.] 43 Ib 45.28N 91.07W
Ladyžin 16 Fe 48.40N 29.13 E
Lae 58 Fe 6.43S 147.01 E
Lae Atoll 57 Hd 8.56N 166.14 E
La Eduvigis 55 Ch 26.50S 59.05W
Laem, Khao- 25 Kf 14.19N 101.11 E
Laer [Ger.] 12 Jb 52.04N 7.21 E
Laer [Ger.] 12 Kb 52.06N 8.05 E
Lærdalsøyri 7 Bf 61.06N 7.29 E
La Escala/L'Escala 13 Pb 42.07N 3.08 E
La Esmeralda 54 Ec 3.10N 65.33W
Læsø 7 Bh 57.15N 10.00 E
Læsø Rende 8 Dg 57.15N 10.45 E
La Española = Hispaniola (EN) 38 Lh 19.00N 71.00W
La Esperanza [Bol.] 54 Ff 14.34S 62.10W
La Esperanza [Hond.] 49 Cf 14.20N 88.10W
La Estrada 13 Db 42.41N 8.29W
Lafayette [Al.-U.S.] 44 Ei 32.54N 85.24W
Lafayette [In.-U.S.] 43 Jc 40.25N 86.53W
Lafayette [La.-U.S.] 39 Jf 30.14N 92.01W
La Fère 12 Fe 49.40N 3.22 E
La Ferrière-sur-Risle 12 Cf 48.59N 0.48 E
La Ferté-Bernard 11 Gf 48.11N 0.40 E
La Ferté-Frênel 12 Cf 48.50N 0.30 E
La Ferté-Macé 11 Ff 48.36N 0.22W
La Ferté-Milon 12 Fe 49.10N 3.07 E
La Ferté-Saint-Aubin 11 Hg 47.43N 1.56 E
La Ferté-sous-Jouarre 11 Jf 48.57N 3.08 E
Laffān, Ra's- 24 Nj 25.54N 51.35 E
Lafia 34 Gd 8.29N 8.31 E
Lafiagi 34 Gd 8.52N 5.15 E
La Flèche 11 Fg 47.42N 0.05W
Lafnitz 14 Kd 46.57N 16.16 E
La Foa 63b Be 21.43S 165.49 E
La Follette 44 Eg 36.23N 84.07W
La Fria 49 Ki 8.13N 72.15W
Laft 24 Pi 26.54N 55.46 E
La Fuente de San Esteban 13 Fd 40.48N 6.15W
Laga, Monti della- 14 Hh 42.45N 13.35 E
La Galite (EN) = Jāliṭah 30 He 37.32N 8.56 E
La Gallareta 55 Bi 29.34S 60.23W
Lagamar 55 Id 18.13S 46.48W
Lagan 8 Eh 56.33N 12.56 E
Lagan 8 Eh 56.55N 13.59 E
Lagan/Abhainn an Lagáin 9 Hg 54.37N 5.53W
Lagarina, Val- 14 Fe 45.50N 11.10 E
La Garita Mountains 45 Ch 38.00N 106.40W
Lagarto 54 Kf 10.54S 37.41W
Lagash 24 Lg 31.27N 46.13 E
Lagawe 26 Hc 16.49N 121.06 E
Lage 12 Kc 51.59N 8.48 E
Lågen 7 Cf 61.08N 10.25 E
Lagh Bogal 36 Gb 0.42N 40.55 E
Laghmān [3] 23 Lb 35.00N 70.15 E
Laghouat 31 He 33.48N 2.53 E
Laghouat [3] 32 Hc 33.30N 3.15 E
La Gloria 49 Ki 8.38N 73.48W
Lagny 11 If 48.52N 2.43 E
Lagoa 13 Dg 37.08N 8.27W
Lagôa 55 Eb 14.08S 55.20W
Lagoa da Prata 55 Je 20.01S 45.33W
Lagoa Vermelha 56 Jc 28.13S 51.32W
Lagodehi 16 Oi 41.50N 46.14 E
La Gomera 49 Bf 14.05N 91.03W
Lagonegro 14 Jj 40.07N 15.46 E
Lagonoy Gulf 26 Hd 13.35N 123.45 E
Lagoon 64n Ab 10.23S 161.05W
Lagos 13 Dg 37.06N 8.40W
Lagos 31 Hh 6.27N 3.23 E
Lágos 15 Ih 41.01N 25.07 E
Lagos [2] 34 Fd 6.30N 3.30 E
Lagos, Baía de- 13 Dg 37.06N 8.39W
Lagosa 36 Ed 5.57S 29.53 E
Lagos de Moreno 47 Dd 21.21N 101.55W
La Grand-Combe 11 Kj 44.13N 4.02 E
La Grande 43 Db 45.20N 118.05W
La Grande Fosse 9 Kl 49.40N 3.00W
La Grande-Motte 11 Kk 43.34N 4.07 E
La Grande Rivière 38 Ld 53.50N 79.00W
La Grande Trench (EN) = Hurd Deep 9 Kl 49.40N 3.00W
La Grange 44 Ef 38.24N 85.23W
Lagrange 44 Ee 41.39N 85.25W
La Grange [Ga.-U.S.] 43 Je 33.02N 85.02W
La Grange [Tx.-U.S.] 45 Hl 29.54N 96.52W
La Gran Sabana 54 Fb 5.30N 61.30W
La Grita 54 Db 8.08N 71.59W
Lagskär 8 He 59.50N 20.00 E
La Guaira 53 Jd 10.36N 66.56W
La Guajira [2] 54 Da 11.30N 72.30W
Lagua Lichan, Puntan- 64b Ba 15.16N 145.50 E
Laguardia 13 Jb 42.33N 2.35W
La Guardia [Sp.] 13 Dc 41.54N 8.53W
La Guardia [Sp.] 13 Ie 39.47N 3.29W
La Guasima 48 Kg 21.06N 97.49W
La Guerche-sur-l'Aubois 11 Ih 46.57N 2.57 E
Laguiole 11 Ij 44.41N 2.51 E
Laguna 56 Kc 28.29S 48.47W
Laguna Alsina 55 Am 36.49S 62.13W
Laguna Beach 46 Gj 33.33N 117.51W
Laguna Blanca 55 Cg 25.08S 58.15W
Laguna de Bay 26 Hd 14.23N 121.15 E
Laguna Limpia 55 Ch 26.29S 59.41W
Laguna Mountains 46 Gj 32.55N 116.25W
Laguna Paiva 56 Hd 31.19S 60.39W
Laguna Superior 47 Fe 16.20N 94.25W
Laguna Veneta 14 Ge 45.25N 12.20 E
Laguna Yema 55 Bg 24.15S 61.15W
Lagunillas [Bol.] 54 Fg 19.38S 63.43W
Lagunillas [Mex.] 48 Ii 17.50N 101.44W
Lagunillas [Ven.] 49 Lh 10.08N 71.16W
Lagunillas [Ven.] 49 Li 8.31N 71.24W
Laha 27 Lb 48.13N 124.36 E
La Habana [3] 49 Fb 22.45N 82.10W
La Habana = Havana (EN) 39 Kg 23.08N 82.22W
Lahad Datu 26 Ge 5.02N 118.19 E
Laham 34 Fc 14.54N 4.25 E
Lahat 26 Dg 3.48S 103.32 E
Lahdenpohja 7 Hf 61.33N 30.13 E
Lahewa 26 Cf 1.24N 97.11 E
Lahij 23 Fg 13.04N 44.53 E
Lāhījān 23 Hb 37.12N 50.01 E
Lahn 10 Df 50.18N 7.37 E
Lahnstein 12 Jd 50.20N 7.29 E
Laholm 7 Ch 56.31N 13.02 E
Laholmsbukten 8 Eh 56.35N 12.50 E
Lahore 22 Jf 31.35N 74.18 E
Lahr 10 Dh 48.20N 7.52 E
Lahti 6 Ic 60.58N 25.40 E
Laï 31 Ih 9.24N 16.18 E
Laiagam 60 Ci 5.31S 143.39 E
Lai'an 28 Eh 32.28N 118.26 E
Lai Chau 25 Kd 22.02N 103.10 E
Laich o'Moray 9 Jd 57.40N 3.30W
Laie 65a Db 21.39N 157.56W
Laifeng 27 If 29.31N 109.23 E
Laighean/Leinster 9 Gh 53.00N 7.00W
L'Aigle 11 Gf 48.45N 0.38 E
Laignes 11 Kg 47.50N 4.22 E
Laihia 7 Fe 62.58N 22.01 E
Lainioälven 7 Fc 67.22N 22.39 E
Lairg 9 Ic 58.01N 4.25W
Lairi 35 Bc 10.49N 17.06 E
Lairi, Batha de- 35 Bc 12.28N 16.45 E
Lais 26 Dg 3.32S 102.03 E
La Isabela 49 Gb 22.57N 80.01W
Laisamis 36 Gb 1.36N 37.48 E
Laiševo 7 Li 55.26N 49.32 E
Laishui 28 Ce 39.23N 115.42 E
Laisvall 7 Dc 66.08N 17.10 E
Laitila 7 Ef 60.53N 21.41 E
Laiwu 28 Df 36.12N 117.40 E
Laiwui 26 Ig 1.22S 127.40 E
Laixi (Shuiji) 28 Ff 36.52N 120.31 E
Laiyang 27 Ld 36.59N 120.39 E
Laiyuan 27 Jd 39.19N 114.43 E
Laizhou Wan 28 Ef 37.30N 119.30 E
Laja 56 Fe 37.16S 72.42W
Laja 17 Hc 66.20N 56.16 E
La Jara 13 He 39.40N 4.55W
Lajeado 55 Gi 29.27S 52.00W
Lajeado, Serra do- 55 Hd 19.08S 49.56W
Lajerd 24 Oe 35.24N 53.04 E
Lajes [Braz.] 54 Ke 5.41S 36.14W
Lajes [Braz.] 53 Kh 27.48S 50.19W
Lajes do Pico 32 Bb 38.23N 28.16W
Lajosmizse 10 Pi 47.01N 19.33 E
La Junta [Co.-U.S.] 43 Gd 37.59N 103.33W
La Junta [Mex.] 48 Fc 28.28N 107.20W
Lak Bor 36 Hb 1.18N 40.40 E
Lake Cargelligo 59 Jf 33.18S 146.23 E
Lake Charles 39 Jf 30.12N 93.12W
Lake City 43 Ke 30.12N 82.38W
Lake District 9 Jg 54.30N 3.10W
Lake Fork Creek 46 Jf 40.13N 110.07W
Lake Geneva 45 Le 42.36N 88.26W
Lake George 44 Kd 43.25N 73.45W
Lake Grace 59 Df 33.06S 118.28 E
Lake Harbour 42 Kd 62.51N 69.53W
Lake Havasu City 46 Hi 34.27N 114.22W
Lake Itasca 45 Ic 46.51N 95.13W
Lake Jackson 45 Il 29.02N 95.27W
Lake King 59 Df 33.05S 119.40 E
Lakeland 43 Kf 28.03N 81.57W
Lake Louise 46 Ga 51.26N 116.11W
Lakemba 63d Cc 18.13S 178.47W
Lakemba Passage 63d Cb 17.53S 178.32W
Lake Mills 45 Je 43.25N 93.32W
Lake Minchumina 40 Ia 63.53N 152.19W
Lake Murray 60 Ci 6.54S 141.28 E
Lake Oswego 46 Dd 45.26N 122.39W
Lake Placid 44 Kc 44.18N 73.59W
Lake Providence 45 Kj 32.48N 91.11W
Lake Pukaki 62 Df 44.11S 170.08 E
Lake Range 46 Ff 40.15N 119.25W
Lake River 42 Jf 54.28N 82.30W
Lakes Entrance 59 Jg 37.53S 147.59 E
Lakeside 46 If 41.13N 112.57W
Lake Tekapo 62 Df 44.00S 170.29 E
Lakeview 43 Cc 42.11N 120.21W
Lakeville 45 Jd 44.39N 93.14W
Lake Wales 44 Gl 27.55N 81.35W
Lakewood [Co.-U.S.] 45 Dg 39.44N 105.06W
Lakewood [Oh.-U.S.] 44 Ge 41.29N 81.50W
Lake Worth 44 Gl 26.37N 80.03W
Lakhdar, Chergui Kef- 13 Pi 35.57N 3.16 E
Lakhdaria 13 Ph 36.34N 3.35 E
Lâki 15 Hh 41.50N 24.50 E
Lakin 45 Fh 37.58N 101.15W
Lakinsk 7 Jh 56.04N 39.58 E
Lákmos Óros 15 Ej 39.40N 21.07 E
Lakon, Ile- 57 Hf 14.17S 167.30 E
Lakonikós Kólpos = Laconia, Gulf of- (EN) 15 Fm 36.35N 22.40 E
Lakota [3] 34 Dd 5.53N 5.42W
Lakota [I.C.] 34 Dd 5.51N 5.41W
Lakota [N.D.-U.S.] 45 Gb 48.02N 98.21W
Lakselv 7 Fa 70.03N 25.01 E
Lakshadweep = Laccadive Islands 21 Jh 11.00N 72.00 E
Lakshadweep [3] 25 Ef 11.00N 72.00 E
La Laguna 55 Bb 14.30S 61.06W
Lalanna 37 Hd 23.28S 45.05 E
Lalapaşa 15 Jh 41.50N 26.44 E
Lāleh Zār, Kūh-e- 21 Hg 29.24N 56.46 E
La Leonesa 55 Ch 27.03S 58.43W
Lālī 24 Mf 32.21N 49.06 E
Lalibela 35 Fc 12.00N 39.04 E
La Libertad [2] 54 Ce 8.00S 78.30W
La Libertad [ElSal.] 47 Gf 13.29N 89.16W
La Libertad [Guat.] 49 Be 16.47N 90.07W
La Libertad [Guat.] 49 Bf 15.30N 91.50W
La Libertad [Hond.] 49 Df 14.43N 87.36W
La Ligua 56 Fd 32.27S 71.14W
Lalin 13 Db 42.39N 8.07W
La Linea 13 Gh 36.10N 5.19W
Lalitpur 25 Fd 24.41N 78.25 E
Lalla Khedidja 13 Qh 36.27N 4.14 E
Lālmanir Hāt 25 Hc 25.54N 89.27 E
La Loche 42 Ge 56.29N 109.27W
La Loupe 11 Hf 48.28N 1.01 E
La Louvière 11 Kd 50.29N 4.11 E
L'Alpe-d'Huez 11 Mi 45.06N 6.04 E
La Lucila 55 Bj 30.25S 61.01W
Lalzit, Gjiri i- 15 Ch 41.31N 19.29 E
La Machine 11 Jh 46.53N 3.28 E
La Maddalena 14 Di 41.13N 9.24 E
La Maiella 5 Hg 42.05N 14.07 E
La Maladeta/Maldítos, Montes- 13 Mb 42.40N 0.50 E
La Malbaie 42 Kg 47.39N 70.10W
La Mancha 5 Fh 39.05N 3.00W
La Manche 5 Fe 50.20N 1.00W
Lamap 61 Cc 16.26S 167.43 E
Lamar 43 Gd 38.05N 102.37W
La Maragateria 13 Fb 42.25N 6.10W
La Marina 13 Lf 38.35N 0.05W
La Marmora 14 Dk 39.59N 9.20 E
La Marque 45 Il 29.22N 94.58W
Lamas 54 Ce 6.25S 76.35W
Lamastre 11 Kj 44.59N 4.35 E
Lamawan 28 Ad 40.05N 111.25 E
Lambach 14 Hb 48.05N 13.53 E
Lamballe 11 Df 48.28N 2.31W
Lambar, Río- 55 Jd 19.30S 45.00W
Lambaréné 31 Ii 0.42S 10.13 E
Lambari 55 Je 21.58S 45.21W
Lambasa 61 Ec 16.26S 179.24 E
Lambay/Reachrainn 9 Gh 53.29N 6.01W
Lambayeque [2] 54 Ce 6.20S 80.00W
Lambayeque 54 Ce 6.42S 79.55W
Lambert Glacier 66 Ff 71.00S 70.00 E
Lambert Land 41 Jc 79.10N 21.00W
Lamberts Bay 31 Il 32.05S 18.17 E
Lambro 14 De 45.08N 9.32 E
Lambsheim 12 Ke 49.31N 8.17 E
Lambton, Cape- 42 Fb 71.04N 123.08W
Lamé 35 Ad 9.15N 14.32 E
Lame Deer 46 Ld 45.37N 106.40W
Lamego 13 Ec 41.06N 7.49W
Lamentin 51e Ab 16.16N 61.38W
La Mesa 46 Gj 32.46N 117.01W
Lamesa 43 Ge 32.44N 101.57W
La Meta 14 Hj 41.41N 13.56 E
Lamezia Terme 14 Kl 38.59N 16.17 E
Lamia 15 Fk 38.54N 22.26 E
Lamina 55 De 20.34S 56.14W
Lamlam, Mount- 64c Bb 13.20N 144.40 E
Lammermuir Hills 9 Kf 55.52N 2.40W
Lammhult 8 Fg 57.10N 14.35 E
Lammi 7 Ff 61.05N 25.01 E
Lamoil 64d Ba 7.39N 151.41 E
Lamon Bay 21 Oh 14.25N 122.00 E
Lamone 14 Gf 44.29N 12.08 E
Lamoni 45 Jf 40.37N 93.56W
Lamont 44 Fj 30.21N 83.50W
La Montaña 52 If 10.00S 72.50W
La Moraña 13 Hd 40.45N 4.55W
La Mosquitia 49 Ef 15.00N 84.20W
La Mothe-Achard 11 Eh 46.37N 1.40W
Lamotrek Atoll 57 Fd 7.30N 146.20 E

Index Symbols

[1] Independent Nation
[2] State, Region
[3] District, County
[4] Municipality
[5] Colony, Dependency
Continent
Physical Region
Historical or Cultural Region
Mount, Mountain
Volcano
Hill
Mountains, Mountain Range
Hills, Escarpment
Plateau, Upland
Pass, Gap
Plain, Lowland
Delta
Salt Flat
Valley, Canyon
Crater, Cave
Karst Features
Depression
Polder
Desert, Dunes
Forest, Woods
Heath, Steppe
Oasis
Cape, Point
Coast, Beach
Cliff
Peninsula
Isthmus
Sandbank
Island
Atoll
Rock, Reef
Islands, Archipelago
Rocks, Reefs
Coral Reef
Well, Spring
Geyser
River, Stream
Waterfall Rapids
River Mouth, Estuary
Lake
Salt Lake
Intermittent Lake
Reservoir
Swamp, Pond
Canal
Glacier
Ice Shelf, Pack Ice
Ocean
Sea
Gulf, Bay
Strait, Fjord
Lagoon
Bank
Seamount
Tablemount
Ridge
Shelf
Basin
Escarpment, Sea Scarp
Fracture
Trench, Abyss
National Park, Reserve
Point of Interest
Recreation Site
Cave, Cavern
Historic Site
Ruins
Wall, Walls
Church, Abbey
Temple
Scientific Station
Airport
Port
Lighthouse
Mine
Tunnel
Dam, Bridge

Lamotte-Beuvron	11	Ig	47.36N	2.01 E
La Moure	45	Gc	46.21N	98.18W
Lampang	25	Je	18.16N	99.34 E
Lampasas	45	Gk	31.03N	98.12W
Lampazos de Naranjo	48	Id	27.01N	100.31W
Lampedusa ◆	14	Go	35.30N	12.35 E
Lampertheim	10	Eg	49.36N	8.28 E
Lampeter	9	Ii	52.07N	4.05W
Lamphun	25	Je	18.35N	99.00 E
Lampione ◆	14	Go	35.35N	12.20 E
Lampung [3]	26	Dg	5.00S	105.00 E
Lamu	31	Li	2.16S	40.54 E
Lamud	54	Ce	6.09S	77.55W
La Mure	11	Lj	44.54N	5.47 E
Lan ∿	16	Ec	52.09N	27.18 E
Lana	14	Fd	46.37N	11.09 E
Lana, Río de la- ∿	48	Li	17.49N	95.09W
Lanai City	65a	Ec	20.50N	156.55W
Lanaihale ▲	65a	Ec	20.49N	156.52W
Lanai Island ◆	57	Lb	20.50N	156.55W
Lanaken	12	Hd	50.53N	5.39 E
Lanark	9	Jf	55.41N	3.48W
Lanbi Kyun ◆	25	Jf	10.50N	98.15 E
Lancang (Menglangba)	27	Gg	22.37N	99.57 E
Lancang Jiang=Mekong (EN) ∿	21	Mh	10.15N	105.55 E
Lancashire [3]	9	Kh	53.55N	2.40W
Lancashire Plain ▭	9	Kh	53.40N	2.45W
Lancaster ▣	9	Kh	53.45N	2.50W
Lancaster [Ca.-U.S.]	43	De	34.42N	118.08W
Lancaster [Eng.-U.K.]	9	Kg	54.03N	2.48W
Lancaster [Mo.-U.S.]	45	Jf	40.31N	92.32W
Lancaster [N.H.-U.S.]	44	Lc	44.29N	71.34W
Lancaster [Oh.-U.S.]	44	Ff	39.43N	82.37W
Lancaster [Ont.-Can.]	44	Jc	45.12N	74.30W
Lancaster [Pa.-U.S.]	43	Lc	40.01N	76.19W
Lancaster [S.C.-U.S.]	44	Gh	34.43N	80.47W
Lancaster Sound ▬	38	Kb	74.13N	84.00W
Lançeiro	55	Fe	20.59S	53.43W
Lancelin	59	Df	31.01S	115.19 E
Lanciano	14	Ih	42.14N	14.23 E
Lančin	15	Ha	48.31N	24.49 E
Lancun	28	Ff	36.25N	120.11 E
Łańcut	10	Sf	50.05N	22.13 E
Land ⧗	8	Cd	60.45N	10.00 E
Lândana	36	Bd	5.15S	12.10 E
Landau an der Isar	10	Ih	48.41N	12.41 E
Landau in der Pfalz	10	Eg	49.12N	8.07 E
Land Bay ◖	66	Mf	75.25S	141.45W
Landeck	14	Ec	47.08N	10.34 E
Landen	12	Hd	50.45N	5.05 E
Lander	43	Fc	42.50N	108.44W
Landerneau	11	Bf	48.27N	4.15W
Lander River ∿	59	Gd	20.25S	132.00 E
Landeryd	8	Eg	57.05N	13.16 E
Landes ⧗	11	Fj	44.15N	1.00W
Landes [3]	11	Fj	44.00N	0.50W
Landesbergen	12	Lb	52.34N	9.08 E
Landeta	55	Ak	32.01S	62.04W
Landete	13	Ke	39.54N	1.22W
Landfallis ◆	25	If	13.40N	93.02 E
Land Glacier ▽	66	Mf	75.40S	141.45W
Landi Kotal	25	Eb	34.06N	71.09 E
Landless Corner	36	Ee	14.53S	28.04 E
Landrecies	12	Fd	50.08N	3.42 E
Landsberg am Lech	10	Gh	48.03N	10.52 E
Landsbro	8	Fg	57.22N	14.54 E
Land's End ►	5	Fe	50.03N	5.44W
Lands End ►	42	Fa	76.25N	122.45W
Landshut	10	Ih	48.32N	12.09 E
Landskrona	8	Ei	55.52N	12.50 E
Landsort ◆	8	Gf	58.45N	17.50 E
Landsortsdjupet ⩡	8	Hf	58.40N	18.30 E
Landstuhl	12	Je	49.25N	7.34 E
Landusky	46	Kc	47.54N	108.37W
La Neuve-Lyre	12	Cf	48.54N	0.45 E
Lanfeng → Lankao	28	Cg	34.49N	114.48 E
Lang	46	Mb	49.56N	104.23W
La'nga Co ≈	27	De	30.41N	81.17 E
Langadhás	15	Gi	40.45N	23.04 E
Langádhia	15	Fl	37.39N	22.03 E
Långan ∿	7	De	63.19N	14.44 E
Langano, Lake- ≈	35	Fd	7.36N	38.43 E
Langao	27	Ie	32.20N	108.53 E
Langara	26	Hg	4.02S	123.00 E
Langarfoss ⇊	7a	Cb	65.35N	14.15W
Langasian	26	Ie	8.16N	125.39 E
Langdon	45	Gb	48.46N	98.22W
Langeac	11	Ji	45.06N	3.29 E
Langeais	11	Gg	47.20N	0.24 E
Langeb ∿	35	Fb	17.46N	36.41 E
Langebaan	37	Bf	33.06S	18.02 E
Langeberg ⛰	37	Cf	33.56S	20.45 E
Langedijk	12	Gb	52.42N	4.48 E
Langeland ◆	7	Ci	55.00N	10.50 E
Langelands Bælt ▬	8	Dj	54.50N	10.55 E
Längelmävesi ≈	8	Kc	61.30N	24.20 E
Langen	12	Ke	49.59N	8.40 E
Langenberg ▲	12	Kc	51.17N	8.34 E
Langenburg	45	Fa	50.50N	101.43W
Langenfeld (Rheinland)	12	Ic	51.06N	6.57 E
Langenhagen	10	Fd	52.27N	9.45 E
Langenselbold	12	Ld	50.11N	9.02 E
Langenthal	14	Bc	47.13N	7.49 E
Langeoog ◆	10	Dc	53.46N	7.32 E
Langeri	20	Jf	50.08N	143.20 E
Langesund	8	Ce	59.00N	9.45 E
Langesundsfjorden ▬	8	Cf	59.00N	9.48 E
Langevåg	8	Bb	62.27N	6.12 E
Langfang → Anci	27	Kd	39.29N	116.40 E
Långfjället ⛰	8	Eb	62.10N	12.20 E
Langfjorden ▬	8	Bb	62.45N	7.30 E
Langhe ⧗	14	Bf	44.30N	8.00 E
Langholm	9	Kf	55.09N	3.00W
Langjökull ▲	5	Ec	64.39N	20.00W
Langkawi, Pulau- ◆	26	Ce	6.22N	99.48 E
Langkon	26	Ge	6.32N	116.42 E
Langlade	44	Ja	48.12N	75.57W
Langnau im Emmental	14	Bd	46.56N	7.46 E
Langogne	11	Jj	44.43N	3.51 E
Langon	11	Fj	44.33N	0.15W
Langorūd	24	Md	37.11N	50.10 E
Langøya ◆	7	Db	68.44N	14.50 E
Langreo	13	Ga	43.18N	5.41W
Langres	11	Lg	47.52N	5.20 E
Langres, Plateau de- ⏢	5	Gf	47.41N	5.03 E
Langrune-sur-Mer	12	Be	49.19N	0.22W
Langsa	22	Li	4.28N	97.58 E
Långsele	8	Ga	63.11N	17.04 E
Långshyttan	8	Gd	60.27N	16.01 E
Lang Son	25	Ld	21.50N	106.44 E
Lang Suan	25	Jg	9.55N	99.07 E
Languedoc ⧗	5	Gg	44.00N	4.00 E
Languedoc ▣	11	Jj	44.00N	4.00 E
Langueyú, Arroyo- ∿	55	Cm	36.39S	58.27W
Langwedel	12	Lb	52.58N	9.13 E
Langxi	28	Ei	31.08N	119.11 E
Langzhong	27	Ie	31.40N	106.04 E
Lan Hsu ◆	27	Lg	22.00N	121.30 E
Laniel	44	Hb	47.06N	79.15W
Lanin, Volcán- △	52	Ii	39.38S	71.30W
Lankao ≈	27	Cd	35.12N	79.50 E
Lankao (Lanfeng) ◆	27	Kg	21.00N	116.00 E
Lankao (Lanfeng)	28	Cg	34.49N	114.48 E
Länkipohja	8	Kc	61.44N	24.48 E
Lannemezan	11	Gk	43.08N	0.23 E
Lannemezan, Plateau de- ⏢	11	Gk	43.09N	0.27 E
Lannion	11	Cf	48.44N	3.28W
Lannion, Baie de- ◖	11	Cf	48.43N	3.34W
La Noria	56	Gb	20.23S	69.53W
Lansdowne House	42	If	52.13N	87.53W
L'Anse	44	Cb	46.45N	88.27W
Lansing [Ia.-U.S.]	45	Ke	43.22N	91.13W
Lansing [Mi.-U.S.]	39	Ke	42.43N	84.34W
Lansjärv	7	Fc	66.39N	22.12 E
Łańskie, Jezioro- ≈	10	Qc	53.33N	20.30 E
Lantar	20	Ie	56.05N	137.35 E
Lanta Yai, Ko- ◆	25	Jg	7.35N	99.03 E
Lanteri	55	Ci	28.50S	59.39W
Lanterne ∿	11	Mg	47.44N	6.03 E
Lanús	55	Cl	34.43S	58.24W
Lanusei	14	Dk	39.53N	9.32 E
Lanvaux, Landes de- ≀	11	Dg	47.47N	2.36W
Lanxi [China]	28	Ej	29.13N	119.28 E
Lanxi [China]	28	Ha	46.15N	126.16 E
Lanxian (Dongcun)	28	Ae	38.17N	111.38 E
Lanyi He ∿	28	Ae	38.40N	110.53 E
Lanzarote ◆	30	Ff	29.00N	13.40W
Lanzhou	22	Mf	36.03N	103.41 E
Lanzo Torinese	14	Be	45.16N	7.28 E
Lao ∿	14	Jk	39.47N	15.48 E
Laoag	22	Oh	18.12N	120.36 E
Laoang	26	Id	12.34N	125.00 E
Lao Cai	22	Mg	22.30N	103.57 E
Laocheng	28	Hc	42.37N	124.04 E
Laoha He ∿	27	Lc	43.24N	120.39 E
Lao He ∿	28	Cj	29.02N	115.47 E
Laohuanghe Kou ⊰	28	Ef	37.39N	119.02 E
Laois [2]	9	Fi	53.00N	7.30W
Laojunmiao → Yumen	22	Lf	39.50N	97.44 E
Laojun Shan ▲	27	Je	33.45N	111.38 E
Lao Ling ⛰	28	Id	41.24N	126.10 E
Laon	11	Je	49.34N	3.37 E
Laona	45	Ld	45.34N	88.40W
Laonnois ⧗	12	Fe	49.35N	3.40 E
La Orchila, Isla- ◆	54	Ea	11.48N	66.10W
La Oroya	53	Ig	11.32S	75.57W
Laos [1]	22	Mh	18.00N	105.00 E
Laoshan (Licun)	28	Ff	36.10N	120.25 E
Laotougou	28	Jc	42.54N	129.09 E
Laou ∿	13	Gi	35.26N	5.05W
Laoye Ling ⛰	28	Kb	44.50N	130.10 E
Lapa	56	Kc	25.45S	49.42W
Lapai	34	Gd	9.03N	6.43 E
Lapalisse	11	Jh	46.15N	3.38 E
La Palma ◆	30	Ff	28.40N	17.52W
La Palma [ElSal.]	49	Cf	14.19N	89.11W
La Palma [Pan.]	47	Ig	8.25N	78.09W
La Palma del Condado	13	Fg	37.23N	6.33W
La Paloma	55	El	34.40S	54.10W
La Pampa [2]	56	Ge	37.00S	66.00W
La Panne/De Panne	12	Ec	51.06N	2.35 E
La Paragua	54	Fb	6.50N	63.20W
La Partida, Isla- ◆	48	De	24.30N	110.25W
La Paz [3]	49	Df	14.15N	87.50W
La Paz [2]	54	Eg	15.00S	68.00W
La Paz [Arg.]	56	Id	30.45S	59.39W
La Paz [Arg.]	56	Gd	33.28S	67.33W
La Paz [Bol.]	53	Jg	16.30S	68.09W
La Paz [Col.]	49	Kh	10.23N	73.10W
La Paz [Hond.]	47	Gf	14.16N	87.40W
La Paz [Mex.]	39	Hg	24.10N	110.18W
La Paz [Ur.]	55	Dl	34.46S	56.13W
La Paz [Ven.]	49	Lh	10.41N	72.00W
La Paz, Bahía de- ◖	47	Bd	24.09N	110.25W
La Paz, Llano de- ▭	48	De	24.00N	110.30W
La Paz Centro	49	Dg	12.20N	86.41W
La Pedrera	54	Ed	1.18S	69.40W
Lapeer	44	Fd	43.03N	83.19W
La Pelada	55	Bj	30.52S	60.59W
La Pérouse, Bahía- ◖	65d	Bb	27.04S	109.18W
La Perouse Strait (EN)= Laperuza, Proliv- ▬	21	Qe	45.30N	142.00 E
La Perouse Strait (EN)= Sōya-Kaikyō ▬	21	Qe	45.30N	142.00 E
Laperuza, Proliv-=La Perouse Strait (EN) ▬	21	Qe	45.30N	142.00 E
La Pesca	47	Ed	23.47N	97.47W
La Petite Pierre	12	Jf	48.52N	7.19 E
La Picasa, Laguna- ≈	55	Al	34.20S	62.14W
La Piedad Cavadas	48	Hg	20.21N	102.00W
La Pine	46	Ee	43.40N	121.30W
Lapinjärvi/Lappträsk	8	Ld	60.36N	26.09 E
Lapinlahti	7	Ge	63.22N	27.30 E
La Plaine	51g	Bb	15.20N	61.15W
La Plana ⧗	13	Ld	40.00N	0.05W
Lapland (EN)=Lappi ⧗	5	Ib	66.50N	22.00 E
Lapland (EN)=Lappland ⧗	5	Ib	66.50N	22.00 E
La Plant	45	Fd	45.10N	100.38W
La Plata	53	Ki	34.55S	57.57W
La Pobla de Lillet	13	Nb	42.15N	1.59 E
La Pobla de Segur/Pobla de Segur	13	Mb	42.15N	0.58 E
La Pocatièr	44	Lb	47.21N	70.02W
La Porte	44	De	41.36N	86.43W
Lapovo	15	Ee	44.11N	21.06 E
Lappajärvi ≈	7	Fe	63.08N	23.40 E
Lappeenranta/Villmanstrand	6	Ic	61.04N	28.11 E
Lappfjärd/Lapväärtti	8	Ib	62.15N	21.32 E
Lappi [2]	7	Gc	67.40N	26.30 E
Lappi	8	Ic	61.06N	21.50 E
Lappi=Lapland (EN) ⧗	5	Ib	66.50N	22.00 E
Lappo/Lapua	7	Fe	62.57N	23.00 E
Lappträsk/Lapinjärvi	8	Ld	60.36N	26.09 E
Lapri	20	He	55.45N	124.59 E
Laprida	56	He	37.33S	60.49W
Lâpseki	24	Bb	40.20N	26.31 E
Lapta	24	Ee	35.20N	33.10 E
Laptev Sea (EN)=Laptevyh, More- ≡	67	Fd	76.00N	126.00 E
Laptevyh, More-=Laptev Sea (EN) ≡	67	Fd	76.00N	126.00 E
Lapua/Lappo	7	Fe	62.57N	23.00 E
La Puebla	13	Pe	39.46N	3.01 E
La Puebla de Cazalla	13	Gg	37.14N	5.19W
Lapuna	55	Ba	13.19S	60.28W
La Puntilla ►	52	Hf	2.11S	81.01W
La Purísima	48	Cd	26.10N	112.04W
Lăpuş	15	Hb	47.30N	24.01 E
Lăpuş ∿	15	Gb	47.39N	23.24 E
La Push	46	Cc	47.55N	124.38W
Lapväärtti/Lappfjärd	8	Ib	62.15N	21.32 E
Łapy	10	Sd	53.00N	22.53 E
Laqīyat al Arba'in	35	Da	20.03N	28.02 E
La Quemada ⁘	48	Hf	22.27N	102.45W
La Quiaca	56	Gb	22.06S	65.37W
L'Aquila	6	Hg	42.22N	13.22 E
Lar	23	Hd	27.41N	54.17 E
Lara [2]	54	Ea	10.10N	69.50W
Larache	32	Fb	35.12N	6.09W
Laragne-Montéglin	11	Lj	44.19N	5.49 E
Lārak ◆	23	Id	26.52N	56.22 E
La Rambla	13	Hg	37.36N	4.44W
Laramie	39	Ie	41.19N	105.35W
Laramie Mountains ⛰	43	Fc	42.00N	105.40W
Laramie Peak ▲	46	Me	42.17N	105.27W
Laramie River ∿	46	Me	42.12N	104.32W
Laranjal, Rio- ∿	55	Ff	23.12S	53.45W
Laranjeiras do Sul	56	Jc	25.25S	52.25W
Larantuka	26	Hh	8.21S	122.59 E
Larat	26	Jh	7.09S	131.45 E
Larat, Pulau- ◆	26	Jh	7.10S	131.50 E
La Raya	49	Ji	8.20N	74.34W
L'Arba	13	Ph	36.34N	3.09 E
L'Arbaa-Naït-Irathen	13	Qh	36.38N	4.12 E
L'Arbresle	11	Ki	45.50N	4.37 E
Lärbro	7	Eh	57.47N	18.47 E
Larche, Col de- ⋎	11	Mj	44.25N	6.53 E
Larde	37	Fc	16.28S	39.43 E
Larderello	14	Eg	43.14N	10.53 E
La Réale	11	Fj	44.35N	0.02W
Laredo [Sp.]	13	Ia	43.24N	3.25W
Laredo [Tx.-U.S.]	39	Jg	27.31N	99.30W
Laren	12	Hb	52.16N	5.16 E
Lārestān ⧗	21	Hg	27.00N	55.30 E
Larestan ▣	24	Pi	27.00N	55.30 E
Large Island ◆	51p	Cb	12.24N	61.30W
Largentière	11	Kj	44.32N	4.18 E
L'Argentière-la-Bessée	11	Mj	44.47N	6.33 E
Largo, Cayo- ◆	49	Gc	21.38N	81.28W
Largs	9	If	55.48N	4.52W
La Ribagorça/Ribagorza ⧗	13	Mb	42.15N	0.30 E
La Ribera ⧗	13	Kb	42.30N	2.00W
Larimore	45	Hc	47.54N	97.38W
Larino	14	Ii	41.48N	14.54 E
La Rioja [2]	56	Gc	30.00S	67.30W
La Rioja ⧗	13	Jb	42.20N	2.20W
La Rioja	53	Jh	29.25S	66.50W
Lárisa	6	Ih	39.38N	22.25 E
La Rivière-Thibouville, Nassandres-	12	Ce	49.07N	0.44 E
Lārkāna	25	Dc	27.33N	68.13 E
Larmor-Plage	11	Cg	47.42N	3.23W
Larnaka/Lárnax	23	Dc	34.55N	33.38 E
Lárnax/Larnaka	23	Dc	34.55N	33.38 E
Larne/Latharna	9	Hg	54.51N	5.49W
Larned	45	Gg	38.11N	99.06W
La Robla	13	Gb	42.48N	5.37W
La Roche	63b	De	21.28S	168.02 E
La Roche-en-Ardenne	11	Ld	50.11N	5.35 E
La Rochefoucauld	11	Gi	45.44N	0.23 E
La Roche-Guyon	12	De	49.05N	1.38 E
La Rochelle	6	Ff	46.10N	1.09W
La Roche-sur-Yon	11	Eh	46.40N	1.26W
La Roda	13	Je	39.13N	2.09W
La Romana	47	Ke	18.25N	68.58W
La Ronge	42	Ge	55.06N	105.17W
La Ronge, Lac- ≈	38	Id	55.05N	104.59W
Larose	45	Kl	29.35N	90.23W
La Rosita	48	Ic	28.24N	101.43W
Larouco ▲	13	Ec	41.56N	7.40W
Larreynaga	49	Dg	12.40N	86.34W
Larrey Point ►	59	Dc	20.00S	119.10 E
Larrimah	58	Ef	15.35S	133.12 E
Larsa ⁘	24	Kg	31.16N	45.49 E
Lars Christensen Kyst ≣	66	Fe	69.30S	68.00 E
Larsen, Mount- ▲	66	Kf	74.51S	162.12 E
Larsen Ice Shelf ❄	66	Qe	68.30S	62.30W
Lartijas Padomju Socialistiska Respublika → Latvija	19	Cd	57.00N	25.00 E
La Rumorosa	48	Aa	32.34N	116.06W
Laruns	11	Fk	43.00N	0.25W
Larvik	7	Bg	59.04N	10.00 E
La Sabana [Arg.]	55	Ch	27.52S	59.57W
La Sabana [Col.]	54	Ec	2.20N	68.32W
Las Adjuntas, Presa de- ⊟	48	Jf	23.55N	98.45W
La Sagra ⧗	13	Id	40.05N	4.00W
La Sagra ▲	13	Jg	37.57N	2.34W
La Salle	45	Lf	41.20N	89.06W
La Salle, Pic- ▲	47	Je	18.22N	71.59W
La Sal Mountains ⛰	46	Kg	38.30N	109.10W
Las Alpujarras ⧗	13	Ih	36.50N	3.25W
La Sanabria ⧗	13	Fb	42.08N	6.30W
Las Animas	45	Eg	38.04N	103.13W
Lās 'ānōd	35	Hd	8.26N	47.24 E
La Sarre	42	Jg	48.48N	79.12W
Las Aves, Islas- ⁂	54	Ea	11.58N	67.33W
Las Avispas	55	Bi	29.53S	61.18W
Las Bardenas ⏢	13	Kb	42.10N	1.25W
Las Bonitas	50	Di	7.52N	65.40W
Las Breñas	56	Hc	27.05S	61.05W
Las Cabezas de San Juan	13	Gh	36.59N	5.56W
Lascahobas	49	Ld	18.50N	71.56W
Lascano	55	Ek	33.40S	54.12W
Las Casitas, Cerro- ▲	47	Cd	23.31N	109.53W
Lascaux, Grotte de- ◓	11	Hi	45.03N	1.11 E
Las Cejas	56	Hc	26.53S	64.44W
Las Chilcas, Arroyo- ∿	55	Cm	37.16S	58.26W
Las Choapas	47	Fe	17.55N	94.05W
Las Cinco Villas ⧗	13	Kb	42.05N	1.07W
Las Cruces	43	Fe	32.23N	106.29W
Lāsdāred	35	Hc	10.10N	46.01 E
Lās Dawa'o	35	Hc	10.22N	49.03 E
La Segarra ⧗	13	Nc	41.30N	1.10 E
La Selva ⧗	13	Oc	41.40N	2.50 E
La Serena ⧗	13	Gf	38.45N	5.30W
La Serena	53	Ih	29.54S	71.16W
La Seu d'Urgell/Seo de Urgel	13	Nb	42.21N	1.28 E
La-Seyne-sur-Mer	11	Lk	43.06N	5.53 E
Las Flores	56	Ie	36.03S	59.07W
Lāsh-e Joveyn	23	Jc	31.43N	61.37 E
Las Heras	56	Gd	32.51S	68.49W
Lashkar Gāh	22	If	31.35N	64.21 E
Las Hurdes ⧗	13	Fd	40.20N	6.20W
La Sila ⛰	5	Hh	39.15N	16.30 E
Łasin	10	Pc	53.32N	19.05 E
Łask	10	Pe	51.36N	19.07 E
Las Lajas	56	Fe	38.31S	70.22W
Las Lomitas	56	Hb	24.42S	60.36W
Las Margaritas	48	Ni	16.19N	91.59W
Las Mariñas ⧗	13	Da	43.20N	8.15W
Las Marismas ψ	13	Fg	37.00N	6.15W
Las Mercedes	54	Eb	9.07N	66.24W
Las Mestenas	48	Gc	28.13N	104.35W
Las Minas, Cerro- ▲	47	Gf	14.33N	88.39W
Las Minas, Sierra de- ⛰	47	Ge	15.05N	90.00W
Las Mixtecas, Sierra del- ⛰	48	Ki	17.45N	97.15W
La Sola, Isla- ◆	54	Fa	11.20N	63.34W
La Solana	13	If	38.56N	3.14W
Lasolo	26	Hg	3.29S	122.04 E
La Sorcière ▲	51k	Bb	13.59N	60.56W
La Souterraine	11	Hh	46.14N	1.29 E
Las Palmas [3]	32	Ed	28.20N	14.20W
Las Palmas de Gran Canaria	31	Ff	28.06N	15.24W
Las Petas	55	Cc	16.23S	59.11W
La Spezia	6	Gg	44.07N	9.50 E
Las Piedras	56	Id	34.45S	56.13W
Las Plumas	53	Jj	43.40S	67.15W
Lās Qoray	35	Hc	11.15N	48.22 E
Las Rosas	55	Bk	32.28S	61.34W
Lassen Peak ▲	43	Cc	40.29N	121.31W
Lassigny	12	Ee	49.35N	2.51 E
Laßnitz ∿	14	Jd	46.46N	15.32 E
Lasso ▲	64b	Ba	15.02N	145.38 E
Las Tablas	49	Gj	7.46N	80.17W
Last Mountain Lake ≈	42	Gf	51.10N	105.15W
Las Toscas	55	Ci	28.21S	59.17W
Lastoursville	36	Bc	0.49S	12.42 E
Lastovo	14	Kh	42.46N	16.55 E
Lastovo ◆	14	Kh	42.45N	16.50 E
Lastovski kanal ▬	14	Kh	42.50N	16.59 E
Las Tres Virgenes, Volcán- △	47	Bc	27.27N	112.34W
Las Tunas [3]	49	Ic	21.00N	77.00W
Las Tunas, Punta- ►	51a	Bb	18.30N	66.37W
Las Varillas	56	Hd	31.52S	62.43W
Las Vegas [N.M.-U.S.]	43	Fd	35.36N	105.13W
Las Vegas [Nv.-U.S.]	39	Hf	36.11N	115.08W
Las Villuercas ⧗	13	Ge	39.33N	5.27W
Łaszczów	10	Tf	50.32N	23.40 E
Lata ▲	65c	Db	14.14S	169.29W
Latacunga	54	Cd	0.55S	78.37W
La Tagua	54	Dd	0.03S	74.40W
Latakia (EN)=Al Lādhiqīyah	22	Ff	35.31N	35.07 E
Latarc, Causse du- ⏢	11	Jk	43.57N	3.11 E
Late Island ◆	61	Gc	18.48S	174.39W
Laterza	14	Kj	40.37N	16.48 E
La Teste	11	Ej	44.38N	1.09W
Latgale ⧗	8	Lh	56.45N	27.30 E
Latgales Augstiene/ Latgalskaja Vozvyšennost ⏢	8	Lh	56.10N	27.30 E
Latgalskaja Vozvyšennost/ Latgales Augstiene ⏢	8	Lh	56.10N	27.30 E
Latharna/Larne	9	Hg	54.51N	5.49W
Lathen	12	Jb	52.52N	7.19 E
La Tigra	55	Bh	27.06S	60.34W
Latina	14	Gi	41.28N	12.52 E
Latisana	14	Ge	45.47N	13.00 E
Latium (EN) = Lazio [2]	14	Gh	42.02N	12.23 E
La Toja	13	Db	42.27N	8.50W
La Toma	56	Gd	33.03S	65.37W
La Tontouta	63b	Ce	22.00S	166.15 E
Latorica ∿	10	Rh	48.28N	21.50 E
La Tortuga, Isla- ◆	54	Ea	10.56N	65.20W
La-Tour-du-Pin	11	Li	45.34N	5.27 E
La Trimouille	11	Hh	46.28N	1.03 E
La Trinidad	49	Dg	12.58N	86.14W
La Trinidad de Orichuna	50	Bi	7.07N	69.45W
La Trinité	50	Fe	14.44N	60.58W
Latronico	14	Kj	40.05N	16.01 E
Lattari, Monti- ⛰	14	Ij	40.40N	14.30 E
La Tuque	42	Kg	47.27N	72.47W
Lātūr	25	Fe	18.24N	76.35 E
Latvia (EN) = Latvija	19	Cd	57.00N	25.00 E
Latvija = Latvia (EN)	19	Cd	57.00N	25.00 E
Latvijas PSR → Latvija	19	Cd	57.00N	25.00 E
Latvijskaja Sovetskaja Socialističeskaja Respublika → Latvija	19	Cd	57.00N	25.00 E
Latvijskaja SSR/Latvijas Padomju Socialistika Respublika → Latvija	19	Cd	57.00N	25.00 E
Lau ∿	30	Kh	6.56N	30.16 E
Laubach	12	Kd	50.33N	8.59 E
Lauchert ∿	10	Fh	48.05N	9.15 E
Lauchhammer	10	Je	51.30N	13.48 E
Lauenburg	10	Gc	53.22N	10.34 E
Lauf an der Pegnitz	10	Hg	49.31N	11.17 E
Laughlan Islands ⁂	63a	Ac	9.15S	153.40 E
Laughlin Peak ▲	45	Dh	36.38N	104.12W
Lau Group ⁂	57	Jf	18.20S	178.30W
Lauhanvuori ▲	8	Jb	62.10N	22.10 E
Laujar de Andarax	13	Jh	36.59N	2.51W
Laukaa	7	Fe	62.25N	25.57 E
Laukuva	8	Ji	55.35N	22.08 E
Laulau, Bahia- ◖	64b	Ba	15.08N	145.46 E
Launceston [Austl.]	58	Fi	41.26S	147.08 E
Launceston [Eng.-U.K.]	9	Ik	50.38N	4.21W
La Unión [Bol.]	55	Bb	15.18S	61.05W
La Unión [Chile]	56	Ff	40.17S	73.05W
La Unión [Col.]	54	Cc	1.37N	77.08W
La Unión [ElSal.]	47	Gf	13.20N	87.51W
La Unión [Mex.]	48	Ii	17.58N	101.49W
La Unión [Peru]	54	Ce	9.46S	76.48W
La Unión [Sp.]	13	Lg	37.37N	0.52W
La Unión [Ven.]	49	Ni	8.13N	67.46W
Laura	59	Ic	15.34S	144.28 E
La Urbana	50	Ci	7.08N	66.56W
Laurel [Ms.-U.S.]	43	Je	31.42N	89.08W
Laurel [Mt.-U.S.]	43	Fb	45.40N	108.46W
Laureles	55	Ej	31.23S	55.52W
Laurel Hill ⌒	44	He	40.02N	79.17W
Laurel Mountain ⛰	44	Hf	39.20N	79.50W
Laurens	44	Fh	34.30N	82.01W
Laurentian Plateau (EN)= Laurentien, Plateau- ⏢	38	Md	50.00N	70.00W
Laurentian Scarp ⌒	44	Ic	45.50N	76.15W
Laurentide Scarp ⌒	44	Kb	46.38N	73.00W
Laurentien, Plateau-= Laurentian Plateau (EN) ⏢	38	Md	50.00N	70.00W
Lauria	14	Jj	40.02N	15.50 E
Lau Ridge (EN) ⋀	3	Kl	25.00S	179.00 E
Laurie River	42	He	56.00N	100.58W
Laurinburg	44	Hh	34.47N	79.27W
Laurium	44	Cb	47.14N	88.26W
Lauro Muller	55	Hi	28.24S	49.23W
Lausanne	6	Gf	46.30N	6.40 E
Lausitzer Gebirge ▲	10	Kf	50.48N	14.40 E
Lausitzer Neiße ∿	10	Kd	52.04N	14.46 E
Laut, Pulau-	26	Ef	4.43N	107.59 E
Laut, Pulau- ◆	21	Nj	3.40S	116.10 E
Lautaret, Col du- ⋎	11	Mi	45.02N	6.24 E
Lautaro	56	Fe	38.31S	72.27W
Lautém	26	Ih	8.22S	126.54 E
Lauter ∿	10	Eg	48.58N	8.11 E
Lauterbach	10	Ff	50.38N	9.24 E
Lauterbourg	12	Kf	48.59N	8.11 E
Lauterecken	12	Je	49.39N	7.36 E
Lauthala ◆	63d	Cb	16.45S	179.41W
Laut Kecil, Kepulauan- ⁂	26	Gg	4.50S	115.45 E
Lautoka	61	Ec	17.37S	177.27 E
Lauvergne Island ◆	64d	Cb	7.00N	152.00 E
Lauwersmeer ≈	12	Ia	53.25N	6.15 E
Lauzerte	11	Hj	44.15N	1.08 E
Lauzon	44	Lb	46.50N	71.10W
Lauzoue ∿	11	Gj	44.03N	0.15 E
Lava ∿	10	Rb	54.37N	21.14 E
Lava, Nosy- [Mad.] ◆	37	Hb	12.49S	48.41 E
Lava, Nosy- [Mad.] ◆	37	Hb	14.33S	47.36 E
Lavaca River ∿	45	Hl	28.50N	96.36W
Lava Flow ⧗	45	Bi	34.45N	108.20W
Laval	11	Ff	48.01N	0.46W
Lavalle	55	Ci	29.01S	59.11W
Lavalleja [2]	55	El	34.00S	55.00W
Lāvān, Jazīreh-ye- ◆	23	Hd	26.48N	53.00 E
Lavanggu	63a	Ed	11.37S	160.15 E
Lavant ∿	14	Id	46.38N	14.56 E
Lavapié, Punta- ►	52	Ii	37.09S	73.35W
Lāvar Meydān ▤	24	Pg	30.20N	54.30 E
Lavassaare	8	Kf	58.29N	24.16 E
Lavaur	11	Hk	43.42N	1.49 E
La Vecilla	13	Gb	42.51N	5.24W
La Vega	47	Je	19.13N	70.31W
La Vela de Coro	49	Mh	11.27N	69.34W
Lavelanet	11	Hl	42.56N	1.51 E
Lavello	14	Ji	41.03N	15.48 E
La Venta ⁘	47	Fe	18.08N	94.03W
Laventie	12	Ed	50.38N	2.46 E
La Ventura	48	Ie	24.37N	100.54W
La Vera ⧗	13	Gd	40.05N	5.30W
L'Averdy, Cape- ►	63a	Ba	5.33S	155.04 E
Laverton	59	Ee	28.38S	122.25 E
Lavia	7	Ff	61.36N	22.36 E
La Victoria	54	Ea	10.14N	67.20W
La Vila Jojosa/Villajoyosa	13	Lf	38.30N	0.14W
La Villita, Presa- ⊟	48	Hh	18.05N	102.05W
La Viña	54	Ce	6.54S	79.28W

Index Symbols

[1] Independent Nation	▣ Historical or Cultural Region	⋎ Pass, Gap	⌣ Depression	≣ Coast, Beach	✳ Rock, Reef	⇊ Waterfall Rapids	═ Canal	⊡ Lagoon	⌐ Escarpment, Sea Scarp	⌂ Historic Site	⚓ Port
[2] State, Region	▲ Mount, Mountain	▭ Plain, Lowland	▥ Polder	◧ Cliff	⁂ Islands, Archipelago	⊰ River Mouth, Estuary	▽ Glacier	⊞ Bank	⚡ Fracture	⁘ Ruins	⛯ Lighthouse
[3] District, County	△ Volcano	◺ Delta	∴ Desert, Dunes	⊐ Peninsula	✴ Rocks, Reefs	≈ Lake	❄ Ice Shelf, Pack Ice	⩟ Seamount	⩡ Trench, Abyss	▙ Wall, Walls	⚒ Mine
[4] Municipality	◠ Hill	▤ Salt Flat	♣ Forest, Woods	⋈ Isthmus	✿ Coral Reef	≋ Salt Lake	☰ Ocean	⊓ Tablemount	✪ National Park, Reserve	✝ Church, Abbey	∩ Tunnel
[5] Colony, Dependency	⛰ Mountains, Mountain Range	∨ Valley, Canyon	≀ Heath, Steppe	⩫ Sandbank	⊙ Well, Spring	┅ Intermittent Lake	≡ Sea	⋀ Ridge	✓ Point of Interest	⛩ Temple	⌿ Dam, Bridge
■ Continent	⌒ Hills, Escarpment	◡ Crater, Cave	☘ Oasis	◆ Island	⊥ Geyser	⊟ Reservoir	◖ Gulf, Bay	⊏ Shelf	✚ Recreation Site	⚗ Scientific Station	
⧗ Physical Region	⏢ Plateau, Upland	✲ Karst Features	► Cape, Point	◎ Atoll	∿ River, Stream	ψ Swamp, Pond	▬ Strait, Fjord	⊔ Basin	◓ Cave, Cavern	✈ Airport	

International Map Index

Index Symbols

[1] Independent Nation
[2] State, Region
[3] District, County
[4] Municipality
[5] Colony, Dependency
Continent
Physical Region

Historical or Cultural Region
Mount, Mountain
Volcano
Hill
Mountains, Mountain Range
Hills, Escarpment
Plateau, Upland

Pass, Gap
Plain, Lowland
Delta
Salt Flat
Valley, Canyon
Crater, Cave
Karst Features

Depression
Polder
Desert, Dunes
Forest, Woods
Heath, Steppe
Oasis
Cape, Point

Coast, Beach
Cliff
Peninsula
Isthmus
Sandbank
Island
Atoll

Rock, Reef
Islands, Archipelago
Rocks, Reefs
Coral Reef
Well, Spring
Geyser
River, Stream

Waterfall Rapids
River Mouth, Estuary
Lake
Salt Lake
Intermittent Lake
Reservoir
Swamp, Pond

Canal
Glacier
Ice Shelf, Pack Ice
Ocean
Sea
Gulf, Bay
Strait, Fjord

Lagoon
Bank
Seamount
Tableland
Ridge
Shelf
Basin

Escarpment, Sea Scarp
Fracture
Trench, Abyss
National Park, Reserve
Point of Interest
Recreation Site
Cave, Cavern

Historic Site
Ruins
Wall, Walls
Church, Abbey
Temple
Scientific Station
Airport

Port
Lighthouse
Mine
Tunnel
Dam, Bridge

Little Scarcies 34 Cd 8.51N 13.09W
Little Sioux River 45 Hf 41.49N 96.04W
Little Sitkin 40a Cb 51.55N 178.30 E
Little Smoky 42 Fe 55.39N 117.37W
Little Snake River 45 Bf 40.27N 108.26W
Littleton [Co.-U.S.] 45 Dg 39.37N 105.01W
Littleton [N.H.-U.S.] 44 Lc 44.18N 71.46W
Little White River [Ont.-Can.] 44 Fb 46.15N 83.00W
Little White River [S.D.-U.S.] 45 Fe 43.44N 100.40W
Littoral [3] 34 He 4.30N 10.00 E
Litvinov 10 Jf 50.36N 13.36 E
Liuba 27 Ie 33.39N 106.53 E
Liuhe 27 Mc 42.16N 125.45 E
Liu He [China] 28 Gd 41.48N 122.43 E
Liu He [China] 28 Ic 42.46N 126.13 E
Liuheng Dao 28 Gj 29.43N 122.08 E
Liujia Xia 27 Hd 35.50N 103.00 E
Liukang Tenggaja, Kepulauan- 26 Gh 6.45 S 118.50 E
Liupai → Tian'e 27 If 25.05N 107.12 E
Liupan Shan 27 Id 35.40N 106.15 E
Liuqu He 28 Fd 40.10N 120.15 E
Liuwa Plain 36 De 14.27 S 22.25 E
Liuyang 28 Bj 28.09N 113.38 E
Liuzhangzhen → Yuanqu 27 Jd 35.19N 111.44 E
Liuzhou 22 Mg 24.22N 109.20 E
Līvāni/Livāny 7 Gh 56.22N 26.12 E
Livanjsko Polje 14 Kg 43.51N 16.50 E
Livany/Līvāni 7 Gh 56.22N 26.12 E
Livarot 12 Ce 49.01N 0.09 E
Livengood 40 Jc 65.32N 148.33W
Livenza 14 Ge 45.35N 12.51 E
Livenzi 15 Ge 44.14N 23.47 E
Live Oak 43 Ke 30.18N 82.59W
Livermore 46 Eh 37.41N 121.46W
Livermore, Mount- 45 Dk 30.37N 104.08W
Liverpool [Eng.-U.K.] 6 Fe 53.25N 2.55W
Liverpool [N.S.-Can.] 42 Lh 44.02N 64.43W
Liverpool, Cape- 42 Jb 73.38N 78.05W
Liverpool Bay [Can.] 42 Ec 70.00N 129.00W
Liverpool Bay [Eng.-U.K.] 9 Jh 53.30N 3.16W
Liverpool Range 59 Kf 31.40 S 150.30 E
Liverpool River 59 Gb 12.00 S 134.00 E
Livigno 14 Ed 46.32N 10.04 E
Livingston [Guat.] 49 Cf 15.50N 88.45W
Livingston [Mt.-U.S.] 43 Eb 45.40N 110.34W
Livingston [Newf.-Can.] 42 Kf 53.40N 66.10W
Livingston [Tn.-U.S.] 44 Eg 36.23N 85.19W
Livingston [Tx.-U.S.] 45 Ik 30.43N 94.56W
Livingston, Lake- 45 Ik 30.45N 95.15W
Livingstone, Chutes de- = Livingstone Falls (EN) 30 Ii 4.50 S 14.30 E
Livingstone Falls (EN) = Livingstone, Chutes de- 30 Ii 4.50 S 14.30 E
Livingstone Memorial 36 Fe 12.19 S 30.18 E
Livingstone Mountains 36 Fd 9.45 S 34.20 E
Livingstonia 36 Fe 10.36 S 34.07 E
Livingston Island 66 Qe 62.36 S 60.30W
Livno 14 Lg 43.50N 17.01 E
Livny 19 De 52.28N 37.37 E
Livonia 44 Fd 42.25N 83.23W
Livonia (EN)=Livonija 5 Id 58.50N 27.30 E
Livonija=Livonia (EN) 5 Id 58.50N 27.30 E
Livorno=Leghorn (EN) 6 Hg 43.33N 10.19 E
Livradois, Monts du- 11 Ji 45.30N 3.33 E
Livramento do Brumado 54 Jf 13.39 S 41.50W
Livron-sur-Drôme 11 Kj 44.46N 4.51 E
Liwale 36 Gd 9.46 S 37.56 E
Liwiec 10 Rd 52.35N 21.33 E
Liwonde 36 Gf 15.01 S 35.13 E
Lixi 27 Hf 26.21N 102.03 E
Lixian [China] 27 Ie 34.11N 105.02 E
Lixian [China] 27 Jf 29.40N 111.45 E
Lixian [China] 28 Ce 38.29N 115.34 E
Lixin 28 Dh 33.09N 116.12 E
Lixoúrion 15 Dk 38.12N 20.26 E
Liyang 28 Ei 31.26N 119.29 E
Lizard 9 Hl 49.57N 5.13W
Lizard Point 5 Ff 49.56N 5.13W
Lizhu 28 Fj 29.58N 120.26 E
Lizy sur Ourcq 12 Fe 49.01N 3.02 E
Ljady 8 Mf 58.35N 28.55 E
Ljahoviči 16 Ec 53.04N 26.15 E
Ljahovskije Ostrova = Lyakhov Islands (EN) 21 Qb 73.30N 141.00 E
Ljalja 17 Jg 59.10N 61.30 E
Ljamin 17 Of 61.18N 71.45 E
Ljangar 18 Ed 40.23N 65.59 E
Ljangasovo 7 Lg 58.33N 49.29 E
Ljapin 17 Je 63.38N 61.58 E
Ljaskelja 8 Nc 61.39N 31.03 E
Ljaskovec 15 If 43.06N 25.43 E
Ljig 15 De 44.14N 20.15 E
Ljuban 16 Ec 52.48N 27.59 E
Ljuban 7 Hg 59.22N 31.13 E
Ljubar 16 Ee 49.55N 27.44 E
Ljubaščevka 15 Nb 47.50N 30.07 E
Ljubelj 14 Id 46.26N 14.16 E
Ljubercy 19 Dd 55.40N 37.55 E
Ljubešov 10 Ve 51.45N 25.37 E
Ljubim 7 Jg 58.22N 40.41 E
Ljubimec 15 Jh 41.50N 26.05 E
Ljubinje 14 Mh 42.57N 18.06 E
Ljubišnja 15 Cf 43.20N 19.07 E
Ljubljana 6 Hf 46.02N 14.30 E
Ljuboml 16 Cd 51.15N 23.59 E
Ljubotin 16 Ie 49.59N 35.55 E
Ljubovija 15 Ce 44.12N 19.22 E
Ljubuški 14 Lg 43.12N 17.33 E
Ljubytino 7 Hg 58.50N 33.25 E
Ljudinovo 19 De 53.51N 34.28 E
Ljugarn 7 Eh 57.19N 18.42 E
Ljungan 5 Hc 62.19N 17.23 E
Ljungaverk 8 Gb 62.29N 16.03 E
Ljungby 7 Ch 56.50N 13.56 E
Ljungbyholm 8 Gh 56.38N 16.10 E
Ljungdalen 7 Ce 62.51N 12.47 E
Ljungsbro 8 Ff 58.31N 15.30 E
Ljungskile 8 Df 58.14N 11.55 E
Ljusdal 7 Df 61.50N 16.05 E
Ljusnan 5 Hc 61.12N 17.08 E
Ljusne 7 Df 61.13N 17.08 E
Ljusterö 8 He 59.30N 18.35 E
Ljuta 8 Mf 58.33N 28.45 E
Llandilo 9 Jj 51.53N 3.59W
Llandovery 9 Jj 51.59N 3.48W
Llandrindod Wells 9 Ji 52.15N 3.23W
Llandudno 9 Jh 53.19N 3.49W
Llanelli 9 Ij 51.42N 4.10W
Llanes 13 Ha 43.25N 4.45W
Llangefni 9 Ih 53.16N 4.18W
Llangollen 9 Ji 52.58N 3.10W
Llano 45 Gk 30.45N 98.41W
Llano Estacado 38 If 33.30N 102.40W
Llano River 45 Gk 30.35N 98.25W
Llanos 52 Je 5.00N 70.00W
Llanos de Sonora 47 Bc 28.20N 111.00W
Llanquihue, Lago- 56 Ff 41.08 S 72.48W
Llata 54 Ce 9.25 S 76.47W
Lleida/Lérida 13 Mc 41.37N 0.37 E
Llerena 13 Ff 38.14N 6.01W
Lleyn 9 Ii 52.54N 4.30W
Llica 54 Eg 19.52 S 68.16W
Llivia 13 Nb 42.28N 1.59 E
Llobregat 13 Oc 41.19N 2.09 E
Lloret de Mar 13 Oc 41.42N 2.51 E
Llorona, Punta- 49 Fi 8.37N 83.44W
Llorri/Orri, Pic d'- 13 Nb 42.23N 1.12 E
Lloydminster 42 Gf 53.17N 110.00W
Lluchmayor 13 Oe 39.29N 2.54 E
Llullaillaco, Volcán- 52 Jh 24.43 S 68.33W
Lo 63b Ca 13.21 S 166.38 E
Loa 46 Jg 38.24N 111.38W
Loa, Rio- 56 Fb 21.26 S 70.04W
Loanatit, Pointe- 63b Dd 19.21 S 169.14 E
Loange 30 Ji 4.17 S 20.02 E
Loango 36 Bc 4.39 S 11.48 E
Loano 14 Cf 44.08N 8.15 E
Loban 7 Mh 56.59N 51.12 E
Lobatse 31 Jk 25.13 S 25.41 E
Löbau/Lubij 10 Ke 51.06N 14.40 E
Lobaye 30 Ih 3.41N 18.35 E
Lobaye [3] 35 Be 4.00N 17.40 E
Lobenstein 10 Hf 50.27N 11.39 E
Loberia 56 Ie 38.09 S 58.47W
Łobez 10 Lc 53.39N 15.36 E
Lobito 31 Ij 12.22 S 13.34 E
Lobo 34 Dd 6.02N 6.47W
Lobos 56 Ie 35.11 S 59.06W
Lobos 32 Ed 28.45N 13.49W
Lobos, Cabo- 48 Cc 29.55N 112.45W
Lobos, Cay- 49 Ib 22.24N 77.32W
Lobos, Cayo- 48 Ph 18.22N 87.24W
Lobos, Isla- 48 Dd 27.20N 110.36W
Lobos, Islas de- 48 Kg 21.27N 97.15W
Lobos de Afuera, Islas- 54 Be 6.57 S 80.42W
Lobos de Tierra, Isla- 54 Be 6.27 S 80.52W
Lobva 19 Gd 59.12N 60.30 E
Łobżonka 10 Nc 53.07N 17.18 E
Locana 14 Be 45.25N 7.27 E
Locarno 14 Cd 46.10N 8.48 E
Loch Aillionn/Allen, Lough- 9 Eg 54.08N 8.08W
Loch Arabhach/Arrow, Lough- 9 Eg 54.05N 8.20W
Lochboisdale 9 Fd 57.09N 7.19W
Loch Cairlinn/Carlingford Lough 9 Gg 54.05N 6.14W
Loch Ce/Key, Lough- 9 Eg 54.00N 8.15W
Loch Coirib/Corrib, Lough- 9 Dh 53.05N 9.10W
Loch Con/Conn, Lough- 9 Dg 54.04N 9.20W
Loch Cuan/Strangford Lough 9 Hg 54.26N 5.36W
Loch Deirgeirt/Derg, Lough- 9 Ei 53.00N 8.20W
Lochearnhead 9 Ie 56.23N 4.18W
Loch Éirne Íochtair/Lower Lough Erne 9 Fg 54.30N 7.50W
Loch Éirne Uachtair/Upper Lough Erne 9 Fg 54.20N 7.30W
Lochem 12 Ib 52.10N 6.25 E
Loches 11 Gg 47.08N 1.00 E
Loch Feabhail/Foyle, Lough- 9 Ff 55.05N 7.10W
Loch Garman/Wexford 9 Fe 52.20N 6.27W
Loch Garman/Wexford [2] 9 Gi 52.20N 6.40W
Lochgilphead 9 He 56.03N 5.26W
Loch Hinninn/Ennell, Lough- 9 Fh 53.28N 7.24W
Lochinver 9 Hc 58.09N 5.15W
Loch Lao/Belfast Lough 9 Hg 54.40N 5.50W
Loch Léin/Leane, Lough- 9 Di 52.05N 9.35W
Loch Leven 9 Je 56.13N 3.10W
Loch Long 9 Ie 56.04N 4.50W
Lochmaddy 9 Fd 57.36N 7.10W
Loch Measca/Mask, Lough- 9 Dh 53.35N 9.20W
Lochnagar 9 Je 56.55N 3.10W
Loch nEathach/Neagh, Lough- 5 Fe 54.38N 6.24W
Loch Ness 9 Id 57.15N 4.30W
Łochów 10 Rd 52.32N 21.48 E
Loch Pholl an Phúca/Poulaphuca Reservoir 9 Gh 53.10N 6.30W
Loch Rí/Ree, Lough- 9 Fh 53.35N 8.00W
Lochsa River 46 Hc 46.08N 115.36W
Loch Sileann/Sheelin, Lough- 9 Fh 53.48N 7.20W
Loch Suili/Swilly, Lough- 9 Ff 55.10N 7.38W
Loch Uí Ghadhra/Gara, Lough- 9 Eh 53.55N 8.30W
Lochy 9 He 56.49N 5.06W
Lochy, Loch- 9 Ie 56.55N 4.55W
Lockerbie 9 Jf 55.07N 3.22W
Lockhart 45 Hl 29.53N 97.41W
Lock Haven 44 Ie 41.09N 77.28W
Löcknitz 10 Hc 53.07N 11.16 E
Lockport 44 Hd 43.11N 78.39W
Locminé 11 Dg 47.53N 2.50W
Locri 14 Kl 38.14N 16.16 E
Lod 24 Fg 31.58N 34.54 E
Lodalskåpa 7 Bf 61.47N 7.12 E
Loddon 12 Db 52.32N 1.29 E
Loddon River 59 Ig 36.41 S 143.55 E
Lodejnoje Pole 19 Dc 60.44N 33.33 E
Lodève 11 Jk 43.43N 3.19 E
Lodi [Ca.-U.S.] 46 Eg 38.08N 121.16W
Lodi [It.] 14 De 45.19N 9.30 E
Lødingen 7 Db 68.25N 16.00 E
Lodja 31 Ji 3.29 S 23.26 E
Lodosa 13 Jb 42.25N 2.05W
Lödöse 8 Ef 58.02N 12.08 E
Lodwar 31 Kh 3.07N 35.36 E
Łódź 6 He 51.46N 19.30 E
Łódź [2] 10 Pe 51.45N 19.30 E
Loei 25 Ke 17.32N 101.34 E
Loeriesfontein 37 Bf 30.56 S 19.26 E
Lofanga 65b Ba 19.50 S 174.33W
Loffa 30 Fh 6.36N 11.05W
Loffa [3] 34 Dd 7.45N 10.00W
Lofoten 5 Hb 68.30N 15.00 E
Lofoten Basin (EN) 5 Ga 70.00N 4.00 E
Lofsdalen 8 Eb 62.07N 13.16 E
Loftahammar 8 Gg 57.52N 16.40 E
Loga 34 Fc 13.37N 3.14 E
Logan [N.M.-U.S.] 45 Ei 35.22N 103.25W
Logan [Oh.-U.S.] 44 Ff 39.32N 82.24W
Logan [Ut.-U.S.] 43 Ec 41.44N 111.50W
Logan [W.V.-U.S.] 44 Gg 37.52N 81.58W
Logan, Mount- [Can.] 38 Ec 60.34N 140.24W
Logan, Mount- [Wa.-U.S.] 46 Eb 48.32N 120.57W
Logan Martin Lake 44 Di 33.40N 86.15W
Logan Mountains 42 Ed 61.00N 128.00W
Logansport 44 De 40.45N 86.21W
Loge 30 Ii 7.49 S 13.06 E
Logojsk 8 Lj 54.12N 27.57 E
Logone 30 Ig 12.06N 15.02 E
Logone Birni 34 Ic 11.47N 15.06 E
Logone Occidental [3] 35 Bd 8.40N 16.00 E
Logone Occidental 35 Bd 9.07N 16.26 E
Logone Oriental [3] 35 Bd 8.20N 16.30 E
Logone Oriental 35 Bd 9.07N 16.26 E
Logroño 13 Jb 42.15N 2.30W
Logroño [Arg.] 55 Bi 29.30 S 61.42W
Logroño [Sp.] 13 Jb 42.28N 2.27W
Logrosán 13 Ge 39.20N 5.29W
Løgstør 7 Bh 56.58N 9.15 E
Logudoro 14 Cj 40.35N 8.40 E
Løgumkloster 8 Ci 55.03N 8.57 E
Lögurinn 7a Cb 65.15N 14.30W
Lohja/Lojo 7 Ff 60.15N 24.05 E
Lohjanjärvi 8 Jd 60.15N 23.55 E
Lohjanselkä/Lojo åsen 8 Kd 60.15N 24.10 E
Löhme 12 Kc 51.41N 8.42 E
Löhne 12 Kb 52.11N 8.41 E
Lohne 12 Kb 52.40N 8.14 E
Lohra 12 Kd 50.44N 8.38 E
Lohr am Main 10 Ff 49.59N 9.35 E
Lohusuu/Lokusu 8 Lf 58.53N 27.01 E
Lohvica 16 Hd 50.22N 33.15 E
Loi, Phou- 25 Kd 20.16N 103.12 E
Loi-Kaw 25 Je 19.41N 97.13 E
Loile 36 Dc 0.52 S 20.12 E
Loimaa 7 Ff 60.51N 23.03 E
Loimijoki 8 Jc 61.13N 22.38 E
Loing 11 If 48.23N 2.48 E
Loir 11 Fg 47.33N 0.32W
Loir, Vaux du- 11 Gg 47.45N 0.25 E
Loire [3] 11 Ji 45.30N 4.00 E
Loire 5 Ff 47.16N 2.11W
Loire, Canal latéral à la- 11 Jh 46.29N 3.59 E
Loire, Val de- 11 Hg 47.40N 1.35 E
Loire-Atlantique [3] 11 Eg 47.15N 1.50W
Loiret [3] 11 Ig 47.55N 2.20 E
Loir-et-Cher [3] 11 Hg 47.30N 1.30 E
Loisach 10 Hi 47.56N 11.27 E
Loison 12 He 49.30N 5.17 E
Loja [Ec.] 53 If 4.00 S 79.13W
Loja [Sp.] 13 Hg 37.10N 4.09W
Lojo/Lohja 7 Ff 60.15N 24.05 E
Lojo åsen/Lohjanselkä 8 Kd 60.15N 24.10 E
Loka 35 Ee 4.16N 31.01 E
Lokači 10 Uf 50.43N 24.44 E
Lokalahti 8 Id 60.41N 21.28 E
Lokandu 36 Ec 2.31 S 25.47 E
Lokantekojärvi 7 Gc 68.56N 27.40 E
Lokbatan 16 Pi 40.21N 49.42 E
Lokčim 17 Ef 61.48N 51.45 E
Løken 8 De 59.48N 11.29 E
Lokeren 11 Jc 51.06N 4.00 E
Lokichar 36 Gb 2.23N 35.39 E
Lokichokio 36 Fb 4.12N 34.21 E
Lokitaung 36 Gb 4.16N 35.45 E
Løkken [Den.] 8 Cg 57.22N 9.43 E
Løkken [Nor.] 7 Be 63.05N 9.36 E
Loknja 7 Hh 56.49N 30.09 E
Loko 34 Gd 8.00N 7.50 E
Lokoja 34 Gd 7.48N 6.44 E
Lokomo 34 Ie 2.41N 15.19 E
Lokoro 36 Cc 1.43 S 18.23 E
Lokossa 34 Fd 6.38N 1.43 E
Lokot 16 Ic 52.33N 34.31 E
Lokoti 34 Hd 6.22N 14.20 E
Loksa 7 Fg 59.34N 25.44 E
Loks Land 42 Ld 62.27N 64.30W
Lokuru 63a Cc 8.35 S 157.20 E
Lokusu/Lohusuu 8 Lf 58.53N 27.01 E
Lokwa Kangole 36 Gb 3.32N 35.54 E
Lol 30 Jh 9.13N 28.59 E
Lola 34 Dd 7.48N 8.32W
Lolimi 35 Ee 4.35N 33.59 E
Loliondo 36 Gc 2.03 S 35.37 E
Lolland 5 He 54.45N 11.30 E
Lollar 12 Kd 50.38N 8.42 E
Lolo 36 Db 2.13N 23.00 E
Lolo 36 Bc 0.40 S 12.28 E
Lolodorf 34 He 3.14N 10.44 E
Lolo Pass 46 Hc 46.40N 114.33W
Loloway 63b Cb 15.17 S 167.58 E
Lom 15 Gf 43.49N 23.14 E
Lom [Afr.] 34 Hd 5.20N 13.24 E
Lom [Bul.] 15 Gf 43.50N 23.15 E
Loma Bonita 48 Lh 18.07N 95.53W
Lomaloma 63d Cb 17.17 S 178.59W
Lomami 30 Jh 0.46N 24.16 E
Loma Mountains 30 Fh 9.10N 11.07W
Lomas de Vallejos 55 Dh 27.44 S 57.56W
Loma Verde 55 Cl 35.16 S 58.24W
Lomba 36 Df 15.36 S 21.32 E
Lombarda, Serra- 54 Hc 2.50N 51.50W
Lombarde, Prealpi- 14 De 46.00N 9.30 E
Lombardia = Lombardy (EN) [2] 14 De 45.40N 9.30 E
Lombardy (EN) = Lombardia [2] 14 De 45.40N 9.30 E
Lomblen, Pulau- 21 Oj 8.25 S 123.30 E
Lombok, Pulau- 21 Nj 8.45 S 116.30 E
Lombok, Selat- 26 Gh 8.30 S 115.50 E
Lomé 31 Hh 6.08N 1.13 E
Lomela 31 Ji 2.18 S 23.17 E
Lomela 30 Ji 0.14 S 20.42 E
Lomellina 14 Ce 45.15N 8.45 E
Loméméti 63b Dd 19.30 S 169.27 E
Lomié 34 He 3.10N 13.37 E
Lomlom 63c Bb 10.19 S 166.16 E
Lomma 8 Ei 55.41N 13.05 E
Lomme 12 Hd 50.08N 5.10 E
Lommel 12 Hc 51.14N 5.18 E
Lomnica 10 Ug 49.02N 24.47 E
Lomond, Loch- 9 Ie 56.08N 4.38W
Lomonosov 19 Cd 59.55N 29.40 E
Lomonosovki 19 Ge 52.50N 66.28 E
Lomonosov Ridge (EN) 67 De 88.00N 140.00 E
Lomont 11 Mg 47.21N 6.36 E
Lompobatang, Gunung- 26 Gh 5.20 S 119.55 E
Lompoc 43 Ce 34.38N 120.27W
Lomsegga 8 Cc 61.49N 8.22 E
Łomża 10 Sc 53.11N 22.05 E
Łomża [2] 10 Sc 53.10N 22.05 E
Lønahorg 8 Bd 60.42N 6.25 E
Loncoche 56 Fe 39.22 S 72.38W
Londa 25 Ee 15.28N 74.31 E
Londerzeel 12 Gc 51.01N 4.18 E
Londiani 36 Gc 0.10 S 35.36 E
Londinières 12 De 49.50N 1.24 E
London [Eng.-U.K.] 6 Fe 51.30N 0.10W
London [Kir.] 64g Bb 1.58N 157.29W
London [Ky.-U.S.] 44 Eg 37.08N 84.05W
London [Ont.-Can.] 39 Ke 42.59N 81.14W
London-Barnet 12 Bc 51.39N 0.12W
London-Bexley 12 Cc 51.26N 0.09 E
London Bridge 51p Bb 12.17N 61.35W
London-Bromley 12 Cc 51.25N 0.01 E
London-Croydon 9 Mj 51.23N 0.07W
Londonderry/Doire 6 Fd 55.00N 7.19W
Londonderry, Cape- 59 Fb 13.45 S 126.55 E
London-Ealing 12 Bc 51.30N 0.19W
London-Enfield 12 Bc 51.40N 0.04W
London-Greenwich 9 Mj 51.28N 0.00
London-Haringey 12 Bc 51.36N 0.06W
London-Harrow 12 Bc 51.36N 0.20W
London-Havering 12 Cc 51.36N 0.11 E
London-Hillingdon 12 Bc 51.31N 0.27W
London-Kingston-upon-Thames 9 Mj 51.28N 0.19W
London-Redbridge 12 Cc 51.35N 0.08 E
London-Sutton 12 Bc 51.21N 0.12W
London-Wandsworth 12 Bc 51.27N 0.12W
London-Westminster 12 Bc 51.30N 0.07W
Londrina 53 Kh 23.18 S 51.09W
Lone Pine 46 Fh 36.36N 118.04W
Longa 36 Ce 14.41 S 18.29 E
Longa [Ang.] 36 Cf 16.25 S 19.04 E
Longa [Ang.] 36 Be 10.15 S 13.30 E
Longa, Proliv- = De Long Strait (EN) 21 Tb 70.20N 178.00 E
Longá, Rio- 54 Jd 3.09 S 41.56W
Long Akah 26 Ff 3.19N 114.47 E
Longarone 14 Gd 46.16N 12.18 E
Longbangun 26 Gf 0.36N 115.11 E
Long Bay [Bar.] 51q Bb 13.04N 59.29W
Long Bay [S.C.-U.S.] 43 Le 33.35N 78.45W
Long Beach [Ca.-U.S.] 39 Hf 33.46N 118.11W
Long Beach [N.Y.-U.S.] 44 Ke 40.35N 73.40W
Long Beach [Wa.-U.S.] 46 Cc 46.21N 124.03W
Long Branch 43 Mc 40.17N 73.59W
Long Buckby 12 Ab 52.18N 1.04W
Long Cay 49 Jb 22.37N 74.20W
Longchuan 27 Kg 24.10N 115.17 E
Long Creek 46 Nb 49.07N 103.00W
Long Eaton 12 Ab 52.54N 1.16W
Longfeng 28 Ha 46.31N 125.02 E
Longford/An Longfort [2] 9 Fh 53.40N 7.40W
Longford/An Longfort 9 Fh 53.44N 7.47W
Long Forties 9 Nd 57.10N 0.05 E
Long Hu 28 Dj 29.37N 116.12 E
Longhua 28 Dd 41.18N 117.44 E
Longido 36 Gc 2.44 S 36.41 E
Long Island [Atg.] 51d Bb 17.08N 61.45W
Long Island [Bah.] 38 Lg 23.10N 75.10W
Long Island [Can.] 42 Jf 54.50N 79.20W
Long Island [Can.] 44 Nc 44.20N 66.15W
Long Island [Pap.N.Gui.] 57 Fe 5.36 S 148.00 E
Long Island [U.S.] 38 Le 40.50N 73.00W
Long Island Sound 44 Ke 41.05N 72.58W
Longjiang 27 Lb 47.20N 123.09 E
Longjuzhai → Danfeng 27 Je 33.44N 110.22 E
Longkou 27 Ld 37.39N 120.20 E
Longlac 42 Ig 49.50N 86.32W
Long Lake [N.D.-U.S.] 45 Fc 46.43N 100.07W
Long Lake [Ont.-Can.] 45 Mb 49.32N 86.45W
Longmalinau 26 Gf 3.30N 116.31 E
Long Men 27 Je 34.40N 110.30 E
Longmont 45 Df 40.10N 105.06W
Longnan 27 Jg 24.54N 114.48 E
Longobucco 14 Kk 39.27N 16.37 E
Longoz 15 Kf 43.02N 27.41 E
Longping → Luodian 27 If 25.26N 106.47 E
Long Point 44 Gd 42.34N 80.15W
Long Point Bay 44 Gd 42.40N 80.14W
Longpujungan 26 Gf 2.34N 115.40 E
Longquan 27 Kf 28.06N 119.05 E
Long Range Mountains 42 Lg 48.00N 58.30W
Longreach 58 Fg 23.26 S 144.15 E
Long Sand 12 Dc 51.37N 1.10 E
Longs Peak 38 Ie 40.15N 105.37W
Long Sutton 12 Cb 52.47N 0.08 E
Longtan 28 Eh 32.10N 119.03 E
Longtown 9 Kf 55.01N 2.58W
Longué 11 Fg 47.23N 0.07W
Longueau 12 Ee 49.52N 2.21 E
Longueville-sur-Scie 12 De 49.48N 1.06 E
Longuyon 11 Le 49.26N 5.36 E
Long Valley 46 Ji 34.37N 111.16W
Longview [Tx.-U.S.] 43 Ie 32.30N 94.44W
Longview [Wa.-U.S.] 43 Cb 46.08N 122.57W
Longwu 27 Hg 24.07N 102.18 E
Longwy 11 Le 49.31N 5.46 E
Longxi 27 Hd 35.01N 104.38 E
Longxian 27 Id 35.00N 106.53 E
Longxian → Wengyuan 27 Jg 24.21N 114.13 E
Longxi Shan 27 Kf 26.35N 117.17 E
Long Xuyen 25 Lf 10.23N 105.25 E
Longyan 27 Kf 25.06N 117.01 E
Longyao 28 Cf 37.21N 114.46 E
Longyearbyen 67 Kd 78.13N 15.38 E
Longyou 28 Ej 29.01N 119.10 E
Longzhou 27 Ig 22.23N 106.49 E
Lonigo 14 Fe 45.23N 11.23 E
Löningen 10 Dd 52.44N 7.46 E
Lonja 14 Ke 45.27N 16.41 E
Lonjsko Polje 14 Ke 45.24N 16.42 E
Lönsboda 8 Fh 56.24N 14.19 E
Lons-le-Saunier 11 Lh 46.40N 5.33 E
Lontra, Ribeirão- 55 Fe 21.28 S 53.37W
Lookout, Cape- [N.C.-U.S.] 43 Le 34.35N 76.32W
Lookout, Cape- [Or.-U.S.] 46 Dd 45.20N 124.00W
Lookout Mountain 44 Eh 34.40N 85.20W
Lookout Pass 43 Db 47.27N 115.42W
Loolmalasin 36 Gc 3.03 S 35.49 E
Loop Head/Ceann Léime 9 Di 52.34N 9.56W
Loosdrechtse Plassen 12 Hb 52.10N 5.08 E
Lop 27 Dd 37.01N 80.16 E
Lopatina, Gora- 21 Qd 50.52N 143.10 E
Lopatino 16 Nc 52.37N 45.47 E
Lopatka, Mys- 21 Rd 50.52N 156.40 E
Lop Buri 25 Kf 14.48N 100.37 E
Lopča 20 He 55.44N 122.45 E
Lopévi 63b Dc 16.30 S 168.21 E
Lopez, Cap- = Lopez, Cape- (EN) 30 Hi 0.37 S 8.43 E
Lopez, Cape- (EN) = Lopez, Cap- 30 Hi 0.37 S 8.43 E
Lop Nur 21 Le 40.30N 90.30 E
Lopnur/Yuli 27 Ec 41.22N 86.09 E
Lopori 30 Ih 1.14N 19.49 E
Loppersum 12 Ia 53.19N 6.45 E
Lopphavet 7 Ea 70.25N 22.00 E
Loppi 8 Kd 60.43N 24.27 E
Lopud 14 Lh 42.41N 17.57 E
Łopuszno 10 Qf 50.57N 20.15 E
Lora del Rio 13 Gg 37.39N 5.32W
Lorain 43 Kc 41.28N 82.11W
Lorán, Boca- 54 Fb 9.00N 60.45W
Lorca 13 Kg 37.40N 1.42W
Lorch 12 Jd 50.03N 7.49 E
Lord Howe Island 57 Gh 31.33 S 159.05 E
Lord Howe Rise (EN) 3 Jm 32.00 S 162.00 E
Lord Mayor Bay 42 Ic 69.45N 92.00W
Lordsburg 45 Bj 32.21N 108.43W
Loreley 12 Jd 50.08N 7.43 E
Lorena 55 Jf 22.44 S 45.08W
Lorengau 60 Dh 2.01 S 147.17 E
Lorestān [3] 23 Gc 33.30N 48.40 E
Loreto [2] 54 Dd 5.00 S 75.00W
Loreto [Arg.] 55 Dh 27.46 S 57.17W
Loreto [Bol.] 54 Fg 15.13 S 64.40W
Loreto [Braz.] 54 Ie 7.05 S 45.09W
Loreto [It.] 14 Hg 43.26N 13.36 E
Loreto [Mex.] 48 If 22.16N 101.58W
Loreto [Mex.] 47 Bc 26.01N 111.21W
Loreto [Par.] 56 Ib 23.16 S 57.11W
Loreto Aprutino 14 Hh 42.26N 13.59 E
Lorica 54 Cb 9.14N 75.49W
Lorient 6 Ff 47.45N 3.22W
Lőrinci 10 Pi 47.44N 19.41 E
Lorn, Firth of- 9 He 56.20N 5.40W
Lorne 59 Ig 38.33 S 143.59 E
Lörrach 10 Di 47.37N 7.40 E
Lorrain, Plateau- 11 Me 49.00N 6.30 E
Lorrain, Rivière du- 51h Ab 14.50N 61.03W
Lorraine 11 Lf 49.00N 6.00 E
Lorraine, Plaine- 11 Lf 48.10N 5.50 E
Lorsch 12 Ke 49.39N 8.34 E
Los 7 Df 61.44N 15.10 E
Los, Iles de- = Los Islands (EN) 34 Cd 9.30N 13.48W

Index Symbols

[1] Independent Nation
[2] State, Region
[3] District, County
[4] Municipality
[5] Colony, Dependency
Continent
Physical Region
Historical or Cultural Region
Mount, Mountain
Volcano
Hill
Mountains, Mountain Range
Hills, Escarpment
Plateau, Upland
Pass, Gap
Plain, Lowland
Delta
Salt Flat
Valley, Canyon
Crater, Cave
Karst Features
Depression
Polder
Desert, Dunes
Forest, Woods
Heath, Steppe
Oasis
Cape, Point
Coast, Beach
Cliff
Peninsula
Isthmus
Sandbank
Island
Atoll
Rock, Reef
Islands, Archipelago
Rocks, Reefs
Coral Reef
Well, Spring
Geyser
River, Stream
Waterfall Rapids
River Mouth, Estuary
Lake
Salt Lake
Intermittent Lake
Reservoir
Swamp, Pond
Canal
Glacier
Ice Shelf, Pack Ice
Ocean
Sea
Gulf, Bay
Strait, Fjord
Lagoon
Bank
Seamount
Tablemount
Ridge
Shelf
Basin
Escarpment, Sea Scarp
Fracture
Trench, Abyss
National Park, Reserve
Point of Interest
Recreation Site
Cave, Cavern
Historic Site
Ruins
Wall, Walls
Church, Abbey
Temple
Scientific Station
Airport
Port
Lighthouse
Mine
Tunnel
Dam, Bridge

Los Alamos 39 If 35.53N 106.19W
Los Amates 49 Cf 15.16N 89.06W
Los Amores 55 Ci 28.06S 59.59W
Los Angeles 39 Hf 34.03N 118.15W
Los Ángeles 53 Ii 37.28S 72.21W
Los Angeles Aqueduct 46 Fi 35.22N 118.05W
Losap Atoll 57 Gd 6.54N 152.44 E
Los Banos 46 Eh 37.04N 120.51W
Los Blancos 56 Hb 23.36S 62.36W
Los Charrúas 55 Cj 31.10S 58.11W
Los Chiles 49 Eh 11.02N 84.43W
Los Conquistadores 55 Cj 30.36S 58.28W
Los Frailes, Islas- 50 Eg 11.12N 63.45W
Los Frentones 55 Bh 26.25S 61.25W
Los Gatos 46 Eh 37.14N 121.59W
Losheim 12 Ie 49.31N 6.45 E
Los Hermanos, Islas- 54 Fa 11.45N 64.25W
Łosice 10 Sd 52.14N 22.43 E
Lošinj 14 If 44.35N 14.28 E
Los Islands (EN)=Los, Iles de- 34 Cd 9.30N 13.48W
Los Juries 55 Ai 28.28S 62.06W
Los Lagos 56 Fe 39.51S 72.50W
Los Lagos [2] 56 Ff 41.20S 73.00W
Los Llanos de Aridane 32 Dd 28.39N 17.54W
Los Médanos, Istmo de- 49 Mh 11.35N 69.45W
Los Mochis 39 Ig 25.45N 108.53W
Los Monegros 13 Lc 41.29N 0.03W
Los Monjes, Islas- 54 Da 12.25N 70.55W
Los Navalmorales 13 He 39.43N 4.38W
Loso 36 Ec 1.10S 27.10 E
Los Palacios 49 Fb 22.35N 83.12W
Los Palacios y Villafranca 13 Gg 37.10N 5.56W
Los Pedroches 13 Hf 38.27N 4.45W
Los Pirpintos 55 Ah 26.08S 62.05W
Los Remedios, Rio de- 48 Fe 24.41N 106.28W
Los Reyes de Salgado 48 Hh 19.35N 102.29W
Los Roques, Islas- 54 Ea 11.50N 66.45W
Los Roques Basin (EN) 50 Cf 12.20N 67.40W
Los Santos [3] 49 Gj 7.45N 80.30W
Los Santos 49 Gj 7.56N 80.25W
Losser 12 Jb 52.16N 7.01 E
Lossiemouth 9 Jd 57.43N 3.18W
Lossnen 8 Eb 62.30N 12.50 E
Los Taques 49 Lh 11.50N 70.16W
Los Telares 56 Hc 28.59S 63.26W
Los Teques 54 Ea 10.21N 67.02W
Los Testigos, Islas- 54 Fa 11.23N 63.06W
Lost River 46 Ef 41.56N 121.30W
Lost River Range 46 Id 44.10N 113.35W
Lost Trail Pass 43 Eb 45.41N 113.57W
Los Vilos 56 Fd 31.55S 71.31W
Lot 5 Gg 44.18N 0.20 E
Lot [3] 11 Hj 44.30N 1.30 E
Lota 56 Fe 37.05S 73.10W
Lotagipi Swamp 35 Ee 4.36N 34.55 E
Løten 8 Dd 60.49N 11.19 E
Lot-et-Garonne [3] 11 Gj 44.20N 0.30 E
Lothair 37 Ee 26.26S 30.27 E
Lothian [3] 9 Jf 55.55N 3.30W
Lothian 9 Jf 55.55N 3.05W
Loto 36 Dc 2.47S 22.30 E
Lotofaga 65c Ba 13.59S 171.50W
Lotoi 36 Cc 1.35S 18.30 E
Lotru 15 Hd 45.20N 24.16 E
Lotrului, Munţii- 15 Gd 45.30N 23.52 E
Lotta 7 Hb 68.39N 30.20 E
Lottefors 8 Gc 61.25N 16.24 E
Löttorp 8 Gg 57.10N 16.59 E
Lotuke, Jabal- 35 Ee 4.07N 33.48 E
Louang Namtha 25 Kd 20.57N 101.25 E
Louangphrabang 22 Mh 19.52N 102.08 E
Loubomo 31 Ii 4.12S 12.41 E
Loučná 10 Lf 50.06N 15.48 E
Loudéac 11 Df 48.10N 2.45W
Loudima 36 Bc 4.07S 13.04 E
Loudon 44 Eh 35.44N 84.20W
Loudun 11 Gh 47.00N 0.04 E
Loué 11 Fg 48.00N 0.09W
Loue 11 Lg 47.01N 5.27 E
Loufan 28 Ae 38.04N 111.47 E
Louga 34 Bb 15.37N 16.13W
Louga [3] 34 Bb 15.00N 15.30W
Louge 11 Hk 43.27N 1.20 E
Loughborough 9 Li 52.47N 1.11W
Lougheed 42 Ha 77.30N 105.00W
Loughrea/Baile Locha Riach 9 Eh 53.12N 8.34W
Louhans 11 Lh 46.38N 5.13 E
Louhi 19 Db 66.04N 33.01 E
Louisa 44 Ff 38.07N 82.36W
Louiseville 44 Kb 46.16N 72.57W
Louisiade Archipelago 57 Gf 11.00S 153.00 E
Louisiana 45 Kg 39.27N 91.03W
Louisiana [2] 43 Ie 31.15N 92.15W
Louis Trichardt 37 Dd 23.01S 29.43 E
Louisville [Ky.-U.S.] 39 Kf 38.16N 85.45W
Louisville [Ms.-U.S.] 45 Lj 33.07N 89.03W
Louis-XIV, Pointe - 42 Jf 54.50N 79.30W
Loukoléla 36 Cc 1.02S 17.07 E
Loulan Yiji 27 Ec 40.32N 89.50 E
Loulé 13 Dg 37.08N 8.02W
Loum 34 Ge 4.43N 9.44 E
Lount Lake 45 Ia 50.10N 94.20W
Louny 10 Jf 50.22N 13.49 E
Loup City 45 Gf 41.17N 98.58W
Loup River 43 Hc 41.24N 97.19W
Loups Marins, Lacs des - 42 Ke 56.40N 74.00W
Lourdes 11 Fk 43.06N 0.03W
Lourenço Marques→Maputo 31 Kk 25.58S 32.34 E
Lousa, Serra da- 13 Dd 40.04N 8.13W
Loushan Guan 27 If 28.02N 106.51 E
Louštín 10 Jf 50.12N 13.48 E
Louth [Austl.] 59 Jf 30.32S 145.07 E
Louth [Eng.-U.K.] 9 Mh 53.22N 0.01W
Louth/Lú [2] 9 Gh 53.55N 6.30W
Loutrá Aidhipsoú 15 Gk 38.51N 23.03 E
Loutrá Killinis 15 El 37.52N 21.07 E
Loutrákion 15 Fl 37.59N 23.00 E
Louvain/Leuven 11 Kd 50.53N 4.42 E
Louvet Point 51k Bb 13.58N 60.53W
Louviers 11 He 49.13N 1.10 E
Lövånger 7 Ed 64.22N 21.18 E
Lovászi 10 Mj 46.33N 16.34 E
Lovat 5 Jd 58.14N 31.28 E
Lovćen 15 Bg 42.24N 18.49 E
Loveč [2] 15 Hf 43.08N 24.43 E
Loveč 15 Hf 43.08N 24.43 E
Loveland 45 Df 40.24N 105.05W
Lovell 43 Fc 44.50N 108.24W
Lovelock 43 Dc 40.11N 118.28W
Lövenich, Köln- 12 Id 50.57N 6.50 E
Lovenske Gorice 14 Jd 46.40N 16.00 E
Lovere 14 Ee 45.49N 10.04 E
Loviisa 7 Gf 60.27N 26.14 E
Loviisa/Lovisa 7 Gf 60.27N 26.14 E
Loving 45 Dj 32.17N 104.06W
Lovington 43 Ge 33.27N 103.21W
Lovisa 7 Gf 60.27N 26.14 E
Lovisa/Loviisa 7 Gf 60.27N 26.14 E
Lovoi 36 Ed 8.05S 26.40 E
Lovosice 10 Kf 50.31N 14.03 E
Lovozero 7 Ib 68.01N 35.01 E
Lovozero, Ozero- 7 Ic 67.50N 35.10 E
Lövstabruk 8 Gd 60.24N 17.53 E
Lövstabukten 8 Gd 60.35N 17.45 E
Lovua 36 Dd 6.07S 20.35 E
Lovua 36 De 11.31S 23.35 E
Low, Cape - 42 Id 63.06N 85.18W
Lowa 30 Ji 1.24S 25.52 E
Lowell 43 Mc 42.39N 71.18W
Löwenberg in der Mark 10 Jd 52.53N 13.09 E
Lower Arrow Lake 46 Fb 49.40N 118.08W
Lower Austria (EN) = Niederösterreich [2] 14 Jb 48.30N 15.45 E
Lower California (EN) → Baja California 38 Hg 28.00N 112.00W
Lower Hutt 62 Fd 41.13S 174.55 E
Lower Lake 46 Ef 41.15N 120.02W
Lower Lake 46 Dg 38.55N 122.36W
Lower Lough Erne/Loch Éirne Iochtair 9 Fg 54.30N 7.50W
Lower Post 42 Ee 59.55N 128.30W
Lower Red Lake 45 Ic 48.00N 94.50W
Lower Rhine (EN) = Neder-Rijn 11 Mc 51.59N 6.20 E
Lower Saxony (EN) = Niedersachsen [2] 10 Fd 52.00N 10.00 E
Lower Trajan's Wall (EN) = Nižni Trajanov Val 15 Ld 45.45N 28.30 E
Lower Tunguska (EN) = Nižnjaja Tunguska 21 Kc 65.48N 88.04 E
Lowestoft 9 Oi 52.29N 1.45 E
Lowestoft Ness 9 Oi 52.28N 1.44 E
Lowgar [3] 23 Kc 33.50N 69.00 E
Łowicz 10 Pd 52.07N 19.56 E
Lowlands 9 Jf 56.00N 4.00W
Lowrah 21 If 31.33N 66.33 E
Lowshān 24 Md 36.39N 49.32 E
Low Tatra (EN) = Nízke Tatry 10 Ph 48.54N 19.40 E
Lowther 42 Hb 74.35N 97.40W
Lowville 44 Jd 43.47N 75.30W
Loxton [Austl.] 59 If 34.27S 140.35 E
Loxton [S.Afr.] 37 Cf 31.30S 22.22 E
Loyalty Islands (EN) = Loyauté, Iles- 57 Hg 21.00S 167.00 E
Loyauté, Iles-=Loyalty Islands (EN) 57 Hg 21.00S 167.00 E
Loyoro 36 Fb 3.21N 34.17 E
Lozère [3] 11 Jj 44.30N 3.30 E
Lozère, Mont- 11 Jj 44.25N 3.46 E
Loznica 15 Ce 44.32N 19.13 E
Lozovaja 19 Df 48.53N 36.15 E
Lozva 19 Gd 59.36N 62.20 E
Lú/Louth [2] 9 Gh 53.55N 6.30W
Lua 36 Cb 2.46N 18.26 E
Luacano 36 De 11.16S 21.38 E
Luachimo 36 Dd 6.33S 20.59 E
Luaha-Sibuha 26 Cg 0.31S 98.28 E
Luahoko 65b Ba 19.40S 174.24W
Luala 37 Fc 17.57S 36.30 E
Lualaba 29 Jh 0.26N 25.20 E
Luama 36 Ec 4.46S 26.53 E
Lua Makika 65a Ec 20.35N 156.34W
Luampa 36 De 14.32S 24.10 E
Lu'an 27 Ke 31.44N 116.30 E
Luanda 31 Ii 8.50S 13.15 E
Luanda [3] 36 Bd 8.30S 13.20 E
Luando 30 Ij 10.19S 16.40 E
Luang, Khao- 25 Jg 8.31N 99.47 E
Luang, Thale- 25 Kg 7.30N 100.15 E
Luang Chiang Dao, Doi- 25 Je 19.23N 98.54 E
Luanginga 30 Jj 15.11S 22.55 E
Luang Prabang Range 25 Ke 18.30N 101.15 E
Luangue 36 Dc 4.17S 20.01 E
Luangwa 36 Kj 15.36S 30.25 E
Luan He 21 Nf 39.20N 119.10 E
Luaniva 64h Bb 13.16S 176.07W
Luannan (Bencheng) 28 Ee 39.30N 118.42 E
Luanping (Anjiangying) 28 Dd 40.55N 117.19 E
Luanshya 31 Jj 13.08S 28.25 E
Luanxian 27 Kd 39.45N 118.44 E
Luanza 36 Ed 8.40S 28.40 E
Luapula 30 Ji 9.26S 28.33 E
Luapula [3] 36 Ee 10.40S 29.15 E
Luarca 13 Fa 43.32N 6.32W
Luashi 36 De 10.56S 23.37 E
Luba 34 Ge 3.28N 8.40 E
Lubaantum 49 Ce 16.17N 88.58W
Lubaczów 10 Tf 50.10N 23.07 E
Lubaczówka 10 Sf 50.08N 22.35 E
Lubalo 36 Cd 7.22S 19.20 E
Lubalo 36 Cd 9.07S 19.15 E
Lubamba 36 Ed 5.14S 26.02 E
Lubań 10 Le 51.08N 15.18 E
Lubāna/Lubana 8 Lh 56.49N 26.49 E
Lubana/Lubāna 8 Lh 56.49N 26.49 E
Lubānas, Ozero-/Lubānas Ezers 8 Lh 56.40N 27.00 E
Lubānas Ezers/Lubanas, Ozero- 8 Lh 56.40N 27.00 E
Lubang Islands 26 Hd 13.45N 120.15 E
Lubango 31 Ij 14.55S 13.28 E
Lubao 31 Ji 5.22S 25.45 E
Lubartów 10 Se 51.28N 22.46 E
Lubawa 10 Pc 53.30N 19.45 E
Lübbecke 10 Ed 52.18N 8.37 E
Lubbeek 12 Gd 50.53N 4.50 E
Lübben/Lubin 10 Je 51.57N 13.54 E
Lübbenau/Lubnjow 10 Je 51.52N 13.58 E
Lubbock 39 If 33.35N 101.51W
Lübeck 6 He 53.52N 10.42 E
Lübecker Bucht 10 Gb 54.00N 10.55 E
Lübeck-Travemünde 10 Gc 53.57N 10.52 E
Lubefu 36 Dc 4.10S 23.00 E
Lubefu 36 Dc 4.43S 24.25 E
Lubei→Jarud Qi 27 Lc 44.30N 120.55 E
Lubelska, Wyżyna- 10 Sf 51.00N 23.00 E
Lubenec 10 Jf 50.08N 13.20 E
Lubenka 16 Sd 50.28N 54.06 E
Lubero 36 Ec 0.06S 29.06 E
Lubéron, Montagne du- 11 Lk 43.48N 5.22 E
Lubi 36 Dc 4.59S 23.26 E
Lubie, Jezioro- 10 Lc 53.30N 15.50 E
Lubień Kujawski 10 Pd 52.25N 19.10 E
Lubij/Löbau 10 Ke 51.06N 14.40 E
Lubilash 29 Ji 6.02S 23.45 E
Lubin 10 Me 51.24N 16.13 E
Lubin/Lübben 10 Je 51.57N 13.54 E
Lublin 6 Ie 51.15N 22.35 E
Lublin [2] 10 Se 51.15N 22.35 E
Lubliniec 10 Of 50.40N 18.41 E
Lubnān=Lebanon (EN) [1] 22 Ff 33.50N 35.50 E
Lubnān, Jabal-=Lebanon Mountains (EN) 23 Ec 34.00N 36.30 E
Lubnjow/Lübbenau 10 Je 51.52N 13.58 E
Lubny 19 De 50.01N 33.00 E
Luboń 10 Md 52.23N 16.54 E
Lubraniec 10 Od 52.33N 18.50 E
Lubsko 10 Ke 51.46N 14.59 E
Lubsza 10 Ke 51.55N 14.45 E
Lubudi 29 Ji 9.13S 25.38 E
Lubudi 36 Ed 9.57S 25.58 E
Lubue 36 Cc 4.10S 19.53 E
Lubuklinggau 26 Dg 3.10S 102.52 E
Lubuksikaping 26 Df 0.08N 100.10 E
Lubumba 36 Ec 3.58S 29.06 E
Lubumbashi 31 Jj 11.40S 27.30 E
Lubuskie, Pojezierze- 10 Ld 52.18N 15.20 E
Lubutu 31 Ji 0.44S 26.35 E
Lucala 36 Bd 6.38S 12.34 E
Lucala 36 Cd 9.16S 15.16 E
Lucania, Mount- 42 Dd 61.01N 140.29W
Lucas 55 Ea 13.05S 55.56W
Lucca 14 Eg 43.50N 10.29 E
Lucea 49 Hd 18.27N 78.10W
Luce Bay 9 Ig 54.47N 4.50W
Lucedale 45 Lk 30.55N 88.35W
Lučegorsk 20 Ig 46.25N 134.20 E
Lucélia 56 Ge 21.44S 51.01W
Lucena [Phil.] 26 Hd 13.56N 121.37 E
Lucena [Sp.] 13 Hg 37.24N 4.29W
Lucena del Cid 13 Ld 40.08N 0.17W
Luc-en-Diois 11 Lj 44.37N 5.27 E
Lučenec 10 Ph 48.20N 19.41 E
Lucera 14 Ji 41.30N 15.20 E
Lucerne (EN) = Luzern 14 Cc 47.05N 8.20 E
Lucerne, Lake- (EN) = Vierwaldstätter-See 14 Cc 47.00N 8.30 E
Lucero 48 Fb 30.49N 106.30W
Lucheng 28 Bf 36.18N 113.15 E
Lucheringo 37 Fb 11.43S 36.15 E
Lucheux 12 Ed 50.12N 2.25 E
Luchico 30 Lj 12.15S 44.25 E
Luchico 36 Cd 6.12S 19.42 E
Lüchow 10 Hd 52.58N 11.09 E
Lüchun 27 Hg 23.02N 102.19 E
Lucipara, Kepulauan- 26 Ih 5.30S 127.33 E
Lucira 36 Be 13.52S 12.32 E
Luck 19 Ce 50.47N 25.20 E
Luckau 10 Je 51.51N 13.43 E
Luckenwalde 10 Jd 52.05N 13.10 E
Lucknow 22 Kg 26.51N 80.55 E
Luçon 11 Eh 46.27N 1.10W
Lucrecia, Cabo- 49 Jc 21.04N 75.37W
Luc-sur-Mer 12 Be 49.18N 0.21W
Lucunga 36 Bd 6.49S 14.35 E
Lucusse 36 De 12.33S 20.51 E
Lüda→Dalian=Dairan (EN) 22 Of 38.55N 121.39 E
Luda Kamčija 15 Kg 43.03N 27.29 E
Ludbreg 14 Kd 46.15N 16.37 E
Lüdenscheid 10 De 51.13N 7.37 E
Lüderitz 31 Ik 26.38S 15.10 E
Lüderitz [3] 37 Be 26.00S 15.00 E
Lüderitz Bay 37 Be 26.35S 15.10 E
Ludhiāna 22 Jf 30.54N 75.51 E
Ludinghausen 12 Jc 51.46N 7.28 E
Ludington 43 Jc 43.57N 86.27W
Ludlow 9 Ki 52.22N 2.43W
Ludogorije 15 Jf 43.46N 26.56 E
Ludogorsko Plato 15 Kf 43.36N 27.03 E
Luduş 15 Hc 46.29N 24.06 E
Ludvika 7 Df 60.09N 15.11 E
Ludwigsburg 10 Fh 48.54N 9.11 E
Ludwigshafen am Rhein 10 Eg 49.29N 8.27 E
Ludwigslust 10 Hc 53.19N 11.30 E
Ludza 7 Gh 56.32N 27.45 E
Luebo 31 Ji 5.21S 21.25 E
Lueki 36 Ec 3.24S 25.57 E
Lueki 36 Ec 3.22S 25.51 E
Luele 36 Dd 7.55S 20.00 E
Luembé 36 Dd 6.43S 24.11 E
Luembe 36 Dd 6.37S 21.06 E
Luena [Ang.] 36 De 12.31S 22.34 E
Luena [Ang.] 31 Ij 11.48S 19.55 E
Luena [Zaire] 36 Ed 9.27S 25.47 E
Luena [Zam.] 36 Df 15.20S 23.30 E
Luengué 36 Df 16.54S 21.52 E
Luenha 37 Ec 16.24S 33.48 E
Luera Peak 45 Cj 33.47N 107.49W
Lueta 36 Dd 7.04S 21.40 E
Lueyang 27 Ie 33.25N 106.14 E
Lufeng 27 Kg 22.57N 115.41 E
Lufico 36 Bd 6.22S 13.30 E
Lufira 29 Ji 8.16S 26.27 E
Lufira, Chutes de la- 36 Ed 9.50S 27.30 E
Lufkin 43 Ie 31.20N 94.44W
Lug 15 De 44.23N 20.45 E
Luga 19 Cd 59.43N 28.18 E
Luga 19 Cd 58.44N 29.50 E
Lugano 14 Cd 46.00N 8.57 E
Lugano, Lago di- 14 Cd 46.00N 9.00 E
Lugansk = Vorošilovgrad 6 Jf 48.34N 39.20 E
Luganville 58 Hf 15.32S 167.10 E
Lügde 12 Lc 51.57N 9.15 E
Lugela 37 Fc 16.26S 36.08 E
Lugenda 30 Kj 11.26S 38.33 E
Lugnaquillia 5 Fe 52.58N 6.27W
Lugo [3] 13 Eb 43.00N 7.30W
Lugo [It.] 14 Ff 44.25N 11.54 E
Lugo [Sp.] 13 Ea 43.00N 7.34W
Lugoj 15 Ed 45.41N 21.55 E
Lugovoj 19 Hg 42.55N 72.47 E
Lugovoj 19 Gd 59.44N 65.55 E
Lugovski 20 Ge 58.05N 112.55 E
Lugulu 36 Ec 2.17S 26.32 E
Luh 7 Kh 56.14N 42.28 E
Luhe 10 Gc 53.18N 10.11 E
Luhe 28 Eh 32.21N 118.50 E
Luhin Sum 27 Kb 46.41N 118.38 E
Luhit 25 Jc 27.48N 95.28 E
Luhovicy 7 Ji 54.59N 39.02 E
Luhuo 27 He 31.21N 100.40 E
Lui 36 Cd 8.41S 17.56 E
Luia 36 Dd 8.26S 21.45 E
Luiana 36 Df 17.22S 22.59 E
Luiana 30 Jj 17.27S 23.14 E
Luie 36 Cc 4.33S 17.41 E
Luik/Liège 6 Ge 50.38N 5.34 E
Luilaka 30 Ji 0.52S 20.12 E
Luilu 36 Dd 6.22S 23.50 E
Luimneach/Limerick 6 Fe 52.40N 8.38W
Luimneach/Limerick [2] 9 Ei 52.30N 9.00W
Luing 9 He 56.13N 5.39W
Luino 14 Cd 46.00N 8.44 E
Luio 36 De 13.15S 21.39 E
Lui Pătru, Vîrful- 15 Gd 45.30N 23.30 E
Luis Correia 54 Jd 2.53S 41.40W
Luishia 36 Ee 11.10S 27.07 E
Luitpold Coast 66 Af 78.30S 32.00W
Luiza 36 Dd 7.12S 22.25 E
Luján [Arg.] 56 Gd 32.22S 65.57W
Luján [Arg.] 56 Id 34.34S 59.07W
Lujiang 28 Di 31.15N 117.17 E
Lukafu 36 Ee 10.30S 27.33 E
Lukanga Swamp 36 Ee 14.25S 27.45 E
Lukavac 14 Mf 44.33N 18.32 E
Lukengo 36 Ed 5.46S 29.06 E
Lukenie 30 Ii 2.44S 18.09 E
Lukeville 46 Ik 31.57N 112.50W
Lukojanov 19 Ed 55.02N 44.30 E
Lukolela 36 Cc 1.03S 17.12 E
Lukonzolwa 36 Ed 8.47S 28.39 E
Lukov 10 Ue 51.14N 24.25 E
Lukovit 15 Hf 43.12N 24.10 E
Łuków 10 Se 51.56N 22.23 E
Lukuga 30 Ji 5.40S 26.55 E
Lukula 36 Bd 5.23S 12.57 E
Lukulu 36 De 14.23S 23.15 E
Lukusashi 36 Fe 14.38S 30.00 E
Luleå 6 Ib 65.34N 22.10 E
Luleälven 6 Ib 65.35N 22.03 E
Lüleburgaz 23 Ca 41.24N 27.21 E
Lüliang Shan 21 Nf 37.45N 111.25 E
Lulimba 36 Ec 4.42S 28.38 E
Luling 45 Hl 29.41N 97.39W
Lulong 28 Ee 39.53N 118.52 E
Lulonga 36 Cb 0.37N 18.23 E
Lulonga 30 Ih 0.43N 18.23 E
Lulua 30 Ji 5.02S 21.07 E
Lulu Fakahega, Mount- 64h Bb 13.16S 176.10W
Luma 65c Db 14.14S 169.32W
Lumajang 26 Fh 8.08S 113.13 E
Lumajangdong Co 27 De 34.00N 81.37 E
Lumbala Kaquengue 31 Jj 14.06S 21.25 E
Lumbala N'guimbo 36 De 12.39S 22.32 E
Lumberton 43 Le 34.37N 79.00W
Lumbo 37 Gc 15.00S 40.44 E
Lumbrales 13 Fd 40.56N 6.43W
Lumbres 12 Ed 50.42N 2.08 E
Lumby 46 Fa 50.15N 118.58W
Lumding 25 Ic 25.45N 93.10 E
Lumege 36 De 11.34S 20.48 E
Lumesule 36 Ge 11.14S 38.06 E
Lumi 60 Ch 3.29S 142.03 E
Lummen 12 Hd 50.59N 5.15 E
Lumparland 8 Id 60.10N 20.15 E
Lumphăt 25 Lf 13.30N 106.59 E
Lumsden [N.Z.] 62 Cf 45.44S 168.26 E
Lumsden [Sask.-Can.] 46 Ma 50.34N 104.53W
Lumuna 36 Ec 3.46S 26.24 E
Lumut 26 Df 4.14N 100.38 E
Luna 13 Gb 42.40N 5.49W
Luna, Laguna de- 55 Di 28.06S 56.46W
Lunan Shan 27 Hf 27.00N 102.30 E
Lunayyr, Harrat- 24 Gj 25.10N 37.50 E
Lunca Ilvei 15 Hb 47.22N 24.59 E
Lund 7 Ci 55.42N 13.11 E
Lunda [3] 36 Cd 9.30S 20.00 E
Lundazi 31 Kj 12.19S 33.13 E
Lunde 8 Gb 62.53N 17.51 E
Lundevatn 8 Bf 58.20N 6.35 E
Lundi 30 Kk 21.19S 32.24 E
Lundu 26 Ef 1.40N 109.51 E
Lundy Island 9 Ij 51.10N 4.40W
Lüneburg 10 Gc 53.15N 10.24 E
Lüneburger Heide 10 Gc 53.10N 10.20 E
Lunel 11 Kk 43.41N 4.08 E
Lünen 10 De 51.37N 7.31 E
Lunéville 11 Mf 48.36N 6.30 E
Lunga 30 Jj 14.34S 26.26 E
Lungué-Bungo 37 Jj 28.38S 16.27 E
Lungwebungu 36 De 14.19S 23.14 E
Lūni 25 Ed 24.41N 71.14 E
Lūni 25 Ec 26.00N 73.00 E
Lunigiana 14 Df 44.20N 9.55 E
Luninec 19 Ce 52.16N 26.50 E
Lunino 16 Nc 53.35N 45.14 E
Lunsemfwa 36 Fe 14.54S 30.12 E
Luntai/Bügür 27 Dc 41.46N 84.10 E
Luobei (Fengxiang) 27 Nb 47.36N 130.58 E
Luobuzhuang 27 Ed 39.30N 88.15 E
Luocheng 27 Ig 24.51N 108.53 E
Luodian (Longping) 27 If 25.26N 106.47 E
Luoding 27 Jg 22.43N 111.33 E
Luohe 27 Je 33.30N 114.08 E
Luo He 27 Id 32.18N 109.12 E
Luoma Hu 28 Eg 34.10N 118.12 E
Luonteri 8 Lc 61.35N 27.45 E
Luoping 27 Hg 24.58N 104.19 E
Luopioinen 8 Kc 61.22N 24.40 E
Luoshan 28 Ch 32.13N 114.32 E
Luotian 28 Ci 30.48N 115.23 E
Luoxiao Shan 27 Jf 26.35N 114.00 E
Luoyang 22 Nf 34.41N 112.25 E
Luoyuan 27 Kf 26.31N 119.32 E
Luozi 36 Bc 4.57S 14.08 E
Lupa 36 Fd 8.39S 33.12 E
Lupane 37 Dc 18.56S 27.48 E
Łupawa 10 Nb 54.42N 17.07 E
Lupeni 15 Gd 45.21N 23.14 E
Luperón 49 Ld 19.54N 70.57W
Łupków 10 Sg 49.12N 22.06 E
Luputa 36 Dd 7.10S 23.42 E
Lūq 31 Lh 3.56N 42.32 E
Luqiao 28 Fj 28.39N 120.05 E
Luqu 27 He 34.36N 102.30 E
Luque 56 Ic 25.16S 57.34W
Luquillo 51a Cb 18.22N 65.43W
Luray 44 Hf 38.40N 78.28W
Lure 11 Mg 47.41N 6.30 E
Lure, Montagne de- 11 Lj 44.07N 5.47 E
Luremo 36 Cd 8.30S 17.51 E
Lurgan/An Lorgain 9 Gg 54.28N 6.20W
Lurín 54 Cf 12.17S 76.52W
Lúrio 37 Gb 13.32S 40.30 E
Lúrio 30 Lj 13.31S 40.42 E
Lusaka 31 Jj 15.25S 28.17 E
Lusambo 31 Ji 4.58S 23.27 E
Lusanga 36 Cc 4.44S 18.58 E
Lusangi 36 Ec 4.37S 27.08 E
Lu Shan 27 Kf 29.30N 115.55 E
Lushan [China] 28 Cj 29.33N 115.58 E
Lushan [China] 28 Bh 33.44N 112.54 E
Lushi 27 Je 34.04N 111.02 E
Lushiko 36 Cd 6.12S 19.42 E
Lushnja 15 Ci 40.56N 19.42 E
Lushoto 36 Gc 4.47S 38.17 E
Lu Shui 28 Bj 29.54N 113.39 E
Lushui (Luzhangjie) 27 Gf 26.00N 98.50 E
Lüshun=Port Arthur (EN) 27 Ld 38.50N 121.13 E
Lusignan 11 Gh 46.26N 0.07 E
Lusk 43 Gc 42.46N 104.27W
Lussac-les-Châteaux 11 Gh 46.24N 0.43 E
Lustrafjorden 8 Bc 61.20N 7.20 E
Lūt, Dasht-e-=Lut, Dasht-i- (EN) 21 Hf 33.00N 57.00 E
Lut, Dasht-i- (EN)=Lūt, Dasht-e- 21 Hf 33.00N 57.00 E
Lu Tao 27 Lg 22.35N 121.30 E
Lutembo 36 De 13.28S 21.22 E
Luti 63a Cb 7.14S 157.00 E
Lütjenburg 10 Gb 54.17N 10.35 E
Luton 9 Mj 51.53N 0.25W
Luton Airport 12 Bc 51.50N 0.22W
Lutong 26 Ff 4.28N 114.00 E
Lutshima 36 Cd 5.22S 18.59 E
Lutshima 36 Cd 5.22S 18.59 E
Lutterworth 12 Ab 52.27N 1.12W
Lutuai 36 De 12.40S 20.12 E
Lutugino 16 Ke 48.23N 39.13 E
Lützow-Holmbukta 66 De 69.10S 37.30 E
Lutzputs 37 Ce 28.22S 20.37 E
Luuk 26 He 5.58N 121.18 E
Luverne 45 He 43.39N 96.13W
Luvidjo 36 Ed 6.26S 26.59 E
Luvua 30 Ji 6.46S 26.58 E
Luvuei 36 De 13.06S 21.12 E
Luwegu 30 Ki 8.31S 37.23 E
Luwingu 36 Ee 10.16S 29.54 E
Luwuk 26 Hg 0.56S 122.47 E
Luxembourg [3] 12 He 50.00N 5.30 E
Luxembourg/Luxemburg [1] 6 Gf 49.45N 6.05 E
Luxembourg/Luxemburg 6 Gf 49.45N 6.05 E
Luxemburg/Luxembourg 6 Gf 49.45N 6.05 E
Luxemburg/Luxembourg [1] 6 Gf 49.45N 6.05 E
Luxeuil-les-Bains 11 Mg 47.49N 6.23 E
Luxi 22 Mg 24.34N 103.44 E
Luxi (Mangshi) 27 Gg 24.29N 98.40 E
Luxor (EN)=Al Uqşur 33 Fd 25.41N 32.39 E
Luy 11 Ek 43.39N 1.08W
Luy de Béarn 11 Fk 43.38N 0.47W

Index Symbols

[1] Independent Nation
[2] State, Region
[3] District, County
[4] Municipality
[5] Colony, Dependency
Continent
Physical Region
Historical or Cultural Region
Mount, Mountain
Volcano
Hill
Mountains, Mountain Range
Hills, Escarpment
Plateau, Upland
Pass, Gap
Plain, Lowland
Delta
Salt Flat
Valley, Canyon
Crater, Cave
Karst Features
Depression
Polder
Desert, Dunes
Forest, Woods
Heath, Steppe
Oasis
Cape, Point
Coast, Beach
Cliff
Peninsula
Isthmus
Sandbank
Island
Atoll
Rock, Reef
Islands, Archipelago
Rocks, Reefs
Coral Reef
Well, Spring
Geyser
River, Stream
Waterfall Rapids
River Mouth, Estuary
Lake
Salt Lake
Intermittent Lake
Reservoir
Swamp, Pond
Canal
Glacier
Ice Shelf, Pack Ice
Ocean
Sea
Gulf, Bay
Strait, Fjord
Lagoon
Bank
Seamount
Tablemount
Ridge
Shelf
Basin
Escarpment, Sea Scarp
Fracture
Trench, Abyss
National Park, Reserve
Point of Interest
Recreation Site
Cave, Cavern
Historic Site
Ruins
Wall, Walls
Church, Abbey
Temple
Scientific Station
Airport
Port
Lighthouse
Mine
Tunnel
Dam, Bridge

Name	Page	Grid	Lat.	Long.
Luy de France	11	Fk	43.38N	0.47W
Luyi	28	Ch	33.51N	115.28 E
Luz	55	Jd	19.48S	45.41W
Luz, Costa de la-	13	Fh	36.40N	6.20W
Luza	19	Ec	60.39N	47.15 E
Luza	5	Kc	60.40N	46.25 E
Luzarches	12	Ee	49.07N	2.25 E
Luzern [2]	14	Cc	47.05N	8.10 E
Luzern = Lucerne (EN)	14	Cc	47.05N	8.20 E
Luzhai	27	Ig	24.31N	109.46 E
Luzhangjie → Lushui	27	Gf	26.00N	98.50 E
Luzhou	22	Mg	28.55N	105.20 E
Luziânia	54	Ig	16.15S	47.56W
Luzická Nisa	10	Kd	52.04N	14.46 E
Luzilândia	54	Jd	3.28S	42.22W
Lužnice	10	Kg	49.16N	14.25 E
Luzon	21	Oh	16.00N	121.00 E
Luzon Sea	26	Gd	12.30N	119.00 E
Luzon Strait (EN)	21	Og	21.00N	122.00 E
Luz-Saint-Sauveur	11	Gl	42.52N	0.01 E
Lužskaja Guba	8	Me	59.35N	28.25 E
Lužskaja Vozvyšennost	8	Mf	58.15N	28.45 E
Luzy	11	Jh	46.47N	3.58 E
Łużyca	10	Oe	51.33N	18.15 E
Lvov	6	If	49.50N	24.00 E
Lvovskaja Oblast [3]	19	Cf	49.45N	24.00 E
Lwowa	60	Hj	10.44S	165.45 E
Lwówek	10	Md	52.28N	16.10 E
Lwówek Śląski	10	Le	51.07N	15.35 E
Lyakhov Islands (EN) = Ljahovskije Ostrova	21	Qb	73.30N	141.00 E
Lyall, Mount-	62	Bf	45.17S	167.33 E
Lyallpur	22	Jf	31.25N	73.05 E
Lychsele	7	Ed	64.36N	18.40 E
Lycia	15	Mm	36.30N	29.30 E
Lyckeby	8	Fh	56.12N	15.39 E
Lyckebyån	8	Fh	56.11N	15.40 E
Lyčkovo	7	Hh	57.57N	32.24 E
Lydd	9	Nk	50.57N	0.55 E
Lydd Airport	12	Cd	50.58N	0.56 E
Lydenburg	37	Ee	25.10S	30.29 E
Lydia	15	Lk	38.35N	28.30 E
Lygna	8	Bf	58.10N	7.02 E
Lygnern	8	Eg	57.29N	12.20 E
Lyme Bay	9	Kk	50.38N	3.00W
Lyminge	12	Dc	51.07N	1.05 E
Lymington	9	Lk	50.46N	1.33W
Łyna	10	Rb	54.37N	21.14 E
Lynchburg	43	Ld	37.24N	79.09W
Lynd	58	Ff	18.56S	144.30 E
Lynden	46	Db	48.57N	122.27W
Lyndon River	59	Cd	23.29S	114.06 E
Lyngdal	7	Bg	58.08N	7.05 E
Lyngen	7	Eb	69.58N	20.30 E
Lyngør	8	Cf	58.38N	9.10 E
Lyngseidet	7	Eb	69.35N	20.13 E
Lynn	44	Ld	42.28N	70.57W
Lynnaj, Gora-	20	Ld	62.55N	163.58 E
Lynn Canal	40	Le	58.50N	135.15W
Lynn Deeps	12	Cb	52.58N	0.20 E
Lynn Lake	39	Id	56.51N	101.03W
Lyntupy	8	Li	55.02N	26.27 E
Lynx Lake	42	Gd	62.25N	106.20W
Lyon	6	Gf	45.45N	4.51 E
Lyon Inlet	42	Jc	66.20N	83.40W
Lyonnais, Monts du-	11	Ki	45.40N	4.30 E
Lyon River	59	De	25.00S	115.20 E
Lyons [Ga.-U.S.]	44	Fi	32.12N	82.19W
Lyons [Ks.-U.S.]	45	Gg	38.21N	98.12W
Lyons, Forêt de-	12	De	49.25N	1.30 E
Lyons-la-Forêt	12	De	49.24N	1.28 E
Lyra Reef	60	Eh	1.50S	153.35 E
Lys	11	Jc	51.03N	3.43 E
Łysa Góra	10	Nd	52.07N	17.33 E
Lysaja, Gora-	8	Lj	54.12N	27.40 E
Lysá nad Labem	10	Kf	50.12N	14.50 E
Lysefjorden	8	Be	59.00N	6.14 E
Lysekil	7	Cf	58.16N	11.26 E
Lyskovo	19	Ed	56.03N	45.03 E
Lyss	14	Bc	47.04N	7.37 E
Lysva	19	Fd	58.07N	57.47 E
Lytham Saint Anne's	9	Jh	53.45N	3.01W
Lyttelton	62	Ee	43.36S	172.43 E
Lytton	46	Ea	50.14N	121.34W
Lyža	17	Hd	65.42N	56.40 E

M

Name	Page	Grid	Lat.	Long.
Ma, Oued el-	32	Fe	24.03N	9.10W
Ma, Song	25	Le	19.45N	105.55 E
Maâdis, Djebel-	13	Qi	35.52N	4.44 E
Maalaea Bay	65a	Ec	20.47N	156.29W
Ma'āmīr	24	Mg	30.04N	48.20 E
Ma'ān	23	Ec	30.12N	35.44 E
Ma'ānīyah	24	Jg	30.44N	43.00 E
Maanselkä	5	Ib	68.07N	28.29 E
Maanselka	7	Ge	63.54N	28.30 E
Ma'anshan	27	Ke	31.38N	118.30 E
Maardu	8	Ke	59.28N	24.56 E
Maarianhamina/Mariehamn	7	Ef	60.06N	19.57 E
Ma 'arrat an Nu 'mān	24	Ge	35.38N	36.40 E
Maarssen	12	Hb	52.08N	5.03 E
Maas = Meuse (EN)	5	Ge	51.49N	5.01 E
Maaseik	11	Lc	51.06N	5.48 E
Maaseik-Neeroeteren	12	Hc	51.05N	5.42 E
Maasin	26	Hd	10.08N	124.50 E
Maasmechelen/Mechelen	12	Hd	50.57N	5.40 E
Maassluis	12	Gc	51.55N	4.17 E
Maastricht	11	Ld	50.52N	5.43 E
Maasupa	63a	Ec	9.18S	161.15 E
Ma'āzah, Al Haḑabat al-	33	Fd	27.44N	31.44 E
Mabalane	37	Ed	23.38S	32.31 E
Mabaruma	50	Gh	8.12N	59.47W
Mabechi-Gawa	29	Ga	40.31N	141.31 E
Mabella	45	Lb	48.37N	89.58W
Mabel Lake	46	Fa	50.35N	118.44W
Mablethorpe	9	Nh	53.21N	0.15 E
Mabote	37	Ed	22.03S	34.08 E
Ma'būs Yūsuf	31	Jf	25.45N	21.00 E
Maçaão	13	Ee	39.33N	8.00W
McAdam	42	Kg	45.36N	67.20W
Macajaí, Rio-	54	Fc	2.25N	60.50W
McAllen	43	Hf	26.12N	98.15W
Macaloge	37	Fb	12.25S	35.25 E
Mac Alpine Lake	42	Hc	66.40N	102.50W
Macambará	55	Di	29.08S	56.03W
Macamic	44	Ha	48.48N	79.01W
Macamic, Lac-	44	Ha	48.46N	79.00W
Macao (EN) = Aomen/Macau [5]	22	Ng	22.10N	113.33 E
Macao (EN) = Aomen/Macau	27	Jg	22.12N	113.33 E
Macao (EN) = Macau/Aomen [5]	22	Ng	22.10N	113.33 E
Macao (EN) = Macau/Aomen	27	Jg	22.12N	113.33 E
Macapá	53	Ke	0.02N	51.03W
Macará	54	Cd	4.21S	79.56W
Macaracas	49	Gj	7.44N	80.33W
Macareo, Caño-	54	Fb	9.47N	61.36W
McArthur	44	Ff	39.14N	82.29W
Mc Arthur River	59	Hc	15.54S	136.40 E
Maçãs	13	Fc	41.29N	6.39W
Macas	54	Cd	2.18S	78.06W
Macatete, Sierra de-	48	Dd	28.00N	110.05W
Macau	53	Mf	5.07S	36.38W
Macau/Aomen = Macao (EN)	27	Jg	22.12N	113.33 E
Macau/Aomen = Macao (EN) [5]	22	Ng	22.10N	113.33 E
Macaúbas	54	Jf	13.02S	42.42W
Macauley Island	57	Ih	30.13S	178.33W
Macaya, Pic de-	47	Je	18.23N	74.02W
McBeth Fiord	42	Kc	69.43N	69.20W
McCamey	45	Ek	31.08N	102.13W
McCammon	46	Ie	42.39N	112.12W
Mc Carthy	40	Kd	61.26N	142.55W
McClellanville	44	Hi	33.06N	79.28W
MacClenny	44	Fj	30.18N	82.07W
Macclesfield	9	Kh	53.16N	2.07W
Macclesfield Bank (EN)	26	Fc	15.50N	114.20 E
McClintock	42	Ie	57.48N	94.12W
McClintock, Mount-	66	Jg	80.13S	157.26 E
Mc Clintock Channel	38	Ib	71.00N	101.00W
McCluer Gulf (EN) = Berau, Teluk-	26	Jg	2.30S	132.30 E
Mc Clure Strait	38	Hb	74.30N	116.00W
McClusky	45	Fc	47.29N	100.27W
McComb	43	Ie	31.14N	90.27W
McConaughy, Lake-	45	Ff	41.18N	101.46W
McConnelsville	44	Gf	39.39N	81.51W
McCook	43	Gc	40.12N	100.38W
McCormick	44	Fi	33.55N	82.19W
McDame	42	Ee	59.13N	129.14W
McDermitt	46	Gf	41.59N	117.36W
Macdhui, Ben-	9	Jd	57.04N	3.40W
Macdonald, Lake-	59	Fd	23.30S	129.00 E
Mc Donald Islands	30	On	52.59S	72.50 E
McDonald Peak [Ca.-U.S.]	46	Ef	40.58N	120.26W
McDonald Peak [Mt.-U.S.]	46	Ic	47.29N	113.46W
Macdonald Range	46	Hb	49.12N	114.46W
Macdonnell Ranges	57	Eg	23.45S	132.20 E
McDouglas Sound	42	Hd	75.15N	97.30W
Macduff	9	Kd	57.40N	2.29W
Macedo de Cavaleiros	13	Fc	41.32N	6.58W
Macedonia (EN) = Makedhonía	5	Ig	41.00N	23.00 E
Macedonia (EN) = Makedhonía	15	Fh	41.00N	23.00 E
Macedonia (EN) = Makedonija	15	Eh	41.50N	22.00 E
Macedonia (EN) = Makedonija	5	Ig	41.00N	23.00 E
Macedonia (EN) = Makedonija	15	Fh	41.00N	23.00 E
Maceió	53	Mf	9.40S	35.43W
Macenta	34	Dd	8.33N	9.28W
Macerata	14	Hg	43.18N	13.27 E
McGehee	45	Kj	33.38N	91.24W
McGill	46	Hg	39.23N	114.47W
Macgillycuddy's Reeks/Na Cruacha Dubha	9	Di	52.00N	9.50W
McGrath	40	Hd	62.58N	155.38W
MacGregor	45	Gb	49.57N	98.49W
McGregor	45	Jc	46.36N	93.19W
McGregor Lake	46	Ia	50.31N	112.53W
Mc Gregor Range	59	Ie	26.40S	142.45 E
McGuire, Mount-	46	Hd	45.10N	114.36W
Machachi	54	Cd	0.30S	78.34W
Machado	55	Je	21.41S	45.56W
Machagai	56	Hc	26.56S	60.03W
Machaila	37	Ed	22.15S	32.58 E
Machaire na Mumhan/Golden Vale	9	Fi	52.30N	8.00W
Machaire Rátha/Maghera	9	Gg	54.51N	6.40W
Machakos	36	Gc	1.31S	37.16 E
Machala	54	Cd	3.16S	79.58W
Machaneng	37	Dd	23.12S	27.30 E
Machareti	54	Fh	20.49S	63.24W
Machar Marshes	35	Ed	9.20N	33.10 E
Machattie, Lake-	59	Hd	24.50S	139.48 E
Machault	12	Ge	49.21N	4.30 E
Macheke	37	Ec	18.05S	31.51 E
Macheng	27	Je	31.10N	115.00 E
Machias	44	Nc	44.43N	67.28W
Machida	29	Fd	35.32N	139.27 E
Machilipatnam (Bandar)	25	Ge	16.10N	81.08 E
Machiques	54	Da	10.04N	72.34W
Machona, Laguna-	48	Mh	18.20N	93.40W
Machów	10	Rf	50.34N	21.40 E
Machupicchu	53	Ig	13.07S	72.34W
Macia	37	Ef	25.02S	33.06 E
Mc Ilwraith Range	59	Ib	13.45S	143.20 E
Măcin	15	Ld	45.15N	28.09 E
Macina	30	Gg	14.30N	5.00W
McIntosh	45	Fd	45.55N	101.21W
Macintyre River	59	Je	29.25S	148.45 E
Maçka	24	Hb	40.50N	39.38 E
Mackay [Austl.]	58	Fg	21.09S	149.11 E
Mackay [Id.-U.S.]	46	Ie	43.55N	113.37W
Mackay, Lake-	57	Dg	22.30S	129.00 E
McKay Lake	45	Mb	49.35N	86.22W
McKean Atoll	57	Je	3.36S	174.08W
McKeand	42	Kd	63.00N	65.05W
McKeesport	44	He	40.21N	79.52W
Mackenzie	38	Fc	69.15N	134.08W
McKenzie	44	Cg	36.08N	88.31W
Mackenzie, District of- [3]	42	Gd	65.00N	115.00W
Mackenzie Bay [Ant.]	66	Fe	68.20S	71.15 E
Mackenzie Bay [Can.]	38	Fc	69.00N	136.30W
McKenzie Island	42	If	51.05N	93.48W
Mackenzie King	38	Hb	77.45N	111.00W
Mackenzie Mountains	38	Gc	64.00N	130.00W
McKenzie River	46	Dd	44.07N	123.06W
Mackenzie River	59	Jd	24.00S	149.55 E
McKerrow, Lake-	62	Cf	44.30S	168.05 E
Mackinac, Straits of-	43	Kb	45.49N	82.45W
Mackinaw City	44	Ec	45.47N	84.44W
McKinley, Mount-	38	Dc	63.30N	151.00W
McKinley Park	40	Jd	63.44N	148.54W
McKinney	45	Hj	33.12N	96.37W
Mackinnon Road	36	Gc	3.44S	39.03 E
McLaughlin	45	Fd	45.49N	100.49W
McLean	45	Fi	35.14N	100.36W
McLeans Town	44	Il	26.39N	77.59W
Maclean Strait	42	Ha	77.30N	103.10W
Maclear	37	Df	31.02S	28.23 E
Macleay River	59	Kf	30.52S	153.01 E
Mc Leod, Lake-	57	Cg	24.10S	113.35 E
McLeod Bay	42	Gd	62.53N	110.15W
McLeod Lake	42	Ff	54.59N	123.02W
McLoughlin, Mount-	46	De	42.27N	122.19W
McLure	46	Ea	51.03N	120.14W
Macmillan	42	Dd	62.52N	135.55W
McMillan, Lake-	45	Dj	32.40N	104.20W
McMillan Pass	42	Ed	63.00N	130.00W
McMinnville [Or.-U.S.]	46	Dd	45.13N	123.12W
McMinnville [Tn.-U.S.]	44	Eh	35.41N	85.46W
McMurdo	66	Kf	77.51S	166.37 E
McNaughton Lake	42	Ff	52.40N	117.50W
Macomb	45	Kf	40.27N	90.40W
Macomer	14	Cj	40.16N	8.47 E
Macomia	37	Gb	12.15S	40.08 E
Mâcon	11	Kh	46.18N	4.50 E
Macon [Ga.-U.S.]	39	Kf	32.50N	83.38W
Macon [Mo.-U.S.]	45	Jg	39.44N	92.28W
Macon [Ms.-U.S.]	45	Lj	33.07N	88.34W
Macondo	36	De	12.36S	23.43 E
Mâconnais, Monts du-	11	Kh	46.18N	4.45 E
Macorís, Cabo-	49	Ld	19.47N	70.28W
Macouba	51h	Ab	14.52N	61.09W
McPherson	43	Hd	38.22N	97.40W
Mc Pherson Range	59	Ke	28.20S	153.00 E
Macquarie	66	Jd	54.30S	158.30 E
Macquarie Harbour	59	Jh	42.20S	145.25 E
Macquarie Ridge (EN)	3	Jo	57.00S	159.00 E
Macquarie River	57	Fh	30.07S	147.24 E
Mac Robertson Land	66	Fe	70.00S	65.00 E
Macroom/Maigh Chromtha	9	Ej	51.54N	8.57W
Macugnaga	14	Be	45.58N	7.58 E
Macujer	54	Dc	0.24N	73.07W
Macuro	50	Fg	10.39N	61.56W
Macusani	54	Df	14.05S	70.26W
Macuspana	48	Mi	17.48N	92.36W
Mačva	15	Ce	44.49N	19.30 E
McVicar Arm	42	Fc	65.10N	120.30W
Ma'dabā	24	Fg	31.43N	35.48 E
Madagali	34	Hc	10.53N	13.38 E
Madagascar	30	Lj	20.00S	47.00 E
Madagascar (EN) = Madagasikara [1]	31	Lj	19.00S	46.00 E
Madagascar Basin (EN)	3	Fl	27.00S	53.00 E
Madagascar Plateau (EN)	3	Fm	30.00S	45.00 E
Madagasikara = Madagascar (EN) [1]	31	Lj	19.00S	46.00 E
Madā'in Şāliḩ	24	Gi	26.48N	37.53 E
Madalai	64a	Ac	7.20N	134.28 E
Madama	34	Ha	21.58N	13.39 E
Madan	15	Hh	41.30N	24.57 E
Madang	58	Fe	5.13S	145.48 E
Madanīyīn	31	Ie	33.21N	10.30 E
Madanīyīn [3]	32	Jc	33.00N	10.45 E
Madaoua	34	Gc	14.05N	5.58 E
Madara	15	Kf	43.17N	27.06 E
Madara-Shima	29	Ae	33.35N	129.45 E
Madaroumfa	34	Gc	13.18N	7.09 E
Madau	63a	Ac	9.00S	152.26 E
Madawaska Highlands	44	Hc	45.20N	78.15W
Maddalena	14	Di	41.15N	9.25 E
Maddalena, Colle della-	11	Mj	44.25N	6.53 E
Maddaloni	14	Ii	41.02N	14.23 E
Made, Made en Drimmelen-	12	Gc	51.41N	4.48 E
Made en Drimmelen	12	Gc	51.41N	4.48 E
Made en Drimmelen-Made	12	Gc	51.41N	4.48 E
Madeir	35	Dd	7.50N	29.12 E
Madeira [5]	31	Fe	32.40N	16.45W
Madeira	30	Fe	32.44N	17.00W
Madeira, Arquipélago da- = Madeira Islands (EN)	30	Fe	32.40N	16.45W
Madeira, Rio-	52	Kf	3.22S	58.45W
Madeira Islands (EN) = Madeira, Arquipélago da-	30	Fe	32.40N	16.45W
Madeleine, Ile de la -	42	Lg	47.26N	61.44W
Madeleine, Monts de la-	11	Jh	46.03N	3.50 E
Maden	24	Hc	38.23N	39.40 E
Madenassa Veld	30	Jj	19.00N	25.30 E
Madera [Ca.-U.S.]	46	Eh	36.57N	120.03W
Madera [Mex.]	47	Cc	29.12N	108.07W
Mader-Chih	13	Ri	35.26N	5.07 E
Madero, Puerto del-	13	Jc	41.48N	2.05W
Madesimo	14	Dd	46.26N	9.21 E
Madgaon	25	Ee	15.22N	73.49 E
Madhya Pradesh [3]	25	Fd	22.00N	79.00 E
Madimba	36	Cc	4.58S	15.08 E
Madina do Boé	34	Cc	11.45N	14.13W
Madinani	34	Dd	9.37N	6.57W
Madīnat al Abyār	33	Dc	32.11N	20.36 E
Madīnat ash Sha'b	22	Gh	12.50N	44.56 E
Madingo-Kayes	36	Bc	4.10S	12.18 E
Madingou	36	Bc	4.09S	13.34 E
Madirovalo	37	Hc	16.29S	46.30 E
Madison [Fl.-U.S.]	44	Fj	30.28N	83.25W
Madison [In.-U.S.]	44	Ef	38.44N	85.23W
Madison [Mn.-U.S.]	45	Hd	45.01N	96.11W
Madison [S.D.-U.S.]	45	He	44.00N	97.07W
Madison [Wi.-U.S.]	39	Ke	43.05N	89.22W
Madison [W.V.-U.S.]	44	Gf	38.03N	81.50W
Madison Range	46	Jd	45.15N	111.20W
Madison River	46	Jd	45.56N	111.30W
Madisonville	43	Jd	37.20N	87.30W
Madiun	26	Fh	7.37S	111.31 E
Mado Gashi	36	Gb	0.44N	39.10 E
Madoi (Huangheyan)	22	Lf	35.00N	98.56 E
Madon	11	Mf	48.36N	6.06 E
Madona	7	Gh	56.53N	26.20 E
Madra Dağı	15	Kj	39.23N	27.12 E
Madrakah, Ra's al-	23	If	18.59N	57.45 E
Madranbaba Dağı	15	Ll	37.38N	28.12 E
Madras [India]	22	Kh	13.05N	80.17 E
Madras [Or.-U.S.]	46	Ed	44.38N	121.08W
Madre, Laguna- [Mex.]	47	Ed	25.00N	97.40W
Madre, Laguna- [Tx.-U.S.]	43	Hf	27.00N	97.35W
Madre, Sierra-	38	Jh	15.20N	92.20W
Madre de Dios [2]	54	Df	12.00S	70.15W
Madre de Dios	54	Df	12.36S	69.59W
Madre de Dios, Isla-	52	Ik	50.15S	75.05W
Madre de Dios, Río-	52	Jg	10.59S	66.08W
Madre del Sur, Sierra- = Southern Sierra Madre (EN)	38	Jj	17.00N	100.00W
Madre Occidental, Sierra- = Western Sierra Madre (EN)	38	Ig	25.00N	105.00W
Madre Oriental, Sierra- = Eastern Sierra Madre (EN)	38	Jg	22.00N	99.30W
Madrid [3]	13	Id	40.30N	3.40W
Madrid	6	Fg	40.24N	3.41W
Madrid-Aravaca	13	Id	40.27N	3.47W
Madridejos	13	Ie	39.28N	3.32W
Madrid-El Pardo	13	Id	40.32N	3.46W
Madrid-Vallecas	13	Id	40.23N	3.37W
Madrid-Villaverde	13	Id	40.21N	3.42W
Madrigal de las Altas Torres	13	Hc	41.05N	5.00W
Mad River	46	Cf	40.57N	124.07W
Madriz [3]	49	Dg	13.30N	86.30W
Madrona, Sierra-	13	Hf	38.25N	4.10W
Madula	36	Eb	0.28N	25.23 E
Madura, Palau-	21	Nj	7.00S	113.20 E
Madurai	22	Ji	9.56N	78.07 E
Madvār, Kūh-e-	23	Hc	30.36N	54.52 E
Madwīn	33	Cd	28.42N	17.31 E
Madyan	21	Fg	27.40N	35.35 E
Madžalis	16	Oh	42.08N	47.50 E
Maebara	29	Be	33.34N	130.13 E
Maebashi	27	Od	36.23N	139.04 E
Mae Hong Son	25	Je	19.16N	97.56 E
Mæl	8	Ce	59.56N	8.48 E
Mae Nam Khong = Mekong (EN)	21	Mh	10.15N	105.55 E
Maesawa	29	Gb	39.03N	141.07 E
Mae Sot	25	Je	16.40N	98.35 E
Maestra, Sierra-	38	Lh	20.00N	76.45W
Maevatanana	37	Hc	16.56S	46.49 E
Maéwo, Ile-	57	Hf	15.10S	168.10 E
Mafeteng	37	De	29.45S	27.18 E
Mafia Channel	36	Gd	7.50S	39.35 E
Mafia Island	30	Ki	7.50S	39.50 E
Mafikeng	31	Jk	25.53S	25.39 E
Mafra [Braz.]	56	Kc	26.07S	49.49W
Mafra [Port.]	13	Cf	38.56N	9.20W
Magadan	22	Rd	59.34N	150.48 E
Magadanskaja Oblast [3]	20	Kd	62.30N	154.00 E
Magadi	36	Gc	1.54S	36.17 E
Magallanes, Estrecho de- = Magellan, Strait of- (EN)	52	Ik	54.00S	71.00W
Magallanes y Antártica Chilena [2]	56	Fh	51.30S	73.30W
Magangué	54	Db	9.14N	74.46W
Maganik	15	Cg	42.44N	19.16 E
Maganoy	26	He	6.51N	124.31 E
Magaria	34	Gc	12.59N	8.50 E
Magazine Mountain	45	Ji	35.10N	93.38W
Magdagači	20	Hf	53.29N	125.55 E
Magdala	55	Bm	36.06S	61.42W
Magdalena [2]	54	Db	10.00N	74.15W
Magdalena [Arg.]	55	Dl	35.04S	57.32W
Magdalena [Bol.]	54	Ff	13.20S	64.08W
Magdalena [Mex.]	47	Bb	30.38N	110.57W
Magdalena [N.M.-U.S.]	45	Ci	34.07N	107.14W
Magdalena, Bahía-	48	Ce	24.35N	112.00W
Magdalena, Isla-	47	Bd	24.55N	112.15W
Magdalena, Llano de la-	47	Bd	24.30N	111.40W
Magdalena, Río- [Col.]	52	Id	11.06N	74.51W
Magdalena, Río- [Mex.]	48	Cb	30.48N	112.32W
Magda Plateau	42	Jb	72.18N	82.55W
Magdeburg	6	He	52.10N	11.40 E
Magdeburger Börde	10	Hd	52.00N	11.30 E
Magdelaine Cays	57	Gf	16.35S	150.15 E
Magee	45	Lk	31.52N	89.44W
Magee, Island-/Oileán Mhic Aodha	9	Hg	54.50N	5.50W
Magelang	26	Fh	7.28S	110.13 E
Magellan, Strait of- (EN) = Magallanes, Estrecho de-	52	Ik	54.00S	71.00W
Magellan Seamounts (EN)	57	Gc	17.30N	152.00 E
Magenta	14	Ce	45.28N	8.53 E
Magerøya	7	Fa	71.03N	25.45 E
Magetan	26	Fh	7.39S	111.20 E
Maggiorasca	14	Df	44.33N	9.29 E
Maggiore, Lago-	14	Ce	45.55N	8.40 E
Maghāghah	33	Fd	28.39N	30.50 E
Maghama	32	Ef	15.31N	12.50W
Maghera/Machaire Rátha	9	Gg	54.51N	6.40W
Maghnia	32	Gc	34.51N	1.44W
Magic Reservoir	46	He	43.20N	114.18W
Mágina, Sierra-	13	Ig	37.45N	3.30W
Magistralny	20	Fe	56.03N	107.35 E
Maglaj	14	Mf	44.33N	18.06 E
Măglenik	15	Ih	41.20N	25.45 E
Maglie	14	Mj	40.07N	18.18 E
Măgliž	15	Ig	42.36N	25.33 E
Magnetawan River	44	Gc	45.46N	80.37W
Magnetic Island	59	Jc	19.10S	146.50 E
Magnitka	17	Ii	55.21N	59.43 E
Magnitnaja, Gora-	17	Ij	53.10N	59.10 E
Magnitogorsk	6	Le	53.27N	59.04 E
Magnolia	45	Jj	33.16N	93.14W
Magnor	7	Cg	59.57N	12.12 E
Magny-en-Vexin	11	He	49.09N	1.47 E
Mago	20	Jf	53.18N	140.20 E
Mágoé	37	Ec	15.48S	31.43 E
Magoebaskloof	37	Ed	23.51S	30.02 E
Magog	44	Kc	45.16N	72.09W
Magosa = Famagusta (EN)	23	Dc	35.07N	33.57 E
Magra [Alg.]	13	Qi	35.29N	4.58 E
Magra [It.]	14	Df	44.03N	9.58 E
Magtá Lahjar	32	Ef	17.50N	13.20W
Maguarinho, Cabo-	54	Id	0.20S	48.20W
Magude	37	Ee	25.02S	32.40 E
Magumeri	34	Hc	12.07N	12.49 E
Magura, Gora-	10	Th	48.50N	23.44 E
Magway	25	Jd	20.00N	95.00 E
Magway	22	Lg	20.09N	94.55 E
Magyarország = Hungary (EN) [1]	6	Hf	47.00N	20.00 E
Mahābād	23	Gb	36.45N	45.53 E
Mahabalipuram	25	Gf	12.37N	80.12 E
Mahabe	37	Hc	17.05S	45.20 E
Mahabo	37	Gd	20.21S	44.39 E
Mahačkala	6	Kg	42.58N	47.30 E
Mahadday Wēyne	35	He	3.00N	45.32 E
Mahādeo Range	25	Ee	17.50N	74.15 E
Mahafaly, Plateau-	37	Gd	24.30S	44.00 E
Mahagi	36	Fb	2.18N	30.59 E
Mahajamba	37	Hc	15.33S	47.08 E
Mahājan	25	Ec	28.47N	73.50 E
Mahajanga	31	Lj	15.17S	46.43 E
Mahajanga [3]	37	Hc	16.30S	47.00 E
Mahajilo	37	Hc	19.42S	45.22 E
Mahakam	21	Nj	0.35S	117.17 E
Mahalapye	37	Dd	23.07S	26.46 E
Mahalevona	37	Hc	15.26S	49.55 E
Mahallāt	24	Nf	33.55N	50.27 E
Mahamid	35	Cb	15.09N	20.25 E
Māhān	24	Qg	30.05N	57.19 E
Mahānadi	21	Kg	20.19N	86.45 E
Mahanoro	37	Hc	19.53S	48.49 E
Mahārāshtra [3]	25	Ee	18.00N	75.00 E
Mahārlū, Daryācheh-ye-	24	Oh	29.25N	52.50 E
Maḩās	35	He	4.24N	46.07 E
Maha Sarakham	25	Ke	16.12N	103.16 E
Mahavavy	30	Lj	15.57S	45.54 E
Mahbés	32	Dd	27.10N	9.50W
Maḩḑah	24	Pj	24.24N	55.59 E
Mahdia	54	Gb	5.16N	59.09W
Mahe	25	Ff	11.42N	75.32 E
Mahébourg	37a	Bb	20.24S	57.42 E
Mahé Island	30	Mi	4.40S	55.28 E
Mahendra Giri	25	Ge	18.58N	84.21 E
Mahenge	31	Ki	8.41S	36.43W
Maheno	62	Df	45.10S	170.50 E
Mahesāna	25	Ed	23.36N	72.24 E
Mahi	25	Ed	22.16N	72.58 E
Mahia Peninsula	61	Eg	39.10S	177.55 E
Mahmudābād	24	Lc	39.25N	47.15 E
Mahmūdābād	24	Od	36.38N	52.15 E
Mahmūd-e 'Erāqī	23	Kb	35.01N	69.20 E
Mahmudiye	24	Dc	39.30N	31.00 E
Mahmutşevketpaşa	15	Mh	41.09N	29.11 E
Māhneshān	24	Ld	36.45N	47.38 E
Mahnevo	17	Jg	58.27N	61.42 E
Mahnomen	45	Ic	47.19N	95.59W
Mahón/Mao	13	Qe	39.53N	4.15 E
Mahoré/Mayotte	30	Lj	12.50S	45.10 E
Mahrāt, Jabal-	35	Ib	17.00N	52.00 E
Mahuan Dao	27	Kd	10.50N	115.47 E
Mahua Point	63a	Fd	10.28S	162.05 E
Maiana Atoll	57	Id	0.55N	173.00 E
Maïao, Ile- (Tubai-Manu)	57	Lf	17.34S	150.35W
Maicao	54	Da	11.23N	72.15W
Maicasagi, Lac-	44	Ia	49.52N	76.48W
Maîche	11	Mg	47.15N	6.48 E
Maicuru, Rio-	54	Hd	2.10S	54.17W
Maidenhead	12	Bc	51.31N	0.42W
Maidstone	9	Nj	51.17N	0.32 E
Maiduguri	31	Ig	11.51N	13.09 E
Maigh Chromtha/Macroom	9	Ej	51.54N	8.57W
Maigudo	35	Fd	7.26N	37.10 E
Maihara	29	Ed	35.20N	136.18 E
Maikala Range	25	Gd	22.30N	81.30 E
Maiko	36	Eb	0.14N	25.33 E
Maikona	36	Gb	2.56N	37.38 E
Maikoor, Pulau-	26	Jh	6.15S	134.15 E
Main	10	Ef	50.00N	8.18 E
Maínalon Óros	15	Fl	37.40N	22.15 E

Index Symbols

[1] Independent Nation	Historical or Cultural Region	Pass, Gap	Depression	Coast, Beach	Rock, Reef	Waterfall Rapids	Canal	Lagoon	Escarpment, Sea Scarp	Historic Site	Port
[2] State, Region	Mount, Mountain	Plain, Lowland	Polder	Cliff	Islands, Archipelago	River Mouth, Estuary	Glacier	Bank	Fracture	Ruins	Lighthouse
[3] District, County	Volcano	Delta	Desert, Dunes	Peninsula	Rocks, Reefs	Lake	Ice Shelf, Pack Ice	Seamount	Trench, Abyss	Wall, Walls	Mine
[4] Municipality	Hill	Salt Flat	Forest, Woods	Isthmus	Coral Reef	Salt Lake	Ocean	Tablemount	National Park, Reserve	Church, Abbey	Tunnel
[5] Colony, Dependency	Mountains, Mountain Range	Valley, Canyon	Heath, Steppe	Sandbank	Well, Spring	Intermittent Lake	Sea	Ridge	Point of Interest	Temple	Dam, Bridge
Continent	Hills, Escarpment	Crater, Cave	Oasis	Island	Geyser	Reservoir	Gulf, Bay	Shelf	Recreation Site	Scientific Station	
Physical Region	Plateau, Upland	Karst Features	Cape, Point	Atoll	River, Stream	Swamp, Pond	Strait, Fjord	Basin	Cave, Cavern	Airport	

Index Symbols

[1] Independent Nation
[2] State, Region
[3] District, County
[4] Municipality
[5] Colony, Dependency
Continent
Physical Region
Historical or Cultural Region
Mount, Mountain
Volcano
Hill
Mountains, Mountain Range
Hills, Escarpment
Plateau, Upland
Pass, Gap
Plain, Lowland
Delta
Salt Flat
Valley, Canyon
Crater, Cave
Karst Features
Depression
Polder
Desert, Dunes
Forest, Woods
Heath, Steppe
Oasis
Cape, Point
Coast, Beach
Cliff
Peninsula
Isthmus
Sandbank
Island
Atoll
Rock, Reef
Islands, Archipelago
Rocks, Reefs
Coral Reef
Well, Spring
Geyser
River, Stream
Waterfall Rapids
River Mouth, Estuary
Lake
Salt Lake
Intermittent Lake
Reservoir
Swamp, Pond
Canal
Glacier
Ice Shelf, Pack Ice
Ocean
Sea
Gulf, Bay
Strait, Fjord
Lagoon
Bank
Seamount
Tablemount
Ridge
Shelf
Basin
Escarpment, Sea Scarp
Fracture
Trench, Abyss
National Park, Reserve
Point of Interest
Recreation Site
Cave, Cavern
Historic Site
Ruins
Wall, Walls
Church, Abbey
Temple
Scientific Station
Airport
Port
Lighthouse
Mine
Tunnel
Dam, Bridge

Manicoré, Rio- 54 Fe 5.51S 61.19W
Manicouagan 42 Kg 49.10N 68.15W
Manicouagan 42 Kf 51.00N 68.20W
Manicouagan, Réservoir- 38 Md 51.30N 68.19W
Manigotagan 45 Ha 51.06N 96.18W
Manihi Atoll 57 Mf 14.24S 145.56W
Manihiki Anchorage 64n Ab 10.23S 161.03W
Manihiki Atoll 57 Kf 10.24S 161.01W
Manika, Plateau de la- 36 Ed 10.00S 26.00 E
Manila [Phil.] 22 Oh 14.35N 121.00 E
Manila [Ut.-U.S.] 46 Kf 40.59N 109.43W
Manila Bay 21 Oh 14.30N 120.45 E
Manilaid/Manilajd 8 Kf 58.08N 24.03 E
Manilajd/Manilaid 8 Kf 58.08N 24.03 E
Manily 20 Ld 62.30N 165.20 E
Maningrida Settlement 59 Gb 12.05S 134.10 E
Maniouro, Pointe- 63b Dc 17.41S 168.35 E
Manipa, Selat- 26 Ig 3.20S 127.23 E
Manipur [3] 25 Id 25.00N 94.00 E
Manipur 25 Id 22.52N 94.05 E
Manisa 23 Cb 38.36N 27.26 E
Manisa Dağı 15 Kk 38.33N 27.28 E
Manises 13 Le 39.29N 0.27W
Manissau a-Missu, Rio- 54 Hf 10.58S 53.20W
Manistee 44 Dc 44.15N 86.18W
Manistee River 44 Dc 44.15N 86.21W
Manistique 43 Jb 45.57N 86.15W
Manitique Lake 44 Eb 46.15N 85.45W
Manitoba [3] 42 Hf 55.00N 97.00W
Manitoba, Lake- 38 Jd 51.00N 98.45W
Manitou Islands 44 Ec 45.10N 86.00W
Manitou Lake 44 Gc 45.48N 82.00W
Manitoulin Island 42 Jg 45.45N 82.30W
Manitou Springs 45 Dg 38.52N 104.55W
Manitouwadge 45 Nb 49.08N 85.47W
Manitowoc 43 Jc 44.06N 87.40W
Manitsoq/Sukkertoppen 41 Ge 65.25N 53.00W
Maniwaki 42 Jg 46.23N 75.58W
Manizales 53 Ie 5.05N 75.32W
Manja 17 Jd 64.23N 60.50 E
Manja 37 Gd 21.23S 44.20 E
Manjača 14 Lf 44.35N 17.05 E
Manjacaze 37 Ed 24.42S 33.33 E
Manjakandriana 37 Hc 18.55S 47.47 E
Manji 29a Bb 43.09N 141.59 E
Manjimup 59 Df 34.14S 116.09 E
Mānjra 25 Fe 18.49N 77.52 E
Män Kät 25 Jd 22.05N 98.01 E
Mankato [Ks.-U.S.] 45 Gg 39.47N 98.12W
Mankato [Mn.-U.S.] 43 Ic 44.10N 94.01W
Mankono 34 Dd 8.04N 6.12W
Mankono [3] 34 Dd 7.58N 6.02W
Mankoya 31 Jj 14.50S 25.00 E
Manley Hot Springs 40 Ic 65.00N 150.37W
Manlleu 13 Ob 42.00N 2.17 E
Manmād 25 Ed 20.15N 74.27 E
Manmanoc, Mount- 26 Hc 17.40N 121.06 E
Manna 26 Dh 4.27S 102.55 E
Mannahill 59 Hf 32.26S 139.59 E
Mannar 25 Fg 8.59N 79.54 E
Mannar, Gulf of- 21 Ji 8.30N 79.00 E
Mannheim 6 Gf 49.29N 8.28 E
Manning [Alta.-Can.] 42 Fe 56.55N 117.33W
Manning [S.C.-U.S.] 44 Gi 33.42N 80.12W
Manning, Cape- 64g Ba 2.02N 157.26W
Manning Strait 63a Db 7.24S 158.04 E
Manningtree 12 Dc 51.57N 1.04 E
Mann Ranges 59 Fe 26.00S 129.30 E
Mann River 59 Gb 12.20S 134.07 E
Mannu, Capo- 14 Cj 40.02N 8.22 E
Mannu, Rio- [It.] 14 Cj 40.50N 8.23 E
Mannu, Rio- [It.] 14 Cj 40.41N 8.59 E
Mano 34 Cd 6.56N 11.31W
Mano [Jap.] 29 Fc 37.58N 138.20 E
Mano [S.L.] 34 Cd 7.55N 12.00W
Manoa 54 Ee 9.40S 65.27W
Man of War, Cayos- 49 Fg 13.02N 83.22W
Manokwari 58 Ee 2.30S 134.36 E
Manombo 37 Gd 22.55S 43.28 E
Manompana 37 Hc 16.41S 49.45 E
Manonga 36 Fc 4.08S 34.12 E
Manono 31 Ji 7.18S 27.25 E
Manono 65c Aa 13.50S 172.05W
Manosque 11 Lk 43.50N 5.47 E
Manouane, Lac- 42 Kf 50.40N 70.45W
Manō-Wan 29 Fc 37.55N 138.15 E
Manp'ojin 28 Id 41.09N 126.17 E
Manra Atoll (Sydney) 57 Je 4.27S 171.15W
Manresa 13 Nc 41.44N 1.50 E
Mansa 31 Jj 11.12S 28.53 E
Mansa Konko 34 Bc 13.28N 15.33W
Mansel 38 Lc 62.00N 79.50W
Mansfield [Austl.] 59 Jg 37.03S 146.05 E
Mansfield [Eng.-U.K.] 9 Lh 53.09N 1.11W
Mansfield [La.-U.S.] 45 Jj 32.02N 93.43W
Mansfield [Oh.-U.S.] 43 Kc 40.46N 82.31W
Mansfield [Pa.-U.S.] 44 Ie 41.47N 77.05W
Mansfield, Mount- 44 Kc 44.33N 72.49W
Mansle 11 Gi 45.52N 0.11 E
Manso, Rio- 55 Db 14.42S 56.16W
Manso, Rio- ou Mortes, Rio das- 52 Kg 11.45S 50.44W
Mansôa 34 Bc 12.04N 15.19W
Mansourah 13 Qh 36.04N 4.28 E
Mansourah, Djebel- 13 Qh 36.02N 4.28 E
Manta 54 Bd 0.57S 80.42W
Manta, Bahía de- 54 Bd 0.50S 80.40W
Mantalingajan, Mount- 26 Ge 8.48N 117.40 E
Manteca 46 Eh 37.48N 121.13W
Mantecal [Ven.] 50 Di 6.52N 65.38W
Mantecal [Ven.] 50 Bi 7.33N 69.09W
Manteigas 13 Ed 40.24N 7.32W
Manteo 44 Jh 35.55N 75.40W
Mantes-la-Jolie 11 Hf 48.59N 1.43 E
Manti 46 Jg 39.16N 111.38W
Mantiqueira, Serra da- 52 Lh 22.00S 44.45W
Manto 49 Df 14.55N 86.23W
Manton 44 Ec 44.24N 85.24W
Mantova 14 Ee 45.09N 10.48 E
Mäntsälä 8 Kd 60.38N 25.20 E
Mänttä 7 Fe 62.02N 24.38 E
Mantua 49 Eb 22.17N 84.17W
Manturovo 19 Ed 58.22N 44.44 E
Mäntyharju 7 Gf 61.25N 26.53 E
Mäntyluoto 8 Ic 61.35N 21.29 E
Manu 54 Df 12.15S 70.50W
Manuae Atoll 57 Lf 19.21S 158.56W
Manua Islands 57 Kf 14.13S 169.35W
Manuangi Atoll 57 Mf 19.12S 141.16W
Manūbah 14 En 36.48N 10.06 E
Manuel 48 Jf 22.44N 98.19W
Manuel Alves, Rio- 54 If 11.19S 48.28W
Manuel Bonavides 48 Hc 29.05N 103.55W
Manuel Derqui 55 Ch 27.50S 58.48W
Manuel J. Cobo 55 Dl 35.49S 57.54W
Manuel Ocampo 55 Bk 33.46S 60.39W
Manuga Reefs 63a Ad 11.00S 153.21 E
Manui, Pulau- 26 Hg 3.35S 123.08 E
Manujān 24 Qi 27.24N 57.32 E
Mānūk, Tell- 24 Hf 33.10N 38.50 E
Manukau 58 Ih 36.56S 174.56 E
Manulu Lagoon 64g Bb 1.56N 157.20W
Manus Island 57 Fe 2.05S 147.00 E
Many 45 Jk 31.34N 93.29W
Manyara, Lake- 36 Gc 3.35S 35.50 E
Manyas 24 Bb 40.02N 27.58 E
Manyč 5 Kf 47.15N 40.00 E
Manyč-Gudilo, Ozero- 5 Kf 46.25N 42.35 E
Manyoni 36 Fd 5.45S 34.50 E
Manzanal, Puerto del- 13 Fb 42.32N 6.10W
Manzanares 13 Ie 39.00N 3.22W
Manzaneda, Cabeza de- 13 Eb 42.20N 7.15W
Manzanilla 13 Fg 37.23N 6.25W
Manzanillo [Cuba] 39 Lg 20.21N 77.07W
Manzanillo [Mex.] 39 Ih 19.03N 104.20W
Manzanillo, Bahía de- [Dom.Rep.] 49 Ld 19.45N 71.46W
Manzanillo, Bahía de- [Mex.] 48 Gh 19.04N 104.25W
Manzanillo, Punta- 49 Hi 9.38N 79.32W
Manzano Mountains 45 Ci 34.45N 106.20W
Manzhouli 22 Ne 49.33N 117.28 E
Manzilah, Buḩayrat al- 24 Eg 31.15N 32.00 E
Manzil Bū Ruqaybah 32 Ib 37.10N 9.48 E
Manzil bū Zalafah 14 En 36.41N 10.35 E
Manzil Tamīn 14 En 36.47N 10.59 E
Manzini 37 Ee 26.29S 31.22 E
Mao 63b Dc 17.29S 168.29 E
Mao [Chad] 31 Ig 14.07N 15.19 E
Mao [Dom.Rep.] 47 Je 19.34N 71.05W
Mao/Mahón 13 Qe 39.53N 4.15 E
Maoke, Pegunungan- 57 Ee 4.00S 138.00 E
Maomao Shan 27 Hd 37.12N 103.10 E
Maoming 22 Ng 21.41N 110.52 E
Maoniu Shan 27 He 32.50N 104.12 E
Maotou Shan 27 Hg 24.31N 100.38 E
Maouri, Dallol- 34 Fc 12.05N 3.32 E
Mapai 37 Ed 22.51S 31.58 E
Mapanda 36 Dd 9.32S 24.16 E
Mapati 36 Bc 3.38S 13.21 E
Mapi 58 Ee 7.07S 139.23 E
Mapi 26 Kh 7.00S 139.16 E
Mapia, Kepulauan- 26 Jf 0.50N 134.20 E
Mapimi, Bolsón de- 38 Ig 27.30N 103.15W
Mapinhane 37 Fd 22.15S 35.07 E
Mapire 50 Di 7.45N 64.42W
Mapiri 54 Eg 15.15S 68.10W
Maple Creek 42 Gg 49.55N 109.27W
Maprik 60 Ch 3.38S 143.03 E
Mapuera, Rio- 54 Gd 1.05S 57.02W
Maputo [3] 37 Ee 26.00S 32.30 E
Maputo (Lourenço Marques) 31 Kk 25.58S 32.34 E
Maputo, Baia de- 30 Kk 26.05S 33.00 E
Maqên (Dawu) 27 He 34.29N 100.01 E
Maqran, Wādī al- 33 Ie 20.55N 47.12 E
Maqu 27 He 34.05N 101.45 E
Maquan He/Damqog Kanbab 27 Df 29.36N 84.09 E
Maquela do Zombo 31 Ii 6.03S 15.08 E
Maquinchao 56 Gf 41.15S 68.44W
Maquoketa 45 Ke 42.04N 90.40W
Mar, Serra do- 52 Lh 25.00S 48.00W
Mara 36 Fc 1.31S 33.56 E
Mara [3] 36 Fc 2.30S 34.00 E
Maraã 54 Ed 1.50S 65.22W
Marab 35 Fc 14.54N 37.55 E
Marabá 54 Ie 5.21S 49.07W
Marabahan 26 Fg 3.00S 114.45 E
Marabá Paulista 55 Gf 22.06S 51.56W
Maraca, Ilha de- 54 Hc 2.05N 50.25W
Maracaibo 53 Id 10.40N 71.37W
Maracaibo, Lago de- = Maracaibo, Lake- (EN) 52 Ie 9.50N 71.30W
Maracaibo, Lake- (EN) = Maracaibo, Lago de- 52 Ie 9.50N 71.30W
Maracaju 54 Gh 21.38S 55.09W
Maracaju, Serra de- [Braz.] 52 Kh 21.00S 55.00W
Maracaju, Serra de- [S.Amer.] 55 Ef 23.57S 55.01W
Maracanã 54 Id 0.46S 47.27W
Maracás 54 Jf 13.26S 40.27W
Maracay 53 Jd 10.15N 67.36W
Marādah 33 Cd 29.14N 19.13 E
Maradi 31 Hg 13.29N 7.06 E
Maradi [2] 34 Gc 14.15N 7.15 E
Marāgheh 23 Gb 37.23N 46.40 E
Marāh 23 Gd 25.04N 45.28 E
Maraho 35 Bb 18.21N 17.28 E
Marahuaca, Cerro- 52 Je 3.34N 65.27W
Marajó, Baía de- 52 Lf 1.00S 48.30W
Marajó, Ilha de- 52 Lf 1.00S 49.30W
Marakei Atoll 57 Id 1.58N 173.25 E
Maralal 36 Gb 1.06N 36.42 E
Maralinga 59 Gf 30.13S 131.35 E
Maralwexi/Bachu 27 Cd 39.46N 78.15 E
Maramag 26 He 7.46N 125.00 E
Maramasike Island 60 Gi 9.30S 161.25 E
Maramba 31 Jj 17.51S 25.52 E
Marampa 34 Cd 8.41N 12.28W
Maramureş [2] 15 Gb 47.40N 24.00 E
Maranchón 13 Jc 41.03N 2.12W
Marānd 23 Gb 38.26N 45.46 E
Marang 26 De 5.12N 103.13 E
Maranhão [2] 54 Je 5.00S 45.00W
Maranhão, Rio- 54 If 14.34S 49.02W
Marano, Laguna di- 14 He 45.44N 13.10 E
Maranoa River 59 Je 27.50S 148.37 E
Marañón, Rio- 52 If 4.30S 73.35W
Marans 11 Fh 46.18N 1.00W
Marão 37 Ed 24.18S 34.07 E
Marão, Serra do- 13 Ec 41.15N 7.55W
Maraoué 34 Dd 6.54N 5.31W
Marapanim 54 Id 0.42S 47.42W
Marapi, Gunung- 26 Dg 0.23S 100.28 E
Marargiu, Capo- 14 Cj 40.20N 8.23 E
Marari, Serra do- 55 Gh 27.30S 51.00W
Mara Rosa 55 Ha 13.58S 49.09W
Mărăşeşti 15 Kd 45.53N 27.14 E
Maratea 14 Jk 39.59N 15.43 E
Marathón 15 Gk 38.09N 23.58 E
Marathon 45 Ek 30.12N 103.15W
Marathon 42 Ig 48.46N 86.26W
Maratua, Pulau- 26 Gf 2.15N 118.36 E
Marau 55 Fi 28.27S 52.12W
Maravari 63a Cb 7.54S 156.44 E
Marāveh Tappeh 24 Pd 37.55N 55.57 E
Maravilha 55 Fh 26.47S 53.09W
Maravillas Creek 45 El 29.34N 102.47W
Maravovo 63a Dc 9.17S 159.38 E
Marāwah 33 Dc 32.29N 21.25 E
Marawi 26 He 8.13N 124.15 E
Marawi 35 Eb 18.29N 31.49 E
Marāwiḩ 24 Oj 24.18N 53.18 E
Marayes 56 Gd 31.29S 67.20W
Marbella 13 Hh 36.31N 4.53W
Marble Bar 59 Dd 21.11S 119.44 E
Marble Canyon 46 Jh 36.30N 111.50W
Marble Falls 45 Gk 30.34N 98.17W
Marble Hall 37 Dd 24.57S 29.13 E
Marburg an der Lahn 10 Ef 50.49N 8.46 E
Marca, Ponta da- 30 Ij 16.31S 11.42 E
Marcal 10 Ni 47.38N 17.32 E
Marcala 49 Df 14.07N 88.00W
Marçal Dağları 15 Kl 37.09N 28.00 E
Marcali 10 Nj 46.35N 17.25 E
March 10 Mh 48.10N 16.59 E
March 9 Ni 52.33N 0.06 E
Marche 11 Hh 46.10N 1.30 E
Marche = Marches (EN) [2] 14 Hh 43.30N 13.15 E
Marche, Plateau de la- 11 Hh 46.16N 1.30 E
Marche-en-Famenne 11 Ld 50.14N 5.20 E
Marchena 13 Gg 37.20N 5.24W
Marchena, Isla- 54a Aa 0.20N 90.30W
Marches (EN) = Marche [2] 14 Hh 43.30N 13.15 E
Marchesato 14 Kk 39.05N 17.00 E
Marchfeld 14 Kb 48.15N 16.40 E
Mar Chiquita, Laguna- 55 Dm 37.37S 57.24W
Mar Chiquita, Laguna- 52 Ji 30.42S 62.36W
Marciana Marina 14 Eh 42.48N 10.12 E
Marcigny 11 Kh 46.16N 4.02 E
Marcilly-sur-Eure 12 Df 48.49N 1.21 E
Marcinelle, Charleroi- 12 Gd 50.25N 4.28 E
Marck 12 Dd 50.57N 1.57 E
Marcoing 12 Fd 50.07N 3.11 E
Marcos Juaréz 56 Hd 32.42S 62.06W
Marcus Baker, Mount- 40 Jd 61.26N 147.45W
Marcus Island (EN) = Minami-Tori-Shima 57 Gb 26.32N 142.09 E
Marcy, Mount- 43 Mc 44.07N 73.56W
Mardakert 16 Oi 40.12N 46.52 E
Mardakjan 16 Qi 40.29N 50.12 E
Mardān 25 Eb 34.12N 71.52 E
Mardarovka 15 Mb 47.30N 29.40 E
Mar del Plata 53 Ki 38.01S 57.35W
Marden 12 Cc 51.10N 0.30 E
Mardin 23 Fb 37.18N 40.44 E
Mardın Dağları 24 Id 37.20N 41.00 E
Maré, Ile- 57 Hg 21.30S 168.00 E
Mare, Muntele- 15 Gc 46.29N 23.14 E
Marechal Cândido Rondon 55 Eg 24.34S 54.04W
Maree, Loch- 9 Hd 57.40N 5.30W
Mareeba 59 Jc 17.00S 145.26 E
Märëg 35 He 3.47N 47.18 E
Maremma 14 Fh 42.30N 11.30 E
Marennes 11 Ei 45.49N 1.07W
Marettimo 14 Gm 37.56N 12.05 E
Mareuil-en-Brie 12 Ff 48.57N 3.45 E
Marfa 43 Ge 30.18N 104.01W
Marfil, Laguna- 55 Bb 15.30S 60.20W
Margai Caka 27 Ed 35.10N 86.55 E
Marganec 19 Df 47.38N 34.40 E
Margaret River 59 Df 33.57S 115.04 E
Margarida 55 De 21.41S 56.44W
Margarita, Isla de- 54 Fa 11.00N 64.00W
Margarita Belén 55 Ch 27.16S 58.58W
Margarition 15 Dj 39.21N 20.26 E
Margate [Eng.-U.K.] 9 Oj 51.24N 1.24 E
Margate [S.Afr.] 37 Ef 30.55S 30.15 E
Marghera, Venezia- 14 Ge 45.28N 12.44 E
Margherita 30 Jh 0.23N 29.54 E
Margherita di Savoia 14 Ki 41.22N 16.09 E
Marghine, Catena del- 14 Cj 40.20N 8.50 E
Marghita 15 Fb 47.21N 22.20 E
Marghūb, Kūh-e- 24 Qf 33.06N 57.30 E
Margilan 19 Hg 40.28N 71.46 E
Margina 15 Fd 45.51N 22.16 E
Marguerite Bay 66 Qe 68.30S 68.30W
Margut 12 He 49.35N 5.16 E
Marha 20 Hd 60.35N 123.10 E
Marha 21 Nc 63.20N 118.50 E
Mari 24 Ie 34.39N 40.53 E
Mari 24 Ee 34.44N 33.18 E
Maria Atoll [W.F.] 57 Ng 22.00S 136.10W
Maria Atoll [W.F.] 57 Lg 21.48S 154.41W
Maria Cleofas, Isla- 48 Fg 21.16N 106.14W
Maria Elena 56 Gb 22.21S 69.40W
Mariager 8 Ch 56.39N 10.00 E
Mariager Fjord 8 Dh 56.40N 10.20 E
Maria Grande, Arroyo- 55 Ci 29.21S 58.45W
Maria Ignacia 55 Cm 37.24S 59.30W
Maria Island [Austl.] 59 Jh 42.40S 148.05 E
Maria Island [Austl.] 59 Hb 14.55S 135.40 E
Maria Island [St.Luc.] 51k Bb 13.44N 60.56W
Mariakani 36 Gc 3.52S 39.28 E
Maria Laach 12 Jd 50.25N 7.15 E
Maria Madre, Isla- 48 Fg 21.35N 106.33W
Maria Magdalena, Isla- 48 Fg 21.25N 106.25W
Mariana Islands 57 Fc 16.00N 145.30 E
Marianao 47 Hd 23.05N 82.26W
Mariana Trench (EN) 3 Ih 14.00N 147.30 E
Marianna [Ar.-U.S.] 45 Ki 34.46N 90.46W
Marianna [Fl.-U.S.] 44 Ej 30.47N 85.14W
Mariannelund 8 Fg 57.37N 15.34 E
Mariano I. Loza 55 Ci 29.22S 58.12W
Mariánské Lázně 10 Ig 49.58N 12.43 E
Marías, Islas- 38 Ig 21.25N 106.28W
Marias Pass 46 Ib 48.19N 113.21W
Marias River 43 Eb 47.56N 110.30W
Maria Theresa Reef 57 Lh 36.58S 151.23W
Mariato, Punta- 47 Hg 7.13N 80.53W
Maria van Diemen, Cape- 62 Ea 34.29S 172.39 E
Mariazell 14 Jc 47.46N 15.19 E
Ma'rib 23 Gf 15.30N 45.20 E
Maribo 8 Dj 54.46N 11.31 E
Maribor 14 Jd 46.33N 15.39 E
Marica 5 Ig 40.52N 26.12 E
Marica 15 Ig 42.02N 25.50 E
Maricao 51a Bb 18.10N 66.58W
Maricopa 46 Ij 33.04N 112.03W
Marīdī [3] 35 Dd 6.05N 29.24 E
Marīdī 35 De 4.55N 29.28 E
Marié, Rio- 54 Ed 0.25S 66.26W
Marie Byrd Land (EN) 66 Nf 80.00S 120.00W
Mariec 7 Lh 56.31N 49.51 E
Marie Galante 47 Le 15.56N 61.16W
Marie-Galante, Canal de- 51e Bc 15.55N 61.25W
Mariehamn/Maarianhamina 7 Ef 60.06N 19.57 E
Marie Louise Island 37b Bb 6.11S 53.09 E
Mariembourg, Couvin- 12 Gd 50.06N 4.31 E
Marienburg 12 Jd 50.04N 7.08 E
Marienmünster 12 Lc 51.50N 9.13 E
Marienstatt 12 Jd 50.40N 7.49 E
Mariental 31 Ik 24.36S 17.59 E
Mariestad 7 Cg 58.43N 13.51 E
Marietta [Ga.-U.S.] 43 Ke 33.57N 84.33W
Marietta [Oh.-U.S.] 44 Gf 39.26N 81.27W
Mariga 34 Gd 9.36N 5.57 E
Marignac 11 Gl 42.55N 0.39 E
Marignane 11 Lk 43.25N 5.13 E
Marigot [Dom.] 50 Fe 15.32N 61.18W
Marigot [Guad.] 50 Ec 18.04N 63.06W
Marigot [Haiti] 49 Kd 18.14N 72.19W
Marigot [Mart.] 51h Ab 14.49N 61.02W
Marigot [St.Luc.] 51k Ab 13.58N 61.02W
Mariinsk 20 De 56.13N 87.45 E
Mariinski Posad 7 Lh 56.08N 47.48 E
Mariinskoje 20 Jf 51.43N 140.19 E
Marijampole (Kapsukas) 7 Fi 54.33N 23.23 E
Marijskaja respublika 19 Ed 56.40N 48.00 E
Marilia 56 Jb 22.13S 50.01W
Mariluz 55 Fg 24.02S 53.13W
Marimba 36 Cd 8.22S 17.02 E
Marimbondo, Cachoeira do- 55 He 20.18S 49.10W
Marín 13 Db 42.23N 8.42W
Marin, Cul-de-Sac du- 51h Bc 14.27N 60.53W
Marina di Catanzaro 14 Kl 38.49N 16.36 E
Marina di Gioiosa Ionica 14 Kl 38.18N 16.20 E
Marina di Pisa 14 Eg 43.40N 10.16 E
Marina di Ravenna 14 Gf 44.29N 12.17 E
Marina Gorka 19 Ce 53.31N 28.12 E
Marinduque 26 Hd 13.24N 121.58 E
Marineland 44 Gk 29.43N 81.12W
Marines 12 De 49.09N 1.59 E
Marinette 43 Jb 45.06N 87.38W
Maringá 53 Kh 23.25S 51.55W
Maringa 30 Ih 1.14N 19.48 E
Marinha Grande 13 De 39.45N 8.56W
Marino [It.] 14 Gi 41.46N 12.39 E
Marino [Van.] 63b Db 14.59S 168.03 E
Marins, Pico dos- 55 Jf 22.27S 45.10W
Marinsko 8 Mf 58.46N 28.39 E
Marion 30 Km 46.36S 37.55 E
Marion [Al.-U.S.] 44 Di 32.32N 87.26W
Marion [Ia.-U.S.] 45 Ke 42.02N 91.36W
Marion [Il.-U.S.] 45 Lh 37.44N 88.56W
Marion [In.-U.S.] 44 Ee 40.33N 85.40W
Marion [Oh.-U.S.] 43 Kc 40.35N 83.08W
Marion [S.C.-U.S.] 44 Hh 34.11N 79.23W
Marion [Va.-U.S.] 44 Gg 36.51N 81.30W
Marion, Lake- 43 Gi 33.30N 80.25W
Marion Reefs 57 Gf 19.10S 152.20 E
Maripa 54 Fa 7.26N 65.09W
Mariposa 46 Fh 37.29N 119.58W
Mariquita, Cerro- 48 Jf 23.13N 98.22W
Marisa 26 Hf 0.28N 121.56 E
Mariscala 55 El 34.03S 54.47W
Mariscal Estigarribia 56 Hb 22.02S 60.38W
Mariupol' 6 Jf 47.06N 37.33 E
Mariusa, Caño 50 Fh 9.43N 61.26W
Mariusa, Isla- 50 Fh 9.39N 61.19W
Marivan 24 Le 35.31N 46.10 E
Märjamaa/Marjamaa 8 Kf 58.54N 24.21 E
Marjamaa/Märjamaa 8 Kf 58.54N 24.21 E
Marjanovka 19 He 54.58N 72.38 E
Marjanovka 10 Uf 50.23N 24.55 E
Mark 12 Gc 51.39N 4.39 E
Mark [Ger.] 12 Jc 51.13N 7.36 E
Mark [Swe.] 8 Eg 57.35N 12.35 E
Marka 31 Lh 1.43N 44.46 E
Markako, Ozero- 19 If 48.45N 85.50 E
Markam (Gartog) 27 Gf 29.32N 98.33 E
Markaryd 7 Ch 56.26N 13.36 E
Markazi [3] 23 Hb 35.30N 51.30 E
Marken 12 Hb 52.27N 5.05 E
Markerwaard 12 Hb 52.31N 5.15 E
Market Deeping 12 Bb 52.40N 0.18W
Market Harborough 9 Mi 52.29N 0.55W
Markham, Mount- 66 Kg 82.51S 161.21 E
Markham Bay 42 Kd 63.30N 71.40W
Markham River 59 Ja 6.35S 146.25 E
Marki 10 Rd 52.20N 21.07 E
Märkische Schweiz 10 Jd 52.35N 14.00 E
Markit 27 Cd 38.53N 77.35 E
Markounda 35 Bd 7.37N 16.59 E
Markovac 15 Ee 44.14N 21.06 E
Markovka 16 Ke 49.31N 39.32 E
Markovo 22 Tc 64.40N 170.25 E
Markoye 34 Fc 14.39N 0.02 E
Marksburg 12 Jd 50.16N 7.40 E
Marksville 45 Jk 31.08N 92.04W
Marktoberdorf 10 Gi 47.47N 10.37 E
Marktredwitz 10 If 50.00N 12.05 E
Markuleşty 15 Lb 47.51N 28.07 E
Marl 10 De 51.39N 7.05 E
Marlagne 12 Gd 50.25N 4.40 E
Marlborough [2] 62 Ed 41.50S 173.40 E
Marlborough [Austl.] 59 Jd 22.49S 149.53 E
Marlborough [Guy.] 50 Gi 7.29N 58.38W
Marle 11 Je 49.44N 3.46 E
Marlin 45 Hk 31.18N 96.53W
Marlinton 44 Gf 38.14N 80.06W
Marlow [Eng.-U.K.] 12 Bc 51.34N 0.46W
Marlow [Ok.-U.S.] 45 Hi 34.39N 97.57W
Marmande 11 Gj 44.30N 0.10 E
Marmara 24 Bb 40.35N 27.33 E
Marmara, Sea of- (EN) = Marmara Denizi 5 Ig 40.40N 28.15 E
Marmara Adasi 24 Bb 40.38N 27.37 E
Marmara Denizi = Marmara, Sea of- (EN) 5 Ig 40.40N 28.15 E
Marmara Ereğlisi 15 Ki 40.58N 27.57 E
Marmara Gölü 15 Lk 38.37N 28.02 E
Marmarica (EN) = Barqah al Bahriyah 30 Je 31.40N 24.30 E
Marmaris 23 Cb 36.51N 28.16 E
Marmelos, Rio- 54 Fe 6.08S 61.47W
Marmion Lake 45 Kb 48.54N 91.30W
Marmolada 14 Fd 46.26N 11.51 E
Marmora 44 Ic 44.29N 77.41W
Marmore, Cascata delle- 14 Gh 42.35N 12.45 E
Marne 10 Ec 53.57N 9.00 E
Marne 5 Gf 48.49N 2.24 E
Marne [3] 11 Kf 48.55N 4.10 E
Marne à la Saône, Canal de la- 11 Kf 48.44N 4.36 E
Marne au Rhin, Canal de la- 11 Nf 48.35N 7.47 E
Mårnes 7 Dc 67.09N 14.06 E
Marneuli 16 Ni 41.29N 44.45 E
Maro 35 Bd 8.25N 18.46 E
Maro 35 Bb 19.23N 16.38 E
Maroa 54 Ec 2.43N 67.33W
Maroantsetra 31 Lj 15.27S 49.44 E
Marokau Atoll 61 Mc 18.02S 142.17W
Marolambo 37 Hd 20.04S 48.08 E
Maromandia 37 Hb 14.11S 48.06 E
Maromme 11 He 49.28N 1.02 E
Maromokotro 37 Hb 14.01S 48.58 E
Maroni, Fleuve- 52 Ke 5.45N 53.58W
Marónia 15 Ii 40.55N 25.31 E
Maronne 11 Hi 45.04N 1.56 E
Maroochydore 59 Ke 26.39S 153.06 E
Maro Reef 57 Jb 25.25N 170.35W
Maros 15 Dc 46.15N 20.12 E
Maros 26 Gg 5.00S 119.34 E
Maroua 31 Ig 10.36N 14.20 E
Marovoay 37 Hc 16.06S 46.37 E
Marowijne River 52 Ke 5.45N 53.58W
Marqādah 24 Ie 35.44N 40.46 E
Mar Qu 27 He 31.58N 101.54 E
Marquard 37 De 28.54S 27.28 E
Marquenterre 12 Dd 50.20N 1.41 E
Marquesas Islands (EN) = Marquises, Iles- 57 Ne 9.00S 139.30W
Marquette 43 Jb 46.33N 87.24W
Marquion 12 Fd 50.13N 3.05 E
Marquis [Gren.] 51p Bb 12.06N 61.37W
Marquis [St.Luc.] 51k Ba 14.02N 60.55W
Marquis, Cape- 51k Ba 14.03N 60.54W
Marquise 12 Dd 50.49N 1.42 E
Marquises, Iles- = Marquesas Islands (EN) 57 Ne 9.00S 139.30W
Marracuene 37 Ee 25.44S 32.41 E
Marradi 14 Ff 44.04N 11.37 E
Marrah, Jabal- 30 Jg 13.04N 24.21 E
Marrak 33 Hf 16.26N 41.54 E
Marrakech 31 Ge 31.38N 8.00W
Marrakech [3] 32 Fc 32.00N 8.00W
Marrawah 59 Ih 40.56S 144.41 E
Marree 58 Eg 29.39S 138.04 E
Marreh, Kūh-e- 24 Oh 29.15N 52.20 E
Marrero 45 Kl 29.54N 90.07W
Marresalja 17 Mb 69.44N 66.59 E
Marresalskije Koški, Ostrova- 17 Mb 69.30N 67.10 E
Marromeu 37 Fc 18.17S 35.56 E
Marrti 7 Gc 67.28N 28.22 E
Marrupa 37 Fb 13.12S 37.30 E
Marsá al 'Alam 33 Fd 25.05N 34.54 E
Marsá al Burayqah 33 Cc 30.25N 19.35 E

Index Symbols

[1] Independent Nation
[2] State, Region
[3] District, County
[4] Municipality
[5] Colony, Dependency
Continent
Physical Region
Historical or Cultural Region
Mount, Mountain
Volcano
Hill
Mountains, Mountain Range
Hills, Escarpment
Plateau, Upland
Pass, Gap
Plain, Lowland
Delta
Salt Flat
Valley, Canyon
Crater, Cave
Karst Features
Depression
Polder
Desert, Dunes
Forest, Woods
Heath, Steppe
Oasis
Cape, Point
Coast, Beach
Cliff
Peninsula
Isthmus
Sandbank
Island
Atoll
Rock, Reef
Islands, Archipelago
Rocks, Reefs
Coral Reef
Well, Spring
Geyser
River, Stream
Waterfall Rapids
River Mouth, Estuary
Lake
Salt Lake
Intermittent Lake
Reservoir
Swamp, Pond
Canal
Glacier
Ice Shelf, Pack Ice
Ocean
Sea
Gulf, Bay
Strait, Fjord
Lagoon
Bank
Seamount
Tablemount
Ridge
Shelf
Basin
Escarpment, Sea Scarp
Fracture
Trench, Abyss
National Park, Reserve
Point of Interest
Recreation Site
Cave, Cavern
Historic Site
Ruins
Wall, Walls
Church, Abbey
Temple
Scientific Station
Airport
Port
Lighthouse
Mine
Tunnel
Dam, Bridge

Marsá al Uwayjah 33 Cc 30.55N 17.52 E
Marsa Ben Mehidi 13 Ji 35.05N 2.11W
Marsabit 31 Kh 2.20N 37.59 E
Marsala 14 Gm 37.48N 12.26 E
Marsá Sha'b 35 Fa 22.52N 35.47 E
Marsá Umm Ghayj 24 Fj 25.38N 34.30 E
Marsberg 10 Ee 51.27N 8.51 E
Marsciano 14 Gh 42.54N 12.20 E
Marsdiep 12 Gb 52.58N 4.45 E
Marseille=Marseilles (EN) 6 Gg 43.18N 5.24 E
Marseille-en-Beauvaisis 11 He 49.35N 1.57 E
Marseilles (EN)=Marseille 6 Gg 43.18N 5.24 E
Marshall [Ak.-U.S.] 40 Gd 61.52N 162.04W
Marshall [Ar.-U.S.] 45 Ji 35.55N 92.38W
Marshall [Il.-U.S.] 45 Mg 39.23N 87.42W
Marshall [Lbr.] 34 Cd 6.09N 10.23W
Marshall [Mn.-U.S.] 43 Hc 44.27N 95.47W
Marshall [Mo.-U.S.] 45 Jg 39.07N 93.12W
Marshall [Tx.-U.S.] 43 Ie 32.33N 94.23W
Marshall Islands [5] 58 Hd 9.00N 168.00 E
Marshall Islands 57 Hd 9.00N 168.00 E
Marshall River 59 Hd 22.59S 136.59 E
Marshalltown 43 Ic 42.03N 92.54W
Marshfield 45 Kd 44.40N 90.10W
Marsh Harbour 47 Ic 26.33N 77.03W
Mārshinān, Kūh-e- 24 Of 32.53N 52.24 E
Marsh Island 45 Kl 29.35N 91.53W
Marsica 14 Hi 41.55N 13.35 E
Marsico Nuovo 14 Jj 40.25N 15.44 E
Marsjaty 17 Jf 60.05N 60.29 E
Marsland 45 Ee 42.29N 103.16W
Mars-la-Tour 12 He 49.06N 5.54 E
Marson 12 Gf 48.55N 4.32 E
Märsta 8 Ge 59.37N 17.51 E
Marstal 8 Dj 54.51N 10.31 E
Marstrand 8 Dg 57.53N 11.35 E
Marta 14 Fh 42.14N 11.42 E
Martaban 25 Je 16.32N 97.37 E
Martaban, Gulf of- (EN) 21 Lh 16.30N 97.00 E
Martap 34 Hd 6.54N 13.03 E
Martapura [Indon.] 26 Dg 4.19S 104.22 E
Martapura [Indon.] 26 Fg 3.25S 114.51 E
Martelange/Martelingen 12 He 49.50N 5.44 E
Martelingen/Martelange 12 He 49.50N 5.44 E
Martés, Sierra de- 13 Le 39.20N 0.57W
Martha's Vineyard 43 Mc 41.25N 70.40W
Martigny 14 Bd 46.06N 7.05 E
Martigues 11 Lk 43.24N 5.03 E
Martil 13 Gi 35.37N 5.17W
Martim Vaz, Ilhas- 52 Nh 20.30S 28.51W
Martin 13 Lc 41.18N 0.19W
Martin [Czech.] 10 Og 49.04N 18.55 E
Martin [S.D.-U.S.] 43 Gc 43.10N 101.44W
Martin [Tn.-U.S.] 44 Cg 36.21N 88.51W
Martina Franca 14 Lj 40.42N 17.20 E
Martinez de Hoz 55 Bl 35.19S 61.37W
Martínez de la Torre 48 Kg 20.04N 97.03W
Martín García, Isla- 55 Cl 34.11S 58.15W
Martin Hills 66 Pg 82.04S 88.01W
Martinho Campos 55 Jd 19.20S 45.13W
Martinique 38 Mh 14.40N 61.00W
Martinique [5] 39 Mh 14.40N 61.00W
Martinique, Canal de la-=Martinique Passage (EN) 47 Le 15.10N 61.20W
Martinique Passage 50 Fe 15.10N 61.20W
Martinique Passage (EN)=Martinique, Canal de la- 47 Le 15.10N 61.20W
Martin Lake 44 Ei 32.50N 85.55W
Martin Peninsula 66 Of 74.25S 114.10W
Martinsburg 44 If 39.28N 77.59W
Martins Ferry 44 Ge 40.07N 80.45W
Martinsville [In.-U.S.] 44 Df 39.26N 86.25W
Martinsville [Va.-U.S.] 43 Ld 36.43N 79.53W
Marton 62 Fd 40.05S 175.23 E
Martos 13 Ig 37.43N 3.58W
Martre, Lac la- 42 Fd 63.20N 118.00W
Martuk 19 Fe 50.47N 56.31 E
Martuni 16 Ni 40.06N 45.18 E
Maru 34 Gc 12.21N 6.24 E
Marud 25 Ee 18.19N 72.58 E
Marudi 26 Ff 4.11N 114.19 E
Marudu, Teluk- 26 Ge 6.45N 116.55 E
Marugame 29 Cd 34.18N 133.47 E
Maruko 29 Fc 36.19N 138.15 E
Mārūn 24 Mg 31.02N 49.36 E
Marungu, Monts- 30 Ji 7.42S 30.00 E
Maruoka 29 Ec 36.09N 136.16 E
Maruseppu 29a Ca 44.01N 143.19 E
Marutea Atoll [W.F.] 57 Ng 21.30S 135.34W
Marutea Atoll [W.F.] 57 Mf 17.00S 143.10W
Maruyama-Gawa 29 Dd 35.40N 134.50 E
Marvão 13 Ee 39.24N 7.23W
Marvast 24 Pg 30.30N 54.15 E
Marvast, Kavīr-e- 24 Pg 30.20N 54.25 E
Mårvatn 8 Cd 60.10N 8.15 E
Marv-Dasht 23 Hd 29.50N 52.40 E
Marvejols 11 Jj 44.33N 3.17 E
Marvine, Mount- 46 Jg 38.40N 111.39W
Marx 16 Od 51.42N 46.46 E
Mary 22 If 37.36N 61.50 E
Maryborough [Austl.] 58 Gg 25.32S 152.42 E
Maryborough [Austl.] 59 Ig 37.03S 143.45 E
Marydale 37 Ce 29.23S 22.05 E
Maryjskaja Oblast [3] 19 Gh 37.15N 62.30 E
Maryland [2] 43 Ld 39.00N 76.45W
Maryland [3] 34 De 4.45N 8.00W
Maryport 9 Jg 54.43N 3.30W
Mary River 59 Gb 12.53S 131.38 E
Marysville [Ca.-U.S.] 46 Eg 39.09N 121.35W
Marysville [Ks.-U.S.] 45 Hg 39.51N 96.39W
Marysville [N.B.-Can.] 44 Nc 45.59N 66.35W
Marysville [Oh.-U.S.] 44 Fe 40.13N 83.22W
Marysville [Wa.-U.S.] 46 Db 48.03N 122.11W
Maryville [Mo.-U.S.] 43 Ic 40.21N 94.52W
Maryville [Tn.-U.S.] 44 Fh 35.46N 83.58W
Marzūq 31 If 25.55N 13.55 E
Marzūq, Ḩamādat- 33 Bd 26.00N 12.30 E
Marzuq, Şaḩrā'- 30 If 24.30N 13.00 E
Masachapa 49 Dh 11.47N 86.31W
Masāhīm, Kūh-e- 24 Pg 30.21N 55.20 E
Masai Steppe 30 Ki 4.45S 37.00 E
Masaka 36 Fc 0.20S 31.44 E
Masākin 32 Jb 35.44N 10.35 E
Masalembo, Kepulauan- 26 Fh 5.30S 114.26 E
Masally 19 Eh 39.01N 48.40 E
Masalog, Puntan- 64b Ba 15.01N 145.41 E
Masan 27 Md 35.11N 128.24 E
Masasi 31 Kj 10.43S 38.48 E
Masaya [3] 49 Dh 12.00N 86.10W
Masaya 47 Gf 11.58N 86.06W
Masbate 21 Oh 12.15N 123.30 E
Masbate 26 Hd 12.10N 123.35 E
Mascara 32 Hb 35.24N 0.08 E
Mascara [3] 32 Hb 35.30N 0.15 E
Mascareignes, Iles-/Mascarene Islands 30 Mk 21.00S 57.00 E
Mascarene Basin (EN) 3 Fk 15.00S 56.00 E
Mascarene Islands/Mascareignes, Iles- 30 Mk 21.00S 57.00 E
Mascarene Plateau (EN) 3 Gk 10.00S 60.00 E
Mascota 48 Gg 20.32N 104.49W
Masela, Pulau- 26 Ih 8.09S 129.50 E
Maseru 31 Jk 29.28S 27.29 E
Maşfūţ 24 Qk 24.48N 56.06 E
Mashābih 24 Gj 25.37N 36.32 E
Mashan 28 Kb 45.12N 130.32 E
Mashava 37 Ed 20.02S 30.29 E
Mashhad 22 Hf 36.18N 59.36 E
Mashike 28 Pc 43.51N 141.31 E
Mashiki 29 Be 32.47N 130.50 E
Mashīz 24 Qh 29.56N 56.37 E
Mashkel 21 Ig 28.02N 63.25 E
Mashonaland North [3] 37 Ec 17.00S 31.00 E
Mashonaland South [3] 37 Ec 18.00S 31.00 E
Mashra' ar Raqq 35 Dd 8.25N 29.16 E
Mashū-Ko 29a Db 43.35N 144.30 E
Masiaca 48 Ed 26.45N 109.18W
Masīlah, Wādī al- 21 Hh 15.10N 51.08 E
Masi-Manimba 36 Cc 4.46S 17.55 E
Masindi 36 Fb 1.42N 31.43 E
Maşīrah, Jazīrat- 21 Hg 20.29N 58.33 E
Maşīrah, Khalīj- 21 Hg 20.15N 57.40 E
Masisi 36 Ec 1.24S 28.49 E
Masjed-Soleymān 23 Gc 31.58N 49.18 E
Mask, Lough-/Loch Measca 9 Dh 53.35N 9.20W
Maskanah 24 Hd 36.01N 38.05 E
Maskelynes, Iles- 63b Cc 16.32S 167.49 E
Maslovare 14 Lf 44.34N 17.33 E
Masoala, Cap- 30 Mj 15.59S 50.13 E
Masoala, Presqu'île de- 37 Ic 15.40S 50.12 E
Mason 45 Gk 30.45N 99.14W
Mason Bay 62 Bg 46.55S 167.45 E
Mason City 39 Je 43.09N 93.12W
Masovia (EN)=Mazowsze 5 Ie 52.40N 20.20 E
Masparro, Río- 49 Mi 8.04N 69.26W
Masqaţ=Muscat (EN) 22 Hg 23.29N 58.33 E
Massa 14 Ef 44.01N 10.09 E
Massachusetts [2] 43 Mc 42.15N 71.50W
Massachusetts Bay 44 Ld 42.20N 70.50W
Massaciuccoli, Lago di- 14 Eg 43.50N 10.20 E
Massafra 14 Lj 40.35N 17.07 E
Massaguet 35 Bc 12.28N 15.26 E
Massakori 35 Bc 13.00N 15.44 E
Massa Marittima 14 Eg 43.03N 10.53 E
Massangano 36 Bd 9.37S 14.17 E
Massangena 37 Ed 21.32S 32.57 E
Massapê 54 Jd 3.31S 40.19W
Massawa (EN)=Mitsiwa 31 Kg 15.37N 39.39 E
Massena 43 Mc 44.56N 74.57W
Massénya 35 Bc 11.24N 16.10 E
Masset 42 Ef 54.02N 132.09W
Masseube 11 Gk 43.26N 0.35 E
Massey Sound 42 Ia 78.00N 94.00W
Massiac 11 Ji 45.15N 3.13 E
Massiaru 8 Kg 57.52N 24.27 E
Massillon 44 Ge 40.48N 81.32W
Massinga 37 Fd 23.20S 35.22 E
Masson Island 66 Ge 66.08S 96.34 E
Massuma 36 De 14.05S 22.00 E
Mastābah 33 Ge 20.49N 39.26 E
Maštaga 16 Pi 40.32N 49.59 E
Masterton 61 Eh 40.57S 175.39 E
Mastūrah 33 Ge 23.06N 38.50 E
Masuda 27 Ne 34.40N 131.51 E
Māsūleh 24 Md 37.10N 48.59 E
Masurai, Gunung- 26 Dg 2.30S 101.51 E
Masuria (EN) 5 Ie 53.50N 21.30 E
Masurian Lakes (EN) 5 Ie 53.45N 21.45 E
Maşyāf 24 Ge 35.03N 36.21 E
Maszewo 10 Lc 53.29N 15.02 E
Mataabé, Cap- 63b Cb 15.38S 166.46 E
Matabeleland North [3] 37 Dc 19.00S 27.30 E
Matabeleland South [3] 37 Dd 21.00S 29.30 E
Matachel 13 Ff 38.50N 6.17W
Matachewan 42 Jg 47.56N 80.39W
Matacu 55 Bc 17.21S 61.28W
Matadi 31 Ii 5.49S 13.27 E
Matador 45 Fi 34.01N 100.49W
Matagalpa [3] 49 Eg 13.00N 85.30W
Matagalpa 39 Kh 12.53N 85.57W
Matagami 42 Jg 49.45N 77.35W
Matagami, Lac- 44 Ia 49.54N 77.32W
Mata Gassīle 35 Ge 2.30N 42.16 E
Matagorda Bay 45 Hl 28.35N 96.20W
Matagorda Island 43 Hf 28.15N 96.30W
Matagorda Peninsula 45 Hl 28.32N 96.07W
Mataiea 65e Fc 17.46S 149.25W
Mataiva Atoll 57 Mf 14.53S 148.40W
Mataj 19 Hf 45.51N 78.43 E
Matak, Pulau- 26 Ef 3.18N 106.16 E
Matakana Island 62 Gb 37.35S 176.05 E
Matala 36 Ce 14.43S 15.02 E
Matalaa, Pointe- 64h Bc 13.20S 176.08W
Matale 25 Gg 7.28N 80.37 E
Mataliele 37 Df 30.24S 28.43 E
Matam 34 Cb 15.40N 13.15W
Matamey 34 Gc 13.26N 8.28 E
Matamoros [Mex.] 47 Dc 25.32N 103.15W
Matamoros [Mex.] 39 Jg 25.53N 97.30W
Matana, Danau- 26 Hg 2.28S 121.20 E
Ma'ţan as Sarra 33 De 21.41N 21.52 E
Matancita 48 De 25.09N 111.59W
Matane 42 Kg 48.51N 67.32W
Matankari 34 Fc 13.46N 4.01 E
Matanza 55 Cl 34.33S 58.35W
Matanzas 39 Kg 23.03N 81.35W
Matanzas [3] 49 Gb 22.40N 81.10W
Matão 55 He 21.35S 48.22W
Matapalo, Cabo- 49 Fi 8.23N 83.19W
Matapan, Cape- (EN)=Taínaron, Ákra- 5 Ih 36.23N 22.29 E
Matape, Río- 48 Dc 28.17N 110.41W
Mata Point 64k Bb 19.07S 169.50W
Matara 35 Fc 14.35N 39.28 E
Matara 25 Gg 5.56N 80.33 E
Mataram 22 Nj 8.35S 116.07 E
Mataranka 59 Gb 14.56S 133.07 E
Mataró 13 Oc 41.32N 2.27 E
Matarraña/Matarranya 13 Mc 41.14N 0.22 E
Matarranya/Matarraña 13 Mc 41.14N 0.22 E
Mataso 63b Dc 17.15S 168.25 E
Matatula, Cape- 65c Cb 14.15S 170.34W
Mataura 62 Cg 46.34S 168.44 E
Mataura 62 Cg 46.12S 168.52 E
Mata-Utu 58 Jf 13.17S 176.08W
Mata-Utu, Baie de- 64h Bb 13.19S 176.07W
Matavai 61 Gb 13.28S 172.35W
Matavera 64p Cb 21.13S 159.44W
Mataverj 65d Ab 27.10S 109.27W
Matawai 62 Gc 38.21S 177.32 E
Matawin, Réservoir- 44 Kb 46.45N 73.50W
Matawin, Rivière- 44 Kb 46.55N 72.55W
Maţāy 24 Dh 28.25N 30.46 E
Maţbakhayn 33 Hf 17.29N 41.48 E
Matca 15 Kd 45.51N 27.32 E
Matemo, Ilha- 37 Gb 12.13S 40.36 E
Matera 14 Kj 40.40N 16.36 E
Matese 14 Ii 41.25N 14.20 E
Mátészalka 10 Si 47.57N 22.20 E
Matfors 7 De 62.21N 17.02 E
Matha 11 Fi 45.52N 0.19W
Mathematicians Seamounts (EN) 47 Be 15.30N 111.00W
Matheson 44 Ga 48.32N 80.28W
Mathis 45 Hl 28.06N 97.50W
Mathrákion 15 Cj 39.46N 19.31 E
Mathura 25 Fc 27.30N 77.41 E
Mati 15 Ch 41.39N 19.34 E
Mati 26 Ie 6.57N 126.13 E
Matias Cardoso 55 Kb 14.52S 43.56W
Matías Romero 47 Ee 16.53N 95.02W
Matícora, Río- 49 Lh 11.01N 71.09W
Matina 49 Fh 10.05N 83.17W
Matinha 54 Id 3.06S 45.02W
Māţir 32 Ib 37.03N 9.40 E
Matiyure, Río- 50 Ci 7.36N 67.39W
Matkaselkja 8 Nc 61.57N 30.33 E
Mātmāţah 32 Ic 33.33N 9.58 E
Matnog 26 Hd 12.35N 124.05 E
Mato, Cerro- 50 Di 7.15N 65.14W
Mato, Río- 50 Di 7.09N 65.07W
Matočkin Šar, Proliv- 19 Fa 73.30N 54.55 E
Mato Grosso [2] 54 Gf 14.00S 56.00W
Mato Grosso [Braz.] 55 Dd 18.18S 57.20W
Mato Grosso [Braz.] 53 Kg 15.00S 59.57W
Mato Grosso, Planalto do-=Mato Grosso, Plateau of- (EN) 52 Kg 15.30S 56.00W
Mato Grosso, Plateau of- (EN)=Mato Grosso, Planalto do- 52 Kg 15.30S 56.00W
Mato Grosso do Sul [2] 54 Hg 20.00S 55.00W
Matos Costa 55 Gh 26.27S 51.09W
Matosinhos 13 Dc 41.11N 8.42W
Matou 28 Cj 29.50N 115.32 E
Matov→Qiuxian 28 Cf 36.47N 114.30 E
Mátra 5 Hf 47.53N 19.57 E
Maţrah 23 Ie 23.29N 58.31 E
Matrei in Osttirol 14 Gc 47.00N 12.32 E
Maţrūḩ 31 Je 31.21N 27.14 E
Matsiatra 37 Hd 21.25S 45.33 E
Matsudo 28 Og 35.48N 139.55 E
Matsue 27 Nd 35.28N 133.04 E
Matsukawa [Jap.] 29 Gc 37.40N 140.28 E
Matsukawa [Jap.] 29 Ed 35.36N 137.53 E
Matsu Liehtao 27 Kf 26.05N 119.56 E
Matsumae 29a Bc 41.26N 140.07 E
Matsumae-Hantō 29a Bc 41.40N 140.15 E
Matsumoto 27 Od 36.14N 137.58 E
Matsuo 29 Gb 39.58N 141.02 E
Matsu-Ōminato 29a Bc 41.16N 141.09 E
Matsusaka 28 Ng 34.34N 136.32 E
Matsushima 29 Gb 38.22N 141.04 E
Matsutō 29 Ec 36.31N 136.33 E
Matsuura 29 Ae 33.22N 129.42 E
Matsuyama 22 Pf 33.50N 132.45 E
Matsuzaki 29 Fd 34.44N 138.45 E
Mattagami Lake 44 Gb 47.57N 81.35W
Mattagami River 42 Jf 50.43N 81.30W
Mattawa 42 Jg 46.19N 78.42W
Matterhorn [Eur.] 14 Be 45.58N 7.39 E
Matterhorn [Nv.-U.S.] 46 Hf 41.49N 115.23W
Matthew, Ile- 57 Ig 22.20S 171.20 E
Matthews Ridge 54 Fb 7.30N 60.10W
Matthew Town 47 Jd 20.57N 73.40W
Maţţī, Sabhat- 35 Ia 23.30N 52.00 E
Mattighofen 14 Hb 48.06N 13.09 E
Mattoon 45 Lg 39.29N 88.22W
Matua, Ostrov- 20 Kg 48.00N 153.10 E
Matucana 54 Cf 11.51S 76.24W
Matuku Island 61 Ec 19.10S 179.46 E
Matundu 36 Db 4.21N 23.40 E
Matundu 36 Gd 8.50S 39.30 E
Maturín 53 Je 9.45N 63.11W
Matvejev Kurgan 16 Kf 47.34N 38.55 E
Maua 37 Fb 13.52S 37.09 E
Maubeuge 11 Jd 50.17N 3.58 E
Ma-ubin 25 Je 16.44N 95.39 E
Maudheimvidda 66 Bf 74.00S 8.00W
Maud Seamount (EN) 66 Ce 65.00S 2.35 E
Maués 54 Gd 3.24S 57.42W
Maués, Rio- 54 Gd 3.22S 57.44W
Mau Escarpment 36 Gc 0.40S 36.02 E
Maug Islands 57 Fb 20.01N 145.13 E
Maui Island 57 Lb 20.45N 156.20W
Mauke Island 57 Lg 20.09S 157.23W
Mau Kyun 25 Jf 12.45N 98.20 E
Mauldre 12 Df 48.59N 1.49 E
Maule [2] 56 Fe 35.45S 72.15W
Mauléon 11 Fh 46.55N 0.45W
Mauléon-Licharre 11 Fk 43.14N 0.53W
Maullin 56 Ff 41.38S 73.37W
Maumee 44 Fe 41.34N 83.39W
Maumere 26 Hh 8.37S 122.14 E
Maun 31 Jj 19.58S 23.26 E
Maun 14 If 44.26N 14.55 E
Mauna Kea 57 Lc 19.50N 155.28W
Maunaloa 65a Db 21.08N 157.13W
Mauna Loa 65a Fd 19.28N 155.36W
Maunath 25 Gc 25.40N 82.38 E
Maunawili 65a Db 21.21N 157.47W
Maunga Roa 64p Bb 21.13S 159.48W
Maungdaw 25 Id 20.49N 92.22 E
Mauncir, Lac - 42 Fc 67.30N 125.00W
Maupihaa Atoll (Mopelia, Atoll-) 57 Lf 16.50S 153.55W
Maupin 46 Ed 45.11N 121.05W
Maupiti, Ile- 57 Lf 16.27S 152.15W
Maurepas, Lake- 45 Kk 30.15N 90.30W
Maures 11 Mk 43.16N 6.23 E
Mauriac 11 Ii 45.13N 2.20 E
Maurice, Lake- 59 Ge 29.30S 131.00 E
Maurienne 11 Mi 45.13N 6.30 E
Mauritania (EN)=Mūrītāniyā [1] 31 Fg 20.00N 12.00W
Mauriti 54 Ke 7.23S 38.46W
Mauritius 30 Mk 20.17S 57.33 E
Mauritius [1] 31 Mj 18.00S 57.40 E
Mauron 11 Df 48.05N 2.18W
Maurs 11 Ij 44.43N 2.12 E
Mauston 45 Ke 43.48N 90.05W
Mauthausen 14 Ib 48.14N 14.31 E
Mauzé-sur-le-Mignon 11 Fh 46.12N 0.40W
Mavinga 36 Df 15.47S 20.24 E
Mavita 37 Ec 19.32S 33.09 E
Mavrovoúni [Grc.] 15 Fj 39.37N 22.47 E
Mavrovoúni [Grc.] 15 Gh 41.07N 23.08 E
Mawchi 25 Je 18.49N 97.09 E
Mawei 27 Kf 26.02N 119.30 E
Mawlaik 25 Id 23.38N 94.25 E
Mawlamyine 22 Le 16.30N 97.38 E
Mawqaq 24 Ii 27.25N 41.08 E
Mawr, Wādī- 23 Ff 15.41N 42.42 E
Mawson 66 Fe 67.36S 62.53 E
Mawson Coast 66 Fe 67.40S 63.30 E
Mawson Escarpment 66 Ff 73.05S 68.10 E
Maxcanú 47 Fd 20.35N 90.01W
Maxixe 37 Fd 23.51S 35.21 E
Maxwell Bay 42 Ib 74.32N 89.00W
May, Isle of- 9 Ke 56.10N 2.30W
Maya, Pulau- 26 Eg 1.10S 109.35 E
Mayaguana Island 47 Jd 22.23N 72.57W
Mayaguana Passage 49 Kb 22.32N 73.15W
Mayagüez 47 Ke 18.12N 67.09W
Mayahi 34 Gc 13.58N 7.40 E
Mayama 36 Bc 3.51S 14.54 E
Mayāmey 24 Pd 36.24N 55.42 E
Maya Mountains 47 Ge 16.40N 88.50W
Mayapan 47 Gd 20.38N 89.27W
Mayarí 49 Jc 20.40N 75.41W
Maybell 45 Bf 40.31N 108.05W
Maychew 35 Fc 12.46N 39.34 E
Mayḑ 35 Hc 10.57N 47.06 E
Maydān 24 Ke 34.55N 45.37 E
Maydena 59 Jh 42.55S 146.30 E
Maydī 23 Ff 16.18N 42.48 E
Mayen 10 Df 50.20N 7.13 E
Mayenne 11 Ff 48.18N 0.37W
Mayenne 11 Fg 47.30N 0.32W
Mayenne [3] 11 Ff 48.05N 0.40W
Mayfa'ah 35 Hc 14.16N 47.35 E
Mayfield 44 Cg 36.44N 88.38W
May Glacier 66 Ie 67.00S 130.00 E
Mayi He 28 Jb 45.52N 128.46 E
Maymyo 25 Jd 22.02N 96.28 E
Maynas 54 Dd 3.00S 75.00W
Mayo 39 Fc 63.35N 135.54W
Mayo/Muigheo [2] 9 Dh 53.50N 9.30W
Mayo, Mountains of- 9 Dg 54.05N 9.30W
Mayo, Río- 48 Ed 26.45N 109.47W
Mayo Darlé 34 Hd 6.30N 11.55 E
Mayo-Kébbi 35 Ad 9.18N 13.33 E
Mayo-Kébbi [3] 35 Bd 10.00N 15.30 E
Mayoko 36 Bc 2.18S 12.49 E
Mayon, Mount- 21 Oh 13.15N 123.41 E
Mayor, Puig-/Major, Puig- 13 Oe 39.48N 2.48 E
Mayor Island 62 Gb 37.15S 176.15 E
Mayor Pablo Lagerenza 56 Ha 19.58S 60.45W
Mayotte [5] 31 Lj 12.50S 45.10 E
Mayotte/Mahoré 30 Lj 12.50S 45.10 E
May Pen 47 Ie 17.58N 77.14W
Mayraira Point 26 Hc 18.39N 120.51 E
Mayran, Laguna de- 48 He 25.45N 102.45W
Mayreau Island 51n Bb 12.39N 61.23W
May-sur-Orne 12 Be 49.06N 0.22W
Maysville 44 Ff 38.39N 83.46W
Mayumba [Gabon] 31 Ii 3.25S 10.39 E
Mayumba [Zaire] 36 Ed 7.16S 27.03 E
Mayum La 27 De 30.35N 82.27 E
Mayville 44 Hd 42.15N 79.32W
Mayyit, Al Baḩr al-=Dead Sea (EN) 21 Ff 31.30N 35.30 E
Mazabuka 36 Ef 15.51S 27.46 E
Mazagão 54 Hd 0.07S 51.17W
Mazamet 11 Ik 43.30N 2.24 E
Māzandarān [3] 23 Hb 36.00N 54.00 E
Māzandarān, Daryā-ye-=Caspian Sea (EN) 5 Lg 42.00N 50.30 E
Mazar 27 Cd 36.27N 77.03 E
Mazara del Vallo 14 Gm 37.39N 12.35 E
Mazār-e Sharīf 22 If 36.42N 67.06 E
Mazarrón, Golfo de- 13 Kg 37.30N 1.18W
Mazartag 27 Dd 38.29N 80.50 E
Mazaruni River 54 Gb 6.25N 58.38W
Mazatenango 47 Ff 14.32N 91.30W
Mazatlán 39 Ig 23.13N 106.25W
Mažeikiai/Mažejkjaj 7 Fh 56.20N 22.22 E
Mažejkjaj/Mážeikiai 7 Fh 56.20N 22.22 E
Mazḩafah, Jabal- 24 Fh 28.48N 34.57 E
Maẓhūr, 'Irq al- 24 Ji 27.25N 43.55 E
Mazinga 51c Ab 17.29N 62.58W
Mazirbe 8 Jg 57.40N 22.10 E
Mazoe 37 Ec 17.30S 30.58 E
Mazoe 30 Kj 16.32S 33.25 E
Mazomeno 36 Ec 4.55S 27.13 E
Mazong Shan 27 Gc 41.33N 97.10 E
Mazowsze 10 Qd 52.40N 20.20 E
Mazowsze=Masovia (EN) 5 Ie 52.40N 20.20 E
Mazsalaca 8 Kg 57.45N 24.59 E
Mazunga 37 Dd 21.44S 29.52 E
Mazurskie, Pojezierze- 10 Qc 53.40N 21.00 E
Mazzarino 14 Im 37.18N 14.13 E
Mba 63d Ab 17.32S 177.42 E
Mbabane 31 Kk 26.18S 31.07 E
Mbabo, Tchabal- 34 Hd 7.16N 12.09 E
Mbacké 34 Bc 14.48N 15.55W
Mbaéré 35 Be 3.47N 17.31 E
Mbaïki 31 Ih 3.53N 18.00 E
Mbakaou 34 Hd 6.19N 12.49 E
Mbakaou, Barrage de- 34 Hd 6.25N 13.00 E
Mbala 31 Ki 8.50S 31.22 E
Mbalam 34 He 2.13N 13.49 E
Mbale 31 Kh 1.05N 34.10 E
Mbali 35 Be 4.27N 18.20 E
Mbalmayo 34 He 3.31N 11.30 E
Mbam 30 Ih 4.24N 11.17 E
Mbamba Bay 36 Fe 11.17S 34.46 E
Mbandaka 31 Ih 0.04N 18.16 E
Mbanga 34 Ge 4.30N 9.34 E
Mbanika 63a Dc 9.05S 159.12 E
M'banza Congo 36 Bd 6.16S 14.15 E
Mbanza-Ngungu 31 Ii 5.35S 14.47 E
Mbarangandu 36 Gd 8.57S 37.24 E
Mbarara 36 Fc 0.36S 30.38 E
Mbari 35 Ce 4.34N 22.43 E
Mbatiki 63d Bb 17.46S 179.08 E
Mbava 63a Cb 7.49S 156.37 E
Mbé 34 Hd 7.51N 13.36 E
Mbengga 63d Bc 18.23S 178.08 E
Mbengwi 34 Hd 6.01N 10.00 E
Mbéré 35 Bd 9.07N 16.26 E
Mbeya 31 Ki 8.54S 33.27 E
Mbeya [3] 36 Fd 8.00S 33.30 E
Mbi 35 Be 4.28N 18.07 E
Mbigou 36 Bc 1.53S 11.56 E
Mbinda 31 Ii 2.07S 12.52 E
Mbinga 36 Ge 10.56S 35.01 E
Mbingué 34 Dc 10.00N 5.54W
Mbini 34 Ge 1.34N 9.37 E
Mbini [3] 34 He 1.30N 10.00 E
Mbini 30 Ih 1.30N 10.30 E
Mboki 35 Dd 5.19N 25.58 E
Mbokonimbeti 63a Ec 8.57S 160.05 E
Mbomo 36 Bb 0.24N 14.44 E
Mbomou=Bomu (EN) [3] 35 Cd 5.30N 23.30 E
Mbomou=Bomu (EN) 30 Jh 4.08N 22.26 E
Mborokua 63a Dc 9.02S 158.44 E
Mbour 34 Bc 14.24N 16.58W
Mbout 32 Ef 16.01N 12.35W
Mbozi 36 Fd 9.02S 32.56 E
Mbrés 35 Bd 6.40N 19.48 E
M'Bridge 36 Bd 7.14S 12.52 E
Mbua 63d Bb 16.48S 178.37 E
Mbuji-Mayi 31 Ji 6.09S 23.33 E
Mbulo 63a Dc 8.46S 158.21 E
Mbulu 36 Gc 3.51S 35.32 E
Mburucuyá 55 Ci 28.03S 58.14W
Mbutha 63d Bb 16.39S 179.51 E
Mbuyuni 36 Gd 7.23S 36.32 E
Mbwemburu 36 Gd 9.29S 39.39 E
Mcalester 43 He 34.56N 95.46W
Mcensk 19 De 53.17N 36.32 E
M'Chedallah 13 Qh 36.22N 4.16 E
Mcherrah 32 Gd 27.00N 4.30W
Mchinga 36 Gd 9.44S 39.42 E
Mchinji 36 Fe 13.48S 32.54 E
Mdandu 36 Fd 9.09S 34.42 E
M'Daourouch 14 Bn 36.05N 7.49 E
Mdennah 32 Gd 25.00N 4.50W
Mdiq 13 Gi 35.41N 5.19W
Mead 44 Fa 49.29N 83.50W
Mead, Lake- 43 Ed 36.05N 114.25W
Meade 40 Hb 70.50N 156.25W
Meade 45 Fh 37.17N 100.20W
Meade Peak 46 Je 42.30N 111.15W
Meadow Lake 42 Gf 54.07N 108.20W
Meadville 44 Ge 41.38N 80.10W
Me-akan-Dake 29a Cb 43.23N 143.59 E
Mealhada 13 Dd 40.22N 8.27W

Index Symbols

- [1] Independent Nation
- [2] State, Region
- [3] District, County
- [4] Municipality
- [5] Colony, Dependency
- Continent
- Physical Region
- Historical or Cultural Region
- Mount, Mountain
- Volcano
- Hill
- Mountains, Mountain Range
- Hills, Escarpment
- Plateau, Upland
- Pass, Gap
- Plain, Lowland
- Delta
- Salt Flat
- Valley, Canyon
- Crater, Cave
- Karst Features
- Depression
- Polder
- Desert, Dunes
- Forest, Woods
- Heath, Steppe
- Oasis
- Cape, Point
- Coast, Beach
- Cliff
- Peninsula
- Isthmus
- Sandbank
- Island
- Atoll
- Rock, Reef
- Islands, Archipelago
- Rocks, Reefs
- Coral Reef
- Well, Spring
- Geyser
- River, Stream
- Waterfall Rapids
- River Mouth, Estuary
- Lake
- Salt Lake
- Intermittent Lake
- Reservoir
- Swamp, Pond
- Canal
- Glacier
- Ice Shelf, Pack Ice
- Ocean
- Sea
- Gulf, Bay
- Strait, Fjord
- Lagoon
- Bank
- Seamount
- Tablemount
- Ridge
- Shelf
- Basin
- Escarpment, Sea Scarp
- Fracture
- Trench, Abyss
- National Park, Reserve
- Point of Interest
- Recreation Site
- Cave, Cavern
- Historic Site
- Ruins
- Wall, Walls
- Church, Abbey
- Temple
- Scientific Station
- Airport
- Port
- Lighthouse
- Mine
- Tunnel
- Dam, Bridge

Mealy Mountains 42 Lf 53.20N 59.30W
Meama 65b Ba 19.45S 174.34W
Méan, Havelange- 12 Hd 50.22N 5.20 E
Meande, Reef 26 Ge 8.09N 119.14 E
Meander River 42 Fe 59.02N 117.42W
Meanguera, Isla- 49 Dg 13.12N 87.43W
Mearim, Rio- 52 Lf 3.04S 44.35W
Meath/An Mhí [2] 9 Gh 53.35N 6.40W
Meaux 11 If 48.57N 2.52 E
Mecca (EN)=Makkah 22 Fg 21.27N 39.49 E
Mechara 35 Gd 8.34N 40.28 E
Mechelen/Maasmechelen 12 Hd 50.57N 5.40 E
Mechelen/Malines 11 Kc 51.02N 4.29 E
Mecheraa-Asfa 13 Ni 35.24N 1.03 E
Mecheria 32 Gc 33.33N 0.17W
Mechernich 12 Id 50.36N 6.39 E
Mechongué 55 Cn 38.09S 58.13W
Mecidiye 15 Ji 40.38N 26.32 E
Mecitözü 24 Fb 40.31N 35.19 E
Mecklemburgischer Höhenrücken 10 Ic 53.40N 12.10 E
Mecklenburg 10 Hc 53.30N 12.00 E
Mecklenburger Bucht 10 Hb 54.20N 11.40 E
Mecklenburger Schweiz 10 Ic 53.45N 12.35 E
Mecoacán, Laguna- 48 Mh 18.20N 93.10W
Meconta 37 Fb 14.59S 39.50 E
Mecsek 10 Oj 46.10N 18.18 E
Mecubúri 37 Gb 14.10S 40.31 E
Mecúfi 37 Gb 13.17S 40.33 E
Mecula 37 Fb 12.05S 37.39 E
Médala 32 Ff 15.30N 5.37W
Medan 22 Li 3.35N 98.40 E
Médanos [Arg.] 56 He 38.50S 62.41W
Médanos [Arg.] 55 Ck 33.24S 59.05W
Medanosa, Punta- 56 Gg 48.06S 65.55W
Mede 14 Ce 45.06N 8.44 E
Médéa 32 Hb 36.16N 2.45 E
Médéa [3] 32 Hb 36.20N 3.25 E
Medebach 12 Kc 51.12N 8.43 E
Medellin 26 Hd 11.08N 123.58 E
Medellín 53 Ie 6.15N 75.35W
Medelpad 8 Gb 62.35N 16.15 E
Medemblik 12 Hb 52.46N 5.06 E
Medenica 10 Tg 49.21N 23.45 E
Mederdra 32 Df 16.54N 15.40W
Medetziz 24 Fd 37.25N 34.40 E
Medford [Or.-U.S.] 39 Ge 42.19N 122.52W
Medford [Wi.-U.S.] 45 Kd 45.09N 90.20W
Medgidia 15 Le 44.15N 28.17 E
Medi 35 Ed 5.06N 30.44 E
Media Luna, Arrecife de la- 49 Ff 15.13N 82.36W
Medianeira 55 Eg 25.17S 54.05W
Mediaş 15 Hc 46.10N 24.21 E
Medical Lake 46 Gc 47.34N 117.41W
Medicine Bow 46 Lf 41.54N 106.12W
Medicine Bow Mountains 46 Lf 41.10N 106.25W
Medicine Butte 46 Jf 41.29N 110.48W
Medicine Hat 39 Hd 50.03N 110.40W
Medicine Lake 46 Mb 48.28N 104.24W
Medicine Lodge 45 Gh 37.17N 98.35W
Međimurje 14 Kd 46.25N 16.30 E
Medina (EN)=Al Madīnah [Sau.Ar.] 22 Fg 24.28N 39.36 E
Medina Az-Zahra 13 Hg 37.52N 4.50W
Medinaceli 13 Jc 41.10N 2.26W
Medina del Campo 13 Hc 41.18N 4.55W
Medina de Rioseco 13 Gc 41.53N 5.02W
Medina-Sidonia 13 Gh 36.27N 5.55W
Medininkai/Medininkaj 8 Kj 54.32N 25.46 E
Medinīpur 25 Hd 22.26N 87.20 E
Medio, Arroyo del- 55 Bk 33.16S 60.15W
Mediterranean Sea (EN)= Akdeniz 5 Hh 35.00N 20.00 E
Mediterranean Sea (EN)= Khatikhon, Yam- 5 Hh 35.00N 20.00 E
Mediterranean Sea (EN)= Méditerranée, Mer- 5 Hh 35.00N 20.00 E
Mediterranean Sea (EN)= Mediterraneo, Mar- 5 Hh 35.00N 20.00 E
Mediterranean Sea (EN)= Mediterráneo, Mar- 5 Hh 35.00N 20.00 E
Mediterranean Sea (EN)= Mesoyéios Thálassa 5 Hh 35.00N 20.00 E
Mediterranean Sea (EN)= Mutawassiţ, Al Baḩr al- 5 Hh 35.00N 20.00 E
Méditerranée, Mer-= Mediterranean Sea (EN) 5 Hh 35.00N 20.00 E
Mediterráneo, Mar-= Mediterranean Sea (EN) 5 Hh 35.00N 20.00 E
Mediterraneo, Mar-= Mediterranean Sea (EN) 5 Hh 35.00N 20.00 E
Medje 36 Eb 2.25N 27.18 E
Medjerda, Monts de la- 32 Ib 36.35N 8.15 E
Mednogorsk 19 Fe 51.26N 57.40 E
Medny, Ostrov- 20 Lf 54.40N 167.50 E
Médoc 11 Fi 45.00N 1.00W
Mêdog 27 Gf 29.18N 95.27 E
Médouneu 36 Bb 1.01N 10.48 E
Medveđa 15 Eg 42.51N 21.36 E
Medvedica 5 Kf 49.35N 42.41 E
Medvedica 7 Ih 57.05N 37.31 E
Medvednica 14 Je 45.55N 15.58 E
Medvedok 7 Mh 57.24N 50.06 E
Medvenka 16 Jd 51.27N 36.08 E
Medveži, Ostrova-=Bear Islands (EN) 21 Sb 70.52N 161.26 E
Medvežjegorsk 19 Dc 62.56N 34.29 E
Medway 12 Cc 51.23N 0.31 E
Medzilaborce 10 Rg 49.16N 21.55 E
Meekatharra 58 Cg 26.36S 118.29 E
Meeker 45 Cf 40.02N 107.55W
Meerane 10 If 50.51N 12.28 E
Meerbusch 12 Ic 51.16N 6.40 E
Meerut 25 Fc 28.59N 77.42 E
Meeteetse 46 Kd 44.09N 108.52W
Mefarlane, Lake- 59 Hf 32.00S 136.40 E
Mega [Eth.] 31 Kh 4.03N 38.20 E
Mega [Indon.] 26 Jg 0.41S 131.53 E
Mega, Pulau- 26 Dg 4.00S 101.02 E
Megalo 35 Gd 6.52N 40.47 E
Megálon Khorion 15 Km 36.27N 27.21 E
Megalópolis 15 Fl 37.24N 22.08 E
Megálo Sofráno 15 Jm 36.04N 26.25 E
Meganision 15 Dk 38.38N 20.43 E
Meganom, Mys- 16 Ig 44.48N 35.05 E
Mégara 15 Gk 38.00N 23.21 E
Megève 11 Mi 45.52N 6.37 E
Meghalaya [3] 25 Ic 26.00N 91.00 E
Megid 33 Dd 28.35N 22.10 E
Megion 19 Hc 61.00N 76.15 E
Megiscane, Lac- 44 Ia 48.30N 76.04W
Megri 16 Oj 38.55N 46.15 E
Mehadia 15 Fe 44.54N 22.22 E
Mehaigne 12 Hd 50.32N 5.13 E
Meharry, Mount- 59 Dd 23.00S 118.35 E
Mehdia 13 Ni 35.25N 1.45 E
Mehdīshahr 24 Oe 35.44N 53.22 E
Mehedinţi [2] 15 Fe 44.30N 23.00 E
Mehetia, Ile- 61 Lc 17.52S 148.03W
Mehrabān 24 Lc 38.05N 47.08 E
Mehrān 24 Pi 26.52N 55.24 E
Mehrān 24 Lf 33.07N 46.10 E
Mehrenga 7 Je 63.17N 41.20 E
Mehrīz 24 Pg 31.35N 54.28 E
Mehtar Lām 23 Lc 34.39N 70.10 E
Mehun-sur-Yèvre 11 Ig 47.09N 2.13 E
Meia Meia 36 Gd 5.49S 35.48 E
Meia Ponte, Rio- 54 Ig 18.32S 49.36W
Meiganga 34 Hd 6.31N 14.18 E
Meighen 42 Ha 79.55N 99.00W
Meihekou→Hailong 27 Mc 42.32N 125.37 E
Meiktila 25 Jd 20.52N 95.52 E
Meilü→Wuchuan 27 Jg 21.28N 110.44 E
Meinerzhagen 12 Jc 51.07N 7.39 E
Meiningen 10 Gf 50.33N 10.25 E
Meio, Rio do- 55 Ja 13.20S 44.34W
Meisenheim 12 Je 49.43N 7.40 E
Meishan [China] 27 He 30.05N 103.48 E
Meishan [China] 28 Ei 31.06N 119.43 E
Meishan → Jinzhai 28 Ci 31.40N 115.52 E
Meißen 10 Je 51.09N 13.29 E
Meißner 10 Fe 51.12N 9.50 E
Meitan (Yiquan) 27 If 27.48N 107.32 E
Meixian 27 Kg 24.21N 116.07 E
Meiyukou 28 Bd 40.01N 113.08 E
Méjean, Causse- 11 Jj 44.16N 3.22 E
Mejillones 56 Fb 23.06S 70.27W
Mékambo 36 Bb 1.01N 13.56 E
Mekdela 35 Fc 11.28N 39.20 E
Mekele=Meqele (EN) 31 Kg 13.30N 39.28 E
Mékhé 34 Bb 15.07N 16.38W
Mekherrhane, Sebkha- 30 Hf 26.22N 1.20 E
Meknès [3] 32 Fc 33.00N 5.30W
Meknès 31 Ge 33.54N 5.32W
Mekong (EN)=Lancang Jiang 21 Mh 10.15N 105.55 E
Mekong (EN)=Mae Nam Khong 21 Mh 10.15N 105.55 E
Mekong (EN)=Mékôngk 21 Mh 10.15N 105.55 E
Mekong (EN)=Mènam Khong 21 Mh 10.15N 105.55 E
Mekong Delta (EN) 21 Mi 10.20N 106.40 E
Mekongga, Gunung- 26 Hg 3.35S 121.15 E
Mékôngk=Mekong (EN) 21 Mh 10.15N 105.55 E
Mekoryuk 40 Fd 60.23N 166.12W
Mékrou 34 Fc 12.24N 2.49 E
Mel, Ilha do- 55 Hg 25.31S 48.20W
Melaab 13 Ni 35.43N 1.20 E
Mēladēn 35 Hc 10.25N 49.52 E
Melaka 22 Mi 2.12N 102.15 E
Melaka, Selat-=Malacca, Strait of- (EN) 21 Mi 2.30N 101.20 E
Melamo, Cabo- 30 Lj 14.24S 40.49 E
Melanesia 57 Hf 13.00S 164.00 E
Melanesian Basin (EN) 3 Jj 0.05S 160.35 E
Melawi 26 Ff 0.05N 111.29 E
Melbourne [Ar.-U.S.] 45 Kh 36.04N 91.54W
Melbourne [Austl.] 58 Fh 37.49S 144.58 E
Melbourne [Eng.-U.K.] 12 Ab 52.49N 1.26W
Melbourne [Fl.-U.S.] 43 Kf 28.05N 80.37W
Melbourne-Dandenong 59 Jg 37.59S 145.12 E
Melchor Múzquiz 47 Dc 27.53N 101.31W
Melchor Ocampo 48 Hi 17.59N 102.11W
Meldorf 10 Fb 54.05N 9.05 E
Mele, Capo- 14 Cg 43.57N 8.10 E
Melekeiok 64a Bc 7.29N 134.38 E
Melela 37 Fc 17.04S 38.36 E
Melenci 15 Dd 45.31N 20.19 E
Melenki 19 Ed 55.23N 41.42 E
Meleto Dağı 24 Ic 38.35N 41.32 E
Meleuz 19 Fe 52.58N 55.59 E
Mélèzes, Rivière aux- 42 Ke 57.00N 69.00W
Melfa 14 Hi 41.30N 13.35 E
Melfi [Chad] 35 Bc 11.04N 17.56 E
Melfi [It.] 14 Jj 41.00N 15.39 E
Melfort 42 Hf 52.52N 104.36W
Melgaço 54 Hd 1.47S 50.44W
Melibocus 10 Eg 49.42N 8.40 E
Melilla [5] 31 Ge 35.19N 2.58W
Melincué, Laguna- 55 Bk 33.42S 61.28W
Melipilla 56 Fd 33.42S 71.13W
Melita 45 Fb 49.16N 101.00W
Melíti 15 Ei 40.50N 21.35 E
Melito di Porto Salvo 14 Jm 37.55N 15.47 E
Melito di Porto Salvo, Punta di- 14 Jm 37.57N 15.45 E
Melitopol 6 Jf 46.50N 35.22 E
Melk 14 Jb 48.13N 15.19 E
Mella 14 Ee 45.13N 10.13 E
Mellakou 13 Ni 35.15N 1.14 E
Mellanfryken 8 Ee 59.40N 13.15 E
Melle [Fr.] 11 Fh 46.13N 0.08W
Melle [Ger.] 12 Kb 52.12N 8.21 E
Mellen 45 Kc 46.20N 90.40W
Mellerud 7 Cg 58.42N 12.28 E
Mellish Reef 59 Lc 17.25S 155.50 E
Mellish Seamount (EN) 57 Ia 34.00N 178.15 E
Mellit 35 Dc 14.08N 25.33 E
Mělník 10 Kf 50.21N 14.30 E
Melnik 15 Gh 41.31N 23.24 E
Melo 53 Ki 32.22S 54.11W
Melo, Rio- 55 De 21.25S 57.55W
Melrhir, Chott- 30 He 34.20N 6.20 E
Melrose 46 Id 45.38N 112.40W
Melsungen 10 Fe 51.08N 9.33 E
Meltaus 7 Fc 66.54N 25.22 E
Melton Constable 12 Db 52.51N 1.02 E
Melton Mowbray 9 Mi 52.46N 0.53W
Meluco 37 Fb 12.33S 39.37 E
Meluli 37 Fc 16.28S 39.44 E
Melun 11 If 48.32N 2.40 E
Melville 38 Ib 75.15N 110.00W
Melville 46 Na 50.55N 102.48W
Melville, Cape- 59 Ib 14.10S 144.30 E
Melville, Lake- 42 Lf 53.42N 59.30W
Melville Bay 59 Hb 12.05S 136.45 E
Melville Bay (EN)=Melville Bugt 67 Od 75.35N 62.30W
Melville Bugt=Melville Bay (EN) 67 Od 75.35N 62.30W
Melville Hills 42 Fc 69.20N 123.00W
Melville Island 57 Ef 11.40S 131.00 E
Melville Peninsula 38 Kc 68.00N 84.00W
Melville Sound 42 Gc 68.05N 107.30W
Melvin, Lough- 9 Eg 54.25N 8.10W
Mélykút 10 Pj 46.13N 19.23 E
Memaliaj 15 Ci 40.20N 19.58 E
Memambetsu 29a Db 43.55N 144.11 E
Memba, Baia de- 37 Gb 14.11S 40.35 E
Memberamo 26 Kg 1.28S 137.52 E
Memboro 26 Gh 9.22S 119.32 E
Mēmele 8 Kh 56.24N 24.10 E
Memmert 10 Cc 53.39N 6.53 E
Memmingen 10 Gi 47.59N 10.10 E
Mempawan 26 Ef 0.22N 108.58 E
Memphis 33 Fd 29.52N 31.15 E
Memphis [Mo.-U.S.] 45 Jf 40.28N 92.10W
Memphis [Tn.-U.S.] 39 Jf 35.08N 90.03W
Memphis [Tx.-U.S.] 45 Fi 34.44N 100.32W
Memrut Dağı 24 Jc 38.40N 42.12 E
Memuro 28 Qc 42.55N 143.03 E
Memuro-Dake 29a Cb 42.52N 142.45 E
Mena 35 Gd 5.30N 41.06 E
Mena [Ar.-U.S.] 45 Ii 34.35N 94.15W
Mena 19 De 51.33N 32.14 E
Menabe 30 Lk 20.00S 44.40 E
Menai Strait 9 Ih 53.12N 4.12W
Ménaka 31 Hg 15.55N 2.26 E
Mènam Khong=Mekong (EN) 21 Mh 10.15N 105.55 E
Menangalaku 26 Gh 9.36S 119.01 E
Menard 45 Gk 30.55N 99.47W
Menawashei 35 Dc 12.40N 25.01 E
Menčul, Gora- 10 Th 48.16N 23:49 E
Mendala, Puncak- 26 Lg 4.44S 140.20 E
Mendanau, Pulau- 26 Eg 2.51S 107.26 E
Mendanha 55 Kd 18.06S 43.30W
Mende 11 Jj 44.31N 3.30 E
Mendebo 30 Kh 6.50N 39.40 E
Mendelejevsk 7 Mi 55.57N 52.22 E
Menden (Sauerland) 10 De 51.26N 7.48 E
Mendes 13 Mi 35.39N 0.52 E
Méndez 48 Je 25.07N 98.34W
Mendi [Eth.] 35 Fd 9.48N 35.05 E
Mendi [Pap.N.Gui.] 60 Ci 6.10S 143.40 E
Mendig 12 Jd 50.22N 7.16 E
Mendip Hills 9 Kj 51.15N 2.40W
Mendocino 46 Dg 39.19N 123.48W
Mendocino, Cape- 38 Ge 40.25N 124.25W
Mendocino Fracture Zone (EN) 3 Lf 40.00N 145.00W
Mendota [Ca.-U.S.] 46 Eh 36.45N 120.23W
Mendota [Il.-U.S.] 45 Lf 41.33N 89.07W
Mendoza 53 Ji 32.54S 68.50W
Mendoza [2] 56 Gd 34.30S 68.30W
Mené, Landes du- 11 Df 48.15N 2.32W
Mene de Mauroa 49 Lh 10.43N 71.01W
Mene Grande 54 Db 9.49S 70.56W
Menemen 24 Bc 38.36N 27.04 E
Menen/Menin 11 Jd 50.48N 3.07 E
Meneng Point 64e Bb 0.33S 166.57 E
Meneses 55 Dj 30.53S 56.30W
Ménez Hom 11 Bf 48.13N 4.16W
Menfi 14 Gm 37.36N 12.58 E
Mengcheng 27 Ke 33.11N 116.30 E
Mengdingjie 27 Gg 23.31N 99.07 E
Menggala 26 Eg 4.28S 105.17 E
Mengíbar 13 Ig 37.58N 3.48W
Mengjin 28 Bg 34.50N 112.26 E
Mengla 27 Hg 21.30N 101.35 E
Menglangba→Lancang 27 Gg 22.37N 99.57 E
Menglian 27 Gg 22.20N 99.27 E
Mengoun Huizu Zizhixian 28 De 38.04N 117.06 E
Mengyin 28 Dg 35.42N 117.56 E
Mengzi 22 Mg 23.23N 103.34 E
Menihek Lakes 42 Kf 54.00N 66.30W
Menin/Menen 11 Jd 50.48N 3.07 E
Menindee 59 If 32.24S 142.26 E
Menindee Lake 59 If 22.00S 142.23 E
Meningie 59 Hg 35.42S 139.20 E
Menjapa, Gunung- 26 Gf 1.05N 116.05 E
Menno 45 He 43.14N 97.34W
Menoíkion Óros 15 Gh 41.11N 23.48 E
Menominee 44 Dc 45.07N 87.39W
Menongue 31 Ij 14.40S 17.39 E
Menor, Mar- 13 Lg 37.43N 0.48W
Menorca=Minorca (EN) 5 Gg 40.00N 4.00 E
Menor do Araguaia, Braço- ou Javaes 54 He 9.50S 50.12W
Mentana 14 Gh 42.02N 12.38 E
Mentasta Lake 40 Kd 62.55N 143.45W
Mentawai, Kepulauan-= Mentawai Islands (EN) 21 Lj 2.00S 99.30 E
Mentawai, Selat- 21 Lj 2.00S 99.30 E
Mentawai Islands (EN)= Mentawai, Kepulauan- 21 Lj 2.00S 99.30 E
Menton 11 Nk 43.47N 7.30 E
Mentougou 28 De 39.56N 116.02 E
Menyuan 27 Hd 37.30N 101.35 E
Menzelinsk 7 Mi 55.45N 53.09 E
Menzies 59 Ee 29.41S 121.02 E
Menzies, Mount- 66 Ff 73.30S 61.50 E
Meon 12 Ad 50.49N 1.15W
Meoqui 47 Cc 28.17N 105.29W
Meponda 37 Eb 13.25S 34.52 E
Meppel 11 Mb 52.42N 6.11 E
Meppen 10 Dd 52.41N 7.19 E
Meqele(EN)=Mekele 31 Kg 13.30N 39.28 E
Mê Qu 27 He 33.58N 102.10 E
Mequinensa, Pantà de-/ Mequinenza, Embalse de- 13 Lc 41.15N 0.02W
Mequinenza, Embalse de-/ Mequinensa, Pantà de- 13 Lc 41.15N 0.02W
Mera 14 Dd 46.11N 9.25 E
Merabello, Gulf of- (EN) = Merabéllou, Kólpos- 15 In 35.14N 25.47 E
Merabéllou, Kólpos- = Merabello, Gulf of- (EN) 15 In 35.14N 25.47 E
Merak 26 Eh 5.56S 106.00 E
Meråker 7 Ce 63.26N 11.45 E
Méralab 63b Db 14.27S 168.03 E
Meramangye, Lake- 59 Ge 28.25S 132.15 E
Meran / Merano 14 Fd 46.40N 11.09 E
Merano / Meran 14 Fd 46.40N 11.09 E
Meratus, Pegunungan- 26 Gg 2.45S 115.40 E
Merauke 58 Fe 8.28S 140.20 E
Mercadal 13 Qe 39.59N 4.05 E
Mercato Saraceno 14 Gg 43.57N 12.12 E
Merced 43 Cd 37.18N 120.29W
Mercedario, Cerro- 52 Ii 31.59S 70.14W
Mercedes [Arg.] 56 Id 34.39S 59.27W
Mercedes [Arg.] 56 Ic 29.12S 58.05W
Mercedes [Arg.] 53 Ji 33.40S 65.30W
Mercedes [Ur.] 53 Ki 33.16S 58.01W
Merchants Bay 42 Lc 67.10N 62.50W
Merchtem 12 Gd 50.58N 4.14 E
Mercury Islands 62 Fb 36.35S 175.50 E
Mercy, Cape - 42 Ld 64.56N 63.40W
Mercy Bay 42 Fb 74.15N 118.10W
Meredith, Cape- 56 Hh 52.12S 60.38W
Meredith, Lake- 45 Fi 35.36N 101.42W
Meredoua 32 Hd 25.20N 2.05 E
Merefa 19 Df 49.51N 36.00 E
Merelbeke 12 Fd 51.00N 3.45 E
Merenga 20 Kd 61.43N 156.05 E
Mergui 22 Lh 12.26N 98.36 E
Mergui Archipelago 21 Lh 12.00N 98.00 E
Méri 34 Hc 10.47N 14.06 E
Meriç 15 Jh 41.11N 26.25 E
Meriç 24 Bb 40.52N 26.12 E
Mérida [2] 54 Db 8.30N 71.10W
Mérida [Mex.] 39 Kg 20.58N 89.37W
Mérida [Sp.] 13 Ff 38.55N 6.20W
Mérida [Ven.] 53 Ie 8.36N 71.08W
Merida, Cordillera de- 52 Ie 8.40N 71.00W
Meridian 39 Kf 32.22N 88.42W
Mérig 63b Cb 14.19S 167.48 E
Mérignac 11 Fj 44.50N 0.38W
Merikarvia 7 Ef 61.51N 21.30 E
Merin, Laguna- 56 Jd 32.45S 52.50W
Meringur 59 If 34.24S 141.29 E
Merir Island 57 Ed 4.19N 132.19 E
Merizo 64c Bb 13.16N 144.40 E
Merke 18 Ic 42.52N 73.12 E
Merkem, Houthulst- 12 Ed 50.57N 2.51 E
Merkine/Merkinė 8 Kj 54.07N 24.20 E
Merkinė/Merkine 8 Kj 54.07N 24.20 E
Merkis/Merkys 7 Fi 54.10N 24.11 E
Merksem, Antwerpen- 12 Gc 51.15N 4.27 E
Merksplas 12 Gc 51.22N 4.52 E
Merkys/Merkis 7 Fi 54.10N 24.11 E
Meroe 35 Eb 16.56N 33.59 E
Meroe 35 Eb 16.05N 33.55 E
Merouane, Chott- 32 Ic 34.00N 6.02 E
Merredin 59 Df 31.29S 118.16 E
Merrick 9 If 55.08N 4.29W
Merrill 43 Jb 45.11N 89.41W
Merriman 45 Fe 42.55N 101.42W
Merritt 42 Ff 50.07N 120.47W
Merritt Island 43 Kf 28.21N 80.42W
Merritt Reservoir 45 Fe 42.35N 100.55W
Mersa Fatma 35 Gc 14.53N 40.19 E
Mersa Teklay 35 Fb 17.25N 38.45 E
Mersea Island 12 Cc 51.47N 0.57 E
Merseburg 10 He 51.22N 12.00 E
Mers el Kebir 13 Li 35.44N 0.43W
Mersey 9 Kh 53.25N 3.00W
Merseyside [3] 9 Kh 53.30N 3.00W
Mersin → İçel 23 Db 36.48N 34.38 E
Mersing 26 Df 2.26N 103.50 E
Mers-les-Bains 12 Dd 50.04N 1.23 E
Mērsrags/Mersrags 8 Jg 57.19N 23.01 E
Mersrags/Mērsrags 8 Jg 57.19N 23.01 E
Merta 25 Ec 26.39N 74.02 E
Merta Road 25 Ec 26.43N 73.55 E
Mertert 12 Ie 49.42N 6.29 E
Merthyr Tydfil 9 Jj 51.46N 3.23W
Merti 36 Gb 1.04N 38.40 E
Mértola 13 Eg 37.38N 7.40W
Mertule Maryam 35 Fc 10.50N 38.15 E
Mertvy Kultuk, Sor- 16 Rg 45.30N 53.40 E
Mertz Glacier 66 Je 67.40S 144.45 E
Meru 36 Gb 0.03N 37.39 E
Méru 11 Ie 49.14N 2.08 E
Meru, Mount- 36 Gc 3.14S 36.45 E
Merure 55 Fb 15.33S 53.05W
Merville 12 Ed 50.38N 2.38 E
Merzifon 23 Ea 40.53N 35.29 E
Merzig 10 Cg 49.27N 6.38 E
Meša 7 Li 55.34N 49.24 E
Mesa [Az.-U.S.] 39 Hf 33.25N 111.50W
Mesa [Co.-U.S.] 45 Bg 39.14N 108.08W
Mesabi Range 45 Jc 47.30N 92.50W
Mesagne 14 Lj 40.34N 17.48 E
Mescalero 45 Dj 33.09N 105.46W
Meščera=Moscow Basin 5 Kd 55.00N 40.30 E
Meschede 10 Ee 51.21N 8.17 E
Mescit Dağı 24 Ib 40.22N 41.11 E
Meščovsk 16 Ib 54.19N 35.18 E
Mesegon 64d Bb 7.09N 151.55 E
Mesfinto 35 Fc 13.28N 37.23 E
Me-Shima 28 Jh 32.01N 128.25 E
Meshkīnshahr 24 Lc 38.24N 47.40 E
Mesima 14 Jl 38.30N 15.55 E
Mesjagutovo 17 Ii 55.35N 58.20 E
Meskiana 14 Bo 35.38N 7.40 E
Meskiana, Oued- 14 Bo 35.48N 7.53 E
Meslo 35 Fd 6.22N 39.50 E
Mesnil-Val, Criel-sur-Mer- 12 Dd 50.03N 1.20 E
Mesola 14 Gf 44.55N 12.14 E
Mesolóngion 15 Ek 38.22N 21.26 E
Mesopotamia 52 Kh 30.00S 58.00W
Mesopotamia (EN) 23 Fc 34.00N 44.00 E
Mesoyéios Thálassa= Mediterranean Sea (EN) 5 Hh 35.00N 20.00 E
Mesquite [Nv.-U.S.] 46 Hh 36.48N 114.04W
Mesquite [Tx.-U.S.] 45 Hj 32.46N 96.36W
Mesra 13 Mi 35.50N 0.10 E
Messaad 32 Hc 34.10N 3.30 E
Messalo 30 Lj 11.40S 40.46 E
Messará, Órmos- 15 Ho 35.00N 24.40 E
Messina [It.] 6 Hh 38.11N 15.34 E
Messina [S.Afr.] 31 Kk 22.23S 30.00 E
Messina, Strait of- (EN) = Messina, Stretto di- 5 Hh 38.15N 15.35 E
Messina, Stretto di- = Messina, Strait of- (EN) 5 Hh 38.15N 15.35 E
Messíni 15 El 37.15N 21.50 E
Messini 15 Fl 37.03N 22.01 E
Messiniakós Kólpos 15 Fm 36.45N 22.10 E
Messojaha 20 Cc 67.52N 77.27 E
Mesta 15 Hi 40.51N 24.44 E
Mestecăniş, Pasul- 15 Ib 47.28N 25.20 E
Mesters Vig 41 Jd 72.15N 24.20W
Mestia 16 Mh 43.03N 42.43 E
Mestre, Espigão- 54 If 12.30S 46.00W
Mestre, Venezia- 14 Ge 45.29N 12.14 E
Mesuji 26 Eg 4.08S 105.52 E
Meta [2] 54 Dc 3.30N 73.00W
Meta, Río- 52 Je 6.12N 67.28W
Meta Incognita Peninsula 38 Mc 62.40N 68.00W
Metairie 45 Kl 29.59N 90.09W
Metaliferi, Munţii- 15 Fc 46.10N 22.50 E
Metallifere, Colline- 14 Eg 43.10N 10.55 E
Metán 56 Hc 25.29S 64.57W
Metangula 37 Eb 12.43S 34.49 E
Metaponto 14 Kj 40.20N 16.50 E
Metauro 14 Hg 43.50N 13.03 E
Metautu 65c Ba 13.57S 171.54W
Meteghan 44 Nc 44.11N 66.10W
Metelen 12 Jb 52.09N 7.12 E
Metéora 15 Ej 39.43N 21.40 E
Meteor Seamount (EN) 30 Hm 48.00S 8.30 E
Meteor Trench (EN) 3 Do 55.00S 27.00 E
Méthana 15 Gl 37.35N 23.23 E
Methánon, Khersónisos- 15 Gl 37.36N 23.22 E
Methven 62 De 43.38S 171.38 E
Methwold 12 Cb 52.31N 0.33 E
Metković 14 Lg 43.03N 17.39 E
Metlakatla 40 Me 55.08N 131.35W
Metlika 14 Je 45.39N 15.19 E
Metlili Chaamba 32 Hc 32.16N 3.38 E
Metmárfag 32 Ed 26.26N 13.26W
Metohija 15 Dg 42.40N 20.27 E
Metro 26 Eh 5.05S 105.20 E
Metropolis 45 Lh 37.09N 88.44W
Métsovon 15 Ej 39.46N 21.11 E
Métsovon, Zigós- = Métsovon Pass (EN) 15 Ej 39.47N 21.15 E
Métsovon Pass (EN) = Métsovon, Zigós- 15 Ej 39.47N 21.15 E
Mettet 12 Gd 50.19N 4.40 E
Mettingen 12 Jb 52.19N 7.47 E
Mettlach 12 Ie 49.30N 6.36 E
Mettmann 12 Ic 51.15N 6.58 E
Metu 31 Kh 8.20N 35.38 E
Metuje 10 Lf 50.20N 15.55 E
Metz 6 Gf 49.08N 6.10 E
Metzervisse 12 Ie 49.19N 6.17 E
Meu 11 Ef 48.02N 1.47W
Meulaboh 26 Cf 4.09N 96.08 E
Meulan 12 De 49.01N 1.54 E
Meulebeke 12 Fd 50.57N 3.17 E
Meureudu 26 Ce 5.16N 96.16 E
Meurthe 11 Mf 48.47N 6.09 E
Meurthe-et-Moselle [3] 11 Mf 48.35N 6.10 E
Meuse [3] 11 Lf 49.00N 5.30 E
Meuse 5 Ge 51.49N 5.01 E
Meuse (EN)=Maas 5 Ge 51.49N 5.01 E
Meuse, Côtes de- 11 Le 49.10N 5.30 E
Meuzenti 35 Bb 18.14N 17.06 E
Mexia 45 Hk 31.41N 96.29W
Mexiana, Ilha 54 Ic 0.00 49.35W
Mexicali 39 Hf 32.40N 115.29W
Mexicana, Altiplanicie-= Mexico, Plateau of- (EN) 38 Ig 25.30N 104.00W
Mexican Hat 46 Kh 37.09N 109.52W
Mexicanos, Laguna de los- 48 Fc 28.09N 106.57W
Mexico 45 Kg 39.10N 91.53W
México [1] 39 Ig 23.00N 102.00W

Index Symbols

[1] Independent Nation
[2] State, Region
[3] District, County
[4] Municipality
[5] Colony, Dependency
Continent
Physical Region
Historical or Cultural Region
Mount, Mountain
Volcano
Hill
Mountains, Mountain Range
Hills, Escarpment
Plateau, Upland
Pass, Gap
Plain, Lowland
Delta
Salt Flat
Valley, Canyon
Crater, Cave
Karst Features
Depression
Polder
Desert, Dunes
Forest, Woods
Heath, Steppe
Oasis
Cape, Point
Coast, Beach
Cliff
Peninsula
Isthmus
Sandbank
Island
Atoll
Rock, Reef
Islands, Archipelago
Rocks, Reefs
Coral Reef
Well, Spring
Geyser
River, Stream
Waterfall Rapids
River Mouth, Estuary
Lake
Salt Lake
Intermittent Lake
Reservoir
Swamp, Pond
Canal
Glacier
Ice Shelf, Pack Ice
Ocean
Sea
Gulf, Bay
Strait, Fjord
Lagoon
Bank
Seamount
Tablemount
Ridge
Shelf
Basin
Escarpment, Sea Scarp
Fracture
Trench, Abyss
National Park, Reserve
Point of Interest
Recreation Site
Cave, Cavern
Historic Site
Ruins
Wall, Walls
Church, Abbey
Temple
Scientific Station
Airport
Port
Lighthouse
Mine
Tunnel
Dam, Bridge

Mitsamiouli 37 Gb 11.23S 43.18 E
Mitsinjo 37 Hc 16.00S 45.52 E
Mitsio, Nosy- 37 Hb 12.54S 48.36 E
Mitsiwa=Massawa (EN) 31 Kg 15.37N 39.39 E
Mitsiwa Channel 35 Fb 15.30N 40.00 E
Mitsuishi 29a Cb 42.15N 142.33 E
Mitsukaido 29 Fc 36.01N 139.59 E
Mitsuke 29 Fc 37.32N 138.56 E
Mitsushima 29 Ad 34.16N 129.20 E
Mittelfranken 10 Gg 49.20N 10.40 E
Mittelland 14 Bd 46.50N 7.05 E
Mittellandkanal 5 He 52.16N 11.41 E
Mittelmark 10 Jd 52.20N 13.20 E
Mittenwald 10 Hi 47.27N 11.15 E
Mittersheim 12 If 48.52N 6.56 E
Mittersill 14 Gc 47.16N 12.29 E
Mittweida 10 If 50.59N 12.59 E
Mitú 53 Ie 1.08N 70.03W
Mitumba, Monts-=Mitumba Range (EN) 30 Ji 6.00S 29.00 E
Mitumba Range (EN)= Mitumba, Monts- 30 Ji 6.00S 29.00 E
Mituva 8 Jj 55.00N 22.45 E
Mitwaba 36 Ed 8.38S 27.20 E
Mitzic 36 Bb 0.47N 11.34 E
Miura 29 Fd 35.08N 139.37 E
Miura-Hantō 29 Fd 35.15N 139.40 E
Mixco Viejo 49 Bf 14.52N 90.40W
Mixian 28 Bg 34.31N 113.22 E
Mixteco, Rio- 48 Jh 18.11N 98.30W
Miya-Gawa 29 Ed 34.32N 136.42 E
Miyagi Ken [2] 28 Pe 38.30N 140.50 E
Miyagusuku-Jima 29b Ab 26.22N 127.59 E
Miyāh, Wādī al- [Eg.] 24 Ej 25.00N 33.23 E
Miyāh, Wādī al- [Sau. Ar.] 24 Gi 26.06N 36.31 E
Miyāh, Wādī al- [Syr.] 24 He 34.44N 39.57 E
Miyake-Jima 27 Oe 34.05N 139.30 E
Miyako 27 Pd 39.38N 141.57 E
Miyako-Jima 27 Mg 24.45N 125.20 E
Miyakonojō 28 Ki 31.44N 131.04 E
Miyako-Rettō 27 Lg 24.25N 125.00 E
Miyako-Wan 29 Hb 39.40N 142.00 E
Miyama 29 Dd 35.17N 135.34 E
Miyanojō 29 Bf 31.54N 130.27 E
Miyanoura-Dake 28 Ki 30.20N 130.29 E
Miyata 29 Be 33.45N 130.45 E
Miyazaki 27 Ne 31.54N 131.26 E
Miyazaki Ken [2] 28 Kh 32.05N 131.20 E
Miyazu 28 Mg 35.32N 135.11 E
Miyazuka-Yama 29 Fd 34.24N 139.16 E
Miyazu-Wan 29 Dd 35.35N 135.13 E
Miyoshi 28 Lg 34.48N 132.51 E
Miyun 27 Kc 40.22N 116.53 E
Miyun Shuiku 28 Dd 40.31N 116.58 E
Mizan Teferi 35 Fd 6.53N 35.28 E
Mizdah 33 Bc 31.26N 12.59 E
Mizen Head/Carn Ui Néid 5 Fe 51.27N 9.49W
Mizil 15 Je 45.01N 26.27 E
Mizorām [3] 25 Id 23.00N 93.00 E
Mizque 54 Eg 17.56S 65.19W
Mizuho 29 Cd 34.50N 132.29 E
Mizuho 66 Ef 70.43S 40.20 E
Mizunami 29 Ed 35.22N 137.15 E
Mizusawa 28 Pe 39.08N 141.08 E
Mjadel 8 Lj 54.54N 27.03 E
Mjakiševo 8 Mh 56.30N 28.54 E
Mjakit 20 Kd 61.23N 152.10 E
Mjällom 8 Ha 62.59N 18.26 E
Mjaundža 20 Jd 63.02N 147.13 E
Mjölby 7 Dg 58.19N 15.08 E
Mjøndalen 8 De 59.45N 10.01 E
Mjorn 8 Eg 57.54N 12.25 E
Mjøsa 5 Hc 60.40N 11.00 E
Mkoani 36 Gd 5.22S 39.39 E
Mkokotoni 36 Gd 5.52S 39.15 E
Mkushi Bona 36 Ee 13.37S 29.23 E
Mkushi River 36 Fe 13.33S 29.40 E
Mkuze 37 Ee 27.10S 32.00 E
Mladá Boleslav 10 Kf 50.21N 14.54 E
Mladenovac 15 De 44.26N 20.42 E
Mlava 15 Ee 44.45N 21.14 E
Mława 10 Qc 53.06N 20.23 E
Mljet 14 Lh 42.45N 17.30 E
Mljetski kanal 14 Lh 42.48N 17.35 E
Mmadinare 37 Dd 21.53S 27.45 E
Mnichovo Hradiště 10 Kf 50.32N 14.59 E
Mnogoveršinny 20 If 53.55N 139.50 E
Moa 49 Jc 20.40N 74.56W
Moa 34 Cd 6.59N 11.36W
Moa, Pulau- 26 Ih 8.10S 127.56 E
Moab 43 Fd 38.35N 109.33W
Moabi 36 Bc 2.24S 10.59 E
Moala 63d Bc 18.36S 179.53 E
Moamba 37 Ee 25.36S 32.15 E
Moanda [Gabon] 36 Bc 1.34S 13.11 E
Moanda [Zaire] 36 Bd 5.56S 12.21 E
Moatize 37 Ec 16.10S 33.46 E
Moba 31 Ji 7.03S 29.47 E
Mobara 29 Gd 35.25N 140.17 E
Mobārakeh 24 Nf 32.20N 51.30 E
Mobaye 31 Jh 4.19N 21.11 E
Mobayi-Mbongo 36 Db 4.18N 21.11 E
Mobeka 36 Cb 1.53N 19.46 E
Moberly 43 Id 39.25N 92.26W
Mobile 39 Kf 30.42N 88.05W
Mobile Bay 43 Je 30.25N 88.00W
Mobridge 43 Gb 45.32N 100.26W
Mobuto Sese Seko, Lac-= Albert, Lake- (EN) 30 Kh 1.40N 31.00 E
Moca 49 Ld 19.24N 70.31W
Moçambique= Mozambique (EN) [1] 31 Kj 18.15S 35.00 E
Moçambique= Mozambique (EN) 31 Lk 15.03S 40.45 E
Moçambique, Canal de-= Mozambique Channel (EN) 30 Lk 20.00S 43.00 E
Moçâmedes → Namibe 36 Bf 15.20S 12.30 E
Moçâmedes → Namibe 31 Ij 15.12S 12.10 E
Mocapra, Rio- 50 Ci 7.56N 66.46W
Mocha, Isla- 56 Fe 38.22S 73.56W
Moc Hoa 25 Lf 10.46N 105.56 E
Mochudi 37 Dd 24.23S 26.08 E
Mocímboa da Praia 31 Lj 11.20S 40.21 E
Möckeln 8 Fh 56.40N 14.10 E
Mockfjärd 8 Fd 60.30N 14.58 E
Môco, Serra- 30 Ij 12.28S 15.10 E
Mocoa 54 Cc 1.09N 76.38W
Mococa 55 Ie 21.28S 47.01W
Mocovi 55 Ci 28.24S 59.42W
Moctezuma [Mex.] 47 Cc 29.48N 109.42W
Moctezuma [Mex.] 48 If 22.45N 101.05W
Moctezuma [Mex.] 48 Fb 30.12N 106.26W
Moctezuma, Rio [Mex.] 48 Ec 29.09N 109.40W
Moctezuma, Rio- [Mex.] 48 Jg 21.59N 98.34W
Mocuba 31 Kj 16.51S 36.56 E
Mocubúri 37 Fb 14.39S 38.54 E
Močurica 15 Jg 42.31N 26.32 E
Modane 11 Mi 45.12N 6.40 E
Modderrivier 37 Ce 29.02S 24.37 E
Modena [It.] 14 Ef 44.40N 10.55 E
Modena [Ut.-U.S.] 46 Ih 37.49N 113.55W
Moder 11 Of 48.49N 8.06 E
Modesto 43 Cd 37.39N 120.59W
Modica 14 In 36.52N 14.46 E
Modjamboli 36 Db 2.28N 22.06 E
Modjigo 34 Hb 17.09N 13.12 E
Mödling 14 Kb 48.05N 16.28 E
Modriča 14 Mf 44.58N 18.18 E
Modum 8 Ce 59.55N 10.00 E
Moe 59 Jg 38.10S 146.15 E
Moelv 7 Cf 60.56N 10.42 E
Moen 64d Bb 7.26N 151.52 E
Moengo 54 Hb 5.37N 54.24W
Moen-jo-Daro 25 Dc 27.19N 68.07 E
Moenkopi Wash 46 Ji 35.54N 111.26W
Moerbeke 12 Fc 51.10N 3.56 E
Moers 10 Ce 51.27N 6.39 E
Moeskroen/Mouscron 11 Jd 50.44N 3.13 E
Moffat 9 Jf 55.20N 3.27W
Moga 36 Ec 2.21S 26.49 E
Mogadishu (EN)= Muqdisho 31 Lh 2.03N 45.22 E
Mogadouro 13 Fc 41.20N 6.43W
Mogadouro, Serra do- 13 Fc 41.19N 6.40W
Mogāl 24 Nd 36.35N 50.35 E
Mogalakwena 37 Dd 22.27S 28.55 E
Mogami 29 Gb 38.45N 140.30 E
Mogami-Gawa 28 Oe 38.54N 139.50 E
Mogami Trench (EN) 29 Fb 39.00N 139.00 E
Mogaung 25 Jc 25.18N 96.56 E
Mogho 35 Ge 4.49N 40.19 E
Mogielnica 10 Qe 51.42N 20.43 E
Mogilev 6 Je 53.56N 30.18 E
Mogilev-Podolski 16 Ee 48.27N 27.48 E
Mogilevskaja Oblast [3] 19 De 53.45N 30.30 E
Mogilno 10 Nd 52.40N 17.58 E
Mogincual 37 Gc 15.34S 40.24 E
Mogoča 22 Nd 53.44N 119.44 E
Mogočin 20 De 57.43N 83.40 E
Mogogh 35 Ed 8.26N 31.19 E
Mogojto 20 Gf 54.25N 110.27 E
Mogojtuj 20 Gf 51.15N 114.58 E
Mogok 25 Jd 22.55N 96.30 E
Mogollon Rim 43 Ee 34.20N 111.00W
Mogotes, Punta- 55 Dn 38.06S 57.33W
Mogotón, Pico- 49 Dg 13.45N 86.23W
Mogrein 31 Ff 25.13N 11.34W
Mogroum 35 Bc 11.06N 15.25 E
Moguer 13 Fg 37.16N 6.50W
Mogzon 20 Gf 51.42N 111.59 E
Mohács 10 Ok 45.59N 18.42 E
Mohaka 62 Gc 39.07S 177.12 E
Mohaka 62 Gc 39.07S 177.12 E
Mohales Hoek 37 Df 30.15S 27.25 E
Mohall 45 Fb 48.46N 101.31W
Moḥammadābād 24 Pg 31.47N 54.27 E
Mohammadia 13 Mi 35.35N 0.04 E
Mohammedia 32 Fc 33.42N 7.24W
Mohanganj 25 Id 24.54N 90.59 E
Mohang-ni 28 If 36.46N 126.08 E
Mohave, Lake- 43 Ed 35.25N 114.38W
Mohawk Mountains 46 Ij 32.25N 113.25W
Mohe 22 Od 53.27N 122.18 E
Moheda 8 Fh 57.00N 14.34 E
Mohéli → Mwali 30 Lj 12.15S 43.45 E
Moher, Cliffs of-/Aillte an Mhothair 9 Di 52.58N 9.27W
Mohican, Cape- 40 Fd 60.12N 167.28W
Mohinora 38 Ig 26.06N 107.04W
Möhnesee 12 Kc 51.29N 8.05 E
Mohns Ridge (EN) 5 Ga 73.00N 5.00 E
Moholm 8 Ff 58.37N 14.02 E
Mohon, Charleville-Mézières- 12 Ge 49.46N 4.43 E
Mohon Peak 46 Ii 34.57N 113.15W
Mohoro 36 Gd 8.08S 39.10 E
Mohotani, Ile- 61 Na 9.59S 138.49W
Mohovaja 62 Kf 53.01N 158.38 E
Moi 8 Bf 58.28N 6.32 E
Moikovac 15 Cg 42.58N 19.35 E
Moimenta da Beira 13 Ed 40.59N 7.37W
Moindou 63b Be 21.42S 165.41 E
Moinești 15 Jc 46.28N 26.29 E
Moirai 15 Hn 35.03N 24.52 E
Mo i Rana 6 Hb 66.18N 14.08 E
Mõisaküla/Myjzakjula 7 Fg 58.07N 25.10 E
Moisés Ville 55 Bj 30.43S 61.29W
Moisie 42 Kf 50.13N 66.06W
Moisie 42 Kf 50.11N 66.06W
Moissac 11 Hj 44.06N 1.05 E
Moissala 35 Bd 8.21N 17.46 E
Moitaco 50 Dh 8.01N 61.21W
Möja 8 He 59.25N 18.55 E
Mojácar 13 Kg 37.08N 1.51W
Mojada, Sierra- 48 Hd 27.15N 103.45W
Mojana, Caño- 49 Ji 9.02N 74.46W
Mojave 43 Dd 35.03N 118.10W
Mojave Desert 38 Hf 35.00N 117.00W
Mojiguaçu, Rio- 55 He 20.53S 48.10W
Moji Mirim 55 If 22.26S 46.57W
Mojjero 20 Fc 68.44N 103.30 E
Mojo 35 Fd 8.36N 39.09 E
Mojo 35 Gd 8.00N 41.50 E
Mojos, Llanos de- 52 Jg 15.00S 65.00W
Moju, Rio- 54 Id 1.40S 48.25W
Mojynty 19 Hf 47.10N 73.18 E
Mokambo 36 Ee 12.25S 28.21 E
Mokapu Peninsula 65a Db 21.26N 157.45W
Mokau 62 Fc 38.42S 174.35 E
Mokau 61 Dg 38.41S 174.37 E
Mokhotlong 37 De 29.17S 29.05 E
Mokil Atoll 57 Gd 6.40N 159.47 E
Moklakan 20 Gf 54.48N 118.56 E
Möklinta 8 Gd 60.05N 16.32 E
Mokochu, Khao- 25 Je 15.56N 99.06 E
Mokohinau Islands 62 Fa 35.55S 175.05 E
Mokolo 34 Hc 10.45N 13.48 E
Mokp'o 27 Of 34.47N 126.23 E
Mokra Gora 15 Dg 42.50N 20.25 E
Mokrany 10 Ue 51.48N 24.23 E
Mokrin 15 Dd 45.56N 20.25 E
Mokša 5 Ke 54.44N 41.53 E
Mokwa 34 Gd 9.17N 5.03 E
Mol 11 Lc 51.11N 5.07 E
Mola di Bari 14 Li 41.04N 17.05 E
Molango 48 Jg 20.47N 98.43W
Moláoi 15 Fm 36.48N 22.51 E
Molara 14 Dj 40.50N 9.45 E
Molas, Punta- 48 Pg 20.35N 86.44W
Molat 14 If 44.13N 14.50 E
Molatón 13 Kf 38.59N 1.24W
Moldau (EN)=Vltava 5 He 50.21N 14.30 E
Moldava nad Bodvou 10 Qh 48.37N 21.00 E
Moldavia (EN) = Moldova 15 Jc 46.30N 27.00 E
Moldavia (EN)=Moldova 5 If 46.30N 27.00 E
Moldavia (EN) = Moldova 19 Cf 47.00N 29.00 E
Moldavskaja Sovetskaja Socialističeskaja Respublika → Moldova 19 Cf 47.00N 29.00 E
Moldavskaja SSR/ Republika Sovetike Socialiste Moldovenjaske → Moldova 19 Cf 47.00N 29.00 E
Moldavskaja SSR → Moldova 19 Cf 47.00N 29.00 E
Molde 6 Gc 62.44N 7.11 E
Moldefjorden 8 Bb 62.45N 7.05 E
Moldova 19 Cf 47.00N 29.00 E
Moldova 15 Jc 46.54N 26.58 E
Moldova = Moldavia (EN) 15 Jc 46.30N 27.00 E
Moldova = Moldavia (EN) 5 If 46.30N 27.00 E
Moldova Nouă 15 Ee 44.44N 21.41 E
Moldoveanu, Vîrful- 5 If 45.36N 24.44 E
Moldoviţa 15 Ib 47.41N 25.32 E
Mole 12 Bc 51.24N 0.20W
Moléne, Ile de- 11 Bf 48.24N 4.58W
Molens van Kinderdijk 12 Gc 51.52N 4.40 E
Molepolole 31 Jk 24.25S 25.30 E
Môle Saint-Nicolas 49 Kd 19.47N 73.22W
Moletai/Moletaj 8 Ki 55.13N 25.36 E
Moletaj/Moletai 8 Ki 55.13N 25.36 E
Molfetta 14 Ki 41.12N 16.36 E
Molihong Shan 28 Hc 42.11N 124.43 E
Molina, Parameras de- 13 Jd 40.55N 2.01W
Molina de Aragón 13 Kd 40.51N 1.53W
Molina de Segura 13 Kf 38.03N 1.12W
Moline 45 Kf 41.30N 90.31W
Moliniere Point 51p Bb 12.05N 61.45W
Molise [2] 14 Ii 41.40N 14.30 E
Molkābād 24 Oe 34.32N 52.35 E
Molkom 8 Ee 59.36N 13.43 E
Möll 14 Hd 46.50N 13.26 E
Moll 55 Cl 35.04S 59.39W
Mollafeneri 15 Mi 40.54N 29.30 E
Mölle 8 Eh 56.17N 12.29 E
Mollendo 53 Ig 17.02S 72.01W
Molliens-Dreuil 12 Ee 49.52N 2.01 E
Mölln 10 Gc 53.38N 10.41 E
Mollösund 8 Df 58.04N 11.28 E
Mölndal 7 Ch 57.39N 12.01 E
Mölnlycke 8 Ef 57.39N 12.09 E
Moločansk 16 If 47.10N 35.36 E
Moločny, Liman- 16 If 46.30N 35.20 E
Molócuè 37 Fc 17.03S 38.52 E
Molodečno 19 Ce 54.19N 26.53 E
Molodežnaja 66 Ee 67.40S 45.51 E
Molodi 8 Mf 58.00N 28.52 E
Molodogvardejskoje 19 He 54.07N 70.50 E
Mologa 5 Jd 58.50N 37.11 E
Molokai Island 57 Lb 21.08N 157.00W
Moloma 7 Lg 58.20N 48.28 E
Molong 9 Jf 33.06S 148.52 E
Molopo 30 Jk 28.31S 20.13 E
Moloundou 34 Ie 2.02N 15.13 E
Molteno 37 Df 31.24S 26.22 E
Molu, Pulau- 26 Jh 6.45S 131.33 E
Moluccas (EN)=Maluku, Kepulauan- 57 De 2.00S 128.00 E
Molucca Sea (EN)=Maluku, Laut- 21 Oj 0.05S 125.00 E
Molygino 20 Ee 58.11N 94.45 E
Moma 20 Jc 66.20N 143.06 E
Moma 37 Fc 16.44S 39.14 E
Mombaça 54 Ke 5.45S 39.28W
Mombasa 31 Ki 4.03S 39.40 E
Mombo 36 Gc 4.53S 38.17 E
Momboyo 36 Cc 0.16S 19.00 E
Mombuca, Serra da- 55 Fd 18.15S 52.26W
Momčilgrad 15 Ih 41.32N 25.25 E
Mömling 12 Le 49.50N 9.09 E
Momotombo, Volcán- 49 Dg 12.26N 86.33W
Mompono 36 Db 0.04N 21.48 E
Mompós 54 Db 9.14N 74.27W
Momski Hrebet 20 Jc 66.00N 145.00 E
Mon [2] 25 Je 17.22N 97.20 E
Møn 7 Ci 55.00N 12.20 E
Mona, Canal de la-=Mona Passage (EN) 38 Mh 18.30N 67.45W
Mona, Isla- 47 Ke 18.05N 67.54W
Mona, Punta- 49 Fi 9.38N 82.37W
Monach Islands 9 Fd 57.32N 7.40W
Monaco [1] 6 Gg 43.42N 7.23 E
Monadhliath Mountains 9 Id 57.15N 4.10W
Monagas [2] 54 Fb 9.20N 63.00W
Monaghan/Muineachán [2] 9 Gg 54.10N 7.00W
Monaghan/Muineachán 9 Gg 54.15N 6.58W
Monahans 45 Ek 31.36N 102.54W
Mona Passage (EN)=Mona, Canal de la- 38 Mh 18.30N 67.45W
Monapo 37 Gb 14.55S 40.18 E
Monarch Mountain 42 Ef 51.54N 125.54W
Monashee Mountains 42 Ff 51.00N 118.43W
Monastyrščina 16 Gb 54.19N 31.48 E
Monatélé 34 He 4.16N 11.12 E
Monbetsu [Jap.] 28 Qc 42.28N 142.07 E
Monbetsu [Jap.] 27 Pc 44.21N 143.22 E
Monbetsu-Shokotsu 29a Ca 44.23N 143.16 E
Moncalieri 14 Be 45.00N 7.41 E
Moncalvo 14 Ce 45.03N 8.16 E
Monção [Braz.] 54 Id 3.30S 45.15W
Monção [Port.] 13 Db 42.05N 8.29W
Moncayo 13 Kc 41.46N 1.50W
Moncayo, Sierra del- 13 Kc 41.45N 1.50W
Mončegorsk 19 Db 67.56N 32.58 E
Mönchengladbach 10 Ce 51.12N 6.26 E
Mönchengladbach-Rheydt 12 Ic 51.10N 6.27 E
Mönchengladbach-Wickrath 12 Ic 51.08N 6.25 E
Mönchgut 10 Jb 54.20N 13.40 E
Monchique 13 Dg 37.19N 8.33W
Monchique, Serra de- 13 Dg 37.19N 8.36W
Monclova 39 Ig 26.54N 101.25W
Moncton 39 Me 46.06N 64.07W
Mondai 55 Fh 27.05S 53.25W
Mondego 13 Dd 40.09N 8.52W
Mondego, Cabo- 13 Dd 40.11N 8.55W
Mondeville 12 Be 49.10N 0.19W
Mondjoko 36 Dc 1.41S 21.12 E
Mondo 35 Bc 13.43N 15.32 E
Mondoñedo 13 Ea 43.26N 7.22W
Mondorf-les-Bains/Bad Mondorf 12 Ie 49.30N 6.17 E
Mondoubleau 11 Gg 47.59N 0.54 E
Mondovi 14 Bf 44.23N 7.49 E
Mondragone 14 Hi 41.07N 13.53 E
Mondy 20 Ff 51.40N 100.59 E
Monemvasía 15 Gm 36.41N 23.03 E
Monessen 44 He 40.09N 79.53W
Monett 45 Jh 36.55N 93.55W
Monfalcone 14 He 45.49N 13.32 E
Monferrato 14 Cf 44.55N 8.05 E
Monforte 13 Ee 39.03N 7.26W
Monforte de Lemos 13 Eb 42.31N 7.30W
Monga 36 Db 4.12N 22.49 E
Mongala 36 Cb 1.53N 19.46 E
Mongalla 35 Ed 5.12N 31.46 E
Mongbwalu 36 Fb 1.57N 30.02 E
Mong Cai 25 Ld 21.32N 107.58 E
Monger, Lake- 59 De 29.15S 117.05 E
Mongga 63a Cb 7.57S 156.59 E
Monggolküre/Zhaosu 27 Dc 43.10N 81.07 E
Monghyr → Munger 25 Hc 25.23N 86.28 E
Monginevro, Colle del- 11 Mj 44.56N 6.44 E
Mongo 31 Ig 12.11N 18.42 E
Mongo 34 Cd 9.34N 12.11W
Mongol Altajn Nuruu → Mongolski Altaj= Mongolian Altai (EN) 21 Le 46.30N 93.00 E
Mongol Ard-Uls=Mongolia (EN) [1] 22 Me 47.00N 104.00 E
Mongolia (EN)=Mongol Ard-Uls [1] 22 Me 47.00N 104.00 E
Mongolian Altai (EN)= Mongol Altajn Nuruu→ Mongolski Altaj 21 Le 46.30N 93.00 E
Mongolian Altai (EN)= Mongolski Altaj (Mongol Altajn Nuruu) 21 Le 46.30N 93.00 E
Mongolski Altaj (Mongol Altajn Nuruu)=Mongolian Altai (EN) 21 Le 46.30N 93.00 E
Mongonu 34 Hc 12.41N 13.36 E
Mongororo 35 Cc 12.01N 22.28 E
Mongoumba 35 Be 3.38N 18.36 E
Mong Pan 25 Jd 20.19N 98.22 E
Mongrove, Punta- 48 Hi 17.56N 102.11W
Mongu 31 Jj 15.17S 23.08 E
Monguel 32 Ef 16.25N 13.08W
Mong Yai 25 Jd 22.25N 98.02 E
Monheim 12 Ic 51.05N 6.53 E
Mönichkirchen 14 Kc 47.30N 16.02 E
Mon Idée, Auvillers-lès-Forges- 12 Ge 49.52N 4.21 E
Monigotes 55 Bj 30.30S 61.39W
Moni Hosiou Louká 15 Fk 38.24N 22.49 E
Monistrol-sur-Loire 11 Ki 45.17N 4.10 E
Monito, Isla- 51a Ab 18.09N 67.56W
Monitor Peak 46 Gg 38.50N 116.32W
Monitor Range 46 Gg 38.45N 116.40W
Monjolos 55 Jd 18.18S 44.05W
Monkayo 26 Ie 7.50N 126.00 E
Monkey Bay 36 Fe 14.05S 34.55 E
Monkey Point 49 Fg 11.36N 83.39W
Monkey River 49 Ce 16.22N 88.29W
Mońki 10 Sc 53.24N 22.49 E
Monkoto 36 Dc 1.38S 20.39 E
Monmouth [Il.-U.S.] 45 Kf 40.55N 90.39W
Monmouth 9 Kj 51.45N 3.00W
Monmouth [Or.-U.S.] 46 Dd 44.51N 123.14W
Monmouth [Wales-U.K.] 9 Kj 51.50N 2.43W
Monmouth Mountain 46 Da 51.00N 123.47W
Mönne 10 De 51.28N 7.30 E
Monnikendam 12 Hb 52.27N 5.02 E
Monnow 9 Kj 51.48N 2.42W
Mono 63a Bb 7.20S 155.35 E
Mono [3] 34 Fd 6.45N 1.50 E
Monobe-Gawa 29 Ce 33.32N 133.42 E
Mono Lake 43 Dd 38.00N 119.00W
Monólithos 15 Km 36.07N 27.45 E
Monopoli 14 Lj 40.57N 17.18 E
Monor 10 Pi 47.21N 19.27 E
Monou 35 Cb 16.24N 22.11 E
Monóvar 13 Lf 38.26N 0.50W
Monowai, Lake- 62 Bf 45.55S 167.25 E
Monreal 12 Jd 50.18N 7.10 E
Monreal del Campo 13 Kd 40.47N 1.21W
Monreale 14 Hl 38.05N 13.17 E
Monroe [Ga.-U.S.] 44 Fi 33.47N 83.43W
Monroe [La.-U.S.] 39 Jf 32.33N 92.07W
Monroe [Mi.-U.S.] 44 Fe 41.55N 83.24W
Monroe [N.C.-U.S.] 44 Gh 34.59N 80.33W
Monroe [Or.-U.S.] 46 Dd 44.19N 123.18W
Monroe [Wi.-U.S.] 45 Le 42.36N 89.38W
Monroe, Lake- 44 Df 39.05N 86.25W
Monroe City 45 Kg 39.39N 91.44W
Monroeville 44 Dj 31.31N 87.20W
Monrovia 31 Fh 6.19N 10.48W
Mons/Bergen 11 Jd 50.27N 3.56 E
Monsanto 13 Ed 40.02N 7.07W
Monschau 10 Cf 50.33N 6.15 E
Monselice 14 Fe 45.14N 11.45 E
Monserrate, Isla- 48 De 25.41N 111.05W
Monsheim 12 Ke 49.38N 8.12 E
Møns Klint 8 Ej 54.58N 12.33 E
Mönsterås 7 Dh 57.02N 16.26 E
Montabaur 10 Df 50.26N 7.50 E
Montagna Grande 14 Gm 37.56N 12.44 E
Montagne 11 Jh 46.10N 3.40 E
Montagu 66 Ad 58.25S 26.20W
Montague 40 Je 60.00N 147.30W
Montague, Isla- 48 Bb 31.45N 114.48W
Montaigu 11 Eh 46.59N 1.19W
Montalbán 13 Ld 40.50N 0.48W
Montalbano Ionico 14 Kj 40.17N 16.34 E
Montalcino 14 Fg 43.03N 11.29 E
Montalegre 13 Ec 41.49N 7.48W
Montalto di Castro 14 Fh 42.21N 11.37 E
Montalto Uffugo 14 Kk 39.24N 16.09 E
Montalvânia 55 Jb 14.28S 44.32W
Montana [2] 43 Eb 47.00N 110.00W
Montana 14 Bd 46.18N 7.30 E
Montánchez 13 Fe 39.13N 6.09W
Montánchez, Sierra de- 13 Ge 39.15N 5.55W
Montargis 11 Ig 48.00N 2.45 E
Montataire 12 Ee 49.16N 2.26 E
Montauban [Fr.] 11 Hj 44.01N 1.21 E
Montauban [Fr.] 11 Df 48.12N 2.03W
Montauk Point 44 Le 41.04N 71.52W
Montbard 11 Kg 47.37N 4.20 E
Montbéliard 11 Mg 47.31N 6.48 E
Montblanc 13 Nc 41.22N 1.10 E
Mont Blanc 5 Gf 45.50N 6.52 E
Montbrison 11 Ki 45.36N 4.03 E
Montceau-les-Mines 11 Kh 46.40N 4.22 E
Mont Cenis, Col du- 5 Gf 45.15N 6.54 E
Montchanin 11 Kh 46.45N 4.27 E
Mont Darwin 37 Ec 16.46S 31.35 E
Mont-de-Marsan 11 Fk 43.53N 0.30W
Montdidier 11 Ie 49.39N 2.34 E
Mont Dore 11 Ii 45.34N 2.49 E
Mont-Dore 63b Cf 22.17S 166.35 E
Monte, Laguna del- 55 Am 37.00S 62.28W
Monteagudo 54 Fg 19.49S 63.59W
Monte Alban 39 Jh 17.02N 96.45W
Monte Alegre 54 Hd 2.01S 54.04W
Monte Alegre, Rio- 55 Gc 17.16S 50.41W
Monte Alegre de Goiás 55 Ia 13.14S 47.10W
Montealegre del Castillo 13 Kf 38.47N 1.19W
Monte Alegre de Minas 55 Hd 18.52S 48.52W
Monte Azul 54 Jg 15.09S 42.53W
Montebello 44 Jc 45.39N 74.56W
Monte Bello Islands 59 Dd 20.25S 115.30 E
Monte Carlo 11 Nk 43.44N 7.25 E
Montecarlo 55 Eh 26.34S 54.47W
Monte Carmelo 55 Id 18.43S 47.29W
Monte Caseros 56 Id 30.15S 57.39W
Montecatini Terme 14 Eg 43.23N 10.45 E
Montecchio Maggiore 14 Fe 45.30N 11.24 E
Monte Comán 56 Gd 34.36S 67.54W
Montecristi 49 Ld 19.52N 71.39W
Montecristo 14 Eh 42.20N 10.20 E
Monte Cristo 55 Bb 14.43S 61.14W
Monte Ermoso 55 Bn 38.55S 61.33W
Monte Escobedo 48 Hf 22.18N 103.35W
Montefalco 14 Gh 42.52N 12.39 E
Montefeltro 14 Gg 43.55N 12.15 E
Montefiascone 14 Gh 42.32N 12.02 E
Montefrio 13 Hg 37.19N 4.01W
Montego Bay 39 Lh 18.30N 77.55W
Monteiro 54 Ke 7.53S 37.07W
Montelíbano 49 Ji 8.02N 75.29W
Montélimar 11 Kj 44.34N 4.45 E
Monte Lindo, Arroyo- 55 Cg 25.28S 59.25W
Monte Lindo, Rio- 56 Ib 23.56S 57.12W
Monte Lindo Chico, Riacho- 55 Dg 25.53S 57.53W

Index Symbols

[1] Independent Nation
[2] State, Region
[3] District, County
[4] Municipality
[5] Colony, Dependency
Continent
Physical Region
Historical or Cultural Region
Mount, Mountain
Volcano
Hill
Mountains, Mountain Range
Hills, Escarpment
Plateau, Upland
Pass, Gap
Plain, Lowland
Delta
Salt Flat
Valley, Canyon
Crater, Cave
Karst Features
Depression
Polder
Desert, Dunes
Forest, Woods
Heath, Steppe
Oasis
Cape, Point
Coast, Beach
Cliff
Peninsula
Isthmus
Sandbank
Island
Atoll
Rock, Reef
Islands, Archipelago
Rocks, Reefs
Coral Reef
Well, Spring
Geyser
River, Stream
Waterfall Rapids
River Mouth, Estuary
Lake
Salt Lake
Intermittent Lake
Reservoir
Swamp, Pond
Canal
Glacier
Ice Shelf, Pack Ice
Ocean
Sea
Gulf, Bay
Strait, Fjord
Lagoon
Bank
Seamount
Tablemount
Ridge
Shelf
Basin
Escarpment, Sea Scarp
Fracture
Trench, Abyss
National Park, Reserve
Point of Interest
Recreation Site
Cave, Cavern
Historic Site
Ruins
Wall, Walls
Church, Abbey
Temple
Scientific Station
Airport
Port
Lighthouse
Mine
Tunnel
Dam, Bridge

Name	Map	Grid	Lat.	Long.
Monte Lindo Grande, Riacho- �River	55	Cg	25.45 S	58.06 W
Montello [Nv.-U.S.]	46	Hf	41.16 N	114.12 W
Montello [Wi.-U.S.]	45	Le	43.48 N	89.20 W
Montemorelos	47	Ec	25.12 N	99.49 W
Montemor-o-Novo	13	Df	38.39 N	8.13 W
Montemor-o-Velho	13	Dd	40.10 N	8.41 W
Montemuro, Serra de- ⌷	13	Dc	40.58 N	8.01 W
Montenegro	56	Jc	29.42 S	51.28 W
Montenegro (EN) = Crna Gora [2]	15	Cg	42.30 N	19.18 E
Montenegro (EN) = Crna Gora [2]	15	Cg	42.30 N	19.18 E
Monte Plata	49	Md	18.48 N	69.47 W
Montepuez ⌷	37	Gb	12.32 S	40.27 E
Montepuez	37	Fb	13.07 S	39.00 E
Montepulciano	14	Fg	43.05 N	11.47 E
Monte Quemado	56	Hc	25.48 S	62.52 W
Monte Real	13	De	39.51 N	8.52 W
Montereale, Passo di- ⌷	14	Hh	42.31 N	13.13 E
Montereau-Faut-Yonne	11	If	48.23 N	2.57 E
Monterey	43	Cd	36.37 N	121.55 W
Monterey Bay ⌷	43	Cd	36.45 N	121.55 W
Monteria	53	Ie	8.46 N	75.53 W
Montero	54	Fg	17.20 S	63.15 W
Monteros	56	Gc	27.10 S	65.30 W
Monterotondo	14	Gh	42.03 N	12.37 E
Monterrey	39	Ig	25.40 N	100.19 W
Montesano	46	Dc	46.59 N	123.36 W
Monte San Savino	14	Fg	43.20 N	11.43 E
Monte Sant'Angelo	14	Ji	41.42 N	15.57 E
Monte Santu, Capo di- ⌷	14	Dj	45.05 N	9.44 E
Montes Claros	53	Lg	16.43 S	43.52 W
Montes Claros de Goiás	55	Gb	15.54 S	51.13 W
Montesilvano	14	Hh	42.31 N	14.09 E
Montevarchi	14	Fg	43.31 N	11.34 E
Montevideo	55	Dl	34.50 S	56.10 W
Montevideo [Mn.-U.S.]	45	Id	44.57 N	95.43 W
Montevideo [Ur.]	53	Ki	34.53 S	56.11 W
Monte Vista	45	Ch	37.35 N	106.09 W
Montfaucon	12	He	49.17 N	5.08 E
Montfort-l'Amaury	12	Df	48.47 N	1.49 E
Montfort-sur-Risle	12	Ce	49.18 N	0.40 E
Montgenèvre, Col de- ⌷	11	Mj	44.56 N	6.44 E
Montgomery	39	Kf	32.23 N	86.18 W
Montgomery Pass ⌷	46	Fh	38.00 N	118.20 W
Montguyon	11	Fi	45.13 N	0.11 W
Monthermé	12	Ge	49.53 N	4.44 E
Monthey	14	Ad	46.15 N	6.56 E
Monthois	12	Ge	49.19 N	4.43 E
Monticello [Ar.-U.S.]	45	Kj	33.38 N	91.47 W
Monticello [Fl.-U.S.]	44	Fj	30.33 N	83.52 W
Monticello [Ia.-U.S.]	45	Ke	42.15 N	91.12 W
Monticello [In.-U.S.]	44	Dd	40.45 N	86.46 W
Monticello [Ky.-U.S.]	44	Eg	36.50 N	84.51 W
Monticello [N.Y.-U.S.]	44	Je	41.39 N	74.41 W
Monticello [Ut.-U.S.]	43	Fd	37.52 N	109.21 W
Montiel	13	Jf	38.42 N	2.52 W
Montiel, Campo de- ⌷	13	Jf	38.46 N	2.44 W
Montiel, Cuchilla de- ⌷	55	Cj	31.05 S	59.10 W
Montignac	11	Hi	45.04 N	1.10 E
Montigny-le-Roi	11	Lf	48.00 N	5.30 E
Montigny-les-Metz	11	Me	49.06 N	6.09 E
Montigny-le-Tilleul	12	Gd	50.23 N	4.22 E
Montijo [Pan.]	49	Gj	7.59 N	81.03 W
Montijo [Port.]	13	Df	38.42 N	8.58 W
Montijo [Sp.]	13	Ff	38.55 N	6.37 W
Montijo, Golfo de- ⌷	49	Gj	7.40 N	81.07 W
Montilla	13	Hg	37.35 N	4.38 W
Montividiu	55	Gc	17.24 S	51.14 W
Montivilliers	11	Ge	49.33 N	0.12 E
Mont Joli	42	Kg	48.35 N	68.11 W
Mont-Laurier	42	Jg	46.33 N	75.30 W
Mont-Louis	44	Oa	49.15 N	65.43 W
Mont-Louis	11	Il	42.31 N	2.07 E
Montluçon	11	Ih	46.20 N	2.36 E
Montmagny	42	Kg	46.59 N	70.33 W
Montmarault	11	Ih	46.19 N	2.57 E
Montmédy	11	Le	49.31 N	5.22 E
Montmirail	11	Jf	48.52 N	3.32 E
Montmorency	12	Ef	49.00 N	2.20 E
Montmorillon	11	Gh	46.26 N	0.52 E
Montmort-Lucy	12	Ff	48.55 N	3.49 E
Monto	59	Kd	24.52 S	151.07 E
Montoire-sur-le-Loir	11	Gg	47.45 N	0.52 E
Montone	14	Gf	44.24 N	12.14 E
Montoro	13	Hf	38.01 N	4.23 W
Montpelier [Id.-U.S.]	43	Ec	42.19 N	111.18 W
Montpelier [Vt.-U.S.]	39	Le	44.16 N	72.35 W
Montpellier	6	Gg	43.36 N	3.53 E
Montpon-Ménestérol	11	Gi	45.01 N	0.10 E
Montréal	39	Le	45.31 N	73.34 W
Montreal Lake ⌷	42	Gf	54.20 N	105.40 W
Montreal River ⌷	44	Hb	47.08 N	79.27 W
Montréjeau	11	Gk	43.05 N	0.35 E
Montreuil [Fr.]	11	Hd	50.28 N	1.46 E
Montreuil [Fr.]	12	Ef	48.52 N	2.26 E
Montreuil-l'Argillé	12	Cf	48.56 N	0.29 E
Montreux	14	Ad	46.26 N	6.55 E
Montrose [Co.-U.S.]	43	Fd	38.29 N	107.53 W
Montrose [Scot.-U.K.]	9	Ke	56.43 N	2.29 W
Monts, Pointe des- ⌷	44	Na	49.19 N	67.23 W
Mont-Saint-Aignan	12	De	49.28 N	1.05 E
Mont-Saint-Michel, Baie du- ⌷	11	Ef	48.40 N	1.40 W
Montsalvy	11	Ij	44.42 N	2.30 E
Montsant, Serra del-/ Montsant, Sierra de- ⌷	13	Mc	41.17 N	0.50 E
Montsant, Serra de-/ Montsant, Sierra de- ⌷	13	Mc	41.17 N	0.50 E
Montsec, Serra del-/ Montsech, Sierra de- ⌷	13	Mb	42.02 N	0.50 E
Montsec, Serra del-/ Montsech, Sierra de- ⌷	13	Mb	42.02 N	0.50 E
Montseny/Pallars, Montsent de- ⌷	13	Nb	42.29 N	1.02 E
Montseny, Sierra de- ⌷	13	Oc	41.48 N	2.24 E
Montserrado [3]	34	Cd	6.35 N	10.35 W
Montserrat [5]	39	Mh	16.45 N	62.12 W
Montserrat, Monasterio de- ⌷	13	Nc	41.35 N	1.49 E
Montserrat, Monèstir de-/ Montserrat, Monasterio de-	13	Nc	41.35 N	1.49 E
Montserrat, Monèstir de- ⌷	13	Nc	41.35 N	1.49 E
Montserrat, Monèstir de-/ Montserrat, Monasterio de-	13	Nc	41.35 N	1.49 E
Montuosa, Isla- ⌷	49	Fj	7.28 N	82.14 W
Montville	12	De	49.33 N	1.07 E
Monument Peak ⌷	46	He	42.07 N	114.14 W
Monument Valley ⌷	46	Jh	36.50 N	110.20 W
Monveda	36	Db	2.57 N	21.27 E
Monviso ⌷	5	Gg	44.40 N	7.07 E
Monywa	25	Jd	22.07 N	95.08 E
Monza	14	De	45.35 N	9.16 E
Monze	36	Ef	16.16 S	27.29 E
Monzen	29	Sc	37.17 N	136.46 E
Monzón	13	Mc	41.55 N	0.12 E
Mo'oka	29	Fc	36.27 N	139.59 E
Moonbeam	44	Fa	49.25 N	82.11 W
Moonie	59	Ke	27.40 S	150.19 E
Moonie River ⌷	59	Je	29.19 S	148.43 E
Moonta	59	Hf	34.04 S	137.35 E
Moora	58	Ch	30.39 S	116.00 E
Moorcroft	46	Md	44.16 N	104.57 W
Moore	45	Hi	35.20 N	97.29 W
Moore, Lake- ⌷	57	Cg	29.50 S	117.35 E
Moorea, Ile- ⌷	57	Mf	17.32 S	149.50 W
Moore's Island ⌷	44	Il	26.18 N	77.33 W
Moorhead	43	Hb	46.53 N	96.45 W
Moormerland	12	Ja	53.18 N	7.26 E
Moormerland-Neermoor	12	Ja	53.18 N	7.26 E
Mooreesburg	37	Bf	33.09 S	18.40 E
Moosburg an der Isar	10	Hh	48.28 N	11.56 E
Moose ⌷	38	Kd	50.48 N	81.18 W
Moosehead Lake ⌷	43	Nb	45.40 N	69.40 W
Moose Jaw	39	Id	50.23 N	105.32 W
Moose Jaw River ⌷	46	Na	50.34 N	105.17 W
Moose Lake	45	Jc	46.25 N	92.45 W
Mooselookmeguntic Lake ⌷	44	Lc	44.53 N	70.48 W
Moose Mountain ⌷	45	Eb	49.45 N	102.37 W
Moose Mountain Creek ⌷	45	Eb	49.12 N	102.10 W
Moosomin	42	Hf	50.09 N	101.40 W
Moosonee	39	Kd	51.17 N	80.39 W
Mopeia	37	Fc	17.59 S	35.43 E
Mopelia, Atoll- → Maupihaa Atoll ⌷	57	Lf	16.50 S	153.55 W
Mopti	31	Gg	14.30 N	4.12 W
Mopti [3]	34	Ec	14.40 N	4.15 W
Moqokorei	35	He	4.04 N	46.08 E
Moquegua [2]	54	Dg	16.50 S	70.55 W
Moquegua	54	Dg	17.12 S	70.56 W
Mór	10	Oi	47.23 N	18.12 E
Mor, Glen- ⌷	9	Id	57.10 N	4.40 W
Mora [Cam.]	34	Hc	11.03 N	14.09 E
Mora [Port.]	13	Df	38.56 N	8.10 W
Mora [Sp.]	13	Ie	39.41 N	3.46 W
Mora [Swe.]	7	Df	61.00 N	14.33 E
Morača ⌷	15	Cg	42.16 N	19.09 E
Morača, Manastir- ⌷	15	Cg	42.46 N	19.24 E
Morādābād	22	Jg	28.50 N	78.47 E
Morada Nova de Minas	55	Jb	18.25 S	45.22 W
Móra d'Ebre/Mora d'Ebro	13	Mc	41.05 N	0.38 E
Mora de Ebro/Móra d'Ebre	13	Mc	41.05 N	0.38 E
Mora de Rubielos	13	Ld	40.15 N	0.45 W
Morafenobe	37	Gc	17.49 S	44.55 E
Morąg	10	Pc	53.56 N	19.56 E
Mórahalom	10	Pj	46.13 N	19.53 E
Moraleda, Canal- ⌷	56	Ff	44.30 S	73.30 W
Moraleja	13	Fd	40.04 N	6.39 W
Morales [Col.]	49	Ki	8.17 N	73.52 W
Morales [Guat.]	49	Cf	15.29 N	88.49 W
Morales, Laguna- ⌷	48	Kf	23.35 N	97.45 W
Moramanga	37	He	18.57 S	48.11 E
Moran	46	Je	43.50 N	110.28 W
Morane Atoll ⌷	57	Ng	23.10 S	137.07 W
Morangas, Ribeirão- ⌷	55	Fd	19.39 S	52.19 W
Morant Bay	49	Ie	17.53 N	76.25 W
Morant Cays ⌷	47	Ie	17.24 N	75.59 W
Morant Point ⌷	49	Ie	17.55 N	76.10 W
Morar, Loch- ⌷	9	He	56.58 N	5.45 W
Morarano	37	Hc	17.46 S	48.10 E
Mora River ⌷	45	Di	35.44 N	104.23 W
Moraska, Góra- ⌷	10	Md	52.30 N	16.52 E
Morat/Murten	14	Bd	46.56 N	7.08 E
Morata, Puerto de- ⌷	13	Kc	41.29 N	1.31 W
Moratalla	13	Kf	38.12 N	1.53 W
Moratuwa	25	Fg	6.46 N	79.53 E
Morava ⌷	5	Hf	48.10 N	16.59 E
Morava = Moravia (EN) ⌷	5	Hf	49.30 N	17.00 E
Morava = Moravia (EN) ⌷	10	Mg	49.30 N	17.00 E
Moravia (EN) = Morava ⌷	5	Hf	49.30 N	17.00 E
Moravia (EN) = Morava ⌷	10	Mg	49.30 N	17.00 E
Moravian Gate (EN) = Moravská Brána ⌷	5	Hf	49.33 N	17.42 E
Moravian Upland (EN) = Českomoravská Vrchovina ⌷	5	Hf	49.20 N	15.30 E
Moravica ⌷	15	Df	43.51 N	20.05 E
Moravská Brána = Moravian Gate (EN) ⌷	5	Hf	49.33 N	17.42 E
Moravské Budějovice	10	Le	49.03 N	15.49 E
Morawa	59	De	29.13 S	116.00 E
Morawhanna	54	Gb	8.16 N	59.45 W
Moray Firth ⌷	5	Fd	57.50 N	3.30 W
Morbach	12	Je	49.49 N	7.07 E
Morbihan [3]	11	Dg	47.35 N	2.50 W
Morbihan ⌷	11	Dg	47.35 N	2.48 W
Mörbylånga	7	Dh	56.31 N	16.23 E
Morcenx	11	Fj	44.02 N	0.55 W
Mordağa	24	Md	37.26 N	49.25 E
Morden	42	Hg	49.11 N	98.05 W
Mordovo	16	Lc	52.05 N	40.46 E
Mordovskaja respublika	19	Ee	54.20 N	44.30 E
Möre	8	Fh	56.25 N	15.55 E
More, Ben- ⌷	9	Ie	56.23 N	4.31 W
Morea	37	Bd	32.41 S	15.54 E
More Assynt, Ben- ⌷	9	Ic	58.07 N	4.51 W
Moreau River ⌷	43	Gb	45.18 N	100.43 W
Morecambe	9	Kg	54.04 N	2.53 W
Morecambe Bay ⌷	9	Kg	54.07 N	3.00 W
Moree	58	Fg	29.28 S	149.51 E
Morehead [Ky.-U.S.]	44	Ff	38.11 N	83.25 W
Morehead [Pap.N.Gui.]	60	Ci	8.50 S	141.57 E
Morehead City ⌷	44	If	34.43 N	76.43 W
Moreira, Gora- ⌷	19	Gb	69.30 N	62.05 E
Morelia	17	Ib	63.20 N	59.45 E
Morella	13	Ld	40.37 N	0.06 W
Morelos	48	Ic	28.25 N	100.53 W
Morelos [2]	47	Ee	18.45 N	99.00 W
Morena, Sierra- ⌷	5	Fh	38.00 N	5.00 W
Moreni	15	Ie	44.59 N	25.39 E
Møre og Romsdal [2]	7	Be	62.40 N	7.50 E
Moresby ⌷	42	Ef	52.45 N	131.50 W
Moreton Bay ⌷	59	Ke	27.20 S	153.15 E
Moreton Island ⌷	59	Ke	27.10 S	153.25 E
Moret-sur-Loing	11	If	48.22 N	2.49 E
Moreuil	11	Ie	49.46 N	2.29 E
Morez	11	Mh	46.31 N	6.02 E
Morezu	15	Hd	45.09 N	24.01 E
Mörfelden	12	Ke	49.59 N	8.34 E
Morgan City	45	Kl	29.42 N	91.12 W
Morganfield	44	Dg	37.41 N	87.55 W
Morganton	44	Gh	35.45 N	81.41 W
Morgantown [Ky.-U.S.]	44	Dg	37.14 N	86.41 W
Morgantown [W.V.-U.S.]	44	Hf	39.38 N	79.57 W
Morges	14	Ad	46.31 N	6.30 E
Morghāb ⌷	23	Jb	38.18 N	61.12 E
Morhange	11	Mf	48.55 N	6.38 E
Mori [China]	27	Fc	43.49 N	90.11 E
Mori [Jap.]	29a	Ab	42.06 N	140.35 E
Moriarty	45	Ci	34.59 N	106.03 W
Morichal Largo, Rio- ⌷	50	Eh	9.27 N	62.25 W
Moriguchi	29	Dd	34.44 N	135.34 E
Morin Dawa (Nirji)	27	Lb	48.30 N	124.28 E
Morioka	22	Qf	39.42 N	141.09 E
Moriyoshi	29	Ga	40.07 N	140.22 E
Moriyoshi-Yama ⌷	29	Ga	39.59 N	140.33 E
Morjärv	7	Fc	66.04 N	22.43 E
Morki	7	Lh	56.28 N	49.00 E
Morko	8	Gf	59.00 N	17.40 E
Morkoka ⌷	20	Gc	65.03 N	115.40 E
Morkøv	8	Di	55.40 N	11.32 E
Morlaix	11	Cf	48.35 N	3.50 W
Morlanwelz	12	Gd	50.27 N	4.14 E
Mörlunda	8	Fg	57.19 N	15.51 E
Mormanno	14	Jk	39.53 N	15.59 E
Morne-à-l'Eau	50	Fd	16.21 N	61.31 W
Morne Diablotin ⌷	47	Le	15.30 N	61.24 W
Mornington, Isla- ⌷	56	Fg	49.45 S	75.23 W
Mornington Island ⌷	59	Hc	16.35 S	139.24 E
Moro	46	Ed	45.29 N	120.44 W
Morobe	58	Ee	7.45 S	147.37 E
Morocco (EN) = Al Maghrib [1]	31	Ge	32.00 N	5.50 W
Morogoro	31	Ki	6.49 S	37.40 E
Morogoro [3]	36	Gd	8.20 S	37.00 E
Moro Gulf ⌷	26	He	6.51 N	123.00 E
Moroléon	48	Ig	20.08 N	101.12 W
Morombe	31	Lk	21.44 S	43.23 E
Morón [Arg.]	55	Cl	34.39 S	58.37 W
Morón [Cuba]	47	Jd	22.06 N	78.38 W
Morón [Ven.]	54	Ea	10.29 N	68.11 W
Morona, Rio- ⌷	54	Cd	4.45 S	77.04 W
Morondava	31	Lk	20.15 S	44.17 E
Morón de la Frontera	13	Gg	37.08 N	5.27 W
Morones, Sierra- ⌷	48	Hg	21.55 N	103.05 W
Moroni	31	Lj	11.41 S	43.16 E
Moron Us He ⌷	21	Lf	34.42 N	94.50 E
Morotai, Pulau- ⌷	57	Dd	2.20 N	128.25 E
Moroto	31	Kh	2.32 N	34.39 E
Moroviţa	15	Kh	45.16 N	21.16 E
Morozov ⌷	15	Ig	42.30 N	25.10 E
Morozovsk	19	Ef	48.00 N	41.50 E
Morpeth	9	Lf	55.10 N	1.41 W
Morphou → Güzelyurt	24	Sc	35.12 N	32.59 E
Morrilton	45	Ji	35.09 N	92.45 W
Morrinhos	54	Jf	17.44 S	49.07 W
Morrinsville	62	Fb	37.39 S	175.32 E
Morris [Il.-U.S.]	45	Lf	41.22 N	88.26 W
Morris [Man.-Can.]	42	Hg	49.21 N	97.22 W
Morris [Mn.-U.S.]	45	Id	45.35 N	95.55 W
Morris, Mount- ⌷	59	Gd	26.09 S	131.04 E
Morris Jesup, Kap- ⌷	67	Me	83.45 N	35.50 W
Morrison Dennis Cays ⌷	49	Gf	14.28 N	82.53 W
Morristown	44	Fg	36.13 N	83.18 W
Morrito	49	Eh	11.37 N	85.05 W
Morro, Punta del- ⌷	48	Kh	19.51 N	96.27 W
Morro Bay	46	Dh	35.22 N	120.51 W
Morro do Chapéu	54	Jf	11.33 S	41.09 W
Morrosquillo, Golfo de- ⌷	49	Ji	9.35 N	75.40 W
Morro Vermelho, Serra do- ⌷	55	Jc	17.45 S	45.20 W
Mörrum	8	Eh	56.11 N	14.45 E
Morrumbala	37	Fc	17.20 S	35.35 E
Morrumbene	37	Fd	23.39 S	35.20 E
Mörrumsån ⌷	8	Eh	56.09 N	14.44 E
Mors ⌷	8	Ch	56.50 N	8.45 E
Moršansk	19	Ee	53.26 N	41.49 E
Morsbach	12	Jd	50.52 N	7.45 E
Morsberg	5	Ge	49.43 N	8.54 E
Mörsil	5	Ge	63.19 N	13.38 E
Mörskom/Myrskylä	8	Kd	60.40 N	25.51 E
Morsott	14	Cn	35.40 N	8.01 E
Mortagne	11	Fj	44.02 N	0.55 W
Mortagne-au-Perche	11	Gf	48.31 N	0.33 E
Mortagne-sur-Sèvre	11	Fg	47.00 N	0.57 W
Mortain	11	Ff	48.39 N	0.56 W
Mortara	14	Ce	45.15 N	8.44 E
Mortcha ⌷	30	Jg	16.00 N	21.10 E
Morteau	11	Mg	47.04 N	6.37 E
Morteaux-Coulibœuf	12	Bf	48.56 N	0.04 W
Morteros	56	Hd	30.42 S	62.00 W
Mortes, Rio das- ⌷	55	Je	21.09 S	44.53 W
Mortesoro	35	Ec	10.12 N	34.09 E
Mortlock Islands ⌷	57	Gd	5.27 N	153.40 E
Morton	46	Dc	46.33 N	122.17 W
Mortsel	12	Gc	51.10 N	4.28 E
Morumbi	55	Ef	23.46 S	54.06 W
Morvan ⌷	11	Jg	47.05 N	4.00 E
Morven	59	Je	26.25 S	147.07 E
Morvern ⌷	9	He	56.35 N	5.50 W
Morvi	25	Ed	22.49 N	70.50 E
Morwell	58	Fh	38.14 S	146.24 E
Morzine	11	Mh	46.11 N	6.43 E
Moržovec, Ostrov- ⌷	7	Kc	66.45 N	42.35 E
Mośa ⌷	7	Fh	38.00 N	5.00 W
Mosbach	10	Fg	49.21 N	9.09 E
Mosby	8	Bf	58.14 N	7.54 E
Mosconi	55	Bl	35.44 S	60.34 W
Moscos Islands ⌷	59	Ke	27.10 S	153.25 E
Moscow [Id.-U.S.]	43	Db	46.44 N	116.59 W
Moscow (EN) = Moskva	5	Jd	55.45 N	37.35 E
Moscow Basin (EN) = Meščera	5	Kd	55.00 N	40.30 E
Moscow Canal (EN) = Moskvy, kanal imeni- ⌷	5	Jd	56.43 N	37.08 E
Moscow Upland (EN) = Moskovskaja Vozvyšennost' ⌷	5	Jd	56.30 N	37.30 E
Mosel = Moselle (EN) ⌷	5	Ge	50.22 N	7.36 E
Moselberge ⌷	12	Ie	49.57 N	6.56 E
Moselle [3]	11	Me	49.00 N	6.20 E
Moselle ⌷	5	Ge	50.22 N	7.36 E
Moselle (EN) = Mosel ⌷	5	Ge	50.22 N	7.36 E
Moses Lake	43	Db	47.08 N	119.17 W
Mosgiel	61	Di	45.53 S	170.22 E
Moshi	31	Ki	3.21 S	37.20 E
Mosina	10	Md	52.16 N	16.51 E
Mosjøen	6	Cd	65.50 N	13.12 E
Moskalvo	20	Jf	53.39 N	142.37 E
Moskenesøy ⌷	7	Cc	67.59 N	13.00 E
Moskovskaja Oblast [3]	19	Dd	55.45 N	37.45 E
Moskovskaja Vozvyšennost' = Moscow Upland (EN) ⌷	5	Jd	56.30 N	37.30 E
Moskovski	18	Gf	37.40 N	69.39 E
Moskva = Moscow (EN)	18	Ee	38.27 N	64.24 E
Moskva, Pik- ⌷	18	He	38.55 N	71.52 E
Moskvy, kanal imeni- = Moscow Canal (EN) ⌷	5	Jd	56.43 N	37.08 E
Moslavačka Gora ⌷	14	Le	45.38 N	16.42 E
Moso ⌷	63b	Ce	21.30 S	168.15 E
Mosomane	37	Dd	24.01 S	26.19 E
Mosoni-Duna ⌷	10	Ni	47.44 N	17.47 E
Mosonmagyaróvár	10	Ni	47.52 N	17.17 E
Mosor ⌷	14	Kg	43.30 N	16.40 E
Mosquero	45	Ei	35.47 N	103.58 W
Mosquito, Baie - ⌷	42	Jd	60.40 N	78.00 W
Mosquito Coast (EN) = Mosquitos, Costa de- ⌷	38	Kh	13.00 N	83.45 W
Mosquitos, Costa de- = Mosquito Coast (EN) ⌷	38	Kh	13.00 N	83.45 W
Mosquitos, Golfo de los- ⌷	49	Hi	9.00 N	81.20 W
Moss	6	Hd	59.26 N	10.42 E
Mossaka	36	Cc	1.13 S	16.48 E
Mossâmedes	55	Gb	16.07 S	50.11 W
Mossbank	46	Mb	49.55 N	105.59 W
Mossburn	61	Ci	45.41 S	168.15 E
Mossel Bay	31	Jl	34.11 S	22.08 E
Mossendjo	36	Bc	2.57 S	12.44 E
Mossman	58	Ff	16.28 S	145.22 E
Mossoró	53	Mf	5.11 S	37.20 W
Moss Point	45	Lk	30.25 N	88.29 W
Mossuril	55	Cf	22.12 S	57.57 W
Most	10	Jd	50.32 N	13.39 E
Mostaganem [3]	32	Hb	35.40 N	0.30 E
Mostaganem	14	Le	45.04 N	17.42 E
Mostar	14	Lg	43.21 N	17.49 E
Mostardas	55	Gj	31.06 S	50.57 W
Møsting, Kap- ⌷	41	Kd	63.45 N	41.00 W
Mostiska	16	Ce	49.48 N	23.09 E
Mostištĕ ⌷	14	Ni	26.54 N	32.28 E
Mostovskoj	16	Hf	44.09 N	13.45 E
Mosty	19	Ce	53.27 N	24.33 E
Mosul (EN) = Al Mawşil	22	Gf	36.20 N	43.08 E
Møsvatn ⌷	7	Bg	59.50 N	8.00 E
Mota	63b	Ca	13.40 S	167.42 E
Motaba ⌷	35	Fc	11.05 N	37.53 E
Motacusito	55	Bc	17.35 S	61.31 W
Mota del Marques	13	Gc	41.38 N	5.10 W
Motagua ⌷	38	Kh	15.44 N	88.14 W
Motajica ⌷	14	Le	45.04 N	17.40 E
Motala	7	Dg	58.33 N	15.03 E
Motala ström ⌷	8	Ef	58.38 N	16.10 E
Motatán	49	Li	9.24 N	70.36 W
Motatán, Rio- ⌷	49	Li	9.32 N	71.02 W
Motegi	29	Gc	36.32 N	140.10 E
Motehuala	47	Dd	23.39 N	100.39 W
Motianling	63d	Ce	34.38 S	178.30 W
Motherwell	9	Jf	55.48 N	4.00 W
Motihāri	25	Gc	26.39 N	84.55 E
Motilla del Palancar	13	Ke	39.34 N	1.53 W
Motiti Island ⌷	62	Gb	37.40 S	176.25 E
Motlav ⌷	63b	Ca	13.40 S	167.40 E
Motobu	29b	Ab	26.40 N	127.55 E
Motol	10	Vd	52.17 N	25.40 E
Motovski Zaliv ⌷	7	Hb	69.30 N	32.30 E
Motoyoshi	29	Gb	38.48 N	141.31 E
Motozintla de Mendoza	48	Mj	15.22 N	92.14 W
Motril	13	Ih	36.45 N	3.31 W
Motru ⌷	15	Ge	44.33 N	23.27 E
Motru	15	Fe	44.48 N	23.00 E
Motsuta-Misaki ⌷	29a	Ab	42.36 N	139.49 E
Mott	45	Ec	46.22 N	102.20 W
Motteville	12	Ce	49.38 N	0.51 E
Motu ⌷	62	Gb	37.51 S	177.35 E
Motueka	62	Ed	41.07 S	173.01 E
Motuhora Island ⌷	62	Gb	37.50 S	177.00 E
Motu-Iti ⌷	65d	Ac	27.11 S	109.27 W
Motu-Iti → Tupai Atoll ⌷	61	Kc	16.17 S	151.50 W
Motul	47	Gd	21.06 N	89.17 W
Motu-Nui ⌷	65d	Ac	27.12 S	109.28 W
Motu One Atoll ⌷	57	Lf	15.48 S	154.33 W
Motupae ⌷	64n	Ac	10.27 S	161.02 W
Motupena Point ⌷	63a	Bb	6.32 S	155.09 E
Moturiki ⌷	63d	Bb	17.46 S	178.45 E
Motutapu ⌷	64p	Cb	21.14 S	159.43 W
Motu Tautara ⌷	65d	Ab	27.05 S	109.26 W
Motutunga Atoll ⌷	57	Mf	17.06 S	144.22 W
Moubray Bay ⌷	66	Kf	72.11 S	170.15 E
Mouchard	11	Lh	46.58 N	5.48 E
Mouchoir Bank (EN) ⌷	47	Jd	20.57 N	70.42 W
Mouchoir Passage ⌷	49	Lc	21.10 N	71.00 W
Moudjéria	32	Ef	17.52 N	12.20 W
Mouila	31	Ii	1.52 S	11.01 E
Mouka	35	Cd	7.16 N	21.52 E
Moul	34	Hb	15.03 N	13.18 E
Mould Bay	39	Hb	76.15 N	119.30 W
Moule	50	Fd	16.20 N	61.21 W
Moule à Chique, Cap- ⌷	51k	Bb	13.43 N	60.57 W
Moulins	11	Jh	46.34 N	3.20 E
Moulmein → Mawlamyine	22	Le	16.30 N	97.38 E
Moulouya ⌷	30	Ge	35.06 N	2.20 W
Moult	12	Be	49.07 N	0.10 W
Moultrie	44	Fj	31.11 N	83.47 W
Moultrie, Lake- ⌷	44	Gi	33.20 N	80.05 W
Mouly, Pointe de- ⌷	63b	Ce	20.43 S	166.23 E
Moundou	31	Ih	8.34 N	16.05 E
Moundsville	44	Gf	39.54 N	80.44 W
Mo'unga'one ⌷	65b	Ba	19.38 S	174.29 W
Mountainair	45	Ci	34.31 N	106.15 W
Mountain Grove	45	Jh	37.08 N	92.16 W
Mountain Home [Ar.-U.S.]	45	Jh	36.21 N	92.23 W
Mountain Home [Id.-U.S.]	43	Dc	43.08 N	115.41 W
Mountain Nile (EN) = Jabal, Baḥr al- ⌷	30	Kh	9.30 N	30.30 E
Mountain Village	40	Gd	62.05 N	163.44 W
Mount Airy	44	Gg	36.31 N	80.37 W
Mount Barker	59	Dd	34.38 S	117.40 E
Mount Carmel	44	Mf	38.25 N	87.46 W
Mount Desert Island ⌷	44	Mc	44.20 N	68.20 W
Mount Douglas	58	Fg	21.30 S	146.50 E
Mount Forest	44	Gd	43.59 N	80.44 W
Mount Frere	37	Df	31.00 S	28.58 E
Mount Gambier	60	Ci	5.52 S	144.13 E
Mount Hagen	59	Hf	34.07 S	135.23 E
Mount Hope	58	Eg	20.44 S	139.30 E
Mount Isa	46	Dc	47.47 N	122.18 W
Mountlake Terrace	44	Ge	40.23 N	80.03 W
Mount Lebanon	59	Hg	35.15 S	138.50 E
Mount Lofty Ranges ⌷	58	Cg	28.04 S	117.49 E
Mount Magnet	61	Gb	37.38 S	176.12 E
Mount Maunganui	59	Gb	11.20 S	132.45 E
Mountnorris Bay ⌷	45	Kf	40.58 N	91.33 W
Mount Pleasant [Ia.-U.S.]	44	Ed	43.35 N	84.47 W
Mount Pleasant [Mi.-U.S.]	44	Hi	32.47 N	79.52 W
Mount Pleasant [S.C.-U.S.]	45	Ij	33.09 N	94.58 W
Mount Pleasant [Tx.-U.S.]	43	Ed	39.33 N	111.27 W
Mount Pleasant [Ut.-U.S.]	9	Hk	50.03 N	5.25 W
Mount's Bay ⌷	62	Cd	43.42 S	171.25 E
Mount Somers	45	Kg	39.59 N	90.45 W
Mount Sterling [Il.-U.S.]	44	Ff	38.04 N	83.56 W
Mount Sterling [Ky.-U.S.]	42	Cd	60.20 N	139.41 W
Mount Vancouver	44	Cj	31.05 N	88.01 W
Mount Vernon [Al.-U.S.]	44	Dg	38.19 N	88.55 W
Mount Vernon [Il.-U.S.]	44	Fg	37.56 N	87.54 W
Mount Vernon [Ky.-U.S.]	44	Fe	40.23 N	82.30 W
Mount Vernon [Oh.-U.S.]	43	Cb	48.25 N	122.20 W
Mount Vernon [Wa.-U.S.]	59	Jd	24.35 S	150.00 E
Moura [Austl.]	13	Ef	38.08 N	7.27 W
Moura [Port.]	13	Ef	38.23 N	7.21 W
Mourão	35	Cb	17.50 N	22.25 E
Mourdi, Dépression du- = Mourdi Depression (EN) ⌷	30	Jg	18.10 N	23.00 E
Mourdiah	34	Dc	14.26 N	7.31 W
Mourdi Depression (EN) = Mourdi, Dépression du- ⌷	30	Jg	18.10 N	23.00 E
Mourmelon-le-Grand	12	Ge	49.08 N	4.22 E
Mourne Mountains/Beanna Boirche ⌷	9	Gg	54.10 N	6.04 W
Mouscron/Moeskroen	11	Id	50.44 N	3.13 E
Moustiers-Sainte-Marie	11	Mj	43.51 N	6.13 E
Moutier/Münster	14	Bd	47.16 N	7.22 E
Moutiers	11	Mi	45.29 N	6.32 E
Mouy	12	Ef	49.19 N	2.19 E
Mouydir ⌷	30	Hf	25.00 N	4.10 E
Mouyondzi	36	Bc	3.58 S	13.57 E
Mouzaia	13	Oh	36.28 N	2.41 E
Mouzon	12	He	49.36 N	5.05 E
Movas	48	Ec	28.10 N	109.25 W

Index Symbols

[1] Independent Nation
[2] State, Region
[3] District, County
[4] Municipality
[5] Colony, Dependency
⌷ Continent
⌷ Physical Region
⌷ Historical or Cultural Region
⌷ Mount, Mountain
⌷ Volcano
⌷ Hill
⌷ Mountains, Mountain Range
⌷ Hills, Escarpment
⌷ Plateau, Upland
⌷ Pass, Gap
⌷ Plain, Lowland
⌷ Delta
⌷ Salt Flat
⌷ Valley, Canyon
⌷ Crater, Cave
⌷ Karst Features
⌷ Depression
⌷ Polder
⌷ Desert, Dunes
⌷ Forest, Woods
⌷ Heath, Steppe
⌷ Oasis
⌷ Cape, Point
⌷ Coast, Beach
⌷ Cliff
⌷ Peninsula
⌷ Isthmus
⌷ Sandbank
⌷ Island
⌷ Atoll
⌷ Rock, Reef
⌷ Islands, Archipelago
⌷ Rocks, Reefs
⌷ Coral Reef
⌷ Well, Spring
⌷ Geyser
⌷ River, Stream
⌷ Waterfall Rapids
⌷ River Mouth, Estuary
⌷ Lake
⌷ Salt Lake
⌷ Intermittent Lake
⌷ Reservoir
⌷ Swamp, Pond
⌷ Canal
⌷ Glacier
⌷ Ice Shelf, Pack Ice
⌷ Ocean
⌷ Sea
⌷ Gulf, Bay
⌷ Strait, Fjord
⌷ Lagoon
⌷ Bank
⌷ Seamount
⌷ Tablemount
⌷ Ridge
⌷ Shelf
⌷ Basin
⌷ Escarpment, Sea Scarp
⌷ Fracture
⌷ Trench, Abyss
⌷ National Park, Reserve
⌷ Point of Interest
⌷ Recreation Site
⌷ Cave, Cavern
⌷ Historic Site
⌷ Ruins
⌷ Church, Abbey
⌷ Temple
⌷ Scientific Station
⌷ Airport
⌷ Port
⌷ Lighthouse
⌷ Mine
⌷ Tunnel
⌷ Dam, Bridge

Moxico [3] 36 De 12.00S 20.00 E
Moxico 36 De 11.51S 20.01 E
Moy/An Mhuaidh 9 Dg 54.12N 9.08W
Moyahua 48 Hg 21.16N 103.10W
Moyale [Eth.] 31 Kh 3.32N 39.04 E
Moyale [Kenya] 36 Gb 3.32N 39.03 E
Moyamba 34 Cd 8.10N 12.26W
Moÿ-de-l'Aisne 12 Fe 49.45N 3.22 E
Moyen Atlas = Middle Atlas (EN) 30 Ge 33.30N 4.30W
Moyen-Chari [3] 35 Bd 9.00N 18.00 E
Moyenne Guinée [3] 34 Cc 11.15N 12.30W
Moyenneville 12 Dd 50.04N 1.45 E
Moyen-Ogooué [3] 36 Bc 0.30S 10.30 E
Moyeuvre-Grande 12 Ie 49.15N 6.02 E
Moyo 36 Fb 3.40N 31.43 E
Moyo, Pulau- 26 Gh 8.15S 117.34 E
Moyobamba 53 If 6.02S 76.58W
Moyowosi 36 Fc 4.50S 31.24 E
Moyto 35 Bc 12.35N 16.33 E
Moyu/Karakax 27 Cd 37.17N 79.42 E
Možajsk 7 Ii 55.32N 36.02 E
Mozambique (EN) = Moçambique [1] 31 Kj 18.15S 35.00 E
Mozambique (EN) = Moçambique 31 Lk 15.03S 40.45 E
Mozambique, Canal de- = Mozambique Channel (EN) 30 Lk 20.00S 43.00 E
Mozambique Channel (EN) = Moçambique, Canal de- 30 Lk 20.00S 43.00 E
Mozambique Channel (EN) = Mozambique, Canal de- 30 Lk 20.00S 43.00 E
Mozambique Plateau (EN) 30 Kl 32.00S 35.00 E
Mozdok 19 Eg 43.44N 44.38 E
Možga 19 Fd 56.28N 52.13 E
Mozuli 8 Mh 56.32N 28.14 E
Mozyr 19 Ce 52.02N 29.16 E
Mpala 36 Ed 6.45S 29.31 E
Mpanda 31 Ki 6.22S 31.02 E
Mpigi 36 Fb 0.15N 32.20 E
Mpika 31 Kj 11.50S 31.27 E
Mpoko 35 Be 4.19N 18.33 E
Mporokoso 36 Fd 9.23S 30.08 E
Mpouia 36 Cc 2.37S 16.13 E
Mpui 36 Fd 8.21S 31.50 E
Mpulungu 36 Fd 8.46S 31.07 E
Mpwapwa 36 Gd 6.21S 36.29 E
Mrągowo 10 Rc 53.52N 21.19 E
Mrakovo 17 Hj 52.43N 56.38 E
Mrkonjić Grad 14 Lf 44.25N 17.06 E
Mrocza 10 Nc 53.14N 17.36 E
Mroga 10 Pd 52.09N 19.42 E
Msangesi 36 Ge 11.40S 36.45 E
Msid, Djebel- 14 Cn 36.25N 8.04 E
Msif 13 Qi 35.23N 4.45 E
M'Sila 13 Qi 35.31N 4.30 E
M'Sila [3] 32 Hb 35.00N 4.30 E
M'Sila 32 Hb 35.42N 4.33 E
Mšinskaja 8 Nf 58.55N 30.03 E
Msta 5 Jd 58.25N 31.20 E
Mstislavl 16 Gc 53.59N 31.45 E
Mszana Dolna 10 Qg 49.42N 20.05 E
Mtakuja 36 Fd 7.22S 30.37 E
Mtama 36 Ge 10.18S 39.22 E
Mtelo 36 Gb 1.39N 35.23 E
Mtera Reservoir 36 Gd 7.01S 35.55 E
Mtito Andei 36 Gc 2.41S 38.10 E
Mtubatuba 37 Ee 28.30S 32.08 E
Mtwara [3] 36 Ge 10.40S 39.00 E
Mtwara 31 Lj 10.16S 40.11 E
Mu, Cerro- 49 Ki 9.29N 73.07W
Mua 64h Ac 13.21S 176.10W
Mu'a 65b Ac 21.11S 175.07W
Mua, Baie de- 64h Bc 13.23S 176.09W
Muaná 54 Id 1.32S 49.13W
Muang Huon 25 Kd 20.09N 101.27 E
Muang Khammouan 25 Ke 17.24N 104.48 E
Muang Không 25 Lf 14.07N 105.51 E
Muang Khôngxédôn 25 Le 15.34N 105.49 E
Muang Khoua 25 Kd 21.05N 102.31 E
Muang Pak Lay 25 Ke 18.12N 101.25 E
Muang Pakxan 25 Ke 18.22N 103.39 E
Muang Pakxong 25 Le 15.11N 106.14 E
Muang Sing 25 Kd 21.11N 101.09 E
Muang Tahoi 25 Le 16.10N 106.38 E
Muang Thai = Thailand (EN) [1] 22 Lh 15.00N 100.00 E
Muang Vangviang 25 Ke 18.56N 102.27 E
Muang Xaignabouri 25 Ke 19.15N 101.45 E
Muang Xay 25 Kd 20.42N 101.59 E
Muang Xépôn 25 Le 16.41N 106.14 E
Muanzanza 36 Dd 6.32S 20.51 E
Muar 26 Df 2.02N 102.34 E
Muaraaman 26 Dg 3.07S 102.12 E
Muarabungo 26 Dg 1.28S 102.07 E
Muaraenim 26 Dg 3.39S 103.48 E
Muaralasan 26 Gf 1.48N 117.12 E
Muarapajang 26 Gg 1.32S 115.48 E
Muarasiberut 26 Cg 1.36S 99.11 E
Muarasiram 26 Gg 0.46S 116.11 E
Muaratebo 26 Dg 1.30S 102.26 E
Muaratewe 26 Fg 0.57S 114.53 E
Muarawahau 26 Gf 1.02N 116.52 E
Mubarek 18 Ee 39.16N 65.07 E
Mubende 36 Fb 0.35N 31.23 E
Mubi 31 Ig 10.16N 13.16 E
Much 12 Jd 50.55N 7.24 E
Muchinga Escarpment 36 Fe 13.40S 34.00 E
Muchinga Mountains 30 Kj 12.00S 31.45 E
Muck 9 Ge 56.50N 6.14W
Mücke 12 Ld 50.37N 9.02 E
Mucojo 37 Gb 12.04S 40.28 E
Muconda 36 De 10.34S 21.20 E
Mucua 37 Ec 18.09S 34.58 E
Mucubela 37 Fc 16.54S 37.49 E
Mucuchies 49 Li 8.45N 70.55W
Mucumbura 37 Ec 16.10S 31.42 E
Mucur 24 Fc 39.04N 34.23 E
Mucusso 36 Df 18.00S 21.25 E
Mudan Jang 21 Oe 46.18N 129.31 E
Mudanjiang 22 Oe 44.35N 129.34 E
Mudanya 24 Cb 40.22N 28.52 E
Muddy Gap 46 Le 42.22N 107.27W
Mudgee 59 Jf 32.36S 149.35 E
Mud Lake 46 Ie 43.53N 112.24W
Mud Lake 46 Gh 37.55N 117.05W
Mudon 25 Je 16.15N 97.44 E
Mudug [3] 35 Hd 6.30N 48.00 E
Mudug 35 Hd 6.20N 47.00 E
Mudurnu 24 Db 40.28N 31.13 E
Muecate 37 Fb 14.53S 39.38 E
Mueda 37 Fb 11.39S 39.33 E
Muerto, Cayo- 49 Ff 14.34N 82.44W
Muerto, Mar- 48 Li 16.10N 94.10W
Mufulira 31 Jj 12.33S 28.14 E
Mufu Shan 27 Jf 29.15N 114.20 E
Mufu Shan 27 Jf 29.00N 113.50 E
Mugello 14 Fg 43.55N 11.25 E
Múggia 14 He 45.36N 13.46 E
Mughshin, Wādī- 35 Ib 19.44N 55.00 E
Mugi 29 De 33.40N 134.25 E
Mu Gia, Deo- 25 Le 17.40N 105.47 E
Mugila, Monts- 36 Ed 6.49S 29.08 E
Muğla 23 Cb 37.12N 28.22 E
Mugodžary 21 He 49.00N 58.40 E
Mugur an Na'ām 24 Ig 31.56N 40.30 E
Muhaiwir 24 If 33.28N 40.59 E
Muḩammad, Ra's- 33 Fd 27.42N 34.13 E
Muḩammad Oawl 35 Fa 20.54N 37.05 E
Muhen 20 Ig 48.10N 136.08 E
Muheza 36 Gd 5.10S 38.47 E
Muhīt, Al Baḩr al- = Atlantic Ocean (EN) 3 Di 2.00N 25.00W
Mühlacker 10 Eh 48.57N 8.50 E
Mühldorf am Inn 10 Ih 48.15N 12.32 E
Mühlhausen in Thüringen 10 Ge 51.13N 10.27 E
Mühlig-Hofmann Gebirge 66 Cf 72.00S 5.20 E
Mühlviertel 14 Ib 48.30N 14.10 E
Muhoršibir → Taksimo 20 Ff 51.01N 107.50 E
Muhos 7 Gd 64.50N 26.01 E
Muhu 7 Fg 58.35N 23.15 E
Muhu 8 Jf 58.37N 23.05 E
Muhu, Proliv-/Muhu Väin 8 Jf 58.45N 23.15 E
Muhulu 36 Ec 1.03S 27.17 E
Muhu Väin/Muhu, Proliv- 8 Jf 58.45N 23.15 E
Muhuwesi 36 Ge 11.16S 37.58 E
Muiderslot 12 Hb 52.20N 5.06 E
Muigheo/Mayo [2] 9 Dh 53.50N 9.30W
Muikamachi 28 Of 37.04N 138.53 E
Muineachán/Monaghan [2] 9 Gg 54.10N 7.00W
Muineachán/Monaghan 9 Gg 54.15N 6.58W
Muine Bheag 9 Gi 52.42N 6.57W
Muir Bhreatan = Saint George's Channel (EN) 5 Fe 52.00N 6.00W
Muir Eireann = Irish Sea (EN) 5 Fe 53.30N 5.20W
Muiron Islands 59 Cd 21.35S 114.20 E
Muir Seamount (EN) 38 Mf 33.41N 63.32W
Muíte 37 Fb 14.02S 39.02 E
Mujeres, Isla- 48 Pg 21.13N 86.43W
Mujezerski 7 He 63.57N 32.01 E
Muji 27 Cd 37.27N 78.33 E
Mujnak 19 Fg 43.44N 59.02 E
Mujnakski Zaliv 18 Bc 43.50N 58.40 E
Mujunkum, Peski- 21 Je 44.00N 70.30 E
Mukačevo 19 Cf 48.26N 22.45 E
Mukah 26 Ff 2.54N 112.06 E
Mukawa 29a Bb 42.35N 141.55 E
Mu-Kawa 29a Bb 42.33N 141.53 E
Mukawwar 35 Fa 20.48N 37.13 E
Mukdahan 25 Ke 16.31N 104.42 E
Mukden → Shenyang 22 Oe 41.48N 123.24 E
Mukeru 64a Bc 7.25N 134.30 E
Mukho 28 Jf 37.33N 129.07 E
Mukinbudin 59 Df 30.54S 118.13 E
Mukojima-Rettō 60 Cb 27.37N 142.10 E
Mukomuko 26 Dg 2.35S 101.07 E
Muksu 18 He 39.17N 71.25 E
Mula 25 Dc 27.57N 67.36 E
Mula 13 Kf 38.03N 1.30W
Mulainagiri 25 Ff 13.24N 75.43 E
Mulaku Atoll 25a Bb 2.57N 73.34 E
Mulaly 19 Hf 45.27N 78.20 E
Mulan 27 Mb 46.00N 128.02 E
Mulanje 30 Kj 16.03S 35.31 E
Mulanje 36 Gf 16.02S 35.30 E
Mulatre, Point- 51g Bb 15.17N 61.15W
Mulatupo Sasardí 49 Ii 8.57N 77.45W
Mulchatna 40 Hd 59.39N 157.08W
Mulchén 56 Fe 37.34S 72.14W
Mulda 17 Kc 67.28N 63.34 E
Mulde 10 Ie 51.48N 12.10 E
Mulebreen 66 Ee 67.28S 59.21 E
Mulegé 47 Bc 26.53N 112.01W
Mulegé, Sierra de- 47 Bc 37.30N 112.40W
Mulenda 36 Dc 4.18S 24.58 E
Muleshoe 45 Ei 34.13N 102.43W
Mulgrave Island 59 Ib 10.05S 142.10 E
Mulhacén 5 Fh 37.03N 3.19W
Mülheim an der Ruhr 12 Ic 51.26N 6.53 E
Mülheim-Kärlich 12 Jd 50.23N 7.30 E
Mulhouse 6 Gf 47.45N 7.20 E
Muli (Bowa) 27 Hf 27.55N 101.13 E
Mulifanua 65c Aa 13.50S 172.02W
Muling 28 Kb 44.34N 130.12 E
Muling (Bamiantong) 28 Kb 44.55N 130.32 E
Muling Guan 28 Ef 36.10N 118.46 E
Muling He 28 Lb 45.53N 133.30 E
Mull, Island of- 5 Fd 56.27N 6.00W
Mull, Sound of- 9 He 56.35N 5.50W
Mullen 45 Fe 42.03N 101.01W
Mullens 44 Gg 37.35N 81.25W
Muller, Pegunungan- 26 Ff 0.40N 113.50 E
Mullet Peninsula/An Muirthead 9 Cg 54.15N 10.04W
Mullett Lake 44 Ec 45.30N 84.30W
Mullewa 59 De 28.33S 115.31 E
Müllheim 10 Di 47.48N 7.38 E
Mullingar/An Muileann gCearr 9 Fh 53.32N 7.20W
Mullsjö 8 Eg 57.55N 13.53 E
Mulobezi 36 Ef 16.47S 25.10 E
Mulock Glacier 66 Jf 79.03S 159.10 E
Mulongo 36 Ed 7.50S 26.57 E
Multān 22 Jf 30.11N 71.29 E
Multé 48 Ni 17.41N 91.24W
Multia 8 Kb 62.25N 24.47 E
Multien 12 Ee 49.05N 2.55 E
Mulu, Gunong- 26 Ff 4.03N 114.56 E
Mulvane 45 Hh 37.29N 97.14W
Mulymja 17 Lf 60.12N 64.32 E
Mumbué 36 Ce 13.53S 17.19 E
Mumbwa 36 Ee 14.59S 27.04 E
Mumhan/Munster 9 Ei 52.30N 9.00W
Mumra 16 Og 45.43N 47.41 E
Mun 21 Mh 15.19N 105.30 E
Muna 48 Og 20.29N 89.43W
Muna 21 Oc 67.52N 123.10 E
Muna, Pulau- 26 Hg 5.00S 122.30 E
Munābāo 25 Ec 25.45N 70.17 E
Munamägi/Munamjagi 8 Lg 57.38N 27.10 E
Munaybarah, Sharm- 24 Gi 26.04N 36.38 E
Muncar 26 Fh 8.29S 114.21 E
Münchberg 10 Hf 50.12N 11.47 E
München = Munich (EN) 6 Hf 48.09N 11.35 E
Münchhausen 12 Kd 50.57N 8.43 E
Muncho Lake 42 Ee 58.56N 125.46W
Munch'ŏn 28 Ie 39.14N 127.22 E
Muncie 43 Jc 40.11N 85.23W
Munda 63a Cc 8.19S 157.15 E
Mundaring, Perth- 59 Df 31.54S 116.10 E
Munday 45 Gj 33.27N 99.38W
Mundemba 34 Ge 4.59N 8.40 E
Münden 10 Fe 51.25N 9.41 E
Mundesley 12 Db 52.52N 1.25 E
Mundford 12 Cb 52.30N 0.39 E
Mundiwindi 58 Dg 23.52S 120.09 E
Mundo 13 Kf 38.19N 1.40W
Mundo Novo 54 Jf 11.52S 40.28W
Munellës, Mali i- 15 Dh 41.58N 20.06 E
Munera 13 Je 39.02N 2.28W
Mungana 59 Ic 17.07S 144.24 E
Mungbere 31 Jh 2.38N 28.30 E
Munger 25 Hc 25.23N 86.28 E
Mungindi 59 Je 28.58S 148.59 E
Munhango 36 Ce 12.10S 18.34 E
Munh-Hajrhan-Ula 21 Le 46.40N 91.30 E
Munich (EN) = München 6 Hf 48.09N 11.35 E
Muniesa 13 Lc 41.02N 0.48W
Munīfah 23 Gd 27.38N 49.00 E
Munising 44 Db 46.25N 86.40W
Munkedal 7 Cg 58.29N 11.41 E
Munkfors 7 Cg 59.50N 13.32 E
Munku Sardik, Gora- 21 Md 51.45N 100.20 E
Muñoz Gamero, Peninsula- 56 Fh 52.30S 73.10W
Munsan 28 If 37.55N 126.22 E
Münsingen 10 Fh 48.25N 9.30 E
Munster 11 Nf 48.03N 7.08 E
Münster [Ger.] 10 De 51.58N 7.38 E
Münster [Ger.] 12 Ke 49.55N 8.52 E
Münster/Moutier 14 Bc 47.16N 7.22 E
Munster/Mumhan 9 Ei 52.30N 9.00W
Münster-Hiltrup 12 Jc 51.54N 7.38 E
Münsterland [Ger.] 10 De 52.00N 7.30 E
Münsterland [Ger.] 12 Kb 52.45N 8.10 E
Münstermaifeld 12 Jd 50.15N 7.22 E
Muntenia 15 Ie 44.00N 26.00 E
Munteni Buzău 15 Je 44.38N 26.59 E
Muntok 26 Eg 2.04S 105.11 E
Munzur Dağları 24 Hc 39.30N 39.10 E
Muojärvi 7 Gd 65.56N 28.36 E
Muong Sen 25 Ke 19.24N 104.08 E
Muonio 6 Ib 67.57N 23.42 E
Muonioälven Muonionijoki 5 Ib 67.11N 23.34 E
Muping 28 Ff 37.23N 121.36 E
Muqaddam 35 Eb 18.04N 31.30 E
Muqayshiţ 24 Oj 24.10N 53.45 E
Muqdisho = Mogadishu (EN) 31 Lh 2.03N 45.22 E
Mur 5 Hf 46.18N 16.55 E
Mura 5 Hf 46.18N 16.55 E
Muradiye [Tur.] 15 Kk 38.39N 27.24 E
Muradiye [Tur.] 24 Jc 39.00N 43.43 E
Murafa 16 Fe 48.13N 28.14 E
Murakami 28 Oe 38.14N 139.29 E
Murallón, Cerro- 52 Ij 49.48S 73.25W
Muráň 10 Qh 48.45N 20.02 E
Mur'aňyo 35 Ic 11.41N 50.27 E
Muraši 19 Ed 59.24N 48.59 E
Murat 21 Ff 38.52N 38.48 E
Murat 11 Ii 45.07N 2.52 E
Murat Dağı 23 Cb 38.55N 29.43 E
Muratlı [Tur.] 24 Ib 41.29N 41.41 E
Muratlı [Tur.] 15 Kh 41.10N 27.30 E
Murau 14 Ic 47.06N 14.10 E
Muravera 14 Dk 39.25N 9.34 E
Murayama 29 Gb 38.29N 140.23 E
Mūrchen Khvort 24 Nf 33.06N 51.30 E
Murchison 62 Ed 41.48S 172.20 E
Murchison, Mount- [Austl.] 59 De 26.46S 116.25 E
Murchison, Mount- [N.Z.] 62 De 43.01S 171.17 E
Murchison River 57 Cg 27.50S 114.00 E
Murcia 6 Fh 37.59N 1.07W
Murcia [3] 13 Kg 38.00N 1.30W
Murcia 13 Kf 38.30N 1.45W
Mur-de-Barrez 11 Ij 44.51N 2.39 E
Murdo 45 Fe 43.53N 100.43W
Mürefte 15 Ki 40.40N 27.14 E
Muren 22 Me 49.38N 100.10 E
Mureş 5 If 46.15N 20.12 E
Mureş [2] 15 Hc 46.30N 24.40 E
Muret 11 Hk 43.28N 1.21 E
Murfreesboro 43 Jd 35.51N 86.23W
Murg 10 Eh 48.55N 8.10 E
Murgab 21 If 38.18N 61.12 E
Murgab 19 Hh 38.10N 73.59 E
Murgab 18 Df 37.32N 62.01 E
Murgaš 15 Gg 42.50N 23.40 E
Murgeni 15 Lc 46.12N 28.01 E
Murgon 59 Ke 26.15S 151.57 E
Muri 64p Cc 21.15S 159.43W
Muriaé 54 Jh 21.08S 42.22W
Murici 54 Ke 9.19S 35.56W
Muriege 36 Dd 9.53S 21.13 E
Murihiti 64n Ab 10.23S 161.02W
Murilo Atoll 57 Gd 8.40N 152.11 E
Mūrītāniyā = Mauritania (EN) [1] 31 Fg 20.00N 12.00W
Müritz 10 Ic 53.25N 12.43 E
Murkong Selek 25 Jc 27.44N 95.18 E
Murmansk 6 Jb 68.58N 33.05 E
Murmanskaja Oblast [3] 19 Db 68.00N 35.30 E
Murmaši 19 Db 68.49N 32.49 E
Murnau 10 Hi 47.41N 11.12 E
Muro 13 Pe 39.44N 3.03 E
Muro, Capo di- 11a Ab 41.44N 8.40 E
Muro Lucano 14 Jj 40.45N 15.29 E
Murom 6 Kd 55.34N 42.02 E
Muromcevo 19 Hd 56.23N 75.14 E
Muroran 22 Qe 42.18N 140.59 E
Muros 13 Cb 42.47N 9.02W
Muros y Noya, Ría de- 13 Db 42.45N 9.00W
Muroto 27 Ne 33.18N 134.09 E
Muroto Zaki 28 Mh 33.16N 134.10 E
Murowana Goślina 10 Nd 52.35N 17.01 E
Murphy [Id.-U.S.] 46 Ge 43.13N 116.33W
Murphy [N.C.-U.S.] 44 Eh 35.05N 84.01W
Murphysboro 45 Lh 37.46N 89.20W
Murrah al Kubrá, Al Buḩayrah al- 24 Eg 30.20N 32.23 E
Murray [Ky.-U.S.] 44 Cg 36.37N 88.19W
Murray [Ut.-U.S.] 46 Jf 40.40N 111.53W
Murray, Lake- [Pap.N.Gui.] 60 Ci 7.00S 141.30 E
Murray, Lake- [S.C.-U.S.] 44 Gh 34.04N 81.23W
Murray Bridge 59 Hg 35.07S 139.17 E
Murray Fracture zone (EN) 3 Lf 34.00N 135.00W
Murray Islands 59 Ia 9.55S 144.05 E
Murray Ridge (EN) 3 Gg 21.00N 61.50 E
Murray River 57 Eh 35.22S 139.22 E
Murraysburg 37 Cf 31.58S 23.47 E
Murro di Porco, Capo- 14 Jm 37.00N 15.20 E
Murrumbidgee River 57 Fh 34.43S 143.12 E
Murrupula 37 Fc 15.27S 38.47 E
Murska Sobota 14 Kd 46.40N 16.10 E
Murten/Morat 14 Bd 46.56N 7.08 E
Murter 14 Jg 43.47N 15.37 E
Murtle Lake 46 Fa 52.08N 119.38W
Murud, Gunong- 26 Gf 3.52N 115.30 E
Murupara 62 Gc 38.27S 176.42 E
Mururoa Atoll 57 Ng 21.52S 138.55W
Murwāra 25 Gd 23.51N 80.24 E
Murwillumbah 59 Ke 28.19S 153.24 E
Mürz 14 Jc 47.24N 15.17 E
Mürzzuschlag 14 Jc 47.36N 15.41 E
Muş 23 Fb 38.44N 41.30 E
Muša/Mūša 7 Fh 56.24N 24.12 E
Mūša/Muša 7 Fh 56.24N 24.12 E
Mūsa, Jabal- = Sinai, Mount- (EN) 24 Eh 28.32N 33.59 E
Musa Ali 35 Gc 12.30N 42.27 E
Musāfī 24 Qk 25.18N 56.10 E
Musā'id 33 Ed 31.36N 25.03 E
Musala 5 Ig 42.11N 23.34 E
Musallam 24 Lg 31.53N 46.56 E
Musan 27 Mc 42.14N 129.13 E
Musandam Peninsula 24 Qi 26.18N 56.24 E
Musay'īd 24 Nj 25.00N 51.33 E
Musaymir 33 Hg 13.27N 44.37 E
Muscat (EN) = Masqaţ 22 Hg 23.29N 58.33 E
Muscat and Oman (EN) → Oman (EN) [1] 22 Hg 21.00N 57.00 E
Muscatine 45 Kf 41.25N 91.03W
Musgrave 58 Ff 14.47S 143.30 E
Musgrave Ranges 57 Eg 26.10S 131.50 E
Mūshā 24 Di 27.07N 31.14 E
Mus-Haja, Gora- 21 Qc 62.35N 140.50 E
Mushāsh al 'Ashawī 24 Mj 24.12N 48.50 E
Mushāsh Ramlān 24 Mj 24.25N 49.15 E
Mushayrib, Ra's- 24 Nj 24.18N 51.44 E
Mushie 36 Cc 3.01S 16.54 E
Mūsi 25 Ge 15.20N 80.06 E
Musi 21 Mj 2.20S 104.56 E
Mūsiān 24 Lf 32.28N 47.26 E
Musicians Seamounts (EN) 57 Kb 29.00N 162.00W
Muskegon 43 Jc 43.14N 86.16W
Muskegon Heights 44 Dd 43.12N 86.12W
Muskegon River 44 Dd 43.14N 86.20W
Muskö 8 He 59.00N 18.05 E
Muskogee 43 Hd 35.45N 95.22W
Muskoka, Lake- 44 Hc 45.00N 79.25W
Musoma 31 Ki 1.30S 33.48 E
Musone 14 Hg 43.28N 13.38 E
Mussaţţaḩah, Al Jazīrah al- 14 Em 37.11N 10.20 E
Mussau Island 60 Dh 1.25S 149.38 E
Musselkanaal, Stadskanaal- 12 Jb 52.56N 7.02 E
Musselshell River 43 Fb 47.21N 107.58W
Mussende 36 Ce 10.31S 16.02 E
Mussidan 11 Gi 45.02N 0.22 E
Mussòmeli 14 Hm 37.35N 13.45 E
Must 27 Fb 46.40N 92.40 E
Muşţafá, Ra's- 14 Fn 36.50N 11.07 E
Mustafakemalpaşa 24 Cb 40.02N 28.24 E
Mustahil 35 Gd 5.15N 44.44 E
Mustāng 25 Gc 29.11N 83.58 E
Mustang Draw 45 Fj 32.00N 101.40W
Mustang Island 45 Hm 28.00N 96.55W
Mustasaari/Korsholm 8 Ia 63.05N 21.43 E
Musters, Lago- 56 Gg 45.27S 69.13W
Mustique Island 50 Ff 12.39N 61.15W
Mustjala 8 Jf 58.25N 22.04 E
Mustla 7 Fg 58.14N 25.52 E
Mustvee 7 Gg 58.52N 26.59 E
Musu-dan 28 Jd 40.50N 129.43 E
Muswellbrook 59 Kf 32.16S 150.53 E
Muszyna 10 Qg 49.21N 20.54 E
Mut 24 Ed 36.39N 33.27 E
Mūţ 33 Ed 25.29N 28.59 E
Mūtaf, Ra's al- 23 Hd 27.41N 51.27 E
Mutalau 64k Ba 18.56S 169.50W
Mutarara 31 Kj 17.27S 35.04 E
Mutatá 54 Cb 7.16N 76.32W
Mutawassiţ, Al Baḩr al- = Mediterranean Sea (EN) 5 Hh 35.00N 20.00 E
Mutha 36 Gc 1.48S 38.26 E
Muting 26 Lh 7.23S 140.20 E
Mutis, Gunung- 26 Hh 9.34S 124.14 E
Mutoraj 20 Fd 61.20N 100.20 E
Mutsamudu 31 Lj 12.09S 44.25 E
Mutshatsha 36 De 10.39S 24.27 E
Mutsu 27 Pc 41.05N 140.55 E
Mutsu-Wan 28 Pd 41.10N 140.55 E
Muttaburra 59 Id 22.36S 144.33 E
Mutterstadt 12 Ke 49.27N 8.21 E
Mutton/Oiléan Coarach 9 Di 52.49N 9.31W
Mutton Bird Islands 62 Bg 47.15S 167.25 E
Mutuali 37 Fb 14.53S 37.00 E
Mutún 55 Dd 19.10S 57.54W
Mutunópolis 55 Ha 13.40S 49.15W
Mutusjärvi 7 Gb 69.31N 26.57 E
Muurame 8 Kb 62.08N 25.40 E
Mu Us Shamo = Ordos Desert (EN) 21 Mf 38.45N 109.10 E
Muxima 36 Bd 9.32S 13.57 E
Muyinga 36 Fc 2.51S 30.20 E
Muy Muy 49 Eg 12.46N 85.38W
Muzaffarābād 25 Eb 34.22N 73.28 E
Muzaffargarh 25 Eb 30.04N 71.12 E
Muzaffarnagar 25 Fc 29.28N 77.41 E
Muzaffarpur 25 Hc 26.07N 85.24 E
Muzambinho 55 Ie 21.22S 46.32W
Muzat He 27 Dc 41.15N 83.27 E
Muži 20 Bc 65.27N 64.40 E
Muzillac 11 Dg 47.33N 2.29W
Mužlja 15 Dd 45.21N 20.25 E
Muztag [China] 21 Kf 35.55N 80.20 E
Muztag [China] 21 Kf 36.25N 87.25 E
Muztagata 27 Cd 38.17N 75.07 E
Mvolo 35 Dd 6.03N 29.56 E
Mvomero 36 Gd 6.20S 37.25 E
Mvoung 36 Bb 0.04N 12.18 E
Mwadingusha 36 Ee 10.45S 27.15 E
Mwali 30 Lj 12.15S 43.45 E
Mwanza [3] 36 Fc 2.30S 32.30 E
Mwanza [Mwi.] 36 Ff 15.37S 34.31 E
Mwanza [Tan.] 31 Ki 2.31S 32.54 E
Mwanza [Zaire] 36 Ed 7.54S 26.45 E
Mwatate 36 Gc 3.30S 38.23 E
Mweelrea 9 Dh 53.38N 9.50W
Mweka 31 Ji 4.51S 21.34 E
Mwene Ditu 31 Ji 7.03S 23.27 E
Mwenga 36 Ec 3.02S 28.26 E
Mweru, Lake- 30 Ji 9.00S 28.45 E
Mweru Wantipa, Lake- 36 Ed 8.42S 29.46 E
Mwimbi 36 Fd 8.39S 31.40 E
Mwinilunga 36 De 11.44S 24.26 E
Mya 30 He 31.40N 5.15 E
Myaing 25 Id 21.37N 94.51 E
Myanaung 25 Je 18.17N 95.19 E
Myanmar-Nainggan-Daw → Burma [1] 22 Lg 22.00N 98.00 E
Myaungmya 25 Ie 16.36N 94.56 E
Mycenae (EN) = Mikínai 15 Fl 37.43N 22.45 E
Myebon 25 Id 20.03N 93.22 E
Myingyan 22 Lg 21.28N 95.23 E
Myinmoletkat Taung 25 Jf 13.28N 98.48 E
Myitta 25 Jf 14.10N 98.31 E
Myjava 10 Mh 48.33N 16.58 E
Myjzakjula/Mõisaküla 7 Fg 58.07N 25.10 E
Mykulkin, Mys- 17 Cc 67.48N 46.40 E
Mylius Erichsens Land 41 Jb 81.40N 24.00W
Myltkyinā 22 Lg 25.23N 97.24 E
Mymensingh 25 Id 24.45N 90.24 E
Mynämäki 7 Ef 60.40N 22.00 E
Mynaral 19 Hf 45.22N 73.39 E
Myōkō-Zan 29 Fc 36.52N 138.06 E
Mýrdalsjökull 7a Bc 63.40N 19.06W
Myre 7 Db 68.51N 15.05 E
Myrskylä/Mörskom 8 Kd 60.40N 25.51 E
Myrtle Beach 43 Le 33.42N 78.54W
Myrtle Point 46 Ce 43.04N 124.08W
Mysen 7 Cg 59.33N 11.20 E
Mysia 15 Kj 39.30N 28.00 E
Myśla 10 Kd 52.40N 14.29 E
Myślenice 10 Pg 49.51N 19.56 E
Myślibórz 10 Kd 52.55N 14.52 E
Mysore 22 Jh 12.18N 76.39 E
Mysore → Karnataka [3] 25 Ff 13.30N 76.00 E
Mys Saryč 16 Hg 44.23N 33.45 E
Myszków 10 Pf 50.36N 19.20 E
Myszyniec 10 Rc 53.24N 21.21 E
My Tho 22 Mh 10.21N 106.21 E
Mytišči 7 Ii 55.56N 37.46 E
Mývatn 7a Cb 65.36N 17.00W

Index Symbols

[1] Independent Nation
[2] State, Region
[3] District, County
[4] Municipality
[5] Colony, Dependency
Continent
Physical Region
Historical or Cultural Region
Mount, Mountain
Volcano
Hill
Mountains, Mountain Range
Hills, Escarpment
Plateau, Upland
Pass, Gap
Plain, Lowland
Delta
Salt Flat
Valley, Canyon
Crater, Cave
Karst Features
Depression
Polder
Desert, Dunes
Forest, Woods
Heath, Steppe
Oasis
Cape, Point
Coast, Beach
Cliff
Peninsula
Isthmus
Sandbank
Island
Atoll
Rock, Reef
Islands, Archipelago
Rocks, Reefs
Coral Reef
Well, Spring
Geyser
River, Stream
Waterfall Rapids
River Mouth, Estuary
Lake
Salt Lake
Intermittent Lake
Reservoir
Swamp, Pond
Canal
Glacier
Ice Shelf, Pack Ice
Ocean
Sea
Gulf, Bay
Strait, Fjord
Lagoon
Bank
Seamount
Tablemount
Ridge
Shelf
Basin
Escarpment, Sea Scarp
Fracture
Trench, Abyss
National Park, Reserve
Point of Interest
Recreation Site
Cave, Cavern
Historic Site
Ruins
Wall, Walls
Church, Abbey
Temple
Scientific Station
Airport
Port
Lighthouse
Mine
Tunnel
Dam, Bridge

Myzeqeja 15 Ci 41.01N 19.36 E
M'Zab 32 Hc 32.35N 3.20 E
Mže 10 Jg 49.46N 13.24 E
Mziha 36 Gd 5.54S 37.47 E
Mzimba 36 Fe 11.54S 33.36 E
Mzuzu 31 Kj 11.27S 33.55 E

N

Naab 10 Ig 49.01N 12.02 E
Naaldwijk 12 Gc 51.59N 4.12 E
Naalehu 65a Fd 19.04N 155.35W
Naantali/Nådendal 7 Ff 60.27N 22.02 E
Naarden 12 Hb 52.18N 5.10 E
Naas/An Nás 9 Gh 53.13N 6.39W
Nabadid 35 Gd 9.38N 43.29 E
Nabão 13 De 39.31N 8.21W
Nabari 29 Ed 34.37N 136.05 E
Naberera 36 Gc 4.12S 38.56 E
Naberežnyje Čelny 6 Ld 55.42N 52.19 E
Nabileque, Rio- 55 De 20.55S 57.49W
Nabire 58 Ee 3.22S 135.29 E
Nabī Shu'ayb, Jabal an- 21 Gh 15.17N 43.59 E
Nabq 24 Fh 28.04N 34.25 E
Nābul 31 Ie 36.27N 10.44 E
Nābul [3] 32 Jb 36.45N 10.45 E
Nābulus 24 Ff 32.13N 35.16 E
Nabusanke 36 Fb 0.01N 32.03 E
Nacala 37 Gb 14.33S 40.40 E
Nacala-a-Velha 31 Lj 14.33S 40.36 E
Nacaome 49 Dg 13.31N 87.30W
Nacaroa 37 Fb 14.23S 39.55 E
Nacereddine 13 Ph 36.08N 3.26 E
Nachikatsuura 29 De 33.39N 135.55 E
Nachingwea 36 Ge 10.23S 38.46 E
Nachi-San 29 De 33.42N 135.51 E
Náchod 10 Mf 50.26N 16.10 E
Nachuge 25 If 10.35N 92.28 E
Nachvak Fiord 42 Le 59.03N 63.45W
Nacka 7 Ee 59.18N 18.10 E
Na Clocha Liatha/Greystones 9 Gh 53.09N 6.04W
Nacogdoches 45 Ik 31.36N 94.39W
Na Comaraigh/Comeragh Mountains 9 Fi 52.13N 7.35W
Nacori, Sierra- 48 Ec 29.50N 108.50W
Nacozari, Rio- 48 Ec 29.48N 109.42W
Nacozari de Garcia 47 Cb 30.24N 109.39W
Na Cruacha/Blue Stack 9 Eg 54.45N 8.06W
Na Cruacha Dubha/Macgillycuddy's Reeks 9 Di 52.00N 9.50W
Nacunday, Rio- 55 Eh 26.03S 54.45W
Nada → Danxian 27 Ih 19.38N 109.32 E
Nådendal/Naantali 7 Ff 60.27N 22.02 E
Nadiād 25 Ed 22.42N 72.52 E
Nădlac 15 Dc 46.10N 20.45 E
Nador [3] 32 Gb 35.00N 3.00W
Nador 32 Gb 35.11N 2.56W
Nădusa 15 Fi 40.38N 22.04 E
Nadvoicy 19 Dc 63.52N 34.20 E
Nadvornaja 16 De 48.38N 24.34 E
Nadym 22 Jc 65.35N 72.42 E
Naeba-San 29 Fc 36.51N 138.41 E
Nærbø 8 Af 58.40N 5.39 E
Næstved 7 Ci 55.14N 11.46 E
Nafada 34 Hc 11.06N 11.20 E
Näfels 14 Dc 47.06N 9.04 E
Nafṭah 14 Dn 36.57N 9.04 E
Naftan Rock 64b Bb 14.50N 145.32 E
Naft-e-Safid 24 Mg 31.40N 49.17 E
Naft-e-Shāh 24 Kf 33.59N 45.30 E
Naft Khāneh 24 Ke 34.02N 45.28 E
Nafūsah, Jabal- 30 Ie 31.50N 12.00 E
Näg 25 Dc 27.24N 65.08 E
Naga 22 Oh 13.28N 123.39 E
Nāga, Kreb en- 32 Fe 24.00N 6.00W
Nagagami Lake 44 Ea 49.28N 85.02W
Nagagami River 45 Na 50.25N 84.20W
Nagahama [Jap.] 29 Ed 35.23N 136.16 E
Nagahama [Jap.] 29 Ce 33.36N 132.29 E
Nagai 29 Gb 38.06N 140.02 E
Nagai 40 Ge 55.11N 159.55W
Na Gaibhlte/Galty Mountains 9 Ei 52.23N 8.11W
Nāgāland [3] 25 Ic 26.30N 94.00 E
Nagano 22 Pf 36.39N 138.11 E
Nagano Ken [2] 28 Nf 36.10N 138.00 E
Nagano-Matsushiro 29 Fc 36.34N 138.10 E
Nagano-Shinonoi 29 Fc 36.35N 138.06 E
Nagaoka 27 Od 37.27N 138.51 E
Nāgappattinam 25 Ff 10.46N 79.50 E
Nagara-Gawa 29 Ed 35.02N 136.43 E
Nagarote 49 Dg 12.16N 86.34W
Nagarzê 27 Ff 28.59N 90.28 E
Nagasaki 27 Of 32.47N 129.56 E
Nagasaki-Hantō 29 Ae 32.40N 129.45 E
Nagasaki Ken [2] 28 Jh 33.00N 129.50 E
Naga-Shima 29 Ce 33.50N 132.05 E
Nagashima 29 Ed 34.12N 136.19 E
Nagashima 29 Be 32.10N 130.10 E
Naga-Shima-Kaikyō 29 Be 32.15N 130.10 E
Nagato 28 Kg 34.21N 131.10 E
Nagayo 29 Ae 32.50N 129.52 E
Nāgda 25 Fd 23.27N 75.25 E
Nāgercoil 25 Fg 8.10N 77.26 E
Naghora Point 60 Gj 10.50S 162.24 E
Nagichot 35 Ee 4.16N 33.34 E
Nagi-San 29 Dd 35.10N 134.10 E
Nagiso 29 Ed 35.36N 137.36 E
Nago 27 Mf 26.35N 128.01 E
Nagold 10 Eh 48.52N 8.42 E
Nagorno-Karabakh 19 Eh 39.55N 46.45 E
Nagorny 20 He 55.45N 124.58 E
Nagorny 20 Md 63.10N 179.05 E
Nagorsk 7 Mg 59.21N 50.48 E
Nago-Wan 29b Ab 26.35N 127.55 E
Nagoya 22 Pf 35.10N 136.55 E
Nāgpur 22 Jg 21.09N 79.06 E
Nagqu 22 Lf 31.30N 92.00 E
Nag's Head 51c Ab 17.13N 62.38W
Nagua 49 Md 19.23N 69.50W
Naguabo 51a Cb 18.13N 65.44W
Nagyatád 10 Nj 46.13N 17.22 E
Nagybajom 10 Mj 46.23N 16.31 E
Nagyecsed 10 Si 47.52N 22.24 E
Nagyhalász 10 Rh 48.08N 21.46 E
Nagykálló 10 Ri 47.53N 21.51 E
Nagykanizsa 10 Mj 46.27N 16.59 E
Nagykáta 10 Pi 47.25N 19.45 E
Nagykőrös 10 Pi 47.02N 19.47 E
Nagykunság 10 Qj 46.55N 20.15 E
Nagy-Milic 10 Rh 48.35N 21.28 E
Naha 22 Og 26.13N 127.40 E
Nahanni Butte 42 Fd 61.04N 123.24W
Nahari 29 De 33.25N 134.01 E
Naharyya 24 Ff 33.00N 35.05 E
Nahāvand 23 Gc 34.12N 48.22 E
Nahe 10 Dg 49.58N 7.57 E
Nahičevan 6 Kh 39.13N 45.27 E
Nahičevanskaja respublika 19 Eh 39.15N 45.35 E
Na'hīmābād 24 Qg 30.51N 56.31 E
Nahodka 22 Pe 42.48N 132.52 E
Nahr al 'Āṣī=Orontes (EN) 23 Eb 36.02N 35.58 E
Nahr Quassel 13 Oi 35.45N 2.46 E
Nahuala, Laguna- 48 Ji 16.50N 99.40W
Nahuel Huapi, Lago- 56 Ff 40.58S 71.30W
Nahunta 44 Gj 31.12N 81.59W
Naie 29a Bb 43.24N 141.52 E
Naiguatá, Pico- 54 Ea 10.33N 66.46W
Naila 10 Hf 50.19N 11.42 E
Naiman Qi (Daqin Tal) 27 Lc 42.49N 120.38 E
Nain 39 Md 57.00N 61.40W
Nā'in 24 Of 32.52N 53.05 E
Na'īnābād 24 Pd 36.14N 54.39 E
Nairai 63d Bb 17.49S 179.24 E
Nairn 9 Jd 57.35N 3.53W
Nairobi 31 Kl 1.17S 36.49 E
Nairobi [3] 36 Gc 1.17S 36.50 E
Naissaar/Najssar 8 Ke 59.35N 24.25 E
Naitamba 63d Cb 17.01S 179.17W
Naizishan 28 Ic 43.41N 127.27 E
Najafābād 23 Hc 32.37N 51.21 E
Najd 23 Fe 25.00N 44.30 E
Najd 21 Gg 25.00N 44.30 E
Nájera 13 Jb 42.25N 2.44W
Najerilla 13 Jb 42.31N 2.42W
Naj' Ḥammādi 33 Fd 26.03N 32.15 E
Najībābād 25 Fc 29.58N 78.10 E
Najin 27 Nc 42.15N 130.18 E
Najō 29 Ec 35.47N 136.12 E
Najrān 33 Hf 17.30N 44.10 E
Najrān 33 Hf 17.30N 44.10 E
Najssar/Naissaar 8 Ke 59.35N 24.25 E
Najstenjarvi 7 He 62.18N 32.42 E
Naju 28 Ig 35.02N 126.43 E
Najzataš, Pereval- 18 If 37.52N 73.46 E
Nakadōri-Jima 28 Jh 32.58N 129.05 E
Nakagawa 29a Ca 44.47N 142.05 E
Naka-Gawa [Jap.] 29 Gc 36.20N 140.36 E
Naka-Gawa [Jap.] 29 De 33.56N 134.42 E
Nakagusuku-Wan 29b Ab 26.15N 127.50 E
Nakahechi 29 De 33.47N 135.29 E
Naka-lō-Jima 60 Cc 24.47N 141.20 E
Naka-Jima 29 Ce 33.58N 132.37 E
Nakajō 28 Oe 38.03N 139.24 E
Naka-Koshiki-Jima 29 Af 31.48N 129.50 E
Nakalele Point 65a Eb 21.02N 156.35W
Nakama 29 Be 33.50N 130.43 E
Nakaminato 29 Gc 36.22N 140.36 E
Nakamura 28 Lh 32.59N 132.56 E
Nakanai Mountains 59 Ka 5.35S 151.10 E
Nakano 29 Fc 36.45N 138.22 E
Naka-no-Dake 29 Fc 37.04N 139.06 E
Nakanojō 29 Fc 36.35N 138.51 E
Naka-no-Shima 28 Lf 36.05N 133.04 E
Naka-no-Shima 27 Mf 29.50N 129.50 E
Nakasato 29a Bc 40.58N 140.26 E
Naka-satsunai 29a Cb 42.42N 143.08 E
Nakashibetsu 28 Rc 43.36N 145.00 E
Nakasongola 36 Fb 1.19N 32.28 E
Nakatonbetsu 29a Ca 44.58N 142.17 E
Nakatsu 28 Kh 33.34N 131.13 E
Nakatsugawa 29 Ed 35.29N 137.30 E
Nakfa 35 Fb 16.40N 38.30 E
Nakhon Pathom 25 Kf 13.49N 100.06 E
Nakhon Phanom 25 Mh 17.22N 104.46 E
Nakhon Ratchasima 22 Mh 14.57N 102.09 E
Nakhon Sawan 22 Mh 15.42N 100.06 E
Nakhon Si Thammarat 22 Li 8.26N 99.58 E
Nakijin 29b Ab 26.42N 127.59 E
Nakina 39 Kd 50.10N 86.42W
Nakkila 8 Ic 61.22N 22.00 E
Naklo nad Notecia 10 Nc 53.08N 17.35 E
Naknek 40 He 58.44N 157.02W
Nakonde 36 Fd 9.19S 32.46 E
Nakskov 7 Ci 54.50N 11.09 E
Näkten 8 Fb 62.50N 14.40 E
Naktong-gang 28 Jg 35.07N 128.57 E
Nakuru 31 Ki 0.20S 35.56 E
Nakusp 46 Ga 50.15N 117.48W
Näl 25 Dc 26.02N 65.29 E
Nalajch → Nalajha 27 Ib 47.45N 107.16 E
Nalajha (Nalajch) 27 Ib 47.45N 107.16 E
Nalčik 6 Kg 43.29N 43.37 E
Nallıhan 24 Db 40.11N 31.21 E
Nalón 13 Fa 43.32N 6.04W
Nālūt 31 Ie 31.52N 10.59 E
Nalwasha 36 Gc 0.43S 36.26 E
Na Machairi/Brandon Head 9 Ci 52.16N 10.15W
Namacurra 37 Fc 17.29S 37.01 E
Namai Bay 64a Bb 7.32N 134.39 E
Namak, Daryācheh-ye-=Namak Lake (EN) 21 Hf 34.45N 51.36 E
Namak Lake (EN)=Namak, Daryācheh-ye- 21 Hf 34.45N 51.36 E
Namakan Lake 45 Jb 48.27N 92.35W
Namak-e Mighān, Kavīr-e- 24 Me 34.13N 49.49 E
Namakia 37 Hc 15.56S 45.48 E
Namakwaland=Little Namamland (EN) 37 Be 29.00S 17.00 E
Namanga 36 Gc 2.33S 36.47 E
Namangan 22 Je 41.00N 71.40 E
Namanganskaja Oblast [3] 19 Hg 41.00N 71.20 E
Namanyere 36 Fd 7.31S 31.03 E
Namapa 37 Fb 13.43S 39.50 E
Namaqua Seamount (EN) 37 Af 31.30S 11.20 E
Namarrói 37 Fc 15.57S 36.51 E
Namasagali 36 Fb 1.01N 32.57 E
Namasale 36 Fb 1.30N 32.37 E
Namatanai 60 Eh 3.40S 152.27 E
Namathu 63d Bb 17.21S 179.26 E
Nambavatu 63d Bb 16.36S 178.55 E
Namber 26 Jg 1.04S 134.49 E
Nambour 59 Ke 26.38S 152.58 E
Nambouwalu 61 Ec 16.59S 178.42 E
Nam Can 25 Kg 8.46N 104.59 E
Namche Bazar 25 Hc 27.49N 86.43 E
Nam Co 21 Lf 30.45N 90.35 E
Namčy 20 Hd 62.35N 129.40 E
Namdalen 7 Cd 64.38N 12.35 E
Nam Dinh 22 Mg 20.25N 106.10 E
Namdō 8 He 59.10N 18.40 E
Nam Du, Quan Dao- 25 Kg 9.42N 104.22 E
Naměche, Andenne- 12 Hd 50.28N 5.00 E
Namelakl Passage 64a Bc 7.24N 134.38 E
Namen/Namur 11 Kd 50.28N 4.52 E
Namerikawa 29 Ec 36.45N 137.20 E
Náměšť nad Oslavou 10 Mg 49.12N 16.09 E
Nametil 37 Fc 15.43S 39.21 E
Namib Desert/Namibwoestyn 30 Ik 23.00S 15.00 E
Namibia (South West Africa) 31 Ik 22.00S 17.00 E
Namibe 31 Ij 15.12S 12.10 E
Namibe 36 Bf 15.20S 12.30 E
Namie 28 Pf 37.29N 140.59 E
Namin 24 Mc 38.25N 48.30 E
Namioka 29 Ga 40.42N 140.35 E
Namiquipa 48 Fc 29.15N 107.40W
Namiranga 37 Gb 10.33S 40.30 E
Namjagbarwa Feng 21 Lg 29.38N 95.04 E
Namja La 27 Df 29.58N 82.34 E
Namkham 25 Jd 23.50N 97.41 E
Namlea 26 Ig 3.18S 127.06 E
Namling 27 Ef 29.44N 89.05 E
Namnoi, Khao- 25 Jf 10.36N 98.38 E
Namoi River 59 Je 30.00S 148.07 E
Namoluk Island 57 Gd 5.55N 153.08 E
Namonuito Atoll 57 Gd 8.46N 150.02 E
Namorik Atoll 57 Hd 5.36N 168.07 E
Namous 32 Gc 30.28N 0.14W
Nampa 43 Dc 43.34N 116.34W
Nampala 34 Db 15.17N 5.33W
Nam Phan=Cochin China (EN) 21 Mg 11.00N 107.00 E
Nam Phong 25 Ke 16.45N 102.52 E
Nampi 28 De 38.02N 116.42 E
Namp'o 27 Md 38.44N 125.25 E
Nampula [3] 37 Fb 15.00S 39.30 E
Nampula 31 Kj 15.07S 39.15 E
Namsê Shankou 27 Df 29.58N 82.34 E
Namsos 6 Hc 64.30N 11.30 E
Namtu 25 Jd 23.05N 97.24 E
Namu 46 Ba 51.49N 127.52W
Namu Atoll 57 Hd 8.00N 168.10 E
Namuka-I-Lau 63d Cc 18.51S 178.38W
Namuli, Serra- 30 Kj 15.21S 37.00 E
Namuno 37 Fb 13.37S 38.48 E
Namur [3] 12 Gd 50.20N 4.50 E
Namur/Namen 11 Kd 50.28N 4.52 E
Namur-Saint Servais 12 Gd 50.28N 4.50 E
Namuruputh 36 Gb 4.34N 35.57 E
Namur-Wépion 12 Gd 50.25N 4.52 E
Namutoni 37 Bc 18.30S 17.55 E
Namwala 36 Ef 15.45S 26.26 E
Namwŏn 28 Ig 35.24N 127.23 E
Namysłów 10 Ne 51.05N 17.42 E
Nan 21 Mh 15.42N 100.09 E
Nan 25 Ke 18.48N 100.46 E
Nana 35 Bd 5.00N 15.50 E
Nana Barya 35 Bd 7.59N 17.43 E
Nanae 29a Bc 41.53N 140.41 E
Nanaimo 42 Fg 49.10N 123.56W
Nanakuli 65a Cb 21.23N 158.08W
Nana-Mambéré [3] 35 Bd 6.00N 16.00 E
Nanango 59 Ke 26.40S 152.00 E
Nanao 27 Od 37.03N 136.58 E
Nanao-Wan 29 Ec 37.10N 137.00 E
Nanatsu-Shima 29 Ec 37.35N 136.50 E
Nancha 27 Mb 47.08N 129.09 E
Nanchang 22 Ng 28.40N 115.58 E
Nancheng 27 Kf 27.32N 116.36 E
Nanchong 22 Mf 30.47N 106.03 E
Nancowry 25 Ig 7.59N 93.32 E
Nancy 6 Gf 48.41N 6.12 E
Nanda Devi 25 Jf 30.23N 79.59 E
Nandaime 49 Dh 11.46N 86.03W
Nandan [China] 27 Ig 24.59N 107.31 E
Nandan [Jap.] 28 Mg 34.15N 134.43 E
Nandaran → Qingyuan 28 Ce 38.46N 115.29 E
Nanded 22 Jh 19.09N 77.20 E
Nandewar Range 59 Kf 30.40S 151.10 E
Nandi 61 Ec 17.48S 177.25 E
Nandu Jiang 27 Jg 20.04N 110.22 E
Nanduri 63d Bb 16.27S 179.09 E
Nandyāl 25 Fe 15.29N 78.29 E
Nanfen 28 Gd 41.06N 123.45 E
Nanfeng 27 Kf 27.15N 116.30 E
Nanga-Eboko 34 He 4.41N 12.22 E
Nanga Parbat 21 Jf 35.15N 74.36 E
Nangapinoh 26 Fg 0.20S 111.44 E
Nangarhār [3] 23 Lc 34.15N 70.30 E
Nangatayap 26 Fg 1.32S 110.34 E
Nangis 11 If 48.33N 3.00 E
Nangnim-san 28 Id 40.21N 126.55 E
Nangnim-Sanmaek 28 Id 40.30N 127.00 E
Nangong 27 Kd 37.22N 115.23 E
Nangqên 27 Ge 32.15N 96.13 E
Nanguan 28 Af 36.42N 111.41 E
Nanguantao → Guantao 28 Cf 36.33N 115.18 E
Nangweshi 36 Df 16.26S 23.20 E
Nan Hai=South China Sea (EN) 21 Ni 10.00N 113.00 E
Nanhaoqian → Shangyi 28 Bd 41.06N 113.58 E
Nanhe 28 Cf 36.58N 114.41 E
Nanhua 27 Hf 25.16N 101.18 E
Nanhui 28 Fi 31.03N 121.46 E
Nan Hulsan Hu 27 Gd 36.45N 95.45 E
Nanjian 27 Hf 25.05N 100.32 E
Nanjiang 27 Ie 32.22N 106.45 E
Nanjing=Nanking (EN) 22 Nf 31.59N 118.51 E
Nankai Trough (EN) 27 Ne 32.00N 135.00 E
Nanking (EN)=Nanjing 22 Nf 31.59N 118.51 E
Nankoku 28 Lh 33.39N 133.44 E
Nanle 28 Cf 36.06N 115.12 E
Nanling 28 Ei 30.55N 118.19 E
Nan Ling 21 Ng 25.00N 112.00 E
Nanlou Shan 28 Ic 43.24N 126.40 E
Nanma → Yiyuan 28 Ef 36.11N 118.10 E
Nanning 22 Mg 22.50N 108.18 E
Nannup 59 Df 33.59S 115.45 E
Nanortalik 41 Hf 60.32N 45.45W
Nanpan Jiang 27 Ig 24.56N 106.12 E
Nānpāra 25 Gc 27.52N 81.30 E
Nanping [China] 22 Ng 26.42N 118.09 E
Nanping [China] 27 He 33.15N 104.13 E
Nanpu 28 Ee 39.16N 118.12 E
Nanqiao → Fengxian 28 Fi 30.55N 121.27 E
Nansei-Shotō=Ryukyu Islands (EN) 21 Og 26.30N 128.00 E
Nansen Cordillera (EN) 67 Ge 87.00N 90.00 E
Nansen Land 41 Hb 83.20N 46.00W
Nanshan Islands (EN)=Nansha Qundao 21 Ni 9.40N 113.30 E
Nansha Qundao=Nanshan Islands (EN) 21 Ni 9.40N 113.30 E
Nansio 36 Fc 2.08S 33.03 E
Nant 11 Jj 44.01N 3.18 E
Nantais, Lac- 42 Kd 61.00N 73.50W
Nanterre 11 If 48.54N 2.12 E
Nantes 6 Ff 47.13N 1.33W
Nantes à Brest, Can. de- 11 Bf 48.12N 4.06W
Nanteuil-le-Haudouin 12 Ee 49.08N 2.48 E
Nanticoke 44 Je 41.13N 76.00W
Nantō 29 Ed 34.17N 136.29 E
Nantong 27 Le 32.00N 120.52 E
Nantong (Jinsha) 28 Fh 32.06N 120.52 E
Nantou 27 Lg 23.54N 120.51 E
Nantua 11 Lh 46.09N 5.37 E
Nantucket 44 Le 41.17N 70.06W
Nantucket Island 43 Mc 41.16N 70.03W
Nantucket Sound 44 Le 41.30N 70.15W
Nanuku Passage 63d Cb 16.45S 179.15W
Nanuku Reef 63d Cb 16.40S 179.26W
Nanumanga Island 57 Ie 6.18S 176.20 E
Nanumea Atoll 57 Ie 5.43S 176.00 E
Nanuque 54 Jg 17.50S 40.21W
Nanusa, Pulau-Pulau- 26 If 4.42N 127.06 E
Nanwan Shuiku 28 Bh 32.02N 113.57 E
Nanwei Dao=Spratly Islands 26 Fe 8.42N 111.40 E
Nanxian 28 Bj 29.22N 112.25 E
Nanxiang 28 Fi 31.18N 121.17 E
Nanxiong 27 Jf 25.13N 114.18 E
Nanxun 28 Fi 30.53N 120.26 E
Nanyandang Shan 27 Lf 27.37N 120.06 E
Nanyang 22 Nf 32.56N 112.32 E
Nanyang Hu 28 Dg 35.15N 116.39 E
Nanyō 28 Pe 38.03N 140.10 E
Nanyuki 31 Kh 0.01N 37.04 E
Nanzhang 27 Je 31.45N 111.53 E
Nanzhao 27 Je 33.28N 112.29 E
Nao, Cabo de la- 5 Gh 38.44N 0.14 E
Naococane, Lac- 42 Kf 52.50N 70.40W
Naoero/Nauru [1] 58 He 0.31S 166.56 E
Naoetsu 29 Fc 37.11N 138.14 E
Não-me-Toque 55 Fi 28.28S 52.49W
Naours, Souterrains de- 12 Ed 50.05N 2.17 E
Napa 46 Dg 38.18N 122.17W
Napanee 44 Ic 44.15N 76.57W
Napassoq 41 Ge 65.45N 52.38W
Napata 35 Eb 18.29N 31.51 E
Na-Peng 25 Lg 23.10N 98.26 E
Napf 14 Bc 47.01N 7.57 E
Napier 58 Ih 39.30S 176.54 E
Napier, Mount- 59 Fc 17.32S 129.10 E
Napier Mountains 66 Ee 66.30S 53.40 E
Naples [Fl.-U.S.] 43 Kf 26.08N 81.48W
Naples [Id.-U.S.] 46 Gb 48.34N 116.24W
Naples (EN)=Napoli 6 Hg 40.50N 14.15 E
Naples, Gulf of- (EN)=Napoli, Golfo di- 14 Ij 40.45N 14.10 E
Napo 27 Ig 23.25N 105.49 E
Napo, Rio- 52 If 3.20S 72.40W
Napoleon 45 Gc 46.30N 99.46W
Napoli=Naples (EN) 6 Hg 40.50N 14.15 E
Napoli, Golfo di-=Naples, Gulf of- (EN) 14 Ij 40.45N 14.10 E
Napostá 55 An 38.26S 62.15W
Napuka, Ile- 57 Mf 14.12S 141.15W
Naqa 35 Eb 16.16N 33.17 E
Naqadeh 23 Gb 36.57N 45.23 E
Naqsh-e-Rostam 24 Og 30.01N 52.50 E
Nar 9 Ni 52.45N 0.24 E
Nāra 25 Dc 24.07N 69.07 E
Nara [Jap.] 27 Oe 34.41N 135.50 E
Nara [Mali] 34 Db 15.11N 7.15W
Naračenskibani 15 Hh 41.54N 24.45 E
Naracoorte 59 Ig 36.58S 140.44 E
Nara-Ken [2] 28 Mg 34.20N 135.55 E
Naranjo 48 Ee 25.48N 108.31W
Naranjos [Bol.] 55 Cd 18.38S 59.09W
Naranjos [Mex.] 48 Kg 21.21N 97.41W
Narao 29 Ae 32.52N 129.04 E
Narathiwat 25 Kg 6.25N 101.48 E
Nārāyanganj 25 Id 23.37N 90.30 E
Narbonne 11 Ik 43.11N 3.00 E
Narca, Ponta da- 36 Bd 6.07S 12.16 E
Narcea 13 Fa 43.28N 6.06W
Narcondam 25 If 13.15N 94.30 E
Nardò 14 Mj 40.11N 18.02 E
Naré 55 Bj 30.58S 60.28W
Nares Land 41 Hb 82.25N 47.30W
Nares Strait 38 Lb 78.50N 73.00W
Narew 10 Td 52.55N 23.29 E
Narew 10 Qd 52.26N 20.42 E
Narian, Pointe- 63b Be 20.05S 164.00 E
Narin Gol 27 Fd 36.54N 92.51 E
Nariño [2] 54 Cc 1.30N 78.00W
Narita 29 Gd 35.47N 140.18 E
Narjan-Mar 6 Lb 67.39N 53.00 E
Närke 8 Ff 59.05N 15.05 E
Narli 24 Gd 37.27N 37.09 E
Narmada 21 Jg 21.38N 72.36 E
Narman 24 Ib 40.21N 41.52 E
Nārnaul 25 Fc 28.03N 76.06 E
Narni 14 Gh 42.31N 12.31 E
Naroč 8 Lj 54.27N 26.45 E
Naroč 8 Lj 54.57N 26.49 E
Naroč, Ozero- 16 Eb 54.50N 26.45 E
Naroda 17 Jd 64.15N 61.00 E
Narodnaja, Gora- 5 Mb 65.04N 60.09 E
Naro-Fominsk 19 Dd 55.24N 36.43 E
Narok 36 Gc 1.05S 35.52 E
Narovlja 16 Fd 51.48N 29.31 E
Närpes/Närpio 8 Ib 62.28N 21.20 E
Närpio/Närpes 8 Ib 62.28N 21.20 E
Narrabri 59 Jf 30.19S 149.47 E
Narrandera 59 Jf 34.45S 146.33 E
Narrogin 59 Df 32.56S 117.10 E
Narromine 59 Jf 32.14S 148.15 E
Narrows, The- 51c Ab 17.12N 62.38W
Narryer, Mount- 59 De 26.30S 116.25 E
Narsimhapur 25 Fd 22.57N 79.12 E
Narssalik 41 Hf 61.42N 49.11W
Narssaq [Grld.] 41 Hf 61.00N 46.00W
Narssaq [Grld.] 41 Gf 64.00N 51.33W
Narssarssuaq 41 Hf 61.10N 45.15W
Narthákion 15 Fj 39.14N 22.22 E
Nartkala 16 Mh 43.32N 43.47 E
Narubis 37 Be 26.55S 18.35 E
Narugo 29 Gb 38.44N 140.43 E
Năruja 15 Jd 45.50N 26.47 E
Naru-Shima 29 Ae 32.50N 128.56 E
Naruto 28 Mg 34.11N 134.37 E
Naruto-Kaikyō 29 Dd 34.15N 134.40 E
Narva 7 Gg 59.29N 28.02 E
Narva 6 Id 59.23N 28.11 E
Narva Jõesuu/Narva-Jyesuu 8 Me 59.21N 28.04 E
Narva-Jyesuu/Narva Jõesuu 8 Me 59.21N 28.04 E
Narva laht 7 Gg 59.30N 27.40 E
Narvik 6 Hb 68.26N 17.25 E
Narvski Zaliv 7 Gg 59.30N 27.40 E
Narvskoje Vodohranilišče 8 Me 59.10N 28.30 E
Narym 20 De 58.58N 81.40 E
Naryn 21 Je 40.54N 71.45 E
Naryn 22 Je 41.26N 75.59 E
Naryncol 19 Ig 42.43N 80.08 E
Narynskaja Oblast [3] 19 Hg 41.20N 75.40 E
Nås 7 Df 60.27N 14.29 E
Na Sailti/Saltee Islands 9 Gi 52.07N 6.36W
Näsåker 7 De 63.23N 16.54 E
Nasarawa 34 Gd 8.32N 7.43 E
Năsăud 15 Hb 47.17N 24.24 E
Nasawa 63b Db 15.12S 168.06 E
Na Sceiri/Skerries 9 Gh 53.35N 6.07W
Nāshik 22 Jg 20.05N 73.48 E
Nash Point 9 Jj 51.24N 3.27W
Nashtärud 24 Nd 36.45N 51.02 E
Nashua 44 Ld 42.44N 71.28W
Nashville [Ar.-U.S.] 45 Jj 33.57N 93.51W
Nashville [Ga.-U.S.] 44 Fj 31.12N 83.15W
Nashville [Il.-U.S.] 45 Lg 38.21N 89.23W
Nashville [In.-U.S.] 44 Df 39.12N 86.15W
Nashville [Tn.-U.S.] 39 Kf 36.09N 86.48W
Nashville Seamount (EN) 38 Nf 35.00N 57.20W
Našice 14 Me 45.30N 18.06 E
Nasielsk 10 Qd 52.36N 20.48 E
Näsijärvi 5 Ic 61.35N 23.40 E
Nāşir 35 Ed 8.36N 33.04 E
Naskaupi 42 Lf 53.47N 60.51W
Nasorolevu 63d Bb 16.38S 179.24 E
Naşr [Eg.] 24 Dg 30.36N 30.23 E
Naşr [Lib.] 33 Dd 28.59N 21.13 E
Naşrābād 24 Of 32.09N 52.08 E
Nass 42 Ee 55.00N 129.50W
Nassandres 12 Ce 49.07N 0.44 E
Nassandres-La Rivière Thibouville 12 Ce 49.07N 0.44 E
Nassau [Bah.] 39 Lg 25.05N 77.21W
Nassau [Ger.] 12 Jd 50.19N 7.48 E
Nassau, Bahia- 56 Gi 55.25S 67.40W
Nassau Island 57 Kf 11.33S 165.25W
Nassau River 59 Ic 15.58S 141.30 E
Nasser, Birkat-=Nasser, Lake-(EN) 30 Kf 22.40N 32.00 E

Index Symbols

[1] Independent Nation
[2] State, Region
[3] District, County
[4] Municipality
[5] Colony, Dependency
Continent
Physical Region
Historical or Cultural Region
Mount, Mountain
Volcano
Hill
Mountains, Mountain Range
Hills, Escarpment
Plateau, Upland
Pass, Gap
Plain, Lowland
Delta
Salt Flat
Valley, Canyon
Crater, Cave
Karst Features
Depression
Polder
Desert, Dunes
Forest, Woods
Heath, Steppe
Oasis
Cape, Point
Coast, Beach
Cliff
Peninsula
Isthmus
Sandbank
Island
Atoll
Rock, Reef
Islands, Archipelago
Rocks, Reefs
Coral Reef
Well, Spring
Geyser
River, Stream
Waterfall Rapids
River Mouth, Estuary
Lake
Salt Lake
Intermittent Lake
Reservoir
Swamp, Pond
Canal
Glacier
Ice Shelf, Pack Ice
Ocean
Sea
Gulf, Bay
Strait, Fjord
Lagoon
Bank
Seamount
Tablemount
Ridge
Shelf
Basin
Escarpment, Sea Scarp
Fracture
Trench, Abyss
National Park, Reserve
Point of Interest
Recreation Site
Cave, Cavern
Historic Site
Ruins
Wall, Walls
Church, Abbey
Temple
Scientific Station
Airport
Port
Lighthouse
Mine
Tunnel
Dam, Bridge

Index Symbols

[1]	Independent Nation
[2]	State, Region
[3]	District, County
[4]	Municipality
■	Colony, Dependency
■	Continent
[X]	Physical Region

- Historical or Cultural Region
- Mount, Mountain
- Volcano
- Hill
- Mountains, Mountain Range
- Hills, Escarpment
- Plateau, Upland
- Pass, Gap
- Plain, Lowland
- Delta
- Salt Flat
- Valley, Canyon
- Crater, Cave
- Karst Features
- Depression
- Polder
- Desert, Dunes
- Forest, Woods
- Heath, Steppe
- Oasis
- Cape, Point
- Coast, Beach
- Cliff
- Peninsula
- Rocks, Reefs
- Sandbank
- Island
- Atoll
- Rock, Reef
- Islands, Archipelago
- River Mouth, Estuary
- Coral Reef
- Well, Spring
- Geyser
- River, Stream
- Waterfall Rapids
- Lake
- Salt Lake
- Intermittent Lake
- Reservoir
- Swamp, Pond
- Canal
- Glacier
- Ice Shelf, Pack Ice
- Ocean
- Sea
- Gulf, Bay
- Strait, Fjord
- Lagoon
- Bank
- Seamount
- Tableland
- Ridge
- Shelf
- Basin
- Escarpment, Sea Scarp
- Fracture
- Trench, Abyss
- National Park, Reserve
- Point of Interest
- Recreation Site
- Cave, Cavern
- Historic Site
- Ruins
- Wall, Walls
- Church, Abbey
- Temple
- Scientific Station
- Airport
- Port
- Lighthouse
- Mine
- Tunnel
- Dam, Bridge

Index Symbols

[1] Independent Nation	◨ Historical or Cultural Region	⤴ Pass, Gap	⬒ Depression	⬓ Coast, Beach	⬗ Rock, Reef	⬖ Waterfall Rapids	⬕ Canal
[2] State, Region	▲ Mount, Mountain	⬚ Plain, Lowland	⬛ Polder	⬜ Cliff	⬝ Islands, Archipelago	⬞ River Mouth, Estuary	⬟ Lagoon

Nižni Oseredok, Ostrov-	16	Pg	45.45N	48.35 E
Nižni Tagil	6	Ld	57.55N	59.57 E
Nižni Trajanov Val=Lower Trajan's Wall (EN)	15	Ld	45.45N	28.30 E
Nižnjaja Omra	17	Ge	62.46N	55.46 E
Nižnjaja Peša	19	Eb	66.43N	47.36 E
Nižnjaja Pojma	20	Ee	56.08N	97.18 E
Nižnjaja Salda	17	Jg	58.05N	60.48 E
Nižnjaja Tavda	19	Gd	57.40N	66.12 E
Nižnjaja Tojma	7	Ke	62.22N	44.15 E
Nižnjaja Tunguska=Lower Tunguska (EN)	21	Kc	65.48N	88.04 E
Nižnjaja Tura	17	Ig	58.37N	59.49 E
Nižnjaja Zolotica	7	Jd	65.41N	40.13 E
Nižny Pjandž	18	Gf	37.14N	68.35 E
Nizza Monferrato	14	Cf	44.46N	8.21 E
Njajs	17	Je	62.25N	60.47 E
Njamunas	5	Id	55.18N	21.23 E
Njandoma	19	Ec	61.43N	40.12 E
Njaris/Neris	8	Kj	54.55N	25.45 E
Njazepetrovsk	17	Ih	56.03N	59.38 E
Njazidja	30	Lj	11.35S	43.20 E
Njegoš	15	Bg	42.53N	18.45 E
Njinjo	36	Gd	8.48S	38.54 E
Njombe	30	Ki	6.56S	35.06 E
Njombe	31	Ki	9.20S	34.46 E
Njudung	8	Fg	57.25N	14.50 E
Njuja	20	Gd	60.32N	116.25 E
Njuk, Ozero-	7	Hd	64.25N	31.45 E
Njuksenica	7	Kf	60.28N	44.15 E
Njukža	20	He	56.30N	121.40 E
Njunes	7	Eb	68.45N	19.30 E
Njurba	22	Nc	63.17N	118.20 E
Njurundabommen	7	De	62.16N	17.22 E
Njutånger	8	Gc	61.37N	17.03 E
Njuvčim	17	Ef	61.22N	50.42 E
Nkambe	34	Hd	6.38N	10.40 E
Nkawkaw	34	Ed	6.33N	0.46W
Nkayi [Con.]	31	Ii	4.05S	13.18 E
Nkayi [Zimb.]	37	Dc	19.00S	28.54 E
Nkhata Bay	36	Fe	11.36S	34.18 E
Nkongsamba	31	Hh	4.57N	9.56 E
Nkota Kota	31	Kj	12.55S	34.18 E
Nkululu	36	Fd	6.26S	32.49 E
Nkusi	36	Fb	1.07N	30.40 E
Nkwalini	37	Ee	28.45S	31.30 E
'Nmai	25	Jc	25.42N	97.30 E
Nmaki	24	Pg	31.16N	55.29 E
Nnewi	34	Gd	6.01N	6.55 E
Nō	29	Ec	37.05N	137.59 E
Noailles	12	Ee	49.20N	2.12 E
Noākhāli	25	Id	22.49N	91.06 E
Noatak	40	Gc	67.34N	162.59W
Nobel	44	Gc	45.25N	80.06W
Nobeoka	27	Ne	32.35N	131.40 E
Noblesville	44	Ee	40.03N	86.00W
Noboribetsu	28	Pc	42.25N	141.11 E
Noce	14	Fd	46.09N	11.04 E
Nocra	35	Fc	15.40N	39.55 E
Nodaway River	45	Ig	39.54N	94.58W
Noēn	27	Hc	43.15N	102.20 E
Noeuf, Ile des-	37b	Bb	6.14S	53.03 E
Noeux-les-Mines	12	Ed	50.29N	2.40 E
Nogajskaja Step	16	Ng	44.15N	46.00 E
Nogales [Az.-U.S.]	43	Ee	31.21N	110.55W
Nogales [Mex.]	39	Hf	31.20N	110.56W
Nogaro	11	Fk	43.46N	0.02W
Nogat	10	Pb	54.11N	19.15 E
Nōgata	29	Be	33.44N	130.44 E
Nogent-le-Rotrou	11	Gf	48.19N	0.50 E
Nogent-sur-Marne	12	Ef	48.50N	2.29 E
Nogent-sur-Oise	12	Ee	49.16N	2.28 E
Nogent-sur-Seine	11	Jf	48.29N	3.30 E
Noginsk	20	Ed	64.25N	91.10 E
Noginsk	19	Dd	55.54N	38.28 E
Nogliki	20	Jf	51.45N	143.15 E
Nōgo-Hakusan	29	Ed	35.46N	136.31 E
Nogoyá	56	Id	32.24S	59.48W
Nogoya, Arroyo-	55	Ck	32.55S	59.59W
Nógrád [2]	10	Ph	48.00N	19.35 E
Nogueira, Serra da-	13	Fc	41.42N	6.52W
Noguera Pallaresa	13	Mb	42.15N	0.54 E
Noguera Ribagorçana/ Noguera Ribagorzana	13	Mc	41.40N	0.43 E
Noguera Ribagorzana/ Noguera Ribagorçana	13	Mc	41.40N	0.43 E
Noh, Laguna-	48	Nh	18.40N	90.20W
Nohain	11	Ig	47.24N	2.55 E
Noheji	28	Pd	40.52N	141.08 E
Nohfelden	12	Je	49.35N	7.09 E
Noidore, Rio-	55	Fb	14.50S	52.34W
Noir, Causse-	11	Jj	44.09N	3.15 E
Noire, Montagne-	11	Ik	43.28N	2.18 E
Noires, Montagnes-	11	Cf	48.09N	3.40W
Noirétable	11	Ji	45.49N	3.46 E
Noirmoutier, Ile de-	11	Dh	46.58N	2.12W
Noirmoutier-en-l'Ile	11	Dg	47.00N	2.15W
Nojima-Zaki	29	Fd	34.54N	139.50 E
Nojiri-Ko	29	Fc	36.49N	138.13 E
Noka	63c	Bb	10.40S	166.03 E
Nokaneng	37	Cc	19.40S	22.12 E
Nokia	7	Ff	61.28N	23.30 E
Nok Kundi	25	Cc	28.48N	62.46 E
Nokomis	46	Ma	51.30N	105.00W
Nokou	35	Ac	14.35N	14.47 E
Nokra	35	Fb	15.42N	39.56 E
Nol	8	Eg	57.55N	12.03 E
Nola [C.A.R.]	35	Be	3.32N	16.04 E
Nola [It.]	14	Ij	40.55N	14.33 E
Nolin Lake	44	Dg	37.20N	86.10W
Nolinsk	19	Ed	57.33N	50.00 E
Nomad	58	Fe	6.21S	142.12 E
Noma Omuramba	37	Cc	19.10S	22.16 E
Noma-Zaki	29	Bf	31.25N	130.06 E
Nombre de Dios	48	Gf	23.51N	104.14W
Nome	39	Cc	64.30N	165.24W
Nomeny	12	If	48.54N	6.14 E
Nomo-Saki	29	Ae	32.35N	129.45 E
Nomozaki	29	Ae	32.35N	129.45 E
Nomuka	65b	Bb	20.15S	174.48W
Nomuka Group	57	Jg	20.20S	174.45W
Nomuka Iki	65b	Bb	20.17S	174.49W
Nomwin Atoll	57	Gd	8.32N	151.47 E
Nonacho Lake	42	Gd	62.40N	109.30W
Nonancourt	12	Df	48.46N	1.12 E
Nonette	12	Ee	49.12N	2.24 E
Nong'an	27	Mc	44.24N	125.08 E
Nong Han	25	Ke	17.21N	103.06 E
Nong Khai	22	Mh	17.52N	102.45 E
Nongoma	37	Ee	27.53S	31.38 E
Nonoava	48	Fd	27.28N	106.44W
Nonouti Atoll	57	Ie	0.40S	174.21 E
Nonsan	28	If	36.12N	127.05 E
Nonsuch Bay	51d	Bb	17.03N	61.42W
Nontron	11	Gi	45.32N	0.40 E
Noord-Beveland	12	Fc	51.35N	3.45 E
Noord-Brabant [3]	12	Gc	51.30N	5.00 E
Noord-Holland [3]	12	Gb	52.40N	4.50 E
Noordhollandskanaal	11	Kb	52.55N	4.50 E
Noordoewer	37	Be	28.45S	17.37 E
Noordoostpolder	11	Lb	52.42N	5.45 E
Noordoostpolder	12	Hb	52.42N	5.44 E
Noordoostpolder-Emmeloord	12	Hb	52.42N	5.44 E
Noordwijk aan Zee	11	Kb	52.14N	4.26 E
Noordwijk aan Zee, Noordwijk-	12	Gb	52.14N	4.26 E
Noordwijk-Noordwijk aan Zee	12	Gb	52.14N	4.26 E
Noordzee=North Sea (EN)	5	Gd	55.20N	3.00 E
Noordzeekanaal	11	Kb	52.30N	4.35 E
Noormarkku/Norrmark	8	Ic	61.35N	21.52 E
Noorvik	40	Gc	66.50N	161.12W
Nootka Island	46	Bb	49.32N	126.42W
Nootka Sound	46	Bb	49.33N	126.38W
Nóqui	36	Bd	5.50S	13.27 E
Nora [It.]	14	Dk	39.00N	9.02 E
Nora [Swe.]	7	Dg	59.31N	15.02 E
Noraskog	8	Fe	59.40N	14.50 E
Norberg	8	Fd	60.04N	15.56 E
Norcia	14	Hh	42.48N	13.05 E
Nord	41	Kb	81.45N	17.30W
Nord [Cam.] [3]	34	Hd	9.00N	13.50 E
Nord [Fr.] [3]	11	Jd	50.20N	3.40 E
Nord [Burkina]	34	Ec	13.40N	2.50W
Nord, Canal du-	11	Id	49.57N	2.55 E
Nord, Mer du-= North Sea (EN)	5	Gd	55.20N	3.00 E
Nordausques	12	Ed	50.49N	2.05 E
Nordaustlandet	67	Jd	79.48N	22.24 E
Nordborg	8	Ci	55.03N	9.45 E
Nordby	8	Ci	55.27N	8.25 E
Norddeutsches Tiefland= North German Plain (EN)	5	He	53.00N	11.00 E
Norden	10	Dc	53.36N	7.12 E
Nordenham	10	Ec	53.39N	8.29 E
Nordenskjölda, Ostrova-= Nordenskjöld, Archipelago (EN)	20	Ea	76.50N	96.00 E
Nordenskjöld Archipelago (EN)=Nordenskjölda, Ostrova-	20	Ea	76.50N	96.00 E
Norderney	10	Dc	53.42N	7.10 E
Norderstedt	10	Fc	53.41N	9.58 E
Nordfjord	8	Bc	61.50N	6.15 E
Nordfjord	7	Af	61.55N	5.10 E
Nordfjordeid	7	Af	61.54N	6.00 E
Nordfold	7	Dc	67.46N	15.12 E
Nordfriesische Inseln= North Frisian Islands (EN)	10	Ea	54.50N	8.30 E
Nordfriesland	10	Eb	54.40N	8.55 E
Nordgau	10	Hg	49.15N	11.50 E
Nordgrønland=North Greenland (EN) [2]	41	Gc	79.30N	50.00W
Nordhausen	10	Ge	51.31N	10.48 E
Nordhordland	8	Ad	60.50N	5.50 E
Nordhorn	10	Dd	52.26N	7.05 E
Nord-Jylland [2]	8	Cg	57.15N	10.00 E
Nordkapp [Nor.] =North Cape (EN)	5	Ia	71.11N	25.48 E
Nordkapp [Sval.]	41	Nb	80.31N	20.00 E
Nordkinn	5	Ia	71.08N	27.39 E
Nordkinnhalvøya	7	Ga	70.55N	27.45 E
Nord-Kvaløy	7	Ea	70.10N	19.11 E
Nordland [3]	7	Cc	67.06N	13.20 E
Nördlingen	10	Gh	48.51N	10.30 E
Nordloher Tief	12	Ja	53.10N	7.45 E
Nordmark	8	Fe	59.50N	14.06 E
Nordmøre	8	Ca	63.00N	8.30 E
Nordostrundingen	67	Le	81.30N	11.00W
Nord-Ostsee Kanal=Kiel Canal (EN)	5	Ge	53.53N	9.08 E
Nord-Ouest [3]	34	Hd	6.30N	10.30 E
Nordøyane	8	Bb	62.40N	6.15 E
Nordreisa	7	Eb	69.46N	21.03 E
Nordre Rønner	8	Dg	57.22N	10.56 E
Nordrhein-Westfalen=North Rhine-Westphalia (EN) [2]	10	De	51.30N	7.30 E
Nordsee=North Sea (EN)	5	Gd	55.20N	3.00 E
Nordsjøen=North Sea (EN)	5	Gd	55.20N	3.00 E
Nordskjobotn	7	Eb	69.13N	19.34 E
Nordsøen=North Sea (EN)	5	Gd	55.20N	3.00 E
Nord Strand	10	Eb	54.30N	8.55 E
Nordtiroler Kalkalpen	10	Hi	47.30N	11.30 E
Nord-Trøndelag [2]	7	Cd	64.25N	12.00 E
Nordwestfjord	41	Jd	71.30N	26.30W
Nore/An Fheoir	9	Gi	52.25N	6.58W
Norefjell	8	Cd	60.16N	9.29 E
Norefjorden	8	Cd	60.10N	9.00 E
Norfolk	9	Oi	52.40N	1.05 E
Norfolk [3]	9	Mi	52.45N	0.40W
Norfolk [Nb.-U.S.]	43	Hc	42.02N	97.25W
Norfolk [Va.-U.S.]	39	Lf	38.40N	76.14W
Norfolk Island [5]	58	Hg	29.05S	167.59 E
Norfolk Island	57	Hg	29.05S	167.59 E
Norfolk Ridge (EN)	57	Hg	29.00S	168.00 E
Norfork Lake	45	Jh	36.25N	92.10W
Norg	12	Ia	53.04N	6.32 E
Norge=Norway (EN) [1]	6	Gc	62.00N	10.00 E
Norheimsund	7	Bf	60.22N	6.08 E
Norikura-Dake	29	Ec	36.06N	137.33 E
Norilsk	22	Kc	69.20N	88.06 E
Normal	45	Lf	40.31N	88.59W
Norman	43	Hd	35.15N	97.26W
Norman, Lake-	44	Gh	35.35N	81.00W
Normanby Island	60	Ej	10.00S	151.00 E
Normanby River	59	Ib	14.25S	144.08 E
Normand, Bocage-	11	Ef	49.00N	1.10W
Normandie=Normandy (EN)	11	Gf	49.00N	0.10 E
Normandie=Normandy (EN)	5	Gf	49.00N	0.10 E
Normandie, Collines de-= Normandy Hills (EN)	5	Ff	48.50N	0.40W
Normandin	44	Ka	48.52N	72.30W
Normandy (EN)= Normandie	11	Gf	49.00N	0.10 E
Normandy (EN)= Normandie	5	Gf	49.00N	0.10 E
Normandy Hills (EN)= Normandie, Collines de-	5	Ff	48.50N	0.40W
Norman Island	51a	Db	18.20N	64.37W
Norman River	59	Ic	17.28S	140.39 E
Normanton	58	Ff	17.40S	141.05 E
Norman Wells	39	Gc	65.17N	126.51W
Norquinco	56	Ff	41.51S	70.54W
Norra Dellen	8	Gc	61.55N	16.40 E
Norrahammar	8	Fg	57.42N	14.06 E
Norrala	8	Gc	61.22N	16.59 E
Norra Midsjöbanken	8	Gh	56.10N	17.30 E
Norra Ny	7	Cf	60.24N	13.15 E
Norra Storfjället	7	Dd	65.53N	15.14 E
Norrbotten [2]	7	Ec	67.26N	19.35 E
Nørre Åby	8	Ci	55.27N	9.54 E
Nørre Alslev	8	Dj	54.54N	11.54 E
Nørre-Nebel	8	Ci	55.47N	8.18 E
Norrent-Fontes	12	Ed	50.35N	2.24 E
Nørresundby	7	Bh	57.04N	9.55 E
Norrhult	7	Dh	57.08N	15.10 E
Norris Lake	44	Fg	36.20N	83.55W
Norristown	44	Je	40.07N	75.20W
Norrköping	6	Hd	58.36N	16.11 E
Norrland	5	Hc	64.27N	17.20 E
Norrland	7	Dd	65.00N	18.00 E
Norrmark/Noormarkku	8	Ic	61.35N	21.52 E
Norrsundet	8	Gd	60.56N	17.08 E
Norrtälje	7	Eg	59.46N	18.42 E
Norseman	58	Dh	32.12S	121.46 E
Norsewood	62	Gd	40.04S	176.13 E
Norsjö	7	Ed	64.55N	19.29 E
Norsjø	8	Ce	59.20N	9.20 E
Norsk	20	Hf	52.20N	129.59 E
Norske Havet=Norwegian, Sea (EN)	5	Gc	70.00N	2.00 E
Norske Øer	41	Kc	79.00N	18.00W
Norsoup	63b	Cc	16.04S	167.23 E
Norte, Baia-	55	Hh	27.30S	48.35W
Norte, Cabo- [Braz.]	54	Ic	1.40N	50.00W
Norte, Cabo- [Pas.]	65d	Ab	27.03S	109.24W
Norte, Canal do-	54	Hc	0.30N	50.30W
Norte, Punta-	56	Hf	42.04S	63.45W
Norte, Serra do-	54	Gf	11.00S	59.00W
Norte del Cabo San Antonio, Punta-	56	Ie	36.17S	56.47W
Norte de Santander [2]	54	Db	8.00N	73.00W
Nortelândia	54	Gf	14.25S	56.48W
North, Cape -	42	Lg	47.02N	60.25W
North Adams	44	Kd	42.42N	73.02W
Northallerton	9	Lg	54.20N	1.26W
Northam [Austl.]	58	Ch	31.39S	116.40 E
Northam [S.Afr.]	37	Dd	24.58S	27.11 E
North America	38	Jf	40.00N	95.00W
North American Basin (EN)	3	Cf	30.00N	60.00W
Northampton	9	Mi	52.30N	1.00W
Northampton [Austl.]	59	Ce	28.21S	114.37 E
Northampton [Eng.-U.K.]	9	Mi	52.14N	0.54W
Northampton [Ma.-U.S.]	44	Kd	42.19N	72.38W
Northampton Seamounts (EN)	57	Jb	25.20N	172.04W
Northamptonshire [3]	9	Mi	52.25N	0.55W
North Andaman	25	If	13.15N	92.55 E
North Arm	42	Gd	62.00N	114.30W
North Astrolabe Reef	63d	Bc	18.39S	178.32 E
North Augusta	44	Gi	33.30N	81.58W
North Aulatsivik	42	Le	59.45N	64.04W
North Australian Basin	3	Hk	14.30S	116.30 E
North Battleford	39	Id	52.47N	108.17W
North Bay	39	Le	46.19N	79.28W
North Belcher Islands	42	Je	56.45N	79.45W
North Berwick	9	Ke	56.04N	2.44W
North Buganda [3]	36	Fb	0.50N	32.10 E
North Caicos	49	Lc	21.56N	71.59W
North Canadian River	43	Hd	35.17N	95.31W
North Cape	57	Ih	34.25S	173.03 E
North Cape (EN)=Nordkapp [Nor.]	5	Ia	71.11N	25.48 E
North Caribou Lake	42	If	52.48N	90.45W
North Carolina [2]	43	Ld	35.30N	80.00W
North Channel	42	Jg	46.02N	82.50W
North Channel/Sruth na Maoile	5	Fd	55.10N	5.40W
Northchapel	12	Bc	51.03N	0.38W
North Charleston	44	Hi	32.53N	80.00W
North Chicago	45	Me	42.20N	87.51W
North Cove	46	Cc	46.47N	124.06W
North Cyprus	22	Ff	35.15N	33.40 E
North Dakota	43	Gb	47.30N	100.15W
North Downs	9	Nj	51.20N	0.10 E
North East	44	Hd	42.13N	79.51W
North-East [3]	37	Dd	21.00S	27.30 E
Northeast Cape	40	Fd	63.18N	168.42W
North-Eastern [3]	36	Hb	1.00N	40.15 E
Northeast Islands	64d	Ba	7.36N	151.57 E
Northeast Pacific Basin (EN)	3	Lg	20.00N	140.00W
Northeast Pass	64d	Ba	7.30N	151.59 E
North East Point	64g	Bb	1.57N	157.16W
Northeast Point [Bah.]	49	Kc	21.18N	72.54W
Northeast Point [Bah.]	49	Kb	22.43N	73.50W
Northeast Providence Channel	47	Ic	25.40N	77.09W
Northeim	10	Fe	51.42N	10.00 E
North Entrance	64a	Bb	7.59N	134.37 E
Northern [Ghana] [3]	34	Ed	9.30N	1.00W
Northern [Mwi.] [3]	36	Fe	11.00S	34.00 E
Northern [S.L.] [3]	34	Cd	9.15N	11.45W
Northern [Ug.] [3]	36	Fb	2.45N	32.45 E
Northern [Zam.] [3]	36	Fe	11.00S	31.00 E
Northern Cay	49	De	17.27N	87.28W
Northern Cook Islands	57	Kf	10.00S	161.00W
Northern Dvina (EN)= Severnaja Dvina	5	Kc	64.32N	40.30 E
Northern Guinea	30	Gh	8.30N	1.00W
Northern Indian Lake	42	He	57.20N	97.17W
Northern Ireland [2]	9	Gg	54.40N	6.45W
Northern Mariana Islands [5]	58	Fc	16.00N	145.30 E
Northern Sporades (EN)= Vórioi Sporádhes, Nisoi-	5	Ih	39.15N	23.55 E
Northern Territory	59	Gc	20.00S	134.00 E
Northern Urals (EN)= Severny Ural	5	Lc	62.00N	59.00 E
Northern Uvals (EN)= Severnyje Uvaly	5	Kd	59.30N	49.00 E
Northfield	45	Jd	44.27N	93.09W
North Fiji Basin (EN)	3	Jk	16.00S	174.00 E
North Foreland	9	Oj	51.23N	1.27 E
North Fork Grand River	45	Ed	45.47N	102.16W
North Fork John Day River	46	Fd	44.45N	119.38W
North Fork Moreau River	45	Ed	45.09N	102.50W
North Fork Pass	42	Dd	64.00N	138.00W
North Fork Powder River	46	Le	43.40N	106.30W
North Fork Red	45	Gi	34.25N	99.14W
North Fort Myers	44	Gl	26.40N	81.54W
North Frisian Islands (EN)= Nordfriesische Inseln	10	Ea	54.50N	8.30 E
North German Plain (EN)= Norddeutsches Tiefland	5	He	53.00N	11.00 E
North Greenland (EN) = Nordgrønland [2]	41	Gc	79.30N	50.00W
North Highlands	46	Eg	38.40N	121.23W
North Horr	36	Gb	3.19N	37.04 E
North Island [N.Z.]	57	Ih	39.00S	176.00 E
North Island [Sey.]	37b	Bc	10.07S	51.11 E
North Kent	42	Ia	76.40N	90.15W
North Korea (EN)=Chosŏn M.I.K. [1]	22	Oe	40.00N	127.30 E
North Lakhimpur	25	Ic	27.14N	94.07 E
Northland [2]	62	Ea	35.30S	173.40 E
North Las Vegas	46	Hh	36.12N	115.07W
North Lincoln Land	42	Ja	76.15N	80.00W
North Little Rock	43	Ie	34.46N	92.14W
North Loup River	45	Gf	41.17N	98.23W
North Magnetic Pole (1980)	67	Qd	77.03N	101.08W
North Malosmadulu Atoll	25a	Ba	5.35N	72.55 E
North Mamm Peak	45	Cg	39.23N	107.52W
North Mayreau Channel	51n	Bb	12.41N	61.20W
North Miami	44	Gm	25.56N	80.09W
North Minch	5	Fd	58.05N	5.55W
North Palisade	46	Fh	37.10N	118.38W
North Pass [F.S.M.]	64d	Ba	7.41N	151.48 E
North Pass [U.S.]	45	Ll	29.10N	89.15W
North Platte	43	Gc	41.08N	100.46W
North Platte	38	Ie	41.15N	100.45W
North Point	64n	Ab	10.22S	161.02W
North Point [Bar.]	51q	Ab	13.20N	59.36W
North Pole	67	Ge	90.00N	0.00
Northport	44	Di	33.14N	87.35W
North Powder	46	Gd	45.03N	117.55W
North Raccoon River	45	Jf	41.35N	93.31W
North Reef	63a	Ee	12.13S	160.04 E
North Rhine-Westphalia (EN)=Nordrhein-Westfalen [2]	10	De	51.30N	7.30 E
North Rim	46	Ih	36.12N	112.03W
North River	42	Ie	58.53N	94.42W
North Rona	9	Hb	59.10N	5.40W
North Ronaldsay	9	Kb	59.25N	2.30W
North Saskatchewan	38	Id	53.15N	105.06W
North Sea	5	Gd	55.20N	3.00 E
North Sea (EN)= Noordzee	5	Gd	55.20N	3.00 E
North Sea (EN)=Nord, Mer du-	5	Gd	55.20N	3.00 E
North Sea (EN)= Nordsee	5	Gd	55.20N	3.00 E
North Sea (EN)= Nordsjøen	5	Gd	55.20N	3.00 E
North Sea (EN)= Nordsøen	5	Gd	55.20N	3.00 E
North Sentinel	25	If	11.33N	92.15 E
North Shoshone Peak	46	Gg	39.10N	117.29W
North Siberian Plain (EN)= Severo-Sibirskaja Niz.	21	Mb	72.00N	104.00 E
North Sound	51d	Bb	17.07N	61.45W
North Sound	49	Gd	19.25N	81.26W
North Stradbroke Island	59	Ke	27.35S	153.30 E
North Taranaki Bight	62	Fc	38.50S	174.25 E
North Thompson	42	Ff	50.41N	120.11W
North Tokelau Trough (EN)	3	Kj	3.00S	165.00W
North Tonawanda	44	Hd	43.02N	78.54W
North Trap	62	Bg	47.20S	167.55 E
North Tyne	9	Kg	54.59N	2.08W
North Uist	9	Fd	57.37N	7.22W
Northumberland [3]	9	Kf	55.15N	2.10W
Northumberland	9	Kf	55.15N	2.05W
Northumberland Islands	57	Gg	21.40S	150.00 E
Northumberland Strait	42	Lg	46.00N	63.30W
North Umpqua River	46	De	43.16N	123.27W
North Vancouver	46	Db	49.19N	123.04W
North Walsham	12	Db	52.49N	1.23 E
Northway	40	Kd	62.59N	141.43W
North West Bluff	51c	Bc	16.49N	62.12W
North West Cape	57	Cg	21.45S	114.10 E
North-Western [3]	36	Ee	13.00S	25.00 E
Northwest Frontier [3]	25	Eb	33.00N	70.30 E
North West Highlands	5	Fd	57.30N	5.00W
Northwest Pacific Basin (EN)	3	Je	40.00N	155.00 E
North West Point	64g	Ab	2.02N	157.30W
Northwest Providence Channel	44	Hl	26.10N	78.20W
Northwest Reef	64a	Bb	7.59N	134.33 E
North West River	42	Lf	53.32N	60.09W
Northwest Territories [3]	42	Hc	66.00N	102.00W
Northwich	9	Kh	53.16N	2.32W
North York Moors	9	Mg	54.25N	0.50W
North Yorkshire [3]	9	Lg	54.15N	1.40W
Norton [Ks.-U.S.]	43	Gd	39.50N	100.01W
Norton [Va.-U.S.]	44	Fg	36.56N	82.37W
Norton [Zimb.]	37	Ec	17.53S	30.41 E
Norton Bay	40	Gd	64.45N	161.15W
Norton Sound	38	Cc	64.45N	161.15W
Norvegia, Kapp-	66	Bf	71.25S	12.18W
Norwalk [Ct.-U.S.]	44	Ke	41.07N	73.27W
Norwalk [Oh.-U.S.]	44	Fe	41.14N	82.37W
Norway	44	Dc	45.47N	87.55W
Norway (EN)=Norge [1]	6	Gc	62.00N	10.00 E
Norway Bay	42	Hb	71.00N	104.35W
Norway House	42	Hf	53.58N	97.50W
Norwegian Basin (EN)	3	Dc	68.00N	2.00W
Norwegian Bay	42	Ij	77.45N	90.30W
Norwegian Sea (EN)= Norske Havet	5	Gc	70.00N	2.00 E
Norwegian Trench (EN)	5	Gd	59.00N	4.30 E
Norwich [Ct.-U.S.]	44	Ke	41.32N	72.05W
Norwich [Eng.-U.K.]	6	Ge	52.38N	1.18 E
Norwich [N.Y.-U.S.]	44	Jd	42.33N	75.33W
Norwich Airport	12	Db	52.40N	1.18 E
Norwood	44	Ef	39.10N	84.28W
Nosappu-Misaki	29a	Db	43.23N	145.47 E
Noshappu-Misaki	29a	Ba	45.27N	141.39 E
Noshiro	27	Pc	40.12N	140.02 E
Nosovaja	19	Fb	68.15N	54.31 E
Nosovka	19	De	50.54N	31.37 E
Nosratābād	23	Id	29.54N	59.59 E
Nossa Senhora das Candeias	54	Kf	12.40S	38.33W
Nossa Senhora do Livramento	55	Db	15.48S	56.22W
Noss Head	9	Jc	58.30N	3.05W
Nossob	30	Jk	26.55S	20.40 E
Nossop	37	Ce	26.55S	20.40 E
Nosy-Be	30	Lj	13.20S	48.15 E
Nosy-Be	31	Lj	13.22S	48.16 E
Nosy-Varika	37	Hd	20.35S	48.30 E
Nota	7	Hb	68.07N	30.10 E
Notch Peak	46	Ig	39.08N	113.24W
Noteć	10	Ld	52.44N	15.26 E
Notecka, Puszcza-	10	Ld	52.45N	16.00 E
Note Kemopla	63c	b	10.55S	165.51 E
Notengo, Laguna de-	48	Ji	16.15N	98.10W
Notia Pindhos	15	Ej	39.30N	21.20 E
Nótioi Sporádhes= Dodecanese (EN)	5	Ih	36.00N	27.00 E
Nótios Evvoïkós Kólpos	15	Gk	38.20N	23.50 E
Nötö	8	Ie	60.00N	21.45 E
Noto [It.]	14	Jn	36.53N	15.04 E
Noto [Jap.]	28	Nf	37.18N	137.09 E
Noto, Golfo di-	14	Jn	36.50N	15.10 E
Notodden	7	Bg	59.34N	9.17 E
Noto-Hantō	27	Od	37.20N	137.00 E
Noto-Jima	29	Ec	37.07N	137.00 E
Notoro-Ko	29a	Da	44.05N	144.10 E
Notoro-Misaki	29a	Da	44.07N	144.15 E
Notranjsko	14	Ie	45.46N	14.26 E
Notre-Dame, Monts-	38	Me	48.00N	69.00W
Notre Dame Bay	42	Mg	49.50N	55.00W
Notre-Dame-de-Courson	12	Cf	48.59N	0.16 E
Notre-Dame-de-Gravenchon	12	Ce	49.29N	0.35 E
Notre Dame-du-Lac	44	Mb	47.38N	68.49W
Notre-Dame-du-Nord	44	Hb	47.36N	79.29W
Notsé	34	Fd	6.59N	1.12 E
Notsuke-Zaki	29a	Db	43.34N	145.19 E
Nottawasaga Bay	44	Gc	44.40N	80.30W
Nottaway	38	Ld	51.25N	79.50W
Notterøy	8	De	59.15N	10.25 E
Nottingham	6	Fe	52.58N	1.10W
Nottingham	42	Jd	63.20N	78.00W
Nottingham	9	Mh	53.05N	1.00W
Nottinghamshire [3]	9	Mh	53.10N	0.55W
Nottoway River	44	Ig	36.33N	76.55W
Nottuln	12	Jc	51.56N	7.21 E
Notukeu Creek	46	Lb	49.55N	106.30W
Nouâdhibou	31	Ff	20.54N	17.01W
Nouâdhibou, Dahklet-	32	De	21.00N	16.50W
Nouâdhibou, Râs-=Blanc Cape- (EN)	30	Ff	20.46N	17.03W
Nouakchott	31	Fg	18.07N	15.59W
Nouakchott, District de- [3]	32	Df	18.06N	15.57W
Nouamrhar	32	Df	19.22N	16.31W
Nouméa	58	Hg	22.16S	166.26 E
Nouna	34	Ec	12.44N	3.52W
Noupoort	37	Cf	31.10S	24.57 E

Index Symbols

[1] Independent Nation
[2] State, Region
[3] District, County
[4] Municipality
[5] Colony, Dependency
Continent
Physical Region
Historical or Cultural Region
Mount, Mountain
Volcano
Hill
Mountains, Mountain Range
Hills, Escarpment
Plateau, Upland
Pass, Gap
Plain, Lowland
Delta
Salt Flat
Valley, Canyon
Crater, Cave
Karst Features
Depression
Polder
Desert, Dunes
Forest, Woods
Heath, Steppe
Oasis
Cape, Point
Coast, Beach
Cliff
Peninsula
Isthmus
Sandbank
Island
Atoll
Rock, Reef
Islands, Archipelago
Rocks, Reefs
Coral Reef
Well, Spring
Geyser
River, Stream
Waterfall Rapids
River Mouth, Estuary
Lake
Salt Lake
Intermittent Lake
Reservoir
Swamp, Pond
Canal
Glacier
Ice Shelf, Pack Ice
Ocean
Sea
Gulf, Bay
Strait, Fjord
Lagoon
Bank
Seamount
Tablemount
Ridge
Shelf
Basin
Escarpment, Sea Scarp
Fracture
Trench, Abyss
National Park, Reserve
Point of Interest
Recreation Site
Cave, Cavern
Historic Site
Ruins
Wall, Walls
Church, Abbey
Temple
Scientific Station
Airport
Port
Lighthouse
Mine
Tunnel
Dam, Bridge

Index Symbols

Symbol	Meaning
[1]	Independent Nation
[2]	State, Region
[3]	District, County
[4]	Municipality
[5]	Colony, Dependency
	Continent
	Physical Region
	Historical or Cultural Region
	Mount, Mountain
	Volcano
	Hill
	Mountains, Mountain Range
	Hills, Escarpment
	Plateau, Upland
	Pass, Gap
	Plain, Lowland
	Delta
	Salt Flat
	Valley, Canyon
	Crater, Cave
	Karst Features
	Depression
	Polder
	Desert, Dunes
	Forest, Woods
	Heath, Steppe
	Oasis
	Cape, Point
	Coast, Beach
	Cliff
	Peninsula
	Isthmus
	Sandbank
	Island
	Atoll
	Rock, Reef
	Islands, Archipelago
	Rocks, Reefs
	Coral Reef
	Well, Spring
	Geyser
	River, Stream
	Waterfall Rapids
	River Mouth, Estuary
	Lake
	Salt Lake
	Intermittent Lake
	Reservoir
	Swamp, Pond
	Canal
	Glacier
	Ice Shelf, Pack Ice
	Ocean
	Sea
	Gulf, Bay
	Strait, Fjord
	Lagoon
	Bank
	Seamount
	Tablemount
	Ridge
	Shelf
	Basin
	Escarpment, Sea Scarp
	Fracture
	Trench, Abyss
	National Park, Reserve
	Point of Interest
	Recreation Site
	Cave, Cavern
	Historic Site
	Ruins
	Wall, Walls
	Church, Abbey
	Temple
	Scientific Station
	Airport
	Port
	Lighthouse
	Mine
	Tunnel
	Dam, Bridge

Ocna Sibiului	15	Hc	45.53N	24.03 E
Ocoa, Bahia de-	49	Ld	18.22N	70.39W
Oconee River	44	Fj	31.58N	82.32W
Oconto	45	Md	44.55N	87.52W
Ocosingo	48	Mi	17.04N	92.15W
Ocotal	49	Dg	13.38N	86.29W
Ocotepeque [3]	49	Cf	14.30N	89.00W
Ocotlán	47	Dd	20.21N	102.46W
Ocotlán de Morelos	48	Ki	16.48N	96.43W
Ocracoke Inlet	44	Ih	35.10N	76.05W
Ocracoke Island	44	Jh	35.09N	75.53W
Ocreza	13	Ee	39.32N	7.50W
Octeville-sur-Mer	12	Ce	49.33N	0.07 E
October Revolution Island (EN)=Oktjabrskoj Revoljuci, Ostrov-	21	Lb	79.30N	97.00 E
Ocú	49	Gj	7.57N	80.47W
Ocumare del Tuy	50	Cg	10.07N	66.46W
Oda [Ghana]	34	Ed	5.55N	0.59W
Oda [Jap.]	29	Ce	33.34N	132.48 E
Ōda	28	Lg	35.11N	132.30 E
Oda, Jabal-	35	Fa	20.21N	36.39 E
Ódádahraun	7a	Cb	65.09N	17.00W
Ōdai	29	Ed	34.24N	136.24 E
Odaigahara-San	29	Ed	34.11N	136.06 E
Odalen	8	Dd	60.15N	11.40 E
Ōdate	28	Pd	40.16N	140.34 E
Odawara	28	Og	35.15N	139.10 E
Odda	7	Bf	60.04N	6.33 E
Odder	8	Di	55.58N	10.10 E
Odeleite	13	Eg	37.21N	7.27W
Odemira	13	Dg	37.36N	8.38W
Ödemiş	24	Bc	38.13N	27.59 E
Odendaalsrus	37	De	27.48 S	26.45 E
Odense	6	Hd	55.24N	10.23 E
Odenthal	12	Jc	51.02N	7.07 E
Odenwald	10	Eg	49.40N	9.00 E
Oder [Eur.]	5	He	53.40N	14.33 E
Oder [Ger.]	10	Ge	51.40N	10.02 E
Oderbruch	10	Kd	52.40N	14.15 E
Oderské vrchy	10	Ng	49.40N	17.45 E
Oderzo	14	Ge	45.47N	12.29 E
Ödeshög	7	Dg	58.14N	14.39 E
Odessa [Tx.-U.S.]	39	If	31.51N	102.22W
Odessa	6	Jf	46.28N	30.44 E
Odessa [Wa.-U.S.]	46	Fc	47.20N	118.41W
Odesskaja Oblast [3]	19	Df	46.45N	30.30 E
Odet	11	Bg	47.52N	4.06W
Odiel	13	Fg	37.10N	6.54W
Odienné	31	Gh	9.30N	7.34W
Odienné [3]	34	Dd	9.45N	7.45W
Odivelas	13	Df	38.12N	8.18W
Ödmården	8	Gc	61.05N	16.40 E
Odobeşti	15	Kd	45.46N	27.03 E
Ŏdŏngk	25	Kf	11.48N	104.45 E
Odoorn	12	Ib	52.51N	6.50 E
Odorheiu Secuiesc	15	Ic	46.18N	25.18 E
Ōdose-Zaki	29a	Bc	40.46N	140.03 E
Odra	5	He	53.40N	14.33 E
Ōdwēyne	35	Hd	9.23N	45.04 E
Odžaci	15	Cd	45.31N	19.16 E
Odžak	14	Me	45.01N	18.18 E
Odzi	37	Ec	19.47 S	32.24 E
Oeiras	13	Eg	37.38N	7.40W
Oeiras [Braz.]	54	Je	7.01 S	42.08W
Oeiras [Port.]	13	Cf	38.41N	9.19W
Oelde	12	Kc	51.49N	8.09 E
Oelerbeek	12	Ib	52.21N	6.38 E
Oelrichs	45	Ee	43.15N	103.10W
Oelsnitz	10	If	50.25N	12.10 E
Oelwein	45	Ke	42.41N	91.55W
Oeno Island	57	Ng	23.56 S	130.44W
Oer-Erkenschwick	12	Jc	51.38N	7.15 E
Oeste, Punta-	51a	Ab	18.05N	67.57W
Oeventrop, Arnsberg-	12	Kc	51.24N	8.08 E
Ōe-Yama	29	Dd	35.27N	135.06 E
Of	24	Ib	40.57N	40.16 E
O'Fallon Creek	46	Mc	46.50N	105.09W
Ofanto	14	Ki	41.21N	16.13 E
Ofaqim	24	Fg	31.17N	34.37 E
Offa	34	Fd	8.09N	4.43 E
Offaly/Uíbh Fhailí [2]	9	Fh	53.20N	7.30W
Offenbach am Main	10	Ef	50.06N	8.46 E
Offenbach-Hundheim	12	Je	49.37N	7.33 E
Offenburg	10	Dh	48.29N	7.56 E
Offida	14	Hh	42.56N	13.41 E
Offoué	36	Bc	0.04 S	11.44 E
Offranville	12	De	49.52N	1.03 E
Ofidhoúsa	15	Jm	36.33N	26.09 E
Ofolanga	65b	Ba	19.36 S	174.27W
Ofu	65c	Db	14.11 S	169.42W
Ōfunato	28	Pe	39.04N	141.43 E
Oga	28	Oe	40.43N	141.18 E
Ogachi	29	Gb	39.05N	140.28 E
Ogaden	30	Lh	7.30N	45.00 E
Oga-Hantō	28	Oe	39.55N	139.50 E
Ōgaki	28	Ng	35.21N	136.37 E
Ogallala	43	Gc	41.08N	101.43W
Ogasawara-Shotō=Bonin Islands (EN)	21	Qg	27.00N	142.10 E
Ogawara-Ko	29a	Bc	40.45N	141.20 E
Ogbomosho	31	Hh	8.08N	4.16 E
Ogden	39	He	41.14N	111.58W
Ogdensburg	44	Jc	44.42N	75.31W
Ogeechee River	44	Gj	31.51N	81.06W
Oghāsh	24	Lc	39.10N	46.55 E
Ogi	29	Fc	37.50N	138.16 E
Ogilvie Mountains	42	Dc	65.00N	140.00W
Ogi-no-Sen	29	Dd	35.26N	134.26 E
Oginski Kanal	16	Dc	52.20N	25.55 E
Oglanly	16	Sj	39.50N	54.33 E
Oglethorpe	44	Ei	31.28N	84.04W
Ogliastra	14	Dk	39.55N	9.35 E
Oglio	14	Ee	45.02N	10.39 E
Ognon	11	Lg	47.20N	5.29 E
Ogo	35	Hd	9.48N	45.35 E
Ogoamas, Bulu-	26	Hf	0.40N	120.12 E
Ogodža	20	If	52.48N	132.40 E
Ogoja	34	Gd	6.40N	8.48 E
Ogoki	42	If	51.38N	85.56W
Ogoki	42	If	51.38N	85.55W
Ogoki Reservoir	42	If	51.35N	86.00W
Ogonëk	20	Ie	59.40N	138.01 E
Ogooué	30	Hi	0.49 S	9.00 E
Ogooué-Ivindo [3]	36	Bb	0.30N	13.00 E
Ogooué-Lolo [3]	36	Bc	1.00 S	13.00 E
Ogooué-Maritime [3]	36	Ac	2.00 S	9.30 E
Ogōri [Jap.]	29	Bd	34.06N	131.25 E
Ogōri [Jap.]	29	Be	33.24N	130.34 E
Ogosta	15	Gf	43.45N	23.51 E
Ogražden	15	Fh	41.30N	22.55 E
Ogre	8	Kh	56.42N	24.33 E
Ogre	7	Fh	56.50N	24.39 E
Ogulin	14	Je	45.16N	15.14 E
Ogun [2]	34	Fd	7.00N	3.40 E
Oguni [Jap.]	29	Fb	38.04N	139.45 E
Oguni [Jap.]	29	Be	33.07N	131.04 E
Ogurčinski, Ostrov-	16	Rj	38.55N	53.05 E
Oğuzeli	24	Gd	37.00N	37.30 E
Oha	22	Qd	53.34N	142.56 E
Ohai	62	Bf	45.56 S	167.57 E
Ohakune	62	Fc	39.25 S	175.25 E
Ohanet	32	Id	28.40N	8.50 E
Ohansk	17	Gh	57.42N	55.25 E
Ōhara	29	Gd	35.15N	140.23 E
Ōhasama	29	Gb	39.28N	141.17 E
Ohata	20	Je	59.20N	143.05 E
Ōhata	28	Pd	41.24N	141.10 E
Ohau, Lake-	62	Cf	44.15 S	169.50 E
Ohey	12	Hd	50.26N	5.08 E
O'Higgins, Cabo-	65d	Bb	27.05 S	109.15W
Ohio	38	Kf	36.59N	89.08W
Ohio [2]	43	Kc	40.15N	82.45W
Ohm	10	Ef	50.51N	8.48 E
Ohmberge	10	Ge	51.30N	10.28 E
'Ohonua	65b	Bc	21.20 S	174.57W
Ohopoho	31	Ij	18.03 S	13.45 E
Ohotsk	22	Qd	59.23N	143.18 E
Ohotskoje More=Okhotsk, Sea of- (EN)	21	Qd	53.00N	150.00 E
Ohre	10	Hd	52.18N	11.47 E
Ohře	10	Kf	50.32N	14.08 E
Ohrid	15	Dh	41.07N	20.48 E
Ohrid, Lake- (EN) = Ohridsko Jezero	5	Ig	41.00N	20.45 E
Ohrid, Lake- (EN) = Ohrit, Liqen i-	5	Ig	41.00N	20.45 E
Ohridsko Jezero=Ohrid, Lake- (EN)	5	Ig	41.00N	20.45 E
Öhringen	10	Fg	49.12N	9.30 E
Ohrit, Liqen i- = Ohrid, Lake- (EN)	5	Ig	41.00N	20.45 E
Ohura	62	Fc	38.51 S	174.59 E
Oiapoque	54	Hc	3.50N	51.50W
Oich	9	Id	57.10N	4.45W
Oi-Gawa	29	Fd	34.46N	138.17 E
Oil City	44	He	41.26N	79.44W
Oildale	46	Fi	35.25N	119.01W
Oiléan Baoi/Dursey	9	Cj	51.36N	10.12W
Oiléan Ciarraí/Castleisland	9	Di	52.14N	9.27W
Oiléan Coarach/Mutton	9	Di	52.49N	9.31W
Oiléan Mhic Aodha/Magee, Island-	9	Hg	54.50N	5.50W
Oinoúsai	15	Jk	38.32N	26.13 E
Oinoúsai, Nisoi-	15	Jk	38.31N	26.14 E
Oirschot	12	Hc	51.30N	5.18 E
Oisans	11	Mi	45.02N	6.02 E
Oise [3]	11	Ie	49.30N	2.30 E
Oise	11	Ie	49.00N	2.04 E
Oise à l'Aisne, Canal de l'-	11	Je	49.36N	3.11 E
Oisemont	12	De	49.57N	1.46 E
Oissel	12	De	49.20N	1.06 E
Oisterwijk	12	Hc	51.35N	5.11 E
Oistins	51q	Ab	13.04N	59.32W
Oistins Bay	51q	Ab	13.03N	59.33W
Ōita	27	Ne	33.14N	131.36 E
Ōita Ken [2]	28	Kh	33.15N	131.20 E
Oíti Óros	15	Fk	38.49N	22.17 E
Oituz, Pasul-	15	Jc	46.03N	26.23 E
Oiwake	29a	Bb	42.52N	141.48 E
Ojat	7	Hf	60.31N	33.05 E
Öje	8	Ed	60.49N	13.51 E
Ojestos de Jalisco	48	Ig	21.50N	101.35W
Ojika-Jima	29	Ae	33.13N	129.03 E
O-Jima	29	Be	34.00N	130.45 E
Ojinaga	47	Dc	29.34N	104.25W
Ojiya	28	Of	37.18N	138.48 E
Ojmjakon	20	Jd	63.28N	142.49 E
Ojocaliente	48	Hf	22.34N	102.15W
Ojo Caliente	48	Fb	30.25N	106.33W
Ojos del Salado, Nevado-	52	Jh	27.06 S	68.32W
Ojos Negros	13	Kd	40.44N	1.30W
Ojtal	19	Hg	42.54N	73.21 E
Oka	21	Md	55.00N	102.03 E
Oka	5	Kd	56.20N	43.59 E
Okaba	26	Kh	8.06 S	139.42 E
Okahandja [3]	37	Bd	21.30 S	17.30 E
Okahandja	31	Ik	21.59 S	16.58 E
Okahukura	62	Fc	38.47 S	175.14 E
Okaihau	62	Ea	35.19 S	173.46 E
Okak Islands	42	Le	57.28N	61.48W
Okanagan Lake	42	Fg	49.55N	119.30W
Okano	36	Bc	0.05 S	10.57 E
Okanogan River	43	Db	48.06N	119.43W
Okapa	59	Ja	6.31 S	145.32 E
Okāra	25	Eb	30.49N	73.27 E
Okarem	19	Fh	38.07N	54.05 E
Okato	62	Ec	39.12 S	173.53 E
Okaukuejo	37	Bc	19.10 S	15.54 E
Okavango	30	Jj	18.53N	22.24 E
Okavango [3]	37	Cc	18.00 S	21.00 E
Okavango Swamp	30	Jj	19.30 S	23.00 E
Ōkawa	29	Be	33.12N	130.23 E
Okaya	28	Of	36.03N	138.03 E
Okayama	22	Pf	34.39N	133.55 E
Okayama Ken [2]	28	Lg	34.50N	133.45 E
Okazaki	28	Ng	34.57N	137.10 E
Okeechobee	44	Gl	27.15N	80.50W
Okeechobee, Lake-	38	Kg	26.55N	80.45W
Okefenokee Swamp	44	Fj	30.42N	82.20W
Okehampton	9	Jk	50.44N	4.00W
Okene	34	Gd	7.33N	6.14 E
Oker	10	Gd	52.30N	10.22 E
Oketo	29a	Cb	43.41N	143.32 E
Okha	25	Dd	22.27N	69.04 E
Ókhi Óros	15	Hk	38.04N	24.28 E
Okhotsk, Sea of- (EN)=Hok-Kai	21	Qd	53.00N	150.00 E
Okhotsk, Sea of- (EN)=Ohotskoje More	21	Qd	53.00N	150.00 E
Okhthonía, Ákra-	15	Hk	38.32N	24.14 E
Oki-Daitō-Jima	27	Ng	24.30N	131.00 E
Okiep	37	Be	29.39 S	17.53 E
Okinawa	29b	Ab	26.20N	127.47 E
Okinawa Islands (EN)=Okinawa-Shotō	21	Og	26.40N	128.00 E
Okinawa-Jima	27	Mf	26.40N	128.20 E
Okinawa Ken [2]	29b	Ab	26.31N	127.59 E
Okinawa-Shotō=Okinawa Islands (EN)	21	Og	26.40N	128.00 E
Okinoerabu-Jima	27	Mf	27.20N	128.35 E
Okino-Shima [Jap.]	29	Ce	32.44N	132.33 E
Okino-Shima [Jap.]	29	Bd	34.15N	130.08 E
Okino-Tori-Shima	21	Pg	20.25N	136.00 E
Oki Ridge (EN)	28	Mf	37.00N	135.00 E
Oki-Shotō	27	Nd	36.00N	132.50 E
Okitipupa	34	Fd	6.30N	4.48 E
Oki Trench (EN)	29	Dc	37.00N	135.30 E
Oklahoma [2]	43	Hd	35.30N	98.00W
Oklahoma City	39	Jf	35.28N	97.32W
Okmulgee	45	Ii	35.37N	95.58W
Oknica	15	Ka	48.22N	27.24 E
Oko	35	Fa	22.20N	35.56 E
Okoko	36	Fb	2.06N	33.53 E
Okolo	36	Fb	2.40N	31.09 E
Okolona	44	Ef	38.08N	85.41W
Okondja	36	Bc	0.41 S	13.47 E
Okonek	10	Mc	53.33N	16.50 E
Okoppe	28	Qb	44.28N	143.08 E
Okotoks	46	Ia	50.44N	113.59W
Okoyo	36	Cc	1.28 S	15.04 E
Okrzeika	10	Re	51.40N	21.30 E
Øksfjord	7	Fa	70.14N	22.22 E
Oksino	17	Fc	67.33N	52.10 E
Okstindane	5	Hb	66.02N	14.10 E
Oktemberjan	16	Ni	40.09N	44.03 E
Oktjabrsk	6	Lf	48.40N	57.11 E
Oktjabrsk	7	Lj	53.13N	48.40 E
Oktjabrski	16	Fc	52.38N	28.54 E
Oktjabrski	17	Kj	52.37N	62.43 E
Oktjabrski	20	Ee	56.05N	99.25 E
Oktjabrski	19	Fe	54.31N	53.28 E
Oktjabrski	17	Hh	56.31N	57.12 E
Oktjabrski	7	Kf	61.05N	43.08 E
Oktjabrski	20	Hf	53.00N	128.42 E
Oktjabrski	20	Kf	52.38N	156.15 E
Oktjabrski	16	Mf	47.56N	43.38 E
Oktjabrskoje	19	Gc	62.28N	66.01 E
Oktjabrskoj Revoljuci, Ostrov-=October Revolution Island (EN)	21	Lb	79.30N	97.00 E
Oku	29b	Bb	26.50N	128.17 E
Ōkuchi	28	Kh	32.04N	130.37 E
Okulovka	7	Hg	58.24N	33.18 E
Okushiri	28	Oc	42.09N	139.29 E
Okushiri-Kaikyō	29a	Ab	42.15N	139.40 E
Okushiri-Tō	27	Oc	42.10N	139.25 E
Okuta	34	Fd	9.13N	3.11 E
Oku Tango-Hantō	29	Dd	35.40N	135.10 E
Okwa	30	Jk	22.26 S	22.58 E
Ola	20	Ke	59.37N	151.20 E
Ólafsfjördur	7a	Ba	66.04N	18.39W
Ólafsvik	7a	Ab	64.53N	23.43W
Ola Grande, Punta-	51a	Bc	17.55N	66.08W
Olaiņe/Olajne	7	Fh	56.49N	23.59 E
Olajne/Olaiņe	7	Fh	56.49N	23.59 E
Olancha	46	Gh	36.17N	117.59W
Olanchito	49	Df	15.30N	86.35W
Olancho [3]	49	Ef	14.45N	86.00W
Öland	5	Hd	56.45N	16.40 E
Ölands norra udde	8	Gg	57.22N	17.05 E
Ölands södra grund	8	Gh	55.40N	17.25 E
Ölands södra udde	8	Gh	56.11N	16.24 E
Olanga	7	Hc	66.08N	30.38 E
Olathe	45	Ig	38.53N	94.49W
Olavarría	53	Ji	36.53 S	60.20W
Oława	10	Nf	50.57N	17.17 E
Oława	10	Nf	50.57N	17.17 E
Olbernhau	10	Jf	50.40N	13.20 E
Olbia	6	Gg	40.55N	9.31 E
Olbia, Golfo di-	14	Dj	40.55N	9.40 E
Old Bahama Channel	49	Ib	22.30N	78.05W
Old Bahama Channel (EN)=Bahamas, Canal Viejo de-	49	Ib	22.30N	78.05W
Old Castile (EN)=Castilla la Vieja	13	Ic	41.30N	4.00W
Old Crow	39	Fc	67.35N	139.50W
Oldeani	36	Gc	3.21 S	35.33 E
Oldebroek	12	Hb	52.26N	5.53 E
Oldenburg	10	Ec	53.10N	8.12 E
Oldenburg in Holstein	10	Gb	54.18N	10.53 E
Oldenzaal	11	Mb	52.19N	6.56 E
Old Faithful Geyser	46	Jd	44.30N	110.45W
Old Fletton	12	Bb	52.34N	0.15W
Oldham	9	Kh	53.33N	2.07W
Old Hickory Lake	44	Dg	36.18N	86.30W
Oldman River	46	Jb	49.56N	111.42W
Old Marsh Bed	59	Gd	20.55 S	130.30 E
Old Mkuski	36	Ee	14.22 S	29.22 E
Old Road	51d	Bb	17.01N	61.50W
Old Road Town	51c	Ab	17.19N	62.48W
Olds	42	Gf	51.47N	114.06W
Old Town	44	Mc	44.56N	68.39W
Old Wives Lake	46	Ma	50.06N	106.00W
Olean	44	Hd	42.05N	78.26W
Olecko	10	Sb	54.03N	22.30 E
Oleiros	13	Ee	39.55N	7.55W
Olëkma	21	Oc	60.22N	120.42 E
Olëkminsk	22	Oc	60.30N	120.15 E
Olëkminski Stanovik	20	Gf	54.00N	119.00 E
Ølen	7	Ag	59.36N	5.48 E
Olenegorsk	19	Db	68.10N	33.13 E
Olenëk	21	Nb	73.00N	119.55 E
Olenëkski Zaliv	20	Hb	73.10N	121.00 E
Olenica	7	Ic	66.29N	35.19 E
Olenj, Ostrov-	20	Cb	72.25N	77.45 E
Olenty	16	Re	49.45N	52.10 E
Oléron, Ile d'-	5	Ff	45.56N	1.18W
Olesko	10	Ug	49.53N	24.58 E
Oleśnica	10	Ne	51.13N	17.23 E
Olesno	10	Of	50.53N	18.25 E
Olevsk	16	Ed	51.13N	27.41 E
Olga	20	Ih	43.46N	135.21 E
Olga, Mount-	59	Ge	25.19 S	130.46 E
Olgastretet	41	Oc	78.30N	24.00 E
Ølgod	8	Ci	55.49N	8.37 E
Olhão	13	Eg	37.02N	7.50W
Olhovatka	16	Kd	50.17N	39.17 E
Oli	34	Fd	9.40N	4.29 E
Oliana	13	Nb	42.04N	1.19 E
Olib	14	If	44.23N	14.47 E
Oliena	14	Dj	40.16N	9.24 E
Olifants [Afr.]	30	Kk	24.03 S	32.40 E
Olifants [Nam.]	37	Be	25.30 S	19.30 E
Olifantshoek	37	Ce	27.57 S	22.42 E
Olimarao Atoll	57	Fd	7.42N	145.53 E
Olimbía	15	El	37.39N	21.38 E
Ólimbos	15	Kn	35.44N	27.13 E
Ólimbos, Óros-=Olympus, Mount- (EN)	5	Ig	40.05N	22.21 E
Ólimbos Óros	15	Jj	39.05N	26.20 E
Olímpia	55	He	20.44 S	48.54W
Olinda	54	Le	8.01 S	34.51W
Olite	13	Kb	42.29N	1.39W
Oliva [Arg.]	56	Hd	32.03 S	63.34W
Oliva [Sp.]	13	Lf	38.55N	0.07W
Oliva, Monasterio de la-	13	Kb	42.20N	1.25W
Oliva de la Frontera	13	Ff	38.16N	6.55W
Oliveira	55	Je	20.41 S	44.49W
Oliveira dos Brejinhos	54	Jf	12.19 S	42.54W
Olivença	37	Fb	11.46 S	35.13 E
Olivenza	13	Ef	38.41N	7.06W
Oliver	46	Fb	49.11N	119.33W
Olivet	11	Hg	47.52N	1.54 E
Olivia	45	Id	44.46N	94.59W
Olja	16	Og	45.47N	47.35 E
Olji Moron He	28	Fb	44.16N	121.42 E
Oljutorski, Mys-	21	Td	59.55N	170.25 E
Oljutorski Zaliv	20	Ld	60.00N	168.00 E
Olkusz	10	Pf	50.17N	19.35 E
Ollan	64d	Bb	7.14N	151.38 E
Ollerton	12	Aa	53.13N	1.01W
Olmedo	13	Hc	41.17N	4.41W
Olmos	54	Ce	5.59 S	79.46W
Olney [Eng.-U.K.]	12	Bb	52.09N	0.42W
Olney [Il.-U.S.]	45	Lg	38.44N	88.05W
Olney [Tx.-U.S.]	45	Gj	33.22N	98.45W
Oloči	20	Gf	51.20N	119.53 E
Olofström	7	Dh	56.16N	14.30 E
Oloitokitok	36	Gc	2.56 S	37.30 E
Oloj	20	Kc	66.20N	159.29 E
Olojski Hrebet	20	Lc	65.50N	162.30 E
Olombo	36	Cc	1.18 S	15.53 E
Ólomburi	63a	Ec	8.59 S	161.09 E
Olomouc	6	Hf	49.36N	17.16 E
Olona	14	De	45.06N	9.21 E
Olonec	19	Dc	61.01N	32.58 E
Olonešty	15	Mc	46.29N	29.52 E
Olongapo	22	Oh	14.50N	120.16 E
Oloron, Gave d'-	11	Ek	43.33N	1.05W
Oloron-Sainte-Marie	11	Fk	43.12N	0.36W
Olosega	65c	Db	14.11 S	169.39W
Olot	13	Ob	42.11N	2.29 E
Olovjannaja	20	Gf	50.56N	115.35 E
Olovo	14	Mf	44.07N	18.35 E
Olpe	10	De	51.02N	7.51 E
Olpoy	63b	Cb	14.52 S	166.33 E
Olroyd River	59	Ib	14.10 S	141.50 E
Olsberg	12	Kc	51.21N	8.30 E
Olshammar	8	Ff	58.45N	14.48 E
Olst	12	Ib	52.20N	6.08 E
Olsztyn	6	Ie	53.48N	20.29 E
Olsztyn [2]	10	Qc	53.50N	20.30 E
Olsztynek	10	Qc	53.36N	20.17 E
Olt [2]	15	He	44.25N	24.30 E
Olt	5	If	43.43N	24.51 E
Oltedal	8	Bf	58.50N	6.02 E
Olten	14	Bc	47.22N	7.55 E
Olteni	15	Ie	44.11N	25.17 E
Oltenia	15	Ge	44.30N	23.30 E
Olteniţa	15	Je	44.05N	26.38 E
Olteţ	15	He	44.14N	24.27 E
Oltu	24	Ib	40.33N	41.59 E
Oluanpi	21	Og	21.54N	120.51 E
Olutanga	26	He	7.22N	122.52 E
Olvera	13	Gh	36.56N	5.16W
Olym	16	Kc	52.27N	38.05 E
Olympia	39	Ge	47.03N	122.53W
Olympic Mountains	46	Dc	47.50N	123.45W
Olympus, Mount-	38	Ge	47.48N	123.43W
Olympus, Mount- (EN)=Ólimbos, Óros-	5	Ig	40.05N	22.21 E
Om	20	Cf	54.59N	73.22 E
Ōma	29a	Bc	41.30N	140.55 E
Oma	17	Cc	66.45N	46.20 E
Ōmachi	28	Nf	36.30N	137.52 E
Omae-Zaki	29	Fd	34.36N	138.14 E
Ōmagari	28	Pe	39.27N	140.29 E
Omagh/An Ómaigh	9	Fg	54.36N	7.18W
Omaha	39	Je	41.16N	95.57W
Omak	46	Fb	48.24N	119.31W
Omakau	62	Cf	45.06 S	169.36 E
Omak Lake	46	Fb	48.16N	119.23W
Oman (EN)='Umān [1]	22	Hg	21.00N	57.00 E
Oman, Gulf of- (EN)='Umān, Khalīj-	21	Hg	25.00N	58.00 E
Omarama	61	Ch	44.29 S	169.58 E
Omar Gambon	35	He	3.10N	45.47 E
Omaru-Gawa	29	Be	32.07N	131.34 E
Omaruru	37	Bd	21.28 S	15.56 E
Omaruru [3]	37	Bd	21.30 S	15.00 E
Omatako	37	Bd	21.07 S	16.43 E
Omatako, Omuramba-	30	Jj	17.57 S	20.25 E
Omate	54	Dg	16.41 S	70.59W
Ōma-Zaki	29a	Bc	41.32N	140.55 E
Ombai, Selat-	26	Hh	8.30 S	125.00 E
Ombella-Mpoko [3]	35	Bd	5.00N	18.00 E
Omberg	8	Ff	58.20N	14.39 E
Ombo	8	Ae	59.15N	6.00 E
Omboué	36	Ac	1.34 S	9.15 E
Ombrone	14	Fh	42.39N	11.01 E
Ombu	27	Ee	31.18N	86.33 E
Omčak	20	Jd	61.38N	147.55 E
Omdurman (EN)=Umm Durmān	31	Kg	15.38N	32.30 E
Ōme	29	Fd	35.47N	139.15 E
Omegna	14	Ce	45.53N	8.24 E
Omeo	59	Jg	37.06 S	147.36 E
Ömerköy	15	Lj	39.50N	28.04 E
Ometepe, Isla de-	47	Gf	11.30N	85.35W
Ometepec	47	Ee	16.41N	98.25W
Omhajer	35	Fc	14.19N	36.40 E
Ōmihachiman	29	Ed	35.08N	136.05 E
Omihi	62	Ee	43.01 S	172.51 E
Omineca	42	Fe	56.05N	124.05W
Omineca Mountains	42	Ee	56.35N	125.55W
Omiš	14	Kg	43.27N	16.42 E
Ōmi-Shima [Jap.]	29	Bd	34.25N	131.15 E
Ōmi-Shima [Jap.]	29	Cd	34.15N	133.00 E
Omitara	37	Bd	22.18 S	18.01 E
Ōmiya	27	Od	35.54N	139.38 E
Ommanney Bay	42	Hb	73.00N	101.00W
Omme Å	8	Ci	55.55N	8.25 E
Ommen	12	Ib	52.31N	6.25 E
Omo	30	Kh	4.32N	36.04 E
Omø	8	Di	55.10N	11.10 E
Omoa, Bahia de-	49	Cf	15.50N	88.10W
Omodeo, Lago-	14	Cj	40.10N	8.55 E
Omoloj	20	Ib	71.08N	132.01 E
Omolon	21	Rc	68.42N	158.36 E
Omolon	20	Lc	65.12N	160.27 E
Omono-Gawa	29	Gb	39.44N	140.04 E
Omont	12	Ge	49.36N	4.44 E
Omoto-Gawa	29	Gb	39.51N	141.58 E
Omsk	22	Jd	55.00N	73.24 E
Omskaja Oblast [3]	19	Hd	56.00N	72.30 E
Omsukčan	20	Kd	62.27N	155.50 E
Omsukčanski Hrebet	20	Kd	63.00N	155.10 E
Ōmu	28	Qb	44.34N	142.58 E
Omu, Vîrful-	15	Id	45.26N	25.25 E
Omulew	10	Rc	53.05N	21.32 E
Ōmura	28	Jh	32.54N	129.57 E
Ōmura-Wan	29	Ae	33.00N	129.50 E
Omurtag	15	Jf	43.06N	26.25 E
Ōmuta	28	Kh	33.02N	130.27 E
Omutinski	19	Gd	56.31N	67.45 E
Omutninsk	19	Fd	58.43N	52.12 E
Oña	13	Ib	42.44N	3.24W
Onagawa	29	Gb	38.26N	141.27 E
Onakayale	37	Bc	17.30 S	15.01 E
Onaman Lake	45	Ma	50.00N	87.29W
Onamia	45	Jc	46.04N	93.40W
Onamue	64d	Bb	7.21N	151.31 E
Onaping Lake	44	Gb	46.57N	81.30W
Onatchiway, Lac-	44	La	49.03N	71.03W
Onawa	45	He	42.02N	96.06W
Onch'ŏn	28	He	38.49N	125.13 E
Oncócua	36	Bf	16.40 S	13.24 E
Onda	13	Le	39.58N	0.15W
Ondangua	31	Ij	17.55 S	16.00 E
Ondàrroa	13	Ja	43.19N	2.25W
Ondava	10	Rh	48.27N	21.48 E
Ondo [2]	34	Gd	7.00N	5.00 E
Ondo [Jap.]	29	Cd	34.12N	132.32 E
Ondo [Nig.]	34	Fd	7.06N	4.50 E
Ondor Sum	28	Bc	42.30N	113.00 E
Ondozero, Ozero-	7	He	63.40N	33.15 E
One and Half Degree Channel	21	Ji	1.30N	73.10 E
Oneata	63d	Cc	18.27 S	178.29W
Oneata Passage	63d	Cc	18.32 S	178.28W
Onega	6	Jc	63.57N	38.05 E
Onega	5	Jc	63.58N	37.55 E
Onega, Lake- (EN)=Onežskoje Ozero	5	Jc	61.30N	35.45 E
Onega Peninsula (EN)=Onežski Poluostrov	5	Jc	64.35N	38.00 E
One Hundred Mile House	42	Ff	51.38N	121.16W
Oneida	44	Jd	43.04N	75.40W
Oneida Lake	44	Jd	43.13N	76.00W
O'Neil	43	Hc	42.27N	98.39W
Ōnejime	29	Bf	31.14N	130.47 E
Onekotan, Ostrov-	21	Re	49.25N	154.45 E
Oneonta [Al.-U.S.]	44	Di	33.57N	86.29W
Oneonta [N.Y.-U.S.]	44	Jd	42.28N	75.04W
Oneroa	64p	Cb	21.15 S	159.43W
Oneşti (Gheorghe Gheorghiu-Dej)	15	Jc	46.12N	26.46 E
Onežskaja guba	5	Jc	64.20N	36.30 E
Onežskoje Ozero=Onega, Lake- (EN)	5	Jc	61.30N	35.45 E
Ongea Levu	63d	Cc	19.08 S	178.24W

Index Symbols

[1] Independent Nation
[2] State, Region
[3] District, County
[4] Municipality
[5] Colony, Dependency
Continent
Physical Region
Historical or Cultural Region
Mount, Mountain
Volcano
Hill
Mountains, Mountain Range
Hills, Escarpment
Plateau, Upland
Pass, Gap
Plain, Lowland
Delta
Salt Flat
Valley, Canyon
Crater, Cave
Karst Features
Depression
Polder
Desert, Dunes
Forest, Woods
Heath, Steppe
Oasis
Cape, Point
Coast, Beach
Cliff
Peninsula
Isthmus
Sandbank
Island
Atoll
Rock, Reef
Islands, Archipelago
Rocks, Reefs
Coral Reef
Well, Spring
Geyser
River, Stream
Waterfall Rapids
River Mouth, Estuary
Lake
Salt Lake
Intermittent Lake
Reservoir
Swamp, Pond
Canal
Glacier
Ice Shelf, Pack Ice
Ocean
Sea
Gulf, Bay
Strait, Fjord
Lagoon
Bank
Seamount
Tablemount
Ridge
Shelf
Basin
Escarpment, Sea Scarp
Fracture
Trench, Abyss
National Park, Reserve
Point of Interest
Recreation Site
Cave, Cavern
Historic Site
Ruins
Wall, Walls
Church, Abbey
Temple
Scientific Station
Airport
Port
Lighthouse
Mine
Tunnel
Dam, Bridge

Ongjin-Gol ⌘	27 Hc 44.30N 103.40 E
Ongjin	27 Md 37.56N 125.22 E
Ongniud Qi (Wudan)	27 Kc 42.58N 119.01 E
Ongole	25 Ge 15.30N 80.03 E
Ongon	27 Jb 45.49N 113.08 E
Onhaye	12 Gd 50.15N 4.50 E
Oni	16 Mh 42.35N 43.27 E
Onigajō-Yama ▲	29 Ce 33.07N 132.41 E
Onilany ⌘	30 Lk 23.34S 43.45 E
Onishibetsu	29a Ca 45.21N 142.06 E
Onitsha	31 Hh 6.10N 6.47 E
Ono	29 Dd 34.51N 134.57 E
Ono ⊕	63d Bc 18.54S 178.29 E
Ōno [Jap.]	28 Ng 35.59N 136.29 E
Ōno [Jap.]	29 Cd 34.18N 132.17 E
Onoda	29 Be 33.59N 131.11 E
Ōno-Gawa ⌘	29 Be 33.15N 131.43 E
Ōnohara-Jima ⊕	29 Fd 34.02N 139.23 E
Onohoj	20 Ff 51.55N 108.01 E
Ono-i-Lau Islands ☐	57 Jg 20.39S 178.42W
Onojō	29 Be 33.34N 130.29 E
Onomichi	28 Lg 34.25N 133.12 E
Onon ⌘	21 Nd 51.42N 115.50 E
Onoto	50 Dh 9.36N 65.12W
Onotoa Atoll ⊙	57 Ie 1.52S 175.34 E
Ons, Isla de- ⊕	13 Db 42.23N 8.56W
Onsala	7 Ch 57.25N 12.01 E
Onseepkans	37 Be 28.45S 19.17 E
Onslow	58 Cg 21.39S 115.06 E
Onslow Bay ◖	43 Le 34.20N 77.20W
On-Take ▲	29 Bf 33.31N 130.39 E
Ontake-San ▲	29 Ed 35.53N 137.29 E
Ontario ③	42 If 50.00N 86.00W
Ontario [Ca.-U.S.]	46 Gi 34.04N 117.39W
Ontario [Or.-U.S.]	43 Dc 44.02N 116.58W
Ontario, Lake- ⊟	38 Le 43.40N 78.00W
Ontario Peninsula ⊨	38 Ke 43.50N 81.00W
Onteniente/Ontinyent	13 Lf 38.49N 0.37W
Ontinyent/Onteniente	13 Lf 38.49N 0.37W
Ontojärvi ⌘	7 Gd 64.08N 29.09 E
Ontonagon	44 Cb 46.52N 89.19W
Ontong Java Atoll ⊙	57 Ge 5.20S 159.30 E
Ō-Numa ⌘	29a Bc 41.59N 140.41 E
Oodnadatta	58 Fg 27.33S 135.28 E
Ooidonk ▲	12 Fc 51.01N 3.35 E
Ookala	65a Fc 20.01N 155.17W
Ooldea	58 Dh 30.27S 131.50 E
Oologah Lake ⊟	45 Ih 36.39N 95.36W
Ooltgensplaat, Oostflakkee-	12 Gc 51.41N 4.21 E
Oostburg	12 Fc 51.20N 3.30 E
Oostelijk Flevoland ⊠	12 Hb 52.30N 5.40 E
Oostende/Ostende	11 Ic 51.14N 2.55 E
Oosterhout	11 Kc 51.38N 4.51 E
Oosterschelde = East Schelde (EN) ⊨	11 Jc 51.30N 4.00 E
Oosterwolde, Oosterstellingwerf-	12 Ha 53.00N 6.18 E
Oosterzele	12 Fd 50.57N 3.48 E
Oostflakkee	12 Gc 51.41N 4.21 E
Oostflakkee-Ooltgensplaat	12 Gc 51.41N 4.21 E
Oostkamp	12 Fc 51.09N 3.14 E
Oost-Souburg, Vlissingen-	12 Fc 51.28N 3.36 E
Ooststellingwerf	12 Ib 53.00N 6.18 E
Ooststellingwerf- Oosterwolde	12 Ha 53.00N 6.18 E
Oost Vieland, Vieland-	12 Ha 53.17N 5.06 E
Oost-Vlaanderen ③	12 Fc 51.00N 3.40 E
Ootmarsum	12 Ib 52.25N 6.54 E
Opala	36 Dc 0.37S 24.21 E
Opalenica	10 Md 52.19N 16.23 E
Opanake	25 Gg 6.36N 80.37 E
Opari	35 Ee 3.56N 32.03 E
Oparino	7 Lg 59.53N 48.25 E
Opasatika	44 Ea 49.31N 82.58W
Opasatika Lake ⊟	44 Fa 49.06N 83.08W
Opasatika River ⌘	44 Fa 50.15N 82.25W
Opatija	14 Ie 45.20N 14.19 E
Opatów	10 Rf 50.49N 21.26 E
Opatówka ⌘	10 Rf 50.42N 21.50 E
Opava	10 Ng 49.57N 17.54 E
Opava ⌘	10 Og 49.51N 18.17 E
Opelika	43 Je 32.39N 85.23W
Opelousas	45 Jk 30.32N 92.05W
Opémisca, Lac- ⊟	44 Ja 49.58N 74.57W
Opheim	46 Lb 48.51N 106.24W
Ophir	40 Hd 63.10N 156.31W
Ophthalmia Range ▲	59 Dd 23.15S 119.30 E
Opienge	36 Eb 0.12N 27.30 E
Opihikao	65a Gd 19.26N 154.53W
Opinaca ⌘	42 Jf 52.14N 78.02W
Opiscotéo, Lac- ⊟	42 Kf 53.09N 68.10W
Opladen, Leverkusen-	10 De 51.04N 7.01 E
Opobo	34 Ge 4.34N 7.27 E
Opočka	19 Cd 56.42N 28.41 E
Opoczno	10 Qe 51.23N 20.17 E
Opole ②	10 Nf 50.40N 17.55 E
Opole	10 Nf 50.41N 17.55 E
Opole Lubelskie	10 Re 51.09N 21.58 E
Oporny	19 Ff 46.13N 54.29 E
Opotiki	62 Gc 38.01S 177.17 E
Opp	44 Dj 31.17N 86.22W
Oppa-Wan ◖	29 Gb 38.35N 141.30 E
Oppdal	7 Be 62.36N 9.40 E
Oppenheim	10 Eg 49.51N 8.21 E
Oppland ②	7 Bf 61.10N 9.40 E
Opportunity	46 Gc 47.39N 117.15W
Opsa	8 Li 55.31N 26.54 E
Opsterland	12 Ia 53.03N 6.04 E
Opsterland-Beetsterzwaag	12 Ia 53.03N 6.04 E
Opua	61 Dg 35.18S 174.07 E
Opunake	62 Ec 39.27S 173.51 E
Oputo	48 Eb 30.03N 109.20W
Oquossoc	44 Lc 45.04N 70.44W
Or ⌘	16 Ud 51.12N 58.33 E
Ōra	33 Cd 28.20N 19.35 E
Oradea	6 If 47.04N 21.56 E
Orahovac	15 Dg 42.24N 20.40 E

Orahovica	14 Le 45.32N 17.53 E
Orai	25 Fc 25.59N 79.28 E
Oraibi Wash ⌘	46 Ji 35.26N 110.49W
Oran	31 Ge 35.42N 0.38W
Oran ③	32 Gb 36.00N 0.35W
Orange [Austl.]	58 Fh 33.17S 149.06 E
Orange [Fr.]	11 Kj 44.08N 4.48 E
Orange [Tx.-U.S.]	43 Ie 30.01N 93.44W
Orange [Va.-U.S.]	44 Hf 38.14N 78.07W
Orange, Cabo- ⊨	30 Ik 28.38N 16.27 E
Orangeburg	52 Ke 4.24N 51.33W
Orange Free State/Oranje Vrystaat ②	43 Ke 33.30N 80.52W
Orange Lake	37 De 29.00S 26.00 E
Orange Park	44 Fk 29.25N 82.13W
Orangeville	44 Gj 30.10N 81.42W
Orange Walk	44 Gd 43.55N 80.06W
Orango ⊕	47 Ge 18.06N 88.33W
Oranienburg	30 Fg 11.05N 16.08W
Oranje/Orange ⌘	10 Jd 52.45N 13.14 E
Oranje Gebergte ▲	30 Ik 28.38N 16.27 E
Oranjemund	54 Hc 3.00N 55.00W
Oranjestad	37 Be 28.38S 16.24 E
Oranje Vrystaat/Orange Free State ②	54 Da 12.33N 70.06W
Oranžerei	37 De 29.00S 26.00 E
Orapa	16 Og 45.50N 47.36 E
Orăştie	37 Dd 21.16S 25.22 E
Orava ⌘	15 Gd 45.50N 23.12 E
Oraviţa	10 Pg 49.08N 19.10 E
Orayská Priehradni Nádrž ⊟	15 Gd 45.02N 21.42 E
Orb ⌘	10 Pg 49.20N 19.35 E
Orba	11 Jk 43.15N 3.18 E
Orba Co ⊟	14 Cf 44.53N 8.37 E
Ørbæk	27 De 34.33N 81.06 E
Orbec	8 Di 55.16N 10.41 E
Orbetello	12 Ce 49.01N 0.25 E
Orbetello, Laguna di- ⊟	14 Fh 42.27N 11.13 E
Orbigo ⌘	14 Fh 42.25N 11.15 E
Orbiquet ⌘	13 Gc 41.58N 5.40W
Orbost	12 Ce 49.09N 0.14 E
Ørbyhus	59 Jg 37.42S 148.27 E
Orcas Island	8 Gd 60.14N 17.42 E
Orchej (Orgejev)	46 Gb 48.39N 122.55W
Orchies	19 Cf 47.23N 28.50 E
Orcia ⌘	12 Fd 50.28N 3.14 E
Orco ⌘	14 Fh 42.58N 11.21 E
Ord, Mount- ▲	14 Be 45.10N 7.52 E
Ordenes	59 Fc 17.20S 125.35 E
Ordos Desert (EN) = Mu Us Shamo ⊠	13 Da 43.04N 8.24W
Ord River ⌘	21 Mf 38.45N 109.10 E
Ordu	57 Dl 35.30S 128.21 E
Ordubad	23 Ea 41.00N 37.53 E
Ordynskoje	16 Oj 38.55N 46.01 E
Ordžonikidze	20 Df 54.22N 81.58 E
Ordžonikidze	16 If 47.40N 34.04 E
Ordžonikidze Vladikavkaz	17 Jj 52.25N 61.45 E
Ordžonikidzeabad	8 Kg 43.03N 44.40 E
Ore aïv ⌘	19 Gh 38.34N 69.02 E
Orebić	8 Fc 61.08N 14.35 E
Örebro	14 Lh 42.58N 17.11 E
Örebro ②	6 Hd 59.17N 15.13 E
Oredež ⌘	7 Dg 59.30N 15.00 E
Oregon	8 Nf 58.50N 30.13 E
Oregon ②	44 Fe 41.38N 83.28W
Oregon City	43 Cc 44.00N 121.00W
Oregon Inlet ◖	43 Cb 45.21N 122.36W
Öregrund	44 Jh 35.50N 75.35W
Orehov	8 Hd 60.20N 18.26 E
Orehovo-Zujevo	16 Hf 47.34N 35.47 E
Orel	8 Jf 55.49N 38.59 E
Orel ⌘	8 Je 52.59N 36.05 E
Orel, Gora- ▲	16 Ie 48.31N 34.55 E
Orellana [Peru]	20 Jf 53.55N 140.01 E
Orellana [Peru]	54 Ce 6.54S 75.04W
Orem	54 Cd 4.40S 78.10W
Ore Mountains (EN) = Erzgebirge ▲	43 Ec 40.19N 111.42W
Ore Mountains (EN) = Krušné Hory ▲	5 He 50.30N 13.15 E
Ören	5 He 50.30N 13.15 E
Orenbel	24 Bd 37.18N 29.17 E
Orenburg	24 Hb 40.00N 39.10 E
Orenburgskaja Oblast ③	16 Le 51.54N 55.06 E
Orencik	19 Fe 52.00N 55.00 E
Orense ③	24 Cc 39.16N 29.34 E
Orense [Arg.]	13 Eb 42.10N 7.30W
Orense [Sp.]	56 Ie 38.40S 59.47W
Oreón, Dhíavlos- ⊨	13 Eb 42.20N 7.51W
Orepuki	15 Fk 38.54N 22.55 E
Orestiás	62 Bg 46.17S 167.44 E
Øresund ⊨	15 Jh 41.30N 26.31 E
Oreti ⌘	5 Hd 55.50N 12.40 E
Orewa	62 Cg 46.28S 168.17 E
Orford	61 Ef 36.35S 174.42 E
Orford Ness ⊨	12 Db 52.05N 1.32 E
Organá/Organyà	9 Oi 52.05N 1.34 E
Organ Needle ▲	13 Nb 42.13N 1.20 E
Organyà/Organá	45 Cj 32.21N 106.33W
Orgaz	13 Nb 42.13N 1.20 E
Orgejev — Orchej	13 Ie 39.39N 3.54W
Orgelet	8 Mf 42.38N 28.50 E
Orgon Tal	11 Lh 46.31N 5.37 E
Orgosolo	28 Bc 43.20N 112.40 E
Orgūn	14 Dd 40.12N 9.21 E
Orhaneli	23 Kc 32.57N 69.11 E
Orhaneli/Koca Çay ⌘	15 Lj 39.54N 29.00 E
Orhangazi	15 Lj 39.56N 28.32 E
Orhaneli	15 Mi 40.30N 29.18 E
Orhei	15 Kh 41.29N 28.99 E
Orhon (Orchon) ⌘	15 Md 50.21N 106.05 E
Orhy, Pico de- ▲	21 Jb 48.24N 2.00W
Oria ⌘	13 Ja 43.17N 2.08W
Orichuna, Río- ⌘	50 Bi 7.30N 68.13W

Orick	46 Cf 41.17N 124.04W
Oriental	48 Kh 19.22N 97.37W
Oriental, Cordillera- ▲	49 Md 18.55N 69.15W
Oriente	56 He 38.44S 60.37W
Orihuela	13 Lf 38.05N 0.57W
Oriku	15 Ci 40.17N 19.25 E
Óri Lekánis ▲	15 Jh 41.08N 24.33 E
Orillia	42 Jh 44.37N 79.25W
Orimattila	7 Ff 60.48N 25.45 E
Orinoco, Río- ⌘	52 Je 8.37N 62.15W
Oripää	8 Jd 60.51N 22.41 E
Orissa ③	25 Gd 21.00N 84.00 E
Orissaare/Orissare	7 Fg 58.34N 23.05 E
Oristano	14 Ck 39.54N 8.36 E
Oristano, Golfo di- ◖	14 Ck 39.50N 8.30 E
Orituco, Río- ⌘	50 Ch 8.45N 67.27W
Orivesi	5 Lc 62.15N 29.25 E
Orivesi ⌘	7 Ff 61.41N 24.21 E
Oriximiná	52 La 1.45S 55.52W
Orizaba	39 Jh 18.51N 97.06W
Orizaba, Pico de- (Citlaltépetl, Volcán-) ▲	38 Jh 19.01N 97.16W
Orizona	55 Hc 17.03S 48.18W
Orjahovo	15 Gf 43.44N 23.58 E
Ørje	8 De 59.29N 11.39 E
Orjen ▲	15 Eg 42.34N 18.33 E
Orjiva	13 Ih 36.54N 3.25W
Orkanger	7 Be 63.19N 9.52 E
Orkdalen ⊠	8 Ca 63.15N 9.50 E
Örkelljunga	8 Eh 56.17N 13.17 E
Orkla ⌘	7 Be 63.19N 9.50 E
Orkney	37 De 27.00S 26.39 E
Orkney ③	9 Kb 59.00N 3.00W
Orkney Islands ☐	5 Fd 59.00N 3.00W
Orländia	55 Ie 20.43S 47.53W
Orlando	39 Kg 28.32N 81.23W
Orlando, Capo d'- ⊨	14 Il 38.10N 14.45 E
Orleáns ⌘	10 Td 52.23N 21.32 E
Orléanais ⊠	11 Hf 48.40N 1.20 E
Orléans	11 Hf 47.55N 1.54 E
Orlice ⌘	10 Lf 50.12N 15.49 E
Orlické Hory ▲	10 Lf 50.13N 16.30 E
Orlik	20 Ef 52.30N 99.55 E
Orlov (Halturin)	19 Ed 58.35N 48.55 E
Orlovskaja oblast	19 De 52.45N 36.30 E
Orlovski	16 Mf 46.52N 42.06 E
Orlovski, mys- ⊨	7 Jc 67.16N 41.18 E
Orly	11 If 48.45N 2.24 E
Ormāra	25 Cc 25.12N 64.38 E
Ormes	11 Mg 49.03N 0.59 E
Ormoc	26 Hd 11.00N 124.37 E
Ormond	62 Gc 38.33S 177.55 E
Ormond Beach	44 Gk 29.17N 81.02W
Ornain ⌘	11 Kf 48.46N 4.47 E
Ornans	11 Mg 47.06N 6.09 E
Ornäs	8 Fd 60.31N 15.32 E
Orne ③	11 Gf 48.40N 0.05 E
Orne [Fr.] ⌘	11 Ie 49.17N 6.11 E
Orne [Fr.] ⌘	11 Be 49.19N 0.14W
Orne Seamount (EN) ☐	61 Je 27.30S 157.30W
Orneta	10 Qb 54.08N 20.08 E
Ornö ⊕	7 Eg 59.05N 18.25 E
Ornsköldsvik	7 Ee 63.18N 18.43 E
Oro	28 Id 40.01N 127.27 E
Oro, Rio de- ⌘	55 Ch 27.04S 58.34W
Oro, Rio del- ⌘	48 Ge 25.35N 105.03W
Orocué	54 Dc 4.48N 71.20W
Orodara	34 Dc 10.59N 4.55W
Orofino	46 Gc 46.29N 116.15W
Orogrande	45 Cj 32.23N 106.08W
Orohena, Mont- ▲	65e Fc 17.31S 149.28W
Oroluk Atoll ⊙	57 Gd 7.32N 155.18 E
Orom	36 Fb 3.20N 33.40 E
Oromocto	42 Kh 45.51N 66.29W
Oron	34 Ge 4.50N 8.14 E
Orona Atoll (Hull) ⊙	57 Je 4.29S 172.10W
Orongo ⊕	65d Ac 27.10S 109.26W
Oronsay ⊕	9 Ge 56.01N 6.14W
Orontes (EN) = Nahr al 'Āsī ⌘	23 Eb 36.02N 35.58 E
Oropesa [Sp.]	13 Ge 39.55N 5.10W
Oropesa [Sp.]	13 Ld 40.06N 0.09W
Oroqen Zizhiqi (Alihe)	27 La 50.35N 123.42 E
Oroquieta	26 He 8.29N 123.48 E
Orós	54 Ke 6.15S 38.55W
Orós, Açude- ⊟	54 Ke 6.15S 39.05W
Orosei	14 Dj 40.23N 9.42 E
Orosei, Golfo di- ◖	14 Dj 40.15N 9.45 E
Orosháza	10 Qj 46.34N 20.40 E
Oro-Shima ⊕	29 Be 33.52N 130.02 E
Oroszlány	10 Oi 47.29N 18.19 E
Orote Peninsula ⊨	64c Bb 13.26N 144.38 E
Orote Point ⊨	64c Bb 13.27N 144.37 E
Orotukan	20 Kd 62.17N 151.50 E
Oroville [Ca.-U.S.]	46 Eg 39.31N 121.33W
Oroville [Wa.-U.S.]	46 Gb 48.56N 119.26W
Orp-Jauche	12 Gd 50.40N 4.57 E
Orqohan	27 Ka 49.36N 121.23 E
Orr	45 Jb 48.03N 92.50W
Orrefors	8 Fh 56.50N 15.45 E
Orri, Pic d'-/Llorri ▲	13 Nb 42.23N 1.13 E
Orsa	8 Ee 54.30N 30.24 E
Orša	8 Fc 61.07N 14.37 E
Orsasjön ⊟	8 Ee 61.05N 14.35 E
Orsay	12 Ef 48.42N 2.11 E
Orsjön ⊟	8 Gc 61.35N 16.52 E
Orsk	6 Le 51.12N 58.34 E
Orşova	15 Fe 44.42N 22.25 E
Ørsta	7 Be 62.12N 6.09 E
Ørsundsbro	8 Ge 59.44N 17.18 E
Orta, Lago d'- ⊟	14 Ce 45.50N 8.25 E
Ortaca	24 Bd 36.49N 28.47 E
Ortaklar	15 Kl 37.53N 27.21 E
Ortaklar	15 Kl 37.53N 27.30 E
Orta Nova	14 Jh 41.19N 15.42 E
Orte	14 Gh 42.27N 12.23 E
Ortegal, Cabo- ⊨	13 Ea 43.45N 7.53W

Ortenberg	12 Ld 50.21N 9.03 E
Orthez	11 Fk 43.29N 0.46W
Orthon, Rio- ⌘	54 Ef 10.50S 66.04W
Ortigueira [Braz.]	56 Jb 24.12S 50.55W
Ortigueira [Sp.]	13 Fa 43.34N 6.44W
Ortisei / Sankt Ulrich	14 Fd 46.34N 11.40 E
Ortiz [Mex.]	48 Dc 28.15N 110.43W
Ortiz [Ven.]	50 Ch 9.37N 67.17W
Ortlergruppe/Ortles ▲	14 Ed 46.30N 10.40 E
Ortles/Ortlergruppe ▲	14 Ed 46.30N 10.40 E
Ortolo ⌘	14a Ab 41.30N 8.55 E
Ortona	14 Ih 42.21N 14.24 E
Ortonville	45 Hd 45.19N 96.27W
Orto-Tokoj	18 Kc 42.20N 76.02 E
Örtze ⌘	10 Fd 52.40N 9.57 E
Orukuizu ⊕	64a Ac 7.10N 134.17 E
Orümiyeh	22 Gf 37.33N 45.04 E
Orümiyeh, Daryācheh-ye = Urmia, Lake- (EN) ⊟	21 Gf 37.40N 45.30 E
Oruro ②	54 Eg 18.40S 67.30W
Oruro	53 Jg 17.59S 67.09W
Orust ⊕	8 Df 58.10N 11.38 E
Orüzgān ③	23 Kc 33.15N 66.00 E
Orüzgān	23 Kc 32.56N 66.38 E
Orval, Abbaye d'- ▲	12 He 49.38N 5.22 E
Orvault	11 Eg 47.16N 1.37W
Orvieto	14 Gh 42.43N 12.07 E
Orville Escarpment ▲	66 Qf 75.45S 65.30W
Orvilos, Óros- ▲	15 Ah 41.23N 23.36 E
Orwell	12 Dc 51.58N 1.18 E
Orwell ⌘	12 Fe 49.08N 3.12 E
Orxois ⊠	12 Ef 49.08N 3.12 E
Orz ⌘	10 Rd 52.50N 21.30 E
Orzinuovi	14 De 45.24N 9.55 E
Orzyc ⌘	10 Rd 52.47N 21.13 E
Orzysz	10 Rc 53.49N 21.56 E
Os	8 Hg 40.32N 72.50 E
Ōsa ⌘	7 Ce 62.30N 11.12 E
Ōsa ⌘	8 Lh 57.17N 55.26 E
Osa, Peninsula de- ⊨	8 Lh 56.21N 26.29 E
Osage	10 Oc 53.33N 18.45 E
Osage River ⌘	47 Hg 8.35N 83.33W
Ōsaka	45 Je 43.17N 92.49W
Ōsaka	43 Id 38.35N 91.57W
Osaka Bay (EN) = Ōsaka- Wan ◖	29 Ed 35.57N 137.14 E
Ōsaka-Fu ②	22 Pf 34.40N 135.30 E
Osakarovka	28 Mg 34.36N 135.27 E
Ōsaka-Wan = Osaka Bay (EN) ◖	28 Mg 34.36N 135.35 E
Osam ⌘	19 He 50.32N 72.39 E
Osan	28 Mg 34.36N 135.27 E
Osasco	15 Hf 43.42N 24.51 E
Osat ⊠	28 If 37.09N 127.04 E
Osawatomie	55 Jf 23.32S 46.46W
Osborne	14 Nf 44.20N 19.20 E
Osburger Hochwald ▲	45 Ig 38.31N 94.57W
Osby	45 Gg 39.26N 98.42W
Osceola [Ar.-U.S.]	12 Le 49.40N 6.50 E
Osceola [Ia.-U.S.]	45 Li 35.42N 89.58W
Osceola [Mo.-U.S.]	43 Jc 41.02N 93.46W
Oschatz	45 Jh 38.03N 93.42W
Oschersleben	10 Je 51.18N 13.07 E
Osen	10 Hd 52.02N 11.15 E
Osered ⌘	7 Cd 64.18N 10.31 E
Osetr ⌘	16 Ld 50.01N 40.48 E
Ōse-Zaki ⊨	16 Kb 55.00N 38.45 E
Osgoode	28 Jh 32.38N 128.42 E
Osh	28 Pc 42.30N 140.22 E
Oshamanbe	42 Jh 43.54N 78.51W
Oshawa	37 Bc 18.08S 15.45 E
Oshima ⌘	29 Gb 38.17N 141.31 E
Oshika	28 Pe 39.20N 141.27 E
Oshika-Hantō ⊨	37 Bc 17.22S 15.55 E
Oshikango	29 Ce 33.38N 132.11 E
Oshima	28 Jh 32.04N 128.26 E
Ō-Shima [Jap.] ⊕	28 Jh 32.04N 128.28 E
Ō-Shima [Jap.] ⊕	28 Ng 34.38N 133.33 E
Ō-Shima [Jap.] ⊕	29 Ae 33.28N 132.33 E
Ō-Shima [Jap.] ⊕	30 Ae 32.34N 128.54 E
Ō-Shima [Jap.] ⊕	29 Ae 33.28N 132.33 E
Ō-Shima [Jap.] ⊕	29 Bf 31.32N 131.25 E
Ō-Shima [Jap.] ⊕	29 Bf 31.33N 130.27 E
Ō-Shima [Jap.] ⊕	29 Bf 31.35N 131.15 E
Ōshima [Jap.] ⊕	28 Jh 32.04N 128.26 E
Oshima-Hantō ⊨	29 Jh 32.04N 128.26 E
Ōshima-Kaikyō ⊨	29 Be 33.52N 130.02 E
Oshkosh [Nb.-U.S.]	45 Ef 41.24N 102.21W
Oshkosh [Wi.-U.S.]	44 Cd 44.01N 88.33W
Oshnaviyeh	24 Kd 37.02N 45.06 E
Oshogbo	31 Hh 7.46N 4.34 E
Oshtorān Kūh ▲	23 Gb 33.20N 49.16 E
Oshtorinān	24 Ke 34.01N 48.38 E
Oshwe	36 Cc 3.24S 19.30 E
Osich'ōn-ni	28 If 37.43N 126.00 E
Osijek	14 Ke 45.33N 18.42 E
Osilo	14 Cj 40.45N 8.40 E
Osimo	14 Hg 43.29N 13.29 E
Osinki	19 Fe 53.10N 49.31 E
Osinniki	20 Dg 53.37N 87.31 E
Osipaonica	15 Ee 44.33N 21.04 E
Osipoviči	8 Mc 53.19N 28.40 E
Osječenica ▲	14 Jf 44.34N 16.17 E
Oskaloosa	45 Ji 41.18N 92.39W
Oskarshamn	6 Hd 57.16N 16.26 E
Oskarström	8 Eh 56.48N 12.58 E
Oskino	20 Fd 60.48N 107.58 E
Öskjuvatn ⊟	7a Cb 65.02N 16.45W
Öskü	24 If 37.55N 46.06 E
Osło ②	15 Mg 40.26N 28.42 E

Oslo ②	7 Cg 59.55N 10.45 E
Oslo	6 Hd 59.55N 10.45 E
Oslofjorden ⊨	5 Hd 59.20N 10.35 E
Osmānābād	25 Fe 18.10N 76.03 E
Osmancik	24 Fb 40.59N 34.49 E
Osmaneli	15 Ni 40.22N 30.01 E
Osmaniye	23 Eb 37.05N 36.14 E
Osmino	8 Mf 58.54N 29.15 E
Ōšmjanskaja Vozvyšennost ▲	8 Kj 54.30N 26.00 E
Ōšmjany	16 Bb 54.25N 25.57 E
Osmo	8 Gf 58.59N 17.54 E
Osmussaar/Osmussaar ⊕	8 Je 59.20N 23.15 E
Osmussar/Osmussaar ⊕	8 Je 59.20N 23.15 E
Osnabrück	6 Ge 52.16N 8.03 E
Osning ▲	12 Kb 52.10N 8.05 E
Oso, Sierra del- ▲	48 Gd 26.00N 105.25W
Osobłoga ⌘	10 Nf 50.27N 17.58 E
Osogovske Planine ▲	15 Fg 42.10N 22.30 E
Osor	14 If 44.42N 14.24 E
Osório	56 Jc 29.54S 50.16W
Osorno	53 Ij 40.34S 73.09W
Osoyoos	42 Fg 49.02N 119.28W
Osøyra	7 Af 60.11N 5.28 E
Ospino	50 Bh 9.18N 69.27W
Osprey Reef ☐	57 Ff 13.55S 146.40 E
Oss	11 Lc 51.46N 5.31 E
Ossa, Mount- ▲	57 Fi 41.54S 146.01 E
Óssa, Óros- ▲	15 Fj 39.49N 22.40 E
Ossabaw Island ⊕	44 Gj 31.47N 81.06W
Ossa de Montiel	13 Jf 38.58N 2.45W
Osse ⌘	11 Gj 44.07N 0.17 E
Ossining	44 Ke 41.10N 73.52W
Ossjøen ⊟	8 Dc 61.15N 11.55 E
Ōskaja Oblast ③	19 Hg 40.45N 73.20 E
Ossora	20 Le 59.15S 163.02 E
Ostanvik	8 Fc 61.10N 15.13 E
Ostaškov	19 Dd 57.09N 33.07 E
Ostbevern	12 Jb 52.03N 7.51 E
Oster	10 Fc 53.33N 9.10 E
Oster	16 Gd 50.55N 30.57 E
Oster	16 Gc 53.47N 31.45 E
Osterburg in der Altmark	10 Hd 52.47N 11.44 E
Österbybruk	8 Gd 60.12N 17.54 E
Österdalälven ⌘	7 Df 60.33N 15.08 E
Østerdalen ⊠	7 Cf 62.00N 10.40 E
Osterfjorden ⊨	8 Ad 60.30N 5.20 E
Osterforse	8 Ga 63.09N 17.01 E
Östergarnsholm ⊕	8 Hg 57.25N 19.00 E
Östergötland ②	6 Hd 58.25N 15.35 E
Östergötland ②	7 Dg 58.25N 15.45 E
Osterholz Scharmbeck	10 Ec 53.14N 8.48 E
Österlen ⊠	8 Fi 55.30N 14.10 E
Ostermark/Teuva	7 Ee 62.29N 21.44 E
Osterode am Harz	10 Ge 51.44N 10.11 E
Østeraya ⊕	7 Af 60.35N 5.13 E
Österreich = Austria (EN) ①	6 Hf 47.30N 14.00 E
Östersjön = Baltic Sea (EN) ⊟	5 Hd 57.00N 19.00 E
Østersøen = Baltic Sea (EN) ⊟	5 Hd 57.00N 19.00 E
Östersund	6 Hc 63.11N 14.39 E
Osterwick, Rosendahl-	12 Jb 52.01N 7.12 E
Østfold ②	7 Cg 59.20N 11.30 E
Ostfriesische Inseln = East Frisian Islands (EN) ☐	41 Id 72.00N 35.00W
Ostfriesland = East Friesland (EN) ⊠	10 Dc 53.45N 7.25 E
Østgrønland = East Greenland (EN) ②	10 Dc 53.20N 7.40 E
Osthammar	8 Ge 60.16N 18.22 E
Osthofen	12 Ke 49.42N 8.20 E
Ostmark	8 Ed 60.17N 12.45 E
Ostrach	10 Fh 48.00N 9.25 E
Östra Silen ⊟	8 De 59.15N 12.20 E
Ostrava	6 Hf 49.50N 18.17 E
Ostrhauerfdehn	12 Ja 53.08N 7.37 E
Ostróda	10 Pc 53.43N 19.59 E
Ostrog	16 Bd 50.19N 26.32 E
Ostrogožsk	19 De 50.52N 39.05 E
Ostrołęka ②	10 Rc 53.05N 21.35 E
Ostrołęka	10 Rc 53.06N 21.34 E
Ostrošicki Gorodok	8 Lj 54.03N 27.46 E
Ostrov	10 Vf 50.18N 12.57 E
Ostrov [Czech.]	10 Id 50.18N 12.57 E
Ostrov [Rom.]	15 Kf 44.07N 27.22 E
Ostrov	16 Cd 47.23N 28.22 E
Ostrov	8 Mf 57.20N 28.22 E
Ostrov	8 Mf 58.28N 28.44 E
Ostrovec	24 Ia 44.01N 88.33W
Ostrovicés, Mali i- ▲	15 Di 40.34N 20.27 E
Ostrovskoje	7 Kh 57.50N 42.13 E
Ostrowiec Świętokrzyski	10 Rf 50.57N 21.23 E
Ostrów Lubelski	10 Se 51.30N 22.52 E
Ostrów Mazowiecka	10 Rd 52.49N 21.54 E
Ostrów Wielkopolski	5 Hf 51.39N 17.49 E
Ostryna	10 Uc 53.41N 24.37 E
Ostrzeszów	10 Oe 51.25N 17.57 E
Ostsee = Baltic Sea (EN) ⊟	5 Hd 57.00N 19.00 E
Oststeirisches Hügelland ⊠	14 Jd 47.00N 15.45 E
Osttirol ⊠	14 Gd 46.50N 12.30 E
Ostuni	14 Lj 40.44N 17.35 E
Ōsumi	29 Bf 31.36N 130.59 E
Ōsumi-Hantō ⊨	29 Bf 31.15N 130.50 E
Ōsumi Islands (EN) = Ōsumi- Shotō ☐	21 Pf 30.35N 130.59 E
Ōsumi-Shotō = Osumi Islands (EN) ☐	21 Pf 30.35N 130.59 E
Osuna	13 Gh 37.14N 5.07W
Osveja	8 Mi 55.59N 28.10 E
Osvejskoje, Ozero- ⊟	8 Mi 55.54N 28.10 E
Oswego	43 Lc 43.27N 76.31W
Oswestry	9 Ji 52.52N 3.04W

Oświęcim	10	Pf	50.03N	19.12 E
Osyka	45	Kk	31.00N	90.28W
Ōta	29	Fc	36.18N	139.22 E
Ota	29	Ec	35.56N	136.03 E
Otago [2]	62	Cf	45.00S	169.10 E
Otago Peninsula ⊏	62	Df	45.50S	170.45 E
Ōtake	28	Lg	34.12N	132.13 E
Otakeho	62	Fc	39.33S	174.03 E
Otaki	62	Fd	40.45S	175.08 E
Ōtakime-Yama ▲	29	Gc	37.22N	140.42 E
Otanoshike	29a	Db	43.01N	144.16 E
Otar	19	Hg	43.31N	75.12 E
Otaru	27	Pc	43.13N	141.00 E
Otautau	62	Bg	46.09S	168.00 E
Otava ∿	10	Kg	49.26N	14.12 E
Otava	8	Lc	61.39N	27.04 E
Otavi	37	Bc	19.39S	17.20 E
Ōtawara	28	Pf	36.52N	140.02 E
Otelu Roşu	15	Fd	45.32N	22.22 E
Otematata	62	Df	44.37S	170.11 E
Otepää/Otepja	7	Gg	58.03N	26.30 E
Otepää, Vozvyšennost-/Otepää Kõrgustik ⊼	8	Lf	58.00N	26.40 E
Otepää Kõrgustik/Otepää, Vozvyšennost- ⊼	8	Lf	58.00N	26.40 E
Otepja/Otepää	7	Gg	58.03N	26.30 E
Oteros ∿	47	Cc	26.55N	108.30W
Othain ∿	12	He	49.31N	5.23 E
Othello	46	Fc	46.50N	119.10W
Othonoi ◆	15	Cj	39.50N	19.25 E
Óthris Óros ⛰	15	Fj	39.02N	22.37 E
Oti ∿	30	Hh	7.48N	0.08 E
Otira	62	De	42.51S	171.33 E
Otish, Monts- ⛰	38	Md	52.45N	69.15W
Otjikondo	37	Bc	19.50S	15.23 E
Otjimbingwe	37	Bd	22.21S	16.08 E
Otjiwarongo	31	Ik	20.29S	16.36 E
Otjiwarongo [3]	37	Bd	20.30S	17.30 E
Otjosondjou, Omuramba- ∿	30	Ij	19.55S	20.00 E
Otjosondu	37	Bd	21.12S	17.58 E
Otmuchowskie, Jezioro- ⊡	10	Nf	50.27N	17.15 E
Otnes	7	Cf	61.46N	11.12 E
Otobe	29a	Bc	41.57N	140.08 E
Otočac	14	Jf	44.52N	15.14 E
Otofuke	29a	Cb	42.59N	143.10 E
Otofuke-Gawa ∿	29a	Cb	42.56N	143.12 E
Otog Qi (Ulan)	27	Id	39.07N	108.00 E
Otoineppu	29a	Ca	44.43N	142.16 E
Otok	14	Me	45.09N	18.53 E
Otopeni	15	Je	44.33N	26.04 E
Otorohanga	62	Fc	38.11S	175.12 E
Otorten, Gora- ▲	17	If	61.50N	59.13 E
Ōtoyo	29	Ce	33.46N	133.40 E
Otra ∿	5	Gd	58.09N	8.00 E
Otradnaja	16	Lg	44.23N	41.31 E
Otradnoje, Ozero- ◍	8	Nd	60.50N	30.25 E
Otradny	7	Mj	53.23N	51.24 E
Otranto	14	Mj	40.09N	18.30 E
Otranto, Canale d'-=Otranto, Strait of- (EN) ⫼	5	Hg	40.00N	19.00 E
Otranto, Capo d'- ►	14	Mj	40.06N	18.31 E
Otranto, Strait of- (EN)=Otranto, Canale d'- ⫼	5	Hg	40.00N	19.00 E
Otranto, Strait of- (EN)=Otrantos, Kanali i- ⫼	15	Bi	40.00N	19.00 E
Otranto, Terra d'- ⧗	14	Mj	40.20N	18.15 E
Otrantos, Kanali i-=Otranto, Strait of- (EN) ⫼	15	Bi	40.00N	19.00 E
Ötscher ▲	14	Jc	47.51N	15.12 E
Ōtsu	28	Mg	35.00N	135.52 E
Ōtsuchi	28	Pe	39.21N	141.54 E
Ōtsuki [Jap.]	29	Fd	35.36N	138.54 E
Ōtsuki [Jap.]	29	Ce	32.50N	132.41 E
Otta ∿	8	Cc	61.46N	9.31 E
Otta	7	Bf	61.46N	9.32 E
Otta ◆	64d	Bb	7.09N	151.54 E
Ottadalen ⧗	8	Bc	61.55N	8.00 E
Ottana	14	Dj	40.15N	9.05 E
Otta Pass ⫼	64d	Bb	7.09N	151.53 E
Ottawa [Il.-U.S.]	45	Lf	41.21N	88.51W
Ottawa [Ks.-U.S.]	43	Hd	38.37N	95.16W
Ottawa [Oh.-U.S.]	44	Ee	41.02N	84.03W
Ottawa [Ont.-Can.]	39	Le	45.25N	75.42W
Ottawa Islands ⁂	38	Kd	59.30N	80.10W
Ottawa River ∿	38	Le	45.20N	73.58W
Ottemby	7	Dh	56.16N	16.24 E
Otterberg	12	Je	49.30N	7.46 E
Otter Creek	44	Fk	29.19N	82.48W
Otterndorf	10	Ec	53.48N	8.54 E
Otteroy ◆	8	Bb	62.40N	6.50 E
Otter Rapids ≋	44	Ga	50.15N	81.45W
Otterup	8	Di	55.31N	10.24 E
Ottumwa	43	Ic	41.01N	92.25W
Ottweiler	12	Je	49.23N	7.10 E
Otukpa	34	Gd	7.05N	7.40 E
Otumpa	55	Ah	27.19S	62.13W
Otuquis, Bañados de- ≋	54	Gg	19.20S	58.30W
Otuquis, Río- ∿	55	Cd	19.41S	58.20W
Oturkpo	34	Gd	7.13N	8.09 E
Otu Tolu Group ⁂	65b	Bb	20.21S	174.32W
Otuzco	54	Ce	7.54S	78.35W
Otway, Cape- ►	59	Ig	38.52S	143.31 E
Otwock	10	Rd	52.07N	21.16 E
Otynja	10	Uh	48.40N	24.57 E
Ötz	14	Ec	47.12N	10.54 E
Ötztaler Ache ∿	14	Ec	47.14N	10.50 E
Ötztaler Alpen ⛰	10	Gi	46.45N	10.55 E
Ou ∿	25	Kd	20.04N	102.13 E
'O'ua ◆	65b	Bb	20.02S	174.41W
Oua ◆	63b	Ce	21.14S	167.05 E
Ouachita, Lake- ◍	45	Ji	34.40N	93.25W
Ouachita Mountains ⛰	38	Jf	34.40N	94.25W
Ouachita River ∿	43	Ie	31.38N	91.49W
Ouadane	31	Ff	20.57N	11.35W
Ouaddaï [3]	35	Cc	13.00N	21.00 E
Ouaddaï ⧗	30	Jg	13.00N	21.00 E
Ouagadougou	31	Gg	12.22N	1.31W
Ouahigouya	31	Gg	13.35N	2.25W
Ouaka [3]	35	Cd	6.00N	21.00 E
Ouaka ∿	30	Ih	4.59N	19.56 E
Oualata	32	Ff	17.18N	7.00W
Oualata, Dahr- ▲	32	Ff	17.48N	7.24W
Oualidia	32	Fc	32.44N	9.02W
Ouallam	34	Fc	14.19N	2.05 E
Ouallene	32	He	24.35N	1.17 E
Ouanda-Djallé	35	Cd	8.54N	22.48 E
Ouandjia	35	Cd	8.35N	23.12 E
Ouandjia ∿	35	Cd	9.35N	21.43 E
Ouango	35	Ce	4.19N	22.33 E
Ouangolodougou	34	Dd	9.58N	5.09W
Ouanne ∿	11	Ig	47.57N	2.47 E
Ouarane ⧗	30	Ff	21.00N	10.00W
Ouargaye	34	Fc	11.32N	0.01 E
Ouargla	31	He	31.57N	5.20 E
Ouargla [3]	32	Id	30.00N	6.30 E
Ouarkziz, Jbel- ⛰	30	Gf	28.00N	8.20W
Ouarra ∿	30	Jh	5.05N	24.26 E
Ouarsenis, Djebel- ▲	13	Ni	35.53N	1.38 E
Ouarsenis, Massif de l'- ⛰	32	Hb	35.50N	2.05 E
Ouarzazate [3]	32	Fc	31.00N	6.30W
Ouarzazate	32	Fc	30.55N	6.55W
Oubangui ∿	30	Ii	0.30S	17.42 E
Ouborré, Pointe- ►	63b	Dd	18.47S	169.16 E
Ouche, Pays d'- ⧗	11	Gf	48.55N	0.45 E
Ōuchi	29	Gb	39.27N	140.06 E
Oud Beijerland	12	Gc	51.50N	4.26 E
Oude IJssel ∿	12	Ic	52.00N	6.10 E
Oudenaarde/Audenarde	11	Jd	50.51N	3.36 E
Oudenbosch	12	Gc	51.35N	4.34 E
Oude Rijn ∿	11	Kb	52.05N	4.20 E
Oudon ∿	11	Fg	47.37N	0.42W
Oudtshoorn	31	Jl	33.35S	22.14 E
Oued Ben Tili	32	Fd	25.48N	9.32W
Oued el Abtal	13	Mi	35.27N	0.41 E
Oued Fodda	13	Nh	36.11N	1.32 E
Oued Lili	13	Ni	35.31N	1.16 E
Oued Rhiou	32	Hb	35.58N	0.55 E
Oued-Taria	13	Mi	35.07N	0.05 E
Oued Tlelat	13	Li	35.33N	0.27W
Oued Zem	31	Ge	32.52N	6.34W
Ouégoa	63b	Be	20.21S	164.26 E
Ouéllé	34	Ed	7.18N	4.01W
Ouémé ∿	30	Hh	6.29N	2.32 E
Ouémé [3]	34	Fd	7.00N	2.35 E
Ouen ◆	63b	Cf	22.26S	166.48 E
Ouenza	32	Ib	35.57N	8.07 E
Ouenza, Djebel- ▲	14	Co	35.57N	8.05 E
Ouessa	34	Ec	11.03N	2.47W
Ouessant, Ile d'- ◆	11	Af	48.28N	5.05W
Ouesso	31	Ih	1.37N	16.04 E
Ouest [3]	34	Hd	5.20N	10.30 E
Ouest, Baie de l'- ◐	64h	Ab	13.15S	176.13W
Ouezzane	32	Fc	34.48N	5.36W
Oughter, Lough- ◍	9	Fg	54.00N	7.29W
Ouham [3]	35	Bd	7.00N	18.00 E
Ouham ∿	30	Ih	9.18N	18.14 E
Ouham-Pendé [3]	35	Bd	7.00N	16.00 E
Ouidah	34	Fd	6.22N	2.05 E
Ouistreham	11	Fe	49.17N	0.15W
Ouistreham-Riva Bella	12	Be	49.17N	0.16W
Oujda [3]	32	Gc	33.00N	2.00W
Oujda	31	Ge	34.40N	1.54W
Oujeft	32	Ee	20.02N	13.03W
Oulainen	7	Fd	64.16N	24.57 E
Oulchy-le-Château	12	Fe	49.12N	3.21 E
Ouled Djellal	32	Ic	34.25N	5.04 E
Ouled Naïl, Monts des- ⛰	32	Hc	34.40N	3.25 E
Oulou, Bahr- ∿	35	Cd	9.48N	21.32 E
Oulu [2]	7	Gd	65.00N	27.00 E
Oulu/Uleåborg	6	Ib	65.01N	25.30 E
Oulu, Lake- (EN)=Oulujärvi ◍	5	Ic	64.20N	27.15 E
Oulujärvi=Oulu, Lake- (EN) ◍	5	Ic	64.20N	27.15 E
Oulujoki ∿	5	Ib	65.01N	25.25 E
Oum Chalouba	31	Jg	15.48N	20.46 E
Oumé [3]	34	Dd	6.25N	5.30W
Oumé	34	Dd	6.23N	5.25W
Oum el Bouaghi [3]	32	Ib	35.30N	7.10 E
Oum el Bouaghi	32	Ib	35.53N	7.07 E
Oum er Rbia ∿	30	Ge	33.19N	8.20W
Oum Hadjer	35	Bc	13.18N	19.41 E
Oumm ed Droûs Guebli, Sebkhet- ◍	32	Ee	24.03N	11.45W
Oumm ed Droûs Telli, Sebkhet- ◍	32	Ee	24.20N	11.30W
Ounasjoki ∿	5	Ib	66.30N	25.45 E
Oundle	12	Bb	52.29N	0.28W
Ounianga ⧗	35	Cb	19.10N	20.30 E
Ounianga Kébir	31	Jg	19.04N	20.29 E
Ountivou	34	Fd	7.21N	1.34 E
Ouolossébougou	34	Dc	12.00N	7.55W
Oupeye	12	Hd	50.42N	5.39 E
Oupu	27	Ma	52.45N	126.00 E
Our ∿	12	Ie	49.53N	6.18 E
Ouray	45	Cg	38.01N	107.40W
Ouray, Mount- ▲	45	Cg	38.25N	106.14W
Ource ∿	11	Kf	48.06N	4.23 E
Ourcq ∿	11	Je	49.01N	3.01 E
Ourcq, Canal de l'- ═	11	If	48.51N	2.22 E
Ourém	54	Id	1.33S	47.06W
Ouricuri	54	Je	7.35S	40.05W
Ourinhos	53	Lh	22.59S	49.52W
Ouro, Rio do- ∿	55	Ha	13.20S	48.59W
Ouro Fino	55	If	22.17S	46.22W
Ouro Prêto	54	Jh	20.23S	43.30W
Ourthe [Bel.] ∿	11	Ld	50.38N	5.35 E
Ourville-en-Caux	12	Ce	49.44N	0.36 E
Ous	19	Gc	60.55N	61.31 E
Ōu-Sanmyaku ⛰	28	Pe	39.00N	141.00 E
Ouse [Eng.-U.K.] ∿	9	Nk	50.47N	0.03 E
Ouse [Eng.-U.K.] ∿	9	Mh	53.42N	0.41W
Oust ∿	11	Dg	47.35N	2.06W
Outagouna	34	Fb	15.11N	0.43 E
Outaouais, Rivière- ∿	38	Le	45.20N	73.58W
Outardes, Rivière aux- ∿	42	Kg	49.05N	68.23W
Outat Oulad El Hajj	32	Gc	33.21N	3.42W
Outer Dowsing ▬	9	Oh	53.25N	1.05 E
Outer Hebrides ⁂	9	Fd	57.50N	7.32W
Outer Santa Barbara Passage ⫼	46	Fj	33.10N	118.30W
Outer Silver Pit ⌣	9	Og	54.05N	2.00 E
Outjo	31	Ik	20.08S	16.08 E
Outjo [3]	37	Ac	19.30S	14.30 E
Outlook	46	La	51.30N	107.03W
Outokumpu	7	Ge	62.44N	29.01 E
Outram Mountain ▲	46	Eb	49.19N	121.05W
Outreau	12	Dd	50.42N	1.35 E
Out Skerries ◆	9	Ma	60.30N	0.50W
Outwell	12	Cb	52.37N	0.14 E
Ouvéa, Ile- ◆	57	Hg	20.35S	166.35 E
Ouvèze ∿	11	Kk	43.59N	4.51 E
Ouxian	28	Ej	28.58N	118.53 E
Ouyen	59	Ig	35.04S	142.20 E
Ouyou Bézédinga	34	Hb	16.32N	13.15 E
Ouzera	13	Oh	36.15N	2.51 E
Ovacık [Tur.]	24	Ed	36.11N	33.40 E
Ovacık [Tur.]	24	Hc	39.22N	39.13 E
Ovada	14	Cf	44.38N	8.38 E
Ova Gölü ◍	15	Mm	36.16N	29.22 E
Ovakent	15	Lk	38.06N	28.02 E
Ovalau Island ◆	63d	Bb	17.40S	178.48 E
Ovalle	53	Ii	30.36S	71.12W
Oval Peak ▲	46	Eb	48.15N	120.25W
Ovamboland ▭	37	Bc	18.30S	16.00 E
Ovamboland [3]	37	Bc	18.00S	16.00 E
Ovan	36	Bb	0.30N	12.10 E
Ovanåker	7	Df	61.21N	15.54 E
Ovar	13	Dd	40.52N	8.38W
Ovau ◆	63a	Cb	6.48S	156.02 E
Ovejas	49	Ji	9.32N	75.14W
Overath	12	Jd	50.57N	7.18 E
Øverbygd	7	Eb	69.01N	19.18 E
Overflakkee ◆	11	Kc	51.45N	4.10 E
Overhalla	7	Cd	64.30N	12.00 E
Overije	12	Gd	50.46N	4.32 E
Overijssel [3]	12	Ib	52.25N	6.30 E
Överkalix	7	Fc	66.19N	22.50 E
Overland Park	45	Ig	38.59N	94.40W
Övermark/Ylimarkku	8	Ib	62.37N	21.28 E
Overpelt	12	Hc	51.12N	5.25 E
Overri	34	Gd	5.29N	7.02 E
Overton	46	Hh	36.33N	114.27W
Övertorneå	7	Fc	66.23N	23.40 E
Överum	8	Gg	57.59N	16.19 E
Ovidiu	15	Le	44.16N	28.34 E
Oviedo [3]	13	Ga	43.20N	6.00W
Oviedo [Dom.Rep.]	49	Le	17.47N	71.22W
Oviedo [Sp.]	6	Fg	43.22N	5.50W
Oviši	8	Ig	57.34N	21.35 E
Ovo, Capo dell'- ►	14	Lj	40.18N	17.30 E
Øvre Årdal	7	Bf	61.19N	7.48 E
Övre Fryken ◍	8	Ed	60.00N	13.05 E
Övre Soppero	7	Eb	68.05N	21.41 E
Ovruč	19	Ce	51.19N	28.50 E
Ovsjanka	20	Hf	53.32N	126.58 E
Owaka	62	Cg	46.27S	169.40 E
Owando	31	Ii	0.29S	15.55 E
Ōwani	28	Pd	40.31N	140.35 E
Owase	28	Ng	34.04N	136.12 E
Owatonna	43	Ic	44.05N	93.14W
Owego	44	Id	42.06N	76.16W
Owen, Mount- ▲	62	Ed	41.33S	172.32 E
Owendo	36	Ab	0.17N	9.30 E
Owen Falls Dam ⌿	36	Fb	0.24N	33.11 E
Owensboro	43	Jd	37.46N	87.07W
Owens Lake ◍	46	Gh	36.25N	117.56W
Owen Sound	42	Jh	44.34N	80.56W
Owens River ∿	46	Gh	36.31N	117.57W
Owen Stanley Range ⛰	57	Fe	9.20S	148.00 E
Owl Creek Mountains ⛰	46	Ke	43.30N	108.35W
Ownay, Kowlal-e- ▲	23	Kc	34.27N	68.22 E
Owo	34	Gd	7.11N	5.35 E
Owosso	44	Ed	43.00N	84.10W
Owyhee	46	Gf	41.57N	116.06W
Owyhee, Lake- ◍	46	Ge	43.28N	117.20W
Owyhee Mountains ⛰	46	Ge	43.00N	116.45W
Owyhee River [U.S.] ∿	46	Ge	43.40N	117.16W
Owyhee River [U.S.] ∿	43	Dc	43.46N	117.02W
Oxberg	8	Fc	61.07N	14.10 E
Oxbow	45	Eb	49.14N	102.11W
Oxelösund	7	Dg	58.40N	17.06 E
Oxford ▭	9	Lj	51.50N	1.30W
Oxford [Eng.-U.K.]	6	Fe	51.46N	1.15W
Oxford [Ms.-U.S.]	45	Li	34.22N	89.32W
Oxford [N.C.-U.S.]	44	Hg	36.19N	78.35W
Oxford [N.Z.]	62	Ee	43.17S	172.11 E
Oxford Lake ◍	42	Hf	54.50N	95.35W
Oxfordshire [3]	9	Lj	51.50N	1.20W
Oxia ◆	15	Ek	38.18N	21.06 E
Oxkutzcab	48	Og	20.18N	89.25W
Oxnard	43	De	34.12N	119.11W
Ox or Slieve Gamph Mountains/Sliabh Gamh ▲	9	Eg	54.10N	8.50W
Oxted	12	Bc	51.14N	0.01W
Oyabe	29	Ec	36.40N	136.52 E
Oyahue	53	Jh	21.08S	68.45W
O-Yama ▲	29	Fd	34.04N	139.31 E
Oyama	28	Of	36.21N	139.50 E
Ōyama	29	Ec	36.35N	137.18 E
Ōyano	29	Be	32.35N	130.27 E
Oyapock, Fleuve- ∿	52	Ke	4.08N	51.40W
Oyem	31	Ih	1.37N	11.35 E
Oyen	46	Ja	51.22N	110.28W
Øyeren ◍	8	De	59.50N	11.14 E
Oykel ∿	9	Id	57.50N	4.25W
Oyo [2]	34	Fd	8.00N	3.50 E
Oyo [Nig.]	34	Fd	7.51N	3.56 E
Oyo [Sud.]	35	Fa	21.55N	36.06 E
Oyodo-Gawa ∿	29	Bf	31.55N	131.28 E
Oyonnax	11	Lh	46.15N	5.40 E
Oyster Bay ◐	59	Jh	42.10S	148.10 E
Øystese	8	Bd	60.23N	6.13 E
Özalp	24	Jc	38.39N	43.59 E
Ozamiz	26	He	8.08N	123.50 E
Ozark	44	Ej	31.28N	85.38W
Ozark Plateau ⊼	38	Jf	37.00N	93.00W
Ozark Reservoir ⊡	45	Ii	35.25N	94.05W
Ozarks, Lake of the- ◍	43	Id	37.39N	92.50W
Ózd	10	Qh	48.13N	20.18 E
Ozeblin ▲	14	Jf	44.35N	15.53 E
Ozernoj, Zaliv- ◐	20	Le	57.00N	163.20 E
Ozernovski	20	Kf	51.21N	156.32 E
Ozerny	16	Vd	51.08N	60.55 E
Ozersk	8	Ij	54.24N	21.59 E
Ozery	10	Uc	53.38N	24.18 E
Ozery	7	Ji	54.54N	38.32 E
Ožezdy	19	Gf	48.03N	67.09 E
Ozieri	14	Cj	40.35N	9.00 E
Ozinki	19	Ee	51.12N	49.47 E
Ožogina ∿	20	Kc	66.12N	151.05 E
Ozona	43	Ge	30.43N	101.12W
Ozorków	10	Pe	51.58N	19.19 E
Ozouri	36	Ac	0.55S	8.55 E
Ozren	14	Mf	44.37N	18.15 E
Ozren	14	Mg	43.59N	18.30 E
Ozren [Yugo.] ⛰	15	Ef	43.36N	21.54 E
Ōzu [Jap.]	29	Be	32.52N	130.52 E
Ōzu [Jap.]	28	Lh	33.30N	132.23 E
Ozurgeti (Maharadze)	19	Eg	41.53N	42.01 E

P

Pääjärvi ◍	8	Kb	62.50N	24.45 E
Paama ◆	63b	Dc	16.28S	168.13 E
Pa-an → Pha-an	25	Je	16.53N	97.38 E
Paar	10	Hh	48.45N	11.35 E
Paarl	31	Il	33.45S	18.56 E
Paauilo	65a	Fc	20.03N	155.22W
Paavola	7	Fd	64.36N	25.12 E
Pabbay ◆	9	Fd	57.47N	7.20W
Pabellón, Ensenada del- ◐	48	Fe	24.27N	107.36W
Pabianice	10	Pe	51.40N	19.22 E
Pābna	25	Hd	24.00N	89.15 E
Pabradė/Pabrade	7	Fi	54.59N	25.50 E
Pabrade/Pabradė	7	Fi	54.59N	25.50 E
Pacaás Novos, Serra dos- ⛰	54	Ff	10.50S	64.00W
Pacajá, Rio- ∿	54	Hd	1.56S	50.55W
Pacajus	54	Kd	4.10S	38.28W
Pacaraima, Serra- ⛰	52	Je	4.30N	60.40W
Pacasmayo	54	Ce	7.24S	79.34W
Paceco	14	Gm	37.59N	12.33 E
Pachala	35	Ed	7.10N	34.06 E
Pacheco	48	Eb	30.06N	108.21W
Pachino	14	Jn	36.43N	15.05 E
Pachitea, Río- ∿	54	De	8.46S	74.32W
Pachuca de Soto	47	Ed	20.07N	98.44W
Pacific-Antarctic Ridge (EN) ⋀	3	Kp	62.00S	157.00W
Pacific City	46	Dd	45.12N	123.57W
Pacific Grove	46	Eh	36.38N	121.56W
Pacific Islands, Trust Territory of the-	58	Ed	7.30N	134.30 E
Pacifico, Océano- = Pacific Ocean (EN) ▩	3	Ki	5.00N	155.00W
Pacific Ocean ▩	3	Ki	5.00N	155.00W
Pacific Ocean (EN)=Kita-Taiheiyō ▩	60	Ch	22.00N	167.00 E
Pacific Ocean (EN)=Pacífico, Océano- ▩	3	Ki	5.00N	155.00W
Pacific Ocean (EN)=Pacifique, Océan- ▩	3	Ki	5.00N	155.00W
Pacific Ocean (EN)=Taiheiyō ▩	3	Ki	5.00N	155.00W
Pacific Ocean (EN)=Tihi Okean ▩	3	Ki	5.00N	155.00W
Pacific Ranges ⛰	42	Ef	50.55N	125.10W
Pacifique, Océan-=Pacific Ocean (EN) ▩	3	Ki	5.00N	155.00W
Packsattel ⋎	14	Id	46.58N	14.58 E
Pacuí, Rio- ∿	55	Jc	16.46S	45.01W
Pacuneiro, Rio- ∿	55	Fa	13.02S	53.25W
Pacy-sur-Eure	12	De	49.01N	1.23 E
Paczków	10	Mf	50.27N	17.00 E
Padana, Pianura-=Po Valley (EN) ▁	5	Gf	45.20N	10.00 E
Padang	22	Mj	0.57S	100.21 E
Padangsidempuan	26	Cf	1.22N	99.16 E
Padangtikar, Pulau- ◆	26	Eg	0.50S	109.30 E
Padany	7	He	63.19N	33.25 E
Padasjoki	8	Kc	61.21N	25.17 E
Padauiri, Rio- ∿	54	Fd	0.15S	64.05W
Paddle Prairie	42	Fe	58.02N	117.50W
Paderborn	10	Ee	51.43N	8.46 E
Paderborn-Elsen	12	Kc	51.44N	8.41 E
Paderborn-Schloß Neuhaus	12	Kc	51.44N	8.42 E
Padeş, Vîrful- ▲	15	Fd	45.40N	22.20 E
Padilla	54	Fg	19.19S	64.20W
Padina	15	Ke	44.50N	27.07 E
Padornelo, Portillo del- ⋎	13	Fb	42.03N	6.50W
Padova = Padua (EN)	14	Fe	45.25N	11.53 E
Padre, Morro do- ▲	55	Ic	16.48S	47.35W
Padre Bernardo	55	Hb	15.21S	48.30W
Padre Island ◆	43	Hf	27.00N	97.15W
Padrón	13	Db	42.44N	8.40W
Padua (EN) = Padova	14	Fe	45.25N	11.53 E
Paducah [Ky.-U.S.]	39	Kf	37.05N	88.36W
Paducah [Tx.-U.S.]	45	Fi	34.01N	100.18W
Padula	14	Jj	40.20N	15.39 E
Paea	65e	Fc	17.41S	149.35W
Paegam-san ▲	28	Id	40.35N	126.15 E
Paengnyong-Do ◆	27	Ld	38.00N	124.40 E
Paeroa	61	Eg	37.23S	175.41 E
Paestum	14	Jj	40.25N	15.01 E
Paeu	63c	Bb	11.22S	166.50 E
Pafuri	37	Ed	22.26S	31.20 E
Pag	14	Jf	44.27N	15.03 E
Pag ◆	14	If	44.30N	15.00 E
Pagadian	26	He	7.49N	123.25 E
Pagai, Kepulauan-=Pagi Islands (EN) ⁂	21	Lj	2.45S	100.00 E
Pagai Selatan ◆	26	Dg	3.00S	100.20 E
Pagai Utara ◆	26	Cg	2.42S	100.07 E
Pagan Island ◆	57	Fc	18.07N	145.46 E
Pagasitikós Kólpos ◐	15	Fj	39.15N	23.00 E
Pagatan	26	Gg	3.36S	115.56 E
Pagat Point ►	64c	Bb	13.30N	144.53 E
Page	46	Jh	36.57N	111.27W
Pagėgiai	8	Ii	55.09N	21.54 E
Paget, Mount- ▲	66	Ad	54.26S	36.33W
Pagi Islands (EN)=Pagai, Kepulauan- ⁂	21	Lj	2.45S	100.00 E
Paglia ∿	14	Gh	42.42N	12.11 E
Pago Bay ◐	64c	Bb	13.25N	144.48 E
Pagoda Point ►	21	Lh	15.57N	94.15 E
Pāgodār	24	Qh	28.10N	57.22 E
Pago Pago	58	Jf	14.16S	170.42W
Pago Pago Harbor ⊜	65c	Cb	14.17S	170.40W
Pago Redondo	55	Ci	29.35S	59.13W
Pagosa Springs	45	Ch	37.16N	107.01W
Pagoua Bay ◐	51g	Ba	15.32N	61.17W
Pagwa River	45	Na	50.01N	85.10W
Pahači	20	Ld	60.30N	169.00 E
Pahala	65a	Fd	19.12N	155.29W
Pàhara, Laguna- ⊜	49	Ff	14.18N	83.15W
Pahiatua	62	Fd	40.27S	175.50 E
Pahkāing Bum ⛰	21	Lg	26.00N	95.30 E
Pahoa	65a	Gd	19.30N	154.57W
Pahokee	44	Gl	26.49N	80.40W
Pahtakor	18	Fd	40.16N	67.55 E
Pahute Mesa ⛰	46	Gh	37.20N	116.40W
Païa	63b	Dc	16.35S	168.12 E
Paide/Pajde	7	Fg	58.57N	25.35 E
Paignton	9	Jk	50.28N	3.30W
Päijänne ◍	5	Ic	61.35N	23.30 E
Páïkon Óros ▲	15	Fi	40.56N	22.21 E
Paila	48	He	25.39N	102.07W
Pailîn	25	Kf	12.51N	102.36 E
Pailitas	49	Ki	8.58N	73.38W
Pailolo Channel ⫼	65a	Eb	21.05N	156.42W
Paimio/Pemar	8	Jd	60.27N	22.42 E
Paimionjoki ∿	8	Jd	60.25N	22.40 E
Paimpol	11	Cf	48.46N	3.03W
Painan	26	Dg	1.21S	100.34 E
Paine, Mount- ▲	66	Mg	86.46S	147.32W
Painel	55	Gh	27.55S	50.06W
Painesville	44	Ge	41.43N	81.15W
Painted Desert ∴	43	Ed	36.00N	111.20W
Paintsville	44	Fg	37.49N	82.48W
País do Vinho ⧗	13	Ec	41.15N	7.55W
Paisley	9	If	55.50N	4.26W
Paita	54	Be	5.06S	81.07W
Païta	63b	Cf	22.08S	166.22 E
Paiva ∿	13	Dc	41.04N	8.16W
Paj	7	If	61.43N	34.28 E
Pajala	7	Fc	67.12N	23.22 E
Pajares, Puerto de- ⋎	13	Ga	43.00N	5.46W
Pajaros, Punta- ►	48	Ph	19.36N	87.25W
Pajaros Point ►	51a	Db	18.31N	64.18W
Pajatén ⌂	54	Ce	7.29S	77.22W
Pajde/Paide	7	Fg	58.57N	25.35 E
Pajęczno	10	Oe	51.09N	19.00 E
Pajer, Gora- ▲	19	Gb	66.40N	64.20 E
Paj-Hoj ⛰	5	Mb	69.00N	62.30 E
Pajule	36	Fb	2.58N	32.56 E
Pakanbaru	22	Mi	0.32N	101.27 E
Pakaraima Mountains ⛰	54	Fb	4.05N	61.30W
Pakch'on	28	He	39.44N	125.35 E
Pakhiá ◆	15	Im	36.16N	25.50 E
Pakhna	24	Ee	34.46N	32.48 E
Pákhnes ▲	15	Gn	35.18N	23.58 E
Paki	34	Gc	11.30N	8.09 E
Pakima	36	Dc	3.21S	24.06 E
Pakin Atoll ◎	57	Gd	7.04N	157.48 E
Pakistan [1]	22	Ig	30.00N	70.00 E
Pakleni Otoci ⁂	14	Kg	43.10N	16.23 E
Pakokku	25	Jd	21.17N	95.06 E
Pakowki Lake ◍	46	Jb	49.22N	110.57W
Pak Phanang	25	Kg	8.21N	100.12 E
Pakrac	14	Le	45.26N	17.12 E
Pakruois/Pakruojis	7	Fi	55.57N	23.50 E
Pakruojis/Pakruois	7	Fi	55.57N	23.50 E
Paks	10	Oj	46.38N	18.52 E
Paktīā [3]	23	Kc	33.30N	69.30 E
Pakwach	36	Fb	2.28N	31.30 E
Pakxé	22	Mh	15.07N	105.47 E
Pakxèng	25	Kd	20.10N	102.40 E
Pala	35	Ad	9.22N	14.54 E
Palacca Point ►	49	Kc	21.15N	73.26W
Palacios [Arg.]	55	Bj	30.43S	61.37W
Palacios [Tx.-U.S.]	45	Hl	28.42N	96.13W
Palafrugell	13	Pc	41.55N	3.10 E
Palagruža ◆	14	Kh	42.24N	16.15 E
Palaiokastrítsa ⌂	15	Cj	39.40N	19.41 E
Palaiokhóra	15	Gn	35.14N	23.41 E
Palaiseau	12	Ef	48.43N	2.15 E
Palamás	15	Fj	39.28N	22.05 E
Palamós	13	Pc	41.51N	3.08 E
Palamuse/Palamuze	8	Lf	58.39N	26.35 E
Palamut	15	Kk	38.59N	27.41 E
Palamuze/Palamuse	8	Lf	58.39N	26.35 E
Palana	22	Rd	59.07N	159.58 E
Palancia ∿	13	Le	39.40N	0.12W
Palanga	19	Cd	55.57N	21.05 E
Palangkaraya	26	Fg	2.16S	113.56 E
Pālanpur	25	Ed	24.10N	72.26 E

Index Symbols

[1] Independent Nation
[2] State, Region
[3] District, County
[4] Municipality
[5] Colony, Dependency
■ Continent
⧗ Physical Region
▭ Historical or Cultural Region
▲ Mount, Mountain
🌋 Volcano
⌒ Hill
⛰ Mountains, Mountain Range
⩚ Hills, Escarpment
⊼ Plateau, Upland
⋎ Pass, Gap
▁ Plain, Lowland
◣ Delta
▤ Salt Flat
⩔ Valley, Canyon
◡ Crater, Cave
✺ Karst Features
▽ Depression
▦ Polder
∴ Desert, Dunes
🌲 Forest, Woods
⩫ Heath, Steppe
🌴 Oasis
► Cape, Point
⌇ Coast, Beach
◧ Cliff
⊏ Peninsula
⋈ Isthmus
⋯ Sandbank
◆ Island
◎ Atoll
✳ Rock, Reef
⁂ Islands, Archipelago
✴ Rocks, Reefs
❋ Coral Reef
⊙ Well, Spring
⛲ Geyser
∿ River, Stream
⫽ Waterfall Rapids
⋔ River Mouth, Estuary
◍ Lake
⊚ Salt Lake
◌ Intermittent Lake
⊡ Reservoir
≋ Swamp, Pond
═ Canal
❄ Glacier
⧆ Ice Shelf, Pack Ice
▩ Ocean
▨ Sea
◐ Gulf, Bay
⫼ Strait, Fjord
⊜ Lagoon
▬ Bank
⩙ Seamount
⊓ Tablemount
⋀ Ridge
⌐ Shelf
⌣ Basin
⌌ Escarpment, Sea Scarp
⚡ Fracture
⋓ Trench, Abyss
♣ National Park, Reserve
★ Point of Interest
☼ Recreation Site
⌓ Cave, Cavern
⛫ Historic Site
⌂ Ruins
▥ Wall, Walls
✝ Church, Abbey
⛩ Temple
⚗ Scientific Station
✈ Airport
⚓ Port
⛯ Lighthouse
⚒ Mine
⋂ Tunnel
⌿ Dam, Bridge

Palaoa Point 65a Ec 20.44N 156.58W
Palapye 31 Jk 22.33S 27.08 E
Palasa 26 Hf 0.29N 120.24 E
Palatka [Fl.-U.S.] 43 Kf 29.39N 81.38W
Palatka 20 Kd 60.05N 151.00 E
Palau (EN) = Belau 58 Ed 7.30N 134.30 E
Palau [5] 58 Ed 7.30N 134.30 E
Palau Islands 57 Ed 7.30N 134.30 E
Palauli 65c Aa 13.44S 172.16W
Palauli Bay 65c Aa 13.47S 172.14W
Palau Trench (EN) 60 Af 6.30N 134.30 E
Palavas-les-Flots 11 Jk 43.32N 3.56 E
Palaw 25 Jf 12.58N 98.39 E
Palawan 21 Ni 9.30N 118.30 E
Palawan Passage 26 Gd 10.00N 118.00 E
Palayan 26 Hc 15.33N 121.06 E
Pālayankottai 25 Fg 8.43N 77.44 E
Palazzo, Punta- 11a Aa 42.22N 8.33 E
Palazzolo Acreide 14 Im 37.04N 14.54 E
Palazzolo sull'Oglio 14 De 45.36N 9.53 E
Paldiski 19 Cd 59.20N 24.06 E
Pale di San Martino 14 Fd 46.14N 11.53 E
Paleleh 26 Hf 1.04N 121.57 E
Palembang 22 Mj 2.55S 104.45 E
Palena 14 Ii 41.59N 14.08 E
Palencia [3] 13 Hb 42.25N 4.30W
Palencia 13 Hb 42.01N 4.32W
Palen Lake 46 Hj 33.46N 115.12W
Palenque 39 Jh 17.30N 92.00W
Palenque [Mex.] 48 Ni 17.31N 91.58W
Palenque [Pan.] 49 Hi 9.13N 79.41W
Palenque, Punta- 49 Ld 18.14N 70.09W
Palermo 6 Hh 38.07N 13.22 E
Palermo, Golfo di- 14 Hl 38.10N 13.25 E
Palestine 43 He 31.46N 95.38W
Palestine (EN) 23 Dc 32.15N 34.47 E
Palestrina 14 Gi 41.50N 12.53 E
Pālghāt 25 Ff 10.47N 76.39 E
Palgrave Point 37 Ad 20.28S 13.16 E
Palhoça 55 Hh 27.38S 48.40W
Pāli 25 Ec 25.46N 73.20 E
Palinuro 14 Jj 40.02N 15.17 E
Palinuro, Capo- 14 Jj 40.02N 15.16 E
Palisades Reservoir 46 Je 43.04N 111.26W
Paliseul 12 He 49.54N 5.08 E
Palivere 8 Jf 59.00N 23.45 E
Palizada 48 Mh 18.15N 92.05W
Paljakka 7 Gd 64.45N 28.07 E
Paljavaam 20 Mc 68.50N 170.50 E
Paljenik 5 Hg 44.15N 17.36 E
Pälkäne 8 Kc 61.20N 24.16 E
Palkino 8 Mg 57.29N 28.10 E
Palk Strait 21 Ji 10.00N 79.45 E
Palla Bianca/Weißkugel 14 Ed 46.48N 10.44 E
Pallars 13 Mb 42.25N 0.55 E
Pallars, Montsent de-/Montseny 13 Nb 42.29N 1.02 E
Pallasovka 19 Ee 50.03N 46.55 E
Pallastunturi 7 Fb 68.06N 24.02 E
Palliser, Cape- 61 Eh 41.37S 175.16 E
Palliser, Iles- 57 Mf 15.30S 146.30W
Palma [Moz.] 37 Gb 10.46S 40.28 E
Palma [Sp.] 6 Gh 39.34N 2.39 E
Palma, Badia de-/Palma, Bahia de- 13 Oe 39.27N 2.35 E
Palma, Bahia de-/Palma, Badia de- 13 Oe 39.27N 2.35 E
Palma, Rio- 54 If 12.33S 47.52W
Palma, Sierra de la- 48 Id 26.00N 101.35W
Palma del Rio 13 Gg 37.42N 5.17W
Palma di Montechiaro 14 Hm 37.11N 13.46 E
Palmar, Laguna del- 55 Bi 29.35S 60.42W
Palmar, Rio- 49 Lh 10.11N 71.52W
Palmar, Salto- 55 Cg 24.18S 59.18W
Palmares 54 Ke 8.41S 35.36W
Palmares do Sul 55 Gj 30.16S 50.31W
Palmarito 54 Db 7.37N 70.10W
Palmarola 14 Gj 40.55N 12.50 E
Palmar Sur 47 Hg 8.58N 83.29W
Palmas 56 Jc 26.30S 52.00W
Palmas, Cape- 30 Gh 4.22N 7.44W
Palmas, Golfo di- 14 Cl 39.00N 8.30 E
Palmas Bellas 49 Gi 9.14N 80.05W
Palma Soriano 47 Id 20.13N 76.00W
Palm Bay 44 Gk 28.01N 80.35W
Palm Beach 43 Kf 26.42N 80.02W
Palmdale 46 Fi 34.35N 118.07W
Palmeira 55 Gg 25.25S 50.00W
Palmeira das Missões 56 Jc 27.55S 53.17W
Palmeira dos Indios 54 Ke 9.25S 36.37W
Palmeirais 54 Je 5.58S 43.04W
Palmeiras, Rio- 55 Gb 15.25S 51.10W
Palmeiras de Goiás 55 Hc 16.47S 49.53W
Palmeirinhas, Ponta das- 30 Ii 9.05S 13.00 E
Palmela 13 Df 38.34N 8.54W
Palmer 40 Jd 61.36N 149.07W
Palmer Archipelago 66 Qe 64.10S 62.00W
Palmer Land (EN) 66 Qf 71.30S 65.00W
Palmer Station 66 Qe 64.46S 64.05W
Palmerston 62 Df 45.29S 170.43 E
Palmerston Atoll 57 Kf 18.04S 163.10W
Palmerston North 58 Ii 40.28S 175.17 E
Palmetto Point 51d Ba 17.35N 61.52W
Palmi 14 Jl 38.21N 15.51 E
Palmira [Col.] 53 Ie 3.32N 76.16W
Palmira [Cuba] 49 Gb 22.14N 80.23W
Palm Islands 59 Jc 18.40S 146.30 E
Palmital 55 Fg 24.39S 52.16W
Palmitas 55 Dk 33.27S 57.48W
Palmito 55 Cd 18.53S 58.22W
Palmitos 55 Fh 27.05S 53.08W
Palm Springs 43 De 33.50N 116.33W
Palmyra 23 Ec 34.33N 38.17 E
Palmyra Atoll 57 Kd 5.52N 162.06W
Palo Alto 43 Cd 37.27N 122.09W
Paloh 26 Ef 1.43N 109.18 E
Paloich 35 Ec 10.28N 32.32 E
Palomani, Nevado- 52 Jg 14.38S 69.14W
Palomar Mountain 43 De 33.22N 116.50W
Palomera, Sierra- 13 Kd 40.40N 1.12W
Palopo 22 Oj 3.00S 120.12 E
Palos, Cabo de- 5 Fh 37.38N 0.41W
Palo Santo 55 Cg 25.34S 59.21W
Palotina 55 Fg 24.17S 53.50W
Palouse River 46 Fc 46.35N 118.13W
Palpa 54 Cf 14.32S 75.11W
Palsa 8 Lg 57.23N 26.24 E
Pålsboda 8 Fe 59.04N 15.20 E
Paltamo 7 Gd 64.25N 27.50 E
Palu [Indon.] 22 Nj 0.53S 119.53 E
Palu [Tur.] 24 Hc 38.42N 39.57 E
Palu, Pulau- 26 Hh 8.20S 121.43 E
Pam 63b Be 20.15S 164.17 E
Pama 34 Fc 11.15N 0.42 E
Påmark/Pomarkku 8 Ic 61.42N 22.00 E
Pambarra 37 Fd 21.56S 35.06 E
Pambeguwa 34 Gc 10.40N 8.17 E
Pamekasan 26 Fh 7.10S 113.28 E
Pamiers 11 Hk 43.07N 1.36 E
Pamir 21 Jf 38.00N 73.00 E
Pamir 19 Hh 37.01N 72.41 E
Påmiut/Frederikshåb 41 Hf 62.00N 49.45W
Pamlico Sound 43 Ld 35.20N 75.55W
Pampa 43 Gd 35.32N 100.58W
Pampa del Indio 55 Ch 26.02S 59.55W
Pampa del Infierno 55 Bh 26.31S 61.10W
Pampa de los Guanacos 56 Hc 26.14S 61.51W
Pampas 54 Df 12.24S 74.54W
Pampas 52 Ji 35.00S 63.00W
Pampeiro 55 Ej 30.38S 55.16W
Pamplona [Col.] 54 Db 7.23N 72.38W
Pamplona [Sp.] 6 Fg 42.49N 1.38W
Pamukkale 15 Ml 37.47N 29.04 E
Pamukova 15 Ni 40.31N 30.09 E
Pamunkey River 44 Ig 37.32N 76.48W
Pan, Tierra del- 13 Gc 41.50N 6.00W
Pana 36 Bc 1.41S 12.39 E
Panagjurište 15 Hg 42.30N 24.11 E
Panaitan, Pulau- 26 Eh 6.36S 105.12 E
Panaitolikón Óros 15 Ek 38.43N 21.39 E
Panaji (Panjim) 22 Jh 15.29N 73.50 E
Panakhaikón Óros 15 Ek 38.12N 21.54 E
Panamá [1] 39 Li 9.00N 80.00W
Panamá = Panama (EN) [3] 49 Hi 9.00N 79.00W
Panamá = Panama City (EN) 39 Li 8.58N 79.31W
Panama (EN) = Panamá [3] 49 Hi 9.00N 79.00W
Panamá, Bahia de- 49 Hi 8.50N 79.15W
Panamá, Canal de- = Panama Canal (EN) 47 Ig 9.20N 79.55W
Panamá, Golfo de- = Panama, Gulf of- (EN) 38 Li 8.00N 79.10W
Panama, Gulf of- (EN) = Panamá, Golfo de- 38 Li 8.00N 79.10W
Panama, Isthmus of- (EN) = Panamá, Istmo de- 38 Li 9.20N 79.30W
Panamá, Istmo de- = Panama, Isthmus of- (EN) 38 Li 9.20N 79.30W
Panama Canal (EN) = Panamá, Canal de- 47 Ig 9.20N 79.55W
Panama City [La.-U.S.] 39 Kf 30.10N 85.41W
Panama City (EN) = Panamá 39 Li 8.58N 79.31W
Panamá La Vieja 49 Hi 9.00N 79.29W
Panambi 55 Fi 28.18S 53.30W
Panamint Range 46 Gh 36.30N 117.20W
Panao 54 Ce 9.49S 76.00W
Panarea 14 Jl 38.40N 15.05 E
Panaro 14 Ff 44.55N 11.25 E
Pana Tinai 63a Ad 11.14S 153.10 E
Pana-Wina 63a Ad 11.11S 153.01 E
Panay 21 Oh 11.15N 122.30 E
Pancake Range 46 Hg 39.00N 115.45W
Pančevo 15 De 44.52N 20.39 E
Pančićev vrh 15 Df 43.15N 20.45 E
Panciu 15 Kd 45.54N 27.05 E
Pancros 63b Db 15.58S 168.12 E
Panda 37 Ed 24.03S 34.43 E
Panda ma Tenga 37 Dc 18.32S 25.38 E
Pandan 26 Hd 11.43N 122.06 E
Pan de Azúcar 55 El 34.48S 55.14W
Pandeiros, Ribeirão- 55 Jb 15.42S 44.36W
Pandelis/Pandélys 8 Kh 56.01N 25.21 E
Pandélys/Pandelis 8 Kh 56.01N 25.21 E
Pandharpur 25 Fe 17.40N 75.20 E
Pändheon 15 Fi 40.05N 22.20 E
Pändhurna 25 Fd 21.36N 78.31 E
Pandivere Kõrgustik/Pandivere Vozvyšennost 8 Le 59.00N 26.15 E
Pandivere Vozvyšennost/Pandivere Kõrgustik 8 Le 59.00N 26.15 E
Pando 56 Id 34.43S 55.57W
Pando [2] 54 Ef 11.20S 67.40W
Pandokrátor 15 Cj 39.45N 19.52 E
Pandora 49 Fi 9.45N 82.57W
Pandrup 8 Cg 57.14N 9.41 E
Pandu 36 Cb 4.59N 19.16 E
Panevežis/Panevėžys 19 Cd 55.44N 24.22 E
Panevėžys/Panevežis 19 Cd 55.44N 24.22 E
Panfilov 19 Ig 44.08N 80.01 E
Panga 36 Eb 1.51N 26.25 E
Pangai 65b Ba 19.48S 174.21W
Pangaion Óros 15 Hi 40.50N 24.05 E
Pangalanes, Canal de- 30 Lk 22.48S 47.50 E
Pangani 36 Gd 5.26S 38.58 E
Pangani or Ruvu 36 Gc 5.26S 38.58 E
Pange 12 Ie 49.05N 6.22 E
Panggoe 58 Ge 7.01S 157.05 E
Pangi 36 Ec 3.11S 26.38 E
Pangkajene 26 Gg 4.50S 119.32 E
Pangkalanberandan 26 Cf 4.01N 98.17 E
Pangkalanbuun 26 Fg 2.41S 111.37 E
Pangkalasiang, Tanjung- 26 Hg 0.42S 123.26 E
Pangkalpinang 26 Eg 2.08S 106.08 E
Pangnirtung 39 Mc 66.08N 65.44W
Pang-Pang 63b Dc 17.41S 168.32 E
Panguitch 43 Ed 37.49N 112.26W
Panguma 34 Cd 8.24N 11.13W
Pangutaran Group 26 He 6.15N 120.30 E
Panhandle 45 Fi 35.21N 101.23W
Pania Mutombo 36 Dd 5.11S 23.51 E
Paniau 65a Ab 21.57N 160.05W
Panié, Mont- 61 Bd 20.36S 164.46 E
Pānīpat 25 Fc 29.23N 76.58 E
Paniza, Puerto de- 13 Kc 41.15N 1.20W
Panjang 26 Eh 5.29S 105.18 E
Panjang, Pulau- 26 Ef 2.44N 108.55 E
Panjgūr 25 Cc 26.58N 64.06 E
Panjim → Panaji 22 Jh 15.29N 73.50 E
Panjwin 24 Ke 35.36N 45.58 E
Pankow, Berlin- 10 Jd 52.34N 13.24 E
Pankshin 34 Gd 9.20N 9.27 E
P'anmunjŏm 28 If 37.57N 126.40 E
Panopah 26 Fg 1.56S 111.11 E
Panorama 56 Jb 21.21S 51.51W
Panshan 28 Gd 41.12N 122.03 E
Panshi 27 Mc 42.56N 126.02 E
Pant 12 Cc 51.53N 0.39 E
Pantanal 52 Kg 18.00S 56.00W
Pantar, Pulau- 26 Hh 8.25S 124.07 E
Pantego 44 Ih 35.34N 76.36W
Pantelleria 14 Fn 36.50N 11.57 E
Pantelleria 5 Hh 36.45N 12.00 E
Pantelleria, Canale di- 14 Fn 36.40N 11.45 E
Pante Makassar 26 Hh 9.12S 124.23 E
Pantoja 54 Cd 0.58S 75.10W
Pánuco 48 Jf 22.03N 98.10W
Pánuco 38 Jg 22.16N 97.47W
Panxian 27 Hf 25.45N 104.39 E
Panyam 34 Gd 9.25N 9.13 E
Panzi 36 Cd 7.13S 17.58 E
Panzós 49 Cf 15.24N 89.40W
Pao, Rio- [Ven.] 50 Bh 8.33N 68.01W
Pao, Rio- [Ven.] 50 Dh 8.06N 64.17W
Paola [It.] 14 Kk 39.21N 16.03 E
Paola [Ks.-U.S.] 45 Ig 38.35N 94.53W
Paoli 44 Df 38.33N 86.28W
Paopao 65e Fc 17.30S 149.49W
Paoua 35 Bd 7.15N 16.26 E
Pápa 10 Ni 47.20N 17.28 E
Papa 65a Fd 19.13N 155.52W
Papaaloa 65a Fd 19.59N 155.13W
Papagaios 55 Jd 19.32S 44.45W
Papagayo, Golfo del- 47 Gf 10.45N 85.45W
Papaikou 65a Fd 19.47N 155.06W
Papakura 62 Fb 37.03S 174.57 E
Papaloapan, Rio- 48 Lh 18.42N 95.38W
Papanduva 55 Gh 26.25S 50.09W
Papangpanjang 26 Dg 0.27S 100.25 E
Papantla de Olarte 47 Ed 20.27N 97.19W
Papar 26 Ge 5.44N 115.56 E
Paparoa Range 62 De 42.05S 171.35 E
Papa Stour 9 La 60.30N 1.40W
Papa Westray 9 Kb 59.22N 2.54W
Papeete 58 Mf 17.32S 149.34W
Papenburg 10 Dc 53.04N 7.24 E
Papenburg-Aschendorf (Ems) 12 Ja 53.04N 7.22 E
Papenoo 65e Fc 17.30S 149.25W
Papes Ezers/Papes Ozero 8 Ih 56.15N 20.55 E
Papes Ozero/Papes Ezers 8 Ih 56.15N 20.55 E
Papetoai 65e Fc 17.30S 149.52W
Papey 7a Cb 64.36N 14.11W
Paphos/Baf 24 Ee 34.50N 32.35 E
Papija 15 Kg 42.07N 27.51 E
Papikion Óros 15 Ih 41.15N 25.18 E
Papilé/Pupile 8 Jh 56.09N 22.45 E
Papile/Papilé 8 Jh 56.09N 22.45 E
Papillion 45 Hf 41.09N 96.03W
Papua, Gulf of- 57 Fe 8.32S 145.00 E
Papua New Guinea [1] 58 Fe 6.00S 150.00 E
Papua Passage 64p Bc 21.15S 159.47W
Papuk 14 Le 45.31N 17.39 E
Papun 25 Je 18.04N 97.27 E
Para 7 Ji 54.23N 40.53 E
Pará [2] 54 Hd 4.00S 53.00W
Pará, Rio- 55 Jd 19.13S 45.07W
Para, Rio- 52 Lf 1.30S 48.55W
Parabel 20 De 58.40N 81.30 E
Parabel 20 De 58.43N 81.31 E
Paraburdoo 59 Dd 23.15S 117.45 E
Paracas 54 Cf 13.49S 76.16W
Paracatu 54 Ig 17.13S 46.52W
Paracatu, Rio- [Braz.] 55 Ic 17.30S 46.32W
Paracatu, Rio- [Braz.] 55 Jc 16.30S 45.04W
Paracel Islands (EN) = Xisha Qundao 21 Nh 16.30N 112.15 E
Pārachinār 25 Eb 33.54N 70.06 E
Paraćin 15 Ef 43.52N 21.25 E
Paracuru 54 Kd 3.24S 39.04W
Parada Km 329 55 Ek 32.30S 55.25W
Paradip 25 Hd 20.19N 86.42 E
Paradise [Ca.-U.S.] 46 Eg 39.46N 121.37W
Paradise [Mi.-U.S.] 44 Eb 46.38N 85.03W
Paragould 45 Kh 36.03N 90.29W
Paragua, Rio- 54 Fb 6.55N 62.55W
Paraguá, Rio- 54 Ff 13.34S 61.53W
Paraguaçu, Rio- 52 Mg 12.45S 38.54W
Paraguaçu Paulista 55 Gf 22.25S 50.34W
Paraguai, Rio 52 Kh 27.18S 58.38W
Paraguaipoa 49 Lh 11.21N 71.57W
Paraguaná, Peninsula de 54 Da 11.55N 70.00W
Paraguari [3] 55 Dg 26.00S 57.10W
Paraguari 56 Ic 25.38S 57.09W
Paraguay [1] 53 Kh 23.00S 58.00W
Paraguay, Rio- 52 Kh 27.18S 58.38W
Paraiba [2] 54 Ke 7.10S 36.30W
Paraiba do Sul, Rio- 52 Lh 21.37S 41.03W
Paraibuna, Represa do- 55 Jf 23.25S 45.35W
Paraibuna, Rio- 55 Jf 23.22S 45.40W
Parainen/Pargas 7 Ff 60.18N 22.18 E
Paraiso [Braz.] 55 Fd 19.03S 52.59W
Paraiso [Mex.] 48 Mh 18.24N 93.14W
Paraiso, Rio- 55 Bb 15.08S 61.52W
Parakou 31 Hh 9.21N 2.37 E
Param 64d Bb 7.22N 151.48 E
Paramaribo 53 Ke 5.50N 55.10W
Paramera, Sierra de la- 13 Hd 40.30N 4.46W
Paramithiá 15 Dj 39.28N 20.31 E
Paramušir, Ostrov- 21 Rd 50.25N 155.50 E
Paraná 53 Ji 31.45S 60.30W
Paraná [2] 56 Jb 24.00S 51.00W
Paraná, Pico- 55 Hg 25.14S 48.48W
Paraná, Rio- 52 Ki 33.43S 59.15W
Paranã, Rio- 52 Lg 12.30S 48.14W
Paraná de las Palmas, Rio- 55 Cl 34.18S 58.33W
Paranaguá 53 Lh 25.31S 48.30W
Paraná-Guazú, Rio- 55 Ck 34.00S 58.25W
Paranaiba 54 Hg 19.40S 51.11W
Paranaiba, Rio- 52 Kh 20.07S 51.05W
Paranaiguara 55 Gd 18.53S 50.28W
Paranapanema, Rio- 52 Kh 22.40S 53.09W
Paranapiacaba, Serra do- 52 Lh 24.20S 49.00W
Paranapuã-Guaçu, Ponta do- 55 Ig 24.24S 47.00W
Paranavai 56 Jb 23.04S 52.28W
Parandak 24 Ne 35.21N 50.42 E
Paranéstion 15 Hh 41.16N 24.30 E
Paranhos 55 Ef 23.55S 55.25W
Paraoa Atoll 57 Mf 19.09S 140.43W
Paraopeba 55 Jd 19.18S 44.25W
Paraopeba, Rio- 55 Jd 18.50S 45.11W
Parapara 63b Ca 13.32S 167.20 E
Paraparaumu 62 Fd 40.55S 175.00 E
Paraspóri 15 Kn 35.54N 27.14 E
Parati 55 Jf 23.13S 44.43W
Paratodos, Serra- 55 Jb 14.40S 44.50W
Paratunka 20 Kf 52.52N 158.12 E
Pārău, Kūh-e- 24 Le 34.37N 47.05 E
Paraúna 55 Gc 17.02S 50.26W
Paravae 64n Bc 10.27S 160.58W
Paray-le-Monial 11 Kh 46.27N 4.07 E
Parbati 25 Fc 25.51N 76.36 E
Parbhani 25 Fe 19.16N 76.47 E
Parchim 10 Hc 53.26N 11.51 E
Parczew 10 Se 51.39N 22.54 E
Pardo 55 Cm 36.15S 59.22W
Pardo, Rio- [Braz.] 55 Fi 29.59S 52.23W
Pardo, Rio- [Braz.] 54 Hh 21.46S 52.09W
Pardo, Rio- [Braz.] 55 He 20.10S 48.38W
Pardo, Rio- [Braz.] 55 Hf 22.55S 49.58W
Pardo, Rio- [Braz.] 55 Jb 15.48S 44.48W
Pardo, Rio- [Braz.] 54 Kg 15.39S 38.57W
Pardubice 10 Lf 50.02N 15.45 E
Parea 65e Eb 16.49S 150.58W
Parecis, Chapada dos- 52 Kg 13.00S 60.00W
Parecis, Rio- 55 Da 12.56S 56.43W
Paredes de Nava 13 Hb 42.09N 4.41W
Parelhas 54 Ke 6.41S 36.39W
Paren 20 Ld 62.28N 163.05 E
Parent 42 Kg 47.55N 74.37W
Parentis-en-Born 11 Ej 44.21N 1.04W
Pareora 62 Df 44.29S 171.13 E
Parepare 22 Nj 4.01S 119.38 E
Párga 15 Dj 39.17N 20.24 E
Pargas/Parainen 7 Ff 60.18N 22.18 E
Pargolovo 8 Nd 60.03N 30.30 E
Parham 51d Bb 17.05N 61.46W
Parhar 19 Gh 37.31N 69.23 E
Pari, Rio- 55 Db 15.36S 56.08W
Paria, Golfo de-/Paria, Gulf of- 54 Fa 10.20N 62.00W
Paria, Gulf of-/Paria, Golfo de- 54 Fa 10.20N 62.00W
Paria, Peninsula de- 50 Eg 10.40N 62.30W
Pariaguán 54 Fb 8.51N 64.43W
Pariaman 26 Dg 0.38S 100.08 E
Paria River 46 Jh 36.52N 111.36W
Paricutin, Volcán- 48 Hh 19.28N 102.15W
Parida, Isla- 49 Fi 8.07N 82.20W
Pari das Pedras 55 Ja 12.45S 44.47W
Parigi 26 Hg 0.48S 120.10 E
Parika 54 Gb 6.52N 58.25W
Parikkala 7 Gf 61.33N 29.30 E
Parima, Serra- 52 Je 3.00N 64.20W
Parinacota 56 Ga 18.12S 69.16W
Pariñas, Punta- 52 Hf 4.40S 81.20W
Paringul Mare, Vîrful- 15 Gd 45.20N 23.30 E
Parintins 53 Kf 2.36S 56.44W
Paris [Fr.] 6 Gf 48.52N 2.20 E
Paris [Il.-U.S.] 45 Mg 39.36N 87.42W
Paris [Kir.] 64g Ab 1.56N 157.31W
Paris [Ky.-U.S.] 44 Ef 38.13N 84.14W
Paris [Tn.-U.S.] 44 Cg 36.19N 88.20W
Paris [Tx.-U.S.] 43 He 33.40N 95.33W
Paris Basin (EN) = Parisien, Bassin- 5 Gf 49.00N 2.00 E
Parisien, Bassin- = Paris Basin (EN) 5 Gf 49.00N 2.00 E
Parita 49 Gi 8.00N 80.31W
Parita, Bahia de- 49 Gi 8.08N 80.24W
Parit Buntar 26 De 5.07N 100.30 E
Parkano 7 Fe 62.01N 23.01 E
Parkent 18 Gd 41.18N 69.40 E
Parker 46 Hi 34.09N 114.17W
Parker, Mount- 59 Fc 17.10S 128.20 E
Parkersburg 43 Kd 39.17N 81.33W
Parker Seamount (EN) 40 If 52.35N 151.15W
Parkes 58 Fh 33.08S 148.11 E
Park Falls 45 Kd 45.56N 90.32W
Parkland 46 Dc 47.09N 122.26W
Park Range 43 Fc 40.00N 106.30W
Park Rapids 45 Ic 46.55N 95.04W
Park River 45 Hb 48.24N 97.45W
Park Valley 46 If 41.50N 113.21W
Parma 14 Ef 44.56N 10.26 E
Parma [It.] 6 Hg 44.48N 10.20 E
Parma [Oh.-U.S.] 44 Ge 41.24N 81.44W
Parnaguá 54 Jf 10.13S 44.38W
Parnaiba 53 Lf 2.54S 41.47W
Parnaiba, Rio- 52 Lf 3.00S 41.50W
Parnamirim [Braz.] 54 Ke 8.05S 39.34W
Parnamirim [Braz.] 54 Ke 5.55S 35.15W
Parnarama 54 Je 5.41S 43.06W
Parnassós Óros = Parnassus (EN) 5 Ih 38.30N 22.37 E
Parnassus 62 Ee 42.43S 173.17 E
Parnassus (EN) = Parnassós Óros 5 Ih 38.30N 22.37 E
Párnis Óros 15 Gk 38.10N 23.40 E
Párnon Óros 15 Fl 37.12N 22.38 E
Pärnu/Pjarnu 6 Id 58.24N 24.32 E
Pärnu-Jaagupi/Pjarnu-Jagupi 8 Kf 58.36N 24.25 E
Pärnu Jõgi/Pjarnu 7 Fg 58.23N 24.34 E
Pärnu Laht/Pjarnu, Zaliv- 7 Fg 58.15N 24.25 E
Parola 8 Kc 61.03N 24.22 E
Paroo River 57 Fh 31.28S 143.32 E
Paropamisus/Salseleh-ye Safid Kūh 21 If 34.30N 63.30 E
Páros 15 Il 37.05N 25.09 E
Páros 15 Il 37.06N 25.12 E
Parowan 46 Ih 37.51N 112.57W
Parpaillon 11 Mj 44.35N 6.40 E
Parque Industrial 55 Jd 19.57S 44.01W
Parral 56 Fe 36.09S 71.50W
Parral, Rio- 48 Gd 27.35N 105.25W
Parras, Sierra de- 48 He 25.25N 102.00W
Parras de la Fuente 47 Dc 25.25N 102.11W
Parravicini 55 Dm 36.27S 57.46W
Parrett 9 Jj 51.13N 3.01W
Parrita 49 Ei 9.30N 84.19W
Parry, Cape- 42 Fb 70.12N 124.35W
Parry, Kap- [Grld.] 41 Jd 72.28N 22.00W
Parry, Kap- [Grld.] 41 Ec 77.00N 71.00W
Parry Bay 42 Jc 68.00N 82.00W
Parry Islands 38 Ib 76.00N 110.00W
Parry Peninsula 42 Fc 69.45N 124.35W
Parry Sound 42 Jg 45.21N 80.02W
Parsęta 10 Lb 54.12N 15.33 E
Parsons [Ks.-U.S.] 43 Hd 37.20N 95.16W
Parsons [W.V.-U.S.] 44 Hf 39.06N 79.43W
Parsons Range 59 Hb 13.30S 135.15 E
Partanna 14 Gm 37.43N 12.53 E
Parthenay 11 Fh 46.39N 0.15W
Partille 8 Eg 57.44N 12.07 E
Partinico 14 Hl 38.03N 13.07 E
Partizansk 20 Ih 43.13N 133.05 E
Partizánske 10 Oh 48.38N 18.23 E
Partizanskoje 20 Ee 55.30N 94.30 E
Paru, Rio- 52 Kf 1.33S 52.38W
Paru de Este, Rio- 54 Hc 1.10N 54.40W
Paru de Oeste, Rio- 52 Kf 1.30S 56.00W
Paruru 63a Ec 9.51S 160.49 E
Parvān [3] 23 Kb 35.15N 69.30 E
Pârvomaj 15 Ig 42.06N 25.13 E
Parys 37 De 27.04S 27.16 E
Paša 7 Hf 60.28N 32.55 E
Pasadena [Ca.-U.S.] 39 Hf 34.09N 118.09W
Pasadena [Tx.-U.S.] 45 Il 29.42N 95.13W
Paşaeli Yarimadası 15 Lh 41.20N 28.25 E
Paşalimani Adası 15 Ki 40.28N 27.37 E
Pasangkaju 26 Gg 1.10S 119.20 E
Păsărgād 24 Og 30.17N 52.55 E
Pasarwajo 26 Hh 5.29S 122.50 E
Pascagoula 43 Je 30.23N 88.31W
Paşcani 15 Jb 47.15N 26.44 E
Pasco 43 Db 46.14N 119.06W
Pasco [2] 54 Cf 10.30S 75.15W
Pascoal 55 Ba 13.38S 61.06W
Pascoal, Monte- 54 Kg 16.54S 39.24W
Pascua, Isla de-/Rapa Nui = Easter Island (EN) 57 Qg 27.07S 109.22W
Pas-de-Calais [3] 11 Id 50.30N 2.20 E
Pas-en-Artois 12 Ed 50.09N 2.30 E
Pasewalk 10 Jc 53.31N 13.59 E
Pasinler 24 Ib 40.00N 41.41 E
Pašino 20 De 55.11N 83.02 E
Pasión, Rio de la- 49 Be 16.28N 90.33W
Pasir Mas 26 De 6.02N 102.08 E
Pasirpengarayan 26 Df 0.51N 100.16 E
Pasir Puteh 26 De 5.50N 102.24 E
Påskallavik 8 Gg 57.10N 16.27 E
Paškovski 16 Kg 45.01N 39.05 E
Pasłęk 10 Pb 54.05N 19.39 E
Pasłęka 10 Pb 54.25N 19.50 E
Pašman 14 Jg 43.57N 15.21 E
Pasni 22 Ig 25.16N 63.28 E
Paso de Indios 56 Gf 43.52S 69.06W
Paso del Cerro 55 Ej 31.31S 55.46W
Paso de los Libres 56 Ic 29.43S 57.05W
Paso de los Toros 56 Id 32.49S 56.31W
Paso Tranqueras 55 Ej 31.12S 55.45W
Passamaquoddy Bay 44 Nc 45.06N 66.59W
Passa Três, Serra- 55 Hb 14.40S 49.30W
Passau 10 Jh 48.35N 13.29 E
Passero, Capo- 14 Jn 36.40N 15.10 E
Passo Fundo 53 Kh 28.15S 52.24W
Passo Fundo, Rio- 55 Fh 27.16S 52.42W
Passos 54 Ig 20.43S 46.37W
Pastaza, Rio- 52 If 4.50S 76.25W
Pasteur 56 He 35.08S 62.14W
Pasto 53 Ie 1.13N 77.17W
Pastora Peak 46 Kh 36.47N 109.10W
Pastoria, Laguna de- 48 Ki 16.00N 97.40W
Pastos Bons 54 Je 6.36S 44.05W
Pastrana 13 Jd 40.25N 2.55W
Paštrik 15 Dg 42.14N 20.32 E
Pasubio 14 Fe 45.47N 11.10 E
Pasvalis/Pasvalys 7 Fh 56.02N 24.28 E
Pasvalys/Pasvalis 7 Fh 56.02N 24.28 E
Pásztó 10 Pi 47.55N 19.42 E

Index Symbols

[1] Independent Nation
[2] State, Region
[3] District, County
[4] Municipality
[5] Colony, Dependency
Continent
Physical Region
Historical or Cultural Region
Mount, Mountain
Volcano
Hill
Mountains, Mountain Range
Hills, Escarpment
Plateau, Upland
Pass, Gap
Plain, Lowland
Delta
Salt Flat
Valley, Canyon
Crater, Cave
Karst Features
Depression
Polder
Desert, Dunes
Forest, Woods
Heath, Steppe
Oasis
Cape, Point
Coast, Beach
Cliff
Peninsula
Isthmus
Sandbank
Island
Atoll
Rock, Reef
Islands, Archipelago
Rocks, Reefs
Coral Reef
Well, Spring
Geyser
River, Stream
Waterfall Rapids
River Mouth, Estuary
Lake
Salt Lake
Intermittent Lake
Reservoir
Swamp, Pond
Canal
Glacier
Ice Shelf, Pack Ice
Ocean
Sea
Gulf, Bay
Strait, Fjord
Lagoon
Bank
Seamount
Tablemount
Ridge
Shelf
Basin
Escarpment, Sea Scarp
Fracture
Trench, Abyss
National Park, Reserve
Point of Interest
Recreation Site
Cave, Cavern
Historic Site
Ruins
Wall, Walls
Church, Abbey
Temple
Scientific Station
Airport
Port
Lighthouse
Mine
Tunnel
Dam, Bridge

Index Symbols

- [1] Independent Nation
- [2] State, Region
- [3] District, County
- [4] Municipality
- [5] Colony, Dependency
- ■ Continent
- [X] Physical Region
- Historical or Cultural Region
- Mount, Mountain
- Volcano
- Hill
- Mountains, Mountain Range
- Hills, Escarpment
- Plateau, Upland
- Pass, Gap
- Plain, Lowland
- Polder
- Delta
- Salt Flat
- Valley, Canyon
- Crater, Cave
- Karst Features
- Depression
- Desert, Dunes
- Forest, Woods
- Heath, Steppe
- Oasis
- Cape, Point
- Coast, Beach
- Cliff
- Peninsula
- Isthmus
- Sandbank
- Island
- Atoll
- Rock, Reef
- Islands, Archipelago
- Rocks, Reefs
- Coral Reef
- Well, Spring
- Geyser
- River, Stream
- Waterfall Rapids
- River Mouth, Estuary
- Lake
- Salt Lake
- Intermittent Lake
- Reservoir
- Swamp, Pond
- Canal
- Glacier
- Ice Shelf, Pack Ice
- Ocean
- Sea
- Gulf, Bay
- Strait, Fjord
- Lagoon
- Bank
- Seamount
- Tablemount
- Ridge
- Shelf
- Basin
- Escarpment, Sea Scarp
- Fracture
- Trench, Abyss
- National Park, Reserve
- Point of Interest
- Recreation Site
- Cave, Cavern
- Historic Site
- Ruins
- Wall, Walls
- Church, Abbey
- Temple
- Scientific Station
- Airport
- Port
- Lighthouse
- Mine
- Tunnel
- Dam, Bridge

Pervari 24 Jd 37.54N 42.36 E
Pervomajsk 19 Ee 54.52N 43.48 E
Pervomajsk 16 Ke 48.36N 38.32 E
Pervomajsk 19 Df 48.03N 30.52 E
Pervomajski 10 Vc 53.52N 25.33 E
Pervomajski 19 Ie 50.15N 81.59 E
Pervomajski 16 Lc 53.18N 40.15 E
Pervomajski 19 Ec 64.26N 40.48 E
Pervomajski 17 Ji 54.52N 61.08 E
Pervomajski 16 Sd 51.34N 54.59 E
Pervomajski 16 Je 49.24N 36.15 E
Pervouralsk 19 Fd 57.00N 60.00 E
Pervy Kurilski Proliv 20 Kf 50.50N 156.50 E
Perwez/Perwijs 12 Gd 50.37N 4.49 E
Perwijs/Perwez 12 Gd 50.37N 4.49 E
Pes 7 Ig 59.10N 35.18 E
Peša 17 Cc 66.50N 47.32 E
Pesaro 14 Gg 43.54N 12.55 E
Pescadores (EN)=Penghu Liehtao 27 Kg 23.30N 119.30 E
Pescadores, Punta- 48 Ef 23.45N 109.45W
Pesčany, Mys- 16 Qh 43.10N 51.18 E
Pesčany, Ostrov 20 Gb 74.20N 115.55 E
Pescara 14 Ih 42.28N 14.13 E
Pescara 6 Hg 42.28N 14.13 E
Pescasseroli 14 Hi 41.48N 13.47 E
Peschici 14 Ki 41.57N 16.01 E
Pescia 14 Eg 43.54N 10.41 E
Pescocostanzo 14 Ii 41.53N 14.04 E
Peshāwar 22 Jf 34.01N 71.33 E
Peshkopia 15 Dh 41.41N 20.26 E
Pesio 14 Bf 44.28N 7.53 E
Peskovka 7 Mg 59.03N 52.22 E
Pesmes 11 Lg 47.17N 5.34 E
Pesočny 8 Nd 60.05N 30.20 E
Peso da Régua 13 Ec 41.10N 7.47W
Pesqueira 54 Ke 8.22S 36.42W
Pesqueria, Rio- 48 Je 25.54N 99.11W
Pessac 11 Fj 44.48N 0.37W
Pest [2] 10 Pi 47.25N 19.20 E
Pešter 15 Df 43.05N 20.02 E
Peštera 15 Hg 42.02N 24.18 E
Pestovo 19 Dd 58.36N 35.47 E
Petacalco, Bahia de- 47 De 17.57N 102.05W
Petaḥ Tiqwa 24 Ff 32.05N 34.53 E
Petäjävesi 8 Kb 62.15N 25.12 E
Petal 45 Lk 31.21N 89.17W
Petalioi 15 Hl 38.01N 24.17 E
Petalioi, Gulf of- (EN) = Petaliōn, Kólpos- 15 Hk 38.00N 24.05 E
Petaliōn, Kólpos- = Petalioi, Gulf of- (EN) 15 Hk 38.00N 24.05 E
Petaluma 46 Dg 38.14N 122.39W
Pétange/Petingen 12 He 49.33N 5.53 E
Petare 54 Ea 10.29N 66.49W
Petatlán 48 Ii 17.31N 101.16W
Petatlán, Rio- 48 Fd 26.09N 107.45W
Petauke 36 Fe 14.15S 31.20 E
Petén 47 Fe 16.15N 89.50W
Petén [3] 49 Be 16.50N 90.00W
Petén Itzá, Lago- 49 Ce 16.59N 89.50W
Petenwell Lake 45 Ld 44.05N 89.45W
Peterborough [Austl.] 59 Hf 32.58S 138.50 E
Peterborough [Eng.-U.K.] 9 Mi 52.35N 0.15W
Peterborough [Ont.-Can.] 42 Jh 44.18N 78.19W
Peterhead 9 Ld 57.30N 1.46W
Peter I, Oy- 66 Pe 68.47S 90.35W
Peter Island 51a Db 18.22N 64.35W
Peterlee 9 Lg 54.46N 1.19W
Petermann Gletscher 41 Fb 80.45N 61.00W
Petermann Ranges 59 Fd 25.00S 129.45 E
Petermanns Bjerg 67 Md 73.10N 28.00W
Peter Pond Lake 42 Ge 55.55N 108.40W
Petersberg 10 He 51.35N 11.57 E
Petersburg [Ak.-U.S.] 40 Me 56.49N 132.57W
Petersburg [In.-U.S.] 44 Df 38.30N 87.16W
Petersburg [Va.-U.S.] 43 Ld 37.14N 77.24W
Petersburg [W.V.-U.S.] 44 Hf 39.01N 79.09W
Petersfield 9 Mk 51.00N 0.56W
Petershagen 12 Kb 52.23N 8.58 E
Peter the Great Bay (EN)= Petra Velikogo, Zaliv- 21 Pe 42.40N 132.00 E
Petilia Policastro 14 Kk 39.07N 16.47 E
Petingen/Pétange 12 He 49.33N 5.53 E
Petit-Bourg 51eAb 16.12N 61.36W
Petit-Canal 51eBb 16.23N 61.29W
Petit Canouan 51nBb 12.47N 61.17W
Petit Cul-de-Sac Marin 51eAb 16.12N 61.33W
Petite Kabylie 13 Rh 36.35N 5.25 E
Petite Rivière de l'Artibonite 49 Kd 19.08N 72.29W
Petites Pyrénées 11 Hk 43.05N 1.10 E
Petite-Terre, Iles de la- 51eBb 16.10N 61.07W
Petit-Goâve 49 Kd 18.26N 72.52W
Petit Martinique Island 51p Ca 12.32N 61.22W
Petit-Mécatina, Rivière du- 42 Lf 50.39N 59.25W
Petit Morin 11 Jf 48.56N 3.07 E
Petit Mustique Island 51nBb 12.51N 61.13W
Petit Nevis Island 51nBb 12.58N 61.15W
Petitot 42 Fd 60.14N 123.29W
Petit Saint-Bernard, Col du- 14 Ae 45.40N 6.55 E
Petit Saint Vincent Island 51nBb 12.33N 61.23W
Petit Savanne 51gBb 15.15N 61.17W
Petitsikapau Lake 42 Kf 54.40N 66.25W
Petkula 7 Gc 67.40N 26.41 E
Petlalcingo 48 Kh 18.05N 97.54W
Peto 47 Gd 20.08N 88.55W
Petorca 56 Fd 32.15S 71.00W
Petoskey 44 Ec 45.22N 84.57W
Petra 24 Fg 30.19N 35.29 E
Petralia Soprana 14 Im 37.47N 14.06 E
Petra Pervogo, Hrebet- 18 He 39.00N 71.10 E
Petra Velikogo, Zaliv- = Peter the Great Bay (EN) 21 Pe 42.40N 132.00 E
Petre, Point- 44 Id 43.50N 77.09W
Petre Bay 62 Je 43.55S 176.40W
Petrel 66 Re 63.28S 56.17W
Petrela 15 Ch 41.15N 19.51 E
Petrella Tifernina 14 Ii 41.41N 14.42 E
Petrič 15 Gh 41.24N 23.13 E
Pétrie, Récif- 61 Bc 18.30S 164.20 E
Petrikov 16 Fc 52.08N 28.31 E
Petrila 15 Gd 45.27N 23.25 E
Petrinja 14 Ke 45.27N 16.17 E
Petrodvorec 7 Gg 59.53N 29.50 E
Petrólea 54 Db 8.30N 72.35W
Petrolia 44 Fd 42.52N 82.09W
Petrolina 54 Je 9.24S 40.30W
Petrolina de Goiás 55 Hc 16.06S 49.20W
Petronanski prohod 15 Gf 43.08N 23.08 E
Petronell 14 Kb 48.07N 16.51 E
Petropavlovka 20 Ff 50.38N 105.19 E
Petropavlovsk 22 Id 54.54N 69.06 E
Petropavlovsk-Kamčatski 22 Rd 53.01N 158.39 E
Petrópolis 53 Lh 22.31S 43.10W
Petroşani 15 Gd 45.25N 23.22 E
Petrovac [Yugo.] 15 Bg 42.12N 18.57 E
Petrovac [Yugo.] 15 Ee 44.22N 21.25 E
Petrova Gora 14 Je 45.17N 15.47 E
Petrovaradin 15 Cd 45.15N 19.53 E
Petrovka 15 Nc 46.55N 30.40 E
Petrovsk 19 Ee 52.18N 45.23 E
Petrovski Jam 7 Ie 63.18N 35.15 E
Petrovsk-Zabajkalski 22 Md 51.17N 108.50 E
Petrov Val 16 Nd 50.10N 45.12 E
Petrozavodsk 6 Jc 61.47N 34.20 E
Petuhovo 19 Gd 55.06N 67.58 E
Petuški 7 Ji 55.59N 39.28 E
Petworth 12 Bd 50.59N 0.36W
Peuetsagoe, Gunung- 26 Cf 4.55N 96.20 E
Peumo 56 Fd 34.24S 71.10W
Peureulak 26 Cf 4.48N 97.53 E
Pevek 22 Tc 69.42N 170.17 E
Pevensey 12 Cd 50.48N 0.21 E
Pevensey Bay 12 Cd 50.48N 0.22 E
Peza 7 Kd 65.34N 44.33 E
Pézenas 11 Jk 43.27N 3.25 E
Pezinok 10 Nh 48.18N 17.16 E
Pfaffenhofen an der Ilm 10 Hh 48.32N 11.31 E
Pfaffenhoffen 12 Jf 48.51N 7.37 E
Pfalz 12 Je 49.20N 7.57 E
Pfalzel, Trier- 12 Ie 49.46N 6.41 E
Pfälzer Bergland 10 Dg 49.35N 7.30 E
Pfälzer Wald 10 Dg 49.15N 7.50 E
Pfarrkirchen 10 Ih 48.26N 12.52 E
Pfinz 12 Ke 49.11N 8.25 E
Pfinztal 12 Ke 49.02N 8.30 E
Pforzheim an der Enz 10 Eh 48.53N 8.42 E
Pfrimm 12 Ke 49.39N 8.22 E
Pfullendorf 10 Fi 47.55N 9.15 E
Pfunds 14 Ed 46.58N 10.33 E
Pfungstadt 12 Ke 49.48N 8.36 E
Phalaborwa 37 Ed 23.55S 31.13 E
Phalodi 25 Ec 27.08N 72.22 E
Pha-an 25 Je 16.53N 97.38 E
Phangnga 25 Jg 8.28N 98.32 E
Phan Ly Cham 25 Lf 11.13N 108.31 E
Phanom 25 Jg 8.49N 98.50 E
Phan Rang 25 Lf 11.34N 108.59 E
Phan Thiet 25 Lf 10.56N 108.06 E
Pharr 45 Gm 26.12N 98.11W
Phatthalung 25 Kg 7.38N 100.04 E
Phayao 25 Ke 18.07N 100.11 E
Phenix City 43 Je 32.29N 85.01W
Phet Buri 25 Jf 13.06N 99.56 E
Phetchabun, Thiu Khao- 25 Ke 16.20N 100.55 E
Phichit 25 Ke 16.24N 100.21 E
Philadelphia [Ms.-U.S.] 45 Lj 32.46N 89.07W
Philadelphia [Pa.-U.S.] 39 Lf 39.57N 75.07W
Philae 33 Fe 23.35N 32.52 E
Philip 45 Fd 44.02N 101.40W
Philippeville 11 Kd 50.12N 4.33 E
Philippi 44 Gf 39.08N 80.03W
Philippi (EN) = Filippoi 15 Hh 41.02N 24.18 E
Philippi, Lake- 59 Hd 24.20S 139.00 E
Philippi Glacier 66 Ge 66.45S 88.20 E
Philippine Basin (EN) 3 Ih 17.00N 132.00 E
Philippine Islands (EN) = Pilipinas 21 Oh 13.00N 122.00 E
Philippines (EN)=Pilipinas [1] 22 Oh 13.00N 122.00 E
Philippine Sea (EN) 21 Oh 20.00N 130.00 E
Philippine Trench (EN) 3 Ii 9.00N 127.00 E
Philippsburg 12 Ke 49.14N 8.27 E
Philipsburg [Mt.-U.S.] 46 Ic 46.20N 113.08W
Philipsburg [Neth.Ant.] 50 Ec 18.01N 63.04W
Philip Smith Mountains 40 Jc 68.30N 148.00W
Philipstown 37 Cf 30.26S 24.29 E
Phillipsburg 45 Gg 39.45N 99.19W
Philpots 42 Jb 74.55N 80.00W
Phitsanulok 22 Mh 16.49N 100.15 E
Phnom Penh (EN)=Phnum Pénh 22 Mh 11.33N 104.55 E
Phnum Penh=Phnom Penh (EN) 22 Mh 11.33N 104.55 E
Phoenix 39 Hf 33.27N 112.05W
Phoenix→Rawaki Atoll 57 Je 3.43S 170.43W
Phoenix Islands 57 Je 4.00S 172.00W
Phôngsali 25 Kd 21.41N 102.06 E
Phrae 25 Ke 18.07N 100.11 E
Phra Nakhom Si Ayutthaya 22 Mh 14.21N 100.33 E
Phrygia 15 Mk 38.30N 29.50 E
Phu Cuong 25 Lf 10.58N 106.39 E
Phuket 22 Li 7.54N 98.24 E
Phuket, Ko- 21 Li 8.00N 98.20 E
Phulbani 25 Gd 20.28N 84.14 E
Phumĭ Mlu Prey 25 Lf 13.48N 105.16 E
Phumĭ Sâmraông 25 Kf 14.11N 103.31 E
Phu My 25 Lf 14.10N 109.03 E
Phuoc Binh 25 Lf 11.50N 106.58 E
Phu Quoc, Dao- 25 Kf 10.12N 104.00 E
Phu Tho 25 Ld 21.24N 105.13 E
Phu Vinh → Tra Vinh 25 Lg 9.56N 106.20 E
Piaanu Pass 64d Ab 7.20N 151.26 E
Piacenza 14 De 45.01N 9.40 E
Piana degli Albanesi 14 Hm 37.59N 13.17 E
Piana Mwanga 36 Ed 7.40S 28.10 E
Piancó 54 Ke 7.12S 37.57W
Pianguan 27 Jd 39.28N 111.32 E
Pianosa [It.] 14 Jh 42.15N 15.45 E
Pianosa [It.] 14 Eh 42.35N 10.05 E
Piaseczno 10 Rd 52.05N 21.01 E
Piaski 10 Se 51.08N 22.51 E
Piątek 10 Pd 52.05N 19.28 E
Piatra 15 If 43.49N 25.10 E
Piatra Neamţ 15 Jc 46.55N 26.20 E
Piatra Olt 15 He 44.22N 24.16 E
Piauí [2] 54 Je 7.00S 43.00W
Piauí, Rio- 52 Lf 6.38S 42.42W
Piave 5 Hf 45.32N 12.44 E
Piaxtla, Punta- 48 Ff 23.38N 106.50W
Piaxtla, Rio- 48 Ff 23.42N 106.49W
Piazza Armerina 14 Im 37.23N 14.22 E
Pibor 35 Ed 8.26N 33.13 E
Pibor Post 35 Ed 6.48N 33.08 E
Pica 56 Gb 20.30S 69.21W
Picachos, Cerro dos- 48 Bc 29.25N 114.10W
Picardie = Picardy (EN) 11 Je 50.00N 3.30 E
Picardy (EN) = Picardie 11 Je 50.00N 3.30 E
Picayune 45 Lk 30.26N 89.41W
Picentini, Monti- 14 Jj 40.45N 15.10 E
Pichanal 53 Jh 23.20S 64.15W
Pichilemu 56 Fd 34.23S 72.00W
Pichilingue 48 De 24.20N 110.20W
Pichna 10 Oe 51.50N 18.40 E
Pichones, Cayos- 49 Ff 15.45N 82.55W
Pichucalco 48 Mi 17.31N 93.04W
Pickering 9 Mg 54.14N 0.46W
Pickering, Vale of- 9 Mg 54.10N 0.45W
Pickle Lake 42 If 51.29N 90.10W
Pickwick Lake 44 Ch 34.55N 88.10W
Pico 30 Ee 38.28N 28.20W
Picos 53 Lf 7.05S 41.28W
Pico Truncado 56 Gg 46.48S 67.58W
Picquigny 12 Ee 49.57N 2.09 E
Picton 61 Dh 41.18S 174.00 E
Pictou 42 Lg 45.41N 62.43W
Picunda 16 Lh 43.12N 40.21 E
Pidurutalagala 21 Ki 7.00N 80.46 E
Piedecuesta 54 Db 6.59N 73.03W
Piedimonte Matese 14 Ii 41.20N 14.22 E
Piedmont [Al.-U.S.] 44 Ei 33.55N 85.37W
Piedmont [Mo.-U.S.] 45 Kh 37.09N 90.42W
Piedmont (EN) = Piemonte [2] 14 Be 45.00N 8.00 E
Piedmont Plateau 38 Kf 35.00N 81.00W
Piedra 13 Kc 41.19N 1.48W
Piedra, Monasterio de- 13 Kc 41.10N 1.50W
Piedrabuena 13 He 39.02N 4.10W
Piedrafita, Puerto de- 13 Fb 42.36N 6.57W
Piedrahita 13 Gd 40.28N 5.19W
Piedras 54 Cd 3.38S 79.54W
Piedras, Punta- 56 Ie 35.25S 57.08W
Piedras, Rio de las- 54 Ef 12.30S 69.14W
Piedras Negras 39 Ig 28.42N 100.31W
Piedras Negras 49 Be 17.12N 91.15W
Piedra Sola 56 Id 32.04S 56.21W
Piekary Śląskie 10 Of 50.24N 18.58 E
Pieksämäki 7 Ge 62.18N 27.08 E
Pielach 14 Jb 48.15N 15.22 E
Pielavesi 7 Ge 63.14N 26.45 E
Pielinen 5 Ic 63.15N 29.40 E
Piemonte = Piedmont (EN) [2] 14 Be 45.00N 8.00 E
Pieniężno 10 Qb 54.15N 20.08 E
Pieni Salpausselkä 5 Lc 61.10N 27.20 E
Piennes 12 He 49.19N 5.47 E
Pienza 14 Fg 43.04N 11.41 E
Pierce 46 Hc 46.29N 115.48W
Piéria Óri 15 Fi 40.12N 22.07 E
Pierre 39 Ie 44.22N 100.21W
Pierrefitte-sur-Aire 12 Hf 48.54N 5.20 E
Pierrefonds 12 Ee 49.21N 2.59 E
Pierrelatte 11 Kj 44.23N 4.42 E
Pieskehaure 7 Dc 66.57N 16.30 E
Piešťany 10 Nh 48.36N 17.50 E
Pietarsaari/Jakobstad 7 Fe 63.40N 22.42 E
Pietermaritzburg 31 Kk 29.37S 30.16 E
Pietersburg 31 Jk 23.54S 29.25 E
Pietraperzia 14 Im 37.25N 14.08 E
Pietrasanta 14 Eg 43.57N 10.14 E
Piet Retief 37 Ee 27.01S 30.50 E
Pietrii, Virful- 15 Fd 45.23N 22.40 E
Pietroşani 15 If 43.43N 25.38 E
Pietrosu, Virful- [Rom.] 15 Ib 47.08N 25.11 E
Pietrosu, Virful- [Rom.] 5 If 47.23N 25.33 E
Pieve di Cadore 14 Gd 46.26N 12.22 E
Pigeon Island 51k Ba 14.06N 60.58W
Pigeon River 45 Lb 48.02N 89.41W
Piggott 45 Kh 36.23N 90.11W
Pigg's Peak 37 Ee 25.58S 31.15 E
Pigs, Bay of- (EN) = Cochinos, Bahia de- 49 Gb 22.07N 81.10W
Pigüé 55 Am 37.37S 62.25W
Pi He 28 Dh 32.26N 116.34 E
Pihkva järv = Pskov, Lake- (EN) 7 Gg 58.00N 28.00 E
Pihlajavesi 7 Gf 61.45N 28.45 E
Pihlava 8 Ic 61.33N 21.36 E
Pihtipudas 7 Fe 63.23N 25.34 E
Piikkiö 8 Jd 60.26N 22.31 E
Piirisaar/Pirissar 8 Lf 58.23N 27.40 E
Pijijiapan 48 Mj 15.42N 93.14W
Pijol, Pico- 49 Df 15.06N 87.35W
Pikalevo 7 Ig 59.32N 34.03 E
Pikangikum 42 If 51.49N 94.00W
Pikelot Island 57 Fd 8.05N 147.38 E
Pikes Peak 43 Fd 38.51N 105.03W
Piketberg 37 Bf 32.54S 18.46 E
Pikiutdleq 41 Hf 64.45N 40.10W
Pikou 28 Ge 39.24N 122.21 E
Pikounda 36 Cb 0.33N 16.42 E
Piła 10 Mc 53.10N 16.44 E
Piła [2] 10 Mc 53.10N 16.45 E
Pila 55 Cm 36.01S 58.08W
Pila, Sierra de la- 13 Kf 38.16N 1.11W
Pilar [Arg.] 55 Bj 31.27S 61.15W
Pilar [Braz.] 54 Ke 9.36S 35.56W
Pilar [Par.] 56 Ic 26.52S 58.23W
Pilas Group 26 He 6.45N 121.35 E
Pilat, Mont- 11 Ki 45.23N 4.35 E
Pilatus 14 Cd 46.59N 8.20 E
Pilaya, Rio- 54 Fh 20.55S 64.04W
Pilcaniyeu 56 Ff 41.08S 70.40W
Pilcomayo, Rio- 52 Kh 25.21S 57.42W
Pile, Jezioro- 10 Mc 53.35N 16.30 E
Pili 15 Ej 39.28N 21.37 E
Pilibhit 25 Fc 28.38N 79.48 E
Pilica 10 Re 51.52N 21.17 E
Pilion Óros 15 Gj 39.24N 23.05 E
Pilipinas=Philippine Islands (EN) 21 Oh 13.00N 122.00 E
Pilipinas=Philippines (EN) [1] 22 Oh 13.00N 122.00 E
Pilis 10 Oi 47.41N 18.53 E
Pillahuincó, Sierra de- 55 Bn 38.18S 60.45W
Pillar, Cape- 59 Jh 43.15S 148.00 E
Pilna 7 Ki 55.33N 45.55 E
Pilões, Rio- 55 Gc 16.14S 50.54W
Pilões, Serra dos- 55 Ic 17.50S 47.13W
Pilón, Rio- 48 Je 25.32N 99.32W
Pilos 15 Em 36.55N 21.42 E
Pilos = Pylos (EN) 15 Em 36.56N 21.40 E
Pilot Peak 46 Hf 41.02N 114.06W
Pilot Rock 46 Fd 45.29N 118.50W
Pilsen (EN)=Plzeň 6 Hf 49.45N 13.24 E
Piltene 7 Eh 57.15N 21.42 E
Pilzno 10 Rg 49.59N 21.17 E
Pim 19 Hc 61.18N 71.57 E
Pimba 59 Hf 31.15S 136.47 E
Pimenteiras 54 Je 6.14S 41.25W
Pimža Jõgi 8 Lg 57.57N 27.59 E
Pina 13 Lc 41.29N 0.32W
Pinacate, Cerro- 48 Cb 31.45N 113.31W
Pinaki Atoll 57 Nf 19.22S 138.44W
Pinamar 55 Dm 37.07S 56.50W
Piñami, Arroyo- 48 Cd 27.44N 113.47W
Pinar 13 Gh 36.46N 5.26W
Pinarbaşi 24 Gc 38.50N 36.30 E
Pinar del Rio 39 Kg 22.25N 83.42W
Pinar del Rio [3] 49 Eb 22.35N 83.40W
Pinarello 11a Bb 41.41N 9.22 E
Pinarhisar 15 Kh 41.37N 27.30 E
Pinchbeck 12 Bb 52.48N 0.09W
Pincher Creek 42 Gg 49.30N 113.48W
Pinçon, Mont- 11 Ff 48.58N 0.37W
Pîncota 15 Ec 46.20N 21.42 E
Pindaíba, Ribeirão 55 Gb 14.48S 52.00W
Pindaré, Rio- 54 Jd 3.17S 44.47W
Pindaré-Mirim 54 Id 3.37S 45.21W
Pindaval 55 Dc 17.08S 56.09W
Pindhos Óros=Pindus Mountains (EN) 5 Ih 39.45N 21.30 E
Pindus Mountains (EN)= Pindhos Óros 5 Ih 39.45N 21.30 E
Pine Bluff 43 Ie 34.13N 92.01W
Pine Bluffs 46 Mf 41.11N 104.04W
Pine Creek 59 Gb 13.49S 131.49 E
Pine Falls 42 Hf 50.35N 96.15W
Pinega 19 Ec 64.42N 43.22 E
Pinega 5 Kc 64.08N 41.54 E
Pine Island Glacier 66 Of 75.00S 101.00W
Pineland 45 Jk 31.15N 93.58W
Pine Mountain [Ga.-U.S.] 44 Ei 32.51N 84.47W
Pine Mountain [U.S.] 44 Fg 36.55N 83.20W
Pine Pass 42 Fe 55.50N 122.30W
Pine Point 39 Hc 61.01N 114.15W
Pine Ridge 45 Ee 43.02N 102.33W
Pinerolo 14 Bf 44.53N 7.21 E
Pines, Isle of- (EN)= Juventud, Isla de la- 38 Kg 21.40N 82.50W
Pines, Isle of- (EN)=Pins, Ile des- 57 Hg 22.37S 167.30 E
Pines, Lake O' The 45 Ij 32.46N 94.35W
Pinetown 37 Ee 29.52S 30.46 E
Ping 21 Mh 15.42N 100.09 E
Pingbian 27 Hg 22.56N 103.46 E
Pingchang 27 Ie 31.38N 107.06 E
Pingding 28 Bf 37.48N 113.37 E
Pingdingbu → Guyuan 28 Cd 41.40N 115.41 E
Pingding Shan 27 Mb 46.39N 128.30 E
Pingdingshan 27 Je 33.41N 113.27 E
Pingdu 28 Ef 36.47N 119.57 E
Pingelap Atoll 57 Hd 6.13N 160.42 E
Pingelly 59 Df 32.32S 117.05 E
Pinggu 28 Dd 40.08N 117.07 E
Pingguo 27 Ig 23.21N 107.34 E
Pinghu 28 Fi 30.42N 121.02 E
Pingjiang 28 Bj 28.45N 113.37 E
Pingle 27 Jg 24.43N 110.42 E
Pingli 27 Ie 32.27N 109.21 E
Pingliang 22 Mf 35.32N 106.41 E
Pinglu (Jingping) 28 Be 39.32N 112.14 E
Pingluo 22 Mf 38.56N 106.34 E
Pingma → Tiandong 27 Ig 23.40N 107.09 E
Pingnan 27 Jg 23.38N 110.23 E
Pingouins, Ile des- 30 Mm 46.25S 50.19 E
Pingquan 27 Kc 41.00N 118.36 E
Pingshan 28 Ce 38.21N 114.01 E
Pingshun 28 Bf 36.12N 113.26 E
Pingtan 27 Kf 25.31N 119.48 E
Pingtung 27 Lg 22.40N 120.29 E
Pingüicas, Cerro- 48 Jg 21.10N 99.42W
Pingvallavatn 7a Bb 64.15N 21.09W
Pingvellir 7a Bb 64.17N 21.03W
Pingwu 27 He 32.27N 104.35 E
Pingxiang [China] 27 Ig 22.11N 106.46 E
Pingxiang [China] 27 Jf 27.43N 113.48 E
Pingyang 27 Lf 27.40N 120.35 E
Pingyao 27 Jd 37.12N 112.13 E
Pingyi 28 Dg 35.30N 117.38 E
Pingyin 28 Df 36.17N 116.26 E
Pingyu 28 Ci 32.58N 114.36 E
Pingyuan 28 Df 37.10N 116.25 E
Pinhal 55 If 22.12S 46.45W
Pinhão 55 Gg 25.43S 51.38W
Pinheir Machado 55 Fj 31.34S 53.23W
Pinhel 13 Ed 40.46N 7.04W
Pini, Pulau- 26 Cf 0.08N 98.40 E
Piniós [Grc.] 15 Fj 39.53N 22.44 E
Piniós [Grc.] 15 El 37.48N 21.14 E
Pinipel 63a Ba 4.24S 154.08 E
Pinjug 7 Lf 60.16N 47.54 E
Pinka 10 Mi 47.00N 16.35 E
Pink Mountain 42 Fe 56.06N 122.35W
Pinnaroo 59 Ig 35.16S 140.55 E
Pinneberg 10 Fc 53.39N 9.48 E
Pinnes, Ákra- 15 Hi 40.07N 24.18 E
Pinolosean 26 Hf 0.23N 124.07 E
Pinos 48 If 22.18N 101.34W
Pinos, Mount- 38 Hf 34.50N 119.09W
Pinos-Puente 13 Ig 37.15N 3.45W
Pinrang 26 Gg 3.48S 119.38 E
Pins, Cap des- 63b Ce 21.04S 167.28 E
Pins, Ile des-=Pines, Isle of- (EN) 57 Hg 22.37S 167.30 E
Pins, Pointe aux- 44 Gd 42.15N 81.51W
Pinsk 19 Ce 52.08N 26.06 E
Pinta, Isla- 54a Aa 0.35N 90.44W
Pintas, Sierra de las- 48 Bb 31.40N 115.10W
Pinto [Arg.] 56 Hc 29.09S 62.39W
Pinto [Sp.] 13 Id 40.14N 3.41W
Pintwater Range 46 Hh 36.55N 115.30W
Pio 63a Ed 10.12S 161.42 E
Pioche 46 Hh 37.56N 114.27W
Piombino 14 Eh 42.55N 10.32 E
Piombino, Canale di- 14 Eh 42.55N 10.30 E
Pioneer Mountains 46 Id 45.40N 113.00W
Pioner, Ostrov- 21 Lb 79.50N 92.30 E
Pionerski 19 Gc 61.12N 62.57 E
Pionerski 7 Ei 54.57N 20.13 E
Pionki 10 Re 51.30N 21.27 E
Piorini, Lago- 54 Fd 3.35S 63.15W
Piorini, Rio- 54 Fd 3.23S 63.30W
Piotrków [2] 10 Pe 51.25N 19.40 E
Piotrków Trybunalski 10 Pe 51.25N 19.42 E
Piove di Sacco 14 Ge 45.18N 12.02 E
Pipa Dingzi 27 Mc 43.57N 128.14 E
Pipéri 15 Hj 39.19N 24.21 E
Pipestone 45 Hd 44.01N 96.19W
Pipestone Creek 45 Fb 49.42N 100.45W
Pipi 35 Cd 7.27N 22.48 E
Pipinas 55 Dl 35.32S 57.20W
Pipmouacan, Réservoir- 42 Kg 49.40N 70.20W
Piqan → Shanshan 27 Fc 42.52N 90.10 E
Piqua 44 Ee 40.08N 84.14W
Piqueras, Puerto de- 13 Jb 42.03N 2.32W
Piquiri, Rio- 56 Jb 24.03S 54.14W
Piquiri, Serra do- 55 Fg 24.53S 52.25W
Piracanjuba 55 Hc 17.18S 49.01W
Piracanjuba, Rio- [Braz.] 55 Hd 18.14S 48.48W
Piracanjuba, Rio- [Braz.] 55 Hc 17.18S 48.13W
Piracema 55 Je 20.31S 44.29W
Piracicaba 56 Kb 22.43S 47.38W
Piracicaba, Rio- 55 Hf 22.36S 48.19W
Piraçununga 55 Ie 21.59S 47.25W
Piracuruca 54 Jd 3.56S 41.42W
Piraeus (EN) = Piraiévs 6 Ih 37.57N 23.38 E
Pirai do Sul 55 Hg 24.31S 49.56W
Piraiévs = Piraeus (EN) 6 Ih 37.57N 23.38 E
Piraju 55 Hf 23.12S 49.23W
Pirajui 55 He 21.59S 49.29W
Piramide, Cerro- 52 Ij 49.01S 73.32W
Piran 14 He 45.32N 13.34 E
Pirané 56 Ic 25.43S 59.06W
Piranhas 55 Gc 16.31S 51.51W
Piranhas, Rio- 55 Gc 16.01S 51.52W
Pirān Shahr 24 Kd 36.40N 45.05 E
Pirapora 53 Lg 17.21S 44.56W
Pirarajá 56 Jd 33.44S 54.45W
Pirate Well 49 Kb 22.26N 73.04W
Piratini 55 Fj 31.27S 53.06W
Piratini, Rio- 55 Fk 32.01S 52.25W
Piratinim, Rio- 55 Ei 28.06S 55.27W
Pirdop 15 Hg 42.42N 24.11 E
Pirenópolis 55 Hb 15.51S 48.57W
Pires do Rio 54 Ig 17.18S 48.17W
Pirgos 15 El 37.41N 21.27 E
Pirgós 15 Fi 40.38N 22.44 E
Piriápolis 55 El 34.54S 55.17W
Pirin 15 Gh 41.40N 23.30 E
Pirineos=Pyrenees (EN) 5 Gg 42.40N 1.00 E
Pirineus, Serra dos- 55 Hc 16.15S 49.10W
Piripiri 54 Jd 4.16S 41.47W
Pirissar/Piirisaar 8 Lf 58.23N 27.40 E
Piritu 50 Bh 9.23N 69.12W
Piritu, Islas- 50 Dg 10.10N 64.56W
Pirizal 55 Dc 16.16S 56.23W
Pirjatin 16 Hd 50.14N 32.30 E
Pirmasens 10 Dg 49.12N 7.36 E
Pirna 10 Jf 50.58N 13.56 E
Piron 63a Ad 11.20S 153.27 E
Pirón 13 Hc 41.23N 4.31W
Pirot 15 Ff 43.09N 22.36 E
Pirre, Cerro- 49 Ij 7.49N 77.43W
Pirrit Hills 66 Pg 81.17S 85.21W
Pirsagat 16 Pj 39.53N 49.19 E
Pir Tāj 24 Me 35.45N 48.07 E
Pirttikylä/Pörtom 8 Ib 62.42N 21.37 E
Piru 26 Ig 3.04S 128.12 E
Pis 64d Ba 7.41N 151.46 E
Pisa 14 Eg 43.43N 10.23 E
Pisa 10 Rc 53.15N 21.52 E
Pisagua 56 Fa 19.36S 70.13W

Index Symbols

[1] Independent Nation
[2] State, Region
[3] District, County
[4] Municipality
[5] Colony, Dependency
Continent
Physical Region
Historical or Cultural Region
Mount, Mountain
Volcano
Hill
Mountains, Mountain Range
Hills, Escarpment
Plateau, Upland
Pass, Gap
Plain, Lowland
Delta
Salt Flat
Valley, Canyon
Crater, Cave
Karst Features
Depression
Polder
Desert, Dunes
Forest, Woods
Heath, Steppe
Oasis
Cape, Point
Coast, Beach
Cliff
Peninsula
Isthmus
Sandbank
Island
Atoll
Rock, Reef
Islands, Archipelago
Rocks, Reefs
Coral Reef
Well, Spring
Geyser
River, Stream
Waterfall Rapids
River Mouth, Estuary
Lake
Salt Lake
Intermittent Lake
Reservoir
Swamp, Pond
Canal
Glacier
Ice Shelf, Pack Ice
Ocean
Sea
Gulf, Bay
Strait, Fjord
Lagoon
Bank
Seamount
Tablemount
Ridge
Shelf
Basin
Escarpment, Sea Scarp
Fracture
Trench, Abyss
National Park, Reserve
Point of Interest
Recreation Site
Cave, Cavern
Historic Site
Ruins
Wall, Walls
Church, Abbey
Temple
Scientific Station
Airport
Port
Lighthouse
Mine
Tunnel
Dam, Bridge

Pisano	14	Eg	43.46N	10.33 E
Pisar	64d	Cb	7.19N	152.01 E
Pisciotta	14	Jj	40.06N	15.14 E
Pisco	53	Ig	13.42S	76.13W
Pişcolt	15	Fb	47.35N	22.18 E
Písek	10	Kg	49.19N	14.10 E
Pishan/Guma	27	Cd	37.38N	78.19 E
Pīsh Qal'eh	24	Qd	37.35N	57.05 E
Pīshvā	24	Ne	35.18N	51.44 E
Piso Firme	55	Ba	13.41S	61.52W
Pissa	7	Ei	54.39N	21.50 E
Pisshiri-Dake	29a	Ba	44.20N	141.55 E
Pista	7	Hd	65.28N	30.45 E
Pisticci	14	Kj	40.23N	16.33 E
Pistoia	14	Eg	43.55N	10.54 E
Pisuerga	13	Hc	41.33N	4.52W
Pisz	10	Rc	53.38N	21.49 E
Pita	34	Cc	11.05N	12.24W
Pitalito	54	Cc	1.53N	76.02W
Pitanga	56	Jb	24.46S	51.44W
Pitanga, Serra da-	55	Gg	24.52S	51.48W
Pitangui	55	Jd	19.40S	44.54W
Pitcairn [5]	58	Og	24.00S	129.00W
Pitcairn Island	57	Ng	25.04S	130.05W
Piteå	7	Ed	65.20N	21.30 E
Piteälven	5	Ib	65.14N	21.32 E
Piteşti	6	Ig	44.51N	24.52 E
Pithiviers	11	If	48.10N	2.15 E
Pithorāgarh	25	Gc	29.35N	80.13 E
Piti	36	Fd	7.00S	32.44 E
Piti	64c	Bb	13.28N	144.41 E
Pitiquito	48	Cb	30.42N	112.02W
Pitkjaranta	19	Dc	61.35N	31.31 E
Pitkkala	8	Jc	61.28N	23.34 E
Pitljar	20	Bc	65.52N	65.55 E
Pitlochry	9	Je	56.43N	3.45W
Pitomača	14	Le	45.57N	17.14 E
Piton, Pointe du-	51e	Ba	16.30N	61.27W
Pit River	43	Cc	40.45N	122.22W
Pitrufquén	56	Fe	38.59S	72.39W
Pitt	42	Ef	53.40N	129.50W
Pitt Island	57	Ji	44.20S	176.10W
Pittsburg	43	Id	37.25N	94.42W
Pittsburgh	39	Le	40.26N	80.00W
Pittsfield [Il.-U.S.]	45	Kg	39.36N	90.48W
Pittsfield [Ma.-U.S.]	44	Kd	42.27N	73.15W
Pittsfield [Me.-U.S.]	44	Mc	44.47N	69.23W
Pitt Strait	62	Jf	44.10S	176.20W
Pitu	26	If	1.41N	128.01 E
Piũi	55	Je	20.28S	45.58W
Piura	53	Hf	5.12S	80.38W
Piura [2]	54	Be	5.00S	80.20W
Piuthān	25	Gc	28.06N	82.52 E
Piva	15	Bf	43.21N	18.51 E
Pivan	20	If	50.27N	137.05 E
Pivijay	49	Jh	10.28N	74.38W
Pižma	7	Lh	57.36N	48.58 E
Pižma	17	Fd	65.24N	52.05 E
Pizzo	14	Kl	38.44N	16.40 E
Pjakupur	20	Cd	65.00N	77.48 E
Pjalica	7	Jc	66.12N	39.32 E
Pjalma	19	Dc	62.27N	35.53 E
Pjana	7	Ki	55.37N	45.58 E
Pjandž	19	Gh	37.15N	69.07 E
Pjandž	21	If	37.06N	68.20 E
Pjaozero, Ozero-	5	Jb	66.05N	30.55 E
Pjarnu/Pärnu	6	Id	58.24N	24.32 E
Pjarnu/Pärnu Jõgi	7	Fg	58.23N	24.34 E
Pjarnu, Zaliv-/Pärnu Laht	7	Fg	58.15N	24.25 E
Pjarnu-Jagupi/Pärnu-Jaagupi	8	Kf	58.36N	24.25 E
Pjasina	21	Kb	73.47N	87.01 E
Pjasino, Ozero-	20	Dc	69.45N	87.30 E
Pjasinski Zaliv	20	Db	74.00N	85.00 E
Pjatigorsk	6	Kg	44.03N	43.04 E
Pjatihatki	16	He	48.27N	33.40 E
Pjórsá	5	Dc	63.45N	20.50W
Pjussi/Püssi	8	Le	59.17N	26.57 E
Pkulagalid	64a	Bb	7.36N	134.33 E
Pkulagasemieg	64a	Ac	7.08N	134.23 E
Pkurengel	64a	Ac	7.27N	134.28 E
Plá	55	Bl	35.07S	60.13W
Placentia	42	Mg	47.14N	53.58W
Placentia Bay	38	Ne	47.15N	54.30W
Placer	26	Hd	11.52N	123.55 E
Placerville	46	Eg	38.43N	120.48W
Placetas	47	Id	22.19N	79.40W
Plácido Rosas	55	Fk	32.45S	53.44W
Plačkovci	15	Ig	42.49N	25.28 E
Plačkovica	15	Fh	41.46N	22.32 E
Plainfield	44	Je	40.37N	74.25W
Plains [Mt.-U.S.]	46	Hc	47.27N	114.53W
Plains [Tx.-U.S.]	45	Ej	33.11N	102.50W
Plainview [Nb.-U.S.]	45	He	42.21N	97.47W
Plainview [Tx.-U.S.]	43	Ge	34.11N	101.43W
Plainville	45	Gg	39.14N	99.18W
Pláka, Akra-	15	Ii	40.02N	25.25 E
Plake	15	Eh	41.14N	21.02 E
Plampang	26	Gh	8.48S	117.48 E
Planá	10	Ig	49.52N	12.44 E
Plana Cays	49	Kb	22.37N	73.33W
Plana o Nueva Tabarca, Isla-	13	Lf	38.10N	0.28W
Planco, Peñón-	48	Ge	24.35N	104.15W
Plane, Ile-	13	Li	35.46N	0.54W
Planeta Rica	54	Cb	8.25N	75.35W
Planet Depth (EN)	3	Hi	10.20S	110.30 E
Planézes	11	Ij	45.00N	2.50 E
Plankinton	45	Ge	43.43N	98.29W
Plantation	44	Gl	26.05N	80.14W
Plantaurel	11	Hk	43.04N	1.30 E
Plant City	44	Fk	28.01N	82.08W
Plasencia	13	Fd	40.02N	6.05W
Plast	19	Ge	54.22N	60.55 E
Plaster Rock	44	Nb	46.54N	67.24W
Plastun	20	Ih	44.48N	136.17 E
Plasy	10	Jg	49.56N	13.24 E
Plata, Rio de la- [P.R.]	51a	Bb	18.30N	66.14W
Plata, Rio de la- [S.Amer.]	52	Ki	35.00S	57.00W
Plataiai	15	Gk	38.13N	23.16 E
Platani	14	Hm	37.24N	13.16 E
Plateau [2]	34	Gd	8.50N	9.00 E
Plateau [3]	36	Cc	2.10S	15.00 E
Plateau, Khorat-	21	Mh	15.30N	102.50 E
Plateaux [3]	34	Fd	7.30N	1.10 E
Platen, Kapp-	41	Ob	80.31N	22.48 E
Plati	15	Fi	40.39N	22.32 E
Plato	54	Db	9.47N	74.47W
Platte	45	Ge	43.23N	98.51W
Platte	38	Je	43.23N	98.51W
Platte Island	30	Mi	5.52S	55.23 E
Platte River	45	Ig	39.16N	94.50W
Platteville	45	Ke	42.44N	90.29W
Plattsburgh	43	Mc	44.42N	73.29W
Plattsmouth	45	If	41.01N	95.53W
Plau	10	Ic	53.27N	12.16 E
Plauen	10	If	50.30N	12.08 E
Plauer See	10	Ic	53.30N	12.20 E
Plav	15	Cg	42.36N	19.57 E
Plavecký Mikuláš	10	Nh	48.30N	17.18 E
Pļaviņas/Pljavinjas	7	Fh	56.38N	25.46 E
Plavsk	16	Jc	53.43N	37.18 E
Playa Azul	47	De	17.59N	102.24W
Playa Noriega, Laguna-	48	Dc	29.10N	111.50W
Playa Vicente	48	Li	17.50N	95.49W
Playón Chico	49	Hi	9.18N	78.14W
Pleasanton [Ks.-U.S.]	45	Ig	38.11N	94.43W
Pleasanton [Tx.-U.S.]	45	Gl	28.58N	98.29W
Pleasant Point	62	Df	44.16S	171.08 E
Pleasant Valley	45	Fi	35.15N	101.48W
Plechý	10	Jh	48.49N	13.53 E
Pleiku	25	Lf	13.59N	108.00 E
Pleiße	10	Ie	51.20N	12.22 E
Plekinge	8	Fh	56.20N	15.05 E
Plenița	15	Ge	44.13N	23.11 E
Plenty, Bay of-	57	Ih	37.45S	177.10 E
Plentywood	43	Gb	48.47N	104.34W
Pleščenicy	16	Eb	54.29N	27.55 E
Pleseck	19	Ec	62.44N	40.18 E
Plešivec	10	Qh	48.33N	20.25 E
Pleşu, Vîrful-	15	Fc	46.32N	22.11 E
Pleszew	10	Ne	51.54N	17.48 E
Plétipi, Lac-	42	Kf	51.42N	70.08W
Plettenberg	12	Jc	51.13N	7.53 E
Plettenbergbaai	37	Cf	34.03S	23.22 E
Pleven [2]	15	Hf	43.25N	24.37 E
Pleven	6	Ig	43.25N	24.37 E
Plibo	34	De	4.35N	7.40W
Pliska	15	Kf	43.22N	27.07 E
Pliszka	10	Kd	52.15N	14.40 E
Plitvice	14	Jf	44.54N	15.36 E
Pljavinjas/Pļaviņas	7	Fh	56.38N	25.46 E
Plješevica	14	Jf	44.45N	15.45 E
Pljevlja	15	Cf	43.21N	19.21 E
Pljusa	7	Gg	58.25N	29.20 E
Pljusa	7	Gg	59.13N	28.11 E
Ploča, Rt-	14	Jg	43.30N	15.58 E
Ploče → Kardeljevo	14	Lg	43.04N	17.26 E
Płock	10	Pd	52.35N	19.45 E
Płock	10	Pd	52.33N	19.43 E
Ploërmel	11	Dg	47.56N	2.24W
Ploieşti	6	Ig	44.57N	26.01 E
Plomárion	15	Jk	38.59N	26.22 E
Plomb du Cantal	11	Ii	45.03N	2.46 E
Plön	10	Gb	54.10N	10.26 E
Płonia	10	Kc	53.25N	14.36 E
Płonka	10	Qd	52.37N	20.30 E
Płońsk	10	Qd	52.38N	20.23 E
Plopana	15	Kc	46.41N	27.13 E
Płoty	10	Lc	53.50N	15.16 E
Plouguerneau	11	Bf	48.36N	4.30W
Plovdiv [2]	15	Hg	42.09N	24.45 E
Plovdiv	6	Ig	42.09N	24.45 E
Plummer	46	Gc	47.20N	116.53W
Plumridge Lakes	59	Fe	29.30S	125.25 E
Plumtree	37	Dd	20.31S	27.48 E
Plungé/Plunge	7	Ei	55.56N	21.48 E
Plunge/Plungé	7	Ei	55.56N	21.48 E
Plymouth [Eng.-U.K.]	6	Fe	50.23N	4.10W
Plymouth [In.-U.S.]	44	De	41.21N	86.19W
Plymouth [Ma.-U.S.]	44	Le	41.58N	70.41W
Plymouth [Mont.]	47	Le	16.42N	62.13W
Plymouth Sound	9	Ik	50.26N	4.05W
Plzeň=Pilsen (EN)	6	Hf	49.45N	13.24 E
Plzeňská pahorkatina	10	Jg	49.50N	13.15 E
Pniewy	10	Md	52.31N	16.15 E
Pô	34	Ec	11.10N	1.09W
Po	5	Hg	44.57N	12.05 E
Po, Colline del-	14	Be	45.05N	7.50 E
Po, Foci del-=Po, Mouths of the- (EN)	14	Gf	44.52N	12.30 E
Po, Mouths of the- (EN)= Po, Foci del-	14	Gf	44.52N	12.30 E
Poarta de Fier a Transilvaniei, Pasul-	15	Fd	45.25N	22.40 E
Poarta Orientală, Pasul-	15	Fd	45.08N	22.20 E
Poás, Volcán-	49	Eh	10.11N	84.13W
Pobé	34	Fd	6.58N	2.41 E
Pobeda, Gora-	21	Qc	65.12N	146.12 E
Pobeda Ice Island	66	Ge	64.30S	97.00 E
Pobedy, Pik-	21	Ke	42.02N	80.05 E
Pobla de Segur/La Pobla de Segur	13	Mb	42.15N	0.58 E
Poblet, Monasterio de-/ Poblet, Monèstir de-	13	Nc	41.20N	1.05 E
Poblet, Monèstir de-/Poblet, Monasterio de-	13	Nc	41.20N	1.05 E
Pobrežije	15	Jf	43.56N	26.21 E
Pocahontas	45	Kh	36.16N	90.58W
Pocatello	39	He	42.52N	112.27W
Počep	16	Hc	52.57N	33.28 E
Pocerina	15	Ce	44.38N	19.35 E
Počinok	19	De	54.23N	32.29 E
Počitelj	14	Lg	43.08N	17.44 E
Pocito, Sierra del-	13	He	39.20N	4.05W
Pocito Casas	48	Dc	28.32N	111.06W
Pocklington Reef	60	Fj	11.00S	155.00 E
Poções	54	Jf	14.31S	40.21W
Poço Fundo, Cachoeira-	55	Jc	16.10S	45.51W
Poconé	54	Gg	16.15S	56.37W
Pocono Mountains	44	Je	41.10N	75.20W
Poços de Caldas	54	Ih	21.48S	46.34W
Pocri	49	Gj	7.40N	80.07W
Podborovje	8	Mg	57.51N	28.46 E
Podborovje	7	Ig	59.32N	35.01 E
Podbrezová	10	Ph	48.49N	19.31 E
Podčerje	17	He	63.55N	57.30 E
Poděbrady	10	Lf	50.09N	15.07 E
Podgajcy	10	Vg	49.12N	25.12 E
Podgorica (Titograd)	6	Hg	42.26N	19.16 E
Po di Volano	14	Gf	44.49N	12.15 E
Podjuga	7	Jf	61.07N	40.54 E
Podkamennaja Tunguska= Stony Tunguska (EN)	21	Lc	61.36N	90.18 E
Podlasie	10	Sd	52.30N	23.00 E
Podlaska, Nizina-	10	Sc	53.00N	22.45 E
Podlužje	15	Ce	44.45N	19.55 E
Podolia (EN)=Podolskaja Vozvyšennost	5	If	49.00N	28.00 E
Podolsk	19	Dd	55.27N	37.33 E
Podolskaja Vozvyšennost= Podolia (EN)	5	If	49.00N	28.00 E
Podor	34	Cb	16.40N	14.57W
Podporožje	19	Dc	60.54N	34.09 E
Podravina	14	Le	45.40N	17.40 E
Podravska Slatina	14	Le	45.42N	17.42 E
Podrima	15	Dg	42.24N	20.33 E
Podromanija	14	Mg	43.54N	18.46 E
Podsvilje	8	Mi	55.09N	28.01 E
Podujevo	15	Eg	42.55N	21.12 E
Podunajská nížina	10	Nh	48.00N	17.40 E
Podvološino	20	Fe	58.15N	108.25 E
Poel	10	Hb	54.00N	11.26 E
Poenița, Vîrful-	15	Gc	46.15N	23.20 E
Pofadder	37	Be	29.10S	19.22 E
Pogăniş	15	Ed	45.41N	21.21 E
Pogar	16	Hc	52.33N	33.16 E
Poggibonsi	14	Fg	43.28N	11.09 E
Pöggstall	14	Jb	48.19N	15.11 E
Pogibi	20	Jf	52.15N	141.45 E
Pogny	12	Gf	48.52N	4.29 E
Pogoanele	15	Je	44.55N	27.00 E
Pogórze Karpackie	10	Qg	49.52N	21.00 E
Pogradeci	15	Di	40.54N	20.39 E
Pograničny	20	Ih	44.26N	131.20 E
Pogrebišče	16	Fe	49.29N	29.14 E
Poguba Xoréu, Rio-	55	Ec	16.29S	54.58W
P'ohang	27	Md	36.02N	129.22 E
Pohja/Pojo	8	Jd	60.06N	23.31 E
Pohjankangas	8	Jc	62.00N	22.30 E
Pohjanlahti=Bothnia, Gulf of- (EN)	5	Hc	63.00N	20.00 E
Pohjanmaa	8	Jb	63.00N	22.30 E
Pohjois-Karjala [2]	7	Ge	63.00N	30.00 E
Pohlheim	12	Kd	50.32N	8.42 E
Pohorje	14	Jd	46.32N	15.28 E
Po Hu	28	Di	30.15N	116.32 E
Pohue Bay	65a	Fd	19.01N	155.48W
Pohvistnevo	19	Fe	53.40N	52.08 E
Poiana Mare	15	Gf	43.55N	23.04 E
Poiana Ruscă, Munții	15	Fd	45.41N	22.30 E
Pöide/Pëjde	8	Jf	58.30N	22.50 E
Poie	36	Dc	2.55S	23.10 E
Poindimié	61	Cd	20.56S	165.20 E
Poindo → Lhünzhub	27	Fe	30.17N	91.20 E
Poinsett, Cape-	66	He	65.42S	113.18 E
Poinsett, Lake-	45	Hd	44.34N	97.05W
Point Arena	46	Dg	38.55N	123.41W
Point au Fer Island	45	Kl	29.15N	91.15W
Pointe-à-Pitre	47	Le	16.14N	61.32W
Pointe Duble	51e	Bb	16.20N	61.00W
Pointe-Noire	51e	Ab	16.14N	61.47W
Pointe Noire	31	Ii	4.48S	11.51 E
Point Hope	40	Fc	68.21N	166.41W
Point Lake	42	Gc	65.15N	113.00W
Point Lay	40	Gc	69.45N	163.03W
Point Pleasant [N.J.-U.S.]	44	Je	40.06N	74.02W
Point Pleasant [W.V.-U.S.]	44	Ff	38.53N	82.07W
Poisson-Blanc, Lac-	44	Jc	46.00N	75.44W
Poissonnier Point	59	Dc	20.00S	119.10 E
Poissy	11	If	48.56N	2.03 E
Poitevin, Marais-	11	Eh	46.22N	1.06W
Poitiers	6	Gf	46.35N	0.20 E
Poitou	11	Fh	46.40N	0.30W
Poitou, Plaines et Seuil du-	11	Gh	46.26N	0.17 E
Poivre Islands	37b	Bb	5.46S	53.19 E
Poix-de-Picardie	11	He	49.47N	1.59 E
Poix-Terron	12	Ge	49.39N	4.39 E
Pojarkovo	20	Hg	49.42N	128.50 E
Pojkovski	20	Hc	60.59N	72.00 E
Pojo/Pohja	8	Jd	60.06N	23.31 E
Pojuba, Rio-	55	Ec	16.30S	54.59W
Pokaran	25	Ec	26.55N	71.55 E
Pokhara	25	Gc	28.14N	83.59 E
Poko	36	Eb	3.09N	26.53 E
Pokoinu	64p	Bb	21.12S	159.49W
Pokój	10	Nf	50.56N	17.50 E
Pokrovka	18	Lc	42.19N	78.01 E
Pokrovsk	20	Hd	61.29N	129.10 E
Pokrovskoje	16	Jc	52.38N	36.51 E
Pokrovskoje	16	Jf	47.59N	36.13 E
Pokšenga	7	Kd	64.01N	44.53 E
Pokutje	15	Ia	48.20N	25.05 E
Pola	7	Hg	58.05N	31.40 E
Polabí	10	Lf	50.10N	15.10 E
Polacca	46	Ji	35.50N	110.23W
Pola de Laviana	13	Ga	43.15N	5.34W
Pola de Lena	13	Ga	43.10N	5.49W
Pola de Siero	13	Ga	43.23N	5.40W
Polanco	55	Ek	33.54S	55.09W
Poland	64g	Ab	1.52N	157.33W
Poland (EN)=Polska [1]	6	He	52.00N	19.00 E
Polanów	10	Mb	54.08N	16.39 E
Polar Plateau	66	Cg	90.00S	0.00
Polar Urals (EN)=Poljarny Ural	5	Mb	66.55N	64.30 E
Polatlı	23	Db	39.36N	32.09 E
Polch	12	Jd	50.18N	7.19 E
Połczyn Zdrój	10	Mc	53.46N	16.06 E
Pol-e Khomrī	23	Kb	35.56N	68.43 E
Pole of Inaccessibility (EN)	66	Eg	82.06S	54.58 E
Pol-e-Safid	24	Od	36.06N	53.01 E
Polesella	14	Ff	44.58N	11.45 E
Polesie Lubelskie	10	Te	51.30N	23.20 E
Polesine	14	Fe	45.00N	11.45 E
Polesje=Polesye (EN)	5	Ie	52.00N	27.00 E
Polessk	8	Ij	54.51N	21.02 E
Polesskoje	16	Fd	51.16N	29.27 E
Polesye (EN)=Polesje	5	Ie	52.00N	27.00 E
Polevskoj	19	Gd	56.28N	60.11 E
Polewali	26	Gg	3.25S	119.20 E
Poležan	15	Gh	41.43N	23.30 E
Polgár	10	Ri	47.52N	21.07 E
Pŏlgyo	28	Ig	34.51N	127.21 E
Poli	34	Hd	8.29N	13.15 E
Poliaigos	15	Hm	36.46N	24.38 E
Poliçani	15	Di	40.08N	20.21 E
Policastro, Golfo di-	14	Jk	40.00N	15.35 E
Police	10	Kc	53.33N	14.35 E
Policoro	14	Kj	40.13N	16.41 E
Poligny	11	Lh	46.50N	5.43 E
Poligus	20	Ed	61.58N	94.40 E
Polikastron	15	Fh	41.00N	22.34 E
Polikhnitos	15	Jj	39.05N	26.11 E
Polillo Islands	21	Oh	14.50N	122.05 E
Pólis	24	Ee	35.02N	32.25 E
Polist	7	Hg	58.07N	31.32 E
Polistena	14	Kl	38.24N	16.04 E
Poliyros	15	Gi	40.23N	23.27 E
Poljarny	19	Db	69.13N	33.28 E
Poljarny	20	Mc	69.01N	178.45 E
Poljarny Ural=Polar Urals (EN)	5	Mb	66.55N	64.30 E
Polkowice	10	Me	51.32N	16.06 E
Pöllau	14	Jc	47.18N	15.50 E
Polle	64d	Bb	7.20N	151.15 E
Pollença/Pollensa	13	Pe	39.53N	3.01 E
Pollensa/Pollença	13	Pe	39.53N	3.01 E
Pollino	5	Hh	39.55N	16.10 E
Polochic, Rio-	49	Cf	15.28N	89.22W
Polock	19	Cd	55.29N	28.52 E
Polog	15	Dh	42.00N	21.00 E
Pologi	19	Df	47.28N	36.15 E
Polonina	10	Jh	48.30N	23.30 E
Polonnaruwa	25	Gg	7.56N	81.00 E
Polonnoje	16	Ed	50.06N	27.29 E
Polousny Krjaž	20	Jc	69.30N	144.00 E
Polska=Poland (EN) [1]	6	He	52.00N	19.00 E
Polski Gradec	15	Jg	42.11N	26.06 E
Polski Trămbeš	15	If	43.22N	25.38 E
Polson	46	Hc	47.41N	114.09W
Poltár	10	Ph	48.27N	19.48 E
Poltava	6	Jf	49.35N	34.34 E
Poltavka	19	He	54.22N	71.45 E
Poltavskaja Oblast [3]	19	Df	49.45N	33.50 E
Põltsamaa/Pyltsamaa	8	Lf	58.23N	26.08 E
Põltsamaa/Pyltsamaa	7	Fg	58.39N	25.59 E
Poluj	20	Bc	66.30N	66.31 E
Polunočnoje	19	Gc	60.52N	60.25 E
Polūr	24	Oe	32.52N	52.03 E
Põlva/Pylva	7	Gg	58.04N	27.06 E
Polvijärvi	7	Ge	62.51N	29.22 E
Polynesia	57	Le	4.00S	156.00W
Polynésie Française=French Polynesia (EN) [5]	58	Mf	16.00S	145.00W
Pom, Laguna de-	48	Mh	18.35N	92.15W
Pomarance	14	Eg	43.18N	10.52 E
Pomarkku/Påmark	8	Ic	61.42N	22.00 E
Pombal [Braz.]	54	Ke	6.46S	37.47W
Pombal [Port.]	13	De	39.55N	8.38W
Pombo, Rio-	55	Fe	20.53S	52.23W
Pomerania (EN)= Pommern	5	He	54.00N	16.00 E
Pomerania (EN)= Pommern	10	Lc	54.00N	16.00 E
Pomeranian Bay (EN)= Pommersche Bucht	10	Kb	54.20N	14.20 E
Pomeranian Bay (EN)= Pomorska, Zatoka-	10	Kb	54.20N	14.20 E
Pomeroy	44	Ff	39.03N	82.03W
Pomio	58	Ge	5.32S	151.30 E
Pomme de Terre Reservoir	45	Jh	37.51N	93.19W
Pommern=Pomerania (EN)	10	Lc	54.00N	16.00 E
Pommern=Pomerania (EN)	5	He	54.00N	16.00 E
Pommersche Bucht= Pomeranian Bay (EN)	10	Kb	54.20N	14.20 E
Pommersfelden	10	Gg	49.46N	10.49 E
Pomona	46	Gi	34.04N	117.45W
Pomona Lake	45	Ig	38.40N	95.35W
Pomorije	15	Kg	42.33N	27.39 E
Pomorska, Zatoka-= Pomeranian Bay (EN)	10	Kb	54.20N	14.20 E
Pomorski Bereg	7	Id	64.00N	36.15 E
Pomorskie, Pojezierze-	10	Mc	53.30N	16.30 E
Pomorski Proliv	19	Eb	68.40N	50.00 E
Pomošnaja	16	Ge	48.14N	31.29 E
Pompano Beach	44	Gl	26.15N	80.07W
Pompei	14	Ij	40.45N	14.30 E
Pompeu	55	Jd	19.12S	44.59W
Ponape	58	Gd	6.52N	158.15 E
Ponape Island	57	Gd	6.55N	158.15 E
Ponca City	43	Hd	36.42N	97.05W
Ponce	39	Mh	18.01N	66.37W
Poncheville, Lac-	44	Ia	50.12N	76.55W
Pondcreek	45	Hh	36.40N	97.48W
Pondicherry	25	Ff	11.56N	79.53 E
Pondicherry [3]	25	Ff	11.55N	79.45 E
Pond Inlet	39	Lb	72.41N	78.00W
Pond Inlet	42	Jb	72.48N	77.00W
Ponea	64n	Ac	10.28S	161.01W
Ponente, Riviera di-	14	Cf	44.10N	8.20 E
Ponérihouen	63b	Be	21.05S	165.24 E
Pones	64d	Bb	7.12N	151.59 E
Ponferrada	13	Fb	42.33N	6.35W
Pongaroa	62	Gd	40.33S	176.11 E
Pongo	30	Jh	8.42N	27.40 E
Pongola	37	Ee	26.52S	32.20 E
Pong Qu	27	Ef	26.49N	87.09 E
Poniatowa	10	Se	51.11N	22.05 E
Ponoj	6	Kb	67.05N	41.07 E
Ponoj	5	Kb	66.59N	41.10 E
Ponomarevka	16	Sc	53.09N	54.12 E
Ponorogo	26	Fh	7.52S	111.27 E
Pons	11	Fi	45.35N	0.33W
Pons/Ponts	13	Nc	41.55N	1.12 E
Ponsul	13	Ee	39.40N	7.31W
Pont-à-Celles	12	Gd	50.30N	4.21 E
Ponta Delgada	31	Ee	37.44N	25.40W
Ponta Delgada [3]	32	Bb	37.48N	25.30W
Ponta Grossa	53	Kh	25.05S	50.09W
Pont-à-Mousson	11	Mf	48.54N	6.04 E
Ponta Porá	53	Kh	22.32S	55.43W
Pontarlier	11	Mh	46.54N	6.22 E
Pontassieve	14	Fg	43.46N	11.26 E
Pont-Audemer	11	Ge	49.21N	0.31 E
Pontaut	55	Bm	37.44S	61.20W
Pontávert	12	Fe	49.25N	3.49 E
Pontchartrain, Lake-	43	Ie	30.10N	90.10W
Pontchâteau	11	Dg	47.26N	2.05W
Pont-de-l'Arche	12	De	49.18N	1.10 E
Pont de Suert	13	Mb	42.24N	0.45 E
Pont-de-Vaux	11	Kh	46.26N	4.56 E
Ponte Alta	55	Gh	27.29S	50.23W
Ponte Alta, Serra da-	55	Id	19.42S	47.40W
Ponte Branca	55	Fc	16.27S	52.40W
Pontecorvo	14	Hi	42.27N	13.40 E
Ponte de Lima	13	Dc	41.46N	8.35W
Ponte de Pedra	55	Ec	17.06S	54.23W
Ponte de Pedrã	55	Da	13.35S	57.21W
Pontedera	14	Eg	43.40N	10.38 E
Ponte de Sor	13	De	39.15N	8.01W
Ponte Firme, Chapada da-	55	Id	18.05S	46.25W
Ponteix	46	Lb	49.49N	107.30W
Ponte Nova	54	Jh	20.24S	42.54W
Pontés e Lacerda	55	Cb	15.11S	59.21W
Pontevedra [3]	13	Db	42.30N	8.30W
Pontevedra	13	Db	42.26N	8.38W
Pontevedra, Ría de-	13	Db	42.22N	8.45W
Ponte Vermelha	55	Ed	19.29S	54.25W
Pont-Farcy	12	Af	48.56N	1.02W
Pontfaverger-Moronvilliers	12	Ge	49.18N	4.19 E
Ponthieu	11	Hd	50.10N	1.55 E
Pontiac [Il.-U.S.]	45	Lf	40.53N	88.38W
Pontiac [Mi.-U.S.]	44	Fd	42.37N	83.18W
Pontianak	22	Mj	0.02S	109.20 E
Pontian Kechil	26	Df	1.29N	103.23 E
Pontine Islands (EN) = Ponziane, Isole-	14	Gj	40.55N	13.00 E
Pontivy	11	Df	48.04N	2.59W
Pontivy, Pays de-	11	Dg	48.00N	3.00W
Pont-l'Abbé	11	Bg	47.52N	4.13W
Pont-l'Evêque	12	Ce	49.18N	0.11 E
Pontoise	11	Ie	49.03N	2.06 E
Pontorson	11	Ef	48.33N	1.31W
Pontremoli	14	Df	44.22N	9.53 E
Pontresina	14	Dd	46.28N	9.53 E
Ponts/Pons	13	Nc	41.55N	1.12 E
Pont-Sainte-Maxence	12	Ee	49.18N	2.36 E
Pont-Saint-Esprit	11	Kj	44.15N	4.39 E
Pontypool	9	Jj	51.43N	3.02W
Ponza	14	Gj	40.54N	12.58 E
Ponza	14	Gj	40.55N	12.55 E
Ponziane, Isole- = Pontine Islands (EN)	14	Gj	40.55N	13.00 E
Pool [3]	36	Bc	3.30S	15.00 E
Poole	9	Lk	50.43N	1.59W
Poona → Pune	22	Jh	18.32N	73.52 E
Poopó	54	Eg	18.23S	66.59W
Poopó, Lago de- = Poopó, Lake- (EN)	52	Jg	18.45S	67.07W
Poopó, Lake- (EN) = Poopó, Lago de-	52	Jg	18.45S	67.07W
Poor Knights Islands	62	Fa	35.30S	174.45 E
Pöösaspea Neem/Pyzaspea	8	Je	59.15N	23.25 E
Popakai	54	Gc	3.22N	55.25W
Popayán	53	Ie	2.27N	76.36W
Poperinge	11	Id	50.51N	2.43 E
Poperinge-Watou	12	Ed	50.51N	2.37 E
Popigaj	20	Gb	71.55N	110.47 E
Popigaj	20	Fb	72.55N	106.00 E
Poplar	46	Mb	48.07N	105.12W
Poplar	42	Hf	53.00N	97.18W
Poplar Bluff	43	Id	36.45N	90.24W
Poplar River	46	Mb	48.05N	105.11W
Popocatépetl, Volcán-	38	Jh	19.02N	98.38W
Popokabaka	36	Cd	5.42S	16.35 E
Popoli	14	Hh	42.10N	13.50 E
Popomanaseu, Mount-	63a	Ec	9.42S	160.03 E
Popondetta	60	Di	8.46S	148.14 E
Popovo	15	Jf	43.21N	26.14 E
Poppberg	10	Hg	49.20N	11.45 E
Poppel, Ravels-	12	Hc	51.27N	5.02 E
Poprad	10	Qg	49.38N	20.42 E
Poprad	6	If	49.03N	20.19 E
Poptún	49	Ce	16.21N	89.26W
Por	10	Tf	50.48N	23.01 E
Porangahau	62	Gd	40.18S	176.38 E

Index Symbols

[1] Independent Nation
[2] State, Region
[3] District, County
[4] Municipality
[5] Colony, Dependency
Continent
Physical Region
Historical or Cultural Region
Mount, Mountain
Volcano
Hill
Mountains, Mountain Range
Hills, Escarpment
Plateau, Upland
Pass, Gap
Plain, Lowland
Delta
Salt Flat
Valley, Canyon
Crater, Cave
Karst Features
Depression
Polder
Desert, Dunes
Forest, Woods
Heath, Steppe
Oasis
Cape, Point
Coast, Beach
Cliff
Peninsula
Isthmus
Sandbank
Island
Atoll
Rock, Reef
Islands, Archipelago
Rocks, Reefs
Coral Reef
Well, Spring
Geyser
River, Stream
Waterfall Rapids
River Mouth, Estuary
Lake
Salt Lake
Intermittent Lake
Reservoir
Swamp, Pond
Canal
Glacier
Ice Shelf, Pack Ice
Ocean
Sea
Gulf, Bay
Strait, Fjord
Lagoon
Bank
Seamount
Tablemount
Ridge
Shelf
Basin
Escarpment, Sea Scarp
Fracture
Trench, Abyss
National Park, Reserve
Point of Interest
Recreation Site
Cave, Cavern
Historic Site
Ruins
Wall, Walls
Church, Abbey
Temple
Scientific Station
Airport
Port
Lighthouse
Mine
Tunnel
Dam, Bridge

Porangatu 55 Ha 13.26S 49.10W
Porbandar 25 Dd 21.38N 69.36E
Porcien 12 Ge 49.40N 4.20E
Porcos, Rio dos- 55 Ja 12.42S 45.07W
Porcuna 13 Hg 37.52N 4.11W
Porcupine 38 Ec 66.35N 145.15W
Porcupine 44 Ga 48.32N 81.10W
Porcupine Bank (EN) 5 Ee 53.20N 13.30W
Porcupine Hills 46 Ha 50.05N 114.10W
Porcupine Plain 42 Dc 67.30N 137.30W
Pordenone 14 Ge 45.57N 12.39E
Poreč 14 He 45.13N 13.37E
Poreč 15 Fe 44.20N 22.05E
Porecatu 55 Gf 22.43S 51.24W
Porečje 8 Kk 53.53N 24.08E
Poreckoje 7 Li 55.13N 46.19E
Porhov 19 Cd 57.45N 29.32E
Pori/Björneborg 6 Ic 61.29N 21.47E
Porion 15 Gn 35.58N 23.16E
Porirua 61 Dh 41.08S 174.50E
Pörisvatn 7a Bb 64.20N 18.55W
Porjus 7 Ec 66.57N 19.49E
Porkkala 8 Ke 59.55N 24.25E
Porlamar 54 Fa 10.57N 63.51W
Porma 13 Gb 42.29N 5.28W
Pornic 11 Dg 47.07N 2.06W
Poronajsk 22 Qe 49.14N 143.04E
Poronin 10 Qg 49.20N 20.04E
Póros 15 Gl 37.30N 23.31E
Póros 15 Gl 37.30N 23.27E
Poroshiri-Dake 28 Qc 42.42N 142.35E
Porosozero 7 He 62.44N 32.42E
Porozovo 10 Ud 52.54N 24.27E
Porpoise Bay 66 Ie 66.30S 128.30E
Porquis Junction 44 Ga 48.43N 80.52W
Porrentruy 14 Bc 47.25N 7.10E
Porreras 13 Oe 39.31N 3.00E
Porretta, Passo della- 14 Ef 44.02N 10.56E
Porretta Terme 14 Ef 44.09N 10.59E
Porsangen 5 Ia 70.50N 26.00E
Porsangerhalvøya 7 Fa 70.50N 25.00E
Porsgrunn 7 Bg 59.09N 9.40E
Pórshöfn 7a Ca 66.10N 15.20W
Porsuk 24 Dc 39.42N 31.59E
Portachuelo 54 Fg 17.21S 63.24W
Portadown/Port an Dúnáin 9 Gg 54.26N 6.27W
Portage 45 Le 43.33N 89.28W
Portage la Prairie 42 Hg 49.57N 98.18W
Port Alberni 42 Fg 49.14N 124.48W
Portalegre 13 Ee 39.17N 7.26W
Portalegre [2] 13 Ee 39.15N 7.35W
Portales 43 Ge 34.11N 103.20W
Port-Alfred 42 Kg 48.20N 70.53W
Port Alfred 37 Df 33.36S 26.55E
Port Alice 42 Ef 50.23N 127.27W
Port Allegany 44 He 41.48N 78.18W
Port an Dúnáin/Portadown 9 Gg 54.26N 6.27W
Port Angeles 43 Cb 48.07N 123.27W
Port Antonio 47 Ie 18.11N 76.28W
Port Arthur [Austl.] 59 Jh 43.09S 147.51E
Port Arthur [Tx.-U.S.] 39 Jg 29.55N 93.55W
Port Arthur (EN)=Lüshun 27 Ld 38.50N 121.13E
Port Augusta 58 Eh 32.30S 137.46E
Port-Au-Prince 39 Lh 18.32N 72.20W
Port-au-Prince, Baie de- 49 Kd 18.40N 72.30W
Port Austin 44 Fc 44.03N 83.01W
Port aux Français 31 Om 49.25S 70.10E
Porta Westfalica 12 Kb 52.15N 8.56E
Port-Bergé-Vao Vao 37 Hc 15.33S 47.38E
Port Blair 22 Lh 11.36N 92.45E
Port-Bou/Portbou 13 Pb 42.25N 3.10E
Portbou/Port-Bou 13 Pb 42.25N 3.10E
Port Burwell [Newf.-Can.] 39 Mc 60.25N 64.49W
Port Burwell [Ont.-Can.] 44 Gd 42.39N 80.49W
Port-Cartier 42 Kf 50.01N 66.53W
Port Chalmers 62 Df 45.49S 170.37E
Port Charlotte 43 Kf 26.59N 82.06W
Port Clinton 44 Fe 41.30N 82.58W
Port Coquitlam 46 Db 49.16N 122.46W
Port-de-Bouc 11 Kk 43.24N 4.59E
Port-de-Paix 49 Kd 19.57N 72.50W
Port Dickson 26 Df 2.31N 101.48E
Port Edward 37 Ef 31.03S 30.13E
Portel [Braz.] 54 Hd 1.57S 50.49W
Portel [Port.] 13 Ef 38.18N 7.42W
Port Elgin 44 Gc 44.26N 81.24W
Port Elizabeth [S.Afr.] 31 Jl 33.58S 25.40E
Port Elizabeth [St.Vin.] 51n Ba 13.00N 61.16W
Port Ellen 9 Gf 55.39N 6.12W
Port-en-Bessin-Huppain 11 Fe 49.21N 0.45W
Port Erin 9 Ig 54.05N 4.43W
Porter Point 51n Ba 13.23N 61.11W
Porterville [Ca.-U.S.] 43 Dd 36.04N 119.01W
Porterville [S.Afr.] 37 Bf 33.00S 19.00E
Portete, Bahia de- 49 Lg 12.13N 71.55W
Port Fairy 59 Ig 38.23S 142.14E
Port Fitzroy 62 Fb 36.10S 175.21E
Port-Gentil 31 Hi 0.43S 8.47E
Port Gibson 45 Kk 31.58N 90.58W
Port Harcourt 31 Hh 4.46N 7.01E
Port Hardy 42 Ef 50.43N 127.29W
Port Hawkesbury 42 Lg 45.37N 61.21W
Porthcawl 9 Jj 51.29N 3.43W
Port Hedland 58 Cg 20.19S 118.34E
Port Heiden 40 He 56.55N 158.41W
Port Hope Simpson 42 Lf 52.30N 56.17W
Port Huron 43 Kc 42.58N 82.27W
Portile de Fier = Iron Gate (EN) 5 Ig 44.41N 22.31E
Port-Ilič 16 Pj 38.53N 48.51E
Portimão 13 Dg 37.08N 8.32W
Port Isabel 45 Hm 26.04N 97.13W
Portița 15 Le 44.41N 29.00E
Port Láirge/Waterford [2] 9 Fi 52.10N 7.40W
Port Láirge/Waterford 6 Fe 52.15N 7.06W
Portland [Austl.] 59 Ig 38.21S 141.36E
Portland [Eng.-U.K.] 9 Kk 50.33N 2.27W
Portland [In.-U.S.] 44 Ee 40.26N 84.59W
Portland [Me.-U.S.] 39 Le 43.39N 70.17W
Portland [N.D.-U.S.] 45 Hc 47.30N 97.22W
Portland [N.Z.] 62 Fa 35.48S 174.20E
Portland [Or.-U.S.] 39 Ge 45.33N 122.36W
Portland [Tx.-U.S.] 45 Hm 27.53N 97.20W
Portland, Bill of- 9 Kk 50.31N 2.28W
Portland, Promontoire- 42 Je 58.41N 78.33W
Portland Bight 49 Ie 17.57N 77.08W
Portland Island 62 Gc 39.20S 177.50E
Portland Point 49 Ie 17.42N 77.11W
Port-la-Nouvelle 11 Jk 43.01N 3.03E
Portlaoise/Port Laoise 9 Fh 53.02N 7.17W
Port Laoise/Portlaoise 9 Fh 53.02N 7.17W
Port Lavaca 43 Hf 28.37N 96.38W
Port Lincoln 58 Eh 34.44S 135.52E
Port Loko 34 Cd 8.46N 12.47W
Port Louis 50 Fd 16.25N 61.32W
Port-Louis 31 Mk 20.10S 57.30E
Port Macquarie 59 Kf 31.26S 152.44E
Portmadoc 9 Ii 52.55N 4.08W
Port Maria 49 Id 18.22N 76.54W
Port-Menier 42 Lg 49.49N 64.20W
Port Moller 40 Ge 55.59N 160.34W
Port Moody 46 Db 49.17N 122.51W
Port Moresby 58 Fe 9.30S 147.07E
Port Nelson 42 Ie 57.04N 92.30W
Portneuf, Rivière- 44 Ma 48.37N 69.05W
Port Nolloth 31 Ik 29.17S 16.51E
Porto [2] 13 Dc 41.15N 8.20W
Porto [Fr.] 11a Aa 42.16N 8.42E
Porto [Port.] 6 Fg 41.09N 8.37W
Porto, Golfe de- 11a Aa 42.16N 8.37E
Pôrto Acre 54 Ee 9.34S 67.31W
Porto Alegre [Braz.] 53 Ki 30.04S 51.11W
Porto Alegre [SaoT.P.] 34 Ge 0.02N 6.32E
Porto Amboim 31 Ij 10.44S 13.45E
Porto Azzurro 14 Eh 42.46N 10.24E
Portobelo 49 Hi 9.33N 79.39W
Porto Cedro 55 Ed 18.17S 55.02W
Porto Cervo 14 Di 41.08N 9.35E
Porto Curupai 55 Ff 22.50S 53.53W
Porto de Moz 53 Kf 1.45S 52.14W
Porto Empedocle 14 Hm 37.17N 13.32E
Porto Esperança [Braz.] 55 Dd 19.37S 57.27W
Porto Esperança [Braz.] 55 Db 14.02S 56.06W
Porto Esperança [Braz.] 55 Dc 17.47S 57.07W
Porto Esperidião 55 Cb 15.51S 58.28W
Porto Estrêla 55 Db 15.20S 57.14W
Portoferraio 14 Eh 42.49N 10.19E
Port of Ness 9 Gc 58.30N 6.15W
Porto Franco 54 Ie 6.20S 47.24W
Port of Spain 53 Jd 10.39N 61.31W
Porto Fundação 55 Ea 13.39S 55.18W
Portogruaro 14 Ge 45.47N 12.50E
Porto Lucena 55 Eh 27.51S 55.01W
Pörtom/Pirttikylä 8 Ib 62.42N 21.37E
Portomaggiore 14 Ff 44.42N 11.48E
Porto Mendes 55 Eg 24.30S 54.20W
Porto Moniz 32 Dc 32.51N 17.10W
Porto Moroco 55 Ea 13.24S 55.35W
Porto Morrinho 55 Dc 16.38S 57.49W
Porto Murtinho 53 Kh 21.42S 57.52W
Porto Novo [Ben.] 31 Hh 6.29N 2.37E
Porto Novo [C.V.] 32 Bf 17.07N 25.04W
Port Orford 46 Ce 42.45N 124.30W
Porto San Giorgio 14 Hg 43.11N 13.48E
Porto Santana 54 Hd 0.03S 51.11W
Porto Sant'Elpidio 14 Hg 43.15N 13.45E
Porto Santo 30 Fe 33.04N 16.20W
Porto Santo Stefano 14 Fh 42.26N 11.07E
Portoscuso 14 Ck 39.12N 8.23E
Pôrto Seguro 54 Kg 16.26S 39.05W
Porto Tolle 14 Gf 44.56N 12.22E
Porto Torres 14 Cj 40.50N 8.24E
Porto União 55 Gh 26.15S 51.05W
Pôrto Válter 54 De 8.15S 72.45W
Porto Vecchio 11a Bb 41.35N 9.17E
Porto Velho 53 Jf 8.46S 63.54W
Portoviejo 53 Hf 1.03S 80.27W
Porto Xavier 55 Eh 27.54S 55.08W
Port Phillip Bay 59 Ig 38.05S 144.50E
Port Pirie 58 Eh 33.11S 138.01E
Portree 9 Gd 57.24N 6.12W
Port Renfrew 46 Cb 48.33N 124.25W
Port Rois/Portrush 9 Gf 55.12N 6.40W
Port Royal 44 If 38.10N 77.12W
Portrush/Port Rois 9 Gf 55.12N 6.40W
Port Said (EN)=Būr Sa'īd 31 Ke 31.16N 32.18E
Port Saint Joe 43 Jf 29.49N 85.18W
Port Saint Johns 37 Df 31.38S 29.33E
Port-Saint-Louis-du-Rhône 11 Kk 43.23N 4.48E
Port-Salut 49 Kd 18.05N 73.55W
Port Saunders 42 Lf 50.39N 57.18W
Port Shepstone 31 Kl 30.46S 30.22E
Portsmouth [Dom.] 50 Fe 15.35N 61.28W
Portsmouth [Eng.-U.K.] 9 Lk 50.48N 1.05W
Portsmouth [N.H.-U.S.] 43 Mc 43.03N 70.47W
Portsmouth [Oh.-U.S.] 43 Kd 38.45N 82.59W
Portsmouth [Va.-U.S.] 43 Ld 36.50N 76.26W
Portsmouth City Airport 12 Ad 50.46N 1.04W
Port Sudan (EN)=Būr Sūdān 31 Kg 19.37N 37.14E
Port Sulphur 45 Ll 29.29N 89.42W
Port Talbot 9 Jj 51.36N 3.47W
Porttipahdantekojärvi 7 Gb 68.06N 26.33E
Port Townsend 46 Db 48.07N 122.46W
Portugal [1] 6 Fh 39.30N 8.00W
Portugalete 13 Ia 43.19N 3.01W
Portuguesa [2] 54 Eb 9.10N 69.15W
Portuguesa, Rio- 54 Eb 7.57N 67.32W
Portuguesa, Sierra de- 50 Bh 9.35N 69.45W
Portuguese Guinea (EN) → Guinea Bissau (EN) [1] 31 Fg 12.00N 15.00W
Portús, Coll del-/Perthus, Col de- 13 Ob 42.28N 2.51E
Port-Vendres 11 Jl 42.31N 3.07E
Port-Vila 58 Hf 17.44S 168.19E
Port Wakefield 59 Hf 34.11S 138.09E
Port Washington 45 Me 43.23N 87.53W
Porvenir [Bol.] 54 Ef 11.15S 68.41W
Porvenir [Bol.] 55 Ba 13.59S 61.39W
Porvenir [Chile] 56 Fh 53.18S 70.22W
Porvenir [Ur.] 55 Dk 32.23S 57.59W
Porvoo/Borgå 7 Ff 60.24N 25.40E
Porvoonjoki 8 Kd 60.23N 25.40E
Porz, Köln- 12 Jd 50.53N 7.03E
Posada, Fiume di- 14 Dj 40.39N 9.45E
Posadas [Arg.] 53 Kh 27.25S 55.50W
Posadas [Sp.] 13 Gg 37.48N 5.06W
Posavina 15 De 44.33N 20.04E
Poschiavo 14 Ed 46.20N 10.04E
Pošehonje 7 Jg 58.30N 39.08E
Posht-e Bādām 24 Pf 33.02N 55.23E
Posio 7 Gc 66.06N 28.09E
Posjet 26 Kc 42.39N 130.48E
Poskam/Zepu 27 Cd 38.12N 77.18E
Poso 22 Oj 1.23S 120.44E
Poso, Danau- 26 Hg 1.52S 120.35E
Posof 24 Jb 41.31N 42.42E
Posŏng 28 Ig 34.46N 127.05E
Pospeliha 20 Df 52.02N 81.56E
Posse 54 If 14.05S 46.22W
Possession, Ile de la- 30 Mm 46.14S 49.55E
Possession Island 37 Be 27.01S 15.30E
Pößneck 10 Hf 50.42N 11.36E
Post 45 Fj 33.12N 101.23W
Posta de San Martín 55 Bk 33.09S 60.31W
Postavy 19 Cd 55.07N 26.50E
Poste Maurice Cortier/Bidon V 32 He 22.18N 1.05E
Poste Weygand 32 He 24.29N 0.40E
Postmasburg 37 Ce 28.18S 23.05E
Postojna 14 Ie 45.47N 14.14E
Posto Simões Lopes 55 Eb 14.14S 54.41W
Postville [Ia.-U.S.] 45 Ke 43.05N 91.34W
Postville [Newf.-Can.] 42 Lf 54.55N 59.58W
Potchefstroom 37 De 26.46S 27.01E
Poteau 45 Ii 35.03N 94.37W
Potenza 14 Hg 43.25N 13.40E
Potenza 14 Jj 40.38N 15.48E
Poteriteri, Lake- 62 Bg 46.05S 167.05E
Potes 13 Ha 43.09N 4.37W
Potgietersrus 37 Dd 24.15S 28.55E
Potholes Reservoir 46 Fc 47.01N 119.19W
Poti 6 Kg 42.08N 41.39E
Poti, Rio- 54 Je 5.02S 42.50W
Potigny 12 Bf 48.58N 0.14W
Potiskum 31 Ig 11.43N 11.04E
Potnarhvin 63b Dd 18.45S 169.12E
Potomac 38 Lf 38.00N 76.18W
Potosí [2] 54 Eh 20.40S 67.00W
Potosí [Bol.] 53 Jg 19.35S 65.45W
Potosí [Mex.] 47 Dd 24.51N 100.19W
Potosí, Bahía- 48 Ii 17.35N 101.30W
Potosí, Cerro- 48 Ie 24.52N 100.13W
Pototan 26 Hd 10.55N 122.40E
Potrerillos 56 Gc 26.26S 69.29W
Potrero, Río- 55 Bc 17.32S 61.35W
Potsdam [Ger.] 10 Jd 52.24N 13.04E
Potsdam [N.Y.-U.S.] 44 Jc 44.40N 75.01W
Pott 63b Ad 19.35S 163.36E
Potters Bar 12 Bc 51.41N 0.10W
Pottstown 44 Je 40.15N 75.38W
Pottsville 44 Ie 40.42N 76.13W
Pouancé 11 Eg 47.45N 1.10W
Pouébo 63b Be 20.24S 164.34E
Pouembout 63b Be 21.08S 164.54E
Poughkeepsie 44 Ke 41.43N 73.56W
Poulaphuca Reservoir/Loch Pholl an Phúca 9 Gh 53.10N 6.30W
Poum 63b Be 20.14S 164.01E
Pourtalé 55 Bm 37.02S 60.36W
Pouso Alegre 54 Ih 22.13S 45.56W
Pouss 34 Ic 10.51N 15.03E
Poutasi 65c Bb 14.01S 171.41W
Pouthisat 25 Kf 12.32N 103.55E
Poutrincourt, Lac- 44 Ja 49.13N 74.04W
Po Valley (EN)=Padana, Pianura- 5 Gf 45.20N 10.00E
Považská Bystrica 10 Og 49.07N 18.28E
Považský Inovec 10 Nh 48.35N 18.00E
Povenec 7 Ie 62.51N 34.45E
Poverty Bay 62 Gc 38.45S 178.00E
Povlen 15 Ce 44.09N 19.44E
Póvoa de Varzim 13 Dc 41.23N 8.46W
Povorino 16 Md 51.12N 42.17E
Povungnituk 42 Jd 60.03N 77.16W
Povungnituk 39 Lc 60.02N 77.10W
Powassan 44 Hb 46.05N 79.22W
Powder River [U.S.] 43 Fb 46.44N 105.26W
Powder River [Or.-U.S.] 46 Gd 44.45N 117.03W
Powell 46 Kd 44.45N 108.46W
Powell, Lake- [U.S.] 43 Ed 37.25N 110.45W
Powell Lake [Can.] 46 Ca 50.11N 124.24W
Powell River 42 Fg 49.52N 124.33W
Powers 44 Dc 45.39N 87.32W
Powers Lake 45 Eb 48.34N 102.39W
Powidzkie, Jezioro- 10 Nc 52.24N 17.57E
Powys [3] 9 Ji 52.25N 3.20W
Poxoréu 54 Hg 15.50S 54.23W
Poxoréu, Rio- [Braz.] 55 Ec 16.32S 54.46W
Poxoréu, Rio- [Braz.] 55 Ec 16.08S 54.14W
Poya 63b Be 21.21S 165.09E
Poyang Hu 21 Ng 29.00N 116.25E
Poza de la Sal 13 Ib 42.40N 3.30W
Pozanti 24 Fd 37.25N 34.52E
Požarevac 15 Ee 44.37N 21.12E
Poza Rica de Hidalgo 39 Jg 20.33N 97.27W
Požarskoje 28 Ma 46.16N 134.04E
Požega 15 Df 43.51N 20.02E
Poznań [2] 10 Pd 52.25N 19.55E
Poznań 6 He 52.25N 16.55E
Pozoblanco 13 Hf 38.22N 4.51W
Pozo Borrado 55 Bi 28.56S 61.41W
Pozo Colorado 55 Cf 23.22S 58.55W
Pozo del Mortero 55 Bg 24.24S 61.02W
Pozo del Tigre 55 Bc 17.34S 61.59W
Pozo Dulce 55 Ai 29.04S 62.02W
Pozos, Punta- 56 Gg 47.57S 65.47W
Pozuelos 54 Fa 10.11N 64.39W
Pozzallo 14 In 36.43N 14.51E
Pozzuoli 14 Ij 40.49N 14.07E
Pra [Ghana] 34 Ed 6.27N 1.47W
Pra 7 Ji 54.45N 41.01E
Prabuty 10 Pc 53.46N 19.10E
Prachatice 10 Jg 49.01N 14.00E
Prachin Buri 25 Kf 14.02N 101.22E
Prachuap Khiri Khan 25 Jf 11.48N 99.47E
Praděd 10 Nf 50.06N 17.14E
Prades 11 Il 42.37N 2.26E
Prado 54 Kg 17.21S 39.13W
Præstø 8 Ei 55.07N 12.03E
Prague (EN)=Praha 6 He 50.05N 14.26E
Praha=Prague (EN) 6 He 50.05N 14.26E
Prahova [2] 15 Id 45.10N 26.00E
Praia 31 Eg 14.55N 23.31W
Praia a Mare 14 Jk 39.54N 15.47E
Praia da Rocha 13 Dg 37.07N 8.32W
Praia Rica 55 Eb 14.51S 55.33W
Praid 15 Ic 46.33N 25.08E
Prainha 54 Hd 1.48S 53.29W
Prairie Dog Town Fork 45 Gi 34.26N 99.21W
Prairie du Chien 45 Ke 43.03N 91.09W
Prangli 8 Ke 59.38N 24.50E
Pránhita 25 Fe 18.49N 79.55E
Prapat 26 Cf 2.40N 98.56E
Prasat 25 Kf 14.38N 103.24E
Praslin 51k Bb 13.53N 60.54W
Praslin, Port- 51k Bb 13.53N 60.54W
Praslin Island 37b Ca 4.19S 55.44E
Prasonision 15 Kn 35.52N 27.46E
Prat, Isla- 56 Fg 48.15S 75.00W
Prata 54 Ig 19.18S 48.55W
Prata, Rio da- 55 Hd 18.49S 49.54W
Pratapgarh 25 Ed 24.02N 74.47E
Prat de Llobregat/El Prat de Llobregat 13 Oc 41.20N 2.06E
Prato 14 Fg 43.53N 11.06E
Pratomagno 14 Fg 43.40N 11.40E
Pratt 43 Hd 37.39N 98.44W
Prättigau 14 Dd 46.55N 9.40E
Pratt Seamount (EN) 40 Ke 56.10N 142.30W
Prattville 44 Di 32.28N 86.29W
Pratudinho, Rio- 55 Ja 13.58S 45.10W
Pravda 18 Cf 36.50N 60.33E
Pravda Coast 66 Ge 67.00S 94.00E
Pravdinsk 8 Ij 54.28N 21.00E
Pravdinsk 7 Kh 56.33N 43.33E
Pravia 13 Fa 43.29N 6.07W
Praxedis G. Guerrero 48 Gb 31.22N 106.00W
Praya 26 Gh 8.42S 116.17E
Prealpi Venete 14 Fd 46.25N 11.50E
Predazzo 14 Fd 46.19N 11.36E
Predeal 15 Id 45.30N 25.34E
Predeal, Pasul- 15 Id 45.28N 25.36E
Predel 14 Hd 46.25N 13.35E
Predivinsk 20 Ee 57.04N 93.37E
Predporožny 20 Jd 65.00N 143.20E
Pré-en-Pail 11 Ff 48.27N 0.12W
Preetz 10 Gb 54.14N 10.17E
Pregolja 7 Ei 54.42N 20.24E
Pregradnaja 16 Lh 43.58N 41.12E
Preilj/Prejli 7 Gh 56.19N 26.48E
Preissac, Lac- 44 Ha 48.25N 78.28W
Prejli/Preilj 7 Gh 56.19N 26.48E
Prekmurje 14 Kd 46.45N 16.15E
Prekornica 15 Cg 42.40N 19.12E
Prekule/Priekule 8 Ii 55.36N 21.12E
Přelouč 10 Lf 50.02N 15.33E
Premià de Mar/Premiá de Mar 13 Oc 41.29N 2.22E
Premiá de Mar/Premià de Mar 13 Oc 41.29N 2.22E
Premnitz 10 Id 52.32N 12.20E
Premuda 14 If 44.21N 14.37E
Prenaj/Prienai 7 Fi 54.39N 23.59E
Prenj 14 Lg 43.32N 17.52E
Prenjasi 15 Dh 41.04N 20.32E
Prentice 45 Kd 45.33N 90.17W
Prentiss 45 Lk 31.36N 89.52W
Prenzlau 10 Jc 53.19N 13.52E
Preobraženije 20 Ih 42.58N 133.55E
Preobraženka 20 Fd 60.04N 107.58E
Preparis Island 25 If 14.52N 93.41E
Preparis North Channel 25 Ie 15.27N 94.05E
Preparis South Channel 25 If 14.55N 94.05E
Přerov 10 Ng 49.27N 17.27E
Prescelly, Mynydd- 9 Ij 51.58N 4.42W
Prescott [Ar.-U.S.] 45 Jj 33.48N 93.23W
Prescott [Az.-U.S.] 43 Ee 34.33N 112.28W
Preševo 15 Eg 42.19N 21.39E
Presho 45 Fe 43.53N 100.04W
Presicce 14 Mk 39.54N 18.16E
Presidencia Roque Sáenz Peña 53 Jh 26.50S 60.30W
Presidente Epitácio 56 Jb 21.46S 52.06W
Presidente Frei 66 Re 62.12S 58.55W
Presidente Hayes [3] 55 Cf 24.00S 59.00W
Presidente Juscelino 55 Jd 18.39S 44.05W
Presidente Murtinho 55 Fb 15.39S 53.54W
Presidente Olegário 55 Id 18.25S 46.25W
Presidente Prudente 56 Jb 22.07S 51.22W
Presidente Venceslau 55 Ge 21.52S 51.50W
President Thiers Seamount (EN) 57 Lg 24.39S 145.51W
Presidio 43 Gf 29.33N 104.23W
Presidio, Rio del- 48 Ff 23.06N 106.17W
Preslav 15 Jf 43.10N 26.49E
Presnovka 17 Mi 54.40N 67.09E
Prešov 10 Rh 49.00N 21.14E
Prespa 15 Hh 41.43N 24.53E
Prespa, Lake- (EN)= Prespansko jezero 5 Ig 40.55N 21.00E
Prespansko jezero=Prespa, Lake- (EN) 5 Ig 40.55N 21.00E
Presque Isle 43 Nb 46.41N 68.01W
Prestea 34 Ed 5.26N 2.09W
Přeštice 10 Jg 49.35N 13.21E
Preston [Eng.-U.K.] 9 Kh 53.46N 2.42W
Preston [Id.-U.S.] 43 Ec 42.06N 111.53W
Preston [Ont.-Can.] 44 Gd 43.23N 80.21W
Prestonsburg 44 Fg 37.40N 82.46W
Preststranda 8 Ce 59.06N 9.04E
Prestwick 9 If 55.30N 4.37W
Prêto, Rio- [Braz.] 54 Jf 11.21S 43.52W
Prêto, Rio- [Braz.] 55 Gd 18.44S 50.23W
Prêto, Rio- [Braz.] 55 Ic 17.00S 46.12W
Prêto, Rio- [Braz.] 55 Ha 13.37S 48.06W
Prêto do Igapó Açu, Rio- 54 Gd 4.26S 59.48W
Pretoria 31 Jk 25.45S 28.10E
Pretty Rock Butte 45 Fc 46.10N 101.42W
Preußisch-Oldendorf 12 Kb 52.18N 8.30E
Préveza 15 Dk 38.57N 20.45E
Prey 12 Df 48.58N 1.13E
Prey Vêng 25 Lf 11.29N 105.19E
Priangarskoje Plato 20 Ee 57.30N 97.00E
Priargunsk 20 Gf 50.27N 119.00E
Pribelski 17 Hi 54.24N 56.29E
Pribilof Islands 38 Cd 57.00N 170.00W
Priboj 15 Cf 43.35N 19.32E
Příbram 10 Kg 49.42N 14.01E
Price [Que.-Can.] 44 Ma 48.39N 68.12W
Price [Ut.-U.S.] 46 Jg 39.36N 110.48W
Price River 46 Jg 39.10N 110.06W
Prichard 44 Cj 30.44N 88.05W
Prickly Pear Cays 51b Ab 18.16N 63.11W
Prickly Point 51p Bc 11.59N 61.45W
Pridneprovskaja Vozvyšennost=Dnepr Upland (EN) 5 Jf 49.00N 32.00E
Priego 13 Jd 40.27N 2.18W
Priego de Córdoba 13 Hg 37.26N 4.11W
Priei, Măgura- 15 Fc 46.58N 22.50E
Priekule 7 Eh 56.29N 21.37E
Priekulė/Prekule 8 Ii 55.36N 21.12E
Prienai/Prenaj 7 Fi 54.39N 23.59E
Priene 24 Bd 37.40N 27.13E
Prieska 31 Jk 29.40S 22.42E
Priest Lake 46 Gb 48.34N 116.52W
Prieta, Peña- 13 Ha 43.01N 4.44W
Prieta, Sierra- 48 Cb 31.15N 112.55W
Prievidza 10 Oh 48.46N 18.39E
Prignitz 10 Hc 53.00N 12.00E
Prijedor 14 Kf 44.59N 16.42E
Prijepolje 15 Cf 43.24N 19.39E
Prijutovo 19 Fe 53.58N 53.58E
Prikaspijskaja Nizmennost=Caspian Depression (EN) 5 Lf 48.00N 52.00E
Prilenskoje Plato = Lena Mountains (EN) 21 Oc 60.45N 125.00E
Prilep 15 Eh 41.21N 21.34E
Priluki 19 De 50.36N 32.24E
Primavera 66 Qe 64.09S 60.57W
Primeira Cruz 54 Jd 2.30S 43.26W
Primorje 8 Hj 54.56N 20.00E
Primorsk 7 Gf 60.22N 28.36E
Primorsk 16 Jf 46.43N 36.22E
Primorski Hrebet 20 Ff 52.30N 106.00E
Primorski Kraj [3] 20 Ig 45.30N 135.30E
Primorsko 15 Kg 42.16N 27.46E
Primorsko-Ahtarsk 19 Df 46.03N 38.11E
Primorskoje 8 Ld 60.32N 27.56E
Primorskoje 15 Nd 45.59N 30.15E
Primošten 14 Jg 43.36N 15.55E
Primrose Lake 42 Gf 54.55N 109.45W
Prims 12 Ie 49.20N 6.44E
Prince Albert 39 Id 53.12N 104.46W
Prince Albert Mountains 66 Jf 76.00S 161.30E
Prince Albert Peninsula 42 Fb 72.30N 116.00W
Prince Albert Road 37 Cf 33.13S 22.02E
Prince Albert Sound 42 Gb 70.25N 115.00W
Prince Alfred, Cape- 42 Fb 74.05N 124.29W
Prince Charles 38 Lc 67.50N 76.00W
Prince Charles Mountains 66 Ff 72.00S 67.00E
Prince-de-Galles, Cap- 42 Kd 61.36N 71.30W
Prince Edward 30 Km 46.33S 37.57E
Prince Edward Island [3] 42 Lg 46.30N 63.00W
Prince Edward Island 38 Me 46.30N 63.00W
Prince Edward Islands 30 Km 46.35S 37.56E
Prince George 39 Gd 53.55N 122.49W
Prince Gustaf Adolf Sea 38 Ib 78.30N 107.00W
Prince of Wales [Ak.-U.S.] 40 Me 55.47N 132.50W
Prince of Wales [Can.] 38 Jb 72.40N 99.00W
Prince of Wales, Cape- 38 Cc 65.40N 168.05W
Prince of Wales Island 59 Ib 10.40S 142.10E
Prince of Wales Mountains 42 Ja 77.45N 78.00W
Prince of Wales Strait 42 Fb 72.45N 118.00W
Prince Patrick 38 Hb 76.45N 119.30W
Prince Regent Inlet 42 Ib 72.45N 90.30W
Prince Rupert 39 Fd 54.19N 130.19W
Prince Rupert Bay 51g Ba 15.34N 61.29W
Prince Rupert Bluff 51g Ba 15.35N 61.29W
Princes Risborough 12 Bc 51.43N 0.49W
Princess Anne 44 Jf 38.12N 75.41W
Princess Charlotte Bay 59 Ib 14.25S 144.00E
Princess Elizabeth Land 66 Ff 70.00S 80.00E

Index Symbols

[1] Independent Nation
[2] State, Region
[3] District, County
[4] Municipality
[5] Colony, Dependency
Continent
Physical Region
Historical or Cultural Region
Mount, Mountain
Volcano
Hill
Mountains, Mountain Range
Hills, Escarpment
Plateau, Upland
Pass, Gap
Plain, Lowland
Delta
Salt Flat
Valley, Canyon
Crater, Cave
Karst Features
Depression
Polder
Desert, Dunes
Forest, Woods
Heath, Steppe
Oasis
Cape, Point
Coast, Beach
Cliff
Peninsula
Isthmus
Sandbank
Island
Atoll
Rock, Reef
Islands, Archipelago
Rocks, Reefs
Coral Reef
Well, Spring
Geyser
River, Stream
Waterfall Rapids
River Mouth, Estuary
Lake
Salt Lake
Intermittent Lake
Reservoir
Swamp, Pond
Canal
Glacier
Ice Shelf, Pack Ice
Ocean
Sea
Gulf, Bay
Strait, Fjord
Lagoon
Bank
Seamount
Tablemount
Ridge
Shelf
Basin
Escarpment, Sea Scarp
Fracture
Trench, Abyss
National Park, Reserve
Point of Interest
Recreation Site
Cave, Cavern
Historic Site
Ruins
Wall, Walls
Church, Abbey
Temple
Scientific Station
Airport
Port
Lighthouse
Mine
Tunnel
Dam, Bridge

Princess Margaret Range	42	Ia	79.00N	88.30W
Princess Royal	42	Ef	52.55N	128.50W
Princeton [B.C.-Can.]	42	Fg	49.27N	120.31W
Princeton [Il.-U.S.]	45	Lf	41.23N	89.28W
Princeton [In.-U.S.]	44	Df	38.21N	87.34W
Princeton [Ky.-U.S.]	44	Dg	37.07N	87.53W
Princeton [Mo.-U.S.]	45	Jf	40.24N	93.35W
Prince William Sound	38	Ec	60.40N	147.00W
Principe	30	Hh	1.37N	7.25 E
Prineville	46	Ed	44.18N	120.51W
Prineville Reservoir	46	Ed	44.08N	120.42W
Prins Christians Sund	41	Hf	60.00N	43.10W
Prinsesse Astrid Kyst	66	Cf	70.45 S	12.30 E
Prinsesse Ragnhild Kyst	66	Df	70.15 S	27.30 E
Prins Harald Kyst	66	De	69.30 S	36.00 E
Prins Karls Forland	41	Nc	78.32N	11.10 E
Prinzapolka	47	Hf	13.24N	83.34W
Prinzapolka, Rio-	49	Fg	13.24N	83.34W
Priora, Mount-	59	Ja	6.51 S	145.58 E
Priozersk	19	Dc	61.04N	30.07 E
Pripet Marshes (EN)	5	Ie	52.00N	27.00 E
Pripjat	5	Je	51.21N	30.09 E
Pripoljarny Ural=Subpolar Urals (EN)	5	Lb	65.00N	60.00 E
Prirečny	19	Db	69.02N	30.15 E
Prišib	16	Pj	39.06N	48.38 E
Prislop, Pasul-	15	Hb	47.37N	24.55 E
Pristan-Prževalsk	18	Lc	42.33N	78.18 E
Pristen	16	Jd	51.15N	36.42 E
Priština	15	Eg	42.40N	21.10 E
Pritzwalk	10	Ic	53.09N	12.11 E
Privas	11	Kj	44.44N	4.36 E
Priverno	14	Hi	41.28N	13.11 E
Privolžkaja Vozvyšennost=Volga Hills (EN)	5	Ke	52.00N	46.00 E
Privolžsk	7	Jh	57.27N	41.16 E
Privolžski	16	Od	51.23N	46.02 E
Prizren	15	Dg	42.13N	20.45 E
Prizzi	14	Hm	37.43N	13.26 E
Prjaža	7	Hf	61.43N	33.37 E
Prnjavor	14	Lf	44.52N	17.40 E
Probolinggo	26	Fh	7.45 S	113.13 E
Prochowice	10	Me	51.17N	16.22 E
Procida	14	Hj	40.45N	14.00 E
Proctor Reservoir	45	Gj	32.02N	98.32W
Proddatur	25	Ff	14.44N	78.33 E
Profitis Ilias [Grc.]	15	Fm	36.53N	22.22 E
Profitis Ilias [Grc.]	15	Fj	39.50N	22.38 E
Profondeville	12	Gd	50.23N	4.52 E
Progonati	15	Ci	40.13N	19.56 E
Prograničnik	18	Dg	35.43N	63.12 E
Progreso [Mex.]	39	Kg	21.17N	89.40W
Progreso [Mex.]	48	Id	27.28N	101.04W
Progress	20	Hg	49.41N	129.40 E
Prohladny	16	Nh	43.45N	44.01 E
Prohorovka	16	Jd	51.02N	36.42 E
Prokopjevsk	22	Kd	53.53N	86.45 E
Prokuplje	15	Ef	43.15N	21.36 E
Proletari	7	Hg	58.26N	31.43 E
Proletarsk	19	Ef	46.41N	41.44 E
Proletarsk	18	Gd	40.10N	69.31 E
Proletarski	16	Id	50.51N	35.46 E
Proletarskoje Vodohranilišče	16	Mf	46.30N	42.10 E
Proliv Soela/Soela Väin	8	Jf	58.40N	22.30 E
Prome	22	Lh	18.49N	95.13 E
Promissão, Represa-	56	Kb	21.32 S	49.52W
Promissão	55	He	21.32 S	49.52W
Promyšlenny	17	Kc	67.35N	63.55 E
Pronja	16	Gc	53.27N	31.03 E
Pronja	16	Lb	54.21N	40.24 E
Pronsfeld	12	Id	50.10N	6.20 E
Prophet	42	Fe	58.46N	122.45W
Propriá	54	Kf	10.13 S	36.51W
Propriano	11a	Ab	41.40N	8.54 E
Prorva	16	Rg	45.57N	53.13 E
Proserpine	59	Jd	20.24 S	148.34 E
Prosna	10	Nd	52.10N	17.39 E
Prosotsáni	15	Gh	41.11N	23.59 E
Prosperidad	26	Ie	8.34N	125.52 E
Prospihino	20	Ee	58.37N	99.20 E
Prosser	46	Fc	46.12N	119.46W
Prostějov	10	Ng	49.29N	17.07 E
Proszowice	10	Qf	50.12N	20.18 E
Próti	15	El	37.03N	21.33 E
Protoka	16	Jg	45.43N	37.46 E
Protva	7	Ii	54.51N	37.16 E
Provadija	15	Kf	43.11N	27.26 E
Prøven	41	Gd	72.15N	55.40W
Provence	11	Lk	44.00N	6.00 E
Provence	5	Gg	44.00N	6.00 E
Providence [Ky.-U.S.]	44	Dg	37.24N	87.39W
Providence [R.I.-U.S.]	39	Le	41.50N	71.25W
Providence, Cape-	62	Bg	46.01 S	166.28 E
Providence Bay	44	Fc	45.44N	82.18W
Providence Island	30	Mi	9.14 S	51.02 E
Providencia, Isla de-	47	Hf	13.21N	81.22W
Providenciales	49	Kc	21.49N	72.15W
Providenija	22	Uc	64.23N	173.18W
Provincetown	44	Ld	42.03N	70.11W
Provins	11	Jf	48.33N	3.18 E
Provo	39	He	40.14N	111.39W
Prozor	14	Lg	43.49N	17.37 E
Prudentópolis	55	Gg	25.12 S	50.57W
Prudhoe Bay	39	Eb	70.20N	148.25W
Prudnik	10	Nf	50.19N	17.34 E
Prüm	12	Ie	49.49N	6.28 E
Prüm	10	Cf	50.13N	6.25 E
Prune Island	51n	Bb	12.35N	61.24W
Prussia (EN)	10	Pc	53.45N	20.00 E
Pruszcz Gdański	10	Ob	54.16N	18.36 E
Pruszków	10	Qd	52.11N	20.48 E
Prut	5	If	45.28N	28.14 E
Pružany	19	Ce	52.36N	24.28 E
Prvić	14	If	44.54N	14.48 E
Prydz Bay	66	Fe	69.00 S	76.00 E
Pryor	45	Ih	36.19N	95.19W
Przasnysz	10	Qc	53.01N	20.55 E
Przedbórz	10	Pe	51.06N	19.53 E
Przemyśl [2]	10	Sg	49.45N	22.45 E
Przemyśl	10	Sg	49.47N	22.47 E
Prževalsk	22	Je	42.29N	78.24 E
Przeworsk	10	Sf	50.05N	22.29 E
Przysucha	10	Qe	51.22N	20.38 E
Psakhná	15	Gk	38.35N	23.38 E
Psará	15	Ik	38.35N	25.37 E
Psathoúra	15	Hj	39.30N	24.11 E
Pščiš	16	Kg	45.03N	39.25 E
Psebaj	16	Lg	44.07N	40.47 E
Psël	5	Jf	49.05N	33.30 E
Psérimos	15	Km	36.56N	27.09 E
Psina	10	Of	50.02N	18.16 E
Pšiš, Gora-	16	Lh	43.24N	41.14 E
Pskem	18	Hd	41.38N	70.01 E
Pskent	18	Gd	40.54N	69.23 E
Pskov	6	Id	57.50N	28.20 E
Pskov, Lake- (EN)=Pihkva järv	7	Gg	58.00N	28.00 E
Pskov, Lake- (EN)=Pskovskoje Ozero	5	Id	58.00N	28.00 E
Pskova	8	Mg	57.47N	28.30 E
Pskovskaja Oblast [3]	19	Cd	57.20N	29.20 E
Pskovskoje Ozero=Pskov, Lake- (EN)	5	Id	58.00N	28.00 E
Psunj	14	Le	45.24N	17.20 E
Ptič	16	Fc	52.09N	28.52 E
Ptolemais	15	Ei	40.31N	21.41 E
Ptuj	14	Jd	46.25N	15.52 E
Pua-a, Cape-	65c	Aa	13.26 S	172.43W
Puah, Pulau-	26	Hg	0.30 S	122.34 E
Puapua	65c	Aa	13.34 S	172.09W
Pucallpa	53	If	8.20 S	74.30W
Pučež	7	Kh	56.59N	43.11 E
Pucheng [China]	27	Kf	27.55N	118.30 E
Pucheng [China]	27	Id	35.00N	109.38 E
Pucho	36	Cf	17.35 S	16.30 E
Pucioasa	15	Id	45.05N	25.25 E
Pučišća	14	Kg	43.21N	16.44 E
Puck	10	Ob	54.44N	18.27 E
Pucka, Zatoka-	10	Ob	54.40N	18.35 E
Pudasjärvi	7	Gd	65.23N	27.00 E
Pudož	19	Dc	61.50N	36.32 E
Pudukkottai	25	Ff	10.23N	78.49 E
Puebla [2]	47	Ee	18.50N	98.00W
Puebla, Sierra de-	48	Kh	19.50N	97.00W
Puebla de Alcocer	13	Gf	38.59N	5.15W
Puebla de Don Fadrique	13	Jg	37.58N	2.26W
Puebla de Guzmán	13	Eg	37.37N	7.15W
Puebla de Sanabria	13	Fb	42.03N	6.38W
Puebla de Trives	13	Eb	42.20N	7.15W
Puebla de Zaragoza	39	Jh	19.03N	98.12W
Pueblo	39	If	38.16N	104.37W
Pueblo Libertador	55	Cj	30.13 S	59.23W
Pueblo Nuevo [Mex.]	48	Gf	23.23N	105.23W
Pueblo Nuevo [Ven.]	49	Mh	11.58N	69.55W
Pueblo Nuevo Tiquisate	49	Bf	14.17N	91.22W
Pueblo Viejo, Laguna de-	48	Kf	22.10N	97.55W
Puelches	56	Ge	38.09 S	65.55W
Puenteáreas	13	Db	42.11N	8.30W
Puente de la Reina	13	Kb	42.40N	1.49W
Puentedeume	13	Da	43.24N	8.10W
Puente-Genil	13	Hg	37.23N	4.47W
Puentelarrá	13	Ib	42.45N	3.03W
Pueo Point	65a	Ab	21.54N	160.04W
Pu'er	27	Hg	23.00N	101.00 E
Puerca, Punta-	51a	Cb	18.15N	65.35W
Puerco, Rio-	45	Ci	34.22N	107.50W
Puerco River	46	Ji	34.52N	110.05W
Puerto Abente	55	Df	22.55 S	57.43W
Puerto Acosta	54	Eg	15.32 S	69.15W
Puerto Adela	55	Eg	24.33 S	54.22W
Puerto Aisén	53	Ij	45.24 S	72.42W
Puerto Alegre	54	Ff	13.53 S	61.36W
Puerto Ángel	47	Ee	15.40N	96.29W
Puerto Arista	48	Mj	15.56N	93.48W
Puerto Armuelles	47	Hg	8.17N	82.52W
Puerto Asis	54	Cc	0.29N	76.32W
Puerto Ayacucho	53	Je	5.40N	67.35W
Puerto Ayora	54a	Ab	0.45 S	90.23W
Puerto Barrios	39	Kh	15.43N	88.36W
Puerto Bermejo	55	Ch	26.56 S	58.30W
Puerto Berrío	54	Db	6.30N	74.25W
Puerto Boyacá	54	Db	5.45N	74.29W
Puerto Caballo	55	Ce	20.12 S	58.12W
Puerto Cabello	53	Jd	10.28N	68.01W
Puerto Cabezas	47	Hf	14.02N	83.23W
Puerto Carreño	53	Je	6.12N	67.22W
Puerto Casado	56	Ib	20.20 S	57.55W
Puerto Colombia	49	Jh	10.59N	74.57W
Puerto Colón	55	Df	23.11 S	57.33W
Puerto Constanza	55	Ck	33.50 S	59.03W
Puerto Cooper	56	Ib	23.03 S	57.43W
Puerto Cortés [C.R.]	49	Fi	8.58N	83.32W
Puerto Cortés [Hond.]	39	Kh	15.48N	87.56W
Puerto Cumarebo	54	Ea	11.29N	69.21W
Puerto de Eten	54	Ce	6.56 S	79.52W
Puerto de la Cruz	32	Dd	28.23N	16.33W
Puerto de Lajas, Cerro-	47	Cc	28.59N	107.02W
Puerto del Rosario	32	Ed	28.30N	13.52W
Puerto de Mazarrón	13	Kg	37.34N	1.15W
Puerto de San José	47	Ff	13.55N	90.49W
Puerto Deseado	53	Jj	47.45 S	65.55W
Puerto de Sóller	13	Oe	39.48N	2.41 E
Puerto Escondido [Mex.]	47	Ee	15.48N	96.57W
Puerto Escondido [Mex.]	48	De	25.48N	111.20W
Puerto Esperanza [Arg.]	55	Eh	26.01 S	54.39W
Puerto Esperanza [Par.]	55	Ce	20.26 S	58.06W
Puerto Estrella	49	Lg	12.14N	71.13W
Puerto Fonciere	55	Df	22.29 S	57.48W
Puerto Francisco de Orellana	54	Cd	0.27 S	76.57W
Puerto Frey	55	Bb	14.42 S	61.10W
Puerto Gaitán	54	Dc	4.20N	72.10W
Puerto General Diaz	55	Eg	25.12 S	54.32W
Puerto Goya	55	Ci	29.09 S	59.20W
Puerto Grether	54	Fg	17.12 S	64.21W
Puerto Guarani	55	De	21.18 S	57.55W
Puerto Heath	54	Ef	12.30 S	68.40W
Puerto Huasco	56	Fc	28.28 S	71.14W
Puerto Huitoto	54	Dc	0.18N	74.03W
Puerto Iguazú	56	Jc	25.34 S	54.34W
Puerto Indio	55	Eg	24.52 S	54.29W
Puerto Ingeniero Ibañez	56	Fg	46.18 S	71.56W
Puerto Isabel	55	Dd	18.11 S	57.37W
Puerto Jesús	49	Eh	10.07N	85.16W
Puerto Juárez	39	Kg	21.11N	86.49W
Puerto la Concordia	54	Dc	2.38N	72.47W
Puerto la Cruz	53	Jd	10.13N	64.38W
Puerto Leguizamo	53	If	0.12 S	74.46W
Puerto Lempira	49	Ff	15.15N	83.46W
Puerto Libertad	47	Bc	29.55N	112.43W
Puerto Limón [Col.]	54	Cc	1.02N	76.32W
Puerto Limón [Col.]	54	Dc	3.23N	73.30W
Puertollano	13	Hf	38.41N	4.07W
Puerto Lopez	47	Jh	4.06N	72.58W
Puerto López	49	Lh	11.56N	71.17W
Puerto Lumbreras	13	Kg	37.34N	1.49W
Puerto Madero	48	Mj	14.44N	92.25W
Puerto Madryn	56	Gf	42.46 S	65.03W
Puerto Magdalena	48	Ce	24.35N	112.05W
Puerto Maldonado	53	Jg	12.36 S	69.11W
Puerto Marangatú	55	Eg	24.39 S	54.21W
Puerto Mayor Otaño	55	Eh	26.19 S	54.44W
Puerto Mihanovich	55	De	20.52 S	57.59W
Puerto Monte Lindo	55	Df	23.57 S	57.12W
Puerto Montt	53	Ij	41.28 S	72.57W
Puerto Morelos	48	Pg	20.50N	86.52W
Puerto Mutis	54	Cb	6.14N	77.25W
Puerto Naranjito	55	Eh	26.57 S	55.18W
Puerto Nariño	54	Ec	4.56N	67.48W
Puerto Natales	53	Ik	51.44 S	72.31W
Puerto Nuevo	55	Ce	20.33 S	58.03W
Puerto Nuevo, Punta-	51a	Bb	18.30N	66.21W
Puerto Ordaz	54	Fb	8.22N	62.41W
Puerto Padre	49	Ic	21.12N	76.36W
Puerto Páez	54	Eb	6.13N	67.28W
Puerto Peñasco	47	Bb	31.20N	113.33W
Puerto Piña	49	Hj	7.35N	78.10W
Puerto Pinasco	56	Ib	22.43 S	57.50W
Puerto Piritu	50	Dg	10.04N	65.03W
Puerto Plata	47	Je	19.48N	70.41W
Puerto Presidente Stroessner	55	Eg	25.33 S	54.39W
Puerto Princesa	22	Ni	9.44N	118.44 E
Puerto Quijarro	55	Dc	17.47 S	57.46W
Puerto Real	13	Fh	36.32N	6.11W
Puerto Rico [5]	39	Mh	18.15N	66.30W
Puerto Rico	38	Mh	18.15N	66.30W
Puerto Rico [Arg.]	56	Jc	26.48 S	54.59W
Puerto Rico [Bol.]	54	Ef	11.05 S	67.38W
Puerto Rico [Col.]	54	Cc	1.54N	75.10W
Puerto Rico Trench (EN)	3	Bg	20.00N	66.00W
Puerto Rondón	54	Db	6.18N	71.06W
Puerto San José	55	Eg	26.32 S	54.50W
Puerto Santa Cruz	53	Jk	50.09 S	68.30W
Puerto Sastre	56	Ib	22.06 S	57.59W
Puerto Siles	54	Ef	12.48 S	65.05W
Puerto Suárez	53	Kg	18.57 S	57.51W
Puerto Tacurú Pytá	55	Df	23.49 S	57.09W
Puerto Tirol	55	Ch	27.23 S	59.05W
Puerto Tres Palmas	55	De	21.43 S	57.58W
Puerto Triunfo	55	Eg	26.45 S	55.06W
Puerto Vallarta	47	Cd	20.37N	105.15W
Puerto Varas	56	Ff	41.19 S	72.59W
Puerto Victoria	55	Eh	26.20 S	54.39W
Puerto Viejo	49	Eh	10.26N	83.59W
Puerto Villamizar	49	Ki	8.19N	72.26W
Puerto Villazón	55	Ba	13.32 S	61.57W
Puerto Wilches	54	Db	7.20N	73.54W
Puerto Ybapobó	55	Df	23.42 S	57.12W
Pueu	65e	Fc	17.44 S	149.13W
Pugačev	19	Ee	52.03N	48.48 E
Puget Sound	46	Dc	48.00N	122.30W
Puglia=Apulia (EN) [2]	14	Ki	41.15N	16.15 E
Pu He	28	Gd	41.21N	122.47 E
Puhja	8	Lf	58.13N	26.17 E
Puigcerdá	13	Nb	42.26N	1.56 E
Puigmal	13	Ob	42.23N	2.07 E
Puir	20	Jf	53.10N	141.25 E
Puisaye, Collines de la-	11	Jg	47.35N	3.18 E
Puisieux	12	Ed	50.07N	2.42 E
Pujehum	34	Cd	7.21N	11.42W
Pujești	15	Kc	46.25N	27.29 E
Puji → Wugong	27	Ie	34.15N	108.14 E
Pujiang	28	Ei	29.28N	119.53 E
Pujili	54	Cd	0.57 S	78.42W
Puka	15	Cg	42.03N	19.54 E
Pukaki, Lake-	62	Df	44.05 S	170.10 E
Pukalani	65a	Ec	20.50N	156.21W
Pukapuka Atoll	57	Kf	10.53 S	165.49W
Pukapuka Atoll [W.F.]	57	Nf	14.49 S	138.48W
Pukaruha Atoll	57	Nf	18.20 S	137.02W
Pukatawagan	42	He	55.44N	101.19W
Pukchin	28	Hd	40.12N	125.45 E
Pukch'ŏng	27	Mc	40.14N	128.19 E
Pukega, Pointe-	64h	Ab	13.17 S	176.13W
Pukekohe	62	Fb	37.12 S	174.54 E
Pukemiro	62	Fb	37.37 S	175.01 E
Pukeuri Junction	62	Df	45.02 S	171.02 E
Pukšenga	7	Je	63.36N	41.55 E
Puksoozero	19	Ec	62.38N	40.32 E
Puksubaek-san	28	Id	40.42N	127.15 E
Pula [It.]	14	Ck	39.01N	9.00 E
Pula	14	Hf	44.52N	13.50 E
Pula, Capo di-	14	Dl	38.59N	9.01 E
Pulandian → Xinjin	27	Ld	39.24N	121.59 E
Pulap Atoll	57	Fd	7.39N	149.25 E
Pulaski [Tn.-U.S.]	44	Dh	35.12N	87.02W
Pulaski [Va.-U.S.]	44	Gg	37.03N	80.47W
Pulau	26	Kh	5.50 S	138.15 E
Pulau Halura	26	Hi	10.19 S	120.11 E
Pulau Irian/New Guinea	57	Fe	5.00 S	140.00 E
Pulau Sapudi	26	Fh	7.06 S	114.20 E
Puławy	10	Re	51.25N	21.57 E
Pulborough	12	Bd	50.57N	0.31W
Pulheim	12	Ic	51.00N	6.48 E
Pulkau	14	Kb	48.43N	16.21 E
Pulkkila	7	Fd	64.16N	25.52 E
Pullman	43	Db	46.44N	117.10W
Pulo Anna Island	57	Ed	4.40N	131.58 E
Pulog, Mount-	21	Oh	16.36N	120.54 E
Pulpito, Punta-	48	Dd	26.30N	111.30W
Pulsano	14	Lj	40.23N	17.21 E
Pułtusk	10	Rd	52.43N	21.05 E
Pülümür	24	Hc	39.30N	39.54 E
Pulusuk Island	57	Fd	6.42N	149.19 E
Puluwat Atoll	57	Fd	7.22N	149.11 E
Puma Yumco	27	Ff	28.35N	90.20 E
Pumpénai/Pumpenaj	8	Ki	55.53N	24.25 E
Pumpenaj/Pumpėnai	8	Ki	55.53N	24.25 E
Pumpkin Creek	46	Mc	46.15N	105.45W
Punā, Isla-	54	Bd	2.50 S	80.10W
Punākha	25	Hc	27.37N	89.52 E
Punaluu	65a	Fd	19.08N	155.30W
Pünch	25	Eb	33.46N	74.06 E
Punda Milia	37	Ed	22.40 S	31.05 E
Pune (Poona)	22	Jh	18.32N	73.52 E
Pünel	24	Md	37.33N	49.07 E
Pungan	18	Hd	40.45N	70.50 E
P'unggi	28	Jf	36.52N	128.32 E
Púngoè	37	Ec	19.50 S	34.48 E
P'ungsan	28	Jd	40.40N	128.05 E
Punia	36	Ec	1.28 S	26.27 E
Punitaqui	56	Fd	30.50 S	71.16W
Punjab [3]	25	Fb	31.00N	76.00 E
Punjab	21	Jf	30.00N	74.00 E
Punjad [3]	25	Eb	30.00N	74.00 E
Punkaharju	8	Mc	61.48N	29.24 E
Punkalaidun	8	Jc	61.07N	23.06 E
Puno	53	Ig	15.50 S	70.02W
Puno [2]	54	Ef	15.00 S	70.00W
Punta, Cerro de-	47	Ke	18.10N	66.36W
Punta Alta	53	Ji	38.53 S	62.04W
Punta Arenas	53	Ik	53.09 S	70.55W
Punta Cardón	54	Da	11.38N	70.14W
Punta de Mata	50	Eh	9.43N	63.38W
Punta Gorda [Blz.]	47	Ge	16.07N	88.48W
Punta Gorda [Fl.-U.S.]	44	Fl	26.56N	82.03W
Punta Gorda [Nic.]	49	Fh	11.31N	83.47W
Punta Gorda, Bahia de-	49	Fh	11.15N	83.45W
Punta Gorda, Rio-	49	Fh	11.30N	83.47W
Punta Indio	55	Dl	35.16 S	57.14W
Punta Prieta	47	Bc	28.58N	114.17W
Puntarenas [3]	49	Ei	9.00N	83.15W
Puntarenas	39	Ki	9.58N	84.50W
Punta Róbalo	49	Fi	9.02N	82.15W
Punto Fijo	54	Da	11.42N	70.13W
Puolanka	7	Gd	64.52N	27.40 E
Puolo Point	65a	Bb	21.54N	159.36W
Puqi	27	Jf	29.43N	113.52 E
Puquio	54	Df	14.42 S	74.08W
Purace, Volcán-	54	Cc	2.21N	76.23W
Purari	60	Ci	7.52 S	145.10 E
Purcell Mountains	42	Fg	49.55N	116.15W
Purdy Islands	57	Fe	2.53 S	146.20 E
Purgatoire River	45	Eg	38.04N	103.10W
Puri	25	He	19.48N	85.51 E
Purificación	47	Ed	23.58N	98.42W
Purikari Neem/Purikarinem	8	Ke	59.36N	25.35 E
Purikarinem/Purikari Neem	8	Ke	59.36N	25.35 E
Purmani/Puurmani	8	Lf	58.30N	26.14 E
Purmerend	11	Kb	52.31N	4.57 E
Purna [India]	25	Fe	19.07N	77.02 E
Purna [India]	25	Fd	21.05N	76.00 E
Purnač	7	Jc	67.00N	40.15 E
Pūrnia	25	Hc	25.47N	87.28 E
Purukcahu	26	Fg	0.35 S	114.35 E
Puruliya	25	Hd	23.20N	86.22 E
Puruni River	50	Gi	6.00N	59.12W
Purus, Rio-	52	Jf	3.42 S	61.28W
Puruvesi	7	Gf	61.50N	29.25 E
Purwakarta	26	Eh	6.34 S	107.26 E
Purwokerto	26	Eh	7.25 S	109.14 E
Pusala Dağı	24	Ed	37.12N	32.54 E
Pusan	22	Of	35.06N	129.03 E
Pusan Si [2]	28	Jg	35.10N	129.05 E
Pushi He	28	Hd	40.17N	124.43 E
Puškin	19	Dd	59.43N	30.24 E
Puškino	16	Pj	39.28N	48.33 E
Puškino	16	Od	51.14N	46.59 E
Puškino	7	Ih	56.02N	37.53 E
Puškinskije Gory	8	Mh	56.59N	28.59 E
Pušlahta	7	Id	64.48N	36.33 E
Püspökladány	10	Ri	47.19N	21.07 E
Püssi/Pjussi	8	Le	59.17N	26.57 E
Pusteci	15	Di	40.47N	20.54 E
Pusteria, Val-/Pustertal	14	Gd	46.45N	12.20 E
Pustertal/Pusteria, Val-	14	Gd	46.45N	12.20 E
Pustomyty	10	Tg	49.37N	23.59 E
Pustoška	7	Gh	56.20N	29.22 E
Putao	25	Jc	27.21N	97.24 E
Putaruru	62	Fc	38.03 S	175.47 E
Putian	27	Kf	25.32N	119.01 E
Putignano	14	Lj	40.51N	17.07 E
Putila	15	Ip	48.00N	25.07 E
Putivl	16	Hd	51.22N	33.55 E
Putjatin	28	Lc	42.52N	132.25 E
Putla de Guerrero	48	Ki	17.02N	97.56W
Putna	15	Kd	45.34N	27.30 E
Putna	15	Ib	47.52N	25.37 E
Putnok	10	Qh	48.18N	20.26 E
Puto	63a	Ba	5.41 S	154.43 E
Putorana, Plato-=Putoran Mountains (EN)	21	Lc	69.00N	95.00 E
Putoran Mountains (EN)=Putorana, Plato-	21	Lc	69.00N	95.00 E
Puttalam	25	Fg	8.02N	79.49 E
Putte	12	Gc	51.04N	4.38 E
Puttelange-aux-Lacs	12	Ie	49.03N	6.56 E
Putten	12	Hb	52.16N	5.35 E
Putten	12	Gc	51.50N	4.15 E
Puttgarden, Burg auf Fehmarn-	10	Hb	54.30N	11.13 E
Püttlingen	12	Ie	49.17N	6.53 E
Putumayo [2]	54	Cc	0.30N	76.00W
Putumayo, Rio-	52	Jf	3.07 S	67.58W
Putuo (Shenjiamen)	28	Gj	29.57N	122.18 E
Putussibau	26	Ff	0.50N	112.56 E
Puu Kukui	65a	Ec	20.54N	156.35W
Puulavesi	5	Ic	61.50N	26.40 E
Puumala	7	Gf	61.32N	28.11 E
Puu o Umi	65a	Fc	20.05N	155.42W
Puurmani/Purmani	8	Lf	58.30N	26.14 E
Puurs	12	Gc	51.05N	4.17 E
Puuwai	65a	Ab	21.54N	160.12W
Puyallup	46	Dc	47.11N	122.18W
Puyang	27	Jd	35.41N	115.00 E
Puy-de-Dôme [3]	11	Ii	45.40N	3.00 E
Puy-l'Évêque	11	Hj	44.30N	1.08 E
Puymorens, Col de-	11	Hl	42.34N	1.49 E
Puyo	54	Cd	1.29 S	77.58W
Puysegur Point	62	Bg	46.10 S	166.37 E
Pwani [3]	36	Gd	7.30 S	39.00 E
Pweto	31	Ji	8.28 S	28.54 E
Pwllheli	9	Ii	52.53N	4.25W
Pyapon	25	Je	16.17N	95.41 E
Pyhäjärvi	7	Fe	63.40N	25.59 E
Pyhäjärvi [Fin.]	7	Ff	61.00N	22.20 E
Pyhäjärvi [Fin.]	7	Fe	63.35N	25.57 E
Pyhäjärvi [Fin.]	8	Kc	62.45N	25.25 E
Pyhäjärvi [Fin.]	8	Jc	61.30N	23.35 E
Pyhäjoki	7	Fd	64.28N	24.13 E
Pyhäjoki	7	Fd	64.28N	24.14 E
Pyhäntä	7	Gd	64.06N	26.19 E
Pyhäranta	8	Id	60.57N	21.27 E
Pyhäselkä	7	Ge	62.30N	29.40 E
Pyhaselkä	8	Mb	62.26N	29.58 E
Pyhätunturi	7	Gc	67.01N	27.09 E
Pyhävesi	8	Lc	61.25N	26.35 E
Pyhävuori	8	Ib	62.17N	21.38 E
Pyhrnpaß	14	Ic	47.38N	14.18 E
Pyhtää/Pyttis	7	Gf	60.29N	26.32 E
Pyinmana	22	Lh	19.44N	96.13 E
Pylos (EN) = Pilos	15	Em	36.56N	21.40 E
Pyltsamaa/Põltsamaa	8	Lf	58.23N	26.08 E
Pyltsamaa/Põltsamaa	7	Fg	58.39N	25.59 E
Pylva/Põlva	7	Gg	58.04N	27.06 E
Pymatuning Reservoir	44	Ge	41.37N	80.30W
P'yŏngan-Namdo [2]	28	Ie	39.20N	126.00 E
P'yŏngan-Pukto [2]	28	Hd	40.00N	125.15 E
P'yŏnggang	27	Md	38.25N	127.17 E
P'yŏngsan	27	Md	38.20N	126.24 E
P'yongt'aek	28	If	36.59N	127.05 E
P'yŏngyang	22	Of	39.01N	125.45 E
P'yŏngyang Si [2]	28	He	39.04N	125.50 E
Pyramiden	41	Nc	77.54N	16.41 E
Pyramid Lake	43	Dc	40.00N	119.35W
Pyramid Mountains	45	Bj	32.00N	108.30W
Pyrénées=Pyrenees (EN)	5	Gg	42.40N	1.00 E
Pyrenees (EN)=Pirineos	5	Gg	42.40N	1.00 E
Pyrenees (EN)=Pyrénées	5	Gg	42.40N	1.00 E
Pyrenees (EN)=Serralada Pirinenca	5	Gg	42.40N	1.00 E
Pyrénées-Atlantiques [3]	11	Fk	43.15N	0.50W
Pyrénées-Orientales [3]	11	Il	42.30N	2.20 E
Pyrzyce	10	Kc	53.10N	14.55 E
Pyšma	19	Gd	57.08N	66.18 E
Pytalovo	7	Gh	57.06N	27.59 E
Pyttegga	8	Bd	62.13N	7.42 E
Pyttis/Pyhtää	7	Gf	60.29N	26.32 E
Pyu	25	Je	18.29N	96.26 E
Pyzaspea/Pöõsaspea Neem	8	Je	59.15N	23.25 E
Pyzdry	10	Nd	52.11N	17.41 E

Q

Qā', Wādī al-	24	Hi	27.04N	38.34 E
Qābis [3]	32	Ic	33.00N	9.30 E
Qābis	31	Ie	33.53N	10.07 E
Qābis, Khalīj-=Gabès, Gulf of-(EN)	30	Ie	34.00N	10.25 E
Qabr Hūd	35	Hb	16.09N	49.34 E
Qāderābād	24	Og	30.17N	53.16 E
Qādir Karam	24	Ke	35.12N	44.53 E
Qāḑub	23	Hg	12.38N	53.57 E
Qā'emshahr	24	Od	36.30N	52.55 E
Qafşah	31	He	34.25N	8.48 E
Qafşah [3]	32	Ic	34.30N	9.00 E
Qa'fūr	14	Dn	36.20N	9.19 E
Qagan	27	Kb	49.16N	118.04 E
Qagan Moron He	28	Ec	43.13N	119.02 E
Qagan Nur	27	Jc	43.20N	112.58 E
Qagan Nur [China]	28	Bd	41.33N	113.48 E
Qagan Nur [China]	27	Jc	43.25N	114.50 E
Qagan Nur [China]	28	Hb	45.14N	124.17 E
Qagan Nur→Zhengxiangbai Qi	27	Jc	42.16N	114.59 E
Qagan Us→Dulan	22	Lf	36.29N	98.29 E
Qagchêng/Xiangcheng	27	Gf	28.56N	99.46 E
Qahar Youyi Houqi (Bayan Qagan)	28	Bd	41.28N	113.10 E
Qahar Youyi Qianqi (Togrog Ul)	28	Bd	40.46N	113.13 E
Qahar Youyi Zhongqi	28	Bd	41.15N	112.36 E
Qahd, Wādī-	24	Ii	26.13N	40.49 E
Qaidam He	27	Gd	36.48N	95.50 E
Qaidam Pendi=Tsaidam Basin (EN)	27	Fd	37.00N	95.00 E

Index Symbols

[1] Independent Nation
[2] State, Region
[3] District, County
[4] Municipality
[5] Colony, Dependency
Continent
Physical Region
Historical or Cultural Region
Mount, Mountain
Volcano
Hill
Mountains, Mountain Range
Hills, Escarpment
Plateau, Upland
Pass, Gap
Plain, Lowland
Delta
Salt Flat
Valley, Canyon
Crater, Cave
Karst Features
Depression
Polder
Desert, Dunes
Forest, Woods
Heath, Steppe
Oasis
Cape, Point
Coast, Beach
Cliff
Peninsula
Isthmus
Sandbank
Island
Atoll
Rock, Reef
Islands, Archipelago
Rocks, Reefs
Coral Reef
Well, Spring
Geyser
River, Stream
Waterfall Rapids
River Mouth, Estuary
Lake
Salt Lake
Intermittent Lake
Reservoir
Swamp, Pond
Canal
Glacier
Ice Shelf, Pack Ice
Ocean
Sea
Gulf, Bay
Strait, Fjord
Lagoon
Bank
Seamount
Tablemount
Ridge
Shelf
Basin
Escarpment, Sea Scarp
Fracture
Trench, Abyss
National Park, Reserve
Point of Interest
Recreation Site
Cave, Cavern
Historic Site
Ruins
Wall, Walls
Church, Abbey
Temple
Scientific Station
Airport
Port
Lighthouse
Mine
Tunnel
Dam, Bridge

Qala'an Naḥl 35 Ec 13.38N 34.57 E
Qalāt 23 Kc 32.07N 66.54 E
Qal'at Abū Ghār 24 Lg 30.25N 46.09 E
Qal'at al Akhḍar 23 Ed 28.06N 37.05 E
Qal 'at al Marqab 24 Fe 35.09N 35.57 E
Qal'at al Mu'aẓẓam 24 Gi 27.45N 37.31 E
Qal'at aş Şanam 14 Co 35.46N 8.21 E
Qal'at Bishah 22 Gh 20.00N 42.36 E
Qal'at Dīzah 24 Kd 36.11N 45.07 E
Qal'at Şāliḥ 24 Lg 31.31N 47.16 E
Qal'at Sukkar 24 Lg 31.53N 46.56 E
Qal'eh Asgar 24 Qh 29.30N 56.35 E
Qal'eh Kūh 24 Mf 33.00N 49.10 E
Qal'eh Mūreh 24 Pe 35.35N 55.58 E
Qal'eh-ye Now 23 Jc 34.59N 63.08 E
Qal'eh-ye Sahar 24 Mg 31.40N 48.33 E
Qalīb ash Shuyūkh 23 Gd 29.12N 47.55 E
Qallābāt 35 Fc 12.58N 36.09 E
Qalmarz, Godār-e- 24 Qf 33.26N 56.14 E
Qalyūb 24 Dg 30.11N 31.13 E
Qamata 37 Df 31.58S 27.24 E
Qamdo 22 Lf 31.15N 97.12 E
Qamīnis 33 Dc 31.40N 20.01 E
Qamsar 24 Nf 33.45N 51.26 E
Qamūdah 32 Ic 35.00N 9.21 E
Qamūdah [3] 32 Ic 34.50N 9.20 E
Qânâq/Thule 67 Od 77.35N 69.40W
Qandahār [3] 23 Kc 31.00N 65.45 E
Qandahār 22 If 31.35N 65.45 E
Qandala 35 Hc 11.23N 49.53 E
Qangdin Gol 28 Cc 43.27N 115.03 E
Qanṭarat al Fahş 14 Dn 36.23N 9.54 E
Qapqal 27 Dc 43.48N 80.47 E
Qaqortoq/Julianehåb 67 Nc 60.50N 46.10W
Qarā Dāgh 24 Lc 38.48N 47.13 E
Qārah 33 Ed 29.37N 26.30 E
Qarah Būlāq 24 Ke 34.32N 45.12 E
Qarah Dagh 24 Jd 37.00N 43.30 E
Qarah Tappah 24 Ke 34.25N 44.56 E
Qarānqū 24 Ld 37.23N 47.43 E
Qardo 31 Lh 9.30N 49.03 E
Qareh Āghāj 24 Ld 36.46N 48.46 E
Qareh Sū [Iran] 23 Ib 37.00N 56.50 E
Qareh Sū [Iran] 23 Hc 34.52N 51.25 E
Qareh Ẕīā'Od Dīn 24 Kc 38.53N 45.02 E
Qarkilik/Ruoqiang 22 Kf 39.02N 88.00 E
Qarnayn, Jazirat al- 24 Oj 24.56N 52.52 E
Qarnayt, Jabal- 23 Fe 21.02N 40.22 E
Qarqan/Qiemo 22 Kf 38.08N 85.32 E
Qarqan He 21 Kf 39.30N 88.15 E
Qarqannah, Juzur-=
Kerkennah Islands (EN) 30 Ie 34.44N 11.12 E
Qartājannah 14 En 36.51N 10.20 E
Qārūn, Birkat- 27 Fd 29.28N 30.40 E
Qaryat Abū Nujaym 33 Cc 30.35N 15.24 E
Qaryat al Gharab 24 Kg 31.27N 44.48 E
Qaryat al Qaddāḥiyah 33 Cc 31.22N 15.14 E
Qaryat al 'Ulyā 23 Gd 27.33N 47.42 E
Qaryat az Zarrūq 33 Cc 32.22N 15.09 E
Qaryat az Zuwaytīnah 33 Dc 30.58N 20.07 E
Qaşabah, Ra's al- 24 Fh 28.02N 34.38 E
Qaşabāt, Hanshīr al- 14 Dn 36.24N 9.54 E
Qasigiánguit/Christianshåb 41 Ge 68.45N 51.30W
Qaşr al Azraq 24 Gg 31.53N 36.49 E
Qaşr Al Hayr 24 Ge 34.23N 37.36 E
Qaşr al Qarahbullī 33 Bc 32.45N 13.43 E
Qaşr 'Amij 24 If 33.30N 41.45 E
Qaşr Bū Hādī 33 Cc 31.03N 16.40 E
Qaşr Burqu' 24 Gf 32.37N 37.58 E
Qasr-e Shīrīn 23 Gc 34.31N 45.35 E
Qaşr Farāfirah 31 Jf 27.15N 28.10 E
Qasr Ḥamān 23 Ge 20.50N 45.50 E
Qaşr Qārūn 24 Dh 29.25N 30.25 E
Qaşş Abū Sa'īd 24 Bi 27.00N 27.35 E
Qatana 24 Gf 33.26N 36.05 E
Qaṭar 21 Hg 25.30N 51.15 E
Qaṭar [1] 22 Hg 25.30N 51.15 E
Qatlīsh 24 Qd 37.50N 57.19 E
Qaṭrānī, Jabal- 24 Dh 29.41N 30.35 E
Qatrūyeh 24 Ph 29.09N 54.43 E
Qattara Depression (EN)=
Qaṭṭārah, Munkhafaḍ al- 30 Je 30.00N 27.30 E
Qawām al Hamzah 24 Kg 31.43N 44.58 E
Qawz Abu Dulū' 35 Eb 16.55N 32.30 E
Qawz Rajab 35 Fb 16.04N 35.34 E
Qaysān 35 Ec 10.45N 34.48 E
Qayyārah 24 Je 35.48N 43.17 E
Qazaqstan =
Kazakhstan (EN) 19 Gf 48.00N 68.00 E
Qazvīn [Iran] 22 Gf 36.16N 50.00 E
Qazvīn [Iraq] 24 Je 34.21N 42.05 E
Qeqertarssuaq/Godhavn 67 Nc 69.20N 53.35W
Qeshm 24 Qi 26.58N 56.16 E
Qeshm 23 Id 26.45N 55.45 E
Qeydār 24 Md 36.07N 48.35 E
Qeys, Jazireh-ye- 23 Hd 26.32N 53.58 E
Qezel Owzan 23 Gb 36.45N 49.22 E
Qian'an [China] 28 Ed 40.01N 118.42 E
Qian'an [China] 28 Hb 44.58N 124.01 E
Qianfangzi 28 Ad 40.01N 111.23 E
Qian Gorlos (Quianguozhen) 27 Lb 45.05N 124.52 E
Qian He 28 Dh 32.55N 117.10 E
Qianjiang [China] 27 Ig 23.37N 108.58 E
Qianjiang [China] 28 Bi 30.25N 112.54 E
Qianjiang [China] 27 If 29.30N 108.45 E
Qianning/Gartar 27 He 30.27N 101.29 E
Qian Shan 27 Lc 40.35N 123.00 E
Qiansuo 27 Hf 25.27N 100.41 E
Qianwei 27 Hf 29.08N 103.56 E
Qianxi [China] 27 If 27.03N 106.04 E
Qianxi [China] 28 Ed 40.08N 118.19 E
Qianyang (Anjiang) 27 Jf 27.19N 110.13 E
Qiaojia 27 Hf 27.00N 103.00 E
Qiaowan 27 Gc 40.36N 96.42 E
Qibilī 32 Ic 33.42N 8.58 E
Qichun (Caojiahe) 28 Ci 30.15N 115.26 E
Qidaogou 28 Id 41.31N 126.18 E
Qidong 28 Fi 31.48N 121.39 E
Qiemo/Qarqan 22 Kf 38.08N 85.32 E
Qift 24 Ei 26.00N 32.49 E
Qijiang 27 If 29.00N 106.39 E
Qijiaojing 27 Fc 43.28N 91.36 E
Qike → Xunke 27 Mb 49.34N 128.28 E
Qili → Shitai 28 Di 30.12N 117.28 E
Qilian (Babao) 27 Hd 38.14N 100.15 E
Qilian Shan 27 Gd 39.12N 98.35 E
Qilian Shan 21 Lf 38.30N 100.00 E
Qimantag 27 Fd 37.00N 91.00 E
Qimen 27 Kf 29.57N 117.39 E
Qinā 31 Kf 26.10N 32.43 E
Qinā, Wādī- 24 Ei 26.12N 32.44 E
Qin'an 27 Ie 34.50N 105.35 E
Qingchengzi 28 Gd 40.44N 123.36 E
Qingchuan 27 Ie 32.32N 105.11 E
Qingdao=Tsingtao (EN) 22 Of 36.05N 120.21 E
Qingduizi 28 Fd 41.27N 121.52 E
Qingfeng 28 Cg 35.54N 115.07 E
Qinggang 27 Mb 46.41N 126.03 E
Qinggil/Qinghe 27 Fb 46.43N 90.24 E
Qinghai Hu=Koko Nor (EN) 21 Mf 37.00N 100.20 E
Qinghai Sheng (Ch'ing-hai Sheng)=Tsinghai (EN) [2] 27 Gd 36.00N 96.00 E
Qing He 28 Hc 42.16N 124.10 E
Qinghe/Qinggil 27 Fb 46.43N 90.24 E
Qinghe (Gexianzhuang) 28 Cf 37.03N 115.39 E
Qinghemen 28 Fd 41.45N 121.25 E
Qingjian 27 Jd 37.10N 110.09 E
Qingjiang 22 Nf 33.31N 119.03 E
Qing Jiang 27 Je 30.24N 111.30 E
Qingjiang (Zhangshuzhen) 27 Kf 28.02N 115.31 E
Qingkou → Ganyu 28 Eg 34.50N 119.07 E
Qinglong 28 Ed 40.26N 118.58 E
Qinglong He 28 Ee 39.51N 118.51 E
Qingshan 28 Ci 30.39N 114.27 E
Qingshuihe 27 Jd 39.56N 111.41 E
Qingshui Jiang 27 If 27.11N 109.48 E
Qingtian 27 Lf 28.12N 120.17 E
Qingxian 28 De 38.35N 116.48 E
Qingxu 28 Bf 37.36N 112.21 E
Qingyang [China] 27 Id 36.01N 107.48 E
Qingyang [China] 28 Di 30.38N 117.50 E
Qingyuan 27 Lc 42.06N 124.56 E
Qingyuan (Nandaran) 28 Ce 38.46N 115.29 E
Qingyun (Xiejiaji) 28 Df 37.46N 117.22 E
Qing Zang Gaoyuan=Tibet, Plateau of- (EN) 21 Kf 32.30N 87.00 E
Qin He 28 Bg 35.01N 113.25 E
Qinhuangdao 27 Kg 40.00N 119.32 E
Qin Ling 21 Mf 34.00N 108.00 E
Qinshui 28 Bg 35.41N 112.10 E
Qintong 28 Fh 32.39N 120.06 E
Qinxian 28 Bf 36.46N 112.42 E
Qinyang 28 Bg 35.05N 112.56 E
Qinyuan 28 Bf 36.29N 112.20 E
Qinzhou 27 Ig 22.02N 108.30 E
Qionghai (Jiaji) 27 Jh 19.25N 110.28 E
Qionglai 27 He 30.24N 103.28 E
Qiongzhou Haixia 21 Ng 20.10N 110.15 E
Qipan Guan 27 Ie 32.45N 106.11 E
Qiqihar 22 Oe 47.21N 123.58 E
Qīr 24 Oh 28.29N 53.04 E
Qira 27 Dd 37.02N 80.53 E
Qiryat Gat 24 Fg 31.36N 34.46 E
Qiryat Shemona 24 Ff 33.13N 35.34 E
Qiryat Yam 24 Ff 32.51N 35.04 E
Qishn 23 Hf 15.26N 51.40 E
Qi Shui 28 Ci 30.09N 115.22 E
Qishuyan 28 Fi 31.41N 120.04 E
Qitai 22 Ke 44.01N 89.28 E
Qitaihe 27 Nb 45.49N 130.51 E
Qiuxian (Matou) 28 Cf 36.50N 115.10 E
Qixia 28 Ff 37.18N 120.50 E
Qixian [China] 28 Bf 37.23N 112.21 E
Qixian [China] 28 Cg 34.33N 114.46 E
Qixian (Zhaoge) 28 Cg 35.35N 114.12 E
Qiyang 27 Jf 26.44N 111.50 E
Qizhou 28 Ci 30.04N 115.20 E
Qogir Feng=Godwin Austen (EN) 21 Jf 35.53N 76.30 E
Qog Qi 27 Ic 41.31N 107.00 E
Qog Ul 27 Kc 44.50N 116.19 E
Qohrūd, Kūhhā-ye- 21 Hf 32.40N 53.00 E
Qoltag 27 Ec 42.20N 88.45 E
Qom 22 Hf 34.39N 50.54 E
Qom 24 Ne 34.48N 51.02 E
Qomolangma Feng=Everest, Mount- (EN) 21 Kg 27.59N 86.56 E
Qomrud 24 Ne 34.43N 51.04 E
Qomsheh 23 Hc 32.00N 51.50 E
Qondūz [3] 23 Kb 36.45N 68.30 E
Qondūz 22 If 36.45N 68.51 E
Qondūz 23 Kb 37.00N 68.16 E
Qoqek/Tacheng 22 Ke 46.45N 82.57 E
Qŏrnoq 41 Gf 64.30N 51.19W
Qorveh 24 Le 35.10N 47.48 E
Qoşbeh-ye Naşşār 23 Gc 30.02N 48.27 E
Qoṭbābād [Iran] 24 Oh 28.39N 53.37 E
Qoṭbābād [Iran] 24 Qi 27.46N 56.06 E
Qoṭūr 24 Kc 38.28N 44.25 E
Qotūr 24 Kc 38.46N 45.16 E
Quadda 31 Jh 8.04N 22.24 E
Quadros, Lagoa dos- 55 Gi 29.42S 50.05W
Quairading 59 Df 32.01S 117.25 E
Quakenbrück 10 Dd 52.41N 7.57 E
Quanah 45 Gi 34.18N 99.44W
Quanbao Shan 27 Je 34.08N 111.26 E
Quang Ngai 25 Le 15.07N 108.48 E
Quang Tri 25 Le 21.02N 106.29 E
Quan He 28 Ch 32.55N 115.52 E
Quanjiao 28 Eh 32.09N 118.16 E
Quan Long 25 Lg 9.11N 105.08 E
Quanzhou [China] 22 Ng 24.57N 118.35 E
Quanzhou [China] 27 Jf 26.01N 111.04 E
Qu'Appelle River 42 Hf 50.27N 101.19W
Quarai 56 Id 30.23S 56.27W
Quarai, Rio- 55 Dj 30.12S 57.36W
Quaregnon 12 Fd 50.26N 3.51 E
Quartu Sant'Elena 14 Dk 39.14N 9.11 E
Quartz Lake 42 Jb 70.57N 80.40W
Quartz Mountain 46 De 43.10N 122.40W
Quartzsite 46 Hj 33.40N 114.13W
Quatre, Isle- 51n Bb 12.57N 61.15W
Quatsino Sound 46 Aa 50.25N 128.10W
Qūchān 22 Hf 37.06N 58.30 E
Qué 36 Ce 14.43S 15.06 E
Queanbeyan 59 Jg 35.21S 149.14 E
Québec 39 Le 46.49N 71.13W
Québec [3] 42 Kf 54.00N 72.00W
Quebó 55 Db 14.36S 56.04W
Quebra Anzol, Rio- 55 Id 19.09S 47.38W
Quebracho 55 Dj 31.57S 57.57W
Quebradillas 51a Bb 18.28N 66.56W
Quedas do Iguaçu 55 Fg 25.31S 52.54W
Quedlinburg 10 He 51.47N 11.09 E
Queen, Cape- 42 Jd 64.43N 78.18W
Queen Alexandra Range 66 Jg 84.00S 168.00 E
Queen Bess, Mount- 42 Ff 51.18N 124.33W
Queenborough 12 Cc 51.25N 0.46 E
Queen Charlotte Islands 38 Gd 51.30N 129.00W
Queen Charlotte Sound 42 Ef 51.30N 129.30W
Queen Charlotte Strait 38 Gd 50.40N 127.25W
Queen Elizabeth Islands 38 Ib 79.00N 105.00W
Queen Elizabeth Range 66 Kg 83.20S 162.00 E
Queen Mary Land 66 Ge 69.00S 96.00 E
Queen Maud Gulf 38 Ic 68.25N 102.30W
Queen Maud Land (EN) 66 Cf 72.30S 12.00 E
Queen Maud Range 66 Lg 86.00S 160.00W
Queens Channel [Austl.] 59 Fb 14.45S 129.25 E
Queens Channel [N.W.T.-Can.] 42 Ha 76.11N 96.00W
Queensland 59 Id 22.00S 145.00 E
Queenstown [Austl.] 59 Jh 42.05S 145.33 E
Queenstown [Guy.] 50 Gi 7.12N 58.29W
Queenstown [N.Z.] 62 Cf 45.02S 168.40 E
Queenstown [S.Afr.] 31 Jl 31.52S 26.52 E
Queguay, Cuchilla del- 55 Dj 31.50S 57.30W
Queguay Grande, Rio- 55 Cj 32.09S 58.09W
Queich 12 Ke 49.14N 8.23 E
Queimadas 54 Kf 10.58S 39.38W
Queiros 55 Gf 21.49S 50.13W
Quela 36 Cd 9.15S 17.05 E
Quelimane 31 Kj 17.51S 36.52 E
Quemado 45 Bi 34.20N 108.30W
Quemado de Güines 49 Gb 22.48N 80.15W
Quembo 36 De 14.57S 20.22 E
Quemú-Quemú 56 He 36.03S 63.33W
Quepos 49 Ei 9.25N 84.09W
Quequén 56 Ie 38.32S 58.42W
Quequén Grande, Rio- 55 Cn 38.34S 58.43W
Quequén Salado, Rio- 55 Bn 38.56S 60.31W
Quercy 11 Hj 44.15N 1.15 E
Querétaro [2] 47 Ed 21.00N 99.55W
Querétaro 39 Ig 20.36N 100.23W
Querobabi 48 Db 30.03N 111.01W
Quesada [C.R.] 49 Eh 10.19N 84.26W
Quesada [Sp.] 13 Ig 37.51N 3.04W
Queshan 27 Je 32.42N 114.04 E
Quesnel 42 Ff 52.59N 122.30W
Quesnel Lake 42 Ff 52.32N 121.05W
Questa 45 Dh 36.42N 105.36W
Quetena 54 Eh 22.10S 67.25W
Quetico Lake 45 Kb 48.37N 91.52W
Quetta 22 If 30.12N 67.00 E
Quevas, Cerro- 48 Dc 29.15N 111.20W
Quevedo 54 Cd 1.02S 79.27W
Queyras 11 Mj 44.44N 6.49 E
Quezaltenango 39 Jh 14.50N 91.31W
Quezaltenango [3] 49 Bf 14.45N 91.40W
Quezon 26 Ge 9.14N 117.56 E
Quezon City 22 Oh 14.38N 121.00 E
Qufu 28 Dg 35.35N 116.59 E
Quianguoshen → Qian Gorlos 27 Lb 45.05N 124.52 E
Quianshan 28 Di 30.38N 116.35 E
Quibala 36 Be 10.44S 14.59 E
Quibaxe 36 Bd 8.30S 14.36 E
Quibdó 54 Cb 5.42N 76.39W
Quiberon, Baie de- 11 Dg 47.32N 3.00W
Quiberon, Presqu'île de- 11 Cg 47.30N 3.08W
Quibor 49 Mi 9.56N 69.37W
Quiché [3] 49 Bf 15.30N 90.55W
Quierschied 12 Je 49.19N 7.03 E
Quiha 35 Fc 13.28N 39.33 E
Quiindy 55 Dh 25.58S 57.16W
Quijarro 55 Cd 19.26S 58.08W
Quilá 48 Fe 24.23N 107.13W
Quilàn, Cabo- 56 Ff 43.16S 74.23W
Quillabamba 54 Df 12.49S 72.43W
Quillacollo 54 Eg 17.26S 66.17W
Quillagua 56 Gb 21.39S 69.33W
Quillan 11 Il 42.52N 2.11 E
Quillebeuf-sur-Seine 12 Ce 49.28N 0.31 E
Quillota 56 Fd 32.53S 71.16W
Quilmes 56 Id 34.44S 58.16W
Quilon 25 Fg 8.53N 76.36 E
Quilpie 59 Ie 26.37S 144.15 E
Quilqué 56 Fd 33.03S 71.27W
Quimarí, Alto de- 49 Ii 8.07N 76.23W
Quimbele 36 Cd 6.30S 16.14 E
Quimilí 56 Hc 27.38S 62.25W
Quimome 55 Bc 17.42S 61.16W
Quimome, Río- 55 Bc 17.36S 61.09W
Quimper 11 Bf 48.00N 4.06W
Quimperlé 11 Cg 47.52N 3.33W
Quinault River 46 Cc 47.23N 124.18W
Quincy [Ca.-U.S.] 46 Eg 39.56N 120.57W
Quincy [Fl.-U.S.] 44 Ej 30.37N 84.32W
Quincy [Il.-U.S.] 43 Id 39.56N 91.23W
Quincy [Ma.-U.S.] 44 Ld 42.15N 71.01W
Quincy [Wa.-U.S.] 46 Fc 47.14N 119.51W
Quindio [2] 54 Cc 4.30N 75.40W
Quingey 11 Lg 47.06N 5.53 E
Quinhagak 40 Ge 59.45N 161.43W
Qui Nhon 22 Mh 13.46N 109.14 E
Quiñihual 55 Bm 37.47S 61.36W
Quiniluban Group 26 Hd 11.27N 120.48 E
Quinn River 46 Ff 40.25N 119.00W
Quiñones 48 De 24.22N 111.25W
Quintanar de la Orden 13 Ie 39.34N 3.03W
Quintana Roo [2] 47 Ge 19.40N 88.30W
Quinze, Lac des- 44 Hb 47.30N 79.00W
Quionga 37 Gb 10.35S 40.33 E
Quipongo 36 Be 14.45S 14.05 E
Quirigua 49 Cf 15.18N 89.07W
Quirihue 56 Fe 36.17S 72.32W
Quirima 36 Ce 10.48S 18.09 E
Quirinópolis 54 Hg 18.32S 50.30W
Quiroga 13 Eb 42.29N 7.16W
Quiros, Cap- 63b Cb 14.56S 167.01 E
Quisiro 49 Lh 10.53N 71.17W
Quissanga 37 Gb 12.25S 40.29 E
Quissico 37 Ed 24.43S 34.45 E
Quita Sueno Bank 47 Hf 14.20N 81.15W
Quitengues 36 Be 14.06S 14.05 E
Quiterage 37 Gb 11.45S 40.27 E
Quitéria, Rio- 55 Ge 20.16S 51.08W
Quitilipi 55 Bh 26.52S 60.13W
Quitman [Ga.-U.S.] 44 Fj 30.47N 83.33W
Quitman [Ms.-U.S.] 45 Lj 32.03N 88.43W
Quito 53 If 0.13S 78.30W
Quitovac 48 Cb 31.32N 112.42W
Quixadá 54 Kd 4.58S 39.01W
Quixeramobim 54 Ke 5.12S 39.17W
Qujiang 28 Cj 28.14N 115.46 E
Qu Jiang [China] 27 Kf 29.32N 119.31 E
Qu Jiang [China] 27 Ie 30.01N 106.24 E
Qujing 27 Hf 25.31N 103.45 E
Qul'ān, Jazā'ir- 24 Fj 24.22N 35.23 E
Qulansiyah 23 Hg 12.41N 53.29 E
Qulaybiah 32 Jb 36.51N 11.06 E
Qulbān al 'Isāwiyah 24 Gg 30.38N 37.53 E
Qulbān an Nabk al Gharbī 24 Gg 31.15N 37.26 E
Qumar He 21 Lf 34.42N 94.50 E
Qumarlêb 27 Ge 34.35N 95.18 E
Qunayfidhah, Nafūd- 24 Kj 24.45N 45.30 E
Quoi 64d Ba 7.32N 151.59 E
Quoich 42 Id 63.56N 93.25W
Quorn 59 Hf 32.21S 138.03 E
Quqên/Jinchuan 27 He 31.02N 102.02 E
Quraitu 24 Ke 34.36N 45.30 E
Qurayyāt, Juzur- 32 Jb 35.48N 11.02 E
Qurbah 14 En 36.35N 10.52 E
Qurdūd 35 Dc 10.17N 29.56 E
Qūr Laban 24 Cg 30.23N 28.59 E
Qurunbāliyah 14 En 36.36N 10.30 E
Qūş 33 Fd 25.55N 32.45 E
Quşay'ir 35 Ic 14.55N 50.20 E
Qutdligssat 41 Gd 70.12N 53.00W
Quthing 37 Df 30.24S 27.42 E
Qutū 33 Hf 18.30N 41.04 E
Quwaiz 33 He 20.27N 44.53 E
Quxian 27 Kf 28.54N 118.53 E
Qūxū 27 Ff 29.23N 90.45 E
Quyang 28 Ce 38.37N 114.41 E
Quy Chau 25 Le 19.33N 105.06 E
Quzhou 28 Cf 36.47N 114.56 E
Qyteti Stalin → Kuçova 15 Ci 40.48N 19.54 E

R

Raab 10 Ni 47.41N 17.38 E
Raahe/Brahestad 7 Fd 64.41N 24.29 E
Rääkkylä 8 Mb 62.19N 29.37 E
Raalte 12 Ib 52.23N 6.17 E
Raamsdonk 12 Gc 51.41N 4.54 E
Raanes Peninsula 42 Ia 78.20N 86.20W
Raasay, Island of- 9 Gd 57.25N 6.04W
Raasay, Sound of- 9 Gd 57.25N 6.05W
Raasiku/Raziku 8 Ke 59.22N 25.11 E
Rab 14 If 44.46N 14.46 E
Rab 14 If 44.45N 14.46 E
Rába 10 Ni 47.41N 17.38 E
Raba 10 Qf 50.09N 20.30 E
Raba 22 Nj 8.27S 118.46 E
Rabāble 35 Hd 8.14N 48.18 E
Rabaçal 13 Ec 41.30N 7.12W
Rabat [Malta] 14 Io 35.50N 14.29 E
Rabat [Mor.] 31 Ge 34.02N 6.50W
Rabat-Salé [2] 32 Fc 34.02N 6.50W
Rabaul 58 Ge 4.12S 152.12 E
Rábca 10 Ni 47.41N 17.37 E
Rabenau 12 Kd 50.40N 8.52 E
Rabī', Ash Shallāl ar-= Fourth Cataract (EN) 30 Kg 18.47N 32.03 E
Rabiah 24 Jd 36.47N 42.07 E
Rábida, Monasterio de- 13 Fg 37.12N 6.55W
Rābigh 23 Ee 22.48N 39.02 E
Rabinal 49 Bf 15.06N 90.27W
Rabka 10 Pg 49.36N 19.56 E
Rabočeostrovsk 7 Id 64.59N 34.44 E
Rabyānah, Şaḥrā'- 30 Jf 24.30N 21.00 E
Rabyānah, Wāḥāt al-= Rebiana Oasis (EN) 33 De 24.14N 21.59 E
Răcăciuni 15 Jc 46.20N 26.59 E
Racalmuto 14 Hm 37.24N 13.44 E
Răcăşdia 15 Ee 44.59N 21.38 E
Racconigi 14 Bf 44.46N 7.46 E
Race, Cape- 38 Ne 46.40N 53.10W
Race Point 44 Ld 42.04N 70.14W
Rach Gia 22 Mh 10.01N 105.05 E
Rachid 32 Ef 18.48N 11.41W
Raciąż 10 Qd 52.47N 20.06 E
Racibórz 10 Of 50.06N 18.13 E
Racine 43 Jc 42.43N 87.48W
Ráckeve 10 Oi 47.10N 18.57 E
Racos 15 Ic 46.03N 25.30 E
Råda 8 Ed 60.00N 13.36 E
Radama, Iles- 37 Hb 14.00S 47.47 E
Radan 15 Ef 43.02N 21.30 E
Rădăuţi 15 Ib 47.51N 25.55 E
Radbuza 10 Jg 49.46N 13.24 E
Radeberg 10 Je 51.07N 13.55 E
Radebeul 10 Je 51.06N 13.39 E
Radeče 14 Jd 46.04N 15.11 E
Radehov 10 Uf 50.13N 24.43 E
Radenthein 14 Hd 46.48N 13.43 E
Radevormwald 12 Jc 51.12N 7.22 E
Radew 10 Lb 54.07N 15.50 E
Radford 44 Gg 37.07N 80.34W
Radnevo 15 Ig 42.18N 25.56 E
Radolfzell 10 Ei 47.44N 8.58 E
Radom [2] 10 Re 51.25N 21.10 E
Radom 6 Ie 51.25N 21.10 E
Radomir 15 Fg 42.33N 22.58 E
Radomka 10 Re 51.43N 21.26 E
Radomsko 10 Pe 51.05N 19.25 E
Radomyśl 16 Fd 50.29N 29.14 E
Radomyśl Wielki 10 Rf 50.12N 21.16 E
Radoškoviči 8 Lj 54.12N 27.17 E
Radotín 10 Kg 49.59N 14.22 E
Radovanu 15 Je 44.12N 26.31 E
Radoviš 15 Fh 41.38N 22.28 E
Radøy 8 Ad 60.40N 5.00 E
Radstadt 14 Hc 47.23N 13.27 E
Radun 10 Vb 54.02N 25.07 E
Radunia 10 Ob 54.25N 18.45 E
Raduša 14 Lg 43.52N 17.29 E
Radvaniči 10 Ue 51.59N 24.09 E
Radviliškis 7 Fi 55.50N 23.33 E
Radymno 10 Sg 49.57N 22.48 E
Radziejów 10 Od 52.38N 18.32 E
Radzyń Podlaski 10 Se 51.48N 22.38 E
Rae 42 Fd 62.50N 116.00W
Rāe Bareli 25 Gc 26.13N 81.14 E
Rae Isthmus 42 Ic 66.55N 86.10W
Raesfeld 12 Ic 51.46N 6.51 E
Raeside, Lake- 59 Ee 29.30S 121.50 E
Raetihi 62 Fc 39.26S 175.17 E
Raevavae, Ile- 57 Mg 23.52S 147.40W
Raevski, Groupe- 61 Mc 16.45S 144.14W
Rāf, Jabal- 24 Hh 29.12N 39.48 E
Rafaela 53 Ji 31.17S 61.30W
Rafai 35 Ce 4.58N 23.56 E
Rafḥā' 23 Fd 29.42N 43.30 E
Rafi 34 Fc 13.28N 4.10 E
Rafkā 24 Qe 35.55N 57.36 E
Rafsanjān 23 Ic 30.24N 56.01 E
Räfsö/Reposaari 8 Ic 61.37N 21.27 E
Raga 31 Jh 8.28N 25.41 E
Ragay Gulf 26 Hd 13.30N 122.45 E
Ragged Island 49 Jb 22.12N 75.44W
Ragged Island Range 47 Id 22.42N 75.55W
Ragged Point 51q Bb 13.10N 59.25W
Raglan 62 Fb 37.48S 174.52 E
Raguencau 44 Ma 49.04N 68.32W
Ragusa 14 In 36.55N 14.44 E
Raguva 8 Ki 55.30N 24.45 E
Raha 26 Hg 4.51S 122.43 E
Raḥā, Ḥarrat ar- 24 Gi 27.40N 36.40 E
Rahad al Bardī 35 Cc 11.18N 23.53 E
Rahama 34 Gc 10.25N 8.41 E
Rahat, Ḥarrat- 33 He 23.00N 40.05 E
Rahat Dağı 15 Ml 37.08N 29.49 E
Rahden 12 Kb 52.26N 8.37 E
Rāhgāmāti 25 Id 22.38N 92.12 E
Rahīmyār Khan 25 Ec 28.25N 70.18 E
Rahmanovskije Ključi 19 If 49.35N 86.35 E
Rahmet 19 Gf 49.19N 65.16 E
Råholt 8 Dd 60.16N 11.11 E
Rahouia 13 Ni 35.32N 1.01 E
Rahov 16 De 48.02N 24.18 E
Rahrbach, Kirchhundem- 12 Jc 51.02N 7.59 E
Raia 13 Df 39.00N 8.17W
Raiatea, Ile- 57 Lf 16.50S 151.25W
Raices 55 Cj 31.54S 59.16W
Rāichūr 22 Jh 16.12N 77.22 E
Raiganj 25 Hc 25.37N 88.07 E
Raigarh 25 Gd 21.54N 83.24 E
Raijua, Pulau- 26 Hi 10.37S 121.36 E
Rainbow Peak 46 Hd 44.55N 115.17W
Rainier, Mount- 38 Ge 46.52N 121.46W
Rainy Lake 43 Ib 48.42N 93.10W
Rainy River 45 Ib 48.43N 94.29W
Rainy River 45 Ib 48.50N 94.41W
Raipur 22 Kg 21.14N 81.38 E
Raisi, Punta- 14 Hl 38.11N 13.06 E
Raisio/Reso 7 Ff 60.29N 22.11 E
Raita Bank (EN) 60 Mb 25.25N 169.30W
Raja Ampat, Kepulauan- 26 Jg 0.50S 130.25 E
Rājahmundry 22 Kh 16.59N 81.47 E
Rajakoski 7 Gb 68.59N 29.07 E
Rajang 21 Ni 2.07N 111.12 E
Rājāpālaiyam 25 Fg 9.27N 77.34 E
Rājasthān [3] 25 Ec 26.00N 74.00 E
Rājasthān Canal 25 Eb 31.10N 75.00 E
Rajbiraj 25 Hc 26.30N 86.50 E
Rajčihinsk 20 Hg 49.43N 129.27 E
Rajevski 17 Gi 54.04N 54.56 E
Rājgarh 25 Fc 28.38N 75.23 E
Rajgródzkie, Jezioro- 10 Sc 53.45N 22.38 E
Rajka 10 Ni 48.00N 17.12 E
Rajkot 22 Jg 22.18N 70.47 E
Raj Nāndgaon 25 Gd 21.06N 81.02 E
Rajony respublikanskogo podčinenija → Čujskaja oblast 19 Hg 42.30N 73.50 E

Index Symbols

[1] Independent Nation
[2] State, Region
[3] District, County
[4] Municipality
[5] Colony, Dependency
Continent
Physical Region
Historical or Cultural Region
Mount, Mountain
Volcano
Hill
Mountains, Mountain Range
Hills, Escarpment
Plateau, Upland
Pass, Gap
Plain, Lowland
Delta
Salt Flat
Valley, Canyon
Crater, Cave
Karst Features
Depression
Polder
Desert, Dunes
Forest, Woods
Heath, Steppe
Oasis
Cape, Point
Coast, Beach
Cliff
Peninsula
Isthmus
Sandbank
Island
Atoll
Rock, Reef
Islands, Archipelago
Rocks, Reefs
Coral Reef
Well, Spring
Geyser
River, Stream
Waterfall Rapids
River Mouth, Estuary
Lake
Salt Lake
Intermittent Lake
Reservoir
Swamp, Pond
Canal
Glacier
Ice Shelf, Pack Ice
Ocean
Sea
Gulf, Bay
Strait, Fjord
Lagoon
Bank
Seamount
Tablemount
Ridge
Shelf
Basin
Escarpment, Sea Scarp
Fracture
Trench, Abyss
National Park, Reserve
Point of Interest
Recreation Site
Cave, Cavern
Historic Site
Ruins
Wall, Walls
Church, Abbey
Temple
Scientific Station
Airport
Port
Lighthouse
Mine
Tunnel
Dam, Bridge

Rājshāhi 25 Hd 24.22N 88.36 E
Rakahanga Atoll 57 Kl 10.02S 161.05W
Rakaia 62 Ee 43.54S 172.13 E
Rakaia 62 Ee 43.45S 172.01 E
Rakan, Ra's- 24 Ni 26.10N 51.13 E
Rakata, Pulau- 26 Eh 6.10S 105.26 E
Raka Zangbo 27 Ef 29.24N 87.58 E
Rakhawt, Wādī- 35 Ib 18.16N 51.50 E
Rakht-e Shāh 24 Mf 33.17N 49.23 E
Rakitnoje 28 Mb 45.36N 134.17 E
Rakitovo 15 Hh 41.59N 24.05 E
Rakkestad 8 De 59.26N 11.21 E
Rakoniewice 10 Md 52.10N 16.16 E
Rakops 37 Cd 21.01S 24.20 E
Rakovnicka panev 10 Jf 50.10N 13.30 E
Rakovnik 10 Jf 50.06N 13.43 E
Rakovski 15 Hg 42.18N 24.58 E
Raków 10 Rf 50.42N 21.03 E
Rakušečny, Mys- 16 Qh 42.52N 51.55 E
Råkvåg 7 Ce 63.46N 10.05 E
Rakvere 7 Gg 59.22N 26.22 E
Raleigh [N.C.-U.S.] 39 Lf 35.47N 78.39W
Raleigh [Ont.-Can.] 45 Kb 49.31N 91.56W
Raleigh Bay 44 Ih 35.00N 76.20W
Ralik Chain 57 Hd 8.00N 167.00 E
Rama 47 Hf 12.09N 84.15W
Rama, Rio- 49 Eg 12.08N 84.13W
Ramādah 32 Jc 32.19N 10.24 E
Ramaḑin, Wādī- 24 Ej 24.57N 32.34 E
Ramales de la Victoria 13 Ia 43.15N 3.27W
Ramalho, Serra do- 55 Ja 13.45S 44.00W
Ramapo Bank (EN) 57 Fb 27.15N 145.10 E
Ramatlabama 37 De 25.37S 25.30 E
Ramberg 10 He 51.45N 11.05 E
Rambervillers 11 Mf 48.21N 6.38 E
Rambi 63d Cb 16.30S 179.59W
Rambouillet 11 Hf 48.39N 1.50 E
Rambutyo Island 57 Fe 2.18S 147.48 E
Rāmhormoz 24 Mg 31.16N 49.36 E
Ramigala/Ramygala 8 Ki 55.28N 24.23 E
Ramis 35 Gd 8.02N 41.36 E
Ramla 24 Fg 31.55N 34.52 E
Ramlīyah, 'Aqabat ar- 24 Di 26.01N 30.42 E
Ramlu 35 Gc 13.20N 41.45 E
Ramm, Jabal- 24 Fh 29.35N 35.24 E
Rammāk, Ghurd ar- 24 Ch 29.40N 29.20 E
Rāmnagar 25 Fc 29.24N 79.07 E
Ramnäs 8 Ge 59.46N 16.12 E
Ramón
Santamarina 55 Cn 38.26S 59.20W
Ramos 63a Ec 8.16S 160.11 E
Ramos, Rio- 48 Ge 25.35N 105.03W
Ramotswa 37 Dd 24.52S 25.50 E
Rāmpur 25 Fc 28.49N 79.02 E
Ramree 25 Ie 19.06N 93.48 E
Rams 24 Oj 25.53N 56.02 E
Ramsele 7 De 63.33N 16.29 E
Ramsey [Eng.-U.K.] 12 Bb 52.27N 0.07W
Ramsey [Ont.-Can.] 44 Fb 47.29N 82.24W
Ramsey [U.K.] 9 Ig 54.20N 4.21W
Ramsey Lake 42 Jg 47.20N 83.00W
Ramsgate 9 Oj 51.20N 1.25 E
Rāmshīr 24 Mg 30.50N 49.30 E
Ramsjö 7 De 62.11N 15.39 E
Ramstein-Miesenbach 12 Je 49.27N 7.32 E
Ramsund 7 Db 68.29N 16.32 E
Ramu 60 Di 4.02S 144.41 E
Ramu 36 Hb 3.56N 41.13 E
Ramvik 7 De 62.49N 17.51 E
Ramville, Ilet- 51h Bb 14.42N 60.53W
Ramygala/Ramigala 8 Ki 55.28N 24.23 E
Rana 7 Dc 66.20N 14.08 E
Rañadoiro, Sierra del- 13 Fa 43.20N 6.45W
Ranai 26 Ef 3.55N 108.23 E
Ranakah, Potjo- 26 Hh 8.38S 120.31 E
Rana Kao, Volcán- 65d Ac 27.11S 109.27W
Rana Roi, Volcán- 65d Ab 27.05S 109.23W
Rana Roraka, Volcán- 65d Bb 27.07S 109.18W
Ranau 26 Ge 5.58N 116.41 E
Ranča 14 Lf 44.24N 17.22 E
Rancagua 53 Ii 34.10S 70.45W
Rance 11 Ef 48.31N 1.59W
Rance, Sivry-Rance- 12 Gd 50.09N 4.16 E
Rancharia 55 Gf 22.15S 50.55W
Rancheria, Rio- 49 Kh 11.34N 72.54W
Rānchī 22 Kg 23.21N 85.20 E
Ranchos 55 Cl 35.32S 58.22W
Ranco, Lago- 56 Ff 40.14S 72.24W
Randa 35 Gc 11.51N 42.40 E
Randaberg 8 Ae 59.00N 5.36 E
Randazzo 14 Im 37.53N 14.57 E
Randers 7 Ch 56.28N 10.03 E
Randers Fjord 8 Dh 56.35N 10.20 E
Randijaure 7 Ec 66.42N 19.18 E
Randow 10 Kc 53.41N 14.04 E
Randsfjorden 7 Cf 60.25N 10.25 E
Ranérou 34 Cb 15.18N 13.58W
Ranfurly 62 Df 45.08S 170.06 E
Rangasa, Tanjung- 26 Gg 3.33S 118.56 E
Ranger 45 Gj 32.28N 98.41W
Rangiora 62 Ee 43.18S 172.36 E
Rangiroa Atoll 57 Mf 15.10S 147.35W
Rangitaiki 62 Gb 37.55S 176.53 E
Rangitata 62 Df 44.10S 171.30 E
Rangitikei 62 Fd 40.17S 175.13 E
Rangkasbitung 26 Eh 6.21S 106.15 E
Rangoon (EN) =
Yangon 22 Lh 16.47N 96.10 E
Rangpur 25 Hc 25.44N 89.16 E
Rāniyah 24 Kd 36.15N 44.53 E
Rankin Inlet 39 Jc 62.45N 92.10W
Rankoshi 29a Bb 42.47N 140.31 E
Rannoch, Loch- 9 Ie 56.41N 4.20W
Ranobe 37 Gc 17.10S 44.08 E
Ranon 63b Dc 16.09S 168.07 E
Ranong 25 Jg 9.59N 98.40 E
Ranongga Island 60 Fi 8.05S 156.34 E
Ranova 16 Lb 54.07N 40.14 E
Ransaren 7 Dd 65.14N 14.59 E
Rantabe 37 Hc 15.42S 49.39 E
Rantasalmi 8 Mb 62.04N 28.18 E
Rantaupanjang 26 Fg 1.23S 112.04 E
Rantauprapat 26 Cf 2.06N 99.50 E
Rantekombola, Bulu- 21 Oj 3.21S 120.01 E
Rantoul 45 Lf 40.19N 88.09W
Ranua 7 Gd 65.55N 26.32 E
Ranyah, Wādī- 33 He 21.18N 43.20 E
Raohe 27 Nb 46.48N 133.58 E
Raon-l'Étape 11 Mf 48.24N 6.51 E
Raoui, Erg er- 32 Gd 29.15N 2.45W
Raoul Island 57 Jg 29.15S 177.52W
Raoyang 28 Ce 38.14N 115.44 E
Raoyang He 28 Gd 41.13N 122.12 E
Rapa, Ile- 57 Mg 27.36S 144.20W
Rapallo 14 Df 44.21N 9.14 E
Rapang 26 Gg 3.50S 119.48 E
Rapa Nui/Pascua, Isla de- =
Easter Island (EN) 57 Qg 27.07S 109.22W
Raper, Cape - 42 Kc 69.41N 67.24W
Rapid City 39 Ie 44.05N 103.14W
Rapid Creek 45 Ee 43.54N 102.37W
Rapid River 44 Dc 45.58N 86.59W
Räpina/Rjapina 8 Lf 58.03N 27.35 E
Rapla 7 Fg 59.02N 24.47 E
Rappahannock River 44 Ig 37.34N 76.18W
Rápulo, Rio- 52 Jg 13.43S 65.32W
Rāqūbah 31 If 28.58N 19.02 E
Raraka Atoll 57 Mf 16.10S 144.54W
Raroia Atoll 57 Mf 16.05S 142.26W
Rarotonga Island 57 Lg 21.14S 159.46W
Rasa, Punta- 52 Jj 40.51S 62.19W
Ra's Abū Daraj 24 Eh 29.23N 32.33 E
Ra's Abū Rudays 24 Eh 28.53N 33.11 E
Ra's Abū Shajarah 24 Fa 21.04N 37.14 E
Ra's Ajdīr 33 Bc 33.09N 11.34 E
Ra's al 'Ayn 24 Id 36.51N 40.04 E
Ra's al-Barr 24 Dg 31.31N 31.50 E
Ra's al Ḩikmah 24 Bg 31.08N 27.50 E
Ra's al Jabal 14 Em 37.13N 10.08 E
Ra's al Khafjī 24 Mh 28.25N 48.30 E
Ra's al Khaymah 23 Id 25.47N 55.57 E
Ra's al Mish'āb 24 Mh 28.12N 48.37 E
Ra's al Unūf 33 Cc 30.31N 18.34 E
Ra's an Naqb 24 Fh 30.00N 35.29 E
Ra's as Sidr 24 Eh 29.36N 32.40 E
Ra's at Tannūrah 24 Ni 26.42N 50.10 E
Ras Beddouza 30 Ge 32.22N 9.18W
Ras Dashen 30 Kg 13.19N 38.20 E
Raseiniai/Rasejnjaj 7 Fi 55.23N 23.07 E
Rasejnjaj/Raseiniai 7 Fi 55.23N 23.07 E
Rās el Mā 34 Eb 16.37N 4.27W
Ras-el-Ma 13 Ji 35.08N 2.29W
Ras el Oued 13 Ri 35.57N 5.02 E
Ra's Ghārib 33 Fd 28.21N 33.06 E
Rashād 35 Ec 11.51N 31.04 E
Rāshayyā 24 Ff 33.30N 35.51 E
Rashīd = Rosetta (EN) 33 Fc 31.24N 30.25 E
Rashid, Maşabb- 24 Dg 31.30N 30.20 E
Rasht 22 Gf 37.16N 49.36 E
Rāsiga 'Alūla 35 Ic 11.59N 50.50 E
Rās Jumbo 35 Gf 1.37S 41.31 E
Raška 15 Df 43.18N 20.38 E
Ra's Madhar, Jabal- 24 Gj 25.46N 37.32 E
Ra's Matārimah 24 Eh 29.27N 32.43 E
Rasmussen Basin 42 Hc 67.56N 95.15W
Rason Lake 59 Ee 28.45S 124.20 E
Rasskazovo 16 Ee 52.39N 41.57 E
Rasšua, Ostrov- 20 Kg 47.40N 153.00 E
Rassvet 20 Ee 57.00N 91.32 E
Ras-Tarf, Cap- 13 Ii 35.17N 3.41W
Rastatt 10 Eh 48.51N 8.12 E
Rastede 12 Ka 53.15N 8.12 E
Rastigaissa 7 Ga 70.03N 26.18 E
Råstojaure 7 Eb 68.45N 20.30 E
Ra's Ţurunbī 24 Fj 25.40N 34.35 E
Rasūl 24 Pi 27.10N 55.30 E
Ra's Zayt 33 Fd 27.56N 33.31 E
Rat 40a Bb 51.55N 178.20 E
Ratak Chain 57 Id 9.00N 171.00 E
Ratangarh 25 Ec 28.05N 74.36 E
Rätansbyn 7 De 62.29N 14.32 E
Rat Buri 25 Jf 13.32N 99.49 E
Rathbun Lake 45 Jf 40.54N 93.05W
Ráth Droma/Rathdrum 9 Gi 52.56N 6.13W
Rathdrum/
Ráth Droma 9 Gi 52.56N 6.13W
Rathenow 10 Id 52.36N 12.20 E
Rathlin Island/
Reachlainn 9 Gf 55.18N 6.13W
Ráth Luirc/An Ráth 9 Ei 52.21N 8.41W
Rathor, Pik- 18 If 37.55N 72.14 E
Rätikon 14 Dc 47.03N 9.40 E
Ratingen 12 Ic 51.18N 6.51 E
Rätische Alpen = Rhaetian
Alps (EN) 14 Dd 46.30N 10.00 E
Rat Islands 38 Ad 52.00N 178.00 E
Ratlām 25 Fd 23.19N 75.04 E
Ratmanova, Ostrov- 20 Lc 35.45N 169.00W
Ratnāgiri 25 Ee 16.59N 73.18 E
Ratnapura 25 Gg 6.41N 80.24 E
Ratno 16 Dd 51.42N 24.31 E
Raton 43 Gd 36.54N 104.24W
Ratqh, Wādī ar- 24 Ie 34.25N 40.55 E
Rätta 20 Dd 63.35N 84.05 E
Rattlesnake Hills 46 Le 42.45N 107.10W
Rattray Head 9 Ld 57.38N 1.46W
Rättvik 7 Df 60.53N 15.06 E
Ratz, Mount- 38 Fd 57.23N 132.19W
Ratzeburg 10 Gc 53.42N 10.46 E
Raub 26 Df 3.48N 101.52 E
Rauch 56 Ie 36.46S 59.06W
Raucourt-et-Flaba 12 Ge 49.36N 4.57 E
Raudeberg 8 Ab 61.59N 5.09 E
Rauer Islands 66 Fe 68.51S 77.50 E
Raufarhöfn 7a Ca 66.27N 15.57W
Raufjellet 8 Dc 61.15N 11.00 E
Raufoss 7 Cf 60.43N 10.37 E
Raukotaha 64n Ac 10.28S 161.01W
Raukumara Range 62 Gc 38.00S 178.00 E
Rauland 8 Be 59.44N 8.00 E
Raúl Leoni, Represa- (Guri)
54 Fb 7.30N 63.00W
Rauma 7 Be 62.33N 7.43 E
Rauma/Raumo 7 Ef 61.08N 21.30 E
Raumo/Rauma 7 Ef 61.08N 21.30 E
Rauna 8 Kg 57.14N 25.39 E
Raunds 12 Bb 52.20N 0.32W
Raurimu 62 Fc 39.07S 175.24 E
Raurkela 22 Kg 22.13N 84.53 E
Rausu 28 Rb 44.01N 145.12 E
Rausu-Dake 29a Da 44.06N 145.07 E
Rautalampi 8 Lb 62.38N 26.50 E
Ravahere Atoll 57 Mf 18.14S 142.09W
Ravan 14 Mf 44.15N 18.16 E
Ravanica, Manastir- 15 Ef 43.58N 21.30 E
Ravānsar 24 Le 34.43N 46.40 E
Ravanusa 14 Hm 37.16N 13.58 E
Rāvar 24 Qg 31.12N 56.53 E
Rava-Russkaja 16 Cd 50.13N 23.37 E
Ravels 12 Gc 51.22N 4.59 E
Ravelsbach 14 Jb 48.30N 15.50 E
Ravels-Poppel 12 Hc 51.27N 5.02 E
Ravenna [It.] 14 Gf 44.25N 12.12 E
Ravenna [Nb.-U.S.] 45 Gf 41.02N 98.55W
Ravensburg 10 Fi 47.47N 9.37 E
Ravenshoe 58 Ff 17.37S 145.29 E
Ravensthorpe 59 Ef 33.35S 120.02 E
Ravi 21 Jf 30.35N 71.49 E
Ravnina 19 Gh 37.57N 62.42 E
Rawaki Atoll (Phoenix) 57 Je 3.43S 170.43W
Rāwalpindi 22 Jf 33.35N 73.03 E
Rawa Mazowiecka 10 Qe 51.46N 20.16 E
Rawāndūz 24 Kd 36.37N 44.31 E
Rawdah 24 Ie 35.15N 41.05 E
Rawene 62 Ea 35.24S 173.30 E
Rawicz 10 Me 51.37N 16.52 E
Rawka 10 Qd 52.07N 20.08 E
Rawlinna 58 Dh 31.01S 125.20 E
Rawlins 43 Fc 41.47N 107.14W
Rawlinson Range 59 Fd 24.50S 128.00 E
Rawson [Arg.] 55 Bl 34.36S 60.04W
Rawson [Arg.] 53 Jj 43.18S 65.06W
Rawura, Ras- 36 He 10.20S 40.30 E
Raxaul 25 Gc 26.59N 84.51 E
Ray, Cape - 42 Lg 47.37N 59.19W
Raya, Bukit- 21 Nj 1.32S 111.05 E
Rayadrug 25 Ff 14.42N 76.52 E
Rayāt 24 Kd 36.40N 44.58 E
Rayleigh 12 Cc 51.35N 0.37 E
Raymond [Alta.-Can.] 46 Ib 49.27N 112.39W
Raymond [Wa.-U.S.] 46 Dc 46.41N 123.44W
Raymondville 43 Hf 26.29N 97.47W
Rayne 45 Jk 30.14N 92.16W
Rayón [Mex.] 48 Jg 21.51N 99.40W
Rayón [Mex.] 48 Dc 29.43N 110.35W
Rayones 48 Ie 25.01N 100.05W
Rayong 25 Kf 12.40N 101.17 E
Raysūt 23 Hf 16.54N 54.02 E
Raytown 45 Ig 39.00N 94.28W
Raz, Pointe du- 11 Bf 48.02N 4.44W
Razan 24 Me 35.23N 49.02 E
Razdan 16 Ni 40.28N 44.43 E
Razdel'naja 16 Gf 46.50N 30.05 E
Razdolinsk 20 Ee 58.25N 94.44 E
Razdol'naja 28 Kc 43.20N 131.49 E
Razdol'noje 28 Kc 43.33N 131.55 E
Razdol'noje 16 Hg 45.47N 33.30 E
Razgrad 15 Jf 43.32N 26.31 E
Razgrad [2] 15 Jf 43.32N 26.31 E
Razī 24 Mc 38.32N 48.08 E
Raziku/Raasiku 8 Ke 59.22N 25.11 E
Razlog 15 Gh 41.53N 23.28 E
Razo 32 Cf 16.37N 24.36W
Ré, Ile de- 5 Ff 46.12N 1.25W
Reachlainn/Rathlin
Island 9 Gf 55.18N 6.13W
Reachrainn/Lambay 9 Gh 53.29N 6.01W
Read 42 Gc 69.12N 114.30W
Reading [Eng.-U.K.] 9 Mj 51.28N 0.59W
Reading [Pa.-U.S.] 43 Lc 40.20N 75.55W
Real, Cordillera- [Bol.] 54 Eg 16.30S 68.30W
Real, Cordillera- [Ec.] 52 If 3.00S 78.00W
Real Audiencia 55 Cm 36.11S 58.35W
Real del Castillo 48 Aa 31.58N 116.19W
Realicó 56 He 35.02S 64.15W
Réalmont 11 Ik 43.47N 2.12 E
Reao Atoll 57 Nf 18.31S 136.23W
Reatini, Monti- 14 Gh 42.35N 12.50 E
Rebais 12 Ff 48.51N 3.14 E
Rebecca, Lake- 59 Ee 29.55S 122.10 E
Rebiana Oasis (EN) =
Rabyānah, Wāḩāt al- 33 De 24.13N 21.59 E
Rebollera 13 Hf 38.24N 4.02W
Reboly 7 He 63.52N 30.47 E
Rebord Manambien 37 Hd 24.05S 46.30 E
Rebun 28 Pb 45.23N 141.02 E
Rebun-Dake 29a Ba 45.22N 141.01 E
Rebun-Suidō 29a Ba 45.15N 141.05 E
Rebun-Tō 27 Pb 45.23N 141.10 E
Recalde 55 Bm 36.39S 61.05W
Recanati 14 Hg 43.24N 13.32 E
Recaş 15 Ed 45.48N 21.30 E
Recherche, Archipelago of
the- 57 Dh 34.06S 122.45 E
Rečica 16 De 52.22N 30.25 E
Recife 53 Mf 8.03S 34.54W
Recife, Cape- 30 Jl 34.02S 25.45 E
Recke 12 Jb 52.23N 7.43 E
Recklinghausen 10 De 51.37N 7.12 E
Recknitz 10 Ib 54.14N 12.28 E
Recoaro Terme 14 Fe 45.42N 11.13 E
Reconquista 56 Ic 29.09S 59.39W
Recovery Glacier 66 Ag 81.10S 28.00W
Recreo 56 Gc 29.16S 65.04W
Recz 10 Lc 53.16N 15.33 E
Reda 10 Ob 54.38N 18.30 E
Redange 12 He 49.46N 5.54 E
Red Bank 44 Eh 35.07N 85.17W
Red Bay 42 Lf 51.44N 56.25W
Red Bluff 43 Cc 40.11N 122.15W
Red Bluff Reservoir 45 Ek 31.57N 103.56W
Redbridge, London- 12 Cc 51.35N 0.08 E
Red Butte 46 Ii 35.55N 112.03W
Redcar 9 Lg 54.37N 1.04W
Red Cliff 51c Ab 17.05N 62.32W
Redcliff 37 Dc 19.02S 29.50 E
Redcliffe, Mount- 59 Ee 28.25S 121.32 E
Red Cloud 45 Gf 40.05N 98.32W
Red Deer 39 Hd 52.16N 113.48W
Red Deer [Can.] 42 Hf 52.55N 101.27W
Red Deer [Can.] 38 Id 50.56N 109.54W
Redding 39 Ge 40.35N 122.24W
Redditch 9 Li 52.19N 1.56W
Rede 9 Kf 55.08N 2.13W
Redenção 54 Kd 4.13S 38.43W
Redfield 43 Hc 44.53N 98.31W
Red Hill 65a Ec 20.43N 156.15W
Red Hills 45 Gh 37.25N 99.25W
Redkino 7 Ih 56.40N 36.19 E
Red Lake 42 If 51.05N 93.55W
Red Lake 42 If 51.03N 93.49W
Red Lake River 45 Hc 47.55N 97.01W
Red Lakes 43 Ib 48.05N 94.45W
Redlands 46 Gi 34.03N 117.11W
Red Lodge 46 Kd 45.11N 109.15W
Redmond 43 Cc 44.17N 121.11W
Red Mountain [Ca.-U.S.] 46 Df 41.35N 123.06W
Red Mountain [Mt.-U.S.] 46 Ic 47.07N 112.44W
Red Oak 45 If 41.01N 95.14W
Redon 11 Dg 47.39N 2.05W
Redonda 50 Ed 16.55N 62.19W
Redondela 13 Db 42.17N 8.36W
Redondo 13 Ef 38.39N 7.33W
Redondo Beach 46 Fj 33.51N 118.23W
Redoubt Volcano 38 Dc 60.29N 152.45W
Red River [N.Amer.] 38 Jd 50.24N 96.48W
Red River [U.S.] 38 Jf 31.00N 91.40W
Red River (EN) = Hông,
Sông- 21 Mg 20.17N 106.34 E
Red River (EN) = Yuan Jiang
[Asia] 21 Mg 20.17N 106.34 E
Red Rock, Lake- 45 Jf 41.30N 93.20W
Red Rock River 46 Id 44.59N 112.52W
Redruth 9 Hk 50.13N 5.14W
Red Sea (EN) = Aḩmar, Al
Baḩr al- 30 Kf 25.00N 38.00 E
Redstone 42 Fd 64.17N 124.33W
Redstone 46 Da 52.08N 123.42W
Red Volta (EN) = Volta
Rouge 30 Gh 10.34N 0.30W
Redwater Creek 46 Mb 48.03N 105.13W
Red Wing 43 Ic 44.34N 92.31W
Redwood City 46 Dh 37.29N 122.13W
Redwood Falls 45 Id 44.32N 95.07W
Ree, Lough-/Loch Rí 9 Fh 53.35N 8.00W
Reed City 44 Ed 43.53N 85.31W
Reedley 46 Fh 36.24N 119.37W
Reeds Peak 45 Cj 33.09N 107.51W
Reedsport 43 Cc 43.42N 124.06W
Reedy Glacier 66 Ng 85.30S 134.00W
Reef Islands 57 Hf 10.15S 166.10 E
Reefton 62 De 42.07S 171.52 E
Reepham 12 Db 52.45N 1.07 E
Rees 12 Ic 51.46N 6.24 E
Reese River 46 Gf 40.39N 116.54W
Refahiye 24 Hc 39.54N 38.46 E
Reforma, Rio- 48 Ed 26.56N 108.12W
Reftele 8 Eg 57.11N 13.35 E
Reftinski 17 Jh 57.10N 61.43 E
Refugio 45 Hl 28.18N 97.17W
Refugio, Punta- 48 Cc 29.30N 113.30W
Rega 10 Lb 54.10N 15.18 E
Regar 19 Gh 38.34N 68.13 E
Regen 10 Jh 48.58N 13.08 E
Regen 10 Ig 49.01N 12.06 E
Regensburg 6 Hf 49.01N 12.06 E
Reggane 31 Hf 26.42N 0.10 E
Regge 12 Ib 52.26N 6.29 E
Reggio di Calabria 6 Hh 38.06N 15.39 E
Reggio nell'Emilia 14 Ef 44.43N 10.36 E
Reghin 15 Hc 46.46N 24.42 E
Regina [Fr.Gui.] 54 Hc 4.19N 52.08W
Regina [Sask.-Can.] 39 Id 50.25N 104.39W
Registan (EN) = Rīgestān 21 If 31.00N 65.00 E
Registro 55 Ig 24.30S 47.50W
Registro do Araguaia 55 Gb 15.44S 51.50W
Regnitz 10 Gg 49.54N 10.49 E
Regocijo 48 Gf 23.35N 105.11W
Reguengos de Monsaraz 13 Ef 38.25N 7.32W
Rehburg-Loccum 12 Lb 52.28N 9.14 E
Rehoboth [3] 37 Bd 23.50S 17.00 E
Rehoboth 37 Bd 23.18S 17.03 E
Reḩovot 24 Fg 31.54N 34.49 E
Reichelsheim (Odenwald) 12 Ke 49.43N 8.51 E
Reichenbach 10 If 50.37N 12.18 E
Reichshoffen 12 Jf 48.56N 7.40 E
Reichshof 12 Jd 50.55N 7.39 E
Reichshof-Denklingen 12 Jd 50.55N 7.39 E
Reidsville 44 Hg 36.21N 79.40W
Reigate 9 Mj 51.14N 0.13W
Reims 6 Gf 49.15N 4.02 E
Rein = Rhine (EN) 5 Ge 51.52N 6.02 E
Reina Adelaida,
Archipiélago- 52 Ik 52.10S 74.25W
Reindeer 42 He 55.34N 103.10W
Reindeer Bank (EN) 51p Ac 11.50N 62.05W
Reindeer Lake 38 Id 57.15N 102.40W
Reineskarvet 8 Cd 60.47N 8.13 E
Reinga, Cape- 62 Ea 34.25S 172.41 E
Reinhardswald 10 Fe 51.30N 9.30 E
Reinheim 12 Je 49.08N 7.11 E
Reinosa 13 Ha 43.00N 4.08W
Reisa 7 Eb 69.48N 21.00 E
Reitoru Atoll 57 Mf 17.52S 143.05W
Reitz 37 De 27.53S 28.31 E
Rejmyra 8 Ff 58.50N 15.55 E
Rejowiec Fabryczny 10 Te 51.08N 23.13 E
Reka Devnja 15 Kf 43.13N 27.36 E
Rekarne 8 Ge 59.20N 16.25 E
Reken 12 Jc 51.48N 7.03 E
Reliance 39 Ic 62.42N 109.08W
Relizane 32 Hb 35.45N 0.33 E
Remagen 12 Jd 50.34N 7.14 E
Remarkable, Mount- 59 Hf 32.48S 138.10 E
Rembang 26 Fh 6.42S 111.20 E
Remedios 56 Mf 8.14N 81.51W
Remedios, Punta- 49 Cg 13.31N 89.49W
Remedios, Rio- 49 Mh 11.01N 69.15W
Remich 12 Ie 49.32N 6.22 E
Rémire 54 Hc 4.53N 52.17W
Remiremont 11 Mf 48.01N 6.35 E
Remire Reef 37b Bb 5.05S 53.22 E
Remontnoje 16 Mf 46.33N 43.40 E
Remoulins 11 Kk 43.56N 4.34 E
Remscheid 10 De 51.11N 7.12 E
Rena 7 Cf 61.08N 11.22 E
Rena 8 Dc 61.08N 11.23 E
Renaix/Ronse 11 Jd 50.45N 3.36 E
Renana, Fossa- 5 Gf 48.40N 7.50 E
Renard Islands 63a Ad 10.50S 153.00 E
Renaud Island 66 Qe 65.40S 66.00W
Rende 14 Kk 39.20N 16.11 E
Rendezvous Bay 51b Ab 18.10N 63.07W
Rend Lake 45 Lg 38.05N 88.58W
Rendova Island 60 Fi 8.32S 157.20 E
Rendsburg 10 Fb 54.18N 9.40 E
Renfrew 42 Jg 45.28N 76.41W
Rengat 26 Dg 0.24S 102.33 E
Rengo 56 Fd 34.25S 70.52W
Reni 16 Fg 45.29N 28.18 E
Renko 8 Kd 60.54N 24.17 E
Renkum 12 Hc 51.58N 5.45 E
Renland 41 Jd 71.15N 27.20W
Renmark 58 Fh 34.11S 140.45 E
Rennell, Islas- 56 Fh 52.00S 74.00W
Rennell Island 57 Hf 11.40S 160.10 E
Rennes 6 Ff 48.05N 1.41W
Rennes, Bassin de- 11 Ef 48.05N 1.40W
Rennesøy 8 Ae 59.05N 5.40 E
Rennick Glacier 66 Kf 70.30S 161.45 E
Rennie Lake 42 Gd 61.10N 105.30W
Reno 39 Hf 39.31N 119.48W
Reno 14 Gf 44.38N 12.16 E
Renqiu 28 De 38.42N 116.06 E
Rensselaer [In.-U.S.] 44 De 40.57N 87.09W
Rensselaer [N.Y.-U.S.] 44 Kd 42.37N 73.44W
Renterría 13 Ka 43.19N 1.54W
Renton 46 Dc 47.30N 122.11W
Renwez 12 Ge 49.50N 4.36 E
Renxian 28 Cf 37.07N 114.41 E
Reo 26 Hh 8.19S 120.30 E
Repartimento, Serra do- 55 Jc 17.40S 44.50W
Repino 8 Md 60.10N 29.58 E
Repong, Pulau- 26 Ef 2.22N 105.53 E
Reposaari/Räfsö 8 Ic 61.37N 21.27 E
Republic 46 Fb 48.39N 118.44W
Republican 38 Jf 39.03N 96.48W
Repulse Bay 39 Kc 66.32N 86.15W
Repulse Bay [Austl.] 59 Jd 20.35S 148.45 E
Repulse Bay [Can.] 42 Ic 66.20N 86.00W
Repvåg 7 Fa 70.45N 25.41 E
Requena [Peru] 54 Dd 5.00S 73.50W
Requena [Sp.] 13 Ke 39.29N 1.06W
Requin Bay 51p Bb 12.02N 61.38W
Réquista 11 Ij 44.02N 2.32 E
Reşadiye Yarimadası 15 Km 36.40N 27.45 E
Reschenpass/Resia, Passo
di- 14 Ed 46.50N 10.30 E
Resen 15 Eh 41.05N 21.01 E
Reserva 55 Gg 24.38S 50.52W
Reserve 45 Bj 33.43N 108.45W
Rešetilovka 16 Ie 49.33N 34.05 E
Reshui 27 Hd 37.38N 100.30 E
Resia, Passo di-/
Reschenpass 14 Ed 46.50N 10.30 E
Resistencia 53 Kh 27.30S 58.59W
Reşiţa 15 Ed 45.18N 21.55 E
Resko 10 Lc 53.47N 15.25 E
Reso/Raisio 7 Ff 60.29N 22.11 E
Resolute 39 Jb 74.41N 94.54W
Resolution 38 Mc 61.30N 65.00W
Resolution Island 42 Ld 61.35N 64.39W
Resolution Island 62 Bf 45.40S 166.35 E
Respublikai Soveth
Socialisti Todžikiston/
Tadžikskaja SSR →
Tajikistan 19 Hh 39.00N 71.00 E
Respublika Sovetike
Sočialiste Moldovenjaske/
Moldavskaja SSR →
Moldova 19 Cf 47.00N 29.00 E
Ressons-sur-Matz 12 Ee 49.33N 2.45 E
Restigouche River 44 Na 48.04N 66.20W
Restinga de Sefton, Isla- 52 Hi 37.00S 83.50W
Restinga Sêca 55 Fi 29.49S 53.23W
Reszel 10 Rb 54.04N 21.09 E
Retalhuleu [3] 49 Bf 14.20N 91.50W
Retalhuleu 47 Ff 14.32N 91.41W
Retavas/Rietavas 8 Ii 55.43N 21.49 E
Retezatului, Munţii- 15 Fd 45.25N 23.00 E
Rethel 11 Ke 49.31N 4.22 E
Rethem (Aller) 12 Lb 52.47N 9.23 E
Réthimnon 15 Hn 35.22N 24.28 E
Retie 12 Hc 51.17N 5.05 E

Index Symbols

[1] Independent Nation
[2] State, Region
[3] District, County
[4] Municipality
[5] Colony, Dependency
Continent
Physical Region
Historical or Cultural Region
Mount, Mountain
Volcano
Hill
Mountains, Mountain Range
Hills, Escarpment
Plateau, Upland
Pass, Gap
Plain, Lowland
Delta
Salt Flat
Valley, Canyon
Crater, Cave
Karst Features
Depression
Polder
Desert, Dunes
Forest, Woods
Heath, Steppe
Oasis
Cape, Point
Coast, Beach
Cliff
Peninsula
Isthmus
Sandbank
Island
Atoll
Rock, Reef
Islands, Archipelago
Rocks, Reefs
Coral Reef
Well, Spring
Geyser
River, Stream
Waterfall Rapids
River Mouth, Estuary
Lake
Salt Lake
Intermittent Lake
Reservoir
Swamp, Pond
Canal
Glacier
Ice Shelf, Pack Ice
Ocean
Sea
Gulf, Bay
Strait, Fjord
Lagoon
Bank
Seamount
Tablemount
Ridge
Shelf
Basin
Escarpment, Sea Scarp
Fracture
Trench, Abyss
National Park, Reserve
Point of Interest
Recreation Site
Cave, Cavern
Historic Site
Ruins
Wall, Walls
Church, Abbey
Temple
Scientific Station
Airport
Port
Lighthouse
Mine
Tunnel
Dam, Bridge

Index Symbols

[1] Independent Nation	◣ Historical or Cultural Region	◻ Pass, Gap	◻ Depression	◻ Coast, Beach	◻ Rock, Reef	◻ Waterfall Rapids	◻ Canal	◻ Lagoon	◻ Escarpment, Sea Scarp	◻ Historic Site
[2] State, Region	▲ Mount, Mountain	▲ Plain, Lowland	◻ Polder	◻ Cliff	◻ Islands, Archipelago	◻ River Mouth, Estuary	◻ Bank	◻ Glacier	◻ Fracture	◻ Ruins
[3] District, County	▲ Volcano	◻ Delta	◻ Desert, Dunes	◻ Peninsula	◻ Rocks, Reefs	◻ Lake	◻ Ice Shelf, Pack Ice	◻ Seamount	◻ Trench, Abyss	◻ Wall, Walls
[4] Municipality	▲ Hill	◻ Salt Flat	◻ Forest, Woods	◻ Isthmus	◻ Coral Reef	◻ Salt Lake	◻ Ocean	◻ Tableland	◻ National Park, Reserve	◻ Church, Abbey
[5] Colony, Dependency	▲ Mountains, Mountain Range	◻ Valley, Canyon	◻ Heath, Steppe	◻ Sandbank	◻ Well, Spring	◻ Intermittent Lake	◻ Ridge	◻ Point of Interest	◻ Temple
◣ Continent	▲ Hills, Escarpment	◻ Crater, Cave	◻ Oasis	◻ Island	◻ Geyser	◻ Reservoir	◻ Sea	◻ Recreation Site	◻ Scientific Station
◣ Physical Region	◻ Plateau, Upland	◻ Karst Features	◻ Cape, Point	◻ Atoll	◻ River, Stream	◻ Swamp, Pond	◻ Gulf, Bay	◻ Shelf	◻ Cave, Cavern	◻ Port
							◻ Strait, Fjord	◻ Basin	◻ Airport	◻ Lighthouse
										◻ Mine
										◻ Tunnel
										◻ Dam, Bridge

Rödeby 8 Fh 56.15N 15.36 E
Rodeio Bonito 55 Fh 27.28S 53.10W
Roden 12 Ia 53.09N 6.26 E
Rodeo [Arg.] 56 Gd 30.12S 69.06W
Rodeo [Mex.] 48 Ge 25.11N 104.34W
Rodeo [N.M.-U.S.] 45 Bk 31.50N 109.02W
Röder 10 Je 51.30N 13.25 E
Rodez 11 Ij 44.20N 2.34 E
Rodgau 12 Kd 50.01N 8.53 E
Rodholivos 15 Gi 40.56N 23.59 E
Ródhos = Rhodes (EN) 6 Ih 36.26N 28.13 E
Ródhos = Rhodes (EN) 5 Ih 36.10N 28.00 E
Rodi Garganico 14 Ji 41.55N 15.53 E
Roding 9 Nj 51.31N 0.06 E
Rodna 15 Hb 47.25N 24.49 E
Rodnei, Munţii- 15 Hb 47.35N 24.40 E
Rodney, Cape- 40 Fd 64.39N 166.24W
Rodniki 7 Jh 57.07N 41.48 E
Rodonit, Gjiri i- 15 Ch 41.35N 19.30 E
Rodonit, Kep i- 15 Ch 41.35N 19.27 E
Rodopi = Rhodope Mountains (EN) 5 Ig 41.30N 24.30 E
Rodrigues Island 30 Nj 19.42S 63.25 E
Roebourne 59 Dd 20.47S 117.09 E
Roebuck Bay 59 Ec 18.04S 122.15 E
Roer 10 Be 51.12N 5.59 E
Roermond 11 Lc 51.12N 6.00 E
Roeselare/Roulers 11 Jd 50.57N 3.08 E
Roes Welcome Sound 42 Id 64.30N 86.45W
Roetgen 12 Id 50.39N 6.12 E
Rogačev 16 Gc 53.09N 30.06 E
Rogačevka 16 Kd 51.31N 39.34 E
Rogagua, Laguna- 54 Ef 13.45S 66.55W
Rogaguado, Laguna- 54 Ef 12.55S 65.45W
Rogaland [2] 7 Bg 59.00N 6.15 E
Rogaška Slatina 14 Jd 46.15N 15.38 E
Rogatica 14 Ng 43.48N 19.01 E
Rogatin 10 Ug 49.19N 24.40 E
Rogers 45 Ih 36.20N 94.07W
Rogers, Mount- 44 Gg 36.39N 81.33W
Rogers City 44 Fc 45.25N 83.49W
Rogers Lake 46 Gi 34.52N 117.51W
Rogers Peak 46 Jg 38.04N 111.32W
Rogersville 44 Fg 36.25N 82.59W
Roggan 42 Jf 54.24N 79.30W
Roggeveldberge 37 Bf 31.50S 19.50 E
Roggewein, Cabo- 65d Bb 27.07S 109.15W
Rognan 7 Dc 67.06N 15.23 E
Rogozhina 15 Ch 41.05N 19.40 E
Rogozna 15 Df 43.04N 20.40 E
Rogožno 10 Md 52.46N 17.00 E
Rogue River 46 Ce 42.26N 124.25W
Rohan, Plateau de- 11 Df 48.10N 3.00W
Rohl 35 Dd 7.05N 29.46 E
Rohrbach in Oberösterreich 14 Hb 48.34N 13.59 E
Rohrbach-lès-Bitche 12 Je 49.03N 7.16 E
Rohri 25 Dc 27.41N 68.54 E
Rohtak 25 Fc 28.54N 76.34 E
Roi, Le Bois du- 11 Kh 46.59N 4.02 E
Roi Et 25 Ke 16.05N 103.42 E
Roi Georges, Iles du- 57 Mf 14.32S 145.08W
Roine 8 Kc 61.25N 24.05 E
Roisel 12 Fe 49.57N 3.06 E
Roja 7 Fh 57.30N 22.51 E
Rojas 56 Hd 34.12S 60.44W
Rojo, Cabo- [Mex.] 47 Ed 21.33N 97.20W
Rojo, Cabo- [P.R.] 49 Nd 18.01N 67.15W
Rokan 26 Df 2.00N 100.52 E
Rokiškis 7 Fi 55.59N 25.37 E
Rokitnoje 16 Ed 51.21N 27.14 E
Rokkasho 29a Bc 40.58N 141.21 E
Rokycany 10 Jg 49.45N 13.36 E
Rokytná 10 Mg 49.05N 16.21 E
Rola Co 27 Ed 35.25N 88.25 E
Rolândia 55 Gf 23.18S 51.22W
Rolla [Mo.-U.S.] 43 Id 37.57N 91.46W
Rolla [N.D.-U.S.] 45 Gb 48.52N 99.37W
Rolleston 62 Ee 43.35S 172.23 E
Rolvsøya 7 Fa 71.00N 24.00 E
Roma [Austl.] 58 Fg 26.35S 148.47 E
Roma [It.] = Rome (EN) 6 Hg 41.54N 12.29 E
Roma [Swe.] 7 Eh 57.32N 18.26 E
Romagna 14 Gf 44.30N 12.15 E
Romaine 42 Lf 50.18N 63.48W
Roman 15 Jc 46.55N 26.55 E
Romanche 11 Li 45.05N 5.43 E
Romanche Gap (EN) 3 Dj 0.10S 18.15W
Romang 55 Ci 29.30S 59.46W
Romang, Pulau- 26 Ih 7.35S 127.26 E
România = Romania (EN) [1] 6 If 46.00N 25.30 E
Romania (EN) = România [1] 6 If 46.00N 25.30 E
Romanija 14 Mg 43.51N 18.43 E
Roman Koš, Gora- 19 Dg 44.36N 34.16 E
Romano, Cayo- 49 Ib 22.04N 77.50W
Romanovka 20 Gf 53.14N 112.46 E
Romans-sur-Isère 11 Li 45.03N 5.03 E
Romanzof, Cape- 38 Cc 61.49N 166.09W
Romanzof Mountains 40 Kc 69.00N 144.00W
Rombas 12 Ie 49.15N 6.05 E
Romblon 26 Hd 12.35N 122.15 E
Rome [Ga.-U.S.] 43 Je 34.16N 85.11W
Rome [N.Y.-U.S.] 44 Lc 43.13N 75.28W
Rome [Or.-U.S.] 46 Ge 42.50N 117.37W
Rome (EN) = Roma [It.] 6 Hg 41.54N 12.29 E
Romeleåsen 8 Ei 55.34N 13.33 E
Romerike 8 Dd 60.05N 11.10 E
Romilly-sur-Seine 11 Jf 48.31N 3.43 E
Rommani 32 Fc 33.32N 6.36W
Romme 8 Fd 60.26N 15.30 E
Rommerskirchen 12 Ic 51.02N 6.41 E
Romney Marsh 12 Cc 51.02N 0.55 E
Romny 19 De 50.45N 33.29 E
Rømø 7 Bi 55.10N 8.30 E
Romodanovo 7 Ki 54.28N 45.18 E
Romont 14 Ad 46.42N 6.55 E
Romorantin-Lanthenay 11 Hg 47.22N 1.45 E
Romsdal 8 Bb 62.35N 7.50 E
Romsdalen 8 Bb 62.30N 7.55 E
Romsdalsfjorden 8 Bb 62.40N 7.15 E
Romsdalshorn 8 Bd 62.29N 7.50 E
Romsey 9 Lk 50.59N 1.30W
Ronas Hill 9 La 60.38N 1.20W
Ronave 64e Ba 0.29S 166.56 E
Roncador, Cayos de- 47 Hf 13.32N 80.03W
Roncador, Serra do- 52 Kg 13.00S 51.50W
Roncador Reef 57 Ge 6.13S 159.22 E
Roncesvalles 13 Ka 43.01N 1.19W
Roncesvalles o Ibañeta, Puerto de- 13 Ka 43.01N 1.19W
Ronciglione 14 Gh 42.17N 12.13 E
Ronco 14 Gf 44.24N 12.12 E
Ronda 13 Gh 36.44N 5.10W
Ronda, Serrania de- 13 Gh 36.45N 5.05W
Ronda do Sul 55 Cb 15.57S 59.42W
Rondane 7 Bf 61.55N 9.45 E
Rønde 7 Ch 56.18N 10.29 E
Ronde, Point- 51g Ba 15.33N 61.29W
Ronde Island 50 Ff 12.18N 61.31W
Rondeslottet 8 Cc 61.55N 9.46 E
Rondon 55 Ff 23.23S 52.48W
Rondón, Pico- 54 Fc 1.36N 63.08W
Rondônia 53 Jg 10.52S 61.57W
Rondônia 54 Ff 11.00S 63.00W
Rondonópolis 53 Kg 16.28S 54.38W
Rong'an (Chang'an) 27 If 25.16N 109.23 E
Rongcheng 28 Ce 39.03N 115.52 E
Rongcheng (Yatou) 28 Gf 37.10N 122.25 E
Rongelap Atoll 57 Hc 11.09N 166.50 E
Rongerik Atoll 57 Hc 11.21N 167.26 E
Rongjiang (Guzhou) 27 If 25.58N 108.30 E
Rongxian 27 Jg 22.48N 110.30 E
Rongzhag/Danba 27 He 30.48N 101.54 E
Rønne 7 Di 55.06N 14.42 E
Ronne Bay 66 Qf 72.30S 74.00W
Ronneby 7 Dh 56.12N 15.18 E
Ronnebyån 8 Fh 56.10N 15.18 E
Ronne Ice Shelf 66 Qf 78.30S 61.00W
Ronse/Renaix 11 Jd 50.45N 3.36 E
Ronuro, Rio- 52 Kg 11.56S 53.33W
Roodepoort 37 De 26.11S 27.54 E
Roof Butte 43 Fd 36.28N 109.05W
Rooiboklaagte 37 Cd 20.20S 21.15 E
Roon, Pulau- 26 Jg 2.23S 134.33 E
Rooniu, Mont- 65e c 17.49S 149.12W
Roorkee 25 Fc 29.52N 77.53 E
Roosendaal 11 Kc 51.32N 4.28 E
Roosevelt [Az.-U.S.] 46 Jj 33.40N 111.09W
Roosevelt [Ut.-U.S.] 46 Kf 40.18N 109.59W
Roosevelt, Mount- 42 Ee 58.23N 125.04W
Roosevelt, Rio- 52 Jf 7.35S 60.20W
Roosevelt Island 66 Lf 79.30S 162.00W
Root Portage 45 Ka 50.53N 91.18W
Ropa 10 Rg 49.46N 21.29 E
Ropar 25 Fb 30.58N 76.20 E
Ropaži 8 Kh 56.58N 24.26 E
Ropczyce 10 Rf 50.03N 21.37 E
Rope, The- 64q Ab 25.04S 130.05W
Roper River 57 Ef 14.43S 135.27 E
Roquefort 11 Fj 44.02N 0.19W
Roque Pérez 55 Cl 35.25S 59.20W
Roquetas de Mar 13 Jh 36.46N 2.36W
Roraima, Monte- 52 Je 5.12N 60.44W
Roraima 54 Fc 1.30N 61.00W
Røros 7 Ce 62.35N 11.24 E
Rorschach 14 Dc 47.30N 9.30 E
Rørvik 7 Cd 64.51N 11.14 E
Ros 16 Ge 49.39N 31.35 E
Rosa, Cap- 14 Cn 36.57N 8.14 E
Rosa, Lake- 49 Kc 20.55N 73.20W
Rosa, Monte- 5 Gf 45.55N 7.53 E
Rošal 7 Ji 55.41N 39.55 E
Rosala 8 Je 59.50N 22.25 E
Rosalia 46 Gc 47.14N 117.22W
Rosalia, Punta- 65d Bb 27.03S 109.19W
Rosalie 51g Bb 15.22N 61.16W
Rosalind Bank (EN) 49 Ge 16.30N 80.30W
Rosamond Lake 46 Fi 34.50N 118.04W
Rosamorada 48 Gf 22.08N 105.12W
Rosana 55 Ff 22.36S 53.01W
Rosario [Arg.] 53 Ji 32.57S 60.40W
Rosario [Braz.] 54 Jd 2.57S 44.14W
Rosario [Mex.] 48 Dd 26.27N 111.38W
Rosario [Mex.] 47 Cd 23.00N 105.52W
Rosario [Par.] 56 Ib 24.27S 57.03W
Rosario [Ven.] 49 Kh 10.19N 72.19W
Rosario, Arroyo- 48 Bb 30.03N 115.45W
Rosario, Bahía- 48 Bc 29.50N 115.45W
Rosario, Cayo del- 49 Gc 21.38N 81.53W
Rosario, Islas de- 49 Jh 10.10N 75.46W
Rosario, Sierra del- 48 He 25.35N 103.50W
Rosario de Arriba 47 Ab 30.01N 115.40W
Rosario de la Frontera 56 Hc 25.48S 64.58W
Rosario de Lerma 56 Gb 24.59S 65.35W
Rosario del Tala 55 Ck 32.18S 59.09W
Rosário do Sul 56 Jd 30.15S 54.55W
Rosário Oeste 54 Gf 14.50S 56.25W
Rosarito 48 Bc 28.38N 114.04W
Rosarno 14 Jl 38.29N 15.58 E
Rosas/Roses 13 Pb 42.16N 3.11 E
Rosas, Golfo de-/Roses, Golf de- 13 Pb 42.10N 3.15 E
Rosa Seamount (EN) 47 Bc 26.12N 114.58W
Rosa Zarate 54 Cc 0.18N 79.27W
Roščino 8 Md 60.13N 29.43 E
Roscoe Glacier 66 Ge 66.30S 95.20 E
Ros Comáin/Roscommon [2] 9 Eh 53.40N 8.30W
Ros Comáin/Roscommon 9 Eh 53.38N 8.11W
Roscommon 44 Ec 44.30N 84.35W
Roscommon/Ros Comáin 9 Eh 53.38N 8.11W
Roscommon/Ros Comáin [2] 9 Eh 53.40N 8.30W
Ros Cré/Roscrea 9 Fi 52.57N 7.47W
Roscrea/Ros Cré 9 Fi 52.57N 7.47W
Rose, Pointe de la- 51h Bb 14.33N 61.03W
Roseau [Dom.] 39 Mh 15.18N 61.24W
Roseau [Dom.] 51g Bb 15.18N 61.24W
Roseau [Mn.-U.S.] 45 Ib 48.51N 95.46W
Roseau [St.Luc.] 51k Ab 13.58N 61.02W
Roseau River 45 Hb 49.08N 97.14W
Rosebery 59 Jh 41.46S 145.32 E
Rosebud 46 Lc 46.16N 106.27W
Rosebud Creek 46 Lc 46.16N 106.28W
Rosebud River 46 Ia 51.25N 112.37W
Roseburg 43 Cc 43.13N 123.20W
Rosemary Bank (EN) 9 Cb 59.15N 10.10W
Rosenberg 43 Hf 29.33N 95.48W
Rosendahl 12 Jb 52.01N 7.12 E
Rosendahl-Osterwick 12 Jb 52.01N 7.12 E
Rosendal 7 Bf 59.59N 6.01 E
Rosenheim 10 Ii 47.51N 12.08 E
Rosental 14 Id 46.33N 14.15 E
Roses/Rosas 13 Pb 42.16N 3.11 E
Roses, Golf de-/Rosas, Golfo de- 13 Pb 42.10N 3.15 E
Roseţi 15 Ke 44.13N 27.26 E
Roseto degli Abruzzi 14 Ih 42.41N 14.01 E
Rosetown 42 Gf 51.33N 108.00W
Rosetta (EN) = Rashīd 33 Fc 31.24N 30.25 E
Roseville 46 Eg 38.45N 121.17W
Roshage 7 Bh 57.07N 8.38 E
Rosica 15 If 43.15N 25.42 E
Rosières-en-Santerre 12 Ee 49.49N 2.43 E
Rosignano Solvay 14 Eg 43.23N 10.26 E
Rosignol 54 Gb 6.17N 57.32W
Roşiori de Vede 15 He 44.07N 24.59 E
Roskilde [2] 8 Ei 55.35N 12.10 E
Roskilde 7 Ci 55.39N 12.05 E
Roslagen 8 He 59.30N 18.40 E
Ros Láir/Rosslare 9 Gi 52.17N 6.23W
Roslavl 19 De 53.58N 32.53 E
Roslyn 46 Ec 47.13N 120.59W
Ros Mhic Thriúin/New Ross 9 Gi 52.24N 6.56W
Røsnæs 8 Di 55.45N 10.55 E
Rosny-sur-Seine 12 Df 49.00N 1.38 E
Rösrath 12 Jd 50.54N 7.12 E
Ross 42 Ed 62.00N 132.25W
Ross [Austl.] 59 Jh 42.02S 147.29 E
Ross 10 Uc 53.16N 24.29 E
Ross [N.Z.] 62 De 42.54S 170.49 E
Ross, Cape- 26 Gd 10.56N 119.13 E
Ross, Mount- 30 Nm 49.25S 69.08 E
Rossano 14 Kk 39.34N 16.38 E
Rossan Point/Ceann Ros Eoghain 9 Eg 54.42N 8.48W
Ross Barnett Reservoir 45 Lj 32.30N 90.00W
Rosseau Lake 44 Hc 45.10N 79.35W
Rossel Island 57 Gf 11.26S 154.07 E
Rossell, Cap- 63b Ce 20.23S 166.36 E
Ross Ice Shelf 66 Lg 81.30S 175.00W
Rossija = Russia (EN) 19 Jc 60.00N 100.00 E
Ross Island 66 Kf 77.30S 168.00 E
Ross Lake 46 Eb 48.53N 121.04W
Rossland 46 Gb 49.05N 117.48W
Rosslare/Ros Láir 9 Gi 52.17N 6.23W
Roßlau 10 Ie 51.53N 12.15 E
Rosso 31 Fg 16.31N 15.49W
Ross-on-Wye 9 Kj 51.55N 2.35W
Rossony 8 Mi 55.53N 28.49 E
Rossoš 19 De 50.11N 39.39 E
Ross River 42 Ed 61.59N 132.27W
Ross Sea (EN) 66 Lf 76.00S 175.00W
Rossvatn 7 Cd 65.45N 14.00 E
Røst 7 Cc 67.31N 12.07 E
Rosta 7 Eb 69.02N 18.40 E
Rostamī 24 Nh 28.52N 51.02 E
Rostan Kalā 24 Od 36.42N 53.27 E
Rösterkopf 12 Ie 49.40N 6.50 E
Rosthern 42 Gf 52.40N 106.20W
Rostock 6 He 54.05N 12.08 E
Rostock-Warnemünde 10 Ib 54.10N 12.05 E
Rostov 19 Dd 57.13N 39.25 E
Rostov-na-Donu 6 Jf 47.14N 39.42 E
Rostovskaja Oblast [3] 19 Ef 47.45N 41.15 E
Roswell [Ga.-U.S.] 44 Eh 34.03N 84.22W
Roswell [N.M.-U.S.] 39 If 33.24N 104.32W
Rot 8 Fc 61.15N 14.02 E
Rota 13 Fh 36.37N 6.21W
Rota Island 57 Fc 14.10N 145.12 E
Rotenburg (Wümme) 10 Fc 53.07N 9.24 E
Rotenburg an der Fulda 10 Ff 50.59N 9.43 E
Roter Main 10 Hf 50.03N 11.27 E
Roth 10 Hg 49.15N 11.06 E
Rothaargebirge 10 Ee 51.05N 8.15 E
Rothenburg ob der Tauber 10 Gg 49.23N 10.11 E
Rother [Eng.-U.K.] 9 Nk 50.57N 0.45 E
Rother [Eng.-U.K.] 12 Bd 50.57N 0.22W
Rothera 66 Qe 67.46S 68.54W
Rotherham 9 Lh 53.26N 1.20W
Rothesay 9 Hf 55.51N 5.03W
Rothorn 14 Cd 46.47N 8.03 E
Rothschild Island 66 Qe 69.25S 72.30W
Rothwell 12 Bb 52.25N 0.48W
Roti, Pulau- 21 Ok 10.45S 123.10 E
Roti, Selat- 26 Hi 10.25S 123.25 E
Rotja, Punta- 13 Nf 38.38N 1.34 E
Rotnes 8 Dd 60.04N 10.53 E
Roto 59 Jf 33.03S 145.29 E
Rotoiti, Lake- 62 Ed 41.50S 172.50 E
Rotondella 14 Kj 40.10N 16.31 E
Rotondo, Monte- 11a Ba 42.13N 9.03 E
Rotoroa, Lake- 62 Ed 41.50S 172.40 E
Rotorua 61 Eg 38.09S 176.15 E
Rotorua, Lake- 62 Gc 38.05S 176.15 E
Rotselaar 12 Gd 50.57N 4.43 E
Rott 10 Jh 48.25N 13.20 E
Rottenburg am Neckar 10 Eh 48.28N 8.56 E
Rotterdam 6 Ge 51.55N 4.28 E
Rottnaälven 8 Ed 59.48N 13.07 E
Rottnen 8 Fh 56.45N 15.05 E
Rottneros 8 Ee 59.48N 13.07 E
Rottnest Island 59 Df 32.00S 115.30 E
Rottumerplaat 11 Ma 53.35N 6.30 E
Rottweil 10 Eh 48.10N 8.37 E
Rotuma Island 57 If 12.30S 177.05 E
Roubaix 11 Jd 50.42N 3.10 E
Roubion 11 Kj 44.31N 4.42 E
Roudnice nad Labem 10 Kf 50.26N 14.16 E
Rouen 6 Gf 49.26N 1.05 E
Rouergue 11 Ij 44.30N 2.56 E
Rouge, Rivière- 44 Jc 45.38N 74.42W
Rouillac 11 Fi 45.47N 0.04W
Roulers/Roeselare 11 Jd 50.57N 3.08 E
Roumois 11 Ge 49.30N 0.30 E
Roundup 43 Fb 46.27N 108.33W
Rousay 9 Jb 59.01N 3.02W
Roussillon 11 Ki 45.22N 4.49 E
Roussillon 11 Il 42.30N 2.30 E
Roussin, Cap- 63b Ce 21.21S 167.59 E
Routot 12 Ce 49.23N 0.44 E
Rouyn-Noranda 39 Le 48.14N 79.01W
Rovaniemi 6 Ib 66.30N 25.43 E
Rovenskaja Oblast [3] 19 Ce 51.00N 26.30 E
Rovereto 14 Fe 45.53N 11.02 E
Rovigo 14 Fe 45.04N 11.47 E
Rovinari 15 Ge 44.55N 23.11 E
Rovinj 14 He 45.05N 13.38 E
Rovkulskoje, Ozero- 7 Hd 64.00N 31.00 E
Rovno 6 Ie 50.37N 26.15 E
Rovnoje 16 Od 50.47N 46.05 E
Rovuma = Ruvuma (EN) 30 Lj 10.29S 40.28 E
Rowa, Iles- 63b Ca 13.37S 167.32 E
Rowley 42 Jc 69.05N 78.55W
Rowley Shoals 57 Cf 17.30S 119.00 E
Roxas [Phil.] 26 Gd 10.28N 119.30 E
Roxas [Phil.] 26 Hd 11.35N 122.45 E
Roxboro 44 Hg 36.24N 78.59W
Roxburgh 62 Cf 45.33S 169.19 E
Roxen 8 Ff 58.30N 15.40 E
Roxo, Cap- 30 Fg 12.20N 16.43W
Roy [N.M.-U.S.] 45 Di 35.57N 104.12W
Roy [Ut.-U.S.] 46 If 41.10N 112.02W
Roya 11 Nk 43.48N 7.35 E
Royal Canal 9 Gh 53.21N 6.15W
Royale, Isle- 43 Jb 48.00N 89.00W
Royal Leamington Spa 9 Li 52.18N 1.31W
Royal Society Range 66 Jf 78.10S 162.36 E
Royal Tunbridge Wells 9 Nj 51.08N 0.16 E
Royan 11 Ei 45.38N 1.02W
Royat 11 Ji 45.46N 3.03 E
Royaumont, Abbaye de- 12 Ee 49.17N 2.28 E
Roye 11 Ie 49.42N 2.48 E
Roy Hill 59 Dd 22.38S 119.57 E
Røyken 8 De 59.45N 10.23 E
Royston 9 Mi 52.03N 0.01W
Rožaj 15 Dg 42.51N 20.10 E
Różan 10 Rd 52.53N 21.25 E
Rozdol 10 Ug 49.24N 24.08 E
Rozewie, Przylądek- 10 Ob 54.51N 18.21 E
Rožišče 16 Dd 50.54N 25.19 E
Rožňava 10 Qh 48.40N 20.32 E
Rožniatov 10 Uh 48.51N 24.14 E
Roznov 15 Jc 46.50N 26.31 E
Rožnov pod Radhoštěm 10 Og 49.28N 18.09 E
Rożnów 10 Qg 49.46N 20.42 E
Rożnowskie, Jezioro- 10 Qg 49.48N 20.45 E
Rozoy-sur-Serre 12 Ge 49.43N 4.08 E
Roztocze 5 Ie 50.30N 23.20 E
Rrësheni 15 Ch 41.47N 19.54 E
RSFSR — Russia (EN) 19 Jc 60.00N 100.00 E
RSFSR — Rossija 19 Jc 60.00N 100.00 E
Rtanj 15 Ef 43.47N 21.54 E
Rtiščevo 19 Ee 52.16N 43.52 E
Ruacana, Quedas- 30 Jj 17.23S 14.15 E
Ruahine Range 62 Gc 39.50S 176.05 E
Ruapehu 57 Ih 39.17S 175.34 E
Ruapuke Island 61 Ci 46.45S 168.30 E
Rua Sura 63a Ec 9.30S 160.36 E
Ruatahuna 62 Gc 38.38S 176.58 E
Rubbestadneset 8 Ae 59.49N 5.17 E
Rubcovsk 22 Kd 51.33N 81.10 E
Rubeho Mountains 36 Gd 6.55S 36.30 E
Rubeshibe 28 Qc 43.47N 143.38 E
Rubežnoje 16 Ke 48.59N 38.26 E
Rubi 36 Db 2.48N 23.54 E
Rubiataba 55 Hb 15.08S 49.48W
Rubiku 15 Ch 41.46N 19.45 E
Rubio 54 Db 7.43N 72.22W
Rubio 13 Ic 41.26N 3.47W
Ruby 40 Hd 64.44N 155.30W
Ruby Lake 46 Hf 40.15N 115.30W
Ruby Mountains 46 Hf 40.25N 115.35W
Ruby Range 46 Id 45.15N 112.15W
Rucăr 15 Id 45.24N 25.10 E
Rucava 8 Ih 56.10N 21.00 E
Ruciane Nida 10 Rc 53.39N 21.35 E
Ruda 10 Of 50.10N 18.18 E
Rudabánya 10 Qh 48.23N 20.38 E
Rūdak 24 Nh 35.51N 51.33 E
Rūdān 24 Qi 27.17N 57.13 E
Ruda Śląska 10 Of 50.18N 18.51 E
Rūdbār [Afg.] 23 Jc 30.09N 62.36 E
Rūdbār [Iran] 24 Md 36.48N 49.24 E
Rüdersdorf bei Berlin 10 Jd 52.27N 13.47 E
Rüdesheim am Rhein 12 Je 49.59N 7.55 E
Rudiškes/Rūdiškės 8 Kj 54.30N 24.58 E
Rūdiškės/Rudiškes 8 Kj 54.30N 24.58 E
Rudki 10 Tg 49.34N 23.30 E
Rudkøbing 7 Ci 54.56N 10.43 E
Rudnaja-Pristan 20 Ih 44.25N 135.49 E
Rudničny 7 Mg 59.38N 52.29 E
Rudnik 15 De 44.08N 20.30 E
Rudnik [Bul.] 15 Kg 42.57N 27.46 E
Rudnik [Pol.] 10 Sf 50.28N 22.15 E
Rudnik [Yugo.] 15 De 44.08N 20.31 E
Rudnja 16 Nd 50.49N 44.36 E
Rudnja 19 De 54.57N 31.07 E
Rudno 10 Tg 49.44N 23.57 E
Rudny 19 Ge 52.57N 63.07 E
Rudny 28 Mb 44.28N 135.00 E
Rudolf, Lake-/Turkana, Lake- 30 Kh 3.30N 36.00 E
Rudolstadt 10 Hf 50.43N 11.20 E
Rudong (Juegang) 28 Fh 32.19N 121.11 E
Rudozem 15 Hh 41.29N 24.51 E
Rūd Sar 23 Hb 37.08N 50.18 E
Rudyard 46 Jb 48.34N 110.33W
Rue 11 Hd 50.16N 1.40 E
Ruecas 13 Ge 39.00N 5.55W
Ruelle-sur-Touvre 11 Gi 45.41N 0.14 E
Rufā'ah 35 Ec 14.46N 33.22 E
Ruffec 11 Gh 46.01N 0.12 E
Ruffing Point 51a Db 18.45N 64.25W
Rufiji 30 Ki 8.00S 39.20 E
Rufino 56 Hd 34.16S 62.42W
Rufisque 34 Bc 14.43N 17.17W
Rufunsa 36 Ef 15.05S 29.40 E
Rugao 28 Fh 32.24N 120.34 E
Rugby [Eng.-U.K.] 9 Li 52.23N 1.15W
Rugby [N.D.-U.S.] 43 Gb 48.22N 99.59W
Rügen 5 He 54.25N 13.24 E
Rugles 12 Cf 48.49N 0.42 E
Ru He 28 Ch 32.55N 114.24 E
Ruhea 25 Hc 26.10N 88.25 E
Ruhengeri 36 Ec 1.30S 29.38 E
Rühlertwist 12 Jb 52.39N 7.06 E
Ruhner Berge 10 Hc 53.17N 11.55 E
Ruhnu, Ostrov-/Ruhnu Saar 7 Fh 57.50N 23.15 E
Ruhnu Saar/Ruhnu, Ostrov- 7 Fh 57.50N 23.15 E
Ruhr 10 Ce 51.27N 6.44 E
Rui'an 27 Lf 27.48N 120.38 E
Ruichang 28 Cj 29.41N 115.38 E
Ruiena/Rūjiena 7 Fh 57.54N 25.17 E
Ruijin 27 Kf 25.59N 116.03 E
Ruili 27 Gg 24.03N 97.46 E
Ruiselede 12 Fc 51.03N 3.24 E
Ruiz 48 Gg 21.57N 105.09W
Ruiz, Nevado del- 54 Cc 4.54N 75.18W
Ruj 15 Fg 42.51N 22.35 E
Ruja/Rūja 8 Kg 57.38N 25.10 E
Rūja/Ruja 8 Kg 57.38N 25.10 E
Rujan 15 Eg 42.23N 21.49 E
Rujen 15 Fg 42.10N 22.31 E
Rūjiena/Ruiena 7 Fh 57.54N 25.17 E
Ruki 30 Ih 0.05N 18.17 E
Rukwa [3] 36 Fd 7.00S 31.20 E
Rukwa, Lake- 30 Ki 8.00S 32.15 E
Rūl Ḍadnah 24 Qk 25.33N 56.21 E
Rülzheim 12 Ke 49.10N 8.18 E
Ruma 15 Cd 45.01N 19.49 E
Rumaylah 35 Fc 12.57N 35.02 E
Rumbek 31 Jh 6.48N 29.41 E
Rumberpon, Pulau- 26 Jg 1.50S 134.15 E
Rum Cay 47 Jd 23.40N 74.53W
Rumes 12 Fd 50.33N 3.18 E
Rumford 44 Lc 44.33N 70.33W
Rumia 10 Ob 54.35N 18.25 E
Rumigny 12 Ge 49.48N 4.16 E
Rumija 15 Cg 42.06N 19.12 E
Rumilly 11 Li 45.52N 5.57 E
Rum Jungle 59 Gb 13.01S 131.00 E
Rummah, Wādī ar- 24 Ki 26.38N 44.18 E
Rumoi 27 Pc 43.56N 141.39 E
Rumphi 36 Fe 11.01S 33.52 E
Run 12 Hc 51.40N 5.20 E
Runan 28 Ci 33.00N 114.21 E
Runanga 62 De 42.24S 171.15 E
Runaway, Cape- 62 Gb 37.32S 177.59 E
Rundēni/Rundeni 8 Lh 56.14N 27.52 E
Rundeni/Rundēni 8 Lh 56.14N 27.52 E
Rundu 31 Ij 17.55S 19.45 E
Rungu 36 Eb 3.11N 27.52 E
Rungwa 31 Ki 6.57S 33.31 E
Rungwa 36 Fd 7.36S 31.50 E
Runmarö 8 He 59.15N 18.45 E
Runn 8 Fd 60.35N 15.40 E
Ruokolahti 7 Gf 61.17N 28.50 E
Ruoqiang/Qarkilik 22 Kf 39.02N 88.00 E
Ruo Shui 21 Le 40.20N 99.40 E
Ruotsalainen 8 Kc 61.15N 25.55 E
Ruotsinpyhtää/Strömfors 8 Ld 60.32N 26.27 E
Ruovesi 7 Ff 61.59N 24.05 E
Ruovesi 8 Kc 61.55N 24.10 E
Rupanco 56 Ff 40.46S 72.42W
Rupea 15 Ic 46.02N 25.13 E
Rupel 12 Gc 51.07N 4.19 E
Rupert 42 Jf 51.30N 78.48W
Rupert 46 Ie 42.37N 113.41W
Rupert, Baie de- 42 Jf 51.35N 79.00W
Ruppert Coast 66 Mf 75.45S 141.00W
Rur 10 Be 51.12N 5.59 E
Rurrenabaque 53 Jg 14.28S 67.34W
Rurstausee 12 Id 50.38N 6.24 E
Rurutu, Ile- 57 Lg 22.26S 151.20W
Rušan 19 Hh 37.57N 71.31 E
Rusape 37 Ec 18.32S 32.07 E
Ruşayriş, Khazzān ar- = Rusayris, Lake- (EN) 35 Ec 11.40N 34.20 E
Rusayris, Lake- (EN) = Ruşayriş, Khazzān ar- 35 Ec 11.40N 34.20 E
Ruse 6 Ig 43.50N 25.57 E
Ruse [2] 15 If 43.50N 25.57 E
Ruşetu 15 Ke 44.57N 27.13 E
Rushan (Xiacun) 28 Ff 36.55N 121.30 E
Rushden 12 Bb 52.17N 0.35W
Rushville 45 Kf 40.07N 90.34W
Rusk 45 Ik 31.48N 95.09W

Index Symbols

[1] Independent Nation
[2] State, Region
[3] District, County
[4] Municipality
[5] Colony, Dependency
Continent
Physical Region
Historical or Cultural Region
Mount, Mountain
Volcano
Hill
Mountains, Mountain Range
Hills, Escarpment
Plateau, Upland
Pass, Gap
Plain, Lowland
Delta
Salt Flat
Valley, Canyon
Crater, Cave
Karst Features
Depression
Polder
Desert, Dunes
Forest, Woods
Heath, Steppe
Oasis
Cape, Point
Coast, Beach
Cliff
Peninsula
Isthmus
Sandbank
Island
Atoll
Rock, Reef
Islands, Archipelago
Rocks, Reefs
Coral Reef
Well, Spring
Geyser
River, Stream
Waterfall Rapids
River Mouth, Estuary
Lake
Salt Lake
Intermittent Lake
Reservoir
Swamp, Pond
Canal
Glacier
Ice Shelf, Pack Ice
Ocean
Sea
Gulf, Bay
Strait, Fjord
Lagoon
Bank
Seamount
Tablemount
Ridge
Shelf
Basin
Escarpment, Sea Scarp
Fracture
Trench, Abyss
National Park, Reserve
Point of Interest
Recreation Site
Cave, Cavern
Historic Site
Ruins
Wall, Walls
Church, Abbey
Temple
Scientific Station
Airport
Port
Lighthouse
Mine
Tunnel
Dam, Bridge

Rusken 8 Fg 57.17N 14.20 E
Rusne/Rusné 8 li 55.19N 21.16 E
Rusné/Rusne 8 li 55.19N 21.16 E
Russel 42 Hb 73.55N 98.35W
Russell [Man. Can.] 42 Hf 50.47N 101.15W
Russell [Ks.-U.S.] 45 Gg 38.54N 98.52W
Russell [N.Z.] 62 Fa 35.16S 174.08 E
Russell Islands 60 Fi 9.04S 159.12 E
Russellville [Al.-U.S.] 44 Dh 34.30N 87.44W
Russellville [Ar.-U.S.] 45 Ji 35.17N 93.08W
Russellville [Ky.-U.S.] 44 Dg 36.51N 86.53W
Russel Range 59 Ef 33.25S 123.30 E
Rüsselsheim 10 Eg 50.00N 8.25 E
Russia (EN) =
  Rossija 19 Jc 60.00N 100.00 E
Russian River 46 Dg 38.27N 123.08W
Rust 14 Kc 47.48N 16.40 E
Rustavi 19 Eg 41.33N 45.02 E
Rustenburg 37 De 25.37S 27.08 E
Ruston 43 le 32.32N 92.38W
Rutaki Passage 64p Bc 21.15S 159.48W
Rutana 36 Fc 3.55S 30.00 E
Rutanzige, Lac- = Edward,
  Lake- (EN) 30 Ji 0.25S 29.30 E
Rute 13 Hg 37.19N 4.22W
Ruteng 26 Hh 8.36S 120.27 E
Rutenga 37 Ed 21.15S 30.44 E
Rüthen 12 Kc 51.29N 8.27 E
Rutherfordton 44 Gh 35.22N 81.57W
Ruthin 9 Jh 53.07N 3.18W
Rutland 9 Mi 52.40N 0.40W
Rutland 44 Kd 43.37N 72.59W
Rutland 25 If 11.25N 92.10 E
Rutog 22 Jf 33.29N 79.42 E
Rutshuru 36 Ec 1.11S 29.27 E
Rutter 44 Gb 46.06N 80.40W
Rutul 16 Oi 41.33N 47.29 E
Ruvo di Puglia 14 Ki 41.09N 16.29 E
Ruvu 36 Gd 6.48S 38.39 E
Ruvuma [3] 36 Ge 10.30S 35.50 E
Ruvuma 30 Lj 10.29S 40.28 E
Ruvuma (EN)
  = Rovuma 30 Lj 10.29S 40.28 E
Ruwayshid, Wādī 24 Hf 32.41N 38.04 E
Ruwer 12 le 49.47N 6.42 E
Ruya 37 Ec 16.34S 33.12 E
Ruyang 28 Bg 34.10N 112.28 E
Ru'yas, Wādī ar- 33 Cd 27.06N 19.24 E
Ruyigi 36 Fc 3.29S 30.15 E
Ruza 7 li 55.39N 36.18 E
Ruzajevka 17 Mj 52.49N 67.01 E
Ruzajevka 19 Ee 54.05N 44.54 E
Ružany 10 Ud 52.48N 24.58 E
Ružomberok 10 Pg 49.05N 19.18 E
Rwanda [1] 31 Ji 2.30S 30.00 E
Ry 8 Ch 56.05N 9.46 E
Ryan 45 Hi 34.01N 97.57W
Rybachi Peninsula (EN) =
  Rybači, Poluostrov- 5 Jb 69.45N 32.35 E
Rybači 8 li 55.09N 20.45 E
Rybači, Poluostrov- =
  Rybachi Peninsula (EN) 5 Jb 69.45N 32.35 E
Rybačje — Issyk-Kul' 19 Hg 42.28N 76.11 E
Rybinsk 6 Jd 58.03N 38.52 E
Rybinskoje Vodohranilišče =
  Rybinsk Reservoir (EN) 5 Jd 58.30N 38.25 E
Rybinsk Reservoir (EN) =
  Rybinskoje
  Vodohranilišče 5 Jd 58.30N 38.25 E
Rybnica 16 Ff 47.45N 29.01 E
Rybnik 10 Of 50.06N 18.32 E
Rybnoje 19 De 54.46N 39.33 E
Rybnovsk 20 Jf 53.15N 141.55 E
Rychnov nad Kněžnou 10 Nd 50.10N 16.17 E
Rychwał 10 Od 52.05N 18.09 E
Ryd 8 Fh 56.28N 14.41 E
Rydaholm 8 Fh 56.59N 14.16 E
Ryde 12 Ad 50.43N 1.10W
Rye 9 Mg 54.10N 0.45W
Rye 9 Nk 50.57N 0.44 E
Rye Bay 12 Cd 50.55N 0.48 E
Ryegate 46 Kc 46.18N 109.15W
Rye Patch Reservoir 46 Ff 40.38N 118.18W
Ryes 12 Be 59.30N 0.37W
Ryfylke 8 Be 59.30N 6.30 E
Ryki 10 Re 51.39N 21.56 E
Rylsk 19 De 51.36N 34.43 E
Rymanów 10 Rg 49.34N 21.53 E
Rymättylä/Rimito 8 Jd 60.25N 21.55 E
Ryn 10 Rc 53.56N 21.33 E
Ryńskie, Jezioro- 10 Rc 53.53N 21.30 E
Ryōhaku-Sanchi 29 Ec 36.05N 136.45 E
Ryōsō-Yosui 29 Gd 35.22N 140.25 E
Ryōtsu 29 Oe 38.05N 138.26 E
Ryōtsu-Wan 29 Fb 38.10N 138.30 E
Ryō-Zen 29 Gc 37.46N 140.41 E
Rypin 10 Pc 53.05N 19.25 E
Ryškany 16 Ef 47.57N 27.32 E
Ryssby 8 Fh 56.52N 14.10 E
Rytterknægten 8 Fi 55.06N 14.54 E
Ryūgasaki 29 Gd 35.54N 140.10 E
Ryukyu Islands (EN) =
  Nansei-Shotō 21 Og 26.30N 128.00 E
Ryūkyū-Shotō 21 Mf 25.30N 126.30 E
Ryukyu Trench (EN) 3 Ig 25.45N 128.00 E
Rzepin 10 Kd 52.22N 14.50 E
Rzeszów [6] 6 le 50.03N 22.00 E
Rzeszów [2] 10 Rf 50.05N 22.00 E
Ržev 6 Jd 56.16N 34.20 E

S

Šaa, Gora- 16 Nh 42.39N 44.43 E
Sa'ādatābād [Iran] 24 Ph 28.02N 55.50 E

Sa'ādatābād [Iran] 24 Og 30.08N 52.38 E
Sa'ādatābād [Iran] 24 Og 30.06N 53.08 E
Sääksjarvi 8 Jc 61.24N 22.24 E
Saalbach 12 Ke 49.15N 8.27 E
Saale 10 He 51.57N 11.55 E
Saaler Bodden 10 Ib 54.20N 12.28 E
Saalfeld 10 Hf 50.39N 11.22 E
Saalfelden am Steinernen
  Meer 14 Gc 47.25N 12.51 E
Saaminki 8 Mc 61.52N 28.50 E
Sääne 12 Ce 49.54N 0.56 E
Saane 14 Bd 46.59N 7.16 E
Saar 14 Bd 46.30N 7.15 E
Saar 10 Cg 49.42N 6.34 E
Saar-Bergland 12 le 49.27N 6.45 E
Saarbrücken 6 Gf 49.14N 7.00 E
Saarbrücken-Dudweiler 12 le 49.17N 7.02 E
Saarburg 10 Cg 49.36N 6.33 E
Sääre/Sjare 8 Ig 57.57N 21.53 E
Saaremaa/Sarema 5 Id 58.25N 22.30 E
Saarijärvi 7 Fe 62.43N 25.16 E
Saaristomeri 8 Id 60.20N 21.10 E
Saarland [2] 10 Cg 49.20N 7.00 E
Saarlouis 10 Cg 49.19N 6.45 E
Šaartuz 19 Gh 37.16N 68.06 E
Saarwellingen 12 le 49.21N 6.49 E
Saas Fee 14 Bd 46.07N 7.55 E
Saatly 16 Pj 39.57N 48.26 E
Saavedra 55 Am 37.45S 62.22W
Sab, Tônlé- 25 Kf 11.34N 104.57 E
Saba 47 Le 17.38N 63.10W
Saba 8 Me 59.05N 29.10 E
Saba Bank (EN) 50 Ed 17.30N 63.30W
Šabac 15 Ce 44.45N 19.43 E
Sabadell 13 Oc 41.33N 2.06 E
Sabae 28 Ng 35.57N 136.11 E
Sabah [2] 26 Ge 5.30N 117.00 E
Sab'ah, Qārat as- 33 Cd 27.20N 17.10 E
Sabak Bernam 26 Df 3.46N 100.59 E
Sabalán, Kūhhā-ye- 21 Jd 38.15N 47.49 E
Sab'ān 24 li 27.04N 41.58 E
Sabana, Archipiélago de- 49 Hb 22.30N 79.00W
Sabana de la Mar 49 Md 19.04N 69.23W
Sabanagrande 49 Dg 13.50N 87.15W
Sabanalarga 54 Da 10.38N 74.56W
Sabancuy 48 Nh 18.58N 91.11W
Sabaneta 49 Ld 19.12N 70.58W
Sabaneta, Pʉntan- 64b Ba 15.17N 145.49 E
Sabang [Indon.] 26 Gf 0.11N 119.51 E
Sabang [Indon.] 26 Ce 5.55N 95.19 E
Šabanözü 24 Eb 40.29N 33.18 E
Šābāoani 15 Ab 47.01N 26.51 E
Sabarei 36 Gb 4.20N 36.55 E
Sab'Atayn, Ramlat as- 33 If 15.30N 46.10 E
Sabatini, Monti- 14 Gh 42.10N 12.15 E
Sabaudia 14 Hi 41.18N 13.01 E
Sabaudia, Lago di- 14 Hi 41.15N 13.05 E
Šabbāgh, Jabal- 24 Fh 28.12N 34.04 E
Sab 'Bi 'Ãr 24 Gf 33.46N 37.41 E
Sabbioneta 14 Ee 45.00N 10.39 E
Sa Bec 25 Lf 10.18N 105.46 E
Sabhā [3] 33 Bd 26.00N 14.00 E
Sabhā 31 If 27.02N 14.26 E
Šabhā 22 Oh 32.20N 36.30 E
Sābhā, Wāhāt- = Sebha
  Oasis (EN) 30 If 27.00N 14.25 E
Sabi 30 Kk 21.00S 35.02 E
Sabidana, Jabal- 35 Fb 18.04N 36.50 E
Sabile 8 Jg 57.05N 22.29 E
Sabina [3] 14 Gh 42.20N 12.45 E
Sabinal 48 Fb 30.57N 107.30W
Sabinal, Peninsula de- 49 Ic 21.40N 77.18W
Sabiñánigo 13 Lb 42.31N 0.22W
Sabinas 47 Dc 27.51N 101.07W
Sabinas, Rio- 48 Id 27.37N 100.42W
Sabinas Hidalgo 47 Dc 26.30N 100.10W
Sabine Lake 45 Jl 29.50N 93.50W
Sabine Pass 45 Jl 29.44N 93.52W
Sabine Peninsula 42 Ga 76.25N 109.50W
Sabine River 43 le 30.00N 93.45W
Sabini, Monti- 14 Gh 42.15N 12.50 E
Šabir, Jabal- 23 Tg 13.30N 44.03 E
Sabirabad 16 Pj 39.59N 48.29 E
Šabla 15 If 43.32N 28.32 E
Sable, Anse de- 51e b 16.07N 61.34W
Sable, Cape- [Can.] 38 Md 43.25N 65.35W
Sable, Cape- [U.S.] 38 Kg 25.12N 81.05W
Sable, Ile de- 57 Gc 19.15S 159.56 E
Sable Island 38 Ne 43.55N 59.55W
Sablé-sur-Sarthe 11 Mf 47.50N 0.20W
Sablūkah, Ash Shallāl as- =
  Sixth Cataract (EN) 30 Kg 16.20N 32.42 E
Sabonetau, Serra da- 55 Kb 15.20S 43.50W
Sabonkafi 49 Mj 14.38N 8.45 E
Sabór 13 Ec 41.10N 7.07W
Şabrātah 33 Bc 32.47N 12.29 E
Sabres 11 Kf 44.09N 0.44W
Sabrina Coast 66 He 67.00S 119.30 E
Sabtang 26 Hb 20.19N 121.52 E
Sabunçi 16 Pi 40.27N 49.57 E
Şabya 23 Tf 17.09N 42.37 E
Sabzevār 22 Hf 36.13N 57.42 E
Saca, Virful- 15 Ic 46.30N 25.16 E
Sacajawea Peak 43 Db 45.15N 117.17W
Sacandica 36 Cd 5.58S 15.56 E
Sacatepéquez [3] 49 Cf 14.35N 90.45W
Sacavém 13 Cf 38.46N 9.05W
Sa'gya 48 Jf 42.25N 95.00W
Sacco 14 Hi 41.31N 13.32 E
Sacedón 13 Jd 40.29N 2.43W
Săcel 15 Hb 47.38N 24.26 E
Săcele 15 Id 45.37N 25.42 E
Sachayoj 55 Bh 26.41S 61.50W
Sachère 16 Mh 42.00N 43.20 E
Sachigo 42 le 55.05N 89.00W
Sachsen = Saxony (EN) 10 Jf 51.00N 13.30 E

Sachsenhagen 12 Lb 52.24N 9.16 E
Sachs Harbour 42 Eb 72.00N 125.08W
Šack 7 Ja 54.04N 41.42 E
Šack 10 Je 51.30N 24.00 E
Sackets Harbor 44 Id 43.57N 76.07W
Saco [Me.-U.S.] 44 Ld 43.29N 70.28W
Saco [Mt.-U.S.] 46 Lb 48.28N 107.21W
Sacramento 38 Gf 38.03N 121.56W
Sacramento [Braz.] 54 lg 19.53S 47.27W
Sacramento [Ca.-U.S.] 39 Gf 38.35N 121.30W
Sacramento, Pampa del- 54 Ce 8.00S 75.50W
Sacramento Mountains 38 If 33.10N 105.50W
Sacramento Valley 43 Cd 39.15N 122.00W
Sacre ou Timalacia, Rio- 55 Ca 13.55S 58.02W
Săcueni 15 Fb 47.21N 22.06 E
Sacuriuiná ou Ponte de
  Pedra, Rio- 55 Da 13.58S 57.18W
Sa'dābād 24 Nh 29.53N 51.07 E
Sa'dah 22 Re 16.57N 43.44 E
Sada-Misaki 29b Ce 33.22N 132.01 E
Sada-Misaki-Hantō 29 Ce 33.23N 132.00 E
Sadani 36 Gd 6.03S 38.47 E
Sadao 25 Kg 6.39N 100.31 E
Sadd al 'Āli 33 Fe 23.54N 32.52 E
Saddle Mountains 46 Cc 46.50N 119.55W
Saddle Peak [India] 25 If 13.09N 93.01 E
Saddle Peak [Mt.-U.S.] 46 Jd 45.57N 110.58W
Sad-e Eskandar 24 Pd 37.10N 55.00 E
Sadiya 25 Jc 27.50N 95.40 E
Sa'diyah, Hawr as- 24 Lf 32.00N 46.45 E
Sado 29 Df 38.29N 8.55W
Sado-Kaikyō 29 Pf 38.00N 138.25 E
Sado-Shima 28 Be 38.04N 131.26 E
Sadowara 19 Gd 56.05N 63.38 E
Šadrinsk 7 Ch 57.20N 10.32 E
Saeby 26 Gh 8.00S 117.30 E
Saengcheon 12 Jb 52.11N 7.38 E
Saerbeck 24 Hi 26.30N 39.30 E
Safājah 21 Ei 26.45N 33.59 E
Şafājah, Jazirat- 34 Ec 12.08N 3.13W
Safané 31 le 34.30N 10.30 E
Şafāqis = Sfax (EN) [3] 31 le 34.44N 10.46 E
Şafāqis = Sfax (EN) 65c Bb 10.45N 171.50W
Safata Harbour 23 Qd 27.59N 48.37 E
Saffānīyah, Ra's as- 26 Gf 0.11N 119.51 E
Säffle 26 Ce 5.55N 95.19 E
Safford 9 Ni 52.01N 0.15 E
Saffron Walden 15 Ab 47.01N 26.51 E
Safi 36 Gb 4.20N 36.55 E
Safi [3] 32 Fc 31.55N 9.00W
Safia, Hamāda- 34 Ea 23.10N 4.15W
Şafiābād 24 Qd 36.45N 57.58 E
Safid 23 Hb 37.23N 50.11 E
Safid, Kūh-e 25 Lf 10.45N 47.30 E
Safid Kūh, Salseleh-ye- 23 Jc 34.30N 63.30 E
Safonovo 19 Dd 55.06N 33.14 E
Safonovo 7 Id 65.41N 47.43 E
Şafrā' al Asyāḥ 21 Jd 26.50N 43.57 E
Şafrā' as Sark 24 Kj 25.25N 44.20 E
Safranbolu 24 Eb 41.15N 32.42 E
Şafwān 24 Lg 30.07N 47.43 E
Saga [Jap.] 27 Ne 33.15N 130.18 E
Saga [Jap.] 28 Je 33.05N 133.06 E
Saga (Gya'gya) 19 Fe 50.30N 64.14 E
Sagae 27 Ef 29.22N 85.15 E
Sagaing [3] 25 Jd 23.30N 95.30 E
Sagaing 22 Jf 21.52N 95.59 E
Saga Ken [2] 28 Jh 33.15N 130.15 E
Sagamihara 27 Fd 35.34N 139.22 E
Sagami-Nada 27 Ne 35.00N 139.30 E
Sagami-Wan 27 Fd 35.15N 139.20 E
Sagan 35 Tf 36.57N 46.57 E
Saganaga Lake 45 Jb 48.14N 90.52W
Saganoseki 29 Be 33.15N 131.53 E
Şagany, Ozero- 15 Md 45.45N 29.55 E
Sāgar [India] 25 Ff 14.10N 75.02 E
Sāgar [India] 22 Jg 23.50N 78.42 E
Sagara 27 Fd 34.40N 138.12 E
Sagaredžo 16 Ni 41.43N 45.16 E
Sagavanirktok 40 Jb 70.20N 148.00W
Sagawa 29 Ce 33.29N 133.16 E
Sage 46 Jf 41.50N 110.56W
Saghād 24 Og 31.12N 52.30 E
Saginaw 39 Kb 43.25N 83.58W
Saginaw Bay 43 Kc 43.50N 83.40W
Sagiz 19 Ff 47.32N 53.45 E
Sagiz 19 Ff 48.12N 54.56 E
Saglek Bay 16 Rf 47.32N 53.27 E
Saglouc → Salluit 42 Le 62.12N 75.38W
Şagone, Golfe de- 20 Ef 51.32N 92.51 E
Sagres 11 aa 36.56N 44.21W
Şagu 26 Mh 20.19N 121.52 E
Sagu/Sauvo 15 Ge 46.03N 21.17 E
Saguache 8 Pi 40.27N 49.57 E
Sagua de Tánamo 49 Cg 38.05N 106.08W
Sagua la Grande 47 Hd 22.49N 80.05W
Saguenay 38 Me 48.10N 69.45W
Saguia el-Hamra 32 Be 26.50N 12.00W
Sagunto/Sagunt 13 Le 39.41N 0.16W
Sagunto/Sagunt 13 Cf 39.41N 0.16W
Sagunto-Grao de Sagunto 13 Le 39.40N 0.16W
Sa'gya 27 Ef 28.53N 88.10 E
Saha (Jakutija),
  respublika 20 Hc 67.00N 130.00 E
Sahagún [Col.] 54 Cb 8.57N 75.27W
Sahagún [Sp.] 13 Gb 42.22N 5.02W
Sahalin, Ostrov- = Sakhalin
  (EN) 21 Qd 50.00N 143.00 E
Sahalinskaja Oblast [3] 20 Jf 50.00N 143.00 E
Sahalinski Zaliv 20 Jf 53.45N 141.30 E

Sahara 30 Hf 21.00N 6.00 E
Saharan Atlas (EN) = Atlas
  Saharien 30 He 34.00N 2.00 E
Sahāranpur 22 Jg 29.58N 77.23 E
Sahel [3] 34 Ec 14.10N 0.50W
Sahel 30 Gg 15.40N 8.30W
Şahin 15 Jh 41.01N 26.50 E
Sāhiwāl [Pak.] 25 Eb 30.41N 72.57 E
Sāhiwāl [Pak.] 25 Eb 31.58N 72.20 E
Sahlābād 23 Ic 32.10N 59.51 E
Sahneh 24 Le 34.29N 47.41 E
Sahovščina 16 le 49.09N 35.57 E
Sahoa Kosa, Mys- 18 Qi 40.13N 50.22 E
Sahrihan 18 Jd 40.40N 72.03 E
Šahrisabz 19 Gh 39.03N 66.41 E
Šahristan, Pereval- 18 Ge 39.35N 68.38 E
Šahtersk 20 Jg 49.13N 142.09 E
Šahterski 20 Md 64.46N 177.47 E
Šahtinsk 19 Hf 49.40N 72.37 E
Šahty 19 Ef 47.42N 40.13 E
Sahuaripa 47 Eb 29.03N 109.14W
Sahuayo de Diaz 47 Dd 20.04N 102.43W
Šahunja 19 Ed 57.43N 46.35 E
Sahūq, Wādī- 24 Jj 25.18N 42.20 E
Šahy 10 Oh 48.05N 18.58 E
Sahyadri/Western Ghats 21 Jh 14.00N 75.00 E
Sai Buri 25 Kg 6.42N 101.37 E
Saïda [3] 32 Hc 35.35N 0.30 E
Saïda 31 He 34.50N 0.09 E
Saïda, Monts de- 31 le 34.44N 10.58 E
Sa'īdābād 23 Id 29.30N 55.42 E
Saidaiji 29 Dd 34.39N 134.02 E
Said Bundas 35 Cd 8.35N 24.30 E
Saidia 13 Ji 35.04N 2.13W
Saidor 60 Di 5.37S 146.28 E
Saidu 25 Eb 34.45N 72.21 E
Saigō 26 Gh 3.16N 133.20 E
Saigon → Ho Chi Minh 22 Mh 10.45N 106.40 E
Saihan Tal → Sonid Youqi 27 Jc 42.45N 112.36 E
Saihan Toroi 41 Kc 41.54N 100.24 E
Saijō 29 Ce 33.55N 133.10 E
Saikai 29 Ae 33.03N 129.44 E
Sai-Kawa 29 Fc 36.37N 138.14 E
Saiki 28 Kh 32.57N 131.54 E
Saiki-Wan 29 Be 33.00N 131.55 E
Sail Rock 51b Bb 12.37N 61.16W
Saimaa 5 Ic 61.15N 28.15 E
Saimaa Canal (EN) =
  Sajmenski Kanal 8 Mc 61.05N 28.18 E
Sain Alto 48 Hf 23.35N 103.15W
Sā in Dezh 24 Ld 36.40N 46.33 E
Sains-Richaumont 12 Fe 49.49N 3.42 E
Saint Abb's Head 9 Kf 55.54N 2.09W
Saint-Affrique 11 Ik 43.57N 2.53 E
Saint Agnes Head 9 Hk 50.23N 5.07W
Saint-Agrève 11 Ki 45.01N 4.24 E
Saint Albans [Eng.-U.K.] 9 Mj 51.46N 0.21W
Saint Albans [Vt.-U.S.] 44 Kc 44.49N 73.05W
Saint Albans [W.V.-U.S.] 44 Gf 38.24N 81.53W
Saint Alban's Head 9 Kk 50.34N 2.04W
Saint Albert 42 Gf 53.38N 113.38W
Saint-Amand-les-Eaux 11 Jd 50.26N 3.26 E
Saint-Amand-Mont-Rond 11 le 46.43N 2.31 E
Saint-André, Cap- 30 Lj 16.11S 44.27 E
Saint-André, Plaine de- 11 Hf 48.55N 1.10 E
Saint-André-de-Cubzac 11 Kh 45.00N 0.27W
Saint-André-de-l'Eure 12 Df 48.54N 1.17 E
Saint-André-sur-Cailly 12 Df 49.30N 1.13 E
Saint Andrews [N.B.-Can.] 44 Nc 45.06N 67.02W
Saint Andrews [Scot.-U.K.] 9 Ke 56.20N 2.48W
Saint Anne 49 Kd 49.40N 2.10W
Saint Ann's Bay 49 Id 18.26N 77.16W
Saint Ann's Head 9 Hj 51.41N 5.10W
Saint Anthony [Id.-U.S.] 46 Jc 43.58N 111.41W
Saint Anthony [Newf.-Can.] 42 Lf 51.22N 55.35W
Saint-Antonin 35 Tf 51.57N 36.57 E
Saint Arnaud 19 Fe 50.37N 79.15 E
Saint-Aubert 44 Lb 47.14N 70.15W
Saint-Aubin-sur-Mer 12 Be 49.20N 0.24W
Saint Augustine 39 Kf 29.51N 81.25W
Saint-Augustin-Saguenay 42 Lf 51.14N 58.39W
Saint Austell 9 Ik 50.20N 4.48W
Saint-Avold 11 Me 49.06N 6.42 E
Saint Barthélemy 47 Le 17.55N 62.50W
Saint-Barthélemy 11 Hl 42.49N 1.45 E
Saint Barthélemy, Canal de- 51b Bb 18.00N 63.00W
Saint Barthélemy, Kanaal
  Van- 51b Bb 18.00N 63.00W
Saint Bees Head 9 Jg 54.32S 3.38W
Saint-Benoit 37a b 21.02S 55.43 E
Saint-Benoît-sur-Loire 11 Hg 47.49N 2.18 E
Saint-Bonnet 11 Mj 44.41N 6.05 E
Saint-Brévin-les-Pins 11 Dg 47.15N 2.10W
Saint Brides Bay 9 Hj 51.48N 5.15W
Saint-Brieuc 11 Df 48.31N 2.47W
Saint-Brieuc, Baie de- 11 Df 48.38N 2.40W
Saint-Calais 11 Gg 47.55N 0.45 E
Saint-Camille 44 Jh 43.10N 79.15W
Saint Catharines 39 Gb 38.05N 106.08W
Saint Catherine, Monastery
  of- (EN) = Dayr Kātrinā 33 Eb 28.31N 33.57 E
Saint Catherine, Mount- 51p Bb 12.10N 61.40W
Saint Catherines Island 45 Jj 31.38N 81.10W
Saint Catherine's Point 9 Lk 50.34N 1.15W
Saint-Céré 11 Hj 44.52N 1.54 E
Saint-Chamond 11 Ki 45.28N 4.30 E
Saint Charles 43 Jd 38.47N 90.29W
Saint-Chély-d'Apcher 11 Jj 44.48N 3.17 E
Saint-Christol, Plateau de- 11 Lj 44.00N 5.50 E
Saint Christopher/Saint
  Kitts 13 Gb 42.22N 5.02W
Saint Christopher-Nevis [5] 38 Mh 17.21N 62.48W
Saint-Cirq-Lapopie 11 Hj 44.28N 1.40 E
Saint Clair, Lake- 44 Gc 42.25N 82.41W
Saint Clair River 44 Fd 42.37N 82.31W

Saint Clair Shores 44 Fd 42.30N 82.54W
Saint-Clair-sur-l'Elle 12 Ae 49.12N 1.02W
Saint-Claud 11 Gi 45.54N 0.28 E
Saint-Claude [Fr.] 11 Lh 46.23N 5.52 E
Saint Claude 45 Gb 49.40N 98.22W
Saint-Claude [Guad.] 51eAb 16.02N 61.42W
Saint Cloud 39 Je 45.33N 94.10W
Saint Croix 47 Le 17.45N 64.45W
Saint Croix Falls 45 Jd 45.24N 92.38W
Saint Croix River 43 Ic 44.45N 92.49W
Saint-Cyr-l'Ecole 12 Ef 48.48N 2.04 E
Saint-Cyr-sur-Loire 11 Gg 47.24N 0.40 E
Saint David Bay 51 Bb 12.04N 61.39W
Saint David's [Gren.] 51p Bb 12.04N 61.39W
Saint David's [Wales-U.K.] 9 Hj 51.54N 5.16W
Saint David's Head 9 Hj 51.55N 5.19W
Saint David's Point 51p Bb 12.01N 61.40W
Saint-Denis [Fr.] 11 If 48.56N 2.22 E
Saint-Denis [May.] 31 Mk 20.52S 55.28 E
Saint-Dié 11 Mf 48.17N 6.57 E
Saint-Dizier 11 Kf 48.38N 4.57 E
Saint-Adresse 12 Ce 49.30N 0.05 E
Sainte-Anne [Guad.] 51eBb 16.14N 61.23W
Sainte-Anne [Mart.] 51h Bc 14.26N 60.53W
Sainte-Anne-des-Monts 44 Na 49.07N 66.29W
Sainte Baume, Chaîne de la- 11 Lk 43.20N 5.45 E
Sainte-Énimie 11 Jj 44.22N 3.25 E
Sainte Geneviève 45 Kh 37.59N 90.03W
Sainte-Geneviève 12 Ee 49.17N 2.12 E
Saint Elias, Mount- 38 Ec 60.18N 140.55W
Saint Elias Mountains 38 Dc 60.30N 139.30W
Saint-Elie 54 Hc 4.50N 53.17W
Sainte-Livrade-sur-Lot 11 Gj 44.24N 0.36 E
Saint-Eloy-les-Mines 11 Ih 46.09N 2.50 E
Sainte Luce 37 Hd 24.46S 47.12 E
Sainte Luce 51h Bc 14.28N 60.56W
Sainte-Lucie, Canal de- =
  Saint Lucia Channel (EN) 50 Fe 14.09N 60.57W
Sainte-Marcellin 11 Li 45.09N 5.19 E
Sainte-Marie [Guad.] 51eAb 16.06N 61.34W
Sainte-Marie, Cap- = Sainte-
  Marie, Cape-(EN) 51h Ab 14.47N 61.00W
Sainte-Marie, Cap- 30 Lk 25.36S 45.08 E
Sainte-Marie, Ile- 30 Lk 25.36S 45.08 E
Sainte-Marie-aux-Mines 11 Nf 48.15N 7.11 E
Sainte-Maure-de-Touraine 11 Gg 47.06N 0.37 E
Sainte-Maxime 11 Mk 43.18N 6.38 E
Sainte-Menehould 11 Ke 49.05N 4.54 E
Sainte-Rose 51eAb 16.20N 61.42W
Sainte-Rose-du-Dégelé 44 Mb 47.30N 68.39W
Sainte Rose du Lac 45 Ga 51.03N 99.32W
Saintes 11 Fi 45.45N 0.38W
Saintes, Canal des- 51eAc 15.55N 61.40W
Saintes, Iles des- 50 Fe 15.52N 61.37W
Sainte-Savine 11 Kf 48.18N 4.03 E
Saintes-Maries-de-la-Mer 11 Kk 43.27N 4.26 E
Sainte-Thérèse 44 Kc 45.22N 73.15W
Saint-Étienne 6 Gf 45.26N 4.24 E
Saint-Étienne-du-Rouvray 11 Df 49.23N 1.06 E
Sainte Victoire, Montagne- 11 Lk 43.32N 5.39 E
Saint-Félicien 44 Ka 48.39N 72.28W
Saint-Florent 11 Nj 44.31N 9.18 E
Saint-Florent, Golfe de- 11a Ba 42.45N 9.16 E
Saint-Florent-sur-Cher 11 Jf 48.00N 3.44 E
Saint-Flour 11 Ih 46.59N 2.15 E
Saint-Four 11 Ih 45.02N 3.05 E
Saint Francis 45 Fg 39.46N 101.48W
Saint Francis River 45 Ki 34.38N 90.35W
Saint Francisville 45 Kk 30.47N 91.23W
Saint-François 51eBb 16.15N 61.17W
Saint François Island 37b Bb 7.10S 52.44 E
Saint François
  Mountains 45 Kh 37.30N 90.35W
Saint-Gaudens 11 Gk 43.07N 0.44 E
Saint George 40 Fe 39.56N 169.35W
Saint George [Austl.] 58 Jf 28.02S 148.35 E
Saint George [N.B.-Can.] 44 Nc 45.10N 66.48W
Saint George [Ut.-U.S.] 43 Ed 37.06N 113.35W
Saint George, Cape-
  [Newf.-Can.] 42 Lm 48.28N 59.16W
Saint George, Cape-
  [Pap.N.Gui.] 60 Eh 4.52S 152.52 E
Saint George, Point- 46 Cf 41.47N 124.15W
Saint George Harbour 44 Nc 43.15N 66.10W
Saint George's 39 Mh 12.03N 61.45W
Saint George's 46 Hc 46.10N 70.38W
Saint George's Bay 42 Lg 48.20N 59.10W
Saint George's Channel 5 Fe 52.00N 6.00W
Saint George's Channel (EN)
  = Muir Bhreatan 5 Fe 52.00N 6.00W
Saint-Georges-du-Vièvre 12 Ce 49.15N 0.35 E
Saint-Germain-en-Laye 11 If 48.54N 2.05 E
Saint-Gervais-d'Auvergne 11 Mi 46.02N 2.49 E
Saint-Gervais-les-Bains 11 Mi 45.54N 6.43 E
Saint-Ghislain 12 Ed 50.27N 3.49 E
Saint-Ghislain-Baudour 12 Ed 50.29N 3.49 E
Saint-Gildas, Pointe de- 11 Dg 47.08N 2.15W
Saint-Gilles 11 Kk 43.41N 4.26 E
Saint-Gilles-Croix-de-Vie 11 Eh 46.41N 1.55W
Saint-Girons 11 Hl 42.59N 1.09 E
Saint-Gobain 11 Je 49.36N 3.23 E
Saint Gotthard Pass (EN) =
  San Gottardo/Sankt
  Gotthard 5 Gf 46.30N 8.30 E
Saint Gotthard Pass (EN) = Sankt
  Gotthard/San Gottardo 5 Gf 46.30N 8.30 E
Saint Govan's Head 9 Ij 51.36N 4.55W
Saint Helena 31 Jj 15.57S 5.42W
Saint Helena Bay 30 Il 32.45S 18.05 E
Saint Helena Island 44 Gi 32.30N 80.30W

Index Symbols

[1] Independent Nation
[2] State, Region
[3] District, County
[4] Municipality
[5] Colony, Dependency
[●] Continent
[◆] Physical Region

Historical or Cultural Region
Mount, Mountain
Volcano
Hill
Mountains, Mountain Range
Hills, Escarpment
Plateau, Upland

Pass, Gap
Plain, Lowland
Delta
Salt Flat
Valley, Canyon
Crater, Cave
Karst Features

Depression
Polder
Desert, Dunes
Forest, Woods
Heath, Steppe
Oasis
Cape, Point

Coast, Beach
Cliff
Peninsula
Isthmus
Sandbank
Island
Atoll

Rock, Reef
Islands, Archipelago
Rocks, Reefs
Coral Reef
Well, Spring
Geyser
River, Stream

Waterfall Rapids
River Mouth, Estuary
Lake
Salt Lake
Intermittent Lake
Reservoir
Swamp, Pond

Canal
Glacier
Ice Shelf, Pack Ice
Ocean
Sea
Gulf, Bay
Strait, Fjord

Lagoon
Bank
Seamount
Tablemount
Ridge
Shelf
Basin

Escarpment, Sea Scarp
Fracture
Trench, Abyss
National Park, Reserve
Point of Interest
Recreation Site
Cave, Cavern

Historic Site
Ruins
Wall, Walls
Church, Abbey
Temple
Scientific Station
Airport

Port
Lighthouse
Mine
Tunnel
Dam, Bridge

Index Symbols

[1] Independent Nation
[2] State, Region
[3] District, County
[4] Municipality
[5] Colony, Dependency
Continent
Physical Region
Historical or Cultural Region
Mount, Mountain
Volcano
Hill
Mountains, Mountain Range
Hills, Escarpment
Plateau, Upland
Pass, Gap
Plain, Lowland
Delta
Salt Flat
Valley, Canyon
Crater, Cave
Karst Features
Depression
Polder
Desert, Dunes
Forest, Woods
Heath, Steppe
Oasis
Cape, Point
Coast, Beach
Cliff
Peninsula
Isthmus
Sandbank
Island
Atoll
Rock, Reef
Islands, Archipelago
Rocks, Reefs
Coral Reef
Well, Spring
Geyser
River, Stream
Waterfall Rapids
River Mouth, Estuary
Lake
Salt Lake
Intermittent Lake
Reservoir
Swamp, Pond
Canal
Glacier
Ice Shelf, Pack Ice
Ocean
Sea
Gulf, Bay
Strait, Fjord
Ridge
Shelf
Basin
Lagoon
Bank
Seamount
Tablemount
Trench, Abyss
Fracture
National Park, Reserve
Point of Interest
Recreation Site
Cave, Cavern
Escarpment, Sea Scarp
Ruins
Wall, Walls
Church, Abbey
Temple
Scientific Station
Airport
Historic Site
Port
Lighthouse
Mine
Tunnel
Dam, Bridge

Index Symbols

① Independent Nation	Historical or Cultural Region	Pass, Gap	Depression	Coast, Beach
② State, Region	Mount, Mountain	Plain, Lowland	Polder	Cliff
③ District, County	Volcano	Delta	Desert, Dunes	Peninsula
④ Municipality	Hill	Salt Flat	Forest, Woods	Isthmus
⑤ Colony, Dependency	Mountains, Mountain Range	Valley, Canyon	Heath, Steppe	Sandbank
Continent	Hills, Escarpment	Crater, Cave	Oasis	Island
Physical Region	Plateau, Upland	Karst Features	Cape, Point	Atoll

Rock, Reef	Waterfall Rapids	Canal	Lagoon
Islands, Archipelago	River Mouth, Estuary	Glacier	Bank
Rocks, Reefs	Lake	Ice Shelf, Pack Ice	Seamount
Coral Reef	Salt Lake	Ocean	Tablemount
Well, Spring	Intermittent Lake	Sea	Ridge
Geyser	Reservoir	Gulf, Bay	Shelf
River, Stream	Swamp, Pond	Strait, Fjord	Basin

Escarpment, Sea Scarp	Historic Site	Port
Fracture	Ruins	Lighthouse
Trench, Abyss	Wall, Walls	Mine
National Park, Reserve	Church, Abbey	Tunnel
Point of Interest	Temple	Dam, Bridge
Recreation Site	Scientific Station	
Cave, Cavern	Airport	

San Marcial, Punta- 48 De 25.30N 111.00W
San Marco, Capo- 14 Hm 37.30N 13.01 E
San Marcos [3] 49 Bf 15.00N 91.55W
San Marcos [Col.] 54 Cb 8.39N 75.08W
San Marcos [Guat.] 49 Bf 14.58N 91.48W
San Marcos [Hond.] 49 Cf 14.24N 88.56W
San Marcos [Mex.] 48 Gg 20.47N 104.11W
San Marcos [Mex.] 48 Ji 16.48N 99.21W
San Marcos [Nic.] 49 Dh 11.55N 86.12W
San Marcos [Tx.-U.S.] 43 Hf 29.53N 97.57W
San Marcos, Isla- 48 Cd 27.13N 112.06W
San Marcos, Sierra de- 48 Hd 26.30N 101.55W
San Marino 14 Gg 43.55N 12.28 E
San Marino [1] 6 Hg 43.55N 12.28 E
San Martín 56 Gd 33.04S 68.28W
San Martín 66 Qe 68.11S 67.00W
San Martín 48 Ab 30.30N 116.05W
San Martín [2] 54 Ce 7.00S 76.50W
San Martín, Cerro- 48 Lh 18.19N 94.48W
San Martín, Lago- 56 Fg 48.52S 72.40W
San Martín, Río- 54 Ff 13.08S 63.43W
San Martín de los Andes 56 Ff 40.10S 71.21W
San Martín de Valdeiglesias 13 Hd 40.21N 4.24W
San Martino di Castrozza 14 Fd 46.16N 11.48 E
San Mateo [Ca.-U.S.] 46 Dh 37.35N 122.19W
San Mateo [Ven.] 50 Dh 9.45N 64.33W
San Mateo/Sant Mateu del Maestrat 13 Md 40.28N 0.11 E
San Mateo Ixtatán 49 Bf 15.50N 91.29W
San Mateo Mountains 45 Cj 33.10N 107.20W
San Matías 55 Cc 16.22S 58.24W
San Matías, Golfo- 52 Jj 41.30S 64.15W
Sanmen (Haiyou) 27 Lf 29.08N 121.22 E
Sanmen Wan 28 Fj 29.00N 121.45 E
Sanmenxia 27 Je 34.44N 111.19 E
San Miguel [Arg.] 55 Dh 27.59S 57.36W
San Miguel [Bol.] 55 Bc 16.42S 61.01W
San Miguel [Ca.-U.S.] 46 Ei 35.45N 120.42W
San Miguel [ElSal.] 39 Kh 13.29N 88.11W
San Miguel [Pan.] 49 Hi 8.27N 78.56W
San Miguel, Golfo de- 49 Hi 8.22N 78.17W
San Miguel, Río- [Bol.] 52 Jg 13.52S 63.56W
San Miguel, Río- [Mex.] 48 Dc 29.16N 110.53W
San Miguel, Río- [Mex.] 48 Fd 26.59N 107.58W
San Miguel, Río- [S.Amer.] 55 Cd 19.25S 58.20W
San Miguel, Salinas de- 55 Bd 19.12S 60.45W
San Miguel, Volcán de- 47 Gf 13.26N 88.16W
San Miguel Bay 26 Hd 13.50N 123.10 E
San Miguel de Allende 48 Ig 20.55N 100.45W
San Miguel de Horcasitas 48 Dc 29.29N 110.45W
San Miguel del Monte 55 Cl 35.27S 58.48W
San Miguel del Padrón 49 Fb 23.05N 82.19W
San Miguel de Tucumán 53 Jh 26.49S 65.13W
San Miguel Island 46 Ei 34.02N 120.22W
San Miguel Islands 26 Ge 7.45N 118.28 E
San Miguelito 55 Bc 17.20S 60.59W
San Miguel River 45 Bg 38.23N 108.48W
San Miguel Sola de Vega 48 Ki 16.31N 96.59W
San Millán 13 Ib 42.18N 3.12W
Sanming 27 Kf 26.11N 117.37 E
San Miniato 14 Eg 43.41N 10.51 E
Sannan 29 Dd 35.04N 135.03 E
Sannār 31 Kg 13.33N 33.38 E
Sannicandro Garganico 14 Ji 41.50N 15.34 E
San Nicolás, Río- [Bol.] 55 Bc 17.08S 61.17W
San Nicolás, Río- [Mex.] 48 Gh 19.40N 105.14W
San Nicolas de los Arroyos 56 Hd 33.20S 60.13W
San Nicolás de los Garzas 48 Ie 25.45N 100.18W
San Nicolas Island 46 Fj 33.15N 119.31W
Sannikova, Proliv- 20 Ib 74.30N 140.00 E
Sannio 14 Ii 41.20N 14.30 E
San'nohe 29 Ga 40.22N 141.15 E
San'nō-Tōge 29 Fc 37.06N 139.44 E
Sannūr, Wādī- 24 Dh 28.59N 31.03 E
Sanok 10 Sg 49.34N 22.13 E
Sanok-Zagórz 10 Sg 49.31N 22.17 E
San Onofre 54 Cb 9.45N 75.32W
San Pablo 22 Oh 14.04N 121.19 E
San Pablo, Punta- 48 Bd 27.15N 114.30W
San Pedro 56 Ib 24.07S 56.59W
San-Pédro 34 De 4.44N 6.37W
San Pedro [3] 55 Dg 24.15S 56.30W
San Pedro [Arg.] 56 Hb 24.14S 64.52W
San Pedro [Arg.] 55 Ck 33.40S 59.40W
San Pedro [Arg.] 56 Jc 26.38S 54.08W
San Pedro, Río- [Guat.] 49 Be 17.46N 91.26W
San Pedro, Río- [Mex.] 48 Gg 21.45N 105.30W
San Pedro, Sierra de- 13 Fe 39.20N 6.35W
San Pedro Carchá 49 Bf 15.29N 90.16W
San Pedro Channel 46 Fj 33.43N 118.23W
San Pedro de Alcántara 13 Hh 36.29N 5.00W
San Pedro de Atacama 56 Gb 22.55S 68.13W
San Pedro de Lloc 54 Ce 7.26S 79.31W
San Pedro de Macorís 49 Md 18.27N 69.18W
San Pedro Mártir, Sierra de- 47 Ab 30.45N 115.13W
San Pedro Nolasco, Isla- 48 Dd 27.58N 111.25W
San Pedro Pochutla 48 Kj 15.44N 96.28W
San Pedros de las Colonias 47 Dc 25.45N 102.59W
San Pedro Sula 39 Kh 15.27N 88.02W
San Pedro Tapanatepec 48 Li 16.21N 94.12W
San Pedro Tututepec 48 Ki 16.09N 97.38W
San Pellegrino Terme 14 De 45.50N 9.40 E
San Pietro 14 Ck 39.10N 8.15 E
San Quentin, Bahía de- 48 Ab 30.20N 116.00W
San Quintín 47 Ab 30.29N 115.57W
San Rafael [Arg.] 53 Ji 34.40S 68.21W
San Rafael [Bol.] 55 Bc 16.45S 60.34W
San Rafael [Ca.-U.S.] 46 Dg 38.00N 122.31W
San Rafael [Mex.] 48 He 24.40N 102.01W
San Rafael [Mex.] 48 Ie 25.01N 100.33W
San Rafael [Ven.] 49 Lh 10.58N 71.44W
San Rafael, Cabo- 49 Md 19.01N 68.57W
San Rafael, Río- 55 Cd 18.26S 59.37W
San Rafael de Atamaica 50 Ci 7.32N 67.24W
San Rafael del Norte 49 Dg 13.12N 86.06W
San Rafael Knob 46 Jg 38.50N 110.48W
San Rafael Mountains 46 Fi 34.45N 119.50W
San Rafael River 46 Jg 38.47N 110.07W
San Ramón [Peru] 54 Cf 11.08S 75.20W
San Ramón [Ur.] 55 El 34.18S 55.58W
San Ramón, Río- 55 Bb 14.03S 61.35W
San Ramón de la Nueva Orán 56 Hb 23.08S 64.20W
San Raymundo, Arroyo- 48 Cd 26.21N 112.37W
San Remo 14 Bg 43.49N 7.46 E
Sanriku 29 Gb 39.08N 141.48 E
San Román, Cabo- 54 Ea 12.12N 70.00W
San Roque [Arg.] 55 Cj 28.34S 58.43W
San Roque [Sp.] 13 Gh 36.13N 5.24W
San Saba 45 Gk 31.12N 98.43W
Sansalé 34 Cc 11.07N 14.51W
San Salvador 13 Pe 39.27N 3.11 E
San Salvador [Arg.] 55 Di 29.16S 57.31W
San Salvador [Arg.] 56 Id 31.37S 58.30W
San Salvador [ElSal.] 39 Kh 13.42N 89.12W
San Salvador [Par.] 55 Dg 25.51S 56.28W
San Salvador (Watling) 47 Jd 24.02N 74.28W
San Salvador, Cuchilla- 55 Dk 33.56S 57.45W
San Salvador, Isla- 52 Gf 0.14S 90.45W
San Salvador, Río- 55 Ck 33.29S 58.23W
San Salvador de Jujuy 53 Jh 24.10S 65.20W
Sansanné-Mango 34 Fc 10.21N 0.28 E
San Sebastián [Col.] 49 Ji 9.13N 74.18W
San Sebastián [P.R.] 51a Bb 18.21N 67.00W
San Sebastián [Sp.] 6 Fg 43.19N 1.59W
San Sebastián, Bahía- 56 Gh 53.15S 68.23W
San Sebastián, Isla- 49 Cg 13.11N 88.26W
San Sebastián de la Gomera 32 Dd 28.06N 17.06W
Sansepolcro 14 Gg 43.34N 12.08 E
San Severo 14 Ji 41.41N 15.23 E
San Silvestre 49 Li 8.15N 70.02W
San Simeon 46 Ei 35.39N 121.11W
Sanski Most 14 Kf 44.46N 16.40 E
Santa Agueda 48 Cd 27.13N 112.20W
Santa Ana 63a Fd 10.50S 162.28 E
Santa Ana [Arg.] 55 Eh 27.22S 55.34W
Santa Ana [Bol.] 55 Bc 16.37S 60.43W
Santa Ana [Bol.] 54 Eg 15.31S 67.30W
Santa Ana [Bol.] 55 Cd 18.43S 58.44W
Santa Ana [Ca.-U.S.] 43 De 33.43N 117.54W
Santa Ana [ElSal.] 39 Kh 13.59N 89.34W
Santa Ana [Mex.] 47 Bb 30.33N 111.07W
Santa Ana [Ven.] 50 Dh 9.19N 64.39W
Santa Ana, Río- 49 Li 9.30N 71.57W
Santa Ana, Volcán de- 38 Kh 13.50N 89.39W
Santa Bárbara [3] 49 Cf 15.10N 88.20W
Santa Barbara 39 Hf 34.03N 118.15W
Santa Bárbara [Hond.] 49 Cf 14.53N 88.14W
Santa Bárbara [Mex.] 47 Cc 26.48N 105.49W
Santa Bárbara [Ven.] 49 Lj 7.47N 71.10W
Santa Bárbara, Puerto de- 13 Lb 42.30N 0.50W
Santa Bárbara, Serra de- 55 Fe 21.45S 53.23W
Santa Barbara Channel 46 Fi 34.15N 119.55W
Santa Catalina 63a Fd 10.54S 162.27 E
Santa Catalina [Col.] 49 Jh 10.37N 75.33W
Santa Catalina [Ven.] 50 Fh 8.33N 61.51W
Santa Catalina, Gulf of- 46 Gj 33.20N 117.45W
Santa Catalina, Isla- 48 De 25.40N 110.45W
Santa Catalina Island 46 Fj 33.23N 118.24W
Santa Catarina 48 Ie 25.41N 100.28W
Santa Catarina [2] 56 Kc 27.00S 50.00W
Santa Catarina, Ilha de- 52 Lh 27.36S 48.30W
Santa Catarina, Sierra- 48 Fc 29.40N 107.30W
Santa Cecília 55 Gh 26.56S 50.27W
Santa Cesarea Terme 14 Mj 40.02N 18.28 E
Santa Clara [Ca.-U.S.] 46 Eh 37.21N 121.59W
Santa Clara [Cuba] 39 Lg 22.24N 79.58W
Santa Clara [Gabon] 36 Ab 0.34N 9.17 E
Santa Clara [Mex.] 48 Fc 29.17N 107.01W
Santa Clara [Ur.] 55 Ek 32.55S 54.58W
Santa Clara, Barragem do- 13 Dg 37.30N 8.20W
Santa Clara, Isla- 56 Ed 33.42S 79.00W
Santa Clara de Saguier 55 Bj 31.21S 61.50W
Santa Coloma de Farners/Santa Coloma de Farnés 13 Oc 41.52N 2.40 E
Santa Coloma de Farnés/Santa Coloma de Farners 13 Oc 41.52N 2.40 E
Santa Coloma de Gramanet 13 Oc 41.27N 2.13 E
Santa Coloma de Queralt 13 Nc 41.32N 1.23 E
Santa Comba 13 Da 43.02N 8.49W
Santa Croce Camerina 14 In 36.50N 14.31 E
Santa Cruz [Arg.] [2] 56 Gg 49.00S 70.00W
Santa Cruz [Azr.] 32 Bb 39.05N 28.01W
Santa Cruz [Azr.] 32 Ab 39.27N 31.07W
Santa Cruz [Bol.] 53 Jg 17.48S 63.10W
Santa Cruz [Bol.] [2] 54 Fg 17.30S 61.30W
Santa Cruz [Braz.] 54 Id 0.36S 49.11W
Santa Cruz [Braz.] 55 Dd 18.32S 57.12W
Santa Cruz [Ca.-U.S.] 43 Cd 36.58N 122.01W
Santa Cruz [Chile] 56 Fd 34.38S 71.22W
Santa Cruz [C.R.] 49 Eh 10.01N 84.02W
Santa Cruz [Phil.] 26 Hd 14.01N 121.21 E
Santa Cruz, Isla- 52 Gf 0.38S 90.23W
Santa Cruz, Isla de- 48 De 25.17N 110.43W
Santa Cruz, Río- 56 Gh 50.08S 68.20W
Santa Cruz, Serra da- 55 Jc 17.05S 45.17W
Santa Cruz Cabrália 54 Kg 16.17S 39.02W
Santa Cruz de la Palma 32 Dd 28.41N 17.45W
Santa Cruz de la Zarza 13 Ie 39.58N 3.10W
Santa Cruz del Quiché 49 Bf 15.02N 91.08W
Santa Cruz del Sur 47 Id 20.43N 78.00W
Santa Cruz de Mudela 13 If 38.38N 3.28W
Santa Cruz de Tenerife [3] 32 Dd 28.10N 17.20W
Santa Cruz de Tenerife 31 Ff 28.27N 16.14W
Santa Cruz do Rio Pardo 55 Hf 22.55S 49.37W
Santa Cruz do Sul 56 Jc 29.43S 52.26W
Santa Cruz Island 46 Fi 34.01N 119.45W
Santa Cruz Islands 57 Hf 10.45S 165.55 E
Santadi 14 Ck 39.05N 8.43 E
Santa Elena [Arg.] 55 Bm 37.21S 60.37W
Santa Elena [Arg.] 56 Id 30.57S 59.48W
Santa Elena [Ec.] 54 Bd 2.14S 80.52W
Santa Elena, Bahía de- [C.R.] 49 Eh 10.59N 85.50W
Santa Elena, Bahía de- [Ec.] 54 Bd 2.05S 80.55W
Santa Elena, Cabo- 47 Gf 10.55N 85.57W
Santa Elena de Uairén 54 Fc 4.37N 61.08W
Santa Eulalia 13 Kd 40.34N 1.19W
Santa Eulalia del Río 13 Nf 38.59N 1.31 E
Santa Fé 49 Fc 21.45N 82.45W
Santa Fe [2] 56 Hd 31.00S 61.00W
Santafé 13 Ig 37.11N 3.43W
Santa Fe [Arg.] 53 Ji 31.40S 60.40W
Santa Fe [N.M.-U.S.] 39 If 35.42N 106.57W
Santa Fe de Bogotá (Bogotá) 53 Ie 4.36N 74.05W
Santa Fé de Minas 55 Jc 16.41S 45.28W
Santa Fé do Sul 55 Ge 20.13S 50.56 N
Sant'Agata di Militello 14 Il 38.04N 14.38 E
Santa Helena [Braz.] 55 Eg 24.56S 54.23W
Santa Helena [Braz.] 54 Id 2.14S 45.18W
Santa Helena de Goiás 54 Hg 17.43S 50.35W
Santa Inês 54 Id 3.39S 45.22W
Santa Inés 49 Mh 10.37N 69.18W
Santa Ines, Bahía- 48 Dd 27.00N 111.55W
Santa Inés, Isla- 52 Ik 53.45S 72.45W
Santa Isabel [Arg.] 55 Bk 33.54S 61.42W
Santa Isabel [Arg.] 56 Ge 36.15S 66.56W
Santa Isabel [Braz.] 55 Ba 13.40S 60.44W
Santa Isabel [P.R.] 51a Bc 17.58N 66.25W
Santa Isabel, Pico de- 34 Ge 3.35N 8.46 E
Santa Isabel Island 57 Ge 8.00S 159.00 E
Santa Izabel do Ivaí 55 Ff 22.58S 53.14W
Santa Juliana 55 Id 19.19S 47.32W
Santa Lucía [Arg.] 56 Gd 31.32S 68.29W
Santa Lucía [Ur.] 55 Dl 34.27S 56.24W
Santa Lucía, Esteros del- 55 Ci 28.15S 58.20W
Santa Lucía, Río- [Arg.] 55 Ci 29.05S 59.13W
Santa Lucía, Río- [Ur.] 55 Dl 34.48S 56.22W
Santa Lucia Cotzumalguapa 49 Bf 14.20N 91.01W
Santa Lucia Range 43 Cd 36.00N 121.20W
Santa Luzia 32 Cf 16.46N 24.45W
Santa Luzia, Ribeirão- 55 Fe 21.31S 53.53W
Santa Margarita 55 Bi 28.18S 61.33W
Santa Margarita, Isla de- 47 Bd 24.27N 111.50W
Santa Margherita Ligure 14 Df 44.20N 9.12 E
Santa Maria [Braz.] 53 Kh 29.41S 53.48W
Santa Maria 10 Ee 36.58N 25.06W
Santa Maria [Ca.-U.S.] 43 Ce 34.57N 120.26W
Santa Maria 56 Gc 26.41S 66.02W
Santa Maria 47 Cb 31.00N 107.14W
Santa Maria 55 Bc 17.08S 61.01W
Santa Maria, Bahía de- 48 Ee 25.05N 108.10W
Santa Maria, Cabo de- [Ang.] 30 Ij 13.25S 12.32 E
Santa Maria, Cabo de- [Port.] 13 Eh 36.58N 7.54W
Santa Maria, Cape- 49 Jb 23.41N 75.19W
Santa Maria, Cayo- 49 Hb 22.40N 79.00W
Santa Maria, Isla- [Chile] 56 Fe 37.02S 73.33W
Santa Maria, Isla- [Ec.] 54a Ab 1.15S 90.25W
Santa Maria, Laguna de- 48 Fb 31.10N 107.15W
Santa Maria, Río- [Mex.] 48 Jg 21.37N 99.15W
Santa Maria, Río- [Pan.] 49 Gi 8.06N 80.29W
Santa Maria, Rio- [Braz.] 55 Ee 21.50S 54.53W
Santa Maria, Rio- [Braz.] 55 Ib 14.19S 46.49W
Santa Maria Asunción Tlaxiaco 48 Ki 17.16N 97.41W
Santa Maria Capua Vetere 14 Ii 41.05N 14.15 E
Santa Maria da Vitória 55 Ja 13.24S 44.12W
Santa Maria de Cuevas 48 Fd 27.55N 106.23W
Santa Maria de Ipire 50 Dh 8.49N 65.19W
Santa Maria del Oro 48 Ge 25.56N 105.22W
Santa Maria del Río 48 Ig 21.48N 100.45W
Santa Maria la Real de Nieva 13 Hc 41.04N 4.24W
Santa Maria Zacatepec 48 Ki 16.46N 98.00W
Santa Marinella 14 Fh 42.02N 11.51 E
Santa Marta 53 Id 11.15N 74.13W
Santa Marta, Cabo de- 36 Be 13.52S 12.25 E
Santa Marta, Ria de- 13 Ea 43.42N 7.51W
Santa Marta Grande, Cabo de- 55 Hi 28.38S 48.45W
Santa Monica 43 De 34.01N 118.30W
Santan 26 Gg 0.03S 117.28 E
Santana 55 Ja 12.59S 44.03W
Santana, Coxilha de- 55 Ej 31.15S 55.15W
Santana, Rio- 55 Gd 19.43S 51.02W
Santana da Boa Vista 55 Fj 30.52S 53.07W
Santana do Livramento 56 Id 30.53S 55.31W
Santander [3] 13 Ia 43.10N 4.00W
Santander [2] 54 Db 6.35N 73.20W
Santander [Col.] 54 Cc 3.01N 76.29W
Santander [Phil.] 26 He 9.25N 123.20 E
Santander [Sp.] 6 Fg 43.28N 3.48W
Santander, Bahía de- 13 Ia 43.27N 3.48W
Santander Jiménez 47 Ed 24.13N 98.28W
Sant'Andrea 14 Lj 40.05N 17.55 E
Sant'Antioco 14 Ck 39.04N 8.27 E
Sant'Antioco 5 Gh 39.05N 8.25 E
Sant Antoni, Cap-/San Antonio, Cabo de- 13 Mf 38.48N 0.12 E
Santañy 13 Pe 39.22N 3.07 E
Santa Olalla 13 Hd 40.01N 4.26W
Santa Olalla del Cala 13 Fg 37.54N 6.13W
Santa Paula 46 Fi 34.21N 119.04W
Santa Pola 13 Lf 38.11N 0.33W
Sant'Arcangelo 14 Kj 40.15N 16.16 E
Santarcangelo di Romagna 14 Gf 44.04N 12.27 E
Santarém [3] 13 De 39.15N 8.35W
Santarém [Braz.] 53 Kf 2.26S 54.42W
Santarém [Port.] 13 De 39.14N 8.41W
Santaren Channel 47 Id 24.00N 79.30W
Santa Rita [Braz.] 55 Cc 16.15S 59.00W
Santa Rita [Col.] 54 Ec 4.55N 68.20W
Santa Rita [Guam] 64c Bb 13.23N 144.40 E
Santa Rita [Hond.] 49 Df 15.09N 87.53W
Santa Rita [Ven.] 50 Ch 8.08N 66.16W
Santa Rita [Ven.] 49 Lh 10.32N 71.32W
Santa Rita do Araguaia 55 Fc 17.20S 53.12W
Santa Rosa [3] 49 Bf 14.10N 90.18W
Santa Rosa [Arg.] 56 Gd 31.31S 65.04W
Santa Rosa [Arg.] 53 Ji 36.40S 64.15W
Santa Rosa [Braz.] 56 Jc 27.52S 54.29W
Santa Rosa [Ca.-U.S.] 43 Cd 38.26N 122.43W
Santa Rosa [Ec.] 54 Cd 3.27S 79.58W
Santa Rosa [N.M.-U.S.] 43 Ge 34.57N 104.41W
Santa Rosa [Par.] 55 Dh 26.52S 56.49W
Santa Rosa [Ven.] 49 Mi 8.26N 69.42W
Santa Rosa [Ven.] 50 Dh 9.38N 64.18W
Santa Rosa, Mount- 64c Ba 13.32N 144.55 E
Santa Rosa de Copán 49 Cf 14.47N 88.46W
Santa Rosa de la Roca 55 Bc 16.04S 61.32W
Santa Rosa Island 46 Ej 33.58N 120.06W
Santa Rosalía 39 Hg 27.19N 112.17W
Santa Rosalía 50 Bh 9.02N 69.01W
Santa Rosalía, Punta- 48 Bc 28.40N 114.20W
Santa Rosa Range 46 Gf 41.00N 117.40W
Santa Rosa Wash 46 Ij 33.10N 112.05W
Šantarskije Ostrova=Shantar Islands (EN) 21 Pd 55.00N 137.36 E
Santas Creus/Santes Creus 13 Nc 41.19N 1.18 E
Santa Sylvina 56 Hc 27.49S 61.09W
Santa Teresa [Arg.] 55 Bk 33.26S 60.47W
Santa Teresa [Mex.] 48 Ke 25.17N 97.51W
Santa Teresa [Peru] 54 Df 13.01S 72.39W
Santa Teresa, Rio- 55 Ha 12.40S 48.47W
Santa Teresa di Riva 14 Jm 37.57N 15.22 E
Santa Teresa Gallura 14 Di 41.14N 9.11 E
Santa Teresita 55 Dm 36.32S 56.41W
Santa Vitória do Palmar 56 Jd 33.31S 53.21W
Santa Vitória 55 Gd 18.50S 50.08W
Sant Barbara Island 46 Fj 33.23N 119.01W
Sant Boi de Llobregat/San Baudilio de Llobregat 13 Oc 41.21N 2.03 E
Sant Carles de la Ràpita/San Carlos de la Rápita 13 Md 40.37N 0.36 E
Santee River 43 Le 33.14N 79.28W
Santeh 24 Ld 36.10N 46.32 E
San Telmo 48 Ab 30.58N 116.06W
San Telmo, Bahía de- 48 Hh 18.45N 103.40W
San Telmo, Punta- 47 De 18.19N 103.30W
Santerno 14 Ff 44.34N 11.58 E
Santerre 11 Ie 49.55N 2.30 E
Santes Creus/Santas Creus 13 Nc 41.19N 1.18 E
Sant'Eufemia, Golfo di- 14 Kl 38.50N 16.05 E
Sant'Eufemia Lamezia 14 Kl 38.55N 16.15 E
Sant Feliu de Llobregat/San Feliú de Llobregat 13 Oc 41.23N 2.03 E
Santhià 14 Ce 45.22N 8.10 E
Santiago [2] 56 Fd 33.30S 70.50W
Santiago [Bol.] 54 Gg 18.19S 59.34W
Santiago [Bol.] 55 Bd 19.22S 60.51W
Santiago [Braz.] 56 Jc 29.11S 54.53W
Santiago [Chile] 53 Ii 33.27S 70.40W
Santiago [Dom.Rep.] 39 Lh 19.27N 70.42W
Santiago [Mex.] 48 Ie 25.25N 100.09W
Santiago [Mex.] 48 Cd 27.32N 112.49W
Santiago [Pan.] 39 Ki 8.05N 80.59W
Santiago [Par.] 55 Dh 27.09S 56.47W
Santiago, Cerro- 49 Gi 8.33N 81.44W
Santiago, Rio- 54 Cd 4.27S 77.36W
Santiago, Río de- 48 Ge 25.11N 105.26W
Santiago, Serranía- 55 Cd 18.25S 59.25W
Santiago de Chuco 54 Ce 8.09S 78.11W
Santiago de Compostela 13 Db 42.53N 8.33W
Santiago de Cuba 39 Lg 20.01N 75.49W
Santiago de Cuba [3] 49 Ic 20.10N 76.10W
Santiago de la Ribera 13 Lg 37.48N 0.48W
Santiago del Estero 53 Jh 27.50S 64.15W
Santiago del Estero [2] 56 Hc 28.00S 63.30W
Santiago de Papasquiaro 48 Ge 25.03N 105.25W
Santiago do Cacém 13 Df 38.01N 8.42W
Santiago Ixcuintla 47 Cd 21.49N 105.13W
Santiago Mountains 45 El 29.40N 103.15W
Santiago Pinotepa Nacional 47 Ee 16.19N 98.01W
Santiaguillo, Isla- 48 Lh 19.05N 95.50W
Santiaguillo, Laguna de- 48 Ge 24.50N 104.50W
Santiam River 46 Dd 44.42N 123.55W
Santillana 13 Ha 43.23N 4.06W
San Timoteo 49 Li 9.48N 71.04W
Säntis 14 Dc 47.15N 9.20 E
Santisteban del Puerto 13 If 38.15N 3.12W
Sant Jordi, Golf de-/San Jorge, Golfe de- 13 Md 40.53N 1.00 E
Sant Mateu del Maestrat/San Mateo 13 Md 40.28N 0.11 E
Santo, Ile- 57 Hf 15.15S 166.50 E
Santo Anastácio 55 Ge 21.58S 51.39W
Santo André 55 If 23.40S 46.31W
Santo Ângelo 56 Jc 28.18S 54.16W
Santo Antão 30 Eg 17.05N 25.10W
Santo Antônio 56 Jc 26.03S 53.12W
Santo Antonio 34 Ge 1.39N 7.25 E
Santo Antônio de Jesus 54 Kf 12.58S 39.16W
Santo Antônio do Içá 54 Ed 3.05S 67.57W
Santo Antônio do Leverger 54 Gg 15.52S 56.05W
Santo Corazón 54 Gg 17.59S 58.51W
Santo Corazón, Río- 55 Cc 17.23S 58.23W
Santo Domingo [Cuba] 49 Gb 22.35N 80.15W
Santo Domingo [Dom.Rep.] 39 Mh 18.28N 69.54W
Santo Domingo [Mex.] 48 Bb 30.43N 115.56W
Santo Domingo [Mex.] 48 Bc 28.12N 114.02W
Santo Domingo [Mex.] 48 If 23.20N 101.44W
Santo Domingo [Nic.] 49 Eg 12.16N 85.05W
Santo Domingo, Cay- 49 Jc 21.42N 75.46W
Santo Domingo, Punta- 48 Cd 26.20N 112.40W
Santo Domingo, Río- [Mex.] 48 Kh 18.10N 96.08W
Santo Domingo, Río- [Ven.] 49 Mi 8.01N 69.33W
Santo Domingo de la Calzada 13 Jb 42.26N 2.57W
Santo Domingo de los Colorados 54 Cd 0.15S 79.10W
Santo Domingo de Silos 13 Ic 41.58N 3.25W
Santo Domingo Pueblo 45 Ci 35.31N 106.22W
San Tomé 50 Dh 8.58N 64.08W
Santoña 13 Ia 43.27N 3.27W
Santos 53 Lh 23.57S 46.20W
Santos, Sierra de los- 13 Gf 38.15N 5.20W
Santos Dumont 55 Ke 21.28S 43.34W
Santos Unzué 55 Bl 35.45S 60.51W
Santo Tirso 13 Dc 41.21N 8.28W
Santo Tomás [Bol.] 55 Cc 17.46S 58.55W
Santo Tomás [Mex.] 48 Ab 31.33N 116.24W
Santo Tomás [Nic.] 49 Eg 12.04N 85.05W
Santo Tomás, Punta- 48 Ab 31.34N 116.42W
Santo Tomé 56 Ic 28.33S 56.03W
Santu Lussurgiu 14 Cj 40.08N 8.39 E
Santurce-Antiguo 13 Ia 43.20N 3.02W
Sanuki-Sanmyaku 29 Cd 34.05N 134.00 E
San Valentín, Cerro- 52 Ij 46.36S 73.20W
San Vicente [Arg.] 55 Cl 35.01S 58.25W
San Vicente [Mex.] 48 Ab 31.20N 116.15W
San Vicente [Phil.] 26 Hc 18.30N 122.09 E
San Vicente, Sierra de- 13 Hd 40.10N 4.45W
San Vicente de Cañete 54 Cf 13.05S 79.24W
San Vicente de la Barquera 13 Ha 43.26N 4.24W
San Vicente del Caguán 54 Dc 2.07N 74.46W
San Vicente de Raspeig 13 Lf 38.24N 0.31W
San Vincente 47 Gf 13.38N 88.48W
San Vincenzo 14 Eg 43.06N 10.32 E
San Vito [C.R.] 49 Fi 8.50N 82.58W
San Vito [It.] 14 Dk 39.26N 9.32 E
San Vito, Capo- 14 Gl 38.11N 12.44 E
Sanya→Yaxian 22 Mh 18.27N 109.28 E
Sanyati 37 Dc 16.49S 28.45 E
San'yō 29 Bd 34.03N 131.10 E
Sanza 14 Jj 40.15N 15.33 E
Sanza Pombo 36 Cd 7.20S 16.00 E
São Bartolomeu, Rio- 55 Ic 16.48S 47.55W
São Benedito 54 Jd 4.03S 40.53W
São Bento 54 Jd 2.42S 44.50W
São Bento do Sul 55 Hh 26.15S 49.23W
São Borja 56 Ic 28.39S 56.00W
São Brás de Alportel 13 Eg 37.09N 7.53W
São Caetano do Sul 56 Kb 23.36S 46.34W
São Carlos [Braz.] 56 Kb 22.01S 47.54W
São Carlos [Braz.] 55 Ej 33.47N 55.30W
São Domingos [Braz.] 55 Ia 13.24S 46.19W
São Domingos [Gui.Bis.] 34 Bc 12.24N 16.12W
São Domingos, Rio- [Braz.] 55 Fe 20.03S 53.13W
São Domingos, Rio- [Braz.] 55 Ia 13.24S 47.12W
São Domingos, Rio- [Braz.] 55 Gd 19.13S 50.44W
São Domingos, Rio- [Braz.] 55 Ib 15.37S 46.14W
São Félix 54 Hf 11.36S 50.39W
São Félix do Xingu 54 He 6.38S 51.59W
São Filipe 32 Cf 14.54N 24.31W
São Francisco [Braz.] 54 Jg 15.57S 44.52W
São Francisco [Braz.] 55 Dd 18.45S 56.55W
São Francisco, Ilha de- 55 Lh 26.18S 48.37W
São Francisco, Rio- 52 Mg 10.30S 36.24W
São Francisco de Assis 55 Ei 29.33S 55.08W
São Francisco de Paula 55 Gi 29.27S 50.35W
São Francisco de Sales 55 Hd 19.52S 49.46W
São Francisco do Sul 56 Kc 26.14S 48.39W
São Gabriel 56 Jd 30.20S 54.19W
São Gonçalo 54 Jh 22.51S 43.04W
São Gonçalo, Canal de- 55 Fk 32.10S 52.38W
São Gonçalo do Abaete 55 Jd 18.20S 45.49W
São Gonçalo do Sapucaí 55 Je 21.54S 45.36W
São Gotardo 55 Id 19.19S 46.03W
Sao Hill 36 Gd 8.20S 35.12 E
São Jerônimo, Serra de- 55 Ec 16.20S 54.55W
São João da Barra 54 Jh 21.38S 41.03W
São João da Boa Vista 55 Ie 21.58S 46.47W
São João d'Aliança 55 Ib 14.42S 47.31W
São João da Madeira 13 Dd 40.54N 8.30W
São João da Ponte 55 Kb 15.56S 44.01W
São João del Rei 54 Jh 21.09S 44.16W
São João de Meriti 55 Kf 22.48S 43.22W
São João do Araguaia 54 Ie 5.23S 48.46W
São João do Piauí 54 Je 8.21S 42.15W
São João dos Patos 54 Je 6.30S 43.42W
São João do Triunfo 55 Gg 25.41S 50.18W
São Joaquim 56 Kc 28.18S 49.56W
São Joaquim da Barra 55 Ie 20.35S 47.53W
São Jorge 30 Ee 38.38N 28.03W
São José da Serra 55 Eb 15.40S 55.18W
São José do Cerrito 55 Gh 27.40S 50.35W
São José do Norte 55 Fk 32.01S 52.03W
São José do Rio Pardo 56 Kb 21.36S 46.54W
São José do Rio Prêto 53 Lh 20.48S 49.23W
São José dos Campos 56 Kb 23.11S 45.53W
São José dos Dourados, Rio- 55 Ge 20.22S 51.21W
Saolat, Buku- 26 If 0.45N 127.59 E
São Leopoldo 56 Jc 29.46S 51.09W
São Lourenço 55 Ec 16.32S 55.02W
São Lourenço, Pantanal de- 54 Gg 17.45S 56.15W
São Lourenço, Rio- 54 Gg 17.53S 57.27W
São Lourenço, Serra de- 55 Ec 17.30S 54.50W
São Lourenço do Sul 56 Jd 31.22S 51.58W
São Luis 53 Lf 2.31S 44.16W
São Luis Gonzaga 56 Jc 28.24S 54.58W
São Mamede, Serra de- 13 Ee 39.19N 7.19W
São Manuel 55 Hf 22.44S 48.34W
São Marcos 55 Gi 28.58S 51.04W
São Marcos, Baía de- 52 Lf 2.30S 44.30W
São Marcos, Rio- 55 Id 18.15S 47.37W
São Mateus [Braz.] 54 Kg 18.44S 39.51W
São Mateus [Braz.] 55 Gg 25.52S 50.23W

Index Symbols

[1] Independent Nation
[2] State, Region
[3] District, County
[4] Municipality
[5] Colony, Dependency
Continent
Physical Region
Historical or Cultural Region
Mount, Mountain
Volcano
Hill
Mountains, Mountain Range
Hills, Escarpment
Plateau, Upland
Pass, Gap
Plain, Lowland
Delta
Salt Flat
Valley, Canyon
Crater, Cave
Karst Features
Depression
Polder
Desert, Dunes
Forest, Woods
Heath, Steppe
Oasis
Cape, Point
Coast, Beach
Cliff
Peninsula
Isthmus
Sandbank
Island
Atoll
Rock, Reef
Islands, Archipelago
Rocks, Reefs
Coral Reef
Well, Spring
Geyser
River, Stream
Waterfall Rapids
River Mouth, Estuary
Lake
Salt Lake
Intermittent Lake
Reservoir
Swamp, Pond
Canal
Glacier
Ice Shelf, Pack Ice
Ocean
Sea
Gulf, Bay
Strait, Fjord
Lagoon
Bank
Seamount
Tablemount
Ridge
Shelf
Basin
Escarpment, Sea Scarp
Fracture
Trench, Abyss
National Park, Reserve
Point of Interest
Recreation Site
Cave, Cavern
Historic Site
Ruins
Wall, Walls
Church, Abbey
Temple
Scientific Station
Airport
Port
Lighthouse
Mine
Tunnel
Dam, Bridge

São Mateus, Rio- 55 Ia 13.48 S 46.54 W
São Miguel 30 Ee 37.47 N 25.30 W
São Miguel, Rio- 55 Ic 16.03 S 46.07 W
São Miguel do Araguaia 55 Ga 13.19 S 50.13 W
São Miguel d'Oeste 55 Fh 26.45 S 53.34 W
Saona, Isla- 49 Md 18.09 N 68.40 W
Saône 5 Gf 45.44 N 4.50 E
Saône-et-Loire [3] 11 Kh 46.40 N 4.30 E
Saonek 26 Jg 0.28 S 130.47 E
São Nicolau 30 Eg 16.35 N 24.15 W
São Nicolau [Braz.] 55 Ei 28.11 S 55.16 W
São Patricio, Rio- 55 Hb 15.02 S 49.15 W
São Paulo 53 Lh 23.32 S 46.37 W
São Paulo [2] 56 Kb 22.00 S 49.00 W
São Paulo de Olivença 54 Ed 3.27 S 68.48 W
São Pedro, Ribeirão 55 Ic 16.54 S 46.32 W
São Pedro do Sul [Braz.] 55 Ei 29.37 S 54.10 W
São Pedro do Sul [Port.] 13 Dd 40.45 N 8.04 W
São Pedro e São Paulo, Penedos de- 52 Ne 0.56 N 29.22 W
São Raimundo Nonato 54 Je 9.01 S 42.42 W
São Romão [Braz.] 55 Ed 18.33 S 54.27 W
São Romão [Braz.] 54 Ig 16.22 S 45.04 W
São Roque 55 De 21.43 S 57.46 W
São Roque, Cabo de- 52 Mf 5.29 S 35.16 W
São Roque, Serra de- 55 Ib 14.40 S 46.50 W
São Sebastião 55 Jf 23.48 S 45.25 W
São Sebastião, Ilha de- 52 Lh 23.50 S 45.18 W
São Sebastião, Ponta- 30 Kk 22.05 S 35.24 E
São Sebastião da Boa Vista 54 Id 1.42 S 49.31 W
São Sebastião do Paraiso 54 Ih 20.55 S 47.00 W
São Sepé 55 Fj 30.10 S 53.34 W
São Simão 54 Hg 18.56 S 50.30 W
São Tiago 30 Eg 15.05 N 23.40 W
São Tomé 30 Hh 0.12 N 6.39 E
São Tomé 31 Hh 0.20 N 6.44 E
São Tomé, Cabo de- 54 Jh 22.00 S 40.59 W
Sao Tome and Principe (EN) = São Tomé e Principe [1] 31 Hh 1.00 N 7.00 E
São Tomé e Príncipe = Sao Tome and Principe (EN) [1] 31 Hh 1.00 N 7.00 E
Saoura 32 Gd 27.50 N 2.50 W
Saoura 30 Gf 28.48 N 0.50 W
São Vicente 30 Eg 16.50 N 25.00 W
São Vicente [Braz.] 55 Ia 13.38 S 46.31 W
São Vicente [Braz.] 56 Kb 23.58 S 46.23 W
São Vicente, Cabo de- 5 Fh 37.01 N 9.00 W
São Xavier, Serra de- 55 Ei 29.15 S 54.15 W
Sápai 15 Ih 41.02 N 25.42 E
Sapanca 15 Ni 40.41 N 30.16 E
Sapanca Gölü 15 Ni 40.43 N 30.15 E
Sape [Braz.] 54 Ke 7.06 S 35.13 W
Sape [Indon.] 26 Gh 8.34 S 118.59 E
Sape, Selat- 26 Gh 8.39 S 119.18 E
Sapele 34 Gd 5.55 N 5.42 E
Sapelo Island 44 Gj 31.28 N 81.15 W
Şaphane 15 Mj 39.01 N 29.14 E
Şaphane Dağı 15 Mj 39.03 N 29.16 E
Sapiéntza 15 Em 36.45 N 21.42 E
Šapkina 17 Fc 66.44 N 52.25 E
Sapo, Serrania del- 49 Hi 7.50 N 78.17 W
Saponé 34 Ec 12.03 N 1.36 W
Sapopema 55 Gf 23.55 S 50.35 W
Saposoa 54 Ce 6.56 S 76.48 W
Sapphire Mountains 46 Ic 46.20 N 113.45 W
Sapporo 22 Qe 43.03 N 141.21 E
Sapri 14 Jj 40.04 N 15.38 E
Saptajev (Nikolski) 19 Gf 47.55 N 67.33 E
Sapulpa 43 Hd 36.00 N 96.06 W
Sapulut 26 Gf 4.42 N 116.29 E
Sāqiyat Sīdī Yūsuf 14 Cn 36.13 N 8.21 E
Saqqez 23 Gb 36.14 N 46.16 E
Sarāb 23 Gb 37.56 N 47.32 E
Saraburi 25 Kf 14.30 N 100.55 E
Saraf Doungous 35 Bc 12.33 N 19.42 E
Sarafjagān 24 Ne 34.28 N 50.28 E
Saragmatha = Everest, Mount- (EN) 21 Kg 27.59 N 86.56 E
Saragossa (EN) = Zaragoza [Sp.] 6 Fg 41.38 N 0.53 W
Sarai 7 Jj 53.44 N 41.03 E
Sarajevo 6 Hg 43.50 N 18.25 E
Saraji Mine 59 Jd 22.30 S 148.20 E
Sarakhs 23 Jb 36.32 N 61.11 E
Sarakiná 15 Hk 38.40 N 24.37 E
Šarakol 17 Kj 52.03 N 62.47 E
Saraktaš 19 Fe 51.47 N 56.18 E
Saraland 44 Cj 30.49 N 88.02 W
Saramati 25 Jc 25.44 N 95.02 E
Saran 19 Hf 49.46 N 72.52 E
Saran, Gunung- 26 Fg 0.25 S 111.18 E
Saranac Lake 44 Jc 44.20 N 74.08 W
Saranci 15 Gg 42.43 N 23.46 E
Saranda 15 Cj 39.52 N 20.00 E
Sarandi 55 Fh 27.56 S 52.55 W
Sarandi, Arroyo- 55 Cj 30.13 S 59.19 W
Sarandi del Yí 55 Ek 33.21 S 55.38 W
Sarandi Grande 55 Dk 33.44 S 56.20 W
Saranga 7 Lh 57.12 N 46.34 E
Sarangani Bay 26 Ie 5.57 N 125.11 E
Sarangani Islands 26 Ie 5.25 N 125.26 E
Saranley 35 Ge 2.23 N 42.16 E
Saransk 6 Ke 54.11 N 45.11 E
Sarapul 6 Ld 56.28 N 53.48 E
Sarapulskoje 20 Ig 48.50 N 135.58 E
Sarare 49 Mi 9.47 N 69.10 W
Sararé, Rio- 55 Cb 14.51 S 59.58 W
Sarasota 43 Kf 27.20 N 82.34 W
Sarata 16 Ff 46.01 N 29.41 E
Sărăţel 15 Kb 47.03 N 27.25 E
Saratoga 46 Lf 41.27 N 106.48 W
Saratoga Springs 43 Mc 43.04 N 73.47 W
Saratok 26 Ff 1.24 N 111.31 E
Saratov 6 Ke 51.34 N 46.02 E
Saratov Reservoir (EN) = Saratovskoje Vodohranilišče 5 Ke 52.50 N 47.50 E
Saratovskaja Oblast [3] 19 Ee 51.30 N 47.00 E
Saratovskoje Vodohranilišče = Saratov Reservoir (EN) 5 Ke 52.50 N 47.50 E
Saravan 25 Le 15.43 N 106.25 E
Sarawak [2] 26 Ff 2.30 N 113.30 E
Saray 24 Bb 41.26 N 27.55 E
Saraya 34 Cc 12.50 N 11.45 W
Sarāyā 24 Fe 35.47 N 35.58 E
Sarayköy 24 Cd 37.55 N 28.56 E
Sarbāz 23 Jd 26.39 N 61.15 E
Sárbogárd 10 Oj 46.53 N 18.38 E
Sarca 14 Ee 45.52 N 10.52 E
Sarcelle, Passe de la- 63b Cf 22.28 S 167.13 E
Sarcelles 12 Ef 49.00 N 2.23 E
Sarcidano 14 Dk 39.40 N 9.15 E
Sardara 14 Ck 39.37 N 8.49 E
Sar Dasht [Iran] 24 Mf 32.32 N 48.52 E
Sar Dasht [Iran] 24 Kd 36.09 N 45.28 E
Sardegna [2] 14 Cj 40.00 N 9.00 E
Sardegna = Sardinia (EN) 5 Gh 40.00 N 9.00 E
Sardegna, Mar di- 14 Bk 40.00 N 7.30 E
Sardes 15 Lk 38.29 N 28.03 E
Sardinal 49 Eh 10.31 N 85.39 W
Sardinata 54 Db 8.07 N 72.48 W
Sardinia (EN) = Sardegna 5 Gh 40.00 N 9.00 E
Sardis Lake 45 Li 34.27 N 89.43 W
Sarektjåkkå 7 Dc 67.25 N 17.46 E
Sarema/Saaremaa 5 Id 58.25 N 22.30 E
Sar-e Pol 23 Kb 36.14 N 65.55 E
Sar Eskand Khān 24 Ld 37.29 N 47.04 E
Sar-e Yazd 24 Pg 31.36 N 54.35 E
Sargasso Sea 38 Mg 29.00 N 65.00 W
Sargatskoje 19 Hd 55.37 N 73.30 E
Sargodha 25 Eb 32.05 N 72.40 E
Šargun 18 Fe 38.31 N 67.59 E
Sarh 31 Ih 9.09 N 18.23 E
Sarhe 11 Fg 47.30 N 0.32 W
Sarhro, Jebel- 32 Fc 31.00 N 6.00 W
Sāri [Iran] 22 Hf 36.34 N 53.04 E
Sāri [Iraq] 24 Je 34.42 N 45.28 E
Sariá 15 Kn 35.50 N 27.15 E
Sarıçakaya 24 Db 40.02 N 30.31 E
Sarigan Island 57 Fc 16.42 N 145.47 E
Sarıgöl 24 Cc 38.14 N 28.43 E
Sarıkamış 24 Jb 40.15 N 42.35 E
Sarıkaya 24 Fc 39.48 N 35.24 E
Sarikei 26 Ff 2.07 N 111.31 E
Sarıköy 15 Ki 40.12 N 27.36 E
Sarina 59 Jd 21.26 S 149.13 E
Sarine 14 Bd 46.59 N 7.16 E
Sariñena 13 Lc 41.48 N 0.10 W
Sarıoğlan 24 Fc 39.05 N 35.59 E
Sarir 33 Dd 27.30 N 22.30 E
Sariwŏn 27 Md 38.30 N 125.45 E
Sarıyer 24 Cb 41.10 N 29.03 E
Sarj, Jabal as- 14 Do 35.56 N 9.32 E
Šarja 6 Kd 58.24 N 45.30 E
Sark 9 Kl 49.26 N 2.21 W
Sarkad 10 Rj 46.45 N 21.23 E
Sarkand 19 Hf 45.25 N 79.54 E
Şarkîkaraağaç 24 Dc 38.04 N 31.23 E
Şarkışla 24 Gc 39.21 N 36.26 E
Šarkovščina 8 Li 55.22 N 27.32 E
Şarköy 24 Bb 40.37 N 27.06 E
Sarlat-la-Canéda 11 Hj 44.53 N 1.13 E
Šarlyk 16 Sc 52.54 N 54.42 E
Sarmi 58 Ee 1.51 S 138.44 E
Sarmiento 53 Jj 45.35 S 69.05 W
Sarmizegetuza 15 Fd 45.31 N 22.47 E
Särna 8 Ec 61.41 N 13.08 E
Sarnen 14 Cd 46.54 N 8.15 E
Sărnena Gora 15 Ig 42.35 N 25.30 E
Sarnia 42 Jh 42.58 N 82.23 W
Sarny 19 Ce 51.21 N 26.36 E
Saroako 26 Hg 2.31 S 121.22 E
Sarolangun 26 Dg 2.18 S 102.42 E
Saroma 29a Ca 44.02 N 143.45 E
Saroma-Ko 28 Qb 44.10 N 143.40 E
Šaromy 20 Kf 54.23 N 158.14 E
Saronic Gulf (EN) = Saronikós Kólpos 15 Gl 37.45 N 23.30 E
Saronikós Kólpos = Saronic Gulf (EN) 15 Gl 37.45 N 23.30 E
Saronno 14 De 45.38 N 9.02 E
Saros, Gulf of- (EN) = Saros Körfezi 24 Bb 40.30 N 26.20 E
Saros Körfezi = Saros, Gulf of- (EN) 24 Bb 40.30 N 26.20 E
Sárospatak 10 Rh 48.19 N 21.35 E
Sar Passage 64a Ac 7.12 N 134.23 E
Sarpinskije Ozera 16 Nf 47.45 N 45.00 E
Šar Planina 15 Dg 42.05 N 20.50 E
Sarpsborg 8 De 59.17 N 11.07 E
Sarqaq 41 Gd 70.00 N 51.39 W
Sarrabus 14 Dk 39.20 N 9.30 E
Sarralbe 11 Ne 49.00 N 7.01 E
Sarrāt, Wādī- 14 Co 35.59 N 8.23 E
Sarre 10 Cg 49.42 N 6.34 E
Sarrebourg 11 Nf 48.44 N 7.03 E
Sarreguemines 11 Ne 49.06 N 7.03 E
Sarre-Union 12 Jf 48.56 N 7.05 E
Sarria 13 Eb 42.47 N 7.24 W
Sarstún, Rio- 49 Cf 15.54 N 88.54 W
Sartang 20 Ic 67.30 N 133.20 E
Sartène 11a Ab 41.37 N 8.59 E
Sarthe [3] 11 Gf 48.00 N 0.05 E
Sartu → Anda 28 Ha 46.35 N 125.00 E
Sarufutsu 29a Ca 45.18 N 142.13 E
Saru-Gawa 29a Cb 42.30 N 142.00 E
Saruhanlı 24 Bc 38.44 N 27.34 E
Sarukaishi-Gawa 29 Gb 39.25 N 141.08 E
Särüq 24 Me 34.25 N 49.30 E
Saruyama-Misaki 29 Ec 37.18 N 136.43 E
Sárvár 10 Mi 47.15 N 16.56 E
Sarvestān 24 Oh 29.16 N 53.13 E
Sárvíz 10 Oj 46.22 N 18.48 E
Saryagač 18 Gd 41.28 N 69.11 E
Sarybarak 18 Hc 43.24 N 71.29 E
Sary-Bulak 18 Jd 41.54 N 75.47 E
Saryč, Mys- 5 Jg 44.25 N 33.45 E
Saryg-Sep 20 Ef 51.30 N 95.40 E
Sary-Iškotrau 18 Kb 45.15 N 76.25 E
Sarykamys 19 Ff 46.00 N 53.41 E
Sarykamyšskoje, Ozero- 19 Fg 41.58 N 57.58 E
Sarykolski Hrebet 18 Je 38.30 N 74.15 E
Šaryn-Gol 27 Ib 49.20 N 106.30 E
Saryozek 19 Hg 44.22 N 77.54 E
Saryšagan 19 Hf 46.05 N 73.38 E
Saryšiganak, Zaliv- 18 Ca 46.35 N 61.25 E
Sarysu 21 Ie 45.12 N 66.36 E
Sary-Taš 19 Hh 39.44 N 73.16 E
Saryžaz 18 Lc 42.54 N 79.31 E
Sarzana 14 Df 44.07 N 9.58 E
Sasabe 48 Db 31.27 N 111.31 W
Sasabeneh 35 Gd 8.00 N 43.44 E
Sasa-ga-Mine 29 Ce 33.49 N 133.17 E
Sasago-Tōge 29 Fd 35.37 N 138.45 E
Sasamungga 63a Cb 7.02 S 156.47 E
Sasarām 25 Gd 24.57 N 84.02 E
Sasari, Mount- 63a Dc 8.11 S 159.33 E
Sascut 15 Kc 46.11 N 27.04 E
Sásd 10 Oj 46.15 N 18.07 E
Sasebo 27 Me 33.12 N 129.44 E
Saseginaga, Lac- 44 Hb 47.05 N 78.34 W
Saskatchewan [3] 42 Gf 54.00 N 106.00 W
Saskatchewan 38 Jd 53.12 N 99.16 W
Saskatoon 39 Id 52.07 N 106.38 W
Saskylah 20 Gb 72.00 N 114.00 E
Saslaya, Cerro- 49 Eg 13.45 N 85.03 W
Sasovo 19 Ee 54.22 N 41.54 E
Sassafras Mountain 44 Fh 35.03 N 82.48 W
Sassandra 30 Gh 4.58 N 6.05 W
Sassandra [3] 34 Dd 5.20 N 6.10 W
Sassandra 31 Gh 4.57 N 6.05 W
Sassari 6 Gg 40.43 N 8.34 E
Sassenberg 12 Kc 51.59 N 8.03 E
Sassenheim 12 Gb 52.14 N 4.33 E
Sassetot-le-Mauconduit 12 Ce 49.48 N 0.32 E
Saßnitz 10 Jb 54.31 N 13.39 E
Sasso Marconi 14 Ff 44.24 N 11.15 E
Sassuolo 14 Ef 44.33 N 10.47 E
Sastobe 18 Hc 42.34 N 70.03 E
Sastre 55 Bj 31.45 S 61.50 W
Sasyk, Ozero- (Kunduk) 16 Fg 45.45 N 29.40 E
Sasykkol, Ozero- 19 If 46.40 N 81.00 E
Sata 29 Bf 31.04 N 130.42 E
Sata, Cape- (EN) = Sata Misaki 21 Pf 30.59 N 130.37 E
Satakunta 8 Jc 61.30 N 23.00 E
Sata-Misaki = Sata, Cape- (EN) 21 Pf 30.59 N 130.37 E
Satan, Pointe de- 63b Dd 19.00 S 169.17 E
Sātāra 25 Ee 17.41 N 73.59 E
Sataua 65c Aa 13.28 S 172.40 W
Satawal Island 57 Fd 7.21 N 147.02 E
Satawan Atoll 57 Gd 5.25 N 153.35 E
Satellite Bay 42 Fa 77.25 N 117.15 W
Säter 7 Df 60.21 N 15.45 E
Satihaure 7 Ec 67.30 N 18.45 E
Satipo 54 Df 11.16 S 74.37 W
Satīt 35 Fc 14.20 N 35.50 E
Satka 19 Fd 55.03 N 59.01 E
Šatki 7 Ki 55.11 N 44.08 E
Sātmāla Range 25 Fe 19.30 N 78.45 E
Satna 25 Gd 24.35 N 80.50 E
Šator 14 Kf 44.09 N 16.37 E
Sátoraljaújhely 10 Rh 48.24 N 21.40 E
Sātpura Range 21 Jg 21.25 N 76.10 E
Satsuma-Hantō 29 Bf 31.25 N 130.25 E
Satsunai-Gawa 29a Cb 42.55 N 143.15 E
Satsunan-Shotō 27 Mf 29.00 N 130.00 E
Sattahip 25 Kf 12.39 N 100.54 E
Satulung 15 Gb 47.34 N 23.26 E
Satu Mare 15 Fb 47.48 N 22.53 E
Satu Mare [2] 15 Fb 47.46 N 22.56 E
Satun 25 Kg 6.39 N 100.03 E
Saturniná ou Papagaio, Rio- 55 Ca 13.55 S 58.18 W
Saualpe 14 Id 46.50 N 14.40 E
Sauce 56 Ic 30.05 S 58.46 W
Sauce Corto, Arroyo- 55 Bm 36.55 S 61.48 W
Sauceda Mountains 46 Ij 32.30 N 112.30 W
Sauce Grande, Rio- 55 Bn 38.59 S 61.07 W
Saucillo 47 Cc 28.01 N 105.17 W
Sauda 8 Be 59.39 N 6.20 E
Saudade, Serra da- [Braz.] 55 Jd 19.20 S 45.50 W
Saudade, Serra da- [Braz.] 55 Fc 16.20 S 53.53 W
Saudarkrókur 7a Bb 65.45 N 19.39 W
Saudi Arabia (EN) = Al 'Arabiyah As-Su'ūdīyah [1] 22 Gg 25.00 N 45.00 E
Sauer [Eur.] 10 Cg 49.44 N 6.31 E
Sauer [Fr.] 12 Kf 48.55 N 8.10 E
Sauerland 10 De 51.10 N 8.00 E
Sauêruiná, Rio- 54 Gf 12.00 S 58.40 W
Sauga Jõgi 8 Kf 58.19 N 24.25 E
Saugatuck 44 Dd 42.40 N 86.12 W
Saugues 11 Jj 44.58 N 3.33 E
Sauk Centre 45 Id 45.44 N 94.57 W
Sauk Rapids 45 Id 45.34 N 94.09 W
Saül 54 Hc 3.37 N 53.12 W
Šaulder 18 Gc 42.47 N 68.24 E
Sauldre 11 Hg 47.16 N 1.30 E
Saulieu 11 Kg 47.16 N 4.14 E
Saulkrasti/Saulkrasty 7 Fh 57.17 N 24.29 E
Saulkrasty/Saulkrasti 7 Fh 57.17 N 24.29 E
Saulnois 12 If 48.52 N 6.30 E
Sault 11 Lj 44.05 N 5.25 E
Sault Sainte Marie [Mi.-U.S.] 43 Kb 46.30 N 84.21 W
Sault Sainte Marie [Ont.-Can.] 39 Ke 46.31 N 84.20 W
Saumarez Reefs 57 Gg 21.50 S 153.40 E
Saumâtre, Étang- 49 Kd 18.35 N 72.00 W
Saumlaki 26 Jh 7.57 S 131.19 E
Saumur 11 Fg 47.16 N 0.05 W
Saunders 66 Ad 57.47 S 26.27 W
Saunders Coast 66 Mf 77.45 S 150.00 W
Saurimo 31 Ji 9.38 S 20.24 E
Sauro 14 Kj 40.18 N 16.21 E
Sautar 36 Ce 11.09 S 18.25 E
Sauteurs 51p Bb 12.14 N 61.38 W
Sauveterre, Causse de- 11 Jj 44.22 N 3.17 E
Sauveterre-de-Guyenne 11 Fj 44.42 N 0.05 W
Sauvo/Sagu 8 Jd 60.21 N 22.42 E
Sauwald 14 Hb 48.28 N 13.40 E
Sava 5 Ig 44.50 N 20.28 E
Savage River 59 Jh 41.33 S 145.09 E
Savai'i Island 57 Jf 13.35 S 172.25 W
Savala 16 Ld 51.06 N 41.29 E
Savalou 34 Fd 7.56 N 1.58 E
Savanes [3] 34 Fc 10.30 N 0.30 E
Savan Island 51n Bb 12.48 N 61.12 W
Savanna 45 Ke 42.05 N 90.08 W
Savannah 38 Kf 32.02 N 80.53 W
Savannah [Ga.-U.S.] 39 Kf 32.04 N 81.05 W
Savannah [Tn.-U.S.] 44 Ch 35.14 N 88.14 W
Savannah Beach 44 Gi 32.01 N 80.51 W
Savannakhét 22 Mh 16.33 N 104.45 E
Savanna-la-Mar 47 Ie 18.13 N 78.08 W
Savanne 45 Kb 48.59 N 90.12 W
Savannes Bay 51k Bb 13.45 N 60.56 W
Savant Lake 42 If 50.15 N 90.42 W
Savant Lake 45 Ka 50.30 N 90.20 W
Savaştepe 24 Bc 39.22 N 27.40 E
Savdirí 35 Dc 14.25 N 29.05 E
Savé 31 Hh 8.02 N 2.29 E
Save [Afr.] 30 Kk 21.00 S 35.02 E
Save [Fr.] 11 Hk 43.47 N 1.17 E
Saveån 8 Dg 57.43 N 11.59 E
Säveh 23 Hb 35.01 N 50.20 E
Săveni 15 Jb 47.57 N 26.52 E
Saverdun 11 Hk 43.14 N 1.35 E
Saverne 11 Nf 48.44 N 7.22 E
Savigliano 14 Bf 44.38 N 7.40 E
Savigsivik 41 Fc 76.00 N 64.45 W
Săvineşti 15 Jc 46.51 N 26.28 E
Savinjske Alpe 14 Id 46.20 N 14.30 E
Savinski 19 Ec 62.57 N 40.13 E
Savino 14 Gf 44.19 N 12.20 E
Săvîrşin 15 Fc 46.01 N 22.14 E
Savitaipale 7 Gf 61.12 N 27.42 E
Šavnik 15 Cg 42.57 N 19.06 E
Savo 63a Dc 9.08 S 159.48 E
Savo 8 Lb 62.30 N 27.30 E
Savoie [3] 11 Mi 45.30 N 6.25 E
Savoie = Savoy (EN) 11 Mi 45.24 N 6.30 E
Savona 14 Cf 44.17 N 8.30 E
Savonlinna/Nyslott 7 Gf 61.52 N 28.53 E
Savonranta 7 Ge 62.11 N 29.12 E
Savonselkä 8 Lb 62.05 N 27.20 E
Savoonga 40 Ed 63.42 N 170.27 W
Savoy (EN) = Savoie 11 Mi 45.24 N 6.30 E
Şavşat 24 Jb 41.15 N 42.20 E
Savsjö 7 Dh 57.25 N 14.40 E
Savudrija, Rt- 14 He 45.30 N 13.31 E
Savukoski 7 Gc 67.17 N 28.10 E
Savur 24 Id 37.33 N 40.53 E
Savusavu 61 Ec 17.34 S 178.15 E
Savusavu Bay 63d Bb 16.45 S 179.15 E
Savu Sea (EN) = Sawu, Laut- 21 Oj 9.40 S 122.00 E
Savuto 14 Kk 39.02 N 16.06 E
Sawahlunto 26 Dg 0.40 S 100.47 E
Sawai Mādhopur 25 Fc 25.59 N 76.22 E
Sawākin 31 Kg 19.07 N 37.20 E
Sawākin, Jazā'ir- = Suakin Archipelago (EN) 30 Kg 19.07 N 37.20 E
Sawankhalok 25 Je 17.19 N 99.54 E
Sawara 29 Gd 35.53 N 140.29 E
Sawasaki-Hana 28 Of 37.47 N 138.12 E
Sawatch Range 45 Cg 39.10 N 106.25 W
Sawbā = Sobat (EN) 30 Kh 9.45 N 31.45 E
Sawbridgeworth 12 Cc 51.49 N 0.09 E
Sawdā', Jabal as- 33 Cd 28.40 N 15.30 E
Sawfajjin 33 Cc 31.54 N 15.07 E
Sawhāj = Sohag (EN) 31 Kf 26.33 N 31.42 E
Sawkanah 33 Cd 29.04 N 15.47 E
Sawla 34 Ed 9.17 N 2.25 W
Sawqirah 23 If 18.10 N 56.30 E
Şawqirah, Ghubbat- 23 If 18.35 N 56.45 E
Sawtooth Mountains 46 He 44.00 N 115.00 W
Sawu, Kepulauan- 26 Hi 10.30 S 121.50 E
Sawu, Laut- = Savu Sea (EN) 21 Oj 9.40 S 122.00 E
Sawu, Pulau- 21 Ok 10.30 S 121.54 E
Şawwān, Ard as- 24 Gg 31.00 N 37.00 E
Sax 13 Lf 38.32 N 0.49 W
Saxby River 59 Ic 18.25 S 140.53 E
Saxmundham 12 Db 52.13 N 1.30 E
Saxony (EN) = Sachsen 10 Jf 51.00 N 13.30 E
Say 34 Fc 13.07 N 2.21 E
Sayabec 44 Na 48.36 N 67.37 W
Saya de Malha Bank (EN) 30 Nj 11.00 S 61.00 E
Sayago 13 Fc 41.20 N 6.10 W
Sayan 54 Cf 11.08 S 77.12 W
Sayang, Pulau- 26 If 0.18 N 129.54 E
Sayaxché 49 Be 16.31 N 90.10 W
Saydā 23 Ec 33.33 N 35.22 E
Sayhūt 22 Hh 15.12 N 51.14 E
Saylorville Lake 45 Jf 41.48 N 93.46 W
Säynätsalo 8 Kb 62.08 N 25.46 E
Sayō 29 Dd 35.01 N 134.22 E
Sayram Hu 27 Dc 44.35 N 81.10 E
Sayula 48 Hh 19.52 N 103.37 W
Saywūn 35 Hb 15.56 N 48.47 E
Sazanit, Ishull i- 15 Ci 40.30 N 19.16 E
Sázava 10 Kg 49.53 N 14.24 E
Sázava 10 Kg 49.52 N 14.54 E
Sbaa 32 Gd 28.13 N 0.10 W
Sbisseb 13 Pi 35.42 N 3.51 E
Sbruč 16 Ee 48.32 N 26.25 E
Scaër 11 Cf 48.02 N 3.42 W
Scafell Pike 9 Jg 54.27 N 3.12 W
Scalea 14 Jk 39.49 N 15.47 E
Scalone, Passo dello- 14 Jk 39.38 N 15.57 E
Scammon, Laguna- 48 Bd 27.45 N 114.15 W
Scammon Bay 40 Fd 61.53 N 165.38 W
Scandinavia (EN) 5 Hc 65.00 N 16.00 E
Scanno 14 Hi 41.54 N 13.53 E
Scansano 14 Fh 42.41 N 11.20 E
Scapa Flow 9 Jc 58.54 N 3.05 W
Scapegoat Mountain 46 Ic 47.19 N 112.50 W
Ščapino 20 Ke 55.15 N 159.25 E
Ščara 16 Dc 53.27 N 24.44 E
Scaramia, Capo- 14 In 36.47 N 14.29 E
Scarba 9 He 56.11 N 5.42 W
Scarborough [Eng.-U.K.] 9 Mg 54.17 N 0.24 W
Scarborough [Trin.] 54 Fa 11.11 N 60.44 W
Scarpe 11 Jd 50.30 N 3.27 E
Ščastje 16 Ke 48.44 N 39.14 E
Sceaux 12 Ef 48.47 N 2.17 E
Ščekino 16 Jb 54.01 N 37.29 E
Ščekurja 17 Jd 64.15 N 60.52 E
Ščeljajur 19 Fb 65.21 N 53.25 E
Scenic 45 Ee 43.47 N 102.30 W
Ščerbakty 19 He 52.29 N 78.14 E
Schaalsee 10 Gc 53.35 N 10.57 E
Schaarbeek/Schaerbeek 12 Gd 50.51 N 4.23 E
Schaerbeek/Schaarbeek 12 Gd 50.51 N 4.23 E
Schaffhausen [2] 14 Cc 47.45 N 8.40 E
Schaffhausen 14 Cc 47.40 N 8.40 E
Schagen 12 Gb 52.48 N 4.48 E
Schärding 14 Hb 48.27 N 13.26 E
Scharmützelsee 10 Kd 52.15 N 14.03 E
Scharnhörn 10 Ec 53.57 N 8.25 E
Scheeßel 12 La 53.10 N 9.29 E
Schefferville 39 Md 54.47 N 64.49 W
Scheibbs 14 Jb 48.00 N 15.10 E
Schela 15 Gd 45.10 N 23.18 E
Schelde 11 Kc 51.22 N 4.15 E
Schelde (EN) = Escaut 11 Kc 51.22 N 4.15 E
Schell Creek Range 43 Ed 39.10 N 114.40 W
Schenectady 43 Mc 42.48 N 73.57 W
Scheno 35 Fd 9.35 N 39.25 E
Scherfede, Warburg- 12 Lc 51.32 N 9.02 E
Scherpenheuvel-Zichem 12 Gd 50.59 N 4.59 E
Scheveningen, 's-Gravenhage- 11 Kb 52.06 N 4.18 E
Schiedam 11 Kc 51.55 N 4.24 E
Schiermonnikoog 11 Ma 53.28 N 6.15 E
Schifferstadt 12 Ke 49.23 N 8.22 E
Schiffgraben 10 Hd 52.02 N 11.10 E
Schifflange 12 Ie 49.30 N 6.01 E
Schijndel 12 Hc 51.37 N 5.28 E
Schiltigheim 11 Nf 48.36 N 7.45 E
Schio 14 Fe 45.43 N 11.21 E
Schipbeek 12 Ib 52.15 N 6.14 E
Schladming 14 Hc 47.23 N 13.41 E
Schlei 10 Fb 54.35 N 9.50 E
Schleiden 10 Cf 50.32 N 6.28 E
Schleiz 10 Hf 50.35 N 11.49 E
Schleswig 10 Fb 54.31 N 9.33 E
Schleswig Holstein [2] 10 Gb 54.00 N 10.30 E
Schlitz 10 Ff 50.40 N 9.34 E
Schloß Holte-Stukenbrock 12 Kc 51.55 N 8.38 E
Schloß Neuhaus, Paderborn- 12 Kc 51.44 N 8.42 E
Schluchsee 10 Ei 47.49 N 8.10 E
Schlüchtern 10 Ff 50.21 N 9.31 E
Schmallenberg 12 Kc 51.09 N 8.18 E
Schmallenberg-Bödefeld-Freiheit 12 Kc 51.15 N 8.24 E
Schmallenberg-Oberkirchen 12 Kc 51.09 N 8.18 E
Schmelz 12 Ie 49.26 N 6.51 E
Schmida 14 Kb 48.20 N 16.14 E
Schneeberg 10 If 50.36 N 12.38 E
Schneeberg [Aus.] 14 Jc 47.46 N 15.52 E
Schneeberg [Ger.] 10 Hf 50.00 N 11.51 E
Schneifel 12 Id 50.16 N 6.23 E
Schoberpaß 14 Ic 47.27 N 14.40 E
Schoberspitze 14 Ic 47.17 N 14.09 E
Schœlcher 51h Ab 14.37 N 61.06 W
Schönebeck 10 Hd 52.01 N 11.45 E
Schönecken 12 Id 50.10 N 6.28 E
Schongau 10 Gi 47.49 N 10.54 E
Schöningen 10 Gd 52.08 N 10.57 E
Schoondijke 12 Fc 51.21 N 3.33 E
Schoonebeek 12 Ib 52.40 N 6.53 E
Schoonhoven 12 Gc 51.55 N 4.51 E
Schorfheide 10 Jd 52.55 N 13.35 E
Schoten 12 Gc 51.15 N 4.30 E
Schotten 12 Ld 50.30 N 9.08 E
Schouten Islands 57 Fe 3.30 S 144.30 E
Schouwen 11 Jc 51.43 N 3.50 E
Schramberg 10 Eh 48.14 N 8.23 E
Schreiber 42 Ig 48.48 N 87.15 W
Schriesheim 12 Ke 49.29 N 8.40 E
Schrobenhausen 10 Hh 48.33 N 11.16 E
Schruns 14 Dc 47.04 N 9.55 E
Schuls/Scuol 14 Ed 46.48 N 10.17 E
Schultz Lake 42 Hd 64.45 N 97.30 W
Schurz 46 Fg 38.58 N 118.46 W
Schussen 10 Fi 47.37 N 9.32 E
Schüttorf 12 Jb 52.19 N 7.14 E
Schwabach 10 Hg 49.20 N 11.02 E
Schwaben = Swabia (EN) 10 Gh 48.20 N 10.30 E
Schwäbisch-Bayerisches Alpenvorland = Swabian-Bavarian Plateau (EN) 5 Hf 48.15 N 10.30 E
Schwäbische Alb = Swabian Jura (EN) 5 Gf 48.25 N 9.30 E

Index Symbols

[1] Independent Nation
[2] State, Region
[3] District, County
[4] Municipality
[5] Colony, Dependency
Continent
Physical Region
Historical or Cultural Region
Mount, Mountain
Volcano
Hill
Mountains, Mountain Range
Hills, Escarpment
Plateau, Upland
Pass, Gap
Plain, Lowland
Delta
Salt Flat
Valley, Canyon
Crater, Cave
Karst Features
Depression
Polder
Desert, Dunes
Forest, Woods
Heath, Steppe
Oasis
Cape, Point
Coast, Beach
Cliff
Peninsula
Isthmus
Sandbank
Island
Atoll
Rock, Reef
Islands, Archipelago
Rocks, Reefs
Coral Reef
Well, Spring
Geyser
River, Stream
Waterfall Rapids
River Mouth, Estuary
Lake
Salt Lake
Intermittent Lake
Reservoir
Swamp, Pond
Canal
Glacier
Ice Shelf, Pack Ice
Ocean
Sea
Gulf, Bay
Strait, Fjord
Lagoon
Bank
Seamount
Tablemount
Ridge
Shelf
Basin
Escarpment, Sea Scarp
Fracture
Trench, Abyss
National Park, Reserve
Point of Interest
Recreation Site
Cave, Cavern
Historic Site
Ruins
Wall, Walls
Church, Abbey
Temple
Scientific Station
Airport
Port
Lighthouse
Mine
Tunnel
Dam, Bridge

Schwäbisch Gmünd 10 Fh 48.48N 9.47 E
Schwäbisch Hall 10 Fg 49.06N 9.44 E
Schwalbach (Saar) 12 Ie 49.18N 6.49 E
Schwalm 12 Lc 51.07N 9.24 E
Schwalm 10 Ff 50.45N 9.25 E
Schwalmstadt 10 Ff 50.55N 9.12 E
Schwalmtal 12 Ic 51.15N 6.15 E
Schwandorf 10 Ig 49.20N 12.07 E
Schwaner, Pegunungan- 26 Fg 0.40S 112.40 E
Schwanewede 12 Ka 53.14N 8.36 E
Schwarzach 10 Ig 49.30N 12.10 E
Schwarzbach 12 Je 49.17N 7.40 E
Schwarze Elster 10 Ie 51.49N 12.51 E
Schwarzer Mann 12 Id 50.15N 6.22 E
Schwarzrand 37 Be 26.00S 17.10 E
Schwarzwald=Black Forest (EN) 5 Gf 48.00N 8.15 E
Schwarzwalder Hochwald 12 Ie 49.39N 6.55 E
Schwatka Mountains 40 Hc 67.25N 157.00W
Schwaz 14 Fc 47.20N 11.42 E
Schwechat 14 Kb 48.08N 16.28 E
Schwechat 14 Kb 48.08N 16.28 E
Schwedt 10 Kc 53.04N 14.18 E
Schweich 12 Ie 49.49N 6.45 E
Schweinfurt 10 Gf 50.03N 10.14 E
Schweiz / Suisse / Svizra / Svizzera = Switzerland (EN) [1] 6 Gf 46.00N 8.30 E
Schweizer-Reneke 37 De 27.11S 25.18 E
Schwelm 12 Jc 51.17N 7.17 E
Schwerin 10 Hc 53.38N 11.23 E
Schweriner See 10 Hc 53.45N 11.28 E
Schwerte 12 Jc 51.27N 7.34 E
Schwetzingen 12 Ke 49.23N 8.34 E
Schwielochsee 10 Kd 52.03N 14.12 E
Schwyz [2] 14 Cc 47.10N 8.50 E
Schwyz 14 Cc 47.03N 8.40 E
Sciacca 14 Hm 37.31N 13.03 E
Scicli 14 In 36.47N 14.42 E
Ščigry 19 De 51.53N 36.55 E
Scilly, Isles of- 5 Ff 49.57N 6.15W
Scioto River 44 Ff 38.44N 83.01W
Ščirec 10 Tg 49.34N 23.54 E
Scobey 46 Mb 48.47N 105.25W
Scordia 14 Im 37.18N 14.51 E
Scoresby Land 41 Jd 71.45N 26.30W
Scoresbysund 67 Md 70.35N 21.40W
Scoresby Sund 67 Md 70.20N 23.30W
Scorff 11 Cg 47.46N 3.21W
Ščors 19 De 51.48N 31.59 E
Scotia Ridge (EN) 3 Co 57.00S 45.00W
Scotia Sea (EN) 52 Mk 57.00S 40.00W
Scotland [2] 9 Ie 56.30N 4.30W
Scotland 5 Fd 56.30N 4.30W
Scotlandville 45 Kk 30.31N 91.11W
Scotstown 44 Lc 45.31N 71.17W
Scott 42 Gf 52.27N 108.23W
Scott, Cape- [Austl.] 59 Fb 13.30S 129.50 E
Scott, Cape - [B.C.-Can.] 42 Ef 50.47N 128.25W
Scott, Mount- 46 De 42.56N 122.01W
Scott Base 66 Kf 77.51S 166.46 E
Scottburgh 37 Ef 30.19S 30.40 E
Scott Channel 46 Aa 50.45N 128.30W
Scott City 45 Fg 38.29N 100.54W
Scott Coast 66 Kf 76.30S 162.30 E
Scott Glacier [Ant.] 66 He 66.15S 100.05 E
Scott Glacier [Ant.] 66 Mg 85.45S 153.00W
Scott Inlet 42 Kb 71.05N 71.05W
Scott Island 66 Le 67.24S 179.55W
Scott Islands 46 Aa 50.48N 128.40W
Scott Peak 46 Id 44.21N 112.50W
Scott Reef 59 Eb 14.00S 121.50 E
Scottsbluff 39 Ie 41.52N 103.40W
Scottsboro 44 Dh 34.40N 86.01W
Scottsburg 44 Ef 38.41N 85.46W
Scottsdale [Austl.] 59 Jh 41.10S 147.31 E
Scottsdale [Az.-U.S.] 43 Ee 33.30N 111.56W
Scotts Head 51g Bb 15.13N 61.23W
Scottsville 44 Dg 36.45N 86.11W
Scottville 44 Dd 43.59N 86.17W
Scranton 39 Le 41.24N 75.40W
Scrivia 14 Ce 45.03N 8.54 E
Scrub Cays 49 Ia 24.07N 76.55W
Scrub Island 51b Bb 18.17N 62.57W
Ščučin 16 Dc 53.39N 24.48 E
Ščučinsk 19 He 53.00N 70.11 E
Ščučja 17 Nc 66.45N 68.20 E
Ščučje 19 Gd 55.15N 62.43 E
Scugog, Lake- 44 Hc 44.10N 78.51W
Ščugor 17 Hd 64.12N 57.32 E
Scunthorpe 9 Mh 53.36N 0.38W
Scuol / Schuls 14 Ed 46.48N 10.17 E
Scutari, Lake- (EN)= Shkodrës, Liqen i- 5 Hg 42.10N 19.20 E
Scutari, Lake- (EN)= Skadarsko Jezero 5 Hg 42.10N 19.20 E
Seaford 9 Nk 50.46N 0.06 E
Seahorse Point 42 Jd 63.47N 80.10W
Sea Islands 43 Ke 31.20N 81.20W
Seal 42 Ie 59.04N 94.47W
Seal Island 44 Nd 43.30N 66.01W
Sealpunt 30 Jl 34.06S 23.24 E
Searcy 45 Ki 35.15N 91.44W
Searles Lake 46 Gi 35.43N 117.20W
Seaside [Ca.-U.S.] 46 Eh 36.37N 121.50W
Seaside [Or.-U.S.] 46 Dc 46.01N 123.55W
Seattle 39 Ge 47.36N 122.20W
Seaward Kaikoura Range 62 Ee 42.15S 173.35 E
Seba 26 Hi 10.29S 121.50 E
Sébaco 49 Dg 12.51N 86.06W
Sebago Lake 44 Ld 43.50N 70.35W
Sebaiera 32 Ee 24.51N 13.02W
Sebaou 13 Ph 36.55N 3.51 E
Sebastian, Cape- 46 Ce 42.19N 124.26W
Sebastián Vizcaíno, Bahía- 38 Hg 28.00N 114.30W
Sebastopol 46 Dg 38.24N 122.49W
Sebatik, Pulau- 26 Gf 4.10N 117.45 E
Sebba 34 Fc 13.26N 0.32 E
Sebderat 35 Fb 15.27N 36.39 E
Sébé 36 Bc 1.02S 13.06 E
Šebekino 19 De 50.27N 37.00 E
Sébékoro 34 Dc 12.49N 8.50W
Seberi 55 Fh 27.29S 53.24W
Sebeş 15 Gd 45.58N 23.34 E
Sebeş 15 Gd 46.00N 23.34 E
Sebes-Körös 15 Dc 46.55N 20.59 E
Sebeşului, Munţii- 15 Gd 45.38N 23.27 E
Sebewaing 44 Fd 43.44N 83.27W
Sebež 19 Cd 56.19N 28.31 E
Sebha Oasis (EN)=Sabhā, Wāḥāt 30 If 27.00N 14.25 E
Şebinkarahisar 24 Hb 40.18N 38.26 E
Sebiş 15 Fc 46.22N 22.07 E
Sebou 30 Ge 34.16N 6.41W
Sebring 44 Gl 27.30N 81.26W
Sebugal 13 Ed 40.21N 7.05W
Sebuku, Pulau- 26 Gg 3.30S 116.22 E
Šebunino 20 Jg 46.24N 141.56 E
Secas, Islas- 49 Gi 7.58N 82.02W
Secchia 14 Ee 45.04N 11.00 E
Sechura 54 Be 5.33S 80.51W
Sechura, Bahía de- 54 Be 5.40S 81.00W
Sechura, Desierto de- 54 Be 6.00S 80.30W
Seckau 14 Ic 47.16N 14.47 E
Seclin 12 Fd 50.33N 3.02 E
Secondigny 11 Fh 46.37N 0.25W
Secos, Ilhéus- 32 Cf 14.58N 24.40W
Secretary Island 62 Bf 45.15S 166.55 E
Sécure, Río- 54 Fg 15.10S 64.52W
Seda 8 Kg 57.38N 25.12 E
Sêda 13 Df 38.56N 8.03W
Seda [Lat.] 8 Kg 57.32N 25.43 E
Seda [Lith.] 8 Jh 56.10N 22.00 E
Sedalia 43 Id 38.42N 93.14W
Sedan 11 Ke 49.42N 4.57 E
Sedanka 40a Eb 53.50N 166.10W
Sedano 13 Ib 42.43N 3.45W
Sedbergh 9 Kg 54.20N 2.31W
Seddenga 35 Ea 20.33N 30.18 E
Seddon 62 Fd 41.40S 174.04 E
Seddon, Kap- 41 Gc 75.20N 58.45W
Seddonville 62 Dd 41.33S 171.59 E
Seddülbahir 15 Ji 40.03N 26.10 E
Sedelnikovo 19 Hd 56.57N 75.18 E
Séderon 11 Lj 44.12N 5.32 E
Sédhiou 34 Bc 12.44N 15.33W
Sedini 14 Ci 40.51N 8.49 E
Šedok 16 Lg 44.13N 40.52 E
Sedom 24 Fg 31.04N 35.24 E
Sedona 46 Ji 34.52N 111.46W
Sedrada 14 Bn 36.08N 7.32 E
Šédro 14 Kg 43.05N 16.42 E
Sedro Woolley 46 Db 48.30N 122.14W
Šeduva 7 Fi 55.48N 23.45 E
Sée 11 Ef 48.39N 1.26W
Seeheim [Ger.] 12 Ke 49.46N 8.40 E
Seeheim [Nam.] 37 Be 26.50S 17.45 E
Seeis 37 Bd 22.29S 17.39 E
Seeland 14 Bc 47.05N 7.05 E
Seeling, Mount- 66 Og 82.28S 103.00W
Seelow 10 Kd 52.31N 14.23 E
Sées 11 Gf 48.36N 0.10 E
Seesen 10 Ge 51.54N 10.11 E
Seewarte Seamounts (EN) 30 Ee 33.00N 28.30W
Şefaatli 24 Fc 39.31N 34.46 E
Sefadu 34 Cd 8.39N 10.59W
Seferihisar 24 Bc 38.11N 26.51 E
Séféto 34 Dc 14.08N 9.51W
Sefid Dasht 24 Nf 32.09N 51.10 E
Sefrou 32 Gc 33.50N 4.50W
Sefuri-San 29 Be 33.26N 130.22 E
Segaf, Kepulauan- 26 Jg 2.10S 130.28 E
Ségalas 11 Ij 44.09N 2.30 E
Segamat 26 Df 2.30N 102.49 E
Segangane 13 Ii 35.10N 3.01W
Şegarcea 15 Ge 44.06N 23.45 E
Šegarka 20 De 57.16N 84.02 E
Segbana 34 Fc 10.56N 3.42 E
Segeg 35 Gd 7.40N 42.50 E
Segesta 14 Gm 37.55N 12.50 E
Segeža 6 Jc 63.44N 34.19 E
Seghe 63a Cc 8.25S 157.51 E
Seglinge 8 Id 60.15N 20.40 E
Segmon 8 Ee 59.17N 13.01 E
Segorbe 13 Le 39.51N 0.29W
Ségou [3] 34 Dc 14.00N 6.20W
Ségou 31 Gg 13.27N 6.15W
Segovia 13 Hd 40.57N 4.07W
Segovia [3] 13 Ic 41.10N 4.00W
Segozero, Ozero- 5 Jc 63.18N 33.45 E
Segré 11 Fg 47.41N 0.52W
Segre 13 Mc 41.40N 0.43 E
Seguam 40a Db 52.17N 172.30W
Séguédine 34 Ha 20.12N 12.59 E
Séguéla 34 Dd 7.57N 6.40W
Séguéla [3] 34 Dd 8.05N 6.32W
Seguin 43 Hf 29.34N 97.58W
Segula 40a Bb 52.01N 178.07 E
Segura 13 Lf 38.06N 0.38W
Segura, Sierra de- 13 Jf 38.00N 2.45W
Segura de la Sierra 13 Jf 38.18N 2.39W
Sehithwa 37 Cd 20.27S 22.42 E
Seia 13 Ed 40.25N 7.42W
Seibal 49 Be 16.27N 90.05W
Seiche 11 Eg 48.00N 1.46W
Seiland 7 Fa 70.25N 23.15 E
Seiling 45 Gh 36.09N 98.56W
Seille [Fr.] 11 Me 49.07N 6.11 E
Seille [Fr.] 11 Kh 46.31N 4.56 E
Sein, Ile de- 11 Bf 48.02N 4.51W
Seinäjoki 7 Fe 62.47N 22.50 E
Seine 5 Gf 49.26N 0.26 E
Seine, Baie de la-=Seine, Bay of the- (EN) 5 Ff 49.30N 0.30W
Seine, Bay of the- (EN)= Seine, Baie de la- 5 Ff 49.30N 0.30W
Seine, Val de- 11 Jf 48.30N 3.20 E
Seine-et-Marne [3] 11 If 48.30N 3.00 E
Seine-Maritime [3] 11 Ge 49.45N 1.00 E
Seine-Saint-Denis [3] 11 If 48.55N 2.30 E
Seine Seamount (EN) 5 Ei 33.45N 14.25W
Seini 15 Gb 47.45N 23.17 E
Seistan (EN)=Sīstān 21 If 30.30N 62.00 E
Seixal 13 Cf 38.38N 9.06W
Sëjaha 20 Cb 70.10N 72.30 E
Sejerø 8 Di 55.55N 11.10 E
Sejerø Bugt 8 Di 55.50N 11.15 E
Sejm 5 Je 51.27N 32.34 E
Sejmčan 20 Kd 62.52N 152.27 E
Sejny 10 Tb 54.07N 23.20 E
Sekakes 37 Df 30.04S 28.21 E
Sekenke 36 Fc 4.16S 34.10 E
Šeki 19 Eg 41.10N 47.11 E
Seki [Jap.] 29 Ed 35.28N 136.54 E
Seki [Tur.] 24 Cd 36.44N 29.33 E
Sekincau, Gunung- 26 Dh 5.05S 104.18 E
Seki-Zaki 29b Be 33.16N 131.54 E
Sekoma 37 Cd 24.36S 23.58 E
Sekondi-Takoradi 31 Gh 4.53N 1.45W
Sekota 35 Fc 12.37N 39.03 E
Šeksna 19 Dd 59.13N 38.32 E
Šelagski, Mys- 20 Mb 70.10N 170.45 E
Selah 46 Ec 46.39N 120.32W
Selajar, Pulau- 26 Hh 6.05S 120.30 E
Selajar, Selat- 26 Hh 5.42S 120.28 E
Selaön 8 Ge 59.25N 17.10 E
Selaru, Pulau- 26 Jh 8.09S 131.00 E
Selatan, Cape- (EN)= Selatan, Tanjung- 21 Nj 4.10S 113.48 E
Selatan, Tanjung-=Selatan, Cape- (EN) 21 Nj 4.10S 113.48 E
Selawik 40 Gc 66.37N 160.03W
Selawik Lake 40 Hc 66.30N 160.40W
Selb 10 If 50.10N 12.08 E
Selbjørn 8 Ae 60.00N 5.10 E
Selbjørnsfjorden 8 Ae 59.55N 5.10 E
Selbu 8 Da 63.13N 11.02 E
Selbukta 66 Bf 71.40S 12.25W
Selbusjøen 8 Da 63.15N 10.55 E
Selby [Eng.-U.K.] 9 Lh 53.48N 1.04W
Selby [S.D.-U.S.] 45 Fd 45.31N 100.02W
Selco 16 Ic 53.23N 34.05 E
Selçuk 24 Bd 37.56N 27.22 E
Seldovia 40 Ie 59.27N 151.43W
Sele 14 Ij 40.29N 14.56 E
Sele, Piana del- 14 Ij 40.30N 14.55 E
Selebi-Pikwe 31 Jk 22.13S 27.58 E
Selečka Planina 15 Eh 41.05N 21.35 E
Šelehov 20 Ff 52.10N 104.01 E
Selemdža 21 Od 51.49N 128.53 E
Selencia 24 Kf 33.04N 44.33 E
Selendi 15 Lk 38.40N 28.41 E
Selendi 15 Lk 38.45N 28.53 E
Selenduma 20 Ff 50.55N 106.10 E
Selenga (Selenge) 21 Md 52.16N 106.16 E
Selenge [Mong.] 27 Hb 49.25N 103.59 E
Selenge [Zaire] 36 Cc 1.58S 18.11 E
Selenge → Selenga 21 Md 52.16N 106.16 E
Selenginsk 20 Ff 51.59N 106.57 E
Selenica 15 Ci 40.32N 19.38 E
Selennjah 20 Jc 67.55N 145.00 E
Sélestat 11 Nf 48.16N 7.27 E
Selety 19 He 53.06N 73.00 E
Seletyteniz, Ozero- 19 He 53.15N 73.15 E
Selevac 15 De 44.30N 20.53 E
Seleznevo 8 Md 60.44N 28.37 E
Selfoss 7a Bc 63.56N 21.00W
Seli 34 Cd 8.33N 12.48W
Sélibabi 32 Ef 15.10N 12.11W
Seliger, Ozero- 19 Dd 57.20N 33.05 E
Seligman 46 Ii 35.20N 112.53W
Šelihova, Zaliv-=Shelikhov Gulf (EN) 21 Rc 60.00N 158.00 E
Selimağa 15 Lj 39.35N 28.33 E
Selimiye 24 Bd 37.24N 27.40 E
Selingenstadt 12 Kd 50.03N 8.59 E
Selinunte 14 Gm 37.35N 12.48 E
Seližarovo 7 Hh 56.51N 33.29 E
Seljatin 15 Ib 47.52N 25.14 E
Selje 8 Ab 62.03N 5.22 E
Seljord 7 Bg 59.29N 8.37 E
Selkirk [Man.-Can.] 45 Ha 50.09N 96.52W
Selkirk [Scot.-U.K.] 9 Kf 55.33N 2.50W
Selkirk Mountains 42 Ff 50.00N 117.00W
Sella 13 Ga 43.28N 5.04W
Sellasia 15 Fl 37.10N 22.25 E
Selle 12 Fd 50.19N 3.23 E
Selles-sur-Cher 11 Hg 47.16N 1.33 E
Sells 46 Jk 31.55N 111.53W
Selm 12 Jc 51.42N 7.28 E
Selma [Al.-U.S.] 43 Je 32.25N 87.01W
Selma [Ca.-U.S.] 46 Fh 36.34N 119.37W
Selmer 44 Ch 35.11N 88.36W
Selmeț Wielki, Jezioro- 10 Sc 53.50N 22.30 E
Šelon 7 Hg 58.14N 30.50 E
Selong 26 Gh 8.39S 116.32 E
Selsey 12 Bd 50.44N 0.47W
Selsey Bill 9 Mk 50.43N 0.48W
Seltz 12 Kf 48.53N 8.06 E
Selu, Pulau- 26 Jh 7.32S 130.54 E
Sélune 11 Ef 48.39N 1.26W
Selva 55 Ai 29.46S 62.03W
Selvagens, Ilhas- 30 Fe 30.05N 15.55W
Selvānā 24 Kd 37.25N 44.51 E
Selvas 52 Jf 5.00S 68.00W
Selway River 46 Hc 46.08N 115.36W
Selwyn, Détroit de- 63b Dc 16.04S 168.11 E
Selwyn Lake 42 He 60.00N 104.30W
Selwyn Mountains 38 Fc 63.10N 130.20W
Selwyn Range 57 Fg 21.35S 140.35 E
Selz 12 Ke 49.59N 8.02 E
Šemaha 16 Pi 40.39N 48.38 E
Semani 15 Ci 40.54N 19.26 E
Semara 31 Ff 26.44N 11.41W
Semarang 22 Nj 6.58S 110.25 E
Sematan 26 Ef 1.48N 109.46 E
Semau, Pulau- 26 Hi 10.13S 123.22 E
Sembakung 26 Gf 3.47N 117.30 E
Sembé 36 Bb 1.39N 14.36 E
Semberija 14 Nf 44.45N 19.10 E
Sembuan 26 Gg 0.19S 115.30 E
Semenicului, Munţii- 15 Fd 45.05N 22.05 E
Semenov 7 Kh 56.49N 44.29 E
Semenovka 16 Hc 52.11N 32.40 E
Semeru, Gunung- 21 Nj 7.58S 113.35 E
Semichi Islands 40a Db 52.42N 174.00 E
Semidi Islands 40 He 56.07N 156.44W
Semiluki 19 De 51.43N 39.02 E
Semily 10 Lf 50.36N 15.20 E
Seminoe Reservoir 46 Le 42.00N 106.50W
Seminole [Ok.-U.S.] 45 Hi 35.14N 96.14W
Seminole [Tx.-U.S.] 45 Ej 32.43N 102.39W
Seminole, Lake- 43 Ke 30.46N 84.50W
Semipalatinsk 22 Kd 50.28N 80.13 E
Semipalatinskaja Oblast [3] 19 If 48.30N 80.10 E
Semirara Islands 26 Hd 11.57N 121.27 E
Semīrom 24 Ng 31.22N 51.47 E
Semisopochnoi 40a Cb 52.00N 179.35 E
Semitau 26 Ff 0.33N 111.58 E
Semiun, Pulau- 26 Ef 4.31N 107.44 E
Semizbugy 19 He 50.12N 74.48 E
Semliki 30 Kh 1.14N 30.28 E
Semmering 14 Jc 47.38N 15.49 E
Semnām [3] 23 Hb 35.00N 53.30 E
Semnān 22 Hf 35.33N 53.24 E
Semnon 11 Eg 47.54N 1.45W
Semois 11 Ke 49.53N 4.45 E
Šemonaiha 19 Ie 50.39N 81.54 E
Semporna 26 Gf 4.28N 118.36 E
Semuda 26 Fg 2.51S 112.58 E
Semur-en-Auxois 11 Kg 47.29N 4.20 E
Senador Mourão 55 Kc 17.51S 43.22W
Senador Pompeu 54 Ke 5.35S 39.22W
Senaja 26 Ge 6.45N 117.03 E
Senaki (Miha Chakaja) 19 Eg 42.17N 42.02 E
Sena Madureira 54 Ee 9.04S 68.40W
Senanga 36 Df 16.07S 23.16 E
Senarpont 12 De 49.53N 1.43 E
Senatobia 45 Li 34.39N 89.58W
Sendai [Jap.] 28 Ki 31.49N 130.18 E
Sendai [Jap.] 22 Qf 38.15N 140.53 E
Sendai-Gawa [Jap.] 29 Bf 31.51N 130.12 E
Sendai-Gawa [Jap.] 29 Dd 35.34N 134.11 E
Sendai-Wan 28 Pe 38.10N 141.15 E
Senden 12 Jc 51.51N 7.30 E
Sendenhorst 12 Jc 51.50N 7.50 E
Senderg 24 Qi 26.52N 57.37 E
Seneca 45 Hg 39.50N 96.04W
Seneca Lake 44 Id 42.40N 76.57W
Sénégal=Senegal (EN) 30 Fg 15.48N 16.32W
Sénégal=Senegal (EN) [1] 31 Fg 14.00N 14.00W
Senegal (EN)=Sénégal [1] 31 Fg 14.00N 14.00W
Senegal (EN)=Sénégal 30 Fg 15.48N 16.32W
Sénégal Oriental [3] 34 Cc 13.30N 13.00W
Senekal 37 De 28.30S 27.32 E
Senetosa, Punta di- 11a Ab 41.33N 8.47 E
Seney 44 Eb 46.21N 85.56W
Senftenberg/Zły Komorow 10 Ke 51.31N 14.01 E
Sengata 22 Ni 0.28N 117.33 E
Sengilej 7 Lj 53.58N 48.46 E
Senguerr, Río- 56 Gg 45.32S 68.54W
Sengwa 37 Dc 17.05S 28.03 E
Senhor do Bonfim 53 Lg 10.27S 40.11W
Senica 10 Nh 48.41N 17.23 E
Senigallia 14 Hg 43.43N 13.13 E
Senirkent 24 Dc 38.07N 30.33 E
Senj 14 If 45.00N 14.54 E
Senja 5 Hb 69.20N 17.30 E
Senjsko Bilo 14 Jf 44.55N 15.03 E
Senkaku-Shotō 27 Lf 25.45N 124.00 E
Şenkaya 24 Jb 40.35N 42.21 E
Senkevičevka 10 Vf 50.29N 25.05 E
Šenkursk 19 Ec 62.08N 42.53 E
Senlin Shan 28 Kc 43.12N 130.38 E
Senlis 11 Ie 49.12N 2.35 E
Senmonorom 25 Lf 12.27N 107.12 E
Senn, Dahr Ou- 32 Ef 17.55N 11.00W
Sennestadt, Bielefeld- 12 Kc 51.57N 8.35 E
Senneterre 42 Jg 48.24N 77.14W
Senno 7 Gi 54.47N 29.41 E
Sennoj 16 Oc 52.07N 46.59 E
Senorbi 14 Dk 39.32N 9.08 E
Senqu 37 Be 28.38S 16.27 E
Sens 11 Jf 48.12N 3.17 E
Sensée 12 Fd 50.16N 3.06 E
Sensuntepeque 49 Cg 13.52N 88.38W
Senta 15 Dd 45.56N 20.05 E
Sentinel Peak 42 Ff 54.58N 122.00W
Sentinel Range 66 Pf 78.10S 85.30W
Senyavin Islands 57 Gd 6.55N 158.00 E
Şenyurt 24 Id 37.06N 40.40 E
Senzaki-Wan 29 Bd 34.25N 131.20 E
Senžarka 17 Mi 54.45N 67.50 E
Seo de Urgel/La Seu d'Urgell 13 Nb 42.21N 1.28 E
Seoni 25 Fd 22.05N 79.32 E
Seoul (EN)=Sŏul 22 Of 37.34N 127.00 E
Séoune 11 Gj 44.10N 0.41 E
Sepanjang, Pulau- 26 Gh 7.10S 115.50 E
Separation Point 62 Ed 40.47S 173.00 E
Sepetovka 19 Ce 50.12N 27.04 E
Sepik River 57 Fe 3.51S 144.34 E
Sępólno Krajeńskie 10 Nc 53.28N 17.32 E
Sępopol 10 Qb 54.15N 21.00 E
Sępopolska, Nizina- 10 Rb 54.15N 21.10 E
Septemvri 15 Hg 42.13N 24.06 E
Septentrional, Cordillera- 49 Ld 19.35N 70.45W
Septeuil 12 Df 48.54N 1.41 E
Sept-Iles 39 Md 50.12N 66.23W
Sepúlveda 13 Ic 41.18N 3.45W
Sequeros 13 Fd 40.31N 6.01W
Sequillo 13 Gc 41.45N 5.30W
Sera 29 Cd 34.36N 133.01 E
Sera, Pulau- 26 Jh 7.40S 131.05 E
Šerabad 19 Gh 37.43N 66.59 E
Šerabad 18 Ff 37.22N 67.03 E
Serafettın Dağları 24 Ic 39.05N 41.10 E
Serafimovič 16 Me 49.36N 42.47 E
Serahs 19 Gh 36.30N 61.13 E
Seraidi 14 Bn 36.55N 7.40 E
Seraing 11 Ld 50.36N 5.31 E
Seram 57 De 3.00S 129.00 E
Seram, Laut-=Ceram Sea (EN) 57 De 2.30S 128.00 E
Serang 26 Eh 6.07S 106.09 E
Serasan, Pulau- 26 Ef 2.30N 109.03 E
Serasan, Selat- 26 Ef 2.20S 109.00 E
Serbia (EN) = Srbija [2] 15 Df 44.00N 21.00 E
Serbia (EN) = Srbija 5 Ig 43.00N 21.00 E
Serbia (EN)=Srbija 15 Df 44.00N 21.00 E
Şercaia 15 Id 45.50N 25.08 E
Serchio 14 Eg 43.47N 10.16 E
Serdo 35 Gc 11.58N 41.18 E
Serdoba 16 Nc 52.34N 44.01 E
Serdobsk 19 Ee 52.29N 44.16 E
Sereba 35 Gc 13.12N 40.32 E
Serebrjansk 19 If 49.43N 83.20 E
Serebrjanski 7 Ib 68.52N 35.32 E
Sered' 10 Nh 48.17N 17.45 E
Seredka 8 Mf 58.10N 28.25 E
Şereflikoçhisar 24 Ec 38.56N 33.33 E
Serein 11 Jg 47.55N 3.31 E
Seremban 26 Df 2.43N 101.56 E
Serengeti Plain 36 Fc 2.50S 35.00 E
Serenje 36 Fe 13.14S 30.14 E
Šereševo 10 Ud 52.31N 24.19 E
Seret 16 De 48.38N 25.52 E
Serfopoúla 15 Hl 37.15N 24.36 E
Sergač 19 Ed 55.33N 45.28 E
Sergeievka 28 Lc 43.23N 133.22 E
Sergeja Kirova, Ostrova- 20 Da 77.10N 90.00 E
Sergejevka 19 Ge 53.51N 67.28 E
Sergejevka 28 Kb 44.20N 131.40 E
Sergijev Posad (Zagorsk) 6 Jd 56.18N 38.08 E
Sergino 22 Ic 62.30N 65.40 E
Sergipe [2] 54 Kf 10.30S 37.10W
Sergokala 16 Oh 42.30N 47.40 E
Sergozero, Ozero- 7 Ic 66.45N 36.50 E
Seria 26 Ff 4.37N 114.19 E
Serian 26 Ff 1.10N 110.34 E
Seriana, Val- 14 De 45.50N 9.50 E
Seribu, Kepulauan- 26 Fh 5.36S 106.33 E
Sérifontaine 12 De 49.21N 1.46 E
Sérifos 15 Hl 37.09N 24.30 E
Sérifos 15 Hl 37.10N 24.30 E
Serifou, Stenón- 15 Hl 37.15N 24.30 E
Serik 24 Dd 36.55N 31.06 E
Seringapatam Reef 59 Eb 13.40S 122.05 E
Serio 14 De 45.16N 9.45 E
Šerlovaja Gora 20 Gf 50.34N 116.18 E
Sermata, Kepulauan- 26 Ih 8.10S 128.40 E
Sermilik 41 Ie 66.00N 38.45W
Sernovodsk 7 Mj 53.54N 51.09 E
Sernur 7 Lh 56.57N 49.11 E
Sernyje Vody 7 Mj 53.53N 50.59 E
Sero 24 Kd 37.33N 44.40 E
Serock 10 Rd 52.31N 21.03 E
Serodino 55 Bk 32.37S 60.57W
Serov 22 Id 59.29N 60.31 E
Serowe 31 Jk 22.23S 26.43 E
Serpa 13 Eg 37.56N 7.36W
Serpent, Vallée du- 34 Dc 14.50N 8.00W
Serpentine Lakes 59 Fe 28.30S 129.10 E
Serpent's Mouth/Serpiente, Boca de la- 54 Fa 10.10N 61.58W
Serpiente, Boca de la-/ Serpent's Mouth 54 Fa 10.10N 61.58W
Serpnevoje 15 Lc 46.23N 28.59 E
Serpuhov 6 Je 54.55N 37.25 E
Serra, Aparados da- 55 Hi 28.45S 49.45W
Serra Bonita 55 Ib 15.13S 46.49W
Serra das Araras 55 Jb 15.30S 45.21W
Serra do Navio 53 Ke 0.59N 52.03W
Serra do Salitre 55 Id 19.06S 46.41W
Serra Dourada 55 Ka 12.50S 43.56W
Sérrai 15 Gh 41.05N 23.33 E
Serralada Litoral Catalana/ Cadena Costero Catalana= Catalan Coastal Range (EN) 5 Gg 41.35N 1.40 E
Serralada Pirinenca= Pyrenees (EN) 5 Gg 42.40N 1.00 E
Serrana Bank 47 Hf 14.23N 80.12W
Serranilla Bank 47 Ie 15.50N 79.50W
Serranópolis 55 Fd 18.16S 52.00W
Serra San Bruno 14 Kl 38.35N 16.20 E
Serrat, Cap- 32 Ib 37.14N 9.13 E
Serra Talhada 54 Ke 7.59S 38.18W
Serre 11 Je 49.41N 3.23 E
Serre, Massif de la- 11 Lg 47.10N 5.35 E
Serre-Ponçon, Réservoir de- 11 Mj 44.27N 6.16 E
Serres 11 Lj 44.26N 5.43 E
Serrezuela 56 Gd 30.38S 65.23W
Serrinha 54 Kf 11.39S 39.00W
Serriola, Bocca- 14 Gg 43.31N 12.21 E
Serro 55 Kd 18.37S 43.23W
Serrota 13 Gd 40.30N 5.04W
Serrote, Rio- 55 Ee 21.27S 54.40W

Index Symbols

[1] Independent Nation
[2] State, Region
[3] District, County
[4] Municipality
[5] Colony, Dependency
Continent
Physical Region
Historical or Cultural Region
Mount, Mountain
Volcano
Hill
Mountains, Mountain Range
Hills, Escarpment
Plateau, Upland
Pass, Gap
Plain, Lowland
Delta
Salt Flat
Valley, Canyon
Crater, Cave
Karst Features
Depression
Polder
Desert, Dunes
Forest, Woods
Heath, Steppe
Oasis
Cape, Point
Coast, Beach
Cliff
Peninsula
Isthmus
Sandbank
Island
Atoll
Rock, Reef
Islands, Archipelago
Rocks, Reefs
Coral Reef
Well, Spring
Geyser
River, Stream
Waterfall Rapids
River Mouth, Estuary
Lake
Salt Lake
Intermittent Lake
Reservoir
Swamp, Pond
Canal
Glacier
Ice Shelf, Pack Ice
Ocean
Sea
Gulf, Bay
Strait, Fjord
Lagoon
Bank
Seamount
Tablemount
Ridge
Shelf
Basin
Escarpment, Sea Scarp
Fracture
Trench, Abyss
National Park, Reserve
Point of Interest
Recreation Site
Cave, Cavern
Historic Site
Ruins
Wall, Walls
Church, Abbey
Temple
Scientific Station
Airport
Port
Lighthouse
Mine
Tunnel
Dam, Bridge

Index Symbols

[1] Independent Nation	Historical or Cultural Region	Pass, Gap
[2] State, Region	Mount, Mountain	Plain, Lowland
[3] District, County	Volcano	Delta
[4] Municipality	Hill	Salt Flat
[5] Colony, Dependency	Mountains, Mountain Range	Valley, Canyon
[6] Continent	Hills, Escarpment	Crater, Cave
[7] Physical Region	Plateau, Upland	Karst Features

Depression	Coast, Beach	Rock, Reef	Waterfall Rapids	Canal	Lagoon	Escarpment, Sea Scarp	Historic Site	Port
Polder	Cliff	Islands, Archipelago	River Mouth, Estuary	Glacier	Bank	Fracture	Ruins	Lighthouse
Desert, Dunes	Peninsula	Rocks, Reefs	Lake	Ice Shelf, Pack Ice	Seamount	Trench, Abyss	Wall, Walls	Mine
Forest, Woods	Isthmus	Coral Reef	Salt Lake	Ocean	Tablemount	National Park, Reserve	Church, Abbey	Tunnel
Heath, Steppe	Sandbank	Well, Spring	Intermittent Lake	Sea	Ridge	Point of Interest	Temple	Dam, Bridge
Oasis	Island	Geyser	Reservoir	Gulf, Bay	Shelf	Recreation Site	Scientific Station	
Cape, Point	Atoll	River, Stream	Swamp, Pond	Strait, Fjord	Basin	Cave, Cavern	Airport	

Shiping 27 Hg 23.44N 102.28 E
Shipki La 27 Ce 31.49N 78.45 E
Shippegan 42 Lg 47.45N 64.42W
Shiprock 45 Bh 36.47N 108.41W
Shipshaw, Rivière- 44 La 48.30N 71.15W
Shipu 28 Fj 29.17N 121.57 E
Shipugi Shankou 27 Ce 31.49N 78.45 E
Shiquan 27 Ie 33.05N 108.15 E
Shiquanhe 22 Jf 32.24N 79.52 E
Shiquan He 27 Ce 32.28N 79.44 E
Shiragami Dake 29 Ga 40.30N 140.12 E
Shiragami-Misaki 29 Pd 41.25N 140.12 E
Shirahama 29 De 33.40N 135.20 E
Shirakawa [Jap.] 29 Ed 35.36N 137.12 E
Shirakawa [Jap.] 29 Ec 36.17N 136.53 E
Shirakawa [Jap.] 28 Pf 37.07N 140.13 E
Shirane-San [Jap.] 27 Od 36.48N 139.22 E
Shirane-San [Jap.] 29 Fd 35.40N 138.13 E
Shirane-San [Jap.] 29 Fc 36.38N 138.32 E
Shiranuka 28 Rc 42.57N 144.05 E
Shiraoi 28 Pc 42.31N 141.16 E
Shirase Coast 66 Mf 78.30S 156.00W
Shirataka 29 Gb 38.11N 140.06 E
Shirataki 29a Cb 43.53N 143.09 E
Shīrāz 22 Hg 29.36N 52.32 E
Shirbīn 24 Dg 31.11N 31.32 E
Shire 30 Kj 17.42S 35.19 E
Shiren 28 Id 41.54N 126.34 E
Shiretoko-Dake 29a Da 44.15N 145.14 E
Shiretoko-Hantō 29a Da 44.00N 145.00 E
Shiretoko-Misaki 27 Qc 44.21N 145.20 E
Shīrgāh 24 Od 36.17N 52.54 E
Shiribetsu-Gawa 29a Bb 42.52N 140.21 E
Shiriha-Misaki 29a Db 42.56N 144.45 E
Shirikishinai 29a Bc 41.48N 141.05 E
Shīrīn 24 Qi 27.10N 56.41 E
Shīrīn sū 24 Me 35.29N 48.27 E
Shiriya-Zaki 27 Pc 41.26N 141.28 E
Shīr Kūh 21 Hf 31.37N 54.04 E
Shirley Mountains 46 Le 42.15N 106.30W
Shiroishi 28 Pe 38.00N 140.37 E
Shirone 29 Fc 37.46N 139.00 E
Shirotori 29 Ed 35.53N 136.52 E
Shirouma-Dake 29 Ec 36.45N 137.46 E
Shirshov Ridge (EN) 20 Me 57.30N 171.00 E
Shīrvān 24 Lf 33.33N 46.49 E
Shirwan Mazīn 24 Kd 37.03N 44.10 E
Shishaldin Volcano 38 Cd 54.45N 163.57W
Shishi-Jima 29 Be 32.17N 130.15 E
Shishmaref 40 Fc 66.14N 166.09W
Shishou 27 Jf 29.42N 112.23 E
Shitai (Qili) 28 Di 30.12N 117.28 E
Shitara 29 Ed 35.05N 137.34 E
Shitou Shan 27 Ma 51.02N 125.12 E
Shivwits Plateau 46 Ih 36.10N 113.40W
Shiwa 28 Pe 39.33N 141.35 E
Shiwan Dashan 27 Ig 21.45N 107.35 E
Shiwa Ngandu 36 Fe 11.12S 31.43 E
Shiwpuri 25 Fc 25.26N 77.39 E
Shixian 28 Jc 43.05N 129.46 E
Shiyan 27 Je 32.34N 110.48 E
Shiyang He 27 Hd 39.00N 103.25 E
Shizilu → Junan 28 Eg 35.10N 118.50 E
Shizugawa 29 Gb 38.40N 141.28 E
Shizui 28 Ic 43.03N 126.09 E
Shizuishan (Dawukou) 27 Id 39.03N 106.24 E
Shizukuishi 29 Gb 39.42N 140.59 E
Shizunai 28 Qc 42.20N 142.22 E
Shizunai-Gawa 29a Cb 42.20N 142.22 E
Shizuoka 22 Pf 34.58N 138.23 E
Shizuoka Ken [2] 28 Og 35.00N 138.25 E
Shkodra 6 Hg 42.05N 19.30 E
Shkodrës, Liqen i-=Scutari, Lake- (EN) 5 Hg 42.10N 19.20 E
Shkumbini 15 Ch 41.01N 19.26 E
Shoal Lake 45 Fa 50.26N 100.34W
Shoal Lake 45 Ib 49.32N 95.00W
Shoal Lakes 45 Ha 50.20N 97.40W
Shōbara 28 Lg 34.51N 133.01 E
Shodo-Shima 29 Dd 34.30N 134.15 E
Shō-Gawa 29 Ec 36.47N 137.04 E
Shokanbetsu-Dake 29a Bb 43.43N 141.31 E
Shokotsu-Gawa 29a Ca 44.23N 143.17 E
Sholāpur → Solāpur 22 Jh 17.41N 75.55 E
Shoqān 24 Qd 37.20N 56.58 E
Shoranūr 25 Ff 10.46N 76.17 E
Shoreham-by-Sea 9 Mk 50.49N 0.16W
Shortland Islands 60 Fi 6.55S 155.53 E
Shosambetsu 29a Ba 44.32N 141.46 E
Shoshone 46 He 42.56N 114.24W
Shoshone Mountains 43 Dd 39.15N 117.25W
Shoshone Peak 46 Gh 36.56N 116.16W
Shoshone River 46 Kd 44.52N 108.11W
Shoshong 37 Dd 23.02S 26.31 E
Shoshoni 46 Ke 43.14N 108.07W
Shotor Khūn 23 Jc 34.20N 64.55 E
Shouchang 28 Ej 29.23N 119.12 E
Shouguang 28 Ef 36.53N 118.44 E
Shouxian (Shouyang) 28 Dh 32.35N 116.47 E
Shouyang → Shouxian 28 Dh 32.35N 116.47 E
Shōwa 29 Gb 39.51N 140.03 E
Show Low 46 Ji 34.15N 110.02W
Shqiperia=Albania (EN) [1] 6 Hg 41.00N 20.00 E
Shreveport 39 Jf 32.30N 93.45W
Shrewsbury 9 Ki 52.43N 2.45W
Shuangcheng 27 Mb 45.21N 126.17 E
Shuangjiang 27 Gg 23.27N 99.50 E
Shuangjiang → Tongdao 27 If 26.14N 109.45 E
Shuangliao 27 Lc 43.30N 123.30 E
Shuangyang 27 Mc 43.31N 125.28 E
Shuangyashan 22 Pe 46.37N 131.10 E
Shucheng 28 Di 31.28N 116.57 E
Shufu 27 Cd 39.27N 75.52 E
Shuguri Falls 36 Gd 8.31S 37.23 E
Shu He 28 Eg 34.07N 118.30 E
Shuicheng 27 Hf 26.34N 104.52 E
Shuiding → Huocheng 27 Dc 44.03N 80.49 E
Shuiji → Laixi 28 Ff 36.52N 120.31 E
Shuijiahu → Changfeng 28 Dh 32.29N 117.10 E
Shuikou → Jianghua 27 Jg 24.58N 111.56 E
Shuiye 28 Cf 36.08N 114.06 E
Shuizhai → Xiangcheng 28 Ch 33.27N 114.53 E
Shūl 24 Ng 30.10N 51.38 E
Shulan 27 Mc 44.26N 126.55 E
Shule 27 Cd 39.25N 76.06 E
Shule He 21 Le 40.20N 92.50 E
Shulu (Xinji) 28 Cf 37.56N 115.14 E
Shumagin Islands 40 He 55.07N 159.45W
Shumarinai-Ko 29a Ca 44.20N 142.13 E
Shunayn, Sabkhat- 33 Dc 30.10N 21.00 E
Shungnak 40 Hc 66.53N 157.02W
Shunyi 28 Dd 40.09N 116.38 E
Shuolong 27 Ig 22.51N 106.55 E
Shuoxian 27 Jd 39.18N 112.25 E
Shūr [Iran] 24 Pi 26.59N 55.47 E
Shūr [Iran] 24 Oh 28.12N 52.09 E
Shūr [Iran] 24 Ne 35.09N 51.30 E
Shūr [Iran] 24 Oh 28.33N 53.12 E
Shūr Āb 24 Pg 31.45N 55.15 E
Shurāb 23 Ic 33.07N 55.18 E
Shūsf 23 Jc 31.48N 60.01 E
Shūsh 24 Mf 32.12N 48.17 E
Shushica 15 Ci 40.34N 19.34 E
Shūshtar 23 Gc 32.03N 48.51 E
Shuswap Lake 46 Fa 50.57N 119.15W
Shūt 24 Oe 34.44N 52.53 E
Shuwak 35 Fc 14.23N 35.52 E
Shuyang 27 Ke 34.01N 118.52 E
Shuzenji 29 Fd 34.58N 138.55 E
Shwebo 25 Jd 22.34N 95.42 E
Shwell 25 Jd 23.56N 96.17 E
Shyok 25 Fa 35.13N 75.53 E
Sia 26 Jh 6.49S 134.19 E
Siagne 11 Mk 43.32N 6.57 E
Siāh Band 23 Kc 33.25N 65.21 E
Siāh-Chashmeh 24 Kc 39.04N 44.23 E
Siāh-Kūh 24 Oe 34.38N 52.16 E
Siak 26 Df 1.13N 102.09 E
Sialkot [Pak.] 25 Ea 35.15N 73.17 E
Sialkot [Pak.] 22 Jf 32.30N 74.31 E
Sianów 10 Mb 54.15N 16.16 E
Siantan, Pulau- 26 Ef 3.10N 106.15 E
Siargao 26 Ie 9.53N 126.02 E
Šiaškotan, Ostrov- 21 Re 48.49N 154.06 E
Siátista 15 Ei 40.16N 21.33 E
Siau, Pulau- 26 If 2.42N 125.24 E
Šiauliai/Šjauljaj 6 Id 55.53N 23.19 E
Siavonga 36 Ef 16.32S 28.43 E
Siazan 19 Eg 41.04N 49.06 E
Sibā'i, Jabal as- 33 Fd 25.43N 34.09 E
Sibaj 19 Fe 52.42N 58.39 E
Sibari 14 Kk 39.45N 16.27 E
Sibasa 37 Ed 22.56S 30.29 E
Šibenik 14 Jg 43.44N 15.53 E
Siberimanua 26 Cg 2.09S 99.34 E
Siberut, Pulau- 21 Lj 1.20S 98.55 E
Siberut, Selat- 26 Cg 0.42S 98.35 E
Sibi 25 Dc 29.33N 67.53 E
Sibigo 26 Cf 2.51N 95.55 E
Sibillini, Monti- 14 Hh 42.55N 13.15 E
Sibircatajaha 17 Lb 69.05N 64.43 E
Sibircevo 20 Ih 44.16N 132.20 E
Sibirjakova, Ostrov- 20 Cb 72.50N 79.00 E
Sibiti 36 Bc 3.41S 13.21 E
Sibiu [2] 15 Hd 45.46N 24.12 E
Sibiu 6 If 45.48N 24.09 E
Sibolga 22 Li 1.45N 98.48 E
Sibsāgar 25 Ic 26.59N 94.38 E
Sibu 22 Ni 2.18N 111.49 E
Sibuguey Bay 26 He 7.30N 122.40 E
Sibut 31 Ih 5.44N 19.05 E
Sibutu Islands 26 Gf 4.45N 119.20 E
Sibutu Passage 26 Gf 4.56N 119.36 E
Sibuyan 26 Hd 12.25N 122.34 E
Sibuyan Sea 26 Hd 12.50N 122.40 E
Siby 34 Dc 12.22N 8.22W
Sibyllenstein 10 Ke 51.12N 14.05 E
Sicani, Monti- 14 Hm 37.40N 13.15 E
Sicasica 54 Eg 17.22S 67.45W
Si Chon 25 Jg 9.00N 99.56 E
Sichuan Pendi 21 Mf 30.01N 105.00 E
Sichuan Sheng (Ssu-ch'uan Sheng)=Szechwan (EN) [2] 27 He 30.00N 103.00 E
Sicilia [2] 14 Im 37.45N 14.15 E
Sicilia = Sicily (EN) 5 Hh 37.30N 14.00 E
Sicilia, Canale di-=Sicily, Strait of- (EN) 5 Hh 37.20N 11.20 E
Sicilia, Mar di- 14 Gn 36.30N 13.00 E
Sicily (EN) = Sicilia 5 Hh 37.30N 14.00 E
Sicily, Strait of- (EN)= Sicilia, Canale di- 5 Hh 37.20N 11.20 E
Sicily, Strait of- (EN)= Tūnis, Canal de- 5 Hh 37.20N 11.20 E
Sico Tinto, Rio- 49 Ef 15.58N 84.58W
Sicuani 53 Ig 14.15S 71.15W
Šid 15 Cd 45.08N 19.14 E
Sidamo [3] 35 Fd 5.48N 38.50 E
Siddipet 25 Fe 18.06N 78.51 E
Side 24 Dd 36.46N 31.22 E
Sidéradougou 34 Ec 10.40N 4.15W
Siderno 14 Kl 38.16N 16.18 E
Siders/Sierre 14 Bd 46.17N 7.32 E
Sīderty 19 He 52.32N 74.50 E
Šiderty 19 He 51.40N 74.50 E
Sidheros, Ákra- 15 Jn 35.19N 26.19 E
Sidhirókastron 15 Gh 41.14N 23.23 E
Sīdī 'Abd ar Raḥmān 24 Cg 30.58N 28.44 E
Sidi Aïch 13 Qh 36.37N 4.41 E
Sidi-Akacha 13 Nh 36.28N 1.18 E
Sidi Ali 13 Mh 36.06N 0.25 E
Sīdī 'Alī al Makkī, Ra's- 14 Em 37.11N 10.17 E
Sīdī Barrānī 33 Ec 31.36N 25.55 E
Sidi Bel Abbes [3] 32 Gc 34.45N 0.35W
Sidi Bel Abbes 32 Gb 35.12N 0.38W
Sidi Bennour 32 Fc 32.39N 8.26W
Sidi di Daoud 13 Ph 36.51N 3.52 E
Sidi Ifni 31 Ff 29.33N 10.10W
Sidi Kacem 32 Fc 34.13N 5.42W
Sidikalang 26 Cf 2.45N 98.19 E
Sidi Lakhdar 13 Mh 36.10N 0.27 E
Sīdī Zayd, Jabal- 14 En 36.29N 10.20 E
Sidlaw Hills 9 Ke 56.30N 3.00W
Sidmouth 9 Jk 50.41N 3.15W
Sidney [B.C.-Can.] 42 Fg 48.39N 123.24W
Sidney [Mt.-U.S.] 43 Gb 47.43N 104.09W
Sidney [Nb.-U.S.] 43 Gc 41.09N 102.59W
Sidney [Oh.-U.S.] 44 Ee 40.16N 84.10W
Sidney Lanier, Lake- 44 Fh 34.15N 83.57W
Sidobre 11 Ik 43.40N 2.30 E
Sidorovsk 20 Dc 66.35N 82.30 E
Sidra 10 Tc 53.33N 23.30 E
Sidra, Gulf of-(EN)=Surt, Khalīj- 30 Ie 31.30N 18.00 E
Sidrolândia 55 Ee 20.55S 54.58W
Siedlce [2] 10 Sd 52.10N 22.15 E
Siedlce 10 Sd 52.11N 22.16 E
Siedlecka, Wysoczyzna- 10 Sd 52.10N 22.15 E
Sieg [Ger.] 10 Df 50.45N 7.05 E
Sieg [Ger.] 12 Kd 50.55N 8.01 E
Siegburg 10 Df 50.48N 7.12 E
Siegen 10 Ef 50.52N 8.02 E
Siemiatycze 10 Sd 52.26N 22.53 E
Siĕmréab 25 Kf 13.22N 103.51 E
Siena 14 Fg 43.19N 11.21 E
Sieniawa 10 Sf 50.11N 22.36 E
Sienne 11 Ee 49.00N 1.34W
Sieradz 10 Oe 51.36N 18.45 E
Sieradz [2] 10 Oe 51.35N 18.45 E
Sieradzka, Niecka- 10 Oe 51.35N 18.50 E
Sierck-les-Bains 12 Ie 49.26N 6.21 E
Sierpc 10 Pd 52.52N 19.41 E
Sierra Blanca 45 Dk 31.11N 105.21W
Sierra Blanca Peak 43 Fe 33.23N 105.48W
Sierra Colorada 56 Gf 40.35S 67.48W
Sierra Leone [1] 31 Fh 8.30N 11.30W
Sierra Leone Basin (EN) 3 Di 5.00N 17.00W
Sierra Leone Rise (EN) 3 Di 5.30N 21.00W
Sierra Madre 21 Oh 16.20N 122.00 E
Sierra Mojada 47 Dc 27.17N 103.42W
Sierre/Siders 14 Bd 46.17N 7.32 E
Siete Palmas 55 Cg 25.13S 58.20W
Siete Puntas, Rio- 55 Df 23.34S 57.20W
Šieu 15 Hb 47.11N 24.13 E
Sīfah 34 Dd 7.59N 6.55W
Sifnos 15 Hm 37.00N 24.40 E
Sig 32 Gb 35.32N 0.11W
Sığacık Körfezi 15 Jk 38.12N 26.45 E
Sigean 11 Ik 43.02N 2.59 E
Sighetu Marmaţiei 15 Gb 47.56N 23.53 E
Sighişoara 15 Hc 46.13N 24.48 E
Sigli 26 Ce 5.23N 95.57 E
Siglufjördur 7a Ba 66.09N 18.55W
Sigmaringen 10 Fh 48.05N 9.13 E
Signal Peak 46 Hj 33.22N 114.03W
Signy Island 66 Re 60.43S 45.38W
Signy-l'Abbaye 12 Ge 49.42N 4.25 E
Signy-le-Petit 12 Ge 49.54N 4.17 E
Sigtuna 7 Dg 59.37N 17.43 E
Siguanea, Ensenada de la- 49 Fc 21.38N 83.05W
Siguatepeque 49 Df 14.32N 87.49W
Sigüenza 13 Jc 41.04N 2.38W
Siguiri 31 Gg 11.25N 9.10W
Sigulda 7 Fh 57.09N 24.53 E
Si He 28 Dg 35.11N 116.42 E
Sihong 28 Eh 33.28N 118.13 E
Sihote-Alin 21 Pe 48.00N 138.00 E
Sihou → Changdao 28 Ff 37.56N 120.42 E
Sihuas 54 Ce 8.34S 77.37W
Siikainen 8 Ic 61.52N 21.50 E
Siilinjärvi 7 Ge 63.02N 27.40 E
Siirt 23 Fb 37.56N 41.57 E
Sijunjung 26 Dg 0.42S 100.58 E
Sikaiana 63a Fc 8.22S 162.45 E
Sikakap 26 Dg 2.46S 100.13 E
Sikanni Chief 42 Fe 58.17N 121.46W
Sikar 25 Fc 27.37N 75.09 E
Sikasso 31 Gg 11.20N 5.40W
Sikasso [3] 34 Dc 10.55N 7.00W
Sikéa [Grc.] 15 Fm 36.46N 22.56 E
Sikéa [Grc.] 15 Gi 40.03N 23.58 E
Sikeston 43 Jd 36.53N 89.35W
Sikinos 15 Im 36.50N 25.05 E
Sikkim [3] 25 Hc 27.50N 88.30 E
Siklós 10 Ok 45.51N 18.18 E
Sikonge 36 Fd 5.38S 32.46 E
Šikotan, Ostrov/Tō, Shikotan- 20 Jh 43.47N 146.45 E
Siktjah 20 Hc 69.55N 125.10 E
Sil 13 Eb 42.27N 7.43W
Sila Grande 14 Kk 39.20N 16.30 E
Sila Greca 14 Kk 39.30N 16.30 E
Šilale/Šilalė 7 Fi 55.29N 22.12 E
Šilalė/Šilale 7 Fi 55.29N 22.12 E
Silao 48 Ig 20.56N 101.26W
Silaogou 28 Be 39.59N 113.03 E
Sila Piccola 14 Kk 39.05N 16.35 E
Silba 14 If 44.23N 14.42 E
Silchar 25 Id 24.49N 92.48 E
Silda 16 Ud 51.47N 59.50 E
Sildagapet 8 Ab 62.05N 5.10 E
Sile 14 Ge 45.28N 12.35 E
Şile 24 Cb 41.05N 29.35 E
Šilega 17 Ec 64.03N 44.02 E
Silesia (EN)=Śląsk 5 He 51.00N 16.45 E
Silesia (EN)=Śląsk 5 He 51.00N 16.45 E
Silet 32 He 22.39N 4.35 E
Silhouette Island 37b Ca 4.29S 55.14 E
Silifke 23 Db 36.22N 33.56 E
Siligir 20 Gc 68.27N 114.50 E
Siling Co 21 Kf 31.50N 89.00 E
Siling Jiao 27 Ke 8.20N 115.27 E
Silisili, Mauga- 65c Aa 13.35S 172.27W
Silistra [2] 15 Kf 44.07N 27.16 E
Silistra 15 Ke 44.07N 27.16 E
Silivri 24 Cb 41.04N 28.15 E
Siljan 7 Df 60.50N 14.45 E
Šilka 20 Gf 51.51N 116.02 E
Šilka 21 Od 53.22N 121.32 E
Silkeborg 7 Bh 56.10N 9.34 E
Sillamäe/Sillamjae 7 Gg 59.24N 27.43 E
Sillamjae/Sillamäe 7 Gg 59.24N 27.43 E
Sillaro 14 Ff 44.34N 11.51 E
Silleiro, Cabo- 13 Db 42.07N 8.54W
Sillé-le-Guillaume 11 Ff 48.12N 0.08W
Sillian 14 Gd 46.45N 12.25 E
Sillil 35 Gc 11.00N 43.26 E
Siloam Springs 45 Ih 36.11N 94.32W
Siloana Plains 36 Df 17.15S 23.10 E
Šilovo 19 Ee 54.24N 40.52 E
Silsbee 45 Ik 30.21N 94.11W
Siltou 35 Bb 16.52N 15.43 E
Šilutė/Šilute 19 Cd 55.21N 21.30 E
Šilute/Šilutė 19 Cd 55.21N 21.30 E
Silvan 24 Ic 38.08N 41.01 E
Silvassa 25 Ed 20.20N 73.05 E
Silver Bank (EN) 49 Mc 20.30N 69.45W
Silver Bay 43 Ib 47.17N 91.16W
Silver City 43 Fe 32.46N 108.17W
Silverdalen 8 Fg 57.32N 15.44 E
Silver Lake 46 Ee 43.06N 120.53W
Silver Spring 44 If 39.02N 77.03W
Silver Springs 46 Fg 39.25N 119.13W
Silverthrone Mountain 46 Ba 51.31N 126.06W
Silverton [Co.-U.S.] 45 Ch 37.49N 107.40W
Silverton [Tx.-U.S.] 45 Fi 34.28N 101.19W
Silves [Braz.] 54 Gd 2.54S 58.27W
Silves [Port.] 13 Dg 37.11N 8.26W
Silvi 14 Ih 42.34N 14.06 E
Silvia 54 Cc 2.37N 76.24W
Silviers River 46 Fe 43.22N 118.48W
Silvretta 14 Ed 46.50N 10.15 E
Silyānah [3] 32 Ib 36.00N 9.30 E
Silyānah 32 Ib 36.05N 9.22 E
Silyānah, Wādī- 14 Dn 36.33N 9.25 E
Sim 17 Hi 54.59N 57.41 E
Sim 17 Hi 54.32N 56.30 E
Sim, Cap- 32 Fc 31.23N 9.51W
Simanggang 26 Ff 1.15N 111.26 E
Šimanovsk 20 Hf 52.01N 127.36 E
Simao 27 Hg 22.40N 101.02 E
Simard, Lac- 44 Hb 47.38N 78.40W
Simareh 24 Mf 32.08N 48.03 E
Simav 23 Ca 40.23N 28.31 E
Simav 24 Cc 39.05N 28.59 E
Simav Dağ 15 Lj 39.04N 28.54 E
Simav Gölü 15 Lj 39.09N 28.55 E
Simayama-Jima 29 Ae 32.40N 128.38 E
Simba 36 Db 0.36N 22.55 E
Simbo 36 Fc 4.53S 29.44 E
Simbo 63a Cc 8.18S 156.34 E
Simbruini, Monti- 14 Hj 41.55N 13.15 E
Simcoe 42 Jh 42.50N 80.18W
Simcoe, Lake- 42 Jh 44.27N 79.20W
Simen 35 Fc 13.25N 38.00 E
Simenti 34 Cc 13.00N 13.25W
Simeria 15 Gd 45.51N 23.01 E
Simeto 14 Jm 37.24N 15.06 E
Simeulue, Pulau- 21 Li 2.35N 96.05 E
Simferopol 6 Jf 44.57N 34.06 E
Simhah, Jabal- 23 Hf 17.20N 54.50 E
Simi 15 Km 36.36N 27.50 E
Simi 15 Km 36.35N 27.50 E
Simiti 49 Kj 7.58N 73.58W
Simitli 15 Gh 41.53N 23.06 E
Şimleu Silvaniei 15 Fb 47.14N 22.48 E
Simmental 14 Bd 46.35N 7.25 E
Simmerath 12 Id 50.36N 6.18 E
Simmerbach 12 Je 49.48N 7.31 E
Simmern 10 Dg 49.59N 7.31 E
Simmertal 12 Je 49.48N 7.33 E
Simnas 8 Jj 54.20N 23.45 E
Simo 7 Fd 65.39N 24.55 E
Simojärvi 7 Gc 66.06N 27.03 E
Simojoki 7 Fd 65.37N 25.03 E
Simojovel de Allende 48 Mi 17.12N 92.38W
Simonstown 37 Bf 34.14S 18.26 E
Simpele 7 Gf 61.26N 29.22 E
Simpeléjärvi 8 Mc 61.30N 29.25 E
Simplon 14 Bd 46.15N 8.00 E
Simpson Desert 57 Eg 25.00S 137.00 E
Simpson Hill 59 Fe 26.30S 126.30 E
Simpson Peninsula 42 Ic 68.45N 89.10W
Simrishamn 7 Di 55.33N 14.20 E
Simsonbaai 51b Ab 18.02N 63.08W
Simušir, Ostrov- 21 Re 46.58N 152.02 E
Sina 25 Fe 17.22N 75.54 E
Sīnā'=Sinai Peninsula (EN) 30 Kf 29.30N 34.00 E
Sinabang 26 Cf 2.29N 96.23 E
Sinadaqo 35 Hd 5.22N 46.22 E
Sinai, Mount- (EN)=Mūsa, Jabal- 24 Eh 28.32N 33.59 E
Sinaia 15 Id 45.21N 25.33 E
Sinai Peninsula (EN)= Sīnā' 30 Kf 29.30N 34.00 E
Sinajana 64c Bb 13.28N 144.45W
Sinaloa [2] 47 Cc 25.00N 107.30W
Sinaloa, Llanos de- 47 Cc 25.00N 107.30W
Sinaloa, Rio- 48 Ee 25.18N 108.30W
Sinaloa de Leyva 48 Ee 25.50N 108.14W
Sinalunga 14 Fg 43.12N 11.44 E
Sinamaica 54 Da 11.05N 71.51W
Sinan 27 If 27.56N 108.11 E
Sinara 17 Kh 56.17N 62.23 E
Sināwin 33 Bc 31.02N 10.36 E
Sinazongwe 36 Ef 17.15S 27.28 E
Şincai 15 Hc 46.39N 24.23 E
Sincanli 24 Dc 38.45N 30.15 E
Sincé 49 Ji 9.14N 75.06W
Sincelejo 53 Ie 9.18N 75.24W
Sinch'am 28 Jc 42.07N 129.25 E
Sinch'ang 28 Jd 40.07N 128.28 E
Sinch'on 28 He 38.28N 125.27 E
Sinclair, Lake- 44 Fi 33.11N 83.16W
Sind [3] 25 Cc 25.30N 69.00 E
Sind 21 Ig 25.30N 69.00 E
Sindal 8 Dg 57.28N 10.13 E
Sindangbarang 26 Eh 7.27S 107.08 E
Sindara 36 Bc 1.02S 10.40 E
Sindelfingen-Böblingen 10 Fh 48.41N 9.01 E
Sindfeld 12 Kc 51.32N 8.48 E
Sindi 7 Fg 58.24N 24.42 E
Sındırgı 24 Cc 39.14N 28.10 E
Sindirgi Geçidi 15 Lj 39.10N 28.04 E
Sindominic 15 Ic 46.35N 25.47 E
Sindri 25 Hd 23.42N 86.29 E
Sinegorje 20 Kd 62.03N 150.25 E
Sinegorski 16 Le 48.00N 40.53 E
Sine-Ider 27 Gb 48.56N 99.33 E
Sinekli 15 Lh 41.14N 28.12 E
Sinelnikovo 16 Ie 48.18N 35.31 E
Sines 13 Dg 37.57N 8.52W
Sines, Cabo de- 13 Dg 37.57N 8.53W
Sine-Saloum [3] 34 Bc 14.00N 15.50W
Singako 35 Bd 9.50N 19.29 E
Singapore / Singapura 22 Mi 1.17N 103.51 E
Singapore Strait (EN)= Singapura, Selat- 26 Df 1.15N 104.00 E
Singapura / Singapore 22 Mi 1.17N 103.51 E
Singapura, Selat-= Singapore Strait (EN) 26 Df 1.15N 104.00 E
Singaraja 26 Gh 8.07S 115.06 E
Singatoka 63d Ac 18.08S 177.30 E
Sing Buri 25 Kf 14.53N 100.25 E
Singen 10 Ei 47.46N 8.50 E
Singeroz Băi 15 Hb 47.22N 24.41 E
Singida [3] 36 Fd 5.30S 34.30 E
Singida 31 Ki 4.49S 34.45 E
Singitic Gulf (EN) = Singitikós Kólpos 15 Gi 40.10N 23.55 E
Singitikós Kólpos = Singitic Gulf (EN) 15 Gi 40.10N 23.55 E
Singkaling Hkamti 25 Jc 26.00N 95.42 E
Singkang 26 Hg 4.08S 120.01 E
Singkawang 26 Ef 0.54N 109.00 E
Singkep, Pulau- 26 Dg 0.30S 104.25 E
Singkil 26 Cf 2.17N 97.49 E
Singleton [Austl.] 59 Kf 32.34S 151.10 E
Singleton [Eng.-U.K.] 12 Bd 50.55N 0.44W
Singleton, Mount- 59 De 29.28S 117.18 E
Singö 8 Hd 60.10N 18.45 E
Siniscola 14 Dj 40.34N 9.41 E
Sini vrăh 15 Ih 41.51N 25.01 E
Sinj 14 Kg 43.42N 16.38 E
Sinjah 35 Ec 13.09N 33.56 E
Sinjai 26 Hh 5.07S 120.15 E
Sinjaja 8 Mg 57.05N 28.33 E
Sinjajevina 15 Cf 43.00N 19.18 E
Sinjār 24 Id 36.19N 41.52 E
Sinjār, Jabal- 24 Id 36.23N 41.52 E
Sinjuža 16 Ge 48.03N 30.50 E
Sinkiang (EN)= Hsin-chiang-wei-wu-erh Tzu-chih-ch'ü → Xinjiang Uygur Zizhiqu [2] 27 Ec 42.00N 86.00 E
Sinkiang (EN)= Xinjiang Uygur Zizhiqu (Hsin-chiang-wei-wu-erh Tzu-chih-ch'ü) [2] 27 Ec 42.00N 86.00 E
Sin-le-Noble 12 Fd 50.22N 3.07 E
Sinmi-Do 28 He 39.33N 124.53 E
Sinn 12 Kd 50.39N 8.20 E
Sinn al Kadhdhāb 33 Fe 23.30N 32.05 E
Sinnamary 54 Hb 5.23N 53.00W
Sinni 14 Kj 40.08N 16.41 E
Sinnicolau Mare 15 Dc 46.05N 20.38 E
Sinnūris 24 Dh 29.25N 30.52 E
Sinnyŏng 28 Jf 36.02N 128.47 E
Sinoe [3] 34 Dd 5.20N 8.40W
Sinoe, Lacul- 15 Le 44.38N 28.53 E
Sinop 23 Ea 41.59N 35.09 E
Sinop Burun 24 Fa 42.02N 35.12 E
Sinp'o 28 Jd 40.02N 128.12 E
Sinsang 28 Ie 39.39N 127.25 E
Sinsheim 10 Eg 49.15N 8.53 E
Sint-Amandsberg, Gent- 12 Fc 51.04N 3.45 E
Sintana 15 Ec 46.21N 21.30 E
Sint-Andries, Brugge- 12 Fc 51.12N 3.10 E
Sintang 26 Ff 0.04N 111.30 E
Sint Eustatius 47 Le 17.30N 62.59W
Sint-Gillis-Waas 12 Gc 51.13N 4.08 E
Sint Kruis 50 Bf 12.18N 69.08W
Sint Laureins 12 Fc 51.15N 3.31 E
Sint Maarten 50 Ec 18.04N 63.04W
Sint Nicolaas 50 Bf 12.26N 69.55W
Sint Niklaas/Saint-Nicolas 11 Kc 51.10N 4.08 E
Sint-Oedenrode 12 Hc 51.34N 5.28 E
Sinton 45 Hl 28.02N 97.33W
Sint-Pieters-Leeuw 12 Gd 50.47N 4.14 E
Sintra 13 Cf 38.48N 9.23W
Sint-Truiden/Saint-Trond 11 Ld 50.49N 5.12 E
Sintu 35 Fd 8.12N 36.56 E
Sinú, Rio- 49 Ji 9.24N 75.49W
Sinŭiju 22 Oe 40.06N 124.24 E
Sinujīf 35 Hd 8.30N 48.59 E
Sinzig 12 Jd 50.33N 7.15 E
Sió 10 Oj 46.23N 18.40 E
Siocon 26 He 7.42N 122.08 E
Siófok 10 Oj 46.54N 18.03 E
Sioma 36 Df 16.40S 23.35 E

Index Symbols

[1] Independent Nation
[2] State, Region
[3] District, County
[4] Municipality
[5] Colony, Dependency
Continent
Physical Region
Historical or Cultural Region
Mount, Mountain
Volcano
Hill
Mountains, Mountain Range
Hills, Escarpment
Plateau, Upland
Pass, Gap
Plain, Lowland
Delta
Salt Flat
Valley, Canyon
Crater, Cave
Karst Features
Depression
Polder
Desert, Dunes
Forest, Woods
Heath, Steppe
Oasis
Cape, Point
Coast, Beach
Cliff
Peninsula
Isthmus
Sandbank
Island
Atoll
Rock, Reef
Islands, Archipelago
Rocks, Reefs
Coral Reef
Well, Spring
Geyser
River, Stream
Waterfall Rapids
River Mouth, Estuary
Lake
Salt Lake
Intermittent Lake
Reservoir
Swamp, Pond
Canal
Glacier
Ice Shelf, Pack Ice
Ocean
Sea
Gulf, Bay
Strait, Fjord
Lagoon
Bank
Seamount
Tablemount
Ridge
Shelf
Basin
Escarpment, Sea Scarp
Fracture
Trench, Abyss
National Park, Reserve
Point of Interest
Recreation Site
Cave, Cavern
Historic Site
Ruins
Wall, Walls
Church, Abbey
Temple
Scientific Station
Airport
Port
Lighthouse
Mine
Tunnel
Dam, Bridge

Sion/Sitten 14 Bd 46.15N 7.20 E
Siorapaluk 41 Ec 77.39N 71.00W
Sioule 11 Jh 46.22N 3.19 E
Sioux City 39 Je 42.30N 96.23W
Sioux Falls 39 Je 43.32N 96.44W
Sioux Lookout 42 If 50.06N 91.55W
Sipalay 26 He 9.45N 122.24 E
Šipan 14 Lh 42.43N 17.54 E
Siparia 50 Fg 10.08N 61.30W
Šipčenski prohod 15 Ig 42.46N 25.19 E
Siping 22 Oe 43.11N 124.24 E
Sipiwesk 42 He 55.27N 97.24W
Sipiwesk Lake 42 He 55.05N 97.35W
Siple, Mount- 66 Nf 73.15S 126.06W
Siple Coast 66 Mg 82.00S 153.00W
Siple Island 66 Nf 73.39S 125.00W
Siple Station 66 Pf 75.55S 83.55W
Sipora, Pulau- 26 Cg 2.12S 99.40 E
Sippola 8 Ld 60.44N 27.00 E
Siqueira Campos 55 Hf 23.42S 49.50W
Siquia, Río- 49 Eg 12.09N 84.13W
Siquijor 26 He 9.13N 123.31 E
Siquisique 54 Ea 10.34N 69.42W
Šira 20 Ef 54.29N 90.02 E
Sira 8 Be 58.17N 6.24 E
Sira 7 Bg 58.25N 6.38 E
Şīr Abū Nu'Ayr 24 Pj 25.13N 54.13 E
Si Racha 25 Kf 13.10N 100.57 E
Siracusa=Syracuse (EN) 6 Hh 37.04N 15.18 E
Sir Alexander, Mount - 42 Ff 53.56N 120.23W
Sirasso 34 Dd 9.16N 6.06W
Şirāţ, Jabal- 33 Hf 17.00N 43.50 E
Sirba 34 Fc 13.46N 1.40 E
Şīr Banī Yās 24 Oj 24.19N 52.37 E
Sirdalen 8 Bf 58.50N 6.40 E
Sirdalsvatn 8 Bf 58.35N 6.40 E
Sire [Eth.] 35 Fd 8.58N 37.00 E
Sire [Eth.] 35 Fd 8.16N 39.30 E
Sir Edward Pellew Group 59 Hc 15.40S 136.50 E
Siret 5 If 45.24N 28.01 E
Siret 15 Jb 47.57N 26.04 E
Sirevåg 7 Ag 58.30N 5.47 E
Sīrīk 23 Id 26.29N 57.09 E
Sirik, Tanjong- 26 Ff 2.46N 111.19 E
Sirina 15 Jm 36.21N 26.41 E
Sirino 14 Jj 40.07N 15.50 E
Sirius Seamount (EN) 40 Gf 52.00N 160.50W
Širjajevo 16 Gf 47.24N 30.13 E
Sir James Mac Brian, Mount- 42 Ed 62.08N 127.40W
Sirjān, Kavīr-e- 24 Ph 29.30N 55.30 E
Sirmione 14 Ee 45.29N 10.36 E
Şırnak 24 Jd 37.32N 42.28 E
Širokaja Pad 20 Jf 50.15N 142.11 E
Široki 20 Jd 63.04N 148.01 E
Širokoje 16 Hf 47.38N 33.14 E
Sironcha 25 Fe 18.50N 79.58 E
Siros 15 Hl 37.26N 24.55 E
Sirpsindiği 15 Jh 41.50N 26.29 E
Sirr, Nafūd as- 24 Kj 25.15N 44.45 E
Sirrayn 33 Hf 19.38N 40.36 E
Sirretta Peak 46 Fi 35.59N 118.20W
Sīrrī, Jazīreh-ye- 24 Pj 25.55N 54.32 E
Sirsa 25 Fc 29.32N 75.01 E
Sir Sandford, Mount- 46 Ga 51.40N 117.52W
Sirte Desert (EN)=As Sidrah 30 Ie 30.30N 17.30 E
Sir Thomas, Mount- 59 Fe 27.11S 129.46 E
Širvintos 7 Fi 55.03N 25.01 E
Sir Wilfrid Laurier, Mount - 42 Ff 52.48N 119.45W
Sisak 14 Ke 45.29N 16.22 E
Si Sa Ket 25 Ke 15.07N 104.19 E
Sīsakht 24 Ng 30.47N 51.33 E
Sisal 48 Ng 21.10N 90.02W
Sisante 13 Je 39.25N 2.13W
Sisargas, Islas- 13 Da 43.22N 8.50W
Šišchid-Gol 27 Ga 51.30N 97.10 E
Sishen 37 Ce 27.55S 22.59 E
Sishui 28 Dg 35.40N 117.17 E
Sisian 16 Oj 39.31N 46.03 E
Sisili 34 Ec 10.16N 1.15W
Sisimiut/Holsteinsborg 67 Nc 67.05N 53.45W
Siskiyou Mountains 46 Df 41.55N 123.15W
Sisŏphŏn 25 Kf 13.35N 102.59 E
Sissano 60 Ch 3.00S 142.03 E
Sisseton 45 Hd 45.40N 97.03W
Sissonne 12 Fe 49.34N 3.54 E
Sīstān=Seistan (EN) 21 If 30.30N 62.00 E
Sistema Central 5 Fg 40.30N 5.00W
Sistema Ibérico=Iberian Mountains (EN) 5 Fg 41.30N 2.30W
Sistemas Béticos 5 Fh 37.35N 3.30W
Sisteron 11 Lj 44.12N 5.56 E
Sisters 46 Ed 44.17N 121.33W
Sistranda 7 Be 63.43N 8.50 E
Sitāpur 25 Gc 27.34N 80.41 E
Sitasjaure 7 Dc 68.00N 17.25 E
Siteki 37 Ee 26.27S 31.57 E
Sitges 13 Nc 41.14N 1.49 E
Sithonía 15 Gi 40.05N 23.55 E
Sitia 15 Jn 35.12N 26.07 E
Sitio d'Abadia 55 Ib 14.48S 46.16W
Sitio Nuevo 49 Jh 10.46N 74.43W
Sitka 39 Fd 57.03N 135.14W
Sitkalidak 40 Ie 57.10N 153.14W
Sitna 15 Kb 47.30N 27.10 E
Sitnica 15 Dg 42.53N 20.52 E
Sitona 35 Fc 14.23N 37.22 E
Sitrah [Bhr.] 24 Ni 26.10N 50.40 E
Sitrah [Eg.] 24 Bh 28.42N 26.54 E
Sittard 11 Ld 51.00N 5.53 E
Sittee Point 49 Ce 16.48N 88.15W
Sitten/Sion 14 Bd 46.15N 7.20 E
Sittingbourne 12 Cc 51.20N 0.45 E
Sittoung 25 Je 17.10N 96.58 E
Sittwe (Akyab) 22 Lg 20.09N 92.54 E
Siuna 49 Eg 13.44N 84.46W
Siuslaw River 46 Cd 44.01N 124.08W
Siva 7 Mh 56.49N 53.55 E
Sivac 15 Cd 45.42N 19.23 E
Sivaki 20 Hf 52.38N 126.45 E
Sivas 22 Ff 39.50N 37.03 E
Sivaš, Ozero- 16 Ig 45.50N 34.40 E
Sivasli 15 Mk 38.30N 29.42 E
Šiveluč, Vulkan- 20 Le 56.33N 161.25 E
Sīvera, Ozero-/Sivera Ezers 8 Li 55.58N 27.25 E
Sivera Ezers/Sivera, Ozero- 8 Li 55.58N 27.25 E
Siverek 23 Eb 37.45N 39.19 E
Siverski 7 Hg 59.22N 30.02 E
Sivomaskinski 17 Kc 66.40N 62.31 E
Sivrice 24 Hc 38.27N 39.19 E
Sivrihisar 24 Dc 39.27N 31.34 E
Sivry-Rance 12 Gd 50.10N 4.16 E
Sivry Rance-Rance 12 Gd 50.09N 4.16 E
Sivry-sur-Meuse 12 He 49.19N 5.16 E
Sīwah 31 Jf 29.12N 25.31 E
Sīwah, Wāḩāt-=Siwa Oasis (EN) 30 Jf 29.10N 25.40 E
Siwalik Range 21 Jg 29.00N 80.00 E
Siwān 25 Gc 26.13N 84.22 E
Siwa Oasis (EN)=Sīwah, Wāḩāt- 30 Jf 29.10N 25.40 E
Sixaola, Río- 49 Fi 9.35N 82.34W
Six Cross Road 51q Bb 13.07N 59.28W
Six-Fours-la-Plage 11 Lk 43.06N 5.51 E
Sixian 28 Dh 33.29N 117.53 E
Six Men's Bay 51q Ab 13.16N 59.38W
Sixth Cataract (EN)=Sablūkah, Ash Shallāl as- 30 Kg 16.20N 32.42 E
Siyah-Chaman 24 Ld 37.35N 47.10 E
Siyang (Zhongxing) 28 Eh 33.43N 118.40 E
Siziwang Qi (Ulan Hua) 28 Ad 41.31N 111.41 E
Sjaelland=Zealand (EN) 5 Hd 55.30N 11.45 E
Sjamozero, Ozero- 7 Hf 61.55N 33.15 E
Sjare/Sääre 8 Ig 57.57N 21.53 E
Sjas 7 Hf 60.10N 32.31 E
Sjasstroj 7 Hf 60.09N 32.36 E
Šjašupe 7 Fi 55.00N 22.10 E
Šjauljaj/Šiauliai 6 Id 55.53N 23.19 E
Sjenica 15 Cf 43.16N 20.00 E
Sjnjaja 20 Hd 61.00N 126.57 E
Sjoa 8 Cc 61.41N 9.33 E
Sjöbo 8 Ei 55.38N 13.42 E
Sjøholt 7 Be 62.29N 6.50 E
Sjujutlijka 15 Ig 42.17N 25.55 E
Sjun 17 Gi 55.43N 54.17 E
Sjuøyane 41 Ob 80.43N 20.45 E
Skadarsko Jezero=Scutari, Lake- (EN) 5 Hg 42.10N 19.20 E
Skadovsk 19 Df 46.07N 32.56 E
Skælskør 8 Di 55.15N 11.19 E
Skærbæk 8 Ci 55.09N 8.46 E
Skagatá 7a Ba 66.07N 20.06W
Skagen 7 Ch 57.44N 10.36 E
Skagern 8 Ff 59.00N 14.15 E
Skagerrak 5 Gd 57.45N 9.00 E
Skaget 8 Cc 61.17N 9.12 E
Skagit River 46 Db 48.20N 122.25W
Skagway 39 Fd 59.28N 135.19W
Skaidi 7 Fa 70.26N 24.30 E
Skaland 7 Db 69.27N 17.18 E
Skälderviken 8 Eh 56.20N 12.40 E
Skålevik 8 Bf 58.04N 8.00 E
Skalisty Golec, gora- 20 Ge 56.20N 119.10 E
Skalisty Golec, gora- 20 Ie 55.55N 130.35 E
Skanderborg 7 Bh 56.02N 9.56 E
Skåne 5 Hd 56.00N 13.30 E
Skånevik 8 Ae 59.44N 5.59 E
Skänninge 8 Ff 58.24N 15.05 E
Skanör 8 Ei 55.25N 12.52 E
Skántzoura 15 Hj 39.05N 24.07 E
Skara 7 Cg 58.22N 13.25 E
Skaraborg [2] 7 Cg 58.20N 13.30 E
Skärblacka 8 Ff 58.34N 15.54 E
Skārdu 25 Fa 35.18N 75.37 E
Skärhamn 8 Dg 57.59N 11.33 E
Skarnes 8 Dd 60.15N 11.41 E
Skarsstind 8 Cb 62.03N 8.35 E
Skarsvåg 7 Fa 71.06N 25.56 E
Skarszewy 10 Ob 54.05N 18.27 E
Skarvdalsegga 8 Cb 62.09N 8.03 E
Skaryszew 10 Re 51.19N 21.15 E
Skarżysko-Kamienna 10 Qe 51.08N 20.53 E
Skasøy 8 Ca 63.20N 8.35 E
Şkăt 15 Gf 43.44N 23.51 E
Skattkärr 8 Ee 59.25N 13.41 E
Skattungbyn 8 Fc 61.12N 14.52 E
Skaudvile/Skaudvilė 7 Fi 55.27N 22.33 E
Skaudvilė/Skaudvile 7 Fi 55.27N 22.33 E
Skaulen 8 Be 59.38N 6.35 E
Skawa 10 Pf 50.02N 19.26 E
Skawina 10 Pg 49.59N 19.49 E
Skee 8 Df 58.56N 11.19 E
Skeena 38 Fd 54.09N 130.02W
Skeena Mountains 42 Ee 56.45N 128.40W
Skegness 9 Nh 53.10N 0.21 E
Skeidararsandur 7a Cc 63.54N 17.14W
Skeldon 54 Gb 5.53N 57.08W
Skeleton Coast 37 Ac 17.50S 12.45 E
Skellefteå 6 Ic 64.46N 20.57 E
Skellefteälven 5 Ic 64.42N 21.06 E
Skelleftehamn 7 Ed 64.41N 21.14 E
Skëndërbeut, Mali i- 15 Ch 41.35N 19.50 E
Skene 8 Eg 57.29N 12.38 E
Skerki Bank (EN) 32 Jb 37.45N 10.50 E
Skerries/Na Sceiri 9 Gh 53.35N 6.07W
Skerryvore 9 Fe 56.20N 7.05W
Skhíza 15 Em 36.44N 21.46 E
Skhoinoúsa 15 Im 36.50N 25.30 E
Ski 7 Cg 59.43N 10.50 E
Skíathos 15 Gj 39.10N 23.28 E
Skiathos 15 Gj 39.10N 23.29 E
Skibbereen/An Sciobairin 9 Dj 51.33N 9.15W
Skibotn 7 Eb 69.24N 20.16 E
Skidel 16 Dc 53.38N 24.17 E
Skien 6 Gd 59.12N 9.36 E
Skierniewice 10 Qe 51.58N 20.08 E
Skierniewice [2] 10 Qe 52.00N 20.10 E
Skiftet/Kihti 8 Id 60.15N 21.05 E
Skikda 31 He 36.52N 6.54 E
Skikda [3] 32 Ib 36.45N 6.50 E
Skillet Fork 45 Lg 38.08N 88.07W
Skillingaryd 8 Fg 57.26N 14.05 E
Skinári, Ákra- 15 Dl 37.56N 20.42 E
Skinnskatteberg 8 Fe 59.50N 15.41 E
Skipton 9 Kh 53.58N 2.01W
Skiptvet 8 De 59.28N 11.11 E
Skiropoúla 15 Hk 38.50N 24.21 E
Skiros 15 Hk 38.54N 24.34 E
Skiros 15 Hk 38.53N 24.32 E
Skive 7 Bh 56.34N 9.02 E
Skive Å 8 Ch 56.34N 9.04 E
Skjærhalden 8 De 59.02N 11.02 E
Skjåk 8 Cc 61.52N 8.22 E
Skjálfandafljót 7a Cb 65.59N 17.38W
Skjeberg 8 De 59.14N 11.12 E
Skjern 7 Bi 55.57N 8.30 E
Skjern Å 7 Bi 55.55N 8.24 E
Skjervøy 7 Ea 70.02N 20.59 E
Skjoldungen 41 Hf 63.20N 41.20W
Sklad 20 Hb 71.52N 123.35 E
Šklov 16 Gb 54.14N 30.18 E
Skobeleva, Pik- 18 Ie 39.51N 72.47 E
Skœrfjorden 41 Kc 77.30N 19.10W
Škofja Loka 14 Id 46.10N 14.18 E
Skog 8 Gc 61.10N 16.55 E
Skógafoss 7a Bc 63.32N 19.31W
Skoghall 8 Ee 59.19N 13.26 E
Skogshorn 8 Cd 60.53N 8.42 E
Skokie 45 Me 42.02N 87.46W
Skole 10 Th 48.58N 23.32 E
Skópelos 15 Gj 39.07N 23.44 E
Skópelos 15 Gj 39.10N 23.40 E
Skopi 15 Jn 35.11N 26.02 E
Skopin 7 Jj 53.52N 39.37 E
Skopje 6 Ig 42.00N 21.29 E
Skórcz 10 Oc 53.48N 18.32 E
Skorovatn 7 Cd 64.39N 13.07 E
Skorpa 8 Ac 61.35N 4.50 E
Skørping 8 Ch 56.50N 9.53 E
Skorpiós 15 Dk 38.42N 20.45 E
Škotovo 28 Lc 43.20N 132.21 E
Skotselv 8 Ce 59.51N 9.53 E
Skoura 32 Fc 31.04N 6.43W
Skövde 7 Cg 58.24N 13.50 E
Skovorodino 22 Od 53.59N 123.55 E
Skowhegan 44 Mc 44.46N 69.43W
Skradin 14 Jg 43.49N 15.56 E
Skreia 8 Dd 60.34N 11.04 E
Skreia 8 Dd 60.39N 10.56 E
Skrekken 8 Bd 60.13N 7.49 E
Skridulaupen 8 Bc 61.55N 7.35 E
Skrimkolla 8 Cb 62.23N 9.04 E
Skrīveri/Skriveri 8 Kh 56.37N 25.10 E
Skriveri/Skrīveri 8 Kh 56.37N 25.10 E
Skrunda 7 Eh 56.41N 22.00 E
Skrwa 10 Pd 52.33N 19.32 E
Skudenesfjorden 8 Ae 59.05N 5.20 E
Skudeneshavn 7 Ag 59.09N 5.17 E
Skuodas 7 Eh 56.17N 21.31 E
Skurup 8 Ei 55.28N 13.30 E
Skutskär 8 Gd 60.38N 17.25 E
Skvira 16 Fe 49.44N 29.42 E
Skwierzyna 10 Ld 52.35N 15.30 E
Skye, Island of- 5 Fd 57.15N 6.10W
Slagelse 7 Ci 55.24N 11.22 E
Slagnäs 7 Ed 65.36N 18.10 E
Slamet, Gunung- 21 Mj 7.14S 109.12 E
Slaná 10 Ri 47.56N 21.08 E
Slancy 19 Cd 59.08N 28.02 E
Slaney/An tSláine 9 Gi 52.21N 6.30W
Slănic 15 Id 45.15N 25.56 E
Slănic Moldova 15 Jc 46.12N 26.26 E
Slannik 15 Jf 43.06N 26.13 E
Slano 14 Lh 42.47N 17.54 E
Slaný 10 Kf 50.14N 14.06 E
Śląsk=Silesia (EN) 10 Me 51.00N 16.45 E
Śląsk=Silesia (EN) 5 He 51.00N 16.45 E
Śląska, Wyżyna- 10 Of 50.28N 18.40 E
Slate Islands 45 Mb 48.34N 86.45W
Slatina 15 He 44.26N 24.22 E
Slatina 10 Ph 48.32N 19.10 E
Slaton 45 Fj 33.26N 101.39W
Slave Coast 30 Hh 6.00N 3.30 E
Slave Lake 42 Ge 55.17N 114.46W
Slave River 38 Hc 61.18N 113.39W
Slavgorod 16 Gc 53.27N 31.01 E
Slavgorod 20 Cf 53.03N 78.48 E
Slavičin 10 Ng 49.06N 17.53 E
Slavjanka 20 Ih 42.55N 131.20 E
Slavjanka 15 Gh 41.23N 23.36 E
Slavjansk 6 Jf 48.52N 37.37 E
Slavjansk-na-Kubani 19 Df 45.15N 38.08 E
Slavkoje 10 Th 48.45N 23.31 E
Slavkoviči 8 Mg 57.37N 29.10 E
Slavonia (EN) = Slavonija 5 Hf 45.00N 18.00 E
Slavonia (EN)=Slavonija 14 Le 45.00N 18.00 E
Slavonija=Slavonia (EN) 14 Le 45.00N 18.00 E
Slavonija = Slavonia (EN) 5 Hf 45.00N 18.00 E
Slavonska Požega 14 Le 45.20N 17.41 E
Slavonski Brod 14 Me 45.09N 18.02 E
Slavsk 8 Ii 55.01N 21.37 E
Slavuta 19 Ce 50.18N 26.52 E
Sława 10 Me 51.53N 16.04 E
Sławatycze 10 Te 51.43N 23.30 E
Sławno 10 Mb 54.22N 16.40 E
Slayton 45 Id 44.01N 95.45W
Sleaford 9 Mh 53.00N 0.24W
Slea Head/Ceann Sléibhe 9 Ci 52.06N 10.27W
Sleat, Sound of- 9 Hd 57.10N 5.50W
Sleen 12 Ib 52.47N 6.49 E
Sleeper Islands 42 Je 57.25N 79.50W
Sléibhte Chill Mhantáin/Wicklow Mountains 9 Gh 53.02N 6.24W
Sleidinge, Evergem- 12 Fc 51.08N 3.41 E
Slesin 10 Od 52.23N 18.19 E
Slessor Glacier 66 Af 79.50S 28.30W
Slessor Peak 66 Qe 66.31S 64.58W
Slettefjell 8 Cc 61.13N 8.44 E
Sletterhage 8 Dh 56.06N 10.31 E
Ślęża 10 Me 51.10N 16.58 E
Ślęża 10 Mf 50.52N 16.45 E
Sliabh Bearnach/Slieve Bernagh 9 Ei 52.50N 8.35W
Sliabh Bladhma/Slieve Bloom 9 Fh 53.10N 7.35W
Sliabh Eachtai/Slieve Aughty 9 Eh 53.10N 8.30W
Sliabh Gamh/Ox or Slieve Gamph Mountains 9 Eg 54.10N 8.50W
Sliabh Mis/Slieve Mish 9 Di 52.10N 9.50W
Sliabh Speirin/Sperrin Mountains 9 Fg 54.50N 7.05W
Slidell 45 Lk 30.17N 89.47W
Slide Mountain 44 Jd 42.00N 74.23W
Slidre 8 Cc 61.10N 9.00 E
Sliedrecht 12 Gc 51.50N 4.46 E
Slieve Aughty/Sliabh Eachtai 9 Eh 53.10N 8.30W
Slieve Bernagh/Sliabh Bearnach 9 Ei 52.50N 8.35W
Slieve Bloom/Sliabh Bladhma 9 Fh 53.10N 7.35W
Slievefelim Mountains 9 Ei 52.45N 8.15W
Slieve Mish/Sliabh Mis 9 Di 52.10N 9.50W
Sligeach/Sligo [2] 9 Eg 54.10N 8.40W
Sligeach/Sligo 6 Fe 54.17N 8.28W
Sligo/Sligeach [2] 9 Eg 54.10N 8.40W
Sligo/Sligeach 6 Fe 54.17N 8.28W
Sligo Bay/Cuan Shligigh 9 Eg 54.20N 8.40W
Slinge 12 Ib 52.08N 6.31 E
Slingebeek 12 Ic 51.59N 6.18 E
Slite 8 Hg 57.43N 18.48 E
Sliven 15 Jg 42.40N 26.19 E
Sliven [2] 15 Jg 42.40N 26.19 E
Slivnica 15 Gg 42.51N 23.02 E
Sljudjanka 20 Ff 51.38N 103.40 E
Slobodka 15 Mb 47.54N 29.12 E
Slobodskoj 19 Fd 58.47N 50.12 E
Slobodzeja 16 Ff 46.43N 29.43 E
Slobozia [Rom.] 15 Ke 44.34N 27.22 E
Slobozia [Rom.] 15 Ie 44.30N 25.11 E
Slochteren 12 Ia 53.12N 6.50 E
Slocum Mountain 46 Gi 35.18N 117.13W
Slonim 19 Ce 53.05N 25.18 E
Sloten 12 Hb 52.54N 5.40 E
Slotermeer 12 Hb 52.55N 5.40 E
Slough 9 Mj 51.31N 0.36W
Slovakia (EN) = Slovenská Republika 6 Hf 48.00N 17.00 E
Slovakia (EN) = Slovensko 5 Hf 48.45N 19.30 E
Slovečna 16 Fd 51.41N 29.42 E
Slovenia (EN) = Slovenija 5 Hf 46.00N 15.00 E
Slovenia (EN) = Slovenija 14 Id 46.00N 15.00 E
Slovenia (EN) = Slovenija 14 Id 46.00N 15.00 E
Slovenija=Slovenia (EN) 14 Id 46.00N 15.00 E
Slovenija = Slovenia (EN) 14 Id 46.00N 15.00 E
Slovenija = Slovenia (EN) 5 Hf 46.00N 15.00 E
Slovenska Bistrica 14 Jd 46.24N 15.34 E
Slovenská Republika = Slovakia (EN) 6 Hf 48.00N 17.00 E
Slovenske Gorice 14 Jd 46.35N 15.55 E
Slovenské rudohorie 10 Ph 48.45N 20.00 E
Slovenský kras 10 Qh 48.35N 20.40 E
Słubice 10 Kd 52.20N 14.35 E
Sluč 16 Ec 52.08N 27.32 E
Sluč 16 Ed 51.37N 26.38 E
Sluck 19 Ce 53.02N 27.31 E
Slunj 14 Je 45.07N 15.35 E
Słupca 10 Nd 52.19N 17.52 E
Słupia 10 Mb 54.35N 16.50 E
Słupsk 10 Nb 54.28N 17.01 E
Słupsk [2] 10 Mb 54.30N 17.00 E
Slyne Head/Ceann Gólaim 9 Ch 53.24N 10.13W
Småland 7 Dh 57.20N 15.05 E
Smålandsfarvandet 8 Di 55.06N 11.20 E
Smålandsstenar 8 Eg 57.10N 13.24 E
Smalininkaj/Smalininkaj 8 Ji 55.01N 22.32 E
Smalininkaj/Smalininkai 8 Ji 55.01N 22.32 E
Smallingerland-Drachten 11 Ma 53.06N 6.05 E
Smallwood Reservoir 38 Md 54.00N 64.30W
Smederevo 15 De 44.39N 20.56 E
Smederevska Palanka 15 De 44.22N 20.58 E
Smedjebacken 7 Df 60.08N 15.25 E
Smela 19 Df 49.13N 31.53 E
Smidovič 20 Ig 48.36N 133.50 E
Šmidta, Mys- 20 Nc 68.45N 178.40W
Šmidta, Ostrov- 21 La 81.08N 90.48 E
Šmidta, Poluostrov- 20 Jf 54.15N 142.40 E
Śmigiel 10 Md 52.01N 16.32 E
Smilde 12 Ib 52.56N 6.28 E
Smiltene 7 Fh 57.28N 25.56 E
Smirnovo 17 Ni 54.31N 69.28 E
Smirnyh 20 Jg 49.45N 142.53 E
Smith 55 Bl 35.30S 61.36W
Smith Arm 42 Fc 66.15N 124.00W
Smith Bay [Ak.-U.S.] 40 Ib 70.51N 154.25W
Smith Bay [Can.] 42 Ja 77.15N 79.00W
Smith Center 45 Gg 39.47N 98.47W
Smithers 42 Ef 54.47N 127.10W
Smithfield [S.Afr.] 37 Df 30.09S 26.30 E
Smithfield [Ut.-U.S.] 46 Jf 41.50N 111.50W
Smith Knoll 9 Pi 52.50N 2.10 E
Smith Mountain Lake 44 Hg 37.10N 79.40W
Smith Peak 46 Gb 48.50N 116.39W
Smith River 46 Jc 47.25N 111.29W
Smiths Falls 42 Jh 44.54N 76.01W
Smith Sound 46 Ba 51.18N 127.48W
Smithton 58 Fi 40.51S 145.07 E
Smjadovo 15 Kf 43.04N 27.01 E
Smjörfjoll 7a Cb 65.35N 14.46W
Smögen 8 Df 58.21N 11.13 E
Smoke Creek Desert 46 Ff 40.30N 119.40W
Smokey Dome 46 He 43.29N 114.56W
Smoky Bay 59 Gf 32.20S 133.45 E
Smoky Cape 59 Kf 30.56S 153.05 E
Smoky Falls 42 Jf 50.03N 82.10W
Smoky Hill 38 Jf 39.03N 96.48W
Smoky Hills 45 Gg 39.15N 99.00W
Smoky River 42 Fe 56.11N 117.19W
Smøla 7 Be 63.25N 8.00 E
Smolensk 6 Je 54.47N 32.03 E
Smolenskaja Oblast [3] 19 De 55.00N 33.00 E
Smolenskaja Vozvyšennost =Smolensk Upland (EN) 5 Je 54.40N 33.00 E
Smolensk Upland (EN)=Smolenskaja Vozvyšennost 5 Je 54.40N 33.00 E
Smoleviči 16 Fb 54.03N 28.02 E
Smolianica 10 Ud 52.40N 24.40 E
Smólikas Óros 5 Ig 40.06N 20.55 E
Smoljan 15 Hh 41.35N 24.41 E
Smoljan [2] 15 Hh 41.40N 24.40 E
Smooth Rock Falls 44 Ga 49.20N 81.39W
Smorgon 19 Ce 54.31N 26.23 E
Smørstabbren 8 Cc 61.32N 8.06 E
Smrdeš 15 Fh 41.34N 22.28 E
Smygehamn 8 Ei 55.21N 13.22 E
Smygehuk 8 Ei 55.21N 13.23 E
Smyley, Cape- 66 Qf 72.00S 78.50W
Smyrna 44 Ei 33.53N 84.31W
Smyrna (EN)=İzmir 22 Ef 38.25N 27.09 E
Smyšljajevka 7 Mj 53.17N 50.24 E
Smythe, Mount- 38 Gd 57.50N 124.59W
Snacke Point 51b Bb 18.17N 62.58W
Snæfell 7a Cb 64.48N 15.34W
Snaefell 9 Ig 54.16N 4.27W
Snæfellsjökull 7a Ab 64.49N 23.46W
Snag 42 Dd 62.23N 140.22W
Snake Bay Settlement 59 Gb 11.25S 130.40 E
Snake Range 46 Hg 39.00N 114.15W
Snake River [Can.] 42 Ec 65.57N 134.13W
Snake River [U.S.] 38 He 46.12N 119.02W
Snake River Plain 43 Ec 42.45N 114.30W
Snare 42 Fd 63.15N 116.08W
Snares Islands 61 Ci 48.00S 166.35 E
Snarumselva 8 Cc 59.57N 9.58 E
Snåsa 7 Cd 64.15N 12.22 E
Sneek 11 La 53.02N 5.40 E
Snekermeer 11 La 52.59N 5.40 E
Snežnaja, Gora- 20 Lc 65.18N 165.30 E
Snežnik 14 Ie 45.26N 14.36 E
Snežnogorsk 20 Dc 68.15N 87.35 E
Šnežnoje 16 Kf 47.59N 38.50 E
Śniardwy, Jezioro- 10 Rc 53.46N 21.44 E
Śnieżka 5 He 50.45N 15.43 E
Śnieżnik 10 Mf 50.12N 16.50 E
Snigirevka 16 Hf 47.04N 32.45 E
Snillfjord 8 Ca 63.24N 9.30 E
Snina 10 Sh 48.59N 22.08 E
Snizort, Loch- 9 Gd 57.30N 6.25W
Snjatyn 16 De 48.29N 25.34 E
Snøhetta 5 Gc 62.20N 9.17 E
Snohomish 46 Dc 47.55N 122.06W
Snønuten 8 Be 59.31N 6.54 E
Snøonipa 8 Bc 61.42N 6.41 E
Snota 8 Cb 62.51N 9.06 E
Snov 16 Gd 51.32N 31.33 E
Snowbird Lake 42 Hd 60.40N 102.50W
Snowdon 5 Fe 53.04N 4.05W
Snowdonia 9 Jh 53.05N 3.55W
Snowdrift 42 Gd 62.23N 110.47W
Snowflake 46 Ji 34.30N 110.05W
Snow Hill 44 Jf 38.11N 75.24W
Snow Lake 42 Hf 54.53N 100.02W
Snow Mountain 43 Cd 39.23N 122.46W
Snowshoe Peak 46 Hb 48.13N 115.41W
Snowville 46 If 41.58N 112.43W
Snowy Mountain [B.C.-Can.] 46 Fb 49.02N 119.57W
Snowy Mountain [N.Y.-U.S.] 44 Jd 43.42N 74.23W
Snowy Mountains 59 Jg 36.30S 148.20 E
Snowy River 59 Jg 37.48S 148.32 E
Snudy, Ozero- 8 Li 55.40N 27.15 E
Snug Corner 49 Kb 22.32N 73.53W
Snuŏl 25 Lf 12.04N 106.26 E
Snyder 43 Ge 32.44N 100.55W
Soalala 37 Hc 16.07S 45.21 E
Soalara 37 Gd 23.35S 43.44 E
Soanierana-Ivongo 37 Hc 16.54S 49.34 E
Soar 12 Ab 52.52N 1.17W
Şoarş 15 Hd 45.56N 24.55 E
Soavinandriana 37 Hc 19.10S 46.43 E
Sob 17 Mc 66.20N 66.02 E

Index Symbols

[1] Independent Nation
[2] State, Region
[3] District, County
[4] Municipality
[5] Colony, Dependency
Continent
Physical Region
Historical or Cultural Region
Mount, Mountain
Volcano
Hill
Mountains, Mountain Range
Hills, Escarpment
Plateau, Upland
Pass, Gap
Plain, Lowland
Delta
Salt Flat
Valley, Canyon
Crater, Cave
Karst Features
Depression
Polder
Desert, Dunes
Forest, Woods
Heath, Steppe
Oasis
Cape, Point
Coast, Beach
Cliff
Peninsula
Isthmus
Sandbank
Island
Atoll
Rock, Reef
Islands, Archipelago
Rocks, Reefs
Coral Reef
Well, Spring
Geyser
River, Stream
Waterfall Rapids
River Mouth, Estuary
Lake
Salt Lake
Intermittent Lake
Reservoir
Swamp, Pond
Canal
Glacier
Ice Shelf, Pack Ice
Ocean
Sea
Gulf, Bay
Strait, Fjord
Lagoon
Bank
Seamount
Tablemount
Ridge
Shelf
Basin
Escarpment, Sea Scarp
Fracture
Trench, Abyss
National Park, Reserve
Point of Interest
Recreation Site
Cave, Cavern
Historic Site
Ruins
Wall, Walls
Church, Abbey
Temple
Scientific Station
Airport
Port
Lighthouse
Mine
Tunnel
Dam, Bridge

Sob	16	Fe	48.41N	29.17 E
Soba	34	Gc	10.59N	8.04 E
Sobaek-Sanmaek	28	Jf	36.00N	128.00 E
Sobat (EN)=Sawbā	30	Kh	9.45N	31.45 E
Sobernheim	12	Je	49.48N	7.39 E
Soběslav	10	Kg	49.16N	14.44 E
Sōbetsu	29a	Bb	42.33N	140.51 E
Sobinka	7	Jh	56.01N	40.07 E
Sobolevo	16	Qd	51.59N	51.48 E
Sobolevo	20	Kf	54.17N	156.00 E
Sobolew	10	Re	51.41N	21.40 E
Sobo-San	29	Be	32.47N	131.21 E
Sobradinho	55	Fi	29.24S	53.03W
Sobral	53	Lf	3.42S	40.21W
Sobrarbe	13	Mb	42.20N	0.05 E
Soca	55	El	34.41S	55.41W
Soča=Isonzo (EN)	14	He	45.43N	13.33 E
Sochaczew	10	Qd	52.14N	20.14 E
Soči	6	Jg	43.35N	39.45 E
Société, Iles de la-=Society Islands (EN)	57	Lf	17.00S	150.00W
Society Islands (EN)=Société, Iles de la-	57	Lf	17.00S	150.00W
Socompa, Paso-	52	Jh	24.27S	68.18W
Socorro [Col.]	54	Db	6.27N	73.16W
Socorro [N.M.-U.S.]	43	Fe	34.04N	106.54W
Socotra (EN) = Suquṭrá	21	Hh	12.30N	54.00 E
Soc Trang	25	Lg	9.36N	105.58 E
Socuéllamos	13	Je	39.17N	2.48W
Soda Lake	46	Gi	35.08N	116.04W
Sodankylä	7	Gc	67.25N	26.36 E
Soda Springs	46	Je	42.39N	111.36W
Söderåsen	8	Eh	56.04N	13.05 E
Söderfors	7	Df	60.23N	17.14 E
Söderhamn	7	Df	61.18N	17.03 E
Söderköping	8	Gf	58.29N	16.18 E
Södermanland	8	Ge	59.10N	16.50 E
Södermanland [2]	7	Dg	59.15N	16.40 E
Söderslätt	8	Ei	55.30N	13.15 E
Södertälje	7	Dg	59.12N	17.37 E
Södertörn	8	Ge	59.05N	18.00 E
Sodo	35	Fd	6.51N	37.45 E
Södra Dellen	8	Gc	61.50N	16.45 E
Södra Gloppet	8	Ia	63.05N	21.00 E
Södra Kvarken	8	Hd	60.20N	19.08 E
Södra-Midsjöbanken	8	Gi	55.40N	17.20 E
Södra Vi	8	Fg	57.45N	15.48 E
Soe	26	Hh	9.52S	124.17 E
Soekmekaar	37	Dd	23.28S	29.58 E
Soela, proliv-/Soela Väin	8	Jf	58.40N	22.30 E
Soela Väin/Soela, proliv-	8	Jf	58.40N	22.30 E
Soest [Ger.]	10	Ee	51.35N	8.07 E
Soest [Neth.]	12	Hb	52.10N	5.20 E
Soeste	12	Ja	53.10N	7.44 E
Soester Borde	12	Kc	51.38N	8.03 E
Soestwetering	12	Ib	51.30N	6.09 E
Sofádhes	15	Fj	39.20N	22.06 E
Sofala [3]	37	Ec	19.30S	34.40 E
Sofala, Baia de-	30	Kk	20.11S	34.45 E
Sofia	37	Hc	15.27S	47.23 E
Sofia [Bul.] [2]	15	Gg	42.43N	23.25 E
Sofia [Grc.] [2]	15	Gg	42.41N	23.19 E
Sofia (EN)=Sofija	6	Ig	42.41N	23.19 E
Sofija=Sofia (EN)	6	Ig	42.41N	23.19 E
Sofijsk	20	If	52.20N	134.01 E
Sofporog	19	Db	65.48N	31.28 E
Sofrána, Nisídhes-	15	Jm	36.04N	26.24 E
Sōfu-Gan	27	Pf	29.50N	140.20 E
Sogamoso	54	Db	5.43N	72.56W
Soganlı	24	Eb	41.11N	32.38 E
Sogara, Lake-	36	Fd	5.15S	31.00 E
Sogda	20	If	50.24N	132.18 E
Sögel	10	Dd	52.51N	7.31 E
Sogeri	60	Di	9.10S	147.32 E
Sogn	8	Ac	61.05N	5.55 E
Sogndalsfjøra	8	Bc	61.14N	7.06 E
Søgne	8	Bf	58.05N	7.49 E
Sognefjell	8	Bc	61.35N	7.55 E
Sognefjorden	5	Gc	61.05N	5.10 E
Sognesjøen	8	Ac	61.05N	5.00 E
Sogn og Fjordane [2]	7	Bf	61.30N	6.50 E
Sogod	26	Hd	10.23N	124.59 E
Sogo Nur	27	Hc	42.20N	101.20 E
Sogoža	7	Jg	58.30N	39.06 E
Söğüt	15	Nj	40.00N	30.11 E
Söğütalan	15	Li	40.03N	28.34 E
Söğüt Gölü	24	Cd	37.03N	29.53 E
Sog Xian	27	Fe	31.51N	93.42 E
Soh	18	He	39.57N	71.08 E
Sohag (EN)=Sawhāj	31	Kf	26.33N	31.42 E
Sohano	60	Ei	5.29S	154.41 E
Sohŭksan-Do	28	Hg	34.04N	125.07 E
Soignies/Zinnik	11	Kd	50.35N	4.04 E
Soini	8	Kb	62.52N	24.13 E
Soisalo	8	Mb	62.40N	28.10 E
Soissonnais, Plateau du-	11	Je	49.15N	3.10 E
Soissons	11	Je	49.22N	3.20 E
Sōja	29	Cd	34.40N	133.44 E
Sojana	7	Kd	65.53N	43.30 E
Sojma	17	Ec	67.00N	51.00 E
Šojna	17	Bc	67.52N	44.08 E
Sŏjosŏn-man=Korea Bay (EN)	21	Of	39.15N	125.00 E
Sojuznoje	16	Vd	50.50N	60.10 E
Sok	19	Fe	53.25N	50.10 E
Sokal	16	Dd	50.29N	24.17 E
Šokalskogo, Proliv-	20	Ea	79.00N	100.00 E
Sokch'o	27	Md	38.12N	128.36 E
Söke	23	Cb	37.45N	27.24 E
Sokele	36	Dd	9.55S	24.36 E
Sokirjany	16	Ee	48.28N	27.25 E
Sokna	7	Bf	60.14N	9.54 E
Soko Banja	15	Ef	43.39N	21.53 E
Sokodé	31	Hh	8.59N	1.08 E
Sokol	19	Ed	59.29N	40.13 E
Sokol	15	Ce	44.18N	19.25 E
Sokółka	10	Tc	53.25N	23.31 E
Sokolo	34	Dc	14.44N	6.07W
Sokolov	10	If	50.11N	12.38 E
Sokołów Podlaski	10	Sd	52.25N	22.15 E
Sokone	34	Bc	13.53N	16.22W
Sokosti	7	Gb	68.20N	28.01 E
Sokoto	30	Hg	11.24N	4.07 E
Sokoto [2]	34	Gc	12.20N	5.20 E
Sokoto	31	Hg	13.04N	5.15 E
Sokourala	34	Dd	9.13N	8.05W
Sōl	35	Hd	9.20N	49.25 E
Sōl	35	Hd	9.40N	48.30 E
Sol, Costa del-	13	Ih	36.46N	3.55W
Sol, Pico do-	55	Ke	20.07S	43.28W
Soła	10	Pf	50.04N	19.13 E
Sola	63b	Ca	13.53S	167.33 E
Solai	36	Gb	0.02N	36.09 E
Solakrossen	8	Af	58.53N	5.36 E
Solander Island	61	Ci	46.35S	166.50 E
Solanet	55	Cm	36.51S	58.31W
Solāpur	22	Jh	17.41N	75.55 E
Solbad Hall in Tirol	14	Fc	47.17N	11.31 E
Solcy	19	Dd	58.09N	30.20 E
Sölden	14	Ed	46.58N	11.00 E
Soldier Point	51d	Bb	17.02N	61.41W
Soldotna	40	Id	60.29N	151.04W
Solec Kujawski	10	Oc	53.06N	18.14 E
Soledad [Arg.]	55	Bj	30.37S	60.55W
Soledad [Ca.-U.S.]	46	Eh	36.26N	121.19W
Soledad [Col.]	54	Da	10.55N	74.46W
Soledad [Ven.]	54	Fb	8.10N	63.34W
Soledad, Boca de-	48	Ce	25.17N	112.09W
Soledad, Isla-/East Falkland	52	Kk	51.45S	58.50W
Soledade	56	Jc	28.50S	52.30W
Sølen	8	Dc	61.55N	11.30 E
Sølensjøen	8	Dc	61.55N	11.35 E
Solentiname, Archipiélago de-	49	Fh	11.10N	85.00W
Solenzara	11a	Bb	41.51N	9.24 E
Solesmes	12	Fd	50.11N	3.30 E
Solferino	14	Ee	45.23N	10.34 E
Solgen	8	Fg	57.33N	15.07 E
Solgne	12	Ie	48.58N	6.18 E
Soligalič	7	Kg	59.07N	42.13 E
Soligorsk	19	Ce	52.49N	27.31 E
Solihull	9	Li	52.25N	1.45W
Solikamsk	19	Fd	59.39N	56.47 E
Sol-Ileck	6	Le	51.12N	55.03 E
Solimán, Punta-	48	Ph	19.50N	87.27W
Solimoes → Amazonas, Rio-=Amazon (EN)	52	Lf	0.10S	49.00W
Solingen	10	De	51.11N	7.05 E
Solińskie, Jezioro-	10	Sg	49.22N	22.30 E
Solis, Presa-	48	Ig	20.05N	100.36W
Sollebrunn	8	Ef	58.07N	12.32 E
Sollefteå	7	De	63.10N	17.16 E
Sollentuna	8	Ge	59.28N	17.54 E
Sóller	13	Oe	39.46N	2.42 E
Sollerön	8	Fd	60.55N	14.37 E
Solling	10	Fe	51.45N	9.35 E
Solms	12	Kd	50.46N	9.36 E
Solna	8	He	59.22N	18.01 E
Solnečnogorsk	7	Ih	56.10N	37.00 E
Solnečny	20	Id	60.10N	137.35 E
Sologne	11	Hg	47.50N	2.00 E
Sologne Bourbonnaise	11	Jh	46.40N	3.30 E
Solok	26	Dg	0.48S	100.39 E
Sololá [3]	49	Bf	14.40N	91.15W
Sololá	49	Bf	14.46N	91.11W
Solomon Islands [1]	58	Ge	8.00S	159.00 E
Solomon Islands	57	Ge	8.00S	159.00 E
Solomon Islands (British Solomon Islands) [1]	58	Ge	8.00S	159.00 E
Solomon River	43	Hd	38.54N	97.22W
Solomon Sea	57	Ge	8.00S	155.00 E
Solon Springs	45	Kc	46.22N	91.48W
Solør	8	Dd	60.30N	11.55 E
Solor, Kepulauan-	26	Hh	8.25S	123.30 E
Solothurn	14	Bc	47.15N	7.30 E
Solothurn [2]	14	Bc	47.20N	7.40 E
Solotvin	10	Uh	48.38N	24.31 E
Soloveckije Ostrova	7	Id	65.05N	35.45 E
Solovjevka	8	Nd	60.44N	30.20 E
Solovjevsk	20	Hf	54.15N	124.30 E
Solovjevsk	20	Gg	49.54N	115.43 E
Sölöz	15	Mi	40.23N	29.25 E
Solre-le-Château	12	Gd	50.10N	4.05 E
Solsona	13	Nc	41.59N	1.31 E
Solt	10	Oj	46.48N	19.00 E
Solta	14	Kg	43.23N	16.17 E
Soltānābād [Iran]	24	Mg	31.03N	49.42 E
Soltānābād [Iran]	24	Rd	36.23N	58.02 E
Solţānī, Khowr-e-	24	Nh	29.00N	50.50 E
Soltāniyeh	24	Md	36.26N	48.48 E
Soltau	10	Fd	52.59N	9.50 E
Soltvadkert	10	Pj	46.35N	19.23 E
Solvang	46	Ei	34.36N	120.08W
Sölvesborg	7	Dh	56.03N	14.33 E
Solvyčegodsk	7	Lf	61.21N	46.52 E
Solway Firth	9	Jg	54.50N	3.35W
Solwezi	31	Jj	12.11S	26.24 E
Sōma	28	Pf	37.48N	140.57 E
Soma	24	Bc	39.10N	27.36 E
Somain	12	Fd	50.22N	3.17 E
Somalia (EN)=Soomaaliya [1]	31	Lh	10.00N	49.00 E
Somali Basin (EN)	3	Fi	0.00	52.00 E
Sombo	36	Dd	8.42S	20.57 E
Sombor	15	Cd	45.46N	19.07 E
Sombrerete	47	Dd	23.38N	103.39W
Sombrero	47	Le	18.36N	63.26W
Sombrero Channel	25	Ig	7.41N	93.35 E
Sombrio	55	Hi	29.07S	49.40W
Sombrio, Lagoa do-	55	Hi	29.12S	49.42W
Somcuţa Mare	15	Gb	47.31N	23.28 E
Someren	12	Hc	51.23N	5.43 E
Somero	8	Jd	60.37N	23.32 E
Somerset	38	Jb	73.30N	93.30W
Somerset [3]	9	Jk	51.10N	3.10W
Somerset	9	Kj	51.00N	3.00W
Somerset [Austl.]	59	Ib	10.35S	142.15 E
Somerset [Ky.-U.S.]	43	Kd	37.05N	84.36W
Somerset [Pa.-U.S.]	44	He	40.02N	79.05W
Somerset East	37	Df	32.42S	25.35 E
Somerton	46	Hj	32.36N	114.43W
Somerville Lake	45	Hk	30.18N	96.40W
Someş	15	Fa	48.07N	22.20 E
Someşu Mare	15	Gb	47.09N	23.55 E
Someşu Mic	15	Gb	47.09N	23.55 E
Somme [3]	11	Id	49.55N	2.30 E
Somme	11	Hd	50.11N	1.39 E
Somme, Baie de-	12	Dd	50.14N	1.33 E
Somme, Bassurelle de la-	12	Dd	50.15N	1.10 E
Somme, Canal de la-	11	He	50.11N	1.39 E
Somme-Leuze	12	Hd	50.20N	5.22 E
Somme-Leuze-Hogne	12	Hd	50.15N	5.17 E
Sommen	7	Dh	58.00N	15.15 E
Sommen	8	Ff	58.08N	14.58 E
Sommepy-Tahure	12	Ge	49.15N	4.33 E
Sömmerda	10	He	51.09N	11.06 E
Somogy [2]	10	Nj	46.25N	17.35 E
Somontano	13	Lc	42.02N	0.20W
Somosierra, Puerto de-	13	Ic	41.09N	3.35W
Somosomo Strait	63d	Bb	16.47S	179.58 E
Somotillo	49	Dg	13.02N	86.53W
Somoto	47	Gf	13.28N	86.35W
Somovo	16	Kd	51.45N	39.25 E
Sompolno	10	Od	52.24N	18.31 E
Somport, Puerto de-	13	Lb	42.48N	0.31W
Son	21	Kg	25.50N	84.55 E
Sona	10	Qd	52.33N	20.35 E
Soná	49	Gi	8.01N	81.19W
Sonaguera	49	Df	15.38N	86.20W
Sonári, Ákra	15	Lm	36.27N	28.13 E
Sŏnch'on	28	He	39.48N	124.55 E
Søndeled	7	Bg	58.46N	9.05 E
Sønderborg	7	Bi	54.55N	9.47 E
Sønder-Jylland [2]	8	Ci	55.00N	9.00 E
Sønder-Omme	8	Ci	55.50N	8.54 E
Sondershausen	10	Ge	51.22N	10.52 E
Søndre Strømfjord	67	Nc	66.59N	50.40W
Søndre Strømfjord	41	Ge	66.10N	53.10W
Søndre Upernavik	41	Gd	72.10N	55.38W
Sondrio	14	Dd	46.10N	9.52 E
Sonepat	25	Fc	28.59N	77.01 E
Song	34	Hd	9.50N	12.37 E
Songa	8	Be	59.47N	7.43 E
Songavatn	8	Be	59.50N	7.35 E
Song Cau	25	Lf	13.27N	109.13 E
Songe	8	Cf	58.41N	9.01 E
Songea	31	Kj	10.41S	35.39 E
Songeons	12	De	49.33N	1.52 E
Songhua Hu	28	Ic	43.30N	126.51 E
Songhua Jiang=Sungari (EN)	21	Pe	47.42N	132.30 E
Songjiang	27	Le	31.01N	121.14 E
Songjiang → Antu	28	Jc	42.33N	128.20 E
Songjianghe	28	Ic	42.10N	127.30 E
Sŏngjin → Kimch'aek	27	Mc	40.41N	129.12 E
Songjŏng	28	Ig	35.08N	126.48 E
Songkhla	22	Mi	7.13N	100.34 E
Songling	27	Lb	48.02N	121.08 E
Songnim	28	He	38.44N	125.38 E
Songo [Ang.]	36	Bd	7.21S	14.50 E
Songo [Moz.]	37	Ec	15.33S	32.48 E
Songololo	36	Bd	5.42S	14.02 E
Songpan (Sungqu)	27	He	32.37N	103.34 E
Songsa-dong	28	Hd	39.49N	124.49 E
Song Shan	27	Je	34.31N	113.00 E
Songshuzhen	28	Ic	42.01N	127.09 E
Songueur	13	Ni	35.11N	1.30 E
Songxian	28	Bg	34.12N	112.09 E
Songzi (Xinjiangkou)	28	Ai	30.10N	116.46 E
Sonid Youqi (Saihan Tal)	27	Jc	42.45N	112.36 E
Sonid Zuoqi (Mandalt)	27	Kc	43.50N	116.45 E
Sonkari	8	Lb	62.50N	26.35 E
Sonkël, Ozero-	18	Jd	41.50N	75.10 E
Sonkovo	7	Ih	57.47N	37.09 E
Son La	22	Mg	21.19N	103.54 E
Sonmiāni Bay	25	Dc	25.15N	66.30 E
Sonneberg	10	Hf	50.21N	11.10 E
Sono, Rio do- [Braz.]	55	Jc	17.02S	45.32W
Sono, Rio do- [Braz.]	54	Ie	9.00S	48.11W
Sonobe	29	Dd	35.07N	135.28 E
Sonoita	47	Bb	31.51N	112.50W
Sonoma Peak	46	Gf	40.52N	117.36W
Sonora [2]	47	Bc	29.20N	110.40W
Sonora	47	Bc	28.48N	111.49W
Sonora [Ca.-U.S.]	46	Eh	37.59N	120.23W
Sonora [Tx.-U.S.]	45	Fk	30.34N	100.39W
Sonqor	24	Le	34.47N	47.36 E
Sonsbeck	12	Ic	51.37N	6.22 E
Sonsonate	47	Gf	13.43N	89.44W
Sonsorol Islands	57	Ed	5.20N	132.13 E
Sonthofen	10	Gi	47.31N	10.17 E
Sontra	10	Fe	51.04N	9.56 E
Soomaaliya=Somalia (EN) [1]	31	Lh	10.00N	49.00 E
Soomenlaht=Finland, Gulf of- (EN)	5	Ic	60.00N	27.00 E
Soonwald	12	Je	49.56N	7.35 E
Søørværøy	7	Cc	67.38N	12.40 E
Sopi, Tanjung-	26	If	2.39N	128.34 E
Sopo	35	Dd	8.51N	26.11 E
Sopockin	10	Tc	53.50N	23.42 E
Sopot [Bul.]	15	Hg	42.39N	24.45 E
Sopot [Pol.]	10	Ob	54.28N	18.34 E
Sopron	10	Mi	47.41N	16.36 E
Sopur	25	Eb	34.18N	74.28 E
Sor	13	De	39.00N	8.17W
Sora	14	Hi	41.43N	13.37 E
Sorachi-Gawa	29a	Bb	43.32N	141.52 E
Söråker	8	Gb	62.31N	17.30 E
Sorak-san	27	Md	38.07N	128.28 E
Sorano	14	Fh	42.41N	11.43 E
Soratteld	12	Kc	51.40N	8.55 E
Sorbas	13	Jg	37.07N	2.07W
Sorbe	13	Id	40.51N	3.08W
Sörberget	8	Gb	62.31N	17.22 E
Sore	11	Fj	44.19N	0.35W
Sorel	42	Kg	46.03N	73.07W
Sorell, Cape-	59	Jh	42.10S	145.10 E
Soresina	14	De	45.17N	9.51 E
Sorezaru Point	63a	Cb	7.37S	156.38 E
Sørfjorden	8	Bd	60.25N	6.40 E
Sørfold	7	Dc	67.28N	15.28 E
Sorgues	11	Kj	44.00N	4.52 E
Sorgun	24	Fc	39.50N	35.19 E
Soria [3]	13	Jc	41.40N	2.40W
Soria	13	Jc	41.46N	2.28W
Soriano [2]	55	Dk	33.30S	57.45W
Sørkapp	67	Kd	76.28N	16.36 E
Sorkh, Godār-e-	24	Pf	33.05N	55.05 E
Sorkh, Kūh-e-	24	Pf	33.05N	55.05 E
Sorkheh	24	Oe	35.28N	53.13 E
Sorø	8	Di	55.26N	11.34 E
Sorocaba	53	Lh	23.29S	47.27W
Soroči Gory	7	Li	55.24N	49.55 E
Soročinsk	19	Fe	52.26N	53.10 E
Soroka	16	Fe	48.07N	28.16 E
Sorol Atoll	57	Fd	8.08N	140.23 E
Sorong	58	Ee	0.53S	131.15 E
Soroti	31	Kh	1.43N	33.37 E
Sørøya	5	Ia	70.36N	22.46 E
Sørøyane	8	Ab	62.20N	5.45 E
Sorraia	13	Df	38.56N	8.53W
Sørreisa	7	Eb	69.09N	18.10 E
Sorrentina, Penisola-	14	Ij	40.35N	14.30 E
Sorrento	14	Ij	40.37N	14.22 E
Sør Rondane	66	Df	72.00S	25.00 E
Sorsatunturi	7	Gc	67.24N	29.38 E
Sorsavesi	8	Lb	62.30N	27.35 E
Sorsele	7	Dd	65.32N	17.30 E
Sorsk	20	Ef	54.00N	90.20 E
Sorso	14	Cj	40.48N	8.34 E
Sorsogon	26	Hd	12.58N	124.00 E
Sort	13	Nb	42.24N	1.08 E
Šortandi	19	He	51.42N	71.05 E
Sortavala	19	Dc	61.44N	30.41 E
Sortland	7	Db	68.42N	15.24 E
Sør-Trøndelag [2]	7	Ce	63.00N	10.40 E
Sorum	17	Ne	63.50N	68.05 E
Sørumsand	8	De	59.58N	11.15 E
Šoša	7	Ih	56.33N	36.09 E
Sŏsan	28	If	36.47N	126.27 E
Sösdala	8	Eh	56.02N	13.40 E
Sos del Rey Católico	13	Kb	42.30N	1.13W
Sosna	16	Kc	52.42N	38.55 E
Sosnogorsk	6	Lc	63.37N	53.51 E
Sosnovka	16	Lc	53.14N	41.22 E
Sosnovka	7	Mh	56.18N	51.17 E
Sosnovka	7	Jc	66.31N	40.33 E
Sosnovka	16	Dd	50.15N	24.13 E
Sosnovo	8	Nd	60.31N	30.29 E
Sosnovo-Ozerskoje	20	Gf	52.31N	111.35 E
Sosnovy Bor	8	Me	59.48N	29.10 E
Sosnowiec	10	Pf	50.18N	19.08 E
Sospel	11	Nk	43.53N	7.27 E
Šostka	19	De	51.52N	33.31 E
Sosumav	37	Hb	13.03S	48.54 E
Sosva	19	Gd	59.32N	62.20 E
Sosva	19	Gc	63.40N	62.02 E
Sosva	19	Gd	59.10N	61.50 E
Sotavento [3]	32	Cf	14.40N	23.25W
Sotavento, Islas de- = Windward Islands (EN)	52	Jd	11.10N	67.00W
Sotik	36	Gc	0.41S	35.07 E
Sotkamo	7	Gd	64.08N	28.25 E
Soto la Marina	48	Jf	23.48N	98.13W
Soto la Marina, Río-	48	Kf	23.45N	97.45W
Sotonera, Embalse de la-	13	Lb	42.05N	0.48W
Sotouboua	34	Fd	8.34N	0.59 E
Sotra	8	Ad	60.20N	5.05 E
Sotsudaka-Zaki	29b	Ba	28.15N	129.10 E
Sottern	8	Fe	59.05N	15.30 E
Sotteville-lès-Rouen	11	He	49.25N	1.06 E
Sottrum	12	La	53.07N	9.14 E
Sottunga	8	Id	60.10N	20.40 E
Sotuf, Adrar-	32	De	21.42N	15.36W
Sotuta	48	Og	20.36N	89.01W
Souanké	36	Bb	2.05N	14.03 E
Soubré	34	Dd	5.47N	6.36W
Soubré [3]	34	Dd	5.47N	6.38W
Soúdha	15	Hn	35.29N	24.04 E
Souf	30	He	33.25N	6.50 E
Soufflenheim	12	Jf	48.50N	7.58 E
Souflion	15	Jh	41.12N	26.18 E
Soufrière	50	Ff	13.52N	61.04W
Soufrière [Guad.]	47	Le	16.03N	61.40W
Soufrière [St.Vin.]	47	Lf	13.21N	61.11W
Soufrière Bay	51g	Bb	15.13N	61.22W
Soufrière Hills	51c	Bc	16.43N	62.10W
Souillac	11	Hj	44.54N	1.29 E
Souilly	11	Le	49.01N	5.17 E
Souk Ahras	32	Ib	36.17N	7.57 E
Souk el Arba du Rharb	32	Fc	34.41N	5.59W
Sŏul=Seoul (EN)	22	Of	37.34N	127.00 E
Soulac-sur-Mer	11	Ei	45.30N	1.06W
Sŏul Si [2]	28	If	37.35N	127.00 E
Soultz-sous-Forêts	12	Jf	48.56N	7.53 E
Soumagne	12	Hd	50.37N	5.45 E
Soummam	13	Rh	36.44N	5.04 E
Sounding Creek	46	Ja	52.06N	110.28W
Soúnion	15	Hl	37.39N	24.02 E
Soúnion, Ákra-	15	Hl	37.39N	24.01 E
Sources, Mont aux-	30	Jk	28.46S	28.52 E
Soure [Braz.]	54	Id	0.44S	48.31W
Soure [Port.]	13	Dd	40.03N	8.38W
Sour el Ghozlane	32	Hb	36.09N	3.41 E
Souris	42	Hg	49.38N	100.15W
Souris	38	Je	49.39N	99.34W
Sous	32	Fc	30.22N	9.37W
Sous	32	Fc	30.25N	9.30W
Sousa	53	Mf	6.45S	38.14W
Sousel	13	Ef	38.57N	7.40W
Sous le Vent, Iles-=Leeward Islands (EN)	57	Lf	16.38S	151.30W
Sousse (EN)=Sūsah [3]	32	Jb	35.45N	10.30 E
Sousse (EN)=Sūsah [Tun.]	31	Ie	35.49N	10.38 E
Sout	37	Cf	33.03S	23.29 E
South Africa / Suid Africa [1]	31	Jl	30.00S	26.00 E
South Alligator River	59	Gb	12.15S	132.24 E
Southam	12	Ab	52.15N	1.23W
South America (EN)	52	Jg	15.00S	60.00W
Southampton	38	Kc	64.20N	84.40W
Southampton [Eng.-U.K.]	6	Fe	50.55N	1.25W
Southampton [N.Y.-U.S.]	44	Ke	40.54N	72.23W
Southampton, Cape -	42	Jd	62.08N	83.44W
Southampton Airport	12	Ad	50.55N	1.23W
Southampton Water	12	Ad	50.52N	1.20W
South Andaman	25	If	11.45N	92.45 E
Southard, Cape-	66	Ie	66.33S	122.04 E
South Auckland-Bay of Plenty [2]	62	Fb	38.00S	176.00 E
South Aulatsivik	42	Le	56.47N	61.30W
South Australia [2]	59	Ge	30.00S	135.00 E
South Australian Basin (EN)	3	Im	40.00S	128.00 E
Southaven	45	Li	35.00N	90.00W
South Baldy	45	Cj	33.59N	107.11W
South Bay	42	Jd	64.00N	83.25W
South Bend	43	Jc	41.41N	86.15W
South Benfleet	12	Cc	51.32N	0.33 E
Southborough	12	Cc	51.09N	0.15 E
South Boston	44	Hg	36.42N	78.58W
Southbridge	62	Ee	43.48S	172.15 E
South Buganda [3]	36	Fc	0.30S	32.00 E
South Caicos	49	Lc	21.31N	71.30W
South Carolina [2]	43	Ke	34.00N	81.00W
South China Basin (EN)	3	Hh	15.00N	115.00 E
South China Sea (EN)=Bien Dong	21	Ni	10.00N	113.00 E
South China Sea (EN)=Cina Selatan, Laut-	21	Ni	10.00N	113.00 E
South China Sea (EN)=Nan Hai	21	Ni	10.00N	113.00 E
South Dakota [2]	43	Gc	44.15N	100.00W
South Downs	9	Mk	50.55N	0.25W
South-East [3]	37	De	25.00S	25.45 E
South East Cape	57	Fi	43.39S	146.50 E
Southeast Indian Ridge (EN)	3	Ho	50.00S	110.00 E
Southeast Pacific Basin (EN)	3	Mp	60.00S	115.00W
South East Point [Austl.]	57	Fh	39.00S	146.20 E
South East Point [Kir.]	64g	Bb	1.40N	157.10W
Southend	42	He	56.20N	103.14W
Southend-on-Sea	9	Nj	51.33N	0.43 E
Southern [Mwi.] [3]	36	Gf	15.30S	35.00 E
Southern [S.L.] [3]	34	Cd	7.40N	12.15W
Southern [Ug.] [3]	36	Fc	0.30S	30.30 E
Southern [Zam.] [3]	36	Ef	16.00S	27.00 E
Southern Alps	57	Ii	43.30S	170.35 E
Southern Cook Island	57	Lg	20.00S	159.00W
Southern Cross	58	Ch	31.13S	119.19 E
Southern Desert (EN)=Janūbīyah, Aş Şaḩrā' al-	30	Jf	24.00N	30.00 E
Southern Ghats	25	Ff	10.00N	76.50 E
Southern Gilbert Islands	60	Jh	1.30S	175.30 E
Southern Indian Lake	38	Jd	57.10N	98.40W
Southern Pines	44	Hh	35.11N	79.24W
Southern Region (EN)=Iglim al Janūbīyah [2]	35	Dd	6.00N	30.00 E
Southern Sierra Madre (EN)=Madre del Sur, Sierra-	38	Jj	17.00N	100.00W
Southern Uplands	5	Fd	55.30N	3.30W
Southern Urals (EN)=Južny Ural	5	Le	54.00N	58.30 E
Southern Yemen (EN) → Yemen, People's Democratic Republic of- (EN) [1]	22	Gh	14.00N	46.00 E
South Esk	9	Ke	56.43N	2.28W
South Fiji Basin (EN)	3	Jl	26.00S	175.00 E
South Foreland	9	Oj	51.09N	1.23 E
South Fork	46	Ge	42.26N	116.53W
South Fork Flathead River	46	Ib	48.07N	113.45W
South Fork Grand River	45	Ed	45.43N	102.17W
South Fork Kern River	46	Fi	35.40N	118.27W
South Fork Moreau River	45	Ed	45.09N	102.50W
South Fork Powder River	46	Le	43.40N	106.30W
South Fork Republican River	45	Ff	40.03N	101.31W
South Georgia/Georgia del Sur, Islas-	66	Ad	54.15S	36.45W
South Glamorgan [3]	9	Jj	51.30N	3.15W
South Haven	44	Dd	42.24N	86.16W
South Honshu Ridge (EN)	3	Ig	24.00N	142.00 E
South Horr	36	Gb	2.06N	36.55 E
South Indian Basin (EN)	3	Ho	60.00S	120.00 E
South Island [F.S.M.]	64d	Bc	6.59N	151.59 E
South Island [Kenya]	36	Gb	2.38N	36.36 E
South Island [N.Z.]	57	Ii	44.00S	171.00 E
South Island [Sey.]	37b	Ab	9.26S	46.23 E
South Island [Sey.]	37b	Bc	10.10S	51.10 E

Index Symbols

[1] Independent Nation · [2] State, Region · [3] District, County · [4] Municipality · [5] Colony, Dependency · Continent · Physical Region · Historical or Cultural Region · Mount, Mountain · Volcano · Hill · Mountains, Mountain Range · Hills, Escarpment · Plateau, Upland · Pass, Gap · Plain, Lowland · Delta · Salt Flat · Valley, Canyon · Crater, Cave · Karst Features · Depression · Polder · Desert, Dunes · Forest, Woods · Heath, Steppe · Oasis · Cape, Point · Coast, Beach · Cliff · Peninsula · Isthmus · Sandbank · Island · Atoll · Rock, Reef · Islands, Archipelago · Rocks, Reefs · Coral Reef · Well, Spring · Geyser · River, Stream · Waterfall Rapids · River Mouth, Estuary · Lake · Salt Lake · Intermittent Lake · Reservoir · Swamp, Pond · Canal · Glacier · Ice Shelf, Pack Ice · Ocean · Sea · Gulf, Bay · Strait, Fjord · Lagoon · Bank · Seamount · Tablemount · Ridge · Shelf · Basin · Escarpment, Sea Scarp · Fracture · Trench, Abyss · National Park, Reserve · Point of Interest · Recreation Site · Cave, Cavern · Historic Site · Ruins · Wall, Walls · Church, Abbey · Temple · Scientific Station · Airport · Port · Lighthouse · Mine · Tunnel · Dam, Bridge

Index Symbols

Store Bælt=Great Belt (EN) 5 Hd 55.30N 11.00 E
Storebro 8 Fg 57.35N 15.51 E
Storefiskbank 9 Qe 56.50N 4.00 E
Store Heddinge 8 Ei 55.19N 12.25 E
Store Hellefiske Bank (EN) 41 Ge 67.30N 55.00W
Store Koldewey 41 Kc 76.20N 18.30W
Store Kvien 8 Dc 61.34N 10.33 E
Støren 7 Ce 63.02N 10.18 E
Store Nupsfonn 8 Be 59.54N 7.08 E
Store Sølnkletten 8 Dc 61.59N 10.18 E
Storfjorden [Nor.] 8 Bb 62.25N 6.30 E
Storfjorden [Sval.] 41 Nc 77.30N 20.00 E
Storfors 8 Fe 59.32N 14.16 E
Storis Passage 42 Hc 67.40N 98.30W
Storkerson Bay 42 Fb 73.00N 124.00W
Storkerson Peninsula 42 Gb 73.00N 106.30W
Storlien 7 Ce 63.19N 12.06 E
Stormarn 10 Gc 53.45N 10.20 E
Storm Bay 59 Jh 43.10S 147.30 E
Storm Lake 43 Hc 42.39N 95.13W
Stornoway 9 Gc 58.12N 6.23W
Storøya 41 Ob 80.08N 27.50 E
Storožinec 16 De 48.10N 25.46 E
Storsjøen [Nor.] 8 Dd 60.25N 11.40 E
Storsjøen [Nor.] 8 Dd 61.35N 11.15 E
Storsjön [Swe.] 8 Gd 60.35N 16.45 E
Storsjön [Swe.] 5 Hc 63.15N 14.20 E
Storsteinfjellet 7 Db 68.14N 17.52 E
Storstrøm [2] 8 Dj 55.00N 11.50 E
Storstrømmen 41 Jc 77.20N 23.00W
Storsudret 8 Hh 57.00N 18.15 E
Storuman 7 Dd 65.14N 16.54 E
Storuman 6 Hb 65.06N 17.06 E
Storvätteshågna 8 Eb 62.07N 12.27 E
Storvigelen 8 Eb 62.32N 12.04 E
Storvik 8 Gd 60.35N 16.32 E
Storvreta 8 Ge 59.58N 17.42 E
Stöttingfjället 7 Dd 64.38N 17.44 E
Stoughton 46 Nb 49.41N 103.03W
Stour [Eng.-U.K.] 9 Lk 50.43N 1.46W
Stour [Eng.-U.K.] 9 Oj 51.52N 1.16 E
Stourbridge 9 Ki 52.27N 2.09W
Støvring 8 Ch 56.53N 9.51 E
Stowmarket 12 Cb 52.11N 0.59 E
Strabane/An Srath Bán 9 Fg 54.49N 7.27W
Stradella 14 De 45.05N 9.18 E
Straelen 12 Ic 51.27N 6.16 E
Strakonice 10 Jg 49.16N 13.55 E
Straldža 15 Jg 42.36N 26.41 E
Stralsund 6 He 54.18N 13.06 E
Strand 37 Bf 34.06S 18.50 E
Stranda 7 Be 62.19N 6.54 E
Strand Bay 42 Ia 79.00N 94.00W
Strangford Lough/Loch Cuan 9 Hg 54.26N 5.36W
Strängnäs 8 Ge 59.23N 17.02 E
Stranraer 9 Hg 54.54N 5.02W
Strasbourg [Fr.] 6 Gf 48.35N 7.45 E
Strasbourg [Sask.-Can.] 46 Ma 51.04N 104.57W
Strašeny 16 Ff 47.06N 28.34 E
Straßwalchen 14 Hc 47.59N 13.15 E
Stratford [N.Z.] 62 Fc 39.21S 174.17 E
Stratford [Ont.-Can.] 44 Gd 43.22N 80.57W
Stratford [Tx.-U.S.] 45 Eh 36.20N 102.04W
Stratford-upon-Avon 9 Li 52.12N 1.41W
Strathclyde [3] 9 If 55.50N 4.50W
Strathgordon 59 Jh 42.54S 146.10 E
Strathmore 9 Je 56.40N 3.05W
Strathmore 46 Ia 51.03N 113.23W
Strathroy 44 Gd 42.57N 81.38W
Strathy Point 9 Ic 58.35N 4.01W
Straubenhardt 12 Kf 48.50N 8.34 E
Straubing 10 Ih 48.53N 12.34 E
Straumnes 7a Aa 66.26N 23.08W
Straumsjøen 7 Db 68.41N 14.30 E
Strausberg 10 Jd 52.35N 13.53 E
Strawberry Mountain 46 Fd 44.19N 118.43W
Strawberry River 46 Jf 40.10N 110.24W
Straža 15 Fg 42.15N 22.14 E
Stražica 15 If 43.14N 25.58 E
Strážiště 10 Kg 49.32N 14.58 E
Strážovské vrchy 10 Oh 48.55N 18.30 E
Streaky Bay 59 Gf 32.48S 134.13 E
Streaky Bay 59 Gf 32.35S 134.10 E
Streator 45 Lf 41.07N 88.50W
Středočeská pahorkatina 10 Kg 49.30N 14.15 E
Středočeský kraj [3] 10 Kg 49.55N 14.30 E
Středoslovenský kraj [3] 10 Ph 48.50N 19.10 E
Strehaia 15 Ge 44.37N 23.12 E
Strei 15 Gd 45.51N 23.03 E
Střela 10 Jg 49.54N 13.32 E
Strelasund 10 Jb 54.20N 13.05 E
Strelka 20 Ee 58.03N 93.05 E
Strelna 7 Jc 66.04N 38.39 E
Strenči 7 Fh 57.39N 25.38 E
Stresa 14 Ce 45.53N 8.32 E
Streževoj 20 Cd 60.42N 77.35 E
Stříbro 10 Ig 49.46N 13.00 E
Strickland River 59 Ia 6.00S 142.05 E
Strîmbeni 15 He 44.28N 24.58 E
Strimón 15 Gi 40.47N 23.51 E
Strimonikós Kólpos 15 Gi 40.40N 23.50 E
Strjama 15 Hg 42.10N 24.56 E
Strofádhes, Nisoi- 15 Dl 37.15N 21.00 E
Ströhen, Wagenfeld- 12 Kb 52.32N 8.39 E
Stromberg 12 Je 49.57N 7.46 E
Stromboli 14 Jl 38.45N 15.15 E
Strömfors/Ruotsinpyhtää 8 Ld 60.32N 26.27 E
Stromness 9 Jc 58.57N 3.18W
Strömsbro 8 Gd 60.42N 17.10 E
Strömsbruk 7 Dc 61.53N 17.19 E
Strömsnäsbruk 8 Eh 56.33N 13.43 E
Strömstad 7 Cf 58.56N 11.10 E
Strömsund 7 De 63.51N 15.35 E
Strongili 15 Hm 36.58N 24.55 E
Stròngoli 14 Lk 39.16N 17.03 E
Stronsay 9 Kb 59.08N 2.38W
Stropkov 10 Rg 49.12N 21.40 E
Stroud 9 Kj 51.45N 2.12W
Struer 7 Bh 56.29N 8.37 E
Struga 15 Dh 41.11N 20.41 E
Strugi-Krasnyje 7 Gg 58.17N 29.08 E
Strule 9 Fg 54.40N 7.20W
Struma 5 Ig 40.47N 23.51 E
Strumble Head 9 Hi 52.02N 5.04W
Strumica 15 Fh 41.26N 22.39 E
Stry 16 De 49.24N 24.13 E
Stry 16 Cd 49.14N 23.49 E
Strydenburg 37 Ce 29.58S 23.40 E
Stryn 7 Bf 61.55N 6.47 E
Strynsvatn 8 Bc 61.55N 7.05 E
Strzegom 10 Mf 50.57N 16.21 E
Strzegomka 10 Me 51.08N 16.50 E
Strzelce Krajeńskie 10 Ld 52.53N 15.32 E
Strzelce Opolskie 10 Of 50.31N 18.19 E
Strzelin 10 Nf 50.47N 17.03 E
Strzelno 10 Od 52.38N 18.11 E
Strzyżów 10 Rg 49.52N 21.47 E
Stuart 40 Gd 63.35N 162.30W
Stuart, Mount- 46 Ec 47.29N 120.54W
Stuart Bluff Range 59 Gd 22.45S 132.15 E
Stuart Lake 42 Ff 54.35N 124.35W
Stuart Range 59 Ge 29.10S 134.55 E
Stubaier Alpen 14 Fc 47.10N 11.05 E
Stubbekøbing 8 Ej 54.43N 12.03 E
Stubbenkammer 10 Jb 54.35N 13.40 E
Stubbs Bay 51n Ba 13.08N 61.10W
Štubik 15 Fe 44.18N 22.21 E
Studenica, Manastir- 15 Df 43.28N 20.37 E
Studholme Junction 62 Df 44.44S 171.08 E
Stugun 7 De 63.10N 15.36 E
Stuhr 12 Ka 53.02N 8.45 E
Stupino 7 Ji 54.57N 38.03 E
Stura di Demonte 14 Bf 44.40N 7.44 E
Stura di Lanzo 14 Be 45.06N 7.44 E
Sturge Island 66 Ke 67.27S 164.18 E
Sturgeon Bay 45 Md 44.50N 87.23W
Sturgeon Falls 42 Jg 46.22N 79.55W
Sturgeon Lake 45 Kb 50.00N 90.45W
Sturgis [Mi.-U.S.] 44 Ee 41.48N 85.25W
Sturgis [S.D.-U.S.] 45 Ed 44.25N 103.31W
Sturkö 8 Fh 56.05N 15.40 E
Sturt Creek 59 Fd 20.08S 127.24 E
Sturt Desert 59 Ie 28.30S 141.00 E
Stutterheim 37 Df 32.33S 27.28 E
Stuttgart [Ar.-U.S.] 45 Ki 34.30N 91.33W
Stuttgart [Ger.] 6 Gf 48.46N 9.11 E
Stviga 16 Ec 52.04N 27.55 E
Stykkishólmur 7a Ab 65.04N 22.44W
Styr 19 Ce 52.07N 26.35 E
Styria (EN) = Steiermark 14 Ic 47.15N 15.00 E
Styria (EN) = Steiermark [2] 14 Ic 47.15N 15.00 E
Styrsö 8 Dg 57.37N 11.46 E
Suafa Point 63a Ec 8.19S 160.41 E
Suai 26 Ih 9.21S 125.17 E
Suakin Archipelago (EN) = Sawākin, Jazā'ir- 30 Kg 19.07N 37.20 E
Suao 27 Lg 24.36N 121.51 E
Suardi 55 Bj 30.32S 61.58W
Suavanao 60 Fi 7.34S 158.44 E
Subačius/Subačjus 8 Ki 55.44N 24.53 E
Subačjus/Subačius 8 Ki 55.44N 24.53 E
Subang 26 Eh 6.34S 107.45 E
Subansiri 25 Jc 26.48N 93.49 E
Subao Ding 27 Jf 27.10N 110.18 E
Šubarkuduk 19 Ff 49.09N 56.31 E
Šubarši 16 Te 48.38N 57.12 E
Subate 8 Lh 56.01N 26.04 E
Subay', 'Urūq- 33 He 22.15N 43.05 E
Subaytilah 35 Ib 35.14N 9.08 E
Subbético, Sistema- 13 Jf 38.30N 2.30W
Subei (Dangchengwan) 27 Fd 39.36N 94.58 E
Subi, Pulau- 26 Ef 2.55N 108.50 E
Subiaco 14 Hi 41.55N 13.06 E
Sublette 45 Fh 37.29N 100.50W
Submeseta Norte 5 Fg 42.20N 4.50W
Submeseta Sur 5 Fh 39.30N 3.30W
Subotica 15 Cc 46.06N 19.40 E
Subpolar Urals (EN) = Pripoljarny Ural 5 Lb 65.00N 60.00 E
Subugo 36 Gc 1.40S 35.49 E
Suceava [3] 15 Jb 47.32N 26.32 E
Suceava [2] 15 Ib 47.40N 25.45 E
Suceava 15 Jb 47.38N 26.15 E
Sucha Beskidzka 10 Pg 49.44N 19.36 E
Süchbaatar → Suhe-Bator 22 Md 50.15N 106.12 E
Suchedniów 10 Qe 51.03N 20.51 E
Suchiapa, Río- 48 Mi 16.36N 93.01W
Suchitepéquez [3] 49 Bf 14.25N 91.20W
Sucia, Bahía- 51a Ac 17.57N 67.10W
Sucio, Río- 49 Ij 7.27N 77.07W
Suck/An tSuca 9 Eh 53.16N 8.03W
Suckling, Mount- 59 Ja 9.45S 148.55 E
Sucre [Bol.] 53 Jg 19.02S 65.17W
Sucre [Col.] [2] 54 Db 9.00N 75.00W
Sucre [Col.] 54 Db 8.50N 74.43W
Sucre [Ven.] [2] 54 Fa 10.25N 63.30W
Suçuarana, Serra da- 55 Jb 14.25S 45.00W
Sucunduri, Rio- 54 Ge 5.30S 59.40W
Sućuraj 14 Lg 43.08N 17.12 E
Sucuriú, Rio- 54 Hh 20.47S 51.38W
Sud, Canal du- 49 Kd 18.40N 73.05W
Sud, Massif du- 49 Kd 18.25N 73.55W
Suda 7 Ig 59.11N 37.33 E
Suda 7 Ig 59.12N 37.30 E
Sudak 19 Dg 44.50N 34.59 E
Sudan 30 Ig 11.30N 15.00 E
Sudan (EN) = As Sūdān [1] 31 Jg 15.00N 30.00 E
Sudbury [Eng.-U.K.] 9 Ni 52.02N 0.44 E
Sudbury [Ont.-Can.] 39 Ke 46.30N 81.00W
Suddie 50 Gi 7.07N 58.29W
Sude 10 Gc 53.22N 10.45 E
Sudeten (EN) 5 He 50.30N 16.00 E
Sudirman, Pegunungan- 26 Kg 4.12S 137.00 E
Sudočje, Ozero- 18 Bc 43.25N 58.30 E
Sudogda 7 Ji 55.59N 40.50 E
Sudost 16 Hc 52.19N 33.24 E
Sud-Ouest [Cam.] [3] 34 Gd 5.20N 9.20 E
Sud-Ouest [U.V.] [3] 34 Ec 10.30N 3.15W
Sudovaja Višnja 10 Tg 49.43N 23.26 E
Südradde 12 Jb 52.41N 7.34 E
Südtirol / Trentino-Alto Adige [2] 14 Fd 46.30N 11.20 E
Sudža 16 Id 51.13N 35.16 E
Sue 30 Jh 7.41N 28.03 E
Sueca 13 Le 39.12N 0.19W
Suess Land 41 Jd 72.45N 26.00W
Suez (EN) = As Suways 31 Kf 29.58N 32.33 E
Suez, Gulf of-(EN) = Suways, Khalīj as- 30 Kf 28.10N 33.27 E
Suez Canal (EN) = Suways, Qanāt as- 30 Ke 29.55N 32.33 E
Suffolk 9 Ni 52.25N 1.00 E
Suffolk 43 Ld 36.44N 76.37W
Suffolk [3] 9 Li 52.10N 1.05W
Sufiān 24 Kc 38.17N 45.59 E
Sugana, Val- 14 Fd 46.00N 11.40 E
Suga-no-Sen 29 Dd 35.22N 134.31 E
Sugar Island 44 Eb 46.25N 84.12W
Sugarloaf Mountain 44 Lc 45.01N 70.22W
Suğla Gölü 24 Ed 37.20N 32.02 E
Sugoj 20 Kd 64.15N 154.29 E
Suguta 36 Gb 2.03N 36.33 E
Suha 15 Ke 44.08N 27.36 E
Suhai Hu 27 Fd 38.55N 94.05 E
Şuḩār 23 Ie 24.22N 56.45 E
Suhe-Bator (Süchbaatar) 22 Md 50.15N 106.12 E
Suhiniči 16 Ib 54.06N 35.20 E
Suhl 10 Gf 50.36N 10.42 E
Suhodolskoje, Ozero- 8 Nd 60.35N 30.30 E
Suhoj Log 17 Kh 56.55N 62.01 E
Suhona 5 Kc 60.46N 46.24 E
Suhr 14 Cc 47.25N 8.04 E
Suhumi 6 Kg 43.01N 41.02 E
Suhurlui 15 Kd 45.25N 27.35 E
Suiá-Missu, Rio- 54 Hf 11.13S 53.15W
Suibara 29 Fc 37.50N 139.12 E
Suichang 27 Kf 28.34N 119.15 E
Suid Africa / South Africa [1] 31 Jl 30.00S 26.00 E
Suide 27 Jd 37.28N 110.15 E
Suifen He 28 Kc 43.20N 131.49 E
Suifenhe 27 Nc 44.25N 131.09 E
Sui He 28 Eh 33.29N 118.06 E
Suihua 27 Mb 46.38N 126.57 E
Suijiang 27 Hf 28.37N 104.00 E
Suileng 27 Mb 47.17N 127.08 E
Suining [China] 27 Ie 30.30N 105.34 E
Suining [China] 28 Dh 33.54N 117.56 E
Suipacha 55 Cl 34.45S 59.41W
Suiping 28 Bh 33.09N 113.59 E
Suippe 11 Je 49.25N 3.57 E
Suippes 11 Ke 49.08N 4.32 E
Suir/An tSiúir 9 Gi 52.15N 7.00W
Suisse / Svizra / Svizzera / Schweiz = Switzerland (EN) [1] 6 Gf 46.00N 8.30 E
Suisse Normande 12 Bf 48.53N 0.50W
Suita 29 Dd 34.45N 135.32 E
Suixi 28 Dh 33.55N 116.47 E
Suixian [China] 28 Cg 34.25N 115.04 E
Suixian [China] 27 Je 31.44N 113.25 E
Suiyang 28 Kb 44.26N 130.53 E
Suizhong 27 Lc 40.21N 120.20 E
Suj 27 Ic 42.12N 108.01 E
Šuja 7 If 61.54N 34.15 E
Šuja 7 If 61.59N 34.15 E
Šuja 19 Ed 56.52N 41.23 E
Sujer 17 Li 55.59N 65.47 E
Suji → Haixing 28 De 38.10N 117.29 E
Sujstamo 8 Nc 61.49N 31.05 E
Sukabumi 26 Eh 6.55S 106.56 E
Sukadana 26 Eg 1.15S 109.57 E
Sukagawa 28 Pf 37.17N 140.23 E
Sukaraja 26 Fg 7.27S 108.12 E
Sukeva 7 Ge 63.54N 27.26 E
Sukhothai 25 Je 17.01N 99.49 E
Suki 35 Ec 13.23N 33.58 E
Sukkertoppen/Manitsoq 41 Ge 65.25N 53.00W
Sukkozero 19 Dc 63.09N 32.23 E
Sukkur 22 Ig 27.42N 68.52 E
Sukon 26 Hg 0.56S 123.10 E
Sukses 37 Bd 21.01S 16.52 E
Suksun 17 Hh 57.07N 57.24 E
Sukumo 28 Ne 32.56N 132.44 E
Sukumo-Wan 29 Ce 32.55N 132.40 E
Sul, Baia- 55 Hh 27.40S 48.35W
Sul, Canal do- 54 Id 0.10S 49.30W
Sula [Nor.] 7 Af 61.10N 4.55 E
Sula [Nor.] 8 Bb 62.25N 6.10 E
Sula 7 Ld 64.41N 47.46 E
Sula 17 Fc 67.16N 52.07 E
Sula 16 He 49.40N 32.43 E
Sula, Kepulauan- = Sulu Islands (EN) 57 De 1.52S 125.22 E
Sūlāmāniya 23 Gb 35.33N 45.26 E
Sūlaimaniya [3] 24 Ke 35.40N 45.30 E
Sulaimān Range 21 Jf 30.30N 70.10 E
Sulak 16 Oh 43.17N 47.31 E
Sulak 19 Eg 43.17N 47.34 E
Sula Sgeir 9 Gb 59.05N 6.10W
Sulawesi/Celebes 21 Oj 2.00S 121.10 E
Sulawesi, Laut- = Celebes Sea (EN) 21 Oj 3.00N 122.00 E
Sulawesi Selatan [3] 26 Gg 4.00S 120.00 E
Sulawesi Tengah [3] 26 Hg 1.00S 121.00 E
Sulawesi Tenggara [3] 26 Hg 4.00S 122.30 E
Sulawesi Utara [3] 26 Hf 1.00N 123.00 E
Sulaymān 14 En 36.42N 10.30 E
Sulb 35 Ea 20.26N 30.20 E
Sulcis 14 Ck 39.05N 8.40 E
Suldalsvatn 8 Be 59.35N 6.45 E
Süldeh 24 Od 36.34N 52.01 E
Sulechów 10 Ld 52.06N 15.37 E
Sulęcin 10 Ld 52.26N 15.08 E
Suleja 17 Ii 55.11N 58.50 E
Sulejów 10 Pe 51.22N 19.53 E
Süleoğlu 15 Jh 41.46N 26.55 E
Sule Skerry 9 Ib 59.10N 4.10W
Sulima 34 Cd 6.58N 11.35W
Sulina 15 Md 45.09N 29.40 E
Sulina, Braţul- 15 Md 45.09N 29.41 E
Sulingen 12 Ed 52.41N 8.48 E
Sulitjelma 7 Dc 67.09N 16.03 E
Sulitjelma 7 Dc 67.08N 16.24 E
Suljukta 19 Gh 39.56N 69.37 E
Sulkava 7 Gf 61.47N 28.23 E
Sullana 53 Hf 4.53S 80.42W
Süller 15 Mk 38.09N 29.29 E
Sullivan [In.-U.S.] 44 Df 39.06N 87.24W
Sullivan [Mo.-U.S.] 45 Kg 38.13N 91.10W
Sullivan Lake 46 Ja 52.00N 112.00W
Sully-sur-Loire 11 Ig 47.46N 2.22 E
Sulmona 14 Hh 42.03N 13.55 E
Sulphur [La.-U.S.] 45 Jk 30.14N 93.23W
Sulphur [Ok.-U.S.] 45 Hi 34.31N 96.58W
Sulphur Creek 45 Ed 44.46N 102.25W
Sulphur River 45 Jj 33.07N 93.52W
Sulphur Springs 45 Ij 33.08N 95.36W
Sulphur Springs Draw 45 Fj 32.12N 101.36W
Sultandağı 24 Dc 38.32N 31.14 E
Sultan Dağları 24 Dc 38.20N 31.20 E
Sultanhanı 24 Ec 38.15N 33.33 E
Sultanhisar 15 Ll 37.53N 28.10 E
Sultānpur 25 Gc 26.16N 82.04 E
Sulu Archipelago 21 Oi 6.00N 121.00 E
Sulu Basin (EN) 26 Ge 8.00N 121.30 E
Sulu Islands (EN) = Sula, Kepulauan- 57 De 1.52S 125.22 E
Suluova 24 Fb 40.47N 35.42 E
Sulūq 33 Dc 31.40N 20.15 E
Sulu Sea 21 Ni 9.00N 120.00 E
Sulz am Neckar 10 Eh 48.21N 8.37 E
Sulzbach (Saar) 12 Je 49.18N 7.04 E
Sulzbach-Rosenberg 10 Hg 49.30N 11.45 E
Sulzberger Bay 66 Mf 77.00S 152.00W
Šumadija 15 De 44.20N 20.40 E
Sumalata 26 Hf 0.59N 122.30 E
Sumāmus 24 Nd 36.50N 50.30 E
Šumanaj 18 Bc 42.37N 58.55 E
Sumatera = Sumatra (EN) 21 Mj 0.01N 102.00 E
Sumatera Barat [3] 26 Dg 1.00S 100.30 E
Sumatera Selatan [3] 26 Dg 3.30S 104.00 E
Sumatera Utara [3] 26 Cf 2.00N 99.00 E
Sumatra (EN) = Sumatera 21 Mj 0.01N 102.00 E
Šumava = Bohemian Forest (EN) 5 Hf 49.00N 13.30 E
Sumayr 33 Hf 17.47N 41.26 E
Sumba, Pulau- 21 Nj 10.00S 120.00 E
Sumba, Selat- = Sumba Strait (EN) 26 Hh 9.05S 120.00 E
Sumbar 16 Jj 38.00N 55.15 E
Sumba Strait (EN) = Sumba, Selat- 26 Hh 9.05S 120.00 E
Sumbawa, Pulau- 21 Nj 8.40S 118.00 E
Sumbawa Besar 26 Gh 8.30S 117.26 E
Sumbawanga 36 Fd 7.58S 31.37 E
Sumber 27 Ib 46.21N 108.20 E
Sumbi Point 63a Cb 7.19S 157.04 E
Sumbu 36 Fd 8.31S 30.29 E
Sumburgh Head 9 Lb 59.51N 1.16W
Sumedang 26 Eh 6.52S 107.55 E
Šume'eh Sarā 24 Md 37.18N 49.19 E
Sümeg 10 Nj 46.59N 17.17 E
Šumen 15 Jf 43.16N 26.55 E
Šumen [2] 15 Jf 43.20N 27.00 E
Sumenep 26 Fh 7.01S 113.52 E
Šumerlja 6 Kd 55.30N 46.26 E
Sumgait 16 Pi 40.37N 49.37 E
Sumgait 6 Kg 40.33N 49.40 E
Sumidouro, Rio- 55 Da 13.28S 56.39W
Šumiha 19 Gd 55.14N 63.19 E
Sumkino 19 Gd 58.09N 68.21 E
Summer, Lake- [N.M.-U.S.] 45 Di 34.38N 104.26W
Summer, Lake- [N.Z.] 62 Ee 42.40S 172.15 E
Summer Lake 46 Ee 42.50N 120.45W
Summerland 46 Fb 49.39N 119.33W
Summerside 42 Lg 46.24N 63.47W
Summersville 44 Gf 38.17N 80.52W
Summerville 44 Eh 34.29N 85.21W
Summit Lake 42 Fe 54.17N 122.38W
Summit Mountain 46 Gg 39.23N 116.28W
Summit Peak 45 Ch 37.21N 106.42W
Sumoto 29 Dd 34.20N 134.54 E
Šumperk 10 Mg 49.58N 16.59 E
Sumprabum 25 Jc 26.33N 97.34 E
Sumsar 18 Hd 41.13N 71.23 E
Šumskaja Oblast [3] 19 De 51.00N 34.15 E
Šumšu, Ostrov- 20 Kf 50.45N 156.20 E
Sumter 43 Ke 33.55N 80.20W
Sumustā al Waqf 24 Dh 28.55N 30.51 E
Sumy 6 Je 50.54N 34.48 E
Suna 7 Mh 57.53N 50.07 E
Suna 7 Ie 62.08N 34.12 E
Sunagawa 28 Pc 43.29N 141.55 E
Šunak, Gora- 19 Hf 47.05N 72.35 E
Sunan 28 He 39.15N 125.40 E
Sunan (Hongwansi) 27 Gd 38.59N 99.25 E
Sunart, Loch- 9 He 56.45N 5.45W
Sunaysilah 24 Ie 35.35N 41.53 E
Sunburst 46 Jb 48.53N 111.55W
Sunbury 44 Ie 40.52N 76.47W
Sunchales 56 Hd 30.56S 61.34W
Suncho Corral 56 Hc 27.56S 63.27W
Sunch'ŏn [N. Kor.] 27 Me 34.57N 127.29 E
Sunch'ŏn [S. Kor.] 27 Md 39.25N 125.56 E
Sun City 46 Ij 33.36N 112.17W
Suncun → Xinwen 27 Kd 35.49N 117.38 E
Sunda, Selat- = Sunda Strait (EN) 21 Mj 6.00S 105.45 E
Sundance 46 Md 44.24N 104.23W
Sundarbans 25 Hd 22.00N 89.00 E
Sundargarh 25 Gd 22.07N 84.02 E
Sunda Strait (EN) = Sunda, Selat- 21 Mj 6.00S 105.45 E
Sunday Strait 59 Ec 16.20S 123.15 E
Sundborn 8 Fd 60.39N 15.46 E
Sundbron 8 Ha 63.01N 18.11 E
Sundbyberg 8 Ge 59.22N 17.58 E
Sunde 7 Ag 59.50N 5.43 E
Sunderland 9 Lg 54.55N 1.23W
Sundern (Sauerland) 12 Kc 51.20N 8.00 E
Sundgau 11 Ng 47.40N 7.15 E
Sündiken Dağları 24 Dc 39.55N 31.00 E
Sundridge 44 Hc 45.46N 79.24W
Sundsvall 6 Hc 62.23N 17.18 E
Sundsvallsbukten 8 Gb 62.20N 17.35 E
Sunflower, Mount- 45 Eg 39.04N 102.01W
Sungaidareh 26 Dg 0.58S 101.30 E
Sungaigerong 26 Dg 2.59S 104.52 E
Sungaiguntung 26 Df 0.18N 103.37 E
Sungai Kolok 25 Kg 6.02N 101.58 E
Sungai Lembing 26 Df 3.55N 103.02 E
Sungailiat 26 Eg 1.51S 106.08 E
Sungaipenuh 26 Dg 2.05S 101.23 E
Sungai Petani 26 De 5.39N 100.30 E
Sungai Siput 26 Df 4.49N 101.04 E
Sungari (EN) = Songhua Jiang 21 Pe 47.42N 132.30 E
Sungqu → Songpan 27 He 32.37N 103.34 E
Sungurlu 24 Fb 40.10N 34.23 E
Sunharon Roads 64b Bb 14.57N 145.36 E
Suning 28 Ce 38.25N 115.50 E
Sunja 14 Ke 45.21N 16.33 E
Sunjiapuzi 28 Ic 42.02N 126.34 E
Sunkar, Gora- 18 Ib 44.12N 73.55 E
Sun Kosi 25 Hc 26.55N 87.09 E
Sunnadalsøra 7 Be 62.40N 8.33 E
Sunnan 7 Cd 64.04N 11.38 E
Sunndalen 8 Cb 62.40N 8.45 E
Sunndalsfjorden 8 Cb 62.45N 8.25 E
Sunne 7 Cg 59.50N 13.09 E
Sunnerbo 8 Eh 56.45N 13.50 E
Sunnersta 8 Ge 59.48N 17.39 E
Sunnfjord 8 Ac 61.25N 5.20 E
Sunnhordland 8 Ae 59.55N 6.00 E
Sunnmøre 8 Bb 62.20N 6.40 E
Sunnyside 46 Fc 46.20N 120.00W
Sunnyvale 46 Dh 37.23N 122.01W
Su-no-Zaki 29 Fd 34.58N 139.45 E
Sun River 46 Jc 47.30N 111.25W
Sunsas, Serranía de- 55 Cc 17.57S 59.35W
Suntar 20 Gd 62.04N 117.40 E
Suntar-Hajata, Hrebet- = Suntar-Khayata Range (EN) 21 Qc 62.00N 143.00 E
Suntar-Khayata Range (EN) = Suntar-Hajata, Hrebet- 21 Qc 62.00N 143.00 E
Suntaži 8 Kh 56.49N 24.57 E
Sun Valley 43 Ec 43.42N 114.21W
Sunwu 27 Mb 49.27N 127.19 E
Sunyani 31 Gh 7.20N 2.20W
Sunža 16 Oh 43.26N 46.08 E
Suojarvi 19 Dc 62.04N 32.21 E
Suokonmäki 8 Kb 62.47N 24.30 E
Suolahti 7 Fe 62.34N 25.52 E
Suomenlahti = Finland, Gulf of- (EN) 5 Ic 60.00N 27.00 E
Suomenniemi 8 Lc 61.19N 27.27 E
Suomenselkä 5 Ic 62.50N 25.00 E
Suomi/Finland [1] 6 Ic 64.00N 26.00 E
Suomussalmi 7 Gd 64.54N 29.00 E
Suō-Nada 29 Be 33.50N 131.30 E
Suonenjoki 7 Ge 62.37N 27.08 E
Suontee 8 Lc 61.40N 26.35 E
Suordah 20 Ic 66.43N 132.04 E
Suozhen → Huantai 28 Ef 36.57N 118.05 E
Supamo, Río- 50 Fi 6.48N 61.50W
Superior [Az.-U.S.] 46 Jj 33.18N 110.06W
Superior [Mt.-U.S.] 46 Hc 47.12N 114.53W
Superior [Nb.-U.S.] 45 Gf 40.01N 98.04W
Superior [Wi.-U.S.] 39 Je 46.44N 92.05W
Superior, Lake- 38 Ke 48.00N 88.00W
Suphan Buri 25 Kf 14.29N 100.10 E
Süphan Dağı 23 Fb 38.54N 42.48 E
Supiori, Pulau- 26 Kg 0.45S 135.30 E
Supoj 16 Ge 49.38N 31.50 E
Support Force Glacier 66 Rg 83.05S 47.30W
Suprasl 10 Tc 53.13N 23.20 E
Supraśl 10 Sc 53.12N 22.55 E
Sup'ung 27 Lc 40.27N 124.57 E
Sup'ung-chosuji 28 Hd 40.30N 125.05 E
Suq ash Shuyūkh 24 Lg 30.53N 46.28 E
Suqian 27 Ke 33.55N 118.13 E
Sūq Suwayq 24 Hj 24.23N 38.27 E
Suquṭrā = Socotra (EN) 21 Hh 12.30N 54.00 E
Şūr 22 Hg 22.31N 59.30 E
Şūr 23 Ec 33.16N 35.11 E
Sur, Cabo- 65d Ac 27.12S 109.26W
Sur, Point- 46 Eh 36.18N 121.54W
Sura 16 Nc 53.53N 45.44 E
Sura 5 Kd 56.06N 46.00 E
Šurab 18 Hd 40.03N 70.33 E
Surabaya 22 Nj 7.15S 112.45 E

Index Symbols

- [1] Independent Nation
- [2] State, Region
- [3] District, County
- [4] Municipality
- [5] Colony, Dependency
- Continent
- Physical Region
- Historical or Cultural Region
- Mount, Mountain
- Volcano
- Hill
- Mountains, Mountain Range
- Hills, Escarpment
- Plateau, Upland
- Pass, Gap
- Plain, Lowland
- Delta
- Salt Flat
- Valley, Canyon
- Crater, Cave
- Karst Features
- Depression
- Polder
- Desert, Dunes
- Forest, Woods
- Heath, Steppe
- Oasis
- Cape, Point
- Coast, Beach
- Cliff
- Peninsula
- Isthmus
- Sandbank
- Island
- Atoll
- Rock, Reef
- Islands, Archipelago
- Rocks, Reefs
- Coral Reef
- Well, Spring
- Geyser
- River, Stream
- Waterfall Rapids
- River Mouth, Estuary
- Lake
- Salt Lake
- Intermittent Lake
- Reservoir
- Swamp, Pond
- Canal
- Glacier
- Ice Shelf, Pack Ice
- Ocean
- Sea
- Gulf, Bay
- Strait, Fjord
- Lagoon
- Bank
- Seamount
- Tablemount
- Ridge
- Shelf
- Basin
- Escarpment, Sea Scarp
- Fracture
- Trench, Abyss
- National Park, Reserve
- Point of Interest
- Recreation Site
- Cave, Cavern
- Historic Site
- Ruins
- Wall, Walls
- Church, Abbey
- Temple
- Scientific Station
- Airport
- Port
- Lighthouse
- Mine
- Tunnel
- Dam, Bridge

Surahammar 8 Ge 59.43N 16.13 E
Sūrak 23 Id 25.43N 58.48 E
Surakarta 22 Nj 7.35S 110.50 E
Şūrān 24 Ge 35.17N 36.45 E
Šurany 10 Oh 48.06N 18.11 E
Surar 35 Gd 7.29N 40.54 E
Surat 22 Jg 21.10N 72.50 E
Surat Thani 22 Li 9.06N 99.20 E
Suraž 7 Hi 55.26N 30.43 E
Suraž 19 De 53.02N 32.29 E
Surčin 15 De 44.47N 20.17 E
Sur del Cabo San Antonio, Punta- 56 Ie 36.52S 56.40W
Surduc 15 Gb 47.15N 23.21 E
Sûre 10 Cg 49.44N 6.31 E
Surendranagar 25 Ed 22.42N 71.41 E
Surgères 11 Fh 46.06N 0.45W
Surgut 22 Jc 61.14N 73.20 E
Surgutiha 20 Dd 63.47N 87.20 E
Surhandarinskaja Oblast [3] 19 Gh 38.00N 67.30 E
Surhandarja 18 Ff 37.14N 67.20 E
Surhob 19 Hh 38.54N 70.04 E
Surigao 26 Ie 9.45N 125.30 E
Surin 25 Kf 14.53N 103.30 E
Suriname [1] 53 Ke 4.00N 56.00W
Suripá, Rio- 49 Mj 7.47N 69.53W
Sūrīyah=Syria (EN) [1] 22 Ff 35.00N 38.00 E
Sürmaq 24 Og 31.03N 52.48 E
Surmelin 12 Fe 49.04N 3.31 E
Sürmene 24 Ib 40.55N 40.07 E
Surna 8 Cb 62.59N 8.40 E
Surnadalsøra 8 Cb 62.59N 8.39 E
Surovikino 19 Ef 48.36N 42.54 E
Surovo 20 Fe 55.39N 105.36 E
Sur-Pakri/Suur-Pakri 8 Je 59.50N 23.45 E
Surprise, Ile- 63b Ad 18.32S 163.02 E
Surprise, Lac- 44 Ja 49.20N 74.57W
Surrey [3] 9 Mj 51.25N 0.30W
Surrey 9 Mj 51.20N 0.05W
Sursee 14 Cc 47.10N 8.07 E
Sursk 16 Nc 53.04N 45.42 E
Surskoje 7 Li 54.31N 46.44 E
Surt 31 Ie 31.13N 16.35 E
Surt, Khalīj-=Sidra, Gulf of-(EN) 30 Ie 31.30N 18.00 E
Surte 8 Eg 57.49N 12.01 E
Surtsey 7a Bc 63.20N 20.38W
Sürüç 24 Hd 36.58N 38.24 E
Surud Ad 30 Lg 10.42N 47.09 E
Suruga-Wan 28 Og 34.55N 138.35 E
Surulangun 26 Dg 2.37S 102.45 E
Survey Pass 40 Ic 67.52N 154.10W
Sur-Vjajn/Suur Väin 8 Jf 58.30N 23.20 E
Surwold 12 Jb 52.57N 7.31 E
Susā 8 Di 55.11N 11.46 E
Šuša 16 Oj 39.43N 46.44 E
Susa [It.] 14 Be 45.08N 7.03 E
Susa [Jap.] 29 Bd 34.37N 131.36 E
Susa, Val di- 14 Be 45.10N 7.10 E
Sušac 14 Kh 42.46N 16.30 E
Sūsah [Lib.] 33 Dc 32.54N 21.58 E
Sūsah [Tun.]=Sousse (EN) 31 Ie 35.49N 10.38 E
Sūsah=Sousse (EN) [3] 32 Jb 35.45N 10.30 E
Susak 14 If 44.31N 14.18 E
Susaki 27 Ne 33.22N 133.17 E
Susami 29 De 33.33N 135.29 E
Susamyr 18 Ic 42.09N 73.59 E
Susanville 43 Cc 40.25N 120.39W
Suşehri 24 Hb 40.11N 38.06 E
Suseja 8 Kh 56.23N 25.00 E
Šušenskoje 20 Ef 53.19N 92.01 E
Sušice 10 Jg 49.14N 13.30 E
Susitna 40 Id 61.16N 150.30W
Suslonger 7 Lh 56.18N 48.12 E
Susoh 26 Cf 3.43N 96.50 E
Susong 28 Di 30.10N 116.06 E
Suspiro 55 Ej 30.38S 54.22W
Suspiro del Moro, Puerto del- 13 Ig 37.08N 3.40W
Susquehanna River 43 Ld 39.33N 76.05W
Susques 56 Gb 23.25S 66.29W
Sussex 9 Mk 50.55N 0.30W
Sussex 44 Oc 45.43N 65.31W
Sussex, Vale of- 9 Mk 51.00N 0.15W
Susubona 63a Dc 8.19S 159.27 E
Susuman 22 Qc 62.47N 148.10 E
Susurluk 24 Cc 39.54N 28.10 E
Susuzmüsellim 15 Kh 41.06N 27.03 E
Šušvė 8 Ji 55.08N 23.53 E
Susz 10 Pc 53.44N 19.20 E
Suţeşti 15 Kd 45.13N 27.26 E
Sutherland 37 Cf 32.24S 20.40 E
Sutherland Falls 62 Bf 44.48S 167.44 E
Sutherlin 46 De 43.25N 123.19W
Sutla 14 Je 45.51N 15.41 E
Sutlej 21 Jg 29.23N 71.02 E
Sutton 44 Gf 38.41N 80.43W
Sutton, London- 12 Bc 51.21N 0.12W
Sutton Bridge 12 Cb 52.46N 0.11 E
Sutton in Ashfield 12 Aa 53.07N 1.16W
Sutton Scotney 12 Ac 51.09N 1.20W
Suttor River 59 Jd 21.25S 147.45 E
Suttsu 28 Pc 42.48N 140.14 E
Sütçüler 24 Dd 37.30N 30.59 E
Sutwik 40 He 56.34N 157.05W
Su'uholo 63a Ec 9.46S 161.58 E
Suunduk 16 Ud 51.46N 58.46 E
Suure-Jaani 7 Fg 58.31N 25.29 E
Suur-Pakri/Sur-Pakri 8 Je 59.50N 23.45 E
Suur Väin/Sur-Vjajn 8 Jf 58.30N 23.20 E
Suva 58 If 18.08S 178.25 E
Suvadiva Atoll 21 Ji 0.30N 73.13 E
Suva Gora 15 Eh 41.51N 21.03 E
Suva Planina 15 Ff 43.08N 22.13 E
Suvasvesi 7 Ge 62.40N 28.10 E
Suvorov 16 Jb 54.08N 36.32 E
Suvorovo 15 Mc 46.33N 29.35 E
Suvorovo 15 Ld 45.35N 29.00 E
Suvorovskaja 16 Mg 44.10N 42.38 E
Suwa 28 Of 36.02N 138.08 E
Suwa-Ko 29 Fc 36.03N 138.05 E
Suwałki 10 Sb 54.07N 22.56 E
Suwałki [2] 10 Sb 54.05N 22.55 E
Suwalskie, Pojezierze- 10 Sb 54.15N 23.00 E
Suwannee River 44 Fk 29.18N 83.09W
Suwanose-Jima 27 Mf 29.40N 129.45 E
Suwarrow Atoll 57 Kf 13.15S 163.05W
Suwayqiyah, Hawr as- 24 Lf 32.40N 46.03 E
Suways, Khalīj as-=Suez, Gulf of-(EN) 30 Kf 28.10N 33.27 E
Suways, Qanāt as-=Suez Canal (EN) 30 Ke 29.55N 32.33 E
Suwŏn 27 Md 37.16N 127.01 E
Suxian 27 Ke 33.36N 116.58 E
Suzaka 29 Fc 36.39N 138.18 E
Suzdal 7 Jh 56.28N 40.27 E
Suzhou 22 Of 31.16N 120.37 E
Suzhou/Jiuquan 22 Lf 39.46N 98.34 E
Suzi He 28 Hd 41.56N 124.20 E
Suzu 27 Od 37.25N 137.17 E
Suzuka 29 Ed 34.51N 136.35 E
Suzuka-Sanmyaku 29 Ed 35.10N 136.20 E
Suzu-Misaki 28 Nf 37.28N 137.20 E
Suzun 20 Df 53.47N 82.19 E
Suzzara 14 Ef 45.00N 10.45 E
Sværholthalvøya 7 Ga 70.30N 26.05 E
Svågan 8 Gc 61.54N 16.33 E
Svalbard [5] 67 Kd 78.00N 20.00 E
Svaljava 16 Ce 48.32N 22.59 E
Svalöv 8 Ei 55.55N 13.06 E
Svaneholm 8 Ee 59.11N 12.33 E
Svaneke 7 Di 55.08N 15.09 E
Svängsta 8 Fh 56.16N 14.46 E
Svanøy 8 Ac 61.30N 5.05 E
Svapa 16 Id 51.44N 34.59 E
Svappavaara 7 Ec 67.39N 21.04 E
Svärdsjö 8 Fd 60.45N 15.55 E
Svartå 8 Fe 59.08N 14.31 E
Svartälven 8 Fe 59.20N 14.35 E
Svartån [Swe.] 8 Fe 59.17N 15.15 E
Svartån [Swe.] 8 Ff 58.28N 15.33 E
Svartån [Swe.] 8 Ge 59.37N 16.33 E
Svartenhuk Halvø=Svartenhuk Peninsula (EN) 41 Gd 71.30N 55.20W
Svartenhuk Peninsula (EN)=Svartenhuk Halvø 41 Gd 71.30N 55.20W
Svartisen 7 Cc 66.38N 13.58 E
Svatoj Nos, Mys- 20 Jb 72.45N 140.45 E
Svatovo 19 Df 49.24N 38.13 E
Svay Riĕng 25 Lf 11.05N 105.48 E
Sveabreen 66 Cf 72.08S 1.53 E
Sveagruva 41 Nc 78.39N 16.25 E
Svealand 7 Dd 60.30N 15.30 E
Svealand 5 Hc 60.30N 15.30 E
Svedala 8 Ei 55.30N 13.14 E
Sveg 7 De 62.02N 14.21 E
Švėkšna 8 Ii 55.32N 21.30 E
Svelgen 7 Af 61.45N 5.18 E
Svelvik 8 De 59.37N 10.24 E
Švenčeneliaj/Švenčioneliai 7 Gi 55.09N 26.02 E
Švenčėnis/Švenčionys 7 Gi 55.07N 26.12 E
Švenčioneliai/Švenčeneliaj 7 Gi 55.09N 26.02 E
Švenčionys/Švenčėnis 7 Gi 55.07N 26.12 E
Svendborg 7 Ci 55.03N 10.37 E
Svendsen Peninsula 42 Ja 77.50N 84.00W
Svenljunga 7 Ch 57.30N 13.07 E
Svenska högarna 8 He 59.35N 19.35 E
Svenskøya 41 Oc 78.43N 26.30 E
Svenstavik 7 De 62.46N 14.27 E
Šventoj/Šventoji 8 Ih 56.04N 20.59 E
Šventoji/Šventoj 8 Ih 56.04N 20.59 E
Sverdlovsk → Jekaterinburg 22 Id 56.51N 60.36 E
Sverdrup, Ostrov- 20 Cb 74.30N 79.35 E
Sverdrup Channel 42 Ha 80.00N 96.30W
Sverdrup Islands 38 Jb 79.00N 98.00W
Sverige=Sweden (EN) [1] 6 Hc 62.00N 15.00 E
Svetac 14 Jg 43.02N 15.45 E
Svēte/Svete 8 Jh 56.40N 23.38 E
Svete/Svēte 8 Jh 56.40N 23.38 E
Sveti Naum 15 Di 40.55N 20.45 E
Sveti Nikola, Prohod- 15 Ff 43.27N 22.36 E
Sveti Nikole 15 Eh 41.52N 21.57 E
Sveti Stefan 15 Bg 42.16N 18.54 E
Svetlaja 20 Ig 46.31N 138.18 E
Svetli 20 Ge 58.34N 116.00 E
Svetlogorsk 19 Ce 52.38N 29.42 E
Svetlogorsk 8 Ij 54.55N 20.08 E
Svetlograd 19 Ef 45.19N 42.40 E
Svetlovodsk 16 He 49.02N 33.15 E
Svetly 19 Ge 50.51N 60.53 E
Svetly 7 Ei 54.41N 20.08 E
Svetly Jar 16 Ne 48.29N 44.46 E
Svetogorsk 7 Gf 61.07N 28.58 E
Svetozarevo 15 Ef 43.59N 21.15 E
Sviča 10 Ug 49.04N 24.06 E
Svid 7 Jf 61.13N 38.45 E
Svidnik 10 Rg 49.18N 21.35 E
Svidník 10 Kg 49.23N 14.58 E
Svijaga 19 Ed 55.48N 48.28 E
Svilaja 14 Kg 43.50N 16.26 E
Svilengrad 15 Jh 41.46N 26.12 E
Svincovy Rudnik 18 Ff 37.52N 66.28 E
Svinecea Mare, Vîrful- 15 Fe 44.48N 22.09 E
Svir 5 Jc 60.30N 32.48 E
Svir 8 Lj 54.50N 26.34 E
Svirica 7 Hf 60.30N 32.54 E
Svirsk 20 Ff 53.04N 103.18 E
Svisloč 16 Fc 53.27N 28.59 E
Svisloč 16 Dc 53.03N 24.07 E
Svištov 15 If 43.37N 25.20 E
Svit 10 Qg 49.03N 20.12 E
Svitava 10 Mg 49.11N 16.38 E
Svitavy 10 Mg 49.46N 16.27 E
Svizra / Svizzera / Schweiz / Suisse = Switzerland (EN) [1] 6 Gf 46.00N 8.30 E
Svizzera / Schweiz / Suisse / Svizra = Switzerland (EN) [1] 6 Gf 46.00N 8.30 E
Svjatoj Nos, Mys- 5 Jb 68.10N 39.43 E
Svobodny 22 Od 51.24N 128.07 E
Svoge 15 Gg 42.58N 23.21 E
Svolvær 7 Db 68.14N 14.34 E
Svratka 10 Mh 48.52N 16.38 E
Svrljig 15 Ff 43.25N 22.08 E
Svulrya 8 Ed 60.25N 12.24 E
Svytaya Anna Trough (EN) 67 He 80.00N 70.00 E
Swabia (EN)=Schwaben 10 Gh 48.20N 10.30 E
Swabian-Bavarian Plateau (EN)=Schwäbisch-Bayerisches Alpenvorland 5 Hf 48.15N 10.30 E
Swabian Jura (EN)=Schwäbische Alb 5 Gf 48.25N 9.30 E
Swaffham 12 Cb 52.39N 0.41 E
Swain Reefs 57 Gg 21.40S 152.15 E
Swains Atoll 57 Jf 11.03S 171.05W
Swainsboro 44 Fi 32.36N 82.20W
Swakop 37 Ad 22.41S 14.31 E
Swakopmund [3] 37 Ad 22.30S 15.00 E
Swakopmund 31 Ik 22.41S 14.34 E
Swale 9 Lg 54.06N 1.20W
Swalmen 12 Ic 51.14N 6.02 E
Swanage 9 Lk 50.37N 1.58W
Swan Hill 59 Ig 35.21S 143.34 E
Swan Range 46 Ic 47.50N 113.40W
Swan River 42 Hf 52.06N 101.16W
Swansboro 44 Ih 34.41N 77.07W
Swansea [Austl.] 59 Jh 42.08S 148.04 E
Swansea [Wales-U.K.] 6 Fe 51.38N 3.57W
Swansea Bay 9 Jj 51.35N 3.52W
Swans Island 44 Mc 44.10N 68.25W
Swanson Lake 45 Ff 40.09N 101.06W
Swan Valley 46 Je 43.28N 111.20W
Swartberge 30 Jl 33.23S 21.48 E
Swarzędz 10 Nd 52.26N 17.05 E
Swastika 44 Ga 48.07N 80.12W
Swaziland [1] 31 Kk 26.30S 31.30 E
Sweden (EN)=Sverige [1] 6 Hc 62.00N 15.00 E
Swedru 34 Ed 5.32N 0.42W
Sweet Grass Hills 46 Jb 48.55N 111.30W
Sweet Home 46 Dd 44.24N 122.44W
Sweetwater 43 Ge 32.28N 100.25W
Sweetwater River 43 Fc 42.31N 107.02W
Swellendam 37 Cf 34.02S 20.26 E
Świder 10 Rd 52.08N 21.12 E
Świdnica 10 Mf 50.51N 16.29 E
Świdnik 10 Se 51.14N 22.41 E
Świdwin 10 Lc 53.47N 15.47 E
Świebodzin 10 Ld 52.15N 15.32 E
Świecie 10 Oc 53.25N 18.28 E
Świętej Anny, Góra- 10 Of 50.28N 18.13 E
Świętokrzyskie, Góry- 10 Qf 50.55N 21.00 E
Swift Current 42 Gf 50.17N 107.50W
Swift Current Creek 46 La 50.40N 107.44W
Swift River 42 Ed 60.05N 131.11W
Swilly, Lough-/Loch Suili 9 Ff 55.10N 7.38W
Swinburne, Cape- 42 Hb 71.14N 98.33W
Swindon 9 Lj 51.34N 1.47W
Swinford/Béal Átha na Muice 9 Eh 53.57N 8.57W
Świnoujście 10 Kc 53.53N 14.14 E
Swischenahner Meer 12 Ka 53.12N 8.01 E
Swisttal 12 Id 50.44N 6.54 E
Switzerland (EN) = Schweiz / Suisse / Svizra / Svizzera [1] 6 Gf 46.00N 8.30 E
Switzerland (EN) = Suisse / Svizra / Svizzera / Schweiz [1] 6 Gf 46.00N 8.30 E
Switzerland (EN) = Svizra / Svizzera / Schweiz / Suisse [1] 6 Gf 46.00N 8.30 E
Switzerland (EN) = Svizzera / Schweiz / Suisse / Svizra [1] 6 Gf 46.00N 8.30 E
Syčevka 16 Ib 55.51N 34.15 E
Syców 10 Ne 51.19N 17.43 E
Sydfalster-Gedser 7 Ci 54.35N 11.57 E
Sydkap Ice Cap 42 Ja 76.30N 85.00W
Sydney [Austl.] 58 Gh 33.52S 151.13 E
Sydney [N.S.-Can.] 39 Me 46.09N 60.11W
Sydney → Manra Atoll 57 Je 4.27S 171.15W
Sydney-Campbelltown 59 Kf 34.04S 150.49 E
Sydney Lake 45 Ia 50.40N 94.24W
Sydney Mines 42 Lg 46.14N 60.12W
Sydney-Penrith 59 Kf 33.45S 150.42 E
Syktyvkar 6 Lc 61.40N 50.46 E
Sylacauga 44 Di 33.10N 86.15W
Sylane 7 Ce 63.02N 12.13 E
Sylarna 7 Ce 63.02N 12.13 E
Sylhet 25 Id 24.54N 91.52 E
Sylling 8 De 59.54N 10.17 E
Sylt 10 Eb 54.55N 8.20 E
Sylva 17 Hh 57.40N 56.57 E
Sylvania 44 Gi 32.45N 81.38W
Sylvania Tablemount (EN) 60 Ge 11.58N 165.00 E
Sylvan Pass 43 Ec 44.28N 110.08W
Sylvester 44 Fj 31.32N 83.49W
Sylvester, Lake- 59 Hc 18.50S 135.50 E
Sym 20 Ed 60.15N 90.02 E
Syndassko 20 Fb 73.14N 108.05 E
Synja 17 Ld 65.12N 64.45 E
Synnfjell 8 Cc 61.05N 9.45 E
Syowa 66 De 69.00S 39.35 E
Syracuse [Ks.-U.S.] 45 Fh 37.59N 101.45W
Syracuse [N.Y.-U.S.] 39 Le 43.03N 76.09W
Syracuse (EN)=Siracusa 6 Hh 37.04N 15.18 E
Syrdarinskaja Oblast [3] 19 Gg 40.30N 68.40 E
Syrdarja 19 Gg 40.52N 68.38 E
Syrdarja=Syr Darya (EN) 21 Ie 46.03N 61.00 E
Syr Darya (EN)=Syrdarja 21 Ie 46.03N 61.00 E
Syria (EN) 21 Ff 35.00N 38.00 E
Syria (EN)=Sūrīyah [1] 22 Ff 35.00N 38.00 E
Syriam 25 Je 16.46N 96.15 E
Syrian Desert- (EN)=Shām, Bādiyat ash- 21 Ff 32.00N 40.00 E
Syrkovoje, Ozero- 17 Lf 60.40N 65.00 E
Syrski 16 Kc 52.36N 39.28 E
Sysert 17 Jh 56.31N 60.49 E
Sysmä 7 Ff 61.30N 25.41 E
Sysola 19 Fc 61.42N 50.58 E
Syssleback 8 Ed 60.44N 12.52 E
Sysulp, Gora- 15 Ha 48.29N 24.17 E
Syverma, Plato- 21 Lc 67.00N 99.00 E
Syzran 6 Ke 53.09N 48.27 E
Szabolcs-Szatmár-Bereg 10 Sh 48.00N 22.10 E
Szamocin 10 Nc 53.02N 17.08 E
Szamos 15 Fa 48.07N 22.20 E
Szamotuły 10 Md 52.37N 16.35 E
Szarvas 10 Qj 46.52N 20.33 E
Szczawnica Krościenko 10 Qg 49.26N 20.30 E
Szczebrzeszyn 10 Sf 50.42N 22.59 E
Szczecin [2] 10 Kc 52.35N 14.30 E
Szczecin=Stettin (EN) 6 He 53.24N 14.32 E
Szczecinek 10 Mc 53.43N 16.42 E
Szczeciński, Zalew- 10 Kc 53.46N 14.14 E
Szczekociny 10 Pf 50.38N 19.50 E
Szczerców 10 Pe 51.18N 19.09 E
Szczucin 10 Rf 50.18N 21.04 E
Szczuczyn 10 Sc 53.34N 22.18 E
Szczytno 10 Qc 53.34N 21.00 E
Szechwan (EN)=Sichuan Sheng (Ssu-ch'uan Sheng) [2] 27 He 30.00N 103.00 E
Szechwan (EN)=Ssu-ch'uan Sheng → Sichuan Sheng [2] 27 He 30.00N 103.00 E
Szécsény 10 Ph 48.05N 19.31 E
Szeged 6 If 46.15N 20.10 E
Szeged [2] 10 Qj 46.16N 20.08 E
Szeghalom 10 Ri 47.02N 21.10 E
Székesfehérvár 6 Hf 47.12N 18.25 E
Szekszárd 10 Oj 46.21N 18.43 E
Szendrő 10 Qh 48.24N 20.44 E
Szentendre 10 Pi 47.40N 19.05 E
Szentes 10 Qj 46.39N 20.16 E
Szentgotthárd 10 Mj 46.57N 16.17 E
Szerencs 10 Rh 48.10N 21.12 E
Szeskie Wzgórza 10 Sb 54.14N 22.22 E
Szigetvár 10 Nj 46.03N 17.48 E
Szkwa 10 Rc 53.10N 21.45 E
Szlichtyngowa 10 Me 51.43N 16.15 E
Szob 10 Oi 47.49N 18.52 E
Szolnok 10 Qi 47.11N 20.12 E
Szolnok → Jász-Nagykun-Szolnok 10 Qi 47.15N 20.30 E
Szombathely 10 Mi 47.14N 16.37 E
Szprotawa 10 Le 51.34N 15.33 E
Sztum 10 Pc 53.56N 19.01 E
Szubin 10 Nc 53.00N 17.44 E
Szydłów 10 Rf 50.35N 21.01 E
Szydłowiec 10 Qe 51.14N 20.51 E

T

Taakoka 64p Cc 21.15S 159.43W
Taalintendas/Dalsbruk 8 Jd 60.02N 22.31 E
Taavetti 8 Ld 60.55N 27.34 E
Tab 10 Oj 46.44N 18.02 E
Tabacal 56 Hb 23.16S 64.15W
Ṭābah 24 Ji 27.02N 42.08 E
Tabaqah 24 He 35.52N 38.34 E
Tabar Islands 57 Ge 2.50S 152.00 E
Ṭabarqah 32 Ib 36.57N 8.45 E
Ṭabas 24 Qf 33.36N 56.54 E
Tabasará, Serrania de- 49 Gi 8.33N 81.40W
Tabasco [2] 47 Fe 18.00N 92.40W
Tabasco y Campeche, Llanos de- 47 Fe 18.15N 91.00W
Tabašino 7 Lh 56.59N 47.43 E
Tābask, Kūh-e- 24 Nh 29.52N 51.49 E
Tabay 55 Ci 28.18S 58.17W
Tabelbala 32 Gd 29.24N 3.15W
Taber 42 Gg 49.47N 112.08W
Taberg 8 Fg 57.41N 14.05 E
Taberg 8 Fg 57.41N 14.05 E
Tabernacle 51c Ab 17.23N 62.46W
Tabernas 13 Jg 37.03N 2.23W
Tabernes de Valldigna 13 Le 39.04N 0.16W
Tabiteuea Atoll 57 Ie 1.20S 174.50 E
Tabla 34 Fc 13.46N 3.01 E
Tablas 26 Hd 12.24N 122.02 E
Tablas Strait 26 Hd 12.40N 121.48 E
Tablat 13 Ph 36.25N 3.19 E
Tablazo, Bahía del- 49 Lh 10.52N 71.35W
Table Cape 62 Gc 39.06S 178.00 E
Table Rock Lake 45 Jh 36.35N 93.30W
Tabocas 55 Jb 14.39S 45.28W
Taboco, Rio- 55 Ed 19.53S 55.58W
Tabola 16 Pg 45.53N 48.20 E
Tábor 10 Kg 49.25N 14.41 E
Tabora 31 Ki 5.01S 32.48 E
Tabora [3] 36 Fd 5.20S 32.30 E
Tabory 17 Lg 58.31N 64.33 E
Tabou 31 Gh 4.25N 7.21W
Tabrīz 22 Gf 38.05N 46.18 E
Tábua 13 Dd 40.21N 8.02W
Tabuaeran Atoll (Fanning) 57 Ld 3.52N 159.20W
Tabūk 22 Fg 28.23N 36.35 E
Tabuk 26 Hc 17.24N 121.25 E
Ṭaburbah 14 Dn 36.50N 9.50 E
Tabursuq 14 Dn 36.28N 9.15 E
Tabursuq, Monts de- 14 Dn 36.25N 9.05 E
Tabusintac 44 Ob 47.24N 65.02W
Tabwemasana 63b Cb 15.22S 166.45 E
Täby 7 Eg 59.30N 18.03 E
Tacámbaro de Codallos 48 Ih 19.14N 101.28W
Tacarcuna, Cerro- 49 Ij 8.05N 77.17W
Tacarigua, Laguna de- 50 Dg 10.15N 65.50W
Tacheng/Qoqek 22 Ke 46.45N 82.57 E
Tachibana-Wan 29 Be 32.45N 130.05 E
Tachichilte, Isla de- 48 Ee 24.59N 108.04W
Tachikawa [Jap.] 29 Fd 35.42N 139.23 E
Tachikawa [Jap.] 29 Fb 38.48N 139.58 E
Táchira [2] 54 Db 7.50N 72.05W
Tachiumet 33 Bd 26.19N 10.03 E
Tachov 10 Ig 49.48N 12.40 E
Tachungnya 64b Bb 14.58N 145.36 E
Tacinski 16 Le 48.13N 41.17 E
Tacir 15 Mi 40.32N 29.44 E
Tacloban 22 Oh 11.15N 125.00 E
Tacna 53 Ig 18.01S 70.15W
Tacna [2] 54 Dg 17.40S 70.20W
Tacoma 39 Ge 47.15N 122.27W
Tacotalpa, Rio- 48 Mi 17.50N 92.52W
Tacuaral 55 Cd 18.59S 58.07W
Tacuarembó [2] 55 Ek 32.10S 55.30W
Tacuarembó, Rio- 55 Ek 32.25S 55.29W
Tacuari, Rio- 55 Fk 32.46S 53.18W
Tacuati 55 Df 23.27S 56.35W
Tadami 29 Fc 37.21N 139.17 E
Tadarimana, Rio- 55 Ec 16.29S 54.31W
Tademaït, Plateau du- 30 Hf 28.30N 2.15 E
Tadine 63b Ce 21.33S 167.53 E
Tadjeraout 32 He 21.17N 1.20 E
Tadjetaret 32 Ie 22.00N 7.30 E
Tadjourah 35 Gc 11.45N 42.54 E
Tadjourah, Golfe de- 35 Gc 11.45N 43.00 E
Tadoule Lake 42 He 58.35N 98.20W
Tadoussac 44 Ma 48.09N 69.43W
Tadžikskaja Sovetskaja Socialističeskaja Respublika → Tajikistan 19 Hh 39.00N 71.00 E
Tadžikskaja SSR/Respublikai Soveth Socialisti Todžikiston → Tajikistan 19 Hh 39.00N 71.00 E
Tadžikskaya SSR → Tajikistan 19 Hh 39.00N 71.00 E
T'aebaek-Sanmaek 21 Of 37.40N 128.50 E
Taechon 28 If 36.21N 126.36 E
T'aech'on 28 Hc 39.55N 125.30 E
Taedong-gang 28 He 38.42N 125.15 E
Taegu 22 Of 35.52N 128.36 E
Taeha-dong 28 Kf 37.31N 130.48 E
Taehan-Haehyŏp=Korea Strait (EN) 21 Of 34.40N 129.00 E
Taehan-Min' guk=South Korea (EN) [1] 22 Of 38.00N 127.30 E
Taehuksan-Do 28 Hg 34.40N 125.25 E
Taejŏn 22 Of 36.20N 127.26 E
Tafahi Island 57 Jf 15.52S 173.55W
Tafalla 13 Kb 42.31N 1.40W
Tafassasset 30 If 21.56N 10.12 E
Tafassasset, Ténéré du- 34 Ha 21.20N 11.00 E
Taff 9 Jj 51.27N 3.09W
Tafilalt 32 Gc 31.18N 4.18W
Tafiré 34 Dd 9.04N 5.10W
Tafi Viejo 56 Gc 26.44S 65.16W
Taflan 24 Gb 41.25N 36.09 E
Tafna 13 Ki 35.18N 1.28W
Tafraout 32 Fd 29.43N 9.00W
Tafresh 24 Ne 34.41N 50.01 E
Taft 24 Pg 31.45N 54.14 E
Taftān, Kūh-e- 21 Ig 28.36N 61.06 E
Taftanāz 24 Ge 35.59N 36.47 E
Taga 65c Aa 13.46S 172.28W
Taga Dzong 25 Hc 27.04N 89.53 E
Tagajō 29 Gb 38.18N 140.58 E
Tagama 30 Hg 15.50N 8.12 E
Taganrog 6 Jf 47.12N 38.56 E
Taganrogski Zaliv 16 Kf 46.50N 38.25 E
Tagant [3] 32 Ef 18.30N 10.30W
Tagant 30 Fg 17.31N 12.07W
Tagarev, Gora- 18 Ae 38.19N 57.18 E
Tagawa 29 Be 33.39N 130.48 E
Tagbilaran 26 He 9.39N 123.51 E
Tageru, Jabal- 35 Db 16.25N 27.10 E
Taggia 14 Bg 43.52N 7.51 E
Taghit 32 Gc 30.55N 2.02W
Tagil 17 Kg 58.33N 62.30 E
Tagish Lake 42 Ed 60.00N 134.00W
Tagliamento 14 He 45.38N 13.06 E
Taglio di Po 14 Ge 45.00N 12.12 E
Tagomago, Isla de- 13 Ne 39.02N 1.39 E
Tagounit 32 Fd 29.58N 5.35W
Tagpochau, Ogso- 64b Ba 15.11N 145.45 E
Tāgrīfat 33 Cd 29.12N 17.21 E
Taguatinga 55 If 12.25S 46.26W
Taguersimet 32 De 24.09N 15.07W
Tagula 63a Ad 11.20S 153.00 E
Tagula Island 57 Gf 11.30S 153.30 E
Tagum 26 Ie 7.21N 125.50 E
Tagus (EN)=Tajo 5 Fh 38.40N 9.24W
Tagus (EN)=Tejo 5 Fh 38.40N 9.24W
Tah 32 Ed 27.37N 12.50W
Tahaa, Ile- 61 Kc 16.38S 151.30W
Tahakopa 62 Cg 46.31S 169.23 E
Tahan, Gunong- 21 Mi 4.39N 102.14 E
Tahanea Atoll 57 Mf 16.52S 144.45W

Index Symbols

- [1] Independent Nation
- [2] State, Region
- [3] District, County
- [4] Municipality
- [5] Colony, Dependency
- Continent
- Physical Region
- Historical or Cultural Region
- Mount, Mountain
- Volcano
- Hill
- Mountains, Mountain Range
- Hills, Escarpment
- Plateau, Upland
- Pass, Gap
- Plain, Lowland
- Delta
- Salt Flat
- Valley, Canyon
- Crater, Cave
- Karst Features
- Depression
- Polder
- Desert, Dunes
- Forest, Woods
- Heath, Steppe
- Oasis
- Cape, Point
- Coast, Beach
- Cliff
- Peninsula
- Isthmus
- Sandbank
- Island
- Atoll
- Rock, Reef
- Islands, Archipelago
- Rocks, Reefs
- Coral Reef
- Well, Spring
- Geyser
- River, Stream
- Waterfall Rapids
- River Mouth, Estuary
- Lake
- Salt Lake
- Intermittent Lake
- Reservoir
- Swamp, Pond
- Canal
- Glacier
- Ice Shelf, Pack Ice
- Ocean
- Sea
- Gulf, Bay
- Strait, Fjord
- Lagoon
- Bank
- Seamount
- Tablemount
- Ridge
- Shelf
- Basin
- Escarpment, Sea Scarp
- Fracture
- Trench, Abyss
- National Park, Reserve
- Point of Interest
- Recreation Site
- Cave, Cavern
- Historic Site
- Ruins
- Wall, Walls
- Church, Abbey
- Temple
- Scientific Station
- Airport
- Port
- Lighthouse
- Mine
- Tunnel
- Dam, Bridge

Index Symbols

[1] Independent Nation	Historical or Cultural Region	Pass, Gap
[2] State, Region	Mount, Mountain	Plain, Lowland
[3] District, County	Volcano	Delta
[4] Municipality	Hill	Salt Flat
[5] Colony, Dependency	Mountains, Mountain Range	Valley, Canyon
Continent	Hills, Escarpment	Crater, Cave
Physical Region	Plateau, Upland	Karst Features

Depression	Coast, Beach	Rock, Reef
Polder	Cliff	Islands, Archipelago
Desert, Dunes	Peninsula	Rocks, Reefs
Forest, Woods	Isthmus	Coral Reef
Heath, Steppe	Sandbank	Well, Spring
Oasis	Island	Geyser
Cape, Point	Atoll	River, Stream

Waterfall Rapids	Canal	Lagoon
River Mouth, Estuary	Bank	Glacier
Lake	Seamount	Ice Shelf, Pack Ice
Salt Lake	Tablemount	Ocean
Intermittent Lake	Ridge	Sea
Reservoir	Shelf	
Swamp, Pond	Gulf, Bay	
	Strait, Fjord	
	Basin	

Escarpment, Sea Scarp	Historic Site	Port
Fracture	Ruins	Lighthouse
Trench, Abyss	Wall, Walls	Mine
National Park, Reserve	Church, Abbey	Tunnel
Point of Interest	Temple	Dam, Bridge
Recreation Site	Scientific Station	
Cave, Cavern	Airport	

Tarauacá 54 De 8.10S 70.46W
Tarauacá, Rio 52 Jf 6.42S 69.48W
Taravao 65e Fc 17.44S 149.19W
Taravao, Baie de- 65e Fc 17.43S 149.17W
Taravo 11a Ab 41.42N 8.48 E
Tarawa Atoll 57 Id 1.25N 173.00 E
Tarawera 62 Gc 39.02S 176.35 E
Tarazi 24 Mg 31.05N 48.18 E
Tarazona 13 Kc 41.54N 1.44W
Tarazona de la Mancha 13 Ke 39.15N 1.55W
Tarbagataj, Hrebet 21 Ke 47.10N 83.00 E
Tarbagatay Shan 27 Db 47.10N 83.00 E
Tarbat Ness 9 Jd 57.50N 3.40W
Tarbert [Scot.-U.K.] 9 Gd 57.54N 6.49W
Tarbert [Scot.-U.K.] 9 Hf 55.52N 5.26W
Tarbes 11 Gk 43.14N 0.05 E
Tarboro 44 Ih 35.54N 77.32W
Tarcăului, Munţii- 15 Jc 46.45N 26.20 E
Tarcoola 59 Gf 30.41S 134.33 E
Tardenois 12 Fe 49.12N 3.40 E
Tardienta 13 Lc 41.59N 0.32W
Tardoire 11 Gi 45.52N 0.14 E
Tardoki-Jani, Gora- 20 Ig 48.50N 137.55 E
Taree 58 Gh 31.54S 152.28 E
Taremert-n-Akli 32 Id 25.53N 5.18 E
Tarentaise 11 Mi 45.30N 6.30 E
Ţarfā', Ra's aţ- 33 Hf 17.02N 42.22 E
Ţarfā', Wādī aţ- 24 Dh 28.38N 30.43 E
Ţarfah, Jazirat aţ- 33 Hg 14.37N 42.55 E
Tarfaya 31 Ff 27.57N 12.55W
Targa 13 Qi 35.41N 4.09 E
Tîrgovişki prohod 15 Jf 43.12N 26.30 E
Tărgovište 15 Jf 43.15N 26.34 E
Tărgovište [2] 15 Jf 43.15N 26.34 E
Tarhankut, Mys- 16 Hg 45.21N 32.30 E
Tarhăus, Vîrful- 15 Jc 46.38N 26.10 E
Tarhūnah 33 Bc 32.26N 13.38 E
Tarhūnī, Jabal at- 33 De 22.12N 22.25 E
Táriba 49 Kj 7.49N 72.13W
Tarīf 23 He 24.01N 53.45 E
Tarifa 13 Gh 36.01N 5.36W
Tarifa, Punta de- 13 Ih 36.00N 3.37W
Tarija 53 Jh 21.31S 64.45W
Tarija [2] 54 Fh 21.30S 64.00W
Tarik 64d Bb 7.21N 151.47 E
Tariku 26 Kg 2.55S 138.26 E
Tarīm [Yem.] 23 Gf 16.03N 49.00 E
Tarīm [Sau.Ar.] 24 Fi 27.54N 35.24 E
Tarim Basin (EN) = Tarim Pendi 21 Ke 41.00N 84.00 E
Tarime 36 Fc 1.21S 34.22 E
Tarim He 21 Ke 41.05N 86.40 E
Tarim Pendi = Tarim Basin (EN) 21 Ke 41.00N 84.00 E
Tarin Kowt 23 Kc 32.52N 65.38 E
Taritatu 26 Kg 2.54S 138.27 E
Tarjalan 27 Hb 49.38N 101.59 E
Tarjannevesi 8 Kb 62.10N 24.05 E
Tarjat 27 Gb 48.10N 99.40 E
Tarka, Vallée de- 34 Gc 14.30N 6.30 E
Tarkastad 37 Df 32.00S 26.16 E
Tarkio 45 If 40.27N 95.23W
Tarko-Sale 20 Cd 64.55N 78.05 E
Tarkwa 34 Ed 5.18N 1.59W
Tarlac 22 Oh 15.29N 120.35 E
Tarm 8 Ci 55.55N 8.32 E
Tarma 54 Cf 11.25S 75.42W
Tarn 11 Hj 44.06N 1.02 E
Tarn [3] 11 Hk 43.50N 2.00 E
Tarna 10 Pi 47.31N 19.59 E
Tärnaby 7 Dd 65.43N 15.16 E
Tarn-et-Garonne [3] 11 Hj 44.00N 1.10 E
Tarnica 10 Sg 49.06N 22.47 E
Tarnobrzeg 10 Rf 50.35N 21.41 E
Tarnobrzeg [2] 10 Rf 50.35N 21.40 E
Tarnogród 10 Sf 50.23N 22.45 E
Tarnos 11 Ek 43.32N 1.28W
Tarnów 6 Ie 50.01N 21.00 E
Tarnów [2] 10 Qf 50.00N 21.00 E
Tarnowskie Góry 10 Of 50.27N 18.52 E
Tärnsjö 8 Gd 60.09N 16.56 E
Taro 14 Ef 45.00N 10.15 E
Taron 63a Aa 4.28S 153.04 E
Taroom 58 Fg 25.39S 149.49 E
Taroudant 32 Fc 30.29N 8.52W
Tarpon Springs 44 Fk 28.09N 82.45W
Tarquinia 14 Fh 42.15N 11.45 E
Tarra, Rio- 49 Ki 9.04N 72.27W
Tarrafal 32 Cf 15.17N 23.46W
Tarragona 6 Gg 41.07N 1.15 E
Tarragona [3] 13 Mc 41.10N 1.00 E
Tarraleah 59 Jh 42.10S 146.30 E
Tarrant 44 Di 33.38N 86.46W
Tarrasa 13 Oc 41.34N 2.01 E
Tárrega 13 Nc 41.39N 1.09 E
Tarsus 23 Db 36.55N 34.53 E
Tart 27 Fd 37.07N 92.57 E
Tartagal 56 Hb 22.32S 63.49W
Tartaro 14 Fe 45.02N 11.30 E
Tartas 11 Fk 43.50N 0.48W
Tartas 20 Ce 55.37N 76.44 E
Tartu 6 Id 58.23N 26.45 E
Tartūs 23 Ec 34.53N 35.53 E
Tarumae-Yama 29a Bb 42.41N 141.23 E
Tarumizu 28 Ki 31.29N 130.42 E
Tarusa 16 Jb 54.43N 37.11 E
Tārūt 24 Ni 26.34N 50.04 E
Tarutau, Ko- 25 Jg 6.35N 99.40 E
Tarutino 16 Ff 46.12N 29.09 E
Tarutung 26 Cf 2.01N 98.58 E
Tarvisio 14 Hd 46.30N 13.35 E
Tarvo 55 Bb 15.06S 60.34W
Tarvo, Rio- 55 Bb 14.47S 61.03W
Tasajera, Sierra- 48 Gc 29.35N 105.35W
Tašanta 20 Dg 49.43N 89.11 E
Tasaral, Ostrov- 18 Ja 46.15N 74.05 E
Tašauz 19 Fg 41.52N 59.59 E
Tašauzskaja Oblast [3] 19 Fg 41.00N 58.40 E
Tasāwah 33 Bd 25.59N 13.29 E
Tasbuget 19 Gg 44.48N 65.38 E
Tasejeva 20 Ee 58.06N 94.01 E
Taseko Lake 46 Da 51.15N 123.35W
Tasendjanet 32 Hd 25.40N 0.59 E
Tashk, Daryācheh-ye- 23 Hd 29.45N 53.35 E
Tasikmalaya 22 Mj 7.20S 108.12 E
Tåsinge 8 Di 55.00N 10.36 E
Tašir (Kalinino) 16 Ni 41.08N 44.14 E
Tasiussaq 41 Gd 73.18N 56.00W
Taskan 20 Kd 62.58N 150.20 E
Taškent 22 Ie 41.20N 69.18 E
Taškentskaja Oblast [3] 19 Gg 41.20N 69.40 E
Taškepri 19 Gh 36.17N 62.38 E
Taškeprinskoje, Vodohranilišče- 18 Df 36.15N 62.40 E
Tasker 34 Hb 15.04N 10.42 E
Taşköprü 24 Fb 41.30N 34.14 E
Taš-Kumyr 18 Hd 41.20N 72.14 E
Taşlıçay 24 Jc 39.38N 43.23 E
Tasman, Mount- 62 De 43.34S 170.09 E
Tasman Basin (EN) 3 Jn 43.00S 158.00 E
Tasman Bay 61 Dh 41.10S 173.15 E
Tasmania 59 Jh 43.00S 147.00 E
Tasmania 57 Fi 43.00S 147.00 E
Tasman Peninsula 59 Jh 43.05S 147.50 E
Tasman Plateau (EN) 3 In 48.00S 148.00 E
Tasman Sea 57 Hh 40.00S 163.00 E
Tășnad 15 Fb 47.29N 22.35 E
Taşova 24 Gb 40.46N 36.20 E
Tassah, Wādī- 14 Cn 36.35N 8.54 E
Tassara 34 Gb 16.01N 5.39 E
Taštagol 20 Df 52.47N 88.00 E
Tåstrup 8 Ei 55.39N 12.19 E
Tastür 14 Dn 36.33N 9.27 E
Tasty-Taldy 19 Ge 50.47N 66.31 E
Ţasūj 24 Kc 38.19N 45.21 E
Taşucu 24 Ed 36.19N 33.53 E
Tata [3] 32 Fd 29.40N 8.00W
Tata [Hun.] 10 Oi 47.39N 18.19 E
Tata [Mor.] 32 Fd 29.45N 7.59W
Tataba 26 Hg 1.18S 122.49 E
Tatabánya 10 Oi 47.34N 18.25 E
Tatakoto Atoll 57 Nf 17.20S 138.23W
Tata Mailau 26 Ih 8.55S 125.30 E
Tatarbunary 16 Fg 45.49N 29.35 E
Tatarsk 22 Jd 55.13N 75.58 E
Tatarstan, respublika 19 Fd 55.20N 50.50 E
Tatar Strait (EN) = Tatarski Proliv 21 Qd 50.00N 141.15 E
Tatau 26 Ff 2.53N 112.51 E
Taţāwīn 32 Jc 32.56N 10.27 E
Tateyama 28 Og 34.59N 139.52 E
Tathlina Lake 42 Fd 60.30N 117.30W
Tathlīth 23 Ff 19.32N 43.30 E
Tatiščevo 16 Nd 51.40N 45.35 E
Tatla Lake 46 Ca 51.58N 124.25W
Tatla Lake 46 Ca 51.55N 123.52W
Tatlow, Mount- 46 Da 51.23N 123.52W
Tatnam, Cape - 42 Ie 57.16N 91.00W
Tatra Mountains (EN) 5 Hf 49.15N 20.00 E
Tatsuno [Jap.] 29 Dd 34.52N 134.33 E
Tatsuno [Jap.] 29 Ed 35.58N 137.58 E
Tatsuruhama 29 Ec 37.04N 136.53 E
Tatta 25 Dd 24.45N 67.55 E
Tatui 55 If 23.21S 47.51W
Tatum 45 Ej 33.16N 103.19W
Tatvan 23 Fb 38.30N 42.16 E
Tau 8 Ae 59.04N 5.54 E
Tau [Am.Sam.] 65c Db 14.15S 169.30W
Tau [Ton.] 65b Bc 21.01S 175.00W
Tauá 54 Je 6.01S 40.26W
Taubaté 53 Lh 23.02S 45.33W
Tauberbischofsheim 10 Fg 49.37N 9.40 E
Taučik 19 Fg 44.15N 51.20 E
Tauere Atoll 57 Mf 17.22S 141.30W
Tauern 5 Hf 47.15N 13.15 E
Taufstein 10 Ff 50.31N 9.14 E
Tauhunu 64n Ac 10.25S 161.03W
Tauhunu 64n Ac 10.25S 161.03W
Taujsk 20 Je 59.46N 149.20 E
Taujskaja Guba 20 Je 59.15N 150.00 E
Taukum 18 Jb 44.50N 75.30 E
Taumako 63c Ba 9.57S 167.13 E
Taumarunui 62 Fc 38.52S 175.15 E
Taum Sauk Mountain 45 Kh 37.34N 90.44W
Taunay 55 De 20.18S 56.05W
Taung 37 Ce 27.33S 24.47 E
Taungdwingyi 25 Jd 20.01N 95.33 E
Taunggyi 25 Jd 20.47N 97.02 E
Taungthonlon 25 Jd 24.58N 95.48 E
Taungup 25 Ie 18.51N 94.14 E
Taunton [Eng.-U.K.] 9 Jj 51.01N 3.06W
Taunton [Ma.-U.S.] 44 Le 41.54N 71.06W
Taunus 10 Ef 50.10N 8.15 E
Taunusstein 12 Kd 50.08N 8.10 E
Taupo 61 Eg 38.41S 176.05 E
Taupo, Lake- 61 Eg 38.50S 175.55 E
Tauragė/Taurage 7 Fi 55.16N 22.19 E
Taurage/Tauragė 7 Fi 55.16N 22.19 E
Tauranga 58 Ih 37.42S 176.10 E
Taurianova 14 Kl 38.21N 16.01 E
Taurion 11 Hi 45.53N 1.24 E
Taurisano 14 Mk 39.57N 18.13 E
Tauroa Point 62 Ea 35.10S 173.04 E
Taurus Mountains (EN) = Toros Dağları 21 Ff 37.00N 33.00 E
Tauste 13 Kc 41.55N 1.15W
Tauu Islands 57 Ge 4.45S 157.00 E
Tauz 19 Eg 41.01N 45.35 E
Tavālesh, Kūhhā-Ye- 24 Mc 38.42N 48.18 E
Tavas [Tur.] 24 Dc 39.54N 30.03 E
Tavas [Tur.] 24 Cd 37.34N 29.04 E
Tavas Ovasi 15 Ll 37.30N 28.55 E
Tavastehus/Hämeenlinna 7 Ff 61.00N 24.27 E
Tavau/Davos 14 Dd 46.47N 9.50 E
Tavda 19 Gd 58.03N 65.15 E
Tavda 21 Id 57.47N 67.16 E
Tavendroua 63b Cc 16.21S 167.22 E
Taveta 36 Gc 3.24S 37.41 E
Taveuni Island 61 Fc 16.51S 179.58W
Taviano 14 Mk 39.59N 18.05 E
Tavignano 11a Ba 42.06N 9.33 E
Tavira 13 Eg 37.07N 7.39W
Tavistock 9 Ik 50.33N 4.08W
Tavolara 14 Dj 40.55N 9.40 E
Tavoliere 14 Ji 41.35N 15.25 E
Tavolžan 19 He 52.44N 77.30 E
Tavoy → Dawei 22 Lh 14.05N 98.12 E
Tavričanka 28 Kc 43.20N 131.52 E
Tavropoú, Tekhnití Límni- 15 Ej 39.15N 21.40 E
Tavşan Adaları 15 Jj 39.55N 26.05 E
Tavşanlı 24 Cc 39.35N 29.30 E
Tavua 61 Ec 17.27S 177.51 E
Taw 9 Ij 51.04N 4.11W
Tawakoni, Lake- 45 Ij 32.55N 96.00W
Tawas City 43 Kc 44.16N 83.31W
Tawau 22 Ni 4.15N 117.54 E
Tawfiqiyah 35 Ed 9.26N 31.37 E
Ţawīlah, Juzur- 24 Ei 27.35N 33.46 E
Tawitawi Group 26 He 5.10N 120.15 E
Ţawkar 31 Kg 18.26N 37.44 E
Ţāwūq 24 Ke 35.08N 44.27 E
Tawūq Chāy 24 Ke 34.35N 44.31 E
Ţāwurghā', Sabkhat- 33 Cc 31.10N 15.15 E
Tawzar 32 Ic 33.55N 8.08 E
Taxco de Alarcón 48 Jh 18.33N 99.36W
Taxkorgan 27 Cd 37.47N 75.14 E
Tay 9 Je 56.30N 3.30W
Tay, Firth of- 9 Ke 56.28N 3.00W
Tay, Loch- 9 Ie 56.30N 4.10W
Tayandu, Kepulauan- 26 Jh 5.30S 132.15 E
Tayëgle 35 Ge 4.02N 44.36 E
Taylor [Nb.-U.S.] 45 Gf 41.46N 99.23W
Taylor [Tx.-U.S.] 43 He 30.34N 97.25W
Taylor, Mount- 43 Fd 35.14N 107.37W
Taylorville 45 Lg 39.33N 89.18W
Taymā' 23 Ed 27.38N 38.29 E
Taymyr Peninsula (EN) = Tajmyr, Poluostrov- 21 Mb 76.00N 104.00 E
Tay Ninh 25 Lf 11.18N 106.06 E
Tayside [3] 9 Je 56.30N 3.40W
Taytay 26 Gd 10.49N 119.31 E
Taza [3] 32 Gc 34.00N 4.00W
Taza [Mor.] 31 Ge 34.13N 4.01W
Taza 20 Gf 54.55N 111.05 E
Tāzah Khurmātū 24 Ke 35.18N 44.20 E
Tazawa-Ko 29 Gb 39.43N 140.40 E
Tazawako 29 Gb 39.42N 140.44 E
Tazenakht 32 Fc 30.35N 7.12W
Tazerbo Oasis (EN) = Tāzirbū, Wāḩāt al- 30 Jf 25.45N 21.00 E
Tazewell [Tn.-U.S.] 44 Fg 36.27N 83.34W
Tazewell [Va.-U.S.] 44 Gg 37.07N 81.34W
Tāzīāzet 32 De 20.55N 15.40W
Tazin Lake 42 Ge 59.48N 109.05W
Tāzirbū, Wāḩāt al- = Tazerbo Oasis (EN) 30 Jf 25.45N 21.00 E
Tazlău 15 Jc 46.16N 26.47 E
Tazmalt 13 Qh 36.43N 4.08 E
Tazouikert 34 Ea 21.46N 1.13W
Tazovskaja Guba 17 Qb 69.05N 76.00 E
Tazovski 20 Cc 67.28N 78.42 E
Tazrouk 32 Ie 23.26N 6.14 E
Tazumal 49 Cg 14.00N 89.40W
Tbilisi 6 Kg 41.43N 44.49 E
Tchad = Chad (EN) [1] 31 Ig 15.00N 19.00 E
Tchad, Lac- = Chad, Lake- (EN) 30 Ig 13.20N 14.00 E
Tchamba [Cam.] 34 Hd 8.37N 12.48 E
Tchamba [Togo] 34 Fd 9.02N 1.25 E
Tchibanga 36 Bc 2.51S 11.02 E
Tchien 34 Dd 6.04N 8.08W
Tchigaï, Plateau du- 30 If 21.30N 14.50 E
Tchin Tabaraden 34 Gb 15.58N 5.50 E
Tcholliré 34 Hd 8.24N 14.10 E
Tczew 10 Ob 54.06N 18.47 E
Tea, Rio- 54 Ed 0.30S 65.09W
Teaca 15 Hc 46.55N 24.31 E
Teacapán 48 Gf 22.33N 105.45W
Teaiti Point 64p Bb 21.11S 159.47W
Te Anau 62 Bf 45.25S 167.43 E
Te Anau, Lake- 61 Ci 45.15S 167.45 E
Teano 14 Ii 41.15N 14.04 E
Teapa 48 Mi 17.33N 92.57W
Te Araroa 61 Eg 37.38S 178.22 E
Te Aroha 62 Fb 37.32S 175.42 E
Tea Tree 59 Gd 22.11S 133.17 E
Te Atu Kura 64p Bb 21.14S 159.45W
Te Awamutu 62 Fc 38.00S 175.19 E
Teberda 16 Lh 43.28N 41.43 E
Tébessa 31 He 35.24N 8.07 E
Tébessa [3] 32 Ic 35.00N 7.45 E
Tébessa, Oued- 14 Bo 35.48N 7.53 E
Tebicuary, Rio- [Par.] 55 Ch 26.36S 58.16W
Tebicuary, Rio- [Par.] 55 Dh 26.26S 56.51W
Tebingtinggi [Indon.] 26 Dg 3.36S 103.05 E
Tebingtinggi [Indon.] 26 Cf 3.20N 99.09 E
Tebulosmta, Gora- 16 Nh 42.33N 45.16 E
Teča 17 Kh 56.17N 62.59 E
Tecate 47 Ab 32.34N 116.38W
Tecer Dağları 24 Gc 39.27N 37.11 E
Techirghiol 15 Le 44.03N 28.36 E
Tecka 56 Ff 43.29S 70.48W
Tecklenburg 12 Jb 52.13N 7.50 E
Tecomán 47 De 18.55N 103.53W
Tecomate, Laguna- 48 Ji 16.45N 99.25W
Tecoripa 48 Ec 28.37N 109.57W
Tecpan de Galeana 47 De 17.15N 100.41W
Tecuala 47 Cd 22.23N 105.27W
Tecuci 15 Kd 45.52N 27.25 E
Tedegra 35 Ba 20.46N 19.34 E
Tedori-Gawa 29 Ec 36.29N 136.28 E
Tedžen 21 If 37.24N 60.38 E
Tedženstroj 19 Gh 36.54N 60.53 E
Teeli 20 Ef 50.57N 90.18 E
Teenuse Jõgi/Tenuze 7 Jf 58.44N 23.58 E
Tees 9 Lg 54.34N 1.16W
Tees Bay 9 Lg 54.35N 1.05W
Teesside → Middlesbrough 6 Fe 54.35N 1.14W
Tefé 53 Jf 3.22S 64.42W
Tefé, Rio- 54 Fd 3.35S 64.47W
Tefedest 32 Ie 24.40N 5.30 E
Tefenni 24 Cd 37.18N 29.47 E
Tegal 22 Mj 6.52S 109.08 E
Tegea (EN) = Teyéa 15 Fl 37.27N 22.25 E
Tegelen 12 Ic 51.20N 6.08 E
Tegernsee 10 Hi 47.43N 11.46 E
Tegina 34 Gc 10.04N 6.11 E
Tégoua 63b Ca 13.15S 166.37 E
Tegucigalpa 39 Kh 14.06N 87.13W
Teguidda I-n-Tessoum 34 Gb 17.26N 6.39 E
Teguldet 20 De 57.20N 88.20 E
Tehachapi 46 Fi 35.08N 118.27W
Tehachapi Mountains 46 Fi 34.56N 118.40W
Tehamiyam 35 Fb 18.20N 36.32 E
Te Hapua 61 Df 34.30S 172.55 E
Tehaupoo 65e Fc 17.49S 149.18W
Tehek Lake 42 Hd 64.55N 95.30W
Téhini 34 Ed 9.36N 3.40W
Tehi-n-Isser 32 Ie 24.48N 8.08 E
Tehoru 26 Ig 3.23S 129.30 E
Tehrān 22 Hf 35.40N 51.26 E
Tehrān → Markazī [3] 23 Hb 35.30N 51.30 E
Tehuacán 47 Ee 18.27N 97.23W
Tehuantepec 47 Ee 16.20N 95.14W
Tehuantepec, Golfo de- = Tehuantepec, Gulf of- (EN) 38 Jh 16.00N 94.50W
Tehuantepec, Gulf of- (EN) = Tehuantepec, Golfo de- 38 Jh 16.00N 94.50W
Tehuantepec, Isthmus of- (EN) = Tehuantepec, Istmo de- 38 Jh 17.00N 94.30W
Tehuantepec, Istmo de- = Tehuantepec, Isthmus of- (EN) 38 Jh 17.00N 94.30W
Tehuantepec Ridge (EN) 47 Ef 13.30N 98.00W
Tehuata Atoll 57 Mf 16.50S 141.55W
Teiga Plateau 35 Db 15.38N 25.40 E
Teignmouth 9 Jk 50.33N 3.30W
Teili/Delet 8 Id 60.15N 20.35 E
Teith 9 Ie 56.14N 4.20W
Teiuş 15 Gc 46.12N 23.41 E
Teixeira Pinto 34 Bc 12.04N 16.02W
Teja 20 Ed 60.27N 92.38 E
Tejkovo 19 Ed 56.50N 40.34 E
Tejo = Tagus (EN) 5 Fh 38.40N 9.24W
Teju 25 Jc 27.55N 96.10 E
Te Kaha 62 Gb 37.44S 177.41 E
Te Kao 62 Ea 34.39S 172.58 E
Tekapo, Lake- 62 De 43.50S 170.30 E
Te Karaka 62 Gc 38.28S 177.52 E
Tekax 48 Og 20.12N 89.17W
Teke 15 Mh 41.04N 29.39 E
Teke 15 Jh 41.21N 26.57 E
Teke Burun [Tur.] 15 Ji 40.02N 26.10 E
Teke Burun [Tur.] 15 Jk 38.05N 26.36 E
Tekeli 19 Hg 44.48N 78.57 E
Tekes 27 Dc 43.10N 81.43 E
Tekes He 27 Dc 43.35N 82.30 E
Tekeze 35 Fc 14.20N 35.50 E
Tekija 15 Fe 44.41N 22.25 E
Tekiliktag 27 Dd 36.35N 80.20 E
Tekirdağ 23 Ca 40.59N 27.31 E
Tekman 24 Ic 39.38N 41.31 E
Te Kopuru 62 Eb 36.02S 173.55 E
Te Kou 64p Bb 21.14S 159.46W
Tekouiat 32 He 22.20N 2.30 E
Tekro 35 Cb 19.34N 20.57 E
Te Kuiti 62 Fc 38.20S 175.10 E
Tela 47 Ge 15.44N 87.27W
Telagh 32 Gc 34.47N 0.34W
Telatai 34 Fb 16.31N 1.30 E
Telavåg 7 Af 60.16N 4.49 E
Telavi 19 Eg 41.55N 45.29 E
Tel Aviv-Yafo 22 Ff 32.04N 34.46 E
Telč 10 Lg 49.11N 15.27 E
Telchac Puerto 48 Og 21.21N 89.16W
Telciu 15 Hb 47.26N 24.24 E
Tele 36 Db 2.48N 23.54 E
Teleac 15 Hc 46.41N 24.48 E
Telečkoje Ozero 20 Df 51.30N 87.45 E
Telefomin 60 Ci 5.08S 141.31 E
Telegraph Creek 42 Ee 57.54N 131.09W
Telekitonga 65b Bb 20.24S 174.32W
Telekivavu'u 65b Bb 20.19S 174.32W
Telêmaco Borba 55 Gg 24.23S 50.28W
Telemark [2] 7 Bg 59.30N 8.40 E
Telemark 8 Ce 59.30N 8.45 E
Telén 56 Ge 36.16S 65.30W
Telen 26 Gf 0.26N 116.42 E
Telenešty 15 Lb 47.30N 28.16 E
Teleno 13 Fb 42.21N 6.23W
Teleorman 15 If 43.52N 25.26 E
Teleorman [2] 15 If 44.10N 25.15 E
Telerhteba, Djebel- 32 Ie 24.10N 6.51 E
Telescope Peak 46 Gh 36.10N 117.05W
Telescope Point 51p Bb 12.08N 61.36W
Telese 14 Ii 41.13N 14.32 E
Teles Pires, Rio- o São Manuel, Rio- 52 Kf 7.21S 58.03W
Telfān, Hadjer- 35 Bc 12.05N 18.57 E
Telford 9 Ki 52.40N 2.30W
Telgte 12 Jc 51.59N 7.47 E
Télimélé 34 Cc 10.54N 13.02W
Teljo, Jabal- 35 Dc 14.42N 25.56 E
Tell al Ubaid 24 Lg 30.59N 46.01 E
Tellaro 14 Jn 36.50N 15.06 E
Tell Atlas (EN) = Atlas Tellien 30 He 36.00N 2.00 E
Tell City 44 Dg 37.57N 86.46W
Teller 40 Fc 65.16N 166.22W
Telok Anson 26 Df 4.02N 101.01 E
Teloloapan 48 Jh 18.21N 99.51W
Telposiz, Gora- 5 Lc 63.54N 59.10 E
Telsen 56 Gf 42.24S 66.57W
Telšiai/Telšjaj 19 Cd 55.59N 22.17 E
Telšjaj/Telšiai 19 Cd 55.59N 22.17 E
Teltow 10 Jd 52.24N 13.16 E
Telukbetung 22 Mj 5.27S 105.16 E
Telukbutun 26 Ef 4.13N 108.12 E
Telukdalem 26 Cf 0.34N 97.49 E
Téma 31 Gh 5.37N 0.01W
Temacine 32 Ic 33.01N 6.01 E
Te Manga 64p Bb 21.13S 159.45W
Tematangi Atoll 57 Mg 21.41S 140.40W
Tembenči 20 Ed 64.36N 99.58 E
Témbi 15 Fj 39.53N 22.35 E
Tembilahan 26 Dg 0.19S 103.09 E
Temblador 50 Eh 8.59N 62.44W
Tembleque 13 Ie 39.42N 3.30W
Temblor Range 46 Fi 35.30N 119.55W
Tembo 36 Cd 7.42S 17.17 E
Tembo, Chutes- 30 Ii 8.50S 15.20 E
Tembo, Mont- 36 Bb 1.50N 12.00 E
Tembué 37 Eb 14.51S 32.50 E
Teme 9 Ki 52.09N 2.18W
Temerin 15 Cd 45.25N 19.53 E
Temerloh 26 Df 3.27N 102.25 E
Teminabuan 26 Jg 1.26S 132.01 E
Temir 19 Ff 49.08N 57.09 E
Temir 16 Te 48.31N 57.29 E
Temirlanovka 18 Gc 42.36N 69.17 E
Temirtau 22 Jd 50.05N 72.56 E
Témiscaming 44 Hb 46.44N 79.06W
Témiscouata, Lac- 44 Mb 47.40N 68.50W
Temki 35 Bc 11.29N 18.13 E
Temnikov 7 Ki 54.40N 43.13 E
Temo 14 Cj 40.17N 8.28 E
Temoe, Ile- 57 Ng 23.20S 134.29W
Temores 48 Ed 27.16N 108.15W
Tempe 46 Jj 33.25N 111.56W
Tempio Pausania 14 Dj 40.54N 9.06 E
Temple 43 He 31.06N 97.21W
Templeman, Mount- 46 Ga 50.43N 117.14W
Templemore/An Teampall Mór 9 Fi 52.48N 7.50W
Templin 10 Jc 53.07N 13.30 E
Tempoal, Rio- 48 Jg 21.47N 98.27W
Tempué 36 Ce 13.27S 18.53 E
Temrjuk 16 Jg 45.15N 37.23 E
Temse/Tamise 12 Gc 51.08N 4.13 E
Temuco 53 Ii 38.44S 72.36W
Temuka 62 Df 44.15S 171.16 E
Tena 54 Cd 0.59S 77.48W
Tenacatita, Bahia de- 48 Gh 19.10N 104.50W
Tenala/Tenhola 8 Jd 60.04N 23.18 E
Tenāli 25 Ge 16.15N 80.35 E
Tenancingo de Degollado 48 Jh 18.58N 99.36W
Tenasserim 25 Jf 12.05N 99.01 E
Tenasserim 25 Jf 12.24N 98.37 E
Tenasserim 21 Lh 12.35N 97.52 E
Tenby 9 Ij 51.41N 4.43W
Tence 11 Ki 45.07N 4.17 E
Tench Island 60 Eh 1.38S 150.42 E
Tenda, Col di- 14 Bf 44.09N 7.34 E
Tendaho 35 Gc 11.38N 41.00 E
Tende 11 Nj 44.05N 7.36 E
Tende, Col de- 14 Bf 44.09N 7.34 E
Ten Degree Channel 21 Lh 10.00N 92.30 E
Tendō 29 Gb 38.22N 140.22 E
Tendrara 32 Gc 33.03N 2.00W
Tendre, Mont- 14 Ad 46.36N 6.19 E
Tendrovskaja Kosa 16 Gf 46.15N 31.45 E
Ténenkou 34 Ec 14.28N 4.55W
Tenente Lira, Rio- 55 Db 15.56S 57.39W
Ténéré 30 Ig 17.35N 10.55 E
Tenéré, 'Erg du- 34 Hb 17.35N 10.55 E
Tenerife 30 Ff 28.19N 16.34W
Ténès 32 Hb 36.31N 1.18 E
Ténès, Cap- 13 Nh 36.33N 1.21 E
Teng 25 Je 19.52N 97.45 E
Tengah, Kepulauan- 26 Gh 7.30S 117.30 E
Tengchong 27 Gg 24.59N 98.32 E
Te Nggano, Lake- 60 Gj 11.45S 160.25 E
Tenggarong 26 Gg 0.24S 116.58 E
Tengger Shamo 21 Mf 38.00N 104.10 E
Tengiz, Ozero- 21 Id 50.25N 69.00 E
Tengréla 34 Dc 10.29N 6.24W
Tengréla [3] 34 Dc 10.27N 6.25W
Tengxian [China] 27 Jg 23.18N 110.49 E
Tengxian [China] 28 Dg 35.07N 117.10 E
Tenhola/Tenala 8 Jd 60.04N 23.18 E
Teniente General Rosendo M. Fraga 55 Af 23.45S 62.09W
Tenkāsi 25 Fg 8.58N 77.18 E
Tenke 36 Ee 10.33S 26.08 E
Tenkeli 20 Jb 70.01N 140.55 E
Tenkodogo 34 Ec 11.47N 0.22W
Tenna 14 Hg 43.14N 13.47 E
Tennant Creek 58 Ef 19.40S 134.10 E
Tennessee 38 Kf 37.04N 88.33W
Tennessee [2] 43 Jd 35.50N 85.30W
Tenneville 12 Hd 50.06N 5.32 E
Tenoïoki 7 Ga 70.28N 28.18 E
Tenom 26 Ge 5.08N 115.57 E
Tenosique de Pino Suárez 47 Fe 17.29N 91.26W
Tenri 29 Dd 34.36N 135.49 E
Tenryū 29 Ed 34.52N 137.47 E
Tenryū-Gawa 28 Ng 34.35N 137.48 E
Tensift 32 Fc 32.02N 9.21W
Ten Sleep 46 Ld 44.02N 107.27W
Tenterden 12 Cc 51.03N 0.42 E

Index Symbols

[1] Independent Nation
[2] State, Region
[3] District, County
[4] Municipality
[5] Colony, Dependency
Continent
Physical Region
Historical or Cultural Region
Mount, Mountain
Volcano
Hill
Mountains, Mountain Range
Hills, Escarpment
Plateau, Upland
Pass, Gap
Plain, Lowland
Delta
Salt Flat
Valley, Canyon
Crater, Cave
Karst Features
Depression
Polder
Desert, Dunes
Forest, Woods
Heath, Steppe
Oasis
Cape, Point
Coast, Beach
Cliff
Peninsula
Isthmus
Sandbank
Island
Atoll
Rock, Reef
Islands, Archipelago
Rocks, Reefs
Coral Reef
Well, Spring
Geyser
River, Stream
Waterfall Rapids
River Mouth, Estuary
Lake
Salt Lake
Intermittent Lake
Reservoir
Swamp, Pond
Canal
Glacier
Ice Shelf, Pack Ice
Ocean
Sea
Gulf, Bay
Strait, Fjord
Lagoon
Bank
Seamount
Tablemount
Ridge
Shelf
Basin
Escarpment, Sea Scarp
Fracture
Trench, Abyss
National Park, Reserve
Point of Interest
Recreation Site
Cave, Cavern
Historic Site
Ruins
Wall, Walls
Church, Abbey
Temple
Scientific Station
Airport
Port
Lighthouse
Mine
Tunnel
Dam, Bridge

Tenterfield 59 Ke 29.03S 152.01 E
Tenuku 25 Ge 81.40N 16.45 E
Tenuze/Teenuse Jõgi 7 Jf 58.44N 23.58 E
Ten-Zan 29 Be 33.20N 130.08 E
Teocaltiche 48 Hg 21.26N 102.35W
Teodelina 55 Bl 34.11S 61.32W
Teodoro Sampaio 55 Ff 22.31S 52.10W
Teófilo Otoni 53 Lg 17.51S 41.30W
Teotepec, Cerro- 38 Ih 16.50N 100.50W
Teotihuacan 47 Ee 19.44N 98.50W
Teotilán del Camino 48 Kh 18.08N 97.05W
Tepa [Indon.] 26 Ih 7.52S 129.31 E
Tepa [W.F.] 64h Bb 13.19S 176.09W
Te Pae Roa Ngake o Tuko 64n Bb 10.23S 161.00W
Tepako, Pointe- 64h Bb 13.16S 176.08W
Tepalcatepec, Río- 48 Ih 18.35N 101.59W
Tepa Point 64k Bb 19.07S 169.56W
Tepatitlán de Morelos 48 Hg 20.49N 102.44W
Tepehuanes 47 Cc 25.21N 105.44W
Tepehuanes, Río- 48 Ge 25.11N 105.26W
Tepehuanes, Sierra de- 47 Cc 25.00N 105.40W
Tepelena 15 Di 40.18N 20.01 E
Tepi 35 Fd 7.03N 35.30 E
Tepic 39 Ig 21.30N 104.54W
Teplá 10 Ig 49.59N 12.52 E
Teplá 10 If 50.14N 12.52 E
Teplice 10 Jf 50.39N 13.50 E
Tepoca, Bahía de- 48 Cb 30.15N 112.50W
Tepopa, Cabo- 48 Cc 29.20N 112.25W
Te Puka 64n Ac 10.26S 161.02W
Te Puke 62 Gb 37.47S 176.20 E
Tequepa, Bahía de- 48 Ii 17.17N 101.05W
Tequila 48 Hg 20.54N 103.47W
Tequisquiapan 48 Jg 20.31N 99.52W
Ter 13 Pb 42.01N 3.12 E
Téra 31 Hg 14.01N 0.45 E
Tera [Port.] 13 Df 38.56N 8.03W
Tera [Sp.] 13 Gc 41.54N 5.44W
Teradomari 29 Fc 37.38N 138.45 E
Terai 21 Kg 26.30N 85.15 E
Teraina Island (Washington) 57 Kd 4.43N 160.24W
Terakeka 35 Ed 5.26N 31.45 E
Teramo 14 Hh 42.39N 13.42 E
Terampa 26 Ef 3.14N 106.14 E
Ter Apel, Vlagtwedde- 12 Jb 52.52N 7.06 E
Terborg, Wisch- 12 Ic 51.55N 6.22 E
Tercan 24 Ic 39.47N 40.24 E
Terceira 30 Ee 38.43N 27.13W
Tercero, Río- 56 Hd 32.55S 62.19W
Terebovlja 16 De 49.18N 25.42 E
Terehovka 28 Kc 43.38N 131.55 E
Terek 16 Nh 43.29N 44.08 E
Terek 5 Kg 43.44N 47.30 E
Térékolé 34 Cb 15.07N 10.53W
Terek-Saj 18 Hd 41.29N 71.13 E
Terenos 55 Ee 20.26S 54.50W
Teresa Cristina 55 Gg 24.48S 51.07W
Teresina 53 Lf 5.05S 42.49W
Teresinha 54 Hc 0.58N 52.02W
Tereška 16 Od 51.50N 46.45 E
Terespol 10 Td 52.05N 23.36 E
Teressa 25 Ig 8.15N 93.10 E
Teresva 16 Cf 47.59N 23.15 E
Terevaka, Cerro- 65d Ab 27.05S 109.23W
Tergnier 11 Je 49.39N 3.18 E
Terhazza 34 Ea 23.36N 4.56W
Teriberka 7 Ib 69.10N 35.10 E
Teriberka 7 Ib 69.09N 35.08 E
Terlingua Creek 45 El 29.10N 103.36W
Termas de Rio Hondo 56 Hc 27.29S 64.52W
Terme 24 Gb 41.12N 36.59 E
Termez 22 If 37.14N 67.16 E
Termini Imerese 14 Hm 37.59N 13.42 E
Termini Imerese, Golfo di- 14 Hl 38.00N 13.45 E
Terminillo 14 Hh 42.28N 13.01 E
Términos, Laguna de- 47 Fe 18.37N 91.33W
Termit, Massif de- 34 Hb 16.15N 11.17 E
Termit-Kaoboul 34 Hb 15.43N 11.37 E
Termoli 14 Ii 42.00N 15.00 E
Termonde/Dendermonde 12 Gc 51.02N 4.07 E
Ternaard, Westdongeradeel- 12 Ha 53.23N 5.58 E
Ternate 25 If 0.48N 127.24 E
Ternej 20 Ig 45.05N 136.35 E
Terneuzen 11 Jc 51.20N 3.50 E
Terni 14 Gh 42.34N 12.37 E
Ternitz 14 Kc 47.43N 16.02 E
Ternois 12 Ed 50.25N 2.19 E
Ternopol 6 If 49.34N 25.38 E
Ternopolskaja Oblast [3] 19 Cf 49.20N 25.35 E
Terpenija, Mys- 20 Jg 48.38N 144.40 E
Terpenija, Zaliv- 21 Qe 49.00N 143.30 E
Terrace 42 Ef 54.31N 128.35W
Terrace Bay 45 Mb 48.47N 87.09W
Terracina 14 Hi 41.17N 13.15 E
Terra de Basto 13 Ec 41.25N 8.00W
Terra Firma 37 Ce 25.36S 23.24 E
Terråk 7 Cd 65.05N 12.25 E
Terralba 14 Ck 39.43N 8.39 E
Terra Rica 55 Ff 22.43S 52.38W
Terrebonne Bay 45 Kl 29.09N 90.35W
Terre-de-Bas 51e Ac 15.51N 61.39W
Terre-de-Haut 51e Ac 15.58N 61.35W
Terre Froides 11 Li 45.30N 5.30 E
Terre Haute 43 Jd 39.28N 87.24W
Terrell 45 Hj 32.44N 96.17W
Terre Plaine 11 Jg 47.25N 4.00 E
Terril 13 Gh 37.00N 5.11W
Territoire de Belfort [3] 11 Mg 47.45N 7.00 E
Terruca 13 Fc 41.45N 6.25W
Terry 46 Mc 46.47N 105.19W
Tersa 16 Nd 50.46N 44.42 E
Terschelling 12 Ha 53.21N 5.13 E
Terschelling 11 La 53.24N 5.20 E
Terschelling-West-Terschelling 12 Ha 53.21N 5.13 E
Tersef 35 Bc 12.55N 16.49 E
Terskej-Alatau, Hrebet- 19 Hg 42.10N 78.45 E
Terski Bereg 7 Jc 66.10N 39.30 E
Tersko-Kumski Kanal 16 Ng 44.47N 44.37 E
Terter (Mir-Bašir) 16 Oi 40.19N 46.58 E
Teruel 13 Kd 40.21N 1.06W
Teruel [3] 13 Ld 40.40N 0.40W
Tervakoski 8 Kd 60.48N 24.37 E
Tervel 15 Kf 43.45N 27.24 E
Tervo 8 Lb 62.57N 26.45 E
Tervola 7 Fc 66.05N 24.48 E
Tes 27 Fa 50.27N 93.30 E
Teša 7 Ki 55.38N 42.10 E
Tesalia 54 Cc 2.29N 75.44W
Tesaret 32 Hd 25.40N 2.43 E
Tesdrero, Cerro- 48 Hf 22.47N 103.04W
Teseney 35 Fb 15.07N 36.40 E
Teshekpuk Lake 40 Ib 70.35N 153.30W
Teshikaga 28 Rc 43.29N 144.28 E
Teshio 28 Pb 44.53N 141.44 E
Teshio-Dake 28 Qc 43.58N 142.50 E
Teshio-Gawa 28 Pb 44.53N 141.44 E
Teshio-Sanchi 29a Ba 44.20N 142.00 E
Tesijn→Tesijn Gol 21 Ld 50.28N 93.04 E
Tesijn Gol (Tesijn) 21 Ld 50.28N 93.04 E
Teslić 14 Lf 44.37N 17.52 E
Teslin 42 Ed 61.34N 134.50W
Teslin 42 Ed 60.09N 132.45W
Teslin Lake 42 Ed 60.00N 132.30W
Tesluí 15 He 44.09N 24.29 E
Tesocoma 48 Ed 27.41N 109.16W
Tesouras, Rio- 55 Gb 14.36S 50.51W
Tesouro 55 Fc 16.04S 53.34W
Tessala, Monts du- 13 Li 35.15N 0.45W
Tessalit 31 Hf 20.14N 0.59 E
Tessaoua 34 Gc 13.45N 7.59 E
Tessenderlo 12 Hc 51.04N 5.05 E
Test 9 Lk 50.55N 1.29W
Test, Tizi n'- 32 Fc 30.50N 8.20W
Testa, Capo- 14 Di 41.14N 9.08 E
Têt 11 Jl 42.44N 3.02 E
Tetari, Cerro- 49 Ki 9.59N 72.55W
Tetas, Punta- 56 Fc 23.31S 70.38W
Tete 31 Kj 16.10S 33.36 E
Tete [3] 37 Ec 15.30S 33.00 E
Te Teko 62 Gc 38.02S 176.48 E
Tetepare Island 63a Cc 8.45S 157.35 E
Téterchen 12 Ie 49.14N 6.34 E
Tetere 63a Ec 9.25S 160.15 E
Teterev 16 Gd 51.01N 30.08 E
Teterow 10 Ic 53.47N 12.34 E
Teteven 15 Hg 42.55N 24.16 E
Tetiaroa Atoll 57 Mf 17.05S 149.32W
Tetijev 16 Fe 49.23N 29.41 E
Tetjuši 7 Li 54.57N 48.49 E
Teton Peak 46 Ic 47.55N 112.48W
Teton Range 46 Je 43.50N 110.55W
Teton River 46 Jc 47.56N 110.31W
Tétouan 31 Ge 35.34N 5.22W
Tétouan [3] 32 Fb 35.35N 5.30W
Tetovo 15 Dg 42.01N 20.58 E
Tetri-Ckaro 16 Ni 41.33N 44.27 E
Teuco, Río- 55 Bg 25.38S 60.12W
Teufelskopf 12 Ie 49.36N 6.49 E
Teulada 14 Cl 38.58N 8.46 E
Teulada, Capo- 5 Gh 38.52N 8.38 E
Téul de Gonzales Ortega 48 Hg 21.28N 103.29W
Teun, Pulau- 26 Ih 6.59S 129.08 E
Teupasenti 49 Df 14.13N 86.42W
Teuquito, Río- 55 Bg 24.22S 61.09W
Teuri-Tō 29a Ba 44.25N 141.20 E
Teutoburger Wald 10 Ee 52.10N 8.15 E
Teuva/Östermark 7 Ee 62.29N 21.44 E
Teuz 15 Ec 46.39N 21.33 E
Tevai 63c Bb 11.37S 166.55 E
Tevaitoa 65e Db 16.46S 151.28W
Tevere = Tiber (EN) 5 Hg 41.44N 12.14 E
Teverya 24 Ff 32.47N 35.32 E
Teviot 9 Kf 55.36N 2.26W
Tevli 10 Ud 52.19N 24.23 E
Tevriz 19 Hd 57.34N 72.24 E
Tevšruleh 27 Hb 47.25N 101.55 E
Te Waewae Bay 62 Bg 46.15S 167.30 E
Tewkesbury 9 Kj 51.59N 2.09W
Têwo (Dêngkagoin) 27 He 34.03N 103.21 E
Texada Island 46 Cb 49.40N 124.24W
Texarkana [Ar.-U.S.] 43 Ie 33.26N 94.02W
Texarkana [Tx.-U.S.] 39 Jf 33.26N 94.03W
Texas 59 Ke 28.51S 151.11 E
Texas [2] 43 He 31.30N 99.00W
Texas City 43 If 29.23N 94.54W
Texcoco 48 Jh 19.31N 98.53W
Texel 12 Ga 53.03N 4.47 E
Texel 11 Ka 53.05N 4.45 E
Texel-De Koog 12 Ga 53.07N 4.46 E
Texel-Den Burg 12 Ga 53.03N 4.47 E
Texoma, Lake- 43 He 33.55N 96.37W
Teyéa = Tegea (EN) 15 Fl 37.27N 22.25 E
Teza 7 Jh 56.32N 41.57 E
Teze-Jel 19 Gh 37.55N 60.22 E
Teziutlán 47 Ee 19.49N 97.21W
Tezpur 25 Ic 26.38N 92.48 E
Tha-anne 42 Id 60.31N 94.37W
Thabana Ntlenyana 30 Jk 29.30S 29.15 E
Thabazimbi 37 Dd 24.41S 27.21 E
Thai, Ao-=Thailand, Gulf of-(EN) 21 Mh 10.00N 102.00 E
Thai Binh 25 Ld 20.27N 106.20 E
Thailand (EN)=Muang Thai [1] 22 Mh 15.00N 100.00 E
Thailand, Gulf of- (EN)= Thai, Ao- 21 Mh 10.00N 102.00 E
Thai Nguyen 25 Ld 21.36N 105.50 E
Thal 25 Eb 31.30N 71.40 E
Thālith, Ash Shallāl ath-= Third Cataract (EN) 30 Kg 19.49N 30.19 E
Thamad Bū Hashīshah 33 Cd 25.50N 18.05 E
Thamarīd 35 Ib 17.39N 54.02 E
Thame 12 Bc 51.45N 0.59W
Thames 61 Eg 37.08S 175.33 E
Thames 5 Ge 51.28N 0.43 E
Thames River 44 Fd 42.19N 82.28W
Thamūd 23 Gf 17.15N 49.54 E
Thāna 22 Jh 19.12N 72.58 E
Thandaung 25 Je 19.04N 96.41 E
Thanh Hoa 22 Mh 19.48N 105.46 E
Thanh Pho Ho Chi Minh (Saigon) 22 Mh 10.45N 106.40 E
Thanjāvūr 25 Ff 10.48N 79.08 E
Thanlwin = Salween (EN) 21 Lg 16.31N 97.37 E
Thann 11 Ng 47.49N 7.05 E
Thaon-les-Vosges 11 Mf 48.15N 6.25 E
Thap Sakae 25 Jf 11.14N 99.31 E
Thar/Great Indian Desert 21 Ig 27.00N 70.00 E
Thargomindah 59 Ie 28.00S 143.49 E
Tharrawaddy 25 Je 17.39N 95.48 E
Tharros 14 Ck 39.54N 8.28 E
Tharthār, Bahr ath- 23 Fc 33.59N 43.12 E
Tharthār, Wādī ath- 23 Fc 33.59N 43.12 E
Thasi Gang Dzong 25 Ic 27.19N 91.34 E
Thásos 5 Ig 40.49N 24.42 E
Thásos 15 Hi 40.47N 24.43 E
Thásou, Dhiavlos- 15 Hi 40.49N 24.42 E
Thathlīth, Wādī- 33 He 20.25N 44.55 E
Thau, Bassin de- 11 Jk 43.23N 3.36 E
Thaxted 12 Cc 51.57N 0.22 E
Thaya 10 Mh 48.37N 16.56 E
Thayetchaung 25 Jf 13.52N 98.16 E
Thayetmyo 25 Je 19.19N 95.11 E
Thaywthadangyi Kyun 25 Jf 12.20N 98.00 E
The Alberga River 59 He 27.06S 135.33 E
The Aldermen Islands 62 Gb 37.00S 176.05 E
Thebai=Thebes (EN) 33 Fd 25.43N 32.35 E
Thebes (EN)=Thebai 33 Fd 25.43N 32.35 E
Thebes (EN) = Thivai 15 Gk 38.19N 23.19 E
The Black Sugarloaf 59 Kf 31.20S 151.33 E
The Borders 9 Kf 55.35N 2.50W
The Bottom 50 Ed 17.38N 63.15W
The Broads 9 Oi 52.40N 1.30 E
The Cheviot 9 Kf 55.28N 2.09W
The Cheviot Hills 9 Kf 55.30N 2.10W
The Crane 51q Bb 13.06N 59.26W
The Dalles 43 Cb 45.36N 121.10W
Thedford 45 Gf 41.59N 100.35W
The Entrance 59 Kf 33.21S 151.30 E
The Everglades 43 Kf 26.00N 81.00W
The Fens 9 Mi 52.38N 0.02W
The Gap 46 Jh 36.25N 111.30W
The Granites 59 Gd 20.35S 130.21 E
The Hague (EN)=Den Haag/'s-Gravenhage 6 Ge 52.06N 4.18 E
The Little Minch 9 Gd 57.35N 6.55W
Thelle 12 De 49.23N 1.51 E
Thelon 38 Jc 64.16N 96.05W
The Macumba River 57 Eg 27.45S 136.50 E
The Merse 9 Kf 55.50N 2.10W
The Naze 12 Dc 51.42N 1.47 E
The Neales River 59 He 28.08S 136.47 E
The Needles 9 Lk 50.39N 1.34W
Theniet el Had 13 Oi 35.32N 2.01 E
Theodore 59 Kd 24.57S 150.05 E
Theológos 15 Hi 40.40N 24.42 E
The Pas 39 Id 53.50N 101.15W
The Pillories 51n Bb 12.54N 61.12W
Thérain 11 Ie 49.15N 2.27 E
Thermaïkós Kólpos = Salonika, Gulf of- (EN) 5 Ig 40.20N 22.45 E
Thermopilai = Thermopylae (EN) 15 Fk 38.48N 22.32 E
Thermopolis 43 Fc 43.39N 108.13W
Thermopylae (EN) = Thermopilai 15 Fk 38.48N 22.32 E
Thérouanne 12 Ed 50.38N 2.15 E
The Round Mountain 59 Kf 30.27S 152.16 E
The Sandlings 9 Oi 52.10N 1.30 E
Thesiger Bay 42 Fb 71.30N 124.00W
The Slot→New Georgia Sound 60 Fi 8.00S 158.10 E
The Solent Spithead 9 Lk 50.46N 1.20W
Thessalía [2] 15 Fj 39.30N 22.10 E
Thessalía=Thessaly (EN) 5 Ih 39.30N 22.10 E
Thessalía = Thessaly (EN) 15 Fj 39.30N 22.10 E
Thessalon 44 Fb 46.15N 83.34W
Thessaloníki = Salonika (EN) 6 Ig 40.38N 22.56 E
Thessaly (EN) = Thessalía 15 Fj 39.30N 22.10 E
Thessaly (EN)= Thessalía 5 Ih 39.30N 22.10 E
The Stevenson River 59 He 27.06S 135.33 E
Thet 12 Cb 52.24N 0.45 E
Thetford 9 Ni 52.25N 0.45 E
Thetford Mines 44 Lb 46.05N 71.18W
The Twins 62 Ed 41.14S 172.40 E
Theux 12 Hd 50.33N 5.49 E
The Valley 47 Le 18.03N 63.04W
The Warburton River 59 He 27.55S 137.28 E
The Wash 5 Ge 52.55N 0.15 E
The Weald 9 Nj 51.05N 0.05 E
The Witties 49 Ff 14.10N 82.45W
The Wolds 9 Mh 53.20N 0.10W
Thiaucourt-Regniéville 12 Hf 48.57N 5.52 E
Thiberville 12 Ce 49.08N 0.27 E
Thibodaux 45 Kl 29.48N 90.49W
Thief River Falls 43 Hb 48.07N 96.10W
Thiel Mountains 66 Pg 85.15S 91.00W
Thiene 14 Fe 45.42N 11.29 E
Thiérache, Collines de la- 11 Je 49.48N 3.55 E
Thiers 11 Ji 45.51N 3.34 E
Thiès 31 Fg 14.48N 16.56W
Thiès [3] 34 Bc 14.45N 16.50W
Thiesi 14 Cj 40.31N 8.43 E
Thika 36 Gc 1.03S 37.05 E
Thikombia 61 Fc 15.44S 179.55W
Thimerais 11 Hf 48.40N 1.20 E
Thimphu 22 Kg 27.28N 89.39 E
Thio 61 Cd 21.37S 166.14 E
Thionville 11 Me 49.22N 6.10 E
Thiou 34 Ec 13.48N 2.40W
Thira 15 Im 36.25N 25.26 E
Thira = Thira (EN) 15 Im 36.24N 25.26 E
Thira (EN) = Thira 15 Im 36.24N 25.26 E
Thirasia 15 Im 36.25N 25.20 E
Third Cataract (EN)= Thālith, Ash Shallāl ath- 30 Kg 19.49N 30.19 E
Thirsk 9 Lg 54.14N 1.20W
Thisted 7 Bh 56.57N 8.42 E
Thithia 63d Cb 17.45S 179.18W
Thiu Khao Phetchabun 25 Ke 16.20N 100.55 E
Thivai = Thebes (EN) 15 Gk 38.19N 23.19 E
Thiviers 11 Gi 45.25N 0.55 E
Thlewiaza 42 Id 60.28N 94.42W
Thoa 42 Gd 60.31N 109.45W
Tho Chu, Dao- 25 Kg 9.00N 103.50 E
Thoen 25 Je 17.41N 99.14 E
Tholen 12 Gc 51.32N 4.13 E
Tholen 11 Kc 51.35N 4.05 E
Tholey 12 Je 49.29N 7.04 E
Thomasset, Rocher- 57 Nf 10.21S 138.25W
Thomaston 44 Ei 32.54N 84.20W
Thomasville [Al.-U.S.] 44 Dj 32.18N 87.47W
Thomasville [Ga.-U.S.] 43 Ke 30.50N 83.59W
Thomasville [N.C.-U.S.] 44 Gh 35.53N 80.05W
Thompson 42 He 55.45N 97.45W
Thompson Falls 46 Hc 47.36N 115.21W
Thompson River 45 Jg 39.45N 93.36W
Thompson Sound 62 Bf 45.10S 167.00 E
Thomsen 42 Fb 73.40N 119.30W
Thomson 44 Fi 33.28N 82.30W
Thomson River 59 Ie 25.11S 142.53 E
Thomson's Falls 36 Gb 0.02N 36.22 E
Thon 12 Fe 49.53N 3.55 E
Thon Buri 22 Mh 13.43N 100.24 E
Thong Pha Phum 25 Jf 14.44N 98.38 E
Thongwa 25 Je 16.46N 96.32 E
Thonon-les-Bains 11 Mh 46.22N 6.29 E
Thoreau 45 Bi 35.24N 108.13W
Thornaby-on-Tees 9 Lg 54.34N 1.18W
Thornbury 61 Ci 46.17S 168.06 E
Thorney 12 Bb 52.37N 0.06W
Thornhill 9 Jf 55.18N 3.40W
Thorshavn 6 Fc 62.01N 6.46W
Thouars 11 Fh 46.58N 0.13W
Thouet 11 Fg 47.17N 0.06W
Thrace (EN) = Thráki 15 Jh 41.20N 26.45 E
Thrace (EN) = Thráki 5 Ig 41.20N 26.45 E
Thrace (EN) = Trakya 15 Jh 41.20N 26.45 E
Thrace (EN) = Trakya 5 Ig 41.20N 26.45 E
Thráki [2] 15 Ih 41.10N 25.30 E
Thráki = Thrace (EN) 5 Ig 41.20N 26.45 E
Thráki=Thrace (EN) 15 Jh 41.20N 26.45 E
Thrakikón Pélagos 15 Hi 40.30N 25.00 E
Thrapston 12 Bb 52.24N 0.32W
Three Forks 43 Eb 45.54N 111.33W
Three Kings Islands 57 Ih 34.10S 172.10 E
Three Kings Trough (EN) 3 Jm 32.00S 170.30 E
Three Points, Cape- 30 Gh 4.45N 2.06W
Three Rivers 44 Ee 41.57N 85.38W
Three Sisters Islands 63a Ed 10.10S 161.57 E
Throckmorton 45 Gj 33.11N 99.11W
Throssel, Lake- 59 Ee 27.25S 124.15 E
Thua 36 Gc 1.17S 40.00 E
Thuin 11 Kd 50.20N 4.17 E
Thule 66 Ad 59.27S 27.19W
Thule/Qânâq 67 Od 77.35N 69.40W
Thule, Mount- 42 Jb 73.00N 78.27W
Thun 14 Bd 46.45N 7.40 E
Thunder Bay 39 Ke 48.23N 89.15W
Thunder Bay [Mi.-U.S.] 44 Fc 45.04N 83.25W
Thunder Bay [Ont.-Can.] 45 Lb 48.24N 89.00W
Thunder Butte 45 Fd 45.19N 101.53W
Thuner See 14 Bd 46.40N 7.45 E
Thung Song 25 Jg 8.11N 99.41 E
Thur 14 Cc 47.36N 8.35 E
Thurgau [2] 14 Dc 47.40N 9.10 E
Thüringen 10 Gf 50.40N 11.00 E
Thüringer Wald=Thuringian Forest (EN) 5 He 50.30N 11.00 E
Thuringian Forest (EN)= Thüringer Wald 5 He 50.30N 11.00 E
Thurles/Durlas 9 Fi 52.41N 7.49W
Thurrock 9 Nj 51.28N 0.20 E
Thursday Island 59 Ib 10.35S 142.13 E
Thurso 6 Fd 58.35N 3.32W
Thurso 9 Jc 58.35N 3.30W
Thurston Island 66 Pf 72.06S 99.00W
Thury-Harcourt 12 Bf 48.59N 0.29W
Thusis/Tusaun 14 Dd 46.42N 9.26 E
Thuwayrāt, Nafūd ath- 24 Kj 26.00N 44.50 E
Thuy Phong 25 Lf 11.14N 108.43 E
Thwaites Iceberg Tongue 66 Of 74.00S 108.30W
Thy 8 Ch 57.00N 8.30 E
Thyborøn 8 Ch 56.42N 8.13 E
Tianbaoshan 28 Jc 42.57N 128.57 E
Tianchang 27 Ke 32.37N 119.00 E
Tiandong (Pingma) 27 Ig 23.40N 107.09 E
Tian'e (Liupai) 27 If 25.05N 107.12 E
Tianguá 54 Jd 3.44S 40.59W
Tianjin=Tientsin (EN) 22 Nf 39.08N 117.12 E
Tianjin Shi (T'ien-chin Shih) [4] 27 Kd 39.08N 117.12 E
Tianjun (Xinyuan) 22 Lf 37.18N 99.15 E
Tianlin (Leli) 27 Ig 24.22N 106.11 E
Tian Ling 28 Kb 44.24N 130.10 E
Tianmen 27 Je 30.40N 113.10 E
Tianmu Shan 28 Ei 30.31N 119.36 E
Tianmu Xi 28 Ej 29.59N 119.24 E
Tianqiaoling 27 Mc 43.35N 129.35 E
Tian Shan 21 Ke 42.00N 80.01 E
Tianshan → Ar Horqin Qi 27 Lc 43.55N 120.05 E
Tianshifu 27 Lc 41.15N 124.20 E
Tianshui 22 Mf 34.35N 105.43 E
Tiantai 28 Fj 29.08N 121.00 E
Tianwangsi 28 Ei 31.45N 119.12 E
Tianyi → Ningcheng 27 Kc 41.34N 119.25 E
Tianzhen 28 Cd 40.24N 114.05 E
Tianzhen→Gaoqing 28 Df 37.10N 117.50 E
Tianzhuangtai 28 Gd 40.49N 122.06 E
Tiaraju 55 Ej 30.15S 54.23W
Tiarei 65e Fc 17.32S 149.20W
Tiaret [3] 32 Hc 34.50N 1.30 E
Tiaret 31 He 35.20N 1.14 E
Tiaret, Monts de- 13 Ni 35.26N 1.15 E
Tiassalé 34 Ed 5.54N 4.50W
Tiavea 65c Ba 13.57S 171.24W
Tīb, Ra's at-=Bon, Cape- (EN) 30 Ie 37.05N 11.03 E
Tibaji 55 Gg 24.30S 50.24W
Tibaji, Rio- 55 Gf 22.47S 51.01W
Tibasti, Sarīr- 33 Bd 24.00N 17.00 E
Tibati 31 Ih 6.28N 12.38 E
Tiber (EN) = Tevere 5 Hg 41.44N 12.14 E
Tiberina, Val- 14 Gg 43.30N 12.10 E
Tibesti 30 If 21.30N 17.30 E
Tibet (EN)=Xizang Zizhiqu (Hsi-tsang Tzu-chih-ch'ü) [2] 27 Ee 32.00N 90.00 E
Tibet, Plateau of- (EN)= Qing Zang Gaoyuan 21 Kf 32.30N 87.00 E
Tibidabo 13 Oc 41.25N 2.07 E
Tibni 24 He 35.35N 30.49 E
Tibro 8 Ff 58.26N 14.10 E
Tibú 49 Ki 8.40N 72.42W
Tibugà, Golfo de- 54 Cb 5.45N 77.20W
Tiburón, Capo- 49 Ii 8.42N 77.21W
Tiburon, Isla- 47 Bc 29.00N 112.25W
Ticao 26 Hd 12.31N 123.42 E
Tice 44 Gl 26.41N 81.49W
Tichá Orlice 10 Mf 50.09N 16.05 E
Tichît 31 Gg 18.26N 9.31W
Tichît, Dahr- 32 Ff 18.30N 9.25W
Tichka, Tizi n'- 32 Fc 31.17N 7.21W
Tichla 32 Ee 21.36N 14.58W
Ticino [2] 14 Cd 46.20N 9.00 E
Ticino 14 De 45.09N 9.14 E
Ticul 47 Gd 20.24N 89.32W
Tidaholm 7 Cg 58.11N 13.57 E
Tidan 8 Ef 58.42N 13.48 E
Tiddim 25 Id 23.22N 93.40 E
Tidikelt, Plaine du- 32 Hd 27.00N 1.30 E
Tidirhine 32 Gc 34.51N 4.31W
Tidjikja 31 Fg 18.32N 11.27W
Tidore 26 If 0.40N 127.26 E
Tidra, Ile- 30 Fg 19.44N 16.24W
Tiebissou 34 Dd 7.10N 5.13W
Tiechang 28 Id 41.40N 126.12 E
Tiel 11 Lc 51.54N 5.25 E
Tieli 27 Mb 47.04N 128.02 E
Tieling 28 Gc 42.18N 123.51 E
Tielt 11 Jc 51.00N 3.20 E
Tienba 34 Dd 8.30N 7.10W
T'ien-chin Shih→Tianjin Shi [4] 27 Kd 39.08N 117.12 E
Tienen/Tirlemont 12 Gd 50.48N 4.57 E
Tiengemeten 12 Gc 51.45N 5.20 E
Tientsin (EN)=Tianjin 22 Nf 39.08N 117.12 E
Tieroko, Tarso- 35 Ba 20.45N 17.52 E
Tierp 7 Df 60.20N 17.30 E
Tierra Amarilla [Chile] 56 Fc 27.29S 70.17W
Tierra Amarilla [N.M.-U.S.] 45 Ch 36.42N 106.33W
Tierra Blanca 47 Ee 18.27N 96.21W
Tierra Colorada 48 Ji 17.10N 99.35W
Tierra del Fuego [2] 56 Gh 54.00S 67.00W
Tierra del Fuego (EN) = Tierra del Fuego, Isla Grande de- 52 Jk 54.00S 69.00W
Tierra del Fuego, Isla Grande de-=Tierra del Fuego (EN) 52 Jk 54.00S 69.00W
Tierralta 54 Cb 8.10N 76.04W
Tiétar 13 Fe 39.50N 6.01W
Tietê, Rio- 52 Kh 20.40S 51.35W
Tietjerksteradeel 12 Ia 53.12N 6.00 E
Tietjerksteradeel-Bergum 12 Hb 52.17N 5.58 E
Tifariti 32 Ed 26.09N 10.33W
Tiffany Mountain 46 Fb 48.40N 119.56W
Tiffin 44 Fe 41.07N 83.11W
Tifton 43 Ke 31.27N 83.31W
Tiga 63b Ce 21.08S 167.49 E
Tigalda 40a Fb 54.05N 165.05W
Tigănești 15 If 43.54N 25.22 E
Tighennif 13 Mi 35.25N 0.15 E
Tigil 20 Ke 57.57N 158.20 E
Tigil 20 Ke 57.48N 158.40 E
Tignère 34 Hd 7.22N 12.39 E
Tigray [3] 35 Fc 14.00N 39.00 E
Tigre 48 Hh 19.53N 102.59W
Tigre, Cerro del- 48 Jf 23.03N 99.16W
Tigre, Rio- [S.Amer.] 52 If 4.30S 74.10W
Tigre, Rio- [Ven.] 50 Eh 9.20N 62.30W
Tigris (EN)=Dicle 21 Gf 31.00N 47.25 E
Tigris (EN)=Dijlah 21 Gf 31.00N 47.25 E
Tigrovy Hvost, Mys- 18 Bc 43.57N 58.45 E
Tiguent 32 Df 17.15N 16.00W
Tiguentourine 32 Id 27.43N 9.33 E
Tigui 35 Bb 18.38N 18.47 E
Tigzirt 13 Qh 36.54N 4.07 E
Tih, Jabal at- 33 Fd 29.35N 34.00 E
Tih, Şahrā' at-=At Tih Desert (EN) 33 Fc 30.05N 34.00 E
Tihāmat 23 Ff 18.30N 41.30 E
Tihāmat Ash Shām 33 Hf 19.15N 41.10 E

Index Symbols

[1] Independent Nation
[2] State, Region
[3] District, County
[4] Municipality
[5] Colony, Dependency
Continent
Physical Region
Historical or Cultural Region
Mount, Mountain
Volcano
Hill
Mountains, Mountain Range
Hills, Escarpment
Plateau, Upland
Pass, Gap
Plain, Lowland
Delta
Salt Flat
Valley, Canyon
Crater, Cave
Karst Features
Depression
Polder
Desert, Dunes
Forest, Woods
Heath, Steppe
Oasis
Cape, Point
Coast, Beach
Cliff
Peninsula
Isthmus
Sandbank
Island
Atoll
Rock, Reef
Islands, Archipelago
Rocks, Reefs
Coral Reef
Well, Spring
Geyser
River, Stream
Waterfall Rapids
River Mouth, Estuary
Lake
Salt Lake
Intermittent Lake
Reservoir
Swamp, Pond
Canal
Glacier
Ice Shelf, Pack Ice
Ocean
Sea
Gulf, Bay
Strait, Fjord
Lagoon
Bank
Seamount
Tablemount
Ridge
Shelf
Basin
Escarpment, Sea Scarp
Fracture
Trench, Abyss
National Park, Reserve
Point of Interest
Recreation Site
Cave, Cavern
Historic Site
Ruins
Wall, Walls
Church, Abbey
Temple
Scientific Station
Airport
Port
Lighthouse
Mine
Tunnel
Dam, Bridge

Tihāmat 'Asīr	33	Hf	17.30N	42.20 E
Tihi Okean=Pacific Ocean (EN)	3	Ki	5.00N	155.00W
Tihoreck	6	Kf	45.51N	40.09 E
Tihuța, Pasul-	15	Hb	47.15N	25.00 E
Tihvin	19	Dd	59.38N	33.31 E
Tiirismaa	8	Kc	61.01N	25.31 E
Tiji	33	Bc	32.01N	11.22 E
Tijirīt	32	Ee	20.30N	15.00W
Tijuana	39	Hf	32.32N	117.01W
Tijucas	55	Hh	27.14S	48.38W
Tijucas, Baia do-	55	Hh	27.15S	48.31W
Tijucas, Rio-	55	Hh	27.15S	48.38W
Tijucas, Serra do-	55	Hh	27.16S	49.10W
Tijucas do Sul	55	Hg	25.56S	49.10W
Tijuco, Rio-	55	Gd	18.40S	50.05W
Tikal	39	Kh	17.20N	89.39W
Tikanlik	27	Ec	40.42N	87.38 E
Tikchik Lakes	40	Hd	60.07N	158.35W
Tikehau Atoll	61	Lb	15.00S	148.10W
Tikei, Ile-	61	Mb	14.58S	144.32W
Tikitiki	62	Hb	37.47S	178.25 E
Tikkakoski	8	Kb	62.24N	25.38 E
Tikkurila	8	Kd	60.18N	25.03 E
Tiko	34	Ge	4.05N	9.22 E
Tikopia Island	57	Hf	12.19S	168.49 E
Tikrit	23	Fc	34.36N	43.42 E
Tikšeozero, Ozero-	7	Hc	66.15N	31.45 E
Tiksi	22	Ob	71.36N	128.48 E
Tiladummati Atoll	25a	Ba	6.50N	73.05 E
Tilamuta	26	Hf	0.30N	122.20 E
Tilburg	11	Lc	51.34N	5.05 E
Tilbury, Gravesend-	9	Nj	51.28N	0.23 E
Tilcara	56	Gb	23.34S	65.22W
Til-Châtel	11	Lg	47.31N	5.10 E
Tileagd	15	Fb	47.04N	22.12 E
Tilemsès	34	Fb	15.37N	4.44 E
Tilemsi, Vallée du-	30	Hg	19.00N	0.02 E
Tilia	32	Gd	27.22N	0.02W
Tiličiki	20	Ld	60.20N	166.03 E
Tiligul	16	Gf	47.07N	30.57 E
Tiligulski Liman	16	Gf	46.50N	31.10 E
Till	9	Kf	55.41N	2.12W
Tillabéry	34	Fc	14.13N	1.27 E
Tillamook	46	Dd	45.27N	123.51W
Tillamook Bay	46	Dd	45.30N	123.53W
Tillanchong	25	Ig	8.30N	93.37 E
Tillberga	8	Ge	59.41N	16.37 E
Tille	11	Lg	47.07N	5.21 E
Tillia	34	Fb	16.08N	4.47 E
Tillières-sur-Avre	12	Df	48.46N	1.04 E
Tillingham	12	Cd	50.58N	0.44 E
Tillsonburg	44	Gd	42.51N	80.44W
Tilly-sur-Seulles	12	Be	49.11N	0.37W
Tiloa	34	Fb	15.04N	2.03 E
Tilos	15	Km	36.25N	27.25 E
Tilpa	59	If	30.57S	144.24 E
Tim	16	Jd	51.37N	37.11 E
Tim	16	Jc	52.15N	37.22 E
Ţimā	33	Fd	26.54N	31.26 E
Timagami	44	Gb	47.00N	80.05W
Timagami, Lake-	42	Jg	46.57N	80.05W
Timane, Rio-	55	Be	20.16S	60.08W
Timan Ridge (EN)= Timanski Krjaž	5	Lc	65.00N	51.00 E
Timanski Bereg	17	Eb	68.20N	51.45 E
Timanski Krjaž=Timan Ridge (EN)	5	Lc	65.00N	51.00 E
Timaru	58	Ii	44.24S	171.15 E
Timaševsk	19	Df	45.35N	38.58 E
Timbalier Bay	45	Kl	29.10N	90.20W
Timbalier Island	45	Kl	29.04N	90.28W
Timbaúba	54	Ke	7.31S	35.19W
Timbédra	32	Ff	16.14N	8.10W
Timbó	55	Hh	26.50S	49.18W
Timbuktu (EN)= Tombouctou	31	Gg	16.46N	2.59W
Timedouine, Ras-	13	Qh	36.28N	4.09 E
Timétrine	34	Eb	19.20N	0.42W
Timétrine	34	Eb	19.27N	0.26W
Timfi Óros	15	Dj	39.57N	20.50 E
Timfristós	15	Ek	38.57N	21.49 E
Timia	34	Gb	18.04N	8.40 E
Timimoun	31	Hf	29.15N	0.15 E
Timimoun, Sebkha de-	32	Hd	29.00N	0.05 E
Timiris, Cap—	32	Df	19.23N	16.32W
Timirjazevo	19	Ge	53.45N	66.33 E
Timiş	15	De	44.51N	20.39 E
Timiş [2]	15	Ed	45.38N	21.13 E
Timiskaming, Lake-	44	Hb	47.35N	79.35W
Timişoara	6	If	45.45N	21.13 E
Ti-m-Merhsoi	34	Gb	18.00N	5.40 E
Timmins	39	Ke	48.28N	81.20W
Timmoudi	32	Gd	29.19N	1.08W
Timms Hill	45	Kd	45.27N	90.11W
Timok	15	Fe	44.13N	22.40 E
Timon	54	Je	5.06S	42.49W
Timor, Laut-=Timor Sea (EN)	57	Df	11.00S	128.00 E
Timor, Pulau-	21	Oj	8.50S	126.00 E
Timor Sea (EN)=Timor, Laut-	57	Df	11.00S	128.00 E
Timor Timur [3]	26	Ih	8.35S	126.00 E
Timor Trough (EN)	3	Ij	9.50S	126.00 E
Timote	56	He	35.21S	62.14W
Timotes	54	Db	8.59N	70.44W
Timpton	20	He	58.43N	127.12 E
Timrå	7	De	62.29N	17.18 E
Tims Ford Lake	44	Dh	35.15N	86.10W
Tin, Ra's at-	33	Dc	32.37N	23.08 E
Tinaca Point	21	Oi	5.33N	125.20 E
Tinaco	50	Bh	9.42N	68.26W
Tinakula	63c	Ab	10.24S	165.47 E
Ti-n-Alkoum	32	Je	24.31N	10.11 E
Ti-n-Amzi [Alg.]	32	He	20.32N	4.37 E
Ti-n-Amzi [Niger]	34	Fb	17.54N	4.32 E
Tinaquillo	50	Bh	9.55N	68.18W
Tinchebray	12	Bf	48.46N	0.44W
Tindalo	35	Ed	5.39N	31.03 E
Tindari	14	Jl	38.10N	15.04 E
Tindila	34	Dc	10.16N	8.15W
Tindouf	31	Gf	27.42N	8.09W
Tindouf, Hamada de-	32	Fd	27.45N	8.25W
Tindouf, Sebkha de-	32	Fd	27.45N	7.35W
Tinée	11	Nk	43.55N	7.11 E
Tineo	13	Fa	43.20N	6.25W
Ti-n-Essako	34	Fb	18.27N	2.29 E
Tin Fouye	32	Id	28.15N	7.45 E
Tinghert, Ḩamādat-	30	Hf	28.50N	10.00 E
Tinglev	8	Cj	54.56N	9.15 E
Tingmiarmiut	41	Hf	62.25N	42.15W
Tingo Maria	54	Ce	9.10S	76.00W
Tingri (Xêgar)	27	Ef	28.41N	87.00 E
Tingsryd	7	Dh	56.32N	14.59 E
Tingstäde	8	Hg	57.44N	18.36 E
Tingvoll	7	Be	62.54N	8.12 E
Tinian Channel	64b	Bb	14.54N	145.37 E
Tinian Island	57	Fc	15.00N	145.38 E
Tini Wells	35	Cb	15.02N	22.48 E
Tinkisso	34	Dc	11.21N	9.10W
Tinnelva	8	Ce	59.34N	9.15 E
Tinniswood, Mount-	46	Da	50.19N	123.50W
Tinnoset	8	Ce	59.43N	9.02 E
Tinnsjo	8	Ce	59.54N	8.55 E
Tinogasta	56	Gc	28.04S	67.34W
Tinos	15	Il	37.35N	25.10 E
Tinos	15	Il	37.32N	25.10 E
Tinou, Stenón-	15	Il	37.38N	25.10 E
Tinrhert, Hamada de-	30	Hf	28.50N	10.00 E
Tinrhir	32	Fc	31.31N	5.32W
Tinsukia	25	Jc	27.30N	95.22 E
Tintagel Head	9	Ik	50.41N	4.46W
Tintamarre, Ile-	51b	Bb	18.07N	63.00W
Ti-n-Tarabine	32	Ie	21.16N	7.24 E
Tintâreni	15	Ge	44.36N	23.29 E
Tintina	56	Hc	27.02S	62.43W
Tinto	13	Fg	37.12N	6.55W
Ti-n-toumma	30	Ig	16.04N	12.40 E
Tinwald	62	De	43.55S	171.43 E
Ti-n-Zaouâtene	31	Hg	19.56N	2.55 E
Tiobraid Árann/Tipperary	9	Ei	52.29N	8.10W
Tiobraid Árann/Tipperary [2]	9	Ei	52.40N	8.20W
Tioga	45	Eb	48.24N	102.56W
Tioman, Pulau-	26	Df	2.48N	104.11 E
Tione di Trento	14	Ed	46.02N	10.43 E
Tioro, Selat-=Tioro, Strait (EN)	26	Hg	4.40S	122.20 E
Tioro Strait (EN)=Tioro, Selat-	26	Hg	4.40S	122.20 E
Tiøtta	7	Cd	65.50N	12.24 E
Tiouilit	32	Df	18.52N	16.10W
Tipasa	13	Oh	36.35N	2.27 E
Tipitapa	47	Gf	12.12N	86.06W
Tipperary/Tiobraid Árann	9	Ei	52.29N	8.10W
Tipperary/Tiobraid Árann [2]	9	Ei	52.40N	8.20W
Tipton, Mount-	46	Hi	35.32N	114.12W
Tip Top Mountain	45	Nb	48.16N	85.59W
Tiptree	12	Cc	51.49N	0.45 E
Tiracambu, Serra do-	54	Id	3.15S	46.30W
Tirahart	32	He	23.45N	2.30 E
Tirān	24	Nf	32.42N	51.09 E
Tirān, Maḑīq-	24	Fi	27.55N	34.28 E
Tirana	6	Hg	41.20N	19.50 E
Tirania	32	Ie	23.08N	9.01 E
Tirano	14	Ed	46.13N	10.10 E
Tiraspol	19	Cf	46.50N	29.37 E
Tirat Karmel	24	Ff	32.46N	34.58 E
Tire	23	Cb	38.04N	27.45 E
Tirebolu	24	Hb	41.00N	38.50 E
Tiree	9	Ge	56.31N	6.49W
Tiree, Passage of-	9	Ge	56.30N	6.30W
Tîrgovişte	15	Ie	44.56N	25.27 E
Tîrgu Bujor	15	Kd	45.52N	27.54 E
Tîrgu Cărbuneşti	15	Ge	44.57N	23.31 E
Tîrgu Frumos	15	Jb	47.12N	27.00 E
Tîrgu Jiu	15	Gd	45.03N	23.17 E
Tîrgu Lăpuş	15	Gb	47.27N	23.52 E
Tîrgu Mureş	6	If	46.33N	24.34 E
Tîrgu Neamţ	15	Jb	47.12N	26.22 E
Tîrgu Ocna	15	Jc	46.17N	26.37 E
Tîrgu Secuiesc	15	Jd	46.00N	26.08 E
Tîrguşor	15	Le	44.27N	28.25 E
Tirich Mir	21	Jf	36.15N	71.50 E
Tirins	15	Fl	37.36N	22.48 E
Tiririca, Serra da-	55	Ic	17.06S	47.06W
Tiris	30	Ff	23.10N	13.30W
Tiris Zemmour [3]	32	Fe	24.00N	10.00W
Tirlemont/Tienen	12	Gd	50.48N	4.57 E
Tirljanski	17	Ii	54.12N	58.33 E
Tîrnava Mare	15	Gc	46.09N	23.42 E
Tîrnava Mică	15	Gc	46.11N	23.55 E
Tîrnăveni	15	Hc	46.20N	24.17 E
Tírnavos	15	Fj	39.45N	22.17 E
Tiro	34	Cd	9.45N	10.39W
Tirol/Tirolo=Tyrol (EN)	14	Fd	47.00N	11.20 E
Tirol=Tyrol (EN) [2]	14	Fc	47.10N	11.25 E
Tirolo/Tirol=Tyrol (EN)	14	Fd	47.00N	11.20 E
Tiros	55	Jd	19.00S	45.58W
Tirreno, Mar-=Tyrrhenian Sea (EN)	5	Hh	40.00N	12.00 E
Tirschenreuth	10	Ig	49.53N	12.21 E
Tirso	14	Ck	39.53N	8.32 E
Tirstrup	8	Dh	56.18N	10.42 E
Tirua Point	62	Fc	38.23S	174.38 E
Tiruchchirappalli	22	Jh	10.49N	78.41 E
Tiruliai/Tiruliaj	8	Ji	55.44N	23.18 E
Tiruliaj/Tiruliai	8	Ji	55.44N	23.18 E
Tirunelveli	22	Ji	8.44N	77.42 E
Tirupati	25	Ff	13.39N	79.25 E
Tirza	8	Lg	57.09N	26.37 E
Tisa=Tisza (EN)	5	If	45.15N	20.17 E
Tis Abay	35	Fc	11.20N	37.40 E
Tisdale	42	Hf	52.51N	104.04W
Tisnaren	8	Ff	58.55N	15.55 E
Tisovec	10	Ph	48.42N	19.57 E
Tissemsilt	32	Hb	35.36N	1.49 E
Tissø	8	Di	55.35N	11.20 E
Tisza	5	If	45.15N	20.17 E
Tisza (EN)=Tisa	5	If	45.15N	20.17 E
Tiszaföldvár	10	Qj	46.59N	20.15 E
Tiszafüred	10	Qi	47.37N	20.46 E
Tiszakécske	10	Qj	46.56N	20.06 E
Tiszántúl	10	Qj	47.00N	21.00 E
Tiszaújváros (Leninváros)	10	Ri	47.56N	21.05 E
Tiszavasvári	10	Ri	47.58N	21.21 E
Titao	34	Ec	13.46N	2.04W
Titarisios	15	Fj	39.47N	22.23 E
Tit-Ary	20	Hb	71.55N	127.01 E
Titicaca, Lago-	52	Jg	15.50S	69.20W
Titikaveka	64p	Bc	21.15S	159.45W
Titlagarh	25	Gd	20.18N	83.09 E
Titlis	14	Cd	46.47N	8.26 E
Titograd → Podgorica	6	Hg	42.26N	19.16 E
Titova Korenica	14	Jf	44.45N	15.42 E
Titovo Užice → Užice	15	Cf	43.52N	19.51 E
Titov Veles	15	Eh	41.42N	21.48 E
Titov vrh	15	Dh	41.58N	20.50 E
Titran	7	Be	63.40N	8.18 E
Titteri	13	Pi	35.59N	3.15 E
Titule	36	Eb	3.17N	25.32 E
Titusville [Fl.-U.S.]	43	Kf	28.37N	80.49W
Titusville [Pa.-U.S.]	44	He	41.37N	79.42W
Tituvenaj/Tytuvėnai	8	Ji	55.33N	23.09 E
Tiva	36	Gc	2.20S	39.55 E
Tivaouane	34	Bc	14.57N	16.49W
Tiveden	8	Ff	58.45N	14.40 E
Tiverton	9	Jk	50.55N	3.29W
Tivoli [Gren.]	51p	Bb	12.10N	61.37W
Tivoli [It.]	14	Gi	41.58N	12.48 E
Ţiwāl	35	Cc	10.22N	22.43 E
Tiwi	36	Gc	4.14S	39.35 E
Tiyo	35	Gc	14.41N	40.57 E
Tizatlán	48	Jh	19.21N	98.15W
Tizimin	47	Gd	21.09N	88.09W
Tizi Ouzou [3]	32	Hb	36.35N	4.05 E
Tizi Ouzou	32	Hb	36.42N	4.03 E
Tiznados, Río-	50	Ch	8.16N	67.47W
Tiznit	32	Fd	29.43N	9.43W
Tiznit [3]	32	Fd	29.07N	9.04W
Tjačev	10	Th	48.02N	23.36 E
Tjanšan	27	Dc	42.00N	80.01 E
Tjasmin	16	He	49.03N	32.50 E
Tjeggelvas	7	Dc	66.35N	17.40 E
Tjeukemeer	11	Lb	52.54N	5.50 E
Tjøme	8	De	59.10N	10.25 E
Tjorn	8	Df	58.00N	11.38 E
Tjub-Karagan, Mys-	16	Qg	44.38N	50.20 E
Tjubuk	17	Jh	56.03N	60.58 E
Tjuhtet	20	De	56.32N	89.29 E
Tjukalinsk	19	Hd	55.52N	72.12 E
Tjuleni, Ostrov-	16	Og	44.30N	47.30 E
Tjuleni, Ostrova-	16	Og	44.55N	50.10 E
Tjulgan	19	Fe	52.22N	56.12 E
Tjumen	22	Id	57.09N	65.32 E
Tjumenskaja Oblast [3]	19	Gd	57.00N	69.00 E
Tjung	20	Hd	63.42N	121.30 E
Tjup	18	Lc	42.44N	78.20 E
Tjuri/Türi	7	Fg	58.50N	25.27 E
Tjust	8	Gg	57.50N	16.15 E
Tjuters Maly, Ostrov-	8	Le	59.45N	26.53 E
Tjuzašu, Pereval-	18	Ic	42.10N	73.50 E
Tkibuli	16	Mh	42.19N	42.59 E
Tkvarčeli	16	Lh	42.52N	41.40 E
Tlacolula	48	Ki	16.57N	96.29W
Tlacotalpan	48	Lh	18.37N	95.40W
Tlahualilo, Sierra del-	48	Hd	26.30N	103.20W
Tlalnepantla	48	Jh	19.33N	99.12W
Tlapa de Comonfort	48	Ji	17.33N	98.33W
Tlapaneco, Río-	48	Jh	18.00N	98.48W
Tlaquepaque	48	Hg	20.39N	103.19W
Tlaxcala [2]	47	Ee	19.25N	98.10W
Tlaxcala	47	Ee	19.19N	98.14W
Tlemcen	32	Gc	34.52N	1.19W
Tlemcen [3]	32	Gc	34.45N	1.30W
Tleń	10	Oc	53.38N	18.20 E
Tleta Rissana	13	Gi	35.14N	5.59W
Tletat ed Douair	13	Oi	35.59N	2.55 E
Tljarata	16	Oh	42.06N	46.22 E
Tlumač	10	Vh	48.46N	25.06 E
Tłuszcz	10	Rd	52.26N	21.26 E
Tmassah	33	Cd	26.22N	15.48 E
Tō, Shikotan-/Šikotan, Ostrov-	20	Jh	43.47N	146.45 E
Toaca, Vîrful-	15	Ic	46.55N	25.59 E
Toagel Mlungui	64a	Ab	7.32N	134.28 E
Toamasina	31	Lj	18.10S	49.24 E
Toamasina [3]	37	Hc	18.00S	48.40 E
Toau Atoll	61	Lc	15.55S	146.00W
Toay	56	He	36.40S	64.21W
Toba	28	Ng	34.29N	136.51 E
Toba, Danau-=Toba, Lake- (EN)	26	Li	2.35N	98.50 E
Tobago	52	Jd	11.15N	60.40W
Tobago Basin (EN)	50	Ff	12.30N	60.30W
Tobago Cays	51n	Bb	12.39N	61.22W
Toba Kākar Range	25	Db	31.15N	68.00 E
Tobarra	13	Kf	38.35N	1.41W
Tobe	29	Ce	33.44N	132.47 E
Tobejuba, Isla-	50	Fh	9.20N	60.52W
Tobelo	26	If	1.25N	127.31 E
Tobermory [Ont.-Can.]	44	Gc	45.15N	81.40W
Tobermory [Scot.-U.K.]	9	Ge	56.37N	6.05W
Tōbetsu	29a	Bb	43.14N	141.29 E
Tobi Island	57	Ed	3.00N	131.10 E
Tobin, Kap-	41	Jd	70.30N	21.30W
Tobin, Mount-	46	Gf	40.22N	117.32W
Tobin Lake [Austl.]	59	Fd	21.45S	125.50 E
Tobin Lake [Sask.-Can.]	42	Hf	53.40N	103.20W
Tobi-Shima	29	Fb	39.12N	139.32 E
Toblach / Dobbiaco	14	Gd	46.44N	12.14 E
Toboali	26	Eg	3.00S	106.30 E
Tobol	19	Ge	52.40N	62.39 E
Tobol	21	Id	58.10N	68.12 E
Tobolsk	22	Id	58.12N	68.16 E
Tobruk (EN)=Ţubruq	31	Je	32.05N	23.59 E
Tobseda	19	Fb	68.36N	52.20 E
Tocantinópolis	53	Lf	6.20S	47.25W
Tocantins	54	If	10.30S	48.00W
Tocantins, Rio-	52	Lf	1.45S	49.10W
Tocantinzinho, Rio-	55	Ha	13.57S	48.20W
Toccoa	44	Fh	34.35N	83.19W
Toce	14	Ce	45.56N	8.29 E
Tochigi	29	Fc	36.23N	139.44 E
Tochigi Ken [2]	28	Of	36.50N	139.50 E
Tochio	29	Fc	37.29N	138.58 E
Töcksfors	8	De	59.31N	11.50 E
Toco	50	Fg	10.50N	60.57W
Tocoa	49	Df	15.41N	86.03W
Toconao	56	Gb	23.11S	68.01W
Tocopilla	53	Ih	22.05S	70.12W
Tocumen	49	Hi	9.05N	79.23W
Tocuyo, Río-	49	Mh	11.03N	68.20W
Todd Mountain	44	Nb	46.32N	66.43W
Todi	14	Gh	42.47N	12.24 E
Tōdi	14	Cd	46.49N	8.55 E
Todo-ga-Saki	27	Pd	39.33N	142.05 E
Todos os Santos, Baia de-	52	Mg	12.48S	38.38W
Todos Santos	47	Bd	23.27N	110.13W
Todos Santos, Bahia-	48	Ab	31.48N	116.42W
Tofino	42	Eg	49.09N	125.54W
Tofte	8	De	59.33N	10.34 E
Toftlund	8	Ci	55.11N	9.04 E
Tofua Island	61	Fc	19.45S	175.05W
Toga	63b	Ca	13.26S	166.41 E
Tōgane	29	Gd	35.33N	140.21 E
Tog Ḑarōr	35	Hc	10.25N	50.00 E
Togdere	35	Hd	9.01N	47.07 E
Tog-Dheer [3]	35	Hd	9.50N	45.50 E
Togi	29	Ec	37.08N	136.43 E
Togiak	40	Ge	59.04N	160.24W
Togian Islands (EN)= Togian, Kepulauan-	26	Hg	0.20S	122.00 E
Togliatti	6	Ke	53.31N	49.26 E
Togni	35	Fb	18.05N	35.10 E
Togo [1]	31	Hh	8.00N	1.10 E
Togrog Ul → Qahar Youyi Qianqi	28	Bd	40.46N	113.13 E
Togtoh	27	Jc	40.17N	111.15 E
Togučin	20	De	55.16N	84.33 E
Toguzak	17	Ki	54.05N	62.48 E
Togwotee Pass	43	Ec	43.45N	110.04W
Tohen	35	Ic	11.44N	51.15 E
Tohma	24	Hc	38.31N	38.25 E
Tohmajärvi	7	He	62.11N	30.23 E
Tohopekaliga, Lake-	44	Gk	28.12N	81.23W
Toi	29	Fd	34.54N	138.47 E
Toijala	7	Ff	61.10N	23.52 E
Toi-Misaki	28	Ki	31.26N	131.19 E
Toisvesi	8	Jb	62.20N	23.45 E
Tojikiston = Tajikistan (EN)	19	Hh	39.00N	71.00 E
Tōjō	29	Cd	34.53N	133.16 E
Tojtepa	18	Gd	41.03N	69.22 E
Tok	19	Jg	49.43N	13.50 E
Tok	16	Rc	52.46N	52.22 E
Tok	40	Kd	63.20N	142.59W
Tokachi-Dake	29a	Cb	43.25N	142.41 E
Tokachi-Gawa	29a	Cb	42.41N	143.37 E
Tokachi-Heiya	29a	Cb	43.00N	143.20 E
Tokachimitsumata	29a	Cb	43.31N	143.07 E
Tōkai [Jap.]	29	Gc	36.27N	140.34 E
Tōkai [Jap.]	29	Ed	35.01N	136.51 E
Tokaj	16	Ld	51.18N	41.04 E
Tokaj	10	Rh	48.07N	21.25 E
Tokamachi	28	Of	37.08N	138.46 E
Tokanui	62	Cg	46.34S	168.57 E
Tokara Islands (EN)= Tokara-Rettō	21	Og	29.35N	129.45 E
Tokara-Kaikyō	28	Ki	30.10N	130.15 E
Tokara-Rettō=Tokara Islands (EN)	21	Og	29.35N	129.45 E
Tokashiki-Jima	29b	Ab	26.13N	127.21 E
Tokat	23	Ea	40.19N	36.34 E
Tŏkch'ŏn	28	Ie	39.45N	126.15 E
Tok-Do	28	Kf	37.22N	131.58 E
Tokelau [5]	58	Je	9.00S	171.46W
Tokelau/Union Islands	57	Je	9.00S	171.45W
Toki	29	Ed	35.22N	137.11 E
Tokke	8	Ce	59.00N	9.15 E
Tokke	8	Be	59.27N	7.58 E
Tokkuztara/Gongliu	27	Dc	43.30N	82.15 E
Tokmak	19	Hg	42.49N	75.19 E
Tokmak	19	Df	47.13N	35.43 E
Tokomaru Bay	61	Eg	38.08S	178.20 E
Tokoname	29	Ed	34.53N	136.49 E
Tokoro	29a	Da	44.08N	144.03 E
Tokoroa	61	Eg	38.13S	175.52 E
Tokoro-Gawa	29a	Da	44.08N	144.04 E
Toksovo	8	Nd	60.10N	30.42 E
Toksu/Xinhe	27	Dc	41.34N	82.38 E
Toksun	27	Ec	42.47N	88.38 E
Toktogul	19	Hg	41.50N	73.01 E
Toktogulskoje Vodohranilišče	18	Id	41.45N	73.00 E
Tokuji	29	Bd	34.11N	131.39 E
Tokulu	65b	Bb	20.06S	174.48W
Toku-no-Shima	27	Mf	27.45N	128.50 E
Tokunoshima	29b	Bb	27.45N	128.58 E
Tokur	20	If	53.09N	132.50 E
Tokushima	27	Ne	34.04N	134.34 E
Tokushima Ken [2]	28	Mh	33.50N	134.10 E
Tokuyama [Jap.]	28	Ed	35.43N	136.27 E
Tokuyama [Jap.]	28	Kg	34.03N	131.49 E
Tokwe	37	Ed	20.09S	31.54 E
Tōkyō	22	Pf	35.40N	139.46 E
Tokyo Bay (EN)=Tōkyō-Wan	28	Og	35.38N	139.57 E
Tōkyō To [2]	28	Og	35.40N	139.20 E
Tōkyō-Wan=Tokyo Bay (EN)	28	Og	35.38N	139.57 E
Tola	21	Me	48.57N	104.48 E
Tolaga Bay	62	Hc	38.22S	178.18 E
Tolbazy	17	Gi	54.02N	55.59 E
Tolbuhin [2]	15	Kf	43.34N	27.50 E
Tolbuhin → Dobrič	15	Kf	43.34N	27.50 E
Toledo	13	Ie	39.50N	4.00W
Toledo [Blz.]	49	Ce	16.25N	88.50W
Toledo [Braz.]	56	Jb	24.44S	53.45W
Toledo [Oh.-U.S.]	39	Ke	41.39N	83.32W
Toledo [Phil.]	26	Hd	10.23N	123.38 E
Toledo [Sp.]	6	Fh	39.52N	4.01W
Toledo, Montes de-	13	He	39.35N	4.20W
Toledo Bend Reservoir	43	Ie	31.30N	93.45W
Tolentino	14	Hg	43.12N	13.17 E
Tolfa	14	Fh	42.09N	11.56 E
Tolfa, Monti della-	14	Fh	42.10N	11.55 E
Tolga	7	Ce	62.25N	11.00 E
Toli	27	Db	45.56N	83.37 E
Toliara	37	Gd	22.00S	44.00 E
Toliara	31	Lk	23.21S	43.39 E
Tolima [2]	54	Cc	3.45N	75.15W
Tolima, Nevado del-	52	Ie	4.40N	75.19W
Toling → Zanda	27	Ce	31.28N	79.50 E
Tolitoli	26	Hf	1.02N	120.49 E
Toll	64d	Bb	7.22N	151.37 E
Tollarp	8	Ei	55.56N	13.59 E
Tollja, Zaliv-	20	Ea	76.40N	100.00 E
Tolmačevo	8	Nf	58.48N	30.01 E
Tolmezzo	14	Hd	46.24N	13.01 E
Tolmin	14	Hd	46.11N	13.44 E
Tolna	10	Oj	46.26N	18.47 E
Tolna [2]	10	Oj	46.30N	18.35 E
Tolo	36	Cc	2.56S	18.34 E
Tolo, Gulf of- (EN)=Tolo, Teluk-	21	Oj	2.00S	122.30 E
Tolo, Teluk-=Tolo, Gulf of- (EN)	21	Oj	2.00S	122.30 E
Toločin	7	Gi	54.25N	29.41 E
Tolosa	13	Ja	43.08N	2.04W
Tolstoj, Mys-	5	Rd	59.10N	155.05 E
Toltén	56	Fe	39.13S	73.14W
Tolú	54	Cb	9.32N	75.34W
Toluca, Nevado de-	38	Jh	19.08N	99.44W
Toluca de Lerdo	39	Jh	19.17N	99.40W
Tom	21	Kd	56.50N	84.27 E
Toma	34	Ec	12.46N	2.53W
Tomah	45	Ke	43.59N	90.30W
Tomakomai	27	Pc	42.38N	141.36 E
Tomamae	29a	Ba	44.18N	141.39 E
Tomanivi	63d	Bb	17.37S	178.01 E
Tomar	13	De	39.36N	8.25W
Tómaros	15	Dj	39.32N	20.45 E
Tomaševka	16	Cd	51.33N	23.40 E
Tomás Young	55	Ai	28.36S	62.11W
Tomaszów Lubelski	10	Tf	50.28N	23.25 E
Tomaszów Mazowiecki	10	Qe	51.32N	20.01 E
Tomatlán	48	Gh	19.56N	105.15W
Tombador, Serra dos-	54	Gf	12.00S	57.40W
Tombigbee River	43	Je	31.04N	87.58W
Tomboco	36	Bd	6.45S	13.18 E
Tombouctou=Timbuktu (EN)	31	Gg	16.46N	2.59W
Tombstone	46	Jk	31.43N	110.04W
Tombua	31	Ij	15.48S	11.52 E
Tomé	56	Fe	36.37S	72.57W
Tomé-Açu	54	Id	2.25S	48.09W
Tomelilla	7	Ci	55.33N	13.57 E
Tomelloso	13	Ie	39.10N	3.01W
Tomichi Creek	45	Cg	38.31N	106.58W
Tomie	29	Ae	32.37N	128.46 E
Tomini, Gulf of- (EN)= Tomini, Teluk-	21	Oj	0.20S	121.00 E
Tomini, Teluk-=Tomini, Gulf of- (EN)	21	Oj	0.20S	121.00 E
Tominian	34	Ec	13.17N	4.35W
Tomioka [Jap.]	29	Gc	37.20N	140.59 E
Tomioka [Jap.]	29	Fc	36.15N	138.52 E
Tomkinson Ranges	59	Fe	26.10S	129.05 E
Tomma	7	Cc	66.15N	12.48 E
Tomo, Río-	54	Eb	5.20N	67.48W
Tomochic	48	Fc	28.20N	107.51W
Tomorit, Mali i-	15	Di	40.40N	20.09 E
Tomotu Neo	63c	Ab	10.41S	165.47 E
Tomotu Noi	63c	Bb	10.50S	166.02 E
Tompa	10	Pj	46.12N	19.33 E
Tompe	26	Gg	0.12S	119.48 E
Tompo	20	Id	62.50N	134.47 E
Tompo	20	Id	64.00N	136.00 E
Tom Price	59	Dd	22.40S	117.55 E
Tomsk	22	Kd	56.30N	84.58 E
Tomskaja Oblast [3]	20	De	58.20N	81.30 E
Tomtabacken	8	Fg	57.30N	14.28 E
Tomur Feng	21	Ke	42.02N	80.05 E
Tom White, Mount-	40	Kd	60.40N	143.40W
Tonaki-Shima	29b	Ab	26.21N	127.09 E
Tonalá	47	Fe	16.04N	93.45W
Tonale, Passo del-	14	Ed	46.16N	10.35 E
Tonami	29	Ec	36.38N	136.57 E
Tonara	14	Dj	40.02N	9.10 E
Tonasket	46	Fb	48.42N	119.26W
Tonb-e Bozorg	24	Pi	26.15N	55.03 E
Tonbetsu-Gawa	29a	Ca	45.08N	142.23 E
Tonbridge	9	Nj	51.12N	0.16 E
Tondano	26	Hf	1.19N	124.54 E
Tondela	13	Dd	40.31N	8.05W
Tønder	7	Bi	54.56N	8.54 E
Tone-Gawa	29	Gd	35.44N	140.51 E
Tonekābon	23	Hb	36.53N	50.56 E
Toney	66	Of	75.50S	115.48W
Tonga [1]	58	Jf	20.00S	175.00W
Tonga	35	Ed	9.28N	31.03 E

Index Symbols

- [1] Independent Nation
- [2] State, Region
- [3] District, County
- [4] Municipality
- [5] Colony, Dependency
- Continent
- Physical Region
- Historical or Cultural Region
- Mount, Mountain
- Volcano
- Hill
- Mountains, Mountain Range
- Hills, Escarpment
- Plateau, Upland
- Pass, Gap
- Plain, Lowland
- Delta
- Salt Flat
- Valley, Canyon
- Crater, Cave
- Karst Features
- Depression
- Polder
- Desert, Dunes
- Forest, Woods
- Heath, Steppe
- Oasis
- Cape, Point
- Coast, Beach
- Cliff
- Peninsula
- Isthmus
- Sandbank
- Island
- Atoll
- Rock, Reef
- Islands, Archipelago
- Rocks, Reefs
- Coral Reef
- Well, Spring
- Geyser
- River, Stream
- Waterfall Rapids
- River Mouth, Estuary
- Lake
- Salt Lake
- Intermittent Lake
- Reservoir
- Swamp, Pond
- Canal
- Glacier
- Ice Shelf, Pack Ice
- Ocean
- Sea
- Gulf, Bay
- Strait, Fjord
- Lagoon
- Bank
- Seamount
- Tablemount
- Ridge
- Shelf
- Basin
- Escarpment, Sea Scarp
- Fracture
- Trench, Abyss
- National Park, Reserve
- Point of Interest
- Recreation Site
- Cave, Cavern
- Historic Site
- Ruins
- Wall, Walls
- Church, Abbey
- Temple
- Scientific Station
- Airport
- Port
- Lighthouse
- Mine
- Tunnel
- Dam, Bridge

International Map Index

Index Symbols

[1]	Independent Nation
[2]	State, Region
[3]	District, County
[4]	Municipality
[5]	Colony, Dependency
[6]	Continent
[7]	Physical Region

- Historical or Cultural Region
- Mount, Mountain
- Volcano
- Hill
- Mountains, Mountain Range
- Hills, Escarpment
- Plateau, Upland
- Pass, Gap
- Plain, Lowland
- Delta
- Salt Flat
- Valley, Canyon
- Crater, Cave
- Karst Features
- Depression
- Polder
- Desert, Dunes
- Forest, Woods
- Heath, Steppe
- Oasis
- Cape, Point
- Coast, Beach
- Cliff
- Peninsula
- Isthmus
- Sandbank
- Island
- Atoll
- Rock, Reef
- Islands, Archipelago
- Rocks, Reefs
- Coral Reef
- Well, Spring
- Geyser
- River, Stream
- Waterfall Rapids
- River Mouth, Estuary
- Lake
- Salt Lake
- Intermitent Lake
- Reservoir
- Swamp, Pond
- Canal
- Bank
- Seamount
- Tablemount
- Ridge
- Shelf
- Strait, Fjord
- Lagoon
- Glacier
- Ice Shelf, Pack Ice
- Ocean
- Sea
- Gulf, Bay
- Basin
- Escarpment, Sea Scarp
- Fracture
- Trench, Abyss
- National Park, Reserve
- Point of Interest
- Recreation Site
- Cave, Cavern
- Historic Site
- Ruins
- Wall, Walls
- Church, Abbey
- Temple
- Scientific Station
- Airport
- Port
- Lighthouse
- Mine
- Tunnel
- Dam, Bridge

Tuy Hoa 25 Lf 13.05N 109.18 E
Tüyserkān 24 Me 34.33N 48.27 E
Tuz, Lake- (EN)=Tuz Gölü 21 Ff 38.45N 33.25 E
Tuzkan, Ozero- 18 Fd 40.35N 67.30 E
Tūz Khurmātū 23 Fc 34.53N 44.38 E
Tuzla 14 Mf 44.33N 18.41 E
Tuzlov 16 Lf 47.23N 40.08 E
Tuzluca 24 Jb 40.03N 43.39 E
Tuzly 15 Nd 45.56N 30.05 E
Tvååker 8 Eg 57.03N 12.24 E
Tvărdica 15 Ig 42.42N 25.54 E
Tvedestrand 7 Bg 58.37N 8.55 E
Tver' (Kalinin) 6 Jd 56.52N 35.55 E
Tver'skaja oblast 19 Dd 57.20N 34.40 E
Tweed 9 Lf 55.46N 2.00W
Tweedsmuir Hills 9 Jf 55.30N 3.22W
Tweerivier 37 Be 25.35S 19.37 E
Twello, Voorst- 12 Ib 52.14N 6.07 E
Twente 11 Mb 52.17N 6.40 E
Twentekanaal 12 Ib 52.13N 6.53 E
Twilight Cove 59 Ff 32.20S 126.00 E
Twin Buttes Reservoir 45 Fk 31.20N 100.35W
Twin Falls 39 He 42.34N 114.28W
Twin Islands 42 Jf 53.50N 80.00W
Twin Peaks 46 Hd 44.35N 114.29W
Twisp 46 Eb 48.22N 120.07W
Twiste 12 Lc 51.29N 9.09 E
Twistringen 10 Ed 52.48N 8.39 E
Two Butte Creek 45 Eg 38.02N 102.08W
Two Harbors 45 Kc 47.01N 91.40W
Two Rivers 45 Md 44.09N 87.34W
Two Thumb Range 62 De 43.45S 170.40 E
Tychy 10 Of 50.09N 18.59 E
Tyczyn 10 Sg 49.58N 22.02 E
Tydal 7 Ce 63.04N 11.34 E
Tygda 20 Hf 53.07N 126.20 E
Tyin 8 Cc 61.15N 8.15 E
Tyin 8 Cc 61.14N 8.14 E
Tyler 43 He 32.21N 95.18W
Tylertown 45 Kk 31.07N 90.09W
Tylösand 8 Eh 56.39N 12.44 E
Tylöskog 8 Ff 58.40N 15.10 E
Tym 20 De 59.30N 80.07 E
Tymovskoje 20 Jf 50.50N 142.41 E
Tympákion 15 Hn 35.06N 24.45 E
Tynda 22 Od 53.07N 126.20 E
Tyne 9 Lf 55.01N 1.26W
Tyne and Wear [3] 9 Lg 55.00N 1.35W
Tynemouth 9 Lf 55.01N 1.24W
Týn nad Vltavou 10 Kg 49.14N 14.26 E
Tynset 7 Ce 62.17N 10.47 E
Tyra, Cayos- 49 Fg 12.50N 83.20W
Tyrifjorden 8 De 60.05N 10.10 E
Tyringe 8 Eh 56.10N 13.35 E
Tyrma 20 If 50.01N 132.10 E
Tyrnyauz 16 Mh 43.23N 42.56 E
Tyrol (EN)=Tirol [2] 14 Fc 47.10N 11.25 E
Tyrol (EN)=Tirol/Tirolo 14 Fd 47.00N 11.20 E
Tyrol (EN)=Tirolo/Tirol 14 Fd 47.00N 11.20 E
Tyrone 44 He 40.41N 78.15W
Tyrrell, Lake- 59 Ig 35.20S 142.50 E
Tyrrel Lake 42 Gd 63.05N 105.30W
Tyrrhenian Basin (EN) 5 Hh 40.00N 13.00 E
Tyrrhenian Sea (EN)= Tirreno, Mar- 5 Hh 40.00N 12.00 E
Tyrva/Tõrva 7 Fg 58.01N 25.59 E
Tyrvää 8 Jc 61.21N 22.53 E
Tysmenica 10 Uh 48.49N 24.56 E
Tyśmienica 10 Se 51.33N 22.30 E
Tysnesøy 7 Af 60.00N 5.35 E
Tysse 8 Ad 60.22N 5.45 E
Tyssedal 8 Bd 60.07N 6.34 E
Tystama/Tõstamaa 8 Jf 58.17N 23.52 E
Tystberga 8 Gf 58.52N 17.15 E
Tyszowce 10 Tf 50.36N 23.41 E
Tytuvėnai/Tituvenaj 8 Ji 55.33N 23.09 E
Tywyn 9 Ii 52.35N 4.05W
Tzanconeja, Rio- 48 Ni 16.51N 91.47W
Tzaneen 37 Ed 23.50S 30.09 E
Tzintzuntzan 48 Ih 19.38N 101.34W
Tzucacab 48 Og 20.04N 89.05W

U

Uaboe 64e Ab 0.31S 166.54 E
Uacurizal, Ilha do- 55 Dc 16.25S 56.05W
Ua Huka, Ile- 57 Ne 8.54S 139.33W
Uanukuhahaki 65b Ba 19.58S 174.29W
Ua Pou, Ile- 57 Me 9.23S 140.03W
Uaroo 59 Dd 23.00S 115.10 E
Uatumã, Rio- 52 Kf 2.26S 57.37W
Uaupés 53 Jf 0.08S 67.05W
Uaupés, Rio- 52 Je 0.02N 67.16W
Uaxactún 47 Ge 17.25N 89.29W
Ub 15 De 44.27N 20.05 E
Ubá 54 Jh 21.07S 42.56W
Übach-Palenberg [Ger.] 10 Cf 50.56N 6.05 E
Ubagan 19 Ge 54.23N 64.40 E
Ubaila 24 If 33.06N 40.15 E
Ubaitaba 54 Kf 14.18S 39.20W
Ubajay 55 Cj 31.47S 58.18W
Ubangi 30 Ii 0.30S 17.42 E
Ubatuba 55 Jf 23.26S 45.04W
Ubay 26 Hd 10.03N 124.28 E
Ubaye 11 Mj 44.28N 6.18 E
Ubayyiḑ, Wādī al- 23 Fc 32.34N 43.48 E
Ube 28 Kh 33.56N 131.15 E
Ubeda 13 If 38.01N 3.22W
Ubekendt Ejland 41 Gd 71.10N 53.45W
Uberaba 53 Lg 19.45S 47.55W
Uberaba, Lagoa- 55 Dc 17.30S 57.45W
Uberlândia 53 Lg 18.56S 48.18W
Überlingen 10 Fi 47.46N 9.10 E
Ubiaja 34 Gd 6.39N 6.23 E
Ubiña, Peña- 13 Ga 43.01N 5.57W
Ubiratã 55 Fg 24.32S 52.56W
Ubon Ratchathani 22 Mh 15.15N 104.54 E
Ubort 16 Fc 52.06N 28.30 E
Ubrique 13 Gh 36.41N 5.27W
Ubsu-Nur (Uvs nuur) 21 Ld 50.20N 92.45 E
Ubundu 31 Ji 0.21S 25.29 E
Učaly 19 Fe 54.20N 59.31 E
Učami 20 Ed 63.50N 96.39 E
Učaral 19 If 46.08N 80.52 E
Ucayali, Rio- 52 If 4.30S 73.30W
Uccle/Ukkel 12 Gd 50.48N 4.19 E
Üçdoruk Tepe 24 Ib 40.45N 41.05 E
Ucero 13 Ic 41.31N 3.04W
Uchiko 29 Ce 33.34N 132.38 E
Uchi Lake 45 Ja 51.05N 92.35W
Uchinomi 29 Dd 34.30N 134.19 E
Uchinoura 29 Bf 31.16N 131.05 E
Uchiura-Wan 28 Pc 42.18N 140.35 E
Uchte 10 Ed 52.30N 8.55 E
Učka 14 Ie 45.17N 14.12 E
Uckange 12 Ie 49.18N 6.09 E
Uckermark 10 Jc 53.10N 13.35 E
Uckfield 12 Cd 50.58N 0.06 E
Učkuduk 19 Gg 42.10N 63.30 E
Učkurgan 18 Id 41.01N 72.04 E
Ucrainskaja Sovetskaja Socialističeskaja Respublika → Ukrayina 19 Df 49.00N 32.00 E
Ucross 46 Ld 44.33N 106.31W
Ucua 36 Bd 8.40S 14.12 E
Učur 21 Pd 58.48N 130.35 E
Uda 21 Pd 54.42N 135.14 E
Uda 20 Ff 51.45N 107.25 E
Uda 20 Ee 56.05N 99.34 E
Udačny 20 Gc 66.25N 112.20 E
Udaipur 22 Jg 24.35N 73.41 E
Udaj 16 Hd 50.05N 33.07 E
Udaquiola 55 Cm 36.34S 58.31W
Udbina 14 Jf 44.32N 15.46 E
Uddevalla 7 Cg 58.21N 11.55 E
Uddjaure 5 Hb 65.58N 17.50 E
Uden 12 Hc 51.40N 5.37 E
Udgir 25 Fe 18.23N 77.06 E
Udhampur 25 Fb 32.56N 75.08 E
Udimskij 7 Kf 61.09N 45.52 E
Udine 14 Hd 46.03N 13.14 E
Udipi 25 Ef 13.21N 74.45 E
Udmurtskaja respublika 19 Fd 57.20N 52.50 E
Udoha 8 Mg 57.58N 29.50 E
Udomlja 7 Ih 57.56N 35.02 E
Udone-Jima 29 Fd 34.28N 139.17 E
Udon Thani 25 Ke 17.25N 102.48 E
Udot 64d Bb 7.23N 151.43 E
Udskaja Guba 21 Pd 55.00N 136.00 E
Udskoje 20 If 54.36N 134.30 E
Udy 16 Je 49.47N 36.35 E
Udžary 16 Oi 40.31N 47.40 E
Udzungwa Range 36 Gd 8.05S 35.50 E
Uebonti 26 Hg 0.55S 121.38 E
Uecker 10 Kc 53.45N 14.04 E
Ueckermünde 10 Kc 53.44N 14.03 E
Ueda 27 Od 36.24N 138.16 E
Uele 30 Jh 4.09N 22.26 E
Uelen 20 Oc 66.13N 169.48W
Uelzen 10 Gd 52.58N 10.34 E
Ueno 28 Ed 34.46N 136.06 E
Uere 30 Jh 3.42N 25.24 E
Ufa 5 Le 54.40N 56.00 E
Ufa 6 Le 54.44N 55.56 E
Uftjuga 7 Lf 61.28N 46.12 E
Ugab 30 Ik 21.12S 13.38 E
Ugale/Ugāle 8 Ig 57.19N 21.52 E
Ugāle/Ugale 8 Ig 57.19N 21.52 E
Ugalla 36 Fd 5.08S 30.42 E
Uganda [1] 31 Kh 1.00N 32.00 E
Ugărčin 15 Hf 43.06N 24.25 E
Ugashik 40 He 57.32N 157.25W
Ughelli 34 Gd 5.30N 5.59 E
Ugijar 13 Ih 36.57N 3.03W
Uglegorsk 20 Jg 49.05N 142.06 E
Uglekamensk 20 Ih 43.18N 133.08 E
Ugleuralski 17 Hg 58.59N 57.38 E
Uglič 19 Dd 57.33N 38.23 E
Ugljan 14 Jf 44.05N 15.10 E
Uglovoje 28 Lc 43.20N 132.06 E
Ugnev 10 Tf 50.20N 23.45 E
Ugo 29 Gb 39.13N 140.23 E
Ugolnyje Kopi 20 Md 64.42N 177.50 E
Ugoma 36 Ec 4.55S 26.50 E
Ugra 19 De 54.30N 36.07 E
Ugtal-Cajdam 27 Ib 48.25N 105.30 E
Uh 10 Rh 48.33N 22.00 E
Uherské Hradiště 10 Ng 49.04N 17.27 E
Úhlava 10 Jg 49.45N 13.23 E
Uhlenhorst 37 Bd 23.45S 17.55 E
Uhta 6 Lc 63.33N 53.40 E
Uibh Fhaili/Offaly [2] 9 Fh 53.20N 7.30W
Uig 9 Gd 57.30N 6.20W
Uige 31 Ii 7.35S 15.04 E
Uige [3] 36 Cd 7.00S 15.30 E
'Uiha 65b Ba 19.54S 174.25W
Uijec 64d Bb 7.10N 151.57 E
Üijŏngbu 28 If 37.44N 127.02 E
Uiju 28 Hd 40.12N 124.32 E
Uil 19 Ff 48.36N 52.30 E
Uil 19 Ff 49.04N 54.42 E
Uilpata, Gora- 16 Mh 42.47N 43.44 E
Uinta Mountains 43 Ec 40.45N 110.05W
Uinta River 46 Kf 40.14N 109.51W
Uis 37 Ad 21.08S 14.49 E
Üisŏng 28 Jf 36.21N 128.42 E
Uitenhage 31 Jl 33.40S 25.28 E
Uithoorn 12 Gb 52.14N 4.52 E
Uithuizen 12 Ia 53.25N 6.42 E
Uithuizerwad 12 Ia 53.30N 6.40 E
Ujae Atoll 57 Hd 9.05N 165.40 E
Ūjān 24 Og 30.45N 52.05 E
Ujandina 20 Jc 68.23N 145.50 E
Ujar 20 Ee 55.48N 94.20 E
Ujarrás 49 Fi 9.50N 83.40W
Ujedinenija, Ostrov- 20 Da 77.30N 82.30 E
Ujelang Atoll 57 Hd 9.49N 160.55 E
Újfehértó 10 Ri 47.48N 21.41 E
Uji 29 Dd 34.53N 135.47 E
Uji 19 Ge 54.20N 63.58 E
Uji-Guntō 28 Ji 31.10N 129.28 E
Ujiie 29 Fc 36.41N 139.57 E
Ujiji 31 Ji 4.55S 29.41 E
Ujjain 22 Jg 23.11N 75.46 E
Ujunglamuru 26 Gg 4.40S 119.58 E
Ujung Pandang (Makasar) 22 Nj 5.07S 119.24 E
Uk 20 Ee 55.04N 98.52 E
Ukata 34 Gc 10.50N 5.50 E
Ukeng, Bukit- 26 Gf 1.45N 115.08 E
Ukerewe Island 36 Fc 2.03S 33.00 E
Uke-Shima 29b Ba 28.02N 129.15 E
Ukhaydir 24 Jf 32.26N 43.36 E
Ukiah [Ca.-U.S.] 43 Cd 39.09N 123.13W
Ukiah [Or.-U.S.] 46 Fd 45.08N 118.56W
Uki Ni Masi 63a Ed 10.15S 161.44 E
Ukkel/Uccle 12 Gd 50.48N 4.19 E
Ukmergė/Ukmerge 7 Fi 55.14N 24.47 E
Ukmerge/Ukmergė 7 Fi 55.14N 24.47 E
Ukraine (EN) 5 Jf 49.00N 32.00 E
Ukraine (EN) = Ukrayina 19 Df 49.00N 32.00 E
Ukrainskaja SSR/Ukrainska Radyanska Socialistična Respublika → Ukrayina 19 Df 49.00N 32.00 E
Ukrainska Radyanska Socialistična Respublika/ Ukrainskaja SSR → Ukrayina 19 Df 49.00N 32.00 E
Ukrayina = Ukraine (EN) 19 Df 49.00N 32.00 E
Ukrina 14 Le 45.05N 17.56 E
Uku-Jima 29 Ae 33.16N 129.07 E
Ula 24 Cd 37.05N 28.26 E
Ulah Lake 45 Hh 36.58N 96.10W
Ulaidh/Ulster 9 Gg 54.30N 7.00W
Ulalu 64d Bb 7.25N 151.40 E
Ulan (Xiligou) 27 Gd 36.55N 98.16 E
Ulan → Otog Qi 27 Id 39.07N 108.00 E
Ulanbaatar → Ulan-Bator 22 Me 47.55N 106.53 E
Ulan-Badrah 28 Ac 43.58N 110.37 E
Ulan-Bator (Ulaanbaatar) 22 Me 47.55N 106.53 E
Ulanbel 19 Hg 44.49N 71.10 E
Ulan-Burgasy, Hrebet- 20 Ff 52.30N 108.30 E
Ulangom 22 Le 49.58N 92.02 E
Ulanhad/Chifeng 27 Kc 42.16N 118.57 E
Ulan Hol 19 Ef 45.27N 46.46 E
Ulan Hot/Horqin Youyi Qianqi 22 Oe 46.04N 122.00 E
Ulan Hua → Siziwang Qi 28 Ad 41.31N 111.41 E
Ulan-Hus 27 Eb 49.02N 89.23 E
Ulanów 10 Sf 50.30N 22.16 E
Ulansuhai Nur 27 Ic 40.56N 108.49 E
Ulan-Tajga 27 Ga 50.45N 98.30 E
Ulan-Ude 22 Md 51.50N 107.37 E
Ulan Ul Hu 27 Fe 34.45N 90.25 E
Ulas 24 Gc 39.27N 37.03 E
Ulawa Island 60 Gi 9.46S 161.57 E
Ulbeja 20 Je 59.20N 144.25 E
Ulchin 28 Jf 36.59N 129.24 E
Ulcinj 15 Ch 41.56N 19.13 E
Uleåborg/Oulu 6 Ib 65.01N 25.30 E
Ulefoss 8 Bg 59.17N 9.16 E
Ulegej 22 Ke 48.56N 89.57 E
Ulety 20 Gf 51.22N 112.30 E
Uleza 15 Ch 41.40N 19.53 E
Ulfborg 8 Ch 56.16N 8.20 E
Ulflingen/Troisvierges 12 Hd 50.07N 6.00 E
Ulft, Gendringen- 12 Ic 51.54N 6.24 E
Ulgain Gol 27 Kb 45.31N 117.50 E
Ulhāsnagar 25 Ee 19.10N 73.07 E
Uliastai → Dong Ujimqin Qi 27 Kc 45.31N 116.58 E
Uliga 58 Id 7.09N 171.13 E
Ulindi 30 Ji 1.40S 25.52 E
Ulithi Atoll 57 Ed 9.58N 139.40 E
Ulja 20 Je 58.48N 141.40 E
Uljanovka 8 Ne 59.37N 30.55 E
Uljanovka 16 Ge 48.20N 30.13 E
Uljanovsk 6 Ke 54.20N 48.24 E
Uljanovskaja Oblast [3] 19 Ee 54.00N 48.00 E
Uljanovskij 19 He 50.05N 73.45 E
Uljasutaj 22 Le 47.45N 96.49 E
Ulkan 20 Fe 55.55N 107.55 E
Ulla 13 Db 42.39N 8.44W
Ullapool 9 Hd 57.54N 5.10W
Ullared 7 Ch 57.08N 12.43 E
Ulldecona 13 Md 40.36N 0.27 E
Ullsfjorden 7 Eb 69.58N 20.00 E
Ullswater 9 Kg 54.34N 2.54W
Ullŭng-Do 28 Kf 37.29N 130.52 E
Ullvettern 8 Fe 59.25N 14.15 E
Ulm 10 Fh 48.25N 10.00 E
Ulmen 12 Id 50.13N 6.59 E
Ulmeni 15 Jd 45.04N 26.39 E
Ulmu 15 Je 44.16N 26.55 E
Ulongwé 37 Eb 14.43S 34.21 E
Ulricehamn 7 Ch 57.47N 13.25 E
Ulrichstein 12 Ld 50.35N 9.12 E
Ulrum 12 Ia 53.22N 6.20 E
Ulrum-Zoutkamp 12 Ia 53.20N 6.18 E
Ulsan 27 Md 35.33N 129.19 E
Ulsteinvik 7 Ae 62.20N 5.53 E
Ulster 10 Ff 50.51N 9.59 E
Ulster/Ulaidh 9 Gg 54.30N 7.00W
Ulster Canal 9 Gg 54.27N 6.40W
Ulu 35 Ec 10.43N 33.29 E
Ulu/Uulu 8 Kf 58.13N 24.29 E
Ulúa, Río- 47 Ge 15.56N 87.43W
Ulubat Gölü 24 Cb 40.10N 28.35 E
Ulubey 24 Cc 38.09N 29.33 E
Uludağ 23 Ca 40.04N 29.13 E
Uludere 24 Jd 37.27N 42.51 E
Uluqqat/Wuqia 27 Cd 39.40N 75.07 E
Ulukışla 24 Fd 37.33N 34.30 E
Ulungur He 21 Ke 46.58N 87.28 E
Ulungur Hu 27 Eb 47.20N 87.10 E
Ulus 24 Eb 41.35N 32.39 E
Ulus Dağ 15 Lj 39.18N 28.24 E
Ulva 9 Ge 56.28N 6.12W
Ulverston 9 Jg 54.12N 3.06W
Ulverstone 59 Jh 41.09S 146.10 E
Ulvik 8 Bd 60.34N 6.54 E
Ulvön 8 Ha 63.05N 18.40 E
Ulysses 45 Fh 37.35N 101.22W
Ulytau 19 Gf 48.35N 67.05 E
Ulytau, Gora- 19 Gf 48.45N 67.00 E
Uly-Žilanšik 19 Gf 48.51N 63.47 E
Uma 27 La 52.36N 120.38 E
Umag 14 He 45.25N 13.32 E
Umala 54 Eg 17.24S 67.58W
Umán 48 Og 20.53N 89.45W
Uman 64d Bb 7.18N 151.53 E
Uman 19 Df 48.47N 30.09 E
'Umān 21 Hg 22.10N 58.00 E
'Umān=Oman (EN) [1] 22 Hg 21.00N 57.00 E
'Umān, Khalīj-=Oman, Gulf of- (EN) 21 Hg 25.00N 58.00 E
Umanak 41 Gd 70.36N 52.15W
Ūmánarssuaq/Farvel, Kap- 67 Nb 59.50N 43.50W
Umatac 64c Bb 13.18N 144.40 E
Umba 19 Db 66.41N 34.17 E
Umbelasha 35 Cd 9.51N 24.50 E
Umbertide 14 Gg 43.18N 12.20 E
Umberto de Campos 54 Jd 2.37S 43.27W
Umboi Island 57 Fe 5.36S 148.00 E
Umbozero, Ozero- 7 Ic 67.45N 34.20 E
Umbria [2] 14 Gh 43.00N 12.30 E
Ume 37 Dc 17.15S 28.20 E
Umeå 6 Ic 63.50N 20.15 E
Umeälven 5 Ic 63.47N 20.16 E
Umm al Arānib 33 Bd 26.08N 14.45 E
Umm al Hayf, Wādī- 23 Hf 18.37N 53.59 E
Umm al Jamāājim 24 Ki 26.59N 45.19 E
Umm al Qaywayn 24 Pj 25.35N 55.34 E
Ummanz 10 Jb 54.30N 13.10 E
Umm ar Rizam 33 Dc 32.32N 23.00 E
Umm as Samīm 23 Ie 21.30N 56.45 E
Umm Bāb 24 Nj 25.12N 50.48 E
Umm Bel 35 Dc 13.32N 28.04 E
Umm Buru 35 Cb 15.01N 23.36 E
Umm Dhibbān 35 Dc 14.14N 29.37 E
Umm Durmān=Omdurman (EN) 31 Kg 15.38N 32.30 E
Umm Inderaba 35 Eb 15.12N 31.54 E
Umm Kaddādah 35 Dc 13.36N 26.42 E
Umm Lajj 23 Ed 25.04N 37.13 E
Umm Naqqāţ, Jabal- 24 Fj 25.30N 34.14 E
Umm Qam'ul 24 Pj 24.47N 54.42 E
Umm Ruwābah 31 Kg 12.54N 31.13 E
Umm Sayyālah 35 Ec 14.25N 31.00 E
Umm Urūmah 24 Gj 25.46N 36.33 E
Umnak 38 Cd 58.25N 168.10W
Umne-Gobi 27 Fb 49.06N 91.43 E
Umpqua River 46 Ce 43.42N 124.03W
Umpulu 36 Ce 12.42S 17.40 E
Umsini, Gunung- 26 Jg 1.35S 133.30 E
Umtata 31 Jl 31.35S 28.47 E
Umuarama 56 Jb 23.45S 53.20W
Umurbey 15 Ji 40.14N 26.36 E
Umvukwes 37 Ec 17.01S 30.52 E
Umvuma 37 Ec 19.19S 30.35 E
Umzingwani 37 Dd 22.12S 29.56 E
Una 14 Ke 45.16N 16.55 E
Unabetsu-Dake 29a Db 43.52N 144.51 E
Unac 14 Kf 44.29N 16.08 E
Unai 54 Ig 16.23S 46.53W
Unalakleet 40 Gd 63.53N 160.47W
Unalaska 38 Cd 53.45N 166.45W
Unare, Río- 50 Dg 10.06N 65.12W
Unauna, Pulau- 26 Hg 0.10S 121.35 E
'Unayzah [Jor.] 24 Fg 30.29N 35.48 E
'Unayzah [Sau. Ar.] 22 Gg 26.06N 43.56 E
Uncia 54 Eg 18.27S 66.37W
Uncompahgre Peak 43 Fd 38.04N 107.28W
Uncompahgre Plateau 45 Bg 38.30N 108.25W
Unden 8 Ff 58.45N 14.25 E
Underberg 37 De 29.50S 29.22 E
Under-Han 22 Ne 47.19N 110.39 E
Undjuljung 20 Hc 66.20N 124.40 E
Undu Point 63d Cb 16.08S 179.57W
Undva Neem/Kiprarenukk, Mys- 8 If 58.25N 21.45 E
Uneča 16 Hc 52.50N 32.44 E
'Ung, Jabal al- 14 Dn 36.45N 9.35 E
Unga 40 Ge 55.15N 160.45W
Ungava, Péninsule d'-= Ungava Peninsula (EN) 38 Lc 60.00N 74.00W
Ungava Bay 38 Md 59.30N 67.30W
Ungava Peninsula (EN)= Ungava, Péninsule d'- 38 Lc 60.00N 74.00W
Ungen' 16 Ef 47.13N 27.50 E
Unggi 28 Kc 42.21N 130.23 E
Ungureni 15 Jb 47.53N 26.47 E
Ungwatiri 35 Fb 16.55N 36.05 E
União 54 Jd 4.35S 42.52W
União da Vitória 56 Jc 26.13S 51.05W
União dos Palmares 54 Ke 9.10S 36.02W
Uničov 10 Ng 49.49N 17.07 E
Uniejów 10 Oe 51.58N 18.49 E
Unije 14 If 44.38N 14.15 E
Unimak 38 Cd 54.50N 164.00W
Unimak Pass 40 Gf 54.35N 164.43W
Unini, Rio- 54 Fd 1.41S 61.30W
Union [Mo.-U.S.] 45 Kg 38.27N 91.00W
Union [S.C.-U.S.] 44 Gh 34.42N 81.37W
Union City 44 Cg 36.26N 89.03W
Uniondale 37 Cf 33.40S 23.08 E
Unión de Reyes 49 Gb 22.48N 81.32W
Unión de Tula 48 Gh 19.58N 104.16W
Union Island 50 Ff 12.36N 61.26W
Union Islands/Tokelau 57 Je 9.00S 171.45W
Union Seamount (EN) 42 Eg 49.35N 132.45W
Union Springs 44 Ei 32.09N 85.49W
Uniontown 44 Hf 39.54N 79.44W
Unionville 45 Jf 40.29N 93.01W
United Arab Emirates (EN) =Al Imārāt al 'Arabīyah al Muttaḩidah [1] 22 Hg 24.00N 54.00 E
United Arab Republic (EN) → Egypt (EN) [1] 31 Jf 27.00N 30.00 E
United Kingdom [1] 6 Fe 54.00N 2.00W
United Kingdom of Great Britain and Northern Ireland [1] 6 Fe 54.00N 2.00W
United States [1] 39 Jf 38.00N 97.00W
United States of America [1] 39 Jf 38.00N 97.00W
Unity [Or.-U.S.] 46 Fd 44.29N 118.13W
Unity [Sask.-Can.] 42 Gf 52.27N 109.10W
Universales, Montes- 13 Kd 40.18N 1.33W
University City 45 Kg 38.39N 90.19W
Unna 10 De 51.32N 7.41 E
Unnāb, Wādī al- 24 Gg 30.11N 36.39 E
Unnukka 8 Lb 62.25N 27.55 E
Unst 5 Fc 60.45N 0.55W
Unstrut 10 He 51.10N 11.48 E
Unterfranken 10 Fg 50.00N 10.00 E
Unterwalden-Nidwalden [2] 14 Cd 46.55N 8.30 E
Unterwalden-Obwalden [2] 14 Cd 46.50N 8.20 E
Unuli Horog 27 Fd 35.12N 91.58 E
Ünye 23 Ea 41.08N 37.17 E
Unža 5 Kd 57.20N 43.08 E
Unzen-Dake 29 Be 32.45N 130.17 E
Uoleva 65b Ba 19.51S 174.24W
Uozu 28 Nf 36.48N 137.24 E
Úpa 10 Lf 50.22N 15.54 E
Upata 54 Fb 8.01N 62.24W
Upemba, Lac- 36 Ed 8.36S 26.26 E
Upernavik 41 Gd 72.40N 56.00W
Upin 26 Ig 2.56S 129.11 E
Upington 31 Jk 28.25S 21.15 E
Upland 12 Kc 51.18N 8.42 E
Upolu Island 57 Jf 13.55S 171.45W
Upolu Point 60 Oc 20.16N 155.52W
Upper [3] 34 Ec 10.30N 1.30W
Upper Arlington 44 Fe 40.01N 83.03W
Upper Arrow Lake 46 Ga 50.30N 117.55W
Upper Austria (EN) = Oberösterreich [2] 14 Hb 48.15N 14.00 E
Upper Hutt 62 Fd 41.07S 175.04 E
Upper Klamath Lake 43 Cc 42.23N 122.00W
Upper Lake 46 Ef 41.44N 120.08W
Upper Lough Erne/Loch Éirne Uachtair 9 Fg 54.20N 7.30W
Upper Red Lake 45 Ib 48.10N 94.40W
Upper Sandusky 44 Fe 40.48N 83.17W
Upper Sheik 35 Hd 9.57N 45.09 E
Upper Thames Valley 9 Lj 51.40N 1.40W
Upper Trajan's Wall (EN)= Verhni Traijanov Val 15 Lc 46.40N 29.00 E
Upper Volta→ Burkina Faso [1] 31 Gg 13.00N 2.00W
Uppingham 12 Bb 52.35N 0.43W
Uppland 8 Gd 60.00N 17.50 E
Upplands Väsby 8 Ge 59.31N 17.54 E
Uppsala [2] 7 Df 60.00N 17.45 E
Uppsala 6 Hd 59.52N 17.38 E
Upsala 45 Kb 49.02N 90.29W
Upshi 25 Fb 33.50N 77.49 E
Upton 46 Md 44.06N 104.38W
Uqbān 33 Hf 15.30N 42.23 E
'Uqlat aş Şuqūr 24 Jj 25.53N 42.15 E
Uqturpan/Wushi 27 Cc 41.10N 79.16 E
Ur 23 Gc 30.58N 46.06 E
Urabá, Golfo de- 54 Cb 8.25N 77.00W
Uracoa 50 Eh 9.00N 62.21W
Uracoa, Rio- 50 Eh 9.08N 62.20W
Uradarja 18 Fe 38.51N 66.02 E
Urad Qianqi 27 Ic 40.49N 108.37 E
Urad Zhonghou Lianheqi (Haliut) 27 Ic 41.34N 108.32 E
Uraga-Suido 29 Fd 35.15N 139.45 E
Ura-Guba 7 Hb 69.18N 32.48 E
Urahoro 29a Cb 42.48N 143.38 E
Urahoro-Gawa 29a Cb 42.44N 143.40 E
Uraj 19 Gc 60.08N 64.40 E
Urakawa 28 Qc 42.09N 142.47 E
Ural 5 Lf 47.00N 51.48 E
Ural Mountains (EN)= Uralskije Gory 5 Ld 57.00N 60.00 E
Uralsk 6 Le 51.14N 51.22 E
Uralskaja Oblast [3] 19 Ff 49.45N 51.00 E
Uralskije Gory=Ural Mountains (EN) 5 Ld 57.00N 60.00 E
Urambo 36 Fd 5.04S 32.03 E
Uranium City 39 Id 59.34N 108.36W
Uraricoera 54 Fc 3.27N 60.59W
Uraricoera, Rio- 52 Je 3.02N 60.30W
Ura-Tjube 19 Gh 39.53N 69.01 E
Urawa 28 Og 35.51N 139.39 E
'Uray'irah 24 Mj 25.57N 48.53 E
Urayq, Nafūd al- 24 Jj 25.17N 42.25 E
Urbana [Il.-U.S.] 45 Lf 40.07N 88.12W
Urbana [Oh.-U.S.] 44 Fe 40.06N 83.45W
Urbandale 45 Jf 41.38N 93.48W
Urbania 14 Gg 43.40N 12.31 E

Index Symbols

[1] Independent Nation
[2] State, Region
[3] District, County
[4] Municipality
[5] Colony, Dependency
Continent
Physical Region
Historical or Cultural Region
Mount, Mountain
Volcano
Hill
Mountains, Mountain Range
Hills, Escarpment
Plateau, Upland
Pass, Gap
Plain, Lowland
Delta
Salt Flat
Valley, Canyon
Crater, Cave
Karst Features
Depression
Polder
Desert, Dunes
Forest, Woods
Heath, Steppe
Oasis
Cape, Point
Coast, Beach
Cliff
Peninsula
Isthmus
Sandbank
Island
Atoll
Rock, Reef
Islands, Archipelago
Rocks, Reefs
Coral Reef
Well, Spring
Geyser
River, Stream
Waterfall Rapids
River Mouth, Estuary
Lake
Salt Lake
Intermittent Lake
Reservoir
Swamp, Pond
Canal
Glacier
Ice Shelf, Pack Ice
Ocean
Sea
Gulf, Bay
Strait, Fjord
Lagoon
Bank
Seamount
Tablemount
Ridge
Shelf
Basin
Escarpment, Sea Scarp
Fracture
Trench, Abyss
National Park, Reserve
Point of Interest
Recreation Site
Cave, Cavern
Historic Site
Ruins
Wall, Walls
Church, Abbey
Temple
Scientific Station
Airport
Port
Lighthouse
Mine
Tunnel
Dam, Bridge

Name	Page	Grid	Lat.	Long.
Urbano Santos	54	Jd	3.12S	43.23W
Urbino	14	Gg	43.43N	12.38 E
Urbino, Étang d'-	11a	Ba	42.02N	9.28 E
Urbión, Picos de-	13	Jb	42.01N	2.52W
Urcel	12	Fe	49.30N	3.33 E
Urcos	54	Df	13.42S	71.38W
Urdinarrain	55	Ck	32.41S	58.53W
Urdoma	7	Lf	61.47N	48.29 E
Urdžar	19	If	47.05N	81.37 E
Ure	9	Lg	54.01N	1.12W
Uré	49	Jj	7.46N	75.31W
Uren	19	Ed	57.29N	45.48 E
Urenui	62	Fc	39.00S	174.23 E
Ures	47	Bc	29.26N	110.24W
Ureshino	29	Ab	33.06N	129.59 E
'Urf, Jabal al-	24	Ei	27.49N	32.55 E
Urfa → Şanlıurfa	23	Eb	37.08N	38.46 E
Urfa Platosu	24	Hd	37.10N	38.50 E
Urgal	20	If	51.00N	132.50 E
Urgel, Llanos de-	13	Lc	41.25N	0.36W
Urgel, Llanos de-/Urgell, Pla d'-	13	Lc	41.25N	0.36W
Urgell, Pla d'-	13	Lc	41.25N	0.36W
Urgell, Pla d'-/Urgel, Llanos de-	13	Lc	41.25N	0.36W
Urgen	28	Ab	44.45N	110.40 E
Urgenč	22	Ie	41.33N	60.38 E
Ürgüp	24	Fc	38.38N	35.56 E
Urgut	19	Gh	39.23N	67.14 E
Uri	25	Eb	34.05N	74.02 E
Uri [2]	14	Cd	46.40N	8.30 E
Uribia	54	Da	11.42N	72.17W
Uricki	19	Ge	53.19N	65.34 E
Urique, Río-	48	Fd	26.29N	107.58W
Urjala	8	Jc	61.05N	23.32 E
Urjupinsk	19	Ee	50.48N	42.02 E
Urk	11	Lb	52.39N	5.36 E
Urkan	20	Hf	53.27N	126.56 E
Urla	24	Bc	38.18N	26.46 E
Urlaţi	15	Je	44.59N	26.14 E
Urluk	20	Ff	50.03N	107.55 E
Urmi	20	Ig	48.43N	134.16 E
Urmia, Lake- (EN) = Orumiyeh, Daryācheh-ye	21	Gf	37.40N	45.30 E
Uromi	34	Gd	6.42N	6.20 E
Uroševac	15	Eg	42.22N	21.10 E
Urshult	8	Fh	56.32N	14.47 E
Ursus	10	Qd	52.12N	20.53 E
Urtazym	17	Ij	52.15N	58.50 E
Urtigueira, Serra da-	55	Gg	24.15S	51.00W
Uru, Rio-	55	Hb	15.24S	49.36W
Uruaçu	54	If	14.30S	49.10W
Uruana	55	Hb	15.30S	49.41W
Uruapan del Progreso	47	De	19.25N	101.58W
Uruará, Rio-	54	Hd	2.00S	53.38W
Urubamba, Rio-	52	Ig	10.43S	73.48W
Urubici	55	Hi	28.02S	49.37W
Urubú, Cachoeira do-	55	Ha	12.52S	48.13W
Urucará	54	Gd	2.32S	57.45W
Uruçuí	54	Je	7.14S	44.33W
Urucuia, Rio- [Braz.]	55	Ib	15.38S	46.10W
Urucuia, Rio- [Braz.]	55	Jc	16.08S	45.05W
Urucum, Serra do-	55	Dd	19.13S	57.33W
Urucurituba	54	Gd	2.41S	57.40W
Uruguai, Rio-	52	Ki	34.12S	58.18W
Uruguaiana	53	Kh	29.45S	57.05W
Uruguay [1]	53	Ki	33.00S	56.00W
Uruguay, Río-	52	Ki	34.12S	58.18W
Urukthapel	64a	Ac	7.15N	134.24 E
Urumbaba Dağı	15	Lj	38.25N	28.49 E
Ürümqi	22	Ke	43.48N	87.35 E
Urup	16	Lg	44.59N	41.10 E
Urup, Ostrov-	21	Qe	46.00N	150.00 E
Uruša	20	Hf	54.03N	122.55 E
Urussu	7	Mi	54.38N	53.24 E
Uruwira	36	Fd	6.27S	31.21 E
Urville, Cape D'- (EN) = Perkam, Tanjung-	26	Kg	1.28S	137.54 E
Uryū	29a	Bb	43.39N	141.51 E
Uryū-Gawa	29a	Bb	43.40N	141.54 E
Urziceni	15	Je	44.43N	26.38 E
Uržum	19	Fd	57.10N	50.01 E
Usa	29	Be	33.31N	131.22 E
Usa	16	Nc	53.02N	45.18 E
Usa	5	Lb	65.57N	56.55 E
Uşak	23	Cb	38.41N	29.25 E
Usakos	37	Bd	22.01S	15.32 E
Ušakovo	20	Hf	51.54N	126.35 E
Ušakovskoje	20	Nb	71.00N	178.35W
Usambara Mountains	30	Ki	4.45S	38.30 E
Usarp Mountains	66	Jf	71.10S	160.00 E
Usas Escarpment	66	Nf	76.00S	125.00W
Ušba, Gora-	16	Mh	43.06N	42.40 E
Usborne, Mount-	56	Ih	51.42S	58.50W
Ušće	15	Df	43.29N	20.38 E
Usedom	10	Jb	54.00N	14.00 E
Useldange	12	He	49.46N	5.59 E
'Ushayrah [Sau. Ar.]	23	He	21.46N	40.38 E
'Ushayrah [Sau. Ar.]	24	Kj	25.35N	45.46 E
Ushibuka	29	Be	32.13N	130.01 E
Ushikubi-Misaki	29a	Bc	41.08N	140.48 E
Ushimado	29	Dd	34.37N	134.09 E
'Ushsh, Wādī al-	24	Fd	27.18N	42.15 E
Ushuaia	53	Jk	54.47S	68.20W
Usingen	12	Kd	50.20N	8.32 E
Usinsk	19	Fb	65.57N	57.29 E
Usküdar	24	Cb	41.01N	29.03 E
Üsküp	15	Kh	41.44N	27.24 E
Uslar	10	Fe	51.40N	9.39 E
Úslava	10	Jg	49.54N	13.32 E
Usman	16	Kd	51.54N	39.20 E
Usman	16	De	52.00N	39.43 E
Usmas, Ozero-/Usmas Ezers	8	Ig	57.13N	22.00 E
Usmas Ezers/Usmas, Ozero-	8	Ig	57.13N	22.00 E
Usogorsk	19	Ec	63.28N	48.35 E
Usoke	36	Fd	5.06S	32.20 E
Usolje	19	Fd	59.25N	56.41 E
Usolje-Sibirskoje	20	Ff	52.48N	103.38 E
Usora	14	Mf	44.43N	18.04 E
Ussel	11	Ii	45.33N	2.09 E
Ussuri	21	Pe	48.28N	135.02 E
Ussurijsk	22	Pe	43.48N	131.59 E
Usta	7	Kh	56.53N	45.28 E
Ust-Barguzin	20	Ff	53.27N	108.59 E
Ust-Bolšereck	20	Kf	52.40N	156.18 E
Ust-Cilma	19	Fb	65.27N	52.06 E
Ust-Čorna	10	Uh	48.17N	24.02 E
Ust-Donecki	16	Lf	47.39N	40.55 E
Ust-Dželguta	16	Mg	44.05N	42.01 E
Uster	14	Cc	47.20N	8.43 E
Ustevatn	8	Bd	60.30N	8.00 E
Ust-Hajrjuzovo	20	Ke	57.04N	156.50 E
Ustica	5	Hh	38.40N	13.10 E
Ustica	14	Hl	38.42N	13.11 E
Ust-Ilimsk	22	Md	58.03N	102.43 E
Ustilug	10	Uf	50.50N	24.09 E
Ústí nad Labem	10	Kf	50.40N	14.02 E
Ústí nad Orlicí	10	Mg	49.58N	16.24 E
Ustinov → Iževsk	6	Ld	56.51N	53.14 E
Ust-Išim	19	Hd	57.44N	71.10 E
Ust-Judoma	20	Ie	59.10N	135.02 E
Ustjurt, Plato	21	He	43.00N	56.00 E
'Ustjužna	7	Ig	58.53N	36.28 E
Ustka	10	Mb	54.35N	16.50 E
Ust-Kamčatsk	22	Sd	56.15N	162.30 E
Ust-Kamenogorsk	22	Ke	49.58N	82.38 E
Ust-Kan	20	Df	50.57N	84.55 E
Ust-Kara	19	Gb	69.15N	64.59 E
Ust-Karsk	20	Gf	52.41N	118.45 E
Ust-Katav	17	Ii	54.56N	58.10 E
Ust-Kujga	22	Pc	70.00N	135.36 E
Ust-Kut	22	Md	56.46N	105.40 E
Ust-Labinsk	19	Df	45.13N	39.40 E
Ust-Luga	7	Gg	59.39N	28.15 E
Ust-Maja	22	Pc	60.25N	134.32 E
Ust-Muja	20	Ge	56.28N	115.30 E
Ust-Nera	22	Qc	64.34N	143.12 E
Ust-Njukža	20	He	56.30N	121.48 E
Uštobe	19	Hf	45.13N	77.59 E
Ust-Olenëk	20	Gb	72.58N	119.42 E
Ust-Omčug	20	Jd	61.05N	149.30 E
Ust-Ordynski	20	Ff	52.48N	104.45 E
Ust-Ordynski Burjatski avtonomnyj okrug	20	Ff	53.30N	104.00 E
Ustovo	15	Hh	41.34N	24.47 E
Ust-Pinega	7	Jd	64.10N	41.58 E
Ust-Pit	20	Ee	58.59N	92.00 E
Ust-Port	20	Dc	69.45N	84.25 E
Ust-Požva	17	Hg	59.05N	56.05 E
Ustrzyki Dolne	10	Sg	49.26N	22.37 E
Ust-Sobolevka	20	Ig	46.10N	137.59 E
Ust-Šonoša	7	Jf	61.11N	41.20 E
Ust-Uda	20	Ff	54.10N	103.03 E
Ust-Ujskoje	17	Ki	54.15N	63.57 E
Ust-Umalta	20	If	51.42N	133.18 E
Ustupo	49	Ii	9.08N	77.56W
Usū	22	Ke	44.27N	84.37 E
Usui-Tōge	29	Fc	36.22N	138.38 E
Usuki	28	Kh	33.08N	131.49 E
Usuki-Wan	29	Be	33.10N	131.50 E
Usulután	49	Cg	13.21N	88.27W
Usumacinta	38	Jh	18.22N	92.40W
Ušumun	20	Hf	52.46N	126.37 E
Usu-San	29a	Bb	42.32N	140.49 E
Usva	17	Hg	58.40N	57.35 E
Usva	17	Hg	58.17N	57.47 E
Utah [2]	43	Ed	39.30N	111.30W
Utah Lake	43	Ec	40.13N	111.49W
Utajärvi	7	Gd	64.45N	26.23 E
Utashinai	29a	Cb	43.31N	142.03 E
Utata	20	Ff	50.51N	102.45 E
Ute Creek	45	Ei	35.21N	103.50W
Utembo	30	Jj	17.06S	22.01 E
Utena	7	Fi	55.29N	25.40 E
Ute Reservoir	45	Ei	35.21N	103.31W
Utete	36	Gd	7.59S	38.47 E
Uthai Thani	25	Ke	15.20N	100.02 E
Utiariti	55	Ca	13.02S	58.17W
Utica	43	Lc	43.06N	75.15W
Utiel	13	Ke	39.34N	1.12W
Utiel, Sierra de-	13	Ke	39.36N	1.08W
Utila	49	De	16.06N	86.54W
Utila, Isla de-	49	De	16.06N	86.56W
Utique	14	Em	37.04N	10.04 E
Utirik Atoll	57	Hc	11.15N	169.48 E
Utlängan	8	Fh	56.00N	15.45 E
Utljukskij Liman	16	If	46.20N	35.15 E
Uto	28	Kh	32.40N	130.41 E
Utö [Fin.]	8	Ie	59.45N	21.25 E
Utö [Swe.]	7	Eg	58.55N	18.15 E
Utoro	29a	Da	44.06N	144.58 E
Utrata	10	Qd	52.13N	20.15 E
Utrecht [3]	12	Hb	52.05N	5.08 E
Utrecht [Neth.]	6	Ge	52.05N	5.08 E
Utrecht [S.Afr.]	37	Ee	27.28S	30.20 E
Utrera	13	Gg	37.11N	5.47W
Utsira	8	Ae	59.20N	4.55 E
Utsjoki	7	Gb	69.53N	27.00 E
Utsunomiya	22	Pf	36.33N	139.52 E
Uttaradit	25	Ke	17.38N	100.06 E
Uttar Pradesh [3]	25	Fc	28.00N	80.00 E
Utuado	49	Nd	18.16N	66.42W
Utukok	40	Gb	70.04N	162.18W
Utuloa	64h	Ab	13.16S	176.11W
Utupua Island	57	Hf	11.20S	166.36 E
Uturoa	65e	Db	16.44S	151.26W
Utva	16	Rd	51.29N	52.40 E
Uudenmaa [2]	7	Ff	60.30N	25.00 E
Uukuniemi	8	Nc	61.47N	30.01 E
Uulu/Ulu	8	Kf	58.13N	24.29 E
Uusikaupunki/Nystad	7	Ef	60.48N	21.25 E
Uusimaa	8	Kd	60.30N	25.00 E
Uva	19	Fd	56.58N	52.14 E
Uvac	15	Cf	43.36N	19.30 E
Uvalde	43	Hf	29.13N	99.47W
Uvarovo	19	Ee	52.00N	42.15 E
Uvdal	8	Cd	60.20N	8.30 E
Uvéa, Ile-	57	Jf	13.18S	176.10W
Uvelka	17	Ji	54.05N	61.35 E
Uvelski	17	Ji	54.26N	61.27 E
Uvildy, Ozero-	17	Ji	55.35N	60.30 E
Uvinza	36	Fd	5.06S	30.22 E
Uvira	31	Ji	3.24S	29.08 E
Uvs nuur → Ubsu-Nur	21	Ld	50.20N	92.45 E
Uwa	29	Ce	33.21N	132.30 E
Uwajima	27	Ne	33.13N	132.34 E
Uwajima-Wan	29	Ce	33.15N	132.30 E
Uwa-Kai	29	Ce	33.20N	132.15 E
Uwayl	35	Dd	8.46N	27.24 E
'Uwaynāt, Jabal al- = Uweinat, Gebel- (EN)	30	Jf	21.54N	24.58 E
'Uwaynat Wannin	33	Bd	28.05N	12.59 E
Uweinat, Gebel- (EN) = 'Uwaynāt, Jabal al-	30	Jf	21.54N	24.58 E
Uwekuli	26	Hg	1.25S	121.06 E
Uwi, Pulau-	26	Ef	1.05N	107.24 E
Uxin Qi (Dabqig)	27	Id	38.27N	109.08 E
Uxmal	39	Kg	20.20N	89.46W
Uyo	34	Gd	5.07N	7.57 E
Uyuni	53	Jh	20.28S	66.50W
Uyuni, Salar de-	52	Jh	20.20S	67.42W
Už [Eur.]	10	Rh	48.33N	22.00 E
Už	16	Gd	51.15N	30.12 E
Uzbekistan (EN) = Ŭzbekiston	19	Gg	41.00N	64.00 E
Uzbekiston Sovet Socialistik Respublikasy/Uzbekskaja SSR → Ŭzbekiston	19	Gg	41.00N	64.00 E
Uzbekskaja Sovetskaja Socialističeskaja Respublika → Ŭzbekiston	19	Gg	41.00N	64.00 E
Uzbekskaja SSR/Uzbekiston Sovet Socialistik Respublikasy → Ŭzbekiston	19	Gg	41.00N	64.00 E
Ŭzbekiston = Uzbekistan (EN)	19	Gg	41.00N	64.00 E
Uzbel Shankou	27	Bd	38.42N	73.48 E
Uzen	19	Fg	43.22N	52.50 E
Uzerche	11	Hi	45.25N	1.34 E
Uzès	11	Kj	44.01N	4.25 E
Uzgen	18	Id	40.44N	73.21 E
Užgorod	19	Cf	48.37N	22.22 E
Užice (Titovo Užice)	15	Cf	43.52N	19.51 E
Uzin	16	Ge	49.52N	30.27 E
Uzlovaja	16	Kb	54.01N	38.12 E
Uzlovoje	10	Sh	48.23N	22.27 E
Užokski, pereval-	16	Ce	49.02N	22.58 E
Uzümlü	15	Mm	36.44N	29.14 E
Uzun Ada	15	Jk	38.28N	26.42 E
Uzunagač	18	Kc	43.08N	76.20 E
Uzunagač	18	Kc	43.36N	76.19 E
Uzunköprü	24	Bb	41.16N	26.41 E
Užur	20	De	55.20N	90.00 E
Užventis	8	Ji	55.44N	22.37 E
Uzynkair, Mys-	18	Bb	45.47N	59.20 E
V				
Vääksy	8	Kc	61.11N	25.33 E
Vaal	30	Jk	29.24S	23.38 E
Vaala	7	Gd	64.34N	26.50 E
Vaals	12	Id	50.46N	6.01 E
Vaalwater	37	Dd	24.20S	28.03 E
Vaasa [2]	7	Fe	63.12N	23.00 E
Vaasa/Vasa	6	Ic	63.06N	21.36 E
Vaassen, Epe-	12	Hb	52.17N	5.58 E
Vabalninkas	8	Ki	55.58N	24.49 E
Vác	10	Pi	47.47N	19.08 E
Vacacai, Rio-	55	Fi	29.55S	53.06W
Vacaria	56	Jc	28.30S	50.56W
Vacaria, Rio-	55	Fe	21.55S	53.59W
Vacaville	46	Eg	38.21N	121.59W
Vaccarès, Étang de-	11	Kk	43.32N	4.34 E
Vache, Ile à-	49	Kd	18.04N	73.38W
Väddö	8	Hd	60.00N	18.50 E
Vadehavet	8	Ci	55.15N	8.40 E
Vădeni	15	Kd	45.22N	27.56 E
Vadheim	8	Ac	61.13N	5.49 E
Vadodara	22	Jg	22.18N	73.12 E
Vado Ligure	14	Cf	44.17N	8.27 E
Vadsø	6	Ia	70.05N	29.46 E
Vadstena	7	Dg	58.27N	14.54 E
Vaduz	6	Gf	47.08N	9.30 E
Værlandet	8	Ac	61.20N	4.45 E
Vaga	5	Kc	62.48N	42.56 E
Vagaj	17	Mh	56.28N	67.18 E
Vagaj	17	Nh	57.55N	69.01 E
Vågåmo	7	Bf	61.53N	9.06 E
Vaganjski vrh	14	Jf	44.21N	15.30 E
Vågåvatn	8	Cc	61.50N	8.50 E
Vaggeryd	7	Dh	57.30N	14.07 E
Vaghena	63a	Cb	7.25S	157.43 E
Vagil	17	Kg	59.45N	62.40 E
Vagis, Gora-	20	Jf	52.20N	142.15 E
Vagnhärad	8	Gf	58.57N	17.31 E
Vågsøy	8	Ac	62.00N	5.05 E
Váh	10	Ni	47.55N	18.00 E
Vah	21	Jc	60.45N	76.45 E
Vahitahi Atoll	57	Nf	18.44S	138.52W
Vahruši	7	Mg	58.43N	50.02 E
Vahš	18	Gf	37.43N	68.49 E
Vahsel Bay → Herzog-Ernst-Bucht	66	Af	77.48S	34.39W
Vahtan	7	Lh	57.59N	46.42 E
Vaiaau	65e	Db	16.52S	151.28W
Vaigat	41	Gd	70.30N	54.00W
Vaihingen an der Enz	12	Kf	48.56N	8.58 E
Vaihú	65d	Ab	27.10S	109.23W
Väike-Maarja/Vjaike-Maarja	8	Le	59.04N	26.12 E
Väike-Pakri/Vjajke-Pakri	8	Je	59.20N	23.50 E
Väike Väin/Vjajke-Vjajn	8	Jf	58.30N	23.10 E
Vaiala	64h	Bb	13.13S	176.09W
Vaiala, Pointe-	64h	Ab	13.13S	176.10W
Vaileka	63d	Bb	17.23S	178.09 E
Vailheu, Récif-	37	Gb	11.48S	43.04 E
Vailly-sur-Aisne	12	Fe	49.25N	3.31 E
Vainikkala	8	Md	60.52N	28.18 E
Vainode/Vajnëde	8	Ih	56.26N	21.45 E
Vairaatea Atoll	57	Nf	19.19S	139.20W
Vaison-la-Romaine	11	Lj	44.14N	5.04 E
Vaitape	65e	Db	16.31S	151.45W
Vaitoare	65e	Db	16.41S	151.28W
Vaitupu Island	57	Ie	7.28S	178.41 E
Vajgač, Ostrov-	5	La	70.00N	59.30 E
Vajnëde/Vainode	8	Ih	56.26N	21.45 E
Vakaga [3]	35	Cd	10.00N	23.30 E
Vakfıkebir	24	Hb	41.03N	39.20 E
Vaksdal	8	Ad	60.29N	5.44 E
Val	20	Jf	52.19N	143.09 E
Vala	7	Mh	56.59N	51.16 E
Valaam	7	Hf	61.24N	30.59 E
Valaam, Ostrov-	8	Nc	61.20N	31.05 E
Valahia = Walachia (EN)	15	He	44.00N	25.00 E
Valahia = Walachia (EN)	5	Ig	44.00N	25.00 E
Valais [2]	14	Bd	46.15N	7.30 E
Valamares, Mali i-	15	Di	40.47N	20.28 E
Valamaz	7	Mh	57.36N	52.14 E
Valandovo	15	Fh	41.19N	22.34 E
Valašské Meziříčí	10	Ng	49.29N	17.58 E
Valáxa	15	Hk	38.49N	24.29 E
Vålberg	8	Ee	59.24N	13.12 E
Valburg	12	Hc	51.55N	5.49 E
Valcabra	13	Jg	37.30N	2.43W
Vâlcedrăm	15	Gf	43.42N	23.27 E
Valcheta	56	Gf	40.42S	66.09W
Valdagno	14	Fe	45.39N	11.18 E
Valdahon	11	Mg	47.09N	6.21 E
Valdai Hills (EN) = Valdajskaja Vozvyšennost	5	Jd	57.00N	33.30 E
Valdaj	19	Dd	57.59N	33.14 E
Valdajskaja Vozvyšennost = Valdai Hills (EN)	5	Jd	57.00N	33.30 E
Valdarno	14	Fg	43.45N	11.15 E
Valdavia	13	Hb	42.24N	4.16W
Valdecañas, Embalse de-	13	Ge	39.45N	5.30W
Valdeganga	13	Ke	39.09N	1.40W
Val-de-Marne [3]	11	If	48.47N	2.29 E
Valdemārpils/Valdemarpils	7	Fh	57.24N	22.39 E
Valdemarpils/Valdemārpils	7	Fh	57.24N	22.39 E
Valdemarsvik	7	Dg	58.12N	16.32 E
Valdepeñas	13	If	38.46N	3.23W
Valderaduey	13	Gc	41.31N	5.42W
Valderas	13	Gb	42.05N	5.27W
Valderrama, Cienaga de-	49	Ki	8.56N	72.10W
Valderrobres/Vall-de-roures	13	Ld	40.53N	0.09W
Valdés, Peninsula-	52	Jj	42.30S	64.00W
Valdez	39	Ec	61.07N	146.16W
Val d'Isère	11	Mi	45.27N	6.59 E
Valdivia	53	Ii	39.48S	73.14W
Valdivia Seamount (EN)	30	Hk	25.20S	6.15 E
Valdobbiadene	14	Fe	45.54N	12.00 E
Val-d'Oise [3]	11	Ie	49.10N	2.10 E
Val-d'Or	39	Le	48.07N	77.47W
Valdosta	39	Kf	30.50N	83.17W
Valdres	8	Cc	60.55N	9.10 E
Vale	16	Mi	41.36N	42.51 E
Vale [Or.-U.S.]	46	Gd	44.01N	117.15W
Valea Ierii	15	Gc	46.39N	23.21 E
Valea lui Mihai	15	Fb	47.31N	22.09 E
Valea Vişeului	15	Hb	47.51N	24.10 E
Valença [Braz.]	55	Kf	22.15S	43.43W
Valença [Braz.]	54	Kf	13.22S	39.05W
Valença do Minho	13	Db	42.02N	8.38W
Valença do Piauí	54	Je	6.24S	41.45W
Valençay	11	Hg	47.09N	1.34 E
Valence [Fr.]	11	Gj	44.06N	0.55 E
Valence [Fr.]	11	Kj	44.56N	4.54 E
Valencia	6	Fh	39.28N	0.22W
Valencia [3]	13	Le	39.20N	0.50W
Valencia	13	Le	39.30N	0.40W
València/Valencia	6	Fh	39.28N	0.22W
Valencia/València	6	Fh	39.28N	0.22W
València, Golf de-/Valencia, Golfo de-	5	Fh	39.30N	0.00
Valencia, Golfo de-/València, Golf de-	5	Fh	39.30N	0.00
Valencia, Lago de-	50	Cg	10.11N	67.45W
Valencia de Alcántara	13	Ee	39.25N	7.14W
Valencia de Don Juan	13	Gb	42.18N	5.31W
Valencia-El Grao	13	Le	39.27N	0.20W
Valenciennes	11	Jd	50.21N	3.32 E
Vălenii de Munte	15	Jd	45.11N	26.02 E
Valentia/Dairbhre	9	Cj	51.55N	10.20W
Valentin	28	Mc	43.07N	134.19 E
Valentine	43	Gc	42.52N	100.33W
Valenza	14	Ce	45.01N	8.38 E
Våler	8	Cf	60.40N	11.50 E
Valera	54	Db	9.19N	70.37W
Valerie Seamount (EN)	57	Ki	42.00S	163.30W
Valga	19	Cd	57.49N	26.05 E
Valge Jõgi	8	Ke	59.32N	25.36 E
Valhalla Mountains	46	Gb	49.45N	117.48W
Valiente, Peninsula-	49	Gi	9.05N	81.51W
Valier	46	Ib	48.18N	112.15W
Valinco, Golfe de-	11a	Ab	41.40N	8.49 E
Valjevo	15	Ce	44.16N	19.53 E
Valka	7	Gh	57.47N	26.01 E
Valkeakoski	7	Ff	61.16N	24.02 E
Valkeala	8	Ld	60.57N	26.48 E
Valkenswaard	12	Hc	51.21N	5.28 E
Valkininkai/Valkininkaj	8	Kj	54.18N	25.55 E
Valkininkaj/Valkininkai	8	Kj	54.18N	25.55 E
Valko/Valkom	8	Ld	60.25N	26.15 E
Valkom/Valko	8	Ld	60.25N	26.15 E
Valkumej	20	Mc	69.41N	170.30 E
Valladolid [3]	13	Hc	41.35N	4.40W
Valladolid [Mex.]	47	Gd	20.41N	88.12W
Valladolid [Sp.]	6	Fg	41.39N	4.43W
Valldal	8	Bb	62.20N	7.21 E
Vall-de-Roures/Valderrobres	13	Ld	40.53N	0.09W
Vall de Uxó	13	Le	39.49N	0.14W
Valle [2]	54	Cc	3.40N	76.30W
Valle [3]	49	Dg	13.30N	87.35W
Valle	7	Bg	59.12N	7.32 E
Vallecas, Madrid-	13	Id	40.23N	3.37W
Valle d'Aosta / Vallée d'Aoste [2]	14	Be	45.45N	7.15 E
Valle de Cabuerniga	13	Ha	43.14N	4.18W
Valle de Guanape	50	Dh	9.54N	65.41W
Valle dei Templi	14	Hm	37.18N	13.35 E
Valle de la Pascua	54	Eb	9.13N	66.00W
Valle de Santiago	48	Ig	20.23N	101.12W
Valle de Topia	48	Fe	25.13N	106.25W
Valle de Zaragoza	48	Gd	27.28N	105.49W
Valledupar	54	Da	10.28N	73.15W
Vallée d'Aoste / Valle d'Aosta [2]	14	Be	45.45N	7.15 E
Vallée Jonction	44	Lb	46.23N	70.55W
Valle Hermoso	48	Ke	25.39N	97.52W
Vallejera, Puerto de-	13	Gd	40.30N	5.42W
Vallejo	43	Cd	38.07N	122.14W
Vallejo, Sierra de-	48	Gg	20.55N	105.20W
Valle Nacional	48	Ki	17.47N	96.19W
Vallenar	53	Ih	28.35S	70.46W
Vallentuna	8	He	59.32N	18.05 E
Valles/El Valles	13	Oc	41.35N	2.15 E
Valles de los Daidos	13	Hd	40.39N	4.09W
Valletta	6	Hh	35.54N	14.31 E
Valley City	43	Hb	46.55N	97.59W
Valley Falls	46	Ee	42.31N	120.15W
Valleyfield	42	Kg	45.15N	74.08W
Valley Station	44	Ef	38.06N	85.52W
Valleyview	42	Fe	55.02N	117.08W
Vallgrund	7	Ee	63.12N	21.14 E
Vallhagar	8	Hg	57.20N	18.10 E
Vallimanca	55	Bm	36.21S	61.02W
Vallimanca, Arroyo-	55	Bl	35.40S	60.02W
Vallo della Lucania	14	Jj	40.14N	15.16 E
Valloires, Abbaye de-	12	Dd	50.20N	1.47 E
Vallorbe	14	Ad	46.43N	6.23 E
Valls	13	Nc	41.17N	1.15 E
Valls d'Andorra → Andorra [1]	6	Gg	42.30N	1.30 E
Vallsta	8	Gc	61.32N	16.22 E
Vallvik	8	Gc	61.11N	17.11 E
Valmaseda	13	Ia	43.12N	3.12W
Valmiera	19	Cd	57.32N	25.29 E
Valmont	12	Ce	49.44N	0.31 E
Valnera	13	Ia	43.10N	3.45W
Valognes	11	Ee	49.31N	1.28W
Valois, Plaine du-	11	Ie	49.10N	2.45 E
Valoria la Buena	13	Hc	41.48N	4.32W
Valpaços	13	Ec	41.36N	7.19W
Valparaiso	44	De	41.28N	87.03W
Valparaíso [Braz.]	55	Ge	21.13S	50.51W
Valparaíso [Chile]	53	Ii	33.02S	71.38W
Valparaíso [Mex.]	48	Hf	22.46N	103.34W
Valpovo	14	Me	45.39N	18.25 E
Valréas	11	Kj	44.23N	4.59 E
Vals	30	Jk	27.23S	26.31 E
Vals, Tanjung-	26	Kh	8.26S	137.38 E
Valsjöbyn	7	Dd	64.04N	14.08 E
Valtellina	14	Dd	46.10N	9.55 E
Valtimo	7	Ge	63.40N	28.48 E
Váltou, Óri-	15	Ej	39.10N	21.20 E
Valujki	19	De	50.12N	38.08 E
Valul-Lui Traian	15	Le	44.15N	28.30 E
Valverde	32	Dd	27.48N	17.55W
Valverde de Júcar	13	Je	39.43N	2.12W
Valverde del Camino	13	Fg	37.34N	6.45W
Valverde del Fresno	13	Ff	40.13N	6.52W
Vamdrup	8	Ci	55.25N	9.17 E
Våmhus	7	Df	61.08N	14.28 E
Vamizi, Ilha-	37	Gb	11.02S	40.40 E
Vammala	7	Ff	61.20N	22.54 E
Vámos	15	Hn	35.25N	24.12 E
Van	23	Fb	38.28N	43.20 E
Van, Lake- (EN) = Van Gölü	21	Gf	38.33N	42.46 E
Vanajanselkä	7	Ff	61.09N	24.15 E
Vanak	24	Ng	31.41N	50.52 E
Vanak	24	Nq	31.32N	51.19 E
Vanån	8	Fd	60.31N	14.14 E
Vanault-les-Dames	12	Gf	48.51N	4.46 E
Vanavana Atoll	57	Ng	20.47S	139.09W
Vanavara	20	Fd	60.22N	102.16 E
Van Buren [Ar.-U.S.]	45	Ii	35.26N	94.21W
Van Buren [Me.-U.S.]	44	Nb	47.09N	67.56W
Vanč	18	He	38.23N	71.29 E
Vanceburg	44	Ff	38.36N	83.19W
Vancouver [B.C.-Can.]	39	Ge	49.16N	123.07W
Vancouver [Wa.-U.S.]	43	Cb	45.39N	122.40W
Vancouver Island	38	Ge	49.45N	126.00W
Vandalia [Il.-U.S.]	45	Lg	38.58N	89.06W
Vandalia [Oh.-U.S.]	44	Ef	39.53N	84.12W
Vanderbijl Park	37	De	26.42S	27.54 E
Vanderhoof	42	Ff	54.01N	124.01W
Vanderlin Island	59	Hc	15.45S	137.00 E
Van Diemen, Cape-	59	Gb	11.10S	130.25 E
Van Diemen Gulf	59	Gb	11.50S	132.00 E
Vandmtor, Ozero-	17	Le	62.15N	65.45 E
Vändra/Vjandra	7	Fg	58.40N	25.01 E
Vänern	5	Hd	58.55N	13.30 E
Vänersborg	7	Cg	58.22N	12.19 E

Index Symbols

[1] Independent Nation
[2] State, Region
[3] District, County
[4] Municipality
[5] Colony, Dependency
Continent
Physical Region
Historical or Cultural Region
Mount, Mountain
Volcano
Hill
Mountains, Mountain Range
Hills, Escarpment
Plateau, Upland
Pass, Gap
Plain, Lowland
Delta
Salt Flat
Valley, Canyon
Crater, Cave
Karst Features
Depression
Polder
Desert, Dunes
Forest, Woods
Heath, Steppe
Oasis
Cape, Point
Coast, Beach
Cliff
Peninsula
Isthmus
Sandbank
Island
Atoll
Rock, Reef
Islands, Archipelago
Rocks, Reefs
Coral Reef
Well, Spring
Geyser
River, Stream
Waterfall Rapids
River Mouth, Estuary
Lake
Salt Lake
Intermittent Lake
Reservoir
Swamp, Pond
Canal
Glacier
Ice Shelf, Pack Ice
Ocean
Sea
Gulf, Bay
Strait, Fjord
Lagoon
Bank
Seamount
Tablemount
Ridge
Shelf
Basin
Escarpment, Sea Scarp
Fracture
Trench, Abyss
National Park, Reserve
Point of Interest
Recreation Site
Cave, Cavern
Historic Site
Ruins
Wall, Walls
Church, Abbey
Temple
Scientific Station
Airport
Port
Lighthouse
Mine
Tunnel
Dam, Bridge

Name	Page	Key	Lat.	Long.
Vang	8	Cc	61.08N	8.35 E
Vangaindrano	37	Hd	23.23 S	47.33 E
Van Gölü = Van, Lake- (EN)	21	Gf	38.33N	42.46 E
Vangunu Island	57	Ge	8.40 S	158.05 E
Van Horn	43	Ge	31.03N	104.50W
Vanick, Rio-	55	Fa	13.06 S	52.52W
Vanier	42	Ha	76.00N	103.50W
Vanikolo	63c	Bb	11.37 S	166.58 E
Vanikolo Islands	57	Hf	11.37 S	167.03 E
Vanimo	60	Ch	2.40 S	141.18 E
Vanino	20	Jg	49.11N	140.19 E
Vankavesi	8	Jc	61.50N	23.50 E
Vanna	7	Ea	70.09N	19.51 E
Vännäs	7	Ee	63.55N	19.45 E
Vanne	11	Jf	48.12N	3.16 E
Vannes	11	Dg	47.40N	2.45W
Van Ninh	25	Lf	12.42N	109.14 E
Vannsjø	8	De	59.25N	10.50 E
Vanoise, Massif de la-	11	Mi	45.20N	6.40 E
Vanona Lava, Ile-	57	Hf	14.00 S	167.30 E
Van Phong, Vung-	25	Lf	12.33N	109.18 E
Van Rees, Pegunungan-	26	Kg	2.35 S	138.15 E
Vanrhynsdorp	37	Bf	31.36 S	18.44 E
Vansbro	7	Df	60.31N	14.13 E
Vanse	8	Bf	58.07N	6.42 E
Vansittart	42	Jc	65.50N	84.00W
Vantaa	8	Kd	60.13N	24.59 E
Vänte Litets grund	8	Hb	62.35N	18.12 E
Vanua Levu	57	If	17.28 S	177.03 E
Vanua Mbalavu	61	Fc	17.14 S	178.57W
Vanuatu	58	Hf	16.00 S	167.00 E
Vanua Vatu	63d	Cc	18.22 S	179.16W
Van Wert	44	Ee	40.53N	84.36W
Van Wyksviei	37	Cf	30.18 S	21.49 E
Vanzylsrus	37	Ce	26.52 S	22.04 E
Vao	63b	Cf	22.40 S	167.29 E
Vao, Nosy-	37	Gc	17.30 S	43.45 E
Vão das Almas	55	Ia	13.42 S	47.27W
Vapnjarka	16	Fe	48.32N	28.46 E
Var	11	Mk	43.30N	6.20 E
Var	11	Nk	43.39N	7.12 E
Vara	14	Df	44.09N	9.53 E
Vara	8	Ef	58.16N	12.57 E
Varaita	14	Bf	44.49N	7.36 E
Varakļāni/Varakljany	7	Gh	56.36N	26.48 E
Varakljany/Varakļāni	7	Gh	56.36N	26.48 E
Varaldsøy	8	Ad	60.10N	6.00 E
Varalé	34	Ed	9.40N	3.17W
Varallo	14	Ce	45.49N	8.15 E
Varāmīn	24	Ne	35.20N	51.39 E
Vārānasi (Benares)	22	Kg	25.20N	83.00 E
Varangerfjorden	5	Ia	70.00N	30.00 E
Varangerhalvøya = Varanger Peninsula (EN)	5	Ia	70.25N	29.30 E
Varanger Peninsula (EN) = Varangerhalvøya	5	Ia	70.25N	29.30 E
Varano, Lago di-	14	Ji	41.53N	15.45 E
Varāvī	24	Oi	27.25N	53.06 E
Varaždin	14	Kd	46.18N	16.20 E
Varazze	14	Cf	44.22N	8.34 E
Varberg	7	Ch	57.06N	12.15 E
Vardak	23	Kc	34.15N	68.00 E
Vardar	5	Ig	40.35N	22.50 E
Varde	7	Bi	55.38N	8.29 E
Varde Å	8	Ci	55.35N	8.20 E
Vardhoúsia Óri	15	Fk	38.40N	22.10 E
Vårdo	8	Id	60.15N	20.20 E
Vardø	7	Ha	70.22N	31.06 E
Varel	10	Ec	53.24N	8.08 E
Varėna/Varena	7	Fi	54.15N	24.39 E
Varena/Varėna	7	Fi	54.15N	24.39 E
Värend	8	Fh	56.45N	14.55 E
Varengeville-sur-Mer	12	Ce	49.55N	0.59 E
Varenikovskaja	16	Jg	45.06N	37.37 E
Varenne	11	Ff	48.24N	0.39W
Varennes-en-Argonne	12	He	49.14N	5.02 E
Varennes-sur-Allier	11	Jh	46.19N	3.24 E
Vareš	14	Mf	44.10N	18.20 E
Varese	14	Ce	45.48N	8.50 E
Varese, Lago di-	14	Ce	45.50N	8.45 E
Vårgårda	8	Ef	58.02N	12.48 E
Vargaši	19	Gd	55.23N	65.48 E
Vargem Grande	54	Jd	3.33 S	43.56W
Varginha	54	Ih	21.33 S	45.26W
Vargön	8	Ef	58.21N	12.22 E
Varhaug	8	Af	58.37N	5.39 E
Varjão	55	Hc	17.03 S	49.37W
Varkaus	6	Ic	62.19N	27.55 E
Värmdö	8	He	59.20N	18.35 E
Värmeln	8	Ee	59.30N	12.55 E
Värmland	8	Ee	59.50N	13.05 E
Värmland	7	Cg	59.45N	13.15 E
Värmlandsnäs	8	Ee	59.00N	13.10 E
Varna	15	Kf	43.10N	27.35 E
Varna [Bul.]	6	Ig	43.13N	27.55 E
Varna	17	Jj	53.24N	60.58 E
Värnamo	7	Dh	57.11N	14.02 E
Varnenski Zaliv	15	Kf	43.11N	27.56 E
Varniai/Varnjaj	8	Ji	55.44N	22.17 E
Varnjaj/Varniai	8	Ji	55.44N	22.17 E
Varnsdorf	10	Kf	50.54N	14.38 E
Várpalota	10	Oi	47.12N	18.08 E
Văršec	15	Gf	43.12N	23.17 E
Varsinais-Suomi/Egentliga Finland	8	Jd	60.40N	22.30 E
Värska	8	Lg	57.58N	27.38 E
Vartašen	16	Oi	41.05N	47.29 E
Varto	24	Ic	39.10N	41.28 E
Vartofta	8	Ef	58.06N	13.38 E
Värtsilä	8	Nb	62.15N	30.40 E
Varzaneh	24	Of	32.25N	52.39 E
Varzaqān	24	Lc	38.31N	46.39 E
Varzarīn, Kūh-e-	23	Gc	33.24N	46.48 E
Várzea, Rio da-	55	Fh	27.13 S	53.19W
Várzea da Palma	55	Jc	17.36 S	44.44W
Varzea Grande	54	Gg	15.39 S	56.08W
Varzelândia	55	Jb	15.42 S	44.02W
Varzi	14	Df	44.49N	9.12 E
Varzuga	7	Ic	66.17N	36.50 E
Varzy	11	Jg	47.22N	3.23 E
Vas	10	Mi	47.10N	16.45 E
Vasa/Vaasa	6	Ic	63.06N	21.36 E
Vasai (Bassein)	25	Ee	19.21N	72.48 E
Vasalemma/Vazalemma	8	Ke	59.15N	24.11 E
Vásárosnamény	10	Sh	48.08N	22.19 E
Vascão	13	Eg	37.31N	7.31W
Vaşcău	15	Fc	46.28N	22.28 E
Vascoeuil	12	De	49.27N	1.23 E
Vascongadas/Euzkadi = Basque Provinces (EN)	13	Ja	43.00N	2.30W
Vascos, Montes-	13	Jb	42.50N	2.10W
Vasgūn	24	Qe	34.55N	56.30 E
Vasileviči	16	Fc	52.14N	29.47 E
Vasiliká	15	Gi	40.28N	23.08 E
Vasiljevka	16	If	47.23N	35.18 E
Vasilkov	19	De	50.12N	30.22 E
Vasilkovka	16	Je	48.13N	36.03 E
Vasiss	19	Hd	57.30N	74.55 E
Vasjugan	20	De	59.10N	80.50 E
Vasjuganje	21	Jd	58.00N	77.00 E
Vaška	19	Ec	64.53N	45.47 E
Vaškovcy	15	Ia	48.16N	25.34 E
Vaslui	15	Kc	46.38N	27.44 E
Vaslui	15	Kc	46.37N	27.44 E
Vaslui	15	Kc	46.41N	27.43 E
Väsman	8	Fd	60.11N	15.04 E
Vassako	35	Bd	8.36N	19.07 E
Vassdalsegga	7	Bg	59.46N	7.07 E
Vassy	12	Bf	48.51N	0.40W
Västeras	6	Hd	59.37N	16.33 E
Västerbotten	7	Dd	64.58N	17.28 E
Västerdalälven	7	Df	60.33N	15.08 E
Västergötland	8	Eg	58.00N	13.05 E
Västerhaninge	8	He	59.07N	18.06 E
Västernorrland	7	De	63.00N	17.30 E
Västervik	7	Dh	57.45N	16.38 E
Västmanland	8	Fe	59.40N	15.15 E
Västmanland	7	Dg	59.45N	16.20 E
Vasto	14	Ih	42.07N	14.42 E
Västra Silen	8	Ee	59.15N	12.10 E
Vasvár	10	Mi	47.03N	16.48 E
Vatan	11	Hg	47.04N	1.49 E
Vatersay	9	Fe	56.53N	7.28W
Vatican City (EN) = Città del Vaticano	6	Hg	41.54N	12.27 E
Vaticano, Capo-	14	Jl	38.37N	15.50 E
Vatilau	63a	Ec	8.53 S	160.01 E
Vatnajökull	5	Ec	64.24N	16.48W
Vatneyri	7a	Ab	65.35N	24.00W
Vatoa Island	57	Jf	19.50 S	178.13W
Vatomandry	37	Hc	19.20 S	48.59 E
Vatra Dornei	15	Ib	47.21N	25.22 E
Vättern	5	Hd	58.25N	14.35 E
Vatu-i-Ra Channel	63d	Bb	17.24 S	178.29 E
Vatulele	63d	Ac	18.33 S	177.38 E
Vatutino	16	Ge	49.02N	31.09 E
Vatu Vara	61	Fc	17.26 S	179.32W
Vaubecourt	12	Hf	48.56N	5.07 E
Vauclin, Pointe du-	51h	Bb	14.34N	60.50W
Vaucluse	11	Lj	44.00N	5.10 E
Vaucluse, Montagne du-	11	Lk	44.32N	5.11 E
Vaucouleurs	11	Lf	48.36N	5.40 E
Vaud	14	Ad	46.35N	6.30 E
Vaudemont, Butte de-	11	Lf	48.25N	6.00 E
Vaughn	43	Fe	34.36N	105.13W
Vaupés	54	Dc	1.00N	71.00W
Vaupés, Río-	52	Je	0.02N	67.16W
Vauvilliers	63b	Ce	21.09 S	167.35 E
Vaux	12	Ge	49.31N	4.17 E
Vaux-le-Vicomte	11	If	48.34N	2.43 E
Vavatenina	37	Hc	17.26 S	49.22 E
Vava'u Group	57	Jf	18.40 S	174.00W
Vava'u Island	61	Gc	18.36 S	174.00W
Vavoua	34	Dd	7.23N	6.29W
Vavuniya	25	Gg	8.45N	80.30 E
Vaxholm	8	He	59.24N	18.20 E
Växjö	6	Hd	56.53N	14.49 E
Vaza-Barris, Rio-	54	Kf	11.10 S	37.10W
Vazalemma/Vasalemma	8	Ke	59.15N	24.11 E
Vazante	54	Ig	18.00 S	46.54W
Vazuza	16	Ia	56.10N	34.35 E
Vding Skovhøj	8	Ch	56.01N	9.48 E
Veadeiros, Chapada dos-	54	If	14.05 S	47.28W
Vecht	10	Cd	52.35N	6.05 E
Vechta	10	Ed	52.43N	8.17 E
Vechte	10	Cd	52.35N	6.05 E
Vecpiebalga	8	Kh	56.57N	25.50 E
Vecsés	10	Pi	47.24N	19.17 E
Vedavågen	8	Ae	59.19N	5.12 E
Veddige	8	Eg	57.16N	12.19 E
Vedea	15	He	44.47N	24.37 E
Vedea	15	Ie	43.59N	25.59 E
Vedeno	16	Oh	42.57N	46.05 E
Vedia	55	Bl	34.30 S	61.32W
Vedrá Isla-	13	Nf	38.52N	1.12 E
Veendam	11	Ma	53.06N	6.58 E
Veenendaal	12	Hb	52.02N	5.35 E
Veere	12	Fc	51.33N	3.40 E
Vega	7	Cd	65.39N	11.50 E
Vega	45	Ei	35.15N	102.26W
Vega Baja	51a	Bb	18.25N	66.23W
Veganj	14	Kg	43.50N	16.45 E
Vegår	8	Cf	58.48N	8.47 E
Vegårshei	8	Cf	58.46N	8.48 E
Veghel	12	Hc	51.37N	5.32 E
Veglie	14	Lj	40.20N	17.58 E
Vegorrítis, Límni-	15	Ei	40.45N	21.48 E
Vègre	11	Fg	47.51N	0.14W
Vegreville	42	Gf	53.30N	112.03W
Vehmersalmi	8	Mb	62.46N	28.02 E
Vehnemoor	12	Ka	53.04N	8.02 E
Veinge	8	Eh	56.34N	13.05 E
Veinticinco de Mayo [Arg.]	56	He	35.26 S	60.10W
Veinticinco de Mayo [Ur.]	55	Dl	34.12 S	56.22W
Veio	14	Gh	42.02N	12.23 E
Veisiejai/Vejsejaj	8	Jj	54.03N	23.46 E
Vejen	7	Bi	55.29N	9.09 E
Vejer de la Frontera	13	Gh	36.15N	5.58W
Vejle	8	Ci	55.45N	9.20 E
Vejle	7	Bi	55.42N	9.32 E
Vejsejaj/Veisiejai	8	Jj	54.03N	23.46 E
Vel	7	Kf	61.06N	42.10 E
Vela, Cabo de la-	49	Kg	12.13N	72.11W
Vela Luka	14	Kh	42.58N	16.44 E
Velas	32	Bb	38.41N	28.13W
Velas, Cabo-	49	Eh	10.22N	85.53W
Velásquez	55	El	34.02 S	54.17W
Velay, Plateaux du-	11	Ji	45.10N	3.50 E
Velaz	55	Ch	26.42 S	58.40W
Velbăždski prohod	15	Fg	42.14N	22.28 E
Velbert	10	De	51.20N	7.02 E
Velddrif	37	Bf	32.47 S	18.10 E
Velden am Wörthersee	14	Id	46.37N	14.03 E
Veldhoven	12	Hc	51.24N	5.24 E
Velebit	5	Hg	44.17N	15.12 E
Velebitski kanal	14	If	44.45N	14.50 E
Veleka	15	Kg	42.04N	27.58 E
Velencei-tó	10	Oi	47.13N	18.36 E
Velenje	14	Jd	46.22N	15.07 E
Velestinon	15	Fj	39.23N	22.45 E
Veleta	13	Ig	37.04N	3.22W
Velež	14	Lg	43.20N	18.00 E
Vélez Blanco	13	Jg	37.41N	2.05W
Vélez de La Gomera, Peñón de-	13	Hi	35.11N	4.54W
Vélez-Málaga	13	Hh	36.47N	4.06W
Vélez Rubio	13	Jg	37.39N	2.04W
Velhas, Rio das-	52	Lg	17.13 S	44.49W
Velika Gorica	14	Ke	45.44N	16.04 E
Velikaja	20	Md	64.35N	176.03 E
Velikaja-Gluša	10	Ve	51.49N	25.11 E
Velikaja Guba	7	Ie	62.17N	35.06 E
Velikaja Kema	20	Ig	45.29N	137.08 E
Velikaja Lepetiha	16	Hf	47.09N	33.59 E
Velikaja Mihajlovka	16	Ff	47.04N	29.52 E
Velika Kapela	14	Je	45.13N	15.02 E
Velika Kladuša	14	Je	45.11N	15.49 E
Velika Morava	15	Ee	44.43N	21.03 E
Velika Plana	15	Ee	44.20N	21.05 E
Veliki Berezny	10	Sh	48.54N	22.30 E
Veliki Byčkov	10	Ui	47.58N	24.04 E
Veliki Drvenik	14	Kg	43.27N	16.09 E
Veliki Jastrebac	15	Ef	43.24N	21.26 E
Velikije Luki	6	Jd	56.20N	30.32 E
Velikije Mosty	10	Uf	50.10N	24.12 E
Veliki kanal	15	Bd	45.52N	18.52 E
Veliki Ljuben	10	Tg	49.37N	23.45 E
Veliki Trnovac	15	Eg	42.29N	21.45 E
Veliki Ustjug	6	Kc	60.46N	46.20 E
Velikodolinskoje	15	Nc	46.20N	30.29 E
Veliko Gradište	15	Ee	44.46N	21.32 E
Veliko Tărnovo	15	If	43.04N	25.39 E
Veliko Tărnovo	6	Ig	43.04N	25.39 E
Velikovisočnoje	19	Fb	67.16N	52.01 E
Veli Lošinj	14	If	44.31N	14.31 E
Vélingara	34	Cc	13.09N	14.07W
Velingrad	15	Gg	42.01N	24.00 E
Velino	14	Hh	42.09N	13.23 E
Velino	14	Gh	42.33N	12.43 E
Veliž	16	Gb	55.36N	31.12 E
Vel'ká Fatra	10	Ph	49.00N	19.05 E
Velké Meziříčí	10	Lg	49.21N	16.00 E
Vel'ký Krtíš	10	Ph	48.13N	19.20 E
Vel'ký Meder (Čalovo)	10	Ni	47.52N	17.47 E
Vella Lavella Island	57	Ge	7.45 S	156.40 E
Velletri	14	Gi	41.41N	12.47 E
Vellinge	8	Ei	55.28N	13.01 E
Vellore	22	Jh	14.26N	79.58 E
Velmerstot	10	Ee	51.50N	9.00 E
Velmo	20	Ed	61.43N	92.25 E
Velopoúla	15	Gm	36.55N	23.28 E
Vels	17	If	60.45N	58.45 E
Velsen-IJmuiden [Neth.]	11	Kb	52.27N	4.39 E
Velsk	19	Ec	61.05N	42.05 E
Veluwe	11	Lb	52.20N	5.50 E
Veluwemeer	12	Hb	52.23N	5.40 E
Velva	45	Fb	48.04N	100.56W
Velvendós	15	Fi	40.15N	22.04 E
Veman	8	Fb	62.02N	14.16 E
Vema Seamount (EN)	30	Hl	31.38 S	8.19 E
Vemdalen	8	Eb	62.27N	13.52 E
Ven	8	Ei	55.55N	12.40 E
Venable Ice Shelf	66	Pf	73.03 S	87.20W
Venado	48	If	22.56N	101.05W
Venado, Cerro-	50	Ei	6.17N	62.45W
Venado Tuerto	56	Hd	33.45 S	61.58W
Venafro	14	Ii	41.29N	14.02 E
Venamo, Río-	50	Fi	6.43N	61.07W
Vence	11	Nk	43.43N	7.07 E
Venceslau Brás	55	Hf	23.51 S	49.48W
Venda	37	Ed	22.35 S	30.45 E
Venda Nova	54	Jg	19.45 S	43.50W
Vendas Novas	13	Df	38.41N	8.27W
Vendée	11	Eh	46.40N	1.20W
Vendée	11	Hh	46.40N	1.10 E
Vendée	11	Fh	46.19N	0.58W
Vendéen, Bocage-	11	Eh	46.50N	1.20W
Vendéenne, Plaine-	11	Eh	46.40N	1.20W
Vendel	8	Gd	60.10N	17.36 E
Vendeuvre-sur-Barse	11	Kf	48.14N	4.29 E
Vendôme	11	Hg	47.48N	1.04 E
Vendrell/El Vendrell	13	Nc	41.13N	1.32 E
Vendsyssel	8	Cg	57.20N	10.00 E
Venetia (EN) = Veneto	14	Fe	45.30N	12.00 E
Venétiko [Grc.]	15	Jk	38.08N	26.01 E
Venétiko [Grc.]	15	Em	36.42N	21.53 E
Veneto = Venetia (EN)	14	Fe	45.30N	12.00 E
Venev	16	Kb	54.22N	38.18 E
Venezia = Venice (EN)	6	Hf	45.27N	12.21 E
Venezia, Golfo di- = Venice, Gulf of- (EN)	5	Hf	45.15N	13.00 E
Venezia-Lido	14	Ge	45.25N	12.22 E
Venezia-Marghera	14	Ge	45.28N	12.44 E
Venezia-Mestre	14	Ge	45.29N	12.14 E
Venezuela	53	Je	8.00N	65.00W
Venezuela, Golfo de- = Venezuela, Gulf of- (EN)	52	Id	11.30N	71.00W
Venezuela, Gulf of- (EN) = Venezuela, Golfo de-	52	Id	11.30N	71.00W
Venezuelan Basin (EN)	38	Mh	15.00N	68.00W
Vengerovo	20	Ce	55.41N	76.55 E
Veniaminof, Mount-	40	He	56.13N	159.18W
Venice	44	Fl	27.06N	82.27W
Venice (EN) = Venezia	6	Hf	45.27N	12.21 E
Venice, Gulf of- (EN) = Venezia, Golfo di-	5	Hf	45.15N	13.00 E
Vénissieux	11	Ki	45.41N	4.53 E
Venjan	8	Ed	60.57N	13.55 E
Venjansjön	8	Ed	60.55N	14.00 E
Venlo	11	Mc	51.24N	6.10 E
Venlock River	59	Ib	12.15 S	142.00 E
Vennesla	7	Bg	58.17N	7.59 E
Venosa	14	Jj	40.58N	15.49 E
Venosta, Val-/Vintschgau	14	Ed	46.40N	10.35 E
Venraij	11	Lc	51.32N	5.59 E
Vent, Canal du- = Windward Passage (EN)	49	Lh	20.00N	73.50W
Vent, Iles du- = Windward Islands (EN)	57	Mf	17.30 S	149.30W
Venta	7	Eh	57.23N	21.32 E
Venta de Baños	13	Hc	41.55N	4.30W
Ventana, Cerro-	48	Fe	24.15N	106.20W
Ventersdorp	37	De	26.17 S	26.48 E
Venterstad	37	Df	30.47 S	25.48 E
Venticinco de Diciembre	55	Dg	24.42 S	56.33W
Ventimiglia	14	Bg	43.47N	7.36 E
Ventnor	12	Ad	50.36N	1.11W
Ventotene	14	Hj	40.45N	13.25 E
Ventoux, Mont-	11	Lj	44.10N	5.17 E
Ventspils	19	Cd	57.24N	21.33 E
Ventuari, Río-	52	Je	3.58N	67.02W
Ventura	43	De	34.17N	119.18W
Vénus, Pointe-	65e	Fc	17.29 S	149.29W
Venus Bay	59	Jg	38.40 S	145.45 E
Venustiano Carranza	48	Mi	16.21N	92.33W
Venustiano Carranza, Presa-	48	Id	27.30N	100.40W
Ver	12	Bc	51.31N	0.27W
Vera [Arg.]	56	Hc	29.28 S	60.13W
Vera [Sp.]	13	Kg	37.15N	1.52W
Verá, Laguna-	55	Dh	26.05 S	57.39W
Veracruz	47	Ee	19.20N	96.40W
Veracruz Llave	39	Jh	19.12N	96.08W
Veraguas	49	Gj	8.30N	81.00W
Verāval	25	Ed	20.54N	70.22 E
Vera y Pintado	55	Bj	30.09 S	60.21W
Verbania	14	Ce	45.56N	8.33 E
Verbovski	7	Ji	55.29N	41.59 E
Vercelli	14	Ce	45.19N	8.25 E
Vercors	11	Lj	44.57N	5.25 E
Verdalsøra	7	Ce	63.48N	11.29 E
Verde, Cape-	49	Jb	22.50N	74.52W
Verde, Cay-	49	Jb	22.02N	75.12W
Verde, Costa-	13	Ga	43.40N	5.40W
Verde, Río-	52	Kh	23.09 S	57.37W
Verde, Rio- [Braz.]	54	Hh	21.12 S	51.53W
Verde, Rio- [Braz.]	55	Hb	15.07 S	48.40W
Verde, Rio- [Braz.]	55	Hd	19.50 S	49.45W
Verde, Rio- [Braz.]	55	Ge	21.12 S	51.53W
Verde, Rio- [Braz.]	55	Gd	18.01 S	50.14W
Verde, Rio- [Braz.]	55	Je	21.27 S	45.40W
Verde, Rio- [Braz.]	55	Ca	13.33 S	58.01W
Verde, Rio- [Braz.]	54	Gf	11.54 S	55.50W
Verde, Rio- [Braz.]	54	Hg	19.11 S	50.44W
Verde, Río- [Mex.]	48	Jg	21.37N	99.15W
Verde, Río- [Mex.]	48	Hg	20.42N	103.14W
Verde, Río- [S.Amer.]	55	Ba	13.59 S	60.20W
Verde Grande, Rio-	55	Kb	14.35 S	43.53W
Verden (Aller)	10	Fd	52.55N	9.14 E
Verde River	43	Ee	33.33N	111.40W
Verdigris River	45	Ii	35.48N	95.18W
Verdinho, Rio-	55	Gc	17.29 S	50.27W
Verdon	11	Lk	43.43N	5.46 E
Verdun [Fr.]	11	Le	49.10N	5.23 E
Verdun [Que.-Can.]	44	Kc	45.28N	73.34W
Verdura	14	Hm	37.28N	13.12 E
Vereeniging	37	De	26.38 S	27.57 E
Vereščagino	19	Fd	58.05N	54.40 E
Verga, Cap-	34	Cc	10.12N	14.27W
Vergara [Arg.]	55	Dl	35.23 S	57.48W
Vergara [Sp.]	13	Ja	43.07N	2.25W
Vergara [Ur.]	55	Fk	32.56 S	53.57W
Vergato	14	Ff	44.17N	11.07 E
Verhnedneprovsk	16	Ie	48.39N	34.21 E
Verhnedneprovski	16	Hb	55.01N	33.21 E
Verhnedvinsk	7	Gi	55.46N	27.59 E
Verhneimbatsk	20	Dd	63.02N	88.00 E
Verhne-Karabahski Kanal	16	Oj	39.44N	47.57 E
Verhnespasskoje	7	Kg	58.45N	45.28 E
Verhnetulomski	7	Hb	68.38N	31.48 E
Verhnetulomskoje Vodohranilišče	7	Hb	68.35N	31.00 E
Verhneuralsk	17	Ij	53.53N	59.13 E
Verhneviljujsk	20	Hd	63.20N	120.25 E
Verhni At-Urjah	20	Kd	62.38N	150.03 E
Verhni Avzjan	17	Hj	53.32N	57.33 E
Verhni Kujto, Ozero-	7	Hd	65.00N	30.40 E
Verhni Most	8	Mg	57.29N	29.00 E
Verhni Tagil	17	Jh	57.22N	60.01 E
Verhni Trajanov Val = Upper Trajan's Wall (EN)	15	Lc	46.40N	29.00 E
Verhni Ufalej	19	Gd	56.04N	60.14 E
Verhnjaja Inta	17	Jd	65.59N	60.29 E
Verhnjaja Pyšma	17	Jh	56.59N	60.37 E
Verhnjaja Salda	17	Jg	58.02N	60.33 E
Verhnjaja Tojma	19	Ec	62.13N	45.01 E
Verhnjaja Tura	17	Ig	58.22N	59.49 E
Verhnj Uslon	7	Li	55.47N	48.58 E
Verhnoje Sinevidnoje	10	Tg	49.02N	23.36 E
Verhojansk	22	Pc	67.35N	133.27 E
Verhojanski Hrebet = Verhoyansk Mountains (EN)	21	Oc	67.00N	129.00 E
Verhoturje	17	Jg	58.52N	60.48 E
Verhovcevo	16	Ie	48.31N	34.12 E
Verhovina	15	Ha	48.08N	24.48 E
Verhovje	16	Jc	52.49N	37.14 E
Verhoyansk Mountains (EN) = Verhojanski Hrebet	21	Oc	67.00N	129.00 E
Verin	13	Ec	41.56N	7.26W
Veriora	8	Lg	58.00N	27.21 E
Verissimo, Rio-	55	Hd	18.23 S	48.20W
Verissimo, Serra do-	55	Hd	19.33 S	48.25W
Verl	12	Kc	51.53N	8.31 E
Vermand	12	Fe	49.52N	3.09 E
Vermeille, Côte-	11	Jl	42.30N	3.20 E
Vermelho, Rio- [Braz.]	55	Ib	14.26 S	46.26W
Vermelho, Rio- [Braz.]	55	Ed	19.36 S	55.58W
Vermelho, Rio- [Braz.]	55	Gb	14.54 S	51.06W
Vermenton	11	Jg	47.40N	3.44 E
Vermilion Bay	42	Ig	49.51N	93.24W
Vermilion Cliffs	46	Ih	37.10N	112.35W
Vermilion Lake	45	Jc	47.53N	92.25W
Vermilion River	44	Gb	46.16N	81.41W
Vermillion	45	He	42.47N	96.56W
Vermillion River	45	He	42.44N	96.53W
Vermillon, Rivière-	44	Kb	47.38N	72.59W
Vérmion Óros	15	Ei	40.30N	22.00 E
Vermont	43	Mc	43.50N	72.45W
Vernal	43	Fc	40.27N	109.32W
Verneuil-sur-Avre	11	Gf	48.44N	0.56 E
Vernhi Barskunčak	16	Oe	48.14N	46.42 E
Vernon [B.C.-Can.]	42	Ff	50.16N	119.16W
Vernon [Fr.]	11	He	49.05N	1.29 E
Vernon [Tx.-U.S.]	43	He	34.09N	99.17W
Vérnon Óros	15	Ei	40.39N	21.22 E
Vernou	51e	Ab	16.11N	61.39W
Verny	12	Ie	49.01N	6.12 E
Vero	13	Mb	42.00N	0.10 E
Vero Beach	43	Kf	27.38N	80.24W
Véroia	15	Fi	40.31N	22.12 E
Verona	6	Hf	45.27N	11.00 E
Verónica	56	Ie	35.22 S	57.20W
Versailles [Fr.]	11	If	48.48N	2.08 E
Versailles [In.-U.S.]	44	Ef	39.04N	85.15W
Versilia	14	Eg	43.55N	10.15 E
Veršino-Darasunski	20	Gf	52.18N	115.32 E
Veršino-Šahtaminski	20	Gf	51.16N	117.55 E
Versmold	12	Kb	52.03N	8.09 E
Verson	12	Be	49.09N	0.27W
Vert, Cap- = Vert, Cape- (EN)	30	Fg	14.43N	17.30W
Vert, Cape- (EN) = Vert, Cap-	30	Fg	14.43N	17.30W
Vertentes, Serra das-	55	Je	20.56 S	44.00W
Vértes	10	Oi	47.25N	18.20 E
Vertientes	49	Hc	21.16N	78.09W
Vertiskos Óros	15	Gi	40.50N	23.19 E
Verviers	11	Ld	50.36N	5.52 E
Vervins	12	Fe	49.50N	3.54 E
Vesanto	8	Lb	62.56N	26.25 E
Vescovato	11a	Ba	42.29N	9.26 E
Vesder/Vesdre	12	Hd	50.37N	5.37 E
Vesdre/Vesder	12	Hd	50.37N	5.37 E
Veselí nad Lužnici	10	Kg	49.11N	14.43 E
Veselovskoje Vodohranilišče	16	Lf	47.00N	41.15 E
Vešenskaja	19	Ef	49.38N	41.46 E
Vesgre	12	Df	48.53N	1.28 E
Vesijarvi	8	Kc	61.05N	25.30 E
Vesjegonsk	7	Ig	58.41N	37.16 E
Veškajma	7	Li	54.03N	47.08 E
Vesle	11	Je	49.23N	3.28 E
Vesljana	17	Gf	60.20N	54.03 E
Vesoul	11	Mg	47.38N	6.10 E
Vessigebro	8	Eh	56.59N	12.39 E
Vest-Agder	7	Bg	58.30N	7.10 E
Vestbygd	7	Bg	58.06N	6.35 E
Vesterålen	5	Hb	68.45N	15.00 E
Vesterøhavn	8	Dg	57.18N	10.56 E
Vestfjorden	5	Hb	68.35N	14.30 E
Vestfold	7	Cg	59.15N	10.10 E
Vestfonna	41	Oc	79.58N	20.15 E
Vestgrønland = West Greenland (EN)	41	He	69.00N	49.30W
Véstia	55	Ge	20.23 S	51.25W
Vestmannæyjar	7a	Bc	63.26N	20.16W
Vestnes	8	Bb	62.38N	7.06 E
Vestre Jakobselv	7	Ga	70.07N	29.25 E
Vestsjælland	8	Di	55.30N	11.30 E
Vestvågøy	7	Cb	68.15N	13.50 E
Vésubie	11	Nk	43.52N	7.12 E
Vesuvio = Vesuvius (EN)	5	Hg	40.49N	14.26 E
Vesuvius (EN) = Vesuvio	5	Hg	40.49N	14.26 E
Veszprém	10	Ni	47.10N	17.40 E
Veszprém	10	Ni	47.06N	17.55 E
Vésztő	10	Rj	46.55N	21.16 E
Vétaoundé, Ile-	57	Hf	13.15 S	167.38 E
Vetauua	63d	Ca	15.57 S	179.24W
Vétê, Pointe-	63b	Ca	13.27 S	166.41 E
Vetka	16	Gc	52.34N	31.13 E
Vetlanda	7	Dh	57.26N	15.04 E
Vetljanka	7	Mj	52.52N	51.09 E
Vetluga	5	Kd	56.18N	46.24 E
Vetluga	7	Kh	57.52N	45.46 E

Index Symbols

Independent Nation · State, Region · District, County · Municipality · Colony, Dependency · Continent · Physical Region · Historical or Cultural Region · Mount, Mountain · Volcano · Hill · Mountains, Mountain Range · Hills, Escarpment · Plateau, Upland · Pass, Gap · Plain, Lowland · Delta · Salt Flat · Valley, Canyon · Crater, Cave · Karst Features · Depression · Polder · Desert, Dunes · Forest, Woods · Heath, Steppe · Oasis · Cape, Point · Coast, Beach · Cliff · Peninsula · Isthmus · Sandbank · Island · Atoll · Rock, Reef · Islands, Archipelago · Rocks, Reefs · Coral Reef · Well, Spring · Geyser · River, Stream · Waterfall Rapids · River Mouth, Estuary · Lake · Salt Lake · Intermittent Lake · Reservoir · Swamp, Pond · Canal · Glacier · Ice Shelf, Pack Ice · Ocean · Sea · Gulf, Bay · Strait, Fjord · Lagoon · Bank · Seamount · Tablemount · Ridge · Shelf · Basin · Escarpment, Sea Scarp · Fracture · Trench, Abyss · National Park, Reserve · Point of Interest · Recreation Site · Cave, Cavern · Historic Site · Ruins · Wall, Walls · Church, Abbey · Temple · Scientific Station · Airport · Port · Lighthouse · Mine · Tunnel · Dam, Bridge

Index Symbols

Independent Nation	Historical or Cultural Region	Pass, Gap	Depression	Coast, Beach
State, Region	Mount, Mountain	Plain, Lowland	Polder	Cliff
District, County	Volcano	Delta	Desert, Dunes	Peninsula
Municipality	Hill	Salt Flat	Forest, Woods	Isthmus
Colony, Dependency	Mountains, Mountain Range	Valley, Canyon	Heath, Steppe	Sandbank
Continent	Hills, Escarpment	Crater, Cave	Oasis	Island
Physical Region	Plateau, Upland	Karst Features	Cape, Point	Atoll

Rock, Reef	Waterfall Rapids	Canal	Lagoon	Escarpment, Sea Scarp	Historic Site
Islands, Archipelago	River Mouth, Estuary	Glacier	Bank	Fracture	Ruins
Rocks, Reefs	Lake	Ice Shelf, Pack Ice	Seamount	Trench, Abyss	Wall, Walls
Coral Reef	Salt Lake	Ocean	Tablemount	National Park, Reserve	Church, Abbey
Well, Spring	Intermittent Lake	Sea	Ridge	Point of Interest	Temple
Geyser	Reservoir	Gulf, Bay	Shelf	Recreation Site	Scientific Station
River, Stream	Swamp, Pond	Strait, Fjord	Basin	Cave, Cavern	Airport
					Port
					Lighthouse
					Mine
					Tunnel
					Dam, Bridge

Index Symbols

[1] Independent Nation
[2] State, Region
[3] District, County
[4] Municipality
[5] Colony, Dependency
■ Continent
☒ Physical Region

Mount, Mountain
Volcano
Hill
Mountains, Mountain Range
Hills, Escarpment
Plateau, Upland

Pass, Gap
Plain, Lowland
Delta
Salt Flat
Valley, Canyon
Crater, Cave
Karst Features

Depression
Polder
Desert, Dunes
Forest, Woods
Heath, Steppe
Oasis
Cape, Point

Coast, Beach
Cliff
Peninsula
Isthmus
Sandbank
Island
Atoll

Rock, Reef
Islands, Archipelago
Rocks, Reefs
Coral Reef
Well, Spring
Geyser
River, Stream

Waterfall Rapids
River Mouth, Estuary
Lake
Salt Lake
Intermittent Lake
Sea
Gulf, Bay
Strait, Fjord

Canal
Glacier
Ice Shelf, Pack Ice
Ocean
Reservoir
Ridge
Shelf
Basin

Lagoon
Bank
Seamount
Tablemount
National Park, Reserve
Point of Interest
Recreation Site
Cave, Cavern

Escarpment, Sea Scarp
Fracture
Trench, Abyss
Wall, Walls
Church, Abbey
Temple
Scientific Station
Airport

Historic Site
Ruins
Wall, Walls
Church, Abbey
Temple
Scientific Station
Airport
Port
Lighthouse
Mine
Tunnel
Dam, Bridge

Wake Island [5] 58 Jd 19.18N 166.36W
Wake Island 57 Hc 19.18N 166.36 E
Wakkanai 22 Qe 45.25N 141.40 E
Wakunai 63a Ba 5.52S 155.13 E
Wakuya 29 Gb 38.33N 141.05 E
Wala 36 Fd 5.46S 32.04 E
Walachia (EN) = Valahia 5 Ig 44.00N 25.00 E
Walachia (EN) = Valahia 15 He 44.00N 25.00 E
Wałbrzych [2] 10 Mf 50.45N 16.15 E
Wałbrzych 6 He 50.46N 16.17 E
Walchensee 10 Hi 47.35N 11.20 E
Walcheren 11 Jc 51.33N 3.35 E
Walcott, Lake- 46 Ie 42.40N 113.23W
Walcourt 12 Gd 50.15N 4.25 E
Walcourt-Fraire 12 Gd 50.16N 4.30 E
Wałcz 10 Mc 53.17N 16.28 E
Waldböckelheim 12 Je 49.49N 7.43 E
Waldbröl 10 Df 50.53N 7.37 E
Waldeck 12 Kc 51.17N 8.50 E
Waldeck 12 Lc 51.12N 9.05 E
Waldems 12 Kd 50.15N 8.18 E
Walden 45 Cf 40.44N 106.17W
Waldfischbach-Burgalben 12 Je 49.17N 7.40 E
Waldkirchen 10 Jh 48.44N 13.36 E
Waldkraiburg 10 Ih 48.12N 12.25 E
Wald-Michelbach 12 Ke 49.34N 8.49 E
Waldnaab 10 Ig 49.35N 12.07 E
Waldorf 44 If 38.37N 76.54W
Waldrach 12 Ie 49.45N 6.45 E
Waldron 45 Ii 34.54N 94.05W
Waldshut 10 Ei 47.37N 8.13 E
Waldviertel 14 Jb 48.30N 15.30 E
Waleabahi, Pulau- 26 Hg 0.15S 122.20 E
Wales 40 Fc 65.36N 168.05W
Wales 42 Ic 67.50N 86.40W
Wales 5 Fe 52.30N 3.30W
Wales [2] 9 Ji 52.30N 3.30W
Walewale 34 Ec 10.21N 0.48W
Walferdange 12 Ie 49.39N 6.08 E
Walgett 58 Fh 30.01S 148.07 E
Walgreen Coast 66 Of 75.15S 105.00W
Walhalla 45 Hb 48.55N 97.55W
Walikale 36 Ec 1.25S 28.03 E
Walker 45 Ic 47.06N 94.35W
Walker Lake 43 Dd 38.40N 118.43W
Walkerston 59 Jd 21.10S 149.10 E
Wall 45 Ed 44.01N 102.14W
Wallace 46 Hc 47.28N 115.56W
Wallaceburg 44 Fd 42.36N 82.23W
Wallangarra 59 Ke 28.56S 151.56 E
Wallaroo 59 Hf 33.56S 137.38 E
Wallary Island 59 Ic 15.05S 141.50 E
Wallasey 9 Jh 53.26N 3.03W
Walla Walla 43 Db 46.08N 118.20W
Walldorf 12 Ke 49.20N 8.39 E
Wallenhorst 12 Kb 52.21N 8.01 E
Wallibu 51n Ba 13.19N 61.15W
Wallingford 12 Ac 51.36N 1.08W
Wallis, Iles- = Wallis Islands (EN) 57 Jf 13.18S 176.10W
Wallis and Futuna (EN) = Wallis-et-Futuna, Iles- [5] 58 Jf 14.00S 177.00W
Walliser Alpen/Alpes Valaisannes 14 Bd 46.10N 7.30 E
Wallis-et-Futuna, Iles- = Wallis and Futuna (EN) [5] 58 Jf 14.00S 177.00W
Wallis Islands (EN) = Wallis, Iles- 57 Jf 13.18S 176.10W
Wallowa 46 Gd 45.34N 117.32W
Wallowa Mountains 46 Gd 45.10N 117.30W
Walmer 12 Dc 51.12N 1.24 E
Walney, Isle of- 9 Jg 54.07N 3.15W
Walnut Ridge 43 Id 36.04N 90.57W
Walpole, Ile- 57 Hg 22.37S 168.57 E
Walrus Islands 40 Ge 58.45N 160.20W
Walsall 9 Li 52.35N 1.58W
Walsenburg 43 Gd 37.37N 104.47W
Walsrode 10 Fd 52.52N 9.35 E
Walterboro 44 Gi 32.54N 80.39W
Walter F. George Lake 44 Ej 31.49N 85.08W
Walter Lake 43 Dd 38.44N 118.43W
Walters 45 Gi 34.22N 98.19W
Waltershausen 10 Gf 50.54N 10.34 E
Waltham 44 Ic 45.58N 76.57W
Walton-on-the-Naze 12 Dc 51.51N 1.17 E
Waltrop 12 Jc 51.38N 7.24 E
Walvisbaai/Walvis Bay [3] 37 Ad 23.00S 14.30 E
Walvisbaai = Walvis Bay (EN) 31 Ik 22.59S 14.31 E
Walvisbaai = Walvis Bay (EN) [5] 31 Ik 22.59S 14.31 E
Walvisbaai = Walvis Bay (EN) 30 Ik 22.57S 14.30 E
Walvis Bay/Walvisbaai [3] 37 Ad 23.00S 14.30 E
Walvis Bay (EN) = Walvisbaai 30 Ik 22.57S 14.30 E
Walvis Bay (EN) = Walvisbaai 31 Ik 22.59S 14.31 E
Walvis Ridge (EN) 3 El 28.00S 3.00 E
Wamba 30 Ii 3.56S 17.12 E
Wamba [Kenya] 36 Gb 0.59N 37.19 E
Wamba [Nig.] 34 Gd 8.56N 8.36 E
Wamba [Zaire] 36 Eb 2.09N 28.00 E
Wamena 26 Kg 4.00S 138.57 E
Wami 30 Ki 6.08S 38.49 E
Wampusirpi 49 Ef 15.15N 84.37W
Wamsutter 46 Lf 41.40N 107.58W
Wan 26 Kh 8.23S 137.56 E
Wana 25 Db 32.17N 69.35 E
Wanaka 58 Hi 44.42S 169.08 E
Wanaka, Lake- 62 Cf 44.30S 169.10 E
Wan'an 27 Jf 26.32N 114.48 E
Wanapiri 26 Kg 4.33S 135.59 E
Wanapitei Lake 44 Gb 46.45N 80.45W
Wandel Hav = Wandel Sea (EN) 41 Gb 83.00N 15.00W
Wandel Sea (EN) = Wandel Hav 41 Gb 83.00N 15.00W
Wandsworth, London- 12 Bc 51.27N 0.12W
Wanganui 62 Fc 39.58S 175.00 E
Wanganui 61 Eg 39.56S 175.02 E
Wangaratta 59 Jg 36.22S 146.20 E
Wangcun [China] 28 Df 36.41N 117.42 E
Wangcun [China] 27 Jd 39.58N 112.53 E
Wangda/Zogang 27 Gf 29.37N 97.58 E
Wangdu 28 Ce 38.43N 115.09 E
Wangen in Allgäu 10 Fi 47.41N 9.50 E
Wangerooge 10 Dc 53.46N 7.55 E
Wanggameti, Gunung- 26 Hi 10.07S 120.14 E
Wanggezhuang → Jiaonan 28 Eg 35.53N 119.58 E
Wangiwangi, Pulau- 26 Hh 5.20S 123.35 E
Wangjiang 28 Di 30.08N 116.41 E
Wangkui 27 Mb 46.50N 126.29 E
Wangpan Yang 21 Of 30.33N 121.26 E
Wangping 27 Mc 43.18N 129.46 E
Wangying → Huaiyin 28 Eh 33.35N 119.02 E
Wani, Laguna- 49 Ff 14.50N 83.25W
Wanie-Rukula 36 Eb 0.14N 25.34 E
Wanitsuka-Yama 29 Bf 31.45N 131.17 E
Wanlewēyn 35 Ge 2.35N 44.55 E
Wan Namton 25 Jd 22.03N 99.33 E
Wannian (Chenying) 28 Dj 28.42N 117.04 E
Wanning 27 Jh 18.59N 110.24 E
Wanquan 28 Cd 40.52N 114.44 E
Wansbeck 9 Lf 55.10N 1.34W
Wan Shui 28 Di 30.30N 117.01 E
Wanxian 22 Mf 30.48N 108.21 E
Wanyuan 27 Ie 32.03N 108.04 E
Wanzai 28 Cj 28.06N 114.27 E
Wanzhi → Wuhu 28 Ei 31.21N 118.23 E
Wapato 46 Ec 46.27N 120.25W
Wapiti 46 Kd 44.28N 109.28W
Wapiti 42 Fe 55.08N 118.19W
Wapsipinicon River 45 Kf 41.44N 90.20W
Waqooyi Galbeed [3] 35 Gc 10.00N 44.00 E
Warangal 22 Jh 18.18N 79.35 E
Waratah Bay 59 Jg 38.50S 146.05 E
Warburg 10 Fe 51.30N 9.10 E
Warburger Borde 12 Lc 51.35N 9.12 E
Warburg-Scherfede 12 Lc 51.32N 9.02 E
Warburton Bay 42 Gd 63.50N 111.30W
Warburton Mission 59 Fe 26.10S 126.35 E
Warburton Range 59 Fe 26.10S 126.40 E
Ward 62 Fd 41.50S 174.08 E
Warden 37 De 27.56S 29.00 E
Wardenburg 12 Ka 53.04N 8.12 E
Wardha 25 Fd 20.45N 78.37 E
Ward Hunt Strait 59 Ja 9.25S 149.55 E
Ware [B.C.-Can.] 42 Ee 57.27N 125.38W
Ware [Eng.-U.K.] 12 Bc 51.49N 0.01W
Waregem 12 Fd 50.53N 3.25 E
Waremme/Borgworm 11 Ld 50.42N 5.15 E
Waren [Ger.] 10 Ic 53.31N 12.41 E
Waren [Indon.] 58 Ee 2.16S 136.20 E
Warendorf 10 De 51.57N 7.59 E
Warin Chamrap 25 Ke 15.14N 104.52 E
Warka 10 Re 51.47N 21.10 E
Warkworth 62 Fb 36.24S 174.40 E
Warmbad [3] 37 Be 28.00S 18.30 E
Warmbad [Nam.] 37 Be 28.29S 18.41 E
Warmbad [S.Afr.] 37 Dd 24.53S 28.17 E
Warming Land 41 Gb 81.50N 52.45W
Warmington 12 Ab 52.08N 1.24W
Warminster 9 Kj 51.13N 2.12W
Warm Springs [Nv.-U.S.] 46 Gg 38.13N 116.20W
Warm Springs [Or.-U.S.] 46 Ed 44.46N 121.16W
Warnemünde, Rostock- 10 Ib 54.10N 12.05 E
Warner, Mount- 46 Da 51.03N 123.12W
Warner Mountains 43 Cc 41.40N 120.20W
Warner Peak 46 Fe 42.27N 119.44W
Warner Robins 43 Ke 32.37N 83.36W
Warner Valley 46 Fe 42.30N 119.55W
Warnes 54 Fg 17.30S 63.10W
Warnow 10 Ib 54.06N 12.09 E
Waroona 59 Df 32.50S 115.55 E
Warragul 59 Jg 38.10S 145.56 E
Warrego Range 59 Je 25.00S 145.45 E
Warrego River 57 Fh 30.24S 145.21 E
Warren [Ar.-U.S.] 45 Jj 33.38N 92.05W
Warren [Mi.-U.S.] 44 Fd 42.28N 83.01W
Warren [Mn.-U.S.] 45 Hb 48.12N 96.46W
Warren [Oh.-U.S.] 43 Kc 41.15N 80.49W
Warren [Pa.-U.S.] 44 He 41.52N 79.09W
Warrenpoint/An Pointe 9 Gg 54.06N 6.15W
Warrensburg 45 Jg 38.46N 93.44W
Warrenton 37 Ce 28.09S 24.47 E
Warri 34 Gd 5.31N 5.45 E
Warrington [Eng.-U.K.] 9 Kh 53.24N 2.37W
Warrington [Fl.-U.S.] 44 Dj 30.23N 87.16W
Warrior Reefs 59 Ia 9.35S 143.10 E
Warrnambool 58 Fh 38.23S 142.29 E
Warroad 43 Hb 48.54N 95.19W
Warrumbungle Range 59 Jf 31.30S 149.40 E
Warsaw [In.-U.S.] 44 Ee 41.14N 85.51W
Warsaw [Mo.-U.S.] 45 Jg 38.15N 93.23W
Warsaw [N.Y.-U.S.] 44 Hd 42.45N 78.07W
Warsaw (EN) = Warszawa 6 Ie 52.15N 21.00 E
Warshīkh 35 He 2.18N 45.48 E
Warstein 12 Kc 51.27N 8.22 E
Warstein-Belecke 12 Kc 51.29N 8.20 E
Warszawa [2] 10 Qd 52.15N 21.00 E
Warszawa = Warsaw (EN) 6 Ie 52.15N 21.00 E
Warta 5 He 52.35N 14.39 E
Waru 26 Jg 3.24S 130.40 E
Warwich 59 Ke 28.13S 152.02 E
Warwick 9 Li 52.25N 1.30W
Warwick [Eng.-U.K.] 9 Li 52.17N 1.34W
Warwick [R.I.-U.S.] 44 Le 41.42N 71.23W
Warwickshire [3] 9 Li 52.10N 1.35W
Wasagu 34 Gc 11.22N 5.48 E
Wasatch Range 38 He 41.15N 111.30W
Wascana Creek 46 Ma 50.40N 104.55W
Wasco 46 Fi 35.36N 119.20W
Waseca 45 Jd 44.05N 93.30W
Washburn 45 Fc 47.17N 101.02W
Washess Bay 64g Ab 1.49N 157.31W
Wāshim 25 Fd 20.10N 76.58 E
Washington [2] 43 Cb 47.30N 120.30W
Washington [D.C.-U.S.] 39 Lf 38.54N 77.01W
Washington [Eng.-U.K.] 9 Lg 54.54N 1.31W
Washington [Ga.-U.S.] 44 Fi 33.44N 82.44W
Washington [Ia.-U.S.] 45 Kf 41.18N 91.42W
Washington [In.-U.S.] 44 Df 38.40N 87.10W
Washington [N.C.-U.S.] 44 Ih 35.33N 77.03W
Washington [Pa.-U.S.] 44 Ge 40.11N 80.16W
Washington → Teraina Island 57 Kd 4.43N 160.24W
Washington, Mount- 38 Le 44.15N 71.15W
Washington Court House 44 Ff 39.32N 83.29W
Washington Island 45 Md 45.23N 86.55W
Washington Land 41 Fb 80.15N 65.00W
Washita River 45 Hi 34.12N 96.50W
Washtucna 46 Fc 46.45N 118.19W
Wasile 26 If 1.04N 127.59 E
Wasilków 10 Tc 53.12N 23.12 E
Wasior 26 Jg 2.43S 134.30 E
Wāsiț [3] 24 Lf 32.35N 46.00 E
Waskaganish 39 Ld 51.25N 78.45W
Wąsosz 10 Me 51.34N 16.42 E
Waspán 47 Hf 14.44N 83.58W
Wassamu 29a Ca 44.02N 142.24 E
Wassenaar 12 Gb 52.09N 4.24 E
Wassènberg 12 Ic 51.06N 6.09 E
Wasserburg am Inn 10 Ih 48.04N 12.14 E
Wasserkuppe 10 Ff 50.30N 9.56 E
Wassigny 12 Fd 50.01N 3.36 E
Wassuk Range 46 Fg 38.40N 118.50W
Wassy 11 Kf 48.30N 4.57 E
Waswanipi, Lac- 44 Ia 49.32N 76.29W
Watampone 22 Oj 4.32S 120.20 E
Watansoppeng 26 Gg 4.21S 119.53 E
Watari 29 Gb 38.02N 140.51 E
Waterbeach 12 Cb 52.16N 0.12 E
Waterberg 37 Bd 20.25S 17.15 E
Waterbury 43 Mc 41.33N 73.02W
Water Cays 49 Ib 23.40N 77.45W
Wateree Pond 44 Gh 34.25N 80.50W
Waterford/Port Láirge 6 Fe 52.15N 7.06W
Waterford/Port Láirge [2] 9 Fi 52.10N 7.40W
Waterford Harbour/Cuan Phort Láirge 9 Gi 52.10N 6.57W
Wateringues 11 Ic 51.00N 2.30 E
Waterloo [Bel.] 11 Kd 50.43N 4.24 E
Waterloo [Ia.-U.S.] 43 Ic 42.30N 92.20W
Waterloo [Il.-U.S.] 45 Kg 38.20N 90.09W
Waterlooville 12 Ad 50.52N 1.01W
Watersmeet 44 Cb 46.18N 89.11W
Watertown [N.Y.-U.S.] 43 Lc 43.57N 75.56W
Watertown [S.D.-U.S.] 43 Hc 44.54N 97.07W
Watertown [Wi.-U.S.] 45 Le 43.12N 88.43W
Waterville 43 Nc 44.33N 69.38W
Watford 9 Mj 51.40N 0.25W
Watford City 45 Ec 47.48N 103.17W
Wa'th 35 Ed 8.10N 32.07 E
Watheroo 59 Df 30.17S 116.04 E
Watīr, Wādī- 24 Fh 29.01N 34.40 E
Watkins Glen 44 Id 42.23N 76.53W
Watling → San Salvador 47 Jd 24.02N 74.28W
Watlington 12 Ac 51.38N 1.00W
Watonga 45 Gi 35.51N 98.25W
Watou, Poperinge- 12 Ed 50.51N 2.37 E
Watrous 42 Gf 51.40N 105.28W
Watsa 31 Jh 3.03N 29.32 E
Watseka 45 Mf 40.47N 87.44W
Watsi [C.R.] 49 Fi 9.37N 82.52W
Watsi [Zaire] 36 Dc 0.19S 21.04 E
Watsi Kengo 36 Dc 0.48S 20.33 E
Watson Lake 39 Gc 60.07N 128.48W
Watsonville 46 Eh 36.55N 121.45W
Watt, Morne- 51g Bb 15.19N 61.19W
Watton 12 Cb 52.34N 0.50 E
Watts Bar Lake 44 Eh 35.48N 84.39W
Wattwil 14 Dc 47.18N 9.05 E
Watubela, Kepulauan- 26 Jg 4.35S 131.40 E
Wau 59 Ja 7.20S 146.45 E
Waubay Lake 45 Hd 45.25N 97.25W
Wauchope 59 Kf 31.27S 152.44 E
Wauchula 44 Gl 27.33N 81.49W
Waucoba Mountain 46 Fh 37.00N 118.01W
Waukara, Gunung- 26 Gg 1.15S 119.42 E
Waukarlycarly, Lake- 59 Ed 21.25S 121.50 E
Waukegan 43 Jc 42.22N 87.50W
Waukesha 45 Le 43.01N 88.14W
Waupaca 45 Ld 44.21N 89.05W
Wausau 43 Jc 44.59N 89.39W
Wauseon 44 Ee 41.33N 84.09W
Wauwatosa 45 Me 43.03N 88.00W
Wave Hill 59 Gc 17.29S 130.57 E
Waveney 9 Oi 52.28N 1.45 E
Waver/Wavre 11 Kd 50.43N 4.37 E
Waverly [Ia.-U.S.] 45 Je 42.44N 92.29W
Waverly [Oh.-U.S.] 44 Ff 39.07N 82.59W
Waverly [Tn.-U.S.] 44 Dg 36.05N 87.48W
Waves 44 Jh 35.37N 75.29W
Wavre/Waver 11 Kd 50.43N 4.37 E
Wāw 31 Jh 7.42N 28.00 E
Wawa [Nig.] 34 Fd 9.55N 4.27 E
Wawa [Ont.-Can.] 42 Jg 47.59N 84.47W
Wawa, Rio- 49 Fg 13.53N 83.28W
Wāw al Kabīr 31 If 25.20N 16.43 E
Wāw an Nāmūs 33 Ce 24.55N 19.45 E
Wāw Nahr 35 Dd 7.03N 27.13 E
Wawo 26 Hg 3.41S 121.02 E
Wawotobi 26 Hg 3.51S 122.06 E
Waxahachie 45 Hj 32.24N 96.51W
Waxweiler 12 Id 50.06N 6.22 E
Waxxari 27 Ed 38.37N 87.22 E
Way, Lake- 59 Ee 26.50S 120.20 E
Waya 63d Ab 17.18S 177.08 E
Wayabula 26 If 2.17N 128.12 E
Wayan 46 Je 43.00N 111.22W
Waycross 43 Ke 31.13N 82.21W
Wayne [Nb.-U.S.] 45 He 42.14N 97.01W
Wayne [W.V.-U.S.] 44 Ff 38.14N 82.27W
Waynesboro [Ga.-U.S.] 44 Fi 33.06N 82.01W
Waynesboro [Ms.-U.S.] 45 Lk 31.40N 88.39W
Waynesboro [Pa.-U.S.] 44 If 39.45N 77.36W
Waynesboro [Va.-U.S.] 44 Hf 38.04N 78.54W
Waynesville [Mo.-U.S.] 45 Jh 37.50N 92.12W
Waynesville [N.C.-U.S.] 44 Fh 35.29N 83.00W
Waynoka 45 Gh 36.35N 98.53W
Waziers 12 Fd 50.23N 3.07 E
Wda 10 Oc 53.25N 18.29 E
Wdzydze, Jezioro- 10 Nc 54.00N 17.50 E
Wé 61 Cd 20.55S 167.16 E
We, Pulau- 26 Ce 5.51N 95.18 E
Wear 9 Lg 54.55N 1.22W
Weatherford [Ok.-U.S.] 45 Gi 35.32N 98.42W
Weatherford [Tx.-U.S.] 43 He 32.46N 97.48W
Weaverville 46 Df 40.44N 122.56W
Weber 62 Gd 40.24S 176.20 E
Webster 45 Hd 45.20N 97.31W
Webster City 45 Je 42.28N 93.49W
Webster Springs 44 Gf 38.29N 80.25W
Weda 26 If 0.21N 127.52 E
Weda, Teluk- 26 If 0.20N 128.00 E
Weddell Island 56 Hh 51.50S 61.00W
Weddel Sea (EN) 66 Rf 72.00S 45.00W
Wedel 10 Fc 53.35N 9.41 E
Wedgeport 44 Od 43.44N 65.59W
Wedza 37 Ec 18.35S 31.35 E
Weed 46 Df 41.25N 122.27W
Weener 10 Dc 53.10N 7.21 E
Weerdinge, Emmen- 12 Ib 52.49N 6.57 E
Weert 11 Lc 51.15N 5.43 E
Weesp 12 Hb 52.18N 5.02 E
Wegberg 12 Ic 51.09N 6.16 E
Węgliniec 10 Le 51.17N 15.13 E
Węgorzewo 10 Rb 54.14N 21.44 E
Wegrów 10 Sd 52.25N 22.01 E
Wehni 35 Fc 12.40N 36.42 E
Weichang (Zhuizishan) 28 Kc 41.55N 117.45 E
Weida 10 If 50.46N 12.04 E
Weiden in der Oberpfalz 10 Ig 49.41N 12.10 E
Weifang 22 Nf 36.43N 119.06 E
Weihai 27 Ld 37.27N 122.02 E
Weihe 28 Jb 44.55N 128.23 E
Wei He 21 Nf 34.36N 110.10 E
Weilburg 10 Ef 50.29N 8.15 E
Weilerbach 12 Je 49.29N 7.38 E
Weilerswist 12 Id 50.46N 6.50 E
Weilheim in Oberbayern 10 Hi 47.50N 11.09 E
Weilmünster 12 Kd 50.26N 8.21 E
Weimar [Ger.] 12 Kd 50.46N 8.43 E
Weimar [Ger.] 10 Hf 50.59N 11.19 E
Weinan 27 Ie 34.30N 109.34 E
Weingarten 10 Fi 47.48N 9.38 E
Weinheim 10 Eg 49.33N 8.40 E
Weining 27 Hf 26.46N 104.18 E
Weinsberger Wald 14 Ib 48.25N 15.00 E
Weinstraße 12 Ke 49.20N 8.05 E
Weinviertel 14 Kb 48.35N 16.30 E
Weipa 58 Ff 12.41S 141.52 E
Weirton 44 Ge 40.24N 80.37W
Weiser 46 Gd 44.15N 116.58W
Weiser River 46 Gd 44.15N 116.59W
Weishan Hu 27 Ke 34.35N 117.15 E
Weishi 28 Cg 34.25N 114.10 E
Weishui → Jingxing 28 Ce 38.03N 114.09 E
Weiße Elster 10 He 51.26N 11.57 E
Weißenberg 12 Je 49.15N 7.49 E
Weißenburg in Bayern 10 Gg 49.02N 10.59 E
Weißenfels 10 He 51.12N 11.58 E
Weißer Main 10 Hf 50.05N 11.24 E
Weißerstein 12 Id 50.24N 6.22 E
Weißkugel/Palla Bianca 14 Ed 46.48N 10.44 E
Weiss Lake 44 Eh 34.15N 85.35W
Weißwasser/Běła Woda 10 Ke 51.31N 14.38 E
Weitra 14 Ib 48.42N 14.53 E
Weixi 27 Gf 27.13N 99.19 E
Weixian 28 Cf 36.59N 115.15 E
Weixin (Zhaxi) 27 If 27.46N 105.04 E
Weiz 14 Jc 47.13N 15.37 E
Wejherowo 10 Ob 54.37N 18.15 E
Welbourn Hill 58 Eg 27.21S 134.06 E
Welch 44 Gg 37.26N 81.36W
Weldiya 35 Fc 11.48N 39.35 E
Weld Range 59 De 26.55S 117.25 E
Welega [3] 35 Fd 8.38N 35.40 E
Welel 35 Ed 8.56N 34.52 E
Weligama 25 Gg 5.58N 80.25 E
Welkenraedt 12 Hd 50.39N 5.58 E
Welker Seamount (EN) 40 Ke 55.07N 140.20W
Welkite 35 Fd 8.17N 37.49 E
Welkom 31 Jk 27.59S 26.45 E
Welland 42 Jh 42.59N 79.15W
Welland 9 Ni 52.53N 0.02 E
Welland Canal 44 Hd 43.14N 79.13W
Wellesley Islands 57 Ef 16.45S 139.30 E
Wellin 12 Hd 50.05N 5.07 E
Wellingborough 9 Mi 52.19N 0.42W
Wellington [2] 62 Fd 40.10S 175.30 E
Wellington [Austl.] 59 Jf 32.33S 148.57 E
Wellington [Eng.-U.K.] 9 Jk 50.59N 3.14W
Wellington [Ks.-U.S.] 45 Hh 37.16N 97.24W
Wellington [Nv.-U.S.] 46 Fg 38.45N 119.22W
Wellington [N.Z.] 58 Ii 41.17S 174.46 E
Wellington, Isla- 52 Ij 49.20S 74.40W
Wellington, Lake- 59 Jg 38.10S 147.15 E
Wellington Channel 42 Ia 75.10N 93.00W
Wells [Eng.-U.K.] 9 Kj 51.13N 2.39W
Wells [Nv.-U.S.] 43 Dc 41.07N 115.01W
Wells, Lake- 59 Ee 26.45S 123.15 E
Wells, Mount- 59 Fc 17.26S 127.14 E
Wellsboro 44 Ie 41.45N 77.18W
Wellsford 62 Fb 36.18S 174.31 E
Wells-next-the-Sea 9 Ni 52.58N 0.51 E
Wellton 46 Hj 32.40N 114.08W
Welmel 35 Gd 5.35N 40.55 E
Wełna 10 Md 52.36N 16.50 E
Welo [3] 35 Fc 12.00N 40.00 E
Wels 14 Ib 48.10N 14.02 E
Welshpool 9 Ji 52.40N 3.09W
Welver 12 Jc 51.37N 7.58 E
Welwitschia 37 Ad 20.21S 14.57 E
Welwyn Garden City 9 Mj 51.48N 0.13W
Wema 36 Dc 0.26S 21.38 E
Wemding 10 Gh 48.52N 10.43 E
Wen'an 28 De 38.52N 116.30 E
Wenatchee 43 Cb 47.25N 120.19W
Wenatchee Mountains 46 Ec 47.20N 120.45W
Wenchang 27 Jh 19.43N 110.44 E
Wenchi 34 Ed 7.44N 2.06W
Wenchit 35 Fc 10.03N 38.35 E
Wenden 12 Jd 50.58N 7.52 E
Wendeng 27 Ld 37.10N 122.01 E
Wendland 10 Gc 53.10N 11.00 E
Wendo 35 Fd 6.37N 38.25 E
Wengyuan (Longxian) 27 Jg 24.21N 114.13 E
Wen He 28 Ef 37.06N 119.29 E
Wenling 27 Lf 28.23N 121.22 E
Wenquan 27 Fe 33.15N 91.55 E
Wenquan/Arixang 27 Dc 44.59N 81.04 E
Wenshan 27 Hg 23.22N 104.23 E
Wenshui 28 Bf 37.26N 112.01 E
Wensu 27 Dc 41.15N 80.14 E
Wensum 12 Db 52.37N 1.22 E
Wentworth 59 If 34.07S 141.55 E
Wenxian 27 He 32.52N 104.40 E
Wenzhou 22 Og 27.57N 120.38 E
Wenzhu 27 Jf 27.00N 114.00 E
Wepener 37 De 29.46S 27.00 E
Wépion, Namur- 12 Gd 50.25N 4.52 E
Werda 37 Ce 25.16S 23.17 E
Werder 31 Lh 7.00N 45.21 E
Werder 10 Jc 53.40N 13.25 E
Werdohl 12 Jc 51.16N 7.46 E
Were Ilu 35 Fc 10.38N 39.23 E
Werkendam 12 Gc 51.49N 4.55 E
Werl 12 Jc 51.33N 7.55 E
Werlte 12 Jb 52.51N 7.41 E
Wermelskirchen 12 Jc 51.09N 7.13 E
Werne 12 Jc 51.40N 7.38 E
Wernigerode 10 Ge 51.50N 10.47 E
Werra 5 Ge 51.26N 9.39 E
Werribee 59 Ig 37.54S 144.40 E
Werris Creek 59 Kf 31.21S 150.39 E
Werse 12 Jb 52.02N 7.41 E
Wertach 10 Gh 48.24N 10.53 E
Wertheim 10 Fg 49.45N 9.31 E
Wesel 10 Ce 51.40N 6.37 E
Weser 5 Ge 53.32N 8.34 E
Weserbergland 10 Fe 51.55N 9.30 E
Wesergebirge 10 Fd 52.15N 9.10 E
Weslaco 45 Gm 26.09N 98.01W
Wesley 51g Ba 15.34N 61.19W
Wesleyville 42 Mg 49.09N 53.34W
Wessel, Cape- 59 Hb 11.00S 136.45 E
Wesseling 12 Id 50.50N 6.59 E
Wessel Islands 57 Ef 12.00S 136.45 E
Wessington Springs 45 Gd 44.05N 98.34W
West Allis 45 Me 43.01N 88.00W
West Baines River 59 Gc 15.26S 130.08 E
West Bay 45 Ll 29.00N 89.30W
West Bend 45 Le 43.25N 88.11W
West Bengal [3] 25 Hd 24.00N 88.00 E
West Berlin (EN) = Berlin 6 He 52.31N 13.24 E
West Branch 44 Ec 44.17N 84.14W
West Bridgford 12 Ab 52.55N 1.07W
West Bromwich 9 Li 52.31N 1.59W
Westbrook 44 Ld 43.41N 70.21W
West Burra 9 La 60.05N 1.10W
West Caicos 49 Kc 21.47N 72.17W
West Cape 57 Hi 45.55S 166.26 E
West Caroline Basin (EN) 3 Ii 4.00N 138.00 E
West Carpathians (EN) = Západné Karpaty 10 Og 49.30N 19.00 E
West Des Moines 45 Jf 41.35N 93.43W
Westdongeradeel 12 Ha 53.23N 5.58 E
Westdongeradeel-Holwerd 12 Ha 53.22N 5.54 E
Westdongeradeel-Ternaard 12 Ha 53.23N 5.58 E
Westeinderplassen 12 Gb 52.15N 4.30 E
West Elk Mountains 45 Cg 38.40N 107.15W
West End 44 Hl 26.41N 78.58W
Westende, Middelkerke- 12 Ec 51.10N 2.46 E
West End Village 51b Ab 18.11N 63.09W
West Entrance 64a Bb 7.57N 134.30 E
Westerbork 12 Ib 52.51N 6.36 E
Westerburg 12 Jd 50.34N 7.59 E
Westerland 10 Eb 54.54N 8.18 E
Westerlo 12 Gc 51.05N 4.55 E
Western [Ghana] [3] 34 Ed 5.30N 2.30W
Western [Kenya] [3] 36 Fb 0.30N 34.35 E
Western [S.L.] [3] 34 Cd 8.20N 13.00W
Western [Ug.] [3] 36 Fb 1.00N 31.00 E
Western [Zam.] [3] 36 Df 15.00S 24.00 E
Western Australia [2] 59 Ed 25.00S 122.00 E
Western Desert (EN) = Gharbīyah, Aş' Şaḩrā' Al- 30 Jf 27.30N 28.00 E
Western Dvina (EN) = Zapadnaja Dvina 5 Id 57.04N 24.03 E
Western Entrance 63a Bb 6.55S 155.40 E
Western Ghats/Sahyadri 21 Jh 14.00N 75.00 E
Western Isles [3] 9 Fd 57.40N 7.10W
Western Port 59 Jg 38.25S 145.10 E
Western River 42 Gc 66.22N 107.15W
Western Sahara (EN) [5] 31 Ff 24.30N 13.00W

Index Symbols

[1] Independent Nation
[2] State, Region
[3] District, County
[4] Municipality
[5] Colony, Dependency
Continent
Physical Region
Historical or Cultural Region
Mount, Mountain
Volcano
Hill
Mountains, Mountain Range
Hills, Escarpment
Plateau, Upland
Pass, Gap
Plain, Lowland
Delta
Salt Flat
Valley, Canyon
Crater, Cave
Karst Features
Depression
Polder
Desert, Dunes
Forest, Woods
Heath, Steppe
Oasis
Cape, Point
Coast, Beach
Cliff
Peninsula
Isthmus
Sandbank
Island
Atoll
Rock, Reef
Islands, Archipelago
Rocks, Reefs
Coral Reef
Well, Spring
Geyser
River, Stream
Waterfall Rapids
River Mouth, Estuary
Lake
Salt Lake
Intermittent Lake
Reservoir
Swamp, Pond
Canal
Glacier
Ice Shelf, Pack Ice
Ocean
Sea
Gulf, Bay
Strait, Fjord
Lagoon
Bank
Seamount
Tablemount
Ridge
Shelf
Basin
Escarpment, Sea Scarp
Fracture
Trench, Abyss
National Park, Reserve
Point of Interest
Recreation Site
Cave, Cavern
Historic Site
Ruins
Wall, Walls
Church, Abbey
Temple
Scientific Station
Airport
Port
Lighthouse
Mine
Tunnel
Dam, Bridge

Western Samoa (EN)= Samoa I Sisifo [1] 58 Jf 13.40S 172.30W
Western Sayans (EN)= Zapadny Sajan 21 Ld 53.00N 94.00 E
Western Sierra Madre (EN) =Madre Occidental, Sierra- 38 Ig 25.00N 105.00W
Western Turkistan (EN) 21 He 41.00N 60.00 E
Westerschelde=West Schelde (EN) 11 Jc 51.25N 3.45 E
Westerschouwen 12 Fc 51.41N 3.43 E
Westerschouwen-Haamstede 12 Fc 51.42N 3.45 E
Westerstede 10 Dc 53.15N 7.56 E
Westerwald 10 Df 50.40N 7.55 E
Westerwoldse A 12 Ja 53.10N 7.10 E
West European Basin (EN) 3 De 47.00N 15.00W
West Falkland 52 Kk 51.40S 60.00W
West Falkland/Gran Malvina, Isla- 52 Kk 51.40S 60.00W
West Fayu Island 57 Fd 8.05N 146.44 E
West Fork Big Blue River 45 Hf 40.42N 96.59W
Westfriesland=West Friesland (EN) 11 Kb 52.45N 4.50 E
West Friesland (EN)= Westfriesland 11 Kb 52.45N 4.50 E
West Frisian Islands (EN)= Waddeneilanden 11 Ka 53.30N 5.00 E
Westgate-on-Sea 12 Dc 51.22N 1.21 E
West Glacier 46 Ib 48.30N 113.59W
West Glamorgan [3] 9 Jj 51.40N 3.55W
West Grand Lake 44 Nc 45.15N 67.52W
West Greenland (EN) = Vestgrønland [2] 41 He 69.00N 49.30W
West Helena 45 Ki 34.33N 90.39W
West Hollywood 44 Gm 25.59N 80.11W
Westhope 45 Fb 48.55N 101.01W
West Ice Shelf 66 Ge 67.00S 85.00 E
West Indies 47 Je 19.00N 70.00W
West Indies (EN)=Indias Occidentales 47 Je 19.00N 70.00W
West Island 37b Ab 9.22S 46.13 E
Westkapelle 12 Fc 51.31N 3.26 E
Westkapelle, Knokke- 12 Fc 51.19N 3.18 E
West Lafayette 44 De 40.27N 86.55W
Westland [2] 62 De 43.10S 170.30 E
West Liberty 44 Fg 37.55N 83.16W
Westlock 42 Gf 54.09N 113.52W
West Lunga 36 De 13.06S 24.39 E
Westmalle 12 Gc 51.18N 4.41 E
West Mariana Basin (EN) 3 Ih 15.00N 137.00 E
Westmeath/An Iarmhí [2] 9 Fh 53.30N 7.30W
West Melanesian Trench (EN) 60 Dh 1.00S 150.00 E
West Memphis 43 Id 35.08N 90.11W
West Mersea 12 Cc 51.46N 0.54 E
West Midlands [3] 9 Li 52.30N 2.00W
Westminster 44 If 39.35N 76.59W
Westminster, London- 12 Bc 51.30N 0.07W
West Monroe 45 Jj 32.31N 92.09W
Westmorland 9 Kg 54.30N 2.40W
West Nicholson 31 Jk 21.03S 29.22 E
West Nueces River 45 Gl 29.16N 99.56W
Weston [Mala.] 26 Ge 5.13N 115.36 E
Weston [W.V.-U.S.] 44 Gf 39.03N 80.28W
Weston [Wy.-U.S.] 46 Md 44.42N 105.18W
Weston-super-Mare 9 Kj 51.21N 2.59W
Westoverledingen 12 Ja 53.10N 7.27 E
Westoverledingen - Ihrhove 12 Ja 53.10N 7.27 E
West Palm Beach 39 Kg 26.43N 80.04W
West Pensacola 44 Dj 30.27N 87.15W
West Plains 43 Id 36.44N 91.51W
West Point [Ms.-U.S.] 45 Lj 33.36N 88.39W
West Point [Nb.-U.S.] 45 Hf 41.51N 96.43W
Westport 58 Ii 41.45S 171.36 E
Westport/Cathair na Mart 9 Dh 53.48N 9.32W
Westray 9 Kb 59.20N 3.00W
Westree 44 Gb 47.27N 81.32W
Westrich 12 Je 49.20N 7.25 E
West Road 12 Cd 50.52N 0.50 E
West Schelde (EN)= Westerschelde 11 Jc 51.25N 3.45 E
West Scotia Basin (EN) 52 Kk 57.00S 53.00W
West Siberian Plain (EN)= Zapadno Sibirskaja Ravnina 21 Jc 60.00N 75.00 E
Weststellingwerf 12 Ib 52.53N 6.00 E
Weststellingwerf-Wolvega 12 Ib 52.53N 6.00 E
West Sussex [3] 9 Mk 51.00N 0.40W
West Tavaputs Plateau 46 Jf 40.00N 110.25W
West-Terschelling, Terschelling- 12 Ha 53.21N 5.13 E
West Union [Ia.-U.S.] 45 Ke 42.57N 91.49W
West Union [Oh.-U.S.] 44 Ff 38.48N 83.33W
West Virginia [2] 43 Kd 38.45N 80.30W
West-Vlaanderen [3] 12 Ec 51.00N 3.00 E
Westwood 46 Ef 40.18N 121.00W
West Wyalong 59 Jf 33.55S 147.13 E
West Yellowstone 43 Eb 44.30N 111.05W
West Yorkshire [3] 9 Lh 53.40N 1.30W
Wetar, Pulau- 57 De 7.48S 126.18 E
Wetaskiwin 42 Gf 52.58N 113.22W
Wete 36 Gd 5.04S 39.43 E
Wětošow/Vetschau 10 Ke 51.47N 14.04 E
Wetter 12 Kd 50.18N 8.49 E
Wetter (Hessen) 12 Kd 50.54N 8.43 E
Wetter (Ruhr) 12 Jc 51.23N 7.24 E
Wetterau 10 Ef 50.15N 8.50 E
Wetteren 11 Jc 51.00N 3.53 E
Wetzlar 10 Ef 50.33N 8.30 E
Wevelgem 12 Fd 50.48N 3.10 E
Wewahitchka 44 Ej 30.07N 85.12W
Wewak 58 Fe 3.34S 143.38 E
Wexford/Loch Garman [2] 9 Gi 52.20N 6.40W
Wexford/Loch Garman 6 Fe 52.20N 6.27W
Wexford Harbour/Cuan Loch Garman 9 Gi 52.20N 6.25W
Wey 9 Mj 51.23N 0.28W
Weyburn 42 Hg 49.41N 103.52W
Weyhe 12 Kb 52.59N 8.52 E
Weyhe-Leeste 12 Kb 52.59N 8.50 E
Weymouth 9 Kk 50.36N 2.28W
Wezet/Visé 12 Hd 50.44N 5.42 E
Whakatane 61 Eg 37.58S 177.00 E
Whale Cove 42 Id 62.14N 92.10W
Whalsay 9 Ma 60.22N 0.59W
Whangarei 58 Ih 35.43S 174.19 E
Wharfe 9 Lh 53.51N 1.07W
Wharton 45 Hl 29.19N 96.06W
Wharton Basin (EN) 3 Hk 19.00S 100.00 E
Wharton Lake 42 Hd 64.00N 99.55W
Whataroa 62 De 43.16S 170.22 E
Wheatland 46 Me 42.03N 104.57W
Wheat Ridge 45 Dg 39.46N 105.07W
Wheeler 42 Ke 57.02N 67.14W
Wheeler 46 Dd 45.42N 123.52W
Wheeler Lake 44 Dh 34.40N 87.05W
Wheeler Peak [N.M.-U.S.] 43 Fd 36.34N 105.25W
Wheeler Peak [U.S.] 38 Hf 38.59N 114.19W
Wheeling 43 Kc 40.05N 80.43W
Whidbey Island 46 Db 48.15N 122.40W
Whitby 9 Mg 54.29N 0.37W
Whitchurch [Eng.-U.K.] 9 Ki 52.58N 2.41W
Whitchurch [Eng.-U.K.] 12 Bc 51.53N 0.50W
Whitchurch [Eng.-U.K.] 12 Ac 51.13N 1.20W
White 42 Jc 65.50N 85.00W
White, Lake- 59 Fd 21.05S 129.00 E
White Bay 38 Nd 50.00N 56.30W
White Bear Lake 45 Jd 45.04N 93.01W
White Butte 45 Ec 46.23N 103.19W
White Carpathians (EN) = Bílé Karpaty 10 Nh 48.55N 17.50 E
White Cliffs 59 If 30.51S 143.05 E
White Cloud 44 Ed 43.33N 85.46W
Whitecourt 42 Ff 54.09N 115.41W
Whitefish 43 Eb 48.25N 114.20W
Whitefish Bay 43 Kb 46.40N 84.50W
Whitefish Point 44 Eb 46.45N 85.00W
Whitefish Range 46 Hb 48.40N 114.26W
Whitehall [Mi.-U.S.] 44 Dd 43.24N 86.21W
Whitehall [Mt.-U.S.] 46 Id 45.52N 112.06W
Whitehall [Oh.-U.S.] 44 Ff 39.58N 82.54W
Whitehall [Wi.-U.S.] 45 Kd 44.22N 91.19W
Whitehaven 9 Jg 54.33N 3.35W
Whitehorse 39 Fc 60.43N 135.03W
White Island [Ant.] 66 Ee 66.44S 48.35 E
White Island [N.Z.] 62 Gb 37.30S 177.10 E
White Lake 45 Jl 29.45N 92.30W
White Lake (EN)=Beloje Ozero 5 Jc 60.11N 37.35 E
Whiteman Range 59 Ja 5.50S 149.55 E
Whitemark 59 Jh 40.07S 148.01 E
White Mountain 40 Db 64.35N 163.04W
White Mountain Peak 43 Dd 37.38N 118.15W
White Mountains [Ak.-U.S.] 40 Jc 65.30N 147.00W
White Mountains [U.S.] 46 Fh 37.30N 118.15W
White Mountains [U.S.] 43 Mc 44.10N 71.35W
Whitemouth Lake 45 Ib 49.14N 95.40W
Whitemouth River 45 Ha 50.07N 96.02W
White Nile (EN)=Abyaḍ, Al Baḥr al- 30 Kg 15.38N 32.31 E
White Nile (EN)=Abyaḍ, Al Baḥr al- [3] 35 Ec 12.40N 32.30 E
White Pass [N.Amer.] 40 Le 59.37N 135.08W
White Pass [Wa.-U.S.] 46 Ec 46.38N 121.24W
Whiteriver 46 Kj 33.50N 109.58W
White River [In.-U.S.] 44 Df 38.25N 87.44W
White River [Nv.-U.S.] 46 Hh 37.18N 115.08W
White River [Ont.-Can.] 42 Ig 48.35N 85.17W
White River [S.D.-U.S.] 45 Fe 43.34N 100.45W
White River [Tx.-U.S.] 45 Fj 33.14N 100.56W
White River [U.S.] 46 Kf 40.04N 109.41W
White River [U.S.] 43 Hc 43.45N 99.30W
White River [U.S.] 38 Jf 33.53N 91.03W
White River [Yuk.-Can.] 42 Dd 63.10N 139.32W
White Salmon 46 Ed 45.44N 121.29W
Whitesand Bay 9 Ik 50.20N 4.35W
White Sea (EN)=Beloje More 5 Kb 66.00N 44.00 E
White sea-Baltic Canal (EN) =Belomorsko-Baltijski Kanal 5 Jc 63.30N 34.48 E
White Settlement 45 Hj 32.45N 97.27W
White Sulphur Springs 46 Jc 46.33N 110.54W
Whiteville 44 Hh 34.20N 78.42W
White Volta 30 Gh 8.38N 0.59W
White Volta (EN)=Volta Blanche 30 Gh 8.38N 0.59W
Whitewater 45 Bg 38.59N 108.27W
Whitewater Baldy 45 Bj 33.20N 108.39W
Whitewater Bay 44 Gm 25.16N 81.00W
Whitewater Lake 45 La 50.50N 89.10W
Whitewood 45 Ea 50.20N 102.15W
Whitianga 62 Fb 36.50S 175.42 E
Whitmore Mountains 66 Og 82.35S 104.30W
Whitney 44 Hc 45.30N 78.14W
Whitney, Lake- 45 Hk 31.55N 97.23W
Whitney, Mount- 38 Hf 36.35N 118.18W
Whitstable 12 Dc 51.21N 1.06 E
Whitsunday Island 59 Jd 20.15S 149.00 E
Whittier 40 Jd 60.46N 148.41W
Whittlesea 59 Jg 37.31S 145.07 E
Whittlesey 12 Bb 52.33N 0.08W
Wholdaia Lake 42 Hd 60.45N 104.10W
Whyalla 59 Hf 33.02S 137.35 E
Wiarton 44 Gc 44.45N 81.09W
Wiawso 34 Ed 6.12N 2.29W
Wibaux 46 Mc 46.59N 104.11W
Wichita 39 Jf 37.41N 97.20W
Wichita Falls 39 Jf 33.54N 98.30W
Wichita Mountains 45 Gi 34.45N 98.40W
Wichita River 45 Gi 34.07N 98.10W
Wick 9 Jc 58.26N 3.06W
Wick 9 Jc 58.25N 3.05W
Wickenburg 46 Ij 33.58N 112.44W
Wickepin 59 Df 32.46S 117.30 E
Wickham 12 Ad 50.54N 1.10W
Wickham Market 12 Db 52.09N 1.22 E
Wickiup Reservoir 46 Ee 43.40N 121.43W
Wickliffe 44 Cg 36.58N 89.05W
Wicklow/Cill Mhantáin [2] 9 Gi 53.00N 6.30W
Wicklow/Cill Mhantáin 9 Gi 52.59N 6.03W
Wicklow Head/Ceann Chill Mhantáin 9 Hi 52.58N 6.00W
Wicklow Mountains/ Sléibhte Chill Mhantáin 9 Gh 53.02N 6.24W
Wicko, Jezioro- 10 Mb 54.33N 16.35 E
Wickrath, Mönchengladbach- 12 Ic 51.08N 6.25 E
Widawa 10 Me 51.13N 16.55 E
Wide Bay 59 Ka 5.05S 152.05 E
Widefield 45 Dg 38.42N 104.40W
Widgiemooltha 59 Ef 31.30S 121.34 E
Wi-Do 28 Ig 35.38N 126.17 E
Więcbork 10 Nc 53.22N 17.30 E
Wied 12 Jd 50.27N 7.28 E
Wiedenbrück 12 Kc 50.51N 8.19 E
Wiehengebirge 12 Ed 52.20N 8.40 E
Wiehl 12 Jd 50.57N 7.32 E
Wieliczka 10 Qg 49.59N 20.04 E
Wielimie, Jezioro- 10 Mc 53.47N 16.50 E
Wielki Dział 10 Tf 50.18N 23.25 E
Wielkopolska 10 Ne 51.50N 17.20 E
Wielkopolskie-Kujawskie, Pojezierze- 10 Md 52.25N 16.30 E
Wieluń 10 Oe 51.14N 18.34 E
Wien [2] 14 Kb 48.15N 16.25 E
Wien = Vienna (EN) 6 Hf 48.12N 16.22 E
Wiener Becken 14 Kc 48.00N 16.28 E
Wiener Neustadt 14 Kc 47.48N 16.15 E
Wienerwald=Vienna Woods (EN) 14 Jb 48.10N 16.00 E
Wieprz 10 Re 51.32N 21.49 E
Wieprza 10 Mb 54.26N 16.22 E
Wieprz-Krzna, Kanał- 10 Se 51.56N 22.56 E
Wierden 12 Ib 52.22N 6.36 E
Wieringen 12 Hb 52.56N 5.02 E
Wieringen-Den Oever 12 Hb 52.56N 5.02 E
Wieringen-Hippolytushoef 12 Gb 52.54N 4.59 E
Wieringermeer 12 Hb 52.51N 5.01 E
Wieringermeer Polder 12 Gb 52.50N 5.00 E
Wieringermeer-Wieringerwerf 12 Hb 52.51N 5.01 E
Wieringerwerf, Wieringermeer- 12 Hb 52.51N 5.01 E
Wieruszów 10 Oe 51.18N 18.08 E
Wierzchowo, Jezioro- 10 Mc 53.50N 16.45 E
Wierzyca 10 Oc 53.51N 18.50 E
Wiesbaden 6 Ge 50.05N 8.15 E
Wiese 10 Di 47.35N 7.35 E
Wieslautern 12 Je 49.05N 7.49 E
Wiesloch 10 Eg 49.18N 8.42 E
Wietingsmoor 12 Kb 52.39N 8.39 E
Wietmarschen 12 Jb 52.32N 7.08 E
Wieżyca 10 Ob 54.17N 18.10 E
Wigan 9 Kh 53.32N 2.35W
Wigger 14 Bc 47.15N 7.55 E
Wiggins 45 Lk 30.51N 89.08W
Wight, Isle of- 5 Fe 50.40N 1.20W
Wigry, Jezioro- 10 Tb 54.05N 23.07 E
Wigston 12 Ab 52.35N 1.06W
Wigtown 9 Ig 54.52N 4.26W
Wigtown Bay 9 Ig 54.46N 4.15W
Wijchen 12 Hc 51.48N 5.44 E
Wijdefjorden 41 Nc 79.50N 15.30 E
Wijk bij Duurstede 12 Hc 51.59N 5.22 E
Wil 14 Dc 47.27N 9.05 E
Wilbur 46 Fc 47.46N 118.42W
Wilburton 45 Ii 34.55N 95.19W
Wilcannia 58 Fh 31.34S 143.23 E
Wild Coast 30 Jl 32.00S 29.50 E
Wilder Seamount (EN) 57 Jd 9.00N 173.00W
Wildeshausen 10 Ed 52.54N 8.26 E
Wild Horse 46 Jb 49.01N 110.12W
Wildspitze 14 Ed 46.53N 10.52 E
Wilga 10 Re 51.50N 21.20 E
Wilhelm-II-Land 66 Ge 69.00S 90.00 E
Wilhelminakanaal 12 Gc 51.43N 4.53 E
Wilhelmshaven 10 Ec 53.31N 8.08 E
Wilhelmstal 37 Bd 21.54S 16.20 E
Wilkes-Barre 43 Lc 41.15N 75.50W
Wilkesboro 44 Gg 36.09N 81.09W
Wilkes Land (EN) 66 Hf 71.00S 120.00 E
Wilkins Coast 66 Qe 69.40S 63.00W
Wilkins Sound 66 Qf 70.15S 73.00W
Willamette River 46 Dd 45.39N 122.46W
Willandra Billabong Creek 59 If 33.08S 144.06 E
Willapa Bay 46 Dc 46.37N 124.00W
Willard 45 Ci 34.36N 106.02W
Willards, Punta- 48 Cc 28.50N 112.35W
Willcox 46 Kj 32.15N 109.50W
Willebadessen 12 Lc 51.38N 9.02 E
Willebadessen-Peckelsheim 12 Lc 51.36N 9.08 E
Willebroek 12 Gc 51.04N 4.22 E
Willemstad [Neth.] 12 Gc 51.41N 4.26 E
Willemstad [Neth.Ant.] 53 Jd 12.06N 68.56W
Willeroo 59 Gc 15.17S 131.35 E
William Bill Dannelly Reservoir 44 Di 32.15N 86.45W
Williams 43 Ed 35.15N 112.11W
Williamsburg [Ky.-U.S.] 44 Eg 36.44N 84.10W
Williamsburg [Va.-U.S.] 44 Ig 37.17N 76.43W
Williams Lake 42 Ff 52.08N 122.09W
Williamson Glacier 66 He 66.30S 114.30 E
Williamsport 43 Lc 41.16N 77.03W
Williamston 44 Ih 35.50N 77.06W
Williamstown 44 Ef 38.38N 84.34W
Willich 12 Ic 51.16N 6.33 E
Willikie's 51d Bb 17.03N 61.42W
Willingdon, Mount- 46 Ga 51.48N 116.17W
Willis Group 57 Gf 16.20S 150.00 E
Williston [N.D.-U.S.] 43 Gb 48.09N 103.37W
Williston [S.Afr.] 37 Cf 31.20S 20.53 E
Williston Lake 38 Gd 50.57N 122.23W
Willits 46 Dg 39.25N 123.21W
Willmar 43 Hb 45.07N 95.03W
Willoughby Bay 51d Bb 17.02N 61.44W
Willow Bunch Lake 46 Mb 49.27N 105.28W
Willowlake 42 Fd 62.42N 123.08W
Willowmore 37 Cf 33.17S 23.29 E
Willows 46 Dg 39.31N 122.12W
Willow Springs 45 Kh 36.59N 91.58W
Wills, Lake- 59 Fd 21.20S 128.40 E
Wills Point 45 Ij 32.43N 95.57W
Wilma Glacier 66 Ee 67.12S 56.00 E
Wilmington [De.-U.S.] 43 Ld 39.44N 75.33W
Wilmington [N.C.-U.S.] 39 Lf 34.14N 77.55W
Wilmington [Oh.-U.S.] 44 Ff 39.28N 83.50W
Wilnsdorf 12 Kd 50.49N 8.06 E
Wilseder Berg 10 Fc 53.10N 9.56 E
Wilson 43 Ld 35.44N 77.55W
Wilson, Cape- 42 Jc 66.59N 81.27W
Wilson, Mount- 45 Ch 37.51N 107.59W
Wilson Bluff 66 Ff 74.20S 66.47 E
Wilson Lake [Al.-U.S.] 44 Dh 34.49N 87.30W
Wilson Lake [Ks.-U.S.] 45 Gg 38.57N 98.40W
Wilsons Promontory 59 Jg 38.55S 146.20 E
Wilton River 59 Gb 14.45S 134.33 E
Wilts 9 Lj 51.20N 2.00W
Wiltshire [3] 9 Lj 51.30N 2.00W
Wiltz 11 Le 49.58N 5.55 E
Wiluna 59 Ee 26.36S 120.13 E
Wimereux 12 Dd 50.46N 1.37 E
Winamac 44 De 41.03N 86.36W
Winburg 37 De 28.37S 27.00 E
Winchelsea 12 Cd 50.55N 0.43 E
Winchester [Eng.-U.K.] 9 Lj 51.04N 1.19W
Winchester [In.-U.S.] 44 Ee 40.10N 84.59W
Winchester [Ky.-U.S.] 44 Ef 38.01N 84.11W
Winchester [Va.-U.S.] 43 Ld 39.11N 78.12W
Windeck 12 Jd 50.49N 7.34 E
Windemin, Pointe- 63b Cc 16.34S 167.27 E
Winder 44 Fi 34.00N 83.47W
Windermere 9 Kg 54.22N 2.56W
Windermere [B.C.-Can.] 46 Ha 50.30N 115.58W
Windermere [Eng.-U.K.] 9 Kg 54.23N 2.54W
Windhoek 31 Ik 22.34S 17.06 E
Windhoek [3] 37 Bd 22.30S 17.00 E
Windischgarsten 14 Ic 47.43N 14.20 E
Wind Mountain 45 Dj 32.02N 105.34W
Windom 45 Ie 43.52N 95.07W
Windom Mountain 45 Ch 37.37N 107.35W
Windorah 59 Ie 25.26S 142.39 E
Window Rock 46 Ki 35.41N 109.03W
Wind River 46 Ke 43.08N 108.12W
Wind River Peak 46 Ke 42.42N 109.07W
Wind River Range 43 Fc 43.05N 109.25W
Windrush 9 Lj 51.42N 1.25W
Windsor [Eng.-U.K.] 9 Mj 51.29N 0.38W
Windsor [N.S.-Can.] 42 Lh 44.59N 64.09W
Windsor [Ont.-Can.] 42 Jh 42.18N 83.01W
Windsor Forest 44 Gj 31.58N 81.10W
Windward Islands 47 Lf 13.00N 61.00W
Windward Islands (EN)= Barlovento, Islas de- 38 Mh 15.00N 61.00W
Windward Islands (EN) = Sotavento, Islas de- 52 Jd 11.10N 67.00W
Windward Islands (EN)= Vent, Îles du- 57 Mf 17.30S 149.30W
Windward Passage (EN)= Vent, Canal du- 49 Lh 20.00N 73.50W
Windward Passage (EN)= Vientos, Paso de los- 38 Lh 20.00N 73.50W
Winfield [Al.-U.S.] 44 Di 33.56N 87.49W
Winfield [Ks.-U.S.] 43 Hd 37.15N 96.59W
Wingene 12 Fc 51.04N 3.16 E
Wingen-sur-Moder 12 Jf 48.55N 7.22 E
Winisk 38 Kd 55.17N 85.05W
Winisk 39 Kd 55.15N 85.12W
Winisk Lake 42 If 52.55N 87.20W
Winkler 45 Hb 49.11N 97.56W
Winklern 14 Gd 46.52N 12.52 E
Winneba 34 Ed 5.20N 0.37W
Winnebago, Lake- 43 Jc 44.00N 88.25W
Winnemucca 43 Dc 40.58N 117.44W
Winnemucca Lake 46 Ff 40.10N 119.20W
Winner 43 Hc 43.22N 99.51W
Winnett 46 Kc 47.00N 108.21W
Winnfield 45 Jk 31.55N 92.38W
Winnibigoshish, Lake- 45 Ic 47.27N 94.12W
Winnipeg 39 Je 49.53N 97.09W
Winnipeg 38 Jd 50.38N 96.19W
Winnipeg, Lake- 38 Jd 52.00N 97.00W
Winnipeg Beach 45 Ha 50.31N 96.58W
Winnipegosis 42 Hf 51.39N 99.56W
Winnipegosis, Lake- 38 Jd 52.30N 100.00W
Winnipesaukee, Lake- 44 Ld 43.35N 71.20W
Winnsboro 45 Kj 32.10N 91.43W
Winnweiler 12 Je 49.34N 7.51 E
Winona [Mn.-U.S.] 43 Ic 44.03N 91.39W
Winona [Mo.-U.S.] 45 Kh 37.06N 91.19W
Winona [Ms.-U.S.] 45 Lj 33.29N 89.44W
Winschoten 11 Na 53.08N 7.02 E
Winsen 10 Gc 53.22N 10.13 E
Winslow [Az.-U.S.] 43 Ed 35.01N 110.42W
Winslow [Eng.-U.K.] 12 Bc 51.57N 0.52W
Winslow Reef 57 Je 1.36S 174.57W
Winston-Salem 43 Kd 36.06N 80.15W
Winterberg 10 Ee 51.12N 8.32 E
Winter Harbour 42 Gb 74.46N 110.40W
Winter Haven 43 Kf 28.01N 81.44W
Winter Park [Co.-U.S.] 45 Dg 39.47N 105.45W
Winter Park [Fl.-U.S.] 44 Gk 28.36N 81.20W
Winters 45 Gk 31.57N 99.58W
Winterset 45 If 41.20N 94.01W
Winterswijk 11 Mc 51.58N 6.44 E
Winterthur 14 Cc 47.30N 8.45 E
Winton [Austl.] 58 Fg 22.23S 143.02 E
Winton [N.C.-U.S.] 44 Ig 36.24N 76.56W
Winton [N.Z.] 62 Cg 46.09S 168.20 E
Wipper [Ger.] 10 He 51.20N 11.10 E
Wipper [Ger.] 10 He 51.47N 11.42 E
Wisbech 9 Ni 52.40N 0.10 E
Wiscasset 44 Mc 44.00N 69.40W
Wisch 12 Ic 51.55N 6.22 E
Wisch-Terborg 12 Ic 51.55N 6.22 E
Wisconsin [2] 43 Jc 44.45N 89.30W
Wisconsin 38 Je 43.00N 91.15W
Wisconsin Range 66 Ng 85.45S 125.00W
Wisconsin Rapids 43 Jc 44.23N 89.49W
Wiseman 40 Ic 67.25N 150.06W
Wisła 10 Og 49.39N 18.50 E
Wisła=Vistula (EN) 5 He 54.22N 18.55 E
Wiślana, Mierzeja- 10 Pb 54.25N 19.30 E
Wiślane, Żuławy- 10 Ob 54.10N 19.00 E
Wiślany, Zalew- 10 Pb 54.27N 19.40 E
Wisłok 10 Sf 50.13N 22.32 E
Wisłoka 10 Rf 50.27N 21.23 E
Wismar 10 Hc 53.54N 11.28 E
Wismarbucht 10 Hc 53.57N 11.25 E
Wissant 12 Dd 50.53N 1.40 E
Wissembourg 11 Ne 49.02N 7.57 E
Wissen 10 Df 50.47N 7.45 E
Wissenkerke 12 Fc 51.35N 3.45 E
Wissey 12 Cb 52.34N 0.21 E
Witbank 31 Jk 25.56S 29.07 E
Witchekan Lake 45 Fb 49.15N 100.16W
Witdraai 37 Ce 26.58S 20.41 E
Witham 12 Cc 51.47N 0.38 E
Witham 9 Ni 52.56N 0.04 E
Withernsea 9 Nh 53.44N 0.02 E
Witkowo 10 Nd 52.27N 17.47 E
Witmarsum, Wonseradeel- 12 Ha 53.06N 5.28 E
Witney 9 Lj 51.48N 1.29W
Witnica 10 Kd 52.40N 14.55 E
Witputz 37 Be 27.37S 16.42 E
Witten 10 De 51.26N 7.20 E
Wittenberg [Ger.] 10 Ie 51.52N 12.39 E
Wittenberg [Wi.-U.S.] 45 Ld 44.49N 89.10W
Wittenberge 10 Hc 53.00N 11.45 E
Wittenoom 59 Dd 22.17S 118.19 E
Wittingen 10 Gd 52.44N 10.43 E
Wittlich 10 Cg 49.59N 6.53 E
Wittmund 10 Dc 53.34N 7.47 E
Wittow 10 Jb 54.38N 13.19 E
Wittstock 10 Ic 53.09N 12.30 E
Witu 36 Hc 2.23S 40.26 E
Witu Islands 60 Dh 4.40S 149.18 E
Witvlei 37 Bd 22.23S 18.32 E
Witzenhausen 10 Fe 51.20N 9.52 E
Wivenhoe 12 Cc 51.51N 0.58 E
Wizard Reef 30 Mi 8.57S 51.01 E
Wizna 10 Sc 53.13N 22.26 E
Wjdawka 10 Oe 51.32N 18.52 E
W. J. Van Blommestein Meer 54 Hc 4.45N 55.00W
Wkra 10 Qd 52.27N 20.44 E
Władysławowo 10 Ob 54.49N 18.25 E
Włocławek 10 Pd 52.39N 19.02 E
Włocławek [2] 10 Od 52.40N 19.00 E
Włodawa 10 Te 51.34N 23.32 E
Włoszczowa 10 Pf 50.25N 19.59 E
Wodonga 59 Jg 36.17S 146.54 E
Wodzisław Śląski 10 Of 50.00N 18.28 E
Woensdrecht 12 Gc 51.25N 4.18 E
Woerden 12 Gb 52.05N 4.52 E
Woerth 12 Jf 48.56N 7.45 E
Woëvre, Plaine de la- 11 Le 49.15N 5.50 E
Wohlthat-Massif 66 Cf 71.35S 12.20 E
Woippy 12 Ie 49.09N 6.09 E
Wojerecy/Hoyerswerda 10 Ke 51.26N 14.15 E
Wokam, Pulau- 26 Jh 5.37S 134.30 E
Woken He 28 Ja 46.19N 129.34 E
Woking 9 Mj 51.20N 0.34W
Wokingham 12 Bc 51.25N 0.50W
Wolbrom 10 Pf 50.24N 19.46 E
Wolcott 44 Id 43.13N 76.42W
Wołczyn 10 Oe 51.01N 18.03 E
Woldberg 12 Hb 52.25N 5.55 E
Woleai Atoll 57 Fd 7.21N 143.52 E
Woleu-Ntem [3] 36 Bb 2.00N 12.00 E
Wolf, Isla- 54a Aa 1.23N 91.49W
Wolf, Volcán- 54a Ab 0.01S 91.20W
Wolfach 10 Eh 48.18N 8.13 E
Wolf Creek 45 Gh 36.35N 99.30W
Wolf Creek 46 Ic 47.00N 112.04W
Wolfen 10 Ie 51.40N 12.17 E
Wolfenbüttel 10 Gd 52.10N 10.33 E
Wolfhagen 10 Fe 51.19N 9.10 E
Wolf Point 43 Fb 48.05N 105.39W
Wolfratshausen 10 Hi 47.54N 11.25 E
Wolf River 45 Ld 44.11N 88.48W
Wolfsberg 14 Id 46.50N 14.50 E
Wolfsburg 10 Gd 52.26N 10.48 E
Wolfstein 12 Je 49.35N 7.36 E
Wolgast 10 Jb 54.03N 13.46 E
Wolica 10 Tf 50.54N 23.12 E
Wolin 10 Kc 53.51N 14.38 E
Wolin 10 Kc 53.50N 14.35 E
Wollaston 12 Bb 52.15N 0.40W
Wollaston, Islas- 56 Gi 55.40S 67.30W
Wollaston Forland 41 Jd 74.35N 20.15W
Wollaston Lake 38 Id 58.15N 103.20W
Wollaston Lake 42 He 58.05N 103.38W
Wollaston Peninsula 38 Hc 70.00N 115.00W
Wollongong 58 Gh 34.25S 150.54 E
Wöllstein 12 Je 49.49N 7.58 E
Wolmaransstad 37 De 27.12S 26.13 E
Wołomin 10 Rd 52.21N 21.14 E
Wołów 10 Me 51.29N 16.55 E

Index Symbols

[1] Independent Nation
[2] State, Region
[3] District, County
[4] Municipality
[5] Colony, Dependency
Continent
Physical Region
Historical or Cultural Region
Mount, Mountain
Volcano
Hill
Mountains, Mountain Range
Hills, Escarpment
Plateau, Upland
Pass, Gap
Plain, Lowland
Delta
Salt Flat
Valley, Canyon
Crater, Cave
Karst Features
Depression
Polder
Desert, Dunes
Forest, Woods
Heath, Steppe
Oasis
Cape, Point
Coast, Beach
Cliff
Peninsula
Isthmus
Sandbank
Island
Atoll
Rock, Reef
Islands, Archipelago
Rocks, Reefs
Coral Reef
Well, Spring
Geyser
River, Stream
Waterfall Rapids
River Mouth, Estuary
Lake
Salt Lake
Intermittent Lake
Reservoir
Swamp, Pond
Canal
Glacier
Ice Shelf, Pack Ice
Ocean
Sea
Gulf, Bay
Strait, Fjord
Lagoon
Bank
Seamount
Tablemount
Ridge
Shelf
Basin
Escarpment, Sea Scarp
Fracture
Trench, Abyss
National Park, Reserve
Point of Interest
Recreation Site
Cave, Cavern
Historic Site
Ruins
Wall, Walls
Church, Abbey
Temple
Scientific Station
Airport
Port
Lighthouse
Mine
Tunnel
Dam, Bridge

Wolseley 42 Hf 50.25N 103.19W
Wolstenholme, Cap - 42 Jd 62.34N 77.30W
Wolstenholme Fjord 41 Ec 76.40N 69.45W
Wolsztyn 10 Md 52.08N 16.06 E
Wolvega, Weststellingwerf- 12 Ib 52.53N 6.00 E
Wolverhampton 9 Ki 52.36N 2.08W
Wolverton 9 Mi 52.04N 0.50W
Wŏnju 27 Md 37.21N 127.58 E
Wŏnsan 22 Of 39.10N 127.26 E
Wonseradeel 12 Ha 53.06N 5.28 E
Wonseradeel-Witmarsum 12 Ha 53.06N 5.28 E
Wonthaggi 59 Jg 38.36S 145.35 E
Woodall Mountain 45 Li 34.45N 88.11W
Woodbridge 9 Oi 52.06N 1.19 E
Woodbridge Bay 51g Bb 15.19N 61.25W
Woodhall Spa 12 Ba 53.09N 0.13W
Woodland [Ca.-U.S.] 46 Eg 38.41N 121.46W
Woodland [Wa.-U.S.] 46 Dd 45.54N 122.45W
Woodlark Island 57 Ge 9.05S 152.50 E
Wood Mountain 46 Lb 49.14N 106.20W
Woodridge 45 Hb 49.17N 96.09W
Wood River 46 Lb 50.08N 106.10W
Wood River Lakes 40 He 59.30N 158.45W
Woodroffe, Mount- 59 Ge 26.20S 131.45 E
Woods, Lake- 59 Gc 17.50S 133.30 E
Woods, Lake of the- 38 Je 49.15N 94.45W
Woods Hole 44 Le 41.31N 70.40W
Woodside 46 Jg 39.21N 110.18W
Woodstock [Eng.-U.K.] 9 Lj 51.52N 1.21W
Woodstock [N.B.-Can.] 42 Kg 46.09N 67.34W
Woodstock [Ont.-Can.] 44 Gd 43.08N 80.45W
Woodstock [Vt.-U.S.] 44 Kd 43.37N 72.31W
Woodville [Ms.-U.S.] 45 Kk 31.01N 91.18W
Woodville [N.Z.] 62 Fd 40.20S 175.52 E
Woodville [Tx.-U.S.] 45 Ik 30.46N 94.25W
Woodward 43 Hd 36.26N 99.24W
Wooler 9 Kf 55.33N 2.01W
Woomera 59 Hf 31.11S 137.10 E
Wooramel River 59 Ce 25.47S 114.10 E
Wooster 44 Ge 40.46N 81.57W
Worcester 9 Ki 52.15N 2.10W
Worcester [Eng.-U.K.] 9 Ki 52.11N 2.13W
Worcester [Ma.-U.S.] 43 Mc 42.16N 71.48W
Worcester [S.Afr.] 31 Il 33.39S 19.27 E
Worcester Range 66 Jf 78.50S 161.00 E
Wörgl 14 Gc 47.29N 12.04 E
Workai, Pulau- 26 Jh 6.40S 134.40 E
Workington 9 Jg 54.39N 3.33W
Worksop 9 Lh 53.18N 1.07W
Workum 12 Hb 52.59N 5.27 E
Worland 43 Fc 44.01N 107.57W
Wormer 12 Gb 52.30N 4.52 E
Wormhout 12 Ed 50.53N 2.28 E
Worms 10 Eg 49.38N 8.21 E
Worms Head 9 Ij 51.34N 4.20W
Wörrstadt 12 Ke 49.50N 8.06 E
Wörth am Rhein 12 Ke 49.03N 8.16 E
Wörther-See 14 Id 46.37N 14.10 E
Worthing 9 Mk 50.48N 0.23W
Worthington 43 Hc 43.37N 95.36W
Wosi 26 Ig 0.11S 127.58 E
Wotho Atoll 57 Hc 10.06N 165.59 E
Wotje Atoll 57 Id 9.27N 170.02 E
Woudenberg 12 Hb 52.05N 5.25 E
Wounnioné, Pointe- 63b Db 14.54S 168.02 E
Wounta, Laguna de- 49 Fg 13.38N 83.34W
Wour 35 Ba 21.21N 15.57 E
Wousi 63b Cb 15.22S 166.39 E
Wowoni, Pulau- 26 Hg 4.08S 123.06 E
Woy Woy 59 Kf 33.30S 151.20 E
Wrangel, Ostrov- = Wrangel Island (EN) 21 Tb 71.00N 179.30 E
Wrangel Island (EN) = Wrangel, Ostrov- 21 Tb 71.00N 179.30 E
Wrangell 39 Fd 56.28N 132.23W
Wrangell, Cape- 40a Ab 52.50N 172.26 E
Wrangell Mountains 38 Ec 62.00N 143.00W
Wrath, Cape- 5 Fd 58.37N 5.01W
Wray 43 Gc 40.05N 102.13W
Wreake 12 Ab 52.41N 1.05W
Wreck Reef 57 Gg 22.15S 155.10 E
Wrecks, Bay of- 64g Bb 1.52N 157.17W
Wrexham 9 Kh 53.03N 3.00W
Wright Island 66 Of 74.03S 116.45W
Wright Patman Lake 45 Ij 33.16N 94.14W
Wrightson, Mount- 46 Jk 31.42N 110.50W
Wrigley 42 Fd 63.19N 123.38W
Wrigley Gulf 66 Nf 74.00S 129.00W
Wrocław [2] 10 Me 51.05N 17.00 E
Wrocław = Breslau (EN) 6 He 51.06N 17.00 E
Wronki 10 Md 52.43N 16.23 E
Wrotham 12 Cc 51.18N 0.19 E
Wroxham 12 Db 52.42N 1.24 E
Września 10 Nd 52.20N 17.34 E
Wschowa 10 Me 51.48N 16.19 E
Wu'an 28 Cf 36.42N 114.12 E
Wuchale 35 Fc 11.31N 39.37 E
Wuchang 28 Ib 44.55N 127.11 E
Wuchang, Wuhan- 28 Ci 30.32N 114.18 E
Wucheng (Jiucheng) 28 Df 37.12N 116.04 E
Wuchiu Hsu 27 Kg 25.00N 119.27 E
Wuchuan 28 Ad 41.08N 111.25 E
Wuchuan (Duru) 27 If 28.28N 107.57 E
Wuchuan (Meilü) 27 Jg 21.28N 110.44 E
Wuda 27 Id 39.30N 106.33 E
Wudan → Ongniud Qi 27 Kc 42.58N 119.01 E
Wudao 27 Ld 39.28N 121.30 E
Wudaoliang 27 Fd 35.15N 93.14 E
Wudi 28 Df 37.44N 117.36 E
Wudil 34 Gc 11.49N 8.51 E
Wuding 27 Hf 25.36N 102.27 E
Wudu 27 He 33.24N 105.00 E
Wugang 27 Jf 26.48N 110.32 E
Wugong (Puji) 27 Ie 34.15N 108.14 E
Wuhai 27 Id 39.32N 106.55 E
Wuhan 22 Nf 30.30N 114.20 E
Wuhan-Hankou 28 Ci 30.35N 114.16 E
Wuhan-Hanyang 28 Ci 30.33N 114.16 E
Wuhan- Wuchang 28 Ci 30.32N 114.18 E
Wuhe 27 Ke 33.08N 117.51 E
Wuhu 22 Nf 31.18N 118.27 E
Wuhu (Wanzhi) 28 Ei 31.21N 118.23 E
Wujia He 27 Ic 40.56N 108.52 E
Wu Jiang 21 Mg 29.43N 107.24 E
Wujiang 28 Fi 31.09N 120.38 E
Wukari 31 Hh 7.51N 9.47 E
Wukro 35 Fc 13.48N 39.37 E
Wular 25 Eb 34.30N 74.30 E
Wulff Land 41 Hb 82.19N 50.00W
Wulian (Hongning) 28 Eg 35.45N 119.13 E
Wuliang Shan 27 Hg 24.00N 101.00 E
Wuliaru, Pulau- 26 Jh 7.27S 131.04 E
Wuling Shan 21 Mg 28.20N 110.00 E
Wulongbei 28 Hd 40.15N 124.16 E
Wulongji → Huaibin 28 Ci 32.27N 115.23 E
Wulur 26 Ih 7.09S 128.39 E
Wum 34 Hd 6.23N 10.04 E
Wumei Shan 28 Cj 28.47N 114.50 E
Wümme 12 Ka 53.10N 8.40 E
Wuning 28 Cj 29.17N 115.05 E
Wünnenberg 12 Kc 51.31N 8.42 E
Wünnenberg-Haaren 12 Kc 51.34N 8.44 E
Wunnummin Lake 42 If 52.55N 89.10W
Wun Rog 35 Dd 9.00N 28.21 E
Wunstrof 10 Fd 52.26N 9.25 E
Wuntho 25 Jd 23.54N 95.41 E
Wupper 10 Ce 51.05N 7.00 E
Wuppertal 10 De 51.16N 7.11 E
Wuqi 27 Id 36.57N 108.15 E
Wuqia/Ulugqat 27 Cd 39.40N 75.07 E
Wuqiao (Sangyuan) 28 Df 37.38N 116.23 E
Wuqing (Yangcun) 28 De 39.23N 117.04 E
Würm 12 Kf 48.53N 8.42 E
Wurno 34 Gc 13.18N 5.26 E
Würselen 12 Id 50.49N 6.08 E
Würzburg 6 Gf 49.48N 9.56 E
Wurzen 10 Ie 51.22N 12.44 E
Wu Shan 27 Ie 31.00N 110.00 E
Wushaoling 27 Hd 37.15N 102.50 E
Wuski/Uqturpan 27 Cc 41.10N 79.16 E
Wusong 28 Fi 31.23N 121.29 E
Wüst Seamount (EN) 30 Gl 34.00S 3.40W
Wusuli Jiang 27 Ob 48.28N 135.02 E
Wutach 12 Ke 47.37N 8.15 E
Wutai [China] 28 Be 38.43N 113.14 E
Wutai [China] 27 Dc 44.38N 82.06 E
Wutai Shan 27 Jd 39.04N 113.28 E
Wuustwezel 12 Gc 51.23N 4.36 E
Wuvulu Island 57 Fe 1.43S 142.50 E
Wuwei 28 Di 31.17N 117.54 E
Wuwei (Liangzhou) 22 Mf 37.58N 102.48 E
Wuxi [China] 22 Of 31.32N 120.18 E
Wuxi [China] 27 Ie 31.27N 109.34 E
Wu Xia 27 Je 31.02N 110.10 E
Wuxiang (Duancun) 28 Bf 36.50N 112.51 E
Wuxing (Huzhou) 27 Le 30.47N 120.07 E
Wuxue → Guangji 27 Kf 29.58N 115.32 E
Wuyang [China] 28 Bh 33.26N 113.35 E
Wuyang [China] 27 Jd 36.29N 113.07 E
Wuyang → Zhenyuan 27 If 27.05N 108.26 E
Wuyi [China] 28 Cf 37.49N 115.54 E
Wuyi [China] 28 Ej 28.54N 119.50 E
Wuyiling 27 Mb 48.37N 129.20 E
Wuyi Shan 21 Ng 27.00N 117.00 E
Wuyuan [China] 22 Me 41.08N 108.17 E
Wuyuan [China] 28 Dj 29.15N 117.52 E
Wuyuanzhen → Haiyan 28 Fi 30.31N 120.56 E
Wuzhai 28 Ae 38.54N 111.49 E
Wuzhen 28 Ai 31.42N 112.00 E
Wuzhi Shan [China] 28 Ed 40.31N 118.02 E
Wuzhi Shan [China] 27 Ih 18.54N 109.40 E
Wuzhong 27 Id 38.00N 106.10 E
Wuzhou 22 Ng 23.32N 111.21 E
Wyalkatchem 59 Df 31.10S 117.22 E
Wyandotte 44 Fd 42.12N 83.10W
Wyandra 59 Je 27.15S 145.59 E
Wye 9 Kj 51.37N 2.39W
Wye 12 Cc 51.11N 0.56 E
Wyemandoo, Mount- 59 De 28.31S 118.32 E
Wyk auf Föhr 10 Eb 54.42N 8.34 E
Wylie, Lake- 44 Gh 35.07N 81.02W
Wymondham 9 Oi 52.34N 1.07 E
Wyndham [Austl.] 58 Df 15.28S 128.06 E
Wyndham [N.Z.] 62 Cg 46.20S 168.51 E
Wyndmere 45 Hc 46.16N 97.08W
Wynne 45 Ki 35.14N 90.47W
Wynniatt Bay 42 Gb 72.50N 111.00W
Wynyard [Austl.] 59 Jh 40.59S 145.41 E
Wynyard [Sask.-Can.] 42 Hf 51.47N 104.10W
Wyoming 44 Ed 42.54N 85.42W
Wyoming [2] 43 Fc 43.00N 107.30W
Wyoming Peak 43 Ec 42.36N 110.37W
Wyśmierzyce 10 Qe 51.38N 20.49 E
Wysoka 10 Nc 53.11N 17.05 E
Wysokie Mazowieckie 10 Sd 52.56N 22.32 E
Wyszków 10 Rd 52.36N 21.28 E
Wyszogród 10 Qd 52.23N 20.11 E
Wytheville 44 Gg 36.57N 81.07W
Wyville Thomson Ridge (EN) 9 Fa 60.10N 8.00W
Wyvis, Ben- 9 Id 57.42N 4.30W

X

Xaintrie 11 Ii 45.00N 2.10 E
Xainza 27 Ee 30.50N 88.37 E
Xaitongmoin 27 Ef 29.26N 88.08 E
Xai-Xai 31 Kk 25.04S 33.39 E
Xamba → Hanggin Houqi 27 Ic 40.59N 107.07 E
Xam Nua 25 Kd 20.25N 104.02 E
Xangongo 31 Ij 16.46S 14.59 E
Xang Qu 27 Ef 29.22N 89.09 E
Xanten 10 Ce 51.40N 6.27 E
Xánthi 15 Hh 41.08N 24.53 E
Xanthos 24 Cd 36.20N 29.20 E
Xanxerê 56 Jc 26.53S 52.23W
Xapuri 54 Ef 10.39S 68.31W
Xar Hudag 27 Jb 45.06N 114.30 E
Xar Moron 28 Ac 42.37N 111.02 E
Xar Moron He 27 Lc 43.24N 120.39 E
Xarrama 13 Df 38.14N 8.20W
Xátiva/Játiva 13 Lf 38.59N 0.31W
Xau, Lake- 37 Cd 21.15S 24.44 E
Xavantes, Represa de- 55 Hf 23.20S 49.35W
Xavantina 55 Fe 21.15S 52.48W
Xayar 27 Dc 41.15N 82.50 E
Xebert 28 Fc 44.00N 122.00 E
Xégar → Tingri 27 Ef 28.41N 87.00 E
Xenia 44 Ff 39.41N 83.56W
Xiabin Ansha 27 Ke 9.48N 116.38 E
Xiachengzi 28 Kb 44.41N 130.26 E
Xiacun → Rushan 28 Ff 36.55N 121.30 E
Xiaguan 27 Hf 25.32N 100.12 E
Xiahe (Labrang) 27 Hd 35.18N 102.30 E
Xiajin 28 Cf 36.57N 116.00 E
Xiamen 22 Ng 24.32N 118.06 E
Xi'an 22 Mf 34.15N 108.50 E
Xianfeng 27 If 29.41N 109.09 E
Xiangcheng 28 Bh 33.51N 113.29 E
Xiangcheng/Qagchêng 27 Gf 28.56N 99.46 E
Xiangcheng (Shuizhai) 28 Ch 33.27N 114.53 E
Xiangfan 22 Nf 32.03N 112.05 E
Xianggang/Hong Kong [5] 22 Ng 22.15N 114.10 E
Xianghua Ling 27 Jf 25.26N 112.32 E
Xianghuang Qi (Xin Bulag) 27 Jc 42.12N 113.59 E
Xiang Jiang 21 Ng 29.26N 113.08 E
Xiangkhoang 25 Ke 19.20N 103.22 E
Xiangkhoang, Plateau de- 25 Ke 19.30N 103.10 E
Xiangquan He 27 Ce 32.05N 79.20 E
Xiangshan (Dancheng) 27 Lf 29.29N 121.52 E
Xiangshan Gang 28 Fj 29.35N 121.38 E
Xiangtan 22 Ng 27.54N 112.55 E
Xiangtang 28 Cj 28.26N 115.59 E
Xiangyin 28 Bj 28.41N 112.53 E
Xiangyuan 28 Bf 36.32N 113.02 E
Xianju 27 Lf 28.50N 120.42 E
Xianning 28 Cj 29.52N 114.17 E
Xiannümiao → Jiangdu 28 Eh 32.30N 119.33 E
Xiantaozhen → Mianyang 28 Bi 30.22N 113.27 E
Xianxia Ling 27 Kf 28.24N 118.40 E
Xianxian 28 De 38.12N 116.07 E
Xianyang 27 Ie 34.26N 108.40 E
Xiaobole Shan 27 La 51.46N 124.09 E
Xiao'ergou 27 Lb 49.10N 123.43 E
Xiaogan 27 Je 30.52N 113.58 E
Xiao He 28 Bf 37.38N 112.24 E
Xiao Hinggan Ling = Lesser Khingan Range (EN) 21 Oe 48.45N 127.00 E
Xiaoling He 28 Fd 40.55N 121.12 E
Xiaoluan He 28 Dd 41.36N 117.05 E
Xiaoqing He 28 Ef 37.19N 118.59 E
Xiaowutai Shan 28 Cf 39.57N 114.59 E
Xiaoxian 28 Dg 34.11N 116.56 E
Xiaoyi 28 Af 37.07N 111.48 E
Xiaoyi → Gongxian 28 Bg 34.46N 112.57 E
Xiapu 27 Kf 26.57N 119.59 E
Xiawa 28 Fc 42.36N 120.33 E
Xiayi 28 Dg 34.14N 116.07 E
Xiazhuang → Linshu 28 Eg 34.56N 118.38 E
Xicalango, Punta- 48 Nh 19.41N 92.00W
Xichang 22 Mg 27.52N 102.15 E
Xicheng → Yangyuan 28 Cd 40.08N 114.10 E
Xicoténcatl 48 Jf 23.00N 98.56W
Xicotepec de Juárez 48 Kg 20.17N 97.57W
Xiejiaji → Qingyun 28 Df 37.46N 117.22 E
Xifei He 28 Dh 32.38N 116.39 E
Xifeng 28 Hc 42.45N 124.44 E
Xifengzhen 27 Id 35.40N 107.42 E
Xigazê 22 Kg 29.15N 88.52 E
Xi He [China] 27 Hc 42.23N 101.03 E
Xi He [China] 28 Dj 29.38N 116.53 E
Xiheying 28 Ce 39.53N 114.42 E
Xihua 28 Ch 33.48N 114.31 E
Xi Jang 21 Ng 23.05N 114.23 E
Xiji [China] 27 Id 35.52N 105.35 E
Xiji [China] 28 Ia 46.09N 127.08 E
Xi Jiang 27 Jg 23.05N 114.23 E
Xijir,Ulan Hu 27 Fd 35.12N 90.18 E
Xikouzi 27 La 42.58N 120.29 E
Xiligou → Ulan 27 Gd 36.55N 98.16 E
Xilin 27 Ig 24.30N 105.05 E
Xilin Gol 28 Dc 43.55N 116.05 E
Xilin Hot → Abagnar Qi 22 Ne 43.58N 116.08 E
Xilitla 48 Jg 21.20N 98.58W
Xilókastron 15 Fk 38.05N 22.38 E
Ximiao 27 Hc 41.04N 100.14 E
Xin'an 28 Bg 34.43N 112.09 E
Xin'anjiang 28 Ei 29.27N 119.15 E
Xin'anjiang Shuiku 27 Kf 29.25N 119.05 E
Xin'anzhen → Guannan 28 Eg 34.04N 119.21 E
Xin'anzhen → Xinyi 27 Ke 34.17N 118.14 E
Xin Barag Youqi (Altan-Emel) 27 Kb 48.41N 116.47 E
Xin Barag Zuoqi (Amgalang) 27 Kb 48.13N 118.14 E
Xinbin 28 Hd 41.44N 125.02 E
Xin Bulag → Xianghuang Qi 27 Jc 42.12N 113.59 E
Xincai 27 Je 32.40N 114.57 E
Xinchang 28 Fj 29.30N 120.54 E
Xincheng [China] 28 Bf 37.57N 112.33 E
Xincheng [China] 27 Ig 24.04N 108.39 E
Xincheng [China] 28 Id 38.33N 106.10 E
Xincheng (Gaobeidian) 28 Ce 39.20N 115.50 E
Xindi → Honghu 28 Bj 29.50N 113.28 E
Xing'an → Ankang 22 Mf 32.37N 109.03 E
Xingcheng 28 Fd 40.38N 120.43 E
Xingguo 27 Kf 26.22N 115.21 E
Xinghai 27 Gd 35.45N 99.59 E
Xinghe 27 Jc 40.52N 113.56 E
Xinghua 28 Eh 32.56N 119.49 E
Xingkai Hu = Khanka Lake (EN) 21 Pe 45.00N 132.24 E
Xinglong 28 Dd 40.25N 117.31 E
Xinglongzhen 28 Ia 46.26N 127.03 E
Xingren 27 If 25.26N 105.08 E
Xingtai 22 Nf 37.00N 114.30 E
Xingtang 28 Ce 38.26N 114.33 E
Xingu, Rio- 52 Kf 1.30S 51.53W
Xingxingxia 27 Gc 41.47N 95.07 E
Xingyang 28 Bg 34.47N 113.21 E
Xinryi (Huangcaoba) 27 Hf 25.03N 104.55 E
Xingzi 28 Dj 29.28N 116.03 E
Xinhe 28 Cf 37.32N 115.14 E
Xinhe/Toksu 27 Dc 41.34N 82.38 E
Xin Hot → Abag Qi 27 Jc 44.01N 114.59 E
Xinhuai He 28 Fg 34.23N 120.05 E
Xinhui → Aohan Qi 28 Ec 42.18N 119.53 E
Xining 22 Mf 36.37N 101.46 E
Xinji → Shulu 28 Cf 37.56N 115.14 E
Xinjian 28 Cj 28.41N 115.50 E
Xin Jiang 28 Dj 28.37N 116.40 E
Xinjiangkou → Songzi 28 Ai 30.10N 116.46 E
Xinjiang Uygur Zizhiqu (Hsin-chiang-wei-wu-erh Tzu-chih-ch'ü) = Sinkiang (EN) [2] 27 Ec 42.00N 86.00 E
Xinjin 27 He 30.25N 103.46 E
Xinjin (Pulandian) 27 Ld 39.24N 121.59 E
Xinkai He 28 Gc 43.36N 122.31 E
Xinle 28 Ce 38.15N 114.40 E
Xinlin 28 Ec 43.58N 118.03 E
Xinlitun [China] 27 Ma 50.58N 126.39 E
Xinlitun [China] 28 Gc 42.01N 122.11 E
Xinlong/Nyagrong 27 He 30.57N 100.12 E
Xinmin 28 Gc 42.00N 122.50 E
Xinpu → Lianyungang 22 Nf 34.34N 119.15 E
Xinqing 27 Mb 48.15N 129.31 E
Xintai 28 Dg 35.54N 117.44 E
Xinwen (Suncun) 28 Dg 35.49N 117.38 E
Xinxian [China] 27 Jd 38.24N 112.43 E
Xinxian [China] 28 Ci 31.42N 114.50 E
Xinxiang 22 Nf 35.17N 113.50 E
Xinyang 27 Je 32.05N 114.07 E
Xinye 28 Bh 32.30N 112.22 E
Xinyi (Xin'anzhen) 27 Ke 34.17N 118.14 E
Xinyi He 28 Eg 34.29N 119.49 E
Xinyuan/Künes 27 Dc 43.24N 83.18 E
Xinyuan → Tianjun 22 Lf 37.18N 99.15 E
Xinzhan 28 Ic 43.52N 127.20 E
Xin Zhen → Hanggin Qi 27 Id 39.54N 108.55 E
Xinzheng 28 Bg 34.25N 113.46 E
Xinzhou 28 Ci 30.51N 114.49 E
Xioashan 28 Fi 30.10N 120.16 E
Xiong Xian 28 De 38.59N 116.06 E
Xionyuecheng 28 Gd 40.12N 122.08 E
Xiping [China] 28 Ej 28.27N 119.29 E
Xiping [China] 28 Bh 33.22N 114.00 E
Xisha Qundao = Paracel Islands (EN) 21 Nh 16.30N 112.15 E
Xishuangbanna 27 Gg 22.15N 100.00 E
Xishuanghe → Kenli 28 Ef 37.35N 118.30 E
Xishui 28 Ci 30.28N 115.15 E
Xitianmu Shan 27 Ke 30.21N 119.25 E
Xiuanzi → Chongli 28 Cd 40.57N 115.12 E
Xi Ujimqin Qi (Bayan Ul Hot) 27 Kc 44.31N 117.33 E
Xiuning 28 Ej 29.47N 118.11 E
Xiushan 27 If 28.29N 108.58 E
Xiu Shui 28 Cj 29.13N 116.00 E
Xiushui 27 Jf 29.02N 114.33 E
Xiuwu 28 Bg 35.13N 113.27 E
Xiuyan 27 Lc 40.18N 123.10 E
Xiwanzi → Chongli 28 Cf 36.50N 115.10 E
Xixabangma Feng 27 Ef 28.21N 85.47 E
Xixian 28 Ch 32.21N 114.43 E
Xixiang 27 Ie 32.58N 107.45 E
Xiyang 28 Bf 37.38N 113.41 E
Xizang Zizhiqu (Hsi-tsang Tzu-chih-ch'ü) = Tibet (EN) [2] 27 Ee 32.00N 90.00 E
Xizhong Dao 28 Fe 39.25N 121.18 E
Xi Taijnar Hu 27 Fd 37.15N 93.30 E
Xochicalco 48 Jh 18.45N 99.20W
Xochimilco 48 Jh 19.16N 99.06W
Xorkol 27 Fd 39.04N 91.05 E
Xpujil 48 Oh 18.35N 89.25W
Xuancheng 28 Ei 30.56N 118.44 E
Xuande Qundao 26 Fc 17.08N 111.30 E
Xuan'en 27 Ie 30.02N 109.30 E
Xuanhan 27 Ie 31.23N 107.39 E
Xuanhua 27 Kc 40.39N 115.05 E
Xuanwei 27 Hf 26.19N 104.05 E
Xuchang 22 Nf 34.00N 113.58 E
Xuecheng (Lincheng) 28 Dg 34.38N 117.14 E
Xuefeng Shan 27 Jf 27.35N 110.50 E
Xue Shan 27 Gf 27.30N 99.55 E
Xugezhuang → Fengnan 28 Ee 39.34N 118.05 E
Xugou 28 Eg 34.37N 119.08 E
Xugui 27 Gd 35.45N 96.08 E
Xuguit Qi (Yakeshi) 27 Lb 49.16N 120.41 E
Xümatang 27 Ge 33.57N 97.00 E
Xun Jiang 23 Hf 23.28N 111.18 E
Xunke (Qike) 27 Mb 49.34N 128.28 E
Xunwu 27 Kg 24.59N 115.33 E
Xunxian 28 Cg 35.40N 114.33 E
Xupu 27 Jf 27.54N 110.35 E
Xúquer/Júcar 5 Fh 39.09N 0.14W
Xushui 28 Ce 39.02N 115.40 E
Xuwen 27 Jg 20.22N 110.10 E
Xuyi 27 Ke 32.58N 118.33 E
Xuyong (Yongning) 27 If 28.13N 105.26 E
Xuzhou 22 Nf 34.12N 117.13 E

Y

Ya'an 22 Mg 30.00N 102.57 E
Yabassi 34 Ge 4.28N 9.58 E
Yabe 29 Be 32.42N 130.59 E
Yabebyry 55 Dh 27.24S 57.11W
Yabelo 35 Fe 4.53N 38.07 E
Yablonovy Range (EN) = Jablonovy Hrebet 21 Nd 53.30N 115.00 E
Yabrai Shan 27 Hc 40.00N 103.10 E
Yabrīn 35 Ha 23.13N 48.59 E
Yabrūd 24 Gf 33.58N 36.40 E
Yabucoa 51a Cb 18.03N 65.53W
Yabuli 27 Mc 44.56N 128.37 E
Yabulu 59 Jc 19.00S 146.40 E
Yacaré Cururú, Cuchilla- 55 Dj 30.30S 56.33W
Yacaré Norte, Riacho- 55 Cf 22.43S 58.14W
Yacaré Sur, Riacho- 55 Cf 22.43S 58.14W
Yachats 46 Cd 44.20N 124.03W
Yacuma, Rio- 54 Ef 13.38S 65.23W
Yacyretá, Isla- 55 Dh 27.25S 56.30W
Yadé, Massif du- 35 Bd 7.00N 15.30 E
Yādgīr 25 Fe 16.46N 77.08 E
Yadong/Chomo 27 Ef 27.38N 89.03 E
Yae-Dake 29b Ab 26.38N 127.56 E
Yaeyama-Rettō 27 Lg 24.20N 124.00 E
Yafran 33 Bc 32.04N 12.31 E
Yağcilar 15 Lj 39.25N 28.23 E
Yagishiri-Tō 29a Ba 44.26N 141.25 E
Yagoua 34 Ic 10.20N 15.14 E
Yagradagzê Shan 27 Gd 35.09N 95.39 E
Yaguajay 49 Hb 22.19N 79.14W
Yaguari 55 Ej 31.31S 54.58W
Yaguari, Arroyo- 55 Di 29.44S 57.37W
Yahalica de Gonzáles Gallo 48 Hg 21.08N 102.51W
Yahuma 36 Db 1.06N 23.10 E
Yaita 29 Fc 36.50N 139.55 E
Yaizu 29 Fd 34.51N 138.19 E
Yajiang/Nyagquka 27 He 30.07N 100.58 E
Yakacik 24 Ed 36.05N 32.45 E
Yake-Dake 29 Ec 36.14N 137.35 E
Yakeishi-Dake 29 Gb 39.10N 140.50 E
Yakeshi → Xuguit Qi 27 Lb 49.16N 120.41 E
Yake-Yama 29 Gb 39.58N 140.48 E
Yakima 39 Ge 46.36N 120.31W
Yakima River 46 Fc 46.15N 119.02W
Yako 34 Ec 12.58N 2.16W
Yakumo 27 Pc 42.15N 140.16 E
Yaku-Shima 27 Ne 30.20N 130.30 E
Yakutat 40 Le 59.33N 139.44W
Yakutat Bay 40 Ke 59.45N 140.45W
Yala 25 Kg 6.32N 101.19 E
Yalahán, Laguna de- 48 Pg 21.30N 87.15W
Yalcubul, Punta- 48 Og 21.35N 88.35W
Yale Point 46 Kh 36.25N 109.48W
Yalewa Kalou 63d Ab 16.40S 177.46 E
Yalgoo 59 De 28.20S 116.41 E
Yalikavak 15 Kl 37.06N 27.18 E
Yaliköy 15 Lh 41.29N 28.17 E
Yalinga 35 Cd 6.31N 23.13 E
Yaloké 35 Bd 5.19N 17.05 E
Yalong Jiang 21 Mg 26.37N 101.48 E
Yalova 24 Cb 40.39N 29.15 E
Yalu Jiang 21 Of 39.55N 124.20 E
Yalvaç 24 Dc 38.17N 31.11 E
Yām, Ramlat- 33 If 17.42N 45.09 E
Yamada [Jap.] 28 Pe 39.28N 141.57 E
Yamada [Jap.] 29 Be 33.33N 130.45 E
Yamada-Wan 29 Hb 39.30N 142.00 E
Yamaga 29 Be 33.01N 130.41 E
Yamagata 27 Pd 38.15N 140.15 E
Yamagata Ken [2] 28 Pe 38.30N 140.00 E
Yamagawa 29 Bf 31.12N 130.39 E
Yamaguchi 27 Ne 34.10N 131.29 E
Yamaguchi Ken [2] 28 Kh 34.10N 131.30 E
Yamakuni 29 Be 33.24N 131.02 E
Yamal Peninsula (EN) = Jamal, Poluostrov- 21 Ib 70.00N 70.00 E
Yamamoto 29 Ga 40.06N 140.03 E
Yamanaka 29 Ec 36.15N 136.22 E
Yamanashi Ken [2] 28 Og 35.30N 138.45 E
Yamashiro 29 Ce 33.57N 133.43 E
Yamato Rise (EN) 28 Me 39.30N 134.30 E
Yamatsuri 29 Gc 36.53N 140.25 E
Yamazaki 29 Dd 35.00N 134.33 E
Yambi, Mesa de- 54 Dc 1.30N 71.20W
Yambio 31 Jh 4.34N 28.23 E
Yambo 35 Fd 8.25N 36.00 E
Yambu Head 51n Ba 13.09N 61.09W
Yambuya 36 Db 1.16N 24.33 E
Yame 29 Be 33.13N 130.34 E
Yamethin 25 Jd 20.26N 96.09 E
Yamma Yamma, Lake- 59 Ie 26.20S 141.25 E
Yamoto 29 Gb 38.25N 141.13 E
Yamoussoukro 34 Dd 6.49N 5.17W
Yampa River 43 Fc 40.32N 108.59W
Yampi Sound 59 Ec 16.11S 123.40 E
Yamuna 21 Kg 25.30N 81.53 E
Yamunanagar 25 Fb 30.08N 76.59 E
Yamzho Yumco 27 Ff 29.00N 90.40 E
Yanagawa 29 Be 33.10N 130.24 E
Yanahara 29 Dd 34.57N 134.05 E
Yanahuanca 54 Cf 10.30S 76.30W
Yanai 29 Ce 33.58N 132.07 E
Yanam 25 Ge 16.51N 82.15 E
Yan'an 22 Mf 36.35N 109.30 E
Yanaoca 54 Df 14.13S 71.26W
Yanbian 27 Hf 26.51N 101.32 E
Yanbu' 23 Ee 24.05N 38.03 E
Yanchang 27 Jd 36.39N 110.03 E
Yancheng [China] 28 Bh 33.35N 114.00 E
Yancheng [China] 27 Le 33.16N 120.10 E
Yanchi 27 Id 37.47N 107.24 E
Yandé 63b Ae 20.03S 163.48 E
Yandina 63a Dc 9.07S 159.13 E
Yandja 36 Cc 1.41S 17.43 E

Index Symbols

[1] Independent Nation
[2] State, Region
[3] District, County
[4] Municipality
[5] Colony, Dependency
Continent
Physical Region
Historical or Cultural Region
Mount, Mountain
Volcano
Hill
Mountains, Mountain Range
Hills, Escarpment
Plateau, Upland
Pass, Gap
Plain, Lowland
Delta
Salt Flat
Valley, Canyon
Crater, Cave
Karst Features
Depression
Polder
Desert, Dunes
Forest, Woods
Heath, Steppe
Oasis
Cape, Point
Coast, Beach
Cliff
Peninsula
Isthmus
Sandbank
Island
Atoll
Rock, Reef
Islands, Archipelago
Rocks, Reefs
Coral Reef
Well, Spring
Geyser
River, Stream
Waterfall Rapids
River Mouth, Estuary
Lake
Salt Lake
Intermittent Lake
Reservoir
Swamp, Pond
Canal
Glacier
Ice Shelf, Pack Ice
Ocean
Sea
Gulf, Bay
Strait, Fjord
Lagoon
Bank
Seamount
Tablemount
Ridge
Shelf
Basin
Escarpment, Sea Scarp
Fracture
Trench, Abyss
National Park, Reserve
Point of Interest
Recreation Site
Cave, Cavern
Historic Site
Ruins
Wall, Walls
Church, Abbey
Temple
Scientific Station
Airport
Port
Lighthouse
Mine
Tunnel
Dam, Bridge

Index Symbols

[1] Independent Nation	⊟ Historical or Cultural Region	⊟ Pass, Gap	⊟ Depression
[2] State, Region	▲ Mount, Mountain	⊟ Plain, Lowland	⊟ Polder
[3] District, County	▲ Volcano	⊟ Delta	⊟ Desert, Dunes
[4] Municipality	▲ Hill	⊟ Salt Flat	⊟ Forest, Woods
[5] Colony, Dependency	⊟ Mountains, Mountain Range	⊟ Valley, Canyon	⊟ Heath, Steppe
■ Continent	⊟ Hills, Escarpment	⊠ Crater, Cave	⊟ Oasis
⊠ Physical Region	⊟ Plateau, Upland	⊠ Karst Features	⊟ Cape, Point

⊟ Coast, Beach	⊠ Rock, Reef	⊟ Waterfall Rapids	⊟ Canal
⊟ Cliff	⊠ Islands, Archipelago	⊟ River Mouth, Estuary	⊟ Bank
⊟ Peninsula	⊟ Rocks, Reefs	⊟ Lake	⊟ Seamount
⊟ Isthmus	⊟ Coral Reef	⊟ Salt Lake	⊟ Tablemount
⊟ Sandbank	⊟ Well, Spring	⊟ Intermittent Lake	⊟ Ridge
⊟ Island	⊟ Geyser	⊟ Reservoir	⊟ Shelf
⊟ Atoll	⊟ River, Stream	⊟ Swamp, Pond	⊟ Basin

⊟ Lagoon	⊟ Escarpment, Sea Scarp	⊠ Historic Site	⊟ Port
⊟ Glacier	⊟ Fracture	⊟ Ruins	⊟ Lighthouse
⊟ Ice Shelf, Pack Ice	⊟ Trench, Abyss	⊟ Wall, Walls	⊟ Mine
⊟ Ocean	⊟ National Park, Reserve	⊟ Church, Abbey	⊟ Tunnel
⊟ Sea	⊟ Point of Interest	⊟ Temple	⊟ Dam, Bridge
⊟ Gulf, Bay	⊟ Recreation Site	⊟ Scientific Station	
⊟ Strait, Fjord	⊟ Cave, Cavern	⊟ Airport	

Index Symbols

- [1] Independent Nation
- [2] State, Region
- [3] District, County
- Municipality
- Colony, Dependency
- Continent
- Physical Region
- Historical or Cultural Region
- Mount, Mountain
- Volcano
- Hill
- Mountains, Mountain Range
- Hills, Escarpment
- Plateau, Upland
- Pass, Gap
- Plain, Lowland
- Delta
- Salt Flat
- Valley, Canyon
- Crater, Cave
- Karst Features
- Depression
- Polder
- Desert, Dunes
- Forest, Woods
- Heath, Steppe
- Oasis
- Cape, Point
- Coast, Beach
- Cliff
- Peninsula
- Isthmus
- Sandbank
- Island
- Atoll
- Rock, Reef
- Islands, Archipelago
- Rocks, Reefs
- Coral Reef
- Well, Spring
- Geyser
- River, Stream
- Waterfall Rapids
- River Mouth, Estuary
- Lake
- Salt Lake
- Intermittent Lake
- Reservoir
- Swamp, Pond
- Canal
- Glacier
- Ice Shelf, Pack Ice
- Ocean
- Sea
- Gulf, Bay
- Strait, Fjord
- Lagoon
- Bank
- Seamount
- Tablemount
- Ridge
- Shelf
- Basin
- Escarpment, Sea Scarp
- Fracture
- Trench, Abyss
- National Park, Reserve
- Point of Interest
- Recreation Site
- Cave, Cavern
- Historic Site
- Ruins
- Wall, Walls
- Church, Abbey
- Temple
- Scientific Station
- Airport
- Port
- Lighthouse
- Mine
- Tunnel
- Dam, Bridge

International Map Index

Index Symbols

- [1] Independent Nation
- [2] State, Region
- [3] District, County
- [4] Municipality
- [5] Colony, Dependency
- Continent
- Physical Region
- Historical or Cultural Region
- Mount, Mountain
- Volcano
- Hill
- Mountains, Mountain Range
- Hills, Escarpment
- Plateau, Upland
- Pass, Gap
- Plain, Lowland
- Delta
- Salt Flat
- Valley, Canyon
- Crater, Cave
- Karst Features
- Depression
- Polder
- Desert, Dunes
- Forest, Woods
- Heath, Steppe
- Oasis
- Cape, Point
- Coast, Beach
- Cliff
- Peninsula
- Isthmus
- Sandbank
- Island
- Atoll
- Rock, Reef
- Islands, Archipelago
- Rocks, Reefs
- Coral Reef
- Well, Spring
- Geyser
- River, Stream
- Waterfall Rapids
- River Mouth, Estuary
- Lake
- Salt Lake
- Intermittent Lake
- Reservoir
- Swamp, Pond
- Canal
- Glacier
- Ice Shelf, Pack Ice
- Ocean
- Sea
- Gulf, Bay
- Strait, Fjord
- Lagoon
- Bank
- Seamount
- Tablemount
- Ridge
- Shelf
- Basin
- Escarpment, Sea Scarp
- Fracture
- Trench, Abyss
- National Park, Reserve
- Point of Interest
- Recreation Site
- Historic Site
- Ruins
- Wall, Walls
- Church, Abbey
- Temple
- Cave, Cavern
- Scientific Station
- Airport
- Port
- Lighthouse
- Mine
- Tunnel
- Dam, Bridge